RANDOM HOUSE

CROSSWORD ANSWER BOOK

Random House Puzzles & Games

COMPILED BY
STANLEY NEWMAN
AND
DANIEL STARK

 Published in the United States by Random House, Inc., New York, NY, and simultaneously in Canada by Random House of Canada Limited, Toronto.

This work was originally published in different form and in hardcover by Times Books, a division of Random House, Inc., in 1996 as *The Crossword Answer Book*.

ISBN 0-8129-3214-5

Random House Puzzles & Games website address:
www.puzzlesatrandom.com

Text design and typography by Daniel Stark
Manufactured in the United States of America
2 4 6 8 9 7 5 3
First Mass Market Edition

INTRODUCTION

Welcome to *The Random House Crossword Answer Book.* Our objective in compiling it has been to fill what we know is an important need for crossword fans – a comprehensive one-volume source for finding troublesome puzzle answers.

If you've used crossword dictionaries, like we have, you've probably discovered that, while these books pack a lot of information, all too often the answer you're looking for just isn't there. The reason why: These books, as good as they are, have been compiled from standard reference sources (dictionaries, thesauruses, and atlases) and bear no direct relationship to the words that actually appear in crosswords.

This gap – between the true "crossword lexicon" and the information available in crossword dictionaries – has been apparent to us for a long time. So, we decided to do something about it. This is the first in what we hope will be a series of "populist" crossword references, designed to be more useful to puzzlers than the books that are currently available.

The first thing you'll notice when you open this book is that it's not organized like crossword dictionaries, where the answers are alphabetized by keywords in the clue. *The Random House Crossword Answer Book* has no clues, only *answers*. It is this emphasis on answers and, more importantly, how we've compiled these answers, that makes this book unique.

So you can see what we mean, let's describe the process by which we selected the words for this book. First, the many thousands of crosswords we've created or edited were examined and their answers compiled. Thus, the majority of the words and phrases included here come from *actual* crosswords. This initial word list was supplemented by the latest editions of standard reference sources, *plus* "popular culture" reference books – covering such things as television, movies, literature, music and the business world. This use of "non-traditional" reference books is crucial in the quest for comprehensiveness. Today's crosswords, as exemplified by the *New York Times*, are filled with contemporary phrases, names and titles that can't be found in dictionaries and atlases.

Once all of these words were compiled, our next job was to decide which words to keep. Space considerations led us to include words up to six letters long. This is not as limiting as you might think, because over 90% of the answers appearing in crosswords are seven letters long or less. Next, we deleted those words that, due to propriety or obscurity, are unlikely to appear in crosswords. Other categories of words that were excluded were: plurals of personal names (like HARRYS), multi-word partial phrases (like A HAT and IS MY), and uncommon forms of common words (such as ZINCS).

Once we were finished deleting, we started adding again. In addition to ourselves, three other puzzle professionals examined our word list for completeness and consistency, and suggested words to be added. (Special thanks to Henry Hook, Trip Payne, and Rebecca Kornbluh.) As a result of this word-selection process, we can say with complete confidence that no other reference of *any* kind contains all the words found here.

A special thank you to the people who suggested new words that we added to this edition: Diane Baldwin, Ramsey Chaffey, Philip Cohen, Chuck Deodene, Harvey Estes, Ray Hamel, Francis Heaney, Henry Hook, Phyllis Jackson, Maura Jacobson, Matt Jones, Rich Norris, Trip Payne, Mel Rosen, Robert A. Shaw, and Richard Silvestri.

For their help in the preparation of this edition, we'd like to thank the following Random House folks: Beth Levy, Ellen Reed, Lisa Arrington, Heidi North and Helen Chang.

Your comments on any aspect of this book are most welcome. In particular, we'd like to know how useful you find this book, as well as your suggestions for words to include in future editions. You may write to us at: Random House Puzzles & Games, 280 Park Avenue, New York, NY 10017. E-mail: xwords@randomhouse.com. We will thank the first sender of any new word we include in future editions by including his or her name in the introduction.

May all your puzzles be completely solved – with or without our help.

Stanley Newman
Daniel Stark

HOW TO USE THIS BOOK

The Random House Crossword Answer Book is arranged first by word length, then alphabetically by the position of two given letters. So, once you have two letters of an answer filled in, you can quickly find a list of words and phrases that have those two letters in those two positions.

For example, on page 525, startingr at the bottom of the third column, you will find six-letter answers whose third letter is S and sixth letter is A, including: BOSNIA, CESSNA, DESICA, RUSSIA and URSULA. The context of the clue, as well as any additional letters you fill in, will help you determine which of the listed choices is the correct one.

We recognize that, unlike traditional crossword dictionaries, this book does not give additional information about words you're not familiar with. For this reason, we recommend that you do what many crossword fans do: use new words as a "springboard" to learn more about a particular subject.

3

AA•
AAA
AAH
AAR
AAS
AAU

A•A
AAA
ABA
ACA
ADA
AEA
AGA
AHA
AIA
AKA
ALA
AMA
ANA
APA
ARA
ASA
ATA
AVA

•AA
AAA
BAA
CAA
FAA
MAA

AB•
ABA
ABB
ABC
ABD
ABE
ABM
ABN
ABO
ABP
ABR
ABS
ABT
ABU
ABY

A•B
ABB
AFB
ALB
AMB
APB
ARB

•AB
BAB
CAB
DAB
FAB
GAB
HAB
JAB
KAB
LAB
MAB
NAB
RAB
SAB
TAB
WAB

AC•
ACA
ACC
ACE
ACH
ACK
ACP
ACR
ACS
ACT
ACU
ACV
ACY

A•C
ABC
ACC
ADC
AEC
AFC
AKC
ALC
AMC
ANC
APC
ARC
ASC
AUC
AVC

•AC
BAC
FAC
LAC
MAC
PAC
SAC
TAC
VAC
WAC

AD•
ADA
ADC
ADD
ADE
ADJ
ADL
ADM
ADO
ADP
ADS
ADV
ADZ

A•D
ABD
ADD
AID
ALD
AND
ARD
AUD

•AD
BAD
CAD
DAD
EAD
FAD
GAD
HAD
LAD
MAD
NAD
PAD
RAD
SAD
TAD
WAD
YAD

AE•
AEA
AEC
AEE
AEF
AER
AES
AET

A•E
ABE
ACE
ADE
AEE
AGE
ALE
AME
ANE
APE
ARE
ASE
ATE
AVE
AWE
AXE
AYE

•AE
BAE
HAE
LAE
MAE
NAE
RAE
SAE
TAE
UAE
VAE

AF•
AFB
AFC
AFF
AFG
AFL
AFM
AFR
AFS
AFT

A•F
AEF
AFF
ALF
AMF
ARF
ATF
AUF

•AF
KAF
OAF
QAF
RAF
WAF

AG•
AGA
AGE
AGO
AGR
AGS
AGT

A•G
AFG
ALG
ANG
ARG
AUG
AVG

•AG
BAG
DAG
GAG
HAG
JAG
LAG
MAG
NAG
PAG
RAG
SAG
TAG
WAG
YAG
ZAG

AH•
AHA
AHS
AHU

A•H
AAH
ACH
AOH
ASH
AYH

•AH
AAH
BAH
DAH
HAH
LAH
MAH
NAH
PAH
RAH
WAH
YAH

AI•
AIA
AID
AIL
AIM
AIN
AIR
AIS
AIT
AIX

A•I
ALI
AMI
ANI
API
ARI
ASI
AVI

•AI
CAI
DAI
GAI
HAI
JAI
KAI
LAI
MAI
RAI
TAI

A•J
ADJ

•AJ
HAJ
MAJ
RAJ
TAJ

AK•
AKA
AKC
AKU

A•K
ACK
ALK
AOK
ARK
ASK
AUK
AWK

•AK
DAK
OAK
PAK
YAK

AL•
ALA
ALB
ALC
ALD
ALE
ALF
ALG
ALI
ALK
ALL
ALP
ALS
ALT
ALY

A•L
ADL
AFL
AIL
ALL
AOL
APL
ASL
ATL
AWL
AXL

•AL
BAL
CAL
DAL
GAL
HAL
IAL
JAL
MAL
PAL
SAL
TAL
UAL
VAL
WAL
ZAL

AM•
AMA
AMB
AMC
AME
AMF
AMI
AMN
AMO
AMP
AMR
AMS
AMT
AMU
AMY

A•M
ABM
ADM
AFM
AIM
ARM
ATM
AUM

•AM
BAM
CAM
DAM
EAM
FAM
GAM
HAM
IAM
JAM
KAM
LAM
NAM
PAM
RAM
SAM
TAM
YAM

AN•
ANA
ANC
AND
ANE
ANG
ANI
ANN
ANO
ANS
ANT
ANU
ANY

A•N
ABN
AIN
AMN
ANN
ARN
ASN
AVN
AWN
AYN

•AN
BAN
CAN
DAN
FAN
HAN
IAN
JAN
KAN
LAN
MAN
NAN
PAN
RAN
SAN
TAN
VAN
WAN

AO•
AOH
AOK
AOL
AOR

A•O
ABO
ADO
AGO
AMO
ANO
APO
ARO
ASO
AVO
AZO

•AO
BAO
FAO
GAO
HAO
LAO
MAO
PAO
SAO
TAO
YAO

AP•
APA
APB
APC
APE
API
APL
APO
APP
APR
APS
APT
APU

A•P
ABP
ACP
ADP
ALP
AMP
APP
ARP
ASP
ATP

•AP
BAP
CAP
DAP
EAP
GAP
HAP
LAP
MAP
NAP
OAP
PAP
RAP
SAP
TAP
YAP
ZAP

•AQ
FAQ

AR•
ARA
ARB
ARC
ARD
ARE
ARF
ARG
ARI
ARK
ARM
ARN
ARO
ARP
ARR
ARS
ART
ARU
ARY

A•R
AAR
ABR
ACR
AER
AFR
AGR
AIR
AMR
AOR
APR
ARR
ASR
AYR

•AR
AAR
BAR
CAR
DAR
EAR
FAR
GAR
HAR
JAR
LAR
MAR
OAR
PAR
SAR
TAR
UAR
VAR
WAR
YAR

AS•
ASA
ASC
ASE
ASH
ASI
ASK
ASL
ASN
ASO
ASP
ASR
ASS
AST
ASU
ASV

A•S
AAS
ABS
ACS
ADS
AES
AFS
AGS
AHS
AIS
ALS
AMS
ANS
APS
ARS
ASS
AUS
AVS

•AS
AAS
BAS
CAS
DAS
FAS
GAS
HAS
JAS
KAS
LAS
MAS
NAS
OAS

PAS RAS SAS TAS VAS WAS YAS ZAS

AT• ATA ATE ATF ATL ATM ATP ATT ATV

A•T ABT ACT AET AFT AGT AIT ALT AMT ANT APT ART AST ATT AUT

•AT BAT CAT DAT EAT FAT GAT HAT JAT KAT LAT MAT NAT OAT PAT QAT RAT SAT TAT VAT WAT XAT YAT

AU• AUC AUD AUF AUG AUK AUM AUS AUT AUX

A•U AAU ABU ACU AHU AKU AMU ANU APU ARU ASU

•AU AAU DAU EAU PAU RAU SAU TAU

AV• AVA AVC AVE AVG AVI AVN AVO AVS

A•V ACV ADV ASV ATV

•AV CAV DAV JAV LAV MAV NAV TAV VAV

AW• AWE AWK AWL AWN

•AW CAW DAW GAW HAW JAW KAW LAW MAW NAW PAW RAW SAW TAW UAW WAW YAW

AX• AXE AXL

A•X AIX AUX

•AX BAX DAX FAX LAX MAX PAX RAX SAX TAX WAX ZAX

AY• AYE AYH AYN AYR

A•Y ABY ACY ALY AMY ANY ARY

•AY BAY CAY DAY FAY GAY HAY JAY KAY LAY MAY NAY PAY RAY SAY TAY VAY WAY YAY

AZ• AZO

A•Z ADZ

•AZ GAZ PAZ YAZ

BA• BAA BAB BAC BAD BAE BAG BAH BAL BAM BAN BAO BAP BAR BAS BAT BAX BAY

B•A BAA BBA BEA BFA BHA BIA BLA BOA BRA BSA

•BA ABA BBA CBA DBA MBA NBA OBA PBA SBA TBA WBA

BB• BBA BBB BBC BBL BBQ BBS

B•B BAB BBB BIB BOB BUB

•BB ABB BBB EBB

BC• BCE BCG

B•C BAC BBC BHC BIC BSC BUC

•BC ABC BBC CBC NBC RBC WBC

BD• BDL BDS

B•D BAD BED BHD BID BOD BPD BUD BVD

•BD ABD MBD

BE• BEA BED BEE BEF BEG BEI BEL BEM BEN BES BET BEV BEY

B•E BAE BCE BEE BLE BME BPE BRE BYE

•BE ABE CBE DBE GBE MBE NBE OBE SBE UBE

BF• BFA

B•F BEF

BG• BGH BGS

B•G BAG BCG BEG BIG BKG BOG BUG

BH• BHA BHC BHD BHP BHT

B•H BAH BGH BPH BSH BTH

BI• BIA BIB BIC BID BIG BIL BIN BIO BIP BIS BIT BIV BIX BIZ

B•I BEI BMI BPI BWI

•BI FBI OBI RBI UBI

•BJ LBJ OBJ PBJ

BK• BKG BKS BKT

B•K BLK BOK

BL• BLA BLE BLK BLS BLT BLU BLY

B•L BAL BBL BDL BEL BIL BOL BPL BTL BUL

•BL BBL DBL OBL

BM• BME BMI BMR BMS BMW BMX

B•M BAM BEM BUM BVM

•BM ABM IBM

B•N BAN BEN BIN BON BUN

•BN ABN EBN IBN WBN

BO• BOA BOB BOD BOG BOK BOL BON BOO BOP BOR BOS BOT BOW BOX BOY BOZ

B•O BAO BIO BOO BRO BYO

•BO ABO EBO HBO IBO LBO

BP• BPD BPE BPH BPI BPL BPS

B•P BAP BHP BIP BOP

•BP ABP QBP

B•Q BBQ BXQ

•BQ BBQ

BR• BRA BRE BRO BRR BRS BRV

B•R BAR BMR BOR BRR BUR

•BR ABR

BS• BSA BSC BSH

B•S BAS BBS BDS BES BGS BIS BKS BLS BMS BOS BPS BRS BTS BUS

•BS ABS BBS CBS DBS EBS FBS GBS LBS NBS OBS PBS QBS TBS VBS WBS YBS

BT• BTH BTL BTS BTU BTW

B•T BAT BET BHT BIT BKT BLT BOT BUT BVT

•BT ABT

BU• BUB BUC BUD BUG BUL BUM BUN BUR BUS BUT BUY

B•U BLU BTU BYU

•BU ABU

BV• BVD BVM BVT

B•V BEV BIV BRV

•BV OBV

BW• BWI

B•W BMW BOW BTW

•BW NBW SBW

BX• BXQ

B•X BAX BIX BMX BOX

•BX PBX

BY• BYE BYO BYU BYZ

B•Y BAY BEY BLY BOY BUY

•BY ABY

B•Z BIZ BOZ BYZ

CA• CAA CAB CAD CAI CAL CAM CAN CAP CAR CAS CAT CAV CAW CAY

C•A CAA CBA CEA CFA CHA CIA CMA COA CPA CSA

•CA ACA FCA GCA ICA MCA OCA RCA

CB• CBA CBC CBE CBS

C•B CAB COB CPB CUB

•CB PCB

CC• CCC CCD CCI CCL CCS CCU CCV CCW CCX

C•C CBC CCC CDC CIC CSC CXC

•CC ACC CCC DCC FCC ICC JCC MCC NCC

CD• CDC CDE CDI CDL CDR CDS CDT CDV CDX

C•D CAD CCD CID CLD CMD COD CPD CUD CYD

•CD CCD GCD JCD LCD MCD RCD SCD

CE• CEA CEE CEL CEN CEO CEP CES CET CEY

C•E CBE CDE CEE CHE CIE CLE COE CUE

•CE ACE BCE GCE ICE

CF• CFA CFI CFL CFO CFS

C•F CIF CTF

•CF GCF HCF MCF

CG• CGM CGS

C•G CHG COG

•CG BCG ECG MCG

CH• CHA CHE CHG CHI CHM

•CH ACH HCH ICH OCH SCH

CI• CIA CIC CID CIE CIF CII CIM CIO CIP CIR CIS CIT CIV CIX

C•I CAI CCI CDI CFI CHI CII CLI CMI CPI CRI CUI CVI CXI

•CI CCI DCI ICI MCI SCI XCI

CK• CKW

C•K CLK CSK

•CK ACK ECK ICK OCK

CL• CLD CLE CLI CLK CLR CLS CLU CLV CLX

C•L CAL CCL CDL CEL CFL CML COL CPL CUL CXL CYL

•CL CCL DCL JCL KCL MCL

CM• CMA CMD CMI CML CMS CMV CMX

C•M CAM CGM CHM CIM COM CPM CUM CWM

•CM DCM ECM LCM MCM SCM

CN• CNN CNO CNS

C•N CAN CEN CNN CON CTN

•CN RCN

CO• COA COB COD COE COG COL COM CON COO COP

COQ	CRU	CTS	DCV	**DA•**	**D•C**	**D•E**	DIG	**D•L**	DOE	**D•R**	**D•T**	**DW•**	ENA	FEC	EKE
COR	CRY		MCV	DAB	DCC	DBE	DII	DAL	DOG	DAR	DAT	DWT	EPA	JEC	EME
COS		**C•T**	PCV	DAD	DEC	DDE	DIK	DBL	DOH	DDR	DDT		ERA	NEC	ENE
COT	**C•R**	CAT	XCV	DAG	DFC	DEE	DIL	DCL	DOI	DER	DET	**D•W**	ESA	PEC	EOE
COW	CAR	CDT		DAH	DOC	DIE	DIM	DEL	DOJ	DIR	DIT	DAW	ETA	REC	ERE
COX	CDR	CET	**CW•**	DAI	DSC	DOE	DIN	DHL	DOL	DLR	DOT	DEW	EVA	SEC	ESE
COY	CIR	CIT	CWM	DAK	DUC	DRE	DIO	DIL	DOM	DNR	DPT	DOW		TEC	ETE
COZ	CLR	COT	CWO	DAL	DXC	DUE	DIP	DKL	DON	DOR	DST	DPW	**•EA**		EVE
	COR	CPT	CWP	DAM		DYE	DIR	DML	DOO		DWT		AEA	**ED•**	EWE
C•O	CPR	CRT	CWT	DAN	**•DC**		DIS	DOL	DOP	**•DR**		**•DW**	BEA	EDA	EXE
CEO	CTR	CST		DAP	ADC	**•DE**	DIT	DPL	DOR	CDR	**•DT**	HDW	CEA	EDB	EYE
CFO	CUR	CUT	**C•W**	DAR	CDC	ADE	DIU	DXL	DOS	DDR	CDT		DEA	EDD	
CIO	CYR	CWT	CAW	DAS	LDC	CDE	DIV		DOT	FDR	DDT	**DX•**	KEA	EDE	**•EE**
CNO			CCW	DAT	MDC	DDE	DIX	**•DL**	DOU	GDR	EDT	DXC	LEA	EDH	AEE
COO	**•CR**	**•CT**	CKW	DAU	UDC	EDE	DIY	ADL	DOW	LDR	MDT	DXI	MEA	EDM	BEE
CPO	ACR	ACT	COW	DAV		IDE		BDL	DOZ	MDR	PDT	DXL	NEA	EDO	CEE
CRO	NCR	ECT		DAW	**DD•**	ODE	**D•I**	CDL			VDT	DXV	PEA	EDP	DEE
CTO	OCR	JCT	**•CW**	DAX	DDE	RDE	DAI	HDL	**D•O**	**DS•**		DXX	REA	EDS	EEE
CWO	VCR	LCT	CCW	DAY	DDR		DCI	LDL	DEO	DSC	**DU•**		SEA	EDT	FEE
CYO		OCT			DDS	**DF•**	DEI	MDL	DIO	DSM	DUB	**D•X**	TEA	EDU	GEE
	CS•	PCT	**CX•**	**D•A**	DDT	DFA	DII		DLO	DSO	DUC	DAX	YEA		HEE
•CO	CSA	RCT	CXC	DBA		DFC	DLI	**DM•**	DOO	DST	DUD	DCX	ZEA	**E•D**	LEE
ECO	CSC		CXI	DEA	**D•D**	DFM	DOI	DMA	DSO		DUE	DEX		EAD	NEE
NCO	CSK	**CU•**	CXL	DFA	DAD		DPI	DMD	DUO	**D•S**	DUG	DIX	**EB•**	EDD	REE
	CST	CUB	CXV	DHA	DED	**D•F**	DVI	DML		DAS	DUH	DLX	EBB	ELD	SEE
CP•	CSX	CUD	CXX	DIA	DID	DEF	DXI	DMS	**•DO**	DBS	DUM	DUX	EBN	END	TEE
CPA		CUE		DMA	DMD	DIF		DMV	ADO	DDS	DUN	DXX	EBO	ESD	VEE
CPB	**C•S**	CUI	**C•X**	DNA	DOD		**•DI**	DMZ	EDO	DES	DUO		EBS	ETD	WEE
CPD	CAS	CUL	CCX	DOA	DUD	**•DF**	CDI		IDO	DHS	DUP	**•DX**			ZEE
CPI	CBS	CUM	CDX		DVD	RDF	IDI	**D•M**	ODO	DIS	DUX	CDX	**E•B**	**•ED**	
CPL	CCS	CUP	CIX	**•DA**			MDI	DAM	UDO	DJS	DUZ	MDX	EBB	BED	**EF•**
CPM	CDS	CUR	CLX	ADA	**•DD**	**D•G**	SDI	DCM		DLS			EDB	DED	EFF
CPO	CES	CUT	CMX	EDA	ADD	DAG		DEM	**DP•**	DMS	**D•U**	**DY•**	EMB	FED	EFG
CPR	CFS		COX	FDA	EDD	DEG	**DJ•**	DFM	DPH	DOS	DAU	DYE		GED	EFS
CPS	CGS	**C•U**	CSX	IDA	ODD	DIG	DJS	DIM	DPI	DPS	DHU	DYN	**•EB**	HED	EFT
CPT	CIS	CCU	CXX	ODA	PDD	DKG		DKM	DPL	DRS	DIU	DYS	DEB	JED	
CPU	CLS	CLU		RDA	RDD	DOG	**D•J**	DOM	DPS	DTS	DOU		FEB	KED	**E•F**
	CMS	CPU	**•CX**		TDD	DUG	DOJ	DSM	DPT	DYS	DRU	**D•Y**	HEB	LED	EFF
C•P	CNS	CRU	CCX	**DB•**			DRJ	DUM	DPW			DAY	JEB	MED	EHF
CAP	COS		DCX	DBA	**DE•**	**•DG**		DVM		**•DS**	**•DU**	DEY	LEB	NED	ELF
CEP	CPS	**•CU**	MCX	DBE	DEA	LDG	**•DJ**		**D•P**	ADS	EDU	DIY	NEB	OED	EMF
CIP	CRS	ACU		DBL	DEB		ADJ	**•DM**	DAP	BDS	VDU	DRY	REB	PED	EOF
COP	CTS	CCU	**CY•**	DBS	DEC	**DH•**		ADM	DEP	CDS			WEB	QED	
CUP	CVS	ECU	CYD		DED	DHA	**DK•**	EDM	DIP	DDS	**DV•**	**D•Z**		RED	**•EF**
CWP		ICU	CYL	**D•B**	DEE	DHL	DKG	PDM	DOP	EDS	DVD	DMZ	**EC•**	TED	AEF
	•CS	TCU	CYO	DAB	DEF	DHS	DKL		DTP	FDS	DVI	DOZ	ECG	WED	BEF
•CP	ACS		CYR	DEB	DEG	DHU	DKM	**DN•**	DUP	GDS	DVM	DUZ	ECK	XED	DEF
ACP	CCS	**CV•**		DIB	DEI			DNA		HDS			ECM	ZED	HEF
FCP	FCS	CVI	**C•Y**	DOB	DEK	**D•H**	**D•K**	DNR	**•DP**	IDS	**D•V**	**•DZ**	ECO		KEF
MCP	ICS	CVS	CAY	DUB	DEL	DAH	DAK		ADP	LDS	DAV	ADZ	ECT	**EE•**	NEF
RCP	JCS		CEY		DEM	DOH	DEK	**D•N**	EDP	MDS	DCV		ECU	EEC	QEF
	LCS	**C•V**	COY	**•DB**	DEN	DPH	DIK	DAN	IDP	ODS	DEV	**EA•**		EEE	REF
C•Q	MCS	CAV	CRY	EDB	DEO	DUH	DRK	DEN		RDS	DIV	EAD	**E•C**	EEG	
COQ	OCS	CCV		PDB	DEP			DIN	**•DQ**	SDS	DLV	EAM	EEC	EEK	**EG•**
	PCS	CDV	**•CY**		DER	**•DH**	**DL•**	DON	PDQ	TDS	DMV	EAP	ENC	EEL	EGG
•CQ	RCS	CIV	ACY	**DC•**	DES	EDH	DLI	DUN		WDS	DXV	EAR	ESC	EEN	EGO
MCQ	WCS	CLV	FCY	DCC	DET		DLO	DYN	**DR•**	YDS		EAT	ETC	EEO	EGR
		CMV	ICY	DCI	DEV	**DI•**	DLR		DRE		**•DV**	EAU	EXC	EER	
CR•	**CT•**	CXV		DCL	DEW	DIA	DLS	**DO•**	DRJ	**DT•**	ADV			EES	**E•G**
CRI	CTF		**C•Z**	DCM	DEX	DIB	DLV	DOA	DRK	DTP	CDV	**E•A**	**•EC**		ECG
CRO	CTN	**•CV**	COZ	DCV	DEY	DID	DLX	DOB	DRS	DTS	MDV	EDA	AEC	**E•E**	EEG
CRS	CTO	ACV		DCX		DIE		DOC	DRU			EKA	DEC	EDE	EFG
CRT	CTR	CCV				DIF		DOD	DRY			ELA	EEC	EEE	EGG

EKG EMG ENG ERG EVG
•EG BEG DEG EEG KEG LEG MEG NEG PEG REG TEG VEG ZEG
EH• EHF EHV
E•H EDH EPH ETH
•EH HEH NEH PEH TEH VEH
EI• EIN EIS
E•I ELI EMI EPI ERI
•EI BEI DEI LEI PEI REI SEI WEI
EK• EKA EKE EKG
E•K ECK EEK

ELK ERK ESK
•EK DEK EEK LEK
EL• ELA ELD ELF ELI ELK ELL ELM ELO ELS ELY
E•L EEL ELL ENL ESL
•EL BEL CEL DEL EEL GEL HEL KEL MEL REL SEL TEL VEL
EM• EMB EME EMF EMG EMI EMO EMP EMS EMT EMU
E•M EAM ECM EDM ELM EOM
•EM BEM DEM

FEM GEM HEM LEM MEM OEM REM SEM TEM
EN• ENA ENC END ENE ENG ENL ENO ENS ENT ENV
E•N EBN EEN EIN EON ERN
•EN BEN CEN DEN EEN FEN GEN HEN KEN LEN MEN OEN PEN REN SEN TEN VEN WEN XEN YEN ZEN
EO• EOE EOF EOM EON EOS
E•O EBO ECO EDO EEO

EGO ELO EMO ENO ESO ETO EXO
•EO CEO DEO EEO GEO LEO MEO NEO OEO REO YEO
EP• EPA EPH EPI EPS
E•P EAP EDP EMP ESP EXP
•EP CEP DEP HEP NEP PEP REP SEP YEP
E•Q ESQ
•EQ REQ SEQ
ER• ERA ERE ERG ERI ERK ERN ERR ERS ERY ERZ

E•R EAR EER EGR ERR EUR EXR EZR
•ER AER DER EER FER GER HER IER JER KER LER MER NER OER PER SER TER VER XER YER
ES• ESA ESC ESD ESE ESK ESL ESO ESP ESQ ESS EST ESU
E•S EBS EDS EES EFS EIS ELS EMS ENS EOS EPS ERS ESS ETS EVS
•ES AES BES

CES DES EES HES LES MES NES PES RES SES TES WES XES YES
ET• ETA ETC ETD ETE ETH ETO ETS ETV
E•T EAT ECT EDT EFT EMT ENT EST EXT
•ET AET BET CET DET FET GET HET JET KET LET MET NET PET RET SET TET VET WET YET
EU• EUR
E•U EAU ECU EDU

EMU ESU
•EU FEU JEU LEU NEU PEU
EV• EVA EVE EVG EVS
E•V EHV ENV ETV
•EV BEV DEV GEV KEV LEV MEV NEV REV ZEV
EW• EWE
•EW DEW FEW HEW JEW KEW LEW MEW NEW PEW SEW YEW
EX• EXC EXE EXO EXP EXR EXT
•EX DEX HEX LEX MEX REX SEX

TEX VEX
EY• EYE
E•Y ELY ERY
•EY BEY CEY DEY FEY GEY HEY KEY LEY NEY REY TEY UEY
EZ• EZR
E•Z ERZ
•EZ FEZ NEZ PEZ SEZ
FA• FAA FAB FAC FAD FAM FAN FAO FAQ FAR FAS FAT FAX FAY
F•A FAA FCA FDA FFA FHA FLA FPA FRA
•FA BFA

CFA DFA FFA MFA UFA
FB• FBI FBS
F•B FAB FEB FIB FMB FOB FRB FUB
•FB AFB LFB RFB
FC• FCA FCC FCP FCS FCY
F•C FAC FCC FEC FIC FMC FPC FTC
•FC AFC DFC KFC NFC PFC SFC
FD• FDA FDR FDS
F•D FAD FED FID FLD FTD FWD
•FD MFD

NFD PFD RFD VFD
FE• FEB FEC FED FEE FEM FEN FER FET FEU FEW FEY FEZ
F•E FEE FIE FOE
•FE IFE RFE
FF• FFA FFF FFV
F•F FFF
•FF AFF EFF FFF IFF OFF
F•G FIG FOG FRG FUG
•FG AFG EFG MFG PFG
FH• FHA
F•H FTH
•FH MFH

FI• FIB FIC FID FIE FIG FIL FIN FIR FIS FIT FIX
F•I FBI FRI FYI
•FI CFI RFI
•FK JFK RFK
FL• FLA FLD FLO FLU FLY
F•L FIL FOL FPL FRL FUL
•FL AFL CFL NFL
FM• FMB FMC FMS
F•M FAM FEM FPM FUM
•FM AFM DFM
FN• FNS

F•N FAN FEN FIN FON FUN FYN
FO• FOB FOE FOG FOL FON FOO FOP FOR FOU FOX FOY
F•O FAO FLO FOO FPO FRO
•FO CFO SFO UFO
FP• FPA FPC FPL FPM FPO FPS
F•P FCP FOP
F•Q FAQ
•FQ RFQ
FR• FRA FRB FRG FRI FRL FRO FRS FRT FRY

F•R FAR FDR FER FIR FOR FUR
•FR AFR MFR TFR
FS• FSU
F•S FAS FBS FCS FDS FIS FMS FNS FPS FRS
•FS AFS CFS EFS IFS LFS
FT• FTC FTD FTH
F•T FAT FET FIT FRT FUT
•FT AFT EFT OFT UFT
FU• FUB FUG FUL FUM FUN FUR FUT
F•U FEU

FLU FOU FSU
F•V FFV
•FV FFV
FW• FWD
F•W FEW
•FW UFW VFW
F•X FAX FIX FOX
FY• FYI FYN
F•Y FAY FCY FEY FLY FOY FRY
•FY IFY
F•Z FEZ
•FZ SFZ
GA• GAB GAD GAG GAI GAL GAM GAO GAP GAR GAS GAT GAW GAY GAZ

G•A GCA GIA GMA GOA GPA GSA
•GA AGA IGA PGA VGA
GB• GBE GBS
G•B GAB GIB GOB
•GB KGB RGB
GC• GCA GCD GCE GCF
G•C GMC GTC
•GC NGC
GD• GDR GDS
G•D GAD GCD GED GLD GOD GPD GTD
•GD MGD SGD
GE• GED GEE GEL GEM GEN

GEO GER GET GEV GEY
G•E GBE GCE GEE GIE GRE GTE
•GE AGE LGE
G•F GCF GRF
•GF KGF NGF
G•G GAG GIG GOG
•GG EGG IGG
GH• GHI GHQ GHZ
•GH BGH HGH UGH
GI• GIA GIB GIE GIG GIL GIN GIP GIS GIT
G•I GAI GHI GUI
GL• GLD

GLO	EGO	**GT•**	**G•Y**	**H•C**	HEF	**•HI**	HOT	HIS	**H•V**	**•IA**	**ID•**	IFY	III	CIM	ION
	IGO	GTC	GAY	HIC	HMF	CHI	HOV	HMS	HOV	AIA	IDA		LII	DIM	IOR
G•L	UGO	GTD	GEY	HOC	HOF	GHI	HOW	HOS		BIA	IDE	**I•F**	MII	HIM	IOS
GAL		GTE	GUY			NHI	HOY	HQS	**•HV**	CIA	IDI	IFF	VII	JIM	IOU
GEL	**GP•**	GTO		**•HC**	**•HF**	PHI		HRS	EHV	DIA	IDO	IMF	XII	KIM	
GIL	GPA	GTP	**•GY**	BHC	EHF	THI	**H•O**	HTS		GIA	IDP	INF		LIM	**I•O**
	GPD	GTT	IGY	MHC	SHF		HAO	HUS	**HW•**	LIA	IDS		**IK•**	MIM	IBO
GM•	GPM			OHC	UHF	**H•J**	HBO		HWM	MIA		**•IF**	IKE	NIM	IDO
GMA	GPO	**G•T**	**G•Z**		VHF	HAJ	HMO	**•HS**	HWY	NIA	**I•D**	CIF		PIM	IGO
GMC	GPS	GAT	GAZ	**HD•**	WHF		HOO	AHS		PIA	IND	DIF	**I•K**	RIM	ILO
GMS		GET	GHZ	HDL		**H•L**		DHS	**H•W**	RIA	IOD	JIF	ICK	SIM	INO
GMT	**G•P**	GIT		HDS	**HG•**	HAL	**•HO**	HHS	HAW	TIA	ITD	KIF	ILK	TIM	IPO
GMW	GAP	GMT	**HA•**	HDW	HGH	HDL	MHO	IHS	HDW	VIA		RIF	INK	VIM	IRO
	GIP	GOT	HAB		HGT	HEL	OHO	JHS	HEW	XIA	**•ID**	ZIF	IRK	WIM	ISO
G•M	GNP	GST	HAD	**H•D**	HGW	HOL	RHO	LHS	HGW	ZIA	AID				ITO
GAM	GOP	GTT	HAE	HAD			SHO	NHS	HOW		BID	**IG•**	**•IK**	**IN•**	IVO
GEM	GTP	GUT	HAG	HED	**H•G**	**•HL**	THO	OHS		**IB•**	CID	IGA	DIK	INA	IWO
GPM	GYP		HAH	HHD	HAG	DHL	WHO	VHS	**•HW**	IBM	DID	IGG	NIK	INC	
GUM		**•GT**	HAI	HID	HOG	NHL		WHS	MHW	IBN	FID	IGN	OIK	IND	**•IO**
GYM	**G•Q**	AGT	HAJ	HOD	HUG		**H•P**			IBO	HID	IGO	PIK	INE	BIO
	GHQ	HGT	HAL	HUD		**HM•**	HAP	**HT•**	**H•X**		KID	IGY		INF	CIO
•GM		MGT	HAM	HYD	**•HG**	HMF	HEP	HTS	HEX	**•IB**	LID		**IL•**	ING	DIO
CGM	**GR•**	RGT	HAN		CHG	HMM	HIP			BIB	MID	**I•G**	ILA	INK	MIO
KGM	GRE	SGT	HAO	**•HD**		HMO	HOP	**H•T**	**•HX**	DIB	OID	IGG	ILE	INN	RIO
MGM	GRF		HAP	BHD	**HH•**	HMS	HUP	HAT	THX	FIB	QID	ING	ILK	INO	TIO
	GRO	**GU•**	HAR	HHD	HHD		HYP	HET		GIB	RID		ILL	INQ	
GN•	GRR	GUI	HAS	LHD	HHH	**H•M**		HGT	**HY•**	JIB	SID	**•IG**	ILO	INS	**IP•**
GNP		GUM	HAT	PHD	HHS	HAM	**•HP**	HIT	HYD	LIB	TID	BIG	ILS	INT	IPA
GNU	**G•R**	GUN	HAW	THD		HEM	BHP	HOT	HYP	MIB		DIG		INV	IPM
	GAR	GUR	HAY		**H•H**	HIM		HST		NIB	**IE•**	FIG	**I•L**		IPO
G•N	GDR	GUS		**HE•**	HAH	HMM	**HQ•**	HUT	**H•Y**	RIB	IER	GIG	IAL	**I•N**	IPS
GEN	GER	GUT	**H•A**	HEB	HCH	HOM	HQS		HAY	SIB		JIG	ILL	IAN	
GIN	GOR	GUV	HUA	HED	HEH	HUM		**•HT**	HEY		**I•E**	MIG	ISL	IBN	**I•P**
GON	GRR	GUY		HEE	HGH	HWM	**•HQ**	BHT	HOY	**IC•**	ICE	NIG		IGN	IDP
GUN	GUR		**•HA**	HEF	HHH		GHQ	SHT	HVY	ICA	IDE	PIG	**•IL**	INN	IMP
GYN		**G•U**	AHA	HEH	HIH	**•HM**			HWY	ICC	IFE	RIG	AIL	ION	
	•GR	GNU	BHA	HEL	HRH	CHM	**HR•**	**HU•**		ICE	IKE	SIG	BIL		**•IP**
•GN	AGR		CHA	HEM	HSH	OHM	HRE	HUA	**•HY**	ICH	ILE	WIG	DIL	**•IN**	BIP
IGN	EGR	**GV•**	DHA	HEN	HUH	PHM	HRH	HUB	SHY	ICI	INE	ZIG	FIL	AIN	CIP
	MGR	GVW	FHA	HEP		THM	HRS	HUD	THY	ICK	IRE		GIL	BIN	DIP
GO•			KHA	HER	**•HH**			HUE	WHY	ICS	ISE	**IH•**	KIL	DIN	GIP
GOA	**GS•**	**G•V**	SHA	HES	HHH	**H•N**	**H•R**	HUG		ICU	ITE	IHR	LIL	EIN	HIP
GOB	GSA	GEV	THA	HET	SHH	HAN	HAR	HUH	**•HZ**	ICY	IVE	IHS	MIL	FIN	KIP
GOD	GST	GOV	WHA	HEW	WHH	HEN	HER	HUI	GHZ		IZE		NIL	GIN	LIP
GOG		GUV		HEX		HIN	HOR	HUM	KHZ	**I•C**		**I•H**	OIL	HIN	MIP
GON	**G•S**		**HB•**	HEY	**HI•**	HON	HUR	HUN	MHZ	ICC	**•IE**	ICH	SIL	JIN	NIP
GOO	GAS	**•GV**	HBO		HIC	HUN		HUP		INC	CIE	ISH	TIL	KIN	PIP
GOP	GBS	TGV		**H•E**	HID		**•HR**	HUR	**IA•**	IOC	DIE		VIL	LIN	RIP
GOR	GDS		**H•B**	HAE	HIE	**HO•**	IHR	HUS	IAL		FIE	**•IH**	WIL	MIN	SIP
GOT	GIS	**G•W**	HAB	HEE	HIH	HOB	PHR	HUT	IAM	**•IC**	GIE	HIH		NIN	TIP
GOV	GMS	GAW	HEB	HIE	HIM	HOC	SHR		IAN	BIC	HIE	NIH	**IM•**	PIN	VIP
	GPS	GMW	HOB	HOE	HIN	HOD	WHR	**•HU**		CIC	LIE		IMF	QIN	WIP
G•O	GUS	GVW	HUB	HRE	HIP	HOE		AHU	**I•A**	FIC	NIE	**II•**	IMP	RIN	YIP
GAO				HUE	HIS	HOF	**HS•**	DHU	ICA	HIC	PIE	III		SIN	ZIP
GEO	**•GS**	**•GW**	**•HB**		HIT	HOG	HSH	JHU	IDA	LIC	SIE		**I•M**	TIN	
GLO	AGS	HGW	LHB	**•HE**		HOI	HSI	PHU	IGA	MIC	TIE	**I•I**	IAM	VIN	**IQ•**
GOO	BGS		PHB	CHE	**H•I**	HOL	HST	SHU	ILA	PIC	VIE	ICI	IBM	WIN	IQS
GPO	CGS	**GY•**	RHB	RHE	HAI	HOM		THU	INA	RIC	WIE	IDI	IPM	XIN	
GRO	JGS	GYM	THB	SHE	HOI	HON	**H•S**		IPA	SIC		III	ISM	YIN	**I•Q**
GTO	LGS	GYN		THE	HSI	HOO	HAS	**HV•**	IRA	TIC	**IF•**		IUM		INQ
	MGS	GYP	**HC•**		HUI	HOP	HDS	HVY	ISA	VIC	IFE	**•II**		**IO•**	
•GO	PGS		HCF	**H•F**		HOR	HES		IVA		IFF	CII	**•IM**	IOC	**•IQ**
AGO	RGS		HCH	HCF		HOS	HHS				IFS	DII	AIM	IOD	LIQ

IR• IRA IRE IRK IRO IRR IRS IRT IRV

I•R IER IHR IOR IRR ISR

•IR AIR CIR DIR FIR KIR MIR PIR SIR VIR

IS• ISA ISE ISH ISL ISM ISO ISR ISS IST

I•S ICS IDS IFS IHS ILS INS IOS IPS IQS IRS ISS ITS IVS

•IS AIS BIS CIS DIS EIS FIS GIS HIS LIS MIS NIS PIS SIS TIS VIS WIS XIS

IT• ITD ITE ITO ITS ITT ITV ITY

I•T INT IRT IST ITT

•IT AIT BIT CIT DIT FIT GIT HIT KIT LIT MIT NIT PIT RIT SIT UIT WIT ZIT

IU• IUM

I•U ICU IOU

•IU DIU LIU NIU PIU TIU

IV• IVA IVE IVO IVS IVY

I•V INV IRV ITV

•IV BIV CIV DIV LIV MIV RIV TIV VIV XIV ZIV

IW• IWO IWW

I•W IWW

•IX AIX BIX CIX DIX FIX KIX LIX MIX NIX PIX SIX XIX

I•Y ICY IFY IGY ITY IVY

•IY DIY

IZ• IZE

•IZ BIZ LIZ VIZ WIZ

JA• JAB JAG JAI JAL JAM JAN JAR JAS JAT JAV JAW JAY

J•B JAB JEB JIB JOB

JC• JCC JCD JCL JCS JCT

J•C JCC JEC JRC JSC JVC

J•D JCD JED JSD JUD

•JD SJD

JE• JEB JEC JED JER JET JEU JEW

J•E JOE

JF• JFK

J•F JIF

JG• JGS

J•G JAG JIG JOG JUG

JH• JHS JHU

JI• JIB JIF JIG JIM JIN

J•I JAI JOI

JK• JKP

J•K JFK

J•L JAL JCL JUL

J•M JAM JIM

•JM WJM

JN• JNT

J•N JAN JIN JON JPN JUN

JO• JOB JOE JOG JOI JON JOS JOT JOY

•JO OJO

JP• JPN JPS

J•P JKP

JR• JRC JRS

J•R JAR JER

•JR RJR

JS• JSC JSD

J•S JAS JCS JGS JHS JOS JPS JRS JUS

•JS DJS PJS VJS

J•T JAT JCT JET JNT JOT JUT

•JT OJT

JU• JUD JUG JUL JUN JUS JUT JUV

J•U JEU JHU

JV• JVC

J•V JAV JUV

•JV KJV

J•W JAW JEW

J•Y JAY JOY

KA• KAB KAF KAI KAM KAN KAS KAT KAW KAY

K•A KEA KHA KOA KRA KWA

•KA AKA EKA OKA SKA

K•B KAB KGB KOB

KC• KCL

K•C KFC

•KC AKC

K•D KED KID KOD KYD

•KD OKD

KE• KEA KED KEF KEG KEL KEN KER KET KEV KEW KEY

K•E KUE KYE

•KE EKE IKE OKE UKE XKE

KF• KFC

K•F KAF KEF KGF KIF

KG• KGB KGF KGM

K•G KEG

•KG BKG DKG EKG PKG

KH• KHA KHZ

K•H KPH KWH

KI• KID KIF KIL KIM KIN KIP KIR KIT KIX

K•I KAI KOI

•KI OKI SKI

KJ• KJV

KK• KKT

KL• KLM

K•L KCL KEL KIL KOL KUL

•KL DKL

K•M KAM KGM KIM KLM KUM

•KM DKM

KN• KNP KNT

K•N KAN KEN KIN KON KUN

KO• KOA KOB KOD KOI KOL KON KOO KOP KOR KOS

K•O KOO

•KO RKO TKO

KP• KPH KPS

K•P KIP KNP KOP KRP

•KP JKP

KR• KRA KRP

K•R KER KIR KOR KUR

K•S KAS KOS KPS KTS

•KS BKS MKS OKS PKS WKS

KT• KTS

K•T KAT KET KIT KKT KNT

•KT BKT KKT MKT PKT QKT SKT TKT

KU• KUE KUL KUM KUN KUR

•KU AKU PKU SKU

K•V KEV KJV

KW• KWA KWH

K•W KAW KEW

•KW CKW

K•X KIX

KY• KYD KYE

K•Y KAY KEY

•KY SKY

K•Z KHZ

LA• LAB LAC LAD LAE LAG LAH LAI LAM LAN LAO LAP LAR LAS LAT LAV LAW LAX LAY

L•A LEA LIA LOA

•LA ALA BLA ELA FLA ILA MLA OLA SLA

LB• LBJ LBO LBS

L•B LAB LEB LFB LHB LIB LLB LOB LUB

•LB ALB LLB

LC• LCD LCM LCS LCT

L•C LAC LDC LIC LOC LSC LTC LUC

•LC ALC PLC TLC

LD• LDC LDG LDL LDR LDS

L•D LAD LCD LED LHD LID LLD LSD LTD

•LD ALD CLD ELD FLD GLD LLD OLD SLD YLD

LE• LEA LEB LED LEE LEG LEI LEK LEM LEN LEO LER LES LET LEU LEV LEW LEX LEY

L•E LAE LEE LGE LIE LYE

•LE ALE BLE CLE ILE OLE ULE

LF• LFB LFS

•LF ALF ELF NLF PLF ULF VLF

LG• LGE LGS

L•G LAG LDG LEG LNG LOG LPG LUG

•LG ALG

LH• LHB LHD LHS

L•H LAH

LI• LIA LIB LIC LID LIE LII LIL LIM LIN LIP LIQ LIS LIT LIU LIV LIX LIZ

L•I LAI LEI LII LOI LSI LUI LVI LXI

•LI ALI CLI DLI ELI MLI XLI

L•J LBJ

L•K LEK

•LK ALK BLK CLK ELK ILK MLK

LL• LLB LLD LLM

L•L LDL LIL

•LL ALL ELL ILL

L•M LAM LCM LEM LIM LLM LOM LPM LUM

•LM ELM KLM LLM ULM

LN• LNG

L•N LAN LEN LIN LON LPN LYN

LO• LOA LOB LOC LOG LOI LOM LON LOO LOP LOQ LOS LOT LOU LOW LOX LOY

L•O LAO LBO LEO LOO LUO LYO

•LO DLO ELO FLO GLO ILO PLO SLO

LP• LPG LPM LPN LPS

L•P LAP LIP LOP

•LP ALP

L•Q LIQ LOQ

LR• LRS LRT

L•R LAR LDR LER LTR

•LR CLR DLR SLR

LS• LSC LSD LSI LST LSU

L•S LAS LBS LCS LDS LES LFS LGS LHS LIS LOS LPS LRS LTS LYS

•LS ALS BLS CLS DLS ELS ILS MLS PLS RLS WLS XLS

LT• LTC LTD LTR LTS

L•T LAT LCT LET LIT LOT LRT LST

•LT ALT BLT ULT

LU• LUB LUC LUG LUI LUM LUO LUV LUX LUZ

L•U LEU LIU LOU LSU

•LU BLU CLU FLU PLU ULU

LV• LVI

L•V LAV LEV LIV LUV LWV LXV

•LV CLV DLV MLV XLV

LW• LWV

L•W LAW LEW LOW

•LW MLW

LX• LXI LXV LXX

L•X LAX LEX LIX LOX LUX LXX

•LX CLX DLX MLX

LY• LYE LYN LYO LYS

L•Y LAY LEY LOY

•LY ALY BLY ELY FLY PLY SLY

L•Z LIZ LUZ

MA• MAA MAB MAC MAD MAE MAG MAH MAI MAJ MAL MAN MAO MAP MAR MAS MAT MAV MAW MAX MAY

M•A MAA MBA MCA MEA MFA MIA MLA MOA MPA MTA

•MA AMA CMA DMA GMA SMA UMA YMA

MB• MBA MBD MBE

M•B MAB MIB MOB

•MB AMB EMB FMB OMB

MC• MCA MCC MCD MCF MCG MCI MCL MCM MCP MCQ MCS MCV MCX

M•C MAC MCC MDC MHC MIC MMC MOC MSC MVC MXC MYC

•MC AMC FMC GMC MMC QMC

MD• MDC MDI MDL MDR MDS MDT MDV MDX

M•D MAD MBD MCD MED MFD MGD MID MMD MOD MUD MXD

•MD CMD DMD MMD VMD

ME• MEA MED MEG MEL MEM MEN MEO MER MES MET MEV MEW MEX

M•E MAE MBE MME MOE MPE MRE

•ME AME BME EME MME UME

MF• MFA MFD MFG MFH MFR

M•F MCF MMF

•MF AMF EMF HMF IMF MMF

MG• MGD MGM MGR MGS MGT

M•G MAG MCG MEG MFG MIG MPG MSG MTG MUG

•MG EMG PMG QMG

MH• MHC MHO MHW MHZ

M•H MAH MFH MPH

MI• MIA MIB MIC MID MIG MII MIL MIM MIN MIO MIP MIR MIS MIT MIV MIX

M•I MAI MCI MDI MII MLI MMI MOI MRI MVI MXI

•MI AMI BMI CMI EMI MMI NMI OMI TMI VMI

M•J MAJ

•MJ TMJ

MK• MKS MKT

M•K MLK

•MK PMK WMK

ML• MLA MLI MLK MLS MLV MLW MLX

M•L MAL MCL MDL MEL MIL MML MOL MSL MXL

•ML CML DML MML SML

MM• MMC MMD MME MMF MMI MML MMM MMV MMX

M•M MCM MEM MGM MIM MMM MOM MTM MUM

•MM HMM MMM

MN• MNO

M•N MAN MEN MIN MON MSN MTN MUN

•MN AMN RMN

MO• MOA MOB MOC MOD MOE MOI MOL MOM MON MOO MOP MOR MOS MOT MOW

M•O MAO MEO MHO MIO MNO MOO MYO

•MO AMO EMO HMO

MP• MPA MPE MPG MPH MPS

M•P MAP MCP MIP MOP MVP

•MP AMP EMP IMP UMP

M•Q MCQ

MR• MRE MRI MRS MRT MRX

M•R MAR MDR MER MFR MGR MIR MOR

•MR AMR BMR NMR

MS• MSC MSG MSL MSN MSS MST MSU MSW

M•S MAS MCS MDS MES MGS MIS MKS MLS MOS MPS MRS MSS MTS MUS

•MS AMS BMS CMS DMS EMS FMS GMS HMS OMS RMS SMS TMS

MT• MTA MTG MTM MTN MTS MTV

M•T MAT MDT MET MGT MIT MKT MOT MRT MST MUT

•MT AMT EMT GMT PMT

MU• MUD MUG MUM MUN MUS MUT MUX MUY

M•U MSU

•MU AMU EMU NMU SMU

MV• MVC MVI MVP

M•V MAV MCV MDV MEV MIV MLV MMV MTV MXV

•MV CMV DMV MMV

M•W MAW MEW MHW MLW MOW MSW

•MW BMW GMW UMW

MX• MXC MXD MXI MXL MXV MXX

M•X MAX MCX MDX MEX MIX MLX MMX MRX MUX MXX MYX

•MX BMX CMX MMX

MY• MYC MYO MYX

M•Y MAY MUY

•MY AMY

M•Z MHZ

•MZ DMZ

NA• NAB NAD NAE NAG NAH NAM NAN NAP NAS NAT NAV NAW NAY

N•A NBA NEA NIA NRA NSA

•NA ANA DNA ENA INA ONA RNA UNA

NB• NBA NBC NBE NBS NBW

N•B NAB NEB NIB NOB NUB

NC• NCC NCO NCR

N•C NBC NCC NEC NFC NGC NRC NSC NYC

•NC ANC ENC INC UNC

N•D NAD NED NFD NOD

•ND AND END IND RND UND

NE• NEA NEB NEC NED NEE NEF NEG NEH NEO NEP NER NES NET NEU NEV NEW NEY NEZ

N•E NAE NBE NEE NIE NNE NOE NYE

•NE ANE ENE INE NNE ONE UNE

NF• NFC NFD NFL

N•F NEF NGF NLF NSF

•NF INF

NG• NGC NGF

N•G NAG NEG NIG NOG

•NG ANG ENG ING LNG SNG UNG

NH• NHI NHL NHS

N•H NAH NEH NIH NOH NTH

•NH UNH

NI• NIA NIB NIE NIG NIH NIK NIL NIM NIN NIP NIS NIT NIU NIX

N•I NHI NMI NUI

•NI ANI ONI UNI

N•K NIK NPK

•NK INK

NL• NLF

N•L NFL NHL NIL NOL NUL

•NL ENL SNL

NM• NMI NMR NMU

N•M NAM NIM NOM NUM

NN• NNE NNW

N•N NAN NIN NON NUN

•NN ANN CNN INN TNN

NO• NOB NOD NOE NOG NOH NOL NOM NON NOP NOR NOS NOT NOV NOW NOX

N•O NCO NEO

•NO ANO CNO ENO INO MNO ONO SNO UNO

NP• NPK NPR NPS

N•P NAP NEP NIP NOP

•NP GNP KNP QNP RNP UNP

•NQ INQ UNQ

NR• NRA NRC

N•R NCR NER

NMR
NOR
NPR

•NR
DNR

NS•
NSA
NSC
NSF
NSW

N•S
NAS
NBS
NES
NHS
NIS
NOS
NPS
NUS

•NS
ANS
CNS
ENS
FNS
INS
ONS
PNS
RNS
TNS
UNS

NT•
NTH

N•T
NAT
NET
NIT
NOT
NUT
NWT

•NT
ANT
ENT
INT
JNT
KNT
ONT
TNT

NU•
NUB
NUI
NUL
NUM
NUN
NUS
NUT

N•U
NEU
NIU
NMU
NWU
NYU

•NU
ANU
GNU
UNU

N•V
NAV
NEV
NOV

•NV
ENV
INV

NW•
NWT
NWU

N•W
NAW
NBW
NEW
NNW
NOW
NSW

•NW
NNW
WNW

N•X
NIX
NOX
NYX

NY•
NYC
NYE
NYU
NYX

N•Y
NAY
NEY

•NY
ANY
SNY

N•Z
NEZ

OA•
OAF
OAK
OAP
OAR
OAS
OAT

O•A
OBA
OCA
ODA
OKA
OLA
ONA
OPA
ORA
OSA
OTA
OVA

•OA
BOA
COA
DOA
GOA
KOA
LOA
MOA
VOA
ZOA

OB•
OBA
OBE
OBI
OBJ
OBL
OBS
OBV

O•B
OMB
ORB
OSB
OTB

•OB
BOB
COB
DOB
FOB
GOB
HOB
JOB
KOB
LOB
MOB
NOB
POB
ROB
SOB
TOB
YOB

OC•
OCA
OCH
OCK
OCR
OCS
OCT

O•C
OHC
ORC
OTC

•OC
DOC
HOC
IOC
LOC
MOC
POC
ROC
SOC
VOC

OD•
ODA
ODD
ODE
ODO
ODS

O•D
ODD
OED
OID
OKD
OLD
OOD
ORD
OUD

•OD
BOD
COD
DOD
GOD
HOD
IOD
KOD
MOD
NOD
OOD
POD
ROD
SOD
TOD
YOD
ZOD

OE•
OED
OEM
OEN
OEO
OER

O•E
OBE
ODE
OKE
OLE
ONE
OPE
ORE
OSE
OTE
OWE

•OE
COE
DOE
EOE
FOE
HOE
JOE
MOE
NOE
POE
ROE
TOE
WOE
ZOE

OF•
OFF
OFT

O•F
OAF
OFF
OOF
OSF

•OF
EOF
HOF
OOF
SOF

O•G
ORG

•OG
BOG
COG
DOG
FOG
GOG
HOG
JOG
LOG
NOG
POG
SOG
TOG
ZOG

OH•
OHC
OHM
OHO
OHS

O•H
OCH
OOH
OSH

•OH
AOH
DOH
NOH
OOH

OI•
OID
OIK
OIL

O•I
OBI
OKI
OMI
ONI
OUI
OVI
OWI

•OI
DOI
HOI
JOI
KOI
LOI
MOI
POI
ROI
SOI
TOI

OJ•
OJO
OJT

O•J
OBJ

•OJ
DOJ

OK•
OKA
OKD
OKE
OKI
OKS

O•K
OAK
OCK
OIK
ORK

•OK
AOK
BOK
ROK
WOK

OL•
OLA
OLD
OLE

O•L
OBL
OIL
OWL
OYL

•OL
AOL
BOL
COL
DOL
FOL
HOL
KOL
MOL
NOL
POL
SOL
VOL

OM•
OMB
OMI
OMS

O•M
OEM
OHM
OPM

•OM
COM
DOM
EOM
HOM
LOM
MOM
NOM
POM
QOM
ROM
TOM
YOM

ON•
ONA
ONE
ONI
ONO
ONS
ONT

O•N
OEN
OON
OWN

•ON
BON
CON
DON
EON
FON
GON
HON
ION
JON
KON
LON
MON
NON
OON
RON
SON
TON
VON
WON
YON

OO•
OOD
OOF
OOH
OON
OOO
OOP
OOX

O•O
ODO
OEO
OHO
OJO
ONO
OOO
ORO
OSO
OTO
OVO
OXO
OYO
OZO

•OO
BOO
COO
DOO
FOO
GOO
HOO
KOO
LOO
MOO
OOO
ROO
SOO
TOO
WOO
XOO
YOO
ZOO

OP•
OPA
OPE
OPM
OPP
OPR
OPS
OPT

O•P
OAP
OOP
OPP

•OP
BOP
COP
DOP
FOP
GOP
HOP
KOP
LOP
MOP
NOP
OOP
POP
SOP
TOP

•OQ
COQ
LOQ

OR•
ORA
ORB
ORC
ORD
ORE
ORG
ORK
ORO
ORR
ORS
ORT
ORV
ORY

O•R
OAR
OCR
OER
OPR
ORR
OUR

•OR
AOR
BOR
COR
DOR
FOR
GOR
HOR
IOR
KOR
MOR
NOR
POR
SOR
TOR
XOR

OS•
OSA
OSB
OSE
OSF
OSH
OSO
OSS
OST
OSU

O•S
OAS
OBS
OCS
ODS
OHS
OKS
OMS
ONS
OPS
ORS
OSS
OTS
OUS
OZS

•OS
BOS
COS
DOS
EOS
HOS
IOS
JOS
KOS
LOS
MOS
NOS
POS
SOS
VOS

OT•
OTA
OTB
OTC
OTE
OTO
OTS
OTT

O•T
OAT
OCT
OFT
OJT
ONT
OPT
ORT
OST
OTT
OUT
OZT

•OT
BOT
COT
DOT
GOT
HOT
JOT
LOT
MOT
NOT
POT
ROT
SOT
TOT
WOT

OU•
OUD
OUI
OUR
OUS
OUT

O•U
OSU

•OU
DOU
FOU
IOU
LOU
SOU
VOU
YOU

OV•
OVA
OVI
OVO

O•V
OBV
ORV

•OV
GOV
HOV
NOV
POV
SOV
TOV

OW•
OWE
OWI
OWL
OWN

•OW
BOW
COW
DOW
HOW
LOW
MOW
NOW
POW
ROW
SOW
TOW
VOW
WOW
YOW

OX•
OXO
OXX
OXY

O•X
OOX
OXX

•OX
BOX
COX
FOX
LOX
NOX
OOX
POX
SOX
TOX
VOX
XOX

OY•
OYL
OYO

O•Y
ORY
OXY

•OY
BOY
COY
FOY
HOY
JOY
LOY
ROY
SOY
TOY

OZ•
OZO
OZS
OZT

•OZ
BOZ
COZ
DOZ
ROZ

PA•
PAC
PAD
PAG
PAH
PAK
PAL
PAM
PAN
PAO
PAP
PAR
PAS
PAT
PAU
PAW
PAX
PAY
PAZ

P•A
PBA
PEA
PGA
PIA
PSA
PTA
PWA
PYA

•PA
APA
CPA
EPA
FPA
GPA
IPA
MPA
OPA
SPA
TPA
WPA

PB•
PBA
PBJ
PBS
PBX

P•B
PCB
PDB
PHB
POB
PPB
PUB

•PB
APB
CPB
PPB

PC•
PCB
PCS
PCT
PCV

P•C
PAC
PEC
PFC
PIC
PLC
POC
PRC
PSC
PTC
PUC
PVC

•PC
APC
FPC
UPC

PD•
PDB
PDD
PDM
PDQ
PDT

P•D
PAD
PDD
PED
PFD
PHD
POD
PPD

•PD
BPD
CPD
GPD
PPD

PE•
PEA
PEC
PED
PEG
PEH
PEI
PEN
PEP
PER
PES
PET
PEU
PEW
PEZ

P•E
PIE
POE
PRE
PYE

•PE
APE
BPE
MPE
OPE

PF•
PFC
PFD
PFG

P•F
PLF
PRF
PSF

•PF
SPF

PG•
PGA
PGS

P•G
PAG
PEG
PFG
PIG
PKG
PMG
POG
PPG
PTG
PUG

•PG
LPG
MPG
PPG
RPG
ZPG

PH•
PHB
PHD
PHI
PHM
PHR
PHU

P•H
PAH
PEH
PPH
PTH

•PH
BPH
DPH
EPH
KPH
MPH
PPH

PI•
PIA
PIC
PIE
PIG
PIK
PIM
PIN
PIP
PIR
PIS
PIT
PIU
PIX

P•I
PEI
PHI
POI
PSI

•PI
API
BPI
CPI
DPI
EPI
RPI
UPI

PJ•
PJS

P•J
PBJ

PK•
PKG

PKS	**P•N**	PRP	PPS	RPT	**PY•**	**QM•**	**Q•T**	**RB•**	**RE•**	PRF	**RJ•**	**•RN**	**R•Q**	**RT•**	**R•W**
PKT	PAN	PUP	PRS	SPT	PYA	QMC	QAT	RBC	REA		RJR	ARN	REQ	RTE	RAW
PKU	PEN		PSS		PYE	QMG	QKT	RBI	REB	**RG•**		ERN	RFQ	RTS	ROW
	PIN	**•PP**	PTS	**PU•**	PYM				REC	RGB	**R•J**	PRN	RPQ	RTW	RTW
P•K	PRN	APP	PXS	PUB	PYR	**Q•M**	**QU•**	**R•B**	RED	RGS	RAJ	URN			
PAK	PUN	OPP		PUC	PYX	QOM	QUA	RAB	REE	RGT			**RR•**	**R•T**	**•RW**
PIK		PPP	**•PS**	PUG		QUM	QUE	REB	REF		**•RJ**	**RO•**	RRR	RAT	TRW
PMK	**•PN**	SPP	APS	PUL	**P•Y**		QUI	RFB	REG	**R•G**	DRJ	ROB	RRS	RCT	
	JPN		BPS	PUN	PAY	**QN•**	QUM	RGB	REI	RAG		ROC		RET	**R•X**
•PK	LPN	**P•Q**	CPS	PUP	PLY	QNP	QUO	RHB	REL	REG	**RK•**	ROD	**R•R**	RGT	RAX
NPK	UPN	PDQ	DPS	PUR	PRY			RIB	REM	RIG	RKO	ROE	RJR	RIT	REX
TPK	WPN		EPS	PUT		**Q•N**	**QV•**	ROB	REN	RPG		ROI	RRR	ROT	
		•PQ	FPS		**•PY**	QIN	QVC	RUB	REO	RUG	**R•K**	ROK	RUR	RPT	**•RX**
PL•	**PO•**	RPQ	GPS	**P•U**	SPY				REP		RFK	ROM		RST	MRX
PLC	POB		IPS	PAU		**QO•**	**Q•V**	**•RB**	REQ	**•RG**	ROK	RON	**•RR**	RUT	
PLF	POC	**PR•**	JPS	PEU	**P•Z**	QOM	QQV	ARB	RES	ARG		ROO	ARR		**RY•**
PLO	POD	PRC	KPS	PHU	PAZ			FRB	RET	ERG	**•RK**	ROT	BRR	**•RT**	RYA
PLS	POE	PRE	LPS	PIU	PEZ	**Q•O**	**•QV**	ORB	REV	FRG	ARK	ROW	ERR	ART	RYE
PLU	POG	PRF	MPS	PKU		QSO	QQV	URB	REX	ORG	DRK	ROY	GRR	CRT	
PLY	POI	PRN	NPS	PLU	**QA•**	QTO			REY		ERK	ROZ	IRR	FRT	**R•Y**
	POL	PRO	OPS		QAF	QUO	**Q•Y**	**RC•**		**RH•**	IRK		ORR	IRT	RAY
P•L	POM	PRP	PPS	**•PU**	QAT		QTY	RCA	**R•E**	RHB	ORK	**R•O**	RRR	LRT	REY
PAL	POP	PRS	QPS	APU		**QP•**		RCD	RAE	RHE		REO		MRT	ROY
POL	POR	PRY	RPS	CPU	**Q•A**	QPS	**RA•**	RCN	RDE	RHO	**RL•**	RHO	**RS•**	ORT	RWY
PTL	POS		SPS		QUA		RAB	RCP	REE		RLS	RIO	RSA		
PUL	POT	**P•R**	TPS	**PV•**		**Q•P**	RAD	RCS	RFE	**R•H**		RKO	RST	**RU•**	**•RY**
	POV	PAR	UPS	PVC	**QB•**	QBP	RAE	RCT	RHE	RAH	**R•L**	ROO	RSV	RUB	ARY
•PL	POW	PER	VPS	PVT	QBP	QNP	RAF		ROE		REL			RUD	CRY
APL	POX	PHR			QBS	QRP	RAG	**R•C**	RTE	**•RH**		**•RO**	**R•S**	RUE	DRY
BPL		PIR	**PT•**	**P•V**			RAH	RBC	RUE	HRH	**•RL**	ARO	RAS	RUG	ERY
CPL	**P•O**	POR	PTA	PCV	**Q•C**	**QQ•**	RAI	REC	RYE		FRL	BRO	RCS	RUM	FRY
DPL	PAO	PUR	PTC	POV	QMC	QQV	RAJ	RIC		**RI•**	URL	CRO	RDS	RUN	ORY
FPL	PLO	PWR	PTG	PPV	QVC		RAM	ROC	**•RE**	RIA		FRO	RES	RUR	PRY
	PPO	PYR	PTH	PTV		**•QQ**	RAN		ARE	RIB	**RM•**	GRO	RGS	RUS	TRY
PM•	PRO		PTL		**Q•D**	SQQ	RAP	**•RC**	BRE	RIC	RMN	IRO	RLS	RUT	WRY
PMG	PTO	**•PR**	PTO	**•PV**	QED		RAS	ARC	DRE	RID	RMS	ORO	RMS		
PMK		APR	PTS	PPV	QID	**QR•**	RAT	JRC	ERE	RIF		PRO	RNS	**R•U**	**R•Z**
PMT	**•PO**	CPR	PTT			QRP	RAU	NRC	GRE	RIG	**R•M**	SRO	RPS	RAU	ROZ
	APO	NPR	PTV	**PW•**	**QE•**	QRS	RAW	ORC	HRE	RIM	RAM	URO	RRS		
P•M	CPO	OPR		PWA	QED		RAX	PRC	IRE	RIN	REM		RTS	**•RU**	**•RZ**
PAM	FPO	SPR	**P•T**	PWR	QEF	**Q•R**	RAY		MRE	RIO	RIM	**RP•**	RUS	ARU	ERZ
PDM	GPO	TPR	PAT	PWT		QTR		**RD•**	ORE	RIP	ROM	RPG	RVS	CRU	
PHM	IPO		PCT		**Q•E**		**R•A**	RDA	PRE	RIT	RPM	RPI		DRU	**SA•**
PIM	PPO	**PS•**	PDT	**P•W**	QUE	**QS•**	RCA	RDD	TRE	RIV	RUM	RPM	**•RS**	TRU	SAB
POM		PSA	PET	PAW		QSO	RDA	RDE	URE			RPQ	ARS	URU	SAC
PPM	**PP•**	PSC	PIT	PEW	**Q•F**		REA	RDF		**R•I**	**•RM**	RPS	BRS		SAD
PYM	PPB	PSF	PKT	POW	QAF	**Q•S**	RIA	RDS	**RF•**	RAI	ARM	RPT	CRS	**RV•**	SAE
	PPD	PSI	PMT		QEF	QBS	RNA		RFB	RBI	VRM		DRS	RVS	SAG
•PM	PPG	PSS	POT	**•PW**		QPS	RSA	**R•D**	RFD	REI		**R•P**	ERS		SAL
CPM	PPH	PST	PPT	DPW	**Q•G**	QRS	RYA	RAD	RFE	RFI	**RN•**	RAP	FRS	**R•V**	SAM
FPM	PPM		PST		QMG	QTS		RCD	RFI	ROI	RNA	RCP	HRS	REV	SAN
GPM	PPO	**P•S**	PTT	**PX•**			**•RA**	RDD	RFK	RPI	RND	REP	IRS	RIV	SAO
IPM	PPP	PAS	PUT	PXS	**QI•**	**•QS**	ARA	RED	RFQ		RNP	RIP	JRS	RSV	SAP
LPM	PPS	PBS	PVT	PXT	QID	HQS	BRA	RFD		**•RI**	RNS	RNP	LRS		SAR
OPM	PPT	PCS	PWT		QIN	IQS	ERA	RID	**R•F**	ARI			MRS	**•RV**	SAS
PPM	PPV	PES	PXT	**P•X**			FRA	RND	RAF	CRI	**R•N**	**•RP**	ORS	BRV	SAT
RPM		PGS		PAX	**Q•I**	**QT•**	IRA	ROD	RDF	ERI	RAN	ARP	PRS	IRV	SAU
WPM	**P•P**	PIS	**•PT**	PBX	QUI	QTO	KRA	RUD	REF	FRI	RCN	KRP	QRS	ORV	SAW
	PAP	PJS	APT	PIX		QTR	NRA		RIF	MRI	REN	PRP	RRS		SAX
PN•	PEP	PKS	CPT	POX	**QK•**	QTS	ORA	**•RD**		SRI	RIN	QRP	SRS	**RW•**	SAY
PNS	PIP	PLS	DPT	PYX	QKT	QTY	SRA	ARD	**•RF**	TRI	RMN	TRP	TRS	RWY	
	POP	PNS	OPT				TRA	ORD	ARF	URI	RON		YRS		**S•A**
	PPP	POS	PPT					URD	GRF		RUN				SBA

SEA SHA SKA SLA SMA SPA SRA SSA STA SUA SWA

•SA ASA BSA CSA ESA GSA ISA NSA OSA PSA RSA SSA USA

SB• SBA SBE SBW

S•B SAB SIB SOB STB SUB

•SB OSB

SC• SCD SCH SCI SCM

S•C SAC SEC SFC SIC SOC SVC

•SC ASC BSC CSC DSC ESC JSC LSC MSC NSC PSC USC

SD• SDI SDS

S•D SAD SCD SGD SID SJD SLD SOD STD SUD SYD

•SD ESD JSD LSD

SE• SEA SEC SEE SEI SEL SEM SEN SEP SEQ SER SES SET SEW SEX SEZ

S•E SAE SBE SEE SHE SIE SSE STE SUE

•SE ASE ESE ISE OSE SSE TSE USE

SF• SFC SFO SFZ

S•F SHF SOF SPF SUF

•SF NSF OSF PSF

SG• SGD SGT

S•G SAG SIG SNG SOG STG SUG

•SG MSG

SH• SHA SHE SHF SHH SHO SHR SHT SHU SHY

S•H SCH SHH

•SH ASH BSH HSH ISH OSH USH

SI• SIB SIC SID SIE SIG SIL SIM SIN SIP SIR SIS SIT SIX

S•I SCI SDI SEI SKI SOI SRI SSI SUI

•SI ASI HSI LSI PSI SSI

SJ• SJD

SK• SKA SKI SKT SKU SKY

S•K STK SUK

•SK ASK CSK ESK TSK

SL• SLA SLD SLO SLR SLY

S•L SAL SEL SIL SML SNL SOL STL SYL

•SL ASL ESL ISL MSL YSL

SM• SMA SML SMS SMU

S•M SAM SCM SEM SIM STM SUM SYM

•SM DSM ISM USM

SN• SNG SNL SNO SNY

S•N SAN SEN SIN SON SSN STN SUN SYN

•SN ASN MSN SSN USN

SO• SOB SOC SOD SOF SOG SOI SOL SON SOO SOP SOR SOS SOT SOU SOV SOW SOX SOY

S•O SAO SFO SHO SLO SNO SOO SRO SUO

•SO ASO DSO ESO ISO OSO QSO USO

SP• SPA SPF SPP SPR SPS SPT SPY

S•P SAP SEP SIP SOP SPP STP SUP

•SP ASP ESP TSP USP

SQ• SQQ

S•Q SEQ SQQ SUQ

•SQ ESQ

SR• SRA SRI SRO SRS

S•R SAR SER SHR SIR SLR SOR SPR SSR STR SUR SVR SYR

•SR ASR ISR SSR TSR

SS• SSA SSE SSI SSN SSR SSS SST SSW

S•S SAS SDS SES SIS SMS SOS SPS SRS SSS STS SUS SYS

•SS ASS ESS ISS MSS OSS PSS SSS USS VSS

ST• STA STB STD STE STG STK STL STM STN STP STR STS STU STY

S•T SAT SET SGT SHT SIT SKT SOT SPT SST

•ST AST CST DST EST GST HST IST LST MST OST PST RST SST

SU• SUA SUB SUD SUE SUF SUG SUI SUK SUM SUN SUO SUP SUQ SUR SUS SUV

S•U SAU SHU SKU SMU SOU STU

•SU ASU ESU FSU LSU MSU OSU TSU USU

SV• SVC SVR

S•V SOV SUV

•SV ASV RSV

SW• SWA SWY

S•W SAW SBW SEW SOW SSW

•SW MSW NSW SSW USW WSW

S•X SAX SEX SIX SOX

•SX CSX USX

SY• SYD SYL SYM SYN SYR SYS

S•Y SAY SHY SKY SLY SNY SOY SPY STY SWY

S•Z SEZ SFZ

TA• TAB TAC TAD TAE TAG TAI TAJ TAL TAM TAN TAO TAP TAR TAS TAT TAU TAV TAW TAX TAY

T•A TBA TEA THA TIA TPA TRA TVA TWA

•TA ATA ETA MTA OTA PTA STA UTA

TB• TBA TBS

T•B TAB THB TOB TUB

•TB OTB STB

TC• TCU

T•C TAC TEC TIC TLC

•TC ETC FTC GTC LTC OTC PTC

TD• TDD TDS

T•D TAD TDD TED THD TID TOD

•TD ETD FTD GTD ITD LTD STD YTD

TE• TEA TEC TED TEE TEG TEH TEL TEM TEN TER TES TET TEX TEY

T•E TAE TEE THE TIE TOE TRE TSE TUE TYE

•TE ATE ETE GTE ITE OTE RTE STE UTE

TF• TFR

•TF ATF CTF

TG• TGV

T•G TAG TEG TOG TUG TVG

•TG MTG PTG STG

TH• THA THB THD THE THI THM THO THU THX THY

T•H TEH

•TH BTH ETH FTH NTH PTH

TI• TIA TIC TID TIE TIL TIM TIN TIO TIP TIS TIU TIV

T•I TAI THI TMI TOI TRI TUI TWI

T•J TAJ TMJ

TK• TKO TKT

T•K TPK TSK

•TK STK

TL• TLC

T•L TAL TEL TIL

•TL ATL BTL PTL STL

TM• TMI TMJ TMS

T•M TAM TEM THM TIM TOM TUM TVM

•TM ATM MTM STM

TN• TNN TNS TNT

T•N TAN TEN TIN TNN TON TUN

•TN CTN MTN STN

TO• TOB TOD TOE TOG TOI TOM TON TOO TOP TOR TOT TOV TOW TOX TOY

T•O TAO THO TIO TKO TOO TWO

•TO CTO ETO GTO ITO OTO PTO QTO UTO

TP• TPA TPK TPR TPS

T•P TAP TIP TOP TRP TSP TUP TVP TWP TYP

•TP ATP DTP GTP STP

TR• TRA TRE TRI TRP TRS TRU TRW TRY

T•R TAR TER TFR TOR TPR TSR TYR

•TR CTR LTR QTR STR VTR

TS• TSE TSK TSP TSR TSU

T•S TAS TBS TDS TES TIS TMS TNS TPS TRS TVS

•TS BTS CTS DTS ETS HTS ITS KTS LTS MTS OTS PTS QTS RTS STS UTS WTS

TT• TTY

T•T TAT TET TKT TNT TOT TUT

•TT ATT GTT ITT OTT PTT

TU• TUB TUE TUG TUI TUM TUN TUP TUT TUX TUZ

T•U TAU TCU THU TIU TRU TSU TZU

•TU BTU STU UTU

TV• TVA TVG TVM TVP TVS

TVY

T•V
TAV
TGV
TIV
TOV

•TV
ATV
ETV
ITV
MTV
PTV

TW•
TWA
TWI
TWO
TWP
TWX

T•W
TAW
TOW
TRW

•TW
BTW
RTW

T•X
TAX
TEX
THX
TOX
TUX
TWX

TY•
TYE
TYP
TYR

T•Y
TAY
TEY
THY
TOY
TRY
TTY
TVY

•TY
ITY
QTY
STY
TTY

TZ•
TZU

T•Z
TUZ

UA•
UAE
UAL
UAR
UAW

U•A
UFA
UMA
UNA
USA
UTA
UVA

•UA
HUA
QUA
SUA

UB•
UBE
UBI

U•B
URB

•UB
BUB
CUB
DUB
FUB
HUB
LUB
NUB
PUB
RUB
SUB
TUB

U•C
UDC
UNC
UPC
USC

•UC
AUC
BUC
DUC
LUC
PUC

UD•
UDC
UDO

U•D
UND
URD

•UD
AUD
BUD
CUD
DUD
HUD
JUD
MUD
OUD
RUD
SUD
WUD

UE•
UEY

U•E
UAE
UBE
UKE
ULE
UME
UNE
URE
USE
UTE

•UE
CUE
DUE
HUE
KUE
QUE
RUE
SUE
TUE
YUE

UF•
UFA
UFO
UFT
UFW

U•F
UHF
ULF

•UF
AUF
SUF

UG•
UGH
UGO

U•G
UNG

•UG
AUG
BUG
DUG
FUG
HUG
JUG
LUG
MUG
PUG
RUG
SUG
TUG
VUG
ZUG

UH•
UHF

U•H
UGH
UNH
USH

•UH
DUH
HUH

UI•
UIT

U•I
UBI
UNI
UPI
URI
UZI

•UI
CUI
GUI
HUI
LUI
NUI
OUI
QUI
SUI
TUI

UK•
UKE

•UK
AUK
SUK
YUK

UL•
ULE
ULF
ULM
ULT
ULU

U•L
UAL
URL

•UL
BUL
CUL
FUL
JUL
KUL
NUL
PUL
VUL
YUL

UM•
UMA
UME
UMP
UMW

U•M
ULM
USM

•UM
AUM
BUM
CUM
DUM
FUM
GUM
HUM
IUM
KUM
LUM
MUM
NUM
QUM
RUM
SUM
TUM
YUM

UN•
UNA
UNC
UND
UNE
UNG
UNH
UNI
UNO
UNP
UNQ
UNS
UNU

U•N
UPN
URN
USN

•UN
BUN
DUN
FUN
GUN
HUN
JUN
KUN
MUN
NUN
PUN
RUN
SUN
TUN

U•O
UDO
UFO
UGO
UNO
URO
USO
UTO

•UO
DUO
LUO
QUO
SUO

UP•
UPC
UPI
UPN
UPS

U•P
UMP
UNP
USP

•UP
CUP
DUP
HUP
PUP
SUP
TUP
YUP

U•Q
UNQ

•UQ
SUQ

UR•
URB
URD
URE
URI
URL
URN
URO
URU

U•R
UAR

•UR
BUR
CUR
EUR
FUR
GUR
HUR
KUR
OUR
PUR
RUR
SUR

US•
USA
USC
USE
USH
USM
USN
USO
USP
USS
USU
USW
USX

U•S
UNS
UPS
USS
UTS

•US
AUS
BUS
GUS
HUS
JUS
MUS
NUS
OUS
RUS
SUS

UT•
UTA
UTE
UTO
UTS
UTU

U•T
UFT
UIT
ULT

•UT
AUT
BUT
CUT
FUT
GUT
HUT
JUT
MUT
NUT
OUT
PUT
RUT
TUT

U•U
ULU
UNU
URU
USU
UTU

UV•
UVA

•UV
GUV
JUV
LUV
SUV

U•W
UAW
UFW
UMW
USW

U•X
USX

•UX
AUX
DUX
LUX
MUX
TUX

U•Y
UEY

•UY
BUY
GUY
MUY

UZ•
UZI

•UZ
DUZ
LUZ
TUZ

VA•
VAC
VAE
VAL
VAN
VAR
VAS
VAT
VAV
VAY

V•A
VGA
VIA
VOA

•VA
AVA
EVA
IVA
OVA
TVA
UVA
WVA

VB•
VBS

VC•
VCR

V•C
VAC
VIC
VOC

•VC
AVC
JVC
MVC
PVC
QVC
SVC

VD•
VDT
VDU

V•D
VFD
VMD

•VD
BVD
DVD

VE•
VEE
VEG
VEH
VEL
VEN
VER
VET
VEX

V•E
VAE
VEE
VIE

•VE
AVE
EVE
IVE

VF•
VFD
VFW

V•F
VHF
VLF

VG•
VGA

V•G
VEG
VUG

•VG
AVG
EVG
TVG

VH•
VHF
VHS

V•H
VEH

VI•
VIA
VIC
VIE
VII
VIL
VIM
VIN
VIP
VIR
VIS
VIV
VIZ

V•I
VII
VMI

•VI
AVI
CVI
DVI
LVI
MVI
OVI
XVI

VJ•
VJS

VL•
VLF

V•L
VAL
VEL
VIL
VOL
VUL

VM•
VMD
VMI

V•M
VIM
VRM

•VM
BVM
DVM
TVM

V•N
VAN
VEN
VIN
VON

•VN
AVN

VO•
VOA
VOC
VOL
VON
VOS
VOU
VOW
VOX

•VO
AVO
IVO
OVO

VP•
VPS

V•P
VIP

•VP
MVP
TVP

VR•
VRM

V•R
VAR
VCR
VER
VIR
VTR

•VR
SVR

VS•
VSS

V•S
VAS
VBS
VHS
VIS
VJS
VOS
VPS
VSS
VWS

•VS
AVS
CVS
EVS
IVS
RVS
TVS

VT•
VTR

V•T
VAT
VDT
VET

•VT
BVT
PVT

VU•
VUG
VUL

V•U
VDU
VOU

V•V
VAV
VIV

VW•
VWS

V•W
VFW
VOW

•VW
GVW

V•X
VEX
VOX

V•Y
VAY

•VY
HVY
IVY
TVY

V•Z
VIZ

WA•
WAB
WAC
WAD
WAF
WAG
WAH
WAL
WAN
WAR
WAS
WAT
WAW
WAX
WAY

W•A
WBA
WHA
WPA
WVA

•WA
KWA
PWA
SWA
TWA

WB•
WBA
WBC
WBN
WBS

W•B
WAB
WEB

WC•
WCS

W•C
WAC
WBC

WD•
WDS

W•D
WAD
WED
WUD

•WD
FWD

WE•
WEB
WED
WEE
WEI
WEN
WES
WET

W•E
WEE
WIE
WOE
WYE

•WE
AWE
EWE
OWE

W•F
WAF
WHF
WWF

•WF
WWF

W•G
WAG
WIG

WH•
WHA
WHF
WHH
WHO
WHR
WHS
WHY

W•H
WAH
WHH

•WH
KWH

WI•
WIE
WIG
WIL
WIM
WIN
WIP
WIS
WIT
WIZ

W•I
WEI
WWI

•WI
BWI
OWI
TWI
WWI

WJ•
WJM

WK•
WKS

W•K
WMK
WOK

•WK
AWK

WL•
WLS

W•L
WAL
WIL

•WL
AWL
OWL

WM•
WMK

W•M
WIM
WJM
WPM

•WM
CWM
HWM

WN•
WNW

W•N
WAN
WBN
WEN
WIN
WON
WPN

•WN
AWN
OWN

WO•
WOE
WOK
WON
WOO
WOT
WOW

W•O
WHO
WOO
WYO

•WO
CWO
IWO
TWO

WP•
WPA
WPM
WPN

W•P
WIP

•WP
CWP
TWP

WR•
WRY

W•R
WAR
WHR

•WR
PWR

WS•
WSW

W•S
WAS
WBS
WCS
WDS
WES
WHS
WIS
WKS
WLS
WTS

•WS
VWS

WT•	WWW	•XC	XVI	X•O	XV•	•XY	YD•	RYE	SYL	YOW	SYR	NYU	ZE•	Z•L	•ZS
WTS		CXC	XXI	XOO	XVI	OXY	YDS	TYE	XYL		TYR		ZEA	ZAL	OZS
	•WW	DXC		XXO				WYE		Y•O		Y•W	ZED		
W•T	IWW	EXC	•XI		X•V	YA•	Y•D		YM•	YAO	YS•	YAW	ZEE	Z•M	Z•T
WAT	WWW	MXC	CXI	•XO	XCV	YAD	YAD	Y•G	YMA	YEO	YSL	YEW	ZEG	ZYM	ZIT
WET			DXI	EXO	XIV	YAG	YLD	YAG		YOO		YOW	ZEN		
WIT	W•X	X•D	LXI	OXO	XLV	YAH	YOD		Y•M		Y•S		ZEV	Z•N	•ZT
WOT	WAX	XED	MXI	XXO	XXV	YAK	YTD	•YG	YAM	•YO	YAS	•YX		ZEN	OZT
			XXI			YAM		ZYG	YOM	BYO	YBS	MYX	Z•E		
•WT	•WX	•XD		•XP	•XV	YAO	•YD		YUM	CYO	YDS	NYX	ZEE	ZO•	ZU•
CWT	TWX	MXD	XK•	EXP	CXV	YAP	CYD	Y•H		LYO	YES	PYX	ZOE	ZOA	ZUG
DWT			XKE		DXV	YAR	HYD	YAH	•YM	MYO	YRS			ZOD	
NWT	WY•	XE•		•XQ	LXV	YAS	KYD		GYM	OYO		Y•Y	•ZE	ZOE	•ZU
PWT	WYE	XED	XL•	BXQ	MXV	YAT	SYD	•YH	PYM	WYO	•YS	YAY	IZE	ZOG	TZU
	WYO	XEN	XLI		XXV	YAW		AYH	SYM		DYS			ZOO	
WU•		XER	XLS	X•R		YAY	YE•		ZYM	Y•P	LYS	Y•Z	Z•F		Z•V
WUD	W•Y	XES	XLV	XER	XX•	YAZ	YEA	YI•		YAP	SYS	YAZ	ZIF	Z•O	ZEV
	WAY			XOR	XXI		YEN	YIN	Y•N	YEP				ZOO	ZIV
•WU	WHY	X•E	X•L		XXO	Y•A	YEO	YIP	YEN	YIP	YT•	•YZ	Z•G		
NWU	WRY	XKE	XYL	•XR	XXV	YEA	YEP		YIN	YUP	YTD	BYZ	ZAG	•ZO	Z•X
				EXR	XXX	YMA	YER	•YI	YON				ZEG	AZO	ZAX
WV•	•WY	•XE	•XL				YES	FYI		•YP	Y•T	ZA•	ZIG	OZO	
WVA	HWY	AXE	AXL	X•S	X•X	•YA	YET		•YN	GYP	YAT	ZAG	ZOG		ZY•
	RWY	EXE	CXL	XES	XIX	PYA	YEW	Y•K	AYN	HYP	YET	ZAL	ZPG	ZP•	ZYG
•WV	SWY		DXL	XIS	XOX	RYA		YAK	DYN	TYP		ZAP	ZUG	ZPG	ZYM
LWV		XI•	MXL	XLS	XXX		Y•E	YUK	FYN		YU•	ZAS	ZYG		
	W•Z	XIA				YB•	YUE		GYN	YR•	YUE	ZAX		Z•P	ZZ•
WW•	WIZ	XII	X•N	•XS	•XX	YBS		YL•	LYN	YRS	YUK		ZI•	ZAP	ZZZ
WWF		XIN	XEN	PXS	CXX		•YE	YLD	SYN		YUL	Z•A	ZIA	ZIP	
WWI	XA•	XIS	XIN		DXX	Y•B	AYE			Y•R	YUM	ZEA	ZIF		Z•Z
WWW	XAT	XIV		X•T	LXX	YOB	BYE	Y•L	YO•	YAR	YUP	ZIA	ZIG	•ZR	ZZZ
		XIX	XO•	XAT	MXX		DYE	YSL	YOB	YER		ZOA	ZIP	EZR	
W•W	X•A		XOO		OXX	•YC	EYE	YUL	YOD		Y•U		ZIT		•ZZ
WAW	XIA	X•I	XOR	•XT	XXX	MYC	KYE		YOM	•YR	YOU	Z•D	ZIV	Z•S	ZZZ
WNW		XCI	XOX	EXT		NYC	LYE	•YL	YON	AYR		ZED		ZAS	
WOW	XC•	XII		PXT	XY•		NYE	CYL	YOO	CYR	•YU	ZOD	•ZI		
WSW	XCI	XLI			XYL		PYE	OYL	YOU	PYR	BYU		UZI		
	XCV														

4

AA••
AAHS
AARE
AARP

A•A•
ABAS
ACAD
ADAH
ADAK
ADAM
ADAR
AFAR
AGAR
AGAS
AHAB
AHAZ
AJAR
AJAX
AKAN
ALAE
ALAI
ALAN
ALAR
ALAS
AMAH
AMAS
AMAT
ANAS
ANAT
ARAB
ARAD
ARAK
ARAL
ARAM
ARAN
ARAS
ASAP
AVAL
AVAR
AWAY
AYAH
AZAN

A••A
ABBA
ACEA
ACTA
AFTA
AGFA
AGHA
AGRA
AGUA
AIDA
AIEA
AIWA
ALBA
ALDA
ALEA
ALFA
ALGA
ALIA
ALKA
ALLA
ALMA
ALTA
ALVA
AMIA
ANKA
ANNA
ANOA
ANSA
ANTA
ANYA
ANZA
APIA
AQUA
ARCA
AREA
ARIA
ARMA
ARPA
ARRA
ASEA
ASIA
ASTA
ATKA
ATRA
ATTA
AULA
AURA
AVIA
AYLA

•AA•
BAAL
BAAS
CAAN
HAAG
MAAM
MAAR
MAAS
MAAT
PAAR
SAAB
SAAR
TAAL
VAAL
WAAC
WAAF
WAAL

•A•A
BABA
BAJA
BAMA
BARA
BAYA
CAMA
CANA
CAPA
CARA
CASA
CATA
CAVA
DADA
DAMA
DANA
DATA
FALA
FATA
FAVA
GABA
GAEA
GAGA
GAIA
GALA
GAMA
GAPA
GAYA
GAZA
HAHA
HAMA
HANA
IANA
JADA
JAVA
KAKA
KAMA
KANA
KARA
KAVA
LALA
LAMA
LANA
LARA
LAVA
MAIA
MAJA
MALA
MAMA
MANA
MARA
MATA
MAYA
NADA
NAHA
NANA
NAPA
NARA
NASA
PABA
PACA
PAPA
PARA
PASA
RAGA
RAJA
RAMA
RANA
RAPA
RARA
RASA
RATA
SABA
SADA
SAGA
SALA
SANA
SARA
SAVA
TADA
TAKA
TALA
TAMA
TANA
TAPA
TARA
TATA
TAXA
VACA
VARA
VAYA
WAKA
WAWA
YADA
YAMA
YANA
ZAMA

••AA
MPAA
NCAA
NOAA

AB••
ABAS
ABBA
ABBE
ABBR
ABBS
ABBY
ABCS
ABED
ABEL
ABER
ABET
ABIB
ABIE
ABLE
ABLY
ABMS
ABOU
ABRI
ABUT
ABYE
ABYS

A•B•
ABBA
ABBE
ABBR
ABBS
ABBY
ALBA
ALBI
ALBS
AMBI
AMBO
AMBS
APBS
ARBS
AUBE

A••B
ABIB
AHAB
ARAB

•AB•
BABA
BABE
BABI
BABS
BABU
BABY
CABS
DABO
DABS
GABA
GABE
GABO
GABS
GABY
HABE
JABS
KABS
LABS
NABE
NABS
PABA
RABE
RABI
RABS
SABA
SABE
SABU
TABI
TABS
TABU
WABS

•A•B
BARB
CARB
DAUB
GARB
IAMB
JAMB
KALB
LAMB
SAAB

••AB
AHAB
ARAB
BLAB
CRAB
DRAB
FLAB
GRAB
JOAB
MOAB
SAAB
SCAB
SLAB
STAB
SWAB

AC••
ACAD
ACCS
ACCT
ACDC
ACEA
ACED
ACER
ACES
ACET
ACEY
ACHE
ACHT
ACHY
ACID
ACIS
ACLU
ACME
ACNE
ACRE
ACRO
ACTA
ACTE
ACTG
ACTH
ACTI
ACTS
ACTV
ACYL

A•C•
ABCS
ACCS
ACCT
ADCS
AGCY
ANCE
ANCY
ARCA
ARCH
ARCO
ARCS
ASCH
ASCI
ASCO

A••C
ACDC
ALEC
AMIC
APOC
AVEC

•AC•
BACH
BACK
BACS
BACT
CACO
DACE
EACH
FACE
FACP
FACS
FACT
HACK
JACK
LACE
LACK
LACS
LACT
LACY
MACC
MACE
MACH
MACK
MACS
MACY
NACL
PACA
PACE
PACK
PACS
PACT
RACE
RACK
RACY
SACK
SACS
TACH
TACK
TACO
TACT
VACA
VACS
WACE
WACK
WACO
WACS
YACK
ZACK

•A•C
BANC
BASC
CALC
CANC
DARC
LAIC
MACC
MARC
MASC
NARC
PARC
TALC
WAAC

••AC
BOAC
BRAC
GMAC
HUAC
WAAC
WRAC

AD••
ADAH
ADAK
ADAM
ADAR
ADCS
ADDN
ADDS
ADDY
ADEN
ADES
ADIN
ADIT
ADJS
ADJT
ADMS
ADOS
ADUE
ADVT
ADZE

A•D•
ACDC
ADDN
ADDS
ADDY
AIDA
AIDE
AIDS
ALDA
ALDO
ANDS
ANDY
AUDE
AUDI
AVDP

A••D
ABED
ACAD
ACED
ACID
AGED
AMID
APED
ARAD
ARID
AULD
AVID
AWED
AXED

•AD•
BADE
CADE
CADI
CADS
DADA
DADE
DADO
DADS
EADS
FADE
FADO
FADS
GADS
HADE
HADJ
JADA
JADE
LADD
LADE
LADS
LADY
MADD
MADE
NADA
NADH
NADP
PADS
QADI
RADM
RADS
SADA
SADD
SADE
SADI
SADR
TADA
TADS
VADE
VADM
WADE
WADI
WADS
YADA

•A•D
BALD
BAND
BARD
BAUD
CARD
DARD
DASD
FAHD
GAUD
HAND
HARD
LADD
LAID
LAND
LAPD
LARD
LAUD
MADD
MAID
MAUD
NARD
NASD
PAID
PARD
PATD
QAID
RAID
RAND
SADD
SAID
SAND
SARD

SAUD
VAUD
WALD
WAND
WARD
YARD
YAZD

••AD
ACAD
ARAD
BEAD
BRAD
CHAD
CLAD
DEAD
DUAD
DYAD
EGAD
FUAD
GLAD
GOAD
GRAD
HEAD
HOAD
JOAD
LEAD
LOAD
MEAD
OBAD
ORAD
QUAD
READ
ROAD
SCAD
SHAD
SPAD
TOAD
WOAD

AE••
AEON
AERO
AERY

A•E•
ABED
ABEL
ABER
ABET
ACEA
ACED
ACER
ACES
ACET
ACEY
ADEN
ADES
AGED
AGEE
AGER
AGES
AHEM
AIEA
AKEE
ALEA
ALEC
ALEE
ALEF
ALEP
ALES
ALEX
AMEN
AMER
AMES
AMEX
ANEW
APED
APER
APES
APEX
AREA
AREO
ARES
ASEA
ATEN
ATES
AUEL
AUER
AVEC
AVER
AVES
AWED
AWES
AXED
AXEL
AXER
AXES
AYER
AYES

A••E
AARE
ABBE
ABIE
ABLE
ABYE
ACHE
ACME
ACNE
ACRE
ACTE
ADUE
ADZE
AGEE
AGUE
AIDE
AIME
AIRE
AKEE
ALAE
ALEE
ALLE
ALOE
ALTE
AMIE
ANCE
ANGE
ANNE
ANTE
AONE
APSE
ARME
ARNE
ARTE
ASHE
AUBE
AUDE
AUGE
AUNE
AXLE
AYME

•AE•
BAER
BAEZ
CAEN
GAEA
GAEL
JAEL
JAEN
KAEL
NAES
TAEL

•A•E
AARE
BABE
BADE
BAKE
BALE
BANE
BARE
BASE
BATE
CADE
CAFE
CAGE
CAKE
CALE
CAME
CANE
CAPE
CARE
CASE
CATE
CAVE
DACE
DADE
DALE
DAME
DANE
DARE
DATE
DAVE
DAZE
EASE
EAVE
FACE
FADE
FAKE
FAME
FANE
FARE
FATE
FAVE
FAYE
FAZE
GABE
GAGE
GALE
GAME
GAPE
GARE
GATE
GAVE
GAYE
GAZE
HABE
HADE
HAKE
HALE
HAME
HARE
HATE
HAVE
HAZE
JADE
JAKE
JANE
JAPE
JAYE
KALE
KAME
KANE
KATE
KAYE
LACE
LADE
LAKE
LAME
LANE
LASE
LATE
LAUE
LAVE
LAZE
MACE
MADE
MAGE
MAKE
MALE
MAME
MANE
MARE
MATE
MAZE
NABE
NAME
NAPE
NATE
NAVE
PACE
PAGE
PALE
PANE
PARE
PASE
PATE
PAVE
RABE
RACE
RAGE
RAKE
RARE
RASE
RATE
RAVE
RAYE
RAZE
SABE
SADE
SAFE
SAGE
SAKE
SALE
SAME
SANE
SASE
SATE
SAVE
SAXE
TAKE
TALE
TAME
TANE
TAPE
TARE
TATE
VADE
VALE
VANE
VASE
WACE
WADE
WAGE
WAKE
WALE
WANE
WARE
WAVE
YALE
YARE
ZANE

••AE
ALAE
BLAE
BRAE
FRAE
IDAE
IRAE

AF••
AFAR
AFGH
AFRO
AFTA
AFTS

A•F•
AGFA
ALFA
AMFM

A••F
ALEF
ALIF
ASIF
ASOF

•AF•
BAFF
CAFE
DAFF
DAFT
GAFF
HAFT
KAFS
OAFS
QAFS
RAFF
RAFT
SAFE
SAFR
TAFT
WAFS
WAFT

•A•F
BAFF
CALF
CANF
DAFF
GAFF
HALF
NAIF
RAFF
TAIF
WAAF
WAIF
ZARF

••AF
DEAF
GRAF
LEAF
LOAF
OLAF
PIAF
RCAF
USAF
WAAF
WRAF

AG••
AGAR
AGAS
AGCY
AGED
AGEE
AGER
AGES
AGFA
AGHA
AGIN
AGIO
AGLY
AGNI
AGOG
AGON
AGRA
AGRI
AGRO
AGTS
AGUA
AGUE

A•G•
AFGH
ALGA
ALGO
ALGY
ANGE
ANGL
ARGO
ARGY
AUGE
AVGS

A••G
ACTG
AGOG

•AG•
BAGS
CAGE
CAGY
DAGS
GAGA
GAGE
GAGS
HAGI
HAGS
IAGO
JAGR
JAGS
LAGO
LAGS
MAGE
MAGI
MAGS
NAGS
NAGY
PAGE
PAGO
RAGA
RAGE
RAGG
RAGS
RAGU
SAGA
SAGE
SAGO
SAGS
TAGS
WAGE
WAGS
YAGI
ZAGS

•A•G
BANG
DANG
DAWG
FANG
GANG
HAAG
HAIG
HANG
HAWG
LANG
MARG
NANG
PANG
RAGG
RANG
SANG
TANG
VANG
WANG
YANG

••AG
BRAG
CRAG
DIAG
DRAG
FLAG
HAAG
PEAG
QUAG
SHAG
SLAG
SNAG
STAG
SWAG

AH••
AHAB
AHAZ
AHEM
AHOY
AHSO

A•H•
AAHS
ACHE
ACHT
ACHY
AGHA
ASHE
ASHY

A••H
ACTH
ADAH
AFGH
ALPH
AMAH
ANKH
ANTH
ARCH
ASCH
AUTH
AYAH

•AH•
AAHS
BAHN
BAHR
BAHS
BAHT
CAHN
DAHL
DAHS
FAHD
FAHR
HAHA
HAHN
HAHS
JAHR
KAHN
LAHR
MAHI
NAHA
OAHU
PAHO
PAHS
SAHL
TAHR
WAHL
ZAHN

•A•H
BACH
BASH
BATH
CASH
CATH
DASH
EACH
FATH
GASH
GATH
HASH
HATH
KAPH
LAKH
LASH
LATH
MACH
MASH
MATH
NADH
NAOH
NASH
OATH
PASH
PATH
RASH
RATH
SASH
TACH
TANH
WASH

••AH
ADAH
AMAH
AYAH
BLAH
ETAH
EVAH
LEAH
NOAH
OPAH
PTAH
SHAH
UTAH
YEAH

AI••
AIDA
AIDE
AIDS
AIEA
AILS
AIME
AIMS
AINS
AINT
AINU
AIRE
AIRS
AIRT
AIRY
AITS
AIWA

A•I•
ABIB
ABIE
ACID
ACIS
ADIN
ADIT
AGIN
AGIO
AKIM
AKIN
ALIA
ALIF
ALII
ALIS
ALIT
AMIA
AMIC
AMID
AMIE
AMIN
AMIR
AMIS
ANIL
ANIM
ANIS
APIA
APIS
ARIA
ARID
ARIL
ARIZ
ASIA
ASIF
ASIR
ASIS
ATIT
AVIA
AVID
AVIS
AVIV
AXIL
AXIS
AYIN
AZIZ

A••I
ABRI
ACTI
AGNI
AGRI
ALAI
ALBI
ALII
ALTI
ALUI
AMBI
AMOI
ANSI
ANTI
AOKI
AQUI
ASCI
ASTI
ATLI
ATOI
ATRI
AUDI
AURI

•AI•
BAIL
BAIN
BAIO
BAIT
CAIN
DAIN
DAIS
FAIL
FAIN
FAIR
FAIT
GAIA
GAIL
GAIN
GAIT
HAIG
HAIK
HAIL
HAIM
HAIR
JAIL
JAIN
KAIN
LAIC
LAID
LAIN
LAIR
LAIT
MAIA
MAID
MAIL
MAIN
MAIS
NAIF
NAIL
PAID
PAIL
PAIN
PAIR
PAIX
QAID
RAID
RAIL
RAIN
SAID
SAIL
SAIS
TAIF
TAIL
TAIN
TAIT
TAIZ
VAIL
VAIN
VAIR
WAIF
WAIL
WAIN
WAIT

•A•I
BABI
BALI
BANI
BARI
CADI
CALI
CAMI
DALI
DARI
HAGI
HAJI
HAPI
HARI
IASI
KAKI
KALI
KAMI
LARI
MAGI
MAHI
MALI
MARI
MAUI
MAXI
MAYI
NAOI
PALI
PARI
QADI
RABI
RAKI
RAMI
RANI
RAVI
SADI
SAKI
SARI
TABI
TALI
TATI
TAVI
TAXI
WADI
YAGI

••AI
ALAI
BNAI
ESAI
KWAI
OJAI
QUAI
THAI
VRAI

AJ••
AJAR
AJAX

A•J•
ADJS
ADJT

•AJ•
BAJA
HAJI
HAJJ
MAJA
RAJA
TAJS

•A•J
HADJ
HAJJ

AK••
AKAN
AKEE
AKIM
AKIN

A•K•
ALKA
ANKA
ANKH
AOKI
ARKS
ASKS
ATKA
AUKS

A••K
ADAK
AMOK
ARAK

•AK•
BAKE
BAKR
BAKU
CAKE
CAKY
FAKE
HAKE
JAKE
KAKA
KAKI
LAKE
LAKH
LAKY
MAKE
MAKO
OAKS
RAKE
RAKI
RAKU
SAKE
SAKI
SAKS
TAKA
TAKE
WAKA
WAKE
YAKS

•A•K
BACK
BALK
BANK
BARK
BASK
CALK
CARK
CASK
DANK
DARK
FALK
GAWK
HACK
HAIK

HANK	ALEE	APPL	PALL	NATL	WAAL	ATUM	**•A•M**	ANDS	AVON	PANS	LAIN	SCAN	ALDO
HARK	ALEF	ARAL	PALM	PAIL	WEAL	AXUM	BALM	ANDY	AXON	PANT	LAWN	SEAN	ALGO
HAWK	ALEP	ARIL	PALO	PALL	ZEAL		BARM	ANEW	AYIN	RANA	MAIN	SHAN	ALLO
JACK	ALES	ARYL	PALP	PARL		**•AM•**	BAUM	ANGE	AZAN	RAND	MANN	SPAN	ALPO
LACK	ALEX	AUEL	PALS	PAUL	**AM••**	BAMA	CALM	ANGL		RANG	PAIN	STAN	ALSO
LANK	ALFA	AVAL	PALY	PAWL	AMAH	BAMS	FARM	ANIL	**•AN•**	RANI	PAWN	SWAN	ALTO
LARK	ALGA	AWOL	RALL	RAIL	AMAS	CAMA	GAUM	ANIM	BANC	RANK	RAIN	THAN	AMBO
MACK	ALGO	AXEL	SALA	RALL	AMAT	CAME	HAIM	ANIS	BAND	RANT	SAWN	TMAN	AMMO
MARK	ALGY	AXIL	SALE	RAUL	AMBI	CAMI	HALM	ANKA	BANE	SANA	TAIN	TUAN	ANNO
MASK	ALIA	AZUL	SALK	SAHL	AMBO	CAMO	HAMM	ANKH	BANG	SAND	TARN	ULAN	APSO
NARK	ALIF		SALP	SAIL	AMBS	CAMP	HARM	ANNA	BANI	SANE	VAIN	WEAN	AQUO
PACK	ALII	**•AL•**	SALS	SAML	AMEN	CAMS	MAAM	ANNE	BANK	SANG	WAIN	XIAN	ARCO
PARK	ALIS	BALD	SALT	SAUL	AMER	DAMA	MALM	ANNO	BANS	SANK	WARN	YEAN	AREO
RACK	ALIT	BALE	TALA	TAAL	AMES	DAME	PALM	ANOA	CANA	SANO	YARN	YUAN	ARGO
RANK	ALKA	BALI	TALC	TAEL	AMEX	DAMN	RADM	ANON	CANC	SANS	YAWN		ARLO
RASK	ALLA	BALK	TALE	TAIL	AMFM	DAMP	TAMM	ANSA	CANE	SANT	ZAHN	**AO••**	ARNO
SACK	ALLE	BALL	TALI	TALL	AMIA	DAMS	VADM	ANSI	CANF	TANA		AOKI	AROO
SALK	ALLO	BALM	TALK	VAAL	AMIC	FAME	WARM	ANTA	CANS	TANE	**••AN**	AONE	ASCO
SANK	ALLS	BALT	TALL	VAIL	AMID	GAMA		ANTE	CANT	TANG	AKAN	AOUT	ASTO
SARK	ALLY	CALC	VALE	WAAL	AMIE	GAME	**••AM**	ANTH	CANY	TANH	ALAN		ATMO
SASK	ALMA	CALE	WALD	WAHL	AMIN	GAMO	ADAM	ANTI	DANA	TANK	ARAN	**A•O•**	ATNO
SAUK	ALMS	CALF	WALE	WAIL	AMIR	GAMP	ARAM	ANTS	DANE	TANS	AZAN	ABOU	ATTO
TACK	ALOE	CALI	WALK	WALL	AMIS	GAMS	BEAM	ANYA	DANG	VANE	BEAN	ADOS	AUTO
TALK	ALOU	CALK	WALL	YALL	AMMO	GAMY	BRAM	ANZA	DANK	VANG	BRAN	AEON	
TANK	ALOW	CALL	WALT	YAWL	AMNT	HAMA	CHAM		DANL	VANS	CAAN	AGOG	**•AO•**
TASK	ALPH	CALM	YALE		AMOI	HAME	CLAM	**A•N•**	DANO	WAND	CHAN	AGON	GAOL
WACK	ALPO	CALS	YALL	**••AL**	AMOK	HAMM	CRAM	ACNE	DANU	WANE	CLAN	AHOY	HAOS
WALK	ALPS	CALX	YALU	ARAL	AMON	HAMS	DIAM	AGNI	FANE	WANG	CYAN	ALOE	KAON
YACK	ALSO	DALE	ZALS	AVAL	AMOR	IAMB	DRAM	AINS	FANG	WANT	DEAN	ALOU	LAOS
YANK	ALTA	DALI		BAAL	AMOS	JAMB	EDAM	AINT	FANS	WANY	DIAN	ALOW	NAOH
ZACK	ALTE	DALS	**•A•L**	BEAL	AMOY	JAMS	ELAM	AINU	GANG	YANA	DWAN	AMOI	NAOI
	ALTI	DALY	BAAL	COAL	AMPS	KAMA	EXAM	AMNT	GANN	YANG	DYAN	AMOK	NAOS
••AK	ALTO	FALA	BAIL	DEAL	AMTS	KAME	FLAM	ANNA	HANA	YANK	EBAN	AMON	TAOS
ADAK	ALTS	FALK	BALL	DHAL	AMUR	KAMI	FOAM	ANNE	HAND	ZANE	EGAN	AMOR	YAOS
ARAK	ALUI	FALL	BAWL	DIAL	AMYL	LAMA	FRAM	ANNO	HANG	ZANY	ELAN	AMOS	
BEAK	ALUM	FALX	CALL	DUAL		LAMB	GLAM	AONE	HANK		EVAN	AMOY	**•A•O**
BIAK	ALVA	GALA	CARL	EGAL	**A•M•**	LAME	GRAM	ARNE	HANS	**•A•N**	FLAN	ANOA	BAIO
DOAK		GALE	CAUL	ELAL	ABMS	LAMP	GUAM	ARNO	IANA	BAHN	FRAN	ANON	BARO
DYAK	**A•L•**	GALL	DAHL	ETAL	ACME	LAMS	IMAM	ATNO	JANE	BAIN	GIAN	APOC	CACO
FLAK	ABLE	GALS	DANL	FOAL	ADMS	LAMY	LIAM	AUNE	KANA	BARN	GMAN	APOS	CAMO
ISAK	ABLY	GALV	EARL	GOAL	AIME	MAMA	LOAM	AUNT	KANE	CAAN	GRAN	ARON	CAPO
LEAK	ACLU	HALE	FAIL	HEAL	AIMS	MAME	MAAM	AWNS	KANO	CAEN	GUAN	AROO	CARO
NDAK	AGLY	HALF	FALL	ICAL	ALMA	NAME	NOAM		KANS	CAHN	IBAN	ASOF	CATO
PEAK	AILS	HALL	GAEL	ITAL	ALMS	RAMA	PRAM	**A••N**	KANT	CAIN	IMAN	ASOR	DABO
SDAK	ALLA	HALM	GAIL	KCAL	AMMO	RAMI	QUAM	ADDN	LANA	CAPN	IRAN	ATOI	DADO
SOAK	ALLE	HALO	GALL	LEAL	ARMA	RAMP	REAM	ADEN	LAND	DAIN	IVAN	ATOM	DANO
SWAK	ALLO	HALS	GAOL	MEAL	ARME	RAMS	ROAM	ADIN	LANE	DAMN	JEAN	ATON	DAYO
TEAK	ALLS	HALT	GAUL	NEAL	ARMS	SAME	SCAM	AEON	LANG	DARN	JOAN	ATOP	FADO
WEAK	ALLY	KALB	HAIL	OPAL	ARMY	SAML	SEAM	AGIN	LANK	DAWN	JUAN	ATOR	FARO
	ARLO	KALE	HALL	ORAL	ATMO	SAMO	SHAM	AGON	MANA	EARN	KEAN	AVON	FASO
AL••	ATLI	KALI	HAUL	OVAL	ATMS	SAMP	SIAM	AKAN	MANE	FAIN	KHAN	AVOS	GABO
ALAE	AULA	KALT	JAEL	PEAL	AYME	TAMA	SLAM	AKIN	MANN	FAUN	KOAN	AVOW	GAMO
ALAI	AULD	LALA	JAIL	REAL		TAME	SPAM	ALAN	MANO	FAWN	KWAN	AWOL	GATO
ALAN	AWLS	LALO	JARL	RIAL	**A••M**	TAMM	SWAM	AMEN	MANS	GAIN	LEAN	AXON	HALO
ALAR	AXLE	MALA	KAEL	RYAL	ADAM	TAMO	TEAM	AMIN	MANU	GANN	LOAN	AZOV	IAGO
ALAS	AYLA	MALE	KARL	SEAL	AHEM	TAMP	TRAM	AMON	MANX	GARN	MEAN		JATO
ALBA		MALI	MAIL	SIAL	AKIM	TAMS	WHAM	ANON	MANY	HAHN	MOAN	**A••O**	KANO
ALBI	**A••L**	MALL	MALL	TAAL	ALUM	VAMP		ARAN	NANA	HAWN	OLAN	ACRO	KARO
ALBS	ABEL	MALM	MARL	TEAL	AMFM	YAMA	**AN••**	ARON	NANG	JAEN	OMAN	AERO	KATO
ALDA	ACYL	MALO	MAUL	URAL	ANIM	YAMS	ANAS	ASSN	NANO	JAIN	ORAN	AFRO	KAYO
ALDO	AMYL	MALT	NACL	VAAL	ARAM	ZAMA	ANAT	ATEN	NANU	KAHN	PLAN	AGIO	LAGO
ALEA	ANGL	PALE	NAIL	VEAL	ARUM		ANCE	ATON	PANE	KAIN	ROAN	AGRO	LALO
ALEC	ANIL	PALI	NASL	VIAL	ATOM		ANCY	ATTN	PANG	KAON	RYAN	AHSO	MAKO

MALO
MANO
MAYO
MAZO
NANO
NASO
NATO
PAGO
PAHO
PALO
PASO
PAVO
SAGO
SAMO
SANO
SATO
TACO
TAMO
TARO
TAXO
WACO

••AO
BIAO
CIAO
ISAO
JIAO
LIAO
PIAO

AP••
APBS
APED
APER
APES
APEX
APIA
APIS
APOC
APOS
APPL
APPS
APPT
APRS
APSE
APSO
APTS

A•P•
ALPH
ALPO
ALPS
AMPS
APPL
APPS
APPT
ARPA
ASPS

A••P
AARP
ALEP
ASAP
ATOP
AVDP

•AP•
BAPS
BAPT
CAPA
CAPE
CAPN
CAPO
CAPP
CAPS
CAPT
DAPS
GAPA
GAPE
GAPS
HAPI
HAPS
JAPE
KAPH
LAPD
LAPP
LAPS
MAPS
NAPA
NAPE
NAPS
PAPA
PAPP
RAPA
RAPP
RAPS
RAPT
SAPS
TAPA
TAPE
TAPS
YAPP
YAPS
ZAPS

•A•P
AARP
CAMP
CAPP
CARP
DAMP
EARP
FACP
GAMP
GARP
GASP
GAWP
HARP
HASP
LAMP
LAPP
NADP
PALP
PAPP
RAMP
RAPP
RASP
SALP
SAMP
TAMP
TARP
VAMP
WARP
WASP
YAPP
YAWP

••AP
ASAP
CHAP
CLAP
EVAP
FLAP
FRAP
HEAP
KNAP
LEAP
NEAP
REAP
SLAP
SNAP
SOAP
SWAP
TRAP
WRAP

AQ••
AQUA
AQUI
AQUO

•AQ•
FAQS

••AQ
IRAQ
SHAQ

AR••
ARAB
ARAD
ARAK
ARAL
ARAM
ARAN
ARAS
ARBS
ARCA
ARCH
ARCO
ARCS
AREA
AREO
ARES
ARGO
ARGY
ARIA
ARID
ARIL
ARIZ
ARKS
ARLO
ARMA
ARME
ARMS
ARMY
ARNE
ARNO
ARON
AROO
ARPA
ARRA
ARRS
ARTE
ARTS
ARTY
ARUM
ARYL

A•R•
AARE
AARP
ABRI
ACRE
ACRO
AERO
AERY
AFRO
AGRA
AGRI
AGRO
AIRE
AIRS
AIRT
AIRY
APRS
ARRA
ARRS
ATRA
ATRI
AURA
AURI
AWRY

A••R
ABBR
ABER
ACER
ADAR
AFAR
AGAR
AGER
AJAR
ALAR
AMER
AMIR
AMOR
AMUR
APER
ASIR
ASOR
ASTR
ATOR
AUER
AVAR
AVER
AXER
AYER
AZUR

•AR•
AARE
AARP
BARA
BARB
BARD
BARE
BARI
BARK
BARM
BARN
BARO
BARR
BARS
BART
CARA
CARB
CARD
CARE
CARK
CARL
CARO
CARP
CARR
CARS
CART
CARY
DARC
DARD
DARE
DARI
DARK
DARN
DART
EARL
EARN
EARP
EARS
FARE
FARM
FARO
FARR
FARS
GARB
GARE
GARN
GARP
GARR
GARS
GARY
HARD
HARE
HARI
HARK
HARM
HARP
HART
HARZ
JARL
JARS
KARA
KARL
KARO
KART
LARA
LARD
LARI
LARK
LARS
MARA
MARC
MARE
MARG
MARI
MARK
MARL
MARS
MART
MARU
MARV
MARX
MARY
NARA
NARC
NARD
NARK
NARY
NARZ
OARS
PARA
PARC
PARD
PARE
PARI
PARK
PARL
PARR
PARS
PART
RARA
RARE
SARA
SARD
SARI
SARK
TARA
TARE
TARN
TARO
TARP
TARS
TART
VARA
VARY
WARD
WARE
WARM
WARN
WARP
WARS
WART
WARY
YARD
YARE
YARN
ZARF

•A•R
BAER
BAHR
BAKR
BARR
CARR
FAHR
FAIR
FARR
GARR
GAUR
HAIR
JAGR
JAHR
LAHR
LAIR
MAAR
MAWR
PAAR
PAIR
PARR
SAAR
SADR
SAFR
SAUR
TAHR
VAIR

••AR
ADAR
AFAR
AGAR
AJAR
ALAR
AVAR
BEAR
BOAR
CHAR
CLAR
CZAR
DEAR
FEAR
GEAR
GNAR
GUAR
HEAR
HOAR
IBAR
ISAR
ITAR
IYAR
IZAR
JBAR
KNAR
LBAR
LEAR
LIAR
MAAR
NEAR
OMAR
OSAR
PAAR
PEAR
PHAR
QUAR
REAR
ROAR
SAAR
SCAR
SEAR
SOAR
SPAR
STAR
TBAR
TEAR
THAR
TSAR
TZAR
USAR
WEAR
YEAR
ZBAR
ZOAR

AS••
ASAP
ASCH
ASCI
ASCO
ASEA
ASHE
ASHY
ASIA
ASIF
ASIR
ASIS
ASKS
ASOF
ASOR
ASPS
ASSN
ASST
ASTA
ASTI
ASTO
ASTR

A•S•
AHSO
ALSO
ANSA
ANSI
APSE
APSO
ASSN
ASST
AUST

A••S
AAHS
ABAS
ABBS
ABCS
ABMS
ABYS
ACCS
ACES
ACIS
ACTS
ADCS
ADDS
ADES
ADJS
ADMS
ADOS
AFTS
AGAS
AGES
AGTS
AIDS
AILS
AIMS
AINS
AIRS
AITS
ALAS
ALBS
ALES
ALIS
ALLS
ALMS
ALPS
ALTS
AMAS
AMBS
AMES
AMIS
AMOS
AMPS
AMTS
ANAS
ANDS
ANIS
ANTS
APBS
APES
APIS
APOS
APPS
APRS
APTS
ARAS
ARBS
ARCS
ARES
ARKS
ARMS
ARRS
ARTS
ASIS
ASKS
ASPS
ATES
ATMS
ATTS
ATVS
AUKS
AVES
AVGS
AVIS
AVOS
AWES
AWLS
AWNS
AXES
AXIS
AYES

•AS•
BASC
BASE
BASH
BASK
BASS
BAST
CASA
CASE
CASH
CASK
CASS
CAST
DASD
DASH
EASE
EAST
EASY
FASO
FAST
GASH
GASP
GAST
HASH
HASP
HAST
IASI
LASE
LASH
LASS
LAST
MASC
MASH
MASK
MASS
MAST
NASA
NASD
NASH
NASL
NASO
NAST
OAST
PASA
PASE
PASH
PASO
PASS
PAST
RASA
RASE
RASH
RASK
RASP
SASE
SASH
SASK
SASS
TASK
TASS
VASE
VAST
WASH
WASP
WAST
ZASU

•A•S
AAHS
BAAS
BABS
BACS
BAGS
BAHS
BAMS
BANS
BAPS
BARS
BASS
BATS
BAYS
CABS
CADS
CALS
CAMS
CANS
CAPS
CARS
CASS
CATS
CAUS
CAVS
CAWS
CAYS
DABS
DADS
DAGS
DAHS
DAIS
DALS
DAMS
DAPS
DATS
DAWS
DAYS
EADS
EARS
EATS
FACS
FADS
FANS
FAQS
FARS
FATS
FAYS
GABS
GADS
GAGS
GALS
GAMS
GAPS
GARS
GATS
HAGS
HAHS
HALS
HAMS
HANS
HAOS
HAPS
HATS
HAUS
HAWS
HAYS
JABS
JAGS
JAMS
JARS
JAWS
JAYS
KABS
KAFS
KANS
LABS
LACS
LADS
LAGS
LAMS
LAOS
LAPS
LARS
LASS
LATS
LAVS
LAWS
LAYS
MAAS
MACS
MAGS
MAIS
MANS
MAPS
MARS
MASS
MATS
MAVS
MAWS
MAYS
NABS
NAES
NAGS
NAOS
NAPS
NAYS
OAFS
OAKS
OARS
OATS
PACS
PADS
PAHS
PALS
PANS
PARS
PASS
PATS
PAWS
PAYS
QAFS
QATS
RABS
RADS
RAGS
RAMS
RAPS
RATS
RAYS
SACS
SAGS
SAIS
SAKS
SALS
SANS
SAPS
SASS
SATS
SAWS
SAYS
TABS
TADS
TAGS
TAJS
TAMS
TANS
TAOS
TAPS
TARS
TASS
TATS
TAUS
TAWS
VACS
VANS
VATS
VAVS
WABS
WACS
WADS
WAFS
WAGS
WARS
WATS
WAWS
WAYS
XATS
YAKS
YAMS
YAOS
YAPS
YAWS
ZAGS
ZALS
ZAPS

••AS
ABAS
AGAS
ALAS
AMAS
ANAS
ARAS
BAAS
BEAS
BIAS
BLAS
BOAS
BRAS
CHAS
CPAS
DIAS
ERAS
ESAS
ETAS
EYAS
FRAS
GRAS
IRAS
KEAS
KHAS
LEAS
MAAS
MBAS
MEAS
MFAS
MOAS
OCAS
ODAS
PEAS
PTAS
RDAS
RIAS
RYAS
SEAS
SPAS
SRAS
STAS
TEAS
THAS
TIAS
TWAS
UPAS
XMAS
YEAS

AT••
ATEN
ATES
ATIT

ATKA ATLI ATMO ATMS ATNO ATOI ATOM ATON ATOP ATOR ATRA ATRI ATTA ATTN ATTO ATTS ATTU ATTY ATUM ATVS ATWT

A•T•
ACTA ACTE ACTG ACTH ACTI ACTS ACTV AFTA AFTS AGTS AITS ALTA ALTE ALTI ALTO ALTS AMTS ANTA ANTE ANTH ANTI ANTS APTS ARTE ARTS ARTY ASTA ASTI ASTO ASTR ATTA ATTN ATTO ATTS ATTU ATTY AUTH AUTO

A••T
ABET ABUT ACCT ACET ACHT ADIT ADJT ADVT AINT AIRT ALIT AMAT AMNT ANAT AOUT APPT ASST ATIT ATWT AUNT AUST

•AT•
BATE BATH BATS BATT CATA CATE CATH CATO CATS CATT CATV DATA DATE DATS EATS FATA FATE FATH FATS GATE GATH GATO GATS GATT HATE HATH HATS JATO KATE KATO KATY KATZ LATE LATH LATS MATA MATE MATH MATS MATT MATU NATE NATL NATO OATH OATS OATY PATD PATE PATH PATS QATS RATA RATE RATH RATS RATT SATE SATO SATS TATA TATE TATI TATS VATS VATU WATS WATT XATS

•A•T
BACT BAHT BAIT BALT BAPT BART BAST BATT CANT CAPT CART CAST CATT DAFT DART EAST FACT FAIT FAST FAUT GAIT GAST GATT HAFT HALT HART HAST HAUT KALT KANT KART LACT LAIT LAST MAAT MALT MART MAST MATT NAST NAUT OAST PACT PANT PART PAST PAYT RAFT RANT RAPT RATT SALT SANT TACT TAFT TAIT TART TAUT VAST WAFT WAIT WALT WANT WART WAST WATT

••AT
AMAT ANAT BEAT BLAT BOAT BRAT CHAT COAT CRAT DRAT ERAT ETAT FEAT FIAT FLAT FRAT GHAT GMAT GNAT GOAT HEAT KHAT KYAT LIAT LSAT MAAT MCAT MEAT MOAT NEAT NLAT PEAT PHAT PLAT PSAT SCAT SEAT SKAT SLAT SPAT STAT SWAT THAT TOAT WHAT

AU••
AUBE AUDE AUDI AUEL AUER AUGE AUKS AULA AULD AUNE AUNT AURA AURI AUST AUTH AUTO

A•U•
ABUT ADUE AGUA AGUE ALUI ALUM AMUR AOUT AQUA AQUI AQUO ARUM ATUM AXUM AZUL AZUR

A••U
ABOU ACLU AINU ALOU ATTU

•AU•
BAUD BAUM CAUL CAUS DAUB EAUX FAUN FAUT FAUX GAUD GAUL GAUM GAUR HAUL HAUS HAUT LAUD LAUE MAUD MAUI MAUL NAUT PAUL RAUL SAUD SAUK SAUL SAUR TAUS TAUT VAUD VAUX

•A•U
BABU BAKU DANU MANU MARU MATU NANU OAHU RAGU RAKU SABU TABU VATU YALU ZASU

••AU
BEAU BLAU ESAU FRAU GRAU LUAU PEAU UNAU VEAU

AV••
AVAL AVAR AVDP AVEC AVER AVES AVGS AVIA AVID AVIS AVIV AVON AVOS AVOW

A•V•
ADVT ALVA ATVS

A••V
ACTV AVIV AZOV

•AV•
CAVA CAVE CAVS CAVY DAVE DAVY EAVE FAVA FAVE GAVE HAVE JAVA KAVA LAVA LAVE LAVS MAVS NAVE NAVY PAVE PAVO RAVE RAVI SAVA SAVE TAVI VAVS WAVE WAVY

•A•V
CATV GALV MARV

••AV
FLAV OLAV OZAV SLAV

AW••
AWAY AWED AWES AWLS AWNS AWOL AWRY

A•W•
AIWA ATWT

A••W
ALOW ANEW AVOW

•AW•
BAWL CAWS DAWG DAWN DAWS FAWN GAWK GAWP HAWG HAWK HAWN HAWS JAWS LAWN LAWS MAWR MAWS PAWL PAWN PAWS SAWN SAWS TAWS WAWA WAWS YAWL YAWN YAWP YAWS

••AW
BRAW CHAW CLAW CRAW DRAW FLAW GNAW SHAW SKAW SLAW THAW

AX••
AXED AXEL AXER AXES AXIL AXIS AXLE AXON AXUM

A••X
AJAX ALEX AMEX APEX

•AX•
MAXI SAXE TAXA TAXI TAXO WAXY

•A•X
CALX EAUX FALX FAUX MANX MARX PAIX VAUX

••AX
AJAX COAX EDAX FLAX HOAX PLAX SFAX TRAX

AY••
AYAH AYER AYES AYIN AYLA AYME

A•Y•
ABYE ABYS ACYL AMYL ANYA ARYL

A••Y
ABBY ABLY ACEY ACHY ADDY AERY AGCY AGLY AHOY AIRY ALGY ALLY AMOY ANCY ANDY ARGY ARMY ARTY ASHY ATTY AWAY AWRY

•AY•
BAYA BAYS CAYS DAYO DAYS FAYE FAYS GAYA GAYE HAYS JAYE JAYS KAYE KAYO LAYS MAYA MAYI MAYO MAYS NAYS PAYS PAYT RAYE RAYS SAYS VAYA WAYS

•A•Y
BABY CAGY CAKY CANY CARY CAVY DALY DAVY EASY GABY GAMY GARY HAZY KATY LACY LADY LAKY LAMY LAZY MACY MANY MARY MAZY NAGY NARY NAVY OATY PALY RACY VARY WANY WARY WAVY WAXY ZANY

••AY
AWAY BRAY CLAY CRAY DDAY DRAY FLAY FRAY GDAY GRAY ISAY ODAY OKAY OLAY PLAY PRAY QUAY SHAY SLAY SPAY STAY SWAY TRAY VDAY WRAY XRAY

AZ••
AZAN AZIZ AZOV AZUL AZUR

A•Z•
ADZE ANZA

A••Z
AHAZ ARIZ AZIZ

•AZ•
DAZE FAZE GAZA GAZE HAZE HAZY JAZZ LAZE LAZY MAZE MAZO MAZY RAZE RAZZ YAZD

•A•Z
BAEZ HARZ JAZZ KATZ NARZ RAZZ TAIZ

••AZ
AHAZ BOAZ BRAZ CHAZ DIAZ GRAZ

BA••
BAAL BAAS BABA BABE BABI BABS BABU BABY BACH BACK BACS BACT BADE BAER BAEZ BAFF BAGS BAHN BAHR BAHS BAHT BAIL BAIN BAIO BAIT BAJA BAKE BAKR BAKU BALD BALE BALI BALK BALL BALM BALT BAMA BAMS BANC BAND BANE BANG BANI BANK BANS BAPS BAPT BARA BARB BARD BARE BARI BARK BARM BARN BARO BARR BARS BART BASC BASE BASH BASK BASS BAST BATE BATH BATS BATT BAUD BAUM BAWL BAYA BAYS

B•A•
BAAL BAAS BEAD BEAK BEAL BEAM BEAN BEAR BEAS BEAT BEAU BIAK BIAO BIAS BLAB BLAE BLAH BLAS BLAT BLAU BNAI BOAC BOAR BOAS BOAT BOAZ BRAC BRAD BRAE BRAG BRAM BRAN BRAS BRAT BRAW BRAY BRAZ

B••A
BABA BAJA BAMA BARA BAYA BELA BEMA BETA BIWA BOCA BOLA BOMA BONA BORA BOTA BOVA BREA BUNA

•BA•
ABAS EBAN IBAN IBAR JBAR LBAR MBAS OBAD

TBAR
ZBAR

•B•A
ABBA
EBLA

••BA
ABBA
ALBA
BABA
CUBA
ELBA
GABA
ISBA
IZBA
JUBA
LUBA
PABA
REBA
SABA
TUBA
YUBA

BB••
BBLS
BBOY
BBQS

B•B•
BABA
BABE
BABI
BABS
BABU
BABY
BEBE
BIBB
BIBI
BIBL
BIBS
BOBS
BUBU

B••B
BARB
BEEB
BIBB
BLAB
BLEB
BLOB
BOMB
BOOB
BULB
BURB
BYOB

•BB•
ABBA
ABBE
ABBR
ABBS
ABBY
EBBS

•B•B
ABIB
DBIB

••BB
BIBB
COBB
GIBB
ROBB
TUBB
WEBB

B•C•
BACH
BACK
BACS
BACT
BECK
BICE
BICS
BOCA
BOCK
BUCK
BUCO
BUCS

B••C
BANC
BASC
BLOC
BMOC
BOAC
BOSC
BRAC
BRIC
BSEC

•BC•
ABCS

BD••
BDRM

B•D•
BADE
BEDE
BEDS
BIDE
BIDS
BLDG
BLDR
BODE
BODO
BODS
BODY
BUDD
BUDS
BVDS

B••D
BALD
BAND
BARD
BAUD
BEAD
BEND
BIGD
BIND
BIRD
BLED
BLVD
BOLD
BOND
BOYD
BRAD
BRED
BSED
BUDD
BUND
BYRD

•B•D
ABED
IBID
OBAD

••BD
STBD

BE••
BEAD
BEAK
BEAL
BEAM
BEAN
BEAR
BEAS
BEAT
BEAU
BEBE
BECK
BEDE
BEDS
BEEB
BEEF
BEEN
BEEP
BEER
BEES
BEET
BEGS
BEIN
BELA
BELG
BELL
BELO
BELS
BELT
BELY
BEMA
BEMS
BEND
BENE
BENG
BENI
BENT
BENU
BENZ
BERG
BERM
BERN
BERT
BESO
BESS
BEST
BETA
BETE
BETH
BETS
BETZ
BEVY
BEYS

B•E•
BAER
BAEZ
BEEB
BEEF
BEEN
BEEP
BEER
BEES
BEET
BIEL
BIEN
BLEB
BLED
BLEU
BLEW
BOER
BREA
BRED
BREE
BREL
BREN
BRER
BRET
BREV
BREW
BSEC
BSED
BYES

B••E
BABE
BADE
BAKE
BALE
BANE
BARE
BASE
BATE
BEBE
BEDE
BENE
BETE
BICE
BIDE
BIKE
BILE
BINE
BISE
BITE
BLAE
BLUE
BODE
BOLE
BONE
BORE
BOSE
BOWE
BPOE
BRAE
BREE
BRIE
BUTE
BYME
BYRE
BYTE

•BE•
ABED
ABEL
ABER
ABET
CBER
EBEN
IBET
IBEX
MBES
OBEY
UBER

•B•E
ABBE
ABIE
ABLE
ABYE
IBLE
OBIE
OBOE

••BE
ABBE
AUBE
BABE
BEBE
CUBE
ELBE
GABE
GIBE
GYBE
HABE
HEBE
JIBE
KOBE
LOBE
LUBE
NABE
NEBE
RABE
ROBE
RUBE
SABE
SEBE
TOBE
TUBE
URBE
VIBE

B•F•
BAFF
BIFF
BOFF
BUFF

B••F
BAFF
BEEF
BIFF
BOFF
BUFF
BUMF

B•G•
BAGS
BEGS
BIGD
BOGS
BOGY
BUGS

B••G
BANG
BELG
BENG
BERG
BING
BIOG
BKPG
BLDG
BONG
BORG
BRAG
BRIG
BULG
BUNG
BURG
BYNG

B•H•
BAHN
BAHR
BAHS
BAHT
BOHM
BOHR
BUHL
BUHR

B••H
BACH
BASH
BATH
BETH
BLAH
BOSH
BOTH
BUSH

••BH
COBH

BI••
BIAK
BIAO
BIAS
BIBB
BIBI
BIBL
BIBS
BICE
BICS
BIDE
BIDS
BIEL
BIEN
BIFF
BIGD
BIKE
BIKO
BILE
BILK
BILL
BIND
BINE
BING
BINS
BIOG
BIOL
BION
BIOS
BIRD
BIRK
BIRL
BIRR
BISE
BISK
BITE
BITS
BITT
BIWA

B•I•
BAIL
BAIN
BAIO
BAIT
BEIN
BLIN
BLIP
BLIT
BOIL
BOIS
BRIC
BRIE
BRIG
BRIM
BRIO
BRIT
BRIX

B••I
BABI
BALI
BANI
BARI
BENI
BIBI
BNAI
BONI
BURI

•BI•
ABIB
ABIE
DBIB
IBID
IBIS
OBIE
OBIS
OBIT
RBIS

•B•I
ABRI

••BI
ALBI
AMBI
BABI
BIBI
DEBI
GOBI
ORBI
RABI
TABI
URBI

B•J•
BAJA

••BJ
SUBJ

BK••
BKPG
BKPR

B•K•
BAKE
BAKR
BAKU
BIKE
BIKO

B••K
BACK
BALK
BANK
BARK
BASK
BEAK
BECK
BIAK
BILK
BIRK
BISK
BOCK
BONK
BOOK
BORK
BOSK
BUCK
BULK
BUNK
BUSK

••BK
HDBK

BL••
BLAB
BLAE
BLAH
BLAS
BLAT
BLAU
BLDG
BLDR
BLEB
BLED
BLEU
BLEW
BLIN
BLIP
BLIT
BLOB
BLOC
BLOT
BLOW
BLTS
BLUE
BLUM
BLUR
BLVD

B•L•
BALD
BALE
BALI
BALK
BALL
BALM
BALT
BBLS
BELA
BELG
BELL
BELO
BELS
BELT
BELY
BILE
BILK
BILL
BOLA
BOLD
BOLE
BOLL
BOLO
BOLT
BULB
BULG
BULK
BULL

B••L
BAAL
BAIL
BALL
BAWL
BEAL
BELL
BIBL
BIEL
BILL
BIOL
BIRL
BOIL
BOLL
BOWL
BREL
BUHL
BULL
BURL

•BL•
ABLE
ABLY
BBLS
EBLA
IBLE

•B•L
ABEL
OBOL

••BL
BIBL
PUBL

BM••
BMOC
BMUS
BMWS

B•M•
BAMA
BAMS
BEMA
BEMS
BOMA
BOMB
BOMP
BOMU
BSMT
BUMF
BUMP
BUMS
BYME

B••M
BALM
BARM
BAUM
BDRM
BEAM
BERM
BLUM
BOHM
BOOM
BRAM
BRIM
BROM

•BM•
ABMS

••BM
ICBM
IRBM
SLBM

BN••
BNAI

B•N•
BANC
BAND
BANE
BANG
BANI
BANK
BANS
BEND
BENE
BENG
BENI
BENT
BENU
BENZ
BIND
BINE
BING
BINS
BONA
BOND
BONE
BONG
BONI
BONK
BONN
BONO
BONY
BRNO
BUNA
BUND
BUNG
BUNK
BUNS
BUNT
BYNG

B••N
BAHN
BAIN
BARN
BEAN
BEEN
BEIN
BERN
BIEN
BION
BLIN
BONN
BOON
BORN
BOSN
BRAN
BREN
BRYN
BUON
BURN

•B•N
EBAN
EBEN
EBON
IBAN

••BN
ISBN
NEBN
NWBN

BO••
BOAC
BOAR
BOAS
BOAT
BOAZ
BOBS
BOCA
BOCK
BODE
BODO
BODS
BODY
BOER
BOFF
BOGS
BOGY
BOHM
BOHR
BOIL
BOIS
BOLA
BOLD
BOLE
BOLL
BOLO
BOLT
BOMA
BOMB
BOMP
BOMU
BONA
BOND
BONE
BONG
BONI
BONK
BONN
BONO
BONY
BOOB
BOOK
BOOM
BOON
BOOP
BOOR
BOOS
BOOT
BOPP
BOPS
BORA
BORE
BORG
BORK
BORN
BORO
BORS
BORT
BOSC
BOSE
BOSH
BOSK
BOSN
BOSS
BOTA
BOTH
BOTS
BOTT
BOUT
BOVA
BOWE
BOWL
BOWS
BOXY
BOYD
BOYO
BOYS
BOYZ
BOZO

B•O•
BBOY
BIOG
BIOL
BION
BIOS
BLOB
BLOC
BLOT
BLOW
BMOC
BOOB
BOOK
BOOM
BOON
BOOP
BOOR
BOOS
BOOT
BPOE
BROM
BROS
BROW
BROZ
BUON
BUOY
BYOB

B••O
BAIO
BARO
BELO
BESO
BIAO
BIKO
BODO
BOLO
BONO
BORO
BOYO
BOZO
BRIO
BRNO
BRYO
BUCO

•BO•
ABOU
BBOY
EBON
IBOS
LBOS
MBOY
OBOE
OBOL

•B•O
EBRO

••BO
AMBO
DABO
GABO
GOBO
HOBO
IGBO
KOBO
LOBO
NEBO
ROBO
UMBO

ZIBO

BP••
BPOE

B•P•
BAPS
BAPT
BKPG
BKPR
BOPP
BOPS

B••P
BEEP
BLIP
BOMP
BOOP
BOPP
BUMP
BURP

•B•P
TBSP

B•Q•
BBQS

•BQ•
BBQS

BR••
BRAC
BRAD
BRAE
BRAG
BRAM
BRAN
BRAS
BRAT
BRAW
BRAY
BRAZ
BREA
BRED
BREE
BREL
BREN
BRER
BRET
BREV
BREW
BRIC
BRIE
BRIG
BRIM
BRIO
BRIT
BRIX
BRNO
BROM
BROS
BROW
BROZ
BRUT
BRUX
BRYN
BRYO

B•R•
BARA
BARB
BARD
BARE
BARI
BARK
BARM
BARN
BARO
BARR
BARS
BART
BDRM
BERG
BERM
BERN
BERT
BIRD
BIRK
BIRL
BIRR
BORA
BORE
BORG
BORK
BORN
BORO
BORS
BORT
BURB
BURG
BURI
BURL
BURN
BURP
BURR
BURS
BURT
BURY
BYRD
BYRE

B••R
BAER
BAHR
BAKR
BARR
BEAR
BEER
BIRR
BKPR
BLDR
BLUR
BOAR
BOER
BOHR
BOOR
BRER
BUHR
BURR

•BR•
ABRI
EBRO

•B•R
ABBR
ABER
CBER
IBAR
JBAR
LBAR
TBAR
UBER
ZBAR

••BR
ABBR
GRBR
GTBR
HEBR
NEBR

BS••
BSEC
BSED
BSMT

B•S•
BASC
BASE
BASH
BASK
BASS
BAST
BESO
BESS
BEST
BISE
BISK
BOSC
BOSE
BOSH
BOSK
BOSN
BOSS
BUSH
BUSK
BUSS
BUST
BUSY

B••S
BAAS
BABS
BACS
BAGS
BAHS
BAMS
BANS
BAPS
BARS
BASS
BATS
BAYS
BBLS
BBQS
BEAS
BEDS
BEES
BEGS
BELS
BEMS
BESS
BETS
BEYS
BIAS
BIBS
BICS
BIDS
BINS
BIOS
BITS
BLAS
BLTS
BMUS
BMWS
BOAS
BOBS
BODS
BOGS
BOIS
BOOS
BOPS
BORS
BOSS
BOTS
BOWS
BOYS
BRAS
BROS
BTUS
BUCS
BUDS
BUGS
BUMS
BUNS
BURS
BUSS
BUTS
BUYS
BVDS
BYES

•BS•
TBSP

•B•S
ABAS
ABBS
ABCS
ABMS
ABYS
BBLS
BBQS
EBBS
IBIS
IBOS
LBOS
MBAS
MBES
OBIS
RBIS

••BS
ABBS
ALBS
AMBS
APBS
ARBS
BABS
BIBS
BOBS
CABS
COBS
CUBS
DABS
DEBS
DIBS
DUBS
EBBS
FIBS
FOBS
FUBS
GABS
GIBS
GOBS
HOBS
HUBS
JABS
JIBS
JOBS
KABS
KOBS
LABS
LHBS
LIBS
LLBS
LOBS
MIBS
MOBS
NABS
NEBS
NIBS
NOBS
NUBS
ORBS
PCBS
PUBS
RABS
REBS
RHBS
RIBS
ROBS
RUBS
SEBS
SIBS
SOBS
SUBS
SWBS
TABS
TUBS
URBS
WABS
WEBS
YOBS

BT••
BTUS

B•T•
BATE
BATH
BATS
BATT
BETA
BETE
BETH
BETS
BETZ
BITE
BITS
BITT
BLTS
BOTA
BOTH
BOTS
BOTT
BUTE
BUTS
BUTT
BYTE

B••T
BACT
BAHT
BAIT
BALT
BAPT
BART
BAST
BATT
BEAT
BEET
BELT
BENT
BERT
BEST
BITT
BLAT
BLIT
BLOT
BOAT
BOLT
BOOT
BORT
BOTT
BOUT
BRAT
BRET
BRIT
BRUT
BSMT
BUNT
BURT
BUST
BUTT

•B•T
ABET
ABUT
IBET
OBIT

••BT
DEBT

BU••
BUBU
BUCK
BUCO
BUCS
BUDD
BUDS
BUFF
BUGS
BUHL
BUHR
BULB
BULG
BULK
BULL
BUMF
BUMP
BUMS
BUNA
BUND
BUNG
BUNK
BUNS
BUNT
BUON
BUOY
BURB
BURG
BURI
BURL
BURN
BURP
BURR
BURS
BURT
BURY
BUSH
BUSK
BUSS
BUST
BUSY
BUTE
BUTS
BUTT
BUYS
BUZZ

B•U•
BAUD
BAUM
BLUE
BLUM
BLUR
BMUS
BOUT
BRUT
BRUX
BTUS

B••U
BABU
BAKU
BEAU
BENU
BLAU
BLEU
BOMU
BUBU

•BU•
ABUT

•B•U
ABOU

••BU
BABU
BUBU
CEBU
SABU
TABU
ZEBU

BV••
BVDS

B•V•
BEVY
BLVD
BOVA

B••V
BREV

B•W•
BAWL
BIWA
BMWS
BOWE
BOWL
BOWS

B••W
BLEW
BLOW
BRAW
BREW
BROW

••BW
NWBW
SWBW

B•X•
BOXY

B••X
BRIX
BRUX

•B•X
IBEX

BY••
BYES
BYME
BYNG
BYOB
BYRD
BYRE
BYTE

B•Y•
BAYA
BAYS
BEYS
BOYD
BOYO
BOYS
BOYZ
BRYN
BRYO
BUYS

B••Y
BABY
BBOY
BELY
BEVY
BODY
BOGY
BONY
BOXY
BRAY
BUOY
BURY
BUSY

•BY•
ABYE
ABYS

•B•Y
ABBY
ABLY
BBOY
MBOY
OBEY

••BY
ABBY
BABY
DOBY
GABY
GOBY
MOBY
RUBY
TCBY
TOBY

B•Z•
BOZO
BUZZ

B••Z
BAEZ
BENZ
BETZ
BOAZ
BOYZ
BRAZ
BROZ
BUZZ

CA••
CAAN
CABS
CACO
CADE
CADI
CADS
CAEN
CAFE
CAGE
CAGY
CAHN
CAIN
CAKE
CAKY
CALC
CALE
CALF
CALI
CALK
CALL
CALM
CALS
CALX
CAMA
CAME
CAMI
CAMO
CAMP
CAMS
CANA
CANC
CANE
CANF
CANS
CANT
CANY
CAPA
CAPE
CAPN
CAPO
CAPP
CAPS
CAPT
CARA
CARB
CARD
CARE
CARK
CARL
CARO
CARP
CARR
CARS
CART
CARY
CASA
CASE
CASH
CASK
CASS
CAST
CATA
CATE
CATH
CATO
CATS
CATT
CATV
CAUL
CAUS
CAVA
CAVE
CAVS
CAVY
CAWS
CAYS

C•A•
CAAN
CHAD
CHAM
CHAN
CHAP
CHAR
CHAS
CHAT
CHAW
CHAZ
CIAO
CLAD
CLAM
CLAN
CLAP
CLAR
CLAW
CLAY
COAL
COAT
COAX
CPAS
CRAB
CRAG
CRAM
CRAT
CRAW
CRAY
CYAN
CZAR

C••A
CAMA
CANA
CAPA
CARA
CASA
CATA
CAVA
CELA
CENA
CERA
CETA
CHIA
COCA
CODA
COLA
COMA
CORA
COSA
COXA
CUBA
CUNA
CYMA

•CA•
ACAD
ICAL
KCAL
MCAT
NCAA
OCAS
RCAF
SCAB
SCAD
SCAM
SCAN
SCAR
SCAT

•C•A
ACEA
ACTA
ECUA
NCAA
OCTA
UCLA

••CA
ARCA
BOCA
COCA
DECA
FICA
INCA
MICA
ORCA
PACA
PICA
RICA
ROCA
SOCA
SPCA
VACA
YMCA
YWCA

CB••
CBER

C•B•
CABS
CEBU
COBB
COBH
COBS
CUBA
CUBE
CUBS

C••B
CARB
CHUB
CLUB
COBB
COMB
CRAB
CRIB
CURB

•CB•
ICBM
PCBS
TCBY

•C•B
SCAB

CC••
CCCI
CCCL
CCCP
CCCV
CCCX
CCII
CCIV
CCIX
CCLI
CCLV
CCLX
CCTV
CCVI
CCXC
CCXI
CCXL
CCXV
CCXX

C•C•
CACO
CCCI
CCCL
CCCP
CCCV
CCCX
COCA
COCK
COCO
CXCI
CXCV
CYCL

C••C
CALC
CANC
CCXC
CDXC
CHIC
CHOC
CINC
CIRC
CMXC
COFC
CONC
CROC

•CC•
ACCS
ACCT
CCCI
CCCL
CCCP
CCCV
CCCX
DCCC
DCCI
DCCL
DCCV
DCCX
ECCE
ECCL
MCCC
MCCI
MCCL
MCCV
MCCX

•C•C
ACDC
CCXC
DCCC
DCXC
MCCC
MCXC
SCLC

••CC
DCCC
MACC
MCCC
MDCC

MLCC
MMCC
SNCC
SPCC

CD••
CDII
CDIV
CDIX
CDLI
CDLV
CDLX
CDRS
CDVI
CDXC
CDXI
CDXL
CDXV
CDXX

C•D•
CADE
CADI
CADS
CEDE
CEDI
CIDE
CMDG
CMDR
CODA
CODE
CODS
CODY
CUDS

C••D
CARD
CHAD
CHID
CLAD
CLOD
COED
COLD
COMD
COND
CORD
CRUD
CUED
CURD

•CD•
ACDC
LCDS
MCDI
MCDL
MCDV
MCDX

•C•D
ACAD
ACED
ACID
ICED
SCAD
SCUD

••CD
MMCD
RECD

CE••
CEBU
CEDE
CEDI
CEES
CEIL
CELA
CELL
CELS
CELT
CENA
CENE
CENO
CENS
CENT
CEOS
CEPE
CEPS
CERA
CERE
CERF
CERN
CERO
CERT
CESS
CEST
CETA
CETE

C•E•
CAEN
CBER
CEES
CHEE
CHEF
CHEM
CHEN
CHER
CHET
CHEW
CHEX
CHEZ
CIEL
CLEF
CLEM
CLEO
CLEW
COED
COEL
COEN
CREE
CREW
CUED
CUER
CUES

C••E
CADE
CAFE
CAGE
CAKE
CALE
CAME
CANE
CAPE
CARE
CASE
CATE
CAVE
CEDE
CENE
CEPE
CERE
CETE
CHEE
CIDE
CINE
CIRE
CITE
CLUE
CODE
COKE
COLE
COME
CONE
COPE
CORE
COTE
COUE
COVE
CREE
CRUE
CTGE
CUBE
CUKE
CULE
CURE
CUTE
CYME
CYTE

•CE•
ACEA
ACED
ACER
ACES
ACET
ACEY
ICED
ICEL
ICER
ICES
ICET

•C•E
ACHE
ACME
ACNE
ACRE
ACTE
ECCE

••CE
ANCE
BICE
DACE
DICE
DUCE
DYCE
ECCE
ENCE
ESCE
FACE
FICE
INCE
LACE
LICE
LUCE
MACE
MICE
NICE
ONCE
PACE
PUCE
RACE
RICE
SYCE
VICE
VOCE
WACE

C•F•
CAFE
COFC
COFS
CUFF
CUFT

C••F
CALF
CANF
CERF
CHEF
CLEF
COIF
CONF
CORF
CUFF

•C•F
RCAF

C•G•
CAGE
CAGY
CHGS
CIGS
COGS
CTGE

C••G
CHUG
CLOG
CMDG
CONG
CRAG

•C•G
ACTG

••CG
USCG

CH••
CHAD
CHAM
CHAN
CHAP
CHAR
CHAS
CHAT
CHAW
CHAZ
CHEE
CHEF
CHEM
CHEN
CHER
CHET
CHEW
CHEX
CHEZ
CHGS
CHIA
CHIC
CHID
CHIN
CHIP
CHIS
CHIT
CHMN
CHOC
CHOL
CHON
CHOP
CHOU
CHOW
CHOY
CHUB
CHUG
CHUM
CHUR

C•H•
CAHN
COHN
COHO

C••H
CASH
CATH
COBH
COSH
CUSH

•CH•
ACHE
ACHT
ACHY
ECHO
ECHT
OCHO
OCHS
TCHR

•C•H
ACTH

••CH
ARCH
ASCH
BACH
DICH
EACH
ETCH
EXCH
FOCH
HOCH
INCH
ITCH
KOCH
LECH
LOCH
MACH
MECH
MICH
MUCH
ORCH
OUCH
RICH
SECH
SUCH
TACH
TECH
WYCH
YECH
ZECH

CI••
CIAO
CIDE
CIEL
CIGS
CIII
CINC
CINE
CINQ
CION
CIRC
CIRE
CIST
CITE
CITS
CITY

C•I•
CAIN
CCII
CCIV
CCIX
CDII
CDIV
CDIX
CEIL
CHIA
CHIC
CHID
CHIN
CHIP
CHIS
CHIT
CIII
CLII
CLIN
CLIO
CLIP
CLIV
CLIX
CMII
CMIV
CMIX
COIF
COIL
COIN
COIR
CRIB
CRIM
CRIN
CRIT
CUIN
CVII
CXII
CXIV
CXIX

C••I
CADI
CALI
CAMI
CCCI
CCII
CCLI
CCVI
CCXI
CDII
CDLI
CDVI
CDXI
CEDI
CIII
CLII
CLVI
CLXI
CMII
CMLI
CMVI
CMXI
CORI
COSI
CVII
CXCI
CXII
CXLI
CXVI
CXXI

•CI•
ACID
ACIS
CCII
CCIV
CCIX
DCII
DCIV
DCIX
MCII
MCIV
MCIX
SCIL
XCII
XCIV
XCIX

•C•I
ACTI
CCCI
CCII
CCLI
CCVI
CCXI
DCCI
DCII
DCLI
DCVI
DCXI
MCCI
MCDI
MCII
MCLI
MCMI
MCVI
MCXI
SCSI
XCII
XCVI

••CI
ASCI
CCCI
CXCI
DCCI
DECI
DXCI
FOCI
LOCI
LUCI
MCCI
MDCI
MMCI
MXCI
UNCI
VICI

C•J•
CUJO

C••J
CONJ

C•K•
CAKE
CAKY
COKE
COKY
CUKE

C••K
CALK
CARK
CASK
COCK
CONK
COOK
CORK
CUSK

•CK•
ICKY

••CK
BACK
BECK
BOCK
BUCK
COCK
DECK
DICK
DOCK
DUCK
DYCK
EYCK
GUCK
HACK
HECK
HICK
HOCK
HUCK
JACK
JOCK
KICK
LACK
LICK
LOCK
LUCK
MACK
MICK
MOCK
MUCK
NECK
NICK
NOCK
PACK
PECK
PICK
PUCK
RACK
RICK
ROCK
RUCK
SACK
SICK
SOCK
SUCK
TACK
TICK
TOCK
TUCK
WACK
WICK
YACK
YUCK
ZACK

CL••
CLAD
CLAM
CLAN
CLAP
CLAR
CLAW
CLAY
CLEF
CLEM
CLEO
CLEW
CLII
CLIN
CLIO
CLIP
CLIV
CLIX
CLOD
CLOG
CLOP
CLOT
CLOY
CLUB
CLUE
CLVI
CLXI
CLXV
CLXX

C•L•
CALC
CALE
CALF
CALI
CALK
CALL
CALM
CALS
CALX
CCLI
CCLV
CCLX
CDLI
CDLV
CDLX
CELA
CELL
CELS
CELT
CMLI
CMLV
CMLX
COLA
COLD
COLE
COLL
COLO
COLS
COLT
COLY
CPLS
CULE
CULL
CULM
CULP
CULS
CULT
CXLI
CXLV

C••L
CALL
CARL
CAUL
CCCL
CCXL
CDXL
CEIL
CELL
CHOL
CIEL
CMXL
COAL
COEL
COIL
COLL
COML
COOL
COWL
CULL
CURL
CYCL

•CL•
ACLU
CCLI
CCLV
CCLX
DCLI
DCLV
DCLX
MCLI
MCLV
MCLX
SCLC
UCLA

•C•L
ACYL
CCCL
CCXL
DCCL
DCXL
ECCL
ECOL
ICAL
ICEL
KCAL
MCCL
MCDL
MCML
MCXL
SCIL

••CL
CCCL
CYCL
DCCL
DECL
ECCL
ENCL
EXCL
INCL
MCCL
MDCL
MMCL
NACL

CM••
CMDG
CMDR
CMII
CMIV
CMIX
CMLI
CMLV
CMLX
CMON
CMOS
CMVI
CMXC
CMXI
CMXL
CMXV
CMXX

C•M•
CAMA
CAME
CAMI
CAMO
CAMP
CAMS
CHMN
COMA
COMB
COMD
COME
COML
COMM
COMO
COMP
COMR
CWMS
CYMA
CYME

C••M
CALM
CHAM
CHEM
CHUM
CLAM
CLEM
COMM
CORM
COSM
CRAM
CRIM
CULM

•CM•
ACME
MCMI
MCML
MCMV
MCMX
RCMP

•C•M
ICBM
SCAM
SCUM

••CM
MMCM

CN••
CNUT

C•N•
CANA
CANC
CANE
CANF
CANS
CANT
CANY
CENA
CENE
CENO
CENS
CENT
CINC
CINE
CINQ
CONC
COND
CONE
CONF
CONG
CONJ
CONK
CONN
CONS
CONT
CONV
CONY
CTNS
CUNA
CUNY

C••N
CAAN
CAEN
CAHN
CAIN
CAPN
CERN
CHAN
CHEN
CHIN
CHMN
CHON
CION
CLAN
CLIN
CMON
COEN
COHN
COIN
CONN
COON
CORN
CRIN
CUIN
CYAN

•CN•
ACNE

•C•N
DCON
ECON
ICON
SCAN

CO••
COAL
COAT
COAX
COBB
COBH
COBS
COCA
COCK
COCO
CODA
CODE
CODS
CODY
COED
COEL
COEN
COFC
COFS

COGS	COSI	**•CO•**	CCCP	CARO	TCHR	COTS	RECS	CURT	CULS	CAVY	MXCV	CCCX	CYME
COHN	COSM	DCON	CHAP	CARP		COWS	ROCS		CULT	CCVI		CCIX	CYTE
COHO	COST	ECOL	CHIP	CARR	**••CR**	CPAS	SACS	**•CT•**	CUNA	CDVI	**CW••**	CCLX	CYTO
COIF	COSY	ECON	CHOP	CARS	INCR	CPLS	SECS	ACTA	CUNY	CLVI	CWMS	CCXX	
COIL	COTE	ICON	CLAP	CART	MICR	CPOS	SICS	ACTE	CUPR	CMVI	CWOS	CDIX	**C•Y•**
COIN	COTS	ICOS	CLIP	CARY		CRTS	TECS	ACTG	CUPS	COVE		CDLX	CAYS
COIR	COTY	NCOS	CLOP	CDRS	**C•S•**	CRUS	TICS	ACTH	CURB	CXVI	**C•W•**	CDXX	CRYO
COKE	COUE	SCOP	COMP	CERA	CASA	CTNS	VACS	ACTI	CURD		CAWS	CHEX	
COKY	COUP	SCOT	COOP	CERE	CASE	CUBS	WACS	ACTS	CURE	**C••V**	COWL	CLIX	**C••Y**
COLA	COVE	SCOW	CORP	CERF	CASH	CUDS		ACTV	CURL	CATV	COWS	CLXX	CAGY
COLD	COWL		COUP	CERN	CASK	CUES	**CT••**	CCTV	CURR	CCCV		CMIX	CAKY
COLE	COWS	**•C•O**	CROP	CERO	CASS	CULS	CTGE	ECTO	CURS	CCIV	**C••W**	CMLX	CANY
COLL	COXA	ACRO	CULP	CERT	CAST	CUPS	CTNS	OCTA	CURT	CCLV	CHAW	CMXX	CARY
COLO	COZY	ECHO	CUSP	CIRC	CESS	CURS		OCTO	CUSH	CCTV	CHEW	COAX	CAVY
COLS		ECTO		CIRE	CEST	CUSS	**C•T•**	RCTS	CUSK	CCXV	CHOW	CRUX	CHOY
COLT	**C•O•**	OCHO	**•CP•**	CORA	CIST	CUTS	CATA	SCTV	CUSP	CDIV	CLAW	CXIX	CITY
COLY	CEOS	OCTO	RCPT	CORD	COSA	CWMS	CATE	WCTU	CUSS	CDLV	CLEW	CXXX	CLAY
COMA	CHOC			CORE	COSH	CWOS	CATH		CUTE	CDXV	CRAW		CLOY
COMB	CHOL	**••CO**	**•C•P**	CORF	COSI		CATO	**•C•T**	CUTS	CLIV	CREW	**•CX•**	CODY
COMD	CHON	ARCO	CCCP	CORI	COSM	**•CS•**	CATS	ACCT		CLXV	CROW	CCXC	COKY
COME	CHOP	ASCO	RCMP	CORK	COST	SCSI	CATT	ACET	**C•U•**	CMIV		CCXI	COLY
COML	CHOU	BUCO	SCOP	CORM	COSY		CATV	ACHT	CAUL	CMLV	**•C•W**	CCXL	CONY
COMM	CHOW	CACO	SCUP	CORN	CUSH	**•C•S**	CCTV	ECHT	CAUS	CMXV	SCOW	CCXV	COPY
COMO	CHOY	COCO		CORO	CUSK	ACCS	CETA	ICET	CHUB	CONV		CCXX	CORY
COMP	CION	DECO	**••CP**	CORP	CUSP	ACES	CETE	MCAT	CHUG	CXCV	**CX••**	DCXC	COSY
COMR	CLOD	EKCO	CCCP	CORR	CUSS	ACIS	CITE	RCPT	CHUM	CXIV	CXCI	DCXI	COTY
CONC	CLOG	LOCO	FACP	CORS		ACTS	CITS	SCAT	CHUR	CXLV	CXCV	DCXL	COZY
COND	CLOP	MECO	FRCP	CORY	**C••S**	ECUS	CITY	SCOT	CLUB	CXXV	CXII	DCXV	CRAY
CONE	CLOT	MYCO		CURB	CABS	ICES	COTE	SCUT	CLUE		CXIV	DCXX	CUNY
CONF	CLOY	PICO	**C••Q**	CURD	CADS	ICOS	COTS		CNUT	**•CV•**	CXIX	MCXC	
CONG	CMON	POCO	CINQ	CURE	CALS	ICUS	COTY	**••CT**	COUE	CCVI	CXLI	MCXI	**•CY•**
CONJ	CMOS	RICO		CURL	CAMS	LCDS	CRTS	ACCT	COUP	DCVI	CXLV	MCXL	ACYL
CONK	COOK	TACO	**CR••**	CURR	CANS	NCOS	CUTE	BACT	CRUD	MCVI	CXVI	MCXV	
CONN	COOL	TICO	CRAB	CURS	CAPS	OCAS	CUTS	DICT	CRUE	XCVI	CXXI	MCXX	**•C•Y**
CONS	COON	VICO	CRAG	CURT	CARS	OCHS	CYTE	DUCT	CRUS		CXXV		ACEY
CONT	COOP	WACO	CRAM		CASS	PCBS	CYTO	FACT	CRUX	**•C•V**	CXXX	**•C•X**	ACHY
CONV	COOS		CRAT	**C••R**	CATS	RCTS		FICT	CRUZ	ACTV		CCCX	ICKY
CONY	COOT	**CP••**	CRAW	CARR	CAUS	VCRS	**C••T**	HECT		CCCV	**C•X•**	CCIX	SCRY
COOK	CPOS	CPAS	CRAY	CBER	CAVS		CANT	LACT	**C••U**	CCIV	CCXC	CCLX	TCBY
COOL	CROC	CPLS	CREE	CHAR	CAWS	**••CS**	CAPT	LECT	CEBU	CCLV	CCXI	CCXX	
COON	CROP	CPOS	CREW	CHER	CAYS	ABCS	CART	PACT	CHOU	CCTV	CCXL	DCCX	**••CY**
COOP	CROW		CRIB	CHUR	CDRS	ACCS	CAST	PICT		CCXV	CCXV	DCIX	AGCY
COOS	CWOS	**C•P•**	CRIM	CLAR	CEES	ADCS	CATT	RECT	**•CU•**	DCCV	CCXX	DCLX	ANCY
COOT		CAPA	CRIN	CMDR	CELS	ARCS	CELT	SECT	ECUA	DCIV	CDXC	DCXX	ENCY
COPE	**C••O**	CAPE	CRIT	COIR	CENS	BACS	CENT	TACT	ECUS	DCLV	CDXI	MCCX	LACY
COPS	CACO	CAPN	CROC	COMR	CEOS	BICS	CERT		ICUS	DCXV	CDXL	MCDX	LUCY
COPT	CAMO	CAPO	CROP	CORR	CEPS	BUCS	CEST	**CU••**	SCUD	MCCV	CDXV	MCIX	MACY
COPY	CAPO	CAPP	CROW	CUER	CESS	DOCS	CHAT	CUBA	SCUM	MCDV	CDXX	MCLX	RACY
CORA	CARO	CAPS	CRTS	CUPR	CHAS	DSCS	CHET	CUBE	SCUP	MCIV	CLXI	MCMX	SECY
CORD	CATO	CAPT	CRUD	CURR	CHGS	ENCS	CHIT	CUBS	SCUT	MCLV	CLXV	MCXX	
CORE	CENO	CEPE	CRUE	CZAR	CHIS	FACS	CIST	CUDS		MCMV	CLXX	XCIX	**CZ••**
CORF	CERO	CEPS	CRUS		CIGS	FRCS	CLOT	CUED	**•C•U**	MCXV	CMXC		CZAR
CORI	CIAO	COPE	CRUX	**•CR•**	CITS	LACS	CNUT	CUER	ACLU	SCTV	CMXI	**••CX**	
CORK	CLEO	COPS	CRUZ	ACRE	CMOS	LDCS	COAT	CUES	ECRU	XCIV	CMXL	CCCX	**C•Z•**
CORM	CLIO	COPT	CRYO	ACRO	COBS	MACS	COLT	CUFF	WCTU		CMXV	DCCX	COZY
CORN	COCO	COPY		ECRU	CODS	MICS	CONT	CUFT		**••CV**	CMXX	MCCX	
CORO	COHO	CUPR	**C•R•**	SCRY	COFS	MOCS	COOT	CUIN	**CV••**	CCCV	COXA	MDCX	**C••Z**
CORP	COLO	CUPS	CARA	VCRS	COGS	ORCS	COPT	CUJO	CVII	CXCV	CXXI	MMCX	CHAZ
CORR	COMO		CARB		COLS	PACS	COST	CUKE		DCCV	CXXV		CHEZ
CORS	CORO	**C••P**	CARD	**•C•R**	CONS	PECS	CRAT	CULE	**C•V•**	DXCV	CXXX	**CY••**	CRUZ
CORY	CRYO	CAMP	CARE	ACER	COOS	PFCS	CRIT	CULL	CAVA	MCCV		CYAN	
COSA	CUJO	CAPP	CARK	ICER	COPS	PICS	CUFT	CULM	CAVE	MDCV	**C••X**	CYCL	**DA••**
COSH	CYTO	CARP	CARL	SCAR	CORS	PLCS	CULT	CULP	CAVS	MMCV	CALX	CYMA	DABO

DABS DACE DADA DADE DADO DADS DAFF DAFT DAGS DAHL DAHS DAIN DAIS DALE DALI DALS DALY DAMA DAME DAMN DAMP DAMS DANA DANE DANG DANK DANL DANO DANU DAPS DARC DARD DARE DARI DARK DARN DART DASD DASH DATA DATE DATS DAUB DAVE DAVY DAWG DAWN DAWS DAYO DAYS DAZE

D•A•
DDAY DEAD DEAF DEAL DEAN DEAR DHAL DIAG DIAL DIAM DIAN DIAS DIAZ DOAK DRAB DRAG DRAM DRAT DRAW DRAY DUAD DUAL DWAN DYAD DYAK DYAN

D••A
DADA DAMA DANA DATA DECA DEJA DEKA DEVA DINA DIVA DOHA DONA DOPA DORA DUMA DUNA DURA DYNA

•DA•
ADAH ADAK ADAM ADAR DDAY EDAM EDAX GDAY IDAE NDAK ODAS ODAY RDAS SDAK VDAY

•D•A
EDDA EDNA EDTA IDEA KDKA ODEA

••DA
AIDA ALDA CODA DADA EDDA ERDA JADA LEDA NADA PODA SADA SODA TADA USDA VEDA VIDA YADA YODA

DB••
DBIB

D•B•
DABO DABS DEBI DEBS DEBT DIBS DOBY DUBS

D••B
DAUB DBIB DRAB DRIB DRUB DUMB

•DB•
HDBK

DC••
DCCC DCCI DCCL DCCV DCCX DCII DCIV DCIX DCLI DCLV DCLX DCON DCVI DCXC DCXI DCXL DCXV DCXX

D•C•
DACE DCCC DCCI DCCL DCCV DCCX DECA DECI DECK DECL DECO DICE DICH DICK DICT DOCK DOCS DSCS DUCE DUCK DUCT DXCI DXCV DYCE DYCK

D••C
DARC DCCC DCXC DESC DISC

•DC•
ADCS LDCS MDCC MDCI MDCL MDCV MDCX

•D•C
CDXC EDUC FDIC MDCC MDXC ODIC

••DC
ACDC MMDC

DD••
DDAY

D•D•
DADA DADE DADO DADS DIDO DMDS DODD DODO DUDE DUDS DVDS

D••D
DARD DASD DEAD DEED DIED DODD DOOD DOWD DRED DUAD DYAD DYED

•DD•
ADDN ADDS ADDY EDDA EDDO EDDS EDDY ODDS

••DD
BUDD DODD FUDD JUDD KIDD LADD MADD MUDD REDD RIDD RUDD SADD SUDD TODD

DE••
DEAD DEAF DEAL DEAN DEAR DEBI DEBS DEBT DECA DECI DECK DECL DECO DEED DEEM DEEP DEER DEES DEET DEFS DEFT DEFY DEGS DEIL DEJA DEKA DEKE DELE DELI DELL DELS DELY DEME DEMI DEMO DEMS DEMY DENE DENG DENS DENT DENY DEPP DEPT DERM DERN DESC DESI DESK DETS DEUM DEUS DEUT DEUX DEVA DEVI DEVO DEWS DEWY DEYS

D•E•
DEED DEEM DEEP DEER DEES DEET DIED DIEM DIEN DIES DIET DIEU DOER DOES DRED DREE DREG DREI DREW DUEL DUES DUET DYED DYER DYES

D••E
DACE DADE DALE DAME DANE DARE DATE DAVE DAZE DEKE DELE DEME DENE DICE DIKE DIME DINE DIRE DIVE DOGE DOLE DOME DONE DOPE DORE DOSE DOTE DOVE DOZE DREE DUCE DUDE DUKE DUNE DUPE DUSE DUVE DYCE DYNE

•DE•
ADEN ADES EDEN EDER IDEA IDEE IDEM IDEO IDES ODEA ODER ODES

•D•E
ADUE ADZE EDGE EDIE HDWE IDAE IDEE IDLE MDSE ODIE

••DE
AIDE AUDE BADE BEDE BIDE BODE CADE CEDE CIDE CODE DADE DUDE ENDE ERDE FADE FIDE GIDE HADE HIDE HYDE JADE JUDE LADE LODE MADE MEDE MODE NIDE NODE NUDE OLDE PODE REDE RIDE RODE RUDE SADE SIDE TIDE TUDE VADE VIDE WADE WIDE

D•F•
DAFF DAFT DEFS DEFT DEFY DIFF DOFF DUFF DUFY

D••F
DAFF DEAF DIFF DOFF DOLF DUFF

D•G•
DAGS DEGS DIGS DOGE DOGG DOGS DOGY

D••G
DANG DAWG DENG DIAG DING DOGG DONG DOUG DRAG DREG DRUG

•DG•
EDGE EDGY

••DG
BLDG CMDG JUDG

DH••
DHAL DHOW

D•H•
DAHL DAHS DOHA

D••H
DASH DICH DISH DOTH

•DH•
EDHS

•D•H
ADAH

••DH
NADH SIDH YODH

DI••
DIAG DIAL DIAM DIAN DIAS DIAZ DIBS DICE DICH DICK DICT DIDO DIED DIEM DIEN DIES DIET DIEU DIFF DIGS DIII DIKE DILL DIME DIMS DINA DINE DING DINK DINO DINS DINT DION DIOR DIOS DIPL DIPS DIRE DIRK DIRS DIRT DISC DISH DISK DISS DIST DITS DITZ DIVA DIVE DIVS

D•I•
DAIN DAIS DBIB DCII DCIV DCIX DEIL DIII DLII DLIT DLIV DLIX DOIL DOIN DOIT DRIB DRIN DRIP DRIQ DVII DXII DXIV DXIX

D••I
DALI DARI DCCI DCII DCLI DCVI DCXI DEBI DECI DELI DEMI DESI DEVI DIII DLII DLVI DLXI DREI DVII DXCI DXII DXLI DXVI DXXI

•DI•
ADIN ADIT CDII CDIV CDIX EDIE EDIT FDIC IDIO MDII MDIV MDIX ODIC ODIE ODIN XDIN XDIV

•D•I
CDII CDLI CDVI CDXI MDCI MDII MDLI MDVI MDXI

••DI
AUDI CADI CEDI JEDI LODI MCDI MIDI MMDI NIDI NODI NUDI PEDI QADI REDI RIDI RUDI SADI VIDI WADI

D•J•
DEJA DOJO

•DJ•
ADJS ADJT

••DJ
HADJ

DK••
DKNY

D•K•
DEKA DEKE DIKE DUKE

D••K
DANK DARK DECK DESK DICK DINK DIRK DISK DOAK DOCK DUCK DUNK DUSK DYAK DYCK

•DK•
KDKA

•D•K
ADAK HDBK NDAK SDAK

DL••
DLII DLIT DLIV DLIX DLVI DLXI DLXV DLXX

D•L•
DALE DALI DALS DALY DCLI DCLV DCLX DELE DELI DELL DELS DELY DILL DOLE DOLF DOLL DOLT DULL DULY DXLI DXLV

D••L
DAHL DANL DCCL DCXL DEAL DECL DEIL DELL DHAL DIAL DILL DIPL DOIL DOLL DUAL DUEL DULL

•DL•
CDLI CDLV CDLX IDLE IDLY MDLI MDLV MDLX

•D•L
CDXL IDOL IDYL MDCL MDXL

••DL
MCDL MMDL

DM••
DMDS DMSO

D•M•
DAMA DAME DAMN DAMP DAMS DEME DEMI DEMO DEMS DEMY DIME DIMS DOME DOMO DOMS DPMS DSMS DUMA DUMB DUMP DVMS

D••M
DEEM DERM DEUM

DIAM
DIEM
DOOM
DORM
DRAM
DRUM

•DM•
ADMS

•D•M
ADAM
BDRM
EDAM
EDOM
IDEM
ODOM

••DM
RADM
VADM

D•N•
DANA
DANE
DANG
DANK
DANL
DANO
DANU
DENE
DENG
DENS
DENT
DENY
DINA
DINE
DING
DINK
DINO
DINS
DINT
DKNY
DONA
DONE
DONG
DONS
DONT
DRNO
DUNA
DUNE
DUNK
DUNN
DUNS
DYNA
DYNE

D••N
DAIN
DAMN
DARN
DAWN
DCON
DEAN
DERN
DIAN
DIEN
DION
DOIN
DOON
DORN
DOWN
DRIN
DUNN
DURN
DWAN
DYAN

•DN•
EDNA

•D•N
ADDN
ADEN
ADIN
EDEN
IDUN
ODIN
XDIN

••DN
ADDN
MIDN

DO••
DOAK
DOBY
DOCK
DOCS
DODD
DODO
DOER
DOES
DOFF
DOGE
DOGG
DOGS
DOGY
DOHA
DOIL
DOIN
DOIT
DOJO
DOLE
DOLF
DOLL
DOLT
DOME
DOMO
DOMS
DONA
DONE
DONG
DONS
DONT
DOOD
DOOM
DOON
DOOR
DOPA
DOPE
DOPY
DORA
DORE
DORM
DORN
DORP
DORR
DORS
DORT
DORY
DOSE
DOSS
DOST
DOTE
DOTH
DOTS
DOUG
DOUP
DOUR
DOUW
DOUX
DOVE
DOWD
DOWN
DOZE
DOZY

D•O•
DCON
DHOW
DION
DIOR
DIOS
DOOD
DOOM
DOON
DOOR
DROP
DSOS
DUOS

D••O
DABO
DADO
DANO
DAYO
DECO
DEMO
DEVO
DIDO
DINO
DMSO
DODO
DOJO
DOMO
DRNO
DURO

•DO•
ADOS
EDOM
IDOL
IDOS
ODOM
ODOR
UDOS

•D•O
EDDO
IDEO
IDIO

••DO
ALDO
BODO
DADO
DIDO
DODO
EDDO
ENDO
FADO
FIDO
INDO
IODO
JUDO
LIDO
ORDO
PEDO
PPDO
REDO
TODO
UNDO
UPDO
YEDO

DP••
DPMS

D•P•
DAPS
DEPP
DEPT
DIPL
DIPS
DOPA
DOPE
DOPY
DUPE

D••P
DAMP
DEEP
DEPP
DORP
DOUP
DRIP
DROP
DUMP

••DP
AVDP
NADP

D••Q
DRIQ

DR••
DRAB
DRAG
DRAM
DRAT
DRAW
DRAY
DRED
DREE
DREG
DREI
DREW
DRIB
DRIN
DRIP
DRIQ
DRNO
DROP
DRUB
DRUG
DRUM
DRYS

D•R•
DARC
DARD
DARE
DARI
DARK
DARN
DART
DERM
DERN
DIRE
DIRK
DIRS
DIRT
DORA
DORE
DORM
DORN
DORP
DORR
DORS
DORT
DORY
DURA
DURN
DURO

D••R
DEAR
DEER
DIOR
DOER
DOOR
DORR
DOUR
DYER

•DR•
BDRM
CDRS
LDRS

•D•R
ADAR
EDER
ODER
ODOR

••DR
BLDR
CMDR
FLDR
HYDR
RMDR
SADR

DS••
DSCS
DSMS
DSOS

D•S•
DASD
DASH
DESC
DESI
DESK
DISC
DISH
DISK
DISS
DIST
DMSO
DOSE
DOSS
DOST
DUSE
DUSK
DUST

D••S
DABS
DADS
DAGS
DAHS
DAIS
DALS
DAMS
DAPS
DATS
DAWS
DAYS
DEBS
DEES
DEFS
DEGS
DELS
DEMS
DENS
DETS
DEUS
DEWS
DEYS
DIAS
DIBS
DIES
DIGS
DIMS
DINS
DIOS
DIPS
DIRS
DISS
DITS
DIVS
DMDS
DOCS
DOES
DOGS
DOMS
DONS
DORS
DOSS
DOTS
DPMS
DRYS
DSCS
DSMS
DSOS
DUBS
DUDS
DUES
DUNS
DUOS
DVDS
DVMS
DYES

•DS•
MDSE

•D•S
ADCS
ADDS
ADES
ADJS
ADMS
ADOS
CDRS
EDDS
EDHS
IDES
IDOS
LDCS
LDRS
ODAS
ODDS
ODES
RDAS
UDOS
VDTS

••DS
ADDS
AIDS
ANDS
BEDS
BIDS
BODS
BUDS
BVDS
CADS
CODS
CUDS
DADS
DMDS
DUDS
DVDS
EADS
EDDS
ENDS
ETDS
FADS
FEDS
FIDS
GADS
GODS
HODS
INDS
KEDS
KIDS
LADS
LCDS
LEDS
LIDS
LLDS
LTDS
MEDS
MODS
MUDS
NODS
ODDS
OLDS
OUDS
PADS
PEDS
PHDS
PODS
RADS
REDS
RFDS
RIDS
RNDS
RODS
SODS
STDS
SUDS
TADS
TEDS
TODS
WADS
WEDS
YODS
ZEDS

D•T•
DATA
DATE
DATS
DETS
DITS
DITZ
DOTE
DOTH
DOTS
DUTY

D••T
DAFT
DART
DEBT
DEET
DEFT
DENT
DEPT
DEUT
DICT
DIET
DINT
DIRT
DIST
DLIT
DOIT
DOLT
DONT
DORT
DOST
DRAT
DUCT
DUET
DUST

•DT•
EDTA
HDTV
VDTS

•D•T
ADIT
ADJT
ADVT
EDIT

DU••
DUAD
DUAL
DUBS
DUCE
DUCK
DUCT
DUDE
DUDS
DUEL
DUES
DUET
DUFF
DUFY
DUKE
DULL
DULY
DUMA
DUMB
DUMP
DUNA
DUNE
DUNK
DUNN
DUNS
DUOS
DUPE
DURA
DURN
DURO
DUSE
DUSK
DUST
DUTY
DUVE

D•U•
DAUB
DEUM
DEUS
DEUT
DEUX
DOUG
DOUP
DOUR
DOUW
DOUX
DRUB
DRUG
DRUM

D••U
DANU
DIEU

•DU•
ADUE
EDUC
IDUN

••DU
KUDU
PUDU
URDU

DV••
DVDS
DVII
DVMS

D•V•
DAVE
DAVY
DCVI
DEVA
DEVI
DEVO
DIVA
DIVE
DIVS
DLVI
DOVE
DUVE
DXVI

D••V
DCCV
DCIV
DCLV
DCXV
DLIV
DLXV
DXCV
DXIV
DXLV
DXXV

•DV•
ADVT
CDVI
MDVI

•D•V
CDIV
CDLV
CDXV
HDTV
MDCV
MDIV
MDLV
MDXV
XDIV

••DV
MCDV
MMDV

DW••
DWAN

D•W•
DAWG
DAWN
DAWS
DEWS
DEWY
DOWD
DOWN

D••W
DHOW
DOUW
DRAW
DREW

•DW•
HDWE

DX••
DXCI
DXCV
DXII
DXIV
DXIX
DXLI
DXLV
DXVI
DXXI
DXXV
DXXX

D•X•
DCXC
DCXI
DCXL
DCXV
DCXX
DLXI
DLXV
DLXX
DXXI
DXXV
DXXX

D••X
DCCX
DCIX
DCLX
DCXX
DEUX
DLIX
DLXX
DOUX
DXIX
DXXX

•DX•
CDXC
CDXI
CDXL
CDXV
CDXX
MDXC
MDXI
MDXL
MDXV
MDXX

•D•X
CDIX
CDLX
CDXX
EDAX
MDCX
MDIX
MDLX
MDXX

••DX
MCDX
MMDX

DY••
DYAD
DYAK
DYAN
DYCE
DYCK
DYED
DYER
DYES
DYNA
DYNE

D•Y•
DAYO
DAYS
DEYS
DRYS

D••Y
DALY
DAVY
DDAY
DEFY
DELY
DEMY
DENY
DEWY
DKNY
DOBY
DOGY
DOPY
DORY
DOZY
DRAY
DUFY
DULY
DUTY

•DY•
IDYL

•D•Y
ADDY
DDAY
EDDY
EDGY
GDAY
IDLY
ODAY
VDAY

••DY
ADDY
ANDY
BODY
CODY
EDDY
HEDY
INDY
JODY
JUDY
LADY
RUDY
TIDY
TODY

D•Z•
DAZE
DOZE
DOZY

D••Z
DIAZ
DITZ

•DZ•
ADZE

••DZ
LODZ

EA••
EACH
EADS
EARL
EARN
EARP
EARS
EASE
EAST
EASY
EATS
EAUX
EAVE

E•A•
EBAN
EDAM
EDAX
EGAD
EGAL
EGAN
ELAL
ELAM
ELAN
ERAS
ERAT
ESAI
ESAS
ESAU
ETAH
ETAL
ETAS
ETAT
EVAH
EVAN
EVAP
EXAM
EYAS

E••A
EBLA
ECUA
EDDA
EDNA
EDTA
ELBA
ELEA
ELIA

ELLA
ELSA
EMIA
EMMA
ENNA
ENYA
EPHA
ERDA
ERMA
ESSA
ESTA
ETNA
ETTA
EYRA
EZRA

•EA•
BEAD
BEAK
BEAL
BEAM
BEAN
BEAR
BEAS
BEAT
BEAU
DEAD
DEAF
DEAL
DEAN
DEAR
FEAR
FEAT
GEAR
HEAD
HEAL
HEAP
HEAR
HEAT
JEAN
KEAN
KEAS
LEAD
LEAF
LEAH
LEAK
LEAL
LEAN
LEAP
LEAR
LEAS
MEAD
MEAL
MEAN
MEAS
MEAT
NEAL
NEAP
NEAR
NEAT
PEAG
PEAK
PEAL
PEAR
PEAS
PEAT
PEAU
READ
REAL
REAM
REAP
REAR
SEAL
SEAM
SEAN
SEAR
SEAS
SEAT
TEAK
TEAL
TEAM
TEAR
TEAS
VEAL
VEAU
WEAK
WEAL
WEAN
WEAR
YEAH
YEAN
YEAR
YEAS
ZEAL

•E•A
BELA
BEMA
BETA
CELA
CENA
CERA
CETA
DECA
DEJA
DEKA
DEVA
FEMA
FETA
GENA
GERA
GETA
HEMA
HERA
HEXA
JENA
LEDA
LEIA
LEMA
LENA
MEGA
MESA
META
NEVA
PENA
PEPA
PETA
REBA
REZA
SEGA
SELA
SERA
SETA
TEMA
TERA
TEWA
VEDA
VEGA
VELA
VENA
VERA
WEKA
XENA
ZETA

••EA
ACEA
AIEA
ALEA
AREA
ASEA
BREA
ELEA
FLEA
GAEA
IDEA
ITEA
ODEA
ONEA
PLEA
RHEA
SHEA
THEA
TOEA
UMEA
UVEA
ZOEA

EB••
EBAN
EBBS
EBEN
EBLA
EBON
EBRO

E•B•
EBBS
ELBA
ELBE

•EB•
BEBE
CEBU
DEBI
DEBS
DEBT
HEBE
HEBR
NEBE
NEBN
NEBO
NEBR
NEBS
REBA
REBS
SEBE
SEBS
WEBB
WEBS
ZEBU

•E•B
BEEB
HERB
KERB
SERB
VERB
WEBB
WEEB

••EB
BEEB
BLEB
LIEB
LOEB
PLEB
SHEB
WEEB

EC••
ECCE
ECCL
ECHO
ECHT
ECOL
ECON
ECRU
ECTO
ECUA
ECUS

E•C•
EACH
ECCE
ECCL
EKCO
ENCE
ENCL
ENCS
ENCY
ESCE
ETCH
EXCH
EXCL
EYCK

E••C
EDUC
EEOC
ELEC
EMIC
EPIC
ERIC
ETIC
EXEC

•EC•
BECK
DECA
DECI
DECK
DECL
DECO
HECK
HECT
LECH
LECT
MECH
MECO
NECK
PECK
PECS
RECD
RECS
RECT
SECH
SECS
SECT
SECY
TECH
TECS
YECH
ZECH

•E•C
DESC
EEOC

••EC
ALEC
AVEC
BSEC
ELEC
EXEC
MSEC
OPEC
PREC
PSEC
SPEC

ED••
EDAM
EDAX
EDDA
EDDO
EDDS
EDDY
EDEN
EDER
EDGE
EDGY
EDHS
EDIE
EDIT
EDNA
EDOM
EDTA
EDUC

E•D•
EADS
EDDA
EDDO
EDDS
EDDY
ENDE
ENDO
ENDS
ERDA
ERDE
ETDS

E••D
EGAD
EKED
ENID
EXOD
EYED

•ED•
BEDE
BEDS
CEDE
CEDI
FEDS
HEDY
JEDI
KEDS
LEDA
LEDS
MEDE
MEDS
PEDI
PEDO
PEDS
REDD
REDE
REDI
REDO
REDS
TEDS
VEDA
WEDS
YEDO
ZEDS

•E•D
BEAD
BEND
DEAD
DEED
FEED
FEND
FEUD
GEED
HEAD
HEED
HELD
HERD
LEAD
LEND
LEWD
MEAD
MEED
MELD
MEND
NEED
NEJD
NERD
PEND
READ
RECD
REDD
REED
REGD
REID
REND
RETD
SEED
SEND
TEED
TEND
VELD
VEND
VERD
WEED
WELD
WEND
ZEND

••ED
ABED
ACED
AGED
APED
AWED
AXED
BLED
BRED
BSED
COED
CUED
DEED
DIED
DRED
DYED
EKED
EYED
FEED
FLED
FRED
GEED
HEED
HIED
HOED
HUED
ICED
IRED
LIED
MEED
MRED
NEED
OHED
OKED
OPED
OWED
PIED
PLED
PRED
REED
RUED
SEED
SHED
SKED
SLED
SPED
SUED
SWED
TEED
TIED
TOED
USED
VIED
WEED

EE••
EEEE
EEGS
EEKS
EELS
EELY
EENY
EEOC
EERO
EERY

E•E•
EBEN
EDEN
EDER
EEEE
EGER
EKED
EKES
ELEA
ELEC
ELEM
ELEV
EMES
EPEE
ESEL
ETES
EVEL
EVEN
EVER
EVES
EWEN
EWER
EWES
EXEC
EXES
EYED
EYER
EYES
EZEK

E••E
EASE
EAVE
ECCE
EDGE
EDIE
EEEE
EINE
EIRE
ELBE
ELIE
ELKE
ELLE
ELSE
ENCE
ENDE
ENNE
ENSE
EPEE
ERDE
ERIE
ERLE
ERNE
ERSE
ERTE
ESCE
ESME
ESNE
ESSE
ESTE
ETRE
ETTE
EVOE
EYRE

•EE•
BEEB
BEEF
BEEN
BEEP
BEER
BEES
BEET
CEES
DEED
DEEM
DEEP
DEER
DEES
DEET
EEEE
FEED
FEEL
FEES
FEET
GEED
GEEK
GEER
GEES
GEEZ
HEED
HEEL
HEEP
HEER
HEET
JEEP
JEER
JEEZ
KEEL
KEEN
KEEP
KEET
LEEK
LEER
LEES
LEET
MEED
MEEK
MEER
MEET
NEED
NEEL
NEEM
NEER
NEET
PEEK
PEEL
PEEN
PEEP
PEER
REED
REEF
REEK
REEL
REES
SEED
SEEK
SEEL
SEEM
SEEN
SEEP
SEER
SEES
TEED
TEEM
TEEN
TEES
VEEP
VEER
VEES
WEEB
WEED
WEEK
WEEN
WEEP
ZEES

•E•E
BEBE
BEDE
BENE
BETE
CEDE
CENE
CEPE
CERE
CETE
DEKE
DELE
DEME
DENE
EEEE
FEME
FERE
FETE
GENE
GERE
HEBE
HEME
HERE
JEFE
JETE
LESE
MEDE
MEME
MERE
METE
NEBE
NENE
NEVE
PEKE
PELE
PEPE
PERE
PETE
REDE
RENE
RETE
REVE
SEBE
SEME
SENE
SERE
SEVE
TELE
TENE
TETE
UELE
VERE
WERE
WEVE
ZEKE

••EE
AGEE
AKEE
ALEE
BREE
CHEE
CREE
DREE
EEEE
EPEE
FLEE
FREE
GHEE
GLEE
GREE
IDEE
INEE
ISEE
KLEE
KNEE
OGEE
OSEE
RHEE
SKEE
SMEE
SNEE
SPEE
THEE
TREE
TWEE
ULEE
USEE
WHEE

EF••
EFFS
EFIK
EFTS

E•F•
EFFS

E••F
ENUF

•EF•
DEFS
DEFT
DEFY
HEFT
JEFE
JEFF
LEFT
NEFF
REFL
REFS
REFT
TEFF
WEFT

•E•F
BEEF
CERF
DEAF
JEFF
KERF
LEAF
LEIF
NEFF
NERF
NEUF
NEWF
OEUF
PELF
PERF
REEF
SELF
SERF
TEFF

••EF
ALEF
BEEF
CHEF
CLEF
FIEF
LIEF
PREF
REEF
TREF

EG••
EGAD
EGAL
EGAN
EGER
EGGO
EGGS
EGGY
EGIS
EGON
EGOS

E•G•
EDGE
EDGY
EEGS
EGGO
EGGS
EGGY
ENGR
ENGS
ERGO
ERGS

•EG•
BEGS
DEGS
EEGS
KEGS
LEGO
LEGS
MEGA
NEGS
PEGS
REGD
REGS
REGT
SEGA
SEGO
TEGS
VEGA
YEGG

•E•G
BELG
BENG
BERG
DENG
GEOG
PEAG
WENG
YEGG

••EG
DREG
GLEG
GREG
OLEG
OREG
ROEG
SKEG

E•H•
ECHO
ECHT
EDHS
ELHI
EPHA
ETHS

E••H
EACH
ESTH
ETAH
ETCH
EVAH
EXCH

•EH•
JEHU
LEHR
NEHI
PEHS
SEHR

•E•H
BETH
HETH
IEOH
LEAH
LECH
MECH
MESH
METH
NETH
PENH
PERH
RESH
SECH
SETH
TECH
TESH
TETH
YEAH
YECH
ZECH
ZEPH

EI••
EINE
EINS

EIRE

E•I•
EDIE
EDIT
EFIK
EGIS
ELIA
ELIE
ELIS
ELIZ
EMIA
EMIC
EMIL
EMIR
EMIT
ENID
EPIC
EPIS
ERIC
ERIE
ERIK
ERIN
ERIQ
ERIS
ETIC
EVIL
EXIT
EZIO

E••I
ELHI
ELOI
EQUI
ESAI
ETUI

•EI•
BEIN
CEIL
DEIL
FEIN
GEIN
HEIN
HEIR
LEIA
LEIF
LEIS
MEIN
MEIR
NEIL
NEIN
OEIL
QEII
REID
REIN
REIS
REIT
SEIN
SEIS
VEII
VEIL
VEIN
WEIL
WEIR
ZEIN

•E•I
BENI
CEDI
DEBI
DECI
DELI
DEMI
DESI
DEVI
HELI
HEMI
JEDI
KEPI
LENI
LEOI
LEVI
NEHI
NERI
NEVI
PEDI
PERI
QEII
REDI
RENI
SEMI
SETI
TERI
VEII
VENI
YETI

••EI
DREI
FREI
ZWEI

•EJ•
DEJA
NEJD
SEJM

EK••
EKCO
EKED
EKES

E•K•
EEKS
ELKE
ELKO
ELKS
ERKS

E••K
EFIK
ERIK
EWOK
EYCK
EZEK

•EK•
DEKA
DEKE
EEKS
LEKS
PEKE
WEKA
ZEKE

•E•K
BEAK
BECK
DECK
DESK
GEEK
HECK
JERK
LEAK
LEEK
LEUK
MEEK
NECK
PEAK
PECK
PEEK
PERK
REEK
SEEK
TEAK
WEAK
WEEK
WELK
YERK

••EK
EZEK
GEEK
LEEK
MEEK
PEEK
PREK
REEK
SEEK
TREK
WEEK

EL••
ELAL
ELAM
ELAN
ELBA
ELBE
ELEA
ELEC
ELEM
ELEV
ELHI
ELIA
ELIE
ELIS
ELIZ
ELKE
ELKO
ELKS
ELLA
ELLE
ELLS
ELLY
ELMO
ELMS
ELOI
ELON
ELSA
ELSE
ELUL

E•L•
EBLA
EELS
EELY
ELLA
ELLE
ELLS
ELLY
EMLY
ERLE

E••L
EARL
ECCL
ECOL
EGAL
ELAL
ELUL
EMIL
ENCL
ENOL
ESEL
ETAL
EVEL
EVIL
EXCL

•EL•
BELA
BELG
BELL
BELO
BELS
BELT
BELY
CELA
CELL
CELS
CELT
DELE
DELI
DELL
DELS
DELY
EELS
EELY
FELL
FELT
GELL
GELS
GELT
HELD
HELI
HELL
HELM
HELO
HELP
JELL
KELP
LELY
MELD
MELL
MELT
NELL
PELE
PELF
PELL
PELT
RELS
RELY
SELA
SELF
SELL
TELE
TELL
TELO
UELE
VELA
VELD
WELD
WELK
WELL
WELT
YELL
YELP

•E•L
BEAL
BELL
CEIL
CELL
DEAL
DECL
DEIL
DELL
FEEL
FELL
GELL
GENL
GEOL
HEAL
HEEL
HELL
HERL
JELL
KEEL
LEAL
MEAL
MELL
MERL
MEWL
NEAL
NEEL
NEIL
NELL
OEIL
PEAL
PEEL
PELL
REAL
REEL
REFL
REPL
SEAL
SEEL
SELL
SEUL
TEAL
TELL
VEAL
VEIL
WEAL
WEIL
WELL
YELL
ZEAL

••EL
ABEL
AUEL
AXEL
BIEL
BREL
CIEL
COEL
DUEL
ESEL
EVEL
FEEL
FUEL
GAEL
HEEL
ICEL
JAEL
JOEL
KAEL
KEEL
KIEL
KTEL
NEEL
NOEL
OPEL
OREL
PEEL
QUEL
REEL
RIEL
SEEL
SHEL
TAEL

EM••
EMES
EMIA
EMIC
EMIL
EMIR
EMIT
EMLY
EMMA
EMMY
EMPS
EMTS
EMUS

E•M•
ELMO
ELMS
EMMA
EMMY
ERMA
ESME

E••M
EDAM
EDOM
ELAM
ELEM
ETYM
EXAM

•EM•
BEMA
BEMS
DEME
DEMI
DEMO
DEMS
DEMY
FEMA
FEME
FEMS
GEMS
HEMA
HEME
HEMI
HEMO
HEMP
HEMS
KEMO
KEMP
LEMA
LEMS
MEME
MEMO
MEMS
NEMO
REMO
REMS
SEME
SEMI
SEMS
TEMA
TEMP

•E•M
BEAM
BERM
DEEM
DERM
DEUM
GEOM
GERM
GEUM
HELM
HERM
MEUM
NEEM
PERM
REAM
SEAM
SEEM
SEJM
TEAM
TEEM
TERM

••EM
AHEM
CHEM
CLEM
DEEM
DIEM
ELEM
FLEM
IDEM
ITEM
NEEM
OREM
POEM
PREM
QUEM
SEEM
SHEM
STEM
TEEM
THEM
YLEM

EN••
ENCE
ENCL
ENCS
ENCY
ENDE
ENDO
ENDS
ENGR
ENGS
ENID
ENNA
ENNE
ENOL
ENOS
ENOW
ENRY
ENSE
ENTO
ENTR
ENTS
ENUF
ENVS
ENVY
ENYA
ENYO
ENZO

E•N•
EDNA
EENY
EINE
EINS
ENNA
ENNE
EONS
ERNE
ERNO
ERNS
ESNE
ETNA

E••N
EARN
EBAN
EBEN
EBON
ECON
EDEN
EGAN
EGON
ELAN
ELON
ERIN
ESPN
ETON
EVAN
EVEN
EWEN
EXON

•EN•
BEND
BENE
BENG
BENI
BENT
BENU
BENZ
CENA
CENE
CENO
CENS
CENT
DENE
DENG
DENS
DENT
DENY
EENY
FEND
FENN
FENS
GENA
GENE
GENL
GENS
GENT
GENU
GENX
GENY
HENS
HENT
JENA
JENS
KENO
KENS
KENT
LENA
LEND
LENI
LENO
LENS
LENT
LENZ
MEND
MENS
MENT
MENU
NENE
OENO
PENA
PEND
PENH
PENN
PENS
PENT
REND
RENE
RENI
RENO
RENT
SEND
SENE
SENS
SENT
TEND
TENE
TENN
TENO
TENS
TENT
VENA
VEND
VENI
VENN
VENT
WEND
WENG
WENS
WENT
XENA
XENO
YENS
ZEND
ZENO

•E•N
AEON
BEAN
BEEN
BEIN
BERN
CERN
DEAN
DERN
FEIN
FENN
FERN
GEIN
HEIN
HERN
HEWN
JEAN
KEAN
KEEN
KERN
LEAN
LEON
MEAN
MEIN
NEBN
NEIN
NEON
NEUN
PEEN
PENN
PEON
REIN
SEAN
SEEN
SEIN
SEWN
TEEN
TENN
TERN
VEIN
VENN
VERN
WEAN
WEEN
YEAN
ZEIN

••EN
ADEN
AMEN
ATEN
BEEN
BIEN
BREN
CAEN
CHEN
COEN
DIEN
EBEN
EDEN
EVEN
EWEN
GLEN
GMEN
GWEN
JAEN
KEEN
LIEN
MIEN
OLEN
OMEN
OPEN
OVEN
OWEN
OXEN
PEEN
RIEN
SEEN
STEN
SVEN
TEEN
THEN
TMEN
WEEN
WHEN
WIEN
WREN
XMEN

EO••
EONS
EOUS

E•O•
EBON
ECOL
ECON
EDOM
EEOC
EGON
EGOS
ELOI
ELON
ENOL
ENOS
ENOW
EPOS
EROO
EROS
ESOP
ESOS
ETON
EVOE
EWOK
EXOD
EXON
EXOR
EYOT

E••O
EBRO
ECHO
ECTO
EDDO
EERO
EGGO
EKCO
ELKO
ELMO
ENDO
ENTO
ENYO
ENZO
ERGO
ERNO
EROO
ESPO
ESSO
ESTO
EURO
EXPO
EZIO

•EO•
AEON
CEOS
EEOC
GEOG
GEOL
GEOM
IEOH
KEOS
LEOI
LEON
LEOS
MEOW
NEON
PEON
REOS

•E•O
AERO
BELO
BESO
CENO
CERO
DECO
DEMO
DEVO
EERO
HELO
HEMO
HERO
KEMO
KENO
KETO
LEGO
LENO
LETO
LEVO
MECO
MEMO
MERO
MESO
NEBO
NEMO
NERO
OENO
PEDO
PEPO
PESO
PETO
REDO
REMO
RENO
REPO
SEGO
SERO
TELO
TENO
VERO
VETO
XENO
XERO
YEDO
ZENO
ZERO

••EO
AREO
CLEO
IDEO
OLEO
OREO
PLEO
RHEO
THEO

EP••
EPEE
EPHA
EPIC
EPIS
EPOS

E•P•
EMPS
ESPN
ESPO
ESPS
ESPY
EXPO
EXPT

E••P
EARP
ESOP
EVAP

•EP•
CEPE
CEPS
DEPP
DEPT
HEPT
KEPI
KEPT
PEPA
PEPE
PEPO
PEPS
REPL
REPO
REPP

REPS REPT SEPT TEPP WEPT ZEPH

•E•P
BEEP DEEP DEPP HEAP HEEP HELP HEMP JEEP KEEP KELP KEMP LEAP NEAP PEEP PERP REAP REPP RESP REUP SEEP TEMP TEPP TERP VEEP WEEP YELP

••EP
ALEP BEEP DEEP HEEP JEEP KEEP PEEP PREP SEEP SHEP SKEP STEP UTEP VEEP WEEP

EQ••
EQUI

E•Q•
ESQS

E••Q
ERIQ

•EQ•
SEQQ

•E•Q
SEQQ

••EQ
FREQ

ER••
ERAS ERAT ERDA ERDE ERGO ERGS ERIC ERIE ERIK ERIN ERIQ ERIS ERKS ERLE ERMA ERNE ERNO ERNS EROO EROS ERRS ERSE ERST ERTE

E•R•
EARL EARN EARP EARS EBRO ECRU EERO EERY EIRE ENRY ERRS ETRE EURO EURY EWRY EYRA EYRE EYRY EZRA

E••R
EDER EGER EMIR ENGR ENTR EVER EWER EXOR EYER

•ER•
AERO AERY BERG BERM BERN BERT CERA CERE CERF CERN CERO CERT DERM DERN EERO EERY FERE FERN GERA GERE GERM HERA HERB HERD HERE HERL HERM HERN HERO HERR HERS JERK KERB KERF KERN KERR KERT MERE MERL MERO MERS MERV NERD NERF NERI NERO PERE PERF PERH PERI PERK PERM PERP PERS PERT PERU SERA SERB SERE SERF SERO SERS SERT SERV TERA TERI TERM TERN TERP TERR VERA VERB VERD VERE VERN VERO VERS VERT VERY WERE WERT XERO YERK ZERO

•E•R
BEAR BEER DEAR DEER FEAR GEAR GEER HEAR HEBR HEER HEIR HERR JEER KERR LEAR LEER LEHR MEER MEIR NEAR NEBR NEER PEAR PEER REAR SEAR SEER SEHR TEAR TERR VEER WEAR WEIR YEAR

••ER
ABER ACER AGER AMER APER AUER AVER AXER AYER BAER BEER BOER BRER CBER CHER CUER DEER DOER DYER EDER EGER EVER EWER EYER GEER GOER HEER HIER HOER HYER ICER ITER JEER LEER MEER NEER NLER ODER OMER ONER OPER OVER OWER OYER PEER PIER PUER RUER SEER STER SUER TIER UBER USER VEER VIER YSER

ES••
ESAI ESAS ESAU ESCE ESEL ESME ESNE ESOP ESOS ESPN ESPO ESPS ESPY ESQS ESSA ESSE ESSO ESTA ESTE ESTH ESTO ESUS

E•S•
EASE EAST EASY ELSA ELSE ENSE ERSE ERST ESSA ESSE ESSO

E••S
EADS EARS EATS EBBS ECUS EDDS EDHS EEGS EEKS EELS EFFS EFTS EGGS EGIS EGOS EINS EKES ELIS ELKS ELLS ELMS EMES EMPS EMTS EMUS ENCS ENDS ENGS ENOS ENTS ENVS EONS EOUS EPIS EPOS ERAS ERGS ERIS ERKS ERNS EROS ERRS ESAS ESOS ESPS ESQS ESUS ETAS ETDS ETES ETHS EVES EWES EXES EXTS EYAS EYES

•ES•
BESO BESS BEST CESS CEST DESC DESI DESK FESS FEST GEST HESS HEST JESS JEST JESU LESE LESS LEST MESA MESH MESO MESS NESS NEST PESO PEST RESH RESP REST SESS TESH TESS TEST VEST WEST ZEST

•E•S
BEAS BEDS BEES BEGS BELS BEMS BESS BETS BEYS CEES CELS CENS CEOS CEPS CESS DEBS DEES DEFS DEGS DELS DEMS DENS DETS DEUS DEWS DEYS EEGS EEKS EELS FEDS FEES FEMS FENS FESS GEES GELS GEMS GENS GETS HEMS HENS HERS HESS HEWS JENS JESS JETS JEWS KEAS KEDS KEGS KENS KEOS KEYS LEAS LEDS LEES LEGS LEIS LEKS LEMS LENS LEOS LESS LETS MEAS MEDS MEMS MENS MERS MESS METS MEWS NEBS NEGS NESS NETS NEWS PEAS PECS PEDS PEGS PEHS PENS PEPS PERS PETS PEWS REBS RECS REDS REES REFS REGS REIS RELS REMS REOS REPS RETS REVS REYS SEAS SEBS SECS SEES SEIS SEMS SENS SERS SESS SETS SEWS TEAS TECS TEDS TEES TEGS TENS TESS TETS UEYS VEES VERS VETS WEBS WEDS WENS WETS YEAS YENS YEWS ZEDS ZEES ZEUS

••ES
ACES ADES AGES ALES AMES APES ARES ATES AVES AWES AXES AYES BEES BYES CEES CUES DEES DIES DOES DUES DYES EKES EMES ETES EVES EWES EXES EYES FEES FOES GEES GOES HIES HOES HRES HUES ICES IDES ILES INES IRES ITES IVES JOES KYES LEES LIES LYES MBES MIES MMES NAES NOES ODES OLES ONES OPES ORES OWES PIES PRES QUES REES RHES ROES RTES RUES RYES SEES SHES STES SUES TEES TIES TOES TRES TUES UKES UNES USES UTES VEES VIES WOES WYES YVES ZEES

ET••
ETAH ETAL ETAS ETAT ETCH ETDS ETES ETHS ETIC ETNA ETON ETRE ETTA ETTE ETUI ETUX ETYM

E•T•
EATS ECTO EDTA EFTS EMTS ENTO ENTR ENTS ERTE ESTA ESTE ESTH ESTO ETTA ETTE EXTS

E••T
EAST ECHT EDIT EMIT ERAT ERST ETAT EXIT EXPT EYOT

•ET•
BETA BETE BETH BETS BETZ CETA CETE DETS FETA FETE GETA GETS GETZ HETH JETE JETS JETT KETO KETT LETO LETS LETT META METE METH METS METZ NETH NETS PETA PETE PETO PETS RETD RETE RETS SETA SETH SETI SETS SETT TETE TETH TETS VETO VETS WETS YETI ZETA

•E•T
BEAT BEET BELT BENT BERT BEST CELT CENT CERT CEST DEBT DEET DEFT DENT DEPT DEUT FEAT FEET FELT FEST GELT GENT GEST HEAT HECT HEET HEFT HENT HEPT HEST JEST JETT KEET KENT KEPT KERT KETT LECT LEET LEFT LENT LEST LETT MEAT MEET MELT MENT NEAT NEET NEST NEUT NEWT NEXT PEAT PELT PENT PERT PEST RECT REFT REGT REIT RENT REPT REST SEAT SECT SENT SEPT SERT SETT SEXT TENT TEST TEUT TEXT VENT VERT VEST WEFT WELT WENT WEPT WERT WEST ZEST

••ET
ABET ACET BEET BRET CHET DEET DIET DUET FEET FRET HEET IBET ICET KEET LEET MEET NEET NYET PIET POET PRET RHET SPET STET SUET TRET

VIET
WHET

EU••
EURO
EURY

E•U•
EAUX
ECUA
ECUS
EDUC
ELUL
EMUS
ENUF
EOUS
EQUI
ESUS
ETUI
ETUX

E••U
ECRU
ESAU

•EU•
DEUM
DEUS
DEUT
DEUX
FEUD
GEUM
JEUX
LEUK
MEUM
NEUF
NEUN
NEUT
OEUF
REUP
SEUL
TEUT
YEUX
ZEUS

•E•U
BEAU
BENU
CEBU
GENU
JEHU
JESU
LEVU
MENU
PEAU
PERU
VEAU
ZEBU

••EU
BLEU
DIEU
LIEU

EV••
EVAH
EVAN
EVAP
EVEL
EVEN
EVER
EVES
EVIL
EVOE

E•V•
EAVE
ENVS
ENVY

E••V
ELEV

•EV•
BEVY
DEVA
DEVI
DEVO
LEVI
LEVO
LEVU
LEVY
NEVA
NEVE
NEVI
REVE
REVS
SEVE
WEVE

•E•V
MERV
SERV

••EV
BREV
ELEV
KIEV
PREV

EW••
EWEN
EWER
EWES
EWOK
EWRY

E••W
ENOW

•EW•
DEWS
DEWY
HEWN
HEWS
JEWS
LEWD
MEWL
MEWS
NEWF
NEWS
NEWT
PEWS
SEWN
SEWS
TEWA
YEWS

•E•W
MEOW

••EW
ANEW
BLEW
BREW
CHEW
CLEW
CREW
DREW
FLEW
GREW
KNEW
LOEW
PHEW
PLEW
SKEW
SLEW
SMEW
SPEW
STEW
THEW
VIEW
WHEW

EX••
EXAM
EXCH
EXCL
EXEC
EXES
EXIT
EXOD
EXON
EXOR
EXPO
EXPT
EXTS

E••X
EAUX
EDAX
ETUX

•EX•
HEXA
NEXT
SEXT
SEXY
TEXT

•E•X
DEUX
GENX
JEUX
YEUX

••EX
ALEX
AMEX
APEX
CHEX
FLEX
GREX
IBEX
ILEX
NMEX
PLEX
TREX

EY••
EYAS
EYCK
EYED
EYER
EYES
EYOT
EYRA
EYRE
EYRY

E•Y•
ENYA
ENYO
ETYM

E••Y
EASY
EDDY
EDGY
EELY
EENY
EERY
EGGY
ELLY
EMLY
EMMY
ENCY
ENRY
ENVY
ESPY
EURY
EWRY
EYRY

•EY•
BEYS
DEYS
KEYS
REYS
UEYS

•E•Y
AERY
BELY
BEVY
DEFY
DELY
DEMY
DENY
DEWY
EELY
EENY
EERY
GENY
HEDY
LELY
LEVY
RELY
SECY
SEXY
VERY

••EY
ACEY
FLEY
FREY
GLEY
GREY
HUEY
IVEY
JOEY
OBEY
OKEY
PREY
SUEY
THEY
TREY
UREY
WHEY

EZ••
EZEK
EZIO
EZRA

E•Z•
ENZO

E••Z
ELIZ

•EZ•
REZA

•E•Z
BENZ
BETZ
GEEZ
GETZ
JEEZ
LENZ
METZ

••EZ
BAEZ
CHEZ
GEEZ
INEZ
JEEZ
OYEZ
PREZ
SUEZ

FA••
FACE
FACP
FACS
FACT
FADE
FADO
FADS
FAHD
FAHR
FAIL
FAIN
FAIR
FAIT
FAKE
FALA
FALK
FALL
FALX
FAME
FANE
FANG
FANS
FAQS
FARE
FARM
FARO
FARR
FARS
FASO
FAST
FATA
FATE
FATH
FATS
FAUN
FAUT
FAUX
FAVA
FAVE
FAWN
FAYE
FAYS
FAZE

F•A•
FEAR
FEAT
FIAT
FLAB
FLAG
FLAK
FLAM
FLAN
FLAP
FLAT
FLAV
FLAW
FLAX
FLAY
FOAL
FOAM
FRAE
FRAM
FRAN
FRAP
FRAS
FRAT
FRAU
FRAY
FUAD

F••A
FALA
FATA
FAVA
FEMA
FETA
FICA
FILA
FINA
FLEA
FNMA
FORA
FRIA
FULA

•FA•
AFAR
MFAS
SFAX

•F•A
AFTA

••FA
AGFA
ALFA
SOFA
TUFA
URFA

F•B•
FIBS
FOBS
FUBS

F••B
FLAB
FLUB
FORB
FTLB

F•C•
FACE
FACP
FACS
FACT
FICA
FICE
FICT
FOCH
FOCI
FRCP
FRCS

F••C
FDIC
FISC
FLIC
FLOC

•FC•
PFCS

••FC
COFC
KOFC

FD••
FDIC

F•D•
FADE
FADO
FADS
FEDS
FIDE
FIDO
FIDS
FLDR
FUDD

F••D
FAHD
FEED
FEND
FEUD
FIND
FLED
FOLD
FOND
FOOD
FORD
FRED
FUAD
FUDD
FUND

•FD•
RFDS

•F•D
NFLD
SFPD

FE••
FEAR
FEAT
FEDS
FEED
FEEL
FEES
FEET
FEIN
FELL
FELT
FEMA
FEME
FEMS
FEND
FENN
FENS
FERE
FERN
FESS
FEST
FETA
FETE
FEUD

F•E•
FEED
FEEL
FEES
FEET
FIEF
FLEA
FLED
FLEE
FLEM
FLEW
FLEX
FLEY
FOES
FRED
FREE
FREI
FREQ
FRET
FREY
FUEL

F••E
FACE
FADE
FAKE
FAME
FANE
FARE
FATE
FAVE
FAYE
FAZE
FEME
FERE
FETE
FICE
FIDE
FIFE
FILE
FINE
FIRE
FIVE
FIXE
FLEE
FLOE
FLUE
FOIE
FORE
FOXE
FRAE
FREE
FROE
FRYE
FUME
FUSE
FUZE
FYKE

••FE
CAFE
FIFE
JEFE
LIFE
RIFE
SAFE
WIFE

F•F•
FIFE
FIFI
FIFO

F••F
FIEF
FUNF

•FF•
EFFS
IFFY
OFFS
PFFT

••FF
BAFF
BIFF
BOFF
BUFF
CUFF
DAFF
DIFF
DOFF
DUFF
GAFF
GUFF
HOFF
HUFF
JEFF
JIFF
LUFF
MIFF
MUFF
NEFF
ORFF
PUFF
RAFF
RIFF
RUFF
SUFF
TEFF
TIFF
TOFF
TUFF

F•G•
FIGS
FOGG
FOGS
FOGY
FUGS
FUGU

F••G
FANG
FLAG
FLOG
FOGG
FROG
FRUG

•FG•
AFGH

F•H•
FAHD
FAHR
FOHN

F••H
FATH
FISH
FOCH

•F•H
AFGH

FI••
FIAT
FIBS
FICA
FICE
FICT
FIDE
FIDO
FIDS
FIEF
FIFE
FIFI
FIFO
FIGS
FIJI
FILA
FILE
FILL
FILM
FILS
FINA
FIND
FINE
FINI
FINK
FINN
FINO
FINS
FIRE
FIRM
FIRN
FIRS
FISC
FISH
FISK
FIST
FITS
FITZ
FIVE
FIXE
FIZZ

F•I•
FAIL
FAIN
FAIR
FAIT
FDIC
FEIN
FLIC
FLIM
FLIP
FLIT
FLIX
FOIE
FOIL
FOIN
FOIS
FRIA
FRIO
FRIS
FRIT
FRIZ
FWIW

F••I
FIFI
FIJI
FINI
FOCI
FREI
FUJI

•FI•
EFIK

•F•I
IFNI
PFUI

••FI
FIFI
HIFI
KOFI
SUFI

F•J•
FIJI
FUJI

F•K•
FAKE
FYKE

F••K
FALK
FINK
FISK
FLAK
FOLK
FORK
FUNK

•F•K
EFIK

FL••
FLAB
FLAG
FLAK
FLAM
FLAN
FLAP
FLAT
FLAV
FLAW
FLAX
FLAY
FLDR
FLEA
FLED
FLEE
FLEM
FLEW
FLEX
FLEY
FLIC
FLIM
FLIP
FLIT
FLIX
FLOC
FLOE
FLOG
FLOP
FLOR
FLOW
FLOZ
FLUB
FLUE
FLUS
FLUX

F•L•
FALA
FALK
FALL
FALX
FELL
FELT
FILA
FILE
FILL
FILM
FILS
FOLD
FOLK
FTLB
FULA
FULL

F••L
FAIL
FALL
FEEL
FELL
FILL
FOAL
FOIL
FOOL
FOUL
FOWL
FUEL
FULL
FURL

•FL•
NFLD

••FL
INFL
REFL

F•M•
FAME
FEMA
FEME
FEMS
FNMA
FUME
FUMY

F••M
FARM
FILM
FIRM
FLAM
FLEM
FLIM
FOAM
FORM
FRAM
FROM

••FM
AMFM

FN••
FNMA

F•N•
FANE

FANG	FOPS	FLOP	FORE	FOBS	FEAT	FUND	**F•X•**	GABE	GIAN	GAGA	**G•D•**	GEER	CTGE
FANS	FORA	FRAP	FORK	FOES	FEET	FUNF	FIXE	GABO	GLAD	GIGA	GADS	GEES	DOGE
FEND	FORB	FRCP	FORM	FOGS	FELT	FUNK	FOXE	GABS	GLAM	INGA	GIDE	GEEZ	EDGE
FENN	FORD		FORT	FOIS	FEST	FUNT	FOXX	GABY	GMAC	JUGA	GODS	GHEE	GAGE
FENS	FORE	**•FP•**	FURL	FONS	FIAT	FURL	FOXY	GADS	GMAN	LPGA		GLEE	HUGE
FINA	FORK	SFPD	FURO	FOPS	FICT	FURO		GAEA	GMAT	MEGA	**G••D**	GLEG	INGE
FIND	FORM		FURS	FOSS	FIST	FURS	**F••X**	GAEL	GNAR	OLGA	GAUD	GLEN	LOGE
FINE	FORT	**••FP**	FURY	FOYS	FLAT	FURY	FALX	GAFF	GNAT	RAGA	GEED	GLEY	LUGE
FINI	FOSS	KOFP		FRAS	FLIT	FUSE	FAUX	GAGA	GNAW	RIGA	GILD	GMEN	MAGE
FINK	FOUL		**F••R**	FRCS	FONT	FUSS	FLAX	GAGE	GOAD	RUGA	GIRD	GOER	MTGE
FINN	FOUR	**F•Q•**	FAHR	FRIS	FOOT	FUST	FLEX	GAGS	GOAL	SAGA	GLAD	GOES	PAGE
FINO	FOWL	FAQS	FAIR	FUBS	FORT	FUTZ	FLIX	GAIA	GOAT	SEGA	GOAD	GREE	RAGE
FINS	FOXE		FARR	FUGS	FOYT	FUZE	FLUX	GAIL	GRAB	TOGA	GOLD	GREG	SAGE
FOND	FOXX	**F••Q**	FEAR	FURS	FRAT	FUZZ	FOXX	GAIN	GRAD	URGA	GOND	GREW	STGE
FONS	FOXY	FREQ	FLDR	FUSS	FRET			GAIT	GRAF	USGA	GOOD	GREX	TIGE
FONT	FOYS		FLOR		FRIT	**F•U•**	**•F•X**	GALA	GRAM	VEGA	GRAD	GREY	URGE
FONZ	FOYT	**•FQ•**	FOUR	**•FS•**	FUNT	FAUN	SFAX	GALE	GRAN	VIGA	GRID	GWEN	WAGE
FUND		RFQS		IFSO	FUST	FAUT		GALL	GRAS	YOGA			
FUNF	**F•O•**		**•FR•**			FAUX	**FY••**	GALS	GRAU	YUGA	**•G•D**	**G••E**	**G•F•**
FUNK	FLOC	**FR••**	AFRO	**•F•S**	**•FT•**	FEUD	FYKE	GALV	GRAY		AGED	GABE	GAFF
FUNT	FLOE	FRAE	MFRS	AFTS	AFTA	FLUB		GAMA	GRAZ	**G•B•**	EGAD	GAGE	GIFT
	FLOG	FRAM		EFFS	AFTS	FLUE	**F•Y•**	GAME	GUAM	GABA		GALE	GIFU
F••N	FLOP	FRAN	**•F•R**	EFTS	EFTS	FLUS	FAYE	GAMO	GUAN	GABE	**••GD**	GAME	GUFF
FAIN	FLOR	FRAP	AFAR	MFAS		FLUX	FAYS	GAMP	GUAR	GABO	BIGD	GAPE	
FAUN	FLOW	FRAS		MFRS	**•F•T**	FOUL	FOYS	GAMS		GABS	REGD	GARE	**G••F**
FAWN	FLOZ	FRAT	**••FR**	OFFS	PFFT	FOUR	FOYT	GAMY	**G••A**	GABY		GATE	GAFF
FEIN	FOOD	FRAU	SAFR	PFCS		FRUG	FRYE	GANG	GABA	GIBB	**GE••**	GAVE	GOLF
FENN	FOOL	FRAY		RFDS	**••FT**			GANN	GAEA	GIBE	GEAR	GAYE	GOOF
FERN	FOOT	FRCP	**F•S•**	RFQS	CUFT	**F••U**	**F••Y**	GAOL	GAGA	GIBS	GEED	GAZE	GRAF
FINN	FROE	FRCS	FASO	UFOS	DAFT	FRAU	FLAY	GAPA	GAIA	GOBI	GEEK	GENE	GUFF
FIRN	FROG	FRED	FAST		DEFT	FUGU	FLEY	GAPE	GALA	GOBO	GEER	GERE	GULF
FLAN	FROM	FREE	FESS	**••FS**	GIFT		FOGY	GAPS	GAMA	GOBS	GEES	GHEE	
FOHN	FROW	FREI	FEST	COFS	HAFT	**•FU•**	FOXY	GARB	GAPA	GOBY	GEEZ	GIBE	**•GF•**
FOIN		FREQ	FISC	DEFS	HEFT	PFUI	FRAY	GARE	GAYA	GRBR	GEIN	GIDE	AGFA
FRAN	**F••O**	FRET	FISH	EFFS	LEFT		FREY	GARN	GAZA	GTBR	GELL	GIVE	
	FADO	FREY	FISK	INFS	LIFT	**••FU**	FUMY	GARP	GENA	GYBE	GELS	GLEE	**•G•F**
•FN•	FARO	FRIA	FIST	KAFS	LOFT	GIFU	FURY	GARR	GERA		GELT	GLUE	TGIF
IFNI	FASO	FRIO	FOSS	OAFS	LUFT	TOFU		GARS	GETA	**G••B**	GEMS	GONE	
	FIDO	FRIS	FUSE	OFFS	PFFT	TUFU	**•F•Y**	GARY	GHIA	GARB	GENA	GORE	**G•G•**
FO••	FIFO	FRIT	FUSS	QAFS	RAFT		IFFY	GASH	GIGA	GIBB	GENE	GREE	GAGA
FOAL	FINO	FRIZ	FUST	REFS	REFT	**F•V•**		GASP	GILA	GLIB	GENL	GYBE	GAGE
FOAM	FRIO	FROE		RIFS	RIFT	FAVA	**••FY**	GAST	GINA	GLOB	GENS	GYRE	GAGS
FOBS	FURO	FROG	**F••S**	WAFS	SIFT	FAVE	DEFY	GATE	GITA	GRAB	GENT	GYVE	GIGA
FOCH		FROM	FACS		SOFT	FIVE	DUFY	GATH	GIZA	GRUB	GENU		GIGI
FOCI	**•FO•**	FROW	FADS	**FT••**	SQFT		IFFY	GATO	GLIA		GENX	**•GE•**	GIGO
FOES	UFOS	FRUG	FANS	FTLB	TAFT	**F••V**		GATS	GNMA	**•GB•**	GENY	AGED	GIGS
FOGG		FRYE	FAQS		TOFT	FLAV	**F•Z•**	GATT	GOYA	IGBO	GEOG	AGEE	GOGH
FOGS	**•F•O**		FARS	**F•T•**	TUFT		FAZE	GAUD			GEOL	AGER	GOGI
FOGY	AFRO	**F•R•**	FATS	FATA	WAFT	**FW••**	FIZZ	GAUL	**•GA•**	**G•C•**	GEOM	AGES	GOGO
FOHN	IFSO	FARE	FAYS	FATE	WEFT	FWIW	FUZE	GAUM	AGAR	GUCK	GERA	EGER	
FOIE		FARM	FEDS	FATH			FUZZ	GAUR	AGAS		GERE	OGEE	**G••G**
FOIL	**••FO**	FARO	FEES	FATS	**FU••**	**F•W•**		GAVE	EGAD	**G••C**	GERM		GANG
FOIN	FIFO	FARR	FEMS	FETA	FUAD	FAWN	**F••Z**	GAWK	EGAL	GLUC	GEST	**•G•E**	GEOG
FOIS	INFO	FARS	FENS	FETE	FUBS	FOWL	FITZ	GAWP	EGAN	GLYC	GETA	AGEE	GLEG
FOLD	LIFO	FERE	FESS	FITS	FUDD		FIZZ	GAYA		GMAC	GETS	AGUE	GLUG
FOLK		FERN	FIBS	FITZ	FUEL	**F••W**	FLOZ	GAYE	**•G•A**		GETZ	OGEE	GONG
FOND	**F•P•**	FIRE	FIDS	FUTZ	FUGS	FLAW	FONZ	GAZA	AGFA	**•GC•**	GEUM	OGLE	GREG
FONS	FOPS	FIRM	FIGS		FUGU	FLEW	FRIZ	GAZE	AGHA	AGCY		OGRE	GRIG
FONT		FIRN	FILS	**F••T**	FUJI	FLOW	FUTZ		AGRA		**G•E•**		GROG
FONZ	**F••P**	FIRS	FINS	FACT	FULA	FROW	FUZZ	**G•A•**	AGUA	**GD••**	GAEA	**••GE**	GUNG
FOOD	FACP	FORA	FIRS	FAIT	FULL	FWIW		GDAY		GDAY	GAEL	ANGE	
FOOL	FLAP	FORB	FITS	FAST	FUME		**GA••**	GEAR	**••GA**		GEED	AUGE	**•GG•**
FOOT	FLIP	FORD	FLUS	FAUT	FUMY		GABA	GHAT	ALGA		GEEK	CAGE	EGGO

EGGS EGGY IGGY OGGI

•G•G
AGOG

••GG
DOGG FOGG HOGG RAGG RIGG YEGG

GH••
GHAT GHEE GHIA

G••H
GASH GATH GISH GOGH GOSH GOTH GUSH

•GH•
AGHA UGHS

•G•H
LGTH

••GH
AFGH GOGH HIGH HUGH NIGH PUGH SIGH YOGH

GI••
GIAN GIBB GIBE GIBS GIDE GIFT GIFU GIGA GIGI GIGO GIGS GILA GILD GILL GILT GIMP GINA GINO GINS GIPS GIRD GIRL GIRN GIRO GIRT GISH GIST GITA GITS GIVE GIZA

G•I•
GAIA GAIL GAIN GAIT GEIN GHIA GLIA GLIB GLIM GOIN GRID GRIG GRIM GRIN GRIP GRIS GRIT GUIN GUIS

G••I
GIGI GOBI GOGI GYRI

•GI•
AGIN AGIO EGIS TGIF

•G•I
AGNI AGRI OGGI UGLI

••GI
GIGI GOGI HAGI MAGI OGGI RIGI YAGI YOGI ZOGI

G••K
GAWK GEEK GOWK GROK GUCK GUNK

GL••
GLAD GLAM GLEE GLEG GLEN GLEY GLIA GLIB GLIM GLOB GLOM GLOP GLOT GLOW GLUC GLUE GLUG GLUM GLUT GLYC GLYN

G•L•
GALA GALE GALL GALS GALV GELL GELS GELT GILA GILD GILL GILT GOLD GOLF GULF GULL GULP

G••L
GAEL GAIL GALL GAOL GAUL GELL GENL GEOL GILL GIRL GOAL GULL

•GL•
AGLY IGLU OGLE UGLI UGLY

•G•L
EGAL

••GL
ANGL

GM••
GMAC GMAN GMAT GMEN

G•M•
GAMA GAME GAMO GAMP GAMS GAMY GEMS GIMP GNMA GUMM GUMP GUMS GYMS

G••M
GAUM GEOM GERM GEUM GLAM GLIM GLOM GLUM GRAM GRIM GUAM GUMM

•GM•
MGMT

GN••
GNAR GNAT GNAW GNMA GNUS

G•N•
GANG GANN GENA GENE GENL GENS GENT GENU GENX GENY GINA GINO GINS GOND GONE GONG GONY GUNG GUNK GUNN GUNS GYNT

G••N
GAIN GANN GARN GEIN GIAN GIRN GLEN GLYN GMAN GMEN GOIN GOON GOWN GRAN GRIN GUAN GUIN GUNN GWEN GWYN

•GN•
AGNI

•G•N
AGIN AGON EGAN EGON

••GN
SIGN

GO••
GOAD GOAL GOAT GOBI GOBO GOBS GOBY GODS GOER GOES GOGH GOGI GOGO GOIN GOLD GOLF GOND GONE GONG GONY GOOD GOOF GOON GOOP GOOS GORE GORP GORY GOSH GOTH GOUP GOUT GOVT GOWK GOWN GOYA

G•O•
GAOL GEOG GEOL GEOM GLOB GLOM GLOP GLOT GLOW GOOD GOOF GOON GOOP GOOS GPOS GROG GROK GROS GROT GROW GTOS GYOR

G••O
GABO GAMO GATO GIGO GINO GIRO GOBO GOGO GYRO

•GO•
AGOG AGON EGON EGOS IGOR

•G•O
AGIO AGRO EGGO IGBO

••GO
ALGO ARGO EGGO ERGO GIGO GOGO HUGO IAGO LAGO LEGO LOGO NOGO PAGO POGO SAGO SEGO TOGO VIGO YUGO ZYGO

GP••
GPOS

G•P•
GAPA GAPE GAPS GIPS GYPS

G••P
GAMP GARP GASP GAWP GIMP GLOP GOOP GORP GOUP GRIP GULP GUMP

GR••
GRAB GRAD GRAF GRAM GRAN GRAS GRAU GRAY GRAZ GRBR GREE GREG GREW GREX GREY GRID GRIG GRIM GRIN GRIP GRIS GRIT GROG GROK GROS GROT GROW GRUB GRUS GRWT

G•R•
GARB GARE GARN GARP GARR GARS GARY GERA GERE GERM GIRD GIRL GIRN GIRO GIRT GORE GORP GORY GURU GYRE GYRI GYRO

G••R
GARR GAUR GEAR GEER GNAR GOER GRBR GTBR GUAR GYOR

•GR•
AGRA AGRI AGRO MGRS OGRE

•G•R
AGAR AGER EGER IGOR

••GR
ENGR JAGR MNGR MSGR SPGR

G•S•
GASH GASP GAST GEST GISH GIST GOSH GUSH GUST

G••S
GABS GADS GAGS GALS GAMS GAPS GARS GATS GEES GELS GEMS GENS GETS GIBS GIGS GINS GIPS GITS GNUS GOBS GODS GOES GOOS GPOS GRAS GRIS GROS GRUS GTOS GUIS GUMS GUNS GUTS GUVS GUYS GYMS GYPS

•G•S
AGAS AGES AGTS EGGS EGIS EGOS MGRS RGTS SGTS UGHS

••GS
AVGS BAGS BEGS BOGS BUGS CHGS CIGS COGS DAGS DEGS DIGS DOGS EEGS EGGS ENGS ERGS FIGS FOGS FUGS GAGS GIGS HAGS HOGS HUGS JAGS JIGS JOGS JUGS KEGS LAGS LEGS LOGS LUGS MAGS MIGS MSGS MTGS MUGS NAGS NEGS NOGS ORGS PEGS PIGS PKGS POGS PUGS RAGS REGS RIGS RUGS SAGS SVGS TAGS TEGS TOGS TUGS VUGS WAGS WIGS ZAGS ZIGS

GT••
GTBR GTOS

G•T•
GATE GATH GATO GATS GATT GETA GETS GETZ GITA GITS GOTH GUTS GWTW

G••T
GAIT GAST GATT GELT GENT GEST GHAT GIFT GILT GIRT GIST GLOT GLUT GMAT GNAT GOAT GOUT GOVT GRIT GROT GRWT GUST GYNT

•GT•
AGTS LGTH RGTS SGTS

•G•T
MGMT

••GT
MSGT REGT SSGT TSGT

GU••
GUAM GUAN GUAR GUCK GUFF GUIN GUIS GULF GULL GULP GUMM GUMP GUMS GUNG GUNK GUNN GUNS GURU GUSH GUST GUTS GUVS GUYS

G•U•
GAUD GAUL GAUM GAUR GEUM GLUC GLUE GLUG GLUM GLUT GNUS GOUP GOUT GRUB GRUS

G••U
GENU GIFU GRAU GURU

•GU•
AGUA AGUE

•G•U
IGLU

••GU
FUGU RAGU

G•V•
GAVE GIVE GOVT GUVS GYVE

G••V
GALV

GW••
GWEN GWTW GWYN

G•W•
GAWK GAWP GOWK GOWN GRWT

G••W
GLOW GNAW GREW GROW GWTW

•GW•
HGWY

G••X
GENX GREX

GY••
GYBE GYMS GYNT GYOR GYPS GYRE GYRI GYRO GYVE

G•Y•
GAYA GAYE GLYC GLYN GOYA GUYS GWYN

G••Y
GABY GAMY GARY GDAY GENY GLEY GOBY GONY GORY GRAY GREY

•G•Y
AGCY AGLY EGGY HGWY IGGY UGLY

••GY
ALGY ARGY BOGY CAGY DOGY EDGY EGGY FOGY IGGY LOGY NAGY ORGY POGY

G•Z•
GAZA GAZE GIZA

G••Z
GEEZ GETZ GRAZ

HA••
HAAG HABE HACK HADE HADJ HAFT HAGI

HAGS
HAHA
HAHN
HAHS
HAIG
HAIK
HAIL
HAIM
HAIR
HAJI
HAJJ
HAKE
HALE
HALF
HALL
HALM
HALO
HALS
HALT
HAMA
HAME
HAMM
HAMS
HANA
HAND
HANG
HANK
HANS
HAOS
HAPI
HAPS
HARD
HARE
HARI
HARK
HARM
HARP
HART
HARZ
HASH
HASP
HAST
HATE
HATH
HATS
HAUL
HAUS
HAUT
HAVE
HAWG
HAWK
HAWN
HAWS
HAYS
HAZE
HAZY

H•A•
HAAG
HEAD
HEAL
HEAP
HEAR
HEAT
HOAD
HOAR
HOAX
HUAC

H••A
HAHA
HAMA
HANA
HEMA
HERA
HEXA
HIJA
HILA
HOLA
HORA
HOYA
HSIA
HULA
HUPA
HYLA

•HA•
AHAB
AHAZ
CHAD
CHAM
CHAN
CHAP
CHAR
CHAS
CHAT
CHAW
CHAZ
DHAL
GHAT
KHAN
KHAS
KHAT
PHAR
PHAT
SHAD
SHAG
SHAH
SHAM
SHAN
SHAQ
SHAW
SHAY
THAI
THAN
THAR
THAS
THAT
THAW
WHAM
WHAT

•H•A
CHIA
GHIA
RHEA
SHEA
THEA
WHOA

••HA
AGHA
DOHA
EPHA
HAHA
NAHA
OSHA

H•B•
HABE
HDBK
HEBE
HEBR
HOBO
HOBS
HUBS

H••B
HERB

•HB•
LHBS
RHBS

•H•B
AHAB
CHUB
SHEB

H•C•
HACK
HECK
HECT
HICK
HOCH
HOCK
HUCK

H••C
HUAC

•H•C
CHIC
CHOC

HD••
HDBK
HDTV
HDWE

H•D•
HADE
HADJ
HEDY
HIDE
HODS
HYDE
HYDR

H••D
HAND
HARD
HEAD
HEED
HELD
HERD
HIED
HIND
HOAD
HOED
HOLD
HOND
HOOD
HUED
HUND

•HD•
PHDS

•H•D
CHAD
CHID
OHED
SHAD
SHED
SHOD
THUD
WHOD

••HD
FAHD

HE••
HEAD
HEAL
HEAP
HEAR
HEAT
HEBE
HEBR
HECK
HECT
HEDY
HEED
HEEL
HEEP
HEER
HEET
HEFT
HEIN
HEIR
HELD
HELI
HELL
HELM
HELO
HELP
HEMA
HEME
HEMI
HEMO
HEMP
HEMS
HENS
HENT
HEPT
HERA
HERB
HERD
HERE
HERL
HERM
HERN
HERO
HERR
HERS
HESS
HEST
HETH
HEWN
HEWS
HEXA

H•E•
HEED
HEEL
HEEP
HEER
HEET
HIED
HIER
HIES
HOED
HOER
HOES
HRES
HUED
HUES
HUEY
HYER

H••E
HABE
HADE
HAKE
HALE
HAME
HARE
HATE
HAVE
HAZE
HDWE
HEBE
HEME
HERE
HIDE
HIKE
HIRE
HITE
HIVE
HOKE
HOLE
HOME
HONE
HOPE
HOSE
HOTE
HOVE
HOWE
HUGE
HUME
HYDE
HYPE

•HE•
AHEM
CHEE
CHEF
CHEM
CHEN
CHER
CHET
CHEW
CHEX
CHEZ
GHEE
OHED
PHEW
RHEA
RHEE
RHEO
RHES
RHET
SHEA
SHEB
SHED
SHEL
SHEM
SHEP
SHES
THEA
THEE
THEM
THEN
THEO
THEW
THEY
WHEE
WHEN
WHET
WHEW
WHEY

•H•E
CHEE
GHEE
IHRE
OHNE
RHEE
RHUE
SHOE
SHUE
THEE
WHEE
WHSE

••HE
ACHE
ASHE
ROHE

H•F•
HAFT
HEFT
HIFI
HOFF
HUFF

H••F
HALF
HOFF
HOOF
HUFF

•H•F
CHEF

HG••
HGWY

H•G•
HAGI
HAGS
HIGH
HOGG
HOGS
HUGE
HUGH
HUGO
HUGS

H••G
HAAG
HAIG
HANG
HAWG
HOGG
HONG
HUNG

•HG•
CHGS

•H•G
CHUG
SHAG
THUG
WHIG

H•H•
HAHA
HAHN
HAHS
HOHO

H••H
HASH
HATH
HETH
HIGH
HOCH
HUGH
HUSH

•H•H
OHOH
SHAH
SHIH
UHOH
UHUH

HI••
HICK
HIDE
HIED
HIER
HIES
HIFI
HIGH
HIJA
HIJO
HIKE
HILA
HILL
HILO
HILT
HIND
HINS
HINT
HIPS
HIRE
HIRT
HISS
HIST
HITE
HITS
HIVE
HIYO

H•I•
HAIG
HAIK
HAIL
HAIM
HAIR
HEIN
HEIR
HSIA
HUIS

H••I
HAGI
HAJI
HAPI
HARI
HELI
HEMI
HIFI
HONI
HOPI

•HI•
CHIA
CHIC
CHID
CHIN
CHIP
CHIS
CHIT
GHIA
OHIO
PHIL
PHIS
PHIZ
SHIH
SHIM
SHIN
SHIP
SHIV
THIN
THIO
THIS
WHIG
WHIM
WHIN
WHIP
WHIR
WHIT
WHIZ

•H•I
THAI

••HI
ELHI
MAHI
NEHI

H•J•
HAJI
HAJJ
HIJA
HIJO
HOJO

H••J
HADJ
HAJJ

H•K•
HAKE
HIKE
HOKE

H••K
HACK
HAIK
HANK
HARK
HAWK
HDBK
HECK
HICK
HOCK
HONK
HOOK
HUCK
HULK
HUNK
HUSK

H•L•
HALE
HALF
HALL
HALM
HALO
HALS
HALT
HELD
HELI
HELL
HELM
HELO
HELP
HILA
HILL
HILO
HILT
HOLA
HOLD
HOLE
HOLM
HOLO
HOLP
HOLS
HOLT
HOLY
HULA
HULK
HULL
HYLA

H••L
HAIL
HALL
HAUL
HEAL
HEEL
HELL
HERL
HILL
HOWL
HULL
HURL

•H•L
CHOL
DHAL
PHIL
SHEL
SHUL

••HL
BUHL
DAHL
KOHL
POHL
SAHL
WAHL
WOHL
WUHL

HM••
HMOS

H•M•
HAMA
HAME
HAMM
HAMS
HEMA
HEME
HEMI
HEMO
HEMP
HEMS
HOME
HOMO
HOMS
HOMY
HUME
HUMP
HUMS
HYMN

H••M
HAIM
HALM
HAMM
HARM
HELM
HERM
HOLM

•HM•
CHMN
OHMS
OHMY

•H•M
AHEM
CHAM
CHEM
CHUM
RHUM
SHAM
SHEM
SHIM
THEM
THOM
WHAM
WHIM
WHOM

••HM
BOHM

H•N•
HANA
HAND
HANG
HANK
HANS
HENS
HENT
HIND
HINS
HINT
HOND
HONE
HONG
HONI
HONK
HUND
HUNG
HUNK
HUNS
HUNT

H••N
HAHN
HAWN
HEIN
HERN
HEWN
HORN
HUON
HYMN
HYPN

•HN•
OHNE
OHNO

•H•N
CHAN
CHEN
CHIN
CHMN
CHON
KHAN
PHON
SHAN
SHIN
SHUN
THAN
THEN
THIN
WHEN
WHIN

••HN
BAHN
CAHN
COHN
FOHN
HAHN
JOHN
KAHN
KUHN
SOHN
ZAHN

HO••
HOAD
HOAR
HOAX
HOBO
HOBS
HOCH
HOCK
HODS
HOED
HOER
HOES
HOFF
HOGG
HOGS
HOHO
HOJO
HOKE
HOLA
HOLD
HOLE
HOLM
HOLO
HOLP
HOLS
HOLT
HOLY
HOME
HOMO
HOMS
HOMY
HOND
HONE
HONG
HONI
HONK
HOOD
HOOF
HOOK
HOOP
HOOT
HOPE
HOPI
HOPS
HORA
HORN
HORS
HORT
HOSE
HOSP
HOSS
HOST
HOTE
HOUR
HOVE
HOWE
HOWL
HOWS
HOYA
HOYS
HOYT

H•O•
HAOS
HMOS
HOOD
HOOF
HOOK
HOOP
HOOT
HUON

H••O
HALO
HELO
HEMO
HERO
HIJO
HILO
HIYO
HOBO
HOHO
HOJO
HOLO
HOMO
HUGO
HYPO

•HO•
AHOY
CHOC
CHOL
CHON
CHOP
CHOU
CHOW
CHOY
DHOW
IHOP
MHOS
OHOH
PHON
PHOT
RHOS
SHOD
SHOE
SHOO
SHOP
SHOT
SHOW
THOM
THOR
THOS
THOU
UHOH
WHOA
WHOD
WHOM
WHOP
WHOS
ZHOU

•H•O
AHSO
OHIO
OHNO
RHEO
SHOO

THEO
THIO

••HO
COHO
ECHO
HOHO
IMHO
MOHO
OCHO
OTHO
PAHO
SOHO
TOHO
YOHO

H•P•
HAPI
HAPS
HEPT
HIPS
HOPE
HOPI
HOPS
HUPA
HYPE
HYPN
HYPO

H••P
HARP
HASP
HEAP
HEEP
HELP
HEMP
HOLP
HOOP
HOSP
HTTP
HUMP

•HP•
SHPT

•H•P
CHAP
CHIP
CHOP
IHOP
SHEP
SHIP
SHOP
WHIP
WHOP
WHUP

•H•Q
SHAQ

HR••
HRES

H•R•
HARD
HARE
HARI
HARK
HARM
HARP
HART
HARZ
HERA
HERB
HERD
HERE
HERL
HERM
HERN
HERO
HERR
HERS
HIRE
HIRT
HORA
HORN
HORS
HORT
HURL
HURT

H••R
HAIR
HEAR
HEBR
HEER
HEIR
HERR
HIER
HOAR
HOER
HOUR
HYDR
HYER

•HR•
IHRE
THRU

•H•R
CHAR
CHER
CHUR
PHAR
THAR
THOR
THUR
WHIR

••HR
BAHR
BOHR
BUHR
FAHR
JAHR
KWHR
LAHR
LEHR
RUHR
SEHR
TAHR
TCHR

HS••
HSIA

H•S•
HASH
HASP
HAST
HESS
HEST
HISS
HIST
HOSE
HOSP
HOSS
HOST
HUSH
HUSK
HUSS

H••S
HAGS
HAHS
HALS
HAMS
HANS
HAOS
HAPS
HATS
HAUS
HAWS
HAYS
HEMS
HENS
HERS
HESS
HEWS
HIES
HINS
HIPS
HISS
HITS
HMOS
HOBS
HODS
HOES
HOGS
HOLS
HOMS
HOPS
HORS
HOSS
HOWS
HOYS
HRES
HUBS
HUES
HUGS
HUIS
HUMS
HUNS
HUSS
HUTS
HWYS

•HS•
AHSO
WHSE

•H•S
CHAS
CHGS
CHIS
KHAS
LHBS
MHOS
OHMS
PHDS
PHIS
PHYS
RHBS
RHES
RHOS
RHYS
SHES
THAS
THIS
THOS
THUS
WHOS
WHYS

••HS
AAHS
BAHS
DAHS
EDHS
ETHS
HAHS
MOHS
OCHS
OOHS
PAHS
PEHS
UGHS

HT••
HTTP

H•T•
HATE
HATH
HATS
HDTV
HETH
HITE
HITS
HOTE
HTTP
HUTS
HUTT
HUTU

H••T
HAFT
HALT
HART
HAST
HAUT
HEAT
HECT
HEET
HEFT
HENT
HEPT
HEST
HILT
HINT
HIRT
HIST
HOLT
HOOT
HORT
HOST
HOYT
HUNT
HURT
HUTT

•H•T
CHAT
CHET
CHIT
GHAT
KHAT
PHAT
PHOT
RHET
SHOT
SHPT
SHUT
THAT
WHAT
WHET
WHIT

••HT
ACHT
BAHT
ECHT
SPHT

HU••
HUAC
HUBS
HUCK
HUED
HUES
HUEY
HUFF
HUGE
HUGH
HUGO
HUGS
HUIS
HULA
HULK
HULL
HUME
HUMP
HUMS
HUND
HUNG
HUNK
HUNS
HUNT
HUON
HUPA
HURL
HURT
HUSH
HUSK
HUSS
HUTS
HUTT
HUTU

H•U•
HAUL
HAUS
HAUT
HOUR

H••U
HUTU

•HU•
CHUB
CHUG
CHUM
CHUR
RHUE
RHUM
SHUE
SHUL
SHUN
SHUT
THUD
THUG
THUR
THUS
UHUH
WHUP

•H•U
CHOU
THOU
THRU
ZHOU

••HU
JEHU
OAHU
WUHU

H•V•
HAVE
HIVE
HOVE

H••V
HDTV

•H•V
SHIV

HW••
HWYS

H•W•
HAWG
HAWK
HAWN
HAWS
HDWE
HEWN
HEWS
HGWY
HOWE
HOWL
HOWS

•H•W
CHAW
CHEW
CHOW
DHOW
PHEW
SHAW
SHOW
THAW
THEW
WHEW

H•X•
HEXA

H••X
HOAX

•H•X
CHEX

HY••
HYDE
HYDR
HYER
HYLA
HYMN
HYPE
HYPN
HYPO

H•Y•
HAYS
HIYO
HOYA
HOYS
HOYT
HWYS

H••Y
HAZY
HEDY
HGWY
HOLY
HOMY
HUEY

•HY•
PHYS
RHYS
WHYS

•H•Y
AHOY
CHOY
OHMY
SHAY
THEY
WHEY

••HY
ACHY
ASHY

H•Z•
HAZE
HAZY

H••Z
HARZ

•H•Z
AHAZ
CHAZ
CHEZ
PHIZ
WHIZ

IA••
IAGO
IAMB
IANA
IASI

I•A•
IBAN
IBAR
ICAL
IDAE
IMAM
IMAN
IRAE
IRAN
IRAQ
IRAS
ISAK
ISAO
ISAR
ISAY
ITAL
ITAR
IVAN
IYAR
IZAR

I••A
IANA
IDEA
ILIA
ILKA
ILSA
INCA
INGA
INKA
IOLA
IONA
IOTA
IOWA
IRMA
ISBA
ISLA
ITEA
ITZA
IXIA
IZBA

•IA•
BIAK
BIAO
BIAS
CIAO
DIAG
DIAL
DIAM
DIAN
DIAS
DIAZ
FIAT
GIAN
JIAO
LIAM
LIAO
LIAR
LIAT
PIAF
PIAO
RIAL
RIAS
SIAL
SIAM
TIAS
VIAL
XIAN

•I•A
AIDA
AIEA
AIWA
BIWA
DINA
DIVA
FICA
FILA
FINA
GIGA
GILA
GINA
GITA
GIZA
HIJA
HILA
JIMA
KINA
KIVA
LILA
LIMA
LINA
LIPA
LIRA
LISA
LIZA
MICA
MINA
MIRA
MITA
NINA
NIPA
NITA
OITA
PICA
PIKA
PIMA
PINA
PIPA
PISA
PITA
RICA
RIGA
RIMA
RITA
SIKA
SIMA
TINA
TIWA
VIDA
VIGA
VILA
VINA
VISA
VITA
VIVA
YIMA

••IA
ALIA
AMIA
APIA
ARIA
ASIA
AVIA
CHIA
ELIA
EMIA
FRIA
GAIA
GHIA
GLIA
HSIA
ILIA
IXIA
LEIA
MAIA
OPIA
USIA

IB••
IBAN
IBAR
IBET
IBEX
IBID
IBIS
IBLE
IBOS

I•B•
ICBM
IGBO
IRBM
ISBA
ISBN
IZBA

I••B
IAMB

•IB•
BIBB
BIBI
BIBL
BIBS
DIBS
FIBS
GIBB
GIBE
GIBS
JIBE
JIBS
LIBS
MIBS
NIBS
RIBS
SIBS
VIBE
ZIBO

•I•B
BIBB
GIBB
LIEB
LIMB
LITB

••IB
ABIB
CRIB
DBIB
DRIB
GLIB
TRIB

IC••
ICAL
ICBM
ICED
ICEL
ICER
ICES
ICET
ICKY
ICON
ICOS
ICUS

I•C•
INCA
INCE
INCH
INCL
INCR
ITCH

•IC•
BICE
BICS
DICE
DICH
DICK
DICT
FICA
FICE
FICT
HICK
KICK
LICE
LICK
MICA
MICE
MICH
MICK
MICR
MICS
NICE
NICK
PICA
PICK
PICO
PICS
PICT
RICA
RICE
RICH
RICK
RICO
SICK
SICS
TICK
TICO
TICS
VICE
VICI
VICO
WICK

•I•C
CINC
CIRC
DISC
FISC
MISC
WISC
ZINC

••IC
AMIC
BRIC
CHIC
EMIC
EPIC
ERIC
ETIC
FDIC
FLIC
LAIC
ODIC
OTIC
ZOIC

ID••
IDAE
IDEA
IDEE
IDEM
IDEO
IDES
IDIO
IDLE
IDLY
IDOL
IDOS
IDUN
IDYL

I•D•
INDO
INDS
INDY
IODO

I••D
IBID
ICED
IRED
IRID
IZOD

•ID•
AIDA
AIDE
AIDS
BIDE
BIDS
CIDE
DIDO
FIDE
FIDO
FIDS
GIDE
HIDE
KIDD
KIDS
LIDO
LIDS
MIDI
MIDN
NIDE
NIDI
RIDD
RIDE
RIDI
RIDS
SIDE
SIDH
TIDE
TIDY
VIDA
VIDE
VIDI
WIDE

•I•D
BIGD
BIND
BIRD
DIED
FIND
GILD
GIRD
HIED
HIND
KIDD
KIND
LIED
LIND
LITD
MILD
MIND
PIED
RIDD
RIND
SILD
SIND
TIED
VIED
WILD
WIND

••ID
ACID
AMID
ARID
AVID
CHID
ENID
GRID
IBID
IRID

LAID LOID MAID OLID OOID OVID PAID QAID QUID RAID REID SAID SKID SLID VOID

IE••
IEOH

I•E•
IBET IBEX ICED ICEL ICER ICES ICET IDEA IDEE IDEM IDEO IDES ILES ILEX INEE INES INEZ IRED IRES ISEE ITEA ITEM ITER ITES IVES IVEY

I••E
IBLE IDAE IDEE IDLE IHRE ILIE ILLE IMRE INCE INEE INGE INRE IOLE IONE IPSE IRAE ISEE ISLE

•IE•
AIEA BIEL BIEN CIEL DIED DIEM DIEN DIES DIET DIEU FIEF HIED HIER HIES KIEL KIEV LIEB LIED LIEF LIEN LIES LIEU MIEN MIES PIED PIER PIES PIET RIEL RIEN TIED TIER TIES VIED VIER VIES VIET VIEW WIEN

•I•E
AIDE AIME AIRE BICE BIDE BIKE BILE BINE BISE BITE CIDE CINE CIRE CITE DICE DIKE DIME DINE DIRE DIVE EINE EIRE FICE FIDE FIFE FILE FINE FIRE FIVE FIXE GIBE GIDE GIVE HIDE HIKE HIRE HITE HIVE JIBE JIVE KINE KITE LICE LIFE LIKE LIME LINE LIRE LISE LITE LIVE MICE MIKE MILE MIME MINE MIRE MISE MITE NICE NIDE NIKE NILE NINE NITE NIUE OISE PIKE PILE PINE PIPE PIRE RICE RIDE RIFE RILE RIME RIPE RIRE RISE RITE RIVE SIDE SINE SIRE SITE SIZE TIDE TIGE TIKE TILE TIME TINE TIRE VIBE VICE VIDE VILE VINE VISE VITE VIVE WIDE WIFE WILE WINE WIPE WIRE WISE WITE XIPE YIPE ZINE

••IE
ABIE AMIE BRIE EDIE ELIE ERIE FOIE ILIE JOIE OBIE ODIE OKIE OPIE PLIE PRIE SOIE

IF••
IFFY IFNI IFSO

I•F•
IFFY INFL INFO INFS

I••F
IMPF IOOF

•IF•
BIFF DIFF FIFE FIFI FIFO GIFT GIFU HIFI JIFF LIFE LIFO LIFT MIFF RIFE RIFF RIFS RIFT SIFT TIFF WIFE

•I•F
BIFF DIFF FIEF JIFF LIEF MIFF PIAF RIFF TIFF

••IF
ALIF ASIF COIF LEIF NAIF TAIF TGIF WAIF

IG••
IGBO IGGY IGLU IGOR

I•G•
IAGO IGGY INGA INGE

•IG•
BIGD CIGS DIGS FIGS GIGA GIGI GIGO GIGS HIGH JIGS MIGS NIGH PIGS RIGA RIGG RIGI RIGS SIGH SIGN TIGE VIGA VIGO WIGS ZIGS

•I•G
BING BIOG DIAG DING KING LING MING PING RIGG RING SING TING VING WING XING ZING

••IG
BRIG GRIG HAIG ORIG PRIG SWIG TRIG TWIG WHIG

IH••
IHOP IHRE

I•H•
IMHO

I••H
IEOH INCH IPOH ISTH ITCH

•I•H
DICH DISH FISH GISH HIGH KISH KITH LITH MICH MINH NIGH PISH PITH RICH SIDH SIGH SIKH SINH TISH WISH WITH

••IH
SHIH

II••
IIII IIWI

I•I•
IBID IBIS IDIO IIII ILIA ILIE ILIO IMIT INIT IRID IRIS ISIS ITIS IWIS IXIA

I••I
IASI IFNI IIII IIWI IMPI INRI

•II•
CIII DIII IIII LIII MIII RIIS VIII XIII

•I•I
BIBI CIII DIII FIFI FIJI FINI GIGI HIFI IIII IIWI JIMI KIKI KIRI KIWI LIII LILI MIDI MIII MIMI MINI NIDI NISI PILI RIDI RIGI SIMI SISI TIKI TITI VICI VIDI VIII VINI VITI XIII ZITI

••II
ALII CCII CDII CIII CLII CMII CVII CXII DCII DIII DLII DVII DXII IIII LIII LVII LXII MCII MDII MIII MLII MMII MVII MXII QEII VEII VIII WWII XCII XIII XLII XVII XXII

•IJ•
FIJI HIJA HIJO RIJN

I•K•
ICKY ILKA ILKS INKA INKS INKY IRKS

I••K
ISAK

•IK•
BIKE BIKO DIKE HIKE KIKI LIKE MIKE NIKE OIKS PIKA PIKE SIKA SIKH TIKE TIKI

•I•K
BIAK BILK BIRK BISK DICK DINK DIRK DISK FINK FISK HICK JINK KICK KINK KIRK LICK LINK MICK MILK MINK NICK OINK PICK PINK RICK RINK RISK SICK SILK SINK TICK WICK WINK WISK

••IK
EFIK ERIK HAIK

IL••
ILES ILEX ILIA ILIE ILIO ILKA ILKS ILLE ILLS ILLY ILSA

I•L•
IBLE IDLE IDLY IGLU ILLE ILLS ILLY INLY IOLA IOLE ISLA ISLE ISLS ITLL

I••L
ICAL ICEL IDOL IDYL INCL INFL INTL ITAL ITLL ITOL

•IL•
AILS BILE BILK BILL DILL FILA FILE FILL FILM FILS GILA GILD GILL GILT HILA HILL HILO HILT JILL JILT KILL KILN KILO KILT LILA LILI LILT LILY MILD MILE MILK MILL MILO MILS MILT NILE NILS OILS OILY PILE PILI PILL RILE RILL SILD SILK SILL SILO SILT TILE TILL TILS TILT VILA VILE WILD WILE WILL WILT WILY ZILL

•I•L
BIBL BIEL BILL BIOL BIRL CIEL DIAL DILL DIPL FILL GILL GIRL HILL JILL KIEL KILL MILL PILL RIAL RIEL RILL SIAL SILL TILL VIAL VIOL WILL ZILL

••IL
ANIL ARIL AXIL BAIL BOIL CEIL COIL DEIL DOIL EMIL EVIL FAIL FOIL GAIL HAIL JAIL MAIL MOIL NAIL NEIL NOIL OEIL PAIL PHIL POIL RAIL ROIL SAIL SCIL SKIL SOIL TAIL TOIL UTIL VAIL VEIL WAIL WEIL

IM••
IMAM IMAN IMHO IMIT IMPF IMPI IMPS IMPV IMRE IMUS

I•M•
IAMB IRMA ISMS

I••M
ICBM IDEM IMAM IRBM ITEM

•IM•
AIME AIMS DIME DIMS GIMP JIMA JIMI JIMS LIMA LIMB LIME LIMN LIMO LIMP LIMY MIME MIMI MIMS PIMA RIMA RIME RIMS RIMY SIMA SIMI SIMP SIMS TIME VIMS WIMP YIMA

•I•M
DIAM DIEM FILM FIRM LIAM SIAM

••IM
AKIM ANIM BRIM CRIM FLIM GLIM GRIM HAIM PRIM SHIM SKIM SLIM SWIM TRIM URIM WHIM

IN••
INCA INCE INCH INCL INCR INDO INDS INDY INEE INES INEZ INFL INFO INFS INGA INGE INIT INKA INKS INKY INLY INNS INON INRE INRI INRO INSP INST INTL INTO

INTR
INTS
INXS

I•N•
IANA
IFNI
INNS
IONA
IONE
IONS
ISNT

I••N
IBAN
ICON
IDUN
IMAN
INON
IRAN
IRON
ISBN
ISSN
IVAN

•IN•
AINS
AINT
AINU
BIND
BINE
BING
BINS
CINC
CINE
CINQ
DINA
DINE
DING
DINK
DINO
DINS
DINT
EINE
EINS
FINA
FIND
FINE
FINI
FINK
FINN
FINO
FINS
GINA
GINO
GINS
HIND
HINS
HINT
JINK
JINN
JINX
KINA
KIND
KINE
KING
KINK
KINO
LINA
LIND
LINE
LING
LINK
LINO
LINT
LINY
LINZ
MINA
MIND
MINE
MING
MINH
MINI
MINK
MINN
MINS
MINT
MINX
NINA
NINE
NINO
OINK
PINA
PINE
PING
PINK
PINS
PINT
PINX
PINY
RIND
RING
RINK
SIND
SINE
SING
SINH
SINK
SINO
SINS
TINA
TINE
TING
TINS
TINT
TINY
VINA
VINE
VING
VINI
VINO
VINS
VINY
WIND
WINE
WING
WINK
WINS
WINY
XING
ZINC
ZINE
ZING

•I•N
BIEN
BION
CION
DIAN
DIEN
DION
FINN
FIRN
GIAN
GIRN
JINN
KILN
LIEN
LIMN
LION
MIDN
MIEN
MINN
PION
RIEN
RIJN
SIGN
SION
TION
WIEN
XIAN
ZION

••IN
ADIN
AGIN
AKIN
AMIN
AYIN
BAIN
BEIN
BLIN
CAIN
CHIN
CLIN
COIN
CRIN
CUIN
DAIN
DOIN
DRIN
ERIN
FAIN
FEIN
FOIN
GAIN
GEIN
GOIN
GRIN
GUIN
HEIN
JAIN
JOIN
KAIN
LAIN
LOIN
LYIN
MAIN
MEIN
NEIN
ODIN
OLIN
PAIN
PNIN
PRIN
RAIN
REIN
RUIN
SEIN
SHIN
SKIN
SPIN
SQIN
TAIN
THIN
TWIN
VAIN
VEIN
WAIN
WHIN
XDIN
ZEIN

IO••
IODO
IOLA
IOLE
IONA
IONE
IONS
IOOF
IOTA
IOUS
IOWA

I•O•
IBOS
ICON
ICOS
IDOL
IDOS
IEOH
IGOR
IHOP
INON
IOOF
IPOH
IPOS
IRON
ITOL
IVOR
IZOD

I••O
IAGO
IDEO
IDIO
IFSO
IGBO
ILIO
IMHO
INDO
INFO
INRO
INTO
IODO
IPSO
ISAO

•IO•
BIOG
BIOL
BION
BIOS
CION
DION
DIOR
DIOS
LION
PION
RIOS
RIOT
SION
TION
TIOS
VIOL
ZION

•I•O
BIAO
BIKO
CIAO
DIDO
DINO
FIDO
FIFO
FINO
GIGO
GINO
GIRO
HIJO
HILO
HIYO
JIAO
KILO
KINO
LIAO
LIDO
LIFO
LIMO
LINO
LIPO
MILO
MIRO
MISO
NINO
PIAO
PICO
RICO
SILO
SINO
TICO
TIRO
TITO
VICO
VIGO
VINO
VITO
ZIBO

••IO
AGIO
BAIO
BRIO
CLIO
EZIO
FRIO
IDIO
ILIO
KRIO
OHIO
OLIO
THIO
TRIO

IP••
IPOH
IPOS
IPSE
IPSO

I•P•
IMPF
IMPI
IMPS
IMPV
ISPY

I••P
IHOP
INSP

•IP•
DIPL
DIPS
GIPS
HIPS
KIPS
LIPA
LIPO
LIPS
MIPS
NIPA
NIPS
PIPA
PIPE
PIPS
PIPY
RIPE
RIPS
SIPS
TIPS
VIPS
WIPE
XIPE
YIPE
YIPS
ZIPS

•I•P
GIMP
LIMP
LISP
SIMP
WIMP
WISP

••IP
BLIP
CHIP
CLIP
DRIP
FLIP
GRIP
QTIP
QUIP
SHIP
SKIP
SLIP
SNIP
TRIP
WHIP

I••Q
IRAQ

•I•Q
CINQ

••IQ
DRIQ
ERIQ

IR••
IRAE
IRAN
IRAQ
IRAS
IRBM
IRED
IRES
IRID
IRIS
IRKS
IRMA
IRON

I•R•
IHRE
IMRE
INRE
INRI
INRO

I••R
IBAR
ICER
IGOR
INCR
INTR
ISAR
ITAR
ITER
IVOR
IYAR
IZAR

•IR•
AIRE
AIRS
AIRT
AIRY
BIRD
BIRK
BIRL
BIRR
CIRC
CIRE
DIRE
DIRK
DIRS
DIRT
EIRE
FIRE
FIRM
FIRN
FIRS
GIRD
GIRL
GIRN
GIRO
GIRT
HIRE
HIRT
KIRI
KIRK
KIRS
LIRA
LIRE
MIRA
MIRE
MIRO
MIRS
MIRV
MIRY
PIRE
PIRS
RIRE
SIRE
SIRS
TIRE
TIRO
WIRE
WIRY

•I•R
BIRR
DIOR
HIER
LIAR
MICR
PIER
TIER
VIER

••IR
AMIR
ASIR
COIR
EMIR
FAIR
HAIR
HEIR
LAIR
MEIR
MUIR
NOIR
PAIR
SOIR
STIR
VAIR
VOIR
WEIR
WHIR
YMIR

IS••
ISAK
ISAO
ISAR
ISAY
ISBA
ISBN
ISEE
ISIS
ISLA
ISLE
ISLS
ISMS
ISNT
ISPY
ISSN
ISTH
ISTS

I•S•
IASI
IFSO
ILSA
INSP
INST
IPSE
IPSO
ISSN
ITSY

I••S
IBIS
IBOS
ICES
ICOS
ICUS
IDES
IDOS
ILES
ILKS
ILLS
IMPS
IMUS
INDS
INES
INFS
INKS
INNS
INTS
INXS
IONS
IOUS
IPOS
IRAS
IRES
IRIS
IRKS
ISIS
ISLS
ISMS
ISTS
ITES
ITIS
IVES
IWIS

•IS•
BISE
BISK
CIST
DISC
DISH
DISK
DISS
DIST
FISC
FISH
FISK
FIST
GISH
GIST
HISS
HIST
KISH
KISS
LISA
LISE
LISP
LIST
MISC
MISE
MISO
MISS
MIST
NISI
OISE
PISA
PISH
RISE
RISK
SISI
TISH
VISA
VISE
WISC
WISE
WISH
WISK
WISP

•I•S
AIDS
AILS
AIMS
AINS
AIRS
AITS
BIAS
BIBS
BICS
BIDS
BINS
BIOS
BITS
CIGS
CITS
DIAS
DIBS
DIES
DIGS
DIMS
DINS
DIOS
DIPS
DIRS
DISS
DITS
DIVS
EINS
FIBS
FIDS
FIGS
FILS
FINS
FIRS
FITS
GIBS
GIGS
GINS
GIPS
GITS
HIES
HINS
HIPS
HISS
HITS
JIBS
JIGS
JIMS
KIDS
KIPS
KIRS
KISS
KITS
LIBS
LIDS
LIES
LIPS
LITS
MIBS
MICS
MIES
MIGS
MILS
MIMS
MINS
MIPS
MIRS
MISS
NIBS
NILS
NIPS
NITS
OIKS
OILS
PICS
PIES
PIGS
PINS
PIPS
PIRS
PITS
PIUS
RIAS
RIBS
RIDS
RIFS
RIGS
RIIS
RIMS
RIOS
RIPS
SIBS
SICS
SIMS
SINS
SIPS
SIRS
SITS
TIAS
TICS
TIES
TILS
TINS
TIOS
TIPS
TIVS
VIES
VIMS
VINS
VIPS
WIGS
WINS
WITS
YIPS
ZIGS
ZIPS

••IS
ACIS
ALIS
AMIS
ANIS
APIS
ASIS
AVIS
AXIS
BOIS
CHIS
DAIS
EGIS
ELIS
EPIS
ERIS
FOIS
FRIS
GRIS
GUIS
HUIS
IBIS
IRIS
ISIS
ITIS
IWIS
KOIS
KRIS
LEIS
LOIS
LUIS
MAIS
OBIS
OSIS
OTIS
OVIS
PHIS
POIS
PSIS
RBIS
REIS
RIIS
SAIS
SEIS
SKIS
THIS
TRIS
TUIS
UNIS
URIS
UZIS

IT••
ITAL
ITAR
ITCH
ITEA
ITEM
ITER
ITES
ITIS
ITLL
ITOL
ITSY
ITTY
ITZA

I•T•
INTL
INTO
INTR
INTS
IOTA
ISTH
ISTS
ITTY

I••T
IBET
ICET
IMIT
INIT
INST
ISNT

•IT•
AITS
BITE
BITS
BITT
CITE
CITS
CITY
DITS
DITZ
FITS
FITZ
GITA
GITS
HITE
HITS
KITE
KITH
KITS
KITT
LITB
LITD
LITE
LITH
LITS
MITA
MITE
MITT
NITA
NITE
NITS
OITA
PITA
PITH

PITS	SIFT	**•I•U**	**IW••**	VSIX	**I••Z**	**J••A**	JEEP	JOGS	**••JJ**	JAIN	TOJO	**J•T•**	**J•W•**
PITT	SILT	AINU	IWIS	XCIX	INEZ	JADA	JEER	JUGA	HAJJ	JEAN		JATO	JAWS
PITY	TILT	DIEU		XLIX		JAVA	JEEZ	JUGS		JINN	**J•P•**	JETE	JEWS
RITA	TINT	GIFU	**I•W•**	XXIX	**•IZ•**	JENA	JEFE		**J•K•**	JOAN	JAPE	JETS	JOWL
RITE	VIET	KIVU	IIWI		FIZZ	JIMA	JEFF	**J••G**	JAKE	JOHN		JETT	
RITT	WILT	LIEU	IOWA	**IY••**	GIZA	JUBA	JEHU	JONG	JOKE	JOIN	**J••P**	JOTS	**J••X**
RITZ	WITT	SITU		IYAR	LIZA	JUGA	JELL	JUDG	JOKY	JOON	JEEP	JUTE	JEUX
SITE			**•IW•**		PIZZ	JURA	JENA	JUNG	JUKE	JUAN	JUMP	JUTS	JINX
SITS	**••IT**	**IV••**	AIWA	**I•Y•**	SIZE		JENS						
SITU	ADIT	IVAN	BIWA	IDYL		**•JA•**	JERK	**••JG**	**J••K**	**••JN**	**J•R•**	**J••T**	**•J•X**
TITI	ALIT	IVES	IIWI		**•I•Z**	AJAR	JESS	LTJG	JACK	RIJN	JARL	JEST	AJAX
TITO	ATIT	IVEY	KIWI	**I••Y**	DIAZ	AJAX	JEST		JERK		JARS	JETT	
VITA	BAIT	IVOR	TIWA	ICKY	DITZ	OJAI	JESU	**J•H•**	JINK	**JO••**	JERK	JILT	**J•Y•**
VITE	BLIT			IDLY	FITZ		JETE	JAHR	JOCK	JOAB	JURA	JOLT	JAYE
VITI	BRIT	**I••V**	**•I•W**	IFFY	FIZZ	**••JA**	JETS	JEHU	JUNK	JOAD	JURE	JUST	JAYS
VITO	CHIT	IMPV	VIEW	IGGY	LINZ	BAJA	JETT	JOHN		JOAN	JURY		JOYS
WITE	CRIT			ILLY	PIZZ	DEJA	JEUX		**J•L•**	JOBS		**••JT**	
WITH	DLIT	**•IV•**	**••IW**	INDY	RITZ	HIJA	JEWS	**J••H**	JELL	JOCK	**J••R**	ADJT	**J••Y**
WITS	DOIT	DIVA	FWIW	INKY		MAJA		JOSH	JILL	JODY	JAGR		JIVY
WITT	EDIT	DIVE		INLY	**••IZ**	RAJA	**J•E•**		JILT	JOEL	JAHR	**JU••**	JODY
ZITI	EMIT	DIVS	**IX••**	ISAY	ARIZ		JAEL	**JI••**	JOLI	JOES	JBAR	JUAN	JOEY
	EXIT	FIVE	IXIA	ISPY	AZIZ	**JB••**	JAEN	JIAO	JOLO	JOEY	JEER	JUBA	JOKY
•I•T	FAIT	GIVE		ITSY	ELIZ	JBAR	JEEP	JIBE	JOLT	JOGS	JOUR	JUDD	JUDY
AINT	FLIT	HIVE	**I•X•**	ITTY	FRIZ		JEER	JIBS	JULE	JOHN		JUDE	JULY
AIRT	FRIT	JIVE	INXS	IVEY	PHIZ	**J•B•**	JEEZ	JIFF	JULY	JOIE	**•J•R**	JUDG	JURY
BITT	GAIT	JIVY		IZZY	QUIZ	JABS	JOEL	JIGS		JOIN	AJAR	JUDO	
CIST	GRIT	KIVA	**I••X**		TAIZ	JIBE	JOES	JILL	**J••L**	JOJO		JUDY	**J•Z•**
DICT	IMIT	KIVU	IBEX	**•IY•**	WHIZ	JIBS	JOEY	JILT	JAEL	JOKE	**J•S•**	JUGA	JAZZ
DIET	INIT	LIVE	ILEX	HIYO		JOBS		JIMA	JAIL	JOKY	JESS	JUGS	
DINT	KNIT	LIVY			**JA••**	JUBA	**J••E**	JIMI	JARL	JOLI	JEST	JUJU	**J••Z**
DIRT	LAIT	RIVE	**•IX•**	**•I•Y**	JABS		JADE	JIMS	JELL	JOLO	JESU	JUKE	JAZZ
DIST	NUIT	TIVS	FIXE	AIRY	JACK	**J••B**	JAKE	JINK	JILL	JOLT	JOSE	JULE	JEEZ
FIAT	OBIT	VIVA	MIXT	CITY	JADA	JAMB	JANE	JINN	JOEL	JONG	JOSH	JULY	
FICT	OMIT	VIVE	PIXY	JIVY	JADE	JOAB	JAPE	JINX	JOWL	JONI	JOSS	JUMP	**KA••**
FIST	QUIT			LILY	JAEL		JAYE	JIVE		JOON	JUST	JUNC	KABS
GIFT	REIT	**•I•V**	**•I•X**	LIMY	JAEN	**J•C•**	JEFE	JIVY	**J•M•**	JOSE		JUNE	KAEL
GILT	SKIT	KIEV	JINX	LINY	JAGR	JACK	JETE		JAMB	JOSH	**J••S**	JUNG	KAFS
GIRT	SLIT	MIRV	MINX	LIVY	JAGS	JOCK	JIBE	**J•I•**	JAMS	JOSS	JABS	JUNK	KAHN
GIST	SMIT		PINX	MIRY	JAHR		JIVE	JAIL	JIMA	JOTS	JAGS	JUNO	KAIN
HILT	SNIT	**••IV**		OILY	JAIL	**J••C**	JOIE	JAIN	JIMI	JOUR	JAMS	JURA	KAKA
HINT	SPIT	AVIV	**••IX**	PINY	JAIN	JUNC	JOKE	JOIE	JIMS	JOVE	JARS	JURE	KAKI
HIRT	SUIT	CCIV	BRIX	PIPY	JAKE		JOSE	JOIN	JUMP	JOWL	JAWS	JURY	KALB
HIST	SWIT	CDIV	CCIX	PITY	JAMB	**J•D•**	JOVE			JOYS	JAYS	JUST	KALE
JILT	TAIT	CLIV	CDIX	PIXY	JAMS	JADA	JUDE	**J••I**	**••JM**		JENS	JUTE	KALI
KILT	TWIT	CMIV	CLIX	RIMY	JANE	JADE	JUKE	JEDI	SEJM	**J•O•**	JESS	JUTS	KALT
KITT	UNIT	CXIV	CMIX	TIDY	JAPE	JEDI	JULE	JIMI		JOON	JETS		KAMA
LIAT	WAIT	DCIV	CXIX	TINY	JARL	JODY	JUNE	JOLI	**J•N•**		JEWS	**J•U•**	KAME
LIFT	WHIT	DLIV	DCIX	VINY	JARS	JUDD	JURE	JONI	JANE	**J••O**	JIBS	JEUX	KAMI
LILT	WRIT	DXIV	DLIX	WILY	JATO	JUDE	JUTE		JENA	JATO	JIGS	JOUR	KANA
LINT		LXIV	DXIX	WINY	JAVA	JUDG		**•J•I**	JENS	JIAO	JIMS		KANE
LIST	**I•U•**	MCIV	FLIX	WIRY	JAWS	JUDO	**J•F•**	OJAI	JINK	JOJO	JOBS	**J••U**	KANO
MILT	ICUS	MDIV	LXIX		JAYE	JUDY	JEFE		JINN	JOLO	JOES	JEHU	KANS
MINT	IDUN	MLIV	MCIX	**IZ••**	JAYS		JEFF	**••JI**	JINX	JUDO	JOGS	JESU	KANT
MIST	IMUS	MMIV	MDIX	IZAR	JAZZ	**J••D**	JIFF	FIJI	JONG	JUNO	JOSS	JUJU	KAON
MITT	IOUS	MXIV	MLIX	IZBA		JOAD		FUJI	JONI		JOTS		KAPH
MIXT		PRIV	MMIX	IZOD	**J•A•**	JUDD	**J••F**	HAJI	JUNC	**••JO**	JOYS	**••JU**	KARA
PICT	**I••U**	SHIV	MXIX	IZZY	JBAR		JEFF	KOJI	JUNE	CUJO	JUGS	JUJU	KARL
PIET	IGLU	SPIV	PAIX		JEAN	**••JD**	JIFF		JUNG	DOJO	JUTS		KARO
PINT		UNIV	PRIX	**I•Z•**	JIAO	NEJD		**J•J•**	JUNK	HIJO		**J•V•**	KART
PITT	**•IU•**	XCIV	TRIX	ITZA	JOAB		**J•G•**	JOJO	JUNO	HOJO	**••JS**	JAVA	KATE
RIFT	NIUE	XDIV	TWIX	IZZY	JOAD	**JE••**	JAGR	JUJU		JOJO	ADJS	JIVE	KATO
RIOT	PIUS	XLIV	UNIX		JOAN	JEAN	JAGS		**J••N**	MOJO	TAJS	JIVY	KATY
RITT		XXIV	VOIX		JUAN	JEDI	JIGS		JAEN	ROJO		JOVE	KATZ

KAVA
KAYE
KAYO

K•A•
KCAL
KEAN
KEAS
KHAN
KHAS
KHAT
KNAP
KNAR
KOAN
KWAI
KWAN
KYAT

K••A
KAKA
KAMA
KANA
KARA
KAVA
KDKA
KINA
KIVA
KOLA
KONA
KYRA

•KA•
AKAN
OKAY
SKAT
SKAW

•K•A
MKSA
OKLA
OKRA
SKUA

••KA
ALKA
ANKA
ATKA
DEKA
ILKA
INKA
KAKA
KDKA
PIKA
PUKA
SIKA
TAKA
WAKA
WEKA

K•B•
KABS
KOBE
KOBO
KOBS

K••B
KALB
KERB
KNOB

KC••
KCAL

K•C•
KICK
KOCH

K••C
KOFC
KROC

•KC•
EKCO

KD••
KDKA

K•D•
KEDS
KIDD
KIDS
KUDU

K••D
KIDD
KIND
KNUD
KURD

•K•D
EKED
NKVD
OKED
SKED
SKID

KE••
KEAN
KEAS
KEDS
KEEL
KEEN
KEEP
KEET
KEGS
KELP
KEMO
KEMP
KENO
KENS
KENT
KEOS
KEPI
KEPT
KERB
KERF
KERN
KERR
KERT
KETO
KETT
KEYS

K•E•
KAEL
KEEL
KEEN
KEEP
KEET
KIEL
KIEV
KLEE
KNEE
KNEW
KTEL
KYES

K••E
KALE
KAME
KANE
KATE
KAYE
KINE
KITE
KLEE
KNEE
KOBE
KORE
KYLE

•KE•
AKEE
EKED
EKES
OKED
OKEY
SKED
SKEE
SKEG
SKEP
SKEW
UKES

•K•E
AKEE
OKIE
SKEE
SKYE

••KE
BAKE
BIKE
CAKE
COKE
CUKE
DEKE
DIKE
DUKE
ELKE
FAKE
FYKE
HAKE
HIKE
HOKE
JAKE
JOKE
JUKE
LAKE
LIKE
LUKE
MAKE
MIKE
NIKE
NUKE
PEKE
PIKE
POKE
RAKE
SAKE
SOKE
TAKE
TIKE
TOKE
TYKE
WAKE
WOKE
YOKE
ZEKE

K•F•
KAFS
KOFC
KOFI
KOFP

K••F
KERF
KOPF

K•G•
KEGS

K••G
KING
KONG
KUNG

•KG•
PKGS

•K•G
BKPG
MKTG
SKEG

KH••
KHAN
KHAS
KHAT

K•H•
KAHN
KOHL
KUHN
KWHR

K••H
KAPH
KISH
KITH
KOCH
KOPH
KUSH

••KH
ANKH
LAKH
SIKH

KI••
KICK
KIDD
KIDS
KIEL
KIEV
KIKI
KILL
KILN
KILO
KILT
KINA
KIND
KINE
KING
KINK
KINO
KIPS
KIRI
KIRK
KIRS
KISH
KISS
KITE
KITH
KITS
KITT
KIVA
KIVU
KIWI

K•I•
KAIN
KNIT
KOIS
KRIO
KRIS

K••I
KAKI
KALI
KAMI
KEPI
KIKI
KIRI
KIWI
KOFI
KOJI
KOMI
KWAI

•KI•
AKIM
AKIN
OKIE
SKID
SKIL
SKIM
SKIN
SKIP
SKIS
SKIT

••KI
AOKI
KAKI
KIKI
LOKI
RAKI
SAKI
TIKI

K•J•
KOJI

K•K•
KAKA
KAKI
KDKA
KIKI
KOKO

K••K
KICK
KINK
KIRK
KOOK
KRUK

KL••
KLEE

K•L•
KALB
KALE
KALI
KALT
KELP
KILL
KILN
KILO
KILT
KOLA
KOLN
KOLO
KYLE

K••L
KAEL
KARL
KCAL
KEEL
KIEL
KILL
KOHL
KOOL
KTEL

•KL•
OKLA
WKLY

•K•L
SKIL
SKOL

K•M•
KAMA
KAME
KAMI
KEMO
KEMP
KOMI

•K•M
AKIM
SKIM

KN••
KNAP
KNAR
KNEE
KNEW
KNIT
KNOB
KNOP
KNOT
KNOW
KNOX
KNUD
KNUR
KNUT

K•N•
KANA
KANE
KANO
KANS
KANT
KENO
KENS
KENT
KINA
KIND
KINE
KING
KINK
KINO
KONA
KONG
KUNG

K••N
KAHN
KAIN
KAON
KEAN
KEEN
KERN
KHAN
KILN
KOAN
KOLN
KUHN
KWAN
KWON

•KN•
DKNY

•K•N
AKAN
AKIN
SKIN

KO••
KOAN
KOBE
KOBO
KOBS
KOCH
KOFC
KOFI
KOFP
KOHL
KOIS
KOJI
KOKO
KOLA
KOLN
KOLO
KOMI
KONA
KONG
KOOK
KOOL
KOOP
KOPF
KOPH
KOPS
KORE
KOTO

K•O•
KAON
KEOS
KNOB
KNOP
KNOT
KNOW
KNOX
KOOK
KOOL
KOOP
KROC
KWON

K••O
KANO
KARO
KATO
KAYO
KEMO
KENO
KETO
KILO
KINO
KOBO
KOKO
KOLO
KOTO
KRIO

•KO•
SKOL
TKOS

•K•O
EKCO

••KO
BIKO
ELKO
KOKO
MAKO
YOKO

K•P•
KAPH
KEPI
KEPT
KIPS
KOPF
KOPH
KOPS

K••P
KEEP
KELP
KEMP
KNAP
KNOP
KOFP
KOOP

•KP•
BKPG
BKPR

•K•P
SKEP
SKIP
WKRP

KR••
KRIO
KRIS
KROC
KRUK

K•R•
KARA
KARL
KARO
KART
KERB
KERF
KERN
KERR
KERT
KIRI
KIRK
KIRS
KORE
KURD
KURT
KYRA

K••R
KERR
KNAR
KNUR
KWHR

•KR•
OKRA
WKRP

•K•R
BKPR

••KR
BAKR

K•S•
KISH
KISS
KUSH

K••S
KABS
KAFS
KANS
KEAS
KEDS
KEGS
KENS
KEOS
KEYS
KHAS
KIDS
KIPS
KIRS
KISS
KITS
KOBS
KOIS
KOPS
KRIS
KYES

•KS•
MKSA

•K•S
EKES
PKGS
SKIS
SKUS
SKYS
TKOS
TKTS
UKES

••KS
ARKS
ASKS
AUKS
EEKS
ELKS
ERKS
ILKS
INKS
IRKS
LEKS
LUKS
OAKS
OIKS
SAKS
SUKS
TPKS
TSKS
WOKS
YAKS
YUKS

KT••
KTEL

K•T•
KATE
KATO
KATY
KATZ
KETO
KETT
KITE
KITH
KITS
KITT
KOTO

K••T
KALT
KANT
KART
KEET
KENT
KEPT
KERT
KETT
KHAT
KILT
KITT
KNIT
KNOT
KNUT
KURT
KYAT

•KT•
MKTG
TKTS

•K•T
SKAT
SKIT

KU••
KUDU
KUHN
KUNG
KURD
KURT
KUSH

K•U•
KNUD
KNUR
KNUT
KRUK

K••U
KIVU
KUDU

•KU•
SKUA
SKUS

••KU
BAKU
PUKU
RAKU

K•V•
KAVA
KIVA
KIVU

K••V
KIEV

•KV•
NKVD

KW••
KWAI
KWAN
KWHR
KWON

K•W•
KIWI

K••W
KNEW
KNOW

•KW•
PKWY

•K•W
SKAW
SKEW

K••X
KNOX

KY••
KYAT
KYES
KYLE
KYRA

K•Y•
KAYE
KAYO
KEYS

K••Y
KATY

•KY•
SKYE
SKYS

•K•Y
DKNY
OKAY
OKEY
PKWY
WKLY

••KY
CAKY
COKY
ICKY
INKY
JOKY
LAKY
POKY

K••Z
KATZ

LA••
LABS
LACE
LACK
LACS
LACT
LACY
LADD
LADE
LADS
LADY
LAGO
LAGS
LAHR
LAIC
LAID
LAIN
LAIR
LAIT
LAKE
LAKH
LAKY
LALA
LALO
LAMA
LAMB
LAME
LAMP
LAMS
LAMY
LANA
LAND
LANE
LANG
LANK
LAOS
LAPD
LAPP
LAPS
LARA
LARD
LARI
LARK
LARS
LASE
LASH
LASS
LAST
LATE
LATH
LATS
LAUD
LAUE
LAVA
LAVE
LAVS
LAWN
LAWS
LAYS
LAZE
LAZY

L•A•
LBAR
LEAD
LEAF
LEAH
LEAK
LEAL
LEAN
LEAP
LEAR
LEAS
LIAM
LIAO

LIAR LIAT LOAD LOAF LOAM LOAN LSAT LUAU

L••A

LALA LAMA LANA LARA LAVA LEDA LEIA LEMA LENA LILA LIMA LINA LIPA LIRA LISA LIZA LOLA LOMA LOTA LPGA LUBA LUNA LYRA

•LA•

ALAE ALAI ALAN ALAR ALAS BLAB BLAE BLAH BLAS BLAT BLAU CLAD CLAM CLAN CLAP CLAR CLAW CLAY ELAL ELAM ELAN FLAB FLAG FLAK FLAM FLAN FLAP FLAT FLAV FLAW FLAX FLAY GLAD GLAM NLAT OLAF OLAN OLAV OLAY PLAN PLAT PLAX PLAY SLAB SLAG SLAM SLAP SLAT SLAV SLAW SLAY ULAN

•L•A

ALBA ALDA ALEA ALFA ALGA ALIA ALKA ALLA ALMA ALTA ALVA ELBA ELEA ELIA ELLA ELSA FLEA GLIA ILIA ILKA ILSA OLGA OLLA PLEA ULNA

••LA

ALLA AULA AYLA BELA BOLA CELA COLA EBLA ELLA FALA FILA FULA GALA GILA HILA HOLA HULA HYLA IOLA ISLA KOLA LALA LILA LOLA MALA MOLA NOLA OKLA OLLA POLA PULA SALA SELA SOLA TALA TOLA TULA UCLA VELA VILA ZOLA

LB••

LBAR LBOS

L•B•

LABS LHBS LIBS LLBS LOBE LOBO LOBS LUBA LUBE

L••B

LAMB LIEB LIMB LITB LOEB

•LB•

ALBA ALBI ALBS ELBA ELBE LLBS SLBM

•L•B

BLAB BLEB BLOB CLUB FLAB FLUB GLIB GLOB NLRB PLEB SLAB SLOB SLUB

••LB

BULB FTLB KALB

LC••

LCDS

L•C•

LACE LACK LACS LACT LACY LDCS LECH LECT LICE LICK LOCH LOCI LOCK LOCO LUCE LUCI LUCK LUCY

L••C

LAIC

•LC•

MLCC PLCS

•L•C

ALEC BLOC ELEC FLIC FLOC GLUC GLYC MLCC

••LC

CALC SCLC TALC

LD••

LDCS LDRS

L•D•

LADD LADE LADS LADY LCDS LEDA LEDS LIDO LIDS LLDS LODE LODI LODZ LTDS

L••D

LADD LAID LAND LAPD LARD LAUD LEAD LEND LEWD LIED LIND LITD LOAD LOID LORD LOUD

•LD•

ALDA ALDO BLDG BLDR FLDR LLDS OLDE OLDS

•L•D

BLED BLVD CLAD CLOD FLED GLAD OLID PLED PLOD SLED SLID

••LD

AULD BALD BOLD COLD FOLD GILD GOLD HELD HOLD MELD MILD MOLD NFLD SILD SOLD TOLD VELD WALD WELD WILD WOLD

LE••

LEAD LEAF LEAH LEAK LEAL LEAN LEAP LEAR LEAS LECH LECT LEDA LEDS LEEK LEER LEES LEET LEFT LEGO LEGS LEHR LEIA LEIF LEIS LEKS LELY LEMA LEMS LENA LEND LENI LENO LENS LENT LENZ LEOI LEON LEOS LESE LESS LEST LETO LETS LETT LEUK LEVI LEVO LEVU LEVY LEWD

L•E•

LEEK LEER LEES LEET LIEB LIED LIEF LIEN LIES LIEU LOEB LOEW LYES

L••E

LACE LADE LAKE LAME LANE LASE LATE LAUE LAVE LAZE LESE LICE LIFE LIKE LIME LINE LIRE LISE LITE LIVE LOBE LODE LOGE LOME LONE LOPE LORE LOSE LOVE LOWE LUBE LUCE LUGE LUKE LUNE LUPE LURE LUTE LUXE LYLE LYNE LYRE

•LE•

ALEA ALEC ALEE ALEF ALEP ALES ALEX BLEB BLED BLEU BLEW CLEF CLEM CLEO CLEW ELEA ELEC ELEM ELEV FLEA FLED FLEE FLEM FLEW FLEX FLEY GLEE GLEG GLEN GLEY ILES ILEX KLEE NLER OLEG OLEN OLEO OLES PLEA PLEB PLED PLEO PLEW PLEX SLED SLEW ULEE YLEM

•L•E

ALAE ALEE ALLE ALOE ALTE BLAE BLUE CLUE ELBE ELIE ELKE ELLE ELSE FLEE FLOE FLUE GLEE GLUE ILIE ILLE KLEE MLLE OLDE PLIE SLOE SLUE SLYE ULEE

••LE

ABLE ALLE AXLE BALE BILE BOLE CALE COLE CULE DALE DELE DOLE ELLE ERLE FILE GALE HALE HOLE IBLE IDLE ILLE IOLE ISLE JULE KALE KYLE LYLE MALE MILE MLLE MOLE MULE NILE OGLE ORLE PALE PELE PILE POLE PULE PYLE RILE ROLE RULE RYLE SALE SOLE TALE TELE TILE TOLE TULE UELE VALE VILE VOLE WALE WILE WOLE YALE YULE

L•F•

LEFT LIFE LIFO LIFT LOFT LUFF LUFT

L••F

LEAF LEIF LIEF LOAF LUFF

•LF•

ALFA

•L•F

ALEF ALIF CLEF OLAF

••LF

CALF DOLF GOLF GULF HALF PELF ROLF SELF SULF WOLF

LG••

LGTH

L•G•

LAGO LAGS LEGO LEGS LOGE LOGO LOGS LOGY LPGA LUGE LUGS

L••G

LANG LING LONG LTJG LUNG

•LG•

ALGA ALGO ALGY OLGA

•L•G

BLDG CLOG FLAG FLOG GLEG GLUG OLEG PLUG SLAG SLOG SLUG

••LG

BELG BULG VULG

LH••

LHBS

L•H•

LAHR LEHR

L••H

LAKH LASH LATH LEAH LECH LGTH LITH LOCH LUSH LUTH

•LH•

ELHI

•L•H

ALPH BLAH

LI••

LIAM LIAO LIAR LIAT LIBS LICE LICK LIDO LIDS LIEB LIED LIEF LIEN LIES LIEU LIFE LIFO LIFT LIII LIKE LILA LILI LILT LILY LIMA LIMB LIME LIMN LIMO LIMP LIMY LINA LIND LINE LING LINK LINO LINT LINY LINZ LION LIPA LIPO LIPS LIRA LIRE LISA LISE LISP LIST LITB LITD LITE LITH LITS LIVE LIVY LIZA

L•I•

LAIC LAID LAIN LAIR LAIT LEIA LEIF LEIS LIII LOID LOIN LOIS LUIS LVII LXII LXIV LXIX LYIN

L••I

LARI LENI LEOI LEVI LIII LILI LOCI LODI LOKI LONI LORI LOTI LUCI LVII LXII LXVI LXXI

•LI•

ALIA ALIF ALII ALIS ALIT BLIN BLIP BLIT CLII CLIN CLIO CLIP CLIV CLIX DLII DLIT DLIV DLIX ELIA ELIE ELIS ELIZ FLIC FLIM FLIP FLIT FLIX GLIA GLIB GLIM ILIA ILIE ILIO MLII MLIV MLIX OLID OLIN OLIO PLIE SLID SLIM SLIP SLIT XLII XLIV XLIX

•L•I

ALAI ALBI ALII ALTI ALUI CLII CLVI CLXI DLII DLVI DLXI ELHI ELOI MLII MLVI MLXI XLII XLVI

••LI

ATLI BALI CALI CCLI CDLI CMLI CXLI DALI DCLI DELI

DXLI HELI JOLI KALI LILI MALI MCLI MDLI MMLI MXLI NOLI PALI PILI PULI SOLI TALI UGLI

L•J•
LTJG

L•K•
LAKE LAKH LAKY LEKS LIKE LOKI LUKE LUKS

L••K
LACK LANK LARK LEAK LEEK LEUK LICK LINK LOCK LOOK LUCK LURK

•LK•
ALKA ELKE ELKO ELKS ILKA ILKS

•L•K
FLAK

••LK
BALK BILK BULK CALK FALK FOLK HULK MILK POLK SALK SILK SULK TALK WALK WELK YOLK

LL••
LLBS LLDS LLMS

L•L•
LALA LALO LELY LILA LILI LILT LILY LOLA LOLL LULL LULU LYLE LYLY

L••L
LEAL LOLL LULL

•LL•
ALLA ALLE ALLO ALLS ALLY ELLA ELLE ELLS ELLY ILLE ILLS ILLY MLLE OLLA

•L•L
ELAL ELUL

••LL
BALL BELL BILL BOLL BULL CALL CELL COLL CULL DELL DILL DOLL DULL FALL FELL FILL FULL GALL GELL GILL GULL HALL HELL HILL HULL ITLL JELL JILL KILL LOLL LULL MALL MELL MILL MOLL MULL NELL NOLL NULL PALL PELL PILL POLL PULL RALL RILL ROLL SELL SILL SYLL TALL TELL TILL TOLL TULL WALL WELL WILL YALL YELL ZILL

L•M•
LAMA LAMB LAME LAMP LAMS LAMY LEMA LEMS LIMA LIMB LIME LIMN LIMO LIMP LIMY LLMS LOMA LOME LUMP

L••M
LIAM LOAM LOOM

•LM•
ALMA ALMS ELMO ELMS LLMS

•L•M
ALUM BLUM CLAM CLEM ELAM ELEM FLAM FLEM FLIM GLAM GLIM GLOM GLUM PLUM SLAM SLBM SLIM SLUM YLEM

••LM
BALM CALM CULM FILM HALM HELM HOLM MALM PALM

L•N•
LANA LAND LANE LANG LANK LENA LEND LENI LENO LENS LENT LENZ LINA LIND LINE LING LINK LINO LINT LINY LINZ LONE LONG LONI LUNA LUNE LUNG LUNN LUNT LYNE LYNN LYNX

L••N
LAIN LAWN LEAN LEON LIEN LIMN LION LOAN LOIN LOON LORN LRON LUNN LYIN LYNN LYON

•LN•
ULNA

•L•N
ALAN BLIN CLAN CLIN ELAN ELON FLAN GLEN GLYN OLAN OLEN OLIN PLAN ULAN

••LN
KILN KOLN SOLN

LO••
LOAD LOAF LOAM LOAN LOBE LOBO LOBS LOCH LOCI LOCK LOCO LODE LODI LODZ LOEB LOEW LOFT LOGE LOGO LOGS LOGY LOID LOIN LOIS LOKI LOLA LOLL LOMA LOME LONE LONG LONI LOOK LOOM LOON LOOP LOOS LOOT LOPE LOPS LORD LORE LORI LORN LORY LOSE LOSS LOST LOTA LOTI LOTS LOTT LOUD LOUP LOUT LOVE LOWE LOWS

L•O•
LAOS LBOS LEOI LEON LEOS LION LOOK LOOM LOON LOOP LOOS LOOT LRON LVOV LYON

L••O
LAGO LALO LEGO LENO LETO LEVO LIAO LIDO LIFO LIMO LINO LIPO LOBO LOCO LOGO

•LO•
ALOE ALOU ALOW BLOB BLOC BLOT BLOW CLOD CLOG CLOP CLOT CLOY ELOI ELON FLOC FLOE FLOG FLOP FLOR FLOW FLOZ GLOB GLOM GLOP GLOT GLOW PLOD PLOP PLOT PLOW PLOY SLOB SLOE SLOG SLOP SLOT SLOW

•L•O
ALDO ALGO ALLO ALPO ALSO ALTO CLEO CLIO ELKO ELMO ILIO OLEO OLIO PLEO

••LO
ALLO ARLO BELO BOLO COLO HALO HELO HILO HOLO JOLO KILO KOLO LALO MALO MILO NOLO OSLO PALO POLO SILO SOLO STLO TELO XYLO

LP••
LPGA

L•P•
LAPD LAPP LAPS LIPA LIPO LIPS LOPE LOPS LUPE

L••P
LAMP LAPP LEAP LIMP LISP LOOP LOUP LUMP

•LP•
ALPH ALPO ALPS

•L•P
ALEP BLIP CLAP CLIP CLOP FLAP FLIP FLOP GLOP PLOP SLAP SLIP SLOP

••LP
CULP GULP HELP HOLP KELP PALP PULP SALP YELP

LR••
LRON

L•R•
LARA LARD LARI LARK LARS LDRS LIRA LIRE LORD LORE LORI LORN LORY LURE LURK LYRA LYRE

L••R
LAHR LAIR LBAR LEAR LEER LEHR LIAR LTYR

•LR•
NLRB SLRS

•L•R
ALAR BLDR BLUR CLAR FLDR FLOR NLER PLUR SLUR

LS••
LSAT LSTS

L•S•
LASE LASH LASS LAST LESE LESS LEST LISA LISE LISP LIST LOSE LOSS LOST LUSH LUST

L••S
LABS LACS LADS LAGS LAMS LAOS LAPS LARS LASS LATS LAVS LAWS LAYS LBOS LCDS LDCS LDRS LEAS LEDS LEES LEGS LEIS LEKS LEMS LENS LEOS LESS LETS LHBS LIBS LIDS LIES LIPS LITS LLBS LLDS LLMS LOBS LOGS LOIS LOOS LOPS LOSS LOTS LOWS LSTS LTDS LUGS LUIS LUKS LUVS LYES

•LS•
ALSO ELSA ELSE ILSA

•L•S
ALAS ALBS ALES ALIS ALLS ALMS ALPS ALTS BLAS BLTS ELIS ELKS ELLS ELMS FLUS ILES ILKS ILLS LLBS LLDS LLMS OLDS OLES PLCS PLUS SLRS ULUS

••LS
AILS ALLS AWLS BBLS BELS CALS CELS COLS CPLS CULS DALS DELS EELS ELLS FILS GALS GELS HALS HOLS ILLS ISLS MILS NILS OILS OWLS PALS POLS RELS SALS SOLS SYLS TILS URLS VOLS ZALS

LT••
LTDS LTJG LTYR

L•T•
LATE LATH LATS LETO LETS LETT LGTH LITB LITD LITE LITH LITS LOTA LOTI LOTS LOTT LSTS LUTE LUTH LUTZ

L••T
LACT LAIT LAST LECT LEET LEFT LENT LEST LETT LIAT LIFT LILT LINT LIST LOFT LOOT LOST LOTT LOUT LSAT LUFT LUNT LUST

•LT•
ALTA ALTE ALTI ALTO ALTS BLTS

•L•T
ALIT BLAT BLIT BLOT CLOT DLIT FLAT FLIT GLOT GLUT NLAT PLAT PLOT SLAT SLIT SLOT

••LT
BALT BELT BOLT CELT COLT CULT DOLT FELT GELT GILT HALT HILT HOLT JILT JOLT KALT KILT LILT MALT MELT MILT MOLT PELT SALT SILT TILT VOLT VULT WALT WELT WILT

LU••
LUAU LUBA LUBE LUCE LUCI LUCK LUCY LUFF LUFT LUGE LUGS LUIS LUKE LUKS LULL LULU LUMP LUNA LUNE LUNG LUNN LUNT

LUPE
LURE
LURK
LUSH
LUST
LUTE
LUTH
LUTZ
LUVS
LUXE

L•U•
LAUD
LAUE
LEUK
LOUD
LOUP
LOUT

L••U
LEVU
LIEU
LUAU
LULU

•LU•
ALUI
ALUM
BLUE
BLUM
BLUR
CLUB
CLUE
ELUL
FLUB
FLUE
FLUS
FLUX
GLUC
GLUE
GLUG
GLUM
GLUT
PLUG
PLUM
PLUR
PLUS
SLUB
SLUE
SLUG
SLUM
SLUR
ULUS

•L•U
ALOU
BLAU
BLEU

••LU
ACLU
IGLU
LULU
OULU
SULU
TOLU
YALU
ZULU

LV••
LVII
LVOV

L•V•
LAVA
LAVE
LAVS
LEVI
LEVO
LEVU
LEVY
LIVE
LIVY
LOVE
LUVS
LXVI

L••V
LVOV
LXIV
LXXV

•LV•
ALVA
BLVD
CLVI
DLVI
MLVI
XLVI

•L•V
CLIV
CLXV
DLIV
DLXV
ELEV
FLAV
MLIV
MLXV
OLAV
SLAV
XLIV

••LV
CCLV
CDLV
CMLV
CXLV
DCLV
DXLV
GALV
MCLV
MDLV
MMLV
MXLV
UNLV

L•W•
LAWN
LAWS
LEWD
LOWE
LOWS

L••W
LOEW

•L•W
ALOW
BLEW
BLOW
CLAW
CLEW
FLAW
FLEW
FLOW
GLOW
PLEW
PLOW
SLAW
SLEW
SLOW

LX••
LXII
LXIV
LXIX
LXVI
LXXI
LXXV
LXXX

L•X•
LUXE
LXXI
LXXV
LXXX

L••X
LXIX
LXXX
LYNX

•LX•
CLXI
CLXV
CLXX
DLXI
DLXV
DLXX
MLXI
MLXV
MLXX

•L•X
ALEX
CLIX
CLXX
DLIX
DLXX
FLAX
FLEX
FLIX
FLUX
ILEX
MLIX
MLXX
PLAX
PLEX
XLIX

••LX
CALX
CCLX
CDLX
CMLX
DCLX
FALX
MCLX
MDLX
MMLX

LY••
LYES
LYIN
LYLE
LYLY
LYNE
LYNN
LYNX
LYON
LYRA
LYRE

L•Y•
LAYS
LTYR

L••Y
LACY
LADY
LAKY
LAMY
LAZY
LELY
LEVY
LILY
LIMY
LINY
LIVY
LOGY
LORY
LUCY
LYLY

•LY•
GLYC
GLYN
SLYE

•L•Y
ALGY
ALLY
CLAY
CLOY
ELLY
FLAY
FLEY
GLEY
ILLY
OLAY
PLAY
PLOY
SLAY

••LY
ABLY
AGLY
ALLY
BELY
COLY
DALY
DELY
DULY
EELY
ELLY
EMLY
HOLY
IDLY
ILLY
INLY
JULY
LELY
LILY
LYLY
MOLY
OILY
ONLY
ORLY
PALY
POLY
RELY
ROLY
UGLY
WILY
WKLY

L•Z•
LAZE
LAZY
LIZA

L••Z
LENZ
LINZ
LODZ
LUTZ

•L•Z
ELIZ
FLOZ

MA••
MAAM
MAAR
MAAS
MAAT
MACC
MACE
MACH
MACK
MACS
MACY
MADD
MADE
MAGE
MAGI
MAGS
MAHI
MAIA
MAID
MAIL
MAIN
MAIS
MAJA
MAKE
MAKO
MALA
MALE
MALI
MALL
MALM
MALO
MALT
MAMA
MAME
MANA
MANE
MANN
MANO
MANS
MANU
MANX
MANY
MAPS
MARA
MARC
MARE
MARG
MARI
MARK
MARL
MARS
MART
MARU
MARV
MARX
MARY
MASC
MASH
MASK
MASS
MAST
MATA
MATE
MATH
MATS
MATT
MATU
MAUD
MAUI
MAUL
MAVS
MAWR
MAWS
MAXI
MAYA
MAYI
MAYO
MAYS
MAZE
MAZO
MAZY

M•A•
MAAM
MAAR
MAAS
MAAT
MBAS
MCAT
MEAD
MEAL
MEAN
MEAS
MEAT
MFAS
MOAB
MOAN
MOAS
MOAT
MPAA

M••A
MAIA
MAJA
MALA
MAMA
MANA
MARA
MATA
MAYA
MEGA
MESA
META
MICA
MINA
MIRA
MITA
MKSA
MOLA
MOMA
MONA
MORA
MOTA
MPAA
MRNA
MYNA
MYRA

•MA•
AMAH
AMAS
AMAT
GMAC
GMAN
GMAT
IMAM
IMAN
OMAN
OMAR
TMAN
XMAS

•M•A
AMIA
EMIA
EMMA
SMSA
UMEA
YMCA

••MA
ALMA
ARMA
BAMA
BEMA
BOMA
CAMA
COMA
CYMA
DAMA
DUMA
EMMA
ERMA
FEMA
FNMA
GAMA
GNMA
HAMA
HEMA
IRMA
JIMA
KAMA
LAMA
LEMA
LIMA
LOMA
MAMA
MOMA
PIMA
PUMA
RAMA
RIMA
ROMA
SIMA
SOMA
TAMA
TEMA
TOMA
TVMA
USMA
YAMA
YIMA
YUMA
ZAMA

MB••
MBAS
MBES
MBOY

M•B•
MIBS
MOBS
MOBY

M••B
MOAB
MUSB
MYOB

•MB•
AMBI
AMBO
AMBS
UMBO

••MB
BOMB
COMB
DUMB
IAMB
JAMB
LAMB
LIMB
NUMB
TOMB

MC••
MCAT
MCCC
MCCI
MCCL
MCCV
MCCX
MCDI
MCDL
MCDV
MCDX
MCII
MCIV
MCIX
MCLI
MCLV
MCLX
MCMI
MCML
MCMV
MCMX
MCVI
MCXC
MCXI
MCXL
MCXV
MCXX

M•C•
MACC
MACE
MACH
MACK
MACS
MACY
MCCC
MCCI
MCCL
MCCV
MCCX
MDCC
MDCI
MDCL
MDCV
MDCX
MECH
MECO
MICA
MICE
MICH
MICK
MICR
MICS
MLCC
MMCC
MMCD
MMCI
MMCL
MMCM
MMCV
MMCX
MOCK
MOCS
MUCH
MUCK
MXCI
MXCV
MYCO

M••C
MACC
MARC
MASC
MCCC
MCXC
MDCC
MDXC
MISC
MLCC
MMCC
MMDC
MMMC
MMXC
MSEC

•MC•
MMCC
MMCD
MMCI
MMCL
MMCM
MMCV
MMCX
YMCA

•M•C
AMIC
BMOC
CMXC
EMIC
GMAC
MMCC
MMDC
MMMC
MMXC

••MC
MMMC
USMC

MD••
MDCC
MDCI
MDCL
MDCV
MDCX
MDII
MDIV
MDIX
MDLI
MDLV
MDLX
MDSE
MDVI
MDXC
MDXI
MDXL
MDXV
MDXX

M•D•
MADD
MADE
MCDI
MCDL
MCDV
MCDX
MEDE
MEDS
MIDI
MIDN
MMDC
MMDI
MMDL
MMDV
MMDX
MODE
MODS
MUDD
MUDS

M••D
MADD
MAID
MAUD
MEAD
MEED
MELD
MEND
MILD
MIND
MMCD
MMMD
MOLD
MOOD
MRED
MUDD
MUSD

•MD•
CMDG
CMDR
DMDS
MMDC
MMDI
MMDL
MMDV
MMDX
RMDR

•M•D
AMID
MMCD
MMMD

••MD
COMD
MMMD

ME••
MEAD
MEAL
MEAN
MEAS
MEAT
MECH
MECO
MEDE
MEDS
MEED
MEEK
MEER
MEET
MEGA
MEIN
MEIR
MELD
MELL
MELT
MEME
MEMO
MEMS
MEND
MENS
MENT
MENU
MEOW
MERE
MERL
MERO
MERS
MERV
MESA
MESH
MESO
MESS
META
METE
METH
METS
METZ
MEUM
MEWL
MEWS

M•E•
MBES
MEED
MEEK
MEER
MEET
MIEN
MIES
MMES
MRED
MSEC

M••E
MACE
MADE
MAGE
MAKE
MALE
MAME
MANE
MARE
MATE
MAZE
MDSE
MEDE
MEME
MERE
METE
MICE
MIKE
MILE
MIME
MINE
MIRE
MISE
MITE
MLLE
MODE
MOLE
MOME
MOPE
MORE
MOSE
MOTE
MOUE
MOVE
MTGE
MULE
MUSE
MUTE

•ME•
AMEN
AMER
AMES
AMEX
EMES
GMEN
MMES
NMEX
OMEN
OMER
SMEE
SMEW
TMEN
UMEA
XMEN

•M•E
AMIE
IMRE
SMEE

••ME
ACME
AIME
ARME
AYME
BYME
CAME
COME
CYME
DAME
DEME
DIME
DOME
ESME
FAME
FEME
FUME
GAME
HAME
HEME
HOME
HUME
KAME
LAME
LIME
LOME
MAME
MEME
MIME
MOME
NAME
NOME
POME
RIME
ROME

SAME	MOHO	MIRA	MDXI	OMRI	MALI	CMLX	MEMO	MANX	DAMN	**M•O•**	ELMO	SIMP	**•M•R**
SEME	MOHS	MIRE	MIDI		MALL	EMLY	MEMS	MANY	HYMN	MBOY	GAMO	SUMP	AMER
SOME		MIRO	MIII	**••MI**	MALM	MMLI	MGMT	MEND	LIMN	MEOW	HEMO	TAMP	AMIR
TAME	**M••H**	MIRS	MIMI	CAMI	MALO	MMLV	MIME	MENS		MHOS	HOMO	TEMP	AMOR
TIME	MACH	MIRV	MINI	DEMI	MALT	MMLX	MIMI	MENT	**MO••**	MOOD	KEMO	TUMP	AMUR
TOME	MASH	MIRY	MLII	HEMI	MCLI		MIMS	MENU	MOAB	MOOG	LIMO	TYMP	CMDR
	MATH	MISC	MLVI	JIMI	MCLV	**•M•L**	MMMC	MINA	MOAN	MOON	MEMO	VAMP	EMIR
MF••	MECH	MISE	MLXI	KAMI	MCLX	AMYL	MMMD	MIND	MOAS	MOOR	NEMO	WIMP	OMAR
MFAS	MESH	MISO	MMCI	KOMI	MDLI	CMXL	MMMI	MINE	MOAT	MOOS	POMO		OMER
MFRS	METH	MISS	MMDI	MCMI	MDLV	EMIL	MMML	MING	MOBS	MOOT	REMO	**MR••**	RMDR
	MICH	MIST	MMII	MIMI	MDLX	MMCL	MMMM	MINH	MOBY	MUON	SAMO	MRED	YMIR
M•F•	MINH	MITA	MMLI	MMMI	MELD	MMDL	MMMV	MINI	MOCK	MYOB	SUMO	MRNA	
MIFF	MOSH	MITE	MMMI	RAMI	MELL	MMML	MMMX	MINK	MOCS		TAMO		**••MR**
MUFF	MOTH	MITT	MMVI	SEMI	MELT	MMXL	MOMA	MINN	MODE	**M••O**	ZYMO	**M•R•**	COMR
	MUCH	MIXT	MMXI	SIMI	MILD		MOME	MINS	MODS	MAKO		MARA	
M••F	MUSH		MUNI	SQMI	MILE	**••ML**	MOMS	MINT	MOHO	MALO	**MP••**	MARC	**MS••**
MIFF	MYTH	**M•I•**	MVII		MILK	COML	MUMP	MINX	MOHS	MANO	MPAA	MARE	MSEC
MUFF		MAIA	MXCI	**M•J•**	MILL	MCML	MUMS	MONA	MOIL	MAYO		MARG	MSGR
	•MH•	MAID	MXII	MAJA	MILO	MMML	MYMY	MONK	MOJO	MAZO	**M•P•**	MARI	MSGS
•MF•	IMHO	MAIL	MXLI	MOJO	MILS	SAML		MONO	MOLA	MECO	MAPS	MARK	MSGT
AMFM		MAIN	MXVI		MILT		**M••M**	MONS	MOLD	MEMO	MIPS	MARL	
	•M•H	MAIS	MXXI	**MK••**	MLLE	**MM••**	MAAM	MONT	MOLE	MERO	MOPE	MARS	**M•S•**
•M•F	AMAH	MCII		MKSA	MMLI	MMCC	MALM	MONY	MOLL	MESO	MOPS	MART	MASC
IMPF	UMPH	MCIV	**•MI•**	MKTG	MMLV	MMCD	MEUM	MRNA	MOLT	MILO	MOPY	MARU	MASH
		MCIX	AMIA		MMLX	MMCI	MMCM	MTNS	MOLY	MIRO		MARV	MASK
••MF	**MI••**	MDII	AMIC	**M•K•**	MOLA	MMCL	MMMM	MUNG	MOMA	MISO	**M••P**	MARX	MASS
BUMF	MIBS	MDIV	AMID	MAKE	MOLD	MMCM	MUSM	MUNI	MOME	MOHO	MUMP	MARY	MAST
	MICA	MDIX	AMIE	MAKO	MOLE	MMCV		MYNA	MOMS	MOJO		MERE	MDSE
MG••	MICE	MEIN	AMIN	MIKE	MOLL	MMCX	**•MM•**		MONA	MONO	**•MP•**	MERL	MESA
MGMT	MICH	MEIR	AMIR		MOLT	MMDC	AMMO	**M••N**	MONK	MORO	AMPS	MERO	MESH
MGRS	MICK	MIII	AMIS	**M••K**	MOLY	MMDI	EMMA	MAIN	MONO	MOTO	EMPS	MERS	MESO
	MICR	MLII	CMII	MACK	MULE	MMDL	EMMY	MANN	MONS	MYCO	IMPF	MERV	MESS
M•G•	MICS	MLIV	CMIV	MARK	MULL	MMDV	MMMC	MEAN	MONT	MYXO	IMPI	MFRS	MISC
MAGE	MIDI	MLIX	CMIX	MASK	MXLI	MMDX	MMMD	MEIN	MONY		IMPS	MGRS	MISE
MAGI	MIDN	MMII	EMIA	MEEK	MXLV	MMES	MMMI	MIDN	MOOD	**•MO•**	IMPV	MIRA	MISO
MAGS	MIEN	MMIV	EMIC	MICK		MMII	MMML	MIEN	MOOG	AMOI	UMPH	MIRE	MISS
MEGA	MIES	MMIX	EMIL	MILK	**M••L**	MMIV	MMMM	MINN	MOON	AMOK	UMPS	MIRO	MIST
MIGS	MIFF	MOIL	EMIR	MINK	MAIL	MMIX	MMMV	MOAN	MOOR	AMON		MIRS	MKSA
MNGR	MIGS	MUIR	EMIT	MOCK	MALL	MMLI	MMMX	MOON	MOOS	AMOR	**••MP**	MIRV	MOSE
MSGR	MIII	MVII	IMIT	MONK	MARL	MMLV		MORN	MOOT	AMOS	BOMP	MIRY	MOSH
MSGS	MIKE	MXII	MMII	MORK	MAUL	MMLX	**•M•M**	MOWN	MOPE	AMOY	BUMP	MORA	MOSS
MSGT	MILD	MXIV	MMIV	MUCK	MCCL	MMMC	AMFM	MUON	MOPS	BMOC	CAMP	MORE	MOST
MTGE	MILE	MXIX	MMIX	MURK	MCDL	MMMD	IMAM		MOPY	CMON	COMP	MORK	MUSB
MTGS	MILK		OMIT	MUSK	MCML	MMMI	MMCM	**•MN•**	MORA	CMOS	DAMP	MORN	MUSD
MUGS	MILL	**M••I**	SMIT		MCXL	MMML	MMMM	AMNT	MORE	HMOS	DUMP	MORO	MUSE
	MILO	MAGI	YMIR	**•M•K**	MDCL	MMMM		OMNI	MORK	OMOO	GAMP	MORT	MUSH
M••G	MILS	MAHI		AMOK	MDXL	MMMV	**••MM**		MORN	SMOG	GIMP	MURK	MUSK
MARG	MILT	MALI	**•M•I**	OMSK	MEAL	MMMX	COMM	**•M•N**	MORO		GUMP	MYRA	MUSM
MING	MIME	MARI	AMBI		MELL	MMVI	GUMM	AMEN	MORT	**•M•O**	HEMP		MUSS
MKTG	MIMI	MAUI	AMOI	**ML••**	MERL	MMXC	HAMM	AMIN	MOSE	AMBO	HUMP	**M••R**	MUST
MOOG	MIMS	MAXI	CMII	MLCC	MEWL	MMXI	MMMM	AMON	MOSH	AMMO	JUMP	MAAR	MYST
MUNG	MINA	MAYI	CMLI	MLII	MILL	MMXL	TAMM	CMON	MOSS	DMSO	KEMP	MAWR	
	MIND	MCCI	CMVI	MLIV	MMCL	MMXV		GMAN	MOST	IMHO	LAMP	MEER	**M••S**
•M•G	MINE	MCDI	CMXI	MLIX	MMDL	MMXX	**MN••**	GMEN	MOTA	OMOO	LIMP	MEIR	MAAS
CMDG	MING	MCII	IMPI	MLLE	MMML		MNGR	IMAN	MOTE	UMBO	LUMP	MICR	MACS
SMOG	MINH	MCLI	MMCI	MLVI	MMXL	**M•M•**		OMAN	MOTH		MUMP	MNGR	MAGS
SMUG	MINI	MCMI	MMDI	MLXI	MOIL	MAMA	**M•N•**	OMEN	MOTO	**••MO**	POMP	MOOR	MAIS
	MINK	MCVI	MMII	MLXV	MOLL	MAME	MANA	TMAN	MOTS	AMMO	PUMP	MSGR	MANS
MH••	MINN	MCXI	MMLI	MLXX	MULL	MCMI	MANE	TMEN	MOTT	ATMO	RAMP	MUIR	MAPS
MHOS	MINS	MDCI	MMMI			MCML	MANN	XMEN	MOUE	CAMO	RCMP		MARS
	MINT	MDII	MMVI	**M•L•**	**•ML•**	MCMV	MANO		MOVE	COMO	ROMP	**•MR•**	MASS
M•H•	MINX	MDLI	MMXI	MALA	CMLI	MCMX	MANS	**••MN**	MOWN	DEMO	RUMP	IMRE	MATS
MAHI	MIPS	MDVI	OMNI	MALE	CMLV	MEME	MANU	CHMN	MOWS	DOMO	SAMP	OMRI	MAVS

MAWS MAYS MBAS MBES MEAS MEDS MEMS MENS MERS MESS METS MEWS MFAS MFRS MGRS MHOS MIBS MICS MIES MIGS MILS MIMS MINS MIPS MIRS MISS MMES MOAS MOBS MOCS MODS MOHS MOMS MONS MOOS MOPS MOSS MOTS MOWS MSGS MTGS MTNS MUDS MUGS MUMS MUSS

•MS•
DMSO OMSK SMSA

•M•S
AMAS AMBS AMES AMIS AMOS AMPS AMTS BMUS BMWS CMOS DMDS EMES EMPS EMTS EMUS HMOS IMPS IMUS MMES PMTS UMPS XMAS

••MS
ABMS ADMS AIMS ALMS ARMS ATMS BAMS BEMS BUMS CAMS CWMS DAMS DEMS DIMS DOMS DPMS DSMS DVMS ELMS FEMS GAMS GEMS GUMS GYMS HAMS HEMS HOMS HUMS ISMS JAMS JIMS LAMS LEMS LLMS MEMS MIMS MOMS MUMS NOMS OHMS POMS RAMS REMS RIMS ROMS RPMS RUMS SEMS SIMS SUMS SYMS TAMS TOMS TUMS VIMS YAMS

MT••
MTGE MTGS MTNS

M•T•
MATA MATE MATH MATS MATT MATU META METE METH METS METZ MITA MITE MITT MKTG MOTA MOTE MOTH MOTO MOTS MOTT MUTE MUTT MYTH

M••T
MAAT MALT MART MAST MATT MCAT MEAT MEET MELT MENT MGMT MILT MINT MIST MITT MIXT MOAT MOLT MONT MOOT MORT MOST MOTT MSGT MUST MUTT MYST

•MT•
AMTS EMTS PMTS

•M•T
AMAT AMNT EMIT GMAT IMIT OMIT SMIT SMUT

••MT
BSMT MGMT STMT

MU••
MUCH MUCK MUDD MUDS MUFF MUGS MUIR MULE MULL MUMP MUMS MUNG MUNI MUON MURK MUSB MUSD MUSE MUSH MUSK MUSM MUSS MUST MUTE MUTT MUZZ

M•U•
MAUD MAUI MAUL MEUM MOUE

M••U
MANU MARU MATU MENU

•MU•
AMUR BMUS EMUS IMUS SMUG SMUT

••MU
BOMU

MV••
MVII

M•V•
MAVS MCVI MDVI MLVI MMVI MOVE MXVI

M••V
MARV MCCV MCDV MCIV MCLV MCMV MCXV MDCV MDIV MDLV MDXV MERV MIRV MLIV MLXV MMCV MMDV MMIV MMLV MMMV MMXV MXCV MXIV MXLV MXXV

•MV•
CMVI MMVI

•M•V
CMIV CMLV CMXV IMPV MMCV MMDV MMIV MMLV MMMV MMXV

••MV
MCMV MMMV

M•W•
MAWR MAWS MEWL MEWS MOWN MOWS

M••W
MEOW

•MW•
BMWS

•M•W
SMEW

MX••
MXCI MXCV MXII MXIV MXIX MXLI MXLV MXVI MXXI MXXV MXXX

M•X•
MAXI MCXC MCXI MCXL MCXV MCXX MDXC MDXI MDXL MDXV MDXX MIXT MLXI MLXV MLXX MMXC MMXI MMXL MMXV MMXX MXXI MXXV MXXX MYXO

M••X
MANX MARX MCCX MCDX MCIX MCLX MCMX MCXX MDCX MDIX MDLX MDXX MINX MLIX MLXX MMCX MMDX MMIX MMLX MMMX MMXX MXIX MXXX

•MX•
CMXC CMXI CMXL CMXV CMXX MMXC MMXI MMXL MMXV MMXX

•M•X
AMEX CMIX CMLX CMXX MMCX MMDX MMIX MMLX MMMX MMXX NMEX

••MX
MCMX MMMX

MY••
MYCO MYMY MYNA MYOB MYRA MYST MYTH MYXO

M•Y•
MAYA MAYI MAYO MAYS

M••Y
MACY MANY MARY MAZY MBOY MIRY MOBY MOLY MONY MOPY MYMY

•MY•
AMYL

•M•Y
AMOY EMLY EMMY

••MY
ARMY DEMY EMMY FUMY GAMY HOMY LAMY LIMY MYMY OHMY RIMY ROMY

M•Z•
MAZE MAZO MAZY MUZZ

M••Z
METZ MUZZ

NA••
NABE NABS NACL NADA NADH NADP NAES NAGS NAGY NAHA NAIF NAIL NAME NANA NANG NANO NANU NAOH NAOI NAOS NAPA NAPE NAPS NARA NARC NARD NARK NARY NARZ NASA NASD NASH NASL NASO NAST NATE NATL NATO NAUT NAVE NAVY NAYS

N•A•
NCAA NDAK NEAL NEAP NEAR NEAT NLAT NOAA NOAH NOAM

N••A
NADA NAHA NANA NAPA NARA NASA NCAA NEVA NINA NIPA NITA NOAA NOLA NONA NORA NOTA NOVA

•NA•
ANAS ANAT BNAI GNAR GNAT GNAW KNAP KNAR SNAG SNAP UNAU

•N•A
ANKA ANNA ANOA ANSA ANTA ANYA ANZA ENNA ENYA FNMA GNMA INCA INGA INKA ONEA

••NA
ANNA BONA BUNA CANA CENA CUNA DANA DINA DONA DUNA DYNA EDNA ENNA ETNA FINA GENA GINA HANA IANA IONA JENA KANA KINA KONA LANA LENA LINA LUNA MANA MINA MONA MRNA MYNA NANA NINA NONA OONA PENA PINA PUNA RANA RONA RRNA SANA TANA TINA TRNA TUNA ULNA USNA VENA VINA XENA YANA ZONA

N•B•
NABE NABS NEBE NEBN NEBO NEBR NEBS NIBS NOBS NUBS NWBN NWBW

N••B
NLRB NTSB NUMB

•N•B
KNOB SNOB SNUB

NC••
NCAA NCOS

N•C•
NACL NECK NICE NICK NOCK

N••C
NARC NUNC

•NC•
ANCE ANCY ENCE ENCL ENCS ENCY INCA INCE INCH INCL INCR ONCE SNCC UNCI

•N•C
SNCC

••NC
BANC CANC CINC CONC JUNC NUNC SYNC ZINC

ND••
NDAK

N•D•
NADA NADH NADP NIDE NIDI NODE NODI NODS NUDE NUDI

N••D
NARD NASD NEED NEJD NERD NFLD NKVD NORD

•ND•
ANDS ANDY ENDE ENDO ENDS INDO INDS INDY RNDS UNDO

•N•D
ENID KNUD

••ND
BAND BEND BIND BOND BUND COND FEND FIND FOND FUND GOND HAND HIND HOND HUND KIND LAND LEND LIND MEND MIND PEND POND RAND REND RIND SAND SEND SIND SYND TEND VEND WAND WEND WIND YOND ZEND

NE••
NEAL NEAP NEAR NEAT NEBE NEBN NEBO NEBR NEBS NECK NEED NEEL NEEM NEER NEET NEFF NEGS NEHI NEIL NEIN NEJD NELL NEMO NENE NEON NERD NERF NERI NERO NESS NEST NETH NETS NEUF NEUN NEUT NEVA NEVE NEVI NEWF NEWS NEWT NEXT

N•E•
NAES NEED NEEL NEEM NEER NEET NLER NMEX NOEL NOES NYET

N••E
NABE NAME NAPE NATE NAVE NEBE NENE NEVE NICE NIDE NIKE NILE NINE NITE NIUE NODE NOME

NONE
NOPE
NOSE
NOTE
NUDE
NUKE
NYSE

•NE•
ANEW
INEE
INES
INEZ
KNEE
KNEW
ONEA
ONER
ONES
SNEE
UNES

•N•E
ANCE
ANGE
ANNE
ANTE
ENCE
ENDE
ENNE
ENSE
INCE
INEE
INGE
INRE
KNEE
ONCE
SNEE

••NE
ACNE
ANNE
AONE
ARNE
AUNE
BANE
BENE
BINE
BONE
CANE
CENE
CINE
CONE
DANE
DENE
DINE
DONE
DUNE
DYNE
EINE
ENNE
ERNE
ESNE
FANE
FINE
GENE
GONE
HONE
IONE
JANE
JUNE
KANE
KINE
LANE
LINE
LONE
LUNE
LYNE
MANE
MINE
NENE
NINE
NONE
OHNE
ORNE
PANE
PINE
PONE
RENE
RUNE
RYNE
SANE
SENE
SINE
SONE
SYNE
TANE
TENE
TINE
TONE
TUNE
TYNE
UTNE
VANE
VINE
WANE
WINE
ZANE
ZINE
ZONE

NF••
NFLD

N•F•
NEFF

N••F
NAIF
NEFF
NERF
NEUF
NEWF

•NF•
INFL
INFO
INFS

•N•F
ENUF

••NF
CANF
CONF
FUNF

N•G•
NAGS
NAGY
NEGS
NIGH
NOGO
NOGS

N••G
NANG

•NG•
ANGE
ANGL
ENGR
ENGS
INGA
INGE
MNGR

•N•G
SNAG
SNOG
SNUG

••NG
BANG
BENG
BING
BONG
BUNG
BYNG
CONG
DANG
DENG
DING
DONG
FANG
GANG
GONG
GUNG
HANG
HONG
HUNG
JONG
JUNG
KING
KONG
KUNG
LANG
LING
LONG
LUNG
MING
MUNG
NANG
PANG
PING
PONG
PUNG
RANG
RING
RUNG
SANG
SING
SONG
SUNG
TANG
TING
TONG
TUNG
VANG
VING
WANG
WENG
WING
WONG
XING
YANG
ZING

N•H•
NAHA
NEHI

N••H
NADH
NAOH
NASH
NETH
NIGH
NOAH
NOSH

•N•H
ANKH
ANTH
INCH

••NH
MINH
PENH
SINH
TANH

NI••
NIBS
NICE
NICK
NIDE
NIDI
NIGH
NIKE
NILE
NILS
NINA
NINE
NINO
NIPA
NIPS
NISI
NITA
NITE
NITS
NIUE

N•I•
NAIF
NAIL
NEIL
NEIN
NOIL
NOIR
NUIT

N••I
NAOI
NEHI
NERI
NEVI
NIDI
NISI
NODI
NOLI
NORI
NOTI
NUDI

•NI•
ANIL
ANIM
ANIS
ENID
INIT
KNIT
PNIN
SNIP
SNIT
UNIS
UNIT
UNIV
UNIX

•N•I
ANSI
ANTI
BNAI
INRI
UNCI

••NI
AGNI
BANI
BENI
BONI
FINI
HONI
IFNI
JONI
LENI
LONI
MINI
MUNI
OMNI
RANI
RENI
TONI
VENI
VINI
ZUNI

N•J•
NEJD

••NJ
CONJ

NK••
NKVD

N•K•
NIKE
NUKE

N••K
NARK
NDAK
NECK
NICK
NOCK
NOOK
NYUK

•NK•
ANKA
ANKH
INKA
INKS
INKY

•N•K
TNPK

••NK
BANK
BONK
BUNK
CONK
DANK
DINK
DUNK
FINK
FUNK
GUNK
HANK
HONK
HUNK
JINK
JUNK
KINK
LANK
LINK
MINK
MONK
OINK
PINK
PUNK
RANK
RINK
SANK
SINK
SUNK
TANK
TONK
WINK
WONK
YANK
ZONK

NL••
NLAT
NLER
NLRB

N•L•
NELL
NFLD
NILE
NILS
NOLA
NOLI
NOLL
NOLO
NULL

N••L
NACL
NAIL
NASL
NATL
NEAL
NEEL
NEIL
NELL
NOEL
NOIL
NOLL
NULL

•NL•
INLY
ONLY
UNLV

•N•L
ANGL
ANIL
ENCL
ENOL
INCL
INFL
INTL

••NL
DANL
GENL

NM••
NMEX

N•M•
NAME
NEMO
NOME
NOMS
NUMB

N••M
NEEM
NOAM
NORM

•NM•
FNMA
GNMA

•N•M
ANIM
ONYM
UNUM

N•N•
NANA
NANG
NANO
NANU
NENE
NINA
NINE
NINO
NONA
NONE
NONO
NUNC
NUNN
NUNS

N••N
NEBN
NEIN
NEON
NEUN
NOON
NORN
NOUN
NUNN
NWBN

•NN•
ANNA
ANNE
ANNO
ENNA
ENNE
INNS

•N•N
ANON
INON
PNIN

••NN
BONN
CONN
DUNN
FENN
FINN
GANN
GUNN
JINN
LUNN
LYNN
MANN
MINN
NUNN
PENN
SUNN
TENN
VENN
WYNN

NO••
NOAA
NOAH
NOAM
NOBS
NOCK
NODE
NODI
NODS
NOEL
NOES
NOGO
NOGS
NOIL
NOIR
NOLA
NOLI
NOLL
NOLO
NOME
NOMS
NONA
NONE
NONO
NOOK
NOON
NOOP
NOOR
NOPE
NORA
NORD
NORI
NORM
NORN
NORW
NOSE
NOSH
NOSY
NOTA
NOTE
NOTI
NOTS
NOUN
NOUS
NOVA
NOVO

N•O•
NAOH
NAOI
NAOS
NCOS
NEON
NOOK
NOON
NOOP
NOOR

N••O
NANO
NASO
NATO
NEBO
NEMO
NERO
NINO
NOGO
NOLO
NONO
NOVO
NYRO

•NO•
ANOA
ANON
ENOL
ENOS
ENOW
INON
KNOB
KNOP
KNOT
KNOW
KNOX
SNOB
SNOG
SNOW

•N•O
ANNO
ENDO
ENTO
ENYO
ENZO
INDO
INFO
INRO
INTO
ONTO
UNDO
UNTO

••NO
ANNO
ARNO
ATNO
BONO
BRNO
CENO
DANO
DINO
DRNO
ERNO
FINO
GINO
JUNO
KANO
KENO
KINO
LENO
LINO
MANO
MONO
NANO
NINO
NONO
OENO
OHNO
RENO
SANO
SINO
TENO
VINO
XENO
ZENO

N•P•
NAPA
NAPE
NAPS
NIPA
NIPS
NOPE

N••P
NADP
NEAP
NOOP

•NP•
TNPK

•N•P
INSP
KNAP
KNOP
SNAP
SNIP

••NQ
CINQ

N•R•
NARA
NARC
NARD
NARK
NARY
NARZ
NERD
NERF
NERI
NERO
NLRB
NORA
NORD
NORI
NORM
NORN
NORW
NYRO

N••R
NEAR
NEBR
NEER
NLER
NOIR
NOOR

•NR•
ENRY
INRE
INRI
INRO

•N•R
ENGR
ENTR
GNAR
INCR
INTR
KNAR
KNUR
MNGR
ONER

••NR
USNR

N•S•
NASA
NASD
NASH
NASL
NASO
NAST
NESS
NEST
NISI
NOSE
NOSH
NOSY
NTSB
NYSE

N••S
NABS
NAES
NAGS
NAOS
NAPS
NAYS
NCOS
NEBS
NEGS
NESS
NETS
NEWS
NIBS
NILS
NIPS
NITS
NOBS
NODS
NOES
NOGS
NOMS
NOTS
NOUS
NUBS
NUNS
NUTS
NUYS

•NS•
ANSA
ANSI
ENSE
INSP
INST

•N•S
ANAS
ANDS
ANIS
ANTS
ENCS
ENDS
ENGS
ENOS
ENTS
ENVS
GNUS
INDS
INES
INFS
INKS
INNS
INTS
INXS
ONES
ONUS
RNDS
UNES
UNIS

••NS
AINS
AWNS
BANS
BINS
BUNS
CANS
CENS
CONS
CTNS
DENS
DINS
DONS
DUNS
EINS
EONS
ERNS
FANS
FENS
FINS
FONS
GENS
GINS
GUNS
HANS
HENS
HINS
HUNS
INNS
IONS
JENS
KANS
KENS
LENS
MANS
MENS
MINS
MONS
MTNS
NUNS
OWNS
PANS
PENS
PINS
PONS
PUNS
RUNS
SANS
SENS
SINS
SONS
SSNS
STNS
SUNS
SYNS
TANS
TENS
TINS
TONS
TUNS
URNS
VANS
VINS
WENS
WINS
WONS
WRNS

YENS

NT••
NTSB
NTWT

N•T•
NATE
NATL
NATO
NETH
NETS
NITA
NITE
NITS
NOTA
NOTE
NOTI
NOTS
NUTS
NUTT

N••T
NAST
NAUT
NEAT
NEET
NEST
NEUT
NEWT
NEXT
NLAT
NTWT
NUIT
NUTT
NYET

•NT•
ANTA
ANTE
ANTH
ANTI
ANTS
ENTO
ENTR
ENTS
INTL
INTO
INTR
INTS
ONTO
UNTO

•N•T
ANAT
CNUT
GNAT
INIT
INST
KNIT
KNOT
KNUT
SNIT
TNUT
UNIT

••NT
AINT
AMNT
AUNT
BENT
BUNT
CANT
CENT
CONT
DENT
DINT
DONT
FONT
FUNT
GENT
GYNT
HENT
HINT
HUNT
ISNT
KANT
KENT
LENT
LINT
LUNT
MENT
MINT
MONT
PANT
PENT
PINT
PONT
PUNT
RANT
RENT
RUNT
SANT
SENT
TENT
TINT
VENT
WANT
WENT
WONT

NU••
NUBS
NUDE
NUDI
NUIT
NUKE
NULL
NUMB
NUNC
NUNN
NUNS
NUTS
NUTT
NUYS

N•U•
NAUT
NEUF
NEUN
NEUT
NIUE
NOUN
NOUS
NYUK

N••U
NANU

•NU•
CNUT
ENUF
GNUS
KNUD
KNUR
KNUT
ONUS
SNUB
SNUG
TNUT
UNUM

•N•U
UNAU

••NU
AINU
BENU
DANU
GENU
MANU
MENU
NANU

N•V•
NAVE
NAVY
NEVA
NEVE
NEVI
NKVD
NOVA
NOVO

•NV•
ENVS
ENVY

•N•V
UNIV
UNLV

••NV
CONV

NW••
NWBN
NWBW

N•W•
NEWF
NEWS
NEWT
NTWT

N••W
NORW
NWBW

•N•W
ANEW
ENOW
GNAW
KNEW
KNOW
SNOW

N•X•
NEXT

N••X
NMEX

•NX•
INXS

•N•X
KNOX
ONYX
UNIX

••NX
GENX
JINX
LYNX
MANX
MINX
PINX

NY••
NYET
NYRO
NYSE
NYUK

N•Y•
NAYS
NUYS

N••Y
NAGY
NARY
NAVY
NOSY

•NY•
ANYA
ENYA
ENYO
ONYM
ONYX

•N•Y
ANCY
ANDY
ENCY
ENRY
ENVY
INDY
INKY
INLY
ONLY

••NY
BONY
CANY
CONY
CUNY
DENY
DKNY
EENY
GENY
GONY
LINY
MANY
MONY
PINY
PONY
PUNY
SONY
SUNY
TINY
TONY
VINY
WANY
WINY
ZANY

N••Z
NARZ

•NZ•
ANZA
ENZO

•N•Z
INEZ

••NZ
BENZ
FONZ
LENZ
LINZ

OA••
OAFS
OAHU
OAKS
OARS
OAST
OATH
OATS
OATY

O•A•
OBAD
OCAS
ODAS
ODAY
OJAI
OKAY
OLAF
OLAN
OLAV
OLAY
OMAN
OMAR
OPAH
OPAL
ORAD
ORAL
ORAN
OSAR
OVAL
OZAV

O••A
OCTA
ODEA
OITA
OKLA
OKRA
OLGA
OLLA
ONEA
OONA
OPIA
ORCA
OSHA
OSSA
OTRA

•OA•
BOAC
BOAR
BOAS
BOAT
BOAZ
COAL
COAT
COAX
DOAK
FOAL
FOAM
GOAD
GOAL
GOAT
HOAD
HOAR
HOAX
JOAB
JOAD
JOAN
KOAN
LOAD
LOAF
LOAM
LOAN
MOAB
MOAN
MOAS
MOAT
NOAA
NOAH
NOAM
ROAD
ROAM
ROAN
ROAR
SOAK
SOAP
SOAR
TOAD
TOAT
WOAD
ZOAR

•O•A
BOCA
BOLA
BOMA
BONA
BORA
BOTA
BOVA
COCA
CODA
COLA
COMA
CORA
COSA
COXA
DOHA
DONA
DOPA
DORA
FORA
GOYA
HOLA
HORA
HOYA
IOLA
IONA
IOTA
IOWA
KOLA
KONA
LOLA
LOMA
LOTA
MOLA
MOMA
MONA
MORA
MOTA
NOAA
NOLA
NONA
NORA
NOTA
NOVA
OONA
PODA
POLA
ROCA
ROMA
RONA
ROSA
ROTA
SOCA
SODA
SOFA
SOLA
SOMA
SORA
SOYA
TOEA
TOGA
TOLA
TOMA
TORA
YODA
YOGA
ZOEA
ZOLA
ZONA

••OA
ANOA
PROA
STOA
WHOA

OB••
OBAD
OBEY
OBIE
OBIS
OBIT
OBOE
OBOL

O•B•
ORBI
ORBS

•OB•
BOBS
COBB
COBH
COBS
DOBY
FOBS
GOBI
GOBO
GOBS
GOBY
HOBO
HOBS
JOBS
KOBE
KOBO
KOBS
LOBE
LOBO
LOBS
MOBS
MOBY
NOBS
ROBB
ROBE
ROBO
ROBS
SOBS
TOBE
TOBY
YOBS

•O•B
BOMB
BOOB
COBB
COMB
FORB
JOAB
LOEB
MOAB
ROBB
SORB
TOMB

••OB
BLOB
BOOB
BYOB
GLOB
KNOB
MYOB
PROB
SLOB
SNOB
SWOB

OC••
OCAS
OCHO
OCHS
OCTA
OCTO

O•C•
ONCE
ORCA
ORCH
ORCS
OUCH

O••C
ODIC
OPEC
OTIC

•OC•
BOCA
BOCK
COCA
COCK
COCO
DOCK
DOCS
FOCH
FOCI
HOCH
HOCK
JOCK
KOCH
LOCH
LOCI
LOCK
LOCO
MOCK
MOCS
NOCK
POCO
ROCA
ROCK
ROCS
SOCA
SOCK
TOCK
VOCE

•O•C
BOAC
BOSC
COFC
CONC
KOFC
ROTC
ZOIC

••OC
APOC
BLOC
BMOC
CHOC
CROC
EEOC
FLOC
KROC
PROC

OD••
ODAS
ODAY
ODDS
ODEA
ODER
ODES
ODIC
ODIE
ODIN
ODOM
ODOR

O•D•
ODDS
OLDE
OLDS
ORDO
OUDS

O••D
OBAD
OHED
OKED
OLID
OOID
OPED
ORAD
OVID
OWED

•OD•
BODE
BODO
BODS
BODY
CODA
CODE
CODS
CODY
DODD
DODO
GODS
HODS
IODO
JODY
LODE
LODI
LODZ
MODE
MODS
NODE
NODI
NODS
PODA
PODE
PODS
RODE
RODS
SODA
SODS
TODD
TODO
TODS
TODY
YODA
YODH
YODS

•O•D
BOLD
BOND
BOYD
COED
COLD
COMD
COND
CORD
DODD
DOOD
DOWD
FOLD
FOND
FOOD
FORD
GOAD
GOLD
GOND
GOOD
HOAD
HOED
HOLD
HOND
HOOD
JOAD
LOAD
LOID
LORD
LOUD
MOLD
MOOD
NORD
OOID
POND
POOD
ROAD
ROOD
SOLD
TOAD
TODD
TOED
TOLD
VOID
WOAD
WOLD
WOOD
WORD
YOND
YOUD

••OD
CLOD
DOOD
EXOD
FOOD
GOOD
HOOD
IZOD
MOOD
PLOD
POOD
PROD
QUOD
ROOD
SHOD
TROD
TWOD
WHOD
WOOD

OE••
OEIL
OENO
OEUF

O•E•
OBEY
ODEA
ODER
ODES
OGEE
OHED
OKED
OKEY
OLEG
OLEN
OLEO
OLES
OMEN
OMER
ONEA
ONER
ONES
OPEC
OPED
OPEL
OPEN
OPER
OPES
OREG
OREL
OREM
OREO
ORES
OSEE
OVEN
OVER
OWED
OWEN
OWER
OWES
OXEN
OYER
OYEZ

O••E
OBIE
OBOE
ODIE
OGEE
OGLE
OGRE
OHNE
OISE
OKIE
OLDE
ONCE
OOZE
OPIE
ORLE
ORNE
OSEE
OSTE
OTOE
OUSE

•OE•
BOER
COED
COEL
COEN
DOER
DOES
FOES
GOER
GOES
HOED
HOER
HOES
JOEL
JOES
JOEY
LOEB
LOEW
NOEL
NOES
POEM
POET
ROEG
ROES
TOEA
TOED
TOES
WOES
ZOEA

•O•E
AONE
BODE
BOLE
BONE
BORE
BOSE
BOWE
CODE
COKE
COLE
COME
CONE
COPE
CORE
COTE
COUE
COVE
DOGE
DOLE
DOME
DONE
DOPE
DORE
DOSE
DOTE
DOVE
DOZE
FOIE
FORE
FOXE
GONE
GORE

HOKE	SOKE	**•O•F**	HOGG	**O•H•**	YODH	FOIS	LEOI	COOK	OLID	JOLT	FOOL	OMRI	COSM
HOLE	SOLE	BOFF	HOGS	OAHU	YOGH	GOIN	NAOI	CORK	OLIN	KOLA	FOUL	OMSK	DOOM
HOME	SOME	COIF	JOGS	OCHO		JOIE	QUOI	DOAK	OLIO	KOLN	FOWL		DORM
HONE	SONE	CONF	LOGE	OCHS	**••OH**	JOIN	TROI	DOCK	OLLA	KOLO	GOAL	**O•M•**	FOAM
HOPE	SORE	CORF	LOGO	OOHS	IEOH	KOIS		FOLK		LOLA	HOWL	OHMS	FORM
HOSE	TOBE	DOFF	LOGS	OSHA	IPOH	LOID	**OJ••**	FORK	**O•L•**	LOLL	JOEL	OHMY	HOLM
HOTE	TOKE	DOLF	LOGY	OTHO	NAOH	LOIN	OJAI	GOWK	OGLE	MOLA	JOWL		LOAM
HOVE	TOLE	GOLF	NOGO		OHOH	LOIS		HOCK	OILS	MOLD	KOHL	**O••M**	LOOM
HOWE	TOME	GOOF	NOGS	**O••H**	POOH	MOIL	**•OJ•**	HONK	OILY	MOLE	KOOL	ODOM	NOAM
IOLE	TONE	HOFF	POGO	OATH	UHOH	NOIL	DOJO	HOOK	OKLA	MOLL	LOLL	ONYM	NORM
IONE	TOPE	HOOF	POGS	OHOH		NOIR	HOJO	JOCK	OLLA	MOLT	MOIL	OREM	POEM
JOIE	TORE	IOOF	POGY	OPAH	**OI••**	OOID	JOJO	KOOK	ONLY	MOLY	MOLL	OVUM	ROAM
JOKE	TOTE	KOPF	TOGA	ORCH	OIKS	POIL	KOJI	LOCK	ORLE	NOLA	NOEL		ROOM
JOSE	VOCE	LOAF	TOGO	ORTH	OILS	POIS	MOJO	LOOK	ORLY	NOLI	NOIL	**•OM•**	VOOM
JOVE	VOLE	POOF	TOGS	OUCH	OILY	ROIL	ROJO	MOCK	OSLO	NOLL	NOLL	BOMA	WORM
KOBE	VOTE	POUF	YOGA		OINK	SOIE	TOJO	MONK	OULU	NOLO	POHL	BOMB	ZOOM
KORE	WOKE	ROLF	YOGH	**•OH•**	OISE	SOIL		MORK	OWLS	POLA	POIL	BOMP	
LOBE	WOLE	ROOF	YOGI	BOHM	OITA	SOIR	**•O•J**	NOCK		POLE	POLL	BOMU	**••OM**
LODE	WORE	TOFF	ZOGI	BOHR		TOIL	CONJ	NOOK	**O••L**	POLK	POOL	COMA	ATOM
LOGE	WOVE	WOLF		COHN	**O•I•**	VOID		POLK	OBOL	POLL	ROIL	COMB	BOOM
LOME	YOKE	WOOF	**•O•G**	COHO	OBIE	VOIR	**OK••**	PORK	OEIL	POLO	ROLL	COMD	BROM
LONE	YORE		BONG	DOHA	OBIS	VOIX	OKAY	ROCK	OPAL	POLS	ROTL	COME	DOOM
LOPE	ZONE	**••OF**	BORG	FOHN	OBIT	ZOIC	OKED	ROOK	OPEL	POLY	SOIL	COML	EDOM
LORE		ASOF	CONG	HOHO	ODIC		OKEY	SOAK	ORAL	ROLE	SOUL	COMM	FROM
LOSE	**••OE**	GOOF	DOGG	JOHN	ODIE	**•O•I**	OKIE	SOCK	OREL	ROLF	TOIL	COMO	GEOM
LOVE	ALOE	HOOF	DONG	KOHL	ODIN	AOKI	OKLA	SOUK	OVAL	ROLL	TOLL	COMP	GLOM
LOWE	BPOE	IOOF	DOUG	MOHO	OEIL	BONI	OKRA	TOCK		ROLY	TOOL	COMR	LOOM
MODE	EVOE	POOF	FOGG	MOHS	OHIO	CORI		TONK	**•OL•**	SOLA	WOHL	DOME	ODOM
MOLE	FLOE	PROF	GONG	OOHS	OKIE	COSI	**O•K•**	TOOK	BOLA	SOLD	WOOL	DOMO	PROM
MOME	FROE	ROOF	HOGG	POHL	OLID	FOCI	OAKS	TORK	BOLD	SOLE	YOWL	DOMS	ROOM
MOPE	OBOE	WOOF	HONG	ROHE	OLIN	GOBI	OIKS	WONK	BOLE	SOLI	ZOOL	HOME	THOM
MORE	OTOE		JONG	SOHN	OLIO	GOGI		WORK	BOLL	SOLN		HOMO	VOOM
MOSE	SHOE	**OG••**	KONG	SOHO	OMIT	HONI	**O••K**	WOUK	BOLO	SOLO	**••OL**	HOMS	WHOM
MOTE	SLOE	OGEE	LONG	TOHO	OOID	HOPI	OINK	YOLK	BOLT	SOLS	AWOL	HOMY	ZOOM
MOUE		OGGI	MOOG	WOHL	OPIA	JOLI	OMSK	YORK	COLA	TOLA	BIOL	KOMI	
MOVE	**OF••**	OGLE	PONG	YOHO	OPIE	JONI	ORSK	ZONK	COLD	TOLD	CHOL	LOMA	**ON••**
NODE	OFFS	OGRE	ROEG		ORIG	KOFI		ZOUK	COLE	TOLE	COOL	LOME	ONCE
NOME			SONG	**•O•H**	OSIS	KOJI	**•OK•**		COLL	TOLL	ECOL	MOMA	ONEA
NONE	**O•F•**	**O•G•**	TONG	BOSH	OTIC	KOMI	AOKI	**••OK**	COLO	TOLU	ENOL	MOME	ONER
NOPE	OAFS	OGGI	WONG	BOTH	OTIS	LOCI	COKE	AMOK	COLS	VOLE	FOOL	MOMS	ONES
NOSE	OFFS	OLGA		COBH	OVID	LODI	COKY	BOOK	COLT	VOLS	GAOL	NOME	ONLY
NOTE	ORFF	ORGS	**••OG**	COSH	OVIS	LOKI	HOKE	COOK	COLY	VOLT	GEOL	NOMS	ONTO
OOZE		ORGY	AGOG	DOTH		LONI	JOKE	EWOK	DOLE	WOLD	IDOL	POME	ONUS
PODE	**O••F**		BIOG	FOCH	**O••I**	LORI	JOKY	GROK	DOLF	WOLE	ITOL	POMO	ONYM
POKE	OEUF	**O••G**	CLOG	GOGH	OGGI	LOTI	KOKO	HOOK	DOLL	WOLF	KOOL	POMP	ONYX
POLE	OLAF	OLEG	FLOG	GOSH	OJAI	NODI	LOKI	KOOK	DOLT	YOLK	OBOL	POMS	
POME	ORFF	OREG	FROG	GOTH	OMNI	NOLI	POKE	LOOK	FOLD	ZOLA	POOL	ROMA	**O•N•**
PONE		ORIG	GEOG	HOCH	OMRI	NORI	POKY	NOOK	FOLK		SKOL	ROME	OENO
POPE	**•OF•**		GROG	JOSH	ORBI	NOTI	SOKE	ROOK	GOLD	**•O•L**	STOL	ROMP	OHNE
PORE	BOFF	**•OG•**	MOOG	KOCH		ROTI	TOKE	TOOK	GOLF	BOIL	TOOL	ROMS	OHNO
POSE	COFC	BOGS	PROG	KOPH	**•OI•**	SOLI	WOKE		HOLA	BOLL	VIOL	ROMY	OINK
ROBE	COFS	BOGY	SLOG	LOCH	BOIL	SORI	WOKS	**OL••**	HOLD	BOWL	VTOL	SOMA	OMNI
RODE	DOFF	COGS	SMOG	MOSH	BOIS	TONI	YOKE	OLAF	HOLE	COAL	WOOL	SOME	OONA
ROHE	HOFF	DOGE	SNOG	MOTH	COIF	TOPI	YOKO	OLAN	HOLM	COEL	ZOOL	TOMA	ORNE
ROLE	KOFC	DOGG		NOAH	COIL	TORI		OLAV	HOLO	COIL		TOMB	OWNS
ROME	KOFI	DOGS	**OH••**	NOSH	COIN	YOGI	**•O•K**	OLAY	HOLP	COLL	**OM••**	TOME	
ROPE	KOFP	DOGY	OHED	POOH	COIR	ZOGI	BOCK	OLDE	HOLS	COML	OMAN	TOMS	**O••N**
ROSE	LOFT	FOGG	OHIO	POSH	DOIL	ZORI	BONK	OLDS	HOLT	COOL	OMAR		ODIN
ROTE	SOFA	FOGS	OHMS	QOPH	DOIN		BOOK	OLEG	HOLY	COWL	OMEN	**•O•M**	OLAN
ROUE	SOFT	FOGY	OHMY	ROSH	DOIT	**••OI**	BORK	OLEN	IOLA	DOIL	OMER	BOHM	OLEN
ROVE	TOFF	GOGH	OHNE	ROTH	FOIE	AMOI	BOSK	OLEO	IOLE	DOLL	OMIT	BOOM	OLIN
ROWE	TOFT	GOGI	OHNO	SOPH	FOIL	ATOI	COCK	OLES	JOLI	FOAL	OMNI	COMM	OMAN
SOIE	TOFU	GOGO	OHOH	TOSH	FOIN	ELOI	CONK	OLGA	JOLO	FOIL	OMOO	CORM	OMEN

OPEN	MONT	MOAN	PEON	BOOS	TOON	SOSO	QOPH	SWOP	BORN	SORA	BOOR	OROS	YOST
ORAN	MONY	MOON	PHON	BOOT	TOOT	TODO	ROPE	TROP	BORO	SORB	DIOR	ORTS	
OVEN	NONA	MORN	PION	COOK	VOOM	TOGO	ROPY	VSOP	BORS	SORE	DOOR	ORVS	**•O•S**
OWEN	NONE	MOWN	POON	COOL	WOOD	TOHO	SOPH	WHOP	BORT	SORI	EXOR	OSIS	BOAS
OXEN	NONO	NOON	PRON	COON	WOOF	TOJO	SOPS		CORA	SORT	FLOR	OTIS	BOBS
OXON	OONA	NORN	SION	COOP	WOOL	TOPO	TOPE	**OR••**	CORD	TORA	GYOR	OTOS	BODS
	POND	NOUN	SOON	COOS	WOOS	TORO	TOPI	ORAD	CORE	TORE	IGOR	OUDS	BOGS
•ON•	PONE	POON	TION	COOT	ZOOL	TOTO	TOPO	ORAL	CORF	TORI	IVOR	OURS	BOIS
AONE	PONG	ROAN	TOON	DOOD	ZOOM	YOHO	TOPS	ORAN	CORI	TORK	MOOR	OUTS	BOOS
BONA	PONS	SOHN	TRON	DOOM	ZOON	YOKO		ORBI	CORK	TORN	NOOR	OVIS	BOPS
BOND	PONT	SOLN	UPON	DOON	ZOOS	YOYO	**•O•P**	ORBS	CORM	TORO	ODOR	OWES	BORS
BONE	PONY	SOON	ZION	DOOR	ZOOT		BOMP	ORCA	CORN	TORR	POOR	OWLS	BOSS
BONG	RONA	SOWN	ZOON	FOOD		**••OO**	BOOP	ORCH	CORO	TORS	THOR	OWNS	BOTS
BONI	SONE	TOON		FOOL	**•O•O**	AROO	BOPP	ORCS	CORP	TORT	UXOR	OXUS	BOWS
BONK	SONG	TORN	**OO••**	FOOT	BODO	EROO	COMP	ORDO	CORR	TORY			BOYS
BONN	SONS	TOWN	OOHS	GOOD	BOLO	OMOO	COOP	OREG	CORS	WORD	**OS••**	**•OS•**	COBS
BONO	SONY	WORN	OOID	GOOF	BONO	SHOO	CORP	OREL	CORY	WORE	OSAR	BOSC	CODS
BONY	TONE	ZOON	OONA	GOON	BORO		COUP	OREM	DORA	WORK	OSEE	BOSE	COFS
CONC	TONG	ZORN	OOPS	GOOP	BOYO	**OP••**	DORP	OREO	DORE	WORM	OSHA	BOSH	COGS
COND	TONI		OORT	GOOS	BOZO	OPAH	DOUP	ORES	DORM	WORN	OSIS	BOSK	COLS
CONE	TONK	**••ON**	OOZE	HOOD	COCO	OPAL	GOOP	ORFF	DORN	WORT	OSLO	BOSN	CONS
CONF	TONS	AEON	OOZY	HOOF	COHO	OPEC	GORP	ORGS	DORP	YORE	OSSA	BOSS	COOS
CONG	TONY	AGON		HOOK	COLO	OPED	GOUP	ORGY	DORR	YORK	OSSO	COSA	COPS
CONJ	WONG	AMON	**O•O•**	HOOP	COMO	OPEL	HOLP	ORIG	DORS	ZORI	OSTE	COSH	CORS
CONK	WONK	ANON	OBOE	HOOT	CORO	OPEN	HOOP	ORLE	DORT	ZORN		COSI	COTS
CONN	WONS	ARON	OBOL	IOOF	DODO	OPER	HOSP	ORLY	DORY		**O•S•**	COSM	COWS
CONS	WONT	ATON	ODOM	JOON	DOJO	OPES	KOFP	ORNE	FORA	**•O•R**	OAST	COST	DOCS
CONT	YOND	AVON	ODOR	KOOK	DOMO	OPIA	KOOP	OROS	FORB	BOAR	OISE	COSY	DOES
CONV	ZONA	AXON	OHOH	KOOL	GOBO	OPIE	LOOP	ORSK	FORD	BOER	OMSK	DOSE	DOGS
CONY	ZONE	BION	OMOO	KOOP	GOGO	OPRY	LOUP	ORTH	FORE	BOHR	ORSK	DOSS	DOMS
DONA	ZONK	BOON	OROS	LOOK	HOBO	OPTO	NOOP	ORTS	FORK	BOOR	OSSA	DOST	DONS
DONE		BUON	OTOE	LOOM	HOHO	OPTS	POMP	ORVS	FORM	COIR	OSSO	FOSS	DORS
DONG	**•O•N**	CHON	OTOS	LOON	HOJO	OPUS	POOP	ORYX	FORT	COMR	OUSE	GOSH	DOSS
DONS	BONN	CION	OXON	LOOP	HOLO		ROMP	ORZO	GORE	CORR	OUST	HOSE	DOTS
DONT	BOON	CMON		LOOS	HOMO	**O•P•**	ROUP		GORP	DOER		HOSP	EONS
EONS	BORN	COON	**O••O**	LOOT	IODO	OOPS	SOAP	**O•R•**	GORY	DOOR	**O••S**	HOSS	EOUS
FOND	BOSN	DCON	OCHO	MOOD	JOJO		SOUP	OARS	HORA	DORR	OAFS	HOST	FOBS
FONS	COEN	DION	OCTO	MOOG	JOLO	**•OP•**		OGRE	HORN	DOUR	OAKS	JOSE	FOES
FONT	COHN	DOON	OENO	MOON	KOBO	BOPP	**••OP**	OKRA	HORS	FOUR	OARS	JOSH	FOGS
FONZ	COIN	EBON	OHIO	MOOR	KOKO	BOPS	ATOP	OMRI	HORT	GOER	OATS	JOSS	FOIS
GOND	CONN	ECON	OHNO	MOOS	KOLO	COPE	BOOP	OORT	KORE	HOAR	OBIS	LOSE	FONS
GONE	COON	EGON	OLEO	MOOT	KOTO	COPS	CHOP	OPRY	LORD	HOER	OCAS	LOSS	FOPS
GONG	CORN	ELON	OLIO	NOOK	LOBO	COPT	CLOP	OTRA	LORE	HOUR	OCHS	LOST	FOSS
GONY	DOIN	ETON	OMOO	NOON	LOCO	COPY	COOP	OTRO	LORI	JOUR	ODAS	MOSE	FOYS
HOND	DOON	EXON	ONTO	NOOP	LOGO	DOPA	CROP	OURS	LORN	MOOR	ODDS	MOSH	GOBS
HONE	DORN	GOON	OPTO	NOOR	MOHO	DOPE	DROP		LORY	NOIR	ODES	MOSS	GODS
HONG	DOWN	HUON	ORDO	POOD	MOJO	DOPY	ESOP	**O••R**	MORA	NOOR	OFFS	MOST	GOES
HONI	FOHN	ICON	OREO	POOF	MONO	FOPS	FLOP	ODER	MORE	POOR	OHMS	NOSE	GOOS
HONK	FOIN	INON	ORZO	POOH	MORO	HOPE	GLOP	ODOR	MORK	POUR	OIKS	NOSH	HOBS
IONA	GOIN	IRON	OSLO	POOL	MOTO	HOPI	GOOP	OMAR	MORN	ROAR	OILS	NOSY	HODS
IONE	GOON	JOON	OSSO	POON	NOGO	HOPS	HOOP	OMER	MORO	SOAR	OLDS	POSE	HOES
IONS	GOWN	KAON	OTHO	POOP	NOLO	KOPF	IHOP	ONER	MORT	SOIR	OLES	POSH	HOGS
JONG	HORN	KWON	OTRO	POOR	NONO	KOPH	KNOP	OPER	NORA	SOUR	ONES	POSS	HOLS
JONI	JOAN	LEON	OTTO	ROOD	NOVO	KOPS	KOOP	OSAR	NORD	TORR	ONUS	POST	HOMS
KONA	JOHN	LION	OUZO	ROOF	POCO	LOPE	LOOP	OVER	NORI	TOUR	OOHS	POSY	HOPS
KONG	JOIN	LOON		ROOK	POGO	LOPS	NOOP	OWER	NORM	VOIR	OOPS	ROSA	HORS
LONE	JOON	LRON	**•OO•**	ROOM	POLO	MOPE	PLOP	OYER	NORN	YOUR	OPES	ROSE	HOSS
LONG	KOAN	LYON	BOOB	ROOS	POMO	MOPS	POOP		NORW	ZOAR	OPTS	ROSH	HOWS
LONI	KOLN	MOON	BOOK	ROOT	ROBO	MOPY	PROP	**•OR•**	OORT		OPUS	ROSS	HOYS
MONA	LOAN	MUON	BOOM	SOON	ROJO	NOPE	SCOP	BORA	PORE	**••OR**	ORBS	ROSY	IONS
MONK	LOIN	NEON	BOON	SOOT	ROTO	OOPS	SHOP	BORE	PORK	AMOR	ORCS	SOSO	IOUS
MONO	LOON	NOON	BOOP	TOOK	SOHO	POPE	SLOP	BORG	PORT	ASOR	ORES	TOSH	JOBS
MONS	LORN	OXON	BOOR	TOOL	SOLO	POPS	STOP	BORK	RORY	ATOR	ORGS	TOSS	JOES

JOGS JOSS JOTS JOYS KOBS KOIS KOPS LOBS LOGS LOIS LOOS LOPS LOSS LOTS LOWS MOAS MOBS MOCS MODS MOHS MOMS MONS MOOS MOPS MOSS MOTS MOWS NOBS NODS NOES NOGS NOMS NOTS NOUS OOHS OOPS PODS POGS POIS POLS POMS PONS POPS POSS POTS POWS ROBS ROCS RODS ROES ROMS ROOS ROSS ROTS ROUS ROWS SOBS SODS SOLS SONS SOPS SOTS SOUS SOWS SOYS TODS TOES TOGS TOMS TONS TOPS TORS TOSS TOTS TOWS TOYS VOLS VOUS VOWS WOES WOKS WONS WOOS WOWS YOBS YODS ZOOS

••OS
ADOS AMOS APOS AVOS BIOS BOOS BROS CEOS CMOS COOS CPOS CWOS DIOS DSOS DUOS EGOS ENOS EPOS EROS ESOS GOOS GPOS GROS GTOS HAOS HMOS IBOS ICOS IDOS IPOS KEOS LAOS LBOS LEOS LOOS MHOS MOOS NAOS NCOS OROS OTOS PROS REOS RHOS RIOS ROOS TAOS THOS TIOS TKOS TWOS UDOS UFOS WHOS WOOS YAOS ZOOS

OT••
OTHO OTIC OTIS OTOE OTOS OTRA OTRO OTTO

O•T•
OATH OATS OATY OCTA OCTO OITA ONTO OPTO OPTS ORTH ORTS OSTE OTTO OUTS

O••T
OAST OBIT OMIT OORT OUST

•OT•
BOTA BOTH BOTS BOTT COTE COTS COTY DOTE DOTH DOTS GOTH HOTE IOTA JOTS KOTO LOTA LOTI LOTS LOTT MOTA MOTE MOTH MOTO MOTS MOTT NOTA NOTE NOTI NOTS POTS ROTA ROTC ROTE ROTH ROTI ROTL ROTO ROTS SOTS TOTE TOTO TOTS VOTE ZOTZ

•O•T
AOUT BOAT BOLT BOOT BORT BOTT BOUT COAT COLT CONT COOT COPT COST DOIT DOLT DONT DORT DOST FONT FOOT FORT FOYT GOAT GOUT GOVT HOLT HOOT HORT HOST HOYT JOLT LOFT LOOT LOST LOTT LOUT MOAT MOLT MONT MOOT MORT MOST MOTT OORT POET PONT PORT POST POUT ROOT ROUT SOFT SOOT SORT TOAT TOFT TOOT TORT TOUT VOLT WONT WORT XOUT YOST ZOOT

••OT
BLOT BOOT CLOT COOT EYOT FOOT GLOT GROT HOOT KNOT LOOT MOOT PHOT PLOT PROT QUOT RIOT ROOT RYOT SCOT SHOT SLOT SOOT SPOT STOT TOOT TROT ZOOT

OU••
OUCH OUDS OULU OURS OUSE OUST OUTS OUZO

O•U•
OEUF ONUS OPUS OVUM OXUS

O••U
OAHU OULU

•OU•
AOUT BOUT COUE COUP DOUG DOUP DOUR DOUW DOUX EOUS FOUL FOUR GOUP GOUT HOUR IOUS JOUR LOUD LOUP LOUT MOUE NOUN NOUS POUF POUR POUT ROUE ROUP ROUS ROUT ROUX SOUK SOUL SOUP SOUR SOUS TOUR TOUT VOUS WOUK XOUT YOUD YOUR ZOUK

•O•U
BOMU TOFU TOLU

••OU
ABOU ALOU CHOU THOU ZHOU

OV••
OVAL OVEN OVER OVID OVIS OVUM

O•V•
ORVS

O••V
OLAV OZAV

•OV•
BOVA COVE DOVE GOVT HOVE JOVE LOVE MOVE NOVA NOVO ROVE WOVE

•O•V
CONV

••OV
AZOV LVOV PROV

OW••
OWED OWEN OWER OWES OWLS OWNS

•OW•
BOWE BOWL BOWS COWL COWS DOWD DOWN FOWL GOWK GOWN HOWE HOWL HOWS IOWA JOWL LOWE LOWS MOWN MOWS POWS ROWE ROWS SOWN SOWS TOWN TOWS VOWS WOWS YOWL

•O•W
DOUW LOEW NORW

••OW
ALOW AVOW BLOW BROW CHOW CROW DHOW ENOW FLOW FROW GLOW GROW KNOW MEOW PLOW PROW SCOW SHOW SLOW SNOW STOW

OX••
OXEN OXON OXUS

O••X
ONYX ORYX

•OX•
BOXY COXA FOXE FOXX FOXY

•O•X
COAX DOUX FOXX HOAX ROUX VOIX

••OX
KNOX PROX

OY••
OYER OYEZ

O•Y•
ONYM ONYX ORYX

O••Y
OATY OBEY ODAY OHMY OILY OKAY OKEY OLAY ONLY OOZY OPRY ORGY ORLY OZZY

•OY•
BOYD BOYO BOYS BOYZ FOYS FOYT GOYA HOYA HOYS HOYT JOYS SOYA SOYS TOYS YOYO

•O•Y
BODY BOGY BONY BOXY CODY COKY COLY CONY COPY CORY COSY COTY COZY DOBY DOGY DOPY DORY DOZY FOGY FOXY GOBY GONY GORY HOLY HOMY JODY JOEY JOKY LOGY LORY MOBY MOLY MONY MOPY NOSY OOZY POGY POKY POLY PONY POSY ROLY ROMY ROPY RORY ROSY SONY TOBY TODY TONY TORY

••OY
AHOY AMOY BBOY BUOY CHOY CLOY MBOY PLOY TROY

OZ••
OZAV OZZY

O•Z•
OOZE OOZY ORZO OUZO OZZY

O••Z
OYEZ

•OZ•
BOZO COZY DOZE DOZY OOZE OOZY

•O•Z
BOAZ BOYZ FONZ LODZ ZOTZ

••OZ
BROZ FLOZ

PA••
PAAR PABA PACA PACE PACK PACS PACT PADS PAGE PAGO PAHO PAHS PAID PAIL PAIN PAIR PAIX PALE PALI PALL PALM PALO PALP PALS PALY PANE PANG PANS PANT PAPA PAPP PARA PARC PARD PARE PARI PARK PARL PARR PARS PART PASA PASE PASH PASO PASS PAST PATD PATE PATH PATS PAUL PAVE PAVO PAWL PAWN PAWS PAYS PAYT

P•A•
PAAR PEAG PEAK PEAL PEAR PEAS PEAT PEAU PHAR PHAT PIAF PIAO PLAN PLAT PLAX PLAY PRAM PRAY PSAT PTAH PTAS

P••A
PABA PACA PAPA PARA PASA PENA PEPA PETA PICA PIKA PIMA PINA PIPA PISA PITA PLEA PODA POLA PROA PUKA PULA PUMA PUNA PUPA

•PA•
CPAS MPAA OPAH OPAL SPAD SPAM SPAN SPAR SPAS SPAT SPAY UPAS

•P•A
APIA EPHA LPGA MPAA OPIA SPCA

••PA
ARPA CAPA DOPA GAPA HUPA LIPA NAPA NIPA PAPA PEPA PIPA PUPA RAPA TAPA

P•B•
PABA PCBS PUBL PUBS

P••B
PLEB PROB

•PB•
APBS

PC••
PCBS

P•C•
PACA PACE PACK PACS PACT PECK PECS PFCS PICA PICK PICO PICS PICT PLCS POCO PUCE PUCK

P••C
PARC PREC PROC PSEC

•PC•
SPCA SPCC

•P•C
APOC EPIC OPEC SPCC SPEC

P•D•
PADS PEDI PEDO PEDS PHDS PODA PODE

PODS
PPDO
PUDU

P••D
PAID
PARD
PATD
PEND
PIED
PLED
PLOD
POND
POOD
PRED
PROD

•PD•
PPDO
UPDO

•P•D
APED
OPED
SPAD
SPED
SPUD

••PD
LAPD
SFPD

PE••
PEAG
PEAK
PEAL
PEAR
PEAS
PEAT
PEAU
PECK
PECS
PEDI
PEDO
PEDS
PEEK
PEEL
PEEN
PEEP
PEER
PEGS
PEHS
PEKE
PELE
PELF
PELL
PELT
PENA
PEND
PENH
PENN
PENS
PENT
PEON
PEPA
PEPE
PEPO
PEPS
PERE
PERF
PERH
PERI
PERK
PERM
PERP
PERS
PERT
PERU
PESO
PEST
PETA
PETE
PETO
PETS
PEWS

P•E•
PEEK
PEEL
PEEN
PEEP
PEER
PHEW
PIED
PIER
PIES
PIET
PLEA
PLEB
PLED
PLEO
PLEW
PLEX
POEM
POET
PREC
PRED
PREF
PREK
PREM
PREP
PRES
PRET
PREV
PREY
PREZ
PSEC
PUER

P••E
PACE
PAGE
PALE
PANE
PARE
PASE
PATE
PAVE
PEKE
PELE
PEPE
PERE
PETE
PIKE
PILE
PINE
PIPE
PIRE
PLIE
PODE
POKE
POLE
POME
PONE
POPE
PORE
POSE
PRIE
PUCE
PULE
PURE
PYLE
PYRE

•PE•
APED
APER
APES
APEX
EPEE
OPEC
OPED
OPEL
OPEN
OPER
OPES
SPEC
SPED
SPEE
SPET
SPEW

•P•E
APSE
BPOE
EPEE
IPSE
OPIE
SPEE

••PE
CAPE
CEPE
COPE
DOPE
DUPE
GAPE
HOPE
HYPE
JAPE
LOPE
LUPE
MOPE
NAPE
NOPE
PEPE
PIPE
POPE
RIPE
ROPE
SUPE
TAPE
TOPE
TYPE
WIPE
XIPE
YIPE

PF••
PFCS
PFFT
PFUI

P•F•
PFFT
PUFF

P••F
PELF
PERF
PIAF
POOF
POUF
PREF
PROF
PUFF

••PF
IMPF
KOPF

P•G•
PAGE
PAGO
PEGS
PIGS
PKGS
POGO
POGS
POGY
PUGH
PUGS

P••G
PANG
PEAG
PING
PLUG
PONG
PRIG
PROG
PUNG

•PG•
LPGA
SPGR

••PG
BKPG
TVPG

PH••
PHAR
PHAT
PHDS
PHEW
PHIL
PHIS
PHIZ
PHON
PHOT
PHYS

P•H•
PAHO
PAHS
PEHS
POHL

P••H
PASH
PATH
PENH
PERH
PISH
PITH
POOH
POSH
PTAH
PUGH
PUSH

•PH•
EPHA
SPHT

•P•H
IPOH
OPAH

••PH
ALPH
KAPH
KOPH
QOPH
SOPH
UMPH
ZEPH

PI••
PIAF
PIAO
PICA
PICK
PICO
PICS
PICT
PIED
PIER
PIES
PIET
PIGS
PIKA
PIKE
PILE
PILI
PILL
PIMA
PINA
PINE
PING
PINK
PINS
PINT
PINX
PINY
PION
PIPA
PIPE
PIPS
PIPY
PIRE
PIRS
PISA
PISH
PITA
PITH
PITS
PITT
PITY
PIUS
PIXY
PIZZ

P•I•
PAID
PAIL
PAIN
PAIR
PAIX
PHIL
PHIS
PHIZ
PLIE
PNIN
POIL
POIS
PRIE
PRIG
PRIM
PRIN
PRIV
PRIX
PSIS

P••I
PALI
PARI
PEDI
PERI
PFUI
PILI
PULI
PUYI

•PI•
APIA
APIS
EPIC
EPIS
OPIA
OPIE
SPIN
SPIT
SPIV

••PI
HAPI
HOPI
IMPI
KEPI
TOPI
TUPI

PK••
PKGS
PKWY

P•K•
PEKE
PIKA
PIKE
POKE
POKY
PUKA
PUKU

P••K
PACK
PARK
PEAK
PECK
PEEK
PERK
PICK
PINK
POLK
PORK
PREK
PUCK
PUNK

•PK•
TPKS

••PK
TNPK

PL••
PLAN
PLAT
PLAX
PLAY
PLCS
PLEA
PLEB
PLED
PLEO
PLEW
PLEX
PLIE
PLOD
PLOP
PLOT
PLOW
PLOY
PLUG
PLUM
PLUR
PLUS

P•L•
PALE
PALI
PALL
PALM
PALO
PALP
PALS
PALY
PELE
PELF
PELL
PELT
PILE
PILI
PILL
POLA
POLE
POLK
POLL
POLO
POLS
POLY
PULA
PULE
PULI
PULL
PULP
PYLE

P••L
PAIL
PALL
PARL
PAUL
PAWL
PEAL
PEEL
PELL
PHIL
PILL
POHL
POIL
POLL
POOL
PUBL
PULL
PURL

•PL•
CPLS

•P•L
APPL
OPAL
OPEL

••PL
APPL
DIPL
REPL

PM••
PMTS

P•M•
PIMA
POME
POMO
POMP
POMS
PUMA
PUMP

P••M
PALM
PERM
PLUM
POEM
PRAM
PREM
PRIM
PROM

•PM•
DPMS
RPMS

•P•M
SPAM

PN••
PNIN

P•N•
PANE
PANG
PANS
PANT
PENA
PEND
PENH
PENN
PENS
PENT
PINA
PINE
PING
PINK
PINS
PINT
PINX
PINY
POND
PONE
PONG
PONS
PONT
PONY
PUNA
PUNG
PUNK
PUNS
PUNT
PUNY

P••N
PAIN
PAWN
PEEN
PENN
PEON
PHON
PION
PLAN
PNIN
POON
PRIN
PRON

•P•N
OPEN
SPAN
SPIN
SPUN
UPON

••PN
CAPN
ESPN
HYPN

PO••
POCO
PODA
PODE
PODS
POEM
POET
POGO
POGS
POGY
POHL
POIL
POIS
POKE
POKY
POLA
POLE
POLK
POLL
POLO
POLS
POLY
POME
POMO
POMP
POMS
POND
PONE
PONG
PONS
PONT
PONY
POOD
POOF
POOH
POOL
POON
POOP
POOR
POPE
POPS
PORE
PORK
PORT
POSE
POSH
POSS
POST
POSY
POTS
POUF
POUR
POUT
POWS

P•O•
PEON
PHON
PHOT
PION
PLOD
PLOP
PLOT
PLOW
PLOY
POOD
POOF
POOH
POOL
POON
POOP
POOR
PROA
PROB
PROC
PROD
PROF
PROG
PROM
PRON
PROP
PROS
PROT
PROV
PROW
PROX

P••O
PAGO
PAHO
PALO
PASO
PAVO
PEDO
PEPO
PESO
PETO
PIAO
PICO
PLEO
POCO
POGO
POLO
POMO
PPDO
PUZO
PYRO

•PO•
APOC
APOS
BPOE
CPOS
EPOS
GPOS
IPOH
IPOS
SPOT
UPON

•P•O
APSO
IPSO
OPTO
PPDO
UPDO
UPTO

••PO
ALPO
CAPO
ESPO
EXPO
HYPO
LIPO
PEPO
REPO
TOPO
TYPO
USPO

PP••
PPDO

P•P•
PAPA
PAPP
PEPA
PEPE
PEPO
PEPS
PIPA
PIPE
PIPS
PIPY
POPE
POPS
PUPA
PUPS
PUPU

P••P
PALP
PAPP
PEEP
PERP
PLOP
POMP
POOP
PREP
PROP
PULP
PUMP

•PP•
APPL
APPS
APPT

••PP
BOPP
CAPP
DEPP
LAPP
PAPP
RAPP
REPP
RUPP
SUPP
TEPP
YAPP

•PQ•
RPQS
SPQR

PR••
PRAM
PRAY
PREC
PRED
PREF
PREK
PREM
PREP
PRES
PRET
PREV
PREY
PREZ
PRIE
PRIG
PRIM
PRIN
PRIV
PRIX
PROA
PROB
PROC
PROD
PROF
PROG
PROM
PRON
PROP
PROS
PROT
PROV
PROW
PROX
PRUT

P•R•
PARA
PARC
PARD
PARE
PARI
PARK
PARL
PARR
PARS
PART
PERE
PERF
PERH
PERI
PERK
PERM
PERP
PERS
PERT
PERU
PIRE
PIRS
PORE
PORK
PORT
PURE
PURL
PURR
PYRE
PYRO

P••R
PAAR
PAIR
PARR
PEAR
PEER

PHAR
PIER
PLUR
POOR
POUR
PUER
PURR

•PR•
APRS
OPRY
SPRY

•P•R
APER
OPER
SPAR
SPGR
SPQR
SPUR

••PR
BKPR
CUPR
SUPR

PS••
PSAT
PSEC
PSIS
PSST

P•S•
PASA
PASE
PASH
PASO
PASS
PAST
PESO
PEST
PISA
PISH
POSE
POSH
POSS
POST
POSY
PSST
PUSH
PUSS

P••S
PACS
PADS
PAHS
PALS
PANS
PARS
PASS
PATS
PAWS
PAYS
PCBS
PEAS
PECS
PEDS
PEGS
PEHS
PENS
PEPS
PERS
PETS
PEWS
PFCS
PHDS
PHIS
PHYS
PICS
PIES
PIGS
PINS
PIPS
PIRS
PITS
PIUS
PKGS
PLCS
PLUS
PMTS
PODS
POGS
POIS
POLS
POMS
PONS
POPS
POSS
POTS
POWS
PRES
PROS
PSIS
PTAS
PUBS
PUGS
PUNS
PUPS
PUSS
PUTS
PVTS

•PS•
APSE
APSO
IPSE
IPSO

•P•S
APBS
APES
APIS
APOS
APPS
APRS
APTS
CPAS
CPLS
CPOS
DPMS
EPIS
EPOS
GPOS
IPOS
OPES
OPTS
OPUS
RPMS
RPQS
RPTS
SPAS
TPKS
UPAS

••PS
ALPS
AMPS
APPS
ASPS
BAPS
BOPS
CAPS
CEPS
COPS
CUPS
DAPS
DIPS
EMPS
ESPS
FOPS
GAPS
GIPS
GYPS
HAPS
HIPS
HOPS
IMPS
KIPS
KOPS
LAPS
LIPS
LOPS
MAPS
MIPS
MOPS
NAPS
NIPS
OOPS
PEPS
PIPS
POPS
PUPS
RAPS
REPS
RIPS
SAPS
SIPS
SOPS
SUPS
TAPS
TIPS
TOPS
TSPS
TWPS
UMPS
USPS
VIPS
YAPS
YIPS
ZAPS
ZIPS

PT••
PTAH
PTAS

P•T•
PATD
PATE
PATH
PATS
PETA
PETE
PETO
PETS
PITA
PITH
PITS
PITT
PITY
PMTS
POTS
PUTS
PUTT
PVTS

P••T
PACT
PANT
PART
PAST
PAYT
PEAT
PELT
PENT
PERT
PEST
PFFT
PHAT
PHOT
PICT
PIET
PINT
PITT
PLAT
PLOT
POET
PONT
PORT
POST
POUT
PRET
PROT
PRUT
PSAT
PSST
PUNT
PUTT

•PT•
APTS
OPTO
OPTS
RPTS
UPTO

•P•T
APPT
SPAT
SPET
SPHT
SPIT
SPOT

••PT
APPT
BAPT
CAPT
COPT
DEPT
EXPT
HEPT
KEPT
RAPT
RCPT
REPT
SEPT
SHPT
SUPT
WEPT

PU••
PUBL
PUBS
PUCE
PUCK
PUDU
PUER
PUFF
PUGH
PUGS
PUKA
PUKU
PULA
PULE
PULI
PULL
PULP
PUMA
PUMP
PUNA
PUNG
PUNK
PUNS
PUNT
PUNY
PUPA
PUPS
PUPU
PURE
PURL
PURR
PUSH
PUSS
PUTS
PUTT
PUYI
PUZO

P•U•
PAUL
PFUI
PIUS
PLUG
PLUM
PLUR
PLUS
POUF
POUR
POUT
PRUT

P••U
PEAU
PERU
PUDU
PUKU
PUPU

•PU•
OPUS
SPUD
SPUN
SPUR

••PU
PUPU

PV••
PVTS

P•V•
PAVE
PAVO

P••V
PREV
PRIV
PROV

•P•V
SPIV

••PV
IMPV

P•W•
PAWL
PAWN
PAWS
PEWS
PKWY
POWS

P••W
PHEW
PLEW
PLOW
PROW

•P•W
SPEW

P•X•
PIXY

P••X
PAIX
PINX
PLAX
PLEX
PRIX
PROX

•P•X
APEX

PY••
PYLE
PYRE
PYRO

P•Y•
PAYS
PAYT
PHYS
PUYI

P••Y
PALY
PINY
PIPY
PITY
PIXY
PKWY
PLAY
PLOY
POGY
POKY
POLY
PONY
POSY
PRAY
PREY
PUNY

•P•Y
OPRY
SPAY
SPRY

••PY
COPY
DOPY
ESPY
ISPY
MOPY
PIPY
ROPY
TYPY

P•Z•
PIZZ
PUZO

P••Z
PHIZ
PIZZ
PREZ

QA••
QADI
QAFS
QAID
QATS

Q•A•
QUAD
QUAG
QUAI
QUAM
QUAR
QUAY

•Q•A
AQUA

Q•D•
QADI

Q••D
QAID
QUAD
QUID
QUOD

•Q•D
SQYD

QE••
QEII

Q•E•
QUEL
QUEM
QUES

Q•F•
QAFS

•QF•
SQFT

Q••G
QUAG

Q••H
QOPH

Q•I•
QAID
QEII
QTIP
QUID
QUIP
QUIT
QUIZ

Q••I
QADI
QEII
QUAI
QUOI

•QI•
SQIN

•Q•I
AQUI
EQUI
SQMI

Q••L
QUEL

Q••M
QUAM
QUEM

•QM•
SQMI

•Q•N
SQIN

QO••
QOPH

Q•O•
QUOD
QUOI
QUOT

•Q•O
AQUO

Q•P•
QOPH

Q••P
QTIP
QUIP

••QQ
SEQQ

Q•R•
QTRS

Q••R
QUAR

••QR
SPQR

Q••S
QAFS
QATS
QTRS
QUES

••QS
BBQS
ESQS
FAQS
RFQS
RPQS
SUQS

QT••
QTIP
QTRS

Q•T•
QATS

Q••T
QUIT
QUOT

•Q•T
SQFT

QU••
QUAD
QUAG
QUAI
QUAM
QUAR
QUAY
QUEL
QUEM
QUES
QUID
QUIP
QUIT
QUIZ
QUOD
QUOI
QUOT

•QU•
AQUA
AQUI
AQUO
EQUI

Q••Y
QUAY

•QY•
SQYD

Q••Z
QUIZ

RA••
RABE
RABI
RABS
RACE
RACK
RACY
RADM
RADS
RAFF
RAFT
RAGA
RAGE
RAGG
RAGS
RAGU
RAID
RAIL
RAIN
RAJA
RAKE
RAKI
RAKU
RALL
RAMA
RAMI
RAMP
RAMS
RANA
RAND
RANG
RANI
RANK
RANT
RAPA
RAPP
RAPS
RAPT
RARA
RARE
RASA
RASE
RASH
RASK
RASP
RATA
RATE
RATH
RATS
RATT
RAUL
RAVE
RAVI
RAYE
RAYS
RAZE
RAZZ

R•A•
RCAF
RDAS
READ
REAL
REAM
REAP
REAR
RIAL
RIAS
ROAD
ROAM
ROAN
ROAR
RYAL
RYAN
RYAS

R••A
RAGA
RAJA
RAMA
RANA
RAPA
RARA
RASA
RATA
REBA
REZA
RHEA
RICA
RIGA
RIMA
RITA
ROCA
ROMA
RONA
ROSA
ROTA
RRNA
RUGA
RUTA

•RA•
ARAB
ARAD
ARAK
ARAL
ARAM
ARAN
ARAS
BRAC
BRAD
BRAE
BRAG
BRAM
BRAN
BRAS
BRAT
BRAW
BRAY
BRAZ
CRAB
CRAG
CRAM
CRAT
CRAW
CRAY
DRAB
DRAG
DRAM
DRAT
DRAW
DRAY
ERAS
ERAT
FRAE
FRAM
FRAN
FRAP
FRAS
FRAT
FRAU
FRAY
GRAB
GRAD
GRAF
GRAM
GRAN
GRAS
GRAU
GRAY
GRAZ
IRAE
IRAN
IRAQ
IRAS
ORAD
ORAL
ORAN
PRAM
PRAY
SRAS
TRAM
TRAP
TRAX
TRAY
URAL
VRAI
WRAC
WRAF
WRAP
WRAY
XRAY

•R•A
ARCA
AREA
ARIA
ARMA
ARPA
ARRA
BREA
ERDA
ERMA
FRIA
IRMA
MRNA
ORCA
PROA
RRNA
SRTA
TRNA
URFA
URGA
URSA

••RA
AGRA
ARRA
ATRA
AURA
BARA
BORA
CARA
CERA
CORA
DORA
DURA
EYRA
EZRA
FORA
GERA
HERA
HORA
JURA
KARA
KYRA
LARA
LIRA
LYRA
MARA
MIRA
MORA
MYRA
NARA
NORA
OKRA
OTRA
PARA
RARA
SARA
SERA
SORA
SURA
TARA
TERA
TORA
VARA
VERA

RB••
RBIS

R•B•
RABE
RABI
RABS
REBA

REBS
RHBS
RIBS
ROBB
ROBE
ROBO
ROBS
RUBE
RUBS
RUBY

R••B
ROBB

•RB•
ARBS
GRBR
IRBM
ORBI
ORBS
URBE
URBI
URBS

•R•B
ARAB
CRAB
CRIB
DRAB
DRIB
DRUB
GRAB
GRUB
PROB
TRIB

••RB
BARB
BURB
CARB
CURB
FORB
GARB
HERB
KERB
NLRB
SERB
SORB
VERB

RC••
RCAF
RCMP
RCPT
RCTS

R•C•
RACE
RACK
RACY
RECD
RECS
RECT
RICA
RICE
RICH
RICK
RICO
ROCA
ROCK
ROCS
RUCK

R••C
ROTC

•RC•
ARCA
ARCH
ARCO
ARCS
FRCP
FRCS
ORCA
ORCH
ORCS

•R•C
BRAC
BRIC
CROC
ERIC
KROC
PREC
PROC
WRAC

••RC
CIRC
DARC
MARC
NARC
PARC

RD••
RDAS

R•D•
RADM
RADS
REDD
REDE
REDI
REDO
REDS
RFDS
RIDD
RIDE
RIDI
RIDS
RMDR
RNDS
RODE
RODS
RUDD
RUDE
RUDI
RUDY

R••D
RAID
RAND
READ
RECD
REDD
REED
REGD
REID
REND
RETD
RIDD
RIND
ROAD
ROOD
RUDD
RUED

•RD•
ERDA
ERDE
ORDO
URDU

•R•D
ARAD
ARID
BRAD
BRED
CRUD
DRED
FRED
GRAD
GRID
IRED
IRID
MRED
ORAD
PRED
PROD
TROD

••RD
BARD
BIRD
BYRD
CARD
CORD
CURD
DARD
FORD
GIRD
HARD
HERD
KURD
LARD
LORD
NARD
NERD
NORD
PARD
SARD
SURD
VERD
WARD
WORD
YARD

RE••
READ
REAL
REAM
REAP
REAR
REBA
REBS
RECD
RECS
RECT
REDD
REDE
REDI
REDO
REDS
REED
REEF
REEK
REEL
REES
REFL
REFS
REFT
REGD
REGS
REGT
REID
REIN
REIS
REIT
RELS
RELY
REMO
REMS
REND
RENE
RENI
RENO
RENT
REOS
REPL
REPO
REPP
REPS
REPT
RESH
RESP
REST
RETD
RETE
RETS
REUP
REVE
REVS
REYS
REZA

R•E•
REED
REEF
REEK
REEL
REES
RHEA
RHEE
RHEO
RHES
RHET
RIEL
RIEN
ROEG
ROES
RTES
RUED
RUER
RUES
RYES

R••E
RABE
RACE
RAGE
RAKE
RARE
RASE
RATE
RAVE
RAYE
RAZE
REDE
RENE
RETE
REVE
RHEE
RHUE
RICE
RIDE
RIFE
RILE
RIME
RIPE
RIRE
RISE
RITE
RIVE
ROBE
RODE
ROHE
ROLE
ROME
ROPE
ROSE
ROTE
ROUE
ROVE
ROWE
RUBE
RUDE
RULE
RUNE
RUSE
RYLE
RYNE

•RE•
AREA
AREO
ARES
BREA
BRED
BREE
BREL
BREN
BRER
BRET
BREV
BREW
CREE
CREW
DRED
DREE
DREG
DREI
DREW
FRED
FREE
FREI
FREQ
FRET
FREY
GREE
GREG
GREW
GREX
GREY
HRES
IRED
IRES
MRED
OREG
OREL
OREM
OREO
ORES
PREC
PRED
PREF
PREK
PREM
PREP
PRES
PRET
PREV
PREY
PREZ
TREE
TREF
TREK
TRES
TRET
TREX
TREY
UREY
WREN

•R•E
ARME
ARNE
ARTE
BRAE
BREE
BRIE
CREE
CRUE
DREE
ERDE
ERIE
ERLE
ERNE
ERSE
ERTE
FRAE
FREE
FROE
FRYE
GREE
IRAE
ORLE
ORNE
PRIE
TREE
TRUE
URBE
URGE

••RE
AARE
ACRE
AIRE
BARE
BORE
BYRE
CARE
CERE
CIRE
CORE
CURE
DARE
DIRE
DORE
EIRE
ETRE
EYRE
FARE
FERE
FIRE
FORE
GARE
GERE
GORE
GYRE
HARE
HERE
HIRE
IHRE
IMRE
INRE
JURE
KORE
LIRE
LORE
LURE
LYRE
MARE
MERE
MIRE
MORE
OGRE
PARE
PERE
PIRE
PORE
PURE
PYRE
RARE
RIRE
SERE
SIRE
SORE
SURE
TARE
TIRE
TORE
TYRE
VERE
WARE
WERE
WIRE
WORE
YARE
YORE

RF••
RFDS
RFQS

R•F•
RAFF
RAFT
REFL
REFS
REFT
RIFE
RIFF
RIFS
RIFT
RUFF

R••F
RAFF
RCAF
REEF
RIFF
ROLF
ROOF
RUFF

•RF•
ORFF
URFA

•R•F
GRAF
ORFF
PREF
PROF
TREF
WRAF

••RF
CERF
CORF
KERF
NERF
PERF
SERF
SURF
TURF
ZARF

RG••
RGTS

R•G•
RAGA
RAGE
RAGG
RAGS
RAGU
REGD
REGS
REGT
RIGA
RIGG
RIGI
RIGS
RUGA
RUGS

R••G
RAGG
RANG
RIGG
RING
ROEG
RUNG

•RG•
ARGO
ARGY
ERGO
ERGS
ORGS
ORGY
URGA
URGE

•R•G
BRAG
BRIG
CRAG
DRAG
DREG
DRUG
FROG
FRUG
GREG
GRIG
GROG
OREG
ORIG
PRIG
PROG
TRIG
TRUG

••RG
BERG
BORG
BURG
MARG
SURG

RH••
RHBS
RHEA
RHEE
RHEO
RHES
RHET
RHOS
RHUE
RHUM
RHYS

R•H•
ROHE
RUHR

R••H
RASH
RATH
RESH
RICH
ROSH
ROTH
RUSH
RUTH

•R•H
ARCH
ORCH
ORTH

••RH
PERH

RI••
RIAL
RIAS
RIBS
RICA
RICE
RICH
RICK
RICO
RIDD
RIDE
RIDI
RIDS
RIEL
RIEN
RIFE
RIFF
RIFS
RIFT
RIGA
RIGG
RIGI
RIGS
RIIS
RIJN
RILE
RILL
RIMA
RIME
RIMS
RIMY
RIND
RING
RINK
RIOS
RIOT
RIPE
RIPS
RIRE
RISE
RISK
RITA
RITE
RITT
RITZ
RIVE

R•I•
RAID
RAIL
RAIN
RBIS
REID
REIN
REIS
REIT
RIIS
ROIL
RUIN

R••I
RABI
RAKI
RAMI
RANI
RAVI
REDI
RENI
RIDI
RIGI
ROTI
RUDI

•RI•
ARIA
ARID
ARIL
ARIZ
BRIC
BRIE
BRIG
BRIM
BRIO
BRIT
BRIX
CRIB
CRIM
CRIN
CRIT
DRIB
DRIN
DRIP
DRIQ
ERIC
ERIE
ERIK
ERIN
ERIQ
ERIS
FRIA
FRIO
FRIS
FRIT
FRIZ
GRID
GRIG
GRIM
GRIN
GRIP
GRIS
GRIT
IRID
IRIS
KRIO
KRIS
ORIG
PRIE
PRIG
PRIM
PRIN
PRIV
PRIX
TRIB
TRIG
TRIM
TRIO
TRIP
TRIS
TRIX
URIM
URIS
WRIT

•R•I
DREI
FREI
ORBI
TROI
URBI
VRAI

••RI
ABRI
AGRI
ATRI
AURI
BARI
BURI
CORI
DARI
GYRI
HARI
INRI
KIRI
LARI
LORI
MARI
NERI
NORI
OMRI
PARI
PERI
SARI
SORI
TERI
TORI
YURI
ZORI

R•J•
RAJA
RIJN
ROJO

R•K•
RAKE
RAKI
RAKU

R••K
RACK
RANK
RASK
REEK
RICK
RINK
RISK
ROCK
ROOK
RUCK
RUSK

•RK•
ARKS
ERKS
IRKS

•R•K
ARAK
ERIK
GROK
KRUK
ORSK
PREK
TREK
TRUK
URUK

••RK
BARK
BIRK
BORK
CARK
CORK
DARK
DIRK
FORK
HARK
JERK
KIRK
LARK
LURK
MARK
MORK
MURK
NARK
PARK
PERK
PORK
SARK
TORK
TURK
WORK
YERK
YORK

R•L•
RALL
RELS
RELY
RILE
RILL
ROLE
ROLF
ROLL
ROLY
RULE
RYLE

R••L
RAIL
RALL
RAUL
REAL
REEL
REFL
REPL
RIAL
RIEL
RILL

ROIL
ROLL
ROTL
RYAL

•RL•
ARLO
ERLE
ORLE
ORLY
URLS

•R•L
ARAL
ARIL
ARYL
BREL
ORAL
OREL
URAL

••RL
BIRL
BURL
CARL
CURL
EARL
FURL
GIRL
HERL
HURL
JARL
KARL
MARL
MERL
PARL
PURL

RM••
RMDR

R•M•
RAMA
RAMI
RAMP
RAMS
RCMP
REMO
REMS
RIMA
RIME
RIMS
RIMY
ROMA
ROME
ROMP
ROMS
ROMY
RPMS
RUMP
RUMS

R••M
RADM
REAM
RHUM
ROAM
ROOM

•RM•
ARMA
ARME
ARMS
ARMY
ERMA
IRMA

•R•M
ARAM
ARUM
BRAM
BRIM
BROM
CRAM
CRIM
DRAM
DRUM
FRAM
FROM
GRAM
GRIM
IRBM
OREM
PRAM
PREM
PRIM
PROM
TRAM
TRIM
URIM

••RM
BARM
BDRM
BERM
CORM
DERM
DORM
FARM
FIRM
FORM
GERM
HARM
HERM
NORM
PERM
TERM
WARM
WORM

RN••
RNDS

R•N•
RANA
RAND
RANG
RANI
RANK
RANT
REND
RENE
RENI
RENO
RENT
RIND
RING
RINK
RONA
RRNA
RUNE
RUNG
RUNS
RUNT
RYNE

R••N
RAIN
REIN
RIEN
RIJN
ROAN
RUIN
RYAN
RYUN

•RN•
ARNE
ARNO
BRNO
DRNO
ERNE
ERNO
ERNS
MRNA
ORNE
RRNA
TRNA
URNS
WRNS

•R•N
ARAN
ARON
BRAN
BREN
BRYN
CRIN
DRIN
ERIN
FRAN
GRAN
GRIN
IRAN
IRON
LRON
ORAN
PRIN
PRON
TRON
WREN

••RN
BARN
BERN
BORN
BURN
CERN
CORN
DARN
DERN
DORN
DURN
EARN
FERN
FIRN
GARN
GIRN
HERN
HORN
KERN
LORN
MORN
NORN
TARN
TERN
TORN
TURN
VERN
WARN
WORN
YARN
ZORN

RO••
ROAD
ROAM
ROAN
ROAR
ROBB
ROBE
ROBO
ROBS
ROCA
ROCK
ROCS
RODE
RODS
ROEG
ROES
ROHE
ROIL
ROJO
ROLE
ROLF
ROLL
ROLY
ROMA
ROME
ROMP
ROMS
ROMY
RONA
ROOD
ROOF
ROOK
ROOM
ROOS
ROOT
ROPE
ROPY
RORY
ROSA
ROSE
ROSH
ROSS
ROSY
ROTA
ROTC
ROTE
ROTH
ROTI
ROTL
ROTO
ROTS
ROUE
ROUP
ROUS
ROUT
ROUX
ROVE
ROWE
ROWS

R•O•
REOS
RHOS
RIOS
RIOT
ROOD
ROOF
ROOK
ROOM
ROOS
ROOT
RYOT

R••O
REDO
REMO
RENO
REPO
RHEO
RICO
ROBO
ROJO
ROTO

•RO•
ARON
AROO
BROM
BROS
BROW
BROZ
CROC
CROP
CROW
DROP
EROO
EROS
FROE
FROG
FROM
FROW
GROG
GROK
GROS
GROT
GROW
IRON
KROC
LRON
OROS
PROA
PROB
PROC
PROD
PROF
PROG
PROM
PRON
PROP
PROS
PROT
PROV
PROW
PROX
TROD
TROI
TRON
TROP
TROT
TROY

•R•O
ARCO
AREO
ARGO
ARLO
ARNO
AROO
BRIO
BRNO
BRYO
CRYO
DRNO
ERGO
ERNO
EROO
FRIO
KRIO
ORDO
OREO
ORZO
TRIO

••RO
ACRO
AERO
AFRO
AGRO
BARO
BORO
CARO
CERO
CORO
DURO
EBRO
EERO
EURO
FARO
FURO
GIRO
GYRO
HERO
INRO
KARO
MERO
MIRO
MORO
NERO
NYRO
OTRO
PYRO
SERO
TARO
TIRO
TORO
TYRO
VERO
XERO
ZERO

RP••
RPMS
RPQS
RPTS

R•P•
RAPA
RAPP
RAPS
RAPT
RCPT
REPL
REPO
REPP
REPS
REPT
RIPE
RIPS
ROPE
ROPY
RUPP

R••P
RAMP
RAPP
RASP
RCMP
REAP
REPP
RESP
REUP
ROMP
ROUP
RSVP
RUMP
RUPP

•RP•
ARPA

•R•P
CROP
DRIP
DROP
FRAP
FRCP
GRIP
PREP
PROP
TRAP
TRIP
TROP
WRAP

••RP
AARP
BURP
CARP
CORP
DORP
EARP
GARP
GORP
HARP
PERP
TARP
TERP
WARP
WKRP

R•Q•
RFQS
RPQS

•R•Q
DRIQ
ERIQ
FREQ
IRAQ

RR••
RRNA

R•R•
RARA
RARE
RIRE
RORY

R••R
REAR
RMDR
ROAR
RUER
RUHR

•RR•
ARRA
ARRS
ERRS

•R•R
BRER
GRBR

••RR
BARR
BIRR
BURR
CARR
CORR
CURR
DORR
FARR
GARR
HERR
KERR
PARR
PURR
TERR
TORR

RS••
RSVP

R•S•
RASA
RASE
RASH
RASK
RASP
RESH
RESP
REST
RISE
RISK
ROSA
ROSE
ROSH
ROSS
ROSY
RUSE
RUSH
RUSK
RUSS
RUST

R••S
RABS
RADS
RAGS
RAMS
RAPS
RATS
RAYS
RBIS
RCTS
RDAS
REBS
RECS
REDS
REES
REFS
REGS
REIS
RELS
REMS
REOS
REPS
RETS
REVS
REYS
RFDS
RFQS
RGTS
RHBS
RHES
RHOS
RHYS
RIAS
RIBS
RIDS
RIFS
RIGS
RIIS
RIMS
RIOS
RIPS
RNDS
ROBS
ROCS
RODS
ROES
ROMS
ROOS
ROSS
ROTS
ROUS
ROWS
RPMS
RPQS
RPTS
RTES
RUBS
RUES
RUGS
RUMS
RUNS
RUSS
RUTS
RYAS
RYES

•RS•
ERSE
ERST
ORSK
URSA

•R•S
ARAS
ARBS
ARCS
ARES
ARKS
ARMS
ARRS
ARTS
BRAS
BROS
CRTS
CRUS
DRYS
ERAS
ERGS
ERIS
ERKS
ERNS
EROS
ERRS
FRAS
FRCS
FRIS
GRAS
GRIS
GROS
GRUS
HRES
IRAS
IRES
IRIS
IRKS
KRIS
ORBS
ORCS
ORES
ORGS
OROS
ORTS
ORVS
PRES
PROS
SRAS
TRES
TRIS
URBS
URIS
URLS
URNS
URUS
WRNS

••RS
AIRS
APRS
ARRS
BARS
BORS
BURS
CARS
CDRS
CORS
CURS
DIRS
DORS
EARS
ERRS
FARS
FIRS
FURS
GARS
HERS
HORS
JARS
KIRS
LARS
LDRS
MARS
MERS
MFRS
MGRS
MIRS
OARS
OURS
PARS
PERS
PIRS
QTRS
SERS
SIRS
SLRS
SSRS
STRS
TARS
TORS
TSRS
VCRS
VERS
WARS

RT••
RTES

R•T•
RATA
RATE
RATH
RATS
RATT
RCTS
RETD
RETE
RETS
RGTS
RITA
RITE
RITT
RITZ
ROTA
ROTC
ROTE
ROTH
ROTI
ROTL
ROTO
ROTS
RPTS
RUTA
RUTH
RUTS

R••T
RAFT
RANT
RAPT
RATT
RCPT
RECT
REFT
REGT
REIT
RENT
REPT
REST
RHET
RIFT
RIOT
RITT
ROOT
ROUT
RUNT
RUST
RYOT

•RT•
ARTE
ARTS
ARTY
CRTS
ERTE
ORTH
ORTS
SRTA

•R•T
BRAT
BRET
BRIT
BRUT
CRAT
CRIT
DRAT
ERAT
ERST
FRAT
FRET
FRIT
GRIT
GROT
GRWT
PRET
PROT
PRUT
TRET
TROT
WRIT

••RT
AIRT
BART
BERT
BORT
BURT
CART
CERT
CURT
DART
DIRT
DORT
FORT
GIRT
HART
HIRT
HORT
HURT
KART
KERT
KURT
MART
MORT
OORT
PART
PERT
PORT
SERT
SORT
TART
TORT
VERT
WART
WERT
WORT
YURT

RU••
RUBE
RUBS
RUBY
RUCK
RUDD
RUDE
RUDI
RUDY
RUED
RUER
RUES
RUFF
RUGA
RUGS
RUHR
RUIN
RULE
RUMP
RUMS
RUNE
RUNG
RUNS

RUNT
RUPP
RUSE
RUSH
RUSK
RUSS
RUST
RUTA
RUTH
RUTS

R•U•
RAUL
REUP
RHUE
RHUM
ROUE
ROUP
ROUS
ROUT
ROUX
RYUN

R••U
RAGU
RAKU

•RU•
ARUM
BRUT
BRUX
CRUD
CRUE
CRUS
CRUX
CRUZ
DRUB
DRUG
DRUM
FRUG
GRUB
GRUS
KRUK
PRUT
TRUE
TRUG
TRUK
URUK
URUS

•R•U
FRAU
GRAU
URDU

••RU
ECRU
GURU
MARU
PERU
THRU

R•V•
RAVE
RAVI
REVE
REVS
RIVE
ROVE
RSVP

•RV•
ORVS

•R•V
BREV
PREV
PRIV
PROV

••RV
MARV
MERV
MIRV
SERV
SURV

R•W•
ROWE
ROWS

•RW•
GRWT

•R•W
BRAW
BREW
BROW
CRAW
CREW
CROW
DRAW
DREW
FROW
GREW
GROW
PROW

••RW
NORW

R••X
ROUX

•R•X
BRIX
BRUX
CRUX
GREX
ORYX
PRIX
PROX
TRAX
TREX
TRIX

••RX
MARX

RY••
RYAL
RYAN
RYAS
RYES
RYLE
RYNE
RYOT
RYUN

R•Y•
RAYE
RAYS
REYS
RHYS

R••Y
RACY
RELY
RIMY
ROLY
ROMY
ROPY
RORY
ROSY
RUBY
RUDY

•RY•
ARYL
BRYN
BRYO
CRYO
DRYS
FRYE
ORYX

•R•Y
ARGY
ARMY
ARTY
BRAY
CRAY
DRAY
FRAY
FREY
GRAY
GREY
ORGY
ORLY
PRAY
PREY
TRAY
TREY
TROY
UREY
WRAY
XRAY

••RY
AERY
AIRY
AWRY
BURY
CARY
CORY
DORY
EERY
ENRY
EURY
EWRY
EYRY
FURY
GARY
GORY
JURY
LORY
MARY
MIRY
NARY
OPRY
RORY
SCRY
SPRY
TORY
VARY
VERY
WARY
WIRY

R•Z•
RAZE
RAZZ
REZA

R••Z
RAZZ
RITZ

•RZ•
ORZO

•R•Z
ARIZ
BRAZ
BROZ
CRUZ
FRIZ
GRAZ
PREZ

••RZ
HARZ
NARZ

SA••
SAAB
SAAR
SABA
SABE
SABU
SACK
SACS
SADA
SADD
SADE
SADI
SADR
SAFE
SAFR
SAGA
SAGE
SAGO
SAGS
SAHL
SAID
SAIL
SAIS
SAKE
SAKI
SAKS
SALA
SALE
SALK
SALP
SALS
SALT
SAME
SAML
SAMO
SAMP
SANA
SAND
SANE
SANG
SANK
SANO
SANS
SANT
SAPS
SARA
SARD
SARI
SARK
SASE
SASH
SASK
SASS
SATE
SATO
SATS
SAUD
SAUK
SAUL
SAUR
SAVA
SAVE
SAWN
SAWS
SAXE
SAYS

S•A•
SAAB
SAAR
SCAB
SCAD
SCAM
SCAN
SCAR
SCAT
SDAK
SEAL
SEAM
SEAN
SEAR
SEAS
SEAT
SFAX
SHAD
SHAG
SHAH
SHAM
SHAN
SHAQ
SHAW
SHAY
SIAL
SIAM
SKAT
SKAW
SLAB
SLAG
SLAM
SLAP
SLAT
SLAV
SLAW
SLAY
SNAG
SNAP
SOAK
SOAP
SOAR
SPAD
SPAM
SPAN
SPAR
SPAS
SPAT
SPAY
SRAS
STAB
STAG
STAN
STAR
STAS
STAT
STAY
SWAB
SWAG
SWAK
SWAM
SWAN
SWAP
SWAT
SWAY

S••A
SABA
SADA
SAGA
SALA
SANA
SARA
SAVA
SEGA
SELA
SERA
SETA
SHEA
SIKA
SIMA
SKUA
SMSA
SOCA
SODA
SOFA
SOLA
SOMA
SORA
SOYA
SPCA
SRTA
STOA
SURA
SUSA
SUVA

•SA•
ASAP
ESAI
ESAS
ESAU
ISAK
ISAO
ISAR
ISAY
LSAT
OSAR
PSAT
TSAR
USAF
USAR

•S•A
ASEA
ASIA
ASTA
ESSA
ESTA
HSIA
ISBA
ISLA
OSHA
OSSA
USDA
USGA
USIA
USMA
USNA
USTA

••SA
ANSA
CASA
COSA
ELSA
ESSA
ILSA
LISA
MESA
MKSA
NASA
OSSA
PASA
PISA
RASA
ROSA
SMSA
SUSA
URSA
VISA
WUSA

S•B•
SABA
SABE
SABU
SEBE
SEBS
SIBS
SLBM
SOBS
STBD
SUBJ
SUBS
SWBS
SWBW

S••B
SAAB
SCAB
SERB
SHEB
SLAB
SLOB
SLUB
SNOB
SNUB
SORB
STAB
STUB
SWAB
SWOB

•SB•
ISBA
ISBN

••SB
MUSB
NTSB

SC••
SCAB
SCAD
SCAM
SCAN
SCAR
SCAT
SCIL
SCLC
SCOP
SCOT
SCOW
SCRY
SCSI
SCTV
SCUD
SCUM
SCUP
SCUT

S•C•
SACK
SACS
SECH
SECS
SECT
SECY
SICK
SICS
SNCC
SOCA
SOCK
SPCA
SPCC
SUCH
SUCK
SYCE

S••C
SCLC
SNCC
SPCC
SPEC
SYNC

•SC•
ASCH
ASCI
ASCO
DSCS
ESCE
USCG

•S•C
BSEC
MSEC
PSEC
USMC

••SC
BASC
BOSC
DESC
DISC
FISC
MASC
MISC
WISC

SD••
SDAK

S•D•
SADA
SADD
SADE
SADI
SADR
SIDE
SIDH
SODA
SODS
STDS
SUDD
SUDS

S••D
SADD
SAID
SAND
SARD
SAUD
SCAD
SCUD
SEED
SEND
SFPD
SHAD
SHED
SHOD
SILD
SIND
SKED
SKID
SLED
SLID
SOLD
SPAD
SPED
SPUD
SQYD
STBD
STUD
SUDD
SUED
SURD
SWED
SYND

•SD•
USDA

•S•D
BSED
USED

••SD
DASD
MUSD
NASD

SE••
SEAL
SEAM
SEAN
SEAR
SEAS
SEAT
SEBE
SEBS
SECH
SECS
SECT
SECY
SEED
SEEK
SEEL
SEEM
SEEN
SEEP
SEER
SEES
SEGA
SEGO
SEHR
SEIN
SEIS
SEJM
SELA
SELF
SELL
SEME
SEMI
SEMS
SEND
SENE
SENS
SENT
SEPT
SEQQ
SERA
SERB
SERE
SERF
SERO
SERS
SERT
SERV
SESS
SETA
SETH
SETI
SETS
SETT
SEUL
SEVE
SEWN
SEWS
SEXT
SEXY

S•E•
SEED
SEEK
SEEL
SEEM
SEEN
SEEP
SEER
SEES
SHEA
SHEB
SHED
SHEL
SHEM
SHEP
SHES
SKED
SKEE
SKEG
SKEP
SKEW
SLED
SLEW
SMEE
SMEW
SNEE
SPEC
SPED
SPEE
SPET
SPEW
STEM
STEN
STEP
STER
STES
STET
STEW
SUED
SUER
SUES
SUET
SUEY
SUEZ
SVEN
SWED

S••E
SABE
SADE
SAFE
SAGE
SAKE
SALE
SAME
SANE
SASE
SATE
SAVE
SAXE
SEBE
SEME
SENE
SERE
SEVE
SHOE
SHUE
SIDE
SINE
SIRE
SITE
SIZE
SKEE
SKYE
SLOE
SLUE
SLYE
SMEE
SNEE
SOIE
SOKE
SOLE
SOME
SONE
SORE
SPEE
STGE
SUPE
SURE
SYCE
SYNE

•SE•
ASEA
BSEC
BSED
ESEL
ISEE
MSEC
OSEE
PSEC
USED
USEE
USER
USES
YSER

•S•E
ASHE
ESCE
ESME
ESNE
ESSE
ESTE
ISEE
ISLE
OSEE
OSTE
USEE

••SE
APSE
BASE
BISE
BOSE
CASE
DOSE
DUSE
EASE
ELSE
ENSE
ERSE
ESSE
FUSE
HOSE
IPSE
JOSE
LASE
LESE
LISE
LOSE
MDSE
MISE
MOSE
MUSE
NOSE
NYSE
OISE
OUSE
PASE
POSE
RASE
RISE
ROSE
RUSE
SASE
VASE
VISE
WHSE
WISE

SF••
SFAX
SFPD

S•F•
SAFE
SAFR
SIFT
SOFA
SOFT
SQFT
SUFF
SUFI

S••F
SELF
SERF
SUFF
SULF
SURF

•S•F
ASIF
ASOF
USAF

SG••
SGTS

S•G•
SAGA SAGE SAGO SAGS SEGA SEGO SIGH SIGN SPGR SSGT STGE SVGS

S••G
SANG SHAG SING SKEG SLAG SLOG SLUG SMOG SMUG SNAG SNOG SNUG SONG STAG SUNG SURG SWAG SWIG

•SG•
MSGR MSGS MSGT SSGT TSGT USGA

•S•G
USCG

SH••
SHAD SHAG SHAH SHAM SHAN SHAQ SHAW SHAY SHEA SHEB SHED SHEL SHEM SHEP SHES SHIH SHIM SHIN SHIP SHIV SHOD SHOE SHOO SHOP SHOT SHOW SHPT SHUE SHUL SHUN SHUT

S•H•
SAHL SEHR SOHN SOHO SPHT

S••H
SASH SECH SETH SHAH SHIH SIDH SIGH SIKH SINH SOPH SUCH

•SH•
ASHE ASHY OSHA

•S•H
ASCH ESTH ISTH

••SH
BASH BOSH BUSH CASH COSH CUSH DASH DISH FISH GASH GISH GOSH GUSH HASH HUSH JOSH KISH KUSH LASH LUSH MASH MESH MOSH MUSH NASH NOSH PASH PISH POSH PUSH RASH RESH ROSH RUSH SASH TESH TISH TOSH TUSH WASH WISH

SI••
SIAL SIAM SIBS SICK SICS SIDE SIDH SIFT SIGH SIGN SIKA SIKH SILD SILK SILL SILO SILT SIMA SIMI SIMP SIMS SIND SINE SING SINH SINK SINO SINS SION SIPS SIRE SIRS SISI SITE SITS SITU SIZE

S•I•
SAID SAIL SAIS SCIL SEIN SEIS SHIH SHIM SHIN SHIP SHIV SKID SKIL SKIM SKIN SKIP SKIS SKIT SLID SLIM SLIP SLIT SMIT SNIP SNIT SOIE SOIL SOIR SPIN SPIT SPIV SQIN STIR SUIT SWIG SWIM SWIT

S••I
SADI SAKI SARI SCSI SEMI SETI SIMI SISI SOLI SORI SQMI SUFI SUZI

•SI•
ASIA ASIF ASIR ASIS HSIA ISIS OSIS PSIS USIA VSIX

•S•I
ASCI ASTI ESAI

••SI
ANSI COSI DESI IASI NISI SCSI SISI

S•J•
SEJM

S••J
SUBJ

SK••
SKAT SKAW SKED SKEE SKEG SKEP SKEW SKID SKIL SKIM SKIN SKIP SKIS SKIT SKOL SKUA SKUS SKYE SKYS

S•K•
SAKE SAKI SAKS SIKA SIKH SOKE SUKS

S••K
SACK SALK SANK SARK SASK SAUK SDAK SEEK SICK SILK SINK SOAK SOCK SOUK SUCK SULK SUNK SWAK

•SK•
ASKS TSKS

•S•K
ISAK

••SK
BASK BISK BOSK BUSK CASK CUSK DESK DISK DUSK FISK HUSK MASK MUSK OMSK ORSK RASK RISK RUSK SASK TASK TUSK WISK

SL••
SLAB SLAG SLAM SLAP SLAT SLAV SLAW SLAY SLBM SLED SLEW SLID SLIM SLIP SLIT SLOB SLOE SLOG SLOP SLOT SLOW SLRS SLUB SLUE SLUG SLUM SLUR SLYE

S•L•
SALA SALE SALK SALP SALS SALT SCLC SELA SELF SELL SILD SILK SILL SILO SILT SOLA SOLD SOLE SOLI SOLN SOLO SOLS STLO SULF SULK SULU SYLL SYLS

S••L
SAHL SAIL SAML SAUL SCIL SEAL SEEL SELL SEUL SHEL SHUL SIAL SILL SKIL SKOL SOIL SOUL STOL SYLL

•SL•
ISLA ISLE ISLS OSLO

•S•L
ESEL

••SL
NASL

SM••
SMEE SMEW SMIT SMOG SMSA SMUG SMUT

S•M•
SAME SAML SAMO SAMP SEME SEMI SEMS SIMA SIMI SIMP SIMS SOMA SOME SQMI STMT SUMO SUMP SUMS SYMS

S••M
SCAM SCUM SEAM SEEM SEJM SHAM SHEM SHIM SIAM SKIM SLAM SLBM SLIM SLUM SPAM STEM STUM SUUM SWAM SWIM SWUM

•SM•
BSMT DSMS ESME ISMS USMA USMC

••SM
COSM MUSM

SN••
SNAG SNAP SNCC SNEE SNIP SNIT SNOB SNOG SNOW SNUB SNUG

S•N•
SANA SAND SANE SANG SANK SANO SANS SANT SEND SENE SENS SENT SIND SINE SING SINH SINK SINO SINS SONE SONG SONS SONY SSNS STNS SUNG SUNK SUNN SUNS SUNY SYNC SYND SYNE SYNS

S••N
SAWN SCAN SEAN SEEN SEIN SEWN SHAN SHIN SHUN SIGN SION SKIN SOHN SOLN SOON SOWN SPAN SPIN SPUN SQIN STAN STEN STUN SUNN SVEN SWAN

•SN•
ESNE ISNT SSNS USNA USNR

•S•N
ASSN ESPN ISBN ISSN

••SN
ASSN BOSN ISSN

SO••
SOAK SOAP SOAR SOBS SOCA SOCK SODA SODS SOFA SOFT SOHN SOHO SOIE SOIL SOIR SOKE SOLA SOLD SOLE SOLI SOLN SOLO SOLS SOMA SOME SONE SONG SONS SONY SOON SOOT SOPH SOPS SORA SORB SORE SORI SORT SOSO SOTS SOUK SOUL SOUP SOUR SOUS SOWN SOWS SOYA SOYS

S•O•
SCOP SCOT SCOW SHOD SHOE SHOO SHOP SHOT SHOW SION SKOL SLOB SLOE SLOG SLOP SLOT SLOW SMOG SNOB SNOG SNOW SOON SOOT SPOT STOA STOL STOP STOT STOW SWOB SWOP

S••O
SAGO SAMO SANO SATO SEGO SERO SHOO SILO SINO SOHO SOLO SOSO STLO SUMO

•SO•
ASOF ASOR DSOS ESOP ESOS VSOP

•S•O
ASCO ASTO ESPO ESSO ESTO ISAO OSLO OSSO USPO

••SO
AHSO ALSO APSO BESO DMSO ESSO FASO IFSO IPSO MESO MISO NASO OSSO PASO PESO SOSO

SP••
SPAD SPAM SPAN SPAR SPAS SPAT SPAY SPCA SPCC SPEC SPED SPEE SPET SPEW SPGR SPHT SPIN SPIT SPIV SPOT SPQR SPRY SPUD SPUN SPUR

S•P•
SAPS SEPT SFPD SHPT SIPS SOPH SOPS SUPE SUPP SUPR SUPS SUPT

S••P
SALP SAMP SCOP SCUP SEEP SHEP SHIP SHOP SIMP SKEP SKIP SLAP SLIP SLOP SNAP SNIP SOAP SOUP STEP STOP SUMP SUPP SWAP SWOP

•SP•
ASPS ESPN ESPO ESPS ESPY ISPY TSPS USPO USPS

•S•P
ASAP ESOP RSVP VSOP

••SP
CUSP GASP HASP HOSP INSP LISP RASP RESP TBSP WASP WISP

SQ••
SQFT SQIN SQMI SQYD

S•Q•
SEQQ SPQR SUQS

S••Q
SEQQ SHAQ

•SQ•
ESQS

SR••
SRAS SRTA

S•R•
SARA SARD SARI SARK SCRY SERA SERB SERE SERF SERO SERS SERT

SERV
SIRE
SIRS
SLRS
SORA
SORB
SORE
SORI
SORT
SPRY
SSRS
STRS
SURA
SURD
SURE
SURF
SURG
SURV

S••R
SAAR
SADR
SAFR
SAUR
SCAR
SEAR
SEER
SEHR
SLUR
SOAR
SOIR
SOUR
SPAR
SPGR
SPQR
SPUR
STAR
STER
STIR
SUER
SUPR

•SR•
SSRS
TSRS

•S•R
ASIR
ASOR
ASTR
ISAR
MSGR
OSAR
TSAR
USAR
USER
USNR
USSR
YSER

••SR
USSR

SS••
SSGT
SSNS
SSRS
SSTS

S•S•
SASE
SASH
SASK
SASS
SCSI
SESS
SISI
SMSA
SOSO
SUSA
SUSS
SYST

S••S
SACS
SAGS
SAIS
SAKS
SALS
SANS
SAPS
SASS
SATS
SAWS
SAYS
SEAS
SEBS
SECS
SEES
SEIS
SEMS
SENS
SERS
SESS
SETS
SEWS
SGTS
SHES
SIBS
SICS
SIMS
SINS
SIPS
SIRS
SITS
SKIS
SKUS
SKYS
SLRS
SOBS
SODS
SOLS
SONS
SOPS
SOTS
SOUS
SOWS
SOYS
SPAS
SRAS
SSNS
SSRS
SSTS
STAS
STDS
STES
STNS
STRS
SUBS
SUDS
SUES
SUKS
SUMS
SUNS
SUPS
SUQS
SUSS
SUVS
SVGS
SWBS
SYLS
SYMS
SYNS

•SS•
ASSN
ASST
ESSA
ESSE
ESSO
ISSN
OSSA
OSSO
PSST
USSR

•S•S
ASIS
ASKS
ASPS
DSCS
DSMS
DSOS
ESAS
ESOS
ESPS
ESQS
ESUS
ISIS
ISLS
ISMS
ISTS
LSTS
MSGS
OSIS
PSIS
SSNS
SSRS
SSTS
TSKS
TSPS
TSRS
USES
USPS

••SS
BASS
BESS
BOSS
BUSS
CASS
CESS
CUSS
DISS
DOSS
FESS
FOSS
FUSS
HESS
HISS
HOSS
HUSS
JESS
JOSS
KISS
LASS
LESS
LOSS
MASS
MESS
MISS
MOSS
MUSS
NESS
PASS
POSS
PUSS
ROSS
RUSS
SASS
SESS
SUSS
TASS
TESS
TOSS
WUSS
WYSS

ST••
STAB
STAG
STAN
STAR
STAS
STAT
STAY
STBD
STDS
STEM
STEN
STEP
STER
STES
STET
STEW
STGE
STIR
STLO
STMT
STNS
STOA
STOL
STOP
STOT
STOW
STRS
STUB
STUD
STUM
STUN
STYX

S•T•
SATE
SATO
SATS
SCTV
SETA
SETH
SETI
SETS
SETT
SGTS
SITE
SITS
SITU
SOTS
SRTA
SSTS

S••T
SALT
SANT
SCAT
SCOT
SCUT
SEAT
SECT
SENT
SEPT
SERT
SETT
SEXT
SHOT
SHPT
SHUT
SIFT
SILT
SKAT
SKIT
SLAT
SLIT
SLOT
SMIT
SMUT
SNIT
SOFT
SOOT
SORT
SPAT
SPET
SPHT
SPIT
SPOT
SQFT
SSGT
STAT
STET
STMT
STOT
SUET
SUIT
SUPT
SWAT
SWIT
SYST

•ST•
ASTA
ASTI
ASTO
ASTR
ESTA
ESTE
ESTH
ESTO
ISTH
ISTS
LSTS
OSTE
SSTS
USTA

•S•T
ASST
BSMT
ISNT
LSAT
MSGT
PSAT
PSST
SSGT
TSGT

••ST
ASST
AUST
BAST
BEST
BUST
CAST
CEST
CIST
COST
DIST
DOST
DUST
EAST
ERST
FAST
FEST
FIST
FUST
GAST
GEST
GIST
GUST
HAST
HEST
HIST
HOST
INST
JEST
JUST
LAST
LEST
LIST
LOST
LUST
MAST
MIST
MOST
MUST
MYST
NAST
NEST
OAST
OUST
PAST
PEST
POST
PSST
REST
RUST
SYST
TEST
VAST
VEST
WAST
WEST
YOST
ZEST

SU••
SUBJ
SUBS
SUCH
SUCK
SUDD
SUDS
SUED
SUER
SUES
SUET
SUEY
SUEZ
SUFF
SUFI
SUIT
SUKS
SULF
SULK
SULU
SUMO
SUMP
SUMS
SUNG
SUNK
SUNN
SUNS
SUNY
SUPE
SUPP
SUPR
SUPS
SUPT
SUQS
SURA
SURD
SURE
SURF
SURG
SURV
SUSA
SUSS
SUUM
SUVA
SUVS
SUZI
SUZY

S•U•
SAUD
SAUK
SAUL
SAUR
SCUD
SCUM
SCUP
SCUT
SEUL
SHUE
SHUL
SHUN
SHUT
SKUA
SKUS
SLUB
SLUE
SLUG
SLUM
SLUR
SMUG
SMUT
SNUB
SNUG
SOUK
SOUL
SOUP
SOUR
SOUS
SPUD
SPUN
SPUR
STUB
STUD
STUM
STUN
SUUM
SWUM

S••U
SABU
SITU
SULU

•SU•
ESUS

•S•U
ESAU

••SU
JESU
ZASU

SV••
SVEN
SVGS

S•V•
SAVA
SAVE
SEVE
SUVA
SUVS

S••V
SCTV
SERV
SHIV
SLAV
SPIV
SURV

•SV•
RSVP

SW••
SWAB
SWAG
SWAK
SWAM
SWAN
SWAP
SWAT
SWAY
SWBS
SWBW
SWED
SWIG
SWIM
SWIT
SWOB
SWOP
SWUM

S•W•
SAWN
SAWS
SEWN
SEWS
SOWN
SOWS

S••W
SCOW
SHAW
SHOW
SKAW
SKEW
SLAW
SLEW
SLOW
SMEW
SNOW
SPEW
STEW
STOW
SWBW

S•X•
SAXE
SEXT
SEXY

S••X
SFAX
STYX

•S•X
VSIX

SY••
SYCE
SYLL
SYLS
SYMS
SYNC
SYND
SYNE
SYNS
SYST

S•Y•
SAYS
SKYE
SKYS
SLYE
SOYA
SOYS
SQYD
STYX

S••Y
SCRY
SECY
SEXY
SHAY
SLAY
SONY
SPAY
SPRY
STAY
SUEY
SUNY
SUZY
SWAY

•S•Y
ASHY
ESPY
ISAY
ISPY

••SY
BUSY
COSY
EASY
ITSY
NOSY
POSY
ROSY

S•Z•
SIZE
SUZI
SUZY

S••Z
SUEZ

TA••
TAAL
TABI
TABS
TABU
TACH
TACK
TACO
TACT
TADA
TADS
TAEL
TAFT
TAGS
TAHR
TAIF
TAIL
TAIN
TAIT
TAIZ
TAJS
TAKA
TAKE
TALA
TALC
TALE
TALI
TALK
TALL
TAMA
TAME
TAMM
TAMO
TAMP
TAMS
TANA
TANE
TANG
TANH
TANK
TANS
TAOS
TAPA
TAPE
TAPS
TARA
TARE
TARN
TARO
TARP
TARS
TART
TASK
TASS
TATA
TATE
TATI
TATS
TAUS
TAUT
TAVI
TAWS
TAXA
TAXI
TAXO

T•A•
TAAL
TBAR
TEAK
TEAL
TEAM
TEAR
TEAS
THAI
THAN
THAR
THAS
THAT
THAW
TIAS
TMAN
TOAD
TOAT
TRAM
TRAP
TRAX
TRAY
TSAR
TUAN
TWAS
TZAR

T••A
TADA
TAKA
TALA
TAMA
TANA
TAPA
TARA
TATA
TAXA
TEMA
TERA
TEWA
THEA
TINA
TIWA
TOEA
TOGA
TOLA
TOMA
TORA
TRNA
TUBA
TUFA
TULA
TUNA
TVMA

•TA•
ETAH
ETAL
ETAS
ETAT
ITAL
ITAR
PTAH
PTAS
STAB
STAG
STAN
STAR
STAS
STAT
STAY
UTAH

•T•A
ATKA
ATRA
ATTA
ETNA
ETTA
ITEA
ITZA
OTRA
STOA

••TA
ACTA
AFTA
ALTA
ANTA
ASTA
ATTA
BETA
BOTA
CATA
CETA
DATA
EDTA
ESTA
ETTA
FATA
FETA
GETA
GITA
IOTA
LOTA
MATA
META
MITA
MOTA
NITA
NOTA
OCTA
OITA
PETA
PITA
RATA
RITA
ROTA
RUTA
SETA
SRTA
TATA
USTA
VITA
ZETA

TB••
TBAR
TBSP

T•B•
TABI
TABS
TABU
TCBY
TOBE
TOBY
TUBA
TUBB
TUBE
TUBS

T••B
TOMB
TRIB
TUBB

•TB•
GTBR
STBD

•T•B
FTLB

NTSB STAB STUB

••TB
LITB

TC••
TCBY TCHR

T•C•
TACH TACK TACO TACT TECH TECS TICK TICO TICS TOCK TUCK

T••C
TALC

•TC•
ETCH ITCH

•T•C
ETIC OTIC

••TC
ROTC

T•D•
TADA TADS TEDS TIDE TIDY TODD TODO TODS TODY TUDE

T••D
TEED TEND THUD TIED TOAD TODD TOED TOLD TROD TWOD

•TD•
ETDS LTDS STDS

•T•D
STBD STUD

••TD
LITD PATD RETD

TE••
TEAK TEAL TEAM TEAR TEAS TECH TECS TEDS TEED TEEM TEEN TEES TEFF TEGS TELE TELL TELO TEMA TEMP TEND TENE TENN TENO TENS TENT TEPP TERA TERI TERM TERN TERP TERR TESH TESS TEST TETE TETH TETS TEUT TEWA TEXT

T•E•
TAEL TEED TEEM TEEN TEES THEA THEE THEM THEN THEO THEW THEY TIED TIER TIES TMEN TOEA TOED TOES TREE TREF TREK TRES TRET TREX TREY TUES TWEE

T••E
TAKE TALE TAME TANE TAPE TARE TATE TELE TENE TETE THEE TIDE TIGE TIKE TILE TIME TINE TIRE TOBE TOKE TOLE TOME TONE TOPE TORE TOTE TREE TRUE TUBE TUDE TULE TUNE TWEE TYKE TYNE TYPE TYRE

•TE•
ATEN ATES ETES ITEA ITEM ITER ITES KTEL RTES STEM STEN STEP STER STES STET STEW UTEP UTES

•T•E
CTGE ETRE ETTE MTGE OTOE STGE UTNE

••TE
ACTE ALTE ANTE ARTE BATE BETE BITE BUTE BYTE CATE CETE CITE COTE CUTE CYTE DATE DOTE ERTE ESTE ETTE FATE FETE GATE HATE HITE HOTE JETE JUTE KATE KITE LATE LITE LUTE MATE METE MITE MOTE MUTE NATE NITE NOTE OSTE PATE PETE RATE RETE RITE ROTE SATE SITE TATE TETE TOTE VITE VOTE WITE

T•F•
TAFT TEFF TIFF TOFF TOFT TOFU TUFA TUFF TUFT TUFU

T••F
TAIF TEFF TGIF TIFF TOFF TREF TUFF TURF

TG••
TGIF

T•G•
TAGS TEGS TIGE TOGA TOGO TOGS TSGT TUGS

T••G
TANG THUG TING TONG TRIG TRUG TUNG TVPG TWIG

•TG•
CTGE MTGE MTGS STGE

•T•G
LTJG STAG

••TG
ACTG MKTG

TH••
THAI THAN THAR THAS THAT THAW THEA THEE THEM THEN THEO THEW THEY THIN THIO THIS THOM THOR THOS THOU THRU THUD THUG THUR THUS

T•H•
TAHR TCHR TOHO

T••H
TACH TANH TECH TESH TETH TISH TOSH TUSH

•TH•
ETHS OTHO

•T•H
ETAH ETCH ITCH PTAH UTAH

••TH
ACTH ANTH AUTH BATH BETH BOTH CATH DOTH ESTH FATH GATH GOTH HATH HETH ISTH KITH LATH LGTH LITH LUTH MATH METH MOTH MYTH NETH OATH ORTH PATH PITH RATH ROTH RUTH SETH TETH WITH

TI••
TIAS TICK TICO TICS TIDE TIDY TIED TIER TIES TIFF TIGE TIKE TIKI TILE TILL TILS TILT TIME TINA TINE TING TINS TINT TINY TION TIOS TIPS TIRE TIRO TISH TITI TITO TIVS TIWA

T•I•
TAIF TAIL TAIN TAIT TAIZ TGIF THIN THIO THIS TOIL TRIB TRIG TRIM TRIO TRIP TRIS TRIX TUIS TWIG TWIN TWIT TWIX

T••I
TABI TALI TATI TAVI TAXI TERI THAI TIKI TITI TONI TOPI TORI TROI TUPI

•TI•
ATIT ETIC ITIS OTIC OTIS QTIP STIR UTIL

•T•I
ATLI ATOI ATRI ETUI

••TI
ACTI ALTI ANTI ASTI LOTI NOTI ROTI SETI TATI TITI VITI YETI ZITI

T•J•
TAJS TOJO

•TJ•
LTJG

TK••
TKOS TKTS

T•K•
TAKA TAKE TIKE TIKI TOKE TPKS TSKS TYKE

T••K
TACK TALK TANK TASK TEAK TICK TNPK TOCK TONK TOOK TORK TREK TRUK TUCK TURK TUSK

•TK•
ATKA

T•L•
TALA TALC TALE TALI TALK TALL TELE TELL TELO TILE TILL TILS TILT TOLA TOLD TOLE TOLL TOLU TULA TULE TULL

T••L
TAAL TAEL TAIL TALL TEAL TELL TILL TOIL TOLL TOOL TULL

•TL•
ATLI FTLB ITLL STLO

•T•L
ETAL ITAL ITLL ITOL KTEL STOL UTIL VTOL

••TL
INTL NATL ROTL

TM••
TMAN TMEN

T•M•
TAMA TAME TAMM TAMO TAMP TAMS TEMA TEMP TIME TOMA TOMB TOME TOMS TUMP TUMS TVMA TYMP

T••M
TAMM TEAM TEEM TERM THEM THOM TRAM TRIM TUUM

•TM•
ATMO ATMS STMT

•T•M
ATOM ATUM ETYM ITEM STEM STUM

TN••
TNPK TNUT

T•N•
TANA TANE TANG TANH TANK TANS TEND TENE TENN TENO TENS TENT TINA TINE TING TINS TINT TINY TONE TONG TONI TONK TONS TONY TRNA TUNA TUNE TUNG TUNS TYNE

T••N
TAIN TARN TEEN TENN TERN THAN THEN THIN TION TMAN TMEN TOON TORN TOWN TRON TUAN TURN TWIN

•TN•
ATNO CTNS ETNA MTNS STNS UTNE

•T•N
ATEN ATON ATTN ETON STAN STEN STUN

••TN
ATTN

TO••
TOAD TOAT TOBE TOBY TOCK TODD TODO TODS TODY TOEA TOED TOES TOFF TOFT TOFU TOGA TOGO TOGS TOHO TOIL TOJO TOKE TOLA TOLD TOLE TOLL TOLU TOMA TOMB TOME TOMS TONE TONG TONI TONK TONS TONY TOOK TOOL TOON TOOT TOPE TOPI TOPO TOPS TORA TORE TORI TORK TORN TORO TORR TORS TORT TORY TOSH TOSS TOTE TOTO TOTS TOUR TOUT TOWN TOWS TOYS

T•O•
TAOS THOM THOR THOS THOU TION TIOS TKOS TOOK TOOL TOON TOOT TROD TROI TRON TROP TROT TROY TWOD TWOS

T••O
TACO TAMO TARO TAXO TELO TENO THEO THIO TICO TIRO TITO TODO TOGO TOHO TOJO TOPO TORO TOTO TRIO TYPO TYRO

•TO•
ATOI ATOM ATON ATOP ATOR ETON GTOS ITOL OTOE OTOS STOA STOL STOP

STOT STOW VTOL

•T•O
ATMO ATNO ATTO OTHO OTRO OTTO STLO

••TO
ALTO ASTO ATTO AUTO CATO CYTO ECTO ENTO ESTO GATO INTO JATO KATO KETO KOTO LETO MOTO NATO OCTO ONTO OPTO OTTO PETO ROTO SATO TITO TOTO UNTO UPTO VETO VITO

TP••
TPKS

T•P•
TAPA TAPE TAPS TEPP TIPS TNPK TOPE TOPI TOPO TOPS TSPS TUPI TVPG TWPS TYPE TYPO TYPY

T••P
TAMP TARP TBSP TEMP TEPP TERP TRAP TRIP TROP TUMP TYMP

•T•P
ATOP HTTP QTIP STEP STOP UTEP

••TP
HTTP

TR••
TRAM TRAP TRAX TRAY TREE TREF TREK TRES TRET TREX TREY TRIB TRIG TRIM TRIO TRIP TRIS TRIX TRNA TROD TROI TRON TROP TROT TROY TRUE TRUG TRUK

T•R•
TARA TARE TARN TARO TARP TARS TART TERA TERI TERM TERN TERP TERR THRU TIRE TIRO TORA TORE TORI TORK TORN TORO TORR TORS TORT TORY TSRS TURF TURK TURN TYRE TYRO

T••R
TAHR TBAR TCHR TEAR TERR THAR THOR THUR TIER TORR TOUR TSAR TZAR

•TR•
ATRA ATRI ETRE OTRA OTRO QTRS STRS

•T•R
ATOR GTBR ITAR ITER LTYR STAR STER STIR

••TR
ASTR ENTR INTR

TS••
TSAR TSGT TSKS TSPS TSRS

T•S•
TASK TASS TBSP TESH TESS TEST TISH TOSH TOSS TUSH TUSK

T••S
TABS TADS TAGS TAJS TAMS TANS TAOS TAPS TARS TASS TATS TAUS TAWS TEAS TECS TEDS TEES TEGS TENS TESS TETS THAS THIS THOS THUS TIAS TICS TIES TILS TINS TIOS TIPS TIVS TKOS TKTS TODS TOES TOGS TOMS TONS TOPS TORS TOSS TOTS TOWS TOYS TPKS TRES TRIS TSKS TSPS TSRS TUBS TUES TUGS TUIS TUMS TUNS TUTS TWAS TWOS TWPS

•TS•
ITSY NTSB

•T•S
ATES ATMS ATTS ATVS BTUS CTNS ETAS ETDS ETES ETHS GTOS ITES ITIS LTDS MTGS MTNS OTIS OTOS PTAS QTRS RTES STAS STDS STES STNS STRS UTES

••TS
ACTS AFTS AGTS AITS ALTS AMTS ANTS APTS ARTS ATTS BATS BETS BITS BLTS BOTS BUTS CATS CITS COTS CRTS CUTS DATS DETS DITS DOTS EATS EFTS EMTS ENTS EXTS FATS FITS GATS GETS GITS GUTS HATS HITS HUTS INTS ISTS JETS JOTS JUTS KITS LATS LETS LITS LOTS LSTS MATS METS MOTS NETS NITS NOTS NUTS OATS OPTS ORTS OUTS PATS PETS PITS PMTS POTS PUTS PVTS QATS RATS RCTS RETS RGTS ROTS RPTS RUTS SATS SETS SGTS SITS SOTS SSTS TATS TETS TKTS TOTS TUTS VATS VDTS VETS WATS WETS WITS XATS

T•T•
TATA TATE TATI TATS TETE TETH TETS TITI TITO TKTS TOTE TOTO TOTS TUTS TUTU

T••T
TACT TAFT TAIT TART TAUT TENT TEST TEUT TEXT THAT TILT TINT TNUT TOAT TOFT TOOT TORT TOUT TRET TROT TSGT TUFT TWIT

•TT•
ATTA ATTN ATTO ATTS ATTU ATTY ETTA ETTE HTTP ITTY OTTO

•T•T
ATIT ATWT ETAT NTWT STAT STET STMT STOT

••TT
BATT BITT BOTT BUTT CATT GATT HUTT JETT KETT KITT LETT LOTT MATT MITT MOTT MUTT NUTT PITT PUTT RATT RITT SETT WATT WITT

TU••
TUAN TUBA TUBB TUBE TUBS TUCK TUDE TUES TUFA TUFF TUFT TUFU TUGS TUIS TULA TULE TULL TUMP TUMS TUNA TUNE TUNG TUNS TUPI TURF TURK TURN TUSH TUSK TUTS TUTU TUUM

T•U•
TAUS TAUT TEUT THUD THUG THUR THUS TNUT TOUR TOUT TRUE TRUG TRUK TUUM

T••U
TABU THOU THRU TOFU TOLU TUFU TUTU

•TU•
ATUM BTUS ETUI ETUX STUB STUD STUM STUN

•T•U
ATTU

••TU
ATTU HUTU MATU SITU TUTU VATU WCTU

TV••
TVMA TVPG

T•V•
TAVI TIVS

•TV•
ATVS

••TV
ACTV CATV CCTV HDTV SCTV

TW••
TWAS TWEE TWIG TWIN TWIT TWIX TWOD TWOS TWPS

T•W•
TAWS TEWA TIWA TOWN TOWS

T••W
THAW THEW

•TW•
ATWT NTWT

•T•W
STEW STOW

••TW
GWTW

T•X•
TAXA TAXI TAXO TEXT

T••X
TRAX TREX TRIX TWIX

•T•X
ETUX STYX

TY••
TYKE TYMP TYNE TYPE TYPO TYPY TYRE TYRO

T•Y•
TOYS

T••Y
TCBY THEY TIDY TINY TOBY TODY TONY TORY TRAY TREY TROY TYPY

•TY•
ETYM LTYR STYX

•T•Y
ATTY ITSY ITTY STAY

••TY
ARTY ATTY CITY COTY DUTY ITTY KATY OATY PITY

TZ••
TZAR

T••Z
TAIZ

•TZ•
ITZA

••TZ
BETZ DITZ FITZ FUTZ GETZ KATZ LUTZ METZ RITZ ZOTZ

U•A•
ULAN UNAU UPAS URAL USAF USAR UTAH

U••A
UCLA ULNA UMEA URFA URGA URSA USDA USGA USIA USMA USNA USTA UVEA

•UA•
DUAD DUAL FUAD GUAM GUAN GUAR HUAC JUAN LUAU QUAD QUAG QUAI QUAM QUAR QUAY TUAN YUAN

•U•A
AULA AURA BUNA CUBA CUNA DUMA DUNA DURA FULA HULA HUPA JUBA JUGA JURA LUBA LUNA PUKA PULA PUMA PUNA PUPA RUGA RUTA SURA SUSA SUVA TUBA TUFA TULA TUNA WUSA YUBA YUGA YUMA

••UA
AGUA AQUA ECUA SKUA

UB••
UBER

U•B•
UMBO URBE URBI URBS

•UB•
AUBE BUBU CUBA CUBE CUBS DUBS FUBS HUBS JUBA LUBA LUBE NUBS PUBL PUBS RUBE RUBS RUBY SUBJ SUBS TUBA TUBB TUBE TUBS YUBA

•U•B
BULB BURB CURB DUMB MUSB NUMB TUBB

••UB
CHUB CLUB DAUB DRUB FLUB GRUB SLUB SNUB STUB

UC••
UCLA

U•C•
UNCI USCG

U••C
USMC

•UC•
BUCK BUCO BUCS DUCE DUCK DUCT GUCK HUCK LUCE LUCI LUCK LUCY MUCH MUCK OUCH

PUCE
PUCK
RUCK
SUCH
SUCK
TUCK
YUCK

•U•C
HUAC
JUNC
NUNC

••UC
EDUC
GLUC

UD••
UDOS

U•D•
UNDO
UPDO
URDU
USDA

U••D
USED

•UD•
AUDE
AUDI
BUDD
BUDS
CUDS
DUDE
DUDS
FUDD
JUDD
JUDE
JUDG
JUDO
JUDY
KUDU
MUDD
MUDS
NUDE
NUDI
OUDS
PUDU
RUDD
RUDE
RUDI
RUDY
SUDD
SUDS
TUDE

•U•D
AULD
BUDD
BUND
CUED
CURD
DUAD
FUAD
FUDD
FUND
HUED
HUND
JUDD
KURD
MUDD
MUSD
QUAD
QUID
QUOD
RUDD
RUED
SUDD
SUED
SURD

••UD
BAUD
CRUD
FEUD
GAUD
KNUD
LAUD
LOUD
MAUD
SAUD
SCUD
SPUD
STUD
THUD
VAUD
YOUD

UE••
UELE
UEYS

U•E•
UBER
UKES
ULEE
UMEA
UNES
UREY
USED
USEE
USER
USES
UTEP
UTES
UVEA

U••E
UELE
ULEE
URBE
URGE
USEE
UTNE

•UE•
AUEL
AUER
CUED
CUER
CUES
DUEL
DUES
DUET
FUEL
HUED
HUES
HUEY
PUER
QUEL
QUEM
QUES
RUED
RUER
RUES
SUED
SUER
SUES
SUET
SUEY
SUEZ
TUES

•U•E
AUBE
AUDE
AUGE
AUNE
BUTE
CUBE
CUKE
CULE
CURE
CUTE
DUCE
DUDE
DUKE
DUNE
DUPE
DUSE
DUVE
FUME
FUSE
FUZE
HUGE
HUME
JUDE
JUKE
JULE
JUNE
JURE
JUTE
LUBE
LUCE
LUGE
LUKE
LUNE
LUPE
LURE
LUTE
LUXE
MULE
MUSE
MUTE
NUDE
NUKE
OUSE
PUCE
PULE
PURE
RUBE
RUDE
RULE
RUNE
RUSE
SUPE
SURE
TUBE
TUDE
TULE
TUNE
YULE

••UE
ADUE
AGUE
BLUE
CLUE
COUE
CRUE
FLUE
GLUE
LAUE
MOUE
NIUE
RHUE
ROUE
SHUE
SLUE
TRUE

UF••
UFOS

U•F•
URFA

U••F
USAF

•UF•
BUFF
CUFF
CUFT
DUFF
DUFY
GUFF
HUFF
LUFF
LUFT
MUFF
PUFF
RUFF
SUFF
SUFI
TUFA
TUFF
TUFT
TUFU

•U•F
BUFF
BUMF
CUFF
DUFF
FUNF
GUFF
GULF
HUFF
LUFF
MUFF
PUFF
RUFF
SUFF
SULF
SURF
TUFF
TURF

••UF
ENUF
NEUF
OEUF
POUF

UG••
UGHS
UGLI
UGLY

U•G•
URGA
URGE
USGA

U••G
USCG

•UG•
AUGE
BUGS
FUGS
FUGU
HUGE
HUGH
HUGO
HUGS
JUGA
JUGS
LUGE
LUGS
MUGS
PUGH
PUGS
RUGA
RUGS
TUGS
VUGS
YUGA
YUGO

•U•G
BULG
BUNG
BURG
GUNG
HUNG
JUDG
JUNG
KUNG
LUNG
MUNG
PUNG
QUAG
RUNG
SUNG
SURG
TUNG
VULG

••UG
CHUG
DOUG
DRUG
FRUG
GLUG
PLUG
SLUG
SMUG
SNUG
THUG
TRUG

UH••
UHOH
UHUH

U•H•
UGHS

U••H
UHOH
UHUH
UMPH
UTAH

•UH•
BUHL
BUHR
KUHN
RUHR
WUHL
WUHU

•U•H
AUTH
BUSH
CUSH
GUSH
HUGH
HUSH
KUSH
LUSH
LUTH
MUCH
MUSH
OUCH
PUGH
PUSH
RUSH
RUTH
SUCH
TUSH

••UH
UHUH

U•I•
UNIS
UNIT
UNIV
UNIX
URIM
URIS
USIA
UTIL
UZIS

U••I
UGLI
UNCI
URBI

•UI•
CUIN
GUIN
GUIS
HUIS
LUIS
MUIR
NUIT
QUID
QUIP
QUIT
QUIZ
RUIN
SUIT
TUIS

•U•I
AUDI
AURI
BURI
FUJI
LUCI
MUNI
NUDI
PULI
PUYI
QUAI
QUOI
RUDI
SUFI
SUZI
TUPI
WUXI
YURI
ZUNI

••UI
ALUI
AQUI
EQUI
ETUI
MAUI
PFUI

•UJ•
CUJO
FUJI
JUJU

•U•J
SUBJ

UK••
UKES

U••K
URUK

•UK•
AUKS
CUKE
DUKE
JUKE
LUKE
LUKS
NUKE
PUKA
PUKU
SUKS
YUKS

•U•K
BUCK
BULK
BUNK
BUSK
CUSK
DUCK
DUNK
DUSK
FUNK
GUCK
GUNK
HUCK
HULK
HUNK
HUSK
JUNK
LUCK
LURK
MUCK
MURK
MUSK
PUCK
PUNK
RUCK
RUSK
SUCK
SULK
SUNK
TUCK
TURK
TUSK
YUCK

••UK
KRUK
LEUK
NYUK
SAUK
SOUK
TRUK
URUK
WOUK
ZOUK

UL••
ULAN
ULEE
ULNA
ULUS

U•L•
UCLA
UELE
UGLI
UGLY
UNLV
URLS

U••L
URAL
UTIL

•UL•
AULA
AULD
BULB
BULG
BULK
BULL
CULE
CULL
CULM
CULP
CULS
CULT
DULL
DULY
FULA
FULL
GULF
GULL
GULP
HULA
HULK
HULL
JULE
JULY
LULL
LULU
MULE
MULL
NULL
OULU
PULA
PULE
PULI
PULL
PULP
RULE
SULF
SULK
SULU
TULA
TULE
TULL
VULG
VULT
YULE
ZULU

•U•L
AUEL
BUHL
BULL
BURL
CULL
CURL
DUAL
DUEL
DULL
FUEL
FULL
FURL
GULL
HULL
HURL
LULL
MULL
NULL
PUBL
PULL
PURL
QUEL
TULL
WUHL

••UL
AZUL
CAUL
ELUL
FOUL
GAUL
HAUL
MAUL
PAUL
RAUL
SAUL
SEUL
SHUL
SOUL

UM••
UMBO
UMEA
UMPH
UMPS

U•M•
USMA
USMC

U••M
UNUM
URIM

•UM•
BUMF
BUMP
BUMS
DUMA
DUMB
DUMP
FUME
FUMY
GUMM
GUMP
GUMS
HUME
HUMP
HUMS
JUMP
LUMP
MUMP
MUMS
NUMB
PUMA
PUMP
RUMP
RUMS
SUMO
SUMP
SUMS
TUMP
TUMS
YUMA

•U•M
CULM
GUAM
GUMM
MUSM
QUAM
QUEM
SUUM
TUUM

••UM
ALUM
ARUM
ATUM
AXUM
BAUM
BLUM
CHUM
DEUM
DRUM
GAUM
GEUM
GLUM
MEUM
OVUM
PLUM
RHUM
SCUM
SLUM
STUM
SUUM
SWUM
TUUM
UNUM

UN••
UNAU
UNCI
UNDO
UNES
UNIS
UNIT
UNIV
UNIX
UNLV
UNTO
UNUM

U•N•
ULNA
URNS
USNA
USNR
UTNE

U••N
ULAN
UPON

•UN•
AUNE
AUNT
BUNA
BUND
BUNG
BUNK
BUNS
BUNT
CUNA
CUNY
DUNA
DUNE
DUNK
DUNN
DUNS
FUND
FUNF
FUNK
FUNT
GUNG
GUNK
GUNN
GUNS
HUND
HUNG
HUNK
HUNS
HUNT
JUNC
JUNE
JUNG
JUNK
JUNO
KUNG
LUNA
LUNE
LUNG
LUNN
LUNT
MUNG
MUNI
NUNC
NUNN
NUNS
PUNA
PUNG
PUNK
PUNS
PUNT
PUNY
RUNE
RUNG
RUNS
RUNT
SUNG
SUNK
SUNN
SUNS
SUNY
TUNA
TUNE
TUNG
TUNS
ZUNI

•U•N
BUON
BURN
CUIN
DUNN
DURN
GUAN
GUIN
GUNN
HUON
JUAN
KUHN
LUNN
MUON
NUNN
RUIN
SUNN
TUAN
TURN
YUAN

••UN
FAUN
IDUN
NEUN
NOUN
RYUN
SHUN
SPUN
STUN

U•O•
UDOS
UFOS
UHOH
UPON
UXOR

U••O
UMBO
UNDO
UNTO
UPDO
UPTO
USPO

•UO•
BUON
BUOY
DUOS
HUON
MUON
QUOD
QUOI
QUOT

•U•O
AUTO
BUCO
CUJO
DURO
EURO
FURO
HUGO
JUDO
JUNO
OUZO
PUZO
SUMO
YUGO

••UO
AQUO

UP••
UPAS
UPDO
UPON
UPTO

U•P•
UMPH
UMPS
USPO
USPS

U••P
UTEP

•UP•
CUPR
CUPS
DUPE
HUPA
LUPE
PUPA
PUPS
PUPU
RUPP
SUPE
SUPP
SUPR
SUPS
SUPT
TUPI

•U•P
BUMP
BURP
CULP
CUSP
DUMP
GULP
GUMP
HUMP
JUMP
LUMP
MUMP
PULP
PUMP
QUIP
RUMP
RUPP
SUMP
SUPP
TUMP

••UP
COUP
DOUP
GOUP
LOUP
REUP
ROUP
SCUP
SOUP
WHUP

•UQ•
SUQS

UR••
URAL
URBE
URBI
URBS
URDU
UREY
URFA
URGA
URGE
URIM
URIS
URLS
URNS
URSA
URUK
URUS

U••R
UBER
USAR
USER
USNR
USSR
UXOR

•UR•
AURA
AURI
BURB
BURG
BURI
BURL
BURN
BURP
BURR
BURS
BURT
BURY
CURB
CURD
CURE
CURL
CURR
CURS
CURT
DURA
DURN
DURO
EURO
EURY
FURL
FURO
FURS
FURY
GURU
HURL
HURT
JURA
JURE
JURY
KURD
KURT
LURE
LURK
MURK
OURS
PURE
PURL
PURR
SURA
SURD
SURE
SURF
SURG
SURV
TURF
TURK
TURN
YURI
YURT

•U•R
AUER
BUHR
BURR
CUER
CUPR
CURR
GUAR
MUIR
PUER
PURR
QUAR
RUER
RUHR
SUER
SUPR

••UR
AMUR
AZUR
BLUR
CHUR
DOUR
FOUR
GAUR
HOUR
JOUR
KNUR
PLUR
POUR
SAUR
SLUR
SOUR
SPUR
THUR
TOUR
YOUR

US••
USAF
USAR
USCG
USDA
USED
USEE
USER
USES
USGA
USIA
USMA
USMC
USNA
USNR
USPO
USPS
USSR
USTA

U•S•
URSA
USSR

U••S
UDOS
UEYS
UFOS
UGHS
UKES
ULUS
UMPS
UNES
UNIS
UPAS
URBS
URIS
URLS
URNS
URUS
USES
USPS
UTES
UZIS

•US•
AUST
BUSH
BUSK
BUSS
BUST
BUSY
CUSH
CUSK
CUSP
CUSS
DUSE
DUSK
DUST
FUSE
FUSS
FUST
GUSH
GUST
HUSH
HUSK
HUSS
JUST
KUSH
LUSH
LUST
MUSB
MUSD
MUSE
MUSH
MUSK
MUSM
MUSS
MUST
OUSE
OUST
PUSH
PUSS
RUSE
RUSH
RUSK
RUSS
RUST
SUSA
SUSS
TUSH
TUSK
WUSA
WUSS

•U•S
AUKS
BUCS
BUDS
BUGS
BUMS
BUNS
BURS
BUSS
BUTS
BUYS
CUBS
CUDS
CUES
CULS
CUPS
CURS
CUSS
CUTS
DUBS
DUDS
DUES
DUNS
DUOS
FUBS
FUGS
FURS
FUSS
GUIS
GUMS
GUNS
GUTS
GUVS
GUYS
HUBS
HUES
HUGS
HUIS
HUMS
HUNS
HUSS
HUTS
JUGS
JUTS
LUGS
LUIS
LUKS
LUVS
MUDS
MUGS
MUMS
MUSS
NUBS
NUNS
NUTS
NUYS
OUDS
OURS
OUTS
PUBS
PUGS
PUNS
PUPS
PUSS
PUTS
QUES
RUBS
RUES
RUGS
RUMS
RUNS
RUSS
RUTS
SUBS
SUDS
SUES
SUKS
SUMS
SUNS
SUPS
SUQS
SUSS
SUVS
TUBS
TUES
TUGS
TUIS
TUMS
TUNS
TUTS
VUGS
WUSS
YUKS

••US
BMUS
BTUS
CAUS
CRUS
DEUS
ECUS
EMUS
EOUS
ESUS
FLUS
GNUS
GRUS
HAUS
ICUS
IMUS
IOUS
NOUS
ONUS
OPUS
OXUS
PIUS
PLUS
ROUS
SKUS
SOUS
TAUS
THUS
ULUS
URUS
VOUS
ZEUS

UT••
UTAH
UTEP
UTES
UTIL
UTNE

U•T•
UNTO
UPTO
USTA

U••T
UNIT

•UT•
AUTH
AUTO
BUTE
BUTS
BUTT
CUTE
CUTS
DUTY
FUTZ
GUTS
HUTS
HUTT
HUTU
JUTE
JUTS
LUTE
LUTH
LUTZ
MUTE
MUTT
NUTS
NUTT
OUTS
PUTS
PUTT
RUTA
RUTH
RUTS
TUTS
TUTU

•U•T
AUNT
AUST
BUNT
BURT
BUST
BUTT
CUFT
CULT
CURT
DUCT
DUET
DUST
FUNT
FUST
GUST
HUNT
HURT
HUTT
JUST
KURT
LUFT
LUNT
LUST
MUST
MUTT
NUIT
NUTT
OUST
PUNT
PUTT
QUIT
QUOT
RUNT
RUST
SUET
SUIT
SUPT
TUFT
VULT
YURT

••UT
ABUT
AOUT
BOUT
BRUT
CNUT
DEUT
FAUT
GLUT
GOUT
HAUT
KNUT
LOUT
NAUT
NEUT
POUT
PRUT
ROUT
SCUT
SHUT
SMUT
TAUT
TEUT
TNUT
TOUT
XOUT

U•U•
UHUH
ULUS
UNUM
URUK
URUS

U••U
UNAU
URDU

•UU•
SUUM
TUUM

•U•U
BUBU
FUGU
GURU
HUTU
JUJU
KUDU
LUAU
LULU
OULU
PUDU
PUKU
PUPU
SULU
TUFU
TUTU
WUHU
ZULU

UV••
UVEA

U••V
UNIV
UNLV

•UV•
DUVE
GUVS
LUVS
SUVA
SUVS

•U•V
SURV

••UW
DOUW

UX••
UXOR

U••X
UNIX

•UX•
LUXE
WUXI

••UX
BRUX
CRUX
DEUX
DOUX
EAUX
ETUX
FAUX
FLUX
JEUX
ROUX
VAUX
YEUX

U•Y•
UEYS

U••Y
UGLY
UREY

•UY•
BUYS
GUYS
NUYS
PUYI

•U•Y
BUOY
BURY
BUSY
CUNY
DUFY
DULY
DUTY
EURY
FUMY
FURY
HUEY
JUDY
JULY
JURY
LUCY
PUNY
QUAY
RUBY
RUDY
SUEY
SUNY
SUZY

UZ••
UZIS

•UZ•
BUZZ
FUZE
FUZZ
MUZZ
OUZO
PUZO
SUZI
SUZY

•U•Z
BUZZ
FUTZ
FUZZ
LUTZ
MUZZ
QUIZ
SUEZ

••UZ
CRUZ

VA••
VAAL
VACA
VACS
VADE
VADM
VAIL
VAIN
VAIR
VALE
VAMP
VANE
VANG
VANS
VARA
VARY
VASE
VAST
VATS
VATU
VAUD
VAUX
VAVS
VAYA

V•A•
VAAL
VDAY
VEAL
VEAU
VIAL
VRAI

V••A
VACA
VARA
VAYA
VEDA
VEGA
VELA
VENA
VERA
VIDA
VIGA
VILA
VINA
VISA
VITA
VIVA

•VA•
AVAL
AVAR
EVAH
EVAN
EVAP
IVAN
OVAL

•V•A
AVIA
TVMA
UVEA

••VA
ALVA
BOVA
CAVA
DEVA
DIVA
FAVA
JAVA
KAVA
KIVA
LAVA
NEVA
NOVA
SAVA
SUVA
VIVA

V•B•
VIBE

V••B
VERB

VC••
VCRS

V•C•
VACA
VACS
VICE
VICI
VICO
VOCE

•V•C
AVEC

VD••
VDAY
VDTS

V•D•
VADE
VADM
VEDA
VIDA
VIDE
VIDI

V••D
VAUD
VELD
VEND
VERD
VIED
VOID

•VD•
AVDP
BVDS
DVDS

•V•D
AVID
OVID

••VD
BLVD
NKVD

VE••
VEAL
VEAU
VEDA
VEEP
VEER
VEES
VEGA
VEII
VEIL
VEIN
VELA
VELD
VENA
VEND
VENI
VENN
VENT
VERA
VERB
VERD
VERE
VERN
VERO
VERS
VERT
VERY
VEST
VETO
VETS

V•E•
VEEP
VEER
VEES
VIED
VIER
VIES
VIET
VIEW

V••E
VADE
VALE
VANE
VASE
VERE
VIBE
VICE
VIDE
VILE
VINE
VISE
VITE
VIVE
VOCE
VOLE
VOTE

•VE•
AVEC
AVER
AVES
EVEL
EVEN
EVER
EVES
IVES
IVEY
OVEN
OVER
SVEN
UVEA
YVES

•V•E
EVOE

••VE
CAVE
COVE
DAVE
DIVE
DOVE

DUVE	VIET	**•V•I**	**V••M**	VETO	AVER	VAVS	**V•W•**	WALL	TWAS	WELD	WIEN	**W••F**	WISH
EAVE	VIEW	CVII	VADM	VICO	EVER		VOWS	WALT		WEND	WOES	WAAF	WITH
FAVE	VIGA	DVII	VOOM	VIGO	IVOR	**VT••**		WAND	**•W•A**	WHOD	WREN	WAIF	WYCH
FIVE	VIGO	LVII		VINO	OVER	VTOL	**V••W**	WANE	YWCA	WILD	WYES	WOLF	
GAVE	VIII	MVII	**•VM•**	VITO			VIEW	WANG		WIND		WOOF	**•WH•**
GIVE	VILA	XVII	DVMS		**VS••**	**V•T•**		WANT	**••WA**	WOAD	**W••E**	WRAF	KWHR
GYVE	VILE		TVMA	**•VO•**	VSIX	VATS	**•V•W**	WANY	AIWA	WOLD	WACE		
HAVE	VIMS	**••VI**		AVON	VSOP	VATU	AVOW	WARD	BIWA	WOOD	WADE	**••WF**	**WI••**
HIVE	VINA	CCVI	**•V•M**	AVOS		VDTS		WARE	IOWA	WORD	WAGE	NEWF	WICK
HOVE	VINE	CDVI	OVUM	AVOW	**V•S•**	VETO	**V••X**	WARM	TEWA		WAKE		WIDE
JIVE	VING	CLVI		EVOE	VASE	VETS	VAUX	WARN	TIWA	**•W•D**	WALE	**W•G•**	WIEN
JOVE	VINI	CMVI	**V•N•**	IVOR	VAST	VITA	VOIX	WARP	WAWA	AWED	WANE	WAGE	WIFE
LAVE	VINO	CXVI	VANE	LVOV	VEST	VITE	VSIX	WARS		OWED	WARE	WAGS	WIGS
LIVE	VINS	DCVI	VANG		VISA	VITI		WART	**W•B•**	SWED	WAVE	WIGS	WILD
LOVE	VINY	DEVI	VANS	**••VO**	VISE	VITO	**V•Y•**	WARY	WABS	TWOD	WERE		WILE
MOVE	VIOL	DLVI	VENA	DEVO		VOTE	VAYA	WASH	WEBB		WEVE	**W••G**	WILL
NAVE	VIPS	DXVI	VEND	LEVO	**V••S**			WASP	WEBS	**••WD**	WHEE	WANG	WILT
NEVE	VISA	LEVI	VENI	NOVO	VACS	**V••T**	**V••Y**	WAST		DOWD	WHSE	WENG	WILY
PAVE	VISE	LXVI	VENN	PAVO	VANS	VAST	VARY	WATS	**W••B**	LEWD	WIDE	WHIG	WIMP
RAVE	VITA	MCVI	VENT		VATS	VENT	VDAY	WATT	WEBB		WIFE	WING	WIND
REVE	VITE	MDVI	VINA	**V•P•**	VAVS	VERT	VERY	WAVE	WEEB	**WE••**	WILE	WONG	WINE
RIVE	VITI	MLVI	VINE	VIPS	VCRS	VEST	VINY	WAVY		WEAK	WINE		WING
ROVE	VITO	MMVI	VING		VDTS	VIET		WAWA	**•WB•**	WEAL	WIPE	**•W•G**	WINK
SAVE	VIVA	MXVI	VINI	**V••P**	VEES	VOLT	**•V•Y**	WAWS	NWBN	WEAN	WIRE	SWAG	WINS
SEVE	VIVE	NEVI	VINO	VAMP	VERS	VULT	IVEY	WAXY	NWBW	WEAR	WISE	SWIG	WINY
VIVE		RAVI	VINS	VEEP	VETS			WAYS	SWBS	WEBB	WITE	TWIG	WIPE
WAVE	**V•I•**	TAVI	VINY	VSOP	VIES	**•VT•**	**••VY**		SWBW	WEBS	WOKE		WIRE
WEVE	VAIL	XCVI			VIMS	PVTS	BEVY	**W•A•**		WEDS	WOLE	**••WG**	WIRY
WOVE	VAIN	XLVI	**V••N**	**•VP•**	VINS		CAVY	WAAC	**•W•B**	WEEB	WORE	DAWG	WISC
	VAIR	XXVI	VAIN	TVPG	VIPS	**••VT**	DAVY	WAAF	SWAB	WEED	WOVE	HAWG	WISE
V•G•	VEII		VEIN		VOLS	ADVT	ENVY	WAAL	SWOB	WEEK			WISH
VEGA	VEIL	**V•L•**	VENN	**•V•P**	VOUS	GOVT	JIVY	WEAK		WEEN	**•WE•**	**WH••**	WISK
VIGA	VEIN	VALE	VERN	AVDP	VOWS		LEVY	WEAL	**WC••**	WEEP	AWED	WHAM	WISP
VIGO	VIII	VELA		EVAP	VUGS	**VU••**	LIVY	WEAN	WCTU	WEFT	AWES	WHAT	WITE
VUGS	VOID	VELD	**•V•N**			VUGS	NAVY	WEAR		WEIL	EWEN	WHEE	WITH
	VOIR	VILA	AVON	**••VP**	**•V•S**	VULG	WAVY	WHAM	**W•C•**	WEIR	EWER	WHEN	WITS
V••G	VOIX	VILE	EVAN	RSVP	AVES	VULT		WHAT	WACE	WEKA	EWES	WHET	WITT
VANG	VSIX	VOLE	EVEN		AVGS		**WA••**	WOAD	WACK	WELD	GWEN	WHEW	
VING		VOLS	IVAN	**VR••**	AVIS	**V•U•**	WAAC	WRAC	WACO	WELK	OWED	WHEY	**W•I•**
VULG	**V••I**	VOLT	OVEN	VRAI	AVOS	VAUD	WAAF	WRAF	WACS	WELL	OWEN	WHIG	WAIF
	VEII	VULG	SVEN		BVDS	VAUX	WAAL	WRAP	WICK	WELT	OWER	WHIM	WAIL
•VG•	VENI	VULT		**V•R•**	DVDS	VOUS	WABS	WRAY	WYCH	WEND	OWES	WHIN	WAIN
AVGS	VICI		**VO••**	VARA	DVMS		WACE			WENG	SWED	WHIP	WAIT
SVGS	VIDI	**V••L**	VOCE	VARY	EVES	**V••U**	WACK	**W••A**	**W••C**	WENS	TWEE	WHIR	WEIL
	VIII	VAAL	VOID	VCRS	IVES	VATU	WACO	WAKA	WAAC	WENT	ZWEI	WHIT	WEIR
•V•G	VINI	VAIL	VOIR	VERA	OVIS	VEAU	WACS	WAWA	WISC	WEPT		WHIZ	WHIG
TVPG	VITI	VEAL	VOIX	VERB	PVTS		WADE	WEKA	WRAC	WERE	**•W•E**	WHOA	WHIM
	VRAI	VEIL	VOLE	VERD	SVGS	**•VU•**	WADI	WHOA		WERT	TWEE	WHOD	WHIN
•V•H		VIAL	VOLS	VERE	YVES	OVUM	WADS	WUSA	**•WC•**	WEST		WHOM	WHIP
EVAH	**•VI•**	VIOL	VOLT	VERN			WAFS		YWCA	WETS	**••WE**	WHOP	WHIR
	AVIA	VTOL	VOOM	VERO	**••VS**	**••VU**	WAFT	**•WA•**		WEVE	BOWE	WHOS	WHIT
VI••	AVID		VOTE	VERS	ATVS	KIVU	WAGE	AWAY	**W•D•**		HDWE	WHSE	WHIZ
VIAL	AVIS	**•V•L**	VOUS	VERT	CAVS	LEVU	WAGS	DWAN	WADE	**W•E•**	HOWE	WHUP	WRIT
VIBE	AVIV	AVAL	VOWS	VERY	DIVS		WAHL	KWAI	WADI	WEEB	LOWE	WHYS	WWII
VICE	CVII	EVEL			ENVS	**V•V•**	WAIF	KWAN	WADS	WEED	ROWE		
VICI	DVII	EVIL	**V•O•**	**V••R**	GUVS	VAVS	WAIL	SWAB	WEDS	WEEK		**W•H•**	**W••I**
VICO	EVIL	OVAL	VIOL	VAIR	LAVS	VIVA	WAIN	SWAG	WIDE	WEEN	**W•F•**	WAHL	WADI
VIDA	LVII		VOOM	VEER	LUVS	VIVE	WAIT	SWAK		WEEP	WAFS	WOHL	WUXI
VIDE	MVII	**V•M•**	VSOP	VIER	MAVS		WAKA	SWAM	**W••D**	WHEE	WAFT	WUHL	WWII
VIDI	OVID	VAMP	VTOL	VOIR	ORVS	**•V•V**	WAKE	SWAN	WALD	WHEN	WEFT	WUHU	
VIED	OVIS	VIMS			REVS	AVIV	WALD	SWAP	WAND	WHET	WIFE		**•WI•**
VIER	XVII		**V••O**	**•V•R**	SUVS	LVOV	WALE	SWAT	WARD	WHEW		**W••H**	FWIW
VIES			VERO	AVAR	TIVS		WALK	SWAY	WEED	WHEY		WASH	IWIS

SWIG
SWIM
SWIT
TWIG
TWIN
TWIT
TWIX
WWII

•W•I
KWAI
WWII
ZWEI

••WI
IIWI
KIWI

WK••
WKLY
WKRP

W•K•
WAKA
WAKE
WEKA
WOKE
WOKS

W••K
WACK
WALK
WEAK
WEEK
WELK
WICK
WINK
WISK
WONK
WORK
WOUK

•W•K
EWOK
SWAK

••WK
GAWK
GOWK
HAWK

W•L•
WALD
WALE
WALK
WALL
WALT
WELD
WELK
WELL
WELT
WILD
WILE
WILL
WILT
WILY
WKLY
WOLD
WOLE
WOLF

W••L
WAAL
WAHL
WAIL
WALL
WEAL
WEIL
WELL
WILL
WOHL
WOOL
WUHL

•WL•
AWLS
OWLS

•W•L
AWOL

••WL
BAWL
BOWL
COWL
FOWL
HOWL
JOWL
MEWL
PAWL
YAWL
YOWL

W•M•
WIMP

W••M
WARM
WHAM
WHIM
WHOM
WORM

•WM•
CWMS

•W•M
SWAM
SWIM
SWUM

W•N•
WAND
WANE
WANG
WANT
WANY
WEND
WENG
WENS
WENT
WIND
WINE
WING
WINK
WINS
WINY
WONG
WONK
WONS
WONT
WRNS
WYNN

W••N
WAIN
WARN
WEAN
WEEN
WHEN
WHIN
WIEN
WORN
WREN
WYNN

•WN•
AWNS
OWNS

•W•N
DWAN
EWEN
GWEN
GWYN
KWAN
KWON
NWBN
OWEN
SWAN
TWIN

••WN
DAWN
DOWN
FAWN
GOWN
HAWN
HEWN
LAWN
MOWN
PAWN
SAWN
SEWN
SOWN
TOWN
YAWN

WO••
WOAD
WOES
WOHL
WOKE
WOKS
WOLD
WOLE
WOLF
WONG
WONK
WONS
WONT
WOOD
WOOF
WOOL
WOOS
WORD
WORE
WORK
WORM
WORN
WORT
WOUK
WOVE
WOWS

W•O•
WHOA
WHOD
WHOM
WHOP
WHOS
WOOD
WOOF
WOOL
WOOS

W••O
WACO

•WO•
AWOL
CWOS
EWOK
KWON
SWOB
SWOP
TWOD
TWOS

W•P•
WEPT
WIPE

W••P
WARP
WASP
WEEP
WHIP
WHOP
WHUP
WIMP
WISP
WKRP
WRAP

•WP•
TWPS

•W•P
SWAP
SWOP

••WP
GAWP
YAWP

WR••
WRAC
WRAF
WRAP
WRAY
WREN
WRIT
WRNS

W•R•
WARD
WARE
WARM
WARN
WARP
WARS
WART
WARY
WERE
WERT
WIRE
WIRY
WKRP
WORD
WORE
WORK
WORM
WORN
WORT

W••R
WEAR
WEIR
WHIR

•WR•
AWRY
EWRY

•W•R
EWER
KWHR
OWER

••WR
MAWR

W•S•
WASH
WASP
WAST
WEST
WHSE
WISC
WISE
WISH
WISK
WISP
WUSA
WUSS
WYSS

W••S
WABS
WACS
WADS
WAFS
WAGS
WARS
WATS
WAWS
WAYS
WEBS
WEDS
WENS
WETS
WHOS
WHYS
WIGS
WINS
WITS
WOES
WOKS
WONS
WOOS
WOWS
WRNS
WUSS
WYES
WYSS

•W•S
AWES
AWLS
AWNS
CWMS
CWOS
EWES
HWYS
IWIS
OWES
OWLS
OWNS
SWBS
TWAS
TWOS
TWPS

••WS
BMWS
BOWS
CAWS
COWS
DAWS
DEWS
HAWS
HEWS
HOWS
JAWS
JEWS
LAWS
LOWS
MAWS
MEWS
MOWS
NEWS
PAWS
PEWS
POWS
ROWS
SAWS
SEWS
SOWS
TAWS
TOWS
VOWS
WAWS
WOWS
YAWS
YEWS

W•T•
WATS
WATT
WCTU
WETS
WITE
WITH
WITS
WITT

W••T
WAFT
WAIT
WALT
WANT
WART
WAST
WATT
WEFT
WELT
WENT
WEPT
WERT
WEST
WHAT
WHET
WHIT
WILT
WITT
WONT
WORT
WRIT

•WT•
GWTW

•W•T
SWAT
SWIT
TWIT

••WT
ATWT
GRWT
NEWT
NTWT

WU••
WUHL
WUHU
WUSA
WUSS
WUXI

W•U•
WHUP
WOUK

W••U
WCTU
WUHU

•WU•
SWUM

W•V•
WAVE
WAVY
WEVE
WOVE

WW••
WWII

W•W•
WAWA
WAWS
WOWS

W••W
WHEW

•W•W
FWIW
GWTW
NWBW
SWBW

W•X•
WAXY
WUXI

•W•X
TWIX

WY••
WYCH
WYES
WYNN
WYSS

W•Y•
WAYS
WHYS

W••Y
WANY
WARY
WAVY
WAXY
WHEY
WILY
WINY
WIRY
WKLY
WRAY

•WY•
GWYN
HWYS

•W•Y
AWAY
AWRY
EWRY
SWAY

••WY
DEWY
HGWY
PKWY

W••Z
WHIZ

XA••
XATS

X•A•
XIAN
XMAS
XRAY

X••A
XENA

•XA•
EXAM

•X•A
IXIA

••XA
COXA
HEXA
TAXA

XC••
XCII
XCIV
XCIX
XCVI

•XC•
CXCI
CXCV
DXCI
DXCV
EXCH
EXCL
MXCI
MXCV

•X•C
EXEC

••XC
CCXC
CDXC
CMXC
DCXC
MCXC
MDXC
MMXC

XD••
XDIN
XDIV

•X•D
AXED
EXOD

XE••
XENA
XENO
XERO

X•E•
XMEN

X••E
XIPE

•XE•
AXED
AXEL
AXER
AXES
EXEC
EXES
OXEN

•X•E
AXLE

••XE
FIXE
FOXE
LUXE
SAXE

X••G
XING

•X•H
EXCH

XI••
XIAN
XIII
XING
XIPE

X•I•
XCII
XCIV
XCIX
XDIN
XDIV
XIII
XLII
XLIV
XLIX
XVII
XXII
XXIV
XXIX

X••I
XCII
XCVI
XIII
XLII
XLVI
XVII
XXII
XXVI
XXXI

•XI•
AXIL
AXIS
CXII
CXIV
CXIX
DXII
DXIV
DXIX
EXIT
IXIA
LXII
LXIV
LXIX
MXII
MXIV
MXIX
XXII
XXIV
XXIX

•X•I
CXCI
CXII
CXLI
CXVI
CXXI
DXCI
DXII
DXLI
DXVI
DXXI
LXII
LXVI
LXXI
MXCI
MXII
MXLI
MXVI
MXXI
XXII
XXVI
XXXI

••XI
CCXI
CDXI
CLXI
CMXI
CXXI
DCXI
DLXI
DXXI
LXXI
MAXI
MCXI
MDXI
MLXI
MMXI
MXXI
TAXI
WUXI
XXXI

XL••
XLII
XLIV
XLIX
XLVI

X•L•
XYLO

•XL•
AXLE
CXLI
CXLV
DXLI
DXLV
MXLI
MXLV

•X•L
AXEL
AXIL
EXCL

••XL
CCXL
CDXL
CMXL
DCXL
MCXL
MDXL
MMXL

XM••
XMAS
XMEN

•X•M
AXUM
EXAM

X•N•
XENA
XENO
XING

X••N
XDIN
XIAN
XMEN

•X•N
AXON
EXON
OXEN
OXON

XO••
XOUT

X••O
XENO
XERO
XYLO

•XO•
AXON
EXOD
EXON
EXOR
OXON
UXOR

•X•O
EXPO

••XO
MYXO
TAXO

X•P•
XIPE

•XP•
EXPO
EXPT

XR••
XRAY

X•R•
XERO

•X•R
AXER
EXOR
UXOR

X••S
XATS
XMAS

•X•S
AXES
AXIS
EXES
EXTS
OXUS

••XS
INXS

X•T•
XATS

X••T
XOUT

•XT•
EXTS

•X•T
EXIT
EXPT

••XT
MIXT
NEXT
SEXT
TEXT

X•U•
XOUT

•XU•
AXUM
OXUS

XV••
XVII

X•V•
XCVI
XLVI
XXVI

X••V
XCIV
XDIV
XLIV

XXIV XXXV

•XV•
CXVI DXVI LXVI MXVI XXVI

•X•V
CXCV CXIV CXLV CXXV DXCV DXIV DXLV DXXV LXIV LXXV MXCV MXIV MXLV MXXV XXIV XXXV

••XV
CCXV CDXV CLXV CMXV CXXV DCXV DLXV DXXV LXXV MCXV MDXV MLXV MMXV MXXV XXXV

XX••
XXII XXIV XXIX XXVI XXXI XXXV XXXX

X•X•
XXXI XXXV XXXX

X••X
XCIX XLIX XXIX XXXX

•XX•
CXXI CXXV CXXX DXXI DXXV DXXX LXXI LXXV LXXX MXXI MXXV MXXX XXXI XXXV XXXX

•X•X
CXIX CXXX DXIX DXXX LXIX LXXX MXIX MXXX XXIX XXXX

••XX
CCXX CDXX CLXX CMXX CXXX DCXX DLXX DXXX FOXX LXXX MCXX MDXX MLXX MMXX MXXX XXXX

XY••
XYLO

X••Y
XRAY

••XY
BOXY FOXY PIXY SEXY WAXY

YA••
YACK YADA YAGI YAKS YALE YALL YALU YAMA YAMS YANA YANG YANK YAOS YAPP YAPS YARD YARE YARN YAWL YAWN YAWP YAWS YAZD

Y•A•
YEAH YEAN YEAR YEAS YUAN

Y••A
YADA YAMA YANA YIMA YMCA YODA YOGA YUBA YUGA YUMA YWCA

•YA•
AYAH CYAN DYAD DYAK DYAN EYAS IYAR KYAT RYAL RYAN RYAS

•Y•A
AYLA CYMA DYNA EYRA HYLA KYRA LYRA MYNA MYRA

••YA
ANYA BAYA ENYA GAYA GOYA HOYA MAYA SOYA VAYA

Y•B•
YOBS YUBA

•YB•
GYBE

•Y•B
BYOB MYOB

Y•C•
YACK YECH YMCA YUCK YWCA

•YC•
CYCL DYCE DYCK EYCK MYCO SYCE WYCH

•Y•C
SYNC

••YC
GLYC

Y•D•
YADA YEDO YODA YODH YODS

Y••D
YARD YAZD YOND YOUD

•YD•
HYDE HYDR

•Y•D
BYRD DYAD DYED EYED SYND

••YD
BOYD SQYD

YE••
YEAH YEAN YEAR YEAS YECH YEDO YEGG YELL YELP YENS YERK YETI YEUX YEWS

Y•E•
YLEM YSER YVES

Y••E
YALE YARE YIPE YOKE YORE YULE

•YE•
AYER AYES BYES DYED DYER DYES EYED EYER EYES HYER KYES LYES NYET OYER OYEZ RYES WYES

•Y•E
AYME BYME BYRE BYTE CYME CYTE DYCE DYNE EYRE FYKE GYBE GYRE GYVE HYDE HYPE KYLE LYLE LYNE LYRE NYSE PYLE PYRE RYLE RYNE SYCE SYNE TYKE TYNE TYPE TYRE

••YE
ABYE FAYE FRYE GAYE JAYE KAYE RAYE SKYE SLYE

Y•G•
YAGI YEGG YOGA YOGH YOGI YUGA YUGO

Y••G
YANG YEGG

•YG•
ZYGO

•Y•G
BYNG

Y•H•
YOHO

Y••H
YEAH YECH YODH YOGH

•Y•H
AYAH MYTH WYCH

YI••
YIMA YIPE YIPS

Y•I•
YMIR

Y••I
YAGI YETI YOGI YURI

•YI•
AYIN LYIN

•Y•I
GYRI

••YI
MAYI PUYI

Y•K•
YAKS YOKE YOKO YUKS

Y••K
YACK YANK YERK YOLK YORK YUCK

•YK•
FYKE TYKE

•Y•K
DYAK DYCK EYCK NYUK

YL••
YLEM

Y•L•
YALE YALL YALU YELL YELP YOLK YULE

Y••L
YALL YAWL YELL YOWL

•YL•
AYLA HYLA KYLE LYLE LYLY PYLE RYLE SYLL SYLS XYLO

•Y•L
CYCL RYAL SYLL

••YL
ACYL AMYL ARYL IDYL

YM••
YMCA YMIR

Y•M•
YAMA YAMS YIMA YUMA

Y••M
YLEM

•YM•
AYME BYME CYMA CYME GYMS HYMN MYMY SYMS TYMP ZYMO

••YM
ETYM ONYM

Y•N•
YANA YANG YANK YENS YOND

Y••N
YARN YAWN YEAN YUAN

•YN•
BYNG DYNA DYNE GYNT LYNE LYNN LYNX MYNA RYNE SYNC SYND SYNE SYNS TYNE WYNN

•Y•N
AYIN CYAN DYAN HYMN HYPN LYIN LYNN LYON RYAN RYUN WYNN

••YN
BRYN GLYN GWYN

YO••
YOBS YODA YODH YODS YOGA YOGH YOGI YOHO YOKE YOKO YOLK YOND YORE YORK YOST YOUD YOUR YOWL YOYO

Y•O•
YAOS

Y••O
YEDO YOHO YOKO YOYO YUGO

•YO•
BYOB EYOT GYOR LYON MYOB RYOT

•Y•O
CYTO GYRO HYPO MYCO MYXO NYRO PYRO TYPO TYRO XYLO ZYGO ZYMO

••YO
BOYO BRYO CRYO DAYO ENYO HIYO KAYO MAYO YOYO

Y•P•
YAPP YAPS YIPE YIPS

Y••P
YAPP YAWP YELP

•YP•
GYPS HYPE HYPN HYPO TYPE TYPO TYPY

•Y•P
TYMP

Y•R•
YARD YARE YARN YERK YORE YORK YURI YURT

Y••R
YEAR YMIR YOUR YSER

•YR•
BYRD BYRE EYRA EYRE EYRY GYRE GYRI GYRO KYRA LYRA LYRE MYRA NYRO PYRE PYRO TYRE TYRO

•Y•R
AYER DYER EYER GYOR HYDR HYER IYAR OYER

••YR
LTYR

YS••
YSER

Y•S•
YOST

Y••S
YAKS YAMS YAOS YAPS YAWS YEAS YENS YEWS YIPS YOBS YODS YUKS YVES

•YS•
MYST NYSE SYST WYSS

•Y•S
AYES BYES DYES EYAS EYES GYMS GYPS KYES LYES RYAS RYES SYLS SYMS SYNS WYES WYSS

••YS
ABYS BAYS BEYS BOYS BUYS CAYS DAYS DEYS DRYS FAYS FOYS GUYS HAYS HOYS HWYS JAYS JOYS KEYS LAYS MAYS NAYS NUYS PAYS PHYS RAYS REYS RHYS SAYS SKYS SOYS TOYS UEYS WAYS WHYS

Y•T•
YETI

Y••T
YOST YURT

•YT•
BYTE CYTE CYTO MYTH

•Y•T
EYOT GYNT KYAT MYST NYET RYOT SYST

••YT
FOYT HOYT PAYT

YU••
YUAN YUBA YUCK YUGA YUGO YUKS YULE YUMA YURI YURT

Y•U•
YEUX YOUD YOUR

Y••U
YALU

•YU•
NYUK RYUN

YV••
YVES

•YV•
GYVE

YW••
YWCA

Y•W•
YAWL YAWN YAWP YAWS YEWS YOWL

Y••X
YEUX

•YX•
MYXO

•Y•X
LYNX

••YX
ONYX ORYX STYX

Y•Y•
YOYO

•Y•Y
EYRY LYLY MYMY TYPY

Y•Z•
YAZD

•Y•Z
OYEZ

••YZ
BOYZ

ZA••
ZACK ZAGS ZAHN ZALS

ZAMA	IZBA	Z•D•	Z•E•	Z••F	ZING	Z••K	Z•N•	ZOIC	ZIBO	ZORI	ZIGS	ZHOU	DOZY
ZANE		ZEDS	ZEES	ZARF	ZION	ZACK	ZANE	ZOLA	ZYGO	ZORN	ZIPS	ZULU	HAZY
ZANY	••ZA		ZOEA		ZIPS	ZONK	ZANY	ZONA	ZYMO		ZOOS		IZZY
ZAPS	ANZA	Z••D	ZWEI	Z•G•	ZITI	ZOUK	ZEND	ZONE		Z••R		•ZU•	LAZY
ZARF	GAZA	ZEND		ZAGS			ZENO	ZONK	•ZO•	ZBAR	•Z•S	AZUL	MAZY
ZASU	GIZA		Z••E	ZIGS	Z•I•	•Z•K	ZINC	ZOOL	AZOV	ZOAR	UZIS	AZUR	OOZY
	ITZA	•Z•D	ZANE	ZOGI	ZEIN	EZEK	ZINE	ZOOM	IZOD				OZZY
Z•A•	LIZA	IZOD	ZEKE	ZYGO	ZOIC		ZING	ZOON		•ZR•	Z•T•	•Z•V	SUZY
ZBAR	REZA		ZINE			Z•L•	ZONA	ZOOS	•Z•O	EZRA	ZETA	AZOV	
ZEAL		••ZD	ZONE	Z••G	Z••I	ZALS	ZONE	ZOOT	EZIO		ZITI	OZAV	Z••Z
ZOAR	ZB••	YAZD		ZING	ZITI	ZILL	ZONK	ZORI		•Z•R	ZOTZ		ZOTZ
	ZBAR		•ZE•		ZOGI	ZOLA	ZUNI	ZORN	••ZO	AZUR		ZW••	
Z••A		ZE••	EZEK	ZH••	ZORI	ZULU		ZOTZ	BOZO	CZAR	Z••T	ZWEI	•ZZ•
ZAMA	Z•B•	ZEAL		ZHOU	ZUNI		Z••N	ZOUK	ENZO	IZAR	ZEST		IZZY
ZETA	ZEBU	ZEBU	••ZE		ZWEI	Z••L	ZAHN		MAZO	TZAR	ZOOT	ZY••	OZZY
ZOEA	ZIBO	ZECH	ADZE	Z•H•		ZEAL	ZEIN	Z•O•	ORZO			ZYGO	
ZOLA		ZEDS	DAZE	ZAHN	•ZI•	ZILL	ZION	ZHOU	OUZO	Z•S•	ZU••	ZYMO	•Z•Z
ZONA	•ZB•	ZEES	DOZE		AZIZ	ZOOL	ZOON	ZION	PUZO	ZASU	ZULU		AZIZ
	IZBA	ZEIN	FAZE	Z••H	EZIO		ZORN	ZOOL		ZEST	ZUNI	Z••Y	
•ZA•		ZEKE	FUZE	ZECH	UZIS	•Z•L		ZOOM	Z•P•			ZANY	••ZZ
AZAN	Z•C•	ZEND	GAZE	ZEPH		AZUL	•Z•N	ZOON	ZAPS	Z••S	Z•U•		BUZZ
CZAR	ZACK	ZENO	HAZE		••ZI		AZAN	ZOOS	ZEPH	ZAGS	ZEUS	•Z•Y	FIZZ
IZAR	ZECH	ZEPH	LAZE	ZI••	SUZI	Z•M•		ZOOT	ZIPS	ZALS	ZOUK	IZZY	FUZZ
OZAV		ZERO	MAZE	ZIBO		ZAMA	ZO••			ZAPS		OZZY	JAZZ
TZAR	Z••C	ZEST	OOZE	ZIGS	Z•K•	ZYMO	ZOAR	Z••O	Z•R•	ZEDS	Z••U		MUZZ
	ZINC	ZETA	RAZE	ZILL	ZEKE		ZOEA	ZENO	ZARF	ZEES	ZASU	••ZY	PIZZ
•Z•A	ZOIC	ZEUS	SIZE	ZINC		Z••M	ZOGI	ZERO	ZERO	ZEUS	ZEBU	COZY	RAZZ
EZRA				ZINE		ZOOM							

5

AA•••
AAHED
AAIUN
AALII
AALTO
AAMES
AANDE
AANDM
AARGH
AARON

A•A••
ABABA
ABACA
ABACI
ABACK
ABACO
ABAFT
ABASE
ABASH
ABATE
ABAYA
ACADS
ACARI
ADAGE
ADAIR
ADAMA
ADAMS
ADANA
ADANO
ADAPT
AEAEA
AFAIK
AFARS
AGAIN
AGALS
AGAMA
AGANA
AGAPE
AGARN
AGARS
AGASP
AGATE
AGAVE
AGAZE
ALACK
ALAIN
ALAMO
ALANA
ALAND
ALARM
ALATE
ALAVA
AMADO
AMAHL
AMAHS
AMAIN
AMANA
AMAPA
AMARA
AMASS
AMATI
AMATO
AMAZE
ANAIS
APACE
APART
AQABA
ARABS
ARABY
ARAMA
ARAME
ASAMA
ASANA
ATALL
ATARI
AVAIL
AVANT
AVARS
AVAST
AWACS
AWAIT
AWAJI
AWAKE
AWARD
AWARE
AWASH
AYAHS
AZANS

A••A•
ABBAS
ABEAM
ABRAM
ACTAS
ADDAX
ADLAI
ADMAN
ADVAL
AETAT
AFLAT
AGHAS
AHEAD
AHMAD
AIDAN
AIMAT
AKBAR
AKKAD
ALBAN
ALCAN
ALDAN
ALFAS
ALGAE
ALGAL
ALIAS
ALLAH
ALLAN
ALLAY
ALMAY
ALTAI
ALTAR
ALVAR
AMMAN
AMPAS
AMWAY
ANEAR
ANNAL
ANNAM
ANNAN
ANOAS
ANSAE
ANTAE
ANTAL
ANTAS
ANWAR
ANZAC
AODAI
AOKAY
APEAK
APIAN
APPAL
AQUAE
AQUAS
AREAL
AREAR
AREAS
ARHAT
ARIAN
ARIAS
ARNAZ
AROAR
ARPAD
ARRAN
ARRAS
ARRAU
ARRAY
ARTAL
ARYAN
ASCAP
ASIAN
ASSAD
ASSAI
ASSAM
ASSAY
ASWAN
ATBAT
ATBAY
ATEAM
ATLAS
ATMAN
ATPAR
ATTAR
ATWAR
AURAE
AURAL
AURAR
AURAS
AVGAS
AVIAN
AXIAL

A•••A
ABABA
ABACA
ABAYA
ABUJA
ACCRA
ACOMA
ACURA
ADAMA
ADANA
ADELA
ADUWA
ADYTA
AEAEA
AECIA
AETNA
AFTRA
AGAMA
AGANA
AGENA
AGITA
AGORA
AHORA
AISHA
AKELA
AKIRA
AKITA
ALANA
ALAVA
ALCOA
ALETA
ALIDA
ALOHA
ALPHA
ALULA
AMANA
AMAPA
AMARA
AMEBA
AMIGA
AMNIA
ANIMA
ANITA
ANTRA
AORTA
APNEA
AQABA
ARAMA
ARECA
ARENA
ARICA
AROMA
ARUBA
ASAMA
ASANA
ASOKA
ASPCA
ASTRA
ASYLA
ATRIA
ATSEA
AUDRA
AVENA
AVILA
AZUSA

•AA••
BAAED
BAALS
KAABA
NAACP
PAAVO
SAABS
WAAFS
WAALS

•A•A•
BABAR
BABAS
BAHAI
BALAS
BANAL
BANAT
BARAB
BASAL
BATAK
BAYAR
CABAL
CACAO
CAMAY
CANAD
CANAL
CARAT
CASAS
CAVAE
DAKAR
DALAI
DAMAN
DAMAR
DANAE
DAVAO
DAYAK
DAYAN
EAGAN
EATAT
FARAD
FARAH
FATAL
GALAH
GALAS
GALAX
GAMAL
GAMAY
GAYAL
HADAR
HADAT
HAGAR
HAHAS
HALAS
HAMAL
HAMAN
HARAR
HASAT
HAZAN
JAMAL
JAPAN
JAVAS
KADAR
KAKAS
KARAN
KARAT
KAUAI
KAVAS
KAYAK
KAZAK
KAZAN
LABAN
LAGAN
LAHAR
LALAW
LAMAR
LAMAS
LANAI
LAPAZ
LARAM
LARAS
LAVAL
LAVAS
LAZAR
MACAO
MACAW
MADAM
MAHAL
MAHAN
MALAN
MALAR
MALAY
MAMAS
MARAS
MARAT
MASAI
MAYAN
MAYAS
NAIAD
NANAK
NANAS
NARAS
NASAL
NATAL
NAVAL
NAWAB
PACAS
PAEAN
PAGAN
PALAE
PALAU
PANAM
PANAY
PAPAL
PAPAS
PAPAW
PAWAT
QATAR
RABAT
RADAR
RAGAS
RAHAB
RAHAL
RAJAH
RAJAS
RAMAN
RAMAR
RANAT
SABAH
SADAT
SAGAL
SAGAN
SAGAS
SAJAK
SAKAI
SALAD
SALAL
SALAM
SAMAR
SANAA
SARAH
SARAN
SATAN
TAKAS
TAPAS
TATAR
VARAS

•A••A
BABKA
BAHIA
BAIZA
BALSA
BANDA
BARCA
BASRA
CALLA
CANEA
CANNA
CAPRA
CARIA
CARLA
CARTA
CASCA
CAUSA
DACCA
DACHA
DACIA
DAIWA
DANZA
DARLA
DARYA
FACIA
FALLA
FANTA
FATHA
FATWA
FAUNA
GALBA
GALEA
GAMBA
GAMMA
GARDA
HABLA
HAEMA
HAIDA
HAIFA
HANNA
HANSA
HASTA
HAUSA
JABBA
JAFFA
KAABA
KAFKA
KANGA
KANSA
KAPPA
KARLA
KARMA
KASHA
LAIKA
LAMIA
LANKA
LANZA
LARVA

LAURA
LAYLA
MAGDA
MAGMA
MAGNA
MAKUA
MALTA
MAMBA
MAMMA
MANIA
MANNA
MANTA
MARIA
MARLA
MARTA
MAUNA
MAZDA
NADIA
NADJA
NAFTA
NAHUA
NAINA
NAIRA
NAMPA
NANNA
PADUA
PAISA
PALEA
PALMA
PAMPA
PANDA
PANGA
PANZA
PAPUA
PARCA
PARKA
PARMA
PASHA
PASTA
PATNA
PAULA
PAVIA
QANDA
RAISA
RASTA
SABRA
SACHA
SACRA
SAIGA
SALPA
SALSA
SALTA
SAMBA
SAMOA
SANAA
SANKA
SANTA
SASHA
SAUNA
TABLA
TAIGA
TALIA
TAMPA
TANKA
TANYA
TATRA
TAYRA
TAZZA
VACUA
VANNA
VANYA
VARIA
VARNA
WAJDA
WALLA
WANDA
WANNA
YABBA
YALTA
YAMPA
ZAMIA
ZAPPA

••AA•
ISAAC
IZAAK
KRAAL
SPAAK

••A•A
ABABA
ABACA
ABAYA
ADAMA
ADANA
AEAEA
AGAMA
AGANA
ALANA
ALAVA
AMANA
AMAPA
AMARA
AQABA
ARAMA
ASAMA
ASANA
BRAGA
BRAVA
BWANA
CHAKA
CLARA
DHAKA
DIANA
DRAMA
DRAVA
GHANA
GRAMA
GRATA
GUAVA
IPANA
IVANA
KAABA
KOALA
KUALA
LHASA
LIANA
LLAMA
MEARA
MIATA
NYALA
NYASA
OCALA
OHARA
OMAHA
OMASA
ORAMA
OSAKA
OZAWA
PLATA
PLAYA
PLAZA
PRAIA
REATA
RIATA
RUANA
SCALA
SCAPA
SHANA
TIARA
TRALA
UZALA

•••AA
SANAA

AB•••
ABABA
ABACA
ABACI
ABACK
ABACO
ABAFT
ABASE
ABASH
ABATE
ABAYA
ABBAS
ABBES
ABBEY
ABBIE
ABBOT
ABBRS
ABCTV
ABDUL
ABEAM
ABEBE
ABELE
ABEND
ABETS
ABHOR
ABIDE
ABLER
ABNER
ABODE
ABOHM
ABOIL
ABOMB
ABORT
ABOUT
ABOVE
ABOVO
ABRAM
ABRIL
ABRIS
ABUJA
ABUSE
ABUTS
ABUZZ
ABYES
ABYSM
ABYSS
ABZUG

A•B••
ABBAS
ABBES
ABBEY
ABBIE
ABBOT
ABBRS
AKBAR
ALBAN
ALBEE
ALBEN
ALBUM
AMBER
AMBIT
AMBLE
AMBOS
AMBOY
AMBRY
ARBER
ARBOR
ARBRE
ATBAT
ATBAY
AUBER

A••B•
ABABA
ABEBE
ADOBE
ALIBI
AMEBA
AQABA
ARABS
ARABY
ARUBA
ASHBY

A•••B
ABOMB
ACERB
ADLIB

•AB••
BABAR
BABAS
BABEL
BABER
BABES
BABIS
BABKA
BABUL
BABYS
CABAL
CABBY
CABER
CABIN
CABLE
CABOT
FABER
FABIO
FABLE
GABBY
GABLE
GABON
GABOR
HABER
HABIT
HABLA
JABBA
JABOT
KABOB
KABUL
LABAN
LABEL
LABIO
LABOR
MABEL
NABES
NABOB
PABLO
PABST
RABAT
RABBI
RABID
RABIN
SABAH
SABER
SABIN
SABLE
SABOT
SABRA
SABRE
TABBY
TABIS
TABLA
TABLE
TABOO
TABOR
YABBA

•A•B•
BAMBI
BARBQ
BARBS
CABBY
CANBY
CARBO
CARBS
DARBY
DAUBS
GABBY
GALBA
GAMBA
GARBO
GARBS
IAMBI
IAMBS
JABBA
JAMBS
KAABA
LAMBS
LAYBY
MAMBA
MAMBO
MAYBE
NAMBY
NASBY
PAMBY
RABBI
RAMBO
SAABS
SAMBA
SATBY
TABBY
TAMBO
YABBA

•A••B
BANDB
BARAB
CALEB
CARIB
CAROB
JACOB
KABOB
NABOB
NAMIB
NAWAB
RAHAB
RANDB
SAHIB

••AB•
ABABA
AQABA
ARABS
ARABY
BLABS
CRABS
DHABI
DRABS
GRABS
KAABA
PEABO
SAABS
SCABS
SLABS
STABS
SWABS

••A•B
PLANB

•••AB
BARAB
DCCAB
ESTAB
KEBAB
NAWAB
RAHAB
REHAB
SQUAB

AC•••
ACADS
ACARI
ACCEL
ACCRA
ACCTS
ACERB
ACERS
ACETO
ACHED
ACHES
ACHOO
ACIDS
ACIDY
ACING
ACMES
ACOMA
ACORN
ACRED
ACRES
ACRID
ACTAS
ACTED
ACTER
ACTII
ACTIN
ACTIV
ACTON
ACTOR
ACTUP
ACUFF
ACURA
ACUTE
ACYLS

A•C••
ABCTV
ACCEL
ACCRA
ACCTS
AECIA
ALCAN
ALCOA
ALCOR
ANCON
ARCED
ARCHI
ARCHY
ASCAP
ASCII
ASCOT
ASCUS

A••C•
ABACA
ABACI
ABACK
ABACO
AITCH
ALACK
ALECK
ALICE
ALYCE
AMICE
AMOCO
AMUCK
APACE
ARECA
ARICA
ASPCA
AWACS

A•••C
ADHOC
ADLOC
AFRIC
AGRIC
ANTIC
ANZAC
ASDIC
ASPIC
ASSOC
ATTIC
AURIC
AZOIC
AZTEC

•AC••
BACHS
BACKS
BACON
CACAO
CACHE
CACTI
DACCA
DACES
DACHA
DACHE
DACIA
FACED
FACER
FACES
FACET
FACIA
FACIE
FACIT
FACTO
FACTS
HACEK
HACKS
JACET
JACKS
JACKY
JACOB
LACED
LACER
LACES
LACEY
LACKS
LACTI
LACTO
MACAO
MACAW
MACED
MACES
MACHE
MACHO
MACHU
MACHY
MACLE
MACON
MACRO
MACYS
NACHO
NACHT
NACRE
PACAS
PACED
PACER
PACES
PACKS
PACTS
RACED
RACER
RACES
RACKS
RACON
SACCO
SACHA
SACHS
SACKS
SACRA
SACRE
SACRO
TACET
TACHO
TACHY
TACIT
TACKS
TACKY
TACOS
VACUA
WACKO
WACKY
XACTO
YACHT
YACKS

•A•C•
BALCH
BANCO
BANCS
BARCA
BATCH
CALCI
CASCA
CASCO
CATCH
CAYCE
DACCA
DANCE
DANCY
FANCY
FARCE
FARCI
HATCH
LAICS
LANCE
LARCH
LATCH
MANCY
MARCH
MARCO
MARCY
MATCH
NAACP
NANCY
NARCO
NARCS
NATCH
PARCA
PARCH
PASCH
PASCO
PATCH
RANCH
RATCH
SACCO
SAUCE
SAUCY
TAXCO
VANCE
VASCO
WATCH

•A••C
BARIC
BASIC
HARDC
HAVOC
MAGIC
MALIC
MANIC
PANIC
SALIC
VATIC

••AC•
ABACA
ABACI
ABACK
ABACO
ALACK
APACE
AWACS
BEACH
BLACK
BRACE
BRACT
CHACO
CLACK
COACH
COACT
CRACK
CRACY
DRACO
ENACT
EPACT
EXACT
FLACK
GLACE
GRACE
GUACO
KEACH
KNACK
KYACK
LEACH
LOACH
NAACP
NYACK
ORACH
ORACY
PEACE
PEACH
PLACE
POACH
QUACK
REACH
REACT
ROACH
SHACK
SLACK
SMACK
SNACK
SPACE
SPACY
STACK
STACY
TEACH
TRACE
TRACK
TRACT
TRACY
WHACK
WRACK
WRACS

••A•C
BLANC
FRANC
ISAAC

•••AC
ANZAC
DIRAC
ENIAC
ILIAC
ISAAC
LILAC
SERAC
SUMAC

AD•••
ADAGE
ADAIR

ADAMA
ADAMS
ADANA
ADANO
ADAPT
ADDAX
ADDED
ADDER
ADDIE
ADDIN
ADDIS
ADDLE
ADDNL
ADDON
ADDTO
ADDUP
ADEEM
ADELA
ADELE
ADENO
ADEPT
ADEUX
ADFIN
ADHEM
ADHOC
ADIEU
ADIGE
ADINT
ADIOS
ADIPO
ADITS
ADLAI
ADLER
ADLIB
ADLOC
ADMAN
ADMEN
ADMIN
ADMIT
ADMIX
ADOBE
ADOLF
ADOPT
ADORE
ADORN
ADOUT
ADREM
ADSUM
ADULT
ADUST
ADUWA
ADVAL
ADVIL
ADYTA
ADZES

A•D••

ABDUL
ADDAX
ADDED
ADDER
ADDIE
ADDIN
ADDIS
ADDLE
ADDNL
ADDON
ADDTO
ADDUP
AEDES
AIDAN
AIDED
AIDES
ALDAN
ALDEN
ALDER
ALDOL
ALDUS
ANDES
ANDIE
ANDOR
ANDRE
ANDRO
ANDRY
ANDUP
AODAI
ARDEN
ARDOR
ASDIC
AUDEN
AUDIE
AUDIO
AUDIS
AUDIT
AUDRA

A••D•

AANDE
AANDM
ABIDE
ABODE
ACADS
ACIDS
ACIDY
ALIDA
AMADO
AMIDE
AMIDO
ANODE
ASIDE
AZIDE

A•••D

AAHED
ABEND
ACHED
ACRED
ACRID
ACTED
ADDED
AHEAD
AHMAD
AHMED
AIDED
AILED
AIMED
AIRED
AKKAD
ALAND
ALGID
ALKYD
ALOUD
AMEND
AMPED
ANTED
APHID
APPTD
APTED
ARCED
ARMED
AROID
ARPAD
ASKED
ASSAD
ASSTD
AVOID
AWARD
AWNED

•AD••

BADDY
BADEN
BADER
BADGE
BADLY
CADDO
CADDY
CADET
CADGE
CADIS
CADIZ
CADRE
DADDY
DADOS
FADED
FADES
FADOS
HADAR
HADAT
HADES
HADJI
HADNT
HADON
HADST
HADTO
JADED
JADES
KADAR
LADED
LADEN
LADER
LADES
LADLE
LADON
LADYS
MADAM
MADGE
MADLY
MADRE
NADER
NADIA
NADIR
NADJA
PADDY
PADRE
PADUA
RADAR
RADII
RADIO
RADIX
RADON
SADAT
SADHE
SADHU
SADIE
SADIS
SADLY
VADER
VADIM
VADIS
VADUZ
WADDY
WADED
WADER
WADES
WADIS
WADUP
YADIM

•A•D•

AANDE
AANDM
BADDY
BALDS
BANDA
BANDB
BANDO
BANDS
BANDW
BANDY
BARDS
BAWDY
CADDO
CADDY
CANDO
CANDW
CANDY
CARDI
CARDS
DADDY
DANDY
FALDO
GANDY
GARDA
GARDE
GAUDS
GAUDY
HAIDA
HANDS
HANDY
HARDC
HARDG
HARDY
HAYDN
KANDY
LANDI
LANDO
LANDS
LARDS
LARDY
LAUDE
LAUDS
MAGDA
MAHDI
MAIDS
MAIDU
MANDY
MARDI
MAUDE
MAZDA
NALDI
NARDS
PADDY
PANDA
PANDL
PARDI
PARDO
PARDS
QANDA
RAIDS
RANDB
RANDD
RANDI
RANDR
RANDS
RANDY
SANDE
SANDH
SANDL
SANDS
SANDY
SARDS
SAUDI
TANDE
TANDY
TARDE
TARDY
WADDY
WAJDA
WALDO
WANDA
WANDS
WARDS
YARDS

•A••D

AAHED
BAAED
BAIRD
BAKED
BALED
BARED
BASED
BATED
BAYED
CAGED
CAKED
CANAD
CANED
CANID
CAPED
CARED
CASED
CAVED
CAWED
DARED
DATED
DAVID
DAZED
EARED
EASED
EAVED
FACED
FADED
FAKED
FAMED
FARAD
FARED
FATED
FAXED
FAZED
GAGED
GAMED
GAPED
GATED
GAZED
HALED
HARED
HASID
HATED
HAWED
HAYED
HAZED
JADED
JAPED
JAWED
LACED
LADED
LAIRD
LAMED
LASED
LAVED
LAZED
MACED
MANED
MATED
MAUND
MAXED
NAIAD
NAKED
NAMED
OARED
PACED
PAGED
PALED
PANED
PARED
PATED
PAVED
PAVID
PAWED
PAYED
RABID
RACED
RAGED
RAKED
RANDD
RANID
RAPID
RASED
RATED
RAVED
RAYED
RAZED
SALAD
SALUD
SAPID
SAROD
SATED
SAVED
SAWED
TAMED
TAPED
TAXED
VALID
VAPID
WADED
WAGED
WAKED
WALED
WANED
WAVED
WAXED
YAWED

••AD•

ACADS
AMADO
BEADS
BEADY
BLADE
BRADS
BRADY
DUADS
DYADS
EGADI
EGADS
EVADE
GLADE
GLADS
GOADS
GRADE
GRADS
GRADY
HEADS
HEADY
IRADE
LEADS
LEADY
LOADS
MEADE
MEADS
PRADO
QUADR
QUADS
READE
READS
READY
ROADS
SCADS
SHADE
SHADS
SHADY
SLADE
SPADE
SPADS
STADT
TOADS
TOADY
TRADE
TSADE
WOADS

••A•D

ALAND
AWARD
BAAED
BEARD
BLAND
BOARD
BRAID
BRAND
CHARD
CHAUD
ELAND
FRAUD
GLAND
GRAND
GUARD
HEARD
HOARD
IZARD
LIARD
OLAND
PLAID
QUAID
QUAND
ROALD
SCALD
SCAND
SHARD
SKALD
STAID
STAND
SWARD
VIAND
WHATD

•••AD

AHEAD
AHMAD
AKKAD
ARPAD
ASSAD
BREAD
BROAD
CANAD
CYCAD
DREAD
DRYAD
FARAD
GOBAD
HEXAD
HODAD
ILIAD
INBAD
JIHAD
KNEAD
MONAD
NAIAD
NICAD
NOMAD
NORAD
OCTAD
OREAD
PLEAD
QUOAD
REPAD
SALAD
SNEAD
SQUAD
STEAD
STRAD
TREAD
TRIAD

AE•••

AEAEA
AECIA
AEDES
AEGIR
AEGIS
AEIOU
AEONS
AERIE
AERON
AEROS
AESIR
AESOP
AETAT
AETNA

A•E••

ABEAM
ABEBE
ABELE
ABEND
ABETS
ACERB
ACERS
ACETO
ADEEM
ADELA
ADELE
ADENO
ADEPT
ADEUX
AGENA
AGENT
AGERS
AHEAD
AKEEM
AKEES
AKELA
AKENE
ALECK
ALEFS
ALENE
ALEPH
ALERT
ALETA
ALEUT
ALEVE
AMEBA
AMEER
AMEND
AMENS
AMENT
ANEAR
ANELE
ANEMO
ANENT
ANETO
APEAK
APERS
APERY
AREAL
AREAR
AREAS
ARECA
ARENA
ARENS
ARENT
ARETE
ATEAM
ATEIN
ATEUP
AVENA
AVENS
AVERS
AVERT
AVERY
AXELS
AXERS
AYERS

A••E•

AAHED
AAMES
ABBES
ABBEY
ABLER
ABNER
ABYES
ACCEL
ACHED
ACHES
ACMES
ACRED
ACRES
ACTED
ACTER
ADDED
ADDER
ADEEM
ADHEM
ADIEU
ADLER
ADMEN
ADREM
ADZES
AEAEA
AEDES
AFTER
AGLET
AGLEY
AGNES
AGNEW
AGREE
AGUES
AHMED
AIDED
AIDES
AIKEN
AILED
AILER
AILEY
AIMED
AIMEE
AIMER
AIRED
AIRES
AJMER
AKEEM
AKEES
ALBEE
ALBEN
ALDEN
ALDER
ALGER
ALIEN
ALLEE
ALLEN
ALLER
ALLES
ALLEY
ALLEZ
ALOES
ALTER
AMBER
AMEER
AMIES
AMPED
AMVET
ANDES
ANGEL
ANGER
ANGES
ANNEE
ANNES
ANNEX
ANSEL
ANSER

ANTED ANTES APFEL APLEY APNEA APPEL APRES APSES APTED APTER ARBER ARCED ARDEN ARIEL ARIES ARLEN ARLES ARMED ARMEE ARMET ARNEL ARPEL ARRET ARTEL ARTES ASHEN ASHER ASHES ASKED ASKER ASKEW ASNER ASPEN ASSES ASSET ASSEZ ASTER ASYET ATSEA AUBER AUDEN AUGER AUREI AWNED AXLES AYRES AZTEC

A•••E

AANDE ABASE ABATE ABBIE ABEBE ABELE ABIDE ABODE ABOVE ABUSE ACUTE ADAGE ADDIE ADDLE ADELE ADIGE ADOBE ADORE AERIE AFIRE AFORE AGAPE AGATE AGAVE AGAZE AGGIE AGILE AGREE AIMEE AINGE AISLE AISNE AKENE ALATE ALBEE ALENE ALEVE ALFIE ALFRE ALGAE ALICE ALIKE ALINE ALIVE ALLEE ALLIE ALONE ALYCE AMAZE AMBLE AMICE AMIDE AMINE AMOLE AMORE AMPLE AMUSE ANDIE ANDRE ANELE ANGIE ANGLE ANIME ANISE ANKLE ANNEE ANNIE ANODE ANOLE ANSAE ANTAE ANTRE APACE APPLE APURE AQUAE ARAME ARBRE ARETE ARGUE ARISE ARMEE ARNIE AROSE ARTIE ASIDE ASONE ASTRE ATIVE ATONE ATQUE AUDIE AURAE AUTRE AWAKE AWARE AWOKE AXONE AZIDE AZINE AZOTE AZURE

•AE••

CAELO FAERY GAELS HAEMA HAEMO PAEAN PAEON SAENS TAEGU TAELS

•A•E•

AAHED AAMES BAAED BABEL BABER BABES BADEN BADER BAGEL BAKED BAKER BAKES BALED BALER BALES BANES BARED BARER BARES BASED BASEL BASER BASES BATED BATES BAUER BAYED BAYER CABER CADET CAFES CAGED CAGER CAGES CAGEY CAKED CAKES CAKEY CALEB CAMEL CAMEO CANEA CANED CANEM CANER CANES CAPED CAPEK CAPER CAPES CAPET CARED CARER CARES CARET CAREW CAREY CASED CASES CASEY CATER CATES CAVED CAVER CAVES CAWED DACES DALES DALEY DAMES DANES DARED DARER DARES DATED DATER DATES DAWES DAZED DAZES EAGER EAMES EARED EASED EASEL EASES EATEN EATER EAVED EAVES FABER FACED FACER FACES FACET FADED FADES FAHEY FAKED FAKER FAKES FAMED FAMES FANES FARED FARER FARES FATED FATES FAVES FAXED FAXES FAZED FAZES GAGED GAGES GALEA GALEN GALES GAMED GAMER GAMES GAMEY GANEF GAPED GAPER GAPES GASES GATED GATES GAVEL GAYER GAZED GAZER GAZES HABER HACEK HADES HAGEN HAKES HALED HALER HALES HALEY HAMEL HAMES HANES HARED HAREM HARES HATED HATER HATES HAUER HAVEL HAVEN HAVER HAVES HAWED HAYED HAYEK HAYES HAZED HAZEL HAZER HAZES JACET JADED JADES JAKES JAMES JANET JAPED JAPES JASEY JAWED KALEL KALES KAREL KAREN KASEM LABEL LACED LACER LACES LACEY LADED LADEN LADER LADES LAGER LAKER LAKES LAMED LAMER LAMES LANES LAPEL LARES LASED LASER LASES LATEN LATER LATEX LAUER LAVED LAVER LAVES LAWES LAXER LAYER LAZED LAZES MABEL MACED MACES MAGEE MAGES MAHER MAKER MAKES MALES MAMET MANED MANES MANET MARES MASER MATED MATEO MATER MATES MATEY MAVEN MAXED MAXES MAYER MAZEL MAZER MAZES NABES NADER NAGEL NAKED NAMED NAMER NAMES NAPES NARES NAREW NAVEL NAVES OAKEN OAKES OARED OASES OATEN OATER OATES PACED PACER PACES PAGED PAGER PAGES PAGET PALEA PALED PALEO PALER PALES PALEY PANED PANEL PANES PAPER PARED PAREE PAREN PARER PARES PAREU PASEO PASES PATED PATEK PATEN PATER PATES PAVED PAVER PAVES PAWED PAWER PAYED PAYEE PAYER RACED RACER RACES RAFER RAGED RAGES RAKED RAKER RAKES RAMEE RAMEN RAMET RANEE RAPEE RAREE RARER RARES RASED RASER RASES RATED RATEL RATER RATES RAVED RAVEL RAVEN RAVER RAVES RAWER RAYED RAZED RAZES SABER SAFER SAFES SAGER SAGES SAGET SAHEL SAKER SAKES SALEM SALEP SALES SANER SASES SATED SATES SAVED SAVER SAVES SAWED SAXES SAYER TACET TAKEI TAKEN TAKER TAKES TALER TALES TAMED TAMER TAMES TANEY TAPED TAPER TAPES TARES TASER TATER TAXED TAXER TAXES VADER VALES VALET VANES VASES VATER WADED WADER WADES WAFER WAGED WAGER WAGES WAKED WAKEN WAKES WALED WALER WALES WALEY WANED WANER WANES WANEY WARES WATER WAVED WAVER WAVES WAXED WAXEN WAXER WAXES XAXES YARER YATES YAWED YAXES ZAXES ZAZEN

•A••E

AANDE BADGE BAIZE BARGE BARRE BASIE BASTE BATHE BAUME BAYLE CABLE CACHE CADGE CADRE CAFFE CAINE CALPE CALVE CANOE CARLE CARNE CARPE CARRE CARTE CARVE CASTE CAUSE CAVAE CAYCE DACHE DAFOE DAMME DANAE DANCE DANKE DANSE DANTE DAVIE DAYNE EAGLE EAGRE EARLE FABLE FACIE FAIRE FALSE FARCE FAROE FAURE FAUVE FAVRE GABLE GAFFE GARDE GASPE GAUGE GAUZE GAYLE HAGUE HAILE HALLE HALVE HANSE HAOLE HARTE HASTE HAUTE HAVRE HAWKE HAWSE JAFFE JAHRE JAIME JAMIE JANIE JARRE JAUNE JAYNE KAFUE KATIE LADLE LAINE LAKME LANCE LANGE LAPSE LARGE LARUE LATHE LATKE LATTE LAUDE LAYNE MACHE MACLE MADGE MADRE MAGEE MAHRE MAILE MAINE MAIZE MALLE MAMIE MANSE MAPLE MARGE MARIE MARNE MASSE MATTE MAUDE MAUVE

MAXIE
MAYBE
NACRE
NAIVE
NAPPE
NASHE
OAKIE
PADRE
PAIGE
PAINE
PALAE
PALME
PANNE
PAREE
PARLE
PARSE
PARTE
PASSE
PASTE
PATHE
PAUSE
PAYEE
PAYNE
RAISE
RAMEE
RAMIE
RANEE
RANGE
RANKE
RAPEE
RAPHE
RAREE
SABLE
SABRE
SACRE
SADHE
SADIE
SALLE
SALVE
SANDE
SANTE
SAONE
SARGE
SATIE
SAUCE
SAUTE
TABLE
TAHOE
TAINE
TANDE
TANTE
TARDE
TARGE
TASSE
TASTE
TAUPE
VAGUE
VALLE
VALSE
VALUE
VALVE
VANCE
WAITE
WAIVE
WASTE
WAYNE
YALIE
ZAIRE
ZANTE

••AE•
AEAEA
BAAED
BRAES
SHAEF
STAEL

••A•E
ABASE
ABATE
ADAGE
AGAPE
AGATE
AGAVE
AGAZE
ALATE
AMAZE
APACE
ARAME
AWAKE
AWARE
BLADE
BLAKE
BLAME
BLARE
BLASE
BLAZE
BRACE
BRAHE
BRAKE
BRAVE
BRAZE
CEASE
CHAFE
CHASE
CLARE
CLAVE
CRAKE
CRANE
CRAPE
CRATE
CRAVE
CRAZE
DEANE
DIANE
DNASE
DRAKE
DRAPE
DUANE
ELATE
ENATE
ERASE
ETAGE
ETAPE
EVADE
FLAKE
FLAME
FLARE
FRAME
GLACE
GLADE
GLARE
GLAZE
GOAPE
GRACE
GRADE
GRAPE
GRATE
GRAVE
GRAZE
HEAVE
IMAGE
INANE
INAWE
IRADE
IRATE
JEANE
KEANE
KNAVE
LEASE
LEAVE
LIANE
MEADE
NEALE
OFAGE
OHARE
ONATE
ORALE
ORATE
OSAGE
OVATE
PEACE
PEALE
PEASE
PHAGE
PHASE
PLACE
PLAGE
PLANE
PLATE
PRASE
PRATE
QUAKE
QUALE
QUARE
READE
RNASE
SCALE
SCAPE
SCARE
SEALE
SHADE
SHAKE
SHALE
SHAME
SHANE
SHAPE
SHARE
SHAVE
SKATE
SLADE
SLAKE
SLATE
SLAVE
SMAZE
SNAKE
SNARE
SOAVE
SPACE
SPADE
SPAKE
SPARE
SPATE
STAGE
STAKE
STALE
STARE
STATE
STAVE
SUAVE
SWAGE
SWALE
TEASE
THANE
TRACE
TRADE
TRAVE
TSADE
UKASE
USAGE
WEAVE
WHALE

•••AE
ALGAE
ANSAE
ANTAE
AQUAE
AURAE
CAVAE
COMAE
COXAE
CUMAE
CYMAE
DANAE
HORAE
MCRAE
MORAE
NOVAE
NUGAE
PALAE
PUPAE
RUGAE
SETAE
STOAE
TOGAE
ULNAE
VENAE
VITAE
ZOEAE

AF•••
AFAIK
AFARS
AFFIX
AFIRE
AFLAT
AFOFL
AFOOT
AFORE
AFOUL
AFRIC
AFRIT
AFROS
AFTER
AFTON
AFTRA

A•F••
ADFIN
AFFIX
ALFAS
ALFIE
ALFRE
APFEL
AWFUL

A••F•
ABAFT
ACUFF
AFOFL
ALEFS
ALIFS
ALOFT

A•••F
ACUFF
ADOLF
ALOOF

•AF••
CAFES
CAFFE
DAFFS
DAFFY
DAFOE
GAFFE
GAFFS
HAFIZ
HAFTS
HAFUN
JAFFA
JAFFE
KAFIR
KAFKA
KAFUE
NAFTA
RAFER
RAFFI
RAFTS
SAFER
SAFES
TAFFY
WAFER
WAFTS

•A•F•
BANFF
CAFFE
DAFFS
DAFFY
GAFFE
GAFFS
HAIFA
HANFF
JAFFA
JAFFE
RAFFI
TAFFY
WAAFS
WAIFS
ZARFS

•A••F
BANFF
CALIF
GANEF
HANFF

••AF•
ABAFT
CHAFE
CHAFF
CRAFT
DRAFT
GRAFT
KRAFT
LEAFS
LEAFY
LOAFS
QUAFF
SHAFT
SNAFU
STAFF
WAAFS
WRAFS

••A•F
CHAFF
DWARF
QUAFF
SCARF
SHAEF
STAFF
SWARF
WHARF

•••AF
DECAF
PILAF
SHEAF

AG•••
AGAIN
AGALS
AGAMA
AGANA
AGAPE
AGARN
AGARS
AGASP
AGATE
AGAVE
AGAZE
AGENA
AGENT
AGERS
AGGIE
AGGRO
AGHAS
AGILE
AGING
AGIOS
AGITA
AGLET
AGLEY
AGLOW
AGNES
AGNEW
AGNON
AGNUS
AGOGO
AGONY
AGORA
AGREE
AGRIC
AGRON
AGUES

A•G••
AEGIR
AEGIS
AGGIE
AGGRO
ALGAE
ALGAL
ALGER
ALGID
ALGIN
ALGOL
ANGEL
ANGER
ANGES
ANGIE
ANGIO
ANGLE
ANGLO
ANGRY
ANGST
ANGUS
ARGIL
ARGOL
ARGON
ARGOS
ARGOT
ARGUE
ARGUS
AUGER
AUGHT
AUGUR
AVGAS

A••G•
AARGH
ADAGE
ADIGE
AGOGO
AINGE
ALIGN
AMIGA
AMIGO

A•••G
ABZUG
ACING
AGING
ALONG
AMONG
APING
AWING
AXING

•AG••
BAGEL
BAGGY
BAGIT
CAGED
CAGER
CAGES
CAGEY
DAGON
EAGAN
EAGER
EAGLE
EAGRE
FAGIN
FAGOT
GAGED
GAGES
HAGAR
HAGEN
HAGIO
HAGUE
JAGGY
LAGAN
LAGER
LAGOS
MAGDA
MAGEE
MAGES
MAGIC
MAGMA
MAGNA
MAGOG
MAGOO
MAGOT
MAGUS
NAGEL
NAGGY
PAGAN
PAGED
PAGER
PAGES
PAGET
RAGAS
RAGED
RAGES
SAGAL
SAGAN
SAGAS
SAGER
SAGES
SAGET
SAGGY
SAGOS
TAGUP
TAGUS
VAGUE
VAGUS
WAGED
WAGER
WAGES
WAGON

•A•G•
AARGH
BADGE
BAGGY
BANGS
BARGE
BARGY
BAUGH
CADGE
CARGO
DANGS
FANGS
FARGO
GANGS
GAUGE
HANGS
HAWGS
JAGGY
KANGA
LANGE
LARGE
LARGO
LAUGH
MADGE
MANGO
MANGY
MARGE
MARGO
NAGGY
PAIGE
PANGA
PANGS
RANGE
RANGY
SAGGY
SAIGA
SARGE
SARGO
TAEGU
TAIGA
TANGO
TANGS
TANGY
TARGE
WAUGH

•A••G
HARDG
LAING
MAGOG
NAVIG
VARIG

••AG•
ADAGE
BRAGA
BRAGG
BRAGS
CRAGS
DRAGS
ETAGE
FLAGG
FLAGS
HOAGY
IMAGE
IMAGO
OFAGE
OSAGE
PHAGE
PHAGO
PHAGY
PLAGE
QUAGS
SHAGS
SLAGS
SNAGS
STAGE
STAGG
STAGS
STAGY
SWAGE
SWAGS
USAGE

••A•G
BRAGG
CHANG
CLANG
CRAIG
DRANG
FLAGG
GRAIG
KIANG
LIANG
ORANG
PRANG
SLANG
SPANG
STAGG
STANG
TWANG
WHANG

•••AG
DORAG
GULAG
IDTAG
REBAG
RETAG
SCRAG
SPRAG

AH•••
AHEAD
AHMAD
AHMED
AHORA
AHOYS
AHSIN

A•H••
AAHED
ABHOR
ACHED
ACHES
ACHOO
ADHEM
ADHOC
AGHAS
ANHUI
APHID
APHIS
ARHAT
ARHUS
ASHBY
ASHEN
ASHER
ASHES
ASHUR
ATHOL
ATHON
ATHOS

A••H•
ABOHM
AISHA
ALOHA
ALPHA
ALTHO
AMAHL
AMAHS
AMPHI
AMPHR
ANKHS
ANTHO
ARCHI
ARCHY
ARTHR
AUGHT
AYAHS

A•••H
AARGH
ABASH
AITCH
ALEPH
ALLAH
AMISH

APISH
ARITH
AWASH
AZOTH

•AH••

AAHED
BAHAI
BAHIA
BAHTS
FAHEY
HAHAS
JAHRE
KAHLO
LAHAR
LAHTI
MAHAL
MAHAN
MAHDI
MAHER
MAHON
MAHRE
NAHUA
NAHUM
RAHAB
RAHAL
SAHEL
SAHIB
TAHOE
TAHRS
WAHOO
YAHOO

•A•H•

BACHS
BASHO
BATHE
BATHO
BATHS
BATHY
CACHE
CATHY
DACHA
DACHE
DASHI
FATHA
KAPHS
KASHA
KATHY
LATHE
LATHS
LATHY
MACHE
MACHO
MACHU
MACHY
MASHY
MATHS
NACHO
NACHT
NASHE
OATHS
PASHA
PATHE
PATHO
PATHS
PATHY
RAPHE
RASHT
RATHS
SACHA
SACHS
SADHE
SADHU
SASHA
TACHO
TACHY
WASHY
YACHT

•A••H

AARGH
BALCH
BALKH
BARTH
BATCH
BAUGH
CATCH
DARTH
EARTH
FAITH
FARAH
GALAH
GARTH
HARSH
HATCH
KARSH
LARCH
LATCH
LAUGH
MARCH
MARSH
MATCH
NAISH
NATCH
PARCH
PASCH
PATCH
RAJAH
RALPH
RANCH
RATCH
SABAH
SAITH
SANDH
SARAH
WALSH
WATCH
WAUGH

••AH•

AMAHL
AMAHS
AYAHS
BLAHS
BRAHE
ICAHN
IDAHO
LEAHY
NOAHS
OMAHA
OPAHS
SHAHN
SHAHS
SPAHI
SPAHN
STAHL
UTAHN

••A•H

ABASH
AWASH
BEACH
BRASH
CLASH
COACH
CRASH
ELATH
FLASH
GNASH
GRAPH
HEATH
KEACH
LEACH
LEASH
LOACH
LOATH
NEATH
ORACH
PEACH
PLASH
PLATH
POACH
QUASH
REACH
ROACH
SLASH
SMASH
SNATH
STASH
SWASH
SWATH
TEACH
TRASH
WRATH

•••AH

ALLAH
BORAH
DINAH
EPHAH
FARAH
GALAH
GERAH
JONAH
JUDAH
LOTAH
MICAH
MYNAH
NORAH
OBEAH
OPRAH
RAJAH
SABAH
SARAH
SELAH
SHOAH
SURAH
TORAH
URIAH

AI•••

AIDAN
AIDED
AIDES
AIKEN
AILED
AILER
AILEY
AIMAT
AIMED
AIMEE
AIMER
AIMTO
AINGE
AINUS
AIOLI
AIRED
AIRES
AISHA
AISLE
AISNE
AITCH

A•I••

AAIUN
ABIDE
ACIDS
ACIDY
ACING
ADIEU
ADIGE
ADINT
ADIOS
ADIPO
ADITS
AEIOU
AFIRE
AGILE
AGING
AGIOS
AGITA
AKINS
AKIRA
AKITA
ALIAS
ALIBI
ALICE
ALIDA
ALIEN
ALIFS
ALIGN
ALIKE
ALINE
ALIOS
ALIST
ALIVE
AMICE
AMIDE
AMIDO
AMIES
AMIGA
AMIGO
AMINE
AMINO
AMIRS
AMISH
AMISS
AMITY
ANILS
ANIMA
ANIME
ANION
ANISE
ANISO
ANITA
APIAN
APING
APISH
ARIAN
ARIAS
ARICA
ARIEL
ARIES
ARILS
ARION
ARISE
ARITH
ARIUM
ARIUS
ASIAN
ASIDE
ATILT
ATION
ATIVE
AVIAN
AVILA
AVION
AVISO
AWING
AXIAL
AXILS
AXING
AXIOM
AXION
AYINS
AZIDE
AZINE

A••I•

AALII
ABBIE
ABOIL
ABRIL
ABRIS
ACRID
ACTII
ACTIN
ACTIV
ADAIR
ADDIE
ADDIN
ADDIS
ADFIN
ADLIB
ADMIN
ADMIT
ADMIX
ADVIL
AECIA
AEGIR
AEGIS
AERIE
AESIR
AFAIK
AFFIX
AFRIC
AFRIT
AGAIN
AGGIE
AGRIC
AHSIN
ALAIN
ALFIE
ALGID
ALGIN
ALLIE
ALLIN
ALVIN
AMAIN
AMBIT
AMNIA
ANAIS
ANDIE
ANGIE
ANGIO
ANNIE
ANNIV
ANTIC
ANTIQ
ANTIS
ANVIL
ANZIO
APHID
APHIS
APRIL
APSIS
ARGIL
ARKIN
ARMIS
ARNIE
AROID
ARRIS
ARSIS
ARTIE
ARTIS
ASCII
ASDIC
ASKIN
ASPIC
ASTIN
ASTIR
ATEIN
ATRIA
ATRIP
ATTIC
AUDIE
AUDIO
AUDIS
AUDIT
AULIS
AURIC
AUXIL
AUXIN
AVAIL
AVOID
AVOIR
AVRIL
AWAIT
AZOIC

A•••I

AALII
ABACI
ACARI
ACTII
ADLAI
AIOLI
ALIBI
ALTAI
AMATI
AMPHI
ANHUI
AODAI
ARCHI
ASCII
ASSAI
ATARI
AUREI
AUSSI
AWAJI

•AI••

AAIUN
BAILS
BAIRD
BAIRN
BAITS
BAIUL
BAIZA
BAIZE
CAINE
CAIRN
CAIRO
DAILY
DAIRY
DAISY
DAIWA
FAILS
FAINT
FAIRE
FAIRS
FAIRY
FAITH
GAILY
GAINS
GAITS
GAIUS
HAIDA
HAIFA
HAIKS
HAIKU
HAILE
HAILS
HAIRS
HAIRY
HAITI
JAILS
JAIME
JAINS
LAICS
LAIKA
LAINE
LAING
LAIRD
LAIRS
LAITY
LAIUS
MAIDS
MAIDU
MAILE
MAILS
MAINE
MAINS
MAINZ
MAIZE
NAIAD
NAILS
NAINA
NAIRA
NAIRN
NAISH
NAIVE
PAIGE
PAILS
PAINE
PAINS
PAINT
PAIRS
PAISA
RAIDS
RAILS
RAINS
RAINY
RAISA
RAISE
RAITT
SAIGA
SAILS
SAINT
SAITH
TAIGA
TAILS
TAINE
TAINO
TAINT
WAIFS
WAILS
WAINS
WAIST
WAITE
WAITS
WAITZ
WAIVE
ZAIRE

•A•I•

AALII
BABIS
BAGIT
BAHIA
BALIN
BARIC
BARIT
BASIC
BASIE
BASIL
BASIN
BASIS
BATIK
CABIN
CADIS
CADIZ
CALIF
CALIX
CAMIS
CANID
CANIS
CANIT
CARIA
CARIB
CASIO
CAVIL
DACIA
DANIO
DARIN
DARIO
DAVID
DAVIE
DAVIS
DAVIT
EATIN
EATIT
FABIO
FACIA
FACIE
FACIT
FAGIN
FAKIR
GAMIN
GAVIN
HABIT
HAFIZ
HAGIO
HAJIS
HAKIM
HASID
JAMIE
JAMIN
JANIE
JANIS
KAFIR
KAKIS
KANIN
KATIE
LABIO
LAMIA
LAPIN
LAPIS
LARIS
LATIN
LAVIN
LAYIN
MAGIC
MALIC
MAMIE
MANIA
MANIC
MARIA
MARIE
MARIN
MARIO
MARIS
MATIN
MAVIS
MAXIE
MAXIM
MAXIS
NADIA
NADIR
NAMIB
NARIS
NAVIG
OAKIE
OASIS
PALIN
PAMIR
PANIC
PARIS
PATIO
PAVIA
PAVID
PAVIS
PAYIN
RABID
RABIN
RADII
RADIO
RADIX
RAJIV
RAKIS
RAMIE
RAMIS
RANID
RANIN
RANIS
RAPID
RATIO
RAVIN
SABIN
SADIE
SADIS
SAHIB
SALIC
SAPID
SAPIR
SARIS
SATIE
SATIN
SAWIN
TABIS
TACIT
TAKIN
TALIA
TAMIL
TAPIN
TAPIR
TAXIS
VADIM
VADIS
VALID
VANIR
VAPID
VARIA
VARIG
VARIX
VATIC
WADIS
XAXIS
YADIM
YALIE
YASIR
YAXIS
ZAMIA
ZAXIS
ZAYIN

•A••I

AALII
BAHAI
BAMBI
BAOJI
BASSI
CACTI
CALCI
CALLI
CAPRI
CARDI
CARPI
DALAI
DASHI
FARCI
FARSI
GALLI
GARNI
HADJI
HAITI
HAJJI
HANOI
IAMBI
KANJI
KAUAI
KAURI

LACTI
LAHTI
LANAI
LANDI
MAHDI
MAORI
MAQUI
MARDI
MARTI
MASAI
MATRI
NALDI
NAMOI
NAOMI
PALPI
PAOLI
PAPPI
PARDI
PARTI
PATRI
PATTI
RABBI
RADII
RAFFI
RANDI
SAKAI
SALMI
SAUDI
TAKEI
TARSI
VALLI
YANNI
YAQUI

••AI•
ADAIR
AFAIK
AGAIN
ALAIN
AMAIN
ANAIS
AVAIL
AWAIT
BLAIR
BRAID
BRAIL
BRAIN
CHAIM
CHAIN
CHAIR
CLAIM
CLAIR
CRAIG
CRAIN
DRAIL
DRAIN
EMAIL
FLAIL
FLAIR
FRAIL
FRAIS
GHAIN
GLAIR
GRAIG
GRAIL
GRAIN
KRAIT
NGAIO
OHAIR
ONAIR
PLAID
PLAIN
PLAIT
PRAIA
QUAID
QUAIL
REAIM
REAIR
SLAIN
SMAIL
SNAIL
SPAIN
STAID
STAIN
STAIR
SWAIN
THAIS
TRAIL
TRAIN
TRAIT
TWAIN
USAIR

••A•I
ABACI
ACARI
AMATI
ATARI
AWAJI
COATI
DHABI
EGADI
ELAZI
GHALI
GHAZI
GRANI
INARI
IRANI
IRAQI
KHAKI
MIAMI
NGAMI
OKAPI
OMANI
PIAUI
PLANI
QUASI
SHARI
SPAHI
SWAMI
SWAZI

•••AI
ADLAI
ALTAI
AODAI
ASSAI
BAHAI
BOHAI
DALAI
DOUAI
DUBAI
ENLAI
KAUAI
KENAI
LANAI
MASAI
POHAI
SAKAI
SERAI
SINAI

AJ•••
AJMER

A•J••
ANJOU
AUJUS

A••J•
ABUJA
AWAJI

•AJ••
CAJUN
HAJIS
HAJJI
MAJOR
RAJAH
RAJAS
RAJIV
SAJAK
WAJDA

•A•J•
BANJO
BAOJI
HADJI
HAJJI
KANJI
NADJA

••AJ•
AWAJI

AK•••
AKBAR
AKEEM
AKEES
AKELA
AKENE
AKINS
AKIRA
AKITA
AKKAD
AKRON
AKSUM

A•K••
AIKEN
AKKAD
ALKYD
ALKYL
ANKHS
ANKLE
AOKAY
ARKIN
ASKED
ASKER
ASKEW
ASKIN

A••K•
ALIKE
ASOKA
AWAKE
AWOKE

A•••K
ABACK
AFAIK
ALACK
ALECK
AMUCK
ANOUK
APEAK

•AK••
BAKED
BAKER
BAKES
BAKST
CAKED
CAKES
CAKEY
DAKAR
FAKED
FAKER
FAKES
FAKIR
HAKES
HAKIM
JAKES
KAKAS
KAKIS
LAKER
LAKES
LAKME
MAKER
MAKES
MAKOS
MAKUA
NAKED
OAKEN
OAKES
OAKIE
OAKUM
RAKED
RAKER
RAKES
RAKIS
SAKAI
SAKER
SAKES
TAKAS
TAKEI
TAKEN
TAKER
TAKES
TAKIN
WAKED
WAKEN
WAKES
YAKOV
YAKUT

•A•K•
BABKA
BACKS
BALKH
BALKS
BALKY
BANKS
BANKY
BARKS
BARKY
BASKS
CALKS
CARKS
CASKS
DANKE
DARKS
GAWKS
GAWKY
HACKS
HAIKS
HAIKU
HANKS
HANKY
HARKS
HAWKE
HAWKS
JACKS
JACKY
KAFKA
LACKS
LAIKA
LANKA
LANKY
LARKS
LARKY
LATKE
MARKS
MASKS
NARKS
PACKS
PANKY
PARKA
PARKS
PAWKY
RACKS
RANKE
RANKS
SACKS
SANKA
SARKY
SAUKS
TACKS
TACKY
TALKS
TALKY
TANKA
TANKS
TASKS
WACKO
WACKY
WALKS
YACKS
YANKS

•A••K
BATAK
BATIK
BAULK
CAPEK
CAULK
DAYAK
HACEK
HAYEK
KAPOK
KAYAK
KAZAK
NANAK
PATEK
SAJAK
TAROK
YAPOK

••AK•
AWAKE
BEAKS
BLAKE
BRAKE
CHAKA
CRAKE
DHAKA
DRAKE
FLAKE
FLAKY
KHAKI
LEAKS
LEAKY
OSAKA
PEAKS
QUAKE
QUAKY
SHAKE
SHAKO
SHAKY
SLAKE
SNAKE
SNAKY
SOAKS
SPAKE
STAKE
TEAKS

••A•K
ABACK
AFAIK
ALACK
BLACK
BLANK
CHALK
CLACK
CLANK
CLARK
CRACK
CRANK
DMARK
DRANK
FLACK
FLANK
FLASK
FRANK
IZAAK
KNACK
KYACK
NYACK
OZARK
PLANK
PRANK
QUACK
QUARK
RUARK
SHACK
SHANK
SHARK
SKANK
SLACK
SMACK
SNACK
SNARK
SPAAK
SPANK
SPARK
STACK
STALK
STANK
STARK
SWANK
THANK
TRACK
WHACK
WRACK

•••AK
APEAK
BATAK
BLEAK
BREAK
CLOAK
CREAK
CROAK
DAYAK
FREAK
IZAAK
KAYAK
KAZAK
KODAK
KOJAK
KULAK
MUZAK
NANAK
NOVAK
SAJAK
SNEAK
SPAAK
SPEAK
STEAK
TILAK
TWEAK
UMIAK
WREAK

AL•••
ALACK
ALAIN
ALAMO
ALANA
ALAND
ALARM
ALATE
ALAVA
ALBAN
ALBEE
ALBEN
ALBUM
ALCAN
ALCOA
ALCOR
ALDAN
ALDEN
ALDER
ALDOL
ALDUS
ALECK
ALEFS
ALENE
ALEPH
ALERT
ALETA
ALEUT
ALEVE
ALFAS
ALFIE
ALFRE
ALGAE
ALGAL
ALGER
ALGID
ALGIN
ALGOL
ALIAS
ALIBI
ALICE
ALIDA
ALIEN
ALIFS
ALIGN
ALIKE
ALINE
ALIOS
ALIST
ALIVE
ALKYD
ALKYL
ALLAH
ALLAN
ALLAY
ALLEE
ALLEN
ALLER
ALLES
ALLEY
ALLEZ
ALLIE
ALLIN
ALLOT
ALLOW
ALLOY
ALLYL
ALMAY
ALOES
ALOFT
ALOHA
ALONE
ALONG
ALOOF
ALORS
ALOUD
ALPHA
ALSOP
ALTAI
ALTAR
ALTER
ALTHO
ALTON
ALTOS
ALTUS
ALULA
ALUMS
ALVAR
ALVIN
ALYCE

A•L••
AALII
AALTO
ABLER
ADLAI
ADLER
ADLIB
ADLOC
AFLAT
AGLET
AGLEY
AGLOW
AILED
AILER
AILEY
ALLAH
ALLAN
ALLAY
ALLEE
ALLEN
ALLER
ALLES
ALLEY
ALLEZ
ALLIE
ALLIN
ALLOT
ALLOW
ALLOY
ALLYL
APLEY
APLUS
ARLEN
ARLES
ATLAS
AULIS
AXLES

A••L•
ABELE
ACYLS
ADDLE
ADELA
ADELE
ADOLF
ADULT
AGALS
AGILE
AIOLI
AISLE
AKELA
ALULA
AMBLE
AMOLE
AMPLE
AMPLY
AMYLO
AMYLS
ANELE
ANGLE
ANGLO
ANILS
ANKLE
ANOLE
APPLE
APPLY
APTLY
ARILS
ASYLA
ATALL
ATILT
ATOLL
AVILA
AWOLS
AXELS
AXILS

A•••L
ABDUL
ABOIL
ABRIL
ACCEL
ADDNL
ADVAL
ADVIL
AFOFL
AFOUL
ALDOL
ALGAL
ALGOL
ALKYL
ALLYL
AMAHL
AMPUL
ANGEL
ANNAL
ANNUL
ANSEL
ANTAL
ANVIL
APFEL
APPAL
APPEL
APRIL
AREAL
ARGIL
ARGOL
ARIEL
ARNEL
ARPEL
ARTAL
ARTEL
ATALL
ATHOL
ATOLL
AURAL
AUXIL
AVAIL
AVRIL
AWFUL
AXIAL

•AL••
AALII
AALTO
BALAS
BALCH
BALDS
BALED
BALER
BALES
BALIN
BALKH
BALKS
BALKY
BALLS
BALLY
BALMS
BALMY
BALSA
BALTO
BALTS
CALCI
CALEB
CALIF
CALIX

CALKS
CALLA
CALLI
CALLS
CALMS
CALPE
CALVE
CALYX
DALAI
DALES
DALEY
DALLY
FALDO
FALLA
FALLS
FALSE
GALAH
GALAS
GALAX
GALBA
GALEA
GALEN
GALES
GALLI
GALLO
GALLS
GALOP
HALAS
HALED
HALER
HALES
HALEY
HALLE
HALLO
HALLS
HALMS
HALON
HALOS
HALTS
HALVE
KALEL
KALES
LALAW
MALAN
MALAR
MALAY
MALES
MALIC
MALLE
MALLS
MALMO
MALTA
MALTS
MALTY
NALDI
PALAE
PALAU
PALEA
PALED
PALEO
PALER
PALES
PALEY
PALIN
PALLS
PALLY
PALMA
PALME
PALMS
PALMY
PALOS
PALPI
PALPS
PALSY
RALLY
RALPH
SALAD
SALAL
SALAM
SALEM
SALEP
SALES
SALIC
SALLE
SALLY
SALMI
SALON
SALPA
SALPS
SALSA
SALTA
SALTS
SALTY
SALUD
SALUT
SALVE
SALVO
TALER
TALES
TALIA
TALKS
TALKY
TALLY
TALON
TALOS
TALUS
VALES
VALET
VALID
VALLE
VALLI
VALOR
VALSE
VALUE
VALVE
WALDO
WALED
WALER
WALES
WALEY
WALKS
WALLA
WALLS
WALLY
WALSH
WALSY
WALTZ
YALIE
YALOW
YALTA

•A•L•

BAALS
BADLY
BAILS
BALLS
BALLY
BAULK
BAWLS
BAYLE
CABLE
CAELO
CALLA
CALLI
CALLS
CARLA
CARLE
CARLO
CARLY
CAULK
CAULS
DAILY
DALLY
DARLA
EAGLE
EARLE
EARLS
EARLY
FABLE
FAILS
FALLA
FALLS
FATLY
FAULT
GABLE
GAELS
GAILY
GALLI
GALLO
GALLS
GAOLS
GAULS
GAYLE
GAYLY
HABLA
HAILE
HAILS
HALLE
HALLO
HALLS
HAOLE
HAPLO
HAPLY
HATLO
HAULM
HAULS
JAILS
JARLS
KAHLO
KARLA
LADLE
LAXLY
LAYLA
MACLE
MADLY
MAILE
MAILS
MALLE
MALLS
MANLY
MAPLE
MARLA
MARLO
MARLS
MARLY
MAULS
NAILS
PABLO
PAILS
PALLS
PALLY
PAOLI
PAOLO
PARLE
PATLY
PAULA
PAULO
PAWLS
RAILS
RALLY
RAWLS
RAWLY
SABLE
SADLY
SAILS
SALLE
SALLY
SAULT
TABLA
TABLE
TAELS
TAILS
TALLY
VALLE
VALLI
VAULT
WAALS
WAILS
WALLA
WALLS
WALLY
WANLY
YAWLS

•A••L

BABEL
BABUL
BAGEL
BAIUL
BANAL
BASAL
BASEL
BASIL
CABAL
CAMEL
CANAL
CAROL
CAVIL
DARYL
EASEL
FATAL
GAMAL
GAVEL
GAYAL
HAMAL
HAMEL
HAVEL
HAZEL
JAMAL
KABUL
KALEL
KAREL
KAROL
LABEL
LAPEL
LAVAL
MABEL
MAHAL
MAZEL
NAGEL
NASAL
NATAL
NAVAL
NAVEL
PANDL
PANEL
PAPAL
PAROL
RAHAL
RAOUL
RATEL
RAVEL
SAGAL
SAHEL
SALAL
SANDL
TAMIL

••AL•

AGALS
ATALL
BAALS
BBALL
BEALL
BEALS
BIALY
CHALK
COALS
DEALS
DEALT
DHALS
DIALS
EXALT
FOALS
GHALI
GOALS
HEALS
HEALY
INALL
ITALO
ITALS
ITALY
KOALA
KUALA
MEALS
MEALY
NEALE
NYALA
OCALA
OPALS
ORALE
ORALS
OVALS
PEALE
PEALS
PSALM
QUALE
QUALM
REALM
REALS
RIALS
ROALD
SCALA
SCALD
SCALE
SCALP
SCALY
SEALE
SEALS
SEALY
SHALE
SHALL
SHALT
SIALS
SKALD
SMALL
SMALT
SPALL
STALE
STALK
STALL
SWALE
TBALL
TEALS
TRALA
UDALL
URALS
UZALA
VEALY
VIALS
WAALS
WEALS
WHALE
ZEALS

••A•L

AMAHL
ATALL
AVAIL
BBALL
BEALL
BRAIL
BRAWL
CRAWL
DRAIL
DRAWL
EMAIL
FLAIL
FRAIL
GNARL
GRAIL
INALL
KRAAL
PEARL
QUAIL
SHALL
SHAWL
SMAIL
SMALL
SNAIL
SNARL
SPALL
STAEL
STAHL
STALL
TBALL
TRAIL
TRAWL
UDALL
UHAUL

•••AL

ADVAL
ALGAL
ANNAL
ANTAL
APPAL
AREAL
ARTAL
AURAL
AXIAL
BANAL
BASAL
BINAL
CABAL
CANAL
COPAL
CORAL
COXAL
DECAL
DORAL
DOTAL
DUCAL
EQUAL
FATAL
FERAL
FETAL
FINAL
FOCAL
FUGAL
GAMAL
GAYAL
GLIAL
GORAL
GYRAL
HAMAL
HORAL
IDEAL
JAMAL
JOUAL
JUBAL
JUGAL
JURAL
KEMAL
KRAAL
LAVAL
LEGAL
LOCAL
LOYAL
MAHAL
MEDAL
METAL
MODAL
MORAL
MURAL
NASAL
NATAL
NAVAL
NEPAL
NIVAL
NOCAL
NODAL
NOPAL
OCTAL
OFFAL
ONEAL
PAPAL
PEDAL
PENAL
PETAL
PHIAL
PIPAL
PUPAL
RAHAL
REGAL
RENAL
RIVAL
RIYAL
ROYAL
RURAL
SAGAL
SALAL
SEGAL
SEPAL
SERAL
SHOAL
SISAL
SKOAL
STEAL
SURAL
TEPAL
TICAL
TIDAL
TIKAL
TONAL
TOTAL
TRIAL
URIAL
USUAL
UXMAL
VENAL
VIDAL
VIRAL
VITAL
VOCAL
WHEAL
ZOEAL
ZONAL

AM•••

AMADO
AMAHL
AMAHS
AMAIN
AMANA
AMAPA
AMARA
AMASS
AMATI
AMATO
AMAZE
AMBER
AMBIT
AMBLE
AMBOS
AMBOY
AMBRY
AMEBA
AMEER
AMEND
AMENS
AMENT
AMICE
AMIDE
AMIDO
AMIES
AMIGA
AMIGO
AMINE
AMINO
AMIRS
AMISH
AMISS
AMITY
AMMAN
AMMON
AMMOS
AMNIA
AMOCO
AMOLE
AMONG
AMORE
AMORT
AMORY
AMOUR
AMPAS
AMPED
AMPHI
AMPHR
AMPLE
AMPLY
AMPUL
AMUCK
AMUSE
AMVET
AMWAY
AMYLO
AMYLS

A•M••

AAMES
ACMES
ADMAN
ADMEN
ADMIN
ADMIT
ADMIX
AHMAD
AHMED
AIMAT
AIMED
AIMEE
AIMER
AIMTO
AJMER
ALMAY
AMMAN
AMMON
AMMOS
ARMED
ARMEE
ARMET
ARMIS
ARMOR
ATMAN
ATMOS

A••M•

ABOMB
ACOMA
ADAMA
ADAMS
AGAMA
ALAMO
ALUMS
ANEMO
ANIMA
ANIME
ANOMY
ARAMA
ARAME
AROMA
ARUMS
ASAMA
ATOMS
ATOMY

A•••M

AANDM
ABEAM
ABOHM
ABRAM
ABYSM
ADEEM
ADHEM
ADREM
ADSUM
AKEEM
AKSUM
ALARM
ALBUM
ANNAM
ANNUM
ARIUM
ASSAM
ATEAM
AURUM
AXIOM

•AM••

AAMES
BAMBI
CAMAY
CAMEL
CAMEO
CAMIS
CAMOS
CAMPO
CAMPS
CAMPY
CAMRY
CAMUS
DAMAN
DAMAR
DAMES
DAMME
DAMNS
DAMON
DAMPS
DAMUP
EAMES
EAMON
FAMED
FAMES
GAMAL
GAMAY
GAMBA
GAMED
GAMER
GAMES
GAMEY
GAMIN
GAMMA
GAMMY
GAMOW
GAMPS
GAMUT
HAMAL
HAMAN
HAMEL
HAMES
HAMMY
IAMBI

IAMBS	ZAMIA	ADAMS	CLAIM	ANGEL	ABNER	ARENA	ANTON	CANIT	LANTZ	SANDH
JAMAL		AGAMA	GRAMM	ANGER	AGNES	ARENS	APIAN	CANNA	LANZA	SANDL
JAMBS	•A•M•	ALAMO	PHARM	ANGES	AGNEW	ARENT	APRON	CANNY	MANCY	SANDS
JAMES	BALMS	ARAMA	PLASM	ANGIE	AGNON	ASANA	ARDEN	CANOE	MANDY	SANDY
JAMIE	BALMY	ARAME	PSALM	ANGIO	AGNUS	ASONE	ARGON	CANON	MANED	SANER
JAMIN	BARMS	ASAMA	QUALM	ANGLE	AINGE	ASSNS	ARIAN	CANSO	MANES	SANKA
JAMMY	BARMY	BEAMS	REAIM	ANGLO	AINUS	ATONE	ARION	CANST	MANET	SANTA
JAMUP	BAUME	BEAMY	REALM	ANGRY	AMNIA	ATONY	ARKIN	CANTO	MANGO	SANTE
LAMAR	CALMS	BLAME	REARM	ANGST	ANNAL	AVANT	ARLEN	CANTS	MANGY	SANTO
LAMAS	DAMME	CHAMP	SHAWM	ANGUS	ANNAM	AVENA	ARRAN	CANTY	MANIA	SANYO
LAMBS	FARMS	CLAMP	SPASM	ANHUI	ANNAN	AVENS	ARSON	DANAE	MANIC	TANDE
LAMED	GAMMA	CLAMS	SWARM	ANILS	ANNEE	AWING	ARYAN	DANCE	MANLY	TANDY
LAMER	GAMMY	CRAMP	UNARM	ANIMA	ANNES	AXING	ASHEN	DANCY	MANNA	TANEY
LAMES	GAUMS	CRAMS		ANIME	ANNEX	AXONE	ASIAN	DANDY	MANNY	TANGO
LAMIA	HAEMA	DRAMA	•••AM	ANION	ANNIE	AXONS	ASKIN	DANES	MANON	TANGS
LAMPS	HAEMO	DRAMS	ABEAM	ANISE	ANNIV	AYINS	ASPEN	DANGS	MANOR	TANGY
MAMAS	HALMS	EDAMS	ABRAM	ANISO	ANNOY	AZANS	ASTIN	DANIO	MANOS	TANKA
MAMBA	HAMMY	EXAMS	ANNAM	ANITA	ANNUL	AZINE	ASTON	DANKE	MANSE	TANKS
MAMBO	HARMS	FLAME	ASSAM	ANJOU	ANNUM		ASWAN	DANNY	MANTA	TANSY
MAMET	JAIME	FLAMS	ATEAM	ANKHS	ANNUS	A•••N	ATEIN	DANSE	NANAK	TANTE
MAMIE	JAMMY	FLAMY	BREAM	ANKLE	APNEA	AAIUN	ATHON	DANTE	NANAS	TANTO
MAMMA	KARMA	FOAMS	CERAM	ANNAL	ARNAZ	AARON	ATION	DANZA	NANCY	TANYA
MAMMY	LAKME	FOAMY	CREAM	ANNAM	ARNEL	ACORN	ATMAN	FANCY	NANNA	VANCE
NAMBY	MAGMA	FRAME	DREAM	ANNAN	ARNIE	ACTIN	AUDEN	FANES	NANNY	VANES
NAMED	MALMO	GRAMA	GLEAM	ANNEE	ASNER	ACTON	AUXIN	FANGS	PANAM	VANIR
NAMER	MAMMA	GRAMM	GLOAM	ANNES	ATNOS	ADDIN	AVIAN	FANNY	PANAY	VANNA
NAMES	MAMMY	GRAMP	HBEAM	ANNEX	AUNTS	ADDON	AVION	FANON	PANDA	VANYA
NAMIB	NAOMI	GRAMS	HIRAM	ANNIE	AUNTY	ADFIN	AXION	FANTA	PANDL	WANDA
NAMOI	PALMA	HYAMS	IBEAM	ANNIV	AWNED	ADMAN		GANDY	PANED	WANDS
NAMPA	PALME	IMAMS	ISLAM	ANNOY		ADMEN	•AN••	GANEF	PANEL	WANED
NAMUR	PALMS	ISAMU	LARAM	ANNUL	A••N•	ADMIN	AANDE	GANGS	PANES	WANER
PAMBY	PALMY	LLAMA	MADAM	ANNUM	ABEND	ADORN	AANDM	HANDS	PANGA	WANES
PAMIR	PARMA	LOAMS	MOHAM	ANNUS	ACING	AERON	BANAL	HANDY	PANGS	WANEY
PAMPA	SALMI	LOAMY	NIZAM	ANOAS	ADANA	AFTON	BANAT	HANES	PANIC	WANLY
RAMAN	SAMMS	MIAMI	OCCAM	ANODE	ADANO	AGAIN	BANCO	HANFF	PANKY	WANNA
RAMAR	SAMMY	NGAMI	OGHAM	ANOLE	ADDNL	AGARN	BANCS	HANGS	PANNE	WANTS
RAMBO	TAMMY	ORAMA	ONEAM	ANOMY	ADENO	AGNON	BANDA	HANKS	PANSY	YANKS
RAMEE	WARMS	PRAMS	PANAM	ANOUK	ADINT	AGRON	BANDB	HANKY	PANTO	YANNI
RAMEN		REAMS	PRIAM	ANSAE	AEONS	AHSIN	BANDO	HANNA	PANTS	ZANTE
RAMET	•A••M	ROAMS	PROAM	ANSEL	AETNA	AIDAN	BANDS	HANNO	PANZA	
RAMIE	AANDM	SCAMP	SALAM	ANSER	AGANA	AIKEN	BANDW	HANOI	QANDA	•A•N•
RAMIS	CANEM	SCAMS	SCRAM	ANSON	AGENA	AKRON	BANDY	HANSA	RANAT	BANNS
RAMON	CAROM	SEAMS	SIXAM	ANTAE	AGENT	ALAIN	BANES	HANSE	RANCH	BARNS
RAMOS	DATUM	SEAMY	STEAM	ANTAL	AGING	ALBAN	BANFF	HANTS	RANDB	CAINE
RAMPS	HAKIM	SHAME	TENAM	ANTAS	AGONY	ALBEN	BANGS	JANET	RANDD	CANNA
SAMAR	HAREM	SHAMS	TWOAM	ANTED	AISNE	ALCAN	BANJO	JANIE	RANDI	CANNY
SAMBA	HARUM	SHAMU	UNJAM	ANTES	AKENE	ALDAN	BANKS	JANIS	RANDR	CARNE
SAMMS	HAULM	SLAMS		ANTHO	AKINS	ALDEN	BANKY	JANUS	RANDS	CARNY
SAMMY	KASEM	SPAMS	AN•••	ANTIC	ALANA	ALGIN	BANNS	KANDY	RANDY	DAMNS
SAMOA	LARAM	STAMP	ANAIS	ANTIQ	ALAND	ALIEN	BANTU	KANGA	RANEE	DANNY
SAMOS	MADAM	SWAMI	ANCON	ANTIS	ALENE	ALIGN	CANAD	KANIN	RANGE	DARNS
SAMPS	MAXIM	SWAMP	ANDES	ANTON	ALINE	ALLAN	CANAL	KANJI	RANGY	DAUNT
TAMBO	NAHUM	TEAMS	ANDIE	ANTRA	ALONE	ALLEN	CANBY	KANSA	RANID	DAWNS
TAMED	OAKUM	TRAMP	ANDOR	ANTRE	ALONG	ALLIN	CANDO	KANZU	RANIN	DAYNE
TAMER	PANAM	TRAMS	ANDRE	ANTSY	AMANA	ALTON	CANDW	LANAI	RANIS	EARNS
TAMES	SALAM	WHAMO	ANDRO	ANVIL	AMEND	ALVIN	CANDY	LANCE	RANKE	FAINT
TAMIL	SALEM	WHAMS	ANDRY	ANWAR	AMENS	AMAIN	CANEA	LANDI	RANKS	FANNY
TAMMY	TATUM		ANDUP	ANZAC	AMENT	AMMAN	CANED	LANDO	RANON	FAUNA
TAMPA	VADIM	••A•M	ANEAR	ANZIO	AMINE	AMMON	CANEM	LANDS	RANTO	FAUNS
TAMPS	YADIM	ALARM	ANELE		AMINO	ANCON	CANER	LANES	RANTS	FAWNS
VAMOS		CHAIM	ANEMO	A•N••	AMONG	ANION	CANES	LANGE	RANUP	GAINS
VAMPS	••AM•	CHARM	ANENT	AANDE	ANENT	ANNAN	CANID	LANKA	SANAA	GARNI
YAMPA	ADAMA	CHASM	ANETO	AANDM	APING	ANSON	CANIS	LANKY	SANDE	GAUNT

HADNT
HANNA
HANNO
HASNT
HAUNT
JAINS
JAUNE
JAUNT
JAYNE
KAONS
LAINE
LAING
LAWNS
LAWNY
LAYNE
MAGNA
MAINE
MAINS
MAINZ
MANNA
MANNY
MARNE
MAUNA
MAUND
MAYNT
NAINA
NANNA
NANNY
PAINE
PAINS
PAINT
PANNE
PATNA
PAWNS
PAYNE
RAINS
RAINY
SAENS
SAINT
SAONE
SAUNA
TAINE
TAINO
TAINT
TARNS
TAUNT
TAWNY
VANNA
VARNA
VAUNT
WAINS
WANNA
WARNS
WASNT
WAYNE
YANNI
YARNS
YAWNS

•A••N

AAIUN
AARON
BACON
BADEN
BAIRN
BALIN
BARON
BASIN
BATON
CABIN
CAIRN
CAJUN
CANON
CAPON
CARON
DAGON
DAMAN
DAMON
DARIN
DAYAN
EAGAN
EAMON
EATEN
EATIN
EATON
FAGIN
FANON
FARON
GABON
GALEN
GAMIN
GATUN
GAVIN
HADON
HAFUN
HAGEN
HALON
HAMAN
HASON
HAVEN
HAYDN
HAZAN
JAMIN
JAPAN
JASON
KANIN
KARAN
KAREN
KAZAN
LABAN
LADEN
LADON
LAGAN
LAPIN
LATEN
LATIN
LAVIN
LAYIN
LAYON
MACON
MAHAN
MAHON
MALAN
MANON
MARIN
MASON
MATIN
MAVEN
MAYAN
MAYON
NAIRN
OAKEN
OATEN
PAEAN
PAEON
PAGAN
PALIN
PAREN
PATEN
PATON
PAYIN
RABIN
RACON
RADON
RAMAN
RAMEN
RAMON
RANIN
RANON
RATON
RAVEN
RAVIN
RAYON
SABIN
SAGAN
SALON
SARAN
SATAN
SATIN
SATON
SAWIN
SAXON
TAKEN
TAKIN
TALON
TAPIN
TAUON
TAXON
WAGON
WAKEN
WAXEN
ZAYIN
ZAZEN

••AN•

ADANA
ADANO
AGANA
ALANA
ALAND
AMANA
ASANA
AVANT
AZANS
BEANO
BEANS
BEANY
BLANC
BLAND
BLANK
BRAND
BRANS
BRANT
BWANA
CHANG
CHANT
CLANG
CLANK
CLANS
CRANE
CRANK
CYANO
DEANE
DEANS
DIANA
DIANE
DRANG
DRANK
DRANO
DUANE
ELAND
EVANS
FLANK
FLANS
FRANC
FRANK
FRANS
FRANZ
GHANA
GIANT
GLAND
GRAND
GRANI
GRANT
INANE
IPANA
IRANI
IVANA
JEANE
JEANS
KEANE
KEANU
KHANS
KIANG
KOANS
LEANS
LEANT
LIANA
LIANE
LIANG
LLANO
LOANS
MEANS
MEANT
MEANY
MOANS
OLAND
OMANI
ORANG
ORANT
PHANY
PIANO
PLANB
PLANE
PLANI
PLANK
PLANO
PLANS
PLANT
PRANG
PRANK
QUAND
QUANT
RIANT
ROANS
RUANA
SCAND
SCANS
SCANT
SHANA
SHANE
SHANK
SHANS
SHANT
SKANK
SLANG
SLANT
SPANG
SPANK
SPANS
STAND
STANG
STANK
SWANK
SWANN
SWANS
THANE
THANK
THANT
TIANT
TRANS
TWANG
VIAND
WEANS
WHANG
YEANS
YUANS

••A•N

AGAIN
AGARN
ALAIN
AMAIN
BRAIN
BRAUN
BRAWN
CHAIN
CRAIN
DRAIN
DRAWN
GHAIN
GRAIN
HEARN
ICAHN
LEARN
PLAIN
PRAWN
SHAHN
SHAUN
SHAWN
SLAIN
SPAHN
SPAIN
SPAWN
STAIN
SWAIN
SWANN
TRAIN
TWAIN
UTAHN
YEARN

•••AN

ADMAN
AIDAN
ALBAN
ALCAN
ALDAN
ALLAN
AMMAN
ANNAN
APIAN
ARIAN
ARRAN
ARYAN
ASIAN
ASWAN
ATMAN
AVIAN
BEGAN
BEHAN
BRIAN
BRYAN
CLEAN
COHAN
CONAN
COPAN
CUBAN
DAMAN
DAYAN
DEWAN
DIVAN
DORAN
DUGAN
DURAN
DYLAN
EAGAN
ELMAN
ETHAN
EVIAN
FURAN
GLEAN
GOLAN
GROAN
HAMAN
HAZAN
HEMAN
HENAN
HOBAN
HOGAN
HONAN
HUMAN
HUNAN
HYMAN
INCAN
IOWAN
JAPAN
KARAN
KAZAN
KORAN
LABAN
LAGAN
LEXAN
LOGAN
LOMAN
LORAN
LUCAN
LYMAN
MAHAN
MALAN
MAYAN
MEGAN
MELAN
MIKAN
MILAN
MORAN
NEMAN
NISAN
NOLAN
OCEAN
OLEAN
ORGAN
OSCAN
OSMAN
PAEAN
PAGAN
PECAN
PERAN
PISAN
PUSAN
RAMAN
REDAN
REGAN
REHAN
REMAN
RENAN
RERAN
RODAN
ROMAN
ROWAN
SAGAN
SARAN
SATAN
SEDAN
SHEAN
SIVAN
SKEAN
SLOAN
SOLAN
SUDAN
SUSAN
TEXAN
TIRAN
TITAN
TYNAN
UCLAN
UHLAN
UNMAN
URBAN
VEGAN
WIGAN
WOMAN
WOTAN
WUHAN
WYMAN
YUMAN

AO•••

AODAI
AOKAY
AORTA

A•O••

ABODE
ABOHM
ABOIL
ABOMB
ABORT
ABOUT
ABOVE
ABOVO
ACOMA
ACORN
ADOBE
ADOLF
ADOPT
ADORE
ADORN
ADOUT
AEONS
AFOFL
AFOOT
AFORE
AFOUL
AGOGO
AGONY
AGORA
AHORA
AHOYS
AIOLI
ALOES
ALOFT
ALOHA
ALONE
ALONG
ALOOF
ALORS
ALOUD
AMOCO
AMOLE
AMONG
AMORE
AMORT
AMORY
AMOUR
ANOAS
ANODE
ANOLE
ANOMY
ANOUK
APORT
AROAR
AROID
AROMA
AROSE
ASOKA
ASONE
ATOLL
ATOMS
ATOMY
ATONE
ATONY
AVOID
AVOIR
AVOWS
AWOKE
AWOLS
AXONE
AXONS
AZOIC
AZOTE
AZOTH

A••O•

AARON
ABBOT
ABHOR
ACHOO
ACTON
ACTOR
ADDON
ADHOC
ADIOS
ADLOC
AEIOU
AERON
AEROS
AESOP
AFOOT
AFROS
AFTON
AGIOS
AGLOW
AGNON
AGRON
AKRON
ALCOA
ALCOR
ALDOL
ALGOL
ALIOS
ALLOT
ALLOW
ALLOY
ALOOF
ALSOP
ALTON
ALTOS
AMBOS
AMBOY
AMMON
AMMOS
ANCON
ANDOR
ANION
ANJOU
ANNOY
ANSON
ANTON
APRON
APSOS
ARBOR
ARDOR
ARGOL
ARGON
ARGOS
ARGOT
ARION
ARMOR
ARROW
ARROZ
ARSON
ARTOO
ASCOT
ASSOC
ASTON
ASTOR
ATHOL
ATHON
ATHOS
ATION
ATMOS
ATNOS
AUTOS
AVION
AXIOM
AXION

A•••O

AALTO
ABACO
ABOVO
ACETO
ACHOO
ADANO
ADDTO
ADENO
ADIPO
AGGRO
AGOGO
AIMTO
ALAMO
ALTHO
AMADO
AMATO
AMIDO
AMIGO
AMINO
AMOCO
AMYLO
ANDRO
ANEMO
ANETO
ANGIO
ANGLO
ANISO
ANTHO
ANZIO
ARTOO
ASTRO
AUDIO
AVISO

•AO••

BAOJI
GAOLS
HAOLE
KAONS
MAORI
NAOMI
PAOLI
PAOLO
RAOUL
SAONE

•A•O•

AARON
BACON
BARON
BASOV
BATON
BATOR
BAYOU
CABOT
CAMOS
CANOE
CANON
CAPON
CAPOS
CAROB
CAROL
CAROM
CARON
DADOS
DAFOE
DAGON
DAMON
DAVOS
EAMON
EATON
FADOS
FAGOT
FANON
FAROE
FARON
FAROS
FAVOR
GABON
GABOR
GALOP
GAMOW
GAROU
GATOR

GATOS
GAVOT
HADON
HALON
HALOS
HANOI
HASON
HAVOC
JABOT
JACOB
JASON
JATOS
KABOB
KAPOK
KAROL
KAYOS
KAZOO
LABOR
LADON
LAGOS
LAYON
MACON
MAGOG
MAGOO
MAGOT
MAHON
MAJOR
MAKOS
MANON
MANOR
MANOS
MASON
MAYON
MAYOR
NABOB
NAMOI
NAXOS
PAEON
PALOS
PAROL
PAROS
PATON
RACON
RADON
RAMON
RAMOS
RANON
RATON
RAYON
RAZOR
SABOT
SAGOS
SALON
SAMOA
SAMOS
SAPOR
SAROD
SAROS
SATON
SAVOR
SAVOY
SAXON
TABOO
TABOR
TACOS
TAHOE
TALON
TALOS
TAROK
TAROT
TAUON
TAXON
VALOR
VAMOS
VAPOR
WAGON
WAHOO
YAHOO
YAKOV
YALOW
YAPOK
YAZOO

•A••O
AALTO
BALTO
BANCO
BANDO
BANJO
BASHO
BASSO
BATHO
CACAO
CADDO
CAELO
CAIRO
CAMEO
CAMPO
CANDO
CANSO
CANTO
CARBO
CARGO
CARLO
CARPO
CASCO
CASIO
DANIO
DARIO
DAVAO
FABIO
FACTO
FALDO
FARGO
GALLO
GARBO
HADTO
HAEMO
HAGIO
HALLO
HANNO
HAPLO
HARPO
HASSO
HASTO
HATLO
IATRO
KAHLO
KAZOO
LABIO
LACTO
LANDO
LARGO
LASSO
LAYTO
MACAO
MACHO
MACRO
MAGOO
MALMO
MAMBO
MANGO
MARCO
MARGO
MARIO
MARLO
MATEO
MATRO
MATZO
MAYPO
NACHO
NARCO
PAAVO
PABLO
PALEO
PANTO
PAOLO
PARDO
PARVO
PASCO
PASEO
PASTO
PATHO
PATIO
PAULO
RADIO
RAMBO
RANTO
RATIO
RATSO
SACCO
SACRO
SALVO
SANTO
SANYO
SARGO
SARTO
SAWTO
SAYSO
TABOO
TACHO
TAINO
TAMBO
TANGO
TANTO
TASSO
TAUPO
TAURO
TAUTO
TAXCO
VASCO
WACKO
WAHOO
WALDO
XACTO
YAHOO
YAZOO

••AO•
CHAOS
MIAOW

••A•O
ABACO
ADANO
ALAMO
AMADO
AMATO
BEANO
BRAVO
CHACO
CHARO
CLARO
CYANO
DIAZO
DRACO
DRANO
ERATO
GLAXO
GUACO
IDAHO
IMAGO
ITALO
LLANO
NEATO
NGAIO
PAAVO
PEABO
PHAGO
PIANO
PLANO
PLATO
PRADO
PRATO
SEATO
SHAKO
WHAMO

•••AO
CACAO
DAVAO
DRLAO
MACAO

AP•••
APACE
APART
APEAK
APERS
APERY
APFEL
APHID
APHIS
APIAN
APING
APISH
APLEY
APLUS
APNEA
APORT
APPAL
APPEL
APPLE
APPLY
APPTD
APPTS
APRES
APRIL
APRON
APSES
APSIS
APSOS
APTED
APTER
APTLY
APURE

A•P••
ALPHA
AMPAS
AMPED
AMPHI
AMPHR
AMPLE
AMPLY
AMPUL
APPAL
APPEL
APPLE
APPLY
APPTD
APPTS
ARPAD
ARPEL
ASPCA
ASPEN
ASPIC
ATPAR

A••P•
ADAPT
ADEPT
ADIPO
ADOPT
AGAPE
ALEPH
AMAPA

A•••P
ACTUP
ADDUP
AESOP
AGASP
ALSOP
ANDUP
ASCAP
ATEUP
ATRIP

•AP••
CAPED
CAPEK
CAPER
CAPES
CAPET
CAPON
CAPOS
CAPRA
CAPRI
CAPTS
GAPED
GAPER
GAPES
HAPLO
HAPLY
HAPPY
JAPAN
JAPED
JAPES
KAPHS
KAPOK
KAPPA
KAPUT
LAPAZ
LAPEL
LAPIN
LAPIS
LAPPS
LAPSE
LAPUP
MAPLE
NAPES
NAPPE
NAPPY
PAPAL
PAPAS
PAPAW
PAPER
PAPPI
PAPPY
PAPUA
RAPEE
RAPHE
RAPID
SAPID
SAPIR
SAPOR
SAPPY
TAPAS
TAPED
TAPER
TAPES
TAPIN
TAPIR
VAPID
VAPOR
YAPOK
ZAPPA
ZAPPY

•A•P•
CALPE
CAMPO
CAMPS
CAMPY
CARPE
CARPI
CARPO
CARPS
DAMPS
GAMPS
GASPE
GASPS
GAWPS
HAPPY
HARPO
HARPS
HARPY
HASPS
KAPPA
LAMPS
LAPPS
MAYPO
NAMPA
NAPPE
NAPPY
PALPI
PALPS
PAMPA
PAPPI
PAPPY
RALPH
RAMPS
RASPS
RASPY
SALPA
SALPS
SAMPS
SAPPY
TAMPA
TAMPS
TARPS
TAUPE
TAUPO
VAMPS
WARPS
WASPS
WASPY
YAMPA
YAWPS
ZAPPA
ZAPPY

•A••P
DAMUP
EATUP
GALOP
GASUP
JAMUP
LAPUP
LAYUP
NAACP
PAYUP
RANUP
SALEP
SATUP
TAGUP
WADUP

••AP•
ADAPT
AGAPE
AMAPA
CHAPS
CLAPS
COAPT
CRAPE
CRAPS
DRAPE
ETAPE
FLAPS
FRAPS
GOAPE
GRAPE
GRAPH
GRAPY
HEAPS
INAPT
KNAPS
LEAPS
LEAPT
NEAPS
OKAPI
REAPS
SCAPA
SCAPE
SHAPE
SLAPS
SNAPS
SOAPS
SOAPY
SWAPS
TRAPP
TRAPS
UNAPT
WRAPS
WRAPT

••A•P
AGASP
CHAMP
CLAMP
CLASP
CRAMP
GRAMP
GRASP
NAACP
SCALP
SCAMP
SCARP
SCAUP
SHARP
STAMP
SWAMP
THARP
TRAMP
TRAPP

•••AP
ASCAP
CHEAP
ONTAP
PTRAP
RECAP
REMAP
RETAP
SCRAP
STRAP
UNCAP

AQ•••
AQABA
AQUAE
AQUAS

A•Q••
ATQUE

A•••Q
ANTIQ

•AQ••
MAQUI
YAQUI

•A•Q•
BARQS

•A••Q
BARBQ

••AQ•
IRAQI

AR•••
ARABS
ARABY
ARAMA
ARAME
ARBER
ARBOR
ARBRE
ARCED
ARCHI
ARCHY
ARDEN
ARDOR
AREAL
AREAR
AREAS
ARECA
ARENA
ARENS
ARENT
ARETE
ARGIL
ARGOL
ARGON
ARGOS
ARGOT
ARGUE
ARGUS
ARHAT
ARHUS
ARIAN
ARIAS
ARICA
ARIEL
ARIES
ARILS
ARION
ARISE
ARITH
ARIUM
ARIUS
ARKIN
ARLEN
ARLES
ARMED
ARMEE
ARMET
ARMIS
ARMOR
ARNAZ
ARNEL
ARNIE
AROAR
AROID
AROMA
AROSE
ARPAD
ARPEL
ARRAN
ARRAS
ARRAU
ARRAY
ARRET
ARRIS
ARROW
ARROZ
ARSIS
ARSON
ARTAL
ARTEL
ARTES
ARTHR
ARTIE
ARTIS
ARTOO
ARTSY
ARTUR
ARUBA
ARUMS
ARYAN

A•R••
AARGH
AARON
ABRAM
ABRIL
ABRIS
ACRED
ACRES
ACRID
ADREM
AERIE
AERON
AEROS
AFRIC
AFRIT
AFROS
AGREE
AGRIC
AGRON
AIRED
AIRES
AKRON
AORTA
APRES
APRIL
APRON
ARRAN
ARRAS
ARRAU
ARRAY
ARRET
ARRIS
ARROW
ARROZ
ATRIA
ATRIP
AURAE
AURAL
AURAR
AURAS
AUREI
AURIC
AURUM
AVRIL
AYRES

A••R•
ABBRS
ABORT
ACARI
ACCRA
ACERB
ACERS
ACORN
ACURA
ADORE
ADORN
AFARS
AFIRE
AFORE
AFTRA
AGARN
AGARS
AGERS
AGGRO
AGORA
AHORA
AKIRA

ALARM
ALERT
ALFRE
ALORS
AMARA
AMBRY
AMIRS
AMORE
AMORT
AMORY
ANDRE
ANDRO
ANDRY
ANGRY
ANTRA
ANTRE
APART
APERS
APERY
APORT
APURE
ARBRE
ASTRA
ASTRE
ASTRO
ATARI
AUDRA
AUTRE
AUTRY
AVARS
AVERS
AVERT
AVERY
AWARD
AWARE
AXERS
AYERS
AZURE

A•••R

ABHOR
ABLER
ABNER
ACTER
ACTOR
ADAIR
ADDER
ADLER
AEGIR
AESIR
AFTER
AILER
AIMER
AJMER
AKBAR
ALCOR
ALDER
ALGER
ALLER
ALTAR
ALTER
ALVAR
AMBER
AMEER
AMOUR
AMPHR
ANDOR
ANEAR
ANGER
ANSER
ANWAR
APTER
ARBER
ARBOR
ARDOR
AREAR
ARMOR
AROAR
ARTHR
ARTUR
ASHER
ASHUR
ASKER
ASNER
ASSUR
ASSYR
ASTER
ASTIR
ASTOR
ATPAR
ATTAR
ATWAR
AUBER
AUGER
AUGUR
AURAR
AUSTR
AVOIR

•AR••

AARGH
AARON
BARAB
BARBQ
BARBS
BARCA
BARDS
BARED
BARER
BARES
BARGE
BARGY
BARIC
BARIT
BARKS
BARKY
BARMS
BARMY
BARNS
BARON
BARQS
BARRE
BARRY
BARTH
BARTS
BARTY
CARAT
CARBO
CARBS
CARDI
CARDS
CARED
CARER
CARES
CARET
CAREW
CAREY
CARGO
CARIA
CARIB
CARKS
CARLA
CARLE
CARLO
CARLY
CARNE
CARNY
CAROB
CAROL
CAROM
CARON
CARPE
CARPI
CARPO
CARPS
CARRE
CARRY
CARTA
CARTE
CARTS
CARVE
DARBY
DARED
DARER
DARES
DARIN
DARIO
DARKS
DARLA
DARNS
DARTH
DARTS
DARYA
DARYL
EARED
EARLE
EARLS
EARLY
EARNS
EARTH
FARAD
FARAH
FARCE
FARCI
FARED
FARER
FARES
FARGO
FARMS
FAROE
FARON
FAROS
FARSI
GARBO
GARBS
GARDA
GARDE
GARNI
GAROU
GARRY
GARTH
HARAR
HARDC
HARDG
HARDY
HARED
HAREM
HARES
HARKS
HARMS
HARPO
HARPS
HARPY
HARRY
HARSH
HARTE
HARTS
HARUM
JARLS
JARRE
KARAN
KARAT
KAREL
KAREN
KARLA
KARMA
KAROL
KARSH
LARAM
LARAS
LARCH
LARDS
LARDY
LARES
LARGE
LARGO
LARIS
LARKS
LARKY
LARRY
LARUE
LARVA
MARAS
MARAT
MARCH
MARCO
MARCY
MARDI
MARES
MARGE
MARGO
MARIA
MARIE
MARIN
MARIO
MARIS
MARKS
MARLA
MARLO
MARLS
MARLY
MARNE
MARRY
MARSH
MARTA
MARTI
MARTS
MARTY
MARVY
MARYS
NARAS
NARCO
NARCS
NARDS
NARES
NAREW
NARIS
NARKS
OARED
PARCA
PARCH
PARDI
PARDO
PARDS
PARED
PAREE
PAREN
PARER
PARES
PAREU
PARIS
PARKA
PARKS
PARLE
PARMA
PAROL
PAROS
PARRY
PARSE
PARTE
PARTI
PARTS
PARTY
PARVO
RAREE
RARER
RARES
SARAH
SARAN
SARDS
SARGE
SARGO
SARIS
SARKY
SAROD
SAROS
SARTO
TARDE
TARDY
TARES
TARGE
TARNS
TAROK
TAROT
TARPS
TARRY
TARSI
TARTS
TARTU
VARAS
VARIA
VARIG
VARIX
VARNA
WARDS
WARES
WARMS
WARNS
WARPS
WARTS
WARTY
YARDS
YARER
YARNS
ZARFS

•A•R•

BAIRD
BAIRN
BARRE
BARRY
BASRA
CADRE
CAIRN
CAIRO
CAMRY
CAPRA
CAPRI
CARRE
CARRY
DAIRY
EAGRE
FAERY
FAIRE
FAIRS
FAIRY
FAURE
FAVRE
GARRY
GAURS
HAIRS
HAIRY
HARRY
HAVRE
IATRO
IATRY
JAHRE
JARRE
KAURI
LAIRD
LAIRS
LARRY
LATRY
LAURA
MACRO
MADRE
MAHRE
MAORI
MARRY
MATRI
MATRO
MAURY
NACRE
NAIRA
NAIRN
NAURU
PADRE
PAIRS
PARRY
PATRI
SABRA
SABRE
SACRA
SACRE
SACRO
SAURY
TAHRS
TARRY
TATRA
TAURO
TAYRA
ZAIRE

•A••R

BABAR
BABER
BADER
BAKER
BALER
BARER
BASER
BATOR
BAUER
BAYAR
BAYER
CABER
CAGER
CANER
CAPER
CARER
CATER
CAVER
DAKAR
DAMAR
DARER
DATER
EAGER
EATER
FABER
FACER
FAKER
FAKIR
FARER
FAVOR
GABOR
GAMER
GAPER
GASTR
GATOR
GAYER
GAZER
HABER
HADAR
HAGAR
HALER
HARAR
HATER
HAUER
HAVER
HAZER
KADAR
KAFIR
LABOR
LACER
LADER
LAGER
LAHAR
LAKER
LAMAR
LAMER
LASER
LATER
LAUER
LAVER
LAXER
LAYER
LAZAR
MAHER
MAJOR
MAKER
MALAR
MANOR
MASER
MASUR
MATER
MAYER
MAYOR
MAZER
NADER
NADIR
NAMER
NAMUR
OATER
PACER
PAGER
PALER
PAMIR
PAPER
PARER
PATER
PAVER
PAWER
PAYER
QATAR
RACER
RADAR
RAFER
RAKER
RAMAR
RANDR
RARER
RASER
RATER
RAVER
RAWER
RAZOR
SABER
SAFER
SAGER
SAKER
SAMAR
SANER
SAPIR
SAPOR
SATYR
SAVER
SAVOR
SAYER
TABOR
TAKER
TALER
TAMER
TAPER
TAPIR
TASER
TATAR
TATER
TAXER
VADER
VALOR
VANIR
VAPOR
VATER
WADER
WAFER
WAGER
WALER
WANER
WATER
WAVER
WAXER
YARER
YASIR

••AR•

ACARI
AFARS
AGARN
AGARS
ALARM
AMARA
APART
ATARI
AVARS
AWARD
AWARE
BEARD
BEARS
BLARE
BOARD
BOARS
CHARD
CHARM
CHARO
CHARS
CHART
CHARY
CLARA
CLARE
CLARK
CLARO
CLARY
CZARS
DEARS
DEARY
DIARY
DMARK
DWARF
FEARS
FLARE
GEARS
GEARY
GLARE
GLARY
GNARL
GNARS
GUARD
GUARS
HEARD
HEARN
HEARS
HEART
HOARD
HOARS
HOARY
IBARS
INARI
IZARD
IZARS
JBARS
KMART
KNARS
LEARN
LEARS
LEARY
LIARD
LIARS
MEARA
NEARS
OHARA
OHARE
OMARR
OPART
OTARU
OTARY
OZARK
PEARL
PEARS
PEARY
PHARM
QUARE
QUARK
QUART
REARM
REARS
ROARS
RUARK
SCARE
SCARF
SCARP
SCARS
SCARY
SEARS
SHARD
SHARE
SHARI
SHARK
SHARP
SMART
SNARE
SNARK
SNARL
SOARS
SPARE
SPARK
SPARS
STARE
STARK
STARR
STARS
START
STARZ
SWARD
SWARF
SWARM
SWART
TBARS
TEARS
TEARY
THARP
TIARA
TSARS
TZARS
UNARM
WEARS
WEARY
WHARF
YEARN
YEARS
ZBARS

••A•R

ADAIR
BLAIR
CHAIR
CLAIR
FLAIR
GLAIR
OHAIR
OMARR
ONAIR
QUADR
REAIR

STAIR
STARR
USAIR

•••AR
AKBAR
ALTAR
ALVAR
ANEAR
ANWAR
AREAR
AROAR
ATPAR
ATTAR
ATWAR
AURAR
BABAR
BAYAR
BIHAR
BLEAR
BOYAR
BRIAR
BYFAR
CEDAR
CESAR
CIGAR
CLEAR
DAKAR
DAMAR
DEBAR
DEWAR
DINAR
DREAR
EDGAR
EGGAR
ELGAR
EMBAR
FILAR
FRIAR
GOFAR
GULAR
HADAR
HAGAR
HARAR
HOWAR
KADAR
LAHAR
LAMAR
LAZAR
LEHAR
LEVAR
LUNAR
MALAR
MIZAR
MOLAR
MYLAR
NOPAR
OSCAR
OSKAR
PILAR
POLAR
QATAR
RADAR
RAMAR
REBAR
RETAR
SAMAR
SEGAR
SHEAR
SITAR
SMEAR
SOFAR
SOLAR
SONAR
SPEAR
SUGAR
SWEAR
TATAR
UNBAR
VELAR
VICAR
VOLAR
ZOHAR

AS•••
ASAMA
ASANA
ASCAP
ASCII
ASCOT
ASCUS
ASDIC
ASHBY
ASHEN
ASHER
ASHES
ASHUR
ASIAN
ASIDE
ASKED
ASKER
ASKEW
ASKIN
ASNER
ASOKA
ASONE
ASPCA
ASPEN
ASPIC
ASSAD
ASSAI
ASSAM
ASSAY
ASSES
ASSET
ASSEZ
ASSNS
ASSOC
ASSTD
ASSTS
ASSUR
ASSYR
ASTER
ASTIN
ASTIR
ASTON
ASTOR
ASTRA
ASTRE
ASTRO
ASWAN
ASYET
ASYLA
ASYUT

A•S••
ADSUM
AESIR
AESOP
AHSIN
AISHA
AISLE
AISNE
AKSUM
ALSOP
ANSAE
ANSEL
ANSER
ANSON
APSES
APSIS
APSOS
ARSIS
ARSON
ASSAD
ASSAI
ASSAM
ASSAY
ASSES
ASSET
ASSEZ
ASSNS
ASSOC
ASSTD
ASSTS
ASSUR
ASSYR
ATSEA
AUSSI
AUSTR

A••S•
ABASE
ABASH
ABUSE
ABYSM
ABYSS
ADUST
AGASP
ALIST
AMASS
AMISH
AMISS
AMUSE
ANGST
ANISE
ANISO
ANTSY
APISH
ARISE
AROSE
ARTSY
AUSSI
AVAST
AVISO
AWASH
AZUSA

A•••S
AAMES
ABBAS
ABBES
ABBRS
ABETS
ABRIS
ABUTS
ABYES
ABYSS
ACADS
ACCTS
ACERS
ACHES
ACIDS
ACMES
ACRES
ACTAS
ACYLS
ADAMS
ADDIS
ADIOS
ADITS
ADZES
AEDES
AEGIS
AEONS
AEROS
AFARS
AFROS
AGALS
AGARS
AGERS
AGHAS
AGIOS
AGNES
AGNUS
AGUES
AHOYS
AIDES
AINUS
AIRES
AKEES
AKINS
ALDUS
ALEFS
ALFAS
ALIAS
ALIFS
ALIOS
ALLES
ALOES
ALORS
ALTOS
ALTUS
ALUMS
AMAHS
AMASS
AMBOS
AMENS
AMIES
AMIRS
AMISS
AMMOS
AMPAS
AMYLS
ANAIS
ANDES
ANGES
ANGUS
ANILS
ANKHS
ANNES
ANNUS
ANOAS
ANTAS
ANTES
ANTIS
APERS
APHIS
APLUS
APPTS
APRES
APSES
APSIS
APSOS
AQUAS
ARABS
AREAS
ARENS
ARGOS
ARGUS
ARHUS
ARIAS
ARIES
ARILS
ARIUS
ARLES
ARMIS
ARRAS
ARRIS
ARSIS
ARTES
ARTIS
ARUMS
ASCUS
ASHES
ASSES
ASSNS
ASSTS
ATHOS
ATLAS
ATMOS
ATNOS
ATOMS
ATTYS
AUDIS
AUJUS
AULIS
AUNTS
AURAS
AUTOS
AVARS
AVENS
AVERS
AVGAS
AVOWS
AWACS
AWOLS
AXELS
AXERS
AXILS
AXLES
AXONS
AYAHS
AYERS
AYINS
AYRES
AZANS

•AS••
BASAL
BASED
BASEL
BASER
BASES
BASHO
BASIC
BASIE
BASIL
BASIN
BASIS
BASKS
BASOV
BASRA
BASSI
BASSO
BASTE
CASAS
CASCA
CASCO
CASED
CASES
CASEY
CASIO
CASKS
CASTE
CASTS
CASUS
DASHI
EASED
EASEL
EASES
EASTS
FASTS
GASES
GASPE
GASPS
GASSY
GASTR
GASUP
HASAT
HASID
HASNT
HASON
HASPS
HASSO
HASTA
HASTE
HASTO
HASTY
JASEY
JASON
JASSY
KASEM
KASHA
LASED
LASER
LASES
LASSO
LASTS
MASAI
MASER
MASHY
MASKS
MASON
MASSE
MASSY
MASTS
MASUR
NASAL
NASBY
NASHE
NASTY
OASES
OASIS
OASTS
PASCH
PASCO
PASEO
PASES
PASHA
PASSE
PASSU
PASSY
PASTA
PASTE
PASTO
PASTS
PASTY
RASED
RASER
RASES
RASHT
RASPS
RASPY
RASTA
SASES
SASHA
SASSY
TASER
TASKS
TASSE
TASSO
TASTE
TASTY
VASCO
VASES
VASTY
WASHY
WASNT
WASPS
WASPY
WASTE
YASIR

•A•S•
BAKST
BALSA
BASSI
BASSO
CANSO
CANST
CAUSA
CAUSE
DAISY
DANSE
FALSE
FARSI
FAUST
GASSY
GAUSS
HADST
HANSA
HANSE
HARSH
HASSO
HAUSA
HAWSE
JASSY
KANSA
KARSH
LAPSE
LASSO
MANSE
MARSH
MASSE
MASSY
MATSU
MAYST
NAISH
PABST
PAISA
PALSY
PANSY
PARSE
PASSE
PASSU
PASSY
PATSY
PAUSE
RAISA
RAISE
RATSO
SALSA
SASSY
SAYSO
TANSY
TARSI
TASSE
TASSO
VALSE
WAIST
WALSH
WALSY

•A••S
AAMES
BAALS
BABAS
BABES
BABIS
BABYS
BACHS
BACKS
BAHTS
BAILS
BAITS
BAKES
BALAS
BALDS
BALES
BALKS
BALLS
BALMS
BALTS
BANCS
BANDS
BANES
BANGS
BANKS
BANNS
BARBS
BARDS
BARES
BARKS
BARMS
BARNS
BARQS
BARTS
BASES
BASIS
BASKS
BATES
BATHS
BATTS
BAWLS
CADIS
CAFES
CAGES
CAKES
CALKS
CALLS
CALMS
CAMIS
CAMOS
CAMPS
CAMUS
CANES
CANIS
CANTS
CAPES
CAPOS
CAPTS
CARBS
CARDS
CARES
CARKS
CARPS
CARTS
CASAS
CASES
CASKS
CASTS
CASUS
CATES
CAULS
CAVES
DACES
DADOS
DAFFS
DALES
DAMES
DAMNS
DAMPS
DANES
DANGS
DARES
DARKS
DARNS
DARTS
DATES
DAUBS
DAVIS
DAVOS
DAVYS
DAWES
DAWNS
DAZES
EAMES
EARLS
EARNS
EASES
EASTS
EAVES
FACES
FACTS
FADES
FADOS
FAILS
FAIRS
FAKES
FALLS
FAMES
FANES
FANGS
FARES
FARMS
FAROS
FASTS
FATES
FAUNS
FAVES
FAWNS
FAXES
FAZES
GAELS
GAFFS
GAGES
GAINS
GAITS
GAIUS
GALAS
GALES
GALLS
GAMES
GAMPS
GANGS
GAOLS
GAPES
GARBS
GASES
GASPS
GATES
GATOS
GAUDS
GAULS
GAUMS
GAURS
GAUSS
GAWKS
GAWPS
GAZES
HACKS
HADES
HAFTS
HAHAS
HAIKS
HAILS
HAIRS
HAJIS
HAKES
HALAS
HALES
HALLS
HALMS
HALOS
HALTS
HAMES
HANDS
HANES
HANGS
HANKS
HANTS
HARES
HARKS
HARMS
HARPS
HARTS
HASPS
HATES
HAULS
HAVES
HAWGS
HAWKS

HAYES
HAZES
IAMBS
JACKS
JADES
JAILS
JAINS
JAKES
JAMBS
JAMES
JANIS
JANUS
JAPES
JARLS
JATOS
JAVAS
KAKAS
KAKIS
KALES
KAONS
KAPHS
KAVAS
KAYOS
LACES
LACKS
LADES
LADYS
LAGOS
LAICS
LAIRS
LAIUS
LAKES
LAMAS
LAMBS
LAMES
LAMPS
LANDS
LANES
LAPIS
LAPPS
LARAS
LARDS
LARES
LARIS
LARKS
LASES
LASTS
LATHS
LAUDS
LAVAS
LAVES
LAWES
LAWNS
LAZES
MACES
MACYS
MAGES
MAGUS
MAIDS
MAILS
MAINS
MAKES
MAKOS
MALES
MALLS
MALTS
MAMAS
MANES
MANOS
MARAS
MARES
MARIS
MARKS
MARLS
MARTS
MARYS
MASKS
MASTS
MATES
MATHS
MAULS
MAVIS
MAXES
MAXIS
MAYAS
MAZES
NABES
NAILS
NAMES
NANAS
NAPES
NARAS
NARCS
NARDS
NARES
NARIS
NARKS
NAVES
NAXOS
OAKES
OASES
OASIS
OASTS
OATES
OATHS
PACAS
PACES
PACKS
PACTS
PAGES
PAILS
PAINS
PAIRS
PALES
PALLS
PALMS
PALOS
PALPS
PANES
PANGS
PANTS
PAPAS
PARDS
PARES
PARIS
PARKS
PAROS
PARTS
PASES
PASTS
PATES
PATHS
PAVES
PAVIS
PAWLS
PAWNS
RACES
RACKS
RAFTS
RAGAS
RAGES
RAIDS
RAILS
RAINS
RAJAS
RAKES
RAKIS
RAMIS
RAMOS
RAMPS
RANDS
RANIS
RANKS
RANTS
RARES
RASES
RASPS
RATES
RATHS
RAVES
RAWLS
RAZES
SAABS
SACHS
SACKS
SADIS
SAENS
SAFES
SAGAS
SAGES
SAGOS
SAILS
SAKES
SALES
SALPS
SALTS
SAMMS
SAMOS
SAMPS
SANDS
SARDS
SARIS
SAROS
SASES
SATES
SAUKS
SAVES
SAXES
TABIS
TACKS
TACOS
TAELS
TAGUS
TAHRS
TAILS
TAKAS
TAKES
TALES
TALKS
TALOS
TALUS
TAMES
TAMPS
TANGS
TANKS
TAPAS
TAPES
TARES
TARNS
TARPS
TARTS
TASKS
TAXES
TAXIS
VADIS
VAGUS
VALES
VAMOS
VAMPS
VANES
VARAS
VASES
WAAFS
WAALS
WADES
WADIS
WAFTS
WAGES
WAIFS
WAILS
WAINS
WAITS
WAKES
WALES
WALKS
WALLS
WANDS
WANES
WANTS
WARDS
WARES
WARMS
WARNS
WARPS
WARTS
WASPS
WATTS
WAVES
WAXES
XAXES
XAXIS
YACKS
YANKS
YARDS
YARNS
YATES
YAWLS
YAWNS
YAWPS
YAXES
YAXIS
ZARFS
ZAXES
ZAXIS

••AS•

ABASE
ABASH
AGASP
AMASS
AVAST
AWASH
BEAST
BLASE
BLASS
BLAST
BOAST
BRASH
BRASS
CEASE
CHASE
CHASM
CLASH
CLASP
CLASS
COAST
CRASH
CRASS
DNASE
ERASE
FEAST
FLASH
FLASK
GLASS
GNASH
GRASP
GRASS
IPASS
KVASS
LEASE
LEASH
LEAST
LHASA
NYASA
OMASA
PEASE
PHASE
PLASH
PLASM
PRASE
QUASH
QUASI
RNASE
ROAST
SLASH
SMASH
SPASM
STASH
SWASH
TEASE
TOAST
TRASH
UKASE
YEAST

••A•S

ACADS
ADAMS
AFARS
AGALS
AGARS
AMAHS
AMASS
ANAIS
ARABS
AVARS
AWACS
AYAHS
AZANS
BAALS
BEADS
BEAKS
BEALS
BEAMS
BEANS
BEARS
BEATS
BEAUS
BLABS
BLAHS
BLASS
BLATS
BOARS
BOATS
BRADS
BRAES
BRAGS
BRANS
BRASS
BRATS
BRAYS
CHAOS
CHAPS
CHARS
CHATS
CHAWS
CLAMS
CLANS
CLAPS
CLASS
CLAUS
CLAWS
CLAYS
COALS
COATS
CRABS
CRAGS
CRAMS
CRAPS
CRASS
CRAWS
CZARS
DEALS
DEANS
DEARS
DHALS
DIALS
DRABS
DRAGS
DRAMS
DRATS
DRAWS
DRAYS
DUADS
DYADS
EDAMS
EGADS
ETATS
EVANS
EXAMS
FEARS
FEATS
FIATS
FLAGS
FLAMS
FLANS
FLAPS
FLATS
FLAWS
FLAYS
FOALS
FOAMS
FRAIS
FRANS
FRAPS
FRATS
FRAYS
GEARS
GHATS
GLADS
GLASS
GMATS
GNARS
GNATS
GNAWS
GOADS
GOALS
GOATS
GRABS
GRADS
GRAMS
GRASS
GRAYS
GUARS
HEADS
HEALS
HEAPS
HEARS
HEATS
HOARS
HYAMS
IBARS
IMAMS
IPASS
ITALS
IZARS
JBARS
JEANS
KEATS
KHANS
KLAUS
KNAPS
KNARS
KOANS
KRAUS
KVASS
KYATS
LEADS
LEAFS
LEAKS
LEANS
LEAPS
LEARS
LIARS
LOADS
LOAFS
LOAMS
LOANS
LSATS
LUAUS
MEADS
MEALS
MEANS
MEATS
MOANS
MOATS
NEAPS
NEARS
NEATS
NOAHS
OKAYS
OPAHS
OPALS
ORALS
OVALS
PEAKS
PEALS
PEARS
PEATS
PLANS
PLATS
PLAYS
PRAMS
PRAUS
PRAYS
PSATS
QUADS
QUAGS
QUAYS
READS
REALS
REAMS
REAPS
REARS
RIALS
ROADS
ROAMS
ROANS
ROARS
SAABS
SCABS
SCADS
SCAMS
SCANS
SCARS
SCATS
SEALS
SEAMS
SEARS
SEATS
SHADS
SHAGS
SHAHS
SHAMS
SHANS
SHAYS
SIALS
SLABS
SLAGS
SLAMS
SLAPS
SLATS
SLAVS
SLAWS
SLAYS
SNAGS
SNAPS
SOAKS
SOAPS
SOARS
SPADS
SPAMS
SPANS
SPARS
SPATS
SPAYS
STABS
STAGS
STARS
STATS
STAYS
SWABS
SWAGS
SWANS
SWAPS
SWATS
SWAYS
TBARS
TEAKS
TEALS
TEAMS
TEARS
THAIS
THATS
THAWS
TOADS
TRAMS
TRANS
TRAPS
TRAYS
TSARS
TZARS
UNAUS
URALS
VIALS
WAAFS
WAALS
WEALS
WEANS
WEARS
WHAMS
WHATS
WOADS
WRACS
WRAFS
WRAPS
XRAYS
YEANS
YEARS
YEATS
YUANS
ZBARS
ZEALS

•••AS

ABBAS
ACTAS
AGHAS
ALFAS
ALIAS
AMPAS
ANOAS
ANTAS
AQUAS
AREAS
ARIAS
ARRAS
ATLAS
AURAS
AVGAS
BABAS
BALAS
BEMAS
BETAS
BOLAS
BORAS
CASAS
CHIAS
CODAS
COLAS
COMAS
CUNAS
CYMAS
DEGAS
DIVAS
DONAS
DUKAS
DUMAS
EDDAS
ELIAS
EPHAS
ESTAS
ETNAS
EYRAS
FETAS
FLEAS
FULAS
GALAS
GETAS
HAHAS
HALAS
HORAS
HOYAS
HULAS
HYLAS
IDEAS
INCAS
IOTAS
ISLAS
IZBAS
JAVAS
JONAS
JOTAS
JUDAS
KAKAS
KAVAS
KINAS
KIVAS
KOLAS
LAMAS
LARAS
LAVAS
LIMAS
LIRAS
LOTAS
LUBAS
LUCAS
LUKAS
MAMAS
MARAS
MAYAS
MESAS
MICAS
MIDAS
MIMAS
MINAS
MOLAS
MORAS
MYNAS
NANAS
NARAS
NINAS
NIPAS
NOVAS
OCCAS
OKRAS
OLLAS
ORCAS
PACAS
PAPAS
PICAS
PIKAS
PIMAS

PITAS
PLEAS
PROAS
PSOAS
PULAS
PUMAS
PUNAS
PUPAS
RAGAS
RAJAS
RHEAS
ROTAS
SAGAS
SIKAS
SILAS
SKUAS
SODAS
SOFAS
SOMAS
SORAS
SOYAS
SRTAS
STOAS
SURAS
TAKAS
TAPAS
TEXAS
TOGAS
TUBAS
TUNAS
ULNAS
UNCAS
VARAS
VEDAS
VEGAS
VILAS
VINAS
VISAS
VITAS
WEKAS
YMCAS
YOGAS
YUGAS
YUMAS
YWCAS
ZETAS
ZOEAS

AT•••

ATALL
ATARI
ATBAT
ATBAY
ATEAM
ATEIN
ATEUP
ATHOL
ATHON
ATHOS
ATILT
ATION
ATIVE
ATLAS
ATMAN
ATMOS
ATNOS
ATOLL
ATOMS
ATOMY
ATONE
ATONY
ATPAR
ATQUE
ATRIA
ATRIP
ATSEA
ATTAR
ATTIC
ATTYS
ATWAR

A•T••

ACTAS
ACTED
ACTER
ACTII
ACTIN
ACTIV
ACTON
ACTOR
ACTUP
AETAT
AETNA
AFTER
AFTON
AFTRA
AITCH
ALTAI
ALTAR
ALTER
ALTHO
ALTON
ALTOS
ALTUS
ANTAE
ANTAL
ANTAS
ANTED
ANTES
ANTHO
ANTIC
ANTIQ
ANTIS
ANTON
ANTRA
ANTRE
ANTSY
APTED
APTER
APTLY
ARTAL
ARTEL
ARTES
ARTHR
ARTIE
ARTIS
ARTOO
ARTSY
ARTUR
ASTER
ASTIN
ASTIR
ASTON
ASTOR
ASTRA
ASTRE
ASTRO
ATTAR
ATTIC
ATTYS
AUTOS
AUTRE
AUTRY
AZTEC

A••T•

AALTO
ABATE
ABCTV
ABETS
ABUTS
ACCTS
ACETO
ACUTE
ADDTO
ADITS
ADYTA
AGATE
AGITA
AIMTO
AKITA
ALATE
ALETA
AMATI
AMATO
AMITY
ANETO
ANITA
AORTA
APPTD
APPTS
ARETE
ARITH
ASSTD
ASSTS
AUNTS
AUNTY
AUSTR
AZOTE
AZOTH

A•••T

ABAFT
ABBOT
ABORT
ABOUT
ADAPT
ADEPT
ADINT
ADMIT
ADOPT
ADOUT
ADULT
ADUST
AETAT
AFLAT
AFOOT
AFRIT
AGENT
AGLET
AIMAT
ALERT
ALEUT
ALIST
ALLOT
ALOFT
AMBIT
AMENT
AMORT
AMVET
ANENT
ANGST
APART
APORT
ARENT
ARGOT
ARHAT
ARMET
ARRET
ASCOT
ASSET
ASYET
ASYUT
ATBAT
ATILT
AUDIT
AUGHT
AVANT
AVAST
AVERT
AWAIT

•AT••

BATAK
BATCH
BATED
BATES
BATHE
BATHO
BATHS
BATHY
BATIK
BATON
BATOR
BATTS
BATTY
CATCH
CATER
CATES
CATHY
CATTY
DATED
DATER
DATES
DATUM
EATAT
EATEN
EATER
EATIN
EATIT
EATON
EATUP
FATAL
FATED
FATES
FATHA
FATLY
FATTY
FATWA
GATED
GATES
GATOR
GATOS
GATUN
HATCH
HATED
HATER
HATES
HATLO
IATRO
IATRY
JATOS
KATHY
KATIE
LATCH
LATEN
LATER
LATEX
LATHE
LATHS
LATHY
LATIN
LATKE
LATRY
LATTE
MATCH
MATED
MATEO
MATER
MATES
MATEY
MATHS
MATIN
MATRI
MATRO
MATSU
MATTE
MATZO
NATAL
NATCH
NATTY
OATEN
OATER
OATES
OATHS
PATCH
PATED
PATEK
PATEN
PATER
PATES
PATHE
PATHO
PATHS
PATHY
PATIO
PATLY
PATNA
PATON
PATRI
PATSY
PATTI
PATTY
QATAR
RATCH
RATED
RATEL
RATER
RATES
RATHS
RATIO
RATON
RATSO
RATTY
SATAN
SATBY
SATED
SATES
SATIE
SATIN
SATON
SATUP
SATYR
TATAR
TATER
TATRA
TATTY
TATUM
VATER
VATIC
WATCH
WATER
WATTS
YATES

•A•T•

AALTO
BAHTS
BAITS
BALTO
BALTS
BANTU
BARTH
BARTS
BARTY
BASTE
BATTS
BATTY
CACTI
CANTO
CANTS
CANTY
CAPTS
CARTA
CARTE
CARTS
CASTE
CASTS
CATTY
DANTE
DARTH
DARTS
EARTH
EASTS
FACTO
FACTS
FAITH
FANTA
FASTS
FATTY
GAITS
GARTH
GASTR
HADTO
HAFTS
HAITI
HALTS
HANTS
HARTE
HARTS
HASTA
HASTE
HASTO
HASTY
HAUTE
LACTI
LACTO
LAHTI
LAITY
LANTZ
LASTS
LATTE
LAYTO
MALTA
MALTS
MALTY
MANTA
MARTA
MARTI
MARTS
MARTY
MASTS
MATTE
NAFTA
NASTY
NATTY
OASTS
PACTS
PANTO
PANTS
PARTE
PARTI
PARTS
PARTY
PASTA
PASTE
PASTO
PASTS
PASTY
PATTI
PATTY
PAYTV
RAFTS
RAITT
RANTO
RANTS
RASTA
RATTY
SAITH
SALTA
SALTS
SALTY
SANTA
SANTE
SANTO
SARTO
SAUTE
SAWTO
TANTE
TANTO
TARTS
TARTU
TASTE
TASTY
TATTY
TAUTO
VASTY
WAFTS
WAITE
WAITS
WAITZ
WALTZ
WANTS
WARTS
WARTY
WASTE
WATTS
XACTO
YALTA
ZANTE

•A••T

BAGIT
BAKST
BANAT
BARIT
CABOT
CADET
CANIT
CANST
CAPET
CARAT
CARET
DAUNT
DAVIT
EATAT
EATIT
FACET
FACIT
FAGOT
FAINT
FAULT
FAUST
GAMUT
GAUNT
GAVOT
HABIT
HADAT
HADNT
HADST
HASAT
HASNT
HAUNT
JABOT
JACET
JANET
JAUNT
KAPUT
KARAT
MAGOT
MAMET
MANET
MARAT
MAYNT
MAYST
NACHT
PABST
PAGET
PAINT
PAWAT
RABAT
RAITT
RAMET
RANAT
RASHT
SABOT
SADAT
SAGET
SAINT
SALUT
SAULT
TACET
TACIT
TAINT
TAROT
TAUNT
VALET
VAULT
VAUNT
WAIST
WASNT
YACHT
YAKUT

••AT•

ABATE
AGATE
ALATE
AMATI
AMATO
BEATS
BLATS
BOATS
BRATS
CHATS
COATI
COATS
CRATE
DRATS
ELATE
ELATH
ENATE
ERATO
ETATS
FEATS
FIATS
FLATS
FLATT
FRATS
GHATS
GMATS
GNATS
GOATS
GRATA
GRATE
HEATH
HEATS
HYATT
IRATE
KEATS
KYATS
LOATH
LSATS
MEATS
MEATY
MIATA
MOATS
NEATH
NEATO
NEATS
ONATE
ORATE
OVATE
PEATS
PEATY
PLATA
PLATE
PLATH
PLATO
PLATS
PLATT
PLATY
PRATE
PRATO
PRATT
PSATS
REATA
RIATA
SCATS
SEATO
SEATS
SHATT
SKATE
SLATE
SLATS
SLATY
SNATH
SPATE
SPATS
STATE
STATS
SWATH
SWATS
THATS
WHATD
WHATS
WRATH
WYATT
YEATS

••A•T

ABAFT
ADAPT
APART
AVANT
AVAST
AWAIT
BEAST
BEAUT
BLAST
BOAST
BRACT
BRANT
CHANT
CHART
COACT
COAPT
COAST
CRAFT
DEALT
DRAFT
ENACT
EPACT
EXACT
EXALT
FEAST
FLATT
GIANT
GRAFT
GRANT
HEART
HYATT
INAPT
KMART
KRAFT
KRAIT
KRAUT
LEANT
LEAPT
LEAST
MEANT
OPART
ORANT

PLAIT
PLANT
PLATT
PRATT
QUANT
QUART
REACT
RIANT
ROAST
SCANT
SHAFT
SHALT
SHANT
SHATT
SLANT
SMALT
SMART
STADT
START
SWART
THANT
TIANT
TOAST
TRACT
TRAIT
UNAPT
WRAPT
WYATT
YEAST

•••AT
AETAT
AFLAT
AIMAT
ARHAT
ATBAT
BANAT
BEGAT
BFLAT
BLEAT
BLOAT
CARAT
CERAT
CFLAT
CHEAT
CLEAT
CROAT
CUGAT
DEFAT
DERAT
DETAT
DFLAT
DITAT
DONAT
DUCAT
EATAT
EBOAT
ECLAT
EFLAT
EILAT
ESBAT
FFLAT
FLOAT
FLYAT
GETAT
GFLAT
GLOAT
GOTAT
GREAT
GROAT
HADAT
HASAT
HERAT
JURAT
KARAT
KERAT
LEMAT
LETAT
LOFAT
LOPAT
MARAT
MURAT
NEMAT
NIPAT
NOFAT
PAWAT
PLEAT
RABAT
RANAT
RUNAT
SADAT
SENAT
SETAT
SHOAT
SKEAT
SPLAT
SPRAT
SQUAT
STOAT
STPAT
SURAT
SWEAT
TREAT
UBOAT
VOLAT
WHEAT

AU•••
AUBER
AUDEN
AUDIE
AUDIO
AUDIS
AUDIT
AUDRA
AUGER
AUGHT
AUGUR
AUJUS
AULIS
AUNTS
AUNTY
AURAE
AURAL
AURAR
AURAS
AUREI
AURIC
AURUM
AUSSI
AUSTR
AUTOS
AUTRE
AUTRY
AUXIL
AUXIN

A•U••
ABUJA
ABUSE
ABUTS
ABUZZ
ACUFF
ACURA
ACUTE
ADULT
ADUST
ADUWA
AGUES
ALULA
ALUMS
AMUCK
AMUSE
APURE
AQUAE
AQUAS
ARUBA
ARUMS
AZURE
AZUSA

A••U•
AAIUN
ABDUL
ABOUT
ABZUG
ACTUP
ADDUP
ADEUX
ADOUT
ADSUM
AFOUL
AGNUS
AINUS
AKSUM
ALBUM
ALDUS
ALEUT
ALOUD
ALTUS
AMOUR
AMPUL
ANDUP
ANGUS
ANHUI
ANNUL
ANNUM
ANNUS
ANOUK
APLUS
ARGUE
ARGUS
ARHUS
ARIUM
ARIUS
ARTUR
ASCUS
ASHUR
ASSUR
ASYUT
ATEUP
ATQUE
AUGUR
AUJUS
AURUM
AWFUL

A•••U
ADIEU
AEIOU
ANJOU
ARRAU

•AU••
BAUER
BAUGH
BAULK
BAUME
CAULK
CAULS
CAUSA
CAUSE
DAUBS
DAUNT
FAULT
FAUNA
FAUNS
FAURE
FAUST
FAUVE
GAUDS
GAUDY
GAUGE
GAULS
GAUMS
GAUNT
GAURS
GAUSS
GAUZE
GAUZY
HAUER
HAULM
HAULS
HAUNT
HAUSA
HAUTE
JAUNE
JAUNT
KAUAI
KAURI
LAUDE
LAUDS
LAUER
LAUGH
LAURA
MAUDE
MAULS
MAUNA
MAUND
MAURY
MAUVE
NAURU
PAULA
PAULO
PAUSE
SAUCE
SAUCY
SAUDI
SAUKS
SAULT
SAUNA
SAURY
SAUTE
TAUNT
TAUON
TAUPE
TAUPO
TAURO
TAUTO
VAULT
VAUNT
WAUGH

•A•U•
AAIUN
BABUL
BAIUL
CAJUN
CAMUS
CASUS
DAMUP
DATUM
EATUP
GAIUS
GAMUT
GASUP
GATUN
HAFUN
HAGUE
HARUM
JAMUP
JANUS
KABUL
KAFUE
KAPUT
LAIUS
LAPUP
LARUE
LAYUP
MAGUS
MAKUA
MAQUI
MASUR
NAHUA
NAHUM
NAMUR
OAKUM
PADUA
PAPUA
PAYUP
RANUP
RAOUL
SALUD
SALUT
SATUP
TAGUP
TAGUS
TALUS
TATUM
VACUA
VADUZ
VAGUE
VAGUS
VALUE
WADUP
YAKUT
YAQUI

•A••U
BANTU
BAYOU
GAROU
HAIKU
KANZU
MACHU
MAIDU
MATSU
NAURU
PALAU
PAREU
PASSU
SADHU
TAEGU
TARTU

••AU•
BEAUS
BEAUT
BEAUX
BRAUN
CHAUD
CLAUS
FRAUD
KLAUS
KRAUS
KRAUT
LUAUS
PIAUI
PRAUS
SCAUP
SHAUN
UHAUL
UNAUS

••A•U
ISAMU
KEANU
OTARU
SHAMU
SNAFU

•••AU
ARRAU
DONAU
PALAU

AV•••
AVAIL
AVANT
AVARS
AVAST
AVENA
AVENS
AVERS
AVERT
AVERY
AVGAS
AVIAN
AVILA
AVION
AVISO
AVOID
AVOIR
AVOWS
AVRIL

A•V••
ADVAL
ADVIL
ALVAR
ALVIN
AMVET
ANVIL

A••V•
ABOVE
ABOVO
AGAVE
ALAVA
ALEVE
ALIVE
ATIVE

A•••V
ABCTV
ACTIV
ANNIV

•AV••
CAVAE
CAVED
CAVER
CAVES
CAVIL
DAVAO
DAVID
DAVIE
DAVIS
DAVIT
DAVOS
DAVYS
EAVED
EAVES
FAVES
FAVOR
FAVRE
GAVEL
GAVIN
GAVOT
HAVEL
HAVEN
HAVER
HAVES
HAVOC
HAVRE
JAVAS
KAVAS
LAVAL
LAVAS
LAVED
LAVER
LAVES
LAVIN
MAVEN
MAVIS
NAVAL
NAVEL
NAVES
NAVIG
NAVVY
PAVED
PAVER
PAVES
PAVIA
PAVID
PAVIS
RAVED
RAVEL
RAVEN
RAVER
RAVES
RAVIN
SAVED
SAVER
SAVES
SAVOR
SAVOY
SAVVY
WAVED
WAVER
WAVES

•A•V•
CALVE
CARVE
FAUVE
HALVE
LARVA
MARVY
MAUVE
NAIVE
NAVVY
PAAVO
PARVO
SALVE
SALVO
SAVVY
VALVE
WAIVE

•A••V
BASOV
PAYTV
RAJIV
YAKOV

••AV•
AGAVE
ALAVA
BRAVA
BRAVE
BRAVO
CLAVE
CRAVE
DRAVA
GRAVE
GRAVY
GUAVA
HEAVE
HEAVY
KNAVE
LEAVE
PAAVO
PEAVY
SHAVE
SLAVE
SLAVS
SOAVE
STAVE
SUAVE
TRAVE
WEAVE

•••AV
SCHAV

AW•••
AWACS
AWAIT
AWAJI
AWAKE
AWARD
AWARE
AWASH
AWFUL
AWING
AWNED
AWOKE
AWOLS

A•W••
AMWAY
ANWAR
ASWAN
ATWAR

A••W•
ADUWA
AVOWS

A•••W
AGLOW
AGNEW
ALLOW
ARROW
ASKEW

•AW••
BAWDY
BAWLS
CAWED
DAWES
DAWNS
FAWNS
GAWKS
GAWKY
GAWPS
HAWED
HAWGS
HAWKE
HAWKS
HAWSE
JAWED
LAWES
LAWNS
LAWNY
NAWAB
PAWAT
PAWED
PAWER
PAWKY
PAWLS
PAWNS
RAWER
RAWLS
RAWLY
SAWED
SAWIN
SAWTO
TAWNY
YAWED
YAWLS
YAWNS
YAWPS

•A•W•
DAIWA
FATWA

•A••W
BANDW
CANDW
CAREW
GAMOW
LALAW
MACAW
NAREW
PAPAW
YALOW

••AW•
BRAWL
BRAWN
CHAWS
CLAWS
CRAWL
CRAWS
DRAWL
DRAWN
DRAWS
FLAWS
FLAWY
GNAWS
INAWE
OZAWA
PRAWN
SHAWL
SHAWM
SHAWN
SLAWS
SPAWN
THAWS
TRAWL

••A•W
MIAOW

•••AW
BYLAW
INLAW
LALAW
MACAW
PAPAW
PSHAW
RESAW
STRAW

AX•••
AXELS
AXERS
AXIAL
AXILS
AXING
AXIOM
AXION
AXLES
AXONE
AXONS

A•X••
AUXIL
AUXIN

A•••X
ADDAX
ADEUX
ADMIX
AFFIX
ANNEX

•AX••
FAXED
FAXES

LAXER
LAXLY
MAXED
MAXES
MAXIE
MAXIM
MAXIS
NAXOS
SAXES
SAXON
TAXCO
TAXED
TAXER
TAXES
TAXIS
TAXON
WAXED
WAXEN
WAXER
WAXES
XAXES
XAXIS
YAXES
YAXIS
ZAXES
ZAXIS

•A••X
CALIX
CALYX
GALAX
LATEX
RADIX
VARIX

••AX•
FLAXY
GLAXO

••A•X
BEAUX

•••AX
ADDAX
BORAX
GALAX
HYRAX
ICEAX
LOMAX
LORAX
RELAX
RETAX
REWAX

AY•••
AYAHS
AYERS
AYINS
AYRES

A•Y••
ABYES
ABYSM
ABYSS
ACYLS
ADYTA
ALYCE
AMYLO
AMYLS
ARYAN
ASYET
ASYLA
ASYUT

A••Y•
ABAYA
AHOYS
ALKYD
ALKYL
ALLYL
ASSYR
ATTYS

A•••Y
ABBEY
ACIDY
AGLEY
AGONY
AILEY
ALLAY
ALLEY
ALLOY
ALMAY
AMBOY
AMBRY
AMITY
AMORY
AMPLY
AMWAY
ANDRY
ANGRY
ANNOY
ANOMY
ANTSY
AOKAY
APERY
APLEY
APPLY
APTLY
ARABY
ARCHY
ARRAY
ARTSY
ASHBY
ASSAY
ATBAY
ATOMY
ATONY
AUNTY
AUTRY
AVERY

•AY••
BAYAR
BAYED
BAYER
BAYLE
BAYOU
CAYCE
DAYAK
DAYAN
DAYNE
GAYAL
GAYER
GAYLE
GAYLY
HAYDN
HAYED
HAYEK
HAYES
JAYNE
KAYAK
KAYOS
LAYBY
LAYER
LAYIN
LAYLA
LAYNE
LAYON
LAYTO
LAYUP
MAYAN
MAYAS
MAYBE
MAYER
MAYNT
MAYON
MAYOR
MAYPO
MAYST
PAYED
PAYEE
PAYER
PAYIN
PAYNE
PAYTV
PAYUP
RAYED
RAYON
SAYER
SAYSO
TAYRA
WAYNE
ZAYIN

•A•Y•
BABYS
CALYX
DARYA
DARYL
DAVYS
LADYS
MACYS
MARYS
SANYO
SATYR
TANYA
VANYA

•A••Y
BADDY
BADLY
BAGGY
BALKY
BALLY
BALMY
BANDY
BANKY
BARGY
BARKY
BARMY
BARRY
BARTY
BATHY
BATTY
BAWDY
CABBY
CADDY
CAGEY
CAKEY
CAMAY
CAMPY
CAMRY
CANBY
CANDY
CANNY
CANTY
CAREY
CARLY
CARNY
CARRY
CASEY
CATHY
CATTY
DADDY
DAFFY
DAILY
DAIRY
DAISY
DALEY
DALLY
DANCY
DANDY
DANNY
DARBY
EARLY
FAERY
FAHEY
FAIRY
FANCY
FANNY
FATLY
FATTY
GABBY
GAILY
GAMAY
GAMEY
GAMMY
GANDY
GARRY
GASSY
GAUDY
GAUZY
GAWKY
GAYLY
HAIRY
HALEY
HAMMY
HANDY
HANKY
HAPLY
HAPPY
HARDY
HARPY
HARRY
HASTY
IATRY
JACKY
JAGGY
JAMMY
JASEY
JASSY
JAZZY
KANDY
KATHY
LACEY
LAITY
LANKY
LARDY
LARKY
LARRY
LATHY
LATRY
LAWNY
LAXLY
LAYBY
MACHY
MADLY
MALAY
MALTY
MAMMY
MANCY
MANDY
MANGY
MANLY
MANNY
MARCY
MARLY
MARRY
MARTY
MARVY
MASHY
MASSY
MATEY
MAURY
NAGGY
NAMBY
NANCY
NANNY
NAPPY
NASBY
NASTY
NATTY
NAVVY
PADDY
PALEY
PALLY
PALMY
PALSY
PAMBY
PANAY
PANKY
PANSY
PAPPY
PARRY
PARTY
PASSY
PASTY
PATHY
PATLY
PATSY
PATTY
PAWKY
RAINY
RALLY
RANDY
RANGY
RASPY
RATTY
RAWLY
SADLY
SAGGY
SALLY
SALTY
SAMMY
SANDY
SAPPY
SARKY
SASSY
SATBY
SAUCY
SAURY
SAVOY
SAVVY
TABBY
TACHY
TACKY
TAFFY
TALKY
TALLY
TAMMY
TANDY
TANEY
TANGY
TANSY
TARDY
TARRY
TASTY
TATTY
TAWNY
VASTY
WACKY
WADDY
WALEY
WALLY
WALSY
WANEY
WANLY
WARTY
WASHY
WASPY
ZAPPY

••AY•
ABAYA
BRAYS
CLAYS
DRAYS
FLAYS
FRAYS
GRAYS
OKAYS
PLAYA
PLAYS
PRAYS
QUAYS
SHAYS
SLAYS
SPAYS
STAYS
SWAYS
TRAYS
XRAYS

••A•Y
ARABY
BEADY
BEAMY
BEANY
BIALY
BRADY
CHARY
CLARY
CRACY
CRAZY
DEARY
DIARY
FLAKY
FLAMY
FLAWY
FLAXY
FOAMY
GEARY
GLARY
GRADY
GRAPY
GRAVY
HEADY
HEALY
HEAVY
HOAGY
HOARY
ITALY
KRAZY
LEADY
LEAFY
LEAHY
LEAKY
LEARY
LOAMY
MEALY
MEANY
MEATY
ORACY
OTARY
PEARY
PEATY
PEAVY
PHAGY
PHANY
PLATY
QUAKY
READY
SCALY
SCARY
SEALY
SEAMY
SHADY
SHAKY
SLATY
SNAKY
SOAPY
SPACY
STACY
STAGY
TEARY
TOADY
TRACY
VEALY
WEARY

•••AY
ALLAY
ALMAY
AMWAY
AOKAY
ARRAY
ASSAY
ATBAY
BELAY
BYWAY
CAMAY
COPAY
DECAY
DELAY
DOUAY
DUFAY
ELWAY
EMBAY
ESSAY
FORAY
GAMAY
INLAY
IXNAY
LEFAY
LEMAY
LURAY
MALAY
MCKAY
MORAY
MYWAY
NOWAY
OHKAY
ONLAY
OTWAY
OYVAY
PANAY
POWAY
RELAY
REPAY
SPLAY
SPRAY
STRAY
TODAY
TOKAY
UNLAY
UNSAY
VEDAY
VJDAY

AZ•••
AZANS
AZIDE
AZINE
AZOIC
AZOTE
AZOTH
AZTEC
AZURE
AZUSA

A•Z••
ABZUG
ADZES
ANZAC
ANZIO

A••Z•
ABUZZ
AGAZE
AMAZE

A•••Z
ABUZZ
ALLEZ
ARNAZ
ARROZ
ASSEZ

•AZ••
DAZED
DAZES
FAZED
FAZES
GAZED
GAZER
GAZES
HAZAN
HAZED
HAZEL
HAZER
HAZES
JAZZY
KAZAK
KAZAN
KAZOO
LAZAR
LAZED
LAZES
MAZDA
MAZEL
MAZER
MAZES
RAZED
RAZES
RAZOR
TAZZA
YAZOO
ZAZEN

•A•Z•
BAIZA
BAIZE
DANZA
GAUZE
GAUZY
JAZZY
KANZU
LANZA
MAIZE
MATZO
PANZA
TAZZA

•A••Z
CADIZ
HAFIZ
LANTZ
LAPAZ
MAINZ
VADUZ
WAITZ
WALTZ

••AZ•
AGAZE
AMAZE
BLAZE
BRAZE
CHAZZ
CRAZE
CRAZY
DIAZO
ELAZI
GHAZI
GLAZE
GRAZE
KRAZY
PLAZA
SMAZE
SWAZI

••A•Z
CHAZZ
FRANZ
STARZ

•••AZ
ARNAZ
HEJAZ
HIJAZ
LAPAZ
TOPAZ

BA•••
BAAED
BAALS
BABAR
BABAS
BABEL
BABER
BABES
BABIS
BABKA
BABUL
BABYS
BACHS
BACKS
BACON
BADDY
BADEN
BADER
BADGE
BADLY
BAGEL
BAGGY
BAGIT
BAHAI
BAHIA
BAHTS
BAILS
BAIRD
BAIRN
BAITS
BAIUL
BAIZA
BAIZE
BAKED
BAKER
BAKES
BAKST
BALAS
BALCH
BALDS
BALED
BALER
BALES
BALIN
BALKH
BALKS
BALKY
BALLS
BALLY
BALMS
BALMY
BALSA
BALTO
BALTS
BAMBI
BANAL
BANAT
BANCO
BANCS

BANDA
BANDB
BANDO
BANDS
BANDW
BANDY
BANES
BANFF
BANGS
BANJO
BANKS
BANKY
BANNS
BANTU
BAOJI
BARAB
BARBQ
BARBS
BARCA
BARDS
BARED
BARER
BARES
BARGE
BARGY
BARIC
BARIT
BARKS
BARKY
BARMS
BARMY
BARNS
BARON
BARQS
BARRE
BARRY
BARTH
BARTS
BARTY
BASAL
BASED
BASEL
BASER
BASES
BASHO
BASIC
BASIE
BASIL
BASIN
BASIS
BASKS
BASOV
BASRA
BASSI
BASSO
BASTE
BATAK
BATCH
BATED
BATES
BATHE
BATHO
BATHS
BATHY
BATIK
BATON
BATOR
BATTS
BATTY
BAUER
BAUGH
BAULK
BAUME
BAWDY
BAWLS
BAYAR
BAYED
BAYER
BAYLE
BAYOU

B•A••
BAAED
BAALS
BBALL
BEACH
BEADS
BEADY
BEAKS
BEALL
BEALS
BEAMS
BEAMY
BEANO
BEANS
BEANY
BEARD
BEARS
BEAST
BEATS
BEAUS
BEAUT
BEAUX
BIALY
BLABS
BLACK
BLADE
BLAHS
BLAIR
BLAKE
BLAME
BLANC
BLAND
BLANK
BLARE
BLASE
BLASS
BLAST
BLATS
BLAZE
BOARD
BOARS
BOAST
BOATS
BRACE
BRACT
BRADS
BRADY
BRAES
BRAGA
BRAGG
BRAGS
BRAHE
BRAID
BRAIL
BRAIN
BRAKE
BRAND
BRANS
BRANT
BRASH
BRASS
BRATS
BRAUN
BRAVA
BRAVE
BRAVO
BRAWL
BRAWN
BRAYS
BRAZE
BWANA

B••A•
BABAR
BABAS
BAHAI
BALAS
BANAL
BANAT
BARAB
BASAL
BATAK
BAYAR
BEGAN
BEGAT
BEHAN
BELAY
BEMAS
BETAS
BFLAT
BIHAR
BINAL
BLEAK
BLEAR
BLEAT
BLOAT
BOHAI
BOLAS
BORAH
BORAS
BORAX
BOYAR
BREAD
BREAK
BREAM
BRIAN
BRIAR
BROAD
BRYAN
BYFAR
BYLAW
BYWAY

B•••A
BABKA
BAHIA
BAIZA
BALSA
BANDA
BARCA
BASRA
BELLA
BELVA
BEREA
BERRA
BETTA
BIOTA
BOHEA
BOOLA
BOSSA
BOTHA
BRAGA
BRAVA
BREDA
BROCA
BUBBA
BUENA
BUFFA
BULBA
BULLA
BURMA
BURSA
BWANA

•BA••
ABABA
ABACA
ABACI
ABACK
ABACO
ABAFT
ABASE
ABASH
ABATE
ABAYA
BBALL
IBARS
JBARS
TBALL
TBARS
ZBARS

•B•A•
ABBAS
ABEAM
ABRAM
EBOAT
HBEAM
IBEAM
OBEAH
UBOAT

•B••A
ABABA
ABACA
ABAYA
ABUJA
IBIZA
MBIRA

••BA•
ABBAS
AKBAR
ALBAN
ATBAT
ATBAY
BABAR
BABAS
CABAL
CUBAN
DEBAR
DUBAI
EMBAR
EMBAY
ESBAT
GOBAD
HOBAN
INBAD
IZBAS
JUBAL
KEBAB
LABAN
LUBAS
RABAT
REBAG
REBAR
SABAH
TUBAS
UNBAR
URBAN

••B•A
BABKA
BUBBA
COBIA
COBRA
DEBRA
DOBLA
DOBRA
HABLA
HUBBA
JABBA
LIBRA
LIBYA
NUBIA
SABRA
TABLA
TIBIA
UMBRA
YABBA
ZEBRA

•••BA
ABABA
AMEBA
AQABA
ARUBA
BUBBA
BULBA
CEIBA
CHIBA
GALBA
GAMBA
HUBBA
JABBA
KAABA
MAMBA
MELBA
PEMBA
RUMBA
SAMBA
SCUBA
SHEBA
SIMBA
SUMBA
VERBA
YABBA
YERBA
YORBA
ZORBA

BB•••
BBALL
BBGUN
BBOYS

B•B••
BABAR
BABAS
BABEL
BABER
BABES
BABIS
BABKA
BABUL
BABYS
BEBOP
BIBBS
BIBLE
BOBBY
BOBUP
BUBBA
BUBER
BUBUS

B••B•
BAMBI
BARBQ
BARBS
BEEBE
BIBBS
BILBO
BILBY
BIXBY
BLABS
BLEBS
BLOBS
BOBBY
BOMBE
BOMBS
BOOBS
BOOBY
BRIBE
BUBBA
BULBA
BULBS
BURBS
BUSBY

B•••B
BANDB
BARAB
BLURB

•BB••
ABBAS
ABBES
ABBEY
ABBIE
ABBOT
ABBRS
EBBED

•B•B•
ABABA
ABEBE

•B••B
ABOMB
HBOMB

••BB•
BIBBS
BOBBY
BUBBA
CABBY
CUBBY
DEBBY
DOBBY
GABBY
GIBBS
HOBBS
HOBBY
HUBBA
HUBBY
JABBA
LIBBY
LOBBY
NOBBY
NUBBY
RABBI
REBBE
RIBBY
ROBBY
TABBY
TIBBS
TUBBY
WEBBY
YABBA
YOBBO

••B•B
CUBEB
KABOB
KEBAB
KEBOB
NABOB

BC•••
BCELL

B•C••
BACHS
BACKS
BACON
BECHE
BECKS
BECKY
BOCCE
BOCCI
BUCKO
BUCKS
BUCKY

B••C•
BALCH
BANCO
BANCS
BARCA
BATCH
BEACH
BEECH
BELCH
BENCH
BIRCH
BLACK
BLOCH
BLOCK
BLOCS
BOCCE
BOCCI
BONCE
BOSCH
BOSCO
BOSCS
BOTCH
BRACE
BRACT
BRECK
BRICE
BRICK
BROCA
BROCK
BRUCE
BRUCH
BRYCE
BUICK
BUNCH
BUSCH
BUTCH

B•••C
BARIC
BASIC
BLANC
BORIC
BRONC

•BC••
ABCTV
NBCTV

•B•C•
ABACA
ABACI
ABACK
ABACO

••B•C
CUBIC
REBEC
SUBIC
XEBEC

•••BC
MSNBC

B•D••
BADDY
BADEN
BADER
BADGE
BADLY
BEDEW
BEDIM
BIDDY
BIDED
BIDEN
BIDES
BIDIN
BIDON
BIDUP
BLDGS
BODED
BODES
BUDDY
BUDGE

B••D•
BADDY
BALDS
BANDA
BANDB
BANDO
BANDS
BANDW
BANDY
BARDS
BAWDY
BEADS
BEADY
BENDS
BENDY
BIDDY
BINDS
BIRDS
BIRDY
BLADE
BLVDS
BONDI
BONDS
BRADS
BRADY
BREDA
BRIDE
BRODY
BSIDE
BUDDY
BUNDS
BUNDT
BUNDY
BYRDS

B•••D
BAAED
BAIRD
BAKED
BALED
BARED
BASED
BATED
BAYED
BEARD
BIDED
BIFID
BIKED
BIPED
BIPOD
BLAND
BLEED
BLEND
BLIND
BLOND
BLOOD
BLUED
BOARD
BODED
BONED
BOOED
BORED
BOUND
BOVID
BOWED
BOXED
BRAID
BRAND
BREAD
BREED
BROAD
BROOD
BUILD
BUSED

•BD••
ABDUL

•B•D•
ABIDE
ABODE

•B••D
ABEND
EBBED
EBOND
TBIRD
TBOND

••B•D
CUBED
EBBED
EMBED
GIBED
GOBAD
GYBED
INBAD
INBED
JIBED
LOBED
LUBED
NOBID
RABID
REBID
ROBED
TUBED
UNBID

BE•••
BEACH
BEADS
BEADY
BEAKS
BEALL
BEALS
BEAMS
BEAMY
BEANO
BEANS
BEANY
BEARD
BEARS
BEAST
BEATS
BEAUS
BEAUT
BEAUX
BEBOP
BECHE
BECKS
BECKY
BEDEW
BEDIM
BEEBE
BEECH
BEEFS
BEEFY
BEENE
BEEPS
BEERS
BEERY
BEETS
BEFIT
BEFOG
BEGAN

BEGAT
BEGET
BEGIN
BEGOT
BEGUM
BEGUN
BEHAN
BEIGE
BEING
BEINS
BELAY
BELCH
BELEM
BELIE
BELLA
BELLE
BELLI
BELLS
BELLY
BELOW
BELTS
BELVA
BEMAS
BENCH
BENDS
BENDY
BENES
BENET
BENIN
BENJI
BENNY
BENTS
BENUE
BENXI
BENZO
BEREA
BERET
BERGH
BERGS
BERLE
BERME
BERMS
BERNE
BERRA
BERRY
BERTH
BERYL
BESET
BESOM
BESOT
BESTS
BETAS
BETEL
BETHS
BETON
BETSY
BETTA
BETTE
BETTY
BEVEL
BEVIN
BEYLE
BEZEL

B•E••
BCELL
BEEBE
BEECH
BEEFS
BEEFY
BEENE
BEEPS
BEERS
BEERY
BEETS
BLEAK
BLEAR
BLEAT
BLEBS
BLEED
BLEEP
BLEND
BLENT
BLESS
BLEST
BOEHM
BOERS
BOEUF
BREAD
BREAK
BREAM
BRECK
BREDA
BREED
BREEN
BRENT
BRERS
BREST
BRETT
BREVE
BREWS
BUELL
BUENA
BUENO

B••E•
BAAED
BABEL
BABER
BABES
BADEN
BADER
BAGEL
BAKED
BAKER
BAKES
BALED
BALER
BALES
BANES
BARED
BARER
BARES
BASED
BASEL
BASER
BASES
BATED
BATES
BAUER
BAYED
BAYER
BEDEW
BEGET
BELEM
BENES
BENET
BEREA
BERET
BESET
BETEL
BEVEL
BEZEL
BIDED
BIDEN
BIDES
BIKED
BIKEL
BIKER
BIKES
BINES
BINET
BIPED
BISES
BITER
BITES
BIZET
BLEED
BLEEP
BLUED
BLUER
BLUES
BLUET
BLUEY
BODED
BODES
BOGEY
BOHEA
BOLES
BONED
BONER
BONES
BONET
BOOED
BOOER
BORED
BORER
BORES
BOTEL
BOWED
BOWEN
BOWER
BOWES
BOXED
BOXER
BOXES
BOYER
BRAES
BREED
BREEN
BRIEF
BRIER
BRIES
BUBER
BUSED
BUSES
BUSEY
BUTEO
BUYER
BYNER
BYRES
BYTES

B•••E
BADGE
BAIZE
BARGE
BARRE
BASIE
BASTE
BATHE
BAUME
BAYLE
BECHE
BEEBE
BEENE
BEIGE
BELIE
BELLE
BENUE
BERLE
BERME
BERNE
BETTE
BEYLE
BIBLE
BILGE
BINGE
BIOME
BIRSE
BITTE
BLADE
BLAKE
BLAME
BLARE
BLASE
BLAZE
BLIGE
BLOKE
BLUME
BOCCE
BOGIE
BOGLE
BOHME
BOISE
BOITE
BOMBE
BONCE
BONNE
BONZE
BOOLE
BOONE
BOOZE
BORGE
BORNE
BOTHE
BOULE
BOUSE
BOWIE
BOYLE
BOYNE
BRACE
BRAHE
BRAKE
BRAVE
BRAZE
BREVE
BRIBE
BRICE
BRIDE
BRINE
BRITE
BROKE
BROME
BRUCE
BRULE
BRUME
BRUTE
BRYCE
BSIDE
BUDGE
BUGLE
BULGE
BURKE
BURSE
BUTTE
BYRNE

•BE••
ABEAM
ABEBE
ABELE
ABEND
ABETS
CBERS
EBERT
HBEAM
IBEAM
IBERT
OBEAH
OBELI
OBESE
OBEYS

•B•E•
ABBES
ABBEY
ABLER
ABNER
ABYES
EBBED
EBSEN
IBSEN
OBIES
OBJET
OBOES

•B••E
ABASE
ABATE
ABBIE
ABEBE
ABELE
ABIDE
ABODE
ABOVE
ABUSE
OBESE
TBONE

••BE•
ABBES
ABBEY
ALBEE
ALBEN
AMBER
ARBER
AUBER
BABEL
BABER
BABES
BUBER
CABER
CUBEB
CUBED
CUBES
CYBER
EBBED
EMBED
EMBER
FABER
FIBER
GIBED
GIBER
GIBES
GOBEL
GYBED
GYBES
HABER
INBED
JIBED
JIBES
KIBEI
LABEL
LIBEL
LOBED
LOBES
LUBED
LUBES
MABEL
NABES
NOBEL
OMBER
REBEC
REBEL
ROBED
ROBES
RUBEN
RUBES
SABER
SOBER
TIBER
TIBET
TOBES
TOBEY
TUBED
TUBER
TUBES
UMBEL
UMBER
UZBEK
VIBES
WEBER
XEBEC
ZIBET

••B•E
ABBIE
ALBEE
AMBLE
ARBRE
BIBLE
CABLE
DOBIE
DOBLE
EUBIE
FABLE
FIBRE
GABLE
IMBUE
LIBRE
NOBLE
OMBRE
REBBE
ROBLE
RUBLE
SABLE
SABRE
TABLE

•••BE
ABEBE
ADOBE
BEEBE
BOMBE
BRIBE
COMBE
FROBE
GLEBE
GLOBE
GREBE
LETBE
MAYBE
NIOBE
PHOBE
PLEBE
PROBE
REBBE
THEBE
TRIBE

BF•••
BFLAT

B•F••
BEFIT
BEFOG
BIFFS
BIFFY
BIFID
BOFFO
BOFFS
BUFFA
BUFFI
BUFFO
BUFFS
BUFFY
BYFAR

B••F•
BANFF
BEEFS
BEEFY
BIFFS
BIFFY
BLUFF
BOFFO
BOFFS
BUFFA
BUFFI
BUFFO
BUFFS
BUFFY

B•••F
BANFF
BLUFF
BOEUF
BRIEF

•B•F•
ABAFT

BG•••
BGIRL

B•G••
BAGEL
BAGGY
BAGIT
BBGUN
BEGAN
BEGAT
BEGET
BEGIN
BEGOT
BEGUM
BEGUN
BIGGY
BIGHT
BIGLY
BIGON
BIGOS
BIGOT
BOGEY
BOGGS
BOGGY
BOGIE
BOGLE
BOGOR
BOGUS
BUGGY
BUGLE
BUGSY
BYGUM

B••G•
BADGE
BAGGY
BANGS
BARGE
BARGY
BAUGH
BEIGE
BERGH
BERGS
BIGGY
BILGE
BILGY
BINGE
BINGO
BINGS
BIOGS
BLDGS
BLIGE
BLIGH
BOGGS
BOGGY
BONGO
BONGS
BORGE
BOUGH
BRAGA
BRAGG
BRAGS
BRIGS
BUDGE
BUGGY
BULGE
BULGY
BUNGS
BURGS

B•••G
BEFOG
BEING
BOING
BOURG
BRAGG
BRING
BRUNG

•BG••
BBGUN
OBGYN

•B••G
ABZUG

••B•G
DEBUG
INBIG
MRBIG
REBAG
SOBIG

B•H••
BAHAI
BAHIA
BAHTS
BEHAN
BIHAR
BOHAI
BOHEA
BOHME
BUHLS

B••H•
BACHS
BASHO
BATHE
BATHO
BATHS
BATHY
BECHE
BETHS
BIGHT
BISHO
BLAHS
BOEHM
BOTHA
BOTHE
BRAHE
BRUHN
BUSHY

B•••H
BALCH
BALKH
BARTH
BATCH
BAUGH
BEACH
BEECH
BELCH
BENCH
BERGH
BERTH
BIRCH
BIRTH
BLIGH
BLOCH
BLUSH
BLUTH
BLYTH
BOOTH
BORAH
BOSCH
BOTCH
BOUGH
BRASH
BRITH
BROTH
BRUCH
BRUSH
BUNCH
BUSCH
BUTCH

•BH••
ABHOR

•B•H•
ABOHM

•B••H
ABASH
OBEAH

••B•H
SABAH

BI•••
BIALY
BIBBS
BIBLE
BIDDY
BIDED
BIDEN
BIDES
BIDIN
BIDON
BIDUP
BIFFS
BIFFY
BIFID
BIGGY
BIGHT
BIGLY
BIGON
BIGOS
BIGOT
BIHAR
BIJOU
BIKED
BIKEL
BIKER
BIKES
BILBO
BILBY
BILGE
BILGY
BILKO
BILKS
BILLS
BILLY
BINAL
BINDS
BINES
BINET
BINGE
BINGO
BINGS
BIOGS
BIOKO

BIOME
BIONT
BIOTA
BIPED
BIPOD
BIRCH
BIRDS
BIRDY
BIRLS
BIRRS
BIRSE
BIRTH
BISES
BISHO
BISON
BITER
BITES
BITSY
BITTE
BITTS
BITTY
BIXBY
BIZET

B•I••

BAILS
BAIRD
BAIRN
BAITS
BAIUL
BAIZA
BAIZE
BEIGE
BEING
BEINS
BGIRL
BLIGE
BLIGH
BLIMP
BLIND
BLINI
BLINK
BLIPS
BLISS
BLITT
BLITZ
BOILS
BOING
BOISE
BOITE
BOITO
BRIAN
BRIAR
BRIBE
BRICE
BRICK
BRIDE
BRIEF
BRIER
BRIES
BRIGS
BRILL
BRIMS
BRINE
BRING
BRINK
BRINY
BRISK
BRITE
BRITH
BRITS
BRITT
BSIDE
BUICK
BUILD
BUILT

B••I•

BABIS
BAGIT
BAHIA
BALIN
BARIC
BARIT
BASIC
BASIE
BASIL
BASIN
BASIS
BATIK
BEDIM
BEFIT
BEGIN
BELIE
BENIN
BEVIN
BIDIN
BIFID
BLAIR
BLOIS
BOGIE
BORIC
BORIS
BOVID
BOWIE
BOXIN
BRAID
BRAIL
BRAIN
BROIL
BRUIN
BRUIT
BUNIN
BURIN

B•••I

BAHAI
BAMBI
BAOJI
BASSI
BELLI
BENJI
BENXI
BLINI
BOCCI
BOHAI
BONDI
BUFFI
BUZZI

•BI••

ABIDE
IBIZA
MBIRA
OBIES
TBILL
TBIRD

•B•I•

ABBIE
ABOIL
ABRIL
ABRIS
QBVII

•B••I

ABACI
EBOLI
OBELI
OBOLI
QBVII

••BI•

ABBIE
AMBIT
BABIS
CABIN
COBIA
CUBIC
CUBIT
DEBIT
DOBIE
DUBIN
ERBIL
EUBIE
FABIO
HABIT
INBIG
LABIO
MOBIL
MRBIG
NOBID
NOBIS
NUBIA
ORBIT
RABID
RABIN
REBID
ROBIN
RUBIK
RUBIN
SABIN
SOBIG
SUBIC
SYBIL
TABIS
TIBIA
TOBIT
UNBID
URBIS
ZUBIN

••B•I

DUBAI
KIBEI
RABBI

•••BI

ALIBI
BAMBI
DHABI
IAMBI
LIMBI
NIMBI
ORIBI
RABBI

BJ•••

BJORN

B•J••

BIJOU

B••J•

BANJO
BAOJI
BENJI

•BJ••

OBJET

•B•J•

ABUJA

B•K••

BAKED
BAKER
BAKES
BAKST
BIKED
BIKEL
BIKER
BIKES

B••K•

BABKA
BACKS
BALKH
BALKS
BALKY
BANKS
BANKY
BARKS
BARKY
BASKS
BEAKS
BECKS
BECKY
BILKO
BILKS
BIOKO
BLAKE
BLOKE
BONKS
BOOKS
BOSKS
BOSKY
BRAKE
BROKE
BUCKO
BUCKS
BUCKY
BULKS
BULKY
BUNKO
BUNKS
BURKE
BUSKS

B•••K

BATAK
BATIK
BAULK
BLACK
BLANK
BLEAK
BLINK
BLOCK
BREAK
BRECK
BRICK
BRINK
BRISK
BROCK
BROOK
BUICK

•B••K

ABACK

••BK•

BABKA

••B•K

RUBIK
UZBEK

BL•••

BLABS
BLACK
BLADE
BLAHS
BLAIR
BLAKE
BLAME
BLANC
BLAND
BLANK
BLARE
BLASE
BLASS
BLAST
BLATS
BLAZE
BLDGS
BLEAK
BLEAR
BLEAT
BLEBS
BLEED
BLEEP
BLEND
BLENT
BLESS
BLEST
BLIGE
BLIGH
BLIMP
BLIND
BLINI
BLINK
BLIPS
BLISS
BLITT
BLITZ
BLOAT
BLOBS
BLOCH
BLOCK
BLOCS
BLOIS
BLOKE
BLOND
BLOOD
BLOOM
BLOOP
BLOTS
BLOWN
BLOWS
BLOWY
BLUED
BLUER
BLUES
BLUET
BLUEY
BLUFF
BLUME
BLUNT
BLURB
BLURS
BLURT
BLUSH
BLUTH
BLUTO
BLVDS
BLYTH

B•L••

BALAS
BALCH
BALDS
BALED
BALER
BALES
BALIN
BALKH
BALKS
BALKY
BALLS
BALLY
BALMS
BALMY
BALSA
BALTO
BALTS
BELAY
BELCH
BELEM
BELIE
BELLA
BELLE
BELLI
BELLS
BELLY
BELOW
BELTS
BELVA
BFLAT
BILBO
BILBY
BILGE
BILGY
BILKO
BILKS
BILLS
BILLY
BOLAS
BOLES
BOLLS
BOLOS
BOLTS
BOLUS
BPLUS
BULBA
BULBS
BULGE
BULGY
BULKS
BULKY
BULLA
BULLS
BULLY
BULOW
BYLAW

B••L•

BAALS
BADLY
BAILS
BALLS
BALLY
BAULK
BAWLS
BAYLE
BBALL
BCELL
BEALL
BEALS
BELLA
BELLE
BELLI
BELLS
BELLY
BERLE
BEYLE
BIALY
BIBLE
BIGLY
BILLS
BILLY
BIRLS
BOGLE
BOILS
BOLLS
BOOLA
BOOLE
BOULE
BOULT
BOWLS
BOYLE
BRILL
BRULE
BUELL
BUGLE
BUHLS
BUILD
BUILT
BULLA
BULLS
BULLY
BURLS
BURLY

B•••L

BABEL
BABUL
BAGEL
BAIUL
BANAL
BASAL
BASEL
BASIL
BBALL
BCELL
BEALL
BERYL
BETEL
BEVEL
BEZEL
BGIRL
BIKEL
BINAL
BOTEL
BRAIL
BRAWL
BRILL
BROIL
BUELL
BUTYL

•BL••

ABLER

•B•L•

ABELE
BBALL
EBOLI
OBELI
OBOLI
OBOLS
TBALL
TBILL
UBOLT

•B••L

ABDUL
ABOIL
ABRIL
BBALL
TBALL
TBILL

••BL•

AMBLE
BIBLE
CABLE
DOBLA
DOBLE
FABLE
GABLE
HABLA
NOBLE
NOBLY
PABLO
ROBLE
RUBLE
SABLE
TABLA
TABLE

••B•L

BABEL
BABUL
CABAL
COBOL
ERBIL
GOBEL
JUBAL
KABUL
LABEL
LIBEL
MABEL
MOBIL
NOBEL
REBEL
SIBYL
SYBIL
TOBOL
UMBEL

B•M••

BAMBI
BEMAS
BOMBE
BOMBS
BUMPS
BUMPY

B••M•

BALMS
BALMY
BARMS
BARMY
BAUME
BEAMS
BEAMY
BERME
BERMS
BIOME
BLAME
BLIMP
BLUME
BOHME
BOOMS
BOOMY
BRIMS
BROME
BROMO
BRUME
BURMA

B•••M

BEDIM
BEGUM
BELEM
BESOM
BLOOM
BOEHM
BOSOM
BREAM
BROOM
BYGUM

•B•M•

ABOMB
HBOMB
MBOMU

•B••M

ABEAM
ABOHM
ABRAM
ABYSM
HBEAM
IBEAM

••BM•

ICBMS

••B•M

ALBUM
SEBUM

B•N••

BANAL
BANAT
BANCO
BANCS
BANDA
BANDB
BANDO
BANDS
BANDW
BANDY
BANES
BANFF
BANGS
BANJO
BANKS
BANKY
BANNS
BANTU
BENCH
BENDS
BENDY
BENES
BENET
BENIN
BENJI
BENNY
BENTS
BENUE
BENXI
BENZO
BINAL
BINDS
BINES
BINET
BINGE
BINGO
BINGS
BONCE
BONDI
BONDS
BONED
BONER
BONES
BONET
BONGO
BONGS
BONKS
BONNE
BONNY
BONUS
BONZE
BONZO
BUNCH
BUNDS
BUNDT
BUNDY
BUNGS
BUNIN
BUNKO
BUNKS
BUNNY
BUNTS
BYNER
BYNOW

B••N•

BANNS
BARNS

BEANO
BEANS
BEANY
BEENE
BEING
BEINS
BENNY
BERNE
BIONT
BLANC
BLAND
BLANK
BLEND
BLENT
BLIND
BLINI
BLINK
BLOND
BLUNT
BOING
BONNE
BONNY
BOONE
BOONS
BORNE
BOSNS
BOUND
BOYNE
BRAND
BRANS
BRANT
BRENT
BRINE
BRING
BRINK
BRINY
BRONC
BRONX
BRUNG
BRUNO
BRUNT
BUENA
BUENO
BUNNY
BUONO
BURNS
BURNT
BWANA
BYRNE

B•••N

BACON
BADEN
BAIRN
BALIN
BARON
BASIN
BATON
BBGUN
BEGAN
BEGIN
BEGUN
BEHAN
BENIN
BETON
BEVIN
BIDEN
BIDIN
BIDON
BIGON
BISON
BJORN
BLOWN
BORON
BOSON
BOURN
BOWEN
BOXIN
BRAIN
BRAUN
BRAWN
BREEN
BRIAN
BROUN
BROWN
BRUHN
BRUIN
BRYAN
BUNIN
BURIN
BYRON

•BN••

ABNER

•B•N•

ABEND
EBOND
EBONS
EBONY
TBOND
TBONE

•B••N

BBGUN
EBSEN
IBSEN
OBGYN

••B•N

ALBAN
ALBEN
CABIN
CUBAN
DUBIN
GABON
HOBAN
LABAN
RABIN
ROBIN
RUBEN
RUBIN
SABIN
URBAN
ZUBIN

BO•••

BOARD
BOARS
BOAST
BOATS
BOBBY
BOBUP
BOCCE
BOCCI
BODED
BODES
BOEHM
BOERS
BOEUF
BOFFO
BOFFS
BOGEY
BOGGS
BOGGY
BOGIE
BOGLE
BOGOR
BOGUS
BOHAI
BOHEA
BOHME
BOILS
BOING
BOISE
BOITE
BOITO
BOLAS
BOLES
BOLLS
BOLOS
BOLTS
BOLUS
BOMBE
BOMBS
BONCE
BONDI
BONDS
BONED
BONER
BONES
BONET
BONGO
BONGS
BONKS
BONNE
BONNY
BONUS
BONZE
BONZO
BOOBS
BOOBY
BOOED
BOOER
BOOKS
BOOLA
BOOLE
BOOMS
BOOMY
BOONE
BOONS
BOORS
BOOST
BOOTH
BOOTS
BOOTY
BOOZE
BORAH
BORAS
BORAX
BORED
BORER
BORES
BORGE
BORIC
BORIS
BORNE
BORON
BOSCH
BOSCO
BOSCS
BOSKS
BOSKY
BOSNS
BOSOM
BOSON
BOSOX
BOSSA
BOSSY
BOTCH
BOTEL
BOTHA
BOTHE
BOUGH
BOULE
BOULT
BOUND
BOURG
BOURN
BOUSE
BOUTS
BOVID
BOWED
BOWEN
BOWER
BOWES
BOWIE
BOWLS
BOXED
BOXER
BOXES
BOXIN
BOXUP
BOYAR
BOYER
BOYLE
BOYNE
BOYOS
BOZOS

B•O••

BAOJI
BBOYS
BIOGS
BIOKO
BIOME
BIONT
BIOTA
BJORN
BLOAT
BLOBS
BLOCH
BLOCK
BLOCS
BLOIS
BLOKE
BLOND
BLOOD
BLOOM
BLOOP
BLOTS
BLOWN
BLOWS
BLOWY
BOOBS
BOOBY
BOOED
BOOER
BOOKS
BOOLA
BOOLE
BOOMS
BOOMY
BOONE
BOONS
BOORS
BOOST
BOOTH
BOOTS
BOOTY
BOOZE
BROAD
BROCA
BROCK
BRODY
BROIL
BROKE
BROME
BROMO
BRONC
BRONX
BROOD
BROOK
BROOM
BROTH
BROUN
BROWN
BROWS
BUONO
BUOYS

B••O•

BACON
BARON
BASOV
BATON
BATOR
BAYOU
BEBOP
BEFOG
BEGOT
BELOW
BESOM
BESOT
BETON
BIDON
BIGON
BIGOS
BIGOT
BIJOU
BIPOD
BISON
BLOOD
BLOOM
BLOOP
BOGOR
BOLOS
BORON
BOSOM
BOSON
BOSOX
BOYOS
BOZOS
BROOD
BROOK
BROOM
BULOW
BYNOW
BYRON

B•••O

BALTO
BANCO
BANDO
BANJO
BASHO
BASSO
BATHO
BEANO
BENZO
BILBO
BILKO
BINGO
BIOKO
BISHO
BLUTO
BOFFO
BOITO
BONGO
BONZO
BOSCO
BRAVO
BROMO
BRUNO
BUCKO
BUENO
BUFFO
BUNKO
BUONO
BURRO
BUTEO

•BO••

ABODE
ABOHM
ABOIL
ABOMB
ABORT
ABOUT
ABOVE
ABOVO
BBOYS
EBOAT
EBOLI
EBOND
EBONS
EBONY
HBOMB
MBOMU
OBOES
OBOLI
OBOLS
TBOND
TBONE
UBOAT
UBOLT

•B•O•

ABBOT
ABHOR

•B••O

ABACO
ABOVO

••BO•

ABBOT
AMBOS
AMBOY
ARBOR
BEBOP
CABOT
COBOL
DUBOS
ELBOW
GABON
GABOR
HOBOS
INBOX
JABOT
KABOB
KEBOB
KOBOS
LABOR
LOBOS
NABOB
OHBOY
OXBOW
POBOX
POBOY
ROBOT
SABOT
TABOO
TABOR
TOBOL
UMBOS
UNBOX
UPBOW

••B•O

DOBRO
FABIO
FIBRO
LABIO
PABLO
TABOO
YOBBO

•••BO

BILBO
CARBO
COMBO
DUMBO
GARBO
GUMBO
JUMBO
LIMBO
MAMBO
MUMBO
PEABO
RAMBO
TAMBO
TURBO
YOBBO

BP•••

BPLUS

B•P••

BIPED
BIPOD

B••P•

BEEPS
BLIPS
BUMPS
BUMPY
BURPS

B•••P

BEBOP
BIDUP
BLEEP
BLIMP
BLOOP
BOBUP
BOXUP
BUYUP

•B•P•

TBSPS

••B•P

BEBOP
BOBUP

B••Q•

BARQS

B•••Q

BARBQ

•••BQ

BARBQ

BR•••

BRACE
BRACT
BRADS
BRADY
BRAES
BRAGA
BRAGG
BRAGS
BRAHE
BRAID
BRAIL
BRAIN
BRAKE
BRAND
BRANS
BRANT
BRASH
BRASS
BRATS
BRAUN
BRAVA
BRAVE
BRAVO
BRAWL
BRAWN
BRAYS
BRAZE
BREAD
BREAK
BREAM
BRECK
BREDA
BREED
BREEN
BRENT
BRERS
BREST
BRETT
BREVE
BREWS
BRIAN
BRIAR
BRIBE
BRICE
BRICK
BRIDE
BRIEF
BRIER
BRIES
BRIGS
BRILL
BRIMS
BRINE
BRING
BRINK
BRINY
BRISK
BRITE
BRITH
BRITS
BRITT
BROAD
BROCA
BROCK
BRODY
BROIL
BROKE
BROME
BROMO
BRONC
BRONX
BROOD
BROOK
BROOM
BROTH
BROUN
BROWN
BROWS
BRUCE
BRUCH
BRUHN
BRUIN
BRUIT
BRULE
BRUME
BRUNG
BRUNO
BRUNT
BRUSH
BRUTE
BRUTS
BRYAN
BRYCE

B•R••

BARAB
BARBQ
BARBS
BARCA
BARDS
BARED
BARER
BARES
BARGE
BARGY
BARIC
BARIT
BARKS
BARKY
BARMS
BARMY
BARNS
BARON
BARQS
BARRE
BARRY
BARTH
BARTS
BARTY
BEREA
BERET
BERGH
BERGS
BERLE
BERME
BERMS
BERNE
BERRA
BERRY
BERTH
BERYL
BIRCH
BIRDS
BIRDY
BIRLS
BIRRS
BIRSE
BIRTH
BORAH
BORAS
BORAX
BORED
BORER
BORES
BORGE
BORIC
BORIS
BORNE
BORON
BURBS
BURGS
BURIN
BURKE
BURLS
BURLY
BURMA
BURNS
BURNT
BURPS
BURRO
BURRS
BURRY
BURSA
BURSE
BURST
BYRDS
BYRES
BYRNE
BYRON

B••R•

BAIRD
BAIRN
BARRE
BARRY
BASRA
BEARD

BEARS
BEERS
BEERY
BERRA
BERRY
BGIRL
BIRRS
BJORN
BLARE
BLURB
BLURS
BLURT
BOARD
BOARS
BOERS
BOORS
BOURG
BOURN
BRERS
BURRO
BURRS
BURRY

B•••R
BABAR
BABER
BADER
BAKER
BALER
BARER
BASER
BATOR
BAUER
BAYAR
BAYER
BIHAR
BIKER
BITER
BLAIR
BLEAR
BLUER
BOGOR
BONER
BOOER
BORER
BOWER
BOXER
BOYAR
BOYER
BRIAR
BRIER
BUBER
BUYER
BYFAR
BYNER

•BR••
ABRAM
ABRIL
ABRIS

•B•R•
ABBRS
ABORT
CBERS
EBERT
IBARS
IBERT
JBARS
MBIRA
TBARS
TBIRD
ZBARS

•B••R
ABHOR
ABLER
ABNER

••BR•
ABBRS
AMBRY
ARBRE
COBRA
DEBRA
DOBRA
DOBRO
FIBRE
FIBRO
LIBRA
LIBRE
OMBRE
SABRA
SABRE
UMBRA
ZEBRA

••B•R
AKBAR
AMBER
ARBER
ARBOR
AUBER
BABAR
BABER
BUBER
CABER
CYBER
DEBAR
EMBAR
EMBER
FABER
FIBER
GABOR
GIBER
HABER
LABOR
OMBER
REBAR
SABER
SOBER
TABOR
TIBER
TUBER
UMBER
UNBAR
WEBER

BS•••
BSIDE

B•S••
BASAL
BASED
BASEL
BASER
BASES
BASHO
BASIC
BASIE
BASIL
BASIN
BASIS
BASKS
BASOV
BASRA
BASSI
BASSO
BASTE
BESET
BESOM
BESOT
BESTS
BISES
BISHO
BISON
BOSCH
BOSCO
BOSCS
BOSKS
BOSKY
BOSNS
BOSOM
BOSON
BOSOX
BOSSA
BOSSY
BUSBY
BUSCH
BUSED
BUSES
BUSEY
BUSHY
BUSKS
BUSTS

B••S•
BAKST
BALSA
BASSI
BASSO
BEAST
BETSY
BIRSE
BITSY
BLASE
BLASS
BLAST
BLESS
BLEST
BLISS
BLUSH
BOAST
BOISE
BOOST
BOSSA
BOSSY
BOUSE
BRASH
BRASS
BREST
BRISK
BRUSH
BUGSY
BURSA
BURSE
BURST

B•••S
BAALS
BABAS
BABES
BABIS
BABYS
BACHS
BACKS
BAHTS
BAILS
BAITS
BAKES
BALAS
BALDS
BALES
BALKS
BALLS
BALMS
BALTS
BANCS
BANDS
BANES
BANGS
BANKS
BANNS
BARBS
BARDS
BARES
BARKS
BARMS
BARNS
BARQS
BARTS
BASES
BASIS
BASKS
BATES
BATHS
BATTS
BAWLS
BBOYS
BEADS
BEAKS
BEALS
BEAMS
BEANS
BEARS
BEATS
BEAUS
BECKS
BEEFS
BEEPS
BEERS
BEETS
BEINS
BELLS
BELTS
BEMAS
BENDS
BENES
BENTS
BERGS
BERMS
BESTS
BETAS
BETHS
BIBBS
BIDES
BIFFS
BIGOS
BIKES
BILKS
BILLS
BINDS
BINES
BINGS
BIOGS
BIRDS
BIRLS
BIRRS
BISES
BITES
BITTS
BLABS
BLAHS
BLASS
BLATS
BLDGS
BLEBS
BLESS
BLIPS
BLISS
BLOBS
BLOCS
BLOIS
BLOTS
BLOWS
BLUES
BLURS
BLVDS
BOARS
BOATS
BODES
BOERS
BOFFS
BOGGS
BOGUS
BOILS
BOLAS
BOLES
BOLLS
BOLOS
BOLTS
BOLUS
BOMBS
BONDS
BONES
BONGS
BONKS
BONUS
BOOBS
BOOKS
BOOMS
BOONS
BOORS
BOOTS
BORAS
BORES
BORIS
BOSCS
BOSKS
BOSNS
BOUTS
BOWES
BOWLS
BOXES
BOYOS
BOZOS
BPLUS
BRADS
BRAES
BRAGS
BRANS
BRASS
BRATS
BRAYS
BRERS
BREWS
BRIES
BRIGS
BRIMS
BRITS
BROWS
BRUTS
BUBUS
BUCKS
BUFFS
BUHLS
BULBS
BULKS
BULLS
BUMPS
BUNDS
BUNGS
BUNKS
BUNTS
BUOYS
BURBS
BURGS
BURLS
BURNS
BURPS
BURRS
BUSES
BUSKS
BUSTS
BUTTS
BYRDS
BYRES
BYTES

•BS••
CBSTV
EBSEN
IBSEN
TBSPS

•B•S•
ABASE
ABASH
ABUSE
ABYSM
ABYSS
OBESE

•B••S
ABBAS
ABBES
ABBRS
ABETS
ABRIS
ABUTS
ABYES
ABYSS
BBOYS
CBERS
EBONS
IBARS
JBARS
OBEYS
OBIES
OBOES
OBOLS
TBARS
TBSPS
ZBARS

••BS•
FUBSY
PABST

••B•S
ABBAS
ABBES
ABBRS
AMBOS
BABAS
BABES
BABIS
BABYS
BIBBS
BUBUS
CUBES
DEBTS
DUBOS
GIBBS
GIBES
GYBES
HOBBS
HOBOS
ICBMS
IZBAS
JIBES
KOBOS
LOBES
LOBOS
LUBAS
LUBES
NABES
NOBIS
REBUS
ROBES
RUBES
TABIS
TIBBS
TOBES
TUBAS
TUBES
UMBOS
URBIS
VIBES
ZEBUS

•••BS
ARABS
BARBS
BIBBS
BLABS
BLEBS
BLOBS
BOMBS
BOOBS
BULBS
BURBS
CARBS
CHUBS
CLUBS
COMBS
CRABS
CRIBS
CURBS
DAUBS
DRABS
DRIBS
DRUBS
DUMBS
FLUBS
FORBS
FTLBS
GARBS
GIBBS
GLOBS
GRABS
GRUBS
HERBS
HOBBS
IAMBS
JAMBS
KERBS
KNOBS
KREBS
LAMBS
LIMBS
NUMBS
PLEBS
PROBS
SAABS
SCABS
SERBS
SLABS
SLOBS
SNOBS
SNUBS
SORBS
STABS
STUBS
SWABS
SWOBS
TIBBS
VERBS

B•T••
BATAK
BATCH
BATED
BATES
BATHE
BATHO
BATHS
BATHY
BATIK
BATON
BATOR
BATTS
BATTY
BETAS
BETEL
BETHS
BETON
BETSY
BETTA
BETTE
BETTY
BITER
BITES
BITSY
BITTE
BITTS
BITTY
BOTCH
BOTEL
BOTHA
BOTHE
BUTCH
BUTEO
BUTTE
BUTTS
BUTTY
BUTUT
BUTYL
BYTES

B••T•
BAHTS
BAITS
BALTO
BALTS
BANTU
BARTH
BARTS
BARTY
BASTE
BATTS
BATTY
BEATS
BEETS
BELTS
BENTS
BERTH
BESTS
BETTA
BETTE
BETTY
BIOTA
BIRTH
BITTE
BITTS
BITTY
BLATS
BLITT
BLITZ
BLOTS
BLUTH
BLUTO
BLYTH
BOATS
BOITE
BOITO
BOLTS
BOOTH
BOOTS
BOOTY
BOUTS
BRATS
BRETT
BRITE
BRITH
BRITS
BRITT
BROTH
BRUTE
BRUTS
BUNTS
BUSTS
BUTTE
BUTTS
BUTTY

B•••T
BAGIT
BAKST
BANAT
BARIT
BEAST
BEAUT
BEFIT
BEGAT
BEGET
BEGOT
BENET
BERET
BESET
BESOT
BFLAT
BIGHT
BIGOT
BINET
BIONT
BIZET
BLAST
BLEAT
BLENT
BLEST
BLITT
BLOAT
BLUET
BLUNT
BLURT
BOAST
BONET
BOOST
BOULT
BRACT
BRANT
BRENT
BREST
BRETT
BRITT
BRUIT
BRUNT
BUILT
BUNDT
BURNT
BURST
BUTUT

•B•T•
ABATE
ABCTV
ABETS
ABUTS
CBSTV
NBCTV

•B••T
ABAFT
ABBOT
ABORT
ABOUT
EBERT
EBOAT
IBERT
OBJET
UBOAT
UBOLT

••BT•
DEBTS

••B•T
ABBOT AMBIT ATBAT CABOT CUBIT DEBIT DEBUT ESBAT HABIT JABOT ORBIT PABST RABAT REBUT ROBOT SABOT TIBET TOBIT ZIBET

•••BT
DOUBT

BU•••
BUBBA BUBER BUBUS BUCKO BUCKS BUCKY BUDDY BUDGE BUELL BUENA BUENO BUFFA BUFFI BUFFO BUFFS BUFFY BUGGY BUGLE BUGSY BUHLS BUICK BUILD BUILT BULBA BULBS BULGE BULGY BULKS BULKY BULLA BULLS BULLY BULOW BUMPS BUMPY BUNCH BUNDS BUNDT BUNDY BUNGS BUNIN BUNKO BUNKS BUNNY BUNTS BUONO BUOYS BURBS BURGS BURIN BURKE BURLS BURLY BURMA BURNS BURNT BURPS BURRO BURRS BURRY BURSA BURSE BURST BUSBY BUSCH BUSED BUSES BUSEY BUSHY BUSKS BUSTS BUTCH BUTEO BUTTE BUTTS BUTTY BUTUT BUTYL BUYER BUYUP BUZZI

B•U••
BAUER BAUGH BAULK BAUME BLUED BLUER BLUES BLUET BLUEY BLUFF BLUME BLUNT BLURB BLURS BLURT BLUSH BLUTH BLUTO BOUGH BOULE BOULT BOUND BOURG BOURN BOUSE BOUTS BRUCE BRUCH BRUHN BRUIN BRUIT BRULE BRUME BRUNG BRUNO BRUNT BRUSH BRUTE BRUTS

B••U•
BABUL BAIUL BBGUN BEAUS BEAUT BEAUX BEGUM BEGUN BENUE BIDUP BOBUP BOEUF BOGUS BOLUS BONUS BOXUP BPLUS BRAUN BROUN BUBUS BUTUT BUYUP BYGUM

B•••U
BANTU BAYOU BIJOU

•BU••
ABUJA ABUSE ABUTS ABUZZ

•B•U•
ABDUL ABOUT ABZUG BBGUN

•B••U
MBOMU

••BU•
ALBUM BABUL BOBUP BUBUS DEBUG DEBUT IMBUE KABUL REBUS REBUT SEBUM ZEBUS

B•V••
BEVEL BEVIN BLVDS BOVID

B••V•
BELVA BRAVA BRAVE BRAVO BREVE

B•••V
BASOV

•BV••
QBVII

•B•V•
ABOVE ABOVO

•B••V
ABCTV CBSTV NBCTV

BW•••
BWANA

B•W••
BAWDY BAWLS BOWED BOWEN BOWER BOWES BOWIE BOWLS BYWAY

B••W•
BLOWN BLOWS BLOWY BRAWL BRAWN BREWS BROWN BROWS

B•••W
BANDW BEDEW BELOW BULOW BYLAW BYNOW

••B•W
ELBOW OXBOW UPBOW

B•X••
BIXBY BOXED BOXER BOXES BOXIN BOXUP

B••X•
BENXI

B•••X
BEAUX BORAX BOSOX BRONX

••B•X
INBOX POBOX UNBOX

BY•••
BYFAR BYGUM BYLAW BYNER BYNOW BYRDS BYRES BYRNE BYRON BYTES BYWAY

B•Y••
BAYAR BAYED BAYER BAYLE BAYOU BEYLE BLYTH BOYAR BOYER BOYLE BOYNE BOYOS BRYAN BRYCE BUYER BUYUP

B••Y•
BABYS BBOYS BERYL BRAYS BUOYS BUTYL

B•••Y
BADDY BADLY BAGGY BALKY BALLY BALMY BANDY BANKY BARGY BARKY BARMY BARRY BARTY BATHY BATTY BAWDY BEADY BEAMY BEANY BECKY BEEFY BEERY BELAY BELLY BENDY BENNY BERRY BETSY BETTY BIALY BIDDY BIFFY BIGGY BIGLY BILBY BILGY BILLY BIRDY BITSY BITTY BIXBY BLOWY BLUEY BOBBY BOGEY BOGGY BONNY BOOBY BOOMY BOOTY BOSKY BOSSY BRADY BRINY BRODY BUCKY BUDDY BUFFY BUGGY BUGSY BULGY BULKY BULLY BUMPY BUNDY BUNNY BURLY BURRY BUSBY BUSEY BUSHY BUTTY BYWAY

•BY••
ABYES ABYSM ABYSS

•B•Y•
ABAYA BBOYS OBEYS OBGYN

•B••Y
ABBEY EBONY

••BY•
BABYS LIBYA SIBYL

••B•Y
ABBEY AMBOY AMBRY ATBAY BOBBY CABBY CUBBY DEBBY DOBBY EMBAY FUBSY GABBY HOBBY HUBBY LIBBY LOBBY NOBBY NOBLY NUBBY OHBOY POBOY RIBBY ROBBY TABBY TOBEY TUBBY WEBBY

•••BY
ARABY ASHBY BILBY BIXBY BOBBY BOOBY BUSBY CABBY CANBY COLBY CORBY COSBY CUBBY DARBY DEBBY DERBY DIDBY DIGBY DOBBY DOLBY FLYBY GABBY GETBY GOTBY GUMBY HERBY HOBBY HUBBY KIRBY LAYBY LIBBY LIEBY LOBBY LOOBY MOSBY NAMBY NASBY NIMBY NOBBY NUBBY PAMBY PUTBY RIBBY RIGBY ROBBY RUGBY SATBY SETBY SITBY TABBY TUBBY VISBY WEBBY WELBY

B•Z••
BEZEL BIZET BOZOS BUZZI

B••Z•
BAIZA BAIZE BENZO BLAZE BONZE BONZO BOOZE BRAZE BUZZI

B•••Z
BLITZ

•BZ••
ABZUG

•B•Z•
ABUZZ IBIZA

•B••Z
ABUZZ

CA•••
CABAL CABBY CABER CABIN CABLE CABOT CACAO CACHE CACTI CADDO CADDY CADET CADGE CADIS CADIZ CADRE CAELO CAFES CAFFE CAGED CAGER CAGES CAGEY CAINE CAIRN CAIRO CAJUN CAKED CAKES CAKEY CALCI CALEB CALIF CALIX CALKS CALLA CALLI CALLS CALMS CALPE CALVE CALYX CAMAY CAMEL CAMEO CAMIS CAMOS CAMPO CAMPS CAMPY CAMRY CAMUS CANAD CANAL CANBY CANDO CANDW CANDY CANEA CANED CANEM CANER CANES CANID CANIS CANIT CANNA CANNY CANOE CANON CANSO CANST CANTO CANTS CANTY CAPED CAPEK CAPER CAPES CAPET CAPON CAPOS CAPRA CAPRI CAPTS CARAT CARBO CARBS CARDI CARDS CARED CARER CARES CARET CAREW CAREY CARGO CARIA CARIB CARKS CARLA CARLE CARLO CARLY CARNE CARNY CAROB CAROL CAROM CARON CARPE CARPI CARPO CARPS CARRE CARRY CARTA CARTE CARTS CARVE CASAS CASCA CASCO CASED CASES CASEY CASIO CASKS CASTE CASTS CASUS CATCH CATER CATES CATHY CATTY CAULK CAULS CAUSA CAUSE CAVAE CAVED CAVER CAVES CAVIL CAWED

CAYCE

C•A••

CEASE
CHACO
CHAFE
CHAFF
CHAIM
CHAIN
CHAIR
CHAKA
CHALK
CHAMP
CHANG
CHANT
CHAOS
CHAPS
CHARD
CHARM
CHARO
CHARS
CHART
CHARY
CHASE
CHASM
CHATS
CHAUD
CHAWS
CHAZZ
CLACK
CLAIM
CLAIR
CLAMP
CLAMS
CLANG
CLANK
CLANS
CLAPS
CLARA
CLARE
CLARK
CLARO
CLARY
CLASH
CLASP
CLASS
CLAUS
CLAVE
CLAWS
CLAYS
COACH
COACT
COALS
COAPT
COAST
COATI
COATS
CRABS
CRACK
CRACY
CRAFT
CRAGS
CRAIG
CRAIN
CRAKE
CRAMP
CRAMS
CRANE
CRANK
CRAPE
CRAPS
CRASH
CRASS
CRATE
CRAVE
CRAWL
CRAWS
CRAZE
CRAZY
CYANO
CZARS

C••A•

CABAL
CACAO
CAMAY
CANAD
CANAL
CARAT
CASAS
CAVAE
CEDAR
CERAM
CERAT
CESAR
CFLAT
CHEAP
CHEAT
CHIAS
CIGAR
CLEAN
CLEAR
CLEAT
CLOAK
CODAS
COHAN
COLAS
COMAE
COMAS
CONAN
COPAL
COPAN
COPAY
CORAL
COXAE
COXAL
CREAK
CREAM
CROAK
CROAT
CUBAN
CUGAT
CUMAE
CUNAS
CYCAD
CYMAE
CYMAS

C•••A

CALLA
CANEA
CANNA
CAPRA
CARIA
CARLA
CARTA
CASCA
CAUSA
CEIBA
CELIA
CELLA
CERIA
CESTA
CEUTA
CHAKA
CHEKA
CHELA
CHIBA
CHINA
CHITA
CHULA
CIERA
CILIA
CILLA
CIRCA
CLARA
CNIDA
COBIA
COBRA
COCOA
COMMA
CONGA
COOSA
COPRA
COREA
CORIA
COSTA
COTTA
CRURA
CULPA
CUPPA
CURIA

•CA••

ACADS
ACARI
ICAHN
OCALA
SCABS
SCADS
SCALA
SCALD
SCALE
SCALP
SCALY
SCAMP
SCAMS
SCAND
SCANS
SCANT
SCAPA
SCAPE
SCARE
SCARF
SCARP
SCARS
SCARY
SCATS
SCAUP

•C•A•

ACTAS
DCCAB
ECLAT
ICEAX
MCKAY
MCRAE
OCCAM
OCCAS
OCEAN
OCTAD
OCTAL
SCHAV
SCRAG
SCRAM
SCRAP
UCLAN

•C••A

ACCRA
ACOMA
ACURA
ICOSA
OCALA
OCHOA
OCREA
SCALA
SCAPA
SCENA
SCHWA
SCUBA
SCUTA

••CA•

ALCAN
ASCAP
CACAO
CYCAD
DCCAB
DECAF
DECAL
DECAY
DUCAL
DUCAT
FOCAL
INCAN
INCAS
LOCAL
LUCAN
LUCAS
MACAO
MACAW
MICAH
MICAS
NICAD
NOCAL
OCCAM
OCCAS
ORCAS
OSCAN
OSCAR
PACAS
PECAN
PICAS
RECAP
TICAL
UNCAP
UNCAS
VICAR
VOCAL
YMCAS
YWCAS

••C•A

ACCRA
AECIA
ALCOA
COCOA
DACCA
DACHA
DACIA
DECCA
DICTA
FACIA
LICIA
LUCCA
LUCIA
LYCRA
MECCA
MICRA
MOCHA
NUCHA
SACHA
SACRA
SUCKA
USCGA
VACUA
WICCA
YUCCA

•••CA

ABACA
ARECA
ARICA
ASPCA
BARCA
BROCA
CASCA
CIRCA
DACCA
DECCA
ERICA
FINCA
LEICA
LORCA
LUCCA
MECCA
MUSCA
PARCA
PLICA
PONCA
SPICA
THECA
TOSCA
UTICA
WICCA
YUCCA

CB•••

CBERS
CBSTV

C•B••

CABAL
CABBY
CABER
CABIN
CABLE
CABOT
COBIA
COBOL
COBRA
CUBAN
CUBBY
CUBEB
CUBED
CUBES
CUBIC
CUBIT
CYBER

C••B•

CABBY
CANBY
CARBO
CARBS
CEIBA
CHIBA
CHUBS
CLUBS
COLBY
COMBE
COMBO
COMBS
CORBY
COSBY
CRABS
CRIBS
CUBBY
CURBS

C•••B

CALEB
CARIB
CAROB
CELEB
CLIMB
CRUMB
CUBEB

•CB••

ICBMS

•C•B•

SCABS
SCUBA

•C••B

ACERB
DCCAB
MCJOB
SCRUB

••C•B

DCCAB
JACOB

CC•••

CCCII
CCCIV
CCCIX
CCCLI
CCCLV
CCCLX
CCCVI
CCCXC
CCCXI
CCCXL
CCCXV
CCCXX
CCIII
CCLEF
CCLII
CCLIV
CCLIX
CCLVI
CCLXI
CCLXV
CCLXX
CCVII
CCXCI
CCXCV
CCXII
CCXIV
CCXIX
CCXLI
CCXLV
CCXVI
CCXXI
CCXXV
CCXXX

C•C••

CACAO
CACHE
CACTI
CCCII
CCCIV
CCCIX
CCCLI
CCCLV
CCCLX
CCCVI
CCCXC
CCCXI
CCCXL
CCCXV
CCCXX
CECHY
CECIL
COCKS
COCKY
COCOA
COCOS
CXCII
CXCIV
CXCIX
CXCVI
CYCAD
CYCLE
CYCLO

C••C•

CALCI
CASCA
CASCO
CATCH
CAYCE
CCXCI
CCXCV
CDXCI
CDXCV
CENCI
CHACO
CHECK
CHICK
CHICO
CHOCK
CHUCK
CINCH
CINCO
CIRCA
CIRCE
CIRCS
CISCO
CLACK
CLICK
CLOCK
CLUCK
CMXCI
CMXCV
COACH
COACT
CONCH
COUCH
CRACK
CRACY
CRECY
CRICK
CROCE
CROCI
CROCK
CROCS
CULCH
CURCI
CUZCO
CZECH

C•••C

CCCXC
CIVIC
COMIC
CONIC
COSEC
CRESC
CUBIC
CYNIC

•CC••

ACCEL
ACCRA
ACCTS
CCCII
CCCIV
CCCIX
CCCLI
CCCLV
CCCLX
CCCVI
CCCXC
CCCXI
CCCXL
CCCXV
CCCXX
DCCAB
DCCCI
DCCCL
DCCCV
DCCCX
DCCII
DCCIV
DCCIX
DCCLI
DCCLV
DCCLX
DCCVI
DCCXC
DCCXI
DCCXL
DCCXV
DCCXX
MCCCI
MCCCL
MCCCV
MCCCX
MCCII
MCCIV
MCCIX
MCCLI
MCCLV
MCCLX
MCCOO
MCCOY
MCCVI
MCCXC
MCCXI
MCCXL
MCCXV
MCCXX
OCCAM
OCCAS
OCCUR

•C•C•

CCXCI
CCXCV
DCCCI
DCCCL
DCCCV
DCCCX
DCXCI
DCXCV
MCCCI
MCCCL
MCCCV
MCCCX
MCXCI
MCXCV

•C••C

CCCXC
DCCXC
MCCXC
MCDXC
MCMXC

••CC•

BOCCE
BOCCI
DACCA
DCCCI
DCCCL
DCCCV
DCCCX
DECCA
GUCCI
LUCCA
LUCCI
MCCCI
MCCCL
MCCCV
MCCCX
MDCCC
MDCCI
MDCCL
MDCCV
MDCCX
MECCA
MMCCC
MMCCI
MMCCL
MMCCV
MMCCX
PUCCI
RECCE
RICCI
ROCCO
SACCO
SECCO
WICCA
YECCH
YUCCA

••C•C

CCCXC
DCCXC
ENCYC
MCCXC
MDCCC
MDCXC
MMCCC
MMCXC

•••CC

MDCCC
MMCCC
MMDCC
MMMCC

CD•••

CDIII
CDLII
CDLIV
CDLIX
CDLVI
CDLXI
CDLXV
CDLXX
CDROM
CDVII
CDXCI
CDXCV
CDXII
CDXIV
CDXIX
CDXLI
CDXLV
CDXVI
CDXXI
CDXXV
CDXXX

C•D••

CADDO
CADDY
CADET
CADGE
CADIS
CADIZ
CADRE
CEDAR
CEDED
CEDES
CEDIS
CIDER
CMDRS
CODAS
CODED
CODER
CODES
CODEX
CUDDY
CYDER

C••D•
CADDO CADDY CANDO CANDW CANDY CARDI CARDS CHIDE CINDY CLODS CLYDE CNIDA COEDS COLDS CONDE CONDO CORDS CREDO CRUDE CUDDY CURDS CURDY CYNDI

C•••D
CAGED CAKED CANAD CANED CANID CAPED CARED CASED CAVED CAWED CEDED CERED CHARD CHAUD CHILD CHORD CITED CLOUD CLUED CLWYD CODED COKED CONTD COOED COPED CORED COULD COWED COXED CREED CRIED CROWD CUBED CUPID CURED CYCAD

•CD••
MCDII MCDIV MCDIX MCDLI MCDLV MCDLX MCDVI MCDXC MCDXI MCDXL MCDXV MCDXX

•C•D•
ACADS ACIDS ACIDY SCADS SCUDI SCUDO SCUDS

•C••D
ACHED ACRED ACRID ACTED OCTAD SCALD SCAND SCEND SCHED SCOLD SCROD

••CD•
MMCDI MMCDL MMCDV MMCDX

••C•D
ARCED CYCAD DICED ELCID FACED LACED LUCID MACED NICAD PACED RACED RICED

•••CD
MMMCD SPECD

CE•••
CEASE CECHY CECIL CEDAR CEDED CEDES CEDIS CEIBA CEILS CELEB CELIA CELIE CELLA CELLI CELLO CELLS CELTS CENCI CENSE CENTI CENTO CENTS CEORL CEPES CERAM CERAT CERED CERES CERIA CEROS CERRO CERTS CESAR CESTA CESTI CETUS CEUTA

C•E••
CAELO CBERS CHEAP CHEAT CHECK CHEEK CHEEP CHEER CHEFS CHEJU CHEKA CHELA CHERE CHERI CHERT CHESS CHEST CHETH CHEVY CHEWS CHEWY CIERA CLEAN CLEAR CLEAT CLEEK CLEFS CLEFT CLEON CLERK CLEWS COEDS COEUR CREAK CREAM CRECY CREDO CREED CREEK CREEL CREEP CREES CREME CREON CREPE CREPT CRESC CRESS CREST CRETE CREWS CUEIN CZECH

C••E•
CABER CADET CAFES CAGED CAGER CAGES CAGEY CAKED CAKES CAKEY CALEB CAMEL CAMEO CANEA CANED CANEM CANER CANES CAPED CAPEK CAPER CAPES CAPET CARED CARER CARES CARET CAREW CAREY CASED CASES CASEY CATER CATES CAVED CAVER CAVES CAWED CCLEF CEDED CEDES CELEB CEPES CERED CERES CHEEK CHEEP CHEER CHIEF CHIEN CIDER CINES CIRES CITED CITER CITES CIVET CLEEK CLUED CLUES CODED CODER CODES CODEX COHEN COKED COKES COLES COLET COMER COMES COMET COMEX CONES CONEY COOED COOEE COOER COPED COPES COREA CORED CORER CORES COREY COSEC COTES COVEN COVER COVES COVET COVEY COWED COWER COWES COXED COXES COXEY COYER COZEN COZES CREED CREEK CREEL CREEP CREES CRIED CRIER CRIES CRUEL CRUET CRYER CUBEB CUBED CUBES CUKES CULET CULEX CUNEO CUPEL CURED CURER CURES CUTER CUTEX CUTEY CUVEE CYBER CYDER CYMES

C•••E
CABLE CACHE CADGE CADRE CAFFE CAINE CALPE CALVE CANOE CARLE CARNE CARPE CARRE CARTE CARVE CASTE CAUSE CAVAE CAYCE CEASE CELIE CENSE CHAFE CHASE CHERE CHIDE CHILE CHIME CHINE CHIVE CHLOE CHOKE CHORE CHOSE CHUTE CIRCE CLARE CLAVE CLIME CLINE CLIVE CLONE CLOSE CLOVE CLYDE CNOTE COMAE COMBE COMME COMTE CONDE CONGE CONTE COOEE COOKE COPSE COUPE COXAE CRAKE CRANE CRAPE CRATE CRAVE CRAZE CREME CREPE CRETE CRIME CROCE CRONE CROZE CRUDE CRUSE CUMAE CURIE CURSE CURVE CUTIE CUVEE CYCLE CYMAE

•CE••
ACERB ACERS ACETO BCELL ICEAX ICEIN ICENI ICERS ICEUP OCEAN SCENA SCEND SCENE SCENT

•C•E•
ACCEL ACHED ACHES ACMES ACRED ACRES ACTED ACTER CCLEF FCLEF GCLEF ICIER ICKES MCGEE OCHER OCREA OCTET SCHED SCREE SCREW

•C••E
ACUTE ECOLE MCGEE MCRAE MCVIE OCHRE SCALE SCAPE SCARE SCENE SCONE SCOPE SCORE SCREE SCUTE

••CE•
ACCEL ARCED DACES DECEM DICED DICER DICES DICEY DUCES EMCEE EXCEL FACED FACER FACES FACET FICES HACEK JACET LACED LACER LACES LACEY LICET LYCEE MACED MACES NICER PACED PACER PACES RACED RACER RACES RICED RICER RICES SYCEE SYCES TACET ULCER VICES

••C•E
BECHE BOCCE CACHE CYCLE DACHE EMCEE FACIE FICHE HECHE LOCKE LUCIE LUCRE LYCEE MACHE MACLE NACRE NICHE ONCLE ONCUE RECCE RICHE ROCHE RUCHE SACRE SOCLE SUCRE SYCEE TYCHE UNCLE

•••CE
ALICE ALYCE AMICE APACE BOCCE BONCE BRACE BRICE BRUCE BRYCE CAYCE CIRCE CROCE DANCE DEICE DEUCE DOLCE DUNCE EDUCE FARCE FENCE FORCE GLACE GRACE HENCE HULCE JOYCE JUICE LANCE MERCE MINCE NIECE NONCE NOSCE ONICE OUNCE PEACE PENCE PERCE PIECE PINCE PLACE PONCE PRICE PRYCE RECCE ROYCE SAUCE SINCE SLICE SPACE SPICE TRACE TRICE TRUCE TWICE VANCE VINCE VOICE WINCE

CF•••
CFLAT

C•F••
CAFES CAFFE CUFFS

C••F•
CAFFE CHAFE CHAFF CHEFS CHUFF CLEFS CLEFT CLIFF CLIFT COIFS COMFY CORFU CRAFT CROFT CUFFS

C•••F
CALIF CCLEF CHAFF CHIEF CHUFF CLIFF

•CF••
MCFLY

•C•F•
ACUFF SCIFI SCOFF SCUFF

•C••F
ACUFF CCLEF FCLEF GCLEF SCARF SCOFF SCUFF SCURF

••C•F
DECAF

C•G••
CAGED CAGER CAGES CAGEY CIGAR CUGAT

C••G•
CADGE CARGO CHUGS CLOGS COIGN CONGA CONGE

CONGO
CORGI
COUGH
CRAGS

C•••G

CHANG
CHING
CHONG
CHUNG
CLANG
CLING
CLUNG
CRAIG
CUING

•CG••

MCGEE

•C••G

ACING
ICING
SCRAG

••CG•

USCGA

••C•G

INCOG

CH•••

CHACO
CHAFE
CHAFF
CHAIM
CHAIN
CHAIR
CHAKA
CHALK
CHAMP
CHANG
CHANT
CHAOS
CHAPS
CHARD
CHARM
CHARO
CHARS
CHART
CHARY
CHASE
CHASM
CHATS
CHAUD
CHAWS
CHAZZ
CHEAP
CHEAT
CHECK
CHEEK
CHEEP
CHEER
CHEFS
CHEJU
CHEKA
CHELA
CHERE
CHERI
CHERT
CHESS
CHEST
CHETH
CHEVY
CHEWS
CHEWY
CHIAS
CHIBA
CHICK
CHICO
CHIDE
CHIEF
CHIEN
CHILD
CHILE
CHILI
CHILL
CHILO
CHIME
CHIMP
CHINA
CHINE
CHING
CHINK
CHINO
CHINS
CHIOS
CHIPS
CHIRO
CHIRP
CHIRR
CHITA
CHITS
CHIVE
CHIVY
CHLOE
CHLOR
CHOCK
CHOIR
CHOKE
CHOKY
CHOLO
CHOMP
CHONG
CHOPS
CHORD
CHORE
CHOSE
CHOWS
CHRIS
CHROM
CHRON
CHRYS
CHUBS
CHUCK
CHUFF
CHUGS
CHULA
CHUMP
CHUMS
CHUNG
CHUNK
CHURL
CHURN
CHUTE

C•H••

COHAN
COHEN
COHOS

C••H•

CACHE
CATHY
CECHY
CUSHY

C•••H

CATCH
CHETH
CINCH
CLASH
CLOTH
COACH
CONCH
COUCH
COUGH
COUTH
CRASH
CRUSH
CULCH
CZECH

•CH••

ACHED
ACHES
ACHOO
ECHIN
ICHOR
ICHTH
OCHER
OCHOA
OCHRE
SCHAV
SCHED
SCHMO
SCHON
SCHWA
VCHIP

•C•H•

ICAHN

•C••H

ICHTH

••CH•

ARCHI
ARCHY
BACHS
BECHE
CACHE
CECHY
DACHA
DACHE
DICHO
DUCHY
FICHE
FICHU
FUCHS
HECHE
HECHT
ITCHY
KOCHI
LOCHS
MACHE
MACHO
MACHU
MACHY
MOCHA
NACHO
NACHT
NICHE
NUCHA
ORCHS
RICHE
ROCHE
RUCHE
SACHA
SACHS
SOCHI
TACHO
TACHY
TECHS
TECHY
TYCHE
TYCHO
VICHY
YACHT

••C•H

MICAH
RICOH
YECCH

•••CH

AITCH
BALCH
BATCH
BEACH
BEECH
BELCH
BENCH
BIRCH
BLOCH
BOSCH
BOTCH
BRUCH
BUNCH
BUSCH
BUTCH
CATCH
CINCH
COACH
CONCH
COUCH
CULCH
CZECH
DITCH
DUTCH
ENOCH
EPOCH
ERICH
FETCH
FILCH
FINCH
FITCH
GULCH
HATCH
HENCH
HITCH
HOOCH
HUNCH
HUTCH
ILICH
KEACH
KENCH
KETCH
KOTCH
LARCH
LATCH
LEACH
LEECH
LOACH
LUNCH
LURCH
LYNCH
MARCH
MATCH
MILCH
MITCH
MOOCH
MULCH
MUNCH
NATCH
NOTCH
ORACH
PARCH
PASCH
PATCH
PEACH
PERCH
PINCH
PITCH
POACH
PONCH
POOCH
PORCH
POUCH
PSYCH
PUNCH
RANCH
RATCH
REACH
REICH
ROACH
STICH
TEACH
TENCH
TORCH
TOUCH
URICH
VETCH
VOUCH
WATCH
WELCH
WENCH
WHICH
WINCH
WITCH
YECCH
ZILCH

CI•••

CIDER
CIERA
CIGAR
CILIA
CILLA
CINCH
CINCO
CINDY
CINES
CIRCA
CIRCE
CIRCS
CIRES
CIRRI
CIRRO
CISCO
CISSY
CITED
CITER
CITES
CIVET
CIVIC
CIVIL

C•I••

CAINE
CAIRN
CAIRO
CCIII
CDIII
CEIBA
CEILS
CHIAS
CHIBA
CHICK
CHICO
CHIDE
CHIEF
CHIEN
CHILD
CHILE
CHILI
CHILL
CHILO
CHIME
CHIMP
CHINA
CHINE
CHING
CHINK
CHINO
CHINS
CHIOS
CHIPS
CHIRO
CHIRP
CHIRR
CHITA
CHITS
CHIVE
CHIVY
CLICK
CLIFF
CLIFT
CLIII
CLIMB
CLIME
CLINE
CLING
CLINK
CLINT
CLIOS
CLIPS
CLIPT
CLIVE
CMIII
CNIDA
COIFS
COIGN
COILS
COINS
COIRS
CRIBS
CRICK
CRIED
CRIER
CRIES
CRIME
CRIMP
CRISP
CRISS
CRIST
CUING
CVIII
CXIII

C••I•

CABIN
CADIS
CADIZ
CALIF
CALIX
CAMIS
CANID
CANIS
CANIT
CARIA
CARIB
CASIO
CAVIL
CCCII
CCCIV
CCCIX
CCIII
CCLII
CCLIV
CCLIX
CCVII
CCXII
CCXIV
CCXIX
CDIII
CDLII
CDLIV
CDLIX
CDVII
CDXII
CDXIV
CDXIX
CECIL
CEDIS
CELIA
CELIE
CERIA
CHAIM
CHAIN
CHAIR
CHOIR
CHRIS
CILIA
CIVIC
CIVIL
CLAIM
CLAIR
CLIII
CLVII
CLXII
CLXIV
CLXIX
CMIII
CMLII
CMLIV
CMLIX
CMVII
CMXII
CMXIV
CMXIX
COBIA
COLIN
COMIC
COMIX
CONIC
CORIA
CRAIG
CRAIN
CROIX
CUBIC
CUBIT
CUEIN
CUMIN
CUPID
CURIA
CURIE
CURIO
CUTIE
CUTIN
CUTIS
CVIII
CXCII
CXCIV
CXCIX
CXIII
CXLII
CXLIV
CXLIX
CXVII
CXXII
CXXIV
CXXIX
CYNIC
CYRIL

C•••I

CACTI
CALCI
CALLI
CAPRI
CARDI
CARPI
CCCII
CCCLI
CCCVI
CCCXI
CCIII
CCLII
CCLVI
CCLXI
CCVII
CCXCI
CCXII
CCXLI
CCXVI
CCXXI
CDIII
CDLII
CDLVI
CDLXI
CDVII
CDXCI
CDXII
CDXLI
CDXVI
CDXXI
CELLI
CENCI
CENTI
CESTI
CHERI
CHILI
CIRRI
CLIII
CLVII
CLXII
CLXVI
CLXXI
CMIII
CMLII
CMLVI
CMLXI
CMVII
CMXCI
CMXII
CMXLI
CMXVI
CMXXI
COATI
CONTI
CORGI
CROCI
CUPRI
CURCI
CVIII
CXCII
CXCVI
CXIII
CXLII
CXLVI
CXVII
CXXII
CXXVI
CXXXI
CYNDI

•CI••

ACIDS
ACIDY
ACING
CCIII
DCIII
ICIER
ICILY
ICING
MCIII
SCIFI
SCION
XCIII

•C•I•

ACRID
ACTII
ACTIN
ACTIV
CCCII
CCCIV
CCCIX
CCIII
CCLII
CCLIV
CCLIX
CCVII
CCXII
CCXIV
CCXIX
DCCII
DCCIV
DCCIX
DCIII
DCLII
DCLIV
DCLIX
DCVII
DCXII
DCXIV
DCXIX
ECHIN
ICEIN
MCCII
MCCIV
MCCIX
MCDII
MCDIV
MCDIX
MCIII
MCLII
MCLIV
MCLIX
MCMII
MCMIV
MCMIX
MCVIE
MCVII
MCXII
MCXIV
MCXIX
SCRIM
SCRIP
VCHIP
XCIII
XCVII

•C••I

ACARI
ACTII
CCCII
CCCLI
CCCVI
CCCXI
CCIII
CCLII
CCLVI
CCLXI
CCVII
CCXCI
CCXII
CCXLI
CCXVI
CCXXI
DCCCI
DCCII
DCCLI
DCCVI
DCCXI
DCIII
DCLII
DCLVI
DCLXI
DCVII
DCXCI
DCXII
DCXLI

DCXVI
DCXXI
ECOLI
ICENI
ICOSI
MCCCI
MCCII
MCCLI
MCCVI
MCCXI
MCDII
MCDLI
MCDVI
MCDXI
MCIII
MCLII
MCLVI
MCLXI
MCMII
MCMLI
MCMVI
MCMXI
MCVII
MCXCI
MCXII
MCXLI
MCXVI
MCXXI
SCIFI
SCUDI
XCIII
XCVII

••CI•
AECIA
ASCII
CCCII
CCCIV
CCCIX
CECIL
CXCII
CXCIV
CXCIX
DACIA
DCCII
DCCIV
DCCIX
DXCII
DXCIV
DXCIX
ELCID
FACIA
FACIE
FACIT
LICIA
LICIT
LUCIA
LUCID
LUCIE
MCCII
MCCIV
MCCIX
MDCII
MDCIV
MDCIX
MMCII
MMCIV
MMCIX
MUCIN
MXCII
MXCIV
MXCIX
MYCIN
OPCIT
RECIP
SOCIO
TACIT

••C•I
ARCHI
ASCII
BOCCI
CACTI
CCCII
CCCLI
CCCVI
CCCXI
CXCII
CXCVI
DCCCI
DCCII
DCCLI
DCCVI
DCCXI
DXCII
DXCVI
GUCCI
KOCHI
LACTI
LUCCI
MCCCI
MCCII
MCCLI
MCCVI
MCCXI
MDCCI
MDCII
MDCLI
MDCVI
MDCXI
MMCCI
MMCDI
MMCII
MMCLI
MMCMI
MMCVI
MMCXI
MXCII
MXCVI
NOCTI
PUCCI
RECTI
RICCI
RICKI
SOCHI
VICKI

•••CI
ABACI
BOCCI
CALCI
CCXCI
CDXCI
CENCI
CMXCI
CROCI
CURCI
DCCCI
DCXCI
FARCI
GUCCI
LUCCI
MCCCI
MCXCI
MDCCI
MDXCI
MERCI
MMCCI
MMDCI
MMMCI
MMXCI
PESCI
PISCI
PUCCI
RICCI
SULCI
VINCI
VOICI

C•J••
CAJUN

C••J•
CHEJU

•CJ••
MCJOB

C•K••
CAKED
CAKES
CAKEY
COKED
COKES
CUKES
CUKOR

C••K•
CALKS
CARKS
CASKS
CHAKA
CHEKA
CHOKE
CHOKY
COCKS
COCKY
CONKS
COOKE
COOKS
COOKY
CORKS
CORKY
CRAKE
CUSKS

C•••K
CAPEK
CAULK
CHALK
CHECK
CHEEK
CHICK
CHINK
CHOCK
CHUCK
CHUNK
CLACK
CLANK
CLARK
CLEEK
CLERK
CLICK
CLINK
CLOAK
CLOCK
CLONK
CLUCK
CLUNK
CRACK
CRANK
CREAK
CREEK
CRICK
CROAK
CROCK
CROOK

•CK••
ICKES
MCKAY

••CK•
BACKS
BECKS
BECKY
BUCKO
BUCKS
BUCKY
COCKS
COCKY
DECKS
DICKS
DICKY
DOCKS
DUCKS
DUCKY
GECKO
HACKS
HECKS
HICKS
HOCKS
JACKS
JACKY
JOCKO
JOCKS
KICKS
KICKY
LACKS
LECKY
LICKS
LOCKE
LOCKS
LUCKS
LUCKY
MOCKS
MUCKS
MUCKY
NECKS
NICKS
NOCKS
OICKS
PACKS
PECKS
PECKY
PICKS
PICKY
PUCKS
RACKS
RICKI
RICKS
RICKY
ROCKS
ROCKY
RUCKS
SACKS
SOCKO
SOCKS
SUCKA
SUCKS
TACKS
TACKY
TICKS
TICKY
TUCKS
VICKI
VICKS
WACKO
WACKY
WICKS
YACKS
YUCKY

••C•K
HACEK

•••CK
ABACK
ALACK
ALECK
AMUCK
BLACK
BLOCK
BRECK
BRICK
BROCK
BUICK
CHECK
CHICK
CHOCK
CHUCK
CLACK
CLICK
CLOCK
CLUCK
CRACK
CRICK
CROCK
FLACK
FLECK
FLICK
FLOCK
FRICK
FROCK
GLICK
GLUCK
KNACK
KNICK
KNOCK
KYACK
MERCK
MONCK
NYACK
PLUCK
PRICK
QUACK
QUICK
SHACK
SHOCK
SHUCK
SLACK
SLICK
SMACK
SMOCK
SNACK
SNICK
SNUCK
SPECK
SPOCK
STACK
STICK
STOCK
STUCK
THICK
TRACK
TRICK
TRUCK
VNECK
WHACK
WRACK
WRECK

CL•••
CLACK
CLAIM
CLAIR
CLAMP
CLAMS
CLANG
CLANK
CLANS
CLAPS
CLARA
CLARE
CLARK
CLARO
CLARY
CLASH
CLASP
CLASS
CLAUS
CLAVE
CLAWS
CLAYS
CLEAN
CLEAR
CLEAT
CLEEK
CLEFS
CLEFT
CLEON
CLERK
CLEWS
CLICK
CLIFF
CLIFT
CLIII
CLIMB
CLIME
CLINE
CLING
CLINK
CLINT
CLIOS
CLIPS
CLIPT
CLIVE
CLOAK
CLOCK
CLODS
CLOGS
CLOMP
CLONE
CLONK
CLOPS
CLOSE
CLOTH
CLOTS
CLOUD
CLOUT
CLOVE
CLOWN
CLOYS
CLUBS
CLUCK
CLUED
CLUES
CLUMP
CLUNG
CLUNK
CLUNY
CLVII
CLWYD
CLXII
CLXIV
CLXIX
CLXVI
CLXXI
CLXXV
CLXXX
CLYDE

C•L••
CALCI
CALEB
CALIF
CALIX
CALKS
CALLA
CALLI
CALLS
CALMS
CALPE
CALVE
CALYX
CCLEF
CCLII
CCLIV
CCLIX
CCLVI
CCLXI
CCLXV
CCLXX
CDLII
CDLIV
CDLIX
CDLVI
CDLXI
CDLXV
CDLXX
CELEB
CELIA
CELIE
CELLA
CELLI
CELLO
CELLS
CELTS
CFLAT
CHLOE
CHLOR
CILIA
CILLA
CMLII
CMLIV
CMLIX
CMLVI
CMLXI
CMLXV
CMLXX
COLAS
COLBY
COLDS
COLES
COLET
COLIN
COLON
COLOR
COLTS
COLUM
CPLUS
CULCH
CULET
CULEX
CULLS
CULLY
CULMS
CULPA
CULTS
CXLII
CXLIV
CXLIX
CXLVI

C••L•
CABLE
CAELO
CALLA
CALLI
CALLS
CARLA
CARLE
CARLO
CARLY
CAULK
CAULS
CCCLI
CCCLV
CCCLX
CCXLI
CCXLV
CDXLI
CDXLV
CEILS
CELLA
CELLI
CELLO
CELLS
CHALK
CHELA
CHILD
CHILE
CHILI
CHILL
CHILO
CHOLO
CHULA
CILLA
CMXLI
CMXLV
COALS
COILS
COOLS
COULD
COWLS
COYLY
CROLY
CULLS
CULLY
CURLS
CURLY
CYCLE
CYCLO

C•••L
CABAL
CAMEL
CANAL
CAROL
CAVIL
CCCXL
CECIL
CEORL
CHILL
CHURL
CIVIL
COBOL
COPAL
CORAL
COXAL
CRAWL
CREEL
CRUEL
CUMUL
CUPEL
CYRIL

•CL••
CCLEF
CCLII
CCLIV
CCLIX
CCLVI
CCLXI
CCLXV
CCLXX
DCLII
DCLIV
DCLIX
DCLVI
DCLXI
DCLXV
DCLXX
ECLAT
FCLEF
GCLEF
MCLII
MCLIV
MCLIX
MCLVI
MCLXI
MCLXV
MCLXX
UCLAN

•C•L•
ACYLS
BCELL
CCCLI
CCCLV
CCCLX
CCXLI
CCXLV
DCCLI
DCCLV
DCCLX
DCXLI
DCXLV
ECOLE
ECOLI
ICILY
MCCLI
MCCLV
MCCLX
MCDLI
MCDLV
MCDLX
MCFLY
MCMLI
MCMLV
MCMLX
MCXLI
MCXLV
OCALA
OCULO
SCALA
SCALD
SCALE
SCALP
SCALY
SCOLD
SCULL

•C••L
ACCEL
BCELL
CCCXL
DCCCL
DCCXL
MCCCL
MCCXL
MCDXL
MCMXL
OCTAL
SCOWL
SCULL

••CL•
CCCLI
CCCLV
CCCLX
CYCLE
CYCLO
DCCLI
DCCLV
DCCLX
MACLE
MCCLI
MCCLV
MCCLX
MDCLI
MDCLV
MDCLX
MMCLI

MMCLV
MMCLX
ONCLE
SOCLE
UNCLE

••C•L
ACCEL
CCCXL
CECIL
DCCCL
DCCXL
DECAL
DUCAL
EXCEL
FOCAL
LOCAL
LTCOL
MCCCL
MCCXL
MDCCL
MDCXL
MMCCL
MMCDL
MMCML
MMCXL
NICOL
NOCAL
PICUL
TICAL
VOCAL

•••CL
DCCCL
MCCCL
MDCCL
MMCCL
MMDCL
MMMCL

CM•••
CMDRS
CMIII
CMLII
CMLIV
CMLIX
CMLVI
CMLXI
CMLXV
CMLXX
CMVII
CMXCI
CMXCV
CMXII
CMXIV
CMXIX
CMXLI
CMXLV
CMXVI
CMXXI
CMXXV
CMXXX

C•M••
CAMAY
CAMEL
CAMEO
CAMIS
CAMOS
CAMPO
CAMPS
CAMPY
CAMRY
CAMUS
COMAE
COMAS
COMBE
COMBO
COMBS
COMER
COMES
COMET
COMEX
COMFY
COMIC
COMIX
COMMA
COMME
COMPO
COMPS
COMTE
COMUS
CUMAE
CUMIN
CUMUL
CYMAE
CYMAS
CYMES
CYMRY

C••M•
CALMS
CHAMP
CHIME
CHIMP
CHOMP
CHUMP
CHUMS
CLAMP
CLAMS
CLIMB
CLIME
CLOMP
CLUMP
COMMA
COMME
CORMS
COSMO
CRAMP
CRAMS
CREME
CRIME
CRIMP
CRUMB
CRUMP
CULMS
CUOMO

C•••M
CANEM
CAROM
CDROM
CERAM
CHAIM
CHARM
CHASM
CHROM
CLAIM
COLUM
CREAM

•CM••
ACMES
MCMII
MCMIV
MCMIX
MCMLI
MCMLV
MCMLX
MCMVI
MCMXC
MCMXI
MCMXL
MCMXV
MCMXX

•C•M•
ACOMA
ICBMS
SCAMP
SCAMS
SCHMO
SCUMS

•C••M
OCCAM
SCRAM
SCRIM
SCRUM

••CM•
MMCMI
MMCML
MMCMV
MMCMX

••C•M
DECEM
LOCUM
MECUM
OCCAM

CN•••
CNIDA
CNOTE

C•N••
CANAD
CANAL
CANBY
CANDO
CANDW
CANDY
CANEA
CANED
CANEM
CANER
CANES
CANID
CANIS
CANIT
CANNA
CANNY
CANOE
CANON
CANSO
CANST
CANTO
CANTS
CANTY
CENCI
CENSE
CENTI
CENTO
CENTS
CINCH
CINCO
CINDY
CINES
CONAN
CONCH
CONDE
CONDO
CONES
CONEY
CONGA
CONGE
CONGO
CONIC
CONKS
CONTD
CONTE
CONTI
CONTR
CONUS
CUNAS
CUNEO
CYNDI
CYNIC

C••N•
CAINE
CANNA
CANNY
CARNE
CARNY
CHANG
CHANT
CHINA
CHINE
CHING
CHINK
CHINO
CHINS
CHONG
CHUNG
CHUNK
CLANG
CLANK
CLANS
CLINE
CLING
CLINK
CLINT
CLONE
CLONK
CLUNG
CLUNK
CLUNY
COINS
COONS
CORNO
CORNS
CORNU
CORNY
COUNT
CRANE
CRANK
CRONE
CRONY
CUING
CYANO

C•••N
CABIN
CAIRN
CAJUN
CANON
CAPON
CARON
CHAIN
CHIEN
CHRON
CHURN
CLEAN
CLEON
CLOWN
COHAN
COHEN
COIGN
COLIN
COLON
CONAN
COPAN
COVEN
COZEN
CRAIN
CREON
CROON
CROWN
CUBAN
CUEIN
CUMIN
CUTIN

•C•N•
ACING
ICENI
ICING
ICONO
ICONS
SCAND
SCANS
SCANT
SCENA
SCEND
SCENE
SCENT
SCONE

•C••N
ACORN
ACTIN
ACTON
ECHIN
ICAHN
ICEIN
OCEAN
SCHON
SCION
SCORN
UCLAN

••C•N
ALCAN
ANCON
BACON
INCAN
LUCAN
MACON
MUCIN
MYCIN
OSCAN
PECAN
RACON
RECON

CO•••
COACH
COACT
COALS
COAPT
COAST
COATI
COATS
COBIA
COBOL
COBRA
COCKS
COCKY
COCOA
COCOS
CODAS
CODED
CODER
CODES
CODEX
COEDS
COEUR
COHAN
COHEN
COHOS
COIFS
COIGN
COILS
COINS
COIRS
COKED
COKES
COLAS
COLBY
COLDS
COLES
COLET
COLIN
COLON
COLOR
COLTS
COLUM
COMAE
COMAS
COMBE
COMBO
COMBS
COMER
COMES
COMET
COMEX
COMFY
COMIC
COMIX
COMMA
COMME
COMPO
COMPS
COMTE
COMUS
CONAN
CONCH
CONDE
CONDO
CONES
CONEY
CONGA
CONGE
CONGO
CONIC
CONKS
CONTD
CONTE
CONTI
CONTR
CONUS
COOED
COOEE
COOER
COOKE
COOKS
COOKY
COOLS
COONS
COOPS
COOPT
COORS
COOSA
COOTS
COPAL
COPAN
COPAY
COPED
COPES
COPRA
COPSE
COPTS
CORAL
CORBY
CORDS
COREA
CORED
CORER
CORES
COREY
CORFU
CORGI
CORIA
CORKS
CORKY
CORMS
CORNO
CORNS
CORNU
CORNY
COROT
CORPS
COSBY
COSEC
COSMO
COSTA
COSTS
COTES
COTTA
COUCH
COUGH
COULD
COUNT
COUPE
COUPS
COURT
COUSY
COUTH
COVEN
COVER
COVES
COVET
COVEY
COWED
COWER
COWES
COWLS
COWRY
COXAE
COXAL
COXED
COXES
COXEY
COYER
COYLY
COYPU
COZEN
COZES

C•O••
CEORL
CHOCK
CHOIR
CHOKE
CHOKY
CHOLO
CHOMP
CHONG
CHOPS
CHORD
CHORE
CHOSE
CHOWS
CLOAK
CLOCK
CLODS
CLOGS
CLOMP
CLONE
CLONK
CLOPS
CLOSE
CLOTH
CLOTS
CLOUD
CLOUT
CLOVE
CLOWN
CLOYS
CNOTE
COOED
COOEE
COOER
COOKE
COOKS
COOKY
COOLS
COONS
COOPS
COOPT
COORS
COOSA
COOTS
CROAK
CROAT
CROCE
CROCI
CROCK
CROCS
CROFT
CROIX
CROLY
CRONE
CRONY
CROOK
CROON
CROPS
CROSS
CROUP
CROWD
CROWN
CROWS
CROZE
CUOMO

C••O•
CABOT
CAMOS
CANOE
CANON
CAPON
CAPOS
CAROB
CAROL
CAROM
CARON
CDROM
CEROS
CHAOS
CHIOS
CHLOE
CHLOR
CHROM
CHRON
CLEON
CLIOS
COBOL
COCOA
COCOS
COHOS
COLON
COLOR
COROT
CREON
CROOK
CROON
CSPOT
CUKOR

C•••O
CACAO
CADDO
CAELO
CAIRO
CAMEO
CAMPO
CANDO
CANSO
CANTO
CARBO
CARGO
CARLO
CARPO
CASCO
CASIO
CELLO
CENTO
CERRO
CHACO
CHARO
CHICO
CHILO
CHINO
CHIRO
CHOLO
CINCO
CIRRO
CISCO
CLARO
COMBO
COMPO
CONDO
CONGO
CORNO
COSMO
CREDO
CUNEO
CUOMO
CUPRO
CURIO
CUZCO
CYANO
CYCLO

•CO••
ACOMA
ACORN
ECOLE
ECOLI
ICONO
ICONS
ICOSA
ICOSI
SCOFF
SCOLD
SCONE
SCOOP
SCOOT
SCOPE
SCOPS
SCOPY
SCORE
SCORN
SCOTS
SCOTT
SCOUR
SCOUT
SCOWL
SCOWS

•C•O•
ACHOO
ACTON
ACTOR
ICHOR
MCCOO
MCCOY
MCJOB
OCHOA
SCHON
SCION

SCOOP
SCOOT
SCROD

•C••O
ACETO
ACHOO
ICONO
MCCOO
OCULO
SCHMO
SCUDO

••CO•
ALCOA
ALCOR
ANCON
ASCOT
BACON
COCOA
COCOS
DECOR
DECOY
DICOT
EPCOT
INCOG
JACOB
LOCOS
LTCOL
MACON
MCCOO
MCCOY
NICOL
PECOS
PICOT
RACON
RECON
RICOH
TACOS

••C•O
BUCKO
CACAO
CYCLO
DICHO
FACTO
GECKO
HECTO
JOCKO
LACTO
MACAO
MACHO
MACRO
MCCOO
MICRO
MUCRO
NACHO
PICRO
RECTO
ROCCO
SACCO
SACRO
SECCO
SOCIO
SOCKO
TACHO
TYCHO
WACKO
XACTO

•••CO
ABACO
AMOCO
BANCO
BOSCO
CASCO
CHACO
CHICO
CINCO
CISCO
CUZCO
DELCO
DISCO
DRACO
GLUCO
GLYCO
GRECO
GUACO
JUNCO
MARCO
NARCO
PASCO
PHYCO
PISCO
ROCCO
SACCO
SECCO
TAXCO
VASCO
WILCO

CP•••
CPLUS

C•P••
CAPED
CAPEK
CAPER
CAPES
CAPET
CAPON
CAPOS
CAPRA
CAPRI
CAPTS
CEPES
COPAL
COPAN
COPAY
COPED
COPES
COPRA
COPSE
COPTS
CSPOT
CUPEL
CUPID
CUPPA
CUPRI
CUPRO

C••P•
CALPE
CAMPO
CAMPS
CAMPY
CARPE
CARPI
CARPO
CARPS
CHAPS
CHIPS
CHOPS
CLAPS
CLIPS
CLIPT
CLOPS
COAPT
COMPO
COMPS
COOPS
COOPT
CORPS
COUPE
COUPS
COYPU
CRAPE
CRAPS
CREPE
CREPT
CROPS
CRYPT
CULPA
CUPPA
CUSPS

C•••P
CHAMP
CHEAP
CHEEP
CHIMP
CHIRP
CHOMP
CHUMP
CLAMP
CLASP
CLOMP
CLUMP
CRAMP
CREEP
CRIMP
CRISP
CROUP
CRUMP
CUTUP

•C•P•
SCAPA
SCAPE
SCOPE
SCOPS
SCOPY
SCUPS

•C••P
ACTUP
ICEUP
SCALP
SCAMP
SCARP
SCAUP
SCOOP
SCRAP
SCRIP
VCHIP

••C•P
ASCAP
RECAP
RECIP
UNCAP

•••CP
NAACP

CR•••
CRABS
CRACK
CRACY
CRAFT
CRAGS
CRAIG
CRAIN
CRAKE
CRAMP
CRAMS
CRANE
CRANK
CRAPE
CRAPS
CRASH
CRASS
CRATE
CRAVE
CRAWL
CRAWS
CRAZE
CRAZY
CREAK
CREAM
CRECY
CREDO
CREED
CREEK
CREEL
CREEP
CREES
CREME
CREON
CREPE
CREPT
CRESC
CRESS
CREST
CRETE
CREWS
CRIBS
CRICK
CRIED
CRIER
CRIES
CRIME
CRIMP
CRISP
CRISS
CRIST
CROAK
CROAT
CROCE
CROCI
CROCK
CROCS
CROFT
CROIX
CROLY
CRONE
CRONY
CROOK
CROON
CROPS
CROSS
CROUP
CROWD
CROWN
CROWS
CROZE
CRUDE
CRUEL
CRUET
CRUMB
CRUMP
CRURA
CRUSE
CRUSH
CRUST
CRYER
CRYPT

C•R••
CARAT
CARBO
CARBS
CARDI
CARDS
CARED
CARER
CARES
CARET
CAREW
CAREY
CARGO
CARIA
CARIB
CARKS
CARLA
CARLE
CARLO
CARLY
CARNE
CARNY
CAROB
CAROL
CAROM
CARON
CARPE
CARPI
CARPO
CARPS
CARRE
CARRY
CARTA
CARTE
CARTS
CARVE
CDROM
CERAM
CERAT
CERED
CERES
CERIA
CEROS
CERRO
CERTS
CHRIS
CHROM
CHRON
CHRYS
CIRCA
CIRCE
CIRCS
CIRES
CIRRI
CIRRO
CORAL
CORBY
CORDS
COREA
CORED
CORER
CORES
COREY
CORFU
CORGI
CORIA
CORKS
CORKY
CORMS
CORNO
CORNS
CORNU
CORNY
COROT
CORPS
CURBS
CURCI
CURDS
CURDY
CURED
CURER
CURES
CURIA
CURIE
CURIO
CURLS
CURLY
CURRY
CURSE
CURST
CURVE
CURVY
CYRIL
CYRUS

C••R•
CADRE
CAIRN
CAIRO
CAMRY
CAPRA
CAPRI
CARRE
CARRY
CBERS
CEORL
CERRO
CHARD
CHARM
CHARO
CHARS
CHART
CHARY
CHERE
CHERI
CHERT
CHIRO
CHIRP
CHIRR
CHORD
CHORE
CHURL
CHURN
CIERA
CIRRI
CIRRO
CLARA
CLARE
CLARK
CLARO
CLARY
CLERK
CMDRS
COBRA
COIRS
COORS
COPRA
COURT
COWRY
CRURA
CUPRI
CUPRO
CURRY
CYMRY
CZARS

C•••R
CABER
CAGER
CANER
CAPER
CARER
CATER
CAVER
CEDAR
CESAR
CHAIR
CHEER
CHIRR
CHLOR
CHOIR
CIDER
CIGAR
CITER
CLAIR
CLEAR
CODER
COEUR
COLOR
COMER
CONTR
COOER
CORER
COVER
COWER
COYER
CRIER
CRYER
CUKOR
CURER
CUTER
CYBER
CYDER

•CR••
ACRED
ACRES
ACRID
ECRUS
MCRAE
OCREA
SCRAG
SCRAM
SCRAP
SCREE
SCREW
SCRIM
SCRIP
SCROD
SCRUB
SCRUM

•C•R•
ACARI
ACCRA
ACERB
ACERS
ACORN
ACURA
ICERS
OCHRE
SCARE
SCARF
SCARP
SCARS
SCARY
SCORE
SCORN
SCURF

•C••R
ACTER
ACTOR
ICHOR
ICIER
OCCUR
OCHER
SCOUR

••CR•
ACCRA
DECRY
LUCRE
LYCRA
MACRO
MICRA
MICRO
MUCRO
NACRE
PICRO
SACRA
SACRE
SACRO
SUCRE

••C•R
ALCOR
DECOR
DICER
FACER
INCUR
LACER
NICER
OCCUR
OSCAR
PACER
RACER
RECUR
RICER
ULCER
VICAR

CS•••
CSPOT

C•S••
CASAS
CASCA
CASCO
CASED
CASES
CASEY
CASIO
CASKS
CASTE
CASTS
CASUS
CBSTV
CESAR
CESTA
CESTI
CISCO
CISSY
COSBY
COSEC
COSMO
COSTA
COSTS
CUSHY
CUSKS
CUSPS

C••S•
CANSO
CANST
CAUSA
CAUSE
CEASE
CENSE
CHASE
CHASM
CHESS
CHEST
CHOSE
CISSY
CLASH
CLASP
CLASS
CLOSE
COAST
COOSA
COPSE
COUSY
CRASH
CRASS
CRESC
CRESS
CREST
CRISP
CRISS
CRIST
CROSS
CRUSE
CRUSH
CRUST
CURSE
CURST

C•••S
CADIS
CAFES
CAGES
CAKES
CALKS
CALLS
CALMS
CAMIS
CAMOS
CAMPS
CAMUS
CANES
CANIS
CANTS
CAPES
CAPOS
CAPTS
CARBS
CARDS
CARES
CARKS
CARPS
CARTS
CASAS
CASES
CASKS
CASTS
CASUS
CATES
CAULS
CAVES
CBERS
CEDES
CEDIS
CEILS
CELLS
CELTS
CENTS
CEPES
CERES
CEROS
CERTS
CETUS
CHAOS
CHAPS
CHARS
CHATS
CHAWS
CHEFS
CHESS
CHEWS
CHIAS
CHINS
CHIOS
CHIPS
CHITS
CHOPS
CHOWS
CHRIS
CHRYS
CHUBS
CHUGS
CHUMS
CINES
CIRCS
CIRES

CITES CLAMS CLANS CLAPS CLASS CLAUS CLAWS CLAYS CLEFS CLEWS CLIOS CLIPS CLODS CLOGS CLOPS CLOTS CLOYS CLUBS CLUES CMDRS COALS COATS COCKS COCOS CODAS CODES COEDS COHOS COIFS COILS COINS COIRS COKES COLAS COLDS COLES COLTS COMAS COMBS COMES COMPS COMUS CONES CONKS CONUS COOKS COOLS COONS COOPS COORS COOTS COPES COPTS CORDS CORES CORKS CORMS CORNS CORPS COSTS COTES COUPS COVES

COWES COWLS COXES COZES CPLUS CRABS CRAGS CRAMS CRAPS CRASS CRAWS CREES CRESS CREWS CRIBS CRIES CRISS CROCS CROPS CROSS CROWS CUBES CUFFS CUKES CULLS CULMS CULTS CUNAS CURBS CURDS CURES CURLS CUSKS CUSPS CUTIS CYMAS CYMES CYRUS CZARS

•C•S•
ICOSA ICOSI

•C••S
ACADS ACCTS ACERS ACHES ACIDS ACMES ACRES ACTAS ACYLS ECRUS ICBMS ICERS ICKES ICONS ICTUS OCCAS SCABS SCADS SCAMS SCANS SCARS SCATS SCOPS SCOTS SCOWS SCUDS SCUMS SCUPS SCUTS

••C•S
ACCTS ASCUS BACHS BACKS BECKS BUCKS COCKS COCOS DACES DECKS DICES DICKS DICTS DOCKS DUCES DUCKS DUCTS FACES FACTS FICES FICUS FOCUS FUCHS HACKS HECKS HICKS HOCKS HOCUS INCAS INCUS JACKS JOCKS KICKS LACES LACKS LICKS LOCHS LOCKS LOCOS LOCUS LUCAS LUCKS MACES MACYS MICAS MOCKS MUCKS NECKS NICKS NOCKS OCCAS OICKS ORCAS ORCHS ORCUS PACAS PACES PACKS PACTS PECKS PECOS PICAS PICKS PICTS POCUS PUCKS RACES RACKS RICES RICKS ROCKS RUCKS SACHS SACKS SECTS SOCKS SUCKS SYCES TACKS TACOS TECHS TICKS TUCKS UNCAS VICES VICKS WICKS YACKS YMCAS YWCAS

•••CS
AWACS BANCS BLOCS BOSCS CIRCS CROCS DISCS EPICS EXECS FISCS FLICS LAICS NARCS SPECS SYNCS WRACS ZINCS

C•T••
CATCH CATER CATES CATHY CATTY CETUS CITED CITER CITES COTES COTTA CUTER CUTEX CUTEY CUTIE CUTIN CUTIS CUTUP

C••T•
CACTI CANTO CANTS CANTY CAPTS CARTA CARTE CARTS CASTE CASTS CATTY CBSTV CELTS CENTI CENTO CENTS CERTS CESTA CESTI CEUTA CHATS CHETH CHITA CHITS CHUTE CLOTH CLOTS CNOTE COATI COATS COLTS COMTE CONTD CONTE CONTI CONTR COOTS COPTS COSTA COSTS COTTA COUTH CRATE CRETE CULTS

C•••T
CABOT CADET CANIT CANST CAPET CARAT CARET CERAT CFLAT CHANT CHART CHEAT CHERT CHEST CIVET CLEAT CLEFT CLIFT CLINT CLIPT CLOUT COACT COAPT COAST COLET COMET COOPT COROT COUNT COURT COVET CRAFT CREPT CREST CRIST CROAT CROFT CRUET CRUST CRYPT CSPOT CUBIT CUGAT CULET CURST

•CT••
ACTAS ACTED ACTER ACTII ACTIN ACTIV ACTON ACTOR ACTUP ICTUS OCTAD OCTAL OCTET

•C•T•
ACCTS ACETO ACUTE ICHTH SCATS SCOTS SCOTT SCUTA SCUTE SCUTS

•C••T
ECLAT OCTET SCANT SCENT SCOOT SCOTT SCOUT

••CT•
ABCTV ACCTS CACTI DICTA DICTS DICTU DUCTS FACTO FACTS HECTO LACTI LACTO NBCTV NOCTI PACTS PICTS RECTI RECTO SECTS XACTO

••C•T
ASCOT DICOT DUCAT EPCOT FACET FACIT HECHT JACET LICET LICIT NACHT OPCIT PICOT TACET TACIT UNCUT YACHT

•••CT
BRACT COACT EDICT EDUCT EJECT ELECT ENACT EPACT ERECT ERUCT EVICT EXACT MULCT REACT TINCT TRACT

CU•••
CUBAN CUBBY CUBEB CUBED CUBES CUBIC CUBIT CUDDY CUEIN CUFFS CUGAT CUING CUKES CUKOR CULCH CULET CULEX CULLS CULLY CULMS CULPA CULTS CUMAE CUMIN CUMUL CUNAS CUNEO CUOMO CUPEL CUPID CUPPA CUPRI CUPRO CURBS CURCI CURDS CURDY CURED CURER CURES CURIA CURIE CURIO CURLS CURLY CURRY CURSE CURST CURVE CURVY CUSHY CUSKS CUSPS CUTER CUTEX CUTEY CUTIE CUTIN CUTIS CUTUP CUVEE CUZCO

C•U••
CAULK CAULS CAUSA CAUSE CEUTA CHUBS CHUCK CHUFF CHUGS CHULA CHUMP CHUMS CHUNG CHUNK CHURL CHURN CHUTE CLUBS CLUCK CLUED CLUES CLUMP CLUNG CLUNK CLUNY COUCH COUGH COULD COUNT COUPE COUPS COURT COUSY COUTH CRUDE CRUEL CRUET CRUMB CRUMP CRURA CRUSE CRUSH CRUST

C••U•
CAJUN CAMUS CASUS CETUS CHAUD CLAUS CLOUD CLOUT COEUR COLUM COMUS CONUS CPLUS CROUP CUMUL CUTUP CYRUS

C•••U
CHEJU CORFU CORNU COYPU

•CU••
ACUFF ACURA ACUTE OCULO SCUBA SCUDI SCUDO SCUDS SCUFF SCULL SCUMS SCUPS SCURF SCUTA SCUTE SCUTS SCUZZ

•C•U•
ACTUP ECRUS ICEUP ICTUS OCCUR SCAUP SCOUR SCOUT SCRUB SCRUM

••CU•
ASCUS FICUS FOCUS HOCUS INCUR INCUS LOCUM LOCUS MECUM OCCUR ONCUE ORCUS PICUL POCUS RECUR UNCUT VACUA

••C•U
DICTU FICHU MACHU

CV•••
CVIII

C•V••
CAVAE CAVED CAVER CAVES CAVIL CCVII CDVII CIVET CIVIC CIVIL CLVII CMVII COVEN COVER COVES COVET COVEY CUVEE CXVII

C••V•
CALVE CARVE CCCVI CCLVI CCXVI CDLVI CDXVI CHEVY CHIVE CHIVY CLAVE CLIVE CLOVE CLXVI CMLVI CMXVI CRAVE CURVE CURVY CXCVI CXLVI

CXXVI

C•••V
CBSTV
CCCIV
CCCLV
CCCXV
CCLIV
CCLXV
CCXCV
CCXIV
CCXLV
CCXXV
CDLIV
CDLXV
CDXCV
CDXIV
CDXLV
CDXXV
CLXIV
CLXXV
CMLIV
CMLXV
CMXCV
CMXIV
CMXLV
CMXXV
CXCIV
CXLIV
CXXIV
CXXXV

•CV••
CCVII
DCVII
MCVIE
MCVII
XCVII

•C•V•
CCCVI
CCLVI
CCXVI
DCCVI
DCLVI
DCXVI
MCCVI
MCDVI
MCLVI
MCMVI
MCXVI

•C••V
ACTIV
CCCIV
CCCLV
CCCXV
CCLIV
CCLXV
CCXCV
CCXIV
CCXLV
CCXXV
DCCCV
DCCIV
DCCLV
DCCXV
DCLIV
DCLXV
DCXCV
DCXIV
DCXLV
DCXXV
MCCCV
MCCIV
MCCLV
MCCXV
MCDIV
MCDLV
MCDXV
MCLIV
MCLXV
MCMIV
MCMLV
MCMXV
MCXCV
MCXIV
MCXLV
MCXXV
SCHAV

••CV•
CCCVI
CXCVI
DCCVI
DXCVI
MCCVI
MDCVI
MMCVI
MXCVI

••C•V
ABCTV
CCCIV
CCCLV
CCCXV
CXCIV
DCCCV
DCCIV
DCCLV
DCCXV
DXCIV
MCCCV
MCCIV
MCCLV
MCCXV
MDCCV
MDCIV
MDCLV
MDCXV
MMCCV
MMCDV
MMCIV
MMCLV
MMCMV
MMCXV
MXCIV
NBCTV

•••CV
CCXCV
CDXCV
CMXCV
DCCCV
DCXCV
MCCCV
MCXCV
MDCCV
MDXCV
MMCCV
MMDCV
MMMCV
MMXCV

C•W••
CAWED
CLWYD
COWED
COWER
COWES
COWLS
COWRY

C••W•
CHAWS
CHEWS
CHEWY
CHOWS
CLAWS
CLEWS
CLOWN
CRAWL
CRAWS
CREWS
CROWD
CROWN
CROWS

C•••W
CANDW
CAREW

•C•W•
SCHWA
SCOWL
SCOWS

•C••W
SCREW

••C•W
MACAW

CX•••
CXCII
CXCIV
CXCIX
CXCVI
CXIII
CXLII
CXLIV
CXLIX
CXLVI
CXVII
CXXII
CXXIV
CXXIX
CXXVI
CXXXI
CXXXV

C•X••
CCXCI
CCXCV
CCXII
CCXIV
CCXIX
CCXLI
CCXLV
CCXVI
CCXXI
CCXXV
CCXXX
CDXCI
CDXCV
CDXII
CDXIV
CDXIX
CDXLI
CDXLV
CDXVI
CDXXI
CDXXV
CDXXX
CLXII
CLXIV
CLXIX
CLXVI
CLXXI
CLXXV
CLXXX
CMXCI
CMXCV
CMXII
CMXIV
CMXIX
CMXLI
CMXLV
CMXVI
CMXXI
CMXXV
CMXXX
COXAE
COXAL
COXED
COXES
COXEY
CXXII
CXXIV
CXXIX
CXXVI
CXXXI
CXXXV

C••X•
CCCXC
CCCXI
CCCXL
CCCXV
CCCXX
CCLXI
CCLXV
CCLXX
CCXXI
CCXXV
CCXXX
CDLXI
CDLXV
CDLXX
CDXXI
CDXXV
CDXXX
CLXXI
CLXXV
CLXXX
CMLXI
CMLXV
CMLXX
CMXXI
CMXXV
CMXXX
CXXXI
CXXXV

C•••X
CALIX
CALYX
CCCIX
CCCLX
CCCXX
CCLIX
CCLXX
CCXIX
CCXXX
CDLIX
CDLXX
CDXIX
CDXXX
CLXIX
CLXXX
CMLIX
CMLXX
CMXIX
CMXXX
CODEX
COMEX
COMIX
CROIX
CULEX
CUTEX
CXCIX
CXLIX
CXXIX

•CX••
CCXCI
CCXCV
CCXII
CCXIV
CCXIX
CCXLI
CCXLV
CCXVI
CCXXI
CCXXV
CCXXX
DCXCI
DCXCV
DCXII
DCXIV
DCXIX
DCXLI
DCXLV
DCXVI
DCXXI
DCXXV
DCXXX
MCXCI
MCXCV
MCXII
MCXIV
MCXIX
MCXLI
MCXLV
MCXVI
MCXXI
MCXXV
MCXXX

•C•X•
CCCXC
CCCXI
CCCXL
CCCXV
CCCXX
CCLXI
CCLXV
CCLXX
CCXXI
CCXXV
CCXXX
DCCXC
DCCXI
DCCXL
DCCXV
DCCXX
DCLXI
DCLXV
DCLXX
DCXXI
DCXXV
DCXXX
MCCXC
MCCXI
MCCXL
MCCXV
MCCXX
MCDXC
MCDXI
MCDXL
MCDXV
MCDXX
MCLXI
MCLXV
MCLXX
MCMXC
MCMXI
MCMXL
MCMXV
MCMXX
MCXXI
MCXXV
MCXXX

•C••X
CCCIX
CCCLX
CCCXX
CCLIX
CCLXX
CCXIX
CCXXX
DCCCX
DCCIX
DCCLX
DCCXX
DCLIX
DCLXX
DCXIX
DCXXX
ICEAX
MCCCX
MCCIX
MCCLX
MCCXX
MCDIX
MCDLX
MCDXX
MCLIX
MCLXX
MCMIX
MCMLX
MCMXX
MCXIX
MCXXX

••CX•
CCCXC
CCCXI
CCCXL
CCCXV
CCCXX
DCCXC
DCCXI
DCCXL
DCCXV
DCCXX
MCCXC
MCCXI
MCCXL
MCCXV
MCCXX
MDCXC
MDCXI
MDCXL
MDCXV
MDCXX
MMCXC
MMCXI
MMCXL
MMCXV
MMCXX

••C•X
CCCIX
CCCLX
CCCXX
CXCIX
DCCCX
DCCIX
DCCLX
DCCXX
DXCIX
MCCCX
MCCIX
MCCLX
MCCXX
MDCCX
MDCIX
MDCLX
MDCXX
MMCCX
MMCDX
MMCIX
MMCLX
MMCMX
MMCXX
MXCIX

•••CX
DCCCX
MCCCX
MDCCX
MMCCX
MMDCX
MMMCX

CY•••
CYANO
CYBER
CYCAD
CYCLE
CYCLO
CYDER
CYMAE
CYMAS
CYMES
CYMRY
CYNDI
CYNIC
CYRIL
CYRUS

C•Y••
CAYCE
CLYDE
COYER
COYLY
COYPU
CRYER
CRYPT

C••Y•
CALYX
CHRYS
CLAYS
CLOYS
CLWYD

C•••Y
CABBY
CADDY
CAGEY
CAKEY
CAMAY
CAMPY
CAMRY
CANBY
CANDY
CANNY
CANTY
CAREY
CARLY
CARNY
CARRY
CASEY
CATHY
CATTY
CECHY
CHARY
CHEVY
CHEWY
CHIVY
CHOKY
CINDY
CISSY
CLARY
CLUNY
COCKY
COLBY
COMFY
CONEY
COOKY
COPAY
CORBY
COREY
CORKY
CORNY
COSBY
COUSY
COVEY
COWRY
COXEY
COYLY
CRACY
CRAZY
CRECY
CROLY
CRONY
CUBBY
CUDDY
CULLY
CURDY
CURLY
CURRY
CURVY
CUSHY
CUTEY
CYMRY

•CY••
ACYLS

•C••Y
ACIDY
ICILY
MCCOY
MCFLY
MCKAY
SCALY
SCARY
SCOPY

••CY•
ENCYC
MACYS

••C•Y
ARCHY
BECKY
BUCKY
CECHY
COCKY
DECAY
DECOY
DECRY
DICEY
DICKY
DUCHY
DUCKY
ITCHY
JACKY
KICKY
LACEY
LECKY
LUCKY
MACHY
MCCOY
MUCKY
ORCZY
PECKY
PICKY
RICKY
ROCKY
TACHY
TACKY
TECHY
TICKY
VICHY
WACKY
YUCKY

•••CY
CRACY
CRECY
DANCY
DEUCY
FANCY
JUICY
MANCY
MARCY
MERCY
NANCY
ORACY
PERCY
PRICY
SAUCY
SPACY
SPICY
STACY
TRACY
ZINCY

CZ•••
CZARS
CZECH

C•Z••
COZEN
COZES
CUZCO

C••Z•
CHAZZ
CRAZE
CRAZY
CROZE

C•••Z
CADIZ
CHAZZ

•C•Z•
SCUZZ

•C••Z
SCUZZ

••CZ•
ORCZY

DA•••
DACCA
DACES
DACHA
DACHE
DACIA
DADDY
DADOS
DAFFS
DAFFY
DAFOE

DAGON DAILY DAIRY DAISY DAIWA DAKAR DALAI DALES DALEY DALLY DAMAN DAMAR DAMES DAMME DAMNS DAMON DAMPS DAMUP DANAE DANCE DANCY DANDY DANES DANGS DANIO DANKE DANNY DANSE DANTE DANZA DARBY DARED DARER DARES DARIN DARIO DARKS DARLA DARNS DARTH DARTS DARYA DARYL DASHI DATED DATER DATES DATUM DAUBS DAUNT DAVAO DAVID DAVIE DAVIS DAVIT DAVOS DAVYS DAWES DAWNS DAYAK DAYAN DAYNE DAZED DAZES

D•A••

DEALS DEALT DEANE DEANS DEARS DEARY DHABI DHAKA DHALS DIALS DIANA DIANE DIARY DIAZO DMARK DNASE DRABS DRACO DRAFT DRAGS DRAIL DRAIN DRAKE DRAMA DRAMS DRANG DRANK DRANO DRAPE DRATS DRAVA DRAWL DRAWN DRAWS DRAYS DUADS DUANE DWARF DYADS

D••A•

DAKAR DALAI DAMAN DAMAR DANAE DAVAO DAYAK DAYAN DCCAB DEBAR DECAF DECAL DECAY DEFAT DEGAS DELAY DERAT DETAT DEWAN DEWAR DFLAT DINAH DINAR DIRAC DITAT DIVAN DIVAS DONAS DONAT DONAU DORAG DORAL DORAN DOTAL DOUAI DOUAY DREAD DREAM DREAR DRLAO DRYAD DUBAI DUCAL DUCAT DUFAY DUGAN DUKAS DUMAS DURAN DYLAN

D•••A

DACCA DACHA DACIA DAIWA DANZA DARLA DARYA DEBRA DECCA DELLA DELTA DERMA DESNA DHAKA DIANA DICTA DITKA DOBLA DOBRA DOGMA DOLMA DONNA DORSA DRAMA DRAVA DRINA DURRA DVINA

•DA••

ADAGE ADAIR ADAMA ADAMS ADANA ADANO ADAPT EDAMS IDAHO UDALL

•D•A•

ADDAX ADLAI ADMAN ADVAL EDDAS EDGAR IDEAL IDEAS IDTAG

•D••A

ADAMA ADANA ADELA ADUWA ADYTA EDEMA EDINA NDOLA

••DA•

ADDAX AIDAN ALDAN AODAI CEDAR CODAS EDDAS HADAR HADAT HODAD JUDAH JUDAS KADAR KODAK MADAM MEDAL MIDAS MODAL NODAL PEDAL RADAR REDAN RODAN SADAT SEDAN SODAS SUDAN TIDAL TODAY VEDAS VEDAY VIDAL VJDAY

••D•A

AUDRA HEDDA HYDRA INDIA INDRA JIDDA JUDEA LYDIA MEDEA MEDIA MUDRA NADIA NADJA PADUA PODIA SIDEA SIDRA SUDRA VEDDA VODKA

•••DA

ALIDA BANDA BREDA CNIDA FONDA FREDA FULDA GARDA GILDA GOLDA GOUDA HAIDA HEDDA HILDA HONDA JIDDA KINDA KORDA LINDA LYNDA MAGDA MAZDA OUIDA PANDA QANDA RHODA SKODA SUNDA THEDA VEDDA VENDA WAJDA WANDA ZELDA ZENDA

D•B••

DEBAR DEBBY DEBIT DEBRA DEBTS DEBUG DEBUT DOBBY DOBIE DOBLA DOBLE DOBRA DOBRO DUBAI DUBIN DUBOS

D••B•

DARBY DAUBS DEBBY DERBY DHABI DIDBY DIGBY DOBBY DOLBY DOUBT DRABS DRIBS DRUBS DUMBO DUMBS

D•••B

DCCAB DEMOB DENEB DWEEB

•D•B•

ADOBE

•D••B

ADLIB

••DB•

DIDBY

••D•B

REDUB SIDEB

•••DB

BANDB RANDB

DC•••

DCCAB DCCCI DCCCL DCCCV DCCCX DCCII DCCIV DCCIX DCCLI DCCLV DCCLX DCCVI DCCXC DCCXI DCCXL DCCXV DCCXX DCIII DCLII DCLIV DCLIX DCLVI DCLXI DCLXV DCLXX DCVII DCXCI DCXCV DCXII DCXIV DCXIX DCXLI DCXLV DCXVI DCXXI DCXXV DCXXX

D•C••

DACCA DACES DACHA DACHE DACIA DCCAB DCCCI DCCCL DCCCV DCCCX DCCII DCCIV DCCIX DCCLI DCCLV DCCLX DCCVI DCCXC DCCXI DCCXL DCCXV DCCXX DECAF DECAL DECAY DECCA DECEM DECKS DECOR DECOY DECRY DICED DICER DICES DICEY DICHO DICKS DICKY DICOT DICTA DICTS DICTU DOCKS DUCAL DUCAT DUCES DUCHY DUCKS DUCKY DUCTS DXCII DXCIV DXCIX DXCVI

D••C•

DACCA DANCE DANCY DCCCI DCCCL DCCCV DCCCX DCXCI DCXCV DECCA DEICE DELCO DEUCE DEUCY DISCO DISCS DITCH DOLCE DRACO DUNCE DUTCH

D•••C

DCCXC DIRAC DORIC DUROC

•DC••

MDCCC MDCCI MDCCL MDCCV MDCCX MDCII MDCIV MDCIX MDCLI MDCLV MDCLX MDCVI MDCXC MDCXI MDCXL MDCXV MDCXX

•D•C•

CDXCI CDXCV EDICT EDUCE EDUCT MDCCC MDCCI MDCCL MDCCV MDCCX MDXCI MDXCV

•D••C

ADHOC ADLOC EDDIC MDCCC MDCXC

••DC•

MMDCC MMDCI MMDCL MMDCV MMDCX

••D•C

ASDIC EDDIC INDIC IODIC LUDIC MCDXC MEDIC MEDOC MMDCC MMDXC MODOC VEDIC

•••DC

HARDC MMMDC

D•D••

DADDY DADOS DIDBY DIDIN DIDNT DIDOS DIDST DIDUP DODGE DODGY DODOS DRDRE DUDDY DUDES

D••D•

DADDY DANDY DEEDS DENDR DINDY DIODE DONDI DOODY DOWDY DREDD DUADS DUDDY DYADS

D•••D

DARED DATED DAVID DAZED DEKED DELED DEWED DICED DIKED DIMED DINED DIVED DOLED DOMED DOPED DOSED DOTED DOZED DREAD DREDD DRIED DROID DROOD DRUID DRYAD DUKED DUPED DYFED

•DD••

ADDAX ADDED ADDER ADDIE ADDIN ADDIS ADDLE ADDNL ADDON ADDTO ADDUP EDDAS EDDIC EDDIE ODDER ODDLY UDDER

•D••D

ADDED EDGED IDLED

••DD•

BADDY BIDDY BUDDY CADDO CADDY CUDDY DADDY DUDDY FUDDY GIDDY HEDDA JIDDA KIDDO KIDDY LIDDY MIDDY MUDDY NEDDY NODDY PADDY REDDY RODDY RUDDS RUDDY SODDY SUDDS TEDDY TODDY VEDDA WADDY

••D•D

ADDED AIDED BIDED BODED CEDED CODED ENDED FADED HODAD JADED LADED REDED REDID

SIDED
TIDED
UNDID
WADED

•••DD
DREDD
RANDD

DE•••
DEALS
DEALT
DEANE
DEANS
DEARS
DEARY
DEBAR
DEBBY
DEBIT
DEBRA
DEBTS
DEBUG
DEBUT
DECAF
DECAL
DECAY
DECCA
DECEM
DECKS
DECOR
DECOY
DECRY
DEEDS
DEEMS
DEEPS
DEERE
DEERS
DEFAT
DEFER
DEFOE
DEFOG
DEGAS
DEICE
DEIFY
DEIGN
DEILS
DEION
DEISM
DEIST
DEITY
DEKED
DEKES
DEKKO
DELAY
DELCO
DELED
DELES
DELFT
DELHI
DELIS
DELLA
DELLS
DELON
DELOS
DELTA
DELTS
DELVE
DEMES
DEMIT
DEMME
DEMOB
DEMON
DEMOS
DEMUR
DENDR
DENEB
DENES
DENIM
DENIS
DENNY
DENOM
DENSE
DENTE
DENTI
DENTS
DENYS
DEOXY
DEPEW
DEPOT
DEPTH
DEPTS
DERAT
DERBY
DEREK
DERIV
DERMA
DERMO
DERRY
DERSU
DESKS
DESNA
DESTE
DETAT
DETER
DETOO
DETRE
DEUCE
DEUCY
DEUTO
DEVIL
DEVON
DEVRY
DEWAN
DEWAR
DEWED
DEWEY
DEXTR

D•E••
DEEDS
DEEMS
DEEPS
DEERE
DEERS
DIEGO
DIEMS
DIENE
DIETS
DOERS
DOEST
DOETH
DREAD
DREAM
DREAR
DREDD
DREGS
DRESS
DUELS
DUETO
DUETS
DWEEB
DWELL
DWELT
DYERS

D••E•
DACES
DALES
DALEY
DAMES
DANES
DARED
DARER
DARES
DATED
DATER
DATES
DAWES
DAZED
DAZES
DECEM
DEFER
DEKED
DEKES
DELED
DELES
DEMES
DENEB
DENES
DEPEW
DEREK
DETER
DEWED
DEWEY
DICED
DICER
DICES
DICEY
DIKED
DIKES
DIMED
DIMES
DINED
DINER
DINES
DIRER
DIVED
DIVER
DIVES
DIYER
DIZEN
DOGES
DOGEY
DOLED
DOLES
DOMED
DOMES
DONEE
DONEN
DOPED
DOPES
DOPEY
DOREN
DOSED
DOSER
DOSES
DOTED
DOTER
DOTES
DOVER
DOVES
DOVEY
DOWEL
DOWER
DOYEN
DOZED
DOZEN
DOZER
DOZES
DRIED
DRIER
DRIES
DRYER
DUCES
DUDES
DUKED
DUKES
DUNES
DUPED
DUPES
DURER
DUVET
DUXES
DWEEB
DYFED
DYNEL
DYNES

D•••E
DACHE
DAFOE
DAMME
DANAE
DANCE
DANKE
DANSE
DANTE
DAVIE
DAYNE
DEANE
DEERE
DEFOE
DEICE
DELVE
DEMME
DENSE
DENTE
DESTE
DETRE
DEUCE
DHOLE
DHOTE
DIANE
DIENE
DINGE
DIODE
DIONE
DIRGE
DISME
DIXIE
DNASE
DOBIE
DOBLE
DODGE
DOGIE
DOLCE
DONEE
DONNE
DOONE
DOUSE
DOWSE
DOYLE
DRAKE
DRAPE
DRDRE
DRIVE
DROME
DRONE
DROVE
DRUPE
DRUSE
DRUZE
DUANE
DULSE
DUNCE
DUNNE
DUPLE
DUPRE

•DE••
ADEEM
ADELA
ADELE
ADENO
ADEPT
ADEUX
EDEMA
EDENS
IDEAL
IDEAS
IDEST
ODELL
ODETS
ODEUM

•D•E•
ADDED
ADDER
ADEEM
ADHEM
ADIEU
ADLER
ADMEN
ADREM
ADZES
EDGED
EDGER
EDGES
EDSEL
IDLED
IDLER
IDLES
ODDER
UDDER

•D••E
ADAGE
ADDIE
ADDLE
ADELE
ADIGE
ADOBE
ADORE
EDDIE
EDILE
EDUCE
IDINE
ODILE
UDINE

••DE•
ADDED
ADDER
AEDES
AIDED
AIDES
ALDEN
ALDER
ANDES
ARDEN
AUDEN
BADEN
BADER
BEDEW
BIDED
BIDEN
BIDES
BODED
BODES
CADET
CEDED
CEDES
CIDER
CODED
CODER
CODES
CODEX
CYDER
DUDES
EIDER
ELDER
EMDEN
ENDED
ENDER
FADED
FADES
FEDEX
FIDEI
FIDEL
FIDES
GODEL
GODET
GODEY
HADES
HIDER
HIDES
INDEF
INDEX
JADED
JADES
JUDEA
JUDEO
LADED
LADEN
LADER
LADES
LODEN
LODES
MEDEA
MEDES
MODEL
MODEM
MODES
NADER
NIDES
NODES
NUDER
NUDES
ODDER
OGDEN
OLDEN
OLDER
ORDER
REDED
REDES
RIDER
RIDES
RODEO
RUDER
RYDER
SEDER
SIDEA
SIDEB
SIDED
SIDER
SIDES
TIDED
TIDES
UDDER
UNDER
VADER
VIDEO
WADED
WADER
WADES
WEDEL
WIDEN
WIDER
WODEN
YODEL

••D•E
ADDIE
ADDLE
ANDIE
ANDRE
AUDIE
BADGE
BUDGE
CADGE
CADRE
DODGE
DRDRE
EDDIE
ENDUE
EYDIE
FUDGE
HEDGE
INDIE
JODIE
JUDGE
KEDGE
LADLE
LEDGE
LODGE
MADGE
MADRE
MIDGE
NIDRE
NUDGE
OLDIE
PADRE
REDYE
RIDGE
RUDGE
SADHE
SADIE
SEDGE
SIDHE
SIDLE
UNDUE
WEDGE
WODGE

•••DE
AANDE
ABIDE
ABODE
AMIDE
ANODE
ASIDE
AZIDE
BLADE
BRIDE
BSIDE
CHIDE
CLYDE
CONDE
CRUDE
DIODE
ELIDE
ELUDE
EPODE
ERODE
ETUDE
EVADE
EXUDE
FERDE
GARDE
GEODE
GLADE
GLEDE
GLIDE
GOLDE
GRADE
GUIDE
HORDE
IMIDE
IRADE
LAUDE
LYNDE
MAUDE
MEADE
MONDE
OXIDE
PRIDE
PRUDE
READE
RHODE
SANDE
SHADE
SLADE
SLIDE
SNIDE
SONDE
SPADE
SPODE
SUEDE
SWEDE
TANDE
TARDE
TEIDE
TILDE
TRADE
TSADE
VERDE
WILDE

DF•••
DFLAT

D•F••
DAFFS
DAFFY
DAFOE
DEFAT
DEFER
DEFOE
DEFOG
DOFFS
DUFAY
DUFFS
DUFFY
DYFED

D••F•
DAFFS
DAFFY
DEIFY
DELFT
DOFFS
DRAFT
DRIFT
DUFFS
DUFFY

D•••F
DECAF
DWARF

•DF••
ADFIN

•D•F•
EDIFY

•D••F
ADOLF

••D•F
INDEF
RIDOF

D•G••
DAGON
DEGAS
DIGBY
DIGIN
DIGIT
DIGUP
DOGES
DOGEY
DOGGO
DOGGY
DOGIE
DOGIT
DOGMA
DOGON
DUGAN
DUGIN
DUGUP

D••G•
DANGS
DEIGN
DIEGO
DINGE
DINGO
DINGS
DINGY
DIRGE
DODGE
DODGY
DOGGO
DOGGY
DONGS
DOUGH
DRAGS
DREGS
DRUGS

D•••G
DEBUG
DEFOG
DOING
DORAG
DRANG
DYING

•DG••
EDGAR
EDGED
EDGER
EDGES

•D•G•
ADAGE
ADIGE

•D••G
IDTAG

••DG•
BADGE
BLDGS
BUDGE
CADGE
DODGE
DODGY
FUDGE
HEDGE
HEDGY
JUDGE
KEDGE
LEDGE
LEDGY
LODGE
MADGE
MIDGE
NUDGE
PODGY
PUDGY
RIDGE
RIDGY
RUDGE
SEDGE
SEDGY
WEDGE
WEDGY
WODGE

•••DG
HARDG

DH•••
DHABI
DHAKA
DHALS
DHOLE
DHOTE
DHOTI
DHOWS

D••H•
DACHA
DACHE
DASHI
DELHI
DICHO
DISHY
DONHO
DUCHY

D•••H
DARTH
DEPTH
DINAH
DITCH
DOETH
DOLPH
DOUGH
DUTCH

•DH••
ADHEM
ADHOC

•D•H•
IDAHO

•D••H
EDITH

••DH•
SADHE
SADHU
SIDHE
YODHS

••D•H
JUDAH
WIDTH

•••DH
SANDH

DI•••
DIALS
DIANA
DIANE
DIARY
DIAZO
DICED
DICER
DICES
DICEY
DICHO
DICKS
DICKY
DICOT
DICTA
DICTS
DICTU
DIDBY
DIDIN
DIDNT
DIDOS
DIDST
DIDUP
DIEGO
DIEMS
DIENE
DIETS
DIGBY
DIGIN
DIGIT
DIGUP
DIJON
DIKED
DIKES
DILLS
DILLY
DIMED
DIMES
DIMLY
DINAH
DINAR
DINDY
DINED
DINER
DINES
DINGE
DINGO
DINGS
DINGY
DINKS
DINKY
DINTS
DINTY
DIODE
DIONE
DIPLO
DIPPY
DIRAC
DIRER
DIRGE
DIRKS
DIRTY
DISCO
DISCS
DISHY
DISKS
DISME
DISTR
DITAT
DITCH
DITKA
DITSY
DITTO
DITTY
DITZY
DIVAN
DIVAS
DIVED
DIVER
DIVES
DIVOT
DIVVY
DIXIE
DIXIT
DIXON
DIYER
DIZEN
DIZZY

D•I••
DAILY
DAIRY
DAISY
DAIWA
DCIII
DEICE
DEIFY
DEIGN
DEILS
DEION
DEISM
DEIST
DEITY
DJINN
DLIII
DOILY
DOING
DOITS
DRIBS
DRIED
DRIER
DRIES
DRIFT
DRILL
DRILY
DRINA
DRINK
DRIPS
DRIVE
DVIII
DVINA
DXIII
DYING

D••I•
DACIA
DANIO
DARIN
DARIO
DAVID
DAVIE
DAVIS
DAVIT
DCCII
DCCIV
DCCIX
DCIII
DCLII
DCLIV
DCLIX
DCVII
DCXII
DCXIV
DCXIX
DEBIT
DELIS
DEMIT
DENIM
DENIS
DERIV
DEVIL
DIDIN
DIGIN
DIGIT
DIXIE
DIXIT
DLIII
DLVII
DLXII
DLXIV
DLXIX
DOBIE
DOGIE
DOGIT
DORIC
DORIS
DRAIL
DRAIN
DROID
DROIT
DRUID
DUBIN
DUGIN
DVIII
DXCII
DXCIV
DXCIX
DXIII
DXLII
DXLIV
DXLIX
DXVII
DXXII
DXXIV
DXXIX

D•••I
DALAI
DASHI
DCCCI
DCCII
DCCLI
DCCVI
DCCXI
DCIII
DCLII
DCLVI
DCLXI
DCVII
DCXCI
DCXII
DCXLI
DCXVI
DCXXI
DELHI
DENTI
DHABI
DHOTI
DLIII
DLVII
DLXII
DLXVI
DLXXI
DONDI
DORSI
DOUAI
DUBAI
DVIII
DXCII
DXCVI
DXIII
DXLII
DXLVI
DXVII
DXXII
DXXVI
DXXXI

•DI••
ADIEU
ADIGE
ADINT
ADIOS
ADIPO
ADITS
CDIII
EDICT
EDIFY
EDILE
EDINA
EDITH
EDITS
IDINE
IDIOM
IDIOT
MDIII
ODILE
ODIST
ODIUM
UDINE

•D•I•
ADAIR
ADDIE
ADDIN
ADDIS
ADFIN
ADLIB
ADMIN
ADMIT
ADMIX
ADVIL
CDIII
CDLII
CDLIV
CDLIX
CDVII
CDXII
CDXIV
CDXIX
EDDIC
EDDIE
EDWIN
MDCII
MDCIV
MDCIX
MDIII
MDLII
MDLIV
MDLIX
MDVII
MDXII
MDXIV
MDXIX

•D••I
ADLAI
CDIII
CDLII
CDLVI
CDLXI
CDVII
CDXCI
CDXII
CDXLI
CDXVI
CDXXI
MDCCI
MDCII
MDCLI
MDCVI
MDCXI
MDIII
MDLII
MDLVI
MDLXI
MDVII
MDXCI
MDXII
MDXLI
MDXVI
MDXXI

••DI•
ADDIE
ADDIN
ADDIS
ANDIE
ASDIC
AUDIE
AUDIO
AUDIS
AUDIT
BEDIM
BIDIN
CADIS
CADIZ
CEDIS
DIDIN
EDDIC
EDDIE
EYDIE
HEDIN
INDIA
INDIC
INDIE
INDIO
INDIV
IODIC
JODIE
LEDIN
LUDIC
LYDIA
MCDII
MCDIV
MCDIX
MEDIA
MEDIC
MEDIT
MIDIS
MMDII
MMDIV
MMDIX
NADIA
NADIR
OLDIE
ONDIT
PODIA
RADII
RADIO
RADIX
REDID
RODIN
SADIE
SADIS
UNDID
VADIM
VADIS
VEDIC
WADIS
XEDIN
YADIM

••D•I
AODAI
FIDEI
HADJI
INDRI
MCDII
MCDLI
MCDVI
MCDXI
MMDCI
MMDII
MMDLI
MMDVI
MMDXI
RADII

•••DI
BONDI
CARDI
CYNDI
DONDI
EGADI
GONDI
HEIDI
HINDI
JEUDI
LANDI
LUNDI
MAHDI
MARDI
MMCDI
MMMDI
MUNDI
NALDI
PARDI
RANDI
SAUDI
SCUDI
SOLDI
TONDI
VERDI

DJ•••
DJINN

D•J••
DIJON
DOJOS

••DJ•
HADJI
NADJA

D•K••
DAKAR
DEKED
DEKES
DEKKO
DIKED
DIKES
DUKAS
DUKED
DUKES

D••K•
DANKE
DARKS
DECKS
DEKKO
DESKS
DHAKA
DICKS
DICKY
DINKS
DINKY
DIRKS
DISKS
DITKA
DOCKS
DRAKE
DUCKS
DUCKY
DUNKS
DUSKS
DUSKY

D•••K
DAYAK
DEREK
DMARK
DRANK
DRINK
DRUNK

••DK•
VODKA

••D•K
KODAK

DL•••
DLIII
DLVII
DLXII
DLXIV
DLXIX
DLXVI
DLXXI
DLXXV
DLXXX

D•L••
DALAI
DALES
DALEY
DALLY
DCLII
DCLIV
DCLIX
DCLVI
DCLXI
DCLXV
DCLXX
DELAY
DELCO
DELED
DELES
DELFT
DELHI
DELIS
DELLA
DELLS
DELON
DELOS
DELTA
DELTS
DELVE
DFLAT
DILLS
DILLY
DOLBY
DOLCE
DOLED
DOLES
DOLLS
DOLLY
DOLMA
DOLOR
DOLPH
DOLTS
DPLUS
DRLAO
DULLS
DULLY
DULSE
DXLII
DXLIV
DXLIX
DXLVI
DYLAN

D••L•
DAILY
DALLY
DARLA
DCCLI
DCCLV
DCCLX
DCXLI
DCXLV
DEALS
DEALT
DEILS
DELLA
DELLS
DHALS
DHOLE
DIALS
DILLS
DILLY
DIMLY
DIPLO
DOBLA
DOBLE
DOILY
DOLLS
DOLLY
DOYLE
DOYLY
DRILL
DRILY
DROLL
DRYLY
DUELS
DULLS
DULLY
DUPLE
DWELL
DWELT

D•••L
DARYL
DCCCL
DCCXL
DECAL
DEVIL
DORAL
DOTAL
DOWEL
DRAIL
DRAWL
DRILL
DROLL
DROOL
DUCAL
DWELL
DYNEL

•DL••
ADLAI
ADLER
ADLIB
ADLOC
CDLII
CDLIV
CDLIX
CDLVI
CDLXI
CDLXV
CDLXX
IDLED
IDLER
IDLES
MDLII
MDLIV
MDLIX
MDLVI
MDLXI
MDLXV
MDLXX

•D•L•
ADDLE
ADELA
ADELE
ADOLF
ADULT
CDXLI
CDXLV
EDILE
IDOLS
IDYLL
IDYLS
MDCLI
MDCLV
MDCLX
MDXLI
MDXLV
NDOLA
ODDLY
ODELL
ODILE
UDALL

•D••L
ADDNL
ADVAL
ADVIL

EDSEL IDEAL IDYLL MDCCL MDCXL ODELL UDALL

••DL•
ADDLE BADLY GODLY LADLE MADLY MCDLI MCDLV MCDLX MMDLI MMDLV MMDLX ODDLY REDLY SADLY SIDLE

••D•L
ABDUL ADDNL ALDOL FIDEL GODEL MCDXL MEDAL MMDCL MMDXL MODAL MODEL NODAL PEDAL TIDAL VIDAL WEDEL YODEL

•••DL
LENDL MMCDL MMMDL PANDL SANDL

DM•••
DMARK

D•M••
DAMAN DAMAR DAMES DAMME DAMNS DAMON DAMPS DAMUP DEMES DEMIT DEMME DEMOB DEMON DEMOS DEMUR DIMED DIMES DIMLY DOMED DOMES DUMAS DUMBO DUMBS DUMMY DUMPS DUMPY

D••M•
DAMME DEEMS DEMME DERMA DERMO DIEMS DISME DOGMA DOLMA DOOMS DORMS DRAMA DRAMS DROME DRUMS DUMMY DUOMO

D•••M
DATUM DECEM DEISM DENIM DENOM DREAM DURUM

•DM••
ADMAN ADMEN ADMIN ADMIT ADMIX

•D•M•
ADAMA ADAMS EDAMS EDEMA

•D••M
ADEEM ADHEM ADREM ADSUM CDROM IDIOM ODEUM ODIUM

••D•M
BEDIM MADAM MODEM SEDUM SODOM VADIM YADIM

•••DM
AANDM

DN•••
DNASE

D•N••
DANAE DANCE DANCY DANDY DANES DANGS DANIO DANKE DANNY DANSE DANTE DANZA DENDR DENEB DENES DENIM DENIS DENNY DENOM DENSE DENTE DENTI DENTS DENYS DINAH DINAR DINDY DINED DINER DINES DINGE DINGO DINGS DINGY DINKS DINKY DINTS DINTY DONAS DONAT DONAU DONDI DONEE DONEN DONGS DONHO DONNA DONNE DONNY DONOR DONUT DUNCE DUNES DUNKS DUNNE DUNNO DYNEL DYNES

D••N•
DAMNS DANNY DARNS DAUNT DAWNS DAYNE DEANE DEANS DENNY DESNA DIANA DIANE DIDNT DIENE DIONE DJINN DOING DONNA DONNE DONNY DOONE DOWNS DOWNY DRANG DRANK DRANO DRINA DRINK DRONE DRUNK DUANE DUNNE DUNNO DURNS DVINA DYING

D•••N
DAGON DAMAN DAMON DARIN DAYAN DEIGN DEION DELON DEMON DEVON DEWAN DIDIN DIGIN DIJON DIVAN DIXON DIZEN DJINN DOGON DONEN DORAN DOREN DOYEN DOZEN DRAIN DRAWN DROWN DUBIN DUGAN DUGIN DURAN DYLAN

•D•N•
ADANA ADANO ADDNL ADENO ADINT EDENS EDINA IDINE ODONT UDINE

•D••N
ADDIN ADDON ADFIN ADMAN ADMEN ADMIN ADORN EDWIN

••DN•
ADDNL DIDNT HADNT

••D•N
ADDIN ADDON AIDAN ALDAN ALDEN ARDEN AUDEN BADEN BIDEN BIDIN BIDON DIDIN EMDEN ENDON FEDON HADON HEDIN LADEN LADON LEDIN LEDON LODEN OGDEN OLDEN RADON REDAN REDON RODAN RODIN SEDAN SIDON SUDAN WIDEN WODEN XEDIN

•••DN
HAYDN

DO•••
DOBBY DOBIE DOBLA DOBLE DOBRA DOBRO DOCKS DODGE DODGY DODOS DOERS DOEST DOETH DOFFS DOGES DOGEY DOGGO DOGGY DOGIE DOGIT DOGMA DOGON DOILY DOING DOITS DOJOS DOLBY DOLCE DOLED DOLES DOLLS DOLLY DOLMA DOLOR DOLPH DOLTS DOMED DOMES DONAS DONAT DONAU DONDI DONEE DONEN DONGS DONHO DONNA DONNE DONNY DONOR DONUT DOODY DOOMS DOONE DOORS DOOZY DOPED DOPES DOPEY DORAG DORAL DORAN DOREN DORIC DORIS DORMS DORPS DORSA DORSI DORSO DOSED DOSER DOSES DOTAL DOTED DOTER DOTES DOTTO DOTTY DOUAI DOUAY DOUBT DOUGH DOURO DOUSE DOVER DOVES DOVEY DOWDY DOWEL DOWER DOWNS DOWNY DOWRY DOWSE DOYEN DOYLE DOYLY DOZED DOZEN DOZER DOZES

D•O••
DEOXY DHOLE DHOTE DHOTI DHOWS DIODE DIONE DOODY DOOMS DOONE DOORS DOOZY DROID DROIT DROLL DROME DRONE DROOD DROOL DROOP DROPS DROSS DROVE DROWN DUOMO

D••O•
DADOS DAFOE DAGON DAMON DAVOS DECOR DECOY DEFOE DEFOG DEION DELON DELOS DEMOB DEMON DEMOS DENOM DEPOT DETOO DEVON DICOT DIDOS DIJON DIVOT DIXON DODOS DOGON DOJOS DOLOR DONOR DROOD DROOL DROOP DUBOS DUROC DUROS

D•••O
DANIO DARIO DAVAO DEKKO DELCO DERMO DETOO DEUTO DIAZO DICHO DIEGO DINGO DIPLO DISCO DITTO DOBRO DOGGO DONHO DORSO DOTTO DOURO DRACO DRANO DRLAO DUETO DUMBO DUNNO DUOMO

•DO••
ADOBE ADOLF ADOPT ADORE ADORN ADOUT IDOLS NDOLA ODONT ODORS ODOUR XDOUT

•D•O•
ADDON ADHOC ADIOS ADLOC CDROM IDIOM IDIOT

•D••O
ADANO ADDTO ADENO ADIPO IDAHO

••DO•
ADDON ALDOL ANDOR ARDOR BIDON DADOS DIDOS DODOS ENDON ENDOR ENDOW FADOS FEDON FODOR GODOT HADON KUDOS LADON LEDON LIDOS MEDOC MODOC MSDOS NODOZ ORDOS RADON REDON REDOX RIDOF SIDON SODOM SYDOW TODOS TUDOR UPDOS VIDOR WIDOW

••D•O
ADDTO ANDRO AUDIO CADDO HADTO HYDRO INDIO JUDEO KIDDO LEDTO PEDRO RADIO RODEO VIDEO

•••DO
AMADO AMIDO BANDO CADDO CANDO CONDO CREDO EJIDO FALDO FORDO FRODO GORDO GUIDO HONDO IMIDO IRIDO KENDO KIDDO LANDO LINDO MISDO MONDO OUTDO PARDO PRADO RHODO RONDO SCUDO SOLDO TONDO WALDO ZENDO

DP•••
DPLUS

D•P••
DEPEW DEPOT DEPTH DEPTS DIPLO DIPPY DOPED DOPES DOPEY DUPED DUPES DUPLE DUPRE

D••P•
DAMPS DEEPS DIPPY DOLPH DORPS DRAPE DRIPS DROPS DRUPE DUMPS

DUMPY

D•••P
DAMUP
DIDUP
DIGUP
DROOP
DRYUP
DUGUP

•D•P•
ADAPT
ADEPT
ADIPO
ADOPT

•D••P
ADDUP

••D•P
ADDUP
ANDUP
BIDUP
DIDUP
ENDUP
FEDUP
WADUP

DR•••
DRABS
DRACO
DRAFT
DRAGS
DRAIL
DRAIN
DRAKE
DRAMA
DRAMS
DRANG
DRANK
DRANO
DRAPE
DRATS
DRAVA
DRAWL
DRAWN
DRAWS
DRAYS
DRDRE
DREAD
DREAM
DREAR
DREDD
DREGS
DRESS
DRIBS
DRIED
DRIER
DRIES
DRIFT
DRILL
DRILY
DRINA
DRINK
DRIPS
DRIVE
DRLAO
DROID
DROIT
DROLL
DROME
DRONE
DROOD
DROOL
DROOP
DROPS
DROSS
DROVE
DROWN
DRUBS
DRUGS
DRUID
DRUMS
DRUNK
DRUPE
DRURY
DRUSE
DRUZE
DRYAD
DRYER
DRYLY
DRYUP

D•R••
DARBY
DARED
DARER
DARES
DARIN
DARIO
DARKS
DARLA
DARNS
DARTH
DARTS
DARYA
DARYL
DERAT
DERBY
DEREK
DERIV
DERMA
DERMO
DERRY
DERSU
DIRAC
DIRER
DIRGE
DIRKS
DIRTY
DORAG
DORAL
DORAN
DOREN
DORIC
DORIS
DORMS
DORPS
DORSA
DORSI
DORSO
DURAN
DURER
DURNS
DUROC
DUROS
DURRA
DURST
DURUM

D••R•
DAIRY
DEARS
DEARY
DEBRA
DECRY
DEERE
DEERS
DERRY
DETRE
DEVRY
DIARY
DMARK
DOBRA
DOBRO
DOERS
DOORS
DOURO
DOWRY
DRDRE
DRURY
DUPRE
DURRA
DWARF
DYERS

D•••R
DAKAR
DAMAR
DARER
DATER
DEBAR
DECOR
DEFER
DEMUR
DENDR
DETER
DEWAR
DEXTR
DICER
DINAR
DINER
DIRER
DISTR
DIVER
DIYER
DOLOR
DONOR
DOSER
DOTER
DOVER
DOWER
DOZER
DREAR
DRIER
DRYER
DURER

•DR••
ADREM
CDROM

•D•R•
ADORE
ADORN
ODORS

•D••R
ADAIR
ADDER
ADLER
EDGAR
EDGER
IDLER
ODDER
ODOUR
UDDER

••DR•
ANDRE
ANDRO
ANDRY
AUDRA
CADRE
CMDRS
DRDRE
HYDRA
HYDRO
INDRA
INDRI
MADRE
MUDRA
NIDRE
PADRE
PEDRO
SIDRA
SUDRA

••D•R
ADDER
ALDER
ANDOR
ARDOR
BADER
CEDAR
CIDER
CODER
CYDER
EIDER
ELDER
ENDER
ENDOR
FODOR
HADAR
HIDER
KADAR
LADER
NADER
NADIR
NUDER
ODDER
OLDER
ORDER
RADAR
RIDER
RUDER
RYDER
SEDER
SIDER
TUDOR
UDDER
UNDER
VADER
VIDOR
WADER
WIDER

•••DR
DENDR
QUADR
RANDR

D•S••
DASHI
DESKS
DESNA
DESTE
DISCO
DISCS
DISHY
DISKS
DISME
DISTR
DOSED
DOSER
DOSES
DUSKS
DUSKY
DUSTS
DUSTY

D••S•
DAISY
DANSE
DEISM
DEIST
DENSE
DERSU
DIDST
DITSY
DNASE
DOEST
DORSA
DORSI
DORSO
DOUSE
DOWSE
DRESS
DROSS
DRUSE
DULSE
DURST

D•••S
DACES
DADOS
DAFFS
DALES
DAMES
DAMNS
DAMPS
DANES
DANGS
DARES
DARKS
DARNS
DARTS
DATES
DAUBS
DAVIS
DAVOS
DAVYS
DAWES
DAWNS
DAZES
DEALS
DEANS
DEARS
DEBTS
DECKS
DEEDS
DEEMS
DEEPS
DEERS
DEGAS
DEILS
DEKES
DELES
DELIS
DELLS
DELOS
DELTS
DEMES
DEMOS
DENES
DENIS
DENTS
DENYS
DEPTS
DESKS
DHALS
DHOWS
DIALS
DICES
DICKS
DICTS
DIDOS
DIEMS
DIETS
DIKES
DILLS
DIMES
DINES
DINGS
DINKS
DINTS
DIRKS
DISCS
DISKS
DIVAS
DIVES
DOCKS
DODOS
DOERS
DOFFS
DOGES
DOITS
DOJOS
DOLES
DOLLS
DOLTS
DOMES
DONAS
DONGS
DOOMS
DOORS
DOPES
DORIS
DORMS
DORPS
DOSES
DOTES
DOVES
DOWNS
DOZES
DPLUS
DRABS
DRAGS
DRAMS
DRATS
DRAWS
DRAYS
DREGS
DRESS
DRIBS
DRIES
DRIPS
DROPS
DROSS
DRUBS
DRUGS
DRUMS
DUADS
DUBOS
DUCES
DUCKS
DUCTS
DUDES
DUELS
DUETS
DUFFS
DUKAS
DUKES
DULLS
DUMAS
DUMBS
DUMPS
DUNES
DUNKS
DUPES
DURNS
DUROS
DUSKS
DUSTS
DUXES
DYADS
DYERS
DYNES

•DS••
ADSUM
EDSEL

•D•S•
ADUST
IDEST
ODIST

•D••S
ADAMS
ADDIS
ADIOS
ADITS
ADZES
EDAMS
EDDAS
EDENS
EDGES
EDITS
IDEAS
IDLES
IDOLS
IDYLS
ODETS
ODORS

••DS•
DIDST
HADST
MIDST
SUDSY

••D•S
ADDIS
AEDES
AIDES
ALDUS
ANDES
AUDIS
BIDES
BLDGS
BODES
CADIS
CEDES
CEDIS
CMDRS
CODAS
CODES
DADOS
DIDOS
DODOS
DUDES
EDDAS
FADES
FADOS
FIDES
HADES
HIDES
INDUS
JADES
JUDAS
KUDOS
KUDUS
LADES
LADYS
LIDOS
LODES
MEDES
MIDAS
MIDIS
MODES
MODUS
MSDOS
NIDES
NIDUS
NODES
NODUS
NUDES
ORDOS
PUDUS
REDES
RIDES
RUDDS
SADIS
SIDES
SODAS
SUDDS
TIDES
TODOS
UPDOS
VADIS
VEDAS
WADES
WADIS
YODHS

•••DS
ACADS
ACIDS
BALDS
BANDS
BARDS
BEADS
BENDS
BINDS
BIRDS
BLVDS
BONDS
BRADS
BUNDS
BYRDS
CARDS
CLODS
COEDS
COLDS
CORDS
CURDS
DEEDS
DUADS
DYADS
EGADS
FEEDS
FENDS
FEUDS
FINDS
FOLDS
FONDS
FOODS
FORDS
FUNDS
GAUDS
GILDS
GIRDS
GLADS
GOADS
GOLDS
GONDS
GOODS
GRADS
GRIDS
HANDS
HEADS
HEEDS
HERDS
HINDS
HOLDS
HOODS
KINDS
KURDS
LANDS
LARDS
LAUDS
LEADS
LEEDS
LENDS
LOADS
LORDS
MAIDS
MEADS
MEEDS
MELDS
MENDS
MINDS
MOLDS
MOODS
NARDS
NEEDS
NERDS
OPEDS
PARDS
PENDS
PIEDS
PLODS
PONDS
POODS
PRODS
QUADS
QUIDS
QUODS
RAIDS
RANDS
READS
REEDS
RENDS
RINDS
ROADS
ROODS
RUDDS
SANDS
SARDS
SCADS
SCUDS
SEEDS
SENDS
SHADS
SHEDS
SKIDS
SLEDS
SPADS
SPUDS
STUDS
SUDDS
SURDS
TENDS
THUDS
TOADS
VELDS
VENDS
VOIDS
WANDS
WARDS
WEEDS
WELDS
WENDS
WILDS
WINDS
WOADS
WOLDS
WOODS
WORDS
YARDS
ZENDS

D•T••
DATED
DATER
DATES
DATUM
DETAT
DETER
DETOO
DETRE
DITAT

DITCH
DITKA
DITSY
DITTO
DITTY
DITZY
DOTAL
DOTED
DOTER
DOTES
DOTTO
DOTTY
DUTCH

D••T•
DANTE
DARTH
DARTS
DEBTS
DEITY
DELTA
DELTS
DENTE
DENTI
DENTS
DEPTH
DEPTS
DESTE
DEUTO
DEXTR
DHOTE
DHOTI
DICTA
DICTS
DICTU
DIETS
DINTS
DINTY
DIRTY
DISTR
DITTO
DITTY
DOETH
DOITS
DOLTS
DOTTO
DOTTY
DRATS
DUCTS
DUETO
DUETS
DUSTS
DUSTY

D•••T
DAUNT
DAVIT
DEALT
DEBIT
DEBUT
DEFAT
DEIST
DELFT
DEMIT
DEPOT
DERAT
DETAT
DFLAT
DICOT
DIDNT
DIDST
DIGIT
DITAT
DIVOT
DIXIT
DOEST
DOGIT
DONAT
DONUT
DOUBT
DRAFT
DRIFT
DROIT
DUCAT
DURST
DUVET
DWELT

•DT••
IDTAG

•D•T•
ADDTO
ADITS
ADYTA
EDITH
EDITS
ODETS

•D••T
ADAPT
ADEPT
ADINT
ADMIT
ADOPT
ADOUT
ADULT
ADUST
EDICT
EDUCT
IDEST
IDIOT
ODIST
ODONT
XDOUT

••DT•
ADDTO
HADTO
LEDTO
WIDTH

••D•T
AUDIT
CADET
DIDNT
DIDST
GODET
GODOT
HADAT
HADNT
HADST
MEDIT
MIDST
ONDIT
SADAT

•••DT
BUNDT
HEIDT
STADT
VEIDT
VELDT
WENDT

DU•••
DUADS
DUANE
DUBAI
DUBIN
DUBOS
DUCAL
DUCAT
DUCES
DUCHY
DUCKS
DUCKY
DUCTS
DUDDY
DUDES
DUELS
DUETO
DUETS
DUFAY
DUFFS
DUFFY
DUGAN
DUGIN
DUGUP
DUKAS
DUKED
DUKES
DULLS
DULLY
DULSE
DUMAS
DUMBO
DUMBS
DUMMY
DUMPS
DUMPY
DUNCE
DUNES
DUNKS
DUNNE
DUNNO
DUOMO
DUPED
DUPES
DUPLE
DUPRE
DURAN
DURER
DURNS
DUROC
DUROS
DURRA
DURST
DURUM
DUSKS
DUSKY
DUSTS
DUSTY
DUTCH
DUVET
DUXES

D•U••
DAUBS
DAUNT
DEUCE
DEUCY
DEUTO
DOUAI
DOUAY
DOUBT
DOUGH
DOURO
DOUSE
DRUBS
DRUGS
DRUID
DRUMS
DRUNK
DRUPE
DRURY
DRUSE
DRUZE

D••U•
DAMUP
DATUM
DEBUG
DEBUT
DEMUR
DIDUP
DIGUP
DONUT
DPLUS
DRYUP
DUGUP
DURUM

D•••U
DERSU
DICTU
DONAU

•DU••
ADULT
ADUST
ADUWA
EDUCE
EDUCT

•D•U•
ADDUP
ADEUX
ADOUT
ADSUM
ODEUM
ODIUM
ODOUR
XDOUT

•D••U
ADIEU

••DU•
ABDUL
ADDUP
ALDUS
ANDUP
BIDUP
DIDUP
ENDUE
ENDUP
FEDUP
INDUS
KUDUS
MODUS
NIDUS
NODUS
PADUA
PUDUS
REDUB
REDUX
SEDUM
UNDUE
VADUZ
WADUP

••D•U
KUDZU
SADHU

•••DU
FONDU
HINDU
MAIDU
PERDU

DV•••
DVIII
DVINA

D•V••
DAVAO
DAVID
DAVIE
DAVIS
DAVIT
DAVOS
DAVYS
DCVII
DEVIL
DEVON
DEVRY
DIVAN
DIVAS
DIVED
DIVER
DIVES
DIVOT
DIVVY
DLVII
DOVER
DOVES
DOVEY
DUVET
DXVII

D••V•
DCCVI
DCLVI
DCXVI
DELVE
DIVVY
DLXVI
DRAVA
DRIVE
DROVE
DXCVI
DXLVI
DXXVI

D•••V
DCCCV
DCCIV
DCCLV
DCCXV
DCLIV
DCLXV
DCXCV
DCXIV
DCXLV
DCXXV
DERIV
DLXIV
DLXXV
DXCIV
DXLIV
DXXIV
DXXXV

•DV••
ADVAL
ADVIL
CDVII
MDVII

•D•V•
CDLVI
CDXVI
MDCVI
MDLVI
MDXVI

•D••V
CDLIV
CDLXV
CDXCV
CDXIV
CDXLV
CDXXV
MDCCV
MDCIV
MDCLV
MDCXV
MDLIV
MDLXV
MDXCV
MDXIV
MDXLV
MDXXV

••DV•
MCDVI
MMDVI

••D•V
INDIV
MCDIV
MCDLV
MCDXV
MMDCV
MMDIV
MMDLV
MMDXV

•••DV
MMCDV
MMMDV

DW•••
DWARF
DWEEB
DWELL
DWELT

D•W••
DAWES
DAWNS
DEWAN
DEWAR
DEWED
DEWEY
DOWDY
DOWEL
DOWER
DOWNS
DOWNY
DOWRY
DOWSE

D••W•
DAIWA
DHOWS
DRAWL
DRAWN
DRAWS
DROWN

D•••W
DEPEW

•DW••
EDWIN

•D•W•
ADUWA

••D•W
BEDEW
ENDOW
SYDOW
WIDOW

•••DW
BANDW
CANDW

DX•••
DXCII
DXCIV
DXCIX
DXCVI
DXIII
DXLII
DXLIV
DXLIX
DXLVI
DXVII
DXXII
DXXIV
DXXIX
DXXVI
DXXXI
DXXXV

D•X••
DCXCI
DCXCV
DCXII
DCXIV
DCXIX
DCXLI
DCXLV
DCXVI
DCXXI
DCXXV
DCXXX
DEXTR
DIXIE
DIXIT
DIXON
DLXII
DLXIV
DLXIX
DLXVI
DLXXI
DLXXV
DLXXX
DUXES
DXXII
DXXIV
DXXIX
DXXVI
DXXXI
DXXXV

D••X•
DCCXC
DCCXI
DCCXL
DCCXV
DCCXX
DCLXI
DCLXV
DCLXX
DCXXI
DCXXV
DCXXX
DEOXY
DLXXI
DLXXV
DLXXX
DXXXI
DXXXV

D•••X
DCCCX
DCCIX
DCCLX
DCCXX
DCLIX
DCLXX
DCXIX
DCXXX
DLXIX
DLXXX
DXCIX
DXLIX
DXXIX

•DX••
CDXCI
CDXCV
CDXII
CDXIV
CDXIX
CDXLI
CDXLV
CDXVI
CDXXI
CDXXV
CDXXX
MDXCI
MDXCV
MDXII
MDXIV
MDXIX
MDXLI
MDXLV
MDXVI
MDXXI
MDXXV
MDXXX

•D•X•
CDLXI
CDLXV
CDLXX
CDXXI
CDXXV
CDXXX
MDCXC
MDCXI
MDCXL
MDCXV
MDCXX
MDLXI
MDLXV
MDLXX
MDXXI
MDXXV
MDXXX

•D••X
ADDAX
ADEUX
ADMIX
CDLIX
CDLXX
CDXIX
CDXXX
MDCCX
MDCIX
MDCLX
MDCXX
MDLIX
MDLXX
MDXIX
MDXXX

••DX•
MCDXC
MCDXI
MCDXL
MCDXV
MCDXX
MMDXC
MMDXI
MMDXL
MMDXV
MMDXX

••D•X
ADDAX
CODEX
FEDEX
INDEX
MCDIX
MCDLX
MCDXX
MMDCX
MMDIX
MMDLX
MMDXX
RADIX
REDOX
REDUX

•••DX
MMCDX
MMMDX

DY•••
DYADS
DYERS
DYFED
DYING
DYLAN
DYNEL
DYNES

D•Y••
DAYAK
DAYAN
DAYNE
DIYER
DOYEN
DOYLE
DOYLY
DRYAD
DRYER
DRYLY
DRYUP

D••Y•
DARYA
DARYL
DAVYS
DENYS
DRAYS

D•••Y
DADDY
DAFFY
DAILY
DAIRY
DAISY
DALEY
DALLY
DANCY
DANDY
DANNY
DARBY
DEARY
DEBBY
DECAY
DECOY
DECRY
DEIFY
DEITY
DELAY
DENNY
DEOXY
DERBY
DERRY
DEUCY
DEVRY
DEWEY

DIARY
DICEY
DICKY
DIDBY
DIGBY
DILLY
DIMLY
DINDY
DINGY
DINKY
DINTY
DIPPY
DIRTY
DISHY
DITSY
DITTY
DITZY
DIVVY
DIZZY
DOBBY
DODGY
DOGEY
DOGGY
DOILY
DOLBY
DOLLY
DONNY
DOODY
DOOZY
DOPEY
DOTTY
DOUAY
DOVEY
DOWDY
DOWNY
DOWRY
DOYLY
DRILY
DRURY
DRYLY
DUCHY
DUCKY
DUDDY
DUFAY
DUFFY
DULLY
DUMMY
DUMPY
DUSKY
DUSTY

•DY••
ADYTA
IDYLL
IDYLS

•D••Y
EDIFY
ODDLY

••DY•
LADYS
REDYE

••D•Y
ANDRY
BADDY
BADLY
BIDDY
BUDDY
CADDY
CUDDY
DADDY
DIDBY
DODGY
DUDDY
FUDDY
GIDDY
GODEY
GODLY
HEDGY
KIDDY
LEDGY
LIDDY
MADLY
MIDDY
MUDDY
NEDDY
NODDY
ODDLY
PADDY
PODGY
PUDGY
REDDY
REDLY
RIDGY
RODDY
RUDDY
SADLY
SEDGY
SODDY
SUDSY
TEDDY
TODAY
TODDY
VEDAY
VJDAY
WADDY
WEDGY

•••DY
ACIDY
BADDY
BANDY
BAWDY
BEADY
BENDY
BIDDY
BIRDY
BRADY
BRODY
BUDDY
BUNDY
CADDY
CANDY
CINDY
CUDDY
CURDY
DADDY
DANDY
DINDY
DOODY
DOWDY
DUDDY
FUDDY
FUNDY
GANDY
GAUDY
GIDDY
GOODY
GORDY
GOUDY
GOWDY
GRADY
GRODY
GURDY
HANDY
HARDY
HEADY
HOWDY
HURDY
KANDY
KIDDY
LARDY
LEADY
LIDDY
LINDY
LUNDY
MANDY
MIDDY
MINDY
MOLDY
MOODY
MUDDY
NEDDY
NEEDY
NERDY
NODDY
PADDY
RANDY
READY
REDDY
REEDY
RINDY
RODDY
ROWDY
RUDDY
SANDY
SEEDY
SHADY
SODDY
STUDY
TANDY
TARDY
TEDDY
TOADY
TODDY
WADDY
WEEDY
WENDY
WINDY
WOODY
WORDY

D•Z••
DAZED
DAZES
DIZEN
DIZZY
DOZED
DOZEN
DOZER
DOZES

D••Z•
DANZA
DIAZO
DITZY
DIZZY
DOOZY
DRUZE

•DZ••
ADZES

••DZ•
KUDZU

••D•Z
CADIZ
NODOZ
VADUZ

EA•••
EAGAN
EAGER
EAGLE
EAGRE
EAMES
EAMON
EARED
EARLE
EARLS
EARLY
EARNS
EARTH
EASED
EASEL
EASES
EASTS
EATAT
EATEN
EATER
EATIN
EATIT
EATON
EATUP
EAVED
EAVES

E•A••
EDAMS
EGADI
EGADS
ELAND
ELATE
ELATH
ELAZI
EMAIL
ENACT
ENATE
EPACT
ERASE
ERATO
ETAGE
ETAPE
ETATS
EVADE
EVANS
EXACT
EXALT
EXAMS

E••A•
EAGAN
EATAT
EBOAT
ECLAT
EDDAS
EDGAR
EFLAT
EGGAR
EILAT
ELGAR
ELIAS
ELMAN
ELWAY
EMBAR
EMBAY
ENIAC
ENLAI
EPHAH
EPHAS
EQUAL
ESBAT
ESSAY
ESTAB
ESTAS
ETHAN
ETNAS
EVIAN
EYRAS

E•••A
EDEMA
EDINA
ELENA
ELIZA
ENNEA
ENOLA
ENTIA
ERICA
ERIKA
ERISA
ETYMA
EVITA
EVORA
EXTRA

•EA••
AEAEA
BEACH
BEADS
BEADY
BEAKS
BEALL
BEALS
BEAMS
BEAMY
BEANO
BEANS
BEANY
BEARD
BEARS
BEAST
BEATS
BEAUS
BEAUT
BEAUX
CEASE
DEALS
DEALT
DEANE
DEANS
DEARS
DEARY
FEARS
FEAST
FEATS
GEARS
GEARY
HEADS
HEADY
HEALS
HEALY
HEAPS
HEARD
HEARN
HEARS
HEART
HEATH
HEATS
HEAVE
HEAVY
JEANE
JEANS
KEACH
KEANE
KEANU
KEATS
LEACH
LEADS
LEADY
LEAFS
LEAFY
LEAHY
LEAKS
LEAKY
LEANS
LEANT
LEAPS
LEAPT
LEARN
LEARS
LEARY
LEASE
LEASH
LEAST
LEAVE
MEADE
MEADS
MEALS
MEALY
MEANS
MEANT
MEANY
MEARA
MEATS
MEATY
NEALE
NEAPS
NEARS
NEATH
NEATO
NEATS
PEABO
PEACE
PEACH
PEAKS
PEALE
PEALS
PEARL
PEARS
PEARY
PEASE
PEATS
PEATY
PEAVY
REACH
REACT
READE
READS
READY
REAIM
REAIR
REALM
REALS
REAMS
REAPS
REARM
REARS
REATA
SEALE
SEALS
SEALY
SEAMS
SEAMY
SEARS
SEATO
SEATS
TEACH
TEAKS
TEALS
TEAMS
TEARS
TEARY
TEASE
VEALY
WEALS
WEANS
WEARS
WEARY
WEAVE
YEANS
YEARN
YEARS
YEAST
YEATS
ZEALS

•E•A•
AETAT
BEGAN
BEGAT
BEHAN
BELAY
BEMAS
BETAS
CEDAR
CERAM
CERAT
CESAR
DEBAR
DECAF
DECAL
DECAY
DEFAT
DEGAS
DELAY
DERAT
DETAT
DEWAN
DEWAR
FERAL
FETAL
FETAS
GERAH
GETAS
GETAT
HEJAZ
HEMAN
HENAN
HERAT
HEXAD
KEBAB
KEMAL
KENAI
KERAT
LEFAY
LEGAL
LEHAR
LEMAT
LEMAY
LETAT
LEVAR
LEXAN
MEDAL
MEGAN
MELAN
MESAS
METAL
NEMAN
NEMAT
NEPAL
PECAN
PEDAL
PENAL
PERAN
PETAL
REBAG
REBAR
RECAP
REDAN
REGAL
REGAN
REHAB
REHAN
RELAX
RELAY
REMAN
REMAP
RENAL
RENAN
REPAD
REPAY
RERAN
RESAW
RETAG
RETAP
RETAR
RETAX
REWAX
SEDAN
SEGAL
SEGAR
SELAH
SENAT
SEPAL
SERAC
SERAI
SERAL
SETAE
SETAT
TENAM
TEPAL
TEXAN
TEXAS
VEDAS
VEDAY
VEGAN
VEGAS
VELAR
VENAE
VENAL
WEKAS
ZETAS

•E••A
AEAEA
AECIA
AETNA
BELLA
BELVA
BEREA
BERRA
BETTA
CEIBA
CELIA
CELLA
CERIA
CESTA
CEUTA
DEBRA
DECCA
DELLA
DELTA
DERMA
DESNA
FELLA
FERIA
FESTA
GEENA
GEMMA
GENOA
GENUA
HEDDA
HEKLA
HELGA
HENNA
HEPTA
KENYA
LEEZA
LEHUA
LEICA
LEILA
LEMMA
LENYA
LEONA
LEORA
LEPTA
MEARA
MECCA
MEDEA
MEDIA
MEHTA
MELBA
MENSA
MESTA
NEMEA
PELLA
PEMBA
PENNA
PENTA
PENZA
PEPLA
PETRA
REATA
REGIA
REINA
RENTA
RETIA
SEEYA
SEHNA
SELMA
SELVA
SENNA
SEPIA
SEPTA
SERRA
SERTA
TEENA
TERRA
TERZA
TESLA
TESTA
TETRA
VEDDA
VENDA
VERBA
VERSA
VESTA
XENIA
YENTA
YERBA
ZEBRA
ZELDA
ZENDA

••EA•
ABEAM
AHEAD
ANEAR
APEAK
AREAL
AREAR
AREAS
ATEAM
BLEAK
BLEAR
BLEAT
BREAD
BREAK
BREAM
CHEAP
CHEAT
CLEAN
CLEAR
CLEAT
CREAK
CREAM
DREAD
DREAM
DREAR
FLEAS
FREAK
GLEAM
GLEAN
GREAT
HBEAM
IBEAM
ICEAX
IDEAL
IDEAS

KNEAD
OBEAH
OCEAN
OLEAN
ONEAL
ONEAM
OREAD
PAEAN
PLEAD
PLEAS
PLEAT
RHEAS
SHEAF
SHEAN
SHEAR
SKEAN
SKEAT
SMEAR
SNEAD
SNEAK
SPEAK
SPEAR
STEAD
STEAK
STEAL
STEAM
SWEAR
SWEAT
TREAD
TREAT
TWEAK
WHEAL
WHEAT
WREAK
ZOEAE
ZOEAL
ZOEAS

••E•A
ADELA
AGENA
AKELA
ALETA
AMEBA
ARECA
ARENA
AVENA
BREDA
BUENA
CHEKA
CHELA
CIERA
EDEMA
ELENA
FREDA
FRENA
FREYA
GEENA
GRETA
HAEMA
HIERA
HYENA
LEEZA
OMEGA
ONEGA
OPERA
OVETA
PIETA
PLENA
SCENA
SEEYA
SHEBA
SHEMA
SIENA
SNEVA
STELA
TEENA
THECA
THEDA
THEMA
THERA
THETA

•••EA
AEAEA
APNEA
ATSEA
BEREA
BOHEA
CANEA
COREA
ENNEA
FOVEA
GALEA
HOSEA
JUDEA
KOREA
LULEA
MEDEA
NEMEA
OCREA
OSHEA
PALEA
PILEA
SIDEA
TYPEA

EB•••
EBBED
EBERT
EBOAT
EBOLI
EBOND
EBONS
EBONY
EBSEN

E•B••
EBBED
ELBOW
EMBAR
EMBAY
EMBED
EMBER
ERBIL
ESBAT
EUBIE

E•••B
ESTAB
EXURB

•EB••
BEBOP
DEBAR
DEBBY
DEBIT
DEBRA
DEBTS
DEBUG
DEBUT
KEBAB
KEBOB
REBAG
REBAR
REBBE
REBEC
REBEL
REBID
REBUS
REBUT
SEBUM
WEBBY
WEBER
XEBEC
ZEBRA
ZEBUS

•E•B•
BEEBE
CEIBA
DEBBY
DERBY
GETBY
HERBS
HERBY
KERBS
LETBE
MELBA
PEABO
PEMBA
REBBE
SERBS
SETBY
VERBA
VERBS
WEBBY
WELBY
YERBA

•E••B
CELEB
DEMOB
DENEB
KEBAB
KEBOB
REDUB
REHAB

••EB•
ABEBE
AMEBA
BEEBE
BLEBS
GLEBE
GREBE
KREBS
LIEBY
PLEBE
PLEBS
SHEBA
THEBE

••E•B
ACERB
DWEEB

•••EB
CALEB
CELEB
CUBEB
DENEB
DWEEB
HOREB
SIDEB
STIEB
TYPEB

EC•••
ECHIN
ECLAT
ECOLE
ECOLI
ECRUS

E•C••
ELCID
EMCEE
ENCYC
EPCOT
EXCEL

E••C•
EDICT
EDUCE
EDUCT
EJECT
ELECT
ENACT
ENOCH
EPACT
EPICS
EPOCH
ERECT
ERICA
ERICH
ERUCT
EVICT
EXACT
EXECS

E•••C
EDDIC
ENCYC
ENIAC
EPISC
ETHIC

•EC••
AECIA
BECHE
BECKS
BECKY
CECHY
CECIL
DECAF
DECAL
DECAY
DECCA
DECEM
DECKS
DECOR
DECOY
DECRY
GECKO
HECHE
HECHT
HECKS
HECTO
LECKY
MECCA
MECUM
NECKS
PECAN
PECKS
PECKY
PECOS
RECAP
RECCE
RECIP
RECON
RECTI
RECTO
RECUR
SECCO
SECTS
TECHS
TECHY
YECCH

•E•C•
BEACH
BEECH
BELCH
BENCH
CENCI
DECCA
DEICE
DELCO
DEUCE
DEUCY
FENCE
FETCH
HENCE
HENCH
KEACH
KENCH
KETCH
LEACH
LEECH
LEICA
MECCA
MERCE
MERCI
MERCK
MERCY
PEACE
PEACH
PENCE
PERCE
PERCH
PERCY
PESCI
REACH
REACT
RECCE
REICH
SECCO
TEACH
TENCH
VETCH
WELCH
WENCH
YECCH

•E••C
GENIC
HELIC
MEDIC
MEDOC
MELIC
MESIC
REBEC
RELIC
SERAC
TELIC
VEDIC
XEBEC
XERIC
ZENIC

••EC•
ALECK
ARECA
BEECH
BRECK
CHECK
CRECY
CZECH
EJECT
ELECT
ERECT
EXECS
FLECK
GRECO
LEECH
NIECE
PIECE
SPECD
SPECK
SPECS
THECA
VNECK
WRECK

••E•C
CRESC
OLEIC

•••EC
AZTEC
COSEC
OLMEC
REBEC
XEBEC

ED•••
EDAMS
EDDAS
EDDIC
EDDIE
EDEMA
EDENS
EDGAR
EDGED
EDGER
EDGES
EDICT
EDIFY
EDILE
EDINA
EDITH
EDITS
EDSEL
EDUCE
EDUCT
EDWIN

E•D••
EDDAS
EDDIC
EDDIE
EIDER
ELDER
EMDEN
ENDED
ENDER
ENDON
ENDOR
ENDOW
ENDUE
ENDUP
EYDIE

E••D•
EGADI
EGADS
EJIDO
ELIDE
ELUDE
EPODE
ERODE
ETUDE
EVADE
EXUDE

E•••D
EARED
EASED
EAVED
EBBED
EBOND
EDGED
EELED
EGGED
ELAND
ELCID
EMBED
EMEND
ENDED
EPHOD
ERRED

•ED••
AEDES
BEDEW
BEDIM
CEDAR
CEDED
CEDES
CEDIS
FEDEX
FEDON
FEDUP
HEDDA
HEDGE
HEDGY
HEDIN
KEDGE
LEDGE
LEDGY
LEDIN
LEDON
LEDTO
MEDAL
MEDEA
MEDES
MEDIA
MEDIC
MEDIT
MEDOC
NEDDY
PEDAL
PEDRO
REDAN
REDDY
REDED
REDES
REDID
REDLY
REDON
REDOX
REDUB
REDUX
REDYE
SEDAN
SEDER
SEDGE
SEDGY
SEDUM
TEDDY
VEDAS
VEDAY
VEDDA
VEDIC
WEDEL
WEDGE
WEDGY
XEDIN

•E•D•
BEADS
BEADY
BENDS
BENDY
DEEDS
DENDR
FEEDS
FENDS
FERDE
FEUDS
GEODE
HEADS
HEADY
HEDDA
HEEDS
HEIDI
HEIDT
HERDS
JEUDI
KENDO
LEADS
LEADY
LEEDS
LENDL
LENDS
MEADE
MEADS
MEEDS
MELDS
MENDS
NEDDY
NEEDS
NEEDY
NERDS
NERDY
PENDS
PERDU
READE
READS
READY
REDDY
REEDS
REEDY
RENDS
SEEDS
SEEDY
SENDS
TEDDY
TEIDE
TENDS
VEDDA
VEIDT
VELDS
VELDT
VENDA
VENDS
VERDE
VERDI
WEEDS
WEEDY
WELDS
WENDS
WENDT
WENDY
ZELDA
ZENDA
ZENDO
ZENDS

•E••D
BEARD
CEDED
CERED
DEKED
DELED
DEWED
EELED
FELID
FETED
FETID
GELID
GEOID
HEARD
HEROD
HEWED
HEXAD
HEXED
KEYED
METED
MEWED
NEFUD
REBID
REDED
REDID
REPAD
RESOD
REWED
SEWED
TEPID
VEXED
WEIRD

••ED•
BREDA
COEDS
CREDO
DEEDS
DREDD
FEEDS
FREDA
GLEDE
HEEDS
LEEDS
MEEDS
NEEDS
NEEDY
OPEDS
PIEDS
REEDS
REEDY
SEEDS
SEEDY
SHEDS
SLEDS
SUEDE
SWEDE
THEDA
WEEDS
WEEDY

••E•D
ABEND
AHEAD
AMEND
BLEED
BLEND
BREAD
BREED
CREED
DREAD
DREDD
EMEND
FIELD
FIEND
FJELD
FREED
FREUD
GREED
KNEAD
KNEED
NOEND
ONEND
OREAD
PLEAD
PSEUD
SCEND
SHEED
SNEAD
SNEED
SNERD
SPECD
SPEED
SPEND
STEAD
STEED
THEYD
TREAD
TREED
TREND
TWEED
UPEND

WIELD
YIELD

•••ED

AAHED
ACHED
ACRED
ACTED
ADDED
AHMED
AIDED
AILED
AIMED
AIRED
AMPED
ANTED
APTED
ARCED
ARMED
ASKED
AWNED
BAAED
BAKED
BALED
BARED
BASED
BATED
BAYED
BIDED
BIKED
BIPED
BLEED
BLUED
BODED
BONED
BOOED
BORED
BOWED
BOXED
BREED
BUSED
CAGED
CAKED
CANED
CAPED
CARED
CASED
CAVED
CAWED
CEDED
CERED
CITED
CLUED
CODED
COKED
COOED
COPED
CORED
COWED
COXED
CREED
CRIED
CUBED
CURED
DARED
DATED
DAZED
DEKED
DELED
DEWED
DICED
DIKED
DIMED
DINED
DIVED
DOLED
DOMED
DOPED
DOSED
DOTED
DOZED
DRIED
DUKED
DUPED
DYFED
EARED
EASED
EAVED
EBBED
EDGED
EELED
EGGED
EMBED
ENDED
ERRED
FACED
FADED
FAKED
FAMED
FARED
FATED
FAXED
FAZED
FETED
FIFED
FILED
FINED
FIRED
FIXED
FLIED
FOXED
FREED
FRIED
FUMED
FUSED
FUZED
GAGED
GAMED
GAPED
GATED
GAZED
GIBED
GLUED
GORED
GREED
GUYED
GYBED
GYVED
HALED
HARED
HATED
HAWED
HAYED
HAZED
HEWED
HEXED
HIKED
HIRED
HIVED
HOKED
HOLED
HOMED
HONED
HOPED
HOSED
HYPED
IDLED
IMPED
INBED
INKED
IRKED
IVIED
JADED
JAPED
JAWED
JIBED
JIVED
JOKED
JUKED
KEYED
KITED
KNEED
LACED
LADED
LAMED
LASED
LAVED
LAZED
LIKED
LIMED
LINED
LIVED
LOBED
LOPED
LOVED
LOWED
LUBED
LURED
MACED
MANED
MATED
MAXED
METED
MEWED
MIKED
MIMED
MINED
MIRED
MIXED
MOOED
MOPED
MOVED
MOWED
MUSED
MUTED
NAKED
NAMED
NIXED
NOSED
NOTED
NUKED
OARED
OGLED
OILED
OOHED
OOZED
OPTED
OUTED
OWNED
PACED
PAGED
PALED
PANED
PARED
PATED
PAVED
PAWED
PAYED
PIKED
PILED
PINED
PIPED
PLIED
POKED
POLED
PORED
POSED
PRIED
PULED
RACED
RAGED
RAKED
RASED
RATED
RAVED
RAYED
RAZED
REDED
REWED
RICED
RILED
RIMED
RIVED
ROBED
ROPED
ROVED
ROWED
RULED
SATED
SAVED
SAWED
SCHED
SEWED
SHEED
SHIED
SHOED
SHRED
SIDED
SIRED
SITED
SIXED
SIZED
SKIED
SLUED
SNEED
SOLED
SOWED
SPEED
SPIED
STEED
TAMED
TAPED
TAXED
TIDED
TILED
TIMED
TINED
TIRED
TONED
TOPED
TOTED
TOWED
TOYED
TREED
TRIED
TRUED
TUBED
TUNED
TWEED
TYPED
UMPED
UNFED
UNLED
UNWED
UPPED
URGED
USHED
USTED
VEXED
VINED
VOTED
VOWED
WADED
WAGED
WAKED
WALED
WANED
WAVED
WAXED
WILED
WINED
WIPED
WIRED
WIVED
WOOED
WOWED
YAWED
YOKED
ZONED

EE•••

EELED
EELER
EERIE

E•E••

EBERT
EDEMA
EDENS
EGEST
EIEIO
EJECT
ELECT
ELEGY
ELEMI
ELENA
ELENI
ELEVE
EMEER
EMEND
EMERY
ENEMY
ENERO
EPEES
ERECT
EVENS
EVENT
EVERS
EVERT
EVERY
EWELL
EWERS
EXECS
EXERT
EYERS

E••E•

EAGER
EAMES
EARED
EASED
EASEL
EASES
EATEN
EATER
EAVED
EAVES
EBBED
EBSEN
EDGED
EDGER
EDGES
EDSEL
EELED
EELER
EFREM
EGGED
EGRET
EIDER
EIGEN
ELDER
ELIEL
ELLEN
ELLER
ELLES
ELMER
ELVER
ELVES
ELWES
EMBED
EMBER
EMCEE
EMDEN
EMEER
EMMER
EMMET
ENDED
ENDER
ENGEL
ENNEA
ENTER
EPEES
ERIES
ERNES
ERRED
ESKER
ESNES
ESSEN
ESSES
ESSEX
ESTEE
ESTER
ESTES
ETHEL
ETHER
ETSEQ
ETZEL
EULER
EXCEL
EXPEL
EYRES

E•••E

EAGLE
EAGRE
EARLE
ECOLE
EDDIE
EDILE
EDUCE
EERIE
EFFIE
ELATE
ELEVE
ELIDE
ELISE
ELITE
ELLIE
ELOPE
ELSIE
ELUDE
ELUTE
ELYSE
EMCEE
EMILE
EMOTE
ENATE
ENDUE
ENSUE
ENTRE
ENURE
EPODE
ERASE
ERNIE
ERODE
EROSE
ESQUE
ESTEE
ETAGE
ETAPE
ETUDE
EUBIE
EVADE
EVOKE
EXILE
EXUDE
EYDIE
EYRIE

•EE••

BEEBE
BEECH
BEEFS
BEEFY
BEENE
BEEPS
BEERS
BEERY
BEETS
DEEDS
DEEMS
DEEPS
DEERE
DEERS
FEEDS
FEELS
FEELY
FEETS
GEEKS
GEEKY
GEENA
GEESE
HEEDS
HEELS
JEEPS
JEERS
KEELS
KEENE
KEENS
KEEPS
KEETS
LEECH
LEEDS
LEEKS
LEERS
LEERY
LEETS
LEEZA
MEEDS
MEESE
MEETS
NEEDS
NEEDY
PEEKS
PEELE
PEELS
PEENS
PEEPS
PEERS
PEETE
PEEVE
REEDS
REEDY
REEFS
REEKS
REEKY
REELS
REESE
REEVE
SEEDS
SEEDY
SEEIN
SEEKS
SEELS
SEELY
SEEMS
SEEPS
SEEPY
SEERS
SEETO
SEEYA
TEEMS
TEENA
TEENS
TEENY
TEETH
TEEUP
VEEPS
VEERS
VEERY
WEEDS
WEEDY
WEEKS
WEEMS
WEENY
WEEPS
WEEPY
WEEST

•E•E•

AEAEA
AEDES
BEDEW
BEGET
BELEM
BENES
BENET
BEREA
BERET
BESET
BETEL
BEVEL
BEZEL
CEDED
CEDES
CELEB
CEPES
CERED
CERES
DECEM
DEFER
DEKED
DEKES
DELED
DELES
DEMES
DENEB
DENES
DEPEW
DEREK
DETER
DEWED
DEWEY
EELED
EELER
FEDEX
FETED
FETES
FEVER
FEWER
FEYER
GELEE
GENES
GENET
HEFEI
HEGEL
HELEN
HEMEN
HEMET
HERES
HEWED
HEWER
HEXED
HEXER
HEXES
JEREZ
JETER
JETES
JEWEL
KESEY
KEVEL
KEYED
KEYES
LEGER
LEVEE
LEVEL
LEVER
LEWES
MEDEA
MEDES
MELEE
MEMEL
MENES
MERES
METED
METER
METES
MEWED
MEYER
NEGEV
NEMEA
NENES
NEVER
NEVES
NEWEL
NEWER
PEKES
PELEE
PELEG
PERES
PEREZ
PETER
PETES
PEWEE
REBEC
REBEL
REDED
REDES
REFER
REHEM
REKEY
RELEE
RELET
REMET
REMEX
RENEE
RENEW
REPEG
REPEL
RESEE
RESET
RESEW
REUEL
REVEL
REVET
REWED
REXES
REYES
SEDER
SEGER
SELES
SERES
SEVEN
SEVER
SEWED
SEWER
SEXES
TEHEE
TELEO
TELES
TELEX
TENET
TEPEE

TETES
TEVET
VELEZ
VENEZ
VESEY
VEXED
VEXER
VEXES
WEBER
WEDEL
WESER
XEBEC
YEMEN
YESES

•E••E
AERIE
BECHE
BEEBE
BEENE
BEIGE
BELIE
BELLE
BENUE
BERLE
BERME
BERNE
BETTE
BEYLE
CEASE
CELIE
CENSE
DEANE
DEERE
DEFOE
DEICE
DELVE
DEMME
DENSE
DENTE
DESTE
DETRE
DEUCE
EERIE
FEMME
FENCE
FERDE
GEESE
GELEE
GENIE
GENRE
GEODE
GESTE
GETME
HEAVE
HECHE
HEDGE
HEINE
HELVE
HENCE
HENGE
HENIE
HERNE
HERVE
HESSE
HEURE
HEUTE
HEYSE
JEANE
JESSE
JEUNE
KEANE
KEDGE
KEENE
LEASE
LEAVE
LEDGE
LEMME
LEONE
LETBE
LETHE
LEVEE
LEYTE
MEADE
MEESE
MELEE
MERCE
MERGE
MERLE
MEROE
MESNE
METRE
MEUSE
NEALE
NEIGE
NERVE
NEUME
PEACE
PEALE
PEASE
PEELE
PEETE
PEEVE
PEKOE
PELEE
PELLE
PENCE
PENNE
PENTE
PERCE
PERLE
PERSE
PEWEE
READE
REBBE
RECCE
REDYE
REESE
REEVE
RELEE
RENEE
RESEE
RETIE
REUNE
REUSE
REVUE
SEALE
SEDGE
SEGUE
SEINE
SEIZE
SENSE
SENTE
SERGE
SERVE
SETAE
SETTE
SEULE
TEASE
TEHEE
TEIDE
TEMPE
TENSE
TEPEE
TERNE
TERRE
TERSE
TEVYE
VENAE
VENUE
VERDE
VERGE
VERNE
VERRE
VERSE
VERTE
VERVE
WEAVE
WEDGE
YENTE

••EE•
ADEEM
AKEEM
AKEES
AMEER
BLEED
BLEEP
BREED
BREEN
CHEEK
CHEEP
CHEER
CLEEK
CREED
CREEK
CREEL
CREEP
CREES
DWEEB
EMEER
EPEES
FLEER
FLEES
FLEET
FREED
FREER
FREES
GHEES
GLEES
GREED
GREEK
GREEN
GREER
GREES
GREET
KNEED
KNEEL
KNEES
OGEES
PREEN
QUEEG
QUEEN
QUEER
SHEED
SHEEN
SHEEP
SHEER
SHEET
SKEET
SLEEK
SLEEP
SLEET
SNEED
SNEER
SPEED
STEED
STEEL
STEEN
STEEP
STEER
SWEEP
SWEET
TREED
TREEN
TREES
TWEED
TWEEN
TWEER
TWEET
WHEEL
WHEEN

••E•E
ABEBE
ABELE
ADELE
AKENE
ALENE
ALEVE
ANELE
ARETE
BEEBE
BEENE
BREVE
CHERE
CREME
CREPE
CRETE
DEERE
DIENE
ELEVE
FRERE
GEESE
GLEBE
GLEDE
GREBE
GRETE
ILENE
IRENE
ISERE
KEENE
LIEGE
LOEWE
MEESE
MNEME
MYEYE
NIECE
OBESE
OPERE
OXEYE
PEELE
PEETE
PEEVE
PIECE
PLEBE
POEME
POETE
QUEUE
REESE
REEVE
SCENE
SHERE
SIEGE
SIETE
SIEVE
SKETE
SPEKE
STELE
STERE
STEVE
SUEDE
SUEME
SWEDE
THEBE
THEME
THERE
THESE
TWERE
WHERE
ZOEAE

•••EE
AGREE
AIMEE
ALBEE
ALLEE
ANNEE
ARMEE
COOEE
CUVEE
DONEE
EMCEE
ESTEE
FUSEE
FUZEE
GELEE
GOSEE
LEVEE
LYCEE
MAGEE
MCGEE
MELEE
NGWEE
PAREE
PAYEE
PELEE
PEWEE
PUREE
RAMEE
RANEE
RAPEE
RAREE
RELEE
RENEE
RESEE
RONEE
RUPEE
SCREE
SPREE
SYCEE
TEHEE
TEPEE
THREE
TUTEE
TYPEE

EF•••
EFFIE
EFIKS
EFLAT
EFREM

E•F••
EFFIE
ELFIN
ENFIN

E••F•
EDIFY

•EF••
BEFIT
BEFOG
DEFAT
DEFER
DEFOE
DEFOG
HEFEI
HEFTS
HEFTY
KEFIR
LEFAY
LEFTS
LEFTY
NEFUD
REFER
REFIT
REFRY
WEFTS

•E•F•
BEEFS
BEEFY
DEIFY
DELFT
FEOFF
LEAFS
LEAFY
REEFS
REIFY
SERFS

•E••F
DECAF
FEOFF
SERIF

••EF•
ALEFS
BEEFS
BEEFY
CHEFS
CLEFS
CLEFT
FIEFS
REEFS
THEFT

••E•F
BOEUF
SHEAF
SHELF

•••EF
BRIEF
CCLEF
CHIEF
FCLEF
GANEF
GCLEF
GRIEF
INDEF
JOSEF
SHAEF
THIEF

EG•••
EGADI
EGADS
EGEST
EGGAR
EGGED
EGGON
EGRET
EGYPT

E•G••
EAGAN
EAGER
EAGLE
EAGRE
EDGAR
EDGED
EDGER
EDGES
EGGAR
EGGED
EGGON
EIGEN
EIGHT
ELGAR
ELGIN
ENGEL
ENGRS
ERGOT

E••G•
ELEGY
ENUGU
ETAGE

E•••G
EKING
EWING

•EG••
AEGIR
AEGIS
BEGAN
BEGAT
BEGET
BEGIN
BEGOT
BEGUM
BEGUN
DEGAS
HEGEL
LEGAL
LEGER
LEGGS
LEGGY
LEGIS
LEGIT
LEGOS
LEGUP
MEGAN
NEGEV
NEGRI
NEGUS
PEGGY
REGAL
REGAN
REGIA
REGIS
REGNI
REGUM
SEGAL
SEGAR
SEGER
SEGNI
SEGNO
SEGOS
SEGUE
VEGAN
VEGAS
YEGGS

•E•G•
BEIGE
BERGH
BERGS
DEIGN
FEIGN
GETGO
HEDGE
HEDGY
HEIGH
HELGA
HENGE
KEDGE
KEOGH
LEDGE
LEDGY
LEGGS
LEGGY
LEIGH
LETGO
MERGE
NEIGE
NEIGH
PEGGY
PENGO
REIGN
SEDGE
SEDGY
SENGI
SERGE
VERGE
WEDGE
WEDGY
WEIGH
YEGGS

•E••G
BEFOG
BEING
DEBUG
DEFOG
GEORG
PELEG
REBAG
RELIG
REPEG
RERIG
RETAG
SELIG
ZELIG

••EG•
DIEGO
DREGS
ELEGY
FUEGO
GREGG
LIEGE
LUEGO
OMEGA
ONEGA
PREGO
SIEGE
SKEGS
TAEGU
TIEGS

••E•G
GREGG
QUEEG
ZWEIG

•••EG
GRIEG
IRREG
KLIEG
PELEG
QUEEG
REPEG
UNPEG

E•H••
ECHIN
EPHAH
EPHAS
EPHOD
EPHOR
ETHAN
ETHEL
ETHER
ETHIC
ETHNO
ETHOS
ETHYL

E••H•
EIGHT
ELIHU

E•••H
EARTH
EDITH
ELATH
ENOCH
EPHAH
EPOCH
ERICH

•EH••
BEHAN
LEHAR
LEHUA
MEHTA
NEHIS
NEHRU
REHAB
REHAN
REHEM
SEHNA
TEHEE

•E•H•
BECHE
BETHS
CECHY
DELHI
HECHE
HECHT
HETHS
LEAHY
LETHE
MESHY
TECHS
TECHY
TETHS

•E••H
BEACH
BEECH
BELCH
BENCH
BERGH
BERTH
DEPTH
FETCH
GERAH
HEATH
HEIGH
HENCH
KEACH
KEITH
KENCH
KEOGH
KETCH
LEACH
LEASH
LEECH
LEIGH
LEITH
NEATH
NEIGH
PEACH
PERCH
PERTH
REACH
REICH
SELAH
TEACH
TEETH
TENCH
TENTH
VETCH
WEIGH
WELCH
WELSH
WENCH
YECCH

••EH•
BOEHM
FOEHN
RUEHL

••E•H
ALEPH
BEECH
CHETH
CZECH
DOETH
FLESH
FRESH
LEECH
OBEAH
TEETH
WYETH

EI•••
EIDER
EIEIO
EIGEN
EIGHT
EILAT

E•I••
EDICT
EDIFY
EDILE
EDINA
EDITH
EDITS
EFIKS
EJIDO
EKING
ELIAS
ELIDE
ELIEL
ELIHU
ELION
ELIOT
ELISE
ELITE
ELIZA
EMILE
EMILY
EMIRS
EMITS
ENIAC
EPICS
EPISC
ERICA
ERICH
ERIES
ERIKA
ERISA
EVIAN
EVICT
EVILS
EVITA
EWING
EXILE
EXIST
EXITS

E••I•
EATIN
EATIT
ECHIN
EDDIC
EDDIE
EDWIN
EERIE
EFFIE
EIEIO
ELCID
ELFIN
ELGIN
ELLIE
ELLIS
ELSIE
ELVIN
ELVIS
EMAIL
ENFIN
ENNIO
ENNIS
ENTIA
EOSIN
EQUIP
EQUIV
ERBIL
ERNIE
ERVIL
ERVIN
ERWIN
ETHIC
ETUIS
ETVIR
EUBIE
EYDIE
EYRIE
EYRIR

E•••I
EBOLI
ECOLI
EGADI
ELAZI
ELEMI
ELENI
ENLAI
ENNUI
ENVOI

•EI••
AEIOU
BEIGE
BEING
BEINS
CEIBA
CEILS
DEICE
DEIFY
DEIGN
DEILS
DEION
DEISM
DEIST
DEITY
FEIGN
FEINT
FEIST
HEIDI
HEIDT
HEIGH
HEINE
HEINZ
HEIRS
HEISS
HEIST
KEITH
LEICA
LEIGH
LEILA
LEITH
MEIJI
MEINY
NEIGE
NEIGH
NEILL
REICH
REIFY
REIGN
REIMS
REINA
REINK
REINS
SEIJI
SEIKO
SEINE
SEISM
SEIZE
TEIDE
VEIDT
VEILS
VEINS
VEINY
WEIGH
WEILL
WEIRD
WEIRS
WEISS
ZEINS
ZEISS
ZEIST

•E•I•
AECIA
AEGIR
AEGIS
AERIE
AESIR
BEDIM
BEFIT
BEGIN
BELIE
BENIN
BEVIN
CECIL
CEDIS
CELIA
CELIE
CERIA
DEBIT
DELIS
DEMIT
DENIM
DENIS
DERIV
DEVIL
EERIE
FELID
FELIS
FELIX
FELIZ
FERIA
FETID
GELID
GENIC
GENIE
GENII
GEOID
GETIN
GETIT
HEDIN
HELIC
HELIO
HELIX
HEMIN
HENIE
KEFIR
KEPIS
KEVIN
KEYIN
LEDIN
LEGIS
LEGIT
LENIN
LENIS
LETIN
LEVIN
LEVIS
LEWIS
LEXIS
MEDIA
MEDIC
MEDIT
MELIC
MERIT
MESIC
METIS
NEHIS
NEVIL
NEVIN
NEVIS
NEXIS
PEKIN
PEPIN
PERIL
PERIS
PETIT
PEWIT
REAIM
REAIR
REBID
RECIP
REDID
REFIT
REGIA
REGIS
RELIC
RELIG
RELIT
REMIT
REMIX
RENIN
REOIL
REPIN
RERIG
RESIN
RETIA
RETIE
REWIN
SEEIN
SELIG
SEMIS
SEPIA
SERIF
SERIN
SETIN
TELIC
TEPID
VEDIC
VENIN
XEDIN
XENIA
XERIC
YETIS
ZELIG
ZENIC

•E••I
BELLI
BENJI
BENXI
CELLI
CENCI
CENTI
CESTI
DELHI
DENTI
FERMI
FERRI
GENII
HEFEI
HEIDI
HENRI
JEUDI
KENAI
KERRI
LEONI
LEROI
MEIJI
MERCI
NEGRI
PENNI
PEPSI
PESCI
PETRI
PETTI
RECTI
REGNI
SEGNI
SEIJI
SENGI
SERAI
TEMPI
TERRI
VERDI
VERMI

••EI•
ATEIN
CUEIN
EIEIO
ICEIN
KLEIN
LIEIN
OLEIC
OLEIN
ONEIL
PLEIO
SEEIN
SHEIK
SKEIN
STEIN
THEIR
TIEIN
TOEIN
ZWEIG

••E•I
CHERI
ELEMI
ELENI
FLEXI
ICENI
OBELI
SIEPI
TREVI
UMEKI

•••EI
AUREI
FIDEI
HEFEI
IMPEI
ISSEI
KIBEI
NISEI
PILEI
TAKEI
TOMEI

EJ•••
EJECT
EJIDO

E•J••
ENJOY

•EJ••
HEJAZ

•E•J•
BENJI
MEIJI
SEIJI

••EJ•
CHEJU
VIEJO

EK•••
EKING

E•K••
ESKER

E••K•
EFIKS
ENSKY
ERIKA
EVOKE
EWOKS

•EK••
DEKED
DEKES
DEKKO
HEKLA
PEKES
PEKIN
PEKOE
REKEY
WEKAS

•E•K•
BEAKS
BECKS
BECKY
DECKS
DEKKO
DESKS
GECKO
GEEKS
GEEKY
HECKS
HERKY
JERKS
JERKY
LEAKS
LEAKY
LECKY
LEEKS
NECKS
PEAKS
PECKS
PECKY
PEEKS
PERKS
PERKY
PESKY
REEKS
REEKY
SEEKS
SEIKO
TEAKS
WEEKS
YERKS

•E••K
DEREK
MERCK
REINK

••EK•
CHEKA
GEEKS
GEEKY
LEEKS
PEEKS
REEKS
REEKY
SEEKS
SPEKE
TREKS
UMEKI
WEEKS

••E•K
ALECK
APEAK
BLEAK
BREAK
BRECK
CHECK
CHEEK
CLEEK
CLERK
CREAK
CREEK
FLECK
FREAK
GREEK
SHEIK
SLEEK
SNEAK
SPEAK
SPECK
STEAK
TWEAK
VNECK
WHELK
WREAK
WRECK

•••EK
CAPEK
CHEEK
CLEEK
CREEK
DEREK
GREEK
HACEK
HAYEK
KOPEK
PATEK
SLEEK
UZBEK

EL•••
ELAND
ELATE
ELATH
ELAZI
ELBOW
ELCID
ELDER
ELECT
ELEGY
ELEMI
ELENA
ELENI
ELEVE
ELFIN
ELGAR
ELGIN
ELIAS
ELIDE
ELIEL
ELIHU
ELION
ELIOT
ELISE
ELITE
ELIZA
ELLEN
ELLER
ELLES
ELLIE
ELLIS
ELMAN
ELMER
ELMOS
ELOPE
ELROY
ELSIE
ELTON
ELUDE
ELUTE
ELVER
ELVES
ELVIN
ELVIS
ELWAY
ELWES
ELYSE

E•L••
ECLAT
EELED
EELER
EFLAT
EILAT
ELLEN
ELLER
ELLES
ELLIE
ELLIS
EMLYN
ENLAI
EOLUS
EULER

E••L•
EAGLE
EARLE
EARLS
EARLY
EBOLI
ECOLE
ECOLI
EDILE
EMILE
EMILY
ENOLA
ENOLS
EVILS
EWELL
EXALT
EXILE
EXULT

E•••L
EASEL
EDSEL
ELIEL
EMAIL
ENGEL
ENROL
EQUAL
ERBIL
ERROL
ERVIL
ETHEL
ETHYL
ETZEL
EWELL
EXCEL
EXPEL
EXTOL

•EL••
BELAY
BELCH
BELEM
BELIE
BELLA
BELLE
BELLI
BELLS
BELLY
BELOW
BELTS
BELVA
CELEB
CELIA
CELIE
CELLA
CELLI
CELLO
CELLS
CELTS
DELAY
DELCO
DELED
DELES
DELFT
DELHI
DELIS
DELLA
DELLS
DELON
DELOS
DELTA
DELTS
DELVE
EELED
EELER
FELID
FELIS
FELIX
FELIZ
FELLA
FELLS
FELLY
FELON
FELTS
GELEE
GELID
HELEN
HELGA
HELIC
HELIO
HELIX
HELLO
HELLS
HELMS
HELOS
HELOT
HELPS
HELVE
JELLO
JELLS
JELLY
KELLY
KELPS
KELPY
KELSO
MELAN
MELBA
MELDS
MELEE
MELIC
MELON
MELOS
MELTS
MELTY
NELLY
PELEE
PELEG
PELLA
PELLE
PELTS
RELAX

RELAY
RELEE
RELET
RELIC
RELIG
RELIT
SELAH
SELES
SELIG
SELLS
SELMA
SELVA
TELEO
TELES
TELEX
TELIC
TELLS
TELLY
TELOS
VELAR
VELDS
VELDT
VELEZ
VELUM
WELBY
WELCH
WELDS
WELLS
WELSH
WELTS
WELTY
YELLS
YELPS
ZELDA
ZELIG

•E•L•

BEALL
BEALS
BELLA
BELLE
BELLI
BELLS
BELLY
BERLE
BEYLE
CEILS
CELLA
CELLI
CELLO
CELLS
DEALS
DEALT
DEILS
DELLA
DELLS
FEELS
FEELY
FELLA
FELLS
FELLY
FEYLY
HEALS
HEALY
HEELS
HEKLA
HELLO
HELLS
HERLS
JELLO
JELLS
JELLY
KEELS
KELLY
LEILA
MEALS
MEALY
MENLO
MERLE
MERLS
MEWLS
NEALE
NEILL
NELLY
NEWLY
PEALE
PEALS
PEELE
PEELS
PELLA
PELLE
PEPLA
PERLE
REALM
REALS
REDLY
REELS
REPLY
SEALE
SEALS
SEALY
SEELS
SEELY
SELLS
SEULE
TEALS
TELLS
TELLY
TESLA
VEALY
VEILS
WEALS
WEILL
WELLS
WETLY
YELLS
ZEALS

•E••L

BEALL
BERYL
BETEL
BEVEL
BEZEL
CECIL
CEORL
DECAL
DEVIL
FERAL
FETAL
HEGEL
HERZL
HEXYL
JEWEL
KEMAL
KEVEL
LEGAL
LENDL
LEVEL
MEDAL
MEMEL
MERYL
METAL
NEILL
NEPAL
NEROL
NEVIL
NEWEL
PEARL
PEDAL
PENAL
PERIL
PETAL
REBEL
REGAL
RENAL
REOIL
REPEL
REUEL
REVEL
SEGAL
SEOUL
SEPAL
SERAL
TEPAL
VENAL
WEDEL
WEILL
YENTL

••EL•

ABELE
ADELA
ADELE
AKELA
ANELE
AXELS
BCELL
BUELL
CAELO
CHELA
DUELS
DWELL
DWELT
EWELL
FEELS
FEELY
FIELD
FJELD
FUELS
GAELS
HEELS
KEELS
KNELL
KNELT
KVELL
LYELL
MYELO
NIELS
NOELS
OBELI
ODELL
OPELS
PEELE
PEELS
PRELL
QUELL
REELS
RIELS
SEELS
SEELY
SHELF
SHELL
SMELL
SMELT
SNELL
SPELL
SPELT
STELA
STELE
SWELL
SZELL
TAELS
WHELK
WHELM
WHELP
WIELD
YIELD

••E•L

AREAL
BCELL
BUELL
CREEL
DWELL
EWELL
IDEAL
KNEEL
KNELL
KVELL
LYELL
ODELL
ONEAL
ONEIL
PRELL
QUELL
RUEHL
SHELL
SMELL
SNELL
SPELL
STEAL
STEEL
SWELL
SZELL
THEOL
WHEAL
WHEEL
ZOEAL

•••EL

ACCEL
ANGEL
ANSEL
APFEL
APPEL
ARIEL
ARNEL
ARPEL
ARTEL
BABEL
BAGEL
BASEL
BETEL
BEVEL
BEZEL
BIKEL
BOTEL
CAMEL
CREEL
CRUEL
CUPEL
DOWEL
DYNEL
EASEL
EDSEL
ELIEL
ENGEL
ETHEL
ETZEL
EXCEL
EXPEL
FIDEL
GAVEL
GIMEL
GOBEL
GODEL
GOMEL
GRUEL
HAMEL
HAVEL
HAZEL
HEGEL
HOSEL
HOTEL
HOVEL
IMPEL
INTEL
JEWEL
JOREL
KALEL
KAREL
KEVEL
KNEEL
KUGEL
LABEL
LAPEL
LEVEL
LIBEL
MABEL
MAZEL
MEMEL
MODEL
MONEL
MOREL
MOTEL
NAGEL
NAVEL
NEWEL
NIGEL
NOBEL
NOVEL
ORIEL
OUSEL
OUZEL
PANEL
PIXEL
RATEL
RAVEL
REBEL
REPEL
REUEL
REVEL
RIGEL
ROWEL
SAHEL
SOREL
SPIEL
STAEL
STEEL
TOWEL
UMBEL
URIEL
URKEL
VOWEL
WEDEL
WHEEL
YODEL
YOKEL

EM•••

EMAIL
EMBAR
EMBAY
EMBED
EMBER
EMCEE
EMDEN
EMEER
EMEND
EMERY
EMILE
EMILY
EMIRS
EMITS
EMLYN
EMMER
EMMET
EMMYS
EMORY
EMOTE
EMPTY

E•M••

EAMES
EAMON
ELMAN
ELMER
ELMOS
EMMER
EMMET
EMMYS

E••M•

EDAMS
EDEMA
ELEMI
ENEMY
ETYMA
EXAMS

E•••M

EFREM
ENORM
ENTOM
EPROM
EPSOM

•EM••

BEMAS
DEMES
DEMIT
DEMME
DEMOB
DEMON
DEMOS
DEMUR
FEMME
FEMTO
FEMUR
GEMMA
GEMMY
GEMOT
HEMAN
HEMEN
HEMET
HEMIN
HEMPS
JEMMY
KEMAL
KEMPS
KEMPT
LEMAT
LEMAY
LEMMA
LEMME
LEMON
LEMUR
MEMEL
MEMOS
NEMAN
NEMAT
NEMEA
PEMBA
REMAN
REMAP
REMET
REMEX
REMIT
REMIX
REMOP
REMOW
REMUS
SEMIS
TEMPE
TEMPI
TEMPO
TEMPS
TEMPT
YEMEN

•E•M•

BEAMS
BEAMY
BERME
BERMS
DEEMS
DEMME
DERMA
DERMO
FEMME
FERMI
GEMMA
GEMMY
GERMS
GERMY
GETME
GEUMS
HELMS
HERMS
JEMMY
LEMMA
LEMME
NEUME
PERMS
REAMS
REIMS
SEAMS
SEAMY
SEEMS
SELMA
TEAMS
TEEMS
TERMS
VERMI
WEEMS

•E••M

BEDIM
BEGUM
BELEM
BESOM
CERAM
DECEM
DEISM
DENIM
DENOM
MECUM
REAIM
REALM
REARM
REGUM
REHEM
RERUM
SEBUM
SEDUM
SEISM
SERUM
TENAM
TENPM
VELUM
VENOM

••EM•

ANEMO
CREME
DEEMS
DIEMS
EDEMA
ELEMI
ENEMY
HAEMA
HAEMO
ITEMS
MNEME
POEME
POEMS
SEEMS
SHEMA
SHEMP
STEMS
SUEME
TEEMS
THEMA
THEME
THEMS
WEEMS

••E•M

ABEAM
ADEEM
AKEEM
ATEAM
BOEHM
BREAM
CREAM
DREAM
GLEAM
HBEAM
IBEAM
ODEUM
OLEUM
ONEAM
ONEPM
RHEUM
STEAM
THERM
WHELM

•••EM

ADEEM
ADHEM
ADREM
AKEEM
BELEM
CANEM
DECEM
EFREM
GOLEM
HAREM
INREM
KASEM
MODEM
PROEM
REHEM
ROREM
SALEM
TOTEM
XYLEM

EN•••

ENACT
ENATE
ENCYC
ENDED
ENDER
ENDON
ENDOR
ENDOW
ENDUE
ENDUP
ENEMY
ENERO
ENFIN
ENGEL
ENGRS
ENIAC
ENJOY
ENLAI
ENNEA
ENNIO
ENNIS
ENNUI
ENOCH
ENOLA
ENOLS
ENORM
ENROL
ENSKY
ENSOR
ENSUE
ENTER
ENTIA
ENTOM
ENTRE
ENTRY
ENUGU
ENURE
ENVOI
ENVOY

E•N••

ENNEA
ENNIO
ENNIS
ENNUI
ERNES
ERNIE
ERNST
ESNES
ETNAS

E••N•

EARNS
EBOND
EBONS
EBONY
EDENS
EDINA
EKING
ELAND
ELENA
ELENI
EMEND
ETHNO
ETONS
EVANS
EVENS
EVENT
EWING
EXONS

E•••N

EAGAN
EAMON
EATEN
EATIN
EATON
EBSEN
ECHIN
EDWIN
EGGON
EIGEN
ELFIN
ELGIN
ELION
ELLEN
ELMAN
ELTON
ELVIN
EMDEN
EMLYN
ENDON
ENFIN
EOSIN
EPSON
ERVIN
ERWIN
ESSEN
ETHAN
EVIAN
EXXON

•EN••

BENCH
BENDS
BENDY
BENES
BENET
BENIN
BENJI
BENNY
BENTS
BENUE
BENXI
BENZO
CENCI
CENSE
CENTI
CENTO
CENTS
DENDR
DENEB
DENES
DENIM
DENIS
DENNY
DENOM
DENSE
DENTE
DENTI
DENTS
DENYS
FENCE
FENDS
FENNY
GENES
GENET
GENIC
GENIE
GENII
GENOA
GENRE
GENRO
GENTS
GENUA
GENUS
HENAN
HENCE
HENCH
HENGE
HENIE
HENNA
HENNY
HENRI
HENRY
HENTS
JENNY
KENAI
KENCH
KENDO
KENNY
KENOS
KENYA
LENDL
LENDS
LENIN
LENIS
LENNY
LENOS
LENOX
LENTO
LENTS
LENYA
MENDS
MENES
MENLO
MENSA
MENUS
NENES
PENAL
PENCE
PENDS
PENGO
PENNA
PENNE
PENNI
PENNY
PENTA
PENTE
PENZA
RENAL
RENAN
RENDS
RENEE
RENEW
RENIN
RENTA
RENTS
SENAT
SENDS
SENGI
SENNA
SENOR
SENSE
SENTE
TENAM
TENCH
TENDS
TENET
TENON
TENOR
TENPM
TENSE
TENTH
TENTS
VENAE
VENAL
VENDA
VENDS
VENEZ
VENIN
VENOM
VENTS
VENUE
VENUS
WENCH
WENDS
WENDT
WENDY
XENIA
XENON
YENTA
YENTE
YENTL
ZENDA
ZENDO
ZENDS
ZENIC

•E•N•

AEONS
AETNA
BEANO
BEANS
BEANY
BEENE
BEING
BEINS
BENNY
BERNE
DEANE
DEANS
DENNY
DESNA
FEINT
FENNY
FERNS
FERNY
GEENA
HEINE
HEINZ
HENNA
HENNY
HERNE
HERNS
JEANE
JEANS
JENNY
JEUNE
KEANE
KEANU
KEENE
KEENS
KENNY
KERNS
LEANS
LEANT
LENNY
LEONA
LEONE
LEONI
MEANS
MEANT
MEANY
MEINY
MESNE
NEONS
PEENS
PENNA
PENNE
PENNI
PENNY
PEONS
PEONY
REGNI
REINA
REINK
REINS
REUNE
SEGNI
SEGNO
SEHNA
SEINE
SENNA
TEENA
TEENS
TEENY
TERNE
TERNS
VEINS
VEINY
VERNE
WEANS
WEENY
YEANS
YESNO
ZEINS

•E••N

AERON
BEGAN
BEGIN
BEGUN
BEHAN
BENIN
BETON
BEVIN
DEIGN
DEION
DELON
DEMON
DEVON
DEWAN
FEDON
FEIGN
FELON
GETIN
GETON
HEARN
HEDIN
HELEN
HEMAN
HEMEN
HEMIN
HENAN
HERON
KEVIN
KEYIN
LEARN
LEDIN
LEDON
LEMON
LENIN
LETIN
LETON
LEVIN
LEVON
LEXAN
MEGAN
MELAN
MELON
MESON
NEMAN
NEVIN
PECAN
PEKIN
PEPIN
PERAN
PERON
RECON
REDAN
REDON
REGAN
REHAN
REIGN
REMAN
RENAN
RENIN
REPIN
RERAN
RERUN
RESIN
REWIN
REWON
SEDAN
SEEIN
SERIN
SETIN
SETON
SEVEN
SEWON
TENON
TETON
TEXAN
VEGAN
VENIN
XEDIN
XENON
YEARN
YEMEN
ZEVON

••EN•

ABEND
ADENO
AGENA
AGENT
AKENE
ALENE
AMEND
AMENS
AMENT
ANENT
ARENA
ARENS
ARENT
AVENA
AVENS
BEENE
BLEND
BLENT
BRENT
BUENA
BUENO
DIENE
EDENS
ELENA
ELENI
EMEND
EVENS
EVENT
FIEND
FRENA
GEENA
GHENT
GLENN
GLENS
GWENN
GWENT
HYENA
ICENI
ILENE
IRENE
KEENE
KEENS
LIENS
MIENS
NOEND
OMENS
ONEND
OPENS
OVENS
OWENS
PEENS
PHENO
PLENA
SAENS
SCENA
SCEND
SCENE
SCENT
SIENA
SPEND
SPENT
STENO
STENS
TEENA
TEENS
TEENY
TREND
TRENT
UPEND
WEENY
WRENS

••E•N

ATEIN
BREEN
CLEAN
CLEON
CREON
CUEIN
FOEHN
FREON
GLEAN
GLENN
GREEN
GWENN
ICEIN
KLEIN
LIEIN
OCEAN
OLEAN
OLEIN
PAEAN
PAEON
PLEON
PREEN
QUEEN
QUERN
SEEIN
SHEAN
SHEEN
SKEAN
SKEIN
STEEN
STEIN
STERN
TIEIN
TOEIN
TREEN
TWEEN
WHEEN

•••EN

ADMEN
AIKEN
ALBEN
ALDEN
ALIEN
ALLEN
ARDEN
ARLEN
ASHEN
ASPEN
AUDEN
BADEN
BIDEN
BOWEN
BREEN
CHIEN
COHEN
COVEN
COZEN
DIZEN
DONEN
DOREN
DOYEN
DOZEN
EATEN
EBSEN
EIGEN
ELLEN
EMDEN
ESSEN
GALEN
GIVEN
GOREN
GREEN
GUTEN
HAGEN
HAVEN
HELEN
HEMEN
IBSEN
KAREN
LADEN
LATEN
LIKEN
LIMEN
LINEN
LIVEN
LODEN
LOREN
LTGEN
LUMEN
MAVEN
NIVEN
NOMEN
NUMEN
NUYEN
OAKEN
OATEN
OFTEN
OGDEN
OLDEN
OLSEN
PAREN
PATEN
PHREN
PREEN
QUEEN
QUIEN
RAMEN
RAVEN
RIPEN
RISEN
RIVEN
ROSEN
ROUEN
ROWEN
RUBEN
RUMEN
SEVEN
SHEEN
SIREN
SOREN
STEEN
TAKEN
TOKEN
TREEN
TWEEN
UNPEN
VIXEN
WAKEN
WAXEN
WHEEN
WIDEN
WIZEN
WODEN
WOKEN
WOMEN
WOVEN
YEMEN
ZAZEN

EO•••

EOLUS
EOSIN

E•O••

EBOAT
EBOLI
EBOND
EBONS
EBONY
ECOLE
ECOLI
ELOPE
EMORY
EMOTE
ENOCH
ENOLA
ENOLS
ENORM
EPOCH
EPODE
EPOXY
ERODE
EROSE
ETONS
EVOKE
EVORA
EWOKS
EXONS
EYOTS

E••O•

EAMON
EATON
EGGON
ELBOW
ELION
ELIOT
ELMOS
ELROY
ELTON
ENDON
ENDOR
ENDOW
ENJOY
ENROL
ENSOR
ENTOM
ENVOI
ENVOY
EPCOT
EPHOD
EPHOR
EPROM
EPSOM
EPSON
ERGOT
ERROL
ERROR
ESPOO
ESTOP
ETHOS
EUROS
EXPOS
EXTOL
EXXON

E•••O

EIEIO
EJIDO
ENERO
ENNIO
ERATO
ESPOO
ETHNO
EXTRO

•EO••

AEONS
CEORL
DEOXY
FEOFF
GEODE
GEOID
GEORG
KEOGH
LEONA
LEONE
LEONI
LEORA
MEOWS
NEONS
PEONS
PEONY
REOIL
SEOUL

•E•O•

AEIOU
AERON
AEROS
AESOP
BEBOP
BEFOG
BEGOT
BELOW
BESOM
BESOT
BETON
CEROS
DECOR
DECOY
DEFOE
DEFOG
DEION
DELON
DELOS
DEMOB
DEMON
DEMOS
DENOM
DEPOT
DETOO
DEVON
FEDON
FELON
FETOR
GEMOT
GENOA
GETON
HELOS
HELOT
HEROD
HERON
HEROS
KEBOB
KENOS
LEDON
LEGOS
LEMON
LENOS
LENOX
LEROI
LEROY
LETON
LEVON
MEDOC
MELON
MELOS
MEMOS
MEROE
MESON
METOO
NEPOS
NEROL
PECOS
PEKOE
PEPOS
PERON
PEROT
PESOS
RECON
REDON
REDOX
REMOP
REMOW
REPOS
REPOT
RESOD
RETOP
RETOW
REWON
SEGOS
SENOR
SEPOY
SEROW
SETON
SEWON
TELOS

TENON
TENOR
TETON
VENOM
XENON
XEROX
ZEROS
ZEVON

•E••O
BEANO
BENZO
CELLO
CENTO
CERRO
DEKKO
DELCO
DERMO
DETOO
DEUTO
FEMTO
FERRO
GECKO
GENRO
GESSO
GETGO
GETTO
HECTO
HELIO
HELLO
JELLO
KELSO
KENDO
LEDTO
LENTO
LEPTO
LETGO
MENLO
METOO
METRO
MEZZO
NEATO
NEURO
PEABO
PEDRO
PENGO
PESTO
PETRO
RECTO
REPRO
RETRO
SEATO
SECCO
SEETO
SEGNO
SEIKO
SERVO
SETTO
TELEO
TEMPO
VERSO
YESNO
ZENDO
ZEPPO

••EO•
CLEON
CREON
FREON
OLEOS
OREOS
PAEON
PLEON
THEOL

••E•O
ACETO
ADENO
ANEMO
ANETO
BUENO
CAELO
CREDO
DIEGO
DUETO
EIEIO
ENERO
FIERO
FUEGO
GRECO
HAEMO
HIERO
HUEVO
LIETO
LUEGO
MYELO
PHENO
PLEIO
PREGO
PTERO
SEETO
SPERO
STENO
TIETO
VIEJO

•••EO
BUTEO
CAMEO
CUNEO
HOMEO
JUDEO
MATEO
MIMEO
MINEO
ORFEO
OSSEO
OSTEO
PALEO
PASEO
RODEO
ROLEO
ROMEO
TELEO
VIDEO
VIREO

EP•••
EPACT
EPCOT
EPEES
EPHAH
EPHAS
EPHOD
EPHOR
EPICS
EPISC
EPOCH
EPODE
EPOXY
EPROM
EPSOM
EPSON

E•P••
EMPTY
ESPOO
EXPEL
EXPOS

E••P•
EGYPT
ELOPE
ERUPT
ETAPE

E•••P
EATUP
ENDUP
EQUIP
ESTOP

•EP••
CEPES
DEPEW
DEPOT
DEPTH
DEPTS
HEPTA
KEPIS
LEPPY
LEPTA
LEPTO
LEPUS
NEPAL
NEPOS
PEPIN
PEPLA
PEPOS
PEPPY
PEPSI
PEPUP
PEPYS
REPAD
REPAY
REPEG
REPEL
REPIN
REPLY
REPOS
REPOT
REPPS
REPRO
SEPAL
SEPIA
SEPOY
SEPTA
TEPAL
TEPEE
TEPID
ZEPPO

•E•P•
BEEPS
DEEPS
HEAPS
HELPS
HEMPS
JEEPS
KEEPS
KELPS
KELPY
KEMPS
KEMPT
LEAPS
LEAPT
LEPPY
NEAPS
PEEPS
PEPPY
PERPS
REAPS
REPPS
REUPS
SEEPS
SEEPY
TEMPE
TEMPI
TEMPO
TEMPS
TEMPT
TENPM
TERPS
VEEPS
WEEPS
WEEPY
YELPS
ZEPPO

•E••P
AESOP
BEBOP
FEDUP
GETUP
HETUP
KEYUP
LEGUP
LETUP
PEPUP
RECAP
RECIP
REMAP
REMOP
RETAP
RETOP
REVUP
SETUP
SEWUP
TEEUP

••EP•
ADEPT
ALEPH
BEEPS
CREPE
CREPT
DEEPS
INEPT
JEEPS
KEEPS
ONEPM
PEEPS
PREPS
SEEPS
SEEPY
SIEPI
SKEPS
SLEPT
STEPS
SWEPT
VEEPS
WEEPS
WEEPY

••E•P
ATEUP
BLEEP
CHEAP
CHEEP
CREEP
ICEUP
ONEUP
SHEEP
SHEMP
SLEEP
STEEP
SWEEP
TEEUP
TIEUP
TWERP
USEUP
WHELP

•••EP
BLEEP
CHEEP
CREEP
JULEP
SALEP
SHEEP
SLEEP
STEEP
STREP
SWEEP

EQ•••
EQUAL
EQUIP
EQUIV
EQUUS

E•Q••
ESQUE

E••Q•
ETSQQ

E•••Q
ETSEQ
ETSQQ

•••EQ
ETSEQ

ER•••
ERASE
ERATO
ERBIL
ERECT
ERGOT
ERICA
ERICH
ERIES
ERIKA
ERISA
ERNES
ERNIE
ERNST
ERODE
EROSE
ERRED
ERROL
ERROR
ERUCT
ERUPT
ERVIL
ERVIN
ERWIN

E•R••
EARED
EARLE
EARLS
EARLY
EARNS
EARTH
ECRUS
EERIE
EFREM
EGRET
ELROY
ENROL
EPROM
ERRED
ERROL
ERROR
EUROS
EURUS
EYRAS
EYRES
EYRIE
EYRIR

E••R•
EAGRE
EBERT
EMERY
EMIRS
EMORY
ENERO
ENGRS
ENORM
ENTRE
ENTRY
ENURE
EVERS
EVERT
EVERY
EVORA
EWERS
EXERT
EXTRA
EXTRO
EXURB
EYERS

E•••R
EAGER
EATER
EDGAR
EDGER
EELER
EGGAR
EIDER
ELDER
ELGAR
ELLER
ELMER
ELVER
EMBAR
EMBER
EMEER
EMMER
ENDER
ENDOR
ENSOR
ENTER
EPHOR
ERROR
ESKER
ESTER
ETHER
ETVIR
EULER
EYRIR

•ER••
AERIE
AERON
AEROS
BEREA
BERET
BERGH
BERGS
BERLE
BERME
BERMS
BERNE
BERRA
BERRY
BERTH
BERYL
CERAM
CERAT
CERED
CERES
CERIA
CEROS
CERRO
CERTS
DERAT
DERBY
DEREK
DERIV
DERMA
DERMO
DERRY
DERSU
EERIE
FERAL
FERDE
FERIA
FERMI
FERNS
FERNY
FERRI
FERRO
FERRY
GERAH
GERMS
GERMY
GERRY
HERAT
HERBS
HERBY
HERDS
HERES
HERKY
HERLS
HERMS
HERNE
HERNS
HEROD
HERON
HEROS
HERTZ
HERVE
HERZL
JEREZ
JERKS
JERKY
JERRY
JERZY
KERAT
KERBS
KERNS
KERRI
KERRY
LEROI
LEROY
MERCE
MERCI
MERCK
MERCY
MERES
MERGE
MERIT
MERLE
MERLS
MEROE
MERRY
MERTZ
MERYL
NERDS
NERDY
NEROL
NERTS
NERTZ
NERVE
NERVY
PERAN
PERCE
PERCH
PERCY
PERDU
PERES
PEREZ
PERIL
PERIS
PERKS
PERKY
PERLE
PERMS
PERON
PEROT
PERPS
PERRY
PERSE
PERTH
RERAN
RERIG
RERUM
RERUN
SERAC
SERAI
SERAL
SERBS
SERES
SERFS
SERGE
SERIF
SERIN
SEROW
SERRA
SERRY
SERTA
SERUM
SERVE
SERVO
TERMS
TERNE
TERNS
TERPS
TERRA
TERRE
TERRI
TERRY
TERSE
TERZA
VERBA
VERBS
VERDE
VERDI
VERGE
VERMI
VERNE
VERRE
VERSA
VERSE
VERSO
VERST
VERTE
VERTS
VERVE
XERIC
XEROX
XERUS
YERBA
YERKS
ZEROS

•E•R•
BEARD
BEARS
BEERS
BEERY
BERRA
BERRY
CEORL
CERRO
DEARS
DEARY
DEBRA
DECRY
DEERE
DEERS
DERRY
DETRE
DEVRY
FEARS
FERRI
FERRO
FERRY
GEARS
GEARY
GENRE
GENRO
GEORG
GERRY
HEARD
HEARN
HEARS
HEART
HEIRS
HENRI
HENRY
HEURE
JEERS
JERRY
KERRI
KERRY
LEARN
LEARS
LEARY
LEERS
LEERY
LEORA
MEARA
MERRY
METRE
METRO
METRY
NEARS
NEGRI
NEHRU
NEURO
PEARL
PEARS
PEARY
PEDRO
PEERS
PERRY
PETRA
PETRI
PETRO
REARM
REARS
REFRY
REPRO
RETRO
RETRY
SEARS
SEERS
SERRA
SERRY
TEARS
TEARY
TERRA
TERRE
TERRI
TERRY
TETRA
VEERS
VEERY
VERRE
WEARS
WEARY
WEIRD
WEIRS
YEARN
YEARS
ZEBRA

•E••R
AEGIR
AESIR
CEDAR
CESAR
DEBAR
DECOR
DEFER
DEMUR
DENDR
DETER
DEWAR
DEXTR
EELER
FEMUR
FETOR
FEVER
FEWER
FEYER
HEWER
HEXER
JETER
KEFIR
LEGER
LEHAR
LEMUR
LEVAR
LEVER
METER
MEYER
NEVER
NEWER
PETER
REAIR
REBAR
RECUR
REFER
RETAR
SEDER
SEGAR
SEGER
SENOR
SEVER
SEWER
TENOR
VELAR
VEXER
WEBER
WESER

••ER•
ACERB
ACERS
AGERS
ALERT
APERS
APERY
AVERS
AVERT
AVERY
AXERS
AYERS
BEERS
BEERY
BOERS
BRERS
CBERS
CHERE
CHERI
CHERT
CIERA
CLERK
DEERE
DEERS
DOERS
DYERS
EBERT
EMERY
ENERO
EVERS
EVERT
EVERY
EWERS
EXERT
EYERS
FAERY
FIERO
FIERY
FRERE
GOERS
HIERA
HIERO
HOERS
IBERT
ICERS
INERT
ISERE
ITERS
JEERS
LEERS
LEERY
MYERS
NLERS
OMERS
ONERS
OPERA
OPERE
OVERS
OVERT
OWERS
PEERS
PIERS
PTERO
QUERN
QUERY
RUERS
SEERS
SHERE
SNERD
SNERT
SPERO
STERE
STERN
SUERS
THERA
THERE
THERM
TIERS
TWERE
TWERP
USERS
VEERS
VEERY
VIERS
WHERE

••E•R
AMEER
ANEAR
AREAR
BLEAR
CHEER
CLEAR
COEUR
DREAR
EMEER
FLEER
FLEUR
FREER
GREER
QUEER
SHEAR
SHEER
SIEUR
SMEAR
SNEER
SOEUR
SPEAR
STEER
SWEAR
THEIR
TWEER

•••ER
ABLER
ABNER
ACTER
ADDER
ADLER
AFTER
AILER
AIMER
AJMER
ALDER
ALGER
ALLER
ALTER
AMBER
AMEER
ANGER
ANSER
APTER
ARBER
ASHER
ASKER
ASNER
ASTER
AUBER
AUGER
BABER
BADER
BAKER
BALER
BARER
BASER
BAUER
BAYER
BIKER
BITER
BLUER
BONER
BOOER
BORER
BOWER
BOXER
BOYER
BRIER
BUBER
BUYER
BYNER
CABER
CAGER
CANER
CAPER
CARER
CATER
CAVER
CHEER
CIDER
CITER
CODER
COMER
COOER
CORER
COVER
COWER
COYER
CRIER
CRYER
CURER
CUTER
CYBER
CYDER
DARER
DATER
DEFER
DETER
DICER
DINER
DIRER
DIVER
DIYER
DOSER
DOTER
DOVER
DOWER
DOZER
DRIER
DRYER
DURER
EAGER
EATER
EDGER
EELER
EIDER
ELDER
ELLER
ELMER
ELVER
EMBER
EMEER
EMMER
ENDER
ENTER
ESKER
ESTER
ETHER
EULER
FABER
FACER
FAKER
FARER
FEVER
FEWER
FEYER
FIBER
FIFER
FILER
FINER
FIRER
FIVER
FIXER
FLEER
FLIER
FLYER
FOYER
FREER
FRIER
FRYER
GAMER
GAPER
GAYER
GAZER
GIBER
GIVER
GLUER
GOFER
GOMER
GONER
GOWER
GREER
GRIER
HABER
HALER
HATER
HAUER
HAVER
HAZER
HEWER
HEXER
HIDER
HIKER
HIRER
HOMER
HOPER
HOVER
HUGER
HYPER
ICIER
IDLER
ILLER
INFER
INGER
INKER
INNER
INTER
JETER
JIVER
JOKER
KHMER
KINER
KITER
KYSER
LACER
LADER
LAGER
LAKER
LAMER
LASER
LATER
LAUER
LAVER
LAXER
LAYER
LEGER
LEVER
LIGER
LINER
LITER
LIVER
LONER
LOPER
LOSER
LOVER
LOWER
LUGER
MAHER
MAKER
MASER
MATER
MAYER
MAZER
METER
MEYER
MILER
MIMER
MINER
MISER
MITER
MIXER
MOPER
MOVER
MOWER
MUSER
MUTER
NADER
NAMER
NEVER
NEWER
NFLER
NHLER
NICER
NIGER
NINER
NITER
NIZER
NOTER
NUDER
OATER
OCHER
ODDER
OFFER
OGLER
OILER
OLDER
OMBER
ORDER
ORSER
OSIER
OSLER
OTHER
OTTER
OUTER
OWNER
PACER
PAGER
PALER
PAPER
PARER
PATER
PAVER
PAWER
PAYER
PETER
PIKER
PIPER
POKER
POLER
POSER
POWER
PRIER
PURER
QUEER
RACER
RAFER
RAKER
RARER
RASER
RATER
RAVER
RAWER
REFER
RICER
RIDER
RIFER
RIKER
RIPER
RISER
RIVER
ROGER
ROMER
ROPER
ROVER
ROWER
RUDER
RULER
RYDER
SABER
SAFER
SAGER
SAKER
SANER
SAVER
SAYER
SEDER
SEGER
SEVER
SEWER
SHEER
SHIER
SHOER
SHYER
SIDER
SIXER
SIZER
SKIER
SLIER
SLYER
SNEER
SOBER
SOLER
SORER
SOWER
SOXER
STEER
SUMER
SUPER
SURER
TAKER
TALER
TAMER
TAPER
TASER
TATER
TAXER
TIBER
TIGER
TILER
TIMER
TITER
TOLER
TONER
TOPER
TOTER
TOWER
TRIER
TRUER
TUBER
TUNER
TWEER
TYLER
TYPER
UDDER
ULCER
UMBER
UNDER
UNGER
UNSER
UNTER
UPPER
URGER
USHER
UTHER
UTTER
VADER
VATER
VEXER
VILER
VIPER
VOTER
VOWER
WADER
WAFER
WAGER
WALER
WANER
WATER
WAVER
WAXER
WEBER
WESER
WIDER
WIPER
WIRER
WISER
WOOER
WRIER
WRYER
WYLER
YARER

ES•••
ESBAT
ESKER
ESNES
ESPOO
ESQUE
ESSAY
ESSEN
ESSES
ESSEX
ESTAB
ESTAS
ESTEE
ESTER
ESTES
ESTOP

E•S••
EASED
EASEL
EASES
EASTS
EBSEN
EDSEL
ELSIE
ENSKY
ENSOR
ENSUE
EOSIN
EPSOM
EPSON
ESSAY
ESSEN
ESSES
ESSEX
ETSEQ
ETSQQ

E••S•
EGEST
ELISE
ELYSE
EPISC
ERASE
ERISA
ERNST
EROSE
EXIST

E•••S
EAMES
EARLS
EARNS
EASES
EASTS
EAVES
EBONS
ECRUS
EDAMS
EDDAS
EDENS
EDGES
EDITS
EFIKS
EGADS
ELIAS
ELLES
ELLIS
ELMOS
ELVES
ELVIS
ELWES
EMIRS
EMITS
EMMYS
ENGRS
ENNIS
ENOLS
EOLUS
EPEES
EPHAS
EPICS
EQUUS
ERIES
ERNES
ESNES
ESSES
ESTAS
ESTES
ETATS
ETHOS
ETNAS
ETONS
ETUIS
EUROS
EURUS
EVANS
EVENS
EVERS
EVILS
EWERS
EWOKS
EXAMS
EXECS
EXITS
EXONS
EXPOS
EYERS
EYOTS
EYRAS
EYRES

•ES••
AESIR
AESOP
BESET
BESOM
BESOT
BESTS
CESAR
CESTA
CESTI
DESKS
DESNA
DESTE
FESTA
FESTS
GESSO
GESTE
GESTS
HESSE
HESTS
JESSE
JESTS
KESEY
MESAS
MESHY
MESIC
MESNE
MESON
MESSY
MESTA
NESTS
PESCI
PESKY
PESOS
PESTO
PESTS
RESAW
RESEE
RESET
RESEW

RESIN
RESOD
RESTS
TESLA
TESTA
TESTS
TESTY
VESEY
VESTA
VESTS
WESER
WESTS
YESES
YESNO
ZESTS
ZESTY

•E•S•

BEAST
BETSY
CEASE
CENSE
DEISM
DEIST
DENSE
DERSU
FEAST
FEIST
GEESE
GESSO
HEISS
HEIST
HESSE
HEYSE
JESSE
KELSO
LEASE
LEASH
LEAST
MEESE
MENSA
MESSY
MEUSE
NEWSY
PEASE
PEPSI
PERSE
REESE
REUSE
SEISM
SENSE
SEUSS
TEASE
TENSE
TERSE
VERSA
VERSE
VERSO
VERST
WEEST
WEISS
WELSH
YEAST
ZEISS
ZEIST

•E••S

AEDES
AEGIS
AEONS
AEROS
BEADS
BEAKS
BEALS
BEAMS
BEANS
BEARS
BEATS
BEAUS
BECKS
BEEFS
BEEPS
BEERS
BEETS
BEINS
BELLS
BELTS
BEMAS
BENDS
BENES
BENTS
BERGS
BERMS
BESTS
BETAS
BETHS
CEDES
CEDIS
CEILS
CELLS
CELTS
CENTS
CEPES
CERES
CEROS
CERTS
CETUS
DEALS
DEANS
DEARS
DEBTS
DECKS
DEEDS
DEEMS
DEEPS
DEERS
DEGAS
DEILS
DEKES
DELES
DELIS
DELLS
DELOS
DELTS
DEMES
DEMOS
DENES
DENIS
DENTS
DENYS
DEPTS
DESKS
FEARS
FEATS
FEEDS
FEELS
FEETS
FELIS
FELLS
FELTS
FENDS
FERNS
FESTS
FETAS
FETES
FEUDS
GEARS
GEEKS
GENES
GENTS
GENUS
GERMS
GESTS
GETAS
GEUMS
HEADS
HEALS
HEAPS
HEARS
HEATS
HECKS
HEEDS
HEELS
HEFTS
HEIRS
HEISS
HELLS
HELMS
HELOS
HELPS
HEMPS
HENTS
HERBS
HERDS
HERES
HERLS
HERMS
HERNS
HEROS
HESTS
HETHS
HEXES
JEANS
JEEPS
JEERS
JELLS
JERKS
JESTS
JETES
KEATS
KEELS
KEENS
KEEPS
KEETS
KELPS
KEMPS
KENOS
KEPIS
KERBS
KERNS
KEYES
LEADS
LEAFS
LEAKS
LEANS
LEAPS
LEARS
LEEDS
LEEKS
LEERS
LEETS
LEFTS
LEGGS
LEGIS
LEGOS
LENDS
LENIS
LENOS
LENTS
LEPUS
LETTS
LEVIS
LEWES
LEWIS
LEXIS
LEXUS
MEADS
MEALS
MEANS
MEATS
MEDES
MEEDS
MEETS
MELDS
MELOS
MELTS
MEMOS
MENDS
MENES
MENUS
MEOWS
MERES
MERLS
MESAS
METES
METIS
MEWLS
NEAPS
NEARS
NEATS
NECKS
NEEDS
NEGUS
NEHIS
NENES
NEONS
NEPOS
NERDS
NERTS
NESTS
NEVES
NEVIS
NEVUS
NEWTS
NEXIS
NEXUS
PEAKS
PEALS
PEARS
PEATS
PECKS
PECOS
PEEKS
PEELS
PEENS
PEEPS
PEERS
PEKES
PELTS
PENDS
PEONS
PEPOS
PEPYS
PERES
PERIS
PERKS
PERMS
PERPS
PESOS
PESTS
PETES
READS
REALS
REAMS
REAPS
REARS
REBUS
REDES
REEDS
REEFS
REEKS
REELS
REGIS
REIMS
REINS
REMUS
RENDS
RENTS
REPOS
REPPS
RESTS
REUPS
REXES
REYES
SEALS
SEAMS
SEARS
SEATS
SECTS
SEEDS
SEEKS
SEELS
SEEMS
SEEPS
SEERS
SEGOS
SELES
SELLS
SEMIS
SENDS
SERBS
SERES
SERFS
SEUSS
SEXES
SEXTS
TEAKS
TEALS
TEAMS
TEARS
TECHS
TEEMS
TEENS
TELES
TELLS
TELOS
TEMPS
TENDS
TENTS
TERMS
TERNS
TERPS
TESTS
TETES
TETHS
TEXAS
TEXTS
VEDAS
VEEPS
VEERS
VEGAS
VEILS
VEINS
VELDS
VENDS
VENTS
VENUS
VERBS
VERTS
VESTS
VEXES
WEALS
WEANS
WEARS
WEEDS
WEEKS
WEEMS
WEEPS
WEFTS
WEIRS
WEISS
WEKAS
WELDS
WELLS
WELTS
WENDS
WESTS
XERUS
YEANS
YEARS
YEATS
YEGGS
YELLS
YELPS
YERKS
YESES
YETIS
ZEALS
ZEBUS
ZEINS
ZEISS
ZENDS
ZEROS
ZESTS
ZETAS

••ES•

BLESS
BLEST
BREST
CHESS
CHEST
CRESC
CRESS
CREST
DOEST
DRESS
EGEST
FLESH
FRESH
GEESE
GLESS
GOEST
GUESS
GUEST
IDEST
LOESS
MEESE
OBESE
POESY
PRESS
PREST
QUEST
REESE
THESE
TRESS
WEEST
WIEST
WREST

••E•S

ABETS
ACERS
AGERS
AKEES
ALEFS
AMENS
APERS
AREAS
ARENS
AVENS
AVERS
AXELS
AXERS
AYERS
BEEFS
BEEPS
BEERS
BEETS
BLEBS
BLESS
BOERS
BRERS
BREWS
CBERS
CHEFS
CHESS
CHEWS
CLEFS
CLEWS
COEDS
CREES
CRESS
CREWS
DEEDS
DEEMS
DEEPS
DEERS
DIEMS
DIETS
DOERS
DREGS
DRESS
DUELS
DUETS
DYERS
EDENS
EPEES
EVENS
EVERS
EWERS
EXECS
EYERS
FEEDS
FEELS
FEETS
FIEFS
FLEAS
FLEES
FLEWS
FLEYS
FREES
FRETS
FUELS
GAELS
GEEKS
GHEES
GLEES
GLENS
GLESS
GLEYS
GOERS
GREES
GREYS
GUESS
HEEDS
HEELS
HOERS
ICERS
IDEAS
ITEMS
ITERS
JEEPS
JEERS
JOEYS
KEELS
KEENS
KEEPS
KEETS
KNEES
KREBS
LEEDS
LEEKS
LEERS
LEETS
LIENS
LIEUS
LOESS
MEEDS
MEETS
MIENS
MYERS
NEEDS
NIELS
NLERS
NOELS
NYETS
OBEYS
ODETS
OGEES
OLEOS
OMENS
OMERS
ONERS
OPEDS
OPELS
OPENS
OREOS
OVENS
OVERS
OWENS
OWERS
PEEKS
PEELS
PEENS
PEEPS
PEERS
PIEDS
PIERS
PLEAS
PLEBS
PLEWS
POEMS
POETS
PREPS
PRESS
PREYS
REEDS
REEFS
REEKS
REELS
RHEAS
RIELS
RUERS
SAENS
SEEDS
SEEKS
SEELS
SEEMS
SEEPS
SEERS
SHEDS
SKEGS
SKEPS
SKEWS
SLEDS
SLEWS
SMEWS
SPECS
SPETS
SPEWS
STEMS
STENS
STEPS
STETS
STEWS
SUERS
SUETS
TAELS
TEEMS
TEENS
THEMS
THEWS
TIEGS
TIERS
TREES
TREKS
TRESS
TREWS
TREYS
USERS
VEEPS
VEERS
VIERS
VIEWS
WEEDS
WEEKS
WEEMS
WEEPS
WHETS
WHEYS
WRENS
ZOEAS

•••ES

AAMES
ABBES
ABYES
ACHES
ACMES
ACRES
ADZES
AEDES
AGNES
AGUES
AIDES
AIRES
AKEES
ALLES
ALOES
AMIES
ANDES
ANGES
ANNES
ANTES
APRES
APSES
ARIES
ARLES
ARTES
ASHES
ASSES
AXLES
AYRES
BABES
BAKES
BALES
BANES
BARES
BASES
BATES
BENES
BIDES
BIKES
BINES
BISES
BITES
BLUES
BODES
BOLES
BONES
BORES
BOWES
BOXES
BRAES
BRIES
BUSES
BYRES
BYTES
CAFES
CAGES
CAKES

CANES
CAPES
CARES
CASES
CATES
CAVES
CEDES
CEPES
CERES
CINES
CIRES
CITES
CLUES
CODES
COKES
COLES
COMES
CONES
COPES
CORES
COTES
COVES
COWES
COXES
COZES
CREES
CRIES
CUBES
CUKES
CURES
CYMES
DACES
DALES
DAMES
DANES
DARES
DATES
DAWES
DAZES
DEKES
DELES
DEMES
DENES
DICES
DIKES
DIMES
DINES
DIVES
DOGES
DOLES
DOMES
DOPES
DOSES
DOTES
DOVES
DOZES
DRIES
DUCES
DUDES
DUKES
DUNES
DUPES
DUXES
DYNES
EAMES
EASES
EAVES
EDGES
ELLES
ELVES
ELWES
EPEES
ERIES
ERNES
ESNES
ESSES
ESTES
EYRES
FACES
FADES
FAKES
FAMES
FANES
FARES
FATES
FAVES
FAXES
FAZES
FETES
FICES
FIDES
FIFES
FILES
FINES
FIRES
FIVES
FIXES
FLEES
FLIES
FLOES
FLUES
FORES
FOXES
FREES
FRIES
FROES
FUMES
FUSES
FYKES
GAGES
GALES
GAMES
GAPES
GASES
GATES
GAZES
GENES
GHEES
GIBES
GILES
GIVES
GLEES
GLUES
GORES
GREES
GULES
GYBES
GYRES
GYVES
HADES
HAKES
HALES
HAMES
HANES
HARES
HATES
HAVES
HAYES
HAZES
HERES
HEXES
HIDES
HIKES
HINES
HIRES
HIVES
HOKES
HOLES
HOMES
HONES
HOPES
HOSES
HYPES
ICKES
IDLES
IGNES
ISLES
IVIES
JADES
JAKES
JAMES
JAPES
JETES
JIBES
JIVES
JOKES
JONES
JUKES
JULES
JUTES
KALES
KEYES
KITES
KNEES
LACES
LADES
LAKES
LAMES
LANES
LARES
LASES
LAVES
LAWES
LAZES
LEWES
LIKES
LIMES
LINES
LITES
LIVES
LOBES
LODES
LOGES
LOPES
LORES
LOSES
LOVES
LOWES
LOXES
LUBES
LUGES
LUNES
LURES
LUTES
LYRES
MACES
MAGES
MAKES
MALES
MANES
MARES
MATES
MAXES
MAZES
MEDES
MENES
MERES
METES
MIKES
MILES
MIMES
MINES
MIRES
MITES
MIXES
MLLES
MODES
MOLES
MOPES
MORES
MOSES
MOTES
MOUES
MOVES
MULES
MUSES
MUTES
MYLES
NABES
NAMES
NAPES
NARES
NAVES
NENES
NEVES
NIDES
NIKES
NILES
NIMES
NINES
NITES
NIXES
NODES
NONES
NOSES
NOTES
NOYES
NUDES
NUKES
OAKES
OASES
OATES
OBIES
OBOES
OGEES
OGLES
OGRES
OKIES
OOZES
ORLES
OTOES
PACES
PAGES
PALES
PANES
PARES
PASES
PATES
PAVES
PEKES
PERES
PETES
PIKES
PILES
PINES
PIPES
PLIES
POKES
POLES
POMES
PONES
POPES
PORES
POSES
PRIES
PULES
PYRES
RACES
RAGES
RAKES
RARES
RASES
RATES
RAVES
RAZES
REDES
REXES
REYES
RICES
RIDES
RILES
RIMES
RISES
RITES
RIVES
ROBES
ROLES
ROPES
ROSES
ROTES
ROUES
ROVES
RUBES
RULES
RUNES
RUSES
SAFES
SAGES
SAKES
SALES
SASES
SATES
SAVES
SAXES
SELES
SERES
SEXES
SHIES
SHOES
SIDES
SIKES
SINES
SIRES
SITES
SIXES
SIZES
SKIES
SLOES
SLUES
SOKES
SOLES
SONES
SORES
SPIES
STIES
SUPES
SYCES
TAKES
TALES
TAMES
TAPES
TARES
TAXES
TELES
TETES
TIDES
TIKES
TILES
TIMES
TINES
TIRES
TOBES
TOMES
TONES
TOPES
TOTES
TOVES
TREES
TRIES
TRUES
TUBES
TULES
TUNES
TUXES
TYKES
TYNES
TYPES
TYRES
URGES
VALES
VANES
VASES
VEXES
VIBES
VICES
VINES
VISES
VOLES
VOTES
WADES
WAGES
WAKES
WALES
WANES
WARES
WAVES
WAXES
WILES
WINES
WIPES
WIRES
WIVES
XAXES
YATES
YAXES
YESES
YIKES
YIPES
YOKES
YPRES
ZAXES
ZINES
ZONES

ET•••

ETAGE
ETAPE
ETATS
ETHAN
ETHEL
ETHER
ETHIC
ETHNO
ETHOS
ETHYL
ETNAS
ETONS
ETSEQ
ETSQQ
ETUDE
ETUIS
ETVIR
ETYMA
ETZEL

E•T••

EATAT
EATEN
EATER
EATIN
EATIT
EATON
EATUP
ELTON
ENTER
ENTIA
ENTOM
ENTRE
ENTRY
ESTAB
ESTAS
ESTEE
ESTER
ESTES
ESTOP
EXTOL
EXTRA
EXTRO

E••T•

EARTH
EASTS
EDITH
EDITS
ELATE
ELATH
ELITE
ELUTE
EMITS
EMOTE
EMPTY
ENATE
ERATO
ETATS
EVITA
EXITS
EYOTS

E•••T

EATAT
EATIT
EBERT
EBOAT
ECLAT
EDICT
EDUCT
EFLAT
EGEST
EGRET
EGYPT
EIGHT
EILAT
EJECT
ELECT
ELIOT
EMMET
ENACT
EPACT
EPCOT
ERECT
ERGOT
ERNST
ERUCT
ERUPT
ESBAT
EVENT
EVERT
EVICT
EXACT
EXALT
EXERT
EXIST
EXULT

•ET••

AETAT
AETNA
BETAS
BETEL
BETHS
BETON
BETSY
BETTA
BETTE
BETTY
CETUS
DETAT
DETER
DETOO
DETRE
FETAL
FETAS
FETCH
FETED
FETES
FETID
FETOR
GETAS
GETAT
GETBY
GETGO
GETIN
GETIT
GETME
GETON
GETTO
GETTY
GETUP
HETHS
HETTY
HETUP
JETER
JETES
JETTY
KETCH
LETAT
LETBE
LETGO
LETHE
LETIN
LETON
LETTS
LETUP
METAL
METED
METER
METES
METIS
METOO
METRE
METRO
METRY
PETAL
PETER
PETES
PETIT
PETRA
PETRI
PETRO
PETTI
PETTY
RETAG
RETAP
RETAR
RETAX
RETIA
RETIE
RETOP
RETOW
RETRO
RETRY
SETAE
SETAT
SETBY
SETIN
SETON
SETTE
SETTO
SETUP
TETES
TETHS
TETON
TETRA
VETCH
WETLY
YETIS
ZETAS

•E•T•

BEATS
BEETS
BELTS
BENTS
BERTH
BESTS
BETTA
BETTE
BETTY
CELTS
CENTI
CENTO
CENTS
CERTS
CESTA
CESTI
CEUTA
DEBTS
DEITY
DELTA
DELTS
DENTE
DENTI
DENTS
DEPTH
DEPTS
DESTE
DEUTO
DEXTR
FEATS
FEETS
FELTS
FEMTO
FESTA
FESTS
GENTS
GESTE
GESTS
GETTO
GETTY
HEATH
HEATS
HECTO
HEFTS
HEFTY
HENTS
HEPTA
HERTZ
HESTS
HETTY
HEUTE
JESTS
JETTY
KEATS
KEETS
KEITH
LEDTO
LEETS
LEFTS
LEFTY
LEITH
LENTO
LENTS
LEPTA
LEPTO
LETTS
LEYTE
MEATS
MEATY
MEETS
MEHTA
MELTS
MELTY
MERTZ

MESTA
NEATH
NEATO
NEATS
NERTS
NERTZ
NESTS
NEWTS
PEATS
PEATY
PEETE
PELTS
PENTA
PENTE
PERTH
PESTO
PESTS
PETTI
PETTY
REATA
RECTI
RECTO
RENTA
RENTS
RESTS
SEATO
SEATS
SECTS
SEETO
SENTE
SEPTA
SERTA
SETTE
SETTO
SEXTS
TEETH
TENTH
TENTS
TESTA
TESTS
TESTY
TEXTS
VENTS
VERTE
VERTS
VESTA
VESTS
WEFTS
WELTS
WELTY
WESTS
YEATS
YENTA
YENTE
YENTL
ZESTS
ZESTY

•E••T
AETAT
BEAST
BEAUT
BEFIT
BEGAT
BEGET
BEGOT
BENET
BERET
BESET
BESOT
CERAT
DEALT
DEBIT
DEBUT
DEFAT
DEIST
DELFT
DEMIT
DEPOT
DERAT
DETAT
FEAST
FEINT
FEIST
GEMOT
GENET
GETAT
GETIT
HEART
HECHT
HEIDT
HEIST
HELOT
HEMET
HERAT
KEMPT
KERAT
LEANT
LEAPT
LEAST
LEGIT
LEMAT
LETAT
MEANT
MEDIT
MERIT
NEMAT
PEROT
PETIT
PEWIT
REACT
REBUT
REFIT
RELET
RELIT
REMET
REMIT
REPOT
RESET
REVET
SENAT
SETAT
TEMPT
TENET
TEVET
VEIDT
VELDT
VERST
WEEST
WENDT
YEAST
ZEIST

••ET•
ABETS
ACETO
ALETA
ANETO
ARETE
BEETS
BRETT
CHETH
CRETE
DIETS
DOETH
DUETO
DUETS
FEETS
FRETS
GRETA
GRETE
KEETS
LEETS
LIETO
MEETS
NYETS
ODETS
OVETA
OVETT
PEETE
PIETA
PIETY
POETE
POETS
RHETT
SEETO
SIETE
SKETE
SPETS
STETS
SUETS
SUETY
TEETH
THETA
TIETO
WHETS
WYETH

••E•T
ADEPT
AGENT
ALERT
ALEUT
AMENT
ANENT
ARENT
AVERT
BLEAT
BLENT
BLEST
BRENT
BREST
BRETT
CHEAT
CHERT
CHEST
CLEAT
CLEFT
CREPT
CREST
DOEST
DWELT
EBERT
EGEST
EJECT
ELECT
ERECT
EVENT
EVERT
EXERT
FLEET
GHENT
GOEST
GREAT
GREET
GUEST
GWENT
IBERT
IDEST
INEPT
INERT
KNELT
LIEUT
OVERT
OVETT
PLEAT
PREST
QUEST
RHETT
SCENT
SHEET
SKEAT
SKEET
SLEET
SLEPT
SMELT
SNERT
SPELT
SPENT
SWEAT
SWEET
SWEPT
THEFT
TREAT
TRENT
TWEET
WEEST
WHEAT
WIEST
WREST

•••ET
AGLET
AMVET
ARMET
ARRET
ASSET
ASYET
BEGET
BENET
BERET
BESET
BINET
BIZET
BLUET
BONET
CADET
CAPET
CARET
CIVET
COLET
COMET
COVET
CRUET
CULET
DUVET
EGRET
EMMET
FACET
FILET
FLEET
GENET
GODET
GREET
HEMET
INLET
INSET
ISLET
JACET
JANET
LICET
LUMET
MAMET
MANET
MONET
MOTET
NONET
NYMET
OBJET
OCTET
ONSET
OWLET
PAGET
PUGET
QUIET
RAMET
RELET
REMET
RESET
REVET
RIVET
ROGET
SAGET
SHEET
SKEET
SLEET
SWEET
TACET
TENET
TEVET
TIBET
TOLET
TVSET
TWEET
UNMET
UNSET
UPSET
VALET
ZIBET

EU•••
EUBIE
EULER
EUROS
EURUS

E•U••
EDUCE
EDUCT
ELUDE
ELUTE
ENUGU
ENURE
EQUAL
EQUIP
EQUIV
EQUUS
ERUCT
ERUPT
ETUDE
ETUIS
EXUDE
EXULT
EXURB

E••U•
EATUP
ECRUS
ENDUE
ENDUP
ENNUI
ENSUE
EOLUS
EQUUS
ESQUE
EURUS

E•••U
ELIHU
ENUGU

•EU••
CEUTA
DEUCE
DEUCY
DEUTO
FEUDS
GEUMS
HEURE
HEUTE
JEUDI
JEUNE
MEUSE
NEUME
NEURO
REUEL
REUNE
REUPS
REUSE
SEULE
SEUSS

•E•U•
BEAUS
BEAUT
BEAUX
BEGUM
BEGUN
BENUE
CETUS
DEBUG
DEBUT
DEMUR
FEDUP
FEMUR
GENUA
GENUS
GETUP
HETUP
KEYUP
LEGUP
LEHUA
LEMUR
LEPUS
LETUP
LEXUS
MECUM
MENUS
NEFUD
NEGUS
NEVUS
NEXUS
PEPUP
REBUS
REBUT
RECUR
REDUB
REDUX
REGUM
REMUS
RERUM
RERUN
REVUE
REVUP
SEBUM
SEDUM
SEGUE
SEOUL
SERUM
SETUP
SEWUP
TEEUP
VELUM
VENUE
VENUS
XERUS
ZEBUS

•E••U
AEIOU
DERSU
KEANU
NEHRU
PERDU

••EU•
ADEUX
ALEUT
ATEUP
BOEUF
COEUR
FLEUR
FREUD
ICEUP
LIEUS
LIEUT
ODEUM
OLEUM
ONEUP
PSEUD
QUEUE
RHEUM
SIEUR
SOEUR
TEEUP
TIEUP
USEUP

••E•U
CHEJU
TAEGU

•••EU
ADIEU
PAREU

EV•••
EVADE
EVANS
EVENS
EVENT
EVERS
EVERT
EVERY
EVIAN
EVICT
EVILS
EVITA
EVOKE
EVORA

E•V••
EAVED
EAVES
ELVER
ELVES
ELVIN
ELVIS
ENVOI
ENVOY
ERVIL
ERVIN
ETVIR

E••V•
ELEVE

E•••V
EQUIV

•EV••
BEVEL
BEVIN
DEVIL
DEVON
DEVRY
FEVER
KEVEL
KEVIN
LEVAR
LEVEE
LEVEL
LEVER
LEVIN
LEVIS
LEVON
NEVER
NEVES
NEVIL
NEVIN
NEVIS
NEVUS
REVEL
REVET
REVUE
REVUP
SEVEN
SEVER
TEVET
TEVYE
ZEVON

•E•V•
BELVA
DELVE
HEAVE
HEAVY
HELVE
HERVE
LEAVE
NERVE
NERVY
PEAVY
PEEVE
REEVE
SELVA
SERVE
SERVO
VERVE
WEAVE

•E••V
DERIV
NEGEV

••EV•
ALEVE
BREVE
CHEVY
ELEVE
HUEVO
PEEVE
REEVE
SIEVE
SNEVA
STEVE
TREVI

•••EV
NEGEV

EW•••
EWELL
EWERS
EWING
EWOKS

E•W••
EDWIN
ELWAY
ELWES
ERWIN

E•••W
ELBOW
ENDOW

•EW••
DEWAN
DEWAR
DEWED
DEWEY
FEWER
HEWED
HEWER
JEWEL
LEWES
LEWIS
MEWED
MEWLS
NEWEL
NEWER
NEWLY
NEWSY
NEWTS
PEWEE
PEWIT
REWAX
REWED
REWIN
REWON
SEWED
SEWER
SEWON
SEWUP

•E•W•
MEOWS

•E••W
BEDEW
BELOW
DEPEW
REMOW
RENEW
RESAW
RESEW
RETOW
SEROW

••EW•
BREWS
CHEWS
CHEWY
CLEWS
CREWS
FLEWS
LOEWE
LOEWY
PLEWS
SKEWS
SLEWS
SMEWS
SPEWS
STEWS
THEWS
THEWY
TREWS
VIEWS
VIEWY

•••EW
AGNEW
ASKEW
BEDEW
CAREW
DEPEW
NAREW
RENEW
RESEW
SCREW
SHREW
SINEW
STREW
THREW

EX•••
EXACT
EXALT
EXAMS
EXCEL
EXECS

EXERT EXILE EXIST EXITS EXONS EXPEL EXPOS EXTOL EXTRA EXTRO EXUDE EXULT EXURB EXXON

E•X••
EXXON

E••X•
EPOXY

E•••X
ESSEX

•EX••
DEXTR HEXAD HEXED HEXER HEXES HEXYL LEXAN LEXIS LEXUS NEXIS NEXUS REXES SEXES SEXTS TEXAN TEXAS TEXTS VEXED VEXER VEXES

•E•X•
BENXI DEOXY

•E••X
BEAUX FEDEX FELIX HELIX LENOX REDOX REDUX RELAX REMEX REMIX RETAX REWAX TELEX XEROX

••EX•
FLEXI PREXY

••E•X
ADEUX ICEAX

•••EX
ANNEX CODEX COMEX CULEX CUTEX ESSEX FEDEX INDEX LATEX LUREX MUREX NYNEX PUREX PYREX REMEX ROLEX SILEX TELEX TIMEX TRUEX

EY•••
EYDIE EYERS EYOTS EYRAS EYRES EYRIE EYRIR

E•Y••
EGYPT ELYSE ETYMA

E••Y•
EMLYN EMMYS ENCYC ETHYL

E•••Y
EARLY EBONY EDIFY ELEGY ELROY ELWAY EMBAY EMERY EMILY EMORY EMPTY ENEMY ENJOY ENSKY ENTRY ENVOY EPOXY ESSAY EVERY

•EY••
BEYLE FEYER FEYLY HEYSE KEYED KEYES KEYIN KEYUP LEYTE MEYER REYES

•E•Y•
BERYL DENYS HEXYL KENYA LENYA MERYL PEPYS REDYE SEEYA TEVYE

•E••Y
BEADY BEAMY BEANY BECKY BEEFY BEERY BELAY BELLY BENDY BENNY BERRY BETSY BETTY CECHY DEARY DEBBY DECAY DECOY DECRY DEIFY DEITY DELAY DENNY DEOXY DERBY DERRY DEUCY DEVRY DEWEY FEELY FELLY FENNY FERNY FERRY FEYLY GEARY GEEKY GEMMY GERMY GERRY GETBY GETTY HEADY HEALY HEAVY HEDGY HEFTY HENNY HENRY HERBY HERKY HETTY JELLY JEMMY JENNY JERKY JERRY JERZY JETTY KELLY KELPY KENNY KERRY KESEY LEADY LEAFY LEAHY LEAKY LEARY LECKY LEDGY LEERY LEFAY LEFTY LEGGY LEMAY LENNY LEPPY LEROY MEALY MEANY MEATY MEINY MELTY MERCY MERRY MESHY MESSY METRY NEDDY NEEDY NELLY NERDY NERVY NEWLY NEWSY PEARY PEATY PEAVY PECKY PEGGY PENNY PEONY PEPPY PERCY PERKY PERRY PESKY PETTY READY REDDY REDLY REEDY REEKY REFRY REIFY REKEY RELAY REPAY REPLY RETRY SEALY SEAMY SEDGY SEEDY SEELY SEEPY SEPOY SERRY SETBY TEARY TECHY TEDDY TEENY TELLY TERRY TESTY VEALY VEDAY VEERY VEINY VESEY WEARY WEBBY WEDGY WEEDY WEENY WEEPY WELBY WELTY WENDY WETLY ZESTY

••EY•
FLEYS FREYA GLEYS GREYS JOEYS MYEYE OBEYS OXEYE PREYS SEEYA THEYD TREYS WHEYS

••E•Y
APERY AVERY BEEFY BEERY CHEVY CHEWY CRECY ELEGY EMERY ENEMY EVERY FAERY FEELY FIERY GEEKY LEERY LIEBY LOEWY NEEDY PIETY POESY PREXY QUERY REEDY REEKY SEEDY SEELY SEEPY SUETY TEENY THEWY VEERY VIEWY WEEDY WEENY WEEPY

•••EY
ABBEY AGLEY AILEY ALLEY APLEY BLUEY BOGEY BUSEY CAGEY CAKEY CAREY CASEY CONEY COREY COVEY COXEY CUTEY DALEY DEWEY DICEY DOGEY DOPEY DOVEY FAHEY FOGEY FOLEY GAMEY GLUEY GODEY GOOEY HALEY HOKEY HOLEY HOMEY HONEY HOOEY HOVEY ISLEY JASEY JIVEY JOKEY KESEY KILEY LACEY LIMEY LINEY LOVEY MATEY MIKEY MONEY MOPEY MOREY MOSEY MULEY NOSEY ONKEY PALEY PINEY POKEY PUSEY REKEY RILEY ROPEY ROSEY SKYEY SOOEY TANEY TOBEY TONEY TYPEY UTLEY VESEY WALEY WANEY WILEY WINEY ZOOEY

E•Z••
ETZEL

E••Z•
ELAZI ELIZA

•EZ••
BEZEL MEZZO

•E•Z•
BENZO HERZL JERZY LEEZA MEZZO PENZA SEIZE TERZA

•E••Z
FELIZ HEINZ HEJAZ HERTZ JEREZ MERTZ NERTZ PEREZ VELEZ VENEZ

••EZ•
LEEZA

•••EZ
ALLEZ ASSEZ GOMEZ JEREZ LOPEZ PEREZ VELEZ VENEZ

FA•••
FABER FABIO FABLE FACED FACER FACES FACET FACIA FACIE FACIT FACTO FACTS FADED FADES FADOS FAERY FAGIN FAGOT FAHEY FAILS FAINT FAIRE FAIRS FAIRY FAITH FAKED FAKER FAKES FAKIR FALDO FALLA FALLS FALSE FAMED FAMES FANCY FANES FANGS FANNY FANON FANTA FARAD FARAH FARCE FARCI FARED FARER FARES FARGO FARMS FAROE FARON FAROS FARSI FASTS FATAL FATED FATES FATHA FATLY FATTY FATWA FAULT FAUNA FAUNS FAURE FAUST FAUVE FAVES FAVOR FAVRE FAWNS FAXED FAXES FAZED FAZES

F•A••
FEARS FEAST FEATS FIATS FLACK FLAGG FLAGS FLAIL FLAIR FLAKE FLAKY FLAME FLAMS FLAMY FLANK FLANS FLAPS FLARE FLASH FLASK FLATS FLATT FLAWS FLAWY FLAXY FLAYS FOALS FOAMS FOAMY FRAIL FRAIS FRAME FRANC FRANK FRANS FRANZ FRAPS FRATS FRAUD FRAYS

F••A•
FARAD FARAH FATAL FERAL FETAL FETAS FFLAT FILAR FINAL FLEAS FLOAT FLYAT FOCAL FORAY FREAK FRIAR FUGAL FULAS FURAN

F•••A
FACIA FALLA FANTA FATHA FATWA FAUNA FELLA FERIA FESTA FINCA FIONA FIRMA FLORA FOLIA FONDA FORMA FOSSA FOVEA FREDA FRENA FREYA FULDA

•FA••
AFAIK AFARS OFAGE

•F•A•
AFLAT BFLAT CFLAT DFLAT EFLAT FFLAT GFLAT OFFAL

•F••A
AFTRA

••FA•
ALFAS BYFAR DEFAT DUFAY GOFAR LEFAY LOFAT NOFAT OFFAL SOFAR SOFAS

••F•A
BUFFA

HOFFA
INFRA
JAFFA
KAFKA
NAFTA
SOFIA

•••FA
BUFFA
HAIFA
HOFFA
JAFFA
LOOFA
SOLFA
SULFA
USOFA

F•B••
FABER
FABIO
FABLE
FIBER
FIBRE
FIBRO
FUBSY

F••B•
FLUBS
FLYBY
FORBS
FROBE
FTLBS

FC•••
FCLEF

F•C••
FACED
FACER
FACES
FACET
FACIA
FACIE
FACIT
FACTO
FACTS
FICES
FICHE
FICHU
FICUS
FOCAL
FOCUS
FUCHS

F••C•
FANCY
FARCE
FARCI
FENCE
FETCH
FILCH
FINCA
FINCH
FISCS
FITCH
FLACK
FLECK
FLICK
FLICS
FLOCK
FORCE
FRICK
FROCK

F•••C
FOLIC
FRANC
FSLIC

•F••C
AFRIC

••F•C
SOFTC

F•D••
FADED
FADES
FADOS
FEDEX
FEDON
FEDUP
FIDEI
FIDEL
FIDES
FODOR
FUDDY
FUDGE

F••D•
FALDO
FEEDS
FENDS
FERDE
FEUDS
FINDS
FOLDS
FONDA
FONDS
FONDU
FOODS
FORDO
FORDS
FREDA
FRODO
FUDDY
FULDA
FUNDS
FUNDY

F•••D
FACED
FADED
FAKED
FAMED
FARAD
FARED
FATED
FAXED
FAZED
FELID
FETED
FETID
FIELD
FIEND
FIFED
FILED
FINED
FIORD
FIRED
FIXED
FJELD
FJORD
FLIED
FLOOD
FLOYD
FLUID
FOUND
FOXED
FRAUD
FREED
FREUD
FRIED
FROID
FROND
FUMED
FUSED
FUZED

••F•D
BIFID
DYFED
FIFED
NEFUD
UNFED

FE•••
FEARS
FEAST
FEATS
FEDEX
FEDON
FEDUP
FEEDS
FEELS
FEELY
FEETS
FEIGN
FEINT
FEIST
FELID
FELIS
FELIX
FELIZ
FELLA
FELLS
FELLY
FELON
FELTS
FEMME
FEMTO
FEMUR
FENCE
FENDS
FENNY
FEOFF
FERAL
FERDE
FERIA
FERMI
FERNS
FERNY
FERRI
FERRO
FERRY
FESTA
FESTS
FETAL
FETAS
FETCH
FETED
FETES
FETID
FETOR
FEUDS
FEVER
FEWER
FEYER
FEYLY

F•E••
FAERY
FEEDS
FEELS
FEELY
FEETS
FIEFS
FIELD
FIEND
FIERO
FIERY
FJELD
FLEAS
FLECK
FLEER
FLEES
FLEET
FLESH
FLEUR
FLEWS
FLEXI
FLEYS
FOEHN
FREAK
FREDA
FREED
FREER
FREES
FRENA
FREON
FRERE
FRESH
FRETS
FREUD
FREYA
FUEGO
FUELS

F••E•
FABER
FACED
FACER
FACES
FACET
FADED
FADES
FAHEY
FAKED
FAKER
FAKES
FAMED
FAMES
FANES
FARED
FARER
FARES
FATED
FATES
FAVES
FAXED
FAXES
FAZED
FAZES
FCLEF
FEDEX
FETED
FETES
FEVER
FEWER
FEYER
FIBER
FICES
FIDEI
FIDEL
FIDES
FIFED
FIFER
FIFES
FILED
FILER
FILES
FILET
FINED
FINER
FINES
FIRED
FIRER
FIRES
FIVER
FIVES
FIXED
FIXER
FIXES
FLEER
FLEES
FLEET
FLIED
FLIER
FLIES
FLOES
FLUES
FLYER
FOGEY
FOLEY
FORES
FOVEA
FOXED
FOXES
FOYER
FREED
FREER
FREES
FRIED
FRIER
FRIES
FROES
FRYER
FUMED
FUMES
FUSED
FUSEE
FUSES
FUZED
FUZEE
FYKES

F•••E
FABLE
FACIE
FAIRE
FALSE
FARCE
FAROE
FAURE
FAUVE
FAVRE
FEMME
FENCE
FERDE
FIBRE
FICHE
FILLE
FISKE
FLAKE
FLAME
FLARE
FLUKE
FLUME
FLUTE
FOOTE
FORCE
FORGE
FORTE
FOSSE
FOYLE
FRAME
FRERE
FRISE
FROBE
FROME
FROZE
FUDGE
FUGUE
FURZE
FUSEE
FUZEE

•F•E•
AFTER
EFREM
NFLER
OFFER
OFTEN

•F••E
AFIRE
AFORE
EFFIE
MFUME
OFAGE
OFUSE

••FE•
APFEL
CAFES
DEFER
DYFED
FIFED
FIFER
FIFES
GOFER
HEFEI
INFER
OFFER
ORFEO
RAFER
REFER
RIFER
SAFER
SAFES
UNFED
WAFER

••F•E
ALFIE
ALFRE
CAFFE
DAFOE
DEFOE
EFFIE
GAFFE
JAFFE
KAFUE
RIFLE

•••FE
CAFFE
CHAFE
GAFFE
GROFE
JAFFE
KNIFE
PHYFE
ROLFE
WOLFE

FF•••
FFLAT

F•F••
FIFED
FIFER
FIFES
FIFTH
FIFTY

F••F•
FEOFF
FIEFS
FLUFF

F•••F
FCLEF
FEOFF
FLUFF

•FF••
AFFIX
EFFIE
OFFAL
OFFER

•F•F•
AFOFL

••FF•
BIFFS
BIFFY
BOFFO
BOFFS
BUFFA
BUFFI
BUFFO
BUFFS
BUFFY
CAFFE
CUFFS
DAFFS
DAFFY
DOFFS
DUFFS
DUFFY
GAFFE
GAFFS
HOFFA
HUFFS
HUFFY
JAFFA
JAFFE
JIFFY
LUFFS
MIFFS
MIFFY
MOFFO
MUFFS
PUFFS
PUFFY
RAFFI
RIFFI
RIFFS
RUFFS
TAFFY
TIFFS
TOFFS
TOFFY

•••FF
ACUFF
BANFF
BLUFF
CHAFF
CHUFF
CLIFF
FEOFF
FLUFF
GOOFF
GRUFF
HANFF
ONOFF
QUAFF
SCOFF
SCUFF
SKIFF
SNIFF
SNUFF
SPIFF
STAFF
STIFF
STUFF
WHIFF
WOLFF

F•G••
FAGIN
FAGOT
FIGHT
FOGEY
FOGGY
FOGIN
FOGUP
FUGAL
FUGGY
FUGIT
FUGUE
FUGUS

F••G•
FANGS
FARGO
FEIGN
FLAGG
FLAGS
FLOGS
FOGGY
FORGE
FORGO
FRIGG
FROGS
FUDGE
FUEGO
FUGGY
FUNGI
FUNGO

F•••G
FLAGG
FLING
FLUNG
FRIGG

•F•G•
OFAGE

••F•G
BEFOG
DEFOG
SOFTG

F•H••
FAHEY
FOHNS

F••H•
FATHA
FICHE
FICHU
FIGHT
FISHY
FOEHN
FUCHS

F•••H
FAITH
FARAH
FETCH
FIFTH
FILCH
FILTH
FINCH
FIRTH
FITCH
FLASH
FLESH
FLUSH
FORTH
FOURH
FRESH
FROSH
FROTH
FURTH

••F•H
FIFTH

FI•••
FIATS
FIBER
FIBRE
FIBRO
FICES
FICHE
FICHU
FICUS
FIDEI
FIDEL
FIDES
FIEFS
FIELD
FIEND
FIERO
FIERY
FIFED
FIFER
FIFES
FIFTH
FIFTY
FIGHT
FILAR
FILCH
FILED
FILER
FILES
FILET
FILLE
FILLS
FILLY
FILMS
FILMY
FILTH
FILUM
FINAL
FINCA
FINCH
FINDS
FINED
FINER
FINES
FINIS
FINKS
FINNO
FINNS
FINNY
FIONA
FIORD
FIRED
FIRER
FIRES
FIRMA
FIRMS
FIRNS
FIRPO
FIRRY
FIRST
FIRTH
FISCS
FISHY
FISKE
FISTS
FITCH
FITIN
FITLY
FIVER
FIVES

FIXED
FIXER
FIXES
FIXIT
FIXUP
FIZZY

F•I••
FAILS
FAINT
FAIRE
FAIRS
FAIRY
FAITH
FEIGN
FEINT
FEIST
FLICK
FLICS
FLIED
FLIER
FLIES
FLING
FLINT
FLIPS
FLIRT
FLITS
FOILS
FOINS
FOIST
FRIAR
FRICK
FRIED
FRIER
FRIES
FRIGG
FRILL
FRIML
FRISE
FRISK
FRITO
FRITS
FRITZ
FRIZZ

F••I•
FABIO
FACIA
FACIE
FACIT
FAGIN
FAKIR
FELID
FELIS
FELIX
FELIZ
FERIA
FETID
FINIS
FITIN
FIXIT
FLAIL
FLAIR
FLUID
FLYIN
FOGIN
FOLIA
FOLIC
FOLIO
FRAIL
FRAIS
FROID
FRUIT
FSLIC
FUGIT
FUSIL

F•••I
FARCI
FARSI
FERMI
FERRI
FIDEI
FLEXI
FORLI
FUNGI

•FI••
AFIRE
EFIKS

•F•I•
AFAIK
AFFIX
AFRIC
AFRIT
EFFIE

••FI•
ADFIN
AFFIX
ALFIE
BEFIT
BIFID
EFFIE
ELFIN
ENFIN
HAFIZ
HIFIS
INFIN
INFIX
KAFIR
KEFIR
REFIT
SOFIA
SUFIS
UNFIT
UNFIX

••F•I
BUFFI
HEFEI
MUFTI
RAFFI
RIFFI

•••FI
BUFFI
RAFFI
RIFFI
SCIFI

FJ•••
FJELD
FJORD

•F•J•
JFKJR

F•K••
FAKED
FAKER
FAKES
FAKIR
FYKES

F••K•
FINKS
FISKE
FLAKE
FLAKY
FLUKE
FLUKY
FOLKS
FOLKY
FORKS
FORKY
FUNKS
FUNKY

F•••K
FLACK
FLANK
FLASK
FLECK
FLICK
FLOCK
FLUNK
FRANK
FREAK
FRICK
FRISK
FROCK

•FK••
JFKJR

•F•K•
EFIKS

•F••K
AFAIK

••FK•
KAFKA

FL•••
FLACK
FLAGG
FLAGS
FLAIL
FLAIR
FLAKE
FLAKY
FLAME
FLAMS
FLAMY
FLANK
FLANS
FLAPS
FLARE
FLASH
FLASK
FLATS
FLATT
FLAWS
FLAWY
FLAXY
FLAYS
FLEAS
FLECK
FLEER
FLEES
FLEET
FLESH
FLEUR
FLEWS
FLEXI
FLEYS
FLICK
FLICS
FLIED
FLIER
FLIES
FLING
FLINT
FLIPS
FLIRT
FLITS
FLOAT
FLOCK
FLOES
FLOGS
FLOOD
FLOOR
FLOPS
FLORA
FLORY
FLOSS
FLOUR
FLOUT
FLOWN
FLOWS
FLOYD
FLUBS
FLUES
FLUFF
FLUID
FLUKE
FLUKY
FLUME
FLUNG
FLUNK
FLUOR
FLUSH
FLUTE
FLUTY
FLYAT
FLYBY
FLYER
FLYIN
FLYNN

F•L••
FALDO
FALLA
FALLS
FALSE
FCLEF
FELID
FELIS
FELIX
FELIZ
FELLA
FELLS
FELLY
FELON
FELTS
FFLAT
FILAR
FILCH
FILED
FILER
FILES
FILET
FILLE
FILLS
FILLY
FILMS
FILMY
FILTH
FILUM
FOLDS
FOLEY
FOLIA
FOLIC
FOLIO
FOLKS
FOLKY
FOLLY
FSLIC
FTLBS
FULAS
FULDA
FULLY

F••L•
FABLE
FAILS
FALLA
FALLS
FATLY
FAULT
FEELS
FEELY
FELLA
FELLS
FELLY
FEYLY
FIELD
FILLE
FILLS
FILLY
FITLY
FJELD
FOALS
FOILS
FOLLY
FOOLS
FORLI
FOULS
FOWLS
FOYLE
FRILL
FUELS
FULLY
FURLS

F•••L
FATAL
FERAL
FETAL
FIDEL
FINAL
FLAIL
FOCAL
FRAIL
FRILL
FRIML
FUGAL
FUSIL

•FL••
AFLAT
BFLAT
CFLAT
DFLAT
EFLAT
FFLAT
GFLAT
NFLER

•F••L
AFOFL
AFOUL
OFFAL

••FL•
MCFLY
NOFLY
RIFLE

••F•L
APFEL
AWFUL
OFFAL

•••FL
AFOFL

F•M••
FAMED
FAMES
FEMME
FEMTO
FEMUR
FUMED
FUMES

F••M•
FARMS
FEMME
FERMI
FILMS
FILMY
FIRMA
FIRMS
FLAME
FLAMS
FLAMY
FLUME
FOAMS
FOAMY
FORMA
FORMS
FRAME
FRIML
FROME
FROMM
FRUMP

F•••M
FILUM
FORUM
FROMM

•F•M•
MFUME

•F••M
EFREM

F•N••
FANCY
FANES
FANGS
FANNY
FANON
FANTA
FENCE
FENDS
FENNY
FINAL
FINCA
FINCH
FINDS
FINED
FINER
FINES
FINIS
FINKS
FINNO
FINNS
FINNY
FONDA
FONDS
FONDU
FONTS
FUNDS
FUNDY
FUNGI
FUNGO
FUNKS
FUNKY
FUNNY

F••N•
FAINT
FANNY
FAUNA
FAUNS
FAWNS
FEINT
FENNY
FERNS
FERNY
FIEND
FINNO
FINNS
FINNY
FIONA
FIRNS
FLANK
FLANS
FLING
FLINT
FLUNG
FLUNK
FLYNN
FOHNS
FOINS
FOUND
FOUNT
FRANC
FRANK
FRANS
FRANZ
FRENA
FROND
FRONT
FUNNY

F•••N
FAGIN
FANON
FARON
FEDON
FEIGN
FELON
FITIN
FLOWN
FLYIN
FLYNN
FOEHN
FOGIN
FREON
FROWN
FURAN
FUTON

•FN••
IFNOT

•F••N
AFTON
OFTEN

••F•N
ADFIN
ELFIN
ENFIN
HAFUN
INFIN
INFUN

FO•••
FOALS
FOAMS
FOAMY
FOCAL
FOCUS
FODOR
FOEHN
FOGEY
FOGGY
FOGIN
FOGUP
FOHNS
FOILS
FOINS
FOIST
FOLDS
FOLEY
FOLIA
FOLIC
FOLIO
FOLKS
FOLKY
FOLLY
FONDA
FONDS
FONDU
FONTS
FOODS
FOOLS
FOOTE
FOOTS
FORAY
FORBS
FORCE
FORDO
FORDS
FORES
FORGE
FORGO
FORKS
FORKY
FORLI
FORMA
FORMS
FORTE
FORTH
FORTS
FORTY
FORUM
FOSSA
FOSSE
FOULS
FOUND
FOUNT
FOURH
FOURS
FOUTS
FOVEA
FOWLS
FOXED
FOXES
FOXTV
FOYER
FOYLE

F•O••
FEOFF
FIONA
FIORD
FJORD
FLOAT
FLOCK
FLOES
FLOGS
FLOOD
FLOOR
FLOPS
FLORA
FLORY
FLOSS
FLOUR
FLOUT
FLOWN
FLOWS
FLOYD
FOODS
FOOLS
FOOTE
FOOTS
FROBE
FROCK
FRODO
FROES
FROGS
FROID
FROME
FROMM
FROND
FRONT
FROSH
FROST
FROTH
FROWN
FROWS
FROZE

F••O•
FADOS
FAGOT
FANON
FAROE
FARON
FAROS
FAVOR
FEDON
FELON
FETOR
FLOOD
FLOOR
FLUOR
FODOR
FREON
FSTOP
FUROR
FUROS
FUTON

F•••O
FABIO
FACTO
FALDO
FARGO
FEMTO
FERRO
FIBRO
FIERO
FINNO
FIRPO
FOLIO
FORDO
FORGO
FRITO
FRODO
FUEGO
FUNGO

•FO••
AFOFL
AFOOT
AFORE
AFOUL

•F•O•
AFOOT
AFROS
AFTON
IFNOT

••FO•
BEFOG
DAFOE
DEFOE
DEFOG
GOFOR

••F•O
BOFFO
BUFFO
MOFFO
ORFEO

•••FO
BOFFO
BUFFO
MOFFO

F••P•
FIRPO
FLAPS
FLIPS
FLOPS
FRAPS

F•••P
FEDUP
FIXUP
FOGUP
FRUMP
FSTOP

FR•••
FRAIL
FRAIS
FRAME
FRANC
FRANK
FRANS
FRANZ
FRAPS
FRATS
FRAUD
FRAYS
FREAK
FREDA
FREED
FREER
FREES
FRENA
FREON
FRERE
FRESH
FRETS
FREUD
FREYA
FRIAR
FRICK
FRIED
FRIER
FRIES
FRIGG
FRILL
FRIML
FRISE
FRISK
FRITO
FRITS
FRITZ
FRIZZ
FROBE
FROCK
FRODO
FROES
FROGS
FROID
FROME
FROMM
FROND
FRONT
FROSH
FROST
FROTH
FROWN
FROWS
FROZE
FRUIT
FRUMP
FRYER

F•R••
FARAD
FARAH
FARCE
FARCI
FARED
FARER
FARES
FARGO
FARMS
FAROE
FARON
FAROS
FARSI
FERAL
FERDE
FERIA
FERMI
FERNS
FERNY
FERRI
FERRO
FERRY
FIRED
FIRER
FIRES
FIRMA
FIRMS
FIRNS
FIRPO
FIRRY
FIRST
FIRTH
FORAY
FORBS
FORCE
FORDO
FORDS
FORES
FORGE
FORGO
FORKS
FORKY
FORLI
FORMA
FORMS
FORTE
FORTH
FORTS
FORTY
FORUM
FURAN
FURLS
FUROR
FUROS
FURRY
FURTH
FURZE

F••R•
FAERY
FAIRE
FAIRS
FAIRY
FAURE
FAVRE
FEARS
FERRI
FERRO
FERRY
FIBRE
FIBRO
FIERO
FIERY
FIORD
FIRRY
FJORD
FLARE
FLIRT
FLORA
FLORY
FOURH
FOURS
FRERE
FURRY

F•••R
FABER
FACER
FAKER
FAKIR
FARER
FAVOR
FEMUR
FETOR
FEVER
FEWER
FEYER
FIBER
FIFER
FILAR
FILER
FINER
FIRER
FIVER
FIXER
FLAIR
FLEER
FLEUR
FLIER
FLOOR
FLOUR
FLUOR
FLYER
FODOR
FOYER
FREER
FRIAR
FRIER
FRYER
FUROR

•FR••
AFRIC
AFRIT
AFROS
EFREM

•F•R•
AFARS
AFIRE
AFORE
AFTRA

•F••R
AFTER
JFKJR
NFLER
OFFER

••FR•
ALFRE
INFRA
REFRY

••F•R
BYFAR
DEFER
FIFER
GOFAR
GOFER
GOFOR
INFER
KAFIR
KEFIR
OFFER
RAFER
REFER
RIFER
RSFSR
SAFER
SOFAR
WAFER

FS•••
FSLIC
FSTOP

F•S••
FASTS
FESTA
FESTS
FISCS
FISHY
FISKE
FISTS
FOSSA
FOSSE
FUSED
FUSEE
FUSES
FUSIL
FUSSY
FUSTY

F••S•
FALSE
FARSI
FAUST
FEAST
FEIST
FIRST
FLASH
FLASK
FLESH
FLOSS
FLUSH
FOIST
FOSSA
FOSSE
FRESH
FRISE
FRISK
FROSH
FROST
FUBSY
FUSSY

F•••S
FACES
FACTS
FADES
FADOS
FAILS
FAIRS
FAKES
FALLS
FAMES
FANES
FANGS
FARES
FARMS
FAROS
FASTS
FATES
FAUNS
FAVES
FAWNS
FAXES
FAZES
FEARS
FEATS
FEEDS
FEELS
FEETS
FELIS
FELLS
FELTS
FENDS
FERNS
FESTS
FETAS
FETES
FEUDS
FIATS
FICES
FICUS
FIDES
FIEFS
FIFES
FILES
FILLS
FILMS
FINDS
FINES
FINIS
FINKS
FINNS
FIRES
FIRMS
FIRNS
FISCS
FISTS
FIVES
FIXES
FLAGS
FLAMS
FLANS
FLAPS
FLATS
FLAWS
FLAYS
FLEAS
FLEES
FLEWS
FLEYS
FLICS
FLIES
FLIPS
FLITS
FLOES
FLOGS
FLOPS
FLOSS
FLOWS
FLUBS
FLUES
FOALS
FOAMS
FOCUS
FOHNS
FOILS
FOINS
FOLDS
FOLKS
FONDS
FONTS
FOODS
FOOLS
FOOTS
FORBS
FORDS
FORES
FORKS
FORMS
FORTS
FOULS
FOURS
FOUTS
FOWLS
FOXES
FRAIS
FRANS
FRAPS
FRATS
FRAYS
FREES
FRETS
FRIES
FRITS
FROES
FROGS
FROWS
FTLBS
FUCHS
FUELS
FUGUS
FULAS
FUMES
FUNDS
FUNKS
FURLS
FUROS
FUSES
FYKES

•F•S•
OFUSE

•F••S
AFARS
AFROS
EFIKS

••FS•
RSFSR

••F•S
ALFAS
BIFFS
BOFFS
BUFFS
CAFES
CUFFS
DAFFS
DOFFS
DUFFS
FIFES
GAFFS
GIFTS
HAFTS
HEFTS
HIFIS
HUFFS
LEFTS
LIFTS
LOFTS
LUFFS
MIFFS
MUFFS
PUFFS
RAFTS
RIFFS
RIFTS
RUFFS
RUFUS
SAFES
SIFTS
SOFAS
SUFIS
TIFFS
TOFFS
TOFTS
TUFTS
WAFTS
WEFTS

•••FS
ALEFS
ALIFS
BEEFS
BIFFS
BOFFS
BUFFS
CHEFS
CLEFS
COIFS
CUFFS
DAFFS
DOFFS
DUFFS
FIEFS
GAFFS
GOLFS
GOOFS
GULFS
HOOFS
HUFFS
LEAFS
LOAFS
LUFFS
MIFFS
MUFFS
POUFS
PROFS
PUFFS
REEFS
RIFFS
ROOFS
RUFFS
SERFS
SURFS
TIFFS
TOFFS
TURFS
WAAFS
WAIFS
WOOFS
WRAFS
ZARFS

FT•••
FTLBS

F•T••
FATAL
FATED
FATES
FATHA
FATLY
FATTY
FATWA
FETAL
FETAS
FETCH
FETED
FETES
FETID
FETOR
FITCH
FITIN
FITLY
FSTOP
FUTON

F••T•
FACTO
FACTS
FAITH
FANTA
FASTS
FATTY
FEATS
FEETS
FELTS
FEMTO
FESTA
FESTS
FIATS
FIFTH
FIFTY
FILTH
FIRTH
FISTS
FLATS
FLATT
FLITS
FLUTE
FLUTY
FONTS
FOOTE
FOOTS
FORTE
FORTH
FORTS
FORTY
FOUTS
FOXTV
FRATS
FRETS
FRITO
FRITS
FRITZ
FROTH
FURTH
FUSTY

F•••T
FACET
FACIT
FAGOT
FAINT
FAULT
FAUST
FEAST
FEINT
FEIST
FFLAT
FIGHT
FILET
FIRST
FIXIT
FLATT
FLEET
FLINT
FLIRT
FLOAT
FLOUT
FLYAT
FOIST
FOUNT
FRONT
FROST
FRUIT
FUGIT

•FT••
AFTER
AFTON
AFTRA
OFTEN

•F••T
AFLAT
AFOOT
AFRIT
BFLAT
CFLAT
DFLAT
EFLAT
FFLAT
GFLAT
IFNOT

••FT•
FIFTH
FIFTY
GIFTS
HAFTS
HEFTS
HEFTY
LEFTS
LEFTY
LIFTS
LOFTS
LOFTY
MUFTI
NAFTA
NIFTY
RAFTS
RIFTS
SIFTS
SOFTC
SOFTG
SOFTY
TOFTS
TUFTS
TUFTY
WAFTS
WEFTS

••F•T
BEFIT
DEFAT
LOFAT
NOFAT
REFIT
UNFIT

•••FT
ABAFT
ALOFT
CLEFT
CLIFT
CRAFT
CROFT
DELFT
DRAFT
DRIFT
GRAFT
GRIFT
KRAFT
SHAFT
SHIFT
SWIFT
THEFT

FU•••
FUBSY
FUCHS
FUDDY
FUDGE
FUEGO
FUELS
FUGAL
FUGGY
FUGIT
FUGUE
FUGUS

FULAS
FULDA
FULLY
FUMED
FUMES
FUNDS
FUNDY
FUNGI
FUNGO
FUNKS
FUNKY
FUNNY
FURAN
FURLS
FUROR
FUROS
FURRY
FURTH
FURZE
FUSED
FUSEE
FUSES
FUSIL
FUSSY
FUSTY
FUTON
FUZED
FUZEE
FUZZY

F•U••
FAULT
FAUNA
FAUNS
FAURE
FAUST
FAUVE
FEUDS
FLUBS
FLUES
FLUFF
FLUID
FLUKE
FLUKY
FLUME
FLUNG
FLUNK
FLUOR
FLUSH
FLUTE
FLUTY
FOULS
FOUND
FOUNT
FOURH
FOURS
FOUTS
FRUIT
FRUMP

F••U•
FEDUP
FEMUR
FICUS
FILUM
FIXUP
FLEUR
FLOUR
FLOUT
FOCUS
FOGUP
FORUM
FRAUD
FREUD
FUGUE
FUGUS

F•••U
FICHU
FONDU

•FU••
MFUME
OFUSE

•F•U•
AFOUL

••FU•
AWFUL
HAFUN
INFUN
KAFUE
NEFUD
RUFUS

•••FU
CORFU
KHUFU
SNAFU

F•V••
FAVES
FAVOR
FAVRE
FEVER
FIVER
FIVES
FOVEA

F••V•
FAUVE

F•••V
FOXTV

F•W••
FAWNS
FEWER
FOWLS

F••W•
FATWA
FLAWS
FLAWY
FLEWS
FLOWN
FLOWS
FROWN
FROWS

F•X••
FAXED
FAXES
FIXED
FIXER
FIXES
FIXIT
FIXUP
FOXED
FOXES
FOXTV

F••X•
FLAXY
FLEXI

F•••X
FEDEX
FELIX

•F••X
AFFIX

••F•X
AFFIX
INFIX
UNFIX

FY•••
FYKES

F•Y••
FEYER
FEYLY
FLYAT
FLYBY
FLYER
FLYIN
FLYNN
FOYER
FOYLE
FRYER

F••Y•
FLAYS
FLEYS
FLOYD
FRAYS
FREYA

F•••Y
FAERY
FAHEY
FAIRY
FANCY
FANNY
FATLY
FATTY
FEELY
FELLY
FENNY
FERNY
FERRY
FEYLY
FIERY
FIFTY
FILLY
FILMY
FINNY
FIRRY
FISHY
FITLY
FIZZY
FLAKY
FLAMY
FLAWY
FLAXY
FLORY
FLUKY
FLUTY
FLYBY
FOAMY
FOGEY
FOGGY
FOLEY
FOLKY
FOLLY
FORAY
FORKY
FORTY
FUBSY
FUDDY
FUGGY
FULLY
FUNDY
FUNKY
FUNNY
FURRY
FUSSY
FUSTY
FUZZY

••F•Y
BIFFY
BUFFY
DAFFY
DUFAY
DUFFY
FIFTY
HEFTY
HUFFY
JIFFY
LEFAY
LEFTY
LOFTY
MCFLY
MIFFY
NIFTY
NOFLY
PUFFY
REFRY
SOFTY
TAFFY
TOFFY
TUFTY

•••FY
BEEFY
BIFFY
BUFFY
COMFY
DAFFY
DEIFY
DUFFY
EDIFY
GOOFY
HUFFY
JIFFY
LEAFY
MIFFY
PUFFY
REIFY
SURFY
TAFFY
TOFFY
TURFY
UNIFY

F•Z••
FAZED
FAZES
FIZZY
FUZED
FUZEE
FUZZY

F••Z•
FIZZY
FRIZZ
FROZE
FURZE
FUZZY

F•••Z
FELIZ
FRANZ
FRITZ
FRIZZ

••F•Z
HAFIZ

GA•••
GABBY
GABLE
GABON
GABOR
GAELS
GAFFE
GAFFS
GAGED
GAGES
GAILY
GAINS
GAITS
GAIUS
GALAH
GALAS
GALAX
GALBA
GALEA
GALEN
GALES
GALLI
GALLO
GALLS
GALOP
GAMAL
GAMAY
GAMBA
GAMED
GAMER
GAMES
GAMEY
GAMIN
GAMMA
GAMMY
GAMOW
GAMPS
GAMUT
GANDY
GANEF
GANGS
GAOLS
GAPED
GAPER
GAPES
GARBO
GARBS
GARDA
GARDE
GARNI
GAROU
GARRY
GARTH
GASES
GASPE
GASPS
GASSY
GASTR
GASUP
GATED
GATES
GATOR
GATOS
GATUN
GAUDS
GAUDY
GAUGE
GAULS
GAUMS
GAUNT
GAURS
GAUSS
GAUZE
GAUZY
GAVEL
GAVIN
GAVOT
GAWKS
GAWKY
GAWPS
GAYAL
GAYER
GAYLE
GAYLY
GAZED
GAZER
GAZES

G•A••
GEARS
GEARY
GHAIN
GHALI
GHANA
GHATS
GHAZI
GIANT
GLACE
GLADE
GLADS
GLAIR
GLAND
GLARE
GLARY
GLASS
GLAXO
GLAZE
GMATS
GNARL
GNARS
GNASH
GNATS
GNAWS
GOADS
GOALS
GOAPE
GOATS
GRABS
GRACE
GRADE
GRADS
GRADY
GRAFT
GRAIG
GRAIL
GRAIN
GRAMA
GRAMM
GRAMP
GRAMS
GRAND
GRANI
GRANT
GRAPE
GRAPH
GRAPY
GRASP
GRASS
GRATA
GRATE
GRAVE
GRAVY
GRAYS
GRAZE
GUACO
GUARD
GUARS
GUAVA

G••A•
GALAH
GALAS
GALAX
GAMAL
GAMAY
GAYAL
GERAH
GETAS
GETAT
GFLAT
GLEAM
GLEAN
GLIAL
GLOAM
GLOAT
GOBAD
GOFAR
GOLAN
GORAL
GOTAT
GREAT
GROAN
GROAT
GULAG
GULAR
GYRAL

G•••A
GALBA
GALEA
GAMBA
GAMMA
GARDA
GEENA
GEMMA
GENOA
GENUA
GHANA
GILDA
GINZA
GOLDA
GONNA
GOTHA
GOTTA
GOUDA
GRAMA
GRATA
GRETA
GROZA
GUAVA
GUNGA
GUTTA

•GA••
AGAIN
AGALS
AGAMA
AGANA
AGAPE
AGARN
AGARS
AGASP
AGATE
AGAVE
AGAZE
EGADI
EGADS
NGAIO
NGAMI

•G•A•
AGHAS
EGGAR
OGHAM

•G••A
AGAMA
AGANA
AGENA
AGITA
AGORA

••GA•
ALGAE
ALGAL
AVGAS
BEGAN
BEGAT
CIGAR
CUGAT
DEGAS
DUGAN
EAGAN
EDGAR
EGGAR
ELGAR
FUGAL
HAGAR
HOGAN
JUGAL
LAGAN
LEGAL
LOGAN
MEGAN
NUGAE
ORGAN
PAGAN
RAGAS
REGAL
REGAN
RUGAE
SAGAL
SAGAN
SAGAS
SEGAL
SEGAR
SUGAR
TOGAE
TOGAS
VEGAN
VEGAS
WIGAN
YOGAS
YUGAS

••G•A
DOGMA
LOGIA
MAGDA
MAGMA
MAGNA
REGIA
SIGMA

•••GA
AMIGA
BRAGA
CONGA
GUNGA
HELGA
KANGA
KIOGA
KYOGA
LONGA
OMEGA
ONEGA
PANGA
SAIGA
TAIGA
TONGA
USCGA
VIRGA
VOLGA

G•B••
GABBY
GABLE
GABON
GABOR
GIBBS
GIBED
GIBER
GIBES
GOBAD
GOBEL
GYBED
GYBES

G••B•
GABBY
GALBA
GAMBA
GARBO
GARBS
GETBY
GIBBS
GLEBE
GLOBE
GLOBS
GOTBY
GRABS
GREBE
GRUBS
GUMBO
GUMBY

••GB•
DIGBY
RIGBY
RUGBY

GC•••
GCLEF

G•C••
GECKO
GUCCI

G••C•
GLACE
GLICK
GLUCK
GLUCO
GLYCO
GRACE
GRECO
GUACO
GUCCI
GULCH

G•••C
GENIC

•G••C
AGRIC
UGRIC

••G•C
HIGHC
LOGIC
MAGIC
YOGIC

G•D••
GIDDY
GODEL
GODET
GODEY
GODLY
GODOT

G••D•
GANDY
GARDA
GARDE
GAUDS
GAUDY
GEODE
GIDDY
GILDA

GILDS
GIRDS
GLADE
GLADS
GLEDE
GLIDE
GOADS
GOLDA
GOLDE
GOLDS
GONDI
GONDS
GOODS
GOODY
GORDO
GORDY
GOUDA
GOUDY
GOWDY
GRADE
GRADS
GRADY
GRIDS
GRODY
GUIDE
GUIDO
GURDY

G•••D
GAGED
GAMED
GAPED
GATED
GAZED
GELID
GEOID
GIBED
GLAND
GLUED
GOBAD
GORED
GOULD
GOURD
GRAND
GREED
GRIND
GUARD
GUILD
GUYED
GYBED
GYVED

•GD••
OGDEN

•G•D•
EGADI
EGADS

•G••D
EGGED
OGLED

••GD•
MAGDA

••G•D
ALGID
CAGED
EDGED
EGGED
GAGED
OHGOD
PAGED
RAGED
RIGID
URGED
WAGED

GE•••
GEARS
GEARY
GECKO
GEEKS
GEEKY
GEENA
GEESE
GELEE
GELID
GEMMA
GEMMY
GEMOT
GENES
GENET
GENIC
GENIE
GENII
GENOA
GENRE
GENRO
GENTS
GENUA
GENUS
GEODE
GEOID
GEORG
GERAH
GERMS
GERMY
GERRY
GESSO
GESTE
GESTS
GETAS
GETAT
GETBY
GETGO
GETIN
GETIT
GETME
GETON
GETTO
GETTY
GETUP
GEUMS

G•E••
GAELS
GEEKS
GEEKY
GEENA
GEESE
GHEES
GHENT
GLEAM
GLEAN
GLEBE
GLEDE
GLEES
GLENN
GLENS
GLESS
GLEYS
GOERS
GOEST
GREAT
GREBE
GRECO
GREED
GREEK
GREEN
GREER
GREES
GREET
GREGG
GRETA
GRETE
GREYS
GUESS
GUEST
GWENN
GWENT

G••E•
GAGED
GAGES
GALEA
GALEN
GALES
GAMED
GAMER
GAMES
GAMEY
GANEF
GAPED
GAPER
GAPES
GASES
GATED
GATES
GAVEL
GAYER
GAZED
GAZER
GAZES
GCLEF
GELEE
GENES
GENET
GHEES
GIBED
GIBER
GIBES
GILES
GIMEL
GIVEN
GIVER
GIVES
GLEES
GLUED
GLUER
GLUES
GLUEY
GOBEL
GODEL
GODET
GODEY
GOFER
GOLEM
GOMEL
GOMER
GOMEZ
GONER
GOOEY
GORED
GOREN
GORES
GOSEE
GOWER
GREED
GREEK
GREEN
GREER
GREES
GREET
GRIEF
GRIEG
GRIER
GRUEL
GULES
GUTEN
GUYED
GYBED
GYBES
GYRES
GYVED
GYVES

G•••E
GABLE
GAFFE
GARDE
GASPE
GAUGE
GAUZE
GAYLE
GEESE
GELEE
GENIE
GENRE
GEODE
GESTE
GETME
GIGUE
GIJOE
GIMME
GLACE
GLADE
GLARE
GLAZE
GLEBE
GLEDE
GLIDE
GLOBE
GLOVE
GLOZE
GNOME
GOAPE
GOLDE
GOOSE
GORGE
GORME
GORSE
GOSEE
GOSSE
GOUGE
GRACE
GRADE
GRAPE
GRATE
GRAVE
GRAZE
GREBE
GRETE
GRIME
GRIPE
GROFE
GROPE
GROVE
GUIDE
GUILE
GUISE

•GE••
AGENA
AGENT
AGERS
EGEST
OGEES

•G•E•
AGLET
AGLEY
AGNES
AGNEW
AGREE
AGUES
EGGED
EGRET
IGNES
NGWEE
OGDEN
OGEES
OGLED
OGLER
OGLES
OGRES

•G••E
AGAPE
AGATE
AGAVE
AGAZE
AGGIE
AGILE
AGREE
NGWEE
OGIVE

••GE•
ALGER
ANGEL
ANGER
ANGES
AUGER
BAGEL
BEGET
BOGEY
CAGED
CAGER
CAGES
CAGEY
DOGES
DOGEY
EAGER
EDGED
EDGER
EDGES
EGGED
EIGEN
ENGEL
FOGEY
GAGED
GAGES
HAGEN
HEGEL
HUGER
INGER
KUGEL
LAGER
LEGER
LIGER
LOGES
LTGEN
LUGER
LUGES
MAGEE
MAGES
MCGEE
NAGEL
NEGEV
NIGEL
NIGER
PAGED
PAGER
PAGES
PAGET
PUGET
RAGED
RAGES
RIGEL
ROGER
ROGET
SAGER
SAGES
SAGET
SEGER
TIGER
UNGER
URGED
URGER
URGES
WAGED
WAGER
WAGES

••G•E
AGGIE
ALGAE
ANGIE
ANGLE
ARGUE
BOGIE
BOGLE
BUGLE
DOGIE
EAGLE
EAGRE
FUGUE
GIGUE
HAGUE
INGLE
LOGUE
MAGEE
MCGEE
NUGAE
ROGUE
RUGAE
SEGUE
SIGNE
TOGAE
VAGUE
VOGUE

•••GE
ADAGE
ADIGE
AINGE
BADGE
BARGE
BEIGE
BILGE
BINGE
BLIGE
BORGE
BUDGE
BULGE
CADGE
CONGE
DINGE
DIRGE
DODGE
ETAGE
FORGE
FUDGE
GAUGE
GORGE
GOUGE
HEDGE
HENGE
HINGE
IMAGE
JORGE
JUDGE
KEDGE
KLUGE
LANGE
LARGE
LEDGE
LIEGE
LODGE
LONGE
LUNGE
MADGE
MARGE
MERGE
MIDGE
NEIGE
NORGE
NUDGE
OFAGE
OSAGE
PAIGE
PHAGE
PLAGE
PURGE
RANGE
RIDGE
ROUGE
RUDGE
SARGE
SEDGE
SERGE
SIEGE
SINGE
STAGE
SURGE
SWAGE
SYNGE
TARGE
TINGE
USAGE
VERGE
WEDGE
WODGE

GF•••
GFLAT

G•F••
GAFFE
GAFFS
GIFTS
GOFAR
GOFER
GOFOR

G••F•
GAFFE
GAFFS
GOLFS
GOOFF
GOOFS
GOOFY
GRAFT
GRIFT
GROFE
GRUFF
GULFS

G•••F
GANEF
GCLEF
GOOFF
GRIEF
GRUFF

G•G••
GAGED
GAGES
GIGOT
GIGUE
GOGOL
GOGOS

G••G•
GANGS
GAUGE
GETGO
GITGO
GLOGG
GLUGS
GOLGI
GONGS
GORGE
GOUGE
GREGG
GRIGS
GROGS
GUNGA

G•••G
GEORG
GLOGG
GOING
GRAIG
GREGG
GRIEG
GULAG

•GG••
AGGIE
AGGRO
EGGAR
EGGED
EGGON

•G•G•
AGOGO

•G••G
AGING

••GG•
BAGGY
BIGGY
BOGGS
BOGGY
BUGGY
DOGGO
DOGGY
FOGGY
FUGGY
HOGGS
JAGGY
LEGGS
LEGGY
MOGGY
MUGGS
MUGGY
NAGGY
PEGGY
PIGGY
PUGGY
RIGGS
SAGGY
SOGGY
VUGGY
WIGGY
YEGGS
ZIGGY

••G•G
MAGOG

•••GG
BRAGG
FLAGG
FRIGG
GLOGG
GREGG
STAGG

GH•••
GHAIN
GHALI
GHANA
GHATS
GHAZI
GHEES
GHENT
GHOST
GHOUL

G••H•
GOTHA
GOTHS
GUSHY

G•••H
GALAH
GARTH
GERAH
GIRTH
GLYPH
GNASH
GRAPH
GULCH

•GH••
AGHAS
OGHAM

••GH•
AUGHT
BIGHT
EIGHT
FIGHT
HIGHC
HIGHS
LIGHT
MIGHT
MUGHO
NIGHT
OUGHT
RIGHT
SIGHS
SIGHT
TIGHT
WIGHT
YOGHS

•••GH
AARGH
BAUGH
BERGH
BLIGH
BOUGH
COUGH
DOUGH
HEIGH
HOUGH
KEOGH
KROGH
LAUGH
LEIGH
LOUGH
NEIGH
ROUGH
SOUGH
THIGH
TOUGH
WAUGH
WEIGH

GI•••
GIANT
GIBBS
GIBED
GIBER
GIBES
GIDDY

GIFTS
GIGOT
GIGUE
GIJOE
GIJON
GILDA
GILDS
GILES
GILLS
GILLY
GILTS
GIMEL
GIMME
GIMPS
GIMPY
GINNY
GINZA
GIPSY
GIRDS
GIRLS
GIRNS
GIROS
GIRTH
GIRTS
GISTS
GITGO
GIVEN
GIVER
GIVES
GIZMO

G•I••

GAILY
GAINS
GAITS
GAIUS
GLIAL
GLICK
GLIDE
GLIMS
GLINT
GLITZ
GOING
GRIDS
GRIEF
GRIEG
GRIER
GRIFT
GRIGS
GRILL
GRIME
GRIMM
GRIMY
GRIND
GRINS
GRIOT
GRIPE
GRIPS
GRIST
GRITS
GUIDE
GUIDO
GUILD
GUILE
GUILT
GUIRO
GUISE

G••I•

GAMIN
GAVIN
GELID
GENIC
GENIE
GENII
GEOID
GETIN
GETIT
GHAIN
GLAIR
GOTIN
GOTIT
GRAIG
GRAIL
GRAIN
GROIN
GSUIT

G•••I

GALLI
GARNI
GENII
GHALI
GHAZI
GOLGI
GONDI
GORKI
GRANI
GUCCI

•GI••

AGILE
AGING
AGIOS
AGITA
BGIRL
OGIVE

•G•I•

AGAIN
AGGIE
AGRIC
NGAIO
UGRIC

•G••I

EGADI
NGAMI

••GI•

AEGIR
AEGIS
AGGIE
ALGID
ALGIN
ANGIE
ANGIO
ARGIL
BAGIT
BEGIN
BOGIE
DIGIN
DIGIT
DOGIE
DOGIT
DUGIN
ELGIN
FAGIN
FOGIN
FUGIT
HAGIO
LEGIS
LEGIT
LOGIA
LOGIC
LOGIN
MAGIC
REGIA
REGIS
RIGID
SIGIL
VIGIL
YOGIC
YOGIS

••G•I

LIGNI
NEGRI
REGNI
SEGNI

•••GI

CORGI
FUNGI
GOLGI
LONGI
LUIGI
SENGI
SHOGI

G•J••

GIJOE
GIJON

G••K•

GAWKS
GAWKY
GECKO
GEEKS
GEEKY
GORKI
GORKY
GOWKS
GROKS
GUNKY

G•••K

GLICK
GLUCK
GREEK

GL•••

GLACE
GLADE
GLADS
GLAIR
GLAND
GLARE
GLARY
GLASS
GLAXO
GLAZE
GLEAM
GLEAN
GLEBE
GLEDE
GLEES
GLENN
GLENS
GLESS
GLEYS
GLIAL
GLICK
GLIDE
GLIMS
GLINT
GLITZ
GLOAM
GLOAT
GLOBE
GLOBS
GLOGG
GLOMS
GLOOM
GLOPS
GLORY
GLOSS
GLOVE
GLOWS
GLOZE
GLUCK
GLUCO
GLUED
GLUER
GLUES
GLUEY
GLUGS
GLUON
GLUTS
GLYCO
GLYPH

G•L••

GALAH
GALAS
GALAX
GALBA
GALEA
GALEN
GALES
GALLI
GALLO
GALLS
GALOP
GCLEF
GELEE
GELID
GFLAT
GILDA
GILDS
GILES
GILLS
GILLY
GILTS
GOLAN
GOLDA
GOLDE
GOLDS
GOLEM
GOLFS
GOLGI
GOLLY
GULAG
GULAR
GULCH
GULES
GULFS
GULLS
GULLY
GULPS
GULPY

G••L•

GABLE
GAELS
GAILY
GALLI
GALLO
GALLS
GAOLS
GAULS
GAYLE
GAYLY
GHALI
GILLS
GILLY
GIRLS
GOALS
GODLY
GOLLY
GOULD
GRILL
GUILD
GUILE
GUILT
GULLS
GULLY

G•••L

GAMAL
GAVEL
GAYAL
GHOUL
GIMEL
GLIAL
GNARL
GOBEL
GODEL
GOGOL
GOMEL
GORAL
GRAIL
GRILL
GROWL
GRUEL
GYRAL

•GL••

AGLET
AGLEY
AGLOW
IGLOO
IGLUS
OGLED
OGLER
OGLES

•G•L•

AGALS
AGILE

•G••L

BGIRL

••GL•

ANGLE
ANGLO
BIGLY
BOGLE
BUGLE
EAGLE
INGLE

••G•L

ALGAL
ALGOL
ANGEL
ARGIL
ARGOL
BAGEL
ENGEL
FUGAL
GOGOL
HEGEL
JUGAL
KUGEL
LEGAL
MOGUL
NAGEL
NIGEL
REGAL
RIGEL
SAGAL
SEGAL
SIGIL
VIGIL

GM•••

GMATS

G•M••

GAMAL
GAMAY
GAMBA
GAMED
GAMER
GAMES
GAMEY
GAMIN
GAMMA
GAMMY
GAMOW
GAMPS
GAMUT
GEMMA
GEMMY
GEMOT
GIMEL
GIMME
GIMPS
GIMPY
GOMEL
GOMER
GOMEZ
GUMBO
GUMBY
GUMMO
GUMMY
GUMUP
GYMNO

G••M•

GAMMA
GAMMY
GAUMS
GEMMA
GEMMY
GERMS
GERMY
GETME
GEUMS
GIMME
GIZMO
GLIMS
GLOMS
GNOME
GORME
GRAMA
GRAMM
GRAMP
GRAMS
GRIME
GRIMM
GRIMY
GRUMP
GUMMO
GUMMY

G•••M

GLEAM
GLOAM
GLOOM
GOLEM
GRAMM
GRIMM
GROOM

•G•M•

AGAMA
NGAMI

•G••M

OGHAM

••GM•

DOGMA
MAGMA
PYGMY
SIGMA

••G•M

BEGUM
BYGUM
JUGUM
REGUM

GN•••

GNARL
GNARS
GNASH
GNATS
GNAWS
GNOME

G•N••

GANDY
GANEF
GANGS
GENES
GENET
GENIC
GENIE
GENII
GENOA
GENRE
GENRO
GENTS
GENUA
GENUS
GINNY
GINZA
GONDI
GONDS
GONER
GONGS
GONNA
GONZO
GUNGA
GUNKY
GUNNY

G••N•

GAINS
GARNI
GAUNT
GEENA
GHANA
GHENT
GIANT
GINNY
GIRNS
GLAND
GLENN
GLENS
GLINT
GOING
GONNA
GOONS
GOONY
GOWNS
GRAND
GRANI
GRANT
GRIND
GRINS
GRUNT
GUNNY
GWENN
GWENT
GWYNN
GYMNO

G•••N

GABON
GALEN
GAMIN
GATUN
GAVIN
GETIN
GETON
GHAIN
GIJON
GIVEN
GLEAN
GLENN
GLUON
GOLAN
GOREN
GOTIN
GOTON
GRAIN
GREEN
GROAN
GROIN
GROWN
GUTEN
GWENN
GWYNN
GYRON

•GN••

AGNES
AGNEW
AGNON
AGNUS
IGNES

•G•N•

AGANA
AGENA
AGENT
AGING
AGONY

•G••N

AGAIN
AGARN
AGNON
AGRON
EGGON
OGDEN

••GN•

LIGNI
LIGNO
MAGNA
REGNI
SEGNI
SEGNO
SIGNE
SIGNO
SIGNS
VIGNY

••G•N

ALGIN
ARGON
BBGUN
BEGAN
BEGIN
BEGUN
BIGON
DAGON
DIGIN
DOGON
DUGAN
DUGIN
EAGAN
EGGON
EIGEN
ELGIN
FAGIN
FOGIN
HAGEN
HOGAN
LAGAN
LOGAN
LOGIN
LOGON
LTGEN
MEGAN
OBGYN
ORGAN
PAGAN
REGAN
SAGAN
VEGAN
WAGON
WIGAN

•••GN

ALIGN
COIGN
DEIGN
FEIGN
REIGN
VSIGN

GO•••

GOADS
GOALS
GOAPE
GOATS
GOBAD
GOBEL
GODEL
GODET
GODEY
GODLY
GODOT
GOERS
GOEST
GOFAR
GOFER
GOFOR
GOGOL
GOGOS
GOING
GOLAN
GOLDA
GOLDE
GOLDS
GOLEM
GOLFS
GOLGI
GOLLY
GOMEL
GOMER
GOMEZ
GONDI
GONDS
GONER
GONGS
GONNA
GONZO
GOODS
GOODY
GOOEY
GOOFF
GOOFS
GOOFY
GOONS
GOONY
GOOPS
GOOPY
GOOSE
GOOSY
GOOUT
GORAL
GORDO
GORDY
GORED
GOREN

GORES
GORGE
GORKI
GORKY
GORME
GORPS
GORSE
GORSY
GOSEE
GOSSE
GOTAT
GOTBY
GOTHA
GOTHS
GOTIN
GOTIT
GOTON
GOTTA
GOTTO
GOTUP
GOUDA
GOUDY
GOUGE
GOULD
GOURD
GOUTY
GOWDY
GOWER
GOWKS
GOWNS

G•O••

GAOLS
GEODE
GEOID
GEORG
GHOST
GHOUL
GLOAM
GLOAT
GLOBE
GLOBS
GLOGG
GLOMS
GLOOM
GLOPS
GLORY
GLOSS
GLOVE
GLOWS
GLOZE
GNOME
GOODS
GOODY
GOOEY
GOOFF
GOOFS
GOOFY
GOONS
GOONY
GOOPS
GOOPY
GOOSE
GOOSY
GOOUT
GROAN
GROAT
GRODY
GROFE
GROGS
GROIN
GROKS
GROOM
GROPE
GROSS
GROSZ
GROTS
GROUP
GROUT
GROVE
GROWL
GROWN
GROWS
GROZA

G••O•

GABON
GABOR
GALOP
GAMOW
GAROU
GATOR
GATOS
GAVOT
GEMOT
GENOA
GETON
GIGOT
GIJOE
GIJON
GIROS
GLOOM
GLUON
GODOT
GOFOR
GOGOL
GOGOS
GOTON
GRIOT
GROOM
GUYOT
GYRON
GYROS

G•••O

GALLO
GARBO
GECKO
GENRO
GESSO
GETGO
GETTO
GITGO
GIZMO
GLAXO
GLUCO
GLYCO
GONZO
GORDO
GOTTO
GRECO
GUACO
GUIDO
GUIRO
GUMBO
GUMMO
GUSTO
GYMNO

•GO••

AGOGO
AGONY
AGORA

•G•O•

AGIOS
AGLOW
AGNON
AGRON
EGGON
IGLOO

•G••O

AGGRO
AGOGO
IGLOO
NGAIO

••GO•

ALGOL
ARGOL
ARGON
ARGOS
ARGOT
BEGOT
BIGON
BIGOS
BIGOT
BOGOR
DAGON
DOGON
EGGON
ERGOT
FAGOT
GIGOT
GOGOL
GOGOS
HUGOS
INGOT
LAGOS
LEGOS
LOGON
LOGOS
LTGOV
MAGOG
MAGOO
MAGOT
NOGOS
OHGOD
RIGOR
SAGOS
SEGOS
VIGOR
WAGON
YUGOS

••G•O

AGGRO
ANGIO
ANGLO
DOGGO
HAGIO
HYGRO
LIGNO
MAGOO
MUGHO
SEGNO
SIGNO

•••GO

AGOGO
AMIGO
BINGO
BONGO
CARGO
CONGO
DIEGO
DINGO
DOGGO
FARGO
FORGO
FUEGO
FUNGO
GETGO
GITGO
IMAGO
INIGO
JINGO
LARGO
LETGO
LINGO
LONGO
LUEGO
MANGO
MARGO
MONGO
MUNGO
OINGO
OLIGO
OUTGO
PENGO
PHAGO
PINGO
PREGO
RINGO
SARGO
SLIGO
SORGO
TANGO
VIRGO

G•P••

GAPED
GAPER
GAPES
GIPSY
GUPPY
GYPSY

G••P•

GAMPS
GASPE
GASPS
GAWPS
GIMPS
GIMPY
GLOPS
GLYPH
GOAPE
GOOPS
GOOPY
GORPS
GRAPE
GRAPH
GRAPY
GRIPE
GRIPS
GROPE
GULPS
GULPY
GUPPY

G•••P

GALOP
GASUP
GETUP
GOTUP
GRAMP
GRASP
GROUP
GRUMP
GUMUP

•G•P•

AGAPE
EGYPT

•G••P

AGASP

••G•P

DIGUP
DUGUP
FOGUP
LEGUP
RIGUP
TAGUP

GR•••

GRABS
GRACE
GRADE
GRADS
GRADY
GRAFT
GRAIG
GRAIL
GRAIN
GRAMA
GRAMM
GRAMP
GRAMS
GRAND
GRANI
GRANT
GRAPE
GRAPH
GRAPY
GRASP
GRASS
GRATA
GRATE
GRAVE
GRAVY
GRAYS
GRAZE
GREAT
GREBE
GRECO
GREED
GREEK
GREEN
GREER
GREES
GREET
GREGG
GRETA
GRETE
GREYS
GRIDS
GRIEF
GRIEG
GRIER
GRIFT
GRIGS
GRILL
GRIME
GRIMM
GRIMY
GRIND
GRINS
GRIOT
GRIPE
GRIPS
GRIST
GRITS
GROAN
GROAT
GRODY
GROFE
GROGS
GROIN
GROKS
GROOM
GROPE
GROSS
GROSZ
GROTS
GROUP
GROUT
GROVE
GROWL
GROWN
GROWS
GROZA
GRUBS
GRUEL
GRUFF
GRUMP
GRUNT

G•R••

GARBO
GARBS
GARDA
GARDE
GARNI
GAROU
GARRY
GARTH
GERAH
GERMS
GERMY
GERRY
GIRDS
GIRLS
GIRNS
GIROS
GIRTH
GIRTS
GORAL
GORDO
GORDY
GORED
GOREN
GORES
GORGE
GORKI
GORKY
GORME
GORPS
GORSE
GORSY
GURDY
GURUS
GYRAL
GYRES
GYRON
GYROS
GYRUS

G••R•

GARRY
GAURS
GEARS
GEARY
GENRE
GENRO
GEORG
GERRY
GLARE
GLARY
GLORY
GNARL
GNARS
GOERS
GOURD
GUARD
GUARS
GUIRO

G•••R

GABOR
GAMER
GAPER
GASTR
GATOR
GAYER
GAZER
GIBER
GIVER
GLAIR
GLUER
GOFAR
GOFER
GOFOR
GOMER
GONER
GOWER
GREER
GRIER
GULAR

•GR••

AGREE
AGRIC
AGRON
EGRET
OGRES
UGRIC

•G•R•

AGARN
AGARS
AGERS
AGGRO
AGORA
BGIRL

•G••R

EGGAR
OGLER

••GR•

AGGRO
ANGRY
EAGRE
ENGRS
HYGRO
NEGRI

••G•R

AEGIR
ALGER
ANGER
AUGER
AUGUR
BOGOR
CAGER
CIGAR
EAGER
EDGAR
EDGER
EGGAR
ELGAR
HAGAR
HUGER
INGER
LAGER
LEGER
LIGER
LUGER
NIGER
PAGER
RIGOR
ROGER
SAGER
SEGAR
SEGER
SUGAR
TIGER
UIGUR
UNGER
URGER
VIGOR
WAGER

GS•••

GSUIT

G•S••

GASES
GASPE
GASPS
GASSY
GASTR
GASUP
GESSO
GESTE
GESTS
GISTS
GOSEE
GOSSE
GUSHY
GUSSY
GUSTO
GUSTS
GUSTY

G••S•

GASSY
GAUSS
GEESE
GESSO
GHOST
GIPSY
GLASS
GLESS
GLOSS
GNASH
GOEST
GOOSE
GOOSY
GORSE
GORSY
GOSSE
GRASP
GRASS
GRIST
GROSS
GROSZ
GUESS
GUEST
GUISE
GUSSY
GUTSY
GYPSY

G•••S

GAELS
GAFFS
GAGES
GAINS
GAITS
GAIUS
GALAS
GALES
GALLS
GAMES
GAMPS
GANGS
GAOLS
GAPES
GARBS
GASES
GASPS
GATES
GATOS
GAUDS
GAULS
GAUMS
GAURS
GAUSS
GAWKS
GAWPS
GAZES
GEARS
GEEKS
GENES
GENTS
GENUS
GERMS
GESTS
GETAS
GEUMS
GHATS
GHEES
GIBBS
GIBES
GIFTS
GILDS
GILES
GILLS
GILTS
GIMPS
GIRDS
GIRLS
GIRNS
GIROS
GIRTS
GISTS
GIVES
GLADS
GLASS
GLEES
GLENS
GLESS
GLEYS
GLIMS
GLOBS
GLOMS
GLOPS
GLOSS
GLOWS
GLUES
GLUGS
GLUTS
GMATS
GNARS
GNATS
GNAWS
GOADS
GOALS
GOATS
GOERS
GOGOS
GOLDS
GOLFS
GONDS
GONGS
GOODS
GOOFS
GOONS
GOOPS
GORES
GORPS
GOTHS
GOWKS
GOWNS
GRABS
GRADS
GRAMS
GRASS
GRAYS
GREES
GREYS
GRIDS
GRIGS
GRINS
GRIPS
GRITS
GROGS

GROKS
GROSS
GROTS
GROWS
GRUBS
GUARS
GUESS
GULES
GULFS
GULLS
GULPS
GURUS
GUSTS
GYBES
GYRES
GYROS
GYRUS
GYVES

•G•S•
AGASP
EGEST

•G••S
AGALS
AGARS
AGERS
AGHAS
AGIOS
AGNES
AGNUS
AGUES
EGADS
IGLUS
IGNES
OGEES
OGLES
OGRES

••GS•
ANGST
BUGSY

••G•S
AEGIS
ANGES
ANGUS
ARGOS
ARGUS
AVGAS
BIGOS
BOGGS
BOGUS
CAGES
DEGAS
DOGES
EDGES
ENGRS
FUGUS
GAGES
GOGOS
HIGHS
HOGGS
HUGOS
LAGOS
LEGGS
LEGIS
LEGOS
LOGES
LOGOS
LUGES
MAGES
MAGUS
MSGTS
MUGGS
NEGUS
NOGOS
PAGES
RAGAS
RAGES
REGIS
RIGGS
SAGAS
SAGES
SAGOS
SEGOS
SIGHS
SIGNS
SSGTS
TAGUS
TOGAS
TSGTS
URGES
VAGUS
VEGAS
WAGES
YEGGS
YOGAS
YOGHS
YOGIS
YUGAS
YUGOS

•••GS
BANGS
BERGS
BINGS
BIOGS
BLDGS
BOGGS
BONGS
BRAGS
BRIGS
BUNGS
BURGS
CHUGS
CLOGS
CRAGS
DANGS
DINGS
DONGS
DRAGS
DREGS
DRUGS
FANGS
FLAGS
FLOGS
FROGS
GANGS
GLUGS
GONGS
GRIGS
GROGS
HANGS
HAWGS
HOGGS
HONGS
KINGS
LEGGS
LONGS
LUNGS
MINGS
MOOGS
MUGGS
PANGS
PINGS
PLUGS
PONGS
PRIGS
PROGS
PUNGS
QUAGS
RIGGS
RINGS
RUNGS
SHAGS
SINGS
SKEGS
SLAGS
SLOGS
SLUGS
SMOGS
SNAGS
SNOGS
SNUGS
SONGS
STAGS
SWAGS
SWIGS
TANGS
THUGS
TIEGS
TINGS
TONGS
TRIGS
TRUGS
TWIGS
WHIGS
WINGS
YEGGS
ZINGS

G•T••
GATED
GATES
GATOR
GATOS
GATUN
GETAS
GETAT
GETBY
GETGO
GETIN
GETIT
GETME
GETON
GETTO
GETTY
GETUP
GITGO
GOTAT
GOTBY
GOTHA
GOTHS
GOTIN
GOTIT
GOTON
GOTTA
GOTTO
GOTUP
GUTEN
GUTSY
GUTTA
GUTTY

G••T•
GAITS
GARTH
GASTR
GENTS
GESTE
GESTS
GETTO
GETTY
GHATS
GIFTS
GILTS
GIRTH
GIRTS
GISTS
GLITZ
GLUTS
GMATS
GNATS
GOATS
GOTTA
GOTTO
GOUTY
GRATA
GRATE
GRETA
GRETE
GRITS
GROTS
GUSTO
GUSTS
GUSTY
GUTTA
GUTTY

G•••T
GAMUT
GAUNT
GAVOT
GEMOT
GENET
GETAT
GETIT
GFLAT
GHENT
GHOST
GIANT
GIGOT
GLINT
GLOAT
GODET
GODOT
GOEST
GOOUT
GOTAT
GOTIT
GRAFT
GRANT
GREAT
GREET
GRIFT
GRIOT
GRIST
GROAT
GROUT
GRUNT
GSUIT
GUEST
GUILT
GUYOT
GWENT

•G•T•
AGATE
AGITA

•G••T
AGENT
AGLET
EGEST
EGRET
EGYPT

••GT•
MSGTS
SSGTS
TSGTS

••G•T
ANGST
ARGOT
AUGHT
BAGIT
BEGAT
BEGET
BEGOT
BIGHT
BIGOT
CUGAT
DIGIT
DOGIT
EIGHT
ERGOT
FAGOT
FIGHT
FUGIT
GIGOT
INGOT
LEGIT
LIGHT
MAGOT
MIGHT
NIGHT
OUGHT
PAGET
PUGET
RIGHT
ROGET
SAGET
SIGHT
TIGHT
WIGHT

•••GT
VINGT

GU•••
GUACO
GUARD
GUARS
GUAVA
GUCCI
GUESS
GUEST
GUIDE
GUIDO
GUILD
GUILE
GUILT
GUIRO
GUISE
GULAG
GULAR
GULCH
GULES
GULFS
GULLS
GULLY
GULPS
GULPY
GUMBO
GUMBY
GUMMO
GUMMY
GUMUP
GUNGA
GUNKY
GUNNY
GUPPY
GURDY
GURUS
GUSHY
GUSSY
GUSTO
GUSTS
GUSTY
GUTEN
GUTSY
GUTTA
GUTTY
GUYED
GUYOT

G•U••
GAUDS
GAUDY
GAUGE
GAULS
GAUMS
GAUNT
GAURS
GAUSS
GAUZE
GAUZY
GEUMS
GLUCK
GLUCO
GLUED
GLUER
GLUES
GLUEY
GLUGS
GLUON
GLUTS
GOUDA
GOUDY
GOUGE
GOULD
GOURD
GOUTY
GRUBS
GRUEL
GRUFF
GRUMP
GRUNT
GSUIT

G••U•
GAIUS
GAMUT
GASUP
GATUN
GENUA
GENUS
GETUP
GHOUL
GIGUE
GOOUT
GOTUP
GROUP
GROUT
GUMUP
GURUS
GYRUS

G•••U
GAROU

•GU••
AGUES

•G•U•
AGNUS
IGLUS

••GU•
ANGUS
ARGUE
ARGUS
AUGUR
BBGUN
BEGUM
BEGUN
BOGUS
BYGUM
DIGUP
DUGUP
FOGUP
FUGUE
FUGUS
GIGUE
HAGUE
JUGUM
LEGUP
LOGUE
MAGUS
MOGUL
MYGUY
NEGUS
REGUM
RIGUP
ROGUE
SEGUE
TAGUP
TAGUS
UIGUR
VAGUE
VAGUS
VOGUE

••G•U
ILGWU

•••GU
ENUGU
LONGU
TAEGU
XINGU

G•V••
GAVEL
GAVIN
GAVOT
GIVEN
GIVER
GIVES
GYVED
GYVES

G••V•
GLOVE
GRAVE
GRAVY
GROVE
GUAVA

•G•V•
AGAVE
OGIVE

••G•V
LTGOV
NEGEV

GW•••
GWENN
GWENT
GWYNN

G•W••
GAWKS
GAWKY
GAWPS
GOWDY
GOWER
GOWKS
GOWNS

G••W•
GLOWS
GNAWS
GROWL
GROWN
GROWS

G•••W
GAMOW

•GW••
NGWEE

•G••W
AGLOW
AGNEW

••GW•
ILGWU

G••X•
GLAXO

G•••X
GALAX

GY•••
GYBED
GYBES
GYMNO
GYPSY
GYRAL
GYRES
GYRON
GYROS
GYRUS
GYVED
GYVES

G•Y••
GAYAL
GAYER
GAYLE
GAYLY
GLYCO
GLYPH
GUYED
GUYOT
GWYNN

G••Y•
GLEYS
GRAYS
GREYS

G•••Y
GABBY
GAILY
GAMAY
GAMEY
GAMMY
GANDY
GARRY
GASSY
GAUDY
GAUZY
GAWKY
GAYLY
GEARY
GEEKY
GEMMY
GERMY
GERRY
GETBY
GETTY
GIDDY
GILLY
GIMPY
GINNY
GIPSY
GLARY
GLORY
GLUEY
GODEY
GODLY
GOLLY
GOODY
GOOEY
GOOFY
GOONY
GOOPY
GOOSY
GORDY
GORKY
GORSY
GOTBY
GOUDY
GOUTY
GOWDY
GRADY
GRAPY
GRAVY
GRIMY
GRODY
GULLY
GULPY
GUMBY
GUMMY
GUNKY
GUNNY
GUPPY
GURDY
GUSHY
GUSSY
GUSTY
GUTSY
GUTTY
GYPSY

•GY••
EGYPT

•G••Y
AGLEY
AGONY

••GY•
OBGYN

••G•Y
ANGRY
BAGGY
BIGGY
BIGLY
BOGEY
BOGGY
BUGGY
BUGSY
CAGEY
DIGBY
DOGEY
DOGGY
FOGEY
FOGGY
FUGGY
JAGGY
LEGGY
MOGGY
MUGGY
MYGUY
NAGGY
PEGGY
PIGGY
PUGGY
PYGMY
RIGBY
RUGBY
SAGGY
SOGGY
VIGNY

VUGGY
WIGGY
ZIGGY

•••GY
BAGGY
BARGY
BIGGY
BILGY
BOGGY
BUGGY
BULGY
DINGY
DODGY
DOGGY
ELEGY
FOGGY
FUGGY
HEDGY
HOAGY
JAGGY
LEDGY
LEGGY
MANGY
MINGY
MOGGY
MUGGY
NAGGY
OLOGY
PEGGY
PHAGY
PIGGY
PODGY
PORGY
PUDGY
PUGGY
RANGY
RIDGY
SAGGY
SEDGY
SOGGY
STAGY
STOGY
TANGY
VUGGY
WEDGY
WIGGY
ZIGGY
ZINGY

G•Z••
GAZED
GAZER
GAZES
GIZMO

G••Z•
GAUZE
GAUZY
GHAZI
GINZA
GLAZE
GLOZE
GONZO
GRAZE
GROZA

G•••Z
GLITZ
GOMEZ
GROSZ

•G•Z•
AGAZE

HA•••
HABER
HABIT
HABLA
HACEK
HACKS
HADAR
HADAT
HADES
HADJI
HADNT
HADON
HADST
HADTO
HAEMA
HAEMO
HAFIZ
HAFTS
HAFUN
HAGAR
HAGEN
HAGIO
HAGUE
HAHAS
HAIDA
HAIFA
HAIKS
HAIKU
HAILE
HAILS
HAIRS
HAIRY
HAITI
HAJIS
HAJJI
HAKES
HAKIM
HALAS
HALED
HALER
HALES
HALEY
HALLE
HALLO
HALLS
HALMS
HALON
HALOS
HALTS
HALVE
HAMAL
HAMAN
HAMEL
HAMES
HAMMY
HANDS
HANDY
HANES
HANFF
HANGS
HANKS
HANKY
HANNA
HANNO
HANOI
HANSA
HANSE
HANTS
HAOLE
HAPLO
HAPLY
HAPPY
HARAR
HARDC
HARDG
HARDY
HARED
HAREM
HARES
HARKS
HARMS
HARPO
HARPS
HARPY
HARRY
HARSH
HARTE
HARTS
HARUM
HASAT
HASID
HASNT
HASON
HASPS
HASSO
HASTA
HASTE
HASTO
HASTY
HATCH
HATED
HATER
HATES
HATLO
HAUER
HAULM
HAULS
HAUNT
HAUSA
HAUTE
HAVEL
HAVEN
HAVER
HAVES
HAVOC
HAVRE
HAWED
HAWGS
HAWKE
HAWKS
HAWSE
HAYDN
HAYED
HAYEK
HAYES
HAZAN
HAZED
HAZEL
HAZER
HAZES

H•A••
HEADS
HEADY
HEALS
HEALY
HEAPS
HEARD
HEARN
HEARS
HEART
HEATH
HEATS
HEAVE
HEAVY
HOAGY
HOARD
HOARS
HOARY
HYAMS
HYATT

H••A•
HADAR
HADAT
HAGAR
HAHAS
HALAS
HAMAL
HAMAN
HARAR
HASAT
HAZAN
HBEAM
HEJAZ
HEMAN
HENAN
HERAT
HEXAD
HIJAZ
HIRAM
HOBAN
HODAD
HOGAN
HONAN
HORAE
HORAL
HORAS
HOWAR
HOYAS
HULAS
HUMAN
HUNAN
HYLAS
HYMAN
HYRAX

H•••A
HABLA
HAEMA
HAIDA
HAIFA
HANNA
HANSA
HASTA
HAUSA
HEDDA
HEKLA
HELGA
HENNA
HEPTA
HIERA
HIJRA
HILDA
HOFFA
HONDA
HOOHA
HOSEA
HOSTA
HOUMA
HUBBA
HUZZA
HYDRA
HYENA
HYPHA

•HA••
CHACO
CHAFE
CHAFF
CHAIM
CHAIN
CHAIR
CHAKA
CHALK
CHAMP
CHANG
CHANT
CHAOS
CHAPS
CHARD
CHARM
CHARO
CHARS
CHART
CHARY
CHASE
CHASM
CHATS
CHAUD
CHAWS
CHAZZ
DHABI
DHAKA
DHALS
GHAIN
GHALI
GHANA
GHATS
GHAZI
KHAKI
KHANS
LHASA
OHAIR
OHARA
OHARE
PHAGE
PHAGO
PHAGY
PHANY
PHARM
PHASE
SHACK
SHADE
SHADS
SHADY
SHAEF
SHAFT
SHAGS
SHAHN
SHAHS
SHAKE
SHAKO
SHAKY
SHALE
SHALL
SHALT
SHAME
SHAMS
SHAMU
SHANA
SHANE
SHANK
SHANS
SHANT
SHAPE
SHARD
SHARE
SHARI
SHARK
SHARP
SHATT
SHAUN
SHAVE
SHAWL
SHAWM
SHAWN
SHAYS
THAIS
THANE
THANK
THANT
THARP
THATS
THAWS
UHAUL
WHACK
WHALE
WHAMO
WHAMS
WHANG
WHARF
WHATD
WHATS

•H•A•
AHEAD
AHMAD
CHEAP
CHEAT
CHIAS
OHKAY
PHIAL
RHEAS
SHEAF
SHEAN
SHEAR
SHOAH
SHOAL
SHOAT
UHLAN
WHEAL
WHEAT

•H••A
AHORA
CHAKA
CHEKA
CHELA
CHIBA
CHINA
CHITA
CHULA
DHAKA
GHANA
LHASA
OHARA
PHYLA
RHODA
RHYTA
SHANA
SHEBA
SHEMA
SHIVA
SHULA
THECA
THEDA
THEMA
THERA
THETA
THUJA
UHURA
XHOSA

••HA•
AGHAS
ARHAT
BAHAI
BEHAN
BIHAR
BOHAI
COHAN
EPHAH
EPHAS
ETHAN
HAHAS
JIHAD
LAHAR
LEHAR
MAHAL
MAHAN
MOHAM
OGHAM
POHAI
PSHAW
RAHAB
RAHAL
REHAB
REHAN
SCHAV
WUHAN
ZOHAR

••H•A
BAHIA
BOHEA
LEHUA
MEHTA
NAHUA
OCHOA
OSHEA
SCHWA
SEHNA

•••HA
AISHA
ALOHA
ALPHA
BOTHA
DACHA
FATHA
GOTHA
HOOHA
HYPHA
KASHA
MISHA
MOCHA
NUCHA
OMAHA
PASHA
SACHA
SASHA

HB•••
HBEAM
HBOMB

H•B••
HABER
HABIT
HABLA
HOBAN
HOBBS
HOBBY
HOBOS
HUBBA
HUBBY

H••B•
HERBS
HERBY
HOBBS
HOBBY
HUBBA
HUBBY

H•••B
HBOMB
HOREB

•HB••
OHBOY

•H•B•
CHIBA
CHUBS
DHABI
PHOBE
SHEBA
THEBE

•H••B
RHOMB
RHUMB
SHRUB
THROB
THUMB

••HB•
ASHBY

••H•B
RAHAB
REHAB
SAHIB

H•C••
HACEK
HACKS
HECHE
HECHT
HECKS
HECTO
HICKS
HOCKS
HOCUS

H••C•
HATCH
HENCE
HENCH
HITCH
HOOCH
HULCE
HUNCH
HUTCH

H•••C
HARDC
HAVOC
HELIC
HIGHC

•H•C•
CHACO
CHECK
CHICK
CHICO
CHOCK
CHUCK
PHYCO
SHACK
SHOCK
SHUCK
THECA
THICK
WHACK
WHICH

••H•C
ADHOC
ETHIC

•••HC
HIGHC

H•D••
HADAR
HADAT
HADES
HADJI
HADNT
HADON
HADST
HADTO
HEDDA
HEDGE
HEDGY
HEDIN
HIDER
HIDES
HODAD
HYDRA
HYDRO

H••D•
HAIDA
HANDS
HANDY
HARDC
HARDG
HARDY
HAYDN
HEADS
HEADY
HEDDA
HEEDS
HEIDI
HEIDT
HERDS
HILDA
HINDI
HINDS
HINDU
HOLDS
HONDA
HONDO
HOODS
HORDE
HOWDY
HURDY

H•••D
HALED
HARED
HASID
HATED
HAWED
HAYED
HAZED
HEARD
HEROD
HEWED
HEXAD
HEXED
HIKED
HIRED
HIVED
HOARD
HODAD
HOKED
HOLED
HOMED
HONED
HOPED
HOSED
HOUND
HUMID
HYOID
HYPED

•H•D•
CHIDE
RHODA
RHODE
RHODO
SHADE
SHADS
SHADY
SHEDS
THEDA
THUDS

•H••D
AHEAD
AHMAD
AHMED
CHARD

CHAUD
CHILD
CHORD
OHGOD
SHARD
SHEED
SHIED
SHOED
SHRED
THEYD
THIRD
WHATD

••HD•
MAHDI

••H•D
AAHED
ACHED
APHID
EPHOD
JIHAD
OOHED
SCHED
USHED

HE•••
HEADS
HEADY
HEALS
HEALY
HEAPS
HEARD
HEARN
HEARS
HEART
HEATH
HEATS
HEAVE
HEAVY
HECHE
HECHT
HECKS
HECTO
HEDDA
HEDGE
HEDGY
HEDIN
HEEDS
HEELS
HEFEI
HEFTS
HEFTY
HEGEL
HEIDI
HEIDT
HEIGH
HEINE
HEINZ
HEIRS
HEISS
HEIST
HEJAZ
HEKLA
HELEN
HELGA
HELIC
HELIO
HELIX
HELLO
HELLS
HELMS
HELOS
HELOT
HELPS
HELVE
HEMAN
HEMEN
HEMET
HEMIN
HEMPS
HENAN
HENCE
HENCH
HENGE
HENIE
HENNA
HENNY
HENRI
HENRY
HENTS
HEPTA
HERAT
HERBS
HERBY
HERDS
HERES
HERKY
HERLS
HERMS
HERNE
HERNS
HEROD
HERON
HEROS
HERTZ
HERVE
HERZL
HESSE
HESTS
HETHS
HETTY
HETUP
HEURE
HEUTE
HEWED
HEWER
HEXAD
HEXED
HEXER
HEXES
HEXYL
HEYSE

H•E••
HAEMA
HAEMO
HBEAM
HEEDS
HEELS
HIERA
HIERO
HOERS
HUEVO
HYENA

H••E•
HABER
HACEK
HADES
HAGEN
HAKES
HALED
HALER
HALES
HALEY
HAMEL
HAMES
HANES
HARED
HAREM
HARES
HATED
HATER
HATES
HAUER
HAVEL
HAVEN
HAVER
HAVES
HAWED
HAYED
HAYEK
HAYES
HAZED
HAZEL
HAZER
HAZES
HEFEI
HEGEL
HELEN
HEMEN
HEMET
HERES
HEWED
HEWER
HEXED
HEXER
HEXES
HIDER
HIDES
HIKED
HIKER
HIKES
HINES
HIRED
HIRER
HIRES
HIVED
HIVES
HOKED
HOKES
HOKEY
HOLED
HOLES
HOLEY
HOMED
HOMEO
HOMER
HOMES
HOMEY
HONED
HONES
HONEY
HOOEY
HOPED
HOPER
HOPES
HOREB
HOSEA
HOSED
HOSEL
HOSES
HOTEL
HOVEL
HOVER
HOVEY
HUGER
HYPED
HYPER
HYPES

H•••E
HAGUE
HAILE
HALLE
HALVE
HANSE
HAOLE
HARTE
HASTE
HAUTE
HAVRE
HAWKE
HAWSE
HEAVE
HECHE
HEDGE
HEINE
HELVE
HENCE
HENGE
HENIE
HERNE
HERVE
HESSE
HEURE
HEUTE
HEYSE
HINGE
HITME
HOMME
HOOKE
HOPPE
HORAE
HORDE
HORNE
HORSE
HOUSE
HOWIE
HOXIE
HOYLE
HULCE

•HE••
AHEAD
CHEAP
CHEAT
CHECK
CHEEK
CHEEP
CHEER
CHEFS
CHEJU
CHEKA
CHELA
CHERE
CHERI
CHERT
CHESS
CHEST
CHETH
CHEVY
CHEWS
CHEWY
GHEES
GHENT
PHENO
RHEAS
RHETT
RHEUM
SHEAF
SHEAN
SHEAR
SHEBA
SHEDS
SHEED
SHEEN
SHEEP
SHEER
SHEET
SHEIK
SHELF
SHELL
SHEMA
SHEMP
SHERE
THEBE
THECA
THEDA
THEFT
THEIR
THEMA
THEME
THEMS
THEOL
THERA
THERE
THERM
THESE
THETA
THEWS
THEWY
THEYD
WHEAL
WHEAT
WHEEL
WHEEN
WHELK
WHELM
WHELP
WHERE
WHETS
WHEYS

•H•E•
AHMED
CHEEK
CHEEP
CHEER
CHIEF
CHIEN
GHEES
KHMER
NHLER
PHREN
SHAEF
SHEED
SHEEN
SHEEP
SHEER
SHEET
SHIED
SHIER
SHIES
SHOED
SHOER
SHOES
SHRED
SHREW
SHYER
THIEF
THREE
THREW
WHEEL
WHEEN

•H••E
CHAFE
CHASE
CHERE
CHIDE
CHILE
CHIME
CHINE
CHIVE
CHLOE
CHOKE
CHORE
CHOSE
CHUTE
DHOLE
DHOTE
OHARE
PHAGE
PHASE
PHILE
PHOBE
PHONE
PHYFE
PHYLE
RHINE
RHODE
RHONE
RHYME
SHADE
SHAKE
SHALE
SHAME
SHANE
SHAPE
SHARE
SHAVE
SHERE
SHINE
SHIRE
SHONE
SHORE
SHOVE
SHUTE
THANE
THEBE
THEME
THERE
THESE
THINE
THOLE
THOSE
THREE
THROE
THULE
THYME
WHALE
WHERE
WHILE
WHINE
WHITE
WHOLE
WHOSE
WHYME
WHYRE

••HE•
AAHED
ACHED
ACHES
ADHEM
ASHEN
ASHER
ASHES
BOHEA
COHEN
ETHEL
ETHER
FAHEY
MAHER
OCHER
OOHED
OSHEA
OTHER
REHEM
SAHEL
SCHED
TEHEE
USHED
USHER
UTHER

••H•E
BOHME
JAHRE
MAHRE
OCHRE
TAHOE
TEHEE

•••HE
BATHE
BECHE
BOTHE
BRAHE
CACHE
DACHE
FICHE
HECHE
LATHE
LETHE
LITHE
MACHE
MOSHE
NASHE
NICHE
PATHE
RAPHE
RICHE
ROCHE
RUCHE
SADHE
SIDHE
TITHE
TYCHE
WITHE
WYTHE

H•F••
HAFIZ
HAFTS
HAFUN
HEFEI
HEFTS
HEFTY
HIFIS
HOFFA
HUFFS
HUFFY

H••F•
HAIFA
HANFF
HOFFA
HOOFS
HUFFS
HUFFY

H•••F
HANFF

•H•F•
CHAFE
CHAFF
CHEFS
CHUFF
KHUFU
PHYFE
SHAFT
SHIFT
THEFT
WHIFF

•H••F
CHAFF
CHIEF
CHUFF
SHAEF
SHEAF
SHELF
THIEF
WHARF
WHIFF
WHOOF

H•G••
HAGAR
HAGEN
HAGIO
HAGUE
HEGEL
HIGHC
HIGHS
HOGAN
HOGGS
HUGER
HUGOS
HYGRO

H••G•
HANGS
HAWGS
HEDGE
HEDGY
HEIGH
HELGA
HENGE
HINGE
HOAGY
HOGGS
HONGS
HOUGH

H•••G
HARDG
HMONG
HYING

•HG••
OHGOD

•H•G•
CHUGS
PHAGE
PHAGO
PHAGY
SHAGS
SHOGI
THIGH
THUGS
WHIGS

•H••G
CHANG
CHING
CHONG
CHUNG
SHRUG
THING
THONG
WHANG

HH•••
HHOUR

H•H••
HAHAS
HOHOS
HOHUM

H••H•
HECHE
HECHT
HETHS
HIGHC
HIGHS
HOOHA
HYPHA

H•••H
HARSH
HATCH
HEATH
HEIGH
HENCH
HITCH
HOOCH
HOUGH
HUMPH
HUNCH
HUTCH

•HH••
UHHUH

•H•H•
SHAHN
SHAHS

•H••H
CHETH
SHISH
SHOAH
SHUSH
THIGH
THOTH
UHHUH
WHICH
WHISH

••H•H
EPHAH
ICHTH
UHHUH

HI•••
HICKS
HIDER
HIDES
HIERA
HIERO
HIFIS
HIGHC
HIGHS
HIJAZ
HIJRA
HIKED
HIKER
HIKES
HILDA
HILLS
HILLY
HILTS
HILUM
HINDI
HINDS
HINDU
HINES
HINGE
HINNY
HINTS
HIPLY
HIPPO
HIPPY
HIPTO
HIRAM
HIRED
HIRER
HIRES
HISSY
HITCH
HITIT
HITME
HITON
HITUP
HIVED
HIVES

H•I••
HAIDA
HAIFA
HAIKS
HAIKU
HAILE
HAILS
HAIRS
HAIRY
HAITI
HEIDI
HEIDT
HEIGH
HEINE
HEINZ
HEIRS
HEISS
HEIST
HOIST
HOITY
HYING

H••I•
HABIT
HAFIZ
HAGIO
HAJIS
HAKIM
HASID
HEDIN
HELIC
HELIO
HELIX
HEMIN
HENIE
HIFIS
HITIT
HOPIN
HOPIS
HOWIE
HOXIE
HUMID
HYOID

H•••I
HADJI
HAITI
HAJJI
HANOI
HEFEI
HEIDI
HENRI
HINDI
HOSNI
HOURI

•HI••
CHIAS
CHIBA
CHICK
CHICO
CHIDE
CHIEF
CHIEN
CHILD
CHILE
CHILI
CHILL
CHILO
CHIME
CHIMP
CHINA
CHINE
CHING
CHINK
CHINO
CHINS
CHIOS
CHIPS
CHIRO
CHIRP
CHIRR
CHITA
CHITS
CHIVE
CHIVY
PHIAL
PHILE
PHILO
PHILY
RHINE
RHINO
RHIZO
SHIED
SHIER
SHIES
SHIFT
SHILL
SHIMS
SHINE
SHINS
SHINY
SHIPS
SHIRE
SHIRK
SHIRR
SHIRT
SHISH
SHIVA
SHIVS
THICK
THIEF
THIGH
THILL
THINE
THING
THINK
THINS
THIRD
WHICH
WHIFF
WHIGS
WHILE
WHIMS
WHINE
WHINS
WHINY
WHIPS
WHIRL
WHIRR
WHIRS
WHISH
WHISK
WHIST
WHITE
WHITS
WHITY

•H•I•
AHSIN
CHAIM
CHAIN
CHAIR
CHOIR
CHRIS
GHAIN
OHAIR
SHEIK
THAIS
THEIR

•H••I
CHERI
CHILI
DHABI
DHOTI
GHALI
GHAZI
KHAKI
PHYSI
SHARI
SHOGI
SHOJI

••HI•
APHID
APHIS
BAHIA
ECHIN
ETHIC
NEHIS
NIHIL
NOHIT
OPHIR
SAHIB
SOHIO
UNHIP
VCHIP

••H•I
ANHUI
BAHAI
BOHAI
LAHTI
MAHDI
POHAI

•••HI
AMPHI
ARCHI
DASHI
DELHI
KOCHI
RISHI
SOCHI
SPAHI
SUSHI

H•J••
HAJIS
HAJJI
HEJAZ
HIJAZ
HIJRA

H••J•
HADJI
HAJJI

•H•J•
CHEJU
SHOJI
THUJA

H•K••
HAKES
HAKIM
HEKLA
HIKED
HIKER
HIKES
HOKED
HOKES
HOKEY
HOKUM

H••K•
HACKS
HAIKS
HAIKU
HANKS
HANKY
HARKS
HAWKE
HAWKS
HECKS
HERKY
HICKS
HOCKS
HONKS
HOOKE
HOOKS
HOOKY
HULKS
HUNKS
HUSKS
HUSKY

H•••K
HACEK
HAYEK
HUROK

•HK••
OHKAY

•H•K•
CHAKA
CHEKA
CHOKE
CHOKY
DHAKA
KHAKI
SHAKE
SHAKO
SHAKY

•H••K
CHALK
CHECK
CHEEK
CHICK
CHINK
CHOCK
CHUCK
CHUNK
SHACK
SHANK
SHARK
SHEIK
SHIRK
SHOCK
SHOOK
SHUCK
THANK
THICK
THINK
THUNK
WHACK
WHELK
WHISK

H•L••
HALAS
HALED
HALER
HALES
HALEY
HALLE
HALLO
HALLS
HALMS
HALON
HALOS
HALTS
HALVE
HELEN
HELGA
HELIC
HELIO
HELIX
HELLO
HELLS
HELMS
HELOS
HELOT
HELPS
HELVE
HILDA
HILLS
HILLY
HILTS
HILUM
HOLDS
HOLED
HOLES
HOLEY
HOLLY
HOLMS
HOLST
HOLTZ
HULAS
HULCE
HULKS
HULLO
HULLS
HYLAS

H••L•
HABLA
HAILE
HAILS
HALLE
HALLO
HALLS
HAOLE
HAPLO
HAPLY
HATLO
HAULM
HAULS
HEALS
HEALY
HEELS
HEKLA
HELLO
HELLS
HERLS
HILLS
HILLY
HIPLY
HOLLY
HOTLY
HOWLS
HOYLE
HULLO
HULLS
HURLS
HURLY

H•••L
HAMAL
HAMEL
HAVEL
HAZEL
HEGEL
HERZL
HEXYL
HORAL
HOROL
HOSEL
HOTEL
HOVEL

•HL••
CHLOE
CHLOR
NHLER
PHLOX
UHLAN

•H•L•
CHALK
CHELA
CHILD
CHILE
CHILI
CHILL
CHILO
CHOLO
CHULA
DHALS
DHOLE
GHALI
PHILE
PHILO
PHILY
PHYLA
PHYLE
PHYLL
SHALE
SHALL
SHALT
SHELF
SHELL
SHILL
SHULA
SHULS
SHYLY
THILL
THOLE
THULE
WHALE
WHELK
WHELM
WHELP
WHILE
WHOLE
WHOLL
WHYLL

•H••L
CHILL
CHURL
GHOUL
PHIAL
PHYLL
SHALL
SHAWL
SHELL
SHILL
SHOAL
THEOL
THILL
UHAUL
WHEAL
WHEEL
WHIRL
WHOLL
WHORL
WHYLL

••HL•
BUHLS
KAHLO

••H•L
ATHOL
ETHEL
ETHYL
MAHAL
NIHIL
RAHAL
SAHEL

•••HL
AMAHL
RUEHL
STAHL

HM•••
HMONG

H•M••
HAMAL
HAMAN
HAMEL
HAMES
HAMMY
HEMAN
HEMEN
HEMET
HEMIN
HEMPS
HOMED
HOMEO
HOMER
HOMES
HOMEY
HOMME
HUMAN
HUMID
HUMOR
HUMPH
HUMPS
HUMPY
HUMUS
HYMAN
HYMNS

H••M•
HAEMA
HAEMO
HALMS
HAMMY
HARMS
HBOMB
HELMS
HERMS
HITME
HOLMS
HOMME
HOUMA
HYAMS

H•••M
HAKIM
HAREM
HARUM
HAULM
HBEAM
HILUM
HIRAM
HOHUM
HOKUM

•HM••
AHMAD
AHMED
KHMER

•H•M•
CHAMP
CHIME
CHIMP
CHOMP
CHUMP
CHUMS
RHOMB
RHUMB
RHYME
SHAME
SHAMS
SHAMU
SHEMA
SHEMP
SHIMS
THEMA
THEME
THEMS
THUMB
THUMP
THYME
THYMY
WHAMO
WHAMS
WHIMS
WHOMP
WHYME

•H••M
CHAIM
CHARM
CHASM
CHROM
PHARM
PHNOM
RHEUM
SHAWM
THERM
THRUM
WHELM

••HM•
BOHME
SCHMO

••H•M
ADHEM
HOHUM
MOHAM
NAHUM
OGHAM
REHEM

•••HM
ABOHM
BOEHM

H•N••
HANDS
HANDY
HANES
HANFF
HANGS
HANKS
HANKY
HANNA
HANNO
HANOI
HANSA
HANSE
HANTS
HENAN
HENCE
HENCH
HENGE
HENIE
HENNA
HENNY
HENRI
HENRY
HENTS
HINDI
HINDS
HINDU
HINES
HINGE
HINNY
HINTS
HONAN
HONDA
HONDO
HONED
HONES
HONEY
HONGS
HONKS
HONOR
HONUS
HUNAN
HUNCH
HUNKS
HUNTS
HUNTZ

H••N•
HADNT
HANNA
HANNO
HASNT
HAUNT
HEINE
HEINZ
HENNA
HENNY
HERNE
HERNS
HINNY
HMONG
HORNE
HORNS
HOSNI
HOUND
HYENA
HYING
HYMNS
HYPNO

H•••N
HADON
HAFUN
HAGEN
HALON
HAMAN
HASON
HAVEN
HAYDN
HAZAN
HEARN
HEDIN
HELEN
HEMAN
HEMEN
HEMIN
HENAN
HERON
HITON
HOBAN
HOGAN
HONAN
HOPIN
HUMAN
HUNAN
HURON
HYMAN
HYSON

•HN••
PHNOM

•H•N•
CHANG
CHANT

CHINA
CHINE
CHING
CHINK
CHINO
CHINS
CHONG
CHUNG
CHUNK
GHANA
GHENT
KHANS
PHANY
PHENO
PHONE
PHONO
PHONS
PHONY
RHINE
RHINO
RHONE
SHANA
SHANE
SHANK
SHANS
SHANT
SHINE
SHINS
SHINY
SHONE
SHUNS
SHUNT
THANE
THANK
THANT
THINE
THING
THINK
THINS
THONG
THUNK
WHANG
WHINE
WHINS
WHINY

•H••N

AHSIN
CHAIN
CHIEN
CHRON
CHURN
GHAIN
PHREN
SHAHN
SHAUN
SHAWN
SHEAN
SHEEN
SHORN
SHOWN
THORN
UHLAN
WHEEN

••HN•

ETHNO
FOHNS
JOHNS
SEHNA

••H•N

ASHEN
ATHON
BEHAN
COHAN
COHEN
ECHIN
ETHAN
MAHAN
MAHON
REHAN
SCHON
WUHAN

•••HN

BRUHN
FOEHN
ICAHN
SHAHN
SPAHN
UTAHN

HO•••

HOAGY
HOARD
HOARS
HOARY
HOBAN
HOBBS
HOBBY
HOBOS
HOCKS
HOCUS
HODAD
HOERS
HOFFA
HOGAN
HOGGS
HOHOS
HOHUM
HOIST
HOITY
HOKED
HOKES
HOKEY
HOKUM
HOLDS
HOLED
HOLES
HOLEY
HOLLY
HOLMS
HOLST
HOLTZ
HOMED
HOMEO
HOMER
HOMES
HOMEY
HOMME
HONAN
HONDA
HONDO
HONED
HONES
HONEY
HONGS
HONKS
HONOR
HONUS
HOOCH
HOODS
HOOEY
HOOFS
HOOHA
HOOKE
HOOKS
HOOKY
HOOPS
HOOTS
HOPED
HOPER
HOPES
HOPIN
HOPIS
HOPPE
HOPUP
HORAE
HORAL
HORAS
HORDE
HOREB
HORNE
HORNS
HOROL
HORSE
HORST
HORSY
HORUS
HOSEA
HOSED
HOSEL
HOSES
HOSNI
HOSTA
HOSTS
HOTEL
HOTLY
HOUGH
HOUMA
HOUND
HOURI
HOURS
HOUSE
HOVEL
HOVER
HOVEY
HOWAR
HOWDY
HOWIE
HOWLS
HOWSO
HOWTO
HOXIE
HOYAS
HOYLE

H•O••

HAOLE
HBOMB
HHOUR
HMONG
HOOCH
HOODS
HOOEY
HOOFS
HOOHA
HOOKE
HOOKS
HOOKY
HOOPS
HOOTS
HYOID

H••O•

HADON
HALON
HALOS
HANOI
HASON
HAVOC
HELOS
HELOT
HEROD
HERON
HEROS
HITON
HOBOS
HOHOS
HONOR
HOROL
HUGOS
HUMOR
HUROK
HURON
HYPOS
HYSON

H•••O

HADTO
HAEMO
HAGIO
HALLO
HANNO
HAPLO
HARPO
HASSO
HASTO
HATLO
HECTO
HELIO
HELLO
HIERO
HIPPO
HIPTO
HOMEO
HONDO
HOWSO
HOWTO
HUEVO
HULLO
HYDRO
HYGRO
HYPNO
HYPSO

•HO••

AHORA
AHOYS
CHOCK
CHOIR
CHOKE
CHOKY
CHOLO
CHOMP
CHONG
CHOPS
CHORD
CHORE
CHOSE
CHOWS
DHOLE
DHOTE
DHOTI
DHOWS
GHOST
GHOUL
HHOUR
PHOBE
PHONE
PHONO
PHONS
PHONY
PHOTO
PHOTS
RHODA
RHODE
RHODO
RHOMB
RHONE
SHOAH
SHOAL
SHOAT
SHOCK
SHOED
SHOER
SHOES
SHOGI
SHOJI
SHONE
SHOOK
SHOOS
SHOOT
SHOPS
SHORE
SHORN
SHORT
SHOTS
SHOUT
SHOVE
SHOWN
SHOWS
SHOWY
SHOYU
THOLE
THONG
THORN
THORO
THORP
THOSE
THOTH
THOUS
WHOLE
WHOLL
WHOMP
WHOOF
WHOOP
WHOPS
WHORL
WHOSE
WHOSO
XHOSA

•H•O•

CHAOS
CHIOS
CHLOE
CHLOR
CHROM
CHRON
OHBOY
OHGOD
OHWOW
PHLOX
PHNOM
SHOOK
SHOOS
SHOOT
THEOL
THROB
THROE
THROW
WHOOF
WHOOP

•H••O

CHACO
CHARO
CHICO
CHILO
CHINO
CHIRO
CHOLO
PHAGO
PHENO
PHILO
PHONO
PHOTO
PHYCO
PHYTO
RHINO
RHIZO
RHODO
SHAKO
THORO
WHAMO
WHOSO

••HO•

ABHOR
ACHOO
ADHOC
ATHOL
ATHON
ATHOS
COHOS
EPHOD
EPHOR
ETHOS
HOHOS
ICHOR
MAHON
NOHOW
OCHOA
SCHON
TAHOE
WAHOO
YAHOO

••H•O

ACHOO
ETHNO
KAHLO
SCHMO
SOHIO
WAHOO
YAHOO

•••HO

ALTHO
ANTHO
BASHO
BATHO
BISHO
DICHO
DONHO
IDAHO
LITHO
MACHO
MINHO
MUGHO
NACHO
ORTHO
PATHO
SOTHO
TACHO
TYCHO

H•P••

HAPLO
HAPLY
HAPPY
HEPTA
HIPLY
HIPPO
HIPPY
HIPTO
HOPED
HOPER
HOPES
HOPIN
HOPIS
HOPPE
HOPUP
HYPED
HYPER
HYPES
HYPHA
HYPNO
HYPOS
HYPSO

H••P•

HAPPY
HARPO
HARPS
HARPY
HASPS
HEAPS
HELPS
HEMPS
HIPPO
HIPPY
HOOPS
HOPPE
HUMPH
HUMPS
HUMPY

H•••P

HETUP
HITUP
HOPUP

•H•P•

CHAPS
CHIPS
CHOPS
SHAPE
SHIPS
SHOPS
WHIPS
WHOPS
WHUPS

•H••P

CHAMP
CHEAP
CHEEP
CHIMP
CHIRP
CHOMP
CHUMP
SHARP
SHEEP
SHEMP
THARP
THORP
THUMP
WHELP
WHOMP
WHOOP

••H•P

UNHIP
VCHIP

H•R••

HARAR
HARDC
HARDG
HARDY
HARED
HAREM
HARES
HARKS
HARMS
HARPO
HARPS
HARPY
HARRY
HARSH
HARTE
HARTS
HARUM
HERAT
HERBS
HERBY
HERDS
HERES
HERKY
HERLS
HERMS
HERNE
HERNS
HEROD
HERON
HEROS
HERTZ
HERVE
HERZL
HIRAM
HIRED
HIRER
HIRES
HORAE
HORAL
HORAS
HORDE
HOREB
HORNE
HORNS
HOROL
HORSE
HORST
HORSY
HORUS
HURDY
HURLS
HURLY
HUROK
HURON
HURRY
HURST
HURTS
HYRAX

H••R•

HAIRS
HAIRY
HARRY
HAVRE
HEARD
HEARN
HEARS
HEART
HEIRS
HENRI
HENRY
HEURE
HIERA
HIERO
HIJRA
HOARD
HOARS
HOARY
HOERS
HOURI
HOURS
HURRY
HYDRA
HYDRO
HYGRO

H•••R

HABER
HADAR
HAGAR
HALER
HARAR
HATER
HAUER
HAVER
HAZER
HEWER
HEXER
HHOUR
HIDER
HIKER
HIRER
HOMER
HONOR
HOPER
HOVER
HOWAR
HUGER
HUMOR
HYPER

•HR••

CHRIS
CHROM
CHRON
CHRYS
PHREN
SHRED
SHREW
SHRUB
SHRUG
THREE
THREW
THROB
THROE
THROW
THRUM

•H•R•

AHORA
CHARD
CHARM
CHARO
CHARS
CHART
CHARY
CHERE
CHERI
CHERT
CHIRO
CHIRP
CHIRR
CHORD
CHORE
CHURL
CHURN
OHARA
OHARE
PHARM
SHARD
SHARE
SHARI
SHARK
SHARP
SHERE
SHIRE
SHIRK
SHIRR
SHIRT
SHORE
SHORN
SHORT
THARP
THERA
THERE
THERM
THIRD
THORN
THORO
THORP
THURS
UHURA
UHURU
WHARF

WHERE
WHIRL
WHIRR
WHIRS
WHORL
WHYRE

•H••R
CHAIR
CHEER
CHIRR
CHLOR
CHOIR
HHOUR
KHMER
NHLER
OHAIR
SHEAR
SHEER
SHIER
SHIRR
SHOER
SHYER
THEIR
WHIRR

••HR•
JAHRE
MAHRE
NEHRU
OCHRE
TAHRS

••H•R
ABHOR
ASHER
ASHUR
BIHAR
EPHOR
ETHER
ICHOR
LAHAR
LEHAR
MAHER
MOHUR
OCHER
OPHIR
OTHER
USHER
UTHER
ZOHAR

•••HR
AMPHR
ARTHR

H•S••
HASAT
HASID
HASNT
HASON
HASPS
HASSO
HASTA
HASTE
HASTO
HASTY
HESSE
HESTS
HISSY
HOSEA
HOSED
HOSEL
HOSES
HOSNI
HOSTA
HOSTS
HUSKS
HUSKY
HUSSY
HYSON

H••S•
HADST
HANSA
HANSE
HARSH
HASSO
HAUSA
HAWSE
HEISS
HEIST
HESSE
HEYSE
HISSY
HOIST
HOLST
HORSE
HORST
HORSY
HOUSE
HOWSO
HURST
HUSSY
HYPSO

H•••S
HACKS
HADES
HAFTS
HAHAS
HAIKS
HAILS
HAIRS
HAJIS
HAKES
HALAS
HALES
HALLS
HALMS
HALOS
HALTS
HAMES
HANDS
HANES
HANGS
HANKS
HANTS
HARES
HARKS
HARMS
HARPS
HARTS
HASPS
HATES
HAULS
HAVES
HAWGS
HAWKS
HAYES
HAZES
HEADS
HEALS
HEAPS
HEARS
HEATS
HECKS
HEEDS
HEELS
HEFTS
HEIRS
HEISS
HELLS
HELMS
HELOS
HELPS
HEMPS
HENTS
HERBS
HERDS
HERES
HERLS
HERMS
HERNS
HEROS
HESTS
HETHS
HEXES
HICKS
HIDES
HIFIS
HIGHS
HIKES
HILLS
HILTS
HINDS
HINES
HINTS
HIRES
HIVES
HOARS
HOBBS
HOBOS
HOCKS
HOCUS
HOERS
HOGGS
HOHOS
HOKES
HOLDS
HOLES
HOLMS
HOMES
HONES
HONGS
HONKS
HONUS
HOODS
HOOFS
HOOKS
HOOPS
HOOTS
HOPES
HOPIS
HORAS
HORNS
HORUS
HOSES
HOSTS
HOURS
HOWLS
HOYAS
HUFFS
HUGOS
HULAS
HULKS
HULLS
HUMPS
HUMUS
HUNKS
HUNTS
HURLS
HURTS
HUSKS
HUTUS
HYAMS
HYLAS
HYMNS
HYPES
HYPOS

•HS••
AHSIN

•H•S•
CHASE
CHASM
CHESS
CHEST
CHOSE
GHOST
LHASA
PHASE
PHYSI
SHISH
SHUSH
THESE
THOSE
WHISH
WHISK
WHIST
WHOSE
WHOSO
XHOSA

•H••S
AHOYS
CHAOS
CHAPS
CHARS
CHATS
CHAWS
CHEFS
CHESS
CHEWS
CHIAS
CHINS
CHIOS
CHIPS
CHITS
CHOPS
CHOWS
CHRIS
CHRYS
CHUBS
CHUGS
CHUMS
DHALS
DHOWS
GHATS
GHEES
KHANS
PHONS
PHOTS
RHEAS
SHADS
SHAGS
SHAHS
SHAMS
SHANS
SHAYS
SHEDS
SHIES
SHIMS
SHINS
SHIPS
SHIVS
SHOES
SHOOS
SHOPS
SHOTS
SHOWS
SHULS
SHUNS
SHUTS
THAIS
THATS
THAWS
THEMS
THEWS
THINS
THOUS
THUDS
THUGS
THURS
WHAMS
WHATS
WHETS
WHEYS
WHIGS
WHIMS
WHINS
WHIPS
WHIRS
WHITS
WHOPS
WHUPS

••H•S
ACHES
AGHAS
APHIS
ARHUS
ASHES
ATHOS
BAHTS
BUHLS
COHOS
EPHAS
ETHOS
FOHNS
HAHAS
HOHOS
JOHNS
NEHIS
TAHRS

•••HS
AMAHS
ANKHS
AYAHS
BACHS
BATHS
BETHS
BLAHS
FUCHS
GOTHS
HETHS
HIGHS
KAPHS
KOPHS
LATHS
LITHS
LOCHS
MATHS
MOTHS
MYTHS
NOAHS
OATHS
OPAHS
ORCHS
PATHS
PITHS
POOHS
QOPHS
RATHS
SACHS
SHAHS
SIGHS
SIKHS
SOPHS
TECHS
TETHS
YODHS
YOGHS

H•T••
HATCH
HATED
HATER
HATES
HATLO
HETHS
HETTY
HETUP
HITCH
HITIT
HITIT
HITME
HITON
HITUP
HOTEL
HOTLY
HUTCH
HUTUS

H••T•
HADTO
HAFTS
HAITI
HALTS
HANTS
HARTE
HARTS
HASTA
HASTE
HASTO
HASTY
HAUTE
HEATH
HEATS
HECTO
HEFTS
HEFTY
HENTS
HEPTA
HERTZ
HESTS
HETTY
HEUTE
HILTS
HINTS
HIPTO
HOITY
HOLTZ
HOOTS
HOSTA
HOSTS
HOWTO
HUNTS
HUNTZ
HURTS
HYATT

H•••T
HABIT
HADAT
HADNT
HADST
HASAT
HASNT
HAUNT
HEART
HECHT
HEIDT
HEIST
HELOT
HEMET
HERAT
HITIT
HOIST
HOLST
HORST
HURST
HYATT

•H•T•
CHATS
CHETH
CHITA
CHITS
CHUTE
DHOTE
DHOTI
GHATS
PHOTO
PHOTS
PHYTO
RHETT
RHYTA
SHATT
SHOTS
SHUTE
SHUTS
THATS
THETA
THOTH
WHATD
WHATS
WHETS
WHITE
WHITS
WHITY

•H••T
CHANT
CHART
CHEAT
CHERT
CHEST
GHENT
GHOST
RHETT
SHAFT
SHALT
SHANT
SHATT
SHEET
SHIFT
SHIRT
SHOAT
SHOOT
SHORT
SHOUT
SHUNT
THANT
THEFT
WHEAT
WHIST

••HT•
BAHTS
ICHTH
LAHTI
MEHTA

••H•T
ARHAT
NOHIT

•••HT
AUGHT
BIGHT
EIGHT
FIGHT
HECHT
LIGHT
MIGHT
NACHT
NIGHT
OUGHT
RASHT
RIGHT
SIGHT
TIGHT
WIGHT
YACHT

HU•••
HUBBA
HUBBY
HUEVO
HUFFS
HUFFY
HUGER
HUGOS
HULAS
HULCE
HULKS
HULLO
HULLS
HUMAN
HUMID
HUMOR
HUMPH
HUMPS
HUMPY
HUMUS
HUNAN
HUNCH
HUNKS
HUNTS
HUNTZ
HURDY
HURLS
HURLY
HUROK
HURON
HURRY
HURST
HURTS
HUSKS
HUSKY
HUSSY
HUTCH
HUTUS
HUZZA

H•U••
HAUER
HAULM
HAULS
HAUNT
HAUSA
HAUTE
HEURE
HEUTE
HOUGH
HOUMA
HOUND
HOURI
HOURS
HOUSE

H••U•
HAFUN
HAGUE
HARUM
HETUP
HHOUR
HILUM
HITUP
HOCUS
HOHUM
HOKUM
HONUS
HOPUP
HORUS
HUMUS
HUTUS

H•••U
HAIKU
HINDU

•HU••
CHUBS
CHUCK
CHUFF
CHUGS
CHULA
CHUMP
CHUMS
CHUNG
CHUNK
CHURL
CHURN
CHUTE
KHUFU
RHUMB
SHUCK
SHULA
SHULS
SHUNS
SHUNT
SHUSH
SHUTE
SHUTS
THUDS
THUGS
THUJA
THULE
THUMB
THUMP
THUNK
THURS
UHURA
UHURU
WHUPS

•H•U•
CHAUD
GHOUL
HHOUR
RHEUM
SHAUN
SHOUT
SHRUB
SHRUG
THOUS
THRUM
UHAUL
UHHUH

•H••U
CHEJU
KHUFU
SHAMU
SHOYU
UHURU

••HU•
ANHUI
ARHUS
ASHUR
HOHUM
LEHUA
MOHUR
NAHUA
NAHUM
UHHUH

••H•U
NEHRU

•••HU
ELIHU
FICHU
MACHU
SADHU
WUSHU

H•V••
HAVEL
HAVEN
HAVER
HAVES
HAVOC
HAVRE
HIVED
HIVES
HOVEL
HOVER
HOVEY

H••V•
HALVE
HEAVE
HEAVY
HELVE
HERVE
HUEVO

•H•V•
CHEVY
CHIVE
CHIVY
SHAVE
SHIVA
SHIVS
SHOVE

••H•V
SCHAV

H•W••
HAWED
HAWGS
HAWKE
HAWKS
HAWSE
HEWED
HEWER
HOWAR
HOWDY
HOWIE
HOWLS
HOWSO
HOWTO

•HW••
OHWOW

•H•W•
CHAWS
CHEWS
CHEWY
CHOWS
DHOWS
SHAWL
SHAWM
SHAWN
SHOWN
SHOWS
SHOWY
THAWS
THEWS
THEWY

•H••W
OHWOW
SHREW
THREW
THROW

••HW•
SCHWA

••H•W
NOHOW
PSHAW

H•X••
HEXAD
HEXED
HEXER
HEXES
HEXYL
HOXIE

H•••X
HELIX
HYRAX

•H••X
PHLOX

HY•••
HYAMS
HYATT
HYDRA
HYDRO
HYENA
HYGRO
HYING
HYLAS
HYMAN
HYMNS
HYOID
HYPED
HYPER
HYPES
HYPHA
HYPNO
HYPOS
HYPSO
HYRAX
HYSON

H•Y••
HAYDN
HAYED
HAYEK
HAYES
HEYSE
HOYAS
HOYLE

H••Y•
HEXYL

H•••Y
HAIRY
HALEY
HAMMY
HANDY
HANKY
HAPLY
HAPPY
HARDY
HARPY
HARRY
HASTY
HEADY
HEALY
HEAVY
HEDGY
HEFTY
HENNY
HENRY
HERBY
HERKY
HETTY
HILLY
HINNY
HIPLY
HIPPY
HISSY
HOAGY
HOARY
HOBBY
HOITY
HOKEY
HOLEY
HOLLY
HOMEY
HONEY
HOOEY
HOOKY
HORSY
HOTLY
HOVEY
HOWDY
HUBBY
HUFFY
HUMPY
HURDY
HURLY
HURRY
HUSKY
HUSSY

•HY••
PHYCO
PHYFE
PHYLA
PHYLE
PHYLL
PHYSI
PHYTO
RHYME
RHYTA
SHYER
SHYLY
THYME
THYMY
WHYLL
WHYME
WHYRE

•H•Y•
AHOYS
CHRYS
SHAYS
SHOYU
THEYD
WHEYS

•H••Y
CHARY
CHEVY
CHEWY
CHIVY
CHOKY
OHBOY
OHKAY
PHAGY
PHANY
PHILY
PHONY
SHADY
SHAKY
SHINY
SHOWY
SHYLY
THEWY
THYMY
WHINY
WHITY

••HY•
ETHYL

••H•Y
ASHBY
FAHEY

•••HY
ARCHY
BATHY
BUSHY
CATHY
CECHY
CUSHY
DISHY
DUCHY
FISHY
GUSHY
ITCHY
KATHY
LATHY
LEAHY
MACHY
MASHY
MESHY
MOTHY
MUSHY
PATHY
PITHY
PUSHY
RUSHY
SOPHY
TACHY
TECHY
VICHY
WASHY
WISHY
WITHY

H•Z••
HAZAN
HAZED
HAZEL
HAZER
HAZES
HUZZA

H••Z•
HERZL
HUZZA

H•••Z
HAFIZ
HEINZ
HEJAZ
HERTZ
HIJAZ
HOLTZ
HUNTZ

•H•Z•
CHAZZ
GHAZI
RHIZO

•H••Z
CHAZZ

IA•••
IAMBI
IAMBS
IATRO
IATRY

I•A••
IBARS
ICAHN
IDAHO
IMAGE
IMAGO
IMAMS
INALL
INANE
INAPT
INARI
INAWE
IPANA
IPASS
IRADE
IRANI
IRAQI
IRATE
ISAAC
ISAMU
ITALO
ITALS
ITALY
IVANA
IZAAK
IZARD
IZARS

I••A•
IBEAM
ICEAX
IDEAL
IDEAS
IDTAG
ILIAC
ILIAD
INBAD
INCAN
INCAS
INLAW
INLAY
IOTAS
IOWAN
ISAAC
ISLAM
ISLAS
IXNAY
IZAAK
IZBAS

I•••A
IBIZA
ICOSA
ILONA
INDIA
INDRA
INFRA
INTRA
IONIA
IPANA
IRINA
IVANA

•IA••
BIALY
DIALS
DIANA
DIANE
DIARY
DIAZO
FIATS
GIANT
KIANG
LIANA
LIANE
LIANG
LIARD
LIARS
MIAMI
MIAOW
MIATA
PIANO
PIAUI
RIALS
RIANT
RIATA
SIALS
TIANT
TIARA
VIALS
VIAND

•I•A•
AIDAN
AIMAT
BIHAR
BINAL
CIGAR
DINAH
DINAR
DIRAC
DITAT
DIVAN
DIVAS
EILAT
FILAR
FINAL
HIJAZ
HIRAM
JIHAD
KINAS
KIVAS
LILAC
LIMAS
LIRAS
MICAH
MICAS
MIDAS
MIKAN
MILAN
MIMAS
MINAS
MIZAR
NICAD
NINAS
NIPAS
NIPAT
NISAN
NIVAL
NIZAM
PICAS
PIKAS
PILAF
PILAR
PIMAS
PIPAL
PISAN
PITAS
RIVAL
RIYAL
SIKAS
SILAS
SINAI
SISAL
SITAR
SIVAN
SIXAM
TICAL
TIDAL
TIKAL
TILAK
TIRAN
TITAN
VICAR
VIDAL
VILAS
VINAS
VIRAL
VISAS
VITAE
VITAL
VITAS
WIGAN

•I••A
AISHA
BIOTA
CIERA
CILIA
CILLA
CIRCA
DIANA
DICTA
DITKA
FINCA
FIONA
FIRMA
GILDA
GINZA
HIERA
HIJRA
HILDA
JIDDA
KINDA
KIOGA
KIOWA
KISKA
LIANA
LIBRA
LIBYA
LICIA
LINDA
LIVIA
MIATA
MICRA
MILPA
MISHA
MISSA
NINJA
PIETA
PILEA
PINNA
PINTA
PINZA
PIPPA
PITTA
PIURA
PIZZA
RIATA
RIOJA
SIDEA
SIDRA
SIENA
SIGMA
SILVA
SIMBA
SITKA
TIARA
TIBIA
TISZA
UINTA
VILLA
VILMA
VIOLA
VIRGA
VIRNA
VISTA
WICCA
WILLA
WILMA
WIRRA
ZIZKA

••IA•
ALIAS
APIAN
ARIAN
ARIAS
ASIAN
AVIAN
AXIAL
BRIAN
BRIAR
CHIAS
ELIAS
ENIAC
EVIAN
FRIAR
GLIAL
ILIAC
ILIAD
NAIAD
PHIAL
PRIAM
TRIAD
TRIAL
UMIAK
URIAH
URIAL

••I•A
AGITA
AKIRA
AKITA
ALIDA
AMIGA
ANIMA
ANITA
ARICA
AVILA
BAIZA
CEIBA
CHIBA
CHINA
CHITA
CNIDA
DAIWA
DRINA
DVINA
EDINA
ELIZA
ERICA
ERIKA
ERISA
EVITA
HAIDA
HAIFA
IBIZA
IRINA
LAIKA
LEICA
LEILA
LUISA
MBIRA
MOIRA
NAINA
NAIRA
ORIYA
OUIDA
OUIJA
PAISA
PLICA
PRIMA
RAISA
REINA
SAIGA
SHIVA
SLIWA
SPICA
SUITA
TAIGA
UTICA
VOILA

•••IA
AECIA
AMNIA
ATRIA
BAHIA
CARIA
CELIA
CERIA
CILIA
COBIA
CORIA
CURIA
DACIA
ENTIA
FACIA
FERIA
FOLIA
INDIA
IONIA
JULIA
LAMIA
LICIA
LIVIA
LOGIA
LUCIA
LURIA
LYDIA
MANIA
MARIA
MEDIA
NADIA
NORIA
NUBIA
OMNIA
OSSIA
OSTIA
PAVIA
PODIA
PRAIA
REGIA
RETIA
SEPIA
SOFIA
SONIA
STRIA
SYRIA
TALIA
TIBIA
VARIA
XENIA
ZAMIA

IB•••
IBARS
IBEAM
IBERT
IBIZA
IBSEN

I•B••
ICBMS
IMBUE
INBAD
INBED
INBIG
INBOX
IZBAS

I••B•
IAMBI

IAMBS

•IB••
BIBBS
BIBLE
FIBER
FIBRE
FIBRO
GIBBS
GIBED
GIBER
GIBES
JIBED
JIBES
KIBEI
LIBBY
LIBEL
LIBRA
LIBRE
LIBYA
RIBBY
SIBYL
TIBBS
TIBER
TIBET
TIBIA
VIBES
ZIBET

•I•B•
BIBBS
BILBO
BILBY
BIXBY
DIDBY
DIGBY
GIBBS
KIRBY
LIBBY
LIEBY
LIMBI
LIMBO
LIMBS
NIMBI
NIMBY
NIOBE
RIBBY
RIGBY
SIMBA
SITBY
TIBBS
VISBY

•I••B
SIDEB

••IB•
ALIBI
BRIBE
CEIBA
CHIBA
CRIBS
DRIBS
ORIBI
TRIBE

••I•B
CLIMB
STIEB

•••IB
ADLIB
CARIB
NAMIB
SAHIB
SQUIB

IC•••
ICAHN
ICBMS
ICEAX
ICEIN
ICENI
ICERS
ICEUP
ICHOR
ICHTH
ICIER
ICILY
ICING
ICKES
ICONO
ICONS
ICOSA
ICOSI
ICTUS

I•C••
INCAN
INCAS
INCOG
INCUR
INCUS
ITCHY

I••C•
ILICH

I•••C
ILIAC
INDIC
IODIC
IONIC
ISAAC
ISTIC

•IC••
DICED
DICER
DICES
DICEY
DICHO
DICKS
DICKY
DICOT
DICTA
DICTS
DICTU
FICES
FICHE
FICHU
FICUS
HICKS
KICKS
KICKY
LICET
LICIA
LICIT
LICKS
MICAH
MICAS
MICRA
MICRO
NICAD
NICER
NICHE
NICKS
NICOL
OICKS
PICAS
PICKS
PICKY
PICOT
PICRO
PICTS
PICUL
RICCI
RICED
RICER
RICES
RICHE
RICKI
RICKS
RICKY
RICOH
TICAL
TICKS
TICKY
VICAR
VICES
VICHY
VICKI
VICKS
WICCA
WICKS

•I•C•
AITCH
BIRCH
CINCH
CINCO
CIRCA
CIRCE
CIRCS
CISCO
DISCO
DISCS
DITCH
FILCH
FINCA
FINCH
FISCS
FITCH
HITCH
MILCH
MINCE
MITCH
NIECE
PIECE
PINCE
PINCH
PISCI
PISCO
PITCH
RICCI
SINCE
TINCT
VINCE
VINCI
WICCA
WILCO
WINCE
WINCH
WITCH
ZILCH
ZINCS
ZINCY

•I••C
CIVIC
DIRAC
HIGHC
LILAC
MIMIC

••IC•
ALICE
AMICE
ARICA
BRICE
BRICK
BUICK
CHICK
CHICO
CLICK
CRICK
DEICE
EDICT
EPICS
ERICA
ERICH
EVICT
FLICK
FLICS
FRICK
GLICK
ILICH
JUICE
JUICY
KNICK
LAICS
LEICA
ONICE
PLICA
PRICE
PRICK
PRICY
QUICK
REICH
SLICE
SLICK
SNICK
SPICA
SPICE
SPICY
STICH
STICK
THICK
TRICE
TRICK
TWICE
URICH
UTICA
VOICE
VOICI
WHICH

••I•C
ENIAC
EPISC
ILIAC

•••IC
AFRIC
AGRIC
ANTIC
ASDIC
ASPIC
ATTIC
AURIC
AZOIC
BARIC
BASIC
BORIC
CIVIC
COMIC
CONIC
CUBIC
CYNIC
DORIC
EDDIC
ETHIC
FOLIC
FSLIC
GENIC
HELIC
INDIC
IODIC
IONIC
ISTIC
LOGIC
LUDIC
LYRIC
MAGIC
MALIC
MANIC
MEDIC
MELIC
MESIC
MIMIC
MUSIC
OLEIC
OPTIC
OSMIC
OSRIC
PANIC
PUNIC
PYRIC
RELIC
RUNIC
SALIC
SONIC
STOIC
SUBIC
TELIC
TONIC
TOPIC
TORIC
TOXIC
TUNIC
UGRIC
VATIC
VEDIC
XERIC
YOGIC
ZENIC

ID•••
IDAHO
IDEAL
IDEAS
IDEST
IDINE
IDIOM
IDIOT
IDLED
IDLER
IDLES
IDOLS
IDTAG
IDYLL
IDYLS

I•D••
INDEF
INDEX
INDIA
INDIC
INDIE
INDIO
INDIV
INDRA
INDRI
INDUS
IODIC

I••D•
IMIDE
IMIDO
IRADE
IRIDO

I•••D
IDLED
ILIAD
IMPED
INBAD
INBED
INKED
IRKED
IVIED
IZARD

•ID••
AIDAN
AIDED
AIDES
BIDDY
BIDED
BIDEN
BIDES
BIDIN
BIDON
BIDUP
CIDER
DIDBY
DIDIN
DIDNT
DIDOS
DIDST
DIDUP
EIDER
FIDEI
FIDEL
FIDES
GIDDY
HIDER
HIDES
JIDDA
KIDDO
KIDDY
LIDDY
LIDOS
MIDAS
MIDDY
MIDGE
MIDIS
MIDST
NIDES
NIDRE
NIDUS
RIDER
RIDES
RIDGE
RIDGY
RIDOF
SIDEA
SIDEB
SIDED
SIDER
SIDES
SIDHE
SIDLE
SIDON
SIDRA
TIDAL
TIDED
TIDES
VIDAL
VIDEO
VIDOR
WIDEN
WIDER
WIDOW
WIDTH

•I•D•
BIDDY
BINDS
BIRDS
BIRDY
CINDY
DINDY
DIODE
FINDS
GIDDY
GILDA
GILDS
GIRDS
HILDA
HINDI
HINDS
HINDU
JIDDA
KIDDO
KIDDY
KINDA
KINDS
LIDDY
LINDA
LINDO
LINDY
MIDDY
MINDS
MINDY
MISDO
PIEDS
RINDS
RINDY
TILDE
WILDE
WILDS
WINDS
WINDY

•I••D
AIDED
AILED
AIMED
AIRED
BIDED
BIFID
BIKED
BIPED
BIPOD
CITED
DICED
DIKED
DIMED
DINED
DIVED
FIELD
FIEND
FIFED
FILED
FINED
FIORD
FIRED
FIXED
GIBED
HIKED
HIRED
HIVED
JIBED
JIHAD
JIVED
KITED
LIARD
LIKED
LIKUD
LIMED
LINED
LIPID
LIVED
LIVID
MIKED
MIMED
MINED
MIRED
MIXED
NICAD
NIXED
OILED
PIKED
PILED
PINED
PIPED
RICED
RIGID
RILED
RIMED
RIVED
SIDED
SIRED
SITED
SIXED
SIZED
TIDED
TILED
TIMED
TIMID
TINED
TIRED
VIAND
VINED
VIRID
VIVID
WIELD
WILED
WINED
WIPED
WIRED
WIVED
YIELD

••ID•
ABIDE
ACIDS
ACIDY
ALIDA
AMIDE
AMIDO
ASIDE
AZIDE
BRIDE
BSIDE
CHIDE
CNIDA
EJIDO
ELIDE
GLIDE
GRIDS
GUIDE
GUIDO
HAIDA
HEIDI
HEIDT
IMIDE
IMIDO
IRIDO
MAIDS
MAIDU
OUIDA
OXIDE
PRIDE
QUIDS
RAIDS
SKIDS
SLIDE
SNIDE
TEIDE
VEIDT
VOIDS

••I•D
BAIRD
BLIND
BUILD
CHILD
CRIED
DRIED
FLIED
FRIED
GRIND
GUILD
ILIAD
IVIED
LAIRD
NAIAD
PLIED
PRIED
SHIED
SKIED
SPIED
TBIRD
THIRD
TRIAD
TRIED
WEIRD

•••ID
ACRID
ALGID
APHID
AROID
AVOID
BIFID
BOVID
BRAID
CANID
CUPID
DAVID
DROID
DRUID
ELCID
FELID
FETID
FLUID
FROID
GELID
GEOID
HASID
HUMID
HYOID
LIPID
LIVID
LUCID
LURID
NOBID
OOTID
OVOID
PAVID
PLAID
QUAID
RABID
RANID
RAPID
REBID
REDID
RIGID
SAPID
SOLID
SQUID
STAID
TEPID
TIMID
TUMID
UNBID
UNDID
URSID
VALID
VAPID
VIRID

VIVID
ZOOID

I•E••
IBEAM
IBERT
ICEAX
ICEIN
ICENI
ICERS
ICEUP
IDEAL
IDEAS
IDEST
ILENE
INEPT
INERT
IRENE
ISERE
ITEMS
ITERS

I••E•
IBSEN
ICIER
ICKES
IDLED
IDLER
IDLES
IGNES
ILLER
IMPED
IMPEI
IMPEL
INBED
INDEF
INDEX
INFER
INGER
INKED
INKER
INLET
INNER
INREM
INSET
INTEL
INTER
IRKED
IRREG
ISLES
ISLET
ISLEY
ISSEI
IVIED
IVIES

I•••E
IDINE
ILENE
IMAGE
IMBUE
IMIDE
IMINE
INANE
INAWE
INDIE
INGLE
INKLE
INURE
INUSE
IRADE
IRATE
IRENE
ISERE
ISSUE
ISTLE
ITSME

•IE••
CIERA
DIEGO
DIEMS
DIENE
DIETS
EIEIO
FIEFS
FIELD
FIEND
FIERO
FIERY
HIERA
HIERO
LIEBY
LIEGE
LIEIN
LIENS
LIETO
LIEUS
LIEUT
MIENS
NIECE
NIELS
PIECE
PIEDS
PIERS
PIETA
PIETY
RIELS
SIEGE
SIENA
SIEPI
SIETE
SIEUR
SIEVE
TIEGS
TIEIN
TIERS
TIETO
TIEUP
VIEJO
VIERS
VIEWS
VIEWY
WIELD
WIEST
YIELD

•I•E•
AIDED
AIDES
AIKEN
AILED
AILER
AILEY
AIMED
AIMEE
AIMER
AIRED
AIRES
BIDED
BIDEN
BIDES
BIKED
BIKEL
BIKER
BIKES
BINES
BINET
BIPED
BISES
BITER
BITES
BIZET
CIDER
CINES
CIRES
CITED
CITER
CITES
CIVET
DICED
DICER
DICES
DICEY
DIKED
DIKES
DIMED
DIMES
DINED
DINER
DINES
DIRER
DIVED
DIVER
DIVES
DIYER
DIZEN
EIDER
EIGEN
FIBER
FICES
FIDEI
FIDEL
FIDES
FIFED
FIFER
FIFES
FILED
FILER
FILES
FILET
FINED
FINER
FINES
FIRED
FIRER
FIRES
FIVER
FIVES
FIXED
FIXER
FIXES
GIBED
GIBER
GIBES
GILES
GIMEL
GIVEN
GIVER
GIVES
HIDER
HIDES
HIKED
HIKER
HIKES
HINES
HIRED
HIRER
HIRES
HIVED
HIVES
JIBED
JIBES
JIVED
JIVER
JIVES
JIVEY
KIBEI
KILEY
KINER
KITED
KITER
KITES
LIBEL
LICET
LIGER
LIKED
LIKEN
LIKES
LIMED
LIMEN
LIMES
LIMEY
LINED
LINEN
LINER
LINES
LINEY
LITER
LITES
LIVED
LIVEN
LIVER
LIVES
MIKED
MIKES
MIKEY
MILER
MILES
MIMED
MIMEO
MIMER
MIMES
MINED
MINEO
MINER
MINES
MIRED
MIRES
MISER
MITER
MITES
MIXED
MIXER
MIXES
NICER
NIDES
NIGEL
NIGER
NIKES
NILES
NIMES
NINER
NINES
NISEI
NITER
NITES
NIVEN
NIXED
NIXES
NIZER
OILED
OILER
PIKED
PIKER
PIKES
PILEA
PILED
PILEI
PILES
PINED
PINES
PINEY
PIPED
PIPER
PIPES
PIXEL
RICED
RICER
RICES
RIDER
RIDES
RIFER
RIGEL
RIKER
RILED
RILES
RILEY
RIMED
RIMES
RIPEN
RIPER
RISEN
RISER
RISES
RITES
RIVED
RIVEN
RIVER
RIVES
RIVET
SIDEA
SIDEB
SIDED
SIDER
SIDES
SIKES
SILEX
SINES
SINEW
SIRED
SIREN
SIRES
SITED
SITES
SIXED
SIXER
SIXES
SIZED
SIZER
SIZES
TIBER
TIBET
TIDED
TIDES
TIGER
TIKES
TILED
TILER
TILES
TIMED
TIMER
TIMES
TIMEX
TINED
TINES
TIRED
TIRES
TITER
VIBES
VICES
VIDEO
VILER
VINED
VINES
VIPER
VIREO
VISES
VIXEN
WIDEN
WIDER
WILED
WILES
WILEY
WINED
WINES
WINEY
WIPED
WIPER
WIPES
WIRED
WIRER
WIRES
WISER
WIVED
WIVES
WIZEN
YIKES
YIPES
ZIBET
ZINES

•I••E
AIMEE
AINGE
AISLE
AISNE
BIBLE
BILGE
BINGE
BIOME
BIRSE
BITTE
CIRCE
DIANE
DIENE
DINGE
DIODE
DIONE
DIRGE
DISME
DIXIE
FIBRE
FICHE
FILLE
FISKE
GIGUE
GIJOE
GIMME
HINGE
HITME
KINTE
KITWE
LIANE
LIBRE
LIEGE
LILLE
LISLE
LISSE
LITHE
LITRE
LIVRE
MIDGE
MILLE
MILNE
MINCE
MINIE
MINKE
MITRE
NICHE
NIDRE
NIECE
NIOBE
NITRE
NIXIE
PIECE
PINCE
PIQUE
PISTE
PIXIE
RICHE
RIDGE
RIFLE
RILKE
RILLE
RINSE
SIDHE
SIDLE
SIEGE
SIETE
SIEVE
SIGNE
SINCE
SINGE
TILDE
TINGE
TITHE
TITLE
TITRE
VILLE
VINCE
VITAE
VIVRE
WILDE
WINCE
WINZE
WITHE
WITTE

••IE•
ADIEU
ALIEN
AMIES
ARIEL
ARIES
BRIEF
BRIER
BRIES
CHIEF
CHIEN
CRIED
CRIER
CRIES
DRIED
DRIER
DRIES
ELIEL
ERIES
FLIED
FLIER
FLIES
FRIED
FRIER
FRIES
GRIEF
GRIEG
GRIER
ICIER
IVIED
IVIES
KLIEG
OBIES
OKIES
ORIEL
OSIER
PLIED
PLIES
PRIED
PRIER
PRIES
QUIEN
QUIET
SHIED
SHIER
SHIES
SKIED
SKIER
SKIES
SLIER
SPIED
SPIEL
SPIES
STIEB
STIES
THIEF
TRIED
TRIER
TRIES
URIEL
WRIER

••I•E
ABIDE
ADIGE
AFIRE
AGILE
ALICE
ALIKE
ALINE
ALIVE
AMICE
AMIDE
AMINE
ANIME
ANISE
ARISE
ASIDE
ATIVE
AZIDE
AZINE
BAIZE
BEIGE
BLIGE
BOISE
BOITE
BRIBE
BRICE
BRIDE
BRINE
BRITE
BSIDE
CAINE
CHIDE
CHILE
CHIME
CHINE
CHIVE
CLIME
CLINE
CLIVE
CRIME
DEICE
DRIVE
EDILE
ELIDE
ELISE
ELITE
EMILE
EXILE
FAIRE
FRISE
GLIDE
GRIME
GRIPE
GUIDE
GUILE
GUISE
HAILE
HEINE
IDINE
IMIDE
IMINE
JAIME
JUICE
KLINE
KNIFE
KOINE
LAINE
LOIRE
LUISE
MAILE
MAINE
MAIZE
MOIRE
NAIVE
NEIGE
NOIRE
NOISE
ODILE
OGIVE
OLIVE
ONICE
OPINE
OVINE
OXIDE
PAIGE
PAINE
PHILE
POISE
PRICE
PRIDE
PRIME
PRIZE
QUIRE
QUITE
RAISE
RHINE
SEINE
SEIZE
SHINE
SHIRE
SKIVE
SLICE
SLIDE
SLIME
SMILE
SMITE
SNIDE
SNIPE
SPICE
SPIKE
SPILE
SPINE
SPIRE
SPITE
STILE
STIPE
SUITE
SWINE
SWIPE
TAINE
TEIDE
THINE
TOILE
TRIBE
TRICE
TRIKE
TRINE
TRIPE
TRITE
TWICE
TWINE
UDINE
UNITE
UTILE
VOICE
VOILE
WAITE
WAIVE
WHILE
WHINE
WHITE
WRITE
ZAIRE

•••IE	PYXIE	**•I••F**	INBIG	BINGE	HEIGH	GRAIG	SIGHT	SAITH	ISTIC	VISIT
ABBIE	RAMIE	PILAF	INCOG	BINGO	INIGO	INBIG	SIKHS	SHISH	IZMIR	VIVID
ADDIE	RETIE	RIDOF	INORG	BINGS	LEIGH	MRBIG	TIGHT	SMITH	IZMIT	ZITIS
AERIE	ROSIE		IRREG	BIOGS	LUIGI	NAVIG	TITHE	STICH		
AGGIE	ROXIE	**••IF•**		DIEGO	NEIGE	RELIG	VICHY	SWISH	**I•••I**	**•I••I**
ALFIE	SADIE	ALIFS	**•IG••**	DINGE	NEIGH	RERIG	WIGHT	SWITH	IAMBI	AIOLI
ALLIE	SATIE	CLIFF	BIGGY	DINGO	OLIGO	SELIG	WISHY	THIGH	ICENI	CIRRI
ANDIE	SUSIE	CLIFT	BIGHT	DINGS	PAIGE	SOBIG	WITHE	TRISH	ICOSI	FIDEI
ANGIE	TOTIE	COIFS	BIGLY	DINGY	PRIGS	SPRIG	WITHY	URIAH	IMPEI	HINDI
ANNIE	UNTIE	DEIFY	BIGON	DIRGE	REIGN	UNRIG		URICH	INARI	JINNI
ARNIE	WYLIE	DRIFT	BIGOS	GITGO	SAIGA	VARIG	**•I••H**	WEIGH	INDRI	KIBEI
ARTIE	YALIE	EDIFY	BIGOT	HINGE	SLIGO	ZELIG	AITCH	WHICH	IRANI	LIGNI
AUDIE	ZOWIE	GRIFT	CIGAR	JINGO	SWIGS	ZWEIG	BIRCH	WHISH	IRAQI	LIMBI
BASIE		HAIFA	DIGBY	KINGS	TAIGA		BIRTH		ISSEI	LIPPI
BELIE	**IF•••**	KNIFE	DIGIN	KIOGA	THIGH	**I•H••**	CINCH	**I•I••**		MIAMI
BOGIE	IFNOT	REIFY	DIGIT	LIEGE	TRIGS	ICHOR	DINAH	IBIZA	**•I•I•**	MILLI
BOWIE		SCIFI	DIGUP	LINGO	TWIGS	ICHTH	DITCH	ICIER	BIDIN	MISTI
CELIE	**I•F••**	SHIFT	EIGEN	MIDGE	VSIGN		FIFTH	ICILY	BIFID	MITZI
CURIE	INFER	SKIFF	EIGHT	MINGS	WEIGH	**I••H•**	FILCH	ICING	CILIA	NIKKI
CUTIE	INFIN	SNIFF	FIGHT	MINGY	WHIGS	ICAHN	FILTH	IDINE	CIVIC	NIMBI
DAVIE	INFIX	SPIFF	GIGOT	OINGO		IDAHO	FINCH	IDIOM	CIVIL	NISEI
DIXIE	INFRA	STIFF	GIGUE	PIGGY	**••I•G**	ITCHY	FIRTH	IDIOT	DIDIN	NITTI
DOBIE	INFUN	SWIFT	HIGHC	PINGO	ACING		FITCH	ILIAC	DIGIN	PIAUI
DOGIE		UNIFY	HIGHS	PINGS	AGING	**I•••H**	GIRTH	ILIAD	DIGIT	PILEI
EDDIE	**I•••F**	WAIFS	LIGER	RIDGE	APING	ICHTH	HITCH	ILICH	DIXIE	PIPPI
EERIE	INDEF	WHIFF	LIGHT	RIDGY	AWING	ILICH	MICAH	ILION	DIXIT	PISCI
EFFIE			LIGNI	RIGGS	AXING	INISH	MILCH	ILIUM	EIEIO	RICCI
ELLIE	**•IF••**	**••I•F**	LIGNO	RINGO	BEING	IRISH	MIRTH	IMIDE	FINIS	RICKI
ELSIE	BIFFS	BRIEF	MIGHT	RINGS	BOING		MITCH	IMIDO	FITIN	RIFFI
ERNIE	BIFFY	CHIEF	NIGEL	SIEGE	BRING	**•IH••**	NINTH	IMINE	FIXIT	RIKKI
EUBIE	BIFID	CLIFF	NIGER	SINGE	CHING	BIHAR	PINCH	IMINO	HIFIS	RISHI
EYDIE	FIFED	GRIEF	NIGHT	SINGS	CLING	JIHAD	PITCH	INIGO	HITIT	SIEPI
EYRIE	FIFER	SKIFF	PIGGY	TIEGS	CUING	NIHIL	RICOH	INION	KILIM	SINAI
FACIE	FIFES	SNIFF	RIGBY	TINGE	DOING		SIXTH	INISH	KIRIN	TIKKI
GENIE	FIFTH	SPIFF	RIGEL	TINGS	DYING	**•I•H•**	TILTH	INITS	KIWIS	TIPPI
HENIE	FIFTY	STIFF	RIGGS	VINGT	EKING	AISHA	WIDTH	IRIDO	LICIA	VICKI
HOWIE	GIFTS	THIEF	RIGHT	VIRGA	EWING	BIGHT	WINCH	IRINA	LICIT	VIKKI
HOXIE	HIFIS	WHIFF	RIGID	VIRGO	FLING	BISHO	WITCH	IRISH	LIEIN	VILLI
INDIE	JIFFY		RIGOR	WIGGY	FRIGG	DICHO	ZILCH	IVIED	LIMIT	VINCI
JAMIE	LIFTS	**•••IF**	RIGUP	WINGS	GOING	DISHY		IVIES	LIPID	
JANIE	MIFFS	CALIF	SIGHS	XINGU	GRIEG	EIGHT	**••IH•**	IVINS	LIVIA	**••II•**
JODIE	MIFFY	MOTIF	SIGHT	ZIGGY	HYING	FICHE	ELIHU	IXION	LIVID	CCIII
JOLIE	NIFTY	SERIF	SIGIL	ZINGS	ICING	FICHU			MIDIS	CDIII
JULIE	RIFER		SIGMA	ZINGY	KLIEG	FIGHT	**••I•H**	**I••I•**	MIMIC	CLIII
KATIE	RIFFI	**IG•••**	SIGNE		KOING	FISHY	AMISH	ICEIN	MINIE	CMIII
KYRIE	RIFFS	IGLOO	SIGNO	**•I••G**	LAING	HIGHC	APISH	ILLIN	MINIM	CVIII
LOUIE	RIFLE	IGLUS	SIGNS	KIANG	LYING	HIGHS	ARITH	IMMIX	MINIS	CXIII
LUCIE	RIFTS	IGNES	TIGER	LIANG	OKING	LIGHT	BLIGH	INBIG	MIXIN	DCIII
LURIE	SIFTS		TIGHT		ORING	LITHE	BRITH	INDIA	NIHIL	DLIII
MAMIE	TIFFS	**I•G••**	UIGUR	**••IG•**	OWING	LITHO	EDITH	INDIC	NIXIE	DVIII
MARIE		ILGWU	VIGIL	ADIGE	RUING	LITHS	ERICH	INDIE	PIPIT	DXIII
MAXIE	**•I•F•**	INGER	VIGNY	ALIGN	SLING	MIGHT	FAITH	INDIO	PIXIE	LVIII
MCVIE	BIFFS	INGLE	VIGOR	AMIGA	STING	MINHO	HEIGH	INDIV	RIGID	LXIII
MINIE	BIFFY	INGOT	WIGAN	AMIGO	SUING	MISHA	ILICH	INFIN	SIGIL	MCIII
MOVIE	FIEFS		WIGGY	BEIGE	SWING	NICHE	INISH	INFIX	SITIN	MDIII
MOXIE	JIFFY	**I••G•**	WIGHT	BLIGE	THING	NIGHT	IRISH	INUIT	TIBIA	MLIII
NIXIE	MIFFS	IMAGE	ZIGGY	BLIGH	TYING	PITHS	KEITH	IODIC	TIEIN	MMIII
OAKIE	MIFFY	IMAGO		BRIGS	USING	PITHY	KNISH	IONIA	TIKIS	MVIII
OLDIE	RIFFI	INIGO	**•I•G•**	COIGN	VYING	RICHE	LEIGH	IONIC	TIMID	MXIII
OLLIE	RIFFS		AINGE	DEIGN	WRING	RIGHT	LEITH	IQUIT	TIPIN	XCIII
OSSIE	TIFFS	**I•••G**	BIGGY	FEIGN		RISHI	NAISH	IRVIN	TITIS	XLIII
OZZIE		ICING	BILGE	FRIGG	**•••IG**	SIDHE	NEIGH	IRWIN	VIGIL	XVIII
PIXIE		IDTAG	BILGY	GRIGS	CRAIG	SIGHS	REICH	ISLIP	VIRID	XXIII

••I•I
ALIBI
BLINI
CCIII
CDIII
CHILI
CLIII
CMIII
CVIII
CXIII
DCIII
DLIII
DVIII
DXIII
HAITI
HEIDI
LUIGI
LVIII
LXIII
MCIII
MDIII
MEIJI
MLIII
MMIII
MVIII
MXIII
ORIBI
PRIMI
SCIFI
SEIJI
TRINI
VOICI
XCIII
XLIII
XVIII
XXIII

•••II
AALII
ACTII
ASCII
CCCII
CCIII
CCLII
CCVII
CCXII
CDIII
CDLII
CDVII
CDXII
CLIII
CLVII
CLXII
CMIII
CMLII
CMVII
CMXII
CVIII
CXCII
CXIII
CXLII
CXVII
CXXII
DCCII
DCIII
DCLII
DCVII
DCXII
DLIII
DLVII
DLXII
DVIII
DXCII
DXIII
DXLII
DXVII
DXXII
GENII
LVIII
LXIII
LXVII
LXXII
MCCII
MCDII
MCIII
MCLII
MCMII
MCVII
MCXII
MDCII
MDIII
MDLII
MDVII
MDXII
MLIII
MLVII
MLXII
MMCII
MMDII
MMIII
MMLII
MMMII
MMVII
MMXII
MVIII
MXCII
MXIII
MXLII
MXMII
MXVII
MXXII
QBVII
RADII
TORII
XCIII
XCVII
XLIII
XLVII
XVIII
XXIII
XXVII
XXXII

•IJ••
BIJOU
DIJON
GIJOE
GIJON
HIJAZ
HIJRA

•I•J•
NINJA
RIOJA
VIEJO

••IJ•
MEIJI
OUIJA
SEIJI

I•K••
ICKES
INKED
INKER
INKLE
IRKED

I•••K
IZAAK

•IK••
AIKEN
BIKED
BIKEL
BIKER
BIKES
DIKED
DIKES
HIKED
HIKER
HIKES
LIKED
LIKEN
LIKES
LIKUD
MIKAN
MIKED
MIKES
MIKEY
NIKES
NIKKI
NIKKO
NIKON
PIKAS
PIKED
PIKER
PIKES
RIKER
RIKKI
SIKAS
SIKES
SIKHS
TIKAL
TIKES
TIKIS
TIKKI
VIKKI
YIKES

•I•K•
BILKO
BILKS
BIOKO
DICKS
DICKY
DINKS
DINKY
DIRKS
DISKS
DITKA
FINKS
FISKE
HICKS
JINKS
KICKS
KICKY
KINKS
KINKY
KIRKS
KISKA
LICKS
LINKS
MILKS
MILKY
MINKE
MINKS
MIRKY
NICKS
NIKKI
NIKKO
OICKS
OINKS
PICKS
PICKY
PINKS
PINKY
RICKI
RICKS
RICKY
RIKKI
RILKE
RINKS
RINKY
RISKS
RISKY
SILKS
SILKY
SINKS
SITKA
TICKS
TICKY
TIKKI
VICKI
VICKS
VIKKI
WICKS
WINKS
ZIZKA

•I••K
KIOSK
MINSK
MIWOK
PINSK
TILAK

••IK•
ALIKE
EFIKS
ERIKA
HAIKS
HAIKU
LAIKA
SEIKO
SPIKE
SPIKY
TRIKE

••I•K
BLINK
BRICK
BRINK
BRISK
BUICK
CHICK
CHINK
CLICK
CLINK
CRICK
DRINK
FLICK
FRICK
FRISK
GLICK
KNICK
PLINK
PRICK
PRINK
QUICK
QUIRK
REINK
SHIRK
SKINK
SLICK
SLINK
SMIRK
SNICK
STICK
STINK
STIRK
SWINK
THICK
THINK
TRICK
UMIAK
WHISK

•••IK
AFAIK
BATIK
LUNIK
RUBIK
RURIK
SHEIK
YUPIK

IL•••
ILENE
ILGWU
ILIAC
ILIAD
ILICH
ILION
ILIUM
ILLER
ILLIN
ILLUS
ILONA

I•L••
IDLED
IDLER
IDLES
IGLOO
IGLUS
ILLER
ILLIN
ILLUS
INLAW
INLAY
INLET
ISLAM
ISLAS
ISLES
ISLET
ISLEY
ISLIP

I••L•
ICILY
IDOLS
IDYLL
IDYLS
IMPLY
INALL
INGLE
INKLE
ISTLE
ITALO
ITALS
ITALY

I•••L
IDEAL
IDYLL
IMPEL
INALL
INTEL

•IL••
AILED
AILER
AILEY
BILBO
BILBY
BILGE
BILGY
BILKO
BILKS
BILLS
BILLY
CILIA
CILLA
DILLS
DILLY
EILAT
FILAR
FILCH
FILED
FILER
FILES
FILET
FILLE
FILLS
FILLY
FILMS
FILMY
FILTH
FILUM
GILDA
GILDS
GILES
GILLS
GILLY
GILTS
HILDA
HILLS
HILLY
HILTS
HILUM
JILTS
KILEY
KILIM
KILLS
KILLY
KILNS
KILOS
KILTS
LILAC
LILLE
LILLY
LILTS
MILAN
MILCH
MILER
MILES
MILKS
MILKY
MILLE
MILLI
MILLS
MILNE
MILOS
MILPA
MILTS
MILTY
NILES
NILLY
NILOT
OILED
OILER
PILAF
PILAR
PILEA
PILED
PILEI
PILES
PILLS
PILOT
PILUM
PILUS
RILED
RILES
RILEY
RILKE
RILLE
RILLS
SILAS
SILEX
SILKS
SILKY
SILLS
SILLY
SILOS
SILTS
SILTY
SILVA
TILAK
TILDE
TILED
TILER
TILES
TILLS
TILLY
TILTH
TILTS
VILAS
VILER
VILLA
VILLE
VILLI
VILMA
WILCO
WILDE
WILDS
WILED
WILES
WILEY
WILLA
WILLS
WILLY
WILMA
WILTS
ZILCH
ZILLS

•I•L•
AIOLI
AISLE
BIALY
BIBLE
BIGLY
BILLS
BILLY
BIRLS
CILLA
DIALS
DILLS
DILLY
DIMLY
DIPLO
FIELD
FILLE
FILLS
FILLY
FITLY
GILLS
GILLY
GIRLS
HILLS
HILLY
HIPLY
KILLS
KILLY
LILLE
LILLY
LISLE
MILLE
MILLI
MILLS
NIELS
NILLY
PILLS
RIALS
RIELS
RIFLE
RILLE
RILLS
SIALS
SIDLE
SILLS
SILLY
TILLS
TILLY
TITLE
VIALS
VILLA
VILLE
VILLI
VIOLA
VIOLS
WIELD
WILLA
WILLS
WILLY
YIELD
ZILLS

•I••L
BIKEL
BINAL
CIVIL
FIDEL
FINAL
GIMEL
LIBEL
NICOL
NIGEL
NIHIL
NIVAL
PICUL
PIPAL
PIXEL
RIGEL
RIVAL
RIYAL
SIBYL
SIGIL
SISAL
TICAL
TIDAL
TIKAL
VIDAL
VIGIL
VINYL
VIRAL
VITAL

••IL•
AGILE
ANILS
ARILS
ATILT
AVILA
AXILS
BAILS
BOILS
BRILL
BUILD
BUILT
CEILS
CHILD
CHILE
CHILI
CHILL
CHILO
COILS
DAILY
DEILS
DOILY
DRILL
DRILY
EDILE
EMILE
EMILY
EVILS
EXILE
FAILS
FOILS
FRILL
GAILY
GRILL
GUILD
GUILE
GUILT
HAILE
HAILS
ICILY
JAILS
KRILL
LEILA
MAILE
MAILS
MOILS
NAILS
NEILL
NOILS
NOILY
ODILE
PAILS
PHILE
PHILO
PHILY
POILS
POILU
QUILL
QUILP
QUILT
RAILS
ROILS
ROILY
SAILS
SHILL
SKILL
SLILY
SMILE
SOILS
SPILE
SPILL
SPILT
STILE
STILL
STILT
SWILL
TAILS
TBILL
THILL
TOILE
TOILS
TRILL
TWILL
UTILE
VEILS
VOILA
VOILE
WAILS
WEILL
WHILE

••I•L
ARIEL
AXIAL
BAIUL
BGIRL
BRILL
CHILL
DRILL
ELIEL
FRILL
FRIML
GLIAL
GRILL
KRILL
NEILL

ORIEL
PHIAL
QUILL
SHILL
SKILL
SKIRL
SPIEL
SPILL
STILL
SWILL
SWIRL
TBILL
THILL
TRIAL
TRILL
TWILL
TWIRL
URIAL
URIEL
WEILL
WHIRL

•••IL
ABOIL
ABRIL
ADVIL
ANVIL
APRIL
ARGIL
AUXIL
AVAIL
AVRIL
BASIL
BRAIL
BROIL
CAVIL
CECIL
CIVIL
CYRIL
DEVIL
DRAIL
EMAIL
ERBIL
ERVIL
FLAIL
FRAIL
FUSIL
GRAIL
MOBIL
NEVIL
NIHIL
ONEIL
PERIL
PUPIL
QUAIL
REOIL
SIGIL
SMAIL
SNAIL
SPOIL
SYBIL
TAMIL
TRAIL
UNTIL
VIGIL
ZORIL

IM•••
IMAGE
IMAGO
IMAMS
IMBUE
IMIDE
IMIDO
IMINE
IMINO
IMMIX
IMPED
IMPEI
IMPEL
IMPLY

I•M••
IAMBI
IAMBS
IMMIX
IZMIR
IZMIT

I••M•
ICBMS
IMAMS
ISAMU
ITEMS
ITSME

I•••M
IBEAM
IDIOM
ILIUM
INREM
IPSUM
ISLAM

•IM••
AIMAT
AIMED
AIMEE
AIMER
AIMTO
DIMED
DIMES
DIMLY
GIMEL
GIMME
GIMPS
GIMPY
JIMMY
KIMPO
LIMAS
LIMBI
LIMBO
LIMBS
LIMED
LIMEN
LIMES
LIMEY
LIMIT
LIMNS
LIMON
LIMOS
LIMPS
MIMAS
MIMED
MIMEO
MIMER
MIMES
MIMIC
MIMSY
NIMBI
NIMBY
NIMES
NIMOY
PIMAS
RIMED
RIMES
SIMBA
SIMMS
SIMON
SIMPS
TIMED
TIMER
TIMES
TIMEX
TIMID
TIMMY
TIMON
TIMOR
WIMPS
WIMPY

•I•M•
BIOME
DIEMS
DISME
FILMS
FILMY
FIRMA
FIRMS
GIMME
GIZMO
HITME
JIMMY
MIAMI
PISMO
SIGMA
SIMMS
SIXMO
TIMMY
VILMA
WILMA

•I••M
FILUM
HILUM
HIRAM
KILIM
MINIM
NIZAM
PILUM
SIXAM
SIXPM
VISUM

••IM•
ANIMA
ANIME
BLIMP
BRIMS
CHIME
CHIMP
CLIMB
CLIME
CRIME
CRIMP
FRIML
GLIMS
GRIME
GRIMM
GRIMY
JAIME
KLIMT
PRIMA
PRIME
PRIMI
PRIMO
PRIMP
PRIMS
REIMS
SHIMS
SKIMP
SKIMS
SLIME
SLIMS
SLIMY
SWIMS
TRIMS
WHIMS

••I•M
ARIUM
AXIOM
DEISM
GRIMM
IDIOM
ILIUM
ODIUM
OPIUM
PRIAM
PRISM
PRIZM
SEISM

•••IM
BEDIM
CHAIM
CLAIM
DENIM
HAKIM
KILIM
MAXIM
MINIM
PURIM
REAIM
SCRIM
VADIM
YADIM

IN•••
INALL
INANE
INAPT
INARI
INAWE
INBAD
INBED
INBIG
INBOX
INCAN
INCAS
INCOG
INCUR
INCUS
INDEF
INDEX
INDIA
INDIC
INDIE
INDIO
INDIV
INDRA
INDRI
INDUS
INEPT
INERT
INFER
INFIN
INFIX
INFRA
INFUN
INGER
INGLE
INGOT
INIGO
INION
INISH
INITS
INKED
INKER
INKLE
INLAW
INLAY
INLET
INNER
INONU
INORG
INPUT
INREM
INSET
INSTR
INSTS
INTEL
INTER
INTOW
INTRA
INTRO
INTWO
INUIT
INURE
INUSE

I•N••
IFNOT
IGNES
INNER
IONIA
IONIC
IXNAY

I••N•
ICENI
ICING
ICONO
ICONS
IDINE
ILENE
ILONA
IMINE
IMINO
INANE
INONU
IPANA
IRANI
IRENE
IRINA
IRONS
IRONY
IVANA
IVINS

I•••N
IBSEN
ICAHN
ICEIN
ILION
ILLIN
INCAN
INFIN
INFUN
INION
IOWAN
IRVIN
IRWIN
IXION

•IN••
AINGE
AINUS
BINAL
BINDS
BINES
BINET
BINGE
BINGO
BINGS
CINCH
CINCO
CINDY
CINES
DINAH
DINAR
DINDY
DINED
DINER
DINES
DINGE
DINGO
DINGS
DINGY
DINKS
DINKY
DINTS
DINTY
FINAL
FINCA
FINCH
FINDS
FINED
FINER
FINES
FINIS
FINKS
FINNO
FINNS
FINNY
GINNY
GINZA
HINDI
HINDS
HINDU
HINES
HINGE
HINNY
HINTS
JINGO
JINKS
JINNI
JINNS
KINAS
KINDA
KINDS
KINER
KINGS
KINKS
KINKY
KINTE
LINDA
LINDO
LINDY
LINED
LINEN
LINER
LINES
LINEY
LINGO
LINKS
LINOS
LINTS
LINTY
LINUS
MINAS
MINCE
MINDS
MINDY
MINED
MINEO
MINER
MINES
MINGS
MINGY
MINHO
MINIE
MINIM
MINIS
MINKE
MINKS
MINOR
MINOS
MINOT
MINSK
MINTO
MINTS
MINTY
MINUS
NINAS
NINER
NINES
NINJA
NINNY
NINON
NINOS
NINTH
OINGO
OINKS
PINCE
PINCH
PINED
PINES
PINEY
PINGO
PINGS
PINKS
PINKY
PINNA
PINON
PINOT
PINSK
PINTA
PINTO
PINTS
PINUP
PINZA
RINDS
RINDY
RINGO
RINGS
RINKS
RINKY
RINSE
RINSO
SINAI
SINCE
SINES
SINEW
SINGE
SINGS
SINKS
SINUS
TINCT
TINED
TINES
TINGE
TINGS
TINNY
TINTS
UINTA
VINAS
VINCE
VINCI
VINED
VINES
VINGT
VINNY
VINOS
VINYL
WINCE
WINCH
WINDS
WINDY
WINED
WINES
WINEY
WINGS
WINKS
WINZE
XINGU
ZINCS
ZINCY
ZINES
ZINGS
ZINGY

•I•N•
AISNE
BIONT
DIANA
DIANE
DIDNT
DIENE
DIONE
FIEND
FINNO
FINNS
FINNY
FIONA
FIRNS
GIANT
GINNY
GIRNS
HINNY
JINNI
JINNS
KIANG
KILNS
LIANA
LIANE
LIANG
LIENS
LIGNI
LIGNO
LIMNS
LIONS
MIENS
MILNE
NINNY
PIANO
PINNA
PIONS
RIANT
SIENA
SIGNE
SIGNO
SIGNS
TIANT
TINNY
VIAND
VIGNY
VINNY
VIRNA

•I••N
AIDAN
AIKEN
BIDEN
BIDIN
BIDON
BIGON
BISON
DIDIN
DIGIN
DIJON
DIVAN
DIXON
DIZEN
EIGEN
FITIN
GIJON
GIVEN
HITON
KIRIN
LIEIN
LIKEN
LIMEN
LIMON
LINEN
LITON
LIVEN
MIKAN
MILAN
MIXIN
NIKON
NINON
NISAN
NIVEN
NIXON
PINON
PISAN
PITON
RIPEN
RIPON
RISEN
RIVEN
SIDON
SIMON
SIREN
SITIN
SITON
SIVAN
TIEIN
TIMON
TIPIN
TIRAN
TITAN
VIXEN
WIDEN
WIGAN
WIZEN

••IN•
ACING
ADINT
AGING
AKINS
ALINE
AMINE
AMINO
APING
AWING
AXING
AYINS
AZINE
BEING
BEINS
BLIND
BLINI
BLINK
BOING
BRINE
BRING
BRINK
BRINY
CAINE
CHINA
CHINE
CHING
CHINK
CHINO
CHINS
CLINE
CLING
CLINK
CLINT
COINS
CUING
DJINN
DOING
DRINA
DRINK
DVINA
DYING
EDINA
EKING
EWING

FAINT
FEINT
FLING
FLINT
FOINS
GAINS
GLINT
GOING
GRIND
GRINS
HEINE
HEINZ
HYING
ICING
IDINE
IMINE
IMINO
IRINA
IVINS
JAINS
JOINS
JOINT
KLINE
KOINE
KOING
LAINE
LAING
LOINS
LYING
MAINE
MAINS
MAINZ
MEINY
NAINA
OKING
OPINE
ORING
OVINE
OWING
PAINE
PAINS
PAINT
PLINK
PLINY
POINT
PRINK
PRINT
QUINN
QUINO
QUINT
RAINS
RAINY
REINA
REINK
REINS
RHINE
RHINO
RUING
RUINS
SAINT
SEINE
SHINE
SHINS
SHINY
SKINK
SKINS
SKINT
SLING
SLINK
SPINE
SPINS
SPINY
STING
STINK
STINT
SUING
SUINT
SWINE
SWING
SWINK
TAINE
TAINO
TAINT
THINE
THING
THINK
THINS
TRINE
TRINI
TWINE
TWINS
TYING
UDINE
USING
VEINS
VEINY
VYING
WAINS
WHINE
WHINS
WHINY
WRING
ZEINS

••I•N

AAIUN
ALIEN
ALIGN
ANION
APIAN
ARIAN
ARION
ASIAN
ATION
AVIAN
AVION
AXION
BAIRN
BRIAN
CAIRN
CHIEN
COIGN
DEIGN
DEION
DJINN
ELION
EVIAN
FEIGN
ILION
INION
IXION
NAIRN
ONION
ORION
PRION
QUIEN
QUINN
REIGN
SCION
UNION
VSIGN

•••IN

ACTIN
ADDIN
ADFIN
ADMIN
AGAIN
AHSIN
ALAIN
ALGIN
ALLIN
ALVIN
AMAIN
ARKIN
ASKIN
ASTIN
ATEIN
AUXIN
BALIN
BASIN
BEGIN
BENIN
BEVIN
BIDIN
BOXIN
BRAIN
BRUIN
BUNIN
BURIN
CABIN
CHAIN
COLIN
CRAIN
CUEIN
CUMIN
CUTIN
DARIN
DIDIN
DIGIN
DRAIN
DUBIN
DUGIN
EATIN
ECHIN
EDWIN
ELFIN
ELGIN
ELVIN
ENFIN
EOSIN
ERVIN
ERWIN
FAGIN
FITIN
FLYIN
FOGIN
GAMIN
GAVIN
GETIN
GHAIN
GOTIN
GRAIN
GROIN
HEDIN
HEMIN
HOPIN
ICEIN
ILLIN
INFIN
IRVIN
IRWIN
JAMIN
KANIN
KEVIN
KEYIN
KIRIN
KLEIN
LAPIN
LATIN
LAVIN
LAYIN
LEDIN
LENIN
LETIN
LEVIN
LIEIN
LOGIN
LUPIN
LYSIN
MARIN
MATIN
MIXIN
MUCIN
MYCIN
MYSIN
NEVIN
NOTIN
NOWIN
OLEIN
OPSIN
ORRIN
OSLIN
PALIN
PAYIN
PEKIN
PEPIN
PLAIN
POPIN
PUPIN
PUTIN
QUOIN
RABIN
RANIN
RAVIN
RENIN
REPIN
RESIN
REWIN
ROBIN
RODIN
ROSIN
RUBIN
RUNIN
RUTIN
SABIN
SATIN
SAWIN
SEEIN
SERIN
SETIN
SITIN
SKEIN
SLAIN
SPAIN
STAIN
STEIN
SWAIN
TAKIN
TAPIN
TIEIN
TIPIN
TOEIN
TOXIN
TRAIN
TURIN
TWAIN
UNPIN
VENIN
XEDIN
ZAYIN
ZUBIN

IO•••

IODIC
IONIA
IONIC
IOTAS
IOWAN

I•O••

ICONO
ICONS
ICOSA
ICOSI
IDOLS
ILONA
INONU
INORG
IRONS
IRONY
IVORY

I••O•

ICHOR
IDIOM
IDIOT
IFNOT
IGLOO
ILION
INBOX
INCOG
INGOT
INION
INTOW
IXION

I•••O

IATRO
ICONO
IDAHO
IGLOO
IMAGO
IMIDO
IMINO
INDIO
INIGO
INTRO
INTWO
IRIDO
ITALO

•IO••

AIOLI
BIOGS
BIOKO
BIOME
BIONT
BIOTA
DIODE
DIONE
FIONA
FIORD
KIOGA
KIOSK
KIOWA
LIONS
NIOBE
PIONS
PIOUS
RIOJA
RIOTS
SIOUX
VIOLA
VIOLS

•I•O•

BIDON
BIGON
BIGOS
BIGOT
BIJOU
BIPOD
BISON
DICOT
DIDOS
DIJON
DIVOT
DIXON
GIGOT
GIJOE
GIJON
GIROS
HITON
KILOS
KIROV
LIDOS
LIMON
LIMOS
LINOS
LITON
MIAOW
MILOS
MINOR
MINOS
MINOT
MISOS
MIWOK
NICOL
NIKON
NILOT
NIMOY
NINON
NINOS
NIXON
PICOT
PILOT
PINON
PINOT
PITON
PITOT
PIVOT
RICOH
RIDOF
RIGOR
RIPON
SIDON
SILOS
SIMON
SITON
TIMON
TIMOR
TIROS
VIDOR
VIGOR
VINOS
VISOR
WIDOW

•I••O

AIMTO
BILBO
BILKO
BINGO
BIOKO
BISHO
CINCO
CIRRO
CISCO
DIAZO
DICHO
DIEGO
DINGO
DIPLO
DISCO
DITTO
EIEIO
FIBRO
FIERO
FINNO
FIRPO
GITGO
GIZMO
HIERO
HIPPO
HIPTO
JINGO
KIDDO
KIMPO
LIETO
LIGNO
LIMBO
LINDO
LINGO
LIPPO
LITHO
MICRO
MIMEO
MINEO
MINHO
MINTO
MIRRO
MISDO
NIKKO
NITRO
OINGO
PIANO
PICRO
PINGO
PINTO
PISCO
PISMO
RINGO
RINSO
RIZZO
SIGNO
SIXMO
TIETO
VIDEO
VIEJO
VIREO
VIRGO
WILCO

••IO•

ADIOS
AEIOU
AGIOS
ALIOS
ANION
ARION
ATION
AVION
AXIOM
AXION
CHIOS
CLIOS
DEION
ELION
ELIOT
GRIOT
IDIOM
IDIOT
ILION
INION
IXION
OLIOS
ONION
ORION
PRION
PRIOR
SCION
TRIOS
UNION

••I•O

ADIPO
AMIDO
AMIGO
AMINO
ANISO
AVISO
BOITO
CAIRO
CHICO
CHILO
CHINO
CHIRO
EJIDO
FRITO
GUIDO
GUIRO
IMIDO
IMINO
INIGO
IRIDO
OLIGO
PHILO
PRIMO
QUINO
QUITO
RHINO
RHIZO
SEIKO
SLIGO
SPIRO
TAINO

•••IO

ANGIO
ANZIO
AUDIO
CASIO
CURIO
DANIO
DARIO
EIEIO
ENNIO
FABIO
FOLIO
HAGIO
HELIO
INDIO
JULIO
LABIO
MARIO
NGAIO
PATIO
PLEIO
RADIO
RATIO
SOCIO
SOHIO
TONIO

IP•••

IPANA
IPASS
IPSUM

I•P••

IMPED
IMPEI
IMPEL
IMPLY
INPUT

I••P•

INAPT
INEPT

I•••P

ICEUP
ISLIP

•IP••

BIPED
BIPOD
DIPLO
DIPPY
GIPSY
HIPLY
HIPPO
HIPPY
HIPTO
LIPID
LIPPI
LIPPO
LIPPY
NIPAS
NIPAT
NIPPY
NIPUP
PIPAL
PIPED
PIPER
PIPES
PIPIT
PIPPA
PIPPI
RIPEN
RIPER
RIPON
RIPUP
TIPIN
TIPPI
TIPPY
TIPSY
TIPUP
VIPER
WIPED
WIPER
WIPES
YIPES
ZIPPY
ZIPUP

•I•P•

DIPPY
FIRPO
GIMPS
GIMPY
HIPPO
HIPPY
KIMPO
LIMPS
LIPPI
LIPPO
LIPPY
LISPS
MILPA
NIPPY
PIPPA
PIPPI
SIEPI
SIMPS
SIXPM
TIPPI
TIPPY
WIMPS
WIMPY
WISPS
WISPY
ZIPPY

•I••P

BIDUP
DIDUP
DIGUP
FIXUP
HITUP
LITUP
MIXUP
NIPUP
PINUP
RIGUP
RIPUP
SITUP
TIEUP
TIPUP
ZIPUP

••IP•
ADIPO
BLIPS
CHIPS
CLIPS
CLIPT
DRIPS
FLIPS
GRIPE
GRIPS
QTIPS
QUIPS
QUIPU
SHIPS
SKIPS
SLIPS
SLIPT
SNIPE
SNIPS
STIPE
SWIPE
TRIPE
TRIPS
WHIPS

••I•P
BLIMP
CHIMP
CHIRP
CRIMP
CRISP
PRIMP
QUILP
SKIMP

•••IP
ATRIP
EQUIP
ISLIP
JOSIP
OXLIP
RECIP
SCRIP
STRIP
TULIP
UNHIP
UNZIP
VCHIP

IQ•••
IQUIT

I••Q•
IRAQI

•IQ••
PIQUE

•••IQ
ANTIQ

IR•••
IRADE
IRANI
IRAQI
IRATE
IRENE
IRIDO
IRINA
IRISH
IRKED
IRONS
IRONY
IRREG
IRVIN
IRWIN

I•R••
INREM
IRREG

I••R•
IATRO
IATRY
IBARS
IBERT
ICERS
INARI
INDRA
INDRI
INERT
INFRA
INORG
INTRA
INTRO
INURE
ISERE
ITERS
IVORY
IZARD
IZARS

I•••R
ICHOR
ICIER
IDLER
ILLER
INCUR
INFER
INGER
INKER
INNER
INSTR
INTER
IZMIR

•IR••
AIRED
AIRES
BIRCH
BIRDS
BIRDY
BIRLS
BIRRS
BIRSE
BIRTH
CIRCA
CIRCE
CIRCS
CIRES
CIRRI
CIRRO
DIRAC
DIRER
DIRGE
DIRKS
DIRTY
FIRED
FIRER
FIRES
FIRMA
FIRMS
FIRNS
FIRPO
FIRRY
FIRST
FIRTH
GIRDS
GIRLS
GIRNS
GIROS
GIRTH
GIRTS
HIRAM
HIRED
HIRER
HIRES
KIRBY
KIRIN
KIRKS
KIROV
LIRAS
MIRED
MIRES
MIRKY
MIRRO
MIRTH
MIRVS
SIRED
SIREN
SIRES
TIRAN
TIRED
TIRES
TIROS
VIRAL
VIREO
VIRGA
VIRGO
VIRID
VIRNA
VIRTU
VIRUS
WIRED
WIRER
WIRES
WIRRA

•I•R•
BIRRS
CIERA
CIRRI
CIRRO
DIARY
FIBRE
FIBRO
FIERO
FIERY
FIORD
FIRRY
HIERA
HIERO
HIJRA
LIARD
LIARS
LIBRA
LIBRE
LITRE
LIVRE
MICRA
MICRO
MIRRO
MITRE
NIDRE
NITRE
NITRO
PICRO
PIERS
PIURA
SIDRA
TIARA
TIERS
TITRE
VIERS
VIVRE
WIRRA

•I••R
AILER
AIMER
BIHAR
BIKER
BITER
CIDER
CIGAR
CITER
DICER
DINAR
DINER
DIRER
DISTR
DIVER
DIYER
EIDER
FIBER
FIFER
FILAR
FILER
FINER
FIRER
FIVER
FIXER
GIBER
GIVER
HIDER
HIKER
HIRER
JIVER
KINER
KITER
LIGER
LINER
LITER
LIVER
MILER
MIMER
MINER
MINOR
MISER
MITER
MIXER
MIZAR
NICER
NIGER
NINER
NITER
NIZER
OILER
PIKER
PILAR
PIPER
RICER
RIDER
RIFER
RIGOR
RIKER
RIPER
RISER
RIVER
SIDER
SIEUR
SITAR
SIXER
SIZER
TIBER
TIGER
TILER
TIMER
TIMOR
TITER
UIGUR
VICAR
VIDOR
VIGOR
VILER
VIPER
VISOR
WIDER
WIPER
WIRER
WISER

••IR•
AFIRE
AKIRA
AMIRS
BAIRD
BAIRN
BGIRL
CAIRN
CAIRO
CHIRO
CHIRP
CHIRR
COIRS
DAIRY
EMIRS
FAIRE
FAIRS
FAIRY
FLIRT
GUIRO
HAIRS
HAIRY
HEIRS
LAIRD
LAIRS
LOIRE
MBIRA
MOIRA
MOIRE
NAIRA
NAIRN
NOIRE
PAIRS
QUIRE
QUIRK
QUIRT
SHIRE
SHIRK
SHIRR
SHIRT
SKIRL
SKIRR
SKIRT
SMIRK
SPIRE
SPIRO
SPIRY
STIRK
STIRS
SWIRL
TBIRD
THIRD
TWIRL
WEIRD
WEIRS
WHIRL
WHIRR
WHIRS
ZAIRE

••I•R
BRIAR
BRIER
CHIRR
CRIER
DRIER
FLIER
FRIAR
FRIER
GRIER
ICIER
OSIER
PRIER
PRIOR
SHIER
SHIRR
SKIER
SKIRR
SLIER
TRIER
WHIRR
WRIER

•••IR
ADAIR
AEGIR
AESIR
ASTIR
AVOIR
BLAIR
CHAIR
CHOIR
CLAIR
ETVIR
EYRIR
FAKIR
FLAIR
GLAIR
IZMIR
KAFIR
KEFIR
NADIR
NOSIR
OHAIR
ONAIR
OPHIR
PAMIR
REAIR
SAPIR
STAIR
TAPIR
THEIR
USAIR
VANIR
YASIR

IS•••
ISAAC
ISAMU
ISERE
ISLAM
ISLAS
ISLES
ISLET
ISLEY
ISLIP
ISSEI
ISSUE
ISSUS
ISTIC
ISTLE
ISUZU

I•S••
IBSEN
INSET
INSTR
INSTS
IPSUM
ISSEI
ISSUE
ISSUS
ITSME

I••S•
ICOSA
ICOSI
IDEST
INISH
INUSE
IPASS
IRISH

I•••S
IAMBS
IBARS
ICBMS
ICERS
ICKES
ICONS
ICTUS
IDEAS
IDLES
IDOLS
IDYLS
IGLUS
IGNES
ILLUS
IMAMS
INCAS
INCUS
INDUS
INITS
INSTS
IOTAS
IPASS
IRONS
ISLAS
ISLES
ISSUS
ITALS
ITEMS
ITERS
IVIES
IVINS
IZARS
IZBAS

•IS••
AISHA
AISLE
AISNE
BISES
BISHO
BISON
CISCO
CISSY
DISCO
DISCS
DISHY
DISKS
DISME
DISTR
FISCS
FISHY
FISKE
FISTS
GISTS
HISSY
KISKA
LISLE
LISPS
LISSE
LISTS
LISZT
MISDO
MISER
MISHA
MISOS
MISSA
MISSY
MISTI
MISTS
MISTY
NISAN
NISEI
NISUS
PISAN
PISCI
PISCO
PISMO
PISTE
RISEN
RISER
RISES
RISHI
RISKS
RISKY
SISAL
SISSY
TISZA
VISAS
VISBY
VISES
VISIT
VISOR
VISTA
VISUM
WISER
WISHY
WISPS
WISPY

•I•S•
BIRSE
BITSY
CISSY
DIDST
DITSY
FIRST
GIPSY
HISSY
KIOSK
LISSE
MIDST
MIMSY
MINSK
MISSA
MISSY
PINSK
RINSE
RINSO
SISSY
TIPSY
WIEST

•I••S
AIDES
AINUS
AIRES
BIBBS
BIDES
BIFFS
BIGOS
BIKES
BILKS
BILLS
BINDS
BINES
BINGS
BIOGS
BIRDS
BIRLS
BIRRS
BISES
BITES
BITTS
CINES
CIRCS
CIRES
CITES
DIALS
DICES
DICKS
DICTS
DIDOS
DIEMS
DIETS
DIKES
DILLS
DIMES
DINES
DINGS
DINKS
DINTS
DIRKS
DISCS
DISKS
DIVAS
DIVES
FIATS
FICES
FICUS
FIDES
FIEFS
FIFES
FILES
FILLS
FILMS
FINDS
FINES
FINIS
FINKS
FINNS
FIRES
FIRMS
FIRNS
FISCS
FISTS
FIVES
FIXES
GIBBS
GIBES
GIFTS
GILDS
GILES
GILLS
GILTS
GIMPS
GIRDS
GIRLS
GIRNS
GIROS
GIRTS
GISTS
GIVES
HICKS
HIDES
HIFIS
HIGHS
HIKES
HILLS
HILTS
HINDS
HINES
HINTS
HIRES
HIVES
JIBES
JILTS
JINKS
JINNS
JIVES
KICKS
KILLS
KILNS
KILOS
KILTS
KINAS

KINDS
KINGS
KINKS
KIRKS
KITES
KITTS
KIVAS
KIWIS
LIARS
LICKS
LIDOS
LIENS
LIEUS
LIFTS
LIKES
LILTS
LIMAS
LIMBS
LIMES
LIMNS
LIMOS
LIMPS
LINES
LINKS
LINOS
LINTS
LINUS
LIONS
LIRAS
LISPS
LISTS
LITES
LITHS
LIVES
MICAS
MIDAS
MIDIS
MIENS
MIFFS
MIKES
MILES
MILKS
MILLS
MILOS
MILTS
MIMAS
MIMES
MINAS
MINDS
MINES
MINGS
MINIS
MINKS
MINOS
MINTS
MINUS
MIRES
MIRVS
MISOS
MISTS
MITES
MITTS
MIXES
NICKS
NIDES
NIDUS
NIELS
NIKES
NILES
NIMES
NINAS
NINES
NINOS
NIPAS
NISUS
NITES
NIXES
OICKS
OINKS
PICAS
PICKS
PICTS
PIEDS
PIERS
PIKAS
PIKES
PILES
PILLS
PILUS
PIMAS
PINES
PINGS
PINKS
PINTS
PIONS
PIOUS
PIPES
PITAS
PITHS
PITTS
RIALS
RICES
RICKS
RIDES
RIELS
RIFFS
RIFTS
RIGGS
RILES
RILLS
RIMES
RINDS
RINGS
RINKS
RIOTS
RISES
RISKS
RITES
RIVES
SIALS
SIDES
SIFTS
SIGHS
SIGNS
SIKAS
SIKES
SIKHS
SILAS
SILKS
SILLS
SILOS
SILTS
SIMMS
SIMPS
SINES
SINGS
SINKS
SINUS
SIRES
SITES
SITUS
SIXES
SIZES
TIBBS
TICKS
TIDES
TIEGS
TIERS
TIFFS
TIKES
TIKIS
TILES
TILLS
TILTS
TIMES
TINES
TINGS
TINTS
TIRES
TIROS
TITIS
TITUS
VIALS
VIBES
VICES
VICKS
VIERS
VIEWS
VILAS
VINAS
VINES
VINOS
VIOLS
VIRUS
VISAS
VISES
VITAS
VITUS
WICKS
WILDS
WILES
WILLS
WILTS
WIMPS
WINDS
WINES
WINGS
WINKS
WIPES
WIRES
WISPS
WIVES
YIKES
YIPES
ZILLS
ZINCS
ZINES
ZINGS
ZITIS

••IS•

ALIST
AMISH
AMISS
ANISE
ANISO
APISH
ARISE
AVISO
BLISS
BOISE
BRISK
CRISP
CRISS
CRIST
DAISY
DEISM
DEIST
ELISE
EPISC
ERISA
EXIST
FEIST
FOIST
FRISE
FRISK
GRIST
GUISE
HEISS
HEIST
HOIST
INISH
IRISH
JOIST
KNISH
KRISS
LUISA
LUISE
MOIST
NAISH
NOISE
NOISY
ODIST
PAISA
POISE
PRISM
RAISA
RAISE
SEISM
SHISH
SWISH
SWISS
TRISH
TWIST
WAIST
WEISS
WHISH
WHISK
WHIST
WRIST
ZEISS
ZEIST

••I•S

ACIDS
ADIOS
ADITS
AGIOS
AKINS
ALIAS
ALIFS
ALIOS
AMIES
AMIRS
AMISS
ANILS
ARIAS
ARIES
ARILS
ARIUS
AXILS
AYINS
BAILS
BAITS
BEINS
BLIPS
BLISS
BOILS
BRIES
BRIGS
BRIMS
BRITS
CEILS
CHIAS
CHINS
CHIOS
CHIPS
CHITS
CLIOS
CLIPS
COIFS
COILS
COINS
COIRS
CRIBS
CRIES
CRISS
DEILS
DOITS
DRIBS
DRIES
DRIPS
EDITS
EFIKS
ELIAS
EMIRS
EMITS
EPICS
ERIES
EVILS
EXITS
FAILS
FAIRS
FLICS
FLIES
FLIPS
FLITS
FOILS
FOINS
FRIES
FRITS
GAINS
GAITS
GAIUS
GLIMS
GRIDS
GRIGS
GRINS
GRIPS
GRITS
HAIKS
HAILS
HAIRS
HEIRS
HEISS
INITS
IVIES
IVINS
JAILS
JAINS
JOINS
KNITS
KRISS
LAICS
LAIRS
LAIUS
LOINS
MAIDS
MAILS
MAINS
MOILS
NAILS
NOILS
OBIES
OKIES
OLIOS
OMITS
PAILS
PAINS
PAIRS
PLIES
POILS
PRIES
PRIGS
PRIMS
QTIPS
QUIDS
QUIPS
QUITS
RAIDS
RAILS
RAINS
REIMS
REINS
ROILS
RUINS
SAILS
SHIES
SHIMS
SHINS
SHIPS
SHIVS
SKIDS
SKIES
SKIMS
SKINS
SKIPS
SKITS
SLIMS
SLIPS
SLITS
SMITS
SNIPS
SNITS
SOILS
SPIES
SPINS
SPITS
SPIVS
STIES
STIRS
SUITS
SWIGS
SWIMS
SWISS
TAILS
THINS
TOILS
TRIES
TRIGS
TRIMS
TRIOS
TRIPS
TWIGS
TWINS
TWITS
UNITS
UNIVS
VEILS
VEINS
VOIDS
WAIFS
WAILS
WAINS
WAITS
WEIRS
WEISS
WHIGS
WHIMS
WHINS
WHIPS
WHIRS
WHITS
WRITS
ZEINS
ZEISS

•••IS

ABRIS
ADDIS
AEGIS
ANAIS
ANTIS
APHIS
APSIS
ARMIS
ARRIS
ARSIS
ARTIS
AUDIS
AULIS
BABIS
BASIS
BLOIS
BORIS
CADIS
CAMIS
CANIS
CEDIS
CHRIS
CUTIS
DAVIS
DELIS
DENIS
DORIS
ELLIS
ELVIS
ENNIS
ETUIS
FELIS
FINIS
FRAIS
HAJIS
HIFIS
HOPIS
JANIS
KAKIS
KEPIS
KIWIS
LAPIS
LARIS
LEGIS
LENIS
LEVIS
LEWIS
LEXIS
LORIS
LOUIS
MARIS
MAVIS
MAXIS
METIS
MIDIS
MINIS
MUNIS
NARIS
NEHIS
NEVIS
NEXIS
NOBIS
NUMIS
OASIS
OPSIS
ORNIS
ORRIS
PARIS
PAVIS
PERIS
POLIS
PULIS
PYXIS
RAKIS
RAMIS
RANIS
REGIS
SADIS
SARIS
SEMIS
SUFIS
TABIS
TAXIS
THAIS
TIKIS
TITIS
TOPIS
TOTIS
TROIS
TUNIS
URBIS
VADIS
WADIS
XAXIS
YAXIS
YETIS
YOGIS
ZAXIS
ZITIS
ZORIS
ZUNIS

IT•••

ITALO
ITALS
ITALY
ITCHY
ITEMS
ITERS
ITSME

I•T••

IATRO
IATRY
ICTUS
IDTAG
INTEL
INTER
INTOW
INTRA
INTRO
INTWO
IOTAS
ISTIC
ISTLE

I••T•

ICHTH
INITS
INSTR
INSTS
IRATE

I•••T

IBERT
IDEST
IDIOT
IFNOT
INAPT
INEPT
INERT
INGOT
INLET
INPUT
INSET
INUIT
IQUIT
ISLET
IZMIT

•IT••

AITCH
BITER
BITES
BITSY
BITTE
BITTS
BITTY
CITED
CITER
CITES
DITAT
DITCH
DITKA
DITSY
DITTO
DITTY
DITZY
FITCH
FITIN
FITLY
GITGO
HITCH
HITIT
HITME
HITON
HITUP
KITED
KITER
KITES
KITTS
KITTY
KITWE
LITER
LITES
LITHE
LITHO
LITHS
LITON
LITRE
LITUP
MITCH
MITER
MITES
MITRE
MITTS
MITTY
MITZI
NITER
NITES
NITRE
NITRO
NITTI
NITTY
PITAS
PITCH
PITHS
PITHY
PITON
PITOT
PITTA
PITTS
RITES
RITZY
SITAR
SITBY
SITED
SITES
SITIN
SITKA
SITON
SITUP
SITUS
TITAN
TITER
TITHE
TITIS
TITLE
TITRE
TITUS
VITAE
VITAL
VITAS
VITUS
WITCH
WITHE
WITHY
WITTE
WITTY
ZITIS

•I•T•

AIMTO
BIOTA
BIRTH

BITTE	RIATA	RIANT	SMITE	MOIST	KRAIT	•I•U•	••I•U	VIVRE	MDXIV	FIXER
BITTS	RIFTS	RIGHT	SMITH	ODIST	LEGIT	AINUS	ADIEU	WIVED	MLXIV	FIXES
BITTY	RIOTS	RIVET	SMITS	PAINT	LICIT	BIDUP	AEIOU	WIVES	MMCIV	FIXIT
DICTA	SIETE	SIGHT	SNITS	POINT	LIMIT	DIDUP	ELIHU		MMDIV	FIXUP
DICTS	SIFTS	TIANT	SPITE	PRINT	MEDIT	DIGUP	HAIKU	•I•V•	MMLIV	MIXED
DICTU	SILTS	TIBET	SPITS	QUIET	MERIT	FICUS	MAIDU	DIVVY	MMMIV	MIXER
DIETS	SILTY	TIGHT	SPITZ	QUILT	NOHIT	FILUM	POILU	MIRVS	MMXIV	MIXES
DINTS	SIXTH	TINCT	SUITA	QUINT	NOTIT	FIXUP	QUIPU	SIEVE	MXCIV	MIXIN
DINTY	SIXTY	VINGT	SUITE	QUIRT	ONDIT	GIGUE		SILVA	MXLIV	MIXUP
DIRTY	TIETO	VISIT	SUITS	RAITT	OPCIT	HILUM	IV•••		MXMIV	NIXED
DISTR	TILTH	WIEST	SWITH	SAINT	ORBIT	HITUP	IVANA	•I••V	MXXIV	NIXES
DITTO	TILTS	WIGHT	SWITZ	SHIFT	PETIT	LIEUS	IVIED	KIROV	RAJIV	NIXIE
DITTY	TINTS	ZIBET	TOITY	SHIRT	PEWIT	LIEUT	IVIES		XXXIV	NIXON
FIATS	UINTA		TRITE	SKINT	PIPIT	LIKUD	IVINS	••IV•		PIXEL
FIFTH	VIRTU	••IT•	TRITT	SKIRT	PLAIT	LINUS	IVORY	ALIVE	I•W••	PIXIE
FIFTY	VISTA	ADITS	TWITS	SLIPT	POLIT	LITUP		ATIVE	IOWAN	SIXAM
FILTH	WIDTH	AGITA	UNITE	SPILT	POSIT	MINUS	I•V••	CHIVE	IRWIN	SIXED
FIRTH	WILTS	AKITA	UNITS	STILT	QUOIT	MIXUP	IRVIN	CHIVY		SIXER
FISTS	WITTE	AMITY	UNITY	STINT	REFIT	NIDUS		CLIVE	I••W•	SIXES
GIFTS	WITTY	ANITA	WAITE	SUINT	RELIT	NIPUP	I•••V	DRIVE	ILGWU	SIXMO
GILTS		ARITH	WAITS	SWIFT	REMIT	NISUS	INDIV	NAIVE	INAWE	SIXPM
GIRTH	•I••T	BAITS	WAITZ	TAINT	SPLIT	PIAUI		OGIVE	INTWO	SIXTH
GIRTS	AIMAT	BLITT	WHITE	TRITT	SPRIT	PICUL	•IV••	OLIVE		SIXTY
GISTS	BIGHT	BLITZ	WHITS	TWIST	TACIT	PILUM	CIVET	PRIVY	I•••W	VIXEN
HILTS	BIGOT	BOITE	WHITY	TWIXT	TOBIT	PILUS	CIVIC	SHIVA	INLAW	
HINTS	BINET	BOITO	WRITE	VEIDT	TOWIT	PINUP	CIVIL	SHIVS	INTOW	•I••X
HIPTO	BIONT	BRITE	WRITS	WAIST	TRAIT	PIOUS	DIVAN	SKIVE		SILEX
JILTS	BIZET	BRITH		WHIST	UNFIT	PIQUE	DIVAS	SPIVS	•IW••	SIOUX
KILTS	CIVET	BRITS	••I•T	WRIST	UNLIT	RIGUP	DIVED	UNIVS	KIWIS	TIMEX
KINTE	DICOT	BRITT	ADINT	ZEIST	VISIT	RIPUP	DIVER	WAIVE	MIWOK	
KITTS	DIDNT	CHITA	ALIST			SIEUR	DIVES			••IX•
KITTY	DIDST	CHITS	ATILT	•••IT	I•U••	SINUS	DIVOT	•••IV	•I•W•	TWIXT
LIETO	DIGIT	DEITY	BLITT	ADMIT	INUIT	SIOUX	DIVVY	ACTIV	KIOWA	
LIFTS	DITAT	DOITS	BRITT	AFRIT	INURE	SITUP	FIVER	ANNIV	KITWE	•••IX
LILTS	DIVOT	EDITH	BUILT	AMBIT	INUSE	SITUS	FIVES	CCCIV	VIEWS	ADMIX
LINTS	DIXIT	EDITS	CLIFT	AUDIT	IQUIT	TIEUP	GIVEN	CCLIV	VIEWY	AFFIX
LINTY	EIGHT	ELITE	CLINT	AWAIT	ISUZU	TIPUP	GIVER	CCXIV		CALIX
LISTS	EILAT	EMITS	CLIPT	BAGIT		TITUS	GIVES	CDLIV	•I••W	CCCIX
MIATA	FIGHT	EVITA	CRIST	BARIT	I••U•	UIGUR	HIVED	CDXIV	MIAOW	CCLIX
MILTS	FILET	EXITS	DEIST	BEFIT	ICEUP	VIRUS	HIVES	CLXIV	SINEW	CCXIX
MILTY	FIRST	FAITH	DRIFT	BRUIT	ICTUS	VISUM	JIVED	CMLIV	WIDOW	CDLIX
MINTO	FIXIT	FLITS	EDICT	CANIT	IGLUS	VITUS	JIVER	CMXIV		CDXIX
MINTS	GIANT	FRITO	ELIOT	CUBIT	ILIUM	ZIPUP	JIVES	CXCIV	••IW•	CLXIX
MINTY	GIGOT	FRITS	EVICT	DAVIT	ILLUS		JIVEY	CXLIV	DAIWA	CMLIX
MIRTH	HITIT	FRITZ	EXIST	DEBIT	IMBUE	•I••U	KIVAS	CXXIV	SLIWA	CMXIX
MISTI	LICET	GAITS	FAINT	DEMIT	INCUR	BIJOU	LIVED	DCCIV		COMIX
MISTS	LICIT	GLITZ	FEINT	DIGIT	INCUS	DICTU	LIVEN	DCLIV	IX•••	CROIX
MISTY	LIEUT	GRITS	FEIST	DIXIT	INDUS	FICHU	LIVER	DCXIV	IXION	CXCIX
MITTS	LIGHT	HAITI	FLINT	DOGIT	INFUN	HINDU	LIVES	DERIV	IXNAY	CXLIX
MITTY	LIMIT	HOITY	FLIRT	DROIT	INPUT	VIRTU	LIVIA	DLXIV		CXXIX
NIFTY	LISZT	INITS	FOIST	EATIT	IPSUM	XINGU	LIVID	DXCIV	I•••X	DCCIX
NINTH	MIDST	KEITH	GLINT	FACIT	ISSUE		LIVRE	DXLIV	ICEAX	DCLIX
NITTI	MIGHT	KNITS	GRIFT	FIXIT	ISSUS	••IU•	NIVAL	DXXIV	IMMIX	DCXIX
NITTY	MINOT	LAITY	GRIOT	FRUIT		AAIUN	NIVEN	EQUIV	INBOX	DLXIX
PICTS	NIGHT	LEITH	GRIST	FUGIT	I•••U	ARIUM	PIVOT	INDIV	INDEX	DXCIX
PIETA	NILOT	OMITS	GUILT	GETIT	ILGWU	ARIUS	RIVAL	LXXIV	INFIX	DXLIX
PIETY	NIPAT	QUITE	HEIDT	GOTIT	INONU	BAIUL	RIVED	MCCIV		DXXIX
PINTA	PICOT	QUITO	HEIST	GSUIT	ISAMU	GAIUS	RIVEN	MCDIV	•IX••	FELIX
PINTO	PILOT	QUITS	HOIST	HABIT	ISUZU	ILIUM	RIVER	MCLIV	BIXBY	HELIX
PINTS	PINOT	RAITT	IDIOT	HITIT		LAIUS	RIVES	MCMIV	DIXIE	IMMIX
PISTE	PIPIT	SAITH	JOINT	INUIT	•IU••	ODIUM	RIVET	MCXIV	DIXIT	INFIX
PITTA	PITOT	SKITS	JOIST	IQUIT	PIURA	OPIUM	SIVAN	MDCIV	DIXON	KYLIX
PITTS	PIVOT	SLITS	KLIMT	IZMIT			VIVID	MDLIV	FIXED	LXXIX

MCCIX
MCDIX
MCLIX
MCMIX
MCXIX
MDCIX
MDLIX
MDXIX
MLXIX
MMCIX
MMDIX
MMLIX
MMMIX
MMXIX
MXCIX
MXLIX
MXXIX
RADIX
REMIX
UNFIX
VARIX
XXXIX

I•Y••
IDYLL
IDYLS

I•••Y
IATRY
ICILY
IMPLY
INLAY
IRONY
ISLEY
ITALY
ITCHY
IVORY
IXNAY

•IY••
DIYER
RIYAL

•I•Y•
LIBYA
SIBYL
VINYL

•I••Y
AILEY
BIALY
BIDDY
BIFFY
BIGGY
BIGLY
BILBY
BILGY
BILLY
BIRDY
BITSY
BITTY
BIXBY
CINDY
CISSY
DIARY
DICEY
DICKY
DIDBY
DIGBY
DILLY
DIMLY
DINDY
DINGY
DINKY
DINTY
DIPPY
DIRTY
DISHY
DITSY
DITTY
DITZY
DIVVY
DIZZY
FIERY
FIFTY
FILLY
FILMY
FINNY
FIRRY
FISHY
FITLY
FIZZY
GIDDY
GILLY
GIMPY
GINNY
GIPSY
HILLY
HINNY
HIPLY
HIPPY
HISSY
JIFFY
JIMMY
JIVEY
KICKY
KIDDY
KILEY
KILLY
KINKY
KIRBY
KITTY
LIBBY
LIDDY
LIEBY
LILLY
LIMEY
LINDY
LINEY
LINTY
LIPPY
MIDDY
MIFFY
MIKEY
MILKY
MILTY
MIMSY
MINDY
MINGY
MINTY
MIRKY
MISSY
MISTY
MITTY
NIFTY
NILLY
NIMBY
NIMOY
NINNY
NIPPY
NITTY
PICKY
PIETY
PIGGY
PINEY
PINKY
PITHY
RIBBY
RICKY
RIDGY
RIGBY
RILEY
RINDY
RINKY
RISKY
RITZY
SILKY
SILLY
SILTY
SISSY
SITBY
SIXTY
TICKY
TILLY
TIMMY
TINNY
TIPPY
TIPSY
TIZZY
VICHY
VIEWY
VIGNY
VINNY
VISBY
WIGGY
WILEY
WILLY
WIMPY
WINDY
WINEY
WISHY
WISPY
WITHY
WITTY
ZIGGY
ZINCY
ZINGY
ZIPPY

••IY•
ORIYA

••I•Y
ACIDY
AMITY
BRINY
CHIVY
DAILY
DAIRY
DAISY
DEIFY
DEITY
DOILY
DRILY
EDIFY
EMILY
FAIRY
GAILY
GRIMY
HAIRY
HOITY
ICILY
JUICY
LAITY
MEINY
NOILY
NOISY
PHILY
PLINY
PRICY
PRIVY
RAINY
REIFY
ROILY
SHINY
SLILY
SLIMY
SPICY
SPIKY
SPINY
SPIRY
TOITY
UNIFY
UNITY
VEINY
WHINY
WHITY

IZ•••
IZAAK
IZARD
IZARS
IZBAS
IZMIR
IZMIT

I••Z•
IBIZA
ISUZU

•IZ••
BIZET
DIZEN
DIZZY
FIZZY
GIZMO
MIZAR
NIZAM
NIZER
PIZZA
RIZZO
SIZED
SIZER
SIZES
TIZZY
WIZEN
ZIZKA

•I•Z•
DIAZO
DITZY
DIZZY
FIZZY
GINZA
LISZT
MITZI
PINZA
PIZZA
RITZY
RIZZO
TISZA
TIZZY
WINZE

•I••Z
HIJAZ

••IZ•
BAIZA
BAIZE
ELIZA
FRIZZ
IBIZA
MAIZE
PRIZE
PRIZM
RHIZO
SEIZE

••I•Z
BLITZ
FRITZ
FRIZZ
GLITZ
HEINZ
MAINZ
SPITZ
SWITZ
WAITZ

•••IZ
CADIZ
FELIZ
HAFIZ

JA•••
JABBA
JABOT
JACET
JACKS
JACKY
JACOB
JADED
JADES
JAFFA
JAFFE
JAGGY
JAHRE
JAILS
JAIME
JAINS
JAKES
JAMAL
JAMBS
JAMES
JAMIE
JAMIN
JAMMY
JAMUP
JANET
JANIE
JANIS
JANUS
JAPAN
JAPED
JAPES
JARLS
JARRE
JASEY
JASON
JASSY
JATOS
JAUNE
JAUNT
JAVAS
JAWED
JAYNE
JAZZY

J•A••
JBARS
JEANE
JEANS

J••A•
JAMAL
JAPAN
JAVAS
JIHAD
JONAH
JONAS
JOTAS
JOUAL
JUBAL
JUDAH
JUDAS
JUGAL
JURAL
JURAT

J•••A
JABBA
JAFFA
JIDDA
JOLLA
JUDEA
JULIA
JUMNA
JUNTA

•J•A•
VJDAY

••JA•
HEJAZ
HIJAZ
KOJAK
RAJAH
RAJAS
SAJAK
UNJAM

••J•A
HIJRA
WAJDA

•••JA
ABUJA
NADJA
NINJA
OUIJA
RIOJA
SONJA
THUJA

JB•••
JBARS

J•B••
JABBA
JABOT
JIBED
JIBES
JUBAL

J••B•
JABBA
JAMBS
JUMBO

J•••B
JACOB

••J•B
MCJOB

J•C••
JACET
JACKS
JACKY
JACOB
JOCKO
JOCKS

J••C•
JOYCE
JUICE
JUICY
JUNCO

•J•C•
EJECT

J•D••
JADED
JADES
JIDDA
JODIE
JUDAH
JUDAS
JUDEA
JUDEO
JUDGE

J••D•
JEUDI
JIDDA

J•••D
JADED
JAPED
JAWED
JIBED
JIHAD
JIVED
JOKED
JUKED

•JD••
VJDAY

•J•D•
EJIDO

•J••D
FJELD
FJORD

••JD•
WAJDA

JE•••
JEANE
JEANS
JEEPS
JEERS
JELLO
JELLS
JELLY
JEMMY
JENNY
JEREZ
JERKS
JERKY
JERRY
JERZY
JESSE
JESTS
JETER
JETES
JETTY
JEUDI
JEUNE
JEWEL

J•E••
JEEPS
JEERS
JOEYS

J••E•
JACET
JADED
JADES
JAKES
JAMES
JANET
JAPED
JAPES
JASEY
JAWED
JEREZ
JETER
JETES
JEWEL
JIBED
JIBES
JIVED
JIVER
JIVES
JIVEY
JOKED
JOKER
JOKES
JOKEY
JONES
JOREL
JOSEF
JUDEA
JUDEO
JUKED
JUKES
JULEP
JULES
JUTES

J•••E
JAFFE
JAHRE
JAIME
JAMIE
JANIE
JARRE
JAUNE
JAYNE
JEANE
JESSE
JEUNE
JODIE
JOLIE
JORGE
JOULE
JOYCE
JUDGE
JUICE
JULIE
JUSTE

•JE••
EJECT
FJELD

•J•E•
AJMER

••JE•
OBJET

••J•E
GIJOE

•••JE
KOPJE

JF•••
JFKJR

J•F••
JAFFA
JAFFE
JIFFY

J••F•
JAFFA
JAFFE
JIFFY

J•••F
JOSEF

J•G••
JAGGY
JUGAL
JUGUM

J••G•
JAGGY
JINGO
JORGE
JUDGE

J•H••
JAHRE
JIHAD
JOHNS

J•••H
JONAH
JUDAH

••J•H
RAJAH

JI•••
JIBED
JIBES
JIDDA
JIFFY
JIHAD
JILTS
JIMMY
JINGO
JINKS
JINNI
JINNS
JIVED
JIVER
JIVES
JIVEY

J•I••
JAILS
JAIME
JAINS
JOINS
JOINT
JOIST
JUICE
JUICY

J••I•
JAMIE
JAMIN
JANIE
JANIS
JODIE
JOLIE
JOSIP
JULIA
JULIE
JULIO

J•••I
JEUDI
JINNI

•JI••
DJINN
EJIDO

••JI•
HAJIS
RAJIV

••J•I
HAJJI

•••JI
AWAJI
BAOJI
BENJI
HADJI
HAJJI

KANJI
MEIJI
SEIJI
SHOJI

J•J••
JUJUS

J••J•
JFKJR

••JJ•
HAJJI

J•K••
JAKES
JFKJR
JOKED
JOKER
JOKES
JOKEY
JUKED
JUKES

J••K•
JACKS
JACKY
JERKS
JERKY
JINKS
JOCKO
JOCKS
JUNKS
JUNKY

••J•K
KOJAK
SAJAK

J•L••
JELLO
JELLS
JELLY
JILTS
JOLIE
JOLLA
JOLLY
JOLTS
JOLTY
JULEP
JULES
JULIA
JULIE
JULIO

J••L•
JAILS
JARLS
JELLO
JELLS
JELLY
JOLLA
JOLLY
JOULE
JOWLS
JOWLY

J•••L
JAMAL
JEWEL
JOREL
JOUAL
JUBAL
JUGAL
JURAL

•J•L•
FJELD

J•M••
JAMAL
JAMBS
JAMES
JAMIE
JAMIN
JAMMY
JAMUP
JEMMY
JIMMY
JUMBO
JUMNA
JUMPS
JUMPY

J••M•
JAIME
JAMMY
JEMMY
JIMMY

J•••M
JORUM
JUGUM

•JM••
AJMER

••J•M
UNJAM

J•N••
JANET
JANIE
JANIS
JANUS
JENNY
JINGO
JINKS
JINNI
JINNS
JONAH
JONAS
JONES
JUNCO
JUNKS
JUNKY
JUNTA
JUNTO

J••N•
JAINS
JAUNE
JAUNT
JAYNE
JEANE
JEANS
JENNY
JEUNE
JINNI
JINNS
JOHNS
JOINS
JOINT
JUMNA

J•••N
JAMIN
JAPAN
JASON

•J•N•
DJINN

•J••N
BJORN
DJINN

••J•N
CAJUN
DIJON
GIJON

JO•••
JOCKO
JOCKS
JODIE
JOEYS
JOHNS
JOINS
JOINT
JOIST
JOKED
JOKER
JOKES
JOKEY
JOLIE
JOLLA
JOLLY
JOLTS
JOLTY
JONAH
JONAS
JONES
JOREL
JORGE
JORUM
JOSEF
JOSIP
JOTAS
JOUAL
JOULE
JOUST
JOWLS
JOWLY
JOYCE

J••O•
JABOT
JACOB
JASON
JATOS
JUROR

J•••O
JELLO
JINGO
JOCKO
JUDEO
JULIO
JUMBO
JUNCO
JUNTO

•JO••
BJORN
FJORD

•J••O
EJIDO

••JO•
ANJOU
BIJOU
DIJON
DOJOS
ENJOY
GIJOE
GIJON
MAJOR
MCJOB
MOJOS

•••JO
BANJO
VIEJO

J•P••
JAPAN
JAPED
JAPES

J••P•
JEEPS
JUMPS
JUMPY

J•••P
JAMUP
JOSIP
JULEP

J•R••
JARLS
JARRE
JEREZ
JERKS
JERKY
JERRY
JERZY
JOREL
JORGE
JORUM
JURAL
JURAT
JUROR

J••R•
JAHRE
JARRE
JBARS
JEERS
JERRY

J•••R
JETER
JFKJR
JIVER
JOKER
JUROR

•J•R•
BJORN
FJORD

•J••R
AJMER

••JR•
HIJRA

••J•R
MAJOR

•••JR
JFKJR

J•S••
JASEY
JASON
JASSY
JESSE
JESTS
JOSEF
JOSIP
JUSTE

J••S•
JASSY
JESSE
JOIST
JOUST

J•••S
JACKS
JADES
JAILS
JAINS
JAKES
JAMBS
JAMES
JANIS
JANUS
JAPES
JARLS
JATOS
JAVAS
JBARS
JEANS
JEEPS
JEERS
JELLS
JERKS
JESTS
JETES
JIBES
JILTS
JINKS
JINNS
JIVES
JOCKS
JOEYS
JOHNS
JOINS
JOKES
JOLTS
JONAS
JONES
JOTAS
JOWLS
JUDAS
JUJUS
JUKES
JULES
JUMPS
JUNKS
JUTES

••J•S
AUJUS
DOJOS
HAJIS
JUJUS
MOJOS
RAJAS

J•T••
JATOS
JETER
JETES
JETTY
JOTAS
JUTES
JUTTY

J••T•
JESTS
JETTY
JILTS
JOLTS
JOLTY
JUNTA
JUNTO
JUSTE
JUTTY

J•••T
JABOT
JACET
JANET
JAUNT
JOINT
JOIST
JOUST
JURAT

•J••T
EJECT

••J•T
OBJET

JU•••
JUBAL
JUDAH
JUDAS
JUDEA
JUDEO
JUDGE
JUGAL
JUGUM
JUICE
JUICY
JUJUS
JUKED
JUKES
JULEP
JULES
JULIA
JULIE
JULIO
JUMBO
JUMNA
JUMPS
JUMPY
JUNCO
JUNKS
JUNKY
JUNTA
JUNTO
JURAL
JURAT
JUROR
JUSTE
JUTES
JUTTY

J•U••
JAUNE
JAUNT
JEUDI
JEUNE
JOUAL
JOULE
JOUST

J••U•
JAMUP
JANUS
JORUM
JUGUM
JUJUS

••JU•
AUJUS
CAJUN
JUJUS

••J•U
ANJOU
BIJOU

•••JU
CHEJU

J•V••
JAVAS
JIVED
JIVER
JIVES
JIVEY

••J•V
RAJIV

J•W••
JAWED
JEWEL
JOWLS
JOWLY

J•Y••
JAYNE
JOYCE

J••Y•
JOEYS

J•••Y
JACKY
JAGGY
JAMMY
JASEY
JASSY
JAZZY
JELLY
JEMMY
JENNY
JERKY
JERRY
JERZY
JETTY
JIFFY
JIMMY
JIVEY
JOKEY
JOLLY
JOLTY
JOWLY
JUICY
JUMPY
JUNKY
JUTTY

•J••Y
VJDAY

••J•Y
ENJOY

J•Z••
JAZZY

J••Z•
JAZZY
JERZY

J•••Z
JEREZ

••J•Z
HEJAZ
HIJAZ

KA•••
KAABA
KABOB
KABUL
KADAR
KAFIR
KAFKA
KAFUE
KAHLO
KAKAS
KAKIS
KALEL
KALES
KANDY
KANGA
KANIN
KANJI
KANSA
KANZU
KAONS
KAPHS
KAPOK
KAPPA
KAPUT
KARAN
KARAT
KAREL
KAREN
KARLA
KARMA
KAROL
KARSH
KASEM
KASHA
KATHY
KATIE
KAUAI
KAURI
KAVAS
KAYAK
KAYOS
KAZAK
KAZAN
KAZOO

K•A••
KAABA
KEACH
KEANE
KEANU
KEATS
KHAKI
KHANS
KIANG
KLAUS
KMART
KNACK
KNAPS
KNARS
KNAVE
KOALA
KOANS
KRAAL
KRAFT
KRAIT
KRAUS
KRAUT
KRAZY
KUALA
KVASS
KYACK
KYATS

K••A•
KADAR
KAKAS
KARAN
KARAT
KAUAI
KAVAS
KAYAK
KAZAK
KAZAN
KEBAB
KEMAL
KENAI
KERAT
KINAS
KIVAS
KNEAD
KODAK
KOJAK
KOLAS
KORAN
KRAAL
KULAK

K•••A
KAABA
KAFKA
KANGA
KANSA
KAPPA
KARLA
KARMA
KASHA
KENYA
KINDA
KIOGA
KIOWA
KISKA
KOALA
KORDA
KOREA
KRONA
KRUPA
KUALA
KUKLA
KYOGA

•KA••
OKAPI
OKAYS
SKALD
SKANK
SKATE
UKASE

•K•A•
AKBAR
AKKAD
OKRAS
SKEAN
SKEAT
SKOAL
SKUAS

•K••A
AKELA
AKIRA
AKITA
SKODA

••KA•
AKKAD
AOKAY
DAKAR
DUKAS
KAKAS
LUKAS
MCKAY
MIKAN
OHKAY
OSKAR
PIKAS
SAKAI
SIKAS
TAKAS
TIKAL
TOKAY

WEKAS

••K•A
HEKLA
KUKLA
MAKUA
PUKKA

•••KA
ASOKA
BABKA
CHAKA
CHEKA
DHAKA
DITKA
ERIKA
KAFKA
KISKA
LAIKA
LANKA
OSAKA
PARKA
POLKA
PUKKA
SANKA
SITKA
STUKA
SUCKA
TANKA
TONKA
VODKA
ZIZKA

K•B••
KABOB
KABUL
KEBAB
KEBOB
KIBEI
KOBOS

K••B•
KAABA
KERBS
KIRBY
KNOBS
KREBS

K•••B
KABOB
KEBAB
KEBOB

•KB••
AKBAR

K•C••
KICKS
KICKY
KOCHI

K••C•
KEACH
KENCH
KETCH
KNACK
KNICK
KNOCK
KOTCH
KYACK

K•D••
KADAR
KEDGE
KIDDO
KIDDY
KODAK
KUDOS
KUDUS
KUDZU

K••D•
KANDY
KENDO
KIDDO
KIDDY
KINDA
KINDS
KORDA
KURDS

K•••D
KEYED
KITED
KNEAD
KNEED

•K•D•
SKIDS
SKODA

•K••D
AKKAD
SKALD
SKIED

••K•D
AKKAD
ALKYD
ASKED
BAKED
BIKED
CAKED
COKED
DEKED
DIKED
DUKED
FAKED
HIKED
HOKED
INKED
IRKED
JOKED
JUKED
LIKED
LIKUD
MIKED
NAKED
NUKED
PIKED
POKED
RAKED
WAKED
YOKED

KE•••
KEACH
KEANE
KEANU
KEATS
KEBAB
KEBOB
KEDGE
KEELS
KEENE
KEENS
KEEPS
KEETS
KEFIR
KEITH
KELLY
KELPS
KELPY
KELSO
KEMAL
KEMPS
KEMPT
KENAI
KENCH
KENDO
KENNY
KENOS
KENYA
KEOGH
KEPIS
KERAT
KERBS
KERNS
KERRI
KERRY
KESEY
KETCH
KEVEL
KEVIN
KEYED
KEYES
KEYIN
KEYUP

K•E••
KEELS
KEENE
KEENS
KEEPS
KEETS
KLEIN
KNEAD
KNEED
KNEEL
KNEES
KNELL
KNELT
KREBS
KVELL

K••E•
KALEL
KALES
KAREL
KAREN
KASEM
KESEY
KEVEL
KEYED
KEYES
KHMER
KIBEI
KILEY
KINER
KITED
KITER
KITES
KLIEG
KNEED
KNEEL
KNEES
KOPEK
KOREA
KUGEL
KYSER

K•••E
KAFUE
KATIE
KEANE
KEDGE
KEENE
KINTE
KITWE
KLINE
KLUGE
KLUTE
KNAVE
KNIFE
KNUTE
KOINE
KOPJE
KRONE
KYRIE

•KE••
AKEEM
AKEES
AKELA
AKENE
SKEAN
SKEAT
SKEET
SKEGS
SKEIN
SKEPS
SKETE
SKEWS

•K•E•
AKEEM
AKEES
OKIES
SKEET
SKIED
SKIER
SKIES
SKYEY

•K••E
AKENE
SKATE
SKETE
SKIVE
UKASE

••KE•
AIKEN
ASKED
ASKER
ASKEW
BAKED
BAKER
BAKES
BIKED
BIKEL
BIKER
BIKES
CAKED
CAKES
CAKEY
COKED
COKES
CUKES
DEKED
DEKES
DIKED
DIKES
DUKED
DUKES
ESKER
FAKED
FAKER
FAKES
FYKES
HAKES
HIKED
HIKER
HIKES
HOKED
HOKES
HOKEY
ICKES
INKED
INKER
IRKED
JAKES
JOKED
JOKER
JOKES
JOKEY
JUKED
JUKES
LAKER
LAKES
LIKED
LIKEN
LIKES
MAKER
MAKES
MIKED
MIKES
MIKEY
NAKED
NIKES
NUKED
NUKES
OAKEN
OAKES
ONKEY
PEKES
PIKED
PIKER
PIKES
POKED
POKER
POKES
POKEY
RAKED
RAKER
RAKES
REKEY
RIKER
SAKER
SAKES
SIKES
SOKES
TAKEI
TAKEN
TAKER
TAKES
TIKES
TOKEN
TYKES
URKEL
WAKED
WAKEN
WAKES
WOKEN
YIKES
YOKED
YOKEL
YOKES

••K•E
ANKLE
INKLE
LAKME
OAKIE
PEKOE

•••KE
ALIKE
AWAKE
AWOKE
BLAKE
BLOKE
BRAKE
BROKE
BURKE
CHOKE
COOKE
CRAKE
DANKE
DRAKE
EVOKE
FISKE
FLAKE
FLUKE
HAWKE
HOOKE
LATKE
LOCKE
MINKE
QUAKE
RANKE
RILKE
SHAKE
SLAKE
SMOKE
SNAKE
SPAKE
SPEKE
SPIKE
SPOKE
STAKE
STOKE
TRIKE

K•F••
KAFIR
KAFKA
KAFUE
KEFIR

K••F•
KHUFU
KNIFE
KRAFT

K•••F
KNOPF

•K•F•
SKIFF

•K••F
SKIFF

K•G••
KUGEL

K••G•
KANGA
KEDGE
KEOGH
KINGS
KIOGA
KLUGE
KROGH
KYOGA

K•••G
KIANG
KLIEG
KOING

•K•G•
SKEGS

•K••G
EKING
OKING

KH•••
KHAKI
KHANS
KHMER
KHUFU

K•H••
KAHLO

K••H•
KAPHS
KASHA
KATHY
KOCHI
KOPHS

K•••H
KARSH
KEACH
KEITH
KENCH
KEOGH
KETCH
KNISH
KOTCH
KROGH

•K••H
SKOSH

••KH•
ANKHS
SIKHS

•••KH
BALKH

KI•••
KIANG
KIBEI
KICKS
KICKY
KIDDO
KIDDY
KILEY
KILIM
KILLS
KILLY
KILNS
KILOS
KILTS
KIMPO
KINAS
KINDA
KINDS
KINER
KINGS
KINKS
KINKY
KINTE
KIOGA
KIOSK
KIOWA
KIRBY
KIRIN
KIRKS
KIROV
KISKA
KITED
KITER
KITES
KITTS
KITTY
KITWE
KIVAS
KIWIS

K•I••
KEITH
KLIEG
KLIMT
KLINE
KNICK
KNIFE
KNISH
KNITS
KOINE
KOING
KRILL
KRISS

K••I•
KAFIR
KAKIS
KANIN
KATIE
KEFIR
KEPIS
KEVIN
KEYIN
KILIM
KIRIN
KIWIS
KLEIN
KRAIT
KYLIX
KYRIE

K•••I
KANJI
KAUAI
KAURI
KENAI
KERRI
KHAKI
KIBEI
KOCHI

•KI••
AKINS
AKIRA
AKITA
EKING
OKIES
OKING
SKIDS
SKIED
SKIER
SKIES
SKIFF
SKILL
SKIMP
SKIMS
SKINK
SKINS
SKINT
SKIPS
SKIRL
SKIRR
SKIRT
SKITS
SKIVE

•K•I•
SKEIN

•K••I
OKAPI

••KI•
ARKIN
ASKIN
FAKIR
HAKIM
KAKIS
OAKIE
PEKIN
RAKIS
TAKIN
TIKIS

••K•I
NIKKI
RIKKI
SAKAI
TAKEI
TIKKI
VIKKI
YOKOI

•••KI
GORKI
KHAKI
NIKKI
RICKI
RIKKI
TIKKI
UMEKI
VICKI
VIKKI

K•J••
KOJAK

K••J•
KANJI
KOPJE

••KJ•
JFKJR

K•K••
KAKAS
KAKIS
KUKLA

K••K•
KAFKA
KHAKI
KICKS
KICKY
KINKS
KINKY
KIRKS
KISKA
KOOKS
KOOKY

K•••K
KAPOK
KAYAK
KAZAK
KIOSK
KNACK
KNICK
KNOCK
KODAK
KOJAK
KOPEK
KULAK
KURSK
KYACK

•KK••
AKKAD

•K••K
SKANK
SKINK
SKULK
SKUNK

••KK•
DEKKO
NIKKI
NIKKO
PUKKA
RIKKI
TIKKI
VIKKI

KL•••
KLAUS
KLEIN
KLIEG
KLIMT
KLINE
KLUGE
KLUTE
KLUTZ

K•L••
KALEL
KALES
KELLY
KELPS
KELPY
KELSO
KILEY
KILIM
KILLS
KILLY
KILNS
KILOS
KILTS
KOLAS
KULAK
KYLIX

K••L•
KAHLO
KARLA
KEELS
KELLY
KILLS
KILLY
KNELL
KNELT
KNOLL
KOALA
KRILL
KRULL
KUALA
KUKLA
KVELL

K•••L
KABUL
KALEL
KAREL
KAROL
KEMAL
KEVEL
KNEEL
KNELL
KNOLL
KNURL
KRAAL
KRILL
KRULL
KUGEL
KVELL
KYZYL

•K•L•
AKELA
SKALD
SKILL
SKULK
SKULL

•K••L
SKILL
SKIRL
SKOAL
SKULL

••KL•
ANKLE
HEKLA
INKLE
KUKLA

••K•L
ALKYL
BIKEL
TIKAL
URKEL
YOKEL

KM•••
KMART

K•M••
KEMAL
KEMPS
KEMPT
KHMER
KIMPO

K••M•
KARMA
KLIMT

K•••M
KASEM
KILIM

•K•M•
SKIMP
SKIMS

•K••M
AKEEM
AKSUM

••KM•
LAKME

••K•M
HAKIM
HOKUM
OAKUM
YOKUM

KN•••
KNACK
KNAPS
KNARS
KNAVE
KNEAD
KNEED
KNEEL
KNEES
KNELL
KNELT
KNICK
KNIFE
KNISH
KNITS
KNOBS
KNOCK
KNOLL
KNOPF
KNOPS
KNORR
KNOTS
KNOUT
KNOWN
KNOWS
KNURL
KNURS
KNUTE

K•N••
KANDY
KANGA
KANIN
KANJI
KANSA
KANZU
KENAI
KENCH
KENDO
KENNY
KENOS
KENYA
KINAS
KINDA
KINDS
KINER
KINGS
KINKS
KINKY
KINTE

K••N•
KAONS
KEANE
KEANU
KEENE
KEENS
KENNY
KERNS
KHANS
KIANG
KILNS
KLINE
KOANS
KOINE
KOING
KOVNO
KRONA
KRONE

K•••N
KANIN
KARAN
KAREN
KAZAN
KEVIN
KEYIN
KIRIN
KLEIN
KNOWN
KORAN

•KN••
SKNXX

•K•N•
AKENE
AKINS
EKING
OKING
SKANK
SKINK
SKINS
SKINT
SKUNK

•K••N
AKRON
SKEAN
SKEIN

••K•N
AIKEN
ARKIN
ASKIN
LIKEN
MIKAN
NIKON
OAKEN
PEKIN
TAKEN
TAKIN
TOKEN
WAKEN
WOKEN
YUKON

KO•••
KOALA
KOANS
KOBOS
KOCHI
KODAK
KOINE
KOING
KOJAK
KOLAS
KOOKS
KOOKY
KOPEK
KOPHS
KOPJE
KORAN
KORDA
KOREA
KOTCH
KOTOS
KOVNO

K•O••
KAONS
KEOGH
KIOGA
KIOSK
KIOWA
KNOBS
KNOCK
KNOLL
KNOPF
KNOPS
KNORR
KNOTS
KNOUT
KNOWN
KNOWS
KOOKS
KOOKY
KROGH
KRONA
KRONE
KYOGA
KYOTO

K••O•
KABOB
KAPOK
KAROL
KAYOS
KAZOO
KEBOB
KENOS
KILOS
KIROV
KOBOS
KOTOS
KUDOS

K•••O
KAHLO
KAZOO
KELSO
KENDO
KIDDO
KIMPO
KOVNO
KYOTO

•KO••
SKOAL
SKODA
SKORT
SKOSH

•K•O•
AKRON

••KO•
CUKOR
MAKOS
NIKON
PEKOE
YAKOV
YOKOI
YUKON
ZUKOR

••K•O
DEKKO
MOKPO
NIKKO
TOKYO

•••KO
BILKO
BIOKO
BUCKO
BUNKO
DEKKO
GECKO
JOCKO
NIKKO
ROYKO
SEIKO
SHAKO
SOCKO
WACKO

K•P••
KAPHS
KAPOK
KAPPA
KAPUT
KEPIS
KOPEK
KOPHS
KOPJE

K••P•
KAPPA
KEEPS
KELPS
KELPY
KEMPS
KEMPT
KIMPO
KNAPS
KNOPF
KNOPS
KRUPA
KRUPP

K•••P
KEYUP
KRUPP

•K•P•
OKAPI
SKEPS
SKIPS

•K••P
SKIMP

••KP•
MOKPO

KR•••
KRAAL
KRAFT
KRAIT
KRAUS
KRAUT
KRAZY
KREBS
KRILL
KRISS
KROGH
KRONA
KRONE
KRULL
KRUPA
KRUPP

K•R••
KARAN
KARAT
KAREL
KAREN
KARLA
KARMA
KAROL
KARSH
KERAT
KERBS
KERNS
KERRI
KERRY
KIRBY
KIRIN
KIRKS
KIROV
KORAN
KORDA
KOREA
KURDS
KURSK
KURTZ
KYRIE

K••R•
KAURI
KERRI
KERRY
KMART
KNARS
KNORR
KNURL
KNURS

K•••R
KADAR
KAFIR
KEFIR
KHMER
KINER
KITER
KNORR
KYSER

•KR••
AKRON
OKRAS

•K•R•
AKIRA
SKIRL
SKIRR
SKIRT
SKORT

•K••R
AKBAR
SKIER
SKIRR

••K•R
ASKER
BAKER
BIKER
CUKOR
DAKAR
ESKER
FAKER
FAKIR
HIKER
INKER
JFKJR
JOKER
LAKER
MAKER
OSKAR
PIKER
POKER
RAKER
RIKER
SAKER
TAKER
ZUKOR

K•S••
KASEM
KASHA
KESEY
KISKA
KYSER

K••S•
KANSA
KARSH
KELSO
KIOSK
KNISH
KRISS
KURSK
KVASS

K•••S
KAKAS
KAKIS
KALES
KAONS
KAPHS
KAVAS
KAYOS
KEATS
KEELS
KEENS
KEEPS
KEETS
KELPS
KEMPS
KENOS
KEPIS
KERBS
KERNS
KEYES
KHANS
KICKS
KILLS
KILNS
KILOS
KILTS
KINAS
KINDS
KINGS
KINKS
KIRKS
KITES
KITTS
KIVAS
KIWIS
KLAUS
KNAPS
KNARS
KNEES
KNITS
KNOBS
KNOPS
KNOTS
KNOWS
KNURS
KOANS
KOBOS
KOLAS
KOOKS
KOPHS
KOTOS
KRAUS
KREBS
KRISS
KUDOS
KUDUS
KURDS
KVASS
KYATS

•KS••
AKSUM

•K•S•
SKOSH
UKASE

•K••S
AKEES
AKINS
OKAYS
OKIES
OKRAS
SKEGS
SKEPS
SKEWS
SKIDS
SKIES
SKIMS
SKINS
SKIPS
SKITS
SKUAS

••KS•
BAKST

••K•S
ANKHS
BAKES
BIKES
CAKES
COKES
CUKES
DEKES
DIKES
DUKAS
DUKES
FAKES
FYKES
HAKES
HIKES
HOKES
ICKES
JAKES
JOKES
JUKES
KAKAS
KAKIS
LAKES
LIKES
LUKAS
MAKES
MAKOS
MIKES
NIKES
NUKES
OAKES
PEKES
PIKAS
PIKES
POKES
RAKES
RAKIS
SAKES
SIKAS
SIKES
SIKHS
SOKES
TAKAS
TAKES
TIKES
TIKIS
TYKES
WAKES
WEKAS
YIKES
YOKES

•••KS
BACKS
BALKS
BANKS
BARKS
BASKS
BEAKS
BECKS
BILKS
BONKS
BOOKS
BOSKS
BUCKS
BULKS
BUNKS
BUSKS
CALKS
CARKS
CASKS
COCKS
CONKS
COOKS
CORKS
CUSKS
DARKS
DECKS
DESKS
DICKS
DINKS
DIRKS
DISKS
DOCKS
DUCKS
DUNKS
DUSKS
EFIKS

EWOKS
FINKS
FOLKS
FORKS
FUNKS
GAWKS
GEEKS
GOWKS
GROKS
HACKS
HAIKS
HANKS
HARKS
HAWKS
HECKS
HICKS
HOCKS
HONKS
HOOKS
HULKS
HUNKS
HUSKS
JACKS
JERKS
JINKS
JOCKS
JUNKS
KICKS
KINKS
KIRKS
KOOKS
LACKS
LARKS
LEAKS
LEEKS
LICKS
LINKS
LOCKS
LOOKS
LUCKS
LURKS
MARKS
MASKS
MILKS
MINKS
MOCKS
MONKS
MUCKS
MUSKS
NARKS
NECKS
NICKS
NOCKS
NOOKS
OICKS
OINKS
PACKS
PARKS
PEAKS
PECKS
PEEKS
PERKS
PICKS
PINKS
PORKS
PUCKS
PUNKS
RACKS
RANKS
REEKS
RICKS
RINKS
RISKS
ROCKS
ROOKS
RUCKS
RUSKS
SACKS
SAUKS
SEEKS
SILKS
SINKS
SOAKS
SOCKS
SOUKS
SUCKS
SULKS
TACKS
TALKS
TANKS
TASKS
TEAKS
TICKS
TREKS
TUCKS
TURKS
TUSKS
VICKS
WALKS
WEEKS
WICKS
WINKS
WONKS
WORKS
YACKS
YANKS
YERKS
YOLKS
ZONKS
ZOUKS

K•T••
KATHY
KATIE
KETCH
KITED
KITER
KITES
KITTS
KITTY
KITWE
KOTCH
KOTOS

K••T•
KEATS
KEETS
KEITH
KILTS
KINTE
KITTS
KITTY
KLUTE
KLUTZ
KNITS
KNOTS
KNUTE
KURTZ
KYATS
KYOTO

K•••T
KAPUT
KARAT
KEMPT
KERAT
KLIMT
KMART
KNELT
KNOUT
KRAFT
KRAIT
KRAUT

•K•T•
AKITA
SKATE
SKETE
SKITS

•K••T
SKEAT
SKEET
SKINT
SKIRT
SKORT

••K•T
BAKST
YAKUT

KU•••
KUALA
KUDOS
KUDUS
KUDZU
KUGEL
KUKLA
KULAK
KURDS
KURSK
KURTZ

K•U••
KAUAI
KAURI
KHUFU
KLUGE
KLUTE
KLUTZ
KNURL
KNURS
KNUTE
KRULL
KRUPA
KRUPP

K••U•
KABUL
KAFUE
KAPUT
KEYUP
KLAUS
KNOUT
KRAUS
KRAUT
KUDUS

K•••U
KANZU
KEANU
KHUFU
KUDZU

•KU••
SKUAS
SKULK
SKULL
SKUNK

•K•U•
AKSUM

••KU•
HOKUM
LIKUD
MAKUA
OAKUM
YAKUT
YOKUM

•••KU
HAIKU
TURKU

KV•••
KVASS
KVELL

K•V••
KAVAS
KEVEL
KEVIN
KIVAS
KOVNO

K••V•
KNAVE

K•••V
KIROV

•K•V•
SKIVE

••K•V
YAKOV

K•W••
KIWIS

K••W•
KIOWA
KITWE
KNOWN
KNOWS

•K•W•
SKEWS

••K•W
ASKEW

K•••X
KYLIX

•K•X•
SKNXX

•K••X
SKNXX

KY•••
KYACK
KYATS
KYLIX
KYOGA
KYOTO
KYRIE
KYSER
KYZYL

K•Y••
KAYAK
KAYOS
KEYED
KEYES
KEYIN
KEYUP

K••Y•
KENYA
KYZYL

K•••Y
KANDY
KATHY
KELLY
KELPY
KENNY
KERRY
KESEY
KICKY
KIDDY
KILEY
KILLY
KINKY
KIRBY
KITTY
KOOKY
KRAZY

•KY••
SKYEY

•K•Y•
OKAYS

•K••Y
SKYEY

••KY•
ALKYD
ALKYL
TOKYO

••K•Y
AOKAY
CAKEY
HOKEY
JOKEY
MCKAY
MIKEY
OHKAY
ONKEY
POKEY
REKEY
TOKAY

•••KY
BALKY
BANKY
BARKY
BECKY
BOSKY
BUCKY
BULKY
CHOKY
COCKY
COOKY
CORKY
DICKY
DINKY
DUCKY
DUSKY
ENSKY
FLAKY
FLUKY
FOLKY
FORKY
FUNKY
GAWKY
GEEKY
GORKY
GUNKY
HANKY
HERKY
HOOKY
HUSKY
JACKY
JERKY
JUNKY
KICKY
KINKY
KOOKY
LANKY
LARKY
LEAKY
LECKY
LUCKY
MILKY
MIRKY
MUCKY
MURKY
MUSKY
PANKY
PAWKY
PECKY
PERKY
PESKY
PICKY
PINKY
PORKY
PUNKY
QUAKY
REEKY
RICKY
RINKY
RISKY
ROCKY
ROOKY
SARKY
SHAKY
SILKY
SMOKY
SNAKY
SPIKY
SULKY
TACKY
TALKY
TICKY
WACKY
WONKY
YOLKY
YUCKY

K•Z••
KAZAK
KAZAN
KAZOO
KYZYL

K••Z•
KANZU
KRAZY
KUDZU

K•••Z
KLUTZ
KURTZ

LA•••
LABAN
LABEL
LABIO
LABOR
LACED
LACER
LACES
LACEY
LACKS
LACTI
LACTO
LADED
LADEN
LADER
LADES
LADLE
LADON
LADYS
LAGAN
LAGER
LAGOS
LAHAR
LAHTI
LAICS
LAIKA
LAINE
LAING
LAIRD
LAIRS
LAITY
LAIUS
LAKER
LAKES
LAKME
LALAW
LAMAR
LAMAS
LAMBS
LAMED
LAMER
LAMES
LAMIA
LAMPS
LANAI
LANCE
LANDI
LANDO
LANDS
LANES
LANGE
LANKA
LANKY
LANTZ
LANZA
LAPAZ
LAPEL
LAPIN
LAPIS
LAPPS
LAPSE
LAPUP
LARAM
LARAS
LARCH
LARDS
LARDY
LARES
LARGE
LARGO
LARIS
LARKS
LARKY
LARRY
LARUE
LARVA
LASED
LASER
LASES
LASSO
LASTS
LATCH
LATEN
LATER
LATEX
LATHE
LATHS
LATHY
LATIN
LATKE
LATRY
LATTE
LAUDE
LAUDS
LAUER
LAUGH
LAURA
LAVAL
LAVAS
LAVED
LAVER
LAVES
LAVIN
LAWES
LAWNS
LAWNY
LAXER
LAXLY
LAYBY
LAYER
LAYIN
LAYLA
LAYNE
LAYON
LAYTO
LAYUP
LAZAR
LAZED
LAZES

L•A••
LEACH
LEADS
LEADY
LEAFS
LEAFY
LEAHY
LEAKS
LEAKY
LEANS
LEANT
LEAPS
LEAPT
LEARN
LEARS
LEARY
LEASE
LEASH
LEAST
LEAVE
LHASA
LIANA
LIANE
LIANG
LIARD
LIARS
LLAMA
LLANO
LOACH
LOADS
LOAFS
LOAMS
LOAMY
LOANS
LOATH
LSATS
LUAUS

L••A•
LABAN
LAGAN
LAHAR
LALAW
LAMAR
LAMAS
LANAI
LAPAZ
LARAM
LARAS
LAVAL
LAVAS
LAZAR
LEFAY
LEGAL
LEHAR
LEMAT
LEMAY
LETAT
LEVAR
LEXAN
LILAC
LIMAS
LIRAS
LOCAL
LOFAT
LOGAN
LOMAN
LOMAX
LOPAT
LORAN
LORAX
LOTAH
LOTAS
LOYAL
LUBAS
LUCAN
LUCAS
LUKAS
LUNAR
LURAY
LYMAN

L•••A
LAIKA
LAMIA
LANKA
LANZA
LARVA
LAURA
LAYLA
LEEZA
LEHUA
LEICA
LEILA
LEMMA
LENYA
LEONA
LEORA
LEPTA
LHASA
LIANA
LIBRA
LIBYA
LICIA
LINDA
LIVIA
LLAMA
LOGIA
LONGA
LOOFA
LORCA
LORNA
LOTTA
LUCCA
LUCIA
LUISA
LULEA
LURIA
LYCRA
LYDIA
LYNDA
LYTTA

•LA••
ALACK
ALAIN
ALAMO
ALANA
ALAND
ALARM
ALATE
ALAVA

BLABS
BLACK
BLADE
BLAHS
BLAIR
BLAKE
BLAME
BLANC
BLAND
BLANK
BLARE
BLASE
BLASS
BLAST
BLATS
BLAZE
CLACK
CLAIM
CLAIR
CLAMP
CLAMS
CLANG
CLANK
CLANS
CLAPS
CLARA
CLARE
CLARK
CLARO
CLARY
CLASH
CLASP
CLASS
CLAUS
CLAVE
CLAWS
CLAYS
ELAND
ELATE
ELATH
ELAZI
FLACK
FLAGG
FLAGS
FLAIL
FLAIR
FLAKE
FLAKY
FLAME
FLAMS
FLAMY
FLANK
FLANS
FLAPS
FLARE
FLASH
FLASK
FLATS
FLATT
FLAWS
FLAWY
FLAXY
FLAYS
GLACE
GLADE
GLADS
GLAIR
GLAND
GLARE
GLARY
GLASS
GLAXO
GLAZE
KLAUS
LLAMA
LLANO
OLAND
PLACE
PLAGE
PLAID
PLAIN
PLAIT
PLANB
PLANE
PLANI
PLANK
PLANO
PLANS
PLANT
PLASH
PLASM
PLATA
PLATE
PLATH
PLATO
PLATS
PLATT
PLATY
PLAYA
PLAYS
PLAZA
SLABS
SLACK
SLADE
SLAGS
SLAIN
SLAKE
SLAMS
SLANG
SLANT
SLAPS
SLASH
SLATE
SLATS
SLATY
SLAVE
SLAVS
SLAWS
SLAYS

•L•A•

ALBAN
ALCAN
ALDAN
ALFAS
ALGAE
ALGAL
ALIAS
ALLAH
ALLAN
ALLAY
ALMAY
ALTAI
ALTAR
ALVAR
BLEAK
BLEAR
BLEAT
BLOAT
CLEAN
CLEAR
CLEAT
CLOAK
ELGAR
ELIAS
ELMAN
ELWAY
FLEAS
FLOAT
FLYAT
GLEAM
GLEAN
GLIAL
GLOAM
GLOAT
ILIAC
ILIAD
OLEAN
OLLAS
PLEAD
PLEAS
PLEAT
SLOAN
ULNAE
ULNAS

•L••A

ALANA
ALAVA
ALCOA
ALETA
ALIDA
ALOHA
ALPHA
ALULA
CLARA
ELENA
ELIZA
FLORA
ILONA
LLAMA
PLATA
PLAYA
PLAZA
PLENA
PLICA
SLIWA
ULTRA

••LA•

ADLAI
AFLAT
ALLAH
ALLAN
ALLAY
ATLAS
BALAS
BELAY
BFLAT
BOLAS
BYLAW
CFLAT
COLAS
DALAI
DELAY
DFLAT
DRLAO
DYLAN
ECLAT
EFLAT
EILAT
ENLAI
FFLAT
FILAR
FULAS
GALAH
GALAS
GALAX
GFLAT
GOLAN
GULAG
GULAR
HALAS
HULAS
HYLAS
INLAW
INLAY
ISLAM
ISLAS
KOLAS
KULAK
LALAW
LILAC
MALAN
MALAR
MALAY
MELAN
MILAN
MOLAR
MOLAS
MYLAR
NOLAN
OLLAS
ONLAY
PALAE
PALAU
PILAF
PILAR
POLAR
PULAS
RELAX
RELAY
SALAD
SALAL
SALAM
SELAH
SILAS
SOLAN
SOLAR
SPLAT
SPLAY
TILAK
UCLAN
UHLAN
UNLAY
VELAR
VILAS
VOLAR
VOLAT

••L•A

BALSA
BELLA
BELVA
BULBA
BULLA
CALLA
CELIA
CELLA
CILIA
CILLA
CULPA
DELLA
DELTA
DOLMA
FALLA
FELLA
FOLIA
FULDA
GALBA
GALEA
GILDA
GOLDA
HELGA
HILDA
JOLLA
JULIA
LULEA
MALTA
MELBA
MILPA
PALEA
PALMA
PELLA
PILEA
POLKA
SALPA
SALSA
SALTA
SELMA
SELVA
SILVA
SOLFA
SULFA
SULLA
TALIA
TULSA
USLTA
VILLA
VILMA
VOLGA
VOLTA
VOLVA
WALLA
WILLA
WILMA
YALTA
ZELDA

•••LA

ADELA
AKELA
ALULA
ASYLA
AVILA
BELLA
BOOLA
BULLA
CALLA
CARLA
CELLA
CHELA
CHULA
CILLA
DARLA
DELLA
DOBLA
ENOLA
FALLA
FELLA
HABLA
HEKLA
JOLLA
KARLA
KOALA
KUALA
KUKLA
LAYLA
LEILA
MARLA
MOOLA
NDOLA
NYALA
OCALA
OOOLA
PAULA
PELLA
PEPLA
PHYLA
SCALA
SHULA
STELA
STOLA
SULLA
TABLA
TESLA
TRALA
TWYLA
UVULA
UZALA
VILLA
VIOLA
VOILA
WALLA
WILLA

L•B••

LABAN
LABEL
LABIO
LABOR
LIBBY
LIBEL
LIBRA
LIBRE
LIBYA
LOBBY
LOBED
LOBES
LOBOS
LUBAS
LUBED
LUBES

L••B•

LAMBS
LAYBY
LETBE
LIBBY
LIEBY
LIMBI
LIMBO
LIMBS
LOBBY
LOOBY

•LB••

ALBAN
ALBEE
ALBEN
ALBUM
ELBOW

•L•B•

ALIBI
BLABS
BLEBS
BLOBS
CLUBS
FLUBS
FLYBY
GLEBE
GLOBE
GLOBS
PLEBE
PLEBS
SLABS
SLOBS

•L••B

BLURB
CLIMB
PLANB
PLUMB

••LB•

BILBO
BILBY
BULBA
BULBS
COLBY
DOLBY
FTLBS
GALBA
MELBA
WELBY

••L•B

ADLIB
CALEB
CELEB

L•C••

LACED
LACER
LACES
LACEY
LACKS
LACTI
LACTO
LECKY
LICET
LICIA
LICIT
LICKS
LOCAL
LOCHS
LOCKE
LOCKS
LOCOS
LOCUM
LOCUS
LTCOL
LUCAN
LUCAS
LUCCA
LUCCI
LUCIA
LUCID
LUCIE
LUCKS
LUCKY
LUCRE
LYCEE
LYCRA

L••C•

LAICS
LANCE
LARCH
LATCH
LEACH
LEECH
LEICA
LOACH
LORCA
LUCCA
LUCCI
LUNCH
LURCH
LYNCH

L•••C

LILAC
LOGIC
LUDIC
LYRIC

•LC••

ALCAN
ALCOA
ALCOR
ELCID
ULCER

•L•C•

ALACK
ALECK
ALICE
ALYCE
BLACK
BLOCH
BLOCK
BLOCS
CLACK
CLICK
CLOCK
CLUCK
ELECT
FLACK
FLECK
FLICK
FLICS
FLOCK
GLACE
GLICK
GLUCK
GLUCO
GLYCO
ILICH
PLACE
PLICA
PLUCK
SLACK
SLICE
SLICK

•L••C

BLANC
ILIAC
OLEIC
OLMEC

••LC•

BALCH
BELCH
CALCI
CULCH
DELCO
DOLCE
FILCH
GULCH
HULCE
MILCH
MULCH
MULCT
SULCI
WELCH
WILCO
ZILCH

••L•C

ADLOC
FOLIC
FSLIC
HELIC
LILAC
MALIC
MELIC
RELIC
SALIC
TELIC

L•D••

LADED
LADEN
LADER
LADES
LADLE
LADON
LADYS
LEDGE
LEDGY
LEDIN
LEDON
LEDTO
LIDDY
LIDOS
LODEN
LODES
LODGE
LUDIC
LYDIA

L••D•

LANDI
LANDO
LANDS
LARDS
LARDY
LAUDE
LAUDS
LEADS
LEADY
LEEDS
LENDL
LENDS
LIDDY
LINDA
LINDO
LINDY
LOADS
LORDS
LUNDI
LUNDY
LYNDA
LYNDE

L•••D

LACED
LADED
LAIRD
LAMED
LASED
LAVED
LAZED
LIARD
LIKED
LIKUD
LIMED
LINED
LIPID
LIVED
LIVID
LLOYD
LOBED
LOPED
LOVED
LOWED
LUBED
LUCID
LURED
LURID

•LD••

ALDAN
ALDEN
ALDER
ALDOL
ALDUS
BLDGS
ELDER
OLDEN
OLDER
OLDIE

•L•D•

ALIDA
BLADE
BLVDS
CLODS
CLYDE
ELIDE
ELUDE
GLADE
GLADS
GLEDE
GLIDE
PLODS
SLADE
SLEDS
SLIDE

•L••D
ALAND
ALGID
ALKYD
ALOUD
BLAND
BLEED
BLEND
BLIND
BLOND
BLOOD
BLUED
CLOUD
CLUED
CLWYD
ELAND
ELCID
FLIED
FLOOD
FLOYD
FLUID
GLAND
GLUED
ILIAD
LLOYD
OLAND
PLAID
PLEAD
PLIED
SLOYD
SLUED

••LD•
BALDS
COLDS
FALDO
FOLDS
FULDA
GILDA
GILDS
GOLDA
GOLDE
GOLDS
HILDA
HOLDS
MELDS
MOLDS
MOLDY
NALDI
SOLDI
SOLDO
TILDE
VELDS
VELDT
WALDO
WELDS
WILDE
WILDS
WOLDS
ZELDA

••L•D
AILED
BALED
DELED
DOLED
EELED
FELID
FILED
GELID
HALED
HOLED
IDLED
OGLED
OILED
PALED
PILED
POLED
PULED
RILED
RULED
SALAD
SALUD
SOLED
SOLID
TILED
UNLED
VALID
WALED
WILED

•••LD
BUILD
CHILD
COULD
FIELD
FJELD
GOULD
GUILD
MOULD
ROALD
SCALD
SCOLD
SKALD
SZOLD
WIELD
WORLD
WOULD
YIELD

LE•••
LEACH
LEADS
LEADY
LEAFS
LEAFY
LEAHY
LEAKS
LEAKY
LEANS
LEANT
LEAPS
LEAPT
LEARN
LEARS
LEARY
LEASE
LEASH
LEAST
LEAVE
LECKY
LEDGE
LEDGY
LEDIN
LEDON
LEDTO
LEECH
LEEDS
LEEKS
LEERS
LEERY
LEETS
LEEZA
LEFAY
LEFTS
LEFTY
LEGAL
LEGER
LEGGS
LEGGY
LEGIS
LEGIT
LEGOS
LEGUP
LEHAR
LEHUA
LEICA
LEIGH
LEILA
LEITH
LEMAT
LEMAY
LEMMA
LEMME
LEMON
LEMUR
LENDL
LENDS
LENIN
LENIS
LENNY
LENOS
LENOX
LENTO
LENTS
LENYA
LEONA
LEONE
LEONI
LEORA
LEPPY
LEPTA
LEPTO
LEPUS
LEROI
LEROY
LETAT
LETBE
LETGO
LETHE
LETIN
LETON
LETTS
LETUP
LEVAR
LEVEE
LEVEL
LEVER
LEVIN
LEVIS
LEVON
LEWES
LEWIS
LEXAN
LEXIS
LEXUS
LEYTE

L•E••
LEECH
LEEDS
LEEKS
LEERS
LEERY
LEETS
LEEZA
LIEBY
LIEGE
LIEIN
LIENS
LIETO
LIEUS
LIEUT
LOESS
LOEWE
LOEWY
LUEGO
LYELL

L••E•
LABEL
LACED
LACER
LACES
LACEY
LADED
LADEN
LADER
LADES
LAGER
LAKER
LAKES
LAMED
LAMER
LAMES
LANES
LAPEL
LARES
LASED
LASER
LASES
LATEN
LATER
LATEX
LAUER
LAVED
LAVER
LAVES
LAWES
LAXER
LAYER
LAZED
LAZES
LEGER
LEVEE
LEVEL
LEVER
LEWES
LIBEL
LICET
LIGER
LIKED
LIKEN
LIKES
LIMED
LIMEN
LIMES
LIMEY
LINED
LINEN
LINER
LINES
LINEY
LITER
LITES
LIVED
LIVEN
LIVER
LIVES
LOBED
LOBES
LODEN
LODES
LOGES
LONER
LOPED
LOPER
LOPES
LOPEZ
LOREN
LORES
LOSER
LOSES
LOVED
LOVER
LOVES
LOVEY
LOWED
LOWER
LOWES
LOXES
LTGEN
LUBED
LUBES
LUGER
LUGES
LULEA
LUMEN
LUMET
LUNES
LURED
LURES
LUREX
LUTES
LYCEE
LYRES

L•••E
LADLE
LAINE
LAKME
LANCE
LANGE
LAPSE
LARGE
LARUE
LATHE
LATKE
LATTE
LAUDE
LAYNE
LEASE
LEAVE
LEDGE
LEMME
LEONE
LETBE
LETHE
LEVEE
LEYTE
LIANE
LIBRE
LIEGE
LILLE
LISLE
LISSE
LITHE
LITRE
LIVRE
LOCKE
LODGE
LOEWE
LOGUE
LOIRE
LONGE
LOOSE
LORNE
LORRE
LOTTE
LOUIE
LOUPE
LOUSE
LUCIE
LUCRE
LUISE
LUNGE
LURIE
LYCEE
LYNDE
LYNNE

•LE••
ALECK
ALEFS
ALENE
ALEPH
ALERT
ALETA
ALEUT
ALEVE
BLEAK
BLEAR
BLEAT
BLEBS
BLEED
BLEEP
BLEND
BLENT
BLESS
BLEST
CLEAN
CLEAR
CLEAT
CLEEK
CLEFS
CLEFT
CLEON
CLERK
CLEWS
ELECT
ELEGY
ELEMI
ELENA
ELENI
ELEVE
FLEAS
FLECK
FLEER
FLEES
FLEET
FLESH
FLEUR
FLEWS
FLEXI
FLEYS
GLEAM
GLEAN
GLEBE
GLEDE
GLEES
GLENN
GLENS
GLESS
GLEYS
ILENE
KLEIN
NLERS
OLEAN
OLEIC
OLEIN
OLEOS
OLEUM
PLEAD
PLEAS
PLEAT
PLEBE
PLEBS
PLEIO
PLENA
PLEON
PLEWS
SLEDS
SLEEK
SLEEP
SLEET
SLEPT
SLEWS

•L•E•
ALBEE
ALBEN
ALDEN
ALDER
ALGER
ALIEN
ALLEE
ALLEN
ALLER
ALLES
ALLEY
ALLEZ
ALOES
ALTER
BLEED
BLEEP
BLUED
BLUER
BLUES
BLUET
BLUEY
CLEEK
CLUED
CLUES
ELDER
ELIEL
ELLEN
ELLER
ELLES
ELMER
ELVER
ELVES
ELWES
FLEER
FLEES
FLEET
FLIED
FLIER
FLIES
FLOES
FLUES
FLYER
GLEES
GLUED
GLUER
GLUES
GLUEY
ILLER
KLIEG
MLLES
OLDEN
OLDER
OLMEC
OLSEN
PLIED
PLIES
SLEEK
SLEEP
SLEET
SLIER
SLOES
SLUED
SLUES
SLYER
ULCER

•L••E
ALATE
ALBEE
ALENE
ALEVE
ALFIE
ALFRE
ALGAE
ALICE
ALIKE
ALINE
ALIVE
ALLEE
ALLIE
ALONE
ALYCE
BLADE
BLAKE
BLAME
BLARE
BLASE
BLAZE
BLIGE
BLOKE
BLUME
CLARE
CLAVE
CLIME
CLINE
CLIVE
CLONE
CLOSE
CLOVE
CLYDE
ELATE
ELEVE
ELIDE
ELISE
ELITE
ELLIE
ELOPE
ELSIE
ELUDE
ELUTE
ELYSE
FLAKE
FLAME
FLARE
FLUKE
FLUME
FLUTE
GLACE
GLADE
GLARE
GLAZE
GLEBE
GLEDE
GLIDE
GLOBE
GLOVE
GLOZE
ILENE
KLINE
KLUGE
KLUTE
OLDIE
OLIVE
OLLIE
PLACE
PLAGE
PLANE
PLATE
PLEBE
PLUME
SLADE
SLAKE
SLATE
SLAVE
SLICE
SLIDE
SLIME
SLOPE
SLYPE
ULNAE

••LE•
ABLER
ADLER
AGLET
AGLEY
AILED
AILER
AILEY
ALLEE
ALLEN
ALLER
ALLES
ALLEY
ALLEZ
APLEY
ARLEN
ARLES
AXLES
BALED
BALER
BALES
BELEM
BOLES
CALEB
CCLEF
CELEB
COLES
COLET
CULET
CULEX
DALES
DALEY
DELED
DELES
DOLED
DOLES
EELED
EELER
ELLEN
ELLER
ELLES
EULER
FCLEF
FILED
FILER
FILES
FILET
FOLEY
GALEA
GALEN
GALES
GCLEF
GELEE
GILES
GOLEM
GULES
HALED
HALER
HALES
HALEY
HELEN
HOLED
HOLES
HOLEY
IDLED
IDLER
IDLES
ILLER
INLET
ISLES
ISLET
ISLEY
JULEP
JULES
KALEL
KALES
KILEY
LULEA
MALES
MELEE
MILER
MILES
MLLES

MOLES
MULES
MULEY
MYLES
NFLER
NHLER
NILES
OGLED
OGLER
OGLES
OILED
OILER
ORLES
OSLER
OWLET
PALEA
PALED
PALEO
PALER
PALES
PALEY
PELEE
PELEG
PILEA
PILED
PILEI
PILES
POLED
POLER
POLES
PULED
PULES
RELEE
RELET
RILED
RILES
RILEY
ROLEO
ROLES
ROLEX
RULED
RULER
RULES
SALEM
SALEP
SALES
SELES
SILEX
SOLED
SOLER
SOLES
TALER
TALES
TELEO
TELES
TELEX
TILED
TILER
TILES
TOLER
TOLET
TULES
TYLER
UNLED
UTLEY
VALES
VALET
VELEZ
VILER
VOLES
WALED
WALER
WALES
WALEY
WILED
WILES
WILEY
WYLER
XYLEM

••L•E
ALLEE
ALLIE
BELIE
BELLE
BILGE
BULGE
CALPE
CALVE
CELIE
CHLOE
DELVE
DOLCE
DULSE
ELLIE
FALSE
FILLE
GELEE
GOLDE
HALLE
HALVE
HELVE
HULCE
JOLIE
JULIE
LILLE
MALLE
MELEE
MILLE
MILNE
NOLLE
NOLTE
OLLIE
PALAE
PALME
PELEE
PELLE
PULSE
RELEE
RILKE
RILLE
ROLFE
ROLLE
SALLE
SALVE
SOLVE
TILDE
TULLE
VALLE
VALSE
VALUE
VALVE
VILLE
VOLTE
WILDE
WOLFE
WYLIE
YALIE

•••LE
ABELE
ADDLE
ADELE
AGILE
AISLE
AMBLE
AMOLE
AMPLE
ANELE
ANGLE
ANKLE
ANOLE
APPLE
BAYLE
BELLE
BERLE
BEYLE
BIBLE
BOGLE
BOOLE
BOULE
BOYLE
BRULE
BUGLE
CABLE
CARLE
CHILE
CYCLE
DHOLE
DOBLE
DOYLE
DUPLE
EAGLE
EARLE
ECOLE
EDILE
EMILE
EXILE
FABLE
FILLE
FOYLE
GABLE
GAYLE
GUILE
HAILE
HALLE
HAOLE
HOYLE
INGLE
INKLE
ISTLE
JOULE
LADLE
LILLE
LISLE
MACLE
MAILE
MALLE
MAPLE
MERLE
MILLE
NEALE
NOBLE
NOLLE
ODILE
ONCLE
ORALE
OVULE
PARLE
PEALE
PEELE
PELLE
PERLE
PHILE
PHYLE
POOLE
PROLE
QUALE
RIFLE
RILLE
ROBLE
ROLLE
RUBLE
SABLE
SALLE
SCALE
SEALE
SEULE
SHALE
SIDLE
SMILE
SOCLE
SPILE
STALE
STELE
STILE
STOLE
STYLE
SWALE
TABLE
THOLE
THULE
TITLE
TOILE
TULLE
UNCLE
UTILE
VALLE
VILLE
VOILE
WHALE
WHILE
WHOLE

L•F••
LEFAY
LEFTS
LEFTY
LIFTS
LOFAT
LOFTS
LOFTY
LUFFS

L••F•
LEAFS
LEAFY
LOAFS
LOOFA
LUFFS

•LF••
ALFAS
ALFIE
ALFRE
ELFIN

•L•F•
ALEFS
ALIFS
ALOFT
BLUFF
CLEFS
CLEFT
CLIFF
CLIFT
FLUFF

•L••F
ALOOF
BLUFF
CLIFF
FLUFF

••LF•
DELFT
GOLFS
GULFS
ROLFE
SOLFA
SULFA
WOLFE
WOLFF

••L•F
CALIF
CCLEF
FCLEF
GCLEF
PILAF
WOLFF

•••LF
ADOLF
SHELF
WOOLF

L•G••
LAGAN
LAGER
LAGOS
LEGAL
LEGER
LEGGS
LEGGY
LEGIS
LEGIT
LEGOS
LEGUP
LIGER
LIGHT
LIGNI
LIGNO
LOGAN
LOGES
LOGIA
LOGIC
LOGIN
LOGON
LOGOS
LOGUE
LTGEN
LTGOV
LUGER
LUGES

L••G•
LANGE
LARGE
LARGO
LAUGH
LEDGE
LEDGY
LEGGS
LEGGY
LEIGH
LETGO
LIEGE
LINGO
LODGE
LONGA
LONGE
LONGI
LONGO
LONGS
LONGU
LOUGH
LUEGO
LUIGI
LUNGE
LUNGS

L•••G
LAING
LIANG
LYING

•LG••
ALGAE
ALGAL
ALGER
ALGID
ALGIN
ALGOL
ELGAR
ELGIN
ILGWU

•L•G•
ALIGN
BLDGS
BLIGE
BLIGH
CLOGS
ELEGY
FLAGG
FLAGS
FLOGS
GLOGG
GLUGS
KLUGE
OLIGO
OLOGY
PLAGE
PLUGS
SLAGS
SLIGO
SLOGS
SLUGS

•L••G
ALONG
CLANG
CLING
CLUNG
FLAGG
FLING
FLUNG
GLOGG
KLIEG
SLANG
SLING
SLUNG

••LG•
BILGE
BILGY
BULGE
BULGY
GOLGI
HELGA
VOLGA

••L•G
GULAG
PELEG
RELIG
SELIG
ZELIG

LH•••
LHASA

L•H••
LAHAR
LAHTI
LEHAR
LEHUA

L••H•
LATHE
LATHS
LATHY
LEAHY
LETHE
LIGHT
LITHE
LITHO
LITHS
LOCHS

L•••H
LARCH
LATCH
LAUGH
LEACH
LEASH
LEECH
LEIGH
LEITH
LOACH
LOATH
LOTAH
LOUGH
LUNCH
LURCH
LYMPH
LYNCH

•L•H•
ALOHA
ALPHA
ALTHO
BLAHS
ELIHU

•L••H
ALEPH
ALLAH
BLIGH
BLOCH
BLUSH
BLUTH
BLYTH
CLASH
CLOTH
ELATH
FLASH
FLESH
FLUSH
GLYPH
ILICH
PLASH
PLATH
PLUSH
SLASH
SLOSH
SLOTH
SLUSH

••LH•
DELHI

••L•H
ALLAH
BALCH
BALKH
BELCH
CULCH
DOLPH
FILCH
FILTH
GALAH
GULCH
MILCH
MULCH
RALPH
SELAH
SYLPH
TILTH
WALSH
WELCH
WELSH
ZILCH

LI•••
LIANA
LIANE
LIANG
LIARD
LIARS
LIBBY
LIBEL
LIBRA
LIBRE
LIBYA
LICET
LICIA
LICIT
LICKS
LIDDY
LIDOS
LIEBY
LIEGE
LIEIN
LIENS
LIETO
LIEUS
LIEUT
LIFTS
LIGER
LIGHT
LIGNI
LIGNO
LIKED
LIKEN
LIKES
LIKUD
LILAC
LILLE
LILLY
LILTS
LIMAS
LIMBI
LIMBO
LIMBS
LIMED
LIMEN
LIMES
LIMEY
LIMIT
LIMNS
LIMON
LIMOS
LIMPS
LINDA
LINDO
LINDY
LINED
LINEN
LINER
LINES
LINEY
LINGO
LINKS
LINOS
LINTS
LINTY
LINUS
LIONS
LIPID
LIPPI
LIPPO
LIPPY
LIRAS
LISLE
LISPS
LISSE
LISTS
LISZT
LITER
LITES
LITHE
LITHO
LITHS
LITON
LITRE
LITUP
LIVED
LIVEN
LIVER
LIVES
LIVIA
LIVID
LIVRE

L•I••
LAICS
LAIKA
LAINE
LAING
LAIRD
LAIRS
LAITY
LAIUS
LEICA
LEIGH
LEILA
LEITH
LOINS
LOIRE
LUIGI
LUISA
LUISE
LVIII
LXIII
LYING

L••I•
LABIO
LAMIA
LAPIN
LAPIS
LARIS
LATIN
LAVIN
LAYIN
LEDIN
LEGIS
LEGIT
LENIN
LENIS
LETIN
LEVIN
LEVIS
LEWIS
LEXIS
LICIA
LICIT
LIEIN
LIMIT
LIPID
LIVIA
LIVID
LOGIA
LOGIC
LOGIN
LORIS
LOUIE
LOUIS
LUCIA
LUCID
LUCIE
LUDIC
LUNIK
LUPIN
LURIA
LURID
LURIE
LVIII
LXIII
LXVII

LXXII
LXXIV
LXXIX
LYDIA
LYRIC
LYSIN

L•••I
LACTI
LAHTI
LANAI
LANDI
LEONI
LEROI
LIGNI
LIMBI
LIPPI
LONGI
LUCCI
LUIGI
LUNDI
LVIII
LXIII
LXVII
LXXII
LXXVI
LXXXI

•LI••
ALIAS
ALIBI
ALICE
ALIDA
ALIEN
ALIFS
ALIGN
ALIKE
ALINE
ALIOS
ALIST
ALIVE
BLIGE
BLIGH
BLIMP
BLIND
BLINI
BLINK
BLIPS
BLISS
BLITT
BLITZ
CLICK
CLIFF
CLIFT
CLIII
CLIMB
CLIME
CLINE
CLING
CLINK
CLINT
CLIOS
CLIPS
CLIPT
CLIVE
DLIII
ELIAS
ELIDE
ELIEL
ELIHU
ELION
ELIOT
ELISE
ELITE
ELIZA
FLICK
FLICS
FLIED
FLIER
FLIES
FLING
FLINT
FLIPS
FLIRT
FLITS
GLIAL
GLICK
GLIDE
GLIMS
GLINT
GLITZ
ILIAC
ILIAD
ILICH
ILION
ILIUM
KLIEG
KLIMT
KLINE
MLIII
OLIGO
OLIOS
OLIVE
PLICA
PLIED
PLIES
PLINK
PLINY
SLICE
SLICK
SLIDE
SLIER
SLIGO
SLILY
SLIME
SLIMS
SLIMY
SLING
SLINK
SLIPS
SLIPT
SLITS
SLIWA
XLIII

•L•I•
ALAIN
ALFIE
ALGID
ALGIN
ALLIE
ALLIN
ALVIN
BLAIR
BLOIS
CLAIM
CLAIR
CLIII
CLVII
CLXII
CLXIV
CLXIX
DLIII
DLVII
DLXII
DLXIV
DLXIX
ELCID
ELFIN
ELGIN
ELLIE
ELLIS
ELSIE
ELVIN
ELVIS
FLAIL
FLAIR
FLUID
FLYIN
GLAIR
ILLIN
KLEIN
MLIII
MLVII
MLXII
MLXIV
MLXIX
OLDIE
OLEIC
OLEIN
OLLIE
PLAID
PLAIN
PLAIT
PLEIO
SLAIN
XLIII
XLVII

•L••I
ALIBI
ALTAI
BLINI
CLIII
CLVII
CLXII
CLXVI
CLXXI
DLIII
DLVII
DLXII
DLXVI
DLXXI
ELAZI
ELEMI
ELENI
FLEXI
MLIII
MLVII
MLXII
MLXVI
MLXXI
PLANI
XLIII
XLVII

••LI•
AALII
ADLIB
ALLIE
ALLIN
AULIS
BALIN
BELIE
CALIF
CALIX
CCLII
CCLIV
CCLIX
CDLII
CDLIV
CDLIX
CELIA
CELIE
CILIA
CMLII
CMLIV
CMLIX
COLIN
CXLII
CXLIV
CXLIX
DCLII
DCLIV
DCLIX
DELIS
DXLII
DXLIV
DXLIX
ELLIE
ELLIS
FELID
FELIS
FELIX
FELIZ
FOLIA
FOLIC
FOLIO
FSLIC
GELID
HELIC
HELIO
HELIX
ILLIN
ISLIP
JOLIE
JULIA
JULIE
JULIO
KILIM
KYLIX
MALIC
MCLII
MCLIV
MCLIX
MDLII
MDLIV
MDLIX
MELIC
MMLII
MMLIV
MMLIX
MXLII
MXLIV
MXLIX
OLLIE
OSLIN
OXLIP
PALIN
POLIS
POLIT
PULIS
RELIC
RELIG
RELIT
SALIC
SELIG
SOLID
SPLIT
TALIA
TELIC
TULIP
UNLIT
VALID
WYLIE
YALIE
ZELIG

••L•I
AALII
ADLAI
BELLI
CALCI
CALLI
CCLII
CCLVI
CCLXI
CDLII
CDLVI
CDLXI
CELLI
CMLII
CMLVI
CMLXI
CXLII
CXLVI
DALAI
DCLII
DCLVI
DCLXI
DELHI
DXLII
DXLVI
ENLAI
GALLI
GOLGI
MCLII
MCLVI
MCLXI
MDLII
MDLVI
MDLXI
MILLI
MMLII
MMLVI
MMLXI
MULTI
MXLII
MXLVI
NALDI
PALPI
PILEI
SALMI
SOLDI
SOLTI
SULCI
VALLI
VILLI

•••LI
AIOLI
BELLI
CALLI
CCCLI
CCXLI
CDXLI
CELLI
CHILI
CMXLI
DCCLI
DCXLI
EBOLI
ECOLI
FORLI
GALLI
GHALI
MCCLI
MCDLI
MCMLI
MCXLI
MDCLI
MDXLI
MILLI
MMCLI
MMDLI
MMMLI
MMXLI
OBELI
OBOLI
OVOLI
PAOLI
STYLI
VALLI
VILLI

L•K••
LAKER
LAKES
LAKME
LIKED
LIKEN
LIKES
LIKUD
LUKAS

L••K•
LACKS
LAIKA
LANKA
LANKY
LARKS
LARKY
LATKE
LEAKS
LEAKY
LECKY
LEEKS
LICKS
LINKS
LOCKE
LOCKS
LOOKS
LUCKS
LUCKY
LURKS

L•••K
LUNIK

•LK••
ALKYD
ALKYL

•L•K•
ALIKE
BLAKE
BLOKE
FLAKE
FLAKY
FLUKE
FLUKY
SLAKE

•L••K
ALACK
ALECK
BLACK
BLANK
BLEAK
BLINK
BLOCK
CLACK
CLANK
CLARK
CLEEK
CLERK
CLICK
CLINK
CLOAK
CLOCK
CLONK
CLUCK
CLUNK
FLACK
FLANK
FLASK
FLECK
FLICK
FLOCK
FLUNK
GLICK
GLUCK
PLANK
PLINK
PLONK
PLUCK
PLUNK
SLACK
SLEEK
SLICK
SLINK
SLUNK

••LK•
BALKH
BALKS
BALKY
BILKO
BILKS
BULKS
BULKY
CALKS
FOLKS
FOLKY
HULKS
MILKS
MILKY
POLKA
RILKE
SILKS
SILKY
SULKS
SULKY
TALKS
TALKY
WALKS
YOLKS
YOLKY

••L•K
KULAK
TILAK

•••LK
BAULK
CAULK
CHALK
SKULK
STALK
WHELK

LL•••
LLAMA
LLANO
LLOYD

L•L••
LALAW
LILAC
LILLE
LILLY
LILTS
LOLLS
LOLLY
LULEA
LULLS
LULLY
LULUS

L••L•
LADLE
LAXLY
LAYLA
LEILA
LILLE
LILLY
LISLE
LOLLS
LOLLY
LOWLY
LULLS
LULLY
LYELL

L•••L
LABEL
LAPEL
LAVAL
LEGAL
LENDL
LEVEL
LIBEL
LOCAL
LOYAL
LTCOL
LYELL
LYSOL

•LL••
ALLAH
ALLAN
ALLAY
ALLEE
ALLEN
ALLER
ALLES
ALLEY
ALLEZ
ALLIE
ALLIN
ALLOT
ALLOW
ALLOY
ALLYL
ELLEN
ELLER
ELLES
ELLIE
ELLIS
ILLER
ILLIN
ILLUS
MLLES
OLLAS
OLLIE

•L•L•
ALULA
SLILY
SLYLY

•L••L
ALDOL
ALGAL
ALGOL
ALKYL
ALLYL
ELIEL
FLAIL
GLIAL

••LL•
BALLS
BALLY
BELLA
BELLE
BELLI
BELLS
BELLY
BILLS
BILLY
BOLLS
BULLA
BULLS
BULLY
CALLA
CALLI
CALLS
CELLA
CELLI
CELLO
CELLS
CILLA
CULLS
CULLY
DALLY
DELLA
DELLS
DILLS
DILLY
DOLLS
DOLLY
DULLS
DULLY
FALLA
FALLS
FELLA
FELLS
FELLY
FILLE
FILLS
FILLY
FOLLY
FULLY
GALLI
GALLO
GALLS
GILLS
GILLY
GOLLY
GULLS
GULLY
HALLE
HALLO
HALLS
HELLO
HELLS
HILLS
HILLY
HOLLY
HULLO
HULLS
JELLO
JELLS
JELLY
JOLLA
JOLLY
KELLY
KILLS
KILLY
LILLE
LILLY
LOLLS
LOLLY
LULLS
LULLY
MALLE
MALLS
MILLE
MILLI
MILLS
MOLLS
MOLLY
MULLS
NELLY
NILLY
NOLLE
NULLS
PALLS
PALLY
PELLA
PELLE

PILLS
POLLO
POLLS
POLLY
PULLS
RALLY
RILLE
RILLS
ROLLE
ROLLO
ROLLS
SALLE
SALLY
SELLS
SILLS
SILLY
SULLA
SULLY
TALLY
TELLS
TELLY
TILLS
TILLY
TOLLS
TOLLY
TULLE
TULLY
VALLE
VALLI
VILLA
VILLE
VILLI
WALLA
WALLS
WALLY
WELLS
WILLA
WILLS
WILLY
YELLS
ZILLS

••L•L
ALLYL
KALEL
SALAL

•••LL
ATALL
ATOLL
BBALL
BCELL
BEALL
BRILL
BUELL
CHILL
DRILL
DROLL
DWELL
EWELL
FRILL
GRILL
IDYLL
INALL
KNELL
KNOLL
KRILL
KRULL
KVELL
LYELL
NEILL
ODELL
PHYLL
PRELL
QUELL
QUILL
SCULL
SHALL
SHELL
SHILL
SKILL
SKULL
SMALL
SMELL
SNELL
SPALL
SPELL
SPILL
STALL
STILL
STULL
SWELL
SWILL
SZELL
TBALL
TBILL
THILL
TRILL
TROLL
TWILL
UDALL
WEILL
WHOLL
WHYLL
YOULL

L•M••
LAMAR
LAMAS
LAMBS
LAMED
LAMER
LAMES
LAMIA
LAMPS
LEMAT
LEMAY
LEMMA
LEMME
LEMON
LEMUR
LIMAS
LIMBI
LIMBO
LIMBS
LIMED
LIMEN
LIMES
LIMEY
LIMIT
LIMNS
LIMON
LIMOS
LIMPS
LOMAN
LOMAX
LUMEN
LUMET
LUMPS
LUMPY
LYMAN
LYMON
LYMPH

L••M•
LAKME
LEMMA
LEMME
LLAMA
LOAMS
LOAMY
LOOMS

L•••M
LARAM
LOCUM

•LM••
ALMAY
ELMAN
ELMER
ELMOS
OLMEC
OLMOS

•L•M•
ALAMO
ALUMS
BLAME
BLIMP
BLUME
CLAMP
CLAMS
CLIMB
CLIME
CLOMP
CLUMP
ELEMI
FLAME
FLAMS
FLAMY
FLUME
GLIMS
GLOMS
KLIMT
LLAMA
PLUMB
PLUME
PLUMP
PLUMS
PLUMY
SLAMS
SLIME
SLIMS
SLIMY
SLOMO
SLUMP
SLUMS

•L••M
ALARM
ALBUM
BLOOM
CLAIM
GLEAM
GLOAM
GLOOM
ILIUM
OLEUM
PLASM

••LM•
BALMS
BALMY
CALMS
CULMS
DOLMA
FILMS
FILMY
HALMS
HELMS
HOLMS
MALMO
PALMA
PALME
PALMS
PALMY
SALMI
SELMA
VILMA
WILMA

••L•M
BELEM
COLUM
FILUM
GOLEM
HILUM
ISLAM
KILIM
PILUM
SALAM
SALEM
SOLUM
VELUM
XYLEM

•••LM
HAULM
PSALM
QUALM
REALM
WHELM

L•N••
LANAI
LANCE
LANDI
LANDO
LANDS
LANES
LANGE
LANKA
LANKY
LANTZ
LANZA
LENDL
LENDS
LENIN
LENIS
LENNY
LENOS
LENOX
LENTO
LENTS
LENYA
LINDA
LINDO
LINDY
LINED
LINEN
LINER
LINES
LINEY
LINGO
LINKS
LINOS
LINTS
LINTY
LINUS
LONER
LONGA
LONGE
LONGI
LONGO
LONGS
LONGU
LUNAR
LUNCH
LUNDI
LUNDY
LUNES
LUNGE
LUNGS
LUNIK
LYNCH
LYNDA
LYNDE
LYNNE

L••N•
LAINE
LAING
LAWNS
LAWNY
LAYNE
LEANS
LEANT
LENNY
LEONA
LEONE
LEONI
LIANA
LIANE
LIANG
LIENS
LIGNI
LIGNO
LIMNS
LIONS
LLANO
LOANS
LOINS
LOONS
LOONY
LORNA
LORNE
LYING
LYNNE
LYONS

L•••N
LABAN
LADEN
LADON
LAGAN
LAPIN
LATEN
LATIN
LAVIN
LAYIN
LAYON
LEARN
LEDIN
LEDON
LEMON
LENIN
LETIN
LETON
LEVIN
LEVON
LEXAN
LIEIN
LIKEN
LIMEN
LIMON
LINEN
LITON
LIVEN
LODEN
LOGAN
LOGIN
LOGON
LOMAN
LORAN
LOREN
LTGEN
LUCAN
LUMEN
LUPIN
LUZON
LYMAN
LYMON
LYSIN

•LN••
ULNAE
ULNAS

•L•N•
ALANA
ALAND
ALENE
ALINE
ALONE
ALONG
BLANC
BLAND
BLANK
BLEND
BLENT
BLIND
BLINI
BLINK
BLOND
BLUNT
CLANG
CLANK
CLANS
CLINE
CLING
CLINK
CLINT
CLONE
CLONK
CLUNG
CLUNK
CLUNY
ELAND
ELENA
ELENI
FLANK
FLANS
FLING
FLINT
FLUNG
FLUNK
FLYNN
GLAND
GLENN
GLENS
GLINT
ILENE
ILONA
KLINE
LLANO
OLAND
PLANB
PLANE
PLANI
PLANK
PLANO
PLANS
PLANT
PLENA
PLINK
PLINY
PLONK
PLUNK
SLANG
SLANT
SLING
SLINK
SLUNG
SLUNK

•L••N
ALAIN
ALBAN
ALBEN
ALCAN
ALDAN
ALDEN
ALGIN
ALIEN
ALIGN
ALLAN
ALLEN
ALLIN
ALTON
ALVIN
BLOWN
CLEAN
CLEON
CLOWN
ELFIN
ELGIN
ELION
ELLEN
ELMAN
ELTON
ELVIN
FLOWN
FLYIN
FLYNN
GLEAN
GLENN
GLUON
ILION
ILLIN
KLEIN
OLDEN
OLEAN
OLEIN
OLSEN
OLSON
PLAIN
PLEON
SLAIN
SLOAN

••LN•
KILNS
MILNE

••L•N
ALLAN
ALLEN
ALLIN
ARLEN
BALIN
COLIN
COLON
DELON
DYLAN
ELLEN
EMLYN
FELON
GALEN
GOLAN
HALON
HELEN
ILLIN
MALAN
MELAN
MELON
MILAN
NOLAN
NYLON
ORLON
OSLIN
PALIN
PYLON
SALON
SOLAN
SOLON
TALON
UCLAN
UHLAN

LO•••
LOACH
LOADS
LOAFS
LOAMS
LOAMY
LOANS
LOATH
LOBBY
LOBED
LOBES
LOBOS
LOCAL
LOCHS
LOCKE
LOCKS
LOCOS
LOCUM
LOCUS
LODEN
LODES
LODGE
LOESS
LOEWE
LOEWY
LOFAT
LOFTS
LOFTY
LOGAN
LOGES
LOGIA
LOGIC
LOGIN
LOGON
LOGOS
LOGUE
LOINS
LOIRE
LOLLS
LOLLY
LOMAN
LOMAX
LONER
LONGA
LONGE
LONGI
LONGO
LONGS
LONGU
LOOBY
LOOFA
LOOKS
LOOMS
LOONS
LOONY
LOOPS
LOOPY
LOOSE
LOOTS
LOPAT
LOPED
LOPER
LOPES
LOPEZ
LOPPY
LORAN
LORAX
LORCA
LORDS
LOREN
LORES
LORIS
LORNA
LORNE
LORRE
LORRY
LOSER
LOSES
LOSSY
LOTAH
LOTAS
LOTTA
LOTTE
LOTTO
LOTUS
LOUGH
LOUIE
LOUIS
LOUPE
LOUSE
LOUSY
LOUTS
LOVED
LOVER
LOVES
LOVEY
LOWED
LOWER
LOWES
LOWLY
LOWRY
LOXES
LOYAL

L•O••
LEONA
LEONE
LEONI
LEORA
LIONS
LLOYD
LOOBY
LOOFA
LOOKS
LOOMS
LOONS
LOONY
LOOPS
LOOPY
LOOSE
LOOTS
LYONS

L••O•
LABOR
LADON
LAGOS
LAYON
LEDON
LEGOS
LEMON
LENOS
LENOX
LEROI
LEROY
LETON
LEVON
LIDOS
LIMON
LIMOS
LINOS
LITON
LOBOS
LOCOS
LOGON
LOGOS
LTCOL
LTGOV
LUXOR
LUZON
LYMON
LYSOL

L•••O
LABIO
LACTO
LANDO
LARGO
LASSO
LAYTO
LEDTO
LENTO
LEPTO
LETGO
LIETO
LIGNO
LIMBO
LINDO
LINGO
LIPPO
LITHO
LLANO
LONGO
LOTTO
LUEGO

•LO••
ALOES
ALOFT
ALOHA
ALONE
ALONG
ALOOF
ALORS
ALOUD
BLOAT
BLOBS
BLOCH
BLOCK
BLOCS
BLOIS
BLOKE
BLOND
BLOOD
BLOOM
BLOOP
BLOTS
BLOWN
BLOWS
BLOWY
CLOAK
CLOCK
CLODS
CLOGS
CLOMP
CLONE
CLONK
CLOPS
CLOSE
CLOTH
CLOTS
CLOUD
CLOUT
CLOVE
CLOWN
CLOYS
ELOPE
FLOAT
FLOCK
FLOES
FLOGS
FLOOD
FLOOR
FLOPS
FLORA
FLORY
FLOSS
FLOUR
FLOUT
FLOWN
FLOWS
FLOYD
GLOAM
GLOAT
GLOBE
GLOBS
GLOGG
GLOMS
GLOOM
GLOPS
GLORY
GLOSS
GLOVE
GLOWS
GLOZE
ILONA
LLOYD
OLOGY
PLODS
PLONK
PLOPS
PLOTS
PLOWS
PLOYS
SLOAN
SLOBS
SLOES
SLOGS
SLOMO
SLOOP
SLOPE
SLOPS
SLOSH
SLOTH
SLOTS
SLOWS
SLOYD
ZLOTY

•L•O•
ALCOA
ALCOR
ALDOL
ALGOL
ALIOS
ALLOT
ALLOW
ALLOY
ALOOF
ALSOP
ALTON
ALTOS
BLOOD
BLOOM
BLOOP
CLEON
CLIOS
ELBOW
ELION
ELIOT
ELMOS
ELROY
ELTON
FLOOD
FLOOR
FLUOR
GLOOM
GLUON
ILION
OLEOS
OLIOS
OLMOS
OLSON
PLEON
SLOOP

•L••O
ALAMO
ALTHO
BLUTO
CLARO
GLAXO
GLUCO
GLYCO
LLANO
OLIGO
PLANO
PLATO
PLEIO
PLUTO
SLIGO
SLOMO

••LO•
ADLOC
AGLOW
ALLOT
ALLOW
ALLOY
BELOW
BOLOS
BULOW
CHLOE
CHLOR
COLON
COLOR
DELON
DELOS
DOLOR
FELON
GALOP
HALON
HALOS
HELOS
HELOT
IGLOO
KILOS
MELON
MELOS
MILOS
NILOT
NYLON
ONLOW
ORLON
ORLOP
PALOS
PHLOX
PILOT
POLOS
PYLON
SALON
SILOS
SOLON
SOLOS
TALON
TALOS
TELOS
VALOR
YALOW

••L•O
AALTO
BALTO
BILBO
BILKO
CELLO
DELCO
DRLAO
FALDO
FOLIO
GALLO
HALLO
HELIO
HELLO
HULLO
IGLOO
JELLO
JULIO
KELSO
MALMO
MOLTO
PALEO
POLLO
ROLEO
ROLLO
SALVO
SOLDO
TELEO
VOLVO
WALDO
WILCO

•••LO
AMYLO
ANGLO
CAELO
CARLO
CELLO
CHILO
CHOLO
CYCLO
DIPLO
GALLO
HALLO
HAPLO
HATLO
HELLO
HULLO
ITALO
JELLO
KAHLO
MARLO
MENLO
MYELO
OCULO
OVOLO
PABLO
PAOLO
PAULO
PHILO
POLLO
ROLLO
STYLO

L•P••
LAPAZ
LAPEL
LAPIN
LAPIS
LAPPS
LAPSE
LAPUP
LEPPY
LEPTA
LEPTO
LEPUS
LIPID
LIPPI
LIPPO
LIPPY
LOPAT
LOPED
LOPER
LOPES
LOPEZ
LOPPY
LUPIN

L••P•
LAMPS
LAPPS
LEAPS
LEAPT
LEPPY
LIMPS
LIPPI
LIPPO
LIPPY
LISPS
LOOPS
LOOPY
LOPPY
LOUPE
LUMPS
LUMPY
LYMPH

L•••P
LAPUP
LAYUP
LEGUP
LETUP
LITUP

•LP••
ALPHA

•L•P•
ALEPH
BLIPS
CLAPS
CLIPS
CLIPT
CLOPS
ELOPE
FLAPS
FLIPS
FLOPS
GLOPS
GLYPH
PLOPS
SLAPS
SLEPT
SLIPS
SLIPT
SLOPE
SLOPS
SLYPE

•L••P
ALSOP
BLEEP
BLIMP
BLOOP
CLAMP
CLASP
CLOMP
CLUMP
PLUMP
SLEEP
SLOOP
SLUMP
SLURP

••LP•
CALPE
CULPA
DOLPH
GULPS
GULPY
HELPS
KELPS
KELPY
MILPA
PALPI
PALPS
PULPS
PULPY
RALPH
SALPA
SALPS
SYLPH
YELPS

••L•P
GALOP
ISLIP
JULEP
ORLOP
OXLIP
POLYP
SALEP
TULIP

•••LP
QUILP
SCALP
WHELP

L•R••
LARAM
LARAS
LARCH
LARDS
LARDY
LARES
LARGE
LARGO
LARIS
LARKS
LARKY
LARRY
LARUE
LARVA
LEROI
LEROY
LIRAS
LORAN
LORAX
LORCA
LORDS
LOREN
LORES
LORIS
LORNA
LORNE
LORRE
LORRY
LURAY
LURCH
LURED
LURES
LUREX
LURIA
LURID
LURIE
LURKS
LYRES
LYRIC

L••R•
LAIRD
LAIRS
LARRY
LATRY
LAURA
LEARN
LEARS
LEARY
LEERS
LEERY
LEORA
LIARD
LIARS
LIBRA
LIBRE
LITRE
LIVRE
LOIRE
LORRE
LORRY
LOWRY
LUCRE
LYCRA

L•••R
LABOR
LACER
LADER
LAGER
LAHAR
LAKER
LAMAR
LAMER
LASER
LATER
LAUER
LAVER
LAXER
LAYER
LAZAR
LEGER
LEHAR
LEMUR
LEVAR
LEVER
LIGER
LINER
LITER
LIVER
LONER
LOPER
LOSER
LOVER
LOWER
LUGER
LUNAR
LUXOR

•LR••
ELROY

•L•R•
ALARM
ALERT
ALFRE
ALORS
BLARE
BLURB
BLURS
BLURT
CLARA
CLARE
CLARK
CLARO
CLARY
CLERK
FLARE
FLIRT
FLORA
FLORY
GLARE
GLARY
GLORY
NLERS
SLURP
SLURS
ULTRA

•L••R
ALCOR
ALDER
ALGER
ALLER
ALTAR
ALTER
ALVAR
BLAIR
BLEAR
BLUER
CLAIR
CLEAR
ELDER
ELGAR
ELLER
ELMER
ELVER
FLAIR
FLEER
FLEUR
FLIER
FLOOR
FLOUR
FLUOR
FLYER
GLAIR
GLUER
ILLER
OLDER
SLIER
SLYER
ULCER

••L•R
ABLER
ADLER
AILER
ALLER
BALER
CHLOR
COLOR
DOLOR
EELER
ELLER
EULER
FILAR
FILER
GULAR
HALER
IDLER
ILLER
MALAR
MILER
MOLAR
MYLAR
NFLER
NHLER
OGLER
OILER
OSLER
PALER
PILAR
POLAR
POLER
RULER
SOLAR
SOLER
TALER
TILER
TOLER
TYLER
VALOR
VELAR
VILER
VOLAR
WALER
WYLER

LS•••
LSATS

L•S••
LASED
LASER
LASES
LASSO
LASTS
LISLE
LISPS
LISSE
LISTS
LISZT
LOSER
LOSES
LOSSY
LUSTS
LUSTY
LYSIN
LYSOL

L••S•
LAPSE
LASSO
LEASE
LEASH
LEAST
LHASA
LISSE
LOESS
LOOSE
LOSSY
LOUSE
LOUSY
LUISA
LUISE

L•••S
LACES
LACKS
LADES
LADYS
LAGOS
LAICS
LAIRS
LAIUS
LAKES
LAMAS
LAMBS
LAMES
LAMPS
LANDS
LANES
LAPIS
LAPPS
LARAS
LARDS
LARES
LARIS
LARKS
LASES
LASTS
LATHS
LAUDS
LAVAS
LAVES
LAWES
LAWNS
LAZES
LEADS
LEAFS
LEAKS
LEANS
LEAPS
LEARS
LEEDS
LEEKS

LEERS
LEETS
LEFTS
LEGGS
LEGIS
LEGOS
LENDS
LENIS
LENOS
LENTS
LEPUS
LETTS
LEVIS
LEWES
LEWIS
LEXIS
LEXUS
LIARS
LICKS
LIDOS
LIENS
LIEUS
LIFTS
LIKES
LILTS
LIMAS
LIMBS
LIMES
LIMNS
LIMOS
LIMPS
LINES
LINKS
LINOS
LINTS
LINUS
LIONS
LIRAS
LISPS
LISTS
LITES
LITHS
LIVES
LOADS
LOAFS
LOAMS
LOANS
LOBES
LOBOS
LOCHS
LOCKS
LOCOS
LOCUS
LODES
LOESS
LOFTS
LOGES
LOGOS
LOINS
LOLLS
LONGS
LOOKS
LOOMS
LOONS
LOOPS
LOOTS
LOPES
LORDS
LORES
LORIS
LOSES
LOTAS
LOTUS
LOUIS
LOUTS
LOVES
LOWES
LOXES
LSATS
LUAUS
LUBAS
LUBES
LUCAS
LUCKS
LUFFS
LUGES
LUKAS
LULLS
LULUS
LUMPS
LUNES
LUNGS
LURES
LURKS
LUSTS
LUTES
LYONS
LYRES

•LS••

ALSOP
ELSIE
OLSEN
OLSON

•L•S•

ALIST
BLASE
BLASS
BLAST
BLESS
BLEST
BLISS
BLUSH
CLASH
CLASP
CLASS
CLOSE
ELISE
ELYSE
FLASH
FLASK
FLESH
FLOSS
FLUSH
GLASS
GLESS
GLOSS
PLASH
PLASM
PLUSH
SLASH
SLOSH
SLUSH

•L••S

ALDUS
ALEFS
ALFAS
ALIAS
ALIFS
ALIOS
ALLES
ALOES
ALORS
ALTOS
ALTUS
ALUMS
BLABS
BLAHS
BLASS
BLATS
BLDGS
BLEBS
BLESS
BLIPS
BLISS
BLOBS
BLOCS
BLOIS
BLOTS
BLOWS
BLUES
BLURS
BLVDS
CLAMS
CLANS
CLAPS
CLASS
CLAUS
CLAWS
CLAYS
CLEFS
CLEWS
CLIOS
CLIPS
CLODS
CLOGS
CLOPS
CLOTS
CLOYS
CLUBS
CLUES
ELIAS
ELLES
ELLIS
ELMOS
ELVES
ELVIS
ELWES
FLAGS
FLAMS
FLANS
FLAPS
FLATS
FLAWS
FLAYS
FLEAS
FLEES
FLEWS
FLEYS
FLICS
FLIES
FLIPS
FLITS
FLOES
FLOGS
FLOPS
FLOSS
FLOWS
FLUBS
FLUES
GLADS
GLASS
GLEES
GLENS
GLESS
GLEYS
GLIMS
GLOBS
GLOMS
GLOPS
GLOSS
GLOWS
GLUES
GLUGS
GLUTS
ILLUS
KLAUS
MLLES
NLERS
OLEOS
OLIOS
OLLAS
OLMOS
PLANS
PLATS
PLAYS
PLEAS
PLEBS
PLEWS
PLIES
PLODS
PLOPS
PLOTS
PLOWS
PLOYS
PLUGS
PLUMS
SLABS
SLAGS
SLAMS
SLAPS
SLATS
SLAVS
SLAWS
SLAYS
SLEDS
SLEWS
SLIMS
SLIPS
SLITS
SLOBS
SLOES
SLOGS
SLOPS
SLOTS
SLOWS
SLUES
SLUGS
SLUMS
SLURS
ULNAS

••LS•

BALSA
DULSE
FALSE
HOLST
KELSO
PALSY
PULSE
SALSA
TULSA
VALSE
WALSH
WALSY
WELSH

••L•S

ALLES
APLUS
ARLES
ATLAS
AULIS
AXLES
BALAS
BALDS
BALES
BALKS
BALLS
BALMS
BALTS
BELLS
BELTS
BILKS
BILLS
BOLAS
BOLES
BOLLS
BOLOS
BOLTS
BOLUS
BPLUS
BULBS
BULKS
BULLS
CALKS
CALLS
CALMS
CELLS
CELTS
COLAS
COLDS
COLES
COLTS
CPLUS
CULLS
CULMS
CULTS
DALES
DELES
DELIS
DELLS
DELOS
DELTS
DILLS
DOLES
DOLLS
DOLTS
DPLUS
DULLS
ELLES
ELLIS
EOLUS
FALLS
FELIS
FELLS
FELTS
FILES
FILLS
FILMS
FOLDS
FOLKS
FTLBS
FULAS
GALAS
GALES
GALLS
GILDS
GILES
GILLS
GILTS
GOLDS
GOLFS
GULES
GULFS
GULLS
GULPS
HALAS
HALES
HALLS
HALMS
HALOS
HALTS
HELLS
HELMS
HELOS
HELPS
HILLS
HILTS
HOLDS
HOLES
HOLMS
HULAS
HULKS
HULLS
HYLAS
IDLES
IGLUS
ILLUS
ISLAS
ISLES
JELLS
JILTS
JOLTS
JULES
KALES
KELPS
KILLS
KILNS
KILOS
KILTS
KOLAS
LILTS
LOLLS
LULLS
LULUS
MALES
MALLS
MALTS
MELDS
MELOS
MELTS
MILES
MILKS
MILLS
MILOS
MILTS
MLLES
MOLAS
MOLDS
MOLES
MOLLS
MOLTS
MULES
MULLS
MYLES
NILES
NULLS
OGLES
OLLAS
ORLES
PALES
PALLS
PALMS
PALOS
PALPS
PELTS
PILES
PILLS
PILUS
POLES
POLIS
POLLS
POLOS
PULAS
PULES
PULIS
PULLS
PULPS
RILES
RILLS
ROLES
ROLLS
RULES
SALES
SALPS
SALTS
SELES
SELLS
SILAS
SILKS
SILLS
SILOS
SILTS
SOLES
SOLOS
SOLUS
SULKS
TALES
TALKS
TALOS
TALUS
TELES
TELLS
TELOS
TILES
TILLS
TILTS
TOLLS
TULES
VALES
VELDS
VILAS
VOLES
VOLTS
WALES
WALKS
WALLS
WELDS
WELLS
WELTS
WILDS
WILES
WILLS
WILTS
WOLDS
YELLS
YELPS
YOLKS
ZILLS
ZULUS

•••LS

ACYLS
AGALS
AMYLS
ANILS
ARILS
AWOLS
AXELS
AXILS
BAALS
BAILS
BALLS
BAWLS
BEALS
BELLS
BILLS
BIRLS
BOILS
BOLLS
BOWLS
BUHLS
BULLS
BURLS
CALLS
CAULS
CEILS
CELLS
COALS
COILS
COOLS
COWLS
CULLS
CURLS
DEALS
DEILS
DELLS
DHALS
DIALS
DILLS
DOLLS
DUELS
DULLS
EARLS
ENOLS
EVILS
FAILS
FALLS
FEELS
FELLS
FILLS
FOALS
FOILS
FOOLS
FOULS
FOWLS
FUELS
FURLS
GAELS
GALLS
GAOLS
GAULS
GILLS
GIRLS
GOALS
GULLS
HAILS
HALLS
HAULS
HEALS
HEELS
HELLS
HERLS
HILLS
HOWLS
HULLS
HURLS
IDOLS
IDYLS
ITALS
JAILS
JARLS
JELLS
JOWLS
KEELS
KILLS
LOLLS
LULLS
MAILS
MALLS
MARLS
MAULS
MEALS
MERLS
MEWLS
MILLS
MOILS
MOLLS
MULLS
NAILS
NIELS
NOELS
NOILS
NULLS
OBOLS
OPALS
OPELS
ORALS
OVALS
PAILS
PALLS
PAWLS
PEALS
PEELS
PILLS
POILS
POLLS
POOLS
PULLS
PURLS
RAILS
RAWLS
REALS
REELS
RIALS
RIELS
RILLS
ROILS
ROLLS
ROTLS
SAILS
SEALS
SEELS
SELLS
SHULS
SIALS
SILLS
SOILS
SOULS
STOLS
TAELS
TAILS
TEALS
TELLS
TILLS
TOILS
TOLLS
TOOLS
URALS
VEILS
VIALS
VIOLS
VTOLS
WAALS
WAILS
WALLS
WEALS
WELLS
WILLS
WOOLS
YAWLS
YELLS
YOWLS
ZEALS
ZILLS

LT•••

LTCOL
LTGEN
LTGOV

L•T••

LATCH
LATEN
LATER
LATEX
LATHE
LATHS
LATHY
LATIN
LATKE
LATRY
LATTE
LETAT
LETBE
LETGO
LETHE
LETIN
LETON
LETTS

LETUP LITER LITES LITHE LITHO LITHS LITON LITRE LITUP LOTAH LOTAS LOTTA LOTTE LOTTO LOTUS LUTES LYTTA

L••T•

LACTI LACTO LAHTI LAITY LANTZ LASTS LATTE LAYTO LEDTO LEETS LEFTS LEFTY LEITH LENTO LENTS LEPTA LEPTO LETTS LEYTE LIETO LIFTS LILTS LINTS LINTY LISTS LOATH LOFTS LOFTY LOOTS LOTTA LOTTE LOTTO LOUTS LSATS LUSTS LUSTY LYTTA

L•••T

LEANT LEAPT LEAST LEGIT LEMAT LETAT LICET LICIT LIEUT LIGHT LIMIT LISZT LOFAT LOPAT LUMET

•LT••

ALTAI ALTAR ALTER ALTHO ALTON ALTOS ALTUS ELTON ULTRA

•L•T•

ALATE ALETA BLATS BLITT BLITZ BLOTS BLUTH BLUTO BLYTH CLOTH CLOTS ELATE ELATH ELITE ELUTE FLATS FLATT FLITS FLUTE FLUTY GLITZ GLUTS KLUTE KLUTZ PLATA PLATE PLATH PLATO PLATS PLATT PLATY PLOTS PLUTO SLATE SLATS SLATY SLITS SLOTH SLOTS ZLOTY

•L••T

ALERT ALEUT ALIST ALLOT ALOFT BLAST BLEAT BLENT BLEST BLITT BLOAT BLUET BLUNT BLURT CLEAT CLEFT CLIFT CLINT CLIPT CLOUT ELECT ELIOT FLATT FLEET FLINT FLIRT FLOAT FLOUT FLYAT GLINT GLOAT KLIMT PLAIT PLANT PLATT PLEAT SLANT SLEET SLEPT SLIPT

••LT•

AALTO BALTO BALTS BELTS BOLTS CELTS COLTS CULTS DELTA DELTS DOLTS FELTS FILTH GILTS HALTS HILTS HOLTZ JILTS JOLTS JOLTY KILTS LILTS MALTA MALTS MALTY MELTS MELTY MILTS MILTY MOLTO MOLTS MULTI NOLTE PELTS SALTA SALTS SALTY SILTS SILTY SOLTI TILTH TILTS USLTA VOLTA VOLTE VOLTS WALTZ WELTS WELTY WILTS YALTA

••L•T

AFLAT AGLET ALLOT BFLAT CFLAT COLET CULET DELFT DFLAT ECLAT EFLAT EILAT FFLAT FILET GFLAT HELOT HOLST INLET ISLET MULCT NILOT OWLET PILOT POLIT RELET RELIT SALUT SPLAT SPLIT TOLET UNLIT VALET VELDT VOLAT

•••LT

ADULT ATILT BOULT BUILT DEALT DWELT EXALT EXULT FAULT GUILT KNELT MOULT POULT QUILT SAULT SHALT SMALT SMELT SMOLT SOULT SPELT SPILT STILT UBOLT VAULT

LU•••

LUAUS LUBAS LUBED LUBES LUCAN LUCAS LUCCA LUCCI LUCIA LUCID LUCIE LUCKS LUCKY LUCRE LUDIC LUEGO LUFFS LUGER LUGES LUIGI LUISA LUISE LUKAS LULEA LULLS LULLY LULUS LUMEN LUMET LUMPS LUMPY LUNAR LUNCH LUNDI LUNDY LUNES LUNGE LUNGS LUNIK LUPIN LURAY LURCH LURED LURES LUREX LURIA LURID LURIE LURKS LUSTS LUSTY LUTES LUXOR LUZON

L•U••

LAUDE LAUDS LAUER LAUGH LAURA LOUGH LOUIE LOUIS LOUPE LOUSE LOUSY LOUTS

L••U•

LAIUS LAPUP LARUE LAYUP LEGUP LEHUA LEMUR LEPUS LETUP LEXUS LIEUS LIEUT LIKUD LINUS LITUP LOCUM LOCUS LOGUE LOTUS LUAUS LULUS

L•••U

LONGU

•LU••

ALULA ALUMS BLUED BLUER BLUES BLUET BLUEY BLUFF BLUME BLUNT BLURB BLURS BLURT BLUSH BLUTH BLUTO CLUBS CLUCK CLUED CLUES CLUMP CLUNG CLUNK CLUNY ELUDE ELUTE FLUBS FLUES FLUFF FLUID FLUKE FLUKY FLUME FLUNG FLUNK FLUOR FLUSH FLUTE FLUTY GLUCK GLUCO GLUED GLUER GLUES GLUEY GLUGS GLUON GLUTS KLUGE KLUTE KLUTZ PLUCK PLUGS PLUMB PLUME PLUMP PLUMS PLUMY PLUNK PLUSH PLUTO SLUED SLUES SLUGS SLUMP SLUMS SLUNG SLUNK SLURP SLURS SLUSH

•L•U•

ALBUM ALDUS ALEUT ALOUD ALTUS CLAUS CLOUD CLOUT FLEUR FLOUR FLOUT ILIUM ILLUS KLAUS OLEUM

•L••U

ELIHU ILGWU

••LU•

APLUS BOLUS BPLUS COLUM CPLUS DPLUS EOLUS FILUM HILUM IGLUS ILLUS LULUS PILUM PILUS SALUD SALUT SOLUM SOLUS TALUS VALUE VELUM ZULUS

••L•U

PALAU

•••LU

POILU UPOLU

LV•••

LVIII

L•V••

LAVAL LAVAS LAVED LAVER LAVES LAVIN LEVAR LEVEE LEVEL LEVER LEVIN LEVIS LEVON LIVED LIVEN LIVER LIVES LIVIA LIVID LIVRE LOVED LOVER LOVES LOVEY LXVII

L••V•

LARVA LEAVE LXXVI

L•••V

LTGOV LXXIV LXXXV

•LV••

ALVAR ALVIN BLVDS CLVII DLVII ELVER ELVES ELVIN ELVIS MLVII XLVII

•L•V•

ALAVA ALEVE ALIVE CLAVE CLIVE CLOVE CLXVI DLXVI ELEVE GLOVE MLXVI OLIVE SLAVE SLAVS

•L••V

CLXIV CLXXV DLXIV DLXXV MLXIV MLXXV

••LV•

BELVA CALVE CCLVI CDLVI CMLVI CXLVI DCLVI DELVE DXLVI HALVE HELVE MCLVI MDLVI MMLVI MXLVI SALVE SALVO SELVA SILVA SOLVE VALVE VOLVA VOLVO

••L•V

CCLIV CCLXV CDLIV CDLXV CMLIV CMLXV CXLIV DCLIV DCLXV DXLIV MCLIV MCLXV MDLIV MDLXV MMLIV MMLXV MXLIV

•••LV

CCCLV CCXLV CDXLV CMXLV DCCLV DCXLV MCCLV MCDLV MCMLV MCXLV MDCLV MDXLV MMCLV MMDLV MMMLV MMXLV

L•W••

LAWES LAWNS LAWNY LEWES LEWIS LOWED LOWER LOWES LOWLY LOWRY

L••W•

LOEWE LOEWY

L•••W

LALAW

•LW••

CLWYD ELWAY ELWES

•L•W•

BLOWN BLOWS BLOWY CLAWS CLEWS CLOWN FLAWS FLAWY FLEWS FLOWN FLOWS GLOWS ILGWU PLEWS PLOWS SLAWS SLEWS SLIWA SLOWS

•L••W

ALLOW ELBOW

••L•W
AGLOW
ALLOW
BELOW
BULOW
BYLAW
INLAW
LALAW
ONLOW
YALOW

LX•••
LXIII
LXVII
LXXII
LXXIV
LXXIX
LXXVI
LXXXI
LXXXV

L•X••
LAXER
LAXLY
LEXAN
LEXIS
LEXUS
LOXES
LUXOR
LXXII
LXXIV
LXXIX
LXXVI
LXXXI
LXXXV

L••X•
LXXXI
LXXXV

L•••X
LATEX
LENOX
LOMAX
LORAX
LUREX
LXXIX

•LX••
CLXII
CLXIV
CLXIX
CLXVI
CLXXI
CLXXV
CLXXX
DLXII
DLXIV
DLXIX
DLXVI
DLXXI
DLXXV
DLXXX
MLXII
MLXIV
MLXIX
MLXVI
MLXXI
MLXXV
MLXXX

•L•X•
CLXXI
CLXXV
CLXXX
DLXXI
DLXXV
DLXXX
FLAXY
FLEXI
GLAXO
MLXXI
MLXXV
MLXXX

•L••X
CLXIX
CLXXX
DLXIX
DLXXX
MLXIX
MLXXX

••LX•
CCLXI
CCLXV
CCLXX
CDLXI
CDLXV
CDLXX
CMLXI
CMLXV
CMLXX
DCLXI
DCLXV
DCLXX
MCLXI
MCLXV
MCLXX
MDLXI
MDLXV
MDLXX
MMLXI
MMLXV
MMLXX

••L•X
CALIX
CALYX
CCLIX
CCLXX
CDLIX
CDLXX
CMLIX
CMLXX
CULEX
CXLIX
DCLIX
DCLXX
DXLIX
FELIX
GALAX
HELIX
KYLIX
MCLIX
MCLXX
MDLIX
MDLXX
MMLIX
MMLXX
MXLIX
PHLOX
RELAX
ROLEX
SILEX
TELEX

•••LX
CCCLX
DCCLX
MCCLX
MCDLX
MCMLX
MDCLX
MMCLX
MMDLX
MMMLX

LY•••
LYCEE
LYCRA
LYDIA
LYELL
LYING
LYMAN
LYMON
LYMPH
LYNCH
LYNDA
LYNDE
LYNNE
LYONS
LYRES
LYRIC
LYSIN
LYSOL
LYTTA

L•Y••
LAYBY
LAYER
LAYIN
LAYLA
LAYNE
LAYON
LAYTO
LAYUP
LEYTE
LOYAL

L••Y•
LADYS
LENYA
LIBYA
LLOYD

L•••Y
LACEY
LAITY
LANKY
LARDY
LARKY
LARRY
LATHY
LATRY
LAWNY
LAXLY
LAYBY
LEADY
LEAFY
LEAHY
LEAKY
LEARY
LECKY
LEDGY
LEERY
LEFAY
LEFTY
LEGGY
LEMAY
LENNY
LEPPY
LEROY
LIBBY
LIDDY
LIEBY
LILLY
LIMEY
LINDY
LINEY
LINTY
LIPPY
LOAMY
LOBBY
LOEWY
LOFTY
LOLLY
LOOBY
LOONY
LOOPY
LOPPY
LORRY
LOSSY
LOUSY
LOVEY
LOWLY
LOWRY
LUCKY
LULLY
LUMPY
LUNDY
LURAY
LUSTY

•LY••
ALYCE
BLYTH
CLYDE
ELYSE
FLYAT
FLYBY
FLYER
FLYIN
FLYNN
GLYCO
GLYPH
SLYER
SLYLY
SLYPE

•L•Y•
ALKYD
ALKYL
ALLYL
CLAYS
CLOYS
CLWYD
FLAYS
FLEYS
FLOYD
GLEYS
LLOYD
PLAYA
PLAYS
PLOYS
SLAYS
SLOYD

•L••Y
ALLAY
ALLEY
ALLOY
ALMAY
BLOWY
BLUEY
CLARY
CLUNY
ELEGY
ELROY
ELWAY
FLAKY
FLAMY
FLAWY
FLAXY
FLORY
FLUKY
FLUTY
FLYBY
GLARY
GLORY
GLUEY
OLOGY
PLATY
PLINY
PLUMY
SLATY
SLILY
SLIMY
SLYLY
ZLOTY

••LY•
ALLYL
CALYX
EMLYN
POLYP

••L•Y
AGLEY
AILEY
ALLAY
ALLEY
ALLOY
APLEY
BALKY
BALLY
BALMY
BELAY
BELLY
BILBY
BILGY
BILLY
BULGY
BULKY
BULLY
COLBY
CULLY
DALEY
DALLY
DELAY
DILLY
DOLBY
DOLLY
DULLY
FELLY
FILLY
FILMY
FOLEY
FOLKY
FOLLY
FULLY
GILLY
GOLLY
GULLY
GULPY
HALEY
HILLY
HOLEY
HOLLY
INLAY
ISLEY
JELLY
JOLLY
JOLTY
KELLY
KELPY
KILEY
KILLY
LILLY
LOLLY
LULLY
MALAY
MALTY
MELTY
MILKY
MILTY
MOLDY
MOLLY
MULEY
NELLY
NILLY
ONLAY
PALEY
PALLY
PALMY
PALSY
POLLY
PULPY
RALLY
RELAY
RILEY
SALLY
SALTY
SILKY
SILLY
SILTY
SPLAY
SULKY
SULLY
TALKY
TALLY
TELLY
TILLY
TOLLY
TULLY
UNLAY
UTLEY
WALEY
WALLY
WALSY
WELBY
WELTY
WILEY
WILLY
YOLKY

•••LY
AMPLY
APPLY
APTLY
BADLY
BALLY
BELLY
BIALY
BIGLY
BILLY
BULLY
BURLY
CARLY
COYLY
CROLY
CULLY
CURLY
DAILY
DALLY
DILLY
DIMLY
DOILY
DOLLY
DOYLY
DRILY
DRYLY
DULLY
EARLY
EMILY
FATLY
FEELY
FELLY
FEYLY
FILLY
FITLY
FOLLY
FULLY
GAILY
GAYLY
GILLY
GODLY
GOLLY
GULLY
HAPLY
HEALY
HILLY
HIPLY
HOLLY
HOTLY
HURLY
ICILY
IMPLY
ITALY
JELLY
JOLLY
JOWLY
KELLY
KILLY
LAXLY
LILLY
LOLLY
LOWLY
LULLY
MADLY
MANLY
MARLY
MCFLY
MEALY
MOLLY
NELLY
NEWLY
NILLY
NOBLY
NOFLY
NOILY
ODDLY
PALLY
PATLY
PHILY
POLLY
RALLY
RAWLY
REDLY
REPLY
ROILY
SADLY
SALLY
SCALY
SEALY
SEELY
SHYLY
SILLY
SLILY
SLYLY
SULLY
SURLY
TALLY
TELLY
TILLY
TOLLY
TRULY
TULLY
VEALY
WALLY
WANLY
WETLY
WILLY
WOOLY
WRYLY

L•Z••
LAZAR
LAZED
LAZES
LUZON

L••Z•
LANZA
LEEZA
LISZT

L•••Z
LANTZ
LAPAZ
LOPEZ

•L•Z•
BLAZE
ELAZI
ELIZA
GLAZE
GLOZE
PLAZA

•L••Z
ALLEZ
BLITZ
GLITZ
KLUTZ

••L•Z
ALLEZ
FELIZ
HOLTZ
VELEZ
WALTZ

MA•••
MABEL
MACAO
MACAW
MACED
MACES
MACHE
MACHO
MACHU
MACHY
MACLE
MACON
MACRO
MACYS
MADAM
MADGE
MADLY
MADRE
MAGDA
MAGEE
MAGES
MAGIC
MAGMA
MAGNA
MAGOG
MAGOO
MAGOT
MAGUS
MAHAL
MAHAN
MAHDI
MAHER
MAHON
MAHRE
MAIDS
MAIDU
MAILE
MAILS
MAINE
MAINS
MAINZ
MAIZE
MAJOR
MAKER
MAKES
MAKOS
MAKUA
MALAN
MALAR
MALAY
MALES
MALIC
MALLE
MALLS
MALMO
MALTA
MALTS
MALTY
MAMAS
MAMBA
MAMBO
MAMET
MAMIE
MAMMA
MAMMY
MANCY
MANDY
MANED
MANES
MANET
MANGO
MANGY
MANIA
MANIC
MANLY
MANNA
MANNY
MANON
MANOR
MANOS
MANSE
MANTA
MAORI
MAPLE
MAQUI
MARAS
MARAT
MARCH
MARCO
MARCY
MARDI
MARES
MARGE
MARGO
MARIA
MARIE
MARIN
MARIO
MARIS
MARKS
MARLA
MARLO
MARLS
MARLY
MARNE
MARRY
MARSH
MARTA
MARTI
MARTS
MARTY
MARVY
MARYS
MASAI
MASER
MASHY
MASKS
MASON
MASSE
MASSY
MASTS
MASUR

MATCH
MATED
MATEO
MATER
MATES
MATEY
MATHS
MATIN
MATRI
MATRO
MATSU
MATTE
MATZO
MAUDE
MAULS
MAUNA
MAUND
MAURY
MAUVE
MAVEN
MAVIS
MAXED
MAXES
MAXIE
MAXIM
MAXIS
MAYAN
MAYAS
MAYBE
MAYER
MAYNT
MAYON
MAYOR
MAYPO
MAYST
MAZDA
MAZEL
MAZER
MAZES

M•A••

MEADE
MEADS
MEALS
MEALY
MEANS
MEANT
MEANY
MEARA
MEATS
MEATY
MIAMI
MIAOW
MIATA
MOANS
MOATS

M••A•

MACAO
MACAW
MADAM
MAHAL
MAHAN
MALAN
MALAR
MALAY
MAMAS
MARAS
MARAT
MASAI
MAYAN
MAYAS
MCKAY
MCRAE
MEDAL
MEGAN
MELAN
MESAS
METAL
MICAH
MICAS
MIDAS
MIKAN
MILAN
MIMAS
MINAS
MIZAR
MODAL
MOHAM
MOLAR
MOLAS
MONAD
MORAE
MORAL
MORAN
MORAS
MORAY
MURAL
MURAT
MUZAK
MYLAR
MYNAH
MYNAS
MYWAY

M•••A

MAGDA
MAGMA
MAGNA
MAKUA
MALTA
MAMBA
MAMMA
MANIA
MANNA
MANTA
MARIA
MARLA
MARTA
MAUNA
MAZDA
MBIRA
MEARA
MECCA
MEDEA
MEDIA
MEHTA
MELBA
MENSA
MESTA
MIATA
MICRA
MILPA
MISHA
MISSA
MOCHA
MOIRA
MOMMA
MONZA
MOOLA
MOTTA
MUDRA
MURRA
MUSCA
MYRNA

•MA••

AMADO
AMAHL
AMAHS
AMAIN
AMANA
AMAPA
AMARA
AMASS
AMATI
AMATO
AMAZE
DMARK
EMAIL
GMATS
IMAGE
IMAGO
IMAMS
KMART
OMAHA
OMANI
OMARR
OMASA
SMACK
SMAIL
SMALL
SMALT
SMART
SMASH
SMAZE

•M•A•

AMMAN
AMPAS
AMWAY
EMBAR
EMBAY
SMEAR
UMIAK
YMCAS

•M••A

AMANA
AMAPA
AMARA
AMEBA
AMIGA
AMNIA
OMAHA
OMASA
OMEGA
OMNIA
UMBRA

••MA•

ADMAN
AHMAD
AIMAT
ALMAY
AMMAN
ATMAN
BEMAS
CAMAY
COMAE
COMAS
CUMAE
CYMAE
CYMAS
DAMAN
DAMAR
DUMAS
ELMAN
GAMAL
GAMAY
HAMAL
HAMAN
HEMAN
HUMAN
HYMAN
JAMAL
KEMAL
LAMAR
LAMAS
LEMAT
LEMAY
LIMAS
LOMAN
LOMAX
LYMAN
MAMAS
MIMAS
NEMAN
NEMAT
NOMAD
OSMAN
PIMAS
PUMAS
RAMAN
RAMAR
REMAN
REMAP
ROMAN
SAMAR
SOMAS
SUMAC
UNMAN
UXMAL
WOMAN
WYMAN
YUMAN
YUMAS

••M•A

COMMA
GAMBA
GAMMA
GEMMA
JUMNA
LAMIA
LEMMA
MAMBA
MAMMA
MOMMA
NAMPA
NEMEA
PAMPA
PEMBA
RUMBA
SAMBA
SAMOA
SIMBA
SUMBA
SUMMA
TAMPA
YAMPA
ZAMIA

•••MA

ACOMA
ADAMA
AGAMA
ANIMA
ARAMA
AROMA
ASAMA
BURMA
COMMA
DERMA
DOGMA
DOLMA
DRAMA
EDEMA
ETYMA
FIRMA
FORMA
GAMMA
GEMMA
GRAMA
HAEMA
HOUMA
KARMA
LEMMA
LLAMA
MAGMA
MAMMA
MOMMA
NORMA
ORAMA
PALMA
PARMA
PRIMA
SELMA
SHEMA
SIGMA
STOMA
SUMMA
THEMA
VILMA
WILMA

MB•••

MBIRA
MBOMU

M•B••

MABEL
MOBIL
MRBIG

M••B•

MAMBA
MAMBO
MAYBE
MELBA
MOSBY
MSNBC
MUMBO

M•••B

MCJOB

•MB••

AMBER
AMBIT
AMBLE
AMBOS
AMBOY
AMBRY
EMBAR
EMBAY
EMBED
EMBER
IMBUE
OMBER
OMBRE
UMBEL
UMBER
UMBOS
UMBRA

•M•B•

AMEBA

••MB•

BAMBI
BOMBE
BOMBS
COMBE
COMBO
COMBS
DUMBO
DUMBS
GAMBA
GUMBO
GUMBY
IAMBI
IAMBS
JAMBS
JUMBO
LAMBS
LIMBI
LIMBO
LIMBS
MAMBA
MAMBO
MUMBO
NAMBY
NIMBI
NIMBY
NUMBS
PAMBY
PEMBA
RAMBO
RUMBA
SAMBA
SIMBA
SUMBA
TAMBO

••M•B

DEMOB
NAMIB

•••MB

ABOMB
CLIMB
CRUMB
HBOMB
PLUMB
RHOMB
RHUMB
THUMB

MC•••

MCCCI
MCCCL
MCCCV
MCCCX
MCCII
MCCIV
MCCIX
MCCLI
MCCLV
MCCLX
MCCOO
MCCOY
MCCVI
MCCXC
MCCXI
MCCXL
MCCXV
MCCXX
MCDII
MCDIV
MCDIX
MCDLI
MCDLV
MCDLX
MCDVI
MCDXC
MCDXI
MCDXL
MCDXV
MCDXX
MCFLY
MCGEE
MCIII
MCJOB
MCKAY
MCLII
MCLIV
MCLIX
MCLVI
MCLXI
MCLXV
MCLXX
MCMII
MCMIV
MCMIX
MCMLI
MCMLV
MCMLX
MCMVI
MCMXC
MCMXI
MCMXL
MCMXV
MCMXX
MCRAE
MCVIE
MCVII
MCXCI
MCXCV
MCXII
MCXIV
MCXIX
MCXLI
MCXLV
MCXVI
MCXXI
MCXXV
MCXXX

M•C••

MACAO
MACAW
MACED
MACES
MACHE
MACHO
MACHU
MACHY
MACLE
MACON
MACRO
MACYS
MCCCI
MCCCL
MCCCV
MCCCX
MCCII
MCCIV
MCCIX
MCCLI
MCCLV
MCCLX
MCCOO
MCCOY
MCCVI
MCCXC
MCCXI
MCCXL
MCCXV
MCCXX
MDCCC
MDCCI
MDCCL
MDCCV
MDCCX
MDCII
MDCIV
MDCIX
MDCLI
MDCLV
MDCLX
MDCVI
MDCXC
MDCXI
MDCXL
MDCXV
MDCXX
MECCA
MECUM
MICAH
MICAS
MICRA
MICRO
MMCCC
MMCCI
MMCCL
MMCCV
MMCCX
MMCDI
MMCDL
MMCDV
MMCDX
MMCII
MMCIV
MMCIX
MMCLI
MMCLV
MMCLX
MMCMI
MMCML
MMCMV
MMCMX
MMCVI
MMCXC
MMCXI
MMCXL
MMCXV
MMCXX
MOCHA
MOCKS
MUCIN
MUCKS
MUCKY
MUCRO
MXCII
MXCIV
MXCIX
MXCVI
MYCIN

M••C•

MANCY
MARCH
MARCO
MARCY
MATCH
MCCCI
MCCCL
MCCCV
MCCCX
MCXCI
MCXCV
MDCCC
MDCCI
MDCCL
MDCCV
MDCCX
MDXCI
MDXCV
MECCA
MERCE
MERCI
MERCK
MERCY
MILCH
MINCE
MITCH
MMCCC
MMCCI
MMCCL
MMCCV
MMCCX
MMDCC
MMDCI
MMDCL
MMDCV
MMDCX
MMMCC
MMMCD
MMMCI
MMMCL
MMMCV
MMMCX
MMXCI
MMXCV
MONCK
MOOCH
MULCH
MULCT
MUNCH
MUSCA

M•••C

MAGIC
MALIC
MANIC
MCCXC
MCDXC
MCMXC
MDCCC
MDCXC
MEDIC
MEDOC
MELIC
MESIC
MIMIC
MMCCC
MMCXC
MMDCC
MMDXC
MMMCC
MMMDC
MMMXC
MODOC
MSNBC
MUSIC

•MC••

EMCEE
MMCCC
MMCCI
MMCCL
MMCCV
MMCCX
MMCDI
MMCDL
MMCDV
MMCDX
MMCII
MMCIV
MMCIX
MMCLI
MMCLV
MMCLX
MMCMI
MMCML
MMCMV
MMCMX
MMCVI
MMCXC
MMCXI
MMCXL
MMCXV
MMCXX
YMCAS

•M•C•

AMICE
AMOCO
AMUCK
CMXCI
CMXCV
MMCCC

MMCCI
MMCCL
MMCCV
MMCCX
MMDCC
MMDCI
MMDCL
MMDCV
MMDCX
MMMCC
MMMCD
MMMCI
MMMCL
MMMCV
MMMCX
MMXCI
MMXCV
SMACK
SMOCK

•M••C
MMCCC
MMCXC
MMDCC
MMDXC
MMMCC
MMMDC
MMMXC

••MC•
MMMCC
MMMCD
MMMCI
MMMCL
MMMCV
MMMCX

••M•C
COMIC
MCMXC
MIMIC
MMMCC
MMMDC
MMMXC
OLMEC
OSMIC
SUMAC

MD•••
MDCCC
MDCCI
MDCCL
MDCCV
MDCCX
MDCII
MDCIV
MDCIX
MDCLI
MDCLV
MDCLX
MDCVI
MDCXC
MDCXI
MDCXL
MDCXV
MDCXX
MDIII
MDLII
MDLIV
MDLIX
MDLVI
MDLXI
MDLXV
MDLXX
MDVII
MDXCI
MDXCV
MDXII
MDXIV
MDXIX
MDXLI
MDXLV
MDXVI
MDXXI
MDXXV
MDXXX

M•D••
MADAM
MADGE
MADLY
MADRE
MCDII
MCDIV
MCDIX
MCDLI
MCDLV
MCDLX
MCDVI
MCDXC
MCDXI
MCDXL
MCDXV
MCDXX
MEDAL
MEDEA
MEDES
MEDIA
MEDIC
MEDIT
MEDOC
MIDAS
MIDDY
MIDGE
MIDIS
MIDST
MMDCC
MMDCI
MMDCL
MMDCV
MMDCX
MMDII
MMDIV
MMDIX
MMDLI
MMDLV
MMDLX
MMDVI
MMDXC
MMDXI
MMDXL
MMDXV
MMDXX
MODAL
MODEL
MODEM
MODES
MODOC
MODUS
MSDOS
MUDDY
MUDRA

M••D•
MAGDA
MAHDI
MAIDS
MAIDU
MANDY
MARDI
MAUDE
MAZDA
MEADE
MEADS
MEEDS
MELDS
MENDS
MIDDY
MINDS
MINDY
MISDO
MMCDI
MMCDL
MMCDV
MMCDX
MMMDC
MMMDI
MMMDL
MMMDV
MMMDX
MOLDS
MOLDY
MONDE
MONDO
MOODS
MOODY
MUDDY
MUNDI

M•••D
MACED
MANED
MATED
MAUND
MAXED
METED
MEWED
MIKED
MIMED
MINED
MIRED
MIXED
MMMCD
MONAD
MONOD
MOOED
MOPED
MOULD
MOUND
MOVED
MOWED
MUSED
MUTED

•MD••
CMDRS
EMDEN
MMDCC
MMDCI
MMDCL
MMDCV
MMDCX
MMDII
MMDIV
MMDIX
MMDLI
MMDLV
MMDLX
MMDVI
MMDXC
MMDXI
MMDXL
MMDXV
MMDXX

•M•D•
AMADO
AMIDE
AMIDO
IMIDE
IMIDO
MMCDI
MMCDL
MMCDV
MMCDX
MMMDC
MMMDI
MMMDL
MMMDV
MMMDX

•M••D
AMEND
AMPED
EMBED
EMEND
IMPED
MMMCD
UMPED

••MD•
MMMDC
MMMDI
MMMDL
MMMDV
MMMDX

••M•D
AHMAD
AHMED
AIMED
ARMED
DIMED
DOMED
FAMED
FUMED
GAMED
HOMED
HUMID
LAMED
LIMED
MIMED
MMMCD
NAMED
NOMAD
RIMED
TAMED
TIMED
TIMID
TUMID

ME•••
MEADE
MEADS
MEALS
MEALY
MEANS
MEANT
MEANY
MEARA
MEATS
MEATY
MECCA
MECUM
MEDAL
MEDEA
MEDES
MEDIA
MEDIC
MEDIT
MEDOC
MEEDS
MEESE
MEETS
MEGAN
MEHTA
MEIJI
MEINY
MELAN
MELBA
MELDS
MELEE
MELIC
MELON
MELOS
MELTS
MELTY
MEMEL
MEMOS
MENDS
MENES
MENLO
MENSA
MENUS
MEOWS
MERCE
MERCI
MERCK
MERCY
MERES
MERGE
MERIT
MERLE
MERLS
MEROE
MERRY
MERTZ
MERYL
MESAS
MESHY
MESIC
MESNE
MESON
MESSY
MESTA
METAL
METED
METER
METES
METIS
METOO
METRE
METRO
METRY
MEUSE
MEWED
MEWLS
MEYER
MEZZO

M•E••
MEEDS
MEESE
MEETS
MIENS
MNEME
MYELO
MYERS
MYEYE

M••E•
MABEL
MACED
MACES
MAGEE
MAGES
MAHER
MAKER
MAKES
MALES
MAMET
MANED
MANES
MANET
MARES
MASER
MATED
MATEO
MATER
MATES
MATEY
MAVEN
MAXED
MAXES
MAYER
MAZEL
MAZER
MAZES
MCGEE
MEDEA
MEDES
MELEE
MEMEL
MENES
MERES
METED
METER
METES
MEWED
MEYER
MIKED
MIKES
MIKEY
MILER
MILES
MIMED
MIMEO
MIMER
MIMES
MINED
MINEO
MINER
MINES
MIRED
MIRES
MISER
MITER
MITES
MIXED
MIXER
MIXES
MLLES
MODEL
MODEM
MODES
MOLES
MONEL
MONET
MONEY
MOOED
MOPED
MOPER
MOPES
MOPEY
MOREL
MORES
MOREY
MOSES
MOSEY
MOTEL
MOTES
MOTET
MOUES
MOVED
MOVER
MOVES
MOWED
MOWER
MULES
MULEY
MUREX
MUSED
MUSER
MUSES
MUTED
MUTER
MUTES
MYLES

M•••E
MACHE
MACLE
MADGE
MADRE
MAGEE
MAHRE
MAILE
MAINE
MAIZE
MALLE
MAMIE
MANSE
MAPLE
MARGE
MARIE
MARNE
MASSE
MATTE
MAUDE
MAUVE
MAXIE
MAYBE
MCGEE
MCRAE
MCVIE
MEADE
MEESE
MELEE
MERCE
MERGE
MERLE
MEROE
MESNE
METRE
MEUSE
MFUME
MIDGE
MILLE
MILNE
MINCE
MINIE
MINKE
MITRE
MNEME
MOIRE
MONDE
MONTE
MOORE
MOOSE
MORAE
MORSE
MOSHE
MOUSE
MOVIE
MOXIE
MURRE
MYEYE
MYOPE

•ME••
AMEBA
AMEER
AMEND
AMENS
AMENT
EMEER
EMEND
EMERY
OMEGA
OMENS
OMERS
SMEAR
SMELL
SMELT
SMEWS
UMEKI

•M•E•
AMBER
AMEER
AMIES
AMPED
AMVET
EMBED
EMBER
EMCEE
EMDEN
EMEER
EMMER
EMMET
IMPED
IMPEI
IMPEL
OMBER
UMBEL
UMBER
UMPED

•M••E
AMAZE
AMBLE
AMICE
AMIDE
AMINE
AMOLE
AMORE
AMPLE
AMUSE
EMCEE
EMILE
EMOTE
IMAGE
IMBUE
IMIDE
IMINE
OMBRE
SMAZE
SMILE
SMITE
SMOKE
SMOTE

••ME•
AAMES
ACMES
ADMEN
AHMED
AIMED
AIMEE
AIMER
AJMER
ARMED
ARMEE
ARMET
CAMEL
CAMEO
COMER
COMES
COMET
COMEX
CYMES
DAMES
DEMES
DIMED
DIMES
DOMED
DOMES
EAMES
ELMER
EMMER
EMMET
FAMED
FAMES
FUMED
FUMES
GAMED
GAMER
GAMES
GAMEY
GIMEL
GOMEL
GOMER
GOMEZ
HAMEL
HAMES
HEMEN
HEMET
HOMED
HOMEO
HOMER
HOMES
HOMEY
JAMES
KHMER
LAMED
LAMER
LAMES
LIMED
LIMEN
LIMES
LIMEY
LUMEN
LUMET
MAMET
MEMEL
MIMED
MIMEO
MIMER
MIMES
NAMED
NAMER
NAMES
NEMEA
NIMES
NOMEN
NUMEN
NYMET
OLMEC
POMES
RAMEE
RAMEN
RAMET
REMET
REMEX
RIMED
RIMES
ROMEO
ROMER
RUMEN
SUMER
TAMED
TAMER
TAMES
TIMED
TIMER
TIMES
TIMEX
TOMEI
TOMES
UNMET
WOMEN
YEMEN

••M•E
AIMEE
ARMEE
BOMBE
COMAE
COMBE
COMME
COMTE
CUMAE
CYMAE
DAMME
DEMME
FEMME
GIMME
HOMME
JAMIE
LEMME
MAMIE
POMME
RAMEE
RAMIE
SOMME
TEMPE

•••ME
ANIME
ARAME
BAUME
BERME
BIOME
BLAME
BLUME
BOHME
BROME
BRUME
CHIME
CLIME
COMME
CREME
CRIME
DAMME
DEMME
DISME
DROME
FEMME
FLAME
FLUME
FRAME
FROME
GETME
GIMME
GNOME
GORME
GRIME
HITME
HOMME
ITSME
JAIME
LAKME
LEMME
MFUME
MNEME
NEUME
NOTME
PALME
PLUME
POEME
POMME
PRIME
RHYME
SHAME
SLIME
SOMME
SPUME
SUEME
THEME
THYME
TORME
TRYME
WHYME

MF•••
MFUME

M•F••
MCFLY
MIFFS
MIFFY
MOFFO
MUFFS
MUFTI

M••F•
MIFFS
MIFFY
MOFFO
MUFFS

M•••F
MOTIF

•M••F
SMURF

••MF•
COMFY

M•G••
MAGDA
MAGEE
MAGES
MAGIC
MAGMA
MAGNA
MAGOG
MAGOO
MAGOT
MAGUS
MCGEE
MEGAN
MIGHT
MOGGY
MOGUL
MSGTS
MUGGS
MUGGY
MUGHO
MYGUY

M••G•
MADGE
MANGO
MANGY
MARGE
MARGO
MERGE
MIDGE
MINGS
MINGY
MOGGY
MONGO
MOOGS
MUGGS
MUGGY
MUNGO

M•••G
MAGOG
MRBIG

•M•G•
AMIGA
AMIGO
IMAGE
IMAGO
OMEGA
SMOGS

•M••G
AMONG
HMONG

M•H••
MAHAL
MAHAN
MAHDI
MAHER
MAHON
MAHRE
MEHTA
MOHAM
MOHUR

M••H•
MACHE
MACHO
MACHU
MACHY
MASHY
MATHS
MESHY
MIGHT
MINHO
MISHA
MOCHA
MOSHE
MOTHS
MOTHY
MUGHO
MUSHY
MYTHS

M•••H
MARCH
MARSH
MATCH
MICAH
MILCH
MIRTH
MITCH
MONTH
MOOCH
MORPH
MOUTH
MULCH
MUNCH
MYNAH
MYRRH

•M•H•
AMAHL
AMAHS
AMPHI
AMPHR
OMAHA

•M••H
AMISH
SMASH
SMITH
SMYTH

••M•H
HUMPH
LYMPH
NYMPH
OOMPH

MI•••
MIAMI
MIAOW
MIATA
MICAH
MICAS
MICRA
MICRO
MIDAS
MIDDY
MIDGE
MIDIS
MIDST
MIENS
MIFFS
MIFFY
MIGHT
MIKAN
MIKED
MIKES
MIKEY
MILAN
MILCH
MILER
MILES
MILKS
MILKY
MILLE
MILLI
MILLS
MILNE
MILOS
MILPA
MILTS
MILTY
MIMAS
MIMED
MIMEO
MIMER
MIMES
MIMIC
MIMSY
MINAS
MINCE
MINDS
MINDY
MINED
MINEO
MINER
MINES
MINGS
MINGY
MINHO
MINIE
MINIM
MINIS
MINKE
MINKS
MINOR
MINOS
MINOT
MINSK
MINTO
MINTS
MINTY
MINUS
MIRED
MIRES
MIRKY
MIRRO
MIRTH
MIRVS
MISDO
MISER
MISHA
MISOS
MISSA
MISSY
MISTI
MISTS
MISTY
MITCH
MITER
MITES
MITRE
MITTS
MITTY
MITZI
MIWOK
MIXED
MIXER
MIXES
MIXIN
MIXUP
MIZAR

M•I••
MAIDS
MAIDU
MAILE
MAILS
MAINE
MAINS
MAINZ
MAIZE
MBIRA
MCIII
MDIII
MEIJI
MEINY
MLIII
MMIII
MOILS
MOIRA
MOIRE
MOIST
MVIII
MXIII

M••I•
MAGIC
MALIC
MAMIE
MANIA
MANIC
MARIA
MARIE
MARIN
MARIO
MARIS
MATIN
MAVIS
MAXIE
MAXIM
MAXIS
MCCII
MCCIV
MCCIX
MCDII
MCDIV
MCDIX
MCIII
MCLII
MCLIV
MCLIX
MCMII
MCMIV
MCMIX
MCVIE
MCVII
MCXII
MCXIV
MCXIX
MDCII
MDCIV
MDCIX
MDIII
MDLII
MDLIV
MDLIX
MDVII
MDXII
MDXIV
MDXIX
MEDIA
MEDIC
MEDIT
MELIC
MERIT
MESIC
METIS
MIDIS
MIMIC
MINIE
MINIM
MINIS
MIXIN
MLIII
MLVII
MLXII
MLXIV
MLXIX
MMCII
MMCIV
MMCIX
MMDII
MMDIV
MMDIX
MMIII
MMLII
MMLIV
MMLIX
MMMII
MMMIV
MMMIX
MMVII
MMXII
MMXIV
MMXIX
MOBIL
MOTIF
MOVIE
MOXIE
MRBIG
MUCIN
MUNIS
MUSIC
MVIII
MXCII
MXCIV
MXCIX
MXIII
MXLII
MXLIV
MXLIX
MXMII
MXMIV
MXVII
MXXII
MXXIV
MXXIX
MYCIN
MYSIN

M•••I
MAHDI
MAORI
MAQUI
MARDI
MARTI
MASAI
MATRI
MCCCI
MCCII
MCCLI
MCCVI
MCCXI
MCDII
MCDLI
MCDVI
MCDXI
MCIII
MCLII
MCLVI
MCLXI
MCMII
MCMLI
MCMVI
MCMXI
MCVII
MCXCI
MCXII
MCXLI
MCXVI
MCXXI
MDCCI
MDCII
MDCLI
MDCVI
MDCXI
MDIII
MDLII
MDLVI
MDLXI
MDVII
MDXCI
MDXII
MDXLI
MDXVI
MDXXI
MEIJI
MERCI
MIAMI
MILLI
MISTI
MITZI
MLIII
MLVII
MLXII
MLXVI
MLXXI
MMCCI
MMCDI
MMCII
MMCLI
MMCMI
MMCVI
MMCXI
MMDCI
MMDII
MMDLI
MMDVI
MMDXI
MMIII
MMLII
MMLVI
MMLXI
MMMCI
MMMDI
MMMII
MMMLI
MMMVI
MMMXI
MMVII
MMXCI
MMXII
MMXLI
MMXVI
MMXXI
MUFTI
MULTI
MUNDI
MVIII
MXCII
MXCVI
MXIII
MXLII
MXLVI
MXMII
MXVII
MXXII
MXXVI
MXXXI

•MI••
AMICE
AMIDE
AMIDO
AMIES
AMIGA
AMIGO
AMINE
AMINO
AMIRS
AMISH
AMISS
AMITY
CMIII
EMILE
EMILY
EMIRS
EMITS
IMIDE
IMIDO
IMINE
IMINO
MMIII
OMITS
SMILE
SMIRK
SMITE
SMITH
SMITS
UMIAK

•M•I•
AMAIN
AMBIT
AMNIA
CMIII
CMLII
CMLIV
CMLIX
CMVII
CMXII
CMXIV
CMXIX
EMAIL
IMMIX
MMCII
MMCIV
MMCIX
MMDII
MMDIV
MMDIX
MMIII
MMLII
MMLIV
MMLIX
MMMII
MMMIV
MMMIX
MMVII
MMXII
MMXIV
MMXIX
OMNIA
SMAIL

•M••I
AMATI
AMPHI
CMIII
CMLII
CMLVI
CMLXI
CMVII
CMXCI
CMXII
CMXLI
CMXVI
CMXXI
IMPEI
MMCCI
MMCDI
MMCII
MMCLI
MMCMI
MMCVI
MMCXI
MMDCI
MMDII
MMDLI
MMDVI
MMDXI
MMIII
MMLII
MMLVI
MMLXI
MMMCI
MMMDI
MMMII
MMMLI
MMMVI
MMMXI
MMVII
MMXCI
MMXII
MMXLI
MMXVI
MMXXI
OMANI
UMEKI

••MI•
ADMIN
ADMIT
ADMIX
ARMIS
CAMIS
COMIC
COMIX
CUMIN
DEMIT
GAMIN
HEMIN
HUMID
IMMIX
IZMIR
IZMIT
JAMIE
JAMIN
LAMIA
LIMIT
MAMIE
MCMII
MCMIV
MCMIX
MIMIC
MMMII
MMMIV
MMMIX
MXMII
MXMIV
NAMIB

NUMIS
OSMIC
PAMIR
RAMIE
RAMIS
REMIT
REMIX
SEMIS
TAMIL
TIMID
TUMID
ZAMIA

••M•I
BAMBI
IAMBI
LIMBI
MCMII
MCMLI
MCMVI
MCMXI
MMMCI
MMMDI
MMMII
MMMLI
MMMVI
MMMXI
MXMII
NAMOI
NIMBI
SOMNI
TEMPI
TOMEI

•••MI
ELEMI
FERMI
MIAMI
MMCMI
NAOMI
NGAMI
NURMI
OTOMI
PRIMI
SALMI
SUOMI
SWAMI
VERMI

M•J••
MAJOR
MCJOB
MOJOS

M••J•
MEIJI

M•K••
MAKER
MAKES
MAKOS
MAKUA
MCKAY
MIKAN
MIKED
MIKES
MIKEY
MOKPO

M••K•
MARKS
MASKS
MILKS
MILKY
MINKE
MINKS
MIRKY
MOCKS
MONKS
MUCKS
MUCKY
MURKY
MUSKS
MUSKY

M•••K
MERCK
MINSK
MIWOK
MONCK
MUZAK

•M•K•
SMOKE
SMOKY
UMEKI

•M••K
AMUCK
DMARK
SMACK
SMIRK
SMOCK
UMIAK

ML•••
MLIII
MLLES
MLVII
MLXII
MLXIV
MLXIX
MLXVI
MLXXI
MLXXV
MLXXX

M•L••
MALAN
MALAR
MALAY
MALES
MALIC
MALLE
MALLS
MALMO
MALTA
MALTS
MALTY
MCLII
MCLIV
MCLIX
MCLVI
MCLXI
MCLXV
MCLXX
MDLII
MDLIV
MDLIX
MDLVI
MDLXI
MDLXV
MDLXX
MELAN
MELBA
MELDS
MELEE
MELIC
MELON
MELOS
MELTS
MELTY
MILAN
MILCH
MILER
MILES
MILKS
MILKY
MILLE
MILLI
MILLS
MILNE
MILOS
MILPA
MILTS
MILTY
MLLES
MMLII
MMLIV
MMLIX
MMLVI
MMLXI
MMLXV
MMLXX
MOLAR
MOLAS
MOLDS
MOLDY
MOLES
MOLLS
MOLLY
MOLTO
MOLTS
MULCH
MULCT
MULES
MULEY
MULLS
MULTI
MXLII
MXLIV
MXLIX
MXLVI
MYLAR
MYLES

M••L•
MACLE
MADLY
MAILE
MAILS
MALLE
MALLS
MANLY
MAPLE
MARLA
MARLO
MARLS
MARLY
MAULS
MCCLI
MCCLV
MCCLX
MCDLI
MCDLV
MCDLX
MCFLY
MCMLI
MCMLV
MCMLX
MCXLI
MCXLV
MDCLI
MDCLV
MDCLX
MDXLI
MDXLV
MEALS
MEALY
MENLO
MERLE
MERLS
MEWLS
MILLE
MILLI
MILLS
MMCLI
MMCLV
MMCLX
MMDLI
MMDLV
MMDLX
MMMLI
MMMLV
MMMLX
MMXLI
MMXLV
MOILS
MOLLS
MOLLY
MOOLA
MOULD
MOULT
MULLS
MYELO

M•••L
MABEL
MAHAL
MAZEL
MCCCL
MCCXL
MCDXL
MCMXL
MDCCL
MDCXL
MEDAL
MEMEL
MERYL
METAL
MMCCL
MMCDL
MMCML
MMCXL
MMDCL
MMDXL
MMMCL
MMMDL
MMMXL
MOBIL
MODAL
MODEL
MOGUL
MONEL
MORAL
MOREL
MOSUL
MOTEL
MURAL

•ML••
CMLII
CMLIV
CMLIX
CMLVI
CMLXI
CMLXV
CMLXX
EMLYN
MMLII
MMLIV
MMLIX
MMLVI
MMLXI
MMLXV
MMLXX

•M•L•
AMBLE
AMOLE
AMPLE
AMPLY
AMYLO
AMYLS
CMXLI
CMXLV
EMILE
EMILY
IMPLY
MMCLI
MMCLV
MMCLX
MMDLI
MMDLV
MMDLX
MMMLI
MMMLV
MMMLX
MMXLI
MMXLV
SMALL
SMALT
SMELL
SMELT
SMILE
SMOLT

•M••L
AMAHL
AMPUL
EMAIL
IMPEL
MMCCL
MMCDL
MMCML
MMCXL
MMDCL
MMDXL
MMMCL
MMMDL
MMMXL
SMAIL
SMALL
SMELL
UMBEL

••ML•
DIMLY
MCMLI
MCMLV
MCMLX
MMMLI
MMMLV
MMMLX

••M•L
CAMEL
CUMUL
GAMAL
GIMEL
GOMEL
HAMAL
HAMEL
JAMAL
KEMAL
MCMXL
MEMEL
MMMCL
MMMDL
MMMXL
TAMIL
UXMAL

•••ML
FRIML
MMCML

MM•••
MMCCC
MMCCI
MMCCL
MMCCV
MMCCX
MMCDI
MMCDL
MMCDV
MMCDX
MMCII
MMCIV
MMCIX
MMCLI
MMCLV
MMCLX
MMCMI
MMCML
MMCMV
MMCMX
MMCVI
MMCXC
MMCXI
MMCXL
MMCXV
MMCXX
MMDCC
MMDCI
MMDCL
MMDCV
MMDCX
MMDII
MMDIV
MMDIX
MMDLI
MMDLV
MMDLX
MMDVI
MMDXC
MMDXI
MMDXL
MMDXV
MMDXX
MMIII
MMLII
MMLIV
MMLIX
MMLVI
MMLXI
MMLXV
MMLXX
MMMCC
MMMCD
MMMCI
MMMCL
MMMCV
MMMCX
MMMDC
MMMDI
MMMDL
MMMDV
MMMDX
MMMII
MMMIV
MMMIX
MMMLI
MMMLV
MMMLX
MMMVI
MMMXC
MMMXI
MMMXL
MMMXV
MMMXX
MMVII
MMXCI
MMXCV
MMXII
MMXIV
MMXIX
MMXLI
MMXLV
MMXVI
MMXXI
MMXXV
MMXXX

M•M••
MAMAS
MAMBA
MAMBO
MAMET
MAMIE
MAMMA
MAMMY
MCMII
MCMIV
MCMIX
MCMLI
MCMLV
MCMLX
MCMVI
MCMXC
MCMXI
MCMXL
MCMXV
MCMXX
MEMEL
MEMOS
MIMAS
MIMED
MIMEO
MIMER
MIMES
MIMIC
MIMSY
MMMCC
MMMCD
MMMCI
MMMCL
MMMCV
MMMCX
MMMDC
MMMDI
MMMDL
MMMDV
MMMDX
MMMII
MMMIV
MMMIX
MMMLI
MMMLV
MMMLX
MMMVI
MMMXC
MMMXI
MMMXL
MMMXV
MMMXX
MOMMA
MOMMY
MOMUS
MRMOM
MUMBO
MUMMY
MUMPS
MXMII
MXMIV

M••M•
MAGMA
MALMO
MAMMA
MAMMY
MBOMU
MFUME
MIAMI
MMCMI
MMCML
MMCMV
MMCMX
MNEME
MOMMA
MOMMY
MUMMY

M•••M
MADAM
MAXIM
MECUM
MINIM
MODEM
MOHAM
MORUM
MRMOM

•MM••
AMMAN
AMMON
AMMOS
EMMER
EMMET
EMMYS
IMMIX
MMMCC
MMMCD
MMMCI
MMMCL
MMMCV
MMMCX
MMMDC
MMMDI
MMMDL
MMMDV
MMMDX
MMMII
MMMIV
MMMIX
MMMLI
MMMLV
MMMLX
MMMVI
MMMXC
MMMXI
MMMXL
MMMXV
MMMXX

•M•M•
IMAMS
MMCMI
MMCML
MMCMV
MMCMX

••MM•
COMMA
COMME
DAMME
DEMME
DUMMY
FEMME
GAMMA
GAMMY
GEMMA
GEMMY
GIMME
GUMMO
GUMMY
HAMMY
HOMME
JAMMY
JEMMY
JIMMY
LEMMA
LEMME
MAMMA
MAMMY
MOMMA
MOMMY
MUMMY
POMME
RUMMY
SAMMS
SAMMY
SIMMS
SOMME
SUMMA
TAMMY
TIMMY
TOMMY
TUMMY
YUMMY

••M•M
MRMOM

•••MM
FROMM
GRAMM
GRIMM

MN•••
MNEME

M•N••
MANCY
MANDY
MANED
MANES
MANET
MANGO
MANGY
MANIA
MANIC
MANLY
MANNA
MANNY
MANON
MANOR
MANOS
MANSE
MANTA
MENDS
MENES
MENLO
MENSA
MENUS
MINAS
MINCE
MINDS
MINDY
MINED
MINEO
MINER
MINES
MINGS
MINGY
MINHO
MINIE
MINIM
MINIS
MINKE
MINKS
MINOR
MINOS

MINOT
MINSK
MINTO
MINTS
MINTY
MINUS
MONAD
MONCK
MONDE
MONDO
MONEL
MONET
MONEY
MONGO
MONKS
MONOD
MONTE
MONTH
MONTY
MONZA
MSNBC
MUNCH
MUNDI
MUNGO
MUNIS
MUNRO
MYNAH
MYNAS

M••N•
MAGNA
MAINE
MAINS
MAINZ
MANNA
MANNY
MARNE
MAUNA
MAUND
MAYNT
MEANS
MEANT
MEANY
MEINY
MESNE
MIENS
MILNE
MOANS
MOONS
MOONY
MORNS
MOUND
MOUNT
MUONS
MYRNA

M•••N
MACON
MAHAN
MAHON
MALAN
MANON
MARIN
MASON
MATIN
MAVEN
MAYAN
MAYON
MEGAN
MELAN
MELON
MESON
MIKAN
MILAN
MIXIN
MORAN
MORON
MOURN
MUCIN
MYCIN
MYRON
MYSIN

•MN••
AMNIA
OMNIA

•M•N•
AMANA
AMEND
AMENS
AMENT
AMINE
AMINO
AMONG
EMEND
HMONG
IMINE
IMINO
OMANI
OMENS

•M••N
AMAIN
AMMAN
AMMON
EMDEN
EMLYN

••MN•
DAMNS
GYMNO
HYMNS
JUMNA
LIMNS
SOMNI

••M•N
ADMAN
ADMEN
ADMIN
AMMAN
AMMON
ATMAN
CUMIN
DAMAN
DAMON
DEMON
EAMON
ELMAN
GAMIN
HAMAN
HEMAN
HEMEN
HEMIN
HUMAN
HYMAN
JAMIN
LEMON
LIMEN
LIMON
LOMAN
LUMEN
LYMAN
LYMON
NEMAN
NOMEN
NUMEN
OSMAN
RAMAN
RAMEN
RAMON
REMAN
ROMAN
RUMEN
SIMON
TIMON
UNMAN
WOMAN
WOMEN
WOMYN
WYMAN
YEMEN
YUMAN

MO•••
MOANS
MOATS
MOBIL
MOCHA
MOCKS
MODAL
MODEL
MODEM
MODES
MODOC
MODUS
MOFFO
MOGGY
MOGUL
MOHAM
MOHUR
MOILS
MOIRA
MOIRE
MOIST
MOJOS
MOKPO
MOLAR
MOLAS
MOLDS
MOLDY
MOLES
MOLLS
MOLLY
MOLTO
MOLTS
MOMMA
MOMMY
MOMUS
MONAD
MONCK
MONDE
MONDO
MONEL
MONET
MONEY
MONGO
MONKS
MONOD
MONTE
MONTH
MONTY
MONZA
MOOCH
MOODS
MOODY
MOOED
MOOGS
MOOLA
MOONS
MOONY
MOORE
MOORS
MOORY
MOOSE
MOOTS
MOPED
MOPER
MOPES
MOPEY
MOPSY
MOPUP
MORAE
MORAL
MORAN
MORAS
MORAY
MOREL
MORES
MOREY
MORNS
MORON
MOROS
MORPH
MORRO
MORSE
MORTS
MORUM
MOSBY
MOSES
MOSEY
MOSHE
MOSSO
MOSSY
MOSUL
MOTEL
MOTES
MOTET
MOTHS
MOTHY
MOTIF
MOTOR
MOTTA
MOTTO
MOTTS
MOUES
MOULD
MOULT
MOUND
MOUNT
MOURN
MOUSE
MOUSY
MOUTH
MOVED
MOVER
MOVES
MOVIE
MOWED
MOWER
MOXIE

M•O••
MAORI
MBOMU
MEOWS
MOOCH
MOODS
MOODY
MOOED
MOOGS
MOOLA
MOONS
MOONY
MOORE
MOORS
MOORY
MOOSE
MOOTS
MUONS
MYOPE

M••O•
MACON
MAGOG
MAGOO
MAGOT
MAHON
MAJOR
MAKOS
MANON
MANOR
MANOS
MASON
MAYON
MAYOR
MCCOO
MCCOY
MCJOB
MEDOC
MELON
MELOS
MEMOS
MEROE
MESON
METOO
MIAOW
MILOS
MINOR
MINOS
MINOT
MISOS
MIWOK
MODOC
MOJOS
MONOD
MORON
MOROS
MOTOR
MRMOM
MSDOS
MYRON

M•••O
MACAO
MACHO
MACRO
MAGOO
MALMO
MAMBO
MANGO
MARCO
MARGO
MARIO
MARLO
MATEO
MATRO
MATZO
MAYPO
MCCOO
MENLO
METOO
METRO
MEZZO
MICRO
MIMEO
MINEO
MINHO
MINTO
MIRRO
MISDO
MOFFO
MOKPO
MOLTO
MONDO
MONGO
MORRO
MOSSO
MOTTO
MUCRO
MUGHO
MUMBO
MUNGO
MUNRO
MYELO

•MO••
AMOCO
AMOLE
AMONG
AMORE
AMORT
AMORY
AMOUR
EMORY
EMOTE
HMONG
SMOCK
SMOGS
SMOKE
SMOKY
SMOLT
SMOOT
SMOTE

•M•O•
AMBOS
AMBOY
AMMON
AMMOS
SMOOT
UMBOS

•M••O
AMADO
AMATO
AMIDO
AMIGO
AMINO
AMOCO
AMYLO
IMAGO
IMIDO
IMINO

••MO•
AMMON
AMMOS
ARMOR
ATMOS
CAMOS
DAMON
DEMOB
DEMON
DEMOS
EAMON
ELMOS
GAMOW
GEMOT
HUMOR
LEMON
LIMON
LIMOS
LYMON
MEMOS
MRMOM
NAMOI
NIMOY
OLMOS
POMOS
RAMON
RAMOS
REMOP
REMOW
RUMOR
SAMOA
SAMOS
SIMON
TIMON
TIMOR
VAMOS

••M•O
AIMTO
CAMEO
CAMPO
COMBO
COMPO
DUMBO
FEMTO
GUMBO
GUMMO
GYMNO
HOMEO
JUMBO
KIMPO
LIMBO
MAMBO
MIMEO
MUMBO
RAMBO
ROMEO
TAMBO
TEMPO

•••MO
ALAMO
ANEMO
BROMO
COSMO
CUOMO
DERMO
DUOMO
GIZMO
GUMMO
HAEMO
MALMO
OROMO
PISMO
PRIMO
PROMO
SCHMO
SIXMO
SLOMO
WHAMO

M•P••
MAPLE
MOPED
MOPER
MOPES
MOPEY
MOPSY
MOPUP

M••P•
MAYPO
MILPA
MOKPO
MORPH
MUMPS
MYOPE

M•••P
MIXUP
MOPUP

•MP••
AMPAS
AMPED
AMPHI
AMPHR
AMPLE
AMPLY
AMPUL
EMPTY
IMPED
IMPEI
IMPEL
IMPLY
UMPED

•M•P•
AMAPA

••MP•
BUMPS
BUMPY
CAMPO
CAMPS
CAMPY
COMPO
COMPS
DAMPS
DUMPS
DUMPY
GAMPS
GIMPS
GIMPY
HEMPS
HUMPH
HUMPS
HUMPY
JUMPS
JUMPY
KEMPS
KEMPT
KIMPO
LAMPS
LIMPS
LUMPS
LUMPY
LYMPH
MUMPS
NAMPA
NYMPH
OOMPH
PAMPA
PUMPS
RAMPS
ROMPS
RUMPS
SAMPS
SIMPS
SUMPS
TAMPA
TAMPS
TEMPE
TEMPI
TEMPO
TEMPS
TEMPT
TUMPS
VAMPS
WIMPS
WIMPY
YAMPA

••M•P
DAMUP
GUMUP
JAMUP
REMAP
REMOP
SUMUP

•••MP
BLIMP
CHAMP
CHIMP
CHOMP
CHUMP
CLAMP
CLOMP
CLUMP
CRAMP
CRIMP
CRUMP
FRUMP
GRAMP
GRUMP
PLUMP
PRIMP
SCAMP
SHEMP
SKIMP
SLUMP
STAMP
STOMP
STUMP
SWAMP
THUMP
TRAMP
TROMP
TRUMP
WHOMP

M•Q••
MAQUI

MR•••
MRBIG
MRMOM

M•R••
MARAS
MARAT
MARCH
MARCO
MARCY
MARDI
MARES
MARGE
MARGO
MARIA
MARIE
MARIN
MARIO
MARIS
MARKS
MARLA
MARLO
MARLS
MARLY
MARNE
MARRY
MARSH
MARTA
MARTI
MARTS
MARTY
MARVY
MARYS
MCRAE
MERCE
MERCI
MERCK
MERCY
MERES
MERGE
MERIT
MERLE
MERLS
MEROE
MERRY
MERTZ
MERYL
MIRED
MIRES
MIRKY
MIRRO
MIRTH

MIRVS
MORAE
MORAL
MORAN
MORAS
MORAY
MOREL
MORES
MOREY
MORNS
MORON
MOROS
MORPH
MORRO
MORSE
MORTS
MORUM
MURAL
MURAT
MUREX
MURKY
MURRA
MURRE
MYRNA
MYRON
MYRRH

M••R•
MACRO
MADRE
MAHRE
MAORI
MARRY
MATRI
MATRO
MAURY
MBIRA
MEARA
MERRY
METRE
METRO
METRY
MICRA
MICRO
MIRRO
MITRE
MOIRA
MOIRE
MOORE
MOORS
MOORY
MORRO
MOURN
MUCRO
MUDRA
MUNRO
MURRA
MURRE
MYERS
MYRRH

M•••R
MAHER
MAJOR
MAKER
MALAR
MANOR
MASER
MASUR
MATER
MAYER
MAYOR
MAZER
METER
MEYER
MILER
MIMER
MINER
MINOR
MISER
MITER
MIXER
MIZAR
MOHUR
MOLAR
MOPER
MOTOR
MOVER
MOWER
MUSER
MUTER
MYLAR

•M•R•
AMARA
AMBRY
AMIRS
AMORE
AMORT
AMORY
CMDRS
DMARK
EMERY
EMIRS
EMORY
KMART
OMARR
OMBRE
OMERS
SMART
SMIRK
SMURF
UMBRA

•M••R
AMBER
AMEER
AMOUR
AMPHR
EMBAR
EMBER
EMEER
EMMER
OMARR
OMBER
SMEAR
UMBER

••MR•
CAMRY
CYMRY

••M•R
AIMER
AJMER
ARMOR
COMER
DAMAR
DEMUR
ELMER
EMMER
FEMUR
GAMER
GOMER
HOMER
HUMOR
IZMIR
KHMER
LAMAR
LAMER
LEMUR
MIMER
NAMER
NAMUR
PAMIR
RAMAR
ROMER
RUMOR
SAMAR
SUMER
TAMER
TIMER
TIMOR

MS•••
MSDOS
MSGTS
MSNBC

M•S••
MASAI
MASER
MASHY
MASKS
MASON
MASSE
MASSY
MASTS
MASUR
MESAS
MESHY
MESIC
MESNE
MESON
MESSY
MESTA
MISDO
MISER
MISHA
MISOS
MISSA
MISSY
MISTI
MISTS
MISTY
MOSBY
MOSES
MOSEY
MOSHE
MOSSO
MOSSY
MOSUL
MUSCA
MUSED
MUSER
MUSES
MUSHY
MUSIC
MUSKS
MUSKY
MUSSY
MUSTS
MUSTY
MYSIN

M••S•
MANSE
MARSH
MASSE
MASSY
MATSU
MAYST
MEESE
MENSA
MESSY
MEUSE
MIDST
MIMSY
MINSK
MISSA
MISSY
MOIST
MOOSE
MOPSY
MORSE
MOSSO
MOSSY
MOUSE
MOUSY
MUSSY

M•••S
MACES
MACYS
MAGES
MAGUS
MAIDS
MAILS
MAINS
MAKES
MAKOS
MALES
MALLS
MALTS
MAMAS
MANES
MANOS
MARAS
MARES
MARIS
MARKS
MARLS
MARTS
MARYS
MASKS
MASTS
MATES
MATHS
MAULS
MAVIS
MAXES
MAXIS
MAYAS
MAZES
MEADS
MEALS
MEANS
MEATS
MEDES
MEEDS
MEETS
MELDS
MELOS
MELTS
MEMOS
MENDS
MENES
MENUS
MEOWS
MERES
MERLS
MESAS
METES
METIS
MEWLS
MICAS
MIDAS
MIDIS
MIENS
MIFFS
MIKES
MILES
MILKS
MILLS
MILOS
MILTS
MIMAS
MIMES
MINAS
MINDS
MINES
MINGS
MINIS
MINKS
MINOS
MINTS
MINUS
MIRES
MIRVS
MISOS
MISTS
MITES
MITTS
MIXES
MLLES
MOANS
MOATS
MOCKS
MODES
MODUS
MOILS
MOJOS
MOLAS
MOLDS
MOLES
MOLLS
MOLTS
MOMUS
MONKS
MOODS
MOOGS
MOONS
MOORS
MOOTS
MOPES
MORAS
MORES
MORNS
MOROS
MORTS
MOSES
MOTES
MOTHS
MOTTS
MOUES
MOVES
MSDOS
MSGTS
MUCKS
MUFFS
MUGGS
MULES
MULLS
MUMPS
MUNIS
MUONS
MUSES
MUSKS
MUSTS
MUTES
MUTTS
MYERS
MYLES
MYNAS
MYTHS

•M•S•
AMASS
AMISH
AMISS
AMUSE
OMASA
SMASH

•M••S
AMAHS
AMASS
AMBOS
AMENS
AMIES
AMIRS
AMISS
AMMOS
AMPAS
AMYLS
CMDRS
EMIRS
EMITS
EMMYS
GMATS
IMAMS
OMENS
OMERS
OMITS
SMEWS
SMITS
SMOGS
SMUTS
UMBOS
YMCAS

••MS•
MIMSY

••M•S
AAMES
ACMES
AMMOS
ARMIS
ATMOS
BEMAS
BOMBS
BUMPS
CAMIS
CAMOS
CAMPS
CAMUS
COMAS
COMBS
COMES
COMPS
COMUS
CYMAS
CYMES
DAMES
DAMNS
DAMPS
DEMES
DEMOS
DIMES
DOMES
DUMAS
DUMBS
DUMPS
EAMES
ELMOS
EMMYS
FAMES
FUMES
GAMES
GAMPS
GIMPS
HAMES
HEMPS
HOMES
HUMPS
HUMUS
HYMNS
IAMBS
JAMBS
JAMES
JUMPS
KEMPS
LAMAS
LAMBS
LAMES
LAMPS
LIMAS
LIMBS
LIMES
LIMNS
LIMOS
LIMPS
LUMPS
MAMAS
MEMOS
MIMAS
MIMES
MOMUS
MUMPS
NAMES
NIMES
NUMBS
NUMIS
OLMOS
PIMAS
POMES
POMOS
PUMAS
PUMPS
RAMIS
RAMOS
RAMPS
REMUS
RIMES
ROMPS
RUMPS
SAMMS
SAMOS
SAMPS
SEMIS
SIMMS
SIMPS
SOMAS
SUMPS
TAMES
TAMPS
TEMPS
TIMES
TOMES
TUMPS
VAMOS
VAMPS
WIMPS
YUMAS

•••MS
ADAMS
ALUMS
ARUMS
ATOMS
BALMS
BARMS
BEAMS
BERMS
BOOMS
BRIMS
CALMS
CHUMS
CLAMS
CORMS
CRAMS
CULMS
DEEMS
DIEMS
DOOMS
DORMS
DRAMS
DRUMS
EDAMS
EXAMS
FARMS
FILMS
FIRMS
FLAMS
FOAMS
FORMS
GAUMS
GERMS
GEUMS
GLIMS
GLOMS
GRAMS
HALMS
HARMS
HELMS
HERMS
HOLMS
HYAMS
ICBMS
IMAMS
ITEMS
LOAMS
LOOMS
NORMS
PALMS
PERMS
PLUMS
POEMS
PRAMS
PRIMS
PROMS
REAMS
REIMS
ROAMS
ROOMS
SAMMS
SCAMS
SCUMS
SEAMS
SEEMS
SHAMS
SHIMS
SIMMS
SKIMS
SLAMS
SLIMS
SLUMS
SPAMS
STEMS
STUMS
SWIMS
TEAMS
TEEMS
TERMS
THEMS
TRAMS
TRIMS
WARMS
WEEMS
WHAMS
WHIMS
WORMS
ZOOMS

M•T••
MATCH
MATED
MATEO
MATER
MATES
MATEY
MATHS
MATIN
MATRI
MATRO
MATSU
MATTE
MATZO
METAL
METED
METER
METES
METIS
METOO
METRE
METRO
METRY
MITCH
MITER
MITES
MITRE
MITTS
MITTY
MITZI
MOTEL
MOTES
MOTET
MOTHS
MOTHY
MOTIF
MOTOR
MOTTA
MOTTO
MOTTS
MUTED
MUTER
MUTES
MUTTS
MYTHS

M••T•
MALTA
MALTS
MALTY
MANTA
MARTA
MARTI
MARTS
MARTY
MASTS
MATTE
MEATS
MEATY
MEETS
MEHTA
MELTS
MELTY
MERTZ
MESTA
MIATA
MILTS
MILTY
MINTO
MINTS
MINTY
MIRTH
MISTI
MISTS
MISTY
MITTS
MITTY
MOATS
MOLTO
MOLTS
MONTE
MONTH
MONTY
MOOTS
MORTS
MOTTA
MOTTO
MOTTS

MOUTH
MSGTS
MUFTI
MULTI
MUSTS
MUSTY
MUTTS

M•••T
MAGOT
MAMET
MANET
MARAT
MAYNT
MAYST
MEANT
MEDIT
MERIT
MIDST
MIGHT
MINOT
MOIST
MONET
MOTET
MOULT
MOUNT
MULCT
MURAT

•M•T•
AMATI
AMATO
AMITY
EMITS
EMOTE
EMPTY
GMATS
OMITS
SMITE
SMITH
SMITS
SMOTE
SMUTS
SMYTH

•M••T
AMBIT
AMENT
AMORT
AMVET
EMMET
KMART
SMALT
SMART
SMELT
SMOLT
SMOOT

••MT•
AIMTO
COMTE
FEMTO

••M•T
ADMIT
AIMAT
ARMET
COMET
DEMIT
EMMET
GAMUT
GEMOT
HEMET
IZMIT
KEMPT
LEMAT
LIMIT
LUMET
MAMET
NEMAT
NYMET
RAMET
REMET
REMIT
TEMPT
UNMET

•••MT
KLIMT

MU•••
MUCIN
MUCKS
MUCKY
MUCRO
MUDDY
MUDRA
MUFFS
MUFTI
MUGGS
MUGGY
MUGHO
MULCH
MULCT
MULES
MULEY
MULLS
MULTI
MUMBO
MUMMY
MUMPS
MUNCH
MUNDI
MUNGO
MUNIS
MUNRO
MUONS
MURAL
MURAT
MUREX
MURKY
MURRA
MURRE
MUSCA
MUSED
MUSER
MUSES
MUSHY
MUSIC
MUSKS
MUSKY
MUSSY
MUSTS
MUSTY
MUTED
MUTER
MUTES
MUTTS
MUZAK
MUZZY

M•U••
MAUDE
MAULS
MAUNA
MAUND
MAURY
MAUVE
MEUSE
MFUME
MOUES
MOULD
MOULT
MOUND
MOUNT
MOURN
MOUSE
MOUSY
MOUTH

M••U•
MAGUS
MAKUA
MAQUI
MASUR
MECUM
MENUS
MINUS
MIXUP
MODUS
MOGUL
MOHUR
MOMUS
MOPUP
MORUM
MOSUL
MYGUY

M•••U
MACHU
MAIDU
MATSU
MBOMU

•MU••
AMUCK
AMUSE
SMURF
SMUTS

•M•U•
AMOUR
AMPUL
IMBUE

••MU•
CAMUS
COMUS
CUMUL
DAMUP
DEMUR
FEMUR
GAMUT
GUMUP
HUMUS
JAMUP
LEMUR
MOMUS
NAMUR
REMUS
SUMUP

•••MU
ISAMU
MBOMU
SHAMU

MV•••
MVIII

M•V••
MAVEN
MAVIS
MCVIE
MCVII
MDVII
MLVII
MMVII
MOVED
MOVER
MOVES
MOVIE
MXVII

M••V•
MARVY
MAUVE
MCCVI
MCDVI
MCLVI
MCMVI
MCXVI
MDCVI
MDLVI
MDXVI
MIRVS
MLXVI
MMCVI
MMDVI
MMLVI
MMMVI
MMXVI
MXCVI
MXLVI
MXXVI

M•••V
MCCCV
MCCIV
MCCLV
MCCXV
MCDIV
MCDLV
MCDXV
MCLIV
MCLXV
MCMIV
MCMLV
MCMXV
MCXCV
MCXIV
MCXLV
MCXXV
MDCCV
MDCIV
MDCLV
MDCXV
MDLIV
MDLXV
MDXCV
MDXIV
MDXLV
MDXXV
MLXIV
MLXXV
MMCCV
MMCDV
MMCIV
MMCLV
MMCMV
MMCXV
MMDCV
MMDIV
MMDLV
MMDXV
MMLIV
MMLXV
MMMCV
MMMDV
MMMIV
MMMLV
MMMXV
MMXCV
MMXIV
MMXLV
MMXXV
MXCIV
MXLIV
MXMIV
MXXIV
MXXXV

•MV••
AMVET
CMVII
MMVII

•M•V•
CMLVI
CMXVI
MMCVI
MMDVI
MMLVI
MMMVI
MMXVI

•M••V
CMLIV
CMLXV
CMXCV
CMXIV
CMXLV
CMXXV
MMCCV
MMCDV
MMCIV
MMCLV
MMCMV
MMCXV
MMDCV
MMDIV
MMDLV
MMDXV
MMLIV
MMLXV
MMMCV
MMMDV
MMMIV
MMMLV
MMMXV
MMXCV
MMXIV
MMXLV
MMXXV

••MV•
MCMVI
MMMVI

••M•V
MCMIV
MCMLV
MCMXV
MMMCV
MMMDV
MMMIV
MMMLV
MMMXV
MXMIV

•••MV
MMCMV

M•W••
MEWED
MEWLS
MIWOK
MOWED
MOWER
MYWAY

M••W•
MEOWS

M•••W
MACAW
MIAOW

•MW••
AMWAY

•M•W•
SMEWS

••M•W
GAMOW
REMOW

MX•••
MXCII
MXCIV
MXCIX
MXCVI
MXIII
MXLII
MXLIV
MXLIX
MXLVI
MXMII
MXMIV
MXVII
MXXII
MXXIV
MXXIX
MXXVI
MXXXI
MXXXV

M•X••
MAXED
MAXES
MAXIE
MAXIM
MAXIS
MCXCI
MCXCV
MCXII
MCXIV
MCXIX
MCXLI
MCXLV
MCXVI
MCXXI
MCXXV
MCXXX
MDXCI
MDXCV
MDXII
MDXIV
MDXIX
MDXLI
MDXLV
MDXVI
MDXXI
MDXXV
MDXXX
MIXED
MIXER
MIXES
MIXIN
MIXUP
MLXII
MLXIV
MLXIX
MLXVI
MLXXI
MLXXV
MLXXX
MMXCI
MMXCV
MMXII
MMXIV
MMXIX
MMXLI
MMXLV
MMXVI
MMXXI
MMXXV
MMXXX
MOXIE
MXXII
MXXIV
MXXIX
MXXVI
MXXXI
MXXXV

M••X•
MCCXC
MCCXI
MCCXL
MCCXV
MCCXX
MCDXC
MCDXI
MCDXL
MCDXV
MCDXX
MCLXI
MCLXV
MCLXX
MCMXC
MCMXI
MCMXL
MCMXV
MCMXX
MCXXI
MCXXV
MCXXX
MDCXC
MDCXI
MDCXL
MDCXV
MDCXX
MDLXI
MDLXV
MDLXX
MDXXI
MDXXV
MDXXX
MLXXI
MLXXV
MLXXX
MMCXC
MMCXI
MMCXL
MMCXV
MMCXX
MMDXC
MMDXI
MMDXL
MMDXV
MMDXX
MMLXI
MMLXV
MMLXX
MMMXC
MMMXI
MMMXL
MMMXV
MMMXX
MMXXI
MMXXV
MMXXX
MXXXI
MXXXV

M•••X
MCCCX
MCCIX
MCCLX
MCCXX
MCDIX
MCDLX
MCDXX
MCLIX
MCLXX
MCMIX
MCMLX
MCMXX
MCXIX
MCXXX
MDCCX
MDCIX
MDCLX
MDCXX
MDLIX
MDLXX
MDXIX
MDXXX
MLXIX
MLXXX
MMCCX
MMCDX
MMCIX
MMCLX
MMCMX
MMCXX
MMDCX
MMDIX
MMDLX
MMDXX
MMLIX
MMLXX
MMMCX
MMMDX
MMMIX
MMMLX
MMMXX
MMXIX
MMXXX
MUREX
MXCIX
MXLIX
MXXIX

•MX••
CMXCI
CMXCV
CMXII
CMXIV
CMXIX
CMXLI
CMXLV
CMXVI
CMXXI
CMXXV
CMXXX
MMXCI
MMXCV
MMXII
MMXIV
MMXIX
MMXLI
MMXLV
MMXVI
MMXXI
MMXXV
MMXXX

•M•X•
CMLXI
CMLXV
CMLXX
CMXXI
CMXXV
CMXXX
MMCXC
MMCXI
MMCXL
MMCXV
MMCXX
MMDXC
MMDXI
MMDXL
MMDXV
MMDXX
MMLXI
MMLXV
MMLXX
MMMXC
MMMXI
MMMXL
MMMXV
MMMXX
MMXXI
MMXXV
MMXXX

•M••X
CMLIX
CMLXX
CMXIX
CMXXX
IMMIX
MMCCX
MMCDX
MMCIX
MMCLX
MMCMX
MMCXX
MMDCX
MMDIX
MMDLX
MMDXX
MMLIX
MMLXX
MMMCX
MMMDX
MMMIX
MMMLX
MMMXX
MMXIX
MMXXX

••MX•
MCMXC
MCMXI
MCMXL
MCMXV
MCMXX
MMMXC
MMMXI
MMMXL
MMMXV
MMMXX

••M•X
ADMIX
COMEX
COMIX
IMMIX
LOMAX
MCMIX
MCMLX
MCMXX
MMMCX
MMMDX
MMMIX
MMMLX
MMMXX
REMEX
REMIX
TIMEX

•••MX
MMCMX

MY•••
MYCIN
MYELO
MYERS
MYEYE
MYGUY
MYLAR
MYLES
MYNAH
MYNAS
MYOPE
MYRNA
MYRON
MYRRH
MYSIN
MYTHS
MYWAY

M•Y••
MAYAN
MAYAS
MAYBE
MAYER
MAYNT
MAYON
MAYOR
MAYPO
MAYST
MEYER

M••Y•
MACYS
MARYS
MERYL
MYEYE

M•••Y
MACHY
MADLY
MALAY
MALTY
MAMMY
MANCY
MANDY
MANGY
MANLY
MANNY
MARCY
MARLY
MARRY
MARTY
MARVY
MASHY
MASSY
MATEY
MAURY
MCCOY
MCFLY
MCKAY
MEALY
MEANY
MEATY
MEINY
MELTY
MERCY
MERRY
MESHY
MESSY
METRY
MIDDY
MIFFY
MIKEY
MILKY
MILTY
MIMSY
MINDY
MINGY
MINTY
MIRKY
MISSY
MISTY
MITTY
MOGGY
MOLDY
MOLLY
MOMMY
MONEY
MONTY
MOODY
MOONY
MOORY
MOPEY
MOPSY
MORAY
MOREY
MOSBY
MOSEY
MOSSY
MOTHY
MOUSY
MUCKY
MUDDY
MUGGY
MULEY
MUMMY
MURKY
MUSHY
MUSKY
MUSSY
MUSTY
MUZZY
MYGUY
MYWAY

•MY••
AMYLO
AMYLS
SMYTH

•M•Y•
EMLYN
EMMYS

•M••Y
AMBOY
AMBRY
AMITY
AMORY
AMPLY
AMWAY
EMBAY
EMERY
EMILY
EMORY
EMPTY
IMPLY
SMOKY

••MY•
EMMYS
WOMYN

••M•Y
ALMAY
BUMPY
CAMAY
CAMPY
CAMRY
COMFY
CYMRY
DIMLY
DUMMY
DUMPY
GAMAY
GAMEY
GAMMY
GEMMY
GIMPY
GUMBY
GUMMY
HAMMY
HOMEY
HUMPY
JAMMY
JEMMY
JIMMY
JUMPY
LEMAY
LIMEY
LUMPY
MAMMY
MIMSY
MOMMY
MUMMY
NAMBY
NIMBY
NIMOY
PAMBY
RUMMY
SAMMY
TAMMY
TIMMY
TOMMY
TUMMY
WIMPY
YUMMY

•••MY
ANOMY
ATOMY
BALMY
BARMY
BEAMY
BOOMY
DUMMY
ENEMY
FILMY
FLAMY
FOAMY
GAMMY
GEMMY
GERMY
GRIMY
GUMMY
HAMMY
JAMMY
JEMMY
JIMMY
LOAMY
MAMMY
MOMMY
MUMMY
PALMY
PLUMY
PYGMY
ROOMY
RUMMY
SAMMY
SEAMY
SLIMY
SPUMY
STYMY
TAMMY
THYMY
TIMMY
TOMMY
TUMMY
WORMY
YUMMY

M•Z••
MAZDA
MAZEL
MAZER
MAZES
MEZZO
MIZAR
MUZAK
MUZZY

M••Z•
MAIZE
MATZO
MEZZO
MITZI
MONZA
MUZZY

M•••Z
MAINZ
MERTZ

•M•Z•
AMAZE
SMAZE

••M•Z
GOMEZ

NA•••
NAACP
NABES
NABOB
NACHO
NACHT
NACRE
NADER
NADIA
NADIR
NADJA
NAFTA
NAGEL
NAGGY
NAHUA
NAHUM
NAIAD
NAILS
NAINA
NAIRA
NAIRN
NAISH
NAIVE
NAKED
NALDI
NAMBY
NAMED
NAMER
NAMES
NAMIB
NAMOI
NAMPA
NAMUR
NANAK
NANAS
NANCY
NANNA
NANNY
NAOMI
NAPES
NAPPE
NAPPY
NARAS
NARCO
NARCS
NARDS
NARES
NAREW
NARIS
NARKS
NASAL
NASBY
NASHE
NASTY
NATAL
NATCH
NATTY
NAURU
NAVAL
NAVEL
NAVES
NAVIG
NAVVY
NAWAB
NAXOS

N•A••
NAACP
NEALE
NEAPS
NEARS
NEATH
NEATO
NEATS
NGAIO
NGAMI
NOAHS
NYACK
NYALA
NYASA

N••A•
NAIAD
NANAK
NANAS
NARAS
NASAL
NATAL
NAVAL
NAWAB
NEMAN
NEMAT
NEPAL
NICAD
NINAS
NIPAS
NIPAT
NISAN
NIVAL
NIZAM
NOCAL
NODAL
NOFAT
NOLAN
NOMAD
NOPAL
NOPAR
NORAD
NORAH
NOVAE
NOVAK
NOVAS
NOWAY
NUGAE

N•••A
NADIA
NADJA
NAFTA
NAHUA
NAINA
NAIRA
NAMPA
NANNA
NDOLA
NEMEA
NINJA
NORIA
NORMA
NUBIA
NUCHA
NYALA
NYASA

•NA••
ANAIS
DNASE
ENACT
ENATE
GNARL
GNARS
GNASH
GNATS
GNAWS
INALL
INANE
INAPT
INARI
INAWE
KNACK
KNAPS
KNARS
KNAVE
ONAIR
ONATE
RNASE
SNACK
SNAFU
SNAGS
SNAIL
SNAKE
SNAKY
SNAPS
SNARE
SNARK
SNARL
SNATH
UNAPT
UNARM
UNAUS

•N•A•
ANEAR
ANNAL
ANNAM
ANNAN
ANOAS
ANSAE
ANTAE
ANTAL
ANTAS
ANWAR
ANZAC
ENIAC
ENLAI
INBAD
INCAN
INCAS
INLAW
INLAY
KNEAD
ONEAL
ONEAM
ONLAY
ONTAP
SNEAD
SNEAK
UNBAR
UNCAP
UNCAS
UNJAM
UNLAY
UNMAN
UNSAY

•N••A
ANIMA
ANITA
ANTRA
CNIDA
ENNEA
ENOLA
ENTIA
INDIA
INDRA
INFRA
INTRA
ONEGA
SNEVA
UNRRA

••NA•
ANNAL
ANNAM
ANNAN
ARNAZ
BANAL
BANAT
BINAL
CANAD
CANAL
CONAN
CUNAS
DANAE
DINAH
DINAR
DONAS
DONAT
DONAU
ETNAS
FINAL
HENAN
HONAN
HUNAN
IXNAY
JONAH
JONAS
KENAI
KINAS
LANAI
LUNAR
MINAS
MONAD
MYNAH
MYNAS
NANAK
NANAS
NINAS
PANAM
PANAY
PENAL
PUNAS
RANAT
RENAL
RENAN
RUNAT
SANAA
SENAT
SINAI
SONAR
TENAM
TONAL
TUNAS
TYNAN
ULNAE
ULNAS
VENAE
VENAL
VINAS
ZONAL

••N•A
AMNIA
APNEA
BANDA
CANEA
CANNA
CONGA
DANZA
DONNA
ENNEA
FANTA
FINCA
FONDA
GENOA
GENUA
GINZA
GONNA
GUNGA
HANNA
HANSA
HENNA
HONDA
IONIA
JUNTA
KANGA
KANSA
KENYA
KINDA
LANKA
LANZA
LENYA
LINDA
LONGA
LYNDA
MANIA
MANNA
MANTA
MENSA
MONZA
NANNA
NINJA
OMNIA
PANDA
PANGA
PANZA
PENNA
PENTA
PENZA
PINNA
PINTA
PINZA
PONCA
PUNTA
QANDA
RENTA
SANAA
SANKA
SANTA
SENNA
SONIA
SONJA
SONYA
SUNDA
SUNNA
TANKA
TANYA
TONGA
TONKA
TONYA
UINTA
VANNA
VANYA
VENDA
WANDA
WANNA
XENIA
YENTA
ZENDA

•••NA
ADANA
AETNA
AGANA
AGENA
ALANA
AMANA
ARENA
ASANA
AVENA
BUENA
BWANA
CANNA
CHINA
DESNA
DIANA
DONNA
DRINA
DVINA
EDINA
ELENA
FAUNA
FIONA
FRENA
GEENA
GHANA
GONNA
HANNA
HENNA
HYENA
ILONA
IPANA
IRINA
IVANA
JUMNA
KRONA
LEONA
LIANA
LORNA
MAGNA
MANNA
MAUNA
MYRNA
NAINA
NANNA
PATNA
PENNA
PINNA
PLENA
POONA
REINA
RUANA
SAUNA
SCENA
SEHNA
SENNA
SHANA
SIENA
SUNNA
TEENA
VANNA
VARNA
VIRNA
WANNA

NB•••
NBCTV

N•B••
NABES
NABOB
NOBBY

NOBEL
NOBID
NOBIS
NOBLE
NOBLY
NUBBY
NUBIA

N••B•
NAMBY
NASBY
NIMBI
NIMBY
NIOBE
NOBBY
NUBBY
NUMBS

N•••B
NABOB
NAMIB
NAWAB

•NB••
INBAD
INBED
INBIG
INBOX
UNBAR
UNBID
UNBOX

•N•B•
KNOBS
SNOBS
SNUBS

••NB•
CANBY
MSNBC

••N•B
BANDB
DENEB
RANDB

•••NB
PLANB

N•C••
NACHO
NACHT
NACRE
NBCTV
NECKS
NICAD
NICER
NICHE
NICKS
NICOL
NOCAL
NOCKS
NOCTI
NUCHA

N••C•
NAACP
NANCY
NARCO
NARCS
NATCH
NIECE
NONCE
NOSCE
NOTCH
NYACK

•NC••
ANCON
ENCYC
INCAN
INCAS
INCOG
INCUR
INCUS
ONCLE
ONCUE
UNCAP
UNCAS
UNCLE
UNCUT

•N•C•
ENACT
ENOCH
KNACK
KNICK
KNOCK
ONICE
SNACK
SNICK
SNUCK
VNECK

•N••C
ANTIC
ANZAC
ENCYC
ENIAC
INDIC

••NC•
BANCO
BANCS
BENCH
BONCE
BUNCH
CENCI
CINCH
CINCO
CONCH
DANCE
DANCY
DUNCE
FANCY
FENCE
FINCA
FINCH
HENCE
HENCH
HUNCH
JUNCO
KENCH
LANCE
LUNCH
LYNCH
MANCY
MINCE
MONCK
MUNCH
NANCY
NONCE
OUNCE
PENCE
PINCE
PINCH
PONCA
PONCE
PONCH
PUNCH
RANCH
SINCE
SYNCS
TENCH
TINCT
VANCE
VINCE
VINCI
WENCH
WINCE
WINCH
ZINCS
ZINCY

••N•C
CONIC
CYNIC
GENIC
IONIC
MANIC
MSNBC
PANIC
PUNIC
RUNIC
SONIC
TONIC
TUNIC
ZENIC

•••NC
BLANC
BRONC
FRANC

ND•••
NDOLA

N•D••
NADER
NADIA
NADIR
NADJA
NEDDY
NIDES
NIDRE
NIDUS
NODAL
NODDY
NODES
NODOZ
NODUS
NUDER
NUDES
NUDGE

N••D•
NALDI
NARDS
NEDDY
NEEDS
NEEDY
NERDS
NERDY
NODDY

N•••D
NAIAD
NAKED
NAMED
NEFUD
NICAD
NIXED
NOBID
NOEND
NOMAD
NORAD
NOSED
NOTED
NUKED

•ND••
ANDES
ANDIE
ANDOR
ANDRE
ANDRO
ANDRY
ANDUP
ENDED
ENDER
ENDON
ENDOR
ENDOW
ENDUE
ENDUP
INDEF
INDEX
INDIA
INDIC
INDIE
INDIO
INDIV
INDRA
INDRI
INDUS
ONDIT
UNDER
UNDID
UNDUE

•N•D•
ANODE
CNIDA
SNIDE

•N••D
ANTED
ENDED
INBAD
INBED
INKED
KNEAD
KNEED
ONEND
SNEAD
SNEED
SNERD
SNOOD
UNBID
UNDID
UNFED
UNLED
UNWED

••ND•
AANDE
AANDM
BANDA
BANDB
BANDO
BANDS
BANDW
BANDY
BENDS
BENDY
BINDS
BONDI
BONDS
BUNDS
BUNDT
BUNDY
CANDO
CANDW
CANDY
CINDY
CONDE
CONDO
CYNDI
DANDY
DENDR
DINDY
DONDI
FENDS
FINDS
FONDA
FONDS
FONDU
FUNDS
FUNDY
GANDY
GONDI
GONDS
HANDS
HANDY
HINDI
HINDS
HINDU
HONDA
HONDO
KANDY
KENDO
KINDA
KINDS
LANDI
LANDO
LANDS
LENDL
LENDS
LINDA
LINDO
LINDY
LUNDI
LUNDY
LYNDA
LYNDE
MANDY
MENDS
MINDS
MINDY
MONDE
MONDO
MUNDI
PANDA
PANDL
PENDS
PONDS
QANDA
RANDB
RANDD
RANDI
RANDR
RANDS
RANDY
RENDS
RINDS
RINDY
RONDO
SANDE
SANDH
SANDL
SANDS
SANDY
SENDS
SONDE
SUNDA
TANDE
TANDY
TENDS
TONDI
TONDO
VENDA
VENDS
WANDA
WANDS
WENDS
WENDT
WENDY
WINDS
WINDY
ZENDA
ZENDO
ZENDS

••N•D
AWNED
BONED
CANAD
CANED
CANID
CONTD
DINED
FINED
HONED
LINED
MANED
MINED
MONAD
MONOD
OWNED
PANED
PINED
RANDD
RANID
SYNOD
TINED
TONED
TUNED
VINED
WANED
WINED
ZONED

•••ND
ABEND
ALAND
AMEND
BLAND
BLEND
BLIND
BLOND
BOUND
BRAND
EBOND
ELAND
EMEND
FIEND
FOUND
FROND
GLAND
GRAND
GRIND
HOUND
MAUND
MOUND
NOEND
OLAND
ONEND
POUND
QUAND
ROUND
SCAND
SCEND
SOUND
SPEND
STAND
TBOND
TREND
UPEND
VIAND
WOUND

NE•••
NEALE
NEAPS
NEARS
NEATH
NEATO
NEATS
NECKS
NEDDY
NEEDS
NEEDY
NEFUD
NEGEV
NEGRI
NEGUS
NEHIS
NEHRU
NEIGE
NEIGH
NEILL
NELLY
NEMAN
NEMAT
NEMEA
NENES
NEONS
NEPAL
NEPOS
NERDS
NERDY
NEROL
NERTS
NERTZ
NERVE
NERVY
NESTS
NEUME
NEURO
NEVER
NEVES
NEVIL
NEVIN
NEVIS
NEVUS
NEWEL
NEWER
NEWLY
NEWSY
NEWTS
NEXIS
NEXUS

N•E••
NEEDS
NEEDY
NIECE
NIELS
NLERS
NOELS
NOEND
NYETS

N••E•
NABES
NADER
NAGEL
NAKED
NAMED
NAMER
NAMES
NAPES
NARES
NAREW
NAVEL
NAVES
NEGEV
NEMEA
NENES
NEVER
NEVES
NEWEL
NEWER
NFLER
NGWEE
NHLER
NICER
NIDES
NIGEL
NIGER
NIKES
NILES
NIMES
NINER
NINES
NISEI
NITER
NITES
NIVEN
NIXED
NIXES
NIZER
NOBEL
NODES
NOMEN
NONES
NONET
NOSED
NOSES
NOSEY
NOTED
NOTER
NOTES
NOVEL
NOYES
NUDER
NUDES
NUKED
NUKES
NUMEN
NUYEN
NYMET
NYNEX

N•••E
NACRE
NAIVE
NAPPE
NASHE
NEALE
NEIGE
NERVE
NEUME
NGWEE
NICHE
NIDRE
NIECE
NIOBE
NITRE
NIXIE
NOBLE
NOIRE
NOISE
NOLLE
NOLTE
NONCE
NOONE
NOOSE
NORGE
NORSE
NORTE
NOSCE
NOTME
NOTRE
NOVAE
NUDGE
NUGAE
NURSE

•NE••
ANEAR
ANELE
ANEMO
ANENT
ANETO
ENEMY
ENERO
INEPT
INERT
KNEAD
KNEED
KNEEL
KNEES
KNELL
KNELT
MNEME
ONEAL
ONEAM
ONEGA
ONEIL
ONEND
ONEPM
ONERS
ONEUP
SNEAD
SNEAK
SNEED
SNEER
SNELL
SNERD
SNERT
SNEVA
VNECK

•N•E•
ANDES
ANGEL
ANGER
ANGES
ANNEE
ANNES
ANNEX
ANSEL
ANSER
ANTED
ANTES
ENDED
ENDER
ENGEL
ENNEA
ENTER
INBED
INDEF
INDEX
INFER
INGER
INKED
INKER
INLET
INNER
INREM
INSET
INTEL
INTER
KNEED
KNEEL
KNEES
ONKEY
ONSET
SNEED
SNEER
UNDER
UNFED

UNGER
UNLED
UNMET
UNPEG
UNPEN
UNSER
UNSET
UNTER
UNWED

•N••E
ANDIE
ANDRE
ANELE
ANGIE
ANGLE
ANIME
ANISE
ANKLE
ANNEE
ANNIE
ANODE
ANOLE
ANSAE
ANTAE
ANTRE
CNOTE
DNASE
ENATE
ENDUE
ENSUE
ENTRE
ENURE
GNOME
INANE
INAWE
INDIE
INGLE
INKLE
INURE
INUSE
KNAVE
KNIFE
KNUTE
MNEME
ONATE
ONCLE
ONCUE
ONICE
RNASE
SNAKE
SNARE
SNIDE
SNIPE
SNORE
TNOTE
UNCLE
UNDUE
UNITE
UNTIE

••NE•
ABNER
AGNES
AGNEW
ANNEE
ANNES
ANNEX
APNEA
ARNEL
ASNER
AWNED
BANES
BENES
BENET
BINES
BINET
BONED
BONER
BONES
BONET
BYNER
CANEA
CANED
CANEM
CANER
CANES
CINES
CONES
CONEY
CUNEO
DANES
DENEB
DENES
DINED
DINER
DINES
DONEE
DONEN
DUNES
DYNEL
DYNES
ENNEA
ERNES
ESNES
FANES
FINED
FINER
FINES
GANEF
GENES
GENET
GONER
HANES
HINES
HONED
HONES
HONEY
IGNES
INNER
JANET
JONES
KINER
LANES
LINED
LINEN
LINER
LINES
LINEY
LONER
LUNES
MANED
MANES
MANET
MENES
MINED
MINEO
MINER
MINES
MONEL
MONET
MONEY
NENES
NINER
NINES
NONES
NONET
NYNEX
OWNED
OWNER
PANED
PANEL
PANES
PINED
PINES
PINEY
PONES
RANEE
RENEE
RENEW
RONEE
RUNES
SANER
SINES
SINEW
SONES
TANEY
TENET
TINED
TINES
TONED
TONER
TONES
TONEY
TUNED
TUNER
TUNES
TYNES
VANES
VENEZ
VINED
VINES
WANED
WANER
WANES
WANEY
WINED
WINES
WINEY
ZINES
ZONED
ZONES

••N•E
AANDE
AINGE
ANNEE
ANNIE
ARNIE
BENUE
BINGE
BONCE
BONNE
BONZE
CANOE
CENSE
CONDE
CONGE
CONTE
DANAE
DANCE
DANKE
DANSE
DANTE
DENSE
DENTE
DINGE
DONEE
DONNE
DUNCE
DUNNE
ERNIE
FENCE
GENIE
GENRE
HANSE
HENCE
HENGE
HENIE
HINGE
JANIE
KINTE
LANCE
LANGE
LONGE
LUNGE
LYNDE
LYNNE
MANSE
MINCE
MINIE
MINKE
MONDE
MONTE
NONCE
OUNCE
PANNE
PENCE
PENNE
PENTE
PINCE
PONCE
PONTE
RANEE
RANGE
RANKE
RENEE
RINSE
RONEE
SANDE
SANTE
SENSE
SENTE
SINCE
SINGE
SONDE
SYNGE
TANDE
TANTE
TENSE
TINGE
TONNE
ULNAE
VANCE
VENAE
VENUE
VINCE
WINCE
WINZE
YENTE
ZANTE

•••NE
AISNE
AKENE
ALENE
ALINE
ALONE
AMINE
ASONE
ATONE
AXONE
AZINE
BEENE
BERNE
BONNE
BOONE
BORNE
BOYNE
BRINE
BYRNE
CAINE
CARNE
CHINE
CLINE
CLONE
CRANE
CRONE
DAYNE
DEANE
DIANE
DIENE
DIONE
DONNE
DOONE
DRONE
DUANE
DUNNE
HEINE
HERNE
HORNE
IDINE
ILENE
IMINE
INANE
IRENE
JAUNE
JAYNE
JEANE
JEUNE
KEANE
KEENE
KLINE
KOINE
KRONE
LAINE
LAYNE
LEONE
LIANE
LORNE
LYNNE
MAINE
MARNE
MESNE
MILNE
NOONE
OPINE
OVINE
OZONE
PAINE
PANNE
PAYNE
PENNE
PHONE
PLANE
PRONE
PRUNE
REUNE
RHINE
RHONE
ROONE
SAONE
SCENE
SCONE
SEINE
SHANE
SHINE
SHONE
SIGNE
SPINE
STONE
STYNE
SWINE
TAINE
TBONE
TERNE
THANE
THINE
TONNE
TOWNE
TRINE
TWINE
UDINE
VERNE
WAYNE
WHINE

NF•••
NFLER

N•F••
NAFTA
NEFUD
NIFTY
NOFAT
NOFLY

•NF••
ENFIN
INFER
INFIN
INFIX
INFRA
INFUN
UNFED
UNFIT
UNFIX

•N•F•
KNIFE
ONOFF
SNAFU
SNIFF
SNUFF
UNIFY

•N••F
INDEF
KNOPF
ONOFF
SNIFF
SNUFF

••NF•
BANFF
HANFF

••N•F
BANFF
GANEF
HANFF

NG•••
NGAIO
NGAMI
NGWEE

N•G••
NAGEL
NAGGY
NEGEV
NEGRI
NEGUS
NIGEL
NIGER
NIGHT
NOGOS
NUGAE

N••G•
NAGGY
NEIGE
NEIGH
NORGE
NUDGE

N•••G
NAVIG

•NG••
ANGEL
ANGER
ANGES
ANGIE
ANGIO
ANGLE
ANGLO
ANGRY
ANGST
ANGUS
ENGEL
ENGRS
INGER
INGLE
INGOT
UNGER

•N•G•
ENUGU
INIGO
ONEGA
SNAGS
SNOGS
SNUGS

•N••G
INBIG
INCOG
INORG
UNPEG
UNRIG

••NG•
AINGE
BANGS
BINGE
BINGO
BINGS
BONGO
BONGS
BUNGS
CONGA
CONGE
CONGO
DANGS
DINGE
DINGO
DINGS
DINGY
DONGS
FANGS
FUNGI
FUNGO
GANGS
GONGS
GUNGA
HANGS
HENGE
HINGE
HONGS
JINGO
KANGA
KINGS
LANGE
LINGO
LONGA
LONGE
LONGI
LONGO
LONGS
LONGU
LUNGE
LUNGS
MANGO
MANGY
MINGS
MINGY
MONGO
MUNGO
OINGO
PANGA
PANGS
PENGO
PINGO
PINGS
PONGS
PUNGS
RANGE
RANGY
RINGO
RINGS
RUNGS
SENGI
SINGE
SINGS
SONGS
SYNGE
TANGO
TANGS
TANGY
TINGE
TINGS
TONGA
TONGS
VINGT
WINGS
XINGU
ZINGS
ZINGY

•••NG
ACING
AGING
ALONG
AMONG
APING
AWING
AXING
BEING
BOING
BRING
BRUNG
CHANG
CHING
CHONG
CHUNG
CLANG
CLING
CLUNG
CUING
DOING
DRANG
DYING
EKING
EWING
FLING
FLUNG
GOING
HMONG
HYING
ICING
KIANG
KOING
LAING
LIANG
LYING
OKING
ORANG
ORING
OWING
PRANG
PRONG
RUING
SLANG
SLING
SLUNG
SOONG
SPANG
STANG
STING
STUNG
SUING
SWING
SWUNG
THING
THONG
TWANG
TYING
USING
VYING
WHANG
WRING
WRONG
WRUNG
YOUNG

NH•••
NHLER

N•H••
NAHUA
NAHUM
NEHIS
NEHRU
NIHIL
NOHIT
NOHOW

N••H•
NACHO
NACHT
NASHE
NICHE
NIGHT
NOAHS
NUCHA

N•••H
NAISH
NATCH
NEATH
NEIGH
NINTH
NORAH
NORTH
NOTCH
NYMPH

•NH••
ANHUI
UNHIP

•N•H•
ANKHS
ANTHO

•N••H
ENOCH
GNASH
INISH
KNISH
SNATH
UNRUH

••NH•
DONHO
MINHO

••N•H
BENCH
BUNCH
CINCH
CONCH

DINAH FINCH HENCH HUNCH JONAH KENCH LUNCH LYNCH MONTH MUNCH MYNAH NINTH PINCH PONCH PUNCH RANCH SANDH TENCH TENTH WENCH WINCH

NI•••

NICAD NICER NICHE NICKS NICOL NIDES NIDRE NIDUS NIECE NIELS NIFTY NIGEL NIGER NIGHT NIHIL NIKES NIKKI NIKKO NIKON NILES NILLY NILOT NIMBI NIMBY NIMES NIMOY NINAS NINER NINES NINJA NINNY NINON NINOS NINTH NIOBE NIPAS NIPAT NIPPY NIPUP NISAN NISEI NISUS NITER NITES NITRE NITRO NITTI NITTY NIVAL NIVEN NIXED NIXES NIXIE NIXON NIZAM NIZER

N•I••

NAIAD NAILS NAINA NAIRA NAIRN NAISH NAIVE NEIGE NEIGH NEILL NOILS NOILY NOIRE NOISE NOISY

N••I•

NADIA NADIR NAMIB NARIS NAVIG NEHIS NEVIL NEVIN NEVIS NEXIS NGAIO NIHIL NIXIE NOBID NOBIS NOHIT NORIA NOSIR NOTIN NOTIT NOWIN NUBIA NUMIS

N•••I

NALDI NAMOI NAOMI NEGRI NGAMI NIKKI NIMBI NISEI NITTI NOCTI NURMI

•NI••

ANILS ANIMA ANIME ANION ANISE ANISO ANITA CNIDA ENIAC INIGO INION INISH INITS KNICK KNIFE KNISH KNITS ONICE ONION SNICK SNIDE SNIFF SNIPE SNIPS SNITS UNIFY UNION UNITE UNITS UNITY UNIVS

•N•I•

ANAIS ANDIE ANGIE ANGIO ANNIE ANNIV ANTIC ANTIQ ANTIS ANVIL ANZIO ENFIN ENNIO ENNIS ENTIA INBIG INDIA INDIC INDIE INDIO INDIV INFIN INFIX INUIT ONAIR ONDIT ONEIL SNAIL UNBID UNDID UNFIT UNFIX UNHIP UNLIT UNPIN UNRIG UNTIE UNTIL UNZIP

•N••I

ANHUI ENLAI ENNUI ENVOI INARI INDRI

••NI•

AMNIA ANNIE ANNIV ARNIE BENIN BUNIN CANID CANIS CANIT CONIC CYNIC DANIO DENIM DENIS ENNIO ENNIS ERNIE FINIS GENIC GENIE GENII HENIE IONIA IONIC JANIE JANIS KANIN LENIN LENIS LUNIK MANIA MANIC MINIE MINIM MINIS MUNIS OMNIA ORNIS PANIC PUNIC RANID RANIN RANIS RENIN RUNIC RUNIN SONIA SONIC TONIC TONIO TUNIC TUNIS VANIR VENIN XENIA ZENIC ZUNIS

••N•I

BENJI BENXI BONDI CENCI CENTI CONTI CYNDI DENTI DONDI ENNUI FUNGI GENII GONDI HANOI HENRI HINDI JINNI KANJI KENAI LANAI LANDI LONGI LUNDI MUNDI PENNI PONTI PONZI RANDI SENGI SINAI SUNNI TONDI VINCI YANNI

•••NI

BLINI ELENI GARNI GRANI HOSNI ICENI IRANI JINNI LEONI LIGNI OMANI PENNI PLANI REGNI SEGNI SOMNI SUNNI TRINI YANNI

N••J•

NADJA NINJA

•NJ••

ANJOU ENJOY UNJAM

••NJ•

BANJO BENJI KANJI NINJA SONJA

N•K••

NAKED NIKES NIKKI NIKKO NIKON NUKED NUKES

N••K•

NARKS NECKS NICKS NIKKI NIKKO NOCKS NOOKS

N•••K

NANAK NOVAK NYACK

•NK••

ANKHS ANKLE INKED INKER INKLE ONKEY

•N•K•

ENSKY SNAKE SNAKY

•N••K

ANOUK KNACK KNICK KNOCK SNACK SNARK SNEAK SNICK SNOOK SNUCK VNECK

••NK•

BANKS BANKY BONKS BUNKO BUNKS CONKS DANKE DINKS DINKY DUNKS FINKS FUNKS FUNKY GUNKY HANKS HANKY HONKS HUNKS JINKS JUNKS JUNKY KINKS KINKY LANKA LANKY LINKS MINKE MINKS MONKS OINKS PANKY PINKS PINKY PUNKS PUNKY RANKE RANKS RINKS RINKY SANKA SINKS TANKA TANKS TONKA WINKS WONKS WONKY YANKS ZONKS

••N•K

LUNIK MINSK MONCK NANAK PINSK

•••NK

BLANK BLINK BRINK CHINK CHUNK CLANK CLINK CLONK CLUNK CRANK DRANK DRINK DRUNK FLANK FLUNK FRANK PLANK PLINK PLONK PLUNK PRANK PRINK REINK SHANK SKANK SKINK SKUNK SLINK SLUNK SPANK SPUNK STANK STINK STUNK SWANK SWINK SWONK THANK THINK THUNK TRUNK

NL•••

NLERS

N•L••

NALDI NELLY NFLER NHLER NILES NILLY NILOT NOLAN NOLLE NOLTE NULLS NYLON

N••L•

NAILS NDOLA NEALE NEILL NELLY NEWLY NIELS NILLY NOBLE NOBLY NOELS NOFLY NOILS NOILY NOLLE NULLS NYALA

N•••L

NAGEL NASAL NATAL NAVAL NAVEL NEILL NEPAL NEROL NEVIL NEWEL NICOL NIGEL NIHIL NIVAL NOBEL NOCAL NODAL NOPAL NOVEL

•NL••

ENLAI INLAW INLAY INLET ONLAY ONLOW UNLAY UNLED UNLIT

•N•L•

ANELE ANGLE ANGLO ANILS ANKLE ANOLE ENOLA ENOLS INALL INGLE INKLE KNELL KNELT KNOLL ONCLE SNELL UNCLE

•N••L

ANGEL ANNAL ANNUL ANSEL ANTAL ANVIL ENGEL ENROL GNARL INALL INTEL KNEEL KNELL KNOLL KNURL ONEAL ONEIL SNAIL SNARL SNELL UNTIL

••NL•

MANLY MENLO WANLY

••N•L

ANNAL ANNUL ARNEL BANAL BINAL CANAL DYNEL FINAL LENDL MONEL PANDL PANEL PENAL RENAL SANDL TONAL VENAL VINYL YENTL ZONAL

•••NL

ADDNL

N•M••

NAMBY NAMED NAMER NAMES NAMIB NAMOI NAMPA NAMUR NEMAN NEMAT NEMEA NIMBI NIMBY NIMES NIMOY NOMAD NOMEN NUMBS NUMEN NUMIS NYMET NYMPH

N••M•

NAOMI NEUME NGAMI NORMA NORMS NOTME NURMI

N•••M

NAHUM NIZAM

•NM••

UNMAN UNMET

•N•M•

ANEMO ANIMA ANIME ANOMY ENEMY GNOME MNEME

•N••M

ANNAM ANNUM ENORM

ENTOM
INREM
ONEAM
ONEPM
UNARM
UNJAM

••N•M
AANDM
ANNAM
ANNUM
CANEM
DENIM
DENOM
MINIM
PANAM
PHNOM
TENAM
TENPM
VENOM

N•N••
NANAK
NANAS
NANCY
NANNA
NANNY
NENES
NINAS
NINER
NINES
NINJA
NINNY
NINON
NINOS
NINTH
NONCE
NONES
NONET
NONOS
NYNEX

N••N•
NAINA
NANNA
NANNY
NEONS
NINNY
NOEND
NOONE
NOONS
NORNS
NOUNS

N•••N
NAIRN
NEMAN
NEVIN
NIKON
NINON
NISAN
NIVEN
NIXON
NOLAN
NOMEN
NOTIN
NOWIN
NUMEN
NUYEN
NYLON

•NN••
ANNAL
ANNAM
ANNAN
ANNEE
ANNES
ANNEX
ANNIE
ANNIV
ANNOY
ANNUL
ANNUM
ANNUS
ENNEA
ENNIO
ENNIS
ENNUI
INNER

•N•N•
ANENT
INANE
INONU
ONEND

•N••N
ANCON
ANION
ANNAN
ANSON
ANTON
ENDON
ENFIN
INCAN
INFIN
INFUN
INION
KNOWN
ONION
UNION
UNMAN
UNPEN
UNPIN

••NN•
BANNS
BENNY
BONNE
BONNY
BUNNY
CANNA
CANNY
DANNY
DENNY
DONNA
DONNE
DONNY
DUNNE
DUNNO
FANNY
FENNY
FINNO
FINNS
FINNY
FUNNY
GINNY
GONNA
GUNNY
HANNA
HANNO
HENNA
HENNY
HINNY
JENNY
JINNI
JINNS
KENNY
LENNY
LYNNE
MANNA
MANNY
NANNA
NANNY
NINNY
PANNE
PENNA
PENNE
PENNI
PENNY
PINNA
PUNNY
RONNY
RUNNY
SENNA
SONNY
SUNNA
SUNNI
SUNNY
TINNY
TONNE
TUNNY
VANNA
VINNY
WANNA
YANNI

••N•N
AGNON
ANNAN
BENIN
BUNIN
CANON
CONAN
DONEN
FANON
HENAN
HONAN
HUNAN
KANIN
LENIN
LINEN
MANON
NINON
PINON
RANIN
RANON
RENAN
RENIN
RUNIN
RUNON
TENON
TYNAN
VENIN
XENON

•••NN
DJINN
FLYNN
GLENN
GWENN
GWYNN
QUINN
SWANN

NO•••
NOAHS
NOBBY
NOBEL
NOBID
NOBIS
NOBLE
NOBLY
NOCAL
NOCKS
NOCTI
NODAL
NODDY
NODES
NODOZ
NODUS
NOELS
NOEND
NOFAT
NOFLY
NOGOS
NOHIT
NOHOW
NOILS
NOILY
NOIRE
NOISE
NOISY
NOLAN
NOLLE
NOLTE
NOMAD
NOMEN
NONCE
NONES
NONET
NONOS
NOOKS
NOONE
NOONS
NOOSE
NOPAL
NOPAR
NORAD
NORAH
NORGE
NORIA
NORMA
NORMS
NORNS
NORSE
NORTE
NORTH
NORVO
NOSCE
NOSED
NOSES
NOSEY
NOSIR
NOTCH
NOTED
NOTER
NOTES
NOTIN
NOTIT
NOTME
NOTRE
NOTSO
NOTUP
NOUNS
NOVAE
NOVAK
NOVAS
NOVEL
NOWAY
NOWIN
NOYES

N•O••
NAOMI
NDOLA
NEONS
NIOBE
NOOKS
NOONE
NOONS
NOOSE

N••O•
NABOB
NAMOI
NAXOS
NEPOS
NEROL
NICOL
NIKON
NILOT
NIMOY
NINON
NINOS
NIXON
NODOZ
NOGOS
NOHOW
NONOS
NYLON

N•••O
NACHO
NARCO
NEATO
NEURO
NGAIO
NIKKO
NITRO
NORVO
NOTSO

•NO••
ANOAS
ANODE
ANOLE
ANOMY
ANOUK
CNOTE
ENOCH
ENOLA
ENOLS
ENORM
GNOME
INONU
INORG
KNOBS
KNOCK
KNOLL
KNOPF
KNOPS
KNORR
KNOTS
KNOUT
KNOWN
KNOWS
ONOFF
SNOBS
SNOGS
SNOOD
SNOOK
SNOOP
SNOOT
SNORE
SNORT
SNOUT
SNOWS
SNOWY
TNOTE

•N•O•
ANCON
ANDOR
ANION
ANJOU
ANNOY
ANSON
ANTON
ENDON
ENDOR
ENDOW
ENJOY
ENROL
ENSOR
ENTOM
ENVOI
ENVOY
INBOX
INCOG
INGOT
INION
INTOW
ONION
ONLOW
ONTOP
SNOOD
SNOOK
SNOOP
SNOOT
UNBOX
UNION

•N••O
ANDRO
ANEMO
ANETO
ANGIO
ANGLO
ANISO
ANTHO
ANZIO
ENERO
ENNIO
INDIO
INIGO
INTRO
INTWO

••NO•
AGNON
ANNOY
ATNOS
BYNOW
CANOE
CANON
DENOM
DONOR
FANON
GENOA
HANOI
HONOR
IFNOT
KENOS
LENOS
LENOX
LINOS
MANON
MANOR
MANOS
MINOR
MINOS
MINOT
MONOD
NINON
NINOS
NONOS
PHNOM
PINON
PINOT
RANON
RUNON
SENOR
SYNOD
TENON
TENOR
VENOM
VINOS
XENON

••N•O
BANCO
BANDO
BANJO
BENZO
BINGO
BONGO
BONZO
BUNKO
CANDO
CANSO
CANTO
CENTO
CINCO
CONDO
CONGO
CUNEO
DANIO
DINGO
DONHO
DUNNO
ENNIO
FINNO
FUNGO
GENRO
GONZO
HANNO
HONDO
JINGO
JUNCO
JUNTO
KENDO
LANDO
LENTO
LINDO
LINGO
LONGO
MANGO
MENLO
MINEO
MINHO
MINTO
MONDO
MONGO
MUNGO
MUNRO
OINGO
PANTO
PENGO
PINGO
PINTO
RANTO
RINGO
RINSO
RONDO
RUNTO
SANTO
SANYO
TANGO
TANTO
TONDO
TONIO
TONTO
ZENDO

•••NO
ADANO
ADENO
AMINO
BEANO
BRUNO
BUENO
BUONO
CHINO
CORNO
CYANO
DRANO
DUNNO
ETHNO
FINNO
GYMNO
HANNO
HYPNO
ICONO
IMINO
KOVNO
LIGNO
LLANO
ORONO
PHENO
PHONO
PIANO
PLANO
QUINO
RHINO
ROVNO
SEGNO
SIGNO
STENO
TAINO
YESNO

N•P••
NAPES
NAPPE
NAPPY
NEPAL
NEPOS
NIPAS
NIPAT
NIPPY
NIPUP
NOPAL
NOPAR

N••P•
NAMPA
NAPPE
NAPPY
NEAPS
NIPPY
NYMPH

N•••P
NAACP
NIPUP
NOTUP

•NP••
INPUT
UNPEG
UNPEN
UNPIN

•N•P•
INAPT
INEPT
KNAPS
KNOPF
KNOPS
ONEPM
SNAPS
SNIPE
SNIPS
UNAPT

•N••P
ANDUP
ENDUP
ONEUP
ONTAP
ONTOP
SNOOP
UNCAP
UNHIP
UNZIP

••NP•
TENPM

••N•P
OWNUP
PINUP
RANUP
RUNUP
SUNUP

•N••Q
ANTIQ

N•R••
NARAS
NARCO
NARCS
NARDS
NARES
NAREW
NARIS
NARKS
NERDS
NERDY
NEROL
NERTS
NERTZ
NERVE
NERVY
NORAD
NORAH
NORGE
NORIA
NORMA
NORMS
NORNS
NORSE
NORTE
NORTH
NORVO
NURMI
NURSE

N••R•
NACRE
NAIRA
NAIRN
NAURU
NEARS
NEGRI
NEHRU
NEURO
NIDRE
NITRE
NITRO
NLERS
NOIRE
NOTRE

N•••R
NADER
NADIR
NAMER
NAMUR
NEVER
NEWER
NFLER
NHLER
NICER
NIGER
NINER
NITER
NIZER
NOPAR
NOSIR
NOTER

NUDER

•NR••

ENROL
INREM
UNRIG
UNRRA
UNRUH

•N•R•

ANDRE
ANDRO
ANDRY
ANGRY
ANTRA
ANTRE
ENERO
ENGRS
ENORM
ENTRE
ENTRY
ENURE
GNARL
GNARS
INARI
INDRA
INDRI
INERT
INFRA
INORG
INTRA
INTRO
INURE
KNARS
KNORR
KNURL
KNURS
ONERS
SNARE
SNARK
SNARL
SNERD
SNERT
SNORE
SNORT
UNARM
UNRRA

•N••R

ANDOR
ANEAR
ANGER
ANSER
ANWAR
ENDER
ENDOR
ENSOR
ENTER
INCUR
INFER
INGER
INKER
INNER
INSTR
INTER
KNORR
ONAIR
SNEER
UNBAR
UNDER
UNGER
UNSER
UNTER

••NR•

GENRE
GENRO
HENRI
HENRY
MUNRO

••N•R

ABNER
ASNER
BONER
BYNER
CANER
CONTR
DENDR
DINAR
DINER
DONOR
FINER
GONER
HONOR
INNER
KINER
LINER
LONER
LUNAR
MANOR
MINER
MINOR
NINER
OWNER
RANDR
SANER
SENOR
SONAR
TENOR
TONER
TUNER
VANIR
WANER

N•S••

NASAL
NASBY
NASHE
NASTY
NESTS
NISAN
NISEI
NISUS
NOSCE
NOSED
NOSES
NOSEY
NOSIR

N••S•

NAISH
NEWSY
NOISE
NOISY
NOOSE
NORSE
NOTSO
NURSE
NUTSY
NYASA

N•••S

NABES
NAILS
NAMES
NANAS
NAPES
NARAS
NARCS
NARDS
NARES
NARIS
NARKS
NAVES
NAXOS
NEAPS
NEARS
NEATS
NECKS
NEEDS
NEGUS
NEHIS
NENES
NEONS
NEPOS
NERDS
NERTS
NESTS
NEVES
NEVIS
NEVUS
NEWTS
NEXIS
NEXUS
NICKS
NIDES
NIDUS
NIELS
NIKES
NILES
NIMES
NINAS
NINES
NINOS
NIPAS
NISUS
NITES
NIXES
NLERS
NOAHS
NOBIS
NOCKS
NODES
NODUS
NOELS
NOGOS
NOILS
NONES
NONOS
NOOKS
NOONS
NORMS
NORNS
NOSES
NOTES
NOUNS
NOVAS
NOYES
NUDES
NUKES
NULLS
NUMBS
NUMIS
NYETS

•NS••

ANSAE
ANSEL
ANSER
ANSON
ENSKY
ENSOR
ENSUE
INSET
INSTR
INSTS
ONSET
UNSAY
UNSER
UNSET

•N•S•

ANGST
ANISE
ANISO
ANTSY
DNASE
GNASH
INISH
INUSE
KNISH
RNASE

•N••S

ANAIS
ANDES
ANGES
ANGUS
ANILS
ANKHS
ANNES
ANNUS
ANOAS
ANTAS
ANTES
ANTIS
ENGRS
ENNIS
ENOLS
GNARS
GNATS
GNAWS
INCAS
INCUS
INDUS
INITS
INSTS
KNAPS
KNARS
KNEES
KNITS
KNOBS
KNOPS
KNOTS
KNOWS
KNURS
ONERS
SNAGS
SNAPS
SNIPS
SNITS
SNOBS
SNOGS
SNOWS
SNUBS
SNUGS
TNUTS
UNAUS
UNCAS
UNITS
UNIVS

••NS•

CANSO
CANST
CENSE
DANSE
DENSE
ERNST
HANSA
HANSE
KANSA
MANSE
MENSA
MINSK
PANSY
PINSK
RINSE
RINSO
SENSE
TANSY
TENSE

••N•S

AGNES
AGNUS
AINUS
ANNES
ANNUS
ATNOS
AUNTS
BANCS
BANDS
BANES
BANGS
BANKS
BANNS
BENDS
BENES
BENTS
BINDS
BINES
BINGS
BONDS
BONES
BONGS
BONKS
BONUS
BUNDS
BUNGS
BUNKS
BUNTS
CANES
CANIS
CANTS
CENTS
CINES
CONES
CONKS
CONUS
CUNAS
DANES
DANGS
DENES
DENIS
DENTS
DENYS
DINES
DINGS
DINKS
DINTS
DONAS
DONGS
DUNES
DUNKS
DYNES
ENNIS
ERNES
ESNES
ETNAS
FANES
FANGS
FENDS
FINDS
FINES
FINIS
FINKS
FINNS
FONDS
FONTS
FUNDS
FUNKS
GANGS
GENES
GENTS
GENUS
GONDS
GONGS
HANDS
HANES
HANGS
HANKS
HANTS
HENTS
HINDS
HINES
HINTS
HONES
HONGS
HONKS
HONUS
HUNKS
HUNTS
IGNES
JANIS
JANUS
JINKS
JINNS
JONAS
JONES
JUNKS
KENOS
KINAS
KINDS
KINGS
KINKS
LANDS
LANES
LENDS
LENIS
LENOS
LENTS
LINES
LINKS
LINOS
LINTS
LINUS
LONGS
LUNES
LUNGS
MANES
MANOS
MENDS
MENES
MENUS
MINAS
MINDS
MINES
MINGS
MINIS
MINKS
MINOS
MINTS
MINUS
MONKS
MUNIS
MYNAS
NANAS
NENES
NINAS
NINES
NINOS
NONES
NONOS
OINKS
ORNIS
PANES
PANGS
PANTS
PENDS
PINES
PINGS
PINKS
PINTS
PONDS
PONES
PONGS
PONTS
PUNAS
PUNGS
PUNKS
PUNTS
RANDS
RANIS
RANKS
RANTS
RENDS
RENTS
RINDS
RINGS
RINKS
RUNES
RUNGS
RUNTS
SANDS
SENDS
SINES
SINGS
SINKS
SINUS
SONES
SONGS
SYNCS
TANGS
TANKS
TENDS
TENTS
TINES
TINGS
TINTS
TONES
TONGS
TONUS
TONYS
TUNAS
TUNES
TUNIS
TYNES
ULNAS
VANES
VENDS
VENTS
VENUS
VINAS
VINES
VINOS
WANDS
WANES
WANTS
WENDS
WINDS
WINES
WINGS
WINKS
WONKS
WONTS
YANKS
ZENDS
ZINCS
ZINES
ZINGS
ZONES
ZONKS
ZUNIS

•••NS

AEONS
AKINS
AMENS
ARENS
ASSNS
AVENS
AXONS
AYINS
AZANS
BANNS
BARNS
BEANS
BEINS
BOONS
BOSNS
BRANS
BURNS
CHINS
CLANS
COINS
COONS
CORNS
DAMNS
DARNS
DAWNS
DEANS
DOWNS
DURNS
EARNS
EBONS
EDENS
ETONS
EVANS
EVENS
EXONS
FAUNS
FAWNS
FERNS
FINNS
FIRNS
FLANS
FOHNS
FOINS
FRANS
GAINS
GIRNS
GLENS
GOONS
GOWNS
GRINS
HERNS
HORNS
HYMNS
ICONS
IRONS
IVINS
JAINS
JEANS
JINNS
JOHNS
JOINS
KAONS
KEENS
KERNS
KHANS
KILNS
KOANS
LAWNS
LEANS
LIENS
LIMNS
LIONS
LOANS
LOINS
LOONS
LYONS
MAINS
MEANS
MIENS
MOANS
MOONS
MORNS
MUONS
NEONS
NOONS
NORNS
NOUNS
OMENS
OPENS
OVENS
OWENS
PAINS
PAWNS
PEENS
PEONS
PHONS
PIONS
PLANS
POONS
RAINS
REINS
ROANS
RUINS
SAENS
SCANS
SHANS
SHINS
SHUNS
SIGNS
SKINS
SPANS
SPINS
STENS
STUNS
SWANS
TARNS
TEENS
TERNS
THINS
TOONS
TOWNS
TRANS
TURNS
TWINS
VEINS
WAINS
WARNS
WEANS
WHINS
WRENS
YARNS
YAWNS
YEANS
YUANS
ZEINS
ZOONS

N•T••

NATAL
NATCH
NATTY
NITER
NITES
NITRE
NITRO
NITTI
NITTY
NOTCH
NOTED
NOTER
NOTES
NOTIN
NOTIT
NOTME
NOTRE

NOTSO
NOTUP
NUTSY
NUTTY

N••T•
NAFTA
NASTY
NATTY
NBCTV
NEATH
NEATO
NEATS
NERTS
NERTZ
NESTS
NEWTS
NIFTY
NINTH
NITTI
NITTY
NOCTI
NOLTE
NORTE
NORTH
NUTTY
NYETS

N•••T
NACHT
NEMAT
NIGHT
NILOT
NIPAT
NOFAT
NOHIT
NONET
NOTIT
NYMET

•NT••
ANTAE
ANTAL
ANTAS
ANTED
ANTES
ANTHO
ANTIC
ANTIQ
ANTIS
ANTON
ANTRA
ANTRE
ANTSY
ENTER
ENTIA
ENTOM
ENTRE
ENTRY
INTEL
INTER
INTOW
INTRA
INTRO
INTWO
ONTAP
ONTOP
UNTER
UNTIE
UNTIL

•N•T•
ANETO
ANITA
CNOTE
ENATE
GNATS
INITS
INSTR
INSTS
KNITS
KNOTS
KNUTE
ONATE
SNATH
SNITS
TNOTE
TNUTS
UNITE
UNITS
UNITY

•N••T
ANENT
ANGST
ENACT
INAPT
INEPT
INERT
INGOT
INLET
INPUT
INSET
INUIT
KNELT
KNOUT
ONDIT
ONSET
SNERT
SNOOT
SNORT
SNOUT
UNAPT
UNCUT
UNFIT
UNLIT
UNMET
UNSET

••NT•
AUNTS
AUNTY
BANTU
BENTS
BUNTS
CANTO
CANTS
CANTY
CENTI
CENTO
CENTS
CONTD
CONTE
CONTI
CONTR
DANTE
DENTE
DENTI
DENTS
DINTS
DINTY
FANTA
FONTS
GENTS
HANTS
HENTS
HINTS
HUNTS
HUNTZ
JUNTA
JUNTO
KINTE
LANTZ
LENTO
LENTS
LINTS
LINTY
MANTA
MINTO
MINTS
MINTY
MONTE
MONTH
MONTY
NINTH
PANTO
PANTS
PENTA
PENTE
PINTA
PINTO
PINTS
PONTE
PONTI
PONTS
PUNTA
PUNTS
PUNTY
RANTO
RANTS
RENTA
RENTS
RUNTO
RUNTS
RUNTY
SANTA
SANTE
SANTO
SENTE
TANTE
TANTO
TENTH
TENTS
TINTS
TONTO
UINTA
VENTS
WANTS
WONTS
YENTA
YENTE
YENTL
ZANTE

••N•T
BANAT
BENET
BINET
BONET
BUNDT
CANIT
CANST
DONAT
DONUT
ERNST
GENET
IFNOT
JANET
MANET
MINOT
MONET
NONET
PINOT
RANAT
RUNAT
SENAT
TENET
TINCT
VINGT
WENDT

•••NT
ADINT
AGENT
AMENT
ANENT
ARENT
AVANT
BIONT
BLENT
BLUNT
BRANT
BRENT
BRUNT
BURNT
CHANT
CLINT
COUNT
DAUNT
DIDNT
EVENT
FAINT
FEINT
FLINT
FOUNT
FRONT
GAUNT
GHENT
GIANT
GLINT
GRANT
GRUNT
GWENT
HADNT
HASNT
HAUNT
JAUNT
JOINT
LEANT
MAYNT
MEANT
MOUNT
ODONT
ORANT
PAINT
PLANT
POINT
PRINT
QUANT
QUINT
RIANT
SAINT
SCANT
SCENT
SHANT
SHUNT
SKINT
SLANT
SPENT
STINT
STUNT
SUINT
TAINT
TAUNT
THANT
TIANT
TRENT
VAUNT
WASNT
YOUNT

NU•••
NUBBY
NUBIA
NUCHA
NUDER
NUDES
NUDGE
NUGAE
NUKED
NUKES
NULLS
NUMBS
NUMEN
NUMIS
NURMI
NURSE
NUTSY
NUTTY
NUYEN

N•U••
NAURU
NEUME
NEURO
NOUNS

N••U•
NAHUA
NAHUM
NAMUR
NEFUD
NEGUS
NEVUS
NEXUS
NIDUS
NIPUP
NISUS
NODUS
NOTUP

N•••U
NAURU
NEHRU

•NU••
ENUGU
ENURE
INUIT
INURE
INUSE
KNURL
KNURS
KNUTE
SNUBS
SNUCK
SNUFF
SNUGS
TNUTS

•N•U•
ANDUP
ANGUS
ANHUI
ANNUL
ANNUM
ANNUS
ANOUK
ENDUE
ENDUP
ENNUI
ENSUE
INCUR
INCUS
INDUS
INFUN
INPUT
KNOUT
ONCUE
ONEUP
SNOUT
UNAUS
UNCUT
UNDUE
UNRUH

•N••U
ANJOU
ENUGU
INONU
SNAFU

••NU•
AGNUS
AINUS
ANNUL
ANNUM
ANNUS
BENUE
BONUS
CONUS
DONUT
ENNUI
GENUA
GENUS
HONUS
JANUS
LINUS
MENUS
MINUS
OWNUP
PINUP
RANUP
RUNUP
SINUS
SUNUP
TONUS
VENUE
VENUS

••N•U
BANTU
DONAU
FONDU
HINDU
KANZU
LONGU
XINGU

•••NU
CORNU
INONU
KEANU

N•V••
NAVAL
NAVEL
NAVES
NAVIG
NAVVY
NEVER
NEVES
NEVIL
NEVIN
NEVIS
NEVUS
NIVAL
NIVEN
NOVAE
NOVAK
NOVAS
NOVEL

N••V•
NAIVE
NAVVY
NERVE
NERVY
NORVO

N•••V
NBCTV
NEGEV

•NV••
ANVIL
ENVOI
ENVOY

•N•V•
KNAVE
SNEVA
UNIVS

•N••V
ANNIV
INDIV

••N•V
ANNIV

N•W••
NAWAB
NEWEL
NEWER
NEWLY
NEWSY
NEWTS
NGWEE
NOWAY
NOWIN

N•••W
NAREW
NOHOW

•NW••
ANWAR
UNWED

•N•W•
GNAWS
INAWE
INTWO
KNOWN
KNOWS
SNOWS
SNOWY

•N••W
ENDOW
INLAW
INTOW
ONLOW

••N•W
AGNEW
BANDW
BYNOW
CANDW
RENEW
SINEW

N•X••
NAXOS
NEXIS
NEXUS
NIXED
NIXES
NIXIE
NIXON

N•••X
NYNEX

•N••X
ANNEX
INBOX
INDEX
INFIX
UNBOX
UNFIX

••NX•
BENXI
SKNXX

••N•X
ANNEX
LENOX
NYNEX
SKNXX

•••NX
BRONX

NY•••
NYACK
NYALA
NYASA
NYETS
NYLON
NYMET
NYMPH
NYNEX

N•Y••
NOYES
NUYEN

N•••Y
NAGGY
NAMBY
NANCY
NANNY
NAPPY
NASBY
NASTY
NATTY
NAVVY
NEDDY
NEEDY
NELLY
NERDY
NERVY
NEWLY
NEWSY
NIFTY
NILLY
NIMBY
NIMOY
NINNY
NIPPY
NITTY
NOBBY
NOBLY
NODDY
NOFLY
NOILY
NOISY
NOSEY
NOWAY
NUBBY
NUTSY
NUTTY

•N•Y•
ENCYC

•N••Y
ANDRY
ANGRY
ANNOY
ANOMY
ANTSY
ENEMY
ENJOY
ENSKY
ENTRY
ENVOY
INLAY
ONKEY
ONLAY
SNAKY
SNOWY
UNIFY
UNITY
UNLAY
UNSAY

••NY•
DENYS
KENYA
LENYA
SANYO
SONYA
TANYA
TONYA
TONYS
VANYA
VINYL

••N•Y
ANNOY
AUNTY
BANDY
BANKY
BENDY
BENNY
BONNY
BUNDY
BUNNY
CANBY
CANDY
CANNY
CANTY
CINDY
CONEY
DANCY
DANDY
DANNY
DENNY
DINDY
DINGY
DINKY
DINTY
DONNY
FANCY
FANNY
FENNY
FINNY
FUNDY
FUNKY
FUNNY
GANDY
GINNY
GUNKY
GUNNY
HANDY
HANKY
HENNY
HENRY
HINNY
HONEY
IXNAY
JENNY
JUNKY
KANDY
KENNY
KINKY
LANKY
LENNY
LINDY

LINEY
LINTY
LUNDY
MANCY
MANDY
MANGY
MANLY
MANNY
MINDY
MINGY
MINTY
MONEY
MONTY
NANCY
NANNY
NINNY
PANAY
PANKY
PANSY
PENNY
PINEY
PINKY
PUNKY
PUNNY
PUNTY
RANDY
RANGY
RINDY
RINKY
RONNY
RUNNY
RUNTY
SANDY
SONNY
SUNNY
TANDY
TANEY
TANGY
TANSY
TINNY
TONEY
TUNNY
VINNY
WANEY
WANLY
WENDY
WINDY
WINEY
WONKY
ZINCY
ZINGY

•••NY
AGONY
ATONY
BEANY
BENNY
BONNY
BRINY
BUNNY
CANNY
CARNY
CLUNY
CORNY
CRONY
DANNY
DENNY
DONNY
DOWNY
EBONY
FANNY
FENNY
FERNY
FINNY
FUNNY
GINNY
GOONY
GUNNY
HENNY
HINNY
IRONY
JENNY
KENNY
LAWNY
LENNY
LOONY
MANNY
MEANY
MEINY
MOONY
NANNY
NINNY
PENNY
PEONY
PHANY
PHONY
PLINY
PUNNY
RAINY
RONNY
RUNNY
SHINY
SONNY
SPINY
STONY
SUNNY
TAWNY
TEENY
TINNY
TOWNY
TUNNY
VEINY
VIGNY
VINNY
WEENY
WHINY

N•Z••
NIZAM
NIZER

N•••Z
NERTZ
NODOZ

•NZ••
ANZAC
ANZIO
UNZIP

••NZ•
BENZO
BONZE
BONZO
DANZA
GINZA
GONZO
KANZU
LANZA
MONZA
PANZA
PENZA
PINZA
PONZI
WINZE

••N•Z
ARNAZ
HUNTZ
LANTZ
VENEZ

•••NZ
FRANZ
HEINZ
MAINZ

OA•••
OAKEN
OAKES
OAKIE
OAKUM
OARED
OASES
OASIS
OASTS
OATEN
OATER
OATES
OATHS

O•A••
OCALA
OFAGE
OHAIR
OHARA
OHARE
OKAPI
OKAYS
OLAND
OMAHA
OMANI
OMARR
OMASA
ONAIR
ONATE
OPAHS
OPALS
OPART
ORACH
ORACY
ORALE
ORALS
ORAMA
ORANG
ORANT
ORATE
OSAGE
OSAKA
OTARU
OTARY
OVALS
OVATE
OZARK
OZAWA

O••A•
OBEAH
OCCAM
OCCAS
OCEAN
OCTAD
OCTAL
OFFAL
OGHAM
OHKAY
OKRAS
OLEAN
OLLAS
ONEAL
ONEAM
ONLAY
ONTAP
OPRAH
ORCAS
OREAD
ORGAN
OSCAN
OSCAR
OSKAR
OSMAN
OTWAY
OYVAY

O•••A
OCALA
OCHOA
OCREA
OHARA
OMAHA
OMASA
OMEGA
OMNIA
ONEGA
OOOLA
OPERA
ORAMA
ORIYA
OSAKA
OSHEA
OSSIA
OSTIA
OUIDA
OUIJA
OVETA
OZAWA

•OA••
BOARD
BOARS
BOAST
BOATS
COACH
COACT
COALS
COAPT
COAST
COATI
COATS
FOALS
FOAMS
FOAMY
GOADS
GOALS
GOAPE
GOATS
HOAGY
HOARD
HOARS
HOARY
KOALA
KOANS
LOACH
LOADS
LOAFS
LOAMS
LOAMY
LOANS
LOATH
MOANS
MOATS
NOAHS
POACH
ROACH
ROADS
ROALD
ROAMS
ROANS
ROARS
ROAST
SOAKS
SOAPS
SOAPY
SOARS
SOAVE
TOADS
TOADY
TOAST
WOADS

•O•A•
AODAI
AOKAY
BOHAI
BOLAS
BORAH
BORAS
BORAX
BOYAR
CODAS
COHAN
COLAS
COMAE
COMAS
CONAN
COPAL
COPAN
COPAY
CORAL
COXAE
COXAL
DONAS
DONAT
DONAU
DORAG
DORAL
DORAN
DOTAL
DOUAI
DOUAY
FOCAL
FORAY
GOBAD
GOFAR
GOLAN
GORAL
GOTAT
HOBAN
HODAD
HOGAN
HONAN
HORAE
HORAL
HORAS
HOWAR
HOYAS
IOTAS
IOWAN
JONAH
JONAS
JOTAS
JOUAL
KODAK
KOJAK
KOLAS
KORAN
LOCAL
LOFAT
LOGAN
LOMAN
LOMAX
LOPAT
LORAN
LORAX
LOTAH
LOTAS
LOYAL
MODAL
MOHAM
MOLAR
MOLAS
MONAD
MORAE
MORAL
MORAN
MORAS
MORAY
NOCAL
NODAL
NOFAT
NOLAN
NOMAD
NOPAL
NOPAR
NORAD
NORAH
NOVAE
NOVAK
NOVAS
NOWAY
POHAI
POLAR
POWAY
RODAN
ROMAN
ROTAS
ROWAN
ROYAL
SODAS
SOFAR
SOFAS
SOLAN
SOLAR
SOMAS
SONAR
SORAS
SOYAS
TODAY
TOGAE
TOGAS
TOKAY
TONAL
TOPAZ
TORAH
TOTAL
VOCAL
VOLAR
VOLAT
WOMAN
WOTAN
YOGAS
ZOEAE
ZOEAL
ZOEAS
ZOHAR
ZONAL

•O••A
AORTA
BOHEA
BOOLA
BOSSA
BOTHA
COBIA
COBRA
COCOA
COMMA
CONGA
COOSA
COPRA
COREA
CORIA
COSTA
COTTA
DOBLA
DOBRA
DOGMA
DOLMA
DONNA
DORSA
FOLIA
FONDA
FORMA
FOSSA
FOVEA
GOLDA
GONNA
GOTHA
GOTTA
GOUDA
HOFFA
HONDA
HOOHA
HOSEA
HOSTA
HOUMA
IONIA
JOLLA
KOALA
KORDA
KOREA
LOGIA
LONGA
LOOFA
LORCA
LORNA
LOTTA
MOCHA
MOIRA
MOMMA
MONZA
MOOLA
MOTTA
NORIA
NORMA
OOOLA
PODIA
POLKA
PONCA
POONA
POPPA
SOFIA
SOLFA
SONIA
SONJA
SONYA
SORTA
SOUSA
TONGA
TONKA
TONYA
TOSCA
VODKA
VOILA
VOLGA
VOLTA
VOLVA
YORBA
ZORBA

••OA•
ANOAS
AROAR
BLOAT
BROAD
CLOAK
CROAK
CROAT
EBOAT
FLOAT
GLOAM
GLOAT
GROAN
GROAT
PROAM
PROAS
PSOAS
QUOAD
SHOAH
SHOAL
SHOAT
SKOAL
SLOAN
STOAE
STOAS
STOAT
TWOAM
UBOAT

••O•A
ACOMA
AGORA
AHORA
ALOHA
AROMA
ASOKA
BIOTA
BOOLA
BROCA
COOSA
ENOLA
EVORA
FIONA
FLORA
GROZA
HOOHA
ICOSA
ILONA
KIOGA
KIOWA
KRONA
KYOGA
LEONA
LEORA
LOOFA
MOOLA
NDOLA
OOOLA
POONA
QUOTA
RHODA
RIOJA
SKODA
SPOSA
STOLA
STOMA
USOFA
VIOLA
XHOSA

•••OA
ALCOA
COCOA
GENOA
OCHOA
SAMOA

OB•••
OBEAH
OBELI
OBESE
OBEYS
OBGYN
OBIES
OBJET
OBOES
OBOLI
OBOLS

O•B••
OHBOY
OMBER
OMBRE
ORBIT
OXBOW

O••B•
ORIBI

•OB••
BOBBY
BOBUP
COBIA
COBOL
COBRA
DOBBY
DOBIE
DOBLA
DOBLE
DOBRA
DOBRO
GOBAD
GOBEL
HOBAN
HOBBS
HOBBY
HOBOS
KOBOS
LOBBY
LOBED
LOBES
LOBOS
MOBIL
NOBBY
NOBEL
NOBID
NOBIS
NOBLE
NOBLY
POBOX
POBOY
ROBBY
ROBED
ROBES
ROBIN
ROBLE
ROBOT
SOBER
SOBIG
TOBES
TOBEY
TOBIT
TOBOL
YOBBO

•O•B•
BOBBY
BOMBE
BOMBS
BOOBS
BOOBY
COLBY
COMBE
COMBO
COMBS
CORBY
COSBY
DOBBY
DOLBY
DOUBT
FORBS
GOTBY
HOBBS
HOBBY
LOBBY
LOOBY
MOSBY
NOBBY
ROBBY
SORBS
YOBBO
YORBA

ZORBA

•O••B
HOREB

••OB•
ADOBE
BLOBS
BOOBS
BOOBY
FROBE
GLOBE
GLOBS
KNOBS
LOOBY
NIOBE
PHOBE
PROBE
PROBS
SLOBS
SNOBS
SWOBS

••O•B
ABOMB
HBOMB
RHOMB

•••OB
CAROB
DEMOB
JACOB
KABOB
KEBOB
MCJOB
NABOB
THROB

OC•••
OCALA
OCCAM
OCCAS
OCCUR
OCEAN
OCHER
OCHOA
OCHRE
OCREA
OCTAD
OCTAL
OCTET
OCULO

O•C••
OCCAM
OCCAS
OCCUR
OICKS
ONCLE
ONCUE
OPCIT
ORCAS
ORCHS
ORCUS
ORCZY
OSCAN
OSCAR

O••C•
ONICE
ORACH
ORACY
OUNCE

O•••C
OLEIC
OLMEC
OPTIC
OSMIC
OSRIC

•OC••
BOCCE
BOCCI
COCKS
COCKY
COCOA
COCOS
DOCKS
FOCAL
FOCUS
HOCKS
HOCUS
JOCKO
JOCKS
KOCHI
LOCAL
LOCHS
LOCKE
LOCKS
LOCOS
LOCUM
LOCUS
MOCHA
MOCKS
NOCAL
NOCKS
NOCTI
POCUS
ROCCO
ROCHE
ROCKS
ROCKY
SOCHI
SOCIO
SOCKO
SOCKS
SOCLE
VOCAL

•O•C•
BOCCE
BOCCI
BONCE
BOSCH
BOSCO
BOSCS
BOTCH
COACH
COACT
CONCH
COUCH
DOLCE
FORCE
HOOCH
JOYCE
KOTCH
LOACH
LORCA
MONCK
MOOCH
NONCE
NOSCE
NOTCH
POACH
PONCA
PONCE
PONCH
POOCH
PORCH
POUCH
ROACH
ROCCO
ROYCE
TORCH
TOSCA
TOUCH
VOICE
VOICI
VOUCH

•O••C
BORIC
COMIC
CONIC
COSEC
DORIC
FOLIC
IODIC
IONIC
LOGIC
MODOC
SOFTC
SONIC
TONIC
TOPIC
TORIC
TOXIC
YOGIC

••OC•
AMOCO
BLOCH
BLOCK
BLOCS
BROCA
BROCK
CHOCK
CLOCK
CROCE
CROCI
CROCK
CROCS
ENOCH
EPOCH
FLOCK
FROCK
HOOCH
KNOCK
MOOCH
POOCH
SHOCK
SMOCK
SPOCK
STOCK

••O•C
AZOIC
BRONC
STOIC

•••OC
ADHOC
ADLOC
ASSOC
DUROC
HAVOC
MEDOC
MODOC

OD•••
ODDER
ODDLY
ODELL
ODETS
ODEUM
ODILE
ODIST
ODIUM
ODONT
ODORS
ODOUR

O•D••
ODDER
ODDLY
OGDEN
OLDEN
OLDER
OLDIE
ONDIT
ORDER
ORDOS

O••D•
OPEDS
OUIDA
OUTDO
OXIDE

O•••D
OARED
OCTAD
OGLED
OHGOD
OILED
OLAND
ONEND
OOHED
OOTID
OOZED
OPTED
OREAD
OUTED
OVOID
OWNED

•OD••
AODAI
BODED
BODES
CODAS
CODED
CODER
CODES
CODEX
DODGE
DODGY
DODOS
FODOR
GODEL
GODET
GODEY
GODLY
GODOT
HODAD
IODIC
JODIE
KODAK
LODEN
LODES
LODGE
MODAL
MODEL
MODEM
MODES
MODOC
MODUS
NODAL
NODDY
NODES
NODOZ
NODUS
PODGY
PODIA
RODAN
RODDY
RODEO
RODIN
SODAS
SODDY
SODOM
TODAY
TODDY
TODOS
VODKA
WODEN
WODGE
YODEL
YODHS

•O•D•
BONDI
BONDS
COEDS
COLDS
CONDE
CONDO
CORDS
DONDI
DOODY
DOWDY
FOLDS
FONDA
FONDS
FONDU
FOODS
FORDO
FORDS
GOADS
GOLDA
GOLDE
GOLDS
GONDI
GONDS
GOODS
GOODY
GORDO
GORDY
GOUDA
GOUDY
GOWDY
HOLDS
HONDA
HONDO
HOODS
HORDE
HOWDY
KORDA
LOADS
LORDS
MOLDS
MOLDY
MONDE
MONDO
MOODS
MOODY
NODDY
PONDS
POODS
ROADS
RODDY
RONDO
ROODS
ROWDY
SODDY
SOLDI
SOLDO
SONDE
TOADS
TOADY
TODDY
TONDI
TONDO
VOIDS
WOADS
WOLDS
WOODS
WOODY
WORDS
WORDY

•O••D
BOARD
BODED
BONED
BOOED
BORED
BOUND
BOVID
BOWED
BOXED
CODED
COKED
CONTD
COOED
COPED
CORED
COULD
COWED
COXED
DOLED
DOMED
DOPED
DOSED
DOTED
DOZED
FOUND
FOXED
GOBAD
GORED
GOULD
GOURD
HOARD
HODAD
HOKED
HOLED
HOMED
HONED
HOPED
HOSED
HOUND
JOKED
LOBED
LOPED
LOVED
LOWED
MONAD
MONOD
MOOED
MOPED
MOULD
MOUND
MOVED
MOWED
NOBID
NOEND
NOMAD
NORAD
NOSED
NOTED
OOHED
OOTID
OOZED
POKED
POLED
PORED
POSED
POUND
ROALD
ROBED
ROPED
ROUND
ROVED
ROWED
SOLED
SOLID
SOUND
SOWED
TONED
TOPED
TOTED
TOWED
TOYED
VOTED
VOWED
WOOED
WORLD
WOULD
WOUND
WOWED
YOKED
ZONED
ZOOID

••OD•
ABODE
ANODE
BRODY
CLODS
DIODE
DOODY
EPODE
ERODE
FOODS
FRODO
GEODE
GOODS
GOODY
GRODY
HOODS
MOODS
MOODY
PLODS
POODS
PRODS
QUODS
RHODA
RHODE
RHODO
ROODS
SKODA
SPODE
WOODS
WOODY

••O•D
ALOUD
AROID
AVOID
BLOND
BLOOD
BOOED
BROAD
BROOD
CHORD
CLOUD
COOED
CROWD
DROID
DROOD
EBOND
FIORD
FJORD
FLOOD
FLOYD
FROID
FROND
GEOID
HYOID
LLOYD
MOOED
OVOID
PROUD
QUOAD
SCOLD
SHOED
SLOYD
SNOOD
STOOD
SWORD
SZOLD
TBOND
WOOED
ZOOID

•••OD
BIPOD
BLOOD
BROOD
DROOD
EPHOD
FLOOD
HEROD
MONOD
OHGOD
RESOD
SAROD
SCROD
SNOOD
STOOD
SYNOD

O•E••
OBEAH
OBELI
OBESE
OBEYS
OCEAN
ODELL
ODETS
ODEUM
OGEES
OLEAN
OLEIC
OLEIN
OLEOS
OLEUM
OMEGA
OMENS
OMERS
ONEAL
ONEAM
ONEGA
ONEIL
ONEND
ONEPM
ONERS
ONEUP
OPEDS
OPELS
OPENS
OPERA
OPERE
OREAD
OREOS
OVENS
OVERS
OVERT
OVETA
OVETT
OWENS
OWERS
OXEYE

O••E•
OAKEN
OAKES
OARED
OASES
OATEN
OATER
OATES
OBIES
OBJET
OBOES
OCHER
OCREA
OCTET
ODDER
OFFER
OFTEN
OGDEN
OGEES
OGLED
OGLER
OGLES
OGRES
OILED
OILER
OKIES
OLDEN
OLDER
OLMEC
OLSEN
OMBER
ONKEY
ONSET
OOHED
OOZED
OOZES
OPTED
ORDER
ORFEO
ORIEL
ORLES
ORSER
OSHEA
OSIER
OSLER
OSSEO
OSTEO
OTHER
OTOES
OTTER
OUSEL
OUTED
OUTER
OUZEL
OWLET
OWNED
OWNER

O•••E
OAKIE
OBESE
OCHRE
ODILE
OFAGE
OFUSE
OGIVE
OHARE
OLDIE
OLIVE
OLLIE
OMBRE
ONATE
ONCLE
ONCUE
ONICE
OPERE
OPINE
ORALE

ORATE
OSAGE
OSSIE
OUNCE
OUTRE
OVATE
OVINE
OVULE
OXEYE
OXIDE
OZONE
OZZIE

•OE••

BOEHM
BOERS
BOEUF
COEDS
COEUR
DOERS
DOEST
DOETH
FOEHN
GOERS
GOEST
HOERS
JOEYS
LOESS
LOEWE
LOEWY
NOELS
NOEND
POEME
POEMS
POESY
POETE
POETS
SOEUR
TOEIN
ZOEAE
ZOEAL
ZOEAS

•O•E•

BODED
BODES
BOGEY
BOHEA
BOLES
BONED
BONER
BONES
BONET
BOOED
BOOER
BORED
BORER
BORES
BOTEL
BOWED
BOWEN
BOWER
BOWES
BOXED
BOXER
BOXES
BOYER
CODED
CODER
CODES
CODEX
COHEN
COKED
COKES
COLES
COLET
COMER
COMES
COMET
COMEX
CONES
CONEY
COOED
COOEE
COOER
COPED
COPES
COREA
CORED
CORER
CORES
COREY
COSEC
COTES
COVEN
COVER
COVES
COVET
COVEY
COWED
COWER
COWES
COXED
COXES
COXEY
COYER
COZEN
COZES
DOGES
DOGEY
DOLED
DOLES
DOMED
DOMES
DONEE
DONEN
DOPED
DOPES
DOPEY
DOREN
DOSED
DOSER
DOSES
DOTED
DOTER
DOTES
DOVER
DOVES
DOVEY
DOWEL
DOWER
DOYEN
DOZED
DOZEN
DOZER
DOZES
FOGEY
FOLEY
FORES
FOVEA
FOXED
FOXES
FOYER
GOBEL
GODEL
GODET
GODEY
GOFER
GOLEM
GOMEL
GOMER
GOMEZ
GONER
GOOEY
GORED
GOREN
GORES
GOSEE
GOWER
HOKED
HOKES
HOKEY
HOLED
HOLES
HOLEY
HOMED
HOMEO
HOMER
HOMES
HOMEY
HONED
HONES
HONEY
HOOEY
HOPED
HOPER
HOPES
HOREB
HOSEA
HOSED
HOSEL
HOSES
HOTEL
HOVEL
HOVER
HOVEY
JOKED
JOKER
JOKES
JOKEY
JONES
JOREL
JOSEF
KOPEK
KOREA
LOBED
LOBES
LODEN
LODES
LOGES
LONER
LOPED
LOPER
LOPES
LOPEZ
LOREN
LORES
LOSER
LOSES
LOVED
LOVER
LOVES
LOVEY
LOWED
LOWER
LOWES
LOXES
MODEL
MODEM
MODES
MOLES
MONEL
MONET
MONEY
MOOED
MOPED
MOPER
MOPES
MOPEY
MOREL
MORES
MOREY
MOSES
MOSEY
MOTEL
MOTES
MOTET
MOUES
MOVED
MOVER
MOVES
MOWED
MOWER
NOBEL
NODES
NOMEN
NONES
NONET
NOSED
NOSES
NOSEY
NOTED
NOTER
NOTES
NOVEL
NOYES
OOHED
OOZED
OOZES
POKED
POKER
POKES
POKEY
POLED
POLER
POLES
POMES
PONES
POPES
PORED
PORES
POSED
POSER
POSES
POWER
ROBED
ROBES
RODEO
ROGER
ROGET
ROLEO
ROLES
ROLEX
ROMEO
ROMER
RONEE
ROPED
ROPER
ROPES
ROPEY
ROREM
ROSEN
ROSES
ROSEY
ROTES
ROUEN
ROUES
ROVED
ROVER
ROVES
ROWED
ROWEL
ROWEN
ROWER
SOBER
SOKES
SOLED
SOLER
SOLES
SONES
SOOEY
SOREL
SOREN
SORER
SORES
SOWED
SOWER
SOXER
TOBES
TOBEY
TOKEN
TOLER
TOLET
TOMEI
TOMES
TONED
TONER
TONES
TONEY
TOPED
TOPER
TOPES
TOTED
TOTEM
TOTER
TOTES
TOVES
TOWED
TOWEL
TOWER
TOYED
VOLES
VOTED
VOTER
VOTES
VOWED
VOWEL
VOWER
WODEN
WOKEN
WOMEN
WOOED
WOOER
WOVEN
WOWED
YODEL
YOKED
YOKEL
YOKES
ZONED
ZONES
ZOOEY

•O••E

BOCCE
BOGIE
BOGLE
BOHME
BOISE
BOITE
BOMBE
BONCE
BONNE
BONZE
BOOLE
BOONE
BOOZE
BORGE
BORNE
BOTHE
BOULE
BOUSE
BOWIE
BOYLE
BOYNE
COMAE
COMBE
COMME
COMTE
CONDE
CONGE
CONTE
COOEE
COOKE
COPSE
COUPE
COXAE
DOBIE
DOBLE
DODGE
DOGIE
DOLCE
DONEE
DONNE
DOONE
DOUSE
DOWSE
DOYLE
FOOTE
FORCE
FORGE
FORTE
FOSSE
FOYLE
GOAPE
GOLDE
GOOSE
GORGE
GORME
GORSE
GOSEE
GOSSE
GOUGE
HOMME
HOOKE
HOPPE
HORAE
HORDE
HORNE
HORSE
HOUSE
HOWIE
HOXIE
HOYLE
JODIE
JOLIE
JORGE
JOULE
JOYCE
KOINE
KOPJE
LOCKE
LODGE
LOEWE
LOGUE
LOIRE
LONGE
LOOSE
LORNE
LORRE
LOTTE
LOUIE
LOUPE
LOUSE
MOIRE
MONDE
MONTE
MOORE
MOOSE
MORAE
MORSE
MOSHE
MOUSE
MOVIE
MOXIE
NOBLE
NOIRE
NOISE
NOLLE
NOLTE
NONCE
NOONE
NOOSE
NORGE
NORSE
NORTE
NOSCE
NOTME
NOTRE
NOVAE
POEME
POETE
POISE
POMME
PONCE
PONTE
POOLE
PORTE
POSSE
POSTE
ROBLE
ROCHE
ROGUE
ROLFE
ROLLE
RONEE
ROONE
ROQUE
ROSIE
ROUGE
ROUSE
ROUTE
ROXIE
ROYCE
SOAVE
SOCLE
SOLVE
SOMME
SONDE
SOUSE
TOGAE
TOILE
TONNE
TOQUE
TORME
TORRE
TORTE
TOTIE
TOUTE
TOWNE
VOGUE
VOICE
VOILE
VOLTE
VOTRE
WODGE
WOLFE
WORSE
YOURE
YOUSE
YOUVE
ZOEAE
ZOWIE

••OE•

ALOES
BOOED
BOOER
COOED
COOEE
COOER
FLOES
FROES
GOOEY
HOOEY
MOOED
OBOES
OTOES
PROEM
SHOED
SHOER
SHOES
SLOES
SOOEY
WOOED
WOOER
ZOOEY

••O•E

ABODE
ABOVE
ADOBE
ADORE
AFORE
ALONE
AMOLE
AMORE
ANODE
ANOLE
AROSE
ASONE
ATONE
AWOKE
AXONE
AZOTE
BIOME
BLOKE
BOOLE
BOONE
BOOZE
BROKE
BROME
CHOKE
CHORE
CHOSE
CLONE
CLOSE
CLOVE
CNOTE
COOEE
COOKE
CROCE
CRONE
CROZE
DHOLE
DHOTE
DIODE
DIONE
DOONE
DROME
DRONE
DROVE
ECOLE
ELOPE
EMOTE
EPODE
ERODE
EROSE
EVOKE
FOOTE
FROBE
FROME
FROZE
GEODE
GLOBE
GLOVE
GLOZE
GNOME
GOOSE
GROFE
GROPE
GROVE
HAOLE
HOOKE
KRONE
LEONE
LOOSE
MOORE
MOOSE
MYOPE
NIOBE
NOONE
NOOSE
OZONE
PHOBE
PHONE
POOLE
PROBE
PROLE
PRONE
PROSE
PROVE
QUOTE
RHODE
RHONE
ROONE
SAONE
SCONE
SCOPE
SCORE
SHONE
SHORE
SHOVE
SLOPE
SMOKE
SMOTE
SNORE
SPODE
SPOKE
SPORE
STOAE
STOKE
STOLE
STONE
STOPE
STORE
STOVE
STOWE
SWOPE
SWORE
TBONE
THOLE
THOSE
TNOTE
TROPE
TROVE
WHOLE
WHOSE
WROTE

•••OE

CANOE
CHLOE
DAFOE
DEFOE
FAROE
GIJOE
MEROE
PEKOE
TAHOE
THROE

OF•••
OFAGE
OFFAL
OFFER
OFTEN
OFUSE

O•F••
OFFAL
OFFER
ORFEO

O••F•
ONOFF

O•••F
ONOFF

•OF••
BOFFO
BOFFS
DOFFS
GOFAR
GOFER
GOFOR
HOFFA
LOFAT
LOFTS
LOFTY
MOFFO
NOFAT
NOFLY
SOFAR
SOFAS
SOFIA
SOFTC
SOFTG
SOFTY
TOFFS
TOFFY
TOFTS

•O•F•
BOFFO
BOFFS
COIFS
COMFY
CORFU
DOFFS
GOLFS
GOOFF
GOOFS
GOOFY
HOFFA
HOOFS
LOAFS
LOOFA
MOFFO
POUFS
ROLFE
ROOFS
SOLFA
TOFFS
TOFFY
WOLFE
WOLFF
WOOFS

•O••F
BOEUF
GOOFF
JOSEF
MOTIF
WOLFF
WOOLF

••OF•
AFOFL
ALOFT
CROFT
FEOFF
GOOFF
GOOFS
GOOFY
GROFE
HOOFS
LOOFA
ONOFF
PROFS
ROOFS
SCOFF
USOFA
WOOFS

••O•F
ADOLF
ALOOF
FEOFF
GOOFF
KNOPF
ONOFF
PROOF
SCOFF
SPOOF
WHOOF
WOOLF

•••OF
ALOOF
PROOF
RIDOF
SPOOF
WHOOF

OG•••
OGDEN
OGEES
OGHAM
OGIVE
OGLED
OGLER
OGLES
OGRES

O•G••
OBGYN
OHGOD
ORGAN
OUGHT

O••G•
OFAGE
OINGO
OLIGO
OLOGY
OMEGA
ONEGA
OSAGE
OUTGO

O•••G
OKING
ORANG
ORING
OWING

•OG••
BOGEY
BOGGS
BOGGY
BOGIE
BOGLE
BOGOR
BOGUS
DOGES
DOGEY
DOGGO
DOGGY
DOGIE
DOGIT
DOGMA
DOGON
FOGEY
FOGGY
FOGIN
FOGUP
GOGOL
GOGOS
HOGAN
HOGGS
LOGAN
LOGES
LOGIA
LOGIC
LOGIN
LOGON
LOGOS
LOGUE
MOGGY
MOGUL
NOGOS
ROGER
ROGET
ROGUE
SOGGY
TOGAE
TOGAS
VOGUE
YOGAS
YOGHS
YOGIC
YOGIS

•O•G•
BOGGS
BOGGY
BONGO
BONGS
BORGE
BOUGH
COIGN
CONGA
CONGE
CONGO
CORGI
COUGH
DODGE
DODGY
DOGGO
DOGGY
DONGS
DOUGH
FOGGY
FORGE
FORGO
GOLGI
GONGS
GORGE
GOUGE
HOAGY
HOGGS
HONGS
HOUGH
JORGE
LODGE
LONGA
LONGE
LONGI
LONGO
LONGS
LONGU
LOUGH
MOGGY
MONGO
MOOGS
NORGE
PODGY
PONGS
PORGY
ROUGE
ROUGH
SOGGY
SONGS
SORGO
SOUGH
TONGA
TONGS
TOUGH
VOLGA
WODGE

•O••G
BOING
BOURG
DOING
DORAG
GOING
KOING
SOBIG
SOFTG
SOONG
TOPOG
YOUNG

••OG•
AGOGO
BIOGS
CLOGS
FLOGS
FROGS
GLOGG
GROGS
KEOGH
KIOGA
KROGH
KYOGA
MOOGS
OLOGY
PROGS
SHOGI
SLOGS
SMOGS
SNOGS
STOGY

••O•G
ALONG
AMONG
CHONG
GEORG
GLOGG
HMONG
INORG
PRONG
SOONG
THONG
WRONG

•••OG
BEFOG
DEFOG
INCOG
MAGOG
TOPOG

OH•••
OHAIR
OHARA
OHARE
OHBOY
OHGOD
OHKAY
OHWOW

O•H••
OCHER
OCHOA
OCHRE
OGHAM
OOHED
OPHIR
OSHEA
OTHER

O••H•
OATHS
OMAHA
OPAHS
ORCHS
ORTHO
OUGHT

O•••H
OBEAH
OOMPH
OPRAH
ORACH

•OH••
BOHAI
BOHEA
BOHME
COHAN
COHEN
COHOS
FOHNS
HOHOS
HOHUM
JOHNS
MOHAM
MOHUR
NOHIT
NOHOW
OOHED
POHAI
SOHIO
ZOHAR

•O•H•
BOEHM
BOTHA
BOTHE
DONHO
FOEHN
GOTHA
GOTHS
HOOHA
KOCHI
KOPHS
LOCHS
MOCHA
MOSHE
MOTHS
MOTHY
NOAHS
POOHS
QOPHS
ROCHE
SOCHI
SOPHS
SOPHY
SOTHO
YODHS
YOGHS

•O••H
BOOTH
BORAH
BOSCH
BOTCH
BOUGH
COACH
CONCH
COUCH
COUGH
COUTH
DOETH
DOLPH
DOUGH
FORTH
FOURH
HOOCH
HOUGH
JONAH
KOTCH
LOACH
LOATH
LOTAH
LOUGH
MONTH
MOOCH
MORPH
MOUTH
NORAH
NORTH
NOTCH
OOMPH
POACH
PONCH
POOCH
PORCH
POUCH
ROACH
ROUGH
SOOTH
SOUGH
SOUTH
TOOTH
TORAH
TORCH
TOUCH
TOUGH
VOUCH
WORTH
YOUTH

••OH•
ABOHM
ALOHA
HOOHA
POOHS

••O•H
AZOTH
BLOCH
BOOTH
BROTH
CLOTH
ENOCH
EPOCH
FROSH
FROTH
HOOCH
KEOGH
KROGH
MOOCH
POOCH
QUOTH
SHOAH
SKOSH
SLOSH
SLOTH
SOOTH
THOTH
TOOTH
TROTH
WROTH

•••OH
RICOH

OI•••
OICKS
OILED
OILER
OINGO
OINKS

O•I••
OBIES
ODILE
ODIST
ODIUM
OGIVE
OKIES
OKING
OLIGO
OLIOS
OLIVE
OMITS
ONICE
ONION
OPINE
OPIUM
ORIBI
ORIEL
ORING
ORION
ORIYA
OSIER
OUIDA
OUIJA
OVINE
OWING
OXIDE

O••I•
OAKIE
OASIS
OHAIR
OLDIE
OLEIC
OLEIN
OLLIE
OMNIA
ONAIR
ONDIT
ONEIL
OOTID
OPCIT
OPHIR
OPSIN
OPSIS
OPTIC
ORBIT
ORNIS
ORRIN
ORRIS
OSLIN
OSMIC
OSRIC
OSSIA
OSSIE
OSTIA
OVOID
OXLIP
OZZIE

O•••I
OBELI
OBOLI
OKAPI
OMANI
ORIBI
OTOMI
OVOLI

•OI••
BOILS
BOING
BOISE
BOITE
BOITO
COIFS
COIGN
COILS
COINS
COIRS
DOILY
DOING
DOITS
FOILS
FOINS
FOIST
GOING
HOIST
HOITY
JOINS
JOINT
JOIST
KOINE
KOING
LOINS
LOIRE
MOILS
MOIRA
MOIRE
MOIST
NOILS
NOILY
NOIRE
NOISE
NOISY
POILS
POILU
POINT
POISE
ROILS
ROILY
SOILS
TOILE
TOILS
TOITY
VOICE
VOICI
VOIDS
VOILA
VOILE

•O•I•
BOGIE
BORIC
BORIS
BOVID
BOWIE
BOXIN
COBIA
COLIN
COMIC
COMIX
CONIC
CORIA
DOBIE
DOGIE
DOGIT
DORIC
DORIS
EOSIN
FOGIN
FOLIA
FOLIC
FOLIO
GOTIN
GOTIT
HOPIN
HOPIS
HOWIE
HOXIE
IODIC
IONIA
IONIC
JODIE
JOLIE
JOSIP
LOGIA
LOGIC
LOGIN
LORIS
LOUIE
LOUIS
MOBIL
MOTIF
MOVIE
MOXIE
NOBID
NOBIS
NOHIT
NORIA
NOSIR
NOTIN
NOTIT
NOWIN
OOTID
PODIA
POLIS
POLIT
POPIN
POSIT
ROBIN
RODIN
ROSIE
ROSIN
ROXIE
SOBIG
SOCIO
SOFIA
SOHIO
SOLID
SONIA
SONIC
TOBIT
TOEIN
TONIC
TONIO
TOPIC
TOPIS
TORIC
TORII
TOTIE
TOTIS
TOWIT
TOXIC
TOXIN
YOGIC
YOGIS
ZOOID
ZORIL
ZORIS
ZOWIE

•O••I
AODAI

BOCCI
BOHAI
BONDI
COATI
CONTI
CORGI
DONDI
DORSI
DOUAI
FORLI
GOLGI
GONDI
GORKI
HOSNI
HOURI
KOCHI
LONGI
NOCTI
POHAI
PONTI
PONZI
ROSSI
SOCHI
SOLDI
SOLTI
SOMNI
TOMEI
TONDI
TOPOI
TORII
TORSI
VOICI
YOKOI

••OI•
ABOIL
AROID
AVOID
AVOIR
AZOIC
BLOIS
BROIL
CHOIR
CROIX
DROID
DROIT
FROID
GEOID
GROIN
HYOID
OVOID
QUOIN
QUOIT
REOIL
SPOIL
STOIC
TROIS
ZOOID

••O•I
AIOLI
BAOJI
CROCI
DHOTI
EBOLI
ECOLI
ICOSI
LEONI
MAORI
NAOMI
OBOLI
OTOMI
OVOLI
PAOLI
SHOGI
SHOJI
SUOMI

•••OI
ENVOI
HANOI
LEROI
NAMOI
TOPOI
YOKOI

O•J••
OBJET

O••J•
OUIJA

•OJ••
DOJOS
KOJAK
MOJOS

•O•J•
KOPJE
SONJA

••OJ•
BAOJI
RIOJA
SHOJI

OK•••
OKAPI
OKAYS
OKIES
OKING
OKRAS

O•K••
OAKEN
OAKES
OAKIE
OAKUM
OHKAY
ONKEY
OSKAR

O••K•
OICKS
OINKS
OSAKA

O•••K
OZARK

•OK••
AOKAY
COKED
COKES
HOKED
HOKES
HOKEY
HOKUM
JOKED
JOKER
JOKES
JOKEY
MOKPO
POKED
POKER
POKES
POKEY
SOKES
TOKAY
TOKEN
TOKYO
WOKEN
YOKED
YOKEL
YOKES
YOKOI
YOKUM

•O•K•
BONKS
BOOKS
BOSKS
BOSKY
COCKS
COCKY
CONKS
COOKE
COOKS
COOKY
CORKS
CORKY
DOCKS
FOLKS
FOLKY
FORKS
FORKY
GORKI
GORKY
GOWKS
HOCKS
HONKS
HOOKE
HOOKS
HOOKY
JOCKO
JOCKS
KOOKS
KOOKY
LOCKE
LOCKS
LOOKS
MOCKS
MONKS
NOCKS
NOOKS
POLKA
PORKS
PORKY
ROCKS
ROCKY
ROOKS
ROOKY
ROYKO
SOAKS
SOCKO
SOCKS
SOUKS
TONKA
VODKA
WONKS
WONKY
WORKS
YOLKS
YOLKY
ZONKS
ZOUKS

•O••K
KODAK
KOJAK
KOPEK
MONCK
NOVAK
POTOK

••OK•
ASOKA
AWOKE
BIOKO
BLOKE
BOOKS
BROKE
CHOKE
CHOKY
COOKE
COOKS
COOKY
EVOKE
EWOKS
GROKS
HOOKE
HOOKS
HOOKY
KOOKS
KOOKY
LOOKS
NOOKS
ROOKS
ROOKY
SMOKE
SMOKY
SPOKE
STOKE

••O•K
ANOUK
BLOCK
BROCK
BROOK
CHOCK
CLOAK
CLOCK
CLONK
CROAK
CROCK
CROOK
FLOCK
FROCK
KIOSK
KNOCK
PLONK
SHOCK
SHOOK
SMOCK
SNOOK
SPOCK
SPOOK
SPORK
STOCK
STOOK
STORK
SWONK

•••OK
BROOK
CROOK
HUROK
KAPOK
MIWOK
POTOK
SHOOK
SNOOK
SPOOK
STOOK
TAROK
YAPOK
YUROK

OL•••
OLAND
OLDEN
OLDER
OLDIE
OLEAN
OLEIC
OLEIN
OLEOS
OLEUM
OLIGO
OLIOS
OLIVE
OLLAS
OLLIE
OLMEC
OLMOS
OLOGY
OLSEN
OLSON

O•L••
OGLED
OGLER
OGLES
OILED
OILER
OLLAS
OLLIE
ONLAY
ONLOW
ORLES
ORLON
ORLOP
OSLER
OSLIN
OWLET
OXLIP

O••L•
OBELI
OBOLI
OBOLS
OCALA
OCULO
ODDLY
ODELL
ODILE
ONCLE
OOOLA
OPALS
OPELS
ORALE
ORALS
OVALS
OVOLI
OVOLO
OVULE

O•••L
OCTAL
ODELL
OFFAL
ONEAL
ONEIL
ORIEL
OUSEL
OUZEL

•OL••
BOLAS
BOLES
BOLLS
BOLOS
BOLTS
BOLUS
COLAS
COLBY
COLDS
COLES
COLET
COLIN
COLON
COLOR
COLTS
COLUM
DOLBY
DOLCE
DOLED
DOLES
DOLLS
DOLLY
DOLMA
DOLOR
DOLPH
DOLTS
EOLUS
FOLDS
FOLEY
FOLIA
FOLIC
FOLIO
FOLKS
FOLKY
FOLLY
GOLAN
GOLDA
GOLDE
GOLDS
GOLEM
GOLFS
GOLGI
GOLLY
HOLDS
HOLED
HOLES
HOLEY
HOLLY
HOLMS
HOLST
HOLTZ
JOLIE
JOLLA
JOLLY
JOLTS
JOLTY
KOLAS
LOLLS
LOLLY
MOLAR
MOLAS
MOLDS
MOLDY
MOLES
MOLLS
MOLLY
MOLTO
MOLTS
NOLAN
NOLLE
NOLTE
POLAR
POLED
POLER
POLES
POLIS
POLIT
POLKA
POLLO
POLLS
POLLY
POLOS
POLYP
ROLEO
ROLES
ROLEX
ROLFE
ROLLE
ROLLO
ROLLS
SOLAN
SOLAR
SOLDI
SOLDO
SOLED
SOLER
SOLES
SOLFA
SOLID
SOLON
SOLOS
SOLTI
SOLUM
SOLUS
SOLVE
TOLER
TOLET
TOLLS
TOLLY
VOLAR
VOLAT
VOLES
VOLGA
VOLTA
VOLTE
VOLTS
VOLVA
VOLVO
WOLDS
WOLFE
WOLFF
YOLKS
YOLKY

•O•L•
BOGLE
BOILS
BOLLS
BOOLA
BOOLE
BOULE
BOULT
BOWLS
BOYLE
COALS
COILS
COOLS
COULD
COWLS
COYLY
DOBLA
DOBLE
DOILY
DOLLS
DOLLY
DOYLE
DOYLY
FOALS
FOILS
FOLLY
FOOLS
FORLI
FOULS
FOWLS
FOYLE
GOALS
GODLY
GOLLY
GOULD
HOLLY
HOTLY
HOWLS
HOYLE
JOLLA
JOLLY
JOULE
JOWLS
JOWLY
KOALA
LOLLS
LOLLY
LOWLY
MOILS
MOLLS
MOLLY
MOOLA
MOULD
MOULT
NOBLE
NOBLY
NOELS
NOFLY
NOILS
NOILY
NOLLE
OOOLA
POILS
POILU
POLLO
POLLS
POLLY
POOLE
POOLS
POULT
ROALD
ROBLE
ROILS
ROILY
ROLLE
ROLLO
ROLLS
ROTLS
SOCLE
SOILS
SOULS
SOULT
TOILE
TOILS
TOLLS
TOLLY
TOOLS
VOILA
VOILE
WOOLF
WOOLS
WOOLY
WORLD
WOULD
YOULL
YOWLS

•O••L
BOTEL
COBOL
COPAL
CORAL
COXAL
DORAL
DOTAL
DOWEL
FOCAL
GOBEL
GODEL
GOGOL
GOMEL
GORAL
HORAL
HOROL
HOSEL
HOTEL
HOVEL
JOREL
JOUAL
LOCAL
LOYAL
MOBIL
MODAL
MODEL
MOGUL
MONEL
MORAL
MOREL
MOSUL
MOTEL
NOBEL
NOCAL
NODAL
NOPAL
NOVEL
ROWEL
ROYAL
SOREL
SOTOL
TOBOL
TONAL
TOPOL
TOTAL
TOWEL
VOCAL
VOWEL
YODEL
YOKEL
YOULL
ZOEAL
ZONAL
ZORIL

••OL•
ADOLF
AIOLI
AMOLE
ANOLE
ATOLL
AWOLS
BOOLA
BOOLE
CHOLO
COOLS
CROLY
DHOLE
DROLL
EBOLI
ECOLE
ECOLI
ENOLA
ENOLS
FOOLS
GAOLS
HAOLE
IDOLS
KNOLL
MOOLA
NDOLA
OBOLI
OBOLS
OOOLA
OVOLI
OVOLO
PAOLI
PAOLO
POOLE
POOLS
PROLE
SCOLD
SMOLT
STOLA
STOLE
STOLS
SZOLD
THOLE
TOOLS
TROLL
UBOLT
UPOLU
VIOLA
VIOLS
VTOLS

WHOLE
WHOLL
WOOLF
WOOLS
WOOLY

••O•L
ABOIL
AFOFL
AFOUL
ATOLL
BROIL
CEORL
DROLL
DROOL
GHOUL
GROWL
KNOLL
PROWL
RAOUL
REOIL
SCOWL
SEOUL
SHOAL
SKOAL
SPOIL
SPOOL
STOOL
TROLL
WHOLL
WHORL

•••OL
ALDOL
ALGOL
ARGOL
ATHOL
CAROL
COBOL
DROOL
ENROL
ERROL
EXTOL
GOGOL
HOROL
KAROL
LTCOL
LYSOL
NEROL
NICOL
PAROL
SOTOL
SPOOL
STOOL
THEOL
TOBOL
TOPOL
TYROL

OM•••
OMAHA
OMANI
OMARR
OMASA
OMBER
OMBRE
OMEGA
OMENS
OMERS
OMITS
OMNIA

O•M••
OLMEC
OLMOS
OOMPH
OSMAN
OSMIC

O••M•
ORAMA
OROMO
OTOMI

O•••M
OAKUM
OCCAM
ODEUM
ODIUM
OGHAM
OLEUM
ONEAM
ONEPM
OPIUM

•OM••
BOMBE
BOMBS
COMAE
COMAS
COMBE
COMBO
COMBS
COMER
COMES
COMET
COMEX
COMFY
COMIC
COMIX
COMMA
COMME
COMPO
COMPS
COMTE
COMUS
DOMED
DOMES
GOMEL
GOMER
GOMEZ
HOMED
HOMEO
HOMER
HOMES
HOMEY
HOMME
LOMAN
LOMAX
MOMMA
MOMMY
MOMUS
NOMAD
NOMEN
OOMPH
POMES
POMME
POMOS
ROMAN
ROMEO
ROMER
ROMPS
SOMAS
SOMME
SOMNI
TOMEI
TOMES
TOMMY
WOMAN
WOMEN
WOMYN

•O•M•
BOHME
BOOMS
BOOMY
COMMA
COMME
CORMS
COSMO
DOGMA
DOLMA
DOOMS
DORMS
FOAMS
FOAMY
FORMA
FORMS
GORME
HOLMS
HOMME
HOUMA
LOAMS
LOAMY
LOOMS
MOMMA
MOMMY
NORMA
NORMS
NOTME
POEME
POEMS
POMME
ROAMS
ROOMS
ROOMY
SOMME
TOMMY
TORME
WORMS
WORMY
ZOOMS

•O••M
BOEHM
BOSOM
COLUM
FORUM
GOLEM
HOHUM
HOKUM
JORUM
LOCUM
MODEM
MOHAM
MORUM
ROREM
SODOM
SOLUM
TOTEM
YOKUM

••OM•
ABOMB
ACOMA
ANOMY
AROMA
ATOMS
ATOMY
BIOME
BOOMS
BOOMY
BROME
BROMO
CHOMP
CLOMP
CUOMO
DOOMS
DROME
DUOMO
FROME
FROMM
GLOMS
GNOME
HBOMB
LOOMS
MBOMU
NAOMI
OROMO
OTOMI
PROMO
PROMS
RHOMB
ROOMS
ROOMY
SLOMO
STOMA
STOMP
SUOMI
TROMP
WHOMP
ZOOMS

••O•M
ABOHM
BLOOM
BROOM
ENORM
FROMM
GLOAM
GLOOM
GROOM
PROAM
PROEM
STORM
TWOAM
TWOPM
VROOM

•••OM
AXIOM
BESOM
BLOOM
BOSOM
BROOM
CAROM
CDROM
CHROM
DENOM
ENTOM
EPROM
EPSOM
GLOOM
GROOM
IDIOM
MRMOM
PHNOM
SODOM
STROM
VENOM
VROOM

ON•••
ONAIR
ONATE
ONCLE
ONCUE
ONDIT
ONEAL
ONEAM
ONEGA
ONEIL
ONEND
ONEPM
ONERS
ONEUP
ONICE
ONION
ONKEY
ONLAY
ONLOW
ONOFF
ONSET
ONTAP
ONTOP

O•N••
OINGO
OINKS
OMNIA
ORNIS
OUNCE
OWNED
OWNER
OWNUP

O••N•
ODONT
OKING
OLAND
OMANI
OMENS
ONEND
OPENS
OPINE
ORANG
ORANT
ORING
ORONO
OVENS
OVINE
OWENS
OWING
OZONE

O•••N
OAKEN
OATEN
OBGYN
OCEAN
OFTEN
OGDEN
OLDEN
OLEAN
OLEIN
OLSEN
OLSON
ONION
OPSIN
ORGAN
ORION
ORLON
ORRIN
ORSON
ORTON
OSCAN
OSLIN
OSMAN

•ON••
BONCE
BONDI
BONDS
BONED
BONER
BONES
BONET
BONGO
BONGS
BONKS
BONNE
BONNY
BONUS
BONZE
BONZO
CONAN
CONCH
CONDE
CONDO
CONES
CONEY
CONGA
CONGE
CONGO
CONIC
CONKS
CONTD
CONTE
CONTI
CONTR
CONUS
DONAS
DONAT
DONAU
DONDI
DONEE
DONEN
DONGS
DONHO
DONNA
DONNE
DONNY
DONOR
DONUT
FONDA
FONDS
FONDU
FONTS
GONDI
GONDS
GONER
GONGS
GONNA
GONZO
HONAN
HONDA
HONDO
HONED
HONES
HONEY
HONGS
HONKS
HONOR
HONUS
IONIA
IONIC
JONAH
JONAS
JONES
LONER
LONGA
LONGE
LONGI
LONGO
LONGS
LONGU
MONAD
MONCK
MONDE
MONDO
MONEL
MONET
MONEY
MONGO
MONKS
MONOD
MONTE
MONTH
MONTY
MONZA
NONCE
NONES
NONET
NONOS
PONCA
PONCE
PONCH
PONDS
PONES
PONGS
PONTE
PONTI
PONTS
PONZI
RONDO
RONEE
RONNY
SONAR
SONDE
SONES
SONGS
SONIA
SONIC
SONJA
SONNY
SONYA
TONAL
TONDI
TONDO
TONED
TONER
TONES
TONEY
TONGA
TONGS
TONIC
TONIO
TONKA
TONNE
TONTO
TONUS
TONYA
TONYS
WONKS
WONKY
WONTS
ZONAL
ZONED
ZONES
ZONKS

•O•N•
BOING
BONNE
BONNY
BOONE
BOONS
BORNE
BOSNS
BOUND
BOYNE
COINS
COONS
CORNO
CORNS
CORNU
CORNY
COUNT
DOING
DONNA
DONNE
DONNY
DOONE
DOWNS
DOWNY
FOHNS
FOINS
FOUND
FOUNT
GOING
GONNA
GOONS
GOONY
GOWNS
HORNE
HORNS
HOSNI
HOUND
JOHNS
JOINS
JOINT
KOANS
KOINE
KOING
KOVNO
LOANS
LOINS
LOONS
LOONY
LORNA
LORNE
MOANS
MOONS
MOONY
MORNS
MOUND
MOUNT
NOEND
NOONE
NOONS
NORNS
NOUNS
POINT
POONA
POONS
POUND
ROANS
RONNY
ROONE
ROUND
ROVNO
SOMNI
SONNY
SOONG
SOUND
TONNE
TOONS
TOWNE
TOWNS
TOWNY
WOUND
YOUNG
YOUNT
ZOONS

•O••N
BORON
BOSON
BOURN
BOWEN
BOXIN
COHAN
COHEN
COIGN
COLIN
COLON
CONAN
COPAN
COVEN
COZEN
DOGON
DONEN
DORAN
DOREN
DOYEN
DOZEN
EOSIN
FOEHN
FOGIN
GOLAN
GOREN
GOTIN
GOTON
HOBAN
HOGAN
HONAN
HOPIN
IOWAN
KORAN
LODEN
LOGAN
LOGIN
LOGON
LOMAN
LORAN
LOREN
MORAN
MORON
MOURN
NOLAN
NOMEN
NOTIN
NOWIN
POPIN
ROBIN
RODAN
RODIN
ROMAN
ROSEN
ROSIN
ROUEN
ROWAN
ROWEN
SOLAN
SOLON
SOREN
TOEIN
TOKEN
TOXIN
TOYON
WODEN
WOKEN
WOMAN
WOMEN
WOMYN
WOTAN
WOVEN

••ON•
AEONS
AGONY
ALONE
ALONG
AMONG
ASONE
ATONE
ATONY
AXONE
AXONS
BIONT
BLOND
BOONE
BOONS
BRONC
BRONX
BUONO
CHONG
CLONE
CLONK
COONS
CRONE
CRONY
DIONE
DOONE

DRONE
EBOND
EBONS
EBONY
ETONS
EXONS
FIONA
FROND
FRONT
GOONS
GOONY
HMONG
ICONO
ICONS
ILONA
INONU
IRONS
IRONY
KAONS
KRONA
KRONE
LEONA
LEONE
LEONI
LIONS
LOONS
LOONY
LYONS
MOONS
MOONY
MUONS
NEONS
NOONE
NOONS
ODONT
ORONO
OZONE
PEONS
PEONY
PHONE
PHONO
PHONS
PHONY
PIONS
PLONK
POONA
POONS
PRONE
PRONG
RHONE
ROONE
SAONE
SCONE
SHONE
SOONG
STONE
STONY
SWONK
TBOND
TBONE
THONG
TOONS
WRONG
ZOONS

••O•N

ACORN
ADORN
BJORN
BLOWN
BROUN
BROWN
CLOWN
CROON
CROWN
DROWN
FLOWN
FROWN
GROAN
GROIN
GROWN
KNOWN
QUOIN
SCORN
SHORN
SHOWN
SLOAN
SPOON
SWOON
SWORN
THORN

•••ON

AARON
ACTON
ADDON
AERON
AFTON
AGNON
AGRON
AKRON
ALTON
AMMON
ANCON
ANION
ANSON
ANTON
APRON
ARGON
ARION
ARSON
ASTON
ATHON
ATION
AVION
AXION
BACON
BARON
BATON
BETON
BIDON
BIGON
BISON
BORON
BOSON
BYRON
CANON
CAPON
CARON
CHRON
CLEON
COLON
CREON
CROON
DAGON
DAMON
DEION
DELON
DEMON
DEVON
DIJON
DIXON
DOGON
EAMON
EATON
EGGON
ELION
ELTON
ENDON
EPSON
EXXON
FANON
FARON
FEDON
FELON
FREON
FUTON
GABON
GETON
GIJON
GLUON
GOTON
GYRON
HADON
HALON
HASON
HERON
HITON
HURON
HYSON
ILION
INION
IXION
JASON
LADON
LAYON
LEDON
LEMON
LETON
LEVON
LIMON
LITON
LOGON
LUZON
LYMON
MACON
MAHON
MANON
MASON
MAYON
MELON
MESON
MORON
MYRON
NIKON
NINON
NIXON
NYLON
OLSON
ONION
ORION
ORLON
ORSON
ORTON
PAEON
PATON
PERON
PINON
PITON
PLEON
PRION
PUTON
PYLON
RACON
RADON
RAMON
RANON
RATON
RAYON
RECON
REDON
REWON
RIPON
RUNON
SALON
SATON
SAXON
SCHON
SCION
SETON
SEWON
SIDON
SIMON
SITON
SOLON
SPOON
SPYON
SWOON
TALON
TAUON
TAXON
TENON
TETON
TIMON
TOYON
TRYON
TYSON
UNION
UPTON
WAGON
XENON
YUKON
ZEVON

OO•••

OOHED
OOMPH
OOOLA
OOTID
OOZED
OOZES

O•O••

OBOES
OBOLI
OBOLS
ODONT
ODORS
ODOUR
OLOGY
ONOFF
OOOLA
OROMO
ORONO
OTOES
OTOMI
OVOID
OVOLI
OVOLO
OZONE

O••O•

OCHOA
OHBOY
OHGOD
OHWOW
OLEOS
OLIOS
OLMOS
OLSON
ONION
ONLOW
ONTOP
ORDOS
OREOS
ORION
ORLON
ORLOP
ORSON
ORTON
ORZOS
OUZOS
OXBOW

O•••O

OCULO
OINGO
OLIGO
ORFEO
OROMO
ORONO
ORTHO
ORURO
OSSEO
OSTEO
OUTDO
OUTGO
OVOLO

•OO••

BOOBS
BOOBY
BOOED
BOOER
BOOKS
BOOLA
BOOLE
BOOMS
BOOMY
BOONE
BOONS
BOORS
BOOST
BOOTH
BOOTS
BOOTY
BOOZE
COOED
COOEE
COOER
COOKE
COOKS
COOKY
COOLS
COONS
COOPS
COOPT
COORS
COOSA
COOTS
DOODY
DOOMS
DOONE
DOORS
DOOZY
FOODS
FOOLS
FOOTE
FOOTS
GOODS
GOODY
GOOEY
GOOFF
GOOFS
GOOFY
GOONS
GOONY
GOOPS
GOOPY
GOOSE
GOOSY
GOOUT
HOOCH
HOODS
HOOEY
HOOFS
HOOHA
HOOKE
HOOKS
HOOKY
HOOPS
HOOTS
KOOKS
KOOKY
LOOBY
LOOFA
LOOKS
LOOMS
LOONS
LOONY
LOOPS
LOOPY
LOOSE
LOOTS
MOOCH
MOODS
MOODY
MOOED
MOOGS
MOOLA
MOONS
MOONY
MOORE
MOORS
MOORY
MOOSE
MOOTS
NOOKS
NOONE
NOONS
NOOSE
OOOLA
POOCH
POODS
POOHS
POOLE
POOLS
POONA
POONS
POOPS
ROODS
ROOFS
ROOKS
ROOKY
ROOMS
ROOMY
ROONE
ROOST
ROOTS
ROOTY
SOOEY
SOONG
SOOTH
SOOTS
SOOTY
TOOLS
TOONS
TOOTH
TOOTS
WOODS
WOODY
WOOED
WOOER
WOOFS
WOOLF
WOOLS
WOOLY
WOOZY
ZOOEY
ZOOID
ZOOMS
ZOONS

•O•O•

BOGOR
BOLOS
BORON
BOSOM
BOSON
BOSOX
BOYOS
BOZOS
COBOL
COCOA
COCOS
COHOS
COLON
COLOR
COROT
DODOS
DOGON
DOJOS
DOLOR
DONOR
FODOR
GODOT
GOFOR
GOGOL
GOGOS
GOTON
HOBOS
HOHOS
HONOR
HOROL
KOBOS
KOTOS
LOBOS
LOCOS
LOGON
LOGOS
MODOC
MOJOS
MONOD
MORON
MOROS
MOTOR
NODOZ
NOGOS
NOHOW
NONOS
POBOX
POBOY
POLOS
POMOS
POPOV
POTOK
ROBOT
ROTOR
ROTOS
SODOM
SOLON
SOLOS
SOPOR
SOTOL
TOBOL
TODOS
TOPOG
TOPOI
TOPOL
TOPOS
TOROS
TOYON
YOKOI
YOYOS

•O••O

BOFFO
BOITO
BONGO
BONZO
BOSCO
COMBO
COMPO
CONDO
CONGO
CORNO
COSMO
DOBRO
DOGGO
DONHO
DORSO
DOTTO
DOURO
FOLIO
FORDO
FORGO
GONZO
GORDO
GOTTO
HOMEO
HONDO
HOWSO
HOWTO
JOCKO
KOVNO
LONGO
LOTTO
MOFFO
MOKPO
MOLTO
MONDO
MONGO
MORRO
MOSSO
MOTTO
NORVO
NOTSO
POLLO
PORTO
POTTO
ROCCO
RODEO
ROLEO
ROLLO
ROMEO
RONDO
ROVNO
ROYKO
SOCIO
SOCKO
SOHIO
SOLDO
SORGO
SOTHO
SOTTO
TOKYO
TONDO
TONIO
TONTO
TORSO
VOLVO
YOBBO
ZORRO

••OO•

AFOOT
ALOOF
BLOOD
BLOOM
BLOOP
BROOD
BROOK
BROOM
CROOK
CROON
DROOD
DROOL
DROOP
FLOOD
FLOOR
GLOOM
GROOM
PROOF
SCOOP
SCOOT
SHOOK
SHOOS
SHOOT
SLOOP
SMOOT
SNOOD
SNOOK
SNOOP
SNOOT
SPOOF
SPOOK
SPOOL
SPOON
SPOOR
STOOD
STOOK
STOOL
STOOP
SWOON
SWOOP
TROOP
VROOM
WHOOF
WHOOP

••O•O

ABOVO
AGOGO
AMOCO
BIOKO
BROMO
BUONO
CHOLO
CUOMO
DUOMO
FRODO
ICONO
KYOTO
OROMO
ORONO
OVOLO
PAOLO
PHONO
PHOTO
PROMO
PROTO
PROVO
RHODO
SLOMO
THORO
TROPO
WHOSO

•••OO

ACHOO
ARTOO
DETOO
ESPOO
IGLOO
KAZOO
MAGOO
MCCOO
METOO
TABOO
WAHOO
YAHOO
YAZOO

OP•••

OPAHS
OPALS
OPART
OPCIT
OPEDS
OPELS
OPENS
OPERA
OPERE

OPHIR
OPINE
OPIUM
OPRAH
OPSIN
OPSIS
OPTED
OPTIC

O••P•
OKAPI
ONEPM
OOMPH

O•••P
ONEUP
ONTAP
ONTOP
ORLOP
OWNUP
OXLIP

•OP••
COPAL
COPAN
COPAY
COPED
COPES
COPRA
COPSE
COPTS
DOPED
DOPES
DOPEY
HOPED
HOPER
HOPES
HOPIN
HOPIS
HOPPE
HOPUP
KOPEK
KOPHS
KOPJE
LOPAT
LOPED
LOPER
LOPES
LOPEZ
LOPPY
MOPED
MOPER
MOPES
MOPEY
MOPSY
MOPUP
NOPAL
NOPAR
POPES
POPIN
POPOV
POPPA
POPPY
POPUP
QOPHS
ROPED
ROPER
ROPES
ROPEY
SOPHS
SOPHY
SOPOR
SOPPY
SOPUP
TOPAZ
TOPED
TOPER
TOPES
TOPIC
TOPIS
TOPOG
TOPOI
TOPOL
TOPOS
TOPPS
TOPSY

•O•P•
COAPT
COMPO
COMPS
COOPS
COOPT
CORPS
COUPE
COUPS
COYPU
DOLPH
DORPS
GOAPE
GOOPS
GOOPY
GORPS
HOOPS
HOPPE
LOOPS
LOOPY
LOPPY
LOUPE
MOKPO
MORPH
OOMPH
POOPS
POPPA
POPPY
ROMPS
SOAPS
SOAPY
SOPPY
SOUPS
SOUPY
TOPPS

•O••P
BOBUP
BOXUP
FOGUP
GOTUP
HOPUP
JOSIP
MOPUP
NOTUP
POLYP
POPUP
SOPUP
TOTUP

••OP•
ADOPT
CHOPS
CLOPS
COOPS
COOPT
CROPS
DROPS
ELOPE
FLOPS
GLOPS
GOOPS
GOOPY
GROPE
HOOPS
KNOPF
KNOPS
LOOPS
LOOPY
MYOPE
PLOPS
POOPS
PROPS
SCOPE
SCOPS
SCOPY
SHOPS
SLOPE
SLOPS
STOPE
STOPS
SWOPE
SWOPS
TROPE
TROPO
TWOPM
WHOPS

••O•P
BLOOP
CHOMP
CLOMP
CROUP
DROOP
GROUP
SCOOP
SLOOP
SNOOP
STOMP
STOOP
STOUP
SWOOP
THORP
TROMP
TROOP
WHOMP
WHOOP

•••OP
AESOP
ALSOP
BEBOP
BLOOP
DROOP
ESTOP
FSTOP
GALOP
ONTOP
ORLOP
REMOP
RETOP
SCOOP
SLOOP
SNOOP
STOOP
STROP
SWOOP
SYSOP
TROOP
WHOOP
ZZTOP

•OQ••
ROQUE
TOQUE

OR•••
ORACH
ORACY
ORALE
ORALS
ORAMA
ORANG
ORANT
ORATE
ORBIT
ORCAS
ORCHS
ORCUS
ORCZY
ORDER
ORDOS
OREAD
OREOS
ORFEO
ORGAN
ORIBI
ORIEL
ORING
ORION
ORIYA
ORLES
ORLON
ORLOP
ORNIS
OROMO
ORONO
ORRIN
ORRIS
ORSER
ORSON
ORTHO
ORTON
ORURO
ORZOS

O•R••
OARED
OCREA
OGRES
OKRAS
OPRAH
ORRIN
ORRIS
OSRIC

O••R•
OCHRE
ODORS
OHARA
OHARE
OMARR
OMBRE
OMERS
ONERS
OPART
OPERA
OPERE
ORURO
OTARU
OTARY
OUTRE
OVERS
OVERT
OWERS
OZARK

O•••R
OATER
OCCUR
OCHER
ODDER
ODOUR
OFFER
OGLER
OHAIR
OILER
OLDER
OMARR
OMBER
ONAIR
OPHIR
ORDER
ORSER
OSCAR
OSIER
OSKAR
OSLER
OTHER
OTTER
OUTER
OWNER

•OR••
AORTA
BORAH
BORAS
BORAX
BORED
BORER
BORES
BORGE
BORIC
BORIS
BORNE
BORON
CORAL
CORBY
CORDS
COREA
CORED
CORER
CORES
COREY
CORFU
CORGI
CORIA
CORKS
CORKY
CORMS
CORNO
CORNS
CORNU
CORNY
COROT
CORPS
DORAG
DORAL
DORAN
DOREN
DORIC
DORIS
DORMS
DORPS
DORSA
DORSI
DORSO
FORAY
FORBS
FORCE
FORDO
FORDS
FORES
FORGE
FORGO
FORKS
FORKY
FORLI
FORMA
FORMS
FORTE
FORTH
FORTS
FORTY
FORUM
GORAL
GORDO
GORDY
GORED
GOREN
GORES
GORGE
GORKI
GORKY
GORME
GORPS
GORSE
GORSY
HORAE
HORAL
HORAS
HORDE
HOREB
HORNE
HORNS
HOROL
HORSE
HORST
HORSY
HORUS
JOREL
JORGE
JORUM
KORAN
KORDA
KOREA
LORAN
LORAX
LORCA
LORDS
LOREN
LORES
LORIS
LORNA
LORNE
LORRE
LORRY
MORAE
MORAL
MORAN
MORAS
MORAY
MOREL
MORES
MOREY
MORNS
MORON
MOROS
MORPH
MORRO
MORSE
MORTS
MORUM
NORAD
NORAH
NORGE
NORIA
NORMA
NORMS
NORNS
NORSE
NORTE
NORTH
NORVO
PORCH
PORED
PORES
PORGY
PORKS
PORKY
PORTE
PORTO
PORTS
ROREM
SORAS
SORBS
SOREL
SOREN
SORER
SORES
SORGO
SORRY
SORTA
SORTS
SORUS
TORAH
TORCH
TORIC
TORII
TORME
TOROS
TORRE
TORRS
TORSI
TORSO
TORTE
TORTS
TORUS
WORDS
WORDY
WORKS
WORLD
WORMS
WORMY
WORRY
WORSE
WORST
WORTH
WORTS
YORBA
ZORBA
ZORIL
ZORIS
ZORRO

•O•R•
BOARD
BOARS
BOERS
BOORS
BOURG
BOURN
COBRA
COIRS
COORS
COPRA
COURT
COWRY
DOBRA
DOBRO
DOERS
DOORS
DOURO
DOWRY
FOURH
FOURS
GOERS
GOURD
HOARD
HOARS
HOARY
HOERS
HOURI
HOURS
LOIRE
LORRE
LORRY
LOWRY
MOIRA
MOIRE
MOORE
MOORS
MOORY
MORRO
MOURN
NOIRE
NOTRE
POURS
ROARS
SOARS
SORRY
SOURS
TORRE
TORRS
TOURS
VOTRE
WORRY
YOURE
YOURS
ZORRO

•O••R
BOGOR
BONER
BOOER
BORER
BOWER
BOXER
BOYAR
BOYER
CODER
COEUR
COLOR
COMER
CONTR
COOER
CORER
COVER
COWER
COYER
DOLOR
DONOR
DOSER
DOTER
DOVER
DOWER
DOZER
FODOR
FOYER
GOFAR
GOFER
GOFOR
GOMER
GONER
GOWER
HOMER
HONOR
HOPER
HOVER
HOWAR
JOKER
LONER
LOPER
LOSER
LOVER
LOWER
MOHUR
MOLAR
MOPER
MOTOR
MOVER
MOWER
NOPAR
NOSIR
NOTER
POKER
POLAR
POLER
POSER
POWER
ROGER
ROMER
ROPER
ROTOR
ROVER
ROWER
SOBER
SOEUR
SOFAR
SOLAR
SOLER
SONAR
SOPOR
SORER
SOWER
SOXER
TOLER
TONER
TOPER
TOTER
TOWER
VOLAR
VOTER
VOWER
WOOER
ZOHAR

••OR•
ABORT
ACORN
ADORE
ADORN
AFORE
AGORA
AHORA
ALORS
AMORE
AMORT
AMORY
APORT
BJORN
BOORS
CEORL
CHORD
CHORE
COORS
DOORS
EMORY
ENORM
EVORA
FIORD
FJORD
FLORA
FLORY
GEORG
GLORY
INORG
IVORY
KNORR
LEORA
MAORI
MOORE
MOORS
MOORY
ODORS
SCORE
SCORN
SHORE
SHORN
SHORT
SKORT
SNORE
SNORT
SPORE
SPORK
SPORT

STORE
STORK
STORM
STORY
SWORD
SWORE
SWORN
THORN
THORO
THORP
WHORL

••O•R

AMOUR
AROAR
AVOIR
BOOER
CHOIR
COOER
FLOOR
FLOUR
HHOUR
KNORR
ODOUR
SCOUR
SHOER
SPOOR
WOOER

•••OR

ABHOR
ACTOR
ALCOR
ANDOR
ARBOR
ARDOR
ARMOR
ASTOR
BATOR
BOGOR
CHLOR
COLOR
CUKOR
DECOR
DOLOR
DONOR
ENDOR
ENSOR
EPHOR
ERROR
FAVOR
FETOR
FLOOR
FLUOR
FODOR
FUROR
GABOR
GATOR
GOFOR
HONOR
HUMOR
ICHOR
JUROR
LABOR
LUXOR
MAJOR
MANOR
MAYOR
MINOR
MOTOR
PRIOR
PRYOR
RAZOR
RIGOR
ROTOR
RUMOR
SAPOR
SAVOR
SENOR
SOPOR
SPOOR
TABOR
TENOR
TIMOR
TUDOR
TUTOR
VALOR
VAPOR
VIDOR
VIGOR
VISOR
ZUKOR

OS•••

OSAGE
OSAKA
OSCAN
OSCAR
OSHEA
OSIER
OSKAR
OSLER
OSLIN
OSMAN
OSMIC
OSRIC
OSSEO
OSSIA
OSSIE
OSTEO
OSTIA

O•S••

OASES
OASIS
OASTS
OLSEN
OLSON
ONSET
OPSIN
OPSIS
ORSER
ORSON
OSSEO
OSSIA
OSSIE
OUSEL
OUSTS

O••S•

OBESE
ODIST
OFUSE
OMASA

O•••S

OAKES
OASES
OASIS
OASTS
OATES
OATHS
OBEYS
OBIES
OBOES
OBOLS
OCCAS
ODETS
ODORS
OGEES
OGLES
OGRES
OICKS
OINKS
OKAYS
OKIES
OKRAS
OLEOS
OLIOS
OLLAS
OLMOS
OMENS
OMERS
OMITS
ONERS
OOZES
OPAHS
OPALS
OPEDS
OPELS
OPENS
OPSIS
ORALS
ORCAS
ORCHS
ORCUS
ORDOS
OREOS
ORLES
ORNIS
ORRIS
ORZOS
OTOES
OUSTS
OUZOS
OVALS
OVENS
OVERS
OWENS
OWERS

•OS••

BOSCH
BOSCO
BOSCS
BOSKS
BOSKY
BOSNS
BOSOM
BOSON
BOSOX
BOSSA
BOSSY
COSBY
COSEC
COSMO
COSTA
COSTS
DOSED
DOSER
DOSES
EOSIN
FOSSA
FOSSE
GOSEE
GOSSE
HOSEA
HOSED
HOSEL
HOSES
HOSNI
HOSTA
HOSTS
JOSEF
JOSIP
LOSER
LOSES
LOSSY
MOSBY
MOSES
MOSEY
MOSHE
MOSSO
MOSSY
MOSUL
NOSCE
NOSED
NOSES
NOSEY
NOSIR
POSED
POSER
POSES
POSIT
POSSE
POSTE
POSTS
ROSEN
ROSES
ROSEY
ROSIE
ROSIN
ROSSI
TOSCA

•O•S•

BOAST
BOISE
BOOST
BOSSA
BOSSY
BOUSE
COAST
COOSA
COPSE
COUSY
DOEST
DORSA
DORSI
DORSO
DOUSE
DOWSE
FOIST
FOSSA
FOSSE
GOEST
GOOSE
GOOSY
GORSE
GORSY
GOSSE
HOIST
HOLST
HORSE
HORST
HORSY
HOUSE
HOWSO
JOIST
JOUST
LOESS
LOOSE
LOSSY
LOUSE
LOUSY
MOIST
MOOSE
MOPSY
MORSE
MOSSO
MOSSY
MOUSE
MOUSY
NOISE
NOISY
NOOSE
NORSE
NOTSO
POESY
POISE
POSSE
POTSY
ROAST
ROOST
ROSSI
ROUSE
ROUST
SOUSA
SOUSE
TOAST
TOPSY
TORSI
TORSO
WORSE
WORST
YOUSE

•O••S

BOARS
BOATS
BODES
BOERS
BOFFS
BOGGS
BOGUS
BOILS
BOLAS
BOLES
BOLLS
BOLOS
BOLTS
BOLUS
BOMBS
BONDS
BONES
BONGS
BONKS
BONUS
BOOBS
BOOKS
BOOMS
BOONS
BOORS
BOOTS
BORAS
BORES
BORIS
BOSCS
BOSKS
BOSNS
BOUTS
BOWES
BOWLS
BOXES
BOYOS
BOZOS
COALS
COATS
COCKS
COCOS
CODAS
CODES
COEDS
COHOS
COIFS
COILS
COINS
COIRS
COKES
COLAS
COLDS
COLES
COLTS
COMAS
COMBS
COMES
COMPS
COMUS
CONES
CONKS
CONUS
COOKS
COOLS
COONS
COOPS
COORS
COOTS
COPES
COPTS
CORDS
CORES
CORKS
CORMS
CORNS
CORPS
COSTS
COTES
COUPS
COVES
COWES
COWLS
COXES
COZES
DOCKS
DODOS
DOERS
DOFFS
DOGES
DOITS
DOJOS
DOLES
DOLLS
DOLTS
DOMES
DONAS
DONGS
DOOMS
DOORS
DOPES
DORIS
DORMS
DORPS
DOSES
DOTES
DOVES
DOWNS
DOZES
EOLUS
FOALS
FOAMS
FOCUS
FOHNS
FOILS
FOINS
FOLDS
FOLKS
FONDS
FONTS
FOODS
FOOLS
FOOTS
FORBS
FORDS
FORES
FORKS
FORMS
FORTS
FOULS
FOURS
FOUTS
FOWLS
FOXES
GOADS
GOALS
GOATS
GOERS
GOGOS
GOLDS
GOLFS
GONDS
GONGS
GOODS
GOOFS
GOONS
GOOPS
GORES
GORPS
GOTHS
GOWKS
GOWNS
HOARS
HOBBS
HOBOS
HOCKS
HOCUS
HOERS
HOGGS
HOHOS
HOKES
HOLDS
HOLES
HOLMS
HOMES
HONES
HONGS
HONKS
HONUS
HOODS
HOOFS
HOOKS
HOOPS
HOOTS
HOPES
HOPIS
HORAS
HORNS
HORUS
HOSES
HOSTS
HOURS
HOWLS
HOYAS
IOTAS
JOCKS
JOEYS
JOHNS
JOINS
JOKES
JOLTS
JONAS
JONES
JOTAS
JOWLS
KOANS
KOBOS
KOLAS
KOOKS
KOPHS
KOTOS
LOADS
LOAFS
LOAMS
LOANS
LOBES
LOBOS
LOCHS
LOCKS
LOCOS
LOCUS
LODES
LOESS
LOFTS
LOGES
LOGOS
LOINS
LOLLS
LONGS
LOOKS
LOOMS
LOONS
LOOPS
LOOTS
LOPES
LORDS
LORES
LORIS
LOSES
LOTAS
LOTUS
LOUIS
LOUTS
LOVES
LOWES
LOXES
MOANS
MOATS
MOCKS
MODES
MODUS
MOILS
MOJOS
MOLAS
MOLDS
MOLES
MOLLS
MOLTS
MOMUS
MONKS
MOODS
MOOGS
MOONS
MOORS
MOOTS
MOPES
MORAS
MORES
MORNS
MOROS
MORTS
MOSES
MOTES
MOTHS
MOTTS
MOUES
MOVES
NOAHS
NOBIS
NOCKS
NODES
NODUS
NOELS
NOGOS
NOILS
NONES
NONOS
NOOKS
NOONS
NORMS
NORNS
NOSES
NOTES
NOUNS
NOVAS
NOYES
OOZES
POCUS
POEMS
POETS
POILS
POKES
POLES
POLIS
POLLS
POLOS
POMES
POMOS
PONDS
PONES
PONGS
PONTS
POODS
POOHS
POOLS
POONS
POOPS
POPES
PORES
PORKS
PORTS
POSES
POSTS
POTTS
POUFS
POURS
POUTS
POWYS
QOPHS
ROADS
ROAMS
ROANS
ROARS
ROBES
ROCKS
ROILS
ROLES
ROLLS
ROMPS
ROODS
ROOFS
ROOKS
ROOMS
ROOTS
ROPES
ROSES
ROTAS
ROTES
ROTLS
ROTOS
ROUES
ROUTS
ROVES
SOAKS
SOAPS
SOARS
SOCKS
SODAS
SOFAS
SOILS
SOKES
SOLES
SOLOS
SOLUS
SOMAS
SONES
SONGS
SOOTS
SOPHS
SORAS
SORBS
SORES
SORTS
SORUS
SOUKS

SOULS
SOUPS
SOURS
SOYAS
TOADS
TOBES
TODOS
TOFFS
TOFTS
TOGAS
TOILS
TOLLS
TOMES
TONES
TONGS
TONUS
TONYS
TOOLS
TOONS
TOOTS
TOPES
TOPIS
TOPOS
TOPPS
TOROS
TORRS
TORTS
TORUS
TOTES
TOTIS
TOURS
TOUTS
TOVES
TOWNS
VOIDS
VOLES
VOLTS
VOTES
WOADS
WOLDS
WONKS
WONTS
WOODS
WOOFS
WOOLS
WORDS
WORKS
WORMS
WORTS
YODHS
YOGAS
YOGHS
YOGIS
YOKES
YOLKS
YOURS
YOWLS
YOYOS
ZOEAS
ZONES
ZONKS
ZOOMS
ZOONS
ZORIS
ZOUKS

••OS•

AROSE
BOOST
CHOSE
CLOSE
COOSA
CROSS
DROSS
EROSE
FLOSS
FROSH
FROST
GHOST
GLOSS
GOOSE
GOOSY
GROSS
GROSZ
ICOSA
ICOSI
KIOSK
LOOSE
MOOSE
NOOSE
PROSE
PROST
PROSY
ROOST
SKOSH
SLOSH
SPOSA
STOSS
THOSE
WHOSE
WHOSO
XHOSA

••O•S

AEONS
AHOYS
ALOES
ALORS
ANOAS
ATOMS
AVOWS
AWOLS
AXONS
BBOYS
BIOGS
BLOBS
BLOCS
BLOIS
BLOTS
BLOWS
BOOBS
BOOKS
BOOMS
BOONS
BOORS
BOOTS
BROWS
BUOYS
CHOPS
CHOWS
CLODS
CLOGS
CLOPS
CLOTS
CLOYS
COOKS
COOLS
COONS
COOPS
COORS
COOTS
CROCS
CROPS
CROSS
CROWS
DHOWS
DOOMS
DOORS
DROPS
DROSS
EBONS
ENOLS
ETONS
EWOKS
EXONS
EYOTS
FLOES
FLOGS
FLOPS
FLOSS
FLOWS
FOODS
FOOLS
FOOTS
FROES
FROGS
FROWS
GAOLS
GLOBS
GLOMS
GLOPS
GLOSS
GLOWS
GOODS
GOOFS
GOONS
GOOPS
GROGS
GROKS
GROSS
GROTS
GROWS
HOODS
HOOFS
HOOKS
HOOPS
HOOTS
ICONS
IDOLS
IRONS
KAONS
KNOBS
KNOPS
KNOTS
KNOWS
KOOKS
LIONS
LOOKS
LOOMS
LOONS
LOOPS
LOOTS
LYONS
MEOWS
MOODS
MOOGS
MOONS
MOORS
MOOTS
MUONS
NEONS
NOOKS
NOONS
OBOES
OBOLS
ODORS
OTOES
PEONS
PHONS
PHOTS
PIONS
PIOUS
PLODS
PLOPS
PLOTS
PLOWS
PLOYS
POODS
POOHS
POOLS
POONS
POOPS
PROAS
PROBS
PRODS
PROFS
PROGS
PROMS
PROPS
PROTS
PROWS
PSOAS
QUODS
RIOTS
ROODS
ROOFS
ROOKS
ROOMS
ROOTS
RYOTS
SCOPS
SCOTS
SCOWS
SHOES
SHOOS
SHOPS
SHOTS
SHOWS
SLOBS
SLOES
SLOGS
SLOPS
SLOTS
SLOWS
SMOGS
SNOBS
SNOGS
SNOWS
SOOTS
SPOTS
STOAS
STOLS
STOPS
STOSS
STOTS
STOWS
SWOBS
SWOPS
THOUS
TOOLS
TOONS
TOOTS
TROIS
TROTS
VIOLS
VTOLS
WHOPS
WOODS
WOOFS
WOOLS
ZOOMS
ZOONS

•••OS

ADIOS
AEROS
AFROS
AGIOS
ALIOS
ALTOS
AMBOS
AMMOS
APSOS
ARGOS
ATHOS
ATMOS
ATNOS
AUTOS
BIGOS
BOLOS
BOYOS
BOZOS
CAMOS
CAPOS
CEROS
CHAOS
CHIOS
CLIOS
COCOS
COHOS
DADOS
DAVOS
DELOS
DEMOS
DIDOS
DODOS
DOJOS
DUBOS
DUROS
ELMOS
ETHOS
EUROS
EXPOS
FADOS
FAROS
FUROS
GATOS
GIROS
GOGOS
GYROS
HALOS
HELOS
HEROS
HOBOS
HOHOS
HUGOS
HYPOS
JATOS
KAYOS
KENOS
KILOS
KOBOS
KOTOS
KUDOS
LAGOS
LEGOS
LENOS
LIDOS
LIMOS
LINOS
LOBOS
LOCOS
LOGOS
MAKOS
MANOS
MELOS
MEMOS
MILOS
MINOS
MISOS
MOJOS
MOROS
MSDOS
NAXOS
NEPOS
NINOS
NOGOS
NONOS
OLEOS
OLIOS
OLMOS
ORDOS
OREOS
ORZOS
OUZOS
PALOS
PAROS
PECOS
PEPOS
PESOS
POLOS
POMOS
RAMOS
REPOS
ROTOS
SAGOS
SAMOS
SAROS
SEGOS
SHOOS
SILOS
SOLOS
TACOS
TALOS
TELOS
TIROS
TODOS
TOPOS
TOROS
TRIOS
TYPOS
TYROS
UMBOS
UPDOS
VAMOS
VINOS
YOYOS
YUGOS
ZEROS

OT•••

OTARU
OTARY
OTHER
OTOES
OTOMI
OTTER
OTWAY

O•T••

OATEN
OATER
OATES
OATHS
OCTAD
OCTAL
OCTET
OFTEN
ONTAP
ONTOP
OOTID
OPTED
OPTIC
ORTHO
ORTON
OSTEO
OSTIA
OTTER
OUTDO
OUTED
OUTER
OUTGO
OUTRE

O••T•

OASTS
ODETS
OMITS
ONATE
ORATE
OUSTS
OVATE
OVETA
OVETT

O•••T

OBJET
OCTET
ODIST
ODONT
ONDIT
ONSET
OPART
OPCIT
ORANT
ORBIT
OUGHT
OVERT
OVETT
OWLET

•OT••

BOTCH
BOTEL
BOTHA
BOTHE
COTES
COTTA
DOTAL
DOTED
DOTER
DOTES
DOTTO
DOTTY
GOTAT
GOTBY
GOTHA
GOTHS
GOTIN
GOTIT
GOTON
GOTTA
GOTTO
GOTUP
HOTEL
HOTLY
IOTAS
JOTAS
KOTCH
KOTOS
LOTAH
LOTAS
LOTTA
LOTTE
LOTTO
LOTUS
MOTEL
MOTES
MOTET
MOTHS
MOTHY
MOTIF
MOTOR
MOTTA
MOTTO
MOTTS
NOTCH
NOTED
NOTER
NOTES
NOTIN
NOTIT
NOTME
NOTRE
NOTSO
NOTUP
OOTID
POTOK
POTSY
POTTO
POTTS
POTTY
ROTAS
ROTES
ROTLS
ROTOR
ROTOS
SOTHO
SOTOL
SOTTO
TOTAL
TOTED
TOTEM
TOTER
TOTES
TOTIE
TOTIS
TOTUP
VOTED
VOTER
VOTES
VOTRE
WOTAN

•O•T•

AORTA
BOATS
BOITE
BOITO
BOLTS
BOOTH
BOOTS
BOOTY
BOUTS
COATI
COATS
COLTS
COMTE
CONTD
CONTE
CONTI
CONTR
COOTS
COPTS
COSTA
COSTS
COTTA
COUTH
DOETH
DOITS
DOLTS
DOTTO
DOTTY
FONTS
FOOTE
FOOTS
FORTE
FORTH
FORTS
FORTY
FOUTS
FOXTV
GOATS
GOTTA
GOTTO
GOUTY
HOITY
HOLTZ
HOOTS
HOSTA
HOSTS
HOWTO
JOLTS
JOLTY
LOATH
LOFTS
LOFTY
LOOTS
LOTTA
LOTTE
LOTTO
LOUTS
MOATS
MOLTO
MOLTS
MONTE
MONTH
MONTY
MOOTS
MORTS
MOTTA
MOTTO
MOTTS
MOUTH
NOCTI
NOLTE
NORTE
NORTH
POETE
POETS
PONTE
PONTI
PONTS
PORTE
PORTO
PORTS
POSTE
POSTS
POTTO
POTTS
POTTY
POUTS
POUTY
ROOTS
ROOTY
ROUTE
ROUTS
SOFTC
SOFTG
SOFTY
SOLTI
SOOTH
SOOTS
SOOTY
SORTA
SORTS
SOTTO
SOUTH
TOFTS
TOITY
TONTO
TOOTH
TOOTS
TORTE
TORTS
TOUTE
TOUTS
VOLTA
VOLTE
VOLTS
WONTS
WORTH
WORTS
YOUTH

•O••T

BOAST
BONET
BOOST
BOULT
COACT
COAPT
COAST

COLET
COMET
COOPT
COROT
COUNT
COURT
COVET
DOEST
DOGIT
DONAT
DONUT
DOUBT
FOIST
FOUNT
GODET
GODOT
GOEST
GOOUT
GOTAT
GOTIT
HOIST
HOLST
HORST
JOINT
JOIST
JOUST
LOFAT
LOPAT
MOIST
MONET
MOTET
MOULT
MOUNT
NOFAT
NOHIT
NONET
NOTIT
POINT
POLIT
POSIT
POULT
ROAST
ROBOT
ROGET
ROOST
ROUST
SOULT
TOAST
TOBIT
TOLET
TOWIT
VOLAT
WORST
YOUNT

••OT•

AZOTE
AZOTH
BIOTA
BLOTS
BOOTH
BOOTS
BOOTY
BROTH
CLOTH
CLOTS
CNOTE
COOTS
DHOTE
DHOTI
EMOTE
EYOTS
FOOTE
FOOTS
FROTH
GROTS
HOOTS
KNOTS
KYOTO
LOOTS
MOOTS
PHOTO
PHOTS
PLOTS
PROTO
PROTS
QUOTA
QUOTE
QUOTH
RIOTS
ROOTS
ROOTY
RYOTS
SCOTS
SCOTT
SHOTS
SLOTH
SLOTS
SMOTE
SOOTH
SOOTS
SOOTY
SPOTS
STOTS
THOTH
TNOTE
TOOTH
TOOTS
TROTH
TROTS
WROTE
WROTH
ZLOTY

••O•T

ABORT
ABOUT
ADOPT
ADOUT
AFOOT
ALOFT
AMORT
APORT
BIONT
BLOAT
BOOST
CLOUT
COOPT
CROAT
CROFT
DROIT
EBOAT
FLOAT
FLOUT
FRONT
FROST
GHOST
GLOAT
GOOUT
GROAT
GROUT
KNOUT
ODONT
PROST
QUOIT
ROOST
SCOOT
SCOTT
SCOUT
SHOAT
SHOOT
SHORT
SHOUT
SKORT
SMOLT
SMOOT
SNOOT
SNORT
SNOUT
SPORT
SPOUT
STOAT
STOUT
TROUT
UBOAT
UBOLT
XDOUT
XSOUT

•••OT

ABBOT
AFOOT
ALLOT
ARGOT
ASCOT
BEGOT
BESOT
BIGOT
CABOT
COROT
CSPOT
DEPOT
DICOT
DIVOT
ELIOT
EPCOT
ERGOT
FAGOT
GAVOT
GEMOT
GIGOT
GODOT
GRIOT
GUYOT
HELOT
IDIOT
IFNOT
INGOT
JABOT
MAGOT
MINOT
NILOT
PEROT
PICOT
PILOT
PINOT
PITOT
PIVOT
REPOT
ROBOT
SABOT
SCOOT
SHOOT
SMOOT
SNOOT
TAROT

OU•••

OUGHT
OUIDA
OUIJA
OUNCE
OUSEL
OUSTS
OUTDO
OUTED
OUTER
OUTGO
OUTRE
OUZEL
OUZOS

O•U••

OCULO
OFUSE
ORURO
OVULE

O••U•

OAKUM
OCCUR
ODEUM
ODIUM
ODOUR
OLEUM
ONCUE
ONEUP
OPIUM
ORCUS
OWNUP

O•••U

OTARU

•OU••

BOUGH
BOULE
BOULT
BOUND
BOURG
BOURN
BOUSE
BOUTS
COUCH
COUGH
COULD
COUNT
COUPE
COUPS
COURT
COUSY
COUTH
DOUAI
DOUAY
DOUBT
DOUGH
DOURO
DOUSE
FOULS
FOUND
FOUNT
FOURH
FOURS
FOUTS
GOUDA
GOUDY
GOUGE
GOULD
GOURD
GOUTY
HOUGH
HOUMA
HOUND
HOURI
HOURS
HOUSE
JOUAL
JOULE
JOUST
LOUGH
LOUIE
LOUIS
LOUPE
LOUSE
LOUSY
LOUTS
MOUES
MOULD
MOULT
MOUND
MOUNT
MOURN
MOUSE
MOUSY
MOUTH
NOUNS
POUCH
POUFS
POULT
POUND
POURS
POUTS
POUTY
ROUEN
ROUES
ROUGE
ROUGH
ROUND
ROUSE
ROUST
ROUTE
ROUTS
SOUGH
SOUKS
SOULS
SOULT
SOUND
SOUPS
SOUPY
SOURS
SOUSA
SOUSE
SOUTH
TOUCH
TOUGH
TOURS
TOUTE
TOUTS
VOUCH
WOULD
WOUND
YOULL
YOUNG
YOUNT
YOURE
YOURS
YOUSE
YOUTH
YOUVE
ZOUKS

•O•U•

BOBUP
BOEUF
BOGUS
BOLUS
BONUS
BOXUP
COEUR
COLUM
COMUS
CONUS
DONUT
EOLUS
FOCUS
FOGUP
FORUM
GOOUT
GOTUP
HOCUS
HOHUM
HOKUM
HONUS
HOPUP
HORUS
JORUM
LOCUM
LOCUS
LOGUE
LOTUS
MODUS
MOGUL
MOHUR
MOMUS
MOPUP
MORUM
MOSUL
NODUS
NOTUP
POCUS
POPUP
ROGUE
ROQUE
SOEUR
SOLUM
SOLUS
SOPUP
SORUS
SOYUZ
TONUS
TOQUE
TORUS
TOTUP
VOGUE
YOKUM

•O••U

CORFU
CORNU
COYPU
DONAU
FONDU
LONGU
POILU

••OU•

ABOUT
ADOUT
AFOUL
ALOUD
AMOUR
ANOUK
BROUN
CLOUD
CLOUT
CROUP
FLOUR
FLOUT
GHOUL
GOOUT
GROUP
GROUT
HHOUR
KNOUT
ODOUR
PIOUS
PROUD
RAOUL
SCOUR
SCOUT
SEOUL
SHOUT
SIOUX
SNOUT
SPOUT
STOUP
STOUT
THOUS
TROUT
XDOUT
XSOUT

••O•U

INONU
MBOMU
SHOYU
UPOLU

•••OU

AEIOU
ANJOU
BAYOU
BIJOU
GAROU

OV•••

OVALS
OVATE
OVENS
OVERS
OVERT
OVETA
OVETT
OVINE
OVOID
OVOLI
OVOLO
OVULE

O•V••

OYVAY

O••V•

OGIVE
OLIVE

•OV••

BOVID
COVEN
COVER
COVES
COVET
COVEY
DOVER
DOVES
DOVEY
FOVEA
HOVEL
HOVER
HOVEY
KOVNO
LOVED
LOVER
LOVES
LOVEY
MOVED
MOVER
MOVES
MOVIE
NOVAE
NOVAK
NOVAS
NOVEL
ROVED
ROVER
ROVES
ROVNO
TOVES
WOVEN

•O•V•

NORVO
SOAVE
SOLVE
VOLVA
VOLVO
YOUVE

•O••V

FOXTV
POPOV

••OV•

ABOVE
ABOVO
CLOVE
DROVE
GLOVE
GROVE
PROVE
PROVO
SHOVE
STOVE
TROVE

•••OV

BASOV
KIROV
LTGOV
POPOV
YAKOV

OW•••

OWENS
OWERS
OWING
OWLET
OWNED
OWNER
OWNUP

O•W••

OHWOW
OTWAY

O••W•

OZAWA

O•••W

OHWOW
ONLOW
OXBOW

•OW••

BOWED
BOWEN
BOWER
BOWES
BOWIE
BOWLS
COWED
COWER
COWES
COWLS
COWRY
DOWDY
DOWEL
DOWER
DOWNS
DOWNY
DOWRY
DOWSE
FOWLS
GOWDY
GOWER
GOWKS
GOWNS
HOWAR
HOWDY
HOWIE
HOWLS
HOWSO
HOWTO
IOWAN
JOWLS
JOWLY
LOWED
LOWER
LOWES
LOWLY
LOWRY
MOWED
MOWER
NOWAY
NOWIN
POWAY
POWER
POWYS
ROWAN
ROWDY
ROWED
ROWEL
ROWEN
ROWER
SOWED
SOWER
TOWED
TOWEL
TOWER
TOWIT
TOWNE
TOWNS
TOWNY
VOWED
VOWEL
VOWER
WOWED
YOWLS
ZOWIE

•O•W•

LOEWE
LOEWY

•O••W

NOHOW

••OW•

AVOWS
BLOWN
BLOWS
BLOWY
BROWN
BROWS
CHOWS
CLOWN
CROWD
CROWN
CROWS
DHOWS
DROWN
FLOWN
FLOWS
FROWN
FROWS
GLOWS
GROWL
GROWN
GROWS
KIOWA
KNOWN
KNOWS
MEOWS
PLOWS
PROWL
PROWS
SCOWL
SCOWS
SHOWN
SHOWS
SHOWY
SLOWS

SNOWS
SNOWY
STOWE
STOWS

•••OW
AGLOW
ALLOW
ARROW
BELOW
BULOW
BYNOW
ELBOW
ENDOW
GAMOW
INTOW
MIAOW
NOHOW
OHWOW
ONLOW
OXBOW
REMOW
RETOW
SEROW
SYDOW
THROW
TUROW
UPBOW
WIDOW
YALOW

OX•••
OXBOW
OXEYE
OXIDE
OXLIP

•OX••
BOXED
BOXER
BOXES
BOXIN
BOXUP
COXAE
COXAL
COXED
COXES
COXEY
FOXED
FOXES
FOXTV
HOXIE
LOXES
MOXIE
ROXIE
SOXER
TOXIC
TOXIN

•O••X
BORAX
BOSOX
CODEX
COMEX
COMIX
LOMAX
LORAX
POBOX
ROLEX

••OX•
DEOXY
EPOXY
PROXY

••O•X
BRONX
CROIX
SIOUX

•••OX
BOSOX
INBOX
LENOX
PHLOX
POBOX
REDOX
UNBOX
XEROX

OY•••
OYVAY

O••Y•
OBEYS
OBGYN
OKAYS
ORIYA
OXEYE

O•••Y
ODDLY
OHBOY
OHKAY
OLOGY
ONKEY
ONLAY
ORACY
ORCZY
OTARY
OTWAY
OYVAY

•OY••
BOYAR
BOYER
BOYLE
BOYNE
BOYOS
COYER
COYLY
COYPU
DOYEN
DOYLE
DOYLY
FOYER
FOYLE
HOYAS
HOYLE
JOYCE
LOYAL
NOYES
ROYAL
ROYCE
ROYKO
SOYAS
SOYUZ
TOYED
TOYON
YOYOS

•O•Y•
JOEYS
POLYP
POWYS
SONYA
TOKYO
TONYA
TONYS
WOMYN

•O••Y
AOKAY
BOBBY
BOGEY
BOGGY
BONNY
BOOBY
BOOMY
BOOTY
BOSKY
BOSSY
COCKY
COLBY
COMFY
CONEY
COOKY
COPAY
CORBY
COREY
CORKY
CORNY
COSBY
COUSY
COVEY
COWRY
COXEY
COYLY
DOBBY
DODGY
DOGEY
DOGGY
DOILY
DOLBY
DOLLY
DONNY
DOODY
DOOZY
DOPEY
DOTTY
DOUAY
DOVEY
DOWDY
DOWNY
DOWRY
DOYLY
FOAMY
FOGEY
FOGGY
FOLEY
FOLKY
FOLLY
FORAY
FORKY
FORTY
GODEY
GODLY
GOLLY
GOODY
GOOEY
GOOFY
GOONY
GOOPY
GOOSY
GORDY
GORKY
GORSY
GOTBY
GOUDY
GOUTY
GOWDY
HOAGY
HOARY
HOBBY
HOITY
HOKEY
HOLEY
HOLLY
HOMEY
HONEY
HOOEY
HOOKY
HORSY
HOTLY
HOVEY
HOWDY
JOKEY
JOLLY
JOLTY
JOWLY
KOOKY
LOAMY
LOBBY
LOEWY
LOFTY
LOLLY
LOOBY
LOONY
LOOPY
LOPPY
LORRY
LOSSY
LOUSY
LOVEY
LOWLY
LOWRY
MOGGY
MOLDY
MOLLY
MOMMY
MONEY
MONTY
MOODY
MOONY
MOORY
MOPEY
MOPSY
MORAY
MOREY
MOSBY
MOSEY
MOSSY
MOTHY
MOUSY
NOBBY
NOBLY
NODDY
NOFLY
NOILY
NOISY
NOSEY
NOWAY
POBOY
PODGY
POESY
POKEY
POLLY
POPPY
PORGY
PORKY
POTSY
POTTY
POUTY
POWAY
ROBBY
ROCKY
RODDY
ROILY
RONNY
ROOKY
ROOMY
ROOTY
ROPEY
ROSEY
ROWDY
SOAPY
SODDY
SOFTY
SOGGY
SONNY
SOOEY
SOOTY
SOPHY
SOPPY
SORRY
SOUPY
TOADY
TOBEY
TODAY
TODDY
TOFFY
TOITY
TOKAY
TOLLY
TOMMY
TONEY
TOPSY
TOWNY
WONKY
WOODY
WOOLY
WOOZY
WORDY
WORMY
WORRY
YOLKY
ZOOEY

••OY•
AHOYS
BBOYS
BUOYS
CLOYS
FLOYD
LLOYD
PLOYS
SHOYU
SLOYD

••O•Y
AGONY
AMORY
ANOMY
ATOMY
ATONY
BLOWY
BOOBY
BOOMY
BOOTY
BRODY
CHOKY
COOKY
CROLY
CRONY
DEOXY
DOODY
DOOZY
EBONY
EMORY
EPOXY
FLORY
GLORY
GOODY
GOOEY
GOOFY
GOONY
GOOPY
GOOSY
GRODY
HOOEY
HOOKY
IRONY
IVORY
KOOKY
LOOBY
LOONY
LOOPY
MOODY
MOONY
MOORY
OLOGY
PEONY
PHONY
PROSY
PROXY
ROOKY
ROOMY
ROOTY
SCOPY
SHOWY
SMOKY
SNOWY
SOOEY
SOOTY
STOGY
STONY
STORY
WOODY
WOOLY
WOOZY
ZLOTY
ZOOEY

•••OY
ALLOY
AMBOY
ANNOY
DECOY
ELROY
ENJOY
ENVOY
LEROY
MCCOY
NIMOY
OHBOY
POBOY
SAVOY
SEPOY

OZ•••
OZARK
OZAWA
OZONE
OZZIE

O•Z••
OOZED
OOZES
ORZOS
OUZEL
OUZOS
OZZIE

O••Z•
ORCZY

•OZ••
BOZOS
COZEN
COZES
DOZED
DOZEN
DOZER
DOZES
OOZED
OOZES

•O•Z•
BONZE
BONZO
BOOZE
DOOZY
GONZO
MONZA
PONZI
WOOZY

•O••Z
GOMEZ
HOLTZ
LOPEZ
NODOZ
SOYUZ
TOPAZ

••OZ•
BOOZE
CROZE
DOOZY
FROZE
GLOZE
GROZA
WOOZY

••O•Z
GROSZ

•••OZ
ARROZ
NODOZ

PA•••
PAAVO
PABLO
PABST
PACAS
PACED
PACER
PACES
PACKS
PACTS
PADDY
PADRE
PADUA
PAEAN
PAEON
PAGAN
PAGED
PAGER
PAGES
PAGET
PAIGE
PAILS
PAINE
PAINS
PAINT
PAIRS
PAISA
PALAE
PALAU
PALEA
PALED
PALEO
PALER
PALES
PALEY
PALIN
PALLS
PALLY
PALMA
PALME
PALMS
PALMY
PALOS
PALPI
PALPS
PALSY
PAMBY
PAMIR
PAMPA
PANAM
PANAY
PANDA
PANDL
PANED
PANEL
PANES
PANGA
PANGS
PANIC
PANKY
PANNE
PANSY
PANTO
PANTS
PANZA
PAOLI
PAOLO
PAPAL
PAPAS
PAPAW
PAPER
PAPPI
PAPPY
PAPUA
PARCA
PARCH
PARDI
PARDO
PARDS
PARED
PAREE
PAREN
PARER
PARES
PAREU
PARIS
PARKA
PARKS
PARLE
PARMA
PAROL
PAROS
PARRY
PARSE
PARTE
PARTI
PARTS
PARTY
PARVO
PASCH
PASCO
PASEO
PASES
PASHA
PASSE
PASSU
PASSY
PASTA
PASTE
PASTO
PASTS
PASTY
PATCH
PATED
PATEK
PATEN
PATER
PATES
PATHE
PATHO
PATHS
PATHY
PATIO
PATLY
PATNA
PATON
PATRI
PATSY
PATTI
PATTY
PAULA
PAULO
PAUSE
PAVED
PAVER
PAVES
PAVIA
PAVID
PAVIS
PAWAT
PAWED
PAWER
PAWKY
PAWLS
PAWNS
PAYED
PAYEE
PAYER
PAYIN
PAYNE
PAYTV
PAYUP

P•A••
PAAVO
PEABO
PEACE
PEACH
PEAKS
PEALE
PEALS
PEARL
PEARS
PEARY
PEASE
PEATS
PEATY
PEAVY
PHAGE
PHAGO
PHAGY
PHANY
PHARM
PHASE
PIANO
PIAUI
PLACE
PLAGE
PLAID
PLAIN
PLAIT
PLANB
PLANE
PLANI
PLANK
PLANO
PLANS
PLANT
PLASH
PLASM
PLATA
PLATE
PLATH
PLATO
PLATS
PLATT
PLATY
PLAYA
PLAYS
PLAZA
POACH
PRADO

PRAIA
PRAMS
PRANG
PRANK
PRASE
PRATE
PRATO
PRATT
PRAUS
PRAWN
PRAYS
PSALM
PSATS

P••A•
PACAS
PAEAN
PAGAN
PALAE
PALAU
PANAM
PANAY
PAPAL
PAPAS
PAPAW
PAWAT
PECAN
PEDAL
PENAL
PERAN
PETAL
PHIAL
PICAS
PIKAS
PILAF
PILAR
PIMAS
PIPAL
PISAN
PITAS
PLEAD
PLEAS
PLEAT
POHAI
POLAR
POWAY
PRIAM
PROAM
PROAS
PSHAW
PSOAS
PTRAP
PULAS
PUMAS
PUNAS
PUPAE
PUPAL
PUPAS
PUSAN

P•••A
PADUA
PAISA
PALEA
PALMA
PAMPA
PANDA
PANGA
PANZA
PAPUA
PARCA
PARKA
PARMA
PASHA
PASTA
PATNA
PAULA
PAVIA
PELLA
PEMBA
PENNA
PENTA
PENZA
PEPLA
PETRA
PHYLA
PIETA
PILEA
PINNA
PINTA
PINZA
PIPPA
PITTA
PIURA
PIZZA
PLATA
PLAYA
PLAZA
PLENA
PLICA
PODIA
POLKA
PONCA
POONA
POPPA
PRAIA
PRIMA
PUKKA
PUNTA

•PA••
APACE
APART
EPACT
IPANA
IPASS
OPAHS
OPALS
OPART
SPAAK
SPACE
SPACY
SPADE
SPADS
SPAHI
SPAHN
SPAIN
SPAKE
SPALL
SPAMS
SPANG
SPANK
SPANS
SPARE
SPARK
SPARS
SPASM
SPATE
SPATS
SPAWN
SPAYS

•P•A•
APEAK
APIAN
APPAL
EPHAH
EPHAS
OPRAH
SPAAK
SPEAK
SPEAR
SPLAT
SPLAY
SPRAG
SPRAT
SPRAY

•P••A
APNEA
IPANA
OPERA
SPICA
SPOSA

••PA•
AMPAS
APPAL
ARPAD
ATPAR
COPAL
COPAN
COPAY
JAPAN
LAPAZ
LOPAT
NEPAL
NIPAS
NIPAT
NOPAL
NOPAR
PAPAL
PAPAS
PAPAW
PIPAL
PUPAE
PUPAL
PUPAS
REPAD
REPAY
SEPAL
STPAT
TAPAS
TEPAL
TOPAZ

••P•A
ALPHA
ASPCA
CAPRA
COPRA
CUPPA
HEPTA
HYPHA
KAPPA
LEPTA
PAPUA
PEPLA
PIPPA
POPPA
SEPIA
SEPTA
SUPRA
TYPEA
ZAPPA

•••PA
AMAPA
CULPA
CUPPA
KAPPA
KRUPA
MILPA
NAMPA
PAMPA
PIPPA
POPPA
SALPA
SCAPA
STUPA
TAMPA
YAMPA
ZAPPA

P•B••
PABLO
PABST
POBOX
POBOY

P••B•
PAMBY
PEABO
PEMBA
PHOBE
PLEBE
PLEBS
PROBE
PROBS
PUTBY

P•••B
PLANB
PLUMB

•PB••
UPBOW

••P•B
TYPEB

P•C••
PACAS
PACED
PACER
PACES
PACKS
PACTS
PECAN
PECKS
PECKY
PECOS
PICAS
PICKS
PICKY
PICOT
PICRO
PICTS
PICUL
POCUS
PUCCI
PUCKS

P••C•
PARCA
PARCH
PASCH
PASCO
PATCH
PEACE
PEACH
PENCE
PERCE
PERCH
PERCY
PESCI
PHYCO
PIECE
PINCE
PINCH
PISCI
PISCO
PITCH
PLACE
PLICA
PLUCK
POACH
PONCA
PONCE
PONCH
POOCH
PORCH
POUCH
PRICE
PRICK
PRICY
PRYCE
PSYCH
PUCCI
PUNCH

P•••C
PANIC
PUNIC
PYRIC

•PC••
EPCOT
OPCIT

•P•C•
APACE
EPACT
EPICS
EPOCH
SPACE
SPACY
SPECD
SPECK
SPECS
SPICA
SPICE
SPICY
SPOCK

•P••C
EPISC
OPTIC

••PC•
ASPCA

••P•C
ASPIC
TOPIC

P•D••
PADDY
PADRE
PADUA
PEDAL
PEDRO
PODGY
PODIA
PUDGY
PUDUS

P••D•
PADDY
PANDA
PANDL
PARDI
PARDO
PARDS
PENDS
PERDU
PIEDS
PLODS
PONDS
POODS
PRADO
PRIDE
PRODS
PRUDE

P•••D
PACED
PAGED
PALED
PANED
PARED
PATED
PAVED
PAVID
PAWED
PAYED
PIKED
PILED
PINED
PIPED
PLAID
PLEAD
PLIED
POKED
POLED
PORED
POSED
POUND
PRIED
PROUD
PSEUD
PULED

•PD••
UPDOS

•P•D•
EPODE
OPEDS
SPADE
SPADS
SPODE
SPUDS

•P••D
APHID
APPTD
APTED
EPHOD
OPTED
SPECD
SPEED
SPEND
SPIED
UPEND
UPPED

••P•D
AMPED
APPTD
ARPAD
BIPED
BIPOD
CAPED
COPED
CUPID
DOPED
DUPED
GAPED
HOPED
HYPED
IMPED
JAPED
LIPID
LOPED
MOPED
PIPED
RAPID
REPAD
ROPED
SAPID
TAPED
TEPID
TOPED
TYPED
UMPED
UPPED
VAPID
WIPED

•••PD
RSVPD

PE•••
PEABO
PEACE
PEACH
PEAKS
PEALE
PEALS
PEARL
PEARS
PEARY
PEASE
PEATS
PEATY
PEAVY
PECAN
PECKS
PECKY
PECOS
PEDAL
PEDRO
PEEKS
PEELE
PEELS
PEENS
PEEPS
PEERS
PEETE
PEEVE
PEGGY
PEKES
PEKIN
PEKOE
PELEE
PELEG
PELLA
PELLE
PELTS
PEMBA
PENAL
PENCE
PENDS
PENGO
PENNA
PENNE
PENNI
PENNY
PENTA
PENTE
PENZA
PEONS
PEONY
PEPIN
PEPLA
PEPOS
PEPPY
PEPSI
PEPUP
PEPYS
PERAN
PERCE
PERCH
PERCY
PERDU
PERES
PEREZ
PERIL
PERIS
PERKS
PERKY
PERLE
PERMS
PERON
PEROT
PERPS
PERRY
PERSE
PERTH
PESCI
PESKY
PESOS
PESTO
PESTS
PETAL
PETER
PETES
PETIT
PETRA
PETRI
PETRO
PETTI
PETTY
PEWEE
PEWIT

P•E••
PAEAN
PAEON
PEEKS
PEELE
PEELS
PEENS
PEEPS
PEERS
PEETE
PEEVE
PHENO
PIECE
PIEDS
PIERS
PIETA
PIETY
PLEAD
PLEAS
PLEAT
PLEBE
PLEBS
PLEIO
PLENA
PLEON
PLEWS
POEME
POEMS
POESY
POETE
POETS
PREEN
PREGO
PRELL
PREPS
PRESS
PREST
PREXY
PREYS
PSEUD
PTERO

P••E•
PACED
PACER
PACES
PAGED
PAGER
PAGES
PAGET
PALEA
PALED
PALEO
PALER
PALES
PALEY
PANED
PANEL
PANES
PAPER
PARED
PAREE
PAREN
PARER
PARES
PAREU
PASEO
PASES
PATED
PATEK
PATEN
PATER
PATES
PAVED
PAVER
PAVES
PAWED
PAWER
PAYED
PAYEE
PAYER
PEKES
PELEE
PELEG
PERES
PEREZ
PETER
PETES
PEWEE
PHREN
PIKED
PIKER
PIKES
PILEA
PILED
PILEI
PILES
PINED
PINES
PINEY
PIPED
PIPER
PIPES
PIXEL
PLIED
PLIES
POKED
POKER
POKES
POKEY
POLED
POLER
POLES
POMES
PONES
POPES
PORED
PORES
POSED
POSER
POSES
POWER
PREEN
PRIED
PRIER
PRIES

PROEM
PUGET
PULED
PULES
PUREE
PURER
PUREX
PUSEY
PYRES
PYREX

P•••E
PADRE
PAIGE
PAINE
PALAE
PALME
PANNE
PAREE
PARLE
PARSE
PARTE
PASSE
PASTE
PATHE
PAUSE
PAYEE
PAYNE
PEACE
PEALE
PEASE
PEELE
PEETE
PEEVE
PEKOE
PELEE
PELLE
PENCE
PENNE
PENTE
PERCE
PERLE
PERSE
PEWEE
PHAGE
PHASE
PHILE
PHOBE
PHONE
PHYFE
PHYLE
PIECE
PINCE
PIQUE
PISTE
PIXIE
PLACE
PLAGE
PLANE
PLATE
PLEBE
PLUME
POEME
POETE
POISE
POMME
PONCE
PONTE
POOLE
PORTE
POSSE
POSTE
PRASE
PRATE
PRICE
PRIDE
PRIME
PRIZE
PROBE
PROLE
PRONE
PROSE
PROVE
PRUDE
PRUNE
PRYCE
PULSE
PUPAE
PUREE
PURGE
PURSE
PYXIE

•PE••
APEAK
APERS
APERY
EPEES
OPEDS
OPELS
OPENS
OPERA
OPERE
SPEAK
SPEAR
SPECD
SPECK
SPECS
SPEED
SPEKE
SPELL
SPELT
SPEND
SPENT
SPERO
SPETS
SPEWS
UPEND

•P•E•
APFEL
APLEY
APNEA
APPEL
APRES
APSES
APTED
APTER
EPEES
OPTED
SPEED
SPIED
SPIEL
SPIES
SPREE
UPPED
UPPER
UPSET
YPRES

•P••E
APACE
APPLE
APURE
EPODE
OPERE
OPINE
SPACE
SPADE
SPAKE
SPARE
SPATE
SPEKE
SPICE
SPIKE
SPILE
SPINE
SPIRE
SPITE
SPODE
SPOKE
SPORE
SPREE
SPRUE
SPUME

••PE•
AMPED
APPEL
ARPEL
ASPEN
BIPED
CAPED
CAPEK
CAPER
CAPES
CAPET
CEPES
COPED
COPES
CUPEL
DEPEW
DOPED
DOPES
DOPEY
DUPED
DUPES
EXPEL
GAPED
GAPER
GAPES
HOPED
HOPER
HOPES
HYPED
HYPER
HYPES
IMPED
IMPEI
IMPEL
JAPED
JAPES
KOPEK
LAPEL
LOPED
LOPER
LOPES
LOPEZ
MOPED
MOPER
MOPES
MOPEY
NAPES
PAPER
PIPED
PIPER
PIPES
POPES
RAPEE
REPEG
REPEL
RIPEN
RIPER
ROPED
ROPER
ROPES
ROPEY
RUPEE
SUPER
SUPES
TAPED
TAPER
TAPES
TEPEE
TOPED
TOPER
TOPES
TYPEA
TYPEB
TYPED
TYPEE
TYPER
TYPES
TYPEY
UMPED
UNPEG
UNPEN
UPPED
UPPER
VIPER
WIPED
WIPER
WIPES
YIPES

••P•E
AMPLE
APPLE
COPSE
DUPLE
DUPRE
HOPPE
KOPJE
LAPSE
MAPLE
NAPPE
PUPAE
RAPEE
RAPHE
RUPEE
TEPEE
TYPEE

•••PE
AGAPE
CALPE
CARPE
COUPE
CRAPE
CREPE
DRAPE
DRUPE
ELOPE
ETAPE
GASPE
GOAPE
GRAPE
GRIPE
GROPE
HOPPE
LOUPE
MYOPE
NAPPE
SCAPE
SCOPE
SHAPE
SLOPE
SLYPE
SNIPE
STIPE
STOPE
STUPE
SWIPE
SWOPE
TAUPE
TEMPE
TRIPE
TROPE

P•F••
PUFFS
PUFFY

P••F•
PHYFE
POUFS
PROFS
PUFFS
PUFFY

P•••F
PILAF
PROOF

•PF••
APFEL

•P•F•
SPIFF

•P••F
SPIFF
SPOOF

•••PF
KNOPF

P•G••
PAGAN
PAGED
PAGER
PAGES
PAGET
PEGGY
PIGGY
PUGET
PUGGY
PYGMY

P••G•
PAIGE
PANGA
PANGS
PEGGY
PENGO
PHAGE
PHAGO
PHAGY
PIGGY
PINGO
PINGS
PLAGE
PLUGS
PODGY
PONGS
PORGY
PREGO
PRIGS
PROGS
PUDGY
PUGGY
PUNGS
PURGE

P•••G
PELEG
PRANG
PRONG

•P••G
APING
SPANG
SPRAG
SPRIG

••P•G
REPEG
TOPOG
UNPEG

PH•••
PHAGE
PHAGO
PHAGY
PHANY
PHARM
PHASE
PHENO
PHIAL
PHILE
PHILO
PHILY
PHLOX
PHNOM
PHOBE
PHONE
PHONO
PHONS
PHONY
PHOTO
PHOTS
PHREN
PHYCO
PHYFE
PHYLA
PHYLE
PHYLL
PHYSI
PHYTO

P•H••
POHAI
PSHAW

P••H•
PASHA
PATHE
PATHO
PATHS
PATHY
PITHS
PITHY
POOHS
PUSHY

P•••H
PARCH
PASCH
PATCH
PEACH
PERCH
PERTH
PINCH
PITCH
PLASH
PLATH
PLUSH
POACH
PONCH
POOCH
PORCH
POUCH
PSYCH
PUNCH

•PH••
APHID
APHIS
EPHAH
EPHAS
EPHOD
EPHOR
OPHIR

•P•H•
OPAHS
SPAHI
SPAHN

•P••H
APISH
EPHAH
EPOCH
OPRAH

••PH•
ALPHA
AMPHI
AMPHR
HYPHA
KAPHS
KOPHS
QOPHS
RAPHE
SOPHS
SOPHY

••P•H
DEPTH

•••PH
ALEPH
DOLPH
GLYPH
GRAPH
HUMPH
LYMPH
MORPH
NYMPH
OOMPH
RALPH
SYLPH

PI•••
PIANO
PIAUI
PICAS
PICKS
PICKY
PICOT
PICRO
PICTS
PICUL
PIECE
PIEDS
PIERS
PIETA
PIETY
PIGGY
PIKAS
PIKED
PIKER
PIKES
PILAF
PILAR
PILEA
PILED
PILEI
PILES
PILLS
PILOT
PILUM
PILUS
PIMAS
PINCE
PINCH
PINED
PINES
PINEY
PINGO
PINGS
PINKS
PINKY
PINNA
PINON
PINOT
PINSK
PINTA
PINTO
PINTS
PINUP
PINZA
PIONS
PIOUS
PIPAL
PIPED
PIPER
PIPES
PIPIT
PIPPA
PIPPI
PIQUE
PISAN
PISCI
PISCO
PISMO
PISTE
PITAS
PITCH
PITHS
PITHY
PITON
PITOT
PITTA
PITTS
PIURA
PIVOT
PIXEL
PIXIE
PIZZA

P•I••
PAIGE
PAILS
PAINE
PAINS
PAINT
PAIRS
PAISA
PHIAL
PHILE
PHILO
PHILY
PLICA
PLIED
PLIES
PLINK
PLINY
POILS
POILU
POINT
POISE
PRIAM
PRICE
PRICK
PRICY
PRIDE
PRIED
PRIER
PRIES
PRIGS
PRIMA
PRIME
PRIMI
PRIMO
PRIMP
PRIMS
PRINK
PRINT
PRION
PRIOR
PRISM
PRIVY
PRIZE
PRIZM

P••I•
PALIN
PAMIR
PANIC
PARIS
PATIO
PAVIA
PAVID
PAVIS
PAYIN
PEKIN
PEPIN
PERIL
PERIS
PETIT
PEWIT
PIPIT
PIXIE
PLAID
PLAIN
PLAIT
PLEIO
PODIA
POLIS
POLIT
POPIN
POSIT
PRAIA
PULIS
PUNIC
PUPIL
PUPIN
PURIM
PUTIN
PYRIC
PYXIE
PYXIS

P•••I
PALPI
PAOLI
PAPPI
PARDI
PARTI
PATRI
PATTI
PENNI
PEPSI
PESCI
PETRI
PETTI
PHYSI
PIAUI
PILEI
PIPPI
PISCI
PLANI
POHAI
PONTI
PONZI
PRIMI
PUCCI
PUTTI

•PI••
APIAN
APING
APISH

EPICS
EPISC
OPINE
OPIUM
SPICA
SPICE
SPICY
SPIED
SPIEL
SPIES
SPIFF
SPIKE
SPIKY
SPILE
SPILL
SPILT
SPINE
SPINS
SPINY
SPIRE
SPIRO
SPIRY
SPITE
SPITS
SPITZ
SPIVS

•P•I•
APHID
APHIS
APRIL
APSIS
OPCIT
OPHIR
OPSIN
OPSIS
OPTIC
SPAIN
SPLIT
SPOIL
SPRIG
SPRIT

•P••I
SPAHI
SPYRI

••PI•
ASPIC
CUPID
HOPIN
HOPIS
KEPIS
LAPIN
LAPIS
LIPID
LUPIN
PEPIN
PIPIT
POPIN
PUPIL
PUPIN
RAPID
REPIN
SAPID
SAPIR
SEPIA
TAPIN
TAPIR
TEPID
TIPIN
TOPIC
TOPIS
UNPIN
VAPID
YUPIK

••P•I
AMPHI
CAPRI
CUPRI
IMPEI
LIPPI
PAPPI
PEPSI
PIPPI
TIPPI
TOPOI

•••PI
CARPI
LIPPI
OKAPI
PALPI
PAPPI
PIPPI
SIEPI
TEMPI
TIPPI

••PJ•
KOPJE

P•K••
PEKES
PEKIN
PEKOE
PIKAS
PIKED
PIKER
PIKES
POKED
POKER
POKES
POKEY
PUKKA

P••K•
PACKS
PANKY
PARKA
PARKS
PAWKY
PEAKS
PECKS
PECKY
PEEKS
PERKS
PERKY
PESKY
PICKS
PICKY
PINKS
PINKY
POLKA
PORKS
PORKY
PUCKS
PUKKA
PUNKS
PUNKY

P•••K
PATEK
PINSK
PLANK
PLINK
PLONK
PLUCK
PLUNK
POTOK
PRANK
PRICK
PRINK

•P•K•
SPAKE
SPEKE
SPIKE
SPIKY
SPOKE

•P••K
APEAK
SPAAK
SPANK
SPARK
SPEAK
SPECK
SPOCK
SPOOK
SPORK
SPUNK

••P•K
CAPEK
KAPOK
KOPEK
YAPOK
YUPIK

PL•••
PLACE
PLAGE
PLAID
PLAIN
PLAIT
PLANB
PLANE
PLANI
PLANK
PLANO
PLANS
PLANT
PLASH
PLASM
PLATA
PLATE
PLATH
PLATO
PLATS
PLATT
PLATY
PLAYA
PLAYS
PLAZA
PLEAD
PLEAS
PLEAT
PLEBE
PLEBS
PLEIO
PLENA
PLEON
PLEWS
PLICA
PLIED
PLIES
PLINK
PLINY
PLODS
PLONK
PLOPS
PLOTS
PLOWS
PLOYS
PLUCK
PLUGS
PLUMB
PLUME
PLUMP
PLUMS
PLUMY
PLUNK
PLUSH
PLUTO

P•L••
PALAE
PALAU
PALEA
PALED
PALEO
PALER
PALES
PALEY
PALIN
PALLS
PALLY
PALMA
PALME
PALMS
PALMY
PALOS
PALPI
PALPS
PALSY
PELEE
PELEG
PELLA
PELLE
PELTS
PHLOX
PILAF
PILAR
PILEA
PILED
PILEI
PILES
PILLS
PILOT
PILUM
PILUS
POLAR
POLED
POLER
POLES
POLIS
POLIT
POLKA
POLLO
POLLS
POLLY
POLOS
POLYP
PULAS
PULED
PULES
PULIS
PULLS
PULPS
PULPY
PULSE
PYLON

P••L•
PABLO
PAILS
PALLS
PALLY
PAOLI
PAOLO
PARLE
PATLY
PAULA
PAULO
PAWLS
PEALE
PEALS
PEELE
PEELS
PELLA
PELLE
PEPLA
PERLE
PHILE
PHILO
PHILY
PHYLA
PHYLE
PHYLL
PILLS
POILS
POILU
POLLO
POLLS
POLLY
POOLE
POOLS
POULT
PRELL
PROLE
PSALM
PULLS
PURLS

P•••L
PANDL
PANEL
PAPAL
PAROL
PEARL
PEDAL
PENAL
PERIL
PETAL
PHIAL
PHYLL
PICUL
PIPAL
PIXEL
PRELL
PROWL
PUPAL
PUPIL

•PL••
APLEY
APLUS
BPLUS
CPLUS
DPLUS
SPLAT
SPLAY
SPLIT

•P•L•
APPLE
APPLY
APTLY
OPALS
OPELS
SPALL
SPELL
SPELT
SPILE
SPILL
SPILT
UPOLU

•P••L
APFEL
APPAL
APPEL
APRIL
SPALL
SPELL
SPIEL
SPILL
SPOIL
SPOOL

••PL•
AMPLE
AMPLY
APPLE
APPLY
DIPLO
DUPLE
HAPLO
HAPLY
HIPLY
IMPLY
MAPLE
PEPLA
REPLY

••P•L
AMPUL
APPAL
APPEL
ARPEL
COPAL
CUPEL
EXPEL
IMPEL
LAPEL
NEPAL
NOPAL
PAPAL
PIPAL
PUPAL
PUPIL
REPEL
SEPAL
TEPAL
TOPOL

P•M••
PAMBY
PAMIR
PAMPA
PEMBA
PIMAS
POMES
POMME
POMOS
PUMAS
PUMPS

P••M•
PALMA
PALME
PALMS
PALMY
PARMA
PERMS
PISMO
PLUMB
PLUME
PLUMP
PLUMS
PLUMY
POEME
POEMS
POMME
PRAMS
PRIMA
PRIME
PRIMI
PRIMO
PRIMP
PRIMS
PROMO
PROMS
PYGMY

P•••M
PANAM
PHARM
PHNOM
PILUM
PLASM
PRIAM
PRISM
PRIZM
PROAM
PROEM
PSALM
PURIM

•P•M•
SPAMS
SPUME
SPUMY

•P••M
EPROM
EPSOM
IPSUM
OPIUM
SPASM

•••PM
ONEPM
SIXPM
TENPM
TWOPM

P•N••
PANAM
PANAY
PANDA
PANDL
PANED
PANEL
PANES
PANGA
PANGS
PANIC
PANKY
PANNE
PANSY
PANTO
PANTS
PANZA
PENAL
PENCE
PENDS
PENGO
PENNA
PENNE
PENNI
PENNY
PENTA
PENTE
PENZA
PHNOM
PINCE
PINCH
PINED
PINES
PINEY
PINGO
PINGS
PINKS
PINKY
PINNA
PINON
PINOT
PINSK
PINTA
PINTO
PINTS
PINUP
PINZA
PONCA
PONCE
PONCH
PONDS
PONES
PONGS
PONTE
PONTI
PONTS
PONZI
PUNAS
PUNCH
PUNGS
PUNIC
PUNKS
PUNKY
PUNNY
PUNTA
PUNTS
PUNTY

P••N•
PAINE
PAINS
PAINT
PANNE
PATNA
PAWNS
PAYNE
PEENS
PENNA
PENNE
PENNI
PENNY
PEONS
PEONY
PHANY
PHENO
PHONE
PHONO
PHONS
PHONY
PIANO
PINNA
PIONS
PLANB
PLANE
PLANI
PLANK
PLANO
PLANS
PLANT
PLENA
PLINK
PLINY
PLONK
PLUNK
POINT
POONA
POONS
POUND
PRANG
PRANK
PRINK
PRINT
PRONE
PRONG
PRUNE
PUNNY

P•••N
PAEAN
PAEON
PAGAN
PALIN
PAREN
PATEN
PATON
PAYIN
PECAN
PEKIN
PEPIN
PERAN
PERON
PHREN
PINON
PISAN
PITON
PLAIN
PLEON
POPIN
PRAWN
PREEN
PRION
PUPIN
PUSAN
PUTIN
PUTON
PYLON

•PN••
APNEA

•P•N•
APING
IPANA
OPENS
OPINE
SPANG
SPANK
SPANS
SPEND
SPENT
SPINE
SPINS
SPINY
SPUNK
UPEND

•P••N
APIAN
APRON
EPSON
OPSIN
SPAHN
SPAIN
SPAWN
SPOON
SPURN
SPYON
UPTON

••PN•
HYPNO

••P•N
ASPEN
CAPON
COPAN
HOPIN
JAPAN
LAPIN
LUPIN
PEPIN
POPIN
PUPIN
REPIN

RIPEN
RIPON
TAPIN
TIPIN
UNPEN
UNPIN

PO•••
POACH
POBOX
POBOY
POCUS
PODGY
PODIA
POEME
POEMS
POESY
POETE
POETS
POHAI
POILS
POILU
POINT
POISE
POKED
POKER
POKES
POKEY
POLAR
POLED
POLER
POLES
POLIS
POLIT
POLKA
POLLO
POLLS
POLLY
POLOS
POLYP
POMES
POMME
POMOS
PONCA
PONCE
PONCH
PONDS
PONES
PONGS
PONTE
PONTI
PONTS
PONZI
POOCH
POODS
POOHS
POOLE
POOLS
POONA
POONS
POOPS
POPES
POPIN
POPOV
POPPA
POPPY
POPUP
PORCH
PORED
PORES
PORGY
PORKS
PORKY
PORTE
PORTO
PORTS
POSED
POSER
POSES
POSIT
POSSE
POSTE
POSTS
POTOK
POTSY
POTTO
POTTS
POTTY
POUCH
POUFS
POULT
POUND
POURS
POUTS
POUTY
POWAY
POWER
POWYS

P•O••
PAOLI
PAOLO
PEONS
PEONY
PHOBE
PHONE
PHONO
PHONS
PHONY
PHOTO
PHOTS
PIONS
PIOUS
PLODS
PLONK
PLOPS
PLOTS
PLOWS
PLOYS
POOCH
POODS
POOHS
POOLE
POOLS
POONA
POONS
POOPS
PROAM
PROAS
PROBE
PROBS
PRODS
PROEM
PROFS
PROGS
PROLE
PROMO
PROMS
PRONE
PRONG
PROOF
PROPS
PROSE
PROST
PROSY
PROTO
PROTS
PROUD
PROVE
PROVO
PROWL
PROWS
PROXY
PSOAS

P••O•
PAEON
PALOS
PAROL
PAROS
PATON
PECOS
PEKOE
PEPOS
PERON
PEROT
PESOS
PHLOX
PHNOM
PICOT
PILOT
PINON
PINOT
PITON
PITOT
PIVOT
PLEON
POBOX
POBOY
POLOS
POMOS
POPOV
POTOK
PRION
PRIOR
PROOF
PRYOR
PUTON
PYLON

P•••O
PAAVO
PABLO
PALEO
PANTO
PAOLO
PARDO
PARVO
PASCO
PASEO
PASTO
PATHO
PATIO
PAULO
PEABO
PEDRO
PENGO
PESTO
PETRO
PHAGO
PHENO
PHILO
PHONO
PHOTO
PHYCO
PHYTO
PIANO
PICRO
PINGO
PINTO
PISCO
PISMO
PLANO
PLATO
PLEIO
PLUTO
POLLO
PORTO
POTTO
PRADO
PRATO
PREGO
PRIMO
PROMO
PROTO
PROVO
PTERO
PUTTO

•PO••
APORT
EPOCH
EPODE
EPOXY
SPOCK
SPODE
SPOIL
SPOKE
SPOOF
SPOOK
SPOOL
SPOON
SPOOR
SPORE
SPORK
SPORT
SPOSA
SPOTS
SPOUT
UPOLU

•P•O•
APRON
APSOS
EPCOT
EPHOD
EPHOR
EPROM
EPSOM
EPSON
SPOOF
SPOOK
SPOOL
SPOON
SPOOR
SPYON
UPBOW
UPDOS
UPTON

•P••O
SPERO
SPIRO

••PO•
BIPOD
CAPON
CAPOS
CSPOT
DEPOT
ESPOO
EXPOS
HYPOS
KAPOK
NEPOS
PEPOS
POPOV
REPOS
REPOT
RIPON
SAPOR
SEPOY
SOPOR
TOPOG
TOPOI
TOPOL
TOPOS
TYPOS
VAPOR
YAPOK

••P•O
CUPRO
DIPLO
ESPOO
HAPLO
HIPPO
HIPTO
HYPNO
HYPSO
LEPTO
LIPPO
REPRO
ZEPPO

•••PO
ADIPO
CAMPO
CARPO
COMPO
FIRPO
HARPO
HIPPO
KIMPO
LIPPO
MAYPO
MOKPO
TAUPO
TEMPO
TROPO
ZEPPO

P•P••
PAPAL
PAPAS
PAPAW
PAPER
PAPPI
PAPPY
PAPUA
PEPIN
PEPLA
PEPOS
PEPPY
PEPSI
PEPUP
PEPYS
PIPAL
PIPED
PIPER
PIPES
PIPIT
PIPPA
PIPPI
POPES
POPIN
POPOV
POPPA
POPPY
POPUP
PUPAE
PUPAL
PUPAS
PUPIL
PUPIN
PUPPY
PUPUS

P••P•
PALPI
PALPS
PAMPA
PAPPI
PAPPY
PEEPS
PEPPY
PERPS
PIPPA
PIPPI
PLOPS
POOPS
POPPA
POPPY
PREPS
PROPS
PULPS
PULPY
PUMPS
PUPPY

P•••P
PAYUP
PEPUP
PINUP
PLUMP
POLYP
POPUP
PRIMP
PTRAP
PUTUP

•PP••
APPAL
APPEL
APPLE
APPLY
APPTD
APPTS
UPPED
UPPER

••PP•
CUPPA
DIPPY
GUPPY
HAPPY
HIPPO
HIPPY
HOPPE
KAPPA
LAPPS
LEPPY
LIPPI
LIPPO
LIPPY
LOPPY
NAPPE
NAPPY
NIPPY
PAPPI
PAPPY
PEPPY
PIPPA
PIPPI
POPPA
POPPY
PUPPY
REPPS
SAPPY
SOPPY
TIPPI
TIPPY
TOPPS
ZAPPA
ZAPPY
ZEPPO
ZIPPY

••P•P
HOPUP
LAPUP
MOPUP
NIPUP
PEPUP
POPUP
RIPUP
SOPUP
TIPUP
ZIPUP

•••PP
KRUPP
TRAPP

P•Q••
PIQUE

PR•••
PRADO
PRAIA
PRAMS
PRANG
PRANK
PRASE
PRATE
PRATO
PRATT
PRAUS
PRAWN
PRAYS
PREEN
PREGO
PRELL
PREPS
PRESS
PREST
PREXY
PREYS
PRIAM
PRICE
PRICK
PRICY
PRIDE
PRIED
PRIER
PRIES
PRIGS
PRIMA
PRIME
PRIMI
PRIMO
PRIMP
PRIMS
PRINK
PRINT
PRION
PRIOR
PRISM
PRIVY
PRIZE
PRIZM
PROAM
PROAS
PROBE
PROBS
PRODS
PROEM
PROFS
PROGS
PROLE
PROMO
PROMS
PRONE
PRONG
PROOF
PROPS
PROSE
PROST
PROSY
PROTO
PROTS
PROUD
PROVE
PROVO
PROWL
PROWS
PROXY
PRUDE
PRUNE
PRYCE
PRYOR

P•R••
PARCA
PARCH
PARDI
PARDO
PARDS
PARED
PAREE
PAREN
PARER
PARES
PAREU
PARIS
PARKA
PARKS
PARLE
PARMA
PAROL
PAROS
PARRY
PARSE
PARTE
PARTI
PARTS
PARTY
PARVO
PERAN
PERCE
PERCH
PERCY
PERDU
PERES
PEREZ
PERIL
PERIS
PERKS
PERKY
PERLE
PERMS
PERON
PEROT
PERPS
PERRY
PERSE
PERTH
PHREN
PORCH
PORED
PORES
PORGY
PORKS
PORKY
PORTE
PORTO
PORTS
PTRAP
PUREE
PURER
PUREX
PURGE
PURIM
PURLS
PURRS
PURSE
PURSY
PURUS
PYRES
PYREX
PYRIC

P••R•
PADRE
PAIRS
PARRY
PATRI
PEARL
PEARS
PEARY
PEDRO
PEERS
PERRY
PETRA
PETRI
PETRO
PHARM
PICRO
PIERS
PIURA
POURS
PTERO
PURRS

P•••R
PACER
PAGER
PALER
PAMIR
PAPER
PARER
PATER
PAVER
PAWER
PAYER
PETER
PIKER
PILAR
PIPER
POKER
POLAR
POLER
POSER
POWER
PRIER
PRIOR
PRYOR
PURER

•PR••
APRES
APRIL
APRON
EPROM
OPRAH
SPRAG
SPRAT
SPRAY
SPREE
SPRIG
SPRIT
SPRUE
YPRES

•P•R•
APART
APERS
APERY
APORT
APURE
OPART
OPERA
OPERE

SPARE
SPARK
SPARS
SPERO
SPIRE
SPIRO
SPIRY
SPORE
SPORK
SPORT
SPURN
SPURS
SPURT
SPYRI

•P••R

APTER
EPHOR
OPHIR
SPEAR
SPOOR
UPPER

••PR•

CAPRA
CAPRI
COPRA
CUPRI
CUPRO
DUPRE
REPRO
SUPRA

••P•R

AMPHR
ATPAR
CAPER
GAPER
HOPER
HYPER
LOPER
MOPER
NOPAR
PAPER
PIPER
RIPER
ROPER
SAPIR
SAPOR
SOPOR
SUPER
SUPVR
TAPER
TAPIR
TOPER
TYPER
UPPER
VAPOR
VIPER
WIPER

PS•••

PSALM
PSATS
PSEUD
PSHAW
PSOAS
PSYCH

P•S••

PASCH
PASCO
PASEO
PASES
PASHA
PASSE
PASSU
PASSY
PASTA
PASTE
PASTO
PASTS
PASTY
PESCI
PESKY
PESOS
PESTO
PESTS
PISAN
PISCI
PISCO
PISMO
PISTE
POSED
POSER
POSES
POSIT
POSSE
POSTE
POSTS
PUSAN
PUSEY
PUSHY

P••S•

PABST
PAISA
PALSY
PANSY
PARSE
PASSE
PASSU
PASSY
PATSY
PAUSE
PEASE
PEPSI
PERSE
PHASE
PHYSI
PINSK
PLASH
PLASM
PLUSH
POESY
POISE
POSSE
POTSY
PRASE
PRESS
PREST
PRISM
PROSE
PROST
PROSY
PULSE
PURSE
PURSY

P•••S

PACAS
PACES
PACKS
PACTS
PAGES
PAILS
PAINS
PAIRS
PALES
PALLS
PALMS
PALOS
PALPS
PANES
PANGS
PANTS
PAPAS
PARDS
PARES
PARIS
PARKS
PAROS
PARTS
PASES
PASTS
PATES
PATHS
PAVES
PAVIS
PAWLS
PAWNS
PEAKS
PEALS
PEARS
PEATS
PECKS
PECOS
PEEKS
PEELS
PEENS
PEEPS
PEERS
PEKES
PELTS
PENDS
PEONS
PEPOS
PEPYS
PERES
PERIS
PERKS
PERMS
PERPS
PESOS
PESTS
PETES
PHONS
PHOTS
PICAS
PICKS
PICTS
PIEDS
PIERS
PIKAS
PIKES
PILES
PILLS
PILUS
PIMAS
PINES
PINGS
PINKS
PINTS
PIONS
PIOUS
PIPES
PITAS
PITHS
PITTS
PLANS
PLATS
PLAYS
PLEAS
PLEBS
PLEWS
PLIES
PLODS
PLOPS
PLOTS
PLOWS
PLOYS
PLUGS
PLUMS
POCUS
POEMS
POETS
POILS
POKES
POLES
POLIS
POLLS
POLOS
POMES
POMOS
PONDS
PONES
PONGS
PONTS
POODS
POOHS
POOLS
POONS
POOPS
POPES
PORES
PORKS
PORTS
POSES
POSTS
POTTS
POUFS
POURS
POUTS
POWYS
PRAMS
PRAUS
PRAYS
PREPS
PRESS
PREYS
PRIES
PRIGS
PRIMS
PROAS
PROBS
PRODS
PROFS
PROGS
PROMS
PROPS
PROTS
PROWS
PSATS
PSOAS
PUCKS
PUDUS
PUFFS
PULAS
PULES
PULIS
PULLS
PULPS
PUMAS
PUMPS
PUNAS
PUNGS
PUNKS
PUNTS
PUPAS
PUPUS
PURLS
PURRS
PURUS
PUTTS
PYRES
PYXIS

•PS••

APSES
APSIS
APSOS
EPSOM
EPSON
IPSUM
OPSIN
OPSIS
UPSET

•P•S•

APISH
EPISC
IPASS
SPASM
SPOSA

•P••S

APERS
APHIS
APLUS
APPTS
APRES
APSES
APSIS
APSOS
BPLUS
CPLUS
DPLUS
EPEES
EPHAS
EPICS
IPASS
OPAHS
OPALS
OPEDS
OPELS
OPENS
OPSIS
SPADS
SPAMS
SPANS
SPARS
SPATS
SPAYS
SPECS
SPETS
SPEWS
SPIES
SPINS
SPITS
SPIVS
SPOTS
SPUDS
SPURS
UPDOS
YPRES

••PS•

COPSE
GIPSY
GYPSY
HYPSO
LAPSE
MOPSY
PEPSI
TIPSY
TOPSY

••P•S

AMPAS
APPTS
CAPES
CAPOS
CAPTS
CEPES
COPES
COPTS
DEPTS
DOPES
DUPES
EXPOS
GAPES
HOPES
HOPIS
HYPES
HYPOS
JAPES
KAPHS
KEPIS
KOPHS
LAPIS
LAPPS
LEPUS
LOPES
MOPES
NAPES
NEPOS
NIPAS
PAPAS
PEPOS
PEPYS
PIPES
POPES
PUPAS
PUPUS
QOPHS
REPOS
REPPS
ROPES
SOPHS
SUPES
SUPTS
TAPAS
TAPES
TOPES
TOPIS
TOPOS
TOPPS
TYPES
TYPOS
WIPES
YIPES

•••PS

BEEPS
BLIPS
BUMPS
BURPS
CAMPS
CARPS
CHAPS
CHIPS
CHOPS
CLAPS
CLIPS
CLOPS
COMPS
COOPS
CORPS
COUPS
CRAPS
CROPS
CUSPS
DAMPS
DEEPS
DORPS
DRIPS
DROPS
DUMPS
FLAPS
FLIPS
FLOPS
FRAPS
GAMPS
GASPS
GAWPS
GIMPS
GLOPS
GOOPS
GORPS
GRIPS
GULPS
HARPS
HASPS
HEAPS
HELPS
HEMPS
HOOPS
HUMPS
JEEPS
JUMPS
KEEPS
KELPS
KEMPS
KNAPS
KNOPS
LAMPS
LAPPS
LEAPS
LIMPS
LISPS
LOOPS
LUMPS
MUMPS
NEAPS
PALPS
PEEPS
PERPS
PLOPS
POOPS
PREPS
PROPS
PULPS
PUMPS
QTIPS
QUIPS
RAMPS
RASPS
REAPS
REPPS
REUPS
ROMPS
RSVPS
RUMPS
SALPS
SAMPS
SCOPS
SCUPS
SEEPS
SHIPS
SHOPS
SIMPS
SKEPS
SKIPS
SLAPS
SLIPS
SLOPS
SNAPS
SNIPS
SOAPS
SOUPS
STEPS
STOPS
SUMPS
SWAPS
SWOPS
TAMPS
TARPS
TBSPS
TEMPS
TERPS
TOPPS
TRAPS
TRIPS
TUMPS
VAMPS
VEEPS
WARPS
WASPS
WEEPS
WHIPS
WHOPS
WHUPS
WIMPS
WISPS
WRAPS
YAWPS
YELPS

PT•••

PTERO
PTRAP

P•T••

PATCH
PATED
PATEK
PATEN
PATER
PATES
PATHE
PATHO
PATHS
PATHY
PATIO
PATLY
PATNA
PATON
PATRI
PATSY
PATTI
PATTY
PETAL
PETER
PETES
PETIT
PETRA
PETRI
PETRO
PETTI
PETTY
PITAS
PITCH
PITHS
PITHY
PITON
PITOT
PITTA
PITTS
POTOK
POTSY
POTTO
POTTS
POTTY
PUTBY
PUTIN
PUTON
PUTTI
PUTTO
PUTTS
PUTTY
PUTUP

P••T•

PACTS
PANTO
PANTS
PARTE
PARTI
PARTS
PARTY
PASTA
PASTE
PASTO
PASTS
PASTY
PATTI
PATTY
PAYTV
PEATS
PEATY
PEETE
PELTS
PENTA
PENTE
PERTH
PESTO
PESTS
PETTI
PETTY
PHOTO
PHOTS
PHYTO
PICTS
PIETA
PIETY
PINTA
PINTO
PINTS
PISTE
PITTA
PITTS
PLATA
PLATE
PLATH
PLATO
PLATS
PLATT
PLATY
PLOTS
PLUTO
POETE
POETS
PONTE
PONTI
PONTS
PORTE
PORTO
PORTS
POSTE
POSTS
POTTO
POTTS
POTTY
POUTS
POUTY
PRATE
PRATO
PRATT
PROTO
PROTS
PSATS
PUNTA
PUNTS
PUNTY
PUTTI
PUTTO
PUTTS
PUTTY

P•••T

PABST
PAGET

PAINT
PAWAT
PEROT
PETIT
PEWIT
PICOT
PILOT
PINOT
PIPIT
PITOT
PIVOT
PLAIT
PLANT
PLATT
PLEAT
POINT
POLIT
POSIT
POULT
PRATT
PREST
PRINT
PROST
PUGET

•PT••
APTED
APTER
APTLY
OPTED
OPTIC
UPTON

•P•T•
APPTD
APPTS
SPATE
SPATS
SPETS
SPITE
SPITS
SPITZ
SPOTS

•P••T
APART
APORT
EPACT
EPCOT
OPART
OPCIT
SPELT
SPENT
SPILT
SPLAT
SPLIT
SPORT
SPOUT
SPRAT
SPRIT
SPURT
UPSET

••PT•
APPTD
APPTS
CAPTS
COPTS
DEPTH
DEPTS
EMPTY
HEPTA
HIPTO
LEPTA
LEPTO
SEPTA
SUPTS

••P•T
CAPET
CSPOT
DEPOT
INPUT
KAPUT
LOPAT
NIPAT
PIPIT
REPOT
STPAT

•••PT
ADAPT
ADEPT
ADOPT
CLIPT
COAPT
COOPT
CREPT
CRYPT
EGYPT
ERUPT
INAPT
INEPT
KEMPT
LEAPT
SLEPT
SLIPT
SWEPT
TEMPT
UNAPT
WRAPT

PU•••
PUCCI
PUCKS
PUDGY
PUDUS
PUFFS
PUFFY
PUGET
PUGGY
PUKKA
PULAS
PULED
PULES
PULIS
PULLS
PULPS
PULPY
PULSE
PUMAS
PUMPS
PUNAS
PUNCH
PUNGS
PUNIC
PUNKS
PUNKY
PUNNY
PUNTA
PUNTS
PUNTY
PUPAE
PUPAL
PUPAS
PUPIL
PUPIN
PUPPY
PUPUS
PUREE
PURER
PUREX
PURGE
PURIM
PURLS
PURRS
PURSE
PURSY
PURUS
PUSAN
PUSEY
PUSHY
PUTBY
PUTIN
PUTON
PUTTI
PUTTO
PUTTS
PUTTY
PUTUP

P•U••
PAULA
PAULO
PAUSE
PIURA
PLUCK
PLUGS
PLUMB
PLUME
PLUMP
PLUMS
PLUMY
PLUNK
PLUSH
PLUTO
POUCH
POUFS
POULT
POUND
POURS
POUTS
POUTY
PRUDE
PRUNE

P••U•
PADUA
PAPUA
PAYUP
PEPUP
PIAUI
PICUL
PILUM
PILUS
PINUP
PIOUS
PIQUE
POCUS
POPUP
PRAUS
PROUD
PSEUD
PUDUS
PUPUS
PURUS
PUTUP

P•••U
PALAU
PAREU
PASSU
PERDU
POILU

•PU••
APURE
SPUDS
SPUME
SPUMY
SPUNK
SPURN
SPURS
SPURT

•P•U•
APLUS
BPLUS
CPLUS
DPLUS
IPSUM
OPIUM
SPOUT
SPRUE

•P••U
UPOLU

••PU•
AMPUL
HOPUP
INPUT
KAPUT
LAPUP
LEPUS
MOPUP
NIPUP
PAPUA
PEPUP
POPUP
PUPUS
RIPUP
SOPUP
TIPUP
ZIPUP

•••PU
COYPU
QUIPU

P•V••
PAVED
PAVER
PAVES
PAVIA
PAVID
PAVIS
PIVOT

P••V•
PAAVO
PARVO
PEAVY
PEEVE
PRIVY
PROVE
PROVO

P•••V
PAYTV
POPOV

•P•V•
SPIVS

••PV•
SUPVR

••P•V
POPOV

P•W••
PAWAT
PAWED
PAWER
PAWKY
PAWLS
PAWNS
PEWEE
PEWIT
POWAY
POWER
POWYS

P••W•
PLEWS
PLOWS
PRAWN
PROWL
PROWS

P•••W
PAPAW
PSHAW

•P•W•
SPAWN
SPEWS

•P••W
UPBOW

••P•W
DEPEW
PAPAW

P•X••
PIXEL
PIXIE
PYXIE
PYXIS

P••X•
PREXY
PROXY

P•••X
PHLOX
POBOX
PUREX
PYREX

•P•X•
EPOXY

PY•••
PYGMY
PYLON
PYRES
PYREX
PYRIC
PYXIE
PYXIS

P•Y••
PAYED
PAYEE
PAYER
PAYIN
PAYNE
PAYTV
PAYUP
PHYCO
PHYFE
PHYLA
PHYLE
PHYLL
PHYSI
PHYTO
PRYCE
PRYOR
PSYCH

P••Y•
PEPYS
PLAYA
PLAYS
PLOYS
POLYP
POWYS
PRAYS
PREYS

P•••Y
PADDY
PALEY
PALLY
PALMY
PALSY
PAMBY
PANAY
PANKY
PANSY
PAPPY
PARRY
PARTY
PASSY
PASTY
PATHY
PATLY
PATSY
PATTY
PAWKY
PEARY
PEATY
PEAVY
PECKY
PEGGY
PENNY
PEONY
PEPPY
PERCY
PERKY
PERRY
PESKY
PETTY
PHAGY
PHANY
PHILY
PHONY
PICKY
PIETY
PIGGY
PINEY
PINKY
PITHY
PLATY
PLINY
PLUMY
POBOY
PODGY
POESY
POKEY
POLLY
POPPY
PORGY
PORKY
POTSY
POTTY
POUTY
POWAY
PREXY
PRICY
PRIVY
PROSY
PROXY
PUDGY
PUFFY
PUGGY
PULPY
PUNKY
PUNNY
PUNTY
PUPPY
PURSY
PUSEY
PUSHY
PUTBY
PUTTY
PYGMY

•PY••
SPYON
SPYRI

•P•Y•
SPAYS

•P••Y
APERY
APLEY
APPLY
APTLY
EPOXY
SPACY
SPICY
SPIKY
SPINY
SPIRY
SPLAY
SPRAY
SPUMY

••PY•
PEPYS

••P•Y
AMPLY
APPLY
COPAY
DIPPY
DOPEY
EMPTY
GIPSY
GUPPY
GYPSY
HAPLY
HAPPY
HIPLY
HIPPY
IMPLY
LEPPY
LIPPY
LOPPY
MOPEY
MOPSY
NAPPY
NIPPY
PAPPY
PEPPY
POPPY
PUPPY
REPAY
REPLY
ROPEY
SAPPY
SEPOY
SOPHY
SOPPY
TIPPY
TIPSY
TOPSY
TYPEY
ZAPPY
ZIPPY

•••PY
BUMPY
CAMPY
DIPPY
DUMPY
GIMPY
GOOPY
GRAPY
GULPY
GUPPY
HAPPY
HARPY
HIPPY
HUMPY
JUMPY
KELPY
LEPPY
LIPPY
LOOPY
LOPPY
LUMPY
NAPPY
NIPPY
PAPPY
PEPPY
POPPY
PULPY
PUPPY
RASPY
SAPPY
SCOPY
SEEPY
SOAPY
SOPPY
SOUPY
TIPPY
WASPY
WEEPY
WIMPY
WISPY
ZAPPY
ZIPPY

P•Z••
PIZZA

P••Z•
PANZA
PENZA
PINZA
PIZZA
PLAZA
PONZI
PRIZE
PRIZM

P•••Z
PEREZ

•P••Z
SPITZ

••P•Z
LAPAZ
LOPEZ
TOPAZ

QA•••
QANDA
QATAR

Q•A••
QUACK
QUADR
QUADS
QUAFF
QUAGS
QUAID
QUAIL
QUAKE
QUAKY
QUALE
QUALM
QUAND
QUANT
QUARE
QUARK
QUART
QUASH
QUASI
QUAYS

Q••A•
QATAR
QUOAD

Q•••A
QANDA
QUOTA

•QA••
AQABA

•Q•A•
AQUAE
AQUAS
EQUAL
SQUAB
SQUAD
SQUAT

•Q••A
AQABA

QB•••
QBVII

•Q•B•
AQABA

•Q••B
SQUAB
SQUIB

Q••C•
QUACK
QUICK

Q••D•
QANDA
QUADR
QUADS
QUIDS
QUODS

Q•••D
QUAID
QUAND
QUOAD

•Q••D
SQUAD
SQUID

Q•E••
QUEEG
QUEEN
QUEER
QUELL
QUERN
QUERY
QUEST
QUEUE

Q••E•
QUEEG
QUEEN
QUEER
QUIEN
QUIET

Q•••E
QUAKE
QUALE
QUARE
QUEUE
QUIRE
QUITE
QUOTE

•Q••E
AQUAE

••Q•E
ATQUE
ESQUE
PIQUE
ROQUE
TOQUE
TUQUE
USQUE

Q••F•
QUAFF

Q•••F
QUAFF

Q••G•
QUAGS

Q•••G
QUEEG

Q••H•
QOPHS

Q•••H
QUASH
QUOTH

Q•I••
QTIPS
QUICK
QUIDS
QUIEN
QUIET
QUILL
QUILP
QUILT
QUINN
QUINO
QUINT
QUIPS
QUIPU
QUIRE
QUIRK
QUIRT
QUITE
QUITO
QUITS

Q••I•
QBVII
QUAID
QUAIL
QUOIN
QUOIT

Q•••I
QBVII
QUASI

•Q•I•
EQUIP
EQUIV
IQUIT
SQUIB
SQUID

••Q•I
MAQUI
YAQUI

•••QI
IRAQI

Q••K•
QUAKE
QUAKY

Q•••K
QUACK
QUARK
QUICK
QUIRK

Q••L•
QUALE
QUALM
QUELL
QUILL
QUILP
QUILT

Q•••L
QUAIL
QUELL
QUILL

•Q••L
EQUAL

Q•••M
QUALM

Q•N••
QANDA

Q••N•
QUAND
QUANT
QUINN
QUINO
QUINT

Q•••N
QUEEN
QUERN
QUIEN
QUINN
QUOIN

QO•••
QOPHS

Q•O••
QUOAD
QUODS
QUOIN
QUOIT
QUOTA
QUOTE
QUOTH

Q•••O
QUINO
QUITO

Q•P••
QOPHS

Q••P•
QTIPS
QUIPS
QUIPU

Q•••P
QUILP

•Q••P
EQUIP

•••QQ
ETSQQ

Q••R•
QUARE
QUARK
QUART
QUERN
QUERY
QUIRE
QUIRK
QUIRT

Q•••R
QATAR
QUADR
QUEER

Q••S•
QUASH
QUASI
QUEST

Q•••S
QOPHS
QTIPS
QUADS
QUAGS
QUAYS
QUIDS
QUIPS
QUITS
QUODS

•Q••S
AQUAS
EQUUS

•••QS
BARQS

QT•••
QTIPS

Q•T••
QATAR

Q••T•
QUITE
QUITO
QUITS
QUOTA
QUOTE
QUOTH

Q•••T
QUANT
QUART
QUEST
QUIET
QUILT
QUINT
QUIRT
QUOIT

•Q••T
IQUIT
SQUAT

QU•••
QUACK
QUADR
QUADS
QUAFF
QUAGS
QUAID
QUAIL
QUAKE
QUAKY
QUALE
QUALM
QUAND
QUANT
QUARE
QUARK
QUART
QUASH
QUASI
QUAYS
QUEEG
QUEEN
QUEER
QUELL
QUERN
QUERY
QUEST
QUEUE
QUICK
QUIDS
QUIEN
QUIET
QUILL
QUILP
QUILT
QUINN
QUINO
QUINT
QUIPS
QUIPU
QUIRE
QUIRK
QUIRT
QUITE
QUITO
QUITS
QUOAD
QUODS
QUOIN
QUOIT
QUOTA
QUOTE
QUOTH

Q••U•
QUEUE

Q•••U
QUIPU

•QU••
AQUAE
AQUAS
EQUAL
EQUIP
EQUIV
EQUUS
IQUIT
SQUAB
SQUAD
SQUAT
SQUIB
SQUID

•Q•U•
EQUUS

••QU•
ATQUE
ESQUE
MAQUI
PIQUE
ROQUE
TOQUE
TUQUE
USQUE
YAQUI

Q•V••
QBVII

•Q••V
EQUIV

Q••Y•
QUAYS

Q•••Y
QUAKY
QUERY

RA•••
RABAT
RABBI
RABID
RABIN
RACED
RACER
RACES
RACKS
RACON
RADAR
RADII
RADIO
RADIX
RADON
RAFER
RAFFI
RAFTS
RAGAS
RAGED
RAGES
RAHAB
RAHAL
RAIDS
RAILS
RAINS
RAINY
RAISA
RAISE
RAITT
RAJAH
RAJAS
RAJIV
RAKED
RAKER
RAKES
RAKIS
RALLY
RALPH
RAMAN
RAMAR
RAMBO
RAMEE
RAMEN
RAMET
RAMIE
RAMIS
RAMON
RAMOS
RAMPS
RANAT
RANCH
RANDB
RANDD
RANDI
RANDR
RANDS
RANDY
RANEE
RANGE
RANGY
RANID
RANIN
RANIS
RANKE
RANKS
RANON
RANTO
RANTS
RANUP
RAOUL
RAPEE
RAPHE
RAPID
RAREE
RARER
RARES
RASED
RASER
RASES
RASHT
RASPS
RASPY
RASTA
RATCH
RATED
RATEL
RATER
RATES
RATHS
RATIO
RATON
RATSO
RATTY
RAVED
RAVEL
RAVEN
RAVER
RAVES
RAVIN
RAWER
RAWLS
RAWLY
RAYED
RAYON
RAZED
RAZES
RAZOR

R•A••
REACH
REACT
READE
READS
READY
REAIM
REAIR
REALM
REALS
REAMS
REAPS
REARM
REARS
REATA
RIALS
RIANT
RIATA
RNASE
ROACH
ROADS
ROALD
ROAMS
ROANS
ROARS
ROAST
RUANA
RUARK

R••A•
RABAT
RADAR
RAGAS
RAHAB
RAHAL
RAJAH
RAJAS
RAMAN
RAMAR
RANAT
REBAG
REBAR
RECAP
REDAN
REGAL
REGAN
REHAB
REHAN
RELAX
RELAY
REMAN
REMAP
RENAL
RENAN
REPAD
REPAY
RERAN
RESAW
RETAG
RETAP
RETAR
RETAX
REWAX
RHEAS
RIVAL
RIYAL
RODAN
ROMAN
ROTAS
ROWAN
ROYAL
RUGAE
RUNAT
RURAL

R•••A
RAISA
RASTA
REATA
REGIA
REINA
RENTA
RETIA
RHODA
RHYTA
RIATA
RIOJA
RUANA
RUMBA

•RA••
ARABS
ARABY
ARAMA
ARAME
BRACE
BRACT
BRADS
BRADY
BRAES
BRAGA
BRAGG
BRAGS
BRAHE
BRAID
BRAIL
BRAIN
BRAKE
BRAND
BRANS
BRANT
BRASH
BRASS
BRATS
BRAUN
BRAVA
BRAVE
BRAVO
BRAWL
BRAWN
BRAYS
BRAZE
CRABS
CRACK
CRACY
CRAFT
CRAGS
CRAIG
CRAIN
CRAKE
CRAMP
CRAMS
CRANE
CRANK
CRAPE
CRAPS
CRASH
CRASS
CRATE
CRAVE
CRAWL
CRAWS
CRAZE
CRAZY
DRABS
DRACO
DRAFT
DRAGS
DRAIL
DRAIN
DRAKE
DRAMA
DRAMS
DRANG
DRANK
DRANO
DRAPE
DRATS
DRAVA
DRAWL
DRAWN
DRAWS
DRAYS
ERASE
ERATO
FRAIL
FRAIS
FRAME
FRANC
FRANK
FRANS
FRANZ
FRAPS
FRATS
FRAUD
FRAYS
GRABS
GRACE
GRADE
GRADS
GRADY
GRAFT
GRAIG
GRAIL
GRAIN
GRAMA
GRAMM
GRAMP
GRAMS
GRAND
GRANI
GRANT
GRAPE
GRAPH
GRAPY
GRASP
GRASS
GRATA
GRATE
GRAVE
GRAVY
GRAYS
GRAZE
IRADE
IRANI
IRAQI
IRATE
KRAAL
KRAFT
KRAIT
KRAUS
KRAUT
KRAZY
ORACH
ORACY
ORALE
ORALS
ORAMA
ORANG
ORANT
ORATE
PRADO
PRAIA
PRAMS
PRANG
PRANK
PRASE
PRATE
PRATO
PRATT
PRAUS
PRAWN
PRAYS
TRACE
TRACK
TRACT
TRACY
TRADE
TRAIL
TRAIN
TRAIT
TRALA

TRAMP TRAMS TRANS TRAPP TRAPS TRASH TRAVE TRAWL TRAYS URALS WRACK WRACS WRAFS WRAPS WRAPT WRATH XRAYS

•R•A•

AREAL AREAR AREAS ARHAT ARIAN ARIAS ARNAZ AROAR ARPAD ARRAN ARRAS ARRAU ARRAY ARTAL ARYAN BREAD BREAK BREAM BRIAN BRIAR BROAD BRYAN CREAK CREAM CROAK CROAT DREAD DREAM DREAR DRLAO DRYAD FREAK FRIAR GREAT GROAN GROAT KRAAL ORCAS OREAD ORGAN PRIAM PROAM PROAS SRTAS TREAD TREAT TRIAD TRIAL URBAN URIAH URIAL WREAK

•R••A

ARAMA ARECA ARENA ARICA AROMA ARUBA BRAGA BRAVA BREDA BROCA CRURA DRAMA DRAVA DRINA ERICA ERIKA ERISA FREDA FRENA FREYA GRAMA GRATA GRETA GROZA IRINA KRONA KRUPA ORAMA ORIYA PRAIA PRIMA TRALA

••RA•

ABRAM ARRAN ARRAS ARRAU ARRAY AURAE AURAL AURAR AURAS BARAB BORAH BORAS BORAX CARAT CERAM CERAT CORAL DERAT DIRAC DORAG DORAL DORAN DURAN EYRAS FARAD FARAH FERAL FORAY FURAN GERAH GORAL GYRAL HARAR HERAT HIRAM HORAE HORAL HORAS HYRAX JURAL JURAT KARAN KARAT KERAT KORAN LARAM LARAS LIRAS LORAN LORAX LURAY MARAS MARAT MCRAE MORAE MORAL MORAN MORAS MORAY MURAL MURAT NARAS NORAD NORAH OKRAS OPRAH PERAN PTRAP RERAN RURAL SARAH SARAN SCRAG SCRAM SCRAP SERAC SERAI SERAL SORAS SPRAG SPRAT SPRAY STRAD STRAP STRAW STRAY SURAH SURAL SURAS SURAT TIRAN TORAH VARAS VIRAL

••R•A

AORTA ATRIA BARCA BEREA BERRA BURMA BURSA CARIA CARLA CARTA CERIA CIRCA COREA CORIA CURIA DARLA DARYA DERMA DORSA DURRA FERIA FIRMA FORMA GARDA KARLA KARMA KORDA KOREA LARVA LORCA LORNA LURIA MARIA MARLA MARTA MURRA MYRNA NORIA NORMA OCREA PARCA PARKA PARMA SERRA SERTA SORTA STRIA SYRIA TERRA TERZA UNRRA VARIA VARNA VERBA VERSA VIRGA VIRNA WIRRA YERBA YORBA ZORBA

•••RA

ACCRA ACURA AFTRA AGORA AHORA AKIRA AMARA ANTRA ASTRA AUDRA BASRA BERRA CAPRA CIERA CLARA COBRA COPRA CRURA DEBRA DOBRA DURRA EVORA EXTRA FLORA HIERA HIJRA HYDRA INDRA INFRA INTRA LAURA LEORA LIBRA LYCRA MBIRA MEARA MICRA MOIRA MUDRA MURRA NAIRA OHARA OPERA PETRA PIURA SABRA SACRA SERRA SIDRA SUDRA SUPRA SUTRA TATRA TAYRA TERRA TETRA THERA TIARA UHURA ULTRA UMBRA UNRRA WIRRA ZEBRA

R•B••

RABAT RABBI RABID RABIN REBAG REBAR REBBE REBEC REBEL REBID REBUS REBUT RIBBY ROBBY ROBED ROBES ROBIN ROBLE ROBOT RUBEN RUBES RUBIK RUBIN RUBLE

R••B•

RABBI RAMBO REBBE RIBBY RIGBY ROBBY RUGBY RUMBA

R•••B

RAHAB RANDB REDUB REHAB RHOMB RHUMB

•RB••

ARBER ARBOR ARBRE ERBIL MRBIG ORBIT URBAN URBIS

•R•B•

ARABS ARABY ARUBA BRIBE CRABS CRIBS DRABS DRIBS DRUBS FROBE GRABS GREBE GRUBS KREBS ORIBI PROBE PROBS TRIBE

•R••B

CRUMB

••RB•

BARBQ BARBS BURBS CARBO CARBS CORBY CURBS DARBY DERBY FORBS GARBO GARBS HERBS HERBY KERBS KIRBY SERBS SORBS TURBO VERBA VERBS YERBA YORBA ZORBA

••R•B

BARAB CARIB CAROB HOREB SCRUB SHRUB THROB

•••RB

ACERB BLURB EXURB

R•C••

RACED RACER RACES RACKS RACON RECAP RECCE RECIP RECON RECTI RECTO RECUR RICCI RICED RICER RICES RICHE RICKI RICKS RICKY RICOH ROCCO ROCHE ROCKS ROCKY RUCHE RUCKS

R••C•

RANCH RATCH REACH REACT RECCE REICH RICCI ROACH ROCCO ROYCE

R•••C

REBEC RELIC RUNIC

•RC••

ARCED ARCHI ARCHY ORCAS ORCHS ORCUS ORCZY

•R•C•

ARECA ARICA BRACE BRACT BRECK BRICE BRICK BROCA BROCK BRUCE BRUCH BRYCE CRACK CRACY CRECY CRICK CROCE CROCI CROCK CROCS DRACO ERECT ERICA ERICH ERUCT FRICK FROCK GRACE GRECO ORACH ORACY PRICE PRICK PRICY PRYCE TRACE TRACK TRACT TRACY TRICE TRICK TRUCE TRUCK URICH WRACK WRACS WRECK

•R••C

BRONC CRESC FRANC

••RC•

BARCA BIRCH CIRCA CIRCE CIRCS CURCI FARCE FARCI FORCE LARCH LORCA LURCH MARCH MARCO MARCY MERCE MERCI MERCK MERCY NARCO NARCS PARCA PARCH PERCE PERCH PERCY PORCH TORCH

••R•C

AFRIC AGRIC AURIC BARIC BORIC DIRAC DORIC DUROC HARDC LYRIC OSRIC PYRIC SERAC TORIC UGRIC XERIC

R•D••

RADAR RADII RADIO RADIX RADON REDAN REDDY REDED REDES REDID REDLY REDON REDOX REDUB REDUX REDYE RIDER RIDES RIDGE RIDGY RIDOF RODAN RODDY RODEO RODIN RUDDS RUDDY RUDER RUDGE RYDER

R••D•

RAIDS RANDB RANDD RANDI RANDR RANDS RANDY READE READS READY REDDY REEDS REEDY RENDS RHODA RHODE RHODO RINDS RINDY ROADS RODDY RONDO ROODS ROWDY RUDDS RUDDY

R•••D

RABID RACED RAGED RAKED RANDD RANID RAPID RASED RATED RAVED RAYED RAZED REBID REDED REDID REPAD RESOD REWED RICED RIGID RILED RIMED RIVED ROALD ROBED ROPED

ROUND
ROVED
ROWED
RSVPD
RULED

•RD••
ARDEN
ARDOR
DRDRE
ORDER
ORDOS

•R•D•
BRADS
BRADY
BREDA
BRIDE
BRODY
CREDO
CRUDE
DREDD
ERODE
FREDA
FRODO
GRADE
GRADS
GRADY
GRIDS
GRODY
IRADE
IRIDO
PRADO
PRIDE
PRODS
PRUDE
TRADE

•R••D
ARCED
ARMED
AROID
ARPAD
BRAID
BRAND
BREAD
BREED
BROAD
BROOD
CREED
CRIED
CROWD
DREAD
DREDD
DRIED
DROID
DROOD
DRUID
DRYAD
ERRED
FRAUD
FREED
FREUD
FRIED
FROID
FROND
GRAND
GREED
GRIND
IRKED
OREAD
PRIED
PROUD
TREAD
TREED
TREND
TRIAD
TRIED
TRUED
URGED
URSID

••RD•
BARDS
BIRDS
BIRDY
BYRDS
CARDI
CARDS
CORDS
CURDS
CURDY
FERDE
FORDO
FORDS
GARDA
GARDE
GIRDS
GORDO
GORDY
GURDY
HARDC
HARDG
HARDY
HERDS
HORDE
HURDY
KORDA
KURDS
LARDS
LARDY
LORDS
MARDI
NARDS
NERDS
NERDY
PARDI
PARDO
PARDS
PERDU
SARDS
SURDS
TARDE
TARDY
VERDE
VERDI
WARDS
WORDS
WORDY
YARDS

••R•D
ACRED
ACRID
AIRED
BARED
BORED
CARED
CERED
CORED
CURED
DARED
EARED
ERRED
FARAD
FARED
FIRED
GORED
HARED
HEROD
HIRED
LURED
LURID
MIRED
NORAD
OARED
PARED
PORED
SAROD
SCROD
SHRED
SIRED
STRAD
TIRED
VIRID
WIRED
WORLD

•••RD
AWARD
BAIRD
BEARD
BOARD
CHARD
CHORD
FIORD
FJORD
GOURD
GUARD
HEARD
HOARD
IZARD
LAIRD
LIARD
SHARD
SNERD
SWARD
SWORD
TBIRD
THIRD
WEIRD

RE•••
REACH
REACT
READE
READS
READY
REAIM
REAIR
REALM
REALS
REAMS
REAPS
REARM
REARS
REATA
REBAG
REBAR
REBBE
REBEC
REBEL
REBID
REBUS
REBUT
RECAP
RECCE
RECIP
RECON
RECTI
RECTO
RECUR
REDAN
REDDY
REDED
REDES
REDID
REDLY
REDON
REDOX
REDUB
REDUX
REDYE
REEDS
REEDY
REEFS
REEKS
REEKY
REELS
REESE
REEVE
REFER
REFIT
REFRY
REGAL
REGAN
REGIA
REGIS
REGNI
REGUM
REHAB
REHAN
REHEM
REICH
REIFY
REIGN
REIMS
REINA
REINK
REINS
REKEY
RELAX
RELAY
RELEE
RELET
RELIC
RELIG
RELIT
REMAN
REMAP
REMET
REMEX
REMIT
REMIX
REMOP
REMOW
REMUS
RENAL
RENAN
RENDS
RENEE
RENEW
RENIN
RENTA
RENTS
REOIL
REPAD
REPAY
REPEG
REPEL
REPIN
REPLY
REPOS
REPOT
REPPS
REPRO
RERAN
RERIG
RERUM
RERUN
RESAW
RESEE
RESET
RESEW
RESIN
RESOD
RESTS
RETAG
RETAP
RETAR
RETAX
RETIA
RETIE
RETOP
RETOW
RETRO
RETRY
REUEL
REUNE
REUPS
REUSE
REVEL
REVET
REVUE
REVUP
REWAX
REWED
REWIN
REWON
REXES
REYES

R•E••
REEDS
REEDY
REEFS
REEKS
REEKY
REELS
REESE
REEVE
RHEAS
RHETT
RHEUM
RIELS
RUEHL
RUERS

R••E•
RACED
RACER
RACES
RAFER
RAGED
RAGES
RAKED
RAKER
RAKES
RAMEE
RAMEN
RAMET
RANEE
RAPEE
RAREE
RARER
RARES
RASED
RASER
RASES
RATED
RATEL
RATER
RATES
RAVED
RAVEL
RAVEN
RAVER
RAVES
RAWER
RAYED
RAZED
RAZES
REBEC
REBEL
REDED
REDES
REFER
REHEM
REKEY
RELEE
RELET
REMET
REMEX
RENEE
RENEW
REPEG
REPEL
RESEE
RESET
RESEW
REUEL
REVEL
REVET
REWED
REXES
REYES
RICED
RICER
RICES
RIDER
RIDES
RIFER
RIGEL
RIKER
RILED
RILES
RILEY
RIMED
RIMES
RIPEN
RIPER
RISEN
RISER
RISES
RITES
RIVED
RIVEN
RIVER
RIVES
RIVET
ROBED
ROBES
RODEO
ROGER
ROGET
ROLEO
ROLES
ROLEX
ROMEO
ROMER
RONEE
ROPED
ROPER
ROPES
ROPEY
ROREM
ROSEN
ROSES
ROSEY
ROTES
ROUEN
ROUES
ROVED
ROVER
ROVES
ROWED
ROWEL
ROWEN
ROWER
RUBEN
RUBES
RUDER
RULED
RULER
RULES
RUMEN
RUNES
RUPEE
RUSES
RYDER

R•••E
RAISE
RAMEE
RAMIE
RANEE
RANGE
RANKE
RAPEE
RAPHE
RAREE
READE
REBBE
RECCE
REDYE
REESE
REEVE
RELEE
RENEE
RESEE
RETIE
REUNE
REUSE
REVUE
RHINE
RHODE
RHONE
RHYME
RICHE
RIDGE
RIFLE
RILKE
RILLE
RINSE
RNASE
ROBLE
ROCHE
ROGUE
ROLFE
ROLLE
RONEE
ROONE
ROQUE
ROSIE
ROUGE
ROUSE
ROUTE
ROXIE
ROYCE
RUBLE
RUCHE
RUDGE
RUGAE
RUPEE
RUSSE

•RE••
AREAL
AREAR
AREAS
ARECA
ARENA
ARENS
ARENT
ARETE
BREAD
BREAK
BREAM
BRECK
BREDA
BREED
BREEN
BRENT
BRERS
BREST
BRETT
BREVE
BREWS
CREAK
CREAM
CRECY
CREDO
CREED
CREEK
CREEL
CREEP
CREES
CREME
CREON
CREPE
CREPT
CRESC
CRESS
CREST
CRETE
CREWS
DREAD
DREAM
DREAR
DREDD
DREGS
DRESS
ERECT
FREAK
FREDA
FREED
FREER
FREES
FRENA
FREON
FRERE
FRESH
FRETS
FREUD
FREYA
GREAT
GREBE
GRECO
GREED
GREEK
GREEN
GREER
GREES
GREET
GREGG
GRETA
GRETE
GREYS
IRENE
KREBS
OREAD
OREOS
PREEN
PREGO
PRELL
PREPS
PRESS
PREST
PREXY
PREYS
TREAD
TREAT
TREED
TREEN
TREES
TREKS
TREND
TRENT
TRESS
TREVI
TREWS
TREYS
WREAK
WRECK
WRENS
WREST

•R•E•
ARBER
ARCED
ARDEN
ARIEL
ARIES
ARLEN
ARLES
ARMED
ARMEE
ARMET
ARNEL
ARPEL
ARRET
ARTEL
ARTES
BRAES
BREED
BREEN
BRIEF
BRIER
BRIES
CREED
CREEK
CREEL
CREEP
CREES
CRIED
CRIER
CRIES
CRUEL
CRUET
CRYER
DRIED
DRIER
DRIES
DRYER
ERIES
ERNES
ERRED
FREED
FREER
FREES
FRIED
FRIER
FRIES
FROES
FRYER
GREED
GREEK
GREEN
GREER
GREES
GREET
GRIEF
GRIEG
GRIER
GRUEL
IRKED
IRREG
ORDER
ORFEO
ORIEL
ORLES
ORSER
PREEN

PRIED
PRIER
PRIES
PROEM
TREED
TREEN
TREES
TRIED
TRIER
TRIES
TRUED
TRUER
TRUES
TRUEX
URGED
URGER
URGES
URIEL
URKEL
WRIER
WRYER

•R••E

ARAME
ARBRE
ARETE
ARGUE
ARISE
ARMEE
ARNIE
AROSE
ARTIE
BRACE
BRAHE
BRAKE
BRAVE
BRAZE
BREVE
BRIBE
BRICE
BRIDE
BRINE
BRITE
BROKE
BROME
BRUCE
BRULE
BRUME
BRUTE
BRYCE
CRAKE
CRANE
CRAPE
CRATE
CRAVE
CRAZE
CREME
CREPE
CRETE
CRIME
CROCE
CRONE
CROZE
CRUDE
CRUSE
DRAKE
DRAPE
DRDRE
DRIVE
DROME
DRONE
DROVE
DRUPE
DRUSE
DRUZE
ERASE
ERNIE
ERODE
EROSE
FRAME
FRERE
FRISE
FROBE
FROME
FROZE
GRACE
GRADE
GRAPE
GRATE
GRAVE
GRAZE
GREBE
GRETE
GRIME
GRIPE
GROFE
GROPE
GROVE
IRADE
IRATE
IRENE
KRONE
ORALE
ORATE
PRASE
PRATE
PRICE
PRIDE
PRIME
PRIZE
PROBE
PROLE
PRONE
PROSE
PROVE
PRUDE
PRUNE
PRYCE
TRACE
TRADE
TRAVE
TRIBE
TRICE
TRIKE
TRINE
TRIPE
TRITE
TROPE
TROVE
TRUCE
TRYME
WRITE
WROTE

••RE•

ACRED
ACRES
ADREM
AGREE
AIRED
AIRES
APRES
ARRET
AUREI
AYRES
BARED
BARER
BARES
BEREA
BERET
BORED
BORER
BORES
BYRES
CARED
CARER
CARES
CARET
CAREW
CAREY
CERED
CERES
CIRES
COREA
CORED
CORER
CORES
COREY
CURED
CURER
CURES
DARED
DARER
DARES
DEREK
DIRER
DOREN
DURER
EARED
EFREM
EGRET
ERRED
EYRES
FARED
FARER
FARES
FIRED
FIRER
FIRES
FORES
GORED
GOREN
GORES
GYRES
HARED
HAREM
HARES
HERES
HIRED
HIRER
HIRES
HOREB
INREM
IRREG
JEREZ
JOREL
KAREL
KAREN
KOREA
LARES
LOREN
LORES
LURED
LURES
LUREX
LYRES
MARES
MERES
MIRED
MIRES
MOREL
MORES
MOREY
MUREX
NARES
NAREW
OARED
OCREA
OGRES
PARED
PAREE
PAREN
PARER
PARES
PAREU
PERES
PEREZ
PHREN
PORED
PORES
PUREE
PURER
PUREX
PYRES
PYREX
RAREE
RARER
RARES
ROREM
SCREE
SCREW
SERES
SHRED
SHREW
SIRED
SIREN
SIRES
SOREL
SOREN
SORER
SORES
SPREE
STREP
STREW
SURER
TARES
THREE
THREW
TIRED
TIRES
TYRES
VIREO
WARES
WIRED
WIRER
WIRES
YARER
YPRES

••R•E

AERIE
AGREE
AURAE
BARGE
BARRE
BERLE
BERME
BERNE
BIRSE
BORGE
BORNE
BURKE
BURSE
BYRNE
CARLE
CARNE
CARPE
CARRE
CARTE
CARVE
CIRCE
CURIE
CURSE
CURVE
DIRGE
EARLE
EERIE
EYRIE
FARCE
FAROE
FERDE
FORCE
FORGE
FORTE
FURZE
GARDE
GORGE
GORME
GORSE
HARTE
HERNE
HERVE
HORAE
HORDE
HORNE
HORSE
JARRE
JORGE
KYRIE
LARGE
LARUE
LORNE
LORRE
LURIE
MARGE
MARIE
MARNE
MCRAE
MERCE
MERGE
MERLE
MEROE
MORAE
MORSE
MURRE
NERVE
NORGE
NORSE
NORTE
NURSE
PAREE
PARLE
PARSE
PARTE
PERCE
PERLE
PERSE
PORTE
PUREE
PURGE
PURSE
RAREE
SARGE
SCREE
SERGE
SERVE
SPREE
SPRUE
SURGE
TARDE
TARGE
TERNE
TERRE
TERSE
THREE
THROE
TORME
TORRE
TORTE
VERDE
VERGE
VERNE
VERRE
VERSE
VERTE
VERVE
WORSE

•••RE

ADORE
AFIRE
AFORE
ALFRE
AMORE
ANDRE
ANTRE
APURE
ARBRE
ASTRE
AUTRE
AWARE
AZURE
BARRE
BLARE
CADRE
CARRE
CHERE
CHORE
CLARE
DEERE
DETRE
DRDRE
DUPRE
EAGRE
ENTRE
ENURE
FAIRE
FAURE
FAVRE
FIBRE
FLARE
FRERE
GENRE
GLARE
HAVRE
HEURE
INURE
ISERE
JAHRE
JARRE
LIBRE
LITRE
LIVRE
LOIRE
LORRE
LUCRE
MADRE
MAHRE
METRE
MITRE
MOIRE
MOORE
MURRE
NACRE
NIDRE
NITRE
NOIRE
NOTRE
OCHRE
OHARE
OMBRE
OPERE
OUTRE
PADRE
QUARE
QUIRE
SABRE
SACRE
SCARE
SCORE
SHARE
SHERE
SHIRE
SHORE
SNARE
SNORE
SPARE
SPIRE
SPORE
STARE
STERE
STORE
SUCRE
SWORE
TERRE
THERE
TITRE
TORRE
TWERE
VERRE
VIVRE
VOTRE
WHERE
WHYRE
YOURE
ZAIRE

R•F••

RAFER
RAFFI
RAFTS
REFER
REFIT
REFRY
RIFER
RIFFI
RIFFS
RIFLE
RIFTS
RSFSR
RUFFS
RUFUS

R••F•

RAFFI
REEFS
REIFY
RIFFI
RIFFS
ROLFE
ROOFS
RUFFS

R•••F

RIDOF

•RF••

ORFEO

•R•F•

CRAFT
CROFT
DRAFT
DRIFT
GRAFT
GRIFT
GROFE
GRUFF
KRAFT
PROFS
WRAFS

•R••F

BRIEF
GRIEF
GRUFF
PROOF

••RF•

CORFU
SERFS
SURFS
SURFY
TURFS
TURFY
ZARFS

••R•F

SERIF

•••RF

DWARF
SCARF
SCURF
SMURF
SWARF
WHARF

R•G••

RAGAS
RAGED
RAGES
REGAL
REGAN
REGIA
REGIS
REGNI
REGUM
RIGBY
RIGEL
RIGGS
RIGHT
RIGID
RIGOR
RIGUP
ROGER
ROGET
ROGUE
RUGAE
RUGBY

R••G•

RANGE
RANGY
REIGN
RIDGE
RIDGY
RIGGS
RINGO
RINGS
ROUGE
ROUGH
RUDGE
RUNGS

R•••G

REBAG
RELIG
REPEG
RERIG
RETAG
RUING

•RG••

ARGIL
ARGOL
ARGON
ARGOS
ARGOT
ARGUE
ARGUS
ERGOT
ORGAN
URGED
URGER
URGES

•R•G•

BRAGA
BRAGG
BRAGS
BRIGS
CRAGS
DRAGS
DREGS
DRUGS
FRIGG
FROGS
GREGG
GRIGS
GROGS
KROGH
PREGO
PRIGS
PROGS
TRIGS
TRUGS

•R••G

BRAGG
BRING
BRUNG
CRAIG
DRANG
FRIGG
GRAIG
GREGG
GRIEG
IRREG
MRBIG
ORANG
ORING
PRANG
PRONG
WRING
WRONG
WRUNG

••RG•

AARGH
BARGE
BARGY
BERGH
BERGS
BORGE
BURGS
CARGO
CORGI
DIRGE
FARGO
FORGE
FORGO
GORGE
JORGE
LARGE
LARGO
MARGE
MARGO
MERGE
NORGE
PORGY
PURGE
SARGE
SARGO
SERGE
SORGO
SURGE
TARGE
VERGE
VIRGA
VIRGO

••R•G
DORAG
HARDG
IRREG
RERIG
SCRAG
SHRUG
SPRAG
SPRIG
STRUG
UNRIG
VARIG

•••RG
BOURG
GEORG
INORG

RH•••
RHEAS
RHETT
RHEUM
RHINE
RHINO
RHIZO
RHODA
RHODE
RHODO
RHOMB
RHONE
RHUMB
RHYME
RHYTA

R•H••
RAHAB
RAHAL
REHAB
REHAN
REHEM

R••H•
RAPHE
RASHT
RATHS
RICHE
RIGHT
RISHI
ROCHE
RUCHE
RUEHL
RUSHY

R•••H
RAJAH
RALPH
RANCH
RATCH
REACH
REICH
RICOH
ROACH
ROUGH

•RH••
ARHAT
ARHUS

•R•H•
ARCHI
ARCHY
ARTHR
BRAHE
BRUHN
ORCHS
ORTHO

•R••H
ARITH
BRASH
BRITH
BROTH
BRUCH
BRUSH
CRASH
CRUSH
ERICH
FRESH
FROSH
FROTH
GRAPH
IRISH
KROGH
ORACH
TRASH
TRISH
TROTH
TRUTH
URIAH
URICH
WRATH
WROTH

••R•H
AARGH
BARTH
BERGH
BERTH
BIRCH
BIRTH
BORAH
DARTH
EARTH
FARAH
FIRTH
FORTH
FURTH
GARTH
GERAH
GIRTH
HARSH
KARSH
LARCH
LURCH
MARCH
MARSH
MIRTH
MORPH
MYRRH
NORAH
NORTH
OPRAH
PARCH
PERCH
PERTH
PORCH
SARAH
SURAH
TORAH
TORCH
UNRUH
WORTH

•••RH
FOURH
MYRRH

RI•••
RIALS
RIANT
RIATA
RIBBY
RICCI
RICED
RICER
RICES
RICHE
RICKI
RICKS
RICKY
RICOH
RIDER
RIDES
RIDGE
RIDGY
RIDOF
RIELS
RIFER
RIFFI
RIFFS
RIFLE
RIFTS
RIGBY
RIGEL
RIGGS
RIGHT
RIGID
RIGOR
RIGUP
RIKER
RIKKI
RILED
RILES
RILEY
RILKE
RILLE
RILLS
RIMED
RIMES
RINDS
RINDY
RINGO
RINGS
RINKS
RINKY
RINSE
RINSO
RIOJA
RIOTS
RIPEN
RIPER
RIPON
RIPUP
RISEN
RISER
RISES
RISHI
RISKS
RISKY
RITES
RITZY
RIVAL
RIVED
RIVEN
RIVER
RIVES
RIVET
RIYAL
RIZZO

R•I••
RAIDS
RAILS
RAINS
RAINY
RAISA
RAISE
RAITT
REICH
REIFY
REIGN
REIMS
REINA
REINK
REINS
RHINE
RHINO
RHIZO
ROILS
ROILY
RUING
RUINS

R••I•
RABID
RABIN
RADII
RADIO
RADIX
RAJIV
RAKIS
RAMIE
RAMIS
RANID
RANIN
RANIS
RAPID
RATIO
RAVIN
REAIM
REAIR
REBID
RECIP
REDID
REFIT
REGIA
REGIS
RELIC
RELIG
RELIT
REMIT
REMIX
RENIN
REOIL
REPIN
RERIG
RESIN
RETIA
RETIE
REWIN
RIGID
ROBIN
RODIN
ROSIE
ROSIN
ROXIE
RUBIK
RUBIN
RUNIC
RUNIN
RURIK
RUTIN

R•••I
RABBI
RADII
RAFFI
RANDI
RECTI
REGNI
RICCI
RICKI
RIFFI
RIKKI
RISHI
ROSSI

•RI••
ARIAN
ARIAS
ARICA
ARIEL
ARIES
ARILS
ARION
ARISE
ARITH
ARIUM
ARIUS
BRIAN
BRIAR
BRIBE
BRICE
BRICK
BRIDE
BRIEF
BRIER
BRIES
BRIGS
BRILL
BRIMS
BRINE
BRING
BRINK
BRINY
BRISK
BRITE
BRITH
BRITS
BRITT
CRIBS
CRICK
CRIED
CRIER
CRIES
CRIME
CRIMP
CRISP
CRISS
CRIST
DRIBS
DRIED
DRIER
DRIES
DRIFT
DRILL
DRILY
DRINA
DRINK
DRIPS
DRIVE
ERICA
ERICH
ERIES
ERIKA
ERISA
FRIAR
FRICK
FRIED
FRIER
FRIES
FRIGG
FRILL
FRIML
FRISE
FRISK
FRITO
FRITS
FRITZ
FRIZZ
GRIDS
GRIEF
GRIEG
GRIER
GRIFT
GRIGS
GRILL
GRIME
GRIMM
GRIMY
GRIND
GRINS
GRIOT
GRIPE
GRIPS
GRIST
GRITS
IRIDO
IRINA
IRISH
KRILL
KRISS
ORIBI
ORIEL
ORING
ORION
ORIYA
PRIAM
PRICE
PRICK
PRICY
PRIDE
PRIED
PRIER
PRIES
PRIGS
PRIMA
PRIME
PRIMI
PRIMO
PRIMP
PRIMS
PRINK
PRINT
PRION
PRIOR
PRISM
PRIVY
PRIZE
PRIZM
TRIAD
TRIAL
TRIBE
TRICE
TRICK
TRIED
TRIER
TRIES
TRIGS
TRIKE
TRILL
TRIMS
TRINE
TRINI
TRIOS
TRIPE
TRIPS
TRISH
TRITE
TRITT
URIAH
URIAL
URICH
URIEL
WRIER
WRING
WRIST
WRITE
WRITS

•R•I•
ARGIL
ARKIN
ARMIS
ARNIE
AROID
ARRIS
ARSIS
ARTIE
ARTIS
BRAID
BRAIL
BRAIN
BROIL
BRUIN
BRUIT
CRAIG
CRAIN
CROIX
DRAIL
DRAIN
DROID
DROIT
DRUID
ERBIL
ERNIE
ERVIL
ERVIN
ERWIN
FRAIL
FRAIS
FROID
FRUIT
GRAIG
GRAIL
GRAIN
GROIN
IRVIN
IRWIN
KRAIT
MRBIG
ORBIT
ORNIS
ORRIN
ORRIS
PRAIA
TRAIL
TRAIN
TRAIT
TROIS
URBIS
URSID

•R••I
ARCHI
CROCI
GRANI
IRANI
IRAQI
ORIBI
PRIMI
TREVI
TRINI

••RI•
ABRIL
ABRIS
ACRID
AERIE
AFRIC
AFRIT
AGRIC
APRIL
ARRIS
ATRIA
ATRIP
AURIC
AVRIL
BARIC
BARIT
BORIC
BORIS
BURIN
CARIA
CARIB
CERIA
CHRIS
CORIA
CURIA
CURIE
CURIO
CYRIL
DARIN
DARIO
DERIV
DORIC
DORIS
EERIE
EYRIE
EYRIR
FERIA
KIRIN
KYRIE
LARIS
LORIS
LURIA
LURID
LURIE
LYRIC
MARIA
MARIE
MARIN
MARIO
MARIS
MERIT
NARIS
NORIA
ORRIN
ORRIS
OSRIC
PARIS
PERIL
PERIS
PURIM
PYRIC
RERIG
RURIK
SARIS
SCRIM
SCRIP
SERIF
SERIN
SPRIG
SPRIT
STRIA
STRIP
SYRIA
TORIC
TORII
TURIN
UGRIC
UNRIG
VARIA
VARIG
VARIX
VIRID
XERIC
ZORIL
ZORIS

••R•I
AUREI
CARDI
CARPI
CIRRI
CORGI
CURCI
DORSI
FARCI
FARSI
FERMI
FERRI
FORLI
GARNI
GORKI
KERRI
LEROI
MARDI
MARTI
MERCI
NURMI
PARDI
PARTI
SERAI
TARSI
TERRI
TORII
TORSI
VERDI
VERMI

•••RI
ACARI
ATARI
CAPRI
CHERI
CIRRI
CUPRI
FERRI
HENRI
HOURI
INARI
INDRI
KAURI
KERRI
MAORI
MATRI
NEGRI
PATRI
PETRI
SHARI
SPYRI
TERRI

R•J••
RAJAH
RAJAS
RAJIV

R••J•
RIOJA

R•K••
RAKED
RAKER
RAKES
RAKIS
REKEY
RIKER
RIKKI

R••K•
RACKS
RANKE
RANKS
REEKS
REEKY
RICKI
RICKS
RICKY
RIKKI
RILKE
RINKS
RINKY

RISKS
RISKY
ROCKS
ROCKY
ROOKS
ROOKY
ROYKO
RUCKS
RUSKS

R•••K
REINK
RUARK
RUBIK
RURIK

•RK••
ARKIN
IRKED
URKEL

•R•K•
BRAKE
BROKE
CRAKE
DRAKE
ERIKA
GROKS
TREKS
TRIKE

•R••K
BREAK
BRECK
BRICK
BRINK
BRISK
BROCK
BROOK
CRACK
CRANK
CREAK
CREEK
CRICK
CROAK
CROCK
CROOK
DRANK
DRINK
DRUNK
FRANK
FREAK
FRICK
FRISK
FROCK
GREEK
PRANK
PRICK
PRINK
TRACK
TRICK
TRUCK
TRUNK
WRACK
WREAK
WRECK

••RK•
BARKS
BARKY
BURKE
CARKS
CORKS
CORKY
DARKS
DIRKS
FORKS
FORKY
GORKI
GORKY
HARKS
HERKY
JERKS
JERKY
KIRKS
LARKS
LARKY
LURKS
MARKS
MIRKY
MURKY
NARKS
PARKA
PARKS
PERKS
PERKY
PORKS
PORKY
SARKY
TURKS
TURKU
WORKS
YERKS

••R•K
DEREK
HUROK
KURSK
MERCK
RURIK
TAROK
YUROK

•••RK
CLARK
CLERK
DMARK
OZARK
QUARK
QUIRK
RUARK
SHARK
SHIRK
SMIRK
SNARK
SPARK
SPORK
STARK
STIRK
STORK

R•L••
RALLY
RALPH
RELAX
RELAY
RELEE
RELET
RELIC
RELIG
RELIT
RILED
RILES
RILEY
RILKE
RILLE
RILLS
ROLEO
ROLES
ROLEX
ROLFE
ROLLE
ROLLO
ROLLS
RULED
RULER
RULES

R••L•
RAILS
RALLY
RAWLS
RAWLY
REALM
REALS
REDLY
REELS
REPLY
RIALS
RIELS
RIFLE
RILLE
RILLS
ROALD
ROBLE
ROILS
ROILY
ROLLE
ROLLO
ROLLS
ROTLS
RUBLE

R•••L
RAHAL
RAOUL
RATEL
RAVEL
REBEL
REGAL
RENAL
REOIL
REPEL
REUEL
REVEL
RIGEL
RIVAL
RIYAL
ROWEL
ROYAL
RUEHL
RURAL

•RL••
ARLEN
ARLES
DRLAO
ORLES
ORLON
ORLOP

•R•L•
ARILS
BRILL
BRULE
CROLY
DRILL
DRILY
DROLL
DRYLY
FRILL
GRILL
KRILL
KRULL
ORALE
ORALS
PRELL
PROLE
TRALA
TRILL
TROLL
TRULY
URALS
WRYLY

•R••L
AREAL
ARGIL
ARGOL
ARIEL
ARNEL
ARPEL
ARTAL
ARTEL
BRAIL
BRAWL
BRILL
BROIL
CRAWL
CREEL
CRUEL
DRAIL
DRAWL
DRILL
DROLL
DROOL
ERBIL
ERROL
ERVIL
FRAIL
FRILL
FRIML
GRAIL
GRILL
GROWL
GRUEL
KRAAL
KRILL
KRULL
ORIEL
PRELL
PROWL
TRAIL
TRAWL
TRIAL
TRILL
TROLL
URIAL
URIEL
URKEL

••RL•
BERLE
BIRLS
BURLS
BURLY
CARLA
CARLE
CARLO
CARLY
CURLS
CURLY
DARLA
EARLE
EARLS
EARLY
FORLI
FURLS
GIRLS
HERLS
HURLS
HURLY
JARLS
KARLA
MARLA
MARLO
MARLS
MARLY
MERLE
MERLS
PARLE
PERLE
PURLS
SURLY
WORLD

••R•L
ABRIL
APRIL
AURAL
AVRIL
BERYL
CAROL
CORAL
CYRIL
DARYL
DORAL
ENROL
ERROL
FERAL
GORAL
GYRAL
HERZL
HORAL
HOROL
JOREL
JURAL
KAREL
KAROL
MERYL
MORAL
MOREL
MURAL
NEROL
PAROL
PERIL
RURAL
SERAL
SOREL
SURAL
TYROL
VIRAL
ZORIL

•••RL
BGIRL
CEORL
CHURL
GNARL
KNURL
PEARL
SKIRL
SNARL
SWIRL
TWIRL
WHIRL
WHORL

R•M••
RAMAN
RAMAR
RAMBO
RAMEE
RAMEN
RAMET
RAMIE
RAMIS
RAMON
RAMOS
RAMPS
REMAN
REMAP
REMET
REMEX
REMIT
REMIX
REMOP
REMOW
REMUS
RIMED
RIMES
ROMAN
ROMEO
ROMER
ROMPS
RUMBA
RUMEN
RUMMY
RUMOR
RUMPS

R••M•
REAMS
REIMS
RHOMB
RHUMB
RHYME
ROAMS
ROOMS
ROOMY
RUMMY

R•••M
REAIM
REALM
REARM
REGUM
REHEM
RERUM
RHEUM
ROREM

•RM••
ARMED
ARMEE
ARMET
ARMIS
ARMOR
MRMOM

•R•M•
ARAMA
ARAME
AROMA
ARUMS
BRIMS
BROME
BROMO
BRUME
CRAMP
CRAMS
CREME
CRIME
CRIMP
CRUMB
CRUMP
DRAMA
DRAMS
DROME
DRUMS
FRAME
FRIML
FROME
FROMM
FRUMP
GRAMA
GRAMM
GRAMP
GRAMS
GRIME
GRIMM
GRIMY
GRUMP
ORAMA
OROMO
PRAMS
PRIMA
PRIME
PRIMI
PRIMO
PRIMP
PRIMS
PROMO
PROMS
TRAMP
TRAMS
TRIMS
TROMP
TRUMP
TRYME

•R••M
ARIUM
BREAM
BROOM
CREAM
DREAM
FROMM
GRAMM
GRIMM
GROOM
MRMOM
PRIAM
PRISM
PRIZM
PROAM
PROEM
VROOM

••RM•
BARMS
BARMY
BERME
BERMS
BURMA
CORMS
DERMA
DERMO
DORMS
FARMS
FERMI
FIRMA
FIRMS
FORMA
FORMS
GERMS
GERMY
GORME
HARMS
HERMS
KARMA
NORMA
NORMS
NURMI
PARMA
PERMS
TERMS
TORME
VERMI
WARMS
WORMS
WORMY

••R•M
ABRAM
ADREM
AURUM
CAROM
CDROM
CERAM
CHROM
DURUM
EFREM
EPROM
FORUM
HAREM
HARUM
HIRAM
INREM
JORUM
LARAM
MORUM
PURIM
RERUM
ROREM
SCRAM
SCRIM
SCRUM
SERUM
STROM
STRUM
THRUM

•••RM
ALARM
CHARM
ENORM
PHARM
REARM
STORM
STURM
SWARM
THERM
UNARM

RN•••
RNASE

R•N••
RANAT
RANCH
RANDB
RANDD
RANDI
RANDR
RANDS
RANDY
RANEE
RANGE
RANGY
RANID
RANIN
RANIS
RANKE
RANKS
RANON
RANTO
RANTS
RANUP
RENAL
RENAN
RENDS
RENEE
RENEW
RENIN
RENTA
RENTS
RINDS
RINDY
RINGO
RINGS
RINKS
RINKY
RINSE
RINSO
RONDO
RONEE
RONNY
RUNAT
RUNES
RUNGS
RUNIC
RUNIN
RUNNY
RUNON
RUNTO
RUNTS
RUNTY
RUNUP

R••N•
RAINS
RAINY
REGNI
REINA
REINK
REINS
REUNE
RHINE
RHINO
RHONE
RIANT
ROANS
RONNY
ROONE
ROUND
ROVNO
RUANA
RUING
RUINS
RUNNY

R•••N
RABIN
RACON
RADON
RAMAN
RAMEN
RAMON
RANIN
RANON
RATON
RAVEN
RAVIN
RAYON
RECON
REDAN
REDON
REGAN
REHAN
REIGN
REMAN
RENAN
RENIN
REPIN
RERAN
RERUN
RESIN
REWIN
REWON
RIPEN
RIPON
RISEN
RIVEN
ROBIN
RODAN
RODIN
ROMAN
ROSEN
ROSIN
ROUEN
ROWAN
ROWEN

RUBEN
RUBIN
RUMEN
RUNIN
RUNON
RUTIN

•RN••
ARNAZ
ARNEL
ARNIE
ERNES
ERNIE
ERNST
ORNIS

•R•N•
ARENA
ARENS
ARENT
BRAND
BRANS
BRANT
BRENT
BRINE
BRING
BRINK
BRINY
BRONC
BRONX
BRUNG
BRUNO
BRUNT
CRANE
CRANK
CRONE
CRONY
DRANG
DRANK
DRANO
DRINA
DRINK
DRONE
DRUNK
FRANC
FRANK
FRANS
FRANZ
FRENA
FROND
FRONT
GRAND
GRANI
GRANT
GRIND
GRINS
GRUNT
IRANI
IRENE
IRINA
IRONS
IRONY
KRONA
KRONE
ORANG
ORANT
ORING
ORONO
PRANG
PRANK
PRINK
PRINT
PRONE
PRONG
PRUNE
TRANS
TREND
TRENT
TRINE
TRINI
TRUNK
WRENS
WRING
WRONG
WRUNG

•R••N
ARDEN
ARGON
ARIAN
ARION
ARKIN
ARLEN
ARRAN
ARSON
ARYAN
BRAIN
BRAUN
BRAWN
BREEN
BRIAN
BROUN
BROWN
BRUHN
BRUIN
BRYAN
CRAIN
CREON
CROON
CROWN
DRAIN
DRAWN
DROWN
ERVIN
ERWIN
FREON
FROWN
GRAIN
GREEN
GROAN
GROIN
GROWN
IRVIN
IRWIN
ORGAN
ORION
ORLON
ORRIN
ORSON
ORTON
PRAWN
PREEN
PRION
TRAIN
TREEN
TRYON
URBAN

••RN•
BARNS
BERNE
BORNE
BURNS
BURNT
BYRNE
CARNE
CARNY
CORNO
CORNS
CORNU
CORNY
DARNS
DURNS
EARNS
FERNS
FERNY
FIRNS
GARNI
GIRNS
HERNE
HERNS
HORNE
HORNS
KERNS
LORNA
LORNE
MARNE
MORNS
MYRNA
NORNS
TARNS
TERNE
TERNS
TURNS
VARNA
VERNE
VIRNA
WARNS
YARNS

••R•N
AARON
AERON
AGRON
AKRON
APRON
ARRAN
BARON
BORON
BURIN
BYRON
CARON
CHRON
DARIN
DORAN
DOREN
DURAN
FARON
FURAN
GOREN
GYRON
HERON
HURON
KARAN
KAREN
KIRIN
KORAN
LORAN
LOREN
MARIN
MORAN
MORON
MYRON
ORRIN
PAREN
PERAN
PERON
PHREN
RERAN
RERUN
SARAN
SERIN
SIREN
SOREN
TIRAN
TURIN

•••RN
ACORN
ADORN
AGARN
BAIRN
BJORN
BOURN
CAIRN
CHURN
HEARN
LEARN
MOURN
NAIRN
QUERN
SCORN
SHORN
SPURN
STERN
SWORN
THORN
UTURN
YEARN

RO•••
ROACH
ROADS
ROALD
ROAMS
ROANS
ROARS
ROAST
ROBBY
ROBED
ROBES
ROBIN
ROBLE
ROBOT
ROCCO
ROCHE
ROCKS
ROCKY
RODAN
RODDY
RODEO
RODIN
ROGER
ROGET
ROGUE
ROILS
ROILY
ROLEO
ROLES
ROLEX
ROLFE
ROLLE
ROLLO
ROLLS
ROMAN
ROMEO
ROMER
ROMPS
RONDO
RONEE
RONNY
ROODS
ROOFS
ROOKS
ROOKY
ROOMS
ROOMY
ROONE
ROOST
ROOTS
ROOTY
ROPED
ROPER
ROPES
ROPEY
ROQUE
ROREM
ROSEN
ROSES
ROSEY
ROSIE
ROSIN
ROSSI
ROTAS
ROTES
ROTLS
ROTOR
ROTOS
ROUEN
ROUES
ROUGE
ROUGH
ROUND
ROUSE
ROUST
ROUTE
ROUTS
ROVED
ROVER
ROVES
ROVNO
ROWAN
ROWDY
ROWED
ROWEL
ROWEN
ROWER
ROXIE
ROYAL
ROYCE
ROYKO

R•O••
RAOUL
REOIL
RHODA
RHODE
RHODO
RHOMB
RHONE
RIOJA
RIOTS
ROODS
ROOFS
ROOKS
ROOKY
ROOMS
ROOMY
ROONE
ROOST
ROOTS
ROOTY
RYOTS

R••O•
RACON
RADON
RAMON
RAMOS
RANON
RATON
RAYON
RAZOR
RECON
REDON
REDOX
REMOP
REMOW
REPOS
REPOT
RESOD
RETOP
RETOW
REWON
RICOH
RIDOF
RIGOR
RIPON
ROBOT
ROTOR
ROTOS
RUMOR
RUNON

R•••O
RADIO
RAMBO
RANTO
RATIO
RATSO
RECTO
REPRO
RETRO
RHINO
RHIZO
RHODO
RINGO
RINSO
RIZZO
ROCCO
RODEO
ROLEO
ROLLO
ROMEO
RONDO
ROVNO
ROYKO
RUNTO
RUSSO

•RO••
AROAR
AROID
AROMA
AROSE
BROAD
BROCA
BROCK
BRODY
BROIL
BROKE
BROME
BROMO
BRONC
BRONX
BROOD
BROOK
BROOM
BROTH
BROUN
BROWN
BROWS
CROAK
CROAT
CROCE
CROCI
CROCK
CROCS
CROFT
CROIX
CROLY
CRONE
CRONY
CROOK
CROON
CROPS
CROSS
CROUP
CROWD
CROWN
CROWS
CROZE
DROID
DROIT
DROLL
DROME
DRONE
DROOD
DROOL
DROOP
DROPS
DROSS
DROVE
DROWN
ERODE
EROSE
FROBE
FROCK
FRODO
FROES
FROGS
FROID
FROME
FROMM
FROND
FRONT
FROSH
FROST
FROTH
FROWN
FROWS
FROZE
GROAN
GROAT
GRODY
GROFE
GROGS
GROIN
GROKS
GROOM
GROPE
GROSS
GROSZ
GROTS
GROUP
GROUT
GROVE
GROWL
GROWN
GROWS
GROZA
IRONS
IRONY
KROGH
KRONA
KRONE
OROMO
ORONO
PROAM
PROAS
PROBE
PROBS
PRODS
PROEM
PROFS
PROGS
PROLE
PROMO
PROMS
PRONE
PRONG
PROOF
PROPS
PROSE
PROST
PROSY
PROTO
PROTS
PROUD
PROVE
PROVO
PROWL
PROWS
PROXY
TROIS
TROLL
TROMP
TROOP
TROPE
TROPO
TROTH
TROTS
TROUT
TROVE
VROOM
WRONG
WROTE
WROTH

•R•O•
ARBOR
ARDOR
ARGOL
ARGON
ARGOS
ARGOT
ARION
ARMOR
ARROW
ARROZ
ARSON
ARTOO
BROOD
BROOK
BROOM
CREON
CROOK
CROON
DROOD
DROOL
DROOP
ERGOT
ERROL
ERROR
FREON
GRIOT
GROOM
MRMOM
ORDOS
OREOS
ORION
ORLON
ORLOP
ORSON
ORTON
ORZOS
PRION
PRIOR
PROOF
PRYOR
TRIOS
TROOP
TRYON
VROOM

•R••O
ARTOO
BRAVO
BROMO
BRUNO
CREDO
DRACO
DRANO
DRLAO
ERATO
FRITO
FRODO
GRECO
IRIDO
ORFEO
OROMO
ORONO
ORTHO
ORURO
PRADO
PRATO
PREGO
PRIMO
PROMO
PROTO
PROVO
TROPO
TRURO

••RO•
AARON
AERON
AEROS
AFROS
AGRON
AKRON
APRON
ARROW
ARROZ
BARON
BORON
BYRON
CAROB
CAROL
CAROM
CARON
CDROM
CEROS
CHROM
CHRON
COROT
DUROC
DUROS
ELROY
ENROL
EPROM
ERROL
ERROR
EUROS
FAROE
FARON
FAROS
FUROR
FUROS
GAROU
GIROS
GYRON
GYROS
HEROD
HERON
HEROS
HOROL
HUROK
HURON
JUROR
KAROL
KIROV
LEROI
LEROY
MEROE
MORON
MOROS
MYRON
NEROL
PAROL
PAROS
PERON
PEROT

SAROD
SAROS
SCROD
SEROW
STROM
STROP
TAROK
TAROT
THROB
THROE
THROW
TIROS
TOROS
TUROW
TYROL
TYROS
XEROX
YUROK
ZEROS

••R•O
BURRO
CARBO
CARGO
CARLO
CARPO
CERRO
CIRRO
CORNO
CURIO
DARIO
DERMO
DORSO
FARGO
FERRO
FIRPO
FORDO
FORGO
GARBO
GORDO
HARPO
LARGO
MARCO
MARGO
MARIO
MARLO
MIRRO
MORRO
NARCO
NORVO
PARDO
PARVO
PORTO
SARGO
SARTO
SERVO
SORGO
TORSO
TURBO
VERSO
VIREO
VIRGO
ZORRO

•••RO
AGGRO
ANDRO
ASTRO
BURRO
CAIRO
CERRO
CHARO
CHIRO
CIRRO
CLARO
CUPRO
DOBRO
DOURO
ENERO
EXTRO
FERRO
FIBRO
FIERO
GENRO
GUIRO
HIERO
HYDRO
HYGRO
IATRO
INTRO
MACRO
MATRO
METRO
MICRO
MIRRO
MORRO
MUCRO
MUNRO
NEURO
NITRO
ORURO
PEDRO
PETRO
PICRO
PTERO
REPRO
RETRO
SACRO
SPERO
SPIRO
TAURO
THORO
TRURO
ZORRO

R•P••
RAPEE
RAPHE
RAPID
REPAD
REPAY
REPEG
REPEL
REPIN
REPLY
REPOS
REPOT
REPPS
REPRO
RIPEN
RIPER
RIPON
RIPUP
ROPED
ROPER
ROPES
ROPEY
RUPEE

R••P•
RALPH
RAMPS
RASPS
RASPY
REAPS
REPPS
REUPS
ROMPS
RSVPD
RSVPS
RUMPS

R•••P
RANUP
RECAP
RECIP
REMAP
REMOP
RETAP
RETOP
REVUP
RIGUP
RIPUP
RUNUP

•RP••
ARPAD
ARPEL

•R•P•
CRAPE
CRAPS
CREPE
CREPT
CROPS
CRYPT
DRAPE
DRIPS
DROPS
DRUPE
ERUPT
FRAPS
GRAPE
GRAPH
GRAPY
GRIPE
GRIPS
GROPE
KRUPA
KRUPP
PREPS
PROPS
TRAPP
TRAPS
TRIPE
TRIPS
TROPE
TROPO
WRAPS
WRAPT

•R••P
CRAMP
CREEP
CRIMP
CRISP
CROUP
CRUMP
DROOP
DRYUP
FRUMP
GRAMP
GRASP
GROUP
GRUMP
KRUPP
ORLOP
PRIMP
TRAMP
TRAPP
TROMP
TROOP
TRUMP

••RP•
BURPS
CARPE
CARPI
CARPO
CARPS
CORPS
DORPS
FIRPO
GORPS
HARPO
HARPS
HARPY
MORPH
PERPS
TARPS
TERPS
WARPS

••R•P
ATRIP
PTRAP
SCRAP
SCRIP
STRAP
STREP
STRIP
STROP
SYRUP

•••RP
CHIRP
SCARP
SHARP
SLURP
THARP
THORP
TWERP
USURP

R•Q••
ROQUE

•R•Q•
IRAQI

••RQ•
BARQS

••R•Q
BARBQ

R•R••
RAREE
RARER
RARES
RERAN
RERIG
RERUM
RERUN
ROREM
RURAL
RURIK

R••R•
REARM
REARS
REFRY
REPRO
RETRO
RETRY
ROARS
RUARK
RUERS

R•••R
RACER
RADAR
RAFER
RAKER
RAMAR
RANDR
RARER
RASER
RATER
RAVER
RAWER
RAZOR
REAIR
REBAR
RECUR
REFER
RETAR
RICER
RIDER
RIFER
RIGOR
RIKER
RIPER
RISER
RIVER
ROGER
ROMER
ROPER
ROTOR
ROVER
ROWER
RSFSR
RUDER
RULER
RUMOR
RYDER

•RR••
ARRAN
ARRAS
ARRAU
ARRAY
ARRET
ARRIS
ARROW
ARROZ
ERRED
ERROL
ERROR
IRREG
ORRIN
ORRIS

•R•R•
ARBRE
BRERS
CRURA
DRDRE
DRURY
FRERE
ORURO
TRURO

•R••R
ARBER
ARBOR
ARDOR
AREAR
ARMOR
AROAR
ARTHR
ARTUR
BRIAR
BRIER
CRIER
CRYER
DREAR
DRIER
DRYER
ERROR
FREER
FRIAR
FRIER
FRYER
GREER
GRIER
ORDER
ORSER
PRIER
PRIOR
PRYOR
TRIER
TRUER
URGER
WRIER
WRYER

••RR•
BARRE
BARRY
BERRA
BERRY
BIRRS
BURRO
BURRS
BURRY
CARRE
CARRY
CERRO
CIRRI
CIRRO
CURRY
DERRY
DURRA
FERRI
FERRO
FERRY
FIRRY
FURRY
GARRY
GERRY
HARRY
HURRY
JARRE
JERRY
KERRI
KERRY
LARRY
LORRE
LORRY
MARRY
MERRY
MIRRO
MORRO
MURRA
MURRE
MYRRH
PARRY
PERRY
PURRS
SERRA
SERRY
SORRY
TARRY
TERRA
TERRE
TERRI
TERRY
TORRE
TORRS
UNRRA
VERRE
WIRRA
WORRY
ZORRO

••R•R
AURAR
BARER
BORER
CARER
CORER
CURER
DARER
DIRER
DURER
ERROR
EYRIR
FARER
FIRER
FUROR
HARAR
HIRER
JUROR
PARER
PURER
RARER
SORER
SURER
WIRER
YARER

•••RR
CHIRR
KNORR
OMARR
SHIRR
SKIRR
STARR
WHIRR

RS•••
RSFSR
RSVPD
RSVPS

R•S••
RASED
RASER
RASES
RASHT
RASPS
RASPY
RASTA
RESAW
RESEE
RESET
RESEW
RESIN
RESOD
RESTS
RISEN
RISER
RISES
RISHI
RISKS
RISKY
ROSEN
ROSES
ROSEY
ROSIE
ROSIN
ROSSI
RUSES
RUSHY
RUSKS
RUSSE
RUSSO
RUSTS
RUSTY

R••S•
RAISA
RAISE
RATSO
REESE
REUSE
RINSE
RINSO
RNASE
ROAST
ROOST
ROSSI
ROUSE
ROUST
RSFSR
RUSSE
RUSSO

R•••S
RACES
RACKS
RAFTS
RAGAS
RAGES
RAIDS
RAILS
RAINS
RAJAS
RAKES
RAKIS
RAMIS
RAMOS
RAMPS
RANDS
RANIS
RANKS
RANTS
RARES
RASES
RASPS
RATES
RATHS
RAVES
RAWLS
RAZES
READS
REALS
REAMS
REAPS
REARS
REBUS
REDES
REEDS
REEFS
REEKS
REELS
REGIS
REIMS
REINS
REMUS
RENDS
RENTS
REPOS
REPPS
RESTS
REUPS
REXES
REYES
RHEAS
RIALS
RICES
RICKS
RIDES
RIELS
RIFFS
RIFTS
RIGGS
RILES
RILLS
RIMES
RINDS
RINGS
RINKS
RIOTS
RISES
RISKS
RITES
RIVES
ROADS
ROAMS
ROANS
ROARS
ROBES
ROCKS
ROILS
ROLES
ROLLS
ROMPS
ROODS
ROOFS
ROOKS
ROOMS
ROOTS
ROPES
ROSES
ROTAS
ROTES
ROTLS
ROTOS
ROUES
ROUTS
ROVES
RSVPS
RUBES
RUCKS
RUDDS
RUERS
RUFFS
RUFUS
RUINS
RULES
RUMPS
RUNES
RUNGS
RUNTS
RUSES
RUSKS
RUSTS
RYOTS

•RS••
ARSIS
ARSON
ORSER
ORSON
URSID

•R•S•
ARISE
AROSE
ARTSY
BRASH
BRASS
BREST
BRISK
BRUSH
CRASH
CRASS
CRESC
CRESS
CREST
CRISP
CRISS
CRIST
CROSS
CRUSE
CRUSH
CRUST
DRESS
DROSS
DRUSE
ERASE
ERISA
ERNST

EROSE
FRESH
FRISE
FRISK
FROSH
FROST
GRASP
GRASS
GRIST
GROSS
GROSZ
IRISH
KRISS
PRASE
PRESS
PREST
PRISM
PROSE
PROST
PROSY
TRASH
TRESS
TRISH
TRUSS
TRUST
TRYST
WREST
WRIST

•R••S

ARABS
AREAS
ARENS
ARGOS
ARGUS
ARHUS
ARIAS
ARIES
ARILS
ARIUS
ARLES
ARMIS
ARRAS
ARRIS
ARSIS
ARTES
ARTIS
ARUMS
BRADS
BRAES
BRAGS
BRANS
BRASS
BRATS
BRAYS
BRERS
BREWS
BRIES
BRIGS
BRIMS
BRITS
BROWS
BRUTS
CRABS
CRAGS
CRAMS
CRAPS
CRASS
CRAWS
CREES
CRESS
CREWS
CRIBS
CRIES
CRISS
CROCS
CROPS
CROSS
CROWS
DRABS
DRAGS
DRAMS
DRATS
DRAWS
DRAYS
DREGS
DRESS
DRIBS
DRIES
DRIPS
DROPS
DROSS
DRUBS
DRUGS
DRUMS
ERIES
ERNES
FRAIS
FRANS
FRAPS
FRATS
FRAYS
FREES
FRETS
FRIES
FRITS
FROES
FROGS
FROWS
GRABS
GRADS
GRAMS
GRASS
GRAYS
GREES
GREYS
GRIDS
GRIGS
GRINS
GRIPS
GRITS
GROGS
GROKS
GROSS
GROTS
GROWS
GRUBS
IRONS
KRAUS
KREBS
KRISS
ORALS
ORCAS
ORCHS
ORCUS
ORDOS
OREOS
ORLES
ORNIS
ORRIS
ORZOS
PRAMS
PRAUS
PRAYS
PREPS
PRESS
PREYS
PRIES
PRIGS
PRIMS
PROAS
PROBS
PRODS
PROFS
PROGS
PROMS
PROPS
PROTS
PROWS
SRTAS
TRAMS
TRANS
TRAPS
TRAYS
TREES
TREKS
TRESS
TREWS
TREYS
TRIES
TRIGS
TRIMS
TRIOS
TRIPS
TROIS
TROTS
TRUES
TRUGS
TRUSS
URALS
URBIS
URGES
WRACS
WRAFS
WRAPS
WRENS
WRITS
XRAYS

••RS•

BIRSE
BURSA
BURSE
BURST
CURSE
CURST
DERSU
DORSA
DORSI
DORSO
DURST
FARSI
FIRST
GORSE
GORSY
HARSH
HORSE
HORST
HORSY
HURST
KARSH
KURSK
MARSH
MORSE
NORSE
NURSE
PARSE
PERSE
PURSE
PURSY
TARSI
TERSE
TORSI
TORSO
VERSA
VERSE
VERSO
VERST
WORSE
WORST
WURST

••R•S

ABRIS
ACRES
AEROS
AFROS
AIRES
APRES
ARRAS
ARRIS
AURAS
AYRES
BARBS
BARDS
BARES
BARKS
BARMS
BARNS
BARQS
BARTS
BERGS
BERMS
BIRDS
BIRLS
BIRRS
BORAS
BORES
BORIS
BURBS
BURGS
BURLS
BURNS
BURPS
BURRS
BYRDS
BYRES
CARBS
CARDS
CARES
CARKS
CARPS
CARTS
CERES
CEROS
CERTS
CHRIS
CHRYS
CIRCS
CIRES
CORDS
CORES
CORKS
CORMS
CORNS
CORPS
CURBS
CURDS
CURES
CURLS
CYRUS
DARES
DARKS
DARNS
DARTS
DIRKS
DORIS
DORMS
DORPS
DURNS
DUROS
EARLS
EARNS
ECRUS
EUROS
EURUS
EYRAS
EYRES
FARES
FARMS
FAROS
FERNS
FIRES
FIRMS
FIRNS
FORBS
FORDS
FORES
FORKS
FORMS
FORTS
FURLS
FUROS
GARBS
GERMS
GIRDS
GIRLS
GIRNS
GIROS
GIRTS
GORES
GORPS
GURUS
GYRES
GYROS
GYRUS
HARES
HARKS
HARMS
HARPS
HARTS
HERBS
HERDS
HERES
HERLS
HERMS
HERNS
HEROS
HIRES
HORAS
HORNS
HORUS
HURLS
HURTS
JARLS
JERKS
KERBS
KERNS
KIRKS
KURDS
LARAS
LARDS
LARES
LARIS
LARKS
LIRAS
LORDS
LORES
LORIS
LURES
LURKS
LYRES
MARAS
MARES
MARIS
MARKS
MARLS
MARTS
MARYS
MERES
MERLS
MIRES
MIRVS
MORAS
MORES
MORNS
MOROS
MORTS
NARAS
NARCS
NARDS
NARES
NARIS
NARKS
NERDS
NERTS
NORMS
NORNS
OGRES
OKRAS
ORRIS
PARDS
PARES
PARIS
PARKS
PAROS
PARTS
PERES
PERIS
PERKS
PERMS
PERPS
PORES
PORKS
PORTS
PURLS
PURRS
PURUS
PYRES
RARES
SARDS
SARIS
SAROS
SERBS
SERES
SERFS
SIRES
SORAS
SORBS
SORES
SORTS
SORUS
SURAS
SURDS
SURFS
TARES
TARNS
TARPS
TARTS
TERMS
TERNS
TERPS
TIRES
TIROS
TOROS
TORRS
TORTS
TORUS
TURFS
TURKS
TURNS
TYRES
TYROS
VARAS
VERBS
VERTS
VIRUS
WARDS
WARES
WARMS
WARNS
WARPS
WARTS
WIRES
WORDS
WORKS
WORMS
WORTS
XERUS
YARDS
YARNS
YERKS
YPRES
YURTS
ZARFS
ZEROS
ZORIS

•••RS

ABBRS
ACERS
AFARS
AGARS
AGERS
ALORS
AMIRS
APERS
AVARS
AVERS
AXERS
AYERS
BEARS
BEERS
BIRRS
BLURS
BOARS
BOERS
BOORS
BRERS
BURRS
CBERS
CHARS
CMDRS
COIRS
COORS
CZARS
DEARS
DEERS
DOERS
DOORS
DYERS
EMIRS
ENGRS
EVERS
EWERS
EYERS
FAIRS
FEARS
FOURS
GAURS
GEARS
GNARS
GOERS
GUARS
HAIRS
HEARS
HEIRS
HOARS
HOERS
HOURS
IBARS
ICERS
ITERS
IZARS
JBARS
JEERS
KNARS
KNURS
LAIRS
LEARS
LEERS
LIARS
MOORS
MYERS
NEARS
NLERS
ODORS
OMERS
ONERS
OVERS
OWERS
PAIRS
PEARS
PEERS
PIERS
POURS
PURRS
REARS
ROARS
RUERS
SCARS
SEARS
SEERS
SLURS
SOARS
SOURS
SPARS
SPURS
STARS
STIRS
SUERS
TAHRS
TBARS
TEARS
THURS
TIERS
TORRS
TOURS
TSARS
TZARS
USERS
VEERS
VIERS
WEARS
WEIRS
WHIRS
YEARS
YOURS
ZBARS

R•T••

RATCH
RATED
RATEL
RATER
RATES
RATHS
RATIO
RATON
RATSO
RATTY
RETAG
RETAP
RETAR
RETAX
RETIA
RETIE
RETOP
RETOW
RETRO
RETRY
RITES
RITZY
ROTAS
ROTES
ROTLS
ROTOR
ROTOS
RUTIN
RUTTY

R••T•

RAFTS
RAITT
RANTO
RANTS
RASTA
RATTY
REATA
RECTI
RECTO
RENTA
RENTS
RESTS
RHETT
RHYTA
RIATA
RIFTS
RIOTS
ROOTS
ROOTY
ROUTE
ROUTS
RUNTO
RUNTS
RUNTY
RUSTS
RUSTY
RUTTY
RYOTS

R•••T

RABAT
RAITT
RAMET
RANAT
RASHT
REACT
REBUT
REFIT
RELET
RELIT
REMET
REMIT
REPOT
RESET
REVET
RHETT
RIANT
RIGHT
RIVET
ROAST
ROBOT
ROGET
ROOST
ROUST
RUNAT

•RT••

ARTAL
ARTEL
ARTES
ARTHR
ARTIE
ARTIS
ARTOO
ARTSY
ARTUR
ORTHO
ORTON
SRTAS

•R•T•
ARETE
ARITH
BRATS
BRETT
BRITE
BRITH
BRITS
BRITT
BROTH
BRUTE
BRUTS
CRATE
CRETE
DRATS
ERATO
FRATS
FRETS
FRITO
FRITS
FRITZ
FROTH
GRATA
GRATE
GRETA
GRETE
GRITS
GROTS
IRATE
ORATE
PRATE
PRATO
PRATT
PROTO
PROTS
TRITE
TRITT
TROTH
TROTS
TRUTH
WRATH
WRITE
WRITS
WROTE
WROTH

•R••T
ARENT
ARGOT
ARHAT
ARMET
ARRET
BRACT
BRANT
BRENT
BREST
BRETT
BRITT
BRUIT
BRUNT
CRAFT
CREPT
CREST
CRIST
CROAT
CROFT
CRUET
CRUST
CRYPT
DRAFT
DRIFT
DROIT
ERECT
ERGOT
ERNST
ERUCT
ERUPT
FRONT
FROST
FRUIT
GRAFT
GRANT
GREAT
GREET
GRIFT
GRIOT
GRIST
GROAT
GROUT
GRUNT
KRAFT
KRAIT
KRAUT
ORANT
ORBIT
PRATT
PREST
PRINT
PROST
TRACT
TRAIT
TREAT
TRENT
TRITT
TROUT
TRUST
TRYST
WRAPT
WREST
WRIST

••RT•
AORTA
BARTH
BARTS
BARTY
BERTH
BIRTH
CARTA
CARTE
CARTS
CERTS
DARTH
DARTS
DIRTY
EARTH
FIRTH
FORTE
FORTH
FORTS
FORTY
FURTH
GARTH
GIRTH
GIRTS
HARTE
HARTS
HERTZ
HURTS
KURTZ
MARTA
MARTI
MARTS
MARTY
MERTZ
MIRTH
MORTS
NERTS
NERTZ
NORTE
NORTH
PARTE
PARTI
PARTS
PARTY
PERTH
PORTE
PORTO
PORTS
SARTO
SERTA
SORTA
SORTS
TARTS
TARTU
TORTE
TORTS
VERTE
VERTS
VIRTU
WARTS
WARTY
WORTH
WORTS
YURTS

••R•T
AFRIT
ARRET
BARIT
BERET
BURNT
BURST
CARAT
CARET
CERAT
COROT
CURST
DERAT
DURST
EGRET
FIRST
HERAT
HORST
HURST
JURAT
KARAT
KERAT
MARAT
MERIT
MURAT
PEROT
SPRAT
SPRIT
STRUT
SURAT
TAROT
VERST
WORST
WURST

•••RT
ABORT
ALERT
AMORT
APART
APORT
AVERT
BLURT
CHART
CHERT
COURT
EBERT
EVERT
EXERT
FLIRT
HEART
IBERT
INERT
KMART
OPART
OVERT
QUART
QUIRT
SHIRT
SHORT
SKIRT
SKORT
SMART
SNERT
SNORT
SPORT
SPURT
START
SWART

RU•••
RUANA
RUARK
RUBEN
RUBES
RUBIK
RUBIN
RUBLE
RUCHE
RUCKS
RUDDS
RUDDY
RUDER
RUDGE
RUEHL
RUERS
RUFFS
RUFUS
RUGAE
RUGBY
RUING
RUINS
RULED
RULER
RULES
RUMBA
RUMEN
RUMMY
RUMOR
RUMPS
RUNAT
RUNES
RUNGS
RUNIC
RUNIN
RUNNY
RUNON
RUNTO
RUNTS
RUNTY
RUNUP
RUPEE
RURAL
RURIK
RUSES
RUSHY
RUSKS
RUSSE
RUSSO
RUSTS
RUSTY
RUTIN
RUTTY

R•U••
REUEL
REUNE
REUPS
REUSE
RHUMB
ROUEN
ROUES
ROUGE
ROUGH
ROUND
ROUSE
ROUST
ROUTE
ROUTS

R••U•
RANUP
RAOUL
REBUS
REBUT
RECUR
REDUB
REDUX
REGUM
REMUS
RERUM
RERUN
REVUE
REVUP
RHEUM
RIGUP
RIPUP
ROGUE
ROQUE
RUFUS
RUNUP

•RU••
ARUBA
ARUMS
BRUCE
BRUCH
BRUHN
BRUIN
BRUIT
BRULE
BRUME
BRUNG
BRUNO
BRUNT
BRUSH
BRUTE
BRUTS
CRUDE
CRUEL
CRUET
CRUMB
CRUMP
CRURA
CRUSE
CRUSH
CRUST
DRUBS
DRUGS
DRUID
DRUMS
DRUNK
DRUPE
DRURY
DRUSE
DRUZE
ERUCT
ERUPT
FRUIT
FRUMP
GRUBS
GRUEL
GRUFF
GRUMP
GRUNT
KRULL
KRUPA
KRUPP
ORURO
PRUDE
PRUNE
TRUCE
TRUCK
TRUED
TRUER
TRUES
TRUEX
TRUGS
TRULY
TRUMP
TRUNK
TRURO
TRUSS
TRUST
TRUTH
WRUNG

•R•U•
ARGUE
ARGUS
ARHUS
ARIUM
ARIUS
ARTUR
BRAUN
BROUN
CROUP
DRYUP
FRAUD
FREUD
GROUP
GROUT
KRAUS
KRAUT
ORCUS
PRAUS
PROUD
TROUT

•R••U
ARRAU

••RU•
AURUM
CYRUS
DURUM
ECRUS
EURUS
FORUM
GURUS
GYRUS
HARUM
HORUS
JORUM
LARUE
MORUM
PURUS
RERUM
RERUN
SCRUB
SCRUM
SERUM
SHRUB
SHRUG
SORUS
SPRUE
STRUG
STRUM
STRUT
SYRUP
THRUM
TORUS
UNRUH
VIRUS
XERUS

••R•U
ARRAU
CORFU
CORNU
DERSU
GAROU
PAREU
PERDU
TARTU
TURKU
VIRTU

•••RU
NAURU
NEHRU
OTARU
UHURU

R•V••
RAVED
RAVEL
RAVEN
RAVER
RAVES
RAVIN
REVEL
REVET
REVUE
REVUP
RIVAL
RIVED
RIVEN
RIVER
RIVES
RIVET
ROVED
ROVER
ROVES
ROVNO
RSVPD
RSVPS

R••V•
REEVE

R•••V
RAJIV

•RV••
ERVIL
ERVIN
IRVIN

•R•V•
BRAVA
BRAVE
BRAVO
BREVE
CRAVE
DRAVA
DRIVE
DROVE
GRAVE
GRAVY
GROVE
PRIVY
PROVE
PROVO
TRAVE
TREVI
TROVE

••RV•
CARVE
CURVE
CURVY
HERVE
LARVA
MARVY
MIRVS
NERVE
NERVY
NORVO
PARVO
SERVE
SERVO
TURVY
VERVE

••R•V
DERIV
KIROV

R•W••
RAWER
RAWLS
RAWLY
REWAX
REWED
REWIN
REWON
ROWAN
ROWDY
ROWED
ROWEL
ROWEN
ROWER

R•••W
REMOW
RENEW
RESAW
RESEW
RETOW

•RW••
ERWIN
IRWIN

•R•W•
BRAWL
BRAWN
BREWS
BROWN
BROWS
CRAWL
CRAWS
CREWS
CROWD
CROWN
CROWS
DRAWL
DRAWN
DRAWS
DROWN
FROWN
FROWS
GROWL
GROWN
GROWS
PRAWN
PROWL
PROWS
TRAWL
TREWS

•R••W
ARROW

••R•W
ARROW
CAREW
NAREW
SCREW
SEROW
SHREW
STRAW
STREW
THREW
THROW
TUROW

R•X••
REXES
ROXIE

R•••X
RADIX
REDOX
REDUX
RELAX
REMEX
REMIX
RETAX
REWAX
ROLEX

•R•X•
PREXY
PROXY

•R••X
BRONX
CROIX
TRUEX

••R•X
BORAX
HYRAX
LORAX
LUREX
MUREX
PUREX
PYREX
VARIX
XEROX

RY•••
RYDER
RYOTS

R•Y••
RAYED
RAYON
REYES
RHYME
RHYTA
RIYAL
ROYAL
ROYCE
ROYKO

R••Y•
REDYE

R•••Y
RAINY
RALLY
RANDY
RANGY
RASPY
RATTY
RAWLY
READY
REDDY
REDLY
REEDY
REEKY
REFRY
REIFY
REKEY

RELAY REPAY REPLY RETRY RIBBY RICKY RIDGY RIGBY RILEY RINDY RINKY RISKY RITZY ROBBY ROCKY RODDY ROILY RONNY ROOKY ROOMY ROOTY ROPEY ROSEY ROWDY RUDDY RUGBY RUMMY RUNNY RUNTY RUSHY RUSTY RUTTY

•RY••

ARYAN BRYAN BRYCE CRYER CRYPT DRYAD DRYER DRYLY DRYUP FRYER PRYCE PRYOR TRYME TRYON TRYST WRYER WRYLY

•R•Y•

BRAYS DRAYS FRAYS FREYA GRAYS GREYS ORIYA PRAYS PREYS TRAYS TREYS XRAYS

•R••Y

ARABY ARCHY ARRAY ARTSY BRADY BRINY BRODY CRACY CRAZY CRECY CROLY CRONY DRILY DRURY DRYLY GRADY GRAPY GRAVY GRIMY GRODY IRONY KRAZY ORACY ORCZY PREXY PRICY PRIVY PROSY PROXY TRACY TRULY WRYLY

••RY•

BERYL CHRYS DARYA DARYL MARYS MERYL

••R•Y

ARRAY BARGY BARKY BARMY BARRY BARTY BERRY BIRDY BURLY BURRY CAREY CARLY CARNY CARRY CORBY COREY CORKY CORNY CURDY CURLY CURRY CURVY DARBY DERBY DERRY DIRTY EARLY ELROY FERNY FERRY FIRRY FORAY FORKY FORTY FURRY GARRY GERMY GERRY GORDY GORKY GORSY GURDY HARDY HARPY HARRY HERBY HERKY HORSY HURDY HURLY HURRY JERKY JERRY JERZY KERRY KIRBY LARDY LARKY LARRY LEROY LORRY LURAY MARCY MARLY MARRY MARTY MARVY MERCY MERRY MIRKY MORAY MOREY MURKY NERDY NERVY PARRY PARTY PERCY PERKY PERRY PORGY PORKY PURSY SARKY SERRY SORRY SPRAY STRAY SURFY SURLY TARDY TARRY TERRY TURFY TURVY WARTY WORDY WORMY WORRY

•••RY

AMBRY AMORY ANDRY ANGRY APERY AUTRY AVERY BARRY BEERY BERRY BURRY CAMRY CARRY CHARY CLARY COWRY CURRY CYMRY DAIRY DEARY DECRY DERRY DEVRY DIARY DOWRY DRURY EMERY EMORY ENTRY EVERY FAERY FAIRY FERRY FIERY FIRRY FLORY FURRY GARRY GEARY GERRY GLARY GLORY HAIRY HARRY HENRY HOARY HURRY IATRY IVORY JERRY KERRY LARRY LATRY LEARY LEERY LORRY LOWRY MARRY MAURY MERRY METRY MOORY OTARY PARRY PEARY PERRY QUERY REFRY RETRY SAURY SCARY SERRY SORRY SPIRY STORY TARRY TEARY TERRY USURY VEERY WEARY WORRY

R•Z••

RAZED RAZES RAZOR RIZZO

R••Z•

RHIZO RITZY RIZZO

•RZ••

ORZOS

•R•Z•

BRAZE CRAZE CRAZY CROZE DRUZE FRIZZ FROZE GRAZE GROZA KRAZY ORCZY PRIZE PRIZM

•R••Z

ARNAZ ARROZ FRANZ FRITZ FRIZZ GROSZ

••RZ•

FURZE HERZL JERZY TERZA

••R•Z

ARROZ HERTZ JEREZ KURTZ MERTZ NERTZ PEREZ

•••RZ

STARZ

SA•••

SAABS SABAH SABER SABIN SABLE SABOT SABRA SABRE SACCO SACHA SACHS SACKS SACRA SACRE SACRO SADAT SADHE SADHU SADIE SADIS SADLY SAENS SAFER SAFES SAGAL SAGAN SAGAS SAGER SAGES SAGET SAGGY SAGOS SAHEL SAHIB SAIGA SAILS SAINT SAITH SAJAK SAKAI SAKER SAKES SALAD SALAL SALAM SALEM SALEP SALES SALIC SALLE SALLY SALMI SALON SALPA SALPS SALSA SALTA SALTS SALTY SALUD SALUT SALVE SALVO SAMAR SAMBA SAMMS SAMMY SAMOA SAMOS SAMPS SANAA SANDE SANDH SANDL SANDS SANDY SANER SANKA SANTA SANTE SANTO SANYO SAONE SAPID SAPIR SAPOR SAPPY SARAH SARAN SARDS SARGE SARGO SARIS SARKY SAROD SAROS SARTO SASES SASHA SASSY SATAN SATBY SATED SATES SATIE SATIN SATON SATUP SATYR SAUCE SAUCY SAUDI SAUKS SAULT SAUNA SAURY SAUTE SAVED SAVER SAVES SAVOR SAVOY SAVVY SAWED SAWIN SAWTO SAXES SAXON SAYER SAYSO

S•A••

SAABS SCABS SCADS SCALA SCALD SCALE SCALP SCALY SCAMP SCAMS SCAND SCANS SCANT SCAPA SCAPE SCARE SCARF SCARP SCARS SCARY SCATS SCAUP SEALE SEALS SEALY SEAMS SEAMY SEARS SEATO SEATS SHACK SHADE SHADS SHADY SHAEF SHAFT SHAGS SHAHN SHAHS SHAKE SHAKO SHAKY SHALE SHALL SHALT SHAME SHAMS SHAMU SHANA SHANE SHANK SHANS SHANT SHAPE SHARD SHARE SHARI SHARK SHARP SHATT SHAUN SHAVE SHAWL SHAWM SHAWN SHAYS SIALS SKALD SKANK SKATE SLABS SLACK SLADE SLAGS SLAIN SLAKE SLAMS SLANG SLANT SLAPS SLASH SLATE SLATS SLATY SLAVE SLAVS SLAWS SLAYS SMACK SMAIL SMALL SMALT SMART SMASH SMAZE SNACK SNAFU SNAGS SNAIL SNAKE SNAKY SNAPS SNARE SNARK SNARL SNATH SOAKS SOAPS SOAPY SOARS SOAVE SPAAK SPACE SPACY SPADE SPADS SPAHI SPAHN SPAIN SPAKE SPALL SPAMS SPANG SPANK SPANS SPARE SPARK SPARS SPASM SPATE SPATS SPAWN SPAYS STABS STACK STACY STADT STAEL STAFF STAGE STAGG STAGS STAGY STAHL STAID STAIN STAIR STAKE STALE STALK STALL STAMP STAND STANG STANK STARE STARK STARR STARS START STARZ STASH STATE STATS STAVE STAYS SUAVE SWABS SWAGE SWAGS SWAIN SWALE SWAMI SWAMP SWANK SWANN SWANS SWAPS SWARD SWARF SWARM SWART SWASH SWATH SWATS SWAYS SWAZI

S••A•

SABAH SADAT SAGAL SAGAN SAGAS SAJAK SAKAI SALAD SALAL SALAM SAMAR SANAA SARAH SARAN SATAN SCHAV SCRAG SCRAM SCRAP SEDAN SEGAL SEGAR SELAH

SENAT
SEPAL
SERAC
SERAI
SERAL
SETAE
SETAT
SHEAF
SHEAN
SHEAR
SHOAH
SHOAL
SHOAT
SIKAS
SILAS
SINAI
SISAL
SITAR
SIVAN
SIXAM
SKEAN
SKEAT
SKOAL
SKUAS
SLOAN
SMEAR
SNEAD
SNEAK
SODAS
SOFAR
SOFAS
SOLAN
SOLAR
SOMAS
SONAR
SORAS
SOYAS
SPAAK
SPEAK
SPEAR
SPLAT
SPLAY
SPRAG
SPRAT
SPRAY
SQUAB
SQUAD
SQUAT
SRTAS
STEAD
STEAK
STEAL
STEAM
STOAE
STOAS
STOAT
STPAT
STRAD
STRAP
STRAW
STRAY
SUDAN
SUGAR
SUMAC
SURAH
SURAL
SURAS
SURAT
SUSAN
SWEAR
SWEAT

S•••A
SABRA
SACHA
SACRA
SAIGA
SALPA
SALSA
SALTA
SAMBA
SAMOA
SANAA
SANKA
SANTA
SASHA
SAUNA
SCALA
SCAPA
SCENA
SCHWA
SCUBA
SCUTA
SEEYA
SEHNA
SELMA
SELVA
SENNA
SEPIA
SEPTA
SERRA
SERTA
SHANA
SHEBA
SHEMA
SHIVA
SHULA
SIDEA
SIDRA
SIENA
SIGMA
SILVA
SIMBA
SITKA
SKODA
SLIWA
SNEVA
SOFIA
SOLFA
SONIA
SONJA
SONYA
SORTA
SOUSA
SPICA
SPOSA
STELA
STOLA
STOMA
STRIA
STUKA
STUPA
SUCKA
SUDRA
SUITA
SULFA
SULLA
SUMBA
SUMMA
SUNDA
SUNNA
SUPRA
SUTRA
SYRIA

•SA••
ASAMA
ASANA
ISAAC
ISAMU
LSATS
OSAGE
OSAKA
PSALM
PSATS
TSADE
TSARS
USAGE
USAIR

•S•A•
ASCAP
ASIAN
ASSAD
ASSAI
ASSAM
ASSAY
ASWAN
ESBAT
ESSAY
ESTAB
ESTAS
ISAAC
ISLAM
ISLAS
OSCAN
OSCAR
OSKAR
OSMAN
PSHAW
PSOAS
USUAL

•S••A
ASAMA
ASANA
ASOKA
ASPCA
ASTRA
ASYLA
OSAKA
OSHEA
OSSIA
OSTIA
USCGA
USLTA
USOFA

••SA•
ANSAE
ASSAD
ASSAI
ASSAM
ASSAY
BASAL
CASAS
CESAR
ESSAY
HASAT
MASAI
MESAS
NASAL
NISAN
PISAN
PUSAN
RESAW
SISAL
SUSAN
UNSAY
VISAS

••S•A
AISHA
ATSEA
BASRA
BOSSA
CASCA
CESTA
COSTA
DESNA
FESTA
FOSSA
HASTA
HOSEA
HOSTA
KASHA
KISKA
MESTA
MISHA
MISSA
MUSCA
OSSIA
PASHA
PASTA
RASTA
SASHA
TESLA
TESTA
TISZA
TOSCA
VESTA
VISTA

•••SA
AZUSA
BALSA
BOSSA
BURSA
CAUSA
COOSA
DORSA
ERISA
FOSSA
HANSA
HAUSA
ICOSA
KANSA
LHASA
LUISA
MENSA
MISSA
NYASA
OMASA
PAISA
RAISA
SALSA
SOUSA
SPOSA
TULSA
VERSA
XHOSA

S•B••
SABAH
SABER
SABIN
SABLE
SABOT
SABRA
SABRE
SEBUM
SIBYL
SOBER
SOBIG
SUBIC
SYBIL

S••B•
SAABS
SAMBA
SATBY
SCABS
SCUBA
SERBS
SETBY
SHEBA
SIMBA
SITBY
SLABS
SLOBS
SNOBS
SNUBS
SORBS
STABS
STUBS
SUMBA
SWABS
SWOBS

S•••B
SAHIB
SCRUB
SHRUB
SIDEB
SQUAB
SQUIB
STIEB

•SB••
ESBAT

•S•B•
ASHBY
MSNBC

•S••B
ESTAB

••SB•
BUSBY
COSBY
MOSBY
NASBY
VISBY

SC•••
SCABS
SCADS
SCALA
SCALD
SCALE
SCALP
SCALY
SCAMP
SCAMS
SCAND
SCANS
SCANT
SCAPA
SCAPE
SCARE
SCARF
SCARP
SCARS
SCARY
SCATS
SCAUP
SCENA
SCEND
SCENE
SCENT
SCHAV
SCHED
SCHMO
SCHON
SCHWA
SCIFI
SCION
SCOFF
SCOLD
SCONE
SCOOP
SCOOT
SCOPE
SCOPS
SCOPY
SCORE
SCORN
SCOTS
SCOTT
SCOUR
SCOUT
SCOWL
SCOWS
SCRAG
SCRAM
SCRAP
SCREE
SCREW
SCRIM
SCRIP
SCROD
SCRUB
SCRUM
SCUBA
SCUDI
SCUDO
SCUDS
SCUFF
SCULL
SCUMS
SCUPS
SCURF
SCUTA
SCUTE
SCUTS
SCUZZ

S•C••
SACCO
SACHA
SACHS
SACKS
SACRA
SACRE
SACRO
SECCO
SECTS
SOCHI
SOCIO
SOCKO
SOCKS
SOCLE
SUCKA
SUCKS
SUCRE
SYCEE
SYCES

S••C•
SACCO
SAUCE
SAUCY
SECCO
SHACK
SHOCK
SHUCK
SINCE
SLACK
SLICE
SLICK
SMACK
SMOCK
SNACK
SNICK
SNUCK
SPACE
SPACY
SPECD
SPECK
SPECS
SPICA
SPICE
SPICY
SPOCK
STACK
STACY
STICH
STICK
STOCK
STUCK
SULCI
SYNCS

S•••C
SALIC
SERAC
SOFTC
SONIC
STOIC
SUBIC
SUMAC

•SC••
ASCAP
ASCII
ASCOT
ASCUS
OSCAN
OSCAR
USCGA

•S•C•
ASPCA
PSYCH

•S••C
ASDIC
ASPIC
ASSOC
FSLIC
ISAAC
ISTIC
MSNBC
OSMIC
OSRIC

••SC•
BOSCH
BOSCO
BOSCS
BUSCH
CASCA
CASCO
CISCO
DISCO
DISCS
FISCS
MUSCA
NOSCE
PASCH
PASCO
PESCI
PISCI
PISCO
TOSCA
VASCO

••S•C
ASSOC
BASIC
COSEC
MESIC
MUSIC

•••SC
CRESC
EPISC

S•D••
SADAT
SADHE
SADHU
SADIE
SADIS
SADLY
SEDAN
SEDER
SEDGE
SEDGY
SEDUM
SIDEA
SIDEB
SIDED
SIDER
SIDES
SIDHE
SIDLE
SIDON
SIDRA
SODAS
SODDY
SODOM
SUDAN
SUDDS
SUDRA
SUDSY
SYDOW

S••D•
SANDE
SANDH
SANDL
SANDS
SANDY
SARDS
SAUDI
SCADS
SCUDI
SCUDO
SCUDS
SEEDS
SEEDY
SENDS
SHADE
SHADS
SHADY
SHEDS
SKIDS
SKODA
SLADE
SLEDS
SLIDE
SNIDE
SODDY
SOLDI
SOLDO
SONDE
SPADE
SPADS
SPODE
SPUDS
STADT
STUDS
STUDY
SUDDS
SUEDE
SUNDA
SURDS
SWEDE

S•••D
SALAD
SALUD
SAPID
SAROD
SATED
SAVED
SAWED
SCALD
SCAND
SCEND
SCHED
SCOLD
SCROD
SEWED
SHARD
SHEED
SHIED
SHOED
SHRED
SIDED
SIRED
SITED
SIXED
SIZED
SKALD
SKIED
SLOYD
SLUED
SNEAD
SNEED
SNERD
SNOOD
SOLED
SOLID
SOUND
SOWED
SPECD
SPEED
SPEND
SPIED
SQUAD
SQUID
STAID
STAND
STEAD
STEED
STOOD
STRAD
SWARD
SWORD
SYNOD
SZOLD

•SD••
ASDIC
MSDOS

•S•D•
ASIDE
BSIDE
TSADE

•S••D
ASKED
ASSAD
ASSTD
PSEUD
RSVPD
USHED
USTED

••SD•
MISDO

••S•D
ASSAD
ASSTD
BASED
BUSED
CASED
DOSED
EASED
FUSED

HASID
HOSED
LASED
MUSED
NOSED
POSED
RASED
RESOD
URSID

SE•••

SEALE
SEALS
SEALY
SEAMS
SEAMY
SEARS
SEATO
SEATS
SEBUM
SECCO
SECTS
SEDAN
SEDER
SEDGE
SEDGY
SEDUM
SEEDS
SEEDY
SEEIN
SEEKS
SEELS
SEELY
SEEMS
SEEPS
SEEPY
SEERS
SEETO
SEEYA
SEGAL
SEGAR
SEGER
SEGNI
SEGNO
SEGOS
SEGUE
SEHNA
SEIJI
SEIKO
SEINE
SEISM
SEIZE
SELAH
SELES
SELIG
SELLS
SELMA
SELVA
SEMIS
SENAT
SENDS
SENGI
SENNA
SENOR
SENSE
SENTE
SEOUL
SEPAL
SEPIA
SEPOY
SEPTA
SERAC
SERAI
SERAL
SERBS
SERES
SERFS
SERGE
SERIF
SERIN
SEROW
SERRA
SERRY
SERTA
SERUM
SERVE
SERVO
SETAE
SETAT
SETBY
SETIN
SETON
SETTE
SETTO
SETUP
SEULE
SEUSS
SEVEN
SEVER
SEWED
SEWER
SEWON
SEWUP
SEXES
SEXTS

S•E••

SAENS
SCENA
SCEND
SCENE
SCENT
SEEDS
SEEDY
SEEIN
SEEKS
SEELS
SEELY
SEEMS
SEEPS
SEEPY
SEERS
SEETO
SEEYA
SHEAF
SHEAN
SHEAR
SHEBA
SHEDS
SHEED
SHEEN
SHEEP
SHEER
SHEET
SHEIK
SHELF
SHELL
SHEMA
SHEMP
SHERE
SIEGE
SIENA
SIEPI
SIETE
SIEUR
SIEVE
SKEAN
SKEAT
SKEET
SKEGS
SKEIN
SKEPS
SKETE
SKEWS
SLEDS
SLEEK
SLEEP
SLEET
SLEPT
SLEWS
SMEAR
SMELL
SMELT
SMEWS
SNEAD
SNEAK
SNEED
SNEER
SNELL
SNERD
SNERT
SNEVA
SOEUR
SPEAK
SPEAR
SPECD
SPECK
SPECS
SPEED
SPEKE
SPELL
SPELT
SPEND
SPENT
SPERO
SPETS
SPEWS
STEAD
STEAK
STEAL
STEAM
STEED
STEEL
STEEN
STEEP
STEER
STEIN
STELA
STELE
STEMS
STENO
STENS
STEPS
STERE
STERN
STETS
STEVE
STEWS
SUEDE
SUEME
SUERS
SUETS
SUETY
SWEAR
SWEAT
SWEDE
SWEEP
SWEET
SWELL
SWEPT
SZELL

S••E•

SABER
SAFER
SAFES
SAGER
SAGES
SAGET
SAHEL
SAKER
SAKES
SALEM
SALEP
SALES
SANER
SASES
SATED
SATES
SAVED
SAVER
SAVES
SAWED
SAXES
SAYER
SCHED
SCREE
SCREW
SEDER
SEGER
SELES
SERES
SEVEN
SEVER
SEWED
SEWER
SEXES
SHAEF
SHEED
SHEEN
SHEEP
SHEER
SHEET
SHIED
SHIER
SHIES
SHOED
SHOER
SHOES
SHRED
SHREW
SHYER
SIDEA
SIDEB
SIDED
SIDER
SIDES
SIKES
SILEX
SINES
SINEW
SIRED
SIREN
SIRES
SITED
SITES
SIXED
SIXER
SIXES
SIZED
SIZER
SIZES
SKEET
SKIED
SKIER
SKIES
SKYEY
SLEEK
SLEEP
SLEET
SLIER
SLOES
SLUED
SLUES
SLYER
SNEED
SNEER
SOBER
SOKES
SOLED
SOLER
SOLES
SONES
SOOEY
SOREL
SOREN
SORER
SORES
SOWED
SOWER
SOXER
SPEED
SPIED
SPIEL
SPIES
SPREE
STAEL
STEED
STEEL
STEEN
STEEP
STEER
STIEB
STIES
STREP
STREW
SUMER
SUPER
SUPES
SURER
SWEEP
SWEET
SYCEE
SYCES

S•••E

SABLE
SABRE
SACRE
SADHE
SADIE
SALLE
SALVE
SANDE
SANTE
SAONE
SARGE
SATIE
SAUCE
SAUTE
SCALE
SCAPE
SCARE
SCENE
SCONE
SCOPE
SCORE
SCREE
SCUTE
SEALE
SEDGE
SEGUE
SEINE
SEIZE
SENSE
SENTE
SERGE
SERVE
SETAE
SETTE
SEULE
SHADE
SHAKE
SHALE
SHAME
SHANE
SHAPE
SHARE
SHAVE
SHERE
SHINE
SHIRE
SHONE
SHORE
SHOVE
SHUTE
SIDHE
SIDLE
SIEGE
SIETE
SIEVE
SIGNE
SINCE
SINGE
SKATE
SKETE
SKIVE
SLADE
SLAKE
SLATE
SLAVE
SLICE
SLIDE
SLIME
SLOPE
SLYPE
SMAZE
SMILE
SMITE
SMOKE
SMOTE
SNAKE
SNARE
SNIDE
SNIPE
SNORE
SOAVE
SOCLE
SOLVE
SOMME
SONDE
SOUSE
SPACE
SPADE
SPAKE
SPARE
SPATE
SPEKE
SPICE
SPIKE
SPILE
SPINE
SPIRE
SPITE
SPODE
SPOKE
SPORE
SPREE
SPRUE
SPUME
STAGE
STAKE
STALE
STARE
STATE
STAVE
STELE
STERE
STEVE
STILE
STIPE
STOAE
STOKE
STOLE
STONE
STOPE
STORE
STOVE
STOWE
STUPE
STYLE
STYNE
SUAVE
SUCRE
SUEDE
SUEME
SUITE
SURGE
SUSIE
SWAGE
SWALE
SWEDE
SWINE
SWIPE
SWOPE
SWORE
SYCEE
SYNGE

•SE••

ISERE
PSEUD
USERS
USEUP

•S•E•

ASHEN
ASHER
ASHES
ASKED
ASKER
ASKEW
ASNER
ASPEN
ASSES
ASSET
ASSEZ
ASTER
ASYET
ESKER
ESNES
ESSEN
ESSES
ESSEX
ESTEE
ESTER
ESTES
ISLES
ISLET
ISLEY
ISSEI
OSHEA
OSIER
OSLER
OSSEO
OSTEO
USHED
USHER
USTED

•S••E

ASIDE
ASONE
ASTRE
BSIDE
ESQUE
ESTEE
ISERE
ISSUE
ISTLE
OSAGE
OSSIE
TSADE
USAGE
USQUE

••SE•

ANSEL
ANSER
APSES
ASSES
ASSET
ASSEZ
ATSEA
BASED
BASEL
BASER
BASES
BESET
BISES
BUSED
BUSES
BUSEY
CASED
CASES
CASEY
COSEC
DOSED
DOSER
DOSES
EASED
EASEL
EASES
EBSEN
EDSEL
ESSEN
ESSES
ESSEX
ETSEQ
FUSED
FUSEE
FUSES
GASES
GOSEE
HOSEA
HOSED
HOSEL
HOSES
IBSEN
INSET
ISSEI
JASEY
JOSEF
KASEM
KESEY
KYSER
LASED
LASER
LASES
LOSER
LOSES
MASER
MISER
MOSES
MOSEY
MUSED
MUSER
MUSES
NISEI
NOSED
NOSES
NOSEY
OASES
OLSEN
ONSET
ORSER
OSSEO
OUSEL
PASEO
PASES
POSED
POSER
POSES
PUSEY
RASED
RASER
RASES
RESEE
RESET
RESEW
RISEN
RISER
RISES
ROSEN
ROSES
ROSEY
RUSES
SASES
TASER
TVSET
UNSER
UNSET
UPSET
VASES
VESEY
VISES
WESER
WISER
YESES

••S•E

AISLE
AISNE
ANSAE
BASIE
BASTE
CASTE
DESTE
DISME
ELSIE
ENSUE
FISKE
FOSSE
FUSEE
GASPE
GESTE
GOSEE
GOSSE
HASTE
HESSE
ISSUE
ITSME
JESSE
JUSTE
LISLE
LISSE
MASSE
MESNE
MOSHE
NASHE
NOSCE
OSSIE
PASSE
PASTE
PISTE
POSSE
POSTE
RESEE
ROSIE
RUSSE
SUSIE
TASSE
TASTE

WASTE

•••SE
ABASE
ABUSE
AMUSE
ANISE
ARISE
AROSE
BIRSE
BLASE
BOISE
BOUSE
BURSE
CAUSE
CEASE
CENSE
CHASE
CHOSE
CLOSE
COPSE
CRUSE
CURSE
DANSE
DENSE
DNASE
DOUSE
DOWSE
DRUSE
DULSE
ELISE
ELYSE
ERASE
EROSE
FALSE
FOSSE
FRISE
GEESE
GOOSE
GORSE
GOSSE
GUISE
HANSE
HAWSE
HESSE
HEYSE
HORSE
HOUSE
INUSE
JESSE
LAPSE
LEASE
LISSE
LOOSE
LOUSE
LUISE
MANSE
MASSE
MEESE
MEUSE
MOOSE
MORSE
MOUSE
NOISE
NOOSE
NORSE
NURSE
OBESE
OFUSE
PARSE
PASSE
PAUSE
PEASE
PERSE
PHASE
POISE
POSSE
PRASE
PROSE
PULSE
PURSE
RAISE
REESE
REUSE
RINSE
RNASE
ROUSE
RUSSE
SENSE
SOUSE
TASSE
TEASE
TENSE
TERSE
THESE
THOSE
UKASE
VALSE
VERSE
WHOSE
WORSE
YOUSE

S•F••
SAFER
SAFES
SIFTS
SOFAR
SOFAS
SOFIA
SOFTC
SOFTG
SOFTY
SUFIS

S••F•
SCIFI
SCOFF
SCUFF
SERFS
SHAFT
SHIFT
SKIFF
SNAFU
SNIFF
SNUFF
SOLFA
SPIFF
STAFF
STIFF
STUFF
SULFA
SURFS
SURFY
SWIFT

S•••F
SCARF
SCOFF
SCUFF
SCURF
SERIF
SHAEF
SHEAF
SHELF
SKIFF
SMURF
SNIFF
SNUFF
SPIFF
SPOOF
STAFF
STIFF
STUFF
SWARF

•SF••
RSFSR

•S•F•
USOFA

••S•F
JOSEF

S•G••
SAGAL
SAGAN
SAGAS
SAGER
SAGES
SAGET
SAGGY
SAGOS
SEGAL
SEGAR
SEGER
SEGNI
SEGNO
SEGOS
SEGUE
SIGHS
SIGHT
SIGIL
SIGMA
SIGNE
SIGNO
SIGNS
SOGGY
SSGTS
SUGAR

S••G•
SAGGY
SAIGA
SARGE
SARGO
SEDGE
SEDGY
SENGI
SERGE
SHAGS
SHOGI
SIEGE
SINGE
SINGS
SKEGS
SLAGS
SLIGO
SLOGS
SLUGS
SMOGS
SNAGS
SNOGS
SNUGS
SOGGY
SONGS
SORGO
SOUGH
STAGE
STAGG
STAGS
STAGY
STOGY
SURGE
SWAGE
SWAGS
SWIGS
SYNGE

S•••G
SCRAG
SELIG
SHRUG
SLANG
SLING
SLUNG
SOBIG
SOFTG
SOONG
SPANG
SPRAG
SPRIG
STAGG
STANG
STING
STRUG
STUNG
SUING
SWING
SWUNG

•SG••
MSGTS
SSGTS
TSGTS

•S•G•
OSAGE
USAGE
USCGA
VSIGN

•S••G
USING

SH•••
SHACK
SHADE
SHADS
SHADY
SHAEF
SHAFT
SHAGS
SHAHN
SHAHS
SHAKE
SHAKO
SHAKY
SHALE
SHALL
SHALT
SHAME
SHAMS
SHAMU
SHANA
SHANE
SHANK
SHANS
SHANT
SHAPE
SHARD
SHARE
SHARI
SHARK
SHARP
SHATT
SHAUN
SHAVE
SHAWL
SHAWM
SHAWN
SHAYS
SHEAF
SHEAN
SHEAR
SHEBA
SHEDS
SHEED
SHEEN
SHEEP
SHEER
SHEET
SHEIK
SHELF
SHELL
SHEMA
SHEMP
SHERE
SHIED
SHIER
SHIES
SHIFT
SHILL
SHIMS
SHINE
SHINS
SHINY
SHIPS
SHIRE
SHIRK
SHIRR
SHIRT
SHISH
SHIVA
SHIVS
SHOAH
SHOAL
SHOAT
SHOCK
SHOED
SHOER
SHOES
SHOGI
SHOJI
SHONE
SHOOK
SHOOS
SHOOT
SHOPS
SHORE
SHORN
SHORT
SHOTS
SHOUT
SHOVE
SHOWN
SHOWS
SHOWY
SHOYU
SHRED
SHREW
SHRUB
SHRUG
SHUCK
SHULA
SHULS
SHUNS
SHUNT
SHUSH
SHUTE
SHUTS
SHYER
SHYLY

S•H••
SAHEL
SAHIB
SCHAV
SCHED
SCHMO
SCHON
SCHWA
SEHNA
SOHIO

S••H•
SACHA
SACHS
SADHE
SADHU
SASHA
SHAHN
SHAHS
SIDHE
SIGHS
SIGHT
SIKHS
SOCHI
SOPHS
SOPHY
SOTHO
SPAHI
SPAHN
STAHL
SUSHI

S•••H
SABAH
SAITH
SANDH
SARAH
SELAH
SHISH
SHOAH
SHUSH
SIXTH
SKOSH
SLASH
SLOSH
SLOTH
SLUSH
SMASH
SMITH
SMYTH
SNATH
SOOTH
SOUGH
SOUTH
STASH
STICH
SURAH
SWASH
SWATH
SWISH
SWITH
SYLPH

•SH••
ASHBY
ASHEN
ASHER
ASHES
ASHUR
OSHEA
PSHAW
USHED
USHER

•S••H
PSYCH

••SH•
AISHA
BASHO
BISHO
BUSHY
CUSHY
DASHI
DISHY
FISHY
GUSHY
KASHA
MASHY
MESHY
MISHA
MOSHE
MUSHY
NASHE
PASHA
PUSHY
RASHT
RISHI
RUSHY
SASHA
SUSHI
WASHY
WISHY
WUSHU

••S•H
BOSCH
BUSCH
PASCH

•••SH
ABASH
AMISH
APISH
AWASH
BLUSH
BRASH
BRUSH
CLASH
CRASH
CRUSH
FLASH
FLESH
FLUSH
FRESH
FROSH
GNASH
HARSH
INISH
IRISH
KARSH
KNISH
LEASH
MARSH
NAISH
PLASH
PLUSH
QUASH
SHISH
SHUSH
SKOSH
SLASH
SLOSH
SLUSH
SMASH
STASH
SWASH
SWISH
TRASH
TRISH
WALSH
WELSH
WHISH

SI•••
SIALS
SIBYL
SIDEA
SIDEB
SIDED
SIDER
SIDES
SIDHE
SIDLE
SIDON
SIDRA
SIEGE
SIENA
SIEPI
SIETE
SIEUR
SIEVE
SIFTS
SIGHS
SIGHT
SIGIL
SIGMA
SIGNE
SIGNO
SIGNS
SIKAS
SIKES
SIKHS
SILAS
SILEX
SILKS
SILKY
SILLS
SILLY
SILOS
SILTS
SILTY
SILVA
SIMBA
SIMMS
SIMON
SIMPS
SINAI
SINCE
SINES
SINEW
SINGE
SINGS
SINKS
SINUS
SIOUX
SIRED
SIREN
SIRES
SISAL
SISSY
SITAR
SITBY
SITED
SITES
SITIN
SITKA
SITON
SITUP
SITUS
SIVAN
SIXAM
SIXED
SIXER
SIXES
SIXMO
SIXPM
SIXTH
SIXTY
SIZED
SIZER
SIZES

S•I••
SAIGA
SAILS
SAINT
SAITH
SCIFI
SCION
SEIJI
SEIKO
SEINE
SEISM
SEIZE
SHIED
SHIER
SHIES
SHIFT
SHILL
SHIMS
SHINE
SHINS
SHINY
SHIPS
SHIRE
SHIRK
SHIRR
SHIRT
SHISH
SHIVA
SHIVS
SKIDS
SKIED
SKIER
SKIES
SKIFF
SKILL
SKIMP
SKIMS
SKINK
SKINS
SKINT
SKIPS
SKIRL
SKIRR
SKIRT
SKITS
SKIVE
SLICE
SLICK
SLIDE
SLIER
SLIGO
SLILY
SLIME
SLIMS
SLIMY
SLING
SLINK
SLIPS
SLIPT
SLITS
SLIWA
SMILE
SMIRK
SMITE
SMITH
SMITS
SNICK
SNIDE
SNIFF
SNIPE
SNIPS
SNITS
SOILS
SPICA
SPICE
SPICY
SPIED
SPIEL
SPIES
SPIFF
SPIKE
SPIKY
SPILE
SPILL
SPILT

SPINE
SPINS
SPINY
SPIRE
SPIRO
SPIRY
SPITE
SPITS
SPITZ
SPIVS
STICH
STICK
STIEB
STIES
STIFF
STILE
STILL
STILT
STING
STINK
STINT
STIPE
STIRK
STIRS
SUING
SUINT
SUITA
SUITE
SUITS
SWIFT
SWIGS
SWILL
SWIMS
SWINE
SWING
SWINK
SWIPE
SWIRL
SWISH
SWISS
SWITH
SWITZ

S••I•
SABIN
SADIE
SADIS
SAHIB
SALIC
SAPID
SAPIR
SARIS
SATIE
SATIN
SAWIN
SCRIM
SCRIP
SEEIN
SELIG
SEMIS
SEPIA
SERIF
SERIN
SETIN
SHEIK
SIGIL
SITIN
SKEIN
SLAIN
SMAIL
SNAIL
SOBIG
SOCIO
SOFIA
SOHIO
SOLID
SONIA
SONIC
SPAIN
SPLIT
SPOIL
SPRIG
SPRIT
SQUIB
SQUID
STAID
STAIN
STAIR
STEIN
STOIC
STRIA
STRIP
SUBIC
SUFIS
SUSIE
SWAIN
SYBIL
SYRIA

S•••I
SAKAI
SALMI
SAUDI
SCIFI
SCUDI
SEGNI
SEIJI
SENGI
SERAI
SHARI
SHOGI
SHOJI
SIEPI
SINAI
SOCHI
SOLDI
SOLTI
SOMNI
SPAHI
SPYRI
STYLI
SULCI
SUNNI
SUOMI
SUSHI
SWAMI
SWAZI

•SI••
ASIAN
ASIDE
BSIDE
OSIER
USING
VSIGN

•S•I•
ASCII
ASDIC
ASKIN
ASPIC
ASTIN
ASTIR
FSLIC
GSUIT
ISLIP
ISTIC
OSLIN
OSMIC
OSRIC
OSSIA
OSSIE
OSTIA
USAIR

•S••I
ASCII
ASSAI
ISSEI

••SI•
AESIR
AHSIN
APSIS
ARSIS
BASIC
BASIE
BASIL
BASIN
BASIS
CASIO
ELSIE
EOSIN
FUSIL
HASID
JOSIP
LYSIN
MESIC
MUSIC
MYSIN
NOSIR
OASIS
OPSIN
OPSIS
OSSIA
OSSIE
POSIT
RESIN
ROSIE
ROSIN
SUSIE
URSID
VISIT
YASIR

••S•I
ASSAI
AUSSI
BASSI
CESTI
DASHI
HOSNI
ISSEI
MASAI
MISTI
NISEI
PESCI
PISCI
RISHI
ROSSI
SUSHI

•••SI
AUSSI
BASSI
DORSI
FARSI
ICOSI
PEPSI
PHYSI
QUASI
ROSSI
TARSI
TORSI

S•J••
SAJAK

S••J•
SEIJI
SHOJI
SONJA

SK•••
SKALD
SKANK
SKATE
SKEAN
SKEAT
SKEET
SKEGS
SKEIN
SKEPS
SKETE
SKEWS
SKIDS
SKIED
SKIER
SKIES
SKIFF
SKILL
SKIMP
SKIMS
SKINK
SKINS
SKINT
SKIPS
SKIRL
SKIRR
SKIRT
SKITS
SKIVE
SKNXX
SKOAL
SKODA
SKORT
SKOSH
SKUAS
SKULK
SKULL
SKUNK
SKYEY

S•K••
SAKAI
SAKER
SAKES
SIKAS
SIKES
SIKHS
SOKES

S••K•
SACKS
SANKA
SARKY
SAUKS
SEEKS
SEIKO
SHAKE
SHAKO
SHAKY
SILKS
SILKY
SINKS
SITKA
SLAKE
SMOKE
SMOKY
SNAKE
SNAKY
SOAKS
SOCKO
SOCKS
SOUKS
SPAKE
SPEKE
SPIKE
SPIKY
SPOKE
STAKE
STOKE
STUKA
SUCKA
SUCKS
SULKS
SULKY

S•••K
SAJAK
SHACK
SHANK
SHARK
SHEIK
SHIRK
SHOCK
SHOOK
SHUCK
SKANK
SKINK
SKULK
SKUNK
SLACK
SLEEK
SLICK
SLINK
SLUNK
SMACK
SMIRK
SMOCK
SNACK
SNARK
SNEAK
SNICK
SNOOK
SNUCK
SPAAK
SPANK
SPARK
SPEAK
SPECK
SPOCK
SPOOK
SPORK
SPUNK
STACK
STALK
STANK
STARK
STEAK
STICK
STINK
STIRK
STOCK
STOOK
STORK
STUCK
STUNK
SWANK
SWINK
SWONK

•SK••
ASKED
ASKER
ASKEW
ASKIN
ESKER
OSKAR

•S•K•
ASOKA
OSAKA

••SK•
BASKS
BOSKS
BOSKY
BUSKS
CASKS
CUSKS
DESKS
DISKS
DUSKS
DUSKY
ENSKY
FISKE
HUSKS
HUSKY
KISKA
MASKS
MUSKS
MUSKY
PESKY
RISKS
RISKY
RUSKS
TASKS
TUSKS

•••SK
BRISK
FLASK
FRISK
KIOSK
KURSK
MINSK
PINSK
WHISK

SL•••
SLABS
SLACK
SLADE
SLAGS
SLAIN
SLAKE
SLAMS
SLANG
SLANT
SLAPS
SLASH
SLATE
SLATS
SLATY
SLAVE
SLAVS
SLAWS
SLAYS
SLEDS
SLEEK
SLEEP
SLEET
SLEPT
SLEWS
SLICE
SLICK
SLIDE
SLIER
SLIGO
SLILY
SLIME
SLIMS
SLIMY
SLING
SLINK
SLIPS
SLIPT
SLITS
SLIWA
SLOAN
SLOBS
SLOES
SLOGS
SLOMO
SLOOP
SLOPE
SLOPS
SLOSH
SLOTH
SLOTS
SLOWS
SLOYD
SLUED
SLUES
SLUGS
SLUMP
SLUMS
SLUNG
SLUNK
SLURP
SLURS
SLUSH
SLYER
SLYLY
SLYPE

S•L••
SALAD
SALAL
SALAM
SALEM
SALEP
SALES
SALIC
SALLE
SALLY
SALMI
SALON
SALPA
SALPS
SALSA
SALTA
SALTS
SALTY
SALUD
SALUT
SALVE
SALVO
SELAH
SELES
SELIG
SELLS
SELMA
SELVA
SILAS
SILEX
SILKS
SILKY
SILLS
SILLY
SILOS
SILTS
SILTY
SILVA
SOLAN
SOLAR
SOLDI
SOLDO
SOLED
SOLER
SOLES
SOLFA
SOLID
SOLON
SOLOS
SOLTI
SOLUM
SOLUS
SOLVE
SPLAT
SPLAY
SPLIT
SULCI
SULFA
SULKS
SULKY
SULLA
SULLY
SYLPH

S••L•
SABLE
SADLY
SAILS
SALLE
SALLY
SAULT
SCALA
SCALD
SCALE
SCALP
SCALY
SCOLD
SCULL
SEALE
SEALS
SEALY
SEELS
SEELY
SELLS
SEULE
SHALE
SHALL
SHALT
SHELF
SHELL
SHILL
SHULA
SHULS
SHYLY
SIALS
SIDLE
SILLS
SILLY
SKALD
SKILL
SKULK
SKULL
SLILY
SLYLY
SMALL
SMALT
SMELL
SMELT
SMILE
SMOLT
SNELL
SOCLE
SOILS
SOULS
SOULT
SPALL
SPELL
SPELT
SPILE
SPILL
SPILT
STALE
STALK
STALL
STELA
STELE
STILE
STILL
STILT
STOLA
STOLE
STOLS
STULL
STYLE
STYLI
STYLO
SULLA
SULLY
SURLY
SWALE
SWELL
SWILL
SZELL
SZOLD

S•••L
SAGAL
SAHEL
SALAL
SANDL
SCOWL
SCULL
SEGAL
SEOUL
SEPAL
SERAL
SHALL
SHAWL
SHELL
SHILL
SHOAL
SIBYL
SIGIL
SISAL
SKILL
SKIRL
SKOAL
SKULL
SMAIL
SMALL
SMELL
SNAIL
SNARL
SNELL
SOREL
SOTOL
SPALL
SPELL
SPIEL
SPILL
SPOIL
SPOOL
STAEL
STAHL
STALL
STEAL
STEEL
STILL
STOOL
STULL
SURAL
SWELL
SWILL
SWIRL
SYBIL
SZELL

•SL••
FSLIC
ISLAM
ISLAS
ISLES
ISLET
ISLEY
ISLIP
OSLER

OSLIN
USLTA

•S•L•
ASYLA
ISTLE
PSALM

•S••L
USUAL

••SL•
AISLE
LISLE
TESLA

••S•L
ANSEL
BASAL
BASEL
BASIL
EASEL
EDSEL
FUSIL
HOSEL
LYSOL
MOSUL
NASAL
OUSEL
SISAL

SM•••
SMACK
SMAIL
SMALL
SMALT
SMART
SMASH
SMAZE
SMEAR
SMELL
SMELT
SMEWS
SMILE
SMIRK
SMITE
SMITH
SMITS
SMOCK
SMOGS
SMOKE
SMOKY
SMOLT
SMOOT
SMOTE
SMURF
SMUTS
SMYTH

S•M••
SAMAR
SAMBA
SAMMS
SAMMY
SAMOA
SAMOS
SAMPS
SEMIS
SIMBA
SIMMS
SIMON
SIMPS
SOMAS
SOMME
SOMNI
SUMAC
SUMBA
SUMER
SUMMA
SUMPS
SUMUP

S••M•
SALMI
SAMMS
SAMMY
SCAMP
SCAMS
SCHMO
SCUMS
SEAMS
SEAMY
SEEMS
SELMA
SHAME
SHAMS
SHAMU
SHEMA
SHEMP
SHIMS
SIGMA
SIMMS
SIXMO
SKIMP
SKIMS
SLAMS
SLIME
SLIMS
SLIMY
SLOMO
SLUMP
SLUMS
SOMME
SPAMS
SPUME
SPUMY
STAMP
STEMS
STOMA
STOMP
STUMP
STUMS
STYMY
SUEME
SUMMA
SUOMI
SWAMI
SWAMP
SWIMS

S•••M
SALAM
SALEM
SCRAM
SCRIM
SCRUM
SEBUM
SEDUM
SEISM
SERUM
SHAWM
SIXAM
SIXPM
SODOM
SOLUM
SPASM
STEAM
STORM
STROM
STRUM
STURM
SWARM

•SM••
OSMAN
OSMIC

•S•M•
ASAMA
ISAMU

•S••M
ASSAM
ISLAM
PSALM

••SM•
COSMO
DISME
ITSME
PISMO

••S•M
ADSUM
AKSUM
ASSAM
BESOM
BOSOM
EPSOM
IPSUM
KASEM
VISUM

•••SM
ABYSM
CHASM
DEISM
PLASM
PRISM
SEISM
SPASM

SN•••
SNACK
SNAFU
SNAGS
SNAIL
SNAKE
SNAKY
SNAPS
SNARE
SNARK
SNARL
SNATH
SNEAD
SNEAK
SNEED
SNEER
SNELL
SNERD
SNERT
SNEVA
SNICK
SNIDE
SNIFF
SNIPE
SNIPS
SNITS
SNOBS
SNOGS
SNOOD
SNOOK
SNOOP
SNOOT
SNORE
SNORT
SNOUT
SNOWS
SNOWY
SNUBS
SNUCK
SNUFF
SNUGS

S•N••
SANAA
SANDE
SANDH
SANDL
SANDS
SANDY
SANER
SANKA
SANTA
SANTE
SANTO
SANYO
SENAT
SENDS
SENGI
SENNA
SENOR
SENSE
SENTE
SINAI
SINCE
SINES
SINEW
SINGE
SINGS
SINKS
SINUS
SKNXX
SONAR
SONDE
SONES
SONGS
SONIA
SONIC
SONJA
SONNY
SONYA
SUNDA
SUNNA
SUNNI
SUNNY
SUNUP
SYNCS
SYNGE
SYNOD

S••N•
SAENS
SAINT
SAONE
SAUNA
SCAND
SCANS
SCANT
SCENA
SCEND
SCENE
SCENT
SCONE
SEGNI
SEGNO
SEHNA
SEINE
SENNA
SHANA
SHANE
SHANK
SHANS
SHANT
SHINE
SHINS
SHINY
SHONE
SHUNS
SHUNT
SIENA
SIGNE
SIGNO
SIGNS
SKANK
SKINK
SKINS
SKINT
SKUNK
SLANG
SLANT
SLING
SLINK
SLUNG
SLUNK
SOMNI
SONNY
SOONG
SOUND
SPANG
SPANK
SPANS
SPEND
SPENT
SPINE
SPINS
SPINY
SPUNK
STAND
STANG
STANK
STENO
STENS
STING
STINK
STINT
STONE
STONY
STUNG
STUNK
STUNS
STUNT
STYNE
SUING
SUINT
SUNNA
SUNNI
SUNNY
SWANK
SWANN
SWANS
SWINE
SWING
SWINK
SWONK
SWUNG

S•••N
SABIN
SAGAN
SALON
SARAN
SATAN
SATIN
SATON
SAWIN
SAXON
SCHON
SCION
SCORN
SEDAN
SEEIN
SERIN
SETIN
SETON
SEVEN
SEWON
SHAHN
SHAUN
SHAWN
SHEAN
SHEEN
SHORN
SHOWN
SIDON
SIMON
SIREN
SITIN
SITON
SIVAN
SKEAN
SKEIN
SLAIN
SLOAN
SOLAN
SOLON
SOREN
SPAHN
SPAIN
SPAWN
SPOON
SPURN
SPYON
STAIN
STEEN
STEIN
STERN
SUDAN
SUSAN
SWAIN
SWANN
SWOON
SWORN

•SN••
ASNER
ESNES
MSNBC

•S•N•
ASANA
ASONE
ASSNS
USING

•S••N
ASHEN
ASIAN
ASKIN
ASPEN
ASTIN
ASTON
ASWAN
ESSEN
OSCAN
OSLIN
OSMAN
VSIGN

••SN•
AISNE
ASSNS
BOSNS
DESNA
HASNT
HOSNI
MESNE
WASNT
YESNO

••S•N
AHSIN
ANSON
ARSON
BASIN
BISON
BOSON
EBSEN
EOSIN
EPSON
ESSEN
HASON
HYSON
IBSEN
JASON
LYSIN
MASON
MESON
MYSIN
NISAN
OLSEN
OLSON
OPSIN
ORSON
PISAN
PUSAN
RESIN
RISEN
ROSEN
ROSIN
SUSAN
TYSON

SO•••
SOAKS
SOAPS
SOAPY
SOARS
SOAVE
SOBER
SOBIG
SOCHI
SOCIO
SOCKO
SOCKS
SOCLE
SODAS
SODDY
SODOM
SOEUR
SOFAR
SOFAS
SOFIA
SOFTC
SOFTG
SOFTY
SOGGY
SOHIO
SOILS
SOKES
SOLAN
SOLAR
SOLDI
SOLDO
SOLED
SOLER
SOLES
SOLFA
SOLID
SOLON
SOLOS
SOLTI
SOLUM
SOLUS
SOLVE
SOMAS
SOMME
SOMNI
SONAR
SONDE
SONES
SONGS
SONIA
SONIC
SONJA
SONNY
SONYA
SOOEY
SOONG
SOOTH
SOOTS
SOOTY
SOPHS
SOPHY
SOPOR
SOPPY
SOPUP
SORAS
SORBS
SOREL
SOREN
SORER
SORES
SORGO
SORRY
SORTA
SORTS
SORUS
SOTHO
SOTOL
SOTTO
SOUGH
SOUKS
SOULS
SOULT
SOUND
SOUPS
SOUPY
SOURS
SOUSA
SOUSE
SOUTH
SOWED
SOWER
SOXER
SOYAS
SOYUZ

S•O••
SAONE
SCOFF
SCOLD
SCONE
SCOOP
SCOOT
SCOPE
SCOPS
SCOPY
SCORE
SCORN
SCOTS
SCOTT
SCOUR
SCOUT
SCOWL
SCOWS
SEOUL
SHOAH
SHOAL
SHOAT
SHOCK
SHOED
SHOER
SHOES
SHOGI
SHOJI
SHONE
SHOOK
SHOOS
SHOOT
SHOPS
SHORE
SHORN
SHORT
SHOTS
SHOUT
SHOVE
SHOWN
SHOWS
SHOWY
SHOYU
SIOUX
SKOAL
SKODA
SKORT
SKOSH
SLOAN
SLOBS
SLOES
SLOGS
SLOMO
SLOOP
SLOPE
SLOPS
SLOSH
SLOTH
SLOTS
SLOWS
SLOYD
SMOCK
SMOGS
SMOKE
SMOKY
SMOLT
SMOOT
SMOTE
SNOBS
SNOGS
SNOOD
SNOOK
SNOOP
SNOOT
SNORE
SNORT
SNOUT
SNOWS
SNOWY
SOOEY
SOONG
SOOTH
SOOTS
SOOTY
SPOCK
SPODE
SPOIL
SPOKE
SPOOF
SPOOK
SPOOL
SPOON
SPOOR
SPORE
SPORK
SPORT
SPOSA
SPOTS
SPOUT
STOAE
STOAS
STOAT
STOCK
STOGY
STOIC

STOKE
STOLA
STOLE
STOLS
STOMA
STOMP
STONE
STONY
STOOD
STOOK
STOOL
STOOP
STOPE
STOPS
STORE
STORK
STORM
STORY
STOSS
STOTS
STOUP
STOUT
STOVE
STOWE
STOWS
SUOMI
SWOBS
SWONK
SWOON
SWOOP
SWOPE
SWOPS
SWORD
SWORE
SWORN
SZOLD

S••O•

SABOT
SAGOS
SALON
SAMOA
SAMOS
SAPOR
SAROD
SAROS
SATON
SAVOR
SAVOY
SAXON
SCHON
SCION
SCOOP
SCOOT
SCROD
SEGOS
SENOR
SEPOY
SEROW
SETON
SEWON
SHOOK
SHOOS
SHOOT
SIDON
SILOS
SIMON
SITON
SLOOP
SMOOT
SNOOD
SNOOK
SNOOP
SNOOT
SODOM
SOLON
SOLOS
SOPOR
SOTOL
SPOOF
SPOOK
SPOOL
SPOON
SPOOR
SPYON
STOOD
STOOK
STOOL
STOOP
STROM
STROP
SWOON
SWOOP
SYDOW
SYNOD
SYSOP

S•••O

SACCO
SACRO
SALVO
SANTO
SANYO
SARGO
SARTO
SAWTO
SAYSO
SCHMO
SCUDO
SEATO
SECCO
SEETO
SEGNO
SEIKO
SERVO
SETTO
SHAKO
SIGNO
SIXMO
SLIGO
SLOMO
SOCIO
SOCKO
SOHIO
SOLDO
SORGO
SOTHO
SOTTO
SPERO
SPIRO
STENO
STYLO

•SO••

ASOKA
ASONE
PSOAS
USOFA
XSOUT

•S•O•

ASCOT
ASSOC
ASTON
ASTOR
CSPOT
ESPOO
ESTOP
FSTOP
MSDOS

•S••O

ASTRO
ESPOO
OSSEO
OSTEO

••SO•

AESOP
ALSOP
ANSON
APSOS
ARSON
ASSOC
BASOV
BESOM
BESOT
BISON
BOSOM
BOSON
BOSOX
ENSOR
EPSOM
EPSON
HASON
HYSON
JASON
LYSOL
MASON
MESON
MISOS
OLSON
ORSON
PESOS
RESOD
SYSOP
TYSON
VISOR

••S•O

BASHO
BASSO
BISHO
BOSCO
CASCO
CASIO
CISCO
COSMO
DISCO
GESSO
GUSTO
HASSO
HASTO
LASSO
MISDO
MOSSO
OSSEO
PASCO
PASEO
PASTO
PESTO
PISCO
PISMO
RUSSO
TASSO
VASCO
YESNO

•••SO

ANISO
AVISO
BASSO
CANSO
DORSO
GESSO
HASSO
HOWSO
HYPSO
KELSO
LASSO
MOSSO
NOTSO
RATSO
RINSO
RUSSO
SAYSO
TASSO
TORSO
VERSO
WHOSO

SP•••

SPAAK
SPACE
SPACY
SPADE
SPADS
SPAHI
SPAHN
SPAIN
SPAKE
SPALL
SPAMS
SPANG
SPANK
SPANS
SPARE
SPARK
SPARS
SPASM
SPATE
SPATS
SPAWN
SPAYS
SPEAK
SPEAR
SPECD
SPECK
SPECS
SPEED
SPEKE
SPELL
SPELT
SPEND
SPENT
SPERO
SPETS
SPEWS
SPICA
SPICE
SPICY
SPIED
SPIEL
SPIES
SPIFF
SPIKE
SPIKY
SPILE
SPILL
SPILT
SPINE
SPINS
SPINY
SPIRE
SPIRO
SPIRY
SPITE
SPITS
SPITZ
SPIVS
SPLAT
SPLAY
SPLIT
SPOCK
SPODE
SPOIL
SPOKE
SPOOF
SPOOK
SPOOL
SPOON
SPOOR
SPORE
SPORK
SPORT
SPOSA
SPOTS
SPOUT
SPRAG
SPRAT
SPRAY
SPREE
SPRIG
SPRIT
SPRUE
SPUDS
SPUME
SPUMY
SPUNK
SPURN
SPURS
SPURT
SPYON
SPYRI

S•P••

SAPID
SAPIR
SAPOR
SAPPY
SEPAL
SEPIA
SEPOY
SEPTA
SOPHS
SOPHY
SOPOR
SOPPY
SOPUP
STPAT
SUPER
SUPES
SUPRA
SUPTS
SUPVR

S••P•

SALPA
SALPS
SAMPS
SAPPY
SCAPA
SCAPE
SCOPE
SCOPS
SCOPY
SCUPS
SEEPS
SEEPY
SHAPE
SHIPS
SHOPS
SIEPI
SIMPS
SIXPM
SKEPS
SKIPS
SLAPS
SLEPT
SLIPS
SLIPT
SLOPE
SLOPS
SLYPE
SNAPS
SNIPE
SNIPS
SOAPS
SOAPY
SOPPY
SOUPS
SOUPY
STEPS
STIPE
STOPE
STOPS
STUPA
STUPE
SUMPS
SWAPS
SWEPT
SWIPE
SWOPE
SWOPS
SYLPH

S•••P

SALEP
SATUP
SCALP
SCAMP
SCARP
SCAUP
SCOOP
SCRAP
SCRIP
SETUP
SEWUP
SHARP
SHEEP
SHEMP
SITUP
SKIMP
SLEEP
SLOOP
SLUMP
SLURP
SNOOP
SOPUP
STAMP
STEEP
STOMP
STOOP
STOUP
STRAP
STREP
STRIP
STROP
STUMP
SUMUP
SUNUP
SWAMP
SWEEP
SWOOP
SYRUP
SYSOP

•SP••

ASPCA
ASPEN
ASPIC
CSPOT
ESPOO

•S•P•

RSVPD
RSVPS

•S••P

ASCAP
ESTOP
FSTOP
ISLIP
USEUP
USURP

••SP•

CUSPS
GASPE
GASPS
HASPS
LISPS
RASPS
RASPY
TBSPS
WASPS
WASPY
WISPS
WISPY

••S•P

AESOP
ALSOP
GASUP
JOSIP
SYSOP

•••SP

AGASP
CLASP
CRISP
GRASP

SQ•••

SQUAB
SQUAD
SQUAT
SQUIB
SQUID

•SQ••

ESQUE
USQUE

••SQ•

ETSQQ

••S•Q

ETSEQ
ETSQQ

SR•••

SRTAS

S•R••

SARAH
SARAN
SARDS
SARGE
SARGO
SARIS
SARKY
SAROD
SAROS
SARTO
SCRAG
SCRAM
SCRAP
SCREE
SCREW
SCRIM
SCRIP
SCROD
SCRUB
SCRUM
SERAC
SERAI
SERAL
SERBS
SERES
SERFS
SERGE
SERIF
SERIN
SEROW
SERRA
SERRY
SERTA
SERUM
SERVE
SERVO
SHRED
SHREW
SHRUB
SHRUG
SIRED
SIREN
SIRES
SORAS
SORBS
SOREL
SOREN
SORER
SORES
SORGO
SORRY
SORTA
SORTS
SORUS
SPRAG
SPRAT
SPRAY
SPREE
SPRIG
SPRIT
SPRUE
STRAD
STRAP
STRAW
STRAY
STREP
STREW
STRIA
STRIP
STROM
STROP
STRUG
STRUM
STRUT
SURAH
SURAL
SURAS
SURAT
SURDS
SURER
SURFS
SURFY
SURGE
SURLY
SYRIA
SYRUP

S••R•

SABRA
SABRE
SACRA
SACRE
SACRO
SAURY
SCARE
SCARF
SCARP
SCARS
SCARY
SCORE
SCORN
SCURF
SEARS
SEERS
SERRA
SERRY
SHARD
SHARE
SHARI
SHARK
SHARP
SHERE
SHIRE
SHIRK
SHIRR
SHIRT
SHORE
SHORN
SHORT
SIDRA
SKIRL
SKIRR
SKIRT
SKORT
SLURP
SLURS
SMART
SMIRK
SMURF
SNARE
SNARK
SNARL
SNERD
SNERT
SNORE
SNORT
SOARS
SORRY
SOURS
SPARE
SPARK
SPARS
SPERO
SPIRE
SPIRO
SPIRY
SPORE
SPORK
SPORT
SPURN
SPURS
SPURT
SPYRI
STARE
STARK
STARR
STARS
START
STARZ
STERE
STERN
STIRK
STIRS
STORE
STORK
STORM
STORY
STURM
SUCRE
SUDRA
SUERS
SUPRA
SUTRA
SWARD
SWARF
SWARM
SWART
SWIRL

SWORD
SWORE
SWORN

S•••R
SABER
SAFER
SAGER
SAKER
SAMAR
SANER
SAPIR
SAPOR
SATYR
SAVER
SAVOR
SAYER
SCOUR
SEDER
SEGAR
SEGER
SENOR
SEVER
SEWER
SHEAR
SHEER
SHIER
SHIRR
SHOER
SHYER
SIDER
SIEUR
SITAR
SIXER
SIZER
SKIER
SKIRR
SLIER
SLYER
SMEAR
SNEER
SOBER
SOEUR
SOFAR
SOLAR
SOLER
SONAR
SOPOR
SORER
SOWER
SOXER
SPEAR
SPOOR
STAIR
STARR
STEER
SUGAR
SUMER
SUPER
SUPVR
SURER
SWEAR

•SR••
OSRIC

•S•R•
ASTRA
ASTRE
ASTRO
ISERE
TSARS
USERS
USURP
USURY

•S••R
ASHER
ASHUR
ASKER
ASNER
ASSUR
ASSYR
ASTER
ASTIR
ASTOR
ESKER
ESTER
OSCAR
OSIER
OSKAR
OSLER
RSFSR
USAIR
USHER

••SR•
BASRA

••S•R
AESIR
ANSER
ASSUR
ASSYR
AUSTR
BASER
CESAR
DISTR
DOSER
ENSOR
GASTR
INSTR
KYSER
LASER
LOSER
MASER
MASUR
MISER
MUSER
NOSIR
ORSER
POSER
RASER
RISER
TASER
UNSER
VISOR
WESER
WISER
YASIR

•••SR
RSFSR

SS•••
SSGTS

S•S••
SASES
SASHA
SASSY
SISAL
SISSY
SUSAN
SUSHI
SUSIE
SYSOP

S••S•
SALSA
SASSY
SAYSO
SEISM
SENSE
SEUSS
SHISH
SHUSH
SISSY
SKOSH
SLASH
SLOSH
SLUSH
SMASH
SOUSA
SOUSE
SPASM
SPOSA
STASH
STOSS
SUDSY
SWASH
SWISH
SWISS

S•••S
SAABS
SACHS
SACKS
SADIS
SAENS
SAFES
SAGAS
SAGES
SAGOS
SAILS
SAKES
SALES
SALPS
SALTS
SAMMS
SAMOS
SAMPS
SANDS
SARDS
SARIS
SAROS
SASES
SATES
SAUKS
SAVES
SAXES
SCABS
SCADS
SCAMS
SCANS
SCARS
SCATS
SCOPS
SCOTS
SCOWS
SCUDS
SCUMS
SCUPS
SCUTS
SEALS
SEAMS
SEARS
SEATS
SECTS
SEEDS
SEEKS
SEELS
SEEMS
SEEPS
SEERS
SEGOS
SELES
SELLS
SEMIS
SENDS
SERBS
SERES
SERFS
SEUSS
SEXES
SEXTS
SHADS
SHAGS
SHAHS
SHAMS
SHANS
SHAYS
SHEDS
SHIES
SHIMS
SHINS
SHIPS
SHIVS
SHOES
SHOOS
SHOPS
SHOTS
SHOWS
SHULS
SHUNS
SHUTS
SIALS
SIDES
SIFTS
SIGHS
SIGNS
SIKAS
SIKES
SIKHS
SILAS
SILKS
SILLS
SILOS
SILTS
SIMMS
SIMPS
SINES
SINGS
SINKS
SINUS
SIRES
SITES
SITUS
SIXES
SIZES
SKEGS
SKEPS
SKEWS
SKIDS
SKIES
SKIMS
SKINS
SKIPS
SKITS
SKUAS
SLABS
SLAGS
SLAMS
SLAPS
SLATS
SLAVS
SLAWS
SLAYS
SLEDS
SLEWS
SLIMS
SLIPS
SLITS
SLOBS
SLOES
SLOGS
SLOPS
SLOTS
SLOWS
SLUES
SLUGS
SLUMS
SLURS
SMEWS
SMITS
SMOGS
SMUTS
SNAGS
SNAPS
SNIPS
SNITS
SNOBS
SNOGS
SNOWS
SNUBS
SNUGS
SOAKS
SOAPS
SOARS
SOCKS
SODAS
SOFAS
SOILS
SOKES
SOLES
SOLOS
SOLUS
SOMAS
SONES
SONGS
SOOTS
SOPHS
SORAS
SORBS
SORES
SORTS
SORUS
SOUKS
SOULS
SOUPS
SOURS
SOYAS
SPADS
SPAMS
SPANS
SPARS
SPATS
SPAYS
SPECS
SPETS
SPEWS
SPIES
SPINS
SPITS
SPIVS
SPOTS
SPUDS
SPURS
SRTAS
SSGTS
STABS
STAGS
STARS
STATS
STAYS
STEMS
STENS
STEPS
STETS
STEWS
STIES
STIRS
STOAS
STOLS
STOPS
STOSS
STOTS
STOWS
STUBS
STUDS
STUMS
STUNS
SUCKS
SUDDS
SUERS
SUETS
SUFIS
SUITS
SULKS
SUMPS
SUPES
SUPTS
SURAS
SURDS
SURFS
SWABS
SWAGS
SWANS
SWAPS
SWATS
SWAYS
SWIGS
SWIMS
SWISS
SWOBS
SWOPS
SYCES
SYNCS

•SS••
ASSAD
ASSAI
ASSAM
ASSAY
ASSES
ASSET
ASSEZ
ASSNS
ASSOC
ASSTD
ASSTS
ASSUR
ASSYR
ESSAY
ESSEN
ESSES
ESSEX
ISSEI
ISSUE
ISSUS
OSSEO
OSSIA
OSSIE

•S•S•
RSFSR

•S••S
ASCUS
ASHES
ASSES
ASSNS
ASSTS
ESNES
ESSES
ESTAS
ESTES
ISLAS
ISLES
ISSUS
LSATS
MSDOS
MSGTS
PSATS
PSOAS
RSVPS
SSGTS
TSARS
TSGTS
USERS

••SS•
AUSSI
BASSI
BASSO
BOSSA
BOSSY
CISSY
FOSSA
FOSSE
FUSSY
GASSY
GESSO
GOSSE
GUSSY
HASSO
HESSE
HISSY
HUSSY
JASSY
JESSE
LASSO
LISSE
LOSSY
MASSE
MASSY
MESSY
MISSA
MISSY
MOSSO
MOSSY
MUSSY
PASSE
PASSU
PASSY
POSSE
ROSSI
RUSSE
RUSSO
SASSY
SISSY
TASSE
TASSO

••S•S
APSES
APSIS
APSOS
ARSIS
ASSES
ASSNS
ASSTS
BASES
BASIS
BASKS
BESTS
BISES
BOSCS
BOSKS
BOSNS
BUSES
BUSKS
BUSTS
CASAS
CASES
CASKS
CASTS
CASUS
COSTS
CUSKS
CUSPS
DESKS
DISCS
DISKS
DOSES
DUSKS
DUSTS
EASES
EASTS
ESSES
FASTS
FESTS
FISCS
FISTS
FUSES
GASES
GASPS
GESTS
GISTS
GUSTS
HASPS
HESTS
HOSES
HOSTS
HUSKS
INSTS
ISSUS
JESTS
LASES
LASTS
LISPS
LISTS
LOSES
LUSTS
MASKS
MASTS
MESAS
MISOS
MISTS
MOSES
MUSES
MUSKS
MUSTS
NESTS
NISUS
NOSES
OASES
OASIS
OASTS
OPSIS
OUSTS
PASES
PASTS
PESOS
PESTS
POSES
POSTS
RASES
RASPS
RESTS
RISES
RISKS
ROSES
RUSES
RUSKS
RUSTS
SASES
TASKS
TBSPS
TESTS
TUSKS
VASES
VESTS
VISAS
VISES
WASPS
WESTS
WISPS
YESES
ZESTS

•••SS
ABYSS
AMASS
AMISS
BLASS
BLESS
BLISS
BRASS
CHESS
CLASS
CRASS
CRESS
CRISS
CROSS
DRESS
DROSS
FLOSS
GAUSS
GLASS
GLESS
GLOSS
GRASS
GROSS
GUESS
HEISS
IPASS
KRISS
KVASS
LOESS
PRESS
SEUSS
STOSS
SWISS
TRESS
TRUSS
WEISS
ZEISS

ST•••
STABS
STACK
STACY
STADT
STAEL
STAFF
STAGE
STAGG
STAGS
STAGY
STAHL
STAID
STAIN
STAIR
STAKE
STALE
STALK
STALL
STAMP
STAND
STANG
STANK
STARE
STARK
STARR
STARS
START
STARZ
STASH
STATE
STATS
STAVE
STAYS

STEAD	STOVE	SITKA	SNITS	SKEAT	ISTIC	HOSTA	UPSET	TRUST	SURAT	SNUGS
STEAK	STOWE	SITON	SOFTC	SKEET	ISTLE	HOSTS	VISIT	TRYST	SURDS	SOUGH
STEAL	STOWS	SITUP	SOFTG	SKINT	OSTEO	INSTR	WASNT	TWIST	SURER	SOUKS
STEAM	STPAT	SITUS	SOFTY	SKIRT	OSTIA	INSTS		VERST	SURFS	SOULS
STEED	STRAD	SOTHO	SOLTI	SKORT	USTED	JESTS	**•••ST**	WAIST	SURFY	SOULT
STEEL	STRAP	SOTOL	SOOTH	SLANT		JUSTE	ADUST	WEEST	SURGE	SOUND
STEEN	STRAW	SOTTO	SOOTS	SLEET	**•S•T•**	LASTS	ALIST	WHIST	SURLY	SOUPS
STEEP	STRAY	SRTAS	SOOTY	SLEPT	ASSTD	LISTS	ANGST	WIEST	SUSAN	SOUPY
STEER	STREP	SUTRA	SORTA	SLIPT	ASSTS	LUSTS	AVAST	WORST	SUSHI	SOURS
STEIN	STREW		SORTS	SMALT	LSATS	LUSTY	BAKST	WREST	SUSIE	SOUSA
STELA	STRIA	**S••T•**	SOTTO	SMART	MSGTS	MASTS	BEAST	WRIST	SUTRA	SOUSE
STELE	STRIP	SAITH	SOUTH	SMELT	PSATS	MESTA	BLAST	WURST		SOUTH
STEMS	STROM	SALTA	SPATE	SMOLT	SSGTS	MISTI	BLEST	YEAST	**S•U••**	SPUDS
STENO	STROP	SALTS	SPATS	SMOOT	TSGTS	MISTS	BOAST	ZEIST	SAUCE	SPUME
STENS	STRUG	SALTY	SPETS	SNERT	USLTA	MISTY	BOOST		SAUCY	SPUMY
STEPS	STRUM	SANTA	SPITE	SNOOT		MUSTS	BREST	**SU•••**	SAUDI	SPUNK
STERE	STRUT	SANTE	SPITS	SNORT	**•S••T**	MUSTY	BURST	SUAVE	SAUKS	SPURN
STERN	STUBS	SANTO	SPITZ	SNOUT	ASCOT	NASTY	CANST	SUBIC	SAULT	SPURS
STETS	STUCK	SARTO	SPOTS	SOULT	ASSET	NESTS	CHEST	SUCKA	SAUNA	SPURT
STEVE	STUDS	SAUTE	SSGTS	SPELT	ASYET	OASTS	COAST	SUCKS	SAURY	SQUAB
STEWS	STUDY	SAWTO	STATE	SPENT	ASYUT	OUSTS	CREST	SUCRE	SAUTE	SQUAD
STICH	STUFF	SCATS	STATS	SPILT	CSPOT	PASTA	CRIST	SUDAN	SCUBA	SQUAT
STICK	STUKA	SCOTS	STETS	SPLAT	ESBAT	PASTE	CRUST	SUDDS	SCUDI	SQUIB
STIEB	STULL	SCOTT	STOTS	SPLIT	GSUIT	PASTO	CURST	SUDRA	SCUDO	SQUID
STIES	STUMP	SCUTA	STUTZ	SPORT	ISLET	PASTS	DEIST	SUDSY	SCUDS	STUBS
STIFF	STUMS	SCUTE	SUETS	SPOUT	XSOUT	PASTY	DIDST	SUEDE	SCUFF	STUCK
STILE	STUNG	SCUTS	SUETY	SPRAT		PESTO	DOEST	SUEME	SCULL	STUDS
STILL	STUNK	SEATO	SUITA	SPRIT	**••ST•**	PESTS	DURST	SUERS	SCUMS	STUDY
STILT	STUNS	SEATS	SUITE	SPURT	ASSTD	PISTE	EGEST	SUETS	SCUPS	STUFF
STING	STUNT	SECTS	SUITS	SQUAT	ASSTS	POSTE	ERNST	SUETY	SCURF	STUKA
STINK	STUPA	SEETO	SUPTS	STADT	AUSTR	POSTS	EXIST	SUFIS	SCUTA	STULL
STINT	STUPE	SENTE	SWATH	START	BASTE	RASTA	FAUST	SUGAR	SCUTE	STUMP
STIPE	STURM	SEPTA	SWATS	STILT	BESTS	RESTS	FEAST	SUING	SCUTS	STUMS
STIRK	STUTZ	SERTA	SWITH	STINT	BUSTS	RUSTS	FEIST	SUINT	SCUZZ	STUNG
STIRS	STYLE	SETTE	SWITZ	STOAT	CASTE	RUSTY	FIRST	SUITA	SEULE	STUNK
STOAE	STYLI	SETTO		STOUT	CASTS	TASTE	FOIST	SUITE	SEUSS	STUNS
STOAS	STYLO	SEXTS	**S•••T**	STPAT	CBSTV	TASTY	FROST	SUITS	SHUCK	STUNT
STOAT	STYMY	SHATT	SABOT	STRUT	CESTA	TESTA	GHOST	SULCI	SHULA	STUPA
STOCK	STYNE	SHOTS	SADAT	STUNT	CESTI	TESTS	GOEST	SULFA	SHULS	STUPE
STOGY		SHUTE	SAGET	SUINT	COSTA	TESTY	GRIST	SULKS	SHUNS	STURM
STOIC	**S•T••**	SHUTS	SAINT	SURAT	COSTS	VASTY	GUEST	SULKY	SHUNT	STUTZ
STOKE	SATAN	SIETE	SALUT	SWART	DESTE	VESTA	HADST	SULLA	SHUSH	SWUNG
STOLA	SATBY	SIFTS	SAULT	SWEAT	DISTR	VESTS	HEIST	SULLY	SHUTE	
STOLE	SATED	SILTS	SCANT	SWEET	DUSTS	VISTA	HOIST	SUMAC	SHUTS	**S••U•**
STOLS	SATES	SILTY	SCENT	SWEPT	DUSTY	WASTE	HOLST	SUMBA	SKUAS	SALUD
STOMA	SATIE	SIXTH	SCOOT	SWIFT	EASTS	WESTS	HORST	SUMER	SKULK	SALUT
STOMP	SATIN	SIXTY	SCOTT		FASTS	ZESTS	HURST	SUMMA	SKULL	SATUP
STONE	SATON	SKATE	SCOUT	**•ST••**	FESTA	ZESTY	IDEST	SUMPS	SKUNK	SCAUP
STONY	SATUP	SKETE	SENAT	ASTER	FESTS		JOIST	SUMUP	SLUED	SCOUR
STOOD	SATYR	SKITS	SETAT	ASTIN	FISTS	**••S•T**	JOUST	SUNDA	SLUES	SCOUT
STOOK	SETAE	SLATE	SHAFT	ASTIR	FUSTY	ASSET	LEAST	SUNNA	SLUGS	SCRUB
STOOL	SETAT	SLATS	SHALT	ASTON	GASTR	BESET	MAYST	SUNNI	SLUMP	SCRUM
STOOP	SETBY	SLATY	SHANT	ASTOR	GESTE	BESOT	MIDST	SUNNY	SLUMS	SEBUM
STOPE	SETIN	SLITS	SHATT	ASTRA	GESTS	HASAT	MOIST	SUNUP	SLUNG	SEDUM
STOPS	SETON	SLOTH	SHEET	ASTRE	GISTS	HASNT	ODIST	SUOMI	SLUNK	SEGUE
STORE	SETTE	SLOTS	SHIFT	ASTRO	GUSTO	INSET	PABST	SUPER	SLURP	SEOUL
STORK	SETTO	SMITE	SHIRT	ESTAB	GUSTS	LISZT	PREST	SUPES	SLURS	SERUM
STORM	SETUP	SMITH	SHOAT	ESTAS	GUSTY	ONSET	PROST	SUPRA	SLUSH	SETUP
STORY	SITAR	SMITS	SHOOT	ESTEE	HASTA	POSIT	QUEST	SUPTS	SMURF	SEWUP
STOSS	SITBY	SMOTE	SHORT	ESTER	HASTE	RASHT	ROAST	SUPVR	SMUTS	SHAUN
STOTS	SITED	SMUTS	SHOUT	ESTES	HASTO	RESET	ROOST	SURAH	SNUBS	SHOUT
STOUP	SITES	SMYTH	SHUNT	ESTOP	HASTY	TVSET	ROUST	SURAL	SNUCK	SHRUB
STOUT	SITIN	SNATH	SIGHT	FSTOP	HESTS	UNSET	TOAST	SURAS	SNUFF	SHRUG

SIEUR
SINUS
SIOUX
SITUP
SITUS
SNOUT
SOEUR
SOLUM
SOLUS
SOPUP
SORUS
SOYUZ
SPOUT
SPRUE
STOUP
STOUT
STRUG
STRUM
STRUT
SUMUP
SUNUP
SYRUP

S•••U
SADHU
SHAMU
SHOYU
SNAFU

•SU••
GSUIT
ISUZU
USUAL
USURP
USURY

•S•U•
ASCUS
ASHUR
ASSUR
ASYUT
ESQUE
ISSUE
ISSUS
PSEUD
USEUP
USQUE
XSOUT

•S••U
ISAMU
ISUZU

••SU•
ADSUM
AKSUM
ASSUR
CASUS
ENSUE
GASUP
IPSUM
ISSUE
ISSUS
MASUR
MOSUL
NISUS
VISUM

••S•U
PASSU
WUSHU

•••SU
DERSU
MATSU
PASSU

S•V••
SAVED
SAVER
SAVES
SAVOR
SAVOY
SAVVY
SEVEN
SEVER
SIVAN

S••V•
SALVE
SALVO
SAVVY
SELVA
SERVE
SERVO
SHAVE
SHIVA
SHIVS
SHOVE
SIEVE
SILVA
SKIVE
SLAVE
SLAVS
SNEVA
SOAVE
SOLVE
SPIVS
STAVE
STEVE
STOVE
SUAVE
SUPVR

S•••V
SCHAV

•SV••
RSVPD
RSVPS

••S•V
BASOV
CBSTV

SW•••
SWABS
SWAGE
SWAGS
SWAIN
SWALE
SWAMI
SWAMP
SWANK
SWANN
SWANS
SWAPS
SWARD
SWARF
SWARM
SWART
SWASH
SWATH
SWATS
SWAYS
SWAZI
SWEAR
SWEAT
SWEDE
SWEEP
SWEET
SWELL
SWEPT
SWIFT
SWIGS
SWILL
SWIMS
SWINE
SWING
SWINK
SWIPE
SWIRL
SWISH
SWISS
SWITH
SWITZ
SWOBS
SWONK
SWOON
SWOOP
SWOPE
SWOPS
SWORD
SWORE
SWORN
SWUNG

S•W••
SAWED
SAWIN
SAWTO
SEWED
SEWER
SEWON
SEWUP
SOWED
SOWER

S••W•
SCHWA
SCOWL
SCOWS
SHAWL
SHAWM
SHAWN
SHOWN
SHOWS
SHOWY
SKEWS
SLAWS
SLEWS
SLIWA
SLOWS
SMEWS
SNOWS
SNOWY
SPAWN
SPEWS
STEWS
STOWE
STOWS

S•••W
SCREW
SEROW
SHREW
SINEW
STRAW
STREW
SYDOW

•SW••
ASWAN

•S••W
ASKEW
PSHAW

••S•W
RESAW
RESEW

S•X••
SAXES
SAXON
SEXES
SEXTS
SIXAM
SIXED
SIXER
SIXES
SIXMO
SIXPM
SIXTH
SIXTY
SOXER

S••X•
SKNXX

S•••X
SILEX
SIOUX
SKNXX

•S••X
ESSEX

••S•X
BOSOX
ESSEX

SY•••
SYBIL
SYCEE
SYCES
SYDOW
SYLPH
SYNCS
SYNGE
SYNOD
SYRIA
SYRUP
SYSOP

S•Y••
SAYER
SAYSO
SHYER
SHYLY
SKYEY
SLYER
SLYLY
SLYPE
SMYTH
SOYAS
SOYUZ
SPYON
SPYRI
STYLE
STYLI
STYLO
STYMY
STYNE

S••Y•
SANYO
SATYR
SEEYA
SHAYS
SHOYU
SIBYL
SLAYS
SLOYD
SONYA
SPAYS
STAYS
SWAYS

S•••Y
SADLY
SAGGY
SALLY
SALTY
SAMMY
SANDY
SAPPY
SARKY
SASSY
SATBY
SAUCY
SAURY
SAVOY
SAVVY
SCALY
SCARY
SCOPY
SEALY
SEAMY
SEDGY
SEEDY
SEELY
SEEPY
SEPOY
SERRY
SETBY
SHADY
SHAKY
SHINY
SHOWY
SHYLY
SILKY
SILLY
SILTY
SISSY
SITBY
SIXTY
SKYEY
SLATY
SLILY
SLIMY
SLYLY
SMOKY
SNAKY
SNOWY
SOAPY
SODDY
SOFTY
SOGGY
SONNY
SOOEY
SOOTY
SOPHY
SOPPY
SORRY
SOUPY
SPACY
SPICY
SPIKY
SPINY
SPIRY
SPLAY
SPRAY
SPUMY
STACY
STAGY
STOGY
STONY
STORY
STRAY
STUDY
STYMY
SUDSY
SUETY
SULKY
SULLY
SUNNY
SURFY
SURLY

•SY••
ASYET
ASYLA
ASYUT
PSYCH

•S•Y•
ASSYR

•S••Y
ASHBY
ASSAY
ESSAY
ISLEY
USURY

••SY•
ASSYR

••S•Y
ASSAY
BOSKY
BOSSY
BUSBY
BUSEY
BUSHY
CASEY
CISSY
COSBY
CUSHY
DISHY
DUSKY
DUSTY
ENSKY
ESSAY
FISHY
FUSSY
FUSTY
GASSY
GUSHY
GUSSY
GUSTY
HASTY
HISSY
HUSKY
HUSSY
JASEY
JASSY
KESEY
LOSSY
LUSTY
MASHY
MASSY
MESHY
MESSY
MISSY
MISTY
MOSBY
MOSEY
MOSSY
MUSHY
MUSKY
MUSSY
MUSTY
NASBY
NASTY
NOSEY
PASSY
PASTY
PESKY
PUSEY
PUSHY
RASPY
RISKY
ROSEY
RUSHY
RUSTY
SASSY
SISSY
TASTY
TESTY
UNSAY
VASTY
VESEY
VISBY
WASHY
WASPY
WISHY
WISPY
ZESTY

•••SY
ANTSY
ARTSY
BETSY
BITSY
BOSSY
BUGSY
CISSY
COUSY
DAISY
DITSY
FUBSY
FUSSY
GASSY
GIPSY
GOOSY
GORSY
GUSSY
GUTSY
GYPSY
HISSY
HORSY
HUSSY
JASSY
LOSSY
LOUSY
MASSY
MESSY
MIMSY
MISSY
MOPSY
MOSSY
MOUSY
MUSSY
NEWSY
NOISY
NUTSY
PALSY
PANSY
PASSY
PATSY
POESY
POTSY
PROSY
PURSY
SASSY
SISSY
SUDSY
TANSY
TIPSY
TOPSY
WALSY

SZ•••
SZELL
SZOLD

S•Z••
SIZED
SIZER
SIZES

S••Z•
SCUZZ
SEIZE
SMAZE
SWAZI

S•••Z
SCUZZ
SOYUZ
SPITZ
STARZ
STUTZ
SWITZ

•S•Z•
ISUZU

•S••Z
ASSEZ

••SZ•
LISZT
TISZA

••S•Z
ASSEZ

•••SZ
GROSZ

TA•••
TABBY
TABIS
TABLA
TABLE
TABOO
TABOR
TACET
TACHO
TACHY
TACIT
TACKS
TACKY
TACOS
TAEGU
TAELS
TAFFY
TAGUP
TAGUS
TAHOE
TAHRS
TAIGA
TAILS
TAINE
TAINO
TAINT
TAKAS
TAKEI
TAKEN
TAKER
TAKES
TAKIN
TALER
TALES
TALIA
TALKS
TALKY
TALLY
TALON
TALOS
TALUS
TAMBO
TAMED
TAMER
TAMES
TAMIL
TAMMY
TAMPA
TAMPS
TANDE
TANDY
TANEY
TANGO
TANGS
TANGY
TANKA
TANKS
TANSY
TANTE
TANTO
TANYA
TAPAS
TAPED
TAPER
TAPES
TAPIN
TAPIR
TARDE
TARDY
TARES
TARGE
TARNS
TAROK
TAROT
TARPS
TARRY
TARSI
TARTS
TARTU
TASER
TASKS
TASSE
TASSO
TASTE
TASTY
TATAR
TATER
TATRA
TATTY
TATUM
TAUNT
TAUON
TAUPE
TAUPO
TAURO
TAUTO
TAWNY
TAXCO
TAXED
TAXER
TAXES
TAXIS
TAXON
TAYRA
TAZZA

T•A••
TBALL
TBARS
TEACH
TEAKS
TEALS
TEAMS
TEARS
TEARY
TEASE
THAIS
THANE

THANK
THANT
THARP
THATS
THAWS
TIANT
TIARA
TOADS
TOADY
TOAST
TRACE
TRACK
TRACT
TRACY
TRADE
TRAIL
TRAIN
TRAIT
TRALA
TRAMP
TRAMS
TRANS
TRAPP
TRAPS
TRASH
TRAVE
TRAWL
TRAYS
TSADE
TSARS
TWAIN
TWANG
TZARS

T••A•

TAKAS
TAPAS
TATAR
TENAM
TEPAL
TEXAN
TEXAS
TICAL
TIDAL
TIKAL
TILAK
TIRAN
TITAN
TODAY
TOGAE
TOGAS
TOKAY
TONAL
TOPAZ
TORAH
TOTAL
TREAD
TREAT
TRIAD
TRIAL
TUBAS
TUNAS
TWEAK
TWOAM
TYNAN

T•••A

TABLA
TAIGA
TALIA
TAMPA
TANKA
TANYA
TATRA
TAYRA
TAZZA
TEENA
TERRA
TERZA
TESLA
TESTA
TETRA
THECA
THEDA
THEMA
THERA
THETA
THUJA
TIARA
TIBIA
TISZA
TONGA
TONKA
TONYA
TOSCA
TRALA
TULSA
TWYLA
TYPEA

•TA••

ATALL
ATARI
ETAGE
ETAPE
ETATS
ITALO
ITALS
ITALY
OTARU
OTARY
STABS
STACK
STACY
STADT
STAEL
STAFF
STAGE
STAGG
STAGS
STAGY
STAHL
STAID
STAIN
STAIR
STAKE
STALE
STALK
STALL
STAMP
STAND
STANG
STANK
STARE
STARK
STARR
STARS
START
STARZ
STASH
STATE
STATS
STAVE
STAYS
UTAHN

•T•A•

ATBAT
ATBAY
ATEAM
ATLAS
ATMAN
ATPAR
ATTAR
ATWAR
ETHAN
ETNAS
OTWAY
PTRAP
STEAD
STEAK
STEAL
STEAM
STOAE
STOAS
STOAT
STPAT
STRAD
STRAP
STRAW
STRAY

•T••A

ATRIA
ATSEA
ETYMA
STELA
STOLA
STOMA
STRIA
STUKA
STUPA
UTICA

••TA•

ACTAS
AETAT
ALTAI
ALTAR
ANTAE
ANTAL
ANTAS
ARTAL
ATTAR
BATAK
BETAS
DETAT
DITAT
DOTAL
EATAT
ESTAB
ESTAS
FATAL
FETAL
FETAS
GETAS
GETAT
GOTAT
IDTAG
IOTAS
JOTAS
LETAT
LOTAH
LOTAS
METAL
NATAL
OCTAD
OCTAL
ONTAP
PETAL
PITAS
QATAR
RETAG
RETAP
RETAR
RETAX
ROTAS
SATAN
SETAE
SETAT
SITAR
SRTAS
TATAR
TITAN
TOTAL
VITAE
VITAL
VITAS
WOTAN
ZETAS

••T•A

AETNA
AFTRA
ANTRA
ASTRA
BETTA
BOTHA
COTTA
DITKA
ENTIA
EXTRA
FATHA
FATWA
GOTHA
GOTTA
GUTTA
INTRA
LOTTA
LYTTA
MOTTA
OSTIA
PATNA
PETRA
PITTA
RETIA
SITKA
SUTRA
TATRA
TETRA
ULTRA

•••TA

ADYTA
AGITA
AKITA
ALETA
ANITA
AORTA
BETTA
BIOTA
CARTA
CESTA
CEUTA
CHITA
COSTA
COTTA
DELTA
DICTA
EVITA
FANTA
FESTA
GOTTA
GRATA
GRETA
GUTTA
HASTA
HEPTA
HOSTA
JUNTA
LEPTA
LOTTA
LYTTA
MALTA
MANTA
MARTA
MEHTA
MESTA
MIATA
MOTTA
NAFTA
OVETA
PASTA
PENTA
PIETA
PINTA
PITTA
PLATA
PUNTA
QUOTA
RASTA
REATA
RENTA
RHYTA
RIATA
SALTA
SANTA
SCUTA
SEPTA
SERTA
SORTA
SUITA
TESTA
THETA
UINTA
USLTA
VESTA
VISTA
VOLTA
YALTA
YENTA

TB•••

TBALL
TBARS
TBILL
TBIRD
TBOND
TBONE
TBSPS

T•B••

TABBY
TABIS
TABLA
TABLE
TABOO
TABOR
TIBBS
TIBER
TIBET
TIBIA
TOBES
TOBEY
TOBIT
TOBOL
TUBAS
TUBBY
TUBED
TUBER
TUBES

T••B•

TABBY
TAMBO
THEBE
TIBBS
TRIBE
TUBBY
TURBO

T•••B

THROB
THUMB
TYPEB

•TB••

ATBAT
ATBAY

•T•B•

FTLBS
STABS
STUBS

•T••B

STIEB

••TB•

GETBY
GOTBY
LETBE
PUTBY
SATBY
SETBY
SITBY

••T•B

ESTAB

T•C••

TACET
TACHO
TACHY
TACIT
TACKS
TACKY
TACOS
TECHS
TECHY
TICAL
TICKS
TICKY
TUCKS
TYCHE
TYCHO

T••C•

TAXCO
TEACH
TENCH
THECA
THICK
TINCT
TORCH
TOSCA
TOUCH
TRACE
TRACK
TRACT
TRACY
TRICE
TRICK
TRUCE
TRUCK
TWICE

T•••C

TELIC
TONIC
TOPIC
TORIC
TOXIC
TUNIC

•TC••

ITCHY
LTCOL

•T•C•

STACK
STACY
STICH
STICK
STOCK
STUCK
UTICA

•T••C

ATTIC
ETHIC
STOIC

••TC•

AITCH
BATCH
BOTCH
BUTCH
CATCH
DITCH
DUTCH
FETCH
FITCH
HATCH
HITCH
HUTCH
KETCH
KOTCH
LATCH
MATCH
MITCH
NATCH
NOTCH
PATCH
PITCH
RATCH
VETCH
WATCH
WITCH

••T•C

ANTIC
ATTIC
AZTEC
ISTIC
OPTIC
VATIC

•••TC

SOFTC

T•D••

TEDDY
TIDAL
TIDED
TIDES
TODAY
TODDY
TODOS
TUDOR

T••D•

TANDE
TANDY
TARDE
TARDY
TEDDY
TEIDE
TENDS
THEDA
THUDS
TILDE
TOADS
TOADY
TODDY
TONDI
TONDO
TRADE
TSADE

T•••D

TAMED
TAPED
TAXED
TBIRD
TBOND
TEPID
THEYD
THIRD
TIDED
TILED
TIMED
TIMID
TINED
TIRED
TONED
TOPED
TOTED
TOWED
TOYED
TREAD
TREED
TREND
TRIAD
TRIED
TRUED
TUBED
TUMID
TUNED
TWEED
TYPED

•T•D•

ETUDE
STADT
STUDS
STUDY

•T••D

STAID
STAND
STEAD
STEED
STOOD
STRAD

••TD•

OUTDO

••T•D

ACTED
ANTED
APTED
BATED
CITED
DATED
DOTED
FATED
FETED
FETID
GATED
HATED
KITED
MATED
METED
MUTED
NOTED
OCTAD
OOTID
OPTED
OUTED
PATED
RATED
SATED
SITED
TOTED
USTED
VOTED

•••TD

APPTD
ASSTD
CONTD
WHATD

TE•••

TEACH
TEAKS
TEALS
TEAMS
TEARS
TEARY
TEASE
TECHS
TECHY
TEDDY
TEEMS
TEENA
TEENS
TEENY
TEETH
TEEUP
TEHEE
TEIDE
TELEO
TELES
TELEX
TELIC
TELLS
TELLY
TELOS
TEMPE
TEMPI
TEMPO
TEMPS
TEMPT
TENAM
TENCH
TENDS
TENET
TENON
TENOR
TENPM
TENSE
TENTH
TENTS
TEPAL
TEPEE
TEPID
TERMS
TERNE
TERNS
TERPS
TERRA
TERRE
TERRI
TERRY
TERSE
TERZA
TESLA
TESTA
TESTS
TESTY
TETES
TETHS
TETON
TETRA
TEVET
TEVYE
TEXAN
TEXAS
TEXTS

T•E••
TAEGU
TAELS
TEEMS
TEENA
TEENS
TEENY
TEETH
TEEUP
THEBE
THECA
THEDA
THEFT
THEIR
THEMA
THEME
THEMS
THEOL
THERA
THERE
THERM
THESE
THETA
THEWS
THEWY
THEYD
TIEGS
TIEIN
TIERS
TIETO
TIEUP
TOEIN
TREAD
TREAT
TREED
TREEN
TREES
TREKS
TREND
TRENT
TRESS
TREVI
TREWS
TREYS
TWEAK
TWEED
TWEEN
TWEER
TWEET
TWERE
TWERP

T••E•
TACET
TAKEI
TAKEN
TAKER
TAKES
TALER
TALES
TAMED
TAMER
TAMES
TANEY
TAPED
TAPER
TAPES
TARES
TASER
TATER
TAXED
TAXER
TAXES
TEHEE
TELEO
TELES
TELEX
TENET
TEPEE
TETES
TEVET
THIEF
THREE
THREW
TIBER
TIBET
TIDED
TIDES
TIGER
TIKES
TILED
TILER
TILES
TIMED
TIMER
TIMES
TIMEX
TINED
TINES
TIRED
TIRES
TITER
TOBES
TOBEY
TOKEN
TOLER
TOLET
TOMEI
TOMES
TONED
TONER
TONES
TONEY
TOPED
TOPER
TOPES
TOTED
TOTEM
TOTER
TOTES
TOVES
TOWED
TOWEL
TOWER
TOYED
TREED
TREEN
TREES
TRIED
TRIER
TRIES
TRUED
TRUER
TRUES
TRUEX
TUBED
TUBER
TUBES
TULES
TUNED
TUNER
TUNES
TUTEE
TUXES
TVSET
TWEED
TWEEN
TWEER
TWEET
TYKES
TYLER
TYNES
TYPEA
TYPEB
TYPED
TYPEE
TYPER
TYPES
TYPEY
TYRES

T•••E
TABLE
TAHOE
TAINE
TANDE
TANTE
TARDE
TARGE
TASSE
TASTE
TAUPE
TBONE
TEASE
TEHEE
TEIDE
TEMPE
TENSE
TEPEE
TERNE
TERRE
TERSE
TEVYE
THANE
THEBE
THEME
THERE
THESE
THINE
THOLE
THOSE
THREE
THROE
THULE
THYME
TILDE
TINGE
TITHE
TITLE
TITRE
TNOTE
TOGAE
TOILE
TONNE
TOQUE
TORME
TORRE
TORTE
TOTIE
TOUTE
TOWNE
TRACE
TRADE
TRAVE
TRIBE
TRICE
TRIKE
TRINE
TRIPE
TRITE
TROPE
TROVE
TRUCE
TRYME
TSADE
TULLE
TUQUE
TUTEE
TWERE
TWICE
TWINE
TYCHE
TYPEE

•TE••
ATEAM
ATEIN
ATEUP
ITEMS
ITERS
PTERO
STEAD
STEAK
STEAL
STEAM
STEED
STEEL
STEEN
STEEP
STEER
STEIN
STELA
STELE
STEMS
STENO
STENS
STEPS
STERE
STERN
STETS
STEVE
STEWS

•T•E•
ATSEA
ETHEL
ETHER
ETSEQ
ETZEL
LTGEN
OTHER
OTOES
OTTER
STAEL
STEED
STEEL
STEEN
STEEP
STEER
STIEB
STIES
STREP
STREW
UTHER
UTLEY
UTTER

•T••E
ATIVE
ATONE
ATQUE
ETAGE
ETAPE
ETUDE
ITSME
STAGE
STAKE
STALE
STARE
STATE
STAVE
STELE
STERE
STEVE
STILE
STIPE
STOAE
STOKE
STOLE
STONE
STOPE
STORE
STOVE
STOWE
STUPE
STYLE
STYNE
UTILE

••TE•
ACTED
ACTER
AFTER
ALTER
ANTED
ANTES
APTED
APTER
ARTEL
ARTES
ASTER
AZTEC
BATED
BATES
BETEL
BITER
BITES
BOTEL
BUTEO
BYTES
CATER
CATES
CITED
CITER
CITES
COTES
CUTER
CUTEX
CUTEY
DATED
DATER
DATES
DETER
DOTED
DOTER
DOTES
EATEN
EATER
ENTER
ESTEE
ESTER
ESTES
FATED
FATES
FETED
FETES
GATED
GATES
GUTEN
HATED
HATER
HATES
HOTEL
INTEL
INTER
JETER
JETES
JUTES
KITED
KITER
KITES
LATEN
LATER
LATEX
LITER
LITES
LUTES
MATED
MATEO
MATER
MATES
MATEY
METED
METER
METES
MITER
MITES
MOTEL
MOTES
MOTET
MUTED
MUTER
MUTES
NITER
NITES
NOTED
NOTER
NOTES
OATEN
OATER
OATES
OCTET
OFTEN
OPTED
OSTEO
OTTER
OUTED
OUTER
PATED
PATEK
PATEN
PATER
PATES
PETER
PETES
RATED
RATEL
RATER
RATES
RITES
ROTES
SATED
SATES
SITED
SITES
TATER
TETES
TITER
TOTED
TOTEM
TOTER
TOTES
TUTEE
UNTER
USTED
UTTER
VATER
VOTED
VOTER
VOTES
WATER
YATES

••T•E
ANTAE
ANTRE
ARTIE
ASTRE
AUTRE
BATHE
BETTE
BITTE
BOTHE
BUTTE
CUTIE
DETRE
ENTRE
ESTEE
GETME
HITME
ISTLE
KATIE
KITWE
LATHE
LATKE
LATTE
LETBE
LETHE
LITHE
LITRE
LOTTE
MATTE
METRE
MITRE
NITRE
NOTME
NOTRE
OUTRE
PATHE
RETIE
SATIE
SETAE
SETTE
TITHE
TITLE
TITRE
TOTIE
TUTEE
UNTIE
VITAE
VOTRE
WITHE
WITTE
WYTHE

•••TE
ABATE
ACUTE
AGATE
ALATE
ARETE
AZOTE
BASTE
BETTE
BITTE
BOITE
BRITE
BRUTE
BUTTE
CARTE
CASTE
CHUTE
CNOTE
COMTE
CONTE
CRATE
CRETE
DANTE
DENTE
DESTE
DHOTE
ELATE
ELITE
ELUTE
EMOTE
ENATE
FLUTE
FOOTE
FORTE
GESTE
GRATE
GRETE
HARTE
HASTE
HAUTE
HEUTE
IRATE
JUSTE
KINTE
KLUTE
KNUTE
LATTE
LEYTE
LOTTE
MATTE
MONTE
NOLTE
NORTE
ONATE
ORATE
OVATE
PARTE
PASTE
PEETE
PENTE
PISTE
PLATE
POETE
PONTE
PORTE
POSTE
PRATE
QUITE
QUOTE
ROUTE
SANTE
SAUTE
SCUTE
SENTE
SETTE
SHUTE
SIETE
SKATE
SKETE
SLATE
SMITE
SMOTE
SPATE
SPITE
STATE
SUITE
TANTE
TASTE
TNOTE
TORTE
TOUTE
TRITE
UNITE
VERTE
VOLTE
WAITE
WASTE
WHITE
WITTE
WRITE
WROTE
YENTE
ZANTE

T•F••
TAFFY
TIFFS
TOFFS
TOFFY
TOFTS
TUFTS
TUFTY

T••F•
TAFFY
THEFT
TIFFS
TOFFS
TOFFY
TURFS
TURFY

T•••F
THIEF

•T•F•
STAFF
STIFF
STUFF

•T••F
STAFF
STIFF
STUFF

••T•F
MOTIF

T•G••
TAGUP
TAGUS
TIGER
TIGHT
TOGAE
TOGAS
TSGTS

T••G•
TAEGU
TAIGA
TANGO
TANGS
TANGY
TARGE
THIGH
THUGS
TIEGS
TINGE
TINGS
TONGA
TONGS
TOUGH
TRIGS
TRUGS
TWIGS

T•••G
THING
THONG
TOPOG
TWANG
TYING

•TG••
LTGEN
LTGOV

•T•G•
ETAGE
STAGE
STAGG
STAGS
STAGY
STOGY

•T••G
STAGG
STANG

STING
STRUG
STUNG

••TG•
GETGO
GITGO
LETGO
OUTGO

••T•G
IDTAG
RETAG

•••TG
SOFTG

TH•••
THAIS
THANE
THANK
THANT
THARP
THATS
THAWS
THEBE
THECA
THEDA
THEFT
THEIR
THEMA
THEME
THEMS
THEOL
THERA
THERE
THERM
THESE
THETA
THEWS
THEWY
THEYD
THICK
THIEF
THIGH
THILL
THINE
THING
THINK
THINS
THIRD
THOLE
THONG
THORN
THORO
THORP
THOSE
THOTH
THOUS
THREE
THREW
THROB
THROE
THROW
THRUM
THUDS
THUGS
THUJA
THULE
THUMB
THUMP
THUNK
THURS
THYME
THYMY

T•H••
TAHOE
TAHRS
TEHEE

T••H•
TACHO
TACHY
TECHS
TECHY
TETHS
TIGHT
TITHE
TYCHE
TYCHO

T•••H
TEACH
TEETH
TENCH
TENTH
THIGH
THOTH
TILTH
TOOTH
TORAH
TORCH
TOUCH
TOUGH
TRASH
TRISH
TROTH
TRUTH

•TH••
ATHOL
ATHON
ATHOS
ETHAN
ETHEL
ETHER
ETHIC
ETHNO
ETHOS
ETHYL
OTHER
UTHER

•T•H•
ITCHY
STAHL
UTAHN

•T••H
STASH
STICH

••TH•
ALTHO
ANTHO
ARTHR
BATHE
BATHO
BATHS
BATHY
BETHS
BOTHA
BOTHE
CATHY
FATHA
GOTHA
GOTHS
HETHS
KATHY
LATHE
LATHS
LATHY
LETHE
LITHE
LITHO
LITHS
MATHS
MOTHS
MOTHY
MYTHS
OATHS
ORTHO
PATHE
PATHO
PATHS
PATHY
PITHS
PITHY
RATHS
SOTHO
TETHS
TITHE
WITHE
WITHY
WYTHE

••T•H
AITCH
BATCH
BOTCH
BUTCH
CATCH
DITCH
DUTCH
FETCH
FITCH
HATCH
HITCH
HUTCH
KETCH
KOTCH
LATCH
LOTAH
MATCH
MITCH
NATCH
NOTCH
PATCH
PITCH
RATCH
VETCH
WATCH
WITCH

•••TH
ARITH
AZOTH
BARTH
BERTH
BIRTH
BLUTH
BLYTH
BOOTH
BRITH
BROTH
CHETH
CLOTH
COUTH
DARTH
DEPTH
DOETH
EARTH
EDITH
ELATH
FAITH
FIFTH
FILTH
FIRTH
FORTH
FROTH
FURTH
GARTH
GIRTH
HEATH
ICHTH
KEITH
LEITH
LOATH
MIRTH
MONTH
MOUTH
NEATH
NINTH
NORTH
PERTH
PLATH
QUOTH
SAITH
SIXTH
SLOTH
SMITH
SMYTH
SNATH
SOOTH
SOUTH
SWATH
SWITH
TEETH
TENTH
THOTH
TILTH
TOOTH
TROTH
TRUTH
WIDTH
WORTH
WRATH
WROTH
WYETH
YOUTH

TI•••
TIANT
TIARA
TIBBS
TIBER
TIBET
TIBIA
TICAL
TICKS
TICKY
TIDAL
TIDED
TIDES
TIEGS
TIEIN
TIERS
TIETO
TIEUP
TIFFS
TIGER
TIGHT
TIKAL
TIKES
TIKIS
TIKKI
TILAK
TILDE
TILED
TILER
TILES
TILLS
TILLY
TILTH
TILTS
TIMED
TIMER
TIMES
TIMEX
TIMID
TIMMY
TIMON
TIMOR
TINCT
TINED
TINES
TINGE
TINGS
TINNY
TINTS
TIPIN
TIPPI
TIPPY
TIPSY
TIPUP
TIRAN
TIRED
TIRES
TIROS
TISZA
TITAN
TITER
TITHE
TITIS
TITLE
TITRE
TITUS
TIZZY

T•I••
TAIGA
TAILS
TAINE
TAINO
TAINT
TBILL
TBIRD
TEIDE
THICK
THIEF
THIGH
THILL
THINE
THING
THINK
THINS
THIRD
TOILE
TOILS
TOITY
TRIAD
TRIAL
TRIBE
TRICE
TRICK
TRIED
TRIER
TRIES
TRIGS
TRIKE
TRILL
TRIMS
TRINE
TRINI
TRIOS
TRIPE
TRIPS
TRISH
TRITE
TRITT
TWICE
TWIGS
TWILL
TWINE
TWINS
TWIRL
TWIST
TWITS
TWIXT
TYING

T••I•
TABIS
TACIT
TAKIN
TALIA
TAMIL
TAPIN
TAPIR
TAXIS
TELIC
TEPID
THAIS
THEIR
TIBIA
TIEIN
TIKIS
TIMID
TIPIN
TITIS
TOBIT
TOEIN
TONIC
TONIO
TOPIC
TOPIS
TORIC
TORII
TOTIE
TOTIS
TOWIT
TOXIC
TOXIN
TRAIL
TRAIN
TRAIT
TROIS
TULIP
TUMID
TUNIC
TUNIS
TURIN
TWAIN

T•••I
TAKEI
TARSI
TEMPI
TERRI
TIKKI
TIPPI
TOMEI
TONDI
TOPOI
TORII
TORSI
TREVI
TRINI
TUTTI

•TI••
ATILT
ATION
ATIVE
QTIPS
STICH
STICK
STIEB
STIES
STIFF
STILE
STILL
STILT
STING
STINK
STINT
STIPE
STIRK
STIRS
UTICA
UTILE

•T•I•
ATEIN
ATRIA
ATRIP
ATTIC
ETHIC
ETUIS
ETVIR
STAID
STAIN
STAIR
STEIN
STOIC
STRIA
STRIP

•T••I
ATARI
OTOMI
STYLI

••TI•
ACTII
ACTIN
ACTIV
ANTIC
ANTIQ
ANTIS
ARTIE
ARTIS
ASTIN
ASTIR
ATTIC
BATIK
CUTIE
CUTIN
CUTIS
EATIN
EATIT
ENTIA
FETID
FITIN
GETIN
GETIT
GOTIN
GOTIT
HITIT
ISTIC
KATIE
LATIN
LETIN
MATIN
METIS
MOTIF
NOTIN
NOTIT
OOTID
OPTIC
OSTIA
PATIO
PETIT
PUTIN
RATIO
RETIA
RETIE
RUTIN
SATIE
SATIN
SETIN
SITIN
TITIS
TOTIE
TOTIS
UNTIE
UNTIL
VATIC
YETIS
ZITIS

••T•I
ACTII
ALTAI
MATRI
MITZI
NITTI
PATRI
PATTI
PETRI
PETTI
PUTTI
TUTTI

•••TI
AMATI
CACTI
CENTI
CESTI
COATI
CONTI
DENTI
DHOTI
HAITI
LACTI
LAHTI
MARTI
MISTI
MUFTI
MULTI
NITTI
NOCTI
PARTI
PATTI
PETTI
PONTI
PUTTI
RECTI
SOLTI
TUTTI

T••J•
THUJA

T•K••
TAKAS
TAKEI
TAKEN
TAKER
TAKES
TAKIN
TIKAL
TIKES
TIKIS
TIKKI
TOKAY
TOKEN
TOKYO
TYKES

T••K•
TACKS
TACKY
TALKS
TALKY
TANKA
TANKS
TASKS
TEAKS
TICKS
TICKY
TIKKI
TONKA
TREKS
TRIKE
TUCKS
TURKS
TURKU
TUSKS

T•••K
TAROK
THANK
THICK
THINK
THUNK
TILAK
TRACK
TRICK
TRUCK
TRUNK
TWEAK

•T•K•
STAKE
STOKE
STUKA

•T••K
STACK
STALK
STANK
STARK
STEAK
STICK
STINK
STIRK
STOCK
STOOK
STORK
STUCK
STUNK

••TK•
DITKA
LATKE
SITKA

••T•K
BATAK
BATIK
PATEK
POTOK

T•L••
TALER
TALES
TALIA
TALKS
TALKY
TALLY
TALON
TALOS
TALUS
TELEO
TELES
TELEX
TELIC
TELLS
TELLY
TELOS
TILAK
TILDE

TILED
TILER
TILES
TILLS
TILLY
TILTH
TILTS
TOLER
TOLET
TOLLS
TOLLY
TULES
TULIP
TULLE
TULLY
TULSA
TYLER

T••L•
TABLA
TABLE
TAELS
TAILS
TALLY
TBALL
TBILL
TEALS
TELLS
TELLY
TESLA
THILL
THOLE
THULE
TILLS
TILLY
TITLE
TOILE
TOILS
TOLLS
TOLLY
TOOLS
TRALA
TRILL
TROLL
TRULY
TULLE
TULLY
TWILL
TWYLA

T•••L
TAMIL
TBALL
TBILL
TEPAL
THEOL
THILL
TICAL
TIDAL
TIKAL
TOBOL
TONAL
TOPOL
TOTAL
TOWEL
TRAIL
TRAWL
TRIAL
TRILL
TROLL
TWILL
TWIRL
TYROL

•TL••
ATLAS
FTLBS
UTLEY

•T•L•
ATALL
ATILT
ATOLL
ITALO
ITALS
ITALY
STALE
STALK
STALL
STELA
STELE
STILE
STILL
STILT
STOLA
STOLE
STOLS
STULL
STYLE
STYLI
STYLO
UTILE
VTOLS

•T••L
ATALL
ATHOL
ATOLL
ETHEL
ETHYL
ETZEL
LTCOL
STAEL
STAHL
STALL
STEAL
STEEL
STILL
STOOL
STULL

••TL•
APTLY
FATLY
FITLY
HATLO
HOTLY
ISTLE
PATLY
ROTLS
TITLE
WETLY

••T•L
ANTAL
ARTAL
ARTEL
BETEL
BOTEL
BUTYL
DOTAL
EXTOL
FATAL
FETAL
HOTEL
INTEL
METAL
MOTEL
NATAL
OCTAL
PETAL
RATEL
SOTOL
TOTAL
UNTIL
VITAL

•••TL
YENTL

T•M••
TAMBO
TAMED
TAMER
TAMES
TAMIL
TAMMY
TAMPA
TAMPS
TEMPE
TEMPI
TEMPO
TEMPS
TEMPT
TIMED
TIMER
TIMES
TIMEX
TIMID
TIMMY
TIMON
TIMOR
TOMEI
TOMES
TOMMY
TUMID
TUMMY
TUMPS

T••M•
TAMMY
TEAMS
TEEMS
TERMS
THEMA
THEME
THEMS
THUMB
THUMP
THYME
THYMY
TIMMY
TOMMY
TORME
TRAMP
TRAMS
TRIMS
TROMP
TRUMP
TRYME
TUMMY

T•••M
TATUM
TENAM
TENPM
THERM
THRUM
TOTEM
TWOAM
TWOPM

•TM••
ATMAN
ATMOS

•T•M•
ATOMS
ATOMY
ETYMA
ITEMS
ITSME
OTOMI
STAMP
STEMS
STOMA
STOMP
STUMP
STUMS
STYMY

•T••M
ATEAM
STEAM
STORM
STROM
STRUM
STURM

••TM•
GETME
HITME
NOTME

••T•M
DATUM
ENTOM
TATUM
TOTEM

TN•••
TNOTE
TNUTS

T•N••
TANDE
TANDY
TANEY
TANGO
TANGS
TANGY
TANKA
TANKS
TANSY
TANTE
TANTO
TANYA
TENAM
TENCH
TENDS
TENET
TENON
TENOR
TENPM
TENSE
TENTH
TENTS
TINCT
TINED
TINES
TINGE
TINGS
TINNY
TINTS
TONAL
TONDI
TONDO
TONED
TONER
TONES
TONEY
TONGA
TONGS
TONIC
TONIO
TONKA
TONNE
TONTO
TONUS
TONYA
TONYS
TUNAS
TUNED
TUNER
TUNES
TUNIC
TUNIS
TUNNY
TYNAN
TYNES

T••N•
TAINE
TAINO
TAINT
TARNS
TAUNT
TAWNY
TBOND
TBONE
TEENA
TEENS
TEENY
TERNE
TERNS
THANE
THANK
THANT
THINE
THING
THINK
THINS
THONG
THUNK
TIANT
TINNY
TONNE
TOONS
TOWNE
TOWNS
TOWNY
TRANS
TREND
TRENT
TRINE
TRINI
TRUNK
TURNS
TWANG
TWINE
TWINS
TYING

T•••N
TAKEN
TAKIN
TALON
TAPIN
TAUON
TAXON
TENON
TETON
TEXAN
THORN
TIEIN
TIMON
TIPIN
TIRAN
TITAN
TOEIN
TOKEN
TOXIN
TOYON
TRAIN
TREEN
TRYON
TURIN
TWAIN
TWEEN
TYNAN
TYSON

•TN••
ATNOS
ETNAS

•T•N•
ATONE
ATONY
ETHNO
ETONS
STAND
STANG
STANK
STENO
STENS
STING
STINK
STINT
STONE
STONY
STUNG
STUNK
STUNS
STUNT
STYNE

•T••N
ATEIN
ATHON
ATION
ATMAN
ETHAN
LTGEN
STAIN
STEEN
STEIN
STERN
UTAHN
UTURN

••TN•
AETNA
PATNA

••T•N
ACTIN
ACTON
AFTON
ALTON
ANTON
ASTIN
ASTON
BATON
BETON
CUTIN
EATEN
EATIN
EATON
ELTON
FITIN
FUTON
GATUN
GETIN
GETON
GOTIN
GOTON
GUTEN
HITON
LATEN
LATIN
LETIN
LETON
LITON
MATIN
NOTIN
OATEN
OFTEN
ORTON
PATEN
PATON
PITON
PUTIN
PUTON
RATON
RUTIN
SATAN
SATIN
SATON
SETIN
SETON
SITIN
SITON
TETON
TITAN
UPTON
WOTAN

TO•••
TOADS
TOADY
TOAST
TOBES
TOBEY
TOBIT
TOBOL
TODAY
TODDY
TODOS
TOEIN
TOFFS
TOFFY
TOFTS
TOGAE
TOGAS
TOILE
TOILS
TOITY
TOKAY
TOKEN
TOKYO
TOLER
TOLET
TOLLS
TOLLY
TOMEI
TOMES
TOMMY
TONAL
TONDI
TONDO
TONED
TONER
TONES
TONEY
TONGA
TONGS
TONIC
TONIO
TONKA
TONNE
TONTO
TONUS
TONYA
TONYS
TOOLS
TOONS
TOOTH
TOOTS
TOPAZ
TOPED
TOPER
TOPES
TOPIC
TOPIS
TOPOG
TOPOI
TOPOL
TOPOS
TOPPS
TOPSY
TOQUE
TORAH
TORCH
TORIC
TORII
TORME
TOROS
TORRE
TORRS
TORSI
TORSO
TORTE
TORTS
TORUS
TOSCA
TOTAL
TOTED
TOTEM
TOTER
TOTES
TOTIE
TOTIS
TOTUP
TOUCH
TOUGH
TOURS
TOUTE
TOUTS
TOVES
TOWED
TOWEL
TOWER
TOWIT
TOWNE
TOWNS
TOWNY
TOXIC
TOXIN
TOYED
TOYON

T•O••
TBOND
TBONE
THOLE
THONG
THORN
THORO
THORP
THOSE
THOTH
THOUS
TNOTE
TOOLS
TOONS
TOOTH
TOOTS
TROIS
TROLL
TROMP
TROOP
TROPE
TROPO
TROTH
TROTS
TROUT
TROVE
TWOAM
TWOPM

T••O•
TABOO
TABOR
TACOS
TAHOE
TALON
TALOS
TAROK
TAROT
TAUON
TAXON
TELOS
TENON
TENOR
TETON
THEOL
THROB
THROE
THROW
TIMON
TIMOR
TIROS
TOBOL
TODOS
TOPOG
TOPOI
TOPOL
TOPOS
TOROS
TOYON
TRIOS
TROOP
TRYON
TUDOR
TUROW
TUTOR
TYPOS
TYROL
TYROS
TYSON

T•••O
TABOO
TACHO
TAINO
TAMBO
TANGO
TANTO
TASSO
TAUPO
TAURO
TAUTO
TAXCO
TELEO
TEMPO
THORO
TIETO
TOKYO
TONDO
TONIO
TONTO
TORSO
TROPO
TRURO
TURBO
TYCHO

•TO••
ATOLL
ATOMS
ATOMY

ATONE
ATONY
ETONS
OTOES
OTOMI
STOAE
STOAS
STOAT
STOCK
STOGY
STOIC
STOKE
STOLA
STOLE
STOLS
STOMA
STOMP
STONE
STONY
STOOD
STOOK
STOOL
STOOP
STOPE
STOPS
STORE
STORK
STORM
STORY
STOSS
STOTS
STOUP
STOUT
STOVE
STOWE
STOWS
VTOLS

•T•O•
ATHOL
ATHON
ATHOS
ATION
ATMOS
ATNOS
ETHOS
LTCOL
LTGOV
STOOD
STOOK
STOOL
STOOP
STROM
STROP

•T••O
ETHNO
ITALO
PTERO
STENO
STYLO

••TO•
ACTON
ACTOR
AFTON
ALTON
ALTOS
ANTON
ARTOO
ASTON
ASTOR
AUTOS
BATON
BATOR
BETON
DETOO
EATON
ELTON
ENTOM
ESTOP
EXTOL
FETOR
FSTOP
FUTON
GATOR
GATOS
GETON
GOTON
HITON
INTOW
JATOS
KOTOS
LETON
LITON
METOO
MOTOR
ONTOP
ORTON
PATON
PITON
PITOT
POTOK
PUTON
RATON
RETOP
RETOW
ROTOR
ROTOS
SATON
SETON
SITON
SOTOL
TETON
TUTOR
UPTON
ZZTOP

••T•O
ALTHO
ANTHO
ARTOO
ASTRO
BATHO
BUTEO
DETOO
DITTO
DOTTO
EXTRO
GETGO
GETTO
GITGO
GOTTO
HATLO
IATRO
INTRO
INTWO
LETGO
LITHO
LOTTO
MATEO
MATRO
MATZO
METOO
METRO
MOTTO
NITRO
NOTSO
ORTHO
OSTEO
OUTDO
OUTGO
PATHO
PATIO
PETRO
POTTO
PUTTO
RATIO
RATSO
RETRO
SETTO
SOTHO
SOTTO

•••TO
AALTO
ACETO
ADDTO
AIMTO
AMATO
ANETO
BALTO
BLUTO
BOITO
CANTO
CENTO
DEUTO
DITTO
DOTTO
DUETO
ERATO
FACTO
FEMTO
FRITO
GETTO
GOTTO
GUSTO
HADTO
HASTO
HECTO
HIPTO
HOWTO
JUNTO
KYOTO
LACTO
LAYTO
LEDTO
LENTO
LEPTO
LIETO
LOTTO
MINTO
MOLTO
MOTTO
NEATO
PANTO
PASTO
PESTO
PHOTO
PHYTO
PINTO
PLATO
PLUTO
PORTO
POTTO
PRATO
PROTO
PUTTO
QUITO
RANTO
RECTO
RUNTO
SANTO
SARTO
SAWTO
SEATO
SEETO
SETTO
SOTTO
TANTO
TAUTO
TIETO
TONTO
XACTO

T•P••
TAPAS
TAPED
TAPER
TAPES
TAPIN
TAPIR
TEPAL
TEPEE
TEPID
TIPIN
TIPPI
TIPPY
TIPSY
TIPUP
TOPAZ
TOPED
TOPER
TOPES
TOPIC
TOPIS
TOPOG
TOPOI
TOPOL
TOPOS
TOPPS
TOPSY
TYPEA
TYPEB
TYPED
TYPEE
TYPER
TYPES
TYPEY
TYPOS

T••P•
TAMPA
TAMPS
TARPS
TAUPE
TAUPO
TBSPS
TEMPE
TEMPI
TEMPO
TEMPS
TEMPT
TENPM
TERPS
TIPPI
TIPPY
TOPPS
TRAPP
TRAPS
TRIPE
TRIPS
TROPE
TROPO
TUMPS
TWOPM

T•••P
TAGUP
TEEUP
THARP
THORP
THUMP
TIEUP
TIPUP
TOTUP
TRAMP
TRAPP
TROMP
TROOP
TRUMP
TULIP
TWERP

•TP••
ATPAR
STPAT

•T•P•
ETAPE
QTIPS
STEPS
STIPE
STOPE
STOPS
STUPA
STUPE

•T••P
ATEUP
ATRIP
PTRAP
STAMP
STEEP
STOMP
STOOP
STOUP
STRAP
STREP
STRIP
STROP
STUMP

••T•P
ACTUP
CUTUP
EATUP
ESTOP
FSTOP
GETUP
GOTUP
HETUP
HITUP
LETUP
LITUP
NOTUP
ONTAP
ONTOP
PUTUP
RETAP
RETOP
SATUP
SETUP
SITUP
TOTUP
ZZTOP

T•Q••
TOQUE
TUQUE

•TQ••
ATQUE

•T•Q•
ETSQQ

•T••Q
ETSEQ
ETSQQ

••T•Q
ANTIQ

TR•••
TRACE
TRACK
TRACT
TRACY
TRADE
TRAIL
TRAIN
TRAIT
TRALA
TRAMP
TRAMS
TRANS
TRAPP
TRAPS
TRASH
TRAVE
TRAWL
TRAYS
TREAD
TREAT
TREED
TREEN
TREES
TREKS
TREND
TRENT
TRESS
TREVI
TREWS
TREYS
TRIAD
TRIAL
TRIBE
TRICE
TRICK
TRIED
TRIER
TRIES
TRIGS
TRIKE
TRILL
TRIMS
TRINE
TRINI
TRIOS
TRIPE
TRIPS
TRISH
TRITE
TRITT
TROIS
TROLL
TROMP
TROOP
TROPE
TROPO
TROTH
TROTS
TROUT
TROVE
TRUCE
TRUCK
TRUED
TRUER
TRUES
TRUEX
TRUGS
TRULY
TRUMP
TRUNK
TRURO
TRUSS
TRUST
TRUTH
TRYME
TRYON
TRYST

T•R••
TARDE
TARDY
TARES
TARGE
TARNS
TAROK
TAROT
TARPS
TARRY
TARSI
TARTS
TARTU
TERMS
TERNE
TERNS
TERPS
TERRA
TERRE
TERRI
TERRY
TERSE
TERZA
THREE
THREW
THROB
THROE
THROW
THRUM
TIRAN
TIRED
TIRES
TIROS
TORAH
TORCH
TORIC
TORII
TORME
TOROS
TORRE
TORRS
TORSI
TORSO
TORTE
TORTS
TORUS
TURBO
TURFS
TURFY
TURIN
TURKS
TURKU
TURNS
TUROW
TURVY
TYRES
TYROL
TYROS

T••R•
TAHRS
TARRY
TATRA
TAURO
TAYRA
TBARS
TBIRD
TEARS
TEARY
TERRA
TERRE
TERRI
TERRY
TETRA
THARP
THERA
THERE
THERM
THIRD
THORN
THORO
THORP
THURS
TIARA
TIERS
TITRE
TORRE
TORRS
TOURS
TRURO
TSARS
TWERE
TWERP
TWIRL
TZARS

T•••R
TABOR
TAKER
TALER
TAMER
TAPER
TAPIR
TASER
TATAR
TATER
TAXER
TENOR
THEIR
TIBER
TIGER
TILER
TIMER
TIMOR
TITER
TOLER
TONER
TOPER
TOTER
TOWER
TRIER
TRUER
TUBER
TUDOR
TUNER
TUTOR
TWEER
TYLER
TYPER

•TR••
ATRIA
ATRIP
PTRAP
STRAD
STRAP
STRAW
STRAY
STREP
STREW
STRIA
STRIP
STROM
STROP
STRUG
STRUM
STRUT

•T•R•
ATARI
ITERS
OTARU
OTARY
PTERO
STARE
STARK
STARR
STARS
START
STARZ
STERE
STERN
STIRK
STIRS
STORE
STORK
STORM
STORY
STURM
UTURN

•T••R
ATPAR
ATTAR
ATWAR
ETHER
ETVIR
OTHER
OTTER
STAIR
STARR
STEER
UTHER
UTTER

••TR•
AFTRA
ANTRA
ANTRE
ASTRA
ASTRE
ASTRO
AUTRE
AUTRY
DETRE
ENTRE
ENTRY
EXTRA
EXTRO
IATRO
IATRY
INTRA
INTRO
LATRY
LITRE
MATRI
MATRO
METRE
METRO
METRY
MITRE
NITRE
NITRO
NOTRE
OUTRE
PATRI
PETRA
PETRI
PETRO
RETRO
RETRY
SUTRA
TATRA
TETRA
TITRE
ULTRA
VOTRE

••T•R
ACTER
ACTOR
AFTER
ALTAR
ALTER
APTER
ARTHR
ARTUR
ASTER
ASTIR
ASTOR
ATTAR
BATOR
BITER
CATER
CITER
CUTER
DATER
DETER
DOTER
EATER
ENTER
ESTER
FETOR
GATOR
HATER
INTER
JETER
KITER
LATER
LITER
MATER
METER
MITER
MOTOR
MUTER
NITER
NOTER
OATER
OTTER
OUTER
PATER
PETER
QATAR
RATER
RETAR
ROTOR
SATYR
SITAR
TATAR
TATER
TITER
TOTER
TUTOR
UNTER
UTTER
VATER
VOTER
WATER

•••TR
AUSTR
CONTR
DEXTR
DISTR
GASTR
INSTR

TS•••
TSADE
TSARS
TSGTS

T•S••
TASER
TASKS
TASSE
TASSO
TASTE
TASTY
TBSPS
TESLA
TESTA
TESTS
TESTY
TISZA
TOSCA
TUSKS
TVSET
TYSON

T••S•
TANSY
TARSI
TASSE
TASSO
TEASE
TENSE
TERSE
THESE
THOSE
TIPSY
TOAST
TOPSY
TORSI
TORSO
TRASH
TRESS
TRISH
TRUSS
TRUST
TRYST
TULSA
TWIST

T•••S
TABIS
TACKS
TACOS
TAELS
TAGUS
TAHRS
TAILS
TAKAS
TAKES
TALES
TALKS
TALOS
TALUS
TAMES
TAMPS
TANGS
TANKS
TAPAS
TAPES
TARES
TARNS
TARPS
TARTS
TASKS
TAXES
TAXIS
TBARS
TBSPS
TEAKS
TEALS
TEAMS
TEARS
TECHS
TEEMS
TEENS
TELES
TELLS
TELOS
TEMPS
TENDS
TENTS
TERMS
TERNS
TERPS
TESTS
TETES
TETHS
TEXAS
TEXTS
THAIS
THATS
THAWS
THEMS
THEWS
THINS
THOUS
THUDS
THUGS
THURS
TIBBS
TICKS
TIDES
TIEGS
TIERS
TIFFS
TIKES
TIKIS
TILES
TILLS
TILTS
TIMES
TINES
TINGS
TINTS
TIRES
TIROS
TITIS
TITUS
TNUTS
TOADS
TOBES
TODOS
TOFFS
TOFTS
TOGAS
TOILS
TOLLS
TOMES
TONES
TONGS
TONUS
TONYS
TOOLS
TOONS
TOOTS
TOPES
TOPIS
TOPOS
TOPPS
TOROS
TORRS
TORTS
TORUS
TOTES
TOTIS
TOURS
TOUTS
TOVES
TOWNS
TRAMS
TRANS
TRAPS
TRAYS
TREES
TREKS
TRESS
TREWS
TREYS
TRIES
TRIGS
TRIMS
TRIOS
TRIPS
TROIS
TROTS
TRUES
TRUGS
TRUSS
TSARS
TSGTS
TUBAS
TUBES
TUCKS
TUFTS
TULES
TUMPS
TUNAS
TUNES
TUNIS
TURFS
TURKS
TURNS
TUSKS
TUTUS
TUXES
TWIGS
TWINS
TWITS
TYKES
TYNES
TYPES
TYPOS
TYRES
TYROS
TZARS

•TS••
ATSEA
ETSEQ
ETSQQ
ITSME

•T•S•
STASH
STOSS

•T••S
ATHOS
ATLAS
ATMOS
ATNOS
ATOMS
ATTYS
ETATS
ETHOS
ETNAS
ETONS
ETUIS
FTLBS
ITALS
ITEMS
ITERS
OTOES
QTIPS
STABS
STAGS
STARS
STATS
STAYS
STEMS
STENS
STEPS
STETS
STEWS
STIES
STIRS
STOAS
STOLS
STOPS
STOSS
STOTS
STOWS
STUBS
STUDS
STUMS
STUNS
VTOLS

••TS•
ANTSY
ARTSY
BETSY
BITSY
DITSY
GUTSY
MATSU
NOTSO
NUTSY
PATSY
POTSY
RATSO

••T•S
ACTAS
ALTOS
ALTUS
ANTAS
ANTES
ANTIS
ARTES
ARTIS
ATTYS
AUTOS
BATES
BATHS
BATTS
BETAS
BETHS
BITES
BITTS
BUTTS
BYTES
CATES
CETUS
CITES
COTES
CUTIS
DATES
DOTES
ESTAS
ESTES
FATES
FETAS
FETES
GATES
GATOS
GETAS
GOTHS
HATES
HETHS
HUTUS
ICTUS
IOTAS
JATOS
JETES
JOTAS
JUTES
KITES
KITTS
KOTOS
LATHS
LETTS
LITES
LITHS
LOTAS
LOTUS
LUTES
MATES
MATHS
METES
METIS
MITES
MITTS
MOTES
MOTHS
MOTTS
MUTES
MUTTS
MYTHS
NITES
NOTES
OATES
OATHS
PATES
PATHS
PETES
PITAS
PITHS
PITTS
POTTS
PUTTS
RATES
RATHS
RITES
ROTAS
ROTES
ROTLS
ROTOS
SATES
SITES
SITUS
SRTAS
TETES
TETHS
TITIS
TITUS
TOTES
TOTIS
TUTUS
VITAS
VITUS
VOTES
WATTS
YATES
YETIS
ZETAS
ZITIS

•••TS
ABETS
ABUTS
ACCTS
ADITS
APPTS
ASSTS
AUNTS
BAHTS
BAITS
BALTS
BARTS
BATTS
BEATS
BEETS
BELTS
BENTS
BESTS
BITTS
BLATS
BLOTS
BOATS
BOLTS
BOOTS
BOUTS
BRATS
BRITS
BRUTS
BUNTS
BUSTS
BUTTS
CANTS
CAPTS
CARTS
CASTS
CELTS
CENTS
CERTS
CHATS
CHITS
CLOTS
COATS
COLTS
COOTS
COPTS
COSTS
CULTS
DARTS
DEBTS
DELTS
DENTS
DEPTS
DICTS
DIETS
DINTS
DOITS
DOLTS
DRATS
DUCTS
DUETS
DUSTS
EASTS
EDITS
EMITS
ETATS
EXITS
EYOTS
FACTS
FASTS
FEATS
FEETS
FELTS
FESTS
FIATS
FISTS
FLATS
FLITS
FONTS
FOOTS
FORTS
FOUTS
FRATS
FRETS
FRITS
GAITS
GENTS
GESTS
GHATS
GIFTS
GILTS
GIRTS
GISTS
GLUTS
GMATS
GNATS
GOATS
GRITS
GROTS
GUSTS
HAFTS
HALTS
HANTS
HARTS
HEATS
HEFTS
HENTS
HESTS
HILTS
HINTS
HOOTS
HOSTS
HUNTS
HURTS
INITS
INSTS
JESTS
JILTS
JOLTS
KEATS
KEETS
KILTS
KITTS
KNITS
KNOTS
KYATS
LASTS
LEETS
LEFTS
LENTS
LETTS
LIFTS
LILTS
LINTS
LISTS
LOFTS
LOOTS
LOUTS
LSATS
LUSTS
MALTS
MARTS
MASTS
MEATS
MEETS
MELTS
MILTS
MINTS
MISTS
MITTS
MOATS
MOLTS
MOOTS
MORTS
MOTTS
MSGTS
MUSTS
MUTTS
NEATS
NERTS
NESTS
NEWTS
NYETS
OASTS
ODETS
OMITS
OUSTS
PACTS
PANTS
PARTS
PASTS
PEATS
PELTS
PESTS
PHOTS
PICTS
PINTS
PITTS
PLATS
PLOTS
POETS
PONTS
PORTS
POSTS
POTTS
POUTS
PROTS
PSATS
PUNTS
PUTTS
QUITS
RAFTS
RANTS
RENTS
RESTS
RIFTS
RIOTS
ROOTS
ROUTS
RUNTS
RUSTS
RYOTS
SALTS
SCATS
SCOTS
SCUTS
SEATS
SECTS
SEXTS
SHOTS
SHUTS
SIFTS
SILTS
SKITS
SLATS
SLITS
SLOTS
SMITS
SMUTS
SNITS
SOOTS
SORTS
SPATS
SPETS
SPITS
SPOTS
SSGTS
STATS
STETS
STOTS
SUETS
SUITS
SUPTS
SWATS
TARTS
TENTS
TESTS
TEXTS
THATS
TILTS
TINTS
TNUTS
TOFTS
TOOTS
TORTS
TOUTS
TROTS
TSGTS
TUFTS

TWITS
UNITS
VENTS
VERTS
VESTS
VOLTS
WAFTS
WAITS
WANTS
WARTS
WATTS
WEFTS
WELTS
WESTS
WHATS
WHETS
WHITS
WILTS
WONTS
WORTS
WRITS
YEATS
YURTS
ZESTS

T•T••
TATAR
TATER
TATRA
TATTY
TATUM
TETES
TETHS
TETON
TETRA
TITAN
TITER
TITHE
TITIS
TITLE
TITRE
TITUS
TOTAL
TOTED
TOTEM
TOTER
TOTES
TOTIE
TOTIS
TOTUP
TUTEE
TUTOR
TUTTI
TUTUS

T••T•
TANTE
TANTO
TARTS
TARTU
TASTE
TASTY
TATTY
TAUTO
TEETH
TENTH
TENTS
TESTA
TESTS
TESTY
TEXTS
THATS
THETA
THOTH
TIETO
TILTH
TILTS
TINTS
TNOTE
TNUTS
TOFTS
TOITY
TONTO
TOOTH
TOOTS
TORTE
TORTS
TOUTE
TOUTS
TRITE
TRITT
TROTH
TROTS
TRUTH
TSGTS
TUFTS
TUFTY
TUTTI
TWITS

T•••T
TACET
TACIT
TAINT
TAROT
TAUNT
TEMPT
TENET
TEVET
THANT
THEFT
TIANT
TIBET
TIGHT
TINCT
TOAST
TOBIT
TOLET
TOWIT
TRACT
TRAIT
TREAT
TRENT
TRITT
TROUT
TRUST
TRYST
TVSET
TWEET
TWIST
TWIXT

•TT••
ATTAR
ATTIC
ATTYS
OTTER
UTTER

•T•T•
ETATS
STATE
STATS
STETS
STOTS
STUTZ

•T••T
ATBAT
ATILT
STADT
START
STILT
STINT
STOAT
STOUT
STPAT
STRUT
STUNT

••TT•
BATTS
BATTY
BETTA
BETTE
BETTY
BITTE
BITTS
BITTY
BUTTE
BUTTS
BUTTY
CATTY
COTTA
DITTO
DITTY
DOTTO
DOTTY
FATTY
GETTO
GETTY
GOTTA
GOTTO
GUTTA
GUTTY
HETTY
JETTY
JUTTY
KITTS
KITTY
LATTE
LETTS
LOTTA
LOTTE
LOTTO
LYTTA
MATTE
MITTS
MITTY
MOTTA
MOTTO
MOTTS
MUTTS
NATTY
NITTI
NITTY
NUTTY
PATTI
PATTY
PETTI
PETTY
PITTA
PITTS
POTTO
POTTS
POTTY
PUTTI
PUTTO
PUTTS
PUTTY
RATTY
RUTTY
SETTE
SETTO
SOTTO
TATTY
TUTTI
WATTS
WITTE
WITTY

••T•T
AETAT
BUTUT
DETAT
DITAT
EATAT
EATIT
GETAT
GETIT
GOTAT
GOTIT
HITIT
LETAT
MOTET
NOTIT
OCTET
PETIT
PITOT
SETAT

•••TT
BLITT
BRETT
BRITT
FLATT
HYATT
OVETT
PLATT
PRATT
RAITT
RHETT
SCOTT
SHATT
TRITT
WYATT

TU•••
TUBAS
TUBBY
TUBED
TUBER
TUBES
TUCKS
TUDOR
TUFTS
TUFTY
TULES
TULIP
TULLE
TULLY
TULSA
TUMID
TUMMY
TUMPS
TUNAS
TUNED
TUNER
TUNES
TUNIC
TUNIS
TUNNY
TUQUE
TURBO
TURFS
TURFY
TURIN
TURKS
TURKU
TURNS
TUROW
TURVY
TUSKS
TUTEE
TUTOR
TUTTI
TUTUS
TUXES

T•U••
TAUNT
TAUON
TAUPE
TAUPO
TAURO
TAUTO
THUDS
THUGS
THUJA
THULE
THUMB
THUMP
THUNK
THURS
TNUTS
TOUCH
TOUGH
TOURS
TOUTE
TOUTS
TRUCE
TRUCK
TRUED
TRUER
TRUES
TRUEX
TRUGS
TRULY
TRUMP
TRUNK
TRURO
TRUSS
TRUST
TRUTH

T••U•
TAGUP
TAGUS
TALUS
TATUM
TEEUP
THOUS
THRUM
TIEUP
TIPUP
TITUS
TONUS
TOQUE
TORUS
TOTUP
TROUT
TUQUE
TUTUS

T•••U
TAEGU
TARTU
TURKU

•TU••
ETUDE
ETUIS
STUBS
STUCK
STUDS
STUDY
STUFF
STUKA
STULL
STUMP
STUMS
STUNG
STUNK
STUNS
STUNT
STUPA
STUPE
STURM
STUTZ
UTURN

•T•U•
ATEUP
ATQUE
STOUP
STOUT
STRUG
STRUM
STRUT

•T••U
OTARU

••TU•
ACTUP
ALTUS
ARTUR
BUTUT
CETUS
CUTUP
DATUM
EATUP
GATUN
GETUP
GOTUP
HETUP
HITUP
HUTUS
ICTUS
LETUP
LITUP
LOTUS
NOTUP
PUTUP
SATUP
SETUP
SITUP
SITUS
TATUM
TITUS
TOTUP
TUTUS
VITUS

••T•U
MATSU

•••TU
BANTU
DICTU
TARTU
VIRTU

TV•••
TVSET

T•V••
TEVET
TEVYE
TOVES

T••V•
TRAVE
TREVI
TROVE
TURVY

•TV••
ETVIR

•T•V•
ATIVE
STAVE
STEVE
STOVE

•T••V
LTGOV

••T•V
ACTIV

•••TV
ABCTV
CBSTV
FOXTV
NBCTV
PAYTV

TW•••
TWAIN
TWANG
TWEAK
TWEED
TWEEN
TWEER
TWEET
TWERE
TWERP
TWICE
TWIGS
TWILL
TWINE
TWINS
TWIRL
TWIST
TWITS
TWIXT
TWOAM
TWOPM
TWYLA

T•W••
TAWNY
TOWED
TOWEL
TOWER
TOWIT
TOWNE
TOWNS
TOWNY

T••W•
THAWS
THEWS
THEWY
TRAWL
TREWS

T•••W
THREW
THROW
TUROW

•TW••
ATWAR
OTWAY

•T•W•
STEWS
STOWE
STOWS

•T••W
STRAW
STREW

••TW•
FATWA
INTWO
KITWE

••T•W
INTOW
RETOW

T•X••
TAXCO
TAXED
TAXER
TAXES
TAXIS
TAXON
TEXAN
TEXAS
TEXTS
TOXIC
TOXIN
TUXES

T••X•
TWIXT

T•••X
TELEX
TIMEX
TRUEX

••T•X
CUTEX
LATEX
RETAX

TY•••
TYCHE
TYCHO
TYING
TYKES
TYLER
TYNAN
TYNES
TYPEA
TYPEB
TYPED
TYPEE
TYPER
TYPES
TYPEY
TYPOS
TYRES
TYROL
TYROS
TYSON

T•Y••
TAYRA
THYME
THYMY
TOYED
TOYON
TRYME
TRYON
TRYST
TWYLA

T••Y•
TANYA
TEVYE
THEYD
TOKYO
TONYA
TONYS
TRAYS
TREYS

T•••Y
TABBY
TACHY
TACKY
TAFFY
TALKY
TALLY
TAMMY
TANDY
TANEY
TANGY
TANSY
TARDY
TARRY
TASTY
TATTY
TAWNY
TEARY
TECHY
TEDDY
TEENY
TELLY
TERRY
TESTY
THEWY
THYMY
TICKY
TILLY
TIMMY
TINNY
TIPPY
TIPSY
TIZZY
TOADY
TOBEY
TODAY
TODDY
TOFFY
TOITY
TOKAY
TOLLY
TOMMY
TONEY
TOPSY
TOWNY
TRACY
TRULY
TUBBY
TUFTY
TULLY
TUMMY
TUNNY
TURFY
TURVY
TYPEY

•TY••
ETYMA
STYLE
STYLI
STYLO
STYMY
STYNE

•T•Y•
ATTYS
ETHYL
STAYS

•T••Y
ATBAY
ATOMY
ATONY
ITALY
ITCHY
OTARY

OTWAY
STACY
STAGY
STOGY
STONY
STORY
STRAY
STUDY
STYMY
UTLEY

••TY•
ATTYS
BUTYL
SATYR

••T•Y
ANTSY
APTLY
ARTSY
AUTRY
BATHY
BATTY
BETSY
BETTY
BITSY
BITTY
BUTTY
CATHY
CATTY
CUTEY
DITSY
DITTY
DITZY
DOTTY
ENTRY
FATLY
FATTY
FITLY
GETBY
GETTY
GOTBY
GUTSY
GUTTY
HETTY
HOTLY
IATRY
JETTY
JUTTY
KATHY
KITTY
LATHY
LATRY
MATEY
METRY
MITTY
MOTHY
NATTY
NITTY
NUTSY
NUTTY
PATHY
PATLY
PATSY
PATTY
PETTY
PITHY
POTSY
POTTY
PUTBY
PUTTY
RATTY
RETRY
RITZY
RUTTY
SATBY
SETBY
SITBY
TATTY
WETLY
WITHY
WITTY

•••TY
AMITY
AUNTY
BARTY
BATTY
BETTY
BITTY
BOOTY
BUTTY
CANTY
CATTY
DEITY
DINTY
DIRTY
DITTY
DOTTY
DUSTY
EMPTY
FATTY
FIFTY
FLUTY
FORTY
FUSTY
GETTY
GOUTY
GUSTY
GUTTY
HASTY
HEFTY
HETTY
HOITY
JETTY
JOLTY
JUTTY
KITTY
LAITY
LEFTY
LINTY
LOFTY
LUSTY
MALTY
MARTY
MEATY
MELTY
MILTY
MINTY
MISTY
MITTY
MONTY
MUSTY
NASTY
NATTY
NIFTY
NITTY
NUTTY
PARTY
PASTY
PATTY
PEATY
PETTY
PIETY
PLATY
POTTY
POUTY
PUNTY
PUTTY
RATTY
ROOTY
RUNTY
RUSTY
RUTTY
SALTY
SILTY
SIXTY
SLATY
SOFTY
SOOTY
SUETY
TASTY
TATTY
TESTY
TOITY
TUFTY
UNITY
VASTY
WARTY
WELTY
WHITY
WITTY
ZESTY
ZLOTY

TZ•••
TZARS

T•Z••
TAZZA
TIZZY

T••Z•
TAZZA
TERZA
TISZA
TIZZY

T•••Z
TOPAZ

•TZ••
ETZEL

•T••Z
STARZ
STUTZ

••TZ•
DITZY
MATZO
MITZI
RITZY

•••TZ
BLITZ
FRITZ
GLITZ
HERTZ
HOLTZ
HUNTZ
KLUTZ
KURTZ
LANTZ
MERTZ
NERTZ
SPITZ
STUTZ
SWITZ
WAITZ
WALTZ

U•A••
UDALL
UHAUL
UKASE
UNAPT
UNARM
UNAUS
URALS
USAGE
USAIR
UTAHN
UZALA

U••A•
UBOAT
UCLAN
UHLAN
ULNAE
ULNAS
UMIAK
UNBAR
UNCAP
UNCAS
UNJAM
UNLAY
UNMAN
UNSAY
URBAN
URIAH
URIAL
USUAL
UXMAL

U•••A
UHURA
UINTA
ULTRA
UMBRA
UNRRA
USCGA
USLTA
USOFA
UTICA
UVULA
UZALA

•UA••
DUADS
DUANE
GUACO
GUARD
GUARS
GUAVA
KUALA
LUAUS
QUACK
QUADR
QUADS
QUAFF
QUAGS
QUAID
QUAIL
QUAKE
QUAKY
QUALE
QUALM
QUAND
QUANT
QUARE
QUARK
QUART
QUASH
QUASI
QUAYS
RUANA
RUARK
SUAVE
YUANS

•U•A•
AURAE
AURAL
AURAR
AURAS
CUBAN
CUGAT
CUMAE
CUNAS
DUBAI
DUCAL
DUCAT
DUFAY
DUGAN
DUKAS
DUMAS
DURAN
FUGAL
FULAS
FURAN
GULAG
GULAR
HULAS
HUMAN
HUNAN
JUBAL
JUDAH
JUDAS
JUGAL
JURAL
JURAT
KULAK
LUBAS
LUCAN
LUCAS
LUKAS
LUNAR
LURAY
MURAL
MURAT
MUZAK
NUGAE
PULAS
PUMAS
PUNAS
PUPAE
PUPAL
PUPAS
PUSAN
QUOAD
RUGAE
RUNAT
RURAL
SUDAN
SUGAR
SUMAC
SURAH
SURAL
SURAS
SURAT
SUSAN
TUBAS
TUNAS
WUHAN
YUGAS
YUMAN
YUMAS

•U••A
AUDRA
BUBBA
BUENA
BUFFA
BULBA
BULLA
BURMA
BURSA
CULPA
CUPPA
CURIA
DURRA
FULDA
GUAVA
GUNGA
GUTTA
HUBBA
HUZZA
JUDEA
JULIA
JUMNA
JUNTA
KUALA
KUKLA
LUCCA
LUCIA
LUISA
LULEA
LURIA
MUDRA
MURRA
MUSCA
NUBIA
NUCHA
OUIDA
OUIJA
PUKKA
PUNTA
QUOTA
RUANA
RUMBA
SUCKA
SUDRA
SUITA
SULFA
SULLA
SUMBA
SUMMA
SUNDA
SUNNA
SUPRA
SUTRA
TULSA
YUCCA

••UA•
AQUAE
AQUAS
DOUAI
DOUAY
EQUAL
JOUAL
KAUAI
SKUAS
SQUAB
SQUAD
SQUAT
USUAL

••U•A
ABUJA
ACURA
ADUWA
ALULA
ARUBA
AZUSA
CAUSA
CEUTA
CHULA
CRURA
FAUNA
GOUDA
HAUSA
HOUMA
KRUPA
LAURA
MAUNA
PAULA
PIURA
SAUNA
SCUBA
SCUTA
SHULA
SOUSA
STUKA
STUPA
THUJA
UHURA
UVULA

•••UA
GENUA
LEHUA
MAKUA
NAHUA
PADUA
PAPUA
VACUA

UB•••
UBOAT
UBOLT

U•B••
UMBEL
UMBER
UMBOS
UMBRA
UNBAR
UNBID
UNBOX
UPBOW
URBAN
URBIS
UZBEK

•UB••
AUBER
BUBBA
BUBER
BUBUS
CUBAN
CUBBY
CUBEB
CUBED
CUBES
CUBIC
CUBIT
DUBAI
DUBIN
DUBOS
EUBIE
FUBSY
HUBBA
HUBBY
JUBAL
LUBAS
LUBED
LUBES
NUBBY
NUBIA
RUBEN
RUBES
RUBIK
RUBIN
RUBLE
SUBIC
TUBAS
TUBBY
TUBED
TUBER
TUBES
ZUBIN

•U•B•
BUBBA
BULBA
BULBS
BURBS
BUSBY
CUBBY
CURBS
DUMBO
DUMBS
GUMBO
GUMBY
HUBBA
HUBBY
JUMBO
MUMBO
NUBBY
NUMBS
PUTBY
RUGBY
RUMBA
SUMBA
TUBBY
TURBO

•U••B
CUBEB

••UB•
ARUBA
CHUBS
CLUBS
DAUBS
DOUBT
DRUBS
FLUBS
GRUBS
SCUBA
SNUBS
STUBS

••U•B
BLURB
CRUMB
EXURB
PLUMB
RHUMB
SQUAB
SQUIB
THUMB

•••UB
REDUB
SCRUB
SHRUB

UC•••
UCLAN

U•C••
ULCER
UNCAP
UNCAS
UNCLE
UNCUT
USCGA

U••C•
URICH
UTICA

U•••C
UGRIC

•UC••
BUCKO
BUCKS
BUCKY
DUCAL
DUCAT
DUCES
DUCHY
DUCKS
DUCKY
DUCTS
FUCHS
GUCCI
LUCAN
LUCAS
LUCCA
LUCCI
LUCIA
LUCID
LUCIE
LUCKS
LUCKY
LUCRE
MUCIN
MUCKS
MUCKY
MUCRO
NUCHA
PUCCI
PUCKS
RUCHE
RUCKS
SUCKA
SUCKS
SUCRE
TUCKS
YUCCA
YUCKY

•U•C•
BUICK
BUNCH
BUSCH
BUTCH
CULCH
CURCI
CUZCO
DUNCE
DUTCH
GUACO
GUCCI
GULCH
HULCE
HUNCH
HUTCH
JUICE
JUICY
JUNCO
LUCCA
LUCCI
LUNCH
LURCH
MULCH
MULCT
MUNCH
MUSCA
OUNCE
PUCCI
PUNCH
QUACK
QUICK
SULCI
YUCCA

•U••C
AURIC
CUBIC
DUROC
LUDIC
MUSIC
PUNIC
RUNIC
SUBIC

SUMAC
TUNIC

••UC•
AMUCK
BRUCE
BRUCH
CHUCK
CLUCK
COUCH
DEUCE
DEUCY
EDUCE
EDUCT
ERUCT
GLUCK
GLUCO
PLUCK
POUCH
SAUCE
SAUCY
SHUCK
SNUCK
STUCK
TOUCH
TRUCE
TRUCK
VOUCH

UD•••
UDALL
UDDER
UDINE

U•D••
UDDER
UNDER
UNDID
UNDUE
UPDOS

U•••D
UMPED
UNBID
UNDID
UNFED
UNLED
UNWED
UPEND
UPPED
URGED
URSID
USHED
USTED

•UD••
AUDEN
AUDIE
AUDIO
AUDIS
AUDIT
AUDRA
BUDDY
BUDGE
CUDDY
DUDDY
DUDES
FUDDY
FUDGE
JUDAH
JUDAS
JUDEA
JUDEO
JUDGE
KUDOS
KUDUS
KUDZU
LUDIC
MUDDY
MUDRA
NUDER
NUDES
NUDGE
PUDGY
PUDUS
RUDDS
RUDDY
RUDER
RUDGE
SUDAN
SUDDS
SUDRA
SUDSY
TUDOR

•U•D•
BUDDY
BUNDS
BUNDT
BUNDY
CUDDY
CURDS
CURDY
DUADS
DUDDY
FUDDY
FULDA
FUNDS
FUNDY
GUIDE
GUIDO
GURDY
HURDY
KURDS
LUNDI
LUNDY
MUDDY
MUNDI
OUIDA
OUTDO
QUADR
QUADS
QUIDS
QUODS
RUDDS
RUDDY
SUDDS
SUEDE
SUNDA
SURDS

•U••D
BUILD
BUSED
CUBED
CUPID
CURED
DUKED
DUPED
FUMED
FUSED
FUZED
GUARD
GUILD
GUYED
HUMID
JUKED
LUBED
LUCID
LURED
LURID
MUSED
MUTED
NUKED
OUTED
PULED
QUAID
QUAND
QUOAD
RULED
TUBED
TUMID
TUNED

••UD•
CRUDE
ELUDE
ETUDE
EXUDE
FEUDS
GAUDS
GAUDY
GOUDA
GOUDY
JEUDI
LAUDE
LAUDS
MAUDE
PRUDE
SAUDI
SCUDI
SCUDO
SCUDS
SPUDS
STUDS
STUDY
THUDS

••U•D
BLUED
BOUND
CLUED
COULD
DRUID
FLUID
FOUND
GLUED
GOULD
GOURD
HOUND
MAUND
MOULD
MOUND
POUND
ROUND
SLUED
SOUND
SQUAD
SQUID
TRUED
WOULD
WOUND

•••UD
ALOUD
CHAUD
CLOUD
FRAUD
FREUD
LIKUD
NEFUD
PROUD
PSEUD
SALUD

U•E••
UMEKI
UPEND
USERS
USEUP

U••E•
UDDER
ULCER
UMBEL
UMBER
UMPED
UNDER
UNFED
UNGER
UNLED
UNMET
UNPEG
UNPEN
UNSER
UNSET
UNTER
UNWED
UPPED
UPPER
UPSET
URGED
URGER
URGES
URIEL
URKEL
USHED
USHER
USTED
UTHER
UTLEY
UTTER
UZBEK

U•••E
UDINE
UKASE
ULNAE
UNCLE
UNDUE
UNITE
UNTIE
USAGE
USQUE
UTILE

•UE••
BUELL
BUENA
BUENO
CUEIN
DUELS
DUETO
DUETS
FUEGO
FUELS
GUESS
GUEST
HUEVO
LUEGO
QUEEG
QUEEN
QUEER
QUELL
QUERN
QUERY
QUEST
QUEUE
RUEHL
RUERS
SUEDE
SUEME
SUERS
SUETS
SUETY

•U•E•
AUBER
AUDEN
AUGER
AUREI
BUBER
BUSED
BUSES
BUSEY
BUTEO
BUYER
CUBEB
CUBED
CUBES
CUKES
CULET
CULEX
CUNEO
CUPEL
CURED
CURER
CURES
CUTER
CUTEX
CUTEY
CUVEE
DUCES
DUDES
DUKED
DUKES
DUNES
DUPED
DUPES
DURER
DUVET
DUXES
EULER
FUMED
FUMES
FUSED
FUSEE
FUSES
FUZED
FUZEE
GULES
GUTEN
GUYED
HUGER
JUDEA
JUDEO
JUKED
JUKES
JULEP
JULES
JUTES
KUGEL
LUBED
LUBES
LUGER
LUGES
LULEA
LUMEN
LUMET
LUNES
LURED
LURES
LUREX
LUTES
MULES
MULEY
MUREX
MUSED
MUSER
MUSES
MUTED
MUTER
MUTES
NUDER
NUDES
NUKED
NUKES
NUMEN
NUYEN
OUSEL
OUTED
OUTER
OUZEL
PUGET
PULED
PULES
PUREE
PURER
PUREX
PUSEY
QUEEG
QUEEN
QUEER
QUIEN
QUIET
RUBEN
RUBES
RUDER
RULED
RULER
RULES
RUMEN
RUNES
RUPEE
RUSES
SUMER
SUPER
SUPES
SURER
TUBED
TUBER
TUBES
TULES
TUNED
TUNER
TUNES
TUTEE
TUXES

•U••E
AUDIE
AURAE
AUTRE
BUDGE
BUGLE
BULGE
BURKE
BURSE
BUTTE
CUMAE
CURIE
CURSE
CURVE
CUTIE
CUVEE
DUANE
DULSE
DUNCE
DUNNE
DUPLE
DUPRE
EUBIE
FUDGE
FUGUE
FURZE
FUSEE
FUZEE
GUIDE
GUILE
GUISE
HULCE
JUDGE
JUICE
JULIE
JUSTE
LUCIE
LUCRE
LUISE
LUNGE
LURIE
MURRE
NUDGE
NUGAE
NURSE
OUNCE
OUTRE
PULSE
PUPAE
PUREE
PURGE
PURSE
QUAKE
QUALE
QUARE
QUEUE
QUIRE
QUITE
QUOTE
RUBLE
RUCHE
RUDGE
RUGAE
RUPEE
RUSSE
SUAVE
SUCRE
SUEDE
SUEME
SUITE
SURGE
SUSIE
TULLE
TUQUE
TUTEE

••UE•
AGUES
BAUER
BLUED
BLUER
BLUES
BLUET
BLUEY
CLUED
CLUES
CRUEL
CRUET
FLUES
GLUED
GLUER
GLUES
GLUEY
GRUEL
HAUER
LAUER
MOUES
REUEL
ROUEN
ROUES
SLUED
SLUES
TRUED
TRUER
TRUES
TRUEX

••U•E
ABUSE
ACUTE
AMUSE
APURE
AQUAE
AZURE
BAUME
BLUME
BOULE
BOUSE
BRUCE
BRULE
BRUME
BRUTE
CAUSE
CHUTE
COUPE
CRUDE
CRUSE
DEUCE
DOUSE
DRUPE
DRUSE
DRUZE
EDUCE
ELUDE
ELUTE
ENURE
ETUDE
EXUDE
FAURE
FAUVE
FLUKE
FLUME
FLUTE
GAUGE
GAUZE
GOUGE
HAUTE
HEURE
HEUTE
HOUSE
INURE
INUSE
JAUNE
JEUNE
JOULE
KLUGE
KLUTE
KNUTE
LAUDE
LOUIE
LOUPE
LOUSE
MAUDE
MAUVE
MEUSE
MFUME
MOUSE
NEUME
OFUSE
OVULE
PAUSE
PLUME
PRUDE
PRUNE
REUNE
REUSE
ROUGE
ROUSE
ROUTE
SAUCE
SAUTE
SCUTE
SEULE
SHUTE
SOUSE
SPUME
STUPE
TAUPE
THULE
TOUTE
TRUCE
YOURE
YOUSE
YOUVE

•••UE
ARGUE
ATQUE
BENUE
ENDUE
ENSUE
ESQUE
FUGUE
GIGUE
HAGUE
IMBUE
ISSUE
KAFUE
LARUE
LOGUE
ONCUE
PIQUE
QUEUE
REVUE
ROGUE
ROQUE
SEGUE
SPRUE
TOQUE
TUQUE
UNDUE
USQUE
VAGUE
VALUE
VENUE
VOGUE

U•F••
UNFED
UNFIT
UNFIX

U••F•
UNIFY
USOFA

•UF••
BUFFA
BUFFI
BUFFO
BUFFS
BUFFY
CUFFS
DUFAY
DUFFS
DUFFY
HUFFS
HUFFY
LUFFS
MUFFS
MUFTI
PUFFS
PUFFY
RUFFS
RUFUS
SUFIS
TUFTS
TUFTY

•U•F•
BUFFA
BUFFI
BUFFO

BUFFS
BUFFY
CUFFS
DUFFS
DUFFY
GULFS
HUFFS
HUFFY
LUFFS
MUFFS
PUFFS
PUFFY
QUAFF
RUFFS
SULFA
SURFS
SURFY
TURFS
TURFY

•U••F
QUAFF

••UF•
ACUFF
BLUFF
CHUFF
FLUFF
GRUFF
KHUFU
POUFS
SCUFF
SNUFF
STUFF

••U•F
ACUFF
BLUFF
CHUFF
FLUFF
GRUFF
SCUFF
SCURF
SMURF
SNUFF
STUFF

•••UF
BOEUF

UG•••
UGRIC

U•G••
UIGUR
UNGER
URGED
URGER
URGES

U••G•
USAGE
USCGA

U•••G
UNPEG
UNRIG
USING

•UG••
AUGER
AUGHT
AUGUR
BUGGY
BUGLE
BUGSY
CUGAT
DUGAN
DUGIN
DUGUP
FUGAL
FUGGY
FUGIT
FUGUE
FUGUS
HUGER
HUGOS
JUGAL
JUGUM
KUGEL
LUGER
LUGES
MUGGS
MUGGY
MUGHO
NUGAE
OUGHT
PUGET
PUGGY
RUGAE
RUGBY
SUGAR
VUGGY
YUGAS
YUGOS

•U•G•
BUDGE
BUGGY
BULGE
BULGY
BUNGS
BURGS
FUDGE
FUEGO
FUGGY
FUNGI
FUNGO
GUNGA
JUDGE
LUEGO
LUIGI
LUNGE
LUNGS
MUGGS
MUGGY
MUNGO
NUDGE
OUTGO
PUDGY
PUGGY
PUNGS
PURGE
QUAGS
RUDGE
RUNGS
SURGE
VUGGY

•U••G
CUING
GULAG
QUEEG
RUING
SUING

••UG•
BAUGH
BOUGH
CHUGS
COUGH
DOUGH
DRUGS
ENUGU
GAUGE
GLUGS
GOUGE
HOUGH
KLUGE
LAUGH
LOUGH
PLUGS
ROUGE
ROUGH
SLUGS
SNUGS
SOUGH
THUGS
TOUGH
TRUGS
WAUGH

••U•G
BOURG
BRUNG
CHUNG
CLUNG
FLUNG
SLUNG
STUNG
SWUNG
WRUNG
YOUNG

•••UG
ABZUG
DEBUG
SHRUG
STRUG

UH•••
UHAUL
UHHUH
UHLAN
UHURA
UHURU

U•H••
UHHUH
UNHIP
USHED
USHER
UTHER

U••H•
UTAHN

U•••H
UHHUH
UNRUH
URIAH
URICH

•UH••
BUHLS
WUHAN

•U•H•
AUGHT
BUSHY
CUSHY
DUCHY
FUCHS
GUSHY
MUGHO
MUSHY
NUCHA
OUGHT
PUSHY
RUCHE
RUEHL
RUSHY
SUSHI
WUSHU

•U••H
BUNCH
BUSCH
BUTCH
CULCH
DUTCH
FURTH
GULCH
HUMPH
HUNCH
HUTCH
JUDAH
LUNCH
LURCH
MULCH
MUNCH
PUNCH
QUASH
QUOTH
SURAH

••UH•
BRUHN

••U•H
BAUGH
BLUSH
BLUTH
BOUGH
BRUCH
BRUSH
COUCH
COUGH
COUTH
CRUSH
DOUGH
FLUSH
FOURH
HOUGH
LAUGH
LOUGH
MOUTH
PLUSH
POUCH
ROUGH
SHUSH
SLUSH
SOUGH
SOUTH
TOUCH
TOUGH
TRUTH
VOUCH
WAUGH
YOUTH

•••UH
UHHUH
UNRUH

UI•••
UIGUR
UINTA

U•I••
UDINE
UMIAK
UNIFY
UNION
UNITE
UNITS
UNITY
UNIVS
URIAH
URIAL
URICH
URIEL
USING
UTICA
UTILE

U••I•
UGRIC
UNBID
UNDID
UNFIT
UNFIX
UNHIP
UNLIT
UNPIN
UNRIG
UNTIE
UNTIL
UNZIP
URBIS
URSID
USAIR

U•••I
UMEKI

•UI••
BUICK
BUILD
BUILT
CUING
GUIDE
GUIDO
GUILD
GUILE
GUILT
GUIRO
GUISE
JUICE
JUICY
LUIGI
LUISA
LUISE
OUIDA
OUIJA
QUICK
QUIDS
QUIEN
QUIET
QUILL
QUILP
QUILT
QUINN
QUINO
QUINT
QUIPS
QUIPU
QUIRE
QUIRK
QUIRT
QUITE
QUITO
QUITS
RUING
RUINS
SUING
SUINT
SUITA
SUITE
SUITS

•U•I•
AUDIE
AUDIO
AUDIS
AUDIT
AULIS
AURIC
AUXIL
AUXIN
BUNIN
BURIN
CUBIC
CUBIT
CUEIN
CUMIN
CUPID
CURIA
CURIE
CURIO
CUTIE
CUTIN
CUTIS
DUBIN
DUGIN
EUBIE
FUGIT
FUSIL
HUMID
JULIA
JULIE
JULIO
LUCIA
LUCID
LUCIE
LUDIC
LUNIK
LUPIN
LURIA
LURID
LURIE
MUCIN
MUNIS
MUSIC
NUBIA
NUMIS
PULIS
PUNIC
PUPIL
PUPIN
PURIM
PUTIN
QUAID
QUAIL
QUOIN
QUOIT
RUBIK
RUBIN
RUNIC
RUNIN
RURIK
RUTIN
SUBIC
SUFIS
SUSIE
TULIP
TUMID
TUNIC
TUNIS
TURIN
YUPIK
ZUBIN
ZUNIS

•U••I
AUREI
AUSSI
BUFFI
BUZZI
CUPRI
CURCI
DUBAI
FUNGI
GUCCI
LUCCI
LUIGI
LUNDI
MUFTI
MULTI
MUNDI
NURMI
PUCCI
PUTTI
QUASI
SULCI
SUNNI
SUOMI
SUSHI
TUTTI

••UI•
BRUIN
BRUIT
DRUID
EQUIP
EQUIV
ETUIS
FLUID
FRUIT
GSUIT
INUIT
IQUIT
LOUIE
LOUIS
SQUIB
SQUID

••U•I
DOUAI
HOURI
JEUDI
KAUAI
KAURI
SAUDI
SCUDI

•••UI
ANHUI
ENNUI
MAQUI
PIAUI
YAQUI

U•J••
UNJAM

•UJ••
AUJUS
JUJUS

•U•J•
OUIJA

••UJ•
ABUJA
THUJA

UK•••
UKASE

U•K••
URKEL

U••K•
UMEKI

U•••K
UMIAK
UZBEK

•UK••
CUKES
CUKOR
DUKAS
DUKED
DUKES
JUKED
JUKES
KUKLA
LUKAS
NUKED
NUKES
PUKKA
YUKON
ZUKOR

•U•K•
BUCKO
BUCKS
BUCKY
BULKS
BULKY
BUNKO
BUNKS
BURKE
BUSKS
CUSKS
DUCKS
DUCKY
DUNKS
DUSKS
DUSKY
FUNKS
FUNKY
GUNKY
HULKS
HUNKS
HUSKS
HUSKY
JUNKS
JUNKY
LUCKS
LUCKY
LURKS
MUCKS
MUCKY
MURKY
MUSKS
MUSKY
PUCKS
PUKKA
PUNKS
PUNKY
QUAKE
QUAKY
RUCKS
RUSKS
SUCKA
SUCKS
SULKS
SULKY
TUCKS
TURKS
TURKU
TUSKS
YUCKY

•U••K
BUICK
HUROK
KULAK
KURSK
LUNIK
MUZAK
QUACK
QUARK
QUICK
QUIRK
RUARK
RUBIK
RURIK
YUPIK
YUROK

••UK•
FLUKE
FLUKY
SAUKS
SOUKS
STUKA
ZOUKS

••U•K
AMUCK
BAULK
CAULK
CHUCK
CHUNK
CLUCK
CLUNK
DRUNK
FLUNK
GLUCK
PLUCK
PLUNK
SHUCK
SKULK
SKUNK
SLUNK
SNUCK
SPUNK
STUCK
STUNK
THUNK
TRUCK
TRUNK

•••UK
ANOUK

UL•••
ULCER
ULNAE
ULNAS
ULTRA

U•L••
UCLAN
UHLAN
UNLAY
UNLED
UNLIT
USLTA
UTLEY

U••L•
UBOLT
UDALL
UNCLE
UPOLU
URALS
UTILE
UVULA
UZALA

U•••L
UDALL
UHAUL
UMBEL
UNTIL
URIAL
URIEL
URKEL
USUAL
UXMAL

•UL••
AULIS
BULBA
BULBS
BULGE
BULGY
BULKS
BULKY
BULLA
BULLS
BULLY
BULOW
CULCH
CULET
CULEX
CULLS
CULLY
CULMS
CULPA
CULTS
DULLS
DULLY
DULSE
EULER
FULAS
FULDA
FULLY
GULAG
GULAR
GULCH
GULES
GULFS
GULLS
GULLY
GULPS
GULPY
HULAS
HULCE
HULKS
HULLO
HULLS
JULEP
JULES
JULIA
JULIE
JULIO
KULAK
LULEA
LULLS
LULLY
LULUS
MULCH
MULCT
MULES
MULEY
MULLS
MULTI
NULLS
PULAS
PULED
PULES
PULIS
PULLS
PULPS
PULPY
PULSE
RULED
RULER
RULES
SULCI
SULFA
SULKS
SULKY
SULLA
SULLY
TULES
TULIP
TULLE
TULLY
TULSA
ZULUS

•U•L•
BUELL
BUGLE
BUHLS
BUILD
BUILT
BULLA
BULLS
BULLY
BURLS
BURLY
CULLS
CULLY
CURLS
CURLY
DUELS
DULLS
DULLY
DUPLE
FUELS
FULLY
FURLS
GUILD
GUILE
GUILT
GULLS
GULLY
HULLO
HULLS
HURLS
HURLY
KUALA
KUKLA
LULLS
LULLY
MULLS
NULLS
PULLS
PURLS
QUALE
QUALM
QUELL
QUILL
QUILP
QUILT
RUBLE
SULLA
SULLY
SURLY
TULLE
TULLY

•U••L
AURAL
AUXIL
BUELL
BUTYL
CUMUL
CUPEL
DUCAL
FUGAL
FUSIL
JUBAL
JUGAL
JURAL
KUGEL
MURAL
OUSEL
OUZEL
PUPAL
PUPIL
QUAIL
QUELL
QUILL
RUEHL
RURAL
SURAL

••UL•
ADULT
ALULA
BAULK
BOULE
BOULT
BRULE
CAULK
CAULS
CHULA
COULD
EXULT
FAULT
FOULS
GAULS
GOULD
HAULM
HAULS
JOULE
KRULL
MAULS
MOULD
MOULT
OCULO
OVULE
PAULA
PAULO
POULT
SAULT
SCULL
SEULE
SHULA
SHULS
SKULK
SKULL
SOULS
SOULT
STULL
THULE
TRULY
UVULA
VAULT
WOULD
YOULL

••U•L
CHURL
CRUEL
EQUAL
GRUEL
JOUAL
KNURL
KRULL
REUEL
SCULL
SKULL
STULL
USUAL
YOULL

•••UL
ABDUL
AFOUL
AMPUL
ANNUL
AWFUL
BABUL
BAIUL
CUMUL
GHOUL
KABUL
MOGUL
MOSUL
PICUL
RAOUL
SEOUL
UHAUL

UM•••
UMBEL
UMBER
UMBOS
UMBRA
UMEKI
UMIAK
UMPED

U•M••
UNMAN
UNMET
UXMAL

U•••M
UNARM
UNJAM

•UM••
BUMPS
BUMPY
CUMAE
CUMIN
CUMUL
DUMAS
DUMBO
DUMBS
DUMMY
DUMPS
DUMPY
FUMED
FUMES
GUMBO
GUMBY
GUMMO
GUMMY
GUMUP
HUMAN
HUMID
HUMOR
HUMPH
HUMPS
HUMPY
HUMUS
JUMBO
JUMNA
JUMPS
JUMPY
LUMEN
LUMET
LUMPS
LUMPY
MUMBO
MUMMY
MUMPS
NUMBS
NUMEN
NUMIS
PUMAS
PUMPS
RUMBA
RUMEN
RUMMY
RUMOR
RUMPS
SUMAC
SUMBA
SUMER
SUMMA
SUMPS
SUMUP
TUMID
TUMMY
TUMPS
YUMAN
YUMAS
YUMMY

•U•M•
BURMA
CULMS
CUOMO
DUMMY
DUOMO
GUMMO
GUMMY
MUMMY
NURMI
RUMMY
SUEME
SUMMA
SUOMI
TUMMY
YUMMY

•U••M
AURUM
DURUM
JUGUM
PURIM
QUALM

••UM•
ALUMS
ARUMS
BAUME
BLUME
BRUME
CHUMP
CHUMS
CLUMP
CRUMB
CRUMP
DRUMS
FLUME
FRUMP
GAUMS
GEUMS
GRUMP
HOUMA
MFUME
NEUME
PLUMB
PLUME
PLUMP
PLUMS
PLUMY
RHUMB
SCUMS
SLUMP
SLUMS
SPUME
SPUMY
STUMP
STUMS
THUMB
THUMP
TRUMP

••U•M
HAULM
STURM

•••UM
ADSUM
AKSUM
ALBUM
ANNUM
ARIUM
AURUM
BEGUM
BYGUM
COLUM
DATUM
DURUM
FILUM
FORUM
HARUM
HILUM
HOHUM
HOKUM
ILIUM
IPSUM
JORUM
JUGUM
LOCUM
MECUM
MORUM
NAHUM
OAKUM
ODEUM
ODIUM
OLEUM
OPIUM
PILUM
REGUM
RERUM
RHEUM
SCRUM
SEBUM
SEDUM
SERUM
SOLUM
STRUM
TATUM
THRUM
VELUM
VISUM
YOKUM

UN•••
UNAPT
UNARM
UNAUS
UNBAR
UNBID
UNBOX
UNCAP
UNCAS
UNCLE
UNCUT
UNDER
UNDID
UNDUE
UNFED
UNFIT
UNFIX
UNGER
UNHIP
UNIFY
UNION
UNITE
UNITS
UNITY
UNIVS
UNJAM
UNLAY
UNLED
UNLIT
UNMAN
UNMET
UNPEG
UNPEN
UNPIN
UNRIG
UNRRA
UNRUH
UNSAY
UNSER
UNSET
UNTER
UNTIE
UNTIL
UNWED
UNZIP

U•N••
UINTA
ULNAE
ULNAS

U••N•
UDINE
UPEND
USING

U•••N
UCLAN
UHLAN
UNION
UNMAN
UNPEN
UNPIN
UPTON
URBAN
UTAHN
UTURN

•UN••
AUNTS
AUNTY
BUNCH
BUNDS
BUNDT
BUNDY
BUNGS
BUNIN
BUNKO
BUNKS
BUNNY
BUNTS
CUNAS
CUNEO
DUNCE
DUNES
DUNKS
DUNNE
DUNNO
FUNDS
FUNDY
FUNGI
FUNGO
FUNKS
FUNKY
FUNNY
GUNGA
GUNKY
GUNNY
HUNAN
HUNCH
HUNKS
HUNTS
HUNTZ
JUNCO
JUNKS
JUNKY
JUNTA
JUNTO
LUNAR
LUNCH
LUNDI
LUNDY
LUNES
LUNGE
LUNGS
LUNIK
MUNCH
MUNDI
MUNGO
MUNIS
MUNRO
OUNCE
PUNAS
PUNCH
PUNGS
PUNIC
PUNKS
PUNKY
PUNNY
PUNTA
PUNTS
PUNTY
RUNAT
RUNES
RUNGS
RUNIC
RUNIN
RUNNY
RUNON
RUNTO
RUNTS
RUNTY
RUNUP
SUNDA
SUNNA
SUNNI
SUNNY
SUNUP
TUNAS
TUNED
TUNER
TUNES
TUNIC
TUNIS
TUNNY
ZUNIS

•U•N•
BUENA
BUENO
BUNNY
BUONO
BURNS
BURNT
CUING
DUANE
DUNNE
DUNNO
DURNS
FUNNY
GUNNY
JUMNA
MUONS
PUNNY
QUAND
QUANT
QUINN
QUINO
QUINT
RUANA
RUING
RUINS
RUNNY
SUING
SUINT
SUNNA
SUNNI
SUNNY
TUNNY
TURNS
YUANS

•U••N
AUDEN
AUXIN
BUNIN
BURIN
CUBAN
CUEIN
CUMIN
CUTIN
DUBIN
DUGAN
DUGIN
DURAN
FURAN
FUTON
GUTEN
HUMAN
HUNAN
HURON
LUCAN
LUMEN
LUPIN
LUZON
MUCIN
NUMEN
NUYEN
PUPIN
PUSAN
PUTIN
PUTON
QUEEN
QUERN
QUIEN
QUINN
QUOIN
RUBEN
RUBIN
RUMEN
RUNIN
RUNON
RUTIN
SUDAN
SUSAN
TURIN
WUHAN
YUKON
YUMAN
ZUBIN

••UN•
BLUNT
BOUND
BRUNG
BRUNO
BRUNT
CHUNG
CHUNK
CLUNG
CLUNK
CLUNY
COUNT
DAUNT
DRUNK
FAUNA
FAUNS
FLUNG
FLUNK
FOUND
FOUNT
GAUNT
GRUNT
HAUNT
HOUND
JAUNE

JAUNT
JEUNE
MAUNA
MAUND
MOUND
MOUNT
NOUNS
PLUNK
POUND
PRUNE
REUNE
ROUND
SAUNA
SHUNS
SHUNT
SKUNK
SLUNG
SLUNK
SOUND
SPUNK
STUNG
STUNK
STUNS
STUNT
SWUNG
TAUNT
THUNK
TRUNK
VAUNT
WOUND
WRUNG
YOUNG
YOUNT

••U•N
BOURN
BRUHN
BRUIN
CHURN
GLUON
MOURN
ROUEN
SPURN
TAUON
UTURN

•••UN
AAIUN
BBGUN
BEGUN
BRAUN
BROUN
CAJUN
GATUN
HAFUN
INFUN
RERUN
SHAUN

U•O••
UBOAT
UBOLT
UPOLU
USOFA

U••O•
UMBOS
UNBOX
UNION
UPBOW
UPDOS
UPTON

•UO••
BUONO
BUOYS
CUOMO
DUOMO
MUONS
QUOAD
QUODS
QUOIN
QUOIT
QUOTA
QUOTE
QUOTH
SUOMI

•U•O•
AUTOS
BULOW
CUKOR
DUBOS
DUROC
DUROS
EUROS
FUROR
FUROS
FUTON
GUYOT
HUGOS
HUMOR
HUROK
HURON
JUROR
KUDOS
LUXOR
LUZON
OUZOS
PUTON
RUMOR
RUNON
TUDOR
TUROW
TUTOR
YUGOS
YUKON
YUROK
ZUKOR

•U••O
AUDIO
BUCKO
BUENO
BUFFO
BUNKO
BUONO
BURRO
BUTEO
CUNEO
CUOMO
CUPRO
CURIO
CUZCO
DUETO
DUMBO
DUNNO
DUOMO
FUEGO
FUNGO
GUACO
GUIDO
GUIRO
GUMBO
GUMMO
GUSTO
HUEVO
HULLO
JUDEO
JULIO
JUMBO
JUNCO
JUNTO
LUEGO
MUCRO
MUGHO
MUMBO
MUNGO
MUNRO
OUTDO
OUTGO
PUTTO
QUINO
QUITO
RUNTO
RUSSO
TURBO

••UO•
FLUOR
GLUON
TAUON

••U•O
BLUTO
BRUNO
DEUTO
DOURO
GLUCO
NEURO
OCULO
ORURO
PAULO
PLUTO
SCUDO
TAUPO
TAURO
TAUTO
TRURO

UP•••
UPBOW
UPDOS
UPEND
UPOLU
UPPED
UPPER
UPSET
UPTON

U•P••
UMPED
UNPEG
UNPEN
UNPIN
UPPED
UPPER

U••P•
UNAPT

U•••P
UNCAP
UNHIP
UNZIP
USEUP
USURP

•UP••
CUPEL
CUPID
CUPPA
CUPRI
CUPRO
DUPED
DUPES
DUPLE
DUPRE
GUPPY
LUPIN
PUPAE
PUPAL
PUPAS
PUPIL
PUPIN
PUPPY
PUPUS
RUPEE
SUPER
SUPES
SUPRA
SUPTS
SUPVR
YUPIK

•U•P•
BUMPS
BUMPY
BURPS
CULPA
CUPPA
CUSPS
DUMPS
DUMPY
GULPS
GULPY
GUPPY
HUMPH
HUMPS
HUMPY
JUMPS
JUMPY
LUMPS
LUMPY
MUMPS
PULPS
PULPY
PUMPS
PUPPY
QUIPS
QUIPU
RUMPS
SUMPS
TUMPS

•U••P
BUYUP
CUTUP
DUGUP
GUMUP
JULEP
PUTUP
QUILP
RUNUP
SUMUP
SUNUP
TULIP

••UP•
COUPE
COUPS
DRUPE
ERUPT
KRUPA
KRUPP
LOUPE
REUPS
SCUPS
SOUPS
SOUPY
STUPA
STUPE
TAUPE
TAUPO
WHUPS

••U•P
CHUMP
CLUMP
CRUMP
EQUIP
FRUMP
GRUMP
KRUPP
PLUMP
SLUMP
SLURP
STUMP
THUMP
TRUMP
USURP

•••UP
ACTUP
ADDUP
ANDUP
ATEUP
BIDUP
BOBUP
BOXUP
BUYUP
CROUP
CUTUP
DAMUP
DIDUP
DIGUP
DRYUP
DUGUP
EATUP
ENDUP
FEDUP
FIXUP
FOGUP
GASUP
GETUP
GOTUP
GROUP
GUMUP
HETUP
HITUP
HOPUP
ICEUP
JAMUP
KEYUP
LAPUP
LAYUP
LEGUP
LETUP
LITUP
MIXUP
MOPUP
NIPUP
NOTUP
ONEUP
OWNUP
PAYUP
PEPUP
PINUP
POPUP
PUTUP
RANUP
REVUP
RIGUP
RIPUP
RUNUP
SATUP
SCAUP
SETUP
SEWUP
SITUP
SOPUP
STOUP
SUMUP
SUNUP
SYRUP
TAGUP
TEEUP
TIEUP
TIPUP
TOTUP
USEUP
WADUP
ZIPUP

U•Q••
USQUE

•UQ••
TUQUE

UR•••
URALS
URBAN
URBIS
URGED
URGER
URGES
URIAH
URIAL
URICH
URIEL
URKEL
URSID

U•R••
UGRIC
UNRIG
UNRRA
UNRUH

U••R•
UHURA
UHURU
ULTRA
UMBRA
UNARM
UNRRA
USERS
USURP
USURY
UTURN

U•••R
UDDER
UIGUR
ULCER
UMBER
UNBAR
UNDER
UNGER
UNSER
UNTER
UPPER
URGER
USAIR
USHER
UTHER
UTTER

•UR••
AURAE
AURAL
AURAR
AURAS
AUREI
AURIC
AURUM
BURBS
BURGS
BURIN
BURKE
BURLS
BURLY
BURMA
BURNS
BURNT
BURPS
BURRO
BURRS
BURRY
BURSA
BURSE
BURST
CURBS
CURCI
CURDS
CURDY
CURED
CURER
CURES
CURIA
CURIE
CURIO
CURLS
CURLY
CURRY
CURSE
CURST
CURVE
CURVY
DURAN
DURER
DURNS
DUROC
DUROS
DURRA
DURST
DURUM
EUROS
EURUS
FURAN
FURLS
FUROR
FUROS
FURRY
FURTH
FURZE
GURDY
GURUS
HURDY
HURLS
HURLY
HUROK
HURON
HURRY
HURST
HURTS
JURAL
JURAT
JUROR
KURDS
KURSK
KURTZ
LURAY
LURCH
LURED
LURES
LUREX
LURIA
LURID
LURIE
LURKS
MURAL
MURAT
MUREX
MURKY
MURRA
MURRE
NURMI
NURSE
PUREE
PURER
PUREX
PURGE
PURIM
PURLS
PURRS
PURSE
PURSY
PURUS
RURAL
RURIK
SURAH
SURAL
SURAS
SURAT
SURDS
SURER
SURFS
SURFY
SURGE
SURLY
TURBO
TURFS
TURFY
TURIN
TURKS
TURKU
TURNS
TUROW
TURVY
WURST
YUROK
YURTS

•U•R•
AUDRA
AUTRE
AUTRY
BURRO
BURRS
BURRY
CUPRI
CUPRO
CURRY
DUPRE
DURRA
FURRY
GUARD
GUARS
GUIRO
HURRY
LUCRE
MUCRO
MUDRA
MUNRO
MURRA
MURRE
OUTRE
PURRS
QUARE
QUARK
QUART
QUERN
QUERY
QUIRE
QUIRK
QUIRT
RUARK
RUERS
SUCRE
SUDRA
SUERS
SUPRA
SUTRA

•U••R
AUBER
AUGER
AUGUR
AURAR
AUSTR
BUBER
BUYER
CUKOR
CURER
CUTER
DURER
EULER
FUROR
GULAR
HUGER
HUMOR
JUROR
LUGER
LUNAR
LUXOR
MUSER
MUTER
NUDER
OUTER
PURER
QUADR
QUEER
RUDER
RULER
RUMOR
SUGAR
SUMER
SUPER
SUPVR
SURER
TUBER
TUDOR
TUNER
TUTOR
ZUKOR

••UR•
ACURA
APURE
AZURE
BLURB
BLURS
BLURT
BOURG
BOURN
CHURL
CHURN
COURT
CRURA
DOURO
DRURY
ENURE
EXURB
FAURE
FOURH
FOURS
GAURS
GOURD
HEURE
HOURI
HOURS
INURE
KAURI
KNURL
KNURS
LAURA
MAURY
MOURN
NAURU
NEURO
ORURO
PIURA

POURS SAURY SCURF SLURP SLURS SMURF SOURS SPURN SPURS SPURT STURM TAURO THURS TOURS TRURO UHURA UHURU USURP USURY UTURN YOURE YOURS

••U•R

BAUER BLUER FLUOR GLUER HAUER LAUER TRUER

•••UR

AMOUR ARTUR ASHUR ASSUR AUGUR COEUR DEMUR FEMUR FLEUR FLOUR HHOUR INCUR LEMUR MASUR MOHUR NAMUR OCCUR ODOUR RECUR SCOUR SIEUR SOEUR UIGUR

US•••

USAGE USAIR USCGA USERS USEUP USHED USHER USING USLTA USOFA USQUE USTED USUAL USURP USURY

U•S••

UNSAY UNSER UNSET UPSET URSID

U••S•

UKASE

U•••S

ULNAS UMBOS UNAUS UNCAS UNITS UNIVS UPDOS URALS URBIS URGES USERS

•US••

AUSSI AUSTR BUSBY BUSCH BUSED BUSES BUSEY BUSHY BUSKS BUSTS CUSHY CUSKS CUSPS DUSKS DUSKY DUSTS DUSTY FUSED FUSEE FUSES FUSIL FUSSY FUSTY GUSHY GUSSY GUSTO GUSTS GUSTY HUSKS HUSKY HUSSY JUSTE LUSTS LUSTY MUSCA MUSED MUSER MUSES MUSHY MUSIC MUSKS MUSKY MUSSY MUSTS MUSTY OUSEL OUSTS PUSAN PUSEY PUSHY RUSES RUSHY RUSKS RUSSE RUSSO RUSTS RUSTY SUSAN SUSHI SUSIE TUSKS WUSHU

•U•S•

AUSSI BUGSY BURSA BURSE BURST CURSE CURST DULSE DURST FUBSY FUSSY GUESS GUEST GUISE GUSSY GUTSY HURST HUSSY KURSK LUISA LUISE MUSSY NURSE NUTSY PULSE PURSE PURSY QUASH QUASI QUEST RUSSE RUSSO SUDSY TULSA WURST

•U••S

AUDIS AUJUS AULIS AUNTS AURAS AUTOS BUBUS BUCKS BUFFS BUHLS BULBS BULKS BULLS BUMPS BUNDS BUNGS BUNKS BUNTS BUOYS BURBS BURGS BURLS BURNS BURPS BURRS BUSES BUSKS BUSTS BUTTS CUBES CUFFS CUKES CULLS CULMS CULTS CUNAS CURBS CURDS CURES CURLS CUSKS CUSPS CUTIS DUADS DUBOS DUCES DUCKS DUCTS DUDES DUELS DUETS DUFFS DUKAS DUKES DULLS DUMAS DUMBS DUMPS DUNES DUNKS DUPES DURNS DUROS DUSKS DUSTS DUXES EUROS EURUS FUCHS FUELS FUGUS FULAS FUMES FUNDS FUNKS FURLS FUROS FUSES GUARS GUESS GULES GULFS GULLS GULPS GURUS GUSTS HUFFS HUGOS HULAS HULKS HULLS HUMPS HUMUS HUNKS HUNTS HURLS HURTS HUSKS HUTUS JUDAS JUJUS JUKES JULES JUMPS JUNKS JUTES KUDOS KUDUS KURDS LUAUS LUBAS LUBES LUCAS LUCKS LUFFS LUGES LUKAS LULLS LULUS LUMPS LUNES LUNGS LURES LURKS LUSTS LUTES MUCKS MUFFS MUGGS MULES MULLS MUMPS MUNIS MUONS MUSES MUSKS MUSTS MUTES MUTTS NUDES NUKES NULLS NUMBS NUMIS OUSTS OUZOS PUCKS PUDUS PUFFS PULAS PULES PULIS PULLS PULPS PUMAS PUMPS PUNAS PUNGS PUNKS PUNTS PUPAS PUPUS PURLS PURRS PURUS PUTTS QUADS QUAGS QUAYS QUIDS QUIPS QUITS QUODS RUBES RUCKS RUDDS RUERS RUFFS RUFUS RUINS RULES RUMPS RUNES RUNGS RUNTS RUSES RUSKS RUSTS SUCKS SUDDS SUERS SUETS SUFIS SUITS SULKS SUMPS SUPES SUPTS SURAS SURDS SURFS TUBAS TUBES TUCKS TUFTS TULES TUMPS TUNAS TUNES TUNIS TURFS TURKS TURNS TUSKS TUTUS TUXES YUANS YUGAS YUGOS YUMAS YURTS ZULUS ZUNIS

••US•

ABUSE ADUST AMUSE AZUSA BLUSH BOUSE BRUSH CAUSA CAUSE COUSY CRUSE CRUSH CRUST DOUSE DRUSE FAUST FLUSH GAUSS HAUSA HOUSE INUSE JOUST LOUSE LOUSY MEUSE MOUSE MOUSY OFUSE PAUSE PLUSH REUSE ROUSE ROUST SEUSS SHUSH SLUSH SOUSA SOUSE TRUSS TRUST YOUSE

••U•S

ABUTS AGUES ALUMS AQUAS ARUMS BLUES BLURS BOUTS BRUTS CAULS CHUBS CHUGS CHUMS CLUBS CLUES COUPS DAUBS DRUBS DRUGS DRUMS EQUUS ETUIS FAUNS FEUDS FLUBS FLUES FOULS FOURS FOUTS GAUDS GAULS GAUMS GAURS GAUSS GEUMS GLUES GLUGS GLUTS GRUBS HAULS HOURS KNURS LAUDS LOUIS LOUTS MAULS MOUES NOUNS PLUGS PLUMS POUFS POURS POUTS REUPS ROUES ROUTS SAUKS SCUDS SCUMS SCUPS SCUTS SEUSS SHULS SHUNS SHUTS SKUAS SLUES SLUGS SLUMS SLURS SMUTS SNUBS SNUGS SOUKS SOULS SOUPS SOURS SPUDS SPURS STUBS STUDS STUMS STUNS THUDS THUGS THURS TNUTS TOURS TOUTS TRUES TRUGS TRUSS WHUPS YOURS ZOUKS

•••US

AGNUS AINUS ALDUS ALTUS ANGUS ANNUS APLUS ARGUS ARHUS ARIUS ASCUS AUJUS BEAUS BOGUS BOLUS BONUS BPLUS BUBUS CAMUS CASUS CETUS CLAUS COMUS CONUS CPLUS CYRUS DPLUS ECRUS EOLUS EQUUS EURUS FICUS FOCUS FUGUS GAIUS GENUS GURUS GYRUS HOCUS HONUS HORUS HUMUS HUTUS ICTUS IGLUS ILLUS INCUS INDUS ISSUS JANUS JUJUS KLAUS KRAUS KUDUS LAIUS LEPUS LEXUS LIEUS LINUS LOCUS LOTUS LUAUS LULUS MAGUS MENUS MINUS MODUS MOMUS NEGUS NEVUS NEXUS NIDUS NISUS NODUS ORCUS PILUS PIOUS POCUS PRAUS PUDUS PUPUS PURUS REBUS REMUS RUFUS SINUS SITUS SOLUS SORUS TAGUS TALUS THOUS TITUS TONUS TORUS TUTUS UNAUS VAGUS VENUS VIRUS VITUS XERUS ZEBUS ZULUS

UT•••

UTAHN UTHER UTICA UTILE UTLEY UTTER UTURN

U•T••

ULTRA UNTER UNTIE UNTIL UPTON USTED UTTER

U••T•

UINTA UNITE UNITS UNITY USLTA

U•••T
UBOAT
UBOLT
UNAPT
UNCUT
UNFIT
UNLIT
UNMET
UNSET
UPSET

•UT••
AUTOS
AUTRE
AUTRY
BUTCH
BUTEO
BUTTE
BUTTS
BUTTY
BUTUT
BUTYL
CUTER
CUTEX
CUTEY
CUTIE
CUTIN
CUTIS
CUTUP
DUTCH
FUTON
GUTEN
GUTSY
GUTTA
GUTTY
HUTCH
HUTUS
JUTES
JUTTY
LUTES
MUTED
MUTER
MUTES
MUTTS
NUTSY
NUTTY
OUTDO
OUTED
OUTER
OUTGO
OUTRE
PUTBY
PUTIN
PUTON
PUTTI
PUTTO
PUTTS
PUTTY
PUTUP
RUTIN
RUTTY
SUTRA
TUTEE
TUTOR
TUTTI
TUTUS

•U•T•
AUNTS
AUNTY
AUSTR
BUNTS
BUSTS
BUTTE
BUTTS
BUTTY
CULTS
DUCTS
DUETO
DUETS
DUSTS
DUSTY
FURTH
FUSTY
GUSTO
GUSTS
GUSTY
GUTTA
GUTTY
HUNTS
HUNTZ
HURTS
JUNTA
JUNTO
JUSTE
JUTTY
KURTZ
LUSTS
LUSTY
MUFTI
MULTI
MUSTS
MUSTY
MUTTS
NUTTY
OUSTS
PUNTA
PUNTS
PUNTY
PUTTI
PUTTO
PUTTS
PUTTY
QUITE
QUITO
QUITS
QUOTA
QUOTE
QUOTH
RUNTO
RUNTS
RUNTY
RUSTS
RUSTY
RUTTY
SUETS
SUETY
SUITA
SUITE
SUITS
SUPTS
TUFTS
TUFTY
TUTTI
YURTS

•U••T
AUDIT
AUGHT
BUILT
BUNDT
BURNT
BURST
BUTUT
CUBIT
CUGAT
CULET
CURST
DUCAT
DURST
DUVET
FUGIT
GUEST
GUILT
GUYOT
HURST
JURAT
LUMET
MULCT
MURAT
OUGHT
PUGET
QUANT
QUART
QUEST
QUIET
QUILT
QUINT
QUIRT
QUOIT
RUNAT
SUINT
SURAT
WURST

••UT•
ABUTS
ACUTE
BLUTH
BLUTO
BOUTS
BRUTE
BRUTS
CEUTA
CHUTE
COUTH
DEUTO
ELUTE
FLUTE
FLUTY
FOUTS
GLUTS
GOUTY
HAUTE
HEUTE
KLUTE
KLUTZ
KNUTE
LOUTS
MOUTH
PLUTO
POUTS
POUTY
ROUTE
ROUTS
SAUTE
SCUTA
SCUTE
SCUTS
SHUTE
SHUTS
SMUTS
SOUTH
STUTZ
TAUTO
TNUTS
TOUTE
TOUTS
TRUTH
YOUTH

••U•T
ADULT
ADUST
BLUET
BLUNT
BLURT
BOULT
BRUIT
BRUNT
COUNT
COURT
CRUET
CRUST
DAUNT
DOUBT
EDUCT
ERUCT
ERUPT
EXULT
FAULT
FAUST
FOUNT
FRUIT
GAUNT
GRUNT
GSUIT
HAUNT
INUIT
IQUIT
JAUNT
JOUST
MOULT
MOUNT
POULT
ROUST
SAULT
SHUNT
SOULT
SPURT
SQUAT
STUNT
TAUNT
TRUST
VAULT
VAUNT
YOUNT

•••UT
ABOUT
ADOUT
ALEUT
ASYUT
BEAUT
BUTUT
CLOUT
DEBUT
DONUT
FLOUT
GAMUT
GOOUT
GROUT
INPUT
KAPUT
KNOUT
KRAUT
LIEUT
REBUT
SALUT
SCOUT
SHOUT
SNOUT
SPOUT
STOUT
STRUT
TROUT
UNCUT
XDOUT
XSOUT
YAKUT

U•U••
UHURA
UHURU
USUAL
USURP
USURY
UTURN
UVULA

U••U•
UHAUL
UHHUH
UIGUR
UNAUS
UNCUT
UNDUE
UNRUH
USEUP
USQUE

U•••U
UHURU
UPOLU

•U•U•
AUGUR
AUJUS
AURUM
BUBUS
BUTUT
BUYUP
CUMUL
CUTUP
DUGUP
DURUM
EURUS
FUGUE
FUGUS
GUMUP
GURUS
HUMUS
HUTUS
JUGUM
JUJUS
KUDUS
LUAUS
LULUS
PUDUS
PUPUS
PURUS
PUTUP
QUEUE
RUFUS
RUNUP
SUMUP
SUNUP
TUQUE
TUTUS
ZULUS

•U••U
KUDZU
QUIPU
TURKU
WUSHU

••UU•
EQUUS

••U•U
ENUGU
ISUZU
KHUFU
NAURU
UHURU

UV•••
UVULA

U••V•
UNIVS

•UV••
CUVEE
DUVET

•U•V•
CURVE
CURVY
GUAVA
HUEVO
SUAVE
SUPVR
TURVY

••UV•
FAUVE
MAUVE
YOUVE

••U•V
EQUIV

U•W••
UNWED

U•••W
UPBOW

•U••W
BULOW
TUROW

••UW•
ADUWA

UX•••
UXMAL

U•••X
UNBOX
UNFIX

•UX••
AUXIL
AUXIN
DUXES
LUXOR
TUXES

•U••X
CULEX
CUTEX
LUREX
MUREX
PUREX

••U•X
TRUEX

•••UX
ADEUX
BEAUX
REDUX
SIOUX

U•••Y
UNIFY
UNITY
UNLAY
UNSAY
USURY
UTLEY

•UY••
BUYER
BUYUP
GUYED
GUYOT
NUYEN

•U•Y•
BUOYS
BUTYL
QUAYS

•U••Y
AUNTY
AUTRY
BUCKY
BUDDY
BUFFY
BUGGY
BUGSY
BULGY
BULKY
BULLY
BUMPY
BUNDY
BUNNY
BURLY
BURRY
BUSBY
BUSEY
BUSHY
BUTTY
CUBBY
CUDDY
CULLY
CURDY
CURLY
CURRY
CURVY
CUSHY
CUTEY
DUCHY
DUCKY
DUDDY
DUFAY
DUFFY
DULLY
DUMMY
DUMPY
DUSKY
DUSTY
FUBSY
FUDDY
FUGGY
FULLY
FUNDY
FUNKY
FUNNY
FURRY
FUSSY
FUSTY
FUZZY
GULLY
GULPY
GUMBY
GUMMY
GUNKY
GUNNY
GUPPY
GURDY
GUSHY
GUSSY
GUSTY
GUTSY
GUTTY
HUBBY
HUFFY
HUMPY
HURDY
HURLY
HURRY
HUSKY
HUSSY
JUICY
JUMPY
JUNKY
JUTTY
LUCKY
LULLY
LUMPY
LUNDY
LURAY
LUSTY
MUCKY
MUDDY
MUGGY
MULEY
MUMMY
MURKY
MUSHY
MUSKY
MUSSY
MUSTY
MUZZY
NUBBY
NUTSY
NUTTY
PUDGY
PUFFY
PUGGY
PULPY
PUNKY
PUNNY
PUNTY
PUPPY
PURSY
PUSEY
PUSHY
PUTBY
PUTTY
QUAKY
QUERY
RUDDY
RUGBY
RUMMY
RUNNY
RUNTY
RUSHY
RUSTY
RUTTY
SUDSY
SUETY
SULKY
SULLY
SUNNY
SURFY
SURLY
TUBBY
TUFTY
TULLY
TUMMY
TUNNY
TURFY
TURVY
VUGGY
YUCKY
YUMMY

••U•Y
BLUEY
CLUNY
COUSY
DEUCY
DOUAY
DRURY
FLUKY
FLUTY
GAUDY
GAUZY
GLUEY
GOUDY
GOUTY
LOUSY
MAURY
MOUSY
PLUMY
POUTY
SAUCY
SAURY
SOUPY
SPUMY
STUDY
TRULY
USURY

•••UY
MYGUY

UZ•••
UZALA
UZBEK

U•Z••
UNZIP

•UZ••
BUZZI
CUZCO
FUZED
FUZEE
FUZZY
HUZZA
LUZON
MUZAK
MUZZY
OUZEL
OUZOS

•U•Z•
BUZZI
FURZE
FUZZY
HUZZA
KUDZU
MUZZY

•U••Z
HUNTZ
KURTZ

••UZ•
ABUZZ
DRUZE
GAUZE
GAUZY
ISUZU
SCUZZ

••U•Z
ABUZZ
KLUTZ
SCUZZ
STUTZ

•••UZ
SOYUZ
VADUZ

VA•••
VACUA
VADER
VADIM
VADIS
VADUZ
VAGUE
VAGUS
VALES
VALET

VALID
VALLE
VALLI
VALOR
VALSE
VALUE
VALVE
VAMOS
VAMPS
VANCE
VANES
VANIR
VANNA
VANYA
VAPID
VAPOR
VARAS
VARIA
VARIG
VARIX
VARNA
VASCO
VASES
VASTY
VATER
VATIC
VAULT
VAUNT

V•A••

VEALY
VIALS
VIAND

V••A•

VARAS
VEDAS
VEDAY
VEGAN
VEGAS
VELAR
VENAE
VENAL
VICAR
VIDAL
VILAS
VINAS
VIRAL
VISAS
VITAE
VITAL
VITAS
VJDAY
VOCAL
VOLAR
VOLAT

V•••A

VACUA
VANNA
VANYA
VARIA
VARNA
VEDDA
VENDA
VERBA
VERSA
VESTA
VILLA
VILMA
VIOLA
VIRGA
VIRNA
VISTA
VODKA
VOILA
VOLGA
VOLTA
VOLVA

•VA••

AVAIL
AVANT
AVARS
AVAST
EVADE
EVANS
IVANA
KVASS
OVALS
OVATE

•V•A•

AVGAS
AVIAN
EVIAN

•V••A

AVENA
AVILA
DVINA
EVITA
EVORA
IVANA
OVETA
UVULA

••VA•

ADVAL
ALVAR
CAVAE
DAVAO
DIVAN
DIVAS
JAVAS
KAVAS
KIVAS
LAVAL
LAVAS
LEVAR
NAVAL
NIVAL
NOVAE
NOVAK
NOVAS
OYVAY
RIVAL
SIVAN

••V•A

FOVEA
LIVIA
PAVIA

•••VA

ALAVA
BELVA
BRAVA
DRAVA
GUAVA
LARVA
SELVA
SHIVA
SILVA
SNEVA
VOLVA

V•B••

VIBES

V••B•

VERBA
VERBS
VISBY

VC•••

VCHIP

V•C••

VACUA
VICAR
VICES
VICHY
VICKI
VICKS
VOCAL

V••C•

VANCE
VASCO
VETCH
VINCE
VINCI
VNECK
VOICE
VOICI
VOUCH

V•••C

VATIC
VEDIC

•V•C•

EVICT

••V•C

CIVIC
HAVOC

V•D••

VADER
VADIM
VADIS
VADUZ
VEDAS
VEDAY
VEDDA
VEDIC
VIDAL
VIDEO
VIDOR
VJDAY
VODKA

V••D•

VEDDA
VEIDT
VELDS
VELDT
VENDA
VENDS
VERDE
VERDI
VOIDS

V•••D

VALID
VAPID
VEXED
VIAND
VINED
VIRID
VIVID
VOTED
VOWED

•V•D•

EVADE

•V••D

AVOID
IVIED
OVOID

••VD•

BLVDS

••V•D

BOVID
CAVED
DAVID
DIVED
EAVED
GYVED
HIVED
JIVED
LAVED
LIVED
LIVID
LOVED
MOVED
PAVED
PAVID
RAVED
RIVED
ROVED
RSVPD
SAVED
VIVID
WAVED
WIVED

VE•••

VEALY
VEDAS
VEDAY
VEDDA
VEDIC
VEDDA
VEEPS
VEERS
VEERY
VEGAN
VEGAS
VEIDT
VEILS
VEINS
VEINY
VELAR
VELDS
VELDT
VELEZ
VELUM
VENAE
VENAL
VENDA
VENDS
VENEZ
VENIN
VENOM
VENTS
VENUE
VENUS
VERBA
VERBS
VERDE
VERDI
VERGE
VERMI
VERNE
VERRE
VERSA
VERSE
VERSO
VERST
VERTE
VERTS
VERVE
VESEY
VESTA
VESTS
VETCH
VEXED
VEXER
VEXES

V•E••

VEEPS
VEERS
VEERY
VIEJO
VIERS
VIEWS
VIEWY
VNECK

V••E•

VADER
VALES
VALET
VANES
VASES
VATER
VELEZ
VENEZ
VESEY
VEXED
VEXER
VEXES
VIBES
VICES
VIDEO
VILER
VINED
VINES
VIPER
VIREO
VISES
VIXEN
VOLES
VOTED
VOTER
VOTES
VOWED
VOWEL
VOWER

V•••E

VAGUE
VALLE
VALSE
VALUE
VALVE
VANCE
VENAE
VENUE
VERDE
VERGE
VERNE
VERRE
VERSE
VERTE
VERVE
VILLE
VINCE
VITAE
VIVRE
VOGUE
VOICE
VOILE
VOLTE
VOTRE

•VE••

AVENA
AVENS
AVERS
AVERT
AVERY
EVENS
EVENT
EVERS
EVERT
EVERY
KVELL
OVENS
OVERS
OVERT
OVETA
OVETT

•V•E•

IVIED
IVIES
TVSET

•V••E

EVADE
EVOKE
OVATE
OVINE
OVULE

••VE•

AMVET
BEVEL
CAVED
CAVER
CAVES
CIVET
COVEN
COVER
COVES
COVET
COVEY
CUVEE
DIVED
DIVER
DIVES
DOVER
DOVES
DOVEY
DUVET
EAVED
EAVES
ELVER
ELVES
FAVES
FEVER
FIVER
FIVES
FOVEA
GAVEL
GIVEN
GIVER
GIVES
GYVED
GYVES
HAVEL
HAVEN
HAVER
HAVES
HIVED
HIVES
HOVEL
HOVER
HOVEY
JIVED
JIVER
JIVES
JIVEY
KEVEL
LAVED
LAVER
LAVES
LEVEE
LEVEL
LEVER
LIVED
LIVEN
LIVER
LIVES
LOVED
LOVER
LOVES
LOVEY
MAVEN
MOVED
MOVER
MOVES
NAVEL
NAVES
NEVER
NEVES
NIVEN
NOVEL
PAVED
PAVER
PAVES
RAVED
RAVEL
RAVEN
RAVER
RAVES
REVEL
REVET
RIVED
RIVEN
RIVER
RIVES
RIVET
ROVED
ROVER
ROVES
SAVED
SAVER
SAVES
SEVEN
SEVER
TEVET
TOVES
WAVED
WAVER
WAVES
WIVED
WIVES
WOVEN

••V•E

CAVAE
CUVEE
DAVIE
FAVRE
HAVRE
LEVEE
LIVRE
MCVIE
MOVIE
NOVAE
REVUE
TEVYE
VIVRE

•••VE

ABOVE
AGAVE
ALEVE
ALIVE
ATIVE
BRAVE
BREVE
CALVE
CARVE
CHIVE
CLAVE
CLIVE
CLOVE
CRAVE
CURVE
DELVE
DRIVE
DROVE
ELEVE
FAUVE
GLOVE
GRAVE
GROVE
HALVE
HEAVE
HELVE
HERVE
KNAVE
LEAVE
MAUVE
NAIVE
NERVE
OGIVE
OLIVE
PEEVE
PROVE
REEVE
SALVE
SERVE
SHAVE
SHOVE
SIEVE
SKIVE
SLAVE
SOAVE
SOLVE
STAVE
STEVE
STOVE
SUAVE
TRAVE
TROVE
VALVE
VERVE
WAIVE
WEAVE
YOUVE

V•G••

VAGUE
VAGUS
VEGAN
VEGAS
VIGIL
VIGNY
VIGOR
VOGUE
VUGGY

V••G•

VERGE
VINGT
VIRGA
VIRGO
VOLGA
VSIGN
VUGGY

V•••G

VARIG
VYING

•VG••

AVGAS

••V•G

NAVIG

V•H••

VCHIP

V••H•

VICHY

V•••H

VETCH
VOUCH

VI•••

VIALS
VIAND
VIBES
VICAR
VICES
VICHY
VICKI
VICKS
VIDAL
VIDEO
VIDOR
VIEJO
VIERS
VIEWS
VIEWY
VIGIL
VIGNY
VIGOR
VIKKI
VILAS
VILER
VILLA
VILLE
VILLI
VILMA
VINAS
VINCE
VINCI
VINED
VINES
VINGT
VINNY
VINOS
VINYL
VIOLA
VIOLS
VIPER
VIRAL
VIREO
VIRGA
VIRGO
VIRID
VIRNA
VIRTU
VIRUS
VISAS
VISBY
VISES
VISIT
VISOR
VISTA
VISUM
VITAE
VITAL
VITAS
VITUS
VIVID
VIVRE
VIXEN

V•I••

VEIDT

VEILS
VEINS
VEINY
VOICE
VOICI
VOIDS
VOILA
VOILE
VSIGN
VYING

V••I•
VADIM
VADIS
VALID
VANIR
VAPID
VARIA
VARIG
VARIX
VATIC
VCHIP
VEDIC
VENIN
VIGIL
VIRID
VISIT
VIVID

V•••I
VALLI
VERDI
VERMI
VICKI
VIKKI
VILLI
VINCI
VOICI

•VI••
AVIAN
AVILA
AVION
AVISO
CVIII
DVIII
DVINA
EVIAN
EVICT
EVILS
EVITA
IVIED
IVIES
IVINS
LVIII
MVIII
OVINE
XVIII

•V•I•
AVAIL
AVOID
AVOIR
AVRIL
CVIII
DVIII
LVIII
MVIII
OVOID
XVIII

•V••I
CVIII
DVIII
LVIII
MVIII
OVOLI
XVIII

••VI•
ADVIL
ALVIN
ANVIL
BEVIN
BOVID
CAVIL
CCVII
CDVII
CIVIC
CIVIL
CLVII
CMVII
CXVII
DAVID
DAVIE
DAVIS
DAVIT
DCVII
DEVIL
DLVII
DXVII
ELVIN
ELVIS
ERVIL
ERVIN
ETVIR
GAVIN
IRVIN
KEVIN
LAVIN
LEVIN
LEVIS
LIVIA
LIVID
LXVII
MAVIS
MCVIE
MCVII
MDVII
MLVII
MMVII
MOVIE
MXVII
NAVIG
NEVIL
NEVIN
NEVIS
PAVIA
PAVID
PAVIS
QBVII
RAVIN
VIVID
XCVII
XLVII
XXVII

••V•I
CCVII
CDVII
CLVII
CMVII
CXVII
DCVII
DLVII
DXVII
ENVOI
LXVII
MCVII
MDVII
MLVII
MMVII
MXVII
QBVII
XCVII
XLVII
XXVII

•••VI
CCCVI
CCLVI
CCXVI
CDLVI
CDXVI
CLXVI
CMLVI
CMXVI
CXCVI
CXLVI
CXXVI
DCCVI
DCLVI
DCXVI
DLXVI
DXCVI
DXLVI
DXXVI
LXXVI
MCCVI
MCDVI
MCLVI
MCMVI
MCXVI
MDCVI
MDLVI
MDXVI
MLXVI
MMCVI
MMDVI
MMLVI
MMMVI
MMXVI
MXCVI
MXLVI
MXXVI
TREVI
XXXVI

VJ•••
VJDAY

V••J•
VIEJO

V•K••
VIKKI

V••K•
VICKI
VICKS
VIKKI
VODKA

V•••K
VNECK

•V•K•
EVOKE

••V•K
NOVAK

V•L••
VALES
VALET
VALID
VALLE
VALLI
VALOR
VALSE
VALUE
VALVE
VELAR
VELDS
VELDT
VELEZ
VELUM
VILAS
VILER
VILLA
VILLE
VILLI
VILMA
VOLAR
VOLAT
VOLES
VOLGA
VOLTA
VOLTE
VOLTS
VOLVA
VOLVO

V••L•
VALLE
VALLI
VAULT
VEALY
VEILS
VIALS
VILLA
VILLE
VILLI
VIOLA
VIOLS
VOILA
VOILE
VTOLS

V•••L
VENAL
VIDAL
VIGIL
VINYL
VIRAL
VITAL
VOCAL
VOWEL

•V•L•
AVILA
EVILS
KVELL
OVALS
OVOLI
OVOLO
OVULE
UVULA

•V••L
AVAIL
AVRIL
KVELL

••V•L
ADVAL
ADVIL
ANVIL
BEVEL
CAVIL
CIVIL
DEVIL
ERVIL
GAVEL
HAVEL
HOVEL
KEVEL
LAVAL
LEVEL
NAVAL
NAVEL
NEVIL
NIVAL
NOVEL
RAVEL
REVEL
RIVAL

V•M••
VAMOS
VAMPS

V••M•
VERMI
VILMA

V•••M
VADIM
VELUM
VENOM
VISUM
VROOM

VN•••
VNECK

V•N••
VANCE
VANES
VANIR
VANNA
VANYA
VENAE
VENAL
VENDA
VENDS
VENEZ
VENIN
VENOM
VENTS
VENUE
VENUS
VINAS
VINCE
VINCI
VINED
VINES
VINGT
VINNY
VINOS
VINYL

V••N•
VANNA
VARNA
VAUNT
VEINS
VEINY
VERNE
VIAND
VIGNY
VINNY
VIRNA
VYING

V•••N
VEGAN
VENIN
VIXEN
VSIGN

•V•N•
AVANT
AVENA
AVENS
DVINA
EVANS
EVENS
EVENT
IVANA
IVINS
OVENS
OVINE

•V••N
AVIAN
AVION
EVIAN

••VN•
KOVNO
ROVNO

••V•N
ALVIN
BEVIN
COVEN
DEVON
DIVAN
ELVIN
ERVIN
GAVIN
GIVEN
HAVEN
IRVIN
KEVIN
LAVIN
LEVIN
LEVON
LIVEN
MAVEN
NEVIN
NIVEN
RAVEN
RAVIN
RIVEN
SEVEN
SIVAN
WOVEN
ZEVON

VO•••
VOCAL
VODKA
VOGUE
VOICE
VOICI
VOIDS
VOILA
VOILE
VOLAR
VOLAT
VOLES
VOLGA
VOLTA
VOLTE
VOLTS
VOLVA
VOLVO
VOTED
VOTER
VOTES
VOTRE
VOUCH
VOWED
VOWEL
VOWER

V•O••
VIOLA
VIOLS
VROOM
VTOLS

V••O•
VALOR
VAMOS
VAPOR
VENOM
VIDOR
VIGOR
VINOS
VISOR
VROOM

V•••O
VASCO
VERSO
VIDEO
VIEJO
VIREO
VIRGO
VOLVO

•VO••
AVOID
AVOIR
AVOWS
EVOKE
EVORA
IVORY
OVOID
OVOLI
OVOLO

•V•O•
AVION

•V••O
AVISO
OVOLO

••VO•
DAVOS
DEVON
DIVOT
ENVOI
ENVOY
FAVOR
GAVOT
HAVOC
LEVON
PIVOT
SAVOR
SAVOY
ZEVON

••V•O
DAVAO
KOVNO
ROVNO

•••VO
ABOVO
BRAVO
HUEVO
NORVO
PAAVO
PARVO
PROVO
SALVO
SERVO
VOLVO

V•P••
VAPID
VAPOR
VIPER

V••P•
VAMPS
VEEPS

V•••P
VCHIP

••VP•
RSVPD
RSVPS

••V•P
REVUP

VR•••
VROOM

V•R••
VARAS
VARIA
VARIG
VARIX
VARNA
VERBA
VERBS
VERDE
VERDI
VERGE
VERMI
VERNE
VERRE
VERSA
VERSE
VERSO
VERST
VERTE
VERTS
VERVE
VIRAL
VIREO
VIRGA
VIRGO
VIRID
VIRNA
VIRTU
VIRUS

V••R•
VEERS
VEERY
VERRE
VIERS
VIVRE
VOTRE

V•••R
VADER
VALOR
VANIR
VAPOR
VATER
VELAR
VEXER
VICAR
VIDOR
VIGOR
VILER
VIPER
VISOR
VOLAR
VOTER
VOWER

•VR••
AVRIL

•V•R•
AVARS
AVERS
AVERT
AVERY
EVERS
EVERT
EVERY
EVORA
IVORY
OVERS
OVERT

•V••R
AVOIR

••VR•
DEVRY
FAVRE
HAVRE
LIVRE
VIVRE

••V•R
ALVAR
CAVER
COVER
DIVER
DOVER
ELVER
ETVIR
FAVOR
FEVER
FIVER
GIVER
HAVER
HOVER
JIVER
LAVER
LEVAR
LEVER
LIVER
LOVER
MOVER
NEVER
PAVER
RAVER
RIVER
ROVER
SAVER
SAVOR
SEVER
WAVER

•••VR
SUPVR

VS•••
VSIGN

V•S••
VASCO
VASES
VASTY
VESEY
VESTA
VESTS
VISAS
VISBY
VISES
VISIT
VISOR
VISTA
VISUM

V••S•
VALSE
VERSA
VERSE

VERSO
VERST

V•••S
VADIS
VAGUS
VALES
VAMOS
VAMPS
VANES
VARAS
VASES
VEDAS
VEEPS
VEERS
VEGAS
VEILS
VEINS
VELDS
VENDS
VENTS
VENUS
VERBS
VERTS
VESTS
VEXES
VIALS
VIBES
VICES
VICKS
VIERS
VIEWS
VILAS
VINAS
VINES
VINOS
VIOLS
VIRUS
VISAS
VISES
VITAS
VITUS
VOIDS
VOLES
VOLTS
VOTES
VTOLS

•VS••
TVSET

•V•S•
AVAST
AVISO
KVASS

•V••S
AVARS
AVENS
AVERS
AVGAS
AVOWS
EVANS
EVENS
EVERS
EVILS
IVIES
IVINS
KVASS
OVALS
OVENS
OVERS

••V•S
BLVDS
CAVES
COVES
DAVIS
DAVOS
DAVYS
DIVAS
DIVES
DOVES
EAVES
ELVES
ELVIS
FAVES
FIVES
GIVES
GYVES
HAVES
HIVES
JAVAS
JIVES
KAVAS
KIVAS
LAVAS
LAVES
LEVIS
LIVES
LOVES
MAVIS
MOVES
NAVES
NEVES
NEVIS
NEVUS
NOVAS
PAVES
PAVIS
RAVES
RIVES
ROVES
RSVPS
SAVES
TOVES
WAVES
WIVES

•••VS
MIRVS
SHIVS
SLAVS
SPIVS
UNIVS

VT•••
VTOLS

V•T••
VATER
VATIC
VETCH
VITAE
VITAL
VITAS
VITUS
VOTED
VOTER
VOTES
VOTRE

V••T•
VASTY
VENTS
VERTE
VERTS
VESTA
VESTS
VIRTU
VISTA
VOLTA
VOLTE
VOLTS

V•••T
VALET
VAULT
VAUNT
VEIDT
VELDT
VERST
VINGT
VISIT
VOLAT

•V•T•
EVITA
OVATE
OVETA
OVETT

•V••T
AVANT
AVAST
AVERT
EVENT
EVERT
EVICT
OVERT
OVETT
TVSET

••V•T
AMVET
CIVET
COVET
DAVIT
DIVOT
DUVET
GAVOT
PIVOT
REVET
RIVET
TEVET

VU•••
VUGGY

V•U••
VAULT
VAUNT
VOUCH

V••U•
VACUA
VADUZ
VAGUE
VAGUS
VALUE
VELUM
VENUE
VENUS
VIRUS
VISUM
VITUS
VOGUE

V•••U
VIRTU

•VU••
OVULE
UVULA

••VU•
NEVUS
REVUE
REVUP

V•V••
VIVID
VIVRE

V••V•
VALVE
VERVE
VOLVA
VOLVO

••VV•
DIVVY
NAVVY
SAVVY

V•W••
VOWED
VOWEL
VOWER

V••W•
VIEWS
VIEWY

•V•W•
AVOWS

V•X••
VEXED
VEXER
VEXES
VIXEN

V•••X
VARIX

VY•••
VYING

V••Y•
VANYA
VINYL

V•••Y
VASTY
VEALY
VEDAY
VEERY
VEINY
VESEY
VICHY
VIEWY
VIGNY
VINNY
VISBY
VJDAY
VUGGY

•V••Y
AVERY
EVERY
IVORY

••VY•
DAVYS
TEVYE

••V•Y
COVEY
DEVRY
DIVVY
DOVEY
ENVOY
HOVEY
JIVEY
LOVEY
NAVVY
OYVAY
SAVOY
SAVVY

•••VY
CHEVY
CHIVY
CURVY
DIVVY
GRAVY
HEAVY
MARVY
NAVVY
NERVY
PEAVY
PRIVY
SAVVY
TURVY

V•••Z
VADUZ
VELEZ
VENEZ

WA•••
WAAFS
WAALS
WACKO
WACKY
WADDY
WADED
WADER
WADES
WADIS
WADUP
WAFER
WAFTS
WAGED
WAGER
WAGES
WAGON
WAHOO
WAIFS
WAILS
WAINS
WAIST
WAITE
WAITS
WAITZ
WAIVE
WAJDA
WAKED
WAKEN
WAKES
WALDO
WALED
WALER
WALES
WALEY
WALKS
WALLA
WALLS
WALLY
WALSH
WALSY
WALTZ
WANDA
WANDS
WANED
WANER
WANES
WANEY
WANLY
WANNA
WANTS
WARDS
WARES
WARMS
WARNS
WARPS
WARTS
WARTY
WASHY
WASNT
WASPS
WASPY
WASTE
WATCH
WATER
WATTS
WAUGH
WAVED
WAVER
WAVES
WAXED
WAXEN
WAXER
WAXES
WAYNE

W•A••
WAAFS
WAALS
WEALS
WEANS
WEARS
WEARY
WEAVE
WHACK
WHALE
WHAMO
WHAMS
WHANG
WHARF
WHATD
WHATS
WOADS
WRACK
WRACS
WRAFS
WRAPS
WRAPT
WRATH
WYATT

W••A•
WEKAS
WHEAL
WHEAT
WIGAN
WOMAN
WOTAN
WREAK
WUHAN
WYMAN

W•••A
WAJDA
WALLA
WANDA
WANNA
WICCA
WILLA
WILMA
WIRRA

•WA••
AWACS
AWAIT
AWAJI
AWAKE
AWARD
AWARE
AWASH
BWANA
DWARF
SWABS
SWAGE
SWAGS
SWAIN
SWALE
SWAMI
SWAMP
SWANK
SWANN
SWANS
SWAPS
SWARD
SWARF
SWARM
SWART
SWASH
SWATH
SWATS
SWAYS
SWAZI
TWAIN
TWANG

•W•A•
SWEAR
SWEAT
TWEAK
TWOAM
YWCAS

•W••A
BWANA
TWYLA

••WA•
AMWAY
ANWAR
ASWAN
ATWAR
BYWAY
DEWAN
DEWAR
ELWAY
HOWAR
IOWAN
MYWAY
NAWAB
NOWAY
OTWAY
PAWAT
POWAY
REWAX
ROWAN

•••WA
ADUWA
DAIWA
FATWA
KIOWA
OZAWA
SCHWA
SLIWA

W•B••
WEBBY
WEBER

W••B•
WEBBY
WELBY

•W•B•
SWABS
SWOBS

•W••B
DWEEB

••W•B
NAWAB

W•C••
WACKO
WACKY
WICCA
WICKS

W••C•
WATCH
WELCH
WENCH
WHACK
WHICH
WICCA
WILCO
WINCE
WINCH
WITCH
WRACK
WRACS
WRECK

•WC••
YWCAS

•W•C•
AWACS
TWICE

W•D••
WADDY
WADED
WADER
WADES
WADIS
WADUP
WEDEL
WEDGE
WEDGY
WIDEN
WIDER
WIDOW
WIDTH
WODEN
WODGE

W••D•
WADDY
WAJDA
WALDO
WANDA
WANDS
WARDS
WEEDS
WEEDY
WELDS
WENDS
WENDT
WENDY
WILDE
WILDS
WINDS
WINDY
WOADS
WOLDS
WOODS
WOODY
WORDS
WORDY

W•••D
WADED
WAGED
WAKED
WALED
WANED
WAVED
WAXED
WEIRD
WHATD
WIELD
WILED
WINED
WIPED
WIRED
WIVED
WOOED
WORLD
WOULD
WOUND
WOWED

•W•D•
SWEDE

•W••D
AWARD
AWNED
OWNED
SWARD
SWORD
TWEED

••WD•
BAWDY
DOWDY
GOWDY
HOWDY
ROWDY

••W•D
BOWED
CAWED
CLWYD
COWED
DEWED
HAWED
HEWED
JAWED
LOWED
MEWED
MOWED
PAWED
REWED
ROWED
SAWED
SEWED
SOWED
TOWED
UNWED
VOWED
WOWED
YAWED

•••WD
CROWD

WE•••
WEALS
WEANS
WEARS
WEARY
WEAVE
WEBBY
WEBER
WEDEL
WEDGE
WEDGY
WEEDS
WEEDY
WEEKS

WEEMS
WEENY
WEEPS
WEEPY
WEEST
WEFTS
WEIGH
WEILL
WEIRD
WEIRS
WEISS
WEKAS
WELBY
WELCH
WELDS
WELLS
WELSH
WELTS
WELTY
WENCH
WENDS
WENDT
WENDY
WESER
WESTS
WETLY

W•E••
WEEDS
WEEDY
WEEKS
WEEMS
WEENY
WEEPS
WEEPY
WEEST
WHEAL
WHEAT
WHEEL
WHEEN
WHELK
WHELM
WHELP
WHERE
WHETS
WHEYS
WIELD
WIEST
WREAK
WRECK
WRENS
WREST
WYETH

W••E•
WADED
WADER
WADES
WAFER
WAGED
WAGER
WAGES
WAKED
WAKEN
WAKES
WALED
WALER
WALES
WALEY
WANED
WANER
WANES
WANEY
WARES
WATER
WAVED
WAVER
WAVES
WAXED
WAXEN
WAXER
WAXES
WEBER
WEDEL
WESER
WHEEL
WHEEN
WIDEN
WIDER
WILED
WILES
WILEY
WINED
WINES
WINEY
WIPED
WIPER
WIPES
WIRED
WIRER
WIRES
WISER
WIVED
WIVES
WIZEN
WODEN
WOKEN
WOMEN
WOOED
WOOER
WOVEN
WOWED
WRIER
WRYER
WYLER

W•••E
WAITE
WAIVE
WASTE
WAYNE
WEAVE
WEDGE
WHALE
WHERE
WHILE
WHINE
WHITE
WHOLE
WHOSE
WHYME
WHYRE
WILDE
WINCE
WINZE
WITHE
WITTE
WODGE
WOLFE
WORSE
WRITE
WROTE
WYLIE
WYTHE

•WE••
DWEEB
DWELL
DWELT
EWELL
EWERS
GWENN
GWENT
OWENS
OWERS
SWEAR
SWEAT
SWEDE
SWEEP
SWEET
SWELL
SWEPT
TWEAK
TWEED
TWEEN
TWEER
TWEET
TWERE
TWERP
ZWEIG

•W•E•
AWNED
DWEEB
OWLET
OWNED
OWNER
SWEEP
SWEET
TWEED
TWEEN
TWEER
TWEET

•W••E
AWAKE
AWARE
AWOKE
SWAGE
SWALE
SWEDE
SWINE
SWIPE
SWOPE
SWORE
TWERE
TWICE
TWINE

••WE•
BOWED
BOWEN
BOWER
BOWES
CAWED
COWED
COWER
COWES
DAWES
DEWED
DEWEY
DOWEL
DOWER
ELWES
FEWER
GOWER
HAWED
HEWED
HEWER
JAWED
JEWEL
LAWES
LEWES
LOWED
LOWER
LOWES
MEWED
MOWED
MOWER
NEWEL
NEWER
NGWEE
PAWED
PAWER
PEWEE
POWER
RAWER
REWED
ROWED
ROWEL
ROWEN
ROWER
SAWED
SEWED
SEWER
SOWED
SOWER
TOWED
TOWEL
TOWER
UNWED
VOWED
VOWEL
VOWER
WOWED
YAWED

••W•E
BOWIE
DOWSE
HAWKE
HAWSE
HOWIE
NGWEE
PEWEE
TOWNE
ZOWIE

•••WE
INAWE
KITWE
LOEWE
STOWE

W•F••
WAFER
WAFTS
WEFTS

W••F•
WAAFS
WAIFS
WHIFF
WOLFE
WOLFF
WOOFS
WRAFS

W•••F
WHARF
WHIFF
WHOOF
WOLFF
WOOLF

•WF••
AWFUL

•W•F•
SWIFT

•W••F
DWARF
SWARF

W•G••
WAGED
WAGER
WAGES
WAGON
WIGAN
WIGGY
WIGHT

W••G•
WAUGH
WEDGE
WEDGY
WEIGH
WHIGS
WIGGY
WINGS
WODGE

W•••G
WHANG
WRING
WRONG
WRUNG

•W•G•
SWAGE
SWAGS
SWIGS
TWIGS

•W••G
AWING
EWING
OWING
SWING
SWUNG
TWANG
ZWEIG

••WG•
HAWGS

WH•••
WHACK
WHALE
WHAMO
WHAMS
WHANG
WHARF
WHATD
WHATS
WHEAL
WHEAT
WHEEL
WHEEN
WHELK
WHELM
WHELP
WHERE
WHETS
WHEYS
WHICH
WHIFF
WHIGS
WHILE
WHIMS
WHINE
WHINS
WHINY
WHIPS
WHIRL
WHIRR
WHIRS
WHISH
WHISK
WHIST
WHITE
WHITS
WHITY
WHOLE
WHOLL
WHOMP
WHOOF
WHOOP
WHOPS
WHORL
WHOSE
WHOSO
WHUPS
WHYLL
WHYME
WHYRE

W•H••
WAHOO
WUHAN

W••H•
WASHY
WIGHT
WISHY
WITHE
WITHY
WUSHU
WYTHE

W•••H
WALSH
WATCH
WAUGH
WEIGH
WELCH
WELSH
WENCH
WHICH
WHISH
WIDTH
WINCH
WITCH
WORTH
WRATH
WROTH
WYETH

•W••H
AWASH
SWASH
SWATH
SWISH
SWITH

WI•••
WICCA
WICKS
WIDEN
WIDER
WIDOW
WIDTH
WIELD
WIEST
WIGAN
WIGGY
WIGHT
WILCO
WILDE
WILDS
WILED
WILES
WILEY
WILLA
WILLS
WILLY
WILMA
WILTS
WIMPS
WIMPY
WINCE
WINCH
WINDS
WINDY
WINED
WINES
WINEY
WINGS
WINKS
WINZE
WIPED
WIPER
WIPES
WIRED
WIRER
WIRES
WIRRA
WISER
WISHY
WISPS
WISPY
WITCH
WITHE
WITHY
WITTE
WITTY
WIVED
WIVES
WIZEN

W•I••
WAIFS
WAILS
WAINS
WAIST
WAITE
WAITS
WAITZ
WAIVE
WEIGH
WEILL
WEIRD
WEIRS
WEISS
WHICH
WHIFF
WHIGS
WHILE
WHIMS
WHINE
WHINS
WHINY
WHIPS
WHIRL
WHIRR
WHIRS
WHISH
WHISK
WHIST
WHITE
WHITS
WHITY
WRIER
WRING
WRIST
WRITE
WRITS

W••I•
WADIS
WYLIE

•WI••
AWING
EWING
OWING
SWIFT
SWIGS
SWILL
SWIMS
SWINE
SWING
SWINK
SWIPE
SWIRL
SWISH
SWISS
SWITH
SWITZ
TWICE
TWIGS
TWILL
TWINE
TWINS
TWIRL
TWIST
TWITS
TWIXT

•W•I•
AWAIT
SWAIN
TWAIN
ZWEIG

•W••I
AWAJI
SWAMI
SWAZI

••WI•
BOWIE
EDWIN
ERWIN
HOWIE
IRWIN
KIWIS
LEWIS
NOWIN
PEWIT
REWIN
SAWIN
TOWIT
ZOWIE

W•J••
WAJDA

•W•J•
AWAJI

W•K••
WAKED
WAKEN
WAKES
WEKAS
WOKEN

W••K•
WACKO
WACKY
WALKS
WEEKS
WICKS
WINKS
WONKS
WONKY
WORKS

W•••K
WHACK
WHELK
WHISK
WRACK
WREAK
WRECK

•W•K•
AWAKE
AWOKE
EWOKS

•W••K
SWANK
SWINK
SWONK
TWEAK

••WK•
GAWKS
GAWKY
GOWKS
HAWKE
HAWKS
PAWKY

••W•K
MIWOK

W•L••
WALDO
WALED
WALER
WALES
WALEY
WALKS
WALLA
WALLS
WALLY
WALSH
WALSY
WALTZ
WELBY
WELCH
WELDS
WELLS
WELSH
WELTS
WELTY
WILCO
WILDE
WILDS
WILED
WILES
WILEY
WILLA
WILLS
WILLY
WILMA
WILTS
WOLDS
WOLFE
WOLFF
WYLER
WYLIE

W••L•
WAALS
WAILS
WALLA
WALLS
WALLY
WANLY
WEALS
WEILL
WELLS
WETLY
WHALE
WHELK
WHELM
WHELP

WHILE
WHOLE
WHOLL
WHYLL
WIELD
WILLA
WILLS
WILLY
WOOLF
WOOLS
WOOLY
WORLD
WOULD
WRYLY

W•••L
WEDEL
WEILL
WHEAL
WHEEL
WHIRL
WHOLL
WHORL
WHYLL

•WL••
OWLET

•W•L•
AWOLS
DWELL
DWELT
EWELL
SWALE
SWELL
SWILL
TWILL
TWYLA

•W••L
AWFUL
DWELL
EWELL
SWELL
SWILL
SWIRL
TWILL
TWIRL

••WL•
BAWLS
BOWLS
COWLS
FOWLS
HOWLS
JOWLS
JOWLY
LOWLY
MEWLS
NEWLY
PAWLS
RAWLS
RAWLY
YAWLS
YOWLS

••W•L
DOWEL
JEWEL
NEWEL
ROWEL
TOWEL
VOWEL

•••WL
BRAWL
CRAWL
DRAWL
GROWL
PROWL
SCOWL
SHAWL
TRAWL

W•M••
WIMPS
WIMPY
WOMAN
WOMEN
WOMYN
WYMAN

W••M•
WARMS
WEEMS
WHAMO
WHAMS
WHIMS
WHOMP
WHYME
WILMA
WORMS
WORMY

W•••M
WHELM

•W•M•
SWAMI
SWAMP
SWIMS

•W••M
SWARM
TWOAM
TWOPM

•••WM
SHAWM

W•N••
WANDA
WANDS
WANED
WANER
WANES
WANEY
WANLY
WANNA
WANTS
WENCH
WENDS
WENDT
WENDY
WINCE
WINCH
WINDS
WINDY
WINED
WINES
WINEY
WINGS
WINKS
WINZE
WONKS
WONKY
WONTS

W••N•
WAINS
WANNA
WARNS
WASNT
WAYNE
WEANS
WEENY
WHANG
WHINE
WHINS
WHINY
WOUND
WRENS
WRING
WRONG
WRUNG

W•••N
WAGON
WAKEN
WAXEN
WHEEN
WIDEN
WIGAN
WIZEN
WODEN
WOKEN
WOMAN
WOMEN
WOMYN
WOTAN
WOVEN
WUHAN
WYMAN

•WN••
AWNED
OWNED
OWNER
OWNUP

•W•N•
AWING
BWANA
EWING
GWENN
GWENT
GWYNN
OWENS
OWING
SWANK
SWANN
SWANS
SWINE
SWING
SWINK
SWONK
SWUNG
TWANG
TWINE
TWINS

•W••N
GWENN
GWYNN
SWAIN
SWANN
SWOON
SWORN
TWAIN
TWEEN

••WN•
DAWNS
DOWNS
DOWNY
FAWNS
GOWNS
LAWNS
LAWNY
PAWNS
TAWNY
TOWNE
TOWNS
TOWNY
YAWNS

••W•N
ASWAN
BOWEN
DEWAN
EDWIN
ERWIN
IOWAN
IRWIN
NOWIN
REWIN
REWON
ROWAN
ROWEN
SAWIN
SEWON

•••WN
BLOWN
BRAWN
BROWN
CLOWN
CROWN
DRAWN
DROWN
FLOWN
FROWN
GROWN
KNOWN
PRAWN
SHAWN
SHOWN
SPAWN

WO•••
WOADS
WODEN
WODGE
WOKEN
WOLDS
WOLFE
WOLFF
WOMAN
WOMEN
WOMYN
WONKS
WONKY
WONTS
WOODS
WOODY
WOOED
WOOER
WOOFS
WOOLF
WOOLS
WOOLY
WOOZY
WORDS
WORDY
WORKS
WORLD
WORMS
WORMY
WORRY
WORSE
WORST
WORTH
WORTS
WOTAN
WOULD
WOUND
WOVEN
WOWED

W•O••
WHOLE
WHOLL
WHOMP
WHOOF
WHOOP
WHOPS
WHORL
WHOSE
WHOSO
WOODS
WOODY
WOOED
WOOER
WOOFS
WOOLF
WOOLS
WOOLY
WOOZY
WRONG
WROTE
WROTH

W••O•
WAGON
WAHOO
WHOOF
WHOOP
WIDOW

W•••O
WACKO
WAHOO
WALDO
WHAMO
WHOSO
WILCO

•WO••
AWOKE
AWOLS
EWOKS
SWOBS
SWONK
SWOON
SWOOP
SWOPE
SWOPS
SWORD
SWORE
SWORN
TWOAM
TWOPM

•W•O•
SWOON
SWOOP

••WO•
MIWOK
OHWOW
REWON
SEWON

••W•O
HOWSO
HOWTO
SAWTO

•••WO
INTWO

W•P••
WIPED
WIPER
WIPES

W••P•
WARPS
WASPS
WASPY
WEEPS
WEEPY
WHIPS
WHOPS
WHUPS
WIMPS
WIMPY
WISPS
WISPY
WRAPS
WRAPT

W•••P
WADUP
WHELP
WHOMP
WHOOP

•W•P•
SWAPS
SWEPT
SWIPE
SWOPE
SWOPS
TWOPM

•W••P
OWNUP
SWAMP
SWEEP
SWOOP
TWERP

••WP•
GAWPS
YAWPS

••W•P
SEWUP

WR•••
WRACK
WRACS
WRAFS
WRAPS
WRAPT
WRATH
WREAK
WRECK
WRENS
WREST
WRIER
WRING
WRIST
WRITE
WRITS
WRONG
WROTE
WROTH
WRUNG
WRYER
WRYLY

W•R••
WARDS
WARES
WARMS
WARNS
WARPS
WARTS
WARTY
WIRED
WIRER
WIRES
WIRRA
WORDS
WORDY
WORKS
WORLD
WORMS
WORMY
WORRY
WORSE
WORST
WORTH
WORTS
WURST

W••R•
WEARS
WEARY
WEIRD
WEIRS
WHARF
WHERE
WHIRL
WHIRR
WHIRS
WHORL
WHYRE
WIRRA
WORRY

W•••R
WADER
WAFER
WAGER
WALER
WANER
WATER
WAVER
WAXER
WEBER
WESER
WHIRR
WIDER
WIPER
WIRER
WISER
WOOER
WRIER
WRYER
WYLER

•W•R•
AWARD
AWARE
DWARF
EWERS
OWERS
SWARD
SWARF
SWARM
SWART
SWIRL
SWORD
SWORE
SWORN
TWERE
TWERP
TWIRL

•W••R
OWNER
SWEAR
TWEER

••WR•
COWRY
DOWRY
LOWRY

••W•R
ANWAR
ATWAR
BOWER
COWER
DEWAR
DOWER
FEWER
GOWER
HEWER
HOWAR
LOWER
MOWER
NEWER
PAWER
POWER
RAWER
ROWER
SEWER
SOWER
TOWER
VOWER

W•S••
WASHY
WASNT
WASPS
WASPY
WASTE
WESER
WESTS
WISER
WISHY
WISPS
WISPY
WUSHU

W••S•
WAIST
WALSH
WALSY
WEEST
WEISS
WELSH
WHISH
WHISK
WHIST
WHOSE
WHOSO
WIEST
WORSE
WORST
WREST
WRIST
WURST

W•••S
WAAFS
WAALS
WADES
WADIS
WAFTS
WAGES
WAIFS
WAILS
WAINS
WAITS
WAKES
WALES
WALKS
WALLS
WANDS
WANES
WANTS
WARDS
WARES
WARMS
WARNS
WARPS
WARTS
WASPS
WATTS
WAVES
WAXES
WEALS
WEANS
WEARS
WEEDS
WEEKS
WEEMS
WEEPS
WEFTS
WEIRS
WEISS
WEKAS
WELDS
WELLS
WELTS
WENDS
WESTS
WHAMS
WHATS
WHETS
WHEYS
WHIGS
WHIMS
WHINS
WHIPS
WHIRS
WHITS
WHOPS
WHUPS
WICKS
WILDS
WILES
WILLS
WILTS
WIMPS
WINDS
WINES
WINGS
WINKS
WIPES
WIRES
WISPS
WIVES
WOADS
WOLDS
WONKS
WONTS
WOODS
WOOFS
WOOLS
WORDS
WORKS
WORMS
WORTS
WRACS
WRAFS
WRAPS
WRENS
WRITS

•W•S•
AWASH
SWASH
SWISH
SWISS
TWIST

•W••S
AWACS AWOLS EWERS EWOKS OWENS OWERS SWABS SWAGS SWANS SWAPS SWATS SWAYS SWIGS SWIMS SWISS SWOBS SWOPS TWIGS TWINS TWITS YWCAS

••WS•
DOWSE HAWSE HOWSO NEWSY

••W•S
BAWLS BOWES BOWLS COWES COWLS DAWES DAWNS DOWNS ELWES FAWNS FOWLS GAWKS GAWPS GOWKS GOWNS HAWGS HAWKS HOWLS JOWLS KIWIS LAWES LAWNS LEWES LEWIS LOWES MEWLS NEWTS PAWLS PAWNS POWYS RAWLS TOWNS YAWLS YAWNS YAWPS YOWLS

•••WS
AVOWS BLOWS BREWS BROWS CHAWS CHEWS CHOWS CLAWS CLEWS CRAWS CREWS CROWS DHOWS DRAWS FLAWS FLEWS FLOWS FROWS GLOWS GNAWS GROWS KNOWS MEOWS PLEWS PLOWS PROWS SCOWS SHOWS SKEWS SLAWS SLEWS SLOWS SMEWS SNOWS SPEWS STEWS STOWS THAWS THEWS TREWS VIEWS

W•T••
WATCH WATER WATTS WETLY WITCH WITHE WITHY WITTE WITTY WOTAN WYTHE

W••T•
WAFTS WAITE WAITS WAITZ WALTZ WANTS WARTS WARTY WASTE WATTS WEFTS WELTS WELTY WESTS WHATD WHATS WHETS WHITE WHITS WHITY WIDTH WILTS WITTE WITTY WONTS WORTH WORTS WRATH WRITE WRITS WROTE WROTH WYATT WYETH

W•••T
WAIST WASNT WEEST WENDT WHEAT WHIST WIEST WIGHT WORST WRAPT WREST WRIST WURST WYATT

•W•T•
SWATH SWATS SWITH SWITZ TWITS

•W••T
AWAIT DWELT GWENT OWLET SWART SWEAT SWEET SWEPT SWIFT TWEET TWIST TWIXT

••WT•
HOWTO NEWTS SAWTO

••W•T
PAWAT PEWIT TOWIT

WU•••
WUHAN WURST WUSHU

W•U••
WAUGH WHUPS WOULD WOUND WRUNG

W••U•
WADUP

W•••U
WUSHU

•WU••
SWUNG

•W•U•
AWFUL OWNUP

••WU•
SEWUP

•••WU
ILGWU

W•V••
WAVED WAVER WAVES WIVED WIVES WOVEN

W••V•
WAIVE WEAVE

W•W••
WOWED

W•••W
WIDOW

••W•W
OHWOW

W•X••
WAXED WAXEN WAXER WAXES

•W•X•
TWIXT

••W•X
REWAX

WY•••
WYATT WYETH WYLER WYLIE WYMAN WYTHE

W•Y••
WAYNE WHYLL WHYME WHYRE WRYER WRYLY

W••Y•
WHEYS WOMYN

W•••Y
WACKY WADDY WALEY WALLY WALSY WANEY WANLY WARTY WASHY WASPY WEARY WEBBY WEDGY WEEDY WEENY WEEPY WELBY WELTY WENDY WETLY WHINY WHITY WIGGY WILEY WILLY WIMPY WINDY WINEY WISHY WISPY WITHY WITTY WONKY WOODY WOOLY WOOZY WORDY WORMY WORRY WRYLY

•WY••
GWYNN TWYLA

•W•Y•
SWAYS

••WY•
CLWYD POWYS

••W•Y
AMWAY BAWDY BYWAY COWRY DEWEY DOWDY DOWNY DOWRY ELWAY GAWKY GOWDY HOWDY JOWLY LAWNY LOWLY LOWRY MYWAY NEWLY NEWSY NOWAY OTWAY PAWKY POWAY RAWLY ROWDY TAWNY TOWNY

•••WY
BLOWY CHEWY FLAWY LOEWY SHOWY SNOWY THEWY VIEWY

W•Z••
WIZEN

W••Z•
WINZE WOOZY

W•••Z
WAITZ WALTZ

•W•Z•
SWAZI

•W••Z
SWITZ

XA•••
XACTO XAXES XAXIS

X•A••
XRAYS

X•••A
XENIA XHOSA

•XA••
EXACT EXALT EXAMS

•X•A•
AXIAL IXNAY UXMAL

•X••A
EXTRA

••XA•
COXAE COXAL HEXAD LEXAN SIXAM TEXAN TEXAS

X•B••
XEBEC

•XB••
OXBOW

•X••B
EXURB

••XB•
BIXBY

XC•••
XCIII XCVII

X•C••
XACTO

X•••C
XEBEC XERIC

•XC••
CXCII CXCIV CXCIX CXCVI DXCII DXCIV DXCIX DXCVI EXCEL MXCII MXCIV MXCIX MXCVI

•X•C•
EXACT EXECS

••XC•
CCXCI CCXCV CDXCI CDXCV CMXCI CMXCV DCXCI DCXCV MCXCI MCXCV MDXCI MDXCV MMXCI MMXCV TAXCO

••X•C
TOXIC

•••XC
CCCXC DCCXC MCCXC MCDXC MCMXC MDCXC MMCXC MMDXC MMMXC

XD•••
XDOUT

X•D••
XEDIN

•X•D•
EXUDE OXIDE

••X•D
BOXED COXED FAXED FIXED FOXED HEXAD HEXED MAXED MIXED NIXED SIXED TAXED VEXED WAXED

XE•••
XEBEC XEDIN XENIA XENON XERIC XEROX XERUS

X••E•
XAXES XEBEC XYLEM

•XE••
AXELS AXERS EXECS EXERT OXEYE

•X•E•
AXLES EXCEL EXPEL

•X••E
AXONE EXILE EXUDE OXEYE OXIDE

••XE•
BOXED BOXER BOXES COXED COXES COXEY DUXES FAXED FAXES FIXED FIXER FIXES FOXED FOXES HEXED HEXER HEXES LAXER LOXES MAXED MAXES MIXED MIXER MIXES NIXED NIXES PIXEL REXES SAXES SEXES SIXED SIXER SIXES SOXER TAXED TAXER TAXES TUXES VEXED VEXER VEXES VIXEN WAXED WAXEN WAXER WAXES XAXES YAXES ZAXES

••X•E
COXAE DIXIE HOXIE MAXIE MOXIE NIXIE PIXIE PYXIE ROXIE

X••G•
XINGU

•X••G
AXING

XH•••
XHOSA

••X•H
SIXTH

XI•••
XINGU

X•I••
XCIII XLIII XVIII XXIII

X••I•
XAXIS XCIII XCVII XEDIN XENIA XERIC XLIII XLVII XVIII XXIII XXVII XXXII XXXIV XXXIX

X•••I
XCIII XCVII XLIII XLVII XVIII XXIII XXVII XXXII XXXVI

•XI••
AXIAL AXILS AXING AXIOM AXION CXIII DXIII EXILE EXIST EXITS IXION LXIII MXIII OXIDE XXIII

•X•I•
CXCII CXCIV CXCIX

CXIII
CXLII
CXLIV
CXLIX
CXVII
CXXII
CXXIV
CXXIX
DXCII
DXCIV
DXCIX
DXIII
DXLII
DXLIV
DXLIX
DXVII
DXXII
DXXIV
DXXIX
LXIII
LXVII
LXXII
LXXIV
LXXIX
MXCII
MXCIV
MXCIX
MXIII
MXLII
MXLIV
MXLIX
MXMII
MXMIV
MXVII
MXXII
MXXIV
MXXIX
OXLIP
XXIII
XXVII
XXXII
XXXIV
XXXIX

•X••I
CXCII
CXCVI
CXIII
CXLII
CXLVI
CXVII
CXXII
CXXVI
CXXXI
DXCII
DXCVI
DXIII
DXLII
DXLVI
DXVII
DXXII
DXXVI
DXXXI
LXIII
LXVII
LXXII
LXXVI
LXXXI
MXCII
MXCVI
MXIII
MXLII
MXLVI
MXMII
MXVII
MXXII
MXXVI
MXXXI
XXIII
XXVII
XXXII
XXXVI

••XI•
AUXIL
AUXIN
BOXIN
CCXII
CCXIV
CCXIX
CDXII
CDXIV
CDXIX
CLXII
CLXIV
CLXIX
CMXII
CMXIV
CMXIX
CXXII
CXXIV
CXXIX
DCXII
DCXIV
DCXIX
DIXIE
DIXIT
DLXII
DLXIV
DLXIX
DXXII
DXXIV
DXXIX
FIXIT
HOXIE
LEXIS
LXXII
LXXIV
LXXIX
MAXIE
MAXIM
MAXIS
MCXII
MCXIV
MCXIX
MDXII
MDXIV
MDXIX
MIXIN
MLXII
MLXIV
MLXIX
MMXII
MMXIV
MMXIX
MOXIE
MXXII
MXXIV
MXXIX
NEXIS
NIXIE
PIXIE
PYXIE
PYXIS
ROXIE
TAXIS
TOXIC
TOXIN
XAXIS
XXXII
XXXIV
XXXIX
YAXIS
ZAXIS

••X•I
CCXCI
CCXII
CCXLI
CCXVI
CCXXI
CDXCI
CDXII
CDXLI
CDXVI
CDXXI
CLXII
CLXVI
CLXXI
CMXCI
CMXII
CMXLI
CMXVI
CMXXI
CXXII
CXXVI
CXXXI
DCXCI
DCXII
DCXLI
DCXVI
DCXXI
DLXII
DLXVI
DLXXI
DXXII
DXXVI
DXXXI
LXXII
LXXVI
LXXXI
MCXCI
MCXII
MCXLI
MCXVI
MCXXI
MDXCI
MDXII
MDXLI
MDXVI
MDXXI
MLXII
MLXVI
MLXXI
MMXCI
MMXII
MMXLI
MMXVI
MMXXI
MXXII
MXXVI
MXXXI
XXXII
XXXVI

•••XI
BENXI
CCCXI
CCLXI
CCXXI
CDLXI
CDXXI
CLXXI
CMLXI
CMXXI
CXXXI
DCCXI
DCLXI
DCXXI
DLXXI
DXXXI
FLEXI
LXXXI
MCCXI
MCDXI
MCLXI
MCMXI
MCXXI
MDCXI
MDLXI
MDXXI
MLXXI
MMCXI
MMDXI
MMLXI
MMMXI
MMXXI
MXXXI

XL•••
XLIII
XLVII

X•L••
XYLEM

•XL••
AXLES
CXLII
CXLIV
CXLIX
CXLVI
DXLII
DXLIV
DXLIX
DXLVI
MXLII
MXLIV
MXLIX
MXLVI
OXLIP

•X•L•
AXELS
AXILS
EXALT
EXILE
EXULT

•X••L
AXIAL
EXCEL
EXPEL
EXTOL
UXMAL

••XL•
CCXLI
CCXLV
CDXLI
CDXLV
CMXLI
CMXLV
DCXLI
DCXLV
LAXLY
MCXLI
MCXLV
MDXLI
MDXLV
MMXLI
MMXLV

••X•L
AUXIL
COXAL
HEXYL
PIXEL

•••XL
CCCXL
DCCXL
MCCXL
MCDXL
MCMXL
MDCXL
MMCXL
MMDXL
MMMXL

X•••M
XYLEM

•XM••
MXMII
MXMIV
UXMAL

•X•M•
EXAMS

•X••M
AXIOM

••XM•
SIXMO

••X•M
MAXIM
SIXAM
SIXPM

X•N••
XENIA
XENON
XINGU

X•••N
XEDIN
XENON

•XN••
IXNAY

•X•N•
AXING
AXONE
AXONS
EXONS

•X••N
AXION
EXXON
IXION

••X•N
AUXIN
BOXIN
DIXON
EXXON
LEXAN
MIXIN
NIXON
SAXON
TAXON
TEXAN
TOXIN
VIXEN
WAXEN

X•O••
XDOUT
XHOSA
XSOUT

X••O•
XENON
XEROX

X•••O
XACTO

•XO••
AXONE
AXONS
EXONS

•X•O•
AXIOM
AXION
EXPOS
EXTOL
EXXON
IXION
OXBOW

•X••O
EXTRO

••XO•
DIXON
EXXON
LUXOR
NAXOS
NIXON
SAXON
TAXON

••X•O
SIXMO
TAXCO

•••XO
GLAXO

•XP••
EXPEL
EXPOS

•X••P
OXLIP

••XP•
SIXPM

••X•P
BOXUP
FIXUP
MIXUP

XR•••
XRAYS

X•R••
XERIC
XEROX
XERUS

•X•R•
AXERS
EXERT
EXTRA
EXTRO
EXURB

••X•R
BOXER
DEXTR
FIXER
HEXER
LAXER
LUXOR
MIXER
SIXER
SOXER
TAXER
VEXER
WAXER

XS•••
XSOUT

X••S•
XHOSA

X•••S
XAXES
XAXIS
XERUS
XRAYS

•X•S•
EXIST

•X••S
AXELS
AXERS
AXILS
AXLES
AXONS
EXAMS
EXECS
EXITS
EXONS
EXPOS

••X•S
BOXES
COXES
DUXES
FAXES
FIXES
FOXES
HEXES
LEXIS
LEXUS
LOXES
MAXES
MAXIS
MIXES
NAXOS
NEXIS
NEXUS
NIXES
PYXIS
REXES
SAXES
SEXES
SEXTS
SIXES
TAXES
TAXIS
TEXAS
TEXTS
TUXES
VEXES
WAXES
XAXES
XAXIS
YAXES
YAXIS
ZAXES
ZAXIS

X••T•
XACTO

X•••T
XDOUT
XSOUT

•XT••
EXTOL
EXTRA
EXTRO

•X•T•
EXITS

•X••T
EXACT
EXALT
EXERT
EXIST
EXULT

••XT•
DEXTR
FOXTV
SEXTS
SIXTH
SIXTY
TEXTS

••X•T
DIXIT
FIXIT

•••XT
TWIXT

X••U•
XDOUT
XERUS
XSOUT

X•••U
XINGU

•XU••
EXUDE
EXULT
EXURB

••XU•
BOXUP
FIXUP
LEXUS
MIXUP
NEXUS

XV•••
XVIII

X•V••
XCVII
XLVII
XXVII

X••V•
XXXVI

X•••V
XXXIV

•XV••
CXVII
DXVII
LXVII
MXVII
XXVII

•X•V•
CXCVI
CXLVI
CXXVI
DXCVI
DXLVI
DXXVI
LXXVI
MXCVI
MXLVI
MXXVI
XXXVI

•X••V
CXCIV
CXLIV
CXXIV
CXXXV
DXCIV
DXLIV
DXXIV
DXXXV
LXXIV
LXXXV
MXCIV
MXLIV
MXMIV
MXXIV
MXXXV
XXXIV

••XV•
CCXVI
CDXVI
CLXVI
CMXVI
CXXVI
DCXVI
DLXVI
DXXVI
LXXVI
MCXVI
MDXVI
MLXVI
MMXVI
MXXVI
XXXVI

••X•V
CCXCV
CCXIV
CCXLV
CCXXV
CDXCV
CDXIV
CDXLV
CDXXV
CLXIV
CLXXV
CMXCV
CMXIV
CMXLV
CMXXV
CXXIV
CXXXV
DCXCV
DCXIV
DCXLV
DCXXV
DLXIV
DLXXV
DXXIV
DXXXV
FOXTV
LXXIV
LXXXV
MCXCV
MCXIV
MCXLV
MCXXV
MDXCV
MDXIV

MDXLV
MDXXV
MLXIV
MLXXV
MMXCV
MMXIV
MMXLV
MMXXV
MXXIV
MXXXV
XXXIV

•••XV
CCCXV
CCLXV
CCXXV
CDLXV
CDXXV
CLXXV
CMLXV
CMXXV
CXXXV
DCCXV
DCLXV
DCXXV
DLXXV
DXXXV
LXXXV
MCCXV
MCDXV
MCLXV
MCMXV
MCXXV
MDCXV
MDLXV
MDXXV
MLXXV
MMCXV
MMDXV
MMLXV
MMMXV
MMXXV
MXXXV

•X••W
OXBOW

XX•••
XXIII
XXVII
XXXII
XXXIV
XXXIX
XXXVI

X•X••
XAXES
XAXIS
XXXII
XXXIV
XXXIX
XXXVI

X•••X
XEROX
XXXIX

•XX••
CXXII
CXXIV
CXXIX
CXXVI
CXXXI
CXXXV
DXXII
DXXIV
DXXIX
DXXVI
DXXXI
DXXXV
EXXON
LXXII
LXXIV
LXXIX
LXXVI
LXXXI
LXXXV
MXXII
MXXIV
MXXIX
MXXVI
MXXXI
MXXXV
XXXII
XXXIV
XXXIX
XXXVI

•X•X•
CXXXI
CXXXV
DXXXI
DXXXV
LXXXI
LXXXV
MXXXI
MXXXV

•X••X
CXCIX
CXLIX
CXXIX
DXCIX
DXLIX
DXXIX
LXXIX
MXCIX
MXLIX
MXXIX
XXXIX

••XX•
CCXXI
CCXXV
CCXXX
CDXXI
CDXXV
CDXXX
CLXXI
CLXXV
CLXXX
CMXXI
CMXXV
CMXXX
CXXXI
CXXXV
DCXXI
DCXXV
DCXXX
DLXXI
DLXXV
DLXXX
DXXXI
DXXXV
LXXXI
LXXXV
MCXXI
MCXXV
MCXXX
MDXXI
MDXXV
MDXXX
MLXXI
MLXXV
MLXXX
MMXXI
MMXXV
MMXXX
MXXXI
MXXXV

••X•X
CCXIX
CCXXX
CDXIX
CDXXX
CLXIX
CLXXX
CMXIX
CMXXX
CXXIX
DCXIX
DCXXX
DLXIX
DLXXX
DXXIX
LXXIX
MCXIX
MCXXX
MDXIX
MDXXX
MLXIX
MLXXX
MMXIX
MMXXX
MXXIX
XXXIX

•••XX
CCCXX
CCLXX
CCXXX
CDLXX
CDXXX
CLXXX
CMLXX
CMXXX
DCCXX
DCLXX
DCXXX
DLXXX
MCCXX
MCDXX
MCLXX
MCMXX
MCXXX
MDCXX
MDLXX
MDXXX
MLXXX
MMCXX
MMDXX
MMLXX
MMMXX
MMXXX
SKNXX

XY•••
XYLEM

X••Y•
XRAYS

•X•Y•
OXEYE

•X••Y
IXNAY

••XY•
HEXYL

••X•Y
BIXBY
COXEY
LAXLY
SIXTY

•••XY
DEOXY
EPOXY
FLAXY
PREXY
PROXY

YA•••
YABBA
YACHT
YACKS
YADIM
YAHOO
YAKOV
YAKUT
YALIE
YALOW
YALTA
YAMPA
YANKS
YANNI
YAPOK
YAQUI
YARDS
YARER
YARNS
YASIR
YATES
YAWED
YAWLS
YAWNS
YAWPS
YAXES
YAXIS
YAZOO

Y•A••
YEANS
YEARN
YEARS
YEAST
YEATS
YUANS

Y••A•
YMCAS
YOGAS
YUGAS
YUMAN
YUMAS
YWCAS

Y•••A
YABBA
YALTA
YAMPA
YENTA
YERBA
YORBA
YUCCA

•YA••
AYAHS
CYANO
DYADS
HYAMS
HYATT
KYACK
KYATS
NYACK
NYALA
NYASA
WYATT

•Y•A•
BYFAR
BYLAW
BYWAY
CYCAD
CYMAE
CYMAS
DYLAN
EYRAS
GYRAL
HYLAS
HYMAN
HYRAX
LYMAN
MYLAR
MYNAH
MYNAS
MYWAY
OYVAY
TYNAN
WYMAN

•Y••A
HYDRA
HYENA
HYPHA
KYOGA
LYCRA
LYDIA
LYNDA
LYTTA
MYRNA
NYALA
NYASA
SYRIA
TYPEA

••YA•
ARYAN
BAYAR
BOYAR
BRYAN
DAYAK
DAYAN
DRYAD
FLYAT
GAYAL
HOYAS
KAYAK
LOYAL
MAYAN
MAYAS
RIYAL
ROYAL
SOYAS

••Y•A
ADYTA
ASYLA
ETYMA
LAYLA
PHYLA
RHYTA
TAYRA
TWYLA

•••YA
ABAYA
DARYA
FREYA
KENYA
LENYA
LIBYA
ORIYA
PLAYA
SEEYA
SONYA
TANYA
TONYA
VANYA

Y•B••
YABBA
YOBBO

Y••B•
YABBA
YERBA
YOBBO
YORBA

•YB••
CYBER
GYBED
GYBES
SYBIL

•Y••B
TYPEB

••YB•
FLYBY
LAYBY
MAYBE

Y•C••
YACHT
YACKS
YECCH
YMCAS
YUCCA
YUCKY
YWCAS

Y••C•
YECCH
YUCCA

Y•••C
YOGIC

•YC••
CYCAD
CYCLE
CYCLO
LYCEE
LYCRA
MYCIN
SYCEE
SYCES
TYCHE
TYCHO

•Y•C•
KYACK
LYNCH
NYACK
SYNCS

•Y••C
CYNIC
LYRIC
PYRIC

••YC•
ALYCE
BRYCE
CAYCE
GLYCO
JOYCE
PHYCO
PRYCE
PSYCH
ROYCE

•••YC
ENCYC

Y•D••
YADIM
YODEL
YODHS

Y••D•
YARDS

Y•••D
YAWED
YIELD
YOKED

•YD••
CYDER
EYDIE
HYDRA
HYDRO
LYDIA
RYDER
SYDOW

•Y•D•
BYRDS
CYNDI
DYADS
LYNDA
LYNDE

•Y••D
CYCAD
DYFED
GYBED
GYVED
HYOID
HYPED
SYNOD
TYPED

••YD•
CLYDE
HAYDN

••Y•D
BAYED
DRYAD
GUYED
HAYED
KEYED
PAYED
RAYED
TOYED

•••YD
ALKYD
CLWYD
FLOYD
LLOYD
SLOYD
THEYD

YE•••
YEANS
YEARN
YEARS
YEAST
YEATS
YECCH
YEGGS
YELLS
YELPS
YEMEN
YENTA
YENTE
YENTL
YERBA
YERKS
YESES
YESNO
YETIS

Y•E••
YIELD

Y••E•
YARER
YATES
YAWED
YAXES
YEMEN
YESES
YIKES
YIPES
YODEL
YOKED
YOKEL
YOKES
YPRES

Y•••E
YALIE
YENTE
YOURE
YOUSE
YOUVE

•YE••
AYERS
DYERS
EYERS
HYENA
LYELL
MYELO
MYERS
MYEYE
NYETS
WYETH

•Y•E•
AYRES
BYNER
BYRES
BYTES
CYBER
CYDER
CYMES
DYFED
DYNEL
DYNES
EYRES
FYKES
GYBED
GYBES
GYRES
GYVED
GYVES
HYPED
HYPER
HYPES
KYSER
LYCEE
LYRES
MYLES
NYMET
NYNEX
PYRES
PYREX
RYDER
SYCEE
SYCES
TYKES
TYLER
TYNES
TYPEA
TYPEB
TYPED
TYPEE
TYPER
TYPES
TYPEY
TYRES
WYLER
XYLEM

•Y••E
BYRNE
CYCLE
CYMAE
EYDIE
EYRIE
KYRIE
LYCEE
LYNDE
LYNNE
MYEYE
MYOPE
PYXIE
SYCEE
SYNGE
TYCHE
TYPEE
WYLIE
WYTHE

••YE•
ABYES
ASYET
BAYED
BAYER
BOYER
BUYER
COYER
CRYER
DIYER
DOYEN
DRYER
FEYER
FLYER
FOYER
FRYER
GAYER
GUYED
HAYED
HAYEK
HAYES
KEYED
KEYES
LAYER
MAYER
MEYER
NOYES
NUYEN
PAYED
PAYEE
PAYER
RAYED
REYES
SAYER
SHYER
SKYEY
SLYER
TOYED
WRYER

••Y•E
ALYCE
BAYLE
BEYLE
BOYLE
BOYNE
BRYCE
CAYCE
CLYDE
DAYNE
DOYLE
ELYSE
FOYLE
GAYLE
HEYSE
HOYLE
JAYNE
JOYCE
LAYNE
LEYTE
MAYBE
PAYEE
PAYNE
PHYFE
PHYLE
PRYCE
RHYME
ROYCE
SLYPE
STYLE
STYNE
THYME
TRYME
WAYNE
WHYME
WHYRE

•••YE
MYEYE
OXEYE
REDYE
TEVYE

•YF••
BYFAR
DYFED

••YF•
PHYFE

Y•G••
YEGGS
YOGAS
YOGHS
YOGIC
YOGIS
YUGAS
YUGOS

Y••G•
YEGGS

Y•••G
YOUNG

•YG••
BYGUM
HYGRO
MYGUY
PYGMY

•Y•G•
KYOGA
SYNGE

•Y••G
DYING
HYING
LYING
TYING
VYING

Y•H••
YAHOO

Y••H•
YACHT
YODHS
YOGHS

Y•••H
YECCH
YOUTH

•Y•H•
AYAHS
HYPHA
MYTHS
TYCHE
TYCHO
WYTHE

•Y••H
LYMPH
LYNCH
MYNAH
MYRRH
NYMPH
SYLPH
WYETH

••Y•H
BLYTH
GLYPH
PSYCH
SMYTH

YI•••
YIELD
YIKES
YIPES

Y••I•
YADIM
YALIE
YASIR
YAXIS
YETIS
YOGIC
YOGIS
YUPIK

Y•••I
YANNI
YAQUI
YOKOI

•YI••
AYINS
DYING
HYING
LYING
TYING
VYING

•Y•I•
CYNIC
CYRIL
EYDIE
EYRIE
EYRIR
HYOID
KYLIX
KYRIE
LYDIA
LYRIC
LYSIN
MYCIN
MYSIN
PYRIC
PYXIE
PYXIS
SYBIL
SYRIA
WYLIE

•Y••I
CYNDI

••YI•
FLYIN
KEYIN
LAYIN
PAYIN
ZAYIN

••Y•I
PHYSI
SPYRI
STYLI

Y•K••
YAKOV
YAKUT
YIKES
YOKED
YOKEL
YOKES
YOKOI
YOKUM
YUKON

Y••K•
YACKS
YANKS
YERKS
YOLKS
YOLKY
YUCKY

Y•••K
YAPOK
YUPIK
YUROK

•YK••
FYKES
TYKES

•Y••K
KYACK
NYACK

••YK•
ROYKO

••Y•K
DAYAK
HAYEK
KAYAK

Y•L••
YALIE
YALOW
YALTA
YELLS
YELPS
YOLKS
YOLKY

Y••L•
YAWLS
YELLS
YIELD
YOULL
YOWLS

Y•••L
YENTL
YODEL
YOKEL
YOULL

•YL••
BYLAW
DYLAN
HYLAS
KYLIX
MYLAR
MYLES
NYLON
PYLON
SYLPH
TYLER
WYLER
WYLIE
XYLEM

•Y•L•
CYCLE
CYCLO
LYELL
MYELO
NYALA

•Y••L
CYRIL
DYNEL
GYRAL
KYZYL
LYELL
LYSOL
SYBIL
TYROL

••YL•
ACYLS
AMYLO
AMYLS
ASYLA
BAYLE
BEYLE
BOYLE
COYLY
DOYLE
DOYLY
DRYLY
FEYLY
FOYLE
GAYLE
GAYLY
HOYLE
IDYLL
IDYLS
LAYLA
PHYLA
PHYLE
PHYLL
SHYLY
SLYLY
STYLE
STYLI
STYLO
TWYLA
WHYLL
WRYLY

••Y•L
GAYAL
IDYLL
LOYAL
PHYLL
RIYAL
ROYAL
WHYLL

•••YL
ALKYL
ALLYL
BERYL
BUTYL
DARYL
ETHYL
HEXYL
KYZYL
MERYL
SIBYL
VINYL

YM•••
YMCAS

Y•M••
YAMPA
YEMEN
YUMAN
YUMAS
YUMMY

Y••M•
YUMMY

Y•••M
YADIM
YOKUM

•YM••
CYMAE
CYMAS
CYMES
CYMRY
GYMNO
HYMAN
HYMNS
LYMAN
LYMON
LYMPH
NYMET
NYMPH
WYMAN

•Y•M•
HYAMS
PYGMY

•Y••M
BYGUM
XYLEM

••YM•
ETYMA
RHYME
STYMY
THYME
THYMY
TRYME
WHYME

••Y•M
ABYSM

Y•N••
YANKS
YANNI
YENTA
YENTE
YENTL

Y••N•
YANNI
YARNS
YAWNS
YEANS
YESNO
YOUNG
YOUNT
YUANS

Y•••N
YEARN
YEMEN
YUKON
YUMAN

•YN••
BYNER
BYNOW
CYNDI
CYNIC
DYNEL
DYNES
LYNCH
LYNDA
LYNDE
LYNNE
MYNAH
MYNAS
NYNEX
SYNCS
SYNGE
SYNOD
TYNAN
TYNES

•Y•N•
AYINS
BYRNE
CYANO
DYING
GYMNO
HYENA
HYING
HYMNS
HYPNO
LYING
LYNNE
LYONS
MYRNA
TYING
VYING

•Y••N
BYRON
DYLAN
GYRON
HYMAN
HYSON
LYMAN
LYMON
LYSIN
MYCIN
MYRON
MYSIN
NYLON
PYLON
TYNAN
TYSON
WYMAN

••YN•
BOYNE
DAYNE
FLYNN
GWYNN
JAYNE
LAYNE
MAYNT
PAYNE
STYNE
WAYNE

••Y•N
ARYAN
BRYAN
DAYAN
DOYEN
FLYIN
FLYNN
GWYNN
HAYDN
KEYIN
LAYIN
LAYON
MAYAN
MAYON
NUYEN
PAYIN
RAYON
SPYON
TOYON
TRYON
ZAYIN

•••YN
EMLYN
OBGYN
WOMYN

YO•••
YOBBO
YODEL
YODHS
YOGAS
YOGHS
YOGIC
YOGIS
YOKED
YOKEL
YOKES
YOKOI
YOKUM
YOLKS
YOLKY
YORBA
YOULL
YOUNG
YOUNT
YOURE
YOURS
YOUSE
YOUTH
YOUVE
YOWLS
YOYOS

Y••O•
YAHOO
YAKOV
YALOW
YAPOK
YAZOO
YOKOI
YOYOS
YUGOS
YUKON
YUROK

Y•••O
YAHOO
YAZOO
YESNO
YOBBO

•YO••
EYOTS
HYOID
KYOGA
KYOTO
LYONS
MYOPE
RYOTS

•Y•O•
BYNOW
BYRON
GYRON
GYROS
HYPOS
HYSON
LYMON
LYSOL
MYRON
NYLON
PYLON
SYDOW
SYNOD
SYSOP
TYPOS
TYROL
TYROS
TYSON

•Y••O
CYANO
CYCLO
GYMNO
HYDRO
HYGRO
HYPNO
HYPSO
KYOTO
MYELO
TYCHO

••YO•
BAYOU
BOYOS
GUYOT
KAYOS
LAYON
MAYON
MAYOR
PRYOR
RAYON
SPYON
TOYON
TRYON
YOYOS

••Y•O
AMYLO
GLYCO
LAYTO
MAYPO
PHYCO
PHYTO
ROYKO
SAYSO
STYLO

•••YO
SANYO
TOKYO

YP•••
YPRES

Y•P••
YAPOK
YIPES
YUPIK

Y••P•
YAMPA
YAWPS
YELPS

•YP••
GYPSY
HYPED
HYPER
HYPES
HYPHA
HYPNO
HYPOS
HYPSO
TYPEA
TYPEB
TYPED
TYPEE
TYPER
TYPES
TYPEY
TYPOS

•Y•P•
LYMPH
MYOPE
NYMPH
SYLPH

•Y••P
SYRUP
SYSOP

••YP•
COYPU
CRYPT
EGYPT
GLYPH
MAYPO
SLYPE

••Y•P
BUYUP
DRYUP
KEYUP
LAYUP
PAYUP

•••YP
POLYP

Y•Q••
YAQUI

Y•R••
YARDS
YARER
YARNS
YERBA
YERKS
YORBA
YPRES
YUROK
YURTS

Y••R•
YEARN
YEARS
YOURE
YOURS

Y•••R
YARER
YASIR

•YR••
AYRES
BYRDS
BYRES
BYRNE
BYRON
CYRIL
CYRUS
EYRAS
EYRES
EYRIE
EYRIR
GYRAL
GYRES
GYRON
GYROS
GYRUS
HYRAX
KYRIE
LYRES
LYRIC
MYRNA
MYRON
MYRRH
PYRES
PYREX
PYRIC
SYRIA
SYRUP
TYRES
TYROL
TYROS

•Y•R•
AYERS
CYMRY
DYERS
EYERS
HYDRA
HYDRO
HYGRO
LYCRA
MYERS
MYRRH

•Y••R
BYFAR
BYNER
CYBER
CYDER
EYRIR
HYPER
KYSER
MYLAR
RYDER
TYLER
TYPER
WYLER

••YR•
SPYRI
TAYRA
WHYRE

••Y•R
BAYAR
BAYER
BOYAR
BOYER
BUYER
COYER
CRYER
DIYER
DRYER
FEYER
FLYER
FOYER
FRYER
GAYER
LAYER
MAYER
MAYOR
MEYER
PAYER
PRYOR
SAYER
SHYER
SLYER
WRYER

•••YR
ASSYR
SATYR

Y•S••
YASIR
YESES
YESNO

Y••S•
YEAST
YOUSE

Y•••S
YACKS
YANKS
YARDS
YARNS
YATES
YAWLS
YAWNS
YAWPS
YAXES
YAXIS
YEANS
YEARS
YEATS
YEGGS
YELLS
YELPS
YERKS
YESES
YETIS
YIKES
YIPES
YMCAS
YODHS
YOGAS
YOGHS
YOGIS
YOKES
YOLKS
YOURS
YOWLS
YOYOS
YPRES
YUANS
YUGAS
YUGOS
YUMAS
YURTS
YWCAS

•YS••
HYSON
KYSER
LYSIN
LYSOL
MYSIN
SYSOP
TYSON

•Y•S•
GYPSY
HYPSO
NYASA

•Y••S
AYAHS
AYERS
AYINS
AYRES
BYRDS
BYRES
BYTES
CYMAS
CYMES
CYRUS
DYADS
DYERS
DYNES
EYERS
EYOTS
EYRAS
EYRES
FYKES
GYBES
GYRES
GYROS
GYRUS
GYVES
HYAMS
HYLAS
HYMNS
HYPES
HYPOS
KYATS
LYONS
LYRES
MYERS
MYLES
MYNAS
MYTHS
NYETS
PYRES
PYXIS
RYOTS
SYCES
SYNCS
TYKES
TYNES
TYPES
TYPOS
TYRES
TYROS

••YS•
ABYSM
ABYSS
ELYSE
HEYSE
MAYST
PHYSI
SAYSO
TRYST

••Y•S
ABYES
ABYSS
ACYLS
AMYLS
BOYOS
HAYES
HOYAS
IDYLS
KAYOS
KEYES
MAYAS
NOYES
REYES
SOYAS
YOYOS

•••YS
AHOYS
ATTYS
BABYS
BBOYS
BRAYS
BUOYS
CHRYS
CLAYS
CLOYS
DAVYS
DENYS
DRAYS
EMMYS
FLAYS
FLEYS
FRAYS
GLEYS
GRAYS
GREYS
JOEYS
LADYS
MACYS
MARYS
OBEYS
OKAYS
PEPYS
PLAYS
PLOYS
POWYS
PRAYS
PREYS
QUAYS
SHAYS
SLAYS
SPAYS
STAYS
SWAYS
TONYS
TRAYS
TREYS
WHEYS
XRAYS

Y•T••
YATES
YETIS

Y••T•
YALTA
YEATS
YENTA
YENTE
YENTL
YOUTH
YURTS

Y•••T
YACHT
YAKUT
YEAST
YOUNT

•YT••
BYTES
LYTTA
MYTHS
WYTHE

•Y•T•
EYOTS
HYATT
KYATS
KYOTO
LYTTA
NYETS
RYOTS
WYATT
WYETH

•Y••T
HYATT
NYMET
WYATT

••YT•
ADYTA
BLYTH
LAYTO
LEYTE
PAYTV
PHYTO
RHYTA
SMYTH

••Y•T
ASYET
ASYUT
CRYPT
EGYPT
FLYAT
GUYOT
MAYNT
MAYST
TRYST

YU•••
YUANS
YUCCA
YUCKY
YUGAS
YUGOS
YUKON
YUMAN
YUMAS
YUMMY
YUPIK
YUROK
YURTS

Y•U••
YOULL
YOUNG
YOUNT
YOURE
YOURS
YOUSE
YOUTH
YOUVE

Y••U•
YAKUT
YAQUI
YOKUM

•Y•U•
BYGUM
CYRUS
GYRUS
MYGUY
SYRUP

••YU•
ASYUT
BUYUP
DRYUP
KEYUP
LAYUP
PAYUP
SOYUZ

••Y•U
BAYOU
COYPU

•••YU
SHOYU

Y••V•
YOUVE

Y•••V
YAKOV

•YV••
GYVED
GYVES
OYVAY

••Y•V
PAYTV

YW•••
YWCAS

Y•W••
YAWED
YAWLS
YAWNS
YAWPS
YOWLS

Y•••W
YALOW

•YW••
BYWAY
MYWAY

•Y••W
BYLAW
BYNOW
SYDOW

Y•X••
YAXES
YAXIS

•YX••
PYXIE
PYXIS

•Y••X
HYRAX
KYLIX
NYNEX
PYREX

•••YX
CALYX

Y•Y••
YOYOS

Y•••Y
YOLKY
YUCKY
YUMMY

•Y•Y•
KYZYL
MYEYE

•Y••Y
BYWAY
CYMRY
GYPSY
MYGUY
MYWAY
OYVAY
PYGMY
TYPEY

••Y•Y
COYLY
DOYLY
DRYLY
FEYLY
FLYBY
GAYLY
LAYBY
SHYLY
SKYEY
SLYLY
STYMY
THYMY
WRYLY

Y•Z••
YAZOO

•YZ••
KYZYL

••Y•Z
SOYUZ

ZA•••
ZAIRE
ZAMIA
ZANTE
ZAPPA
ZAPPY
ZARFS
ZAXES
ZAXIS
ZAYIN
ZAZEN

Z•A••
ZBARS
ZEALS

Z••A•
ZETAS
ZOEAE
ZOEAL
ZOEAS
ZOHAR
ZONAL

Z•••A
ZAMIA
ZAPPA
ZEBRA
ZELDA
ZENDA
ZIZKA
ZORBA

•ZA••
AZANS
CZARS
IZAAK
IZARD
IZARS
OZARK
OZAWA
TZARS
UZALA

•Z•A•
IZAAK
IZBAS

•Z••A
AZUSA
OZAWA
UZALA

••ZA•
ANZAC
HAZAN
KAZAK
KAZAN
LAZAR
MIZAR
MUZAK
NIZAM

••Z•A
HUZZA
MAZDA
PIZZA
TAZZA
ZIZKA

•••ZA
BAIZA
DANZA
ELIZA
GINZA
GROZA
HUZZA
IBIZA
LANZA
LEEZA
MONZA
PANZA
PENZA
PINZA
PIZZA
PLAZA
TAZZA
TERZA
TISZA

ZB•••
ZBARS

Z•B••
ZEBRA
ZEBUS
ZIBET
ZUBIN

Z••B•
ZORBA

•ZB••
IZBAS
UZBEK

Z••C•
ZILCH
ZINCS
ZINCY

Z•••C
ZENIC

•Z•C•
CZECH

•Z••C
AZOIC
AZTEC

••ZC•
CUZCO

••Z•C
ANZAC

Z••D•
ZELDA
ZENDA
ZENDO
ZENDS

Z•••D
ZONED
ZOOID

•Z•D•
AZIDE

•Z••D
IZARD
SZOLD

••ZD•
MAZDA

••Z•D
DAZED
DOZED
FAZED
FUZED
GAZED
HAZED
LAZED
OOZED
RAZED
SIZED

ZE•••
ZEALS
ZEBRA
ZEBUS
ZEINS
ZEISS
ZEIST
ZELDA
ZELIG
ZENDA
ZENDO
ZENDS
ZENIC
ZEPPO
ZEROS
ZESTS
ZESTY
ZETAS
ZEVON

Z•E••
ZOEAE
ZOEAL
ZOEAS
ZWEIG

Z••E•
ZAXES
ZAZEN
ZIBET
ZINES
ZONED
ZONES
ZOOEY

Z•••E
ZAIRE
ZANTE
ZOEAE
ZOWIE

•ZE••
CZECH
SZELL

•Z•E•
AZTEC
UZBEK

•Z••E
AZIDE
AZINE
AZOTE
AZURE
OZONE
OZZIE

••ZE•
ADZES
BEZEL
BIZET
COZEN
COZES
DAZED
DAZES
DIZEN
DOZED
DOZEN
DOZER
DOZES
ETZEL
FAZED
FAZES
FUZED
FUZEE
GAZED
GAZER
GAZES
HAZED
HAZEL
HAZER
HAZES
LAZED
LAZES
MAZEL
MAZER
MAZES
NIZER
OOZED
OOZES
OUZEL
RAZED
RAZES
SIZED
SIZER
SIZES
WIZEN
ZAZEN

••Z•E
FUZEE
OZZIE

•••ZE
AGAZE
AMAZE
BAIZE
BLAZE
BONZE
BOOZE
BRAZE
CRAZE
CROZE
DRUZE
FROZE
FURZE
GAUZE
GLAZE
GLOZE
GRAZE
MAIZE
PRIZE
SEIZE
SMAZE
WINZE

Z••F•
ZARFS

Z•G••
ZIGGY

Z••G•
ZIGGY
ZINGS
ZINGY

Z•••G
ZELIG
ZWEIG

••Z•G
ABZUG

Z•H••
ZOHAR

Z•••H
ZILCH

•Z••H
AZOTH
CZECH

ZI•••
ZIBET
ZIGGY
ZILCH
ZILLS
ZINCS
ZINCY
ZINES
ZINGS
ZINGY
ZIPPY
ZIPUP
ZITIS
ZIZKA

Z•I••
ZAIRE
ZEINS
ZEISS
ZEIST

Z••I•
ZAMIA
ZAXIS
ZAYIN
ZELIG
ZENIC
ZITIS
ZOOID
ZORIL
ZORIS
ZOWIE
ZUBIN
ZUNIS
ZWEIG

•ZI••
AZIDE
AZINE

•Z•I•
AZOIC
IZMIR
IZMIT
OZZIE

••ZI•
ANZIO
OZZIE
UNZIP

••Z•I
BUZZI

•••ZI
BUZZI
ELAZI
GHAZI
MITZI
PONZI
SWAZI

Z•K••
ZUKOR

Z••K•
ZIZKA
ZONKS
ZOUKS

•Z••K
IZAAK
OZARK
UZBEK

••ZK•
ZIZKA

••Z•K
KAZAK
MUZAK

ZL•••
ZLOTY

Z•L••
ZELDA
ZELIG
ZILCH
ZILLS
ZULUS

Z••L•
ZEALS
ZILLS

Z•••L
ZOEAL
ZONAL
ZORIL

•Z•L•
SZELL
SZOLD
UZALA

•Z••L
SZELL

••Z•L
BEZEL
ETZEL
HAZEL
KYZYL
MAZEL
OUZEL

•••ZL
HERZL

Z•M••
ZAMIA

Z••M•
ZOOMS

•ZM••
IZMIR
IZMIT

••ZM•
GIZMO

••Z•M
NIZAM

•••ZM
PRIZM

Z•N••
ZANTE
ZENDA
ZENDO
ZENDS
ZENIC
ZINCS
ZINCY
ZINES
ZINGS
ZINGY
ZONAL
ZONED
ZONES
ZONKS
ZUNIS

Z••N•
ZEINS
ZOONS

Z•••N
ZAYIN
ZAZEN
ZEVON
ZUBIN

•Z•N•
AZANS
AZINE
OZONE

••Z•N
COZEN
DIZEN
DOZEN
HAZAN
KAZAN
LUZON
WIZEN
ZAZEN

ZO•••
ZOEAE
ZOEAL
ZOEAS
ZOHAR
ZONAL
ZONED
ZONES
ZONKS
ZOOEY
ZOOID
ZOOMS
ZOONS
ZORBA
ZORIL
ZORIS
ZORRO
ZOUKS
ZOWIE

Z•O••
ZLOTY
ZOOEY
ZOOID
ZOOMS
ZOONS

Z••O•
ZEROS
ZEVON
ZUKOR
ZZTOP

Z•••O
ZENDO
ZEPPO
ZORRO

•ZO••
AZOIC
AZOTE
AZOTH
OZONE
SZOLD

•Z•O•
ZZTOP

••ZO•
BOZOS
KAZOO
LUZON
ORZOS
OUZOS
RAZOR
YAZOO

••Z•O
ANZIO
CUZCO
GIZMO
KAZOO
MEZZO
RIZZO
YAZOO

•••ZO
BENZO
BONZO
DIAZO
GONZO
MATZO
MEZZO
RHIZO
RIZZO

Z•P••
ZAPPA
ZAPPY
ZEPPO
ZIPPY
ZIPUP

Z••P•
ZAPPA
ZAPPY
ZEPPO
ZIPPY

Z•••P
ZIPUP
ZZTOP

•Z••P
ZZTOP

••Z•P
UNZIP

Z•R••
ZARFS
ZEROS
ZORBA
ZORIL
ZORIS
ZORRO

Z••R•
ZAIRE
ZBARS
ZEBRA
ZORRO

Z•••R
ZOHAR
ZUKOR

•Z•R•
AZURE
CZARS
IZARD
IZARS
OZARK
TZARS

•Z••R
IZMIR

••Z•R
DOZER
GAZER
HAZER
LAZAR
MAZER
MIZAR
NIZER
RAZOR
SIZER

Z•S••
ZESTS
ZESTY

Z••S•
ZEISS
ZEIST

Z•••S
ZARFS
ZAXES
ZAXIS
ZBARS
ZEALS
ZEBUS
ZEINS
ZEISS
ZENDS
ZEROS
ZESTS
ZETAS
ZILLS
ZINCS
ZINES
ZINGS
ZITIS
ZOEAS
ZONES
ZONKS
ZOOMS
ZOONS
ZORIS
ZOUKS
ZULUS
ZUNIS

•Z•S•
AZUSA

•Z••S
AZANS
CZARS
IZARS
IZBAS
TZARS

••Z•S
ADZES
BOZOS
COZES
DAZES
DOZES
FAZES
GAZES
HAZES
LAZES
MAZES
OOZES
ORZOS
OUZOS
RAZES
SIZES

Z•T••
ZETAS
ZITIS
ZZTOP

Z••T•
ZANTE
ZESTS
ZESTY
ZLOTY

Z•••T
ZEIST
ZIBET

•ZT••
AZTEC
ZZTOP

•Z•T•
AZOTE
AZOTH

•Z••T
IZMIT

••Z•T
BIZET

•••ZT
LISZT

ZU•••
ZUBIN
ZUKOR
ZULUS
ZUNIS

Z•U••
ZOUKS

Z••U•
ZEBUS
ZIPUP
ZULUS

•ZU••
AZURE
AZUSA

••ZU•
ABZUG

•••ZU
ISUZU
KANZU
KUDZU

Z•V••
ZEVON

ZW•••
ZWEIG

Z•W••
ZOWIE

•Z•W•
OZAWA

Z•X••
ZAXES
ZAXIS

Z•Y••
ZAYIN

Z•••Y
ZAPPY
ZESTY
ZIGGY
ZINCY
ZINGY
ZIPPY
ZLOTY
ZOOEY

••ZY•
KYZYL

••Z•Y
DIZZY
FIZZY
FUZZY
JAZZY
MUZZY
TIZZY

•••ZY
CRAZY
DITZY
DIZZY
DOOZY
FIZZY
FUZZY
GAUZY
JAZZY
JERZY
KRAZY
MUZZY
ORCZY
RITZY
TIZZY
WOOZY

ZZ•••
ZZTOP

Z•Z••
ZAZEN
ZIZKA

•ZZ••
OZZIE

••ZZ•
BUZZI
DIZZY
FIZZY
FUZZY
HUZZA
JAZZY
MEZZO
MUZZY
PIZZA
RIZZO
TAZZA
TIZZY

•••ZZ
ABUZZ
CHAZZ
FRIZZ
SCUZZ

6

AA••••

AACHEN
AAFAIR
AAHING

A•A•••

ABACAS
ABACUS
ABASED
ABASES
ABATED
ABATES
ABATIS
ACACIA
ACADIA
ACAJOU
ACARID
ACARUS
ADAGES
ADAGIO
ADAPTS
AGADIR
AGAMAS
AGARIC
AGASSI
AGATES
AGATHA
AGAVES
AJANTA
ALAMOS
ALANIS
ALANON
ALARIC
ALARMS
ALARUM
ALASKA
ALATAU
ALATED
AMADIS
AMADOU
AMAJOR
AMALFI
AMALIE
AMANDA
AMATIS
AMATOL
AMAZED
AMAZES
AMAZON
ANACIN
ANADEM
ANALOG
ANANDA
ANATTO
APACHE
APATHY
ARABIA
ARABIC
ARABLE
ARAFAT
ARAGON
ARALIA
ARALLU
ARAMIS
ARARAT
ARAWAK
ASANAS
ATAMAN
AVAILS
AVALON
AVANTI
AVATAR
AVAUNT
AWAITS
AWAKED
AWAKEN
AWAKES
AWARDS
AZALEA

A••A••

AAFAIR
ABBACY
ABLATE
ABLAUT
ABLAZE
ABOARD
ABRADE
ABRAMS
ACHAEA
ACKACK
ACUATE
ADDAMS
ADJANI
ADMASS
ADNATE
AERATE
AFEARD
AFFAIR
AFLAME
AFLATS
AFRAID
AFRAME
AGHAST
AGLAIA
AGLARE
AGNATE
AIRARM
AKUAKU
ALBANO
ALBANY
ALCAPP
ALEAST
ALKALI
ALLAYS
ALMATY
ALPACA
ALSACE
ALTAIC
ALTAIR
ALTARS
ALWAYS
AMBATO
AMHARA
ANKARA
ANNABA
ANNALS
ANSARA
ANSATE
ANWANG
ANYANG
AODAIS
APIARY
APPALL
APPALS
AQUATE
ARCADE
ARCANA
ARCANE
ARCARO
ARGALI
ARMADA
ARMAGH
ARMAND
ARMANI
ARRACK
ARRANT
ARRAYS
ARVADA
ARYANS
ASGARD
ASHARP
ASIANS
ASKARI
ASLANT
ASMARA
ASSAIL
ASSAYS
ATBATS
ATEAMS
ATEASE
ATHAND
ATLAST
ATLATL
ATTACH
ATTACK
ATTAIN
ATTARS
AUBADE
AUFAIT
AULAIT
AUPAIR
AVIANS
AVIARY
AVIATE
AWEARY
AYEAYE
AYMARA

A•••A•

ABACAS
ABORAL
ABROAD
ABSCAM
ACETAL
ACTSAS
ACTUAL
ADIDAS
ADONAI
ADRIAN
AEGEAN
AENEAS
AERIAL
AFFRAY
AFGHAN
AFLOAT
AGAMAS
AGENAS
AGLEAM
AGORAE
AGORAS
AIMSAT
AIRBAG
AIRDAM
AIRMAN
AIRSAC
AIRWAY
AKELAS
AKITAS
ALATAU
ALEGAR
ALEMAN
ALLDAY
ALLMAN
ALOHAS
ALOMAR
ALPHAS
ALTMAN
ALULAE
ALULAR
AMEBAE
AMEBAS
AMIGAS
AMORAL
AMTRAC
AMTRAK
AMYTAN
ANDEAN
ANIMAL
ANIMAS
ANNEAL
ANNUAL
ANORAK
ANSGAR
ANURAN
ANYDAY
ANYWAY
AORTAE
AORTAL
AORTAS
AOUDAD
APEMAN
APICAL
APODAL
APPEAL
APPEAR
APPIAN
ARAFAT
ARARAT
ARAWAK
ARCTAN
ARECAS
ARENAS
AROMAS
ARREAR
ARUBAN
ASANAS
ASCHAM
ASHCAN
ASHLAR
ASHRAM
ASOSAN
ASTRAL
ASTRAY
ATAMAN
ATONAL
ATRIAL
ATTHAT
AUDIAL
AUGEAN
AVATAR
AVOWAL
AXONAL

A••••A

ABOLLA
ACACIA
ACADIA
ACEDIA
ACHAEA
ADNEXA
AEOLIA
AFRICA
AGATHA
AGENDA
AGLAIA
AHIMSA
AJANTA
ALASKA
ALEXIA
ALICIA
ALPACA
ALTHEA
ALTIMA
ALUMNA
ALYSSA
AMANDA
AMELIA
AMENRA
AMHARA
AMOEBA
ANANDA
ANCONA
ANDREA
ANEMIA
ANGELA
ANGLIA
ANGOLA
ANGORA
ANITRA
ANKARA
ANNABA
ANNIKA
ANSARA
APULIA
AQUILA
ARABIA
ARALIA
ARBELA
ARCANA
AREOLA
ARETHA
ARISTA
ARJUNA
ARMADA
ARNICA
ARRIBA
ARROBA
ARVADA
ASMARA
ASPERA
ATHENA
ATTICA
ATTILA
AURIGA
AURORA
AVESTA
AXILLA
AYESHA
AYMARA
AZALEA

•AA•••

BAAING
LAAGER
PAANGA

•A•A••

AAFAIR
BABALU
BACALL
BAHAMA
BALAAM
BALATA
BAMAKO
BANANA
BASALT
BATAAN
BAYARD
BAZAAR
CABALA
CABALS
CABANA
CACAOS
CALAIS
CALASH
CAMARO
CANAAN
CANADA
CANALS
CANAPE
CANARD
CANARY
CARAFE
CARATS
CASABA
CASALS
CASAVA
DACAPO
DAGAMA
DALASI
DAMAGE
DAMASK
DAMATO
DANANG
DANAUS
DATARY
FACADE
FALANA
FARADS
FATALE
GALAGO
GALAHS
GALATA
GALAXY
GAMAYS
GARAGE
GAWAIN
GAYALS
HABANA
HAMALS
HARALD
HARARE
HARASS
HATARI
HAVANA
HAVASU
HAWAII
HAZANS
HAZARD

JACALS
JACANA
JALAPA
JAMAAL
JAPANS
JAVARI
KAKAPO
KALAKH
KAMALA
KANAKA
KARATE
KARATS
KAYAKS
KAZAKH
KAZAKS
LAGASH
LALALA
LAMARR
LAMAZE
LANAIS
LANARK
LANATE
LARAMS
LAVABO
LAVAGE
MACACO
MACAWS
MADAME
MADAMS
MAKALU
MALABO
MALADY
MALAGA
MALATE
MALAWI
MALAYA
MALAYS
MANAGE
MANAMA
MANANA
MANAUS
MARACA
MARAUD
MASADA
MASAIS
MAYANS
NAGANO
NAIADS
NAMATH
NASALS
NATANT
NAVAHO
NAVAJO
NAWABS
OAXACA
PADANG
PAEANS
PAGANS
PAHANG
PAHARI
PAJAMA
PALACE
PALAEO
PALATE
PANADA
PANAMA
PAPACY
PAPAGO
PAPAIN
PAPAWS
PAPAYA
PARADE
PARANA
PARANG
PARAPH
PATACA
PAVANE
QATARI
RABATO
RAFAEL
RAJAHS
RAMADA
RAMATE
RAVAGE
SABATO
SAFARI
SAHARA
SALAAM
SALADO
SALADS
SALALS
SALAMI
SALARY
SAMARA
SARANS
SATANG
SAVAGE
SAVAII
SAVANT
SAVATE
TABARD
TAMALE
TAMARA
TAMAYO
TANAKA
TANANA
TARAWA
TATAMI
TATARS
UAKARI
VACANT
VACATE
VAGARY
WABASH
WASABI
WAYANS
XANADU
YAMAHA
ZAPATA

•A••A•

BABKAS
BADHAM
BADMAN
BAGDAD
BAHIAN
BAIKAL
BAIZAS
BALAAM
BALKAN
BALLAD
BALSAM
BALZAC
BANTAM
BANYAN
BANZAI
BAOBAB
BARCAR
BARKAT
BARMAN
BARTAB
BATAAN
BATEAU
BATMAN
BATYAM
BAZAAR
CAESAR
CAFTAN
CAGUAS
CAIMAN
CALLAO
CALLAS
CALPAC
CAMEAT
CANAAN
CANCAN
CANNAE
CANTAB
CANVAS
CAPIAS
CAPTAN
CARMAN
CARNAL
CARPAL
CASBAH
CASPAR
CASUAL
CATHAY
CATNAP
CAUDAL
CAUSAL
CAVEAT
CAVIAR
CAYMAN
DACHAS
DAEDAL
DAGMAR
DALLAS
DAMMAR
DANNAY
DARNAY
EARLAP
EARWAX
EATSAT
FABIAN
FABRAY
FACIAL
FACIAS
FAISAL
FANTAN
FARRAH
FARRAR
FATCAT
FATWAS
FAUNAE
FAUNAL
FAUNAS
GAGLAW
GAGMAN
GALEAE
GALPAL
GALWAY
GALYAK
GAMMAS
GASBAG
GASCAP
GASMAN
GASPAR
GATEAU
GAVIAL
HABEAS
HAEMAT
HAGMAN
HAIDAS
HAINAN
HALVAH
HANGAR
HANNAH
HARLAN
HASSAM
HASSAN
HAUSAS
HAVEAT
HAWHAW
JABBAR
JACKAL
JAGUAR
JAMAAL
JARRAH
KALKAN
KALMAR
KANSAN
KANSAS
KAPLAN
KAPPAS
KARNAK
KARRAS
KASBAH
KASDAN
KATMAI
KAUNAS
LABIAL
LAMIAS
LAMMAS
LANDAU
LAPHAM
LARIAT
LARVAE
LARVAL
LARVAS
LASCAR
LAWMAN
LAYMAN
MACRAE
MADCAP
MADMAN
MADMAX
MADRAS
MAENAD
MAGMAS
MAGYAR
MAITAI
MAMBAS
MAMMAL
MAMMAS
MANDAN
MANDAY
MANIAC
MANIAS
MANRAY
MANTAS
MANUAL
MAOTAI
MARGAY
MARIAH
MARIAN
MAUMAU
MAYDAY
MAYHAP
MAYTAG
NAIRAS
NARIAL
NARWAL
NASCAR
NASDAQ
NASSAU
NATHAN
NAYSAY
PACMAN
PADUAN
PAISAS
PALEAE
PALLAS
PALMAS
PAMPAS
PANDAS
PAPPAS
PAPUAN
PARCAE
PARIAH
PARKAS
PARKAY
PARLAY
PASCAL
PASHAS
PASTAS
PATHAN
PAWPAW
PAWSAT
PAYDAY
QANTAS
RACIAL
RADIAL
RADIAN
RAGBAG
RAGLAN
RAGMAN
RAGTAG
RAHRAH
RAILAT
RAMEAU
RAMSAY
RASCAL
RASHAD
RATTAN
SABRAS
SACRAL
SADDAM
SAIGAS
SAIPAN
SALAAM
SALMAN
SALSAS
SAMBAL
SAMBAR
SAMBAS
SAMIAM
SAMOAN
SAMPAN
SANDAL
SASHAY
SATRAP
SAUNAS
TABLAS
TAGDAY
TAIGAS
TAINAN
TAIPAN
TAIWAN
TALKAT
TAMTAM
TANKAS
TANOAK
TANOAN
TAPPAN
TARMAC
TARPAN
TARSAL
TARTAN
TARTAR
TARZAN
TASMAN
TAXMAN
TAYRAS
TAZZAS
VACLAV
VANDAL
VARNAS
VASLAV
VASSAL
VASSAR
WAHWAH
WANTAD
WARSAW
WAUSAU
WAYLAY
ZAMIAS

•A•••A

BAHAMA
BAKULA
BALATA
BALBOA
BANANA
BANGKA
BARBRA
BAROJA
CABALA
CABANA
CAMERA
CANADA
CANOLA
CANOVA
CAPITA
CARINA
CASABA
CASAVA
CASSIA
CATENA
CAYUGA
DAGAMA
DAHLIA
DAKOTA
DAMITA
DATURA
EARTHA
FACULA
FAENZA
FAJITA
FALANA
FARINA
FASCIA
FATIMA
GALATA
GALENA
GALLIA
GAMBIA
GARCIA
HABANA
HAVANA
JACANA
JALAPA
JASCHA
KAGERA
KAHLUA
KAHUNA
KAILUA
KAMALA
KANAKA
KARIBA
KAUNDA
LABREA
LACUNA
LADIDA
LADOGA
LAGUNA
LAKOTA
LALALA
LAMBDA
LAMESA
LAMINA
LAPUTA
LAROSA
LATINA
LATONA
LATOYA
LATVIA
MACULA
MADURA
MAKEBA
MAKUTA
MALAGA
MALAYA
MANAMA
MANANA
MANCHA
MANILA
MANTRA
MANTUA
MARACA
MARCIA
MARINA
MARISA
MARKKA
MARSHA
MARTHA
MASADA
MATTEA
MAURYA
MAXIMA
MAZOLA
MAZUMA
NAGOYA
NARNIA
NASHUA
NATURA
NAUSEA
OAXACA
PAANGA
PAELLA
PAGODA
PAJAMA
PAKULA
PALLIA
PALOMA
PAMELA
PANADA
PANAMA
PAPAYA
PARANA
PARULA
PATACA
PATINA
PAYOLA
RADULA
RAFFIA
RAMADA
RAMBLA
RAMONA
SABENA
SAHARA
SALINA
SALIVA
SALVIA
SAMARA
SAMOSA
SANCTA
SANDIA
SANDRA
SARNIA
TABULA
TACOMA
TAMARA
TANAKA
TANANA
TANTRA
TARAWA
VAISYA
VARUNA
WALESA
YAKIMA
YAKUZA
YAMAHA
ZADORA
ZAMBIA
ZAPATA
ZAREBA

••AA••

KRAALS

••A•A•

ABACAS
AGAMAS
ALATAU
ARAFAT
ARARAT
ARAWAK
ASANAS
ATAMAN
AVATAR
BRAVAS
BWANAS
CRAVAT
DRAMAS
FRACAS
GOAWAY
GRABAT
GRAHAM
GRAMAS
GUAVAS
HIATAL
IBADAN
IMAMAN
INAJAM
INAWAY
ISAIAH
IZABAL
KOALAS
LIANAS
LLAMAS
MCADAM
NYALAS
OMAHAN
OMAHAS
PLAGAL
PLANAR
PLAYAS
PLAYAT
PLAZAS
QUASAR
REAGAN
REATAS
RIATAS
RUANAS
RYAZAN
SCALAR
SCARAB
SEABAG
SEAFAN
SEAGAL
SEALAB
SEAMAN
SEAWAY
SHABAN
SHAMAN
SHAZAM
SNAPAT
SRANAN
STABAT
STALAG
SWARAJ
TEABAG
TEARAT
TIARAS
TOAMAN
TRAJAN
UTAHAN

••A••A

ACACIA
ACADIA
AGATHA
AJANTA
ALASKA
AMANDA
ANANDA
ARABIA
ARALIA
AZALEA
BIAFRA
BIANCA
BLANCA
BLANDA
BRAHMA
BRAILA
BRAZZA
CHACHA
CHACMA
CRANIA
DEANNA
DHARMA
ETALIA
EXACTA
FLAVIA
FRANCA
GOANNA
GRADEA
GRAMPA
GRAPPA

GRATIA
ICARIA
ITALIA
ITASCA
JOANNA
KWACHA
KWANZA
LUANDA
MIAMIA
MIASMA
NYASSA
PAANGA
PIAZZA
PLASMA
PRAJNA
PRAVDA
QUAGGA
QUANTA
REALIA
RUANDA
RWANDA
SCALIA
SHANIA
SHARIA
SHASTA
SPARTA
STADIA
STANZA
THALIA
TRAUMA
UGANDA
URANIA
ZSAZSA

•••AA•

BALAAM
BATAAN
BAZAAR
CANAAN
GSTAAD
JAMAAL
SALAAM

•••A•A

ACHAEA
AGLAIA
ALPACA
AMHARA
ANKARA
ANNABA
ANSARA
ARCANA
ARMADA
ARVADA
ASMARA
AYMARA
BAHAMA
BALATA
BANANA
BEMATA
CABALA
CABANA
CANADA
CASABA
CASAVA
CICADA
CLOACA
COLADA
CUIABA
CUNAXA
DAGAMA
DOUALA
ERRATA
ESPANA
FALANA
GALATA
GELADA
GEMARA
GUIANA
GUYANA
HABANA
HAVANA
HIVAOA
IGUANA
ILEANA
IMPALA
INDABA
ITHACA
JACANA
JALAPA
JICAMA
JUDAEA
JUMADA
KAMALA
KANAKA
KERALA
LALALA
LUSAKA
MALAGA
MALAYA
MANAMA
MANANA
MARACA
MASADA
MEDAKA
MEGARA
MORAVA
MUFASA
NEVADA
NICAEA
OAXACA
OGLALA
OKSANA
OOLALA
ORGANA
ORIANA
OSHAWA
OTTAVA
OTTAWA
PAJAMA
PANADA
PANAMA
PAPAYA
PARANA
PATACA
PESAWA
PICARA
PINATA
PIRANA
POSADA
PYJAMA
RAMADA
RENATA
ROXANA
SAHARA
SAMARA
SEDAKA
SOMATA
SONATA
STRATA
TAMARA
TANAKA
TANANA
TARAWA
TIRANA
TUCANA
UMTATA
URBANA
YAMAHA
YUKATA
YUKAWA
ZAPATA
ZENANA

AB••••

ABACAS
ABACUS
ABASED
ABASES
ABATED
ABATES
ABATIS
ABBACY
ABBESS
ABBEYS
ABBOTS
ABBOTT
ABDUCT
ABELES
ABESSE
ABHORS
ABIDED
ABIDES
ABJECT
ABJURE
ABLATE
ABLAUT
ABLAZE
ABLEST
ABLOOM
ABLUSH
ABOARD
ABODES
ABOHMS
ABOLLA
ABOMBS
ABORAL
ABORTS
ABOUND
ABRADE
ABRAMS
ABROAD
ABRUPT
ABSCAM
ABSENT
ABSORB
ABSURD
ABUKIR
ABUSED
ABUSER
ABUSES
ABYDOS
ABYING
ABYSMS

A•B•••

ABBACY
ABBESS
ABBEYS
ABBOTS
ABBOTT
ALBANO
ALBANY
ALBEDO
ALBEIT
ALBERT
ALBINO
ALBION
ALBOIN
ALBORG
ALBUMS
AMBATO
AMBERS
AMBERY
AMBITS
AMBLED
AMBLER
AMBLES
AMBLIN
AMBUSH
ARBELA
ARBORS
ARBOUR
ASBURY
ATBATS
ATBEST
AUBADE
AUBREY
AUBURN

A••B••

ADOBES
AIRBAG
AIRBUS
ALIBIS
ALIBLE
ALLBUT
AMEBAE
AMEBAS
AMEBIC
ANUBIS
ARABIA
ARABIC
ARABLE
ARUBAN

A•••B•

ABOMBS
ACHEBE
ADLIBS
AEROBE
AKIMBO
AMOEBA
ANNABA
ARDEBS
ARRIBA
ARROBA

A••••B

ABSORB
ADSORB
ADVERB
APLOMB

•AB•••

BABALU
BABBLE
BABELS
BABIED
BABIES
BABKAS
BABOON
BABSON
BABULS
CABALA
CABALS
CABANA
CABBED
CABBIE
CABERS
CABINS
CABLED
CABLER
CABLES
DABBED
DABBLE
DABNEY
FABIAN
FABLED
FABLER
FABLES
FABRAY
FABRIC
GABBED
GABBER
GABBLE
GABBRO
GABIES
GABION
GABLED
GABLER
GABLES
HABANA
HABEAS
HABILE
HABITS
JABBAR
JABBED
JABBER
JABIRU
JABOTS
KABOBS
KABOOM
KABUKI
LABELS
LABIAL
LABILE
LABORS
LABOUR
LABREA
LABRET
LABRUM
MABELL
NABBED
NABBER
NABOBS
NABORS
PABLUM
RABATO
RABBET
RABBIS
RABBIT
RABBLE
RABIES
SABATO
SABENA
SABERS
SABINE
SABINS
SABLES
SABOTS
SABRAS
SABRES
TABARD
TABBED
TABLAS
TABLED
TABLES
TABLET
TABOOS
TABORS
TABRIZ
TABULA
WABASH
YABBER

•A•B••

BABBLE
BADBOY
BALBOA
BAMBOO
BAOBAB
BARBED
BARBEL
BARBER
BARBET
BARBIE
BARBRA
BATBOY
BAUBLE
CABBED
CABBIE
CAMBER
CARBON
CARBOS
CARBOY
CASBAH
DABBED
DABBLE
DAUBED
DAUBER
DAUBES
DAYBED
DAYBOY
GABBED
GABBER
GABBLE
GABBRO
GAMBIA
GAMBIT
GAMBLE
GAMBOL
GARBED
GARBLE
GASBAG
HARBIN
HARBOR
HASBRO
HATBOX
IAMBIC
JABBAR
JABBED
JABBER
KASBAH
LAMBDA
LAMBED
LAYBYS
LAZBOY
MAMBAS
MAMBOS
MARBLE
MARBLY
MAYBES
NABBED
NABBER
PAYBOX
RABBET
RABBIS
RABBIT
RABBLE
RAGBAG
RAMBLA
RAMBLE
SAMBAL
SAMBAR
SAMBAS
TABBED
TALBOT
WAMBLE
WAMBLY
WARBLE
YABBER
ZAMBIA

•A••B•

CAMEBY
CARIBE
CARIBS
CAROBS
CASABA
DANUBE
GATSBY
GAZEBO
HARDBY
JACOBI
KABOBS
KARIBA
LAIDBY
LAVABO
LAYSBY
MAKEBA
MALABO
MALIBU
NABOBS
NASEBY
NAWABS
PASSBY
SAHIBS
SASEBO
WASABI
ZAREBA

•A•••B

BAOBAB
BARTAB
CANTAB
DAYJOB
ZAGREB

••AB••

ARABIA
ARABIC
ARABLE
BLABBY
CRABBE
CRABBY
DIABLO
DOABLE
DRABLY
ENABLE
FLABBY
GRABAT
GRABBY
GRABEN
GRABLE
ISABEL
IZABAL
LIABLE
RHABDO
SCABBY
SEABAG
SEABED
SEABEE
SHABAN
SHABBY
STABAT
STABLE
STABLY
SWABBY
TEABAG
UNABLE
USABLE
USABLY
VIABLE
VIABLY

••A•B•

BLABBY
CRABBE
CRABBY
CRAMBO
FLABBY
FLAMBE
GRABBY
NEARBY
SCABBY
SHABBY
SWABBY

••A••B

SCARAB
SEALAB

•••AB•

ANNABA
CASABA
CUIABA
INDABA
KEBABS
LAVABO
MALABO
MCCABE
MESABI
MUGABE
NAWABS
PICABO
REHABS
SQUABS
STRABO
WASABI

•••A•B

BEDAUB
BICARB
DEKALB
STRAUB

••••AB

BAOBAB
BARTAB
CANTAB
CONFAB
MIHRAB
PREFAB
PUNJAB
SCARAB
SCHWAB
SEALAB
SKYLAB

AC••••

ACACIA
ACADIA
ACAJOU
ACARID
ACARUS
ACCEDE
ACCENT
ACCEPT
ACCESS
ACCORD
ACCOST
ACCRUE
ACCUSE
ACEDIA
ACEOUS
ACEOUT
ACESUP
ACETAL
ACETIC
ACETYL
ACHAEA
ACHEBE
ACHENE
ACHIER
ACHING
ACIDIC
ACIDLY
ACINUS
ACKACK
ACORNS
ACQUIT
ACROSS
ACTIII
ACTING
ACTINO
ACTION
ACTIUM
ACTIVE
ACTONE
ACTORS
ACTOUT
ACTSAS
ACTSON
ACTSUP
ACTTWO
ACTUAL
ACUATE
ACUITY
ACUMEN

A•C•••

AACHEN
ACCEDE
ACCENT
ACCEPT
ACCESS
ACCORD
ACCOST
ACCRUE

ACCUSE
AHCHOO
ALCAPP
ALCOTT
ALCOVE
ALCUIN
ANCHOR
ANCIEN
ANCONA
ARCADE
ARCANA
ARCANE
ARCARO
ARCCOS
ARCHED
ARCHER
ARCHES
ARCHIE
ARCHLY
ARCHON
ARCING
ARCTAN
ARCTIC
ASCEND
ASCENT
ASCHAM
ASCOTS
ATCOST

A••C••

ABACAS
ABACUS
ABSCAM
ACACIA
AFLCIO
ALECKY
ALECTO
ALICIA
AMECHE
AMICES
AMICUS
ANACIN
ANTCOW
APACHE
APICAL
APICES
ARCCOS
ARECAS
ASHCAN
AVOCET

A•••C•

ABBACY
ABDUCT
ABJECT
ACKACK
ADDUCE
ADDUCT
ADVICE
AFFECT
AFRICA
AGENCY
ALNICO
ALPACA
ALSACE
AMERCE
ANTICS
APERCU
APIECE
ARNICA
ARRACK
ASDICS
ASPECT
ASPICS
ATONCE
ATTACH
ATTACK
ATTICA
ATTICS
AVOUCH
AZTECS

A••••C

ACETIC
ACIDIC
AEOLIC
AGARIC
AIRSAC
ALARIC
ALTAIC
AMEBIC
AMTRAC
ANEMIC
ANGLIC
ANODIC
ANOMIC
AORTIC
ARABIC
ARCTIC
ATOMIC
ATONIC

•AC•••

AACHEN
BACALL
BACHED
BACKED
BACKER
BACKIN
BACKUP
BACKUS
CACAOS
CACHED
CACHES
CACHET
CACHOU
CACKLE
CACTUS
DACAPO
DACHAS
DACOIT
DACRON
DACTYL
FACADE
FACETS
FACEUP
FACIAL
FACIAS
FACIES
FACILE
FACING
FACTOR
FACULA
HACEKS
HACKED
HACKER
HACKIE
HACKLE
HACKLY
JACALS
JACANA
JACKAL
JACKED
JACKET
JACKEY
JACKIE
JACKUP
JACLYN
JACOBI
LACERS
LACEUP
LACHES
LACIER
LACILY
LACING
LACKED
LACKEY
LACTIC
LACUNA
MACACO
MACAWS
MACEIO
MACHES
MACHOS
MACOUN
MACRAE
MACRON
MACROS
MACULA
NACHOS
NACRES
PACERS
PACIFY
PACING
PACINO
PACKED
PACKER
PACKET
PACKUP
PACMAN
RACEME
RACERS
RACHEL
RACHIS
RACIAL
RACIER
RACILY
RACINE
RACING
RACKED
RACKET
RACKUP
RACONS
SACHEM
SACHET
SACKED
SACKER
SACQUE
SACRAL
SACRED
SACRUM
TACKED
TACKER
TACKLE
TACKON
TACOMA
TACTIC
VACANT
VACATE
VACHEL
VACLAV
VACUUM
WACKOS
YACHTS
YACKED

•A•C••

BARCAR
BAUCIS
CAICOS
CALCES
CANCAN
CANCEL
CANCUN
CATCHY
CAUCHO
CAUCHY
CAUCUS
DANCED
DANCER
DANCES
FALCES
FALCON
FARCED
FARCES
FARCRY
FASCES
FASCIA
FATCAT
FAUCES
FAUCET
GARCIA
GARCON
GASCAP
GASCON
GAUCHE
GAUCHO
JASCHA
JAYCEE
LANCED
LANCER
LANCES
LANCET
LASCAR
MADCAP
MANCHA
MANCHU
MARCEL
MARCHE
MARCIA
MARCIE
MARCOS
MARCUS
MASCOT
NASCAR
PANCHO
PARCAE
PARCEL
PASCAL
PATCHY
PAUCIS
RANCHO
RANCID
RANCOR
RASCAL
SANCHO
SANCTA
SAUCED
SAUCER
SAUCES
TAICHI
TALCED
TALCUM
WARCRY

•A••C•

BARUCH
BASICS
CALICO
HAUNCH
HAVOCS
JANICE
LAMECH
LAUNCH
MACACO
MALICE
MARACA
NATICK
NAUTCH
OAXACA
PALACE
PANICS
PAPACY
PATACA
PAUNCH
SAMECH
ZANUCK

•A•••C

BALTIC
BALZAC
BARDIC
CADMIC
CALPAC
FABRIC
GAELIC
GALLIC
GARLIC
IAMBIC
IATRIC
KARMIC
LACTIC
MANIAC
MANIOC
MANTIC
MASTIC
PARSEC
TACTIC
TANNIC
TARMAC

••AC••

ABACAS
ABACUS
ACACIA
ANACIN
APACHE
BEACHY
BEACON
BLACKS
BRACED
BRACER
BRACES
BRACHY
BRACTS
CHACHA
CHACMA
CLACKS
CRACKS
CRACKY
DEACON
DRACHM
ENACTS
EXACTA
EXACTO
EXACTS
FIACRE
FLACKS
FLACON
FRACAS
GLACES
GLACIS
GRACED
GRACES
GRACIE
GUACOS
KNACKS
KWACHA
KYACKS
LEACHY
NIACIN
ORACHS
ORACLE
PEACHY
PLACED
PLACER
PLACES
PLACET
PLACID
POACHY
QUACKS
REACTS
SEACOW
SHACKS
SLACKS
SMACKS
SNACKS
SPACED
SPACEK
SPACER
SPACES
SPACEY
STACEY
STACKS
STACTE
TEACUP
TRACED
TRACER
TRACES
TRACEY
TRACHY
TRACKS
TRACTS
URACIL
VIACOM
WHACKS
WHACKY
WRACKS

••A•C•

BIANCA
BLANCA
BLANCH
BRANCH
CHALCO
CHANCE
CHANCY
CLANCY
EPARCH
EXARCH
FIANCE
FIASCO
FRANCA
FRANCE
FRANCK
FRANCO
FRANCS
GLANCE
GRAECO
INARCH
ITASCA
KLATCH
NUANCE
PLAICE
PLANCK
PRANCE
SCARCE
SEANCE
SEARCH
SNATCH
STANCE
STANCH
STARCH
SWATCH
THATCH
TRANCE
USANCE

••A••C

AGARIC
ALARIC
ARABIC
CYANIC
DYADIC
ITALIC
PHATIC
SLAVIC
STATIC
TLALOC
TRAGIC
URALIC
URANIC

•••AC•

ABBACY
ACKACK
ALPACA
ALSACE
ARRACK
ATTACH
ATTACK
BLEACH
BREACH
BROACH
CLOACA
CURACY
CUSACK
DEFACE
DETACH
DIDACT
EFFACE
ENLACE
GOBACK
HIJACK
HORACE
IGNACE
IGUACU
IMPACT
INFACT
INTACT
ITHACA
KOVACS
LEGACY
LILACS
LUNACY
MACACO
MARACA
MENACE
MONACO
OAXACA
ONEACT
ORBACH
OUTACT
PALACE
PAPACY
PATACA
PESACH
PIRACY
PLEACH
POMACE
PREACH
PURACE
REDACT
REFACE
RELACE
SERACS
SOLACE
SUMACS
TENACE
TEXACO
THRACE
THWACK
UNLACE
UNPACK
UNTACK
VIVACE

•••A•C

ALTAIC
JUDAIC
MOSAIC
ROMAIC

••••AC

AIRSAC
AMTRAC
BALZAC
BIGMAC
CALPAC
CHIRAC
COGNAC
CONTAC
IPECAC
MANIAC
MELMAC
MICMAC
OVISAC
PROZAC
SENLAC
TARMAC
TICTAC
TOMBAC
UNIVAC
ZODIAC

AD••••

ADAGES
ADAGIO
ADAPTS
ADDAMS
ADDEND
ADDERS
ADDING
ADDLED
ADDLES
ADDONS
ADDSIN
ADDSON
ADDSTO
ADDSUP
ADDUCE
ADDUCT
ADEEMS
ADELIE
ADELLE
ADEPTS
ADESTE
ADHERE
ADIDAS
ADIEUS
ADIEUX
ADJANI
ADJOIN
ADJURE
ADJUST
ADLIBS
ADMASS
ADMIRE
ADMITS
ADNATE
ADNEXA
ADOBES
ADOLPH
ADONAI
ADONIS
ADOPTS
ADORED
ADOREE
ADORER
ADORES
ADORNS
ADRENO
ADRIAN
ADRIEN
ADRIFT
ADROIT
ADSORB
ADULTS
ADVENT
ADVERB
ADVERT
ADVICE
ADVISE
ADWEEK
ADYTUM
ADZUKI

A•D•••

ABDUCT
ADDAMS
ADDEND
ADDERS
ADDING
ADDLED
ADDLES
ADDONS
ADDSIN
ADDSON
ADDSTO
ADDSUP

ADDUCE
ADDUCT
AEDILE
AIDERS
AIDFUL
AIDING
ALDERS
ALDINE
ALDOSE
ALDOUS
ALDRIN
ANDEAN
ANDHOW
ANDREA
ANDREI
ANDRES
ANDREW
ANDREY
ANDROS
AODAIS
ARDEBS
ARDENT
ARDORS
ARDOUR
ASDICS
AUDENS
AUDIAL
AUDILE
AUDIOS
AUDITS
AUDREY

A••D••

ABIDED
ABIDES
ABODES
ABYDOS
ACADIA
ACEDIA
ACIDIC
ACIDLY
ADIDAS
AGADIR
AIRDAM
AIRDRY
ALLDAY
AMADIS
AMADOU
AMEDEO
AMIDES
AMIDOL
AMIDST
ANADEM
ANODES
ANODIC
ANYDAY
AOUDAD
APODAL
ARIDLY
ASIDES
ATODDS
AVEDON
AVIDLY
AWEDLY
AZIDES
AZODYE

A•••D•

ABRADE
ACCEDE
AGENDA
AIKIDO
ALBEDO
ALKYDS
ALLUDE
AMANDA
AMENDS
ANANDA
ANHYDR
APHIDS
ARCADE
ARENDT
ARMADA
AROIDS
ARVADA
ATODDS
AUBADE
AVOIDS
AWARDS

A••••D

ABASED
ABATED
ABIDED
ABOARD
ABOUND
ABROAD
ABSURD
ABUSED
ACARID
ACCORD
ADDEND
ADDLED
ADORED
AENEID
AFEARD
AFFORD
AFIELD
AFRAID
AGEOLD
AGREED
ALATED
ALFRED
ALLIED
ALMOND
AMAZED
AMBLED
AMPHID
AMUSED
ANELED
ANGLED
ANKLED
ANTEED
AOUDAD
APPEND
ARCHED
ARGUED
ARMAND
ARNOLD
AROUND
ASCEND
ASGARD
ASTRID
ATHAND
ATONED
ATSTUD
ATTEND
ATWOOD
AUFOND
AUGEND
AVOWED
AWAKED
AXSEED

•AD•••

BADBOY
BADDER
BADDIE
BADEGG
BADGER
BADGES
BADGUY
BADHAM
BADLOT
BADMAN
BADMEN
CADDIE
CADDIS
CADENT
CADETS
CADGED
CADGER
CADGES
CADMIC
CADMUS
CADRES
DADDYO
DADOED
DADOES
FADEIN
FADING
GADDED
GADDER
GADFLY
GADGET
HADDIE
HADJES
HADJIS
HADRON
JADING
JADISH
LADDER
LADDIE
LADERS
LADIDA
LADIES
LADING
LADINO
LADLED
LADLER
LADLES
LADOGA
MADAME
MADAMS
MADCAP
MADDEN
MADDER
MADDIE
MADEDO
MADEIT
MADERO
MADEUP
MADMAN
MADMAX
MADMEN
MADRAS
MADRES
MADRID
MADSEN
MADTOM
MADURA
MADURO
NADINE
NADIRS
PADANG
PADDED
PADDER
PADDLE
PADRES
PADUAN
RADDLE
RADIAL
RADIAN
RADIOS
RADISH
RADIUM
RADIUS
RADNER
RADOME
RADULA
SADDAM
SADDEN
SADDER
SADDLE
SADHES
SADHUS
VADOSE
WADDED
WADDLE
WADDLY
WADEIN
WADERS
WADING
WADSUP
ZADDIK
ZADORA

•A•D••

BADDER
BADDIE
BAGDAD
BALDER
BALDLY
BANDED
BANDIT
BANDOG
BARDIC
BARDOT
CADDIE
CADDIS
CALDER
CAMDEN
CANDID
CANDLE
CANDOR
CARDED
CARDER
CARDIN
CARDIO
CAUDAL
CAUDEX
CAUDLE
CAWDOR
DADDYO
DAEDAL
DANDER
DANDIE
DANDLE
DAWDLE
FANDOM
GADDED
GADDER
GANDER
GANDHI
GARDEN
HADDIE
HAGDON
HAIDAS
HANDED
HANDEL
HANDIN
HANDLE
HANDON
HANDUP
HARDBY
HARDEN
HARDER
HARDLY
HARDUP
HAYDEN
KANDER
KASDAN
LADDER
LADDIE
LAIDBY
LAIDIN
LAIDON
LAIDTO
LAIDUP
LANDAU
LANDED
LANDER
LANDHO
LANDIS
LANDON
LANDRY
LAPDOG
LARDED
LARDER
LARDON
LAUDED
LAUDER
MADDEN
MADDER
MADDIE
MAHDIS
MAIDEN
MAIDUS
MALDEN
MANDAN
MANDAY
MARDUK
MAYDAY
NASDAQ
PADDED
PADDER
PADDLE
PAIDIN
PAIDUP
PANDAS
PANDER
PANDIT
PARDON
PAYDAY
RADDLE
RAIDED
RAIDER
RANDOM
RANDRY
SADDAM
SADDEN
SADDER
SADDLE
SANDAL
SANDED
SANDER
SANDIA
SANDRA
SARDIS
SAUDIS
TAGDAY
TANDEM
TAWDRY
VALDEZ
VANDAL
VARDEN
WADDED
WADDLE
WADDLY
WALDEN
WANDER
WARDED
WARDEN
WARDER
YARDED
ZADDIK
ZANDER

•A••D•

CANADA
CANIDS
FACADE
FARADS
HAIRDO
HALIDE
KAUNDA
LADIDA
LAIRDS
LAMBDA
LAMEDH
LAMEDS
LAREDO
MADEDO
MAKEDO
MALADY
MASADA
MAUNDY
NAIADS
PAGODA
PANADA
PARADE
PARODY
RAMADA
RANIDS
RAPIDS
RATEDG
RATEDR
RATEDX
SALADO
SALADS
SARODS
XANADU

•A•••D

BABIED
BACHED
BACKED
BAGDAD
BAGGED
BAILED
BAITED
BALKED
BALLAD
BANDED
BANGED
BANKED
BANNED
BARBED
BARGED
BARKED
BARRED
BASHED
BASKED
BASTED
BATHED
BATTED
BAWLED
BAYARD
CABBED
CABLED
CACHED
CADGED
CALKED
CALLED
CALMED
CALVED
CAMPED
CANARD
CANDID
CANNED
CANOED
CANTED
CAPPED
CAPSID
CARDED
CARKED
CARPED
CARTED
CARVED
CASHED
CATTED
CAUSED
DABBED
DADOED
DAFFED
DAMMED
DAMNED
DAMPED
DANCED
DAPPED
DARNED
DARTED
DASHED
DAUBED
DAWNED
DAYBED
EAGLED
EARNED
FABLED
FAGEND
FAGGED
FAILED
FAIRED
FANGED
FANNED
FARCED
FARMED
FASTED
FATTED
FAWNED
GABBED
GABLED
GADDED
GAFFED
GAGGED
GAINED
GAITED
GALLED
GAMMED
GANGED
GAOLED
GAPPED
GARBED
GASHED
GASPED
GASSED
GAUGED
GAUMED
GAWKED
GAWPED
HACKED
HAFTED
HAILED
HAIRED
HALOED
HALOID
HALTED
HALVED
HAMMED
HANDED
HANGED
HAPPED
HARALD
HARKED
HARMED
HAROLD
HARPED
HASHED
HASPED
HATRED
HATTED
HAULED
HAWKED
HAZARD
JABBED
JACKED
JAGGED
JAILED
JAMMED
JARRED
JAZZED
KAYOED
LACKED
LADLED
LAGGED
LAMBED
LAMMED
LANCED
LANDED
LAPPED
LAPSED
LARDED
LARKED
LASHED
LASTED
LATHED
LAUDED
MADRID
MAENAD
MAILED
MALTED
MANNED
MAPPED
MARAUD
MARKED
MARLED
MARRED
MASHED
MASKED
MASSED
MATTED
MAULED
NABBED
NAGGED
NAILED
NAPPED
PACKED
PADDED
PAINED
PAIRED
PALLED
PALLID
PALMED
PANNED
PANTED
PARKED
PARRED
PARSED
PARTED
PASSED
PASTED
PATTED
PAUSED
PAWNED
RACKED
RAFTED
RAGGED
RAIDED
RAILED
RAINED
RAISED
RAMMED
RAMPED
RAMROD
RANCID
RANGED
RANKED
RANTED
RAPPED
RASHAD
RASHID
RASPED
RATTED
RAZZED
SACKED
SACRED
SAGGED
SAILED
SALTED
SALVED
SANDED
SAPPED
SASHED
SASSED
SAUCED
SAWRED
SAYYID
TABARD
TABBED
TABLED

TACKED
TAGEND
TAGGED
TAILED
TALCED
TALKED
TALMUD
TAMPED
TANGED
TANKED
TANNED
TAPPED
TARRED
TASKED
TASTED
TATTED
TAXIED
VALUED
VALVED
VAMPED
VANNED
VARIED
VATTED
WADDED
WAFTED
WAGGED
WAILED
WAITED
WAIVED
WALKED
WALLED
WANNED
WANTAD
WANTED
WARDED
WARGOD
WARMED
WARNED
WARPED
WARRED
WASHED
WASTED
YACKED
YAKKED
YANKED
YAPPED
YARDED
YARNED
YAWNED
YAWPED
ZAGGED
ZAPPED

••AD••

ACADIA
AGADIR
AMADIS
AMADOU
ANADEM
BEADED
BEADLE
BEADUP
BLADED
BLADER
BLADES
CHADOR
CRADLE
DEADEN
DEADER
DEADLY
DEADON
DIADEM
DYADIC
EVADED
EVADER
EVADES
GLADES
GLADLY
GLADYS
GOADED
GRADEA
GRADED
GRADER
GRADES
GRADIN
GRADUS
HEADED
HEADER
HEADIN
HEADON
HEADUP
HYADES
IBADAN
ISADOR
LEADED
LEADEN
LEADER
LEADIN
LEADON
LEADTO
LEADUP
LOADED
LOADER
MCADAM
MCADOO
MEADOW
QUADRI
READER
READIN
ROADIE
SEADOG
SHADED
SHADES
SHADOW
SPADED
SPADER
SPADES
SPADIX
STADIA
TRADED
TRADER
TRADES

••A•D•

AMANDA
ANANDA
AWARDS
BEARDS
BLANDA
BOARDS
BRAIDS
BRANDO
BRANDS
BRANDT
BRANDX
BRANDY
CIARDI
CLAUDE
ELANDS
FRAIDY
FRAUDS
GLANDS
GRANDE
GRANDS
GUARDS
HOARDS
LUANDA
PLAIDS
PRAVDA
RHABDO
RUANDA
RWANDA
SCALDS
SHANDY
SHARDS
SKALDS
STANDS
SWARDS
UGANDA
VIANDS

••A••D

ABASED
ABATED
ACARID
ALATED
AMAZED
AWAKED
BEADED
BEAKED
BEAMED
BEANED
BIASED
BLADED
BLAMED
BLARED
BLAZED
BOATED
BRACED
BRAKED
BRAVED
BRAYED
BRAZED
CEASED
CHAFED
CHASED
CLAWED
COATED
COAXED
CRANED
CRATED
CRAVED
CRAZED
DIALED
DRAPED
DRAYED
ELAPID
ELATED
ERASED
EVADED
FEARED
FLAKED
FLAMED
FLARED
FLAWED
FLAYED
FOALED
FOAMED
FRAMED
FRAYED
GEARED
GLARED
GLAZED
GNAWED
GOADED
GRACED
GRADED
GRATED
GRAVED
GRAVID
GRAYED
GRAZED
HEADED
HEALED
HEAPED
HEATED
HEAVED
HOAXED
IMAGED
KHALID
LEADED
LEAFED
LEAKED
LEANED
LEAPED
LEASED
LEAVED
LOADED
LOAFED
LOAMED
LOANED
MOANED
MOATED
NEARED
OKAYED
ORATED
PEAKED
PEALED
PEAPOD
PHASED
PLACED
PLACID
PLANED
PLATED
PLAYED
PRATED
PRAYED
QUAKED
REAMED
REAPED
REARED
ROAMED
ROARED
RRATED
SCALED
SCAPED
SCARED
SEABED
SEALED
SEAMED
SEARED
SEATED
SHADED
SHAMED
SHAPED
SHARED
SHAVED
SKATED
SLAKED
SLATED
SLAVED
SLAYED
SNAKED
SNARED
SOAKED
SOAPED
SOARED
SPACED
SPADED
SPARED
SPAYED
STAGED
STAKED
STALED
STARED
STATED
STAVED
STAYED
SWAGED
SWAYED
TEAMED
TEARED
TEASED
THAWED
TRACED
TRADED
UNAGED
UNAWED
WEANED
WEAVED
XRATED
XRAYED
YEANED

•••AD•

ABRADE
ARCADE
ARMADA
ARVADA
AUBADE
BREADS
BROADS
CANADA
CICADA
COLADA
CYCADS
DECADE
DORADO
DREADS
DRYADS
FACADE
FARADS
GELADA
HEXADS
HODADS
INVADE
JIHADS
JUMADA
JURADO
KNEADS
MALADY
MASADA
MENADO
MIKADO
MILADY
MONADS
NAIADS
NEVADA
NOMADS
OCTADS
OREADS
PANADA
PARADE
PLEADS
POMADE
POSADA
RAMADA
REMADE
REPADS
RIYADH
SALADO
SALADS
SQUADS
STEADS
STEADY
STRADS
TIRADE
TREADS
TRIADS
UNLADE
UNMADE
XANADU

•••A•D

ABOARD
AFEARD
AFRAID
ARMAND
ASGARD
ATHAND
BAYARD
BRIAND
BRIARD
BYHAND
CANARD
COWARD
CUNARD
DEMAND
DONALD
DOTARD
EDGARD
EDUARD
EDVARD
EDWARD
ERHARD
ERRAND
EXPAND
EZZARD
FUGARD
GERALD
GERARD
GIRARD
GODARD
GSTAAD
HARALD
HAZARD
HERALD
HOWARD
IDCARD
INHAND
INLAID
INLAND
INWARD
ISLAND
IZZARD
LELAND
LIGAND
LIZARD
MARAUD
ONHAND
ONLAND
ONWARD
OSWALD
OXNARD
PETARD
PICARD
POLAND
REGARD
RELAID
REMAND
REPAID
REPAND
RESAND
RETARD
REWARD
RIBALD
RIBAND
RITARD
ROLAND
RONALD
SEWARD
STRAND
TABARD
TOGAED
TOWARD
UNHAND
UNLAID
UNPAID
UNSAID
UPLAND
UPWARD
VISAED
WIZARD

••••AD

ABROAD
AOUDAD
BAGDAD
BALLAD
BEHEAD
BYROAD
CIUDAD
CONRAD
DOODAD
EMQUAD
ENNEAD
ENQUAD
FORBAD
GETMAD
GILEAD
GOTMAD
GSTAAD
HEPTAD
INROAD
KEYPAD
KONRAD
MAENAD
MSQUAD
MYRIAD
NOLEAD
NOLOAD
NOTBAD
OGDOAD
PENTAD
PLEIAD
RASHAD
RELOAD
REREAD
SINBAD
SINEAD
SPREAD
TETRAD
THREAD
TOOBAD
UNCLAD
UNLEAD
UNLOAD
UNREAD
UPLOAD
WANTAD

AE••••

AEDILE
AEETES
AEGEAN
AENEAS
AENEID
AEOLIA
AEOLIC
AEOLUS
AERATE
AERIAL
AERIES
AERIFY
AERILY
AEROBE
AETHER

A•E•••

ABELES
ABESSE
ACEDIA
ACEOUS
ACEOUT
ACESUP
ACETAL
ACETIC
ACETYL
ADEEMS
ADELIE
ADELLE
ADEPTS
ADESTE
AEETES
AFEARD
AGEING
AGEISM
AGEIST
AGENAS
AGENCY
AGENDA
AGENTS
AGEOLD
AHERNE
AIELLO
AKELAS
AKENES
ALEAST
ALECKY
ALECTO
ALEGAR
ALEGRE
ALEMAN
ALEPHS
ALEPPO
ALERTS
ALEUTS
ALEVEL
ALEXEI
ALEXIA
ALEXIS
AMEBAE
AMEBAS
AMEBIC
AMECHE
AMEDEO
AMEERS
AMELIA
AMENDS
AMENRA
AMENTS
AMERCE
AMERSP
ANELED
ANELES
ANEMIA
ANEMIC
ANERGY
APEMAN
APEMEN
APERCU
APEXES
ARECAS
ARENAS
ARENDT
AREOLA
ARETES
ARETHA
AREZZO
ASEITY
ASEVER
ATEAMS
ATEASE
ATEMPO
ATEOUT
ATERGO
ATESTS
AVEDON
AVENGE
AVENUE
AVERNO
AVERSE
AVERTS
AVESTA
AWEARY
AWEDLY
AWEIGH
AYEAYE
AYESHA

A••E••

ABBESS
ABBEYS
ABJECT
ABLEST
ABSENT
ACCEDE
ACCENT
ACCEPT
ACCESS
ACHEBE
ACHENE
ADDEND
ADDERS
ADEEMS
ADHERE
ADIEUS
ADIEUX
ADNEXA

ADRENO
ADVENT
ADVERB
ADVERT
ADWEEK
AEGEAN
AENEAS
AENEID
AFFECT
AFIELD
AFREET
AFRESH
AGLEAM
AGLETS
AGREED
AGREES
AIDERS
AILEEN
AILERS
ALBEDO
ALBEIT
ALBERT
ALDERS
ALIENS
ALKENE
ALLEES
ALLEGE
ALLELE
ALLEYS
ALPERT
ALTERS
ALWEST
AMBERS
AMBERY
AMEERS
AMIENS
AMOEBA
AMPERE
AMVETS
ANDEAN
ANGELA
ANGELI
ANGELL
ANGELO
ANGELS
ANGERS
ANNEAL
ANNEXE
ANSELM
ANTEED
ANTERO
ANTEUP
APIECE
APPEAL
APPEAR
APPEND
APTEST
ARBELA
ARDEBS
ARDENT
ARGENT
ARLEEN
ARLENE
ARMETS
ARNESS
ARNETT
ARPENT
ARREAR
ARREST
ARSENE
ARTELS
ARTERY
ASCEND
ASCENT
ASKERS
ASLEEP
ASPECT
ASPENS
ASPERA
ASSENT
ASSERT
ASSESS
ASSETS
ASTERN
ASTERS
ASWELL
ATBEST
ATHENA
ATHENE
ATHENS
ATREST
ATREUS
ATTEND
ATTEST
AUDENS
AUGEAN
AUGEND
AUGERS
AUREUS
AUTEUR
AXSEED
AZTECS

A•••E•

AACHEN
ABASED
ABASES
ABATED
ABATES
ABELES
ABIDED
ABIDES
ABODES
ABUSED
ABUSER
ABUSES
ACHAEA
ACHIER
ACUMEN
ADAGES
ADDLED
ADDLES
ADOBES
ADORED
ADOREE
ADORER
ADORES
ADRIEN
ADWEEK
AEETES
AERIES
AETHER
AFREET
AGATES
AGAVES
AGGIES
AGREED
AGREES
AIGRET
AILEEN
AIRIER
AIRMEN
AISLES
AKENES
ALATED
ALEVEL
ALEXEI
ALFRED
ALFVEN
ALINES
ALITER
ALLEES
ALLIED
ALLIES
ALLSET
ALLWET
ALTHEA
AMAZED
AMAZES
AMBLED
AMBLER
AMBLES
AMEDEO
AMICES
AMIDES
AMINES
AMOLES
AMPLER
AMSTEL
AMULET
AMUSED
AMUSES
ANADEM
ANCIEN
ANDREA
ANDREI
ANDRES
ANDREW
ANDREY
ANELED
ANELES
ANGLED
ANGLER
ANGLES
ANIMES
ANKLED
ANKLES
ANKLET
ANNLEE
ANODES
ANOLES
ANSWER
ANTEED
ANTHEM
ANTHER
ANTLER
ANTRES
APEMEN
APEXES
APICES
APOGEE
APPLES
APPLET
ARCHED
ARCHER
ARCHES
ARETES
ARGUED
ARGUER
ARGUES
ARISEN
ARISES
ARLEEN
ARMIES
ARMLET
ARNHEM
ARTIER
ASEVER
ASHIER
ASHLEY
ASIDES
ASLEEP
ATONED
ATONES
ATTLEE
AUBREY
AUDREY
AUKLET
AUSPEX
AUSTEN
AVOCET
AVOWED
AVOWER
AWAKED
AWAKEN
AWAKES
AWOKEN
AXSEED
AZALEA
AZIDES
AZINES
AZORES

A••••E

ABESSE
ABJURE
ABLATE
ABLAZE
ABRADE
ACCEDE
ACCRUE
ACCUSE
ACHEBE
ACHENE
ACTIVE
ACTONE
ACUATE
ADDUCE
ADELIE
ADELLE
ADESTE
ADHERE
ADJURE
ADMIRE
ADNATE
ADOREE
ADVICE
ADVISE
AEDILE
AERATE
AEROBE
AFFINE
AFLAME
AFRAME
AGLARE
AGNATE
AGORAE
AHERNE
ALCOVE
ALDINE
ALDOSE
ALEGRE
ALFINE
ALGORE
ALIBLE
ALKENE
ALLEGE
ALLELE
ALLUDE
ALLURE
ALPINE
ALSACE
ALULAE
AMALIE
AMEBAE
AMECHE
AMERCE
AMPERE
AMPULE
ANNEXE
ANNLEE
ANOMIE
ANSATE
ANYONE
AORTAE
APACHE
APIECE
APLITE
APOGEE
APPOSE
AQUATE
ARABLE
ARCADE
ARCANE
ARCHIE
ARGIVE
ARGYLE
ARIOSE
ARLENE
ARMURE
AROUSE
ARRIVE
ARSENE
ASHORE
ASLOPE
ASPIRE
ASSIZE
ASSUME
ASSURE
ASTUTE
ATEASE
ATHENE
ATHOME
ATONCE
ATTIRE
ATTLEE
ATTUNE
AUBADE
AUDILE
AUNTIE
AUSSIE
AVENGE
AVENUE
AVERSE
AVIATE
AVULSE
AWHILE
AXLIKE
AYEAYE
AZODYE

•AE•••

CAESAR
DAEDAL
FAENZA
FAERIE
FAEROE
GAELIC
HAEMAT
HAEMON
JAEGER
MAENAD
PAEANS
PAELLA
PAEONS

•A•E••

BABELS
BADEGG
BAGELS
BAKERS
BAKERY
BALEEN
BALERS
BAREGE
BARELY
BAREST
BASELY
BASEST
BATEAU
BAYEUX
CABERS
CADENT
CADETS
CAGERS
CAMEAT
CAMEBY
CAMEIN
CAMELS
CAMEON
CAMEOS
CAMERA
CAMETO
CAMEUP
CANERS
CAPERS
CAREEN
CAREER
CARESS
CARETO
CARETS
CASEFY
CASERN
CATENA
CATERS
CAVEAT
CAVEIN
CAVELL
CAVERN
CAVERS
CAVETT
DALETH
DARENT
DARETO
DATERS
EASEIN
EASELS
EASEUP
EATERS
EATERY
FACETS
FACEUP
FADEIN
FAGEND
FAKERS
FAKERY
FARERS
GAIETY
GALEAE
GALENA
GAMELY
GAMEST
GAMETE
GAPERS
GARETH
GATEAU
GATERS
GAVEIN
GAVELS
GAVEUP
GAYEST
GAZEBO
HABEAS
HACEKS
HALERS
HALERU
HALEST
HALEVY
HAMELN
HAREMS
HATERS
HAVEAT
HAVENS
HAVENT
HAVEON
HAVERS
HAZELS
HAZERS
JAPERS
JAPERY
JASEYS
KAGERA
KAREEM
LABELS
LACERS
LACEUP
LADERS
LAGERS
LAKERS
LAMECH
LAMEDH
LAMEDS
LAMELY
LAMENT
LAMESA
LAMEST
LAPELS
LAREDO
LASERS
LATEEN
LATELY
LATENE
LATENS
LATENT
LATEST
LAVERS
LAXEST
LAYERS
MABELL
MACEIO
MADEDO
MADEIT
MADERO
MADEUP
MAKEBA
MAKEDO
MAKEIT
MAKERS
MAKEUP
MANEGE
MASERS
MASERU
MATERS
MATEYS
MAVENS
MAXENE
MAZERS
NAMELY
NAMERS
NAPERY
NASEBY
NAVELS
OATERS
PACERS
PAGERS
PALEAE
PALELY
PALEST
PAMELA
PANELS
PAPERS
PAPERY
PARENS
PARENT
PARERS
PARETO
PAREVE
PASEOS
PATENS
PATENT
PATERS
PAVERS
PAWERS
PAYEES
PAYERS
RACEME
RACERS
RAKEIN
RAKERS
RAKEUP
RAMEAU
RAMETS
RANEES
RAREFY
RARELY
RAREST
RASERS
RATEDG
RATEDR
RATEDX
RATELS
RATERS
RAVELS
RAVENS
RAVERS
RAVEUP
RAWEGG
RAWEST
SABENA
SABERS
SAFELY
SAFEST
SAFETY
SAGELY
SAGEST
SAKERS
SAMECH
SAMEKH
SANELY
SANEST
SASEBO
SATEEN
SAVERS
SAVEUP
SAYERS
TAGEND
TAKEIN
TAKEON
TAKERS
TAKETH
TAKETO
TAKEUP
TALENT
TALERS
TALESE
TAMELY
TAMERS
TAMEST
TAPERS
TASERS
TATERS
TAVERN
TAXERS
VALENS
VALENT
VALERY
VALETS
VARESE
WADEIN
WADERS
WAFERS
WAFERY
WAGERS
WAKENS
WAKEUP
WALERS
WALESA
WANERS
WATERS
WATERY
WAVEIN
WAVERS
WAVERY
WAXERS
YARELY
YAREST
ZAREBA
ZAZENS

•A••E•

AACHEN
BABIED
BABIES
BACHED
BACKED
BACKER
BADDER
BADGER
BADGES
BADMEN

BAGGED	CACHET	CARVEY	EARNED	GANGES	HARDEN	LADLED	MAILER	NANSEN	PAWNED
BAGGER	CADGED	CASHED	EARNER	GANNET	HARDER	LADLER	MAILES	NANTES	PAWNEE
BAILED	CADGER	CASHES	EASIER	GAOLED	HARKED	LADLES	MAIZES	NAPIER	PAWNER
BAILEE	CADGES	CASHEW	EASTER	GAOLER	HARKEN	LAFFER	MAJGEN	NAPLES	PAYEES
BAILER	CADRES	CASPER	FABLED	GAPPED	HARKER	LAGGED	MALDEN	NAPPED	RABBET
BAILEY	CAGIER	CASTER	FABLER	GARBED	HARLEM	LAGGER	MALLEE	NAPPER	RABIES
BAINES	CAGNEY	CASTES	FABLES	GARDEN	HARLEY	LAKIER	MALLEI	NAPPES	RACHEL
BAITED	CAHIER	CATHER	FACIES	GARNER	HARMED	LAMBED	MALLET	NASSER	RACIER
BALDER	CAKIER	CATTED	FAGGED	GARNET	HARPED	LAMMED	MALTED	NATTER	RACKED
BALEEN	CALCES	CAUDEX	FAILED	GARRET	HARPER	LANCED	MANGER	NAUSEA	RACKET
BALKED	CALDER	CAUSED	FAIRED	GARTER	HARVEY	LANCER	MANNED	NAVIES	RADNER
BALLET	CALKED	CAUSES	FAIRER	GARVEY	HASHED	LANCES	MANNER	OAKLEY	RAFAEL
BANDED	CALLED	DABBED	FALCES	GASHED	HASHES	LANCET	MANSES	OATIER	RAFTED
BANGED	CALLER	DABNEY	FALLEN	GASHES	HASPED	LANDED	MANTEL	PACKED	RAFTER
BANGER	CALLES	DADOED	FALSER	GASJET	HASTEN	LANDER	MANUEL	PACKER	RAGGED
BANKED	CALMED	DADOES	FALTER	GASKET	HASTES	LANIER	MAPLES	PACKET	RAGMEN
BANKER	CALMER	DAFFED	FANGED	GASMEN	HATRED	LANKER	MAPPED	PADDED	RAIDED
BANNED	CALVED	DAFTER	FANJET	GASPED	HATTED	LAPPED	MAPPER	PADDER	RAIDER
BANNER	CALVES	DAGGER	FANNED	GASPER	HATTER	LAPPET	MARCEL	PADRES	RAILED
BANTER	CALXES	DAILEY	FARCED	GASSED	HAULED	LAPSED	MARGES	PAINED	RAILER
BARBED	CAMBER	DAIREN	FARCES	GASSER	HAULER	LAPSES	MARIEL	PAIRED	RAINED
BARBEL	CAMDEN	DAISES	FARLEY	GASSES	HAWKED	LAPTEV	MARKED	PALAEO	RAINER
BARBER	CAMLET	DALLES	FARMED	GATHER	HAWKER	LARDED	MARKER	PALIER	RAINES
BARBET	CAMPED	DAMIEN	FARMER	GAUGED	HAWSER	LARDER	MARKET	PALLED	RAINEY
BARGED	CAMPER	DAMMED	FASCES	GAUGER	HAWSES	LARGER	MARLED	PALLET	RAISED
BARGES	CANCEL	DAMNED	FASTED	GAUGES	HAYDEN	LARGES	MARLEE	PALMED	RAISER
BARKED	CANIER	DAMPED	FASTEN	GAUMED	HAYLEY	LARKED	MARLEY	PALMER	RAISES
BARKER	CANKER	DAMPEN	FASTER	GAUZES	HAZIER	LARSEN	MARMEE	PALTER	RAMIES
BARLEY	CANNED	DAMPER	FATHER	GAWKED	JABBED	LASHED	MARNER	PAMPER	RAMJET
BARMEN	CANNEL	DAMSEL	FATTED	GAWKER	JABBER	LASHER	MARRED	PANDER	RAMMED
BARNES	CANNER	DANCED	FATTEN	GAWPED	JACKED	LASHES	MARTEL	PANNED	RAMPED
BARNEY	CANNES	DANCER	FATTER	HACKED	JACKET	LASSEN	MARTEN	PANNER	RAMSES
BARRED	CANOED	DANCES	FAUCES	HACKER	JACKEY	LASSER	MARVEL	PANNES	RAMSEY
BARREL	CANOES	DANDER	FAUCET	HADJES	JAEGER	LASSES	MASHED	PANTED	RANEES
BARREN	CANTED	DANGER	FAWKES	HAFTED	JAGGED	LASTED	MASHER	PANZER	RANGED
BARRES	CANTER	DANIEL	FAWNED	HAILED	JAGGER	LASTEX	MASHES	PAPIER	RANGER
BARTER	CAPLET	DANKER	FAWNER	HAILEY	JAILED	LATEEN	MASKED	PARCEL	RANGES
BASHED	CAPPED	DANNER	GABBED	HAINES	JAILER	LATHED	MASKER	PARGET	RANKED
BASHES	CAPPER	DANTES	GABBER	HAIRED	JAMMED	LATHER	MASSED	PARKED	RANKER
BASKED	CARDED	DAPPED	GABIES	HAJJES	JAMMER	LATHES	MASSES	PARKER	RANTED
BASKET	CARDER	DAPPER	GABLED	HALLEL	JANSEN	LATKES	MASSEY	PARLEY	RANTER
BASSES	CAREEN	DARIEN	GABLER	HALLEY	JARRED	LATTEN	MASTER	PARRED	RAPIER
BASSET	CAREER	DARKEN	GABLES	HALOED	JASPER	LATTER	MATHER	PARREL	RAPPED
BASTED	CARIES	DARKER	GADDED	HALOES	JAURES	LAUDED	MATTEA	PARSEC	RAPPEE
BASTER	CARKED	DARNED	GADDER	HALSEY	JAVIER	LAUDER	MATTED	PARSED	RAPPEL
BASTES	CARMEL	DARNEL	GADGET	HALTED	JAYCEE	LAUPER	MATTEL	PARSEE	RAPPER
BATHED	CARMEN	DARNER	GAFFED	HALTER	JAYVEE	LAUREL	MATTER	PARSER	RAQUEL
BATHER	CARNES	DARREN	GAFFER	HALVED	JAZZED	LAUREN	MATTES	PARSES	RASHER
BATHES	CARNET	DARTED	GAFFES	HALVES	JAZZES	LAWMEN	MAULED	PARTED	RASHES
BATMEN	CARNEY	DARTER	GAGGED	HAMLET	KAISER	LAWYER	MAULER	PASSED	RASPED
BATTED	CARPED	DASHED	GAGMEN	HAMMED	KANDER	LAYMEN	MAUMEE	PASSEL	RASPER
BATTEL	CARPEL	DASHER	GAINED	HAMMER	KAREEM	LAZIER	MAUSER	PASSER	RASTER
BATTEN	CARPER	DASHES	GAINER	HAMPER	KAVNER	MACHES	MAUVES	PASSES	RATHER
BATTER	CARPET	DAUBED	GAITED	HANDED	KAYOED	MADDEN	MAYBES	PASTED	RATTED
BAWLED	CARREL	DAUBER	GAITER	HANDEL	LAAGER	MADDER	MAYHEM	PASTEL	RATTER
BAWLER	CARREY	DAUBES	GALLED	HANGED	LABREA	MADMEN	MAZIER	PASTES	RAZZED
BAXTER	CARTED	DAVIES	GALLEY	HANGER	LABRET	MADRES	NABBED	PATTED	RAZZES
CABBED	CARTEL	DAWNED	GAMIER	HANKER	LACHES	MADSEN	NABBER	PATTEN	SABLES
CABLED	CARTER	DAYBED	GAMMED	HANLEY	LACIER	MAGNET	NACRES	PATTER	SABRES
CABLER	CARTES	EAGLED	GAMMER	HANSEL	LACKED	MAGUEY	NAGGED	PAULEY	SACHEM
CABLES	CARVED	EAGLES	GANDER	HAOLES	LACKEY	MAHLER	NAGGER	PAUPER	SACHET
CACHED	CARVER	EAGLET	GANGED	HAPPED	LADDER	MAIDEN	NAILED	PAUSED	SACKED
CACHES	CARVES	EAGRES	GANGER	HAPPEN	LADIES	MAILED	NAILER	PAUSES	SACKER

SACRED
SADDEN
SADDER
SADHES
SAGGED
SAILED
SALLET
SALTED
SALTEN
SALTER
SALVED
SALVER
SALVES
SAMLET
SAMUEL
SANDED
SANDER
SANGER
SANSEI
SANTEE
SAPPED
SAPPER
SARGES
SASHED
SASHES
SASSED
SASSER
SASSES
SATEEN
SAUCED
SAUCER
SAUCES
SAUGER
SAUREL
SAUTES
SAWRED
SAWYER
SAYLES
SAYYES
TABBED
TABLED
TABLES
TABLET
TACKED
TACKER
TAGGED
TAILED
TAIPEI
TALCED
TALKED
TALKER
TALLER
TAMPED
TAMPER
TANDEM
TANGED
TANKED
TANKER
TANNED
TANNER
TANTES
TAPPED
TAPPER
TAPPET
TARGES
TARGET
TARRED
TARTER
TASKED
TASSEL
TASSES
TASTED
TASTER
TASTES
TATTED
TATTER
TAUPES
TAUTEN
TAUTER
TAXIED
TAXIES
TAXMEN
VACHEL
VAGUER
VAINER
VALDEZ
VALLEE
VALLEY
VALUED
VALUES
VALVED
VALVES
VAMPED
VAMPER
VANIER
VANNED
VARDEN
VARIED
VARIES
VARLET
VARNEY
VASTER
VATTED
WADDED
WAFTED
WAGGED
WAGNER
WAILED
WAILER
WAITED
WAITER
WAIVED
WAIVER
WAIVES
WALDEN
WALKED
WALKEN
WALKER
WALLED
WALLER
WALLET
WALTER
WANDER
WANIER
WANNED
WANNER
WANTED
WAPNER
WARDED
WARDEN
WARDER
WARIER
WARMED
WARMER
WARNED
WARNER
WARPED
WARRED
WARREN
WASHED
WASHER
WASHES
WASTED
WASTER
WASTES
WATNEY
WAVIER
WAXIER
XAVIER
YABBER
YACKED
YAHWEH
YAKKED
YAKKER
YALIES
YAMMER
YANKED
YANKEE
YAPPED
YARDED
YARNED
YASSER
YAWNED
YAWNER
YAWPED
YAWPER
ZAFFER
ZAGGED
ZAGREB
ZAIRES
ZANDER
ZANIER
ZANIES
ZAPPED
ZAPPER

•A•••E

BABBLE
BADDIE
BAFFLE
BAGGIE
BAILEE
BANGLE
BARBIE
BAREGE
BARITE
BARQUE
BARRIE
BASQUE
BATTLE
BATTUE
BAUBLE
CABBIE
CACKLE
CADDIE
CAIQUE
CAJOLE
CALQUE
CAMISE
CANAPE
CANDLE
CANINE
CANNAE
CANTLE
CANUTE
CAPONE
CAPOTE
CARAFE
CARIBE
CAROLE
CARRIE
CASQUE
CASTLE
CATTLE
CAUDLE
CAYUSE
DABBLE
DAMAGE
DAMONE
DAMORE
DANDIE
DANDLE
DANGLE
DANGME
DANUBE
DAPHNE
DAPPLE
DARKLE
DATIVE
DAWDLE
DAYONE
DAZZLE
FACADE
FACILE
FAERIE
FAEROE
FAILLE
FALINE
FAMINE
FANNIE
FATALE
FAUNAE
GABBLE
GAGGLE
GALEAE
GALORE
GAMBLE
GAMETE
GAMINE
GANGLE
GANGUE
GARAGE
GARBLE
GARGLE
GAUCHE
HABILE
HACKIE
HACKLE
HADDIE
HAGGLE
HALIDE
HALITE
HAMITE
HANDLE
HANKIE
HARARE
HASSLE
HATTIE
JACKIE
JAMOKE
JANGLE
JANICE
JANINE
JAYCEE
JAYVEE
KALINE
KARATE
KATHIE
LABILE
LADDIE
LAHORE
LAINIE
LAMAZE
LANATE
LANOSE
LAOTSE
LARVAE
LASSIE
LATENE
LAURIE
LAVAGE
MACRAE
MADAME
MADDIE
MAGGIE
MAGPIE
MAISIE
MAITRE
MALATE
MALICE
MALLEE
MALONE
MANAGE
MANEGE
MANGLE
MANQUE
MANTLE
MARBLE
MARCHE
MARCIE
MARGIE
MARINE
MARLEE
MARMEE
MARNIE
MARPLE
MARQUE
MASHIE
MASQUE
MATTIE
MATURE
MAUMEE
MAXENE
MAXINE
MAXIXE
NADINE
NANNIE
NAPPIE
NATIVE
NATURE
PADDLE
PAIUTE
PALACE
PALATE
PALEAE
PARADE
PARCAE
PAREVE
PAROLE
PARSEE
PARURE
PATINE
PAVANE
PAWNEE
RABBLE
RACEME
RACINE
RADDLE
RADOME
RAFFLE
RAMATE
RAMBLE
RAMONE
RAMOSE
RANKLE
RAPINE
RAPPEE
RASSLE
RATINE
RATITE
RATTLE
RAVAGE
RAVINE
RAZZLE
SABINE
SACQUE
SADDLE
SAFIRE
SAINTE
SALINE
SALOME
SALUTE
SAMITE
SAMMIE
SAMPLE
SANTEE
SARTRE
SATIRE
SAVAGE
SAVATE
SAVOIE
TACKLE
TAGORE
TAILLE
TALESE
TALKIE
TAMALE
TANGLE
TATTLE
VACATE
VADOSE
VALISE
VALLEE
VARESE
WADDLE
WAFFLE
WAGGLE
WAHINE
WALKIE
WAMBLE
WANGLE
WARBLE
WASHOE
WATTLE
YANKEE

••AE••

GRAECO
URAEUS

••A•E•

ABASED
ABASES
ABATED
ABATES
ADAGES
AGATES
AGAVES
ALATED
AMAZED
AMAZES
ANADEM
AWAKED
AWAKEN
AWAKES
AZALEA
BEADED
BEAKED
BEAKER
BEAMED
BEANED
BEARER
BEATEN
BEATER
BEAVER
BIASED
BIASES
BLADED
BLADER
BLADES
BLAMED
BLAMES
BLARED
BLARES
BLAZED
BLAZER
BLAZES
BOATED
BOATEL
BOATER
BRACED
BRACER
BRACES
BRAKED
BRAKES
BRAVED
BRAVER
BRAVES
BRAYED
BRAYER
BRAZED
BRAZEN
BRAZER
BRAZES
CEASED
CEASES
CHAFED
CHAFES
CHALET
CHANEL
CHANEY
CHAPEL
CHASED
CHASER
CHASES
CHAVEZ
CLARET
CLAVES
CLAWED
CLAWER
CLAYEY
COALER
COATED
COAXED
COAXER
COAXES
CRAKES
CRANED
CRANES
CRAPES
CRATED
CRATER
CRATES
CRAVED
CRAVEN
CRAVER
CRAVES
CRAZED
CRAZES
DEADEN
DEADER
DEAFEN
DEAFER
DEALER
DEARER
DIADEM
DIALED
DIALER
DIAPER
DLAYER
DRAGEE
DRAKES
DRAPED
DRAPER
DRAPES
DRAWER
DRAYED
EDAMES
ELATED
ELATER
ELATES
ELAYER
ENAMEL
ENATES
ERASED
ERASER
ERASES
ETAPES
EVADED
EVADER
EVADES
FEARED
FEARER
FLAKED
FLAKER
FLAKES
FLAKEY
FLAMED
FLAMES
FLARED
FLARES
FLAWED
FLAXEN
FLAXES
FLAYED
FLAYER
FOALED
FOAMED
FRAMED
FRAMES
FRASER
FRAUEN
FRAYED
FRAZER
GEARED
GLACES
GLADES
GLARED
GLARES
GLASER
GLAZED
GLAZER
GLAZES
GNAWED
GNAWER
GOADED
GOATEE
GRABEN
GRACED
GRACES
GRADEA
GRADED
GRADER
GRADES
GRAPES
GRAPEY
GRATED
GRATER
GRATES
GRAVED
GRAVEL
GRAVEN
GRAVER
GRAVES
GRAYED
GRAYER
GRAZED
GRAZER
GRAZES
HEADED
HEADER
HEALED
HEALER
HEANEY
HEAPED
HEARER
HEATED
HEATER
HEAVED
HEAVEN
HEAVER
HEAVES
HOAXED
HOAXER
HOAXES
HYADES
IMAGED
IMAGER
IMAGES
IMARET
INANER
INAPET
IRATER
ISABEL
JUAREZ
KNAVES
KRAKEN
KRAMER
KRATER
LAAGER
LEADED
LEADEN
LEADER
LEAFED
LEAKED
LEAKER
LEAKEY
LEANED
LEANER
LEAPED

LEAPER	PRAYED	SLATER	TEARED	CHASTE	QUAYLE	AYEAYE	HORACE	OUTAGE	TODATE
LEASED	PRAYER	SLATES	TEASED	CLAIRE	ROADIE	BECAME	HUMANE	OUTATE	TOWAGE
LEASER	QUAKED	SLAVED	TEASEL	CLAQUE	RVALUE	BEDAZE	ICEAGE	PALACE	TRIAGE
LEASES	QUAKER	SLAVER	TEASER	CLARKE	SCARCE	BEHAVE	IDEATE	PALATE	TUBATE
LEAVED	QUAKES	SLAVES	TEASES	CLAUDE	SCARNE	BERATE	IGNACE	PARADE	TULANE
LEAVEN	QUAVER	SLAVEY	TEASET	CLAUSE	SCATHE	BETAKE	IMPALE	PAVANE	TULARE
LEAVES	READER	SLAYED	THALER	COARSE	SEABEE	BEWARE	INCASE	PEDATE	ULLAGE
LIANES	REALER	SLAYER	THALES	CRABBE	SEANCE	BINATE	INHALE	PELAGE	UNCAGE
LOADED	REALES	SNAKED	THAMES	CRADLE	SEARLE	BORAGE	INMATE	PHRASE	UNCASE
LOADER	REAMED	SNAKES	THANES	DEARIE	SHAYNE	BORATE	INNAGE	PIKAKE	UNEASE
LOAFED	REAMER	SNARED	THAWED	DEARME	SNATHE	BUTANE	INNATE	PILATE	UNIATE
LOAFER	REAPED	SNARES	THAYER	DIANNE	SPARGE	BYNAME	INSANE	PIRATE	UNLACE
LOAMED	REAPER	SOAKED	TOATEE	DOABLE	SPARSE	CANAPE	INTAKE	PLEASE	UNLADE
LOANED	REARED	SOAKER	TRACED	DRAGEE	SPATHE	CARAFE	INVADE	POMACE	UNMADE
LOANER	REARER	SOAPED	TRACER	DUARTE	STABLE	CERATE	IODATE	POMADE	UNMAKE
LOAVES	RHAMES	SOAPER	TRACES	DWAYNE	STACTE	CESARE	KARATE	POTAGE	UNSAFE
MEAGER	ROAMED	SOARED	TRACEY	ECARTE	STANCE	CETANE	LAMAZE	PURACE	UPDATE
MEANER	ROAMER	SOARER	TRADED	ELAINE	STAPLE	CHOATE	LANATE	RAMATE	UPTAKE
MOANED	ROARED	SOARES	TRADER	ELAPSE	STARVE	CLEAVE	LAVAGE	RAVAGE	URBANE
MOANER	ROARER	SOAVES	TRADES	ELAYNE	STATUE	COMATE	LEGATE	REBATE	VACATE
MOATED	RRATED	SPACED	TRALEE	ENABLE	SWANEE	CREASE	LENAPE	RECANE	VISAGE
NEARED	SCALED	SPACEK	TRAVEL	FIACRE	SWATHE	CREATE	LESAGE	REDATE	VITALE
NEARER	SCALER	SPACER	TRAVES	FIANCE	SWAYZE	CUBAGE	LIGATE	REFACE	VIVACE
NEATEN	SCALES	SPACES	TUAREG	FLAMBE	TOATEE	CURARE	LINAGE	REGALE	VOLARE
NEATER	SCAPED	SPACEY	UKASES	FLANGE	TRALEE	CURATE	LIPASE	RELACE	VOYAGE
NIAMEY	SCAPES	SPADED	UNAGED	FRAISE	TRANCE	DAMAGE	LOBATE	RELATE	ZONATE
OCASEK	SCARED	SPADER	UNAWED	FRANCE	UNABLE	DEBASE	LOCALE	REMADE	ZOUAVE
OCASEY	SCARER	SPADES	UPASES	FRAPPE	USABLE	DEBATE	LOCATE	REMAKE	ZYMASE
OKAYED	SCARES	SPARED	USAGES	GLANCE	USANCE	DECADE	LOVAGE	RENAME	
ONAGER	SEABED	SPARER	WEAKEN	GOALIE	UVALUE	DEFACE	LUNATE	REPAVE	••••AE
ORALES	SEABEE	SPARES	WEAKER	GOATEE	VIABLE	DEFAME	LUXATE	RERATE	AGORAE
ORATED	SEALED	SPATES	WEANED	GRABLE	WHATVE	DEGAGE	MADAME	RESALE	ALULAE
ORATES	SEALER	SPAYED	WEARER	GRACIE	WRASSE	DELATE	MALATE	RETAKE	AMEBAE
OSAGES	SEAMED	STACEY	WEASEL	GRAMME		DILATE	MANAGE	RETAPE	AORTAE
PEAHEN	SEAMEN	STAGED	WEAVED	GRANDE	•••AE•	DONATE	MCCABE	ROTATE	BULLAE
PEAKED	SEARED	STAGER	WEAVER	GRANGE	ACHAEA	DOSAGE	MCHALE	ROXANE	BURSAE
PEALED	SEATED	STAGES	WEAVES	HEARYE	ISRAEL	DOTAGE	MENACE	ROYALE	CANNAE
PEAVEY	SEATER	STAKED	WHALER	HOAGIE	JUDAEA	EFFACE	MENAGE	RUGATE	CELLAE
PHAGES	SHADED	STAKES	WHALES	HOARSE	NICAEA	ENCAGE	METATE	SAVAGE	CHELAE
PHASED	SHADES	STALED	XIAMEN	JEANNE	PALAEO	ENCASE	MIRAGE	SAVATE	CNIDAE
PHASER	SHAKEN	STALER	XRATED	JOANIE	RAFAEL	ENGAGE	MOHAVE	SCRAPE	COSTAE
PHASES	SHAKER	STALES	XRAYED	JOANNE	TOGAED	ENLACE	MOJAVE	SEDATE	CURIAE
PIAGET	SHAKES	STAMEN	YEAGER	KHAFRE	VISAED	ENRAGE	MORALE	SENATE	FAUNAE
PLACED	SHALES	STAPES	YEANED	LEAGUE		EQUATE	MUGABE	SERAPE	FLORAE
PLACER	SHALEY	STARED		LIABLE	•••A•E	ERGATE	MUTATE	SESAME	FOSSAE
PLACES	SHAMED	STARER	••A••E	LIAISE	ABLATE	ERRARE	NEGATE	SEWAGE	FOVEAE
PLACET	SHAMES	STARES	AMALIE	LOATHE	ABLAZE	ESCAPE	NEWAGE	SHEAVE	GALEAE
PLAGES	SHAPED	STASES	APACHE	MEAGRE	ABRADE	ESTATE	NONAGE	SILAGE	GEMMAE
PLANED	SHAPER	STATED	ARABLE	MEALIE	ACUATE	ETHANE	NONAME	SLEAVE	GUTTAE
PLANER	SHAPES	STATEN	BEADLE	MEANIE	ADNATE	EXHALE	NOSALE	SLEAZE	HYDRAE
PLANES	SHARED	STATER	BEAGLE	NUANCE	AERATE	FACADE	NOTATE	SLOANE	LARVAE
PLANET	SHARER	STATES	BEANIE	OPAQUE	AFLAME	FATALE	NUTATE	SOCAGE	MACRAE
PLATED	SHARES	STAVED	BEATLE	ORACLE	AFRAME	FEMALE	OBLATE	SOLACE	MENSAE
PLATEN	SHAVED	STAVES	BLAINE	ORANGE	AGLARE	FINALE	OCTANE	SQUARE	NUCHAE
PLATER	SHAVEN	STAYED	BLAISE	PIAFFE	AGNATE	FIXATE	OCTAVE	STRAFE	OCREAE
PLATES	SHAVER	SUAVER	BRAISE	PLAGUE	ALSACE	FORAGE	OFLATE	STRAKE	PALEAE
PLAYED	SHAVES	SWAGED	BRAQUE	PLAICE	ANSATE	GARAGE	OLDAGE	TAMALE	PARCAE
PLAYER	SKATED	SWAGES	CHAINE	PLANTE	AQUATE	GREASE	OLEATE	TENACE	PENNAE
PRASES	SKATER	SWALES	CHAISE	PLAQUE	ARCADE	GREAVE	ONSALE	THRACE	PHILAE
PRATED	SKATES	SWANEE	CHANCE	PLATTE	ARCANE	GYRATE	ONTAPE	THRALE	PHYLAE
PRATER	SLAKED	SWAYED	CHANGE	PRAGUE	ATEASE	HARARE	OPIATE	TIRADE	PINNAE
PRATES	SLAKES	SWAYER	CHARGE	PRAISE	AUBADE	HECATE	ORGATE	TIRANE	PLICAE
PRAXES	SLATED	TEAMED	CHASSE	PRANCE	AVIATE	HOMAGE	ORNATE	TISANE	REGGAE

STELAE
STRIAE
SUMMAE
SUNDAE
TESTAE
THECAE
TIBIAE
UMBRAE
UVULAE

AF••••
AFEARD
AFFAIR
AFFECT
AFFINE
AFFIRM
AFFORD
AFFRAY
AFGHAN
AFIELD
AFLAME
AFLATS
AFLCIO
AFLOAT
AFRAID
AFRAME
AFREET
AFRESH
AFRICA
AFRITS

A•F•••
AAFAIR
AFFAIR
AFFECT
AFFINE
AFFIRM
AFFORD
AFFRAY
AJFOYT
ALFINE
ALFRED
ALFVEN
AUFAIT
AUFOND

A••F••
AIDFUL
AIMFOR
AIMFUL
ALLFOR
ARAFAT
ARMFUL
ARTFUL
ASKFOR

A•••F•
ADRIFT
AERIFY
AMALFI
ARGUFY
AURIFY

•AF•••
AAFAIR
BAFFIN
BAFFLE
CAFTAN
DAFFED
DAFTER
DAFTLY
FAFNIR
GAFFED
GAFFER
GAFFES
HAFTED
KAFFIR
KAFIRS
LAFFER
OAFISH
RAFAEL
RAFFIA
RAFFLE
RAFTED
RAFTER
SAFARI
SAFELY
SAFEST
SAFETY
SAFIRE
WAFERS
WAFERY
WAFFLE
WAFFLY
WAFTED
ZAFFER
ZAFTIG

•A•F••
BAFFIN
BAFFLE
BAGFUL
BARFLY
CANFUL
CAPFUL
CARFUL
DAFFED
EARFUL
GADFLY
GAFFED
GAFFER
GAFFES
HATFUL
JARFUL
KAFFIR
LAFFER
LAPFUL
LAWFUL
LAYFOR
MANFUL
MAYFLY
PANFRY
PANFUL
PAYFOR
RAFFIA
RAFFLE
RANFOR
SAWFIT
VATFUL
WAFFLE
WAFFLY
ZAFFER

•A••F•
BASIFY
CANIFF
CARAFE
CASEFY
FAROFF
GASIFY
LAYOFF
PACIFY
PAYOFF
RAMIFY
RANOFF
RAREFY
RARIFY
RATIFY
SALIFY
SAWOFF
TAPOFF
TARIFF

•A•••F
CANIFF
FAROFF
LAYOFF
MASSIF
PAYOFF
RANOFF
SAWOFF
TAPOFF
TARIFF

••AF••
ARAFAT
BIAFRA
CHAFED
CHAFES
CHAFFS
CHAFFY
CRAFTS
CRAFTY
DEAFEN
DEAFER
DEAFLY
DRAFTS
DRAFTY
GRAFTS
INAFIX
INAFOG
KHAFRE
LEAFED
LOAFED
LOAFER
PIAFFE
QUAFFS
SEAFAN
SEAFOX
SHAFTS
SNAFUS
STAFFS

••A•F•
AMALFI
CHAFFS
CHAFFY
DWARFS
PIAFFE
QUAFFS
SCARFS
STAFFS
WHARFS

••A••F
HEAROF
SHARIF
STAPUF
WHATIF

•••AF•
CARAFE
DECAFS
PILAFS
SCLAFF
SHEAFS
STRAFE
UNSAFE

•••A•F
BEHALF
INHALF
SCLAFF

AG••••
AGADIR
AGAMAS
AGARIC
AGASSI
AGATES
AGATHA
AGAVES
AGEING
AGEISM
AGEIST
AGENAS
AGENCY
AGENDA
AGENTS
AGEOLD
AGGIES
AGGROS
AGHAST
AGLAIA
AGLARE
AGLEAM
AGLETS
AGLINT
AGNATE
AGORAE
AGORAS
AGOROT
AGOUTI
AGREED
AGREES
AGUISH

A•G•••
AEGEAN
AFGHAN
AGGIES
AGGROS
AIGRET
ALGORE
ANGELA
ANGELI
ANGELL
ANGELO
ANGELS
ANGERS
ANGKOR
ANGLED
ANGLER
ANGLES
ANGLIA
ANGLIC
ANGLOS
ANGOLA
ANGORA
ARGALI
ARGENT
ARGIVE
ARGOSY
ARGOTS
ARGUED
ARGUER
ARGUES
ARGUFY
ARGYLE
ARGYLL
ASGARD
AUGEAN
AUGEND
AUGERS
AUGHTS
AUGURS
AUGURY
AUGUST

A••G••
ADAGES
ADAGIO
AIRGUN
ALEGAR
ALEGRE
ALIGHT
ALIGNS
AMIGAS
AMIGOS
ANSGAR
APOGEE
ARAGON
ARIGHT
ARTGUM

A•••G•
ALLEGE
ANERGY
ARMAGH
ASSIGN
ATERGO
AURIGA
AVENGE
AWEIGH

A••••G
AAHING
ABYING
ACHING
ACTING
ADDING
AGEING
AIDING
AILING
AIMING
AIRBAG
AIRING
ALBORG
ANALOG
ANWANG
ANYANG
ARCING
ARMING
ASKING
AWNING

•AG•••
BAGDAD
BAGELS
BAGFUL
BAGGED
BAGGER
BAGGIE
BAGSIT
BAGUIO
CAGERS
CAGIER
CAGILY
CAGING
CAGNEY
CAGUAS
DAGAMA
DAGGER
DAGMAR
EAGLED
EAGLES
EAGLET
EAGRES
FAGEND
FAGGED
FAGOTS
GAGGED
GAGGLE
GAGING
GAGLAW
GAGMAN
GAGMEN
HAGDON
HAGGIS
HAGGLE
HAGMAN
JAGGED
JAGGER
JAGUAR
KAGERA
LAGASH
LAGERS
LAGGED
LAGGER
LAGOON
LAGUNA
MAGGIE
MAGGIO
MAGMAS
MAGNET
MAGNON
MAGNUM
MAGNUS
MAGPIE
MAGUEY
MAGYAR
NAGANO
NAGGED
NAGGER
NAGOYA
PAGANS
PAGERS
PAGING
PAGODA
RAGBAG
RAGGED
RAGING
RAGLAN
RAGMAN
RAGMEN
RAGMOP
RAGOUT
RAGRUG
RAGTAG
RAGTOP
SAGELY
SAGEST
SAGGED
TAGDAY
TAGEND
TAGGED
TAGORE
TAGOUT
TAGSUP
VAGARY
VAGUER
WAGERS
WAGGED
WAGGLE
WAGGLY
WAGGON
WAGING
WAGNER
WAGONS
ZAGGED
ZAGREB

•A•G••
BADGER
BADGES
BADGUY
BAGGED
BAGGER
BAGGIE
BANGED
BANGER
BANGKA
BANGLE
BANGOR
BANGUI
BANGUP
BARGED
BARGES
CADGED
CADGER
CADGES
CAPGUN
CARGOS
CATGUT
CAUGHT
DAGGER
DANGER
DANGLE
DANGLY
DANGME
DAYGLO
FAGGED
FANGED
GADGET
GAGGED
GAGGLE
GANGED
GANGER
GANGES
GANGLE
GANGLY
GANGUE
GANGUP
GARGLE
GAUGED
GAUGER
GAUGES
HAGGIS
HAGGLE
HAIGHT
HANGAR
HANGED
HANGER
HANGIN
HANGON
HANGUL
HANGUP
JAEGER
JAGGED
JAGGER
JANGLE
JANGLY
JARGON
LAAGER
LAGGED
LAGGER
LANGUR
LARGER
LARGES
LARGOS
LAUGHS
MAGGIE
MAGGIO
MAJGEN
MANGER
MANGLE
MANGOS
MARGAY
MARGES
MARGIE
MARGIN
MARGOT
NAGGED
NAGGER
NAUGHT
PARGET
RAGGED
RANGED
RANGER
RANGES
RANGUP
RAYGUN
SAGGED
SAIGAS
SAIGON
SANGER
SANGTO
SARGES
SARGON
SARGOS
SAUGER
TAGGED
TAIGAS
TANGED
TANGLE
TANGLY
TANGOS
TANGUY
TARGES
TARGET
TAUGHT
VAUGHN
WAGGED
WAGGLE
WAGGLY
WAGGON
WANGLE
WARGOD
YANGON
ZAGGED

•A••G•
BADEGG
BAREGE
CAYUGA
DAMAGE
GALAGO
GARAGE
LADOGA
LATIGO
LAVAGE
MALAGA
MALIGN
MANAGE
MANEGE
PAANGA
PAPAGO
RAVAGE
RAWEGG
SAVAGE

•A•••G
AAHING
BAAING
BADEGG
BAKING
BALING
BANDOG
BARING
BARONG
BASING
BATING
BAYING
CAGING
CAKING
CANING
CARING
CASING
CATRIG
CAVING
CAWING
DANANG
DANZIG
DARING
DATING
DATONG
DAZING
EALING
EARING
EARWIG
EASING
EATING
FACING
FADING
FAKING
FARING
FAXING
FAZING
GAGING
GAMING
GAPING
GASBAG
GASLOG
GATING
GAZING
HALING
HARING
HATING
HAVING
HAWING
HAYING

HAZING
JADING
JAPING
JAWING
LACING
LADING
LAMING
LAPDOG
LAVING
LAWING
LAYING
LAZING
MAKING
MATING
MAYTAG
NAMING
OARING
PACING
PADANG
PAGING
PAHANG
PALING
PARANG
PARING
PAVING
PAWING
PAYING
RACING
RAGBAG
RAGING
RAGRUG
RAGTAG
RAKING
RARING
RASING
RATEDG
RATING
RAVING
RAWEGG
RAZING
SARONG
SATANG
SATING
SAVING
SAWING
SAWLOG
SAYING
TAKING
TAMING
TAPING
TARING
TAUTOG
TAWING
TAXING
WADING
WAGING
WAKING
WANING
WARING
WAVING
WAXING
YAWING
ZAFTIG

••AG••

ADAGES
ADAGIO
ARAGON
BEAGLE
CRAGGY
DRAGEE
DRAGGY
DRAGIN
DRAGON
FLAGGY
FLAGON
HOAGIE
IMAGED
IMAGER
IMAGES
KNAGGY
LAAGER
LEAGUE
MEAGER
MEAGRE
ONAGER
OSAGES
PHAGES
PIAGET
PLAGAL
PLAGES
PLAGIO
PLAGUE
PRAGUE
QUAGGA
QUAGGY
REAGAN
SEAGAL
SHAGGY
SLAGGY
SNAGGY
STAGED
STAGER
STAGES
SWAGED
SWAGES
TRAGIC
UNAGED
USAGES
YEAGER

••A•G•

CHANGE
CHARGE
CLANGS
CRAGGY
DRAGGY
FLAGGY
FLANGE
GRANGE
KIANGS
KNAGGY
LIANGS
ORANGE
ORANGS
ORANGY
PAANGA
PRANGS
QUAGGA
QUAGGY
QUANGO
SHAGGY
SLAGGY
SLANGS
SLANGY
SNAGGY
SPARGE
TWANGS
TWANGY
UBANGI
WHANGS

••A••G

ANALOG
BAAING
DIALOG
INAFOG
QUAHOG
SEABAG
SEADOG
STALAG
TEABAG
TUAREG

•••AG•

ARMAGH
BORAGE
CUBAGE
DAMAGE
DEGAGE
DORAGS
DOSAGE
DOTAGE
ENCAGE
ENGAGE
ENRAGE
FORAGE
GALAGO
GARAGE
GULAGS
HOMAGE
ICEAGE
IDTAGS
INNAGE
LAVAGE
LESAGE
LINAGE
LOVAGE
MALAGA
MANAGE
MENAGE
MIRAGE
NEWAGE
NONAGE
OLDAGE
OUTAGE
PAPAGO
PELAGE
POTAGE
RAVAGE
REBAGS
RETAGS
SAVAGE
SCRAGS
SEWAGE
SILAGE
SOCAGE
SPRAGS
TOBAGO
TOWAGE
TRIAGE
ULLAGE
UNCAGE
VIRAGO
VISAGE
VOYAGE

•••A•G

ANWANG
ANYANG
CHIANG
DANANG
KDLANG
PADANG
PAHANG
PARANG
PENANG
REHANG
SATANG
SPRANG

••••AG

AIRBAG
DOGTAG
GASBAG
GOSTAG
GYMBAG
ICEBAG
JETLAG
KITBAG
MAYTAG
RAGBAG
RAGTAG
REDTAG
REFLAG
SEABAG
SONTAG
STALAG
TEABAG
UNSNAG
WIGWAG
ZIGZAG

AH••••

AHCHOO
AHERNE
AHIMSA

A•H•••

AAHING
ABHORS
ACHAEA
ACHEBE
ACHENE
ACHIER
ACHING
ADHERE
AGHAST
ALHIRT
AMHARA
ANHYDR
APHIDS
ASHARP
ASHCAN
ASHIER
ASHLAR
ASHLEY
ASHORE
ASHRAM
ATHAND
ATHENA
ATHENE
ATHENS
ATHOME
AWHILE
AWHIRL

A••H••

AACHEN
ABOHMS
AETHER
AFGHAN
AHCHOO
ALOHAS
ALPHAS
ALTHEA
AMPHID
ANCHOR
ANDHOW
ANNHON
ANTHEM
ANTHER
ANYHOW
ARCHED
ARCHER
ARCHES
ARCHIE
ARCHLY
ARCHON
ARNHEM
ARTHRO
ARTHUR
ASCHAM
ATTHAT
AUGHTS
AUTHOR

A•••H•

AGATHA
ALEPHS
ALIGHT
AMECHE
APACHE
APATHY
ARETHA
ARIGHT
AYESHA

A••••H

ABLUSH
ADOLPH
AFRESH
AGUISH
AMBUSH
ARMAGH
ASPISH
ATTACH
AVOUCH
AWEIGH

•AH•••

AAHING
BAHAMA
BAHIAN
CAHIER
CAHOWS
DAHLIA
KAHLIL
KAHLUA
KAHUNA
LAHORE
MAHDIS
MAHLER
MAHOUT
MAHZOR
PAHANG
PAHARI
RAHRAH
SAHARA
SAHIBS
TAHINI
TAHITI
WAHINE
WAHOOS
WAHWAH
YAHOOS
YAHWEH

•A•H••

AACHEN
BACHED
BADHAM
BARHOP
BASHED
BASHES
BATHED
BATHER
BATHES
BATHOS
CACHED
CACHES
CACHET
CACHOU
CARHOP
CASHED
CASHES
CASHEW
CASHIN
CATHAY
CATHER
DACHAS
DAPHNE
DASHED
DASHER
DASHES
DASHIS
FATHER
FATHOM
GASHED
GASHES
GATHER
HASHED
HASHES
HATHOR
HAWHAW
JANHUS
KATHIE
LACHES
LAPHAM
LASHED
LASHER
LASHES
LASHIO
LASHUP
LATHED
LATHER
LATHES
MACHES
MACHOS
MASHED
MASHER
MASHES
MASHIE
MATHER
MATHIS
MAYHAP
MAYHEM
NACHOS
NASHUA
NATHAN
PASHAS
PASHTO
PATHAN
PATHOL
PATHOS
RACHEL
RACHIS
RASHAD
RASHER
RASHES
RASHID
RASHLY
RATHER
SACHEM
SACHET
SADHES
SADHUS
SASHAY
SASHED
SASHES
VACHEL
VASHTI
WARHOL
WASHED
WASHER
WASHES
WASHOE
WASHUP
YACHTS

•A••H•

CANTHI
CATCHY
CAUCHO
CAUCHY
CAUGHT
EARTHA
EARTHY
FAITHS
GALAHS
GANDHI
GARTHS
GAUCHE
GAUCHO
HAIGHT
JASCHA
JAWOHL
LANDHO
LAUGHS
MANCHA
MANCHU
MARCHE
MARSHA
MARSHY
MARTHA
NAUGHT
NAVAHO
PANCHO
PATCHY
RAJAHS
RANCHO
SANCHO
SAPPHO
TAICHI
TAUGHT
VAUGHN
XANTHO
YAMAHA

•A•••H

BANISH
BARISH
BARUCH
CALASH
CALIPH
CASBAH
DALETH
DANISH
FAMISH
FARRAH
GALOSH
GARETH
GARISH
HALVAH
HANNAH
HAUNCH
JADISH
JARRAH
KALAKH
KASBAH
KAZAKH
LAGASH
LAMECH
LAMEDH
LATISH
LAUNCH
LAVISH
MARIAH
MARISH
MATZOH
NAMATH
NAUTCH
OAFISH
PALISH
PARAPH
PARIAH
PARISH
PAUNCH
RADISH
RAHRAH
RAKISH
RAVISH
RAWISH
SALISH
SAMECH
SAMEKH
TAKETH
VANISH
WABASH
WAHWAH
WARMTH
YAHWEH

••AH••

BRAHMA
BRAHMS
GRAHAM
OMAHAN
OMAHAS
PEAHEN
QUAHOG
SPAHIS
UTAHAN

••A•H•

AGATHA
APACHE
APATHY
BEACHY
BRACHY
BRASHY
CHACHA
DRACHM
FLASHY
GRAPHS
GRAPHY
HEATHS
HEATHY
KWACHA
LEACHY
LOATHE
ORACHS
PEACHY
PLASHY
POACHY
SCATHE
SNATHE
SNATHS
SPATHE
SWATHE
SWATHS
TRACHY
TRASHY
WRATHS
WRATHY

••A••H

BLANCH
BRANCH
DEARTH
EPARCH
EXARCH
HEALTH
HEARTH
INARCH
ISAIAH
KLATCH
SEARCH
SNATCH
STANCH
STARCH
SWARTH
SWATCH
THATCH
WEALTH
WRAITH

•••AH•

EPHAHS
GALAHS
GERAHS
JONAHS
LOTAHS
MYNAHS
NAVAHO
OBEAHS
RAJAHS
SURAHS
TORAHS
YAMAHA

•••A•H

ARMAGH
ATTACH
BLEACH
BREACH
BREATH
BROACH
BYPATH
CALASH
DETACH

EMDASH
ENDASH
INCASH
KALAKH
KAZAKH
LAGASH
NAMATH
ORBACH
PARAPH
PESACH
PLEACH
POTASH
PREACH
REHASH
REWASH
RIYADH
SERAPH
SHEATH
SIWASH
SPLASH
SQUASH
TERAPH
THRASH
UNLASH
WABASH
WREATH

••••AH

BEULAH
CASBAH
DOODAH
ELIJAH
FARRAH
FELLAH
GULLAH
HALVAH
HANNAH
HIJRAH
HOOHAH
HOOKAH
HOORAH
HOWDAH
HURRAH
HUZZAH
ISAIAH
JARRAH
JINNAH
JOSIAH
JUBBAH
KASBAH
LOOFAH
MARIAH
MOOLAH
MULLAH
NULLAH
OHYEAH
OOMPAH
PARIAH
PISGAH
PUNKAH
PURDAH
RAHRAH
RUPIAH
SIRRAH
SUKKAH
TUSSAH
UZZIAH
WAHWAH
WHYDAH
ZILPAH

AI••••

AIDERS
AIDFUL
AIDING
AIELLO
AIGRET
AIKIDO
AILEEN
AILERS
AILING
AIMFOR
AIMFUL
AIMING
AIMSAT
AIMSTO
AIRARM
AIRBAG
AIRBUS
AIRDAM
AIRDRY
AIRGUN
AIRIER
AIRILY
AIRING
AIRMAN
AIRMEN
AIROUT
AIRSAC
AIRWAY
AISLES

A•I•••

ABIDED
ABIDES
ACIDIC
ACIDLY
ACINUS
ADIDAS
ADIEUS
ADIEUX
AFIELD
AHIMSA
AKIMBO
AKITAS
ALIBIS
ALIBLE
ALICIA
ALIENS
ALIGHT
ALIGNS
ALINES
ALIOTO
ALISON
ALITER
AMICES
AMICUS
AMIDES
AMIDOL
AMIDST
AMIENS
AMIGAS
AMIGOS
AMINES
AMINOR
AMINUS
ANIMAL
ANIMAS
ANIMES
ANIMUS
ANIONS
ANITRA
APIARY
APICAL
APICES
APIECE
ARIDLY
ARIGHT
ARIOSE
ARIOSO
ARISEN
ARISES
ARISTA
ARISTO
ASIANS
ASIDES
ASIMOV
AVIANS
AVIARY
AVIATE
AVIDLY
AVISOS
AXILLA
AXIOMS
AXIONS
AZIDES
AZINES

A••I••

AAHING
ABYING
ACHIER
ACHING
ACTIII
ACTING
ACTINO
ACTION
ACTIUM
ACTIVE
ACUITY
ADDING
ADLIBS
ADMIRE
ADMITS
ADRIAN
ADRIEN
ADRIFT
ADVICE
ADVISE
AEDILE
AERIAL
AERIES
AERIFY
AERILY
AFFINE
AFFIRM
AFRICA
AFRITS
AGEING
AGEISM
AGEIST
AGGIES
AGLINT
AGUISH
AIDING
AIKIDO
AILING
AIMING
AIRIER
AIRILY
AIRING
ALBINO
ALBION
ALDINE
ALFINE
ALHIRT
ALLIED
ALLIES
ALLIUM
ALNICO
ALOINS
ALPINE
ALTIMA
ALTIUS
AMBITS
AMNION
ANCIEN
ANNIKA
ANOINT
ANTICS
ANVILS
AORIST
APHIDS
APLITE
APPIAN
AQUILA
AQUINO
ARCING
ARGIVE
ARLISS
ARMIES
ARMING
ARNICA
AROIDS
ARRIBA
ARRIVE
ARTIER
ARTILY
ARTIST
ASDICS
ASEITY
ASHIER
ASKING
ASPICS
ASPIRE
ASPISH
ASSIGN
ASSISI
ASSIST
ASSIZE
ASWIRL
ATKINS
ATRIAL
ATRISK
ATRIUM
ATTICA
ATTICS
ATTILA
ATTIRE
ATWILL
AUDIAL
AUDILE
AUDIOS
AUDITS
AURIFY
AURIGA
AUXINS
AVAILS
AVOIDS
AWAITS
AWEIGH
AWHILE
AWHIRL
AWNING
AXLIKE

A•••I•

AAFAIR
ABATIS
ABUKIR
ACACIA
ACADIA
ACARID
ACEDIA
ACETIC
ACIDIC
ACQUIT
ACTIII
ADAGIO
ADDSIN
ADELIE
ADJOIN
ADONIS
ADROIT
AENEID
AEOLIA
AEOLIC
AFFAIR
AFLCIO
AFRAID
AGADIR
AGARIC
AGLAIA
ALANIS
ALARIC
ALBEIT
ALBOIN
ALCUIN
ALDRIN
ALEXIA
ALEXIS
ALIBIS
ALICIA
ALTAIC
ALTAIR
AMADIS
AMALIE
AMATIS
AMBLIN
AMEBIC
AMELIA
AMPHID
ANACIN
ANEMIA
ANEMIC
ANGLIA
ANGLIC
ANNUIT
ANODIC
ANOMIC
ANOMIE
ANTRIM
ANUBIS
AODAIS
AORTIC
APULIA
ARABIA
ARABIC
ARALIA
ARAMIS
ARCHIE
ARCTIC
ARMPIT
ARTOIS
ASKSIN
ASSAIL
ASTRID
ATOMIC
ATONIC
ATTAIN
ATTRIT
AUFAIT
AULAIT
AUNTIE
AUPAIR
AUSSIE
AUSTIN
AZORIN

A••••I

ACTIII
ADJANI
ADONAI
ADZUKI
AGASSI
AGOUTI
ALEXEI
ALKALI
ALUMNI
AMALFI
ANDREI
ANGELI
ANNULI
ARGALI
ARMANI
ASKARI
ASSISI
AVANTI

•AI•••

BAIKAL
BAILED
BAILEE
BAILER
BAILEY
BAILOR
BAINES
BAIRNS
BAITED
BAIZAS
CAICOS
CAIMAN
CAIQUE
CAIRNS
DAIKON
DAILEY
DAIMON
DAIMYO
DAINTY
DAIREN
DAISES
FAILED
FAILLE
FAINTS
FAIRED
FAIRER
FAIRLY
FAIRUP
FAISAL
FAITHS
FAIYUM
GAIETY
GAIJIN
GAINED
GAINER
GAINLY
GAINON
GAINST
GAITED
GAITER
HAIDAS
HAIGHT
HAIKUS
HAILED
HAILEY
HAINAN
HAINES
HAIRDO
HAIRED
JAILED
JAILER
JAIPUR
KAILUA
KAISER
LAIDBY
LAIDIN
LAIDON
LAIDTO
LAIDUP
LAINIE
LAIRDS
MAIDEN
MAIDUS
MAILED
MAILER
MAILES
MAILIN
MAINLY
MAISIE
MAITAI
MAITRE
MAIZES
NAIADS
NAILED
NAILER
NAILIN
NAIRAS
PAIDIN
PAIDUP
PAILOU
PAINED
PAINTS
PAINTY
PAIRED
PAIRUP
PAISAS
PAIUTE
RAIDED
RAIDER
RAILAT
RAILED
RAILER
RAINED
RAINER
RAINES
RAINEY
RAIPUR
RAISED
RAISER
RAISES
RAISIN
SAIGAS
SAIGON
SAILED
SAILOR
SAINTE
SAINTS
SAIPAN
TAICHI
TAIGAS
TAILED
TAILLE
TAILOR
TAINAN
TAINOS
TAINTS
TAIPAN
TAIPEI
TAIWAN
VAINER
VAINLY
VAISYA
WAILED
WAILER
WAISTS
WAITED
WAITER
WAITON
WAITUP
WAIVED
WAIVER
WAIVES
ZAIRES

•A•I••

AAHING
BAAING
BABIED
BABIES
BAHIAN
BAKING
BALING
BANISH
BARING
BARISH
BARITE
BARIUM
BASICS
BASIFY
BASING
BASINS
BATIKS
BATING
BAYING
CABINS
CAGIER
CAGILY
CAGING
CAHIER
CAKIER
CAKING
CALICO
CALIPH
CAMINO
CAMION
CAMISE
CANIDS
CANIER
CANIFF
CANINE
CANING
CAPIAS
CAPITA
CARIBE
CARIBS
CARIES
CARINA
CARING
CASING
CASINO
CATION
CAVIAR
CAVILS
CAVING
CAVITY
CAWING
DAMIEN
DAMITA
DANIEL
DANISH
DARIEN
DARING
DARIUS
DATING
DATIVE
DAVIES
DAVITS
DAZING
EALING
EARING
EASIER
EASILY
EASING
EATING
FABIAN
FACIAL
FACIAS
FACIES
FACILE
FACING
FADING
FAJITA
FAKING
FAKIRS
FALINE
FAMILY
FAMINE
FAMISH
FANION
FARINA
FARING
FATIMA
FAXING
FAZING
GABIES
GABION
GAGING
GAMIER
GAMILY
GAMINE
GAMING
GAMINS
GAPING
GARISH
GASIFY
GATING
GAVIAL
GAZING
HABILE
HABITS

HAKIMS
HALIDE
HALING
HALITE
HAMILL
HAMITE
HARING
HATING
HAVING
HAWING
HAYING
HAZIER
HAZILY
HAZING
JABIRU
JADING
JADISH
JANICE
JANINE
JAPING
JAVIER
JAWING
KAFIRS
KALINE
KARIBA
LABIAL
LABILE
LACIER
LACILY
LACING
LADIDA
LADIES
LADING
LADINO
LAKIER
LAMIAS
LAMINA
LAMING
LANIER
LAPINS
LARIAT
LATIGO
LATINA
LATINI
LATINO
LATINS
LATISH
LATIUM
LAVING
LAVISH
LAWING
LAXITY
LAYING
LAZIER
LAZILY
LAZING
MAKING
MALIBU
MALICE
MALIGN
MANIAC
MANIAS
MANILA
MANIOC
MAOISM
MAOIST
MARIAH
MARIAN
MARIEL
MARIKO
MARILU
MARINA
MARINE
MARINO
MARION
MARISA
MARISH
MARIST
MARIUS
MATING
MATINS
MAXIMA
MAXIMS
MAXINE
MAXIXE
MAZIER
MAZILY
NADINE
NADIRS
NAMING
NAPIER
NARIAL
NATICK
NATION
NATIVE
NAVIES
OAFISH
OARING
OATIER
PACIFY
PACING
PACINO
PAGING
PALIER
PALING
PALISH
PAMIRS
PANICS
PAPIER
PARIAH
PARING
PARISH
PARITY
PATINA
PATINE
PATIOS
PAVING
PAWING
PAYING
RABIES
RACIAL
RACIER
RACILY
RACINE
RACING
RADIAL
RADIAN
RADIOS
RADISH
RADIUM
RADIUS
RAGING
RAKING
RAKISH
RAMIES
RAMIFY
RANIDS
RAPIDS
RAPIER
RAPINE
RAPINI
RARIFY
RARING
RARITY
RASING
RATIFY
RATINE
RATING
RATION
RATIOS
RATITE
RAVINE
RAVING
RAVISH
RAWISH
RAZING
SABINE
SABINS
SAFIRE
SAHIBS
SALIFY
SALINA
SALINE
SALISH
SALIVA
SAMIAM
SAMITE
SANITY
SATING
SATINS
SATINY
SATIRE
SAVING
SAVIOR
SAWING
SAYING
TAHINI
TAHITI
TAKING
TAKINS
TALION
TAMILS
TAMING
TANIST
TAOISM
TAOIST
TAPING
TAPINS
TAPIRS
TARIFF
TARING
TAWING
TAXIED
TAXIES
TAXING
VALISE
VALIUM
VANIER
VANISH
VANITY
VARIED
VARIES
WADING
WAGING
WAHINE
WAKING
WANIER
WANING
WAPITI
WARIER
WARILY
WARING
WAVIER
WAVILY
WAVING
WAXIER
WAXILY
WAXING
XAVIER
YAKIMA
YALIES
YAWING
ZAMIAS
ZANIER
ZANIES
ZANILY
ZAYINS

•A••I•

AAFAIR
BACKIN
BADDIE
BAFFIN
BAGGIE
BAGSIT
BAGUIO
BALTIC
BANDIT
BARBIE
BARDIC
BARKIN
BARRIE
BARRIO
BARRIS
BAUCIS
CABBIE
CADDIE
CADDIS
CADMIC
CALAIS
CALLIN
CALVIN
CAMEIN
CANDID
CANLIT
CAPRIS
CAPSID
CARDIN
CARDIO
CARLIN
CARRIE
CASHIN
CASSIA
CASSIO
CASSIS
CATKIN
CATNIP
CATRIG
CAVEIN
DACOIT
DAHLIA
DANDIE
DANZIG
DARNIT
DARWIN
DASHIS
DASSIN
DAYLIT
EARWIG
EASEIN
EATSIN
FABRIC
FADEIN
FAERIE
FAFNIR
FALLIN
FANNIE
FASCIA
GAELIC
GAIJIN
GALLIA
GALLIC
GALOIS
GAMBIA
GAMBIT
GARCIA
GARLIC
GASKIN
GASLIT
GATLIN
GAVEIN
GAWAIN
HACKIE
HADDIE
HADJIS
HAGGIS
HAJJIS
HALOID
HAMLIN
HANDIN
HANGIN
HANKIE
HARBIN
HARLIN
HARRIS
HATPIN
HATTIE
HAWAII
IAMBIC
IATRIC
JACKIE
JAMSIN
KAFFIR
KAHLIL
KAOLIN
KARMIC
KATHIE
KAURIS
LACTIC
LADDIE
LAIDIN
LAINIE
LANAIS
LANDIS
LANVIN
LASHIO
LASSIE
LATVIA
LAURIE
LAYSIN
MACEIO
MADDIE
MADEIT
MADRID
MAGGIE
MAGGIO
MAGPIE
MAHDIS
MAILIN
MAISIE
MAJLIS
MAKEIT
MALKIN
MALTIN
MANNIX
MANTIC
MANTIS
MAORIS
MAQUIS
MARCIA
MARCIE
MARGIE
MARGIN
MARLIN
MARNIE
MARTIN
MARVIN
MASAIS
MASHIE
MASSIF
MASTIC
MATHIS
MATLIN
MATRIX
MATTIE
NAILIN
NANNIE
NAPKIN
NAPPIE
NARNIA
NARVIK
PAIDIN
PALLIA
PALLID
PANDIT
PAPAIN
PAQUIN
PARNIS
PARRIS
PARVIS
PASSIM
PASTIS
PATOIS
PAUCIS
PAYSIN
RABBIS
RABBIT
RACHIS
RAFFIA
RAISIN
RAKEIN
RANCID
RANKIN
RASHID
RATLIN
SALVIA
SAMMIE
SANDIA
SANTIR
SARDIS
SARNIA
SAUDIS
SAVAII
SAVOIE
SAVOIR
SAWFIT
SAYYID
TABRIZ
TACTIC
TAKEIN
TALKIE
TANNIC
TANNIN
TARPIT
VALOIS
WADEIN
WALKIE
WALKIN
WALLIS
WANTIN
WAVEIN
YAQUIS
ZADDIK
ZAFTIG
ZAMBIA

•A•••I

BANGUI
BANZAI
BATUMI
CANTHI
CARONI
DALASI
GANDHI
HATARI
HAWAII
JACOBI
JAVARI
KABUKI
KATMAI
LATINI
LAZULI
MAITAI
MALAWI
MALLEI
MALOTI
MAOTAI
NAPOLI
PAHARI
PAPYRI
QATARI
RAPINI
SAFARI
SALAMI
SALUKI
SANSEI
SATORI
SAVAII
TAHINI
TAHITI
TAICHI
TAIPEI
TATAMI
UAKARI
VASHTI
WAPITI
WASABI
WATUSI
YANQUI

••AI••

AVAILS
AWAITS
BAAING
BLAINE
BLAISE
BRAIDS
BRAILA
BRAILS
BRAINS
BRAINY
BRAISE
CHAINE
CHAINS
CHAIRS
CHAISE
CLAIMS
CLAIRE
DRAILS
DRAINS
ELAINE
EMAILS
FLAILS
FLAIRS
FRAIDY
FRAISE
GHAINS
GLAIRS
GLAIRY
GRAILS
GRAINS
GRAINY
ISAIAH
KRAITS
LIAISE
PLAICE
PLAIDS
PLAINS
PLAINT
PLAITS
PRAISE
QUAILS
QUAINT
REAIMS
REAIRS
SNAILS
STAINS
STAIRS
SWAINS
TRAILS
TRAINS
TRAITS
WRAITH

••A•I•

ABATIS
ACACIA
ACADIA
ACARID
ADAGIO
AGADIR
AGARIC
ALANIS
ALARIC
AMADIS
AMALIE
AMATIS
ANACIN
ARABIA
ARABIC
ARALIA
ARAMIS
BEANIE
BEATIT
BEAVIS
BRAZIL
CHAPIN
CLAVIN
COATIS
CRANIA
CRANIO
CYANIC
DEALIN
DEARIE
DEASIL
DRAGIN
DRAWIN
DYADIC
ELAPID
ETALIA
ETALII
FLAVIA
GHAZIS
GLACIS
GOALIE
GRACIE
GRADIN
GRATIA
GRATIN
GRATIS
GRAVID
HEADIN
HOAGIE
ICARIA
INAFIX
IRANIS
IRAQIS
ITALIA
ITALIC
JOANIE
KHAKIS
KHALID
LEADIN
MEALIE
MEANIE
MIAMIA
NIACIN
OKAPIS
OMANIS
OXALIS
PHATIC
PLACID
PLAGIO
PRAXIS
READIN
REALIA
ROADIE
SCALIA
SHAMIR
SHANIA
SHARIA
SHARIF
SLAVIC
SPADIX
SPAHIS
SPAVIN
STADIA
STALIN
STASIS
STATIC
SWAMIS
SWAZIS
THALIA
THATIS
TRAGIC
TRAVIS
URACIL
URALIC
URANIA
URANIC

WHATIF

••A••I
AGASSI
AMALFI
AVANTI
BHAKTI
BRAZZI
CIARDI
ETALII
QUADRI
SCAMPI
SHAKTI
SMALTI
UBANGI

•••AI•
AAFAIR
AFFAIR
AFRAID
AGLAIA
ALTAIC
ALTAIR
AODAIS
ASSAIL
ATTAIN
AUFAIT
AULAIT
AUPAIR
BELAIR
BEWAIL
CALAIS
DERAIL
DETAIL
DETAIN
DOMAIN
ECLAIR
ENTAIL
EURAIL
GAWAIN
HAWAII
HOTAIR
IMPAIR
INLAID
INVAIN
JUDAIC
KUWAIT
LANAIS
LCHAIM
LORAIN
MASAIS
MCBAIN
MCLAIN
MCNAIR
MIDAIR
MOHAIR
MOSAIC
OBTAIN
ORDAIN
OXTAIL
PAPAIN
PETAIN
REGAIN
RELAID
REMAIL
REMAIN
RENAIL
REPAID
REPAIR
RETAIL
RETAIN
ROMAIC
SAVAII
SERAIS
SPRAIN
STRAIN
STRAIT
UJJAIN
UNFAIR
UNLAID
UNPAID
UNSAID
USMAIL

•••A•I
ADJANI
ALKALI
ARGALI
ARMANI
ASKARI
BIHARI
BONAMI
DALASI
DENALI
DOMANI
DORATI
ERNANI
FULANI
GELATI
HATARI
HAWAII
HEGARI
ITHAKI
JAVARI
KIGALI
MALAWI
MESABI
NEPALI
PAHARI
QATARI
ROMAJI
RUBATI
SAFARI
SALAMI
SAVAII
SOMALI
SOUARI
STRATI
TATAMI
UAKARI
WASABI

••••AI
ADONAI
BANZAI
BONSAI
KATMAI
KUBLAI
MAITAI
MAOTAI
NILGAI

AJ••••
AJANTA
AJFOYT

A•J•••
ABJECT
ABJURE
ADJANI
ADJOIN
ADJURE
ADJUST
ANJOUS
ARJUNA

A••J••
ACAJOU
AMAJOR

•AJ•••
CAJOLE
CAJUNS
FAJITA
HAJJES
HAJJIS
MAJGEN
MAJLIS
MAJORS
PAJAMA
RAJAHS
RAJPUT

•A•J••
BANJOS
BANJUL
DAYJOB
FANJET
GAIJIN
GASJET
HADJES
HADJIS
HAJJES
HAJJIS
RAMJET

•A••J•
BAROJA
NAVAJO

••AJ••
ACAJOU
AMAJOR
BMAJOR
CMAJOR
DMAJOR
EMAJOR
FMAJOR
GMAJOR
INAJAM
PRAJNA
TRAJAN

••A••J
SWARAJ

•••AJ•
NAVAJO
ROMAJI

••••AJ
SGTMAJ
SWARAJ
THEHAJ

AK••••
AKELAS
AKENES
AKIMBO
AKITAS
AKUAKU

A•K•••
ACKACK
AIKIDO
ALKALI
ALKENE
ALKYDS
ALKYLS
ANKARA
ANKLED
ANKLES
ANKLET
ASKARI
ASKERS
ASKFOR
ASKING
ASKOUT
ASKSIN
ATKINS
AUKLET

A••K••
ABUKIR
ANGKOR
AWAKED
AWAKEN
AWAKES
AWOKEN

A•••K•
ADZUKI
AKUAKU
ALASKA
ALECKY
ANNIKA
AXLIKE

A••••K
ACKACK
ADWEEK
AMTRAK
ANORAK
ARAWAK
ARRACK
ATRISK
ATTACK
ATWORK

•AK•••
BAKERS
BAKERY
BAKING
BAKULA
CAKIER
CAKING
DAKOTA
FAKERS
FAKERY
FAKING
FAKIRS
HAKIMS
KAKAPO
LAKERS
LAKIER
LAKOTA
MAKALU
MAKEBA
MAKEDO
MAKEIT
MAKERS
MAKEUP
MAKING
MAKUTA
OAKLEY
PAKULA
RAKEIN
RAKERS
RAKEUP
RAKING
RAKISH
SAKERS
TAKEIN
TAKEON
TAKERS
TAKETH
TAKETO
TAKEUP
TAKING
TAKINS
UAKARI
WAKENS
WAKEUP
WAKING
YAKIMA
YAKKED
YAKKER
YAKUTS
YAKUZA

•A•K••
BABKAS
BACKED
BACKER
BACKIN
BACKUP
BACKUS
BAIKAL
BALKAN
BALKED
BANKED
BANKER
BANKON
BARKAT
BARKED
BARKER
BARKIN
BASKED
BASKET
CACKLE
CALKED
CANKER
CARKED
CATKIN
DAIKON
DANKER
DANKLY
DARKEN
DARKER
DARKLE
DARKLY
FAWKES
GASKET
GASKIN
GAWKED
GAWKER
HACKED
HACKER
HACKIE
HACKLE
HACKLY
HAIKUS
HANKER
HANKIE
HARKED
HARKEN
HARKER
HAWKED
HAWKER
JACKAL
JACKED
JACKET
JACKEY
JACKIE
JACKUP
KALKAN
LACKED
LACKEY
LANKER
LANKLY
LARKED
LATKES
MALKIN
MARKED
MARKER
MARKET
MARKKA
MARKUP
MASKED
MASKER
NAPKIN
PACKED
PACKER
PACKET
PACKUP
PARKAS
PARKAY
PARKED
PARKER
RACKED
RACKET
RACKUP
RANKED
RANKER
RANKIN
RANKLE
RANKLY
SACKED
SACKER
TACKED
TACKER
TACKLE
TACKON
TALKAT
TALKED
TALKER
TALKIE
TALKTO
TALKUP
TANKAS
TANKED
TANKER
TANKUP
TASKED
WACKOS
WALKED
WALKEN
WALKER
WALKIE
WALKIN
WALKON
WALKUP
YACKED
YAKKED
YAKKER
YANKED
YANKEE

•A••K•
BAMAKO
BANGKA
BATIKS
BAULKS
CAULKS
HACEKS
JAMOKE
JANSKY
KABUKI
KALAKH
KANAKA
KAYAKS
KAZAKH
KAZAKS
MARIKO
MARKKA
SALUKI
SAMEKH
TANAKA
YAPOKS

•A•••K
BARTOK
DAMASK
FAROUK
GALYAK
KARNAK
LANARK
MARDUK
NANOOK
NARVIK
NATICK
TANOAK
ZADDIK
ZANUCK

••AK••
AWAKED
AWAKEN
AWAKES
BEAKED
BEAKER
BHAKTI
BRAKED
BRAKES
CRAKES
DRAKES
FLAKED
FLAKER
FLAKES
FLAKEY
KHAKIS
KRAKEN
KRAKOW
LEAKED
LEAKER
LEAKEY
PEAKED
QUAKED
QUAKER
QUAKES
SHAKEN
SHAKER
SHAKES
SHAKOS
SHAKTI
SLAKED
SLAKES
SNAKED
SNAKES
SOAKED
SOAKER
SOAKUP
STAKED
STAKES
WEAKEN
WEAKER
WEAKLY

••A•K•
ALASKA
BLACKS
BLANKS
CHALKS
CHALKY
CLACKS
CLANKS
CLANKY
CLARKE
CRACKS
CRACKY
CRANKS
CRANKY
DMARKS
FLACKS
FLANKS
FLASKS
FRANKS
KNACKS
KYACKS
OZARKS
PLANKS
PRANKS
QUACKS
QUARKS
SHACKS
SHANKS
SHARKS
SKANKS
SLACKS
SMACKS
SNACKS
SPANKS
SPANKY
SPARKS
SPARKY
STACKS
STALKS
STALKY
STANKY
SWANKS
SWANKY
THANKS
TRACKS
WHACKS
WHACKY
WRACKS

••A••K
ARAWAK
BRATSK
FRANCK
GDANSK
OCASEK
PLANCK
SPACEK
URALSK

•••AK•
AKUAKU
BAMAKO
BETAKE
BREAKS
CLOAKS
CREAKS
CREAKY
CROAKS
CROAKY
FREAKS
FREAKY
INTAKE
ITHAKI
KALAKH
KANAKA
KAYAKS
KAZAKH
KAZAKS
KULAKS
LUSAKA
MEDAKA
PIKAKE
REMAKE
RETAKE
SEDAKA
SNEAKS
SNEAKY
SPEAKS
STEAKS
STRAKE
TANAKA
TILAKS
TWEAKS
UMIAKS
UNMAKE
UPTAKE
WREAKS

•••A•K
ACKACK
ARRACK
ATTACK
BYTALK
CUSACK
DAMASK
DEBARK
EMBANK
EMBARK
GOBACK
HIJACK
LANARK
MOHAWK
NEWARK
REMARK
SHRANK
SQUAWK
STMARK
THWACK
UNMASK
UNPACK
UNTACK
UPTALK

••••AK
AMTRAK
ANORAK
ARAWAK
BUROAK
DEEPAK
DVORAK
GALYAK
ITZHAK
KARNAK
KODIAK
PINOAK
REDOAK
SCREAK
SENDAK
SLEZAK
SLOVAK
SPIVAK
SQUEAK
STREAK
TANOAK

AL••••
ALAMOS
ALANIS
ALANON
ALARIC
ALARMS
ALARUM
ALASKA
ALATAU
ALATED
ALBANO
ALBANY
ALBEDO
ALBEIT
ALBERT
ALBINO
ALBION
ALBOIN
ALBORG
ALBUMS
ALCAPP
ALCOTT
ALCOVE
ALCUIN
ALDERS
ALDINE
ALDOSE
ALDOUS
ALDRIN
ALEAST
ALECKY
ALECTO
ALEGAR
ALEGRE
ALEMAN
ALEPHS
ALEPPO
ALERTS
ALEUTS
ALEVEL
ALEXEI
ALEXIA
ALEXIS
ALFINE
ALFRED
ALFVEN
ALGORE
ALHIRT
ALIBIS
ALIBLE
ALICIA
ALIENS
ALIGHT
ALIGNS
ALINES
ALIOTO
ALISON
ALITER
ALKALI
ALKENE
ALKYDS
ALKYLS
ALLAYS
ALLBUT
ALLDAY
ALLEES
ALLEGE
ALLELE
ALLEYS
ALLFOR
ALLIED
ALLIES
ALLIUM
ALLMAN
ALLOTS
ALLOUT
ALLOWS
ALLOYS
ALLPRO
ALLSET
ALLUDE
ALLURE
ALLWET
ALMATY
ALMOND
ALMOST
ALNICO
ALOHAS
ALOINS
ALOMAR
ALONSO
ALONZO
ALPACA
ALPERT
ALPHAS
ALPINE
ALSACE
ALTAIC
ALTAIR
ALTARS
ALTERS
ALTHEA
ALTIMA
ALTIUS
ALTMAN
ALULAE
ALULAR
ALUMNA
ALUMNI
ALWAYS
ALWEST
ALYSSA

A•L•••
ABLATE
ABLAUT
ABLAZE
ABLEST
ABLOOM
ABLUSH
ADLIBS
AFLAME
AFLATS
AFLCIO
AFLOAT
AGLAIA
AGLARE
AGLEAM
AGLETS
AGLINT
AILEEN
AILERS
AILING
ALLAYS
ALLBUT
ALLDAY
ALLEES
ALLEGE
ALLELE
ALLEYS
ALLFOR
ALLIED
ALLIES
ALLIUM
ALLMAN
ALLOTS
ALLOUT
ALLOWS
ALLOYS
ALLPRO
ALLSET
ALLUDE
ALLURE
ALLWET
APLITE
APLOMB
ARLEEN
ARLENE
ARLISS
ASLANT
ASLEEP
ASLOPE
ATLAST
ATLATL
AULAIT
AXLIKE

A••L••
ABELES
ABOLLA
ADDLED
ADDLES
ADELIE
ADELLE
ADOLPH
ADULTS
AEOLIA
AEOLIC
AEOLUS
AIELLO
AISLES
AKELAS
ALULAE
ALULAR
AMALFI
AMALIE
AMBLED
AMBLER
AMBLES
AMBLIN
AMELIA
AMOLES
AMPLER
AMULET
ANALOG
ANELED
ANELES
ANGLED
ANGLER
ANGLES
ANGLIA
ANGLIC
ANGLOS
ANKLED
ANKLES
ANKLET
ANNLEE
ANOLES
ANTLER
APOLLO
APPLES
APPLET
APULIA
ARALIA
ARALLU
ARMLET
ASHLAR
ASHLEY
ASYLUM
ATOLLS
ATTLEE
AUKLET
AVALON
AVULSE
AXILLA
AZALEA

A•••L•
ABOLLA
ACIDLY
ADELLE
AEDILE
AERILY
AFIELD
AGEOLD
AIELLO
AIRILY
ALIBLE
ALKALI
ALKYLS
ALLELE
AMPULE
AMPULS
ANGELA
ANGELI
ANGELL
ANGELO
ANGELS
ANGOLA
ANNALS
ANNULI
ANNULS
ANSELM
ANVILS
APOLLO
APPALL
APPALS
AQUILA
ARABLE
ARALLU
ARBELA
ARCHLY
AREOLA
ARGALI
ARGYLE
ARGYLL
ARIDLY
ARNOLD
ARTELS
ARTILY
ASWELL
ATOLLS
ATTILA
ATWILL
AUDILE
AVAILS
AVIDLY
AWEDLY
AWHILE
AXILLA

A••••L
ABORAL
ACETAL
ACETYL
ACTUAL
AERIAL
AIDFUL
AIMFUL
ALEVEL
AMATOL
AMIDOL
AMORAL
AMSTEL
ANGELL
ANIMAL
ANNEAL
ANNUAL
AORTAL
APICAL
APODAL
APPALL
APPEAL
ARGYLL
ARMFUL
ARTFUL
ASSAIL
ASTRAL
ASWELL
ASWIRL
ATLATL
ATONAL
ATRIAL
ATWILL
AUDIAL
AVOWAL
AWHIRL
AXONAL

•AL•••
BALAAM
BALATA
BALBOA
BALDER
BALDLY
BALEEN
BALERS
BALING
BALKAN
BALKED
BALLAD
BALLET
BALLON
BALLOT
BALLOU
BALLUP
BALSAM
BALTIC
BALZAC
CALAIS
CALASH
CALCES
CALDER
CALICO
CALIPH
CALKED
CALLAO
CALLAS
CALLED
CALLER
CALLES
CALLIN
CALLON
CALLOW
CALLUP
CALLUS
CALMED
CALMER
CALMLY
CALPAC
CALQUE
CALVED
CALVES
CALVIN
CALXES
DALASI
DALETH
DALLAS
DALLES
DALTON
EALING
FALANA
FALCES
FALCON
FALINE
FALLEN
FALLIN
FALLON
FALLOW
FALLTO
FALSER
FALTER
GALAGO
GALAHS
GALATA
GALAXY
GALEAE
GALENA
GALLED
GALLEY
GALLIA
GALLIC
GALLON
GALLOP
GALLUP
GALOIS
GALOOT
GALOPS
GALORE
GALOSH
GALPAL
GALWAY
GALYAK
HALERS
HALERU
HALEST
HALEVY
HALIDE
HALING
HALITE
HALLEL
HALLEY
HALLOO
HALLOS
HALLOW
HALLUX
HALOED
HALOES
HALOID
HALSEY
HALTED
HALTER
HALVAH
HALVED
HALVES
JALAPA
JALOPY
KALAKH
KALINE
KALKAN
KALMAR
LALALA
MALABO
MALADY
MALAGA
MALATE
MALAWI
MALAYA
MALAYS
MALDEN
MALIBU
MALICE
MALIGN
MALKIN
MALLEE
MALLEI
MALLET
MALLOW
MALONE
MALORY
MALOTI
MALTED
MALTIN
PALACE
PALAEO
PALATE
PALEAE
PALELY
PALEST
PALIER
PALING
PALISH
PALLAS
PALLED
PALLET
PALLIA
PALLID
PALLOR
PALMAS
PALMED
PALMER
PALOMA
PALPUS
PALTER
PALTRY
SALAAM
SALADO
SALADS
SALALS
SALAMI
SALARY
SALIFY
SALINA
SALINE
SALISH
SALIVA
SALLET
SALLOW
SALMAN
SALMON
SALOME
SALONS
SALOON
SALSAS
SALTED
SALTEN
SALTER
SALTON
SALTUM
SALUKI
SALUTE
SALVED
SALVER
SALVES
SALVIA
SALVOR
SALVOS
SALYUT
TALBOT
TALCED
TALCUM
TALENT
TALERS
TALESE
TALION
TALKAT
TALKED
TALKER
TALKIE
TALKTO
TALKUP
TALLER
TALLOW
TALMUD
TALONS
VALDEZ
VALENS
VALENT
VALERY
VALETS
VALISE
VALIUM
VALLEE
VALLEY
VALOIS
VALOUR
VALUED
VALUES
VALVED
VALVES
WALDEN
WALERS
WALESA
WALKED
WALKEN
WALKER
WALKIE
WALKIN
WALKON
WALKUP
WALLED
WALLER
WALLET
WALLIS
WALLOP
WALLOW
WALLUP
WALNUT
WALRUS
WALTER
WALTON
YALIES

•A•L••
BADLOT
BAILED
BAILEE
BAILER
BAILEY
BAILOR
BALLAD
BALLET
BALLON
BALLOT
BALLOU
BALLUP
BANLON
BARLEY
BAULKS
BAWLED
BAWLER
BAYLOR
CABLED
CABLER
CABLES
CALLAO
CALLAS
CALLED
CALLER
CALLES
CALLIN
CALLON
CALLOW
CALLUP
CALLUS
CAMLET
CANLIT
CAPLET
CARLIN
CARLOS
CARLOT
CAULKS
DAHLIA
DAILEY
DALLAS
DALLES
DAYLIT
EAGLED

EAGLES
EAGLET
EARLAP
FABLED
FABLER
FABLES
FAILED
FAILLE
FALLEN
FALLIN
FALLON
FALLOW
FALLTO
FARLEY
FARLOW
FAULTS
FAULTY
FAWLTY
GABLED
GABLER
GABLES
GAELIC
GAGLAW
GALLED
GALLEY
GALLIA
GALLIC
GALLON
GALLOP
GALLUP
GAOLED
GAOLER
GARLIC
GASLIT
GASLOG
GATLIN
HAILED
HAILEY
HALLEL
HALLEY
HALLOO
HALLOS
HALLOW
HALLUX
HAMLET
HAMLIN
HANLEY
HAOLES
HARLAN
HARLEM
HARLEY
HARLIN
HARLOW
HAULED
HAULER
HAULMS
HAULUP
HAYLEY
JACLYN
JAILED
JAILER
KAHLIL
KAHLUA

KAILUA
KAOLIN
KAPLAN
LADLED
LADLER
LADLES
LAYLOW
MAHLER
MAILED
MAILER
MAILES
MAILIN
MAJLIS
MALLEE
MALLEI
MALLET
MALLOW
MAPLES
MARLED
MARLEE
MARLEY
MARLIN
MARLON
MATLIN
MAULED
MAULER
NAILED
NAILER
NAILIN
NAPLES
OAKLEY
PABLUM
PAELLA
PAILOU
PALLAS
PALLED
PALLET
PALLIA
PALLID
PALLOR
PARLAY
PARLEY
PARLOR
PAULEY
PAVLOV
RAGLAN
RAILAT
RAILED
RAILER
RATLIN
SABLES
SAILED
SAILOR
SALLET
SALLOW
SAMLET
SAULTS
SAWLOG
SAYLES
TABLAS
TABLED
TABLES
TABLET

TAILED
TAILLE
TAILOR
TALLER
TALLOW
TAYLOR
VACLAV
VALLEE
VALLEY
VARLET
VASLAV
VAULTS
VAULTY
WAILED
WAILER
WALLED
WALLER
WALLET
WALLIS
WALLOP
WALLOW
WALLUP
WAYLAY
WAYLON

•A••L•

BABALU
BABBLE
BABELS
BABULS
BACALL
BAFFLE
BAGELS
BAKULA
BALDLY
BANGLE
BARELY
BARFLY
BAROLO
BASALT
BASELY
BASSLY
BATTLE
BAUBLE
CABALA
CABALS
CACKLE
CAGILY
CAJOLE
CALMLY
CAMELS
CANALS
CANDLE
CANOLA
CANTLE
CAROLE
CAROLS
CASALS
CASTLE
CATTLE
CAUDLE
CAVELL
CAVILS

DABBLE
DAFTLY
DAMPLY
DANDLE
DANGLE
DANGLY
DANKLY
DAPPLE
DARKLE
DARKLY
DAWDLE
DAYGLO
DAZZLE
EASELS
EASILY
FACILE
FACULA
FAILLE
FAIRLY
FAMILY
FATALE
GABBLE
GADFLY
GAGGLE
GAINLY
GAMBLE
GAMELY
GAMILY
GANGLE
GANGLY
GARBLE
GARGLE
GAVELS
GAYALS
HABILE
HACKLE
HACKLY
HAGGLE
HAMALS
HAMELN
HAMILL
HANDLE
HARALD
HARDLY
HAROLD
HASSLE
HAZELS
HAZILY
JACALS
JANGLE
JANGLY
KAMALA
LABELS
LABILE
LACILY
LALALA
LAMELY
LANKLY
LAPELS
LASTLY
LATELY
LAZILY
LAZULI

MABELL
MACULA
MAINLY
MAKALU
MANGLE
MANILA
MANTLE
MARBLE
MARBLY
MARILU
MARPLE
MAYFLY
MAZILY
MAZOLA
NAMELY
NAPOLI
NASALS
NAVELS
PADDLE
PAELLA
PAKULA
PALELY
PAMELA
PANELS
PAROLE
PARTLY
PARULA
PAYOLA
RABBLE
RACILY
RADDLE
RADULA
RAFFLE
RAMBLA
RAMBLE
RANKLE
RANKLY
RAPTLY
RARELY
RASHLY
RASSLE
RATELS
RATTLE
RATTLY
RAVELS
RAZZLE
SADDLE
SAFELY
SAGELY
SALALS
SAMPLE
SANELY
TABULA
TACKLE
TAILLE
TAMALE
TAMELY
TAMILS
TANGLE
TANGLY
TARTLY
TATTLE
TAUTLY

VAINLY
VASTLY
WADDLE
WADDLY
WAFFLE
WAFFLY
WAGGLE
WAGGLY
WAMBLE
WAMBLY
WANGLE
WARBLE
WARILY
WARMLY
WATTLE
WAVILY
WAXILY
YARELY
ZANILY

•A•••L

BACALL
BAGFUL
BAIKAL
BANJUL
BARBEL
BARREL
BATTEL
CANCEL
CANFUL
CANNEL
CAPFUL
CARFUL
CARMEL
CARNAL
CARPAL
CARPEL
CARREL
CARROL
CARTEL
CASUAL
CAUDAL
CAUSAL
CAVELL
DACTYL
DAEDAL
DAMSEL
DANIEL
DARNEL
DARRYL
EARFUL
FACIAL
FAISAL
FAUNAL
FAZOOL
GALPAL
GAMBOL
GAVIAL
HALLEL
HAMILL
HANDEL
HANGUL
HANSEL

HATFUL
JACKAL
JAMAAL
JARFUL
JAWOHL
KAHLIL
LABIAL
LAPFUL
LARVAL
LAUREL
LAWFUL
MABELL
MAMMAL
MANFUL
MANTEL
MANUAL
MANUEL
MARCEL
MARIEL
MARTEL
MARVEL
MATTEL
NARIAL
NARWAL
PANFUL
PARCEL
PARREL
PASCAL
PASSEL
PASTEL
PATHOL
PATROL
RACHEL
RACIAL
RADIAL
RAFAEL
RAPPEL
RAQUEL
RASCAL
SACRAL
SAMBAL
SAMUEL
SANDAL
SAUREL
TARSAL
TASSEL
VACHEL
VANDAL
VASSAL
VATFUL
WARHOL

••AL••

AMALFI
AMALIE
ANALOG
ARALIA
ARALLU
AVALON
AZALEA
CHALCO
CHALET
CHALKS

CHALKY
COALER
DEALER
DEALIN
DIALED
DIALER
DIALOG
DIALUP
DUALLY
ETALIA
ETALII
EXALTS
FEALTY
FOALED
GOALIE
HEALED
HEALER
HEALTH
ITALIA
ITALIC
KHALID
KOALAS
LEALTY
MEALIE
NYALAS
ORALES
ORALLY
OVALLY
OXALIS
PEALED
PSALMS
QUALMS
REALER
REALES
REALIA
REALLY
REALMS
REALTY
RIALTO
RVALUE
SCALAR
SCALDS
SCALED
SCALER
SCALES
SCALIA
SCALPS
SEALAB
SEALED
SEALER
SEALUP
SHALES
SHALEY
SHALLY
SHALOM
SKALDS
SLALOM
SMALLS
SMALTI
SMALTO
SPALLS
STALAG
STALED

STALER
STALES
STALIN
STALKS
STALKY
STALLS
SWALES
THALER
THALES
THALIA
TLALOC
TRALEE
URALIC
URALSK
UVALUE
WEALTH
WHALER
WHALES
ZEALOT

••A•L•

ARABLE
ARALLU
AVAILS
BEADLE
BEAGLE
BEATLE
BRAILA
BRAILS
BRAWLS
CHARLY
CRADLE
CRAWLS
CRAWLY
DEADLY
DEAFLY
DEARLY
DIABLO
DOABLE
DRABLY
DRAILS
DRAWLS
DRAWLY
DUALLY
EMAILS
ENABLE
FEATLY
FLAILS
FLATLY
GLADLY
GNARLS
GNARLY
GRABLE
GRAILS
GRAYLY
KRAALS
LEANLY
LIABLE
MEANLY
MEASLY
NEARLY
NEATLY
ORACLE

ORALLY
OVALLY
PEARLS
PEARLY
QUAILS
QUAYLE
REALLY
SEARLE
SHALLY
SHAWLS
SMALLS
SNAILS
SNARLS
SNARLY
SPALLS
STABLE
STABLY
STALLS
STAPLE
THATLL
TRAILS
TRAWLS
UNABLE
USABLE
USABLY
VIABLE
VIABLY
WEAKLY
WHATLL
YEARLY

••A••L

AMATOL
BOATEL
BRAZIL
CHANEL
CHAPEL
DEASIL
ENAMEL
GRAVEL
HIATAL
ISABEL
IZABAL
PLAGAL
SEAGAL
TEASEL
THATLL
TRAVEL
URACIL
WEASEL
WHATLL

•••AL•

ALKALI
ANNALS
APPALL
APPALS
ARGALI
BABALU
BACALL
BASALT
BECALM
BEFALL

BEHALF
BYTALK
CABALA
CABALS
CANALS
CASALS
COBALT
CORALS
DECALS
DEKALB
DENALI
DESALT
DONALD
DOUALA
DUVALL
ENDALL
ENHALO
EQUALS
EXHALE
FATALE
FEMALE
FINALE
FINALS
GAYALS
GERALD
GORALS
HAMALS
HARALD
HERALD
IDEALS
IMPALA
IMPALE
INHALE
INHALF
JACALS
KAMALA
KERALA
KIGALI
KODALY
KRAALS
KURALT
LALALA
LEGALS
LOCALE
LOCALS
MAKALU
MCHALE
MEDALS
MEGALO
METALS
MORALE
MORALS
MURALS
NASALS
NEPALI
NOSALE
OGLALA
ONCALL
ONSALE
OOLALA
OSWALD
PEDALS
PETALS
PHIALS
PIPALS
RECALL
REGALE
RESALE
RESALT
RIBALD
RIVALS
RIYALS
ROBALO
RONALD
ROYALE
ROYALS
SALALS
SEPALS
SHOALS
SHOALY
SISALS
SKOALS
SOMALI
SQUALL
STEALS
STMALO
TAMALE
TEPALS
THRALE
THRALL
TICALS
TOTALS
TRIALS
TUVALU
TYBALT
UPTALK
URIALS
USUALS
VITALE
VITALS
VOCALS
WHEALS
YOUALL

•••A•L

APPALL
ASSAIL
ATLATL
BACALL
BEFALL
BEWAIL
DEPAUL
DERAIL
DETAIL
DUVALL
ENDALL
ENTAIL
EURAIL
INHAUL
ISRAEL
JAMAAL
ONCALL
OXTAIL
RAFAEL
RECALL
REMAIL
RENAIL
RETAIL
RUPAUL
SCRAWL
SPRAWL
SQUALL
STPAUL
THRALL
USMAIL
YOUALL

••••AL

ABORAL
ACETAL
ACTUAL
AERIAL
AMORAL
ANIMAL
ANNEAL
ANNUAL
AORTAL
APICAL
APODAL
APPEAL
ASTRAL
ATONAL
ATRIAL
AUDIAL
AVOWAL
AXONAL
BAIKAL
BELIAL
BENGAL
BHOPAL
BOREAL
BRIDAL
BRUMAL
BRUTAL
BUCCAL
BURSAL
CARNAL
CARPAL
CASUAL
CAUDAL
CAUSAL
CEREAL
CHEVAL
CHORAL
COEVAL
CORRAL
COSTAL
CRURAL
CUNEAL
CURIAL
CYMBAL
DAEDAL
DENIAL
DENTAL
DERMAL
DISMAL
DISTAL
DORSAL
DOSSAL
DUCTAL
EPICAL
EPINAL
ESPIAL
FACIAL
FAISAL
FAUNAL
FERIAL
FESTAL
FEUDAL
FILIAL
FINIAL
FISCAL
FLORAL
FOETAL
FONTAL
FORMAL
FRUGAL
GALPAL
GAVIAL
GENIAL
GENUAL
GIMBAL
GLOBAL
HERBAL
HIATAL
HIEMAL
HYETAL
HYMNAL
INSTAL
IRREAL
IZABAL
JACKAL
JAMAAL
JOVIAL
LABIAL
LARVAL
LETHAL
LINEAL
LOREAL
LOWCAL
MAMMAL
MANUAL
MEDIAL
MENIAL
MENSAL
MENTAL
MESCAL
MISSAL
MITRAL
MORTAL
MUSIAL
MUTUAL
MYRDAL
NARIAL
NARWAL
NEURAL
NORMAL
NUCHAL
ORDEAL
OSTEAL
PASCAL
PENPAL
PINEAL
PLAGAL
PLEXAL
PLURAL
PORTAL
POSTAL
PRIMAL
RACIAL
RADIAL
RASCAL
REDEAL
REDIAL
REGNAL
REHEAL
RENTAL
REPEAL
RESEAL
RETIAL
RETRAL
REVEAL
RHINAL
RITUAL
SACRAL
SAMBAL
SANDAL
SEAGAL
SEPTAL
SERIAL
SERVAL
SIGNAL
SOCIAL
SPINAL
SPIRAL
SQUEAL
TARSAL
THECAL
TIBIAL
TIMBAL
TINCAL
TRIBAL
TRINAL
UMBRAL
UNCIAL
UNGUAL
UNITAL
UNOCAL
UNREAL
UNSEAL
VANDAL
VASSAL
VEINAL
VENIAL
VERBAL
VERNAL
VESTAL
VISUAL
WITHAL

AM••••

AMADIS
AMADOU
AMAJOR
AMALFI
AMALIE
AMANDA
AMATIS
AMATOL
AMAZED
AMAZES
AMAZON
AMBATO
AMBERS
AMBERY
AMBITS
AMBLED
AMBLER
AMBLES
AMBLIN
AMBUSH
AMEBAE
AMEBAS
AMEBIC
AMECHE
AMEDEO
AMEERS
AMELIA
AMENDS
AMENRA
AMENTS
AMERCE
AMERSP
AMHARA
AMICES
AMICUS
AMIDES
AMIDOL
AMIDST
AMIENS
AMIGAS
AMIGOS
AMINES
AMINOR
AMINUS
AMNION
AMOEBA
AMOLES
AMORAL
AMOSOZ
AMOUNT
AMOURS
AMPERE
AMPHID
AMPLER
AMPULE
AMPULS
AMSTEL
AMTRAC
AMTRAK
AMULET
AMUSED
AMUSES
AMVETS
AMYTAN

A•M•••

ADMASS
ADMIRE
ADMITS
AIMFOR
AIMFUL
AIMING
AIMSAT
AIMSTO
ALMATY
ALMOND
ALMOST
ARMADA
ARMAGH
ARMAND
ARMANI
ARMETS
ARMFUL
ARMIES
ARMING
ARMLET
ARMORS
ARMORY
ARMOUR
ARMPIT
ARMURE
ASMARA
ATMOST
AUMONT
AYMARA

A••M••

ABOMBS
ACUMEN
AGAMAS
AHIMSA
AIRMAN
AIRMEN
AKIMBO
ALAMOS
ALEMAN
ALLMAN
ALOMAR
ALTMAN
ALUMNA
ALUMNI
ANEMIA
ANEMIC
ANIMAL
ANIMAS
ANIMES
ANIMUS
ANOMIC
ANOMIE
APEMAN
APEMEN
ARAMIS
AROMAS
ASIMOV
ATAMAN
ATEMPO
ATOMIC

A•••M•

ABOHMS
ABRAMS
ABYSMS
ADDAMS
ADEEMS
AFLAME
AFRAME
ALARMS
ALBUMS
ALTIMA
APLOMB
ASSUME
ATEAMS
ATHOME
AUTUMN
AXIOMS

A••••M

ABLOOM
ABSCAM
ACTIUM
ADYTUM
AFFIRM
AGEISM
AGLEAM
AIRARM
AIRDAM
ALARUM
ALLIUM
ANADEM
ANONYM
ANSELM
ANTHEM
ANTRIM
ANTRUM
ARNHEM
ARTGUM
ASCHAM
ASHRAM
ASYLUM
ATRIUM

•AM•••

BAMAKO
BAMBOO
CAMARO
CAMBER
CAMDEN
CAMEAT
CAMEBY
CAMEIN
CAMELS
CAMEON
CAMEOS
CAMERA
CAMETO
CAMEUP
CAMINO
CAMION
CAMISE
CAMLET
CAMPED
CAMPER
CAMPOS
CAMPUS
DAMAGE
DAMASK
DAMATO
DAMIEN
DAMITA
DAMMAR
DAMMED
DAMNED
DAMONE
DAMORE
DAMOUR
DAMPED
DAMPEN
DAMPER
DAMPLY
DAMSEL
DAMSON
DAMSUP
FAMILY
FAMINE
FAMISH
FAMOUS
GAMAYS
GAMBIA
GAMBIT
GAMBLE
GAMBOL
GAMELY
GAMEST
GAMETE
GAMIER
GAMILY
GAMINE
GAMING
GAMINS
GAMMAS
GAMMED
GAMMER
GAMMON
GAMUTS
HAMALS
HAMELN
HAMILL
HAMITE
HAMLET
HAMLIN
HAMMED
HAMMER
HAMPER
IAMBIC
JAMAAL
JAMMED
JAMMER
JAMOKE
JAMSIN
JAMSUP
JAMUPS
KAMALA
LAMARR
LAMAZE
LAMBDA
LAMBED
LAMECH
LAMEDH
LAMEDS
LAMELY
LAMENT
LAMESA
LAMEST
LAMIAS
LAMINA
LAMING
LAMMAS
LAMMED
LAMONT
LAMOUR
MAMBAS
MAMBOS
MAMMAL
MAMMAS
MAMMON
NAMATH
NAMELY
NAMERS
NAMING
PAMELA
PAMIRS
PAMPAS
PAMPER
RAMADA
RAMATE
RAMBLA
RAMBLE
RAMEAU
RAMETS
RAMIES
RAMIFY
RAMJET
RAMMED
RAMONA
RAMONE
RAMOSE
RAMOUS
RAMPED
RAMROD
RAMSAY
RAMSES
RAMSEY
RAMSON
SAMARA
SAMBAL
SAMBAR
SAMBAS
SAMECH
SAMEKH
SAMIAM
SAMITE
SAMLET
SAMMIE
SAMOAN
SAMOSA
SAMPAN
SAMPLE
SAMSON
SAMUEL

TAMALE
TAMARA
TAMAYO
TAMELY
TAMERS
TAMEST
TAMILS
TAMING
TAMMUZ
TAMPED
TAMPER
TAMTAM
VAMPED
VAMPER
WAMBLE
WAMBLY
WAMPUM
YAMAHA
YAMMER
ZAMBIA
ZAMIAS

•A•M••
BADMAN
BADMEN
BARMAN
BARMEN
BATMAN
BATMEN
CADMIC
CADMUS
CAIMAN
CALMED
CALMER
CALMLY
CARMAN
CARMEL
CARMEN
CAYMAN
DAGMAR
DAIMON
DAIMYO
DAMMAR
DAMMED
FARMED
FARMER
GAGMAN
GAGMEN
GAMMAS
GAMMED
GAMMER
GAMMON
GASMAN
GASMEN
GAUMED
HAEMAT
HAEMON
HAGMAN
HAMMED
HAMMER
HARMED
HARMON
HAYMOW
JAMMED
JAMMER
KALMAR
KARMIC
KATMAI
LAMMAS
LAMMED
LAWMAN
LAWMEN
LAYMAN
LAYMEN
MADMAN
MADMAX
MADMEN
MAGMAS
MAMMAL
MAMMAS
MAMMON
MARMEE
MARMOT
MAUMAU
MAUMEE
PACMAN
PALMAS
PALMED
PALMER
PATMOS
RAGMAN
RAGMEN
RAGMOP
RAMMED
SALMAN
SALMON
SAMMIE
TALMUD
TAMMUZ
TARMAC
TASMAN
TAXMAN
TAXMEN
WARMED
WARMER
WARMLY
WARMTH
WARMUP
YAMMER

•A••M•
BAHAMA
BATUMI
CAROMS
DAGAMA
DANGME
FATIMA
GAZUMP
HAKIMS
HAREMS
HAULMS
LARAMS
MADAME
MADAMS
MANAMA
MAXIMA
MAXIMS
MAZUMA
PAJAMA
PALOMA
PANAMA
RACEME
RADOME
SALAMI
SALOME
TACOMA
TATAMI
YAKIMA

•A•••M
BADHAM
BALAAM
BALSAM
BANTAM
BARIUM
BARNUM
BATYAM
BAYRUM
FAIYUM
FANDOM
FATHOM
HANSOM
HARLEM
HASSAM
KABOOM
KAREEM
LABRUM
LAPHAM
LATIUM
MADTOM
MAGNUM
MAOISM
MAYHEM
PABLUM
PASSIM
RADIUM
RANDOM
RANSOM
SACHEM
SACRUM
SADDAM
SALAAM
SALTUM
SAMIAM
TALCUM
TAMTAM
TANDEM
TAOISM
VACUUM
VALIUM
WAMPUM

••AM••
AGAMAS
ALAMOS
ARAMIS
ATAMAN
BEAMED
BEAMON
BEAMUP
BLAMED
BLAMES
CHAMMY
CHAMPS
CLAMMY
CLAMOR
CLAMPS
CLAMUP
CRAMBO
CRAMPS
DRAMAS
EDAMES
ENAMEL
ENAMOR
FLAMBE
FLAMED
FLAMES
FOAMED
FRAMED
FRAMES
GLAMOR
GRAMAS
GRAMME
GRAMMY
GRAMPA
GRAMPS
IMAMAN
KRAMER
LLAMAS
LOAMED
MIAMIA
NIAMEY
REAMED
REAMER
RHAMES
ROAMED
ROAMER
SCAMPI
SCAMPS
SEAMAN
SEAMED
SEAMEN
SEAMUS
SHAMAN
SHAMED
SHAMES
SHAMIR
SHAMUS
STAMEN
STAMPS
SWAMIS
SWAMPS
SWAMPY
TEAMED
TEAMUP
THAMES
TOAMAN
TRAMPS
WHAMMO
WHAMMY
XIAMEN

••A•M•
ALARMS
BRAHMA
BRAHMS
CHACMA
CHAMMY
CHARMS
CHASMS
CLAIMS
CLAMMY
DEARME
DHARMA
GRAMME
GRAMMY
MIASMA
PLASMA
PLASMO
PSALMS
QUALMS
REAIMS
REALMS
REARMS
SHAWMS
SMARMY
SPASMS
SWARMS
TRAUMA
UNARMS
WHAMMO
WHAMMY

••A••M
ALARUM
ANADEM
DIADEM
DIATOM
DRACHM
GRAHAM
INAJAM
MCADAM
OMASUM
SCARUM
SHALOM
SHAZAM
SLALOM
VIACOM

•••AM•
ABRAMS
ADDAMS
AFLAME
AFRAME
ATEAMS
BAHAMA
BECAME
BIGAMY
BONAMI
BREAMS
BYNAME
CCLAMP
CREAMS
CREAMY
DAGAMA
DECAMP
DEFAME
DREAMS
DREAMT
DREAMY
DYNAMO
ENCAMP
GLEAMS
GLEAMY
HBEAMS
IBEAMS
INFAMY
JICAMA
LARAMS
MADAME
MADAMS
MANAMA
NONAME
OGHAMS
PAJAMA
PANAMA
PREAMP
PROAMS
PYJAMA
RENAME
REVAMP
SALAMI
SCRAMS
SESAME
STEAMS
STEAMY
TATAMI
UGGAMS
UNJAMS

•••A•M
AIRARM
BALAAM
BECALM
DISARM
LCHAIM
REWARM
SALAAM

••••AM
ABSCAM
AGLEAM
AIRDAM
ASCHAM
ASHRAM
BADHAM
BALAAM
BALSAM
BANTAM
BATYAM
BEDLAM
BELDAM
COBHAM
DIGRAM
DIRHAM
DUNHAM
DURHAM
ENGRAM
FIVEAM
FOURAM
GOTHAM
GRAHAM
HASSAM
INAJAM
INGRAM
INSEAM
JETSAM
LAPHAM
LOGJAM
MCADAM
MIRIAM
NINEAM
OLDHAM
PUTNAM
RODHAM
SADDAM
SALAAM
SAMIAM
SCREAM
SHAZAM
SILOAM
STREAM
TAMTAM
WIGWAM

AN••••
ANACIN
ANADEM
ANALOG
ANANDA
ANATTO
ANCHOR
ANCIEN
ANCONA
ANDEAN
ANDHOW
ANDREA
ANDREI
ANDRES
ANDREW
ANDREY
ANDROS
ANELED
ANELES
ANEMIA
ANEMIC
ANERGY
ANGELA
ANGELI
ANGELL
ANGELO
ANGELS
ANGERS
ANGKOR
ANGLED
ANGLER
ANGLES
ANGLIA
ANGLIC
ANGLOS
ANGOLA
ANGORA
ANHYDR
ANIMAL
ANIMAS
ANIMES
ANIMUS
ANIONS
ANITRA
ANJOUS
ANKARA
ANKLED
ANKLES
ANKLET
ANNABA
ANNALS
ANNEAL
ANNEXE
ANNHON
ANNIKA
ANNLEE
ANNOYS
ANNUAL
ANNUIT
ANNULI
ANNULS
ANODES
ANODIC
ANOINT
ANOLES
ANOMIC
ANOMIE
ANONYM
ANORAK
ANSARA
ANSATE
ANSELM
ANSGAR
ANSWER
ANTCOW
ANTEED
ANTERO
ANTEUP
ANTHEM
ANTHER
ANTICS
ANTLER
ANTONY
ANTRES
ANTRIM
ANTRON
ANTRUM
ANUBIS
ANURAN
ANVILS
ANWANG
ANYANG
ANYDAY
ANYHOW
ANYONE
ANYWAY

A•N•••
ADNATE
ADNEXA
AENEAS
AENEID
AGNATE
ALNICO
AMNION
ANNABA
ANNALS
ANNEAL
ANNEXE
ANNHON
ANNIKA
ANNLEE
ANNOYS
ANNUAL
ANNUIT
ANNULI
ANNULS
ARNESS
ARNETT
ARNHEM
ARNICA
ARNOLD
AUNTIE
AWNING

A••N••
ACINUS
ADONAI
ADONIS
AGENAS
AGENCY
AGENDA
AGENTS
AJANTA
AKENES
ALANIS
ALANON
ALINES
ALONSO
ALONZO
AMANDA
AMENDS
AMENRA
AMENTS
AMINES
AMINOR
AMINUS
ANANDA
ANONYM
ARENAS
ARENDT
ASANAS
ATONAL
ATONCE
ATONED
ATONES
ATONIC
AVANTI
AVENGE
AVENUE
AXONAL
AZINES

A•••N•
AAHING
ABOUND
ABSENT
ABYING
ACCENT
ACHENE
ACHING
ACORNS
ACTING
ACTINO
ACTONE
ADDEND
ADDING
ADDONS
ADJANI
ADORNS
ADRENO
ADVENT
AFFINE
AGEING
AGLINT
AHERNE
AIDING
AILING
AIMING
AIRING
ALBANO
ALBANY
ALBINO
ALDINE
ALFINE
ALIENS
ALIGNS
ALKENE
ALMOND
ALOINS
ALPINE
ALUMNA
ALUMNI
AMIENS
AMOUNT
ANCONA
ANIONS
ANOINT
ANTONY
ANWANG
ANYANG
ANYONE
APPEND
APRONS
AQUINO
ARCANA
ARCANE
ARCING
ARDENT
ARGENT
ARJUNA
ARLENE
ARMAND
ARMANI
ARMING
AROUND

ARPENT
ARRANT
ARSENE
ARSONS
ARYANS
ASCEND
ASCENT
ASIANS
ASKING
ASLANT
ASPENS
ASSENT
ATHAND
ATHENA
ATHENE
ATHENS
ATKINS
ATTEND
ATTUNE
AUDENS
AUFOND
AUGEND
AUMONT
AUXINS
AVAUNT
AVERNO
AVIANS
AWNING
AXIONS

A••••N

AACHEN
ACTION
ACTSON
ACUMEN
ADDSIN
ADDSON
ADJOIN
ADRIAN
ADRIEN
AEGEAN
AFGHAN
AILEEN
AIRGUN
AIRMAN
AIRMEN
ALANON
ALBION
ALBOIN
ALCUIN
ALDRIN
ALEMAN
ALFVEN
ALISON
ALLMAN
ALTMAN
AMAZON
AMBLIN
AMNION
AMYTAN
ANACIN
ANCIEN
ANDEAN
ANNHON
ANTRON
ANURAN
APEMAN
APEMEN
APPIAN
ARAGON
ARCHON
ARCTAN
ARISEN
ARLEEN
ARUBAN
ASHCAN
ASKSIN
ASOSAN
ASSIGN
ASTERN
ASWOON
ATAMAN
ATTAIN
AUBURN
AUGEAN
AUSTEN
AUSTIN
AUTUMN
AVALON
AVEDON
AWAKEN
AWOKEN
AZORIN

•AN•••

BANANA
BANDED
BANDIT
BANDOG
BANGED
BANGER
BANGKA
BANGLE
BANGOR
BANGUI
BANGUP
BANISH
BANJOS
BANJUL
BANKED
BANKER
BANKON
BANLON
BANNED
BANNER
BANQUO
BANTAM
BANTER
BANTUS
BANYAN
BANZAI
CANAAN
CANADA
CANALS
CANAPE
CANARD
CANARY
CANCAN
CANCEL
CANCUN
CANDID
CANDLE
CANDOR
CANERS
CANFUL
CANIDS
CANIER
CANIFF
CANINE
CANING
CANKER
CANLIT
CANNAE
CANNED
CANNEL
CANNER
CANNES
CANNON
CANNOT
CANOED
CANOES
CANOLA
CANONS
CANOPY
CANOVA
CANTAB
CANTED
CANTER
CANTHI
CANTLE
CANTON
CANTOR
CANTOS
CANUTE
CANVAS
CANYON
DANANG
DANAUS
DANCED
DANCER
DANCES
DANDER
DANDIE
DANDLE
DANGER
DANGLE
DANGLY
DANGME
DANIEL
DANISH
DANKER
DANKLY
DANNAY
DANNER
DANSON
DANTES
DANTON
DANUBE
DANZIG
FANDOM
FANGED
FANION
FANJET
FANNED
FANNIE
FANONS
FANOUT
FANTAN
GANDER
GANDHI
GANGED
GANGER
GANGES
GANGLE
GANGLY
GANGUE
GANGUP
GANNET
GANTRY
HANDED
HANDEL
HANDIN
HANDLE
HANDON
HANDUP
HANGAR
HANGED
HANGER
HANGIN
HANGON
HANGUL
HANGUP
HANKER
HANKIE
HANLEY
HANNAH
HANSEL
HANSOM
HANSON
JANGLE
JANGLY
JANHUS
JANICE
JANINE
JANSEN
JANSKY
KANAKA
KANDER
KANSAN
KANSAS
KANTOR
LANAIS
LANARK
LANATE
LANCED
LANCER
LANCES
LANCET
LANDAU
LANDED
LANDER
LANDHO
LANDIS
LANDON
LANDRY
LANGUR
LANIER
LANKER
LANKLY
LANOSE
LANSON
LANVIN
MANAGE
MANAMA
MANANA
MANAUS
MANCHA
MANCHU
MANDAN
MANDAY
MANEGE
MANFUL
MANGER
MANGLE
MANGOS
MANIAC
MANIAS
MANILA
MANIOC
MANNED
MANNER
MANNIX
MANORS
MANQUE
MANRAY
MANSES
MANTAS
MANTEL
MANTIC
MANTIS
MANTLE
MANTRA
MANTUA
MANUAL
MANUEL
NANNIE
NANOOK
NANSEN
NANTES
PANADA
PANAMA
PANCHO
PANDAS
PANDER
PANDIT
PANELS
PANFRY
PANFUL
PANICS
PANNED
PANNER
PANNES
PANOUT
PANTED
PANTOS
PANTRY
PANZER
QANTAS
RANCHO
RANCID
RANCOR
RANDOM
RANDRY
RANEES
RANFOR
RANGED
RANGER
RANGES
RANGUP
RANIDS
RANKED
RANKER
RANKIN
RANKLE
RANKLY
RANOFF
RANOUT
RANSOM
RANTED
RANTER
SANCHO
SANCTA
SANDAL
SANDED
SANDER
SANDIA
SANDRA
SANELY
SANEST
SANGER
SANGTO
SANITY
SANNUP
SANSEI
SANTEE
SANTIR
SANTOS
TANAKA
TANANA
TANDEM
TANGED
TANGLE
TANGLY
TANGOS
TANGUY
TANIST
TANKAS
TANKED
TANKER
TANKUP
TANNED
TANNER
TANNIC
TANNIN
TANOAK
TANOAN
TANTES
TANTRA
VANDAL
VANIER
VANISH
VANITY
VANNED
VANRYN
WANDER
WANERS
WANGLE
WANIER
WANING
WANNED
WANNER
WANTAD
WANTED
WANTIN
WANTON
WANTTO
XANADU
XANTHO
YANGON
YANKED
YANKEE
YANQUI
ZANDER
ZANIER
ZANIES
ZANILY
ZANUCK

•A•N••

BAINES
BANNED
BANNER
BARNES
BARNEY
BARNUM
CAGNEY
CANNAE
CANNED
CANNEL
CANNER
CANNES
CANNON
CANNOT
CAPNUT
CARNAL
CARNES
CARNET
CARNEY
CARNOT
CATNAP
CATNIP
DABNEY
DAINTY
DAMNED
DANNAY
DANNER
DARNAY
DARNED
DARNEL
DARNER
DARNIT
DAUNTS
DAWNED
DAWNON
EARNED
EARNER
FAENZA
FAFNIR
FAINTS
FANNED
FANNIE
FAUNAE
FAUNAL
FAUNAS
FAUNUS
FAWNED
FAWNER
GAINED
GAINER
GAINLY
GAINON
GAINST
GANNET
GARNER
GARNET
GAYNOR
HAINAN
HAINES
HANNAH
HAUNCH
HAUNTS
JAUNTS
JAUNTY
KARNAK
KAUNAS
KAUNDA
KAVNER
LAINIE
LAUNCH
MAENAD
MAGNET
MAGNON
MAGNUM
MAGNUS
MAINLY
MANNED
MANNER
MANNIX
MARNER
MARNIE
MAUNDY
NANNIE
NARNIA
PAANGA
PAINED
PAINTS
PAINTY
PANNED
PANNER
PANNES
PARNIS
PAUNCH
PAWNED
PAWNEE
PAWNER
RADNER
RAINED
RAINER
RAINES
RAINEY
SAINTE
SAINTS
SANNUP
SARNIA
SAUNAS
TAINAN
TAINOS
TAINTS
TANNED
TANNER
TANNIC
TANNIN
TAUNTS
VAINER
VAINLY
VANNED
VARNAS
VARNEY
VAUNTS
WAGNER
WALNUT
WANNED
WANNER
WAPNER
WARNED
WARNER
WATNEY
YARNED
YAWNED
YAWNER

•A••N•

AAHING
BAAING
BAIRNS
BAKING
BALING
BANANA
BARING
BARONG
BARONS
BARONY
BASING
BASINS
BATING
BATONS
BAYING
CABANA
CABINS
CADENT
CAGING
CAIRNS
CAJUNS
CAKING
CAMINO
CANINE
CANING
CANONS
CAPONE
CAPONS
CARINA
CARING
CARONI
CASING
CASINO
CATENA
CAVING
CAWING
DAMONE
DANANG
DAPHNE
DARENT
DARING
DATING
DATONG
DAYONE
DAZING
EALING
EARING
EASING
EATING
FACING
FADING
FAGEND
FAKING
FALANA
FALINE
FAMINE
FANONS
FARINA
FARING
FAXING
FAZING
GAGING
GALENA
GAMINE
GAMING
GAMINS
GAPING
GATING
GAZING
HABANA
HALING
HARING
HATING
HAVANA
HAVENS
HAVENT
HAVING
HAWING
HAYING
HAZANS
HAZING
JACANA
JADING
JANINE
JAPANS
JAPING
JAWING
KAHUNA

KALINE
LACING
LACUNA
LADING
LADINO
LAGUNA
LAMENT
LAMINA
LAMING
LAMONT
LAPINS
LARYNX
LATENE
LATENS
LATENT
LATINA
LATINI
LATINO
LATINS
LATONA
LAVING
LAWING
LAYING
LAZING
MAKING
MALONE
MANANA
MARINA
MARINE
MARINO
MASONS
MATING
MATINS
MAVENS
MAXENE
MAXINE
MAYANS
NADINE
NAGANO
NAMING
NATANT
OARING
PACING
PACINO
PADANG
PAEANS
PAEONS
PAGANS
PAGING
PAHANG
PALING
PARANA
PARANG
PARENS
PARENT
PARING
PATENS
PATENT
PATINA
PATINE
PAVANE
PAVING
PAWING
PAYING
RACINE
RACING
RACONS
RAGING
RAKING
RAMONA
RAMONE
RAPINE
RAPINI
RARING
RASING
RATINE
RATING
RAVENS
RAVINE
RAVING
RAYONS
RAZING
SABENA
SABINE
SABINS
SALINA
SALINE
SALONS
SARANS
SARONG
SATANG
SATING
SATINS
SATINY
SAVANT
SAVING
SAWING
SAXONS
SAXONY
SAYING
TAGEND
TAHINI
TAKING
TAKINS
TALENT
TALONS
TAMING
TANANA
TAPING
TAPINS
TARING
TAUONS
TAWING
TAXING
VACANT
VALENS
VALENT
VARUNA
WADING
WAGING
WAGONS
WAHINE
WAKENS
WAKING
WANING
WARING
WAVING
WAXING
WAYANS
YAWING
ZAYINS
ZAZENS

•A•••N

AACHEN
BABOON
BABSON
BACKIN
BADMAN
BADMEN
BAFFIN
BAHIAN
BALEEN
BALKAN
BALLON
BANKON
BANLON
BANYAN
BARKIN
BARMAN
BARMEN
BARREN
BARRON
BARTON
BARYON
BARZUN
BATAAN
BATMAN
BATMEN
BATTEN
CAFTAN
CAIMAN
CALLIN
CALLON
CALVIN
CAMDEN
CAMEIN
CAMEON
CAMION
CANAAN
CANCAN
CANCUN
CANNON
CANTON
CANYON
CAPGUN
CAPTAN
CARBON
CARDIN
CAREEN
CARLIN
CARMAN
CARMEN
CARSON
CARTON
CASERN
CASHIN
CASTON
CATION
CATKIN
CATTON
CAVEIN
CAVERN
CAXTON
CAYMAN
DACRON
DAIKON
DAIMON
DAIREN
DALTON
DAMIEN
DAMPEN
DAMSON
DANSON
DANTON
DARIEN
DARKEN
DARREN
DARWIN
DASSIN
DATSUN
DAWNON
DAWSON
DAYTON
EASEIN
EASTON
EATSIN
FABIAN
FADEIN
FALCON
FALLEN
FALLIN
FALLON
FANION
FANTAN
FASTEN
FATTEN
GABION
GAGMAN
GAGMEN
GAIJIN
GAINON
GALLON
GAMMON
GARCON
GARDEN
GARSON
GASCON
GASKIN
GASMAN
GASMEN
GASTON
GATLIN
GAVEIN
GAWAIN
HADRON
HAEMON
HAGDON
HAGMAN
HAINAN
HAMELN
HAMLIN
HANDIN
HANDON
HANGIN
HANGON
HANSON
HAPPEN
HARBIN
HARDEN
HARKEN
HARLAN
HARLIN
HARMON
HARPON
HASSAN
HASTEN
HATPIN
HAVEON
HAYDEN
JACLYN
JAMSIN
JANSEN
JARGON
KALKAN
KANSAN
KAOLIN
KAPLAN
KASDAN
LAGOON
LAIDIN
LAIDON
LANDON
LANSON
LANVIN
LARDON
LARSEN
LARSON
LASSEN
LATEEN
LATTEN
LAUREN
LAWMAN
LAWMEN
LAWSON
LAWTON
LAYMAN
LAYMEN
LAYSIN
LAYSON
MACOUN
MACRON
MADDEN
MADMAN
MADMEN
MADSEN
MAGNON
MAIDEN
MAILIN
MAJGEN
MALDEN
MALIGN
MALKIN
MALTIN
MAMMON
MANDAN
MARGIN
MARIAN
MARION
MARLIN
MARLON
MAROON
MARRON
MARTEN
MARTIN
MARVIN
MATLIN
MATRON
NAILIN
NANSEN
NAPKIN
NATHAN
NATION
NATRON
PACMAN
PADUAN
PAIDIN
PAPAIN
PAPUAN
PAQUIN
PARDON
PARSON
PARTON
PASSON
PATHAN
PATRON
PATTEN
PATTON
PAXTON
PAYSIN
PAYSON
RADIAN
RAGLAN
RAGMAN
RAGMEN
RAISIN
RAKEIN
RAMSON
RANKIN
RATION
RATLIN
RATSON
RATTAN
RAYGUN
SADDEN
SAIGON
SAIPAN
SALMAN
SALMON
SALOON
SALTEN
SALTON
SAMOAN
SAMPAN
SAMSON
SARGON
SARTON
SATEEN
SATURN
TACKON
TAINAN
TAIPAN
TAIWAN
TAKEIN
TAKEON
TALION
TANNIN
TANOAN
TAPPAN
TARPAN
TARPON
TARTAN
TARZAN
TASMAN
TAUTEN
TAVERN
TAXMAN
TAXMEN
VANRYN
VARDEN
VAUGHN
WADEIN
WAGGON
WAITON
WALDEN
WALKEN
WALKIN
WALKON
WALTON
WANTIN
WANTON
WARDEN
WARREN
WATSON
WAVEIN
WAYLON
YANGON
YAUPON

••AN••

AJANTA
ALANIS
ALANON
AMANDA
ANANDA
ASANAS
AVANTI
BEANED
BEANIE
BEANOS
BIANCA
BLANCA
BLANCH
BLANDA
BLANKS
BRANCH
BRANDO
BRANDS
BRANDT
BRANDX
BRANDY
BRANNY
BRANTS
BWANAS
CHANCE
CHANCY
CHANEL
CHANEY
CHANGE
CHANTS
CLANCY
CLANGS
CLANKS
CLANKY
CRANED
CRANES
CRANIA
CRANIO
CRANKS
CRANKY
CRANNY
CYANIC
DEANNA
DIANNE
ELANDS
FIANCE
FLANGE
FLANKS
FRANCA
FRANCE
FRANCK
FRANCO
FRANCS
FRANKS
FRANNY
GDANSK
GIANTS
GLANCE
GLANDS
GOANNA
GRANDE
GRANDS
GRANGE
GRANNY
GRANTS
HEANEY
INANER
IRANIS
JEANNE
JOANIE
JOANNA
JOANNE
KIANGS
KRANTZ
KWANZA
LEANED
LEANER
LEANLY
LEANON
LEANTO
LIANAS
LIANES
LIANGS
LLANOS
LOANED
LOANER
LUANDA
MEANER
MEANIE
MEANLY
MOANED
MOANER
NUANCE
OMANIS
ORANGE
ORANGS
ORANGY
ORANTS
PAANGA
PEANUT
PIANOS
PLANAR
PLANCK
PLANED
PLANER
PLANES
PLANET
PLANKS
PLANON
PLANTE
PLANTS
PRANCE
PRANGS
PRANKS
QUANGO
QUANTA
RUANAS
RUANDA
RWANDA
SCANTS
SCANTY
SEANCE
SHANDY
SHANIA
SHANKS
SHANNY
SHANTY
SKANKS
SLANGS
SLANGY
SLANTS
SPANKS
SPANKY
SRANAN
STANCE
STANCH
STANDS
STANKY
STANZA
SWANEE
SWANKS
SWANKY
THANES
THANKS
TRANCE
TWANGS
TWANGY
UBANGI
UGANDA
URANIA
URANIC
URANUS
USANCE
VIANDS
WEANED
WHANGS
YEANED

••A•N•

AVAUNT
BAAING
BLAINE
BRAINS
BRAINY
BRANNY
BRAWNY
CHAINE
CHAINS
CRANNY
DEANNA
DIANNE
DRAINS
DWAYNE
ELAINE
ELAYNE
FLAUNT
FRANNY
GHAINS
GOANNA
GRAINS
GRAINY
GRANNY
JEANNE
JOANNA
JOANNE
KEARNY
KRASNY
LEARNS
LEARNT
PLAINS
PLAINT
PRAJNA
PRAWNS
QUAINT
SCARNE
SHANNY
SHAYNE
SPAWNS
STAINS
SWAINS
TRAINS
YEARNS

••A••N

ALANON
AMAZON
ANACIN
ARAGON
ATAMAN
AVALON

AWAKEN
BEACON
BEAMON
BEARON
BEATEN
BEATON
BLAZON
BRAZEN
CHAPIN
CHARON
CLAVIN
CRAVEN
CRAYON
DEACON
DEADEN
DEADON
DEAFEN
DEALIN
DRAGIN
DRAGON
DRAWIN
DRAWON
FLACON
FLAGON
FLAXEN
FRAUEN
GRABEN
GRADIN
GRATIN
GRAVEN
HEADIN
HEADON
HEAVEN
IBADAN
IMAMAN
KEATON
KLAXON
KRAKEN
LEADEN
LEADIN
LEADON
LEANON
LEAVEN
NEATEN
NIACIN
OMAHAN
PEAHEN
PLANON
PLATEN
PLAYON
READIN
REAGAN
REASON
RYAZAN
SEAFAN
SEAMAN
SEAMEN
SEASON
SEATON
SHABAN
SHAKEN
SHAMAN
SHARON
SHAVEN
SPAVIN
SRANAN
STALIN
STAMEN
STATEN
STAYON
TOAMAN
TRAJAN
UTAHAN
WEAKEN
WEAPON
XIAMEN

•••AN•

ADJANI
ALBANO
ALBANY
ANWANG
ANYANG
ARCANA
ARCANE
ARMAND
ARMANI
ARRANT
ARYANS
ASIANS
ASLANT
ATHAND
AVIANS
BANANA
BESANT
BEZANT
BOTANY
BRIAND
BRIANS
BRYANT
BUTANE
BYHAND
CABANA
CEDANT
CETANE
CHIANG
CLEANS
CONANT
CYRANO
DANANG
DECANT
DELANO
DELANY
DEMAND
DISANT
DIVANS
DOMANI
DOPANT
DUNANT
DURANT
EMBANK
ENFANT
ERNANI
ERRAND
ERRANT
ESPANA
ETHANE
EXPAND
EXTANT
FALANA
FULANI
GITANO
GLEANS
GROANS
GUIANA
GUYANA
HABANA
HAVANA
HAZANS
HOGANS
HUMANE
HUMANS
IGUANA
ILEANA
INCANS
INFANT
INHAND
INLAND
INSANE
IOWANS
ISLAND
JACANA
JAPANS
JOHANN
KDLANG
LELAND
LEMANS
LEVANT
LIGAND
LITANY
MANANA
MAYANS
MCCANN
MELANO
MILANO
MORANT
MURANO
MUTANT
NAGANO
NATANT
OCEANS
OCTANE
OCTANT
OKSANA
ONHAND
ONLAND
ORGANA
ORGANS
ORIANA
PADANG
PAEANS
PAGANS
PAHANG
PARANA
PARANG
PAVANE
PECANS
PEDANT
PENANG
PIRANA
PISANO
PISANS
PLIANT
POLAND
RECANE
RECANT
REDANT
REHANG
REMAND
REMANS
REPAND
RESAND
RIBAND
ROLAND
ROMANO
ROMANS
ROMANY
ROXANA
ROXANE
SARANS
SATANG
SAVANT
SECANT
SEDANS
SEJANT
SHRANK
SKEANS
SLOANE
SOLANS
SOMANY
SONANT
SPRANG
STRAND
SUSANN
TANANA
TEJANO
TENANT
TEXANS
TIRANA
TIRANE
TISANE
TITANS
TRUANT
TUCANA
TULANE
TYRANT
UCLANS
UHLANS
UNHAND
UNMANS
UPLAND
URBANA
URBANE
UTHANT
VACANT
VEGANS
VIVANT
VOLANS
VOLANT
WAYANS
ZENANA

•••A•N

ATTAIN
BATAAN
CANAAN
DETAIN
DOMAIN
GAWAIN
INVAIN
JOHANN
LORAIN
MCBAIN
MCCANN
MCLAIN
OBTAIN
ORDAIN
PAPAIN
PETAIN
REGAIN
REMAIN
RESAWN
RETAIN
SPRAIN
STRAIN
SUSANN
UJJAIN

••••AN

ADRIAN
AEGEAN
AFGHAN
AIRMAN
ALEMAN
ALLMAN
ALTMAN
AMYTAN
ANDEAN
ANURAN
APEMAN
APPIAN
ARCTAN
ARUBAN
ASHCAN
ASOSAN
ATAMAN
AUGEAN
BADMAN
BAHIAN
BALKAN
BANYAN
BARMAN
BATAAN
BATMAN
BEMOAN
BHUTAN
BORMAN
BOWMAN
BROGAN
BUCHAN
BUNYAN
BURMAN
BUSMAN
CAFTAN
CAIMAN
CANAAN
CANCAN
CAPTAN
CARMAN
CAYMAN
COLMAN
CONMAN
COOGAN
CORBAN
CORMAN
COWMAN
CRETAN
DEMEAN
DESMAN
DOLMAN
DORIAN
DOTHAN
DUNCAN
DURBAN
DURIAN
ELFMAN
ENDMAN
EOLIAN
EONIAN
FABIAN
FANTAN
FBIMAN
FENIAN
FENMAN
FEZZAN
FIJIAN
FINNAN
FIRMAN
FLYMAN
FORMAN
FRYPAN
FUJIAN
GAGMAN
GASMAN
GENOAN
GERMAN
GIBRAN
GUNMAN
HAGMAN
HAINAN
HARLAN
HASSAN
HERMAN
HETMAN
HITMAN
IBADAN
ICEMAN
IMAMAN
INDIAN
INSPAN
IONIAN
JORDAN
JOVIAN
JULIAN
KALKAN
KANSAN
KAPLAN
KASDAN
KEENAN
KENYAN
KERMAN
KIDMAN
KIRMAN
KLIBAN
KOREAN
KORMAN
KURGAN
LAWMAN
LAYMAN
LEGMAN
LIBYAN
LLBEAN
LONGAN
LUCIAN
MADMAN
MANDAN
MARIAN
MCLEAN
MEDIAN
MERMAN
MIDIAN
MINOAN
MINYAN
MORGAN
NATHAN
NETMAN
NEUMAN
NEWMAN
NICEAN
NISSAN
NOONAN
NORMAN
NUBIAN
OBIWAN
OBRIAN
OHIOAN
OILCAN
OILMAN
OILPAN
OLDMAN
OMAHAN
ONEMAN
ONLOAN
ORPHAN
OSSIAN
OUTRAN
PACMAN
PADUAN
PAPUAN
PATHAN
PENMAN
PIEMAN
PIEPAN
PITMAN
QUMRAN
RADIAN
RAGLAN
RAGMAN
RATTAN
REAGAN
REPLAN
RODMAN
RUDMAN
RUTTAN
RYAZAN
RYOKAN
SAIPAN
SALMAN
SAMOAN
SAMPAN
SEAFAN
SEAMAN
SHABAN
SHAMAN
SHORAN
SIMIAN
SIOUAN
SLOGAN
SOLDAN
SRANAN
STEFAN
STJOAN
SULTAN
SUNTAN
SYLVAN
SYRIAN
TAINAN
TAIPAN
TAIWAN
TANOAN
TAPPAN
TARPAN
TARTAN
TARZAN
TASMAN
TAXMAN
TERRAN
TINCAN
TINMAN
TINPAN
TITIAN
TOAMAN
TODMAN
TONGAN
TOUCAN
TRAJAN
TREPAN
TROJAN
TRUMAN
TUBMAN
TULSAN
TUPIAN
TURBAN
TUSCAN
TYRIAN
UGRIAN
ULLMAN
UTAHAN
VIVIAN
VULCAN
WICCAN
WYSTAN
YEOMAN
YESMAN
YUNNAN
ZEEMAN

AO••••

AODAIS
AORIST
AORTAE
AORTAL
AORTAS
AORTIC
AOUDAD

A•O•••

ABOARD
ABODES
ABOHMS
ABOLLA
ABOMBS
ABORAL
ABORTS
ABOUND
ACORNS
ADOBES
ADOLPH
ADONAI
ADONIS
ADOPTS
ADORED
ADOREE
ADORER
ADORES
ADORNS
AEOLIA
AEOLIC
AEOLUS
AGORAE
AGORAS
AGOROT
AGOUTI
ALOHAS
ALOINS
ALOMAR
ALONSO
ALONZO
AMOEBA
AMOLES
AMORAL
AMOSOZ
AMOUNT
AMOURS
ANODES
ANODIC
ANOINT
ANOLES
ANOMIC
ANOMIE
ANONYM
ANORAK
APODAL
APOGEE
APOLLO
AROIDS
AROMAS
AROUND
AROUSE
ASOSAN
ATODDS
ATOLLS
ATOMIC
ATONAL
ATONCE
ATONED
ATONES
ATONIC
AVOCET
AVOIDS
AVOUCH
AVOWAL
AVOWED
AVOWER
AWOKEN
AXONAL
AZODYE
AZORES
AZORIN

A••O••

ABBOTS
ABBOTT
ABHORS
ABLOOM
ABROAD
ABSORB
ACCORD
ACCOST
ACEOUS
ACEOUT
ACROSS
ACTONE
ACTORS
ACTOUT
ADDONS
ADJOIN
ADROIT
ADSORB
AEROBE
AFFORD
AFLOAT
AGEOLD
AIROUT
AJFOYT
ALBOIN
ALBORG
ALCOTT
ALCOVE
ALDOSE
ALDOUS
ALGORE
ALIOTO
ALLOTS
ALLOUT
ALLOWS
ALLOYS
ALMOND
ALMOST
ANCONA

ANGOLA
ANGORA
ANIONS
ANJOUS
ANNOYS
ANTONY
ANYONE
APLOMB
APPOSE
APRONS
ARBORS
ARBOUR
ARDORS
ARDOUR
AREOLA
ARGOSY
ARGOTS
ARIOSE
ARIOSO
ARMORS
ARMORY
ARMOUR
ARNOLD
ARROBA
ARROWS
ARROYO
ARSONS
ARTOIS
ASCOTS
ASHORE
ASKOUT
ASLOPE
ASSORT
ASWOON
ATCOST
ATEOUT
ATHOME
ATMOST
ATWOOD
ATWORK
AUFOND
AUMONT
AURORA
AUROUS
AXIOMS
AXIONS

A•••O•

ABLOOM
ABYDOS
ACAJOU
ACTION
ACTSON
ADDSON
AGGROS
AGOROT
AHCHOO
AIMFOR
ALAMOS
ALANON
ALBION
ALISON
ALLFOR
AMADOU
AMAJOR
AMATOL
AMAZON
AMIDOL
AMIGOS
AMINOR
AMNION
AMOSOZ
ANALOG
ANCHOR
ANDHOW
ANDROS
ANGKOR
ANGLOS
ANNHON
ANTCOW
ANTRON
ANYHOW
ARAGON
ARCCOS
ARCHON
ASIMOV
ASKFOR
ASTROS
ASWOON
ATWOOD
AUDIOS
AUTHOR
AVALON
AVEDON
AVISOS

A••••O

ACTINO
ACTTWO
ADAGIO
ADDSTO
ADRENO
AFLCIO
AHCHOO
AIELLO
AIKIDO
AIMSTO
AKIMBO
ALBANO
ALBEDO
ALBINO
ALECTO
ALEPPO
ALIOTO
ALLPRO
ALNICO
ALONSO
ALONZO
AMBATO
AMEDEO
ANATTO
ANGELO
ANTERO
APOLLO
AQUINO
ARCARO
AREZZO
ARIOSO
ARISTO
ARROYO
ARTHRO
ARTURO
ATEMPO
ATERGO
AUSTRO
AVERNO

•AO•••

BAOBAB
GAOLED
GAOLER
HAOLES
KAOLIN
LAOTSE
LAOTZU
MAOISM
MAOIST
MAORIS
MAOTAI
TAOISM
TAOIST

•A•O••

BABOON
BAROJA
BAROLO
BARONG
BARONS
BARONY
BATONS
BAYOUS
CAHOWS
CAJOLE
CANOED
CANOES
CANOLA
CANONS
CANOPY
CANOVA
CAPONE
CAPONS
CAPOTE
CAROBS
CAROLE
CAROLS
CAROMS
CARONI
CAVORT
DACOIT
DADOED
DADOES
DAKOTA
DAMONE
DAMORE
DAMOUR
DATONG
DAYONE
EATOUT
FAGOTS
FAMOUS
FANONS
FANOUT
FAROFF
FAROUK
FAROUT
FAVORS
FAVOUR
FAZOOL
GALOIS
GALOOT
GALOPS
GALORE
GALOSH
GATORS
HALOED
HALOES
HALOID
HAROLD
HAVOCS
JABOTS
JACOBI
JALOPY
JAMOKE
JAWOHL
KABOBS
KABOOM
KAROSS
KAYOED
KAZOOS
LABORS
LABOUR
LADOGA
LAGOON
LAHORE
LAKOTA
LAMONT
LAMOUR
LANOSE
LAROSA
LATONA
LATOUR
LATOYA
LAYOFF
LAYOUT
MACOUN
MAHOUT
MAJORS
MALONE
MALORY
MALOTI
MANORS
MAROON
MASONS
MAXOUT
MAYORS
MAZOLA
NABOBS
NABORS
NAGOYA
NANOOK
NAPOLI
PAEONS
PAGODA
PALOMA
PANOUT
PARODY
PAROLE
PATOIS
PAYOFF
PAYOLA
PAYOUT
RACONS
RADOME
RAGOUT
RAMONA
RAMONE
RAMOSE
RAMOUS
RANOFF
RANOUT
RAYONS
RAZORS
SABOTS
SALOME
SALONS
SALOON
SAMOAN
SAMOSA
SAPORS
SARODS
SARONG
SATORI
SATOUT
SAVOIE
SAVOIR
SAVORS
SAVORY
SAVOUR
SAWOFF
SAWOUT
SAXONS
SAXONY
TABOOS
TABORS
TACOMA
TAGORE
TAGOUT
TALONS
TANOAK
TANOAN
TAPOFF
TAPOUT
TAROTS
TAUONS
VADOSE
VALOIS
VALOUR
VAPORS
VAPORY
VAPOUR
WAGONS
WAHOOS
WAYOUT
YAHOOS
YAPOKS
ZADORA

•A••O•

BABOON
BABSON
BADBOY
BADLOT
BAILOR
BALBOA
BALLON
BALLOT
BALLOU
BAMBOO
BANDOG
BANGOR
BANJOS
BANKON
BANLON
BARDOT
BARHOP
BARRON
BARROW
BARTOK
BARTON
BARYON
BASSOS
BATBOY
BATHOS
BAYLOR
CACAOS
CACHOU
CAICOS
CALLON
CALLOW
CAMEON
CAMEOS
CAMION
CAMPOS
CANDOR
CANNON
CANNOT
CANTON
CANTOR
CANTOS
CANYON
CAPTOR
CARBON
CARBOS
CARBOY
CARGOS
CARHOP
CARLOS
CARLOT
CARNOT
CARROL
CARROT
CARSON
CARTON
CASTON
CASTOR
CATION
CATTON
CAWDOR
CAXTON
DACRON
DAIKON
DAIMON
DALTON
DAMSON
DANSON
DANTON
DARROW
DAWNON
DAWSON
DAYBOY
DAYJOB
DAYTON
EASTON
FACTOR
FAEROE
FALCON
FALLON
FALLOW
FANDOM
FANION
FARLOW
FARROW
FATHOM
FAZOOL
GABION
GAINON
GALLON
GALLOP
GALOOT
GAMBOL
GAMMON
GARCON
GARSON
GASCON
GASLOG
GASTON
GAYNOR
HADRON
HAEMON
HAGDON
HALLOO
HALLOS
HALLOW
HANDON
HANGON
HANSOM
HANSON
HARBOR
HARLOW
HARMON
HARPON
HARROW
HATBOX
HATHOR
HAVEON
HAYMOW
JARGON
KABOOM
KANTOR
KARPOV
KARROO
KAZOOS
LAGOON
LAIDON
LANDON
LANSON
LAPDOG
LAPTOP
LARDON
LARGOS
LARSON
LASSOS
LAWSON
LAWTON
LAYFOR
LAYLOW
LAYSON
LAZBOY
MACHOS
MACRON
MACROS
MADTOM
MAGNON
MAHZOR
MALLOW
MAMBOS
MAMMON
MANGOS
MANIOC
MARCOS
MARGOT
MARION
MARLON
MARMOT
MAROON
MARRON
MARROW
MASCOT
MATRON
MATZOH
MATZOS
MAYPOP
NACHOS
NANOOK
NARROW
NATION
NATRON
PAILOU
PALLOR
PANTOS
PARDON
PARLOR
PARROT
PARSON
PARTON
PASEOS
PASSON
PASTOR
PATHOL
PATHOS
PATIOS
PATMOS
PATROL
PATRON
PATTON
PAVLOV
PAXTON
PAYBOX
PAYFOR
PAYSON
RADIOS
RAGMOP
RAGTOP
RAMROD
RAMSON
RANCOR
RANDOM
RANFOR
RANSOM
RAPTOR
RATION
RATIOS
RATSON
SAIGON
SAILOR
SALLOW
SALMON
SALOON
SALTON
SALVOR
SALVOS
SAMSON
SANTOS
SARGON
SARGOS
SARTON
SAVIOR
SAWLOG
SAYSOS
TABOOS
TACKON
TAILOR
TAINOS
TAKEON
TALBOT
TALION
TALLOW
TANGOS
TARPON
TATTOO
TAUTOG
TAYLOR
WACKOS
WAGGON
WAHOOS
WAITON
WALKON
WALLOP
WALLOW
WALTON
WANTON
WARGOD
WARHOL
WASHOE
WATSON
WAYLON
YAHOOS
YANGON
YARROW
YAUPON

•A•••O

BAGUIO
BAMAKO
BAMBOO
BANQUO
BAROLO
BARRIO
CALICO
CALLAO
CAMARO
CAMETO
CAMINO
CARDIO
CARETO
CARUSO
CASINO
CASSIO
CASTRO
CAUCHO
DACAPO
DADDYO
DAIMYO
DAMATO
DARETO
DAYGLO
FALLTO
GABBRO
GALAGO
GASTRO
GAUCHO
GAZEBO
HAIRDO
HALLOO
HASBRO
KAKAPO
KARROO
LADINO
LAIDTO
LANDHO
LAREDO
LASHIO
LATIGO
LATINO
LAVABO
LAYSTO
MACACO
MACEIO
MADEDO
MADERO
MADURO
MAGGIO
MAKEDO
MALABO
MAPUTO
MARIKO
MARINO
NAGANO
NAVAHO
NAVAJO

PACINO
PALAEO
PANCHO
PAPAGO
PARETO
PASHTO
RABATO
RANCHO
SABATO
SALADO
SANCHO
SANGTO
SAPPHO
SASEBO
TAKETO
TALKTO
TAMAYO
TATTOO
WANTTO
XANTHO

••A•O•

ACAJOU
ALAMOS
ALANON
AMADOU
AMAJOR
AMATOL
AMAZON
ANALOG
ARAGON
AVALON
BEACON
BEAMON
BEANOS
BEARON
BEATON
BLAZON
BMAJOR
BRASOV
BRAVOS
BRAZOS
CHADOR
CHARON
CLAMOR
CLAROS
CMAJOR
CRAYON
DEACON
DEADON
DIALOG
DIATOM
DMAJOR
DRAGON
DRAWON
EMAJOR
ENAMOR
FLACON
FLAGON
FLAVOR
FMAJOR
GLAMOR
GMAJOR
GUACOS
HEADON
HEAROF
INAFOG
INAROW
ISADOR
KEATON
KLAXON
KRAKOW
LEADON
LEANON
LLANOS
MCADOO
MEADOW
ORATOR
PEAPOD
PHAROS
PIANOS
PLANON
PLAYON
QUAHOG
REASON
SEACOW
SEADOG
SEAFOX
SEASON
SEATON
SHADOW
SHAKOS
SHALOM
SHARON
SLALOM
STATOR
STAYON
TEAPOT
TEAPOY
TLALOC
VIACOM
WEAPON
ZEALOT

••A••O

ADAGIO
ANATTO
BRANDO
CHALCO
CHARRO
CRAMBO
CRANIO
DIABLO
EXACTO
FIASCO
FRANCO
GEARTO
GRAECO
GRASSO
LEADTO
LEANTO
MCADOO
NEARTO
PLAGIO
PLASMO
QUANGO
QUARTO
RHABDO
RIALTO
SMALTO
SNAPTO
SOASTO
WHAMMO

•••AO•

CACAOS
HIVAOA

•••A•O

ALBANO
AMBATO
ARCARO
BAMAKO
BORAXO
CAMARO
CHEAPO
CITATO
CYRANO
DACAPO
DAMATO
DELANO
DORADO
DYNAMO
ELPASO
ENHALO
FIGARO
GALAGO
GELATO
GITANO
HEMATO
JURADO
KAKAPO
LAVABO
LEGATO
MACACO
MALABO
MEGALO
MELANO
MENADO
MIKADO
MILANO
MONACO
MURANO
MUTATO
NAGANO
NAVAHO
NAVAJO
NEMATO
NOVATO
OCTAVO
PALAEO
PAPAGO
PICABO
PICARO
PISANO
POTATO
RABATO
ROBALO
ROMANO
RUBATO
SABATO
SALADO
SOMATO
STMALO
STRABO
STRATO
TAMAYO
TEJANO
TERATO
TEXACO
TOBAGO
TOMATO
VIRAGO

••••AO

BILBAO
CALLAO
TODDAO

AP••••

APACHE
APATHY
APEMAN
APEMEN
APERCU
APEXES
APHIDS
APIARY
APICAL
APICES
APIECE
APLITE
APLOMB
APODAL
APOGEE
APOLLO
APPALL
APPALS
APPEAL
APPEAR
APPEND
APPIAN
APPLES
APPLET
APPOSE
APRONS
APTEST
APULIA

A•P•••

ALPACA
ALPERT
ALPHAS
ALPINE
AMPERE
AMPHID
AMPLER
AMPULE
AMPULS
APPALL
APPALS
APPEAL
APPEAR
APPEND
APPIAN
APPLES
APPLET
APPOSE
ARPENT
ASPECT
ASPENS
ASPERA
ASPICS
ASPIRE
ASPISH
AUPAIR

A••P••

ADAPTS
ADEPTS
ADOPTS
ALEPHS
ALEPPO
ALLPRO
ARMPIT
AUSPEX

A•••P•

ABRUPT
ACCEPT
ADOLPH
ALCAPP
ALEPPO
ASLOPE
ATEMPO

A••••P

ACESUP
ACTSUP
ADDSUP
ALCAPP
AMERSP
ANTEUP
ASHARP
ASLEEP

•AP•••

CAPERS
CAPFUL
CAPGUN
CAPIAS
CAPITA
CAPLET
CAPNUT
CAPONE
CAPONS
CAPOTE
CAPPED
CAPPER
CAPRIS
CAPSID
CAPTAN
CAPTOR
DAPHNE
DAPPED
DAPPER
DAPPLE
GAPERS
GAPING
GAPPED
HAPPED
HAPPEN
JAPANS
JAPERS
JAPERY
JAPING
KAPLAN
KAPPAS
LAPDOG
LAPELS
LAPFUL
LAPHAM
LAPINS
LAPPED
LAPPET
LAPSED
LAPSES
LAPSUP
LAPTEV
LAPTOP
LAPUTA
MAPLES
MAPPED
MAPPER
MAPUTO
NAPERY
NAPIER
NAPKIN
NAPLES
NAPOLI
NAPPED
NAPPER
NAPPES
NAPPIE
PAPACY
PAPAGO
PAPAIN
PAPAWS
PAPAYA
PAPERS
PAPERY
PAPIER
PAPPAS
PAPPUS
PAPUAN
PAPYRI
RAPIDS
RAPIER
RAPINE
RAPINI
RAPPED
RAPPEE
RAPPEL
RAPPER
RAPTLY
RAPTOR
SAPORS
SAPPED
SAPPER
SAPPHO
TAPERS
TAPING
TAPINS
TAPIRS
TAPOFF
TAPOUT
TAPPAN
TAPPED
TAPPER
TAPPET
VAPORS
VAPORY
VAPOUR
WAPITI
WAPNER
YAPOKS
YAPPED
ZAPATA
ZAPPED
ZAPPER

•A•P••

CALPAC
CAMPED
CAMPER
CAMPOS
CAMPUS
CAPPED
CAPPER
CARPAL
CARPED
CARPEL
CARPER
CARPET
CARPUS
CASPAR
CASPER
DAMPED
DAMPEN
DAMPER
DAMPLY
DAPPED
DAPPER
DAPPLE
GALPAL
GAPPED
GASPAR
GASPED
GASPER
GAWPED
HAMPER
HAPPED
HAPPEN
HARPED
HARPER
HARPON
HASPED
HATPIN
JAIPUR
JASPER
KAPPAS
KARPOV
LAPPED
LAPPET
LAUPER
MAGPIE
MAPPED
MAPPER
MARPLE
MAYPOP
NAPPED
NAPPER
NAPPES
NAPPIE
PALPUS
PAMPAS
PAMPER
PAPPAS
PAPPUS
PAUPER
PAWPAW
RAIPUR
RAJPUT
RAMPED
RAPPED
RAPPEE
RAPPEL
RAPPER
RASPED
RASPER
SAIPAN
SAMPAN
SAMPLE
SAPPED
SAPPER
SAPPHO
TAIPAN
TAIPEI
TAMPED
TAMPER
TAPPAN
TAPPED
TAPPER
TAPPET
TARPAN
TARPIT
TARPON
TAUPES
VAMPED
VAMPER
WAMPUM
WARPED
YAPPED
YAUPON
YAWPED
YAWPER
ZAPPED
ZAPPER

•A••P•

CALIPH
CANAPE
CANOPY
DACAPO
GALOPS
JALAPA
JALOPY
JAMUPS
KAKAPO
LAYUPS
PARAPH

•A•••P

BACKUP
BALLUP
BANGUP
BARHOP
CALLUP
CAMEUP
CARHOP
CATNAP
CATNIP
CATSUP
DAMSUP
EARLAP
EASEUP
EATSUP
FACEUP
FAIRUP
GALLOP
GALLUP
GANGUP
GASCAP
GAVEUP
GAZUMP
HANDUP
HANGUP
HARDUP
HAULUP
JACKUP
JAMSUP
JAZZUP
LACEUP
LAIDUP
LAPSUP
LAPTOP
LARRUP
LASHUP
LAYSUP
MADCAP
MADEUP
MAKEUP
MARKUP
MAYHAP
MAYPOP
PACKUP
PAIDUP
PAIRUP
PASSUP
PAYSUP
RACKUP
RAGMOP
RAGTOP
RAKEUP
RANGUP
RAVEUP
SANNUP
SATRAP
SAVEUP
TAGSUP
TAKEUP
TALKUP
TANKUP
WADSUP
WAITUP
WAKEUP
WALKUP
WALLOP
WALLUP
WARMUP
WASHUP

••AP••

ADAPTS
CHAPEL
CHAPIN
COAPTS
CRAPES
DIAPER
DRAPED
DRAPER
DRAPES
ELAPID
ELAPSE
ETAPES
FLAPPY
FRAPPE
GRAPES
GRAPEY
GRAPHS
GRAPHY
GRAPPA
HEAPED
INAPET
LEAPED
LEAPER
OKAPIS
PEAPOD
REAPED
REAPER
SCAPED
SCAPES
SHAPED
SHAPER
SHAPES
SLAPPY
SLAPUP
SNAPAT
SNAPPY
SNAPTO
SNAPUP
SOAPED
SOAPER
STAPES
STAPLE
STAPUF
TEAPOT
TEAPOY
TRAPPY
WEAPON

WRAPUP

••A•P•
CHAMPS
CLAMPS
CLASPS
CRAMPS
FLAPPY
FRAPPE
GRAMPA
GRAMPS
GRAPPA
GRASPS
SCALPS
SCAMPI
SCAMPS
SCARPS
SCAUPS
SHARPS
SLAPPY
SNAPPY
STAMPS
SWAMPS
SWAMPY
TRAMPS
TRAPPY

••A••P
BEADUP
BEAMUP
BEARUP
BEATUP
CHATUP
CLAMUP
DIALUP
DRAWUP
GEARUP
HEADUP
HEATUP
LEADUP
PLAYUP
REARUP
SEALUP
SLAPUP
SNAPUP
SOAKUP
STAYUP
TEACUP
TEAMUP
TEARUP
WRAPUP

•••AP•
ALCAPP
CANAPE
CHEAPO
DACAPO
ENRAPT
ESCAPE
JALAPA
KAKAPO
LENAPE
ONTAPE
PARAPH
PTRAPS
RECAPS
REMAPS
RETAPE
RETAPS
SCRAPE
SCRAPS
SERAPE
SERAPH
STRAPS
TERAPH
UNCAPS

•••A•P
ALCAPP
ASHARP
BSHARP
CCLAMP
CSHARP
DECAMP
DSHARP
ENCAMP
ESCARP
ESHARP
FSHARP
GSHARP
PREAMP
REVAMP

••••AP
BITMAP
BUMRAP
BURLAP
CATNAP
DEWLAP
EARLAP
ENTRAP
ENWRAP
GASCAP
HOTCAP
HUBCAP
ICECAP
KIDNAP
MADCAP
MAYHAP
MILSAP
MISHAP
MOBCAP
NOSOAP
REDCAP
REWRAP
RIPRAP
SATRAP
SKYCAP
TOECAP
TOETAP
UNSNAP
UNTRAP
UNWRAP

AQ••••
AQUATE
AQUILA
AQUINO

A•Q•••
ACQUIT

•AQ•••
MAQUIS
PAQUIN
RAQUEL
YAQUIS

•A•Q••
BANQUO
BARQUE
BASQUE
CAIQUE
CALQUE
CASQUE
MANQUE
MARQUE
MASQUE
SACQUE
YANQUI

•A•••Q
NASDAQ

••AQ••
BRAQUE
CLAQUE
IRAQIS
OPAQUE
PLAQUE

••••AQ
COMPAQ
NASDAQ

AR••••
ARABIA
ARABIC
ARABLE
ARAFAT
ARAGON
ARALIA
ARALLU
ARAMIS
ARARAT
ARAWAK
ARBELA
ARBORS
ARBOUR
ARCADE
ARCANA
ARCANE
ARCARO
ARCCOS
ARCHED
ARCHER
ARCHES
ARCHIE
ARCHLY
ARCHON
ARCING
ARCTAN
ARCTIC
ARDEBS
ARDENT
ARDORS
ARDOUR
ARECAS
ARENAS
ARENDT
AREOLA
ARETES
ARETHA
AREZZO
ARGALI
ARGENT
ARGIVE
ARGOSY
ARGOTS
ARGUED
ARGUER
ARGUES
ARGUFY
ARGYLE
ARGYLL
ARIDLY
ARIGHT
ARIOSE
ARIOSO
ARISEN
ARISES
ARISTA
ARISTO
ARJUNA
ARLEEN
ARLENE
ARLISS
ARMADA
ARMAGH
ARMAND
ARMANI
ARMETS
ARMFUL
ARMIES
ARMING
ARMLET
ARMORS
ARMORY
ARMOUR
ARMPIT
ARMURE
ARNESS
ARNETT
ARNHEM
ARNICA
ARNOLD
AROIDS
AROMAS
AROUND
AROUSE
ARPENT
ARRACK
ARRANT
ARRAYS
ARREAR
ARREST
ARRIBA
ARRIVE
ARROBA
ARROWS
ARROYO
ARSENE
ARSONS
ARTELS
ARTERY
ARTFUL
ARTGUM
ARTHRO
ARTHUR
ARTIER
ARTILY
ARTIST
ARTOIS
ARTURO
ARUBAN
ARVADA
ARYANS

A•R•••
ABRADE
ABRAMS
ABROAD
ABRUPT
ACROSS
ADRENO
ADRIAN
ADRIEN
ADRIFT
ADROIT
AERATE
AERIAL
AERIES
AERIFY
AERILY
AEROBE
AFRAID
AFRAME
AFREET
AFRESH
AFRICA
AFRITS
AGREED
AGREES
AIRARM
AIRBAG
AIRBUS
AIRDAM
AIRDRY
AIRGUN
AIRIER
AIRILY
AIRING
AIRMAN
AIRMEN
AIROUT
AIRSAC
AIRWAY
AORIST
AORTAE
AORTAL
AORTAS
AORTIC
APRONS
ARRACK
ARRANT
ARRAYS
ARREAR
ARREST
ARRIBA
ARRIVE
ARROBA
ARROWS
ARROYO
ATREST
ATREUS
ATRIAL
ATRISK
ATRIUM
AUREUS
AURIFY
AURIGA
AURORA
AUROUS

A••R••
ABORAL
ABORTS
ACARID
ACARUS
ACCRUE
ACORNS
ADORED
ADOREE
ADORER
ADORES
ADORNS
AFFRAY
AGARIC
AGGROS
AGORAE
AGORAS
AGOROT
AHERNE
AIGRET
ALARIC
ALARMS
ALARUM
ALDRIN
ALERTS
ALFRED
AMERCE
AMERSP
AMORAL
AMTRAC
AMTRAK
ANDREA
ANDREI
ANDRES
ANDREW
ANDREY
ANDROS
ANERGY
ANORAK
ANTRES
ANTRIM
ANTRON
ANTRUM
ANURAN
APERCU
ARARAT
ASHRAM
ASTRAL
ASTRAY
ASTRID
ASTROS
ATERGO
ATTRIT
AUBREY
AUDREY
AVERNO
AVERSE
AVERTS
AWARDS
AZORES
AZORIN

A•••R•
ABHORS
ABJURE
ABOARD
ABSORB
ABSURD
ACCORD
ACTORS
ADDERS
ADHERE
ADJURE
ADMIRE
ADSORB
ADVERB
ADVERT
AFEARD
AFFIRM
AFFORD
AGLARE
AIDERS
AILERS
AIRARM
AIRDRY
ALBERT
ALBORG
ALDERS
ALEGRE
ALGORE
ALHIRT
ALLPRO
ALLURE
ALPERT
ALTARS
ALTERS
AMBERS
AMBERY
AMEERS
AMENRA
AMHARA
AMOURS
AMPERE
ANGERS
ANGORA
ANITRA
ANKARA
ANSARA
ANTERO
APIARY
ARBORS
ARCARO
ARDORS
ARMORS
ARMORY
ARMURE
ARTERY
ARTHRO
ARTURO
ASBURY
ASGARD
ASHARP
ASHORE
ASKARI
ASKERS
ASMARA
ASPERA
ASPIRE
ASSERT
ASSORT
ASSURE
ASTERN
ASTERS
ASWIRL
ATTARS
ATTIRE
ATWORK
AUBURN
AUGERS
AUGURS
AUGURY
AURORA
AUSTRO
AVIARY
AWEARY
AWHIRL
AYMARA

A••••R
AAFAIR
ABUKIR
ABUSER
ACHIER
ADORER
AETHER
AFFAIR
AGADIR
AIMFOR
AIRIER
ALEGAR
ALITER
ALLFOR
ALOMAR
ALTAIR
ALULAR
AMAJOR
AMBLER
AMINOR
AMPLER
ANCHOR
ANGKOR
ANGLER
ANHYDR
ANSGAR
ANSWER
ANTHER
ANTLER
APPEAR
ARBOUR
ARCHER
ARDOUR
ARGUER
ARMOUR
ARREAR
ARTHUR
ARTIER
ASEVER
ASHIER
ASHLAR
ASKFOR
AUPAIR
AUTEUR
AUTHOR
AVATAR
AVOWER

•AR•••
BARBED
BARBEL
BARBER
BARBET
BARBIE
BARBRA
BARCAR
BARDIC
BARDOT
BAREGE
BARELY
BAREST
BARFLY
BARGED
BARGES
BARHOP
BARING
BARISH
BARITE
BARIUM
BARKAT
BARKED
BARKER
BARKIN
BARLEY
BARMAN
BARMEN
BARNES
BARNEY
BARNUM
BAROJA
BAROLO
BARONG
BARONS
BARONY
BARQUE
BARRED
BARREL
BARREN
BARRES
BARRIE
BARRIO
BARRIS
BARRON
BARROW
BARTAB
BARTER
BARTOK
BARTON
BARUCH
BARYON
BARZUN
CARAFE
CARATS
CARBON
CARBOS
CARBOY
CARDED
CARDER
CARDIN
CARDIO
CAREEN
CAREER
CARESS
CARETO
CARETS
CARFUL
CARGOS
CARHOP
CARIBE
CARIBS
CARIES
CARINA
CARING
CARKED
CARLIN
CARLOS
CARLOT
CARMAN
CARMEL
CARMEN
CARNAL
CARNES
CARNET
CARNEY
CARNOT
CAROBS
CAROLE
CAROLS

CAROMS
CARONI
CARPAL
CARPED
CARPEL
CARPER
CARPET
CARPUS
CARREL
CARREY
CARRIE
CARROL
CARROT
CARSON
CARTED
CARTEL
CARTER
CARTES
CARTON
CARUSO
CARVED
CARVER
CARVES
CARVEY
DARENT
DARETO
DARIEN
DARING
DARIUS
DARKEN
DARKER
DARKLE
DARKLY
DARNAY
DARNED
DARNEL
DARNER
DARNIT
DARREN
DARROW
DARRYL
DARTED
DARTER
DARWIN
EARFUL
EARING
EARLAP
EARNED
EARNER
EARTHA
EARTHY
EARWAX
EARWIG
FARADS
FARCED
FARCES
FARCRY
FARERS
FARINA
FARING
FARLEY
FARLOW
FARMED
FARMER
FAROFF
FAROUK
FAROUT
FARRAH
FARRAR
FARROW
GARAGE
GARBED
GARBLE
GARCIA
GARCON
GARDEN
GARETH
GARGLE
GARISH
GARLIC
GARNER
GARNET
GARRET
GARSON
GARTER
GARTHS
GARVEY
HARALD
HARARE
HARASS
HARBIN
HARBOR
HARDBY
HARDEN
HARDER
HARDLY
HARDUP
HAREMS
HARING
HARKED
HARKEN
HARKER
HARLAN
HARLEM
HARLEY
HARLIN
HARLOW
HARMED
HARMON
HAROLD
HARPED
HARPER
HARPON
HARRIS
HARROW
HARVEY
JARFUL
JARGON
JARRAH
JARRED
KARATE
KARATS
KAREEM
KARIBA
KARMIC
KARNAK
KAROSS
KARPOV
KARRAS
KARROO
KARSTS
LARAMS
LARDED
LARDER
LARDON
LAREDO
LARGER
LARGES
LARGOS
LARIAT
LARKED
LAROSA
LARRUP
LARSEN
LARSON
LARVAE
LARVAL
LARVAS
LARYNX
MARACA
MARAUD
MARBLE
MARBLY
MARCEL
MARCHE
MARCIA
MARCIE
MARCOS
MARCUS
MARDUK
MARGAY
MARGES
MARGIE
MARGIN
MARGOT
MARIAH
MARIAN
MARIEL
MARIKO
MARILU
MARINA
MARINE
MARINO
MARION
MARISA
MARISH
MARIST
MARIUS
MARKED
MARKER
MARKET
MARKKA
MARKUP
MARLED
MARLEE
MARLEY
MARLIN
MARLON
MARMEE
MARMOT
MARNER
MARNIE
MAROON
MARPLE
MARQUE
MARRED
MARRON
MARROW
MARSHA
MARSHY
MARTEL
MARTEN
MARTHA
MARTIN
MARTYR
MARVEL
MARVIN
NARIAL
NARNIA
NARROW
NARVIK
NARWAL
OARING
PARADE
PARANA
PARANG
PARAPH
PARCAE
PARCEL
PARDON
PARENS
PARENT
PARERS
PARETO
PAREVE
PARGET
PARIAH
PARING
PARISH
PARITY
PARKAS
PARKAY
PARKED
PARKER
PARLAY
PARLEY
PARLOR
PARNIS
PARODY
PAROLE
PARRED
PARREL
PARRIS
PARROT
PARSEC
PARSED
PARSEE
PARSER
PARSES
PARSON
PARTED
PARTLY
PARTON
PARULA
PARURE
PARVIS
RAREFY
RARELY
RAREST
RARIFY
RARING
RARITY
SARANS
SARDIS
SARGES
SARGON
SARGOS
SARNIA
SARODS
SARONG
SARTON
SARTRE
TARAWA
TARGES
TARGET
TARIFF
TARING
TARMAC
TAROTS
TARPAN
TARPIT
TARPON
TARRED
TARSAL
TARSUS
TARTAN
TARTAR
TARTER
TARTLY
TARZAN
VARDEN
VARESE
VARIED
VARIES
VARLET
VARNAS
VARNEY
VARUNA
WARBLE
WARCRY
WARDED
WARDEN
WARDER
WARGOD
WARHOL
WARIER
WARILY
WARING
WARMED
WARMER
WARMLY
WARMTH
WARMUP
WARNED
WARNER
WARPED
WARRED
WARREN
WARSAW
YARDED
YARELY
YAREST
YARNED
YARROW
ZAREBA

•A•R••

BAIRNS
BARRED
BARREL
BARREN
BARRES
BARRIE
BARRIO
BARRIS
BARRON
BARROW
BAYRUM
CADRES
CAIRNS
CAPRIS
CARREL
CARREY
CARRIE
CARROL
CARROT
CATRIG
DACRON
DAIREN
DARREN
DARROW
DARRYL
EAGRES
FABRAY
FABRIC
FAERIE
FAEROE
FAIRED
FAIRER
FAIRLY
FAIRUP
FARRAH
FARRAR
FARROW
GARRET
HADRON
HAIRDO
HAIRED
HARRIS
HARROW
HATRED
IATRIC
JARRAH
JARRED
JAURES
KARRAS
KARROO
KAURIS
LABREA
LABRET
LABRUM
LAIRDS
LARRUP
LAUREL
LAUREN
LAURIE
MACRAE
MACRON
MACROS
MADRAS
MADRES
MADRID
MANRAY
MAORIS
MARRED
MARRON
MARROW
MATRIX
MATRON
MAURYA
NACRES
NAIRAS
NARROW
NATRON
PADRES
PAIRED
PAIRUP
PARRED
PARREL
PARRIS
PARROT
PATROL
PATRON
RAGRUG
RAHRAH
RAMROD
SABRAS
SABRES
SACRAL
SACRED
SACRUM
SATRAP
SAUREL
SAWRED
TABRIZ
TARRED
TAURUS
TAYRAS
VANRYN
WALRUS
WARRED
WARREN
YARROW
ZAGREB
ZAIRES

•A••R•

BAKERS
BAKERY
BALERS
BARBRA
BAYARD
CABERS
CAGERS
CAMARO
CAMERA
CANARD
CANARY
CANERS
CAPERS
CASERN
CASTRO
CATERS
CAVERN
CAVERS
CAVORT
DAMORE
DATARY
DATERS
DATURA
EATERS
EATERY
FAKERS
FAKERY
FAKIRS
FARCRY
FARERS
FAVORS
GABBRO
GALORE
GANTRY
GAPERS
GASTRO
GATERS
GATORS
HALERS
HALERU
HARARE
HASBRO
HATARI
HATERS
HAVERS
HAZARD
HAZERS
JABIRU
JAPERS
JAPERY
JAVARI
KAFIRS
KAGERA
LABORS
LACERS
LADERS
LAGERS
LAHORE
LAKERS
LAMARR
LANARK
LANDRY
LASERS
LAVERS
LAYERS
MADERO
MADURA
MADURO
MAITRE
MAJORS
MAKERS
MALORY
MANORS
MANTRA
MASERS
MASERU
MATERS
MATURE
MAYORS
MAZERS
NABORS
NADIRS
NAMERS
NAPERY
NATURA
NATURE
OATERS
PACERS
PAGERS
PAHARI
PALTRY
PAMIRS
PANFRY
PANTRY
PAPERS
PAPERY
PAPYRI
PARERS
PARURE
PASTRY
PATERS
PAVERS
PAWERS
PAYERS
QATARI
RACERS
RAKERS
RANDRY
RASERS
RATERS
RAVERS
RAZORS
SABERS
SAFARI
SAFIRE
SAHARA
SAKERS
SALARY
SAMARA
SANDRA
SAPORS
SARTRE
SATIRE
SATORI
SATURN
SATYRS
SAVERS
SAVORS
SAVORY
SAYERS
TABARD
TABORS
TAGORE
TAKERS
TALERS
TAMARA
TAMERS
TANTRA
TAPERS
TAPIRS
TASERS
TATARS
TATERS
TAVERN
TAWDRY
TAXERS
UAKARI
VAGARY
VALERY
VAPORS
VAPORY
WADERS
WAFERS
WAFERY
WAGERS
WALERS
WANERS
WARCRY
WATERS
WATERY
WAVERS
WAVERY
WAXERS
ZADORA

•A•••R

AAFAIR
BACKER
BADDER
BADGER
BAGGER
BAILER
BAILOR
BALDER
BANGER
BANGOR
BANKER
BANNER
BANTER
BARBER
BARCAR
BARKER
BARTER
BASTER
BATHER
BATTER
BAWLER
BAXTER
BAYLOR
BAZAAR
CABLER
CADGER
CAESAR

CAGIER
CAHIER
CAKIER
CALDER
CALLER
CALMER
CAMBER
CAMPER
CANDOR
CANIER
CANKER
CANNER
CANTER
CANTOR
CAPPER
CAPTOR
CARDER
CAREER
CARPER
CARTER
CARVER
CASPAR
CASPER
CASTER
CASTOR
CATHER
CAVIAR
CAWDOR
DAFTER
DAGGER
DAGMAR
DAMMAR
DAMOUR
DAMPER
DANCER
DANDER
DANGER
DANKER
DANNER
DAPPER
DARKER
DARNER
DARTER
DASHER
DAUBER
EARNER
EASIER
EASTER
FABLER
FACTOR
FAFNIR
FAIRER
FALSER
FALTER
FARMER
FARRAR
FASTER
FATHER
FATTER
FAVOUR
FAWNER
GABBER
GABLER
GADDER
GAFFER
GAINER
GAITER
GAMIER
GAMMER
GANDER
GANGER
GAOLER
GARNER
GARTER
GASPAR
GASPER
GASSER
GATHER
GAUGER
GAWKER
GAYNOR
HACKER
HALTER
HAMMER
HAMPER
HANGAR
HANGER
HANKER
HARBOR
HARDER
HARKER
HARPER
HATHOR
HATTER
HAULER
HAWKER
HAWSER
HAZIER
JABBAR
JABBER
JAEGER
JAGGER
JAGUAR
JAILER
JAIPUR
JAMMER
JASPER
JAVIER
KAFFIR
KAISER
KALMAR
KANDER
KANTOR
KAVNER
LAAGER
LABOUR
LACIER
LADDER
LADLER
LAFFER
LAGGER
LAKIER
LAMARR
LAMOUR
LANCER
LANDER
LANGUR
LANIER
LANKER
LARDER
LARGER
LASCAR
LASHER
LASSER
LATHER
LATOUR
LATTER
LAUDER
LAUPER
LAWYER
LAYFOR
LAZIER
MADDER
MAGYAR
MAHLER
MAHZOR
MAILER
MANGER
MANNER
MAPPER
MARKER
MARNER
MARTYR
MASHER
MASKER
MASTER
MATHER
MATTER
MAULER
MAUSER
MAZIER
NABBER
NAGGER
NAILER
NAPIER
NAPPER
NASCAR
NASSER
NATTER
OATIER
PACKER
PADDER
PALIER
PALLOR
PALMER
PALTER
PAMPER
PANDER
PANNER
PANZER
PAPIER
PARKER
PARLOR
PARSER
PASSER
PASTOR
PATTER
PAUPER
PAWNER
PAYFOR
RACIER
RADNER
RAFTER
RAIDER
RAILER
RAINER
RAIPUR
RAISER
RANCOR
RANFOR
RANGER
RANKER
RANTER
RAPIER
RAPPER
RAPTOR
RASHER
RASPER
RASTER
RATEDR
RATHER
RATTER
SACKER
SADDER
SAILOR
SALTER
SALVER
SALVOR
SAMBAR
SANDER
SANGER
SANTIR
SAPPER
SASSER
SAUCER
SAUGER
SAVIOR
SAVOIR
SAVOUR
SAWYER
TACKER
TAILOR
TALKER
TALLER
TAMPER
TANKER
TANNER
TAPPER
TARTAR
TARTER
TASTER
TATTER
TAUTER
TAYLOR
VAGUER
VAINER
VALOUR
VAMPER
VANIER
VAPOUR
VASSAR
VASTER
WAGNER
WAILER
WAITER
WAIVER
WALKER
WALLER
WALTER
WANDER
WANIER
WANNER
WAPNER
WARDER
WARIER
WARMER
WARNER
WASHER
WASTER
WAVIER
WAXIER
XAVIER
YABBER
YAKKER
YAMMER
YASSER
YAWNER
YAWPER
ZAFFER
ZANDER
ZANIER
ZAPPER

••AR••

ACARID
ACARUS
AGARIC
ALARIC
ALARMS
ALARUM
ARARAT
AWARDS
BEARDS
BEARER
BEARON
BEARUP
BLARED
BLARES
BOARDS
CHARGE
CHARLY
CHARMS
CHARON
CHARRO
CHARTS
CIARDI
CLARET
CLARKE
CLAROS
COARSE
DEARER
DEARIE
DEARLY
DEARME
DEARTH
DHARMA
DMARKS
DUARTE
DWARFS
ECARTE
EPARCH
EXARCH
FEARED
FEARER
FLARED
FLARES
GEARED
GEARTO
GEARUP
GHARRY
GLARED
GLARES
GNARLS
GNARLY
GUARDS
HEARER
HEAROF
HEARST
HEARTH
HEARTS
HEARTY
HEARYE
HOARDS
HOARSE
ICARIA
ICARUS
IMARET
INARCH
INAROW
INARUT
JUAREZ
KEARNY
KNARRY
LEARNS
LEARNT
NEARBY
NEARED
NEARER
NEARLY
NEARTO
OZARKS
PEARLS
PEARLY
PHAROS
QUARKS
QUARRY
QUARTO
QUARTS
QUARTZ
REARED
REARER
REARMS
REARUP
ROARED
ROARER
SCARAB
SCARCE
SCARED
SCARER
SCARES
SCARFS
SCARNE
SCARPS
SCARRY
SCARUM
SEARCH
SEARED
SEARLE
SHARDS
SHARED
SHARER
SHARES
SHARIA
SHARIF
SHARKS
SHARON
SHARPS
SMARMY
SMARTS
SMARTY
SNARED
SNARES
SNARLS
SNARLY
SOARED
SOARER
SOARES
SPARED
SPARER
SPARES
SPARGE
SPARKS
SPARKY
SPARSE
SPARTA
STARCH
STARED
STARER
STARES
STARRY
STARTS
STARVE
SWARAJ
SWARDS
SWARMS
SWARTH
TEARAT
TEARED
TEARUP
TIARAS
TUAREG
UNARMS
WEARER
WHARFS
YEARLY
YEARNS

••A•R•

BIAFRA
CHAIRS
CHARRO
CLAIRE
FIACRE
FLAIRS
GHARRY
GLAIRS
GLAIRY
GOAWRY
KHAFRE
KNARRY
MEAGRE
QUADRI
QUARRY
REAIRS
SCARRY
STAIRS
STARRY

••A••R

AGADIR
AMAJOR
AVATAR
BEAKER
BEARER
BEATER
BEAVER
BLADER
BLAZER
BMAJOR
BOATER
BRACER
BRAVER
BRAYER
BRAZER
CHADOR
CHASER
CLAMOR
CLAWER
CMAJOR
COALER
COAXER
CRATER
CRAVER
DEADER
DEAFER
DEALER
DEARER
DIALER
DIAPER
DLAYER
DMAJOR
DRAPER
DRAWER
ELATER
ELAYER
EMAJOR
ENAMOR
ERASER
EVADER
FEARER
FLAKER
FLAVOR
FLAYER
FMAJOR
FRASER
FRAZER
GLAMOR
GLASER
GLAZER
GMAJOR
GNAWER
GRADER
GRATER
GRAVER
GRAYER
GRAZER
HEADER
HEALER
HEARER
HEATER
HEAVER
HOAXER
IMAGER
INANER
IRATER
ISADOR
KRAMER
KRATER
LAAGER
LEADER
LEAKER
LEANER
LEAPER
LEASER
LOADER
LOAFER
LOANER
MEAGER
MEANER
MOANER
NEARER
NEATER
ONAGER
ORATOR
PHASER
PLACER
PLANAR
PLANER
PLATER
PLAYER
PRATER
PRAYER
QUAKER
QUASAR
QUAVER
READER
REALER
REAMER
REAPER
REARER
ROAMER
ROARER
SCALAR
SCALER
SCARER
SEALER
SEATER
SHAKER
SHAMIR
SHAPER
SHARER
SHAVER
SKATER
SLATER
SLAVER
SLAYER
SOAKER
SOAPER
SOARER
SPACER
SPADER
SPARER
STAGER
STALER
STARER
STATER
STATOR
SUAVER
SWAYER
TEASER
THALER
THAYER
TRACER
TRADER
WEAKER
WEARER
WEAVER
WHALER
YEAGER

•••AR•

ABOARD
AFEARD
AGLARE
AIRARM
ALTARS
AMHARA
ANKARA
ANSARA
APIARY
ARCARO
ASGARD
ASHARP
ASKARI
ASMARA
ATTARS
AVIARY
AWEARY
AYMARA
BAYARD
BEWARE
BICARB
BIHARI
BINARY
BLEARS
BLEARY
BOGART
BOVARY
BOYARS
BRIARD

BRIARS
BSHARP
CAMARO
CANARD
CANARY
CEDARS
CESARE
CIGARS
CLEARS
COWARD
CSHARP
CUNARD
CURARE
DATARY
DEBARK
DEBARS
DENARY
DEPART
DINARS
DISARM
DOTARD
DREARY
DSHARP
EDGARD
EDGARS
EDUARD
EDVARD
EDWARD
EMBARK
ERHARD
ERRARE
ESCARP
ESHARP
EZZARD
FIGARO
FRIARS
FRIARY
FSHARP
FUGARD
GEMARA
GERARD
GIRARD
GOCART
GODARD
GOKART
GSHARP
HARARE
HATARI
HAZARD
HEGARI
HILARY
HOBART
HOWARD
IDCARD
IMPART
INPART
INWARD
IZZARD
JAVARI
LAMARR
LANARK
LIZARD
MEGARA
MOLARS
MOZART
NEWARK
NONARY
NOTARY
OLEARY
ONWARD
OSCARS
OXCART
OXNARD
PAHARI
PETARD
PICARA
PICARD
PICARO
POPART
QATARI
REBARS
REGARD
REMARK
RETARD
RETARS
REWARD
REWARM
RITARD
ROSARY
ROTARY
SAFARI
SAHARA
SALARY
SAMARA
SENARY
SEWARD
SHEARS
SITARS
SMEARS
SMEARY
SOLARS
SOUARI
SPEARS
SQUARE
STMARK
STUART
SUBARU
SUGARS
SUGARY
SWEARS
TABARD
TAMARA
TATARS
THWART
TOWARD
TULARE
UAKARI
UNBARS
UNWARY
UPWARD
VAGARY
VICARS
VOLARE
VOTARY
WIZARD

•••A•R

AAFAIR
AFFAIR
ALTAIR
AUPAIR
BAZAAR
BELAIR
ECLAIR
HOTAIR
IMPAIR
LAMARR
MCNAIR
MIDAIR
MOHAIR
REPAIR
UNFAIR

••••AR

ALEGAR
ALOMAR
ALULAR
ANSGAR
APPEAR
ARREAR
ASHLAR
AVATAR
BARCAR
BAZAAR
BEGGAR
BOWOAR
BOXCAR
BULGAR
BURSAR
BUSBAR
CAESAR
CASPAR
CAVIAR
CELLAR
CHUKAR
COLLAR
COSTAR
COUGAR
DAGMAR
DAMMAR
DELMAR
DEODAR
DISBAR
DOGEAR
DOLLAR
DUNBAR
DURBAR
ENDEAR
FARRAR
FOLIAR
FULMAR
GASPAR
GUITAR
GUNNAR
HANGAR
HOTCAR
HOTWAR
HUSSAR
INGEAR
INGMAR
INSTAR
ISHTAR
ISOBAR
JABBAR
JAGUAR
KALMAR
KEVLAR
LASCAR
LEKVAR
LINEAR
LOTHAR
LUMBAR
MAGYAR
MEDGAR
MEDLAR
MOLNAR
MORTAR
NASCAR
NECTAR
NEWMAR
OCULAR
OVULAR
PEDLAR
PILLAR
PINDAR
PLANAR
POPLAR
PREWAR
PSYWAR
PULSAR
QINTAR
QUASAR
REHEAR
RETEAR
SAMBAR
SCALAR
SHIKAR
SHOFAR
SIRDAR
STELAR
SUBPAR
TARTAR
THENAR
TINEAR
TOWCAR
TROCAR
UPROAR
UVULAR
VASSAR
VULGAR
WEIMAR
WETBAR
ZEDBAR

AS••••

ASANAS
ASBURY
ASCEND
ASCENT
ASCHAM
ASCOTS
ASDICS
ASEITY
ASEVER
ASGARD
ASHARP
ASHCAN
ASHIER
ASHLAR
ASHLEY
ASHORE
ASHRAM
ASIANS
ASIDES
ASIMOV
ASKARI
ASKERS
ASKFOR
ASKING
ASKOUT
ASKSIN
ASLANT
ASLEEP
ASLOPE
ASMARA
ASOSAN
ASPECT
ASPENS
ASPERA
ASPICS
ASPIRE
ASPISH
ASSAIL
ASSAYS
ASSENT
ASSERT
ASSESS
ASSETS
ASSIGN
ASSISI
ASSIST
ASSIZE
ASSORT
ASSUME
ASSURE
ASTERN
ASTERS
ASTRAL
ASTRAY
ASTRID
ASTROS
ASTUTE
ASWELL
ASWIRL
ASWOON
ASYLUM

A•S•••

ABSCAM
ABSENT
ABSORB
ABSURD
ADSORB
AISLES
ALSACE
AMSTEL
ANSARA
ANSATE
ANSELM
ANSGAR
ANSWER
ARSENE
ARSONS
ASSAIL
ASSAYS
ASSENT
ASSERT
ASSESS
ASSETS
ASSIGN
ASSISI
ASSIST
ASSIZE
ASSORT
ASSUME
ASSURE
ATSTUD
AUSPEX
AUSSIE
AUSTEN
AUSTIN
AUSTRO
AXSEED

A••S••

ABASED
ABASES
ABESSE
ABUSED
ABUSER
ABUSES
ABYSMS
ACESUP
ACTSAS
ACTSON
ACTSUP
ADDSIN
ADDSON
ADDSTO
ADDSUP
ADESTE
AGASSI
AIMSAT
AIMSTO
AIRSAC
ALASKA
ALISON
ALLSET
ALYSSA
AMOSOZ
AMUSED
AMUSES
ARISEN
ARISES
ARISTA
ARISTO
ASKSIN
ASOSAN
ATESTS
AUSSIE
AVESTA
AVISOS
AYESHA

A•••S•

ABBESS
ABESSE
ABLEST
ABLUSH
ACCESS
ACCOST
ACCUSE
ACROSS
ADJUST
ADMASS
ADVISE
AFRESH
AGASSI
AGEISM
AGEIST
AGHAST
AGUISH
AHIMSA
ALDOSE
ALEAST
ALMOST
ALONSO
ALWEST
ALYSSA
AMBUSH
AMERSP
AMIDST
AORIST
APPOSE
APTEST
ARGOSY
ARIOSE
ARIOSO
ARLISS
ARNESS
AROUSE
ARREST
ARTIST
ASPISH
ASSESS
ASSISI
ASSIST
ATBEST
ATCOST
ATEASE
ATLAST
ATMOST
ATREST
ATRISK
ATTEST
AUGUST
AVERSE
AVULSE

A••••S

ABACAS
ABACUS
ABASES
ABATES
ABATIS
ABBESS
ABBEYS
ABBOTS
ABELES
ABHORS
ABIDES
ABODES
ABOHMS
ABOMBS
ABORTS
ABRAMS
ABUSES
ABYDOS
ABYSMS
ACARUS
ACCESS
ACEOUS
ACINUS
ACORNS
ACROSS
ACTORS
ACTSAS
ADAGES
ADAPTS
ADDAMS
ADDERS
ADDLES
ADDONS
ADEEMS
ADEPTS
ADIDAS
ADIEUS
ADLIBS
ADMASS
ADMITS
ADOBES
ADONIS
ADOPTS
ADORES
ADORNS
ADULTS
AEETES
AENEAS
AEOLUS
AERIES
AFLATS
AFRITS
AGAMAS
AGATES
AGAVES
AGENAS
AGENTS
AGGIES
AGGROS
AGLETS
AGORAS
AGREES
AIDERS
AILERS
AIRBUS
AISLES
AKELAS
AKENES
AKITAS
ALAMOS
ALANIS
ALARMS
ALBUMS
ALDERS
ALDOUS
ALEPHS
ALERTS
ALEUTS
ALEXIS
ALIBIS
ALIENS
ALIGNS
ALINES
ALKYDS
ALKYLS
ALLAYS
ALLEES
ALLEYS
ALLIES
ALLOTS
ALLOWS
ALLOYS
ALOHAS
ALOINS
ALPHAS
ALTARS
ALTERS
ALTIUS
ALWAYS
AMADIS
AMATIS
AMAZES
AMBERS
AMBITS
AMBLES
AMEBAS
AMEERS
AMENDS
AMENTS
AMICES
AMICUS
AMIDES
AMIENS
AMIGAS
AMIGOS
AMINES
AMINUS
AMOLES
AMOURS
AMPULS
AMUSES
AMVETS
ANDRES
ANDROS
ANELES
ANGELS
ANGERS
ANGLES
ANGLOS
ANIMAS
ANIMES
ANIMUS
ANIONS
ANJOUS
ANKLES
ANNALS
ANNOYS
ANNULS
ANODES
ANOLES
ANTICS
ANTRES
ANUBIS
ANVILS
AODAIS
AORTAS
APEXES
APHIDS
APICES
APPALS
APPLES
APRONS
ARAMIS
ARBORS
ARCCOS
ARCHES
ARDEBS
ARDORS
ARECAS
ARENAS
ARETES
ARGOTS
ARGUES
ARISES
ARLISS
ARMETS
ARMIES
ARMORS
ARNESS
AROIDS
AROMAS
ARRAYS
ARROWS
ARSONS
ARTELS
ARTOIS
ARYANS
ASANAS
ASCOTS
ASDICS
ASIANS
ASIDES
ASKERS
ASPENS
ASPICS
ASSAYS
ASSESS
ASSETS
ASTERS
ASTROS

ATBATS
ATEAMS
ATESTS
ATHENS
ATKINS
ATODDS
ATOLLS
ATONES
ATREUS
ATTARS
ATTICS
AUDENS
AUDIOS
AUDITS
AUGERS
AUGHTS
AUGURS
AUREUS
AUROUS
AUXINS
AVAILS
AVERTS
AVIANS
AVISOS
AVOIDS
AWAITS
AWAKES
AWARDS
AXIOMS
AXIONS
AZIDES
AZINES
AZORES
AZTECS

•AS•••

BASALT
BASELY
BASEST
BASHED
BASHES
BASICS
BASIFY
BASING
BASINS
BASKED
BASKET
BASQUE
BASSES
BASSET
BASSLY
BASSOS
BASTED
BASTER
BASTES
CASABA
CASALS
CASAVA
CASBAH
CASEFY
CASERN
CASHED
CASHES
CASHEW
CASHIN
CASING
CASINO
CASPAR
CASPER
CASQUE
CASSIA
CASSIO
CASSIS
CASTER
CASTES
CASTLE
CASTON
CASTOR
CASTRO
CASUAL
DASHED
DASHER
DASHES
DASHIS
DASSIN
EASEIN
EASELS
EASEUP
EASIER
EASILY
EASING
EASTER
EASTON
FASCES
FASCIA
FASTED
FASTEN
FASTER
GASBAG
GASCAP
GASCON
GASHED
GASHES
GASIFY
GASJET
GASKET
GASKIN
GASLIT
GASLOG
GASMAN
GASMEN
GASPAR
GASPED
GASPER
GASSED
GASSER
GASSES
GASTON
GASTRO
HASBRO
HASHED
HASHES
HASPED
HASSAM
HASSAN
HASSLE
HASTEN
HASTES
JASCHA
JASEYS
JASPER
KASBAH
KASDAN
LASCAR
LASERS
LASHED
LASHER
LASHES
LASHIO
LASHUP
LASSEN
LASSER
LASSES
LASSIE
LASSOS
LASTED
LASTEX
LASTLY
MASADA
MASAIS
MASCOT
MASERS
MASERU
MASHED
MASHER
MASHES
MASHIE
MASKED
MASKER
MASONS
MASQUE
MASSED
MASSES
MASSEY
MASSIF
MASTER
MASTIC
NASALS
NASCAR
NASDAQ
NASEBY
NASHUA
NASSAU
NASSER
PASCAL
PASEOS
PASHAS
PASHTO
PASSBY
PASSED
PASSEL
PASSER
PASSES
PASSIM
PASSON
PASSUP
PASTAS
PASTED
PASTEL
PASTES
PASTIS
PASTOR
PASTRY
RASCAL
RASERS
RASHAD
RASHER
RASHES
RASHID
RASHLY
RASING
RASPED
RASPER
RASSLE
RASTER
SASEBO
SASHAY
SASHED
SASHES
SASSED
SASSER
SASSES
TASERS
TASKED
TASMAN
TASSEL
TASSES
TASTED
TASTER
TASTES
VASHTI
VASLAV
VASSAL
VASSAR
VASTER
VASTLY
WASABI
WASHED
WASHER
WASHES
WASHOE
WASHUP
WASTED
WASTER
WASTES
YASSER

•A•S••

BABSON
BAGSIT
BALSAM
BASSES
BASSET
BASSLY
BASSOS
CAESAR
CAPSID
CARSON
CASSIA
CASSIO
CASSIS
CATSUP
CAUSAL
CAUSED
CAUSES
DAISES
DAMSEL
DAMSON
DAMSUP
DANSON
DASSIN
DATSUN
DAWSON
EATSAT
EATSIN
EATSUP
FAISAL
FALSER
GARSON
GASSED
GASSER
GASSES
GATSBY
HALSEY
HANSEL
HANSOM
HANSON
HASSAM
HASSAN
HASSLE
HAUSAS
HAWSER
HAWSES
JAMSIN
JAMSUP
JANSEN
JANSKY
KAISER
KANSAN
KANSAS
KARSTS
LANSON
LAPSED
LAPSES
LAPSUP
LARSEN
LARSON
LASSEN
LASSER
LASSES
LASSIE
LASSOS
LAWSON
LAYSBY
LAYSIN
LAYSON
LAYSTO
LAYSUP
MADSEN
MAISIE
MANSES
MARSHA
MARSHY
MASSED
MASSES
MASSEY
MASSIF
MAUSER
NANSEN
NASSAU
NASSER
NAUSEA
NAYSAY
PAISAS
PARSEC
PARSED
PARSEE
PARSER
PARSES
PARSON
PASSBY
PASSED
PASSEL
PASSER
PASSES
PASSIM
PASSON
PASSUP
PAUSED
PAUSES
PAWSAT
PAYSIN
PAYSON
PAYSUP
RAISED
RAISER
RAISES
RAISIN
RAMSAY
RAMSES
RAMSEY
RAMSON
RANSOM
RASSLE
RATSON
SALSAS
SAMSON
SANSEI
SASSED
SASSER
SASSES
SAYSOS
TAGSUP
TARSAL
TARSUS
TASSEL
TASSES
VAISYA
VASSAL
VASSAR
WADSUP
WAISTS
WARSAW
WATSON
WAUSAU
YASSER

•A••S•

BANISH
BAREST
BARISH
BASEST
CALASH
CAMISE
CARESS
CARUSO
CAYUSE
DALASI
DAMASK
DANISH
FAMISH
GAINST
GALOSH
GAMEST
GARISH
GAYEST
HALEST
HARASS
HAVASU
JADISH
KAROSS
LAGASH
LAMESA
LAMEST
LANOSE
LAOTSE
LAROSA
LATEST
LATISH
LAVISH
LAXEST
MAOISM
MAOIST
MARISA
MARISH
MARIST
OAFISH
PALEST
PALISH
PARISH
RADISH
RAKISH
RAMOSE
RAREST
RAVISH
RAWEST
RAWISH
SAFEST
SAGEST
SALISH
SAMOSA
SANEST
TALESE
TAMEST
TANIST
TAOISM
TAOIST
VADOSE
VALISE
VANISH
VARESE
WABASH
WALESA
WATUSI
YAREST

•A•••S

BABELS
BABIES
BABKAS
BABULS
BACKUS
BADGES
BAGELS
BAINES
BAIRNS
BAIZAS
BAKERS
BALERS
BANJOS
BANTUS
BARGES
BARNES
BARONS
BARRES
BARRIS
BASHES
BASICS
BASINS
BASSES
BASSOS
BASTES
BATHES
BATHOS
BATIKS
BATONS
BAUCIS
BAULKS
BAYOUS
CABALS
CABERS
CABINS
CABLES
CACAOS
CACHES
CACTUS
CADDIS
CADETS
CADGES
CADMUS
CADRES
CAGERS
CAGUAS
CAHOWS
CAICOS
CAIRNS
CAJUNS
CALAIS
CALCES
CALLAS
CALLES
CALLUS
CALVES
CALXES
CAMELS
CAMEOS
CAMPOS
CAMPUS
CANALS
CANERS
CANIDS
CANNES
CANOES
CANONS
CANTOS
CANVAS
CAPERS
CAPIAS
CAPONS
CAPRIS
CARATS
CARBOS
CARESS
CARETS
CARGOS
CARIBS
CARIES
CARLOS
CARNES
CAROBS
CAROLS
CAROMS
CARPUS
CARTES
CARVES
CASALS
CASHES
CASSIS
CASTES
CATERS
CAUCUS
CAULKS
CAUSES
CAVERS
CAVILS
DACHAS
DADOES
DAISES
DALLAS
DALLES
DANAUS
DANCES
DANTES
DARIUS
DASHES
DASHIS
DATERS
DAUBES
DAUNTS
DAVIES
DAVITS
EAGLES
EAGRES
EASELS
EATERS
FABLES
FACETS
FACIAS
FACIES
FAGOTS
FAINTS
FAITHS
FAKERS
FAKIRS
FALCES
FAMOUS
FANONS
FARADS
FARCES
FARERS
FASCES
FATWAS
FAUCES
FAULTS
FAUNAS
FAUNUS
FAVORS
FAWKES
GABIES
GABLES
GAFFES
GALAHS
GALOIS
GALOPS
GAMAYS
GAMINS
GAMMAS
GAMUTS
GANGES
GAPERS
GARTHS
GASHES
GASSES
GATERS
GATORS
GAUGES
GAUZES
GAVELS
GAYALS
HABEAS
HABITS
HACEKS
HADJES
HADJIS
HAGGIS
HAIDAS
HAIKUS
HAINES
HAJJES
HAJJIS
HAKIMS
HALERS
HALLOS
HALOES
HALVES
HAMALS
HAOLES
HARASS
HAREMS

HARRIS
HASHES
HASTES
HATERS
HAULMS
HAUNTS
HAUSAS
HAVENS
HAVERS
HAVOCS
HAWSES
HAZANS
HAZELS
HAZERS
JABOTS
JACALS
JAMUPS
JANHUS
JAPANS
JAPERS
JASEYS
JAUNTS
JAURES
JAZZES
KABOBS
KAFIRS
KANSAS
KAPPAS
KARATS
KAROSS
KARRAS
KARSTS
KAUNAS
KAURIS
KAYAKS
KAZAKS
KAZOOS
LABELS
LABORS
LACERS
LACHES
LADERS
LADIES
LADLES
LAGERS
LAIRDS
LAKERS
LAMEDS
LAMIAS
LAMMAS
LANAIS
LANCES
LANDIS
LAPELS
LAPINS
LAPSES
LARAMS
LARGES
LARGOS
LARVAS
LASERS
LASHES
LASSES
LASSOS
LATENS
LATHES
LATINS
LATKES
LAUGHS
LAVERS
LAYBYS
LAYERS
LAYUPS
MACAWS
MACHES
MACHOS
MACROS
MADAMS
MADRAS
MADRES
MAGMAS
MAGNUS
MAHDIS
MAIDUS
MAILES
MAIZES
MAJLIS
MAJORS
MAKERS
MALAYS
MAMBAS
MAMBOS
MAMMAS
MANAUS
MANGOS
MANIAS
MANORS
MANSES
MANTAS
MANTIS
MAORIS
MAPLES
MAQUIS
MARCOS
MARCUS
MARGES
MARIUS
MASAIS
MASERS
MASHES
MASONS
MASSES
MATERS
MATEYS
MATHIS
MATINS
MATTES
MATZOS
MAUVES
MAVENS
MAXIMS
MAYANS
MAYBES
MAYORS
MAZERS
NABOBS
NABORS
NACHOS
NACRES
NADIRS
NAIADS
NAIRAS
NAMERS
NANTES
NAPLES
NAPPES
NASALS
NAVELS
NAVIES
NAWABS
OATERS
PACERS
PADRES
PAEANS
PAEONS
PAGANS
PAGERS
PAINTS
PAISAS
PALLAS
PALMAS
PALPUS
PAMIRS
PAMPAS
PANDAS
PANELS
PANICS
PANNES
PANTOS
PAPAWS
PAPERS
PAPPAS
PAPPUS
PARENS
PARERS
PARKAS
PARNIS
PARRIS
PARSES
PARVIS
PASEOS
PASHAS
PASSES
PASTAS
PASTES
PASTIS
PATENS
PATERS
PATHOS
PATIOS
PATMOS
PATOIS
PAUCIS
PAUSES
PAVERS
PAWERS
PAYEES
PAYERS
QANTAS
RABBIS
RABIES
RACERS
RACHIS
RACONS
RADIOS
RADIUS
RAINES
RAISES
RAJAHS
RAKERS
RAMETS
RAMIES
RAMOUS
RAMSES
RANEES
RANGES
RANIDS
RAPIDS
RASERS
RASHES
RATELS
RATERS
RATIOS
RAVELS
RAVENS
RAVERS
RAYONS
RAZORS
RAZZES
SABERS
SABINS
SABLES
SABOTS
SABRAS
SABRES
SADHES
SADHUS
SAHIBS
SAIGAS
SAINTS
SAKERS
SALADS
SALALS
SALONS
SALSAS
SALVES
SALVOS
SAMBAS
SANTOS
SAPORS
SARANS
SARDIS
SARGES
SARGOS
SARODS
SASHES
SASSES
SATINS
SATYRS
SAUCES
SAUDIS
SAULTS
SAUNAS
SAUTES
SAVERS
SAVORS
SAXONS
SAYERS
SAYLES
SAYSOS
SAYYES
TABLAS
TABLES
TABOOS
TABORS
TAIGAS
TAINOS
TAINTS
TAKERS
TAKINS
TALERS
TALONS
TAMERS
TAMILS
TANGOS
TANKAS
TANTES
TAPERS
TAPINS
TAPIRS
TARGES
TAROTS
TARSUS
TASERS
TASSES
TASTES
TATARS
TATERS
TAUNTS
TAUONS
TAUPES
TAURUS
TAXERS
TAXIES
TAYRAS
TAZZAS
VALENS
VALETS
VALOIS
VALUES
VALVES
VAPORS
VARIES
VARNAS
VAULTS
VAUNTS
WACKOS
WADERS
WAFERS
WAGERS
WAGONS
WAHOOS
WAISTS
WAIVES
WAKENS
WALERS
WALLIS
WALRUS
WANERS
WASHES
WASTES
WATERS
WAVERS
WAXERS
WAYANS
YACHTS
YAHOOS
YAKUTS
YALIES
YAPOKS
YAQUIS
ZAIRES
ZAMIAS
ZANIES
ZAYINS
ZAZENS

••AS••

ABASED
ABASES
AGASSI
ALASKA
BEASTS
BIASED
BIASES
BLASTS
BOASTS
BRASHY
BRASOV
BRASSY
CEASED
CEASES
CHASED
CHASER
CHASES
CHASMS
CHASSE
CHASTE
CLASPS
CLASSY
COASTS
DEASIL
ERASED
ERASER
ERASES
FEASTS
FIASCO
FLASHY
FLASKS
FRASER
GLASER
GLASSY
GRASPS
GRASSO
GRASSY
ITASCA
KRASNY
LEASED
LEASER
LEASES
MEASLY
MIASMA
NYASSA
OCASEK
OCASEY
OMASUM
PHASED
PHASER
PHASES
PLASHY
PLASMA
PLASMO
PLASTY
PRASES
QUASAR
REASON
ROASTS
SEASON
SHASTA
SOASTO
SPASMS
STASES
STASIS
TEASED
TEASEL
TEASER
TEASES
TEASET
TOASTS
TOASTY
TRASHY
UKASES
UPASES
WEASEL
WRASSE
YEASTS
YEASTY

••A•S•

AGASSI
BLAISE
BRAISE
BRASSY
BRATSK
CHAISE
CHASSE
CLASSY
CLAUSE
COARSE
ELAPSE
FRAISE
GDANSK
GLASSY
GRASSO
GRASSY
HEARST
HOARSE
LIAISE
NYASSA
PRAISE
SPARSE
URALSK
WRASSE
ZSAZSA

••A••S

ABACAS
ABACUS
ABASES
ABATES
ABATIS
ACARUS
ADAGES
ADAPTS
AGAMAS
AGATES
AGAVES
ALAMOS
ALANIS
ALARMS
AMADIS
AMATIS
AMAZES
ARAMIS
ASANAS
AVAILS
AWAITS
AWAKES
AWARDS
BEANOS
BEARDS
BEASTS
BEAUTS
BEAVIS
BIASES
BLACKS
BLADES
BLAMES
BLANKS
BLARES
BLASTS
BLAZES
BOARDS
BOASTS
BRACES
BRACTS
BRAHMS
BRAIDS
BRAILS
BRAINS
BRAKES
BRANDS
BRANTS
BRAVAS
BRAVES
BRAVOS
BRAWLS
BRAZES
BRAZOS
BWANAS
CEASES
CHAFES
CHAFFS
CHAINS
CHAIRS
CHALKS
CHAMPS
CHANTS
CHARMS
CHARTS
CHASES
CHASMS
CLACKS
CLAIMS
CLAMPS
CLANGS
CLANKS
CLAROS
CLASPS
CLAVES
COAPTS
COASTS
COATIS
COAXES
CRACKS
CRAFTS
CRAKES
CRAMPS
CRANES
CRANKS
CRAPES
CRATES
CRAVES
CRAWLS
CRAZES
DMARKS
DRAFTS
DRAILS
DRAINS
DRAKES
DRAMAS
DRAPES
DRAWLS
DWARFS
EDAMES
ELANDS
ELATES
EMAILS
ENACTS
ENATES
ERASES
ETAPES
EVADES
EXACTS
EXALTS
FEASTS
FLACKS
FLAILS
FLAIRS
FLAKES
FLAMES
FLANKS
FLARES
FLASKS
FLAXES
FRACAS
FRAMES
FRANCS
FRANKS
FRAUDS
GHAINS
GHAZIS
GIANTS
GLACES
GLACIS
GLADES
GLADYS
GLAIRS
GLANDS
GLARES
GLAZES
GNARLS
GRACES
GRADES
GRADUS
GRAFTS
GRAILS
GRAINS
GRAMAS
GRAMPS
GRANDS
GRANTS
GRAPES
GRAPHS
GRASPS
GRATES
GRATIS
GRAVES
GRAZES
GUACOS
GUARDS
GUAVAS
HEARTS
HEATHS
HEAVES
HIATUS
HOARDS
HOAXES
HYADES
ICARUS
IMAGES
IRANIS
IRAQIS
KHAKIS
KIANGS
KNACKS
KNAVES
KOALAS
KRAALS
KRAITS
KYACKS
LEARNS
LEASES
LEAVES
LIANAS
LIANES
LIANGS
LLAMAS
LLANOS
LOAVES

NYALAS
OKAPIS
OMAHAS
OMANIS
ORACHS
ORALES
ORANGS
ORANTS
ORATES
OSAGES
OXALIS
OZARKS
PEARLS
PHAGES
PHAROS
PHASES
PIANOS
PLACES
PLAGES
PLAIDS
PLAINS
PLAITS
PLANES
PLANKS
PLANTS
PLATES
PLAYAS
PLAZAS
PRANGS
PRANKS
PRASES
PRATES
PRAWNS
PRAXES
PRAXIS
PSALMS
QUACKS
QUAFFS
QUAILS
QUAKES
QUALMS
QUARKS
QUARTS
REACTS
REAIMS
REAIRS
REALES
REALMS
REARMS
REATAS
RHAMES
RIATAS
ROASTS
RUANAS
SCALDS
SCALES
SCALPS
SCAMPS
SCANTS
SCAPES
SCARES
SCARFS
SCARPS
SCAUPS
SEAMUS
SHACKS
SHADES
SHAFTS
SHAKES
SHAKOS
SHALES
SHAMES
SHAMUS
SHANKS
SHAPES
SHARDS
SHARES
SHARKS
SHARPS
SHAVES
SHAWLS
SHAWMS
SKALDS
SKANKS
SKATES
SLACKS
SLAKES
SLANGS
SLANTS
SLATES
SLAVES
SMACKS
SMALLS
SMARTS
SNACKS
SNAFUS
SNAILS
SNAKES
SNARES
SNARLS
SNATHS
SOARES
SOAVES
SPACES
SPADES
SPAHIS
SPALLS
SPANKS
SPARES
SPARKS
SPASMS
SPATES
SPAWNS
STACKS
STAFFS
STAGES
STAINS
STAIRS
STAKES
STALES
STALKS
STALLS
STAMPS
STANDS
STAPES
STARES
STARTS
STASES
STASIS
STATES
STATUS
STAVES
SWAGES
SWAINS
SWALES
SWAMIS
SWAMPS
SWANKS
SWARDS
SWARMS
SWATHS
SWAZIS
TEASES
THALES
THAMES
THANES
THANKS
THATIS
TIARAS
TOASTS
TRACES
TRACKS
TRACTS
TRADES
TRAILS
TRAINS
TRAITS
TRAMPS
TRAVES
TRAVIS
TRAWLS
TWANGS
UKASES
UNARMS
UPASES
URAEUS
URANUS
USAGES
VIANDS
WEAVES
WHACKS
WHALES
WHANGS
WHARFS
WRACKS
WRATHS
YEARNS
YEASTS

•••AS•

ADMASS
AGHAST
ALEAST
ATEASE
ATLAST
BREAST
BYPASS
BYPAST
CALASH
CREASE
CREASY
DALASI
DAMASK
DEBASE
DYNAST
ELPASO
EMDASH
ENCASE
ENDASH
GOEASY
GREASE
GREASY
HARASS
HAVASU
INCASE
INCASH
KUVASZ
LAGASH
LIPASE
MORASS
MUFASA
NLEAST
OBLAST
PHRASE
PLEASE
POTASH
QUEASY
RECAST
REHASH
REPAST
REWASH
SIWASH
SPLASH
SQUASH
STRASS
THRASH
UNCASE
UNEASE
UNEASY
UNLASH
UNMASK
UPCAST
WABASH
ZYMASE

•••A•S

ABRAMS
ADDAMS
ADMASS
AFLATS
ALLAYS
ALTARS
ALWAYS
ANNALS
AODAIS
APPALS
ARRAYS
ARYANS
ASIANS
ASSAYS
ATBATS
ATEAMS
ATTARS
AVIANS
BELAYS
BLEARS
BLEATS
BLOATS
BOYARS
BREADS
BREAKS
BREAMS
BRIANS
BRIARS
BROADS
BYLAWS
BYPASS
BYWAYS
CABALS
CACAOS
CALAIS
CANALS
CARATS
CASALS
CEDARS
CHEATS
CHIAUS
CIGARS
CLEANS
CLEARS
CLEATS
CLOAKS
COPAYS
CORALS
CREAKS
CREAMS
CROAKS
CROATS
CYCADS
DANAUS
DEBARS
DECAFS
DECALS
DECAYS
DEFATS
DELAYS
DINARS
DIVANS
DORAGS
DREADS
DREAMS
DRYADS
DUCATS
EBOATS
ECLATS
EDGARS
EFLATS
EMBAYS
EPHAHS
EQUALS
ESSAYS
FARADS
FINALS
FLOATS
FORAYS
FREAKS
FRIARS
GALAHS
GAMAYS
GAYALS
GERAHS
GLEAMS
GLEANS
GLOATS
GORALS
GREATS
GROANS
GROATS
GULAGS
HAMALS
HARASS
HAZANS
HBEAMS
HEXADS
HODADS
HOGANS
HUMANS
IBEAMS
IDEALS
IDTAGS
INCANS
INLAWS
INLAYS
IOWANS
JACALS
JAPANS
JIHADS
JONAHS
JURATS
KARATS
KAYAKS
KAZAKS
KEBABS
KNEADS
KORATS
KOVACS
KRAALS
KULAKS
LANAIS
LARAMS
LEGALS
LEMANS
LILACS
LOCALS
LOTAHS
MACAWS
MADAMS
MALAYS
MANAUS
MASAIS
MAYANS
MEDALS
METALS
MOLARS
MONADS
MORALS
MORASS
MORAYS
MURALS
MYNAHS
NAIADS
NASALS
NAWABS
NOMADS
OBEAHS
OCEANS
OCTADS
OGHAMS
OREADS
ORGANS
OSCARS
PAEANS
PAGANS
PAPAWS
PECANS
PEDALS
PETALS
PHIALS
PILAFS
PIPALS
PISANS
PLEADS
PLEATS
PROAMS
PTRAPS
RAJAHS
REBAGS
REBARS
RECAPS
REHABS
RELAYS
REMANS
REMAPS
REPADS
REPAYS
RESAWS
RETAGS
RETAPS
RETARS
RIVALS
RIYALS
ROMANS
ROYALS
SALADS
SALALS
SARANS
SCRAGS
SCRAMS
SCRAPS
SEDANS
SEPALS
SERACS
SERAIS
SHEAFS
SHEARS
SHOALS
SHOATS
SISALS
SITARS
SKEANS
SKOALS
SMEARS
SNEAKS
SOLANS
SOLARS
SPEAKS
SPEARS
SPLATS
SPLAYS
SPRAGS
SPRATS
SPRAYS
SQUABS
SQUADS
SQUATS
STEADS
STEAKS
STEALS
STEAMS
STOATS
STRADS
STRAPS
STRASS
STRAUS
STRAWS
STRAYS
SUGARS
SUMACS
SURAHS
SWEARS
SWEATS
TATARS
TEPALS
TEXANS
TICALS
TILAKS
TITANS
TOKAYS
TORAHS
TOTALS
TREADS
TREATS
TRIADS
TRIALS
TWEAKS
UBOATS
UCLANS
UGGAMS
UHLANS
UMIAKS
UNBARS
UNCAPS
UNIATS
UNJAMS
UNMANS
UNSAYS
URIALS
USUALS
VEGANS
VICARS
VITALS
VOCALS
VOLANS
WAYANS
WHEALS
WHEATS
WREAKS

••••AS

ABACAS
ACTSAS
ADIDAS
AENEAS
AGAMAS
AGENAS
AGORAS
AKELAS
AKITAS
ALOHAS
ALPHAS
AMEBAS
AMIGAS
ANIMAS
AORTAS
ARECAS
ARENAS
AROMAS
ASANAS
BABKAS
BAIZAS
BETTAS
BIOGAS
BIOTAS
BOREAS
BRAVAS
BURGAS
BURSAS
BWANAS
CAGUAS
CALLAS
CANVAS
CAPIAS
CEIBAS
CESTAS
CHELAS
COBIAS
COBRAS
COCOAS
COMMAS
CONGAS
COSTAS
COTTAS
CUPPAS
CYCLAS
DACHAS
DALLAS
DEBRAS
DELTAS
DOBLAS
DOBRAS
DOGMAS
DOLMAS
DONNAS
DORCAS
DRAMAS
ESDRAS
EXTRAS
FACIAS
FATWAS
FAUNAS
FELLAS
FERIAS
FESTAS
FLORAS
FORTAS
FOSSAS
FRACAS
GAMMAS
GRAMAS
GUAVAS
HABEAS
HAIDAS
HAUSAS
HELLAS
HENNAS
HOOHAS
HOSTAS
HUZZAS
HYDRAS
HYENAS
JUNTAS
KANSAS
KAPPAS
KARRAS
KAUNAS
KIOWAS
KOALAS
LAMIAS
LAMMAS
LARVAS
LEHUAS
LEMMAS
LIANAS
LLAMAS
LOOFAS
MADRAS
MAGMAS
MAMBAS
MAMMAS
MANIAS
MANTAS
MECCAS
MEDIAS
MENSAS
MILPAS
MOCHAS
MOMMAS
MUDRAS
MULLAS
NAIRAS
NINJAS
NORIAS
NYALAS
OMAHAS
OMEGAS
OPERAS
PAISAS
PALLAS
PALMAS
PAMPAS

PANDAS
PAPPAS
PARKAS
PASHAS
PASTAS
PIETAS
PINNAS
PIZZAS
PLAYAS
PLAZAS
POLKAS
POPPAS
QANTAS
QUOTAS
REATAS
REINAS
RIATAS
RIOJAS
RUANAS
RUMBAS
SABRAS
SAIGAS
SALSAS
SAMBAS
SAUNAS
SCENAS
SCHWAS
SCUBAS
SENNAS
SEPIAS
SIGMAS
SILVAS
SOLFAS
SPICAS
STOMAS
STUPAS
SUCHAS
SUCKAS
SUDRAS
SUMMAS
SUTRAS
TABLAS
TAIGAS
TANKAS
TAYRAS
TAZZAS
TESLAS
TETRAS
THETAS
THOMAS
THUJAS
TIARAS
TIBIAS
TOBIAS
TOKLAS
UINTAS
ULTRAS
UMBRAS
UNITAS
UVULAS
VARNAS
VESTAS
VILLAS
VIOLAS
VISTAS
VODKAS
VOLVAS
XHOSAS
YENTAS
YUCCAS
ZAMIAS
ZEBRAS

AT••••

ATAMAN
ATBATS
ATBEST
ATCOST
ATEAMS
ATEASE
ATEMPO
ATEOUT
ATERGO
ATESTS
ATHAND
ATHENA
ATHENE
ATHENS
ATHOME
ATKINS
ATLAST
ATLATL
ATMOST
ATODDS
ATOLLS
ATOMIC
ATONAL
ATONCE
ATONED
ATONES
ATONIC
ATREST
ATREUS
ATRIAL
ATRISK
ATRIUM
ATSTUD
ATTACH
ATTACK
ATTAIN
ATTARS
ATTEND
ATTEST
ATTHAT
ATTICA
ATTICS
ATTILA
ATTIRE
ATTLEE
ATTRIT
ATTUNE
ATWILL
ATWOOD
ATWORK

A•T•••

ACTIII
ACTING
ACTINO
ACTION
ACTIUM
ACTIVE
ACTONE
ACTORS
ACTOUT
ACTSAS
ACTSON
ACTSUP
ACTTWO
ACTUAL
AETHER
ALTAIC
ALTAIR
ALTARS
ALTERS
ALTHEA
ALTIMA
ALTIUS
ALTMAN
AMTRAC
AMTRAK
ANTCOW
ANTEED
ANTERO
ANTEUP
ANTHEM
ANTHER
ANTICS
ANTLER
ANTONY
ANTRES
ANTRIM
ANTRON
ANTRUM
APTEST
ARTELS
ARTERY
ARTFUL
ARTGUM
ARTHRO
ARTHUR
ARTIER
ARTILY
ARTIST
ARTOIS
ARTURO
ASTERN
ASTERS
ASTRAL
ASTRAY
ASTRID
ASTROS
ASTUTE
ATTACH
ATTACK
ATTAIN
ATTARS
ATTEND
ATTEST
ATTHAT
ATTICA
ATTICS
ATTILA
ATTIRE
ATTLEE
ATTRIT
ATTUNE
AUTEUR
AUTHOR
AUTUMN
AZTECS

A••T••

ABATED
ABATES
ABATIS
ACETAL
ACETIC
ACETYL
ACTTWO
ADYTUM
AEETES
AGATES
AGATHA
AKITAS
ALATAU
ALATED
ALITER
AMATIS
AMATOL
AMSTEL
AMYTAN
ANATTO
ANITRA
AORTAE
AORTAL
AORTAS
AORTIC
APATHY
ARCTAN
ARCTIC
ARETES
ARETHA
ATSTUD
AUNTIE
AUSTEN
AUSTIN
AUSTRO
AVATAR

A•••T•

ABBOTS
ABBOTT
ABLATE
ABORTS
ACUATE
ACUITY
ADAPTS
ADDSTO
ADEPTS
ADESTE
ADMITS
ADNATE
ADOPTS
ADULTS
AERATE
AFLATS
AFRITS
AGENTS
AGLETS
AGNATE
AGOUTI
AIMSTO
AJANTA
ALCOTT
ALECTO
ALERTS
ALEUTS
ALIOTO
ALLOTS
ALMATY
AMBATO
AMBITS
AMENTS
AMVETS
ANATTO
ANSATE
APLITE
AQUATE
ARGOTS
ARISTA
ARISTO
ARMETS
ARNETT
ASCOTS
ASEITY
ASSETS
ASTUTE
ATBATS
ATESTS
ATLATL
AUDITS
AUGHTS
AVANTI
AVERTS
AVESTA
AVIATE
AWAITS

A••••T

ABBOTT
ABDUCT
ABJECT
ABLAUT
ABLEST
ABRUPT
ABSENT
ACCENT
ACCEPT
ACCOST
ACEOUT
ACQUIT
ACTOUT
ADDUCT
ADJUST
ADRIFT
ADROIT
ADVENT
ADVERT
AFFECT
AFLOAT
AFREET
AGEIST
AGHAST
AGLINT
AGOROT
AIGRET
AIMSAT
AIROUT
AJFOYT
ALBEIT
ALBERT
ALCOTT
ALEAST
ALHIRT
ALIGHT
ALLBUT
ALLOUT
ALLSET
ALLWET
ALMOST
ALPERT
ALWEST
AMIDST
AMOUNT
AMULET
ANKLET
ANNUIT
ANOINT
AORIST
APPLET
APTEST
ARAFAT
ARARAT
ARDENT
ARENDT
ARGENT
ARIGHT
ARMLET
ARMPIT
ARNETT
ARPENT
ARRANT
ARREST
ARTIST
ASCENT
ASKOUT
ASLANT
ASPECT
ASSENT
ASSERT
ASSIST
ASSORT
ATBEST
ATCOST
ATEOUT
ATLAST
ATMOST
ATREST
ATTEST
ATTHAT
ATTRIT
AUFAIT
AUGUST
AUKLET
AULAIT
AUMONT
AVAUNT
AVOCET

•AT•••

BATAAN
BATBOY
BATEAU
BATHED
BATHER
BATHES
BATHOS
BATIKS
BATING
BATMAN
BATMEN
BATONS
BATTED
BATTEL
BATTEN
BATTER
BATTLE
BATTUE
BATUMI
BATYAM
CATCHY
CATENA
CATERS
CATGUT
CATHAY
CATHER
CATION
CATKIN
CATNAP
CATNIP
CATRIG
CATSUP
CATTED
CATTLE
CATTON
DATARY
DATERS
DATING
DATIVE
DATONG
DATSUN
DATURA
EATERS
EATERY
EATING
EATOUT
EATSAT
EATSIN
EATSUP
FATALE
FATCAT
FATHER
FATHOM
FATIMA
FATTED
FATTEN
FATTER
FATWAS
GATEAU
GATERS
GATHER
GATING
GATLIN
GATORS
GATSBY
HATARI
HATBOX
HATERS
HATFUL
HATHOR
HATING
HATPIN
HATRED
HATTED
HATTER
HATTIE
IATRIC
KATHIE
KATMAI
LATEEN
LATELY
LATENE
LATENS
LATENT
LATEST
LATHED
LATHER
LATHES
LATIGO
LATINA
LATINI
LATINO
LATINS
LATISH
LATIUM
LATKES
LATONA
LATOUR
LATOYA
LATTEN
LATTER
LATVIA
MATERS
MATEYS
MATHER
MATHIS
MATING
MATINS
MATLIN
MATRIX
MATRON
MATTEA
MATTED
MATTEL
MATTER
MATTES
MATTIE
MATURE
MATZOH
MATZOS
NATANT
NATHAN
NATICK
NATION
NATIVE
NATRON
NATTER
NATURA
NATURE
OATERS
OATIER
PATACA
PATCHY
PATENS
PATENT
PATERS
PATHAN
PATHOL
PATHOS
PATINA
PATINE
PATIOS
PATMOS
PATOIS
PATROL
PATRON
PATTED
PATTEN
PATTER
PATTON
QATARI
RATEDG
RATEDR
RATEDX
RATELS
RATERS
RATHER
RATIFY
RATINE
RATING
RATION
RATIOS
RATITE
RATLIN
RATSON
RATTAN
RATTED
RATTER
RATTLE
RATTLY
SATANG
SATEEN
SATING
SATINS
SATINY
SATIRE
SATORI
SATOUT
SATRAP
SATURN
SATYRS
TATAMI
TATARS
TATERS
TATTED
TATTER
TATTLE
TATTOO
VATFUL
VATTED
WATERS
WATERY
WATNEY
WATSON
WATTLE
WATUSI

•A•T••

BAITED
BALTIC
BANTAM
BANTER
BANTUS
BARTAB
BARTER
BARTOK
BARTON
BASTED
BASTER
BASTES
BATTED
BATTEL
BATTEN
BATTER
BATTLE
BATTUE
BAXTER
CACTUS
CAFTAN
CANTAB
CANTED
CANTER
CANTHI
CANTLE
CANTON
CANTOR
CANTOS
CAPTAN
CAPTOR
CARTED
CARTEL
CARTER
CARTES
CARTON
CASTER
CASTES
CASTLE
CASTON

CASTOR
CASTRO
CATTED
CATTLE
CATTON
CAXTON
DACTYL
DAFTER
DAFTLY
DALTON
DANTES
DANTON
DARTED
DARTER
DAYTON
EARTHA
EARTHY
EASTER
EASTON
FACTOR
FAITHS
FALTER
FANTAN
FASTED
FASTEN
FASTER
FATTED
FATTEN
FATTER
GAITED
GAITER
GANTRY
GARTER
GARTHS
GASTON
GASTRO
HAFTED
HALTED
HALTER
HASTEN
HASTES
HATTED
HATTER
HATTIE
KANTOR
LACTIC
LAOTSE
LAOTZU
LAPTEV
LAPTOP
LASTED
LASTEX
LASTLY
LATTEN
LATTER
LAWTON
MADTOM
MAITAI
MAITRE
MALTED
MALTIN
MANTAS
MANTEL
MANTIC
MANTIS
MANTLE
MANTRA
MANTUA
MAOTAI
MARTEL
MARTEN
MARTHA
MARTIN
MARTYR
MASTER
MASTIC
MATTEA
MATTED
MATTEL
MATTER
MATTES
MATTIE
MAYTAG
NANTES
NATTER
NAUTCH
PALTER
PALTRY
PANTED
PANTOS
PANTRY
PARTED
PARTLY
PARTON
PASTAS
PASTED
PASTEL
PASTES
PASTIS
PASTOR
PASTRY
PATTED
PATTEN
PATTER
PATTON
PAXTON
QANTAS
RAFTED
RAFTER
RAGTAG
RAGTOP
RANTED
RANTER
RAPTLY
RAPTOR
RASTER
RATTAN
RATTED
RATTER
RATTLE
RATTLY
SALTED
SALTEN
SALTER
SALTON
SALTUM
SANTEE
SANTIR
SANTOS
SARTON
SARTRE
SAUTES
TACTIC
TAMTAM
TANTES
TANTRA
TARTAN
TARTAR
TARTER
TARTLY
TASTED
TASTER
TASTES
TATTED
TATTER
TATTLE
TATTOO
TAUTEN
TAUTER
TAUTLY
TAUTOG
VASTER
VASTLY
VATTED
WAFTED
WAITED
WAITER
WAITON
WAITUP
WALTER
WALTON
WANTAD
WANTED
WANTIN
WANTON
WANTTO
WASTED
WASTER
WASTES
WATTLE
XANTHO
ZAFTIG

•A••T•

BALATA
BARITE
CADETS
CAMETO
CANUTE
CAPITA
CAPOTE
CARATS
CARETO
CARETS
CAVETT
CAVITY
DAINTY
DAKOTA
DALETH
DAMATO
DAMITA
DARETO
DAUNTS
DAVITS
FACETS
FAGOTS
FAINTS
FAJITA
FALLTO
FAULTS
FAULTY
FAWLTY
GAIETY
GALATA
GAMETE
GAMUTS
GARETH
HABITS
HALITE
HAMITE
HAUNTS
JABOTS
JAUNTS
JAUNTY
KARATE
KARATS
KARSTS
LAIDTO
LAKOTA
LANATE
LAPUTA
LAXITY
LAYSTO
MAKUTA
MALATE
MALOTI
MAPUTO
NAMATH
PAINTS
PAINTY
PAIUTE
PALATE
PARETO
PARITY
PASHTO
RABATO
RAMATE
RAMETS
RARITY
RATITE
SABATO
SABOTS
SAFETY
SAINTE
SAINTS
SALUTE
SAMITE
SANCTA
SANGTO
SANITY
SAULTS
SAVATE
TAHITI
TAINTS
TAKETH
TAKETO
TALKTO
TAROTS
TAUNTS
VACATE
VALETS
VANITY
VASHTI
VAULTS
VAULTY
VAUNTS
WAISTS
WANTTO
WAPITI
WARMTH
YACHTS
YAKUTS
ZAPATA

•A•••T

BADLOT
BAGSIT
BALLET
BALLOT
BANDIT
BARBET
BARDOT
BAREST
BARKAT
BASALT
BASEST
BASKET
BASSET
CACHET
CADENT
CAMEAT
CAMLET
CANLIT
CANNOT
CAPLET
CAPNUT
CARLOT
CARNET
CARNOT
CARPET
CARROT
CATGUT
CAUGHT
CAVEAT
CAVETT
CAVORT
DACOIT
DARENT
DARNIT
DAYLIT
EAGLET
EATOUT
EATSAT
FANJET
FANOUT
FAROUT
FATCAT
FAUCET
GADGET
GAINST
GALOOT
GAMBIT
GAMEST
GANNET
GARNET
GARRET
GASJET
GASKET
GASLIT
GAYEST
HAEMAT
HAIGHT
HALEST
HAMLET
HAVEAT
HAVENT
JACKET
LABRET
LAMENT
LAMEST
LAMONT
LANCET
LAPPET
LARIAT
LATENT
LATEST
LAXEST
LAYOUT
MADEIT
MAGNET
MAHOUT
MAKEIT
MALLET
MAOIST
MARGOT
MARIST
MARKET
MARMOT
MASCOT
MAXOUT
NATANT
NAUGHT
PACKET
PALEST
PALLET
PANDIT
PANOUT
PARENT
PARGET
PARROT
PATENT
PAWSAT
PAYOUT
RABBET
RABBIT
RACKET
RAGOUT
RAILAT
RAJPUT
RAMJET
RANOUT
RAREST
RAWEST
SACHET
SAFEST
SAGEST
SALLET
SALYUT
SAMLET
SANEST
SATOUT
SAVANT
SAWFIT
SAWOUT
TABLET
TAGOUT
TALBOT
TALENT
TALKAT
TAMEST
TANIST
TAOIST
TAPOUT
TAPPET
TARGET
TARPIT
TAUGHT
VACANT
VALENT
VARLET
WALLET
WALNUT
WAYOUT
YAREST

••AT••

ABATED
ABATES
ABATIS
AGATES
AGATHA
ALATAU
ALATED
AMATIS
AMATOL
ANATTO
APATHY
AVATAR
BEATEN
BEATER
BEATIT
BEATLE
BEATON
BEATTY
BEATUP
BLATTY
BOATED
BOATEL
BOATER
BRATSK
BRATTY
CHATTY
CHATUP
COATED
COATIS
CRATED
CRATER
CRATES
DIATOM
ELATED
ELATER
ELATES
ENATES
FEATLY
FLATLY
GNATTY
GOATEE
GRATED
GRATER
GRATES
GRATIA
GRATIN
GRATIS
HEATED
HEATER
HEATHS
HEATHY
HEATUP
HIATAL
HIATUS
IRATER
KEATON
KLATCH
KRATER
LOATHE
MOATED
NEATEN
NEATER
NEATLY
ORATED
ORATES
ORATOR
PHATIC
PLATED
PLATEN
PLATER
PLATES
PLATTE
PRATED
PRATER
PRATES
REATAS
RIATAS
RRATED
SCATHE
SCATTY
SEATED
SEATER
SEATON
SKATED
SKATER
SKATES
SLATED
SLATER
SLATES
SNATCH
SNATHE
SNATHS
SPATES
SPATHE
STATED
STATEN
STATER
STATES
STATIC
STATOR
STATUE
STATUS
SWATCH
SWATHE
SWATHS
THATCH
THATIS
THATLL
TOATEE
WHATIF
WHATLL
WHATVE
WRATHS
WRATHY
XRATED

••A•T•

ADAPTS
AJANTA
ANATTO
AVANTI
AWAITS
BEASTS
BEATTY
BEAUTS
BEAUTY
BHAKTI
BLASTS
BLATTY
BOASTS
BRACTS
BRANTS
BRATTY
CHANTS
CHARTS
CHASTE
CHATTY
COAPTS
COASTS
CRAFTS
CRAFTY
DEARTH
DRAFTS
DRAFTY
DUARTE
ECARTE
ENACTS
EXACTA
EXACTO
EXACTS
EXALTS
FEALTY
FEASTS
GEARTO
GIANTS
GNATTY
GRAFTS
GRANTS
HEALTH
HEARTH
HEARTS
HEARTY
KRAITS
KRANTZ
LEADTO
LEALTY
LEANTO
NEARTO
ORANTS
PLAITS
PLANTE
PLANTS
PLASTY
PLATTE
QUANTA
QUARTO
QUARTS
QUARTZ
REACTS
REALTY
RIALTO
ROASTS
SCANTS
SCANTY
SCATTY
SHAFTS
SHAKTI
SHANTY
SHASTA
SLANTS
SMALTI
SMALTO
SMARTS
SMARTY
SNAPTO
SOASTO
SPARTA
STACTE
STARTS
SWARTH
TOASTS
TOASTY
TRACTS
TRAITS
WEALTH
WRAITH
YEASTS
YEASTY

••A••T

ARAFAT
ARARAT
AVAUNT
BEATIT

BRANDT
CHALET
CLARET
CRAVAT
FLAUNT
GRABAT
HEARST
IMARET
INAPET
INARUT
LEARNT
PEANUT
PIAGET
PLACET
PLAINT
PLANET
PLAYAT
QUAINT
SNAPAT
STABAT
TEAPOT
TEARAT
TEASET
ZEALOT

•••AT•

ABLATE
ACUATE
ADNATE
AERATE
AFLATS
AGNATE
ALMATY
AMBATO
ANSATE
AQUATE
ATBATS
ATLATL
AVIATE
BALATA
BEMATA
BERATE
BINATE
BLEATS
BLOATS
BORATE
BREATH
BYPATH
CARATS
CERATE
CHEATS
CHOATE
CITATO
CLEATS
COMATE
CREATE
CROATS
CURATE
DAMATO
DEBATE
DEFATS
DELATE
DILATE
DONATE
DORATI
DUCATS
EBOATS
ECLATS
EFLATS
EQUATE
ERGATE
ERRATA
ERSATZ
ESTATE
FIXATE
FLOATS
FLOATY
GALATA
GELATI
GELATO
GLOATS
GREATS
GROATS
GYRATE
HECATE
HEMATO
IDEATE
IGNATZ
INMATE
INNATE
IODATE
JURATS
KARATE
KARATS
KORATS
LANATE
LEGATE
LEGATO
LIGATE
LOBATE
LOCATE
LUNATE
LUXATE
MALATE
METATE
MUTATE
MUTATO
NAMATH
NEGATE
NEMATO
NOTATE
NOVATO
NUTATE
OBLATE
OFLATE
OLEATE
OPIATE
ORGATE
ORNATE
OUTATE
PALATE
PEDATE
PILATE
PINATA
PIRATE
PLEATS
POTATO
RABATO
RAMATE
REBATE
REDATE
RELATE
RENATA
RERATE
ROTATE
RUBATI
RUBATO
RUGATE
SABATO
SAVATE
SEDATE
SENATE
SHEATH
SHOATS
SOMATA
SOMATO
SONATA
SPLATS
SPRATS
SQUATS
STOATS
STRATA
STRATI
STRATO
SWEATS
SWEATY
TERATO
TODATE
TOMATO
TREATS
TREATY
TUBATE
UBOATS
UMTATA
UNIATE
UNIATS
UPDATE
VACATE
WHEATS
WREATH
YUKATA
ZAPATA
ZONATE

•••A•T

ABLAUT
AGHAST
ALEAST
ARRANT
ASLANT
ATLAST
AUFAIT
AULAIT
BASALT
BESANT
BEZANT
BOGART
BREAST
BRYANT
BYPAST
CEDANT
COBALT
CONANT
DECANT
DEPART
DESALT
DIDACT
DISANT
DOPANT
DREAMT
DUNANT
DURANT
DYNAST
ENFANT
ENRAPT
ERRANT
EXTANT
GOCART
GOKART
HOBART
IMPACT
IMPART
INFACT
INFANT
INPART
INTACT
KURALT
KUWAIT
LEVANT
MORANT
MOZART
MUTANT
NATANT
NLEAST
OBLAST
OCTANT
ONEACT
OUTACT
OXCART
PEDANT
PLIANT
POPART
RECANT
RECAST
REDACT
REDANT
REPAST
RESALT
SAVANT
SECANT
SEJANT
SONANT
STRAIT
STUART
TENANT
THWART
TRUANT
TYBALT
TYRANT
UMLAUT
UPCAST
UTHANT
VACANT
VIVANT
VOLANT

••••AT

AFLOAT
AIMSAT
ARAFAT
ARARAT
ATTHAT
BARKAT
BOBCAT
CAMEAT
CAVEAT
COMBAT
COMEAT
COMSAT
CRAVAT
DEFEAT
DIKTAT
DOGSAT
EATSAT
FATCAT
FERMAT
FLEWAT
FOGHAT
FORMAT
GETSAT
GOESAT
GRABAT
HAEMAT
HAVEAT
HEPCAT
HEREAT
HINTAT
HISSAT
HOOTAT
JEERAT
JUMPAT
KEEPAT
KEPTAT
KITKAT
KOMBAT
LARIAT
LEERAT
LESTAT
LETSAT
LOOKAT
LOQUAT
LOWFAT
MEDLAT
MUDCAT
MUSCAT
NIPSAT
NONFAT
NOUGAT
NUMBAT
OLDHAT
ORGEAT
OUTEAT
PAWSAT
PECKAT
PEEKAT
PEERAT
PICKAT
PLAYAT
POKEAT
PTBOAT
RAILAT
RECOAT
REDHAT
REGNAT
REHEAT
REPEAT
RESEAT
REXCAT
RUNSAT
SETSAT
SEURAT
SHEVAT
SHOTAT
SNAPAT
SNOCAT
SOTHAT
SOWHAT
STABAT
STOMAT
TALKAT
TEARAT
THREAT
THROAT
TINHAT
TOMCAT
TOPCAT
TOPHAT
TOREAT
UNSEAT
UPBEAT
WENTAT
WINKAT
WOMBAT

AU••••

AUBADE
AUBREY
AUBURN
AUDENS
AUDIAL
AUDILE
AUDIOS
AUDITS
AUDREY
AUFAIT
AUFOND
AUGEAN
AUGEND
AUGERS
AUGHTS
AUGURS
AUGURY
AUGUST
AUKLET
AULAIT
AUMONT
AUNTIE
AUPAIR
AUREUS
AURIFY
AURIGA
AURORA
AUROUS
AUSPEX
AUSSIE
AUSTEN
AUSTIN
AUSTRO
AUTEUR
AUTHOR
AUTUMN
AUXINS

A•U•••

ABUKIR
ABUSED
ABUSER
ABUSES
ACUATE
ACUITY
ACUMEN
ADULTS
AGUISH
AKUAKU
ALULAE
ALULAR
ALUMNA
ALUMNI
AMULET
AMUSED
AMUSES
ANUBIS
ANURAN
AOUDAD
APULIA
AQUATE
AQUILA
AQUINO
ARUBAN
AVULSE

A••U••

ABDUCT
ABJURE
ABLUSH
ABOUND
ABRUPT
ABSURD
ACCUSE
ACQUIT
ACTUAL
ADDUCE
ADDUCT
ADJURE
ADJUST
ADZUKI
AGOUTI
ALBUMS
ALCUIN
ALEUTS
ALLUDE
ALLURE
AMBUSH
AMOUNT
AMOURS
AMPULE
AMPULS
ANNUAL
ANNUIT
ANNULI
ANNULS
ARGUED
ARGUER
ARGUES
ARGUFY
ARJUNA
ARMURE
AROUND
AROUSE
ARTURO
ASBURY
ASSUME
ASSURE
ASTUTE
ATTUNE
AUBURN
AUGURS
AUGURY
AUGUST
AUTUMN
AVAUNT
AVOUCH

A•••U•

ABACUS
ABLAUT
ACARUS
ACCRUE
ACEOUS
ACEOUT
ACESUP
ACINUS
ACTIUM
ACTOUT
ACTSUP
ADDSUP
ADIEUS
ADIEUX
ADYTUM
AEOLUS
AIDFUL
AIMFUL
AIRBUS
AIRGUN
AIROUT
ALARUM
ALDOUS
ALLBUT
ALLIUM
ALLOUT
ALTIUS
AMICUS
AMINUS
ANIMUS
ANJOUS
ANTEUP
ANTRUM
ARBOUR
ARDOUR
ARMFUL
ARMOUR
ARTFUL
ARTGUM
ARTHUR
ASKOUT
ASYLUM
ATEOUT
ATREUS
ATRIUM
ATSTUD
AUREUS
AUROUS
AUTEUR
AVENUE

A••••U

ACAJOU
AKUAKU
ALATAU
AMADOU
APERCU
ARALLU

•AU•••

BAUBLE
BAUCIS
BAULKS
CAUCHO
CAUCHY
CAUCUS
CAUDAL
CAUDEX
CAUDLE
CAUGHT
CAULKS
CAUSAL
CAUSED
CAUSES
DAUBED
DAUBER
DAUBES
DAUNTS
FAUCES
FAUCET
FAULTS
FAULTY
FAUNAE
FAUNAL
FAUNAS
FAUNUS
GAUCHE
GAUCHO
GAUGED
GAUGER
GAUGES
GAUMED
GAUZES
HAULED
HAULER
HAULMS
HAULUP
HAUNCH
HAUNTS
HAUSAS
JAUNTS
JAUNTY
JAURES
KAUNAS
KAUNDA
KAURIS
LAUDED
LAUDER
LAUGHS
LAUNCH
LAUPER
LAUREL
LAUREN
LAURIE
MAULED
MAULER
MAUMAU
MAUMEE
MAUNDY
MAURYA
MAUSER
MAUVES
NAUGHT
NAUSEA
NAUTCH
PAUCIS
PAULEY
PAUNCH
PAUPER
PAUSED
PAUSES
SAUCED
SAUCER
SAUCES
SAUDIS
SAUGER
SAULTS
SAUNAS
SAUREL
SAUTES
TAUGHT
TAUNTS
TAUONS
TAUPES
TAURUS
TAUTEN
TAUTER
TAUTLY
TAUTOG
VAUGHN
VAULTS
VAULTY
VAUNTS
WAUSAU
YAUPON

•A•U••
BABULS
BAGUIO
BAKULA
BARUCH
BATUMI
CAGUAS
CAJUNS
CANUTE
CARUSO
CASUAL
CAYUGA
CAYUSE
DANUBE
DATURA
FACULA
GAMUTS
GAZUMP
JAGUAR
JAMUPS
KABUKI
KAHUNA
LACUNA
LAGUNA
LAPUTA
LAYUPS
LAZULI
MACULA
MADURA
MADURO
MAGUEY
MAKUTA
MANUAL
MANUEL
MAPUTO
MAQUIS
MATURE
MAZUMA
NATURA
NATURE
PADUAN
PAIUTE
PAKULA
PAPUAN
PAQUIN
PARULA
PARURE
RADULA
RAQUEL
SALUKI
SALUTE
SAMUEL
SATURN
TABULA
VACUUM
VAGUER
VALUED
VALUES
VARUNA
WATUSI
YAKUTS
YAKUZA
YAQUIS
ZANUCK

•A••U•
BACKUP
BACKUS
BADGUY
BAGFUL
BALLUP
BANGUI
BANGUP
BANJUL
BANQUO
BANTUS
BARIUM
BARNUM
BARQUE
BARZUN
BASQUE
BATTUE
BAYEUX
BAYOUS
BAYRUM
CACTUS
CADMUS
CAIQUE
CALLUP
CALLUS
CALQUE
CAMEUP
CAMPUS
CANCUN
CANFUL
CAPFUL
CAPGUN
CAPNUT
CARFUL
CARPUS
CASQUE
CATGUT
CATSUP
CAUCUS
DAMOUR
DAMSUP
DANAUS
DARIUS
DATSUN
EARFUL
EASEUP
EATOUT
EATSUP
FACEUP
FAIRUP
FAIYUM
FAMOUS
FANOUT
FAROUK
FAROUT
FAUNUS
FAVOUR
GALLUP
GANGUE
GANGUP
GAVEUP
HAIKUS
HALLUX
HANDUP
HANGUL
HANGUP
HARDUP
HATFUL
HAULUP
JACKUP
JAIPUR
JAMSUP
JANHUS
JARFUL
JAZZUP
KAHLUA
KAILUA
LABOUR
LABRUM
LACEUP
LAIDUP
LAMOUR
LANGUR
LAPFUL
LAPSUP
LARRUP
LASHUP
LATIUM
LATOUR
LAWFUL
LAYOUT
LAYSUP
MACOUN
MADEUP
MAGNUM
MAGNUS
MAHOUT
MAIDUS
MAKEUP
MANAUS
MANFUL
MANQUE
MANTUA
MARAUD
MARCUS
MARDUK
MARIUS
MARKUP
MARQUE
MASQUE
MAXOUT
NASHUA
PABLUM
PACKUP
PAIDUP
PAIRUP
PALPUS
PANFUL
PANOUT
PAPPUS
PASSUP
PAYOUT
PAYSUP
RACKUP
RADIUM
RADIUS
RAGOUT
RAGRUG
RAIPUR
RAJPUT
RAKEUP
RAMOUS
RANGUP
RANOUT
RAVEUP
RAYGUN
SACQUE
SACRUM
SADHUS
SALTUM
SALYUT
SANNUP
SATOUT
SAVEUP
SAVOUR
SAWOUT
TAGOUT
TAGSUP
TAKEUP
TALCUM
TALKUP
TALMUD
TAMMUZ
TANGUY
TANKUP
TAPOUT
TARSUS
TAURUS
VACUUM
VALIUM
VALOUR
VAPOUR
VATFUL
WADSUP
WAITUP
WAKEUP
WALKUP
WALLUP
WALNUT
WALRUS
WAMPUM
WARMUP
WASHUP
WAYOUT
YANQUI

•A•••U
BABALU
BALLOU
BATEAU
CACHOU
GATEAU
HALERU
HAVASU
JABIRU
LANDAU
LAOTZU
MAKALU
MALIBU
MANCHU
MARILU
MASERU
MAUMAU
NASSAU
PAILOU
RAMEAU
WAUSAU
XANADU

••AU••
AVAUNT
BEAUTS
BEAUTY
CLAUDE
CLAUSE
FLAUNT
FRAUDS
FRAUEN
SCAUPS
TRAUMA

••A•U•
ABACUS
ACARUS
ALARUM
BEADUP
BEAMUP
BEARUP
BEATUP
BRAQUE
CHATUP
CLAMUP
CLAQUE
DIALUP
DRAWUP
GEARUP
GRADUS
HEADUP
HEATUP
HIATUS
ICARUS
INARUT
LEADUP
LEAGUE
OMASUM
OPAQUE
PEANUT
PLAGUE
PLAQUE
PLAYUP
PRAGUE
REARUP
RVALUE
SCARUM
SEALUP
SEAMUS
SHAMUS
SLAPUP
SNAFUS
SNAPUP
SOAKUP
STAPUF
STATUE
STATUS
STAYUP
TEACUP
TEAMUP
TEARUP
URAEUS
URANUS
UVALUE
WRAPUP

••A••U
ACAJOU
ALATAU
AMADOU
ARALLU

•••AU•
ABLAUT
BEDAUB
CHIAUS
DANAUS
DEPAUL
DEPAUW
INHAUL
MANAUS
MARAUD
RUPAUL
STPAUL
STRAUB
STRAUS
UMLAUT

•••A•U
AKUAKU
BABALU
DEJAVU
HAVASU
IGUACU
MAKALU
SUBARU
TUVALU
XANADU

••••AU
ALATAU
BATEAU
BISSAU
BUREAU
GATEAU
JUNEAU
LANDAU
MAUMAU
MOLDAU
MOREAU
NASSAU
NIIHAU
RAMEAU
RESEAU
ROSEAU
WAUSAU

AV••••
AVAILS
AVALON
AVANTI
AVATAR
AVAUNT
AVEDON
AVENGE
AVENUE
AVERNO
AVERSE
AVERTS
AVESTA
AVIANS
AVIARY
AVIATE
AVIDLY
AVISOS
AVOCET
AVOIDS
AVOUCH
AVOWAL
AVOWED
AVOWER
AVULSE

A•V•••
ADVENT
ADVERB
ADVERT
ADVICE
ADVISE
AMVETS
ANVILS
ARVADA

A••V••
AGAVES
ALEVEL
ALFVEN
ASEVER

A•••V•
ACTIVE
ALCOVE
ARGIVE
ARRIVE

A••••V
ASIMOV

•AV•••
CAVEAT
CAVEIN
CAVELL
CAVERN
CAVERS
CAVETT
CAVIAR
CAVILS
CAVING
CAVITY
CAVORT
DAVIES
DAVITS
FAVORS
FAVOUR
GAVEIN
GAVELS
GAVEUP
GAVIAL
HAVANA
HAVASU
HAVEAT
HAVENS
HAVENT
HAVEON
HAVERS
HAVING
HAVOCS
JAVARI
JAVIER
KAVNER
LAVABO
LAVAGE
LAVERS
LAVING
LAVISH
MAVENS
NAVAHO
NAVAJO
NAVELS
NAVIES
PAVANE
PAVERS
PAVING
PAVLOV
RAVAGE
RAVELS
RAVENS
RAVERS
RAVEUP
RAVINE
RAVING
RAVISH
SAVAGE
SAVAII
SAVANT
SAVATE
SAVERS
SAVEUP
SAVING
SAVIOR
SAVOIE
SAVOIR
SAVORS
SAVORY
SAVOUR
TAVERN
WAVEIN
WAVERS
WAVERY
WAVIER
WAVILY
WAVING
XAVIER

•A•V••
CALVED
CALVES
CALVIN
CANVAS
CARVED
CARVER
CARVES
CARVEY
GARVEY
HALVAH
HALVED
HALVES
HARVEY
JAYVEE
LANVIN
LARVAE
LARVAL
LARVAS
LATVIA
MARVEL
MARVIN
MAUVES
NARVIK
PARVIS
SALVED
SALVER
SALVES
SALVIA
SALVOR
SALVOS
VALVED
VALVES
WAIVED
WAIVER
WAIVES

•A••V•
CANOVA
CASAVA
DATIVE
HALEVY
NATIVE
PAREVE
SALIVA

•A•••V
KARPOV
LAPTEV
PAVLOV
VACLAV
VASLAV

••AV••
AGAVES
BEAVER
BEAVIS
BRAVAS
BRAVED
BRAVER
BRAVES
BRAVOS
CHAVEZ
CLAVES
CLAVIN
CRAVAT
CRAVED
CRAVEN
CRAVER
CRAVES
FLAVIA
FLAVOR
GRAVED
GRAVEL
GRAVEN
GRAVER
GRAVES
GRAVID
GUAVAS
HEAVED
HEAVEN
HEAVER
HEAVES
KNAVES
LEAVED
LEAVEN
LEAVES
LOAVES
PEAVEY
PRAVDA
QUAVER
SHAVED
SHAVEN
SHAVER
SHAVES
SLAVED
SLAVER
SLAVES
SLAVEY
SLAVIC
SOAVES
SPAVIN
STAVED
STAVES
SUAVER
TRAVEL
TRAVES
TRAVIS
WEAVED
WEAVER
WEAVES

••A•V•
STARVE
WHATVE

••A••V
BRASOV

•••AV•
BEHAVE
CASAVA
CLEAVE
DEJAVU
GREAVE
MOHAVE

MOJAVE
MORAVA
OCTAVE
OCTAVO
OTTAVA
REPAVE
SHEAVE
SLEAVE
ZOUAVE

••••AV
GUSTAV
MOSHAV
VACLAV
VASLAV

AW••••
AWAITS
AWAKED
AWAKEN
AWAKES
AWARDS
AWEARY
AWEDLY
AWEIGH
AWHILE
AWHIRL
AWNING
AWOKEN

A•W•••
ADWEEK
ALWAYS
ALWEST
ANWANG
ASWELL
ASWIRL
ASWOON
ATWILL
ATWOOD
ATWORK

A••W••
AIRWAY
ALLWET
ANSWER
ANYWAY
ARAWAK
AVOWAL
AVOWED
AVOWER

A•••W•
ACTTWO
ALLOWS
ARROWS

A••••W
ANDHOW
ANDREW
ANTCOW
ANYHOW

•AW•••
BAWLED
BAWLER
CAWDOR
CAWING
DAWDLE
DAWNED
DAWNON
DAWSON
FAWKES
FAWLTY
FAWNED
FAWNER
GAWAIN
GAWKED
GAWKER
GAWPED
HAWAII
HAWHAW
HAWING
HAWKED
HAWKER
HAWSER
HAWSES
JAWING
JAWOHL
LAWFUL
LAWING
LAWMAN
LAWMEN
LAWSON
LAWTON
LAWYER
NAWABS
PAWERS
PAWING
PAWNED
PAWNEE
PAWNER
PAWPAW
PAWSAT
RAWEGG
RAWEST
RAWISH
SAWFIT
SAWING
SAWLOG
SAWOFF
SAWOUT
SAWRED
SAWYER
TAWDRY
TAWING
YAWING
YAWNED
YAWNER
YAWPED
YAWPER

•A•W••
DARWIN
EARWAX
EARWIG
FATWAS
GALWAY
NARWAL
TAIWAN
WAHWAH
YAHWEH

•A••W•
CAHOWS
MACAWS
MALAWI
PAPAWS
TARAWA

•A•••W
BARROW
CALLOW
CASHEW
DARROW
FALLOW
FARLOW
FARROW
GAGLAW
HALLOW
HARLOW
HARROW
HAWHAW
HAYMOW
LAYLOW
MALLOW
MARROW
NARROW
PAWPAW
SALLOW
TALLOW
WALLOW
WARSAW
YARROW

••AW••
ARAWAK
BRAWLS
BRAWNY
CLAWED
CLAWER
CRAWLS
CRAWLY
DRAWER
DRAWIN
DRAWLS
DRAWLY
DRAWON
DRAWUP
FLAWED
GNAWED
GNAWER
GOAWAY
GOAWRY
INAWAY
PRAWNS
SEAWAY
SHAWLS
SHAWMS
SPAWNS
THAWED
TRAWLS
UNAWED

••A••W
INAROW
KRAKOW
MEADOW
SEACOW
SHADOW

•••AW•
BYLAWS
INLAWS
MACAWS
MALAWI
MOHAWK
OSHAWA
OTTAWA
PAPAWS
PESAWA
RESAWN
RESAWS
SCRAWL
SPRAWL
SQUAWK
STRAWS
STRAWY
TARAWA
YUKAWA

•••A•W
DEPAUW

••••AW
BOWSAW
BROKAW
CUSHAW
GAGLAW
GEEGAW
GEWGAW
GUFFAW
HAWHAW
HEEHAW
JIGSAW
MCGRAW
OLDSAW
OUTLAW
PAWPAW
PITSAW
PRELAW
REDRAW
RIPSAW
SEESAW
UNDRAW
WARSAW

AX••••
AXILLA
AXIOMS
AXIONS
AXLIKE
AXONAL
AXSEED

A•X•••
AUXINS

A••X••
ALEXEI
ALEXIA
ALEXIS
APEXES

A•••X•
ADNEXA
ANNEXE

A••••X
ADIEUX
AUSPEX

•AX•••
BAXTER
CAXTON
FAXING
LAXEST
LAXITY
MAXENE
MAXIMA
MAXIMS
MAXINE
MAXIXE
MAXOUT
OAXACA
PAXTON
SAXONS
SAXONY
TAXERS
TAXIED
TAXIES
TAXING
TAXMAN
TAXMEN
WAXERS
WAXIER
WAXILY
WAXING

•A•X••
CALXES

•A••X•
GALAXY
MAXIXE

•A•••X
BAYEUX
CAUDEX
EARWAX
HALLUX
HATBOX
LARYNX
LASTEX
MADMAX
MANNIX
MATRIX
PAYBOX
RATEDX

••AX••
COAXED
COAXER
COAXES
FLAXEN
FLAXES
HOAXED
HOAXER
HOAXES
KLAXON
PRAXES
PRAXIS

••A••X
BRANDX
INAFIX
SEAFOX
SPADIX

•••AX•
BORAXO
CUNAXA
EUTAXY
GALAXY

••••AX
CLIMAX
COLFAX
EARWAX
KOUFAX
MADMAX
PICKAX
POLEAX
PRETAX
PROTAX
SINTAX
SMILAX
SURTAX
SYNTAX
THORAX

AY••••
AYEAYE
AYESHA
AYMARA

A•Y•••
ABYDOS
ABYING
ABYSMS
ADYTUM
ALYSSA
AMYTAN
ANYANG
ANYDAY
ANYHOW
ANYONE
ANYWAY
ARYANS
ASYLUM

A••Y••
ALKYDS
ALKYLS
ANHYDR
ARGYLE
ARGYLL

A•••Y•
ABBEYS
ACETYL
AJFOYT
ALLAYS
ALLEYS
ALLOYS
ALWAYS
ANNOYS
ARRAYS
ARROYO
ASSAYS
AYEAYE
AZODYE

A••••Y
ABBACY
ACIDLY
ACUITY
AERIFY
AERILY
AFFRAY
AGENCY
AIRDRY
AIRILY
AIRWAY
ALBANY
ALECKY
ALLDAY
ALMATY
AMBERY
ANDREY
ANERGY
ANTONY
ANYDAY
ANYWAY
APATHY
APIARY
ARCHLY
ARGOSY
ARGUFY
ARIDLY
ARMORY
ARTERY
ARTILY
ASBURY
ASEITY
ASHLEY
ASTRAY
AUBREY
AUDREY
AUGURY
AURIFY
AVIARY
AVIDLY
AWEARY
AWEDLY

•AY•••
BAYARD
BAYEUX
BAYING
BAYLOR
BAYOUS
BAYRUM
CAYMAN
CAYUGA
CAYUSE
DAYBED
DAYBOY
DAYGLO
DAYJOB
DAYLIT
DAYONE
DAYTON
GAYALS
GAYEST
GAYNOR
HAYDEN
HAYING
HAYLEY
HAYMOW
JAYCEE
JAYVEE
KAYAKS
KAYOED
LAYBYS
LAYERS
LAYFOR
LAYING
LAYLOW
LAYMAN
LAYMEN
LAYOFF
LAYOUT
LAYSBY
LAYSIN
LAYSON
LAYSTO
LAYSUP
LAYUPS
MAYANS
MAYBES
MAYDAY
MAYFLY
MAYHAP
MAYHEM
MAYORS
MAYPOP
MAYTAG
NAYSAY
PAYBOX
PAYDAY
PAYEES
PAYERS
PAYFOR
PAYING
PAYOFF
PAYOLA
PAYOUT
PAYSIN
PAYSON
PAYSUP
RAYGUN
RAYONS
SAYERS
SAYING
SAYLES
SAYSOS
SAYYES
SAYYID
TAYLOR
TAYRAS
WAYANS
WAYLAY
WAYLON
WAYOUT
ZAYINS

•A•Y••
BANYAN
BARYON
BATYAM
CANYON
FAIYUM
GALYAK
LARYNX
LAWYER
MAGYAR
PAPYRI
SALYUT
SATYRS
SAWYER
SAYYES
SAYYID

•A••Y•
DACTYL
DADDYO
DAIMYO
DARRYL
GAMAYS
JACLYN
JASEYS
LATOYA
LAYBYS
MALAYA
MALAYS
MARTYR
MATEYS
MAURYA
NAGOYA
PAPAYA
TAMAYO
VAISYA
VANRYN

•A•••Y
BADBOY
BADGUY
BAILEY
BAKERY
BALDLY
BARELY
BARFLY
BARLEY
BARNEY
BARONY
BASELY
BASIFY
BASSLY
BATBOY
CAGILY
CAGNEY
CALMLY
CAMEBY
CANARY
CANOPY
CARBOY
CARNEY
CARREY
CARVEY
CASEFY
CATCHY
CATHAY
CAUCHY
CAVITY
DABNEY
DAFTLY
DAILEY
DAINTY
DAMPLY
DANGLY
DANKLY
DANNAY
DARKLY
DARNAY
DATARY
DAYBOY
EARTHY
EASILY
EATERY
FABRAY
FAIRLY
FAKERY
FAMILY
FARCRY
FARLEY
FAULTY
FAWLTY
GADFLY
GAIETY
GAINLY
GALAXY
GALLEY
GALWAY
GAMELY
GAMILY
GANGLY
GANTRY

GARVEY
GASIFY
GATSBY
HACKLY
HAILEY
HALEVY
HALLEY
HALSEY
HANLEY
HARDBY
HARDLY
HARLEY
HARVEY
HAYLEY
HAZILY
JACKEY
JALOPY
JANGLY
JANSKY
JAPERY
JAUNTY
LACILY
LACKEY
LAIDBY
LAMELY
LANDRY
LANKLY
LASTLY
LATELY
LAXITY
LAYSBY
LAZBOY
LAZILY
MAGUEY
MAINLY
MALADY
MALORY
MANDAY
MANRAY
MARBLY
MARGAY
MARLEY
MARSHY
MASSEY
MAUNDY
MAYDAY
MAYFLY
MAZILY
NAMELY
NAPERY
NASEBY
NAYSAY
OAKLEY
PACIFY
PAINTY
PALELY
PALTRY
PANFRY
PANTRY
PAPACY
PAPERY
PARITY
PARKAY
PARLAY
PARLEY
PARODY
PARTLY
PASSBY
PASTRY
PATCHY
PAULEY
PAYDAY
RACILY
RAINEY
RAMIFY
RAMSAY
RAMSEY
RANDRY
RANKLY
RAPTLY
RAREFY
RARELY
RARIFY
RARITY
RASHLY
RATIFY
RATTLY
SAFELY
SAFETY
SAGELY
SALARY
SALIFY
SANELY
SANITY
SASHAY
SATINY
SAVORY
SAXONY
TAGDAY
TAMELY
TANGLY
TANGUY
TARTLY
TAUTLY
TAWDRY
VAGARY
VAINLY
VALERY
VALLEY
VANITY
VAPORY
VARNEY
VASTLY
VAULTY
WADDLY
WAFERY
WAFFLY
WAGGLY
WAMBLY
WARCRY
WARILY
WARMLY
WATERY
WATNEY
WAVERY
WAVILY
WAXILY
WAYLAY
YARELY
ZANILY

••AY••

BRAYED
BRAYER
CLAYEY
CRAYON
DLAYER
DRAYED
DWAYNE
ELAYER
ELAYNE
FLAYED
FLAYER
FRAYED
GRAYED
GRAYER
GRAYLY
OKAYED
PLAYAS
PLAYAT
PLAYED
PLAYER
PLAYON
PLAYUP
PRAYED
PRAYER
QUAYLE
SHAYNE
SLAYED
SLAYER
SPAYED
STAYED
STAYON
STAYUP
SWAYED
SWAYER
SWAYZE
THAYER
XRAYED

••A•Y•

GLADYS
HEARYE

••A••Y

APATHY
BEACHY
BEATTY
BEAUTY
BLABBY
BLATTY
BRACHY
BRAINY
BRANDY
BRANNY
BRASHY
BRASSY
BRATTY
BRAWNY
CHAFFY
CHALKY
CHAMMY
CHANCY
CHANEY
CHARLY
CHATTY
CLAMMY
CLANCY
CLANKY
CLASSY
CLAYEY
CRABBY
CRACKY
CRAFTY
CRAGGY
CRANKY
CRANNY
CRAWLY
DEADLY
DEAFLY
DEARLY
DRABLY
DRAFTY
DRAGGY
DRAWLY
DUALLY
FEALTY
FEATLY
FLABBY
FLAGGY
FLAKEY
FLAPPY
FLASHY
FLATLY
FRAIDY
FRANNY
GHARRY
GLADLY
GLAIRY
GLASSY
GNARLY
GNATTY
GOAWAY
GOAWRY
GRABBY
GRAINY
GRAMMY
GRANNY
GRAPEY
GRAPHY
GRASSY
GRAYLY
HEANEY
HEARTY
HEATHY
INAWAY
KEARNY
KNAGGY
KNARRY
KRASNY
LEACHY
LEAKEY
LEALTY
LEANLY
MEANLY
MEASLY
NEARBY
NEARLY
NEATLY
NIAMEY
OCASEY
ORALLY
ORANGY
OVALLY
PEACHY
PEARLY
PEAVEY
PLASHY
PLASTY
POACHY
QUAGGY
QUARRY
REALLY
REALTY
SCABBY
SCANTY
SCARRY
SCATTY
SEAWAY
SHABBY
SHAGGY
SHALEY
SHALLY
SHANDY
SHANNY
SHANTY
SLAGGY
SLANGY
SLAPPY
SLAVEY
SMARMY
SMARTY
SNAGGY
SNAPPY
SNARLY
SNAZZY
SPACEY
SPANKY
SPARKY
STABLY
STACEY
STALKY
STANKY
STARRY
SWABBY
SWAMPY
SWANKY
TEAPOY
TOASTY
TRACEY
TRACHY
TRAPPY
TRASHY
TWANGY
USABLY
VIABLY
WEAKLY
WHACKY
WHAMMY
WRATHY
YEARLY
YEASTY

•••AY•

ALLAYS
ALWAYS
ARRAYS
ASSAYS
AYEAYE
BELAYS
BYWAYS
COPAYS
DECAYS
DELAYS
EMBAYS
ESSAYS
FORAYS
GAMAYS
INLAYS
MALAYA
MALAYS
MORAYS
PAPAYA
RELAYS
REPAYS
SPLAYS
SPRAYS
STRAYS
TAMAYO
TOKAYS
UNSAYS

•••A•Y

ABBACY
ALBANY
ALMATY
APIARY
AVIARY
AWEARY
BIGAMY
BINARY
BLEARY
BOTANY
BOVARY
CANARY
CREAKY
CREAMY
CREASY
CROAKY
CURACY
DATARY
DELANY
DENARY
DREAMY
DREARY
EUTAXY
FLOATY
FREAKY
FRIARY
GALAXY
GLEAMY
GOEASY
GREASY
HILARY
INFAMY
KODALY
LEGACY
LITANY
LUNACY
MALADY
MILADY
NONARY
NOTARY
OLEARY
PAPACY
PIRACY
QUEASY
ROMANY
ROSARY
ROTARY
SALARY
SENARY
SHOALY
SLEAZY
SMEARY
SNEAKY
SOMANY
STEADY
STEAMY
STRAWY
SUGARY
SWEATY
TREATY
UNEASY
UNWARY
VAGARY
VOTARY

••••AY

AFFRAY
AIRWAY
ALLDAY
ANYDAY
ANYWAY
ASTRAY
BELLAY
BENDAY
BENGAY
BETRAY
BEWRAY
BISCAY
BOMBAY
BYPLAY
CATHAY
CONWAY
CORDAY
DANNAY
DARNAY
DEEJAY
DEFRAY
DELRAY
DISMAY
DOGDAY
ESTRAY
FABRAY
FENWAY
FLYWAY
FRIDAY
GALWAY
GOAWAY
HEYDAY
HOORAY
HURRAY
ILLSAY
INAWAY
INPLAY
JETWAY
KEYWAY
LEEWAY
MANDAY
MANRAY
MARGAY
MAYDAY
MIDDAY
MIDWAY
MILLAY
MISLAY
MISSAY
MONDAY
MORNAY
MURRAY
NAYSAY
NETPAY
NORGAY
NORWAY
OFFDAY
ONEDAY
ONEWAY
OUTLAY
PARKAY
PARLAY
PAYDAY
PEDWAY
PREPAY
RAMSAY
REDBAY
REPLAY
RUNWAY
SASHAY
SEAWAY
SKYWAY
SUBWAY
SUNDAY
SUNRAY
TAGDAY
TWOWAY
VEEJAY
WAYLAY

AZ••••

AZALEA
AZIDES
AZINES
AZODYE
AZORES
AZORIN
AZTECS

A•Z•••

ADZUKI

A••Z••

AMAZED
AMAZES
AMAZON
AREZZO

A•••Z•

ABLAZE
ALONZO
AREZZO
ASSIZE

A••••Z

AMOSOZ

•AZ•••

BAZAAR
DAZING
DAZZLE
FAZING
FAZOOL
GAZEBO
GAZING
GAZUMP
HAZANS
HAZARD
HAZELS
HAZERS
HAZIER
HAZILY
HAZING
JAZZED
JAZZES
JAZZUP
KAZAKH
KAZAKS
KAZOOS
LAZBOY
LAZIER
LAZILY
LAZING
LAZULI
MAZERS
MAZIER
MAZILY
MAZOLA
MAZUMA
RAZING
RAZORS
RAZZED
RAZZES
RAZZLE
TAZZAS
ZAZENS

•A•Z••

BAIZAS
BALZAC
BANZAI
BARZUN
DANZIG
DAZZLE
GAUZES
JAZZED
JAZZES
JAZZUP
MAHZOR
MAIZES
MATZOH
MATZOS
PANZER
RAZZED
RAZZES
RAZZLE
TARZAN
TAZZAS

•A••Z•

FAENZA
LAMAZE
LAOTZU
YAKUZA

•A•••Z

TABRIZ
TAMMUZ
VALDEZ

••AZ••

AMAZED
AMAZES
AMAZON
BLAZED
BLAZER
BLAZES
BLAZON
BRAZED
BRAZEN
BRAZER
BRAZES
BRAZIL
BRAZOS
BRAZZA
BRAZZI
CRAZED
CRAZES
FRAZER
GHAZIS
GLAZED
GLAZER
GLAZES
GRAZED
GRAZER
GRAZES
PIAZZA
PLAZAS
RYAZAN
SHAZAM

SNAZZY
SWAZIS
ZSAZSA

••A•Z•
BRAZZA
BRAZZI
KWANZA
PIAZZA
SNAZZY
STANZA
SWAYZE

••A••Z
CHAVEZ
JUAREZ
KRANTZ
QUARTZ

•••AZ•
ABLAZE
BEDAZE
LAMAZE
PIZAZZ
SLEAZE
SLEAZY

•••A•Z
ERSATZ
IGNATZ
KUVASZ
PIZAZZ

••••AZ
SHIRAZ

BA••••
BAAING
BABALU
BABBLE
BABELS
BABIED
BABIES
BABKAS
BABOON
BABSON
BABULS
BACALL
BACHED
BACKED
BACKER
BACKIN
BACKUP
BACKUS
BADBOY
BADDER
BADDIE
BADEGG
BADGER
BADGES
BADGUY
BADHAM
BADLOT
BADMAN
BADMEN
BAFFIN
BAFFLE
BAGDAD
BAGELS
BAGFUL
BAGGED
BAGGER
BAGGIE
BAGSIT
BAGUIO
BAHAMA
BAHIAN
BAIKAL
BAILED
BAILEE
BAILER
BAILEY
BAILOR
BAINES
BAIRNS
BAITED
BAIZAS
BAKERS
BAKERY
BAKING
BAKULA
BALAAM
BALATA
BALBOA
BALDER
BALDLY
BALEEN
BALERS
BALING
BALKAN
BALKED
BALLAD
BALLET
BALLON
BALLOT
BALLOU
BALLUP
BALSAM
BALTIC
BALZAC
BAMAKO
BAMBOO
BANANA
BANDED
BANDIT
BANDOG
BANGED
BANGER
BANGKA
BANGLE
BANGOR
BANGUI
BANGUP
BANISH
BANJOS
BANJUL
BANKED
BANKER
BANKON
BANLON
BANNED
BANNER
BANQUO
BANTAM
BANTER
BANTUS
BANYAN
BANZAI
BAOBAB
BARBED
BARBEL
BARBER
BARBET
BARBIE
BARBRA
BARCAR
BARDIC
BARDOT
BAREGE
BARELY
BAREST
BARFLY
BARGED
BARGES
BARHOP
BARING
BARISH
BARITE
BARIUM
BARKAT
BARKED
BARKER
BARKIN
BARLEY
BARMAN
BARMEN
BARNES
BARNEY
BARNUM
BAROJA
BAROLO
BARONG
BARONS
BARONY
BARQUE
BARRED
BARREL
BARREN
BARRES
BARRIE
BARRIO
BARRIS
BARRON
BARROW
BARTAB
BARTER
BARTOK
BARTON
BARUCH
BARYON
BARZUN
BASALT
BASELY
BASEST
BASHED
BASHES
BASICS
BASIFY
BASING
BASINS
BASKED
BASKET
BASQUE
BASSES
BASSET
BASSLY
BASSOS
BASTED
BASTER
BASTES
BATAAN
BATBOY
BATEAU
BATHED
BATHER
BATHES
BATHOS
BATIKS
BATING
BATMAN
BATMEN
BATONS
BATTED
BATTEL
BATTEN
BATTER
BATTLE
BATTUE
BATUMI
BATYAM
BAUBLE
BAUCIS
BAULKS
BAWLED
BAWLER
BAXTER
BAYARD
BAYEUX
BAYING
BAYLOR
BAYOUS
BAYRUM
BAZAAR

B•A•••
BAAING
BEACHY
BEACON
BEADED
BEADLE
BEADUP
BEAGLE
BEAKED
BEAKER
BEAMED
BEAMON
BEAMUP
BEANED
BEANIE
BEANOS
BEARDS
BEARER
BEARON
BEARUP
BEASTS
BEATEN
BEATER
BEATIT
BEATLE
BEATON
BEATTY
BEATUP
BEAUTS
BEAUTY
BEAVER
BEAVIS
BHAKTI
BIAFRA
BIANCA
BIASED
BIASES
BLABBY
BLACKS
BLADED
BLADER
BLADES
BLAINE
BLAISE
BLAMED
BLAMES
BLANCA
BLANCH
BLANDA
BLANKS
BLARED
BLARES
BLASTS
BLATTY
BLAZED
BLAZER
BLAZES
BLAZON
BMAJOR
BOARDS
BOASTS
BOATED
BOATEL
BOATER
BRACED
BRACER
BRACES
BRACHY
BRACTS
BRAHMA
BRAHMS
BRAIDS
BRAILA
BRAILS
BRAINS
BRAINY
BRAISE
BRAKED
BRAKES
BRANCH
BRANDO
BRANDS
BRANDT
BRANDX
BRANDY
BRANNY
BRANTS
BRAQUE
BRASHY
BRASOV
BRASSY
BRATSK
BRATTY
BRAVAS
BRAVED
BRAVER
BRAVES
BRAVOS
BRAWLS
BRAWNY
BRAYED
BRAYER
BRAZED
BRAZEN
BRAZER
BRAZES
BRAZIL
BRAZOS
BRAZZA
BRAZZI
BWANAS

B••A••
BABALU
BACALL
BAHAMA
BALAAM
BALATA
BAMAKO
BANANA
BASALT
BATAAN
BAYARD
BAZAAR
BECALM
BECAME
BEDAUB
BEDAZE
BEFALL
BEHALF
BEHAVE
BELAIR
BELAYS
BEMATA
BERATE
BESANT
BETAKE
BEWAIL
BEWARE
BEZANT
BICARB
BIGAMY
BIHARI
BINARY
BINATE
BLEACH
BLEARS
BLEARY
BLEATS
BLOATS
BOGART
BONAMI
BORAGE
BORATE
BORAXO
BOTANY
BOVARY
BOYARS
BREACH
BREADS
BREAKS
BREAMS
BREAST
BREATH
BRIAND
BRIANS
BRIARD
BRIARS
BROACH
BROADS
BRYANT
BSHARP
BUTANE
BYHAND
BYLAWS
BYNAME
BYPASS
BYPAST
BYPATH
BYTALK
BYWAYS

B•••A•
BABKAS
BADHAM
BADMAN
BAGDAD
BAHIAN
BAIKAL
BAIZAS
BALAAM
BALKAN
BALLAD
BALSAM
BALZAC
BANTAM
BANYAN
BANZAI
BAOBAB
BARCAR
BARKAT
BARMAN
BARTAB
BATAAN
BATEAU
BATMAN
BATYAM
BAZAAR
BEDLAM
BEGGAR
BEHEAD
BELDAM
BELIAL
BELLAY
BEMOAN
BENDAY
BENGAL
BENGAY
BETRAY
BETTAS
BEULAH
BEWRAY
BHOPAL
BHUTAN
BIGMAC
BILBAO
BIOGAS
BIOTAS
BISCAY
BISSAU
BITMAP
BOBCAT
BOMBAY
BONSAI
BOREAL
BOREAS
BORMAN
BOWMAN
BOWOAR
BOWSAW
BOXCAR
BRAVAS
BRIDAL
BROGAN
BROKAW
BRUMAL
BRUTAL
BUCCAL
BUCHAN
BULGAR
BULLAE
BUMRAP
BUNYAN
BUREAU
BURGAS
BURLAP
BURMAN
BUROAK
BURSAE
BURSAL
BURSAR
BURSAS
BUSBAR
BUSMAN
BWANAS
BYPLAY
BYROAD

B••••A
BAHAMA
BAKULA
BALATA
BALBOA
BANANA
BANGKA
BARBRA
BAROJA
BELUGA
BEMATA
BERTHA
BETCHA
BIAFRA
BIANCA
BIKILA
BITOLA
BLANCA
BLANDA
BODEGA
BOGOTA
BORGIA
BOSNIA
BRAHMA
BRAILA
BRAZZA
BRENDA
BUDDHA
BULOVA
BUQSHA
BUSHWA

•BA•••
ABACAS
ABACUS
ABASED
ABASES
ABATED
ABATES
ABATIS
IBADAN
UBANGI

•B•A••
ABBACY
ABLATE
ABLAUT
ABLAZE
ABOARD
ABRADE
ABRAMS
EBOATS
HBEAMS
IBEAMS
OBEAHS
OBLAST
OBLATE
OBTAIN
UBOATS

•B••A•
ABACAS
ABORAL
ABROAD
ABSCAM
FBIMAN
IBADAN
OBIWAN
OBRIAN

•B•••A
ABOLLA
IBERIA
OBELIA

••BA••
ABBACY
ALBANO
ALBANY
AMBATO
ATBATS
AUBADE
BABALU
CABALA
CABALS
CABANA
COBALT
CUBAGE
DEBARK
DEBARS
DEBASE
DEBATE
EMBANK
EMBARK
EMBAYS
GOBACK
HABANA
HOBART
KEBABS
LOBATE
MCBAIN
ORBACH
RABATO
REBAGS
REBARS
REBATE
RIBALD
RIBAND
ROBALO
RUBATI
RUBATO
SABATO
SUBARU
TABARD
TOBAGO
TUBATE
TYBALT
UNBARS

URBANA
URBANE
WABASH

••B•A•
BABKAS
BOBCAT
COBHAM
COBIAS
COBRAS
DEBRAS
DOBLAS
DOBRAS
FABIAN
FABRAY
GIBRAN
HABEAS
HUBCAP
JABBAR
JUBBAH
KUBLAI
LABIAL
LIBYAN
LLBEAN
MOBCAP
NUBIAN
PTBOAT
SABRAS
SUBPAR
SUBWAY
TABLAS
TIBIAE
TIBIAL
TIBIAS
TOBIAS
TUBMAN
UMBRAE
UMBRAL
UMBRAS
UPBEAT
ZEBRAS

••B••A
ARBELA
CABALA
CABANA
CIBOLA
EUBOEA
FIBULA
HABANA
LABREA
NEBULA
ROBBIA
SABENA
TABULA
UMBRIA
URBANA

•••BA•
AIRBAG
AMEBAE
AMEBAS
ARUBAN
BAOBAB
BILBAO
BOMBAY
BUSBAR
CASBAH
CEIBAS
COMBAT
CORBAN
CYMBAL
DISBAR
DUNBAR
DURBAN
DURBAR
FORBAD
GASBAG
GIMBAL
GLOBAL
GRABAT
GYMBAG
HERBAL
ICEBAG
ISOBAR
IZABAL
JABBAR
JUBBAH
KASBAH
KITBAG
KLIBAN
KOMBAT
LUMBAR
MAMBAS
NOTBAD
NUMBAT
RAGBAG
REDBAY
RUMBAS
SAMBAL
SAMBAR
SAMBAS
SCUBAS
SEABAG
SHABAN
SINBAD
STABAT
TEABAG
TIMBAL
TOMBAC
TOOBAD
TRIBAL
TURBAN
VERBAL
WETBAR
WOMBAT
ZEDBAR

•••B•A
ARABIA
BALBOA
BARBRA
GAMBIA
JERBOA
LAMBDA
LISBOA
OJIBWA
PHOBIA
PUEBLA
RAMBLA
ROBBIA
SERBIA
ZAMBIA

••••BA
AMOEBA
ANNABA
ARRIBA
ARROBA
CASABA
CUIABA
DJERBA
HECUBA
INDABA
JOJOBA
KARIBA
MAKEBA
RHUMBA
YORUBA
ZAREBA

BB••••
BBKING

B•B•••
BABALU
BABBLE
BABELS
BABIED
BABIES
BABKAS
BABOON
BABSON
BABULS
BEBOPS
BIBBED
BIBLES
BIBLIO
BOBBED
BOBBER
BOBBIE
BOBBIN
BOBBLE
BOBCAT
BOBSUP
BUBBLE
BUBBLY

B••B••
BABBLE
BADBOY
BALBOA
BAMBOO
BAOBAB
BARBED
BARBEL
BARBER
BARBET
BARBIE
BARBRA
BATBOY
BAUBLE
BEDBUG
BERBER
BIBBED
BIGBEN
BIGBOY
BILBAO
BIOBIO
BLABBY
BOBBED
BOBBER
BOBBIE
BOBBIN
BOBBLE
BOMBAY
BOMBED
BOMBER
BOMBES
BONBON
BOOBOO
BOUBOU
BOXBOY
BRIBED
BRIBES
BUBBLE
BUBBLY
BULBIL
BULBUL
BUMBLE
BUMBRY
BURBLE
BURBLY
BURBOT
BUSBAR
BUSBOY
BYEBYE

B•••B•
BLABBY
BLURBS
BRUMBY

B••••B
BAOBAB
BARTAB
BEDAUB
BENUMB
BICARB

•BB•••
ABBACY
ABBESS
ABBEYS
ABBOTS
ABBOTT
EBBING

•B•B••
IBIBIO

•B••B•
ABOMBS
HBOMBS

•B•••B
ABSORB

••BB••
BABBLE
BIBBED
BOBBED
BOBBER
BOBBIE
BOBBIN
BOBBLE
BUBBLE
BUBBLY
CABBED
CABBIE
COBBLE
DABBED
DABBLE
DEBBIE
DIBBLE
DOBBER
DOBBIN
DUBBED
DUBBIN
DYBBUK
FIBBED
FIBBER
FOBBED
FUBBED
GABBED
GABBER
GABBLE
GABBRO
GIBBED
GIBBER
GIBBET
GIBBON
GOBBLE
HOBBES
HOBBIT
HOBBLE
HUBBLE
HUBBLY
HUBBUB
JABBAR
JABBED
JABBER
JIBBED
JOBBED
JOBBER
JUBBAH
KIBBLE
LIBBED
LIBBER
LOBBED
LOBBER
LUBBER
MOBBED
NABBED
NABBER
NIBBLE
NOBBLE
NUBBED
NUBBIN
NUBBLE
NUBBLY
PEBBLE
PEBBLY
RABBET
RABBIS
RABBIT
RABBLE
REBBES
RIBBED
RIBBON
ROBBED
ROBBER
ROBBIA
ROBBIE
RUBBED
RUBBER
RUBBLE
RUBBLY
SOBBED
SOBBER
SUBBED
TABBED
TUBBED
WEBBED
WEBBER
WOBBLE
WOBBLY
YABBER
YOBBOS

••B•B•
CUBEBS
IMBIBE
KABOBS
KEBABS
KEBOBS
NABOBS

••B••B
COBWEB
HOBNOB
HUBBUB
SUBDEB
SUBURB

•••BB•
BLABBY
CHUBBY
CLUBBY
CRABBE
CRABBY
FLABBY
GRABBY
GRUBBY
KNOBBY
SCABBY
SHABBY
SLOBBY
SNOBBY
SNUBBY
STUBBY
SWABBY

•••B•B
BAOBAB
HUBBUB
SKIBOB

••••BB
SQUIBB
TYCOBB

BC••••
BCELLS

B•C•••
BACALL
BACHED
BACKED
BACKER
BACKIN
BACKUP
BACKUS
BECALM
BECAME
BECKER
BECKET
BECKON
BECOME
BICARB
BICEPS
BICKER
BICORN
BOCCIE
BOCHCO
BUCCAL
BUCHAN
BUCKED
BUCKET
BUCKLE
BUCKUP

B••C••
BARCAR
BAUCIS
BEACHY
BEACON
BETCHA
BISCAY
BLACKS
BLOCKS
BLOCKY
BOBCAT
BOCCIE
BONCES
BOTCHY
BOUCLE
BOXCAR
BRACED
BRACER
BRACES
BRACHY
BRACTS
BRECHT
BRICKS
BRICKY
BUCCAL
BUNCHE
BUNCHY
BUNCOS

B•••C•
BARUCH
BASICS
BEDECK
BIANCA
BIERCE
BISECT
BLANCA
BLANCH
BLEACH
BLENCH
BLOTCH
BOCHCO
BODICE
BORSCH
BOUNCE
BOUNCY
BRANCH
BREACH
BREECH
BROACH
BRONCO
BRONCS
BROOCH
BRUNCH

B••••C
BALTIC
BALZAC
BARDIC
BELLOC
BIGMAC
BIONIC
BIOTIC

•B•C••
ABACAS
ABACUS
ABSCAM

•B••C•
ABBACY
ABDUCT
ABJECT
OBJECT

••BC••
BOBCAT
DUBCEK
HUBCAP
MOBCAP

••B•C•
ABBACY
CUBICS
GOBACK
LUBECK
ORBACH
REBECS
XEBECS

••B••C
ENBLOC
FABRIC
PUBLIC
RUBRIC

•••B•C
AMEBIC
ARABIC
IAMBIC
PHOBIC
QUEBEC
SORBIC
TOMBAC

B•D•••
BADBOY
BADDER
BADDIE
BADEGG
BADGER
BADGES
BADGUY
BADHAM
BADLOT
BADMAN
BADMEN
BEDAUB
BEDAZE
BEDBUG
BEDECK
BEDEWS
BEDIMS
BEDLAM
BIDDEN
BIDDER
BIDDLE
BIDING
BIDSIN
BIDSON
BIDSUP
BODEGA
BODICE
BODIED
BODIES
BODILY
BODING
BODKIN
BODONI
BUDDED
BUDDHA
BUDGED
BUDGES
BUDGET
BUDGIE

B••D••
BADDER
BADDIE
BAGDAD
BALDER
BALDLY
BANDED
BANDIT
BANDOG
BARDIC
BARDOT
BEADED
BEADLE
BEADUP
BELDAM
BENDAY
BENDED
BENDER
BENDIX
BIDDEN
BIDDER
BIDDLE
BINDER
BINDUP
BIRDED
BIRDER
BIRDIE
BLADED
BLADER
BLADES
BOLDER
BOLDLY
BONDED
BOODLE
BORDEN
BORDER
BOUDIN
BRIDAL
BRIDES
BRIDGE
BRIDLE
BRODIE
BRUDER
BSIDES
BUDDED
BUDDHA
BUNDLE
BURDEN

B•••D•
BEARDS
BESIDE
BETIDE
BIONDI
BIPEDS
BIPODS
BLANDA
BLEEDS
BLENDE
BLENDS
BLINDS

BLONDE
BLONDS
BLOODY
BOARDS
BOLIDE
BORIDE
BOUNDS
BOVIDS
BRAIDS
BRANDO
BRANDS
BRANDT
BRANDX
BRANDY
BREADS
BREEDS
BRENDA
BROADS
BROODS
BROODY
BUILDS

B••••D

BABIED
BACHED
BACKED
BAGDAD
BAGGED
BAILED
BAITED
BALKED
BALLAD
BANDED
BANGED
BANKED
BANNED
BARBED
BARGED
BARKED
BARRED
BASHED
BASKED
BASTED
BATHED
BATTED
BAWLED
BAYARD
BEADED
BEAKED
BEAMED
BEANED
BEEFED
BEEPED
BEGGED
BEHEAD
BEHELD
BEHIND
BEHOLD
BELIED
BELLED
BELTED
BENDED
BESTED
BEYOND
BIASED
BIBBED
BIFFED
BIFOLD
BIGRED
BILKED
BILLED
BINGED
BINNED
BIRDED
BIRLED
BITTED
BLADED
BLAMED
BLARED
BLAZED
BOATED
BOBBED
BODIED
BOFFED
BOGGED
BOILED
BOLTED
BOMBED
BONDED
BONGED
BOOKED
BOOMED
BOOTED
BOPPED
BOSSED
BOUSED
BOWLED
BRACED
BRAKED
BRAVED
BRAYED
BRAZED
BREWED
BRIAND
BRIARD
BRIBED
BRIGID
BRINED
BRUXED
BUCKED
BUDDED
BUDGED
BUFFED
BUGGED
BUGLED
BUJOLD
BULGED
BULKED
BULLED
BUMMED
BUMPED
BUNGED
BUNKED
BUNTED
BUOYED
BURIED
BURLED
BURNED
BURPED
BURRED
BUSHED
BUSIED
BUSKED
BUSSED
BUSTED
BUTTED
BUZZED
BYHAND
BYROAD
BYWORD

•BD•••

ABDUCT

•B•D••

ABIDED
ABIDES
ABODES
ABYDOS
IBADAN
IBIDEM

•B••D•

ABRADE
EBONDS
MBUNDU
TBIRDS
TBONDS

•B•••D

ABASED
ABATED
ABIDED
ABOARD
ABOUND
ABROAD
ABSURD
ABUSED
OBEYED
OBTUND

••BD••

EMBDEN
SUBDEB
SUBDUE

••B•D•

ALBEDO
AUBADE
EMBEDS
EMBODY
LIBIDO
NOBODY
REBIDS

••B••D

AMBLED
BABIED
BIBBED
BOBBED
CABBED
CABLED
CUBOID
DABBED
DUBBED
FABLED
FIBBED
FOBBED
FUBBED
GABBED
GABLED
GIBBED
HYBRID
IMBUED
INBRED
JABBED
JIBBED
JOBBED
KOBOLD
LIBBED
LOBBED
MOBBED
NABBED
NUBBED
REBEND
REBIND
RIBALD
RIBAND
RIBBED
ROBBED
RUBBED
RUBIED
SOBBED
SUBBED
TABARD
TABBED
TABLED
TUBBED
UNBEND
UNBIND
WEBBED

•••BD•

LAMBDA
RHABDO

•••B•D

BARBED
BIBBED
BOBBED
BOMBED
BRIBED
CABBED
COMBED
CURBED
DABBED
DAUBED
DAYBED
DUBBED
FIBBED
FOBBED
FORBAD
FORBID
FUBBED
GABBED
GARBED
GIBBED
GLOBED
HOTBED
JABBED
JIBBED
JOBBED
LAMBED
LIBBED
LIMBED
LOBBED
MOBBED
MORBID
NABBED
NOTBAD
NUBBED
NUMBED
OUTBID
PROBED
REDBUD
RIBBED
ROBBED
RUBBED
SEABED
SINBAD
SOBBED
SUBBED
TABBED
TOOBAD
TUBBED
TURBID
WEBBED

BE••••

BEACHY
BEACON
BEADED
BEADLE
BEADUP
BEAGLE
BEAKED
BEAKER
BEAMED
BEAMON
BEAMUP
BEANED
BEANIE
BEANOS
BEARDS
BEARER
BEARON
BEARUP
BEASTS
BEATEN
BEATER
BEATIT
BEATLE
BEATON
BEATTY
BEATUP
BEAUTS
BEAUTY
BEAVER
BEAVIS
BEBOPS
BECALM
BECAME
BECKER
BECKET
BECKON
BECOME
BEDAUB
BEDAZE
BEDBUG
BEDECK
BEDEWS
BEDIMS
BEDLAM
BEEFED
BEEFUP
BEEGUM
BEEPED
BEEPER
BEETLE
BEEVES
BEFALL
BEFELL
BEFITS
BEFOGS
BEFORE
BEFOUL
BEGETS
BEGGAR
BEGGED
BEGINS
BEGLEY
BEGOFF
BEGONE
BEGUMS
BEHALF
BEHAVE
BEHEAD
BEHELD
BEHEST
BEHIND
BEHOLD
BEHOOF
BEHOVE
BEIGES
BEINGS
BEIRUT
BEKESY
BELAIR
BELAYS
BELDAM
BELFRY
BELIAL
BELIED
BELIEF
BELIES
BELIKE
BELIZE
BELLAY
BELLED
BELLES
BELLOC
BELLOW
BELOIT
BELONG
BELTED
BELUGA
BEMATA
BEMINE
BEMIRE
BEMOAN
BEMUSE
BENDAY
BENDED
BENDER
BENDIX
BENGAL
BENGAY
BENHUR
BENIGN
BENING
BENITO
BENOIT
BENONI
BENSON
BENTON
BENUMB
BENZOL
BERATE
BERBER
BEREFT
BERETS
BERGEN
BERING
BERLIN
BERNIE
BERTHA
BERTHS
BERTIE
BESANT
BESETS
BESIDE
BESOMS
BESOTS
BESSER
BESSIE
BESTED
BESTIR
BESTOW
BETAKE
BETCHA
BETELS
BETHEL
BETIDE
BETISE
BETONY
BETOOK
BETRAY
BETSEY
BETSON
BETTAS
BETTER
BETTOR
BEULAH
BEURRE
BEVELS
BEVIES
BEWAIL
BEWARE
BEWRAY
BEYOND
BEZANT
BEZELS

B•E•••

BCELLS
BEEFED
BEEFUP
BEEGUM
BEEPED
BEEPER
BEETLE
BEEVES
BIERCE
BLEACH
BLEARS
BLEARY
BLEATS
BLEEDS
BLEEPS
BLENCH
BLENDE
BLENDS
BLENNY
BLEWIT
BLEWUP
BOEING
BREACH
BREADS
BREAKS
BREAMS
BREAST
BREATH
BRECHT
BREECH
BREEDS
BREEZE
BREEZY
BREMEN
BRENDA
BRENTS
BRETON
BREUER
BREVES
BREVET
BREVIS
BREWED
BREWER
BREYER
BUENOS
BYEBYE

B••E••

BABELS
BADEGG
BAGELS
BAKERS
BAKERY
BALEEN
BALERS
BAREGE
BARELY
BAREST
BASELY
BASEST
BATEAU
BAYEUX
BEDECK
BEDEWS
BEFELL
BEGETS
BEHEAD
BEHELD
BEHEST
BEKESY
BEREFT
BERETS
BESETS
BETELS
BEVELS
BEZELS
BICEPS
BIKERS
BIPEDS
BIREME
BISECT
BITERS
BLEEDS
BLEEPS
BLUELY
BLUEOX
BLUEST
BLUESY
BLUETS
BLUEYS
BODEGA
BOGEYS
BOLERO
BOLEYN
BONERS
BONEUP
BOPEEP
BOREAL
BOREAS
BOREON
BORERS
BOREUP
BOTELS
BOWERS
BOWERY
BOXERS
BREECH
BREEDS
BREEZE
BREEZY
BRIEFS
BRIENZ
BRIERS
BRIERY
BUREAU
BUTENE
BUTEOS
BUYERS

B•••E•

BABIED
BABIES
BACHED
BACKED
BACKER
BADDER
BADGER
BADGES
BADMEN
BAGGED
BAGGER
BAILED
BAILEE
BAILER
BAILEY
BAINES
BAITED
BALDER
BALEEN
BALKED
BALLET
BANDED
BANGED
BANGER
BANKED
BANKER
BANNED
BANNER
BANTER
BARBED
BARBEL
BARBER
BARBET
BARGED
BARGES
BARKED
BARKER
BARLEY
BARMEN
BARNES
BARNEY
BARRED
BARREL
BARREN
BARRES
BARTER
BASHED
BASHES
BASKED
BASKET
BASSES
BASSET
BASTED
BASTER
BASTES
BATHED

BATHER
BATHES
BATMEN
BATTED
BATTEL
BATTEN
BATTER
BAWLED
BAWLER
BAXTER
BEADED
BEAKED
BEAKER
BEAMED
BEANED
BEARER
BEATEN
BEATER
BEAVER
BECKER
BECKET
BEEFED
BEEPED
BEEPER
BEEVES
BEGGED
BEGLEY
BEIGES
BELIED
BELIEF
BELIES
BELLED
BELLES
BELTED
BENDED
BENDER
BERBER
BERGEN
BESSER
BESTED
BETHEL
BETSEY
BETTER
BEVIES
BIASED
BIASES
BIBBED
BIBLES
BICKER
BIDDEN
BIDDER
BIFFED
BIGBEN
BIGGER
BIGRED
BIGTEN
BILGES
BILKED
BILLED
BILLET
BINDER
BINGED
BINGES
BINNED
BIOMES
BIRDED
BIRDER
BIRLED
BIRNEY
BISSET
BITTED
BITTEN
BITTER
BLADED
BLADER
BLADES
BLAMED
BLAMES
BLARED
BLARES
BLAZED
BLAZER
BLAZES
BLIMEY
BLIXEN
BLOKES
BLOOEY
BLOWER
BOATED
BOATEL
BOATER
BOBBED
BOBBER
BODIED
BODIES
BOFFED
BOGGED
BOGIES
BOGLES
BOILED
BOILER
BOITES
BOLDER
BOLGER
BOLTED
BOMBED
BOMBER
BOMBES
BONCES
BONDED
BONGED
BONIER
BONNES
BONNET
BONZES
BOOKED
BOOKER
BOOMED
BOOMER
BOOTED
BOOTEE
BOOTES
BOPEEP
BOPPED
BOPPER
BORDEN
BORDER
BORNEO
BOSKET
BOSLEY
BOSSED
BOSSES
BOTHER
BOTREE
BOULES
BOULEZ
BOUSED
BOUSES
BOVVER
BOWLED
BOWLER
BOWLES
BOWMEN
BOWNET
BOWSER
BOWYER
BOXIER
BOXSET
BRACED
BRACER
BRACES
BRAKED
BRAKES
BRAVED
BRAVER
BRAVES
BRAYED
BRAYER
BRAZED
BRAZEN
BRAZER
BRAZES
BREMEN
BREUER
BREVES
BREVET
BREWED
BREWER
BREYER
BRIBED
BRIBES
BRIDES
BRINED
BRINES
BROKEN
BROKER
BRUDER
BRUGES
BRULES
BRUMES
BRUNEI
BRUNET
BRUTES
BRUXED
BRUXES
BSIDES
BUCKED
BUCKET
BUDDED
BUDGED
BUDGES
BUDGET
BUFFED
BUFFER
BUFFET
BUGGED
BUGLED
BUGLER
BUGLES
BULGED
BULGES
BULKED
BULLED
BULLET
BULWER
BUMMED
BUMMER
BUMPED
BUMPER
BUNGED
BUNGEE
BUNKED
BUNKER
BUNSEN
BUNTED
BUNTER
BUNUEL
BUOYED
BURDEN
BURGEE
BURGER
BURIED
BURIES
BURLED
BURLEY
BURNED
BURNER
BURNET
BURNEY
BURPED
BURRED
BURSES
BUSHED
BUSHEL
BUSHES
BUSIED
BUSIER
BUSIES
BUSKED
BUSMEN
BUSSED
BUSSES
BUSTED
BUSTER
BUTLER
BUTTED
BUTTER
BUTTES
BUZZED
BUZZER
BUZZES
BYRNES

B••••E

BABBLE
BADDIE
BAFFLE
BAGGIE
BAILEE
BANGLE
BARBIE
BAREGE
BARITE
BARQUE
BARRIE
BASQUE
BATTLE
BATTUE
BAUBLE
BEADLE
BEAGLE
BEANIE
BEATLE
BECAME
BECOME
BEDAZE
BEETLE
BEFORE
BEGONE
BEHAVE
BEHOVE
BELIKE
BELIZE
BEMINE
BEMIRE
BEMUSE
BERATE
BERNIE
BERTIE
BESIDE
BESSIE
BETAKE
BETIDE
BETISE
BEURRE
BEWARE
BIDDLE
BIERCE
BIGGIE
BIGLIE
BIGTOE
BILLIE
BINATE
BIRDIE
BIREME
BISQUE
BLAINE
BLAISE
BLENDE
BLITHE
BLONDE
BLOUSE
BLYTHE
BMOVIE
BOBBIE
BOBBLE
BOCCIE
BODICE
BOGGLE
BOLIDE
BONNIE
BOODLE
BOOGIE
BOOKIE
BOOTEE
BOOTHE
BOOTIE
BORAGE
BORATE
BORIDE
BOTREE
BOTTLE
BOUCLE
BOUFFE
BOULLE
BOUNCE
BOURKE
BOURNE
BOURSE
BOVINE
BOWTIE
BRAISE
BRAQUE
BREEZE
BRIDGE
BRIDLE
BRODIE
BROGUE
BRONTE
BRONZE
BROOKE
BROWNE
BROWSE
BRUISE
BUBBLE
BUCKLE
BUDGIE
BULLAE
BUMBLE
BUNCHE
BUNDLE
BUNGEE
BUNGLE
BURBLE
BURGEE
BURGLE
BURSAE
BUSTLE
BUTANE
BUTENE
BYEBYE
BYGONE
BYJOVE
BYLINE
BYNAME
BYROTE
BYSSHE

•BE•••

ABELES
ABESSE
EBERLY
HBEAMS
IBEAMS
IBERIA
IBEXES
OBEAHS
OBELIA
OBELUS
OBERON
OBEYED

•B•E••

ABBESS
ABBEYS
ABJECT
ABLEST
ABSENT
OBJECT
OBSESS
OBTEST
OBVERT
UBIETY

•B••E•

ABASED
ABASES
ABATED
ABATES
ABELES
ABIDED
ABIDES
ABODES
ABUSED
ABUSER
ABUSES
FBIMEN
IBEXES
IBIDEM
IBISES
OBEYED
OBITER
OBRIEN
OBSTET
TBONES

•B•••E

ABESSE
ABJURE
ABLATE
ABLAZE
ABRADE
OBLATE
OBLIGE
OBTUSE
UBIQUE

••BE••

ABBESS
ABBEYS
ALBEDO
ALBEIT
ALBERT
AMBERS
AMBERY
ARBELA
ATBEST
BABELS
CABERS
CUBEBS
CYBELE
EDBERG
EGBERT
EKBERG
ELBERT
EMBEDS
EMBERS
FIBERS
GIBERS
HABEAS
HUBERT
JOBETH
LABELS
LIBELS
LIBERI
LLBEAN
LUBECK
MABELL
REBECS
REBELS
REBEND
REBENT
RIBEYE
ROBERT
RUBENS
SABENA
SABERS
SEBERG
SOBEIT
SOBERS
TUBERS
UMBELS
UMBERS
UNBELT
UNBEND
UNBENT
UPBEAT
UZBEKS
WEBERN
XEBECS
ZIBETS

••B•E•

AMBLED
AMBLER
AMBLES
AUBREY
BABIED
BABIES
BIBBED
BIBLES
BOBBED
BOBBER
CABBED
CABLED
CABLER
CABLES
COBWEB
DABBED
DABNEY
DOBBER
DUBBED
DUBCEK
EMBDEN
EMBLEM
EUBOEA
FABLED
FABLER
FABLES
FIBBED
FIBBER
FIBRES
FOBBED
FUBBED
GABBED
GABBER
GABIES
GABLED
GABLER
GABLES
GIBBED
GIBBER
GIBBET
GIBLET
GOBIES
GOBLET
HEBREW
HOBBES
HOBOES
IMBUED
IMBUES
INBRED
JABBED
JABBER
JIBBED
JOBBED
JOBBER
LABREA
LABRET
LIBBED
LIBBER
LOBBED
LOBBER
LUBBER
MOBBED
MOBLEY
NABBED
NABBER
NOBLER
NOBLES
NUBBED
RABBET
RABIES
REBBES
RIBBED
ROBBED
ROBBER
ROBLES
RUBBED
RUBBER
RUBIED
RUBIES
RUBLES
RUBLEV
SABLES
SABRES
SOBBED
SOBBER
SUBBED
SUBDEB
SUBLET
SUBSET
TABBED
TABLED
TABLES
TABLET
TOBIES
TUBBED
VEBLEN
WEBBED
WEBBER
YABBER

••B••E

AUBADE
BABBLE
BOBBIE
BOBBLE
BUBBLE
CABBIE
COBBLE
CUBAGE
CYBELE
DABBLE
DEBASE
DEBATE
DEBBIE
DEBONE
DIBBLE
GABBLE
GOBBLE
HABILE
HOBBLE
HUBBLE
IMBIBE
IMBRUE
KIBBLE
LABILE
LOBATE
LOBULE
MOBILE
MRBLUE
NIBBLE
NOBBLE
NUBBLE
NUBILE
PEBBLE
RABBLE
REBATE
REBUKE

RIBEYE
RIBOSE
ROBBIE
RUBBLE
SABINE
SUBDUE
SUBTLE
TIBIAE
TUBATE
UMBRAE
URBANE
WOBBLE

•••BE•
ADOBES
BARBED
BARBEL
BARBER
BARBET
BERBER
BIBBED
BIGBEN
BOBBED
BOBBER
BOMBED
BOMBER
BOMBES
BRIBED
BRIBES
CABBED
CAMBER
COMBED
COMBER
COMBES
CORBEL
CUMBER
CURBED
DABBED
DAUBED
DAUBER
DAUBES
DAYBED
DOBBER
DUBBED
DUMBER
FERBER
FIBBED
FIBBER
FOBBED
FORBES
FUBBED
GABBED
GABBER
GARBED
GERBER
GIBBED
GIBBER
GIBBET
GIMBEL
GLEBES
GLOBED
GLOBES
GOOBER
GRABEN
GREBES
GUMBEL
HOBBES
HOTBED
ISABEL
JABBED
JABBER
JIBBED
JOBBED
JOBBER
KHYBER
LAMBED
LIBBED
LIBBER
LIMBED
LIMBER
LOBBED
LOBBER
LUBBER
LUMBER
MAYBES
MEMBER
MOBBED
NABBED
NABBER
NUBBED
NUMBED
NUMBER
PLEBES
PROBED
PROBER
PROBES
QUEBEC
RABBET
REBBES
REUBEN
RIBBED
ROBBED
ROBBER
RUBBED
RUBBER
SEABED
SEABEE
SIMBEL
SOBBED
SOBBER
SOMBER
SORBET
SUBBED
TABBED
THEBES
TIMBER
TREBEK
TRIBES
TUBBED
WEBBED
WEBBER
YABBER
YOUBET

•••B•E
ALIBLE
AMEBAE
ARABLE
BABBLE
BARBIE
BAUBLE
BOBBIE
BOBBLE
BUBBLE
BUMBLE
BURBLE
BYEBYE
CABBIE
COBBLE
CRABBE
DABBLE
DEBBIE
DIBBLE
DOABLE
DOOBIE
DOUBLE
EDIBLE
ENABLE
FEEBLE
FOIBLE
FUMBLE
GABBLE
GAMBLE
GARBLE
GOBBLE
GRABLE
HEEBIE
HERBIE
HOBBLE
HOMBRE
HUBBLE
HUMBLE
JUMBLE
KIBBLE
LIABLE
MARBLE
MUMBLE
NIBBLE
NIMBLE
NOBBLE
NUBBLE
PEBBLE
RABBLE
RAMBLE
ROBBIE
ROUBLE
RUBBLE
RUMBLE
SEABEE
SOMBRE
STABLE
TIMBRE
TREBLE
TUMBLE
UNABLE
USABLE
VIABLE
WAMBLE
WARBLE
WIMBLE
WOBBLE
ZOMBIE

••••BE
ACHEBE
AEROBE
CARIBE
CRABBE
DANUBE
ENROBE
EPHEBE
FLAMBE
IMBIBE
JUJUBE
LETSBE
MCCABE
MUGABE
PHOEBE
SCRIBE
STROBE
THISBE
UNROBE

B•F•••
BAFFIN
BAFFLE
BEFALL
BEFELL
BEFITS
BEFOGS
BEFORE
BEFOUL
BIFFED
BIFOLD
BOFFED
BOFFIN
BOFFOS
BUFFED
BUFFER
BUFFET
BUFFON
BUFFOS

B••F••
BAFFIN
BAFFLE
BAGFUL
BARFLY
BEEFED
BEEFUP
BELFRY
BIAFRA
BIFFED
BLUFFS
BOFFED
BOFFIN
BOFFOS
BOTFLY
BOUFFE
BOWFIN
BOXFUL
BUFFED
BUFFER
BUFFET
BUFFON
BUFFOS

B•••F•
BASIFY
BEGOFF
BEREFT
BITOFF
BLUFFS
BOUFFE
BRIEFS
BUGOFF
BUYOFF

B••••F
BEGOFF
BEHALF
BEHOOF
BELIEF
BITOFF
BUGOFF
BUYOFF

••BF••
SOBFUL

••B•F•
FOBOFF
REBUFF
RUBIFY
RUBOFF

••B••F
FOBOFF
REBUFF
RUBOFF

BG••••
BGIRLS

B•G•••
BAGDAD
BAGELS
BAGFUL
BAGGED
BAGGER
BAGGIE
BAGSIT
BAGUIO
BEGETS
BEGGAR
BEGGED
BEGINS
BEGLEY
BEGOFF
BEGONE
BEGUMS
BIGAMY
BIGBEN
BIGBOY
BIGGER
BIGGIE
BIGGUN
BIGHTS
BIGLIE
BIGMAC
BIGOTS
BIGRED
BIGSUR
BIGTEN
BIGTOE
BIGTOP
BIGWIG
BOGART
BOGEYS
BOGGED
BOGGLE
BOGIES
BOGLES
BOGONG
BOGOTA
BUGGED
BUGLED
BUGLER
BUGLES
BUGOFF
BUGOUT
BYGONE
BYGOSH

B••G••
BADGER
BADGES
BADGUY
BAGGED
BAGGER
BAGGIE
BANGED
BANGER
BANGKA
BANGLE
BANGOR
BANGUI
BANGUP
BARGED
BARGES
BEAGLE
BEEGUM
BEGGAR
BEGGED
BEIGES
BENGAL
BENGAY
BERGEN
BIGGER
BIGGIE
BIGGUN
BILGES
BINGED
BINGES
BIOGAS
BIRGIT
BLIGHT
BOGGED
BOGGLE
BOIGNY
BOLGER
BONGED
BONGOS
BOOGIE
BORGIA
BOUGHS
BOUGHT
BRIGGS
BRIGHT
BRIGID
BROGAN
BROGUE
BRUGES
BUDGED
BUDGES
BUDGET
BUDGIE
BUGGED
BULGAR
BULGED
BULGES
BULGUR
BUNGED
BUNGEE
BUNGLE
BURGAS
BURGEE
BURGER
BURGHS
BURGLE
BURGOO
BURGOS

B•••G•
BADEGG
BAREGE
BEFOGS
BEINGS
BELUGA
BENIGN
BODEGA
BOINGO
BORAGE
BRIDGE
BRIGGS
BRINGS

B••••G
BAAING
BADEGG
BAKING
BALING
BANDOG
BARING
BARONG
BASING
BATING
BAYING
BBKING
BEDBUG
BELONG
BENING
BERING
BIDING
BIGWIG
BIKING
BITING
BLUING
BODING
BOEING
BOGONG
BONING
BOOING
BORING
BOWING
BOXING
BUSING
BUTUNG
BUYING

•B••G•
OBLIGE
UBANGI

•B•••G
ABYING
BBKING
EBBING
OBLONG

••BG••
SUBGUM

••B•G•
CUBAGE
DEBUGS
REBAGS
TOBAGO

••B••G
ALBORG
COBURG
CUBING
CYBORG
EBBING
EDBERG
EKBERG
GIBING
GYBING
JIBING
LUBING
ORBING
ROBING
SEBERG
TUBING
VYBORG

•••B•G
AIRBAG
BEDBUG
GASBAG
GYMBAG
HUMBUG
ICEBAG
KITBAG
LIEBIG
RAGBAG
SEABAG
SOWBUG
TEABAG

BH••••
BHAKTI
BHOPAL
BHUTAN
BHUTTO

B•H•••
BAHAMA
BAHIAN
BEHALF
BEHAVE
BEHEAD
BEHELD
BEHEST
BEHIND
BEHOLD
BEHOOF
BEHOVE
BIHARI
BSHARP
BYHAND

B••H••
BACHED
BADHAM
BARHOP
BASHED
BASHES
BATHED
BATHER
BATHES
BATHOS
BENHUR
BETHEL
BIGHTS
BISHOP
BOCHCO
BOOHOO
BOTHER
BRAHMA
BRAHMS
BUCHAN
BUSHED
BUSHEL
BUSHES
BUSHWA

B•••H•
BEACHY
BERTHA
BERTHS
BETCHA
BIRTHS
BLIGHT
BLITHE
BLYTHE
BOLSHY
BOOTHE
BOOTHS
BOTCHY
BOUGHS
BOUGHT
BRACHY
BRASHY
BRECHT
BRIGHT
BROTHS
BRUSHY
BUDDHA
BUNCHE
BUNCHY
BUQSHA
BURGHS
BYSSHE

B••••H
BANISH
BARISH
BARUCH
BEULAH
BLANCH
BLEACH
BLENCH
BLOTCH
BLUISH
BORSCH
BOYISH
BRANCH
BREACH
BREATH
BREECH
BROACH
BROOCH
BRUNCH
BYGOSH
BYPATH

•BH•••
ABHORS

•B•H••
ABOHMS

•B••H•
OBEAHS

•B•••H
ABLUSH

••BH••
COBHAM
JOBHOP

••B••H
AMBUSH
JOBETH
JUBBAH
KIBOSH
ORBACH

WABASH

•••B•H
CASBAH
JUBBAH
KASBAH

BI••••
BIAFRA
BIANCA
BIASED
BIASES
BIBBED
BIBLES
BIBLIO
BICARB
BICEPS
BICKER
BICORN
BIDDEN
BIDDER
BIDDLE
BIDING
BIDSIN
BIDSON
BIDSUP
BIERCE
BIFFED
BIFOLD
BIGAMY
BIGBEN
BIGBOY
BIGGER
BIGGIE
BIGGUN
BIGHTS
BIGLIE
BIGMAC
BIGOTS
BIGRED
BIGSUR
BIGTEN
BIGTOE
BIGTOP
BIGWIG
BIHARI
BIJOUX
BIKERS
BIKILA
BIKING
BIKINI
BILBAO
BILGES
BILKED
BILLED
BILLET
BILLIE
BILLON
BILLOW
BILOXI
BIMINI
BINARY
BINATE
BINDER
BINDUP
BINGED
BINGES
BINNED
BIOBIO
BIOGAS
BIOMES
BIONDI
BIONIC
BIOTAS
BIOTIC
BIOTIN
BIPEDS
BIPODS
BIRDED
BIRDER
BIRDIE
BIREME
BIRGIT
BIRLED
BIRNEY
BIRTHS
BISCAY
BISECT
BISHOP
BISONS
BISQUE
BISSAU
BISSET
BISTRO
BITERS
BITING
BITMAP
BITOFF
BITOLA
BITTED
BITTEN
BITTER

B•I•••
BAIKAL
BAILED
BAILEE
BAILER
BAILEY
BAILOR
BAINES
BAIRNS
BAITED
BAIZAS
BEIGES
BEINGS
BEIRUT
BGIRLS
BLIGHT
BLIMEY
BLIMPS
BLINDS
BLINIS
BLINKS
BLINTZ
BLITHE
BLIXEN
BMINOR
BMINUS
BOIGNY
BOILED
BOILER
BOINGO
BOITES
BRIAND
BRIANS
BRIARD
BRIARS
BRIBED
BRIBES
BRICKS
BRICKY
BRIDAL
BRIDES
BRIDGE
BRIDLE
BRIEFS
BRIENZ
BRIERS
BRIERY
BRIGGS
BRIGHT
BRIGID
BRILLO
BRILLS
BRINED
BRINES
BRINGS
BRINKS
BRITON
BSIDES
BUILDS

B••I••
BAAING
BABIED
BABIES
BAHIAN
BAKING
BALING
BANISH
BARING
BARISH
BARITE
BARIUM
BASICS
BASIFY
BASING
BASINS
BATIKS
BATING
BAYING
BBKING
BEDIMS
BEFITS
BEGINS
BEHIND
BELIAL
BELIED
BELIEF
BELIES
BELIKE
BELIZE
BEMINE
BEMIRE
BENIGN
BENING
BENITO
BERING
BESIDE
BETIDE
BETISE
BEVIES
BIDING
BIKILA
BIKING
BIKINI
BIMINI
BITING
BLAINE
BLAISE
BLUING
BLUISH
BODICE
BODIED
BODIES
BODILY
BODING
BOEING
BOGIES
BOLIDE
BONIER
BONING
BONITO
BOOING
BORIDE
BORING
BOVIDS
BOVINE
BOWING
BOXIER
BOXING
BOYISH
BRAIDS
BRAILA
BRAILS
BRAINS
BRAINY
BRAISE
BROILS
BRUINS
BRUISE
BRUITS
BUNION
BURIED
BURIES
BURINS
BUSIED
BUSIER
BUSIES
BUSILY
BUSING
BUYING
BYLINE

B•••I•
BACKIN
BADDIE
BAFFIN
BAGGIE
BAGSIT
BAGUIO
BALTIC
BANDIT
BARBIE
BARDIC
BARKIN
BARRIE
BARRIO
BARRIS
BAUCIS
BEANIE
BEATIT
BEAVIS
BELAIR
BELOIT
BENDIX
BENOIT
BERLIN
BERNIE
BERTIE
BESSIE
BESTIR
BEWAIL
BIBLIO
BIDSIN
BIGGIE
BIGLIE
BIGWIG
BILLIE
BIOBIO
BIONIC
BIOTIC
BIOTIN
BIRDIE
BIRGIT
BLEWIT
BLINIS
BLOWIN
BLOWIT
BMOVIE
BOBBIE
BOBBIN
BOCCIE
BODKIN
BOFFIN
BOLLIX
BONNIE
BOOGIE
BOOKIE
BOOTIE
BORGIA
BOSNIA
BOUDIN
BOWFIN
BOWTIE
BRAZIL
BREVIS
BRIGID
BRODIE
BROLIN
BUDGIE
BULBIL
BUNYIP
BUSKIN
BUSTIN
BUTTIN

B••••I
BANGUI
BANZAI
BATUMI
BENONI
BHAKTI
BIHARI
BIKINI
BILOXI
BIMINI
BIONDI
BODONI
BONAMI
BONSAI
BORZOI
BRAZZI
BRUNEI
BUSONI

•BI•••
ABIDED
ABIDES
FBIMAN
FBIMEN
IBIBIO
IBIDEM
IBISES
OBISPO
OBITER
OBIWAN
TBILLS
TBIRDS
UBIETY
UBIQUE

•B•I••
ABYING
BBKING
EBBING
OBLIGE
OBOIST
OBRIAN
OBRIEN

•B••I•
ABATIS
ABUKIR
IBERIA
IBIBIO
OBELIA
OBTAIN

•B•••I
UBANGI

••BI••
ALBINO
ALBION
AMBITS
BABIED
BABIES
CABINS
COBIAS
CUBICS
CUBING
CUBISM
CUBIST
CUBITS
CYBILL
DEBITS
EBBING
ERBIUM
FABIAN
GABIES
GABION
GIBILL
GIBING
GOBIES
GYBING
HABILE
HABITS
IMBIBE
JABIRU
JIBING
KIBITZ
LABIAL
LABILE
LIBIDO
LUBING
MOBILE
MOBIUS
NUBIAN
NUBILE
ORBING
ORBITS
RABIES
REBIDS
REBIND
ROBING
ROBINS
RUBIED
RUBIES
RUBIFY
SABINE
SABINS
SUBITO
TIBIAE
TIBIAL
TIBIAS
TOBIAS
TOBIES
TUBING
TUBIST
UNBIND

••B•I•
ALBEIT
ALBOIN
AMBLIN
BIBLIO
BOBBIE
BOBBIN
CABBIE
CUBOID
DEBBIE
DEBRIS
DOBBIN
DOBLIN
DUBBIN
DUBLIN
DUBOIS
FABRIC
FIBRIL
FIBRIN
GOBLIN
HOBBIT
HUBRIS
HYBRID
LIBRIS
LUBLIN
MCBAIN
NUBBIN
PUBLIC
RABBIS
RABBIT
REBOIL
ROBBIA
ROBBIE
RUBRIC
RUBSIN
SOBEIT
SUBMIT
TABRIZ
UMBRIA

••B••I
KABUKI
KUBLAI
LIBERI
RUBATI

•••BI•
ALIBIS
AMEBIC
ANUBIS
ARABIA
ARABIC
BARBIE
BIOBIO
BOBBIE
BOBBIN
BULBIL
CABBIE
CORBIN
DEBBIE
DOBBIN
DOOBIE
DUBBIN
DURBIN
FORBID
GAMBIA
GAMBIT
GERBIL
GLOBIN
HARBIN
HEEBIE
HENBIT
HERBIE
HOBBIT
IAMBIC
IBIBIO
LIEBIG
MORBID
NUBBIN
ORIBIS
OUTBID
PHOBIA
PHOBIC
RABBIS
RABBIT
ROBBIA
ROBBIE
SERBIA
SORBIC
TIDBIT
TITBIT
TURBID
TURBIT
TWOBIT
VERBIS
ZAMBIA
ZOMBIE

••••BI
ITURBI
JACOBI
MESABI
RHOMBI
WASABI

B•J•••
BIJOUX
BUJOLD
BYJOVE

B••J••
BANJOS
BANJUL
BMAJOR
BOOJUM

B•••J•
BAROJA

•BJ•••
ABJECT
ABJURE
OBJECT

B•K•••
BAKERS
BAKERY
BAKING
BAKULA
BBKING
BEKESY
BIKERS
BIKILA
BIKING
BIKINI

B••K••
BABKAS
BACKED
BACKER
BACKIN
BACKUP
BACKUS
BAIKAL
BALKAN
BALKED
BANKED
BANKER
BANKON
BARKAT
BARKED
BARKER
BARKIN
BASKED
BASKET
BEAKED
BEAKER
BECKER
BECKET
BECKON
BHAKTI
BICKER
BILKED
BLOKES
BODKIN
BOOKED
BOOKER
BOOKIE
BOSKET
BRAKED
BRAKES
BROKAW
BROKEN
BROKER
BUCKED
BUCKET
BUCKLE
BUCKUP
BULKED
BUNKED
BUNKER
BUNKOS
BUNKUM
BUSKED
BUSKIN

B•••K•
BAMAKO
BANGKA
BATIKS
BAULKS
BELIKE
BETAKE
BLACKS
BLANKS
BLINKS
BLOCKS
BLOCKY
BOURKE
BREAKS
BRICKS
BRICKY
BRINKS
BROOKE
BROOKS
BROOKY

B••••K
BARTOK
BEDECK
BETOOK
BRATSK
BUROAK
BYTALK

•BK•••
BBKING

•B•K••
ABUKIR

••BK••
BABKAS

••B•K•
KABUKI
REBUKE
UZBEKS

••B••K
DEBARK
DEBUNK
DUBCEK
DYBBUK
EMBANK
EMBARK
GOBACK
INBULK
LUBECK
TOBRUK

•••B•K
DYBBUK
LOMBOK
REEBOK
RHEBOK
TREBEK

BL••••
BLABBY
BLACKS
BLADED
BLADER
BLADES
BLAINE
BLAISE
BLAMED
BLAMES
BLANCA
BLANCH
BLANDA
BLANKS
BLARED
BLARES
BLASTS
BLATTY
BLAZED
BLAZER
BLAZES
BLAZON
BLEACH
BLEARS
BLEARY
BLEATS
BLEEDS
BLEEPS
BLENCH
BLENDE
BLENDS
BLENNY
BLEWIT
BLEWUP
BLIGHT
BLIMEY
BLIMPS
BLINDS
BLINIS
BLINKS
BLINTZ
BLITHE
BLIXEN
BLOATS
BLOCKS
BLOCKY
BLOKES
BLONDE
BLONDS
BLOODY
BLOOEY
BLOOMS
BLOOMY
BLOOPS
BLOTCH
BLOTTO
BLOTTY
BLOUSE
BLOWER
BLOWIN
BLOWIT
BLOWSY
BLOWUP
BLOWZY
BLUELY
BLUEOX
BLUEST
BLUESY
BLUETS
BLUEYS
BLUFFS
BLUING
BLUISH
BLUNTS
BLURBS
BLURRY
BLURTS
BLYTHE

B•L•••
BALAAM
BALATA
BALBOA
BALDER
BALDLY
BALEEN
BALERS
BALING
BALKAN
BALKED
BALLAD
BALLET
BALLON
BALLOT
BALLOU
BALLUP
BALSAM
BALTIC
BALZAC
BELAIR
BELAYS
BELDAM
BELFRY
BELIAL
BELIED
BELIEF
BELIES
BELIKE
BELIZE
BELLAY
BELLED
BELLES
BELLOC
BELLOW
BELOIT
BELONG
BELTED
BELUGA
BILBAO
BILGES
BILKED
BILLED
BILLET
BILLIE
BILLON
BILLOW
BILOXI
BOLDER
BOLDLY
BOLERO
BOLEYN
BOLGER
BOLIDE
BOLLIX
BOLSHY
BOLTED
BOLTON
BULBIL
BULBUL
BULGAR
BULGED
BULGES
BULGUR
BULKED
BULLAE
BULLED
BULLET
BULOVA
BULWER
BYLAWS
BYLINE

B••L••
BADLOT
BAILED
BAILEE
BAILER
BAILEY
BAILOR
BALLAD
BALLET
BALLON
BALLOT
BALLOU
BALLUP
BANLON
BARLEY
BAULKS
BAWLED
BAWLER
BAYLOR
BCELLS
BEDLAM
BEGLEY
BELLAY
BELLED
BELLES
BELLOC
BELLOW
BERLIN
BEULAH
BIBLES
BIBLIO
BIGLIE
BILLED
BILLET
BILLIE
BILLON
BILLOW
BIRLED
BOGLES
BOILED
BOILER
BOLLIX
BOSLEY
BOULES
BOULEZ
BOULLE
BOWLED
BOWLER
BOWLES
BRILLO
BRILLS
BROLIN
BROLLY
BRULES
BUGLED
BUGLER
BUGLES
BUILDS
BULLAE
BULLED
BULLET
BURLAP
BURLED
BURLEY
BUTLER
BYPLAY

B•••L•
BABALU
BABBLE
BABELS
BABULS
BACALL
BAFFLE
BAGELS
BAKULA
BALDLY
BANGLE
BARELY
BARFLY
BAROLO
BASALT
BASELY
BASSLY
BATTLE
BAUBLE
BCELLS
BEADLE
BEAGLE
BEATLE
BECALM
BEETLE
BEFALL
BEFELL
BEHALF
BEHELD
BEHOLD
BETELS
BEVELS
BEZELS
BGIRLS
BIDDLE
BIFOLD
BIKILA
BITOLA
BLUELY
BOBBLE
BODILY
BOGGLE
BOLDLY
BOODLE
BOTELS
BOTFLY
BOTTLE
BOUCLE
BOULLE
BRAILA
BRAILS
BRAWLS
BRIDLE
BRILLO
BRILLS
BROILS
BROLLY
BUBBLE
BUBBLY
BUCKLE
BUJOLD
BUMBLE
BUNDLE
BUNGLE
BURBLE
BURBLY
BURGLE
BUSILY
BUSTLE
BYTALK

B••••L
BACALL
BAGFUL
BAIKAL
BANJUL
BARBEL
BARREL
BATTEL
BEFALL
BEFELL
BEFOUL
BELIAL
BENGAL
BENZOL
BETHEL
BEWAIL
BHOPAL
BOATEL
BOREAL
BOXFUL
BRAZIL
BRIDAL
BRUMAL
BRUTAL
BUCCAL
BULBIL
BULBUL
BUNUEL
BURSAL
BUSHEL

•BL•••
ABLATE
ABLAUT
ABLAZE
ABLEST
ABLOOM
ABLUSH
OBLAST
OBLATE
OBLIGE
OBLONG

•B•L••
ABELES
ABOLLA
OBELIA
OBELUS
TBILLS
UBOLTS

•B••L•
ABOLLA
EBERLY
TBILLS

•B•••L
ABORAL

••BL••
AMBLED
AMBLER
AMBLES
AMBLIN
BIBLES
BIBLIO
CABLED
CABLER
CABLES
DOBLAS
DOBLIN
DUBLIN
EMBLEM
ENBLOC
FABLED
FABLER
FABLES
GABLED
GABLER
GABLES
GIBLET
GOBLET
GOBLIN
JOBLOT
KUBLAI
LUBLIN
MOBLEY
MRBLUE
NOBLER
NOBLES
PABLUM
PUBLIC
ROBLES
RUBLES
RUBLEV
SABLES
SUBLET
TABLAS
TABLED
TABLES
TABLET
VEBLEN

••B•L•
ARBELA
BABALU
BABBLE
BABELS
BABULS
BOBBLE
BUBBLE
BUBBLY
CABALA
CABALS
CIBOLA
COBALT
COBBLE
CYBELE
CYBILL
DABBLE
DIBBLE
FIBULA
GABBLE
GIBILL
GOBBLE
HABILE
HOBBLE
HUBBLE
HUBBLY
INBULK
KIBBLE
KOBOLD
LABELS
LABILE
LIBELS
LOBULE
MABELL
MOBILE
NEBULA
NIBBLE
NOBBLE
NUBBLE
NUBBLY
NUBILE
PEBBLE
PEBBLY
RABBLE
REBELS
REBOLT
RIBALD
ROBALO
RUBBLE
RUBBLY
SIBYLS
SUBTLE
SUBTLY
TABULA
TYBALT
UMBELS
UNBELT
UNBOLT
WOBBLE
WOBBLY

••B••L
CYBILL
FIBRIL
GIBILL
LABIAL
MABELL
REBOIL
SOBFUL
TIBIAL
UMBRAL

•••BL•
ALIBLE
ARABLE
BABBLE
BAUBLE
BOBBLE
BUBBLE
BUBBLY
BUMBLE
BURBLE
BURBLY
COBBLE
DABBLE
DIABLO
DIBBLE
DOABLE
DOUBLE
DOUBLY
DRABLY
DUMBLY
EDIBLE
ENABLE
FEEBLE
FEEBLY
FOIBLE
FUMBLE
GABBLE
GAMBLE
GARBLE
GLIBLY
GOBBLE
GRABLE
HOBBLE
HUBBLE
HUBBLY
HUMBLE
HUMBLY
JUMBLE
KIBBLE
LIABLE
MARBLE
MARBLY
MUMBLE
MUMBLY
NIBBLE
NIMBLE
NIMBLY
NOBBLE
NUBBLE
NUBBLY
NUMBLY
PEBBLE
PEBBLY
PUEBLA
PUEBLO
RABBLE
RAMBLA
RAMBLE
ROUBLE
RUBBLE
RUBBLY
RUMBLE
RUMBLY
STABLE
STABLY
TREBLE
TREBLY
TUMBLE
UNABLE
USABLE
USABLY
VIABLE
VIABLY
WAMBLE
WAMBLY
WARBLE
WIMBLE
WOBBLE
WOBBLY

•••B•L
BARBEL
BULBIL
BULBUL
CORBEL
CYMBAL
GAMBOL
GERBIL
GIMBAL
GIMBEL
GLOBAL
GUMBEL
HERBAL
ISABEL
IZABAL
SAMBAL
SIMBEL
SYMBOL
TIMBAL
TRIBAL
TYDBOL
VERBAL

BM••••
BMAJOR
BMINOR
BMINUS
BMOVIE

B•M•••
BAMAKO
BAMBOO
BEMATA
BEMINE
BEMIRE
BEMOAN
BEMUSE
BIMINI
BOMBAY
BOMBED
BOMBER
BOMBES
BUMBLE
BUMBRY
BUMMED
BUMMER
BUMOUT
BUMPED
BUMPER
BUMPPO
BUMPUP
BUMRAP

B••M••
BADMAN
BADMEN
BARMAN
BARMEN
BATMAN
BATMEN
BEAMED
BEAMON
BEAMUP
BIGMAC
BIOMES
BITMAP
BLAMED
BLAMES
BLIMEY
BLIMPS
BONMOT
BOOMED
BOOMER
BORMAN
BOWMAN
BOWMEN
BREMEN
BRUMAL
BRUMBY
BRUMES
BUMMED
BUMMER
BURMAN
BUSMAN
BUSMEN

B•••M•
BAHAMA
BATUMI
BECAME
BECOME
BEDIMS
BEGUMS
BENUMB
BESOMS
BIGAMY
BIREME
BLOOMS
BLOOMY
BONAMI
BRAHMA
BRAHMS
BREAMS
BROOMS
BROOMY
BYNAME

B••••M
BADHAM
BALAAM
BALSAM
BANTAM
BARIUM
BARNUM
BATYAM
BAYRUM
BECALM
BEDLAM
BEEGUM
BELDAM
BOOJUM
BOTTOM
BUNKUM

•B•M••
ABOMBS
FBIMAN
FBIMEN
HBOMBS

•B••M•
ABOHMS
ABRAMS
ABYSMS
HBEAMS
IBEAMS

•B•••M
ABLOOM
ABSCAM
IBIDEM

••BM••
SUBMIT
TUBMAN

••B•M•
ALBUMS

••B••M
COBHAM
CUBISM
EMBLEM
ERBIUM
KABOOM
LABRUM
PABLUM
SHBOOM
SUBGUM

B•N•••
BANANA
BANDED
BANDIT
BANDOG
BANGED
BANGER
BANGKA
BANGLE
BANGOR
BANGUI
BANGUP
BANISH
BANJOS
BANJUL
BANKED
BANKER
BANKON
BANLON
BANNED
BANNER
BANQUO
BANTAM
BANTER
BANTUS
BANYAN
BANZAI
BENDAY
BENDED
BENDER
BENDIX
BENGAL
BENGAY
BENHUR
BENIGN
BENING
BENITO
BENOIT
BENONI
BENSON
BENTON
BENUMB
BENZOL
BINARY
BINATE
BINDER
BINDUP
BINGED
BINGES
BINNED
BONAMI
BONBON
BONCES
BONDED
BONERS
BONEUP
BONGED
BONGOS
BONIER
BONING
BONITO
BONMOT
BONNES
BONNET
BONNIE
BONSAI
BONTON
BONZES
BUNCHE
BUNCHY
BUNCOS
BUNDLE
BUNGED
BUNGEE
BUNGLE
BUNION
BUNKED
BUNKER
BUNKOS
BUNKUM
BUNSEN
BUNTED
BUNTER
BUNUEL
BUNYAN
BUNYIP
BYNAME

B••N••
BAINES
BANNED
BANNER
BARNES
BARNEY
BARNUM
BEANED
BEANIE
BEANOS
BEINGS
BERNIE
BIANCA
BINNED
BIONDI
BIONIC
BIRNEY
BLANCA
BLANCH
BLANDA
BLANKS
BLENCH
BLENDE
BLENDS
BLENNY
BLINDS
BLINIS
BLINKS
BLINTZ
BLONDE
BLONDS
BLUNTS
BMINOR
BMINUS
BOINGO
BONNES
BONNET
BONNIE
BORNEO
BOSNIA
BOUNCE
BOUNCY
BOUNDS
BOUNTY
BOWNET
BRANCH
BRANDO
BRANDS
BRANDT
BRANDX
BRANDY
BRANNY
BRANTS
BRENDA
BRENTS
BRINED
BRINES
BRINGS
BRINKS
BRONCO
BRONCS
BRONTE
BRONZE
BRONZY
BRUNCH
BRUNEI
BRUNET
BRUNTS
BUENOS
BURNED
BURNER
BURNET
BURNEY
BURNUP
BWANAS
BYRNES

B•••N•
BAAING
BAIRNS
BAKING
BALING
BANANA
BARING
BARONG
BARONS
BARONY
BASING
BASINS
BATING
BATONS
BAYING
BBKING
BEGINS
BEGONE
BEHIND
BELONG
BEMINE
BENING
BENONI
BERING
BESANT
BETONY
BEYOND
BEZANT
BIDING
BIKING
BIKINI
BIMINI
BISONS
BITING
BLAINE
BLENNY
BLUING
BODING
BODONI
BOEING
BOGONG
BOIGNY
BONING
BOOING
BORING
BOSONS
BOSUNS
BOTANY
BOURNE
BOVINE
BOWING
BOXING
BRAINS
BRAINY
BRANNY
BRAWNY
BRIAND
BRIANS
BRIENZ
BROWNE
BROWNS
BROWNY
BRUINS
BRYANT
BRYONY
BURINS
BUSING
BUSONI
BUTANE
BUTENE
BUTUNG
BUYING
BYGONE
BYHAND
BYLINE

B••••N
BABOON
BABSON
BACKIN
BADMAN
BADMEN
BAFFIN
BAHIAN
BALEEN
BALKAN
BALLON
BANKON
BANLON
BANYAN
BARKIN
BARMAN
BARMEN
BARREN
BARRON
BARTON
BARYON
BARZUN
BATAAN
BATMAN
BATMEN
BATTEN
BEACON
BEAMON
BEARON
BEATEN
BEATON
BECKON
BEMOAN
BENIGN
BENSON
BENTON
BERGEN
BERLIN
BETSON
BHUTAN
BICORN
BIDDEN
BIDSIN
BIDSON
BIGBEN
BIGGUN
BIGTEN
BILLON
BIOTIN
BITTEN
BLAZON
BLIXEN
BLOWIN
BOBBIN
BODKIN
BOFFIN
BOLEYN
BOLTON
BONBON
BONTON
BORDEN
BOREON
BORMAN
BOSTON
BOUDIN
BOWFIN
BOWMAN
BOWMEN
BRAZEN
BREMEN
BRETON
BRITON
BROGAN
BROKEN
BROLIN
BRYSON
BUCHAN
BUFFON
BUNION
BUNSEN
BUNYAN
BURDEN
BURMAN
BURTON
BUSKIN
BUSMAN
BUSMEN
BUSTIN
BUTTIN
BUTTON

•B•N••
EBONDS
MBUNDU
TBONDS
TBONES
UBANGI

•B••N•
ABOUND
ABSENT
ABYING
BBKING
EBBING
OBLONG
OBTUND

•B•••N
FBIMAN
FBIMEN
IBADAN
OBERON
OBIWAN
OBRIAN
OBRIEN
OBTAIN

••BN••
DABNEY
HOBNOB

••B•N•
ALBANO
ALBANY
ALBINO
CABANA
CABINS
CUBING
DEBONE
DEBUNK
EBBING
EMBANK
GIBING
GYBING
HABANA
JIBING
LUBING
ORBING
REBEND
REBENT
REBIND
RIBAND
ROBING
ROBINS
RUBENS
SABENA
SABINE
SABINS
TUBING
UNBEND
UNBENT
UNBIND
URBANA
URBANE

••B••N
ALBION
ALBOIN
AMBLIN
AUBURN
BABOON
BABSON
BOBBIN
COBURN
DOBBIN
DOBLIN
DOBSON
DUBBIN
DUBLIN
EMBDEN
FABIAN
FIBRIN
GABION
GIBBON
GIBRAN
GIBSON
GOBLIN
HEBRON
HOBSON
INBORN
LEBRUN
LIBYAN
LLBEAN
LUBLIN
MCBAIN
NUBBIN
NUBIAN
OSBORN
REBORN
RIBBON
ROBSON
RUBSIN
SUBORN
TUBMAN
UNBORN
VEBLEN
WEBERN

•••B•N
ARUBAN
BIGBEN
BOBBIN
BONBON
CARBON
CORBAN
CORBIN
DOBBIN
DUBBIN
DURBAN
DURBIN
GIBBON
GLOBIN
GRABEN
HARBIN
KLIBAN
LISBON
NUBBIN
REUBEN
RIBBON
SHABAN
TURBAN

BO••••
BOARDS
BOASTS
BOATED
BOATEL
BOATER
BOBBED
BOBBER
BOBBIE
BOBBIN
BOBBLE
BOBCAT
BOBSUP
BOCCIE
BOCHCO
BODEGA
BODICE
BODIED
BODIES
BODILY
BODING
BODKIN
BODONI
BOEING
BOFFED
BOFFIN
BOFFOS
BOGART
BOGEYS
BOGGED

BOGGLE
BOGIES
BOGLES
BOGONG
BOGOTA
BOIGNY
BOILED
BOILER
BOINGO
BOITES
BOLDER
BOLDLY
BOLERO
BOLEYN
BOLGER
BOLIDE
BOLLIX
BOLSHY
BOLTED
BOLTON
BOMBAY
BOMBED
BOMBER
BOMBES
BONAMI
BONBON
BONCES
BONDED
BONERS
BONEUP
BONGED
BONGOS
BONIER
BONING
BONITO
BONMOT
BONNES
BONNET
BONNIE
BONSAI
BONTON
BONZES
BOOBOO
BOODLE
BOOGIE
BOOHOO
BOOING
BOOJUM
BOOKED
BOOKER
BOOKIE
BOOMED
BOOMER
BOOSTS
BOOTED
BOOTEE
BOOTES
BOOTHE
BOOTHS
BOOTIE
BOOTSY
BOOTUP
BOPEEP
BOPPED
BOPPER
BORAGE
BORATE
BORAXO
BORDEN
BORDER
BOREAL
BOREAS
BOREON
BORERS
BOREUP
BORGIA
BORIDE
BORING
BORMAN
BORNEO
BORROW
BORSCH
BORZOI
BOSKET
BOSLEY
BOSNIA
BOSONS
BOSSED
BOSSES
BOSTON
BOSUNS
BOTANY
BOTCHY
BOTELS
BOTFLY
BOTHER
BOTREE
BOTTLE
BOTTOM
BOUBOU
BOUCLE
BOUDIN
BOUFFE
BOUGHS
BOUGHT
BOULES
BOULEZ
BOULLE
BOUNCE
BOUNCY
BOUNDS
BOUNTY
BOURKE
BOURNE
BOURSE
BOUSED
BOUSES
BOVARY
BOVIDS
BOVINE
BOVVER
BOWERS
BOWERY
BOWFIN
BOWING
BOWLED
BOWLER
BOWLES
BOWMAN
BOWMEN
BOWNET
BOWOAR
BOWOUT
BOWSAW
BOWSER
BOWTIE
BOWWOW
BOWYER
BOXBOY
BOXCAR
BOXERS
BOXFUL
BOXIER
BOXING
BOXSET
BOXTOP
BOYARS
BOYISH

B•O•••

BAOBAB
BHOPAL
BIOBIO
BIOGAS
BIOMES
BIONDI
BIONIC
BIOTAS
BIOTIC
BIOTIN
BLOATS
BLOCKS
BLOCKY
BLOKES
BLONDE
BLONDS
BLOODY
BLOOEY
BLOOMS
BLOOMY
BLOOPS
BLOTCH
BLOTTO
BLOTTY
BLOUSE
BLOWER
BLOWIN
BLOWIT
BLOWSY
BLOWUP
BLOWZY
BMOVIE
BOOBOO
BOODLE
BOOGIE
BOOHOO
BOOING
BOOJUM
BOOKED
BOOKER
BOOKIE
BOOMED
BOOMER
BOOSTS
BOOTED
BOOTEE
BOOTES
BOOTHE
BOOTHS
BOOTIE
BOOTSY
BOOTUP
BROACH
BROADS
BRODIE
BROGAN
BROGUE
BROILS
BROKAW
BROKEN
BROKER
BROLIN
BROLLY
BRONCO
BRONCS
BRONTE
BRONZE
BRONZY
BROOCH
BROODS
BROODY
BROOKE
BROOKS
BROOKY
BROOMS
BROOMY
BROTHS
BROWNE
BROWNS
BROWNY
BROWSE
BUOYED
BUOYUP

B••O••

BABOON
BAROJA
BAROLO
BARONG
BARONS
BARONY
BATONS
BAYOUS
BEBOPS
BECOME
BEFOGS
BEFORE
BEFOUL
BEGOFF
BEGONE
BEHOLD
BEHOOF
BEHOVE
BELOIT
BELONG
BEMOAN
BENOIT
BENONI
BESOMS
BESOTS
BETONY
BETOOK
BEYOND
BICORN
BIFOLD
BIGOTS
BIJOUX
BILOXI
BIPODS
BISONS
BITOFF
BITOLA
BLOODY
BLOOEY
BLOOMS
BLOOMY
BLOOPS
BODONI
BOGONG
BOGOTA
BOSONS
BOWOAR
BOWOUT
BROOCH
BROODS
BROODY
BROOKE
BROOKS
BROOKY
BROOMS
BROOMY
BRYONY
BUGOFF
BUGOUT
BUJOLD
BULOVA
BUMOUT
BUROAK
BUSONI
BUYOFF
BUYOUT
BYGONE
BYGOSH
BYJOVE
BYROAD
BYROTE
BYWORD

B•••O•

BABOON
BABSON
BADBOY
BADLOT
BAILOR
BALBOA
BALLON
BALLOT
BALLOU
BAMBOO
BANDOG
BANGOR
BANJOS
BANKON
BANLON
BARDOT
BARHOP
BARRON
BARROW
BARTOK
BARTON
BARYON
BASSOS
BATBOY
BATHOS
BAYLOR
BEACON
BEAMON
BEANOS
BEARON
BEATON
BECKON
BEHOOF
BELLOC
BELLOW
BENSON
BENTON
BENZOL
BESTOW
BETOOK
BETSON
BETTOR
BIDSON
BIGBOY
BIGTOE
BIGTOP
BILLON
BILLOW
BISHOP
BLAZON
BLUEOX
BMAJOR
BMINOR
BOFFOS
BOLTON
BONBON
BONGOS
BONMOT
BONTON
BOOBOO
BOOHOO
BOREON
BORROW
BORZOI
BOSTON
BOTTOM
BOUBOU
BOWWOW
BOXBOY
BOXTOP
BRASOV
BRAVOS
BRAZOS
BRETON
BRITON
BRYSON
BUENOS
BUFFON
BUFFOS
BUNCOS
BUNION
BUNKOS
BURBOT
BURGOO
BURGOS
BURROS
BURROW
BURTON
BUSBOY
BUTEOS
BUTTON

B••••O

BAGUIO
BAMAKO
BAMBOO
BANQUO
BAROLO
BARRIO
BENITO
BHUTTO
BIBLIO
BIOBIO
BISTRO
BLOTTO
BOCHCO
BOINGO
BOLERO
BONITO
BOOBOO
BOOHOO
BORAXO
BORNEO
BRANDO
BRILLO
BRONCO
BUMPPO
BURGOO

•BO•••

ABOARD
ABODES
ABOHMS
ABOLLA
ABOMBS
ABORAL
ABORTS
ABOUND
EBOATS
EBONDS
HBOMBS
OBOIST
TBONDS
TBONES
UBOATS
UBOLTS

•B•O••

ABBOTS
ABBOTT
ABHORS
ABLOOM
ABROAD
ABSORB
OBLONG

•B••O•

ABLOOM
ABYDOS
OBERON

•B•••O

IBIBIO
OBISPO

••BO••

ABBOTS
ABBOTT
ALBOIN
ALBORG
ARBORS
ARBOUR
BABOON
BEBOPS
CIBOLA
CUBOID
CYBORG
DEBONE
DUBOIS
ELBOWS
EMBODY
EMBOSS
EUBOEA
FOBOFF
HOBOES
INBORN
JABOTS
KABOBS
KABOOM
KEBOBS
KIBOSH
KOBOLD
LABORS
LABOUR
NABOBS
NABORS
NOBODY
OSBORN
OXBOWS
POBOYS
PTBOAT
REBOIL
REBOLT
REBOOT
REBORN
REBOZO
RIBOSE
ROBOTS
RUBOFF
RUBOUT
SABOTS
SHBOOM
SUBORN
TABOOS
TABORS
TOBOOT
UNBOLT
UNBORN
UPBOWS
VYBORG

••B•O•

ALBION
BABOON
BABSON
DEBTOR
DOBROS
DOBSON
ENBLOC
GABION
GIBBON
GIBSON
HEBRON
HOBNOB
HOBSON
JOBHOP
JOBLOT
KABOOM
REBOOT
RIBBON
ROBROY
ROBSON
SHBOOM
TABOOS
TOBOOT
YOBBOS

••B••O

ALBANO
ALBEDO
ALBINO
AMBATO
BIBLIO
EMBRYO
GABBRO
LIBIDO
RABATO
REBOZO
ROBALO
RUBATO
SABATO
SUBITO
TOBAGO

•••BO•

BADBOY
BALBOA
BAMBOO
BATBOY
BIGBOY
BONBON
BOOBOO
BOUBOU
BOXBOY
BURBOT
BUSBOY
CARBON
CARBOS
CARBOY
COMBOS
COWBOY
DAYBOY
FLYBOY
FOGBOW
GAMBOL
GIBBON
GUMBOS
HARBOR
HATBOX
HOTBOX
ICEBOX
IROBOT
JERBOA
JUMBOS
LAZBOY
LESBOS
LIMBOS
LISBOA
LISBON
LOMBOK
LOWBOY
MAMBOS
OLDBOY
OUTBOX
PAYBOX
PHOBOS
REEBOK
RHEBOK
RIBBON
SKIBOB
SKYBOX
SYMBOL
TALBOT
TOMBOY
TURBOS
TURBOT
TYDBOL
YOBBOS

•••B•O

BAMBOO
BILBAO
BIOBIO
BOOBOO
DIABLO
GABBRO
HASBRO
IBIBIO
PUEBLO
RHABDO

••••BO
AKIMBO
CRAMBO
GAZEBO
LAVABO
MALABO
NINGBO
PHLEBO
PICABO
SASEBO
STRABO

B•P•••
BIPEDS
BIPODS
BOPEEP
BOPPED
BOPPER
BYPASS
BYPAST
BYPATH
BYPLAY

B••P••
BEEPED
BEEPER
BHOPAL
BOPPED
BOPPER
BUMPED
BUMPER
BUMPPO
BUMPUP
BURPED

B•••P•
BEBOPS
BICEPS
BLEEPS
BLIMPS
BLOOPS
BUMPPO

B••••P
BACKUP
BALLUP
BANGUP
BARHOP
BEADUP
BEAMUP
BEARUP
BEATUP
BEEFUP
BIDSUP
BIGTOP
BINDUP
BISHOP
BITMAP
BLEWUP
BLOWUP
BOBSUP
BONEUP
BOOTUP
BOPEEP
BOREUP
BOXTOP
BSHARP
BUCKUP
BUMPUP
BUMRAP
BUNYIP
BUOYUP
BURLAP
BURNUP
BUYSUP

•B••P•
ABRUPT
OBISPO

••BP••
SUBPAR

••B•P•
BEBOPS

••B••P
BOBSUP
HUBCAP
JOBHOP
MOBCAP

B•Q•••
BUQSHA

B••Q••
BANQUO
BARQUE
BASQUE
BISQUE
BRAQUE

•B•Q••
UBIQUE

BR••••
BRACED
BRACER
BRACES
BRACHY
BRACTS
BRAHMA
BRAHMS
BRAIDS
BRAILA
BRAILS
BRAINS
BRAINY
BRAISE
BRAKED
BRAKES
BRANCH
BRANDO
BRANDS
BRANDT
BRANDX
BRANDY
BRANNY
BRANTS
BRAQUE
BRASHY
BRASOV
BRASSY
BRATSK
BRATTY
BRAVAS
BRAVED
BRAVER
BRAVES
BRAVOS
BRAWLS
BRAWNY
BRAYED
BRAYER
BRAZED
BRAZEN
BRAZER
BRAZES
BRAZIL
BRAZOS
BRAZZA
BRAZZI
BREACH
BREADS
BREAKS
BREAMS
BREAST
BREATH
BRECHT
BREECH
BREEDS
BREEZE
BREEZY
BREMEN
BRENDA
BRENTS
BRETON
BREUER
BREVES
BREVET
BREVIS
BREWED
BREWER
BREYER
BRIAND
BRIANS
BRIARD
BRIARS
BRIBED
BRIBES
BRICKS
BRICKY
BRIDAL
BRIDES
BRIDGE
BRIDLE
BRIEFS
BRIENZ
BRIERS
BRIERY
BRIGGS
BRIGHT
BRIGID
BRILLO
BRILLS
BRINED
BRINES
BRINGS
BRINKS
BRITON
BROACH
BROADS
BRODIE
BROGAN
BROGUE
BROILS
BROKAW
BROKEN
BROKER
BROLIN
BROLLY
BRONCO
BRONCS
BRONTE
BRONZE
BRONZY
BROOCH
BROODS
BROODY
BROOKE
BROOKS
BROOKY
BROOMS
BROOMY
BROTHS
BROWNE
BROWNS
BROWNY
BROWSE
BRUDER
BRUGES
BRUINS
BRUISE
BRUITS
BRULES
BRUMAL
BRUMBY
BRUMES
BRUNCH
BRUNEI
BRUNET
BRUNTS
BRUSHY
BRUTAL
BRUTES
BRUTUS
BRUXED
BRUXES
BRYANT
BRYONY
BRYSON

B•R•••
BARBED
BARBEL
BARBER
BARBET
BARBIE
BARBRA
BARCAR
BARDIC
BARDOT
BAREGE
BARELY
BAREST
BARFLY
BARGED
BARGES
BARHOP
BARING
BARISH
BARITE
BARIUM
BARKAT
BARKED
BARKER
BARKIN
BARLEY
BARMAN
BARMEN
BARNES
BARNEY
BARNUM
BAROJA
BAROLO
BARONG
BARONS
BARONY
BARQUE
BARRED
BARREL
BARREN
BARRES
BARRIE
BARRIO
BARRIS
BARRON
BARROW
BARTAB
BARTER
BARTOK
BARTON
BARUCH
BARYON
BARZUN
BERATE
BERBER
BEREFT
BERETS
BERGEN
BERING
BERLIN
BERNIE
BERTHA
BERTHS
BERTIE
BIRDED
BIRDER
BIRDIE
BIREME
BIRGIT
BIRLED
BIRNEY
BIRTHS
BORAGE
BORATE
BORAXO
BORDEN
BORDER
BOREAL
BOREAS
BOREON
BORERS
BOREUP
BORGIA
BORIDE
BORING
BORMAN
BORNEO
BORROW
BORSCH
BORZOI
BURBLE
BURBLY
BURBOT
BURDEN
BUREAU
BURGAS
BURGEE
BURGER
BURGHS
BURGLE
BURGOO
BURGOS
BURIED
BURIES
BURINS
BURLAP
BURLED
BURLEY
BURMAN
BURNED
BURNER
BURNET
BURNEY
BURNUP
BUROAK
BURPED
BURRED
BURROS
BURROW
BURSAE
BURSAL
BURSAR
BURSAS
BURSES
BURSTS
BURTON
BYRNES
BYROAD
BYROTE

B••R••
BAIRNS
BARRED
BARREL
BARREN
BARRES
BARRIE
BARRIO
BARRIS
BARRON
BARROW
BAYRUM
BEARDS
BEARER
BEARON
BEARUP
BEIRUT
BETRAY
BEURRE
BEWRAY
BGIRLS
BIERCE
BIGRED
BLARED
BLARES
BLURBS
BLURRY
BLURTS
BOARDS
BORROW
BOTREE
BOURKE
BOURNE
BOURSE
BUMRAP
BURRED
BURROS
BURROW

B•••R•
BAKERS
BAKERY
BALERS
BARBRA
BAYARD
BEFORE
BELFRY
BEMIRE
BEURRE
BEWARE
BIAFRA
BICARB
BICORN
BIHARI
BIKERS
BINARY
BISTRO
BITERS
BLEARS
BLEARY
BLURRY
BOGART
BOLERO
BONERS
BORERS
BOVARY
BOWERS
BOWERY
BOXERS
BOYARS
BRIARD
BRIARS
BRIERS
BRIERY
BSHARP
BUMBRY
BUYERS
BYWORD

B••••R
BACKER
BADDER
BADGER
BAGGER
BAILER
BAILOR
BALDER
BANGER
BANGOR
BANKER
BANNER
BANTER
BARBER
BARCAR
BARKER
BARTER
BASTER
BATHER
BATTER
BAWLER
BAXTER
BAYLOR
BAZAAR
BEAKER
BEARER
BEATER
BEAVER
BECKER
BEEPER
BEGGAR
BELAIR
BENDER
BENHUR
BERBER
BESSER
BESTIR
BETTER
BETTOR
BICKER
BIDDER
BIGGER
BIGSUR
BINDER
BIRDER
BITTER
BLADER
BLAZER
BLOWER
BMAJOR
BMINOR
BOATER
BOBBER
BOILER
BOLDER
BOLGER
BOMBER
BONIER
BOOKER
BOOMER
BOPPER
BORDER
BOTHER
BOVVER
BOWLER
BOWOAR
BOWSER
BOWYER
BOXCAR
BOXIER
BRACER
BRAVER
BRAYER
BRAZER
BREUER
BREWER
BREYER
BROKER
BRUDER
BUFFER
BUGLER
BULGAR
BULGUR
BULWER
BUMMER
BUMPER
BUNKER
BUNTER
BURGER
BURNER
BURSAR
BUSBAR
BUSIER
BUSTER
BUTLER
BUTTER
BUZZER

•BR•••
ABRADE
ABRAMS
ABROAD
ABRUPT
OBRIAN
OBRIEN

•B•R••
ABORAL
ABORTS
EBERLY
IBERIA
OBERON
TBIRDS

•B••R•
ABHORS
ABJURE
ABOARD
ABSORB
ABSURD
OBVERT

•B•••R
ABUKIR
ABUSER
OBITER

••BR••
AUBREY
COBRAS
DEBRAS
DEBRIS
DOBRAS
DOBROS
ELBRUS
EMBRYO
FABRAY
FABRIC
FIBRES
FIBRIL
FIBRIN
GIBRAN
HEBREW
HEBRON
HUBRIS
HYBRID
IMBRUE
INBRED
LABREA
LABRET
LABRUM
LEBRUN
LIBRIS
ROBROY
RUBRIC
SABRAS
SABRES
TABRIZ
TOBRUK
UMBRAE
UMBRAL
UMBRAS
UMBRIA
ZEBRAS

••B•R•
ALBERT
ALBORG
AMBERS

AMBERY
ARBORS
ASBURY
AUBURN
CABERS
COBURG
COBURN
CYBORG
DEBARK
DEBARS
EDBERG
EGBERT
EKBERG
ELBERT
EMBARK
EMBERS
FIBERS
GABBRO
GIBERS
HOBART
HUBERT
INBORN
JABIRU
LABORS
LIBERI
NABORS
OSBORN
REBARS
REBORN
REBURY
ROBERT
SABERS
SEBERG
SOBERS
SUBARU
SUBORN
SUBURB
TABARD
TABORS
TUBERS
UMBERS
UNBARS
UNBORN
VYBORG
WEBERN

••B••R
AMBLER
ARBOUR
BOBBER
CABLER
DEBTOR
DOBBER
FABLER
FIBBER
GABBER
GABLER
GIBBER
JABBAR
JABBER
JOBBER
LABOUR
LIBBER
LOBBER
LUBBER
NABBER
NOBLER
ROBBER
RUBBER
SOBBER
SUBPAR
WEBBER
YABBER

•••BR•
BARBRA
BUMBRY
GABBRO
HASBRO
HOMBRE
SOMBRE
TIMBRE

•••B•R
BARBER
BERBER
BOBBER
BOMBER
BUSBAR
CAMBER
COMBER
CUMBER
DAUBER
DISBAR
DOBBER
DUMBER
DUNBAR
DURBAR
FERBER
FIBBER
GABBER
GERBER
GIBBER
GOOBER
HARBOR
ISOBAR
JABBAR
JABBER
JOBBER
KHYBER
LIBBER
LIMBER
LOBBER
LUBBER
LUMBAR
LUMBER
MEMBER
NABBER
NUMBER
PROBER
ROBBER
RUBBER
SAMBAR
SOBBER
SOMBER
TIMBER
WEBBER
WETBAR
WILBUR
YABBER
ZEDBAR

BS••••
BSHARP
BSIDES

B•S•••
BASALT
BASELY
BASEST
BASHED
BASHES
BASICS
BASIFY
BASING
BASINS
BASKED
BASKET
BASQUE
BASSES
BASSET
BASSLY
BASSOS
BASTED
BASTER
BASTES
BESANT
BESETS
BESIDE
BESOMS
BESOTS
BESSER
BESSIE
BESTED
BESTIR
BESTOW
BISCAY
BISECT
BISHOP
BISONS
BISQUE
BISSAU
BISSET
BISTRO
BOSKET
BOSLEY
BOSNIA
BOSONS
BOSSED
BOSSES
BOSTON
BOSUNS
BUSBAR
BUSBOY
BUSHED
BUSHEL
BUSHES
BUSHWA
BUSIED
BUSIER
BUSIES
BUSILY
BUSING
BUSKED
BUSKIN
BUSMAN
BUSMEN
BUSONI
BUSSED
BUSSES
BUSTED
BUSTER
BUSTIN
BUSTLE
BYSSHE
BYSSUS

B••S••
BABSON
BAGSIT
BALSAM
BASSES
BASSET
BASSLY
BASSOS
BEASTS
BENSON
BESSER
BESSIE
BETSEY
BETSON
BIASED
BIASES
BIDSIN
BIDSON
BIDSUP
BIGSUR
BISSAU
BISSET
BLASTS
BOASTS
BOBSUP
BOLSHY
BONSAI
BOOSTS
BORSCH
BOSSED
BOSSES
BOUSED
BOUSES
BOWSAW
BOWSER
BOXSET
BRASHY
BRASOV
BRASSY
BRUSHY
BRYSON
BUNSEN
BUQSHA
BURSAE
BURSAL
BURSAR
BURSAS
BURSES
BURSTS
BUSSED
BUSSES
BUYSUP
BYSSHE
BYSSUS

B•••S•
BANISH
BAREST
BARISH
BASEST
BEHEST
BEKESY
BEMUSE
BETISE
BLAISE
BLOUSE
BLOWSY
BLUEST
BLUESY
BLUISH
BOOTSY
BOURSE
BOYISH
BRAISE
BRASSY
BRATSK
BREAST
BROWSE
BRUISE
BYGOSH
BYPASS
BYPAST

B••••S
BABELS
BABIES
BABKAS
BABULS
BACKUS
BADGES
BAGELS
BAINES
BAIRNS
BAIZAS
BAKERS
BALERS
BANJOS
BANTUS
BARGES
BARNES
BARONS
BARRES
BARRIS
BASHES
BASICS
BASINS
BASSES
BASSOS
BASTES
BATHES
BATHOS
BATIKS
BATONS
BAUCIS
BAULKS
BAYOUS
BCELLS
BEANOS
BEARDS
BEASTS
BEAUTS
BEAVIS
BEBOPS
BEDEWS
BEDIMS
BEEVES
BEFITS
BEFOGS
BEGETS
BEGINS
BEGUMS
BEIGES
BEINGS
BELAYS
BELIES
BELLES
BERETS
BERTHS
BESETS
BESOMS
BESOTS
BETELS
BETTAS
BEVELS
BEVIES
BEZELS
BGIRLS
BIASES
BIBLES
BICEPS
BIGHTS
BIGOTS
BIKERS
BILGES
BINGES
BIOGAS
BIOMES
BIOTAS
BIPEDS
BIPODS
BIRTHS
BISONS
BITERS
BLACKS
BLADES
BLAMES
BLANKS
BLARES
BLASTS
BLAZES
BLEARS
BLEATS
BLEEDS
BLEEPS
BLENDS
BLIMPS
BLINDS
BLINIS
BLINKS
BLOATS
BLOCKS
BLOKES
BLONDS
BLOOMS
BLOOPS
BLUETS
BLUEYS
BLUFFS
BLUNTS
BLURBS
BLURTS
BMINUS
BOARDS
BOASTS
BODIES
BOFFOS
BOGEYS
BOGIES
BOGLES
BOITES
BOMBES
BONCES
BONERS
BONGOS
BONNES
BONZES
BOOSTS
BOOTES
BOOTHS
BOREAS
BORERS
BOSONS
BOSSES
BOSUNS
BOTELS
BOUGHS
BOULES
BOUNDS
BOUSES
BOVIDS
BOWERS
BOWLES
BOXERS
BOYARS
BRACES
BRACTS
BRAHMS
BRAIDS
BRAILS
BRAINS
BRAKES
BRANDS
BRANTS
BRAVAS
BRAVES
BRAVOS
BRAWLS
BRAZES
BRAZOS
BREADS
BREAKS
BREAMS
BREEDS
BRENTS
BREVES
BREVIS
BRIANS
BRIARS
BRIBES
BRICKS
BRIDES
BRIEFS
BRIERS
BRIGGS
BRILLS
BRINES
BRINGS
BRINKS
BROADS
BROILS
BRONCS
BROODS
BROOKS
BROOMS
BROTHS
BROWNS
BRUGES
BRUINS
BRUITS
BRULES
BRUMES
BRUNTS
BRUTES
BRUTUS
BRUXES
BSIDES
BUDGES
BUENOS
BUFFOS
BUGLES
BUILDS
BULGES
BUNCOS
BUNKOS
BURGAS
BURGHS
BURGOS
BURIES
BURINS
BURROS
BURSAS
BURSES
BURSTS
BUSHES
BUSIES
BUSSES
BUTEOS
BUTTES
BUTUTS
BUYERS
BUZZES
BWANAS
BYLAWS
BYPASS
BYRNES
BYSSUS
BYWAYS

•BS•••
ABSCAM
ABSENT
ABSORB
ABSURD
OBSESS
OBSTET

•B•S••
ABASED
ABASES
ABESSE
ABUSED
ABUSER
ABUSES
ABYSMS
IBISES
OBISPO

•B••S•
ABBESS
ABESSE
ABLEST
ABLUSH
OBLAST
OBOIST
OBSESS
OBTEST
OBTUSE

•B•••S
ABACAS
ABACUS
ABASES
ABATES
ABATIS
ABBESS
ABBEYS
ABBOTS
ABELES
ABHORS
ABIDES
ABODES
ABOHMS
ABOMBS
ABORTS
ABRAMS
ABUSES
ABYDOS
ABYSMS
EBOATS
EBONDS
HBEAMS
HBOMBS
IBEAMS
IBEXES
IBISES
OBEAHS
OBELUS
OBSESS
TBILLS
TBIRDS
TBONDS
TBONES
UBOATS
UBOLTS

••BS••
BABSON
BOBSUP
DOBSON
GIBSON
HOBSON
ROBSON
RUBSIN
SUBSET

••B•S•
ABBESS
AMBUSH
ATBEST
CUBISM
CUBIST
DEBASE
EMBOSS
GOBUST
KIBOSH
RIBOSE
ROBUST
TUBIST
UNBUSY
WABASH

••B••S
ABBESS
ABBEYS
ABBOTS
ALBUMS
AMBERS
AMBITS
AMBLES
ARBORS
ATBATS
BABELS
BABIES
BABKAS
BABULS
BEBOPS
BIBLES
CABALS
CABERS
CABINS
CABLES
COBIAS
COBRAS

CUBEBS
CUBICS
CUBITS
DEBARS
DEBITS
DEBRAS
DEBRIS
DEBUGS
DEBUTS
DOBLAS
DOBRAS
DOBROS
DUBOIS
ELBOWS
ELBRUS
EMBAYS
EMBEDS
EMBERS
EMBOSS
FABLES
FIBERS
FIBRES
GABIES
GABLES
GIBERS
GOBIES
HABEAS
HABITS
HOBBES
HOBOES
HUBRIS
IMBUES
JABOTS
KABOBS
KEBABS
KEBOBS
LABELS
LABORS
LIBELS
LIBRIS
MOBIUS
NABOBS
NABORS
NOBLES
ORBITS
OXBOWS
POBOYS
RABBIS
RABIES
REBAGS
REBARS
REBBES
REBECS
REBELS
REBIDS
REBUTS
ROBINS
ROBLES
ROBOTS
RUBENS
RUBIES
RUBLES
SABERS
SABINS
SABLES
SABOTS
SABRAS
SABRES
SIBYLS
SOBERS
TABLAS
TABLES
TABOOS
TABORS
TIBIAS
TOBIAS
TOBIES
TUBERS
UMBELS
UMBERS
UMBRAS
UNBARS
UPBOWS
UZBEKS
XEBECS
YOBBOS
ZEBRAS
ZIBETS

•••B•S

ADOBES
AIRBUS
ALIBIS
AMEBAS
ANUBIS
BOMBES
BRIBES
CARBOS
CEIBAS
COMBES
COMBOS
DAUBES
DOUBTS
EREBUS
FLYBYS
FORBES
GLEBES
GLOBES
GREBES
GUMBOS
HOBBES
JUMBOS
LAYBYS
LESBOS
LIEBYS
LIMBOS
LIMBUS
MAMBAS
MAMBOS
MAYBES
NIMBUS
ORIBIS
PHOBOS
PLEBES
PROBES
RABBIS
REBBES
RUMBAS
SAMBAS
SCUBAS
THEBES
TRIBES
TURBOS
VERBIS
YOBBOS

••••BS

ABOMBS
ADLIBS
ARDEBS
BLURBS
CARIBS
CAROBS
CELEBS
CLIMBS
CRUMBS
CUBEBS
DEMOBS
DWEEBS
EXURBS
HBOMBS
KABOBS
KEBABS
KEBOBS
MCJOBS
NABOBS
NAWABS
PLUMBS
REDUBS
REHABS
RHOMBS
RHUMBS
SAHIBS
SCRUBS
SHRUBS
SQUABS
SQUIBS
THROBS
THUMBS

B•T•••

BATAAN
BATBOY
BATEAU
BATHED
BATHER
BATHES
BATHOS
BATIKS
BATING
BATMAN
BATMEN
BATONS
BATTED
BATTEL
BATTEN
BATTER
BATTLE
BATTUE
BATUMI
BATYAM
BETAKE
BETCHA
BETELS
BETHEL
BETIDE
BETISE
BETONY
BETOOK
BETRAY
BETSEY
BETSON
BETTAS
BETTER
BETTOR
BITERS
BITING
BITMAP
BITOFF
BITOLA
BITTED
BITTEN
BITTER
BOTANY
BOTCHY
BOTELS
BOTFLY
BOTHER
BOTREE
BOTTLE
BOTTOM
BUTANE
BUTENE
BUTEOS
BUTLER
BUTTED
BUTTER
BUTTES
BUTTIN
BUTTON
BUTUNG
BUTUTS
BYTALK

B••T••

BAITED
BALTIC
BANTAM
BANTER
BANTUS
BARTAB
BARTER
BARTOK
BARTON
BASTED
BASTER
BASTES
BATTED
BATTEL
BATTEN
BATTER
BATTLE
BATTUE
BAXTER
BEATEN
BEATER
BEATIT
BEATLE
BEATON
BEATTY
BEATUP
BEETLE
BELTED
BENTON
BERTHA
BERTHS
BERTIE
BESTED
BESTIR
BESTOW
BETTAS
BETTER
BETTOR
BHUTAN
BHUTTO
BIGTEN
BIGTOE
BIGTOP
BIOTAS
BIOTIC
BIOTIN
BIRTHS
BISTRO
BITTED
BITTEN
BITTER
BLATTY
BLITHE
BLOTCH
BLOTTO
BLOTTY
BLYTHE
BOATED
BOATEL
BOATER
BOITES
BOLTED
BOLTON
BONTON
BOOTED
BOOTEE
BOOTES
BOOTHE
BOOTHS
BOOTIE
BOOTSY
BOOTUP
BOSTON
BOTTLE
BOTTOM
BOWTIE
BOXTOP
BRATSK
BRATTY
BRETON
BRITON
BROTHS
BRUTAL
BRUTES
BRUTUS
BUNTED
BUNTER
BURTON
BUSTED
BUSTER
BUSTIN
BUSTLE
BUTTED
BUTTER
BUTTES
BUTTIN
BUTTON

B•••T•

BALATA
BARITE
BEASTS
BEATTY
BEAUTS
BEAUTY
BEFITS
BEGETS
BEMATA
BENITO
BERATE
BERETS
BESETS
BESOTS
BHAKTI
BHUTTO
BIGHTS
BIGOTS
BINATE
BLASTS
BLATTY
BLEATS
BLINTZ
BLOATS
BLOTTO
BLOTTY
BLUETS
BLUNTS
BLURTS
BOASTS
BOGOTA
BONITO
BOOSTS
BORATE
BOUNTY
BRACTS
BRANTS
BRATTY
BREATH
BRENTS
BRONTE
BRUITS
BRUNTS
BURSTS
BUTUTS
BYPATH
BYROTE

B••••T

BADLOT
BAGSIT
BALLET
BALLOT
BANDIT
BARBET
BARDOT
BAREST
BARKAT
BASALT
BASEST
BASKET
BASSET
BEATIT
BECKET
BEHEST
BEIRUT
BELOIT
BENOIT
BEREFT
BESANT
BEZANT
BILLET
BIRGIT
BISECT
BISSET
BLEWIT
BLIGHT
BLOWIT
BLUEST
BOBCAT
BOGART
BONMOT
BONNET
BOSKET
BOUGHT
BOWNET
BOWOUT
BOXSET
BRANDT
BREAST
BRECHT
BREVET
BRIGHT
BRUNET
BRYANT
BUCKET
BUDGET
BUFFET
BUGOUT
BULLET
BUMOUT
BURBOT
BURNET
BUYOUT
BYPAST

•BT•••

OBTAIN
OBTEST
OBTUND
OBTUSE

•B•T••

ABATED
ABATES
ABATIS
OBITER
OBSTET

•B••T•

ABBOTS
ABBOTT
ABLATE
ABORTS
EBOATS
OBLATE
UBIETY
UBOATS
UBOLTS

•B•••T

ABBOTT
ABDUCT
ABJECT
ABLAUT
ABLEST
ABRUPT
ABSENT
OBJECT
OBLAST
OBOIST
OBSTET
OBTEST
OBVERT

••BT••

DEBTOR
SUBTLE
SUBTLY

••B•T•

ABBOTS
ABBOTT
AMBATO
AMBITS
ATBATS
CUBITS
DEBATE
DEBITS
DEBUTS
HABITS
JABOTS
JOBETH
KIBITZ
LOBATE
ORBITS
RABATO
REBATE
REBUTS
ROBOTS
RUBATI
RUBATO
SABATO
SABOTS
SUBITO
TUBATE
ZIBETS

••B••T

ABBOTT
ALBEIT
ALBERT
ATBEST
BOBCAT
COBALT
CUBIST
EGBERT
ELBERT
GIBBET
GIBLET
GOBLET
GOBUST
HOBART
HOBBIT
HUBERT
JOBLOT
LABRET
PTBOAT
RABBET
RABBIT
REBENT
REBOLT
REBOOT
ROBERT
ROBUST
RUBOUT
SOBEIT
SUBLET
SUBMIT
SUBSET
TABLET
TOBOOT
TUBIST
TYBALT
UNBELT
UNBENT
UNBOLT
UPBEAT

•••BT•

DOUBTS

•••B•T

ALLBUT
BARBET
BURBOT
COMBAT
GAMBIT
GIBBET
GRABAT
HENBIT
HOBBIT
IROBOT
KOMBAT
KORBUT
NUMBAT
RABBET
RABBIT
SORBET
STABAT
TALBOT
TIDBIT
TITBIT
TURBIT
TURBOT
TWOBIT
WOMBAT
YOUBET

••••BT

INDEBT

BU••••

BUBBLE
BUBBLY
BUCCAL
BUCHAN
BUCKED
BUCKET
BUCKLE
BUCKUP
BUDDED
BUDDHA
BUDGED
BUDGES
BUDGET
BUDGIE
BUENOS
BUFFED
BUFFER
BUFFET
BUFFON
BUFFOS
BUGGED
BUGLED
BUGLER
BUGLES
BUGOFF
BUGOUT
BUILDS
BUJOLD
BULBIL
BULBUL
BULGAR
BULGED
BULGES
BULGUR
BULKED
BULLAE
BULLED
BULLET
BULOVA
BULWER
BUMBLE
BUMBRY

BUMMED
BUMMER
BUMOUT
BUMPED
BUMPER
BUMPPO
BUMPUP
BUMRAP
BUNCHE
BUNCHY
BUNCOS
BUNDLE
BUNGED
BUNGEE
BUNGLE
BUNION
BUNKED
BUNKER
BUNKOS
BUNKUM
BUNSEN
BUNTED
BUNTER
BUNUEL
BUNYAN
BUNYIP
BUOYED
BUOYUP
BUQSHA
BURBLE
BURBLY
BURBOT
BURDEN
BUREAU
BURGAS
BURGEE
BURGER
BURGHS
BURGLE
BURGOO
BURGOS
BURIED
BURIES
BURINS
BURLAP
BURLED
BURLEY
BURMAN
BURNED
BURNER
BURNET
BURNEY
BURNUP
BUROAK
BURPED
BURRED
BURROS
BURROW
BURSAE
BURSAL
BURSAR
BURSAS
BURSES
BURSTS
BURTON
BUSBAR
BUSBOY
BUSHED
BUSHEL
BUSHES
BUSHWA
BUSIED
BUSIER
BUSIES
BUSILY
BUSING
BUSKED
BUSKIN
BUSMAN
BUSMEN
BUSONI
BUSSED
BUSSES
BUSTED
BUSTER
BUSTIN
BUSTLE
BUTANE
BUTENE
BUTEOS
BUTLER
BUTTED
BUTTER
BUTTES
BUTTIN
BUTTON
BUTUNG
BUTUTS
BUYERS
BUYING
BUYOFF
BUYOUT
BUYSUP
BUZZED
BUZZER
BUZZES

B•U•••

BAUBLE
BAUCIS
BAULKS
BEULAH
BEURRE
BHUTAN
BHUTTO
BLUELY
BLUEOX
BLUEST
BLUESY
BLUETS
BLUEYS
BLUFFS
BLUING
BLUISH
BLUNTS
BLURBS
BLURRY
BLURTS
BOUBOU
BOUCLE
BOUDIN
BOUFFE
BOUGHS
BOUGHT
BOULES
BOULEZ
BOULLE
BOUNCE
BOUNCY
BOUNDS
BOUNTY
BOURKE
BOURNE
BOURSE
BOUSED
BOUSES
BRUDER
BRUGES
BRUINS
BRUISE
BRUITS
BRULES
BRUMAL
BRUMBY
BRUMES
BRUNCH
BRUNEI
BRUNET
BRUNTS
BRUSHY
BRUTAL
BRUTES
BRUTUS
BRUXED
BRUXES

B••U••

BABULS
BAGUIO
BAKULA
BARUCH
BATUMI
BEAUTS
BEAUTY
BEGUMS
BELUGA
BEMUSE
BENUMB
BLOUSE
BOSUNS
BREUER
BUNUEL
BUTUNG
BUTUTS

B•••U•

BACKUP
BACKUS
BADGUY
BAGFUL
BALLUP
BANGUI
BANGUP
BANJUL
BANQUO
BANTUS
BARIUM
BARNUM
BARQUE
BARZUN
BASQUE
BATTUE
BAYEUX
BAYOUS
BAYRUM
BEADUP
BEAMUP
BEARUP
BEATUP
BEDAUB
BEDBUG
BEEFUP
BEEGUM
BEFOUL
BEIRUT
BENHUR
BIDSUP
BIGGUN
BIGSUR
BIJOUX
BINDUP
BISQUE
BLEWUP
BLOWUP
BMINUS
BOBSUP
BONEUP
BOOJUM
BOOTUP
BOREUP
BOWOUT
BOXFUL
BRAQUE
BROGUE
BRUTUS
BUCKUP
BUGOUT
BULBUL
BULGUR
BUMOUT
BUMPUP
BUNKUM
BUOYUP
BURNUP
BUYOUT
BUYSUP
BYSSUS

B••••U

BABALU
BALLOU
BATEAU
BISSAU
BOUBOU
BUREAU

•BU•••

ABUKIR
ABUSED
ABUSER
ABUSES
MBUNDU

•B•U••

ABDUCT
ABJURE
ABLUSH
ABOUND
ABRUPT
ABSURD
OBTUND
OBTUSE

•B••U•

ABACUS
ABLAUT
OBELUS
UBIQUE

•B•••U

MBUNDU

••BU••

ALBUMS
AMBUSH
ASBURY
AUBURN
BABULS
COBURG
COBURN
DEBUGS
DEBUNK
DEBUTS
FIBULA
GOBUST
IMBUED
IMBUES
INBULK
KABUKI
LOBULE
NEBULA
REBUFF
REBUKE
REBURY
REBUTS
ROBUST
SUBURB
TABULA
UNBUSY

••B•U•

ARBOUR
BOBSUP
DYBBUK
ELBRUS
ERBIUM
HUBBUB
IMBRUE
LABOUR
LABRUM
LEBRUN
MOBIUS
MRBLUE
PABLUM
RUBOUT
SOBFUL
SUBDUE
SUBGUM
TOBRUK

••B••U

BABALU
JABIRU
SUBARU

•••BU•

AIRBUS
ALLBUT
BEDBUG
BULBUL
DYBBUK
EREBUS
HUBBUB
HUMBUG
KORBUT
LIMBUS
NIMBUS
REDBUD
SOWBUG
WILBUR

•••B•U

BOUBOU

••••BU

MALIBU

B•V•••

BEVELS
BEVIES
BOVARY
BOVIDS
BOVINE
BOVVER

B••V••

BEAVER
BEAVIS
BEEVES
BMOVIE
BOVVER
BRAVAS
BRAVED
BRAVER
BRAVES
BRAVOS
BREVES
BREVET
BREVIS

B•••V•

BEHAVE
BEHOVE
BULOVA
BYJOVE

B••••V

BRASOV

•BV•••

OBVERT

••B••V

RUBLEV

BW••••

BWANAS

B•W•••

BAWLED
BAWLER
BEWAIL
BEWARE
BEWRAY
BOWERS
BOWERY
BOWFIN
BOWING
BOWLED
BOWLER
BOWLES
BOWMAN
BOWMEN
BOWNET
BOWOAR
BOWOUT
BOWSAW
BOWSER
BOWTIE
BOWWOW
BOWYER
BYWAYS
BYWORD

B••W••

BIGWIG
BLEWIT
BLEWUP
BLOWER
BLOWIN
BLOWIT
BLOWSY
BLOWUP
BLOWZY
BOWWOW
BRAWLS
BRAWNY
BREWED
BREWER
BROWNE
BROWNS
BROWNY
BROWSE
BULWER

B•••W•

BEDEWS
BUSHWA
BYLAWS

B••••W

BARROW
BELLOW
BESTOW
BILLOW
BORROW
BOWSAW
BOWWOW
BROKAW
BURROW

•B•W••

OBIWAN

••BW••

COBWEB
SUBWAY

••B•W•

ELBOWS
OXBOWS
UPBOWS

••B••W

HEBREW

•••BW•

OJIBWA

•••B•W

FOGBOW

B•X•••

BAXTER
BOXBOY
BOXCAR
BOXERS
BOXFUL
BOXIER
BOXING
BOXSET
BOXTOP

B••X••

BLIXEN
BRUXED
BRUXES

B•••X•

BILOXI
BORAXO

B••••X

BAYEUX
BENDIX
BIJOUX
BLUEOX
BOLLIX
BRANDX

•B•X••

IBEXES

•••B•X

HATBOX
HOTBOX
ICEBOX
OUTBOX
PAYBOX
SKYBOX

BY••••

BYEBYE
BYGONE
BYGOSH
BYHAND
BYJOVE
BYLAWS
BYLINE
BYNAME
BYPASS
BYPAST
BYPATH
BYPLAY
BYRNES
BYROAD
BYROTE
BYSSHE
BYSSUS
BYTALK
BYWAYS
BYWORD

B•Y•••

BAYARD
BAYEUX
BAYING
BAYLOR
BAYOUS
BAYRUM
BEYOND
BLYTHE
BOYARS
BOYISH
BRYANT
BRYONY
BRYSON
BUYERS
BUYING
BUYOFF
BUYOUT
BUYSUP

B••Y••

BANYAN
BARYON
BATYAM
BOWYER
BRAYED
BRAYER
BREYER
BUNYAN
BUNYIP
BUOYED
BUOYUP

B•••Y•

BELAYS
BLUEYS
BOGEYS
BOLEYN
BYEBYE
BYWAYS

B••••Y

BADBOY
BADGUY
BAILEY
BAKERY
BALDLY
BARELY
BARFLY
BARLEY
BARNEY
BARONY
BASELY
BASIFY
BASSLY
BATBOY
BEACHY
BEATTY
BEAUTY
BEGLEY
BEKESY
BELFRY
BELLAY
BENDAY
BENGAY
BETONY
BETRAY
BETSEY
BEWRAY
BIGAMY
BIGBOY
BINARY
BIRNEY
BISCAY
BLABBY
BLATTY
BLEARY
BLENNY
BLIMEY
BLOCKY
BLOODY
BLOOEY
BLOOMY
BLOTTY
BLOWSY
BLOWZY
BLUELY

BLUESY
BLURRY
BODILY
BOIGNY
BOLDLY
BOLSHY
BOMBAY
BOOTSY
BOSLEY
BOTANY
BOTCHY
BOTFLY
BOUNCY
BOUNTY
BOVARY
BOWERY
BOXBOY
BRACHY
BRAINY
BRANDY
BRANNY
BRASHY
BRASSY
BRATTY
BRAWNY
BREEZY
BRICKY
BRIERY
BROLLY
BRONZY
BROODY
BROOKY
BROOMY
BROWNY
BRUMBY
BRUSHY
BRYONY
BUBBLY
BUMBRY
BUNCHY
BURBLY
BURLEY
BURNEY
BUSBOY
BUSILY
BYPLAY

•BY•••
ABYDOS
ABYING
ABYSMS

•B•Y••
OBEYED

•B••Y•
ABBEYS

•B•••Y
ABBACY
EBERLY
UBIETY

••BY••
LIBYAN
SIBYLS

••B•Y•
ABBEYS
EMBAYS
EMBRYO
POBOYS
RIBEYE

••B••Y
ABBACY
ALBANY
AMBERY
ASBURY
AUBREY
BUBBLY
DABNEY
EMBODY
FABRAY
HUBBLY
MOBLEY
NOBODY
NUBBLY
PEBBLY
REBURY
ROBROY
RUBBLY
RUBIFY
SUBTLY
SUBWAY
UNBUSY
WOBBLY

•••BY•
BYEBYE
FLYBYS
LAYBYS
LIEBYS

•••B•Y
BADBOY
BATBOY
BIGBOY
BLABBY
BOMBAY
BOXBOY
BUBBLY
BUMBRY
BURBLY
BUSBOY
CARBOY
CHUBBY
CLUBBY
COWBOY
CRABBY
DAYBOY
DOUBLY
DRABLY
DUMBLY
FEEBLY
FLABBY
FLYBOY
GLIBLY
GRABBY
GRUBBY
HUBBLY
HUMBLY
KNOBBY
LAZBOY
LOWBOY
MARBLY
MUMBLY
NIMBLY
NUBBLY
NUMBLY
OLDBOY
PEBBLY
REDBAY
RUBBLY
RUMBLY
SCABBY
SHABBY
SLOBBY
SNOBBY
SNUBBY
STABLY
STUBBY
SWABBY
TOMBOY
TREBLY
USABLY
VIABLY
WAMBLY
WOBBLY

••••BY
BLABBY
BRUMBY
CAMEBY
CHUBBY
CLUBBY
COMEBY
CRABBY
CROSBY
CRUMBY
DOESBY
DROPBY
FLABBY
GATSBY
GETSBY
GOESBY
GONEBY
GOODBY
GRABBY
GRUBBY
HARDBY
HEREBY
KNOBBY
LAIDBY
LAYSBY
NASEBY
NEARBY
PASSBY
PHILBY
PUTSBY
SCABBY
SETSBY
SHABBY
SITSBY
SLOBBY
SNOBBY
SNUBBY
STUBBY
SWABBY
TRILBY
WENTBY

B•Z•••
BAZAAR
BEZANT
BEZELS
BUZZED
BUZZER
BUZZES

B••Z••
BAIZAS
BALZAC
BANZAI
BARZUN
BENZOL
BLAZED
BLAZER
BLAZES
BLAZON
BONZES
BORZOI
BRAZED
BRAZEN
BRAZER
BRAZES
BRAZIL
BRAZOS
BRAZZA
BRAZZI
BUZZED
BUZZER
BUZZES

B•••Z•
BEDAZE
BELIZE
BLOWZY
BRAZZA
BRAZZI
BREEZE
BREEZY
BRONZE
BRONZY

B••••Z
BLINTZ
BOULEZ
BRIENZ

•B••Z•
ABLAZE

••B•Z•
REBOZO

••B••Z
KIBITZ
TABRIZ

CA••••
CABALA
CABALS
CABANA
CABBED
CABBIE
CABERS
CABINS
CABLED
CABLER
CABLES
CACAOS
CACHED
CACHES
CACHET
CACHOU
CACKLE
CACTUS
CADDIE
CADDIS
CADENT
CADETS
CADGED
CADGER
CADGES
CADMIC
CADMUS
CADRES
CAESAR
CAFTAN
CAGERS
CAGIER
CAGILY
CAGING
CAGNEY
CAGUAS
CAHIER
CAHOWS
CAICOS
CAIMAN
CAIQUE
CAIRNS
CAJOLE
CAJUNS
CAKIER
CAKING
CALAIS
CALASH
CALCES
CALDER
CALICO
CALIPH
CALKED
CALLAO
CALLAS
CALLED
CALLER
CALLES
CALLIN
CALLON
CALLOW
CALLUP
CALLUS
CALMED
CALMER
CALMLY
CALPAC
CALQUE
CALVED
CALVES
CALVIN
CALXES
CAMARO
CAMBER
CAMDEN
CAMEAT
CAMEBY
CAMEIN
CAMELS
CAMEON
CAMEOS
CAMERA
CAMETO
CAMEUP
CAMINO
CAMION
CAMISE
CAMLET
CAMPED
CAMPER
CAMPOS
CAMPUS
CANAAN
CANADA
CANALS
CANAPE
CANARD
CANARY
CANCAN
CANCEL
CANCUN
CANDID
CANDLE
CANDOR
CANERS
CANFUL
CANIDS
CANIER
CANIFF
CANINE
CANING
CANKER
CANLIT
CANNAE
CANNED
CANNEL
CANNER
CANNES
CANNON
CANNOT
CANOED
CANOES
CANOLA
CANONS
CANOPY
CANOVA
CANTAB
CANTED
CANTER
CANTHI
CANTLE
CANTON
CANTOR
CANTOS
CANUTE
CANVAS
CANYON
CAPERS
CAPFUL
CAPGUN
CAPIAS
CAPITA
CAPLET
CAPNUT
CAPONE
CAPONS
CAPOTE
CAPPED
CAPPER
CAPRIS
CAPSID
CAPTAN
CAPTOR
CARAFE
CARATS
CARBON
CARBOS
CARBOY
CARDED
CARDER
CARDIN
CARDIO
CAREEN
CAREER
CARESS
CARETO
CARETS
CARFUL
CARGOS
CARHOP
CARIBE
CARIBS
CARIES
CARINA
CARING
CARKED
CARLIN
CARLOS
CARLOT
CARMAN
CARMEL
CARMEN
CARNAL
CARNES
CARNET
CARNEY
CARNOT
CAROBS
CAROLE
CAROLS
CAROMS
CARONI
CARPAL
CARPED
CARPEL
CARPER
CARPET
CARPUS
CARREL
CARREY
CARRIE
CARROL
CARROT
CARSON
CARTED
CARTEL
CARTER
CARTES
CARTON
CARUSO
CARVED
CARVER
CARVES
CARVEY
CASABA
CASALS
CASAVA
CASBAH
CASEFY
CASERN
CASHED
CASHES
CASHEW
CASHIN
CASING
CASINO
CASPAR
CASPER
CASQUE
CASSIA
CASSIO
CASSIS
CASTER
CASTES
CASTLE
CASTON
CASTOR
CASTRO
CASUAL
CATCHY
CATENA
CATERS
CATGUT
CATHAY
CATHER
CATION
CATKIN
CATNAP
CATNIP
CATRIG
CATSUP
CATTED
CATTLE
CATTON
CAUCHO
CAUCHY
CAUCUS
CAUDAL
CAUDEX
CAUDLE
CAUGHT
CAULKS
CAUSAL
CAUSED
CAUSES
CAVEAT
CAVEIN
CAVELL
CAVERN
CAVERS
CAVETT
CAVIAR
CAVILS
CAVING
CAVITY
CAVORT
CAWDOR
CAWING
CAXTON
CAYMAN
CAYUGA
CAYUSE

C•A•••
CEASED
CEASES
CHACHA
CHACMA
CHADOR
CHAFED
CHAFES
CHAFFS
CHAFFY
CHAINE
CHAINS
CHAIRS
CHAISE
CHALCO
CHALET
CHALKS
CHALKY
CHAMMY
CHAMPS
CHANCE
CHANCY
CHANEL
CHANEY
CHANGE
CHANTS
CHAPEL
CHAPIN
CHARGE
CHARLY
CHARMS
CHARON
CHARRO
CHARTS
CHASED
CHASER
CHASES
CHASMS
CHASSE
CHASTE
CHATTY
CHATUP
CHAVEZ
CIARDI
CLACKS
CLAIMS
CLAIRE
CLAMMY
CLAMOR
CLAMPS
CLAMUP
CLANCY
CLANGS
CLANKS
CLANKY
CLAQUE
CLARET
CLARKE
CLAROS
CLASPS
CLASSY
CLAUDE
CLAUSE
CLAVES
CLAVIN
CLAWED
CLAWER
CLAYEY
CMAJOR
COALER
COAPTS
COARSE
COASTS
COATED
COATIS
COAXED
COAXER
COAXES
CRABBE
CRABBY
CRACKS
CRACKY
CRADLE
CRAFTS
CRAFTY
CRAGGY
CRAKES
CRAMBO

CRAMPS
CRANED
CRANES
CRANIA
CRANIO
CRANKS
CRANKY
CRANNY
CRAPES
CRATED
CRATER
CRATES
CRAVAT
CRAVED
CRAVEN
CRAVER
CRAVES
CRAWLS
CRAWLY
CRAYON
CRAZED
CRAZES
CYANIC

C••A••

CABALA
CABALS
CABANA
CACAOS
CALAIS
CALASH
CAMARO
CANAAN
CANADA
CANALS
CANAPE
CANARD
CANARY
CARAFE
CARATS
CASABA
CASALS
CASAVA
CCLAMP
CEDANT
CEDARS
CERATE
CESARE
CETANE
CHEAPO
CHEATS
CHIANG
CHIAUS
CHOATE
CICADA
CIGARS
CITATO
CLEANS
CLEARS
CLEATS
CLEAVE
CLOACA
CLOAKS
COBALT
COLADA
COMATE
CONANT
COPAYS
CORALS
COWARD
CREAKS
CREAKY
CREAMS
CREAMY
CREASE
CREASY
CREATE
CROAKS
CROAKY
CROATS
CSHARP
CUBAGE
CUIABA
CUNARD
CUNAXA
CURACY
CURARE
CURATE
CUSACK
CYCADS
CYRANO

C•••A•

CAESAR
CAFTAN
CAGUAS
CAIMAN
CALLAO
CALLAS
CALPAC
CAMEAT
CANAAN
CANCAN
CANNAE
CANTAB
CANVAS
CAPIAS
CAPTAN
CARMAN
CARNAL
CARPAL
CASBAH
CASPAR
CASUAL
CATHAY
CATNAP
CAUDAL
CAUSAL
CAVEAT
CAVIAR
CAYMAN
CEIBAS
CELLAE
CELLAR
CEREAL
CESTAS
CHELAE
CHELAS
CHEVAL
CHIRAC
CHORAL
CHUKAR
CIUDAD
CLIMAX
CNIDAE
COBHAM
COBIAS
COBRAS
COCOAS
COEVAL
COGNAC
COLFAX
COLLAR
COLMAN
COMBAT
COMEAT
COMMAS
COMPAQ
COMSAT
CONFAB
CONGAS
CONMAN
CONRAD
CONTAC
CONWAY
COOGAN
CORBAN
CORDAY
CORMAN
CORRAL
COSTAE
COSTAL
COSTAR
COSTAS
COTTAS
COUGAR
COWMAN
CRAVAT
CRETAN
CRURAL
CUNEAL
CUPPAS
CURIAE
CURIAL
CUSHAW
CYCLAS
CYMBAL

C••••A

CABALA
CABANA
CAMERA
CANADA
CANOLA
CANOVA
CAPITA
CARINA
CASABA
CASAVA
CASSIA
CATENA
CAYUGA
CESSNA
CETERA
CHACHA
CHACMA
CHICHA
CHOLLA
CHOPRA
CHROMA
CHUKKA
CIBOLA
CICADA
CINEMA
CLOACA
COLADA
COLIMA
CONCHA
CONTRA
COPULA
CORNEA
CORONA
CORYZA
COULDA
COVINA
COWPEA
CRANIA
CRENNA
CREUSA
CRIMEA
CUESTA
CUIABA
CUNAXA
CUPOLA

•CA•••

ACACIA
ACADIA
ACAJOU
ACARID
ACARUS
ECARTE
ICARIA
ICARUS
MCADAM
MCADOO
OCASEK
OCASEY
SCABBY
SCALAR
SCALDS
SCALED
SCALER
SCALES
SCALIA
SCALPS
SCAMPI
SCAMPS
SCANTS
SCANTY
SCAPED
SCAPES
SCARAB
SCARCE
SCARED
SCARER
SCARES
SCARFS
SCARNE
SCARPS
SCARRY
SCARUM
SCATHE
SCATTY
SCAUPS

•C•A••

ACHAEA
ACKACK
ACUATE
CCLAMP
ECLAIR
ECLATS
ICEAGE
LCHAIM
MCBAIN
MCCABE
MCCANN
MCHALE
MCLAIN
MCNAIR
OCEANS
OCTADS
OCTANE
OCTANT
OCTAVE
OCTAVO
SCLAFF
SCRAGS
SCRAMS
SCRAPE
SCRAPS
SCRAWL
UCLANS

•C••A•

ACETAL
ACTSAS
ACTUAL
ICEBAG
ICECAP
ICEMAN
MCADAM
MCGRAW
MCLEAN
OCREAE
OCULAR
SCALAR
SCARAB
SCENAS
SCHWAB
SCHWAS
SCREAK
SCREAM
SCUBAS

•C•••A

ACACIA
ACADIA
ACEDIA
ACHAEA
ICARIA
MCCREA
RCCOLA
SCALIA
SCHEMA
SCLERA
SCORIA
SCOTIA
SCYLLA

••CA••

ALCAPP
ARCADE
ARCANA
ARCANE
ARCARO
BACALL
BECALM
BECAME
BICARB
CACAOS
CICADA
CYCADS
DACAPO
DECADE
DECAFS
DECALS
DECAMP
DECANT
DECAYS
DUCATS
ENCAGE
ENCAMP
ENCASE
ESCAPE
ESCARP
FACADE
GOCART
HECATE
IDCARD
INCANS
INCASE
INCASH
JACALS
JACANA
JICAMA
LOCALE
LOCALS
LOCATE
MACACO
MACAWS
MCCABE
MCCANN
NICAEA
ONCALL
OSCARS
OXCART
PECANS
PICABO
PICARA
PICARD
PICARO
RECALL
RECANE
RECANT
RECAPS
RECAST
SECANT
SOCAGE
TICALS
TUCANA
UNCAGE
UNCAPS
UNCASE
UPCAST
VACANT
VACATE
VICARS
VOCALS

••C•A•

ARCTAN
ASCHAM
BUCCAL
BUCHAN
COCOAS
CYCLAS
DACHAS
DUCTAL
FACIAL
FACIAS
JACKAL
LUCIAN
MACRAE
MECCAS
MICMAC
MOCHAS
NECTAR
NICEAN
NUCHAE
NUCHAL
PACMAN
PECKAT
PICKAT
PICKAX
RACIAL
RECOAT
SACRAL
SOCIAL
SUCHAS
SUCKAS
TICTAC
UNCIAL
UNCLAD
VACLAV
WICCAN
YUCCAS

••C••A

ANCONA
ARCANA
CICADA
ENCINA
FACULA
HECUBA
ISCHIA
JACANA
JICAMA
LACUNA
MACULA
MCCREA
MUCOSA
NICAEA
NICOLA
OSCULA
PICARA
RCCOLA
TACOMA
TUCANA
VICUNA

•••CA•

ABACAS
ABSCAM
APICAL
ARECAS
ASHCAN
BARCAR
BISCAY
BOBCAT
BOXCAR
BUCCAL
CANCAN
DORCAS
DUNCAN
EPICAL
FATCAT
FISCAL
FRACAS
GASCAP
HEPCAT
HOTCAP
HOTCAR
HUBCAP
ICECAP
IPECAC
LASCAR
LOWCAL
MADCAP
MECCAS
MESCAL
MOBCAP
MUDCAT
MUSCAT
NASCAR
OILCAN
PARCAE
PASCAL
PLICAE
RASCAL
REDCAP
REXCAT
SKYCAP
SNOCAT
SPICAS
THECAE
THECAL
TINCAL
TINCAN
TOECAP
TOMCAT
TOPCAT
TOUCAN
TOWCAR
TROCAR
TUSCAN
UNOCAL
VULCAN
WICCAN
YUCCAS

•••C•A

ACACIA
ALICIA
BETCHA
CHACHA
CHACMA
CHICHA
CONCHA
EJECTA
EXACTA
FASCIA
FLICKA
FULCRA
GARCIA
GOTCHA
JASCHA
KWACHA
MANCHA
MARCIA
MISCHA
MURCIA
PERCHA
SANCTA
TRICIA

••••CA

AFRICA
ALPACA
ARNICA
ATTICA
BIANCA
BLANCA
CLOACA
DESICA
DODECA
EROICA
FRANCA
FRESCA
ITASCA
ITHACA
KONICA
LEXICA
LORICA
MARACA
MONICA
OAXACA
PATACA
SENECA
SILICA
SIRICA
TOLUCA
TUNICA

C•B•••

CABALA
CABALS
CABANA
CABBED
CABBIE
CABERS
CABINS
CABLED
CABLER
CABLES
CIBOLA
COBALT
COBBLE
COBHAM
COBIAS
COBRAS
COBURG
COBURN
COBWEB
CUBAGE
CUBEBS
CUBICS
CUBING
CUBISM
CUBIST
CUBITS
CUBOID
CYBELE
CYBILL
CYBORG

C••B••

CABBED
CABBIE
CAMBER
CARBON
CARBOS
CARBOY
CASBAH
CEIBAS
CHUBBY
CLUBBY
COBBLE
COMBAT
COMBED
COMBER
COMBES
COMBOS
CORBAN
CORBEL
CORBIN
COWBOY
CRABBE
CRABBY
CUMBER

CURBED
CYMBAL

C•••B•
CAMEBY
CARIBE
CARIBS
CAROBS
CASABA
CELEBS
CHUBBY
CLIMBS
CLUBBY
COMEBY
CRABBE
CRABBY
CRAMBO
CROSBY
CRUMBS
CRUMBY
CUBEBS
CUIABA

C••••B
CANTAB
CHERUB
COBWEB
CONFAB
CONJOB

•CB•••
MCBAIN

•C•B••
ICEBAG
ICEBOX
SCABBY
SCUBAS

•C••B•
ACHEBE
MCCABE
MCJOBS
SCABBY
SCRIBE
SCRUBS

•C•••B
SCARAB
SCHWAB

••C•B•
HECUBA
JACOBI
MCCABE
PICABO
TYCOBB

••C••B
BICARB
TYCOBB

CC••••
CCLAMP

C•C•••
CACAOS
CACHED
CACHES
CACHET
CACHOU
CACKLE
CACTUS
CECILE
CECILY
CICADA
CICELY
CICERO
COCCID
COCCUS
COCCYX
COCHIN
COCKED
COCKER
COCKLE
COCOAS
COCOON
CUCKOO
CYCADS
CYCLAS
CYCLED
CYCLER
CYCLES
CYCLIC
CYCLOS

C••C••
CAICOS
CALCES
CANCAN
CANCEL
CANCUN
CATCHY
CAUCHO
CAUCHY
CAUCUS
CHACHA
CHACMA
CHECKS
CHICHA
CHICHI
CHICKS
CHICLE
CHICLY
CHOCKS
CHUCKS
CIRCLE
CIRCUM
CIRCUS
CISCOS
CLACKS
CLICHE
CLICKS
CLOCHE
CLOCKS
CLUCKS
COCCID
COCCUS
COCCYX
CONCHA
CONCHS
CONCUR
CRACKS
CRACKY
CRECHE
CRICKS
CROCKS
CROCUS
CRUCES
CZECHS

C•••C•
CALICO
CHALCO
CHANCE
CHANCY
CHEECH
CHINCH
CHOICE
CHURCH
CIVICS
CLANCY
CLENCH
CLINCH
CLOACA
CLUTCH
COERCE
COMICS
CONICS
CONOCO
CRISCO
CROUCH
CRUNCH
CRUTCH
CUBICS
CURACY
CUSACK
CYNICS

C••••C
CADMIC
CALPAC
CEDRIC
CELTIC
CHIRAC
CITRIC
CLERIC
CLINIC
COGNAC
CONTAC
COPTIC
COSMIC
COURIC
CRITIC
CULTIC
CUPRIC
CYANIC
CYCLIC
CYMRIC

•CC•••
ACCEDE
ACCENT
ACCEPT
ACCESS
ACCORD
ACCOST
ACCRUE
ACCUSE
ECCLES
MCCABE
MCCANN
MCCREA
OCCULT
OCCUPY
OCCURS
RCCOLA

•C•C••
ACACIA
ICECAP
ICICLE

•C••C•
ACKACK
OCLOCK
SCARCE
SCHICK
SCONCE
SCORCH
SCOTCH
SCUTCH

•C•••C
ACETIC
ACIDIC
ECESIC
ECHOIC
ICONIC
SCENIC

••CC••
ARCCOS
BOCCIE
BUCCAL
COCCID
COCCUS
COCCYX
HICCUP
MECCAS
PICCHU
SICCED
SOCCER
SUCCES
SUCCOR
WICCAN
YUCCAS

••C•C•
BOCHCO
DECOCT
MACACO
ROCOCO

••C••C
ARCTIC
CYCLIC
HECTIC
LACTIC
MICMAC
PECTIC
PICNIC
TACTIC
TICTAC
UNCHIC

•••CC•
STUCCO

•••C•C
IPECAC

CD••••
CDROMS

C•D•••
CADDIE
CADDIS
CADENT
CADETS
CADGED
CADGER
CADGES
CADMIC
CADMUS
CADRES
CEDANT
CEDARS
CEDING
CEDRIC
CIDERS
CODDLE
CODERS
CODGER
CODIFY
CODING
CODONS
CUDDLE
CUDDLY
CUDGEL
CYDERS

C••D••
CADDIE
CADDIS
CALDER
CAMDEN
CANDID
CANDLE
CANDOR
CARDED
CARDER
CARDIN
CARDIO
CAUDAL
CAUDEX
CAUDLE
CAWDOR
CHADOR
CHIDED
CHIDER
CHIDES
CINDER
CIUDAD
CLODDY
CNIDAE
CNIDUS
CODDLE
COEDIT
COLDER
COLDLY
CONDOR
CONDOS
COODER
CORDAY
CORDED
CORDON
CRADLE
CREDIT
CREDOS
CRUDDY
CRUDER
CUDDLE
CUDDLY
CURDED
CURDLE

C•••D•
CANADA
CANIDS
CHILDE
CHILDS
CHORDS
CIARDI
CICADA
CLAUDE
CLODDY
CLOUDS
CLOUDY
COLADA
COMEDY
COULDA
CREEDS
CROWDS
CRUDDY
CUPIDS
CYCADS

C••••D
CABBED
CABLED
CACHED
CADGED
CALKED
CALLED
CALMED
CALVED
CAMPED
CANARD
CANDID
CANNED
CANOED
CANTED
CAPPED
CAPSID
CARDED
CARKED
CARPED
CARTED
CARVED
CASHED
CATTED
CAUSED
CEASED
CEILED
CELLED
CENSED
CERVID
CESSED
CHAFED
CHASED
CHEWED
CHIDED
CHIMED
CHOKED
CHOWED
CHUTED
CIUDAD
CLAWED
CLEPED
CLEWED
CLONED
CLOSED
CLOYED
COATED
COAXED
COCCID
COCKED
COGGED
COIFED
COILED
COINED
COMBED
CONFED
CONKED
CONNED
CONOID
CONRAD
COOKED
COOLED
COOPED
COPIED
COPPED
CORDED
CORKED
CORNED
COSHED
COSIED
COWARD
COWLED
COZIED
CRANED
CRATED
CRAVED
CRAZED
CREWED
CROWED
CUBOID
CUFFED
CULLED
CUNARD
CUPPED
CURBED
CURDED
CURLED
CURRED
CURSED
CURVED
CUSPED
CUSPID
CUSSED
CYCLED

•C•D••
ACADIA
ACEDIA
ACIDIC
ACIDLY
ICEDIN
ICEDUP
MCADAM
MCADOO

•C••D•
ACCEDE
OCTADS
SCALDS
SCENDS
SCOLDS
SCRODS

•C•••D
ACARID
ACCORD
ECHOED
SCALED
SCAPED
SCARED
SCOPED
SCORED
SCREED

••C•D•
ACCEDE
ARCADE
CICADA
CYCADS
DECADE
DECIDE
DECODE
ENCODE
ESCUDO
FACADE
RECEDE
RECODE
SECEDE

••C••D
ACCORD
ARCHED
ASCEND
BACHED
BACKED
BUCKED
CACHED
COCCID
COCKED
CYCLED
DECKED
DOCKED
DUCKED
EMCEED
ETCHED
EUCLID
EXCEED
FECUND
HACKED
HOCKED
IDCARD
INCHED
ITCHED
JACKED
JOCUND
KICKED
LACKED
LICKED
LOCKED
LUCKED
MOCKED
MUCKED
NECKED
NICKED
ORCHID
PACKED
PECKED
PICARD
PICKED
RACKED
RECORD
RICKED
ROCKED
RUCKED
SACKED
SACRED
SECOND
SICCED
SOCKED
SUCKED
TACKED
TICKED
TUCKED
UNCLAD
WICKED
YACKED

•••C•D
BRACED
COCCID
DANCED
DEICED
DEUCED
EDUCED
FARCED
FENCED
FORCED
GRACED
JUICED
LANCED
MERCED
MINCED
PIECED
PLACED
PLACID
PRICED
RANCID
SAUCED
SICCED
SLICED
SPACED
SPICED
SYNCED
TALCED
TRACED
TRICED
VISCID
VOICED
WINCED

CE••••
CEASED
CEASES
CECILE
CECILY
CEDANT
CEDARS
CEDING
CEDRIC
CEIBAS
CEILED
CELEBS
CELERY
CELINE
CELLAE
CELLAR
CELLED
CELLOS
CELTIC
CEMENT
CENOTE
CENSED
CENSER
CENSES
CENSOR
CENSUS
CENTER
CENTOS
CENTRE
CENTRI

CENTRO
CEORLS
CERATE
CEREAL
CEREUS
CERIPH
CERISE
CERIUM
CERMET
CERROS
CERTIF
CERUSE
CERVID
CESARE
CESIUM
CESSED
CESSES
CESSNA
CESTAS
CESTOS
CESTUS
CETANE
CETERA
CEYLON

C•E•••

CAESAR
CHEAPO
CHEATS
CHECKS
CHEECH
CHEEKS
CHEEKY
CHEEPS
CHEERS
CHEERY
CHEESE
CHEESY
CHEKOV
CHELAE
CHELAS
CHEMIN
CHENIN
CHEOPS
CHEQUE
CHERIE
CHERRY
CHERTY
CHERUB
CHERYL
CHESTS
CHESTY
CHETHS
CHEVAL
CHEVET
CHEVRE
CHEWED
CHEWER
CHEWUP
CLEANS
CLEARS
CLEATS
CLEAVE
CLEEKS
CLEESE
CLEFTS
CLENCH
CLEPED
CLERGY
CLERIC
CLERKS
CLEVER
CLEVES
CLEVIS
CLEWED
COEDIT
COELOM
COERCE
COEVAL
CREAKS
CREAKY
CREAMS
CREAMY
CREASE
CREASY
CREATE
CRECHE
CREDIT
CREDOS
CREEDS
CREEKS
CREELS
CREEPS
CREEPY
CREMES
CRENEL
CRENNA
CREOLE
CREPES
CRESOL
CRESTS
CRETAN
CRETIN
CREUSA
CREWED
CREWEL
CUESTA
CZECHS
CZERNY

C••E••

CABERS
CADENT
CADETS
CAGERS
CAMEAT
CAMEBY
CAMEIN
CAMELS
CAMEON
CAMEOS
CAMERA
CAMETO
CAMEUP
CANERS
CAPERS
CAREEN
CAREER
CARESS
CARETO
CARETS
CASEFY
CASERN
CATENA
CATERS
CAVEAT
CAVEIN
CAVELL
CAVERN
CAVERS
CAVETT
CELEBS
CELERY
CEMENT
CEREAL
CEREUS
CETERA
CHEECH
CHEEKS
CHEEKY
CHEEPS
CHEERS
CHEERY
CHEESE
CHEESY
CHIEFS
CICELY
CICERO
CIDERS
CINEMA
CITERS
CIVETS
CLEEKS
CLEESE
CLIENT
CLUEIN
CODERS
COGENT
COHEIR
COHERE
COLEUS
COMEAT
COMEBY
COMEDY
COMEIN
COMELY
COMEON
COMERS
COMETH
COMETO
COMETS
COMEUP
CONEYS
COOERS
CORERS
COSELL
COVENS
COVENT
COVERS
COVERT
COVETS
COVEYS
COWENS
COWERS
COYEST
COZENS
CREEDS
CREEKS
CREELS
CREEPS
CREEPY
CRIERS
CRUETS
CRYERS
CUBEBS
CULETS
CUNEAL
CUPELS
CURERS
CUTELY
CUTEST
CUTESY
CUVEES
CYBELE
CYDERS

C•••E•

CABBED
CABLED
CABLER
CABLES
CACHED
CACHES
CACHET
CADGED
CADGER
CADGES
CADRES
CAGIER
CAGNEY
CAHIER
CAKIER
CALCES
CALDER
CALKED
CALLED
CALLER
CALLES
CALMED
CALMER
CALVED
CALVES
CALXES
CAMBER
CAMDEN
CAMLET
CAMPED
CAMPER
CANCEL
CANIER
CANKER
CANNED
CANNEL
CANNER
CANNES
CANOED
CANOES
CANTED
CANTER
CAPLET
CAPPED
CAPPER
CARDED
CARDER
CAREEN
CAREER
CARIES
CARKED
CARMEL
CARMEN
CARNES
CARNET
CARNEY
CARPED
CARPEL
CARPER
CARPET
CARREL
CARREY
CARTED
CARTEL
CARTER
CARTES
CARVED
CARVER
CARVES
CARVEY
CASHED
CASHES
CASHEW
CASPER
CASTER
CASTES
CATHER
CATTED
CAUDEX
CAUSED
CAUSES
CEASED
CEASES
CEILED
CELLED
CENSED
CENSER
CENSES
CENTER
CERMET
CESSED
CESSES
CHAFED
CHAFES
CHALET
CHANEL
CHANEY
CHAPEL
CHASED
CHASER
CHASES
CHAVEZ
CHEVET
CHEWED
CHEWER
CHIDED
CHIDER
CHIDES
CHIMED
CHIMES
CHINES
CHISEL
CHIVES
CHOKED
CHOKER
CHOKES
CHOLER
CHORES
CHOSEN
CHOWED
CHUTED
CHUTES
CINDER
CIPHER
CISKEI
CITIES
CLARET
CLAVES
CLAWED
CLAWER
CLAYEY
CLEPED
CLEVER
CLEVES
CLEWED
CLIMES
CLINES
CLONED
CLONES
CLOSED
CLOSER
CLOSES
CLOSET
CLOVEN
CLOVER
CLOVES
CLOYED
CNOTES
COALER
COATED
COAXED
COAXER
COAXES
COBWEB
COCKED
COCKER
CODGER
COFFEE
COFFER
COGGED
COIFED
COILED
COINED
COINER
COKIER
COLDER
COLIES
COLLET
COLTER
COMBED
COMBER
COMBES
COMPEL
COMTES
CONFED
CONFER
CONGER
CONIES
CONKED
CONKER
CONMEN
CONNED
CONNER
CONTES
CONVEX
CONVEY
COODER
COOKED
COOKER
COOLED
COOLER
COONEY
COOPED
COOPER
COOTER
COPIED
COPIER
COPIES
COPLEY
COPPED
COPPER
COPSES
COPTER
COQUET
CORBEL
CORDED
CORKED
CORKER
CORNEA
CORNED
CORNEL
CORNER
CORNET
CORREL
CORSET
CORTES
CORTEX
CORTEZ
CORVEE
CORVES
COSHED
COSHES
COSIED
COSIER
COSIES
COSSET
COTTEN
COTTER
COULEE
COUPES
COUTER
COWLED
COWLEY
COWMEN
COWPEA
COWPER
COZIED
COZIER
COZIES
CRAKES
CRANED
CRANES
CRAPES
CRATED
CRATER
CRATES
CRAVED
CRAVEN
CRAVER
CRAVES
CRAZED
CRAZES
CREMES
CRENEL
CREPES
CREWED
CREWEL
CRIKEY
CRIMEA
CRIMES
CRIPES
CRISES
CRONES
CROWED
CROWER
CROZES
CRUCES
CRUDER
CRUSES
CRUXES
CUDGEL
CUFFED
CULLED
CULLEN
CULLER
CULLET
CULVER
CUMBER
CUPPED
CURBED
CURDED
CURFEW
CURLED
CURLER
CURLEW
CURLEY
CURRED
CURSED
CURSES
CURTER
CURVED
CURVES
CURVET
CUSPED
CUSSED
CUSSES
CUSTER
CUTIES
CUTLER
CUTLET
CUTTER
CUVEES
CYCLED
CYCLER
CYCLES
CYGNET
CYPHER

C••••E

CABBIE
CACKLE
CADDIE
CAIQUE
CAJOLE
CALQUE
CAMISE
CANAPE
CANDLE
CANINE
CANNAE
CANTLE
CANUTE
CAPONE
CAPOTE
CARAFE
CARIBE
CAROLE
CARRIE
CASQUE
CASTLE
CATTLE
CAUDLE
CAYUSE
CECILE
CELINE
CELLAE
CENOTE
CENTRE
CERATE
CERISE
CERUSE
CESARE
CETANE
CHAINE
CHAISE
CHANCE
CHANGE
CHARGE
CHASSE
CHASTE
CHEESE
CHELAE
CHEQUE
CHERIE
CHEVRE
CHICLE
CHIGOE
CHILDE
CHILOE
CHOATE
CHOICE
CHOOSE
CHROME
CINQUE
CIRCLE
CIRQUE
CLAIRE
CLAQUE
CLARKE
CLAUDE
CLAUSE
CLEAVE
CLEESE
CLICHE
CLIQUE
CLOCHE
CLOQUE
CLOTHE
CNIDAE
COARSE
COBBLE
COCKLE
CODDLE
COERCE
COFFEE
COHERE
COHUNE
COLLIE
COMATE
CONNIE
CONTRE
CONURE
COOKIE
COOTIE
CORVEE
COSINE
COSTAE
COULEE
COUPLE
COURSE
COWRIE
COYOTE
CRABBE
CRADLE
CREASE
CREATE
CRECHE
CREOLE
CRINGE
CROSSE
CROUSE
CROUTE
CRUISE

CRUSOE
CUBAGE
CUDDLE
CUIQUE
CUISSE
CURARE
CURATE
CURDLE
CURIAE
CURULE
CYBELE

•CE•••
ACEDIA
ACEOUS
ACEOUT
ACESUP
ACETAL
ACETIC
ACETYL
BCELLS
ECESIC
ECESIS
ICEAGE
ICEBAG
ICEBOX
ICECAP
ICEDIN
ICEDUP
ICEFOG
ICEMAN
ICEMEN
ICEOUT
ICESIN
ICESUP
OCEANS
OCELLI
OCELOT
SCENAS
SCENDS
SCENES
SCENIC
SCENTS

•C•E••
ACCEDE
ACCENT
ACCEPT
ACCESS
ACHEBE
ACHENE
ICIEST
MCLEAN
OCHERS
OCHERY
OCREAE
OCTETS
SCHELL
SCHEMA
SCHEME
SCLERA
SCLERO
SCREAK
SCREAM
SCREED
SCREEN
SCREES
SCREWS
SCREWY

•C••E•
ACHAEA
ACHIER
ACUMEN
ECCLES
ECHOED
ECHOES
ECOLES
ICEMEN
ICKIER
MCCREA
MCGREW
MCKUEN
OCASEK
OCASEY
OCHRES
SCALED
SCALER
SCALES
SCAPED
SCAPES
SCARED
SCARER
SCARES
SCENES
SCHLEP
SCONES
SCOPED
SCOPES
SCORED
SCORER
SCORES
SCOTER
SCREED
SCREEN
SCREES
SCUTES

•C•••E
ACCEDE
ACCRUE
ACCUSE
ACHEBE
ACHENE
ACTIVE
ACTONE
ACUATE
ECARTE
ECTYPE
ICEAGE
ICICLE
MCCABE
MCHALE
OCREAE
OCTANE
OCTAVE
SCARCE
SCARNE
SCATHE
SCHEME
SCONCE
SCOUSE
SCRAPE
SCRIBE
SCURVE
SCYTHE

••CE••
ACCEDE
ACCENT
ACCEPT
ACCESS
ASCEND
ASCENT
BICEPS
CICELY
CICERO
DECEIT
DECENT
DICERS
DOCENT
EMCEED
EMCEES
EOCENE
ESCENT
EXCEED
EXCELS
EXCEPT
EXCESS
FACETS
FACEUP
HACEKS
INCEPT
LACERS
LACEUP
LUCENT
LYCEES
LYCEUM
MACEIO
NICEAN
NICELY
NICENE
NICEST
NICETY
NOCENT
PACERS
RACEME
RACERS
RECEDE
RECENT
RECESS
RICERS
SECEDE
SECERN
ULCERS

••C•E•
AACHEN
ANCIEN
ARCHED
ARCHER
ARCHES
BACHED
BACKED
BACKER
BECKER
BECKET
BICKER
BUCKED
BUCKET
CACHED
CACHES
CACHET
COCKED
COCKER
CYCLED
CYCLER
CYCLES
DECKED
DECKER
DECREE
DICIER
DICKER
DICKEY
DOCKED
DOCKER
DOCKET
DUCKED
ECCLES
EMCEED
EMCEES
ESCHER
ESCHEW
ETCHED
ETCHER
ETCHES
EXCEED
FACIES
FICHES
HACKED
HACKER
HICKEY
HOCKED
HOCKEY
INCHED
INCHES
ITCHED
ITCHES
JACKED
JACKET
JACKEY
JOCKEY
KICKED
KICKER
KUCHEN
LACHES
LACIER
LACKED
LACKEY
LECTER
LICHEN
LICKED
LOCKED
LOCKER
LOCKET
LUCKED
LYCEES
MACHES
MCCREA
MICHEL
MICKEY
MOCKED
MOCKER
MUCKED
NACRES
NECKED
NICAEA
NICHES
NICKED
NICKEL
NICKER
NUCLEI
NUCLEO
PACKED
PACKER
PACKET
PECKED
PICKED
PICKER
PICKET
POCKET
PUCKER
RACHEL
RACIER
RACKED
RACKET
RICHEN
RICHER
RICHES
RICKED
RICKEY
ROCHET
ROCKED
ROCKER
ROCKET
RUCHES
RUCKED
SACHEM
SACHET
SACKED
SACKER
SACRED
SECKEL
SECRET
SICCED
SICKEN
SICKER
SOCCER
SOCKED
SOCKET
SOCLES
SUCCES
SUCKED
SUCKER
TACKED
TACKER
TICKED
TICKER
TICKET
TUCKED
TUCKER
TUCKET
UNCLES
VACHEL
WICKED
WICKER
WICKET
YACKED

••C••E
ACCEDE
ACCRUE
ACCUSE
ALCOVE
ARCADE
ARCANE
ARCHIE
BECAME
BECOME
BOCCIE
BUCKLE
CACKLE
CECILE
COCKLE
DECADE
DECIDE
DECKLE
DECODE
DECREE
DOCILE
ENCAGE
ENCASE
ENCODE
ENCORE
EOCENE
ESCAPE
EUCHRE
EXCISE
EXCITE
EXCUSE
FACADE
FACILE
FICHTE
FICKLE
FOCSLE
HACKIE
HACKLE
HECATE
HECKLE
INCASE
INCISE
INCITE
INCOME
INCUSE
JACKIE
JECKLE
JOCOSE
LOCALE
LOCATE
LUCITE
MACRAE
MCCABE
NICENE
NICOLE
NUCHAE
OOCYTE
OSCINE
PICKLE
RACEME
RACINE
RECANE
RECEDE
RECIFE
RECIPE
RECITE
RECODE
RECUSE
RICHIE
ROCKNE
SACQUE
SECEDE
SECURE
SICKLE
SOCAGE
TACKLE
TECHIE
TICKLE
UNCAGE
UNCASE
VACATE

•••CE•
AMICES
APICES
AVOCET
BONCES
BRACED
BRACER
BRACES
CALCES
CANCEL
CRUCES
DANCED
DANCER
DANCES
DEICED
DEICER
DEICES
DEUCED
DEUCES
DUBCEK
DULCET
DUNCES
EDUCED
EDUCES
FALCES
FARCED
FARCES
FASCES
FAUCES
FAUCET
FENCED
FENCER
FENCES
FORCED
FORCER
FORCES
GLACES
GRACED
GRACES
GROCER
JAYCEE
JUICED
JUICER
JUICES
LANCED
LANCER
LANCES
LANCET
MARCEL
MERCED
MERCER
MINCED
MINCER
MINCES
NIECES
NUECES
OUNCES
PARCEL
PENCEL
PIECED
PIECER
PIECES
PINCER
PISCES
PLACED
PLACER
PLACES
PLACET
PONCES
PRICED
PRICER
PRICES
PRICEY
SAUCED
SAUCER
SAUCES
SICCED
SLICED
SLICER
SLICES
SOCCER
SPACED
SPACEK
SPACER
SPACES
SPACEY
SPICED
SPICES
STACEY
SUCCES
SYNCED
TALCED
TERCEL
TERCET
TRACED
TRACER
TRACES
TRACEY
TRICED
TRICEP
TRICES
TRUCES
UNICEF
VINCES
VOICED
VOICES
WENCES
WINCED
WINCER
WINCES

•••C•E
AMECHE
APACHE
BOCCIE
BOUCLE
BUNCHE
CHICLE
CIRCLE
CLICHE
CLOCHE
CRECHE
FESCUE
FIACRE
FLECHE
GAUCHE
GRACIE
ICICLE
JAYCEE
LOUCHE
MARCHE
MARCIE
MISCUE
MUNCIE
MUSCLE
ORACLE
PARCAE
PLICAE
PROCNE
PSYCHE
QUICHE
RESCUE
ROSCOE
RUNCIE
SEICHE
SIECLE
SPECIE
STACTE
THECAE
THICKE
TOUCHE
TROCHE

••••CE
ADDUCE
ADVICE
ALSACE
AMERCE
APIECE
ATONCE
BIERCE
BODICE
BOUNCE
CHANCE
CHOICE
COERCE
DEDUCE
DEFACE
DEVICE
DRYICE
EFFACE
ELLICE
ENLACE
ENTICE
EUNICE
EVINCE
FIANCE
FIERCE
FLEECE
FRANCE
GLANCE
GREECE
HORACE
IGNACE
INDUCE
JANICE
JOUNCE
MALICE
MENACE
NODICE
NOTICE
NOVICE
NUANCE
OFFICE
PALACE
PEERCE
PIERCE
PLAICE
POLICE
POMACE
POUNCE
PRANCE
PRINCE
PUMICE
PURACE
QUINCE
REDUCE
REFACE
RELACE
SCARCE
SCONCE
SEANCE
SEDUCE
SLUICE
SOLACE
SOURCE
SPLICE
SPRUCE
STANCE

TENACE
THENCE
THRACE
THRICE
TIERCE
TRANCE
UNLACE
USANCE
VELOCE
VENICE
VIVACE
WHENCE

C•F•••
CAFTAN
COFFEE
COFFER
CUFFED

C••F••
CANFUL
CAPFUL
CARFUL
CHAFED
CHAFES
CHAFFS
CHAFFY
CHUFFY
CLEFTS
CLIFFS
CLIFFY
COFFEE
COFFER
COIFED
COLFAX
COMFIT
CONFAB
CONFED
CONFER
CRAFTS
CRAFTY
CROFTS
CUFFED
CUPFUL
CURFEW

C•••F•
CANIFF
CARAFE
CASEFY
CHAFFS
CHAFFY
CHIEFS
CHUFFY
CITIFY
CLIFFS
CLIFFY
CODIFY
CRYOFF
CUTOFF

C••••F
CANIFF
CERTIF
CRYOFF
CUTOFF

•C•F••
ICEFOG
SCIFIS
SCOFFS
SCUFFS

•C••F•
SCARFS
SCHIFF
SCLAFF
SCOFFS
SCRUFF
SCUFFS
SCURFY

•C•••F
SCHIFF
SCLAFF
SCRUFF

••C•F•
DECAFS
PACIFY
RECIFE

•••C•F
UNICEF

C•G•••
CAGERS
CAGIER
CAGILY
CAGING
CAGNEY
CAGUAS
CIGARS
COGENT
COGGED
COGITO
COGNAC
CYGNET
CYGNUS

C••G••
CADGED
CADGER
CADGES
CAPGUN
CARGOS
CATGUT
CAUGHT
CHIGOE
CLOGGY
CLOGUP
CODGER
COGGED
COIGNS
CONGAS
CONGER
CONGOU
COOGAN
CORGIS
COUGAR
COUGHS
CRAGGY
CUDGEL

C•••G•
CAYUGA
CHANGE
CHARGE
CHOUGH
CLANGS
CLERGY
CLINGS
CLINGY
CLOGGY
COLUGO
COSIGN
CRAGGY
CRINGE
CUBAGE

C••••G
CAGING
CAKING
CANING
CARING
CASING
CATRIG
CAVING
CAWING
CEDING
CHIANG
CITING
CLUING
COBURG
CODING
COMING
COOING
COPING
CORING
COWING
CRYING
CUBING
CURING
CYBORG

•CG•••
MCGRAW
MCGREW

•C••G•
ICEAGE
ICINGS
MCHUGH
SCRAGS

•C•••G
ACHING
ACTING
ICEBAG
ICEFOG
ICHING

••C•G•
ENCAGE
SOCAGE
UNCAGE

••C••G
ARCING
DICING
FACING
LACING
PACING
RACING
RICING
UNCLOG

CH••••
CHACHA
CHACMA
CHADOR
CHAFED
CHAFES
CHAFFS
CHAFFY
CHAINE
CHAINS
CHAIRS
CHAISE
CHALCO
CHALET
CHALKS
CHALKY
CHAMMY
CHAMPS
CHANCE
CHANCY
CHANEL
CHANEY
CHANGE
CHANTS
CHAPEL
CHAPIN
CHARGE
CHARLY
CHARMS
CHARON
CHARRO
CHARTS
CHASED
CHASER
CHASES
CHASMS
CHASSE
CHASTE
CHATTY
CHATUP
CHAVEZ
CHEAPO
CHEATS
CHECKS
CHEECH
CHEEKS
CHEEKY
CHEEPS
CHEERS
CHEERY
CHEESE
CHEESY
CHEKOV
CHELAE
CHELAS
CHEMIN
CHENIN
CHEOPS
CHEQUE
CHERIE
CHERRY
CHERTY
CHERUB
CHERYL
CHESTS
CHESTY
CHETHS
CHEVAL
CHEVET
CHEVRE
CHEWED
CHEWER
CHEWUP
CHIANG
CHIAUS
CHICHA
CHICHI
CHICKS
CHICLE
CHICLY
CHIDED
CHIDER
CHIDES
CHIEFS
CHIGOE
CHILDE
CHILDS
CHILLI
CHILLS
CHILLY
CHILOE
CHIMED
CHIMES
CHIMPS
CHINCH
CHINES
CHINKS
CHINKY
CHINOS
CHINTZ
CHINUP
CHIPIN
CHIRAC
CHIRON
CHIRPS
CHIRPY
CHIRRS
CHISEL
CHISOX
CHITIN
CHITON
CHIVES
CHLORO
CHOATE
CHOCKS
CHOICE
CHOIRS
CHOKED
CHOKER
CHOKES
CHOLER
CHOLLA
CHOLOS
CHOMPS
CHONJU
CHOOSE
CHOOSY
CHOOYU
CHOPIN
CHOPPY
CHOPRA
CHORAL
CHORDS
CHORES
CHORUS
CHOSEN
CHOUGH
CHOWED
CHRISM
CHROMA
CHROME
CHROMO
CHROMY
CHRONO
CHUBBY
CHUCKS
CHUFFY
CHUHSI
CHUKAR
CHUKKA
CHUMMY
CHUMPS
CHUNKS
CHUNKY
CHURCH
CHURLS
CHURNS
CHURRO
CHURRS
CHUTED
CHUTES
CHYRON

C•H•••
CAHIER
CAHOWS
COHEIR
COHERE
COHORT
COHOST
COHUNE
CSHARP

C••H••
CACHED
CACHES
CACHET
CACHOU
CARHOP
CASHED
CASHES
CASHEW
CASHIN
CATHAY
CATHER
CHUHSI
CIPHER
COBHAM
COCHIN
COSHED
COSHES
CUSHAW
CYPHER

C•••H•
CANTHI
CATCHY
CAUCHO
CAUCHY
CAUGHT
CHACHA
CHETHS
CHICHA
CHICHI
CLICHE
CLOCHE
CLOTHE
CLOTHO
CLOTHS
CONCHA
CONCHS
COUGHS
CRECHE
CZECHS

C••••H
CALASH
CALIPH
CASBAH
CERIPH
CHEECH
CHINCH
CHOUGH
CHURCH
CLENCH
CLINCH
CLUTCH
COMETH
COYISH
CROUCH
CRUNCH
CRUTCH

•CH•••
ACHAEA
ACHEBE
ACHENE
ACHIER
ACHING
ECHINO
ECHOED
ECHOES
ECHOIC
ICHING
ICHTHY
LCHAIM
MCHALE
MCHUGH
OCHERS
OCHERY
OCHRES
SCHELL
SCHEMA
SCHEME
SCHICK
SCHIFF
SCHISM
SCHIST
SCHIZY
SCHLEP
SCHMOO
SCHMOS
SCHNOZ
SCHOOL
SCHORL
SCHULZ
SCHUSS
SCHWAB
SCHWAS
VCHIPS

•C••H•
ICHTHY
SCATHE
SCYTHE

•C•••H
MCHUGH
SCORCH
SCOTCH
SCUTCH

••CH••
AACHEN
AHCHOO
ANCHOR
ARCHED
ARCHER
ARCHES
ARCHIE
ARCHLY
ARCHON
ASCHAM
BACHED
BOCHCO
BUCHAN
CACHED
CACHES
CACHET
CACHOU
COCHIN
DACHAS
DUCHIN
ESCHER
ESCHEW
ETCHED
ETCHER
ETCHES
EUCHRE
FICHES
FICHTE
FICHUS
INCHED
INCHES
INCHON
ISCHIA
ITCHED
ITCHES
KUCHEN
LACHES
LICHEN
MACHES
MACHOS
MICHEL
MOCHAS
NACHOS
NICHES
NUCHAE
NUCHAL
ORCHID
ORCHIL
RACHEL
RACHIS
RICHEN
RICHER
RICHES
RICHIE
RICHLY
ROCHET
RUCHES
SACHEM
SACHET
SUCHAS
TECHIE
TECHNO
TUCHUN
UNCHIC
URCHIN
VACHEL
YACHTS

••C•H•
PICCHU

••C••H
INCASH

•••CH•
AMECHE
APACHE
BEACHY
BETCHA
BOTCHY
BRACHY
BRECHT
BUNCHE
BUNCHY
CATCHY
CAUCHO
CAUCHY
CHACHA
CHICHA
CHICHI
CLICHE
CLOCHE
CONCHA
CONCHS
CRECHE
CZECHS
DRACHM
EPOCHS
FLECHE
GAUCHE
GAUCHO
GOTCHA
HONCHO
JASCHA
KIMCHI
KWACHA
LEACHY
LITCHI
LOUCHE
LUNCHY
MANCHA
MANCHU
MARCHE
MISCHA
MUNCHY
NOTCHY
ORACHS
PANCHO
PATCHY
PEACHY
PERCHA
PICCHU
PITCHY
POACHY
PONCHO
POUCHY
PSYCHE
PSYCHO
PSYCHS
PUNCHY
QUICHE
RANCHO
REECHO
SANCHO
SEICHE
TAICHI
TETCHY
TORCHY
TOUCHE

TOUCHY
TRACHY
TRICHO
TROCHE
WITCHY

••••CH
ATTACH
AVOUCH
BARUCH
BLANCH
BLEACH
BLENCH
BLOTCH
BORSCH
BRANCH
BREACH
BREECH
BROACH
BROOCH
BRUNCH
CHEECH
CHINCH
CHURCH
CLENCH
CLINCH
CLUTCH
CROUCH
CRUNCH
CRUTCH
DETACH
DRENCH
EDKOCH
ENRICH
EPARCH
EXARCH
FLETCH
FLINCH
FLITCH
FRENCH
GLITCH
GRINCH
GROUCH
HAUNCH
HIRSCH
HITECH
HOOTCH
INARCH
KIRSCH
KITSCH
KLATCH
KVETCH
LAMECH
LAUNCH
MENSCH
MOLOCH
MUNICH
NAUTCH
ORBACH
PAUNCH
PESACH
PLEACH
PREACH
PUTSCH
QUENCH
SAMECH
SCORCH
SCOTCH
SCUTCH
SEARCH
SKETCH
SKITCH
SLOUCH
SMIRCH
SMOOCH
SMUTCH
SNATCH
SNITCH
SPEECH
STANCH
STARCH
STENCH
STITCH
STORCH
SWATCH
SWITCH
THATCH
TRENCH
TWITCH
VOTECH
WRENCH
WRETCH
ZURICH

CI••••
CIARDI
CIBOLA
CICADA
CICELY
CICERO
CIDERS
CIGARS
CILIUM
CINDER
CINEMA
CINQUE
CIPHER
CIRCLE
CIRCUM
CIRCUS
CIRQUE
CIRRUS
CISCOS
CISKEI
CITATO
CITERS
CITIES
CITIFY
CITING
CITIUS
CITRIC
CITRON
CITRUS
CIUDAD
CIVETS
CIVICS

C•I•••
CAICOS
CAIMAN
CAIQUE
CAIRNS
CEIBAS
CEILED
CHIANG
CHIAUS
CHICHA
CHICHI
CHICKS
CHICLE
CHICLY
CHIDED
CHIDER
CHIDES
CHIEFS
CHIGOE
CHILDE
CHILDS
CHILLI
CHILLS
CHILLY
CHILOE
CHIMED
CHIMES
CHIMPS
CHINCH
CHINES
CHINKS
CHINKY
CHINOS
CHINTZ
CHINUP
CHIPIN
CHIRAC
CHIRON
CHIRPS
CHIRPY
CHIRRS
CHISEL
CHISOX
CHITIN
CHITON
CHIVES
CLICHE
CLICKS
CLIENT
CLIFFS
CLIFFY
CLIMAX
CLIMBS
CLIMES
CLINCH
CLINES
CLINGS
CLINGY
CLINIC
CLINKS
CLIPON
CLIQUE
CLIQUY
CMINOR
CMINUS
CNIDAE
CNIDUS
COIFED
COIGNS
COILED
COILUP
COINED
COINER
CRICKS
CRIERS
CRIKEY
CRIMEA
CRIMES
CRIMPS
CRIMPY
CRINGE
CRIPES
CRISCO
CRISES
CRISIS
CRISPS
CRISPY
CRISTO
CRITIC
CUIABA
CUIQUE
CUISSE

C••I••
CABINS
CAGIER
CAGILY
CAGING
CAHIER
CAKIER
CAKING
CALICO
CALIPH
CAMINO
CAMION
CAMISE
CANIDS
CANIER
CANIFF
CANINE
CANING
CAPIAS
CAPITA
CARIBE
CARIBS
CARIES
CARINA
CARING
CASING
CASINO
CATION
CAVIAR
CAVILS
CAVING
CAVITY
CAWING
CECILE
CECILY
CEDING
CELINE
CERIPH
CERISE
CERIUM
CESIUM
CHAINE
CHAINS
CHAIRS
CHAISE
CHOICE
CHOIRS
CHRISM
CILIUM
CITIES
CITIFY
CITING
CITIUS
CIVICS
CLAIMS
CLAIRE
CLUING
COBIAS
CODIFY
CODING
COGITO
COKIER
COLIES
COLIMA
COMICS
COMING
COMITY
CONICS
CONIES
CONIUM
COOING
COPIED
COPIER
COPIES
COPING
CORING
CORIUM
COSIED
COSIER
COSIES
COSIGN
COSILY
COSINE
COVINA
COWING
COYISH
COZIED
COZIER
COZIES
COZILY
CRUISE
CRYING
CUBICS
CUBING
CUBISM
CUBIST
CUBITS
CUPIDS
CURIAE
CURIAL
CURING
CURIOS
CURIUM
CUTIES
CUTINS
CYBILL
CYNICS

C•••I•
CABBIE
CADDIE
CADDIS
CADMIC
CALAIS
CALLIN
CALVIN
CAMEIN
CANDID
CANLIT
CAPRIS
CAPSID
CARDIN
CARDIO
CARLIN
CARRIE
CASHIN
CASSIA
CASSIO
CASSIS
CATKIN
CATNIP
CATRIG
CAVEIN
CEDRIC
CELTIC
CERTIF
CERVID
CHAPIN
CHEMIN
CHENIN
CHERIE
CHIPIN
CHITIN
CHOPIN
CITRIC
CLAVIN
CLERIC
CLEVIS
CLINIC
CLORIS
CLOVIS
CLUEIN
COATIS
COCCID
COCHIN
COEDIT
COHEIR
COLLIE
COMEIN
COMFIT
COMMIT
COMMIX
CONNIE
CONOID
COOKIE
COOLIT
COOTIE
COPTIC
CORBIN
CORGIS
COSMIC
COURIC
COUSIN
COWRIE
CRANIA
CRANIO
CREDIT
CRETIN
CRISIS
CRITIC
CRONIN
CUBOID
CULKIN
CULLIS
CULTIC
CUPRIC
CURTIN
CURTIS
CURTIZ
CUSPID
CUSTIS
CUTSIN
CYANIC
CYCLIC
CYMRIC

C••••I
CANTHI
CARONI
CENTRI
CHICHI
CHILLI
CHUHSI
CIARDI
CISKEI
CUMULI

•CI•••
ACIDIC
ACIDLY
ACINUS
ICICLE
ICIEST
ICINGS
SCIFIS
SCIONS
SCIPIO

•C•I••
ACHIER
ACHING
ACTIII
ACTING
ACTINO
ACTION
ACTIUM
ACTIVE
ACUITY
ECHINO
ICHING
ICKIER
SCHICK
SCHIFF
SCHISM
SCHIST
SCHIZY
SCRIBE
SCRIMP
SCRIMS
SCRIPS
SCRIPT
VCHIPS

•C••I•
ACACIA
ACADIA
ACARID
ACEDIA
ACETIC
ACIDIC
ACQUIT
ACTIII
ECESIC
ECESIS
ECHOIC
ECLAIR
ICARIA
ICEDIN
ICESIN
ICONIC
LCHAIM
MCBAIN
MCLAIN
MCNAIR
SCALIA
SCENIC
SCIFIS
SCIPIO
SCORIA
SCOTIA

•C•••I
ACTIII
OCELLI
OCTOPI
OCTROI
SCAMPI

••CI••
ANCIEN
ARCING
CECILE
CECILY
DECIDE
DICIER
DICING
DOCILE
ENCINA
ENCINO
EXCISE
EXCITE
FACIAL
FACIAS
FACIES
FACILE
FACING
INCISE
INCITE
LACIER
LACILY
LACING
LUCIAN
LUCITE
LUCIUS
MUCINS
OSCINE
PACIFY
PACING
PACINO
RACIAL
RACIER
RACILY
RACINE
RACING
RECIFE
RECIPE
RECITE
RICING
SICILY
SOCIAL
UNCIAL

••C•I•
ALCUIN
ARCHIE
ARCTIC
BACKIN
BOCCIE
COCCID
COCHIN
CYCLIC
DACOIT
DECEIT
DUCHIN
EUCLID
HACKIE
HECTIC
ISCHIA
JACKIE
KICKIN
LACTIC
LOCKIN
MACEIO
ORCHID
ORCHIL
PECTIC
PECTIN
PICNIC
RACHIS
RECOIL
RICHIE
SOCKIN
SUCKIN
TACTIC
TECHIE
TOCSIN
TUCKIN
UNCHIC
UNCOIL
URCHIN
VICTIM
VICTIS

••C••I
JACOBI
NUCLEI

•••CI•
ACACIA
AFLCIO
ALICIA
ANACIN
BAUCIS
BOCCIE
COCCID
ELICIT
FASCIA
GARCIA
GLACIS
GRACIE
MARCIA
MARCIE
MUNCIE
MURCIA
NIACIN
NUNCIO
PAUCIS
PENCIL
PHOCIS
PLACID
PRECIS
RANCID
RUNCIE
SPECIE
TRICIA
URACIL
VINCIT
VISCID

•••C•I
CHICHI
KIMCHI
LITCHI
TAICHI

••••CI
MEDICI

C•J•••
CAJOLE
CAJUNS

C••J••
CMAJOR
CONJOB

C•••J•
CHONJU

•CJ•••
MCJOBS

•C•J••
ACAJOU

C•K•••
CAKIER
CAKING
COKIER

C••K••
CACKLE
CALKED
CANKER
CARKED
CATKIN
CHEKOV
CHOKED
CHOKER
CHOKES
CHUKAR
CHUKKA
CISKEI
COCKED
COCKER
COCKLE
CONKED
CONKER
COOKED
COOKER
COOKIE
COOKUP
CORKED
CORKER
CRAKES
CRIKEY
CUCKOO
CULKIN

C•••K•
CAULKS
CHALKS
CHALKY
CHECKS
CHEEKS
CHEEKY
CHICKS
CHINKS
CHINKY
CHOCKS
CHUCKS
CHUKKA
CHUNKS
CHUNKY
CLACKS
CLANKS
CLANKY
CLARKE
CLEEKS
CLERKS
CLICKS
CLINKS
CLOAKS
CLOCKS
CLONKS
CLUCKS
CLUNKS
CLUNKY
CRACKS
CRACKY
CRANKS
CRANKY
CREAKS
CREAKY
CREEKS
CRICKS
CROAKS
CROAKY
CROCKS
CROOKS

C••••K
CUSACK

•CK•••
ACKACK
ICKIER
MCKUEN

•C•••K
ACKACK
OCASEK
OCLOCK
SCHICK
SCREAK

••CK••
BACKED
BACKER
BACKIN
BACKUP
BACKUS
BECKER
BECKET
BECKON
BICKER
BUCKED
BUCKET
BUCKLE
BUCKUP
CACKLE
COCKED
COCKER
COCKLE
CUCKOO
DECKED
DECKER
DECKLE
DICKER
DICKEY
DOCKED
DOCKER
DOCKET
DUCKED
FICKLE
GECKOS
HACKED
HACKER
HACKIE
HACKLE
HACKLY
HECKLE
HICKEY
HICKOK
HOCKED
HOCKEY
JACKAL
JACKED
JACKET
JACKEY
JACKIE
JACKUP
JECKLE
JOCKEY
KICKED
KICKER
KICKIN
KICKUP
LACKED
LACKEY
LICKED
LOCKED
LOCKER
LOCKET
LOCKIN
LOCKON
LOCKUP
LUCKED
MICKEY
MOCKED
MOCKER
MOCKUP
MUCKED
MUCKUP
NECKED
NICKED
NICKEL
NICKER
PACKED
PACKER
PACKET
PACKUP
PECKAT
PECKED
PICKAT
PICKAX
PICKED
PICKER
PICKET
PICKLE
PICKON
PICKUP
POCKET
PUCKER
RACKED
RACKET
RACKUP
RECKON
RICKED
RICKEY
ROCKED
ROCKER
ROCKET
ROCKNE
ROCKYV
RUCKED
RUCKUS
SACKED
SACKER
SECKEL
SICKEN
SICKER
SICKLE
SICKLY
SOCKED
SOCKET
SOCKIN
SUCKAS
SUCKED
SUCKER
SUCKIN
TACKED
TACKER
TACKLE
TACKON
TICKED
TICKER
TICKET
TICKLE
TICKLY
TUCKED
TUCKER
TUCKET
TUCKIN
WACKOS
WICKED
WICKER
WICKET
YACKED

••C•K•
HACEKS

••C••K
HICKOK
RECORK
UNCORK

•••CK•
ALECKY
BLACKS
BLOCKS
BLOCKY
BRICKS
BRICKY
CHECKS
CHICKS
CHOCKS
CHUCKS
CLACKS
CLICKS
CLOCKS
CLUCKS
CRACKS
CRACKY
CRICKS
CROCKS
FLACKS
FLECKS
FLECKY
FLICKA
FLICKS
FLOCKS
FLOCKY
FROCKS
KNACKS
KNICKS
KNOCKS
KYACKS
PLUCKS
PLUCKY
PRICKS
QUACKS
SHACKS
SHOCKS
SHUCKS
SLACKS
SLICKS
SMACKS
SMOCKS
SNACKS
SNICKS
SPECKS
STACKS
STICKS
STICKY
STOCKS
STOCKY
THICKE
TRACKS
TRICKS
TRICKY
TRUCKS
VNECKS
WHACKS
WHACKY
WRACKS
WRECKS
YOICKS

•••C•K
DUBCEK
SPACEK

••••CK
ACKACK
ARRACK
ATTACK
BEDECK
CUSACK
FRANCK
GOBACK
HIJACK
INLUCK
KOPECK
LUBECK
MOHOCK
NATICK
OCLOCK
ONDECK
PLANCK
RELOCK
REMICK
SCHICK
SHTICK
STRICK
STRUCK
THWACK
UNLOCK
UNPACK
UNTACK
UPTICK
YORICK
ZANUCK

CL••••
CLACKS
CLAIMS
CLAIRE
CLAMMY
CLAMOR
CLAMPS
CLAMUP
CLANCY
CLANGS
CLANKS
CLANKY
CLAQUE
CLARET
CLARKE
CLAROS
CLASPS
CLASSY
CLAUDE
CLAUSE
CLAVES
CLAVIN
CLAWED
CLAWER
CLAYEY
CLEANS
CLEARS
CLEATS
CLEAVE
CLEEKS
CLEESE
CLEFTS
CLENCH
CLEPED
CLERGY
CLERIC
CLERKS
CLEVER
CLEVES
CLEVIS
CLEWED
CLICHE
CLICKS
CLIENT
CLIFFS
CLIFFY
CLIMAX
CLIMBS
CLIMES
CLINCH
CLINES
CLINGS
CLINGY
CLINIC
CLINKS
CLIPON
CLIQUE
CLIQUY
CLOACA
CLOAKS
CLOCHE
CLOCKS
CLODDY
CLOGGY
CLOGUP
CLOMPS
CLONED
CLONES
CLONKS
CLONUS
CLOQUE
CLORIS
CLOROX
CLOSED
CLOSER
CLOSES
CLOSET
CLOTHE
CLOTHO
CLOTHS
CLOTTY
CLOUDS
CLOUDY
CLOUTS
CLOVEN
CLOVER
CLOVES
CLOVIS
CLOWNS
CLOYED
CLUBBY
CLUCKS
CLUEIN
CLUING
CLUMPS
CLUMPY
CLUMSY
CLUNKS
CLUNKY
CLUTCH

C•L•••
CALAIS
CALASH
CALCES
CALDER
CALICO
CALIPH
CALKED
CALLAO
CALLAS
CALLED
CALLER
CALLES
CALLIN
CALLON
CALLOW
CALLUP
CALLUS
CALMED
CALMER
CALMLY
CALPAC
CALQUE
CALVED
CALVES
CALVIN
CALXES
CCLAMP
CELEBS
CELERY
CELINE
CELLAE
CELLAR
CELLED
CELLOS
CELTIC
CHLORO
CILIUM
COLADA
COLDER
COLDLY
COLEUS
COLFAX
COLIES
COLIMA
COLLAR
COLLET
COLLIE
COLLOP
COLLOQ
COLMAN
COLONS
COLONY
COLORS
COLOUR
COLTER
COLUGO
COLUMN
CULETS
CULKIN
CULLED
CULLEN
CULLER
CULLET
CULLIS
CULTIC
CULVER

C••L••
CABLED
CABLER
CABLES
CALLAO
CALLAS
CALLED
CALLER
CALLES
CALLIN
CALLON
CALLOW
CALLUP
CALLUS
CAMLET
CANLIT
CAPLET
CARLIN
CARLOS
CARLOT
CAULKS
CEILED
CELLAE
CELLAR
CELLED
CELLOS
CEYLON
CHALCO
CHALET
CHALKS
CHALKY
CHELAE
CHELAS
CHILDE
CHILDS
CHILLI
CHILLS
CHILLY
CHILOE
CHOLER
CHOLLA
CHOLOS
COALER
COELOM
COILED
COILUP
COLLAR
COLLET
COLLIE
COLLOP
COLLOQ
COOLED
COOLER
COOLIT
COOLLY
COPLEY
COULDA
COULEE
COWLED
COWLEY
CULLED
CULLEN
CULLER
CULLET
CULLIS
CURLED
CURLER
CURLEW
CURLEY
CURLUP
CUTLER
CUTLET
CYCLAS
CYCLED
CYCLER
CYCLES
CYCLIC
CYCLOS

C•••L•
CABALA
CABALS
CACKLE
CAGILY
CAJOLE
CALMLY
CAMELS
CANALS
CANDLE
CANOLA
CANTLE
CAROLE
CAROLS
CASALS
CASTLE
CATTLE
CAUDLE
CAVELL
CAVILS
CECILE
CECILY
CEORLS
CHARLY
CHICLE
CHICLY
CHILLI
CHILLS
CHILLY
CHOLLA
CHURLS
CIBOLA
CICELY
CIRCLE
COBALT
COBBLE
COCKLE
CODDLE
COLDLY

COMELY
COMPLY
COOLLY
COPULA
CORALS
COSELL
COSILY
COSTLY
COUPLE
COZILY
CRADLE
CRAWLS
CRAWLY
CREELS
CREOLE
CUDDLE
CUDDLY
CUMULI
CUMULO
CUPELS
CUPOLA
CURDLE
CURTLY
CURULE
CUTELY
CYBELE
CYBILL

C••••L
CANCEL
CANFUL
CANNEL
CAPFUL
CARFUL
CARMEL
CARNAL
CARPAL
CARPEL
CARREL
CARROL
CARTEL
CASUAL
CAUDAL
CAUSAL
CAVELL
CEREAL
CHANEL
CHAPEL
CHERYL
CHEVAL
CHISEL
CHORAL
COEVAL
COMPEL
CONSUL
CORBEL
CORNEL
CORRAL
CORREL
COSELL
COSTAL
CRENEL
CRESOL
CREWEL
CRURAL
CUDGEL
CUNEAL
CUPFUL
CURIAL
CYBILL
CYMBAL

•CL•••
CCLAMP
ECLAIR
ECLATS
MCLAIN
MCLEAN
OCLOCK
SCLAFF
SCLERA
SCLERO
UCLANS

•C•L••
BCELLS
ECCLES
ECOLES
OCELLI
OCELOT
OCULAR
SCALAR
SCALDS
SCALED
SCALER
SCALES
SCALIA
SCALPS
SCHLEP
SCOLDS
SCULLS
SCULLY
SCULPT
SCYLLA

•C••L•
ACIDLY
BCELLS
ICICLE
MCHALE
OCCULT
OCELLI
RCCOLA
SCHELL
SCHULZ
SCOWLS
SCROLL
SCULLS
SCULLY
SCYLLA

•C•••L
ACETAL
ACETYL
ACTUAL
SCHELL
SCHOOL
SCHORL
SCRAWL
SCROLL

••CL••
CYCLAS
CYCLED
CYCLER
CYCLES
CYCLIC
CYCLOS
ECCLES
EUCLID
JACLYN
NUCLEI
NUCLEO
SOCLES
UNCLAD
UNCLES
UNCLOG
VACLAV

••C•L•
ARCHLY
BACALL
BECALM
BUCKLE
CACKLE
CECILE
CECILY
CICELY
COCKLE
DECALS
DECKLE
DOCILE
EXCELS
FACILE
FACULA
FICKLE
FOCSLE
HACKLE
HACKLY
HECKLE
INCULT
JACALS
JECKLE
LACILY
LOCALE
LOCALS
MACULA
NICELY
NICOLA
NICOLE
NICOLO
OCCULT
ONCALL
OSCULA
PICKLE
PICULS
RACILY
RCCOLA
RECALL
RICHLY
SICILY
SICKLE
SICKLY
TACKLE
TICALS
TICKLE
TICKLY
VOCALS

••C••L
BACALL
BUCCAL
DACTYL
DUCTAL
FACIAL
JACKAL
MICHEL
MRCOOL
NICKEL
NUCHAL
ONCALL
ORCHIL
RACHEL
RACIAL
RECALL
RECOIL
SACRAL
SECKEL
SOCIAL
UNCIAL
UNCOIL
UNCOOL
UNCURL
VACHEL

•••CL•
BOUCLE
CHICLE
CHICLY
CIRCLE
ICICLE
MUSCLE
MUSCLY
ORACLE
SIECLE

•••C•L
APICAL
BUCCAL
CANCEL
EPICAL
FISCAL
GLYCOL
LOWCAL
MARCEL
MESCAL
PARCEL
PASCAL
PENCEL
PENCIL
RASCAL
TERCEL
THECAL
TINCAL
UNOCAL
URACIL

CM••••
CMAJOR
CMINOR
CMINUS

C•M•••
CAMARO
CAMBER
CAMDEN
CAMEAT
CAMEBY
CAMEIN
CAMELS
CAMEON
CAMEOS
CAMERA
CAMETO
CAMEUP
CAMINO
CAMION
CAMISE
CAMLET
CAMPED
CAMPER
CAMPOS
CAMPUS
CEMENT
COMATE
COMBAT
COMBED
COMBER
COMBES
COMBOS
COMEAT
COMEBY
COMEDY
COMEIN
COMELY
COMEON
COMERS
COMETH
COMETO
COMETS
COMEUP
COMFIT
COMICS
COMING
COMITY
COMMAS
COMMIT
COMMIX
COMMON
COMPAQ
COMPEL
COMPLY
COMPOS
COMSAT
COMTES
CUMBER
CUMULI
CUMULO
CYMBAL
CYMRIC

C••M••
CADMIC
CADMUS
CAIMAN
CALMED
CALMER
CALMLY
CARMAN
CARMEL
CARMEN
CAYMAN
CERMET
CHAMMY
CHAMPS
CHEMIN
CHIMED
CHIMES
CHIMPS
CHOMPS
CHUMMY
CHUMPS
CLAMMY
CLAMOR
CLAMPS
CLAMUP
CLIMAX
CLIMBS
CLIMES
CLOMPS
CLUMPS
CLUMPY
CLUMSY
COLMAN
COMMAS
COMMIT
COMMIX
COMMON
CONMAN
CONMEN
CORMAN
COSMIC
COSMOS
COWMAN
COWMEN
CRAMBO
CRAMPS
CREMES
CRIMEA
CRIMES
CRIMPS
CRIMPY
CRUMBS
CRUMBY
CRUMMY

C•••M•
CAROMS
CCLAMP
CDROMS
CHACMA
CHAMMY
CHARMS
CHASMS
CHROMA
CHROME
CHROMO
CHROMY
CHUMMY
CINEMA
CLAIMS
CLAMMY
COLIMA
COLUMN
CREAMS
CREAMY
CRUMMY

C••••M
CERIUM
CESIUM
CHRISM
CILIUM
CIRCUM
COBHAM
COELOM
CONIUM
CORIUM
CUBISM
CURIUM
CUSTOM

•C•M••
ACUMEN
ICEMAN
ICEMEN
SCAMPI
SCAMPS
SCHMOO
SCHMOS
SCUMMY

•C••M•
CCLAMP
SCHEMA
SCHEME
SCRAMS
SCRIMP
SCRIMS
SCRUMS
SCUMMY

•C•••M
ACTIUM
LCHAIM
MCADAM
SCARUM
SCHISM
SCREAM

••CM••
MICMAC
PACMAN

••C•M•
BECAME
BECOME
DECAMP
ENCAMP
INCOME
JICAMA
RACEME
TACOMA

••C••M
ASCHAM
BECALM
DICTUM
LYCEUM
SACHEM
SACRUM
VACUUM
VICTIM

•••CM•
CHACMA

•••C•M
ABSCAM
CIRCUM
DRACHM
NONCOM
SITCOM
TALCUM
VIACOM

CN••••
CNIDAE
CNIDUS
CNOTES

C•N•••
CANAAN
CANADA
CANALS
CANAPE
CANARD
CANARY
CANCAN
CANCEL
CANCUN
CANDID
CANDLE
CANDOR
CANERS
CANFUL
CANIDS
CANIER
CANIFF
CANINE
CANING
CANKER
CANLIT
CANNAE
CANNED
CANNEL
CANNER
CANNES
CANNON
CANNOT
CANOED
CANOES
CANOLA
CANONS
CANOPY
CANOVA
CANTAB
CANTED
CANTER
CANTHI
CANTLE
CANTON
CANTOR
CANTOS
CANUTE
CANVAS
CANYON
CENOTE
CENSED
CENSER
CENSES
CENSOR
CENSUS
CENTER
CENTOS
CENTRE
CENTRI
CENTRO
CINDER
CINEMA
CINQUE
CONANT
CONCHA
CONCHS
CONCUR
CONDOR
CONDOS
CONEYS
CONFAB
CONFED
CONFER
CONGAS
CONGER
CONGOU
CONICS
CONIES
CONIUM
CONJOB
CONKED
CONKER
CONMAN
CONMEN
CONNED
CONNER
CONNIE
CONNOR
CONOCO
CONOID
CONRAD
CONROY
CONSUL
CONTAC
CONTES
CONTRA
CONTRE
CONURE
CONVEX
CONVEY
CONVOY
CONWAY
CUNARD
CUNAXA
CUNEAL
CYNICS

C••N••
CAGNEY
CANNAE
CANNED
CANNEL
CANNER
CANNES
CANNON
CANNOT
CAPNUT
CARNAL
CARNES
CARNET
CARNEY
CARNOT
CATNAP
CATNIP
CHANCE
CHANCY
CHANEL
CHANEY
CHANGE
CHANTS
CHENIN
CHINCH
CHINES
CHINKS
CHINKY
CHINOS
CHINTZ
CHINUP
CHONJU
CHUNKS
CHUNKY
CLANCY
CLANGS
CLANKS
CLANKY
CLENCH
CLINCH
CLINES
CLINGS
CLINGY
CLINIC

CLINKS
CLONED
CLONES
CLONKS
CLONUS
CLUNKS
CLUNKY
CMINOR
CMINUS
COGNAC
COINED
COINER
CONNED
CONNER
CONNIE
CONNOR
COONEY
CORNEA
CORNED
CORNEL
CORNER
CORNET
COUNTS
COUNTY
CPSNOW
CRANED
CRANES
CRANIA
CRANIO
CRANKS
CRANKY
CRANNY
CRENEL
CRENNA
CRINGE
CRONES
CRONIN
CRONUS
CRONYN
CRUNCH
CYANIC
CYGNET
CYGNUS

C•••N•

CABANA
CABINS
CADENT
CAGING
CAIRNS
CAJUNS
CAKING
CAMINO
CANINE
CANING
CANONS
CAPONE
CAPONS
CARINA
CARING
CARONI
CASING
CASINO
CATENA
CAVING
CAWING
CEDANT
CEDING
CELINE
CEMENT
CESSNA
CETANE
CHAINE
CHAINS
CHIANG
CHRONO
CHURNS
CITING
CLEANS
CLIENT
CLOWNS
CLUING
CODING
CODONS
COGENT
COHUNE
COIGNS
COLONS
COLONY
COMING
CONANT
COOING
COPING
CORING
CORONA
COSINE
COVENS
COVENT
COVINA
COWENS
COWING
COZENS
CRANNY
CRENNA
CROONS
CROWNS
CRYING
CUBING
CURING
CUTINS
CYRANO
CZERNY

C••••N

CAFTAN
CAIMAN
CALLIN
CALLON
CALVIN
CAMDEN
CAMEIN
CAMEON
CAMION
CANAAN
CANCAN
CANCUN
CANNON
CANTON
CANYON
CAPGUN
CAPTAN
CARBON
CARDIN
CAREEN
CARLIN
CARMAN
CARMEN
CARSON
CARTON
CASERN
CASHIN
CASTON
CATION
CATKIN
CATTON
CAVEIN
CAVERN
CAXTON
CAYMAN
CEYLON
CHAPIN
CHARON
CHEMIN
CHENIN
CHIPIN
CHIRON
CHITIN
CHITON
CHOPIN
CHOSEN
CHYRON
CITRON
CLAVIN
CLIPON
CLOVEN
CLUEIN
COBURN
COCHIN
COCOON
COLMAN
COLUMN
COMEIN
COMEON
COMMON
CONMAN
CONMEN
COOGAN
CORBAN
CORBIN
CORDON
CORMAN
COSIGN
COTTEN
COTTON
COUPON
COUSIN
COWMAN
COWMEN
CRAVEN
CRAYON
CRETAN
CRETIN
CRONIN
CRONYN
CROTON
CULKIN
CULLEN
CURTIN
CURZON
CUTSIN

•CN•••

MCNAIR

•C•N••

ACINUS
ICINGS
ICONIC
SCANTS
SCANTY
SCENAS
SCENDS
SCENES
SCENIC
SCENTS
SCHNOZ
SCONCE
SCONES

•C••N•

ACCENT
ACHENE
ACHING
ACORNS
ACTING
ACTINO
ACTONE
ECHINO
ICHING
MCCANN
OCEANS
OCTANE
OCTANT
SCARNE
SCIONS
SCORNS
UCLANS

•C•••N

ACTION
ACTSON
ACUMEN
ICEDIN
ICEMAN
ICEMEN
ICESIN
MCBAIN
MCCANN
MCKUEN
MCLAIN
MCLEAN
SCREEN

••CN••

PICNIC

••C•N•

ACCENT
ANCONA
ARCANA
ARCANE
ARCING
ASCEND
ASCENT
DECANT
DECENT
DICING
DOCENT
ENCINA
ENCINO
EOCENE
ESCENT
FACING
FECUND
INCANS
JACANA
JOCUND
LACING
LACUNA
LUCENT
MCCANN
MUCINS
NICENE
NOCENT
OSCINE
PACING
PACINO
PECANS
POCONO
RACINE
RACING
RACONS
RECANE
RECANT
RECENT
RECONS
RICING
ROCKNE
SECANT
SECOND
TECHNO
TUCANA
VACANT
VICUNA

••C••N

AACHEN
ALCUIN
ANCIEN
ARCHON
ARCTAN
BACKIN
BECKON
BICORN
BUCHAN
COCHIN
COCOON
DACRON
DUCHIN
INCHON
JACLYN
KICKIN
KUCHEN
LICHEN
LOCKIN
LOCKON
LUCIAN
MACOUN
MACRON
MCCANN
MICRON
NICEAN
PACMAN
PECTIN
PICKON
RECKON
RICHEN
SECERN
SICKEN
SOCKIN
SUCKIN
TACKON
TOCSIN
TUCHUN
TUCKIN
TUCSON
TYCOON
URCHIN
WICCAN

•••CN•

PROCNE

•••C•N

ANACIN
ASHCAN
BEACON
CANCAN
CANCUN
DEACON
DUNCAN
FALCON
FLACON
GARCON
GASCON
NIACIN
OILCAN
TINCAN
TOUCAN
TUSCAN
VULCAN
WICCAN
ZIRCON

CO••••

COALER
COAPTS
COARSE
COASTS
COATED
COATIS
COAXED
COAXER
COAXES
COBALT
COBBLE
COBHAM
COBIAS
COBRAS
COBURG
COBURN
COBWEB
COCCID
COCCUS
COCCYX
COCHIN
COCKED
COCKER
COCKLE
COCOAS
COCOON
CODDLE
CODERS
CODGER
CODIFY
CODING
CODONS
COEDIT
COELOM
COERCE
COEVAL
COFFEE
COFFER
COGENT
COGGED
COGITO
COGNAC
COHEIR
COHERE
COHORT
COHOST
COHUNE
COIFED
COIGNS
COILED
COILUP
COINED
COINER
COKIER
COLADA
COLDER
COLDLY
COLEUS
COLFAX
COLIES
COLIMA
COLLAR
COLLET
COLLIE
COLLOP
COLLOQ
COLMAN
COLONS
COLONY
COLORS
COLOUR
COLTER
COLUGO
COLUMN
COMATE
COMBAT
COMBED
COMBER
COMBES
COMBOS
COMEAT
COMEBY
COMEDY
COMEIN
COMELY
COMEON
COMERS
COMETH
COMETO
COMETS
COMEUP
COMFIT
COMICS
COMING
COMITY
COMMAS
COMMIT
COMMIX
COMMON
COMPAQ
COMPEL
COMPLY
COMPOS
COMSAT
COMTES
CONANT
CONCHA
CONCHS
CONCUR
CONDOR
CONDOS
CONEYS
CONFAB
CONFED
CONFER
CONGAS
CONGER
CONGOU
CONICS
CONIES
CONIUM
CONJOB
CONKED
CONKER
CONMAN
CONMEN
CONNED
CONNER
CONNIE
CONNOR
CONOCO
CONOID
CONRAD
CONROY
CONSUL
CONTAC
CONTES
CONTRA
CONTRE
CONURE
CONVEX
CONVEY
CONVOY
CONWAY
COODER
COOERS
COOGAN
COOING
COOKED
COOKER
COOKIE
COOKUP
COOLED
COOLER
COOLIT
COOLLY
COONEY
COOPED
COOPER
COOPTS
COOPUP
COOTER
COOTIE
COPAYS
COPIED
COPIER
COPIES
COPING
COPLEY
COPOUT
COPPED
COPPER
COPSES
COPTER
COPTIC
COPULA
COQUET
CORALS
CORBAN
CORBEL
CORBIN
CORDAY
CORDED
CORDON
CORERS
CORGIS
CORING
CORIUM
CORKED
CORKER
CORMAN
CORNEA
CORNED
CORNEL
CORNER
CORNET
CORONA
CORPUS
CORRAL
CORREL
CORSET
CORTES
CORTEX
CORTEZ
CORVEE
CORVES
CORYZA
COSELL
COSHED
COSHES
COSIED
COSIER
COSIES
COSIGN
COSILY
COSINE
COSMIC
COSMOS
COSSET
COSTAE
COSTAL
COSTAR
COSTAS
COSTLY
COTTAS
COTTEN
COTTER
COTTON
COUGAR
COUGHS
COULDA
COULEE
COUNTS
COUNTY
COUPES
COUPLE
COUPON
COURIC
COURSE
COURTS
COUSIN
COUTER
COVENS
COVENT
COVERS
COVERT
COVETS
COVEYS
COVINA
COWARD
COWBOY
COWENS
COWERS
COWING
COWLED
COWLEY

COWMAN
COWMEN
COWPEA
COWPER
COWPOX
COWRIE
COYEST
COYISH
COYOTE
COYPUS
COZENS
COZIED
COZIER
COZIES
COZILY

C•O•••

CEORLS
CHOATE
CHOCKS
CHOICE
CHOIRS
CHOKED
CHOKER
CHOKES
CHOLER
CHOLLA
CHOLOS
CHOMPS
CHONJU
CHOOSE
CHOOSY
CHOOYU
CHOPIN
CHOPPY
CHOPRA
CHORAL
CHORDS
CHORES
CHORUS
CHOSEN
CHOUGH
CHOWED
CLOACA
CLOAKS
CLOCHE
CLOCKS
CLODDY
CLOGGY
CLOGUP
CLOMPS
CLONED
CLONES
CLONKS
CLONUS
CLOQUE
CLORIS
CLOROX
CLOSED
CLOSER
CLOSES
CLOSET
CLOTHE
CLOTHO
CLOTHS
CLOTTY
CLOUDS
CLOUDY
CLOUTS
CLOVEN
CLOVER
CLOVES
CLOVIS
CLOWNS
CLOYED
CNOTES
COODER
COOERS
COOGAN
COOING
COOKED
COOKER
COOKIE
COOKUP
COOLED
COOLER
COOLIT
COOLLY
COONEY
COOPED
COOPER
COOPTS
COOPUP
COOTER
COOTIE
CROAKS
CROAKY
CROATS
CROCKS
CROCUS
CROFTS
CRONES
CRONIN
CRONUS
CRONYN
CROOKS
CROONS
CROPUP
CROSBY
CROSSE
CROTON
CROUCH
CROUPY
CROUSE
CROUTE
CROWDS
CROWED
CROWER
CROWNS
CROZES

C••O••

CAHOWS
CAJOLE
CANOED
CANOES
CANOLA
CANONS
CANOPY
CANOVA
CAPONE
CAPONS
CAPOTE
CAROBS
CAROLE
CAROLS
CAROMS
CARONI
CAVORT
CDROMS
CENOTE
CHEOPS
CHLORO
CHOOSE
CHOOSY
CHOOYU
CHROMA
CHROME
CHROMO
CHROMY
CHRONO
CIBOLA
COCOAS
COCOON
CODONS
COHORT
COHOST
COLONS
COLONY
COLORS
COLOUR
CONOCO
CONOID
COPOUT
CORONA
COYOTE
CREOLE
CROOKS
CROONS
CRYOFF
CSPOTS
CUBOID
CUPOLA
CUTOFF
CUTOUT
CYBORG

C•••O•

CACAOS
CACHOU
CAICOS
CALLON
CALLOW
CAMEON
CAMEOS
CAMION
CAMPOS
CANDOR
CANNON
CANNOT
CANTON
CANTOR
CANTOS
CANYON
CAPTOR
CARBON
CARBOS
CARBOY
CARGOS
CARHOP
CARLOS
CARLOT
CARNOT
CARROL
CARROT
CARSON
CARTON
CASTON
CASTOR
CATION
CATTON
CAWDOR
CAXTON
CELLOS
CENSOR
CENTOS
CERROS
CESTOS
CEYLON
CHADOR
CHARON
CHEKOV
CHIGOE
CHILOE
CHINOS
CHIRON
CHISOX
CHITON
CHOLOS
CHYRON
CISCOS
CITRON
CLAMOR
CLAROS
CLIPON
CLOROX
CMAJOR
CMINOR
COCOON
COELOM
COLLOP
COLLOQ
COMBOS
COMEON
COMMON
COMPOS
CONDOR
CONDOS
CONGOU
CONJOB
CONNOR
CONROY
CONVOY
CORDON
COSMOS
COTTON
COUPON
COWBOY
COWPOX
CPSNOW
CRAYON
CREDOS
CRESOL
CROTON
CRUSOE
CUCKOO
CURIOS
CURSOR
CURZON
CUSTOM
CUSTOS
CYCLOS

C••••O

CALICO
CALLAO
CAMARO
CAMETO
CAMINO
CARDIO
CARETO
CARUSO
CASINO
CASSIO
CASTRO
CAUCHO
CENTRO
CHALCO
CHARRO
CHEAPO
CHLORO
CHROMO
CHRONO
CHURRO
CICERO
CITATO
CLOTHO
COGITO
COLUGO
COMETO
CONOCO
CRAMBO
CRANIO
CRISCO
CRISTO
CRYPTO
CUCKOO
CUMULO
CYRANO

•CO•••

ACORNS
ECOLES
ICONIC
SCOFFS
SCOLDS
SCONCE
SCONES
SCOOPS
SCOOTS
SCOPED
SCOPES
SCORCH
SCORED
SCORER
SCORES
SCORIA
SCORNS
SCOTCH
SCOTER
SCOTIA
SCOTTO
SCOTTY
SCOURS
SCOUSE
SCOUTS
SCOWLS

•C•O••

ACCORD
ACCOST
ACEOUS
ACEOUT
ACROSS
ACTONE
ACTORS
ACTOUT
ECHOED
ECHOES
ECHOIC
ICEOUT
MCJOBS
OCLOCK
OCTOPI
RCCOLA
SCHOOL
SCHORL
SCIONS
SCOOPS
SCOOTS
SCRODS
SCROLL
SCROOP

•C••O•

ACAJOU
ACTION
ACTSON
ICEBOX
ICEFOG
MCADOO
OCELOT
OCTROI
SCHMOO
SCHMOS
SCHNOZ
SCHOOL
SCROOP

•C•••O

ACTINO
ACTTWO
ECHINO
MCADOO
OCTAVO
SCHMOO
SCIPIO
SCLERO
SCOTTO

••CO••

ACCORD
ACCOST
ALCOTT
ALCOVE
ANCONA
ASCOTS
ATCOST
BECOME
BICORN
COCOAS
COCOON
DACOIT
DECOCT
DECODE
DECORS
DECOYS
DICOTS
ENCODE
ENCORE
ESCORT
INCOME
JACOBI
JOCOSE
MACOUN
MRCOOL
MUCOSA
MUCOUS
NICOLA
NICOLE
NICOLO
PICOTS
POCONO
RACONS
RCCOLA
RECOAT
RECODE
RECOIL
RECONS
RECOPY
RECORD
RECORK
RECOUP
ROCOCO
SECOND
TACOMA
TYCOBB
TYCOON
UNCOIL
UNCOOL
UNCORK
WICOPY

••C•O•

AHCHOO
ANCHOR
ARCCOS
ARCHON
BECKON
CACAOS
CACHOU
COCOON
CUCKOO
CYCLOS
DACRON
DOCTOR
ESCROW
FACTOR
GECKOS
HECTOR
HICKOK
INCHON
LECTOR
LICTOR
LOCKON
MACHOS
MACRON
MACROS
MICRON
MICROS
MRCOOL
NACHOS
PICKON
RECKON
RECTOR
RECTOS
SECTOR
SUCCOR
TACKON
TUCSON
TYCOON
UNCLOG
UNCOOL
VECTOR
VICTOR
WACKOS

••C••O

AHCHOO
ARCARO
BOCHCO
CICERO
CUCKOO
DACAPO
ENCINO
ESCUDO
MACACO
MACEIO
NICOLO
NUCLEO
PACINO
PICABO
PICARO
POCONO
ROCOCO
TECHNO

•••CO•

ANTCOW
ARCCOS
BEACON
BUNCOS
CAICOS
CISCOS
DEACON
DISCOS
FALCON
FLACON
GARCON
GASCON
GLYCOL
GUACOS
JUNCOS
MARCOS
MASCOT
MOSCOW
NONCOM
PESCOW
RANCOR
ROSCOE
SEACOW
SITCOM
SUCCOR
TRICOT
VIACOM
WILCOX
ZIRCON

•••C•O

AFLCIO
ALECTO
CAUCHO
EXACTO
GAUCHO
HONCHO
NUNCIO
PANCHO
PONCHO
PSYCHO
RANCHO
REECHO
SANCHO
STUCCO
TRICHO
VELCRO

••••CO

ALNICO
BOCHCO
BRONCO
CALICO
CHALCO
CONOCO
CRISCO
ENESCO
ENRICO
FIASCO
FRANCO
FRESCO
FRISCO
GRAECO
MACACO
MEDICO
MEJICO
MEXICO
MONACO
OROZCO
ROCOCO
STUCCO
SUNOCO
TEXACO
UNESCO
ZYDECO

CP••••

CPSNOW

C•P•••

CAPERS
CAPFUL
CAPGUN
CAPIAS
CAPITA
CAPLET
CAPNUT
CAPONE
CAPONS
CAPOTE
CAPPED
CAPPER
CAPRIS
CAPSID
CAPTAN
CAPTOR
CIPHER
COPAYS
COPIED
COPIER
COPIES
COPING
COPLEY
COPOUT
COPPED
COPPER
COPSES
COPTER
COPTIC
COPULA
CSPOTS
CUPELS
CUPFUL
CUPIDS
CUPOLA
CUPPAS
CUPPED
CUPRIC
CYPHER
CYPRUS

C••P••

CALPAC
CAMPED
CAMPER

CAMPOS
CAMPUS
CAPPED
CAPPER
CARPAL
CARPED
CARPEL
CARPER
CARPET
CARPUS
CASPAR
CASPER
CHAPEL
CHAPIN
CHIPIN
CHOPIN
CHOPPY
CHOPRA
CLEPED
CLIPON
COAPTS
COMPAQ
COMPEL
COMPLY
COMPOS
COOPED
COOPER
COOPTS
COOPUP
COPPED
COPPER
CORPUS
COUPES
COUPLE
COUPON
COWPEA
COWPER
COWPOX
COYPUS
CRAPES
CREPES
CRIPES
CROPUP
CRYPTO
CRYPTS
CUPPAS
CUPPED
CUSPED
CUSPID

C•••P•

CALIPH
CANAPE
CANOPY
CERIPH
CHAMPS
CHEAPO
CHEEPS
CHEOPS
CHIMPS
CHIRPS
CHIRPY
CHOMPS
CHOPPY
CHUMPS
CLAMPS
CLASPS
CLOMPS
CLUMPS
CLUMPY
CRAMPS
CREEPS
CREEPY
CRIMPS
CRIMPY
CRISPS
CRISPY
CROUPY
CUTUPS

C••••P

CALLUP
CAMEUP
CARHOP
CATNAP
CATNIP
CATSUP
CCLAMP
CHATUP
CHEWUP
CHINUP
CLAMUP
CLOGUP
COILUP
COLLOP
COMEUP
COOKUP
COOPUP
CROPUP
CSHARP
CURLUP
CUTSUP

•C•P••

SCAPED
SCAPES
SCIPIO
SCOPED
SCOPES

•C••P•

ACCEPT
ECTYPE
OCCUPY
OCTOPI
SCALPS
SCAMPI
SCAMPS
SCARPS
SCAUPS
SCOOPS
SCRAPE
SCRAPS
SCRIPS
SCRIPT
SCULPT
VCHIPS

•C•••P

ACESUP
ACTSUP
CCLAMP
ICECAP
ICEDUP
ICESUP
SCHLEP
SCRIMP
SCROOP

••C•P•

ACCEPT
ALCAPP
BICEPS
DACAPO
ESCAPE
EXCEPT
INCEPT
OCCUPY
RECAPS
RECIPE
RECOPY
UNCAPS
WICOPY

••C••P

ALCAPP
BACKUP
BUCKUP
DECAMP
ENCAMP
ESCARP
FACEUP
HICCUP
JACKUP
KICKUP
LACEUP
LOCKUP
MOCKUP
MUCKUP
PACKUP
PICKUP
RACKUP
RECOUP

•••C•P

EGGCUP
EYECUP
GASCAP
HICCUP
HOTCAP
HUBCAP
ICECAP
MADCAP
MOBCAP
REDCAP
SKYCAP
TEACUP
TOECAP
TRICEP

C•Q•••

COQUET

C••Q••

CAIQUE
CALQUE
CASQUE
CHEQUE
CINQUE
CIRQUE
CLAQUE
CLIQUE
CLIQUY
CLOQUE
CUIQUE

C••••Q

COLLOQ
COMPAQ

•CQ•••

ACQUIT

••CQ••

SACQUE

CR••••

CRABBE
CRABBY
CRACKS
CRACKY
CRADLE
CRAFTS
CRAFTY
CRAGGY
CRAKES
CRAMBO
CRAMPS
CRANED
CRANES
CRANIA
CRANIO
CRANKS
CRANKY
CRANNY
CRAPES
CRATED
CRATER
CRATES
CRAVAT
CRAVED
CRAVEN
CRAVER
CRAVES
CRAWLS
CRAWLY
CRAYON
CRAZED
CRAZES
CREAKS
CREAKY
CREAMS
CREAMY
CREASE
CREASY
CREATE
CRECHE
CREDIT
CREDOS
CREEDS
CREEKS
CREELS
CREEPS
CREEPY
CREMES
CRENEL
CRENNA
CREOLE
CREPES
CRESOL
CRESTS
CRETAN
CRETIN
CREUSA
CREWED
CREWEL
CRICKS
CRIERS
CRIKEY
CRIMEA
CRIMES
CRIMPS
CRIMPY
CRINGE
CRIPES
CRISCO
CRISES
CRISIS
CRISPS
CRISPY
CRISTO
CRITIC
CROAKS
CROAKY
CROATS
CROCKS
CROCUS
CROFTS
CRONES
CRONIN
CRONUS
CRONYN
CROOKS
CROONS
CROPUP
CROSBY
CROSSE
CROTON
CROUCH
CROUPY
CROUSE
CROUTE
CROWDS
CROWED
CROWER
CROWNS
CROZES
CRUCES
CRUDDY
CRUDER
CRUETS
CRUISE
CRUMBS
CRUMBY
CRUMMY
CRUNCH
CRURAL
CRUSES
CRUSOE
CRUSTS
CRUSTY
CRUTCH
CRUXES
CRYERS
CRYING
CRYOFF
CRYPTO
CRYPTS

C•R•••

CARAFE
CARATS
CARBON
CARBOS
CARBOY
CARDED
CARDER
CARDIN
CARDIO
CAREEN
CAREER
CARESS
CARETO
CARETS
CARFUL
CARGOS
CARHOP
CARIBE
CARIBS
CARIES
CARINA
CARING
CARKED
CARLIN
CARLOS
CARLOT
CARMAN
CARMEL
CARMEN
CARNAL
CARNES
CARNET
CARNEY
CARNOT
CAROBS
CAROLE
CAROLS
CAROMS
CARONI
CARPAL
CARPED
CARPEL
CARPER
CARPET
CARPUS
CARREL
CARREY
CARRIE
CARROL
CARROT
CARSON
CARTED
CARTEL
CARTER
CARTES
CARTON
CARUSO
CARVED
CARVER
CARVES
CARVEY
CDROMS
CERATE
CEREAL
CEREUS
CERIPH
CERISE
CERIUM
CERMET
CERROS
CERTIF
CERUSE
CERVID
CHRISM
CHROMA
CHROME
CHROMO
CHROMY
CHRONO
CIRCLE
CIRCUM
CIRCUS
CIRQUE
CIRRUS
CORALS
CORBAN
CORBEL
CORBIN
CORDAY
CORDED
CORDON
CORERS
CORGIS
CORING
CORIUM
CORKED
CORKER
CORMAN
CORNEA
CORNED
CORNEL
CORNER
CORNET
CORONA
CORPUS
CORRAL
CORREL
CORSET
CORTES
CORTEX
CORTEZ
CORVEE
CORVES
CORYZA
CURACY
CURARE
CURATE
CURBED
CURDED
CURDLE
CURERS
CURFEW
CURIAE
CURIAL
CURING
CURIOS
CURIUM
CURLED
CURLER
CURLEW
CURLEY
CURLUP
CURRED
CURSED
CURSES
CURSOR
CURTER
CURTIN
CURTIS
CURTIZ
CURTLY
CURTSY
CURULE
CURVED
CURVES
CURVET
CURZON
CYRANO

C••R••

CADRES
CAIRNS
CAPRIS
CARREL
CARREY
CARRIE
CARROL
CARROT
CATRIG
CEDRIC
CEORLS
CERROS
CHARGE
CHARLY
CHARMS
CHARON
CHARRO
CHARTS
CHERIE
CHERRY
CHERTY
CHERUB
CHERYL
CHIRAC
CHIRON
CHIRPS
CHIRPY
CHIRRS
CHORAL
CHORDS
CHORES
CHORUS
CHURCH
CHURLS
CHURNS
CHURRO
CHURRS
CHYRON
CIARDI
CIRRUS
CITRIC
CITRON
CITRUS
CLARET
CLARKE
CLAROS
CLERGY
CLERIC
CLERKS
CLORIS
CLOROX
COARSE
COBRAS
COERCE
CONRAD
CONROY
CORRAL
CORREL
COURIC
COURSE
COURTS
COWRIE
CRURAL
CUPRIC
CURRED
CYMRIC
CYPRUS
CZERNY

C•••R•

CABERS
CAGERS
CAMARO
CAMERA
CANARD
CANARY
CANERS
CAPERS
CASERN
CASTRO
CATERS
CAVERN
CAVERS
CAVORT
CEDARS
CELERY
CENTRE
CENTRI
CENTRO
CESARE
CETERA
CHAIRS
CHARRO
CHEERS
CHEERY
CHERRY
CHEVRE
CHIRRS
CHLORO
CHOIRS
CHOPRA
CHURRO
CHURRS
CICERO
CIDERS
CIGARS
CITERS
CLAIRE
CLEARS
COBURG
COBURN
CODERS
COHERE
COHORT
COLORS
COMERS
CONTRA
CONTRE
CONURE
COOERS
CORERS
COVERS
COVERT
COWARD
COWERS
CRIERS
CRYERS
CSHARP
CUNARD
CURARE
CURERS
CYBORG
CYDERS

C••••R

CABLER
CADGER
CAESAR
CAGIER
CAHIER
CAKIER

CALDER
CALLER
CALMER
CAMBER
CAMPER
CANDOR
CANIER
CANKER
CANNER
CANTER
CANTOR
CAPPER
CAPTOR
CARDER
CAREER
CARPER
CARTER
CARVER
CASPAR
CASPER
CASTER
CASTOR
CATHER
CAVIAR
CAWDOR
CELLAR
CENSER
CENSOR
CENTER
CHADOR
CHASER
CHEWER
CHIDER
CHOKER
CHOLER
CHUKAR
CINDER
CIPHER
CLAMOR
CLAWER
CLEVER
CLOSER
CLOVER
CMAJOR
CMINOR
COALER
COAXER
COCKER
CODGER
COFFER
COHEIR
COINER
COKIER
COLDER
COLLAR
COLOUR
COLTER
COMBER
CONCUR
CONDOR
CONFER
CONGER
CONKER
CONNER
CONNOR
COODER
COOKER
COOLER
COOPER
COOTER
COPIER
COPPER
COPTER
CORKER
CORNER
COSIER
COSTAR
COTTER
COUGAR
COUTER
COWPER
COZIER
CRATER
CRAVER
CROWER
CRUDER
CULLER
CULVER
CUMBER
CURLER
CURSOR
CURTER
CUSTER
CUTLER
CUTTER
CYCLER
CYPHER

•CR•••
ACROSS
OCREAE
SCRAGS
SCRAMS
SCRAPE
SCRAPS
SCRAWL
SCREAK
SCREAM
SCREED
SCREEN
SCREES
SCREWS
SCREWY
SCRIBE
SCRIMP
SCRIMS
SCRIPS
SCRIPT
SCRODS
SCROLL
SCROOP
SCRUBS
SCRUFF
SCRUMS

•C•R••
ACARID
ACARUS
ACCRUE
ACORNS
ECARTE
ICARIA
ICARUS
MCCREA
MCGRAW
MCGREW
OCHRES
OCTROI
SCARAB
SCARCE
SCARED
SCARER
SCARES
SCARFS
SCARNE
SCARPS
SCARRY
SCARUM
SCORCH
SCORED
SCORER
SCORES
SCORIA
SCORNS
SCURFY
SCURRY
SCURVE
SCURVY

•C••R•
ACCORD
ACTORS
OCCURS
OCHERS
OCHERY
SCARRY
SCHORL
SCLERA
SCLERO
SCOURS
SCURRY

•C•••R
ACHIER
ECLAIR
ICKIER
MCNAIR
OCULAR
SCALAR
SCALER
SCARER
SCORER
SCOTER

••CR••
ACCRUE
DACRON
DECREE
ESCROW
MACRAE
MACRON
MACROS
MCCREA
MICRON
MICROS
NACRES
SACRAL
SACRED
SACRUM
SECRET

••C•R•
ACCORD
ARCARO
BICARB
BICORN
CICERO
DECORS
DICERS
ENCORE
ESCARP
ESCORT
EUCHRE
GOCART
IDCARD
INCURS
LACERS
OCCURS
OSCARS
OXCART
PACERS
PICARA
PICARD
PICARO
RACERS
RECORD
RECORK
RECURS
RICERS
SECERN
SECURE
ULCERS
UNCORK
UNCURL
VICARS

••C••R
ANCHOR
ARCHER
BACKER
BECKER
BICKER
COCKER
CYCLER
DECKER
DICIER
DICKER
DOCKER
DOCTOR
ESCHER
ETCHER
FACTOR
HACKER
HECTOR
KICKER
LACIER
LECTER
LECTOR
LICTOR
LOCKER
MOCKER
NECTAR
NICKER
PACKER
PICKER
PUCKER
RACIER
RECTOR
RICHER
ROCKER
SACKER
SECTOR
SICKER
SOCCER
SUCCOR
SUCKER
TACKER
TICKER
TUCKER
VECTOR
VICTOR
WICKER

•••CR•
DESCRY
FARCRY
FIACRE
FULCRA
OUTCRY
VELCRO
WARCRY

•••C•R
BARCAR
BOXCAR
BRACER
CONCUR
DANCER
DEICER
FENCER
FORCER
GROCER
HOTCAR
JUICER
LANCER
LASCAR
MERCER
MINCER
NASCAR
PIECER
PINCER
PLACER
PRICER
RANCOR
SAUCER
SLICER
SOCCER
SPACER
SUCCOR
TOWCAR
TRACER
TROCAR
WINCER

CS••••
CSHARP
CSPOTS

C•S•••
CASABA
CASALS
CASAVA
CASBAH
CASEFY
CASERN
CASHED
CASHES
CASHEW
CASHIN
CASING
CASINO
CASPAR
CASPER
CASQUE
CASSIA
CASSIO
CASSIS
CASTER
CASTES
CASTLE
CASTON
CASTOR
CASTRO
CASUAL
CESARE
CESIUM
CESSED
CESSES
CESSNA
CESTAS
CESTOS
CESTUS
CISCOS
CISKEI
COSELL
COSHED
COSHES
COSIED
COSIER
COSIES
COSIGN
COSILY
COSINE
COSMIC
COSMOS
COSSET
COSTAE
COSTAL
COSTAR
COSTAS
COSTLY
CPSNOW
CUSACK
CUSHAW
CUSPED
CUSPID
CUSSED
CUSSES
CUSTER
CUSTIS
CUSTOM
CUSTOS

C••S••
CAESAR
CAPSID
CARSON
CASSIA
CASSIO
CASSIS
CATSUP
CAUSAL
CAUSED
CAUSES
CEASED
CEASES
CENSED
CENSER
CENSES
CENSOR
CENSUS
CESSED
CESSES
CESSNA
CHASED
CHASER
CHASES
CHASMS
CHASSE
CHASTE
CHESTS
CHESTY
CHISEL
CHISOX
CHOSEN
CLASPS
CLASSY
CLOSED
CLOSER
CLOSES
CLOSET
COASTS
COMSAT
CONSUL
COPSES
CORSET
COSSET
COUSIN
CRESOL
CRESTS
CRISCO
CRISES
CRISIS
CRISPS
CRISPY
CRISTO
CROSBY
CROSSE
CRUSES
CRUSOE
CRUSTS
CRUSTY
CUESTA
CUISSE
CURSED
CURSES
CURSOR
CUSSED
CUSSES
CUTSIN
CUTSUP

C•••S•
CALASH
CAMISE
CARESS
CARUSO
CAYUSE
CERISE
CERUSE
CHAISE
CHASSE
CHEESE
CHEESY
CHOOSE
CHOOSY
CHRISM
CHUHSI
CLASSY
CLAUSE
CLEESE
CLUMSY
COARSE
COHOST
COURSE
COYEST
COYISH
CREASE
CREASY
CREUSA
CROSSE
CROUSE
CRUISE
CUBISM
CUBIST
CUISSE
CURTSY
CUTEST
CUTESY

C••••S
CABALS
CABERS
CABINS
CABLES
CACAOS
CACHES
CACTUS
CADDIS
CADETS
CADGES
CADMUS
CADRES
CAGERS
CAGUAS
CAHOWS
CAICOS
CAIRNS
CAJUNS
CALAIS
CALCES
CALLAS
CALLES
CALLUS
CALVES
CALXES
CAMELS
CAMEOS
CAMPOS
CAMPUS
CANALS
CANERS
CANIDS
CANNES
CANOES
CANONS
CANTOS
CANVAS
CAPERS
CAPIAS
CAPONS
CAPRIS
CARATS
CARBOS
CARESS
CARETS
CARGOS
CARIBS
CARIES
CARLOS
CARNES
CAROBS
CAROLS
CAROMS
CARPUS
CARTES
CARVES
CASALS
CASHES
CASSIS
CASTES
CATERS
CAUCUS
CAULKS
CAUSES
CAVERS
CAVILS
CDROMS
CEASES
CEDARS
CEIBAS
CELEBS
CELLOS
CENSES
CENSUS
CENTOS
CEORLS
CEREUS
CERROS
CESSES
CESTAS
CESTOS
CESTUS
CHAFES
CHAFFS
CHAINS
CHAIRS
CHALKS
CHAMPS
CHANTS
CHARMS
CHARTS
CHASES
CHASMS
CHEATS
CHECKS
CHEEKS
CHEEPS
CHEERS
CHELAS
CHEOPS
CHESTS
CHETHS
CHIAUS
CHICKS
CHIDES
CHIEFS
CHILDS
CHILLS
CHIMES
CHIMPS
CHINES
CHINKS
CHINOS
CHIRPS
CHIRRS
CHIVES
CHOCKS
CHOIRS
CHOKES
CHOLOS
CHOMPS
CHORDS
CHORES
CHORUS
CHUCKS
CHUMPS
CHUNKS
CHURLS

CHURNS
CHURRS
CHUTES
CIDERS
CIGARS
CIRCUS
CIRRUS
CISCOS
CITERS
CITIES
CITIUS
CITRUS
CIVETS
CIVICS
CLACKS
CLAIMS
CLAMPS
CLANGS
CLANKS
CLAROS
CLASPS
CLAVES
CLEANS
CLEARS
CLEATS
CLEEKS
CLEFTS
CLERKS
CLEVES
CLEVIS
CLICKS
CLIFFS
CLIMBS
CLIMES
CLINES
CLINGS
CLINKS
CLOAKS
CLOCKS
CLOMPS
CLONES
CLONKS
CLONUS
CLORIS
CLOSES
CLOTHS
CLOUDS
CLOUTS
CLOVES
CLOVIS
CLOWNS
CLUCKS
CLUMPS
CLUNKS
CMINUS
CNIDUS
CNOTES
COAPTS
COASTS
COATIS
COAXES
COBIAS
COBRAS
COCCUS
COCOAS
CODERS
CODONS
COIGNS
COLEUS
COLIES
COLONS
COLORS
COMBES
COMBOS
COMERS
COMETS
COMICS
COMMAS
COMPOS
COMTES
CONCHS
CONDOS
CONEYS
CONGAS
CONICS
CONIES
CONTES
COOERS
COOPTS
COPAYS
COPIES
COPSES
CORALS
CORERS
CORGIS
CORPUS
CORTES
CORVES
COSHES
COSIES
COSMOS
COSTAS
COTTAS
COUGHS
COUNTS
COUPES
COURTS
COVENS
COVERS
COVETS
COVEYS
COWENS
COWERS
COYPUS
COZENS
COZIES
CRACKS
CRAFTS
CRAKES
CRAMPS
CRANES
CRANKS
CRAPES
CRATES
CRAVES
CRAWLS
CRAZES
CREAKS
CREAMS
CREDOS
CREEDS
CREEKS
CREELS
CREEPS
CREMES
CREPES
CRESTS
CRICKS
CRIERS
CRIMES
CRIMPS
CRIPES
CRISES
CRISIS
CRISPS
CROAKS
CROATS
CROCKS
CROCUS
CROFTS
CRONES
CRONUS
CROOKS
CROONS
CROWDS
CROWNS
CROZES
CRUCES
CRUETS
CRUMBS
CRUSES
CRUSTS
CRUXES
CRYERS
CRYPTS
CSPOTS
CUBEBS
CUBICS
CUBITS
CULETS
CULLIS
CUPELS
CUPIDS
CUPPAS
CURERS
CURIOS
CURSES
CURTIS
CURVES
CUSSES
CUSTIS
CUSTOS
CUTIES
CUTINS
CUTUPS
CUVEES
CYCADS
CYCLAS
CYCLES
CYCLOS
CYDERS
CYGNUS
CYNICS
CYPRUS
CZECHS

•C•S••

ACESUP
ACTSAS
ACTSON
ACTSUP
ECESIC
ECESIS
ICESIN
ICESUP
OCASEK
OCASEY

•C••S•

ACCESS
ACCOST
ACCUSE
ACROSS
ICIEST
SCHISM
SCHIST
SCHUSS
SCOUSE

•C•••S

ACARUS
ACCESS
ACEOUS
ACINUS
ACORNS
ACROSS
ACTORS
ACTSAS
BCELLS
ECCLES
ECESIS
ECHOES
ECLATS
ECOLES
ICARUS
ICINGS
MCJOBS
OCCURS
OCEANS
OCHERS
OCHRES
OCTADS
OCTETS
SCALDS
SCALES
SCALPS
SCAMPS
SCANTS
SCAPES
SCARES
SCARFS
SCARPS
SCAUPS
SCENAS
SCENDS
SCENES
SCENTS
SCHMOS
SCHUSS
SCHWAS
SCIFIS
SCIONS
SCOFFS
SCOLDS
SCONES
SCOOPS
SCOOTS
SCOPES
SCORES
SCORNS
SCOURS
SCOUTS
SCOWLS
SCRAGS
SCRAMS
SCRAPS
SCREES
SCREWS
SCRIMS
SCRIPS
SCRODS
SCRUBS
SCRUMS
SCUBAS
SCUFFS
SCULLS
SCUTES
UCLANS
VCHIPS

••CS••

FOCSLE
TOCSIN
TUCSON

••C•S•

ACCESS
ACCOST
ACCUSE
ATCOST
ENCASE
EXCESS
EXCISE
EXCUSE
INCASE
INCASH
INCISE
INCUSE
JOCOSE
LOCUST
MUCOSA
NICEST
RECAST
RECESS
RECUSE
UNCASE
UPCAST

••C••S

ACCESS
ARCCOS
ARCHES
ASCOTS
BACKUS
BICEPS
CACAOS
CACHES
CACTUS
COCCUS
COCOAS
CYCADS
CYCLAS
CYCLES
CYCLOS
DACHAS
DECAFS
DECALS
DECAYS
DECORS
DECOYS
DICERS
DICOTS
DICTUS
DUCATS
ECCLES
EMCEES
ETCHES
EXCELS
EXCESS
FACETS
FACIAS
FACIES
FICHES
FICHUS
GECKOS
HACEKS
INCANS
INCHES
INCURS
ITCHES
JACALS
LACERS
LACHES
LOCALS
LUCIUS
LYCEES
MACAWS
MACHES
MACHOS
MACROS
MECCAS
MICROS
MOCHAS
MUCINS
MUCOUS
NACHOS
NACRES
NICHES
OCCURS
OSCARS
PACERS
PECANS
PICOTS
PICULS
RACERS
RACHIS
RACONS
RECAPS
RECESS
RECONS
RECTOS
RECTUS
RECURS
RICERS
RICHES
RUCHES
RUCKUS
SOCLES
SUCCES
SUCHAS
SUCKAS
TICALS
ULCERS
UNCAPS
UNCLES
VICARS
VICTIS
VOCALS
WACKOS
YACHTS
YUCCAS

•••C•S

ABACAS
ABACUS
AMICES
AMICUS
APICES
ARCCOS
ARECAS
BAUCIS
BLACKS
BLOCKS
BONCES
BRACES
BRACTS
BRICKS
BUNCOS
CAICOS
CALCES
CAUCUS
CHECKS
CHICKS
CHOCKS
CHUCKS
CIRCUS
CISCOS
CLACKS
CLICKS
CLOCKS
CLUCKS
COCCUS
CONCHS
CRACKS
CRICKS
CROCKS
CROCUS
CRUCES
CZECHS
DANCES
DEICES
DEUCES
DISCOS
DISCUS
DORCAS
DUNCES
EDICTS
EDUCES
EJECTS
ELECTS
ENACTS
EPOCHS
ERECTS
ERUCTS
EVICTS
EXACTS
FALCES
FARCES
FASCES
FAUCES
FENCES
FLACKS
FLECKS
FLICKS
FLOCKS
FORCES
FRACAS
FROCKS
GLACES
GLACIS
GRACES
GUACOS
JUICES
JUNCOS
KNACKS
KNICKS
KNOCKS
KYACKS
LANCES
MARCOS
MARCUS
MECCAS
MINCES
MULCTS
NIECES
NUECES
ORACHS
OUNCES
PAUCIS
PHOCIS
PIECES
PISCES
PLACES
PLUCKS
PONCES
PRECIS
PRICES
PRICKS
PSYCHS
QUACKS
REACTS
SAUCES
SHACKS
SHOCKS
SHUCKS
SLACKS
SLICES
SLICKS
SMACKS
SMOCKS
SNACKS
SNICKS
SPACES
SPECKS
SPICAS
SPICES
STACKS
STICKS
STOCKS
SUCCES
SULCUS
TINCTS
TRACES
TRACKS
TRACTS
TRICES
TRICKS
TRUCES
TRUCKS
VINCES
VNECKS
VOICES
WENCES
WHACKS
WINCES
WRACKS
WRECKS
YOICKS
YUCCAS

••••CS

ANTICS
ASDICS
ASPICS
ATTICS
AZTECS
BASICS
BRONCS
CIVICS
COMICS
CONICS
CUBICS
CYNICS
DUROCS
ETHICS
FRANCS
HAVOCS
IONICS
KOVACS
LILACS
LYRICS
MEDICS
MIMICS
MODOCS
OLMECS
OPTICS
OSMICS
PANICS
REBECS
RELICS
SERACS
SONICS
STOICS
SUMACS
TONICS
TOPICS
TOXICS
TUNICS
XEBECS

C•T•••

CATCHY
CATENA
CATERS
CATGUT
CATHAY
CATHER
CATION
CATKIN
CATNAP
CATNIP
CATRIG
CATSUP
CATTED
CATTLE
CATTON
CETANE
CETERA
CITATO
CITERS
CITIES
CITIFY
CITING
CITIUS
CITRIC
CITRON
CITRUS
COTTAS
COTTEN
COTTER
COTTON
CUTELY
CUTEST
CUTESY
CUTIES
CUTINS
CUTLER
CUTLET
CUTOFF
CUTOUT

CUTSIN
CUTSUP
CUTTER
CUTUPS

C••T••
CACTUS
CAFTAN
CANTAB
CANTED
CANTER
CANTHI
CANTLE
CANTON
CANTOR
CANTOS
CAPTAN
CAPTOR
CARTED
CARTEL
CARTER
CARTES
CARTON
CASTER
CASTES
CASTLE
CASTON
CASTOR
CASTRO
CATTED
CATTLE
CATTON
CAXTON
CELTIC
CENTER
CENTOS
CENTRE
CENTRI
CENTRO
CERTIF
CESTAS
CESTOS
CESTUS
CHATTY
CHATUP
CHETHS
CHITIN
CHITON
CHUTED
CHUTES
CLOTHE
CLOTHO
CLOTHS
CLOTTY
CLUTCH
CNOTES
COATED
COATIS
COLTER
COMTES
CONTAC
CONTES
CONTRA
CONTRE
COOTER
COOTIE
COPTER
COPTIC
CORTES
CORTEX
CORTEZ
COSTAE
COSTAL
COSTAR
COSTAS
COSTLY
COTTAS
COTTEN
COTTER
COTTON
COUTER
CRATED
CRATER
CRATES
CRETAN
CRETIN
CRITIC
CROTON
CRUTCH
CULTIC
CURTER
CURTIN
CURTIS
CURTIZ
CURTLY
CURTSY
CUSTER
CUSTIS
CUSTOM
CUSTOS
CUTTER

C•••T•
CADETS
CAMETO
CANUTE
CAPITA
CAPOTE
CARATS
CARETO
CARETS
CAVETT
CAVITY
CENOTE
CERATE
CHANTS
CHARTS
CHASTE
CHATTY
CHEATS
CHERTY
CHESTS
CHESTY
CHINTZ
CHOATE
CITATO
CIVETS
CLEATS
CLEFTS
CLOTTY
CLOUTS
COAPTS
COASTS
COGITO
COMATE
COMETH
COMETO
COMETS
COMITY
COOPTS
COUNTS
COUNTY
COURTS
COVETS
COYOTE
CRAFTS
CRAFTY
CREATE
CRESTS
CRISTO
CROATS
CROFTS
CROUTE
CRUETS
CRUSTS
CRUSTY
CRYPTO
CRYPTS
CSPOTS
CUBITS
CUESTA
CULETS
CURATE

C••••T
CACHET
CADENT
CAMEAT
CAMLET
CANLIT
CANNOT
CAPLET
CAPNUT
CARLOT
CARNET
CARNOT
CARPET
CARROT
CATGUT
CAUGHT
CAVEAT
CAVETT
CAVORT
CEDANT
CEMENT
CERMET
CHALET
CHEVET
CLARET
CLIENT
CLOSET
COBALT
COEDIT
COGENT
COHORT
COHOST
COLLET
COMBAT
COMEAT
COMFIT
COMMIT
COMSAT
CONANT
COOLIT
COPOUT
COQUET
CORNET
CORSET
COSSET
COVENT
COVERT
COYEST
CRAVAT
CREDIT
CUBIST
CULLET
CURVET
CUTEST
CUTLET
CUTOUT
CYGNET

•CT•••
ACTIII
ACTING
ACTINO
ACTION
ACTIUM
ACTIVE
ACTONE
ACTORS
ACTOUT
ACTSAS
ACTSON
ACTSUP
ACTTWO
ACTUAL
ECTYPE
OCTADS
OCTANE
OCTANT
OCTAVE
OCTAVO
OCTETS
OCTOPI
OCTROI

•C•T••
ACETAL
ACETIC
ACETYL
ACTTWO
ICHTHY
SCATHE
SCATTY
SCOTCH
SCOTER
SCOTIA
SCOTTO
SCOTTY
SCUTCH
SCUTES
SCYTHE

•C••T•
ACUATE
ACUITY
ECARTE
ECLATS
OCTETS
SCANTS
SCANTY
SCATTY
SCENTS
SCOOTS
SCOTTO
SCOTTY
SCOUTS

•C•••T
ACCENT
ACCEPT
ACCOST
ACEOUT
ACQUIT
ACTOUT
ICEOUT
ICIEST
OCCULT
OCELOT
OCTANT
SCHIST
SCRIPT
SCULPT

••CT••
ARCTAN
ARCTIC
CACTUS
DACTYL
DICTUM
DICTUS
DOCTOR
DUCTAL
FACTOR
HECTIC
HECTOR
LACTIC
LECTER
LECTOR
LICTOR
NECTAR
PECTIC
PECTIN
RECTOR
RECTOS
RECTUS
SECTOR
TACTIC
TICTAC
VECTOR
VICTIM
VICTIS
VICTOR

••C•T•
ALCOTT
ASCOTS
DICOTS
DUCATS
EXCITE
FACETS
FICHTE
HECATE
INCITE
LOCATE
LUCITE
NICETY
OOCYTE
PICOTS
RECITE
VACATE
YACHTS

••C••T
ACCENT
ACCEPT
ACCOST
ALCOTT
ASCENT
ATCOST
BECKET
BUCKET
CACHET
DACOIT
DECANT
DECEIT
DECENT
DECOCT
DOCENT
DOCKET
ESCENT
ESCORT
EXCEPT
GOCART
INCEPT
INCULT
JACKET
LOCKET
LOCUST
LUCENT
NICEST
NOCENT
OCCULT
OXCART
PACKET
PECKAT
PICKAT
PICKET
POCKET
RACKET
RECANT
RECAST
RECENT
RECOAT
ROCHET
ROCKET
SACHET
SECANT
SECRET
SOCKET
TICKET
TUCKET
UPCAST
VACANT
WICKET

•••CT•
ALECTO
BRACTS
EDICTS
EJECTA
EJECTS
ELECTS
ENACTS
ERECTS
ERUCTS
EVICTS
EXACTA
EXACTO
EXACTS
HINCTY
MULCTS
REACTS
SANCTA
STACTE
TINCTS
TRACTS

•••C•T
AVOCET
BOBCAT
BRECHT
DULCET
ELICIT
FATCAT
FAUCET
HEPCAT
LANCET
MASCOT
MUDCAT
MUSCAT
PLACET
REXCAT
SNOCAT
TERCET
TOMCAT
TOPCAT
TRICOT
VINCIT

••••CT
ABDUCT
ABJECT
ADDUCT
AFFECT
ASPECT
BISECT
DECOCT
DEDUCT
DEFECT
DEJECT
DELICT
DEPICT
DETECT
DIDACT
DIRECT
EFFECT
EXPECT
IMPACT
INDICT
INDUCT
INFACT
INFECT
INJECT
INSECT
INTACT
OBJECT
ONEACT
OUTACT
REDACT
REJECT
RELICT
RELUCT
RESECT
SELECT
STRICT

CU••••
CUBAGE
CUBEBS
CUBICS
CUBING
CUBISM
CUBIST
CUBITS
CUBOID
CUCKOO
CUDDLE
CUDDLY
CUDGEL
CUESTA
CUFFED
CUIABA
CUIQUE
CUISSE
CULETS
CULKIN
CULLED
CULLEN
CULLER
CULLET
CULLIS
CULTIC
CULVER
CUMBER
CUMULI
CUMULO
CUNARD
CUNAXA
CUNEAL
CUPELS
CUPFUL
CUPIDS
CUPOLA
CUPPAS
CUPPED
CUPRIC
CURACY
CURARE
CURATE
CURBED
CURDED
CURDLE
CURERS
CURFEW
CURIAE
CURIAL
CURING
CURIOS
CURIUM
CURLED
CURLER
CURLEW
CURLEY
CURLUP
CURRED
CURSED
CURSES
CURSOR
CURTER
CURTIN
CURTIS
CURTIZ
CURTLY
CURTSY
CURULE
CURVED
CURVES
CURVET
CURZON
CUSACK
CUSHAW
CUSPED
CUSPID
CUSSED
CUSSES
CUSTER
CUSTIS
CUSTOM
CUSTOS
CUTELY
CUTEST
CUTESY
CUTIES
CUTINS
CUTLER
CUTLET
CUTOFF
CUTOUT
CUTSIN
CUTSUP
CUTTER
CUTUPS
CUVEES

C•U•••
CAUCHO
CAUCHY
CAUCUS
CAUDAL
CAUDEX
CAUDLE
CAUGHT
CAULKS
CAUSAL
CAUSED
CAUSES
CHUBBY
CHUCKS
CHUFFY
CHUHSI
CHUKAR
CHUKKA
CHUMMY
CHUMPS
CHUNKS
CHUNKY
CHURCH
CHURLS
CHURNS
CHURRO
CHURRS
CHUTED
CHUTES
CIUDAD
CLUBBY
CLUCKS
CLUEIN
CLUING
CLUMPS
CLUMPY
CLUMSY
CLUNKS
CLUNKY
CLUTCH
COUGAR
COUGHS
COULDA
COULEE
COUNTS
COUNTY
COUPES
COUPLE
COUPON
COURIC
COURSE
COURTS
COUSIN
COUTER

CRUCES
CRUDDY
CRUDER
CRUETS
CRUISE
CRUMBS
CRUMBY
CRUMMY
CRUNCH
CRURAL
CRUSES
CRUSOE
CRUSTS
CRUSTY
CRUTCH
CRUXES

C••U••
CAGUAS
CAJUNS
CANUTE
CARUSO
CASUAL
CAYUGA
CAYUSE
CERUSE
CHOUGH
CLAUDE
CLAUSE
CLOUDS
CLOUDY
CLOUTS
COBURG
COBURN
COHUNE
COLUGO
COLUMN
CONURE
COPULA
COQUET
CREUSA
CROUCH
CROUPY
CROUSE
CROUTE
CUMULI
CUMULO
CURULE
CUTUPS

C•••U•
CACTUS
CADMUS
CAIQUE
CALLUP
CALLUS
CALQUE
CAMEUP
CAMPUS
CANCUN
CANFUL
CAPFUL
CAPGUN
CAPNUT
CARFUL
CARPUS
CASQUE
CATGUT
CATSUP
CAUCUS
CENSUS
CEREUS
CERIUM
CESIUM
CESTUS
CHATUP
CHEQUE
CHERUB
CHEWUP
CHIAUS
CHINUP
CHORUS
CILIUM
CINQUE
CIRCUM
CIRCUS
CIRQUE
CIRRUS
CITIUS
CITRUS
CLAMUP
CLAQUE
CLIQUE
CLIQUY
CLOGUP
CLONUS
CLOQUE
CMINUS
CNIDUS
COCCUS
COILUP
COLEUS
COLOUR
COMEUP
CONCUR
CONIUM
CONSUL
COOKUP
COOPUP
COPOUT
CORIUM
CORPUS
COYPUS
CROCUS
CRONUS
CROPUP
CUIQUE
CUPFUL
CURIUM
CURLUP
CUTOUT
CUTSUP
CYGNUS
CYPRUS

C••••U
CACHOU
CHONJU
CHOOYU
CONGOU

•CU•••
ACUATE
ACUITY
ACUMEN
OCULAR
SCUBAS
SCUFFS
SCULLS
SCULLY
SCULPT
SCUMMY
SCURFY
SCURRY
SCURVE
SCURVY
SCUTCH
SCUTES
SCUZZY

•C•U••
ACCUSE
ACQUIT
ACTUAL
MCHUGH
MCKUEN
OCCULT
OCCUPY
OCCURS
SCAUPS
SCHULZ
SCHUSS
SCOURS
SCOUSE
SCOUTS
SCRUBS
SCRUFF
SCRUMS

•C••U•
ACARUS
ACCRUE
ACEOUS
ACEOUT
ACESUP
ACINUS
ACTIUM
ACTOUT
ACTSUP
ICARUS
ICEDUP
ICEOUT
ICESUP
SCARUM

•C•••U
ACAJOU

••CU••
ACCUSE
ALCUIN
ESCUDO
EXCUSE
FACULA
FECUND
HECUBA
INCULT
INCURS
INCUSE
JOCUND
LACUNA
LOCUST
MACULA
OCCULT
OCCUPY
OCCURS
OSCULA
PICULS
RECURS
RECUSE
SECURE
UNCURL
VACUUM
VICUNA

••C•U•
ACCRUE
BACKUP
BACKUS
BUCKUP
CACTUS
COCCUS
DICTUM
DICTUS
FACEUP
FICHUS
HICCUP
JACKUP
KICKUP
LACEUP
LOCKUP
LUCIUS
LYCEUM
MACOUN
MOCKUP
MUCKUP
MUCOUS
PACKUP
PICKUP
RACKUP
RECOUP
RECTUS
RUCKUS
SACQUE
SACRUM
TUCHUN
VACUUM

••C••U
CACHOU
PICCHU

•••CU•
ABACUS
AMICUS
CANCUN
CAUCUS
CIRCUM
CIRCUS
COCCUS
CONCUR
CROCUS
DISCUS
EGGCUP
EYECUP
FESCUE
HICCUP
MARCUS
MISCUE
RESCUE
SULCUS
TALCUM
TEACUP

•••C•U
MANCHU
PICCHU

••••CU
APERCU
IGUACU

C•V•••
CAVEAT
CAVEIN
CAVELL
CAVERN
CAVERS
CAVETT
CAVIAR
CAVILS
CAVING
CAVITY
CAVORT
CIVETS
CIVICS
COVENS
COVENT
COVERS
COVERT
COVETS
COVEYS
COVINA
CUVEES

C••V••
CALVED
CALVES
CALVIN
CANVAS
CARVED
CARVER
CARVES
CARVEY
CERVID
CHAVEZ
CHEVAL
CHEVET
CHEVRE
CHIVES
CLAVES
CLAVIN
CLEVER
CLEVES
CLEVIS
CLOVEN
CLOVER
CLOVES
CLOVIS
COEVAL
CONVEX
CONVEY
CONVOY
CORVEE
CORVES
CRAVAT
CRAVED
CRAVEN
CRAVER
CRAVES
CULVER
CURVED
CURVES
CURVET

C•••V•
CANOVA
CASAVA
CLEAVE

C••••V
CHEKOV

•C••V•
ACTIVE
OCTAVE
OCTAVO
SCURVE
SCURVY

••C•V•
ALCOVE

••C••V
ROCKYV
VACLAV

C•W•••
CAWDOR
CAWING
COWARD
COWBOY
COWENS
COWERS
COWING
COWLED
COWLEY
COWMAN
COWMEN
COWPEA
COWPER
COWPOX
COWRIE

C••W••
CHEWED
CHEWER
CHEWUP
CHOWED
CLAWED
CLAWER
CLEWED
CLOWNS
COBWEB
CONWAY
CRAWLS
CRAWLY
CREWED
CREWEL
CROWDS
CROWED
CROWER
CROWNS

C•••W•
CAHOWS

C••••W
CALLOW
CASHEW
CPSNOW
CURFEW
CURLEW
CUSHAW

•C•W••
SCHWAB
SCHWAS
SCOWLS

•C••W•
ACTTWO
SCRAWL
SCREWS
SCREWY

•C•••W
MCGRAW
MCGREW

••C•W•
MACAWS

••C••W
ESCHEW
ESCROW

•••C•W
ANTCOW
MOSCOW
PESCOW
SEACOW

C•X•••
CAXTON

C••X••
CALXES
COAXED
COAXER
COAXES
CRUXES

C•••X•
CUNAXA

C••••X
CAUDEX
CHISOX
CLIMAX
CLOROX
COCCYX
COLFAX
COMMIX
CONVEX
CORTEX
COWPOX

•C•••X
ICEBOX

••C••X
COCCYX
PICKAX

•••C•X
COCCYX
WILCOX

CY••••
CYANIC
CYBELE
CYBILL
CYBORG
CYCADS
CYCLAS
CYCLED
CYCLER
CYCLES
CYCLIC
CYCLOS
CYDERS
CYGNET
CYGNUS
CYMBAL
CYMRIC
CYNICS
CYPHER
CYPRUS
CYRANO

C•Y•••
CAYMAN
CAYUGA
CAYUSE
CEYLON
CHYRON
COYEST
COYISH
COYOTE
COYPUS
CRYERS
CRYING
CRYOFF
CRYPTO
CRYPTS

C••Y••
CANYON
CLAYEY
CLOYED
CORYZA
CRAYON

C•••Y•
CHERYL
CHOOYU
COCCYX
CONEYS
COPAYS
COVEYS
CRONYN

C••••Y
CAGILY
CAGNEY
CALMLY
CAMEBY
CANARY
CANOPY
CARBOY
CARNEY
CARREY
CARVEY
CASEFY
CATCHY
CATHAY
CAUCHY
CAVITY
CECILY
CELERY
CHAFFY
CHALKY
CHAMMY
CHANCY
CHANEY
CHARLY
CHATTY
CHEEKY
CHEERY
CHEESY
CHERRY
CHERTY
CHESTY
CHICLY
CHILLY
CHINKY
CHIRPY
CHOOSY
CHOPPY
CHROMY
CHUBBY
CHUFFY
CHUMMY
CHUNKY
CICELY
CITIFY
CLAMMY
CLANCY
CLANKY
CLASSY
CLAYEY
CLERGY
CLIFFY
CLINGY
CLIQUY
CLODDY
CLOGGY
CLOTTY
CLOUDY
CLUBBY
CLUMPY
CLUMSY
CLUNKY
CODIFY
COLDLY
COLONY
COMEBY
COMEDY
COMELY
COMITY
COMPLY
CONROY
CONVEY
CONVOY
CONWAY
COOLLY
COONEY
COPLEY
CORDAY
COSILY
COSTLY
COUNTY
COWBOY
COWLEY
COZILY
CRABBY
CRACKY
CRAFTY
CRAGGY
CRANKY
CRANNY
CRAWLY
CREAKY
CREAMY
CREASY
CREEPY
CRIKEY
CRIMPY
CRISPY

CROAKY
CROSBY
CROUPY
CRUDDY
CRUMBY
CRUMMY
CRUSTY
CUDDLY
CURACY
CURLEY
CURTLY
CURTSY
CUTELY
CUTESY
CZERNY

•CY•••
SCYLLA
SCYTHE

•C•Y••
ECTYPE

•C••Y•
ACETYL

•C•••Y
ACIDLY
ACUITY
ICHTHY
OCASEY
OCCUPY
OCHERY
SCABBY
SCANTY
SCARRY
SCATTY
SCHIZY
SCOTTY
SCREWY
SCULLY
SCUMMY
SCURFY
SCURRY
SCURVY
SCUZZY

••CY••
OOCYTE

••C•Y•
COCCYX
DACTYL
DECAYS
DECOYS
JACLYN
ROCKYV

••C••Y
ARCHLY
CECILY
CICELY
DICKEY
HACKLY
HICKEY
HOCKEY
JACKEY
JOCKEY
LACILY
LACKEY
MICKEY
NICELY
NICETY
OCCUPY
PACIFY
RACILY
RECOPY
RICHLY
RICKEY
SICILY
SICKLY
TICKLY
WICOPY

•••CY•
COCCYX

•••C•Y
ALECKY
BEACHY
BISCAY
BLOCKY
BOTCHY
BRACHY
BRICKY
BUNCHY
CATCHY
CAUCHY
CHICLY
CRACKY
DESCRY
FARCRY
FLECKY
FLOCKY
HINCTY
LEACHY
LUNCHY
MUNCHY
MUSCLY
NOTCHY
OUTCRY
PATCHY
PEACHY
PITCHY
PLUCKY
POACHY
POUCHY
PRICEY
PUNCHY
SPACEY
STACEY
STICKY
STOCKY
TETCHY
TORCHY
TOUCHY
TRACEY
TRACHY
TRICKY
WARCRY
WHACKY
WITCHY

••••CY
ABBACY
AGENCY
BOUNCY
CHANCY
CLANCY
CURACY
FLEECY
IDIOCY
JOUNCY
LEGACY
LUNACY
PAPACY
PIRACY
POLICY
QUINCY

CZ••••
CZECHS
CZERNY

C•Z•••
COZENS
COZIED
COZIER
COZIES
COZILY

C••Z••
CRAZED
CRAZES
CROZES
CURZON

C•••Z•
CORYZA

C••••Z
CHAVEZ
CHINTZ
CORTEZ
CURTIZ

•C•Z••
SCUZZY

•C••Z•
SCHIZY
SCUZZY

•C•••Z
SCHNOZ
SCHULZ

DA••••
DABBED
DABBLE
DABNEY
DACAPO
DACHAS
DACOIT
DACRON
DACTYL
DADDYO
DADOED
DADOES
DAEDAL
DAFFED
DAFTER
DAFTLY
DAGAMA
DAGGER
DAGMAR
DAHLIA
DAIKON
DAILEY
DAIMON
DAIMYO
DAINTY
DAIREN
DAISES
DAKOTA
DALASI
DALETH
DALLAS
DALLES
DALTON
DAMAGE
DAMASK
DAMATO
DAMIEN
DAMITA
DAMMAR
DAMMED
DAMNED
DAMONE
DAMORE
DAMOUR
DAMPED
DAMPEN
DAMPER
DAMPLY
DAMSEL
DAMSON
DAMSUP
DANANG
DANAUS
DANCED
DANCER
DANCES
DANDER
DANDIE
DANDLE
DANGER
DANGLE
DANGLY
DANGME
DANIEL
DANISH
DANKER
DANKLY
DANNAY
DANNER
DANSON
DANTES
DANTON
DANUBE
DANZIG
DAPHNE
DAPPED
DAPPER
DAPPLE
DARENT
DARETO
DARIEN
DARING
DARIUS
DARKEN
DARKER
DARKLE
DARKLY
DARNAY
DARNED
DARNEL
DARNER
DARNIT
DARREN
DARROW
DARRYL
DARTED
DARTER
DARWIN
DASHED
DASHER
DASHES
DASHIS
DASSIN
DATARY
DATERS
DATING
DATIVE
DATONG
DATSUN
DATURA
DAUBED
DAUBER
DAUBES
DAUNTS
DAVIES
DAVITS
DAWDLE
DAWNED
DAWNON
DAWSON
DAYBED
DAYBOY
DAYGLO
DAYJOB
DAYLIT
DAYONE
DAYTON
DAZING
DAZZLE

D•A•••
DEACON
DEADEN
DEADER
DEADLY
DEADON
DEAFEN
DEAFER
DEAFLY
DEALER
DEALIN
DEANNA
DEARER
DEARIE
DEARLY
DEARME
DEARTH
DEASIL
DHARMA
DIABLO
DIADEM
DIALED
DIALER
DIALOG
DIALUP
DIANNE
DIAPER
DIATOM
DLAYER
DMAJOR
DMARKS
DOABLE
DRABLY
DRACHM
DRAFTS
DRAFTY
DRAGEE
DRAGGY
DRAGIN
DRAGON
DRAILS
DRAINS
DRAKES
DRAMAS
DRAPED
DRAPER
DRAPES
DRAWER
DRAWIN
DRAWLS
DRAWLY
DRAWON
DRAWUP
DRAYED
DUALLY
DUARTE
DWARFS
DWAYNE
DYADIC

D••A••
DACAPO
DAGAMA
DALASI
DAMAGE
DAMASK
DAMATO
DANANG
DANAUS
DATARY
DEBARK
DEBARS
DEBASE
DEBATE
DECADE
DECAFS
DECALS
DECAMP
DECANT
DECAYS
DEFACE
DEFAME
DEFATS
DEGAGE
DEJAVU
DEKALB
DELANO
DELANY
DELATE
DELAYS
DEMAND
DENALI
DENARY
DEPART
DEPAUL
DEPAUW
DERAIL
DESALT
DETACH
DETAIL
DETAIN
DIDACT
DILATE
DINARS
DISANT
DISARM
DIVANS
DOMAIN
DOMANI
DONALD
DONATE
DOPANT
DORADO
DORAGS
DORATI
DOSAGE
DOTAGE
DOTARD
DOUALA
DREADS
DREAMS
DREAMT
DREAMY
DREARY
DRYADS
DSHARP
DUCATS
DUNANT
DURANT
DUVALL
DYNAMO
DYNAST

D•••A•
DACHAS
DAEDAL
DAGMAR
DALLAS
DAMMAR
DANNAY
DARNAY
DEBRAS
DEEJAY
DEEPAK
DEFEAT
DEFRAY
DELMAR
DELRAY
DELTAS
DEMEAN
DENIAL
DENTAL
DEODAR
DERMAL
DESMAN
DEWLAP
DIGRAM
DIKTAT
DIRHAM
DISBAR
DISMAL
DISMAY
DISTAL
DOBLAS
DOBRAS
DOGDAY
DOGEAR
DOGMAS
DOGSAT
DOGTAG
DOLLAR
DOLMAN
DOLMAS
DONNAS
DOODAD
DOODAH
DORCAS
DORIAN
DORSAL
DOSSAL
DOTHAN
DRAMAS
DUCTAL
DUNBAR
DUNCAN
DUNHAM
DURBAN
DURBAR
DURHAM
DURIAN
DVORAK

D••••A
DAGAMA
DAHLIA
DAKOTA
DAMITA
DATURA
DEANNA
DEFLEA
DESICA
DHARMA
DJERBA
DODECA
DODOMA
DOUALA
DUENNA
DULLEA
DUNERA
DURYEA

•DA•••
ADAGES
ADAGIO
ADAPTS
EDAMES
GDANSK

•D•A••
ADDAMS
ADJANI
ADMASS
ADNATE
EDGARD
EDGARS
EDUARD
EDVARD
EDWARD
IDCARD
IDEALS
IDEATE
IDTAGS
KDLANG

•D••A•
ADIDAS
ADONAI
ADRIAN

•D•••A
ADNEXA
EDESSA
ODESSA
ODETTA

••DA••
ADDAMS
AODAIS
BEDAUB
BEDAZE
CEDANT
CEDARS
DIDACT
EMDASH
ENDALL
ENDASH
GODARD
HODADS
INDABA
IODATE
JUDAEA
JUDAIC
KODALY
MADAME
MADAMS
MEDAKA
MEDALS
MIDAIR
OLDAGE
ORDAIN
PADANG
PEDALS
PEDANT
PEDATE
REDACT
REDANT
REDATE
SEDAKA
SEDANS
SEDATE
TODATE
UPDATE

••D•A•
ANDEAN
AUDIAL
BADHAM
BADMAN
BEDLAM
ENDEAR
ENDMAN
ESDRAS
HYDRAE
HYDRAS
INDIAN
KIDMAN
KIDNAP
KODIAK
MADCAP
MADMAN
MADMAX
MADRAS
MEDGAR
MEDIAL
MEDIAN
MEDIAS
MEDLAR
MEDLAT
MIDDAY
MIDIAN
MIDWAY
MUDCAT

MUDRAS
OGDOAD
OLDHAM
OLDHAT
OLDMAN
OLDSAW
ORDEAL
PADUAN
PEDLAR
PEDWAY
RADIAL
RADIAN
REDBAY
REDCAP
REDEAL
REDHAT
REDIAL
REDOAK
REDRAW
REDTAG
RODHAM
RODMAN
RUDMAN
SADDAM
SUDRAS
TODDAO
TODMAN
UNDRAW
VODKAS
ZEDBAR
ZODIAC

••D••A

ANDREA
BODEGA
BUDDHA
DODECA
DODOMA
EIDOLA
ENDORA
EUDORA
FEDORA
GODIVA
INDABA
INDIRA
JUDAEA
JUDOKA
LADIDA
LADOGA
MADURA
MEDAKA
MEDINA
MEDUSA
MODELA
MODENA
OEDEMA
RADULA
REDSEA
SEDAKA
ZADORA

•••DA•

ADIDAS
AIRDAM
ALLDAY
ANYDAY
AOUDAD
APODAL
BAGDAD
BELDAM
BENDAY
BRIDAL
CAUDAL
CIUDAD
CNIDAE
CORDAY
DAEDAL
DEODAR
DOGDAY
DOODAD
DOODAH
FEUDAL
FRIDAY
HAIDAS
HEYDAY
HOWDAH
IBADAN
JORDAN
KASDAN
LANDAU
MANDAN
MANDAY
MAYDAY
MCADAM
MIDDAY
MOLDAU
MONDAY
MYRDAL
NASDAQ
OFFDAY
ONEDAY
PANDAS
PAYDAY
PINDAR
PURDAH
SADDAM
SANDAL
SENDAK
SIRDAR
SOLDAN
SUNDAE
SUNDAY
TAGDAY
TODDAO
VANDAL
WHYDAH

•••D•A

ACADIA
ACEDIA
BUDDHA
EXEDRA
GRADEA
SANDIA
SANDRA
STADIA
TREDIA
TUNDRA

••••DA

AGENDA
AMANDA
ANANDA
ARMADA
ARVADA
BLANDA
BRENDA
CANADA
CICADA
COLADA
COULDA
GELADA
GLENDA
IMELDA
JUMADA
KAUNDA
LADIDA
LAMBDA
LERIDA
LUANDA
MASADA
MERIDA
NERUDA
NEVADA
OLINDA
ONEIDA
OREIDA
PAGODA
PANADA
POSADA
PRAVDA
RAMADA
REMUDA
RESEDA
RHONDA
RUANDA
RWANDA
UGANDA
VIGODA

D•B•••

DABBED
DABBLE
DABNEY
DEBARK
DEBARS
DEBASE
DEBATE
DEBBIE
DEBITS
DEBONE
DEBRAS
DEBRIS
DEBTOR
DEBUGS
DEBUNK
DEBUTS
DIBBLE
DOBBER
DOBBIN
DOBLAS
DOBLIN
DOBRAS
DOBROS
DOBSON
DUBBED
DUBBIN
DUBCEK
DUBLIN
DUBOIS
DYBBUK

D••B••

DABBED
DABBLE
DAUBED
DAUBER
DAUBES
DAYBED
DAYBOY
DEBBIE
DIABLO
DIBBLE
DISBAR
DOABLE
DOBBER
DOBBIN
DOOBIE
DOUBLE
DOUBLY
DOUBTS
DRABLY
DUBBED
DUBBIN
DUMBER
DUMBLY
DUNBAR
DURBAN
DURBAR
DURBIN
DYBBUK

D•••B•

DANUBE
DEMOBS
DJERBA
DOESBY
DROPBY
DWEEBS

D••••B

DAYJOB
DEKALB
DIONEB

•DB•••

EDBERG

•D•B••

ADOBES
EDIBLE

•D••B•

ADLIBS

•D•••B

ADSORB
ADVERB
ODDJOB

••DB••

BADBOY
BEDBUG
OLDBOY
REDBAY
REDBUD
TIDBIT
TYDBOL
ZEDBAR

••D•B•

ARDEBS
INDABA
INDEBT
REDUBS

••D••B

BEDAUB
MIDRIB
ODDJOB

•••DB•

GOODBY
HARDBY
LAIDBY

•••D•B

SUBDEB

D•C•••

DACAPO
DACHAS
DACOIT
DACRON
DACTYL
DECADE
DECAFS
DECALS
DECAMP
DECANT
DECAYS
DECEIT
DECENT
DECIDE
DECKED
DECKER
DECKLE
DECOCT
DECODE
DECORS
DECOYS
DECREE
DICERS
DICIER
DICING
DICKER
DICKEY
DICOTS
DICTUM
DICTUS
DOCENT
DOCILE
DOCKED
DOCKER
DOCKET
DOCTOR
DUCATS
DUCHIN
DUCKED
DUCTAL

D••C••

DANCED
DANCER
DANCES
DEACON
DEICED
DEICER
DEICES
DESCRY
DEUCED
DEUCES
DISCOS
DISCUS
DORCAS
DRACHM
DUBCEK
DULCET
DUNCAN
DUNCES

D•••C•

DECOCT
DEDUCE
DEDUCT
DEFACE
DEFECT
DEJECT
DELICT
DEPICT
DESICA
DETACH
DETECT
DEVICE
DIDACT
DIRECT
DODECA
DRENCH
DRYICE
DUROCS

D••••C

DELTIC
DYADIC

•DC•••

IDCARD

•D•C••

EDICTS
EDUCED
EDUCES

•D••C•

ADDUCE
ADDUCT
ADVICE
EDKOCH
IDIOCY

•D•••C

EDENIC

••DC••

MADCAP
MUDCAT
REDCAP

••D•C•

ABDUCT
ADDUCE
ADDUCT
ASDICS
BEDECK
BODICE
DEDUCE
DEDUCT
DIDACT
DODECA
INDICT
INDUCE
INDUCT
MEDICI
MEDICO
MEDICS
MODOCS
NODICE
ONDECK
REDACT
REDUCE
SEDUCE
ZYDECO

••D••C

CADMIC
CEDRIC
JUDAIC
OLDVIC
ZODIAC

•••D•C

ACIDIC
ANODIC
BARDIC
DYADIC
IRIDIC
NORDIC
OXIDIC
RUNDMC
SYNDIC
ZENDIC

D•D•••

DADDYO
DADOED
DADOES
DEDUCE
DEDUCT
DIDACT
DIDDLE
DIDDLY
DIDIES
DIDION
DODDER
DODECA
DODGED
DODGER
DODGES
DODODO
DODOES
DODOMA
DUDEEN
DUDISH
DUDLEY

D••D••

DADDYO
DAEDAL
DANDER
DANDIE
DANDLE
DAWDLE
DEADEN
DEADER
DEADLY
DEADON
DEEDED
DEEDEE
DEIDRE
DENDRI
DENDRO
DEODAR
DIADEM
DIDDLE
DIDDLY
DIKDIK
DIODES
DODDER
DOGDAY
DOGDOM
DONDER
DOODAD
DOODAH
DOODLE
DREDGE
DRUDGE
DRYDEN
DUMDUM
DUNDEE
DYADIC

D•••D•

DECADE
DECIDE
DECODE
DELUDE
DEMODE
DENUDE
DERIDE
DIPODY
DIRNDL
DIVIDE
DODODO
DORADO
DOSIDO
DREADS
DROIDS
DRUIDS
DRYADS

D••••D

DABBED
DADOED
DAFFED
DAMMED
DAMNED
DAMPED
DANCED
DAPPED
DARNED
DARTED
DASHED
DAUBED
DAWNED
DAYBED
DECKED
DEEDED
DEEMED
DEFEND
DEFIED
DEICED
DELVED
DEMAND
DEMOND
DENIED
DENNED
DENTED
DEPEND
DEUCED
DEVOID
DIALED
DIETED
DIMMED
DINGED
DINNED
DINTED
DIPPED
DISHED
DISKED
DISSED
DOCKED
DODGED
DOFFED
DOGGED
DOGOOD
DOLLED
DONALD
DONNED
DOODAD
DOOMED
DOSSED
DOTARD
DOTTED
DOUSED
DOWNED
DOWSED
DRAPED
DRAYED
DRONED
DUBBED
DUCKED
DUELED
DULLED
DUMPED
DUNKED
DUNNED
DURNED
DUSTED

•DD•••

ADDAMS
ADDEND
ADDERS
ADDING
ADDLED
ADDLES
ADDONS
ADDSIN
ADDSON
ADDSTO
ADDSUP
ADDUCE
ADDUCT
EDDIED
EDDIES
EDDOES
ODDEST
ODDITY
ODDJOB
ODDLOT
ODDSON
UDDERS

•D•D••

ADIDAS

•D••D•

IDOIDO

•D•••D

ADDEND
ADDLED
ADORED
EDDIED
EDGARD
EDITED
EDMOND
EDMUND
EDUARD
EDUCED
EDVARD

EDWARD
EDWOOD
IDCARD

••DD••
BADDER
BADDIE
BIDDEN
BIDDER
BIDDLE
BUDDED
BUDDHA
CADDIE
CADDIS
CODDLE
CUDDLE
CUDDLY
DADDYO
DIDDLE
DIDDLY
DODDER
FIDDLE
FODDER
FUDDLE
GADDED
GADDER
HADDIE
HEDDLE
HIDDEN
HUDDLE
JUDDER
KIDDED
KIDDER
KIDDIE
LADDER
LADDIE
LIDDED
LUDDEN
MADDEN
MADDER
MADDIE
MEDDLE
MIDDAY
MIDDEN
MIDDLE
MUDDED
MUDDER
MUDDLE
NODDED
NODDLE
PADDED
PADDER
PADDLE
PEDDLE
PODDED
PUDDLE
PUDDLY
RADDLE
REDDEN
REDDER
REDDOG
RIDDED
RIDDEN
RIDDLE
RODDED
RUDDER
RUDDLE
SADDAM
SADDEN
SADDER
SADDLE
SIDDUR
SODDED
SODDEN
SUDDEN
TEDDED
TEDDER
TIDDLY
TODDAO
TODDLE
VEDDER
WADDED
WADDLE
WADDLY
WEDDED
ZADDIK

••D•D•
DODODO
HODADS
IODIDE
LADIDA
MADEDO

••D••D
ADDEND
ADDLED
BODIED
BUDDED
BUDGED
CADGED
DADOED
DODGED
EDDIED
ENDUED
FUDGED
GADDED
GODARD
HEDGED
INDEED
JUDGED
KEDGED
KIDDED
KIDVID
LADLED
LIDDED
LODGED
MADRID
MUDDED
NODDED
NUDGED
OGDOAD
PADDED
PODDED
REDBUD
REDYED
RIDDED
RIDGED
RODDED
SIDLED
SODDED
SUDSED
TEDDED
TIDIED
UNDYED
WADDED
WEDDED
WEDGED

•••DD•
ATODDS
CLODDY
CRUDDY
FREDDY
QUIDDE
SHODDY
SKIDDY

•••D•D
ABIDED
AOUDAD
BAGDAD
BANDED
BEADED
BENDED
BIRDED
BLADED
BONDED
BUDDED
CANDID
CARDED
CHIDED
CIUDAD
CORDED
CURDED
DEEDED
DOODAD
ELIDED
ELUDED
ERODED
EVADED
EXUDED
FENDED
FEUDED
FOLDED
FORDED
FUNDED
GADDED
GILDED
GIRDED
GLIDED
GOADED
GRADED
GUIDED
HANDED
HEADED
HEEDED
HERDED
HOODED
KIDDED
LANDED
LARDED
LAUDED
LEADED
LIDDED
LOADED
LORDED
MELDED
MENDED
MINDED
MISDID
MOLDED
MUDDED
NEEDED
NODDED
OUTDID
PADDED
PENDED
PODDED
PRIDED
RAIDED
RIDDED
RODDED
SANDED
SEEDED
SHADED
SODDED
SORDID
SPADED
TEDDED
TENDED
TRADED
VENDED
VOIDED
WADDED
WARDED
WEDDED
WEEDED
WELDED
WENDED
WINDED
WOODED
WORDED
YARDED

DE••••
DEACON
DEADEN
DEADER
DEADLY
DEADON
DEAFEN
DEAFER
DEAFLY
DEALER
DEALIN
DEANNA
DEARER
DEARIE
DEARLY
DEARME
DEARTH
DEASIL
DEBARK
DEBARS
DEBASE
DEBATE
DEBBIE
DEBITS
DEBONE
DEBRAS
DEBRIS
DEBTOR
DEBUGS
DEBUNK
DEBUTS
DECADE
DECAFS
DECALS
DECAMP
DECANT
DECAYS
DECEIT
DECENT
DECIDE
DECKED
DECKER
DECKLE
DECOCT
DECODE
DECORS
DECOYS
DECREE
DEDUCE
DEDUCT
DEEDED
DEEDEE
DEEJAY
DEEMED
DEEPAK
DEEPEN
DEEPER
DEEPLY
DEFACE
DEFAME
DEFATS
DEFEAT
DEFECT
DEFEND
DEFERS
DEFIED
DEFIES
DEFILE
DEFINE
DEFLEA
DEFOGS
DEFORM
DEFRAY
DEFTER
DEFTLY
DEFUSE
DEGAGE
DEGREE
DEGUST
DEHORN
DEICED
DEICER
DEICES
DEIDRE
DEIGNS
DEIMOS
DEISTS
DEJAVU
DEJECT
DEJURE
DEKALB
DEKING
DEKKOS
DELANO
DELANY
DELATE
DELAYS
DELEON
DELETE
DELFTS
DELICT
DELIST
DELIUS
DELMAR
DELONG
DELPHI
DELRAY
DELRIO
DELROY
DELTAS
DELTIC
DELUDE
DELUGE
DELUXE
DELVED
DELVER
DELVES
DEMAND
DEMEAN
DEMIES
DEMISE
DEMITS
DEMOBS
DEMODE
DEMOND
DEMONS
DEMOTE
DEMURE
DEMURS
DENALI
DENARY
DENDRI
DENDRO
DENGUE
DENIAL
DENIED
DENIER
DENIES
DENIMS
DENIRO
DENISE
DENNED
DENNIS
DENOTE
DENOVO
DENSER
DENTAL
DENTED
DENTIL
DENTIN
DENTON
DENUDE
DENVER
DENZEL
DEODAR
DEPART
DEPAUL
DEPAUW
DEPEND
DEPICT
DEPLOY
DEPONE
DEPORT
DEPOSE
DEPOTS
DEPTHS
DEPUTE
DEPUTY
DERAIL
DERIDE
DERIVE
DERMAL
DERMIS
DERRIS
DESALT
DESCRY
DESERT
DESICA
DESIGN
DESILU
DESIRE
DESIST
DESMAN
DESOTO
DESPOT
DESTRY
DETACH
DETAIL
DETAIN
DETECT
DETENT
DETERS
DETEST
DETOUR
DETROP
DEUCED
DEUCES
DEVEIN
DEVEST
DEVICE
DEVILS
DEVINE
DEVISE
DEVITO
DEVOID
DEVOIR
DEVOTE
DEVOTO
DEVOUR
DEVOUT
DEWIER
DEWILY
DEWING
DEWITT
DEWLAP
DEXTER
DEXTRO

D•E•••
DAEDAL
DEEDED
DEEDEE
DEEJAY
DEEMED
DEEPAK
DEEPEN
DEEPER
DEEPLY
DIEOFF
DIEOUT
DIEPPE
DIESEL
DIESES
DIESIS
DIETED
DIETER
DJERBA
DOESBY
DOESIN
DOESNT
DOESUP
DREADS
DREAMS
DREAMT
DREAMY
DREARY
DREDGE
DRENCH
DRESSY
DREWIN
DREWON
DREWUP
DREXEL
DUELED
DUELER
DUELLO
DUENNA
DWEEBS
DWELLS
DYEING
DYELOT

D••E••
DALETH
DARENT
DARETO
DATERS
DECEIT
DECENT
DEFEAT
DEFECT
DEFEND
DEFERS
DEJECT
DELEON
DELETE
DEMEAN
DEPEND
DESERT
DETECT
DETENT
DETERS
DETEST
DEVEIN
DEVEST
DICERS
DIGEST
DINEIN
DINEON
DINERO
DINERS
DIRECT
DIRELY
DIREST
DIVEIN
DIVERS
DIVERT
DIVEST
DIYERS
DIZENS
DOCENT
DODECA
DOGEAR
DOGEYS
DOLENZ
DONEES
DONEIN
DONETS
DONEUP
DOREMI
DOSERS
DOTELL
DOTEON
DOVEIN
DOWELS
DOWERS
DOWERY
DOYENS
DOZENS
DOZERS
DRIERS
DRIEST
DRYERS
DRYEST
DUDEEN
DUNERA
DUPERY
DURESS
DUVETS
DWEEBS

D•••E•
DABBED
DABNEY
DADOED
DADOES
DAFFED
DAFTER
DAGGER
DAILEY
DAIREN
DAISES
DALLES
DAMIEN
DAMMED
DAMNED
DAMPED
DAMPEN
DAMPER
DAMSEL
DANCED
DANCER
DANCES
DANDER
DANGER
DANIEL
DANKER
DANNER
DANTES
DAPPED
DAPPER
DARIEN
DARKEN
DARKER
DARNED
DARNEL
DARNER
DARREN
DARTED
DARTER
DASHED
DASHER
DASHES
DAUBED
DAUBER
DAUBES
DAVIES
DAWNED
DAYBED
DEADEN
DEADER
DEAFEN
DEAFER
DEALER
DEARER
DECKED
DECKER
DECREE
DEEDED
DEEDEE
DEEMED
DEEPEN
DEEPER
DEFIED

DEFIES
DEFLEA
DEFTER
DEGREE
DEICED
DEICER
DEICES
DELVED
DELVER
DELVES
DEMIES
DENIED
DENIER
DENIES
DENNED
DENSER
DENTED
DENVER
DENZEL
DEUCED
DEUCES
DEWIER
DEXTER
DHOLES
DHOTEL
DIADEM
DIALED
DIALER
DIAPER
DICIER
DICKER
DICKEY
DIDIES
DIESEL
DIESES
DIETED
DIETER
DIFFER
DIGGER
DILLER
DILSEY
DIMMED
DIMMER
DINGED
DINKEY
DINNED
DINNER
DINTED
DIODES
DIONEB
DIPPED
DIPPER
DIRGES
DISHED
DISHES
DISKED
DISMES
DISNEY
DISPEL
DISSED
DITHER
DITZES
DLAYER
DOBBER
DOCKED
DOCKER
DOCKET
DODDER
DODGED
DODGER
DODGES
DODOES
DOFFED
DOGGED
DOGGER
DOGIES
DOGLEG
DOLLED
DOLMEN
DOMREP
DONDER
DONEES
DONKEY
DONNED
DONNEE
DONNER
DOOLEY
DOOMED
DOPIER
DORIES
DORMER
DORSET
DORSEY
DOSSED
DOSSEL
DOSSER
DOSSES
DOTTED
DOURER
DOUSED
DOUSES
DOWNED
DOWNER
DOWNEY
DOWSED
DOWSER
DOWSES
DOZIER
DRAGEE
DRAKES
DRAPED
DRAPER
DRAPES
DRAWER
DRAYED
DREXEL
DRIVEL
DRIVEN
DRIVER
DRIVES
DRONED
DRONER
DRONES
DROVER
DROVES
DRUPES
DRUZES
DRYDEN
DUBBED
DUBCEK
DUCKED
DUDEEN
DUDLEY
DUELED
DUELER
DUFFEL
DUFFER
DUIKER
DULCET
DULLEA
DULLED
DULLER
DULLES
DUMBER
DUMPED
DUMPER
DUNCES
DUNDEE
DUNKED
DUNKER
DUNNED
DUPLEX
DURFEY
DURNED
DURYEA
DUSTED
DUSTER
DUTIES

D••••E

DABBLE
DAMAGE
DAMONE
DAMORE
DANDIE
DANDLE
DANGLE
DANGME
DANUBE
DAPHNE
DAPPLE
DARKLE
DATIVE
DAWDLE
DAYONE
DAZZLE
DEARIE
DEARME
DEBASE
DEBATE
DEBBIE
DEBONE
DECADE
DECIDE
DECKLE
DECODE
DECREE
DEDUCE
DEEDEE
DEFACE
DEFAME
DEFILE
DEFINE
DEFUSE
DEGAGE
DEGREE
DEIDRE
DEJURE
DELATE
DELETE
DELUDE
DELUGE
DELUXE
DEMISE
DEMODE
DEMOTE
DEMURE
DENGUE
DENISE
DENOTE
DENUDE
DEPONE
DEPOSE
DEPUTE
DERIDE
DERIVE
DESIRE
DEVICE
DEVINE
DEVISE
DEVOTE
DIANNE
DIBBLE
DIDDLE
DIEPPE
DILATE
DILUTE
DIMPLE
DINGLE
DIONNE
DIPOLE
DIRIGE
DISUSE
DIVIDE
DIVINE
DOABLE
DOCILE
DOGGIE
DOMINE
DONATE
DONGLE
DONNEE
DOOBIE
DOODLE
DOOGIE
DOOZIE
DOSAGE
DOTAGE
DOTTIE
DOTTLE
DOUBLE
DRAGEE
DREDGE
DROGUE
DROWSE
DRUDGE
DRYICE
DUARTE
DUNDEE
DWAYNE

•DE•••

ADEEMS
ADELIE
ADELLE
ADEPTS
ADESTE
EDENIC
EDERLE
EDESSA
IDEALS
IDEATE
ODENSE
ODESSA
ODETTA
ODETTE

•D•E••

ADDEND
ADDERS
ADEEMS
ADHERE
ADIEUS
ADIEUX
ADNEXA
ADRENO
ADVENT
ADVERB
ADVERT
ADWEEK
EDBERG
EDGEIN
EDGERS
EDSELS
IDLERS
IDLEST
ODDEST
UDDERS

•D••E•

ADAGES
ADDLED
ADDLES
ADOBES
ADORED
ADOREE
ADORER
ADORES
ADRIEN
ADWEEK
EDAMES
EDDIED
EDDIES
EDDOES
EDGIER
EDILES
EDITED
EDUCED
EDUCES

•D•••E

ADDUCE
ADELIE
ADELLE
ADESTE
ADHERE
ADJURE
ADMIRE
ADNATE
ADOREE
ADVICE
ADVISE
EDERLE
EDIBLE
IDEATE
ODENSE
ODETTE

••DE••

ADDEND
ADDERS
AIDERS
ALDERS
ANDEAN
ARDEBS
ARDENT
AUDENS
BADEGG
BEDECK
BEDEWS
BODEGA
CADENT
CADETS
CIDERS
CODERS
CYDERS
DODECA
DUDEEN
EIDERS
ELDERS
ELDEST
ENDEAR
ENDERS
FADEIN
GIDEON
GODETS
HIDEHO
HIDEKI
HIDERS
INDEBT
INDEED
INDENE
INDENT
LADERS
LODENS
LUDENS
MADEDO
MADEIT
MADERO
MADEUP
MODELA
MODELS
MODELT
MODEMS
MODENA
MODERN
MODEST
MUDEEL
NUDELY
NUDEST
ODDEST
OEDEMA
OLDEST
ONDECK
ORDEAL
ORDERS
REDEAL
REDEEM
REDENY
REDEYE
RIDENT
RIDERS
RODENT
RODEOS
RUDELY
RUDEST
RYDELL
SEDERS
SIDERO
SIDERS
TEDEUM
UDDERS
VIDEOS
VIDERI
WADEIN
WADERS
WEDELN
WIDELY
WIDENS
WIDEST
YODELS
ZYDECO

••D•E•

ADDLED
ADDLES
ANDREA
ANDREI
ANDRES
ANDREW
ANDREY
AUDREY
BADDER
BADGER
BADGES
BADMEN
BIDDEN
BIDDER
BODIED
BODIES
BUDDED
BUDGED
BUDGES
BUDGET
CADGED
CADGER
CADGES
CADRES
CODGER
CUDGEL
DADOED
DADOES
DIDIES
DODDER
DODGED
DODGER
DODGES
DODOES
DUDEEN
DUDLEY
EDDIED
EDDIES
EDDOES
ENDMEN
ENDUED
ENDUES
FIDGET
FODDER
FUDGED
FUDGES
GADDED
GADDER
GADGET
GIDGET
HADJES
HEDGED
HEDGER
HEDGES
HEDREN
HIDDEN
HODGES
INDEED
INDIES
JUDAEA
JUDDER
JUDGED
JUDGES
KEDGED
KEDGES
KIDDED
KIDDER
KIDNEY
LADDER
LADIES
LADLED
LADLER
LADLES
LEDGER
LEDGES
LIDDED
LODGED
LODGER
LODGES
LUDDEN
MADDEN
MADDER
MADMEN
MADRES
MADSEN
MEDLEY
MIDDEN
MIDGES
MIDGET
MIDLER
MUDDED
MUDDER
MUDEEL
MUDHEN
NODDED
NUDGED
NUDGER
NUDGES
OLDIES
OLDMEN
OODLES
PADDED
PADDER
PADRES
PODDED
RADNER
REDDEN
REDDER
REDEEM
REDOES
REDREW
REDSEA
REDYED
REDYES
RIDDED
RIDDEN
RIDGED
RIDGES
RIDLEY
RODDED
RODNEY
RUDDER
SADDEN
SADDER
SADHES
SEDGES
SIDLED
SIDLES
SIDNEY
SODDED
SODDEN
SUDDEN
SUDSED
SUDSES
SYDNEY
TEDDED
TEDDER
TEDKEY
TIDIED
TIDIER
TIDIES
UNDIES
UNDOER
UNDOES
UNDYED
VEDDER
WADDED
WEDDED
WEDGED
WEDGES
WIDGET
WODGES

••D••E

ADDUCE
AEDILE
ALDINE
ALDOSE
AUDILE
BADDIE
BEDAZE
BIDDLE
BODICE
BUDGIE
CADDIE
CODDLE
CUDDLE
DEDUCE
DIDDLE
ENDIVE
ENDURE
ENDUSE
FIDDLE
FUDDLE
HADDIE
HEDDLE
HUDDLE
HYDRAE
INDENE
INDITE
INDORE
INDUCE
IODATE
IODIDE
IODINE
IODISE
IODIZE
KIDDIE
LADDIE
MADAME
MADDIE
MEDDLE
MIDDLE
MODINE
MODULE
MUDDLE
MUDPIE
NADINE
NODDLE
NODICE
NODOSE
NODULE
OLDAGE
ONDINE
ORDURE
PADDLE

PEDATE
PEDDLE
PUDDLE
RADDLE
RADOME
REDATE
REDEYE
REDONE
REDUCE
RIDDLE
RUDDLE
SADDLE
SEDATE
SEDILE
SEDUCE
TODATE
TODDLE
UNDINE
UNDONE
UPDATE
UPDIKE
VADOSE
WADDLE
WEDGIE

•••DE•

ABIDED
ABIDES
ABODES
AMEDEO
AMIDES
ANADEM
ANODES
ASIDES
AZIDES
BADDER
BALDER
BANDED
BEADED
BENDED
BENDER
BIDDEN
BIDDER
BINDER
BIRDED
BIRDER
BLADED
BLADER
BLADES
BOLDER
BONDED
BORDEN
BORDER
BRIDES
BRUDER
BSIDES
BUDDED
BURDEN
CALDER
CAMDEN
CARDED
CARDER
CAUDEX
CHIDED
CHIDER
CHIDES
CINDER
COLDER
COODER
CORDED
CRUDER
CURDED
DANDER
DEADEN
DEADER
DEEDED
DEEDEE
DIADEM
DIODES
DODDER
DONDER
DRYDEN
DUNDEE
ELIDED
ELIDES
ELUDED
ELUDER
ELUDES
EMBDEN
EPODES
ERODED
ERODES
ETUDES
EVADED
EVADER
EVADES
EXUDED
EXUDES
FEEDER
FENDED
FENDER
FEUDED
FINDER
FODDER
FOLDED
FOLDER
FONDER
FORDED
FUNDED
GADDED
GADDER
GANDER
GARDEN
GENDER
GEODES
GILDED
GILDER
GIRDED
GIRDER
GLADES
GLIDED
GLIDER
GLIDES
GOADED
GOLDEN
GOODEN
GRADEA
GRADED
GRADER
GRADES
GUIDED
GUIDES
HANDED
HANDEL
HARDEN
HARDER
HAYDEN
HEADED
HEADER
HEEDED
HEEDER
HEIDEN
HERDED
HERDER
HIDDEN
HINDER
HOLDEN
HOLDER
HOODED
HORDES
HOYDEN
HYADES
IBIDEM
IRIDES
JUDDER
KANDER
KIDDED
KIDDER
KINDER
LADDER
LANDED
LANDER
LARDED
LARDER
LAUDED
LAUDER
LEADED
LEADEN
LEADER
LEIDEN
LENDER
LEWDER
LEYDEN
LIDDED
LIEDER
LINDEN
LOADED
LOADER
LORDED
LOUDEN
LOUDER
LUDDEN
LUNDEN
MADDEN
MADDER
MAIDEN
MALDEN
MELDED
MENDED
MENDEL
MENDER
MENDES
MIDDEN
MILDER
MILDEW
MINDED
MINDER
MOLDED
MOLDER
MUDDED
MUDDER
MURDER
NEEDED
NODDED
OXIDES
PADDED
PADDER
PANDER
PEEDEE
PENDED
PODDED
POLDER
PONDER
POWDER
PRIDED
PRIDES
PRUDES
RAIDED
RAIDER
READER
REDDEN
REDDER
RENDER
RHODES
RIDDED
RIDDEN
RODDED
RONDEL
RUDDER
SADDEN
SADDER
SANDED
SANDER
SEEDED
SEEDER
SEIDEL
SENDER
SHADED
SHADES
SLIDER
SLIDES
SNIDER
SNYDER
SODDED
SODDEN
SOLDER
SONDES
SPADED
SPADER
SPADES
SPIDER
SUBDEB
SUDDEN
SUEDES
SUNDER
SUNDEW
SWEDEN
SWEDES
TANDEM
TEDDED
TEDDER
TENDED
TENDER
TILDEN
TILDES
TINDER
TRADED
TRADER
TRADES
VALDEZ
VARDEN
VEDDER
VENDED
VENDEE
VOIDED
WADDED
WALDEN
WANDER
WARDED
WARDEN
WARDER
WEDDED
WEEDED
WEEDER
WELDED
WELDER
WENDED
WILDER
WINDED
WINDER
WINDEX
WONDER
WOODED
WOODEN
WORDED
YARDED
YONDER
ZANDER
ZUIDER

•••D•E

AZODYE
BADDIE
BEADLE
BIDDLE
BIRDIE
BOODLE
BRIDGE
BRIDLE
BRODIE
BUNDLE
CADDIE
CANDLE
CAUDLE
CNIDAE
CODDLE
CRADLE
CUDDLE
CURDLE
DANDIE
DANDLE
DAWDLE
DEEDEE
DEIDRE
DIDDLE
DOODLE
DREDGE
DRUDGE
DUNDEE
FIDDLE
FLEDGE
FONDLE
FONDUE
FOODIE
FRIDGE
FUDDLE
GIRDLE
GOLDIE
GOODIE
GORDIE
GRUDGE
HADDIE
HANDLE
HEDDLE
HUDDLE
HURDLE
KIDDIE
KINDLE
KLUDGE
LADDIE
MADDIE
MEDDLE
MIDDLE
MUDDLE
NEEDLE
NODDLE
NOODLE
ONEDGE
PADDLE
PEDDLE
PEEDEE
PERDUE
PHEDRE
PLEDGE
POODLE
PUDDLE
PURDUE
QUIDDE
RADDLE
RIDDLE
ROADIE
RUDDLE
RUNDLE
SADDLE
SLEDGE
SLUDGE
SMUDGE
STODGE
SUBDUE
SUNDAE
TIEDYE
TODDLE
TRUDGE
VENDEE
WADDLE

••••DE

ABRADE
ACCEDE
ALLUDE
ARCADE
AUBADE
BESIDE
BETIDE
BLENDE
BLONDE
BOLIDE
BORIDE
CHILDE
CLAUDE
DECADE
DECIDE
DECODE
DELUDE
DEMODE
DENUDE
DERIDE
DIVIDE
ENCODE
FACADE
GOURDE
GRANDE
HALIDE
IMPEDE
INSIDE
INVADE
IODIDE
ISOLDE
LIPIDE
MRHYDE
ONSIDE
OROIDE
PARADE
POMADE
QUIDDE
RECEDE
RECODE
REMADE
RESIDE
SECEDE
STRIDE
STRODE
TIRADE
TRIODE
UNLADE
UNMADE
UPSIDE

D•F•••

DAFFED
DAFTER
DAFTLY
DEFACE
DEFAME
DEFATS
DEFEAT
DEFECT
DEFEND
DEFERS
DEFIED
DEFIES
DEFILE
DEFINE
DEFLEA
DEFOGS
DEFORM
DEFRAY
DEFTER
DEFTLY
DEFUSE
DIFFER
DOFFED
DUFFEL
DUFFER

D••F••

DAFFED
DEAFEN
DEAFER
DEAFLY
DELFTS
DIFFER
DOFFED
DOOFUS
DRAFTS
DRAFTY
DRIFTS
DRIFTY
DRYFLY
DUFFEL
DUFFER
DURFEY

D•••F•

DECAFS
DIEOFF
DRYOFF
DWARFS

D••••F

DIEOFF
DRYOFF

•D••F•

ADRIFT

••DF••

AIDFUL
GADFLY
MEDFLY
REDFIN
REDFIR
REDFOX

••D•F•

CODIFY
LEDOFF
MODIFY
NIDIFY
NODOFF

••D••F

LEDOFF
NODOFF
RIDSOF
RUDOLF

•••D•F

KINDOF
TOLDOF

D•G•••

DAGAMA
DAGGER
DAGMAR
DEGAGE
DEGREE
DEGUST
DIGEST
DIGGER
DIGITS
DIGLOT
DIGOUT
DIGRAM
DIGSIN
DIGSUP
DOGDAY
DOGDOM
DOGEAR
DOGEYS
DOGGED
DOGGER
DOGGIE
DOGIES
DOGLEG
DOGMAS
DOGONS
DOGOOD
DOGSAT
DOGSIT
DOGTAG
DUGONG
DUGOUT

D••G••

DAGGER
DANGER
DANGLE
DANGLY
DANGME
DAYGLO
DEIGNS
DENGUE
DIGGER
DINGED
DINGHY
DINGLE
DINGUS
DIRGES
DODGED
DODGER
DODGES
DOGGED
DOGGER
DOGGIE
DONGLE
DOOGIE
DOUGHS
DOUGHY
DRAGEE
DRAGGY
DRAGIN
DRAGON
DROGUE
DWIGHT

D•••G•

DAMAGE
DEBUGS
DEFOGS
DEGAGE
DELUGE
DESIGN
DIRIGE
DIRIGO
DOINGS
DORAGS
DOSAGE
DOTAGE
DRAGGY
DREDGE
DRINGS
DRUDGE

D••••G

DANANG
DANZIG
DARING
DATING
DATONG
DAZING
DEKING
DELONG
DEWING
DIALOG
DICING
DIKING
DINING
DIVING
DOGLEG
DOGTAG
DOLING
DOMING
DOPING
DOSING
DOTING
DOZING
DRYING
DUGONG
DUKING

DUPING
DURING
DYEING

•DG•••
EDGARD
EDGARS
EDGEIN
EDGERS
EDGIER
EDGILY
EDGING

•D•G••
ADAGES
ADAGIO

•D••G•
IDTAGS

•D•••G
ADDING
EDBERG
EDGING
IDLING
KDLANG

••DG••
BADGER
BADGES
BADGUY
BUDGED
BUDGES
BUDGET
BUDGIE
CADGED
CADGER
CADGES
CODGER
CUDGEL
DODGED
DODGER
DODGES
FIDGET
FUDGED
FUDGES
GADGET
GIDGET
HEDGED
HEDGER
HEDGES
HODGES
JUDGED
JUDGES
KEDGED
KEDGES
LEDGER
LEDGES
LODGED
LODGER
LODGES
MEDGAR
MIDGES
MIDGET
NUDGED
NUDGER
NUDGES
PIDGIN
REDGUM
RIDGED
RIDGES
SEDGES
WEDGED
WEDGES
WEDGIE
WIDGET
WODGES

••D•G•
BADEGG
BODEGA
INDIGO
LADOGA
OLDAGE

••D••G
ADDING
AIDING
BADEGG
BEDBUG
BIDING
BODING
CEDING
CODING
ENDING
FADING
HIDING
JADING
LADING
LUDWIG
PADANG
REDDOG
REDING
REDTAG
RIDING
SIDING
TIDING
WADING

•••DG•
BRIDGE
DREDGE
DRUDGE
FLEDGE
FLEDGY
FRIDGE
GRUDGE
KLUDGE
ONEDGE
PLEDGE
SLEDGE
SLUDGE
SLUDGY
SMUDGE
SMUDGY
STODGE
STODGY
TRUDGE

•••D•G
BANDOG
GUNDOG
HOTDOG
LAPDOG
PYEDOG
REDDOG
SEADOG
SUNDOG
TOPDOG
TOYDOG

••••DG
RATEDG

DH••••
DHARMA
DHOLES
DHOTEL
DHOTIS

D•H•••
DAHLIA
DEHORN
DRHOOK
DSHARP

D••H••
DACHAS
DAPHNE
DASHED
DASHER
DASHES
DASHIS
DIRHAM
DISHED
DISHES
DITHER
DOTHAN
DUCHIN
DUNHAM
DURHAM

D•••H•
DELPHI
DEPTHS
DINGHY
DOUGHS
DOUGHY
DRACHM
DWIGHT

D••••H
DALETH
DANISH
DEARTH
DETACH
DOODAH
DOVISH
DRENCH
DUDISH
DULUTH

•DH•••
ADHERE

•D•••H
ADOLPH
EDKOCH

••DH••
ANDHOW
BADHAM
MUDHEN
OLDHAM
OLDHAT
REDHAT
REDHOT
RODHAM
SADHES
SADHUS

••D•H•
BUDDHA
HIDEHO
WIDTHS

••D••H
DUDISH
EMDASH
ENDASH
JADISH
JUDITH
MODISH
OLDISH
RADISH
WIDISH

•••DH•
BUDDHA
GANDHI
LANDHO

•••D•H
DOODAH
GOODOH
HOWDAH
PURDAH
WHYDAH

••••DH
LAMEDH
RIYADH

DI••••
DIABLO
DIADEM
DIALED
DIALER
DIALOG
DIALUP
DIANNE
DIAPER
DIATOM
DIBBLE
DICERS
DICIER
DICING
DICKER
DICKEY
DICOTS
DICTUM
DICTUS
DIDACT
DIDDLE
DIDDLY
DIDIES
DIDION
DIEOFF
DIEOUT
DIEPPE
DIESEL
DIESES
DIESIS
DIETED
DIETER
DIFFER
DIGEST
DIGGER
DIGITS
DIGLOT
DIGOUT
DIGRAM
DIGSIN
DIGSUP
DIKDIK
DIKING
DIKTAT
DILATE
DILLER
DILLON
DILSEY
DILUTE
DIMITY
DIMMED
DIMMER
DIMOUT
DIMPLE
DIMPLY
DIMSUM
DIMWIT
DINARS
DINEIN
DINEON
DINERO
DINERS
DINGED
DINGHY
DINGLE
DINGUS
DINING
DINKEY
DINNED
DINNER
DINTED
DIODES
DIONEB
DIONNE
DIOXIN
DIPODY
DIPOLE
DIPPED
DIPPER
DIRECT
DIRELY
DIREST
DIRGES
DIRHAM
DIRIGE
DIRIGO
DIRNDL
DISANT
DISARM
DISBAR
DISCOS
DISCUS
DISHED
DISHES
DISKED
DISMAL
DISMAY
DISMES
DISNEY
DISOWN
DISPEL
DISSED
DISTAL
DISTIL
DISUSE
DITHER
DITTOS
DITZES
DIVANS
DIVEIN
DIVERS
DIVERT
DIVEST
DIVIDE
DIVINE
DIVING
DIVINO
DIVOTS
DIXITS
DIYERS
DIZENS

D•I•••
DAIKON
DAILEY
DAIMON
DAIMYO
DAINTY
DAIREN
DAISES
DEICED
DEICER
DEICES
DEIDRE
DEIGNS
DEIMOS
DEISTS
DMINOR
DMINUS
DMITRI
DOINGS
DRIERS
DRIEST
DRIFTS
DRIFTY
DRILLS
DRINGS
DRINKS
DRIPPY
DRIVEL
DRIVEN
DRIVER
DRIVES
DUIKER
DWIGHT

D••I••
DAMIEN
DAMITA
DANIEL
DANISH
DARIEN
DARING
DARIUS
DATING
DATIVE
DAVIES
DAVITS
DAZING
DEBITS
DECIDE
DEFIED
DEFIES
DEFILE
DEFINE
DEKING
DELICT
DELIST
DELIUS
DEMIES
DEMISE
DEMITS
DENIAL
DENIED
DENIER
DENIES
DENIMS
DENIRO
DENISE
DEPICT
DERIDE
DERIVE
DESICA
DESIGN
DESILU
DESIRE
DESIST
DEVICE
DEVILS
DEVINE
DEVISE
DEVITO
DEWIER
DEWILY
DEWING
DEWITT
DICIER
DICING
DIDIES
DIDION
DIGITS
DIKING
DIMITY
DINING
DIRIGE
DIRIGO
DIVIDE
DIVINE
DIVING
DIVINO
DIXITS
DOCILE
DOGIES
DOLING
DOMINE
DOMING
DOMINI
DOMINO
DONITZ
DOPIER
DOPING
DORIAN
DORIES
DOSIDO
DOSING
DOTING
DOVISH
DOZIER
DOZILY
DOZING
DRAILS
DRAINS
DROIDS
DROITS
DRUIDS
DRYICE
DRYING
DRYINK
DUDISH
DUKING
DUPING
DURIAN
DURING
DUTIES
DYEING

D•••I•
DACOIT
DAHLIA
DANDIE
DANZIG
DARNIT
DARWIN
DASHIS
DASSIN
DAYLIT
DEALIN
DEARIE
DEASIL
DEBBIE
DEBRIS
DECEIT
DELRIO
DELTIC
DENNIS
DENTIL
DENTIN
DERAIL
DERMIS
DERRIS
DETAIL
DETAIN
DEVEIN
DEVOID
DEVOIR
DHOTIS
DIESIS
DIGSIN
DIKDIK
DIMWIT
DINEIN
DIOXIN
DISTIL
DIVEIN
DOBBIN
DOBLIN
DOESIN
DOGGIE
DOGSIT
DOMAIN
DONEIN
DOOBIE
DOOGIE
DOOZIE
DORRIT
DOTTIE
DOVEIN
DRAGIN
DRAWIN
DREWIN
DROPIN
DROPIT
DUBBIN
DUBLIN
DUBOIS
DUCHIN
DUNLIN
DURBIN
DUSTIN
DYADIC

D••••I
DALASI
DELPHI
DENALI
DENDRI
DMITRI
DOMANI
DOMINI
DORATI
DOREMI
DROMOI

•DI•••
ADIDAS
ADIEUS
ADIEUX
EDIBLE
EDICTS
EDILES
EDISON
EDITED
EDITIO
EDITOR
IDIOCY
IDIOMS
IDIOTS
ODIOUS
ODISTS
ODIUMS

•D•I••
ADDING
ADLIBS
ADMIRE
ADMITS
ADRIAN
ADRIEN
ADRIFT
ADVICE
ADVISE
EDDIED
EDDIES
EDGIER
EDGILY
EDGING
IDLING
IDOIDO
ODDITY

•D••I•
ADAGIO
ADDSIN
ADELIE
ADJOIN
ADONIS
ADROIT
EDENIC
EDGEIN
EDITIO

•D•••I
ADJANI
ADONAI
ADZUKI

••DI••
ADDING
AEDILE
AIDING
ALDINE
ASDICS
AUDIAL
AUDILE
AUDIOS
AUDITS
BEDIMS
BIDING
BODICE
BODIED
BODIES
BODILY
BODING
CEDING
CODIFY
CODING
DIDIES
DIDION
DUDISH
EDDIED
EDDIES
ENDING
ENDIVE
FADING
GODIVA
HIDING
INDIAN
INDICT
INDIES
INDIGO
INDIRA
INDITE
INDIUM
IODIDE
IODINE
IODISE
IODIZE
JADING
JADISH
JUDITH
KODIAK
LADIDA
LADIES
LADING
LADINO
MEDIAL
MEDIAN
MEDIAS
MEDICI
MEDICO
MEDICS
MEDINA
MEDIUM
MIDIAN
MODIFY
MODINE
MODISH
NADINE
NADIRS
NIDIFY
NODICE
NUDIST
NUDITY
ODDITY
OLDIES
OLDISH
ONDINE
PODIUM
RADIAL
RADIAN
RADIOS
RADISH
RADIUM
RADIUS
REDIAL
REDING
REDINK
RIDING
SEDILE
SIDING
SODIUM
TEDIUM
TIDIED
TIDIER
TIDIES
TIDILY
TIDING
UNDIES
UNDINE
UPDIKE
WADING
WIDISH
ZODIAC

••D•I•
ADDSIN
ALDRIN
AODAIS
BADDIE
BIDSIN
BODKIN
BUDGIE
CADDIE
CADDIS
CADMIC
CEDRIC
FADEIN
GODWIN
GODWIT
HADDIE
HADJIS
INDRIS
JUDAIC
KIDDIE
KIDVID
LADDIE
LUDWIG
MADDIE
MADEIT
MADRID
MIDAIR
MIDRIB
MUDPIE
NUDNIK
OLDVIC
ORDAIN
PIDGIN
REDFIN
REDFIR
TIDBIT
WADEIN
WEDGIE
ZADDIK

••D••I
ANDREI
BODONI
HIDEKI
MEDICI
MIDORI
VIDERI

•••DI•
ACADIA
ACEDIA
ACIDIC
AGADIR
AMADIS
ANODIC
BADDIE
BANDIT
BARDIC
BENDIX
BIRDIE
BOUDIN
BRODIE
CADDIE
CADDIS
CANDID
CARDIN
CARDIO
COEDIT
CREDIT
DANDIE
DIKDIK
DYADIC
FOODIE
GOLDIE
GOODIE
GORDIE
GRADIN
GRODIN
HADDIE
HANDIN
HEADIN
HELDIN
HOLDIN
HOLDIT
ICEDIN
IRIDIC
KIDDIE
LADDIE
LAIDIN
LANDIS
LEADIN
MADDIE
MAHDIS
MISDID
NORDIC
OUTDID
OXIDIC
PAIDIN
PANDIT
PUNDIT
READIN
REEDIT
ROADIE
SANDIA
SARDIS
SAUDIS
SENDIN
SLIDIN
SORDID
SPADIX
STADIA
STUDIO
SYNDIC
TIEDIN
TOEDIN
TREDIA
VERDIN
ZADDIK
ZENDIC

•••D•I
DENDRI
GANDHI
QUADRI

••••DI
BIONDI
CIARDI
SOLIDI
YEHUDI

DJ••••
DJERBA

D•J•••
DEJAVU
DEJECT
DEJURE

D••J••
DAYJOB
DEEJAY
DMAJOR
DONJON

•DJ•••
ADJANI
ADJOIN
ADJURE
ADJUST

•D•J••
ODDJOB

••DJ••
HADJES
HADJIS
ODDJOB

D•K•••
DAKOTA
DEKALB
DEKING
DEKKOS
DIKDIK
DIKING
DIKTAT
DUKING

D••K••
DAIKON
DANKER
DANKLY
DARKEN
DARKER
DARKLE
DARKLY
DECKED
DECKER
DECKLE
DEKKOS
DICKER
DICKEY
DINKEY
DISKED
DOCKED
DOCKER
DOCKET
DONKEY
DRAKES
DUCKED
DUIKER
DUNKED
DUNKER

D•••K•
DMARKS
DRINKS

D••••K
DAMASK
DEBARK
DEBUNK
DEEPAK
DIKDIK
DRHOOK
DRYINK
DUBCEK
DVORAK
DYBBUK

•DK•••
EDKOCH

•D••K•
ADZUKI

•D•••K
ADWEEK
GDANSK

••DK••
BODKIN
TEDKEY
VODKAS

••D•K•
HIDEKI
JUDOKA
MEDAKA
SEDAKA
UPDIKE

••D••K
BEDECK
KODIAK
NUDNIK
ONDECK
PODUNK
REDINK
REDOAK
ZADDIK

•••D•K
DIKDIK
MARDUK
SENDAK
ZADDIK

DL••••
DLAYER

D•L•••
DALASI
DALETH
DALLAS
DALLES
DALTON
DELANO
DELANY
DELATE
DELAYS
DELEON
DELETE
DELFTS
DELICT
DELIST
DELIUS
DELMAR
DELONG
DELPHI
DELRAY
DELRIO
DELROY
DELTAS
DELTIC
DELUDE
DELUGE
DELUXE
DELVED
DELVER
DELVES
DILATE
DILLER
DILLON
DILSEY
DILUTE
DOLENZ
DOLING
DOLLAR
DOLLED
DOLLOP
DOLLUP
DOLMAN
DOLMAS
DOLMEN
DOLORS
DOLOUR
DULCET
DULLEA
DULLED
DULLER
DULLES
DULUTH

D••L••
DAHLIA
DAILEY
DALLAS
DALLES
DAYLIT
DEALER
DEALIN
DEFLEA
DEPLOY
DEWLAP
DHOLES
DIALED
DIALER
DIALOG
DIALUP
DIGLOT
DILLER
DILLON
DOBLAS
DOBLIN
DOGLEG
DOLLAR
DOLLED
DOLLOP
DOLLUP
DOOLEY
DRILLS
DROLLS
DROLLY
DUALLY
DUBLIN
DUDLEY
DUELED
DUELER
DUELLO
DULLEA
DULLED
DULLER
DULLES
DUNLIN
DUNLOP
DUPLEX
DWELLS
DYELOT

D•••L•
DABBLE
DAFTLY
DAMPLY
DANDLE
DANGLE
DANGLY
DANKLY
DAPPLE
DARKLE
DARKLY
DAWDLE
DAYGLO
DAZZLE
DEADLY
DEAFLY
DEARLY
DECALS
DECKLE
DEEPLY
DEFILE
DEFTLY
DEKALB
DENALI
DESALT
DESILU
DEVILS
DEWILY
DIABLO
DIBBLE
DIDDLE
DIDDLY
DIMPLE
DIMPLY
DINGLE
DIPOLE
DIRELY
DOABLE
DOCILE
DONALD
DONGLE
DOODLE
DOTELL
DOTTLE
DOUALA
DOUBLE
DOUBLY
DOURLY
DOWELS
DOZILY
DRABLY
DRAILS
DRAWLS
DRAWLY
DRILLS
DROLLS
DROLLY
DROOLS
DROOLY
DRYFLY
DUALLY
DUELLO
DUMBLY
DUVALL
DWELLS

D••••L
DACTYL
DAEDAL
DAMSEL
DANIEL
DARNEL
DARRYL
DEASIL
DENIAL
DENTAL
DENTIL
DENZEL
DEPAUL
DERAIL
DERMAL
DETAIL
DHOTEL
DIESEL
DIRNDL
DISMAL
DISPEL
DISTAL
DISTIL
DORSAL
DOSSAL
DOSSEL
DOTELL
DREXEL
DRIVEL
DUCTAL
DUFFEL
DUVALL

•DL•••
ADLIBS
IDLERS
IDLEST
IDLING
KDLANG

•D•L••
ADDLED
ADDLES
ADELIE
ADELLE
ADOLPH
ADULTS
EDILES
IDYLLS
ODDLOT

•D••L•
ADELLE
EDERLE
EDGILY
EDIBLE
EDSELS
IDEALS
IDYLLS

••DL••
ADDLED
ADDLES
BADLOT
BEDLAM
DUDLEY
LADLED
LADLER
LADLES
LUDLUM
MEDLAR
MEDLAT
MEDLEY
MIDLER
ODDLOT
OODLES
PEDLAR
RIDLEY
SIDLED
SIDLES

••D•L•
AEDILE
AUDILE
BIDDLE
BODILY
CODDLE
CUDDLE
CUDDLY
DIDDLE
DIDDLY
EIDOLA
ENDALL
FIDDLE
FUDDLE
GADFLY
HEDDLE
HUDDLE
KODALY
MEDALS
MEDDLE
MEDFLY
MIDDLE
MODELA
MODELS
MODELT
MODULE
MODULO
MUDDLE
NODDLE
NODULE
NUDELY
PADDLE
PEDALS

PEDDLE
PUDDLE
PUDDLY
RADDLE
RADULA
RIDDLE
RUDDLE
RUDELY
RUDOLF
RYDELL
SADDLE
SEDILE
TIDDLY
TIDILY
TODDLE
UNDULY
WADDLE
WADDLY
WEDELN
WIDELY
YODELS

••D••L
AIDFUL
AUDIAL
CUDGEL
ENDALL
MEDIAL
MUDEEL
ORDEAL
RADIAL
REDEAL
REDIAL
RYDELL
TYDBOL

•••DL•
ACIDLY
ARIDLY
AVIDLY
AWEDLY
BALDLY
BEADLE
BIDDLE
BOLDLY
BOODLE
BRIDLE
BUNDLE
CANDLE
CAUDLE
CODDLE
COLDLY
CRADLE
CUDDLE
CUDDLY
CURDLE
DANDLE
DAWDLE
DEADLY
DIDDLE
DIDDLY
DOODLE
FIDDLE
FONDLE
FONDLY
FUDDLE
GIRDLE
GLADLY
GOODLY
HANDLE
HARDLY
HEDDLE
HUDDLE
HURDLE
KINDLE
KINDLY
LEWDLY
LORDLY
LOUDLY
MEDDLE
MIDDLE
MILDLY
MUDDLE
NEEDLE
NODDLE
NOODLE
PADDLE
PEDDLE
POODLE
PUDDLE
PUDDLY
RADDLE
RIDDLE
RUDDLE
RUNDLE
SADDLE
TIDDLY
TODDLE
WADDLE
WADDLY
WILDLY

•••D•L
AMIDOL
APODAL
BRIDAL
CAUDAL
DAEDAL
FEUDAL
HANDEL
MENDEL
MYRDAL
OXYDOL
RONDEL
SANDAL
SEIDEL
VANDAL

••••DL
DIRNDL

DM••••
DMAJOR
DMARKS
DMINOR
DMINUS
DMITRI

D•M•••
DAMAGE
DAMASK
DAMATO
DAMIEN
DAMITA
DAMMAR
DAMMED
DAMNED
DAMONE
DAMORE
DAMOUR
DAMPED
DAMPEN
DAMPER
DAMPLY
DAMSEL
DAMSON
DAMSUP
DEMAND
DEMEAN
DEMIES
DEMISE
DEMITS
DEMOBS
DEMODE
DEMOND
DEMONS
DEMOTE
DEMURE
DEMURS
DIMITY
DIMMED
DIMMER
DIMOUT
DIMPLE
DIMPLY
DIMSUM
DIMWIT
DOMAIN
DOMANI
DOMINE
DOMING
DOMINI
DOMINO
DOMREP
DUMBER
DUMBLY
DUMDUM
DUMONT
DUMPED
DUMPER

D••M••
DAGMAR
DAIMON
DAIMYO
DAMMAR
DAMMED
DEEMED
DEIMOS
DELMAR
DERMAL
DERMIS
DESMAN
DIMMED
DIMMER
DISMAL
DISMAY
DISMES
DOGMAS
DOLMAN
DOLMAS
DOLMEN
DOOMED
DORMER
DRAMAS
DROMOI
DROMOS
DRUMUP
DUOMOS

D•••M•
DAGAMA
DANGME
DEARME
DECAMP
DEFAME
DENIMS
DHARMA
DODOMA
DOREMI
DREAMS
DREAMT
DREAMY
DYNAMO

D••••M
DEFORM
DIADEM
DIATOM
DICTUM
DIGRAM
DIMSUM
DIRHAM
DISARM
DOGDOM
DORSUM
DRACHM
DUMDUM
DUNHAM
DURHAM

•DM•••
ADMASS
ADMIRE
ADMITS
EDMOND
EDMUND

•D•M••
EDAMES

•D••M•
ADDAMS
ADEEMS
CDROMS
IDIOMS
ODIUMS

•D•••M
ADYTUM

••DM••
BADMAN
BADMEN
CADMIC
CADMUS
ENDMAN
ENDMEN
KIDMAN
MADMAN
MADMAX
MADMEN
OLDMAN
OLDMEN
RODMAN
RUDMAN
TODMAN

••D•M•
ADDAMS
BEDIMS
DODOMA
MADAME
MADAMS
MODEMS
OEDEMA
RADOME
SEDUMS

••D••M
BADHAM
BEDLAM
INDIUM
LUDLUM
MADTOM
MEDIUM
OLDHAM
PODIUM
RADIUM
REDEEM
REDGUM
RODHAM
SADDAM
SODIUM
TEDEUM
TEDIUM

•••DM•
RUNDMC

•••D•M
AIRDAM
ANADEM
BELDAM
DIADEM
DOGDOM
DUMDUM
FANDOM
IBIDEM
MCADAM
RANDOM
SADDAM
SELDOM
TANDEM
WINDOM
WISDOM

D•N•••
DANANG
DANAUS
DANCED
DANCER
DANCES
DANDER
DANDIE
DANDLE
DANGER
DANGLE
DANGLY
DANGME
DANIEL
DANISH
DANKER
DANKLY
DANNAY
DANNER
DANSON
DANTES
DANTON
DANUBE
DANZIG
DENALI
DENARY
DENDRI
DENDRO
DENGUE
DENIAL
DENIED
DENIER
DENIES
DENIMS
DENIRO
DENISE
DENNED
DENNIS
DENOTE
DENOVO
DENSER
DENTAL
DENTED
DENTIL
DENTIN
DENTON
DENUDE
DENVER
DENZEL
DINARS
DINEIN
DINEON
DINERO
DINERS
DINGED
DINGHY
DINGLE
DINGUS
DINING
DINKEY
DINNED
DINNER
DINTED
DONALD
DONATE
DONDER
DONEES
DONEIN
DONETS
DONEUP
DONGLE
DONITZ
DONJON
DONKEY
DONNAS
DONNED
DONNEE
DONNER
DONORS
DONUTS
DUNANT
DUNBAR
DUNCAN
DUNCES
DUNDEE
DUNERA
DUNHAM
DUNKED
DUNKER
DUNLIN
DUNLOP
DUNNED
DYNAMO
DYNAST

D••N••
DABNEY
DAINTY
DAMNED
DANNAY
DANNER
DARNAY
DARNED
DARNEL
DARNER
DARNIT
DAUNTS
DAWNED
DAWNON
DEANNA
DENNED
DENNIS
DIANNE
DINNED
DINNER
DIONEB
DIONNE
DIRNDL
DISNEY
DMINOR
DMINUS
DOINGS
DONNAS
DONNED
DONNEE
DONNER
DOWNED
DOWNER
DOWNEY
DOWNON
DRENCH
DRINGS
DRINKS
DRONED
DRONER
DRONES
DUENNA
DUNNED
DURNED

D•••N•
DAMONE
DANANG
DAPHNE
DARENT
DARING
DATING
DATONG
DAYONE
DAZING
DEANNA
DEBONE
DEBUNK
DECANT
DECENT
DEFEND
DEFINE
DEIGNS
DEKING
DELANO
DELANY
DELONG
DEMAND
DEMOND
DEMONS
DEPEND
DEPONE
DETENT
DEVINE
DEWING
DIANNE
DICING
DIKING
DINING
DIONNE
DISANT
DIVANS
DIVINE
DIVING
DIVINO
DIZENS
DOCENT
DOESNT
DOGONS
DOLENZ
DOLING
DOMANI
DOMINE
DOMING
DOMINI
DOMINO
DOPANT
DOPING
DOSING
DOTING
DOYENS
DOZENS
DOZING
DRAINS
DROWNS
DRYING
DRYINK
DUENNA
DUGONG
DUKING
DUMONT
DUNANT
DUPING
DUPONT
DURANT
DURING
DWAYNE
DYEING

D••••N
DACRON
DAIKON
DAIMON
DAIREN
DALTON
DAMIEN
DAMPEN
DAMSON
DANSON
DANTON
DARIEN
DARKEN
DARREN
DARWIN
DASSIN
DATSUN
DAWNON
DAWSON
DAYTON
DEACON
DEADEN
DEADON
DEAFEN
DEALIN
DEEPEN
DEHORN
DELEON
DEMEAN
DENTIN
DENTON
DESIGN
DESMAN
DETAIN
DEVEIN
DIDION
DIGSIN
DILLON
DINEIN
DINEON
DIOXIN
DISOWN
DIVEIN
DOBBIN
DOBLIN
DOBSON
DOESIN
DOLMAN
DOLMEN
DOMAIN
DONEIN
DONJON
DORIAN
DOTEON
DOTHAN
DOVEIN
DOWNON
DRAGIN
DRAGON
DRAWIN
DRAWON
DREWIN
DREWON
DRIVEN
DROPIN
DRYDEN
DRYRUN
DUBBIN
DUBLIN
DUCHIN
DUDEEN
DUNCAN
DUNLIN
DURBAN
DURBIN
DURIAN
DUSTIN

•DN•••
ADNATE
ADNEXA

•D•N••
ADONAI
ADONIS
EDENIC
GDANSK
ODENSE

ODONTO

•D••N•
ADDEND
ADDING
ADDONS
ADJANI
ADORNS
ADRENO
ADVENT
EDGING
EDMOND
EDMUND
EDWYNN
IDLING
KDLANG

•D•••N
ADDSIN
ADDSON
ADJOIN
ADRIAN
ADRIEN
EDGEIN
EDISON
EDWYNN
ODDSON

••DN••
KIDNAP
KIDNEY
NUDNIK
RADNER
RODNEY
SIDNEY
SYDNEY

••D•N•
ADDEND
ADDING
ADDONS
AIDING
ALDINE
ARDENT
AUDENS
BIDING
BODING
BODONI
CADENT
CEDANT
CEDING
CODING
CODONS
ENDING
FADING
HIDING
INDENE
INDENT
IODINE
JADING
LADING
LADINO
LODENS
LUDENS
MEDINA
MODENA
MODINE
NADINE
ONDINE
PADANG
PEDANT
PODUNK
REDANT
REDENY
REDING
REDINK
REDONE
RIDENT
RIDING
RODENT
SEDANS
SIDING
TIDING
UNDINE
UNDONE
WADING
WIDENS

••D••N
ADDSIN
ADDSON
ALDRIN
ANDEAN
BADMAN
BADMEN
BIDDEN
BIDSIN
BIDSON
BODKIN
DIDION
DUDEEN
ENDMAN
ENDMEN
ENDRUN
FADEIN
GIDEON
GODOWN
GODSON
GODWIN
GUDRUN
HADRON
HEDREN
HEDRON
HIDDEN
HUDSON
INDIAN
KIDMAN
LUDDEN
MADDEN
MADMAN
MADMEN
MADSEN
MEDIAN
MIDDEN
MIDIAN
MODERN
MUDHEN
ODDSON
OLDMAN
OLDMEN
ORDAIN
PADUAN
PIDGIN
RADIAN
REDDEN
REDFIN
RIDDEN
RODMAN
RUDMAN
SADDEN
SODDEN
SUDDEN
TODMAN
WADEIN
WEDELN

•••DN•
GRODNO
NEEDNT

•••D•N
AVEDON
BIDDEN
BORDEN
BOUDIN
BURDEN
CAMDEN
CARDIN
CORDON
DEADEN
DEADON
DRYDEN
EMBDEN
FEEDON
FELDON
GARDEN
GOLDEN
GOODEN
GORDON
GRADIN
GRODIN
GUIDON
HAGDON
HANDIN
HANDON
HARDEN
HAYDEN
HEADIN
HEADON
HEIDEN
HELDIN
HELDON
HIDDEN
HOLDEN
HOLDIN
HOLDON
HOYDEN
IBADAN
ICEDIN
JORDAN
KASDAN
LAIDIN
LAIDON
LANDON
LARDON
LEADEN
LEADIN
LEADON
LEIDEN
LEYDEN
LINDEN
LONDON
LOUDEN
LUDDEN
LUNDEN
LYNDON
MADDEN
MAIDEN
MALDEN
MANDAN
MIDDEN
PAIDIN
PARDON
READIN
REDDEN
RIDDEN
SADDEN
SENDIN
SLIDIN
SODDEN
SOLDAN
SOLDON
SUDDEN
SWEDEN
TENDON
TIEDIN
TILDEN
TOEDIN
TOLDON
VARDEN
VERDIN
VERDON
VERDUN
WALDEN
WARDEN
WOODEN

DO••••
DOABLE
DOBBER
DOBBIN
DOBLAS
DOBLIN
DOBRAS
DOBROS
DOBSON
DOCENT
DOCILE
DOCKED
DOCKER
DOCKET
DOCTOR
DODDER
DODECA
DODGED
DODGER
DODGES
DODODO
DODOES
DODOMA
DOESBY
DOESIN
DOESNT
DOESUP
DOFFED
DOGDAY
DOGDOM
DOGEAR
DOGEYS
DOGGED
DOGGER
DOGGIE
DOGIES
DOGLEG
DOGMAS
DOGONS
DOGOOD
DOGSAT
DOGSIT
DOGTAG
DOINGS
DOLENZ
DOLING
DOLLAR
DOLLED
DOLLOP
DOLLUP
DOLMAN
DOLMAS
DOLMEN
DOLORS
DOLOUR
DOMAIN
DOMANI
DOMINE
DOMING
DOMINI
DOMINO
DOMREP
DONALD
DONATE
DONDER
DONEES
DONEIN
DONETS
DONEUP
DONGLE
DONITZ
DONJON
DONKEY
DONNAS
DONNED
DONNEE
DONNER
DONORS
DONUTS
DOOBIE
DOODAD
DOODAH
DOODLE
DOOFUS
DOOGIE
DOOLEY
DOOMED
DOOWOP
DOOZIE
DOPANT
DOPIER
DOPING
DORADO
DORAGS
DORATI
DORCAS
DOREMI
DORIAN
DORIES
DORMER
DORRIT
DORSAL
DORSET
DORSEY
DORSUM
DOSAGE
DOSERS
DOSIDO
DOSING
DOSSAL
DOSSED
DOSSEL
DOSSER
DOSSES
DOTAGE
DOTARD
DOTELL
DOTEON
DOTHAN
DOTING
DOTTED
DOTTIE
DOTTLE
DOUALA
DOUBLE
DOUBLY
DOUBTS
DOUGHS
DOUGHY
DOURER
DOURLY
DOUSED
DOUSES
DOVEIN
DOVISH
DOWELS
DOWERS
DOWERY
DOWNED
DOWNER
DOWNEY
DOWNON
DOWSED
DOWSER
DOWSES
DOYENS
DOZENS
DOZERS
DOZIER
DOZILY
DOZING

D•O•••
DEODAR
DHOLES
DHOTEL
DHOTIS
DIODES
DIONEB
DIONNE
DIOXIN
DOOBIE
DOODAD
DOODAH
DOODLE
DOOFUS
DOOGIE
DOOLEY
DOOMED
DOOWOP
DOOZIE
DROGUE
DROIDS
DROITS
DROLLS
DROLLY
DROMOI
DROMOS
DRONED
DRONER
DRONES
DROOLS
DROOLY
DROOPS
DROOPY
DROPBY
DROPIN
DROPIT
DROVER
DROVES
DROWNS
DROWSE
DROWSY
DUOMOS
DVORAK

D••O••
DACOIT
DADOED
DADOES
DAKOTA
DAMONE
DAMORE
DAMOUR
DATONG
DAYONE
DEBONE
DECOCT
DECODE
DECORS
DECOYS
DEFOGS
DEFORM
DEHORN
DELONG
DEMOBS
DEMODE
DEMOND
DEMONS
DEMOTE
DENOTE
DENOVO
DEPONE
DEPORT
DEPOSE
DEPOTS
DESOTO
DETOUR
DEVOID
DEVOIR
DEVOTE
DEVOTO
DEVOUR
DEVOUT
DICOTS
DIEOFF
DIEOUT
DIGOUT
DIMOUT
DIPODY
DIPOLE
DISOWN
DIVOTS
DODODO
DODOES
DODOMA
DOGONS
DOGOOD
DOLORS
DOLOUR
DONORS
DRHOOK
DROOLS
DROOLY
DROOPS
DROOPY
DRYOFF
DRYOUT
DUBOIS
DUGONG
DUGOUT
DUMONT
DUPONT
DUROCS

D•••O•
DACRON
DAIKON
DAIMON
DALTON
DAMSON
DANSON
DANTON
DARROW
DAWNON
DAWSON
DAYBOY
DAYJOB
DAYTON
DEACON
DEADON
DEBTOR
DEIMOS
DEKKOS
DELEON
DELROY
DENTON
DEPLOY
DESPOT
DETROP
DIALOG
DIATOM
DIDION
DIGLOT
DILLON
DINEON
DISCOS
DITTOS
DMAJOR
DMINOR
DOBROS
DOBSON
DOCTOR
DOGDOM
DOGOOD
DOLLOP
DONJON
DOOWOP
DOTEON
DOWNON
DRAGON
DRAWON
DREWON
DRHOOK
DROMOI
DROMOS
DRYROT
DUNLOP
DUOMOS
DYELOT

D••••O
DACAPO
DADDYO
DAIMYO
DAMATO
DARETO
DAYGLO
DELANO
DELRIO
DENDRO
DENIRO
DENOVO
DESOTO
DEVITO
DEVOTO
DEXTRO
DIABLO
DINERO
DIRIGO
DIVINO
DODODO
DOMINO
DORADO
DOSIDO
DUELLO
DYNAMO

•DO•••
ADOBES
ADOLPH
ADONAI
ADONIS
ADOPTS
ADORED
ADOREE
ADORER
ADORES
ADORNS
IDOIDO
ODONTO
ODOURS

•D•O••
ADDONS
ADJOIN
ADROIT
ADSORB
CDROMS
EDDOES
EDKOCH
EDMOND
EDWOOD
IDIOCY
IDIOMS
IDIOTS
ODIOUS

•D••O•
ADDSON
EDISON
EDITOR
EDWOOD
ODDJOB
ODDLOT
ODDSON

•D•••O
ADAGIO
ADDSTO
ADRENO
EDITIO
IDOIDO

ODONTO
HYDROS
INDOOR
KUDROW
MADTOM
ODDJOB
ODDLOT
ODDSON
OLDBOY
RADIOS
REDDOG
REDFOX
REDHOT
REDSOX
REDTOP
RIDSOF
RODEOS
TYDBOL
VIDEOS

••DO••
ADDONS
ALDOSE
ALDOUS
ARDORS
ARDOUR
BODONI
CODONS
DADOED
DADOES
DODODO
DODOES
DODOMA
EDDOES
EIDOLA
ENDORA
ENDOWS
EUDORA
FEDORA
GODOWN
HIDOUT
INDOOR
INDORE
JUDOKA
KIDORY
LADOGA
LEDOFF
LEDOUT
MIDORI
MODOCS
NODOFF
NODOSE
OGDOAD
RADOME
REDOAK
REDOES
REDONE
RUDOLF
TUDORS
UNDOER
UNDOES
UNDONE
VADOSE
WIDOWS
XEDOUT
ZADORA

••D•O•
ADDSON
ANDHOW
ANDROS
AUDIOS
BADBOY
BADLOT
BIDSON
DIDION
GIDEON
GODSON
HADRON
HEDRON
HUDSON

••D••O
ADDSTO
DADDYO
DODODO
ENDURO
HIDEHO
INDIGO
LADINO
MADEDO
MADERO
MADURO
MEDICO
MODULO
OLDPRO
SIDERO
TODDAO
ZYDECO

•••DO•
ABYDOS
AMADOU
AMIDOL
AVEDON
BANDOG
BARDOT
CANDOR
CAWDOR
CHADOR
CONDOR
CONDOS
CORDON
CREDOS
DEADON
DOGDOM
EJIDOS
FANDOM
FEEDON
FELDON
FYODOR
GOODOH
GORDON
GUIDON
GUNDOG
HAGDON
HANDON
HEADON
HELDON
HOLDON
HOODOO
HOTDOG
ISADOR
KINDOF
LAIDON
LANDON
LAPDOG
LARDON
LEADON
LONDON
LYNDON
MCADOO
MEADOW
OXYDOL
PARDON
PYEDOG
RANDOM
REDDOG
RONDOS
SEADOG
SELDOM
SHADOW
SOLDON
SUNDOG
TENDON
TOLDOF
TOLDON
TONDOS
TOPDOG
TOYDOG
VENDOR
VERDON
VOODOO
WINDOM
WINDOW
WISDOM
ZENDOS

•••D•O
AMEDEO
CARDIO
DADDYO
DENDRO
GRODNO
HELDTO
HOLDTO
HOODOO
LAIDTO
LANDHO
LEADTO
MCADOO
STUDIO
TENDTO
TIEDTO
TODDAO
USEDTO
VOODOO

••••DO
AIKIDO
ALBEDO
BRANDO
DODODO
DORADO
DOSIDO
ESCUDO
HAIRDO
IDOIDO
JURADO
KOMODO
LAREDO
LIBIDO
MADEDO
MAKEDO
MENADO
MIKADO
OVERDO
OVIEDO
PSEUDO
RHABDO
SALADO
SPEEDO
TEREDO
TOLEDO
TUXEDO
WEIRDO

D•P•••
DAPHNE
DAPPED
DAPPER
DAPPLE
DEPART
DEPAUL
DEPAUW
DEPEND
DEPICT
DEPLOY
DEPONE
DEPORT
DEPOSE
DEPOTS
DEPTHS
DEPUTE
DEPUTY
DIPODY
DIPOLE
DIPPED
DIPPER
DOPANT
DOPIER
DOPING
DUPERY
DUPING
DUPLEX
DUPONT

D••P••
DAMPED
DAMPEN
DAMPER
DAMPLY
DAPPED
DAPPER
DAPPLE
DEEPAK
DEEPEN
DEEPER
DEEPLY
DELPHI
DESPOT
DIAPER
DIEPPE
DIMPLE
DIMPLY
DIPPED
DIPPER
DISPEL
DRAPED
DRAPER
DRAPES
DRIPPY
DROPBY
DROPIN
DROPIT
DRUPES
DUMPED
DUMPER

D•••P•
DACAPO
DIEPPE
DRIPPY
DROOPS
DROOPY

D••••P
DAMSUP
DECAMP
DETROP
DEWLAP
DIALUP
DIGSUP
DOESUP
DOLLOP
DOLLUP
DOMREP
DONEUP
DOOWOP
DRAWUP
DREWUP
DRUMUP
DSHARP
DUNLOP
DUSTUP

•D•P••
ADAPTS
ADEPTS
ADOPTS

•D••P•
ADOLPH

•D•••P
ADDSUP

••DP••
MUDPIE
OLDPRO

••D••P
ADDSUP
BIDSUP
ENDSUP
KIDNAP
MADCAP
MADEUP
REDCAP
REDTOP
TIDYUP
WADSUP

•••D•P
BEADUP
BINDUP
FOLDUP
HANDUP
HARDUP
HEADUP
HELDUP
HOLDUP
ICEDUP
LAIDUP
LEADUP
PAIDUP
SENDUP
SPEDUP
TEEDUP
TIEDUP
USEDUP
WINDUP

•••D•Q
NASDAQ

DR••••
DRABLY
DRACHM
DRAFTS
DRAFTY
DRAGEE
DRAGGY
DRAGIN
DRAGON
DRAILS
DRAINS
DRAKES
DRAMAS
DRAPED
DRAPER
DRAPES
DRAWER
DRAWIN
DRAWLS
DRAWLY
DRAWON
DRAWUP
DRAYED
DREADS
DREAMS
DREAMT
DREAMY
DREARY
DREDGE
DRENCH
DRESSY
DREWIN
DREWON
DREWUP
DREXEL
DRHOOK
DRIERS
DRIEST
DRIFTS
DRIFTY
DRILLS
DRINGS
DRINKS
DRIPPY
DRIVEL
DRIVEN
DRIVER
DRIVES
DROGUE
DROIDS
DROITS
DROLLS
DROLLY
DROMOI
DROMOS
DRONED
DRONER
DRONES
DROOLS
DROOLY
DROOPS
DROOPY
DROPBY
DROPIN
DROPIT
DROVER
DROVES
DROWNS
DROWSE
DROWSY
DRUDGE
DRUIDS
DRUMUP
DRUPES
DRUZES
DRYADS
DRYDEN
DRYERS
DRYEST
DRYFLY
DRYICE
DRYING
DRYINK
DRYOFF
DRYOUT
DRYROT
DRYRUN

D•R•••
DARENT
DARETO
DARIEN
DARING
DARIUS
DARKEN
DARKER
DARKLE
DARKLY
DARNAY
DARNED
DARNEL
DARNER
DARNIT
DARREN
DARROW
DARRYL
DARTED
DARTER
DARWIN
DERAIL
DERIDE
DERIVE
DERMAL
DERMIS
DERRIS
DIRECT
DIRELY
DIREST
DIRGES
DIRHAM
DIRIGE
DIRIGO
DIRNDL
DORADO
DORAGS
DORATI
DORCAS
DOREMI
DORIAN
DORIES
DORMER
DORRIT
DORSAL
DORSET
DORSEY
DORSUM
DURANT
DURBAN
DURBAR
DURBIN
DURESS
DURFEY
DURHAM
DURIAN
DURING
DURNED
DUROCS
DURYEA

D••R••
DACRON
DAIREN
DARREN
DARROW
DARRYL
DEARER
DEARIE
DEARLY
DEARME
DEARTH
DEBRAS
DEBRIS
DECREE
DEFRAY
DEGREE
DELRAY
DELRIO
DELROY
DERRIS
DETROP
DHARMA
DIGRAM
DJERBA
DMARKS
DOBRAS
DOBROS
DOMREP
DORRIT
DOURER
DOURLY
DRYROT
DRYRUN
DUARTE
DVORAK
DWARFS

D•••R•
DAMORE
DATARY
DATERS
DATURA
DEBARK
DEBARS
DECORS
DEFERS
DEFORM
DEHORN
DEIDRE
DEJURE
DEMURE
DEMURS
DENARY
DENDRI
DENDRO
DENIRO
DEPART
DEPORT
DESCRY
DESERT
DESIRE
DESTRY
DETERS
DEXTRO
DICERS
DINARS
DINERO
DINERS
DISARM
DIVERS
DIVERT
DIYERS
DMITRI
DOLORS
DONORS
DOSERS
DOTARD
DOWERS
DOWERY
DOZERS
DREARY
DRIERS
DRYERS
DSHARP
DUNERA
DUPERY

D••••R
DAFTER
DAGGER
DAGMAR
DAMMAR
DAMOUR
DAMPER
DANCER
DANDER
DANGER
DANKER
DANNER
DAPPER
DARKER
DARNER
DARTER
DASHER
DAUBER
DEADER
DEAFER
DEALER
DEARER
DEBTOR
DECKER
DEEPER
DEFTER
DEICER
DELMAR
DELVER
DENIER
DENSER
DENVER
DEODAR
DETOUR
DEVOIR
DEVOUR
DEWIER

DEXTER
DIALER
DIAPER
DICIER
DICKER
DIETER
DIFFER
DIGGER
DILLER
DIMMER
DINNER
DIPPER
DISBAR
DITHER
DLAYER
DMAJOR
DMINOR
DOBBER
DOCKER
DOCTOR
DODDER
DODGER
DOGEAR
DOGGER
DOLLAR
DOLOUR
DONDER
DONNER
DOPIER
DORMER
DOSSER
DOURER
DOWNER
DOWSER
DOZIER
DRAPER
DRAWER
DRIVER
DRONER
DROVER
DUELER
DUFFER
DUIKER
DULLER
DUMBER
DUMPER
DUNBAR
DUNKER
DURBAR
DUSTER

•DR•••
ADRENO
ADRIAN
ADRIEN
ADRIFT
ADROIT
CDROMS

•D•R••
ADORED
ADOREE
ADORER
ADORES
ADORNS
EDERLE

•D••R•
ADDERS
ADHERE
ADJURE
ADMIRE
ADSORB
ADVERB
ADVERT
EDBERG
EDGARD
EDGARS
EDGERS
EDUARD
EDVARD
EDWARD
IDCARD
IDLERS
ODOURS
UDDERS

•D•••R
ADORER
EDGIER
EDITOR

••DR••
ALDRIN
ANDREA
ANDREI
ANDRES
ANDREW
ANDREY
ANDROS
AUDREY
CADRES
CEDRIC
ENDRUN
ESDRAS
GUDRUN
HADRON
HEDREN
HEDRON
HYDRAE
HYDRAS
HYDROS
INDRIS
KUDROW
MADRAS
MADRES
MADRID
MIDRIB
MUDRAS
PADRES
REDRAW
REDREW
SUDRAS
UNDRAW

••D•R•
ADDERS
AIDERS
ALDERS
ARDORS
CEDARS
CIDERS
CODERS
CYDERS
EIDERS
ELDERS
ENDERS
ENDORA
ENDURE
ENDURO
EUDORA
FEDORA
GODARD
HIDERS
INDIRA
INDORE
KIDORY
LADERS
MADERO
MADURA
MADURO
MIDORI
MODERN
NADIRS
OLDPRO
ORDERS
ORDURE
RIDERS
SEDERS
SIDERO
SIDERS
TUDORS
UDDERS
VIDERI
WADERS
ZADORA

••D••R
ARDOUR
BADDER
BADGER
BIDDER
CADGER
CODGER
DODDER
DODGER
ENDEAR
FODDER
GADDER
HEDGER
INDOOR
JUDDER
KIDDER
LADDER
LADLER
LEDGER
LODGER
MADDER
MEDGAR
MEDLAR
MIDAIR
MIDLER
MUDDER
NUDGER
PADDER
PEDLAR
RADNER
REDDER
REDFIR
RUDDER
SADDER
SIDDUR
TEDDER
TIDIER
UNDOER
VEDDER
ZEDBAR

•••DR•
AIRDRY
DEIDRE
DENDRI
DENDRO
EXEDRA
LANDRY
PHEDRE
QUADRI
RANDRY
RUNDRY
SANDRA
SUNDRY
TAWDRY
TUNDRA

•••D•R
AGADIR
BADDER
BALDER
BENDER
BIDDER
BINDER
BIRDER
BLADER
BOLDER
BORDER
BRUDER
CALDER
CANDOR
CARDER
CAWDOR
CHADOR
CHIDER
CINDER
COLDER
CONDOR
COODER
CRUDER
DANDER
DEADER
DEODAR
DODDER
DONDER
ELUDER
EVADER
FEEDER
FENDER
FINDER
FODDER
FOLDER
FONDER
FYODOR
GADDER
GANDER
GENDER
GILDER
GIRDER
GLIDER
GRADER
HARDER
HEADER
HEEDER
HERDER
HINDER
HOLDER
ISADOR
JUDDER
KANDER
KIDDER
KINDER
LADDER
LANDER
LARDER
LAUDER
LEADER
LENDER
LEWDER
LIEDER
LOADER
LOUDER
MADDER
MENDER
MILDER
MINDER
MOLDER
MUDDER
MURDER
PADDER
PANDER
PINDAR
POLDER
PONDER
POWDER
RAIDER
READER
REDDER
RENDER
RUDDER
SADDER
SANDER
SEEDER
SENDER
SIDDUR
SIRDAR
SLIDER
SNIDER
SNYDER
SOLDER
SPADER
SPIDER
SUNDER
TEDDER
TENDER
TINDER
TRADER
VEDDER
VENDOR
WANDER
WARDER
WEEDER
WELDER
WILDER
WINDER
WONDER
YONDER
ZANDER
ZUIDER

••••DR
ANHYDR
RATEDR

DS••••
DSHARP

D•S•••
DASHED
DASHER
DASHES
DASHIS
DASSIN
DESALT
DESCRY
DESERT
DESICA
DESIGN
DESILU
DESIRE
DESIST
DESMAN
DESOTO
DESPOT
DESTRY
DISANT
DISARM
DISBAR
DISCOS
DISCUS
DISHED
DISHES
DISKED
DISMAL
DISMAY
DISMES
DISNEY
DISOWN
DISPEL
DISSED
DISTAL
DISTIL
DISUSE
DOSAGE
DOSERS
DOSIDO
DOSING
DOSSAL
DOSSED
DOSSEL
DOSSER
DOSSES
DUSTED
DUSTER
DUSTIN
DUSTUP

D••S••
DAISES
DAMSEL
DAMSON
DAMSUP
DANSON
DASSIN
DATSUN
DAWSON
DEASIL
DEISTS
DENSER
DIESEL
DIESES
DIESIS
DIGSIN
DIGSUP
DILSEY
DIMSUM
DISSED
DOBSON
DOESBY
DOESIN
DOESNT
DOESUP
DOGSAT
DOGSIT
DORSAL
DORSET
DORSEY
DORSUM
DOSSAL
DOSSED
DOSSEL
DOSSER
DOSSES
DOUSED
DOUSES
DOWSED
DOWSER
DOWSES
DRESSY

D•••S•
DALASI
DAMASK
DANISH
DEBASE
DEFUSE
DEGUST
DELIST
DEMISE
DENISE
DEPOSE
DESIST
DETEST
DEVEST
DEVISE
DIGEST
DIREST
DISUSE
DIVEST
DOVISH
DRESSY
DRIEST
DROWSE
DROWSY
DRYEST
DUDISH
DURESS
DYNAST

D••••S
DACHAS
DADOES
DAISES
DALLAS
DALLES
DANAUS
DANCES
DANTES
DARIUS
DASHES
DASHIS
DATERS
DAUBES
DAUNTS
DAVIES
DAVITS
DEBARS
DEBITS
DEBRAS
DEBRIS
DEBUGS
DEBUTS
DECAFS
DECALS
DECAYS
DECORS
DECOYS
DEFATS
DEFERS
DEFIES
DEFOGS
DEICES
DEIGNS
DEIMOS
DEISTS
DEKKOS
DELAYS
DELFTS
DELIUS
DELTAS
DELVES
DEMIES
DEMITS
DEMOBS
DEMONS
DEMURS
DENIES
DENIMS
DENNIS
DEPOTS
DEPTHS
DERMIS
DERRIS
DETERS
DEUCES
DEVILS
DHOLES
DHOTIS
DICERS
DICOTS
DICTUS
DIDIES
DIESES
DIESIS
DIGITS
DINARS
DINERS
DINGUS
DIODES
DIRGES
DISCOS
DISCUS
DISHES
DISMES
DITTOS
DITZES
DIVANS
DIVERS
DIVOTS
DIXITS
DIYERS
DIZENS
DMARKS
DMINUS
DOBLAS
DOBRAS
DOBROS
DODGES
DODOES
DOGEYS
DOGIES
DOGMAS
DOGONS
DOINGS
DOLMAS
DOLORS
DONEES
DONETS
DONNAS
DONORS
DONUTS
DOOFUS
DORAGS
DORCAS
DORIES
DOSERS
DOSSES
DOUBTS
DOUGHS
DOUSES
DOWELS
DOWERS
DOWSES
DOYENS
DOZENS
DOZERS
DRAFTS
DRAILS
DRAINS
DRAKES
DRAMAS
DRAPES
DRAWLS
DREADS
DREAMS
DRIERS
DRIFTS
DRILLS
DRINGS
DRINKS
DRIVES
DROIDS
DROITS
DROLLS
DROMOS
DRONES
DROOLS
DROOPS
DROVES
DROWNS
DRUIDS
DRUPES
DRUZES
DRYADS
DRYERS
DUBOIS
DUCATS
DULLES
DUNCES
DUOMOS
DURESS
DUROCS
DUTIES
DUVETS
DWARFS
DWEEBS
DWELLS

•DS•••
ADSORB
EDSELS

•D•S••

ADDSIN
ADDSON
ADDSTO
ADDSUP
ADESTE
EDESSA
EDISON
ODDSON
ODESSA
ODISTS

•D••S•

ADJUST
ADMASS
ADVISE
EDESSA
GDANSK
IDLEST
ODDEST
ODENSE
ODESSA

•D•••S

ADAGES
ADAPTS
ADDAMS
ADDERS
ADDLES
ADDONS
ADEEMS
ADEPTS
ADIDAS
ADIEUS
ADLIBS
ADMASS
ADMITS
ADOBES
ADONIS
ADOPTS
ADORES
ADORNS
ADULTS
CDROMS
EDAMES
EDDIES
EDDOES
EDGARS
EDGERS
EDICTS
EDILES
EDSELS
EDUCES
IDEALS
IDIOMS
IDIOTS
IDLERS
IDTAGS
IDYLLS
ODIOUS
ODISTS
ODIUMS
ODOURS
UDDERS

••DS••

ADDSIN
ADDSON
ADDSTO
ADDSUP
BIDSIN
BIDSON
BIDSUP
ENDSUP
GODSON
HUDSON
MADSEN
ODDSON
OLDSAW
REDSEA
REDSOX
RIDSOF
SUDSED
SUDSES
WADSUP

••D•S•

ALDOSE
DUDISH
ELDEST
EMDASH
ENDASH
ENDUSE
IODISE
JADISH
MEDUSA
MODEST
MODISH
NODOSE
NUDEST
NUDIST
ODDEST
OLDEST
OLDISH
RADISH
RUDEST
VADOSE
WIDEST
WIDISH

••D••S

ADDAMS
ADDERS
ADDLES
ADDONS
AIDERS
ALDERS
ALDOUS
ANDRES
ANDROS
AODAIS
ARDEBS
ARDORS
ASDICS
AUDENS
AUDIOS
AUDITS
BADGES
BEDEWS
BEDIMS
BODIES
BUDGES
CADDIS
CADETS
CADGES
CADMUS
CADRES
CEDARS
CIDERS
CODERS
CODONS
CYDERS
DADOES
DIDIES
DODGES
DODOES
EDDIES
EDDOES
EIDERS
ELDERS
ENDERS
ENDOWS
ENDUES
ESDRAS
FUDGES
GODETS
HADJES
HADJIS
HEDGES
HIDERS
HODADS
HODGES
HYDRAS
HYDROS
INDIES
INDRIS
JUDGES
KEDGES
KUDZUS
LADERS
LADIES
LADLES
LEDGES
LODENS
LODGES
LUDENS
MADAMS
MADRAS
MADRES
MEDALS
MEDIAS
MEDICS
MIDGES
MODELS
MODEMS
MODOCS
MUDRAS
NADIRS
NUDGES
OLDIES
OODLES
ORDERS
PADRES
PEDALS
RADIOS
RADIUS
REDOES
REDUBS
REDYES
RIDERS
RIDGES
RODEOS
SADHES
SADHUS
SEDANS
SEDERS
SEDGES
SEDUMS
SIDERS
SIDLES
SUDRAS
SUDSES
TIDIES
TUDORS
UDDERS
UNDIES
UNDOES
VIDEOS
VODKAS
WADERS
WEDGES
WIDENS
WIDOWS
WIDTHS
WODGES
YODELS

•••DS•

AMIDST
WOODSY

•••D•S

ABIDES
ABODES
ABYDOS
ADIDAS
AMADIS
AMIDES
ANODES
ASIDES
ATODDS
AZIDES
BLADES
BRIDES
BSIDES
CADDIS
CHIDES
CNIDUS
CONDOS
CREDOS
DIODES
EJIDOS
ELIDES
ELUDES
EPODES
ERODES
ETUDES
EVADES
EXODUS
EXUDES
GEODES
GLADES
GLADYS
GLIDES
GRADES
GRADUS
GUIDES
HAIDAS
HINDUS
HORDES
HYADES
IRIDES
LANDIS
MAHDIS
MAIDUS
MENDES
OXIDES
PANDAS
PINDUS
PRIDES
PRUDES
RHODES
RONDOS
SARDIS
SAUDIS
SHADES
SLIDES
SONDES
SPADES
SUEDES
SWEDES
TILDES
TONDOS
TRADES
VELDTS
ZENDOS

••••DS

ALKYDS
AMENDS
APHIDS
AROIDS
ATODDS
AVOIDS
AWARDS
BEARDS
BIPEDS
BIPODS
BLEEDS
BLENDS
BLINDS
BLONDS
BOARDS
BOUNDS
BOVIDS
BRAIDS
BRANDS
BREADS
BREEDS
BROADS
BROODS
BUILDS
CANIDS
CHILDS
CHORDS
CLOUDS
CREEDS
CROWDS
CUPIDS
CYCADS
DREADS
DROIDS
DRUIDS
DRYADS
EBONDS
ELANDS
EMBEDS
EMENDS
EPHODS
FARADS
FIELDS
FIENDS
FIORDS
FJELDS
FJORDS
FLOODS
FLUIDS
FOUNDS
FRAUDS
FRONDS
GLANDS
GOURDS
GRANDS
GRINDS
GUARDS
GUILDS
HEXADS
HOARDS
HODADS
HOUNDS
JIHADS
KNEADS
LAIRDS
LAMEDS
LIPIDS
LLOYDS
MONADS
MOPEDS
MOULDS
MOUNDS
NAIADS
NOMADS
OCTADS
OREADS
OVOIDS
PLAIDS
PLEADS
POUNDS
PSEUDS
RANIDS
RAPIDS
REBIDS
REPADS
RESODS
REWEDS
ROUNDS
SALADS
SARODS
SCALDS
SCENDS
SCOLDS
SCRODS
SHARDS
SHREDS
SKALDS
SNOODS
SOLIDS
SOUNDS
SPEEDS
SPENDS
SQUADS
SQUIDS
STANDS
STEADS
STEEDS
STRADS
SWARDS
SWORDS
SYNODS
TBIRDS
TBONDS
THIRDS
TREADS
TRENDS
TRIADS
TWEEDS
UPENDS
URSIDS
VIANDS
WIELDS
WORLDS
WOUNDS
YIELDS
ZOOIDS
ZOUNDS

D•T•••

DATARY
DATERS
DATING
DATIVE
DATONG
DATSUN
DATURA
DETACH
DETAIL
DETAIN
DETECT
DETENT
DETERS
DETEST
DETOUR
DETROP
DITHER
DITTOS
DITZES
DOTAGE
DOTARD
DOTELL
DOTEON
DOTHAN
DOTING
DOTTED
DOTTIE
DOTTLE
DUTIES

D••T••

DACTYL
DAFTER
DAFTLY
DALTON
DANTES
DANTON
DARTED
DARTER
DAYTON
DEBTOR
DEFTER
DEFTLY
DELTAS
DELTIC
DENTAL
DENTED
DENTIL
DENTIN
DENTON
DEPTHS
DESTRY
DEXTER
DEXTRO
DHOTEL
DHOTIS
DIATOM
DICTUM
DICTUS
DIETED
DIETER
DIKTAT
DINTED
DISTAL
DISTIL
DITTOS
DMITRI
DOCTOR
DOGTAG
DOTTED
DOTTIE
DOTTLE
DUCTAL
DUSTED
DUSTER
DUSTIN
DUSTUP

D•••T•

DAINTY
DAKOTA
DALETH
DAMATO
DAMITA
DARETO
DAUNTS
DAVITS
DEARTH
DEBATE
DEBITS
DEBUTS
DEFATS
DEISTS
DELATE
DELETE
DELFTS
DEMITS
DEMOTE
DENOTE
DEPOTS
DEPUTE
DEPUTY
DESOTO
DEVITO
DEVOTE
DEVOTO
DEWITT
DICOTS
DIGITS
DILATE
DILUTE
DIMITY
DIVOTS
DIXITS
DONATE
DONETS
DONITZ
DONUTS
DORATI
DOUBTS
DRAFTS
DRAFTY
DRIFTS
DRIFTY
DROITS
DUARTE
DUCATS
DULUTH
DUVETS

D••••T

DACOIT
DARENT
DARNIT
DAYLIT
DECANT
DECEIT
DECENT
DECOCT
DEDUCT
DEFEAT
DEFECT
DEGUST
DEJECT
DELICT
DELIST
DEPART
DEPICT
DEPORT
DESALT
DESERT
DESIST
DESPOT
DETECT
DETENT
DETEST
DEVEST
DEVOUT
DEWITT
DIDACT
DIEOUT
DIGEST
DIGLOT
DIGOUT
DIKTAT
DIMOUT
DIMWIT
DIRECT
DIREST
DISANT
DIVERT
DIVEST
DOCENT
DOCKET
DOESNT
DOGSAT
DOGSIT
DOPANT
DORRIT
DORSET
DREAMT
DRIEST
DROPIT
DRYEST
DRYOUT
DRYROT
DUGOUT
DULCET
DUMONT
DUNANT
DUPONT
DURANT
DWIGHT
DYELOT
DYNAST

•DT•••

IDTAGS

•D•T••

ADYTUM
EDITED
EDITIO
EDITOR

ODETTA
ODETTE

•D••T•
ADAPTS
ADDSTO
ADEPTS
ADESTE
ADMITS
ADNATE
ADOPTS
ADULTS
EDICTS
IDEATE
IDIOTS
ODDITY
ODETTA
ODETTE
ODISTS
ODONTO

•D•••T
ADDUCT
ADJUST
ADRIFT
ADROIT
ADVENT
ADVERT
IDLEST
ODDEST
ODDLOT

••DT••
MADTOM
REDTAG
REDTOP
WIDTHS

••D•T•
ADDSTO
AUDITS
CADETS
GODETS
INDITE
IODATE
JUDITH
NUDITY
ODDITY
PEDATE
REDATE
SEDATE
TODATE
UPDATE

••D••T
ABDUCT
ADDUCT
ARDENT
BADLOT
BUDGET
CADENT
CEDANT
DEDUCT
DIDACT
ELDEST
FIDGET
GADGET
GIDGET
GODWIT
HIDOUT
INDEBT
INDENT
INDICT
INDUCT
LEDOUT
MADEIT
MEDLAT
MIDGET
MODELT
MODEST
MUDCAT
NUDEST
NUDIST
ODDEST
ODDLOT
OLDEST
OLDHAT
PEDANT
REDACT
REDANT
REDHAT
REDHOT
RIDENT
RODENT
RUDEST
TIDBIT
WIDEST
WIDGET
XEDOUT

•••DT•
HELDTO
HOLDTO
LAIDTO
LEADTO
TENDTO
TIEDTO
USEDTO
VELDTS

•••D•T
AMIDST
BANDIT
BARDOT
COEDIT
CREDIT
HOLDIT
NEEDNT
PANDIT
PUNDIT
REEDIT

••••DT
ARENDT
BRANDT

DU••••
DUALLY
DUARTE
DUBBED
DUBBIN
DUBCEK
DUBLIN
DUBOIS
DUCATS
DUCHIN
DUCKED
DUCTAL
DUDEEN
DUDISH
DUDLEY
DUELED
DUELER
DUELLO
DUENNA
DUFFEL
DUFFER
DUGONG
DUGOUT
DUIKER
DUKING
DULCET
DULLEA
DULLED
DULLER
DULLES
DULUTH
DUMBER
DUMBLY
DUMDUM
DUMONT
DUMPED
DUMPER
DUNANT
DUNBAR
DUNCAN
DUNCES
DUNDEE
DUNERA
DUNHAM
DUNKED
DUNKER
DUNLIN
DUNLOP
DUNNED
DUOMOS
DUPERY
DUPING
DUPLEX
DUPONT
DURANT
DURBAN
DURBAR
DURBIN
DURESS
DURFEY
DURHAM
DURIAN
DURING
DURNED
DUROCS
DURYEA
DUSTED
DUSTER
DUSTIN
DUSTUP
DUTIES
DUVALL
DUVETS

D•U•••
DAUBED
DAUBER
DAUBES
DAUNTS
DEUCED
DEUCES
DOUALA
DOUBLE
DOUBLY
DOUBTS
DOUGHS
DOUGHY
DOURER
DOURLY
DOUSED
DOUSES
DRUDGE
DRUIDS
DRUMUP
DRUPES
DRUZES

D••U••
DANUBE
DATURA
DEBUGS
DEBUNK
DEBUTS
DEDUCE
DEDUCT
DEFUSE
DEGUST
DEJURE
DELUDE
DELUGE
DELUXE
DEMURE
DEMURS
DENUDE
DEPUTE
DEPUTY
DILUTE
DISUSE
DONUTS
DULUTH

D•••U•
DAMOUR
DAMSUP
DANAUS
DARIUS
DATSUN
DELIUS
DENGUE
DEPAUL
DEPAUW
DETOUR
DEVOUR
DEVOUT
DIALUP
DICTUM
DICTUS
DIEOUT
DIGOUT
DIGSUP
DIMOUT
DIMSUM
DINGUS
DISCUS
DMINUS
DOESUP
DOLLUP
DOLOUR
DONEUP
DOOFUS
DORSUM
DRAWUP
DREWUP
DROGUE
DRUMUP
DRYOUT
DRYRUN
DUGOUT
DUMDUM
DUSTUP
DYBBUK

D••••U
DEJAVU
DESILU

•DU•••
ADULTS
EDUARD
EDUCED
EDUCES

•D•U••
ADDUCE
ADDUCT
ADJURE
ADJUST
ADZUKI
EDMUND
ODIUMS
ODOURS

•D••U•
ADDSUP
ADIEUS
ADIEUX
ADYTUM
ODIOUS

••DU••
ABDUCT
ADDUCE
ADDUCT
DEDUCE
DEDUCT
ENDUED
ENDUES
ENDURE
ENDURO
ENDUSE
INDUCE
INDUCT
MADURA
MADURO
MEDUSA
MODULE
MODULO
NODULE
ORDURE
PADUAN
PODUNK
RADULA
REDUBS
REDUCE
SEDUCE
SEDUMS
UNDULY

••D•U•
ADDSUP
AIDFUL
ALDOUS
ARDOUR
BADGUY
BEDAUB
BEDBUG
BIDSUP
CADMUS
ENDRUN
ENDSUP
GUDRUN
HIDOUT
INDIUM
KUDZUS
LEDOUT
LUDLUM
MADEUP
MEDIUM
PODIUM
RADIUM
RADIUS
REDBUD
REDGUM
SADHUS
SIDDUR
SODIUM
TEDEUM
TEDIUM
TIDYUP
WADSUP
XEDOUT

•••DU•
BEADUP
BINDUP
CNIDUS
DUMDUM
EXODUS
FOLDUP
FONDUE
GRADUS
HANDUP
HARDUP
HEADUP
HELDUP
HINDUS
HOLDUP
ICEDUP
LAIDUP
LEADUP
MAIDUS
MARDUK
PAIDUP
PERDUE
PINDUS
PURDUE
SENDUP
SIDDUR
SPEDUP
SUBDUE
TEEDUP
TIEDUP
USEDUP
VERDUN
WINDUP

•••D•U
AMADOU
LANDAU
MOLDAU

••••DU
MBUNDU
TELEDU
XANADU

DV••••
DVORAK

D•V•••
DAVIES
DAVITS
DEVEIN
DEVEST
DEVICE
DEVILS
DEVINE
DEVISE
DEVITO
DEVOID
DEVOIR
DEVOTE
DEVOTO
DEVOUR
DEVOUT
DIVANS
DIVEIN
DIVERS
DIVERT
DIVEST
DIVIDE
DIVINE
DIVING
DIVINO
DIVOTS
DOVEIN
DOVISH
DUVALL
DUVETS

D••V••
DELVED
DELVER
DELVES
DENVER
DRIVEL
DRIVEN
DRIVER
DRIVES
DROVER
DROVES

D•••V•
DATIVE
DEJAVU
DENOVO
DERIVE

•DV•••
ADVENT
ADVERB
ADVERT
ADVICE
ADVISE
EDVARD

••DV••
KIDVID
OLDVIC

••D•V•
ENDIVE
GODIVA

DW••••
DWARFS
DWAYNE
DWEEBS
DWELLS
DWIGHT

D•W•••
DAWDLE
DAWNED
DAWNON
DAWSON
DEWIER
DEWILY
DEWING
DEWITT
DEWLAP
DOWELS
DOWERS
DOWERY
DOWNED
DOWNER
DOWNEY
DOWNON
DOWSED
DOWSER
DOWSES

D••W••
DARWIN
DIMWIT
DOOWOP
DRAWER
DRAWIN
DRAWLS
DRAWLY
DRAWON
DRAWUP
DREWIN
DREWON
DREWUP
DROWNS
DROWSE
DROWSY

D•••W•
DISOWN

D••••W
DARROW
DEPAUW

•DW•••
ADWEEK
EDWARD
EDWOOD
EDWYNN

••DW••
GODWIN
GODWIT
LUDWIG
MIDWAY
PEDWAY

••D•W•
BEDEWS
ENDOWS
GODOWN
WIDOWS

••D••W
ANDHOW
ANDREW
KUDROW
OLDSAW
REDRAW
REDREW
UNDRAW

•••D•W
MEADOW
MILDEW
SHADOW
SUNDEW
WINDOW

D•X•••
DEXTER
DEXTRO
DIXITS

D••X••
DIOXIN
DREXEL

D•••X•
DELUXE

D••••X
DUPLEX

•D••X•
ADNEXA

•D•••X
ADIEUX

••D••X
MADMAX
REDFOX
REDSOX

•••D•X
BENDIX
CAUDEX
SPADIX
WINDEX

••••DX
BRANDX
RATEDX

DY••••
DYADIC
DYBBUK
DYEING
DYELOT
DYNAMO
DYNAST

D•Y•••
DAYBED
DAYBOY
DAYGLO
DAYJOB
DAYLIT
DAYONE
DAYTON
DIYERS

DOYENS
DRYADS
DRYDEN
DRYERS
DRYEST
DRYFLY
DRYICE
DRYING
DRYINK
DRYOFF
DRYOUT
DRYROT
DRYRUN

D••Y••
DLAYER
DRAYED
DURYEA
DWAYNE

D•••Y•
DACTYL
DADDYO
DAIMYO
DARRYL
DECAYS
DECOYS
DELAYS
DOGEYS

D••••Y
DABNEY
DAFTLY
DAILEY
DAINTY
DAMPLY
DANGLY
DANKLY
DANNAY
DARKLY
DARNAY
DATARY
DAYBOY
DEADLY
DEAFLY
DEARLY
DEEJAY
DEEPLY
DEFRAY
DEFTLY
DELANY
DELRAY
DELROY
DENARY
DEPLOY
DEPUTY
DESCRY
DESTRY
DEWILY
DICKEY
DIDDLY
DILSEY
DIMITY
DIMPLY
DINGHY
DINKEY
DIPODY
DIRELY
DISMAY
DISNEY
DOESBY
DOGDAY
DONKEY
DOOLEY
DORSEY
DOUBLY
DOUGHY
DOURLY
DOWERY
DOWNEY
DOZILY
DRABLY
DRAFTY
DRAGGY
DRAWLY
DREAMY
DREARY
DRESSY
DRIFTY
DRIPPY
DROLLY
DROOLY
DROOPY
DROPBY
DROWSY
DRYFLY
DUALLY
DUDLEY
DUMBLY
DUPERY
DURFEY

•DY•••
ADYTUM
IDYLLS

•D•Y••
EDWYNN

•D•••Y
EDGILY
IDIOCY
ODDITY

••DY••
REDYED
REDYES
TIDYUP
UNDYED

••D•Y•
DADDYO
REDEYE

••D••Y
ANDREY
AUDREY
BADBOY
BADGUY
BODILY
CODIFY
CUDDLY
DIDDLY
DUDLEY
GADFLY
KIDNEY
KIDORY
KODALY
MEDFLY
MEDLEY
MIDDAY
MIDWAY
MODIFY
NIDIFY
NUDELY
NUDITY
ODDITY
OLDBOY
PEDWAY
PUDDLY
REDBAY
REDENY
RIDLEY
RODNEY
RUDELY
SIDNEY
SYDNEY
TEDKEY
TIDDLY
TIDILY
UNDULY
WADDLY
WIDELY

•••DY•
AZODYE
DADDYO
GLADYS
TIEDYE

•••D•Y
ACIDLY
AIRDRY
ALLDAY
ANYDAY
ARIDLY
AVIDLY
AWEDLY
BALDLY
BENDAY
BOLDLY
CLODDY
COLDLY
CORDAY
CRUDDY
CUDDLY
DEADLY
DIDDLY
DOGDAY
FLEDGY
FONDLY
FREDDY
FRIDAY
GLADLY
GOODBY
GOODLY
HARDBY
HARDLY
HEYDAY
KINDLY
LAIDBY
LANDRY
LEWDLY
LORDLY
LOUDLY
MANDAY
MAYDAY
MIDDAY
MILDLY
MONDAY
OFFDAY
ONEDAY
PAYDAY
PUDDLY
RANDRY
RUNDRY
SHODDY
SKIDDY
SLUDGY
SMUDGY
STODGY
SUNDAY
SUNDRY
TAGDAY
TAWDRY
TIDDLY
WADDLY
WILDLY
WOODSY

••••DY
BLOODY
BRANDY
BROODY
CLODDY
CLOUDY
COMEDY
CRUDDY
DIPODY
EMBODY
FRAIDY
FREDDY
GREEDY
GRUNDY
HOUNDY
MALADY
MAUNDY
MELODY
MILADY
MONODY
MOULDY
NOBODY
PARODY
REMEDY
SHANDY
SHEEDY
SHINDY
SHODDY
SKIDDY
SPEEDY
STEADY
STURDY
TRENDY
TWEEDY
UNTIDY
WEIRDY

D•Z•••
DAZING
DAZZLE
DIZENS
DOZENS
DOZERS
DOZIER
DOZILY
DOZING

D••Z••
DANZIG
DAZZLE
DENZEL
DITZES
DOOZIE
DRUZES

D••••Z
DOLENZ
DONITZ

•DZ•••
ADZUKI

••DZ••
KUDZUS

••D•Z•
BEDAZE
IODIZE

•••D•Z
VALDEZ

EA••••
EAGLED
EAGLES
EAGLET
EAGRES
EALING
EARFUL
EARING
EARLAP
EARNED
EARNER
EARTHA
EARTHY
EARWAX
EARWIG
EASEIN
EASELS
EASEUP
EASIER
EASILY
EASING
EASTER
EASTON
EATERS
EATERY
EATING
EATOUT
EATSAT
EATSIN
EATSUP

E•A•••
ECARTE
EDAMES
ELAINE
ELANDS
ELAPID
ELAPSE
ELATED
ELATER
ELATES
ELAYER
ELAYNE
EMAILS
EMAJOR
ENABLE
ENACTS
ENAMEL
ENAMOR
ENATES
EPARCH
ERASED
ERASER
ERASES
ETALIA
ETALII
ETAPES
EVADED
EVADER
EVADES
EXACTA
EXACTO
EXACTS
EXALTS
EXARCH

E••A••
EBOATS
ECLAIR
ECLATS
EDGARD
EDGARS
EDUARD
EDVARD
EDWARD
EFFACE
EFLATS
ELPASO
EMBANK
EMBARK
EMBAYS
EMDASH
ENCAGE
ENCAMP
ENCASE
ENDALL
ENDASH
ENFANT
ENGAGE
ENHALO
ENLACE
ENRAGE
ENRAPT
ENTAIL
EPHAHS
EQUALS
EQUATE
ERGATE
ERHARD
ERNANI
ERRAND
ERRANT
ERRARE
ERRATA
ERSATZ
ESCAPE
ESCARP
ESHARP
ESPANA
ESSAYS
ESTATE
ETHANE
EURAIL
EUTAXY
EXHALE
EXPAND
EXTANT
EZZARD

E•••A•
EARLAP
EARWAX
EATSAT
ELFMAN
ELIJAH
EMQUAD
ENDEAR
ENDMAN
ENGRAM
ENNEAD
ENQUAD
ENTRAP
ENWRAP
EOLIAN
EONIAN
EPICAL
EPINAL
ESDRAS
ESPIAL
ESTRAY
EXTRAS

E••••A
EARTHA
EDESSA
EGERIA
EGESTA
EIDOLA
EJECTA
ELISHA
ELISSA
ELMIRA
ELVIRA
EMILIA
ENCINA
ENDORA
ENIGMA
EROICA
ERRATA
ESPANA
ESPOSA
ETALIA
EUBOEA
EUDORA
EUPNEA
EUREKA
EUROPA
EXACTA
EXEDRA

•EA•••
BEACHY
BEACON
BEADED
BEADLE
BEADUP
BEAGLE
BEAKED
BEAKER
BEAMED
BEAMON
BEAMUP
BEANED
BEANIE
BEANOS
BEARDS
BEARER
BEARON
BEARUP
BEASTS
BEATEN
BEATER
BEATIT
BEATLE
BEATON
BEATTY
BEATUP
BEAUTS
BEAUTY
BEAVER
BEAVIS
CEASED
CEASES
DEACON
DEADEN
DEADER
DEADLY
DEADON
DEAFEN
DEAFER
DEAFLY
DEALER
DEALIN
DEANNA
DEARER
DEARIE
DEARLY
DEARME
DEARTH
DEASIL
FEALTY
FEARED
FEARER
FEASTS
FEATLY
GEARED
GEARTO
GEARUP
HEADED
HEADER
HEADIN
HEADON
HEADUP
HEALED
HEALER
HEALTH
HEANEY
HEAPED
HEARER
HEAROF
HEARST
HEARTH
HEARTS
HEARTY
HEARYE
HEATED
HEATER
HEATHS
HEATHY
HEATUP
HEAVED
HEAVEN
HEAVER
HEAVES
JEANNE
KEARNY
KEATON
LEACHY
LEADED
LEADEN
LEADER
LEADIN
LEADON
LEADTO
LEADUP
LEAFED
LEAGUE
LEAKED
LEAKER
LEAKEY
LEALTY
LEANED
LEANER
LEANLY
LEANON
LEANTO
LEAPED
LEAPER
LEARNS
LEARNT
LEASED
LEASER
LEASES
LEAVED
LEAVEN
LEAVES
MEADOW
MEAGER
MEAGRE
MEALIE
MEANER
MEANIE
MEANLY
MEASLY
NEARBY
NEARED
NEARER
NEARLY
NEARTO
NEATEN
NEATER
NEATLY
PEACHY
PEAHEN
PEAKED
PEALED
PEANUT
PEAPOD
PEARLS
PEARLY
PEAVEY
REACTS
READER
READIN
REAGAN
REAIMS
REAIRS
REALER
REALES
REALIA
REALLY
REALMS
REALTY
REAMED
REAMER
REAPED
REAPER
REARED

REARER
REARMS
REARUP
REASON
REATAS
SEABAG
SEABED
SEABEE
SEACOW
SEADOG
SEAFAN
SEAFOX
SEAGAL
SEALAB
SEALED
SEALER
SEALUP
SEAMAN
SEAMED
SEAMEN
SEAMUS
SEANCE
SEARCH
SEARED
SEARLE
SEASON
SEATED
SEATER
SEATON
SEAWAY
TEABAG
TEACUP
TEAMED
TEAMUP
TEAPOT
TEAPOY
TEARAT
TEARED
TEARUP
TEASED
TEASEL
TEASER
TEASES
TEASET
WEAKEN
WEAKER
WEAKLY
WEALTH
WEANED
WEAPON
WEARER
WEASEL
WEAVED
WEAVER
WEAVES
YEAGER
YEANED
YEARLY
YEARNS
YEASTS
YEASTY
ZEALOT

•E•A••

AERATE
BECALM
BECAME
BEDAUB
BEDAZE
BEFALL
BEHALF
BEHAVE
BELAIR
BELAYS
BEMATA
BERATE
BESANT
BETAKE
BEWAIL
BEWARE
BEZANT
CEDANT
CEDARS
CERATE
CESARE
CETANE
DEBARK
DEBARS
DEBASE
DEBATE
DECADE
DECAFS
DECALS
DECAMP
DECANT
DECAYS
DEFACE
DEFAME
DEFATS
DEGAGE
DEJAVU
DEKALB
DELANO
DELANY
DELATE
DELAYS
DEMAND
DENALI
DENARY
DEPART
DEPAUL
DEPAUW
DERAIL
DESALT
DETACH
DETAIL
DETAIN
FEMALE
GELADA
GELATI
GELATO
GEMARA
GERAHS
GERALD
GERARD
HECATE
HEGARI
HEMATO
HERALD
HEXADS
KEBABS
KERALA
LEGACY
LEGALS
LEGATE
LEGATO
LELAND
LEMANS
LENAPE
LESAGE
LEVANT
MEDAKA
MEDALS
MEGALO
MEGARA
MELANO
MENACE
MENADO
MENAGE
MESABI
METALS
METATE
NEGATE
NEMATO
NEPALI
NEVADA
NEWAGE
NEWARK
PECANS
PEDALS
PEDANT
PEDATE
PELAGE
PENANG
PESACH
PESAWA
PETAIN
PETALS
PETARD
REBAGS
REBARS
REBATE
RECALL
RECANE
RECANT
RECAPS
RECAST
REDACT
REDANT
REDATE
REFACE
REGAIN
REGALE
REGARD
REHABS
REHANG
REHASH
RELACE
RELAID
RELATE
RELAYS
REMADE
REMAIL
REMAIN
REMAKE
REMAND
REMANS
REMAPS
REMARK
RENAIL
RENAME
RENATA
REPADS
REPAID
REPAIR
REPAND
REPAST
REPAVE
REPAYS
RERATE
RESALE
RESALT
RESAND
RESAWN
RESAWS
RETAGS
RETAIL
RETAIN
RETAKE
RETAPE
RETAPS
RETARD
RETARS
REVAMP
REWARD
REWARM
REWASH
SECANT
SEDAKA
SEDANS
SEDATE
SEJANT
SENARY
SENATE
SEPALS
SERACS
SERAIS
SERAPE
SERAPH
SESAME
SEWAGE
SEWARD
TEJANO
TENACE
TENANT
TEPALS
TERAPH
TERATO
TEXACO
TEXANS
VEGANS
ZENANA

•E••A•

AEGEAN
AENEAS
AERIAL
BEDLAM
BEGGAR
BEHEAD
BELDAM
BELIAL
BELLAY
BEMOAN
BENDAY
BENGAL
BENGAY
BETRAY
BETTAS
BEULAH
BEWRAY
CEIBAS
CELLAE
CELLAR
CEREAL
CESTAS
DEBRAS
DEEJAY
DEEPAK
DEFEAT
DEFRAY
DELMAR
DELRAY
DELTAS
DEMEAN
DENIAL
DENTAL
DEODAR
DERMAL
DESMAN
DEWLAP
FELLAH
FELLAS
FENIAN
FENMAN
FENWAY
FERIAL
FERIAS
FERMAT
FESTAL
FESTAS
FEUDAL
FEZZAN
GEEGAW
GEMMAE
GENIAL
GENOAN
GENUAL
GERMAN
GETMAD
GETSAT
GEWGAW
HEEHAW
HELLAS
HENNAS
HEPCAT
HEPTAD
HERBAL
HEREAT
HERMAN
HETMAN
HEYDAY
JEERAT
JETLAG
JETSAM
JETWAY
KEENAN
KEEPAT
KENYAN
KEPTAT
KERMAN
KEVLAR
KEYPAD
KEYWAY
LEERAT
LEEWAY
LEGMAN
LEHUAS
LEKVAR
LEMMAS
LESTAT
LETHAL
LETSAT
MECCAS
MEDGAR
MEDIAL
MEDIAN
MEDIAS
MEDLAR
MEDLAT
MELMAC
MENIAL
MENSAE
MENSAL
MENSAS
MENTAL
MERMAN
MESCAL
NECTAR
NETMAN
NETPAY
NEUMAN
NEURAL
NEWMAN
NEWMAR
PECKAT
PEDLAR
PEDWAY
PEEKAT
PEERAT
PENMAN
PENNAE
PENPAL
PENTAD
REAGAN
REATAS
RECOAT
REDBAY
REDCAP
REDEAL
REDHAT
REDIAL
REDOAK
REDRAW
REDTAG
REFLAG
REGGAE
REGNAL
REGNAT
REHEAL
REHEAR
REHEAT
REINAS
RELOAD
RENTAL
REPEAL
REPEAT
REPLAN
REPLAY
REREAD
RESEAL
RESEAT
RESEAU
RETEAR
RETIAL
RETRAL
REVEAL
REWRAP
REXCAT
SEABAG
SEAFAN
SEAGAL
SEALAB
SEAMAN
SEAWAY
SEESAW
SENDAK
SENLAC
SENNAS
SEPIAS
SEPTAL
SERIAL
SERVAL
SETSAT
SEURAT
TEABAG
TEARAT
TERRAN
TESLAS
TESTAE
TETRAD
TETRAS
VEEJAY
VEINAL
VENIAL
VERBAL
VERNAL
VESTAL
VESTAS
WEIMAR
WENTAT
WETBAR
YENTAS
YEOMAN
YESMAN
ZEBRAS
ZEDBAR
ZEEMAN

•E•••A

AEOLIA
BELUGA
BEMATA
BERTHA
BETCHA
CESSNA
CETERA
DEANNA
DEFLEA
DESICA
FEDORA
FEMORA
GEISHA
GELADA
GEMARA
GENERA
GENEVA
GEZIRA
HECUBA
HEGIRA
HELENA
HESTIA
JERBOA
KERALA
KESHIA
LERIDA
LEXICA
MEDAKA
MEDINA
MEDUSA
MEGARA
MELINA
MERIDA
NEBULA
NERUDA
NESTEA
NEVADA
OEDEMA
PELOTA
PENNIA
PEORIA
PEPITA
PERCHA
PERSIA
PERUGA
PESAWA
PESETA
PETULA
REALIA
REDSEA
REGINA
REMORA
REMUDA
RENATA
RESEDA
RETINA
SEDAKA
SEGURA
SELENA
SENECA
SENEGA
SENORA
SENTRA
SERBIA
SERENA
SEROSA
TEPHRA
TERESA
VERONA
ZENANA
ZEUGMA

••EA••

AFEARD
ALEAST
ATEAMS
ATEASE
AWEARY
AYEAYE
BLEACH
BLEARS
BLEARY
BLEATS
BREACH
BREADS
BREAKS
BREAMS
BREAST
BREATH
CHEAPO
CHEATS
CLEANS
CLEARS
CLEATS
CLEAVE
CREAKS
CREAKY
CREAMS
CREAMY
CREASE
CREASY
CREATE
DREADS
DREAMS
DREAMT
DREAMY
DREARY
FREAKS
FREAKY
GLEAMS
GLEAMY
GLEANS
GOEASY
GREASE
GREASY
GREATS
GREAVE
HBEAMS
IBEAMS
ICEAGE
IDEALS
IDEATE
ILEANA
KNEADS
NLEAST
OBEAHS
OCEANS
OLEARY
OLEATE
ONEACT
OREADS
PAEANS
PLEACH
PLEADS
PLEASE
PLEATS
PREACH
PREAMP
QUEASY
SHEAFS
SHEARS
SHEATH
SHEAVE
SKEANS
SLEAVE
SLEAZE
SLEAZY
SMEARS
SMEARY
SNEAKS
SNEAKY
SPEAKS
SPEARS
STEADS
STEADY
STEAKS
STEALS
STEAMS
STEAMY
SWEARS
SWEATS
SWEATY
TREADS
TREATS
TREATY
TWEAKS
UNEASE
UNEASY
WHEALS
WHEATS
WREAKS
WREATH

••E•A•

ACETAL
AGENAS
AKELAS
ALEGAR
ALEMAN
AMEBAE
AMEBAS

APEMAN
ARECAS
ARENAS
CAESAR
CHELAE
CHELAS
CHEVAL
COEVAL
CRETAN
DAEDAL
DEEJAY
DEEPAK
FLEWAT
FOETAL
GEEGAW
GOESAT
HAEMAT
HEEHAW
HIEMAL
HYENAS
HYETAL
ICEBAG
ICECAP
ICEMAN
IPECAC
JEERAT
KEENAN
KEEPAT
LEERAT
LEEWAY
MAENAD
OMEGAS
ONEDAY
ONEMAN
ONEWAY
OPERAS
PEEKAT
PEERAT
PIEMAN
PIEPAN
PIETAS
PLEIAD
PLEXAL
PREFAB
PRELAW
PREPAY
PRETAX
PREWAR
SCENAS
SEESAW
SHEVAT
SLEZAK
STEFAN
STELAE
STELAR
THECAE
THECAL
THEHAJ
THENAR
THETAS
TOECAP
TOETAP
TREPAN

VEEJAY
ZEEMAN

••E••A
ACEDIA
AGENDA
ALEXIA
AMELIA
AMENRA
ANEMIA
AREOLA
ARETHA
AVESTA
AYESHA
BRENDA
CRENNA
CREUSA
CUESTA
DJERBA
DUENNA
EDESSA
EGERIA
EGESTA
EJECTA
EXEDRA
FAENZA
FIESTA
FRESCA
GLENDA
GRETNA
IBERIA
ILEANA
ILESHA
IMELDA
OBELIA
ODESSA
ODETTA
OMERTA
ONEIDA
OREIDA
PAELLA
PLEURA
PNEUMA
PUEBLA
QUETTA
SHEENA
SHEILA
SHERPA
SIENNA
SIERRA
SIESTA
STELLA
STERNA
THELMA
THESEA
TIERRA
TREDIA
VIENNA

•••EA•
AEGEAN
AENEAS
AGLEAM
ANDEAN
ANNEAL
APPEAL
APPEAR
ARREAR
AUGEAN
BATEAU
BEHEAD
BOREAL
BOREAS
BUREAU
CAMEAT
CAVEAT
CEREAL
COMEAT
CUNEAL
DEFEAT
DEMEAN
DOGEAR
ENDEAR
ENNEAD
FIVEAM
FOVEAE
GALEAE
GATEAU
GILEAD
HABEAS
HAVEAT
HEREAT
INGEAR
INSEAM
IRREAL
JUNEAU
KOREAN
LINEAL
LINEAR
LLBEAN
LOREAL
MCLEAN
MOREAU
NICEAN
NINEAM
NOLEAD
OCREAE
OHYEAH
ORDEAL
ORGEAT
OSTEAL
OUTEAT
PALEAE
PINEAL
POKEAT
POLEAX
RAMEAU
REDEAL
REHEAL
REHEAR
REHEAT
REPEAL
REPEAT
REREAD
RESEAL
RESEAT
RESEAU
RETEAR
REVEAL
ROSEAU
SCREAK
SCREAM
SINEAD
SPREAD
SQUEAK
SQUEAL
STREAK
STREAM
THREAD
THREAT
TINEAR
TOREAT
UNLEAD
UNREAD
UNREAL
UNSEAL
UNSEAT
UPBEAT

•••E•A
ADNEXA
AMOEBA
ANGELA
ARBELA
ASPERA
ATHENA
BODEGA
CAMERA
CATENA
CETERA
CINEMA
DODECA
DUNERA
EUREKA
GALENA
GENERA
GENEVA
HELENA
KAGERA
KINEMA
LAMESA
MAKEBA
MODELA
MODENA
MONERA
MONETA
MULETA
NOVENA
OEDEMA
ORTEGA
PAMELA
PESETA
RESEDA
RIVERA
ROWENA
SABENA
SCHEMA
SCLERA
SELENA
SENECA
SENEGA
SERENA
SHEENA
SISERA
TERESA
TOPEKA
WALESA
XIMENA
ZAREBA

••••EA
ACHAEA
ALTHEA
ANDREA
AZALEA
CORNEA
COWPEA
CRIMEA
DEFLEA
DULLEA
DURYEA
EUBOEA
EUPNEA
GRADEA
GUINEA
HOTTEA
JUDAEA
LABREA
MATTEA
MCCREA
NAUSEA
NESTEA
NICAEA
NOUMEA
REDSEA
SPIREA
THESEA

EB••••
EBBING
EBERLY
EBOATS
EBONDS

E•B•••
EBBING
EDBERG
EGBERT
EKBERG
ELBERT
ELBOWS
ELBRUS
EMBANK
EMBARK
EMBAYS
EMBDEN
EMBEDS
EMBERS
EMBLEM
EMBODY
EMBOSS
EMBRYO
ENBLOC
ERBIUM
EUBOEA

E••B••
EDIBLE
ENABLE
EREBUS

E•••B•
ENROBE
EPHEBE
EXURBS

•EB•••
BEBOPS
DEBARK
DEBARS
DEBASE
DEBATE
DEBBIE
DEBITS
DEBONE
DEBRAS
DEBRIS
DEBTOR
DEBUGS
DEBUNK
DEBUTS
HEBREW
HEBRON
KEBABS
KEBOBS
LEBRUN
NEBULA
PEBBLE
PEBBLY
REBAGS
REBARS
REBATE
REBBES
REBECS
REBELS
REBEND
REBENT
REBIDS
REBIND
REBOIL
REBOLT
REBOOT
REBORN
REBOZO
REBUFF
REBUKE
REBURY
REBUTS
SEBERG
VEBLEN
WEBBED
WEBBER
WEBERN
XEBECS
ZEBRAS

•E•B••
BEDBUG
BERBER
CEIBAS
DEBBIE
FEEBLE
FEEBLY
FERBER
GERBER
GERBIL
HEEBIE
HENBIT
HERBAL
HERBIE
JERBOA
LESBOS
MEMBER
PEBBLE
PEBBLY
REBBES
REDBAY
REDBUD
REEBOK
REUBEN
SEABAG
SEABED
SEABEE
SERBIA
TEABAG
VERBAL
VERBIS
WEBBED
WEBBER
WETBAR
ZEDBAR

•E••B•
AEROBE
CELEBS
DEMOBS
GETSBY
HECUBA
HEREBY
KEBABS
KEBOBS
LETSBE
MESABI
NEARBY
REDUBS
REHABS
SETSBY
WENTBY

•E•••B
BEDAUB
BENUMB
DEKALB
RESORB
REVERB
SEALAB

••EB••
AMEBAE
AMEBAS
AMEBIC
BYEBYE
EREBUS
FEEBLE
FEEBLY
GLEBES
GREBES
HEEBIE
ICEBAG
ICEBOX
LIEBIG
LIEBYS
PLEBES
PUEBLA
PUEBLO
QUEBEC
REEBOK
RHEBOK
THEBES
TREBEK
TREBLE
TREBLY

••E•B•
DJERBA
DOESBY
DWEEBS
GOESBY

••E••B
CHERUB
PREFAB
THEWEB

•••EB•
ACHEBE
AMOEBA
ARDEBS
CAMEBY
CELEBS
COMEBY
CUBEBS
DWEEBS
EPHEBE
GAZEBO
GONEBY
HEREBY
INDEBT
MAKEBA
NASEBY
PHLEBO
PHOEBE
SASEBO
ZAREBA

•••E•B
ADVERB
REVERB
SUPERB

••••EB
COBWEB
DIONEB
SUBDEB
THEWEB
ZAGREB

EC••••
ECARTE
ECCLES
ECESIC
ECESIS
ECHINO
ECHOED
ECHOES
ECHOIC
ECLAIR
ECLATS
ECOLES
ECTYPE

E•C•••
ECCLES
EMCEED
EMCEES
ENCAGE
ENCAMP
ENCASE
ENCINA
ENCINO
ENCODE
ENCORE
EOCENE
ESCAPE
ESCARP
ESCENT
ESCHER
ESCHEW
ESCORT
ESCROW
ESCUDO
ETCHED
ETCHER
ETCHES
EUCHRE
EUCLID
EXCEED
EXCELS
EXCEPT
EXCESS
EXCISE
EXCITE
EXCUSE

E••C••
EDICTS
EDUCED
EDUCES
EGGCUP
EJECTA
EJECTS
ELECTS
ELICIT
ENACTS
EPICAL
EPOCHS
ERECTS
ERUCTS
EVICTS
EXACTA
EXACTO
EXACTS
EYECUP

E•••C•
EDKOCH
EFFACE
EFFECT
ELLICE
ENESCO
ENLACE
ENRICH
ENRICO
ENTICE
EPARCH
EROICA
ETHICS
EUNICE
EVINCE
EXARCH
EXPECT

E••••C
ECESIC
ECHOIC
EDENIC
ENBLOC
EROTIC
ETHNIC
ETONIC
EXILIC
EXOTIC

•EC•••
BECALM
BECAME
BECKER
BECKET
BECKON
BECOME
CECILE
CECILY
DECADE
DECAFS
DECALS
DECAMP
DECANT
DECAYS
DECEIT
DECENT
DECIDE
DECKED
DECKER
DECKLE
DECOCT
DECODE
DECORS
DECOYS

DECREE
FECUND
GECKOS
HECATE
HECKLE
HECTIC
HECTOR
HECUBA
JECKLE
LECTER
LECTOR
MECCAS
NECKED
NECTAR
PECANS
PECKAT
PECKED
PECTIC
PECTIN
RECALL
RECANE
RECANT
RECAPS
RECAST
RECEDE
RECENT
RECESS
RECIFE
RECIPE
RECITE
RECKON
RECOAT
RECODE
RECOIL
RECONS
RECOPY
RECORD
RECORK
RECOUP
RECTOR
RECTOS
RECTUS
RECURS
RECUSE
SECANT
SECEDE
SECERN
SECKEL
SECOND
SECRET
SECTOR
SECURE
TECHIE
TECHNO
VECTOR

•E•C••

BEACHY
BEACON
BETCHA
DEACON
DEICED
DEICER
DEICES
DESCRY
DEUCED
DEUCES
FENCED
FENCER
FENCES
FESCUE
HEPCAT
LEACHY
MECCAS
MERCED
MERCER
MESCAL
PEACHY
PENCEL
PENCIL
PERCHA
PESCOW
REACTS
REDCAP
REECHO
RESCUE
REXCAT
SEACOW
SEICHE
TEACUP
TERCEL
TERCET
TETCHY
VELCRO
WENCES

•E••C•

BEDECK
DECOCT
DEDUCE
DEDUCT
DEFACE
DEFECT
DEJECT
DELICT
DEPICT
DESICA
DETACH
DETECT
DEVICE
LEGACY
LEXICA
MEDICI
MEDICO
MEDICS
MEJICO
MENACE
MENSCH
MEXICO
PEERCE
PESACH
REBECS
REDACT
REDUCE
REFACE
REJECT
RELACE
RELICS
RELICT
RELOCK
RELUCT
REMICK
RESECT
SEANCE
SEARCH
SEDUCE
SELECT
SENECA
SERACS
TENACE
TEXACO
VELOCE
VENICE
XEBECS

•E•••C

AEOLIC
BELLOC
CEDRIC
CELTIC
DELTIC
FENNEC
FERENC
FERRIC
GESTIC
HECTIC
HEROIC
MELMAC
METRIC
PECTIC
PELVIC
PEPTIC
SENLAC
SEPTIC
TENREC
ZENDIC

••EC••

ALECKY
ALECTO
AMECHE
ARECAS
BRECHT
CHECKS
CRECHE
CZECHS
EJECTA
EJECTS
ELECTS
ERECTS
EYECUP
FLECHE
FLECKS
FLECKY
ICECAP
IPECAC
NIECES
NUECES
PIECED
PIECER
PIECES
PRECIS
REECHO
SIECLE
SPECIE
SPECKS
THECAE
THECAL
TOECAP
VNECKS
WRECKS

••E•C•

AGENCY
AMERCE
APERCU
BIERCE
BLEACH
BLENCH
BREACH
BREECH
CHEECH
CLENCH
COERCE
DRENCH
ENESCO
FIERCE
FLEECE
FLEECY
FLETCH
FRENCH
FRESCA
FRESCO
GREECE
KVETCH
ONEACT
PEERCE
PIERCE
PLEACH
PREACH
QUENCH
SKETCH
SPEECH
STENCH
THENCE
TIERCE
TRENCH
UNESCO
WHENCE
WRENCH
WRETCH

••E••C

ACETIC
AMEBIC
ANEMIC
CLERIC
ECESIC
EDENIC
GAELIC
IPECAC
IRENIC
NOETIC
POETIC
QUEBEC
SCENIC
THETIC

•••EC•

ABJECT
AFFECT
APIECE
ASPECT
AZTECS
BEDECK
BISECT
BREECH
CHEECH
DEFECT
DEJECT
DETECT
DIRECT
DODECA
EFFECT
EXPECT
FLEECE
FLEECY
GRAECO
GREECE
HITECH
INFECT
INJECT
INSECT
KOPECK
LAMECH
LUBECK
OBJECT
OLMECS
ONDECK
REBECS
REJECT
RESECT
SAMECH
SELECT
SENECA
SPEECH
VOTECH
XEBECS
ZYDECO

•••E•C

FERENC
HOMEEC

••••EC

FENNEC
HOMEEC
MIXTEC
ONSPEC
PARSEC
QUEBEC
TENREC
TOLTEC

ED••••

EDAMES
EDBERG
EDDIED
EDDIES
EDDOES
EDENIC
EDERLE
EDESSA
EDGARD
EDGARS
EDGEIN
EDGERS
EDGIER
EDGILY
EDGING
EDIBLE
EDICTS
EDILES
EDISON
EDITED
EDITIO
EDITOR
EDKOCH
EDMOND
EDMUND
EDSELS
EDUARD
EDUCED
EDUCES
EDVARD
EDWARD
EDWOOD
EDWYNN

E•D•••

EDDIED
EDDIES
EDDOES
EIDERS
EIDOLA
ELDERS
ELDEST
EMDASH
ENDALL
ENDASH
ENDEAR
ENDERS
ENDING
ENDIVE
ENDMAN
ENDMEN
ENDORA
ENDOWS
ENDRUN
ENDSUP
ENDUED
ENDUES
ENDURE
ENDURO
ENDUSE
ESDRAS
EUDORA

E••D••

EJIDOS
ELIDED
ELIDES
ELUDED
ELUDER
ELUDES
EMBDEN
EPODES
ERODED
ERODES
ETUDES
EVADED
EVADER
EVADES
EXEDRA
EXODUS
EXUDED
EXUDES

E•••D•

EBONDS
ELANDS
EMBEDS
EMBODY
EMENDS
ENCODE
EPHODS
ESCUDO

E••••D

EAGLED
EARNED
ECHOED
EDDIED
EDGARD
EDITED
EDMOND
EDMUND
EDUARD
EDUCED
EDVARD
EDWARD
EDWOOD
ELAPID
ELATED
ELIDED
ELOPED
ELUDED
ELUTED
ELWOOD
EMCEED
EMOTED
EMQUAD
ENDUED
ENFOLD
ENGIRD
ENNEAD
ENQUAD
ENSUED
ENURED
ENVIED
ERASED
ERHARD
ERODED
ERRAND
ESPIED
ETCHED
EUCLID
EVADED
EVENED
EVOKED
EXCEED
EXILED
EXITED
EXPAND
EXPEND
EXTEND
EXUDED
EYELID
EZZARD

•ED•••

AEDILE
BEDAUB
BEDAZE
BEDBUG
BEDECK
BEDEWS
BEDIMS
BEDLAM
CEDANT
CEDARS
CEDING
CEDRIC
DEDUCE
DEDUCT
FEDORA
HEDDLE
HEDGED
HEDGER
HEDGES
HEDREN
HEDRON
KEDGED
KEDGES
LEDGER
LEDGES
LEDOFF
LEDOUT
MEDAKA
MEDALS
MEDDLE
MEDFLY
MEDGAR
MEDIAL
MEDIAN
MEDIAS
MEDICI
MEDICO
MEDICS
MEDINA
MEDIUM
MEDLAR
MEDLAT
MEDLEY
MEDUSA
OEDEMA
PEDALS
PEDANT
PEDATE
PEDDLE
PEDLAR
PEDWAY
REDACT
REDANT
REDATE
REDBAY
REDBUD
REDCAP
REDDEN
REDDER
REDDOG
REDEAL
REDEEM
REDENY
REDEYE
REDFIN
REDFIR
REDFOX
REDGUM
REDHAT
REDHOT
REDIAL
REDING
REDINK
REDOAK
REDOES
REDONE
REDRAW
REDREW
REDSEA
REDSOX
REDTAG
REDTOP
REDUBS
REDUCE
REDYED
REDYES
SEDAKA
SEDANS
SEDATE
SEDERS
SEDGES
SEDILE
SEDUCE
SEDUMS
TEDDED
TEDDER
TEDEUM
TEDIUM
TEDKEY
VEDDER
WEDDED
WEDELN
WEDGED
WEDGES
WEDGIE
XEDOUT
ZEDBAR

•E•D••

BEADED
BEADLE
BEADUP
BELDAM
BENDAY
BENDED
BENDER
BENDIX
DEADEN
DEADER
DEADLY
DEADON
DEEDED
DEEDEE
DEIDRE
DENDRI
DENDRO
DEODAR
FEEDER
FEEDON
FELDON
FENDED
FENDER
FEUDAL
FEUDED
GENDER
GEODES
HEADED
HEADER
HEADIN
HEADON
HEADUP
HEDDLE
HEEDED
HEEDER
HEIDEN
HELDIN
HELDON
HELDTO
HELDUP
HERDED
HERDER
HEYDAY
LEADED
LEADEN
LEADER
LEADIN
LEADON
LEADTO
LEADUP
LEIDEN
LENDER
LEWDER
LEWDLY
LEYDEN
MEADOW
MEDDLE
MELDED
MENDED
MENDEL

MENDER
MENDES
NEEDED
NEEDLE
NEEDNT
PEDDLE
PEEDEE
PENDED
PERDUE
READER
READIN
REDDEN
REDDER
REDDOG
REEDIT
RENDER
SEADOG
SEEDED
SEEDER
SEIDEL
SELDOM
SENDAK
SENDER
SENDIN
SENDUP
TEDDED
TEDDER
TEEDUP
TENDED
TENDER
TENDON
TENDTO
VEDDER
VELDTS
VENDED
VENDEE
VENDOR
VERDIN
VERDON
VERDUN
WEDDED
WEEDED
WEEDER
WELDED
WELDER
WENDED
ZENDIC
ZENDOS

•E••D•
BEARDS
BESIDE
BETIDE
DECADE
DECIDE
DECODE
DELUDE
DEMODE
DENUDE
DERIDE
GELADA
HEXADS
LERIDA
MELODY
MENADO
MERIDA
NERUDA
NEVADA
REBIDS
RECEDE
RECODE
REMADE
REMEDY
REMUDA
REPADS
RESEDA
RESIDE
RESODS
REWEDS
SECEDE
TELEDU
TEREDO
WEIRDO
WEIRDY
YEHUDI

•E•••D
AENEID
BEADED
BEAKED
BEAMED
BEANED
BEEFED
BEEPED
BEGGED
BEHEAD
BEHELD
BEHIND
BEHOLD
BELIED
BELLED
BELTED
BENDED
BESTED
BEYOND
CEASED
CEILED
CELLED
CENSED
CERVID
CESSED
DECKED
DEEDED
DEEMED
DEFEND
DEFIED
DEICED
DELVED
DEMAND
DEMOND
DENIED
DENNED
DENTED
DEPEND
DEUCED
DEVOID
FEARED
FECUND
FELLED
FELTED
FENCED
FENDED
FERVID
FESSED
FEUDED
GEARED
GELLED
GEMMED
GERALD
GERARD
GERUND
GETMAD
HEADED
HEALED
HEAPED
HEATED
HEAVED
HEDGED
HEEDED
HEELED
HEFTED
HELMED
HELPED
HEMMED
HENTED
HEPTAD
HERALD
HERDED
HESIOD
JEERED
JELLED
JERKED
JESTED
JETTED
KEDGED
KEELED
KEENED
KEGGED
KENNED
KERNED
KEYPAD
LEADED
LEAFED
LEAKED
LEANED
LEAPED
LEASED
LEAVED
LEERED
LEGEND
LEGGED
LELAND
LEMOND
LENSED
LEONID
LETTED
LEVEED
LEVIED
MELDED
MELTED
MENDED
MEOWED
MERCED
MERGED
MESHED
MESSED
METHOD
MEWLED
NEARED
NECKED
NEEDED
NEREID
NESTED
NETTED
PEAKED
PEALED
PEAPOD
PECKED
PEEKED
PEELED
PEENED
PEEPED
PEERED
PEEVED
PEGGED
PELTED
PENDED
PENNED
PENROD
PENTAD
PEPPED
PEQUOD
PERIOD
PERKED
PERMED
PERNOD
PETARD
PETTED
REAMED
REAPED
REARED
REBEND
REBIND
RECORD
REDBUD
REDYED
REEFED
REEKED
REELED
REEVED
REFFED
REFUND
REGARD
REHELD
REINED
RELAID
RELIED
RELOAD
REMAND
REMEND
REMIND
REMOLD
RENTED
REPAID
REPAND
REREAD
RESAND
RESEED
RESEND
RESHOD
RESOLD
RESTED
RETARD
RETIED
RETOLD
REUSED
REVVED
REWARD
REWELD
REWIND
REWORD
SEABED
SEALED
SEAMED
SEARED
SEATED
SECOND
SEEDED
SEEMED
SEEPED
SEERED
SEGUED
SEINED
SEIZED
SENSED
SERVED
SEWARD
TEAMED
TEARED
TEASED
TEDDED
TEEMED
TEHEED
TEMPED
TENDED
TENSED
TENTED
TERMED
TESTED
TETRAD
VEERED
VEGGED
VEILED
VEINED
VENDED
VENTED
VERGED
VERSED
VESPID
VESTED
VETOED
VETTED
WEANED
WEAVED
WEBBED
WEDDED
WEDGED
WEEDED
WELDED
WELLED
WELTED
WENDED
WETTED
YEANED
YELLED
YELPED
YENNED
YERKED
YESSED
ZEROED
ZESTED

••ED••
ACEDIA
AMEDEO
AVEDON
AWEDLY
COEDIT
CREDIT
CREDOS
DAEDAL
DEEDED
DEEDEE
DREDGE
EXEDRA
FEEDER
FEEDON
FLEDGE
FLEDGY
FREDDY
HEEDED
HEEDER
ICEDIN
ICEDUP
LIEDER
NEEDED
NEEDLE
NEEDNT
ONEDAY
ONEDGE
PEEDEE
PHEDRE
PLEDGE
PYEDOG
REEDIT
SEEDED
SEEDER
SLEDGE
SPEDUP
SUEDES
SWEDEN
SWEDES
TEEDUP
TIEDIN
TIEDTO
TIEDUP
TIEDYE
TOEDIN
TREDIA
USEDTO
USEDUP
WEEDED
WEEDER

••E•D•
AGENDA
AMENDS
ARENDT
BLEEDS
BLENDE
BLENDS
BREADS
BREEDS
BRENDA
CREEDS
DREADS
EMENDS
FIELDS
FIENDS
FJELDS
FREDDY
GLENDA
GREEDY
IMELDA
KNEADS
ONEIDA
OREADS
OREIDA
OVERDO
PLEADS
PSEUDO
PSEUDS
SCENDS
SHEEDY
SPEEDO
SPEEDS
SPEEDY
SPENDS
STEADS
STEADY
STEEDS
TREADS
TRENDS
TRENDY
TWEEDS
TWEEDY
UPENDS
WIELDS
YIELDS

••E••D
AFEARD
AGEOLD
ANELED
BEEFED
BEEPED
BREWED
CHEWED
CLEPED
CLEWED
CREWED
DEEDED
DEEMED
DIETED
DUELED
EVENED
EYELID
FLEXED
FLEYED
FOETID
FUELED
GREYED
HEEDED
HEELED
JEERED
KEELED
KEENED
LEERED
MAENAD
NEEDED
OBEYED
OPENED
PEEKED
PEELED
PEENED
PEEPED
PEERED
PEEVED
PIECED
PLEIAD
PREMED
PREYED
QUEUED
REEFED
REEKED
REELED
REEVED
SEEDED
SEEMED
SEEPED
SEERED
SIEGED
SIEVED
SKEWED
SLEWED
SPEWED
STEWED
TEEMED
THEEND
THEFED
THEKID
THEMED
TIERED
TIEROD
TREPID
USERID
VEERED
VIEWED
WEEDED
WHERED

•••ED•
ACCEDE
ALBEDO
BIPEDS
BLEEDS
BREEDS
COMEDY
CREEDS
EMBEDS
GREEDY
IMPEDE
LAMEDH
LAMEDS
LAREDO
MADEDO
MAKEDO
MOPEDS
OVIEDO
RATEDG
RATEDR
RATEDX
RECEDE
REMEDY
RESEDA
REWEDS
SECEDE
SHEEDY
SHREDS
SPEEDO
SPEEDS
SPEEDY
STEEDS
TELEDU
TEREDO
TOLEDO
TUXEDO
TWEEDS
TWEEDY

•••E•D
ADDEND
AENEID
AFIELD
AGREED
ANTEED
APPEND
ASCEND
ATTEND
AUGEND
AXSEED
BEHEAD
BEHELD
DEFEND
DEPEND
EMCEED
ENNEAD
EXCEED
EXPEND
EXTEND
FAGEND
FRIEND
GILEAD
IMPEND
INDEED
INNEED
INTEND
LEGEND
LEVEED
LOWEND
NEREID
NOLEAD
OFFEND
OSTEND
PUREED
REBEND
REHELD
REMEND
REREAD
RESEED
RESEND
REWELD
SCREED
SHIELD
SHREWD
SINEAD
SPREAD
TAGEND
TEHEED
THEEND
THREAD
THREED
UNBEND
UNHEED
UNLEAD
UNREAD
UPHELD

••••ED
ABASED
ABATED
ABIDED
ABUSED
ADDLED
ADORED
AGREED
ALATED
ALFRED
ALLIED
AMAZED
AMBLED
AMUSED
ANELED
ANGLED
ANKLED
ANTEED
ARCHED
ARGUED
ATONED
AVOWED
AWAKED
AXSEED
BABIED
BACHED
BACKED
BAGGED
BAILED
BAITED
BALKED
BANDED

BANGED	BRIBED	CHUTED	DEEDED	ETCHED	FRAYED	GRATED	HOOFED	JUTTED	LODGED
BANKED	BRINED	CLAWED	DEEMED	EVADED	FUBBED	GRAVED	HOOKED	KAYOED	LOFTED
BANNED	BRUXED	CLEPED	DEFIED	EVENED	FUDGED	GRAYED	HOOPED	KEDGED	LOGGED
BARBED	BUCKED	CLEWED	DEICED	EVOKED	FUELED	GRAZED	HOOTED	KEELED	LOLLED
BARGED	BUDDED	CLONED	DELVED	EXCEED	FUNDED	GREYED	HOPPED	KEENED	LONGED
BARKED	BUDGED	CLOSED	DENIED	EXILED	FUNKED	GRIMED	HORNED	KEGGED	LOOKED
BARRED	BUFFED	CLOYED	DENNED	EXITED	FUNNED	GRIPED	HORSED	KENNED	LOOMED
BASHED	BUGGED	COATED	DENTED	EXUDED	FURLED	GROPED	HOSTED	KERNED	LOOPED
BASKED	BUGLED	COAXED	DEUCED	FABLED	FURRED	GUIDED	HOTBED	KICKED	LOOSED
BASTED	BULGED	COCKED	DIALED	FAGGED	FUSSED	GULFED	HOUSED	KIDDED	LOOTED
BATHED	BULKED	COGGED	DIETED	FAILED	FUTZED	GULLED	HOWLED	KILLED	LOPPED
BATTED	BULLED	COIFED	DIMMED	FAIRED	FUZZED	GULPED	HUFFED	KILNED	LORDED
BAWLED	BUMMED	COILED	DINGED	FANGED	GABBED	GUMMED	HUGGED	KILTED	LOTTED
BEADED	BUMPED	COINED	DINNED	FANNED	GABLED	GUNNED	HULKED	KINGED	LOUSED
BEAKED	BUNGED	COMBED	DINTED	FARCED	GADDED	GUSHED	HULLED	KINKED	LUCKED
BEAMED	BUNKED	CONFED	DIPPED	FARMED	GAFFED	GUSTED	HUMMED	KISSED	LUFFED
BEANED	BUNTED	CONKED	DISHED	FASTED	GAGGED	GUTTED	HUMPED	KNIFED	LUGGED
BEEFED	BUOYED	CONNED	DISKED	FATTED	GAINED	GYPPED	HUNTED	LACKED	LULLED
BEEPED	BURIED	COOKED	DISSED	FAWNED	GAITED	HACKED	HURLED	LADLED	LUMPED
BEGGED	BURLED	COOLED	DOCKED	FEARED	GALLED	HAFTED	HUSHED	LAGGED	LUNGED
BELIED	BURNED	COOPED	DODGED	FELLED	GAMMED	HAILED	HUSKED	LAMBED	LURKED
BELLED	BURPED	COPIED	DOFFED	FELTED	GANGED	HAIRED	HUTTED	LAMMED	LUSTED
BELTED	BURRED	COPPED	DOGGED	FENCED	GAOLED	HALOED	HYMNED	LANCED	MAILED
BENDED	BUSHED	CORDED	DOLLED	FENDED	GAPPED	HALTED	HYPOED	LANDED	MALTED
BESTED	BUSIED	CORKED	DONNED	FESSED	GARBED	HALVED	ILLFED	LAPPED	MANNED
BIASED	BUSKED	CORNED	DOOMED	FEUDED	GASHED	HAMMED	IMAGED	LAPSED	MAPPED
BIBBED	BUSSED	COSHED	DOSSED	FIBBED	GASPED	HANDED	IMBUED	LARDED	MARKED
BIFFED	BUSTED	COSIED	DOTTED	FILLED	GASSED	HANGED	INBRED	LARKED	MARLED
BIGRED	BUTTED	COWLED	DOUSED	FILMED	GAUGED	HAPPED	INCHED	LASHED	MARRED
BILKED	BUZZED	COZIED	DOWNED	FINKED	GAUMED	HARKED	INDEED	LASTED	MASHED
BILLED	CABBED	CRANED	DOWSED	FINNED	GAWKED	HARMED	INNEED	LATHED	MASKED
BINGED	CABLED	CRATED	DRAPED	FIRMED	GAWPED	HARPED	INURED	LAUDED	MASSED
BINNED	CACHED	CRAVED	DRAYED	FISHED	GEARED	HASHED	IRONED	LEADED	MATTED
BIRDED	CADGED	CRAZED	DRONED	FISTED	GELLED	HASPED	ISSUED	LEAFED	MAULED
BIRLED	CALKED	CREWED	DUBBED	FITTED	GEMMED	HATRED	ITCHED	LEAKED	MELDED
BITTED	CALLED	CROWED	DUCKED	FIZZED	GIBBED	HATTED	JABBED	LEANED	MELTED
BLADED	CALMED	CUFFED	DUELED	FLAKED	GIFTED	HAULED	JACKED	LEAPED	MENDED
BLAMED	CALVED	CULLED	DULLED	FLAMED	GIGGED	HAWKED	JAGGED	LEASED	MEOWED
BLARED	CAMPED	CUPPED	DUMPED	FLARED	GILDED	HEADED	JAILED	LEAVED	MERCED
BLAZED	CANNED	CURBED	DUNKED	FLAWED	GILLED	HEALED	JAMMED	LEERED	MERGED
BOATED	CANOED	CURDED	DUNNED	FLAYED	GINNED	HEAPED	JARRED	LEGGED	MESHED
BOBBED	CANTED	CURLED	DURNED	FLEXED	GIPPED	HEATED	JAZZED	LENSED	MESSED
BODIED	CAPPED	CURRED	DUSTED	FLEYED	GIRDED	HEAVED	JEERED	LETTED	MEWLED
BOFFED	CARDED	CURSED	EAGLED	FLOWED	GIRNED	HEDGED	JELLED	LEVEED	MIFFED
BOGGED	CARKED	CURVED	EARNED	FLUTED	GIRTED	HEEDED	JERKED	LEVIED	MILKED
BOILED	CARPED	CUSPED	ECHOED	FLUXED	GLARED	HEELED	JESTED	LIBBED	MILLED
BOLTED	CARTED	CUSSED	EDDIED	FOALED	GLAZED	HEFTED	JETTED	LICKED	MINCED
BOMBED	CARVED	CYCLED	EDITED	FOAMED	GLIDED	HELMED	JIBBED	LIDDED	MINDED
BONDED	CASHED	DABBED	EDUCED	FOBBED	GLOBED	HELPED	JIGGED	LIFTED	MINTED
BONGED	CATTED	DADOED	ELATED	FOGGED	GLOVED	HEMMED	JILTED	LILTED	MISLED
BOOKED	CAUSED	DAFFED	ELIDED	FOILED	GLOWED	HENTED	JINKED	LIMBED	MISSED
BOOMED	CEASED	DAMMED	ELOPED	FOINED	GLOZED	HERDED	JINXED	LIMNED	MISTED
BOOTED	CEILED	DAMNED	ELUDED	FOLDED	GNAWED	HILLED	JOBBED	LIMPED	MITRED
BOPPED	CELLED	DAMPED	ELUTED	FOOLED	GOADED	HINGED	JOGGED	LINKED	MOANED
BOSSED	CENSED	DANCED	EMCEED	FOOTED	GOLFED	HINTED	JOINED	LIPPED	MOATED
BOUSED	CESSED	DAPPED	EMOTED	FORCED	GONGED	HIPPED	JOLTED	LISPED	MOBBED
BOWLED	CHAFED	DARNED	ENDUED	FORDED	GOOFED	HISSED	JOSHED	LISTED	MOCKED
BRACED	CHASED	DARTED	ENSUED	FORGED	GOOSED	HOAXED	JOTTED	LOADED	MOILED
BRAKED	CHEWED	DASHED	ENURED	FORKED	GORGED	HOCKED	JUDGED	LOAFED	MOLDED
BRAVED	CHIDED	DAUBED	ENVIED	FORMED	GOUGED	HOGGED	JUGGED	LOAMED	MOLTED
BRAYED	CHIMED	DAWNED	ERASED	FOULED	GOWNED	HONIED	JUICED	LOANED	MONIED
BRAZED	CHOKED	DAYBED	ERODED	FOWLED	GRACED	HONKED	JUMPED	LOBBED	MOONED
BREWED	CHOWED	DECKED	ESPIED	FRAMED	GRADED	HOODED	JUNKED	LOCKED	MOORED

MOOTED
MOPPED
MOSHED
MOSSED
MOUSED
MUCKED
MUDDED
MUFFED
MUGGED
MULLED
MUMMED
MUMPED
MUSHED
MUSSED
MUZZED
NABBED
NAGGED
NAILED
NAPPED
NEARED
NECKED
NEEDED
NESTED
NETTED
NICKED
NIPPED
NODDED
NOISED
NOOSED
NOSHED
NUBBED
NUDGED
NULLED
NUMBED
NURSED
NUTTED
OBEYED
OINKED
OKAYED
OPENED
OPINED
ORATED
OUSTED
PACKED
PADDED
PAINED
PAIRED
PALLED
PALMED
PANNED
PANTED
PARKED
PARRED
PARSED
PARTED
PASSED
PASTED
PATTED
PAUSED
PAWNED
PEAKED
PEALED
PECKED
PEEKED
PEELED
PEENED
PEEPED
PEERED
PEEVED
PEGGED
PELTED
PENDED
PENNED
PEPPED
PERKED
PERMED
PETTED
PHASED
PHONED
PHYSED
PICKED
PIECED
PIGGED
PILLED
PINGED
PINKED
PINNED
PIPPED
PIQUED
PITHED
PITIED
PITTED
PLACED
PLANED
PLATED
PLAYED
PLOWED
PLUMED
PODDED
POISED
POLLED
PONGED
PONIED
POOHED
POOLED
POOPED
POPPED
PORTED
POSTED
POTTED
POURED
POUTED
PRATED
PRAYED
PREMED
PREYED
PRICED
PRIDED
PRIMED
PRIZED
PROBED
PROSED
PROVED
PRUNED
PUFFED
PUGGED
PULLED
PULPED
PULSED
PUMPED
PUNNED
PUNTED
PUREED
PURGED
PURLED
PURRED
PURSED
PUSHED
PUTTED
QUAKED
QUEUED
QUOTED
RACKED
RAFTED
RAGGED
RAIDED
RAILED
RAINED
RAISED
RAMMED
RAMPED
RANGED
RANKED
RANTED
RAPPED
RASPED
RATTED
RAZZED
REAMED
REAPED
REARED
REDYED
REEFED
REEKED
REELED
REEVED
REFFED
REINED
RELIED
RENTED
RESEED
RESTED
RETIED
REUSED
REVVED
RHYMED
RIBBED
RICKED
RIDDED
RIDGED
RIFFED
RIFLED
RIFTED
RIGGED
RIMMED
RINGED
RINSED
RIOTED
RIPPED
RISKED
ROAMED
ROARED
ROBBED
ROCKED
RODDED
ROILED
ROLLED
ROMPED
ROOFED
ROOKED
ROOMED
ROOTED
ROTTED
ROUGED
ROUSED
ROUTED
RRATED
RSVPED
RUBBED
RUBIED
RUCKED
RUFFED
RUGGED
RUINED
RUSHED
RUSTED
RUTTED
SACKED
SACRED
SAGGED
SAILED
SALTED
SALVED
SANDED
SAPPED
SASHED
SASSED
SAUCED
SAWRED
SCALED
SCAPED
SCARED
SCOPED
SCORED
SCREED
SEABED
SEALED
SEAMED
SEARED
SEATED
SEEDED
SEEMED
SEEPED
SEERED
SEGUED
SEINED
SEIZED
SENSED
SERVED
SHADED
SHAMED
SHAPED
SHARED
SHAVED
SHINED
SHOOED
SHORED
SHOVED
SHOWED
SICCED
SIDLED
SIEGED
SIEVED
SIFTED
SIGHED
SIGNED
SILKED
SILOED
SILTED
SINGED
SINNED
SIPPED
SKATED
SKEWED
SKIVED
SLAKED
SLATED
SLAVED
SLAYED
SLEWED
SLICED
SLIMED
SLOPED
SLOWED
SMILED
SMOKED
SNAKED
SNARED
SNIPED
SNORED
SNOWED
SOAKED
SOAPED
SOARED
SOBBED
SOCKED
SODDED
SOILED
SOLOED
SOLVED
SOPPED
SORTED
SOTTED
SOURED
SOUSED
SPACED
SPADED
SPARED
SPAYED
SPEWED
SPICED
SPIKED
SPINED
SPIRED
SPITED
SPOKED
SPUMED
STAGED
STAKED
STALED
STARED
STATED
STAVED
STAYED
STEWED
STOKED
STONED
STORED
STOWED
STYLED
SUBBED
SUCKED
SUDSED
SUITED
SULKED
SUMMED
SUNNED
SUPPED
SURFED
SURGED
SUSSED
SWAGED
SWAYED
SWIPED
SYNCED
TABBED
TABLED
TACKED
TAGGED
TAILED
TALCED
TALKED
TAMPED
TANGED
TANKED
TANNED
TAPPED
TARRED
TASKED
TASTED
TATTED
TAXIED
TEAMED
TEARED
TEASED
TEDDED
TEEMED
TEHEED
TEMPED
TENDED
TENSED
TENTED
TERMED
TESTED
THAWED
THEFED
THEMED
THREED
TICKED
TIDIED
TIERED
TIFFED
TILLED
TILTED
TINGED
TINNED
TINTED
TIPPED
TITHED
TITLED
TITRED
TOGAED
TOGGED
TOILED
TOLLED
TOOLED
TOOTED
TOPPED
TOSSED
TOTTED
TOURED
TOUTED
TRACED
TRADED
TRICED
TROWED
TUBBED
TUCKED
TUFTED
TUGGED
TUMMED
TURFED
TURNED
TUSKED
TUTUED
TWINED
UNAGED
UNAWED
UNDYED
UNHEED
UNITED
UNSHED
UNTIED
UNUSED
VALUED
VALVED
VAMPED
VANNED
VARIED
VATTED
VEERED
VEGGED
VEILED
VEINED
VENDED
VENTED
VERGED
VERSED
VESTED
VETOED
VETTED
VIEWED
VISAED
VOICED
VOIDED
WADDED
WAFTED
WAGGED
WAILED
WAITED
WAIVED
WALKED
WALLED
WANNED
WANTED
WARDED
WARMED
WARNED
WARPED
WARRED
WASHED
WASTED
WEANED
WEAVED
WEBBED
WEDDED
WEDGED
WEEDED
WELDED
WELLED
WELTED
WENDED
WETTED
WHERED
WHILED
WHINED
WICKED
WIGGED
WILLED
WILTED
WINCED
WINDED
WINGED
WINKED
WISHED
WISPED
WITHED
WITTED
WOLFED
WONNED
WONTED
WOODED
WOOFED
WORDED
WORKED
WORMED
XRATED
XRAYED
YACKED
YAKKED
YANKED
YAPPED
YARDED
YARNED
YAWNED
YAWPED
YEANED
YELLED
YELPED
YENNED
YERKED
YESSED
YIPPED
YOLKED
YOWLED
YOYOED
YUKKED
ZAGGED
ZAPPED
ZEROED
ZESTED
ZIGGED
ZINGED
ZIPPED
ZONKED
ZOOMED

EE••••

EELERS
EELIER
EERIER
EERILY
EEYORE

E•E•••

EBERLY
ECESIC
ECESIS
EDENIC
EDERLE
EDESSA
EGERIA
EGESTA
EGESTS
EJECTA
EJECTS
EKEOUT
ELECTS
ELEGIT
ELEMIS
ELEVEN
ELEVES
EMEERS
EMENDS
EMERGE
EMEUTE
ENERGY
ENESCO
EREBUS
ERECTS
ERENOW
ERESTU
ETERNE
EVELYN
EVENED
EVENER
EVENKI
EVENLY
EVENSO
EVENTS
EVENUP
EVERLY
EVERSO
EVERTS
EXEDRA
EXEMPT
EXERTS
EXETER
EXEUNT
EYECUP
EYEFUL
EYEING
EYELET
EYELID

E••E••

EASEIN
EASELS
EASEUP
EATERS
EATERY
EDBERG
EDGEIN
EDGERS
EDSELS
EELERS
EFFECT
EFFETE
EGBERT
EGRESS
EGRETS
EIDERS
EILEEN
EKBERG
ELBERT
ELDERS
ELDEST
ELLERY
ELVERS
EMBEDS
EMBERS
EMCEED
EMCEES
EMEERS
EMMETS
EMMETT
EMPERY
ENDEAR
ENDERS
ENGELS
ENMESH
ENNEAD
ENTERO
ENTERS
EOCENE
EPHEBE
ERNEST
ESCENT
ESKERS
ESSENE

ESTEEM
ESTERS
ETHENE
ETHERS
ETSEQQ
EUGENE
EUREKA
EXCEED
EXCELS
EXCEPT
EXCESS
EXLEGE
EXPECT
EXPELS
EXPEND
EXPERT
EXSERT
EXTEND
EXTENT
EXTERN

E•••E•

EAGLED
EAGLES
EAGLET
EAGRES
EARNED
EARNER
EASIER
EASTER
ECCLES
ECHOED
ECHOES
ECOLES
EDAMES
EDDIED
EDDIES
EDDOES
EDGIER
EDILES
EDITED
EDUCED
EDUCES
EELIER
EERIER
EGGIER
EIFFEL
EILEEN
EISNER
EITHER
ELATED
ELATER
ELATES
ELAYER
ELEVEN
ELEVES
ELIDED
ELIDES
ELITES
ELOPED
ELOPER
ELOPES
ELUDED
ELUDER
ELUDES
ELUTED
ELUTES
ELYSEE
EMBDEN
EMBLEM
EMCEED
EMCEES
EMOTED
EMOTER
EMOTES
ENAMEL
ENATES
ENDMEN
ENDUED
ENDUES
ENSUED
ENSUES
ENTREE
ENURED
ENURES
ENVIED
ENVIER
ENVIES
EPODES
EPOPEE
ERASED
ERASER
ERASES
ERODED
ERODES
ESCHER
ESCHEW
ESPIED
ESPIES
ESTEEM
ESTHER
ETAPES
ETCHED
ETCHER
ETCHES
ETUDES
EUBOEA
EUPNEA
EVADED
EVADER
EVADES
EVENED
EVENER
EVILER
EVOKED
EVOKER
EVOKES
EXCEED
EXETER
EXILED
EXILES
EXITED
EXUDED
EXUDES
EYELET
EYRIES

E••••E

ECARTE
ECTYPE
EDERLE
EDIBLE
EEYORE
EFFACE
EFFETE
EFFUSE
ELAINE
ELAPSE
ELAYNE
ELLICE
ELMORE
ELOISE
ELYSEE
EMERGE
EMEUTE
EMIGRE
EMPIRE
ENABLE
ENCAGE
ENCASE
ENCODE
ENCORE
ENDIVE
ENDURE
ENDUSE
ENGAGE
ENGINE
ENISLE
ENLACE
ENRAGE
ENROBE
ENSILE
ENSURE
ENTICE
ENTIRE
ENTREE
ENZYME
EOCENE
EPHEBE
EPOPEE
EQUATE
EQUINE
ERGATE
ERMINE
ERRARE
ESCAPE
ESSENE
ESTATE
ETERNE
ETHANE
ETHENE
ETOILE
EUCHRE
EUGENE
EUNICE
EUROPE
EVINCE
EVOLVE
EVONNE
EVULSE
EVZONE
EXCISE
EXCITE
EXCUSE
EXHALE
EXLEGE
EXMORE
EXPIRE
EXPOSE
EXWIFE

•EE•••

AEETES
BEEFED
BEEFUP
BEEGUM
BEEPED
BEEPER
BEETLE
BEEVES
DEEDED
DEEDEE
DEEJAY
DEEMED
DEEPAK
DEEPEN
DEEPER
DEEPLY
FEEBLE
FEEBLY
FEEDER
FEEDON
FEEING
FEELER
GEEGAW
GEEGEE
GEEING
GEEZER
HEEBIE
HEEDED
HEEDER
HEEHAW
HEELED
HEELER
JEERAT
JEERED
JEERER
JEETER
JEEVES
KEELED
KEELER
KEENAN
KEENED
KEENEN
KEENER
KEENLY
KEEPAT
KEEPER
KEEPIN
KEEPON
KEEPTO
KEEPUP
LEERAT
LEERED
LEERER
LEEWAY
MEEKER
MEEKLY
MEERUT
MEETER
MEETLY
NEEDED
NEEDLE
NEEDNT
NEESON
PEEDEE
PEEKAT
PEEKED
PEELED
PEELER
PEENED
PEEPED
PEEPER
PEERAT
PEERCE
PEERED
PEERIN
PEEVED
PEEVES
PEEWEE
REEBOK
REECHO
REEDIT
REEFED
REEFER
REEKED
REELED
REELIN
REESES
REEVED
REEVES
SEEDED
SEEDER
SEEFIT
SEEGER
SEEING
SEEKER
SEELEY
SEEMED
SEEMLY
SEENIN
SEENTO
SEEOFF
SEEOUT
SEEPED
SEEPIN
SEERED
SEESAW
SEESIN
SEESTO
SEETHE
TEEDUP
TEEHEE
TEEING
TEEMED
TEENER
TEENSY
TEEOFF
TEESUP
TEETER
TEETHE
TEEVEE
VEEJAY
VEERED
WEEDED
WEEDER
WEEKLY
WEENIE
WEENSY
WEEPER
WEEPIE
WEEVIL
ZEEMAN

•E•E••

AEGEAN
AENEAS
AENEID
BEDECK
BEDEWS
BEFELL
BEGETS
BEHEAD
BEHELD
BEHEST
BEKESY
BEREFT
BERETS
BESETS
BETELS
BEVELS
BEZELS
CELEBS
CELERY
CEMENT
CEREAL
CEREUS
CETERA
DECEIT
DECENT
DEFEAT
DEFECT
DEFEND
DEFERS
DEJECT
DELEON
DELETE
DEMEAN
DEPEND
DESERT
DETECT
DETENT
DETERS
DETEST
DEVEIN
DEVEST
EELERS
FERENC
FEVERS
FEWEST
FEYEST
GELEES
GENERA
GENETS
GENEVA
GENEVE
GERENT
HELENA
HELENE
HELENS
HEREAT
HEREBY
HEREIN
HEREOF
HEREON
HERESY
HERETO
HETERO
HEWERS
HEXERS
JEREMY
JEWELS
JEWETT
KEVELS
LEGEND
LEVEED
LEVEES
LEVELS
LEVENE
LEVERS
LEXEME
MELEES
MERELY
MEREST
METEOR
METERS
NENETS
NEREID
NEREIS
NEREUS
NEVERS
NEWELS
NEWEST
OEDEMA
PELEUS
PESETA
PETERS
PEWEES
REBECS
REBELS
REBEND
REBENT
RECEDE
RECENT
RECESS
REDEAL
REDEEM
REDENY
REDEYE
REFERS
REGENT
REHEAL
REHEAR
REHEAT
REHEEL
REHELD
REHEMS
REJECT
REKEYS
RELENT
RELETS
RELEVY
REMEDY
REMELT
REMEND
RENEGE
RENEWS
REPEAL
REPEAT
REPEGS
REPELS
REPENT
REREAD
RERENT
RESEAL
RESEAT
RESEAU
RESECT
RESEDA
RESEED
RESEEN
RESEES
RESELL
RESEND
RESENT
RESETS
RESEWN
RESEWS
RETEAR
RETELL
RETENE
RETEST
REVEAL
REVELS
REVERB
REVERE
REVERS
REVERT
REVETS
REWEDS
REWELD
SEBERG
SECEDE
SECERN
SEDERS
SELECT
SELENA
SELENE
SELENO
SEMELE
SENECA
SENEGA
SERENA
SERENE
SEVENS
SEVERE
SEVERN
SEVERS
SEVERY
SEWELL
SEWERS
TEDEUM
TEHEED
TEHEES
TELEDU
TENENS
TENETS
TEPEES
TEREDO
TERESA
TERETE
TEREUS
VENEER
VENETO
VEREEN
VEXERS
WEBERN
WEDELN
WERENT
XEBECS
YEMENI

•E••E•

AEETES
AERIES
AETHER
BEADED
BEAKED
BEAKER
BEAMED
BEANED
BEARER
BEATEN
BEATER
BEAVER
BECKER
BECKET
BEEFED
BEEPED
BEEPER
BEEVES
BEGGED
BEGLEY
BEIGES
BELIED
BELIEF
BELIES
BELLED
BELLES
BELTED
BENDED
BENDER
BERBER
BERGEN
BESSER
BESTED
BETHEL
BETSEY
BETTER
BEVIES
CEASED
CEASES
CEILED
CELLED
CENSED
CENSER
CENSES
CENTER
CERMET
CESSED
CESSES
DEADEN
DEADER
DEAFEN
DEAFER
DEALER
DEARER
DECKED
DECKER
DECREE
DEEDED
DEEDEE
DEEMED
DEEPEN
DEEPER
DEFIED
DEFIES
DEFLEA
DEFTER
DEGREE
DEICED
DEICER
DEICES
DELVED
DELVER
DELVES
DEMIES
DENIED
DENIER
DENIES
DENNED
DENSER
DENTED
DENVER
DENZEL
DEUCED
DEUCES
DEWIER
DEXTER
EELIER
EERIER
FEARED
FEARER
FEEDER
FEELER
FELLED
FELLER
FELTED
FEMMES
FENCED
FENCER

FENCES
FENDED
FENDER
FENMEN
FENNEC
FENNEL
FERBER
FERRER
FERRET
FESSED
FESSES
FESTER
FETTER
FEUDED
FEZZES
GEARED
GEEGEE
GEEZER
GEIGER
GEISEL
GELEES
GELLED
GELSEY
GEMMED
GENDER
GENIES
GENRES
GEODES
GERBER
GESTES
GETSET
GETTER
GEYSER
HEADED
HEADER
HEALED
HEALER
HEANEY
HEAPED
HEARER
HEATED
HEATER
HEAVED
HEAVEN
HEAVER
HEAVES
HEBREW
HEDGED
HEDGER
HEDGES
HEDREN
HEEDED
HEEDER
HEELED
HEELER
HEFNER
HEFTED
HEIDEN
HEIFER
HELLER
HELMED
HELMET
HELPED
HELPER
HELTER
HELVES
HEMMED
HEMMER
HENLEY
HENNER
HENTED
HEPPER
HERDED
HERDER
HERMES
HEROES
HERSEY
HESTER
JEERED
JEERER
JEETER
JEEVES
JELLED
JENNER
JENNET
JENNEY
JENSEN
JERKED
JERSEY
JESSEL
JESTED
JESTER
JETSET
JETTED
KEDGED
KEDGES
KEELED
KEELER
KEENED
KEENEN
KEENER
KEEPER
KEGGED
KEGLER
KEITEL
KELLER
KELLEY
KELSEY
KENNED
KENNEL
KENNER
KEPLER
KERMES
KERNED
KERNEL
KERSEE
KERSEY
KEYNES
LEADED
LEADEN
LEADER
LEAFED
LEAKED
LEAKER
LEAKEY
LEANED
LEANER
LEAPED
LEAPER
LEASED
LEASER
LEASES
LEAVED
LEAVEN
LEAVES
LECTER
LEDGER
LEDGES
LEERED
LEERER
LEGGED
LEGMEN
LEGREE
LEHRER
LEIDEN
LEMUEL
LENDER
LENSED
LENSES
LENTEN
LEONES
LERNER
LESLEY
LESSEE
LESSEN
LESSER
LESTER
LETTED
LETTER
LEVEED
LEVEES
LEVIED
LEVIER
LEVIES
LEWDER
LEYDEN
MEAGER
MEANER
MEDLEY
MEEKER
MEETER
MELDED
MELEES
MELTED
MEMBER
MENDED
MENDEL
MENDER
MENDES
MENKEN
MENNEN
MEOWED
MERCED
MERCER
MERGED
MERGER
MERGES
MERKEL
MERMEN
MERSEY
MESHED
MESHES
MESMER
MESSED
MESSES
METIER
METRES
MEWLED
MEWLER
NEARED
NEARER
NEATEN
NEATER
NECKED
NEEDED
NEPHEW
NERVES
NESSES
NESTEA
NESTED
NESTER
NETHER
NETMEN
NETTED
NEUMES
NEUTER
NEWLEY
OERTER
PEAHEN
PEAKED
PEALED
PEAVEY
PECKED
PEEDEE
PEEKED
PEELED
PEELER
PEENED
PEEPED
PEEPER
PEERED
PEEVED
PEEVES
PEEWEE
PEGGED
PEGLER
PEKOES
PELLET
PELMET
PELTED
PELTER
PENCEL
PENDED
PENMEN
PENNED
PENNER
PENNEY
PENSEE
PEPPED
PEPPER
PERKED
PERMED
PERTER
PESTER
PETREL
PETTED
PETTER
PEWEES
PEWTER
READER
REALER
REALES
REAMED
REAMER
REAPED
REAPER
REARED
REARER
REBBES
REDDEN
REDDER
REDEEM
REDOES
REDREW
REDSEA
REDYED
REDYES
REEFED
REEFER
REEKED
REELED
REESES
REEVED
REEVES
REFFED
REFLEX
REFUEL
REGLET
REGRET
REHEEL
REINED
REINER
RELIED
RELIEF
RELIES
RENDER
RENNES
RENNET
RENTED
RENTER
REOPEN
RESEED
RESEEN
RESEES
RESHES
RESTED
RESTER
RETIED
RETIES
REUBEN
REUNES
REUSED
REUSES
REUTER
REVIEW
REVUES
REVVED
SEABED
SEABEE
SEALED
SEALER
SEAMED
SEAMEN
SEARED
SEATED
SEATER
SECKEL
SECRET
SEDGES
SEEDED
SEEDER
SEEGER
SEEKER
SEELEY
SEEMED
SEEPED
SEERED
SEGUED
SEGUES
SEIDEL
SEINED
SEINER
SEINES
SEIZED
SEIZER
SEIZES
SELLER
SELVES
SEMPER
SENDER
SENNET
SENSED
SENSEI
SENSES
SEPTET
SEQUEL
SERGEI
SERGES
SERIES
SERVED
SERVER
SERVES
SESTET
SETTEE
SETTER
SEVRES
SEXIER
SEXTET
TEAMED
TEARED
TEASED
TEASEL
TEASER
TEASES
TEASET
TEDDED
TEDDER
TEDKEY
TEEHEE
TEEMED
TEENER
TEETER
TEEVEE
TEHEED
TEHEES
TELLER
TEMPED
TEMPEH
TEMPER
TENDED
TENDER
TENREC
TENSED
TENSER
TENSES
TENTED
TENTER
TEPEES
TERCEL
TERCET
TERKEL
TERMED
TERNES
TERRET
TERSER
TESTED
TESTEE
TESTER
TETHER
TETZEL
TEXMEX
VEBLEN
VEDDER
VEERED
VEGGED
VEILED
VEINED
VELVET
VENDED
VENDEE
VENEER
VENTED
VENTER
VENUES
VEREEN
VERGED
VERGER
VERGES
VERSED
VERSES
VERTEX
VERVES
VERVET
VESPER
VESSEL
VESTED
VESTEE
VETOED
VETOER
VETOES
VETTED
WEAKEN
WEAKER
WEANED
WEARER
WEASEL
WEAVED
WEAVER
WEAVES
WEBBED
WEBBER
WEDDED
WEDGED
WEDGES
WEEDED
WEEDER
WEEPER
WELDED
WELDER
WELLED
WELLER
WELLES
WELTED
WELTER
WENCES
WENDED
WERFEL
WERNER
WESLEY
WESSEX
WETHER
WETTED
WETTER
XERXES
YEAGER
YEANED
YELLED
YELLER
YELPED
YELPER
YENNED
YEOMEN
YERKED
YERKES
YESMEN
YESSED
YESSES
YESTER
ZENGER
ZEROED
ZEROES
ZESTED

•E•••E

AEDILE
AERATE
AEROBE
BEADLE
BEAGLE
BEANIE
BEATLE
BECAME
BECOME
BEDAZE
BEETLE
BEFORE
BEGONE
BEHAVE
BEHOVE
BELIKE
BELIZE
BEMINE
BEMIRE
BEMUSE
BERATE
BERNIE
BERTIE
BESIDE
BESSIE
BETAKE
BETIDE
BETISE
BEURRE
BEWARE
CECILE
CELINE
CELLAE
CENOTE
CENTRE
CERATE
CERISE
CERUSE
CESARE
CETANE
DEARIE
DEARME
DEBASE
DEBATE
DEBBIE
DEBONE
DECADE
DECIDE
DECKLE
DECODE
DECREE
DEDUCE
DEEDEE
DEFACE
DEFAME
DEFILE
DEFINE
DEFUSE
DEGAGE
DEGREE
DEIDRE
DEJURE
DELATE
DELETE
DELUDE
DELUGE
DELUXE
DEMISE
DEMODE
DEMOTE
DEMURE
DENGUE
DENISE
DENOTE
DENUDE
DEPONE
DEPOSE
DEPUTE
DERIDE
DERIVE
DESIRE
DEVICE
DEVINE
DEVISE
DEVOTE
EEYORE
FEEBLE
FELINE
FELIPE
FELLOE
FEMALE
FERGIE
FERULE
FESCUE
FETTLE
GEEGEE
GEMMAE
GEMOTE
GENEVE
GENOME
GENTLE
GEORGE
GERTIE
HEARYE
HECATE
HECKLE
HEDDLE
HEEBIE
HELENE
HERBIE
HETTIE
JEANNE
JECKLE
JEJUNE
JENNIE
JEROME
JESSIE
KELPIE
KERSEE
KETONE
KETTLE
KEWPIE
LEAGUE
LEFTIE
LEGATE
LEGREE
LEGUME
LENAPE
LENNIE
LENORE
LEONIE
LESAGE
LESLIE
LESSEE
LETSBE
LEVENE

LEVINE
LEVITE
LEXEME
MEAGRE
MEALIE
MEANIE
MEDDLE
MENACE
MENAGE
MENSAE
MEROPE
METATE
METOPE
METTLE
NEEDLE
NEGATE
NEISSE
NELLIE
NESSIE
NESTLE
NETTLE
NEWAGE
OENONE
OEUVRE
PEBBLE
PEDATE
PEDDLE
PEEDEE
PEERCE
PEEWEE
PELAGE
PELIKE
PENNAE
PENSEE
PEOPLE
PERDUE
PERUKE
PERUSE
PESTLE
PETITE
PETRIE
PEYOTE
REBATE
REBUKE
RECANE
RECEDE
RECIFE
RECIPE
RECITE
RECODE
RECUSE
REDATE
REDEYE
REDONE
REDUCE
REFACE
REFILE
REFINE
REFUGE
REFUSE
REFUTE
REGALE
REGGAE
REGGIE
REGIME
REGLUE
REHIRE
RELACE
RELATE
RELINE
RELIVE
RELUME
REMADE
REMAKE
REMISE
REMOTE
REMOVE
RENAME
RENEGE
RENNIE
RENOTE
REPAVE
REPINE
REPOSE
REPUTE
RERATE
RESALE
RESCUE
RESHOE
RESIDE
RESILE
RESOLE
RESUME
RETAKE
RETAPE
RETENE
RETILE
RETIME
RETIRE
RETUNE
RETYPE
REVERE
REVILE
REVISE
REVIVE
REVOKE
REWIRE
REWOVE
REZONE
SEABEE
SEANCE
SEARLE
SECEDE
SECURE
SEDATE
SEDILE
SEDUCE
SEETHE
SEICHE
SELENE
SEMELE
SEMITE
SEMPRE
SENATE
SERAPE
SERENE
SERINE
SESAME
SETOSE
SETTEE
SETTLE
SEVERE
SEWAGE
TECHIE
TEEHEE
TEETHE
TEEVEE
TEMPLE
TENACE
TENURE
TERETE
TESSIE
TESTAE
TESTEE
VEGGIE
VELOCE
VENDEE
VENICE
VENIRE
VENITE
VERITE
VESTEE
WEDGIE
WEENIE
WEEPIE

••EE••

ADEEMS
AMEERS
BLEEDS
BLEEPS
BREECH
BREEDS
BREEZE
BREEZY
CHEECH
CHEEKS
CHEEKY
CHEEPS
CHEERS
CHEERY
CHEESE
CHEESY
CLEEKS
CLEESE
CREEDS
CREEKS
CREELS
CREEPS
CREEPY
DWEEBS
EMEERS
FLEECE
FLEECY
FLEERS
FLEETS
FREELY
FREEST
FREEZE
GREECE
GREEDY
GREEKS
GREENE
GREENS
GREENY
GREETS
KNEELS
OKEEFE
PREENS
QUEENS
SHEEDY
SHEEHY
SHEENA
SHEENS
SHEEPS
SHEERS
SHEETS
SLEEKS
SLEEKY
SLEEPS
SLEEPY
SLEETS
SLEETY
SLEEVE
SNEERS
SNEERY
SNEEZE
SNEEZY
SPEECH
SPEEDO
SPEEDS
SPEEDY
STEEDS
STEELE
STEELS
STEELY
STEEPS
STEERS
STEEVE
SWEEPS
SWEETS
THEEND
TWEEDS
TWEEDY
TWEENS
TWEENY
TWEEST
TWEETS
TWEETY
TWEEZE
WHEELS
WHEEZE
WHEEZY

••E•E•

ABELES
AEETES
AKENES
ALEVEL
ALEXEI
AMEDEO
ANELED
ANELES
APEMEN
APEXES
ARETES
ASEVER
BEEFED
BEEPED
BEEPER
BEEVES
BREMEN
BREUER
BREVES
BREVET
BREWED
BREWER
BREYER
CHEVET
CHEWED
CHEWER
CLEPED
CLEVER
CLEVES
CLEWED
CREMES
CRENEL
CREPES
CREWED
CREWEL
DEEDED
DEEDEE
DEEMED
DEEPEN
DEEPER
DIESEL
DIESES
DIETED
DIETER
DREXEL
DUELED
DUELER
ELEVEN
ELEVES
EVENED
EVENER
EXETER
EYELET
FEEDER
FEELER
FLEXED
FLEXES
FLEYED
FUELED
FUELER
GEEGEE
GEEZER
GLEBES
GREBES
GRETEL
GREYED
GREYER
HEEDED
HEEDER
HEELED
HEELER
IBEXES
ICEMEN
ILEXES
IRENES
JAEGER
JEERED
JEERER
JEETER
JEEVES
JOETEX
KEELED
KEELER
KEENED
KEENEN
KEENER
KEEPER
KIEFER
LEERED
LEERER
LIEDER
LIEFER
LIEGES
LIENEE
MEEKER
MEETER
NEEDED
NIECES
NUECES
OBEYED
OLEVEL
OMELET
OPENED
OPENER
OXEYES
PEEDEE
PEEKED
PEELED
PEELER
PEENED
PEEPED
PEEPER
PEERED
PEEVED
PEEVES
PEEWEE
PIECED
PIECER
PIECES
PIEMEN
PIETER
PLEBES
PREFER
PREMED
PRESET
PRETER
PREYED
QUEBEC
QUEUED
QUEUER
QUEUES
REEFED
REEFER
REEKED
REELED
REESES
REEVED
REEVES
SCENES
SEEDED
SEEDER
SEEGER
SEEKER
SEELEY
SEEMED
SEEPED
SEERED
SHEKEL
SHEREE
SIEGED
SIEGEL
SIEGES
SIEVED
SIEVES
SKEWED
SKEWER
SLEWED
SPEWED
STELES
STEREO
STERES
STEVEN
STEWED
STEWER
SUEDES
SWEDEN
SWEDES
TEEHEE
TEEMED
TEENER
TEETER
TEEVEE
THEBES
THEFED
THEMED
THEMES
THERES
THESEA
THESES
THEWEB
TIERED
TREBEK
UNEVEN
USENET
VEERED
VIEWED
VIEWER
WEEDED
WEEDER
WEEPER
WHERED
WHERES
WIENER
WIESEL

••E••E

ABESSE
ADELIE
ADELLE
ADESTE
AHERNE
ALEGRE
AMEBAE
AMECHE
AMERCE
ATEASE
AVENGE
AVENUE
AVERSE
AYEAYE
BEETLE
BIERCE
BLENDE
BREEZE
BYEBYE
CHEESE
CHELAE
CHEQUE
CHERIE
CHEVRE
CLEAVE
CLEESE
COERCE
CREASE
CREATE
CRECHE
CREOLE
DEEDEE
DIEPPE
DREDGE
EDERLE
EMERGE
EMEUTE
ETERNE
FAERIE
FAEROE
FEEBLE
FIERCE
FLECHE
FLEDGE
FLEECE
FLENSE
FREEZE
GEEGEE
GLENNE
GOETHE
GREASE
GREAVE
GREECE
GREENE
GREIGE
GUERRE
HEEBIE
ICEAGE
IDEATE
INESSE
KPELLE
KRESGE
LIENEE
LIERNE
NEEDLE
ODENSE
ODETTE
OKEEFE
OLEATE
ONEDGE
ORELSE
PEEDEE
PEERCE
PEEWEE
PHEDRE
PIERCE
PIERRE
PLEASE
PLEDGE
PREMIE
PUENTE
SEETHE
SHEAVE
SHELVE
SHEREE
SIECLE
SLEAVE
SLEAZE
SLEDGE
SLEEVE
SNEEZE
SPECIE
STEELE
STEEVE
STELAE
STEPPE
STERNE
STEVIE
SVELTE
SWERVE
TEEHEE
TEETHE
TEEVEE
THECAE
THENCE
THEYRE
THEYVE
TIEDYE
TIERCE
TREBLE
TSETSE
TWEEZE
TWELVE
UNEASE
VIENNE
WEENIE
WEEPIE
WHEEZE
WHENCE
YVETTE

•••EE•

ADWEEK
AFREET
AGREED
AGREES
AILEEN
ALLEES
ANTEED
ARLEEN
ASLEEP
AXSEED
BALEEN
BOPEEP
CAREEN
CAREER
CUVEES
DONEES
DUDEEN
EILEEN
EMCEED
EMCEES
ESTEEM
EXCEED
FUSEES
FUZEES
GELEES
HOMEEC
INDEED
INNEED
KAREEM
LATEEN
LEVEED
LEVEES
LYCEES
MELEES
MOREEN
MUDEEL
PAYEES
PEWEES
POTEEN
PUREED
PUREES
RANEES
REDEEM
REHEEL
RESEED
RESEEN
RESEES
RUPEES
SATEEN
SCREED
SCREEN
SCREES
SPLEEN
SPREES
STREEP
STREET
TEHEED
TEHEES
TEPEES
THREED
THREES
TUREEN
UNHEED
UNMEET
UNREEL
UNSEEN

UPKEEP
VENEER
VEREEN

•••E•E
ACCEDE
ACHEBE
ACHENE
ADHERE
ALKENE
ALLEGE
ALLELE
AMPERE
ANNEXE
APIECE
ARLENE
ARSENE
ATHENE
BAREGE
BIREME
BREEZE
BUTENE
CHEESE
CLEESE
COHERE
CYBELE
DELETE
EFFETE
EOCENE
EPHEBE
ESSENE
ETHENE
EUGENE
EXLEGE
FILENE
FLEECE
FOVEAE
FREEZE
FRIEZE
GALEAE
GAMETE
GENEVE
GREECE
GREENE
GRIEVE
GYRENE
HELENE
IMPEDE
INDENE
INHERE
IRLENE
ISMENE
JOLENE
LATENE
LEVENE
LEXEME
MANEGE
MAXENE
NICENE
OCREAE
OKEEFE
OSSETE
PALEAE
PAREVE
PHOEBE
POPEYE
RACEME
RECEDE
REDEYE
RENEGE
RETENE
REVERE
RIBEYE
SCHEME
SECEDE
SELENE
SEMELE
SERENE
SEVERE
SLEEVE
SNEEZE
SPHERE
STEELE
STEEVE
STPETE
SURETE
TALESE
TERETE
THIEVE
TUYERE
TWEEZE
VARESE
WHEEZE
XYLENE

••••EE
ADOREE
ANNLEE
APOGEE
ATTLEE
BAILEE
BOOTEE
BOTREE
BUNGEE
BURGEE
COFFEE
CORVEE
COULEE
DECREE
DEEDEE
DEGREE
DONNEE
DRAGEE
DUNDEE
ELYSEE
ENTREE
EPOPEE
FRISEE
GEEGEE
GOATEE
HUMVEE
JAYCEE
JAYVEE
KERSEE
LEGREE
LESSEE
LIENEE
LISTEE
MALLEE
MARLEE
MARMEE
MAUMEE
PARSEE
PAWNEE
PEEDEE
PEEWEE
PENSEE
POMMEE
PONGEE
PUGREE
PUTTEE
RAPPEE
RUSHEE
SANTEE
SEABEE
SETTEE
SHEREE
SIGNEE
SIRREE
SOIREE
SWANEE
TEEHEE
TEEVEE
TESTEE
TOATEE
TOFFEE
TOUPEE
TOWHEE
TRALEE
UNFREE
VALLEE
VENDEE
VESTEE
YANKEE
YIPPEE

EF••••
EFFACE
EFFECT
EFFETE
EFFIGY
EFFLUX
EFFORT
EFFUSE
EFLATS

E•F•••
EFFACE
EFFECT
EFFETE
EFFIGY
EFFLUX
EFFORT
EFFUSE
EIFFEL
ELFISH
ELFMAN
ENFANT
ENFOLD
ERFURT

E••F••
EARFUL
EIFFEL
EYEFUL

E•••F•
EXWIFE

E••••F
ENGULF

•EF•••
BEFALL
BEFELL
BEFITS
BEFOGS
BEFORE
BEFOUL
DEFACE
DEFAME
DEFATS
DEFEAT
DEFECT
DEFEND
DEFERS
DEFIED
DEFIES
DEFILE
DEFINE
DEFLEA
DEFOGS
DEFORM
DEFRAY
DEFTER
DEFTLY
DEFUSE
HEFLIN
HEFNER
HEFTED
KEFIRS
LEFTIE
LEFTIN
REFACE
REFERS
REFFED
REFILE
REFILL
REFINE
REFITS
REFLAG
REFLEX
REFLUX
REFORM
REFUEL
REFUGE
REFUND
REFUSE
REFUTE
TEFLON

•E•F••
BEEFED
BEEFUP
BELFRY
DEAFEN
DEAFER
DEAFLY
DELFTS
HEIFER
LEAFED
LETFLY
MEDFLY
PEPFUL
REDFIN
REDFIR
REDFOX
REEFED
REEFER
REFFED
SEAFAN
SEAFOX
SEEFIT
WERFEL
WETFLY

•E••F•
AERIFY
BEGOFF
BEREFT
DECAFS
GETOFF
LEDOFF
LETOFF
REBUFF
RECIFE
SEEOFF
SENUFO
SERIFS
SETOFF
TEEOFF
VERIFY

•E•••F
BEGOFF
BEHALF
BEHOOF
BELIEF
CERTIF
GETOFF
HEAROF
HEREOF
LEDOFF
LETOFF
REBUFF
RELIEF
SEEOFF
SETOFF
TEEOFF
TELLOF

••EF••
BEEFED
BEEFUP
CLEFTS
EYEFUL
ICEFOG
IREFUL
KIEFER
LIEFER
LIEFLY
OLEFIN
PREFAB
PREFER
PREFIX
REEFED
REEFER
RUEFUL
SEEFIT
STEFAN
STEFFI
STEFOY
THEFED
THEFLY
THEFTS
USEFUL
WOEFUL

••E•F•
DIEOFF
OKEEFE
SEEOFF
SHEAFS
STEFFI
TEEOFF

••E••F
DIEOFF
SEEOFF
SHERIF
TEEOFF

•••EF•
BEREFT
BRIEFS
CASEFY
CHIEFS
GRIEFS
OKEEFE
RAREFY
TUMEFY

•••E•F
HEREOF
IMPERF
ITSELF
MYSELF

••••EF
BELIEF
RELIEF
UNICEF

EG••••
EGBERT
EGERIA
EGESTA
EGESTS
EGGCUP
EGGIER
EGGING
EGGNOG
EGGSON
EGMONT
EGOISM
EGOIST
EGRESS
EGRETS

E•G•••
EAGLED
EAGLES
EAGLET
EAGRES
EDGARD
EDGARS
EDGEIN
EDGERS
EDGIER
EDGILY
EDGING
EGGCUP
EGGIER
EGGING
EGGNOG
EGGSON
EIGHTH
EIGHTS
EIGHTY
ENGAGE
ENGELS
ENGINE
ENGIRD
ENGIRT
ENGLUT
ENGRAM
ENGULF
ERGATE
ERGOTS
EUGENE

E••G••
ELEGIT
EMIGRE
ENIGMA

E•••G•
EFFIGY
ELOIGN
EMERGE
ENCAGE
ENERGY
ENGAGE
ENOUGH
ENRAGE
ENSIGN
ERYNGO
EULOGY
EXLEGE

E••••G
EALING
EARING
EARWIG
EASING
EATING
EBBING
EDBERG
EDGING
EGGING
EGGNOG
EKBERG
ENDING
EPILOG
EPPING
ERRING
ERVING
EYEING

•EG•••
AEGEAN
BEGETS
BEGGAR
BEGGED
BEGINS
BEGLEY
BEGOFF
BEGONE
BEGUMS
DEGAGE
DEGREE
DEGUST
HEGARI
HEGIRA
KEGGED
KEGLER
LEGACY
LEGALS
LEGATE
LEGATO
LEGEND
LEGGED
LEGION
LEGIST
LEGMAN
LEGMEN
LEGREE
LEGUIN
LEGUME
MEGALO
MEGARA
MEGILP
MEGOHM
NEGATE
PEGGED
PEGLER
PEGTOP
REGAIN
REGALE
REGARD
REGENT
REGGAE
REGGIE
REGIME
REGINA
REGION
REGIUS
REGLET
REGLUE
REGNAL
REGNAT
REGRET
SEGUED
SEGUES
SEGURA
VEGANS
VEGGED
VEGGIE

•E•G••
BEAGLE
BEEGUM
BEGGAR
BEGGED
BEIGES
BENGAL
BENGAY
BERGEN
DEIGNS
DENGUE
FEIGNS
FERGIE
FERGUS
GEEGAW
GEEGEE
GEIGER
GEWGAW
HEDGED
HEDGER
HEDGES
HEIGHT
JETGUN
KEDGED
KEDGES
KEGGED
LEAGUE
LEDGER
LEDGES
LEGGED
LENGTH
MEAGER
MEAGRE
MEDGAR
MERGED
MERGER
MERGES
NEIGHS
PEGGED
PENGHU
REAGAN
REDGUM
REGGAE
REGGIE
REIGNS
SEAGAL
SEDGES
SEEGER
SERGEI
SERGES
SERGIO
VEGGED
VEGGIE
VEIGHT
VERGED
VERGER
VERGES
WEDGED
WEDGES
WEDGIE
WEIGHS
WEIGHT
YEAGER
ZENGER
ZEUGMA

•E••G•
BEFOGS
BEINGS
BELUGA
BENIGN
DEBUGS
DEFOGS
DEGAGE
DELUGE
DESIGN
GEORGE
GEORGY
LEHIGH
LESAGE
LETSGO
MENAGE
NEWAGE
PELAGE
PERUGA
REBAGS
REFUGE
RENEGE
REPEGS
REPUGN
RESIGN
RETAGS
SENEGA
SEWAGE
TELUGU

•E•••G
BEDBUG
BELONG
BENING
BERING
CEDING
DEKING
DELONG
DEWING
FEEING
FETING
GEEING
GEHRIG
HERZOG

HEWING
HEXING
JETLAG
KENNYG
KEYING
MEKONG
METING
MEWING
PEKING
PENANG
PETROG
REDDOG
REDING
REDTAG
REFLAG
REHANG
REHUNG
RESING
SEABAG
SEADOG
SEBERG
SEEING
SEWING
TEABAG
TEEING
VEXING
WETTIG

••EG••
ALEGAR
ALEGRE
BEEGUM
ELEGIT
GEEGAW
GEEGEE
GREGOR
JAEGER
LIEGES
OMEGAS
OREGON
SEEGER
SIEGED
SIEGEL
SIEGES

••E•G•
ANERGY
ATERGO
AVENGE
AWEIGH
CLERGY
DREDGE
EMERGE
ENERGY
FLEDGE
FLEDGY
GREIGE
ICEAGE
KRESGE
ONEDGE
PLEDGE
SLEDGE
SLEIGH

••E••G
AGEING
BOEING
DYEING
EYEING
FEEING
GEEING
HIEING
HOEING
ICEBAG
ICEFOG
KOENIG
LIEBIG
PYEDOG
SEEING
STENOG
TEEING
TIEING
TOEING

•••EG•
ALLEGE
BADEGG
BAREGE
BODEGA
EXLEGE
FOREGO
MANEGE
NONEGO
ORTEGA
OSWEGO
PHLEGM
RAWEGG
RENEGE
REPEGS
SENEGA
UNPEGS

•••E•G
BADEGG
EDBERG
EKBERG
LIPENG
RATEDG
RAWEGG
SEBERG

••••EG
DOGLEG
MUSKEG
NUTMEG
TUAREG

E•H•••
ECHINO
ECHOED
ECHOES
ECHOIC
ENHALO
EPHAHS
EPHEBE
EPHODS
EPHORI
EPHORS
EPHRON
ERHARD
ESHARP
ETHANE
ETHENE
ETHERS
ETHICS
ETHNIC
ETHNOS
EXHALE
EXHORT

E••H••
EIGHTH
EIGHTS
EIGHTY
EITHER
ELOHIM
ESCHER
ESCHEW
ESTHER
ETCHED
ETCHER
ETCHES
EUCHRE

E•••H•
EARTHA
EARTHY
ELISHA
EPHAHS
EPOCHS

E••••H
EDKOCH
EIGHTH
ELFISH
ELIJAH
ELVISH
EMDASH
ENDASH
ENMESH
ENOUGH
ENRICH
EOLITH
EPARCH
EXARCH

•EH•••
BEHALF
BEHAVE
BEHEAD
BEHELD
BEHEST
BEHIND
BEHOLD
BEHOOF
BEHOVE
DEHORN
GEHRIG
LEHIGH
LEHRER
LEHUAS
REHABS
REHANG
REHASH
REHEAL
REHEAR
REHEAT
REHEEL
REHELD
REHEMS
REHIRE
REHOOK
REHUNG
TEHEED
TEHEES
YEHUDI

•E•H••
AETHER
BENHUR
BETHEL
HEEHAW
JETHRO
KESHIA
LETHAL
MENHIR
MESHED
MESHES
METHOD
METHYL
NEPHEW
NEPHRO
NETHER
PEAHEN
REDHAT
REDHOT
RESHES
RESHIP
RESHOD
RESHOE
RESHOT
SENHOR
TECHIE
TECHNO
TEEHEE
TEPHRA
TETHER
TETHYS
WETHER
ZEPHYR

•E••H•
BEACHY
BERTHA
BERTHS
BETCHA
DELPHI
DEPTHS
GEISHA
GERAHS
HEATHS
HEATHY
HEIGHT
LEACHY
MEGOHM
NEIGHS
PEACHY
PENGHU
PERCHA
REECHO
SEETHE
SEICHE
TEETHE
TENTHS
TETCHY
VEIGHT
WEIGHS
WEIGHT

•E•••H
BEULAH
CERIPH
DEARTH
DETACH
FELLAH
FETISH
HEALTH
HEARTH
JEWISH
LEHIGH
LENGTH
MENSCH
NEWISH
PERISH
PESACH
REHASH
RELISH
REWASH
SEARCH
SERAPH
TEMPEH
TERAPH
WEALTH
ZENITH
ZEROTH

••EH••
FOEHNS
HEEHAW
TEEHEE
THEHAJ

••E•H•
ALEPHS
AMECHE
ARETHA
AYESHA
BRECHT
CHETHS
CRECHE
CZECHS
FLECHE
FLESHY
GOETHE
ILESHA
OBEAHS
REECHO
SEETHE
SHEEHY
TEETHE

••E••H
AWEIGH
BLEACH
BLENCH
BREACH
BREATH
BREECH
CHEECH
CLENCH
DRENCH
FLETCH
FRENCH
GUELPH
KVETCH
PLEACH
PREACH
QUENCH
SHEATH
SKETCH
SLEIGH
SLEUTH
SMERSH
SPEECH
STENCH
TRENCH
WREATH
WRENCH
WRETCH

•••EH•
HIDEHO
SHEEHY

•••E•H
AFRESH
BREECH
CHEECH
COMETH
DALETH
ENMESH
GARETH
HITECH
JOBETH
JOSEPH
LAMECH
LAMEDH
OHYEAH
SAMECH
SAMEKH
SPEECH
TAKETH
THRESH
UNMESH
VOTECH

••••EH
TEMPEH
YAHWEH

EI••••
EIDERS
EIDOLA
EIFFEL
EIGHTH
EIGHTS
EIGHTY
EILEEN
EISNER
EITHER

E•I•••
EDIBLE
EDICTS
EDILES
EDISON
EDITED
EDITIO
EDITOR
EJIDOS
ELICIT
ELIDED
ELIDES
ELIJAH
ELINOR
ELISHA
ELISSA
ELITES
ELIXIR
EMIGRE
EMILIA
EMILIO
EMINOR
ENIGMA
ENISLE
EOIPSO
EPICAL
EPILOG
EPINAL
EPIRUS
ERINYS
EVICTS
EVILER
EVILLY
EVINCE
EXILED
EXILES
EXILIC
EXISTS
EXITED

E••I••
EALING
EARING
EASIER
EASILY
EASING
EATING
EBBING
ECHINO
EDDIED
EDDIES
EDGIER
EDGILY
EDGING
EELIER
EERIER
EERILY
EFFIGY
EGGIER
EGGING
EGOISM
EGOIST
ELAINE
ELFISH
ELLICE
ELLIOT
ELMIRA
ELNINO
ELOIGN
ELOISE
ELVIRA
ELVISH
EMAILS
EMPIRE
ENCINA
ENCINO
ENDING
ENDIVE
ENGINE
ENGIRD
ENGIRT
ENLIST
ENMITY
ENNIUS
ENRICH
ENRICO
ENSIGN
ENSILE
ENTICE
ENTIRE
ENTITY
ENVIED
ENVIER
ENVIES
EOLIAN
EOLITH
EONIAN
EOSINS
EPPING
EQUINE
EQUIPS
EQUITY
ERBIUM
ERMINE
EROICA
ERRING
ERVING
ESKIMO
ESPIAL
ESPIED
ESPIES
ETHICS
ETOILE
EUNICE
EXCISE
EXCITE
EXPIRE
EXPIRY
EXWIFE
EYEING
EYRIES

E•••I•
EARWIG
EASEIN
EATSIN
ECESIC
ECESIS
ECHOIC
ECLAIR
EDENIC
EDGEIN
EDITIO
EGERIA
ELAPID
ELEGIT
ELEMIS
ELICIT
ELIXIR
ELOHIM
EMILIA
EMILIO
ENJOIN
ENOKIS
ENOSIS
ENTAIL
ENVOIS
EROTIC
ESPRIT
ETALIA
ETALII
ETHNIC
ETONIC
EUCLID
EURAIL
EXILIC
EXOTIC
EYELID

E••••I
EPHORI
ERNANI
ETALII
EVENKI

•EI•••
BEIGES
BEINGS
BEIRUT
CEIBAS
CEILED
DEICED
DEICER
DEICES
DEIDRE
DEIGNS
DEIMOS
DEISTS
FEIGNS
FEINTS
FEISTY
GEIGER
GEISEL
GEISHA
HEIDEN
HEIFER
HEIGHT
HEISTS
KEITEL
LEIDEN
NEIGHS
NEISSE
REIGNS
REILLY
REINAS
REINED
REINER
REININ
REINKS
SEICHE
SEIDEL
SEINED
SEINER
SEINES
SEISMO
SEISMS
SEIZED
SEIZER
SEIZES
VEIGHT
VEILED
VEINAL
VEINED
WEIGHS
WEIGHT
WEIMAR
WEIRDO
WEIRDY

•E•I••
AEDILE
AERIAL
AERIES
AERIFY
AERILY
BEDIMS
BEFITS
BEGINS
BEHIND
BELIAL
BELIED
BELIEF
BELIES
BELIKE
BELIZE
BEMINE
BEMIRE
BENIGN
BENING
BENITO
BERING

BESIDE
BETIDE
BETISE
BEVIES
CECILE
CECILY
CEDING
CELINE
CERIPH
CERISE
CERIUM
CESIUM
DEBITS
DECIDE
DEFIED
DEFIES
DEFILE
DEFINE
DEKING
DELICT
DELIST
DELIUS
DEMIES
DEMISE
DEMITS
DENIAL
DENIED
DENIER
DENIES
DENIMS
DENIRO
DENISE
DEPICT
DERIDE
DERIVE
DESICA
DESIGN
DESILU
DESIRE
DESIST
DEVICE
DEVILS
DEVINE
DEVISE
DEVITO
DEWIER
DEWILY
DEWING
DEWITT
EELIER
EERIER
EERILY
FEEING
FELINE
FELIPE
FENIAN
FERIAL
FERIAS
FERITY
FETING
FETISH
GEEING
GEMINI
GENIAL
GENIES
GENIUS
GEZIRA
HEGIRA
HELIOS
HELIUM
HERIOT
HESIOD
HEWING
HEXING
JEWISH
KEFIRS
KEYING
LEGION
LEGIST
LEHIGH
LENITY
LERIDA
LEVIED
LEVIER
LEVIES
LEVINE
LEVITE
LEVITY
LEXICA
MEDIAL
MEDIAN
MEDIAS
MEDICI
MEDICO
MEDICS
MEDINA
MEDIUM
MEGILP
MEJICO
MELINA
MENIAL
MENINX
MERIDA
MERINO
MERITS
METIER
METING
MEWING
MEXICO
NEVINS
NEWISH
PEKING
PEKINS
PELIKE
PELION
PEPINO
PEPITA
PERILS
PERIOD
PERISH
PETITE
PEWITS
REAIMS
REAIRS
REBIDS
REBIND
RECIFE
RECIPE
RECITE
REDIAL
REDING
REDINK
REFILE
REFILL
REFINE
REFITS
REGIME
REGINA
REGION
REGIUS
REHIRE
RELICS
RELICT
RELIED
RELIEF
RELIES
RELINE
RELISH
RELIST
RELIVE
REMICK
REMIND
REMISE
REMISS
REMITS
REOILS
REPINE
REPINS
RESIDE
RESIGN
RESILE
RESING
RESINS
RESINY
RESIST
RETIAL
RETIED
RETIES
RETILE
RETIME
RETINA
RETIRE
REVIEW
REVILE
REVISE
REVIVE
REWIND
REWINS
REWIRE
SEDILE
SEEING
SEMITE
SENIOR
SENITI
SEPIAS
SERIAL
SERIES
SERIFS
SERINE
SERINS
SETINS
SEWING
SEXIER
SEXILY
SEXIST
TEDIUM
TEEING
VENIAL
VENICE
VENIRE
VENITE
VERIFY
VERILY
VERISM
VERITE
VERITY
VEXING
ZENITH

•E••I•

AENEID
AEOLIA
AEOLIC
BEANIE
BEATIT
BEAVIS
BELAIR
BELOIT
BENDIX
BENOIT
BERLIN
BERNIE
BERTIE
BESSIE
BESTIR
BEWAIL
CEDRIC
CELTIC
CERTIF
CERVID
DEALIN
DEARIE
DEASIL
DEBBIE
DEBRIS
DECEIT
DELRIO
DELTIC
DENNIS
DENTIL
DENTIN
DERAIL
DERMIS
DERRIS
DETAIL
DETAIN
DEVEIN
DEVOID
DEVOIR
FELLIN
FERGIE
FERRIC
FERRIS
FERVID
GEHRIG
GERBIL
GERTIE
GESTIC
GETSIN
GETSIT
HEADIN
HECTIC
HEEBIE
HEFLIN
HELDIN
HEMSIN
HENBIT
HENNIN
HENRIK
HERBIE
HEREIN
HERMIT
HEROIC
HESTIA
HETTIE
JENNIE
JERKIN
JESSIE
JESUIT
KEEPIN
KELPIE
KELVIN
KEMPIS
KERMIS
KERMIT
KESHIA
KEWPIE
KEYSIN
LEADIN
LEFTIE
LEFTIN
LEGUIN
LENNIE
LENTIL
LEONID
LEONIE
LESLIE
LETSIN
MEALIE
MEANIE
MELVIL
MELVIN
MEMOIR
MENHIR
MENTIS
MERLIN
METRIC
NELLIE
NEREID
NEREIS
NESSIE
PECTIC
PECTIN
PEERIN
PELVIC
PELVIS
PENCIL
PENNIA
PENNIS
PEORIA
PEPSIN
PEPTIC
PERMIT
PERNIO
PERSIA
PETAIN
PETRIE
PETTIT
READIN
REALIA
REBOIL
RECOIL
REDFIN
REDFIR
REEDIT
REELIN
REGAIN
REGGIE
REININ
REJOIN
RELAID
REMAIL
REMAIN
RENAIL
RENNIE
RENNIN
RENOIR
REPAID
REPAIR
RESHIP
RESNIK
RESPIN
RETAIL
RETAIN
RETRIM
REVOIR
SEEFIT
SEENIN
SEEPIN
SEESIN
SENDIN
SENNIT
SENTIN
SEPTIC
SEQUIN
SERAIS
SERBIA
SERGIO
SERKIN
SETSIN
TECHIE
TENNIS
TENPIN
TESSIE
TETRIS
VEGGIE
VERBIS
VERDIN
VERMIN
VESPID
WEDGIE
WEENIE
WEEPIE
WEEVIL
WELKIN
WENTIN
WESKIT
WETTIG
YESSIR
ZENDIC
ZEROIN
ZEUXIS

•E•••I

BENONI
CENTRI
DELPHI
DENALI
DENDRI
GELATI
GEMINI
HEGARI
JETSKI
KERNOI
MEDICI
MESABI
NEPALI
NEROLI
SENITI
SENSEI
SERGEI
SESQUI
YEHUDI
YEMENI

••EI••

AGEING
AGEISM
AGEIST
ASEITY
AWEIGH
BOEING
DYEING
EYEING
FEEING
GEEING
GNEISS
GREIGE
HIEING
HOEING
KLEIST
KWEISI
ONEIDA
ONEILL
OREIDA
PLEIAD
SEEING
SHEIKS
SHEILA
SKEINS
SLEIGH
STEINS
TEEING
THEIRS
THEISM
THEIST
TIEING
TIEINS
TOEING
TOEINS

••E•I•

ACEDIA
ACETIC
ADELIE
ALEXIA
ALEXIS
AMEBIC
AMELIA
ANEMIA
ANEMIC
BLEWIT
BREVIS
CHEMIN
CHENIN
CHERIE
CLERIC
CLEVIS
COEDIT
CREDIT
CRETIN
DIESIS
DOESIN
DREWIN
ECESIC
ECESIS
EDENIC
EGERIA
ELEGIT
ELEMIS
EYELID
FAERIE
FLEWIN
FOETID
GAELIC
GOESIN
HEEBIE
IBERIA
ICEDIN
ICESIN
IGETIT
IRENIC
ISELIN
KEEPIN
KOENIG
LIEBIG
LIESIN
MYELIN
NOESIS
NOETIC
NOEXIT
OBELIA
OLEFIN
PEERIN
PIETIN
POETIC
PRECIS
PREFIX
PRELIM
PREMIE
PREVIN
REEDIT
REELIN
SCENIC
SEEFIT
SEENIN
SEEPIN
SEESIN
SHERIF
SPECIE
STEPIN
STEVIE
THEKID
THELIP
THESIS
THESIX
THETIC
THETIS
THEWIZ
TIEDIN
TIEPIN
TIESIN
TMESIS
TOEDIN
TOESIN
TREDIA
TREPID
USERID
WEENIE
WEEPIE
WEEVIL

••E••I

ALEXEI
EVENKI
KWEISI
NIELLI
OCELLI
RIENZI
STEFFI

•••EI•

AENEID
ALBEIT
CAMEIN
CAVEIN
CLUEIN
COHEIR
COMEIN
DECEIT
DEVEIN
DINEIN
DIVEIN
DONEIN
DOVEIN
EASEIN
EDGEIN
FADEIN
GAVEIN
GIVEIN
HEREIN
LIVEIN
LOMEIN
LOSEIT
LOVEIN
MACEIO
MADEIT
MAKEIT
MOVEIN
NEREID
NEREIS
OSSEIN
PILEIN
RAKEIN
ROPEIN
SOBEIT
SOLEIL
TAKEIN
TUNEIN
UNVEIL
VOTEIN
WADEIN
WAVEIN

•••E•I

ANGELI
DOREMI
HIDEKI
HUMERI
LIBERI
SILENI
VIDERI
YEMENI

••••EI

ALEXEI
ANDREI
BRUNEI
CISKEI
GLUTEI
MALLEI
NIKKEI
NUCLEI
PROTEI
SANSEI
SENSEI
SERGEI
TAIPEI

EJ••••

EJECTA
EJECTS
EJIDOS

E•J•••

ENJOIN
ENJOYS

E••J••

ELIJAH

EMAJOR

•EJ•••
DEJAVU
DEJECT
DEJURE
JEJUNE
MEJICO
REJECT
REJOIN
SEJANT
TEJANO

•E•J••
DEEJAY
MENJOU
SELJUK
VEEJAY

••EJ••
DEEJAY
VEEJAY

••E••J
THEHAJ

•••E•J
INTERJ

EK••••
EKBERG
EKEOUT

E•K•••
EDKOCH
ESKERS
ESKIMO

E••K••
ENOKIS
EVOKED
EVOKER
EVOKES

E•••K•
EUREKA
EVENKI

E••••K
EMBANK
EMBARK

•EK•••
BEKESY
DEKALB
DEKING
DEKKOS
JEKYLL
LEKVAR
MEKONG
NEKTON
PEKING
PEKINS
PEKOES
REKEYS

•E•K••
BEAKED
BEAKER
BECKER
BECKET
BECKON
DECKED
DECKER
DECKLE
DEKKOS
GECKOS
HECKLE
JECKLE
JERKED
JERKIN
LEAKED
LEAKER
LEAKEY
MEEKER
MEEKLY
MENKEN
MERKEL
NECKED
PEAKED
PECKAT
PECKED
PEEKAT
PEEKED
PERKED
PERKUP
RECKON
REEKED
SECKEL
SEEKER
SERKIN
TEDKEY
TERKEL
WEAKEN
WEAKER
WEAKLY
WEEKLY
WELKIN
WESKIT
YERKED
YERKES

•E••K•
BELIKE
BETAKE
JETSKI
MEDAKA
NEVSKY
PELIKE
PERUKE
REBUKE
REINKS
REMAKE
RETAKE
REVOKE
SEDAKA

•E•••K
BEDECK
BETOOK
DEBARK
DEBUNK
DEEPAK
HENRIK
NEWARK
RECORK
REDINK
REDOAK
REEBOK
REHOOK
RELOCK
REMARK
REMICK
RESNIK
RETOOK
REWORK
SELJUK
SENDAK

••EK••
CHEKOV
MEEKER
MEEKLY
PEEKAT
PEEKED
REEKED
SEEKER
SHEKEL
THEKID
WEEKLY

••E•K•
ALECKY
BREAKS
CHECKS
CHEEKS
CHEEKY
CLEEKS
CLERKS
CREAKS
CREAKY
CREEKS
EVENKI
FLECKS
FLECKY
FREAKS
FREAKY
GREEKS
SHEIKS
SLEEKS
SLEEKY
SNEAKS
SNEAKY
SPEAKS
SPECKS
STEAKS
TWEAKS
VNECKS
WHELKS
WREAKS
WRECKS

••E••K
DEEPAK
REEBOK
RHEBOK
SLEZAK
TREBEK

•••EK•
CHEEKS
CHEEKY
CLEEKS
CREEKS
EUREKA
GREEKS
HACEKS
HIDEKI
KOPEKS
SAMEKH
SLEEKS
SLEEKY
TOPEKA
UZBEKS

•••E•K
ADWEEK
BEDECK
KOPECK
LUBECK
ONDECK
SCREAK
SQUEAK
STREAK

••••EK
ADWEEK
DUBCEK
OCASEK
SHRIEK
SPACEK
TREBEK

EL••••
ELAINE
ELANDS
ELAPID
ELAPSE
ELATED
ELATER
ELATES
ELAYER
ELAYNE
ELBERT
ELBOWS
ELBRUS
ELDERS
ELDEST
ELECTS
ELEGIT
ELEMIS
ELEVEN
ELEVES
ELFISH
ELFMAN
ELICIT
ELIDED
ELIDES
ELIJAH
ELINOR
ELISHA
ELISSA
ELITES
ELIXIR
ELLERY
ELLICE
ELLIOT
ELMIRA
ELMORE
ELNINO
ELOHIM
ELOIGN
ELOISE
ELOPED
ELOPER
ELOPES
ELPASO
ELUDED
ELUDER
ELUDES
ELUTED
ELUTES
ELVERS
ELVIRA
ELVISH
ELWOOD
ELYSEE

E•L•••
EALING
ECLAIR
ECLATS
EELERS
EELIER
EFLATS
EILEEN
ELLERY
ELLICE
ELLIOT
ENLACE
ENLIST
EOLIAN
EOLITH
EULOGY
EXLEGE

E••L••
EAGLED
EAGLES
EAGLET
EARLAP
ECCLES
ECOLES
EDILES
EFFLUX
EMBLEM
EMILIA
EMILIO
EMPLOY
ENBLOC
ENGLUT
EPILOG
ETALIA
ETALII
EUCLID
EVELYN
EVILER
EVILLY
EVOLVE
EVULSE
EXALTS
EXILED
EXILES
EXILIC
EXULTS
EYELET
EYELID

E•••L•
EASELS
EASILY
EBERLY
EDERLE
EDGILY
EDIBLE
EDSELS
EERILY
EIDOLA
EMAILS
ENABLE
ENDALL
ENFOLD
ENGELS
ENGULF
ENHALO
ENISLE
ENROLL
ENROLS
ENSILE
EQUALS
ERROLL
ETOILE
EVENLY
EVERLY
EVILLY
EXCELS
EXHALE
EXPELS
EXTOLS

E••••L
EARFUL
EIFFEL
ENAMEL
ENDALL
ENROLL
ENSOUL
ENTAIL
EPICAL
EPINAL
ERROLL
ESPIAL
ETYMOL
EURAIL
EYEFUL

•EL•••
BELAIR
BELAYS
BELDAM
BELFRY
BELIAL
BELIED
BELIEF
BELIES
BELIKE
BELIZE
BELLAY
BELLED
BELLES
BELLOC
BELLOW
BELOIT
BELONG
BELTED
BELUGA
CELEBS
CELERY
CELINE
CELLAE
CELLAR
CELLED
CELLOS
CELTIC
DELANO
DELANY
DELATE
DELAYS
DELEON
DELETE
DELFTS
DELICT
DELIST
DELIUS
DELMAR
DELONG
DELPHI
DELRAY
DELRIO
DELROY
DELTAS
DELTIC
DELUDE
DELUGE
DELUXE
DELVED
DELVER
DELVES
EELERS
EELIER
FELDON
FELINE
FELIPE
FELLAH
FELLAS
FELLED
FELLER
FELLIN
FELLOE
FELLON
FELLOW
FELLTO
FELONS
FELONY
FELTED
GELADA
GELATI
GELATO
GELEES
GELLED
GELSEY
HELDIN
HELDON
HELDTO
HELDUP
HELENA
HELENE
HELENS
HELIOS
HELIUM
HELLAS
HELLER
HELLOS
HELMED
HELMET
HELMUT
HELOTS
HELPED
HELPER
HELTER
HELVES
JELLED
KELLER
KELLEY
KELPIE
KELSEY
KELVIN
LELAND
MELANO
MELDED
MELEES
MELINA
MELLON
MELLOW
MELMAC
MELODY
MELONS
MELOTT
MELTED
MELTON
MELVIL
MELVIN
MELVYN
NELLIE
NELSON
PELAGE
PELEUS
PELIKE
PELION
PELLET
PELMET
PELOPS
PELOTA
PELTED
PELTER
PELTRY
PELVIC
PELVIS
RELACE
RELAID
RELATE
RELAYS
RELENT
RELETS
RELEVY
RELICS
RELICT
RELIED
RELIEF
RELIES
RELINE
RELISH
RELIST
RELIVE
RELOAD
RELOCK
RELUCT
RELUME
SELDOM
SELECT
SELENA
SELENE
SELENO
SELJUK
SELLER
SELVES
TELEDU
TELLER
TELLOF
TELLON
TELUGU
VELCRO
VELDTS
VELLUM
VELOCE
VELOUR
VELVET
WELDED
WELDER
WELKIN
WELLED
WELLER
WELLES
WELLUP
WELTED
WELTER
YELLED
YELLER
YELLOW
YELPED
YELPER

•E•L••
AEOLIA
AEOLIC
AEOLUS
BEDLAM
BEGLEY
BELLAY
BELLED
BELLES
BELLOC
BELLOW
BERLIN
BEULAH
CEILED
CELLAE
CELLAR
CELLED
CELLOS
CEYLON
DEALER
DEALIN
DEFLEA
DEPLOY
DEWLAP
FEALTY
FEELER
FELLAH
FELLAS
FELLED
FELLER
FELLIN
FELLOE
FELLON
FELLOW
FELLTO
GELLED
HEALED
HEALER
HEALTH
HEELED
HEELER
HEFLIN
HELLAS
HELLER
HELLOS
HENLEY
JELLED
JETLAG
KEELED
KEELER
KEGLER
KELLER
KELLEY
KEPLER
KEVLAR
LEALTY
LESLEY
LESLIE
MEALIE

MEDLAR
MEDLAT
MEDLEY
MELLON
MELLOW
MERLIN
MERLON
MERLOT
MEWLED
MEWLER
NELLIE
NEWLEY
PEALED
PEDLAR
PEELED
PEELER
PEGLER
PELLET
PEPLOS
PEPLUM
REALER
REALES
REALIA
REALLY
REALMS
REALTY
REELED
REELIN
REFLAG
REFLEX
REFLUX
REGLET
REGLUE
REILLY
REPLAN
REPLAY
REPLOW
REVLON
SEALAB
SEALED
SEALER
SEALUP
SEELEY
SELLER
SENLAC
TEFLON
TELLER
TELLOF
TELLON
TESLAS
VEBLEN
VEILED
VELLUM
WEALTH
WELLED
WELLER
WELLES
WELLUP
WESLEY
YELLED
YELLER
YELLOW
ZEALOT

•E••L•

AEDILE
AERILY
BEADLE
BEAGLE
BEATLE
BECALM
BEETLE
BEFALL
BEFELL
BEHALF
BEHELD
BEHOLD
BETELS
BEVELS
BEZELS
CECILE
CECILY
CEORLS
DEADLY
DEAFLY
DEARLY
DECALS
DECKLE
DEEPLY
DEFILE
DEFTLY
DEKALB
DENALI
DESALT
DESILU
DEVILS
DEWILY
EERILY
FEATLY
FEEBLE
FEEBLY
FEMALE
FERULE
FETTLE
GENTLE
GENTLY
GERALD
HECKLE
HEDDLE
HERALD
JECKLE
JEKYLL
JEWELS
KEENLY
KERALA
KETTLE
KEVELS
LEANLY
LEGALS
LETFLY
LEVELS
LEWDLY
MEANLY
MEASLY
MEDALS
MEDDLE
MEDFLY
MEEKLY
MEETLY
MEGALO
MEGILP
MERELY
METALS
METTLE
NEARLY
NEATLY
NEBULA
NEEDLE
NEPALI
NEROLI
NESTLE
NETTLE
NETTLY
NEWELS
PEARLS
PEARLY
PEBBLE
PEBBLY
PEDALS
PEDDLE
PENULT
PEOPLE
PERILS
PERTLY
PESTLE
PETALS
PETULA
REALLY
REBELS
REBOLT
RECALL
REFILE
REFILL
REGALE
REHELD
REILLY
REMELT
REMOLD
REOILS
REPELS
REPOLL
RESALE
RESALT
RESELL
RESILE
RESOLD
RESOLE
RESULT
RETELL
RETILE
RETOLD
REVELS
REVILE
REVOLT
REWELD
SEARLE
SEDILE
SEEMLY
SEMELE
SEPALS
SETTLE
SEWELL
SEXILY
TEMPLE
TEPALS
VERILY
WEAKLY
WEDELN
WEEKLY
WETFLY
YEARLY

•E•••L

AERIAL
BEFALL
BEFELL
BEFOUL
BELIAL
BENGAL
BENZOL
BETHEL
BEWAIL
CEREAL
DEASIL
DENIAL
DENTAL
DENTIL
DENZEL
DEPAUL
DERAIL
DERMAL
DETAIL
FENNEL
FERIAL
FESTAL
FEUDAL
GEISEL
GENIAL
GENUAL
GERBIL
HERBAL
JEKYLL
JESSEL
KEITEL
KENNEL
KERNEL
LEMUEL
LENTIL
LETHAL
MEDIAL
MELVIL
MENDEL
MENIAL
MENSAL
MENTAL
MERKEL
MESCAL
METHYL
NEURAL
NEUROL
PENCEL
PENCIL
PENPAL
PEPFUL
PETREL
PETROL
REBOIL
RECALL
RECOIL
REDEAL
REDIAL
REFILL
REFUEL
REGNAL
REHEAL
REHEEL
REMAIL
RENAIL
RENTAL
REPEAL
REPOLL
RESEAL
RESELL
RETAIL
RETELL
RETIAL
RETOOL
RETRAL
REVEAL
SEAGAL
SECKEL
SEIDEL
SEPTAL
SEQUEL
SERIAL
SERVAL
SEWELL
TEASEL
TERCEL
TERKEL
TETZEL
VEINAL
VENIAL
VERBAL
VERNAL
VESSEL
VESTAL
WEASEL
WEEVIL
WERFEL

••EL••

ABELES
ADELIE
ADELLE
AIELLO
AKELAS
AMELIA
ANELED
ANELES
BCELLS
CHELAE
CHELAS
COELOM
DUELED
DUELER
DUELLO
DWELLS
DYELOT
EVELYN
EYELET
EYELID
FEELER
FIELDS
FJELDS
FUELED
FUELER
GAELIC
GUELPH
HEELED
HEELER
IMELDA
ISELIN
KEELED
KEELER
KNELLS
KPELLE
KVELLS
LIELOW
MYELIN
NIELLI
NIELLO
OBELIA
OBELUS
OCELLI
OCELOT
OKELLY
OMELET
ORELSE
OTELLO
PAELLA
PEELED
PEELER
PRELAW
PRELIM
QUELLS
REELED
REELIN
SEELEY
SHELLS
SHELLY
SHELTY
SHELVE
SMELLS
SMELLY
SMELTS
SNELLS
SPELLS
STELAE
STELAR
STELES
STELLA
STELMO
SVELTE
SWELLS
THELIP
THELMA
TWELVE
WHELKS
WHELMS
WHELPS
WIELDS
YIELDS

••E•L•

ADELLE
AGEOLD
AIELLO
AREOLA
AWEDLY
BCELLS
BEETLE
CREELS
CREOLE
DEEPLY
DUELLO
DWELLS
EBERLY
EDERLE
EVENLY
EVERLY
FEEBLE
FEEBLY
FREELY
GREYLY
IDEALS
ISEULT
KEENLY
KNEELS
KNELLS
KPELLE
KVELLS
LIEFLY
MEEKLY
MEETLY
NEEDLE
NIELLI
NIELLO
OCELLI
OKELLY
ONEILL
OPENLY
OTELLO
OVERLY
PAELLA
PUEBLA
PUEBLO
QUELLS
SEEMLY
SHEILA
SHELLS
SHELLY
SIECLE
SMELLS
SMELLY
SNELLS
SPELLS
STEALS
STEELE
STEELS
STEELY
STELLA
SWELLS
THEFLY
THEYLL
TREBLE
TREBLY
WEEKLY
WHEALS
WHEELS

••E••L

ACETAL
ACETYL
ALEVEL
CHERYL
CHEVAL
COEVAL
CRENEL
CRESOL
CREWEL
DAEDAL
DIESEL
DREXEL
EYEFUL
FOETAL
GRETEL
HIEMAL
HYETAL
IREFUL
OLEVEL
ONEILL
PHENOL
PHENYL
PLEXAL
RUEFUL
SHEKEL
SHERYL
SIEGEL
STEROL
THECAL
THEYLL
USEFUL
WEEVIL
WIESEL
WOEFUL

•••EL•

AFIELD
ALLELE
ANGELA
ANGELI
ANGELL
ANGELO
ANGELS
ANSELM
ARBELA
ARTELS
ASWELL
BABELS
BAGELS
BARELY
BASELY
BEFELL
BEHELD
BETELS
BEVELS
BEZELS
BLUELY
BOTELS
CAMELS
CAVELL
CICELY
COMELY
COSELL
CREELS
CUPELS
CUTELY
CYBELE
DIRELY
DOTELL
DOWELS
EASELS
EDSELS
ENGELS
EXCELS
EXPELS
FINELY
FREELY
GAMELY
GAVELS
GIMELS
GRUELS
HAMELN
HAZELS
HOMELY
HOSELS
HOTELS
HOVELS
HOWELL
HUGELY
IMPELS
ITSELF
JEWELS
KEVELS
KNEELS
LABELS
LAMELY
LAPELS
LATELY
LEVELS
LIBELS
LIKELY
LIVELY
LONELY
LOVELL
LOVELY
LOWELL
MABELL
MERELY
MODELA
MODELS
MODELT
MORELS
MOTELS
MUTELY
MYSELF
NAMELY
NAVELS
NEWELS
NICELY
NOVELS
NUDELY
OHWELL
ORIELS
ORWELL
OUSELS
OUZELS
PALELY
PAMELA
PANELS
PIXELS
POMELO
POWELL
PURELY
RARELY
RATELS
RAVELS
REBELS
REHELD
REMELT
REPELS
RESELL
RETELL
REVELS
REWELD
RIFELY
RIPELY
RONELY
ROWELS
RUDELY
RYDELL
SAFELY
SAGELY
SANELY
SCHELL
SEMELE
SEWELL
SHIELD
SOLELY
SORELY
SPIELS
STEELE
STEELS
STEELY
SURELY
TAMELY
TIMELY
TOWELS
TUPELO
UMBELS
UNBELT
UNWELL
UPHELD
UPWELL
VILELY
VOWELS
VOWELY
WEDELN
WHEELS
WIDELY

WIFELY
WISELY
YARELY
YODELS
YOKELS

•••E•L

ANGELL
ANNEAL
APPEAL
ASWELL
BEFELL
BOREAL
CAVELL
CEREAL
COSELL
CUNEAL
DOTELL
HOWELL
IRREAL
LINEAL
LOREAL
LOVELL
LOWELL
MABELL
MUDEEL
OHWELL
ORDEAL
ORWELL
OSTEAL
PINEAL
POWELL
REDEAL
REHEAL
REHEEL
REPEAL
RESEAL
RESELL
RETELL
REVEAL
RYDELL
SCHELL
SEWELL
SHTETL
SOLEIL
SQUEAL
UNREAL
UNREEL
UNSEAL
UNVEIL
UNWELL
UPWELL

••••EL

ALEVEL
AMSTEL
BARBEL
BARREL
BATTEL
BETHEL
BOATEL
BUNUEL
BUSHEL
CANCEL
CANNEL
CARMEL
CARPEL
CARREL
CARTEL
CHANEL
CHAPEL
CHISEL
COMPEL
CORBEL
CORNEL
CORREL
CRENEL
CREWEL
CUDGEL
DAMSEL
DANIEL
DARNEL
DENZEL
DHOTEL
DIESEL
DISPEL
DOSSEL
DREXEL
DRIVEL
DUFFEL
EIFFEL
ENAMEL
FENNEL
FUNNEL
GEISEL
GIMBEL
GOSPEL
GRAVEL
GRETEL
GROVEL
GUMBEL
GUNNEL
HALLEL
HANDEL
HANSEL
HILLEL
HORMEL
HOSTEL
IJSSEL
ISABEL
ISOHEL
ISRAEL
JESSEL
KEITEL
KENNEL
KERNEL
KOPPEL
KUMMEL
LAUREL
LEMUEL
LINTEL
LIONEL
LISTEL
MANTEL
MANUEL
MARCEL
MARIEL
MARTEL
MARVEL
MATTEL
MENDEL
MERKEL
MICHEL
MIGUEL
MONTEL
MORSEL
MOSTEL
MUDEEL
MURIEL
MUSSEL
NICKEL
OLEVEL
PARCEL
PARREL
PASSEL
PASTEL
PENCEL
PETREL
POMMEL
PROPEL
PUMMEL
RACHEL
RAFAEL
RAPPEL
RAQUEL
REFUEL
REHEEL
ROMMEL
RONDEL
RUNNEL
SAMUEL
SAUREL
SECKEL
SEIDEL
SEQUEL
SHEKEL
SHOVEL
SIEGEL
SIMBEL
SIMNEL
SISKEL
SNIVEL
SORREL
SPINEL
STIPEL
SWIVEL
TASSEL
TEASEL
TERCEL
TERKEL
TETZEL
TINSEL
TRAVEL
TROWEL
TUNNEL
UNREEL
VACHEL
VESSEL
WEASEL
WERFEL
WIESEL

EM••••

EMAILS
EMAJOR
EMBANK
EMBARK
EMBAYS
EMBDEN
EMBEDS
EMBERS
EMBLEM
EMBODY
EMBOSS
EMBRYO
EMCEED
EMCEES
EMDASH
EMEERS
EMENDS
EMERGE
EMEUTE
EMIGRE
EMILIA
EMILIO
EMINOR
EMMETS
EMMETT
EMOTED
EMOTER
EMOTES
EMPERY
EMPIRE
EMPLOY
EMPTOR
EMQUAD

E•M•••

EDMOND
EDMUND
EGMONT
ELMIRA
ELMORE
EMMETS
EMMETT
ENMESH
ENMITY
ERMINE
EXMOOR
EXMORE

E••M••

EDAMES
ELEMIS
ELFMAN
ENAMEL
ENAMOR
ENDMAN
ENDMEN
ETYMOL
ETYMON
EXEMPT

E•••M•

ENCAMP
ENIGMA
ENTOMO
ENZYME
EPROMS
ESKIMO

E••••M

EGOISM
ELOHIM
EMBLEM
ENGRAM
EPONYM
ERBIUM
ESTEEM

•EM•••

BEMATA
BEMINE
BEMIRE
BEMOAN
BEMUSE
CEMENT
DEMAND
DEMEAN
DEMIES
DEMISE
DEMITS
DEMOBS
DEMODE
DEMOND
DEMONS
DEMOTE
DEMURE
DEMURS
FEMALE
FEMMES
FEMORA
FEMURS
GEMARA
GEMINI
GEMMAE
GEMMED
GEMOTE
GEMOTS
HEMATO
HEMMED
HEMMER
HEMSIN
KEMPIS
LEMANS
LEMMAS
LEMMON
LEMNOS
LEMOND
LEMONS
LEMONY
LEMUEL
LEMURS
MEMBER
MEMNON
MEMOIR
MEMORY
NEMATO
REMADE
REMAIL
REMAIN
REMAKE
REMAND
REMANS
REMAPS
REMARK
REMEDY
REMELT
REMEND
REMICK
REMIND
REMISE
REMISS
REMITS
REMOLD
REMOPS
REMORA
REMOTE
REMOVE
REMOWN
REMOWS
REMUDA
SEMELE
SEMITE
SEMPER
SEMPRE
TEMPED
TEMPEH
TEMPER
TEMPLE
TEMPOS
TEMPTS
TEMPUS
YEMENI

•E•M••

BEAMED
BEAMON
BEAMUP
CERMET
DEEMED
DEIMOS
DELMAR
DERMAL
DERMIS
DESMAN
FEMMES
FENMAN
FENMEN
FERMAT
GEMMAE
GEMMED
GERMAN
GETMAD
HELMED
HELMET
HELMUT
HEMMED
HEMMER
HERMAN
HERMES
HERMIT
HERMON
HETMAN
KERMAN
KERMES
KERMIS
KERMIT
LEGMAN
LEGMEN
LEMMAS
LEMMON
MELMAC
MERMAN
MERMEN
MESMER
NETMAN
NETMEN
NEUMAN
NEUMES
NEWMAN
NEWMAR
PELMET
PENMAN
PENMEN
PERMED
PERMIT
REAMED
REAMER
SEAMAN
SEAMED
SEAMEN
SEAMUS
SEEMED
SEEMLY
SERMON
TEAMED
TEAMUP
TEEMED
TERMED
TEXMEX
VERMIN
WEIMAR
WETMOP
YEOMAN
YEOMEN
YESMAN
YESMEN
ZEEMAN

•E••M•

BECAME
BECOME
BEDIMS
BEGUMS
BENUMB
BESOMS
DEARME
DECAMP
DEFAME
DENIMS
GENOME
JEREMY
JEROME
LEGUME
LEXEME
OEDEMA
REAIMS
REALMS
REARMS
REGIME
REHEMS
RELUME
RENAME
RESUME
RETIME
REVAMP
SEDUMS
SEISMO
SEISMS
SERUMS
SESAME
VENOMS
ZEUGMA

•E•••M

BECALM
BEDLAM
BEEGUM
BELDAM
CERIUM
CESIUM
DEFORM
HELIUM
JETSAM
MEDIUM
MEGOHM
PEPLUM
REDEEM
REDGUM
REFORM
RETRIM
REWARM
SELDOM
SEPTUM
TEDEUM
TEDIUM
VELLUM
VERISM

••EM••

ALEMAN
ANEMIA
ANEMIC
APEMAN
APEMEN
ATEMPO
BREMEN
CHEMIN
CREMES
DEEMED
ELEMIS
EXEMPT
HAEMAT
HAEMON
HIEMAL
ICEMAN
ICEMEN
ONEMAN
PIEMAN
PIEMEN
PREMED
PREMIE
QUEMOY
SEEMED
SEEMLY
TEEMED
THEMED
THEMES
TREMOR
ZEEMAN

••E•M•

ADEEMS
ATEAMS
BREAMS
CREAMS
CREAMY
DREAMS
DREAMT
DREAMY
GLEAMS
GLEAMY
HBEAMS
IBEAMS
PNEUMA
PREAMP
RHEUMS
RHEUMY
STEAMS
STEAMY
STELMO
THELMA
THERMO
THERMS
WHELMS

••E••M

AGEISM
BEEGUM
COELOM
FRENUM
PHENOM
PLENUM
PRELIM
THEISM

•••EM•

ADEEMS
BIREME
CINEMA
DOREMI
GOLEMS
HAREMS
JEREMY
KINEMA
LEXEME
MODEMS
OEDEMA
PROEMS
RACEME
REHEMS
SCHEMA
SCHEME
SOLEMN
TOTEMS

•••E•M

AGLEAM
ANSELM
ESTEEM
FIVEAM
FIVEPM
INSEAM
KAREEM
LYCEUM
MUSEUM
NINEAM
NINEPM
PHLEGM
PILEUM
REDEEM
SCREAM
STREAM
TEDEUM

••••EM

ANADEM
ANTHEM
ARNHEM
DIADEM
EMBLEM
ESTEEM
HARLEM
IBIDEM
KAREEM
MAYHEM
MOSLEM
PHLOEM
PROTEM
REDEEM
SACHEM
SHOLEM
SYSTEM
TANDEM
WILLEM

EN••••

ENABLE
ENACTS
ENAMEL
ENAMOR
ENATES
ENBLOC
ENCAGE
ENCAMP
ENCASE
ENCINA
ENCINO
ENCODE
ENCORE

ENDALL
ENDASH
ENDEAR
ENDERS
ENDING
ENDIVE
ENDMAN
ENDMEN
ENDORA
ENDOWS
ENDRUN
ENDSUP
ENDUED
ENDUES
ENDURE
ENDURO
ENDUSE
ENERGY
ENESCO
ENFANT
ENFOLD
ENGAGE
ENGELS
ENGINE
ENGIRD
ENGIRT
ENGLUT
ENGRAM
ENGULF
ENHALO
ENIGMA
ENISLE
ENJOIN
ENJOYS
ENLACE
ENLIST
ENMESH
ENMITY
ENNEAD
ENNIUS
ENOKIS
ENOSIS
ENOUGH
ENQUAD
ENRAGE
ENRAPT
ENRICH
ENRICO
ENROBE
ENROLL
ENROLS
ENROOT
ENSIGN
ENSILE
ENSOUL
ENSUED
ENSUES
ENSURE
ENTAIL
ENTERO
ENTERS
ENTICE
ENTIRE
ENTITY
ENTOMO
ENTRAP
ENTREE
ENURED
ENURES
ENVIED
ENVIER
ENVIES
ENVOIS
ENVOYS
ENWRAP
ENZYME

E•N•••

ELNINO
ENNEAD
ENNIUS
EONIAN
ERNANI
ERNEST
EUNICE

E••N••

EARNED
EARNER
EBONDS
EDENIC
EGGNOG
EISNER
ELANDS
ELINOR
EMENDS
EMINOR
EPINAL
EPONYM
ERENOW
ERINYS
ERYNGO
ETHNIC
ETHNOS
ETONIC
EUPNEA
EVENED
EVENER
EVENKI
EVENLY
EVENSO
EVENTS
EVENUP
EVINCE
EVONNE

E•••N•

EALING
EARING
EASING
EATING
EBBING
ECHINO
EDGING
EDMOND
EDMUND
EDWYNN
EGGING
EGMONT
ELAINE
ELAYNE
ELNINO
EMBANK
ENCINA
ENCINO
ENDING
ENFANT
ENGINE
EOCENE
EOSINS
EPPING
EQUINE
ERMINE
ERNANI
ERRAND
ERRANT
ERRING
ERVING
ESCENT
ESPANA
ESSENE
ETERNE
ETHANE
ETHENE
EUGENE
EVONNE
EVZONE
EXEUNT
EXPAND
EXPEND
EXTANT
EXTEND
EXTENT
EYEING

E••••N

EASEIN
EASTON
EATSIN
EDGEIN
EDISON
EDWYNN
EGGSON
EILEEN
ELEVEN
ELFMAN
ELOIGN
EMBDEN
ENDMAN
ENDMEN
ENDRUN
ENJOIN
ENSIGN
EOLIAN
EONIAN
EPHRON
ETYMON
EVELYN
EXTERN

•EN•••

AENEAS
AENEID
BENDAY
BENDED
BENDER
BENDIX
BENGAL
BENGAY
BENHUR
BENIGN
BENING
BENITO
BENOIT
BENONI
BENSON
BENTON
BENUMB
BENZOL
CENOTE
CENSED
CENSER
CENSES
CENSOR
CENSUS
CENTER
CENTOS
CENTRE
CENTRI
CENTRO
DENALI
DENARY
DENDRI
DENDRO
DENGUE
DENIAL
DENIED
DENIER
DENIES
DENIMS
DENIRO
DENISE
DENNED
DENNIS
DENOTE
DENOVO
DENSER
DENTAL
DENTED
DENTIL
DENTIN
DENTON
DENUDE
DENVER
DENZEL
FENCED
FENCER
FENCES
FENDED
FENDER
FENIAN
FENMAN
FENMEN
FENNEC
FENNEL
FENWAY
GENDER
GENERA
GENETS
GENEVA
GENEVE
GENIAL
GENIES
GENIUS
GENOAN
GENOME
GENRES
GENTLE
GENTLY
GENTRY
GENUAL
HENBIT
HENLEY
HENNAS
HENNER
HENNIN
HENRIK
HENRYV
HENSON
HENTED
JENNER
JENNET
JENNEY
JENNIE
JENSEN
KENNED
KENNEL
KENNER
KENNYG
KENTON
KENYAN
LENAPE
LENDER
LENGTH
LENITY
LENNIE
LENNON
LENNOX
LENORE
LENSED
LENSES
LENTEN
LENTIL
MENACE
MENADO
MENAGE
MENDED
MENDEL
MENDER
MENDES
MENHIR
MENIAL
MENINX
MENJOU
MENKEN
MENNEN
MENSAE
MENSAL
MENSAS
MENSCH
MENTAL
MENTIS
MENTOR
NENETS
OENONE
PENANG
PENCEL
PENCIL
PENDED
PENGHU
PENMAN
PENMEN
PENNAE
PENNED
PENNER
PENNEY
PENNIA
PENNIS
PENNON
PENPAL
PENROD
PENSEE
PENTAD
PENTUP
PENULT
PENURY
RENAIL
RENAME
RENATA
RENDER
RENEGE
RENEWS
RENNES
RENNET
RENNIE
RENNIN
RENOIR
RENOTE
RENOWN
RENTAL
RENTED
RENTER
SENARY
SENATE
SENDAK
SENDER
SENDIN
SENDUP
SENECA
SENEGA
SENHOR
SENIOR
SENITI
SENLAC
SENNAS
SENNET
SENNIT
SENORA
SENORS
SENSED
SENSEI
SENSES
SENSOR
SENTIN
SENTRA
SENTRY
SENTUP
SENUFO
TENACE
TENANT
TENDED
TENDER
TENDON
TENDTO
TENENS
TENETS
TENNIS
TENONS
TENORS
TENPIN
TENREC
TENSED
TENSER
TENSES
TENSOR
TENTED
TENTER
TENTHS
TENURE
TENUTO
VENDED
VENDEE
VENDOR
VENEER
VENETO
VENIAL
VENICE
VENIRE
VENITE
VENOMS
VENOUS
VENTED
VENTER
VENUES
WENCES
WENDED
WENTAT
WENTBY
WENTIN
WENTON
WENTUP
YENNED
YENTAS
ZENANA
ZENDIC
ZENDOS
ZENGER
ZENITH

•E•N••

BEANED
BEANIE
BEANOS
BEINGS
BERNIE
DEANNA
DENNED
DENNIS
FEINTS
FENNEC
FENNEL
HEANEY
HEFNER
HENNAS
HENNER
HENNIN
HEXNUT
JEANNE
JENNER
JENNET
JENNEY
JENNIE
KEENAN
KEENED
KEENEN
KEENER
KEENLY
KENNED
KENNEL
KENNER
KENNYG
KERNED
KERNEL
KERNOI
KERNOS
KEYNES
LEANED
LEANER
LEANLY
LEANON
LEANTO
LEMNOS
LENNIE
LENNON
LENNOX
LEONES
LEONID
LEONIE
LERNER
MEANER
MEANIE
MEANLY
MEMNON
MENNEN
PEANUT
PEENED
PENNAE
PENNED
PENNER
PENNEY
PENNIA
PENNIS
PENNON
PERNIO
PERNOD
REGNAL
REGNAT
REINAS
REINED
REINER
REININ
REINKS
RENNES
RENNET
RENNIE
RENNIN
RESNIK
REUNES
SEANCE
SEENIN
SEENTO
SEINED
SEINER
SEINES
SENNAS
SENNET
SENNIT
SEWNON
SEWNUP
TEENER
TEENSY
TENNIS
TERNES
VEINAL
VEINED
VERNAL
VERNON
WEANED
WEENIE
WEENSY
WERNER
YEANED
YENNED

•E••N•

BEGINS
BEGONE
BEHIND
BELONG
BEMINE
BENING
BENONI
BERING
BESANT
BETONY
BEYOND
BEZANT
CEDANT
CEDING
CELINE
CEMENT
CESSNA
CETANE
DEANNA
DEBONE
DEBUNK
DECANT
DECENT
DEFEND
DEFINE
DEIGNS
DEKING
DELANO
DELANY
DELONG
DEMAND
DEMOND
DEMONS
DEPEND
DEPONE
DETENT
DEVINE
DEWING
FECUND
FEEING
FEIGNS
FELINE
FELONS
FELONY
FERENC
FETING
GEEING
GEMINI
GERENT
GERONT
GERUND
HELENA
HELENE
HELENS
HERONS
HEWING
HEXING
JEANNE
JEJUNE
KEARNY
KETONE
KEYING
LEARNS
LEARNT
LEGEND
LELAND
LEMANS
LEMOND
LEMONS
LEMONY
LEVANT
LEVENE
LEVINE
MEDINA
MEKONG
MELANO
MELINA
MELONS
MENINX
MERINO
MESONS
METING
MEWING
NEEDNT
NEVINS
OENONE

PECANS
PEDANT
PEKING
PEKINS
PENANG
PEPINO
REBEND
REBENT
REBIND
RECANE
RECANT
RECENT
RECONS
REDANT
REDENY
REDING
REDINK
REDONE
REFINE
REFUND
REGENT
REGINA
REHANG
REHUNG
REIGNS
RELENT
RELINE
REMAND
REMANS
REMEND
REMIND
REPAND
REPENT
REPINE
REPINS
RERENT
RERUNS
RESAND
RESEND
RESENT
RESING
RESINS
RESINY
RETENE
RETINA
RETUNE
REWIND
REWINS
REZONE
SECANT
SECOND
SEDANS
SEEING
SEJANT
SELENA
SELENE
SELENO
SERENA
SERENE
SERINE
SERINS
SETINS
SEVENS
SEWING
TECHNO
TEEING
TEJANO
TENANT
TENENS
TENONS
TETONS
TEXANS
VEGANS
VERONA
VEXING
WERENT
YEARNS
YEMENI
ZENANA

•E•••N

AEGEAN
BEACON
BEAMON
BEARON
BEATEN
BEATON
BECKON
BEMOAN
BENIGN
BENSON
BENTON
BERGEN
BERLIN
BETSON
CEYLON
DEACON
DEADEN
DEADON
DEAFEN
DEALIN
DEEPEN
DEHORN
DELEON
DEMEAN
DENTIN
DENTON
DESIGN
DESMAN
DETAIN
DEVEIN
FEEDON
FELDON
FELLIN
FELLON
FENIAN
FENMAN
FENMEN
FEZZAN
GENOAN
GERMAN
GETSIN
GETSON
HEADIN
HEADON
HEAVEN
HEBRON
HEDREN
HEDRON
HEFLIN
HEIDEN
HELDIN
HELDON
HEMSIN
HENNIN
HENSON
HEREIN
HEREON
HERMAN
HERMON
HESTON
HETMAN
JENSEN
JERKIN
JETGUN
JETSON
KEATON
KEENAN
KEENEN
KEEPIN
KEEPON
KELVIN
KENTON
KENYAN
KEPTON
KERMAN
KEYSIN
LEADEN
LEADIN
LEADON
LEANON
LEAVEN
LEBRUN
LEFTIN
LEGION
LEGMAN
LEGMEN
LEGUIN
LEIDEN
LEMMON
LENNON
LENTEN
LEPTON
LESSEN
LESSON
LETSIN
LETSON
LEYDEN
MEDIAN
MELLON
MELTON
MELVIN
MELVYN
MEMNON
MENKEN
MENNEN
MERLIN
MERLON
MERMAN
MERMEN
MERTON
MERVYN
NEATEN
NEESON
NEKTON
NELSON
NETMAN
NETMEN
NETTON
NEUMAN
NEURON
NEWMAN
NEWTON
PEAHEN
PECTIN
PEERIN
PELION
PENMAN
PENMEN
PENNON
PEPSIN
PERSON
PETAIN
PEYTON
READIN
REAGAN
REASON
REBORN
RECKON
REDDEN
REDFIN
REELIN
REGAIN
REGION
REININ
REJOIN
REMAIN
REMOWN
RENNIN
RENOWN
REOPEN
REPLAN
REPUGN
RESAWN
RESEEN
RESEWN
RESIGN
RESPIN
RESTON
RETAIN
RETTON
RETURN
REUBEN
REVLON
REVSON
SEAFAN
SEAMAN
SEAMEN
SEASON
SEATON
SECERN
SEENIN
SEEPIN
SEESIN
SENDIN
SENTIN
SEQUIN
SERKIN
SERMON
SETSIN
SETSON
SEVERN
SEWNON
SEWSON
SEXTON
TEFLON
TELLON
TENDON
TENPIN
TERRAN
TEUTON
VEBLEN
VERDIN
VERDON
VERDUN
VEREEN
VERMIN
VERNON
WEAKEN
WEAPON
WEBERN
WEDELN
WELKIN
WENTIN
WENTON
WESSON
YEOMAN
YEOMEN
YESMAN
YESMEN
ZEEMAN
ZEROIN

••EN••

AGENAS
AGENCY
AGENDA
AGENTS
AKENES
AMENDS
AMENRA
AMENTS
ARENAS
ARENDT
AVENGE
AVENUE
BLENCH
BLENDE
BLENDS
BLENNY
BRENDA
BRENTS
BUENOS
CHENIN
CLENCH
CRENEL
CRENNA
DRENCH
DUENNA
EDENIC
EMENDS
ERENOW
EVENED
EVENER
EVENKI
EVENLY
EVENSO
EVENTS
EVENUP
FAENZA
FIENDS
FLENSE
FRENCH
FRENUM
FRENZY
GLENDA
GLENNE
GUENON
HYENAS
IRENES
IRENIC
KEENAN
KEENED
KEENEN
KEENER
KEENLY
KOENIG
LIENEE
MAENAD
ODENSE
OHENRY
OPENED
OPENER
OPENLY
OPENTO
OPENUP
PEENED
PHENOL
PHENOM
PHENYL
PLENTY
PLENUM
PRENUP
PUENTE
QUENCH
RIENZI
SCENAS
SCENDS
SCENES
SCENIC
SCENTS
SEENIN
SEENTO
SIENNA
SPENDS
STENCH
STENOG
STENOS
TEENER
TEENSY
THENAR
THENCE
TRENCH
TRENDS
TRENDY
TWENTY
UPENDS
USENET
VIENNA
VIENNE
WEENIE
WEENSY
WHENCE
WIENER
WRENCH

••E•N•

AGEING
AHERNE
AVERNO
BLENNY
BOEING
CLEANS
CRENNA
CZERNY
DOESNT
DUENNA
DYEING
ETERNE
EXEUNT
EYEING
FEEING
FOEHNS
FRESNO
GEEING
GLEANS
GLENNE
GREENE
GREENS
GREENY
GRETNA
HIEING
HOEING
ILEANA
LIERNE
NEEDNT
OCEANS
PAEANS
PAEONS
PREENS
QUEENS
QUERNS
SEEING
SHEENA
SHEENS
SIENNA
SKEANS
SKEINS
STEINS
STERNA
STERNE
STERNO
STERNS
TEEING
THEEND
TIEING
TIEINS
TOEING
TOEINS
TWEENS
TWEENY
VIENNA
VIENNE

••E••N

ALEMAN
APEMAN
APEMEN
AVEDON
BREMEN
BRETON
CHEMIN
CHENIN
CRETAN
CRETIN
DEEPEN
DOESIN
DREWIN
DREWON
ELEVEN
EVELYN
FEEDON
FLEWIN
GOESIN
GOESON
GREWON
GUENON
HAEMON
HIERON
ICEDIN
ICEMAN
ICEMEN
ICESIN
ISELIN
KEENAN
KEENEN
KEEPIN
KEEPON
KMESON
LIESIN
MYELIN
NEESON
OBERON
OLEFIN
OLESON
ONEMAN
OREGON
PEERIN
PIEMAN
PIEMEN
PIEPAN
PIETIN
PREVIN
PREYON
QUEZON
REELIN
SEENIN
SEEPIN
SEESIN
STEFAN
STEPIN
STEPON
STEVEN
SWEDEN
TIEDIN
TIEPIN
TIESIN
TOEDIN
TOESIN
TREPAN
UNEVEN
ZEEMAN

•••EN•

ABSENT
ACCENT
ACHENE
ADDEND
ADRENO
ADVENT
ALIENS
ALKENE
AMIENS
APPEND
ARDENT
ARGENT
ARLENE
ARPENT
ARSENE
ASCEND
ASCENT
ASPENS
ASSENT
ATHENA
ATHENE
ATHENS
ATTEND
AUDENS
AUGEND
BRIENZ
BUTENE
CADENT
CATENA
CEMENT
CLIENT
COGENT
COVENS
COVENT
COWENS
COZENS
DARENT
DECENT
DEFEND
DEPEND
DETENT
DIZENS
DOCENT
DOLENZ
DOYENS
DOZENS
EOCENE
ESCENT
ESSENE
ETHENE
EUGENE
EXPEND
EXTEND
EXTENT
FAGEND
FERENC
FILENE
FLUENT
FOMENT
FRIEND
GALENA
GERENT
GIVENS
GREENE
GREENS
GREENY
GYRENE
HAVENS
HAVENT
HELENA
HELENE
HELENS
IMPEND
INDENE
INDENT
INTEND
INTENS
INTENT
INVENT
IRLENE
ISMENE
JOLENE
LAMENT
LATENE
LATENS
LATENT
LEGEND
LEVENE
LIKENS
LIMENS
LINENS
LINENY
LIPENG
LIVENS
LODENS
LORENZ
LOWEND
LUCENT
LUDENS
LUMENS
MAVENS
MAXENE
MIZENS
MODENA
MOMENT
MORENO

NICENE
NOCENT
NOLENS
NOVENA
NUGENT
OFFEND
ORIENT
OSTEND
PARENS
PARENT
PATENS
PATENT
POTENT
PREENS
QUEENS
RAVENS
REBEND
REBENT
RECENT
REDENY
REGENT
RELENT
REMEND
REPENT
RERENT
RESEND
RESENT
RETENE
RIDENT
RIPENS
RODENT
ROWENA
ROWENS
RUBENS
RUMENS
SABENA
SELENA
SELENE
SELENO
SERENA
SERENE
SEVENS
SHEENA
SHEENS
SILENI
SILENT
SIRENS
SOLENT
STHENO
TAGEND
TALENT
TENENS
THEEND
TOKENS
TWEENS
TWEENY
UNBEND
UNBENT
UNPENS
URGENT
VALENS
VALENT
VIXENS
VOLENS
WAKENS
WERENT
WIDENS
WISENT
WIZENS
WOMENS
XIMENA
XYLENE
YEMENI
ZAZENS

•••E•N

AEGEAN
AILEEN
ANDEAN
ARLEEN
ASTERN
AUGEAN
BALEEN
BOLEYN
BOREON
CAMEIN
CAMEON
CAREEN
CASERN
CAVEIN
CAVERN
CLUEIN
COMEIN
COMEON
DELEON
DEMEAN
DEVEIN
DINEIN
DINEON
DIVEIN
DONEIN
DOTEON
DOVEIN
DUDEEN
EASEIN
EDGEIN
EILEEN
EXTERN
FADEIN
GAVEIN
GIDEON
GIVEIN
GOVERN
HAMELN
HAVEON
HEREIN
HEREON
HIREON
INTERN
KOREAN
LATEEN
LIVEIN
LIVEON
LLBEAN
LOMEIN
LOVEIN
MCLEAN
MODERN
MOREEN
MOVEIN
MOVEON
NICEAN
OSSEIN
PIGEON
PILEIN
PILEON
POLEYN
POTEEN
RAKEIN
RESEEN
RESEWN
ROPEIN
RULEON
SATEEN
SCREEN
SECERN
SEVERN
SIMEON
SOLEMN
SPLEEN
STREWN
TAKEIN
TAKEON
TAVERN
TUNEIN
TUREEN
UNSEEN
UNSEWN
VEREEN
VOTEIN
WADEIN
WAVEIN
WEBERN
WEDELN
WOREON
WYVERN

••••EN

AACHEN
ACUMEN
ADRIEN
AILEEN
AIRMEN
ALFVEN
ANCIEN
APEMEN
ARISEN
ARLEEN
AUSTEN
AWAKEN
AWOKEN
BADMEN
BALEEN
BARMEN
BARREN
BATMEN
BATTEN
BEATEN
BERGEN
BIDDEN
BIGBEN
BIGTEN
BITTEN
BLIXEN
BORDEN
BOWMEN
BRAZEN
BREMEN
BROKEN
BUNSEN
BURDEN
BUSMEN
CAMDEN
CAREEN
CARMEN
CHOSEN
CLOVEN
CONMEN
COTTEN
COWMEN
CRAVEN
CULLEN
DAIREN
DAMIEN
DAMPEN
DARIEN
DARKEN
DARREN
DEADEN
DEAFEN
DEEPEN
DOLMEN
DRIVEN
DRYDEN
DUDEEN
EILEEN
ELEVEN
EMBDEN
ENDMEN
FALLEN
FASTEN
FATTEN
FBIMEN
FENMEN
FLAXEN
FLYMEN
FRAUEN
FROZEN
GAGMEN
GARDEN
GASMEN
GLUTEN
GOLDEN
GOODEN
GOSHEN
GOTTEN
GRABEN
GRAVEN
GUNMEN
HAPPEN
HARDEN
HARKEN
HASTEN
HAYDEN
HEAVEN
HEDREN
HEIDEN
HIDDEN
HITMEN
HOLDEN
HOYDEN
HYPHEN
ICEMEN
IMOGEN
JANSEN
JENSEN
KEENEN
KITTEN
KJOLEN
KRAKEN
KUCHEN
LARSEN
LASSEN
LATEEN
LATTEN
LAUREN
LAWMEN
LAYMEN
LEADEN
LEAVEN
LEGMEN
LEIDEN
LENTEN
LESSEN
LEYDEN
LICHEN
LINDEN
LISTEN
LOOSEN
LOUDEN
LUDDEN
LUMPEN
LUNDEN
MADDEN
MADMEN
MADSEN
MAIDEN
MAJGEN
MALDEN
MARTEN
MCKUEN
MENKEN
MENNEN
MERMEN
MIDDEN
MIRREN
MITTEN
MIZZEN
MOLTEN
MOREEN
MORGEN
MUDHEN
NANSEN
NEATEN
NETMEN
NGUYEN
NISSEN
OBRIEN
OILMEN
OLDMEN
ORIGEN
OXYGEN
PATTEN
PEAHEN
PENMEN
PIEMEN
PIGPEN
PINKEN
PITMEN
PLATEN
POLLEN
POTEEN
PROVEN
RAGMEN
REDDEN
REOPEN
RESEEN
REUBEN
RICHEN
RIDDEN
RIPKEN
ROTTEN
SADDEN
SALTEN
SATEEN
SCREEN
SEAMEN
SHAKEN
SHAVEN
SICKEN
SILKEN
SLOVEN
SODDEN
SOFTEN
SPLEEN
SPOKEN
STAMEN
STATEN
STEVEN
STOLEN
SUDDEN
SULLEN
SUNKEN
SWEDEN
TAUTEN
TAXMEN
TILDEN
TINMEN
TOPTEN
TUREEN
UNEVEN
UNOPEN
UNSEEN
USOPEN
VARDEN
VEBLEN
VEREEN
VIVIEN
WALDEN
WALKEN
WARDEN
WARREN
WEAKEN
WHITEN
WOODEN
WOOLEN
WORSEN
XIAMEN
YEOMEN
YESMEN

EO••••

EOCENE
EOIPSO
EOLIAN
EOLITH
EONIAN
EOSINS

E•O•••

EBOATS
EBONDS
ECOLES
EGOISM
EGOIST
ELOHIM
ELOIGN
ELOISE
ELOPED
ELOPER
ELOPES
EMOTED
EMOTER
EMOTES
ENOKIS
ENOSIS
ENOUGH
EPOCHS
EPODES
EPONYM
EPOPEE
ERODED
ERODES
EROICA
EROTIC
ETOILE
ETONIC
EVOKED
EVOKER
EVOKES
EVOLVE
EVONNE
EXODUS
EXOTIC

E••O••

EATOUT
ECHOED
ECHOES
ECHOIC
EDDOES
EDKOCH
EDMOND
EDWOOD
EEYORE
EFFORT
EGMONT
EIDOLA
EKEOUT
ELBOWS
ELMORE
ELWOOD
EMBODY
EMBOSS
ENCODE
ENCORE
ENDORA
ENDOWS
ENFOLD
ENJOIN
ENJOYS
ENROBE
ENROLL
ENROLS
ENROOT
ENSOUL
ENTOMO
ENVOIS
ENVOYS
EPHODS
EPHORI
EPHORS
EPROMS
ERGOTS
ERROLL
ERRORS
ESCORT
ESPOSA
ESPOSO
ESTOPS
EUBOEA
EUDORA
EULOGY
EUROPA
EUROPE
EVZONE
EXHORT
EXMOOR
EXMORE
EXPORT
EXPOSE
EXPOST
EXTOLS
EXTORT
EXVOTO

E•••O•

EASTON
EDISON
EDITOR
EDWOOD
EGGNOG
EGGSON
EJIDOS
ELINOR
ELLIOT
ELWOOD
EMAJOR
EMINOR
EMPLOY
EMPTOR
ENAMOR
ENBLOC
ENROOT
EPHRON
EPILOG
ERENOW
ESCROW
ETHNOS
ETUXOR
ETYMOL
ETYMON
EXMOOR

E••••O

ECHINO
EDITIO
ELNINO
ELPASO
EMBRYO
EMILIO
ENCINO
ENDURO
ENESCO
ENHALO
ENRICO
ENTERO
ENTOMO
EOIPSO
ERYNGO
ESCUDO
ESKIMO
ESPOSO
EVENSO
EVERSO
EXACTO
EXVOTO

•EO•••

AEOLIA
AEOLIC
AEOLUS
CEORLS
DEODAR
GEODES
GEORGE
GEORGY
LEONES
LEONID
LEONIE
MEOWED
PEOPLE
PEORIA
REOILS
REOPEN
YEOMAN
YEOMEN

•E•O••

AEROBE
BEBOPS
BECOME
BEFOGS
BEFORE
BEFOUL
BEGOFF
BEGONE
BEHOLD
BEHOOF
BEHOVE
BELOIT
BELONG
BEMOAN
BENOIT
BENONI
BESOMS
BESOTS
BETONY
BETOOK
BEYOND
CENOTE
DEBONE
DECOCT
DECODE
DECORS
DECOYS
DEFOGS
DEFORM
DEHORN
DELONG
DEMOBS
DEMODE
DEMOND
DEMONS
DEMOTE
DENOTE
DENOVO
DEPONE
DEPORT
DEPOSE
DEPOTS
DESOTO
DETOUR
DEVOID
DEVOIR
DEVOTE
DEVOTO
DEVOUR
DEVOUT
EEYORE
FEDORA
FELONS
FELONY
FEMORA
GEMOTE
GEMOTS
GENOAN
GENOME
GERONT
GETOFF
GETOUT

HELOTS
HEROES
HEROIC
HERONS
JEROME
KEBOBS
KETONE
LEDOFF
LEDOUT
LEMOND
LEMONS
LEMONY
LENORE
LETOFF
LETOUT
MEGOHM
MEKONG
MELODY
MELONS
MELOTT
MEMOIR
MEMORY
MEROPE
MESONS
METOPE
NEROLI
OENONE
PEKOES
PELOPS
PELOTA
PEYOTE
REBOIL
REBOLT
REBOOT
REBORN
REBOZO
RECOAT
RECODE
RECOIL
RECONS
RECOPY
RECORD
RECORK
RECOUP
REDOAK
REDOES
REDONE
REFORM
REHOOK
REJOIN
RELOAD
RELOCK
REMOLD
REMOPS
REMORA
REMOTE
REMOVE
REMOWN
REMOWS
RENOIR
RENOTE
RENOWN
REPOLL
REPORT
REPOSE
REPOST
REPOTS
RESODS
RESOLD
RESOLE
RESORB
RESORT
RETOLD
RETOOK
RETOOL
RETOPS
RETORT
RETOUR
RETOWS
REVOIR
REVOKE
REVOLT
REWORD
REWORK
REWOVE
REZONE
SECOND
SEEOFF
SEEOUT
SENORA
SENORS
SEPOYS
SEROSA
SEROUS
SEROWS
SETOFF
SETOSE
SETOUT
TEEOFF
TENONS
TENORS
TETONS
VELOCE
VELOUR
VENOMS
VENOUS
VERONA
VETOED
VETOER
VETOES
XEDOUT
ZEROED
ZEROES
ZEROIN
ZEROTH

•E••O•

BEACON
BEAMON
BEANOS
BEARON
BEATON
BECKON
BEHOOF
BELLOC
BELLOW
BENSON
BENTON
BENZOL
BESTOW
BETOOK
BETSON
BETTOR
CELLOS
CENSOR
CENTOS
CERROS
CESTOS
CEYLON
DEACON
DEADON
DEBTOR
DEIMOS
DEKKOS
DELEON
DELROY
DENTON
DEPLOY
DESPOT
DETROP
FEEDON
FELDON
FELLOE
FELLON
FELLOW
FERVOR
GECKOS
GETSON
HEADON
HEAROF
HEBRON
HECTOR
HEDRON
HELDON
HELIOS
HELLOS
HENSON
HEREOF
HEREON
HERIOT
HERMON
HERZOG
HESIOD
HESTON
HEYYOU
JERBOA
JETSON
KEATON
KEEPON
KENTON
KEPTON
KERNOI
KERNOS
LEADON
LEANON
LECTOR
LEGION
LEMMON
LEMNOS
LENNON
LENNOX
LEPTON
LESBOS
LESSON
LESSOR
LETSON
MEADOW
MELLON
MELLOW
MELTON
MEMNON
MENJOU
MENTOR
MERLON
MERLOT
MERTON
METEOR
METHOD
METROS
MEZZOS
NEESON
NEKTON
NELSON
NESTOR
NETTON
NEUROL
NEURON
NEWTON
PEAPOD
PEGTOP
PELION
PENNON
PENROD
PEPLOS
PEQUOD
PEQUOT
PERIOD
PERNOD
PERROT
PERSON
PESCOW
PESTOS
PETROG
PETROL
PEYTON
REASON
REBOOT
RECKON
RECTOR
RECTOS
REDDOG
REDFOX
REDHOT
REDSOX
REDTOP
REEBOK
REGION
REHOOK
REPLOW
REPROS
RESHOD
RESHOE
RESHOT
RESTON
RETOOK
RETOOL
RETROS
RETTON
REVLON
REVSON
SEACOW
SEADOG
SEAFOX
SEASON
SEATON
SECTOR
SELDOM
SENHOR
SENIOR
SENSOR
SERMON
SERVOS
SESTOS
SETSON
SETTOS
SEWNON
SEWSON
SEXTON
TEAPOT
TEAPOY
TEFLON
TELLOF
TELLON
TEMPOS
TENDON
TENSOR
TERROR
TEUTON
VECTOR
VENDOR
VERDON
VERNON
VERSOS
WEAPON
WENTON
WESSON
WETMOP
YELLOW
ZEALOT
ZENDOS

•E•••O

BENITO
CENTRO
DELANO
DELRIO
DENDRO
DENIRO
DENOVO
DESOTO
DEVITO
DEVOTO
DEXTRO
FELLTO
GEARTO
GELATO
GETSTO
HELDTO
HEMATO
HERETO
HETERO
JETHRO
KEEPTO
LEADTO
LEANTO
LEGATO
LETSGO
MEDICO
MEGALO
MEJICO
MELANO
MENADO
MERINO
MEXICO
NEARTO
NEMATO
NEPHRO
NEXTTO
PEPINO
PERNIO
REBOZO
REECHO
SEENTO
SEESTO
SEISMO
SELENO
SENUFO
SERGIO
TECHNO
TEJANO
TENDTO
TENUTO
TERATO
TEREDO
TEXACO
VELCRO
VENETO
WEIRDO

••EO••

ACEOUS
ACEOUT
AGEOLD
AREOLA
ATEOUT
CHEOPS
CREOLE
DIEOFF
DIEOUT
EKEOUT
ICEOUT
PAEONS
SEEOFF
SEEOUT
TEEOFF
THEORY

••E•O•

AVEDON
BRETON
BUENOS
CHEKOV
COELOM
CREDOS
CRESOL
DREWON
DYELOT
ERENOW
FAEROE
FEEDON
FLEXOR
FOETOR
GOESON
GREGOR
GREWON
GUENON
HAEMON
HIERON
HUEVOS
ICEBOX
ICEFOG
KEEPON
KMESON
LIELOW
NEESON
OBERON
OCELOT
OLESON
OREGON
PHENOL
PHENOM
PLEXOR
PREYON
PYEDOG
QUEMOY
QUEZON
REEBOK
RHEBOK
RHETOR
STEFOY
STENOG
STENOS
STEPON
STEROL
THETOY
TIEROD
TREMOR
TREVOR

••E••O

AIELLO
ALECTO
ALEPPO
AMEDEO
AREZZO
ATEMPO
ATERGO
AVERNO
CHEAPO
DUELLO
ENESCO
EVENSO
EVERSO
FRESCO
FRESNO
GHETTO
KEEPTO
LIESTO
NIELLO
ONETWO
OPENTO
OTELLO
OVERDO
PIETRO
PRESTO
PSEUDO
PUEBLO
PUERTO
REECHO
SEENTO
SEESTO
SPEEDO
STELMO
STEREO
STERNO
THERMO
TIEDTO
TIESTO
UNESCO
USEDTO

•••EO•

BLUEOX
BOREON
BUTEOS
CAMEON
CAMEOS
COMEON
DELEON
DINEON
DOTEON
GIDEON
HAVEON
HEREOF
HEREON
HIREON
LIVEON
METEOR
MIMEOS
MOVEON
PASEOS
PIGEON
PILEON
RODEOS
ROLEOS
ROMEOS
RULEON
SIMEON
TAKEON
VIDEOS
VIREOS
WOREON

•••E•O

ADRENO
ALBEDO
ANGELO
ANTERO
BOLERO
CAMETO
CARETO
CICERO
COMETO
DARETO
DINERO
ENTERO
FOREGO
GAZEBO
GIVETO
GRAECO
HERETO
HETERO
HIDEHO
HOVETO
LAREDO
MACEIO
MADEDO
MADERO
MAKEDO
MORENO
NONEGO
NUMERO
OSWEGO
OVIEDO
PARETO
PHLEBO
PINERO
POMELO
ROMERO
SASEBO
SCLERO
SELENO
SIDERO
SOWETO
SPEEDO
STHENO
TAKETO
TEREDO
TOLEDO
TORERO
TUPELO
TUXEDO
VENETO
WISETO
ZYDECO

••••EO

AMEDEO
BORNEO
NUCLEO
PALAEO
STEREO

EP••••

EPARCH
EPHAHS
EPHEBE
EPHODS
EPHORI
EPHORS
EPHRON
EPICAL
EPILOG
EPINAL
EPIRUS
EPOCHS
EPODES
EPONYM
EPOPEE
EPPING
EPROMS

E•P•••

ELPASO
EMPERY
EMPIRE
EMPLOY
EMPTOR
EPPING
ESPANA
ESPIAL
ESPIED
ESPIES
ESPOSA
ESPOSO
ESPRIT
EUPNEA
EXPAND
EXPECT
EXPELS
EXPEND
EXPERT
EXPIRE
EXPIRY
EXPORT
EXPOSE
EXPOST

E••P••

ELAPID
ELAPSE
ELOPED
ELOPER
ELOPES
EOIPSO
EPOPEE
ERUPTS
ETAPES

E•••P•

ECTYPE
ENRAPT
EQUIPS
ESCAPE
ESTOPS
EUROPA
EUROPE
EXCEPT
EXEMPT

E••••P
EARLAP
EASEUP
EATSUP
EGGCUP
ENCAMP
ENDSUP
ENTRAP
ENWRAP
ESCARP
ESHARP
EVENUP
EYECUP

•EP•••
DEPART
DEPAUL
DEPAUW
DEPEND
DEPICT
DEPLOY
DEPONE
DEPORT
DEPOSE
DEPOTS
DEPTHS
DEPUTE
DEPUTY
HEPCAT
HEPPER
HEPTAD
KEPLER
KEPTAT
KEPTON
KEPTUP
LEPTON
NEPALI
NEPHEW
NEPHRO
PEPFUL
PEPINO
PEPITA
PEPLOS
PEPLUM
PEPPED
PEPPER
PEPSIN
PEPSUP
PEPTIC
REPADS
REPAID
REPAIR
REPAND
REPAST
REPAVE
REPAYS
REPEAL
REPEAT
REPEGS
REPELS
REPENT
REPINE
REPINS
REPLAN
REPLAY
REPLOW
REPOLL
REPORT
REPOSE
REPOST
REPOTS
REPROS
REPUGN
REPUTE
SEPALS
SEPIAS
SEPOYS
SEPTAL
SEPTET
SEPTIC
SEPTUM
TEPALS
TEPEES
TEPHRA
ZEPHYR

•E•P••
BEEPED
BEEPER
DEEPAK
DEEPEN
DEEPER
DEEPLY
DELPHI
DESPOT
HEAPED
HELPED
HELPER
HEPPER
KEEPAT
KEEPER
KEEPIN
KEEPON
KEEPTO
KEEPUP
KELPIE
KEMPIS
KEWPIE
KEYPAD
LEAPED
LEAPER
NETPAY
PEAPOD
PEEPED
PEEPER
PENPAL
PEOPLE
PEPPED
PEPPER
REAPED
REAPER
REOPEN
RESPIN
SEEPED
SEEPIN
SEMPER
SEMPRE
TEAPOT
TEAPOY
TEMPED
TEMPEH
TEMPER
TEMPLE
TEMPOS
TEMPTS
TEMPUS
TENPIN
VESPER
VESPID
WEAPON
WEEPER
WEEPIE
YELPED
YELPER

•E••P•
BEBOPS
CERIPH
FELIPE
GETUPS
LENAPE
LETUPS
MEROPE
METOPE
PELOPS
RECAPS
RECIPE
RECOPY
REMAPS
REMOPS
RETAPE
RETAPS
RETOPS
RETYPE
SERAPE
SERAPH
SETUPS
TERAPH

•E•••P
BEADUP
BEAMUP
BEARUP
BEATUP
BEEFUP
DECAMP
DETROP
DEWLAP
FESSUP
GEARUP
GETSUP
HEADUP
HEATUP
HELDUP
KEEPUP
KEPTUP
KEYSUP
LEADUP
LETSUP
MEGILP
MESSUP
PEGTOP
PENTUP
PEPSUP
PERKUP
REARUP
RECOUP
REDCAP
REDTOP
RESHIP
RESTUP
REVAMP
REVSUP
REWRAP
SEALUP
SENDUP
SENTUP
SETSUP
SEWNUP
SEWSUP
TEACUP
TEAMUP
TEARUP
TEEDUP
TEESUP
WELLUP
WENTUP
WETMOP

••EP••
ADEPTS
ALEPHS
ALEPPO
BEEPED
BEEPER
CLEPED
CREPES
DEEPAK
DEEPEN
DEEPER
DEEPLY
DIEPPE
KEEPAT
KEEPER
KEEPIN
KEEPON
KEEPTO
KEEPUP
PEEPED
PEEPER
PIEPAN
PREPAY
PREPPY
SEEPED
SEEPIN
STEPIN
STEPON
STEPPE
STEPUP
TIEPIN
TREPAN
TREPID
WEEPER
WEEPIE

••E•P•
ALEPPO
ATEMPO
BLEEPS
CHEAPO
CHEEPS
CHEOPS
CREEPS
CREEPY
DIEPPE
EXEMPT
GUELPH
ONEUPS
PREPPY
SHEEPS
SHERPA
SLEEPS
SLEEPY
STEEPS
STEPPE
SWEEPS
TIEUPS
TWERPS
WHELPS

••E••P
ACESUP
AMERSP
BEEFUP
BLEWUP
CHEWUP
DOESUP
DREWUP
EVENUP
EYECUP
GOESUP
GREWUP
ICECAP
ICEDUP
ICESUP
KEEPUP
OPENUP
PREAMP
PRENUP
SPEDUP
STEPUP
TEEDUP
TEESUP
THELIP
TIEDUP
TIESUP
TOECAP
TOETAP
USEDUP
USESUP

•••EP•
ACCEPT
BICEPS
BLEEPS
CHEEPS
CREEPS
CREEPY
EXCEPT
FIVEPM
INCEPT
JOSEPH
JULEPS
NINEPM
SHEEPS
SLEEPS
SLEEPY
STEEPS
SWEEPS

•••E•P
ANTEUP
ASLEEP
BONEUP
BOPEEP
BOREUP
CAMEUP
COMEUP
DONEUP
EASEUP
FACEUP
FIREUP
GAVEUP
GIVEUP
HIKEUP
HOLEUP
HYPEUP
LACEUP
LINEUP
MADEUP
MAKEUP
MOVEUP
PILEUP
PIPEUP
RAKEUP
RAVEUP
RILEUP
SAVEUP
SIZEUP
STREEP
TAKEUP
TONEUP
TOREUP
TUNEUP
TYPEUP
UPKEEP
WAKEUP
WIPEUP
WISEUP
WOKEUP

••••EP
ASLEEP
BOPEEP
DOMREP
INSTEP
SCHLEP
STREEP
TRICEP
UPKEEP

EQ••••
EQUALS
EQUATE
EQUINE
EQUIPS
EQUITY

E•Q•••
EMQUAD
ENQUAD

E•••Q•
ETSEQQ

E••••Q
ETSEQQ

•EQ•••
PEQUOD
PEQUOT
SEQUEL
SEQUIN

•E•Q••
SESQUI

••EQ••
CHEQUE

•••EQ•
ETSEQQ

•••E•Q
ETSEQQ

••••EQ
SUSIEQ

ER••••
ERASED
ERASER
ERASES
ERBIUM
EREBUS
ERECTS
ERENOW
ERESTU
ERFURT
ERGATE
ERGOTS
ERHARD
ERINYS
ERMINE
ERNANI
ERNEST
ERODED
ERODES
EROICA
EROTIC
ERRAND
ERRANT
ERRARE
ERRATA
ERRING
ERROLL
ERRORS
ERSATZ
ERUCTS
ERUPTS
ERVING
ERYNGO

E•R•••
EARFUL
EARING
EARLAP
EARNED
EARNER
EARTHA
EARTHY
EARWAX
EARWIG
EERIER
EERILY
EGRESS
EGRETS
ENRAGE
ENRAPT
ENRICH
ENRICO
ENROBE
ENROLL
ENROLS
ENROOT
EPROMS
ERRAND
ERRANT
ERRARE
ERRATA
ERRING
ERROLL
ERRORS
EURAIL
EUREKA
EUROPA
EUROPE
EYRIES

E••R••
EAGRES
EBERLY
ECARTE
EDERLE
EGERIA
ELBRUS
EMBRYO
EMERGE
ENDRUN
ENERGY
ENGRAM
ENTRAP
ENTREE
ENURED
ENURES
ENWRAP
EPARCH
EPHRON
EPIRUS
ESCROW
ESDRAS
ESPRIT
ESTRAY
ETERNE
EVERLY
EVERSO
EVERTS
EXARCH
EXERTS
EXTRAS
EXURBS

E•••R•
EATERS
EATERY
EDBERG
EDGARD
EDGARS
EDGERS
EDUARD
EDVARD
EDWARD
EELERS
EEYORE
EFFORT
EGBERT
EIDERS
EKBERG
ELBERT
ELDERS
ELLERY
ELMIRA
ELMORE
ELVERS
ELVIRA
EMBARK
EMBERS
EMEERS
EMIGRE
EMPERY
EMPIRE
ENCORE
ENDERS
ENDORA
ENDURE
ENDURO
ENGIRD
ENGIRT
ENSURE
ENTERO
ENTERS
ENTIRE
EPHORI
EPHORS
ERFURT
ERHARD
ERRARE
ERRORS
ESCARP
ESCORT
ESHARP
ESKERS
ESTERS
ETHERS
EUCHRE
EUDORA
EXEDRA
EXHORT
EXMORE
EXPERT
EXPIRE
EXPIRY
EXPORT
EXSERT
EXTERN
EXTORT
EZZARD

E••••R
EARNER
EASIER
EASTER
ECLAIR
EDGIER
EDITOR
EELIER
EERIER
EGGIER
EISNER
EITHER
ELATER
ELAYER
ELINOR
ELIXIR
ELOPER
ELUDER
EMAJOR
EMINOR
EMOTER
EMPTOR
ENAMOR
ENDEAR
ENVIER
ERASER
ESCHER
ESTHER
ETCHER
ETUXOR
EVADER
EVENER
EVILER
EVOKER
EXETER
EXMOOR

•ER•••
AERATE
AERIAL
AERIES
AERIFY

AERILY
AEROBE
BERATE
BERBER
BEREFT
BERETS
BERGEN
BERING
BERLIN
BERNIE
BERTHA
BERTHS
BERTIE
CERATE
CEREAL
CEREUS
CERIPH
CERISE
CERIUM
CERMET
CERROS
CERTIF
CERUSE
CERVID
DERAIL
DERIDE
DERIVE
DERMAL
DERMIS
DERRIS
EERIER
EERILY
FERBER
FERENC
FERGIE
FERGUS
FERIAL
FERIAS
FERITY
FERMAT
FERRER
FERRET
FERRIC
FERRIS
FERULE
FERVID
FERVOR
GERAHS
GERALD
GERARD
GERBER
GERBIL
GERENT
GERMAN
GERONT
GERTIE
GERUND
HERALD
HERBAL
HERBIE
HERDED
HERDER
HEREAT
HEREBY
HEREIN
HEREOF
HEREON
HERESY
HERETO
HERIOT
HERMAN
HERMES
HERMIT
HERMON
HEROES
HEROIC
HERONS
HERSEY
HERZOG
JERBOA
JEREMY
JERKED
JERKIN
JEROME
JERSEY
KERALA
KERMAN
KERMES
KERMIS
KERMIT
KERNED
KERNEL
KERNOI
KERNOS
KERSEE
KERSEY
LERIDA
LERNER
MERCED
MERCER
MERELY
MEREST
MERGED
MERGER
MERGES
MERIDA
MERINO
MERITS
MERKEL
MERLIN
MERLON
MERLOT
MERMAN
MERMEN
MEROPE
MERSEY
MERTON
MERVYN
NEREID
NEREIS
NEREUS
NEROLI
NERUDA
NERVES
OERTER
PERCHA
PERDUE
PERILS
PERIOD
PERISH
PERKED
PERKUP
PERMED
PERMIT
PERNIO
PERNOD
PERROT
PERSIA
PERSON
PERTER
PERTLY
PERUGA
PERUKE
PERUSE
RERATE
REREAD
RERENT
RERUNS
SERACS
SERAIS
SERAPE
SERAPH
SERBIA
SERENA
SERENE
SERGEI
SERGES
SERGIO
SERIAL
SERIES
SERIFS
SERINE
SERINS
SERKIN
SERMON
SEROSA
SEROUS
SEROWS
SERUMS
SERVAL
SERVED
SERVER
SERVES
SERVOS
TERAPH
TERATO
TERCEL
TERCET
TEREDO
TERESA
TERETE
TEREUS
TERKEL
TERMED
TERNES
TERRAN
TERRET
TERROR
TERSER
VERBAL
VERBIS
VERDIN
VERDON
VERDUN
VEREEN
VERGED
VERGER
VERGES
VERIFY
VERILY
VERISM
VERITE
VERITY
VERMIN
VERNAL
VERNON
VERONA
VERSED
VERSES
VERSOS
VERSTS
VERSUS
VERTEX
VERVES
VERVET
WERENT
WERFEL
WERNER
XERXES
YERKED
YERKES
ZEROED
ZEROES
ZEROIN
ZEROTH

•E•R••

BEARDS
BEARER
BEARON
BEARUP
BEIRUT
BETRAY
BEURRE
BEWRAY
CEDRIC
CEORLS
CERROS
DEARER
DEARIE
DEARLY
DEARME
DEARTH
DEBRAS
DEBRIS
DECREE
DEFRAY
DEGREE
DELRAY
DELRIO
DELROY
DERRIS
DETROP
FEARED
FEARER
FERRER
FERRET
FERRIC
FERRIS
GEARED
GEARTO
GEARUP
GEHRIG
GENRES
GEORGE
GEORGY
HEARER
HEAROF
HEARST
HEARTH
HEARTS
HEARTY
HEARYE
HEBREW
HEBRON
HEDREN
HEDRON
HENRIK
HENRYV
JEERAT
JEERED
JEERER
KEARNY
LEARNS
LEARNT
LEBRUN
LEERAT
LEERED
LEERER
LEGREE
LEHRER
MEERUT
METRES
METRIC
METROS
NEARBY
NEARED
NEARER
NEARLY
NEARTO
NEURAL
NEUROL
NEURON
PEARLS
PEARLY
PEERAT
PEERCE
PEERED
PEERIN
PENROD
PEORIA
PERROT
PETREL
PETRIE
PETROG
PETROL
REARED
REARER
REARMS
REARUP
REDRAW
REDREW
REGRET
REPROS
RETRAL
RETRIM
RETROS
REWRAP
SEARCH
SEARED
SEARLE
SECRET
SEERED
SEURAT
SEVRES
TEARAT
TEARED
TEARUP
TENREC
TERRAN
TERRET
TERROR
TETRAD
TETRAS
TETRIS
VEERED
WEARER
WEIRDO
WEIRDY
YEARLY
YEARNS
ZEBRAS

•E••R•

BEFORE
BELFRY
BEMIRE
BEURRE
BEWARE
CEDARS
CELERY
CENTRE
CENTRI
CENTRO
CESARE
CETERA
DEBARK
DEBARS
DECORS
DEFERS
DEFORM
DEHORN
DEIDRE
DEJURE
DEMURE
DEMURS
DENARY
DENDRI
DENDRO
DENIRO
DEPART
DEPORT
DESCRY
DESERT
DESIRE
DESTRY
DETERS
DEXTRO
EELERS
EEYORE
FEDORA
FEMORA
FEMURS
FEVERS
GEMARA
GENERA
GENTRY
GERARD
GEZIRA
HEGARI
HEGIRA
HETERO
HEWERS
HEXERS
JETHRO
KEFIRS
LEMURS
LENORE
LEVERS
MEAGRE
MEGARA
MEMORY
MESSRS
METERS
NEPHRO
NEVERS
NEWARK
OEUVRE
PELTRY
PENURY
PETARD
PETERS
REAIRS
REBARS
REBORN
REBURY
RECORD
RECORK
RECURS
REFERS
REFORM
REGARD
REHIRE
REMARK
REMORA
REPORT
RESORB
RESORT
RETARD
RETARS
RETIRE
RETORT
RETURN
REVERB
REVERE
REVERS
REVERT
REWARD
REWARM
REWIRE
REWORD
REWORK
SEBERG
SECERN
SECURE
SEDERS
SEGURA
SEMPRE
SENARY
SENORA
SENORS
SENTRA
SENTRY
SEVERE
SEVERN
SEVERS
SEVERY
SEWARD
SEWERS
TENORS
TENURE
TEPHRA
VELCRO
VENIRE
VESTRY
VEXERS
WEBERN

•E•••R

AETHER
BEAKER
BEARER
BEATER
BEAVER
BECKER
BEEPER
BEGGAR
BELAIR
BENDER
BENHUR
BERBER
BESSER
BESTIR
BETTER
BETTOR
CELLAR
CENSER
CENSOR
CENTER
DEADER
DEAFER
DEALER
DEARER
DEBTOR
DECKER
DEEPER
DEFTER
DEICER
DELMAR
DELVER
DENIER
DENSER
DENVER
DEODAR
DETOUR
DEVOIR
DEVOUR
DEWIER
DEXTER
EELIER
EERIER
FEARER
FEEDER
FEELER
FELLER
FENCER
FENDER
FERBER
FERRER
FERVOR
FESTER
FETTER
GEEZER
GEIGER
GENDER
GERBER
GETTER
GEYSER
HEADER
HEALER
HEARER
HEATER
HEAVER
HECTOR
HEDGER
HEEDER
HEELER
HEFNER
HEIFER
HELLER
HELPER
HELTER
HEMMER
HENNER
HEPPER
HERDER
HESTER
JEERER
JEETER
JENNER
JESTER
KEELER
KEENER
KEEPER
KEGLER
KELLER
KENNER
KEPLER
KEVLAR
LEADER
LEAKER
LEANER
LEAPER
LEASER
LECTER
LECTOR
LEDGER
LEERER
LEHRER
LEKVAR
LENDER
LERNER
LESSER
LESSOR
LESTER
LETTER
LEVIER
LEWDER
MEAGER
MEANER
MEDGAR
MEDLAR
MEEKER
MEETER
MEMBER
MEMOIR
MENDER
MENHIR
MENTOR
MERCER
MERGER
MESMER
METEOR
METIER
MEWLER
NEARER
NEATER
NECTAR
NESTER
NESTOR
NETHER
NEUTER
NEWMAR
OERTER
PEDLAR
PEELER
PEEPER
PEGLER
PELTER
PENNER
PEPPER
PERTER
PESTER
PETTER
PEWTER
READER
REALER
REAMER
REAPER
REARER

RECTOR
REDDER
REDFIR
REEFER
REHEAR
REINER
RENDER
RENOIR
RENTER
REPAIR
RESTER
RETEAR
RETOUR
REUTER
REVOIR
SEALER
SEATER
SECTOR
SEEDER
SEEGER
SEEKER
SEINER
SEIZER
SELLER
SEMPER
SENDER
SENHOR
SENIOR
SENSOR
SERVER
SETTER
SEXIER
TEASER
TEDDER
TEENER
TEETER
TELLER
TEMPER
TENDER
TENSER
TENSOR
TENTER
TERROR
TERSER
TESTER
TETHER
VECTOR
VEDDER
VELOUR
VENDOR
VENEER
VENTER
VERGER
VESPER
VETOER
WEAKER
WEARER
WEAVER
WEBBER
WEEDER
WEEPER
WEIMAR
WELDER
WELLER
WELTER
WERNER
WETBAR
WETHER
WETTER
YEAGER
YELLER
YELPER
YESSIR
YESTER
ZEDBAR
ZENGER
ZEPHYR

••ER••

AHERNE
ALERTS
AMERCE
AMERSP
ANERGY
APERCU
ATERGO
AVERNO
AVERSE
AVERTS
BIERCE
CHERIE
CHERRY
CHERTY
CHERUB
CHERYL
CLERGY
CLERIC
CLERKS
COERCE
CZERNY
DJERBA
EBERLY
EDERLE
EGERIA
EMERGE
ENERGY
ETERNE
EVERLY
EVERSO
EVERTS
EXERTS
FAERIE
FAEROE
FIERCE
GUERRE
HIERON
IBERIA
JEERAT
JEERED
JEERER
LEERAT
LEERED
LEERER
LIERNE
MEERUT
OBERON
OMERTA
OPERAS
OVERDO
OVERLY
PEERAT
PEERCE
PEERED
PEERIN
PIERCE
PIERRE
PUERTO
QUERNS
QWERTY
SEERED
SHEREE
SHERIF
SHERPA
SHERRY
SHERYL
SIERRA
SKERRY
SMERSH
SPERRY
STEREO
STERES
STERNA
STERNE
STERNO
STERNS
STEROL
SWERVE
THERES
THERMO
THERMS
TIERCE
TIERED
TIEROD
TIERRA
TWERPS
USERID
VEERED
WHERED
WHERES
WHERRY

••E•R•

AFEARD
ALEGRE
AMEERS
AMENRA
AWEARY
BLEARS
BLEARY
CHEERS
CHEERY
CHERRY
CHEVRE
CLEARS
DREARY
EMEERS
EXEDRA
FLEERS
FLEURY
GUERRE
OHENRY
OLEARY
PHEDRE
PIERRE
PIETRO
PLEURA
POETRY
SHEARS
SHEERS
SHERRY
SIERRA
SKERRY
SMEARS
SMEARY
SNEERS
SNEERY
SOEURS
SPEARS
SPERRY
STEERS
SWEARS
THEIRS
THEORY
THEYRE
TIERRA
WHERRY

••E••R

ALEGAR
ASEVER
BEEPER
BREUER
BREWER
BREYER
CAESAR
CHEWER
CLEVER
DEEPER
DIETER
DUELER
EVENER
EXETER
FEEDER
FEELER
FLEXOR
FOETOR
FUELER
GEEZER
GREGOR
GREYER
HEEDER
HEELER
JAEGER
JEERER
JEETER
KEELER
KEENER
KEEPER
KIEFER
LEERER
LIEDER
LIEFER
MEEKER
MEETER
OPENER
PEELER
PEEPER
PIECER
PIETER
PLEXOR
PREFER
PRETER
PREWAR
QUEUER
REEFER
RHETOR
SEEDER
SEEGER
SEEKER
SKEWER
STELAR
STEWER
TEENER
TEETER
THENAR
TREMOR
TREVOR
VIEWER
WEEDER
WEEPER
WIENER

•••ER•

ADDERS
ADHERE
ADVERB
ADVERT
AIDERS
AILERS
ALBERT
ALDERS
ALPERT
ALTERS
AMBERS
AMBERY
AMEERS
AMPERE
ANGERS
ANTERO
ARTERY
ASKERS
ASPERA
ASSERT
ASTERN
ASTERS
AUGERS
BAKERS
BAKERY
BALERS
BIKERS
BITERS
BOLERO
BONERS
BORERS
BOWERS
BOWERY
BOXERS
BRIERS
BRIERY
BUYERS
CABERS
CAGERS
CAMERA
CANERS
CAPERS
CASERN
CATERS
CAVERN
CAVERS
CELERY
CETERA
CHEERS
CHEERY
CICERO
CIDERS
CITERS
CODERS
COHERE
COMERS
COOERS
CORERS
COVERS
COVERT
COWERS
CRIERS
CRYERS
CURERS
CYDERS
DATERS
DEFERS
DESERT
DETERS
DICERS
DINERO
DINERS
DIVERS
DIVERT
DIYERS
DOSERS
DOWERS
DOWERY
DOZERS
DRIERS
DRYERS
DUNERA
DUPERY
EATERS
EATERY
EDBERG
EDGERS
EELERS
EGBERT
EIDERS
EKBERG
ELBERT
ELDERS
ELLERY
ELVERS
EMBERS
EMEERS
EMPERY
ENDERS
ENTERO
ENTERS
ESKERS
ESTERS
ETHERS
EXPERT
EXSERT
EXTERN
FAKERS
FAKERY
FARERS
FEVERS
FIBERS
FIFERS
FILERS
FINERY
FIRERS
FIVERS
FIXERS
FLEERS
FLIERS
FLYERS
FOYERS
FRIERS
FRYERS
GAPERS
GATERS
GENERA
GIBERS
GIVERS
GLUERS
GOFERS
GONERS
GOVERN
HALERS
HALERU
HATERS
HAVERS
HAZERS
HETERO
HEWERS
HEXERS
HIDERS
HIKERS
HIRERS
HOMERS
HOPERS
HOVERS
HUBERT
HUMERI
IDLERS
IMPERF
INFERS
INHERE
INKERS
INSERT
INTERJ
INTERN
INVERT
JAPERS
JAPERY
JIVERS
JOKERS
KAGERA
KHMERS
KITERS
LACERS
LADERS
LAGERS
LAKERS
LASERS
LAVERS
LAYERS
LEVERS
LIBERI
LIFERS
LIGERS
LINERS
LITERS
LIVERS
LIVERY
LONERS
LOPERS
LOSERS
LOVERS
LOWERS
LOWERY
LUGERS
MADERO
MAKERS
MASERS
MASERU
MATERS
MAZERS
METERS
MILERS
MIMERS
MINERS
MISERS
MISERY
MITERS
MIXERS
MODERN
MONERA
MOPERS
MOPERY
MOVERS
MOWERS
MOYERS
MUSERS
NAMERS
NAPERY
NEVERS
NFLERS
NHLERS
NINERS
NITERS
NITERY
NOTERS
NUMERO
OATERS
OBVERT
OCHERS
OCHERY
OFFERS
OGLERS
OILERS
ORDERS
ORNERY
ORRERY
OSIERS
OTHERS
OTTERS
OWNERS
PACERS
PAGERS
PAPERS
PAPERY
PARERS
PATERS
PAVERS
PAWERS
PAYERS
PETERS
PIKERS
PINERO
PINERY
PIPERS
PLIERS
POKERS
POKERY
POLERS
POSERS
POWERS
PRIERS
RACERS
RAKERS
RASERS
RATERS
RAVERS
REFERS
REVERB
REVERE
REVERS
REVERT
RICERS
RIDERS
RISERS
RIVERA
RIVERS
ROBERT
ROGERS
ROMERO
ROPERS
ROVERS
ROWERS
RULERS
RUPERT
SABERS
SAKERS
SAVERS
SAYERS
SCLERA
SCLERO
SEBERG
SECERN
SEDERS
SEVERE
SEVERN
SEVERS
SEVERY
SEWERS
SHEERS
SHOERS
SIDERO
SIDERS
SISERA
SIXERS
SIZERS
SKIERS
SNEERS
SNEERY
SOBERS
SOLERS
SOMERS
SOWERS
SOXERS
SPHERE
SPHERY
SPIERS
STEERS
SUPERB
SUPERS
TAKERS
TALERS
TAMERS
TAPERS
TASERS
TATERS
TAVERN
TAXERS
TIGERS
TILERS
TIMERS
TITERS
TONERS
TOPERS
TORERO
TOTERS
TOWERS
TOWERY
TRIERS
TUBERS
TUNERS
TUYERE
TYPERS
UDDERS
ULCERS
UMBERS
UPPERS
URGERS
USHERS
UTTERS
VALERY
VEXERS
VIDERI
VINERY
VIPERS

VOTERS
VOWERS
WADERS
WAFERS
WAFERY
WAGERS
WALERS
WANERS
WATERS
WATERY
WAVERS
WAVERY
WAXERS
WEBERN
WINERY
WIPERS
WIRERS
WOOERS
WYVERN

•••E•R

APPEAR
ARREAR
AUTEUR
CAREER
COHEIR
DOGEAR
ENDEAR
INGEAR
LINEAR
METEOR
POSEUR
RATEDR
REHEAR
RETEAR
TINEAR
VENEER

••••ER

ABUSER
ACHIER
ADORER
AETHER
AIRIER
ALITER
AMBLER
AMPLER
ANGLER
ANSWER
ANTHER
ANTLER
ARCHER
ARGUER
ARTIER
ASEVER
ASHIER
AVOWER
BACKER
BADDER
BADGER
BAGGER
BAILER
BALDER
BANGER
BANKER
BANNER
BANTER
BARBER
BARKER
BARTER
BASTER
BATHER
BATTER
BAWLER
BAXTER
BEAKER
BEARER
BEATER
BEAVER
BECKER
BEEPER
BENDER
BERBER
BESSER
BETTER
BICKER
BIDDER
BIGGER
BINDER
BIRDER
BITTER
BLADER
BLAZER
BLOWER
BOATER
BOBBER
BOILER
BOLDER
BOLGER
BOMBER
BONIER
BOOKER
BOOMER
BOPPER
BORDER
BOTHER
BOVVER
BOWLER
BOWSER
BOWYER
BOXIER
BRACER
BRAVER
BRAYER
BRAZER
BREUER
BREWER
BREYER
BROKER
BRUDER
BUFFER
BUGLER
BULWER
BUMMER
BUMPER
BUNKER
BUNTER
BURGER
BURNER
BUSIER
BUSTER
BUTLER
BUTTER
BUZZER
CABLER
CADGER
CAGIER
CAHIER
CAKIER
CALDER
CALLER
CALMER
CAMBER
CAMPER
CANIER
CANKER
CANNER
CANTER
CAPPER
CARDER
CAREER
CARPER
CARTER
CARVER
CASPER
CASTER
CATHER
CENSER
CENTER
CHASER
CHEWER
CHIDER
CHOKER
CHOLER
CINDER
CIPHER
CLAWER
CLEVER
CLOSER
CLOVER
COALER
COAXER
COCKER
CODGER
COFFER
COINER
COKIER
COLDER
COLTER
COMBER
CONFER
CONGER
CONKER
CONNER
COODER
COOKER
COOLER
COOPER
COOTER
COPIER
COPPER
COPTER
CORKER
CORNER
COSIER
COTTER
COUTER
COWPER
COZIER
CRATER
CRAVER
CROWER
CRUDER
CULLER
CULVER
CUMBER
CURLER
CURTER
CUSTER
CUTLER
CUTTER
CYCLER
CYPHER
DAFTER
DAGGER
DAMPER
DANCER
DANDER
DANGER
DANKER
DANNER
DAPPER
DARKER
DARNER
DARTER
DASHER
DAUBER
DEADER
DEAFER
DEALER
DEARER
DECKER
DEEPER
DEFTER
DEICER
DELVER
DENIER
DENSER
DENVER
DEWIER
DEXTER
DIALER
DIAPER
DICIER
DICKER
DIETER
DIFFER
DIGGER
DILLER
DIMMER
DINNER
DIPPER
DITHER
DLAYER
DOBBER
DOCKER
DODDER
DODGER
DOGGER
DONDER
DONNER
DOPIER
DORMER
DOSSER
DOURER
DOWNER
DOWSER
DOZIER
DRAPER
DRAWER
DRIVER
DRONER
DROVER
DUELER
DUFFER
DUIKER
DULLER
DUMBER
DUMPER
DUNKER
DUSTER
EARNER
EASIER
EASTER
EDGIER
EELIER
EERIER
EGGIER
EISNER
EITHER
ELATER
ELAYER
ELOPER
ELUDER
EMOTER
ENVIER
ERASER
ESCHER
ESTHER
ETCHER
EVADER
EVENER
EVILER
EVOKER
EXETER
FABLER
FAIRER
FALSER
FALTER
FARMER
FASTER
FATHER
FATTER
FAWNER
FEARER
FEEDER
FEELER
FELLER
FENCER
FENDER
FERBER
FERRER
FESTER
FETTER
FIBBER
FILLER
FILTER
FINDER
FINGER
FIRMER
FISHER
FITTER
FLAKER
FLAYER
FLOWER
FODDER
FOGGER
FOKKER
FOLDER
FONDER
FOOLER
FOOTER
FORCER
FORGER
FORKER
FORMER
FOSTER
FOULER
FOWLER
FOXIER
FRASER
FRAZER
FUELER
FULLER
FUMIER
GABBER
GABLER
GADDER
GAFFER
GAINER
GAITER
GAMIER
GAMMER
GANDER
GANGER
GAOLER
GARNER
GARTER
GASPER
GASSER
GATHER
GAUGER
GAWKER
GEEZER
GEIGER
GENDER
GERBER
GETTER
GEYSER
GIBBER
GILDER
GINGER
GIPPER
GIRDER
GLASER
GLAZER
GLIDER
GLOVER
GLOWER
GLUIER
GNAWER
GOLFER
GOOBER
GOOIER
GOOVER
GOPHER
GORIER
GOUGER
GRADER
GRATER
GRAVER
GRAYER
GRAZER
GREYER
GRIPER
GROCER
GROVER
GROWER
GULPER
GUNNER
GUNTER
GUSHER
GUTTER
GYPPER
HACKER
HALTER
HAMMER
HAMPER
HANGER
HANKER
HARDER
HARKER
HARPER
HATTER
HAULER
HAWKER
HAWSER
HAZIER
HEADER
HEALER
HEARER
HEATER
HEAVER
HEDGER
HEEDER
HEELER
HEFNER
HEIFER
HELLER
HELPER
HELTER
HEMMER
HENNER
HEPPER
HERDER
HESTER
HIGHER
HILLER
HINDER
HINTER
HIPPER
HISSER
HITHER
HITTER
HOAXER
HOKIER
HOLDER
HOLIER
HOLLER
HOMIER
HONKER
HOOFER
HOOPER
HOOTER
HOOVER
HOPPER
HORNER
HOSIER
HOTTER
HOWLER
HUGGER
HULLER
HUMMER
HUNGER
HUNKER
HUNTER
HURLER
HUSKER
ICKIER
IFFIER
IMAGER
INANER
INKIER
IRATER
IRONER
ISOMER
ISSUER
JABBER
JAEGER
JAGGER
JAILER
JAMMER
JASPER
JAVIER
JEERER
JEETER
JENNER
JESTER
JIGGER
JITTER
JIVIER
JOBBER
JOGGER
JOINER
JOKIER
JOSSER
JOYNER
JUDDER
JUICER
JUMPER
JUNKER
JUSTER
KAISER
KANDER
KAVNER
KEELER
KEENER
KEEPER
KEGLER
KELLER
KENNER
KEPLER
KHYBER
KICKER
KIDDER
KIEFER
KILLER
KILMER
KILTER
KINDER
KIPPER
KISSER
KNOWER
KOHLER
KOSHER
KOTTER
KRAMER
KRATER
KRONER
KRUGER
LAAGER
LACIER
LADDER
LADLER
LAFFER
LAGGER
LAKIER
LANCER
LANDER
LANIER
LANKER
LARDER
LARGER
LASHER
LASSER
LATHER
LATTER
LAUDER
LAUPER
LAWYER
LAZIER
LEADER
LEAKER
LEANER
LEAPER
LEASER
LECTER
LEDGER
LEERER
LEHRER
LENDER
LERNER
LESSER
LESTER
LETTER
LEVIER
LEWDER
LIBBER
LIEDER
LIEFER
LIFTER
LIMBER
LIMIER
LIMNER
LIMPER
LINGER
LINIER
LINKER
LINTER
LISTER
LITTER
LOADER
LOAFER
LOANER
LOBBER
LOCKER
LODGER
LOGGER
LOGIER
LOITER
LONGER
LOOKER
LOOPER
LOOSER
LOOTER
LOPPER
LOUDER
LOUVER
LUBBER
LUGGER
LUMBER
LUMPER
LUNKER
LUSHER
LUSTER
LUTHER
MADDER
MAHLER
MAILER
MANGER
MANNER
MAPPER
MARKER
MARNER
MASHER
MASKER
MASTER
MATHER
MATTER
MAULER

MAUSER
MAZIER
MEAGER
MEANER
MEEKER
MEETER
MEMBER
MENDER
MERCER
MERGER
MESMER
METIER
MEWLER
MIDLER
MILDER
MILKER
MILLER
MILNER
MINCER
MINDER
MINTER
MIRIER
MISTER
MOANER
MOCKER
MOILER
MOLDER
MOLTER
MONGER
MOPIER
MOPPER
MOSHER
MOTHER
MOUSER
MUDDER
MUGGER
MULLER
MUMMER
MURDER
MUSHER
MUSTER
MUTTER
NABBER
NAGGER
NAILER
NAPIER
NAPPER
NASSER
NATTER
NEARER
NEATER
NESTER
NETHER
NEUTER
NICKER
NIGHER
NIPPER
NOBLER
NOSHER
NOSIER
NUDGER
NUMBER
NURSER
NUTTER
OATIER
OBITER
OERTER
OILIER
OLIVER
ONAGER
OOZIER
OPENER
OPINER
OSTLER
OUSTER
OYSTER
PACKER
PADDER
PALIER
PALMER
PALTER
PAMPER
PANDER
PANNER
PANZER
PAPIER
PARKER
PARSER
PASSER
PATTER
PAUPER
PAWNER
PEELER
PEEPER
PEGLER
PELTER
PENNER
PEPPER
PERTER
PESTER
PETTER
PEWTER
PFIZER
PHASER
PICKER
PIECER
PIETER
PILFER
PINCER
PINIER
PINKER
PINNER
PINTER
PIPIER
PITIER
PITTER
PLACER
PLANER
PLATER
PLAYER
PLOVER
PLOWER
POKIER
POLDER
POLLER
PONDER
POORER
POPPER
PORKER
PORTER
POSHER
POSTER
POTHER
POTTER
POURER
POUTER
POWDER
PRATER
PRAYER
PREFER
PRETER
PRICER
PRIMER
PROBER
PROPER
PROSER
PROVER
PRUNER
PUCKER
PUFFER
PUMPER
PUNIER
PUNKER
PUNTER
PURRER
PURSER
PUTTER
QUAKER
QUAVER
QUEUER
QUIVER
QUOTER
RACIER
RADNER
RAFTER
RAIDER
RAILER
RAINER
RAISER
RANGER
RANKER
RANTER
RAPIER
RAPPER
RASHER
RASPER
RASTER
RATHER
RATTER
READER
REALER
REAMER
REAPER
REARER
REDDER
REEFER
REINER
RENDER
RENTER
RESTER
REUTER
RHYMER
RICHER
RIFLER
RIGGER
RIMIER
RINGER
RIOTER
RIPPER
RISKER
RITTER
ROAMER
ROARER
ROBBER
ROCKER
ROHMER
ROLLER
ROMPER
ROOFER
ROOMER
ROOTER
ROPIER
ROSIER
ROSTER
ROTTER
ROUSER
ROUTER
ROZZER
RUBBER
RUDDER
RUINER
RUMMER
RUNNER
RUTGER
SACKER
SADDER
SALTER
SALVER
SANDER
SANGER
SAPPER
SASSER
SAUCER
SAUGER
SAWYER
SCALER
SCARER
SCORER
SCOTER
SEALER
SEATER
SEEDER
SEEGER
SEEKER
SEINER
SEIZER
SELLER
SEMPER
SENDER
SERVER
SETTER
SEXIER
SHAKER
SHAPER
SHARER
SHAVER
SHINER
SHIRER
SHIVER
SHOVER
SHOWER
SICKER
SIFTER
SIGHER
SIGNER
SILVER
SIMMER
SIMPER
SINGER
SINKER
SINNER
SINTER
SIPPER
SISLER
SISTER
SITTER
SKATER
SKEWER
SKIVER
SLATER
SLAVER
SLAYER
SLICER
SLIDER
SLIVER
SLOWER
SMILER
SMOKER
SNIDER
SNIPER
SNORER
SNYDER
SOAKER
SOAPER
SOARER
SOBBER
SOCCER
SOFTER
SOLDER
SOLVER
SOMBER
SOMMER
SOONER
SORTER
SOURER
SOUTER
SPACER
SPADER
SPARER
SPIDER
SPIKER
SPRIER
SPRYER
STAGER
STALER
STARER
STATER
STEWER
STIVER
STOKER
STONER
STORER
STOVER
STUMER
STYLER
SUAVER
SUCKER
SUFFER
SULKER
SUMMER
SUMNER
SUMTER
SUNDER
SUPPER
SURFER
SUTLER
SUTTER
SWAYER
SWIPER
TACKER
TALKER
TALLER
TAMPER
TANKER
TANNER
TAPPER
TARTER
TASTER
TATTER
TAUTER
TEASER
TEDDER
TEENER
TEETER
TELLER
TEMPER
TENDER
TENSER
TENTER
TERSER
TESTER
TETHER
THALER
THAYER
TICKER
TIDIER
TIGGER
TILLER
TILTER
TIMBER
TINDER
TINIER
TINKER
TINNER
TINTER
TIPPER
TITFER
TITHER
TITTER
TOILER
TONIER
TOOTER
TOPPER
TOSSER
TOTHER
TOTTER
TOURER
TOUTER
TOWNER
TRACER
TRADER
TRITER
TUCKER
TUGGER
TURNER
TUSKER
TWOFER
TYPIER
UGLIER
ULSTER
UNDOER
UNITER
USURER
VAGUER
VAINER
VAMPER
VANIER
VASTER
VEDDER
VENEER
VENTER
VERGER
VESPER
VETOER
VIEWER
VINIER
VIZIER
WAGNER
WAILER
WAITER
WAIVER
WALKER
WALLER
WALTER
WANDER
WANIER
WANNER
WAPNER
WARDER
WARIER
WARMER
WARNER
WASHER
WASTER
WAVIER
WAXIER
WEAKER
WEARER
WEAVER
WEBBER
WEEDER
WEEPER
WELDER
WELLER
WELTER
WERNER
WETHER
WETTER
WHALER
WHINER
WHITER
WICKER
WIENER
WILDER
WILIER
WINCER
WINDER
WINGER
WINIER
WINKER
WINNER
WINTER
WIRIER
WISHER
WISTER
WITHER
WOHLER
WOLPER
WONDER
WOOFER
WORKER
WOWSER
WRITER
WYNTER
XAVIER
XYSTER
YABBER
YAKKER
YAMMER
YASSER
YAWNER
YAWPER
YEAGER
YELLER
YELPER
YESTER
YONDER
YORKER
ZAFFER
ZANDER
ZANIER
ZAPPER
ZENGER
ZIMMER
ZINGER
ZIPPER
ZITHER
ZONKER
ZUIDER

ES••••

ESCAPE
ESCARP
ESCENT
ESCHER
ESCHEW
ESCORT
ESCROW
ESCUDO
ESDRAS
ESHARP
ESKERS
ESKIMO
ESPANA
ESPIAL
ESPIED
ESPIES
ESPOSA
ESPOSO
ESPRIT
ESSAYS
ESSENE
ESTATE
ESTEEM
ESTERS
ESTHER
ESTOPS
ESTRAY

E•S•••

EASEIN
EASELS
EASEUP
EASIER
EASILY
EASING
EASTER
EASTON
EDSELS
EISNER
ENSIGN
ENSILE
ENSOUL
ENSUED
ENSUES
ENSURE
EOSINS
ERSATZ
ESSAYS
ESSENE
ETSEQQ
EXSERT

E••S••

EATSAT
EATSIN
EATSUP
ECESIC
ECESIS
EDESSA
EDISON
EGESTA
EGESTS
EGGSON
ELISHA
ELISSA
ELYSEE
ENDSUP
ENESCO
ENISLE
ENOSIS
ERASED
ERASER
ERASES
ERESTU
EXISTS

E•••S•

EDESSA
EFFUSE
EGOISM
EGOIST
EGRESS
ELAPSE
ELDEST
ELFISH
ELISSA
ELOISE
ELPASO
ELVISH
EMBOSS
EMDASH
ENCASE
ENDASH
ENDUSE
ENLIST
ENMESH
EOIPSO
ERNEST
ESPOSA
ESPOSO
EVENSO
EVERSO
EVULSE
EXCESS
EXCISE
EXCUSE
EXPOSE
EXPOST

E••••S

EAGLES
EAGRES
EASELS
EATERS
EBOATS
EBONDS
ECCLES
ECESIS
ECHOES
ECLATS
ECOLES
EDAMES
EDDIES
EDDOES
EDGARS
EDGERS
EDICTS
EDILES
EDSELS

EDUCES
EELERS
EFLATS
EGESTS
EGRESS
EGRETS
EIDERS
EIGHTS
EJECTS
EJIDOS
ELANDS
ELATES
ELBOWS
ELBRUS
ELDERS
ELECTS
ELEMIS
ELEVES
ELIDES
ELITES
ELOPES
ELUDES
ELUTES
ELVERS
EMAILS
EMBAYS
EMBEDS
EMBERS
EMBOSS
EMCEES
EMEERS
EMENDS
EMMETS
EMOTES
ENACTS
ENATES
ENDERS
ENDOWS
ENDUES
ENGELS
ENJOYS
ENNIUS
ENOKIS
ENOSIS
ENROLS
ENSUES
ENTERS
ENURES
ENVIES
ENVOIS
ENVOYS
EOSINS
EPHAHS
EPHODS
EPHORS
EPIRUS
EPOCHS
EPODES
EPROMS
EQUALS
EQUIPS
ERASES
EREBUS
ERECTS
ERGOTS
ERINYS
ERODES
ERRORS
ERUCTS
ERUPTS
ESDRAS
ESKERS
ESPIES
ESSAYS
ESTERS
ESTOPS
ETAPES
ETCHES
ETHERS
ETHICS
ETHNOS
ETUDES
EVADES
EVENTS
EVERTS
EVICTS
EVOKES
EXACTS
EXALTS
EXCELS
EXCESS
EXERTS
EXILES
EXISTS
EXODUS
EXPELS
EXTOLS
EXTRAS
EXUDES
EXULTS
EXURBS
EYRIES

•ES•••

BESANT
BESETS
BESIDE
BESOMS
BESOTS
BESSER
BESSIE
BESTED
BESTIR
BESTOW
CESARE
CESIUM
CESSED
CESSES
CESSNA
CESTAS
CESTOS
CESTUS
DESALT
DESCRY
DESERT
DESICA
DESIGN
DESILU
DESIRE
DESIST
DESMAN
DESOTO
DESPOT
DESTRY
FESCUE
FESSED
FESSES
FESSUP
FESTAL
FESTAS
FESTER
FESTUS
GESTES
GESTIC
HESIOD
HESTER
HESTIA
HESTON
JESSEL
JESSIE
JESTED
JESTER
JESUIT
KESHIA
LESAGE
LESBOS
LESLEY
LESLIE
LESSEE
LESSEN
LESSER
LESSON
LESSOR
LESTAT
LESTER
MESABI
MESCAL
MESHED
MESHES
MESMER
MESONS
MESSED
MESSES
MESSRS
MESSUP
NESSES
NESSIE
NESTEA
NESTED
NESTER
NESTLE
NESTOR
PESACH
PESAWA
PESCOW
PESETA
PESTER
PESTLE
PESTOS
RESALE
RESALT
RESAND
RESAWN
RESAWS
RESCUE
RESEAL
RESEAT
RESEAU
RESECT
RESEDA
RESEED
RESEEN
RESEES
RESELL
RESEND
RESENT
RESETS
RESEWN
RESEWS
RESHES
RESHIP
RESHOD
RESHOE
RESHOT
RESIDE
RESIGN
RESILE
RESING
RESINS
RESINY
RESIST
RESNIK
RESODS
RESOLD
RESOLE
RESORB
RESORT
RESPIN
RESTED
RESTER
RESTON
RESTUP
RESULT
RESUME
SESAME
SESQUI
SESTET
SESTOS
TESLAS
TESSIE
TESTAE
TESTED
TESTEE
TESTER
VESPER
VESPID
VESSEL
VESTAL
VESTAS
VESTED
VESTEE
VESTRY
WESKIT
WESLEY
WESSEX
WESSON
YESMAN
YESMEN
YESSED
YESSES
YESSIR
YESTER
ZESTED

•E•S••

BEASTS
BENSON
BESSER
BESSIE
BETSEY
BETSON
CEASED
CEASES
CENSED
CENSER
CENSES
CENSOR
CENSUS
CESSED
CESSES
CESSNA
DEASIL
DEISTS
DENSER
FEASTS
FEISTY
FESSED
FESSES
FESSUP
GEISEL
GEISHA
GELSEY
GETSAT
GETSBY
GETSET
GETSIN
GETSIT
GETSON
GETSTO
GETSUP
GEYSER
HEISTS
HEMSIN
HENSON
HERSEY
JENSEN
JERSEY
JESSEL
JESSIE
JETSAM
JETSET
JETSKI
JETSON
KELSEY
KERSEE
KERSEY
KEYSIN
KEYSUP
LEASED
LEASER
LEASES
LENSED
LENSES
LESSEE
LESSEN
LESSER
LESSON
LESSOR
LETSAT
LETSBE
LETSGO
LETSIN
LETSON
LETSUP
MEASLY
MENSAE
MENSAL
MENSAS
MENSCH
MERSEY
MESSED
MESSES
MESSRS
MESSUP
NEESON
NEISSE
NELSON
NESSES
NESSIE
NEVSKY
PENSEE
PEPSIN
PEPSUP
PERSIA
PERSON
REASON
REDSEA
REDSOX
REESES
REUSED
REUSES
REVSON
REVSUP
SEASON
SEESAW
SEESIN
SEESTO
SEISMO
SEISMS
SENSED
SENSEI
SENSES
SENSOR
SETSAT
SETSBY
SETSIN
SETSON
SETSUP
SEWSON
SEWSUP
TEASED
TEASEL
TEASER
TEASES
TEASET
TEESUP
TENSED
TENSER
TENSES
TENSOR
TERSER
TESSIE
VERSED
VERSES
VERSOS
VERSTS
VERSUS
VESSEL
WEASEL
WESSEX
WESSON
YEASTS
YEASTY
YESSED
YESSES
YESSIR

•E••S•

BEHEST
BEKESY
BEMUSE
BETISE
CERISE
CERUSE
DEBASE
DEFUSE
DEGUST
DELIST
DEMISE
DENISE
DEPOSE
DESIST
DETEST
DEVEST
DEVISE
FETISH
FEWEST
FEYEST
HEARST
HERESY
JEWISH
LEGIST
MEDUSA
MEREST
NEISSE
NEWEST
NEWISH
PERISH
PERUSE
RECAST
RECESS
RECUSE
REFUSE
REHASH
RELISH
RELIST
REMISE
REMISS
REPAST
REPOSE
REPOST
RESIST
RETEST
REVISE
REWASH
SEROSA
SETOSE
SEXIST
TEENSY
TERESA
VERISM
WEENSY

•E•••S

AEETES
AENEAS
AEOLUS
AERIES
BEANOS
BEARDS
BEASTS
BEAUTS
BEAVIS
BEBOPS
BEDEWS
BEDIMS
BEEVES
BEFITS
BEFOGS
BEGETS
BEGINS
BEGUMS
BEIGES
BEINGS
BELAYS
BELIES
BELLES
BERETS
BERTHS
BESETS
BESOMS
BESOTS
BETELS
BETTAS
BEVELS
BEVIES
BEZELS
CEASES
CEDARS
CEIBAS
CELEBS
CELLOS
CENSES
CENSUS
CENTOS
CEORLS
CEREUS
CERROS
CESSES
CESTAS
CESTOS
CESTUS
DEBARS
DEBITS
DEBRAS
DEBRIS
DEBUGS
DEBUTS
DECAFS
DECALS
DECAYS
DECORS
DECOYS
DEFATS
DEFERS
DEFIES
DEFOGS
DEICES
DEIGNS
DEIMOS
DEISTS
DEKKOS
DELAYS
DELFTS
DELIUS
DELTAS
DELVES
DEMIES
DEMITS
DEMOBS
DEMONS
DEMURS
DENIES
DENIMS
DENNIS
DEPOTS
DEPTHS
DERMIS
DERRIS
DETERS
DEUCES
DEVILS
EELERS
FEASTS
FEIGNS
FEINTS
FELLAS
FELONS
FEMMES
FEMURS
FENCES
FERGUS
FERIAS
FERRIS
FESSES
FESTAS
FESTUS
FEVERS
FEZZES
GECKOS
GELEES
GEMOTS
GENETS
GENIES
GENIUS
GENRES
GEODES
GERAHS
GESTES
GETUPS
HEARTS
HEATHS
HEAVES
HEDGES
HEISTS
HELENS
HELIOS
HELLAS
HELLOS
HELOTS
HELVES
HENNAS
HERMES
HEROES
HERONS
HEWERS
HEXADS
HEXERS
JEEVES
JEWELS
KEBABS
KEBOBS
KEDGES
KEFIRS
KEMPIS
KERMES
KERMIS
KERNOS
KEVELS
KEYNES
LEARNS
LEASES
LEAVES
LEDGES
LEGALS
LEHUAS
LEMANS
LEMMAS
LEMNOS
LEMONS
LEMURS
LENSES
LEONES
LESBOS
LETUPS
LEVEES
LEVELS
LEVERS
LEVIES
MECCAS

MEDALS
MEDIAS
MEDICS
MELEES
MELONS
MENDES
MENSAS
MENTIS
MERGES
MERITS
MESHES
MESONS
MESSES
MESSRS
METALS
METERS
METRES
METROS
MEZZOS
NEIGHS
NENETS
NEREIS
NEREUS
NERVES
NESSES
NEUMES
NEVERS
NEVINS
NEWELS
PEARLS
PECANS
PEDALS
PEEVES
PEKINS
PEKOES
PELEUS
PELOPS
PELVIS
PENNIS
PEPLOS
PERILS
PESTOS
PETALS
PETERS
PEWEES
PEWITS
REACTS
REAIMS
REAIRS
REALES
REALMS
REARMS
REATAS
REBAGS
REBARS
REBBES
REBECS
REBELS
REBIDS
REBUTS
RECAPS
RECESS
RECONS
RECTOS
RECTUS
RECURS
REDOES
REDUBS
REDYES
REESES
REEVES
REFERS
REFITS
REGIUS
REHABS
REHEMS
REIGNS
REINAS
REINKS
REKEYS
RELAYS
RELETS
RELICS
RELIES
REMANS
REMAPS
REMISS
REMITS
REMOPS
REMOWS
RENEWS
RENNES
REOILS
REPADS
REPAYS
REPEGS
REPELS
REPINS
REPOTS
REPROS
RERUNS
RESAWS
RESEES
RESETS
RESEWS
RESHES
RESINS
RESODS
RETAGS
RETAPS
RETARS
RETIES
RETOPS
RETOWS
RETROS
REUNES
REUSES
REVELS
REVERS
REVETS
REVUES
REWEDS
REWINS
SEAMUS
SEDANS
SEDERS
SEDGES
SEDUMS
SEGUES
SEINES
SEISMS
SEIZES
SELVES
SENNAS
SENORS
SENSES
SEPALS
SEPIAS
SEPOYS
SERACS
SERAIS
SERGES
SERIES
SERIFS
SERINS
SEROUS
SEROWS
SERUMS
SERVES
SERVOS
SESTOS
SETINS
SETTOS
SETUPS
SEVENS
SEVERS
SEVRES
SEWERS
TEASES
TEHEES
TEMPOS
TEMPTS
TEMPUS
TENENS
TENETS
TENNIS
TENONS
TENORS
TENSES
TENTHS
TEPALS
TEPEES
TEREUS
TERNES
TESLAS
TETHYS
TETONS
TETRAS
TETRIS
TEXANS
VEGANS
VELDTS
VENOMS
VENOUS
VENUES
VERBIS
VERGES
VERSES
VERSOS
VERSTS
VERSUS
VERVES
VESTAS
VETOES
VEXERS
WEAVES
WEDGES
WEIGHS
WELLES
WENCES
XEBECS
XERXES
YEARNS
YEASTS
YENTAS
YERKES
YESSES
ZEBRAS
ZENDOS
ZEROES
ZEUXIS

••ES••

ABESSE
ACESUP
ADESTE
ATESTS
AVESTA
AYESHA
CAESAR
CHESTS
CHESTY
CRESOL
CRESTS
CUESTA
DIESEL
DIESES
DIESIS
DOESBY
DOESIN
DOESNT
DOESUP
DRESSY
ECESIC
ECESIS
EDESSA
EGESTA
EGESTS
ENESCO
ERESTU
FIESTA
FLESHY
FRESCA
FRESCO
FRESNO
GOESAT
GOESBY
GOESIN
GOESON
GOESUP
GUESTS
ICESIN
ICESUP
ILESHA
INESSE
KMESON
KRESGE
LIESIN
LIESTO
NEESON
NOESIS
ODESSA
OLESON
PRESET
PRESTO
QUESTS
REESES
RHESUS
SEESAW
SEESIN
SEESTO
SIESTA
TEESUP
THESEA
THESES
THESIS
THESIX
TIESIN
TIESTO
TIESUP
TMESIS
TOESIN
UNESCO
USESUP
WIESEL
WRESTS

••E•S•

ABESSE
AGEISM
AGEIST
ALEAST
AMERSP
ATEASE
AVERSE
BREAST
CHEESE
CHEESY
CLEESE
CREASE
CREASY
CREUSA
DRESSY
EDESSA
EVENSO
EVERSO
FLENSE
FREEST
GNEISS
GOEASY
GREASE
GREASY
INESSE
KLEIST
KWEISI
NLEAST
ODENSE
ODESSA
ORELSE
PLEASE
QUEASY
SMERSH
TEENSY
THEISM
THEIST
TSETSE
TWEEST
UNEASE
UNEASY
WEENSY

••E••S

ABELES
ACEOUS
ADEEMS
ADEPTS
AEETES
AGENAS
AGENTS
AKELAS
AKENES
ALEPHS
ALERTS
ALEUTS
ALEXIS
AMEBAS
AMEERS
AMENDS
AMENTS
ANELES
APEXES
ARECAS
ARENAS
ARETES
ATEAMS
ATESTS
AVERTS
BCELLS
BEEVES
BLEARS
BLEATS
BLEEDS
BLEEPS
BLENDS
BREADS
BREAKS
BREAMS
BREEDS
BRENTS
BREVES
BREVIS
BUENOS
CHEATS
CHECKS
CHEEKS
CHEEPS
CHEERS
CHELAS
CHEOPS
CHESTS
CHETHS
CLEANS
CLEARS
CLEATS
CLEEKS
CLEFTS
CLERKS
CLEVES
CLEVIS
CREAKS
CREAMS
CREDOS
CREEDS
CREEKS
CREELS
CREEPS
CREMES
CREPES
CRESTS
CZECHS
DIESES
DIESIS
DREADS
DREAMS
DWEEBS
DWELLS
ECESIS
EGESTS
EJECTS
ELECTS
ELEMIS
ELEVES
EMEERS
EMENDS
EREBUS
ERECTS
EVENTS
EVERTS
EXERTS
FIELDS
FIENDS
FJELDS
FLECKS
FLEERS
FLEETS
FLEXES
FOEHNS
FOETUS
FREAKS
GLEAMS
GLEANS
GLEBES
GNEISS
GREATS
GREBES
GREEKS
GREENS
GREETS
GUESTS
HBEAMS
HUEVOS
HYENAS
IBEAMS
IBEXES
IDEALS
ILEXES
IRENES
JEEVES
KNEADS
KNEELS
KNELLS
KVELLS
LIEBYS
LIEGES
LIEUTS
NIECES
NOESIS
NUECES
OBEAHS
OBELUS
OCEANS
OMEGAS
ONEUPS
OPERAS
OREADS
OXEYES
PAEANS
PAEONS
PEEVES
PIECES
PIETAS
PLEADS
PLEATS
PLEBES
PLEXUS
PRECIS
PREENS
PSEUDS
QUEENS
QUELLS
QUERNS
QUESTS
QUEUES
REESES
REEVES
RHESUS
RHEUMS
SCENAS
SCENDS
SCENES
SCENTS
SHEAFS
SHEARS
SHEENS
SHEEPS
SHEERS
SHEETS
SHEIKS
SHELLS
SIEGES
SIEVES
SKEANS
SKEINS
SLEEKS
SLEEPS
SLEETS
SMEARS
SMELLS
SMELTS
SNEAKS
SNEERS
SNELLS
SOEURS
SPEAKS
SPEARS
SPECKS
SPEEDS
SPELLS
SPENDS
STEADS
STEAKS
STEALS
STEAMS
STEEDS
STEELS
STEEPS
STEERS
STEINS
STELES
STENOS
STERES
STERNS
SUEDES
SWEARS
SWEATS
SWEDES
SWEEPS
SWEETS
SWELLS
THEBES
THEFTS
THEIRS
THEMES
THERES
THERMS
THESES
THESIS
THETAS
THETIS
TIEINS
TIEUPS
TMESIS
TOEINS
TREADS
TREATS
TRENDS
TWEAKS
TWEEDS
TWEENS
TWEETS
TWERPS
UPENDS
VNECKS
WHEALS
WHEATS
WHEELS
WHELKS
WHELMS
WHELPS
WHERES
WIELDS
WREAKS
WRECKS
WRESTS
YIELDS

•••ES•

ABBESS
ABLEST
ACCESS
AFRESH
ALWEST
APTEST
ARNESS
ARREST
ASSESS
ATBEST
ATREST
ATTEST
BAREST
BASEST
BEHEST
BEKESY
BLUEST
BLUESY
CARESS
CHEESE
CHEESY
CLEESE
COYEST
CUTEST
CUTESY
DETEST
DEVEST
DIGEST
DIREST
DIVEST
DRIEST
DRYEST
DURESS
EGRESS
ELDEST
ENMESH
ERNEST
EXCESS
FEWEST
FEYEST
FINEST
FOREST
FREEST
GAMEST
GAYEST
GOWEST
HALEST
HERESY
HONEST
HUGEST
ICIEST
IDLEST
ILLEST

INFEST
INGEST
INJEST
INNESS
INVEST
IQTEST
LAMESA
LAMEST
LATEST
LAXEST
LOWEST
MEREST
MODEST
MOLEST
MUTEST
NEWEST
NICEST
NLWEST
NOLESS
NUDEST
OBSESS
OBTEST
ODDEST
OGRESS
OLDEST
PALEST
PRIEST
PUREST
RAREST
RAWEST
RECESS
RETEST
RIFEST
RIPEST
RUDEST
SAFEST
SAGEST
SANEST
SHIEST
SHYEST
SLIEST
SLYEST
SOREST
STRESS
SUREST
TALESE
TAMEST
TERESA
THRESH
TRUEST
TWEEST
UNLESS
UNMESH
UNREST
VARESE
VILEST
WALESA
WIDEST
WISEST
WRIEST
WRYEST
YAREST

•••E•S

ABBESS
ABBEYS
ACCESS
ADDERS
ADEEMS
ADIEUS
AENEAS
AGLETS
AGREES
AIDERS
AILERS
ALDERS
ALIENS
ALLEES
ALLEYS
ALTERS
AMBERS
AMEERS
AMIENS
AMVETS
ANGELS
ANGERS
ARDEBS
ARMETS
ARNESS
ARTELS
ASKERS
ASPENS
ASSESS
ASSETS
ASTERS
ATHENS
ATREUS
AUDENS
AUGERS
AUREUS
AZTECS
BABELS
BAGELS
BAKERS
BALERS
BEDEWS
BEGETS
BERETS
BESETS
BETELS
BEVELS
BEZELS
BICEPS
BIKERS
BIPEDS
BITERS
BLEEDS
BLEEPS
BLUETS
BLUEYS
BOGEYS
BONERS
BOREAS
BORERS
BOTELS
BOWERS
BOXERS
BREEDS
BRIEFS
BRIERS
BUTEOS
BUYERS
CABERS
CADETS
CAGERS
CAMELS
CAMEOS
CANERS
CAPERS
CARESS
CARETS
CATERS
CAVERS
CELEBS
CEREUS
CHEEKS
CHEEPS
CHEERS
CHIEFS
CIDERS
CITERS
CIVETS
CLEEKS
CODERS
COLEUS
COMERS
COMETS
CONEYS
COOERS
CORERS
COVENS
COVERS
COVETS
COVEYS
COWENS
COWERS
COZENS
CREEDS
CREEKS
CREELS
CREEPS
CRIERS
CRUETS
CRYERS
CUBEBS
CULETS
CUPELS
CURERS
CUVEES
CYDERS
DATERS
DEFERS
DETERS
DICERS
DINERS
DIVERS
DIYERS
DIZENS
DOGEYS
DONEES
DONETS
DOSERS
DOWELS
DOWERS
DOYENS
DOZENS
DOZERS
DRIERS
DRYERS
DURESS
DUVETS
DWEEBS
EASELS
EATERS
EDGERS
EDSELS
EELERS
EGRESS
EGRETS
EIDERS
ELDERS
ELVERS
EMBEDS
EMBERS
EMCEES
EMEERS
EMMETS
ENDERS
ENGELS
ENTERS
ESKERS
ESTERS
ETHERS
EXCELS
EXCESS
EXPELS
FACETS
FAKERS
FARERS
FEVERS
FIBERS
FIFERS
FILERS
FILETS
FIRERS
FIVERS
FIVEWS
FIXERS
FLEERS
FLEETS
FLIERS
FLYERS
FOGEYS
FOYERS
FRIERS
FRYERS
FUSEES
FUZEES
GAPERS
GATERS
GAVELS
GELEES
GENETS
GIBERS
GIMELS
GIVENS
GIVERS
GLUERS
GODETS
GOFERS
GOLEMS
GONERS
GREEKS
GREENS
GREETS
GRIEFS
GRUELS
HABEAS
HACEKS
HALERS
HAREMS
HATERS
HAVENS
HAVERS
HAZELS
HAZERS
HELENS
HEWERS
HEXERS
HIDERS
HIKERS
HIRERS
HOMERS
HONEYS
HOPERS
HOSELS
HOTELS
HOVELS
HOVERS
IDLERS
IMPELS
INFERS
INKERS
INLETS
INNESS
INSETS
INTENS
ISLETS
JAPERS
JASEYS
JEWELS
JIVERS
JOKERS
JULEPS
KEVELS
KHMERS
KITERS
KNEELS
KOPEKS
LABELS
LACERS
LADERS
LAGERS
LAKERS
LAMEDS
LAPELS
LASERS
LATENS
LAVERS
LAYERS
LEVEES
LEVELS
LEVERS
LIBELS
LIFERS
LIGERS
LIKENS
LIMENS
LIMEYS
LINENS
LINERS
LITERS
LIVENS
LIVERS
LODENS
LONERS
LOPERS
LOSERS
LOVERS
LOWERS
LUDENS
LUGERS
LUMENS
LYCEES
MAKERS
MASERS
MATERS
MATEYS
MAVENS
MAZERS
MELEES
METERS
MILERS
MIMEOS
MIMERS
MINERS
MISERS
MITERS
MIXERS
MIZENS
MODELS
MODEMS
MONEYS
MOPEDS
MOPERS
MORELS
MOSEYS
MOTELS
MOTETS
MOVERS
MOWERS
MOYERS
MULEYS
MUSERS
NAMERS
NAVELS
NENETS
NEREIS
NEREUS
NEVERS
NEWELS
NFLERS
NHLERS
NINERS
NITERS
NOLENS
NOLESS
NONETS
NOPETS
NOTERS
NOVELS
NYMETS
OATERS
OBSESS
OCHERS
OCTETS
OFFERS
OGLERS
OGRESS
OILERS
OLMECS
ONSETS
ORDERS
ORIELS
OSIERS
OTHERS
OTTERS
OUSELS
OUZELS
OWLETS
OWNERS
PACERS
PAGERS
PANELS
PAPERS
PARENS
PARERS
PASEOS
PATENS
PATERS
PAVERS
PAWERS
PAYEES
PAYERS
PELEUS
PETERS
PEWEES
PIKERS
PILEUS
PIPERS
PIXELS
PLIERS
POKERS
POKEYS
POLERS
POSERS
POWERS
PREENS
PRIERS
PROEMS
PUREES
QUEENS
QUIETS
RACERS
RAKERS
RAMETS
RANEES
RASERS
RATELS
RATERS
RAVELS
RAVENS
RAVERS
REBECS
REBELS
RECESS
REFERS
REHEMS
REKEYS
RELETS
RENEWS
REPEGS
REPELS
RESEES
RESETS
RESEWS
REVELS
REVERS
REVETS
REWEDS
RICERS
RIDERS
RIPENS
RISERS
RIVERS
RIVETS
RODEOS
ROGERS
ROLEOS
ROMEOS
ROPERS
ROVERS
ROWELS
ROWENS
ROWERS
RUBENS
RULERS
RUMENS
RUPEES
SABERS
SAKERS
SAVERS
SAYERS
SCREES
SCREWS
SEDERS
SEVENS
SEVERS
SEWERS
SHEENS
SHEEPS
SHEERS
SHEETS
SHOERS
SHREDS
SHREWS
SIDERS
SINEWS
SIRENS
SIXERS
SIZERS
SKIERS
SLEEKS
SLEEPS
SLEETS
SNEERS
SOBERS
SOLERS
SOLEUS
SOMERS
SOWERS
SOXERS
SPEEDS
SPIELS
SPIERS
SPREES
STEEDS
STEELS
STEEPS
STEERS
STRESS
STREWS
SUPERS
SWEEPS
SWEETS
TAKERS
TALERS
TAMERS
TAPERS
TASERS
TATERS
TAXERS
TEHEES
TENENS
TENETS
TEPEES
TEREUS
THREES
TIGERS
TILERS
TIMERS
TITERS
TOKENS
TONERS
TOPERS
TOTEMS
TOTERS
TOWELS
TOWERS
TRIERS
TUBERS
TUNERS
TVSETS
TWEEDS
TWEENS
TWEETS
TYPERS
UDDERS
ULCERS
UMBELS
UMBERS
UNLESS
UNPEGS
UNPENS
UNSEWS
UPPERS
UPSETS
URAEUS
URGERS
USHERS
UTTERS
UZBEKS
VALENS
VALETS
VEXERS
VIDEOS
VIPERS
VIREOS
VIXENS
VOLENS
VOTERS
VOWELS
VOWERS
WADERS
WAFERS
WAGERS
WAKENS
WALERS
WANERS
WATERS
WAVERS
WAXERS
WHEELS
WIDENS
WIPERS
WIRERS
WIZENS
WOMENS
WOOERS
XEBECS
YODELS
YOKELS
ZAZENS
ZIBETS

••••ES

ABASES
ABATES
ABELES
ABIDES
ABODES
ABUSES
ADAGES
ADDLES
ADOBES
ADORES
AEETES
AERIES
AGATES
AGAVES

AGGIES	BOGLES	CHORES	DIESES	FARCES	GLOBES	INURES	MAILES	OPUSES	PYXIES
AGREES	BOITES	CHUTES	DIODES	FASCES	GLOVES	IRENES	MAIZES	ORALES	QUAKES
AISLES	BOMBES	CITIES	DIRGES	FAUCES	GLOZES	IRIDES	MANSES	ORATES	QUEUES
AKENES	BONCES	CLAVES	DISHES	FAWKES	GLUTES	IRISES	MAPLES	ORGIES	QUIRES
ALINES	BONNES	CLEVES	DISMES	FEMMES	GNOMES	ISSUES	MARGES	ORTLES	QUOTES
ALLEES	BONZES	CLIMES	DITZES	FENCES	GOBIES	ISTLES	MASHES	ORYXES	RABIES
ALLIES	BOOTES	CLINES	DODGES	FESSES	GOOSES	ITCHES	MASSES	OSAGES	RAINES
AMAZES	BOSSES	CLONES	DODOES	FEZZES	GORGES	JAURES	MATTES	OUNCES	RAISES
AMBLES	BOULES	CLOSES	DOGIES	FIBRES	GORSES	JAZZES	MAUVES	OVULES	RAMIES
AMICES	BOUSES	CLOVES	DONEES	FICHES	GOUGES	JEEVES	MAYBES	OXEYES	RAMSES
AMIDES	BOWLES	CNOTES	DORIES	FILLES	GRACES	JINXES	MELEES	OXIDES	RANEES
AMINES	BRACES	COAXES	DOSSES	FISHES	GRADES	JOSHES	MENDES	PADRES	RANGES
AMOLES	BRAKES	COLIES	DOUSES	FIZZES	GRAPES	JOSSES	MERGES	PANNES	RASHES
AMUSES	BRAVES	COMBES	DOWSES	FLAKES	GRATES	JOULES	MESHES	PARSES	RAZZES
ANDRES	BRAZES	COMTES	DRAKES	FLAMES	GRAVES	JUDGES	MESSES	PASSES	REALES
ANELES	BREVES	CONIES	DRAPES	FLARES	GRAZES	JUICES	METRES	PASTES	REBBES
ANGLES	BRIBES	CONTES	DRIVES	FLAXES	GREBES	JURIES	MIDGES	PAUSES	REDOES
ANIMES	BRIDES	COPIES	DRONES	FLEXES	GRIMES	KEDGES	MINCES	PAYEES	REDYES
ANKLES	BRINES	COPSES	DROVES	FLORES	GRIPES	KERMES	MINKES	PEEVES	REESES
ANODES	BRUGES	CORTES	DRUPES	FLUKES	GROPES	KEYNES	MINXES	PEKOES	REEVES
ANOLES	BRULES	CORVES	DRUZES	FLUMES	GROVES	KISSES	MISSES	PEWEES	RELIES
ANTRES	BRUMES	COSHES	DULLES	FLUTES	GUIDES	KNAVES	MITRES	PHAGES	RENNES
APEXES	BRUTES	COSIES	DUNCES	FLUXES	GUILES	KNIFES	MOINES	PHASES	RESEES
APICES	BRUXES	COUPES	DUTIES	FOGIES	GUISES	KNIVES	MOIRES	PHONES	RESHES
APPLES	BSIDES	COZIES	EAGLES	FORBES	GUSHES	KOPJES	MONIES	PIECES	RETIES
ARCHES	BUDGES	CRAKES	EAGRES	FORCES	HADJES	LACHES	MONTES	PIQUES	REUNES
ARETES	BUGLES	CRANES	ECCLES	FORGES	HAINES	LADIES	MOSHES	PISCES	REUSES
ARGUES	BULGES	CRAPES	ECHOES	FORTES	HAJJES	LADLES	MOSSES	PISTES	REVUES
ARISES	BURIES	CRATES	ECOLES	FOSSES	HALOES	LANCES	MOUSES	PITIES	RHAMES
ARMIES	BURSES	CRAVES	EDAMES	FOWLES	HALVES	LAPSES	MOVIES	PIXIES	RHODES
ASIDES	BUSHES	CRAZES	EDDIES	FRAMES	HAOLES	LARGES	MURRES	PLACES	RHYMES
ATONES	BUSIES	CREMES	EDDOES	FRISES	HASHES	LASHES	MUSHES	PLAGES	RICHES
AWAKES	BUSSES	CREPES	EDILES	FUDGES	HASTES	LASSES	MUSSES	PLANES	RIDGES
AZIDES	BUTTES	CRIMES	EDUCES	FUGUES	HAWSES	LATHES	MUZZES	PLATES	RIFLES
AZINES	BUZZES	CRIPES	ELATES	FURIES	HEAVES	LATKES	MYOPES	PLEBES	RILLES
AZORES	BYRNES	CRISES	ELEVES	FURZES	HEDGES	LEASES	NACRES	PLUMES	RINSES
BABIES	CABLES	CRONES	ELIDES	FUSEES	HELVES	LEAVES	NANTES	PLUSES	ROBLES
BADGES	CACHES	CROZES	ELITES	FUSSES	HERMES	LEDGES	NAPLES	POGIES	ROGUES
BAINES	CADGES	CRUCES	ELOPES	FUTZES	HEROES	LENSES	NAPPES	POISES	ROUGES
BARGES	CADRES	CRUSES	ELUDES	FUZEES	HINGES	LEONES	NAVIES	PONCES	ROUSES
BARNES	CALCES	CRUXES	ELUTES	FUZZES	HISSES	LEVEES	NERVES	PONIES	ROUTES
BARRES	CALLES	CURSES	EMCEES	GABIES	HOAXES	LEVIES	NESSES	PONTES	RUBIES
BASHES	CALVES	CURVES	EMOTES	GABLES	HOBBES	LIANES	NEUMES	POSIES	RUBLES
BASSES	CALXES	CUSSES	ENATES	GAFFES	HOBOES	LIEGES	NICHES	POSSES	RUCHES
BASTES	CANNES	CUTIES	ENDUES	GANGES	HODGES	LILIES	NIECES	PRASES	RUPEES
BATHES	CANOES	CUVEES	ENSUES	GASHES	HOLMES	LISLES	NITRES	PRATES	RUSHES
BEEVES	CARIES	CYCLES	ENURES	GASSES	HOOVES	LITRES	NIXIES	PRAXES	SABLES
BEIGES	CARNES	DADOES	ENVIES	GAUGES	HORDES	LIVRES	NOBLES	PRICES	SABRES
BELIES	CARTES	DAISES	EPODES	GAUZES	HORSES	LOAVES	NOISES	PRIDES	SADHES
BELLES	CARVES	DALLES	ERASES	GELEES	HOUSES	LODGES	NOONES	PRIMES	SALVES
BEVIES	CASHES	DANCES	ERODES	GENIES	HUGHES	LONGES	NOOSES	PRIZES	SARGES
BIASES	CASTES	DANTES	ESPIES	GENRES	HUSHES	LOOIES	NOSHES	PROBES	SASHES
BIBLES	CAUSES	DASHES	ETAPES	GEODES	HYADES	LOOSES	NUDGES	PROLES	SASSES
BILGES	CEASES	DAUBES	ETCHES	GESTES	IBEXES	LORIES	NUECES	PROSES	SAUCES
BINGES	CENSES	DAVIES	ETUDES	GIGUES	IBISES	LOSSES	NURSES	PROVES	SAUTES
BIOMES	CESSES	DEFIES	EVADES	GIJOES	ILEXES	LOUPES	OCHRES	PRUDES	SAYLES
BLADES	CHAFES	DEICES	EVOKES	GIMMES	IMAGES	LOUSES	OGIVES	PRUNES	SAYYES
BLAMES	CHASES	DELVES	EXILES	GLACES	IMBUES	LUNGES	OLDIES	PULSES	SCALES
BLARES	CHIDES	DEMIES	EXUDES	GLADES	INCHES	LUTZES	OLIVES	PUREES	SCAPES
BLAZES	CHIMES	DENIES	EYRIES	GLARES	INDIES	LYCEES	ONUSES	PURGES	SCARES
BLOKES	CHINES	DEUCES	FABLES	GLAZES	INGLES	LYNXES	ONYXES	PURSES	SCENES
BODIES	CHIVES	DHOLES	FACIES	GLEBES	INGRES	MACHES	OODLES	PUSHES	SCONES
BOGIES	CHOKES	DIDIES	FALCES	GLIDES	INKLES	MADRES	OPINES	PUSSES	SCOPES

SCORES
SCREES
SCUTES
SEDGES
SEGUES
SEINES
SEIZES
SELVES
SENSES
SERGES
SERIES
SERVES
SEVRES
SHADES
SHAKES
SHALES
SHAMES
SHAPES
SHARES
SHAVES
SHINES
SHIRES
SHORES
SHOVES
SIDLES
SIEGES
SIEVES
SINGES
SKATES
SKIVES
SLAKES
SLATES
SLAVES
SLICES
SLIDES
SLIMES
SLOPES
SLYPES
SMILES
SMITES
SMOKES
SNAKES
SNARES
SNIPES
SNOPES
SNORES
SOARES
SOAVES
SOCLES
SOLVES
SONDES
SOUSES
SPACES
SPADES
SPARES
SPATES
SPICES
SPIKES
SPILES
SPINES
SPIRES
SPITES
SPOKES
SPORES
SPREES
SPRUES
SPUMES
STAGES
STAKES
STALES
STAPES
STARES
STASES
STATES
STAVES
STELES
STERES
STILES
STIPES
STOKES
STOLES
STONES
STOPES
STORES
STOVES
STUPES
STYLES
SUCCES
SUDSES
SUEDES
SUITES
SURGES
SUSSES
SWAGES
SWALES
SWEDES
SWIPES
TABLES
TANTES
TARGES
TASSES
TASTES
TAUPES
TAXIES
TBONES
TEASES
TEHEES
TENSES
TEPEES
TERNES
THALES
THAMES
THANES
THEBES
THEMES
THERES
THESES
THOLES
THREES
THROES
TIDIES
TILDES
TINGES
TITHES
TITLES
TITRES
TNOTES
TOBIES
TOILES
TONNES
TOQUES
TORIES
TORRES
TORTES
TOSSES
TRACES
TRADES
TRAVES
TRIBES
TRICES
TRIKES
TRINES
TROPES
TROVES
TRUCES
TULLES
TUQUES
TURVES
TWINES
UGLIES
UKASES
UNCLES
UNDIES
UNDOES
UNGUES
UNITES
UNTIES
UPASES
URUSES
USAGES
VALUES
VALVES
VARIES
VENUES
VERGES
VERSES
VERVES
VETOES
VINCES
VOGUES
VOICES
VOILES
VOSGES
VSIXES
WAIVES
WASHES
WASTES
WEAVES
WEDGES
WELLES
WENCES
WHALES
WHERES
WHILES
WHINES
WHITES
WHOLES
WILKES
WINCES
WINZES
WISHES
WITHES
WODGES
WOLVES
WRITES
WUSSES
XERXES
XFILES
YALIES
YERKES
YESSES
ZAIRES
ZANIES
ZEROES

ET••••

ETALIA
ETALII
ETAPES
ETCHED
ETCHER
ETCHES
ETERNE
ETHANE
ETHENE
ETHERS
ETHICS
ETHNIC
ETHNOS
ETOILE
ETONIC
ETSEQQ
ETUDES
ETUXOR
ETYMOL
ETYMON

E•T•••

EATERS
EATERY
EATING
EATOUT
EATSAT
EATSIN
EATSUP
ECTYPE
EITHER
ENTAIL
ENTERO
ENTERS
ENTICE
ENTIRE
ENTITY
ENTOMO
ENTRAP
ENTREE
ESTATE
ESTEEM
ESTERS
ESTHER
ESTOPS
ESTRAY
EUTAXY
EXTANT
EXTEND
EXTENT
EXTERN
EXTOLS
EXTORT
EXTRAS

E••T••

EARTHA
EARTHY
EASTER
EASTON
EDITED
EDITIO
EDITOR
ELATED
ELATER
ELATES
ELITES
ELUTED
ELUTES
EMOTED
EMOTER
EMOTES
EMPTOR
ENATES
EROTIC
EXETER
EXITED
EXOTIC

E•••T•

EBOATS
ECARTE
ECLATS
EDICTS
EFFETE
EFLATS
EGESTA
EGESTS
EGRETS
EIGHTH
EIGHTS
EIGHTY
EJECTA
EJECTS
ELECTS
EMEUTE
EMMETS
EMMETT
ENACTS
ENMITY
ENTITY
EOLITH
EQUATE
EQUITY
ERECTS
ERESTU
ERGATE
ERGOTS
ERRATA
ERSATZ
ERUCTS
ERUPTS
ESTATE
EVENTS
EVERTS
EVICTS
EXACTA
EXACTO
EXACTS
EXALTS
EXCITE
EXERTS
EXISTS
EXULTS
EXVOTO

E••••T

EAGLET
EATOUT
EATSAT
EFFECT
EFFORT
EGBERT
EGMONT
EGOIST
EKEOUT
ELBERT
ELDEST
ELEGIT
ELICIT
ELLIOT
EMMETT
ENFANT
ENGIRT
ENGLUT
ENLIST
ENRAPT
ENROOT
ERFURT
ERNEST
ERRANT
ESCENT
ESCORT
ESPRIT
EXCEPT
EXEMPT
EXEUNT
EXHORT
EXPECT
EXPERT
EXPORT
EXPOST
EXSERT
EXTANT
EXTENT
EXTORT
EYELET

•ET•••

AETHER
BETAKE
BETCHA
BETELS
BETHEL
BETIDE
BETISE
BETONY
BETOOK
BETRAY
BETSEY
BETSON
BETTAS
BETTER
BETTOR
CETANE
CETERA
DETACH
DETAIL
DETAIN
DETECT
DETENT
DETERS
DETEST
DETOUR
DETROP
FETING
FETISH
FETTER
FETTLE
GETMAD
GETOFF
GETOUT
GETSAT
GETSBY
GETSET
GETSIN
GETSIT
GETSON
GETSTO
GETSUP
GETTER
GETUPS
HETERO
HETMAN
HETTIE
JETGUN
JETHRO
JETLAG
JETSAM
JETSET
JETSKI
JETSON
JETTED
JETWAY
KETONE
KETTLE
LETFLY
LETHAL
LETOFF
LETOUT
LETSAT
LETSBE
LETSGO
LETSIN
LETSON
LETSUP
LETTED
LETTER
LETUPS
METALS
METATE
METEOR
METERS
METHOD
METHYL
METIER
METING
METOPE
METRES
METRIC
METROS
METTLE
NETHER
NETMAN
NETMEN
NETPAY
NETTED
NETTLE
NETTLY
NETTON
PETAIN
PETALS
PETARD
PETERS
PETITE
PETREL
PETRIE
PETROG
PETROL
PETTED
PETTER
PETTIT
PETULA
RETAGS
RETAIL
RETAIN
RETAKE
RETAPE
RETAPS
RETARD
RETARS
RETEAR
RETELL
RETENE
RETEST
RETIAL
RETIED
RETIES
RETILE
RETIME
RETINA
RETIRE
RETOLD
RETOOK
RETOOL
RETOPS
RETORT
RETOUR
RETOWS
RETRAL
RETRIM
RETROS
RETTON
RETUNE
RETURN
RETYPE
SETINS
SETOFF
SETOSE
SETOUT
SETSAT
SETSBY
SETSIN
SETSON
SETSUP
SETTEE
SETTER
SETTLE
SETTOS
SETUPS
TETCHY
TETHER
TETHYS
TETONS
TETRAD
TETRAS
TETRIS
TETZEL
VETOED
VETOER
VETOES
VETTED
WETBAR
WETFLY
WETHER
WETMOP
WETTED
WETTER
WETTIG

•E•T••

AEETES
BEATEN
BEATER
BEATIT
BEATLE
BEATON
BEATTY
BEATUP
BEETLE
BELTED
BENTON
BERTHA
BERTHS
BERTIE
BESTED
BESTIR
BESTOW
BETTAS
BETTER
BETTOR
CELTIC
CENTER
CENTOS
CENTRE
CENTRI
CENTRO
CERTIF
CESTAS
CESTOS
CESTUS
DEBTOR
DEFTER
DEFTLY
DELTAS
DELTIC
DENTAL
DENTED
DENTIL
DENTIN
DENTON
DEPTHS
DESTRY
DEXTER
DEXTRO
FEATLY
FELTED
FESTAL
FESTAS
FESTER
FESTUS
FETTER
FETTLE
GENTLE
GENTLY
GENTRY
GERTIE
GESTES
GESTIC
GETTER
HEATED
HEATER
HEATHS
HEATHY
HEATUP
HECTIC
HECTOR
HEFTED
HELTER
HENTED
HEPTAD
HESTER
HESTIA
HESTON
HETTIE
JEETER
JESTED
JESTER
JETTED
KEATON
KEITEL
KENTON
KEPTAT
KEPTON

KEPTUP
KETTLE
LECTER
LECTOR
LEFTIE
LEFTIN
LENTEN
LENTIL
LEPTON
LESTAT
LESTER
LETTED
LETTER
MEETER
MEETLY
MELTED
MELTON
MENTAL
MENTIS
MENTOR
MERTON
METTLE
NEATEN
NEATER
NEATLY
NECTAR
NEKTON
NESTEA
NESTED
NESTER
NESTLE
NESTOR
NETTED
NETTLE
NETTLY
NETTON
NEUTER
NEWTON
NEXTTO
OERTER
PECTIC
PECTIN
PEGTOP
PELTED
PELTER
PELTRY
PENTAD
PENTUP
PEPTIC
PERTER
PERTLY
PESTER
PESTLE
PESTOS
PETTED
PETTER
PETTIT
PEWTER
PEYTON
REATAS
RECTOR
RECTOS
RECTUS
REDTAG
REDTOP
RENTAL
RENTED
RENTER
RESTED
RESTER
RESTON
RESTUP
RETTON
REUTER
SEATED
SEATER
SEATON
SECTOR
SEETHE
SENTIN
SENTRA
SENTRY
SENTUP
SEPTAL
SEPTET
SEPTIC
SEPTUM
SESTET
SESTOS
SETTEE
SETTER
SETTLE
SETTOS
SEXTET
SEXTON
TEETER
TEETHE
TENTED
TENTER
TENTHS
TESTAE
TESTED
TESTEE
TESTER
TEUTON
VECTOR
VENTED
VENTER
VERTEX
VESTAL
VESTAS
VESTED
VESTEE
VESTRY
VETTED
WELTED
WELTER
WENTAT
WENTBY
WENTIN
WENTON
WENTUP
WETTED
WETTER
WETTIG
YENTAS
YESTER
ZESTED

•E••T•

AERATE
BEASTS
BEATTY
BEAUTS
BEAUTY
BEFITS
BEGETS
BEMATA
BENITO
BERATE
BERETS
BESETS
BESOTS
CENOTE
CERATE
DEARTH
DEBATE
DEBITS
DEBUTS
DEFATS
DEISTS
DELATE
DELETE
DELFTS
DEMITS
DEMOTE
DENOTE
DEPOTS
DEPUTE
DEPUTY
DESOTO
DEVITO
DEVOTE
DEVOTO
DEWITT
FEALTY
FEASTS
FEINTS
FEISTY
FELLTO
FERITY
GEARTO
GELATI
GELATO
GEMOTE
GEMOTS
GENETS
GETSTO
HEALTH
HEARTH
HEARTS
HEARTY
HECATE
HEISTS
HELDTO
HELOTS
HEMATO
HERETO
JEWETT
KEEPTO
LEADTO
LEALTY
LEANTO
LEGATE
LEGATO
LENGTH
LENITY
LEVITE
LEVITY
MELOTT
MERITS
METATE
NEARTO
NEGATE
NEMATO
NENETS
NEXTTO
PEDATE
PELOTA
PEPITA
PESETA
PETITE
PEWITS
PEYOTE
REACTS
REALTY
REBATE
REBUTS
RECITE
REDATE
REFITS
REFUTE
RELATE
RELETS
REMITS
REMOTE
RENATA
RENOTE
REPOTS
REPUTE
RERATE
RESETS
REVETS
SEDATE
SEENTO
SEESTO
SEMITE
SENATE
SENITI
TEMPTS
TENDTO
TENETS
TENUTO
TERATO
TERETE
VELDTS
VENETO
VENITE
VERITE
VERITY
VERSTS
WEALTH
YEASTS
YEASTY
ZENITH
ZEROTH

•E•••T

BEATIT
BECKET
BEHEST
BEIRUT
BELOIT
BENOIT
BEREFT
BESANT
BEZANT
CEDANT
CEMENT
CERMET
DECANT
DECEIT
DECENT
DECOCT
DEDUCT
DEFEAT
DEFECT
DEGUST
DEJECT
DELICT
DELIST
DEPART
DEPICT
DEPORT
DESALT
DESERT
DESIST
DESPOT
DETECT
DETENT
DETEST
DEVEST
DEVOUT
DEWITT
FERMAT
FERRET
FEWEST
FEYEST
GERENT
GERONT
GETOUT
GETSAT
GETSET
GETSIT
HEARST
HEIGHT
HELMET
HELMUT
HENBIT
HEPCAT
HEREAT
HERIOT
HERMIT
HEXNUT
JEERAT
JENNET
JESUIT
JETSET
JEWETT
KEEPAT
KEPTAT
KERMIT
LEARNT
LEDOUT
LEERAT
LEGIST
LESTAT
LETOUT
LETSAT
LEVANT
MEDLAT
MEERUT
MELOTT
MEREST
MERLOT
NEEDNT
NEWEST
PEANUT
PECKAT
PEDANT
PEEKAT
PEERAT
PELLET
PELMET
PENULT
PEQUOT
PERMIT
PERROT
PETTIT
REBENT
REBOLT
REBOOT
RECANT
RECAST
RECENT
RECOAT
REDACT
REDANT
REDHAT
REDHOT
REEDIT
REGENT
REGLET
REGNAT
REGRET
REHEAT
REJECT
RELENT
RELICT
RELIST
RELUCT
REMELT
RENNET
REPAST
REPEAT
REPENT
REPORT
REPOST
RERENT
RESALT
RESEAT
RESECT
RESENT
RESHOT
RESIST
RESORT
RESULT
RETEST
RETORT
REVERT
REVOLT
REXCAT
SECANT
SECRET
SEEFIT
SEEOUT
SEJANT
SELECT
SENNET
SENNIT
SEPTET
SESTET
SETOUT
SETSAT
SEURAT
SEXIST
SEXTET
TEAPOT
TEARAT
TEASET
TENANT
TERCET
TERRET
VEIGHT
VELVET
VERVET
WEIGHT
WENTAT
WERENT
WESKIT
XEDOUT
ZEALOT

••ET••

ACETAL
ACETIC
ACETYL
AEETES
ARETES
ARETHA
BEETLE
BRETON
CHETHS
CRETAN
CRETIN
DIETED
DIETER
EXETER
FLETCH
FOETAL
FOETID
FOETOR
FOETUS
FRETTY
GHETTO
GOETHE
GRETEL
GRETNA
HYETAL
IGETIT
JEETER
JOETEX
KVETCH
MEETER
MEETLY
NOETIC
ODETTA
ODETTE
ONETWO
PIETAS
PIETER
PIETIN
PIETRO
POETIC
POETRY
PRETAX
PRETER
PRETTY
QUETTA
RHETOR
SEETHE
SKETCH
TEETER
TEETHE
THETAS
THETIC
THETIS
THETOY
TOETAP
TSETSE
WRETCH
YVETTE

••E•T•

ADEPTS
ADESTE
AGENTS
ALECTO
ALERTS
ALEUTS
AMENTS
ASEITY
ATESTS
AVERTS
AVESTA
BLEATS
BREATH
BRENTS
CHEATS
CHERTY
CHESTS
CHESTY
CLEATS
CLEFTS
CREATE
CRESTS
CUESTA
EGESTA
EGESTS
EJECTA
EJECTS
ELECTS
EMEUTE
ERECTS
ERESTU
EVENTS
EVERTS
EXERTS
FIESTA
FLEETS
FRETTY
GHETTO
GREATS
GREETS
GUESTS
IDEATE
KEEPTO
LIESTO
LIEUTS
ODETTA
ODETTE
OLEATE
OMERTA
OPENTO
PLEATS
PLENTY
PRESTO
PRETTY
PUENTE
PUERTO
QUESTS
QUETTA
QWERTY
SCENTS
SEENTO
SEESTO
SHEATH
SHEETS
SHELTY
SIESTA
SLEETS
SLEETY
SLEUTH
SMELTS
SVELTE
SWEATS
SWEATY
SWEETS
THEFTS
TIEDTO
TIESTO
TREATS
TREATY
TWEETS
TWEETY
TWENTY
USEDTO
WHEATS
WREATH
WRESTS
YVETTE

••E••T

ACEOUT
AGEIST
ALEAST
ARENDT
ATEOUT
BLEWIT
BREAST
BRECHT
BREVET
CHEVET
COEDIT
CREDIT
DIEOUT
DOESNT
DREAMT
DYELOT
EKEOUT
ELEGIT
EXEMPT
EXEUNT
EYELET
FLEWAT
FREEST
GOESAT
HAEMAT
ICEOUT
IGETIT
ISEULT
JEERAT
KEEPAT
KLEIST
LEERAT
MEERUT
NEEDNT
NLEAST
NOEXIT
OCELOT
OMELET
ONEACT
PEEKAT
PEERAT
PRESET
REEDIT
SEEFIT
SEEOUT
SHEVAT
THEIST
TWEEST
USENET

•••ET•

AGLETS
AMVETS
ARMETS
ARNETT
ASSETS
BEGETS

BERETS
BESETS
BLUETS
CADETS
CAMETO
CARETO
CARETS
CAVETT
CIVETS
COMETH
COMETO
COMETS
COVETS
CRUETS
CULETS
DALETH
DARETO
DELETE
DONETS
DUVETS
EFFETE
EGRETS
EMMETS
EMMETT
FACETS
FILETS
FLEETS
GAIETY
GAMETE
GARETH
GENETS
GIVETO
GODETS
GREETS
HERETO
HOVETO
INLETS
INSETS
ISLETS
JEWETT
JOBETH
JOWETT
LOVETT
MOIETY
MONETA
MOTETS
MULETA
NENETS
NICETY
NINETY
NONETS
NOPETS
NYMETS
OCTETS
ONSETS
OSSETE
OWLETS
PARETO
PESETA
QUIETS
RAMETS
RELETS
RESETS
REVETS
RIVETS
SAFETY
SHEETS
SHTETL
SLEETS
SLEETY
SOWETO
STPETE
SURETE
SURETY
SWEETS
TAKETH
TAKETO
TENETS
TERETE
TVSETS
TWEETS
TWEETY
UBIETY
UPSETS
VALETS
VENETO
WISETO
ZIBETS

•••E•T

ABJECT
ABLEST
ABSENT
ACCENT
ACCEPT
ADVENT
ADVERT
AFFECT
AFREET
ALBEIT
ALBERT
ALPERT
ALWEST
APTEST
ARDENT
ARGENT
ARNETT
ARPENT
ARREST
ASCENT
ASPECT
ASSENT
ASSERT
ATBEST
ATREST
ATTEST
BAREST
BASEST
BEHEST
BEREFT
BISECT
BLUEST
CADENT
CAMEAT
CAVEAT
CAVETT
CEMENT
CLIENT
COGENT
COMEAT
COVENT
COVERT
COYEST
CUTEST
DARENT
DECEIT
DECENT
DEFEAT
DEFECT
DEJECT
DESERT
DETECT
DETENT
DETEST
DEVEST
DIGEST
DIRECT
DIREST
DIVERT
DIVEST
DOCENT
DRIEST
DRYEST
EFFECT
EGBERT
ELBERT
ELDEST
EMMETT
ERNEST
ESCENT
EXCEPT
EXPECT
EXPERT
EXSERT
EXTENT
FEWEST
FEYEST
FINEST
FLUENT
FOMENT
FOREST
FREEST
GAMEST
GAYEST
GERENT
GOWEST
HALEST
HAVEAT
HAVENT
HEREAT
HONEST
HUBERT
HUGEST
ICIEST
IDLEST
ILLEST
INCEPT
INDEBT
INDENT
INFECT
INFEST
INGEST
INJECT
INJEST
INSECT
INSERT
INTENT
INVENT
INVERT
INVEST
IQTEST
JEWETT
JOWETT
LAMENT
LAMEST
LATENT
LATEST
LAXEST
LOSEIT
LOVETT
LOWEST
LUCENT
MADEIT
MAKEIT
MEREST
MODELT
MODEST
MOLEST
MOMENT
MUTEST
NEWEST
NICEST
NLWEST
NOCENT
NUDEST
NUGENT
OBJECT
OBTEST
OBVERT
ODDEST
OLDEST
ORGEAT
ORIENT
OUTEAT
PALEST
PARENT
PATENT
POKEAT
POTENT
PRIEST
PUREST
RAREST
RAWEST
REBENT
RECENT
REGENT
REHEAT
REJECT
RELENT
REMELT
REPEAT
REPENT
RERENT
RESEAT
RESECT
RESENT
RETEST
REVERT
RIDENT
RIFEST
RIPEST
ROBERT
RODENT
RUDEST
RUPERT
SAFEST
SAGEST
SANEST
SELECT
SHIEST
SHYEST
SILENT
SLIEST
SLYEST
SOBEIT
SOLENT
SOREST
STREET
SUREST
TALENT
TAMEST
THREAT
TOREAT
TRUEST
TWEEST
UNBELT
UNBENT
UNMEET
UNREST
UNSEAT
UPBEAT
URGENT
URTEXT
VALENT
VILEST
WERENT
WIDEST
WISENT
WISEST
WRIEST
WRYEST
YAREST

••••ET

AFREET
AIGRET
ALLSET
ALLWET
AMULET
ANKLET
APPLET
ARMLET
AUKLET
AVOCET
BALLET
BARBET
BASKET
BASSET
BECKET
BILLET
BISSET
BONNET
BOSKET
BOWNET
BOXSET
BREVET
BRUNET
BUCKET
BUDGET
BUFFET
BULLET
BURNET
CACHET
CAMLET
CAPLET
CARNET
CARPET
CERMET
CHALET
CHEVET
CLARET
CLOSET
COLLET
COQUET
CORNET
CORSET
COSSET
CULLET
CURVET
CUTLET
CYGNET
DOCKET
DORSET
DULCET
EAGLET
EYELET
FANJET
FAUCET
FERRET
FIDGET
FILLET
FLORET
FLYNET
FORGET
GADGET
GANNET
GARNET
GARRET
GASJET
GASKET
GETSET
GIBBET
GIBLET
GIDGET
GIMLET
GOBLET
GORGET
GOTSET
GOULET
GRIVET
GULLET
GUSSET
HAMLET
HELMET
HOGGET
HORNET
ILLMET
IMARET
INAPET
INKJET
JACKET
JENNET
JETSET
JOLIET
JULIET
JUNKET
KISMET
LABRET
LANCET
LAPPET
LIMPET
LINNET
LIONET
LOCKET
MAGNET
MALLET
MARKET
MIDGET
MILLET
MINUET
MOPPET
MULLET
MUPPET
MUSKET
NOTYET
NUGGET
NUTLET
OBSTET
OFFSET
OMELET
OUTLET
OUTSET
PACKET
PALLET
PARGET
PELLET
PELMET
PIAGET
PICKET
PIGLET
PIOLET
PIQUET
PLACET
PLANET
POCKET
POPPET
POSSET
PRESET
PRIPET
PRIVET
PULLET
PUNNET
PUPPET
RABBET
RACKET
RAMJET
REGLET
REGRET
RENNET
RILLET
ROCHET
ROCKET
RUNLET
RUSSET
SACHET
SALLET
SAMLET
SECRET
SENNET
SEPTET
SESTET
SEXTET
SIGNET
SIPPET
SOCKET
SONNET
SORBET
SOVIET
SPINET
STREET
STYLET
SUBLET
SUBSET
SUNSET
SWIVET
TABLET
TAPPET
TARGET
TEASET
TERCET
TERRET
TICKET
TIPPET
TOILET
TRIJET
TRIVET
TUCKET
TUFFET
TURRET
UNMEET
USENET
VARLET
VELVET
VERVET
VIOLET
WALLET
WICKET
WIDGET
WIGLET
WILLET
YOUBET

EU••••

EUBOEA
EUCHRE
EUCLID
EUDORA
EUGENE
EULOGY
EUNICE
EUPNEA
EURAIL
EUREKA
EUROPA
EUROPE
EUTAXY

E•U•••

EDUARD
EDUCED
EDUCES
ELUDED
ELUDER
ELUDES
ELUTED
ELUTES
ENURED
ENURES
EQUALS
EQUATE
EQUINE
EQUIPS
EQUITY
ERUCTS
ERUPTS
ETUDES
ETUXOR
EVULSE
EXUDED
EXUDES
EXULTS
EXURBS

E••U••

EDMUND
EFFUSE
EMEUTE
EMQUAD
ENDUED
ENDUES
ENDURE
ENDURO
ENDUSE
ENGULF
ENOUGH
ENQUAD
ENSUED
ENSUES
ENSURE
ERFURT
ESCUDO
EXCUSE
EXEUNT

E•••U•

EARFUL
EASEUP
EATOUT
EATSUP
EFFLUX
EGGCUP
EKEOUT
ELBRUS
ENDRUN
ENDSUP
ENGLUT
ENNIUS
ENSOUL
EPIRUS
ERBIUM
EREBUS
EVENUP
EXODUS
EYECUP
EYEFUL

E••••U

ERESTU

•EU•••

BEULAH
BEURRE
DEUCED
DEUCES
FEUDAL
FEUDED
NEUMAN
NEUMES
NEURAL
NEUROL
NEURON
NEUTER
OEUVRE
REUBEN
REUNES
REUSED
REUSES
REUTER
SEURAT
TEUTON
ZEUGMA
ZEUXIS

•E•U••

BEAUTS
BEAUTY
BEGUMS
BELUGA
BEMUSE
BENUMB
CERUSE
DEBUGS
DEBUNK
DEBUTS
DEDUCE
DEDUCT
DEFUSE
DEGUST
DEJURE
DELUDE

DELUGE
DELUXE
DEMURE
DEMURS
DENUDE
DEPUTE
DEPUTY
FECUND
FEMURS
FERULE
GENUAL
GERUND
GETUPS
HECUBA
JEJUNE
JESUIT
LEGUIN
LEGUME
LEHUAS
LEMUEL
LEMURS
LETUPS
MEDUSA
NEBULA
NERUDA
PENULT
PENURY
PEQUOD
PEQUOT
PERUGA
PERUKE
PERUSE
PETULA
REBUFF
REBUKE
REBURY
REBUTS
RECURS
RECUSE
REDUBS
REDUCE
REFUEL
REFUGE
REFUND
REFUSE
REFUTE
REHUNG
RELUCT
RELUME
REMUDA
REPUGN
REPUTE
RERUNS
RESULT
RESUME
RETUNE
RETURN
REVUES
SECURE
SEDUCE
SEDUMS
SEGUED
SEGUES
SEGURA
SENUFO
SEQUEL
SEQUIN
SERUMS
SETUPS
TELUGU
TENURE
TENUTO
VENUES
YEHUDI

•E••U•

AEOLUS
BEADUP
BEAMUP
BEARUP
BEATUP
BEDAUB
BEDBUG
BEEFUP
BEEGUM
BEFOUL
BEIRUT
BENHUR
CENSUS
CEREUS
CERIUM
CESIUM
CESTUS
DELIUS
DENGUE
DEPAUL
DEPAUW
DETOUR
DEVOUR
DEVOUT
FERGUS
FESCUE
FESSUP
FESTUS
GEARUP
GENIUS
GETOUT
GETSUP
HEADUP
HEATUP
HELDUP
HELIUM
HELMUT
HEXNUT
JETGUN
KEEPUP
KEPTUP
KEYSUP
LEADUP
LEAGUE
LEBRUN
LEDOUT
LETOUT
LETSUP
MEDIUM
MEERUT
MESSUP
NEREUS
PEANUT
PELEUS
PENTUP
PEPFUL
PEPLUM
PEPSUP
PERDUE
PERKUP
REARUP
RECOUP
RECTUS
REDBUD
REDGUM
REFLUX
REGIUS
REGLUE
RESCUE
RESTUP
RETOUR
REVSUP
SEALUP
SEAMUS
SEEOUT
SELJUK
SENDUP
SENTUP
SEPTUM
SEROUS
SESQUI
SETOUT
SETSUP
SEWNUP
SEWSUP
TEACUP
TEAMUP
TEARUP
TEDEUM
TEDIUM
TEEDUP
TEESUP
TEMPUS
TEREUS
VELLUM
VELOUR
VENOUS
VERDUN
VERSUS
WELLUP
WENTUP
XEDOUT

•E•••U

DEJAVU
DESILU
HEYYOU
MENJOU
PENGHU
RESEAU
TELEDU
TELUGU

••EU••

ALEUTS
BREUER
CREUSA
EMEUTE
EXEUNT
FLEURY
ISEULT
LIEUTS
ONEUPS
PLEURA
PNEUMA
PSEUDO
PSEUDS
QUEUED
QUEUER
QUEUES
RHEUMS
RHEUMY
SLEUTH
SOEURS
TIEUPS

••E•U•

ACEOUS
ACEOUT
ACESUP
ATEOUT
AVENUE
BEEFUP
BEEGUM
BLEWUP
CHEQUE
CHERUB
CHEWUP
DIEOUT
DOESUP
DREWUP
EKEOUT
EREBUS
EVENUP
EYECUP
EYEFUL
FOETUS
FRENUM
GOESUP
GREWUP
ICEDUP
ICEOUT
ICESUP
IREFUL
KEEPUP
MEERUT
OBELUS
OPENUP
PLENUM
PLEXUS
PRENUP
RHESUS
RUEFUL
SEEOUT
SPEDUP
STEPUP
TEEDUP
TEESUP
TIEDUP
TIESUP
USEDUP
USEFUL
USESUP
WOEFUL

••E••U

APERCU
ERESTU

•••EU•

ADIEUS
ADIEUX
ANTEUP
ATREUS
AUREUS
AUTEUR
BAYEUX
BONEUP
BOREUP
CAMEUP
CEREUS
COLEUS
COMEUP
DONEUP
EASEUP
FACEUP
FIREUP
GAVEUP
GIVEUP
HIKEUP
HOLEUP
HYPEUP
LACEUP
LINEUP
LYCEUM
MADEUP
MAKEUP
MOVEUP
MUSEUM
NEREUS
PELEUS
PILEUM
PILEUP
PILEUS
PIPEUP
POSEUR
RAKEUP
RAVEUP
RILEUP
SAVEUP
SIZEUP
SOLEUS
TAKEUP
TEDEUM
TEREUS
TONEUP
TOREUP
TUNEUP
TYPEUP
URAEUS
WAKEUP
WIPEUP
WISEUP
WOKEUP

•••E•U

BATEAU
BUREAU
GATEAU
HALERU
JUNEAU
MASERU
MOREAU
RAMEAU
RESEAU
ROSEAU
TELEDU

••••EU

MILIEU

EV••••

EVADED
EVADER
EVADES
EVELYN
EVENED
EVENER
EVENKI
EVENLY
EVENSO
EVENTS
EVENUP
EVERLY
EVERSO
EVERTS
EVICTS
EVILER
EVILLY
EVINCE
EVOKED
EVOKER
EVOKES
EVOLVE
EVONNE
EVULSE
EVZONE

E•V•••

EDVARD
ELVERS
ELVIRA
ELVISH
ENVIED
ENVIER
ENVIES
ENVOIS
ENVOYS
ERVING
EXVOTO

E••V••

ELEVEN
ELEVES

E•••V•

ENDIVE
EVOLVE

•EV•••

BEVELS
BEVIES
DEVEIN
DEVEST
DEVICE
DEVILS
DEVINE
DEVISE
DEVITO
DEVOID
DEVOIR
DEVOTE
DEVOTO
DEVOUR
DEVOUT
FEVERS
KEVELS
KEVLAR
LEVANT
LEVEED
LEVEES
LEVELS
LEVENE
LEVERS
LEVIED
LEVIER
LEVIES
LEVINE
LEVITE
LEVITY
NEVADA
NEVERS
NEVINS
NEVSKY
REVAMP
REVEAL
REVELS
REVERB
REVERE
REVERS
REVERT
REVETS
REVIEW
REVILE
REVISE
REVIVE
REVLON
REVOIR
REVOKE
REVOLT
REVSON
REVSUP
REVUES
REVVED
SEVENS
SEVERE
SEVERN
SEVERS
SEVERY
SEVRES

•E•V••

BEAVER
BEAVIS
BEEVES
CERVID
DELVED
DELVER
DELVES
DENVER
FERVID
FERVOR
HEAVED
HEAVEN
HEAVER
HEAVES
HELVES
JEEVES
KELVIN
LEAVED
LEAVEN
LEAVES
LEKVAR
MELVIL
MELVIN
MELVYN
MERVYN
NERVES
OEUVRE
PEAVEY
PEEVED
PEEVES
PELVIC
PELVIS
REEVED
REEVES
REVVED
SELVES
SERVAL
SERVED
SERVER
SERVES
SERVOS
TEEVEE
VELVET
VERVES
VERVET
WEAVED
WEAVER
WEAVES
WEEVIL

•E••V•

BEHAVE
BEHOVE
DEJAVU
DENOVO
DERIVE
GENEVA
GENEVE
RELEVY
RELIVE
REMOVE
REPAVE
REVIVE
REWOVE

•E•••V

HENRYV

••EV••

ALEVEL
ASEVER
BEEVES
BREVES
BREVET
BREVIS
CHEVAL
CHEVET
CHEVRE
CLEVER
CLEVES
CLEVIS
COEVAL
ELEVEN
ELEVES
HUEVOS
JEEVES
OLEVEL
PEEVED
PEEVES
PREVIN
REEVED
REEVES
SHEVAT
SIEVED
SIEVES
STEVEN
STEVIE
TEEVEE
TREVOR
UNEVEN
WEEVIL

••E•V•

CLEAVE
GREAVE
SHEAVE
SHELVE
SLEAVE
SLEEVE
STEEVE
SWERVE
THEYVE
TWELVE

••E••V

CHEKOV

•••EV•

GENEVA
GENEVE
GRIEVE
HALEVY
PAREVE
RELEVY
SLEEVE
STEEVE
THIEVE

••••EV

KISLEV
LAPTEV
RUBLEV

E•W•••

EDWARD
EDWOOD
EDWYNN
ELWOOD
ENWRAP
EXWIFE

E••W••

EARWAX
EARWIG

E•••W•

ELBOWS
ENDOWS

E••••W

ERENOW
ESCHEW
ESCROW

•EW•••

BEWAIL
BEWARE
BEWRAY
DEWIER
DEWILY
DEWING
DEWITT
DEWLAP
FEWEST
GEWGAW
HEWERS
HEWING
JEWELS
JEWETT
JEWISH
KEWPIE
LEWDER
LEWDLY
MEWING
MEWLED
MEWLER
NEWAGE
NEWARK
NEWELS
NEWEST

NEWISH
NEWLEY
NEWMAN
NEWMAR
NEWTON
PEWEES
PEWITS
PEWTER
REWARD
REWARM
REWASH
REWEDS
REWELD
REWIND
REWINS
REWIRE
REWORD
REWORK
REWOVE
REWRAP
SEWAGE
SEWARD
SEWELL
SEWERS
SEWING
SEWNON
SEWNUP
SEWSON
SEWSUP

•E•W••
FENWAY
JETWAY
KEYWAY
LEEWAY
MEOWED
PEDWAY
PEEWEE
SEAWAY

•E••W•
BEDEWS
PESAWA
REMOWN
REMOWS
RENEWS
RENOWN
RESAWN
RESAWS
RESEWN
RESEWS
RETOWS
SEROWS

•E•••W
BELLOW
BESTOW
DEPAUW
FELLOW
GEEGAW
GEWGAW
HEBREW
HEEHAW
MEADOW
MELLOW
NEPHEW
PESCOW
REDRAW
REDREW
REPLOW
REVIEW
SEACOW
SEESAW
YELLOW

••EW••
BLEWIT
BLEWUP
BREWED
BREWER
CHEWED
CHEWER
CHEWUP
CLEWED
CREWED
CREWEL
DREWIN
DREWON
DREWUP
FLEWAT
FLEWIN
GREWON
GREWUP
LEEWAY
ONEWAY
PEEWEE
PREWAR
SKEWED
SKEWER
SLEWED
SPEWED
STEWED
STEWER
THEWEB
THEWIZ
VIEWED
VIEWER

••E•W•
ONETWO

••E••W
ERENOW
GEEGAW
HEEHAW
LIELOW
PRELAW
SEESAW

•••EW•
BEDEWS
FIVEWS
RENEWS
RESEWN
RESEWS
SCREWS
SCREWY
SHREWD
SHREWS
SINEWS
SINEWY
STREWN
STREWS
UNSEWN
UNSEWS

••••EW
ANDREW
CASHEW
CURFEW
CURLEW
ESCHEW
HEBREW
MCGREW
MILDEW
NEPHEW
ONVIEW
REDREW
REVIEW
SUNDEW

EX••••
EXACTA
EXACTO
EXACTS
EXALTS
EXARCH
EXCEED
EXCELS
EXCEPT
EXCESS
EXCISE
EXCITE
EXCUSE
EXEDRA
EXEMPT
EXERTS
EXETER
EXEUNT
EXHALE
EXHORT
EXILED
EXILES
EXILIC
EXISTS
EXITED
EXLEGE
EXMOOR
EXMORE
EXODUS
EXOTIC
EXPAND
EXPECT
EXPELS
EXPEND
EXPERT
EXPIRE
EXPIRY
EXPORT
EXPOSE
EXPOST
EXSERT
EXTANT
EXTEND
EXTENT
EXTERN
EXTOLS
EXTORT
EXTRAS
EXUDED
EXUDES
EXULTS
EXURBS
EXVOTO
EXWIFE

E••X••
ELIXIR
ETUXOR

E•••X•
EUTAXY

E••••X
EARWAX
EFFLUX

•EX•••
DEXTER
DEXTRO
HEXADS
HEXERS
HEXING
HEXNUT
LEXEME
LEXICA
MEXICO
NEXTTO
REXCAT
SEXIER
SEXILY
SEXIST
SEXTET
SEXTON
TEXACO
TEXANS
TEXMEX
VEXERS
VEXING

•E•X••
XERXES
ZEUXIS

•E••X•
DELUXE

•E•••X
BENDIX
LENNOX
MENINX
REDFOX
REDSOX
REFLEX
REFLUX
SEAFOX
TEXMEX
VERTEX
WESSEX

••EX••
ALEXEI
ALEXIA
ALEXIS
APEXES
DREXEL
FLEXED
FLEXES
FLEXOR
IBEXES
ILEXES
NOEXIT
PLEXAL
PLEXOR
PLEXUS

••E••X
ICEBOX
JOETEX
PREFIX
PRETAX
THESIX

•••EX•
ADNEXA
ANNEXE
URTEXT

•••E•X
ADIEUX
BAYEUX
BLUEOX
POLEAX
RATEDX

••••EX
AUSPEX
CAUDEX
CONVEX
CORTEX
DUPLEX
JOETEX
LASTEX
POLLEX
REFLEX
SUSSEX
TEXMEX
UNISEX
VERTEX
VORTEX
WESSEX
WINDEX

EY••••
EYECUP
EYEFUL
EYEING
EYELET
EYELID
EYRIES

E•Y•••
EEYORE
ELYSEE
ERYNGO
ETYMOL
ETYMON

E••Y••
ECTYPE
EDWYNN
ELAYER
ELAYNE
ENZYME

E•••Y•
EMBAYS
EMBRYO
ENJOYS
ENVOYS
EPONYM
ERINYS
ESSAYS
EVELYN

E••••Y
EARTHY
EASILY
EATERY
EBERLY
EDGILY
EERILY
EFFIGY
EIGHTY
ELLERY
EMBODY
EMPERY
EMPLOY
ENERGY
ENMITY
ENTITY
EQUITY
ESTRAY
EULOGY
EUTAXY
EVENLY
EVERLY
EVILLY
EXPIRY

•EY•••
BEYOND
CEYLON
EEYORE
FEYEST
GEYSER
HEYDAY
HEYYOU
KEYING
KEYNES
KEYPAD
KEYSIN
KEYSUP
KEYWAY
LEYDEN
PEYOTE
PEYTON

•E•Y••
HEYYOU
JEKYLL
KENYAN
REDYED
REDYES
RETYPE

•E••Y•
BELAYS
DECAYS
DECOYS
DELAYS
HEARYE
HENRYV
KENNYG
MELVYN
MERVYN
METHYL
REDEYE
REKEYS
RELAYS
REPAYS
SEPOYS
TETHYS
ZEPHYR

•E•••Y
AERIFY
AERILY
BEACHY
BEATTY
BEAUTY
BEGLEY
BEKESY
BELFRY
BELLAY
BENDAY
BENGAY
BETONY
BETRAY
BETSEY
BEWRAY
CECILY
CELERY
DEADLY
DEAFLY
DEARLY
DEEJAY
DEEPLY
DEFRAY
DEFTLY
DELANY
DELRAY
DELROY
DENARY
DEPLOY
DEPUTY
DESCRY
DESTRY
DEWILY
EERILY
FEALTY
FEATLY
FEEBLY
FEISTY
FELONY
FENWAY
FERITY
GELSEY
GENTLY
GENTRY
GEORGY
GETSBY
HEANEY
HEARTY
HEATHY
HENLEY
HEREBY
HERESY
HERSEY
HEYDAY
JENNEY
JEREMY
JERSEY
JETWAY
KEARNY
KEENLY
KELLEY
KELSEY
KERSEY
KEYWAY
LEACHY
LEAKEY
LEALTY
LEANLY
LEEWAY
LEGACY
LEMONY
LENITY
LESLEY
LETFLY
LEVITY
LEWDLY
MEANLY
MEASLY
MEDFLY
MEDLEY
MEEKLY
MEETLY
MELODY
MEMORY
MERELY
MERSEY
NEARBY
NEARLY
NEATLY
NETPAY
NETTLY
NEVSKY
NEWLEY
PEACHY
PEARLY
PEAVEY
PEBBLY
PEDWAY
PELTRY
PENNEY
PENURY
PERTLY
REALLY
REALTY
REBURY
RECOPY
REDBAY
REDENY
REILLY
RELEVY
REMEDY
REPLAY
RESINY
SEAWAY
SEELEY
SEEMLY
SENARY
SENTRY
SETSBY
SEVERY
SEXILY
TEAPOY
TEDKEY
TEENSY
TETCHY
VEEJAY
VERIFY
VERILY
VERITY
VESTRY
WEAKLY
WEEKLY
WEENSY
WEIRDY
WENTBY
WESLEY
WETFLY
YEARLY
YEASTY

••EY••
BREYER
FLEYED
GREYED
GREYER
GREYLY
OBEYED
OXEYES
PREYED
PREYON
THEYLL
THEYRE
THEYVE

••E•Y•
ACETYL
AYEAYE
BYEBYE
CHERYL
EVELYN
LIEBYS
PHENYL
SHERYL
TIEDYE

••E••Y
AGENCY
ALECKY
ANERGY
ASEITY
AWEARY
AWEDLY
BLEARY
BLENNY
BREEZY
CHEEKY
CHEERY
CHEESY
CHERRY
CHERTY
CHESTY
CLERGY
CREAKY
CREAMY
CREASY
CREEPY
CZERNY
DEEJAY
DEEPLY
DOESBY
DREAMY
DREARY
DRESSY
EBERLY
ENERGY
EVENLY
EVERLY
FEEBLY
FLECKY
FLEDGY
FLEECY
FLESHY
FLEURY
FREAKY
FREDDY
FREELY
FRENZY
FRETTY
GLEAMY
GOEASY
GOESBY
GREASY
GREEDY
GREENY

GREYLY
KEENLY
LEEWAY
LIEFLY
MEEKLY
MEETLY
OHENRY
OKELLY
OLEARY
ONEDAY
ONEWAY
OPENLY
OVERLY
PLENTY
POETRY
PREPAY
PREPPY
PRETTY
QUEASY
QUEMOY
QWERTY
RHEUMY
SEELEY
SEEMLY
SHEEDY
SHEEHY
SHELLY
SHELTY
SHERRY
SKERRY
SLEAZY
SLEEKY
SLEEPY
SLEETY
SMEARY
SMELLY
SNEAKY
SNEERY
SNEEZY
SPEEDY
SPERRY
STEADY
STEAMY
STEELY
STEFOY
SWEATY
TEENSY
THEFLY
THEORY
THETOY
TREATY
TREBLY
TRENDY
TWEEDY
TWEENY
TWEETY
TWENTY
UNEASY
VEEJAY
WEEKLY
WEENSY
WHEEZY
WHERRY

•••EY•

ABBEYS
ALLEYS
BLUEYS
BOGEYS
BOLEYN
CONEYS
COVEYS
DOGEYS
FOGEYS
HONEYS
JASEYS
LIMEYS
MATEYS
MONEYS
MOSEYS
MULEYS
POKEYS
POLEYN
POPEYE
REDEYE
REKEYS
RIBEYE

•••E•Y

AMBERY
ARTERY
BAKERY
BARELY
BASELY
BEKESY
BLUELY
BLUESY
BOWERY
BREEZY
BRIERY
CAMEBY
CASEFY
CELERY
CHEEKY
CHEERY
CHEESY
CICELY
COMEBY
COMEDY
COMELY
CREEPY
CUTELY
CUTESY
DIRELY
DOWERY
DUPERY
EATERY
ELLERY
EMPERY
FAKERY
FINELY
FINERY
FLEECY
FREELY
GAIETY
GAMELY
GONEBY
GREEDY
GREENY
HALEVY
HEREBY
HERESY
HOMELY
HUGELY
JAPERY
JEREMY
LAMELY
LATELY
LIKELY
LINENY
LIVELY
LIVERY
LONELY
LOVELY
LOWERY
MERELY
MISERY
MOIETY
MOPERY
MUTELY
NAMELY
NAPERY
NASEBY
NICELY
NICETY
NINETY
NITERY
NUDELY
OCHERY
ORNERY
ORRERY
PALELY
PAPERY
PINERY
POKERY
PURELY
RAREFY
RARELY
REDENY
RELEVY
REMEDY
RIFELY
RIPELY
RONELY
RUDELY
SAFELY
SAFETY
SAGELY
SANELY
SCREWY
SEVERY
SHEEDY
SHEEHY
SINEWY
SLEEKY
SLEEPY
SLEETY
SNEERY
SNEEZY
SOLELY
SORELY
SPEEDY
SPHERY
STEELY
SURELY
SURETY
TAMELY
TIMELY
TOWERY
TUMEFY
TWEEDY
TWEENY
TWEETY
UBIETY
VALERY
VILELY
VINERY
VOWELY
WAFERY
WATERY
WAVERY
WHEEZY
WIDELY
WIFELY
WINERY
WISELY
YARELY

••••EY

ANDREY
ASHLEY
AUBREY
AUDREY
BAILEY
BARLEY
BARNEY
BEGLEY
BETSEY
BIRNEY
BLIMEY
BLOOEY
BOSLEY
BURLEY
BURNEY
CAGNEY
CARNEY
CARREY
CARVEY
CHANEY
CLAYEY
CONVEY
COONEY
COPLEY
COWLEY
CRIKEY
CURLEY
DABNEY
DAILEY
DICKEY
DILSEY
DINKEY
DISNEY
DONKEY
DOOLEY
DORSEY
DOWNEY
DUDLEY
DURFEY
FARLEY
FINNEY
FLAKEY
FLOOEY
FLUKEY
FLUTEY
FOSSEY
GALLEY
GARVEY
GELSEY
GOOSEY
GRAPEY
GURLEY
GURNEY
HAILEY
HALLEY
HALSEY
HANLEY
HARLEY
HARVEY
HAYLEY
HEANEY
HENLEY
HERSEY
HICKEY
HOCKEY
HORNEY
HORSEY
HURLEY
HUSSEY
HUXLEY
JACKEY
JENNEY
JERSEY
JITNEY
JOCKEY
KELLEY
KELSEY
KERSEY
KIDNEY
KINSEY
LACKEY
LEAKEY
LESLEY
LINNEY
LINSEY
LOONEY
LOWKEY
LYNLEY
MAGUEY
MARLEY
MASSEY
MEDLEY
MERSEY
MICKEY
MOBLEY
MONKEY
MOONEY
MORLEY
MOTLEY
MOUSEY
MURREY
NEWLEY
NIAMEY
NIPSEY
OAKLEY
OCASEY
OFFKEY
ORKNEY
OSPREY
PARLEY
PAULEY
PEAVEY
PENNEY
PHONEY
PHOOEY
POMPEY
PRICEY
PULLEY
PURVEY
RAINEY
RAMSEY
RICKEY
RIDLEY
RIPLEY
RODNEY
ROMNEY
ROONEY
SEELEY
SHALEY
SIDNEY
SISLEY
SLAVEY
SMILEY
SMOKEY
SPACEY
STACEY
STOREY
SURREY
SURVEY
SYDNEY
TEDKEY
TORREY
TRACEY
TUNNEY
TURKEY
VALLEY
VARNEY
VOLLEY
WATNEY
WESLEY
WHINEY
WIMSEY
WOLSEY
WOOLEY
WURLEY

EZ••••

EZZARD

E•Z•••

ENZYME
EVZONE
EZZARD

E••••Z

ERSATZ

•EZ•••

BEZANT
BEZELS
FEZZAN
FEZZES
GEZIRA
MEZZOS
REZONE

•E•Z••

BENZOL
DENZEL
FEZZAN
FEZZES
GEEZER
HERZOG
MEZZOS
SEIZED
SEIZER
SEIZES
TETZEL

•E••Z•

BEDAZE
BELIZE
REBOZO

••EZ••

AREZZO
GEEZER
QUEZON
SLEZAK

••E•Z•

AREZZO
BREEZE
BREEZY
FAENZA
FREEZE
FRENZY
RIENZI
SLEAZE
SLEAZY
SNEEZE
SNEEZY
TWEEZE
WHEEZE
WHEEZY

••E••Z

THEWIZ

•••EZ•

BREEZE
BREEZY
FREEZE
FRIEZE
SNEEZE
SNEEZY
TWEEZE
WHEEZE
WHEEZY

•••E•Z

BRIENZ
DOLENZ
LORENZ

••••EZ

BOULEZ
CHAVEZ
CORTEZ
JUAREZ
MONTEZ
TROPEZ
VALDEZ

FA••••

FABIAN
FABLED
FABLER
FABLES
FABRAY
FABRIC
FACADE
FACETS
FACEUP
FACIAL
FACIAS
FACIES
FACILE
FACING
FACTOR
FACULA
FADEIN
FADING
FAENZA
FAERIE
FAEROE
FAFNIR
FAGEND
FAGGED
FAGOTS
FAILED
FAILLE
FAINTS
FAIRED
FAIRER
FAIRLY
FAIRUP
FAISAL
FAITHS
FAIYUM
FAJITA
FAKERS
FAKERY
FAKING
FAKIRS
FALANA
FALCES
FALCON
FALINE
FALLEN
FALLIN
FALLON
FALLOW
FALLTO
FALSER
FALTER
FAMILY
FAMINE
FAMISH
FAMOUS
FANDOM
FANGED
FANION
FANJET
FANNED
FANNIE
FANONS
FANOUT
FANTAN
FARADS
FARCED
FARCES
FARCRY
FARERS
FARINA
FARING
FARLEY
FARLOW
FARMED
FARMER
FAROFF
FAROUK
FAROUT
FARRAH
FARRAR
FARROW
FASCES
FASCIA
FASTED
FASTEN
FASTER
FATALE
FATCAT
FATHER
FATHOM
FATIMA
FATTED
FATTEN
FATTER
FATWAS
FAUCES
FAUCET
FAULTS
FAULTY
FAUNAE
FAUNAL
FAUNAS
FAUNUS
FAVORS
FAVOUR
FAWKES
FAWLTY
FAWNED
FAWNER
FAXING
FAZING
FAZOOL

F•A•••

FEALTY
FEARED
FEARER
FEASTS
FEATLY
FIACRE
FIANCE
FIASCO
FLABBY
FLACKS
FLACON
FLAGGY
FLAGON
FLAILS
FLAIRS
FLAKED
FLAKER
FLAKES
FLAKEY
FLAMBE
FLAMED
FLAMES
FLANGE
FLANKS
FLAPPY
FLARED
FLARES
FLASHY
FLASKS
FLATLY
FLAUNT
FLAVIA
FLAVOR
FLAWED
FLAXEN
FLAXES
FLAYED
FLAYER
FMAJOR
FOALED
FOAMED
FRACAS
FRAIDY
FRAISE
FRAMED
FRAMES
FRANCA
FRANCE
FRANCK
FRANCO
FRANCS
FRANKS

FRANNY
FRAPPE
FRASER
FRAUDS
FRAUEN
FRAYED
FRAZER

F••A••
FACADE
FALANA
FARADS
FATALE
FEMALE
FIGARO
FINALE
FINALS
FIXATE
FLOATS
FLOATY
FORAGE
FORAYS
FREAKS
FREAKY
FRIARS
FRIARY
FSHARP
FUGARD
FULANI

F•••A•
FABIAN
FABRAY
FACIAL
FACIAS
FAISAL
FANTAN
FARRAH
FARRAR
FATCAT
FATWAS
FAUNAE
FAUNAL
FAUNAS
FBIMAN
FELLAH
FELLAS
FENIAN
FENMAN
FENWAY
FERIAL
FERIAS
FERMAT
FESTAL
FESTAS
FEUDAL
FEZZAN
FIJIAN
FILIAL
FINIAL
FINNAN
FIRMAN
FISCAL
FIVEAM
FLEWAT
FLORAE
FLORAL
FLORAS
FLYMAN
FLYWAY
FOETAL
FOGHAT
FOLIAR
FONTAL
FORBAD
FORMAL
FORMAN
FORMAT
FORTAS
FOSSAE
FOSSAS
FOURAM
FOVEAE
FRACAS
FRIDAY
FRUGAL
FRYPAN
FUJIAN
FULMAR

F••••A
FACULA
FAENZA
FAJITA
FALANA
FARINA
FASCIA
FATIMA
FEDORA
FEMORA
FIBULA
FIESTA
FLAVIA
FLICKA
FRANCA
FRESCA
FULCRA

•F•A••
AFEARD
AFFAIR
AFLAME
AFLATS
AFRAID
AFRAME
EFFACE
EFLATS
OFLATE

•F••A•
AFFRAY
AFGHAN
AFLOAT
OFFDAY

•F•••A
AFRICA
SFORZA

••FA••
AAFAIR
AFFAIR
AUFAIT
BEFALL
DEFACE
DEFAME
DEFATS
EFFACE
ENFANT
INFACT
INFAMY
INFANT
MUFASA
RAFAEL
REFACE
SAFARI
UNFAIR

••F•A•
AFFRAY
CAFTAN
DEFEAT
DEFRAY
ELFMAN
GUFFAW
OFFDAY
REFLAG

••F••A
DEFLEA
MUFASA
RAFFIA

•••FA•
ARAFAT
COLFAX
CONFAB
GUFFAW
KOUFAX
LOOFAH
LOOFAS
LOWFAT
NONFAT
PREFAB
SEAFAN
SHOFAR
SOLFAS
STEFAN

•••F•A
BIAFRA
RAFFIA

FB••••
FBIMAN
FBIMEN

F•B•••
FABIAN
FABLED
FABLER
FABLES
FABRAY
FABRIC
FIBBED
FIBBER
FIBERS
FIBRES
FIBRIL
FIBRIN
FIBULA
FOBBED
FOBOFF
FUBBED

F••B••
FEEBLE
FEEBLY
FERBER
FIBBED
FIBBER
FLABBY
FLYBOY
FLYBYS
FOBBED
FOGBOW
FOIBLE
FORBAD
FORBES
FORBID
FUBBED
FUMBLE

F•••B•
FLABBY
FLAMBE

•••F•B
CONFAB
PREFAB

F•C•••
FACADE
FACETS
FACEUP
FACIAL
FACIAS
FACIES
FACILE
FACING
FACTOR
FACULA
FECUND
FICHES
FICHTE
FICHUS
FICKLE
FOCSLE

F••C••
FALCES
FALCON
FARCED
FARCES
FARCRY
FASCES
FASCIA
FATCAT
FAUCES
FAUCET
FENCED
FENCER
FENCES
FESCUE
FIACRE
FISCAL
FLACKS
FLACON
FLECHE
FLECKS
FLECKY
FLICKA
FLICKS
FLOCKS
FLOCKY
FORCED
FORCER
FORCES
FRACAS
FROCKS
FULCRA

F•••C•
FIANCE
FIASCO
FIERCE
FLEECE
FLEECY
FLETCH
FLINCH
FLITCH
FRANCA
FRANCE
FRANCK
FRANCO
FRANCS
FRENCH
FRESCA
FRESCO
FRISCO

F••••C
FABRIC
FENNEC
FERENC
FERRIC
FINNIC
FISTIC
FORMIC
FROLIC
FUSTIC

•F•C••
AFLCIO

•F••C•
AFFECT
AFRICA
EFFACE
EFFECT
OFFICE

••F•C•
AFFECT
DEFACE
DEFECT
EFFACE
EFFECT
INFACT
INFECT
OFFICE
REFACE

•••F•C
UNIFIC

F•D•••
FADEIN
FADING
FEDORA
FIDDLE
FIDGET
FODDER
FUDDLE
FUDGED
FUDGES

F••D••
FANDOM
FEEDER
FEEDON
FELDON
FENDED
FENDER
FEUDAL
FEUDED
FIDDLE
FINDER
FLEDGE
FLEDGY
FODDER
FOLDED
FOLDER
FOLDUP
FONDER
FONDLE
FONDLY
FONDUE
FOODIE
FORDED
FREDDY
FRIDAY
FRIDGE
FUDDLE
FUNDED
FYODOR

F•••D•
FACADE
FARADS
FIELDS
FIENDS
FIORDS
FJELDS
FJORDS
FLOODS
FLUIDS
FOUNDS
FRAIDY
FRAUDS
FREDDY
FRONDS

F••••D
FABLED
FAGEND
FAGGED
FAILED
FAIRED
FANGED
FANNED
FARCED
FARMED
FASTED
FATTED
FAWNED
FEARED
FECUND
FELLED
FELTED
FENCED
FENDED
FERVID
FESSED
FEUDED
FIBBED
FILLED
FILMED
FINKED
FINNED
FIRMED
FISHED
FISTED
FITTED
FIZZED
FLAKED
FLAMED
FLARED
FLAWED
FLAYED
FLEXED
FLEYED
FLORID
FLOWED
FLUTED
FLUXED
FLYROD
FOALED
FOAMED
FOBBED
FOETID
FOGGED
FOILED
FOINED
FOLDED
FOOLED
FOOTED
FORBAD
FORBID
FORCED
FORDED
FORGED
FORKED
FORMED
FOULED
FOWLED
FRAMED
FRAYED
FRIEND
FRIGID
FUBBED
FUDGED
FUELED
FUGARD
FUNDED
FUNKED
FUNNED
FURLED
FURRED
FUSSED
FUTZED
FUZZED

•F•D••
OFFDAY

•F•••D
AFEARD
AFFORD
AFIELD
AFRAID
OFFEND

••FD••
OFFDAY

••F••D
AFFORD
ALFRED
AUFOND
BIFFED
BIFOLD
BOFFED
BUFFED
CUFFED
DAFFED
DEFEND
DEFIED
DOFFED
ENFOLD
GAFFED
GIFTED
HAFTED
HEFTED
HUFFED
INFOLD
LIFTED
LOFTED
LUFFED
MIFFED
MUFFED
OFFEND
OXFORD
PUFFED
RAFTED
REFFED
REFUND
RIFFED
RIFLED
RIFTED
RUFFED
SIFTED
TIFFED
TUFTED
UNFOLD
WAFTED

•••F•D
BEEFED
BIFFED
BOFFED
BUFFED
CHAFED
COIFED
CONFED
CUFFED
DAFFED
DOFFED
GAFFED
GOLFED
GOOFED
GULFED
HOOFED
HUFFED
ILLFED
KNIFED
LEAFED
LOAFED
LUFFED
MIFFED
MUFFED
PUFFED
REEFED
REFFED
RIFFED
ROOFED
RUFFED
SURFED
THEFED
TIFFED
TRIFID
TURFED
WOLFED
WOOFED

FE••••
FEALTY
FEARED
FEARER
FEASTS
FEATLY
FECUND
FEDORA
FEEBLE
FEEBLY
FEEDER
FEEDON
FEEING
FEELER
FEIGNS
FEINTS
FEISTY
FELDON
FELINE
FELIPE
FELLAH
FELLAS
FELLED
FELLER
FELLIN
FELLOE
FELLON
FELLOW
FELLTO
FELONS
FELONY
FELTED
FEMALE
FEMMES
FEMORA
FEMURS
FENCED
FENCER
FENCES
FENDED
FENDER
FENIAN
FENMAN
FENMEN
FENNEC
FENNEL
FENWAY
FERBER
FERENC
FERGIE
FERGUS
FERIAL
FERIAS
FERITY
FERMAT
FERRER
FERRET
FERRIC
FERRIS
FERULE
FERVID
FERVOR
FESCUE

FESSED
FESSES
FESSUP
FESTAL
FESTAS
FESTER
FESTUS
FETING
FETISH
FETTER
FETTLE
FEUDAL
FEUDED
FEVERS
FEWEST
FEYEST
FEZZAN
FEZZES

F•E•••

FAENZA
FAERIE
FAEROE
FEEBLE
FEEBLY
FEEDER
FEEDON
FEEING
FEELER
FIELDS
FIENDS
FIERCE
FIESTA
FJELDS
FLECHE
FLECKS
FLECKY
FLEDGE
FLEDGY
FLEECE
FLEECY
FLEERS
FLEETS
FLENSE
FLESHY
FLETCH
FLEURY
FLEWAT
FLEWIN
FLEXED
FLEXES
FLEXOR
FLEYED
FOEHNS
FOETAL
FOETID
FOETOR
FOETUS
FREAKS
FREAKY
FREDDY
FREELY
FREEST
FREEZE
FRENCH
FRENUM
FRENZY
FRESCA
FRESCO
FRESNO
FRETTY
FUELED
FUELER

F••E••

FACETS
FACEUP
FADEIN
FAGEND
FAKERS
FAKERY
FARERS
FERENC
FEVERS
FEWEST
FEYEST
FIBERS
FIFERS
FILENE
FILERS
FILETS
FINELY
FINERY
FINEST
FIRERS
FIREUP
FIVEAM
FIVEPM
FIVERS
FIVEWS
FIXERS
FLEECE
FLEECY
FLEERS
FLEETS
FLIERS
FLUENT
FLYERS
FOGEYS
FOMENT
FOREGO
FOREST
FOVEAE
FOYERS
FREELY
FREEST
FREEZE
FRIEND
FRIERS
FRIEZE
FRYERS
FUSEES
FUZEES

F•••E•

FABLED
FABLER
FABLES
FACIES
FAGGED
FAILED
FAIRED
FAIRER
FALCES
FALLEN
FALSER
FALTER
FANGED
FANJET
FANNED
FARCED
FARCES
FARLEY
FARMED
FARMER
FASCES
FASTED
FASTEN
FASTER
FATHER
FATTED
FATTEN
FATTER
FAUCES
FAUCET
FAWKES
FAWNED
FAWNER
FBIMEN
FEARED
FEARER
FEEDER
FEELER
FELLED
FELLER
FELTED
FEMMES
FENCED
FENCER
FENCES
FENDED
FENDER
FENMEN
FENNEC
FENNEL
FERBER
FERRER
FERRET
FESSED
FESSES
FESTER
FETTER
FEUDED
FEZZES
FIBBED
FIBBER
FIBRES
FICHES
FIDGET
FILLED
FILLER
FILLES
FILLET
FILMED
FILTER
FINDER
FINGER
FINKED
FINNED
FINNEY
FIRMED
FIRMER
FISHED
FISHER
FISHES
FISTED
FITTED
FITTER
FIZZED
FIZZES
FLAKED
FLAKER
FLAKES
FLAKEY
FLAMED
FLAMES
FLARED
FLARES
FLAWED
FLAXEN
FLAXES
FLAYED
FLAYER
FLEXED
FLEXES
FLEYED
FLOOEY
FLORES
FLORET
FLOWED
FLOWER
FLUKES
FLUKEY
FLUMES
FLUTED
FLUTES
FLUTEY
FLUXED
FLUXES
FLYMEN
FLYNET
FOALED
FOAMED
FOBBED
FODDER
FOGGED
FOGGER
FOGIES
FOILED
FOINED
FOKKER
FOLDED
FOLDER
FONDER
FOOLED
FOOLER
FOOTED
FOOTER
FORBES
FORCED
FORCER
FORCES
FORDED
FORGED
FORGER
FORGES
FORGET
FORKED
FORKER
FORMED
FORMER
FORTES
FOSSES
FOSSEY
FOSTER
FOULED
FOULER
FOWLED
FOWLER
FOWLES
FOXIER
FRAMED
FRAMES
FRASER
FRAUEN
FRAYED
FRAZER
FRISEE
FRISES
FROZEN
FUBBED
FUDGED
FUDGES
FUELED
FUELER
FUGUES
FULLER
FUMIER
FUNDED
FUNKED
FUNNED
FUNNEL
FURIES
FURLED
FURRED
FURZES
FUSEES
FUSSED
FUSSES
FUTZED
FUTZES
FUZEES
FUZZED
FUZZES

F••••E

FACADE
FACILE
FAERIE
FAEROE
FAILLE
FALINE
FAMINE
FANNIE
FATALE
FAUNAE
FEEBLE
FELINE
FELIPE
FELLOE
FEMALE
FERGIE
FERULE
FESCUE
FETTLE
FIACRE
FIANCE
FICHTE
FICKLE
FIDDLE
FIERCE
FIGURE
FILENE
FILOSE
FINALE
FINITE
FIPPLE
FIXATE
FIZZLE
FLAMBE
FLANGE
FLECHE
FLEDGE
FLEECE
FLENSE
FLORAE
FOCSLE
FOIBLE
FOLKIE
FONDLE
FONDUE
FOODIE
FOOZLE
FORAGE
FOSSAE
FOVEAE
FOZZIE
FRAISE
FRANCE
FRAPPE
FREEZE
FRIDGE
FRIEZE
FRINGE
FRISEE
FUDDLE
FUMBLE
FURORE
FUTILE
FUTURE

•FE•••

AFEARD

•F•E••

AFFECT
AFIELD
AFREET
AFRESH
EFFECT
EFFETE
NFLERS
OFFEND
OFFERS

•F••E•

AFREET
IFFIER
OFFKEY
OFFSET
PFIZER
XFILES

•F•••E

AFFINE
AFLAME
AFRAME
EFFACE
EFFETE
EFFUSE
OFFICE
OFLATE

••FE••

AFFECT
BEFELL
DEFEAT
DEFECT
DEFEND
DEFERS
EFFECT
EFFETE
FIFERS
GOFERS
INFECT
INFERS
INFEST
LIFERS
OFFEND
OFFERS
REFERS
RIFELY
RIFEST
SAFELY
SAFEST
SAFETY
WAFERS
WAFERY
WIFELY

••F•E•

ALFRED
ALFVEN
BIFFED
BOFFED
BUFFED
BUFFER
BUFFET
COFFEE
COFFER
CUFFED
DAFFED
DAFTER
DEFIED
DEFIES
DEFLEA
DEFTER
DIFFER
DOFFED
DUFFEL
DUFFER
EIFFEL
GAFFED
GAFFER
GAFFES
GIFTED
HAFTED
HEFNER
HEFTED
HUFFED
IFFIER
LAFFER
LIFTED
LIFTER
LOFTED
LUFFED
MIFFED
MUFFED
OFFKEY
OFFSET
PUFFED
PUFFER
RAFAEL
RAFTED
RAFTER
REFFED
REFLEX
REFUEL
RIFFED
RIFLED
RIFLER
RIFLES
RIFTED
RUFFED
SIFTED
SIFTER
SOFTEN
SOFTER
SUFFER
TIFFED
TOFFEE
TUFFET
TUFTED
UNFREE
WAFTED
ZAFFER

••F••E

AFFINE
ALFINE
BAFFLE
BEFORE
COFFEE
DEFACE
DEFAME
DEFILE
DEFINE
DEFUSE
EFFACE
EFFETE
EFFUSE
IMFINE
INFUSE
LEFTIE
MIFUNE
MUFFLE
OFFICE
ONFILE
ONFIRE
PIFFLE
RAFFLE
REFACE
REFILE
REFINE
REFUGE
REFUSE
REFUTE
RIFFLE
RUFFLE
SAFIRE
SOFINE
SOFTIE
TOFFEE
UNFREE
WAFFLE

•••FE•

BEEFED
BIFFED
BOFFED
BUFFED
BUFFER
BUFFET
CHAFED
CHAFES
COFFEE
COFFER
COIFED
CONFED
CONFER
CUFFED
CURFEW
DAFFED
DEAFEN
DEAFER
DIFFER
DOFFED
DUFFEL
DUFFER
DURFEY
EIFFEL
GAFFED
GAFFER
GAFFES
GOLFED
GOLFER
GOOFED
GULFED
HEIFER
HOOFED
HOOFER
HUFFED
ILLFED
KIEFER
KNIFED
KNIFES
LAFFER
LEAFED
LIEFER
LOAFED
LOAFER
LUFFED
MIFFED
MUFFED
PILFER
PREFER
PUFFED
PUFFER
REEFED
REEFER
REFFED
RIFFED
ROOFED
ROOFER
RUFFED
SUFFER
SURFED
SURFER
THEFED
TIFFED
TITFER
TOFFEE
TUFFET
TURFED
TWOFER
WERFEL
WOLFED
WOOFED
WOOFER
ZAFFER

•••F•E

BAFFLE
BOUFFE
COFFEE
KHAFRE
MUFFLE
PIAFFE
PIFFLE

PURFLE
RAFFLE
RIFFLE
RUFFLE
STIFLE
TOFFEE
TRIFLE
WAFFLE

••••FE

BOUFFE
CARAFE
EXWIFE
OKEEFE
PIAFFE
RECIFE
STRAFE
STRIFE
TOLIFE
UNSAFE

F•F•••

FAFNIR
FIFERS
FIFING
FIFTHS

F••F••

FITFUL
FLUFFS
FLUFFY
FULFIL

F•••F•

FAROFF
FLUFFS
FLUFFY
FOBOFF

F••••F

FAROFF
FOBOFF

•FF•••

AFFAIR
AFFECT
AFFINE
AFFIRM
AFFORD
AFFRAY
EFFACE
EFFECT
EFFETE
EFFIGY
EFFLUX
EFFORT
EFFUSE
IFFIER
OFFDAY
OFFEND
OFFERS
OFFICE
OFFING
OFFISH
OFFKEY
OFFSET

••FF••

BAFFIN
BAFFLE
BIFFED
BOFFED
BOFFIN
BOFFOS
BUFFED
BUFFER
BUFFET
BUFFON
BUFFOS
COFFEE
COFFER
CUFFED
DAFFED
DIFFER
DOFFED
DUFFEL
DUFFER
EIFFEL
GAFFED
GAFFER
GAFFES
GUFFAW
HUFFED
KAFFIR
LAFFER
LUFFED
MIFFED
MUFFED
MUFFIN
MUFFLE
PIFFLE
PUFFED
PUFFER
PUFFIN
RAFFIA
RAFFLE
REFFED
RIFFED
RIFFLE
RUFFED
RUFFLE
RUFFLY
SOFFIT
SUFFER
SUFFIX
TIFFED
TIFFIN
TOFFEE
TUFFET
WAFFLE
WAFFLY
ZAFFER

••F•F•

RIFIFI

•••FF•

BLUFFS
BOUFFE
CHAFFS
CHAFFY
CHUFFY
CLIFFS
CLIFFY
FLUFFS
FLUFFY
PIAFFE
QUAFFS
SCOFFS
SCUFFS
SKIFFS
SNIFFS
SNIFFY
SNUFFS
SNUFFY
SPIFFS
SPIFFY
STAFFS
STEFFI
STIFFS
STUFFS
STUFFY
WHIFFS

••••FF

BEGOFF
BITOFF
BUGOFF
BUYOFF
CANIFF
CRYOFF
CUTOFF
DIEOFF
DRYOFF
FAROFF
FOBOFF
GETOFF
GOTOFF
HOPOFF
LAYOFF
LEDOFF
LETOFF
LOGOFF
NODOFF
PAYOFF
POPOFF
PUTOFF
RANOFF
REBUFF
RIPOFF
RUBOFF
RUNOFF
SAWOFF
SCHIFF
SCLAFF
SCRUFF
SEEOFF
SETOFF
TAPOFF
TARIFF
TEEOFF
TIPOFF
TOPOFF

F•G•••

FAGEND
FAGGED
FAGOTS
FIGARO
FIGHTS
FIGURE
FOGBOW
FOGEYS
FOGGED
FOGGER
FOGHAT
FOGIES
FOGSIN
FOGSUP
FUGARD
FUGUES

F••G••

FAGGED
FANGED
FEIGNS
FERGIE
FERGUS
FIDGET
FINGER
FIZGIG
FLAGGY
FLAGON
FLIGHT
FOGGED
FOGGER
FORGED
FORGER
FORGES
FORGET
FORGOT
FOUGHT
FRIGHT
FRIGID
FROGGY
FRUGAL
FUDGED
FUDGES
FUNGUS

F•••G•

FLAGGY
FLANGE
FLEDGE
FLEDGY
FLINGS
FORAGE
FOREGO
FRIDGE
FRINGE
FRINGY
FROGGY

F••••G

FACING
FADING
FAKING
FARING
FAXING
FAZING
FEEING
FETING
FIFING
FILING
FINING
FIRING
FIXING
FIZGIG
FLYING
FOXING
FRYING
FUMING
FUSING
FUZING

•FG•••

AFGHAN

•F••G•

EFFIGY

•F•••G

OFFING

••F•G•

BEFOGS
DEFOGS
EFFIGY
REFUGE

••F••G

FIFING
OFFING
REFLAG
ZAFTIG

•••F•G

ICEFOG
INAFOG

F•H•••

FSHARP

F••H••

FATHER
FATHOM
FICHES
FICHTE
FICHUS
FIGHTS
FISHED
FISHER
FISHES
FOEHNS
FOGHAT
FUZHOU

F•••H•

FAITHS
FIFTHS
FILTHY
FIRTHS
FLASHY
FLECHE
FLESHY
FLIGHT
FOUGHT
FRIGHT
FROTHS
FROTHY

F••••H

FAMISH
FARRAH
FELLAH
FETISH
FINISH
FLETCH
FLINCH
FLITCH
FOURTH
FRENCH

•F•H••

AFGHAN

•F•••H

AFRESH
OFFISH

••F•H•

FIFTHS

••F••H

ELFISH
GOFISH
OAFISH
OFFISH

•••F•H

LOOFAH

FI••••

FIACRE
FIANCE
FIASCO
FIBBED
FIBBER
FIBERS
FIBRES
FIBRIL
FIBRIN
FIBULA
FICHES
FICHTE
FICHUS
FICKLE
FIDDLE
FIDGET
FIELDS
FIENDS
FIERCE
FIESTA
FIFERS
FIFING
FIFTHS
FIGARO
FIGHTS
FIGURE
FIJIAN
FILENE
FILERS
FILETS
FILIAL
FILING
FILIUS
FILLED
FILLER
FILLES
FILLET
FILLIN
FILLIP
FILLUP
FILMED
FILOSE
FILTER
FILTHY
FINALE
FINALS
FINDER
FINELY
FINERY
FINEST
FINGER
FINIAL
FINING
FINISH
FINITE
FINITO
FINKED
FINNAN
FINNED
FINNEY
FINNIC
FIORDS
FIPPLE
FIRERS
FIREUP
FIRING
FIRKIN
FIRMAN
FIRMED
FIRMER
FIRMLY
FIRMUP
FIRSTS
FIRTHS
FISCAL
FISHED
FISHER
FISHES
FISTED
FISTIC
FITFUL
FITSIN
FITTED
FITTER
FIVEAM
FIVEPM
FIVERS
FIVEWS
FIXATE
FIXERS
FIXING
FIXITY
FIXUPS
FIZGIG
FIZZED
FIZZES
FIZZLE

F•I•••

FAILED
FAILLE
FAINTS
FAIRED
FAIRER
FAIRLY
FAIRUP
FAISAL
FAITHS
FAIYUM
FBIMAN
FBIMEN
FEIGNS
FEINTS
FEISTY
FLICKA
FLICKS
FLIERS
FLIGHT
FLIMSY
FLINCH
FLINGS
FLINTS
FLINTY
FLIPUP
FLIRTS
FLIRTY
FLITCH
FMINOR
FOIBLE
FOILED
FOINED
FOISTS
FRIARS
FRIARY
FRIDAY
FRIDGE
FRIEND
FRIERS
FRIEZE
FRIGHT
FRIGID
FRIJOL
FRILLS
FRILLY
FRINGE
FRINGY
FRISCO
FRISEE
FRISES
FRISKS
FRISKY
FRITOS
FRIZZY

F••I••

FABIAN
FACIAL
FACIAS
FACIES
FACILE
FACING
FADING
FAJITA
FAKING
FAKIRS
FALINE
FAMILY
FAMINE
FAMISH
FANION
FARINA
FARING
FATIMA
FAXING
FAZING
FEEING
FELINE
FELIPE
FENIAN
FERIAL
FERIAS
FERITY
FETING
FETISH
FIFING
FIJIAN
FILIAL
FILING
FILIUS
FINIAL
FINING
FINISH
FINITE
FINITO
FIRING
FIXING
FIXITY
FLAILS
FLAIRS
FLUIDS
FLYING
FLYINS
FOGIES
FOLIAR
FOLIOS
FOLIUM
FORINT
FOXIER
FOXILY
FOXING
FRAIDY
FRAISE
FRUITS
FRUITY
FRYING
FUJIAN
FUMIER
FUMING
FURIES
FUSILS
FUSING
FUSION
FUTILE
FUZING

F•••I•

FABRIC
FADEIN
FAERIE
FAFNIR
FALLIN
FANNIE
FASCIA
FELLIN
FERGIE
FERRIC
FERRIS
FERVID
FIBRIL
FIBRIN
FILLIN
FILLIP
FINNIC
FIRKIN
FISTIC
FITSIN
FIZGIG
FLAVIA
FLEWIN
FLORID
FLORIN
FLORIO
FOETID
FOGSIN
FOLKIE
FOODIE
FORBID
FORMIC
FOSSIL
FOZZIE
FRIGID
FROLIC
FULFIL
FUSTIC

F••••I

FRUTTI
FULANI

•FI•••
AFIELD
PFIZER
XFILES

•F•I••
AFFINE
AFFIRM
AFRICA
AFRITS
EFFIGY
IFFIER
OFFICE
OFFING
OFFISH

•F••I•
AFFAIR
AFLCIO
AFRAID

••FI••
AFFINE
AFFIRM
ALFINE
BEFITS
DEFIED
DEFIES
DEFILE
DEFINE
EFFIGY
ELFISH
FIFING
GOFISH
IFFIER
IMFINE
INFIRM
KAFIRS
KEFIRS
OAFISH
OFFICE
OFFING
OFFISH
ONFILE
ONFIRE
REFILE
REFILL
REFINE
REFITS
RIFIFI
SAFIRE
SOFINE
SUFISM
UNFITS

••F•I•
AAFAIR
AFFAIR
AUFAIT
BAFFIN
BOFFIN
FAFNIR
HEFLIN
KAFFIR
LEFTIE
LEFTIN
MUFFIN
MUFTIS
PUFFIN
RAFFIA
SOFFIT
SOFTIE
SUFFIX
TIFFIN
UNFAIR
ZAFTIG

••F••I
RIFIFI
SAFARI

•••FI•
BAFFIN
BOFFIN
BOWFIN
COMFIT
FULFIL
HOOFIT
INAFIX
KAFFIR
MISFIT
MUFFIN
OLEFIN
OUTFIT
PREFIX
PROFIT
PUFFIN
RAFFIA
REDFIN
REDFIR
SAWFIT
SCIFIS
SEEFIT
SOFFIT
SUFFIX
TIFFIN
TRIFID
UNIFIC

•••F•I
STEFFI

••••FI
AMALFI
RIFIFI
STEFFI

FJ••••
FJELDS
FJORDS

F•J•••
FAJITA
FIJIAN
FUJIAN

F••J••
FANJET
FMAJOR
FRIJOL

F•K•••
FAKERS
FAKERY
FAKING
FAKIRS
FOKKER

F••K••
FAWKES
FICKLE
FINKED
FIRKIN
FLAKED
FLAKER
FLAKES
FLAKEY
FLUKES
FLUKEY
FOKKER
FOLKIE
FOLKSY
FORKED
FORKER
FUNKED

F•••K•
FLACKS
FLANKS
FLASKS
FLECKS
FLECKY
FLICKA
FLICKS
FLOCKS
FLOCKY
FLUNKS
FLUNKY
FRANKS
FREAKS
FREAKY
FRISKS
FRISKY
FROCKS

F••••K
FAROUK
FRANCK

•F•K••
OFFKEY

••FK••
OFFKEY

FL••••
FLABBY
FLACKS
FLACON
FLAGGY
FLAGON
FLAILS
FLAIRS
FLAKED
FLAKER
FLAKES
FLAKEY
FLAMBE
FLAMED
FLAMES
FLANGE
FLANKS
FLAPPY
FLARED
FLARES
FLASHY
FLASKS
FLATLY
FLAUNT
FLAVIA
FLAVOR
FLAWED
FLAXEN
FLAXES
FLAYED
FLAYER
FLECHE
FLECKS
FLECKY
FLEDGE
FLEDGY
FLEECE
FLEECY
FLEERS
FLEETS
FLENSE
FLESHY
FLETCH
FLEURY
FLEWAT
FLEWIN
FLEXED
FLEXES
FLEXOR
FLEYED
FLICKA
FLICKS
FLIERS
FLIGHT
FLIMSY
FLINCH
FLINGS
FLINTS
FLINTY
FLIPUP
FLIRTS
FLIRTY
FLITCH
FLOATS
FLOATY
FLOCKS
FLOCKY
FLOODS
FLOOEY
FLOORS
FLOPPY
FLOPSY
FLORAE
FLORAL
FLORAS
FLORES
FLORET
FLORID
FLORIN
FLORIO
FLOSSY
FLOURS
FLOURY
FLOUTS
FLOWED
FLOWER
FLUENT
FLUFFS
FLUFFY
FLUIDS
FLUKES
FLUKEY
FLUMES
FLUNKS
FLUNKY
FLUORO
FLURRY
FLUTED
FLUTES
FLUTEY
FLUXED
FLUXES
FLYBOY
FLYBYS
FLYERS
FLYING
FLYINS
FLYMAN
FLYMEN
FLYNET
FLYOUT
FLYROD
FLYWAY

F•L•••
FALANA
FALCES
FALCON
FALINE
FALLEN
FALLIN
FALLON
FALLOW
FALLTO
FALSER
FALTER
FELDON
FELINE
FELIPE
FELLAH
FELLAS
FELLED
FELLER
FELLIN
FELLOE
FELLON
FELLOW
FELLTO
FELONS
FELONY
FELTED
FILENE
FILERS
FILETS
FILIAL
FILING
FILIUS
FILLED
FILLER
FILLES
FILLET
FILLIN
FILLIP
FILLUP
FILMED
FILOSE
FILTER
FILTHY
FOLDED
FOLDER
FOLDUP
FOLIAR
FOLIOS
FOLIUM
FOLKIE
FOLKSY
FOLLOW
FOLSOM
FULANI
FULCRA
FULFIL
FULLER
FULMAR
FULTON

F••L••
FABLED
FABLER
FABLES
FAILED
FAILLE
FALLEN
FALLIN
FALLON
FALLOW
FALLTO
FARLEY
FARLOW
FAULTS
FAULTY
FAWLTY
FEALTY
FEELER
FELLAH
FELLAS
FELLED
FELLER
FELLIN
FELLOE
FELLON
FELLOW
FELLTO
FIELDS
FILLED
FILLER
FILLES
FILLET
FILLIN
FILLIP
FILLUP
FJELDS
FOALED
FOILED
FOLLOW
FOOLED
FOOLER
FOULED
FOULER
FOULLY
FOULUP
FOWLED
FOWLER
FOWLES
FRILLS
FRILLY
FROLIC
FUELED
FUELER
FULLER
FURLED

F•••L•
FACILE
FACULA
FAILLE
FAIRLY
FAMILY
FATALE
FEATLY
FEEBLE
FEEBLY
FEMALE
FERULE
FETTLE
FIBULA
FICKLE
FIDDLE
FINALE
FINALS
FINELY
FIPPLE
FIRMLY
FIZZLE
FLAILS
FLATLY
FOCSLE
FOIBLE
FONDLE
FONDLY
FOOZLE
FOULLY
FOXILY
FREELY
FRILLS
FRILLY
FUDDLE
FUMBLE
FUSILS
FUTILE

F••••L
FACIAL
FAISAL
FAUNAL
FAZOOL
FENNEL
FERIAL
FESTAL
FEUDAL
FIBRIL
FILIAL
FINIAL
FISCAL
FITFUL
FLORAL
FOETAL
FONTAL
FORMAL
FOSSIL
FRIJOL
FRUGAL
FULFIL
FUNNEL

•FL•••
AFLAME
AFLATS
AFLCIO
AFLOAT
EFLATS
NFLERS
OFLATE

•F•L••
EFFLUX
XFILES

•F••L•
AFIELD

••FL••
DEFLEA
EFFLUX
HEFLIN
INFLOW
INFLUX
REFLAG
REFLEX
REFLUX
RIFLED
RIFLER
RIFLES
TEFLON

••F•L•
BAFFLE
BEFALL
BEFELL
BIFOLD
DAFTLY
DEFILE
DEFTLY
ENFOLD
INFOLD
INFULL
MUFFLE
ONFILE
PIFFLE
RAFFLE
REFILE
REFILL
RIFELY
RIFFLE
RUFFLE
RUFFLY
SAFELY
SOFTLY
UNFOLD
WAFFLE
WAFFLY
WIFELY

••F••L
BEFALL
BEFELL
BEFOUL
DUFFEL
EIFFEL
INFULL
RAFAEL
REFILL
REFUEL
UNFURL

•••FL•
BAFFLE
BARFLY
BOTFLY
DEAFLY
DRYFLY
GADFLY
LETFLY
LIEFLY
MAYFLY
MEDFLY
MUFFLE
OUTFLY
PIFFLE
POPFLY
PURFLE
RAFFLE
RIFFLE
RUFFLE
RUFFLY
STIFLE
THEFLY
TRIFLE
WAFFLE
WAFFLY
WETFLY

•••F•L
AIDFUL
AIMFUL
ARMFUL
ARTFUL
BAGFUL
BOXFUL
CANFUL
CAPFUL
CARFUL
CUPFUL
DUFFEL
EARFUL
EIFFEL
EYEFUL
FITFUL
FULFIL
HATFUL
IREFUL
JARFUL
JOYFUL
JUGFUL
LAPFUL
LAWFUL
MANFUL
PANFUL
PEPFUL
POTFUL
RUEFUL
SINFUL
SOBFUL
USEFUL
VATFUL
WERFEL
WILFUL
WOEFUL

FM••••
FMAJOR
FMINOR

F•M•••
FAMILY
FAMINE
FAMISH
FAMOUS
FEMALE
FEMMES
FEMORA
FEMURS
FOMENT
FUMBLE
FUMIER
FUMING

F••M••
FARMED
FARMER
FBIMAN
FBIMEN
FEMMES
FENMAN
FENMEN
FERMAT
FILMED
FIRMAN
FIRMED
FIRMER
FIRMLY
FIRMUP
FLAMBE
FLAMED
FLAMES
FLIMSY
FLUMES
FLYMAN
FLYMEN
FOAMED
FORMAL
FORMAN
FORMAT
FORMED
FORMER
FORMIC
FRAMED
FRAMES
FRUMPS
FRUMPY
FULMAR

F•••M•
FATIMA
FORUMS

F••••M
FAIYUM
FANDOM
FATHOM
FIVEAM
FIVEPM
FOLIUM
FOLSOM
FOURAM
FOURPM
FRENUM

•F••M•
AFLAME
AFRAME

•F•••M
AFFIRM

••FM••
ELFMAN

••F•M•
DEFAME
INFAMY

••F••M
AFFIRM
DEFORM
INFIRM
INFORM
REFORM
SUFISM

F•N•••
FANDOM
FANGED
FANION
FANJET
FANNED
FANNIE
FANONS
FANOUT
FANTAN
FENCED
FENCER
FENCES
FENDED
FENDER
FENIAN
FENMAN
FENMEN
FENNEC
FENNEL
FENWAY
FINALE
FINALS
FINDER
FINELY
FINERY
FINEST
FINGER
FINIAL
FINING
FINISH
FINITE
FINITO
FINKED
FINNAN
FINNED
FINNEY
FINNIC
FONDER
FONDLE
FONDLY
FONDUE
FONTAL
FUNDED
FUNGUS
FUNKED
FUNNED
FUNNEL

F••N••
FAENZA
FAFNIR
FAINTS
FANNED
FANNIE
FAUNAE
FAUNAL
FAUNAS
FAUNUS
FAWNED
FAWNER
FEINTS
FENNEC
FENNEL
FIANCE
FIENDS
FINNAN
FINNED
FINNEY
FINNIC
FLANGE
FLANKS
FLENSE
FLINCH
FLINGS
FLINTS
FLINTY
FLUNKS
FLUNKY
FLYNET
FMINOR
FOINED
FOUNDS
FOUNTS
FRANCA
FRANCE
FRANCK
FRANCO
FRANCS
FRANKS
FRANNY
FRENCH
FRENUM
FRENZY
FRINGE
FRINGY
FRONDS
FRONTS
FUNNED
FUNNEL

F•••N•
FACING
FADING
FAGEND
FAKING
FALANA
FALINE
FAMINE
FANONS
FARINA
FARING
FAXING
FAZING
FECUND
FEEING
FEIGNS
FELINE
FELONS
FELONY
FERENC
FETING
FIFING
FILENE
FILING
FINING
FIRING
FIXING
FLAUNT
FLUENT
FLYING
FLYINS
FOEHNS
FOMENT
FORINT
FOXING
FRANNY
FRESNO
FRIEND
FROWNS
FRYING
FULANI
FUMING
FUSING
FUTONS
FUZING

F••••N
FABIAN
FADEIN
FALCON
FALLEN
FALLIN
FALLON
FANION
FANTAN
FASTEN
FATTEN
FBIMAN
FBIMEN
FEEDON
FELDON
FELLIN
FELLON
FENIAN
FENMAN
FENMEN
FEZZAN
FIBRIN
FIJIAN
FILLIN
FINNAN
FIRKIN
FIRMAN
FITSIN
FLACON
FLAGON
FLAXEN
FLEWIN
FLORIN
FLYMAN
FLYMEN
FOGSIN
FORMAN
FRAUEN
FROZEN
FRYPAN
FUJIAN
FULTON
FUSION

•F••N•
AFFINE
OFFEND
OFFING

•F•••N
AFGHAN

••FN••
FAFNIR
HEFNER

••F•N•
AFFINE
ALFINE
AUFOND
DEFEND
DEFINE
ENFANT
FIFING
IMFINE
INFANT
MIFUNE
OFFEND
OFFING
REFINE
REFUND
SOFINE

••F••N
ALFVEN
BAFFIN
BOFFIN
BUFFON
CAFTAN
ELFMAN
HEFLIN
LEFTIN
MUFFIN
PUFFIN
SOFTEN
TEFLON
TIFFIN

•••F•N
BAFFIN
BOFFIN
BOWFIN
BUFFON
DEAFEN
MUFFIN
OLEFIN
PUFFIN
REDFIN
SEAFAN
STEFAN
TIFFIN

FO••••
FOALED
FOAMED
FOBBED
FOBOFF
FOCSLE
FODDER
FOEHNS
FOETAL
FOETID
FOETOR
FOETUS
FOGBOW
FOGEYS
FOGGED
FOGGER
FOGHAT
FOGIES
FOGSIN
FOGSUP
FOIBLE
FOILED
FOINED
FOISTS
FOKKER
FOLDED
FOLDER
FOLDUP
FOLIAR
FOLIOS
FOLIUM
FOLKIE
FOLKSY
FOLLOW
FOLSOM
FOMENT
FONDER
FONDLE
FONDLY
FONDUE
FONTAL
FOODIE
FOOLED
FOOLER
FOOTED
FOOTER
FOOZLE
FORAGE
FORAYS
FORBAD
FORBES
FORBID
FORCED
FORCER
FORCES
FORDED
FOREGO
FOREST
FORGED
FORGER
FORGES
FORGET
FORGOT
FORINT
FORKED
FORKER
FORMAL
FORMAN
FORMAT
FORMED
FORMER
FORMIC
FORTAS
FORTES
FORUMS
FOSSAE
FOSSAS
FOSSES
FOSSEY
FOSSIL
FOSTER
FOUGHT
FOULED
FOULER
FOULLY
FOULUP
FOUNDS
FOUNTS
FOURAM
FOURPM
FOURTH
FOVEAE
FOWLED
FOWLER
FOWLES
FOXIER
FOXILY
FOXING
FOYERS
FOZZIE

F•O•••
FIORDS
FJORDS
FLOATS
FLOATY
FLOCKS
FLOCKY
FLOODS
FLOOEY
FLOORS
FLOPPY
FLOPSY
FLORAE
FLORAL
FLORAS
FLORES
FLORET
FLORID
FLORIN
FLORIO
FLOSSY
FLOURS
FLOURY
FLOUTS
FLOWED
FLOWER
FOODIE
FOOLED
FOOLER
FOOTED
FOOTER
FOOZLE
FROCKS
FROGGY
FROLIC
FRONDS
FRONTS
FROSTS
FROSTY
FROTHS
FROTHY
FROWNS
FROWZY
FROZEN
FYODOR

F••O••
FAGOTS
FAMOUS
FANONS
FANOUT
FAROFF
FAROUK
FAROUT
FAVORS
FAVOUR
FAZOOL
FEDORA
FELONS
FELONY
FEMORA
FILOSE
FLOODS
FLOOEY
FLOORS
FLUORO
FLYOUT
FOBOFF
FSTOPS
FTROOP
FURORE
FURORS
FUTONS

F•••O•
FACTOR
FAEROE
FALCON
FALLON
FALLOW
FANDOM
FANION
FARLOW
FARROW
FATHOM
FAZOOL
FEEDON
FELDON
FELLOE
FELLON
FELLOW
FERVOR
FLACON
FLAGON
FLAVOR
FLEXOR
FLYBOY
FLYROD
FMAJOR
FMINOR
FOETOR
FOGBOW
FOLIOS
FOLLOW
FOLSOM
FORGOT
FRIJOL
FRITOS
FTROOP
FULTON
FURROW
FUSION
FUZHOU
FYODOR

F••••O
FALLTO
FELLTO
FIASCO
FIGARO
FINITO
FLORIO
FLUORO
FOREGO
FRANCO
FRESCO
FRESNO
FRISCO

•FO•••
SFORZA

•F•O••
AFFORD
AFLOAT
EFFORT

•F•••O
AFLCIO

••FO••
AFFORD
AJFOYT
AUFOND
BEFOGS
BEFORE
BEFOUL
BIFOLD
DEFOGS
DEFORM
EFFORT
ENFOLD
INFOLD
INFORM
ONFOOT
OXFORD
REFORM
RUFOUS
UNFOLD

••F•O•
BOFFOS
BUFFON
BUFFOS
INFLOW
ONFOOT
TEFLON

•••FO•
AIMFOR
ALLFOR
ASKFOR
BOFFOS
BUFFON
BUFFOS
GUNFOR
ICEFOG
INAFOG
KITFOX
LAYFOR
OPTFOR
OUTFOX
PAYFOR
RANFOR
REDFOX
RUNFOR
SEAFOX
STEFOY
TRYFOR

••••FO
SENUFO

F•P•••
FIPPLE

F••P••
FIPPLE
FLAPPY
FLIPUP
FLOPPY
FLOPSY
FRAPPE
FRYPAN

F•••P•
FELIPE

FIVEPM
FIXUPS
FLAPPY
FLOPPY
FOURPM
FRAPPE
FRUMPS
FRUMPY
FSTOPS

F••••P
FACEUP
FAIRUP
FESSUP
FILLIP
FILLUP
FIREUP
FIRMUP
FLIPUP
FOGSUP
FOLDUP
FOULUP
FSHARP
FTROOP

••F••P
LIFTUP

•••F•P
BEEFUP
GOOFUP

FR••••
FRACAS
FRAIDY
FRAISE
FRAMED
FRAMES
FRANCA
FRANCE
FRANCK
FRANCO
FRANCS
FRANKS
FRANNY
FRAPPE
FRASER
FRAUDS
FRAUEN
FRAYED
FRAZER
FREAKS
FREAKY
FREDDY
FREELY
FREEST
FREEZE
FRENCH
FRENUM
FRENZY
FRESCA
FRESCO
FRESNO
FRETTY
FRIARS
FRIARY
FRIDAY
FRIDGE
FRIEND
FRIERS
FRIEZE
FRIGHT
FRIGID
FRIJOL
FRILLS
FRILLY
FRINGE
FRINGY
FRISCO
FRISEE
FRISES
FRISKS
FRISKY
FRITOS
FRIZZY
FROCKS
FROGGY
FROLIC
FRONDS
FRONTS
FROSTS
FROSTY
FROTHS
FROTHY
FROWNS
FROWZY
FROZEN
FRUGAL
FRUITS
FRUITY
FRUMPS
FRUMPY
FRUTTI
FRYERS
FRYING
FRYPAN

F•R•••
FARADS
FARCED
FARCES
FARCRY
FARERS
FARINA
FARING
FARLEY
FARLOW
FARMED
FARMER
FAROFF
FAROUK
FAROUT
FARRAH
FARRAR
FARROW
FERBER
FERENC
FERGIE
FERGUS
FERIAL
FERIAS
FERITY
FERMAT
FERRER
FERRET
FERRIC
FERRIS
FERULE
FERVID
FERVOR
FIRERS
FIREUP
FIRING
FIRKIN
FIRMAN
FIRMED
FIRMER
FIRMLY
FIRMUP
FIRSTS
FIRTHS
FORAGE
FORAYS
FORBAD
FORBES
FORBID
FORCED
FORCER
FORCES
FORDED
FOREGO
FOREST
FORGED
FORGER
FORGES
FORGET
FORGOT
FORINT
FORKED
FORKER
FORMAL
FORMAN
FORMAT
FORMED
FORMER
FORMIC
FORTAS
FORTES
FORUMS
FTROOP
FURIES
FURLED
FURORE
FURORS
FURRED
FURROW
FURZES

F••R••
FABRAY
FABRIC
FAERIE
FAEROE
FAIRED
FAIRER
FAIRLY
FAIRUP
FARRAH
FARRAR
FARROW
FEARED
FEARER
FERRER
FERRET
FERRIC
FERRIS
FIBRES
FIBRIL
FIBRIN
FIERCE
FIORDS
FJORDS
FLARED
FLARES
FLIRTS
FLIRTY
FLORAE
FLORAL
FLORAS
FLORES
FLORET
FLORID
FLORIN
FLORIO
FLURRY
FLYROD
FOURAM
FOURPM
FOURTH
FURRED
FURROW

F•••R•
FAKERS
FAKERY
FAKIRS
FARCRY
FARERS
FAVORS
FEDORA
FEMORA
FEMURS
FEVERS
FIACRE
FIBERS
FIFERS
FIGARO
FIGURE
FILERS
FINERY
FIRERS
FIVERS
FIXERS
FLAIRS
FLEERS
FLEURY
FLIERS
FLOORS
FLOURS
FLOURY
FLUORO
FLURRY
FLYERS
FOYERS
FRIARS
FRIARY
FRIERS
FRYERS
FSHARP
FUGARD
FULCRA
FURORE
FURORS
FUTURE

F••••R
FABLER
FACTOR
FAFNIR
FAIRER
FALSER
FALTER
FARMER
FARRAR
FASTER
FATHER
FATTER
FAVOUR
FAWNER
FEARER
FEEDER
FEELER
FELLER
FENCER
FENDER
FERBER
FERRER
FERVOR
FESTER
FETTER
FIBBER
FILLER
FILTER
FINDER
FINGER
FIRMER
FISHER
FITTER
FLAKER
FLAVOR
FLAYER
FLEXOR
FLOWER
FMAJOR
FMINOR
FODDER
FOETOR
FOGGER
FOKKER
FOLDER
FOLIAR
FONDER
FOOLER
FOOTER
FORCER
FORGER
FORKER
FORMER
FOSTER
FOULER
FOWLER
FOXIER
FRASER
FRAZER
FUELER
FULLER
FULMAR
FUMIER
FYODOR

•FR•••
AFRAID
AFRAME
AFREET
AFRESH
AFRICA
AFRITS

•F•R••
AFFRAY
SFORZA

•F••R•
AFEARD
AFFIRM
AFFORD
EFFORT
NFLERS
OFFERS

•F•••R
AFFAIR
IFFIER
PFIZER

••FR••
AFFRAY
ALFRED
DEFRAY
UNFREE

••F•R•
AFFIRM
AFFORD
BEFORE
DEFERS
DEFORM
EFFORT
ERFURT
FIFERS
GOFERS
INFERS
INFIRM
INFORM
KAFIRS
KEFIRS
LIFERS
OFFERS
ONFIRE
OXFORD
REFERS
REFORM
SAFARI
SAFIRE
UNFURL
WAFERS
WAFERY

••F••R
AAFAIR
AFFAIR
BUFFER
COFFER
DAFTER
DEFTER
DIFFER
DUFFER
FAFNIR
GAFFER
HEFNER
IFFIER
KAFFIR
LAFFER
LIFTER
PUFFER
RAFTER
RIFLER
SIFTER
SOFTER
SUFFER
UNFAIR
ZAFFER

•••FR•
BELFRY
BIAFRA
KHAFRE
PANFRY

•••F•R
AIMFOR
ALLFOR
ASKFOR
BUFFER
COFFER
CONFER
DEAFER
DIFFER
DUFFER
GAFFER
GOLFER
GUNFOR
HEIFER
HOOFER
KAFFIR
KIEFER
LAFFER
LAYFOR
LIEFER
LOAFER
OPTFOR
PAYFOR
PILFER
PREFER
PUFFER
RANFOR
REDFIR
REEFER
ROOFER
RUNFOR
SHOFAR
SUFFER
SULFUR
SURFER
TITFER
TRYFOR
TWOFER
WOOFER
ZAFFER

FS••••
FSHARP
FSTOPS

F•S•••
FASCES
FASCIA
FASTED
FASTEN
FASTER
FESCUE
FESSED
FESSES
FESSUP
FESTAL
FESTAS
FESTER
FESTUS
FISCAL
FISHED
FISHER
FISHES
FISTED
FISTIC
FOSSAE
FOSSAS
FOSSES
FOSSEY
FOSSIL
FOSTER
FUSEES
FUSILS
FUSING
FUSION
FUSSED
FUSSES
FUSTIC

F••S••
FAISAL
FALSER
FEASTS
FEISTY
FESSED
FESSES
FESSUP
FIASCO
FIESTA
FIRSTS
FITSIN
FLASHY
FLASKS
FLESHY
FLOSSY
FOCSLE
FOGSIN
FOGSUP
FOISTS
FOLSOM
FOSSAE
FOSSAS
FOSSES
FOSSEY
FOSSIL
FRASER
FRESCA
FRESCO
FRESNO
FRISCO
FRISEE
FRISES
FRISKS
FRISKY
FROSTS
FROSTY
FUSSED
FUSSES

F•••S•
FAMISH
FETISH
FEWEST
FEYEST
FILOSE
FINEST
FINISH
FLENSE
FLIMSY
FLOPSY
FLOSSY
FOLKSY
FOREST
FRAISE
FREEST

F••••S
FABLES
FACETS
FACIAS
FACIES
FAGOTS
FAINTS
FAITHS
FAKERS
FAKIRS
FALCES
FAMOUS
FANONS
FARADS
FARCES
FARERS
FASCES
FATWAS
FAUCES
FAULTS
FAUNAS
FAUNUS
FAVORS
FAWKES
FEASTS
FEIGNS
FEINTS
FELLAS
FELONS
FEMMES
FEMURS
FENCES
FERGUS
FERIAS
FERRIS
FESSES
FESTAS
FESTUS
FEVERS
FEZZES
FIBERS
FIBRES
FICHES
FICHUS
FIELDS
FIENDS
FIFERS
FIFTHS
FIGHTS
FILERS
FILETS
FILIUS
FILLES
FINALS
FIORDS
FIRERS
FIRSTS
FIRTHS
FISHES
FIVERS
FIVEWS
FIXERS
FIXUPS

FIZZES
FJELDS
FJORDS
FLACKS
FLAILS
FLAIRS
FLAKES
FLAMES
FLANKS
FLARES
FLASKS
FLAXES
FLECKS
FLEERS
FLEETS
FLEXES
FLICKS
FLIERS
FLINGS
FLINTS
FLIRTS
FLOATS
FLOCKS
FLOODS
FLOORS
FLORAS
FLORES
FLOURS
FLOUTS
FLUFFS
FLUIDS
FLUKES
FLUMES
FLUNKS
FLUTES
FLUXES
FLYBYS
FLYERS
FLYINS
FOEHNS
FOETUS
FOGEYS
FOGIES
FOISTS
FOLIOS
FORAYS
FORBES
FORCES
FORGES
FORTAS
FORTES
FORUMS
FOSSAS
FOSSES
FOUNDS
FOUNTS
FOWLES
FOYERS
FRACAS
FRAMES
FRANCS
FRANKS
FRAUDS
FREAKS
FRIARS
FRIERS
FRILLS
FRISES
FRISKS
FRITOS
FROCKS
FRONDS
FRONTS
FROSTS
FROTHS
FROWNS
FRUITS
FRUMPS
FRYERS
FSTOPS
FUDGES
FUGUES
FUNGUS
FURIES
FURORS
FURZES
FUSEES
FUSILS
FUSSES
FUTONS
FUTZES
FUZEES
FUZZES

•F•S••

OFFSET

•F••S•

AFRESH
EFFUSE
OFFISH

•F•••S

AFLATS
AFRITS
EFLATS
NFLERS
OFFERS
XFILES

••FS••

OFFSET

••F•S•

DEFUSE
EFFUSE
ELFISH
GOFISH
INFEST
INFUSE
MUFASA
OAFISH
OFFISH
REFUSE
RIFEST
SAFEST
SUFISM

••F••S

BEFITS
BEFOGS
BOFFOS
BUFFOS
DEFATS
DEFERS
DEFIES
DEFOGS
FIFERS
FIFTHS
GAFFES
GOFERS
INFERS
KAFIRS
KEFIRS
LIFERS
MUFTIS
OFFERS
REFERS
REFITS
RIFLES
RUFOUS
UNFITS
WAFERS

•••F•S

BLUFFS
BOFFOS
BUFFOS
CHAFES
CHAFFS
CLEFTS
CLIFFS
CRAFTS
CROFTS
DELFTS
DOOFUS
DRAFTS
DRIFTS
FLUFFS
GAFFES
GRAFTS
GRIFTS
KNIFES
LOOFAS
QUAFFS
SCIFIS
SCOFFS
SCUFFS
SHAFTS
SHIFTS
SKIFFS
SNAFUS
SNIFFS
SNUFFS
SOLFAS
SPIFFS
STAFFS
STIFFS
STUFFS
SWIFTS
THEFTS
WHIFFS

••••FS

BLUFFS
BRIEFS
CHAFFS
CHIEFS
CLIFFS
DECAFS
DWARFS
FLUFFS
GRIEFS
KLOOFS
MOTIFS
PILAFS
PROOFS
QUAFFS
SCARFS
SCOFFS
SCUFFS
SERIFS
SHEAFS
SKIFFS
SMURFS
SNIFFS
SNUFFS
SPIFFS
SPOOFS
STAFFS
STIFFS
STUFFS
WHARFS
WHIFFS
WHOOFS

FT••••

FTROOP

F•T•••

FATALE
FATCAT
FATHER
FATHOM
FATIMA
FATTED
FATTEN
FATTER
FATWAS
FETING
FETISH
FETTER
FETTLE
FITFUL
FITSIN
FITTED
FITTER
FSTOPS
FUTILE
FUTONS
FUTURE
FUTZED
FUTZES

F••T••

FACTOR
FAITHS
FALTER
FANTAN
FASTED
FASTEN
FASTER
FATTED
FATTEN
FATTER
FEATLY
FELTED
FESTAL
FESTAS
FESTER
FESTUS
FETTER
FETTLE
FIFTHS
FILTER
FILTHY
FIRTHS
FISTED
FISTIC
FITTED
FITTER
FLATLY
FLETCH
FLITCH
FLUTED
FLUTES
FLUTEY
FOETAL
FOETID
FOETOR
FOETUS
FONTAL
FOOTED
FOOTER
FORTAS
FORTES
FOSTER
FRETTY
FRITOS
FROTHS
FROTHY
FRUTTI
FULTON
FUSTIC

F•••T•

FACETS
FAGOTS
FAINTS
FAJITA
FALLTO
FAULTS
FAULTY
FAWLTY
FEALTY
FEASTS
FEINTS
FEISTY
FELLTO
FERITY
FICHTE
FIESTA
FIGHTS
FILETS
FINITE
FINITO
FIRSTS
FIXATE
FIXITY
FLEETS
FLINTS
FLINTY
FLIRTS
FLIRTY
FLOATS
FLOATY
FLOUTS
FOISTS
FOUNTS
FOURTH
FRETTY
FRONTS
FROSTS
FROSTY
FRUITS
FRUITY
FRUTTI

F••••T

FANJET
FANOUT
FAROUT
FATCAT
FAUCET
FERMAT
FERRET
FEWEST
FEYEST
FIDGET
FILLET
FINEST
FLAUNT
FLEWAT
FLIGHT
FLORET
FLUENT
FLYNET
FLYOUT
FOGHAT
FOMENT
FOREST
FORGET
FORGOT
FORINT
FORMAT
FOUGHT
FREEST
FRIGHT

•F••T•

AFLATS
AFRITS
EFFETE
EFLATS
OFLATE

•F•••T

AFFECT
AFLOAT
AFREET
EFFECT
EFFORT
OFFSET

••FT••

CAFTAN
DAFTER
DAFTLY
DEFTER
DEFTLY
FIFTHS
GIFTED
HAFTED
HEFTED
LEFTIE
LEFTIN
LIFTED
LIFTER
LIFTUP
LOFTED
MUFTIS
RAFTED
RAFTER
RIFTED
SIFTED
SIFTER
SOFTEN
SOFTER
SOFTIE
SOFTLY
TUFTED
WAFTED
ZAFTIG

••F•T•

BEFITS
DEFATS
EFFETE
REFITS
REFUTE
SAFETY
UNFITS

••F••T

AFFECT
AJFOYT
AUFAIT
BUFFET
DEFEAT
DEFECT
EFFECT
EFFORT
ENFANT
ERFURT
INFACT
INFANT
INFECT
INFEST
OFFSET
ONFOOT
RIFEST
SAFEST
SOFFIT
TUFFET

•••FT•

CLEFTS
CRAFTS
CRAFTY
CROFTS
DELFTS
DRAFTS
DRAFTY
DRIFTS
DRIFTY
GRAFTS
GRIFTS
SHAFTS
SHIFTS
SHIFTY
SWIFTS
THEFTS

•••F•T

ARAFAT
BUFFET
COMFIT
HOOFIT
LOWFAT
MISFIT
NONFAT
OUTFIT
PROFIT
SAWFIT
SEEFIT
SOFFIT
TUFFET

••••FT

ADRIFT
BEREFT
GOSOFT
SHRIFT
THRIFT
UPLIFT

FU••••

FUBBED
FUDDLE
FUDGED
FUDGES
FUELED
FUELER
FUGARD
FUGUES
FUJIAN
FULANI
FULCRA
FULFIL
FULLER
FULMAR
FULTON
FUMBLE
FUMIER
FUMING
FUNDED
FUNGUS
FUNKED
FUNNED
FUNNEL
FURIES
FURLED
FURORE
FURORS
FURRED
FURROW
FURZES
FUSEES
FUSILS
FUSING
FUSION
FUSSED
FUSSES
FUSTIC
FUTILE
FUTONS
FUTURE
FUTZED
FUTZES
FUZEES
FUZHOU
FUZING
FUZZED
FUZZES

F•U•••

FAUCES
FAUCET
FAULTS
FAULTY
FAUNAE
FAUNAL
FAUNAS
FAUNUS
FEUDAL
FEUDED
FLUENT
FLUFFS
FLUFFY
FLUIDS
FLUKES
FLUKEY
FLUMES
FLUNKS
FLUNKY
FLUORO
FLURRY
FLUTED
FLUTES
FLUTEY
FLUXED
FLUXES
FOUGHT
FOULED
FOULER
FOULLY
FOULUP
FOUNDS
FOUNTS
FOURAM
FOURPM
FOURTH
FRUGAL
FRUITS
FRUITY
FRUMPS
FRUMPY
FRUTTI

F••U••

FACULA
FECUND
FEMURS
FERULE
FIBULA
FIGURE
FIXUPS
FLAUNT
FLEURY
FLOURS
FLOURY
FLOUTS
FORUMS
FRAUDS
FRAUEN
FUGUES
FUTURE

F•••U•

FACEUP
FAIRUP
FAIYUM
FAMOUS
FANOUT
FAROUK
FAROUT
FAUNUS
FAVOUR
FERGUS
FESCUE
FESSUP
FESTUS
FICHUS
FILIUS
FILLUP
FIREUP
FIRMUP
FITFUL
FLIPUP
FLYOUT
FOETUS

FOGSUP
FOLDUP
FOLIUM
FONDUE
FOULUP
FRENUM
FUNGUS

F••••U
FUZHOU

•F•U••
EFFUSE

•F••U•
EFFLUX

••FU••
DEFUSE
EFFUSE
ERFURT
INFULL
INFUSE
MIFUNE
REFUEL
REFUGE
REFUND
REFUSE
REFUTE
UNFURL

••F•U•
BEFOUL
EFFLUX
INFLUX
LIFTUP
REFLUX
RUFOUS

•••FU•
AIDFUL
AIMFUL
ARMFUL
ARTFUL
BAGFUL
BEEFUP
BOXFUL
CANFUL
CAPFUL
CARFUL
CUPFUL
DOOFUS
EARFUL
EYEFUL
FITFUL
GOOFUP
HATFUL
IREFUL
JARFUL
JOYFUL
JUGFUL
LAPFUL
LAWFUL
MANFUL
PANFUL
PEPFUL
POTFUL
RUEFUL
SINFUL
SNAFUS
SOBFUL
SULFUR
USEFUL
VATFUL
WILFUL
WOEFUL

••••FU
KUNGFU

F•V•••
FAVORS
FAVOUR
FEVERS
FIVEAM
FIVEPM
FIVERS
FIVEWS
FOVEAE

F••V••
FERVID
FERVOR
FLAVIA
FLAVOR

••FV••
ALFVEN

F•W•••
FAWKES
FAWLTY
FAWNED
FAWNER
FEWEST
FOWLED
FOWLER
FOWLES

F••W••
FATWAS
FENWAY
FLAWED
FLEWAT
FLEWIN
FLOWED
FLOWER
FLYWAY
FROWNS
FROWZY

F•••W•
FIVEWS

F••••W
FALLOW
FARLOW
FARROW
FELLOW
FOGBOW
FOLLOW
FURROW

••F••W
GUFFAW
INFLOW

•••F•W
CURFEW
GUFFAW

F•X•••
FAXING
FIXATE
FIXERS
FIXING
FIXITY
FIXUPS
FOXIER
FOXILY
FOXING

F••X••
FLAXEN
FLAXES
FLEXED
FLEXES
FLEXOR
FLUXED
FLUXES

•F•••X
EFFLUX

••F••X
EFFLUX
INFLUX
REFLEX
REFLUX
SUFFIX

•••F•X
COLFAX
INAFIX
KITFOX
KOUFAX
OUTFOX
PREFIX
REDFOX
SEAFOX
SUFFIX

FY••••
FYODOR

F•Y•••
FEYEST
FLYBOY
FLYBYS
FLYERS
FLYING
FLYINS
FLYMAN
FLYMEN
FLYNET
FLYOUT
FLYROD
FLYWAY
FOYERS
FRYERS
FRYING
FRYPAN

F••Y••
FAIYUM
FLAYED
FLAYER
FLEYED
FRAYED

F•••Y•
FLYBYS
FOGEYS
FORAYS

F••••Y
FABRAY
FAIRLY
FAKERY
FAMILY
FARCRY
FARLEY
FAULTY
FAWLTY
FEALTY
FEATLY
FEEBLY
FEISTY
FELONY
FENWAY
FERITY
FILTHY
FINELY
FINERY
FINNEY
FIRMLY
FIXITY
FLABBY
FLAGGY
FLAKEY
FLAPPY
FLASHY
FLATLY
FLECKY
FLEDGY
FLEECY
FLESHY
FLEURY
FLIMSY
FLINTY
FLIRTY
FLOATY
FLOCKY
FLOOEY
FLOPPY
FLOPSY
FLOSSY
FLOURY
FLUFFY
FLUKEY
FLUNKY
FLURRY
FLUTEY
FLYBOY
FLYWAY
FOLKSY
FONDLY
FOSSEY
FOULLY
FOXILY
FRAIDY
FRANNY
FREAKY
FREDDY
FREELY
FRENZY
FRETTY
FRIARY
FRIDAY
FRILLY
FRINGY
FRISKY
FRIZZY
FROGGY
FROSTY
FROTHY
FROWZY
FRUITY
FRUMPY

•F•••Y
AFFRAY
EFFIGY
OFFDAY
OFFKEY

••F•Y•
AJFOYT

••F••Y
AFFRAY
DAFTLY
DEFRAY
DEFTLY
EFFIGY
INFAMY
OFFDAY
OFFKEY
RIFELY
RUFFLY
SAFELY
SAFETY
SOFTLY
WAFERY
WAFFLY
WIFELY

•••F•Y
BARFLY
BELFRY
BOTFLY
CHAFFY
CHUFFY
CLIFFY
CRAFTY
DEAFLY
DRAFTY
DRIFTY
DRYFLY
DURFEY
FLUFFY
GADFLY
LETFLY
LIEFLY
MAYFLY
MEDFLY
OUTFLY
PANFRY
POPFLY
RUFFLY
SHIFTY
SNIFFY
SNUFFY
SPIFFY
STEFOY
STUFFY
THEFLY
WAFFLY
WETFLY

••••FY
AERIFY
ARGUFY
AURIFY
BASIFY
CASEFY
CHAFFY
CHUFFY
CITIFY
CLIFFY
CODIFY
FLUFFY
GASIFY
MINIFY
MODIFY
NIDIFY
NOTIFY
OSSIFY
PACIFY
PURIFY
RAMIFY
RAREFY
RARIFY
RATIFY
RUBIFY
SALIFY
SCURFY
SNIFFY
SNUFFY
SPIFFY
STUFFY
TUMEFY
TYPIFY
UGLIFY
VERIFY
VILIFY
VINIFY
VIVIFY

F•Z•••
FAZING
FAZOOL
FEZZAN
FEZZES
FIZGIG
FIZZED
FIZZES
FIZZLE
FOZZIE
FUZEES
FUZHOU
FUZING
FUZZED
FUZZES

F••Z••
FEZZAN
FEZZES
FIZZED
FIZZES
FIZZLE
FOOZLE
FOZZIE
FRAZER
FRIZZY
FROZEN
FURZES
FUTZED
FUTZES
FUZZED
FUZZES

F•••Z•
FAENZA
FREEZE
FRENZY
FRIEZE
FRIZZY
FROWZY

•F•Z••
PFIZER

•F••Z•
SFORZA

GA••••
GABBED
GABBER
GABBLE
GABBRO
GABIES
GABION
GABLED
GABLER
GABLES
GADDED
GADDER
GADFLY
GADGET
GAELIC
GAFFED
GAFFER
GAFFES
GAGGED
GAGGLE
GAGING
GAGLAW
GAGMAN
GAGMEN
GAIETY
GAIJIN
GAINED
GAINER
GAINLY
GAINON
GAINST
GAITED
GAITER
GALAGO
GALAHS
GALATA
GALAXY
GALEAE
GALENA
GALLED
GALLEY
GALLIA
GALLIC
GALLON
GALLOP
GALLUP
GALOIS
GALOOT
GALOPS
GALORE
GALOSH
GALPAL
GALWAY
GALYAK
GAMAYS
GAMBIA
GAMBIT
GAMBLE
GAMBOL
GAMELY
GAMEST
GAMETE
GAMIER
GAMILY
GAMINE
GAMING
GAMINS
GAMMAS
GAMMED
GAMMER
GAMMON
GAMUTS
GANDER
GANDHI
GANGED
GANGER
GANGES
GANGLE
GANGLY
GANGUE
GANGUP
GANNET
GANTRY
GAOLED
GAOLER
GAPERS
GAPING
GAPPED
GARAGE
GARBED
GARBLE
GARCIA
GARCON
GARDEN
GARETH
GARGLE
GARISH
GARLIC
GARNER
GARNET
GARRET
GARSON
GARTER
GARTHS
GARVEY
GASBAG
GASCAP
GASCON
GASHED
GASHES
GASIFY
GASJET
GASKET
GASKIN
GASLIT
GASLOG
GASMAN
GASMEN
GASPAR
GASPED
GASPER
GASSED
GASSER
GASSES
GASTON
GASTRO
GATEAU
GATERS
GATHER
GATING
GATLIN
GATORS
GATSBY
GAUCHE
GAUCHO
GAUGED
GAUGER
GAUGES
GAUMED
GAUZES
GAVEIN
GAVELS
GAVEUP
GAVIAL
GAWAIN
GAWKED
GAWKER
GAWPED
GAYALS
GAYEST
GAYNOR
GAZEBO
GAZING
GAZUMP

G•A•••
GDANSK
GEARED
GEARTO
GEARUP
GHAINS
GHARRY
GHAZIS
GIANTS
GLACES
GLACIS
GLADES
GLADLY
GLADYS
GLAIRS
GLAIRY
GLAMOR
GLANCE
GLANDS
GLARED
GLARES
GLASER
GLASSY
GLAZED
GLAZER
GLAZES
GMAJOR
GNARLS
GNARLY
GNATTY
GNAWED
GNAWER
GOADED
GOALIE
GOANNA
GOATEE
GOAWAY
GOAWRY
GRABAT

GRABBY GRABEN GRABLE GRACED GRACES GRACIE GRADEA GRADED GRADER GRADES GRADIN GRADUS GRAECO GRAFTS GRAHAM GRAILS GRAINS GRAINY GRAMAS GRAMME GRAMMY GRAMPA GRAMPS GRANDE GRANDS GRANGE GRANNY GRANTS GRAPES GRAPEY GRAPHS GRAPHY GRAPPA GRASPS GRASSO GRASSY GRATED GRATER GRATES GRATIA GRATIN GRATIS GRAVED GRAVEL GRAVEN GRAVER GRAVES GRAVID GRAYED GRAYER GRAYLY GRAZED GRAZER GRAZES GUACOS GUARDS GUAVAS

G••A••

GALAGO GALAHS GALATA GALAXY GAMAYS GARAGE GAWAIN GAYALS GELADA GELATI GELATO GEMARA GERAHS GERALD GERARD GIRARD GITANO GLEAMS GLEAMY GLEANS GLOATS GOBACK GOCART GODARD GOEASY GOKART GORALS GREASE GREASY GREATS GREAVE GROANS GROATS GSHARP GSTAAD GUIANA GULAGS GUYANA GYRATE

G•••A•

GAGLAW GAGMAN GALEAE GALPAL GALWAY GALYAK GAMMAS GASBAG GASCAP GASMAN GASPAR GATEAU GAVIAL GEEGAW GEMMAE GENIAL GENOAN GENUAL GERMAN GETMAD GETSAT GEWGAW GIBRAN GILEAD GIMBAL GLOBAL GOAWAY GOESAT GOSTAG GOTHAM GOTMAD GRABAT GRAHAM GRAMAS GSTAAD GUAVAS GUFFAW GUITAR GULLAH GUNMAN GUNNAR GUSTAV GUTTAE GYMBAG

G••••A

GALATA GALENA GALLIA GAMBIA GARCIA GEISHA GELADA GEMARA GENERA GENEVA GEZIRA GLENDA GLINKA GLORIA GLOSSA GOANNA GODIVA GOTCHA GRADEA GRAMPA GRAPPA GRATIA GRETNA GUIANA GUINEA GURKHA GUYANA

•GA•••

AGADIR AGAMAS AGARIC AGASSI AGATES AGATHA AGAVES UGANDA

•G•A••

AGHAST AGLAIA AGLARE AGNATE IGNACE IGNATZ IGUACU IGUANA OGHAMS OGLALA UGGAMS

•G••A•

AGAMAS AGENAS AGLEAM AGORAE AGORAS OGDOAD SGTMAJ UGRIAN

•G•••A

AGATHA AGENDA AGLAIA EGERIA EGESTA IGUANA OGLALA UGANDA

••GA••

ARGALI ASGARD BIGAMY BOGART CIGARS DAGAMA DEGAGE EDGARD EDGARS ENGAGE ERGATE FIGARO FUGARD HEGARI HOGANS KIGALI LAGASH LEGACY LEGALS LEGATE LEGATO LIGAND LIGATE MEGALO MEGARA MUGABE NAGANO NEGATE ORGANA ORGANS ORGATE PAGANS REGAIN REGALE REGARD RUGATE SUGARS SUGARY TOGAED UGGAMS VAGARY VEGANS

••G•A•

AEGEAN AFGHAN AUGEAN BAGDAD BEGGAR BIGMAC CAGUAS COGNAC DAGMAR DIGRAM DOGDAY DOGEAR DOGMAS DOGSAT DOGTAG ENGRAM FOGHAT GAGLAW GAGMAN HAGMAN INGEAR INGMAR INGRAM JAGUAR JIGSAW LEGMAN LOGJAM MAGMAS MAGYAR MCGRAW ORGEAT RAGBAG RAGLAN RAGMAN RAGTAG REGGAE REGNAL REGNAT SIGMAS SIGNAL TAGDAY UNGUAL WIGWAG WIGWAM ZIGZAG

••G••A

ANGELA ANGLIA ANGOLA ANGORA BOGOTA DAGAMA HEGIRA KAGERA LAGUNA LIGULA LOGGIA MEGARA NAGOYA ORGANA PAGODA REGINA SEGURA VIGODA

•••GA•

ALEGAR AMIGAS ANSGAR BEGGAR BENGAL BENGAY BIOGAS BROGAN BULGAR BURGAS CONGAS COOGAN COUGAR FRUGAL GEEGAW GEWGAW HANGAR KURGAN LONGAN MARGAY MEDGAR MORGAN NILGAI NORGAY NOUGAT OMEGAS PISGAH PLAGAL REAGAN REGGAE SAIGAS SEAGAL SLOGAN TAIGAS TONGAN VULGAR

•••G•A

BANGKA BORGIA ENIGMA LINGUA LOGGIA QUAGGA STIGMA ZEUGMA

••••GA

AURIGA BELUGA BODEGA CAYUGA LADOGA MALAGA ORTEGA PAANGA PERUGA QUAGGA SENEGA

G•B•••

GABBED GABBER GABBLE GABBRO GABIES GABION GABLED GABLER GABLES GIBBED GIBBER GIBBET GIBBON GIBERS GIBILL GIBING GIBLET GIBRAN GIBSON GOBACK GOBBLE GOBIES GOBLET GOBLIN GOBUST GYBING

G••B••

GABBED GABBER GABBLE GABBRO GAMBIA GAMBIT GAMBLE GAMBOL GARBED GARBLE GASBAG GERBER GERBIL GIBBED GIBBER GIBBET GIBBON GIMBAL GIMBEL GLEBES GLIBLY GLOBAL GLOBED GLOBES GLOBIN GOBBLE GOOBER GRABAT GRABBY GRABEN GRABLE GREBES GRUBBY GUMBEL GUMBOS GYMBAG

G•••B•

GATSBY GAZEBO GETSBY GOESBY GONEBY GOODBY GRABBY GRUBBY

•GB•••

EGBERT

••GB••

BIGBEN BIGBOY FOGBOW RAGBAG

••G•B•

MUGABE

••G••B

ZAGREB

•••GB•

NINGBO

G•C•••

GECKOS GOCART

G••C••

GARCIA GARCON GASCAP GASCON GAUCHE GAUCHO GLACES GLACIS GLYCOL GOTCHA GRACED GRACES GRACIE GROCER GUACOS

G•••C•

GLANCE GLITCH GOBACK GRAECO GREECE GRINCH GROUCH

G••••C

GAELIC GALLIC GARLIC GESTIC GNOMIC GOTHIC

•G•C••

EGGCUP

•G••C•

AGENCY IGNACE IGUACU

•G•••C

AGARIC

••GC••

EGGCUP

••G•C•

LEGACY

••G••C

ANGLIC BIGMAC COGNAC

•••G•C

TRAGIC

GD••••

GDANSK

G•D•••

GADDED GADDER GADFLY GADGET GIDEON GIDGET GODARD GODETS GODIVA GODOWN GODSON GODWIN GODWIT GUDRUN

G••D••

GADDED GADDER GANDER GANDHI GARDEN GENDER GEODES GILDED GILDER GIRDED GIRDER GIRDLE GLADES GLADLY GLADYS GLIDED GLIDER GLIDES GOADED GOLDEN GOLDIE GOODBY GOODEN GOODIE GOODLY GOODOH GORDIE GORDON GRADEA GRADED GRADER GRADES GRADIN GRADUS GRODIN GRODNO GRUDGE GUIDED GUIDES GUIDON GUNDOG

G•••D•

GELADA GLANDS GLENDA GOURDE GOURDS GRANDE GRANDS GREEDY GRINDS GRUNDY GUARDS GUILDS

G••••D

GABBED GABLED GADDED GAFFED GAGGED GAINED GAITED

GALLED
GAMMED
GANGED
GAOLED
GAPPED
GARBED
GASHED
GASPED
GASSED
GAUGED
GAUMED
GAWKED
GAWPED
GEARED
GELLED
GEMMED
GERALD
GERARD
GERUND
GETMAD
GIBBED
GIFTED
GIGGED
GILDED
GILEAD
GILLED
GINNED
GIPPED
GIRARD
GIRDED
GIRNED
GIRTED
GLARED
GLAZED
GLIDED
GLOBED
GLOVED
GLOWED
GLOZED
GNAWED
GOADED
GODARD
GOLFED
GONGED
GOOFED
GOOSED
GORGED
GOTMAD
GOUGED
GOUNOD
GOWILD
GOWNED
GRACED
GRADED
GRATED
GRAVED
GRAVID
GRAYED
GRAZED
GREYED
GRIMED
GRIPED
GROPED
GROUND
GSTAAD
GUIDED
GULFED
GULLED
GULPED
GUMMED
GUNNED
GUSHED
GUSTED
GUTTED
GYPPED

•GD•••

OGDOAD

•G•D••

AGADIR

•G••D•

AGENDA
UGANDA

•G•••D

AGEOLD
AGREED
OGDOAD

••GD••

BAGDAD
DOGDAY
DOGDOM
HAGDON
TAGDAY

••G•D•

PAGODA
VIGODA

••G••D

ANGLED
ARGUED
ASGARD
AUGEND
BAGDAD
BAGGED
BEGGED
BIGRED
BOGGED
BUGGED
BUGLED
COGGED
DOGGED
DOGOOD
EAGLED
EDGARD
ENGIRD
FAGEND
FAGGED
FOGGED
FUGARD
GAGGED
GIGGED
HOGGED
HUGGED
INGRID
JAGGED
JIGGED
JOGGED
JUGGED
KEGGED
LAGGED
LEGEND
LEGGED
LIGAND
LOGGED
LUGGED
MUGGED
NAGGED
NOGOOD
OSGOOD
PEGGED
PIGGED
PUGGED
RAGGED
REGARD
RIGGED
RUGGED
SAGGED
SEGUED
SIGHED
SIGNED
SIGURD
TAGEND
TAGGED
TOGAED
TOGGED
TUGGED
UNGIRD
VEGGED
WAGGED
WIGGED
ZAGGED
ZIGGED

•••G•D

BAGGED
BANGED
BARGED
BEGGED
BINGED
BOGGED
BONGED
BRIGID
BUDGED
BUGGED
BULGED
BUNGED
CADGED
COGGED
DINGED
DODGED
DOGGED
FAGGED
FANGED
FOGGED
FORGED
FRIGID
FUDGED
GAGGED
GANGED
GAUGED
GIGGED
GONGED
GORGED
GOUGED
HANGED
HEDGED
HINGED
HOGGED
HUGGED
IMAGED
JAGGED
JIGGED
JOGGED
JUDGED
JUGGED
KEDGED
KEGGED
KINGED
LAGGED
LEGGED
LODGED
LOGGED
LONGED
LUGGED
LUNGED
MERGED
MUGGED
NAGGED
NUDGED
PEGGED
PIGGED
PINGED
PONGED
PONGID
PUGGED
PURGED
RAGGED
RANGED
RIDGED
RIGGED
RINGED
ROUGED
RUGGED
SAGGED
SIEGED
SINGED
STAGED
SUNGOD
SURGED
SWAGED
TAGGED
TANGED
TINGED
TINGOD
TOGGED
TUGGED
TURGID
UNAGED
VEGGED
VERGED
WAGGED
WARGOD
WEDGED
WIGGED
WINGED
ZAGGED
ZIGGED
ZINGED

GE••••

GEARED
GEARTO
GEARUP
GECKOS
GEEGAW
GEEGEE
GEEING
GEEZER
GEHRIG
GEIGER
GEISEL
GEISHA
GELADA
GELATI
GELATO
GELEES
GELLED
GELSEY
GEMARA
GEMINI
GEMMAE
GEMMED
GEMOTE
GEMOTS
GENDER
GENERA
GENETS
GENEVA
GENEVE
GENIAL
GENIES
GENIUS
GENOAN
GENOME
GENRES
GENTLE
GENTLY
GENTRY
GENUAL
GEODES
GEORGE
GEORGY
GERAHS
GERALD
GERARD
GERBER
GERBIL
GERENT
GERMAN
GERONT
GERTIE
GERUND
GESTES
GESTIC
GETMAD
GETOFF
GETOUT
GETSAT
GETSBY
GETSET
GETSIN
GETSIT
GETSON
GETSTO
GETSUP
GETTER
GETUPS
GEWGAW
GEYSER
GEZIRA

G•E•••

GAELIC
GEEGAW
GEEGEE
GEEING
GEEZER
GHETTO
GLEAMS
GLEAMY
GLEANS
GLEBES
GLENDA
GLENNE
GNEISS
GOEASY
GOESAT
GOESBY
GOESIN
GOESON
GOESUP
GOETHE
GREASE
GREASY
GREATS
GREAVE
GREBES
GREECE
GREEDY
GREEKS
GREENE
GREENS
GREENY
GREETS
GREGOR
GREIGE
GRETEL
GRETNA
GREWON
GREWUP
GREYED
GREYER
GREYLY
GUELPH
GUENON
GUERRE
GUESTS

G••E••

GAIETY
GALEAE
GALENA
GAMELY
GAMEST
GAMETE
GAPERS
GARETH
GATEAU
GATERS
GAVEIN
GAVELS
GAVEUP
GAYEST
GAZEBO
GELEES
GENERA
GENETS
GENEVA
GENEVE
GERENT
GIBERS
GIDEON
GILEAD
GIMELS
GIVEIN
GIVENS
GIVERS
GIVETO
GIVEUP
GLUERS
GODETS
GOFERS
GOLEMS
GONEBY
GONERS
GOVERN
GOWEST
GRAECO
GREECE
GREEDY
GREEKS
GREENE
GREENS
GREENY
GREETS
GRIEFS
GRIEVE
GRUELS
GYRENE

G•••E•

GABBED
GABBER
GABIES
GABLED
GABLER
GABLES
GADDED
GADDER
GADGET
GAFFED
GAFFER
GAFFES
GAGGED
GAGMEN
GAINED
GAINER
GAITED
GAITER
GALLED
GALLEY
GAMIER
GAMMED
GAMMER
GANDER
GANGED
GANGER
GANGES
GANNET
GAOLED
GAOLER
GAPPED
GARBED
GARDEN
GARNER
GARNET
GARRET
GARTER
GARVEY
GASHED
GASHES
GASJET
GASKET
GASMEN
GASPED
GASPER
GASSED
GASSER
GASSES
GATHER
GAUGED
GAUGER
GAUGES
GAUMED
GAUZES
GAWKED
GAWKER
GAWPED
GEARED
GEEGEE
GEEZER
GEIGER
GEISEL
GELEES
GELLED
GELSEY
GEMMED
GENDER
GENIES
GENRES
GEODES
GERBER
GESTES
GETSET
GETTER
GEYSER
GIBBED
GIBBER
GIBBET
GIBLET
GIDGET
GIFTED
GIGGED
GIGUES
GIJOES
GILDED
GILDER
GILLED
GIMBEL
GIMLET
GIMMES
GINGER
GINNED
GIPPED
GIPPER
GIRDED
GIRDER
GIRNED
GIRTED
GLACES
GLADES
GLARED
GLARES
GLASER
GLAZED
GLAZER
GLAZES
GLEBES
GLIDED
GLIDER
GLIDES
GLOBED
GLOBES
GLOVED
GLOVER
GLOVES
GLOWED
GLOWER
GLOZED
GLOZES
GLUIER
GLUTEI
GLUTEN
GLUTES
GNAWED
GNAWER
GNOMES
GOADED
GOATEE
GOBIES
GOBLET
GOLDEN
GOLFED
GOLFER
GONGED
GOOBER
GOODEN
GOOFED
GOOIER
GOOSED
GOOSES
GOOSEY
GOOVER
GOPHER
GORGED
GORGES
GORGET
GORIER
GORSES
GOSHEN
GOSPEL
GOTSET
GOTTEN
GOUGED
GOUGER
GOUGES
GOULET
GOWNED
GRABEN
GRACED
GRACES
GRADEA
GRADED
GRADER
GRADES
GRAPES
GRAPEY
GRATED
GRATER
GRATES
GRAVED
GRAVEL
GRAVEN
GRAVER
GRAVES
GRAYED
GRAYER
GRAZED
GRAZER
GRAZES
GREBES
GRETEL
GREYED
GREYER
GRIMED
GRIMES
GRIPED
GRIPER
GRIPES
GRIVET
GROCER
GROPED
GROPES
GROVEL
GROVER

GROVES
GROWER
GUIDED
GUIDES
GUILES
GUINEA
GUISES
GULFED
GULLED
GULLET
GULPED
GULPER
GUMBEL
GUMMED
GUNMEN
GUNNED
GUNNEL
GUNNER
GUNTER
GURLEY
GURNEY
GUSHED
GUSHER
GUSHES
GUSSET
GUSTED
GUTTED
GUTTER
GYPPED
GYPPER

G••••E

GABBLE
GAGGLE
GALEAE
GALORE
GAMBLE
GAMETE
GAMINE
GANGLE
GANGUE
GARAGE
GARBLE
GARGLE
GAUCHE
GEEGEE
GEMMAE
GEMOTE
GENEVE
GENOME
GENTLE
GEORGE
GERTIE
GIGGLE
GILLIE
GIRDLE
GLANCE
GLENNE
GOALIE
GOATEE
GOBBLE
GOETHE
GOGGLE
GOHOME
GOLDIE
GOODIE
GOOGLE
GORDIE
GOURDE
GRABLE
GRACIE
GRAMME
GRANDE
GRANGE
GREASE
GREAVE
GREECE
GREENE
GREIGE
GRIEVE
GRILLE
GRILSE
GRIMKE
GRIPPE
GROOVE
GROSSE
GROUSE
GRUDGE
GRUNGE
GUERRE
GUIMPE
GUNITE
GURGLE
GUTTAE
GUZZLE
GWYNNE
GYRATE
GYRENE
GYROSE

•GE•••

AGEING
AGEISM
AGEIST
AGENAS
AGENCY
AGENDA
AGENTS
AGEOLD
EGERIA
EGESTA
EGESTS
IGETIT

•G•E••

AGLEAM
AGLETS
AGREED
AGREES
EGBERT
EGRESS
EGRETS
OGLERS
OGRESS

•G••E•

AGATES
AGAVES
AGGIES
AGREED
AGREES
EGGIER
NGUYEN
OGIVES
UGLIER
UGLIES

•G•••E

AGLARE
AGNATE
AGORAE
IGNACE
IGNITE
IGNORE
UGSOME

••GE••

AEGEAN
ANGELA
ANGELI
ANGELL
ANGELO
ANGELS
ANGERS
ARGENT
AUGEAN
AUGEND
AUGERS
BAGELS
BEGETS
BOGEYS
CAGERS
COGENT
DIGEST
DOGEAR
DOGEYS
EDGEIN
EDGERS
ENGELS
EUGENE
FAGEND
FOGEYS
HUGELY
HUGEST
INGEAR
INGEST
KAGERA
LAGERS
LEGEND
LIGERS
LUGERS
NUGENT
ORGEAT
PAGERS
PIGEON
REGENT
ROGERS
SAGELY
SAGEST
TAGEND
TIGERS
URGENT
URGERS
WAGERS

••G•E•

AGGIES
AIGRET
ANGLED
ANGLER
ANGLES
ARGUED
ARGUER
ARGUES
BAGGED
BAGGER
BEGGED
BEGLEY
BIGBEN
BIGGER
BIGRED
BIGTEN
BOGGED
BOGIES
BOGLES
BUGGED
BUGLED
BUGLER
BUGLES
CAGIER
CAGNEY
COGGED
CYGNET
DAGGER
DEGREE
DIGGER
DOGGED
DOGGER
DOGIES
DOGLEG
EAGLED
EAGLES
EAGLET
EAGRES
EDGIER
EGGIER
FAGGED
FOGGED
FOGGER
FOGIES
FUGUES
GAGGED
GAGMEN
GIGGED
GIGUES
HIGHER
HOGGED
HOGGET
HUGGED
HUGGER
HUGHES
INGLES
INGRES
JAGGED
JAGGER
JIGGED
JIGGER
JOGGED
JOGGER
JUGGED
KEGGED
KEGLER
LAGGED
LAGGER
LEGGED
LEGMEN
LEGREE
LOGGED
LOGGER
LOGIER
LUGGED
LUGGER
MAGNET
MAGUEY
MCGREW
MIGUEL
MUGGED
MUGGER
NAGGED
NAGGER
NIGHER
NUGGET
ORGIES
PEGGED
PEGLER
PIGGED
PIGLET
PIGPEN
POGIES
PUGGED
PUGREE
RAGGED
RAGMEN
REGLET
REGRET
RIGGED
RIGGER
ROGUES
RUGGED
SAGGED
SEGUED
SEGUES
SIGHED
SIGHER
SIGNED
SIGNEE
SIGNER
SIGNET
TAGGED
TIGGER
TOGAED
TOGGED
TUGGED
TUGGER
UNGUES
VAGUER
VEGGED
VOGUES
WAGGED
WAGNER
WIGGED
WIGLET
ZAGGED
ZAGREB
ZIGGED

••G••E

ALGORE
ARGIVE
ARGYLE
BAGGIE
BEGONE
BIGGIE
BIGLIE
BIGTOE
BOGGLE
BYGONE
DEGAGE
DEGREE
DOGGIE
ENGAGE
ENGINE
ERGATE
EUGENE
FIGURE
GAGGLE
GIGGLE
GOGGLE
HAGGLE
HIGGLE
HOGTIE
JIGGLE
JOGGLE
JUGGLE
LEGATE
LEGREE
LEGUME
LIGATE
LIGURE
MAGGIE
MAGPIE
MIGGLE
MUGABE
NEGATE
NIGGLE
ORGATE
PIGGIE
PUGREE
REGALE
REGGAE
REGGIE
REGIME
REGLUE
RUGATE
RUGOSE
SIGNEE
TAGORE
TOGGLE
UNGLUE
VEGGIE
WAGGLE
WIGGLE
ZYGOTE

•••GE•

ADAGES
APOGEE
BADGER
BADGES
BAGGED
BAGGER
BANGED
BANGER
BARGED
BARGES
BEGGED
BEIGES
BERGEN
BIGGER
BILGES
BINGED
BINGES
BOGGED
BOLGER
BONGED
BRUGES
BUDGED
BUDGES
BUDGET
BUGGED
BULGED
BULGES
BUNGED
BUNGEE
BURGEE
BURGER
CADGED
CADGER
CADGES
CODGER
COGGED
CONGER
CUDGEL
DAGGER
DANGER
DIGGER
DINGED
DIRGES
DODGED
DODGER
DODGES
DOGGED
DOGGER
DRAGEE
FAGGED
FANGED
FIDGET
FINGER
FOGGED
FOGGER
FORGED
FORGER
FORGES
FORGET
FUDGED
FUDGES
GADGET
GAGGED
GANGED
GANGER
GANGES
GAUGED
GAUGER
GAUGES
GEEGEE
GEIGER
GIDGET
GIGGED
GINGER
GONGED
GORGED
GORGES
GORGET
GOUGED
GOUGER
GOUGES
HANGED
HANGER
HEDGED
HEDGER
HEDGES
HINGED
HINGES
HODGES
HOGGED
HOGGET
HUGGED
HUGGER
HUNGER
IMAGED
IMAGER
IMAGES
IMOGEN
JAEGER
JAGGED
JAGGER
JIGGED
JIGGER
JOGGED
JOGGER
JUDGED
JUDGES
JUGGED
KEDGED
KEDGES
KEGGED
KINGED
KRUGER
LAAGER
LAGGED
LAGGER
LARGER
LARGES
LEDGER
LEDGES
LEGGED
LIEGES
LINGER
LODGED
LODGER
LODGES
LOGGED
LOGGER
LONGED
LONGER
LONGES
LUGGED
LUGGER
LUNGED
LUNGES
MAJGEN
MANGER
MARGES
MEAGER
MERGED
MERGER
MERGES
MIDGES
MIDGET
MONGER
MORGEN
MUGGED
MUGGER
NAGGED
NAGGER
NUDGED
NUDGER
NUDGES
NUGGET
ONAGER
ORIGEN
OSAGES
OXYGEN
PARGET
PEGGED
PHAGES
PIAGET
PIGGED
PINGED
PLAGES
PONGED
PONGEE
PUGGED
PURGED
PURGES
RAGGED
RANGED
RANGER
RANGES
RIDGED
RIDGES
RIGGED
RIGGER
RINGED
RINGER
ROUGED
ROUGES
RUGGED
RUTGER
SAGGED
SANGER
SARGES
SAUGER
SEDGES
SEEGER
SERGEI
SERGES
SIEGED
SIEGEL
SIEGES
SINGED
SINGER
SINGES
STAGED
STAGER
STAGES
SURGED
SURGES
SWAGED
SWAGES
TAGGED
TANGED
TARGES
TARGET
TIGGER
TINGED
TINGES
TOGGED
TUGGED
TUGGER
UNAGED
USAGES
VEGGED
VERGED
VERGER
VERGES
VOSGES
WAGGED
WEDGED
WEDGES
WIDGET
WIGGED
WINGED
WINGER
WODGES
YEAGER
ZAGGED
ZENGER
ZIGGED
ZINGED
ZINGER

•••G•E

ALEGRE
APOGEE
BAGGIE
BANGLE
BEAGLE
BIGGIE

BOGGLE
BOOGIE
BROGUE
BUDGIE
BUNGEE
BUNGLE
BURGEE
BURGLE
CHIGOE
DANGLE
DANGME
DENGUE
DINGLE
DOGGIE
DONGLE
DOOGIE
DRAGEE
DROGUE
EMIGRE
FERGIE
GAGGLE
GANGLE
GANGUE
GARGLE
GEEGEE
GIGGLE
GOGGLE
GOOGLE
GURGLE
HAGGLE
HIGGLE
HOAGIE
JANGLE
JIGGLE
JINGLE
JOGGLE
JUGGLE
JUNGLE
KINGME
LEAGUE
LONGUE
MAGGIE
MANGLE
MARGIE
MEAGRE
MIGGLE
MINGLE
NIGGLE
PIGGIE
PLAGUE
PONGEE
PRAGUE
REGGAE
REGGIE
SINGLE
SOIGNE
STOGIE
TANGLE
TINGLE
TOGGLE
TONGUE
VEGGIE
WAGGLE
WANGLE
WEDGIE
WIGGLE
WOOGIE

••••GE
ALLEGE
AVENGE
BAREGE
BORAGE
BRIDGE
CHANGE
CHARGE
CRINGE
CUBAGE
DAMAGE
DEGAGE
DELUGE
DIRIGE
DOSAGE
DOTAGE
DREDGE
DRUDGE
EMERGE
ENCAGE
ENGAGE
ENRAGE
EXLEGE
FLANGE
FLEDGE
FORAGE
FRIDGE
FRINGE
GARAGE
GEORGE
GRANGE
GREIGE
GRUDGE
GRUNGE
HOMAGE
ICEAGE
INNAGE
KLUDGE
KRESGE
LAVAGE
LESAGE
LINAGE
LOUNGE
LOVAGE
MANAGE
MANEGE
MENAGE
MIRAGE
NEWAGE
NONAGE
OBLIGE
OLDAGE
ONEDGE
ORANGE
OUTAGE
PELAGE
PLEDGE
PLUNGE
POTAGE
RAVAGE
REFUGE
RENEGE
SAVAGE
SEWAGE
SILAGE
SLEDGE
SLUDGE
SMUDGE
SOCAGE
SPARGE
SPONGE
SPURGE
STODGE
STOOGE
TOWAGE
TRIAGE
TRUDGE
TWINGE
ULLAGE
UNCAGE
VISAGE
VOYAGE

G•F•••
GAFFED
GAFFER
GAFFES
GIFTED
GOFERS
GOFISH
GUFFAW

G••F••
GADFLY
GAFFED
GAFFER
GAFFES
GOLFED
GOLFER
GOOFED
GOOFUP
GRAFTS
GRIFTS
GUFFAW
GULFED
GUNFOR

G•••F•
GASIFY
GETOFF
GOSOFT
GOTOFF
GRIEFS

G••••F
GETOFF
GOTOFF

•G••F•
UGLIFY

••GF••
BAGFUL
JUGFUL

••G•F•
ARGUFY
BEGOFF
BUGOFF
LOGOFF

••G••F
BEGOFF
BUGOFF
ENGULF
LOGOFF

•••GF•
KUNGFU

G•G•••
GAGGED
GAGGLE
GAGING
GAGLAW
GAGMAN
GAGMEN
GIGGED
GIGGLE
GIGGLY
GIGOLO
GIGOTS
GIGUES
GOGGLE
GOGGLY

G••G••
GADGET
GAGGED
GAGGLE
GANGED
GANGER
GANGES
GANGLE
GANGLY
GANGUE
GANGUP
GARGLE
GAUGED
GAUGER
GAUGES
GEEGAW
GEEGEE
GEIGER
GEWGAW
GIDGET
GIGGED
GIGGLE
GIGGLY
GILGUY
GINGER
GLOGGS
GOGGLE
GOGGLY
GONGED
GOOGLE
GOOGLY
GOOGOL
GOOGOO
GORGED
GORGES
GORGET
GORGON
GOUGED
GOUGER
GOUGES
GREGOR
GRIGRI
GROGGY
GUNGHO
GURGLE

G•••G•
GALAGO
GARAGE
GEORGE
GEORGY
GINKGO
GLOGGS
GOINGS
GONOGO
GRANGE
GREIGE
GRINGO
GROGGY
GRUDGE
GRUNGE
GRUNGY
GULAGS

G••••G
GAGING
GAMING
GAPING
GASBAG
GASLOG
GATING
GAZING
GEEING
GEHRIG
GIBING
GIVING
GLUING
GORING
GOSTAG
GUNDOG
GUYING
GYBING
GYMBAG

•GG•••
AGGIES
AGGROS
EGGCUP
EGGIER
EGGING
EGGNOG
EGGSON
UGGAMS

•G•••G
AGEING
EGGING
EGGNOG
OGLING

••GG••
BAGGED
BAGGER
BAGGIE
BEGGAR
BEGGED
BIGGER
BIGGIE
BIGGUN
BOGGED
BOGGLE
BUGGED
COGGED
DAGGER
DIGGER
DOGGED
DOGGER
DOGGIE
FAGGED
FOGGED
FOGGER
GAGGED
GAGGLE
GIGGED
GIGGLE
GIGGLY
GOGGLE
GOGGLY
HAGGIS
HAGGLE
HIGGLE
HOGGED
HOGGET
HUGGED
HUGGER
JAGGED
JAGGER
JIGGED
JIGGER
JIGGLE
JIGGLY
JOGGED
JOGGER
JOGGLE
JUGGED
JUGGLE
KEGGED
LAGGED
LAGGER
LEGGED
LOGGED
LOGGER
LOGGIA
LUGGED
LUGGER
MAGGIE
MAGGIO
MIGGLE
MUGGED
MUGGER
NAGGED
NAGGER
NIGGLE
NOGGIN
NUGGET
PEGGED
PIGGED
PIGGIE
PUGGED
RAGGED
REGGAE
REGGIE
RIGGED
RIGGER
RUGGED
SAGGED
TAGGED
TIGGER
TOGGED
TOGGLE
TUGGED
TUGGER
VEGGED
VEGGIE
WAGGED
WAGGLE
WAGGLY
WAGGON
WIGGED
WIGGLE
WIGGLY
ZAGGED
ZIGGED

••G•G•
DEGAGE
ENGAGE

••G••G
BIGWIG
BOGONG
CAGING
DOGLEG
DOGTAG
DUGONG
EDGING
EGGING
EGGNOG
GAGING
PAGING
RAGBAG
RAGING
RAGRUG
RAGTAG
URGING
WAGING
WIGWAG
ZIGZAG

•••GG•
BRIGGS
CLOGGY
CRAGGY
DRAGGY
FLAGGY
FROGGY
GLOGGS
GROGGY
KNAGGY
QUAGGA
QUAGGY
SHAGGY
SLAGGY
SLUGGO
SMOGGY
SNAGGY
TWIGGY

•••G•G
FIZGIG

••••GG
BADEGG
RAWEGG

GH••••
GHAINS
GHARRY
GHAZIS
GHETTO
GHOSTS
GHOULS

G•H•••
GEHRIG
GOHOME
GSHARP

G••H••
GASHED
GASHES
GATHER
GOPHER
GOSHEN
GOTHAM
GOTHIC
GRAHAM
GUSHED
GUSHER
GUSHES

G•••H•
GALAHS
GANDHI
GARTHS
GAUCHE
GAUCHO
GEISHA
GERAHS
GIRTHS
GLYPHS
GOETHE
GOTCHA
GRAPHS
GRAPHY
GUNGHO
GUNSHY
GURKHA

G••••H
GALOSH
GARETH
GARISH
GLITCH
GOFISH
GOODOH
GOWITH
GRINCH
GROUCH
GROWTH
GUELPH
GULLAH

•GH•••
AGHAST
OGHAMS

•G••H•
AGATHA

•G•••H
AGUISH
OGRISH

••GH••
AFGHAN
AUGHTS
BIGHTS
EIGHTH
EIGHTS
EIGHTY
FIGHTS
FOGHAT
HIGHER
HIGHIQ
HIGHLY
HIGHUP
HUGHES
LIGHTS
MIGHTY
MUGHOS
NIGHER
NIGHTS
NIGHTY
OUGHTS
RIGHTO
RIGHTS
RIGHTY
SIGHED
SIGHER
SIGHTS
TIGHTS
WIGHTS

••G•H•
MEGOHM

••G••H
BYGOSH
EIGHTH
LAGASH

•••GH•
ALIGHT
ARIGHT
BLIGHT
BOUGHS
BOUGHT
BRIGHT
BURGHS
CAUGHT
COUGHS
DINGHY
DOUGHS
DOUGHY
DWIGHT
FLIGHT
FOUGHT
FRIGHT
GUNGHO
HAIGHT
HEIGHT
HOUGHS
KNIGHT
LAUGHS
LOUGHS
NAUGHT
NEIGHS
NOUGHT
PENGHU
PLIGHT
ROUGHS
ROUGHY
SLIGHT
SOUGHS
SOUGHT
TAUGHT
THIGHS
TOUGHS
TOUGHY
VAUGHN
VEIGHT
VOIGHT
WEIGHS
WEIGHT
WRIGHT

•••G•H
LENGTH
PISGAH

••••GH
ARMAGH
AWEIGH
CHOUGH
ENOUGH
LEHIGH

MCHUGH
ONHIGH
PLOUGH
SLEIGH
SLOUGH
THOUGH
TROUGH

GI••••
GIANTS
GIBBED
GIBBER
GIBBET
GIBBON
GIBERS
GIBILL
GIBING
GIBLET
GIBRAN
GIBSON
GIDEON
GIDGET
GIFTED
GIGGED
GIGGLE
GIGGLY
GIGOLO
GIGOTS
GIGUES
GIJOES
GILDED
GILDER
GILEAD
GILGUY
GILLED
GILLIE
GILLIS
GIMBAL
GIMBEL
GIMELS
GIMLET
GIMMES
GINGER
GINKGO
GINNED
GIOTTO
GIPPED
GIPPER
GIRARD
GIRDED
GIRDER
GIRDLE
GIRNED
GIRTED
GIRTHS
GITANO
GIVEIN
GIVENS
GIVERS
GIVETO
GIVEUP
GIVING
GIZMOS

G•I•••
GAIETY
GAIJIN
GAINED
GAINER
GAINLY
GAINON
GAINST
GAITED
GAITER
GEIGER
GEISEL
GEISHA
GLIBLY
GLIDED
GLIDER
GLIDES
GLINKA
GLINTS
GLITCH
GLITZY
GMINOR
GOINGS
GOINTO
GRIEFS
GRIEVE
GRIFTS
GRIGRI
GRILLE
GRILLS
GRILSE
GRIMED
GRIMES
GRIMKE
GRIMLY
GRINCH
GRINDS
GRINGO
GRIOTS
GRIPED
GRIPER
GRIPES
GRIPPE
GRISLY
GRISON
GRISTS
GRITTY
GRIVET
GUIANA
GUIDED
GUIDES
GUIDON
GUILDS
GUILES
GUILTY
GUIMPE
GUINEA
GUIROS
GUISES
GUITAR
GUITRY

G••I••
GABIES
GABION
GAGING
GAMIER
GAMILY
GAMINE
GAMING
GAMINS
GAPING
GARISH
GASIFY
GATING
GAVIAL
GAZING
GEEING
GEMINI
GENIAL
GENIES
GENIUS
GEZIRA
GHAINS
GIBILL
GIBING
GIVING
GLAIRS
GLAIRY
GLUIER
GLUING
GNEISS
GOBIES
GODIVA
GOFISH
GOLINO
GOOIER
GORIER
GORILY
GORING
GOWILD
GOWITH
GRAILS
GRAINS
GRAINY
GREIGE
GROINS
GSUITS
GUNITE
GUYING
GYBING

G•••I•
GAELIC
GAIJIN
GALLIA
GALLIC
GALOIS
GAMBIA
GAMBIT
GARCIA
GARLIC
GASKIN
GASLIT
GATLIN
GAVEIN
GAWAIN
GEHRIG
GERBIL
GERTIE
GESTIC
GETSIN
GETSIT
GHAZIS
GILLIE
GILLIS
GIVEIN
GLACIS
GLOBIN
GLORIA
GLYNIS
GNOMIC
GNOSIS
GOALIE
GOBLIN
GODWIN
GODWIT
GOESIN
GOLDIE
GOODIE
GORDIE
GOSSIP
GOTHIC
GOTOIT
GRACIE
GRADIN
GRATIA
GRATIN
GRATIS
GRAVID
GRODIN

G••••I
GANDHI
GELATI
GEMINI
GLUTEI
GRIGRI

•GI•••
BGIRLS
OGIVES

•G•I••
AGEING
AGEISM
AGEIST
AGGIES
AGLINT
AGUISH
EGGIER
EGGING
EGOISM
EGOIST
IGNITE
OGLING
OGRISH
UGLIER
UGLIES
UGLIFY
UGLILY
UGRIAN

•G••I•
AGADIR
AGARIC
AGLAIA
EGERIA
IGETIT
IGOTIT

•G•••I
AGASSI
AGOUTI

••GI••
AGGIES
ARGIVE
BEGINS
BOGIES
CAGIER
CAGILY
CAGING
COGITO
DIGITS
DOGIES
EDGIER
EDGILY
EDGING
EGGIER
EGGING
ENGINE
ENGIRD
ENGIRT
FOGIES
GAGING
HEGIRA
LEGION
LEGIST
LOGIER
LOGILY
LOGION
MEGILP
MYGIRL
ORGIES
PAGING
POGIES
RAGING
REGIME
REGINA
REGION
REGIUS
SIGILS
UNGIRD
UNGIRT
URGING
VIGILS
WAGING
YOGINI
YOGISM

••G•I•
ANGLIA
ANGLIC
BAGGIE
BAGSIT
BAGUIO
BIGGIE
BIGLIE
BIGWIG
DIGSIN
DOGGIE
DOGSIT
EDGEIN
FOGSIN
HAGGIS
HIGHIQ
HOGTIE
INGRID
LEGUIN
LIGNIN
LOGGIA
LOGSIN
MAGGIE
MAGGIO
MAGPIE
NOGGIN
PIGGIE
REGAIN
REGGIE
SIGNIN
TIGRIS
TUGRIK
UNGUIS
VEGGIE

••G••I
ANGELI
ARGALI
HEGARI
KIGALI
LUGOSI
YOGINI

•••GI•
ADAGIO
BAGGIE
BIGGIE
BIRGIT
BOOGIE
BORGIA
BRIGID
BUDGIE
CORGIS
DOGGIE
DOOGIE
DRAGIN
ELEGIT
FERGIE
FIZGIG
FRIGID
HAGGIS
HANGIN
HINGIS
HOAGIE
HUNGIN
LOGGIA
MAGGIE
MAGGIO
MARGIE
MARGIN
NOGGIN
ORIGIN
PIDGIN
PIGGIE
PLAGIO
PLUGIN
PONGID
REGGIE
SERGIO
SINGIN
STOGIE
TRAGIC
TURGID
VEGGIE
VIRGIL
VIRGIN
WEDGIE
WINGIT
WOOGIE
XINGIN

•••G•I
BANGUI
GRIGRI
MOWGLI
NILGAI
SERGEI
SNUGLI

••••GI
UBANGI

G•J•••
GIJOES

G••J••
GAIJIN
GASJET
GMAJOR

•G•••J
SGTMAJ

••GJ••
LOGJAM

G•K•••
GOKART

G••K••
GASKET
GASKIN
GAWKED
GAWKER
GECKOS
GINKGO
GURKHA

G•••K•
GLINKA
GREEKS
GRIMKE

G••••K
GALYAK
GDANSK
GOBACK

••GK••
ANGKOR

••G••K
TUGRIK

•••GK•
BANGKA

GL••••
GLACES
GLACIS
GLADES
GLADLY
GLADYS
GLAIRS
GLAIRY
GLAMOR
GLANCE
GLANDS
GLARED
GLARES
GLASER
GLASSY
GLAZED
GLAZER
GLAZES
GLEAMS
GLEAMY
GLEANS
GLEBES
GLENDA
GLENNE
GLIBLY
GLIDED
GLIDER
GLIDES
GLINKA
GLINTS
GLITCH
GLITZY
GLOATS
GLOBAL
GLOBED
GLOBES
GLOBIN
GLOGGS
GLOOMS
GLOOMY
GLOPPY
GLORIA
GLOSSA
GLOSSO
GLOSSY
GLOVED
GLOVER
GLOVES
GLOWED
GLOWER
GLOZED
GLOZES
GLUERS
GLUIER
GLUING
GLUMLY
GLUONS
GLUTEI
GLUTEN
GLUTES
GLYCOL
GLYNIS
GLYPHS

G•L•••
GALAGO
GALAHS
GALATA
GALAXY
GALEAE
GALENA
GALLED
GALLEY
GALLIA
GALLIC
GALLON
GALLOP
GALLUP
GALOIS
GALOOT
GALOPS
GALORE
GALOSH
GALPAL
GALWAY
GALYAK
GELADA
GELATI
GELATO
GELEES
GELLED
GELSEY
GILDED
GILDER
GILEAD
GILGUY
GILLED
GILLIE
GILLIS
GOLDEN
GOLDIE
GOLEMS
GOLFED
GOLFER
GOLINO
GOLLUM
GULAGS
GULFED
GULLAH
GULLED
GULLET
GULPED
GULPER

G••L••
GABLED
GABLER
GABLES
GAELIC
GAGLAW
GALLED
GALLEY
GALLIA
GALLIC
GALLON
GALLOP
GALLUP
GAOLED
GAOLER
GARLIC
GASLIT
GASLOG
GATLIN
GELLED
GIBLET
GILLED
GILLIE
GILLIS
GIMLET
GOALIE
GOBLET
GOBLIN
GOLLUM
GOSLOW
GOULET
GRILLE
GRILLS
GRILSE
GUELPH
GUILDS
GUILES
GUILTY
GULLAH
GULLED
GULLET
GURLEY

G•••L•
GABBLE
GADFLY
GAGGLE
GAINLY
GAMBLE
GAMELY
GAMILY
GANGLE
GANGLY
GARBLE

GARGLE
GAVELS
GAYALS
GENTLE
GENTLY
GERALD
GHOULS
GIBILL
GIGGLE
GIGGLY
GIGOLO
GIMELS
GIRDLE
GLADLY
GLIBLY
GLUMLY
GNARLS
GNARLY
GOBBLE
GOGGLE
GOGGLY
GOODLY
GOOGLE
GOOGLY
GORALS
GORILY
GOWILD
GRABLE
GRAILS
GRAYLY
GREYLY
GRILLE
GRILLS
GRIMLY
GRISLY
GROWLS
GROWLY
GRUELS
GURGLE
GUZZLE

G••••L
GALPAL
GAMBOL
GAVIAL
GEISEL
GENIAL
GENUAL
GERBIL
GIBILL
GIMBAL
GIMBEL
GLOBAL
GLYCOL
GOOGOL
GOSPEL
GRAVEL
GRETEL
GROVEL
GUMBEL
GUNNEL

•GL•••
AGLAIA
AGLARE
AGLEAM
AGLETS
AGLINT
IGLOOS
OGLALA
OGLERS
OGLING
UGLIER
UGLIES
UGLIFY
UGLILY

•G••L•
AGEOLD
BGIRLS
OGLALA
UGLILY

••GL••
ANGLED
ANGLER
ANGLES
ANGLIA
ANGLIC
ANGLOS
BEGLEY
BIGLIE
BOGLES
BUGLED
BUGLER
BUGLES
DIGLOT
DOGLEG
EAGLED
EAGLES
EAGLET
ENGLUT
GAGLAW
INGLES
KEGLER
PEGLER
PIGLET
RAGLAN
REGLET
REGLUE
TIGLON
UNGLUE
WIGLET

••G•L•
ANGELA
ANGELI
ANGELL
ANGELO
ANGELS
ANGOLA
ARGALI
ARGYLE
ARGYLL
BAGELS
BOGGLE
CAGILY
EDGILY
ENGELS
ENGULF
GAGGLE
GIGGLE
GIGGLY
GIGOLO
GOGGLE
GOGGLY
HAGGLE
HIGGLE
HIGHLY
HUGELY
JIGGLE
JIGGLY
JOGGLE
JUGGLE
KIGALI
LEGALS
LIGULA
LOGILY
MEGALO
MEGILP
MIGGLE
MOGULS
NIGGLE
REGALE
SAGELY
SIGILS
TOGGLE
VIGILS
WAGGLE
WAGGLY
WIGGLE
WIGGLY

••G••L
ANGELL
ARGYLL
BAGFUL
JUGFUL
MIGUEL
MYGIRL
REGNAL
SIGNAL
UNGUAL

•••GL•
BANGLE
BEAGLE
BOGGLE
BUNGLE
BURGLE
DANGLE
DANGLY
DAYGLO
DINGLE
DONGLE
GAGGLE
GANGLE
GANGLY
GARGLE
GIGGLE
GIGGLY
GOGGLE
GOGGLY
GOOGLE
GOOGLY
GURGLE
HAGGLE
HIGGLE
JANGLE
JANGLY
JIGGLE
JIGGLY
JINGLE
JINGLY
JOGGLE
JUGGLE
JUNGLE
JUNGLY
KINGLY
LONGLY
MANGLE
MIGGLE
MINGLE
MOWGLI
NIGGLE
SINGLE
SINGLY
SMUGLY
SNUGLI
SNUGLY
TANGLE
TANGLY
TINGLE
TINGLY
TOGGLE
TRIGLY
WAGGLE
WAGGLY
WANGLE
WIGGLE
WIGGLY
YUNGLO

•••G•L
BENGAL
CUDGEL
FRUGAL
GOOGOL
HANGUL
MONGOL
PLAGAL
SEAGAL
SIEGEL
VIRGIL

GM••••
GMAJOR
GMINOR

G•M•••
GAMAYS
GAMBIA
GAMBIT
GAMBLE
GAMBOL
GAMELY
GAMEST
GAMETE
GAMIER
GAMILY
GAMINE
GAMING
GAMINS
GAMMAS
GAMMED
GAMMER
GAMMON
GAMUTS
GEMARA
GEMINI
GEMMAE
GEMMED
GEMOTE
GEMOTS
GIMBAL
GIMBEL
GIMELS
GIMLET
GIMMES
GUMBEL
GUMBOS
GUMMED
GUMSUP
GYMBAG

G••M••
GAGMAN
GAGMEN
GAMMAS
GAMMED
GAMMER
GAMMON
GASMAN
GASMEN
GAUMED
GEMMAE
GEMMED
GERMAN
GETMAD
GIMMES
GIZMOS
GLAMOR
GLUMLY
GNOMES
GNOMIC
GNOMON
GOTMAD
GRAMAS
GRAMME
GRAMMY
GRAMPA
GRAMPS
GRIMED
GRIMES
GRIMKE
GRIMLY
GRUMPS
GRUMPY
GUIMPE
GUMMED
GUNMAN
GUNMEN

G•••M•
GAZUMP
GENOME
GLEAMS
GLEAMY
GLOOMS
GLOOMY
GOHOME
GOLEMS
GRAMME
GRAMMY
GROOMS

G••••M
GOLLUM
GOTHAM
GRAHAM
GYPSUM

•GM•••
EGMONT

•G•M••
AGAMAS
SGTMAJ

•G••M•
OGHAMS
UGGAMS
UGSOME

•G•••M
AGEISM
AGLEAM
EGOISM

••GM••
BIGMAC
DAGMAR
DOGMAS
GAGMAN
GAGMEN
HAGMAN
INGMAR
LEGMAN
LEGMEN
MAGMAS
RAGMAN
RAGMEN
RAGMOP
SIGMAS

••G•M•
BEGUMS
BIGAMY
DAGAMA
LEGUME
REGIME
UGGAMS

••G••M
DIGRAM
DOGDOM
ENGRAM
INGRAM
LOGJAM
MAGNUM
MEGOHM
WIGWAM
YOGISM

•••GM•
DANGME
ENIGMA
KINGME
STIGMA
ZEUGMA

•••G•M
ARTGUM
BEEGUM
REDGUM
SUBGUM

••••GM
PHLEGM

GN••••
GNARLS
GNARLY
GNATTY
GNAWED
GNAWER
GNEISS
GNOMES
GNOMIC
GNOMON
GNOSIS

G•N•••
GANDER
GANDHI
GANGED
GANGER
GANGES
GANGLE
GANGLY
GANGUE
GANGUP
GANNET
GANTRY
GENDER
GENERA
GENETS
GENEVA
GENEVE
GENIAL
GENIES
GENIUS
GENOAN
GENOME
GENRES
GENTLE
GENTLY
GENTRY
GENUAL
GINGER
GINKGO
GINNED
GONEBY
GONERS
GONGED
GONOGO
GUNDOG
GUNFOR
GUNGHO
GUNITE
GUNMAN
GUNMEN
GUNNAR
GUNNED
GUNNEL
GUNNER
GUNSHY
GUNTER

G••N••
GAINED
GAINER
GAINLY
GAINON
GAINST
GANNET
GARNER
GARNET
GAYNOR
GDANSK
GIANTS
GINNED
GIRNED
GLANCE
GLANDS
GLENDA
GLENNE
GLINKA
GLINTS
GLYNIS
GMINOR
GOANNA
GOINGS
GOINTO
GOUNOD
GOWNED
GRANDE
GRANDS
GRANGE
GRANNY
GRANTS
GRINCH
GRINDS
GRINGO
GRUNDY
GRUNGE
GRUNGY
GRUNTS
GUENON
GUINEA
GUNNAR
GUNNED
GUNNEL
GUNNER
GURNEY
GWYNNE

G•••N•
GAGING
GALENA
GAMINE
GAMING
GAMINS
GAPING
GATING
GAZING
GEEING
GEMINI
GERENT
GERONT
GERUND
GHAINS
GIBING
GITANO
GIVENS
GIVING
GLEANS
GLENNE
GLUING
GLUONS
GOANNA
GOLINO
GORING
GRAINS
GRAINY
GRANNY
GREENE
GREENS
GREENY
GRETNA
GROANS
GRODNO
GROINS
GROUND
GROZNY
GUIANA
GUYANA
GUYING
GWYNNE
GYBING
GYRENE
GYRONS

G••••N
GABION
GAGMAN
GAGMEN
GAIJIN
GAINON
GALLON
GAMMON
GARCON
GARDEN
GARSON
GASCON
GASKIN
GASMAN
GASMEN
GASTON
GATLIN
GAVEIN
GAWAIN
GENOAN
GERMAN
GETSIN
GETSON
GIBBON
GIBRAN
GIBSON
GIDEON
GIVEIN
GLOBIN
GLUTEN
GNOMON
GOBLIN
GODOWN
GODSON
GODWIN
GOESIN
GOESON
GOLDEN
GOODEN
GORDON
GORGON
GOSHEN
GOTTEN
GOVERN
GRABEN
GRADIN
GRATIN
GRAVEN
GREWON
GRISON
GRODIN
GROTON
GROWON
GUDRUN
GUENON
GUIDON
GUNMAN
GUNMEN

•GN•••
AGNATE
IGNACE
IGNATZ
IGNITE
IGNORE

•G•N••
AGENAS
AGENCY
AGENDA
AGENTS
EGGNOG
UGANDA

•G••N•
AGEING
AGLINT
EGGING
EGMONT
IGUANA
OGLING

•G•••N
EGGSON
NGUYEN
UGRIAN

••GN••
CAGNEY
COGNAC
CYGNET
CYGNUS
EGGNOG
LIGNIN
LUGNUT
MAGNET
MAGNON
MAGNUM
MAGNUS
MIGNON
PIGNUT
REGNAL
REGNAT
SIGNAL
SIGNED
SIGNEE
SIGNER
SIGNET
SIGNIN
SIGNON
SIGNOR
SIGNUP
WAGNER

••G•N•
ARGENT
AUGEND
BEGINS
BEGONE
BOGONG
BYGONE
CAGING
COGENT
DOGONS
DUGONG
EDGING
EGGING
ENGINE
EUGENE
FAGEND
GAGING
HOGANS
LAGUNA
LEGEND
LIGAND
NAGANO
NUGENT
ORGANA
ORGANS
PAGANS
PAGING
RAGING
REGENT
REGINA
TAGEND
URGENT
URGING
VEGANS
WAGING
WAGONS
YOGINI

••G••N
AEGEAN
AFGHAN
AUGEAN
BIGBEN
BIGGUN
BIGTEN
DIGSIN
EDGEIN
EGGSON
FOGSIN
GAGMAN
GAGMEN
HAGDON
HAGMAN
LAGOON
LEGION
LEGMAN
LEGMEN
LEGUIN
LIGNIN
LOGION
LOGSIN
LOGSON
MAGNON
MIGNON
NOGGIN
PIGEON
PIGPEN
RAGLAN
RAGMAN
RAGMEN
REGAIN
REGION
SIGNIN
SIGNON
TIGLON
WAGGON

•••GN•
ALIGNS
BOIGNY
COIGNS
DEIGNS
FEIGNS
REIGNS
SOIGNE
VSIGNS

•••G•N
AIRGUN
ARAGON
BERGEN
BIGGUN
BROGAN
CAPGUN
COOGAN
DRAGIN
DRAGON
FLAGON
GORGON
HANGIN
HANGON
HUNGIN
HUNGON
IMOGEN
ISOGON
JARGON
JETGUN
KURGAN
LONGAN
MAJGEN
MARGIN
MORGAN
MORGEN
NOGGIN
OREGON
ORIGEN
ORIGIN
OUTGUN
OXYGEN
PIDGIN
PLUGIN
POPGUN
RAYGUN
REAGAN
SAIGON
SARGON
SHOGUN
SINGIN
SIXGUN
SLOGAN
TONGAN
TOPGUN
TRIGON
TROGON
VAUGHN
VIRGIN
WAGGON
XINGIN
YANGON

••••GN
ASSIGN
BENIGN
COSIGN
DESIGN
ELOIGN
ENSIGN
IMPUGN
MALIGN
OPPUGN
REPUGN
RESIGN

GO••••
GOADED
GOALIE
GOANNA
GOATEE
GOAWAY
GOAWRY
GOBACK
GOBBLE
GOBIES
GOBLET
GOBLIN
GOBUST
GOCART
GODARD
GODETS
GODIVA
GODOWN
GODSON
GODWIN
GODWIT
GOEASY
GOESAT
GOESBY
GOESIN
GOESON
GOESUP
GOETHE
GOFERS
GOFISH
GOGGLE
GOGGLY
GOHOME
GOINGS
GOINTO
GOKART
GOLDEN
GOLDIE
GOLEMS
GOLFED
GOLFER
GOLINO
GOLLUM
GONEBY
GONERS
GONGED
GONOGO
GOOBER
GOODBY
GOODEN
GOODIE
GOODLY
GOODOH
GOOFED
GOOFUP
GOOGLE
GOOGLY
GOOGOL
GOOGOO
GOOIER
GOOSED
GOOSES
GOOSEY
GOOVER
GOPHER
GORALS
GORDIE
GORDON
GORGED
GORGES
GORGET
GORGON
GORIER
GORILY
GORING
GORSES
GOSHEN
GOSLOW
GOSOFT
GOSPEL
GOSSIP
GOSTAG
GOTCHA
GOTHAM
GOTHIC
GOTMAD
GOTOFF
GOTOIT
GOTOUT
GOTSET
GOTTEN
GOUGED
GOUGER
GOUGES
GOULET
GOUNOD
GOURDE
GOURDS
GOVERN
GOWEST
GOWILD
GOWITH
GOWNED

G•O•••
GAOLED
GAOLER
GEODES
GEORGE
GEORGY
GHOSTS
GHOULS
GIOTTO
GLOATS
GLOBAL
GLOBED
GLOBES
GLOBIN
GLOGGS
GLOOMS
GLOOMY
GLOPPY
GLORIA
GLOSSA
GLOSSO
GLOSSY
GLOVED
GLOVER
GLOVES
GLOWED
GLOWER
GLOZED
GLOZES
GNOMES
GNOMIC
GNOMON
GNOSIS
GOOBER
GOODBY
GOODEN
GOODIE
GOODLY
GOODOH
GOOFED
GOOFUP
GOOGLE
GOOGLY
GOOGOL
GOOGOO
GOOIER
GOOSED
GOOSES
GOOSEY
GOOVER
GROANS
GROATS
GROCER
GRODIN
GRODNO
GROGGY
GROINS
GROOMS
GROOVE
GROOVY
GROPED
GROPES
GROSSE
GROSSO
GROSZY
GROTON
GROTTO
GROTTY
GROUCH
GROUND
GROUPS
GROUSE
GROUTS
GROUTY
GROVEL
GROVER
GROVES
GROWER
GROWLS
GROWLY
GROWON
GROWTH
GROWUP
GROZNY

G••O••
GALOIS
GALOOT
GALOPS
GALORE
GALOSH
GATORS
GEMOTE
GEMOTS
GENOAN
GENOME
GERONT
GETOFF
GETOUT
GIGOLO
GIGOTS
GIJOES
GLOOMS
GLOOMY
GLUONS
GODOWN
GOHOME
GONOGO
GOSOFT
GOTOFF
GOTOIT
GOTOUT
GRIOTS
GROOMS
GROOVE
GROOVY
GUYOTS
GYRONS
GYROSE

G•••O•
GABION
GAINON
GALLON
GALLOP
GALOOT
GAMBOL
GAMMON
GARCON
GARSON
GASCON
GASLOG
GASTON
GAYNOR
GECKOS
GETSON
GIBBON
GIBSON
GIDEON
GIZMOS
GLAMOR
GLYCOL
GMAJOR
GMINOR
GNOMON
GODSON
GOESON
GOODOH
GOOGOL
GOOGOO
GORDON
GORGON
GOSLOW
GOUNOD
GREGOR
GREWON
GRISON
GROTON
GROWON
GUACOS
GUENON
GUIDON
GUIROS
GUMBOS
GUNDOG
GUNFOR

G••••O
GABBRO
GALAGO
GASTRO
GAUCHO
GAZEBO
GEARTO
GELATO
GETSTO
GHETTO
GIGOLO
GINKGO
GIOTTO
GITANO
GIVETO
GLOSSO
GOINTO
GOLINO
GONOGO
GOOGOO
GRAECO
GRASSO
GRINGO
GRODNO
GROSSO
GROTTO
GUNGHO

•GO•••
AGORAE
AGORAS
AGOROT
AGOUTI
EGOISM
EGOIST
IGOTIT

•G•O••
AGEOLD
EGMONT
IGLOOS
IGNORE
OGDOAD
UGSOME

•G••O•
AGGROS
AGOROT
EGGNOG
EGGSON
IGLOOS

••GO••
ALGORE
ANGOLA
ANGORA
ARGOSY
ARGOTS
BEGOFF
BEGONE
BIGOTS
BOGONG
BOGOTA
BUGOFF
BUGOUT
BYGONE
BYGOSH
DIGOUT
DOGONS
DOGOOD
DUGONG
DUGOUT
ERGOTS
FAGOTS
GIGOLO
GIGOTS
INGOTS
LAGOON
LOGOFF
LOGOUT
LUGOSI
MEGOHM
NAGOYA
NOGOOD
OSGOOD
PAGODA
PIGOUT
RAGOUT
RIGORS
RIGOUR
RUGOSE
TAGORE
TAGOUT
VIGODA
VIGORS
VIGOUR
WAGONS
WIGOUT
ZYGOTE

••G•O•
AGGROS
ANGKOR
ANGLOS
BIGBOY
BIGTOE
BIGTOP
DIGLOT
DOGDOM
DOGOOD
EGGNOG
EGGSON
FOGBOW
HAGDON
LAGOON
LEGION
LOGION
LOGSON
MAGNON
MIGNON
MUGHOS
NOGOOD
OSGOOD
PEGTOP
PIGEON
RAGMOP
RAGTOP
REGION
SIGNON
SIGNOR
TIGLON
WAGGON

••G••O
ANGELO
BAGUIO
COGITO
FIGARO
GIGOLO
LEGATO
MAGGIO
MEGALO
NAGANO
RIGHTO

•••GO•
AMIGOS
ARAGON
BANGOR
BONGOS
BURGOO
BURGOS
CARGOS
CHIGOE
CONGOU
DRAGON
FLAGON

FORGOT
GOOGOL
GOOGOO
GORGON
GREGOR
HANGON
HUNGON
ISOGON
JARGON
LARGOS
MANGOS
MARGOT
MONGOL
MUNGOS
OREGON
SAIGON
SARGON
SARGOS
SPIGOT
SUNGOD
TANGOS
TINGOD
TRIGON
TROGON
TURGOR
WAGGON
WARGOD
YANGON

•••G•O

ADAGIO
BURGOO
DAYGLO
GOOGOO
GUNGHO
MAGGIO
NINGBO
PLAGIO
SANGTO
SERGIO
SINGTO
SLUGGO
YUNGLO

••••GO

ATERGO
BOINGO
COLUGO
DIRIGO
ERYNGO
FOREGO
GALAGO
GINKGO
GONOGO
GRINGO
INDIGO
LATIGO
LETSGO
NONEGO
OLINGO
OSWEGO
PAPAGO
QUANGO
SLUGGO
STINGO
TOBAGO
VIRAGO

G•P•••

GAPERS
GAPING
GAPPED
GIPPED
GIPPER
GOPHER
GYPPED
GYPPER
GYPSUM

G••P••

GALPAL
GAPPED
GASPAR
GASPED
GASPER
GAWPED
GIPPED
GIPPER
GLOPPY
GLYPHS
GOSPEL
GRAPES
GRAPEY
GRAPHS
GRAPHY
GRAPPA
GRIPED
GRIPER
GRIPES
GRIPPE
GROPED
GROPES
GULPED
GULPER
GYPPED
GYPPER

G•••P•

GALOPS
GETUPS
GLOPPY
GRAMPA
GRAMPS
GRAPPA
GRASPS
GRIPPE
GROUPS
GRUMPS
GRUMPY
GUELPH
GUIMPE

G••••P

GALLOP
GALLUP
GANGUP
GASCAP
GAVEUP
GAZUMP
GEARUP
GETSUP
GIVEUP
GOESUP
GOOFUP
GOSSIP
GREWUP
GROWUP
GSHARP
GUMSUP

•G•••P

EGGCUP

••GP••

MAGPIE
PIGPEN

••G••P

BIGTOP
DIGSUP
EGGCUP
FOGSUP
HIGHUP
MEGILP
PEGTOP
RAGMOP
RAGTOP
RIGSUP
SIGNUP
TAGSUP

•••G•P

BANGUP
CLOGUP
GANGUP
HANGUP
HUNGUP
RANGUP
RINGUP
RUNGUP

••G••Q

HIGHIQ

GR••••

GRABAT
GRABBY
GRABEN
GRABLE
GRACED
GRACES
GRACIE
GRADEA
GRADED
GRADER
GRADES
GRADIN
GRADUS
GRAECO
GRAFTS
GRAHAM
GRAILS
GRAINS
GRAINY
GRAMAS
GRAMME
GRAMMY
GRAMPA
GRAMPS
GRANDE
GRANDS
GRANGE
GRANNY
GRANTS
GRAPES
GRAPEY
GRAPHS
GRAPHY
GRAPPA
GRASPS
GRASSO
GRASSY
GRATED
GRATER
GRATES
GRATIA
GRATIN
GRATIS
GRAVED
GRAVEL
GRAVEN
GRAVER
GRAVES
GRAVID
GRAYED
GRAYER
GRAYLY
GRAZED
GRAZER
GRAZES
GREASE
GREASY
GREATS
GREAVE
GREBES
GREECE
GREEDY
GREEKS
GREENE
GREENS
GREENY
GREETS
GREGOR
GREIGE
GRETEL
GRETNA
GREWON
GREWUP
GREYED
GREYER
GREYLY
GRIEFS
GRIEVE
GRIFTS
GRIGRI
GRILLE
GRILLS
GRILSE
GRIMED
GRIMES
GRIMKE
GRIMLY
GRINCH
GRINDS
GRINGO
GRIOTS
GRIPED
GRIPER
GRIPES
GRIPPE
GRISLY
GRISON
GRISTS
GRITTY
GRIVET
GROANS
GROATS
GROCER
GRODIN
GRODNO
GROGGY
GROINS
GROOMS
GROOVE
GROOVY
GROPED
GROPES
GROSSE
GROSSO
GROSZY
GROTON
GROTTO
GROTTY
GROUCH
GROUND
GROUPS
GROUSE
GROUTS
GROUTY
GROVEL
GROVER
GROVES
GROWER
GROWLS
GROWLY
GROWON
GROWTH
GROWUP
GROZNY
GRUBBY
GRUDGE
GRUELS
GRUMPS
GRUMPY
GRUNDY
GRUNGE
GRUNGY
GRUNTS

G•R•••

GARAGE
GARBED
GARBLE
GARCIA
GARCON
GARDEN
GARETH
GARGLE
GARISH
GARLIC
GARNER
GARNET
GARRET
GARSON
GARTER
GARTHS
GARVEY
GERAHS
GERALD
GERARD
GERBER
GERBIL
GERENT
GERMAN
GERONT
GERTIE
GERUND
GIRARD
GIRDED
GIRDER
GIRDLE
GIRNED
GIRTED
GIRTHS
GORALS
GORDIE
GORDON
GORGED
GORGES
GORGET
GORGON
GORIER
GORILY
GORING
GORSES
GURGLE
GURKHA
GURLEY
GURNEY
GYRATE
GYRENE
GYRONS
GYROSE

G••R••

GARRET
GEARED
GEARTO
GEARUP
GEHRIG
GENRES
GEORGE
GEORGY
GHARRY
GIBRAN
GLARED
GLARES
GLORIA
GNARLS
GNARLY
GOURDE
GOURDS
GUARDS
GUDRUN
GUERRE
GUIROS

G•••R•

GABBRO
GALORE
GANTRY
GAPERS
GASTRO
GATERS
GATORS
GEMARA
GENERA
GENTRY
GERARD
GEZIRA
GHARRY
GIBERS
GIRARD
GIVERS
GLAIRS
GLAIRY
GLUERS
GOAWRY
GOCART
GODARD
GOFERS
GOKART
GONERS
GOVERN
GRIGRI
GSHARP
GUERRE
GUITRY

G••••R

GABBER
GABLER
GADDER
GAFFER
GAINER
GAITER
GAMIER
GAMMER
GANDER
GANGER
GAOLER
GARNER
GARTER
GASPAR
GASPER
GASSER
GATHER
GAUGER
GAWKER
GAYNOR
GEEZER
GEIGER
GENDER
GERBER
GETTER
GEYSER
GIBBER
GILDER
GINGER
GIPPER
GIRDER
GLAMOR
GLASER
GLAZER
GLIDER
GLOVER
GLOWER
GLUIER
GMAJOR
GMINOR
GNAWER
GOLFER
GOOBER
GOOIER
GOOVER
GOPHER
GORIER
GOUGER
GRADER
GRATER
GRAVER
GRAYER
GRAZER
GREGOR
GREYER
GRIPER
GROCER
GROVER
GROWER
GUITAR
GULPER
GUNFOR
GUNNAR
GUNNER
GUNTER
GUSHER
GUTTER
GYPPER

•GR•••

AGREED
AGREES
EGRESS
EGRETS
OGRESS
OGRISH
UGRIAN

•G•R••

AGARIC
AGGROS
AGORAE
AGORAS
AGOROT
BGIRLS
EGERIA

•G••R•

AGLARE
EGBERT
IGNORE
OGLERS

•G•••R

AGADIR
EGGIER
UGLIER

••GR••

AGGROS
AIGRET
BIGRED
DEGREE
DIGRAM
EAGRES
ENGRAM
INGRAM
INGRES
INGRID
LEGREE
MCGRAW
MCGREW
PUGREE
RAGRUG
REGRET
TIGRIS
TUGRIK
ZAGREB

••G•R•

ALGORE
ANGERS
ANGORA
ASGARD
AUGERS
AUGURS
AUGURY
BOGART
CAGERS
CIGARS
EDGARD
EDGARS
EDGERS
ENGIRD
ENGIRT
FIGARO
FIGURE
FUGARD
HEGARI
HEGIRA
KAGERA
LAGERS
LIGERS
LIGURE
LUGERS
MEGARA
MYGIRL
PAGERS
REGARD
RIGORS
ROGERS
SEGURA
SIGURD
SUGARS
SUGARY
TAGORE
TIGERS
UIGURS
UNGIRD
UNGIRT
URGERS
VAGARY
VIGORS
WAGERS
YOGURT

••G••R

ANGKOR
ANGLER
ARGUER
BAGGER
BEGGAR
BIGGER
BIGSUR
BUGLER
CAGIER
DAGGER
DAGMAR
DIGGER
DOGEAR
DOGGER
EDGIER
EGGIER
FOGGER
HIGHER
HUGGER
INGEAR
INGMAR
JAGGER
JAGUAR
JIGGER
JOGGER
KEGLER
LAGGER
LOGGER
LOGIER
LUGGER
MAGYAR
MUGGER
NAGGER

NIGHER
PEGLER
RIGGER
RIGOUR
SIGHER
SIGNER
SIGNOR
TIGGER
TUGGER
VAGUER
VIGOUR
WAGNER

•••GR•

ALEGRE
EMIGRE
GRIGRI
HUNGRY
MEAGRE

•••G•R

ALEGAR
ANSGAR
BADGER
BAGGER
BANGER
BANGOR
BEGGAR
BIGGER
BOLGER
BULGAR
BULGUR
BURGER
CADGER
CODGER
CONGER
COUGAR
DAGGER
DANGER
DIGGER
DODGER
DOGGER
FINGER
FOGGER
FORGER
GANGER
GAUGER
GEIGER
GINGER
GOUGER
GREGOR
HANGAR
HANGER
HEDGER
HUGGER
HUNGER
IMAGER
JAEGER
JAGGER
JIGGER
JOGGER
KRUGER
LAAGER
LAGGER
LANGUR
LARGER
LEDGER
LINGER
LODGER
LOGGER
LONGER
LUGGER
MANGER
MEAGER
MEDGAR
MERGER
MONGER
MUGGER
NAGGER
NUDGER
ONAGER
RANGER
RIGGER
RINGER
RUTGER
SANGER
SAUGER
SEEGER
SINGER
STAGER
TIGGER
TUGGER
TURGOR
VERGER
VULGAR
WINGER
YEAGER
ZENGER
ZINGER

GS••••

GSHARP
GSTAAD
GSUITS

G•S•••

GASBAG
GASCAP
GASCON
GASHED
GASHES
GASIFY
GASJET
GASKET
GASKIN
GASLIT
GASLOG
GASMAN
GASMEN
GASPAR
GASPED
GASPER
GASSED
GASSER
GASSES
GASTON
GASTRO
GESTES
GESTIC
GOSHEN
GOSLOW
GOSOFT
GOSPEL
GOSSIP
GOSTAG
GUSHED
GUSHER
GUSHES
GUSSET
GUSTAV
GUSTED

G••S••

GARSON
GASSED
GASSER
GASSES
GATSBY
GEISEL
GEISHA
GELSEY
GETSAT
GETSBY
GETSET
GETSIN
GETSIT
GETSON
GETSTO
GETSUP
GEYSER
GHOSTS
GIBSON
GLASER
GLASSY
GLOSSA
GLOSSO
GLOSSY
GNOSIS
GODSON
GOESAT
GOESBY
GOESIN
GOESON
GOESUP
GOOSED
GOOSES
GOOSEY
GORSES
GOSSIP
GOTSET
GRASPS
GRASSO
GRASSY
GRISLY
GRISON
GRISTS
GROSSE
GROSSO
GROSZY
GUESTS
GUISES
GUMSUP
GUNSHY
GUSSET
GYPSUM

G•••S•

GAINST
GALOSH
GAMEST
GARISH
GAYEST
GDANSK
GLASSY
GLOSSA
GLOSSO
GLOSSY
GNEISS
GOBUST
GOEASY
GOFISH
GOWEST
GRASSO
GRASSY
GREASE
GREASY
GRILSE
GROSSE
GROSSO
GROUSE
GYROSE

G••••S

GABIES
GABLES
GAFFES
GALAHS
GALOIS
GALOPS
GAMAYS
GAMINS
GAMMAS
GAMUTS
GANGES
GAPERS
GARTHS
GASHES
GASSES
GATERS
GATORS
GAUGES
GAUZES
GAVELS
GAYALS
GECKOS
GELEES
GEMOTS
GENETS
GENIES
GENIUS
GENRES
GEODES
GERAHS
GESTES
GETUPS
GHAINS
GHAZIS
GHOSTS
GHOULS
GIANTS
GIBERS
GIGOTS
GIGUES
GIJOES
GILLIS
GIMELS
GIMMES
GIRTHS
GIVENS
GIVERS
GIZMOS
GLACES
GLACIS
GLADES
GLADYS
GLAIRS
GLANDS
GLARES
GLAZES
GLEAMS
GLEANS
GLEBES
GLIDES
GLINTS
GLOATS
GLOBES
GLOGGS
GLOOMS
GLOVES
GLOZES
GLUERS
GLUONS
GLUTES
GLYNIS
GLYPHS
GNARLS
GNEISS
GNOMES
GNOSIS
GOBIES
GODETS
GOFERS
GOINGS
GOLEMS
GONERS
GOOSES
GORALS
GORGES
GORSES
GOUGES
GOURDS
GRACES
GRADES
GRADUS
GRAFTS
GRAILS
GRAINS
GRAMAS
GRAMPS
GRANDS
GRANTS
GRAPES
GRAPHS
GRASPS
GRATES
GRATIS
GRAVES
GRAZES
GREATS
GREBES
GREEKS
GREENS
GREETS
GRIEFS
GRIFTS
GRILLS
GRIMES
GRINDS
GRIOTS
GRIPES
GRISTS
GROANS
GROATS
GROINS
GROOMS
GROPES
GROUPS
GROUTS
GROVES
GROWLS
GRUELS
GRUMPS
GRUNTS
GSUITS
GUACOS
GUARDS
GUAVAS
GUESTS
GUIDES
GUILDS
GUILES
GUIROS
GUISES
GULAGS
GUMBOS
GUSHES
GUYOTS
GYRONS

•GS•••

UGSOME

•G•S••

AGASSI
EGESTA
EGESTS
EGGSON

•G••S•

AGASSI
AGEISM
AGEIST
AGHAST
AGUISH
EGOISM
EGOIST
EGRESS
OGRESS
OGRISH

•G•••S

AGAMAS
AGATES
AGAVES
AGENAS
AGENTS
AGGIES
AGGROS
AGLETS
AGORAS
AGREES
BGIRLS
EGESTS
EGRESS
EGRETS
IGLOOS
OGHAMS
OGIVES
OGLERS
OGRESS
UGGAMS
UGLIES

••GS••

BAGSIT
BIGSUR
DIGSIN
DIGSUP
DOGSAT
DOGSIT
EGGSON
FOGSIN
FOGSUP
JIGSAW
LOGSIN
LOGSON
PIGSTY
RIGSUP
TAGSUP

••G•S•

ARGOSY
AUGUST
BYGOSH
DEGUST
DIGEST
HUGEST
INGEST
LAGASH
LEGIST
LUGOSI
RUGOSE
SAGEST
YOGISM

••G••S

AGGIES
AGGROS
ANGELS
ANGERS
ANGLES
ANGLOS
ARGOTS
ARGUES
AUGERS
AUGHTS
AUGURS
BAGELS
BEGETS
BEGINS
BEGUMS
BIGHTS
BIGOTS
BOGEYS
BOGIES
BOGLES
BUGLES
CAGERS
CAGUAS
CIGARS
CYGNUS
DIGITS
DOGEYS
DOGIES
DOGMAS
DOGONS
EAGLES
EAGRES
EDGARS
EDGERS
EIGHTS
ENGELS
ERGOTS
FAGOTS
FIGHTS
FOGEYS
FOGIES
FUGUES
GIGOTS
GIGUES
HAGGIS
HOGANS
HUGHES
INGLES
INGOTS
INGRES
LAGERS
LEGALS
LIGERS
LIGHTS
LUGERS
MAGMAS
MAGNUS
MOGULS
MUGHOS
NIGHTS
ORGANS
ORGIES
OUGHTS
PAGANS
PAGERS
POGIES
REGIUS
RIGHTS
RIGORS
ROGERS
ROGUES
SEGUES
SIGHTS
SIGILS
SIGMAS
SUGARS
TIGERS
TIGHTS
TIGRIS
UGGAMS
UIGURS
UNGUES
UNGUIS
URGERS
VEGANS
VIGILS
VIGORS
VOGUES
WAGERS
WAGONS
WIGHTS

•••G•S

ADAGES
ALIGNS
AMIGAS
AMIGOS
BADGES
BARGES
BEIGES
BILGES
BINGES
BIOGAS
BONGOS
BOUGHS
BRIGGS
BRUGES
BUDGES
BULGES
BURGAS
BURGHS
BURGOS
CADGES
CARGOS
COIGNS
CONGAS
CORGIS
COUGHS
DEIGNS
DINGUS
DIRGES
DODGES
DOUGHS
FEIGNS
FERGUS
FORGES
FUDGES
FUNGUS
GANGES
GAUGES
GLOGGS
GORGES
GOUGES
HAGGIS
HEDGES
HINGES
HINGIS
HODGES
HOUGHS
IMAGES
JUDGES
KEDGES
LARGES
LARGOS
LAUGHS
LEDGES
LIEGES
LODGES
LONGES
LOUGHS
LUNGES
MANGOS
MARGES
MERGES
MIDGES
MUNGOS
NEIGHS
NUDGES
OMEGAS
OSAGES
PHAGES
PLAGES
PURGES
RANGES
REIGNS
RIDGES
ROUGES
ROUGHS
SAIGAS
SARGES
SARGOS
SEDGES
SERGES
SIEGES
SINGES
SOUGHS
STAGES
SURGES
SWAGES
TAIGAS
TANGOS
TARGES
THIGHS
TINGES

TOUGHS
USAGES
VERGES
VOSGES
VSIGNS
WEDGES
WEIGHS
WODGES

••••GS

BEFOGS
BEINGS
BRIGGS
BRINGS
CLANGS
CLINGS
DEBUGS
DEFOGS
DOINGS
DORAGS
DRINGS
FLINGS
GLOGGS
GOINGS
GULAGS
HMONGS
ICINGS
IDTAGS
KIANGS
LIANGS
ORANGS
ORINGS
PRANGS
PRONGS
REBAGS
REPEGS
RETAGS
SCRAGS
SHRUGS
SLANGS
SLINGS
SPRAGS
SPRIGS
STINGS
SWINGS
THINGS
THONGS
TWANGS
UNPEGS
UNRIGS
WHANGS
WRINGS
WRONGS

G•T•••

GATEAU
GATERS
GATHER
GATING
GATLIN
GATORS
GATSBY
GETMAD
GETOFF
GETOUT
GETSAT
GETSBY
GETSET
GETSIN
GETSIT
GETSON
GETSTO
GETSUP
GETTER
GETUPS
GITANO
GOTCHA
GOTHAM
GOTHIC
GOTMAD
GOTOFF
GOTOIT
GOTOUT
GOTSET
GOTTEN
GSTAAD
GUTTAE
GUTTED
GUTTER

G••T••

GAITED
GAITER
GANTRY
GARTER
GARTHS
GASTON
GASTRO
GENTLE
GENTLY
GENTRY
GERTIE
GESTES
GESTIC
GETTER
GHETTO
GIFTED
GIOTTO
GIRTED
GIRTHS
GLITCH
GLITZY
GLUTEI
GLUTEN
GLUTES
GNATTY
GOATEE
GOETHE
GOSTAG
GOTTEN
GRATED
GRATER
GRATES
GRATIA
GRATIN
GRATIS
GRETEL
GRETNA
GRITTY
GROTON
GROTTO
GROTTY
GUITAR
GUITRY
GUNTER
GUSTAV
GUSTED
GUTTAE
GUTTED
GUTTER

G•••T•

GAIETY
GALATA
GAMETE
GAMUTS
GARETH
GEARTO
GELATI
GELATO
GEMOTE
GEMOTS
GENETS
GETSTO
GHETTO
GHOSTS
GIANTS
GIGOTS
GIOTTO
GIVETO
GLINTS
GLOATS
GNATTY
GODETS
GOINTO
GOWITH
GRAFTS
GRANTS
GREATS
GREETS
GRIFTS
GRIOTS
GRISTS
GRITTY
GROATS
GROTTO
GROTTY
GROUTS
GROUTY
GROWTH
GRUNTS
GSUITS
GUESTS
GUILTY
GUNITE
GUYOTS
GYRATE

G••••T

GADGET
GAINST
GALOOT
GAMBIT
GAMEST
GANNET
GARNET
GARRET
GASJET
GASKET
GASLIT
GAYEST
GERENT
GERONT
GETOUT
GETSAT
GETSET
GETSIT
GIBBET
GIBLET
GIDGET
GIMLET
GOBLET
GOBUST
GOCART
GODWIT
GOESAT
GOKART
GORGET
GOSOFT
GOTOIT
GOTOUT
GOTSET
GOULET
GOWEST
GRABAT
GRIVET
GULLET
GUSSET

•GT•••

SGTMAJ

•G•T••

AGATES
AGATHA
IGETIT
IGOTIT

•G••T•

AGENTS
AGLETS
AGNATE
AGOUTI
EGESTA
EGESTS
EGRETS
IGNATZ
IGNITE

•G•••T

AGEIST
AGHAST
AGLINT
AGOROT
EGBERT
EGMONT
EGOIST
IGETIT
IGOTIT

••GT••

BIGTEN
BIGTOE
BIGTOP
DOGTAG
HOGTIE
PEGTOP
RAGTAG
RAGTOP

••G•T•

ARGOTS
AUGHTS
BEGETS
BIGHTS
BIGOTS
BOGOTA
COGITO
DIGITS
EIGHTH
EIGHTS
EIGHTY
ERGATE
ERGOTS
FAGOTS
FIGHTS
GIGOTS
INGOTS
LEGATE
LEGATO
LIGATE
LIGHTS
MIGHTY
NEGATE
NIGHTS
NIGHTY
ORGATE
OUGHTS
PIGSTY
RIGHTO
RIGHTS
RIGHTY
RUGATE
SIGHTS
TIGHTS
WIGHTS
ZYGOTE

••G••T

AIGRET
ARGENT
AUGUST
BAGSIT
BOGART
BUGOUT
COGENT
CYGNET
DEGUST
DIGEST
DIGLOT
DIGOUT
DOGSAT
DOGSIT
DUGOUT
EAGLET
ENGIRT
ENGLUT
FOGHAT
HOGGET
HUGEST
INGEST
LEGIST
LOGOUT
LUGNUT
MAGNET
NUGENT
NUGGET
ORGEAT
PIGLET
PIGNUT
PIGOUT
RAGOUT
REGENT
REGLET
REGNAT
REGRET
SAGEST
SIGNET
TAGOUT
UNGIRT
URGENT
WIGLET
WIGOUT
YOGURT

•••GT•

LENGTH
SANGTO
SINGTO

•••G•T

ALIGHT
ARIGHT
BIRGIT
BLIGHT
BOUGHT
BRIGHT
BUDGET
CATGUT
CAUGHT
DWIGHT
ELEGIT
FIDGET
FLIGHT
FORGET
FORGOT
FOUGHT
FRIGHT
GADGET
GIDGET
GORGET
HAIGHT
HEIGHT
HOGGET
KNIGHT
MARGOT
MIDGET
NAUGHT
NOUGAT
NOUGHT
NUGGET
PARGET
PIAGET
PLIGHT
ROTGUT
SLIGHT
SOUGHT
SPIGOT
TARGET
TAUGHT
VEIGHT
VOIGHT
WEIGHT
WIDGET
WINGIT
WRIGHT

GU••••

GUACOS
GUARDS
GUAVAS
GUDRUN
GUELPH
GUENON
GUERRE
GUESTS
GUFFAW
GUIANA
GUIDED
GUIDES
GUIDON
GUILDS
GUILES
GUILTY
GUIMPE
GUINEA
GUIROS
GUISES
GUITAR
GUITRY
GULAGS
GULFED
GULLAH
GULLED
GULLET
GULPED
GULPER
GUMBEL
GUMBOS
GUMMED
GUMSUP
GUNDOG
GUNFOR
GUNGHO
GUNITE
GUNMAN
GUNMEN
GUNNAR
GUNNED
GUNNEL
GUNNER
GUNSHY
GUNTER
GURGLE
GURKHA
GURLEY
GURNEY
GUSHED
GUSHER
GUSHES
GUSSET
GUSTAV
GUSTED
GUTTAE
GUTTED
GUTTER
GUYANA
GUYING
GUYOTS
GUZZLE

G•U•••

GAUCHE
GAUCHO
GAUGED
GAUGER
GAUGES
GAUMED
GAUZES
GLUERS
GLUIER
GLUING
GLUMLY
GLUONS
GLUTEI
GLUTEN
GLUTES
GOUGED
GOUGER
GOUGES
GOULET
GOUNOD
GOURDE
GOURDS
GRUBBY
GRUDGE
GRUELS
GRUMPS
GRUMPY
GRUNDY
GRUNGE
GRUNGY
GRUNTS
GSUITS

G••U••

GAMUTS
GAZUMP
GENUAL
GERUND
GETUPS
GHOULS
GIGUES
GOBUST
GROUCH
GROUND
GROUPS
GROUSE
GROUTS
GROUTY

G•••U•

GALLUP
GANGUE
GANGUP
GAVEUP
GEARUP
GENIUS
GETOUT
GETSUP
GILGUY
GIVEUP
GOESUP
GOLLUM
GOOFUP
GOTOUT
GRADUS
GREWUP
GROWUP
GUDRUN
GUMSUP
GYPSUM

G••••U

GATEAU

•GU•••

AGUISH
IGUACU
IGUANA
NGUYEN

•G•U••

AGOUTI

•G••U•

EGGCUP

•G•••U

IGUACU

••GU••

ARGUED
ARGUER
ARGUES
ARGUFY
AUGURS
AUGURY
AUGUST
BAGUIO
BEGUMS
CAGUAS
DEGUST
ENGULF
FIGURE
FUGUES
GIGUES
JAGUAR
LAGUNA
LEGUIN
LEGUME
LIGULA
LIGURE
MAGUEY
MIGUEL
MOGULS
ROGUES
SEGUED
SEGUES
SEGURA
SIGURD
UIGURS
UNGUAL
UNGUES
UNGUIS
VAGUER
VOGUES
YOGURT

••G•U•

BAGFUL
BIGGUN
BIGSUR
BUGOUT
CYGNUS
DIGOUT
DIGSUP
DUGOUT
EGGCUP
ENGLUT
FOGSUP
HIGHUP
JUGFUL
LOGOUT
LUGNUT
MAGNUM
MAGNUS
PIGNUT
PIGOUT
RAGOUT
RAGRUG
REGIUS
REGLUE
RIGOUR
RIGSUP
SIGNUP
TAGOUT
TAGSUP
UNGLUE

VIGOUR
WIGOUT

•••GU•
AIRGUN
ARTGUM
BADGUY
BANGUI
BANGUP
BEEGUM
BIGGUN
BROGUE
BULGUR
CAPGUN
CATGUT
CLOGUP
DENGUE
DINGUS
DROGUE
FERGUS
FUNGUS
GANGUE
GANGUP
GILGUY
HANGUL
HANGUP
HUNGUP
JETGUN
LANGUR
LEAGUE
LINGUA
LONGUE
OUTGUN
PLAGUE
POPGUN
PRAGUE
RANGUP
RAYGUN
REDGUM
RINGUP
ROTGUT
RUNGUP
SHOGUN
SIXGUN
SUBGUM
TANGUY
TONGUE
TOPGUN

•••G•U
CONGOU
HUNGWU
KUNGFU
PENGHU

••••GU
TELUGU

G•V•••
GAVEIN
GAVELS
GAVEUP
GAVIAL
GIVEIN
GIVENS
GIVERS
GIVETO
GIVEUP
GIVING
GOVERN

G••V••
GARVEY
GLOVED
GLOVER
GLOVES
GOOVER
GRAVED
GRAVEL
GRAVEN
GRAVER
GRAVES
GRAVID
GRIVET
GROVEL
GROVER
GROVES
GUAVAS

G•••V•
GENEVA
GENEVE
GODIVA
GREAVE
GRIEVE
GROOVE
GROOVY

G••••V
GUSTAV

•G•V••
AGAVES
OGIVES

••G•V•
ARGIVE

GW••••
GWYNNE

G•W•••
GAWAIN
GAWKED
GAWKER
GAWPED
GEWGAW
GOWEST
GOWILD
GOWITH
GOWNED

G••W••
GALWAY
GLOWED
GLOWER
GNAWED
GNAWER
GOAWAY
GOAWRY
GODWIN
GODWIT
GREWON
GREWUP
GROWER
GROWLS
GROWLY
GROWON
GROWTH
GROWUP

G•••W•
GODOWN

G••••W
GAGLAW
GEEGAW
GEWGAW
GOSLOW
GUFFAW

••GW••
BIGWIG
WIGWAG
WIGWAM

••G••W
FOGBOW
GAGLAW
JIGSAW
MCGRAW
MCGREW

•••GW•
HUNGWU

•••G•W
GEEGAW
GEWGAW

G•••X•
GALAXY

GY••••
GYBING
GYMBAG
GYPPED
GYPPER
GYPSUM
GYRATE
GYRENE
GYRONS
GYROSE

G•Y•••
GAYALS
GAYEST
GAYNOR
GEYSER
GLYCOL
GLYNIS
GLYPHS
GUYANA
GUYING
GUYOTS
GWYNNE

G••Y••
GALYAK
GRAYED
GRAYER
GRAYLY
GREYED
GREYER
GREYLY

G•••Y•
GAMAYS
GLADYS

G••••Y
GADFLY
GAIETY
GAINLY
GALAXY
GALLEY
GALWAY
GAMELY
GAMILY
GANGLY
GANTRY
GARVEY
GASIFY
GATSBY
GELSEY
GENTLY
GENTRY
GEORGY
GETSBY
GHARRY
GIGGLY
GILGUY
GLADLY
GLAIRY
GLASSY
GLEAMY
GLIBLY
GLITZY
GLOOMY
GLOPPY
GLOSSY
GLUMLY
GNARLY
GNATTY
GOAWAY
GOAWRY
GOEASY
GOESBY
GOGGLY
GONEBY
GOODBY
GOODLY
GOOGLY
GOOSEY
GORILY
GRABBY
GRAINY
GRAMMY
GRANNY
GRAPEY
GRAPHY
GRASSY
GRAYLY
GREASY
GREEDY
GREENY
GREYLY
GRIMLY
GRISLY
GRITTY
GROGGY
GROOVY
GROSZY
GROTTY
GROUTY
GROWLY
GROZNY
GRUBBY
GRUMPY
GRUNDY
GRUNGY
GUILTY
GUITRY
GUNSHY
GURLEY
GURNEY

•G•Y••
NGUYEN

•G•••Y
AGENCY
UGLIFY
UGLILY

••GY••
ARGYLE
ARGYLL
MAGYAR

••G•Y•
BOGEYS
DOGEYS
FOGEYS
NAGOYA

••G••Y
ARGOSY
ARGUFY
AUGURY
BEGLEY
BIGAMY
BIGBOY
CAGILY
CAGNEY
DOGDAY
EDGILY
EIGHTY
GIGGLY
GOGGLY
HIGHLY
HUGELY
JIGGLY
LEGACY
LOGILY
MAGUEY
MIGHTY
NIGHTY
PIGSTY
RIGHTY
SAGELY
SUGARY
TAGDAY
VAGARY
WAGGLY
WIGGLY

•••G•Y
BADGUY
BENGAY
BOIGNY
CLOGGY
CRAGGY
DANGLY
DINGHY
DOUGHY
DRAGGY
FLAGGY
FROGGY
GANGLY
GIGGLY
GILGUY
GOGGLY
GOOGLY
GROGGY
HUNGRY
JANGLY
JIGGLY
JINGLY
JUNGLY
KINGLY
KNAGGY
LONGLY
MARGAY
NORGAY
QUAGGY
ROUGHY
SHAGGY
SINGLY
SLAGGY
SMOGGY
SMUGLY
SNAGGY
SNUGLY
TANGLY
TANGUY
TINGLY
TOUGHY
TRIGLY
TWIGGY
WAGGLY
WIGGLY

••••GY
ANERGY
CLERGY
CLINGY
CLOGGY
CRAGGY
DRAGGY
EFFIGY
ENERGY
EULOGY
FLAGGY
FLEDGY
FRINGY
FROGGY
GEORGY
GROGGY
GRUNGY
KNAGGY
OOLOGY
ORANGY
QUAGGY
SHAGGY
SLAGGY
SLANGY
SLUDGY
SMOGGY
SMUDGY
SNAGGY
SPONGY
STINGY
STODGY
SWINGY
SYZYGY
THINGY
TWANGY
TWIGGY

G•Z•••
GAZEBO
GAZING
GAZUMP
GEZIRA
GIZMOS
GUZZLE

G••Z••
GAUZES
GEEZER
GHAZIS
GLAZED
GLAZER
GLAZES
GLOZED
GLOZES
GRAZED
GRAZER
GRAZES
GROZNY
GUZZLE

G•••Z•
GLITZY
GROSZY

•G•••Z
IGNATZ

••GZ••
ZIGZAG

HA••••
HABANA
HABEAS
HABILE
HABITS
HACEKS
HACKED
HACKER
HACKIE
HACKLE
HACKLY
HADDIE
HADJES
HADJIS
HADRON
HAEMAT
HAEMON
HAFTED
HAGDON
HAGGIS
HAGGLE
HAGMAN
HAIDAS
HAIGHT
HAIKUS
HAILED
HAILEY
HAINAN
HAINES
HAIRDO
HAIRED
HAJJES
HAJJIS
HAKIMS
HALERS
HALERU
HALEST
HALEVY
HALIDE
HALING
HALITE
HALLEL
HALLEY
HALLOO
HALLOS
HALLOW
HALLUX
HALOED
HALOES
HALOID
HALSEY
HALTED
HALTER
HALVAH
HALVED
HALVES
HAMALS
HAMELN
HAMILL
HAMITE
HAMLET
HAMLIN
HAMMED
HAMMER
HAMPER
HANDED
HANDEL
HANDIN
HANDLE
HANDON
HANDUP
HANGAR
HANGED
HANGER
HANGIN
HANGON
HANGUL
HANGUP
HANKER
HANKIE
HANLEY
HANNAH
HANSEL
HANSOM
HANSON
HAOLES
HAPPED
HAPPEN
HARALD
HARARE
HARASS
HARBIN
HARBOR
HARDBY
HARDEN
HARDER
HARDLY
HARDUP
HAREMS
HARING
HARKED
HARKEN
HARKER
HARLAN
HARLEM
HARLEY
HARLIN
HARLOW
HARMED
HARMON
HAROLD
HARPED
HARPER
HARPON
HARRIS
HARROW
HARVEY
HASBRO
HASHED
HASHES
HASPED
HASSAM
HASSAN
HASSLE
HASTEN
HASTES
HATARI
HATBOX
HATERS
HATFUL
HATHOR
HATING
HATPIN
HATRED
HATTED
HATTER
HATTIE
HAULED
HAULER
HAULMS
HAULUP
HAUNCH
HAUNTS
HAUSAS
HAVANA
HAVASU
HAVEAT
HAVENS
HAVENT
HAVEON
HAVERS
HAVING
HAVOCS
HAWAII
HAWHAW
HAWING
HAWKED
HAWKER
HAWSER
HAWSES
HAYDEN
HAYING
HAYLEY
HAYMOW
HAZANS
HAZARD
HAZELS
HAZERS
HAZIER
HAZILY
HAZING

H•A•••
HEADED
HEADER
HEADIN
HEADON

HEADUP
HEALED
HEALER
HEALTH
HEANEY
HEAPED
HEARER
HEAROF
HEARST
HEARTH
HEARTS
HEARTY
HEARYE
HEATED
HEATER
HEATHS
HEATHY
HEATUP
HEAVED
HEAVEN
HEAVER
HEAVES
HIATAL
HIATUS
HOAGIE
HOARDS
HOARSE
HOAXED
HOAXER
HOAXES
HYADES

H••A••

HABANA
HAMALS
HARALD
HARARE
HARASS
HATARI
HAVANA
HAVASU
HAWAII
HAZANS
HAZARD
HBEAMS
HECATE
HEGARI
HEMATO
HERALD
HEXADS
HIJACK
HILARY
HIVAOA
HOBART
HODADS
HOGANS
HOMAGE
HORACE
HOTAIR
HOWARD
HUMANE
HUMANS

H•••A•

HABEAS
HAEMAT
HAGMAN
HAIDAS
HAINAN
HALVAH
HANGAR
HANNAH
HARLAN
HASSAM
HASSAN
HAUSAS
HAVEAT
HAWHAW
HEEHAW
HELLAS
HENNAS
HEPCAT
HEPTAD
HERBAL
HEREAT
HERMAN
HETMAN
HEYDAY
HIATAL
HIEMAL
HIJRAH
HINTAT
HISSAT
HITMAN
HOOHAH
HOOHAS
HOOKAH
HOORAH
HOORAY
HOOTAT
HOSTAS
HOTCAP
HOTCAR
HOTWAR
HOWDAH
HUBCAP
HURRAH
HURRAY
HUSSAR
HUZZAH
HUZZAS
HYDRAE
HYDRAS
HYENAS
HYETAL
HYMNAL

H••••A

HABANA
HAVANA
HECUBA
HEGIRA
HELENA
HESTIA
HIVAOA
HOOPLA
HOTTEA
HULLOA

•HA•••

BHAKTI
CHACHA
CHACMA
CHADOR
CHAFED
CHAFES
CHAFFS
CHAFFY
CHAINE
CHAINS
CHAIRS
CHAISE
CHALCO
CHALET
CHALKS
CHALKY
CHAMMY
CHAMPS
CHANCE
CHANCY
CHANEL
CHANEY
CHANGE
CHANTS
CHAPEL
CHAPIN
CHARGE
CHARLY
CHARMS
CHARON
CHARRO
CHARTS
CHASED
CHASER
CHASES
CHASMS
CHASSE
CHASTE
CHATTY
CHATUP
CHAVEZ
DHARMA
GHAINS
GHARRY
GHAZIS
KHAFRE
KHAKIS
KHALID
PHAGES
PHAROS
PHASED
PHASER
PHASES
PHATIC
RHABDO
RHAMES
SHABAN
SHABBY
SHACKS
SHADED
SHADES
SHADOW
SHAFTS
SHAGGY
SHAKEN
SHAKER
SHAKES
SHAKOS
SHAKTI
SHALES
SHALEY
SHALLY
SHALOM
SHAMAN
SHAMED
SHAMES
SHAMIR
SHAMUS
SHANDY
SHANIA
SHANKS
SHANNY
SHANTY
SHAPED
SHAPER
SHAPES
SHARDS
SHARED
SHARER
SHARES
SHARIA
SHARIF
SHARKS
SHARON
SHARPS
SHASTA
SHAVED
SHAVEN
SHAVER
SHAVES
SHAWLS
SHAWMS
SHAYNE
SHAZAM
THALER
THALES
THALIA
THAMES
THANES
THANKS
THATCH
THATIS
THATLL
THAWED
THAYER
WHACKS
WHACKY
WHALER
WHALES
WHAMMO
WHAMMY
WHANGS
WHARFS
WHATIF
WHATLL
WHATVE

•H•A••

CHEAPO
CHEATS
CHIANG
CHIAUS
CHOATE
PHIALS
PHRASE
SHEAFS
SHEARS
SHEATH
SHEAVE
SHOALS
SHOALY
SHOATS
SHRANK
THRACE
THRALE
THRALL
THRASH
THWACK
THWART
UHLANS
WHEALS
WHEATS

•H••A•

BHOPAL
BHUTAN
CHELAE
CHELAS
CHEVAL
CHIRAC
CHORAL
CHUKAR
OHIOAN
OHYEAH
PHILAE
PHYLAE
RHINAL
SHABAN
SHAMAN
SHAZAM
SHEVAT
SHIKAR
SHIRAZ
SHOFAR
SHORAN
SHOTAT
THECAE
THECAL
THEHAJ
THENAR
THETAS
THOMAS
THORAX
THREAD
THREAT
THROAT
THUJAS
WHYDAH
XHOSAS

•H•••A

AHIMSA
CHACHA
CHACMA
CHICHA
CHOLLA
CHOPRA
CHROMA
CHUKKA
DHARMA
PHOBIA
RHONDA
RHUMBA
SHANIA
SHARIA
SHASTA
SHEENA
SHEILA
SHERPA
SHORTA
THALIA
THELMA
THESEA

••HA••

ACHAEA
AGHAST
AMHARA
ASHARP
ATHAND
BAHAMA
BEHALF
BEHAVE
BIHARI
BSHARP
BYHAND
CSHARP
DSHARP
ENHALO
EPHAHS
ERHARD
ESHARP
ETHANE
EXHALE
FSHARP
GSHARP
INHALE
INHALF
INHAND
INHAUL
ITHACA
ITHAKI
JIHADS
JOHANN
LCHAIM
MCHALE
MOHAIR
MOHAVE
MOHAWK
OGHAMS
ONHAND
OSHAWA
PAHANG
PAHARI
REHABS
REHANG
REHASH
SAHARA
UNHAND
UTHANT

••H•A•

ASHCAN
ASHLAR
ASHRAM
BAHIAN
BEHEAD
ISHTAR
LEHUAS
MIHRAB
RAHRAH
REHEAL
REHEAR
REHEAT
SCHWAB
SCHWAS
WAHWAH

••H••A

ACHAEA
AMHARA
ATHENA
BAHAMA
DAHLIA
ITHACA
KAHLUA
KAHUNA
OSHAWA
SAHARA
SCHEMA

•••HA•

AFGHAN
ALOHAS
ALPHAS
ASCHAM
ATTHAT
BADHAM
BUCHAN
CATHAY
COBHAM
CUSHAW
DACHAS
DIRHAM
DOTHAN
DUNHAM
DURHAM
FOGHAT
GOTHAM
GRAHAM
HAWHAW
HEEHAW
HOOHAH
HOOHAS
ITZHAK
LAPHAM
LETHAL
LOTHAR
MAYHAP
MISHAP
MOCHAS
MOSHAV
NATHAN
NIIHAU
NUCHAE
NUCHAL
OLDHAM
OLDHAT
OMAHAN
OMAHAS
ORPHAN
PASHAS
PATHAN
RASHAD
REDHAT
RODHAM
SASHAY
SOTHAT
SOWHAT
SUCHAS
THEHAJ
TINHAT
TOPHAT
UTAHAN
WITHAL

•••H•A

ALTHEA
BRAHMA
BUSHWA
ISCHIA
JOSHUA
KESHIA
MOTHRA
NASHUA
PYTHIA
SOPHIA
TEPHRA

••••HA

AGATHA
ARETHA
AYESHA
BERTHA
BETCHA
BUDDHA
BUQSHA
CHACHA
CHICHA
CONCHA
EARTHA
ELISHA
GEISHA
GOTCHA
GURKHA
ILESHA
JASCHA
KWACHA
MANCHA
MARSHA
MARTHA
MISCHA
PERCHA
QUOTHA
TRISHA
YAMAHA

HB••••

HBEAMS
HBOMBS

H•B•••

HABANA
HABEAS
HABILE
HABITS
HEBREW
HEBRON
HOBART
HOBBES
HOBBIT
HOBBLE
HOBNOB
HOBOES
HOBSON
HUBBLE
HUBBLY
HUBBUB
HUBCAP
HUBERT
HUBRIS
HYBRID

H••B••

HARBIN
HARBOR
HASBRO
HATBOX
HEEBIE
HENBIT
HERBAL
HERBIE
HOBBES
HOBBIT
HOBBLE
HOMBRE
HOTBED
HOTBOX
HUBBLE
HUBBLY
HUBBUB
HUMBLE
HUMBLY
HUMBUG

H•••B•

HARDBY
HBOMBS
HECUBA
HEREBY

H••••B

HOBNOB
HOTTUB
HUBBUB

•HB•••

SHBOOM

•H•B••

CHUBBY
KHYBER
PHOBIA
PHOBIC
PHOBOS
RHABDO
RHEBOK
SHABAN
SHABBY
THEBES

•H••B•

CHUBBY
PHILBY
PHLEBO
PHOEBE
RHOMBI
RHOMBS
RHUMBA
RHUMBS
SHABBY
SHRUBS
THISBE
THROBS
THUMBS

•H•••B

CHERUB
THEWEB

••H•B•

ACHEBE
EPHEBE
REHABS
SAHIBS

••H••B

MIHRAB
SCHWAB

H•C•••

HACEKS
HACKED
HACKER
HACKIE
HACKLE
HACKLY
HECATE
HECKLE
HECTIC

HECTOR
HECUBA
HICCUP
HICKEY
HICKOK
HOCKED
HOCKEY

H••C••
HEPCAT
HICCUP
HINCTY
HONCHO
HOTCAP
HOTCAR
HUBCAP

H•••C•
HAUNCH
HAVOCS
HIJACK
HIRSCH
HITECH
HOOTCH
HORACE

H••••C
HECTIC
HEROIC
HOMEEC

•HC•••
AHCHOO

•H•C••
CHACHA
CHACMA
CHECKS
CHICHA
CHICHI
CHICKS
CHICLE
CHICLY
CHOCKS
CHUCKS
PHOCIS
SHACKS
SHOCKS
SHUCKS
THECAE
THECAL
THICKE
WHACKS
WHACKY

•H••C•
CHALCO
CHANCE
CHANCY
CHEECH
CHINCH
CHOICE
CHURCH
SHTICK
THATCH
THENCE
THRACE
THRICE
THWACK
WHENCE

•H•••C
CHIRAC
PHATIC
PHOBIC
PHONIC
PHOTIC
THETIC

••HC••
ASHCAN

••H•C•
ETHICS
ITHACA
MOHOCK
SCHICK

••H••C
ECHOIC
ETHNIC

•••HC•
BOCHCO

•••H•C
GOTHIC
LITHIC
MYTHIC
ORPHIC
UNCHIC

H•D•••
HADDIE
HADJES
HADJIS
HADRON
HEDDLE
HEDGED
HEDGER
HEDGES
HEDREN
HEDRON
HIDDEN
HIDEHO
HIDEKI
HIDERS
HIDING
HIDOUT
HODADS
HODGES
HUDDLE
HUDSON
HYDRAE
HYDRAS
HYDROS

H••D••
HADDIE
HAGDON
HAIDAS
HANDED
HANDEL
HANDIN
HANDLE
HANDON
HANDUP
HARDBY
HARDEN
HARDER
HARDLY
HARDUP
HAYDEN
HEADED
HEADER
HEADIN
HEADON
HEADUP
HEDDLE
HEEDED
HEEDER
HEIDEN
HELDIN
HELDON
HELDTO
HELDUP
HERDED
HERDER
HEYDAY
HIDDEN
HINDER
HINDUS
HOLDEN
HOLDER
HOLDIN
HOLDIT
HOLDON
HOLDTO
HOLDUP
HOODED
HOODOO
HORDES
HOTDOG
HOWDAH
HOYDEN
HUDDLE
HURDLE
HYADES

H•••D•
HAIRDO
HALIDE
HEXADS
HOARDS
HODADS
HOUNDS
HOUNDY

H••••D
HACKED
HAFTED
HAILED
HAIRED
HALOED
HALOID
HALTED
HALVED
HAMMED
HANDED
HANGED
HAPPED
HARALD
HARKED
HARMED
HAROLD
HARPED
HASHED
HASPED
HATRED
HATTED
HAULED
HAWKED
HAZARD
HEADED
HEALED
HEAPED
HEATED
HEAVED
HEDGED
HEEDED
HEELED
HEFTED
HELMED
HELPED
HEMMED
HENTED
HEPTAD
HERALD
HERDED
HESIOD
HILLED
HINGED
HINTED
HIPPED
HISPID
HISSED
HOAXED
HOCKED
HOGGED
HONIED
HONKED
HOODED
HOOFED
HOOKED
HOOPED
HOOTED
HOPPED
HORNED
HORRID
HORSED
HOSTED
HOTBED
HOTROD
HOUSED
HOWARD
HOWLED
HUFFED
HUGGED
HULKED
HULLED
HUMMED
HUMPED
HUNTED
HURLED
HUSHED
HUSKED
HUTTED
HYBRID
HYMNED
HYPOED

•H•D••
CHADOR
CHIDED
CHIDER
CHIDES
PHEDRE
RHODES
SHADED
SHADES
SHADOW
SHODDY
WHYDAH

•H••D•
CHILDE
CHILDS
CHORDS
RHABDO
RHONDA
SHANDY
SHARDS
SHEEDY
SHINDY
SHODDY
SHREDS
THIRDS

•H•••D
CHAFED
CHASED
CHEWED
CHIDED
CHIMED
CHOKED
CHOWED
CHUTED
KHALID
PHASED
PHONED
PHYSED
RHYMED
SHADED
SHAMED
SHAPED
SHARED
SHAVED
SHIELD
SHINED
SHOOED
SHORED
SHOULD
SHOVED
SHOWED
SHREWD
SHROUD
THAWED
THEEND
THEFED
THEKID
THEMED
THREAD
THREED
WHERED
WHILED
WHINED

••HD••
MAHDIS

••H•D•
ANHYDR
APHIDS
EPHODS
JIHADS
MRHYDE
YEHUDI

••H••D
ATHAND
BEHEAD
BEHELD
BEHIND
BEHOLD
BYHAND
ECHOED
ERHARD
INHAND
ONHAND
ONHOLD
REHELD
TEHEED
UNHAND
UNHEED
UPHELD
UPHOLD

•••H•D
AMPHID
ARCHED
BACHED
BASHED
BATHED
BUSHED
CACHED
CASHED
COSHED
DASHED
DISHED
ETCHED
FISHED
GASHED
GUSHED
HASHED
HUSHED
INCHED
ITCHED
JOSHED
LASHED
LATHED
MASHED
MESHED
METHOD
MOSHED
MUSHED
NOSHED
ORCHID
PITHED
POOHED
PUSHED
RASHAD
RASHID
RESHOD
RUSHED
SASHED
SIGHED
TITHED
UNSHED
UNSHOD
WASHED
WISHED
WITHED

HE••••
HEADED
HEADER
HEADIN
HEADON
HEADUP
HEALED
HEALER
HEALTH
HEANEY
HEAPED
HEARER
HEAROF
HEARST
HEARTH
HEARTS
HEARTY
HEARYE
HEATED
HEATER
HEATHS
HEATHY
HEATUP
HEAVED
HEAVEN
HEAVER
HEAVES
HEBREW
HEBRON
HECATE
HECKLE
HECTIC
HECTOR
HECUBA
HEDDLE
HEDGED
HEDGER
HEDGES
HEDREN
HEDRON
HEEBIE
HEEDED
HEEDER
HEEHAW
HEELED
HEELER
HEFLIN
HEFNER
HEFTED
HEGARI
HEGIRA
HEIDEN
HEIFER
HEIGHT
HEISTS
HELDIN
HELDON
HELDTO
HELDUP
HELENA
HELENE
HELENS
HELIOS
HELIUM
HELLAS
HELLER
HELLOS
HELMED
HELMET
HELMUT
HELOTS
HELPED
HELPER
HELTER
HELVES
HEMATO
HEMMED
HEMMER
HEMSIN
HENBIT
HENLEY
HENNAS
HENNER
HENNIN
HENRIK
HENRYV
HENSON
HENTED
HEPCAT
HEPPER
HEPTAD
HERALD
HERBAL
HERBIE
HERDED
HERDER
HEREAT
HEREBY
HEREIN
HEREOF
HEREON
HERESY
HERETO
HERIOT
HERMAN
HERMES
HERMIT
HERMON
HEROES
HEROIC
HERONS
HERSEY
HERZOG
HESIOD
HESTER
HESTIA
HESTON
HETERO
HETMAN
HETTIE
HEWERS
HEWING
HEXADS
HEXERS
HEXING
HEXNUT
HEYDAY
HEYYOU

H•E•••
HAEMAT
HAEMON
HBEAMS
HEEBIE
HEEDED
HEEDER
HEEHAW
HEELED
HEELER
HIEING
HIEMAL
HIERON
HOEING
HUEVOS
HYENAS
HYETAL

H••E••
HABEAS
HACEKS
HALERS
HALERU
HALEST
HALEVY
HAMELN
HAREMS
HATERS
HAVEAT
HAVENS
HAVENT
HAVEON
HAVERS
HAZELS
HAZERS
HELENA
HELENE
HELENS
HEREAT
HEREBY
HEREIN
HEREOF
HEREON
HERESY
HERETO
HETERO
HEWERS
HEXERS
HIDEHO
HIDEKI
HIDERS
HIKERS
HIKEUP
HIREON
HIRERS
HITECH
HOLEUP
HOMEEC
HOMELY
HOMERS
HONEST
HONEYS
HOPERS
HOSELS
HOTELS
HOVELS
HOVERS
HOVETO
HOWELL
HUBERT
HUGELY
HUGEST
HUMERI
HYPEUP

H•••E•
HACKED
HACKER
HADJES
HAFTED
HAILED
HAILEY
HAINES
HAIRED
HAJJES
HALLEL
HALLEY
HALOED
HALOES

HALSEY
HALTED
HALTER
HALVED
HALVES
HAMLET
HAMMED
HAMMER
HAMPER
HANDED
HANDEL
HANGED
HANGER
HANKER
HANLEY
HANSEL
HAOLES
HAPPED
HAPPEN
HARDEN
HARDER
HARKED
HARKEN
HARKER
HARLEM
HARLEY
HARMED
HARPED
HARPER
HARVEY
HASHED
HASHES
HASPED
HASTEN
HASTES
HATRED
HATTED
HATTER
HAULED
HAULER
HAWKED
HAWKER
HAWSER
HAWSES
HAYDEN
HAYLEY
HAZIER
HEADED
HEADER
HEALED
HEALER
HEANEY
HEAPED
HEARER
HEATED
HEATER
HEAVED
HEAVEN
HEAVER
HEAVES
HEBREW
HEDGED
HEDGER
HEDGES
HEDREN
HEEDED
HEEDER
HEELED
HEELER
HEFNER
HEFTED
HEIDEN
HEIFER
HELLER
HELMED
HELMET
HELPED
HELPER
HELTER
HELVES
HEMMED
HEMMER
HENLEY
HENNER
HENTED
HEPPER
HERDED
HERDER
HERMES
HEROES
HERSEY
HESTER
HICKEY
HIDDEN
HIGHER
HILLED
HILLEL
HILLER
HINDER
HINGED
HINGES
HINTED
HINTER
HIPPED
HIPPER
HISSED
HISSER
HISSES
HITHER
HITMEN
HITTER
HOAXED
HOAXER
HOAXES
HOBBES
HOBOES
HOCKED
HOCKEY
HODGES
HOGGED
HOGGET
HOKIER
HOLDEN
HOLDER
HOLIER
HOLLER
HOLMES
HOMEEC
HOMIER
HONIED
HONKED
HONKER
HOODED
HOOFED
HOOFER
HOOKED
HOOPED
HOOPER
HOOTED
HOOTER
HOOVER
HOOVES
HOPPED
HOPPER
HORDES
HORMEL
HORNED
HORNER
HORNET
HORNEY
HORSED
HORSES
HORSEY
HOSIER
HOSTED
HOSTEL
HOTBED
HOTTEA
HOTTER
HOUSED
HOUSES
HOWLED
HOWLER
HOYDEN
HUFFED
HUGGED
HUGGER
HUGHES
HULKED
HULLED
HULLER
HUMMED
HUMMER
HUMPED
HUMVEE
HUNGER
HUNKER
HUNTED
HUNTER
HURLED
HURLER
HURLEY
HUSHED
HUSHES
HUSKED
HUSKER
HUSSEY
HUTTED
HUXLEY
HYADES
HYMNED
HYPHEN
HYPOED

H••••E

HABILE
HACKIE
HACKLE
HADDIE
HAGGLE
HALIDE
HALITE
HAMITE
HANDLE
HANKIE
HARARE
HASSLE
HATTIE
HEARYE
HECATE
HECKLE
HEDDLE
HEEBIE
HELENE
HERBIE
HETTIE
HIGGLE
HIPPIE
HOAGIE
HOARSE
HOBBLE
HOGTIE
HOMAGE
HOMBRE
HONORE
HOOPLE
HOOPOE
HOOTIE
HOPPLE
HORACE
HUBBLE
HUDDLE
HUMANE
HUMBLE
HUMVEE
HURDLE
HURTLE
HUSTLE
HYDRAE

•HE•••

AHERNE
CHEAPO
CHEATS
CHECKS
CHEECH
CHEEKS
CHEEKY
CHEEPS
CHEERS
CHEERY
CHEESE
CHEESY
CHEKOV
CHELAE
CHELAS
CHEMIN
CHENIN
CHEOPS
CHEQUE
CHERIE
CHERRY
CHERTY
CHERUB
CHERYL
CHESTS
CHESTY
CHETHS
CHEVAL
CHEVET
CHEVRE
CHEWED
CHEWER
CHEWUP
GHETTO
OHENRY
PHEDRE
PHENOL
PHENOM
PHENYL
RHEBOK
RHESUS
RHETOR
RHEUMS
RHEUMY
SHEAFS
SHEARS
SHEATH
SHEAVE
SHEEDY
SHEEHY
SHEENA
SHEENS
SHEEPS
SHEERS
SHEETS
SHEIKS
SHEILA
SHEKEL
SHELLS
SHELLY
SHELTY
SHELVE
SHEREE
SHERIF
SHERPA
SHERRY
SHERYL
SHEVAT
THEBES
THECAE
THECAL
THEEND
THEFED
THEFLY
THEFTS
THEHAJ
THEIRS
THEISM
THEIST
THEKID
THELIP
THELMA
THEMED
THEMES
THENAR
THENCE
THEORY
THERES
THERMO
THERMS
THESEA
THESES
THESIS
THESIX
THETAS
THETIC
THETIS
THETOY
THEWEB
THEWIZ
THEYLL
THEYRE
THEYVE
WHEALS
WHEATS
WHEELS
WHEEZE
WHEEZY
WHELKS
WHELMS
WHELPS
WHENCE
WHERED
WHERES
WHERRY

•H•E••

CHEECH
CHEEKS
CHEEKY
CHEEPS
CHEERS
CHEERY
CHEESE
CHEESY
CHIEFS
KHMERS
NHLERS
OHWELL
OHYEAH
PHLEBO
PHLEGM
PHOEBE
SHEEDY
SHEEHY
SHEENA
SHEENS
SHEEPS
SHEERS
SHEETS
SHIELD
SHIEST
SHOERS
SHREDS
SHREWD
SHREWS
SHTETL
SHYEST
THEEND
THIEVE
THREAD
THREAT
THREED
THREES
THRESH
WHEELS
WHEEZE
WHEEZY

•H••E•

CHAFED
CHAFES
CHALET
CHANEL
CHANEY
CHAPEL
CHASED
CHASER
CHASES
CHAVEZ
CHEVET
CHEWED
CHEWER
CHIDED
CHIDER
CHIDES
CHIMED
CHIMES
CHINES
CHISEL
CHIVES
CHOKED
CHOKER
CHOKES
CHOLER
CHORES
CHOSEN
CHOWED
CHUTED
CHUTES
DHOLES
DHOTEL
KHYBER
PHAGES
PHASED
PHASER
PHASES
PHLOEM
PHONED
PHONES
PHONEY
PHOOEY
PHYSED
RHAMES
RHODES
RHYMED
RHYMER
RHYMES
SHADED
SHADES
SHAKEN
SHAKER
SHAKES
SHALES
SHALEY
SHAMED
SHAMES
SHAPED
SHAPER
SHAPES
SHARED
SHARER
SHARES
SHAVED
SHAVEN
SHAVER
SHAVES
SHEKEL
SHEREE
SHINED
SHINER
SHINES
SHIRER
SHIRES
SHIVER
SHOLEM
SHOOED
SHORED
SHORES
SHOVED
SHOVEL
SHOVER
SHOVES
SHOWED
SHOWER
SHRIEK
THALER
THALES
THAMES
THANES
THAWED
THAYER
THEBES
THEFED
THEMED
THEMES
THERES
THESEA
THESES
THEWEB
THOLES
THREED
THREES
THROES
WHALER
WHALES
WHERED
WHERES
WHILED
WHILES
WHINED
WHINER
WHINES
WHINEY
WHITEN
WHITER
WHITES
WHOLES

•H•••E

AHERNE
CHAINE
CHAISE
CHANCE
CHANGE
CHARGE
CHASSE
CHASTE
CHEESE
CHELAE
CHEQUE
CHERIE
CHEVRE
CHICLE
CHIGOE
CHILDE
CHILOE
CHOATE
CHOICE
CHOOSE
CHROME
KHAFRE
LHOTSE
PHEDRE
PHILAE
PHOEBE
PHRASE
PHYLAE
SHAYNE
SHEAVE
SHELVE
SHEREE
SHIITE
SHOPPE
SHORTE
SHOWME
SHRIKE
SHRINE
SHRIVE
SHROVE
THECAE
THENCE
THEYRE
THEYVE
THICKE
THIEVE
THISBE
THORPE
THRACE
THRALE
THRICE
THRIVE
THRONE
THROVE
WHATVE
WHEEZE
WHENCE

••HE••

ACHEBE
ACHENE
ADHERE
ATHENA
ATHENE
ATHENS
BEHEAD
BEHELD
BEHEST
COHEIR
COHERE
EPHEBE
ETHENE
ETHERS
INHERE
OCHERS
OCHERY
OTHERS
REHEAL
REHEAR
REHEAT
REHEEL
REHELD
REHEMS
SCHELL
SCHEMA
SCHEME
SPHERE
SPHERY
STHENO
TEHEED
TEHEES
UNHEED
UPHELD
USHERS

••H•E•

ACHAEA
ACHIER
ASHIER
ASHLEY
CAHIER
ECHOED
ECHOES
KOHLER
LEHRER
MAHLER
OCHRES
REHEEL
ROHMER

SCHLEP
TEHEED
TEHEES
UNHEED
WOHLER
YAHWEH

••H••E
ACHEBE
ACHENE
ADHERE
ASHORE
ATHENE
ATHOME
AWHILE
BEHAVE
BEHOVE
COHERE
COHUNE
EPHEBE
ETHANE
ETHENE
EXHALE
GOHOME
INHALE
INHERE
JOHORE
LAHORE
MCHALE
MOHAVE
MRHYDE
OPHITE
REHIRE
SCHEME
SPHERE
WAHINE

•••HE•
AACHEN
AETHER
ALTHEA
ANTHEM
ANTHER
ARCHED
ARCHER
ARCHES
ARNHEM
BACHED
BASHED
BASHES
BATHED
BATHER
BATHES
BETHEL
BOTHER
BUSHED
BUSHEL
BUSHES
CACHED
CACHES
CACHET
CASHED
CASHES
CASHEW
CATHER
CIPHER
COSHED
COSHES
CYPHER
DASHED
DASHER
DASHES
DISHED
DISHES
DITHER
EITHER
ESCHER
ESCHEW
ESTHER
ETCHED
ETCHER
ETCHES
FATHER
FICHES
FISHED
FISHER
FISHES
GASHED
GASHES
GATHER
GOPHER
GOSHEN
GUSHED
GUSHER
GUSHES
HASHED
HASHES
HIGHER
HITHER
HUGHES
HUSHED
HUSHES
HYPHEN
INCHED
INCHES
ISOHEL
ITCHED
ITCHES
JOSHED
JOSHES
KOSHER
KUCHEN
LACHES
LASHED
LASHER
LASHES
LATHED
LATHER
LATHES
LICHEN
LUSHER
LUTHER
MACHES
MASHED
MASHER
MASHES
MATHER
MAYHEM
MESHED
MESHES
MICHEL
MOSHED
MOSHER
MOSHES
MOTHER
MUDHEN
MUSHED
MUSHER
MUSHES
NEPHEW
NETHER
NICHES
NIGHER
NOSHED
NOSHER
NOSHES
PEAHEN
PITHED
POOHED
POSHER
POTHER
PUSHED
PUSHES
RACHEL
RASHER
RASHES
RATHER
RESHES
RICHEN
RICHER
RICHES
ROCHET
RUCHES
RUSHED
RUSHEE
RUSHES
SACHEM
SACHET
SADHES
SASHED
SASHES
SIGHED
SIGHER
TEEHEE
TETHER
TITHED
TITHER
TITHES
TOTHER
TOWHEE
UNSHED
VACHEL
WASHED
WASHER
WASHES
WETHER
WISHED
WISHER
WISHES
WITHED
WITHER
WITHES
ZITHER

•••H•E
ARCHIE
DAPHNE
EUCHRE
FICHTE
KATHIE
KISHKE
MASHIE
NUCHAE
RESHOE
RICHIE
RUSHEE
SOPHIE
TECHIE
TEEHEE
TOWHEE
WASHOE

••••HE
AMECHE
APACHE
BLITHE
BLYTHE
BOOTHE
BUNCHE
BYSSHE
CLICHE
CLOCHE
CLOTHE
CRECHE
FLECHE
GAUCHE
GOETHE
LOATHE
LOUCHE
MARCHE
PSYCHE
QUICHE
SCATHE
SCYTHE
SEETHE
SEICHE
SNATHE
SOOTHE
SPATHE
SWATHE
TEETHE
TOUCHE
TROCHE
WRITHE

H•F•••
HAFTED
HEFLIN
HEFNER
HEFTED
HUFFED

H••F••
HATFUL
HEIFER
HOOFED
HOOFER
HOOFIT
HUFFED

H•••F•
HOPOFF

H••••F
HEAROF
HEREOF
HOPOFF

•H•F••
CHAFED
CHAFES
CHAFFS
CHAFFY
CHUFFY
KHAFRE
SHAFTS
SHIFTS
SHIFTY
SHOFAR
THEFED
THEFLY
THEFTS
WHIFFS

•H••F•
CHAFFS
CHAFFY
CHIEFS
CHUFFY
SHEAFS
SHRIFT
THRIFT
WHARFS
WHIFFS
WHOOFS

•H•••F
SHARIF
SHERIF
WHATIF

••H•F•
SCHIFF

••H••F
BEHALF
BEHOOF
INHALF
SCHIFF

H•G•••
HAGDON
HAGGIS
HAGGLE
HAGMAN
HEGARI
HEGIRA
HIGGLE
HIGHER
HIGHIQ
HIGHLY
HIGHUP
HOGANS
HOGGED
HOGGET
HOGTIE
HUGELY
HUGEST
HUGGED
HUGGER
HUGHES

H••G••
HAGGIS
HAGGLE
HAIGHT
HANGAR
HANGED
HANGER
HANGIN
HANGON
HANGUL
HANGUP
HEDGED
HEDGER
HEDGES
HEIGHT
HIGGLE
HINGED
HINGES
HINGIS
HOAGIE
HODGES
HOGGED
HOGGET
HOUGHS
HUGGED
HUGGER
HUNGER
HUNGIN
HUNGON
HUNGRY
HUNGUP
HUNGWU

H•••G•
HMONGS
HOMAGE

H••••G
HALING
HARING
HATING
HAVING
HAWING
HAYING
HAZING
HERZOG
HEWING
HEXING
HIDING
HIEING
HIKING
HIRING
HIVING
HOEING
HOLING
HOMING
HONING
HOPING
HOSING
HOTDOG
HUMBUG
HYPING

•H•G••
CHIGOE
PHAGES
SHAGGY
SHOGUN
THIGHS

•H••G•
CHANGE
CHARGE
CHOUGH
PHLEGM
SHAGGY
SHRUGS
THINGS
THINGY
THONGS
THOUGH
WHANGS

•H•••G
CHIANG
PHOTOG
SHYING
THRONG

••H•G•
LEHIGH
MCHUGH
ONHIGH

••H••G
AAHING
ACHING
GEHRIG
ICHING
OOHING
PAHANG
REHANG
REHUNG

•••H•G
LITHOG
QUAHOG

H•H•••
HLHUNT
HOHOHO

H••H••
HASHED
HASHES
HATHOR
HAWHAW
HEEHAW
HIGHER
HIGHIQ
HIGHLY
HIGHUP
HIPHOP
HITHER
HOOHAH
HOOHAS
HUGHES
HUSHED
HUSHES
HYPHEN

H•••H•
HAIGHT
HEATHS
HEATHY
HEIGHT
HIDEHO
HOHOHO
HONCHO
HONSHU
HOUGHS
HUMPHS

H••••H
HALVAH
HANNAH
HAUNCH
HEALTH
HEARTH
HIJRAH
HIRSCH
HITECH
HOOHAH
HOOKAH
HOORAH
HOOTCH
HOWDAH
HURRAH
HUZZAH

•H•H••
AHCHOO
CHUHSI
THEHAJ

•H••H•
CHACHA
CHETHS
CHICHA
CHICHI
RHYTHM
SHEEHY
THIGHS

•H•••H
CHEECH
CHINCH
CHOUGH
CHURCH
OHYEAH
SHEATH
SHILOH
THATCH
THOUGH
THRASH
THRESH
THRUSH
WHOOSH
WHYDAH

••H•H•
EPHAHS
HOHOHO
ICHTHY
YOHOHO

••H••H
LEHIGH
MCHUGH
ONHIGH
RAHRAH
REHASH
WAHWAH
YAHWEH

•••H•H
EIGHTH
HOOHAH

HI••••
HIATAL
HIATUS
HICCUP
HICKEY
HICKOK
HIDDEN
HIDEHO
HIDEKI
HIDERS
HIDING
HIDOUT
HIEING
HIEMAL
HIERON
HIGGLE
HIGHER
HIGHIQ
HIGHLY
HIGHUP
HIJACK
HIJRAH
HIKERS
HIKEUP
HIKING
HILARY
HILLED
HILLEL
HILLER
HILTON
HINCTY
HINDER
HINDUS
HINGED
HINGES
HINGIS
HINTAT
HINTED
HINTER
HINTON
HIPHOP
HIPPED
HIPPER
HIPPIE
HIPPOS
HIREON
HIRERS
HIRING
HIRSCH
HISPID
HISSAT
HISSED
HISSER
HISSES
HITECH
HITHER
HITMAN
HITMEN
HITOUT
HITSIT
HITSON
HITSUP
HITTER
HIVAOA
HIVING

H•I•••
HAIDAS
HAIGHT
HAIKUS
HAILED
HAILEY
HAINAN
HAINES
HAIRDO
HAIRED
HEIDEN
HEIFER
HEIGHT
HEISTS
HOISTS

H••I••
HABILE
HABITS
HAKIMS
HALIDE
HALING

HALITE
HAMILL
HAMITE
HARING
HATING
HAVING
HAWING
HAYING
HAZIER
HAZILY
HAZING
HEGIRA
HELIOS
HELIUM
HERIOT
HESIOD
HEWING
HEXING
HIDING
HIEING
HIKING
HIRING
HIVING
HOEING
HOKIER
HOLIER
HOLILY
HOLING
HOLISM
HOLIST
HOMIER
HOMILY
HOMING
HOMINY
HONIED
HONING
HOPING
HOSIER
HOSING
HYPING

H•••I•
HACKIE
HADDIE
HADJIS
HAGGIS
HAJJIS
HALOID
HAMLIN
HANDIN
HANGIN
HANKIE
HARBIN
HARLIN
HARRIS
HATPIN
HATTIE
HAWAII
HEADIN
HECTIC
HEEBIE
HEFLIN
HELDIN
HEMSIN
HENBIT
HENNIN
HENRIK
HERBIE
HEREIN
HERMIT
HEROIC
HESTIA
HETTIE
HIGHIQ
HINGIS
HIPPIE
HISPID
HITSIT
HOAGIE
HOBBIT
HOGTIE
HOLDIN
HOLDIT
HOOFIT
HOOTIE
HOPSIN
HORNIN
HORRID
HOTAIR
HOTTIP
HOURIS
HOWLIN
HUBRIS
HUNGIN
HYBRID

H••••I
HATARI
HAWAII
HEGARI
HIDEKI
HUMERI

•HI•••
AHIMSA
CHIANG
CHIAUS
CHICHA
CHICHI
CHICKS
CHICLE
CHICLY
CHIDED
CHIDER
CHIDES
CHIEFS
CHIGOE
CHILDE
CHILDS
CHILLI
CHILLS
CHILLY
CHILOE
CHIMED
CHIMES
CHIMPS
CHINCH
CHINES
CHINKS
CHINKY
CHINOS
CHINTZ
CHINUP
CHIPIN
CHIRAC
CHIRON
CHIRPS
CHIRPY
CHIRRS
CHISEL
CHISOX
CHITIN
CHITON
CHIVES
OHIOAN
PHIALS
PHILAE
PHILBY
PHILIP
PHILLY
PHILOL
PHILOS
RHINAL
RHINOS
SHIELD
SHIEST
SHIFTS
SHIFTY
SHIISM
SHIITE
SHIKAR
SHILLS
SHILLY
SHILOH
SHIMMY
SHIMON
SHINDY
SHINED
SHINER
SHINES
SHINNY
SHINTO
SHIRAZ
SHIRER
SHIRES
SHIRKS
SHIRRS
SHIRTS
SHIRTY
SHIVER
THICKE
THIEVE
THIGHS
THILLS
THINGS
THINGY
THINKS
THINLY
THIRDS
THIRST
THIRTY
THISBE
WHIFFS
WHILED
WHILES
WHILOM
WHILST
WHIMSY
WHINED
WHINER
WHINES
WHINEY
WHINNY
WHIPPY
WHIPUP
WHIRLS
WHIRLY
WHIRRS
WHISKS
WHISKY
WHITEN
WHITER
WHITES
WHITTY
WHIZZO

•H•I••
CHAINE
CHAINS
CHAIRS
CHAISE
CHOICE
CHOIRS
CHRISM
GHAINS
SHEIKS
SHEILA
SHIISM
SHIITE
SHRIEK
SHRIFT
SHRIKE
SHRILL
SHRIMP
SHRINE
SHRINK
SHRIVE
SHTICK
SHYING
THEIRS
THEISM
THEIST
THRICE
THRIFT
THRILL
THRIPS
THRIVE

•H••I•
CHAPIN
CHEMIN
CHENIN
CHERIE
CHIPIN
CHITIN
CHOPIN
DHOTIS
GHAZIS
KHAKIS
KHALID
PHATIC
PHILIP
PHOBIA
PHOBIC
PHOCIS
PHONIC
PHOTIC
PHYSIO
SHAMIR
SHANIA
SHARIA
SHARIF
SHERIF
SHOJIS
SHOOIN
SHOWIN
SHUTIN
THALIA
THATIS
THEKID
THELIP
THESIS
THESIX
THETIC
THETIS
THEWIZ
WHATIF

•H•••I
BHAKTI
CHICHI
CHILLI
CHUHSI
RHOMBI
SHAKTI
SHORTI
THYRSI
WHOOPI

••HI••
AAHING
ACHIER
ACHING
ALHIRT
APHIDS
ASHIER
AWHILE
AWHIRL
BAHIAN
BEHIND
CAHIER
ECHINO
ETHICS
ICHING
LEHIGH
NIHILO
NOHITS
ONHIGH
OOHING
OPHITE
REHIRE
SAHIBS
SCHICK
SCHIFF
SCHISM
SCHIST
SCHIZY
SPHINX
TAHINI
TAHITI
TSHIRT
UPHILL
VCHIPS
WAHINE

••H•I•
COHEIR
DAHLIA
ECHOIC
ETHNIC
GEHRIG
KAHLIL
LCHAIM
MAHDIS
MOHAIR

••H••I
BIHARI
EPHORI
ITHAKI
PAHARI
TAHINI
TAHITI
YEHUDI

•••HI•
AMPHID
ARCHIE
CASHIN
COCHIN
DASHIS
DUCHIN
ELOHIM
GOTHIC
HIGHIQ
ISCHIA
KATHIE
KESHIA
LASHIO
LITHIC
MASHIE
MATHIS
MENHIR
MISHIT
MUZHIK
MYTHIC
ORCHID
ORCHIL
ORPHIC
OUTHIT
PYTHIA
RACHIS
RASHID
RESHIP
RICHIE
SOPHIA
SOPHIE
SPAHIS
TECHIE
UNCHIC
URCHIN
WITHIN
WITHIT

•••H•I
CHUHSI
ISTHMI
MYTHOI
TISHRI
TZUHSI
VASHTI

••••HI
CANTHI
CHICHI
DELPHI
GANDHI
KIMCHI
LITCHI
TAICHI

H•J•••
HAJJES
HAJJIS
HIJACK
HIJRAH

H••J••
HADJES
HADJIS
HAJJES
HAJJIS

•H•J••
SHOJIS
THUJAS

•H••J•
CHONJU

•H•••J
THEHAJ

•••H•J
THEHAJ

H•K•••
HAKIMS
HIKERS
HIKEUP
HIKING
HOKIER
HYKSOS

H••K••
HACKED
HACKER
HACKIE
HACKLE
HACKLY
HAIKUS
HANKER
HANKIE
HARKED
HARKEN
HARKER
HAWKED
HAWKER
HECKLE
HICKEY
HICKOK
HOCKED
HOCKEY
HONKED
HONKER
HOOKAH
HOOKED
HOOKUP
HULKED
HUNKER
HUSKED
HUSKER

H•••K•
HACEKS
HIDEKI

H••••K
HENRIK
HICKOK
HIJACK

•H•K••
BHAKTI
CHEKOV
CHOKED
CHOKER
CHOKES
CHUKAR
CHUKKA
KHAKIS
SHAKEN
SHAKER
SHAKES
SHAKOS
SHAKTI
SHEKEL
SHIKAR
THEKID
ZHUKOV

•H••K•
CHALKS
CHALKY
CHECKS
CHEEKS
CHEEKY
CHICKS
CHINKS
CHINKY
CHOCKS
CHUCKS
CHUKKA
CHUNKS
CHUNKY
SHACKS
SHANKS
SHARKS
SHEIKS
SHIRKS
SHOCKS
SHOOKS
SHRIKE
SHUCKS
THANKS
THICKE
THINKS
THUNKS
WHACKS
WHACKY
WHELKS
WHISKS
WHISKY

•H•••K
RHEBOK
SHRANK
SHRIEK
SHRINK
SHRUNK
SHTICK
THWACK

••H•K•
ITHAKI

••H••K
DRHOOK
MOHAWK
MOHOCK
REHOOK
SCHICK
UNHOOK

•••HK•
KISHKE
ROTHKO

•••H•K
ITZHAK
MUZHIK

HL••••
HLHUNT

H•L•••
HALERS
HALERU
HALEST
HALEVY
HALIDE
HALING
HALITE
HALLEL
HALLEY
HALLOO
HALLOS
HALLOW
HALLUX
HALOED
HALOES
HALOID
HALSEY
HALTED
HALTER
HALVAH
HALVED
HALVES
HELDIN
HELDON
HELDTO
HELDUP
HELENA
HELENE
HELENS
HELIOS
HELIUM
HELLAS
HELLER
HELLOS
HELMED
HELMET
HELMUT
HELOTS
HELPED
HELPER
HELTER
HELVES
HILARY
HILLED
HILLEL
HILLER
HILTON
HOLDEN
HOLDER
HOLDIN
HOLDIT
HOLDON
HOLDTO
HOLDUP
HOLEUP
HOLIER
HOLILY
HOLING
HOLISM
HOLIST
HOLLER
HOLLOW
HOLMES
HULKED

HULLED
HULLER
HULLOA
HULLOS

H••L••
HAILED
HAILEY
HALLEL
HALLEY
HALLOO
HALLOS
HALLOW
HALLUX
HAMLET
HAMLIN
HANLEY
HAOLES
HARLAN
HARLEM
HARLEY
HARLIN
HARLOW
HAULED
HAULER
HAULMS
HAULUP
HAYLEY
HEALED
HEALER
HEALTH
HEELED
HEELER
HEFLIN
HELLAS
HELLER
HELLOS
HENLEY
HILLED
HILLEL
HILLER
HOLLER
HOLLOW
HOWLED
HOWLER
HOWLIN
HULLED
HULLER
HULLOA
HULLOS
HURLED
HURLER
HURLEY
HUXLEY

H•••L•
HABILE
HACKLE
HACKLY
HAGGLE
HAMALS
HAMELN
HAMILL
HANDLE
HARALD
HARDLY
HAROLD
HASSLE
HAZELS
HAZILY
HECKLE
HEDDLE
HERALD
HIGGLE
HIGHLY
HOBBLE
HOLILY
HOMELY
HOMILY
HOOPLA
HOOPLE
HOPPLE
HOSELS
HOSTLY
HOTELS
HOURLY
HOVELS
HOWELL
HUBBLE
HUBBLY
HUDDLE
HUGELY
HUMBLE
HUMBLY
HURDLE
HURTLE
HUSTLE

H••••L
HALLEL
HAMILL
HANDEL
HANGUL
HANSEL
HATFUL
HERBAL
HIATAL
HIEMAL
HILLEL
HORMEL
HOSTEL
HOWELL
HYETAL
HYMNAL

•HL•••
CHLORO
NHLERS
PHLEBO
PHLEGM
PHLOEM
UHLANS

•H•L••
CHALCO
CHALET
CHALKS
CHALKY
CHELAE
CHELAS
CHILDE
CHILDS
CHILLI
CHILLS
CHILLY
CHILOE
CHOLER
CHOLLA
CHOLOS
DHOLES
KHALID
PHILAE
PHILBY
PHILIP
PHILLY
PHILOL
PHILOS
PHYLAE
PHYLLO
PHYLUM
SHALES
SHALEY
SHALLY
SHALOM
SHELLS
SHELLY
SHELTY
SHELVE
SHILLS
SHILLY
SHILOH
SHOLEM
SHOLOM
THALER
THALES
THALIA
THELIP
THELMA
THILLS
THOLES
WHALER
WHALES
WHELKS
WHELMS
WHELPS
WHILED
WHILES
WHILOM
WHILST
WHOLES
WHOLLY

•H••L•
CHARLY
CHICLE
CHICLY
CHILLI
CHILLS
CHILLY
CHOLLA
CHURLS
GHOULS
OHWELL
PHIALS
PHILLY
PHYLLO
SHALLY
SHAWLS
SHEILA
SHELLS
SHELLY
SHIELD
SHILLS
SHILLY
SHOALS
SHOALY
SHOULD
SHRILL
THATLL
THEFLY
THEYLL
THILLS
THINLY
THRALE
THRALL
THRILL
THUSLY
WHATLL
WHEALS
WHEELS
WHIRLS
WHIRLY
WHOLLY
WHORLS

•H•••L
BHOPAL
CHANEL
CHAPEL
CHERYL
CHEVAL
CHISEL
CHORAL
DHOTEL
OHWELL
PHENOL
PHENYL
PHILOL
RHINAL
SHEKEL
SHERYL
SHOVEL
SHRILL
SHTETL
THATLL
THECAL
THEYLL
THRALL
THRILL
WHATLL

••HL••
ASHLAR
ASHLEY
DAHLIA
KAHLIL
KAHLUA
KOHLER
MAHLER
SCHLEP
WOHLER

••H•L•
AWHILE
BEHALF
BEHELD
BEHOLD
ENHALO
EXHALE
INHALE
INHALF
MCHALE
NIHILO
ONHOLD
REHELD
SCHELL
SCHULZ
UNHOLY
UPHELD
UPHILL
UPHOLD

••H••L
AWHIRL
INHAUL
KAHLIL
REHEAL
REHEEL
SCHELL
SCHOOL
SCHORL
UPHILL

•••HL•
ARCHLY
HIGHLY
LUSHLY
POSHLY
RASHLY
RICHLY

•••H•L
BETHEL
BUSHEL
ISOHEL
LETHAL
METHYL
MICHEL
MYTHOL
NUCHAL
ORCHIL
PATHOL
RACHEL
VACHEL
WARHOL
WITHAL

••••HL
JAWOHL

HM••••
HMONGS

H•M•••
HAMALS
HAMELN
HAMILL
HAMITE
HAMLET
HAMLIN
HAMMED
HAMMER
HAMPER
HEMATO
HEMMED
HEMMER
HEMSIN
HOMAGE
HOMBRE
HOMEEC
HOMELY
HOMERS
HOMIER
HOMILY
HOMING
HOMINY
HUMANE
HUMANS
HUMBLE
HUMBLY
HUMBUG
HUMERI
HUMMED
HUMMER
HUMMUS
HUMORS
HUMOUR
HUMPED
HUMPHS
HUMVEE
HYMNAL
HYMNED

H••M••
HAEMAT
HAEMON
HAGMAN
HAMMED
HAMMER
HARMED
HARMON
HAYMOW
HBOMBS
HELMED
HELMET
HELMUT
HEMMED
HEMMER
HERMAN
HERMES
HERMIT
HERMON
HETMAN
HIEMAL
HITMAN
HITMEN
HOLMES
HORMEL
HORMUZ
HUMMED
HUMMER
HUMMUS

H•••M•
HAKIMS
HAREMS
HAULMS
HBEAMS

H••••M
HANSOM
HARLEM
HASSAM
HELIUM
HOLISM

•HM•••
KHMERS

•H•M••
AHIMSA
CHAMMY
CHAMPS
CHEMIN
CHIMED
CHIMES
CHIMPS
CHOMPS
CHUMMY
CHUMPS
RHAMES
RHOMBI
RHOMBS
RHUMBA
RHUMBS
RHYMED
RHYMER
RHYMES
SHAMAN
SHAMED
SHAMES
SHAMIR
SHAMUS
SHIMMY
SHIMON
THAMES
THEMED
THEMES
THOMAS
THUMBS
THUMPS
THYMUS
WHAMMO
WHAMMY
WHIMSY
WHOMPS
WHOMSO

•H••M•
CHACMA
CHAMMY
CHARMS
CHASMS
CHROMA
CHROME
CHROMO
CHROMY
CHUMMY
DHARMA
KHOUMS
RHEUMS
RHEUMY
SHAWMS
SHIMMY
SHOWME
SHRIMP
THELMA
THERMO
THERMS
THRUMS
WHAMMO
WHAMMY
WHELMS

•H•••M
CHRISM
PHENOM
PHLEGM
PHLOEM
PHYLUM
RHYTHM
SHALOM
SHAZAM
SHBOOM
SHIISM
SHOLEM
SHOLOM
THEISM
WHILOM

••HM••
ROHMER
SCHMOO
SCHMOS

••H•M•
ATHOME
BAHAMA
GOHOME
OGHAMS
REHEMS
SCHEMA
SCHEME

••H••M
ASHRAM
LCHAIM
SCHISM

•••HM•
ABOHMS
BRAHMA
BRAHMS
ISTHMI
MYOHMY

•••H•M
ANTHEM
ARNHEM
ASCHAM
BADHAM
COBHAM
DIRHAM
DUNHAM
DURHAM
ELOHIM
FATHOM
GOTHAM
GRAHAM
LAPHAM
MAYHEM
OLDHAM
RODHAM
SACHEM

••••HM
DRACHM
MEGOHM
RHYTHM

H•N•••
HANDED
HANDEL
HANDIN
HANDLE
HANDON
HANDUP
HANGAR
HANGED
HANGER
HANGIN
HANGON
HANGUL
HANGUP
HANKER
HANKIE
HANLEY
HANNAH
HANSEL
HANSOM
HANSON
HENBIT
HENLEY
HENNAS
HENNER
HENNIN
HENRIK
HENRYV
HENSON
HENTED
HINCTY
HINDER
HINDUS
HINGED
HINGES
HINGIS
HINTAT
HINTED
HINTER
HINTON
HONCHO
HONEST
HONEYS
HONIED
HONING
HONKED
HONKER
HONORE
HONORS
HONOUR
HONSHU
HUNGER
HUNGIN
HUNGON
HUNGRY
HUNGUP
HUNGWU
HUNKER
HUNTED
HUNTER

H••N••
HAINAN
HAINES
HANNAH
HAUNCH
HAUNTS
HEANEY
HEFNER
HENNAS
HENNER
HENNIN
HEXNUT
HMONGS
HOBNOB
HORNED
HORNER
HORNET
HORNEY
HORNIN
HOUNDS
HOUNDY
HOWNOW
HYENAS
HYMNAL
HYMNED
HYPNOS

H•••N•
HABANA

HALING
HARING
HATING
HAVANA
HAVENS
HAVENT
HAVING
HAWING
HAYING
HAZANS
HAZING
HELENA
HELENE
HELENS
HERONS
HEWING
HEXING
HIDING
HIEING
HIKING
HIRING
HIVING
HLHUNT
HOEING
HOGANS
HOLING
HOMING
HOMINY
HONING
HOPING
HOSING
HUMANE
HUMANS
HURONS
HYPING

H••••N
HADRON
HAEMON
HAGDON
HAGMAN
HAINAN
HAMELN
HAMLIN
HANDIN
HANDON
HANGIN
HANGON
HANSON
HAPPEN
HARBIN
HARDEN
HARKEN
HARLAN
HARLIN
HARMON
HARPON
HASSAN
HASTEN
HATPIN
HAVEON
HAYDEN
HEADIN
HEADON
HEAVEN
HEBRON
HEDREN
HEDRON
HEFLIN
HEIDEN
HELDIN
HELDON
HEMSIN
HENNIN
HENSON
HEREIN
HEREON
HERMAN
HERMON
HESTON
HETMAN
HIDDEN
HIERON
HILTON
HINTON
HIREON
HITMAN
HITMEN
HITSON
HOBSON
HOLDEN
HOLDIN
HOLDON
HOPSIN
HORNIN
HORTON
HOWLIN
HOYDEN
HUDSON
HUNGIN
HUNGON
HUSTON
HUTTON
HYPHEN

•H•N••
CHANCE
CHANCY
CHANEL
CHANEY
CHANGE
CHANTS
CHENIN
CHINCH
CHINES
CHINKS
CHINKY
CHINOS
CHINTZ
CHINUP
CHONJU
CHUNKS
CHUNKY
OHENRY
PHENOL
PHENOM
PHENYL
PHONED
PHONES
PHONEY
PHONIC
PHONON
PHONOS
RHINAL
RHINOS
RHONDA
SHANDY
SHANIA
SHANKS
SHANNY
SHANTY
SHINDY
SHINED
SHINER
SHINES
SHINNY
SHINTO
SHUNTS
THANES
THANKS
THENAR
THENCE
THINGS
THINGY
THINKS
THINLY
THONGS
THUNKS
WHANGS
WHENCE
WHINED
WHINER
WHINES
WHINEY
WHINNY
WHYNOT

•H••N•
AHERNE
CHAINE
CHAINS
CHIANG
CHRONO
CHURNS
GHAINS
SHANNY
SHAYNE
SHEENA
SHEENS
SHINNY
SHRANK
SHRINE
SHRINK
SHRUNK
SHYING
THEEND
THORNS
THORNY
THRONE
THRONG
UHLANS
WHINNY

•H•••N
BHUTAN
CHAPIN
CHARON
CHEMIN
CHENIN
CHIPIN
CHIRON
CHITIN
CHITON
CHOPIN
CHOSEN
CHYRON
OHIOAN
PHONON
PHOTON
RHYTON
SHABAN
SHAKEN
SHAMAN
SHARON
SHAVEN
SHIMON
SHOGUN
SHOOIN
SHORAN
SHOWIN
SHUTIN
THROWN
WHITEN

••HN••
ETHNIC
ETHNOS
JOHNNY
SCHNOZ

••H•N•
AAHING
ACHENE
ACHING
ATHAND
ATHENA
ATHENE
ATHENS
BEHIND
BYHAND
COHUNE
ECHINO
ETHANE
ETHENE
HLHUNT
ICHING
INHAND
JOHANN
JOHNNY
KAHUNA
ONHAND
OOHING
PAHANG
REHANG
REHUNG
SPHINX
STHENO
TAHINI
UNHAND
UTHANT
WAHINE

••H••N
ASHCAN
BAHIAN
DEHORN
EPHRON
JOHANN

•••HN•
DAPHNE
FOEHNS
TECHNO
VISHNU

•••H•N
AACHEN
AFGHAN
ANNHON
ARCHON
BUCHAN
CASHIN
COCHIN
DOTHAN
DUCHIN
GOSHEN
HYPHEN
INCHON
KUCHEN
LICHEN
MUDHEN
NATHAN
OMAHAN
ORPHAN
PATHAN
PEAHEN
PUSHON
PYTHON
RICHEN
SIPHON
SYPHON
TUCHUN
URCHIN
UTAHAN
WITHIN

••••HN
STJOHN
UPJOHN
VAUGHN

HO••••
HOAGIE
HOARDS
HOARSE
HOAXED
HOAXER
HOAXES
HOBART
HOBBES
HOBBIT
HOBBLE
HOBNOB
HOBOES
HOBSON
HOCKED
HOCKEY
HODADS
HODGES
HOEING
HOGANS
HOGGED
HOGGET
HOGTIE
HOHOHO
HOISTS
HOKIER
HOLDEN
HOLDER
HOLDIN
HOLDIT
HOLDON
HOLDTO
HOLDUP
HOLEUP
HOLIER
HOLILY
HOLING
HOLISM
HOLIST
HOLLER
HOLLOW
HOLMES
HOMAGE
HOMBRE
HOMEEC
HOMELY
HOMERS
HOMIER
HOMILY
HOMING
HOMINY
HONCHO
HONEST
HONEYS
HONIED
HONING
HONKED
HONKER
HONORE
HONORS
HONOUR
HONSHU
HOODED
HOODOO
HOOFED
HOOFER
HOOFIT
HOOHAH
HOOHAS
HOOKAH
HOOKED
HOOKUP
HOOPED
HOOPER
HOOPLA
HOOPLE
HOOPOE
HOORAH
HOORAY
HOOTAT
HOOTCH
HOOTED
HOOTER
HOOTIE
HOOVER
HOOVES
HOPERS
HOPING
HOPOFF
HOPPED
HOPPER
HOPPLE
HOPSIN
HOPSUP
HORACE
HORDES
HORMEL
HORMUZ
HORNED
HORNER
HORNET
HORNEY
HORNIN
HORRID
HORROR
HORSED
HORSES
HORSEY
HORTON
HOSELS
HOSIER
HOSING
HOSTAS
HOSTED
HOSTEL
HOSTLY
HOTAIR
HOTBED
HOTBOX
HOTCAP
HOTCAR
HOTDOG
HOTELS
HOTPOT
HOTROD
HOTTEA
HOTTER
HOTTIP
HOTTUB
HOTWAR
HOUGHS
HOUNDS
HOUNDY
HOURIS
HOURLY
HOUSED
HOUSES
HOVELS
HOVERS
HOVETO
HOWARD
HOWDAH
HOWELL
HOWLED
HOWLER
HOWLIN
HOWNOW
HOWTOS
HOYDEN

H•O•••
HAOLES
HBOMBS
HMONGS
HOODED
HOODOO
HOOFED
HOOFER
HOOFIT
HOOHAH
HOOHAS
HOOKAH
HOOKED
HOOKUP
HOOPED
HOOPER
HOOPLA
HOOPLE
HOOPOE
HOORAH
HOORAY
HOOTAT
HOOTCH
HOOTED
HOOTER
HOOTIE
HOOVER
HOOVES

H••O••
HALOED
HALOES
HALOID
HAROLD
HAVOCS
HELOTS
HEROES
HEROIC
HERONS
HIDOUT
HITOUT
HOBOES
HOHOHO
HONORE
HONORS
HONOUR
HOPOFF
HUMORS
HUMOUR
HURONS
HYPOED

H•••O•
HADRON
HAEMON
HAGDON
HALLOO
HALLOS
HALLOW
HANDON
HANGON
HANSOM
HANSON
HARBOR
HARLOW
HARMON
HARPON
HARROW
HATBOX
HATHOR
HAVEON
HAYMOW
HEADON
HEAROF
HEBRON
HECTOR
HEDRON
HELDON
HELIOS
HELLOS
HENSON
HEREOF
HEREON
HERIOT
HERMON
HERZOG
HESIOD
HESTON
HEYYOU
HICKOK
HIERON
HILTON
HINTON
HIPHOP
HIPPOS
HIREON
HITSON
HIVAOA
HOBNOB
HOBSON
HOLDON
HOLLOW
HOODOO
HOOPOE
HORROR
HORTON
HOTBOX
HOTDOG
HOTPOT
HOTROD
HOWNOW
HOWTOS
HUDSON
HUEVOS
HULLOA
HULLOS
HUNGON
HUSTON
HUTTON
HYDROS
HYKSOS
HYPNOS
HYSSOP

H••••O
HAIRDO
HALLOO
HASBRO
HELDTO
HEMATO
HERETO
HETERO
HIDEHO
HOHOHO
HOLDTO
HONCHO
HOODOO
HOVETO

•HO•••
BHOPAL
CHOATE
CHOCKS
CHOICE
CHOIRS
CHOKED
CHOKER
CHOKES
CHOLER
CHOLLA
CHOLOS
CHOMPS
CHONJU
CHOOSE
CHOOSY
CHOOYU
CHOPIN
CHOPPY
CHOPRA
CHORAL
CHORDS
CHORES
CHORUS
CHOSEN
CHOUGH
CHOWED
DHOLES
DHOTEL
DHOTIS

GHOSTS
GHOULS
KHOUMS
LHOTSE
PHOBIA
PHOBIC
PHOBOS
PHOCIS
PHOEBE
PHONED
PHONES
PHONEY
PHONIC
PHONON
PHONOS
PHOOEY
PHOTIC
PHOTOG
PHOTON
PHOTOS
RHODES
RHOMBI
RHOMBS
RHONDA
SHOALS
SHOALY
SHOATS
SHOCKS
SHODDY
SHOERS
SHOFAR
SHOGUN
SHOJIS
SHOLEM
SHOLOM
SHOOED
SHOOIN
SHOOKS
SHOOTS
SHOPPE
SHORAN
SHORED
SHORES
SHORTA
SHORTE
SHORTI
SHORTO
SHORTS
SHORTU
SHORTY
SHOTAT
SHOTUP
SHOULD
SHOUTS
SHOVED
SHOVEL
SHOVER
SHOVES
SHOWED
SHOWER
SHOWIN
SHOWME
SHOWUP
THOLES
THOMAS
THONGS
THORAX
THORNS
THORNY
THORPE
THORPS
THOUGH
WHOLES
WHOLLY
WHOMPS
WHOMSO
WHOOFS
WHOOPI
WHOOPS
WHOOSH
WHORLS
XHOSAS

•H•O••

CHEOPS
CHLORO
CHOOSE
CHOOSY
CHOOYU
CHROMA
CHROME
CHROMO
CHROMY
CHRONO
OHIOAN
PHLOEM
PHOOEY
SHBOOM
SHOOED
SHOOIN
SHOOKS
SHOOTS
SHROUD
SHROVE
THEORY
THROAT
THROBS
THROES
THRONE
THRONG
THROVE
THROWN
THROWS
WHOOFS
WHOOPI
WHOOPS
WHOOSH

•H••O•

AHCHOO
CHADOR
CHARON
CHEKOV
CHIGOE
CHILOE
CHINOS
CHIRON
CHISOX
CHITON
CHOLOS
CHYRON
PHAROS
PHENOL
PHENOM
PHILOL
PHILOS
PHOBOS
PHONON
PHONOS
PHOTOG
PHOTON
PHOTOS
RHEBOK
RHETOR
RHINOS
RHYTON
SHADOW
SHAKOS
SHALOM
SHARON
SHBOOM
SHILOH
SHIMON
SHOLOM
THETOY
WHILOM
WHYNOT
ZHUKOV

•H•••O

AHCHOO
BHUTTO
CHALCO
CHARRO
CHEAPO
CHLORO
CHROMO
CHRONO
CHURRO
GHETTO
PHLEBO
PHYLLO
PHYSIO
RHABDO
SHINTO
SHORTO
THERMO
WHAMMO
WHIZZO
WHOMSO

••HO••

ABHORS
ASHORE
ATHOME
BEHOLD
BEHOOF
BEHOVE
CAHOWS
COHORT
COHOST
DEHORN
DRHOOK
ECHOED
ECHOES
ECHOIC
EPHODS
EPHORI
EPHORS
EXHORT
GOHOME
HOHOHO
JOHORE
LAHORE
MAHOUT
MOHOCK
ONHOLD
REHOOK
SCHOOL
SCHORL
UNHOLY
UNHOOK
UPHOLD
WAHOOS
YAHOOS
YOHOHO

••H•O•

BEHOOF
DRHOOK
EPHRON
ETHNOS
MAHZOR
REHOOK
SCHMOO
SCHMOS
SCHNOZ
SCHOOL
UNHOOK
WAHOOS
YAHOOS

••H••O

ECHINO
ENHALO
HOHOHO
NIHILO
SCHMOO
STHENO
YOHOHO

•••HO•

AHCHOO
ANCHOR
ANDHOW
ANNHON
ANYHOW
ARCHON
AUTHOR
BARHOP
BATHOS
BISHOP
BOOHOO
CACHOU
CARHOP
FATHOM
FUZHOU
HATHOR
HIPHOP
INCHON
JOBHOP
LITHOG
LITHOS
LUTHOR
MACHOS
METHOD
MUGHOS
MYTHOI
MYTHOL
MYTHOS
NACHOS
NOSHOW
PATHOL
PATHOS
PUSHON
PYTHON
QUAHOG
REDHOT
RESHOD
RESHOE
RESHOT
SENHOR
SIPHON
SYPHON
TVSHOW
UNSHOD
UPSHOT
WARHOL
WASHOE
YOOHOO

•••H•O

AHCHOO
ARTHRO
BOCHCO
BOOHOO
JETHRO
LASHIO
NEPHRO
PASHTO
RIGHTO
ROTHKO
TECHNO
YOOHOO

••••HO

CAUCHO
CLOTHO
GAUCHO
GUNGHO
HIDEHO
HOHOHO
HONCHO
LANDHO
MORPHO
NAVAHO
PANCHO
PONCHO
PSYCHO
RANCHO
REECHO
SANCHO
SAPPHO
TRICHO
XANTHO
YOHOHO

H•P•••

HAPPED
HAPPEN
HEPCAT
HEPPER
HEPTAD
HIPHOP
HIPPED
HIPPER
HIPPIE
HIPPOS
HOPERS
HOPING
HOPOFF
HOPPED
HOPPER
HOPPLE
HOPSIN
HOPSUP
HYPEUP
HYPHEN
HYPING
HYPNOS
HYPOED

H••P••

HAMPER
HAPPED
HAPPEN
HARPED
HARPER
HARPON
HASPED
HATPIN
HEAPED
HELPED
HELPER
HEPPER
HIPPED
HIPPER
HIPPIE
HIPPOS
HISPID
HOOPED
HOOPER
HOOPLA
HOOPLE
HOOPOE
HOPPED
HOPPER
HOPPLE
HOTPOT
HUMPED
HUMPHS

H••••P

HANDUP
HANGUP
HARDUP
HAULUP
HEADUP
HEATUP
HELDUP
HICCUP
HIGHUP
HIKEUP
HIPHOP
HITSUP
HOLDUP
HOLEUP
HOOKUP
HOPSUP
HOTCAP
HOTTIP
HUBCAP
HUNGUP
HYPEUP
HYSSOP

•H•P••

BHOPAL
CHAPEL
CHAPIN
CHIPIN
CHOPIN
CHOPPY
CHOPRA
SHAPED
SHAPER
SHAPES
SHOPPE
WHIPPY
WHIPUP

•H••P•

CHAMPS
CHEAPO
CHEEPS
CHEOPS
CHIMPS
CHIRPS
CHIRPY
CHOMPS
CHOPPY
CHUMPS
SHARPS
SHEEPS
SHERPA
SHOPPE
THORPE
THORPS
THRIPS
THUMPS
WHELPS
WHIPPY
WHOMPS
WHOOPI
WHOOPS

•H•••P

CHATUP
CHEWUP
CHINUP
PHILIP
SHOTUP
SHOWUP
SHRIMP
SHUTUP
THELIP
WHIPUP

••H•P•

VCHIPS

••H••P

ASHARP
BSHARP
CSHARP
DSHARP
ESHARP
FSHARP
GSHARP
SCHLEP

•••H•P

BARHOP
BISHOP
CARHOP
HIGHUP
HIPHOP
JOBHOP
LASHUP
MAYHAP
MISHAP
PUSHUP
RESHIP
WASHUP

H••••Q

HIGHIQ

•H•Q••

CHEQUE

•••H•Q

HIGHIQ

H•R•••

HARALD
HARARE
HARASS
HARBIN
HARBOR
HARDBY
HARDEN
HARDER
HARDLY
HARDUP
HAREMS
HARING
HARKED
HARKEN
HARKER
HARLAN
HARLEM
HARLEY
HARLIN
HARLOW
HARMED
HARMON
HAROLD
HARPED
HARPER
HARPON
HARRIS
HARROW
HARVEY
HERALD
HERBAL
HERBIE
HERDED
HERDER
HEREAT
HEREBY
HEREIN
HEREOF
HEREON
HERESY
HERETO
HERIOT
HERMAN
HERMES
HERMIT
HERMON
HEROES
HEROIC
HERONS
HERSEY
HERZOG
HIREON
HIRERS
HIRING
HIRSCH
HORACE
HORDES
HORMEL
HORMUZ
HORNED
HORNER
HORNET
HORNEY
HORNIN
HORRID
HORROR
HORSED
HORSES
HORSEY
HORTON
HURDLE
HURLED
HURLER
HURLEY
HURONS
HURRAH
HURRAY
HURTLE

H••R••

HADRON
HAIRDO
HAIRED
HARRIS
HARROW
HATRED
HEARER
HEAROF
HEARST
HEARTH
HEARTS
HEARTY
HEARYE
HEBREW
HEBRON
HEDREN
HEDRON
HENRIK
HENRYV
HIERON
HIJRAH
HOARDS
HOARSE
HOORAH
HOORAY
HORRID
HORROR
HOTROD
HOURIS
HOURLY
HUBRIS
HURRAH
HURRAY
HYBRID
HYDRAE
HYDRAS
HYDROS

H•••R•

HALERS
HALERU
HARARE
HASBRO
HATARI
HATERS
HAVERS
HAZARD
HAZERS
HEGARI
HEGIRA
HETERO
HEWERS
HEXERS
HIDERS
HIKERS

HILARY
HIRERS
HOBART
HOMBRE
HOMERS
HONORE
HONORS
HOPERS
HOVERS
HOWARD
HUBERT
HUMERI
HUMORS
HUNGRY

H••••R

HACKER
HALTER
HAMMER
HAMPER
HANGAR
HANGER
HANKER
HARBOR
HARDER
HARKER
HARPER
HATHOR
HATTER
HAULER
HAWKER
HAWSER
HAZIER
HEADER
HEALER
HEARER
HEATER
HEAVER
HECTOR
HEDGER
HEEDER
HEELER
HEFNER
HEIFER
HELLER
HELPER
HELTER
HEMMER
HENNER
HEPPER
HERDER
HESTER
HIGHER
HILLER
HINDER
HINTER
HIPPER
HISSER
HITHER
HITTER
HOAXER
HOKIER
HOLDER
HOLIER
HOLLER
HOMIER
HONKER
HONOUR
HOOFER
HOOPER
HOOTER
HOOVER
HOPPER
HORNER
HORROR
HOSIER
HOTAIR
HOTCAR
HOTTER
HOTWAR
HOWLER
HUGGER
HULLER
HUMMER
HUMOUR
HUNGER
HUNKER
HUNTER
HURLER
HUSKER
HUSSAR

•HR•••

CHRISM
CHROMA
CHROME
CHROMO
CHROMY
CHRONO
PHRASE
SHRANK
SHREDS
SHREWD
SHREWS
SHRIEK
SHRIFT
SHRIKE
SHRILL
SHRIMP
SHRINE
SHRINK
SHRIVE
SHROUD
SHROVE
SHRUBS
SHRUGS
SHRUNK
THRACE
THRALE
THRALL
THRASH
THREAD
THREAT
THREED
THREES
THRESH
THRICE
THRIFT
THRILL
THRIPS
THRIVE
THROAT
THROBS
THROES
THRONE
THRONG
THROVE
THROWN
THROWS
THRUMS
THRUSH
THRUST

•H•R••

AHERNE
CHARGE
CHARLY
CHARMS
CHARON
CHARRO
CHARTS
CHERIE
CHERRY
CHERTY
CHERUB
CHERYL
CHIRAC
CHIRON
CHIRPS
CHIRPY
CHIRRS
CHORAL
CHORDS
CHORES
CHORUS
CHURCH
CHURLS
CHURNS
CHURRO
CHURRS
CHYRON
DHARMA
GHARRY
PHAROS
SHARDS
SHARED
SHARER
SHARES
SHARIA
SHARIF
SHARKS
SHARON
SHARPS
SHEREE
SHERIF
SHERPA
SHERRY
SHERYL
SHIRAZ
SHIRER
SHIRES
SHIRKS
SHIRRS
SHIRTS
SHIRTY
SHORAN
SHORED
SHORES
SHORTA
SHORTE
SHORTI
SHORTO
SHORTS
SHORTU
SHORTY
THERES
THERMO
THERMS
THIRDS
THIRST
THIRTY
THORAX
THORNS
THORNY
THORPE
THORPS
THYRSI
WHARFS
WHERED
WHERES
WHERRY
WHIRLS
WHIRLY
WHIRRS
WHORLS

•H••R•

CHAIRS
CHARRO
CHEERS
CHEERY
CHERRY
CHEVRE
CHIRRS
CHLORO
CHOIRS
CHOPRA
CHURRO
CHURRS
GHARRY
KHAFRE
KHMERS
NHLERS
OHENRY
PHEDRE
SHEARS
SHEERS
SHERRY
SHIRRS
SHOERS
THEIRS
THEORY
THEYRE
THWART
WHERRY
WHIRRS

•H•••R

CHADOR
CHASER
CHEWER
CHIDER
CHOKER
CHOLER
CHUKAR
KHYBER
PHASER
RHETOR
RHYMER
SHAKER
SHAMIR
SHAPER
SHARER
SHAVER
SHIKAR
SHINER
SHIRER
SHIVER
SHOFAR
SHOVER
SHOWER
THALER
THAYER
THENAR
WHALER
WHINER
WHITER

••HR••

ASHRAM
EPHRON
GEHRIG
LEHRER
MIHRAB
OCHRES
RAHRAH

••H•R•

ABHORS
ADHERE
ALHIRT
AMHARA
ASHARP
ASHORE
AWHIRL
BIHARI
BSHARP
COHERE
COHORT
CSHARP
DEHORN
DSHARP
EPHORI
EPHORS
ERHARD
ESHARP
ETHERS
EXHORT
FSHARP
GSHARP
INHERE
JOHORE
LAHORE
MOHURS
OCHERS
OCHERY
OTHERS
PAHARI
REHIRE
SAHARA
SCHORL
SPHERE
SPHERY
TSHIRT
UNHURT
USHERS

••H••R

ACHIER
ANHYDR
ASHIER
ASHLAR
CAHIER
COHEIR
ISHTAR
KOHLER
LEHRER
MAHLER
MAHZOR
MOHAIR
REHEAR
ROHMER
WOHLER

•••HR•

ARTHRO
EUCHRE
JETHRO
MOTHRA
NEPHRO
TEPHRA
TISHRI

•••H•R

AETHER
ANCHOR
ANTHER
ARCHER
ARTHUR
AUTHOR
BATHER
BENHUR
BOTHER
CATHER
CIPHER
CYPHER
DASHER
DITHER
EITHER
ESCHER
ESTHER
ETCHER
FATHER
FISHER
GATHER
GOPHER
GUSHER
HATHOR
HIGHER
HITHER
KOSHER
LASHER
LATHER
LOTHAR
LUSHER
LUTHER
LUTHOR
MASHER
MATHER
MENHIR
MOSHER
MOTHER
MUSHER
NETHER
NIGHER
NOSHER
POSHER
POTHER
RASHER
RATHER
RICHER
SENHOR
SIGHER
TETHER
TITHER
TOTHER
WASHER
WETHER
WISHER
WITHER
ZEPHYR
ZITHER

H•S•••

HASBRO
HASHED
HASHES
HASPED
HASSAM
HASSAN
HASSLE
HASTEN
HASTES
HESIOD
HESTER
HESTIA
HESTON
HISPID
HISSAT
HISSED
HISSER
HISSES
HOSELS
HOSIER
HOSING
HOSTAS
HOSTED
HOSTEL
HOSTLY
HUSHED
HUSHES
HUSKED
HUSKER
HUSSAR
HUSSEY
HUSTLE
HUSTON
HYSSOP

H••S••

HALSEY
HANSEL
HANSOM
HANSON
HASSAM
HASSAN
HASSLE
HAUSAS
HAWSER
HAWSES
HEISTS
HEMSIN
HENSON
HERSEY
HIRSCH
HISSAT
HISSED
HISSER
HISSES
HITSIT
HITSON
HITSUP
HOBSON
HOISTS
HONSHU
HOPSIN
HOPSUP
HORSED
HORSES
HORSEY
HOUSED
HOUSES
HUDSON
HUSSAR
HUSSEY
HYKSOS
HYSSOP

H•••S•

HALEST
HARASS
HAVASU
HEARST
HERESY
HOARSE
HOLISM
HOLIST
HONEST
HUGEST

H••••S

HABEAS
HABITS
HACEKS
HADJES
HADJIS
HAGGIS
HAIDAS
HAIKUS
HAINES
HAJJES
HAJJIS
HAKIMS
HALERS
HALLOS
HALOES
HALVES
HAMALS
HAOLES
HARASS
HAREMS
HARRIS
HASHES
HASTES
HATERS
HAULMS
HAUNTS
HAUSAS
HAVENS
HAVERS
HAVOCS
HAWSES
HAZANS
HAZELS
HAZERS
HBEAMS
HBOMBS
HEARTS
HEATHS
HEAVES
HEDGES
HEISTS
HELENS
HELIOS
HELLAS
HELLOS
HELOTS
HELVES
HENNAS
HERMES
HEROES
HERONS
HEWERS
HEXADS
HEXERS
HIATUS
HIDERS
HIKERS
HINDUS
HINGES
HINGIS
HIPPOS
HIRERS
HISSES
HMONGS
HOARDS
HOAXES
HOBBES
HOBOES
HODADS
HODGES
HOGANS
HOISTS
HOLMES
HOMERS
HONEYS
HONORS
HOOHAS
HOOVES
HOPERS
HORDES
HORSES
HOSELS
HOSTAS
HOTELS
HOUGHS
HOUNDS
HOURIS
HOUSES
HOVELS
HOVERS
HOWTOS
HUBRIS
HUEVOS
HUGHES
HULLOS
HUMANS
HUMMUS
HUMORS
HUMPHS
HURONS
HUSHES
HUZZAS
HYADES
HYDRAS
HYDROS
HYENAS
HYKSOS
HYPNOS

•H•S••

CHASED
CHASER
CHASES
CHASMS
CHASSE
CHASTE
CHESTS
CHESTY
CHISEL

CHISOX
CHOSEN
GHOSTS
PHASED
PHASER
PHASES
PHYSED
PHYSIO
RHESUS
SHASTA
THESEA
THESES
THESIS
THESIX
THISBE
THUSLY
WHISKS
WHISKY
XHOSAS

•H••S•

AHIMSA
CHAISE
CHASSE
CHEESE
CHEESY
CHOOSE
CHOOSY
CHRISM
CHUHSI
LHOTSE
PHRASE
SHIEST
SHIISM
SHYEST
THEISM
THEIST
THIRST
THRASH
THRESH
THRUSH
THRUST
THYRSI
WHILST
WHIMSY
WHOMSO
WHOOSH

•H•••S

CHAFES
CHAFFS
CHAINS
CHAIRS
CHALKS
CHAMPS
CHANTS
CHARMS
CHARTS
CHASES
CHASMS
CHEATS
CHECKS
CHEEKS
CHEEPS
CHEERS
CHELAS
CHEOPS
CHESTS
CHETHS
CHIAUS
CHICKS
CHIDES
CHIEFS
CHILDS
CHILLS
CHIMES
CHIMPS
CHINES
CHINKS
CHINOS
CHIRPS
CHIRRS
CHIVES
CHOCKS
CHOIRS
CHOKES
CHOLOS
CHOMPS
CHORDS
CHORES
CHORUS
CHUCKS
CHUMPS
CHUNKS
CHURLS
CHURNS
CHURRS
CHUTES
DHOLES
DHOTIS
GHAINS
GHAZIS
GHOSTS
GHOULS
KHAKIS
KHMERS
KHOUMS
NHLERS
PHAGES
PHAROS
PHASES
PHIALS
PHILOS
PHOBOS
PHOCIS
PHONES
PHONOS
PHOTOS
RHAMES
RHESUS
RHEUMS
RHINOS
RHODES
RHOMBS
RHUMBS
RHYMES
SHACKS
SHADES
SHAFTS
SHAKES
SHAKOS
SHALES
SHAMES
SHAMUS
SHANKS
SHAPES
SHARDS
SHARES
SHARKS
SHARPS
SHAVES
SHAWLS
SHAWMS
SHEAFS
SHEARS
SHEENS
SHEEPS
SHEERS
SHEETS
SHEIKS
SHELLS
SHIFTS
SHILLS
SHINES
SHIRES
SHIRKS
SHIRRS
SHIRTS
SHOALS
SHOATS
SHOCKS
SHOERS
SHOJIS
SHOOKS
SHOOTS
SHORES
SHORTS
SHOUTS
SHOVES
SHREDS
SHREWS
SHRUBS
SHRUGS
SHUCKS
SHUNTS
THALES
THAMES
THANES
THANKS
THATIS
THEBES
THEFTS
THEIRS
THEMES
THERES
THERMS
THESES
THESIS
THETAS
THETIS
THIGHS
THILLS
THINGS
THINKS
THIRDS
THOLES
THOMAS
THONGS
THORNS
THORPS
THREES
THRIPS
THROBS
THROES
THROWS
THRUMS
THUJAS
THUMBS
THUMPS
THUNKS
THYMUS
UHLANS
WHACKS
WHALES
WHANGS
WHARFS
WHEALS
WHEATS
WHEELS
WHELKS
WHELMS
WHELPS
WHERES
WHIFFS
WHILES
WHINES
WHIRLS
WHIRRS
WHISKS
WHITES
WHOLES
WHOMPS
WHOOFS
WHOOPS
WHORLS
XHOSAS

••H•S•

AGHAST
BEHEST
COHOST
REHASH
SCHISM
SCHIST
SCHUSS

••H••S

ABHORS
APHIDS
ATHENS
CAHOWS
ECHOES
EPHAHS
EPHODS
EPHORS
ETHERS
ETHICS
ETHNOS
JIHADS
LEHUAS
MAHDIS
MOHURS
NOHITS
OCHERS
OCHRES
OGHAMS
OTHERS
REHABS
REHEMS
SAHIBS
SCHMOS
SCHUSS
SCHWAS
TEHEES
USHERS
VCHIPS
WAHOOS
YAHOOS

•••HS•

CHUHSI
TZUHSI

•••H•S

ABOHMS
ALOHAS
ALPHAS
ARCHES
AUGHTS
BASHES
BATHES
BATHOS
BIGHTS
BRAHMS
BUSHES
CACHES
CASHES
COSHES
DACHAS
DASHES
DASHIS
DISHES
EIGHTS
ETCHES
FICHES
FICHUS
FIGHTS
FISHES
FOEHNS
GASHES
GUSHES
HASHES
HOOHAS
HUGHES
HUSHES
INCHES
ITCHES
JANHUS
JOSHES
LACHES
LASHES
LATHES
LIGHTS
LITHOS
MACHES
MACHOS
MASHES
MATHIS
MESHES
MOCHAS
MOSHES
MUGHOS
MUSHES
MYTHOS
NACHOS
NICHES
NIGHTS
NOSHES
OMAHAS
OUGHTS
PASHAS
PATHOS
PUSHES
RACHIS
RASHES
RESHES
RICHES
RIGHTS
RUCHES
RUSHES
SADHES
SADHUS
SASHES
SIGHTS
SPAHIS
SUCHAS
TETHYS
TIGHTS
TITHES
TOPHUS
TYPHUS
WASHES
WIGHTS
WISHES
WITHES
YACHTS

••••HS

ALEPHS
BERTHS
BIRTHS
BOOTHS
BOUGHS
BROTHS
BURGHS
CHETHS
CLOTHS
CONCHS
COUGHS
CZECHS
DEPTHS
DOUGHS
EPHAHS
EPOCHS
FAITHS
FIFTHS
FIRTHS
FROTHS
GALAHS
GARTHS
GERAHS
GIRTHS
GLYPHS
GRAPHS
HEATHS
HOUGHS
HUMPHS
JONAHS
LAUGHS
LOTAHS
LOUGHS
LYMPHS
MONTHS
MORPHS
MOUTHS
MYNAHS
MYRRHS
NEIGHS
NINTHS
NORTHS
NYMPHS
OBEAHS
ORACHS
PSYCHS
RAJAHS
ROUGHS
SIXTHS
SLOTHS
SMITHS
SNATHS
SOUGHS
SOUTHS
SURAHS
SWATHS
SYLPHS
TENTHS
THIGHS
TORAHS
TOUGHS
TROTHS
TRUTHS
WEIGHS
WIDTHS
WORTHS
WRATHS
YOUTHS

H•T•••

HATARI
HATBOX
HATERS
HATFUL
HATHOR
HATING
HATPIN
HATRED
HATTED
HATTER
HATTIE
HETERO
HETMAN
HETTIE
HITECH
HITHER
HITMAN
HITMEN
HITOUT
HITSIT
HITSON
HITSUP
HITTER
HOTAIR
HOTBED
HOTBOX
HOTCAP
HOTCAR
HOTDOG
HOTELS
HOTPOT
HOTROD
HOTTEA
HOTTER
HOTTIP
HOTTUB
HOTWAR
HUTTED
HUTTON

H••T••

HAFTED
HALTED
HALTER
HASTEN
HASTES
HATTED
HATTER
HATTIE
HEATED
HEATER
HEATHS
HEATHY
HEATUP
HECTIC
HECTOR
HEFTED
HELTER
HENTED
HEPTAD
HESTER
HESTIA
HESTON
HETTIE
HIATAL
HIATUS
HILTON
HINTAT
HINTED
HINTER
HINTON
HITTER
HOGTIE
HOOTAT
HOOTCH
HOOTED
HOOTER
HOOTIE
HORTON
HOSTAS
HOSTED
HOSTEL
HOSTLY
HOTTEA
HOTTER
HOTTIP
HOTTUB
HOWTOS
HUNTED
HUNTER
HURTLE
HUSTLE
HUSTON
HUTTED
HUTTON
HYETAL

H•••T•

HABITS
HALITE
HAMITE
HAUNTS
HEALTH
HEARTH
HEARTS
HEARTY
HECATE
HEISTS
HELDTO
HELOTS
HEMATO
HERETO
HINCTY
HOISTS
HOLDTO
HOVETO

H••••T

HAEMAT
HAIGHT
HALEST
HAMLET
HAVEAT
HAVENT
HEARST
HEIGHT
HELMET
HELMUT
HENBIT
HEPCAT
HEREAT
HERIOT
HERMIT
HEXNUT
HIDOUT
HINTAT
HISSAT
HITOUT
HITSIT
HLHUNT
HOBART
HOBBIT
HOGGET
HOLDIT
HOLIST
HONEST
HOOFIT
HOOTAT
HORNET
HOTPOT
HUBERT
HUGEST

•HT•••

SHTETL
SHTICK

•H•T••

BHUTAN
BHUTTO
CHATTY
CHATUP
CHETHS
CHITIN
CHITON
CHUTED
CHUTES
DHOTEL
DHOTIS
GHETTO
LHOTSE
PHATIC
PHOTIC
PHOTOG
PHOTON
PHOTOS
RHETOR
RHYTHM
RHYTON
SHOTAT
SHOTUP
SHUTIN
SHUTUP
THATCH
THATIS
THATLL
THETAS
THETIC
THETIS
THETOY
WHATIF
WHATLL

WHATVE
WHITEN
WHITER
WHITES
WHITTY

•H••T•
BHAKTI
BHUTTO
CHANTS
CHARTS
CHASTE
CHATTY
CHEATS
CHERTY
CHESTS
CHESTY
CHINTZ
CHOATE
GHETTO
GHOSTS
SHAFTS
SHAKTI
SHANTY
SHASTA
SHEATH
SHEETS
SHELTY
SHIFTS
SHIFTY
SHIITE
SHINTO
SHIRTS
SHIRTY
SHOATS
SHOOTS
SHORTA
SHORTE
SHORTI
SHORTO
SHORTS
SHORTU
SHORTY
SHOUTS
SHTETL
SHUNTS
THEFTS
THIRTY
WHEATS
WHITTY

•H•••T
CHALET
CHEVET
SHEVAT
SHIEST
SHOTAT
SHRIFT
SHYEST
THEIST
THIRST
THREAT
THRIFT
THROAT
THRUST
THWART
WHILST
WHYNOT

••HT••
ICHTHY
ISHTAR

••H•T•
NOHITS
OPHITE
TAHITI

••H••T
AGHAST
ALHIRT
BEHEST
COHORT
COHOST
EXHORT
HLHUNT
MAHOUT
REHEAT
SCHIST
TSHIRT
UNHURT
UTHANT

•••HT•
AUGHTS
BIGHTS
EIGHTH
EIGHTS
EIGHTY
FICHTE
FIGHTS
LIGHTS
MIGHTY
NIGHTS
NIGHTY
OUGHTS
PASHTO
RIGHTO
RIGHTS
RIGHTY
SIGHTS
TIGHTS
VASHTI
WIGHTS
YACHTS

•••H•T
ATTHAT
CACHET
FOGHAT
MISHIT
OLDHAT
OUTHIT
REDHAT
REDHOT
RESHOT
ROCHET
SACHET
SOTHAT
SOWHAT
TINHAT
TOPHAT
UPSHOT
WITHIT

••••HT
ALIGHT
ARIGHT
BLIGHT
BOUGHT
BRECHT
BRIGHT
CAUGHT
DWIGHT
FLIGHT
FOUGHT
FRIGHT
HAIGHT
HEIGHT
KNIGHT
NAUGHT
NOUGHT
PLIGHT
SLIGHT
SOUGHT
TAUGHT
VEIGHT
VOIGHT
WEIGHT
WRIGHT

HU••••
HUBBLE
HUBBLY
HUBBUB
HUBCAP
HUBERT
HUBRIS
HUDDLE
HUDSON
HUEVOS
HUFFED
HUGELY
HUGEST
HUGGED
HUGGER
HUGHES
HULKED
HULLED
HULLER
HULLOA
HULLOS
HUMANE
HUMANS
HUMBLE
HUMBLY
HUMBUG
HUMERI
HUMMED
HUMMER
HUMMUS
HUMORS
HUMOUR
HUMPED
HUMPHS
HUMVEE
HUNGER
HUNGIN
HUNGON
HUNGRY
HUNGUP
HUNGWU
HUNKER
HUNTED
HUNTER
HURDLE
HURLED
HURLER
HURLEY
HURONS
HURRAH
HURRAY
HURTLE
HUSHED
HUSHES
HUSKED
HUSKER
HUSSAR
HUSSEY
HUSTLE
HUSTON
HUTTED
HUTTON
HUXLEY
HUZZAH
HUZZAS

H•U•••
HAULED
HAULER
HAULMS
HAULUP
HAUNCH
HAUNTS
HAUSAS
HOUGHS
HOUNDS
HOUNDY
HOURIS
HOURLY
HOUSED
HOUSES

H••U••
HECUBA
HLHUNT

H•••U•
HAIKUS
HALLUX
HANDUP
HANGUL
HANGUP
HARDUP
HATFUL
HAULUP
HEADUP
HEATUP
HELDUP
HELIUM
HELMUT
HEXNUT
HIATUS
HICCUP
HIDOUT
HIGHUP
HIKEUP
HINDUS
HITOUT
HITSUP
HOLDUP
HOLEUP
HONOUR
HOOKUP
HOPSUP
HORMUZ
HOTTUB
HUBBUB
HUMBUG
HUMMUS
HUMOUR
HUNGUP
HYPEUP

H••••U
HALERU
HAVASU
HEYYOU
HONSHU
HUNGWU

•HU•••
BHUTAN
BHUTTO
CHUBBY
CHUCKS
CHUFFY
CHUHSI
CHUKAR
CHUKKA
CHUMMY
CHUMPS
CHUNKS
CHUNKY
CHURCH
CHURLS
CHURNS
CHURRO
CHURRS
CHUTED
CHUTES
RHUMBA
RHUMBS
SHUCKS
SHUNTS
SHUTIN
SHUTUP
THUJAS
THUMBS
THUMPS
THUNKS
THUSLY
ZHUKOV

•H•U••
CHOUGH
GHOULS
KHOUMS
RHEUMS
RHEUMY
SHOULD
SHOUTS
SHRUBS
SHRUGS
SHRUNK
THOUGH
THRUMS
THRUSH
THRUST

•H••U•
CHATUP
CHEQUE
CHERUB
CHEWUP
CHIAUS
CHINUP
CHORUS
PHYLUM
RHESUS
SHAMUS
SHOGUN
SHOTUP
SHOWUP
SHROUD
SHUTUP
THYMUS
WHIPUP

•H•••U
CHONJU
CHOOYU
SHORTU

••HU••
COHUNE
HLHUNT
KAHUNA
LEHUAS
MCHUGH
MOHURS
REHUNG
SCHULZ
SCHUSS
UNHURT
YEHUDI

••H•U•
INHAUL
KAHLUA
MAHOUT

•••HU•
ARTHUR
BENHUR
FICHUS
HIGHUP
JANHUS
JOSHUA
LASHUP
NASHUA
PUSHUP
SADHUS
TOPHUS
TUCHUN
TYPHUS
WASHUP

•••H•U
CACHOU
FUZHOU
NIIHAU
VISHNU

••••HU
HONSHU
KYUSHU
MANCHU
PENGHU
PICCHU

H•V•••
HAVANA
HAVASU
HAVEAT
HAVENS
HAVENT
HAVEON
HAVERS
HAVING
HAVOCS
HIVAOA
HIVING
HOVELS
HOVERS
HOVETO

H••V••
HALVAH
HALVED
HALVES
HARVEY
HEAVED
HEAVEN
HEAVER
HEAVES
HELVES
HOOVER
HOOVES
HUEVOS
HUMVEE

H•••V•
HALEVY

H••••V
HENRYV

•H•V••
CHAVEZ
CHEVAL
CHEVET
CHEVRE
CHIVES
SHAVED
SHAVEN
SHAVER
SHAVES
SHEVAT
SHIVER
SHOVED
SHOVEL
SHOVER
SHOVES

•H••V•
SHEAVE
SHELVE
SHRIVE
SHROVE
THEYVE
THIEVE
THRIVE
THROVE
WHATVE

•H•••V
CHEKOV
ZHUKOV

••H•V•
BEHAVE
BEHOVE
MOHAVE

•••H•V
MOSHAV

H•W•••
HAWAII
HAWHAW
HAWING
HAWKED
HAWKER
HAWSER
HAWSES
HEWERS
HEWING
HOWARD
HOWDAH
HOWELL
HOWLED
HOWLER
HOWLIN
HOWNOW
HOWTOS

H••W••
HOTWAR

H•••W•
HUNGWU

H••••W
HALLOW
HARLOW
HARROW
HAWHAW
HAYMOW
HEBREW
HEEHAW
HOLLOW
HOWNOW

•HW•••
OHWELL
THWACK
THWART

•H•W••
CHEWED
CHEWER
CHEWUP
CHOWED
SHAWLS
SHAWMS
SHOWED
SHOWER
SHOWIN
SHOWME
SHOWUP
THAWED
THEWEB
THEWIZ

•H••W•
SHREWD
SHREWS
THROWN
THROWS

•H•••W
SHADOW

••HW••
SCHWAB
SCHWAS
WAHWAH
YAHWEH

••H•W•
CAHOWS
MOHAWK
OSHAWA

•••HW•
BUSHWA

•••H•W
ANDHOW
ANYHOW
CASHEW
CUSHAW
ESCHEW
HAWHAW
HEEHAW
NEPHEW
NOSHOW
TVSHOW

H•X•••
HEXADS
HEXERS
HEXING
HEXNUT
HUXLEY

H••X••
HOAXED
HOAXER
HOAXES

H••••X
HALLUX
HATBOX
HOTBOX

•H•••X
CHISOX
THESIX
THORAX

••H••X
SPHINX

HY••••
HYADES
HYBRID
HYDRAE
HYDRAS
HYDROS
HYENAS
HYETAL
HYKSOS
HYMNAL
HYMNED
HYPEUP
HYPHEN
HYPING
HYPNOS
HYPOED
HYSSOP

H•Y•••
HAYDEN
HAYING
HAYLEY
HAYMOW

HEYDAY
HEYYOU
HOYDEN

H••Y••
HEYYOU

H•••Y•
HEARYE
HENRYV
HONEYS

H••••Y
HACKLY
HAILEY
HALEVY
HALLEY
HALSEY
HANLEY
HARDBY
HARDLY
HARLEY
HARVEY
HAYLEY
HAZILY
HEANEY
HEARTY
HEATHY
HENLEY
HEREBY
HERESY
HERSEY
HEYDAY
HICKEY
HIGHLY
HILARY
HINCTY
HOCKEY
HOLILY
HOMELY
HOMILY
HOMINY
HOORAY
HORNEY
HORSEY
HOSTLY
HOUNDY
HOURLY
HUBBLY
HUGELY
HUMBLY
HUNGRY
HURLEY
HURRAY
HUSSEY
HUXLEY

•HY•••
CHYRON
KHYBER
OHYEAH
PHYLAE
PHYLLO
PHYLUM
PHYSED
PHYSIO
RHYMED
RHYMER
RHYMES
RHYTHM
RHYTON
SHYEST
SHYING
THYMUS
THYRSI
WHYDAH
WHYNOT

•H•Y••
SHAYNE
THAYER
THEYLL
THEYRE
THEYVE

•H••Y•
CHERYL
CHOOYU
PHENYL
SHERYL

•H•••Y
CHAFFY
CHALKY
CHAMMY
CHANCY
CHANEY
CHARLY
CHATTY
CHEEKY
CHEERY
CHEESY
CHERRY
CHERTY
CHESTY
CHICLY
CHILLY
CHINKY
CHIRPY
CHOOSY
CHOPPY
CHROMY
CHUBBY
CHUFFY
CHUMMY
CHUNKY
GHARRY
OHENRY
PHILBY
PHILLY
PHONEY
PHOOEY
RHEUMY
SHABBY
SHAGGY
SHALEY
SHALLY
SHANDY
SHANNY
SHANTY
SHEEDY
SHEEHY
SHELLY
SHELTY
SHERRY
SHIFTY
SHILLY
SHIMMY
SHINDY
SHINNY
SHIRTY
SHOALY
SHODDY
SHORTY
THEFLY
THEORY
THETOY
THINGY
THINLY
THIRTY
THORNY
THUSLY
WHACKY
WHAMMY
WHEEZY
WHERRY
WHIMSY
WHINEY
WHINNY
WHIPPY
WHIRLY
WHISKY
WHITTY
WHOLLY

••HY••
ANHYDR
MRHYDE

••H••Y
ASHLEY
ICHTHY
JOHNNY
OCHERY
SCHIZY
SPHERY
UNHOLY

•••HY•
METHYL
TETHYS
ZEPHYR

•••H•Y
ARCHLY
CATHAY
EIGHTY
HIGHLY
LUSHLY
MIGHTY
MYOHMY
NIGHTY
POSHLY
RASHLY
RICHLY
RIGHTY
SASHAY

••••HY
APATHY
BEACHY
BOLSHY
BOTCHY
BRACHY
BRASHY
BRUSHY
BUNCHY
CATCHY
CAUCHY
DINGHY
DOUGHY
EARTHY
FILTHY
FLASHY
FLESHY
FROTHY
GRAPHY
GUNSHY
HEATHY
ICHTHY
LEACHY
LUNCHY
MARSHY
MORPHY
MOUTHY
MUNCHY
MURPHY
NOTCHY
PATCHY
PEACHY
PITCHY
PLASHY
PLUSHY
POACHY
POUCHY
PUNCHY
ROUGHY
SHEEHY
SLITHY
SLOSHY
SLUSHY
SMITHY
STITHY
TETCHY
TOOTHY
TORCHY
TOUCHY
TOUGHY
TRACHY
TRASHY
TROPHY
WITCHY
WORTHY
WRATHY

H•Z•••
HAZANS
HAZARD
HAZELS
HAZERS
HAZIER
HAZILY
HAZING
HUZZAH
HUZZAS

H••Z••
HERZOG
HUZZAH
HUZZAS

H••••Z
HORMUZ

•H•Z••
GHAZIS
SHAZAM
WHIZZO

•H••Z•
WHEEZE
WHEEZY
WHIZZO

•H•••Z
CHAVEZ
CHINTZ
SHIRAZ
THEWIZ

••HZ••
MAHZOR

••H•Z•
SCHIZY

••H••Z
SCHNOZ
SCHULZ

IA••••
IAMBIC
IATRIC

I•A•••
IBADAN
ICARIA
ICARUS
IMAGED
IMAGER
IMAGES
IMAMAN
IMARET
INAFIX
INAFOG
INAJAM
INANER
INAPET
INARCH
INAROW
INARUT
INAWAY
IRANIS
IRAQIS
IRATER
ISABEL
ISADOR
ISAIAH
ITALIA
ITALIC
ITASCA
IZABAL

I••A••
IBEAMS
ICEAGE
IDCARD
IDEALS
IDEATE
IDTAGS
IGNACE
IGNATZ
IGUACU
IGUANA
ILEANA
IMPACT
IMPAIR
IMPALA
IMPALE
IMPART
INCANS
INCASE
INCASH
INDABA
INFACT
INFAMY
INFANT
INHALE
INHALF
INHAND
INHAUL
INLAID
INLAND
INLAWS
INLAYS
INMATE
INNAGE
INNATE
INPART
INSANE
INTACT
INTAKE
INVADE
INVAIN
INWARD
IODATE
IOWANS
ISLAND
ISRAEL
ITHACA
ITHAKI
IZZARD

I•••A•
IBADAN
ICEBAG
ICECAP
ICEMAN
ILLSAY
IMAMAN
INAJAM
INAWAY
INDIAN
INGEAR
INGMAR
INGRAM
INPLAY
INROAD
INSEAM
INSPAN
INSTAL
INSTAR
IONIAN
IPECAC
IRREAL
ISAIAH
ISHTAR
ISOBAR
ITZHAK
IZABAL

I••••A
IBERIA
ICARIA
IGUANA
ILEANA
ILESHA
IMELDA
IMPALA
INDABA
INDIRA
INTIMA
ISCHIA
ISTRIA
ITALIA
ITASCA
ITHACA

•IA•••
BIAFRA
BIANCA
BIASED
BIASES
CIARDI
DIABLO
DIADEM
DIALED
DIALER
DIALOG
DIALUP
DIANNE
DIAPER
DIATOM
FIACRE
FIANCE
FIASCO
GIANTS
HIATAL
HIATUS
KIANGS
LIABLE
LIAISE
LIANAS
LIANES
LIANGS
MIAMIA
MIASMA
NIACIN
NIAMEY
PIAFFE
PIAGET
PIANOS
PIAZZA
RIALTO
RIATAS
TIARAS
VIABLE
VIABLY
VIACOM
VIANDS
XIAMEN

•I•A••
AIRARM
BICARB
BIGAMY
BIHARI
BINARY
BINATE
CICADA
CIGARS
CITATO
DIDACT
DILATE
DINARS
DISANT
DISARM
DIVANS
FIGARO
FINALE
FINALS
FIXATE
GIRARD
GITANO
HIJACK
HILARY
HIVAOA
JICAMA
JIHADS
KIGALI
LIGAND
LIGATE
LILACS
LINAGE
LIPASE
LITANY
LIZARD
MIDAIR
MIKADO
MILADY
MILANO
MIRAGE
NICAEA
PICABO
PICARA
PICARD
PICARO
PIKAKE
PILAFS
PILATE
PINATA
PIPALS
PIRACY
PIRANA
PIRATE
PISANO
PISANS
PIZAZZ
RIBALD
RIBAND
RITARD
RIVALS
RIYADH
RIYALS
SILAGE
SISALS
SITARS
SIWASH
TICALS
TILAKS
TIRADE
TIRANA
TIRANE
TISANE
TITANS
VICARS
VIRAGO
VISAED
VISAGE
VITALE
VITALS
VIVACE
VIVANT
WIZARD

•I••A•
AIMSAT
AIRBAG
AIRDAM
AIRMAN
AIRSAC
AIRWAY
BIGMAC
BILBAO
BIOGAS
BIOTAS
BISCAY
BISSAU
BITMAP
CIUDAD
DIGRAM
DIKTAT
DIRHAM
DISBAR
DISMAL
DISMAY
DISTAL
FIJIAN
FILIAL
FINIAL
FINNAN
FIRMAN
FISCAL
FIVEAM
GIBRAN
GILEAD
GIMBAL
HIATAL
HIEMAL
HIJRAH
HINTAT
HISSAT
HITMAN
JIGSAW
JINNAH
KIDMAN
KIDNAP
KIOWAS
KIRMAN
KITBAG
KITKAT
LIANAS
LIBYAN
LINEAL
LINEAR
MICMAC
MIDDAY
MIDIAN
MIDWAY
MIHRAB
MILLAY
MILPAS
MILSAP
MINOAN
MINYAN
MIRIAM
MISHAP
MISLAY
MISSAL
MISSAY
MITRAL
NICEAN
NIIHAU
NILGAI
NINEAM
NINJAS
NIPSAT
NISSAN
OILCAN
OILMAN

OILPAN
PICKAT
PICKAX
PIEMAN
PIEPAN
PIETAS
PILLAR
PINDAR
PINEAL
PINNAE
PINNAS
PINOAK
PISGAH
PITMAN
PITSAW
PIZZAS
QINTAR
RIATAS
RIOJAS
RIPRAP
RIPSAW
RITUAL
SIGMAS
SIGNAL
SILOAM
SILVAS
SIMIAN
SINBAD
SINEAD
SINTAX
SIOUAN
SIRDAR
SIRRAH
TIARAS
TIBIAE
TIBIAL
TIBIAS
TICTAC
TIMBAL
TINCAL
TINCAN
TINEAR
TINHAT
TINMAN
TINPAN
TITIAN
UINTAS
VILLAS
VIOLAS
VISTAS
VISUAL
VIVIAN
WICCAN
WIGWAG
WIGWAM
WINKAT
WITHAL
ZIGZAG
ZILPAH

•I•••A

BIAFRA
BIANCA
BIKILA
BITOLA
CIBOLA
CICADA
CINEMA
EIDOLA
FIBULA
FIESTA
HIVAOA
JICAMA
KINEMA
LIGULA
LINGUA
LIOTTA
LISBOA
MIAMIA
MIASMA
MIKITA
MIMOSA
MINIMA
MISCHA
NICAEA
NICOLA
NIKITA
NIKOLA
PIAZZA
PICARA
PINATA
PIRANA
RIVERA
SIENNA
SIERRA
SIESTA
SILICA
SIRICA
SISERA
SISTRA
TIERRA
TIRANA
VICUNA
VIENNA
VIGODA
VIZSLA
WINONA
XIMENA
ZINNIA

••IA••

APIARY
ASIANS
AVIANS
AVIARY
AVIATE
BRIAND
BRIANS
BRIARD
BRIARS
CHIANG
CHIAUS
CUIABA
FRIARS
FRIARY
GUIANA
NAIADS
OPIATE
ORIANA
PHIALS
PLIANT
TRIADS
TRIAGE
TRIALS
UMIAKS
UNIATE
UNIATS
URIALS

••I•A•

ADIDAS
AKITAS
AMIGAS
ANIMAL
ANIMAS
APICAL
BAIKAL
BAIZAS
BRIDAL
CAIMAN
CEIBAS
CHIRAC
CLIMAX
CNIDAE
ELIJAH
EPICAL
EPINAL
FAISAL
FBIMAN
FRIDAY
GUITAR
HAIDAS
HAINAN
KLIBAN
MAITAI
NAIRAS
NIIHAU
OBIWAN
OHIOAN
OVISAC
PAISAS
PHILAE
PLICAE
PRIMAL
RAILAT
REINAS
RHINAL
SAIGAS
SAIPAN
SHIKAR
SHIRAZ
SMILAX
SPICAS
SPINAL
SPIRAL
SPIVAK
TAIGAS
TAINAN
TAIPAN
TAIWAN
TRIBAL
TRINAL
UNITAL
UNITAS
UNIVAC
VEINAL
WEIMAR

••I••A

AHIMSA
ALICIA
ANITRA
ARISTA
AXILLA
CHICHA
CRIMEA
CUIABA
ELISHA
ELISSA
EMILIA
ENIGMA
FLICKA
GEISHA
GLINKA
GUIANA
GUINEA
KAILUA
OJIBWA
OLINDA
OLIVIA
ORIANA
ORISSA
QUINOA
SPIREA
STIGMA
TRICIA
TRISHA
TRIVIA
VAISYA

•••IA•

ADRIAN
AERIAL
APPIAN
ATRIAL
AUDIAL
BAHIAN
BELIAL
CAPIAS
CAVIAR
COBIAS
CURIAE
CURIAL
DENIAL
DORIAN
DURIAN
EOLIAN
EONIAN
ESPIAL
FABIAN
FACIAL
FACIAS
FENIAN
FERIAL
FERIAS
FIJIAN
FILIAL
FINIAL
FOLIAR
FUJIAN
GAVIAL
GENIAL
INDIAN
IONIAN
ISAIAH
JOSIAH
JOVIAL
JOVIAN
JULIAN
KODIAK
LABIAL
LAMIAS
LARIAT
LUCIAN
MANIAC
MANIAS
MARIAH
MARIAN
MEDIAL
MEDIAN
MEDIAS
MENIAL
MIDIAN
MIRIAM
MUSIAL
MYRIAD
NARIAL
NORIAS
NUBIAN
OBRIAN
OSSIAN
PARIAH
PLEIAD
RACIAL
RADIAL
RADIAN
REDIAL
RETIAL
RUPIAH
SAMIAM
SEPIAS
SERIAL
SIMIAN
SOCIAL
STRIAE
SYRIAN
TIBIAE
TIBIAL
TIBIAS
TITIAN
TOBIAS
TUPIAN
TYRIAN
UGRIAN
UNCIAL
UZZIAH
VENIAL
VIVIAN
ZAMIAS
ZODIAC

•••I•A

AFRICA
ALTIMA
ANNIKA
AQUILA
ARNICA
ARRIBA
ATTICA
ATTILA
AURIGA
BIKILA
BRAILA
CAPITA
CARINA
COLIMA
COVINA
DAMITA
DESICA
ELMIRA
ELVIRA
ENCINA
EROICA
FAJITA
FARINA
FATIMA
GEZIRA
GODIVA
HEGIRA
INDIRA
INTIMA
KARIBA
KONICA
LADIDA
LAMINA
LATINA
LERIDA
LEXICA
LOLITA
LORICA
LOUISA
LUMINA
MANILA
MARINA
MARISA
MAXIMA
MEDINA
MELINA
MERIDA
MIKITA
MINIMA
MONICA
MORITA
NIKITA
NUMINA
ONEIDA
OPTIMA
OREIDA
PATINA
PEPITA
PURINA
REGINA
RETINA
ROSITA
RUMINA
SALINA
SALIVA
SHEILA
SILICA
SIRICA
TROIKA
TUNICA
ULTIMA
YAKIMA

••••IA

ACACIA
ACADIA
ACEDIA
AEOLIA
AGLAIA
ALEXIA
ALICIA
AMELIA
ANEMIA
ANGLIA
APULIA
ARABIA
ARALIA
BORGIA
BOSNIA
CASSIA
CRANIA
DAHLIA
EGERIA
EMILIA
ETALIA
FASCIA
FLAVIA
GALLIA
GAMBIA
GARCIA
GLORIA
GRATIA
HESTIA
IBERIA
ICARIA
ISCHIA
ISTRIA
ITALIA
KESHIA
LATVIA
LOGGIA
MARCIA
MIAMIA
MURCIA
MYOPIA
NARNIA
NUTRIA
OBELIA
OLIVIA
PALLIA
PENNIA
PEORIA
PERSIA
PHOBIA
PORTIA
PYTHIA
RAFFIA
REALIA
ROBBIA
RUSSIA
SALVIA
SANDIA
SARNIA
SCALIA
SCORIA
SCOTIA
SERBIA
SHANIA
SHARIA
SOPHIA
STADIA
STYRIA
SYLVIA
THALIA
TREDIA
TRICIA
TRIVIA
UMBRIA
URANIA
UTOPIA
ZAMBIA
ZINNIA
ZOYSIA

IB••••

IBADAN
IBEAMS
IBERIA
IBEXES
IBIBIO
IBIDEM
IBISES

I•B•••

IMBIBE
IMBRUE
IMBUED
IMBUES
INBORN
INBRED
INBULK

I••B••

IAMBIC
IBIBIO
ICEBAG
ICEBOX
IROBOT
ISABEL
ISOBAR
IZABAL

I•••B•

IMBIBE
INDABA
INDEBT
ITURBI

•IB•••

BIBBED
BIBLES
BIBLIO
CIBOLA
DIBBLE
FIBBED
FIBBER
FIBERS
FIBRES
FIBRIL
FIBRIN
FIBULA
GIBBED
GIBBER
GIBBET
GIBBON
GIBERS
GIBILL
GIBING
GIBLET
GIBRAN
GIBSON
JIBBED
JIBING
KIBBLE
KIBITZ
KIBOSH
LIBBED
LIBBER
LIBELS
LIBERI
LIBIDO
LIBRIS
LIBYAN
NIBBLE
RIBALD
RIBAND
RIBBED
RIBBON
RIBEYE
RIBOSE
SIBYLS
TIBIAE
TIBIAL
TIBIAS
ZIBETS

•I•B••

AIRBAG
AIRBUS
BIBBED
BIGBEN
BIGBOY
BILBAO
BIOBIO
DIABLO
DIBBLE
DISBAR
FIBBED
FIBBER
GIBBED
GIBBER
GIBBET
GIBBON
GIMBAL
GIMBEL
JIBBED
KIBBLE
KITBAG
LIABLE
LIBBED
LIBBER
LIEBIG
LIEBYS
LIMBED
LIMBER
LIMBOS
LIMBUS
LISBOA
LISBON
NIBBLE
NIMBLE
NIMBLY
NIMBUS
RIBBED
RIBBON
SIMBEL
SINBAD
TIDBIT
TIMBAL
TIMBER
TIMBRE
TITBIT
VIABLE
VIABLY
WILBUR
WIMBLE

•I••B•

NINGBO
PICABO
SITSBY

•I•••B

BICARB
DIONEB
MIDRIB
MIHRAB

••IB••

ALIBIS
ALIBLE
BRIBED
BRIBES
CEIBAS
EDIBLE
FOIBLE
GLIBLY
IBIBIO

KLIBAN
OJIBWA
ORIBIS
SKIBOB
TRIBAL
TRIBES

••I•B•
AKIMBO
CLIMBS
CUIABA
LAIDBY
PHILBY
THISBE
TRILBY

••I••B
SKIBOB

•••IB•
ADLIBS
ARRIBA
CARIBE
CARIBS
IMBIBE
KARIBA
MALIBU
SAHIBS
SCRIBE
SQUIBB
SQUIBS

•••I•B
SQUIBB

••••IB
MIDRIB

IC••••
ICARIA
ICARUS
ICEAGE
ICEBAG
ICEBOX
ICECAP
ICEDIN
ICEDUP
ICEFOG
ICEMAN
ICEMEN
ICEOUT
ICESIN
ICESUP
ICHING
ICHTHY
ICICLE
ICIEST
ICINGS
ICKIER
ICONIC

I•C•••
IDCARD
INCANS
INCASE
INCASH
INCEPT
INCHED
INCHES
INCHON
INCISE
INCITE
INCOME
INCULT
INCURS
INCUSE
ISCHIA
ITCHED
ITCHES

I••C••
ICECAP
ICICLE
IPECAC

I•••C•
IDIOCY
IGNACE
IGUACU
IMPACT
INARCH
INDICT
INDUCE
INDUCT
INFACT
INFECT
INJECT
INLUCK
INSECT
INTACT
IONICS
ITASCA
ITHACA

I••••C
IAMBIC
IATRIC
ICONIC
INSYNC
IPECAC
IRENIC
IRIDIC
IRONIC
ITALIC

•IC•••
BICARB
BICEPS
BICKER
BICORN
CICADA
CICELY
CICERO
DICERS
DICIER
DICING
DICKER
DICKEY
DICOTS
DICTUM
DICTUS
FICHES
FICHTE
FICHUS
FICKLE
HICCUP
HICKEY
HICKOK
JICAMA
KICKED
KICKER
KICKIN
KICKUP
LICHEN
LICKED
LICTOR
MICHEL
MICKEY
MICMAC
MICRON
MICROS
NICAEA
NICEAN
NICELY
NICENE
NICEST
NICETY
NICHES
NICKED
NICKEL
NICKER
NICOLA
NICOLE
NICOLO
PICABO
PICARA
PICARD
PICARO
PICCHU
PICKAT
PICKAX
PICKED
PICKER
PICKET
PICKLE
PICKON
PICKUP
PICNIC
PICOTS
PICULS
RICERS
RICHEN
RICHER
RICHES
RICHIE
RICHLY
RICING
RICKED
RICKEY
SICCED
SICILY
SICKEN
SICKER
SICKLE
SICKLY
TICALS
TICKED
TICKER
TICKET
TICKLE
TICKLY
TICTAC
VICARS
VICTIM
VICTIS
VICTOR
VICUNA
WICCAN
WICKED
WICKER
WICKET
WICOPY

•I•C••
BISCAY
CIRCLE
CIRCUM
CIRCUS
CISCOS
DISCOS
DISCUS
FIACRE
FISCAL
HICCUP
HINCTY
KIMCHI
LITCHI
MINCED
MINCER
MINCES
MISCHA
MISCUE
NIACIN
NIECES
OILCAN
PICCHU
PIECED
PIECER
PIECES
PINCER
PISCES
PITCHY
SICCED
SIECLE
SITCOM
TINCAL
TINCAN
TINCTS
VIACOM
VINCES
VINCIT
VISCID
WICCAN
WILCOX
WINCED
WINCER
WINCES
WITCHY
ZIRCON

•I••C•
BIANCA
BIERCE
BISECT
CIVICS
DIDACT
DIRECT
FIANCE
FIASCO
FIERCE
HIJACK
HIRSCH
HITECH
KIRSCH
KITSCH
LILACS
MIMICS
PIERCE
PIRACY
SILICA
SIRICA
TIERCE
VIVACE

•I•••C
AIRSAC
BIGMAC
BIONIC
BIOTIC
CITRIC
FINNIC
FISTIC
LITHIC
MICMAC
MIXTEC
NITRIC
PICNIC
TICTAC
VITRIC
ZIPLOC

••IC••
ALICIA
AMICES
AMICUS
APICAL
APICES
BRICKS
BRICKY
CAICOS
CHICHA
CHICHI
CHICKS
CHICLE
CHICLY
CLICHE
CLICKS
CRICKS
DEICED
DEICER
DEICES
EDICTS
ELICIT
EPICAL
EVICTS
FLICKA
FLICKS
ICICLE
JUICED
JUICER
JUICES
KNICKS
PLICAE
PRICED
PRICER
PRICES
PRICEY
PRICKS
QUICHE
SEICHE
SLICED
SLICER
SLICES
SLICKS
SNICKS
SPICAS
SPICED
SPICES
STICKS
STICKY
TAICHI
THICKE
TRICED
TRICEP
TRICES
TRICHO
TRICIA
TRICKS
TRICKY
TRICOT
UNICEF
VOICED
VOICES
YOICKS

••I•C•
APIECE
CHINCH
CLINCH
CRISCO
EVINCE
FLINCH
FLITCH
FRISCO
GLITCH
GRINCH
IDIOCY
PRINCE
QUINCE
QUINCY
SKITCH
SMIRCH
SNITCH
STITCH
SWITCH
TWITCH

••I••C
ACIDIC
CHIRAC
CLINIC
CRITIC
EXILIC
IRIDIC
OTITIC
OVISAC
OXIDIC
STIVIC
UNIFIC
UNIVAC

•••IC•
ADVICE
AFRICA
ALNICO
ANTICS
ARNICA
ASDICS
ASPICS
ATTICA
ATTICS
BASICS
BODICE
CALICO
CHOICE
CIVICS
COMICS
CONICS
CUBICS
CYNICS
DELICT
DEPICT
DESICA
DEVICE
DRYICE
ELLICE
ENRICH
ENRICO
ENTICE
EROICA
ETHICS
EUNICE
INDICT
IONICS
JANICE
KONICA
LEXICA
LORICA
LYRICS
MALICE
MEDICI
MEDICO
MEDICS
MEJICO
MEXICO
MIMICS
MONICA
MUNICH
NATICK
NODICE
NOTICE
NOVICE
OFFICE
OPTICS
OSMICS
PANICS
PLAICE
POLICE
POLICY
PUMICE
RELICS
RELICT
REMICK
SCHICK
SHTICK
SILICA
SIRICA
SLUICE
SONICS
SPLICE
STOICS
STRICK
STRICT
THRICE
TONICS
TOPICS
TOXICS
TUNICA
TUNICS
UPTICK
VENICE
YORICK
ZURICH

•••I•C
MANIAC
MANIOC
ZODIAC

••••IC
ACETIC
ACIDIC
AEOLIC
AGARIC
ALARIC
ALTAIC
AMEBIC
ANEMIC
ANGLIC
ANODIC
ANOMIC
AORTIC
ARABIC
ARCTIC
ATOMIC
ATONIC
BALTIC
BARDIC
BIONIC
BIOTIC
CADMIC
CEDRIC
CELTIC
CITRIC
CLERIC
CLINIC
COPTIC
COSMIC
COURIC
CRITIC
CULTIC
CUPRIC
CYANIC
CYCLIC
CYMRIC
DELTIC
DYADIC
ECESIC
ECHOIC
EDENIC
EROTIC
ETHNIC
ETONIC
EXILIC
EXOTIC
FABRIC
FERRIC
FINNIC
FISTIC
FORMIC
FROLIC
FUSTIC
GAELIC
GALLIC
GARLIC
GESTIC
GNOMIC
GOTHIC
HECTIC
HEROIC
IAMBIC
IATRIC
ICONIC
IRENIC
IRIDIC
IRONIC
ITALIC
JUDAIC
KARMIC
LACTIC
LITHIC
MANTIC
MASTIC
METRIC
MOSAIC
MYOPIC
MYSTIC
MYTHIC
NITRIC
NOETIC
NORDIC
OLDVIC
ORPHIC
OTITIC
OXIDIC
OZONIC
PECTIC
PELVIC
PEPTIC
PHATIC
PHOBIC
PHONIC
PHOTIC
PICNIC
POETIC
PONTIC
PUBLIC
PYKNIC
ROMAIC
RUBRIC
RUSTIC
SCENIC
SEPTIC
SLAVIC
SORBIC
STATIC
STIVIC
SYNDIC
TACTIC
TANNIC
THETIC
TRAGIC
TROPIC
TURKIC
UNCHIC
UNIFIC
URALIC
URANIC
VITRIC
ZENDIC

ID••••
IDCARD
IDEALS
IDEATE
IDIOCY
IDIOMS
IDIOTS
IDLERS
IDLEST
IDLING
IDOIDO
IDTAGS
IDYLLS

I•D•••
INDABA
INDEBT
INDEED
INDENE

INDENT
INDIAN
INDICT
INDIES
INDIGO
INDIRA
INDITE
INDIUM
INDOOR
INDORE
INDRIS
INDUCE
INDUCT
IODATE
IODIDE
IODINE
IODISE
IODIZE

I••D••

IBADAN
IBIDEM
ICEDIN
ICEDUP
IRIDES
IRIDIC
ISADOR

I•••D•

IDOIDO
IMELDA
IMPEDE
INSIDE
INVADE
IODIDE
ISOLDE

I••••D

IDCARD
ILLFED
IMAGED
IMBUED
IMPEND
INBRED
INCHED
INDEED
INFOLD
INGRID
INHAND
INKIND
INLAID
INLAND
INNEED
INROAD
INTEND
INURED
INWARD
IRONED
ISLAND
ISOPOD
ISSUED
ITCHED
IZZARD

•ID•••

AIDERS
AIDFUL
AIDING
BIDDEN
BIDDER
BIDDLE
BIDING
BIDSIN
BIDSON
BIDSUP
CIDERS
DIDACT
DIDDLE
DIDDLY
DIDIES
DIDION
EIDERS
EIDOLA
FIDDLE
FIDGET
GIDEON
GIDGET
HIDDEN
HIDEHO
HIDEKI
HIDERS
HIDING
HIDOUT
KIDDED
KIDDER
KIDDIE
KIDMAN
KIDNAP
KIDNEY
KIDORY
KIDVID
LIDDED
MIDAIR
MIDDAY
MIDDEN
MIDDLE
MIDGES
MIDGET
MIDIAN
MIDLER
MIDORI
MIDRIB
MIDWAY
NIDIFY
PIDGIN
RIDDED
RIDDEN
RIDDLE
RIDENT
RIDERS
RIDGED
RIDGES
RIDING
RIDLEY
RIDSOF
SIDDUR
SIDERO
SIDERS
SIDING
SIDLED
SIDLES
SIDNEY
TIDBIT
TIDDLY
TIDIED
TIDIER
TIDIES
TIDILY
TIDING
TIDYUP
VIDEOS
VIDERI
WIDELY
WIDENS
WIDEST
WIDGET
WIDISH
WIDOWS
WIDTHS

•I•D••

AIRDAM
AIRDRY
BIDDEN
BIDDER
BIDDLE
BINDER
BINDUP
BIRDED
BIRDER
BIRDIE
CINDER
CIUDAD
DIADEM
DIDDLE
DIDDLY
DIKDIK
DIODES
FIDDLE
FINDER
GILDED
GILDER
GIRDED
GIRDER
GIRDLE
HIDDEN
HINDER
HINDUS
KIDDED
KIDDER
KIDDIE
KINDER
KINDLE
KINDLY
KINDOF
LIDDED
LIEDER
LINDEN
MIDDAY
MIDDEN
MIDDLE
MILDER
MILDEW
MILDLY
MINDED
MINDER
MISDID
PINDAR
PINDUS
RIDDED
RIDDEN
RIDDLE
SIDDUR
SIRDAR
TIDDLY
TIEDIN
TIEDTO
TIEDUP
TIEDYE
TILDEN
TILDES
TINDER
WILDER
WILDLY
WINDED
WINDER
WINDEX
WINDOM
WINDOW
WINDUP
WISDOM

•I••D•

AIKIDO
BIONDI
BIPEDS
BIPODS
CIARDI
CICADA
DIPODY
DIRNDL
DIVIDE
FIELDS
FIENDS
FIORDS
JIHADS
LIBIDO
LIPIDE
LIPIDS
MIKADO
MILADY
RIYADH
TIRADE
VIANDS
VIGODA
WIELDS
YIELDS

•I•••D

BIASED
BIBBED
BIFFED
BIFOLD
BIGRED
BILKED
BILLED
BINGED
BINNED
BIRDED
BIRLED
BITTED
CIUDAD
DIALED
DIETED
DIMMED
DINGED
DINNED
DINTED
DIPPED
DISHED
DISKED
DISSED
FIBBED
FILLED
FILMED
FINKED
FINNED
FIRMED
FISHED
FISTED
FITTED
FIZZED
GIBBED
GIFTED
GIGGED
GILDED
GILEAD
GILLED
GINNED
GIPPED
GIRARD
GIRDED
GIRNED
GIRTED
HILLED
HINGED
HINTED
HIPPED
HISPID
HISSED
JIBBED
JIGGED
JILTED
JINKED
JINXED
KICKED
KIDDED
KIDVID
KILLED
KILNED
KILTED
KINGED
KINKED
KISSED
LIBBED
LICKED
LIDDED
LIFTED
LIGAND
LILTED
LIMBED
LIMNED
LIMPED
LIMPID
LINKED
LIPOID
LIPPED
LIQUID
LISPED
LISTED
LIZARD
MIFFED
MILKED
MILLED
MILORD
MINCED
MINDED
MINTED
MISDID
MISLED
MISSED
MISTED
MITRED
NICKED
NIMROD
NIPPED
OINKED
PICARD
PICKED
PIECED
PIGGED
PILLED
PINGED
PINKED
PINNED
PIPPED
PIQUED
PITHED
PITIED
PITTED
RIBALD
RIBAND
RIBBED
RICKED
RIDDED
RIDGED
RIFFED
RIFLED
RIFTED
RIGGED
RIMMED
RINGED
RINSED
RIOTED
RIPPED
RISKED
RITARD
SICCED
SIDLED
SIEGED
SIEVED
SIFTED
SIGHED
SIGNED
SIGURD
SILKED
SILOED
SILTED
SINBAD
SINEAD
SINGED
SINNED
SIPPED
TICKED
TIDIED
TIERED
TIEROD
TIFFED
TILLED
TILTED
TINGED
TINGOD
TINNED
TINTED
TIPPED
TITHED
TITLED
TITRED
VIEWED
VISAED
VISCID
WICKED
WIGGED
WILLED
WILTED
WINCED
WINDED
WINGED
WINKED
WISHED
WISPED
WITHED
WITTED
WIZARD
YIPPED
ZIGGED
ZINGED
ZIPPED

••ID••

ABIDED
ABIDES
ACIDIC
ACIDLY
ADIDAS
AMIDES
AMIDOL
AMIDST
ARIDLY
ASIDES
AVIDLY
AZIDES
BRIDAL
BRIDES
BRIDGE
BRIDLE
BSIDES
CHIDED
CHIDER
CHIDES
CNIDAE
CNIDUS
DEIDRE
EJIDOS
ELIDED
ELIDES
FRIDAY
FRIDGE
GLIDED
GLIDER
GLIDES
GUIDED
GUIDES
GUIDON
HAIDAS
HEIDEN
IBIDEM
IRIDES
IRIDIC
LAIDBY
LAIDIN
LAIDON
LAIDTO
LAIDUP
LEIDEN
MAIDEN
MAIDUS
OXIDES
OXIDIC
PAIDIN
PAIDUP
PRIDED
PRIDES
QUIDDE
RAIDED
RAIDER
SEIDEL
SKIDDY
SLIDER
SLIDES
SLIDIN
SNIDER
SPIDER
VOIDED
ZUIDER

••I•D•

BLINDS
BUILDS
CHILDE
CHILDS
GRINDS
GUILDS
HAIRDO
LAIRDS
NAIADS
OLINDA
OVIEDO
QUIDDE
SHINDY
SKIDDY
TBIRDS
THIRDS
TRIADS
TRIODE
WEIRDO
WEIRDY

••I••D

ABIDED
AFIELD
BAILED
BAITED
BOILED
BRIAND
BRIARD
BRIBED
BRIGID
BRINED
CEILED
CHIDED
CHIMED
COIFED
COILED
COINED
DEICED
EDITED
ELIDED
EXILED
EXITED
FAILED
FAIRED
FOILED
FOINED
FRIEND
FRIGID
GAINED
GAITED
GLIDED
GRIMED
GRIPED
GUIDED
HAILED
HAIRED
JAILED
JOINED
JUICED
KNIFED
MAILED
MOILED
NAILED
NOISED
OPINED
PAINED
PAIRED
POISED
PRICED
PRIDED
PRIMED
PRIZED
RAIDED
RAILED
RAINED
RAISED
REINED
ROILED
RUINED
SAILED
SEINED
SEIZED
SHIELD
SHINED
SKIVED
SLICED
SLIMED
SMILED
SNIPED
SOILED
SPICED
SPIKED
SPINED
SPIRED
SPITED
SUITED
SWIPED
TAILED
TOILED
TRICED
TRIFID
TRIPOD
TWINED
UNIPOD
UNITED
VEILED
VEINED
VOICED
VOIDED
WAILED
WAITED
WAIVED
WHILED
WHINED

•••ID•

AIKIDO
APHIDS
AROIDS
AVOIDS
BESIDE
BETIDE
BOLIDE
BORIDE
BOVIDS
BRAIDS
CANIDS
CUPIDS
DECIDE
DERIDE
DIVIDE
DOSIDO
DROIDS

DRUIDS
FLUIDS
FRAIDY
HALIDE
IDOIDO
INSIDE
IODIDE
LADIDA
LERIDA
LIBIDO
LIPIDE
LIPIDS
MERIDA
ONEIDA
ONSIDE
OREIDA
OROIDE
OVOIDS
PLAIDS
RANIDS
RAPIDS
REBIDS
RESIDE
SOLIDI
SOLIDS
SQUIDS
STRIDE
UNTIDY
UPSIDE
URSIDS
ZOOIDS

•••I•D

ALLIED
BABIED
BEHIND
BELIED
BODIED
BURIED
BUSIED
COPIED
COSIED
COZIED
DEFIED
DENIED
EDDIED
ENGIRD
ENVIED
ESPIED
GOWILD
HESIOD
HONIED
INKIND
LEVIED
MONIED
MYRIAD
PERIOD
PITIED
PLEIAD
PONIED
REBIND
RELIED
REMIND
RETIED
REWIND
RUBIED
TAXIED
TIDIED
UNBIND
UNGIRD
UNKIND
UNTIED
UNWIND
UPWIND
VARIED

••••ID

ACARID
AENEID
AFRAID
AMPHID
ASTRID
BRIGID
CANDID
CAPSID
CERVID
COCCID
CONOID
CUBOID
CUSPID
DEVOID
ELAPID
EUCLID
EYELID
FERVID
FLORID
FOETID
FORBID
FRIGID
GRAVID
HALOID
HISPID
HORRID
HYBRID
INGRID
INLAID
KHALID
KIDVID
LEONID
LIMPID
LIPOID
LIQUID
MADRID
MISDID
MORBID
NEREID
ORCHID
OUTBID
OUTDID
PALLID
PLACID
PONGID
PUTRID
RANCID
RASHID
RELAID
REPAID
SAYYID
SORDID
STOLID
STUPID
THEKID
TOROID
TORPID
TORRID
TREPID
TRIFID
TURBID
TURGID
UNLAID
UNPAID
UNSAID
USERID
VESPID
VISCID
XYLOID

I•E•••

IBEAMS
IBERIA
IBEXES
ICEAGE
ICEBAG
ICEBOX
ICECAP
ICEDIN
ICEDUP
ICEFOG
ICEMAN
ICEMEN
ICEOUT
ICESIN
ICESUP
IDEALS
IDEATE
IGETIT
ILEANA
ILESHA
ILEXES
IMELDA
INESSE
IPECAC
IREFUL
IRENES
IRENIC
ISELIN
ISEULT

I••E••

ICIEST
IDLERS
IDLEST
ILLEST
IMPEDE
IMPELS
IMPEND
IMPERF
INCEPT
INDEBT
INDEED
INDENE
INDENT
INFECT
INFERS
INFEST
INGEAR
INGEST
INHERE
INJECT
INJEST
INKERS
INLETS
INNEED
INNESS
INSEAM
INSECT
INSERT
INSETS
INTEND
INTENS
INTENT
INTERJ
INTERN
INVENT
INVERT
INVEST
IQTEST
IRLENE
IRREAL
ISLETS
ISMENE
ITSELF

I•••E•

IBEXES
IBIDEM
IBISES
ICEMEN
ICKIER
IFFIER
IJSSEL
ILEXES
ILLFED
ILLMET
IMAGED
IMAGER
IMAGES
IMARET
IMBUED
IMBUES
IMOGEN
INANER
INAPET
INBRED
INCHED
INCHES
INDEED
INDIES
INGLES
INGRES
INKIER
INKJET
INKLES
INNEED
INSTEP
INURED
INURES
IRATER
IRENES
IRIDES
IRISES
IRONED
IRONER
ISABEL
ISOHEL
ISOMER
ISRAEL
ISSUED
ISSUER
ISSUES
ISTLES
ITCHED
ITCHES

I••••E

ICEAGE
ICICLE
IDEATE
IGNACE
IGNITE
IGNORE
ILLUME
ILLUSE
IMBIBE
IMBRUE
IMFINE
IMMUNE
IMMURE
IMPALE
IMPEDE
IMPOSE
IMPURE
IMPUTE
INCASE
INCISE
INCITE
INCOME
INCUSE
INDENE
INDITE
INDORE
INDUCE
INESSE
INFUSE
INHALE
INHERE
INJOKE
INJURE
INLINE
INLOVE
INMATE
INNAGE
INNATE
INOUYE
INSANE
INSIDE
INSOLE
INSURE
INTAKE
INTIME
INTINE
INTONE
INTUNE
INVADE
INVITE
INVOKE
IODATE
IODIDE
IODINE
IODISE
IODIZE
IOLITE
IONISE
IONIZE
IRLENE
IRVINE
ISMENE
ISOLDE

•IE•••

AIELLO
BIERCE
DIEOFF
DIEOUT
DIEPPE
DIESEL
DIESES
DIESIS
DIETED
DIETER
FIELDS
FIENDS
FIERCE
FIESTA
HIEING
HIEMAL
HIERON
KIEFER
LIEBIG
LIEBYS
LIEDER
LIEFER
LIEFLY
LIEGES
LIELOW
LIENEE
LIERNE
LIESIN
LIESTO
LIEUTS
NIECES
NIELLI
NIELLO
PIECED
PIECER
PIECES
PIEMAN
PIEMEN
PIEPAN
PIERCE
PIERRE
PIETAS
PIETER
PIETIN
PIETRO
RIENZI
SIECLE
SIEGED
SIEGEL
SIEGES
SIENNA
SIERRA
SIESTA
SIEVED
SIEVES
TIEDIN
TIEDTO
TIEDUP
TIEDYE
TIEING
TIEINS
TIEPIN
TIERCE
TIERED
TIEROD
TIERRA
TIESIN
TIESTO
TIESUP
TIEUPS
VIENNA
VIENNE
VIEWED
VIEWER
WIELDS
WIENER
WIESEL
YIELDS

•I•E••

AIDERS
AILEEN
AILERS
BICEPS
BIKERS
BIPEDS
BIREME
BISECT
BITERS
CICELY
CICERO
CIDERS
CINEMA
CITERS
CIVETS
DICERS
DIGEST
DINEIN
DINEON
DINERO
DINERS
DIRECT
DIRELY
DIREST
DIVEIN
DIVERS
DIVERT
DIVEST
DIYERS
DIZENS
EIDERS
EILEEN
FIBERS
FIFERS
FILENE
FILERS
FILETS
FINELY
FINERY
FINEST
FIRERS
FIREUP
FIVEAM
FIVEPM
FIVERS
FIVEWS
FIXERS
GIBERS
GIDEON
GILEAD
GIMELS
GIVEIN
GIVENS
GIVERS
GIVETO
GIVEUP
HIDEHO
HIDEKI
HIDERS
HIKERS
HIKEUP
HIREON
HIRERS
HITECH
JIVERS
KINEMA
KITERS
LIBELS
LIBERI
LIFERS
LIGERS
LIKELY
LIKENS
LIMENS
LIMEYS
LINEAL
LINEAR
LINENS
LINENY
LINERS
LINEUP
LIPENG
LITERS
LIVEIN
LIVELY
LIVENS
LIVEON
LIVERS
LIVERY
MILERS
MIMEOS
MIMERS
MINERS
MISERS
MISERY
MITERS
MIXERS
MIZENS
NICEAN
NICELY
NICENE
NICEST
NICETY
NINEAM
NINEPM
NINERS
NINETY
NITERS
NITERY
OILERS
PIGEON
PIKERS
PILEIN
PILEON
PILEUM
PILEUP
PILEUS
PINEAL
PINERO
PINERY
PIPERS
PIPEUP
PIXELS
RIBEYE
RICERS
RIDENT
RIDERS
RIFELY
RIFEST
RILEUP
RIPELY
RIPENS
RIPEST
RISERS
RIVERA
RIVERS
RIVETS
SIDERO
SIDERS
SILENI
SILENT
SIMEON
SINEAD
SINEWS
SINEWY
SIRENS
SISERA
SIXERS
SIZERS
SIZEUP
TIGERS
TILERS
TIMELY
TIMERS
TINEAR
TITERS
VIDEOS
VIDERI
VILELY
VILEST
VINERY
VIPERS
VIREOS
VIXENS
WIDELY
WIDENS
WIDEST
WIFELY
WINERY
WIPERS
WIPEUP
WIRERS
WISELY
WISENT
WISEST
WISETO
WISEUP
WIZENS
XIMENA
ZIBETS

•I••E•

AIGRET
AILEEN
AIRIER
AIRMEN
AISLES
BIASED
BIASES
BIBBED
BIBLES
BICKER
BIDDEN
BIDDER
BIFFED
BIGBEN
BIGGER
BIGRED
BIGTEN
BILGES
BILKED
BILLED
BILLET
BINDER
BINGED
BINGES
BINNED
BIOMES
BIRDED
BIRDER

BIRLED
BIRNEY
BISSET
BITTED
BITTEN
BITTER
CINDER
CIPHER
CISKEI
CITIES
DIADEM
DIALED
DIALER
DIAPER
DICIER
DICKER
DICKEY
DIDIES
DIESEL
DIESES
DIETED
DIETER
DIFFER
DIGGER
DILLER
DILSEY
DIMMED
DIMMER
DINGED
DINKEY
DINNED
DINNER
DINTED
DIODES
DIONEB
DIPPED
DIPPER
DIRGES
DISHED
DISHES
DISKED
DISMES
DISNEY
DISPEL
DISSED
DITHER
DITZES
EIFFEL
EILEEN
EISNER
EITHER
FIBBED
FIBBER
FIBRES
FICHES
FIDGET
FILLED
FILLER
FILLES
FILLET
FILMED
FILTER
FINDER
FINGER
FINKED
FINNED
FINNEY
FIRMED
FIRMER
FISHED
FISHER
FISHES
FISTED
FITTED
FITTER
FIZZED
FIZZES
GIBBED
GIBBER
GIBBET
GIBLET
GIDGET
GIFTED
GIGGED
GIGUES
GIJOES
GILDED
GILDER
GILLED
GIMBEL
GIMLET
GIMMES
GINGER
GINNED
GIPPED
GIPPER
GIRDED
GIRDER
GIRNED
GIRTED
HICKEY
HIDDEN
HIGHER
HILLED
HILLEL
HILLER
HINDER
HINGED
HINGES
HINTED
HINTER
HIPPED
HIPPER
HISSED
HISSER
HISSES
HITHER
HITMEN
HITTER
JIBBED
JIGGED
JIGGER
JILTED
JINKED
JINXED
JINXES
JITNEY
JITTER
JIVIER
KICKED
KICKER
KIDDED
KIDDER
KIDNEY
KIEFER
KILLED
KILLER
KILMER
KILNED
KILTED
KILTER
KINDER
KINGED
KINKED
KINSEY
KIPPER
KISLEV
KISMET
KISSED
KISSER
KISSES
KITTEN
LIANES
LIBBED
LIBBER
LICHEN
LICKED
LIDDED
LIEDER
LIEFER
LIEGES
LIENEE
LIFTED
LIFTER
LILIES
LILTED
LIMBED
LIMBER
LIMIER
LIMNED
LIMNER
LIMPED
LIMPER
LIMPET
LINDEN
LINGER
LINIER
LINKED
LINKER
LINNET
LINNEY
LINSEY
LINTEL
LINTER
LIONEL
LIONET
LIPPED
LISLES
LISPED
LISTED
LISTEE
LISTEL
LISTEN
LISTER
LITRES
LITTER
LIVRES
MICHEL
MICKEY
MIDDEN
MIDGES
MIDGET
MIDLER
MIFFED
MIGUEL
MILDER
MILDEW
MILIEU
MILKED
MILKER
MILLED
MILLER
MILLET
MILNER
MINCED
MINCER
MINCES
MINDED
MINDER
MINKES
MINTED
MINTER
MINUET
MINXES
MIRIER
MIRREN
MISLED
MISSED
MISSES
MISTED
MISTER
MITRED
MITRES
MITTEN
MIXTEC
MIZZEN
NIAMEY
NICAEA
NICHES
NICKED
NICKEL
NICKER
NIECES
NIGHER
NIKKEI
NIPPED
NIPPER
NIPSEY
NISSEN
NITRES
NIXIES
OILIER
OILMEN
OINKED
PIAGET
PICKED
PICKER
PICKET
PIECED
PIECER
PIECES
PIEMEN
PIETER
PIGGED
PIGLET
PIGPEN
PILFER
PILLED
PINCER
PINGED
PINIER
PINKED
PINKEN
PINKER
PINNED
PINNER
PINTER
PIOLET
PIPIER
PIPPED
PIQUED
PIQUES
PIQUET
PISCES
PISTES
PITHED
PITIED
PITIER
PITIES
PITMEN
PITTED
PITTER
PIXIES
RIBBED
RICHEN
RICHER
RICHES
RICKED
RICKEY
RIDDED
RIDDEN
RIDGED
RIDGES
RIDLEY
RIFFED
RIFLED
RIFLER
RIFLES
RIFTED
RIGGED
RIGGER
RILLES
RILLET
RIMIER
RIMMED
RINGED
RINGER
RINSED
RINSES
RIOTED
RIOTER
RIPKEN
RIPLEY
RIPPED
RIPPER
RISKED
RISKER
RITTER
SICCED
SICKEN
SICKER
SIDLED
SIDLES
SIDNEY
SIEGED
SIEGEL
SIEGES
SIEVED
SIEVES
SIFTED
SIFTER
SIGHED
SIGHER
SIGNED
SIGNEE
SIGNER
SIGNET
SILKED
SILKEN
SILOED
SILTED
SILVER
SIMBEL
SIMMER
SIMNEL
SIMPER
SINGED
SINGER
SINGES
SINKER
SINNED
SINNER
SINTER
SIPPED
SIPPER
SIPPET
SIRREE
SISKEL
SISLER
SISLEY
SISTER
SITTER
TICKED
TICKER
TICKET
TIDIED
TIDIER
TIDIES
TIERED
TIFFED
TIGGER
TILDEN
TILDES
TILLED
TILLER
TILTED
TILTER
TIMBER
TINDER
TINGED
TINGES
TINIER
TINKER
TINMEN
TINNED
TINNER
TINSEL
TINTED
TINTER
TIPPED
TIPPER
TIPPET
TITFER
TITHED
TITHER
TITHES
TITLED
TITLES
TITRED
TITRES
TITTER
VIEWED
VIEWER
VINCES
VINIER
VIOLET
VISAED
VIVIEN
VIZIER
WICKED
WICKER
WICKET
WIDGET
WIENER
WIESEL
WIGGED
WIGLET
WILDER
WILIER
WILKES
WILLED
WILLEM
WILLET
WILTED
WIMSEY
WINCED
WINCER
WINCES
WINDED
WINDER
WINDEX
WINGED
WINGER
WINIER
WINKED
WINKER
WINNER
WINTER
WINZES
WIRIER
WISHED
WISHER
WISHES
WISPED
WISTER
WITHED
WITHER
WITHES
WITTED
XIAMEN
YIPPED
YIPPEE
ZIGGED
ZIMMER
ZINGED
ZINGER
ZIPPED
ZIPPER
ZITHER

•I•••E

BIDDLE
BIERCE
BIGGIE
BIGLIE
BIGTOE
BILLIE
BINATE
BIRDIE
BIREME
BISQUE
CINQUE
CIRCLE
CIRQUE
DIANNE
DIBBLE
DIDDLE
DIEPPE
DILATE
DILUTE
DIMPLE
DINGLE
DIONNE
DIPOLE
DIRIGE
DISUSE
DIVIDE
DIVINE
FIACRE
FIANCE
FICHTE
FICKLE
FIDDLE
FIERCE
FIGURE
FILENE
FILOSE
FINALE
FINITE
FIPPLE
FIXATE
FIZZLE
GIGGLE
GILLIE
GIRDLE
HIGGLE
HIPPIE
JIGGLE
JIMMIE
JINGLE
KIBBLE
KIDDIE
KILTIE
KINDLE
KINGME
KIRTLE
KISHKE
LIABLE
LIAISE
LIENEE
LIERNE
LIGATE
LIGURE
LILLIE
LINAGE
LIPASE
LIPIDE
LISTEE
LITTLE
LIZZIE
MIDDLE
MIFUNE
MIGGLE
MILLIE
MILTIE
MINGLE
MINNIE
MINUTE
MIRAGE
MISCUE
MISUSE
MIZZLE
NIBBLE
NICENE
NICOLE
NIGGLE
NIMBLE
PIAFFE
PICKLE
PIERCE
PIERRE
PIFFLE
PIGGIE
PIKAKE
PILATE
PILOSE
PINITE
PINKIE
PINNAE
PINOLE
PINTLE
PIRATE
RIBEYE
RIBOSE
RICHIE
RIDDLE
RIFFLE
RIMOSE
RIMPLE
RIPPLE
RISQUE
SICKLE
SIECLE
SIGNEE
SILAGE
SILONE
SIMILE
SIMONE
SIMPLE
SINGLE
SINISE
SIRREE
SIZZLE
TIBIAE
TICKLE
TIEDYE
TIERCE
TILLIE
TIMBRE
TINGLE
TINKLE
TIPPLE
TIPTOE
TIRADE
TIRANE
TISANE
TISSUE
TITTLE
VIABLE
VIENNE
VINNIE
VIRILE
VIRTUE
VISAGE
VISINE
VITALE
VIVACE
WIGGLE
WILLIE
WIMBLE
WIMPLE
WINKIE
WINKLE
WINNIE
YIPPEE

••IE••

ADIEUS
ADIEUX
AFIELD

ALIENS
AMIENS
APIECE
BRIEFS
BRIENZ
BRIERS
BRIERY
CHIEFS
CLIENT
CRIERS
DRIERS
DRIEST
FLIERS
FRIEND
FRIERS
FRIEZE
GAIETY
GRIEFS
GRIEVE
ICIEST
MOIETY
ORIELS
ORIENT
OSIERS
OVIEDO
PLIERS
PRIERS
PRIEST
QUIETS
SHIELD
SHIEST
SKIERS
SLIEST
SPIELS
SPIERS
THIEVE
TRIERS
UBIETY
WRIEST

••I•E•

ABIDED
ABIDES
ALINES
ALITER
AMICES
AMIDES
AMINES
ANIMES
APICES
ARISEN
ARISES
ASIDES
AZIDES
AZINES
BAILED
BAILEE
BAILER
BAILEY
BAINES
BAITED
BEIGES
BLIMEY
BLIXEN
BOILED
BOILER
BOITES
BRIBED
BRIBES
BRIDES
BRINED
BRINES
BSIDES
CEILED
CHIDED
CHIDER
CHIDES
CHIMED
CHIMES
CHINES
CHISEL
CHIVES
CLIMES
CLINES
COIFED
COILED
COINED
COINER
CRIKEY
CRIMEA
CRIMES
CRIPES
CRISES
DAILEY
DAIREN
DAISES
DEICED
DEICER
DEICES
DRIVEL
DRIVEN
DRIVER
DRIVES
DUIKER
EDILES
EDITED
ELIDED
ELIDES
ELITES
EVILER
EXILED
EXILES
EXITED
FAILED
FAIRED
FAIRER
FBIMEN
FOILED
FOINED
FRISEE
FRISES
GAINED
GAINER
GAITED
GAITER
GEIGER
GEISEL
GLIDED
GLIDER
GLIDES
GRIMED
GRIMES
GRIPED
GRIPER
GRIPES
GRIVET
GUIDED
GUIDES
GUILES
GUINEA
GUISES
HAILED
HAILEY
HAINES
HAIRED
HEIDEN
HEIFER
IBIDEM
IBISES
IRIDES
IRISES
JAILED
JAILER
JOINED
JOINER
JUICED
JUICER
JUICES
KAISER
KEITEL
KNIFED
KNIFES
KNIVES
LEIDEN
LOITER
MAIDEN
MAILED
MAILER
MAILES
MAIZES
MOILED
MOILER
MOINES
MOIRES
NAILED
NAILER
NOISED
NOISES
OBITER
OGIVES
OLIVER
OLIVES
OPINED
OPINER
OPINES
ORIGEN
OXIDES
PAINED
PAIRED
PFIZER
POISED
POISES
PRICED
PRICER
PRICES
PRICEY
PRIDED
PRIDES
PRIMED
PRIMER
PRIMES
PRIPET
PRIVET
PRIZED
PRIZES
QUIRES
QUIVER
RAIDED
RAIDER
RAILED
RAILER
RAINED
RAINER
RAINES
RAINEY
RAISED
RAISER
RAISES
REINED
REINER
ROILED
RUINED
RUINER
SAILED
SEIDEL
SEINED
SEINER
SEINES
SEIZED
SEIZER
SEIZES
SHINED
SHINER
SHINES
SHIRER
SHIRES
SHIVER
SKIVED
SKIVER
SKIVES
SLICED
SLICER
SLICES
SLIDER
SLIDES
SLIMED
SLIMES
SLIVER
SMILED
SMILER
SMILES
SMILEY
SMITES
SNIDER
SNIPED
SNIPER
SNIPES
SNIVEL
SOILED
SOIREE
SPICED
SPICES
SPIDER
SPIKED
SPIKER
SPIKES
SPILES
SPINED
SPINEL
SPINES
SPINET
SPIREA
SPIRED
SPIRES
SPITED
SPITES
STILES
STIPEL
STIPES
STIVER
SUITED
SUITES
SWIPED
SWIPER
SWIPES
SWIVEL
SWIVET
TAILED
TAIPEI
TOILED
TOILER
TOILES
TOILET
TRIBES
TRICED
TRICEP
TRICES
TRIJET
TRIKES
TRINES
TRITER
TRIVET
TWINED
TWINES
UNICEF
UNISEX
UNITED
UNITER
UNITES
VAINER
VEILED
VEINED
VOICED
VOICES
VOIDED
VOILES
VSIXES
WAILED
WAILER
WAITED
WAITER
WAIVED
WAIVER
WAIVES
WHILED
WHILES
WHINED
WHINER
WHINES
WHINEY
WHITEN
WHITER
WHITES
WRITER
WRITES
XFILES
ZAIRES
ZUIDER

••I••E

ALIBLE
APIECE
ARIOSE
AVIATE
BAILEE
BLITHE
BRIDGE
BRIDLE
CAIQUE
CHICLE
CHIGOE
CHILDE
CHILOE
CLICHE
CLIQUE
CNIDAE
CRINGE
CUIQUE
CUISSE
DEIDRE
EDIBLE
EMIGRE
ENISLE
EVINCE
FAILLE
FOIBLE
FRIDGE
FRIEZE
FRINGE
FRISEE
GRIEVE
GRILLE
GRILSE
GRIMKE
GRIPPE
GUIMPE
ICICLE
LAINIE
MAISIE
MAITRE
NEISSE
OPIATE
ORIOLE
OTIOSE
PAIUTE
PHILAE
PLICAE
PLISSE
POINTE
PRINCE
PUISNE
QUICHE
QUIDDE
QUINCE
SAINTE
SEICHE
SHIITE
SOIGNE
SOIREE
STIFLE
SUISSE
TAILLE
THICKE
THIEVE
THISBE
TRIAGE
TRIFLE
TRIODE
TRIPLE
TRISTE
TRIUNE
TRIXIE
TUILLE
TWINGE
UBIQUE
UNIATE
UNIQUE
WRITHE

•••IE•

ACHIER
ADRIEN
AERIES
AGGIES
AIRIER
ALLIED
ALLIES
ANCIEN
ARMIES
ARTIER
ASHIER
BABIED
BABIES
BELIED
BELIEF
BELIES
BEVIES
BODIED
BODIES
BOGIES
BONIER
BOXIER
BURIED
BURIES
BUSIED
BUSIER
BUSIES
CAGIER
CAHIER
CAKIER
CANIER
CARIES
CITIES
COKIER
COLIES
CONIES
COPIED
COPIER
COPIES
COSIED
COSIER
COSIES
COZIED
COZIER
COZIES
CUTIES
DAMIEN
DANIEL
DARIEN
DAVIES
DEFIED
DEFIES
DEMIES
DENIED
DENIER
DENIES
DEWIER
DICIER
DIDIES
DOGIES
DOPIER
DORIES
DOZIER
DUTIES
EASIER
EDDIED
EDDIES
EDGIER
EELIER
EERIER
EGGIER
ENVIED
ENVIER
ENVIES
ESPIED
ESPIES
EYRIES
FACIES
FOGIES
FOXIER
FUMIER
FURIES
GABIES
GAMIER
GENIES
GLUIER
GOBIES
GOOIER
GORIER
HAZIER
HOKIER
HOLIER
HOMIER
HONIED
HOSIER
ICKIER
IFFIER
INDIES
INKIER
JAVIER
JIVIER
JOKIER
JOLIET
JULIET
JURIES
LACIER
LADIES
LAKIER
LANIER
LAZIER
LEVIED
LEVIER
LEVIES
LILIES
LIMIER
LINIER
LOGIER
LOOIES
LORIES
MARIEL
MAZIER
METIER
MILIEU
MIRIER
MONIED
MONIES
MOPIER
MOVIES
MURIEL
NAPIER
NAVIES
NIXIES
NOSIER
OATIER
OBRIEN
OILIER
OLDIES
ONVIEW
OOZIER
ORGIES
PALIER
PAPIER
PINIER
PIPIER
PITIED
PITIER
PITIES
PIXIES
POGIES
POKIER
PONIED
PONIES
POSIES
PUNIER
PYXIES
RABIES
RACIER
RAMIES
RAPIER
RELIED
RELIEF
RELIES
RETIED
RETIES
REVIEW
RIMIER
ROPIER
ROSIER
RUBIED
RUBIES
SERIES
SEXIER
SHRIEK
SOVIET
SPRIER
SUSIEQ
TAXIED
TAXIES
TIDIED
TIDIER
TIDIES
TINIER
TOBIES
TONIER
TORIES
TYPIER
UGLIER
UGLIES
UNDIES
UNTIED
UNTIES
VANIER
VARIED
VARIES
VINIER
VIVIEN
VIZIER
WANIER
WARIER
WAVIER
WAXIER
WILIER
WINIER
WIRIER
XAVIER
YALIES
ZANIER
ZANIES

•••I•E

ACTIVE
ADMIRE
ADVICE
ADVISE
AEDILE
AFFINE
ALDINE
ALFINE
ALPINE
APLITE
ARGIVE
ARRIVE
ASPIRE
ASSIZE
ATTIRE
AUDILE
AWHILE
AXLIKE
BARITE
BELIKE
BELIZE
BEMINE
BEMIRE
BESIDE
BETIDE
BETISE
BLAINE
BLAISE
BODICE
BOLIDE
BORIDE
BOVINE
BRAISE
BRUISE
BYLINE
CAMISE
CANINE
CARIBE
CECILE
CELINE
CERISE
CHAINE
CHAISE
CHOICE
CLAIRE
COSINE
CRUISE
CURIAE
DATIVE
DECIDE
DEFILE
DEFINE
DEMISE
DENISE
DERIDE
DERIVE
DESIRE
DEVICE
DEVINE
DEVISE
DIRIGE
DIVIDE
DIVINE
DOCILE
DOMINE
DRYICE
ELAINE
ELLICE
ELOISE
EMPIRE
ENDIVE
ENGINE
ENSILE
ENTICE
ENTIRE
EQUINE
ERMINE
ETOILE
EUNICE
EXCISE
EXCITE
EXPIRE
EXWIFE
FACILE
FALINE
FAMINE
FELINE
FELIPE
FINITE
FRAISE
FUTILE
GAMINE
GREIGE
GUNITE
HABILE
HALIDE
HALITE
HAMITE
IGNITE
IMBIBE
IMFINE
INCISE
INCITE
INDITE
INLINE
INSIDE
INTIME
INTINE
INVITE
IODIDE
IODINE
IODISE
IODIZE
IOLITE
IONISE
IONIZE
IRVINE
JANICE
JANINE
KALINE
KURILE
LABILE
LEVINE
LEVITE
LIAISE
LIPIDE
LOUISE
LUCITE
LUPINE
LYSINE
MALICE
MARINE
MAXINE
MAXIXE
MOBILE
MODINE
MOLINE
MOTILE
MOTIVE
MURINE
NADINE
NATIVE
NODICE
NOMINE
NOTICE
NOVICE
NOWISE
NUBILE
OBLIGE
OFFICE
ONDINE
ONFILE
ONFIRE
ONLINE
ONSIDE
ONSITE
ONTIME
OOLITE
OPHITE
OROIDE
ORPINE
OSCINE
OXLIKE
PATINE
PELIKE
PETITE
PINITE
PLAICE
POLICE
POLITE
PRAISE
PUMICE
PURINE
PYRITE
RACINE
RAPINE
RATINE
RATITE
RAVINE
RECIFE
RECIPE
RECITE
REFILE
REFINE
REGIME
REHIRE
RELINE
RELIVE
REMISE
REPINE
RESIDE
RESILE
RETILE
RETIME
RETIRE
REVILE
REVISE
REVIVE
REWIRE
RUTILE
SABINE
SAFIRE
SALINE
SAMITE
SATIRE
SCRIBE
SEDILE
SEMITE
SERINE
SHIITE
SHRIKE
SHRINE
SHRIVE
SIMILE
SINISE
SLUICE
SOFINE
SPLICE
SPLINE
SPRITE
SQUIRE
STRIAE
STRIDE
STRIFE
STRIKE
STRINE
STRIPE
STRIVE
SUPINE
THRICE
THRIVE
TIBIAE
TOLIFE
TONITE
UMPIRE
UNDINE
UNLIKE
UNPILE
UNRIPE
UNWISE
UPDIKE
UPRISE
UPSIDE
UPTIME
URSINE
VALISE
VENICE
VENIRE
VENITE
VERITE
VIRILE
VISINE
VOTIVE
WAHINE

••••IE

ADELIE
AMALIE
ANOMIE
ARCHIE
AUNTIE
AUSSIE
BADDIE
BAGGIE
BARBIE
BARRIE
BEANIE
BERNIE
BERTIE
BESSIE
BIGGIE
BIGLIE
BILLIE
BIRDIE
BMOVIE
BOBBIE
BOCCIE
BONNIE
BOOGIE
BOOKIE
BOOTIE
BOWTIE
BRODIE
BUDGIE
CABBIE
CADDIE
CARRIE
CHERIE
COLLIE
CONNIE
COOKIE
COOTIE
COWRIE
DANDIE
DEARIE
DEBBIE
DOGGIE
DOOBIE
DOOGIE
DOOZIE
DOTTIE
FAERIE
FANNIE
FERGIE
FOLKIE
FOODIE
FOZZIE
GERTIE
GILLIE
GOALIE
GOLDIE
GOODIE
GORDIE
GRACIE
HACKIE
HADDIE
HANKIE
HATTIE
HEEBIE
HERBIE
HETTIE
HIPPIE
HOAGIE
HOGTIE
HOOTIE
JACKIE
JENNIE
JESSIE
JIMMIE
JOANIE
JUNKIE
KATHIE
KELPIE
KEWPIE
KIDDIE
KILTIE
KOOKIE
LADDIE
LAINIE
LASSIE
LAURIE
LEFTIE
LENNIE
LEONIE
LESLIE
LILLIE
LIZZIE
LOONIE
MADDIE
MAGGIE
MAGPIE
MAISIE
MARCIE
MARGIE
MARNIE
MASHIE
MATTIE
MEALIE
MEANIE
MILLIE
MILTIE
MINNIE
MOMMIE
MUDPIE
MUNCIE
MUSKIE
NANNIE
NAPPIE
NELLIE
NESSIE
PETRIE
PIGGIE
PINKIE
POTPIE
PREMIE
PUNKIE
REGGIE
RENNIE
RICHIE
ROADIE
ROBBIE
ROLLIE
RONNIE
ROOKIE
ROOMIE
RUNCIE
SAMMIE
SAVOIE
SKOKIE
SOFTIE
SOPHIE
SORTIE
SPECIE
STEVIE
STOGIE
STYMIE
TALKIE
TECHIE
TESSIE
TILLIE
TOONIE
TOWNIE
TRIXIE
VEGGIE
VINNIE
WALKIE
WEDGIE
WEENIE
WEEPIE
WILLIE
WINKIE
WINNIE
WOOGIE
WOOKIE
YORKIE
YUPPIE
ZOMBIE

IF••••

IFFIER

I•F•••

IFFIER
IMFINE
INFACT
INFAMY
INFANT
INFECT
INFERS
INFEST
INFIRM
INFLOW
INFLUX
INFOLD
INFORM
INFULL
INFUSE

I••F••

ICEFOG
ILLFED
INAFIX
INAFOG
IREFUL

I••••F

IMPERF
INHALF
ITSELF

•IF•••

BIFFED
BIFOLD
DIFFER
EIFFEL
FIFERS
FIFING
FIFTHS
GIFTED
LIFERS
LIFTED
LIFTER
LIFTUP
MIFFED
MIFUNE
PIFFLE
RIFELY
RIFEST
RIFFED
RIFFLE
RIFIFI
RIFLED
RIFLER
RIFLES
RIFTED
SIFTED
SIFTER
TIFFED
TIFFIN
WIFELY

•I•F••

AIDFUL
AIMFOR
AIMFUL
BIAFRA
BIFFED
DIFFER
EIFFEL
FITFUL
KIEFER
KITFOX
LIEFER
LIEFLY
MIFFED
MISFIT
PIAFFE
PIFFLE
PILFER
RIFFED
RIFFLE
SINFUL
TIFFED
TIFFIN
TITFER
WILFUL

•I••F•

BITOFF
CITIFY
DIEOFF
MINIFY
NIDIFY
PIAFFE
PILAFS
RIFIFI
RIPOFF
TIPOFF
VILIFY
VINIFY
VIVIFY

•I•••F

BITOFF
DIEOFF
KINDOF
RIDSOF
RIPOFF
TIPOFF

••IF••

CLIFFS
CLIFFY
COIFED
DRIFTS
DRIFTY
GRIFTS
HEIFER
KNIFED
KNIFES
SCIFIS
SHIFTS
SHIFTY
SKIFFS
SNIFFS
SNIFFY
SPIFFS
SPIFFY
STIFFS
STIFLE
SWIFTS
TRIFID
TRIFLE
UNIFIC
WHIFFS

••I•F•

BRIEFS
CHIEFS
CLIFFS
CLIFFY
GRIEFS
SKIFFS
SNIFFS
SNIFFY
SPIFFS
SPIFFY
STIFFS
WHIFFS

••I••F

UNICEF

•••IF•

ADRIFT
AERIFY
AURIFY
BASIFY
CANIFF
CITIFY
CODIFY
EXWIFE
GASIFY
MINIFY
MODIFY
MOTIFS
NIDIFY
NOTIFY
OSSIFY
PACIFY
PURIFY
RAMIFY
RARIFY
RATIFY
RECIFE
RIFIFI
RUBIFY
SALIFY
SCHIFF
SERIFS
SHRIFT
STRIFE
TARIFF
THRIFT
TOLIFE
TYPIFY
UGLIFY
UPLIFT
VERIFY
VILIFY
VINIFY
VIVIFY

•••I•F

BELIEF
CANIFF
RELIEF
SCHIFF
TARIFF

••••IF

CERTIF
MASSIF
SHARIF
SHERIF
WHATIF

IG••••

IGETIT

IGLOOS
IGNACE
IGNATZ
IGNITE
IGNORE
IGOTIT
IGUACU
IGUANA

I•G•••

INGEAR
INGEST
INGLES
INGMAR
INGOTS
INGRAM
INGRES
INGRID

I••G••

IMAGED
IMAGER
IMAGES
IMOGEN
ISOGON

I•••G•

ICEAGE
ICINGS
IDTAGS
IMPUGN
INDIGO
INNAGE

I••••G

ICEBAG
ICEFOG
ICHING
IDLING
IMPING
INAFOG
INKING
INNING
IRKING
IRVING

•IG•••

AIGRET
BIGAMY
BIGBEN
BIGBOY
BIGGER
BIGGIE
BIGGUN
BIGHTS
BIGLIE
BIGMAC
BIGOTS
BIGRED
BIGSUR
BIGTEN
BIGTOE
BIGTOP
BIGWIG
CIGARS
DIGEST
DIGGER
DIGITS
DIGLOT
DIGOUT
DIGRAM
DIGSIN
DIGSUP
EIGHTH
EIGHTS
EIGHTY
FIGARO
FIGHTS
FIGURE
GIGGED
GIGGLE
GIGGLY
GIGOLO
GIGOTS
GIGUES
HIGGLE
HIGHER
HIGHIQ
HIGHLY
HIGHUP
JIGGED
JIGGER
JIGGLE
JIGGLY
JIGSAW
KIGALI
LIGAND
LIGATE
LIGERS
LIGHTS
LIGNIN
LIGULA
LIGURE
MIGGLE
MIGHTY
MIGNON
MIGUEL
NIGGLE
NIGHER
NIGHTS
NIGHTY
PIGEON
PIGGED
PIGGIE
PIGLET
PIGNUT
PIGOUT
PIGPEN
PIGSTY
RIGGED
RIGGER
RIGHTO
RIGHTS
RIGHTY
RIGORS
RIGOUR
RIGSUP
SIGHED
SIGHER
SIGHTS
SIGILS
SIGMAS
SIGNAL
SIGNED
SIGNEE
SIGNER
SIGNET
SIGNIN
SIGNON
SIGNOR
SIGNUP
SIGURD
TIGERS
TIGGER
TIGHTS
TIGLON
TIGRIS
UIGURS
VIGILS
VIGODA
VIGORS
VIGOUR
WIGGED
WIGGLE
WIGGLY
WIGHTS
WIGLET
WIGOUT
WIGWAG
WIGWAM
ZIGGED
ZIGZAG

•I•G••

AIRGUN
BIGGER
BIGGIE
BIGGUN
BILGES
BINGED
BINGES
BIOGAS
BIRGIT
DIGGER
DINGED
DINGHY
DINGLE
DINGUS
DIRGES
FIDGET
FINGER
FIZGIG
GIDGET
GIGGED
GIGGLE
GIGGLY
GILGUY
GINGER
HIGGLE
HINGED
HINGES
HINGIS
JIGGED
JIGGER
JIGGLE
JIGGLY
JINGLE
JINGLY
KINGED
KINGLY
KINGME
LIEGES
LINGER
LINGUA
MIDGES
MIDGET
MIGGLE
MINGLE
NIGGLE
NILGAI
NINGBO
PIAGET
PIDGIN
PIGGED
PIGGIE
PINGED
PISGAH
RIDGED
RIDGES
RIGGED
RIGGER
RINGED
RINGER
RINGUP
SIEGED
SIEGEL
SIEGES
SINGED
SINGER
SINGES
SINGIN
SINGLE
SINGLY
SINGTO
SIXGUN
TIGGER
TINGED
TINGES
TINGLE
TINGLY
TINGOD
VIRGIL
VIRGIN
WIDGET
WIGGED
WIGGLE
WIGGLY
WINGED
WINGER
WINGIT
XINGIN
ZIGGED
ZINGED
ZINGER

•I••G•

DIRIGE
DIRIGO
GINKGO
KIANGS
LIANGS
LINAGE
MIRAGE
SILAGE
VIRAGO
VISAGE

•I•••G

AIDING
AILING
AIMING
AIRBAG
AIRING
BIDING
BIGWIG
BIKING
BITING
CITING
DIALOG
DICING
DIKING
DINING
DIVING
FIFING
FILING
FINING
FIRING
FIXING
FIZGIG
GIBING
GIVING
HIDING
HIEING
HIKING
HIRING
HIVING
JIBING
JIVING
KITBAG
KITING
LIEBIG
LIKING
LIMING
LINING
LIPENG
LITHOG
LIVING
MIKING
MIMING
MINING
MIRING
MIXING
NIXING
OILING
OILRIG
PIKING
PILING
PINING
PIPING
RICING
RIDING
RILING
RIMING
RISING
RIVING
SIDING
SIRING
SITING
SIXING
SIZING
TIDING
TIEING
TILING
TIMING
TIRING
VIKING
VINING
WIGWAG
WILING
WINING
WIPING
WIRING
ZIGZAG

••IG••

ALIGHT
ALIGNS
AMIGAS
AMIGOS
ARIGHT
BEIGES
BLIGHT
BOIGNY
BRIGGS
BRIGHT
BRIGID
CHIGOE
COIGNS
DEIGNS
DWIGHT
EMIGRE
ENIGMA
FEIGNS
FLIGHT
FRIGHT
FRIGID
GEIGER
GRIGRI
HAIGHT
HEIGHT
KNIGHT
NEIGHS
ORIGEN
ORIGIN
PLIGHT
REIGNS
SAIGAS
SAIGON
SLIGHT
SOIGNE
SPIGOT
STIGMA
TAIGAS
THIGHS
TRIGLY
TRIGON
TWIGGY
VEIGHT
VOIGHT
VSIGNS
WEIGHS
WEIGHT
WRIGHT

••I•G•

BEINGS
BOINGO
BRIDGE
BRIGGS
BRINGS
CLINGS
CLINGY
CRINGE
DOINGS
DRINGS
FLINGS
FRIDGE
FRINGE
FRINGY
GOINGS
GRINGO
ICINGS
OLINGO
ORINGS
SLINGS
STINGO
STINGS
STINGY
SWINGS
SWINGY
THINGS
THINGY
TRIAGE
TWIGGY
TWINGE
WRINGS

••I••G

CHIANG
EPILOG
SKIING

•••IG•

ASSIGN
AURIGA
AWEIGH
BENIGN
COSIGN
DESIGN
DIRIGE
DIRIGO
EFFIGY
ELOIGN
ENSIGN
GREIGE
INDIGO
LATIGO
LEHIGH
MALIGN
OBLIGE
ONHIGH
RESIGN
SLEIGH
SPRIGS
UNRIGS

•••I•G

AAHING
ABYING
ACHING
ACTING
ADDING
AGEING
AIDING
AILING
AIMING
AIRING
ARCING
ARMING
ASKING
AWNING
BAAING
BAKING
BALING
BARING
BASING
BATING
BAYING
BBKING
BENING
BERING
BIDING
BIKING
BITING
BLUING
BODING
BOEING
BONING
BOOING
BORING
BOWING
BOXING
BUSING
BUYING
CAGING
CAKING
CANING
CARING
CASING
CAVING
CAWING
CEDING
CITING
CLUING
CODING
COMING
COOING
COPING
CORING
COWING
CRYING
CUBING
CURING
DARING
DATING
DAZING
DEKING
DEWING
DICING
DIKING
DINING
DIVING
DOLING
DOMING
DOPING
DOSING
DOTING
DOZING
DRYING
DUKING
DUPING
DURING
DYEING
EALING
EARING
EASING
EATING
EBBING
EDGING
EGGING
ENDING
EPPING
ERRING
ERVING
EYEING
FACING
FADING
FAKING
FARING
FAXING
FAZING
FEEING
FETING
FIFING
FILING
FINING
FIRING
FIXING
FLYING
FOXING
FRYING
FUMING
FUSING
FUZING
GAGING
GAMING
GAPING
GATING
GAZING
GEEING
GIBING
GIVING
GLUING
GORING
GUYING
GYBING
HALING
HARING
HATING
HAVING
HAWING
HAYING
HAZING
HEWING
HEXING
HIDING
HIEING
HIKING
HIRING
HIVING
HOEING
HOLING
HOMING
HONING
HOPING
HOSING
HYPING
ICHING
IDLING
IMPING
INKING
INNING
IRKING
IRVING
JADING
JAPING
JAWING
JIBING
JIVING
JOKING
JUKING
KEYING
KITING
LACING
LADING
LAMING
LAVING
LAWING
LAYING
LAZING
LIKING
LIMING
LINING
LIVING
LOPING
LOSING
LOVING
LOWING
LUBING
LURING

LUTING
MAKING
MATING
METING
MEWING
MIKING
MIMING
MINING
MIRING
MIXING
MOOING
MOPING
MOVING
MOWING
MUSING
MUTING
NAMING
NIXING
NOSING
NOTING
NUKING
OARING
OFFING
OGLING
OILING
OOHING
OOZING
OPTING
ORBING
OUTING
OWNING
PACING
PAGING
PALING
PARING
PAVING
PAWING
PAYING
PEKING
PIKING
PILING
PINING
PIPING
PLYING
POKING
POLING
PORING
POSING
PRYING
PULING
RACING
RAGING
RAKING
RARING
RASING
RATING
RAVING
RAZING
REDING
RESING
RICING
RIDING
RILING
RIMING
RISING
RIVING
ROBING
ROPING
ROVING
ROWING
RULING
SATING
SAVING
SAWING
SAYING
SEEING
SEWING
SHYING
SIDING
SIRING
SITING
SIXING
SIZING
SKIING
SKYING
SLUING
SOLING
SOWING
SPRING
SPYING
STRING
TAKING
TAMING
TAPING
TARING
TAWING
TAXING
TEEING
TIDING
TIEING
TILING
TIMING
TIRING
TOEING
TONING
TOTING
TOWING
TOYING
TRUING
TRYING
TUBING
TUNING
TURING
TYPING
UPPING
URGING
VEXING
VIKING
VINING
VOTING
VOWING
WADING
WAGING
WAKING
WANING
WARING
WAVING
WAXING
WILING
WINING
WIPING
WIRING
WOOING
WOWING
YAWING
YOKING
ZONING

••••IG

BIGWIG
CATRIG
DANZIG
EARWIG
FIZGIG
GEHRIG
KOENIG
LIEBIG
LUDWIG
OILRIG
WETTIG
ZAFTIG

I•H•••

ICHING
ICHTHY
INHALE
INHALF
INHAND
INHAUL
INHERE
ISHTAR
ITHACA
ITHAKI

I••H••

INCHED
INCHES
INCHON
ISCHIA
ISOHEL
ISTHMI
ITCHED
ITCHES
ITZHAK

I•••H•

ICHTHY
ILESHA

I••••H

IMPISH
INARCH
INCASH
INRUSH
INWITH
IOMOTH
IRTYSH
ISAIAH

•IH•••

BIHARI
JIHADS
MIHRAB
NIHILO

•I•H••

BIGHTS
BISHOP
CIPHER
DIRHAM
DISHED
DISHES
DITHER
EIGHTH
EIGHTS
EIGHTY
EITHER
FICHES
FICHTE
FICHUS
FIGHTS
FISHED
FISHER
FISHES
HIGHER
HIGHIQ
HIGHLY
HIGHUP
HIPHOP
HITHER
KISHKE
LICHEN
LIGHTS
LITHIC
LITHOG
LITHOS
MICHEL
MIGHTY
MISHAP
MISHIT
NICHES
NIGHER
NIGHTS
NIGHTY
NIIHAU
PITHED
RICHEN
RICHER
RICHES
RICHIE
RICHLY
RIGHTO
RIGHTS
RIGHTY
SIGHED
SIGHER
SIGHTS
SIPHON
TIGHTS
TINHAT
TISHRI
TITHED
TITHER
TITHES
VISHNU
WIGHTS
WISHED
WISHER
WISHES
WITHAL
WITHED
WITHER
WITHES
WITHIN
WITHIT
ZITHER

•I••H•

BIRTHS
DINGHY
FIFTHS
FILTHY
FIRTHS
GIRTHS
HIDEHO
KIMCHI
LITCHI
MISCHA
NINTHS
PICCHU
PITCHY
SIXTHS
WIDTHS
WITCHY

•I•••H

EIGHTH
FINISH
HIJRAH
HIRSCH
HITECH
JINNAH
KIBOSH
KIRSCH
KITSCH
LILITH
PISGAH
RIYADH
SIRRAH
SIWASH
WIDISH
WINISH
ZILPAH
ZIZITH

••IH••

NIIHAU

••I•H•

ALIGHT
ARIGHT
BLIGHT
BLITHE
BRIGHT
CHICHA
CHICHI
CLICHE
DWIGHT
ELISHA
FAITHS
FLIGHT
FRIGHT
GEISHA
HAIGHT
HEIGHT
KNIGHT
NEIGHS
PLIGHT
QUICHE
SEICHE
SLIGHT
SLITHY
SMITHS
SMITHY
STITHY
TAICHI
THIGHS
TRICHO
TRISHA
VEIGHT
VOIGHT
WEIGHS
WEIGHT
WRIGHT
WRITHE

••I••H

CHINCH
CLINCH
ELIJAH
FLINCH
FLITCH
GLITCH
GRINCH
PLINTH
SHILOH
SKITCH
SMIRCH
SNITCH
SPILTH
STITCH
SWITCH
TWITCH

•••I•H

AGUISH
ASPISH
AWEIGH
BANISH
BARISH
BLUISH
BOYISH
CALIPH
CERIPH
COYISH
DANISH
DOVISH
DUDISH
ELFISH
ELVISH
ENRICH
EOLITH
FAMISH
FETISH
FINISH
GARISH
GOFISH
GOWITH
IMPISH
INWITH
ISAIAH
JADISH
JEWISH
JOSIAH
JUDITH
JUTISH
LATISH
LAVISH
LEHIGH
LILITH
LOWISH
MARIAH
MARISH
MODISH
MOPISH
MULISH
MUNICH
NEWISH
OAFISH
OFFISH
OGRISH
OLDISH
ONHIGH
OOLITH
ORNITH
OWLISH
PALISH
PARIAH
PARISH
PERISH
POLISH
PUNISH
RADISH
RAKISH
RAVISH
RAWISH
RELISH
RUPIAH
SALISH
SLEIGH
SQUISH
TONISH
UNWISH
UPPISH
UZZIAH
VANISH
WIDISH
WINISH
WRAITH
ZENITH
ZIZITH
ZURICH

I•I•••

IBIBIO
IBIDEM
IBISES
ICICLE
ICIEST
ICINGS
IDIOCY
IDIOMS
IDIOTS
INIONS
INITIO
IRIDES
IRIDIC
IRISES
IRISIN

I••I••

ICHING
ICKIER
IDLING
IDOIDO
IFFIER
IGNITE
ILLINI
ILOILO
IMBIBE
IMFINE
IMPING
IMPISH
INCISE
INCITE
INDIAN
INDICT
INDIES
INDIGO
INDIRA
INDITE
INDIUM
INFIRM
INKIER
INKIND
INKING
INLINE
INNING
INSIDE
INSIST
INSITU
INTIMA
INTIME
INTINE
INUITS
INVITE
INVIVO
INWITH
IODIDE
IODINE
IODISE
IODIZE
IOLITE
IONIAN
IONICS
IONISE
IONIUM
IONIZE
IRKING
IRVINE
IRVING
ISAIAH

I•••I•

IAMBIC
IATRIC
IBERIA
IBIBIO
ICARIA
ICEDIN
ICESIN
ICONIC
IGETIT
IGOTIT
ILORIN
IMPAIR
INAFIX
INDRIS
INGRID
INITIO
INLAID
INSTIL
INTUIT
INVAIN
IRANIS
IRAQIS
IRENIC
IRIDIC
IRISIN
IRONIC
ISCHIA
ISELIN
ISTRIA
ITALIA
ITALIC

I••••I

ILLINI
ISTHMI
ITHAKI
ITURBI

•II•••

NIIHAU

•I•I••

AIDING
AIKIDO
AILING
AIMING
AIRIER
AIRILY
AIRING
BIDING
BIKILA
BIKING
BIKINI
BIMINI
BITING
CILIUM
CITIES
CITIFY
CITING
CITIUS
CIVICS
DICIER
DICING
DIDIES
DIDION
DIGITS
DIKING
DIMITY
DINING
DIRIGE
DIRIGO
DIVIDE
DIVINE
DIVING
DIVINO
DIXITS
FIFING
FIJIAN
FILIAL
FILING
FILIUS
FINIAL
FINING
FINISH
FINITE
FINITO
FIRING
FIXING
FIXITY
GIBILL
GIBING
GIVING
HIDING
HIEING
HIKING
HIRING
HIVING
JIBING
JIMINY
JIVIER
JIVING
KIBITZ
KILIMS
KITING
LIAISE
LIBIDO
LIKING
LILIES
LILITH
LIMIER
LIMING
LIMITS
LINIER
LINING
LIPIDE
LIPIDS

LIVING
MIDIAN
MIKING
MIKITA
MILIEU
MIMICS
MIMING
MINIFY
MINIMA
MINIMS
MINING
MINION
MINIUM
MIRIAM
MIRIER
MIRING
MIXING
NIDIFY
NIHILO
NIKITA
NIMINY
NIMITZ
NIXIES
NIXING
OILIER
OILILY
OILING
PIKING
PILING
PIMINY
PINIER
PINING
PINION
PINITE
PIPIER
PIPING
PIPITS
PITIED
PITIER
PITIES
PIXIES
QIVIUT
RICING
RIDING
RIFIFI
RILING
RIMIER
RIMING
RIMINI
RISING
RIVING
SICILY
SIDING
SIGILS
SILICA
SIMIAN
SIMILE
SINISE
SIRICA
SIRING
SIRIUS
SITING
SITINS
SIXING
SIZING
TIBIAE
TIBIAL
TIBIAS
TIDIED
TIDIER
TIDIES
TIDILY
TIDING
TIEING
TIEINS
TILING
TIMING
TINIER
TINILY
TIPINS
TIRING
TITIAN
VIGILS
VIKING
VILIFY
VINIER
VINIFY
VINING
VIRILE
VISINE
VISION
VISITS
VIVIAN
VIVIEN
VIVIFY
VIZIER
WIDISH
WILIER
WILILY
WILING
WINIER
WINING
WINISH
WIPING
WIRIER
WIRILY
WIRING
ZIZITH

•I••I•

BIBLIO
BIDSIN
BIGGIE
BIGLIE
BIGWIG
BILLIE
BIOBIO
BIONIC
BIOTIC
BIOTIN
BIRDIE
BIRGIT
CITRIC
DIESIS
DIGSIN
DIKDIK
DIMWIT
DINEIN
DIOXIN
DISTIL
DIVEIN
FIBRIL
FIBRIN
FILLIN
FILLIP
FINNIC
FIRKIN
FISTIC
FITSIN
FIZGIG
GILLIE
GILLIS
GIVEIN
HIGHIQ
HINGIS
HIPPIE
HISPID
HITSIT
JIMMIE
KICKIN
KIDDIE
KIDVID
KILTIE
LIBRIS
LIEBIG
LIESIN
LIGNIN
LILLIE
LIMPID
LIPOID
LIQUID
LITHIC
LIVEIN
LIZZIE
MIAMIA
MIDAIR
MIDRIB
MILLIE
MILTIE
MINNIE
MINUIT
MIOSIS
MISDID
MISFIT
MISHIT
MISSIS
NIACIN
NITRIC
NITWIT
OILRIG
PICNIC
PIDGIN
PIETIN
PIGGIE
PILEIN
PINKIE
PINXIT
PINYIN
PIPKIN
PIPPIN
PIRRIP
PISTIL
RICHIE
RIZZIO
SIGNIN
SIKKIM
SINGIN
SINKIN
SISKIN
SITSIN
TIDBIT
TIEDIN
TIEPIN
TIESIN
TIFFIN
TIGRIS
TILLIE
TILLIS
TILSIT
TIPSIN
TITBIT
VICTIM
VICTIS
VINCIT
VINNIE
VIOLIN
VIRGIL
VIRGIN
VISCID
VITRIC
WILLIE
WILLIS
WINGIT
WINKIE
WINNIE
WINWIN
WITHIN
WITHIT
XINGIN
ZINNIA

•I•••I

BIHARI
BIKINI
BILOXI
BIMINI
BIONDI
CIARDI
CISKEI
HIDEKI
KIGALI
KIMCHI
KINSKI
LIBERI
LITCHI
MIDORI
NIELLI
NIKKEI
NILGAI
PILOTI
RIENZI
RIFIFI
RIMINI
SILENI
TISHRI
TIVOLI
VIDERI

••II••

SHIISM
SHIITE
SKIING

••I•I•

ACIDIC
ALIBIS
ALICIA
BLINIS
BRIGID
CHIPIN
CHITIN
CLINIC
CRISIS
CRITIC
EDITIO
ELICIT
ELIXIR
EMILIA
EMILIO
EXILIC
FRIGID
GAIJIN
IBIBIO
INITIO
IRIDIC
IRISIN
JOININ
LAIDIN
LAINIE
MAILIN
MAISIE
NAILIN
OLIVIA
ORIBIS
ORIGIN
OSIRIS
OTITIC
OTITIS
OXIDIC
PAIDIN
PHILIP
QUITIT
RAISIN
REININ
SCIFIS
SCIPIO
SKIPIT
SLIDIN
SLIPIN
SMILIN
SPIRIT
STIRIN
STIVIC
TRICIA
TRIFID
TRIVIA
TRIXIE
TWILIT
UNIFIC

••I••I

CHICHI
CHILLI
DMITRI
GRIGRI
MAITAI
PRIORI
TAICHI
TAIPEI

•••II•

ACTIII

•••I•I

ACTIII
ASSISI
BIKINI
BIMINI
DOMINI
GEMINI
ILLINI
KWEISI
LATINI
MEDICI
RAPINI
RIFIFI
RIMINI
ROTINI
SENITI
SOLIDI
SURIMI
TAHINI
TAHITI
WAPITI
YOGINI

••••II

ACTIII
ETALII
HAWAII
SAVAII

IJ••••

IJSSEL

I•J•••

INJECT
INJEST
INJOKE
INJURE
INJURY

I••J••

INAJAM
INKJET

I••••J

INTERJ

•IJ•••

BIJOUX
FIJIAN
GIJOES
HIJACK
HIJRAH

•I•J••

NINJAS
RIOJAS

••IJ••

ELIJAH
FRIJOL
GAIJIN
TRIJET

I•K•••

ICKIER
INKERS
INKIER
INKIND
INKING
INKJET
INKLES
IRKING

I•••K•

INJOKE
INTAKE
INVOKE
ITHAKI

I••••K

INBULK
INLUCK
ITZHAK

•IK•••

AIKIDO
BIKERS
BIKILA
BIKING
BIKINI
DIKDIK
DIKING
DIKTAT
HIKERS
HIKEUP
HIKING
KIKUYU
LIKELY
LIKENS
LIKING
MIKADO
MIKING
MIKITA
NIKITA
NIKKEI
NIKOLA
PIKAKE
PIKERS
PIKING
SIKKIM
VIKING

•I•K••

BICKER
BILKED
CISKEI
DICKER
DICKEY
DINKEY
DISKED
FICKLE
FINKED
FIRKIN
GINKGO
HICKEY
HICKOK
JINKED
KICKED
KICKER
KICKIN
KICKUP
KINKED
KITKAT
LICKED
LINKED
LINKER
LINKUP
MICKEY
MILKED
MILKER
MINKES
NICKED
NICKEL
NICKER
NIKKEI
OINKED
PICKAT
PICKAX
PICKED
PICKER
PICKET
PICKLE
PICKON
PICKUP
PINKED
PINKEN
PINKER
PINKIE
PIPKIN
RICKED
RICKEY
RIPKEN
RISKED
RISKER
SICKEN
SICKER
SICKLE
SICKLY
SIKKIM
SILKED
SILKEN
SINKER
SINKIN
SISKEL
SISKIN
TICKED
TICKER
TICKET
TICKLE
TICKLY
TINKER
TINKLE
TINKLY
WICKED
WICKER
WICKET
WILKES
WINKAT
WINKED
WINKER
WINKIE
WINKLE

•I••K•

HIDEKI
KINSKI
KIOSKS
KISHKE
MIWOKS
PIKAKE
RIMSKY
TILAKS

•I•••K

DIKDIK
HICKOK
HIJACK
PINOAK

••IK••

BAIKAL
CRIKEY
DAIKON
DUIKER
HAIKUS
SHIKAR
SPIKED
SPIKER
SPIKES
TRIKES

••I•K•

BLINKS
BRICKS
BRICKY
BRINKS
CHICKS
CHINKS
CHINKY
CLICKS
CLINKS
CRICKS
DRINKS
FLICKA
FLICKS
FRISKS
FRISKY
GLINKA
GRIMKE
KNICKS
PLINKS
PRICKS
PRINKS
QUIRKS
QUIRKY
REINKS
SHIRKS
SKINKS
SLICKS
SLINKS
SLINKY
SMIRKS
SMIRKY
SNICKS
SPINKS
STICKS
STICKY
STINKS
STINKY
STIRKS
THICKE
THINKS
TRICKS
TRICKY
UMIAKS
WHISKS
WHISKY
YOICKS

••I••K

SPIVAK

•••IK•

ANNIKA
AXLIKE
BATIKS
BELIKE
MARIKO
OXLIKE
PELIKE
SHEIKS
SHRIKE
STRIKE
TROIKA
UNLIKE
UPDIKE

•••I•K

ATRISK
DRYINK
KODIAK
NATICK
REDINK
REMICK
SCHICK
SHRIEK
SHRINK
SHTICK

STRICK
UNKINK
UNLINK
UPLINK
UPTICK
YORICK

••••IK
DIKDIK
HENRIK
MUZHIK
NARVIK
NUDNIK
RESNIK
SLOVIK
SUSLIK
TUGRIK
ZADDIK

IL••••
ILEANA
ILESHA
ILEXES
ILLEST
ILLFED
ILLINI
ILLMET
ILLSAY
ILLUME
ILLUSE
ILOILO
ILORIN

I•L•••
IDLERS
IDLEST
IDLING
IGLOOS
ILLEST
ILLFED
ILLINI
ILLMET
ILLSAY
ILLUME
ILLUSE
INLAID
INLAND
INLAWS
INLAYS
INLETS
INLINE
INLOVE
INLUCK
IOLITE
IRLENE
ISLAND
ISLETS

I••L••
IDYLLS
IMELDA
INFLOW
INFLUX
INGLES
INKLES
INPLAY
ISELIN
ISOLDE
ISTLES
ITALIA
ITALIC

I•••L•
ICICLE
IDEALS
IDYLLS
ILOILO
IMPALA
IMPALE
IMPELS
INBULK
INCULT
INFOLD
INFULL
INHALE
INHALF
INSOLE
INSULT
ISEULT
ITSELF

I••••L
IJSSEL
INFULL
INHAUL
INSTAL
INSTIL
IREFUL
IRREAL
ISABEL
ISOHEL
ISRAEL
IZABAL

•IL•••
AILEEN
AILERS
AILING
BILBAO
BILGES
BILKED
BILLED
BILLET
BILLIE
BILLON
BILLOW
BILOXI
CILIUM
DILATE
DILLER
DILLON
DILSEY
DILUTE
EILEEN
FILENE
FILERS
FILETS
FILIAL
FILING
FILIUS
FILLED
FILLER
FILLES
FILLET
FILLIN
FILLIP
FILLUP
FILMED
FILOSE
FILTER
FILTHY
GILDED
GILDER
GILEAD
GILGUY
GILLED
GILLIE
GILLIS
HILARY
HILLED
HILLEL
HILLER
HILTON
JILTED
KILIMS
KILLED
KILLER
KILMER
KILNED
KILROY
KILTED
KILTER
KILTIE
LILACS
LILIES
LILITH
LILLIE
LILTED
MILADY
MILANO
MILDER
MILDEW
MILDLY
MILERS
MILIEU
MILKED
MILKER
MILLAY
MILLED
MILLER
MILLET
MILLIE
MILNER
MILORD
MILOSZ
MILPAS
MILSAP
MILTIE
MILTON
NILGAI
OILCAN
OILERS
OILIER
OILILY
OILING
OILMAN
OILMEN
OILPAN
OILRIG
PILAFS
PILATE
PILEIN
PILEON
PILEUM
PILEUP
PILEUS
PILFER
PILING
PILLAR
PILLED
PILLOW
PILOSE
PILOTI
PILOTS
RILEUP
RILING
RILLES
RILLET
SILAGE
SILENI
SILENT
SILICA
SILKED
SILKEN
SILOAM
SILOED
SILONE
SILTED
SILVAS
SILVER
TILAKS
TILDEN
TILDES
TILERS
TILING
TILLED
TILLER
TILLIE
TILLIS
TILSIT
TILTED
TILTER
VILELY
VILEST
VILIFY
VILLAS
VILLON
VILLUS
WILBUR
WILCOX
WILDER
WILDLY
WILFUL
WILIER
WILILY
WILING
WILKES
WILLED
WILLEM
WILLET
WILLIE
WILLIS
WILLOW
WILSON
WILTED
WILTON
ZILPAH

•I•L••
AIELLO
AISLES
BIBLES
BIBLIO
BIGLIE
BILLED
BILLET
BILLIE
BILLON
BILLOW
BIRLED
DIALED
DIALER
DIALOG
DIALUP
DIGLOT
DILLER
DILLON
FIELDS
FILLED
FILLER
FILLES
FILLET
FILLIN
FILLIP
FILLUP
GIBLET
GILLED
GILLIE
GILLIS
GIMLET
HILLED
HILLEL
HILLER
KILLED
KILLER
KISLEV
LIELOW
LILLIE
LISLES
MIDLER
MILLAY
MILLED
MILLER
MILLET
MILLIE
MISLAY
MISLED
NIELLI
NIELLO
PIGLET
PILLAR
PILLED
PILLOW
PIOLET
RIALTO
RIDLEY
RIFLED
RIFLER
RIFLES
RILLES
RILLET
RIPLEY
SIDLED
SIDLES
SISLER
SISLEY
TIGLON
TILLED
TILLER
TILLIE
TILLIS
TITLED
TITLES
VILLAS
VILLON
VILLUS
VIOLAS
VIOLET
VIOLIN
WIELDS
WIGLET
WILLED
WILLEM
WILLET
WILLIE
WILLIS
WILLOW
YIELDS
ZIPLOC

•I••L•
AIELLO
AIRILY
BIDDLE
BIFOLD
BIKILA
BITOLA
CIBOLA
CICELY
CIRCLE
DIABLO
DIBBLE
DIDDLE
DIDDLY
DIMPLE
DIMPLY
DINGLE
DIPOLE
DIRELY
EIDOLA
FIBULA
FICKLE
FIDDLE
FINALE
FINALS
FINELY
FIPPLE
FIRMLY
FIZZLE
GIBILL
GIGGLE
GIGGLY
GIGOLO
GIMELS
GIRDLE
HIGGLE
HIGHLY
JIGGLE
JIGGLY
JINGLE
JINGLY
KIBBLE
KIGALI
KINDLE
KINDLY
KINGLY
KIRTLE
LIABLE
LIBELS
LIEFLY
LIGULA
LIKELY
LIMPLY
LIONLY
LITTLE
LIVELY
MIDDLE
MIGGLE
MILDLY
MINGLE
MIZZLE
NIBBLE
NICELY
NICOLA
NICOLE
NICOLO
NIELLI
NIELLO
NIGGLE
NIHILO
NIKOLA
NIMBLE
NIMBLY
OILILY
PICKLE
PICULS
PIFFLE
PINOLE
PINTLE
PIPALS
PIXELS
RIBALD
RICHLY
RIDDLE
RIFELY
RIFFLE
RIMPLE
RIPELY
RIPPLE
RIPPLY
RIVALS
RIYALS
SIBYLS
SICILY
SICKLE
SICKLY
SIECLE
SIGILS
SIMILE
SIMPLE
SIMPLY
SINGLE
SINGLY
SISALS
SIZZLE
TICALS
TICKLE
TICKLY
TIDDLY
TIDILY
TIMELY
TINGLE
TINGLY
TINILY
TINKLE
TINKLY
TIPPLE
TITTLE
TIVOLI
VIABLE
VIABLY
VIGILS
VILELY
VINYLS
VIRILE
VITALE
VITALS
VIZSLA
WIDELY
WIFELY
WIGGLE
WIGGLY
WILDLY
WILILY
WIMBLE
WIMPLE
WINKLE
WIRILY
WISELY

•I•••L
AIDFUL
AIMFUL
DIESEL
DIRNDL
DISMAL
DISPEL
DISTAL
DISTIL
EIFFEL
FIBRIL
FILIAL
FINIAL
FISCAL
FITFUL
GIBILL
GIMBAL
GIMBEL
HIATAL
HIEMAL
HILLEL
LINEAL
LINTEL
LIONEL
LISTEL
MICHEL
MIGUEL
MISSAL
MITRAL
NICKEL
PINEAL
PISTIL
PISTOL
RITUAL
SIEGEL
SIGNAL
SIMBEL
SIMNEL
SINFUL
SISKEL
TIBIAL
TIMBAL
TINCAL
TINSEL
VIRGIL
VISUAL
WIESEL
WILFUL
WITHAL

••IL••
AXILLA
BAILED
BAILEE
BAILER
BAILEY
BAILOR
BOILED
BOILER
BRILLO
BRILLS
BUILDS
CEILED
CHILDE
CHILDS
CHILLI
CHILLS
CHILLY
CHILOE
COILED
COILUP
DAILEY
DRILLS
EDILES
EMILIA
EMILIO
EPILOG
EVILER
EVILLY
EXILED
EXILES
EXILIC
FAILED
FAILLE
FOILED
FRILLS
FRILLY
GRILLE
GRILLS
GRILSE
GUILDS
GUILES
GUILTY
HAILED
HAILEY
JAILED
JAILER
KAILUA
MAILED
MAILER
MAILES
MAILIN
MOILED
MOILER
NAILED
NAILER
NAILIN
PAILOU
PHILAE
PHILBY
PHILIP
PHILLY
PHILOL
PHILOS
POILUS
QUILLS
QUILTS
RAILAT
RAILED
RAILER
REILLY
ROILED
SAILED
SAILOR
SHILLS
SHILLY
SHILOH
SKILLS
SMILAX
SMILED

SMILER
SMILES
SMILEY
SMILIN
SOILED
SPILES
SPILLS
SPILTH
STILES
STILLS
STILLY
STILTS
SWILLS
TAILED
TAILLE
TAILOR
TBILLS
THILLS
TOILED
TOILER
TOILES
TOILET
TRILBY
TRILLS
TUILLE
TWILIT
TWILLS
VEILED
VOILES
WAILED
WAILER
WHILED
WHILES
WHILOM
WHILST
XFILES

••I•L•

ACIDLY
AFIELD
ALIBLE
ARIDLY
AVIDLY
AXILLA
BGIRLS
BRIDLE
BRILLO
BRILLS
CHICLE
CHICLY
CHILLI
CHILLS
CHILLY
DRILLS
EDIBLE
ENISLE
EVILLY
FAILLE
FAIRLY
FOIBLE
FRILLS
FRILLY
GAINLY
GLIBLY
GRILLE
GRILLS
GRIMLY
GRISLY
ICICLE
MAINLY
ORIELS
ORIOLE
PHIALS
PHILLY
PRIMLY
QUILLS
REILLY
SHIELD
SHILLS
SHILLY
SKILLS
SKIRLS
SLIMLY
SPIELS
SPILLS
STIFLE
STILLS
STILLY
SWILLS
SWIRLS
SWIRLY
TAILLE
TBILLS
THILLS
THINLY
TRIALS
TRIFLE
TRIGLY
TRILLS
TRIMLY
TRIPLE
TRIPLY
TUILLE
TWILLS
TWIRLS
URIALS
VAINLY
WHIRLS
WHIRLY

••I••L

AMIDOL
ANIMAL
APICAL
BAIKAL
BRIDAL
CHISEL
DRIVEL
EPICAL
EPINAL
FAISAL
FRIJOL
GEISEL
KEITEL
PHILOL
PRIMAL
RHINAL
SEIDEL
SNIVEL
SPINAL
SPINEL
SPIRAL
STIPEL
SWIVEL
TRIBAL
TRINAL
UNITAL
VEINAL

•••IL•

AEDILE
AERILY
AIRILY
ANVILS
AQUILA
ARTILY
ATTILA
ATWILL
AUDILE
AVAILS
AWHILE
BIKILA
BODILY
BRAILA
BRAILS
BROILS
BUSILY
CAGILY
CAVILS
CECILE
CECILY
COSILY
COZILY
CYBILL
DEFILE
DESILU
DEVILS
DEWILY
DOCILE
DOZILY
DRAILS
EASILY
EDGILY
EERILY
EMAILS
ENSILE
ETOILE
FACILE
FAMILY
FLAILS
FOXILY
FUSILS
FUTILE
GAMILY
GIBILL
GORILY
GOWILD
GRAILS
HABILE
HAMILL
HAZILY
HOLILY
HOMILY
ILOILO
JOKILY
KURILE
LABILE
LACILY
LAZILY
LOGILY
MANILA
MARILU
MAZILY
MEGILP
MOBILE
MOTILE
NIHILO
NOSILY
NUBILE
OILILY
ONEILL
ONFILE
OOZILY
PERILS
POKILY
PUNILY
PUPILS
QUAILS
RACILY
REFILE
REFILL
REOILS
RESILE
RETILE
REVILE
ROSILY
RUTILE
SEDILE
SEXILY
SHEILA
SHRILL
SICILY
SIGILS
SIMILE
SNAILS
SPOILS
SPOILT
SQUILL
TAMILS
THRILL
TIDILY
TINILY
TRAILS
UGLILY
UNOILY
UNPILE
UNWILY
UPHILL
VERILY
VIGILS
VIRILE
WARILY
WAVILY
WAXILY
WILILY
WIRILY
ZANILY
ZORILS

•••I•L

AERIAL
ASWIRL
ATRIAL
ATWILL
AUDIAL
AWHIRL
BELIAL
CURIAL
CYBILL
DANIEL
DENIAL
ESPIAL
FACIAL
FERIAL
FILIAL
FINIAL
GAVIAL
GENIAL
GIBILL
HAMILL
JOVIAL
LABIAL
MARIEL
MEDIAL
MENIAL
MURIEL
MUSIAL
MYGIRL
NARIAL
ONEILL
RACIAL
RADIAL
REDIAL
REFILL
RETIAL
SERIAL
SHRILL
SOCIAL
SQUILL
THRILL
TIBIAL
UNCIAL
UPHILL
VENIAL

••••IL

ASSAIL
BEWAIL
BRAZIL
BULBIL
DEASIL
DENTIL
DERAIL
DETAIL
DISTIL
ENTAIL
EURAIL
FIBRIL
FOSSIL
FULFIL
GERBIL
INSTIL
KAHLIL
LENTIL
MELVIL
NYQUIL
ORCHIL
OXTAIL
PENCIL
PISTIL
REBOIL
RECOIL
REMAIL
RENAIL
RETAIL
SOLEIL
TONSIL
UNCOIL
UNVEIL
URACIL
USMAIL
VIRGIL
WEEVIL

IM••••

IMAGED
IMAGER
IMAGES
IMAMAN
IMARET
IMBIBE
IMBRUE
IMBUED
IMBUES
IMELDA
IMFINE
IMMUNE
IMMUNO
IMMURE
IMOGEN
IMPACT
IMPAIR
IMPALA
IMPALE
IMPART
IMPEDE
IMPELS
IMPEND
IMPERF
IMPING
IMPISH
IMPORT
IMPOSE
IMPOST
IMPROV
IMPUGN
IMPURE
IMPUTE

I•M•••

IAMBIC
IMMUNE
IMMUNO
IMMURE
INMATE
INMOST
IOMOTH
ISMENE

I••M••

ICEMAN
ICEMEN
ILLMET
IMAMAN
INGMAR
ISOMER

I•••M•

IBEAMS
IDIOMS
ILLUME
INCOME
INFAMY
INTIMA
INTIME
ISTHMI

I••••M

IBIDEM
INAJAM
INDIUM
INFIRM
INFORM
INGRAM
INSEAM
IONIUM

•IM•••

AIMFOR
AIMFUL
AIMING
AIMSAT
AIMSTO
BIMINI
DIMITY
DIMMED
DIMMER
DIMOUT
DIMPLE
DIMPLY
DIMSUM
DIMWIT
GIMBAL
GIMBEL
GIMELS
GIMLET
GIMMES
JIMINY
JIMMIE
JIMSON
KIMCHI
KIMONO
LIMBED
LIMBER
LIMBOS
LIMBUS
LIMENS
LIMEYS
LIMIER
LIMING
LIMITS
LIMNED
LIMNER
LIMPED
LIMPER
LIMPET
LIMPID
LIMPLY
MIMEOS
MIMERS
MIMICS
MIMING
MIMOSA
NIMBLE
NIMBLY
NIMBUS
NIMINY
NIMITZ
NIMROD
PIMINY
RIMIER
RIMING
RIMINI
RIMMED
RIMOSE
RIMPLE
RIMSKY
SIMBEL
SIMEON
SIMIAN
SIMILE
SIMMER
SIMNEL
SIMONE
SIMONY
SIMPER
SIMPLE
SIMPLY
TIMBAL
TIMBER
TIMBRE
TIMELY
TIMERS
TIMING
WIMBLE
WIMPLE
WIMSEY
XIMENA
ZIMMER

•I•M••

AIRMAN
AIRMEN
BIGMAC
BIOMES
BITMAP
DIMMED
DIMMER
DISMAL
DISMAY
DISMES
FILMED
FIRMAN
FIRMED
FIRMER
FIRMLY
FIRMUP
GIMMES
GIZMOS
HIEMAL
HITMAN
HITMEN
JIMMIE
KIDMAN
KILMER
KIRMAN
KISMET
LITMUS
MIAMIA
MICMAC
NIAMEY
OILMAN
OILMEN
PIEMAN
PIEMEN
PITMAN
PITMEN
RIMMED
SIGMAS
SIMMER
TINMAN
TINMEN
XIAMEN
ZIMMER

•I••M•

BIGAMY
BIREME
CINEMA
JICAMA
KILIMS
KINEMA
KINGME
MIASMA
MINIMA
MINIMS

•I•••M

AIRARM
AIRDAM
CILIUM
CIRCUM
DIADEM
DIATOM
DICTUM
DIGRAM
DIMSUM
DIRHAM
DISARM
FIVEAM
FIVEPM
MINIUM
MIRIAM
NINEAM
NINEPM
PILEUM
SIKKIM
SILOAM
SITCOM
VIACOM
VICTIM
WIGWAM
WILLEM
WINDOM
WISDOM

••IM••

AHIMSA
AKIMBO
ANIMAL
ANIMAS
ANIMES
ANIMUS
ASIMOV
BLIMEY
BLIMPS
CAIMAN
CHIMED
CHIMES
CHIMPS
CLIMAX
CLIMBS
CLIMES
CRIMEA
CRIMES
CRIMPS
CRIMPY
DAIMON
DAIMYO
DEIMOS
FBIMAN
FBIMEN
FLIMSY
GRIMED
GRIMES
GRIMKE
GRIMLY
GUIMPE
PRIMAL
PRIMED
PRIMER
PRIMES
PRIMLY
PRIMOS
PRIMPS
PRIMUM
PRIMUS
SHIMMY
SHIMON
SKIMPS
SKIMPY

SLIMED
SLIMES
SLIMLY
SLIMSY
STIMPY
TRIMLY
WEIMAR
WHIMSY

••I•M•
AXIOMS
ENIGMA
IDIOMS
ODIUMS
PRISMS
SEISMO
SEISMS
SHIMMY
STIGMA

••I••M
FAIYUM
IBIDEM
PRIMUM
SHIISM
WHILOM

•••IM•
ALTIMA
BEDIMS
CLAIMS
COLIMA
DENIMS
ESKIMO
FATIMA
HAKIMS
INTIMA
INTIME
KILIMS
MAXIMA
MAXIMS
MINIMA
MINIMS
ONTIME
OPTIMA
REAIMS
REGIME
RETIME
SCRIMP
SCRIMS
SHRIMP
SURIMI
ULTIMA
ULTIMO
UPTIME
YAKIMA

•••I•M
ACTIUM
AFFIRM
AGEISM
ALLIUM
ATRIUM
BARIUM
CERIUM
CESIUM
CHRISM
CILIUM
CONIUM
CORIUM
CUBISM
CURIUM
EGOISM
ERBIUM
FOLIUM
HELIUM
HOLISM
INDIUM
INFIRM
IONIUM
LATIUM
MAOISM
MEDIUM
MINIUM
MIRIAM
MONISM
OMNIUM
OSMIUM
OSTIUM
PODIUM
PURISM
RADIUM
SAMIAM
SCHISM
SHIISM
SODIUM
SQUIRM
SUFISM
TAOISM
TEDIUM
THEISM
TRUISM
VALIUM
VERISM
YOGISM

••••IM
ANTRIM
ELOHIM
LCHAIM
MUSLIM
PASSIM
PRELIM
RETRIM
SIKKIM
VICTIM

IN••••
INAFIX
INAFOG
INAJAM
INANER
INAPET
INARCH
INAROW
INARUT
INAWAY
INBORN
INBRED
INBULK
INCANS
INCASE
INCASH
INCEPT
INCHED
INCHES
INCHON
INCISE
INCITE
INCOME
INCULT
INCURS
INCUSE
INDABA
INDEBT
INDEED
INDENE
INDENT
INDIAN
INDICT
INDIES
INDIGO
INDIRA
INDITE
INDIUM
INDOOR
INDORE
INDRIS
INDUCE
INDUCT
INESSE
INFACT
INFAMY
INFANT
INFECT
INFERS
INFEST
INFIRM
INFLOW
INFLUX
INFOLD
INFORM
INFULL
INFUSE
INGEAR
INGEST
INGLES
INGMAR
INGOTS
INGRAM
INGRES
INGRID
INHALE
INHALF
INHAND
INHAUL
INHERE
INIONS
INITIO
INJECT
INJEST
INJOKE
INJURE
INJURY
INKERS
INKIER
INKIND
INKING
INKJET
INKLES
INLAID
INLAND
INLAWS
INLAYS
INLETS
INLINE
INLOVE
INLUCK
INMATE
INMOST
INNAGE
INNATE
INNEED
INNESS
INNING
INOUYE
INPART
INPLAY
INPORT
INPOUR
INPUTS
INROAD
INRUSH
INSANE
INSEAM
INSECT
INSERT
INSETS
INSIDE
INSIST
INSITU
INSOLE
INSPAN
INSTAL
INSTAR
INSTEP
INSTIL
INSULT
INSURE
INSYNC
INTACT
INTAKE
INTEND
INTENS
INTENT
INTERJ
INTERN
INTIMA
INTIME
INTINE
INTONE
INTOTO
INTOWN
INTROS
INTUIT
INTUNE
INTURN
INUITS
INURED
INURES
INVADE
INVAIN
INVENT
INVERT
INVEST
INVITE
INVIVO
INVOKE
INWARD
INWITH

I•N•••
IGNACE
IGNATZ
IGNITE
IGNORE
INNAGE
INNATE
INNEED
INNESS
INNING
IONIAN
IONICS
IONISE
IONIUM
IONIZE

I••N••
ICINGS
ICONIC
INANER
IRANIS
IRENES
IRENIC
IRONED
IRONER
IRONIC
IRONON

I•••N•
ICHING
IDLING
IGUANA
ILEANA
ILLINI
IMFINE
IMMUNE
IMMUNO
IMPEND
IMPING
INCANS
INDENE
INDENT
INFANT
INHAND
INIONS
INKIND
INKING
INLAND
INLINE
INNING
INSANE
INSYNC
INTEND
INTENS
INTENT
INTINE
INTONE
INTUNE
INVENT
IODINE
IOWANS
IRKING
IRLENE
IRVINE
IRVING
ISLAND
ISMENE

I••••N
IBADAN
ICEDIN
ICEMAN
ICEMEN
ICESIN
ILORIN
IMAMAN
IMOGEN
IMPUGN
INBORN
INCHON
INDIAN
INSPAN
INTERN
INTOWN
INTURN
INVAIN
IONIAN
IRISIN
IRONON
ISELIN
ISOGON

•IN•••
BINARY
BINATE
BINDER
BINDUP
BINGED
BINGES
BINNED
CINDER
CINEMA
CINQUE
DINARS
DINEIN
DINEON
DINERO
DINERS
DINGED
DINGHY
DINGLE
DINGUS
DINING
DINKEY
DINNED
DINNER
DINTED
FINALE
FINALS
FINDER
FINELY
FINERY
FINEST
FINGER
FINIAL
FINING
FINISH
FINITE
FINITO
FINKED
FINNAN
FINNED
FINNEY
FINNIC
GINGER
GINKGO
GINNED
HINCTY
HINDER
HINDUS
HINGED
HINGES
HINGIS
HINTAT
HINTED
HINTER
HINTON
JINGLE
JINGLY
JINKED
JINNAH
JINXED
JINXES
KINDER
KINDLE
KINDLY
KINDOF
KINEMA
KINGED
KINGLY
KINGME
KINKED
KINSEY
KINSKI
LINAGE
LINDEN
LINEAL
LINEAR
LINENS
LINENY
LINERS
LINEUP
LINGER
LINGUA
LINIER
LINING
LINKED
LINKER
LINKUP
LINNET
LINNEY
LINSEY
LINTEL
LINTER
MINCED
MINCER
MINCES
MINDED
MINDER
MINERS
MINGLE
MINIFY
MINIMA
MINIMS
MINING
MINION
MINIUM
MINKES
MINNIE
MINNOW
MINOAN
MINORS
MINTED
MINTER
MINUET
MINUIT
MINUTE
MINXES
MINYAN
NINEAM
NINEPM
NINERS
NINETY
NINGBO
NINJAS
NINTHS
OINKED
PINATA
PINCER
PINDAR
PINDUS
PINEAL
PINERO
PINERY
PINGED
PINIER
PINING
PINION
PINITE
PINKED
PINKEN
PINKER
PINKIE
PINNAE
PINNAS
PINNED
PINNER
PINOAK
PINOLE
PINONS
PINOTS
PINSON
PINTER
PINTLE
PINTOS
PINUPS
PINXIT
PINYIN
PINYON
PINZON
QINTAR
RINGED
RINGER
RINGUP
RINSED
RINSES
SINBAD
SINEAD
SINEWS
SINEWY
SINFUL
SINGED
SINGER
SINGES
SINGIN
SINGLE
SINGLY
SINGTO
SINISE
SINKER
SINKIN
SINNED
SINNER
SINTAX
SINTER
TINCAL
TINCAN
TINCTS
TINDER
TINEAR
TINGED
TINGES
TINGLE
TINGLY
TINGOD
TINHAT
TINIER
TINILY
TINKER
TINKLE
TINKLY
TINMAN
TINMEN
TINNED
TINNER
TINPAN
TINPOT
TINSEL
TINTED
TINTER
UINTAS
VINCES
VINCIT
VINERY
VINIER
VINIFY
VINING
VINNIE
VINOUS
VINTON
VINYLS
WINCED
WINCER
WINCES
WINDED
WINDER
WINDEX
WINDOM
WINDOW
WINDUP
WINERY
WINGED
WINGER
WINGIT
WINIER
WINING
WINISH
WINKAT
WINKED
WINKER
WINKIE
WINKLE
WINNER
WINNIE
WINNOW
WINONA
WINOUT
WINSOR
WINTER
WINTRY
WINWIN
WINZES
XINGIN
ZINGED
ZINGER
ZINNIA

•I•N••
BIANCA
BINNED
BIONDI
BIONIC
BIRNEY
DIANNE
DINNED
DINNER
DIONEB
DIONNE
DIRNDL

DISNEY
EISNER
FIANCE
FIENDS
FINNAN
FINNED
FINNEY
FINNIC
GIANTS
GINNED
GIRNED
JINNAH
JITNEY
KIANGS
KIDNAP
KIDNEY
KILNED
LIANAS
LIANES
LIANGS
LIENEE
LIGNIN
LIMNED
LIMNER
LINNET
LINNEY
LIONEL
LIONET
LIONLY
MIGNON
MILNER
MINNIE
MINNOW
PIANOS
PICNIC
PIGNUT
PINNAE
PINNAS
PINNED
PINNER
RIENZI
SIDNEY
SIENNA
SIGNAL
SIGNED
SIGNEE
SIGNER
SIGNET
SIGNIN
SIGNON
SIGNOR
SIGNUP
SIMNEL
SINNED
SINNER
TINNED
TINNER
VIANDS
VIENNA
VIENNE
VINNIE
WIENER
WINNER
WINNIE
WINNOW
ZINNIA

•I••N•

AIDING
AILING
AIMING
AIRING
BIDING
BIKING
BIKINI
BIMINI
BISONS
BITING
CITING
DIANNE
DICING
DIKING
DINING
DIONNE
DISANT
DIVANS
DIVINE
DIVING
DIVINO
DIZENS
FIFING
FILENE
FILING
FINING
FIRING
FIXING
GIBING
GITANO
GIVENS
GIVING
HIDING
HIEING
HIKING
HIRING
HIVING
JIBING
JIMINY
JIVING
KIMONO
KITING
LIERNE
LIGAND
LIKENS
LIKING
LIMENS
LIMING
LINENS
LINENY
LINING
LIPENG
LITANY
LIVENS
LIVING
MIFUNE
MIKING
MILANO
MIMING
MINING
MIRING
MIXING
MIZENS
NICENE
NIMINY
NIXING
OILING
PIKING
PILING
PIMINY
PINING
PINONS
PIPING
PIRANA
PISANO
PISANS
PITONS
RIBAND
RICING
RIDENT
RIDING
RILING
RIMING
RIMINI
RIPENS
RISING
RIVING
SIDING
SIENNA
SILENI
SILENT
SILONE
SIMONE
SIMONY
SIRENS
SIRING
SITING
SITINS
SIXING
SIZING
TIDING
TIEING
TIEINS
TILING
TIMING
TIPINS
TIRANA
TIRANE
TIRING
TISANE
TITANS
VICUNA
VIENNA
VIENNE
VIKING
VINING
VISHNU
VISINE
VIVANT
VIXENS
WIDENS
WILING
WINING
WINONA
WIPING
WIRING
WISENT
WIZENS
XIMENA

•I•••N

AILEEN
AIRGUN
AIRMAN
AIRMEN
BICORN
BIDDEN
BIDSIN
BIDSON
BIGBEN
BIGGUN
BIGTEN
BILLON
BIOTIN
BITTEN
CITRON
DIDION
DIGSIN
DILLON
DINEIN
DINEON
DIOXIN
DISOWN
DIVEIN
EILEEN
FIBRIN
FIJIAN
FILLIN
FINNAN
FIRKIN
FIRMAN
FITSIN
GIBBON
GIBRAN
GIBSON
GIDEON
GIVEIN
HIDDEN
HIERON
HILTON
HINTON
HIREON
HITMAN
HITMEN
HITSON
JIMSON
KICKIN
KIDMAN
KIRMAN
KITTEN
LIBYAN
LICHEN
LIESIN
LIGNIN
LINDEN
LIPTON
LISBON
LISTEN
LISTON
LIVEIN
LIVEON
MICRON
MIDDEN
MIDIAN
MIGNON
MILTON
MINION
MINOAN
MINYAN
MIRREN
MITTEN
MIZZEN
NIACIN
NICEAN
NIPPON
NISSAN
NISSEN
OILCAN
OILMAN
OILMEN
OILPAN
PICKON
PIDGIN
PIEMAN
PIEMEN
PIEPAN
PIETIN
PIGEON
PIGPEN
PILEIN
PILEON
PINION
PINKEN
PINSON
PINYIN
PINYON
PINZON
PIPKIN
PIPPIN
PISTON
PITMAN
PITMEN
RIBBON
RICHEN
RIDDEN
RIPKEN
SICKEN
SIGNIN
SIGNON
SILKEN
SIMEON
SIMIAN
SINGIN
SINKIN
SIOUAN
SIPHON
SISKIN
SITSIN
SITSON
SIXGUN
TIEDIN
TIEPIN
TIESIN
TIFFIN
TIGLON
TILDEN
TINCAN
TINMAN
TINMEN
TINPAN
TIPSIN
TITIAN
VILLON
VINTON
VIOLIN
VIRGIN
VISION
VIVIAN
VIVIEN
WICCAN
WILSON
WILTON
WINWIN
WITHIN
XIAMEN
XINGIN
ZIRCON

••IN••

ACINUS
ALINES
AMINES
AMINOR
AMINUS
AZINES
BAINES
BEINGS
BLINDS
BLINIS
BLINKS
BLINTZ
BMINOR
BMINUS
BOINGO
BRINED
BRINES
BRINGS
BRINKS
CHINCH
CHINES
CHINKS
CHINKY
CHINOS
CHINTZ
CHINUP
CLINCH
CLINES
CLINGS
CLINGY
CLINIC
CLINKS
CMINOR
CMINUS
COINED
COINER
CRINGE
DAINTY
DMINOR
DMINUS
DOINGS
DRINGS
DRINKS
ELINOR
EMINOR
EPINAL
ERINYS
EVINCE
FAINTS
FEINTS
FLINCH
FLINGS
FLINTS
FLINTY
FMINOR
FOINED
FRINGE
FRINGY
GAINED
GAINER
GAINLY
GAINON
GAINST
GLINKA
GLINTS
GMINOR
GOINGS
GOINTO
GRINCH
GRINDS
GRINGO
GUINEA
HAINAN
HAINES
ICINGS
JOINED
JOINER
JOININ
JOINTS
JOINUP
LAINIE
MAINLY
MOINES
OLINDA
OLINGO
OPINED
OPINER
OPINES
ORINGS
PAINED
PAINTS
PAINTY
PLINKS
PLINTH
POINTE
POINTS
POINTY
PRINCE
PRINKS
PRINTS
QUINCE
QUINCY
QUINOA
QUINTS
RAINED
RAINER
RAINES
RAINEY
REINAS
REINED
REINER
REININ
REINKS
RHINAL
RHINOS
RUINED
RUINER
SAINTE
SAINTS
SEINED
SEINER
SEINES
SHINDY
SHINED
SHINER
SHINES
SHINNY
SHINTO
SKINKS
SKINNY
SLINGS
SLINKS
SLINKY
SPINAL
SPINED
SPINEL
SPINES
SPINET
SPINKS
SPINTO
STINGO
STINGS
STINGY
STINKS
STINKY
STINTS
SWINGS
SWINGY
TAINAN
TAINOS
TAINTS
THINGS
THINGY
THINKS
THINLY
TRINAL
TRINES
TWINED
TWINES
TWINGE
VAINER
VAINLY
VEINAL
VEINED
WHINED
WHINER
WHINES
WHINEY
WHINNY
WRINGS

••I•N•

ALIENS
ALIGNS
AMIENS
ANIONS
ASIANS
AVIANS
AXIONS
BAIRNS
BOIGNY
BRIAND
BRIANS
BRIENZ
CAIRNS
CHIANG
CLIENT
COIGNS
DEIGNS
FEIGNS
FRIEND
GUIANA
INIONS
ONIONS
ONIONY
ORIANA
ORIENT
PLIANT
PRIONS
PUISNE
REIGNS
SCIONS
SHINNY
SKIING
SKINNY
SOIGNE
TRIUNE
UNIONS
VSIGNS
WHINNY

••I••N

ALISON
ARISEN
BLIXEN
BRITON
CAIMAN
CHIPIN
CHIRON
CHITIN
CHITON
CLIPON
DAIKON
DAIMON
DAIREN
DRIVEN
EDISON
FBIMAN
FBIMEN
GAIJIN
GAINON
GRISON
GUIDON
HAINAN
HEIDEN
IRISIN
JOININ
KLIBAN
LAIDIN
LAIDON
LEIDEN
MAIDEN
MAILIN
NAILIN
NOIRON
OBIWAN
OHIOAN
ORIGEN
ORIGIN
ORISON
PAIDIN
POISON
PRISON
RAISIN
REININ
SAIGON
SAIPAN
SHIMON
SKIRUN
SLIDIN
SLIPIN
SLIPON
SMILIN
STIRIN
TAINAN
TAIPAN
TAIWAN
TRIGON
TRITON
UNISON
WAITON
WHITEN

•••IN•

AAHING
ABYING
ACHING
ACTING
ACTINO
ADDING
AFFINE
AGEING
AGLINT

AIDING
AILING
AIMING
AIRING
ALBINO
ALDINE
ALFINE
ALOINS
ALPINE
ANOINT
AQUINO
ARCING
ARMING
ASKING
ATKINS
AUXINS
AWNING
BAAING
BAKING
BALING
BARING
BASING
BASINS
BATING
BAYING
BBKING
BEGINS
BEHIND
BEMINE
BENING
BERING
BIDING
BIKING
BIKINI
BIMINI
BITING
BLAINE
BLUING
BODING
BOEING
BONING
BOOING
BORING
BOVINE
BOWING
BOXING
BRAINS
BRAINY
BRUINS
BURINS
BUSING
BUYING
BYLINE
CABINS
CAGING
CAKING
CAMINO
CANINE
CANING
CARINA
CARING
CASING
CASINO
CAVING
CAWING
CEDING
CELINE
CHAINE
CHAINS
CITING
CLUING
CODING
COMING
COOING
COPING
CORING
COSINE
COVINA
COWING
CRYING
CUBING
CURING
CUTINS
DARING
DATING
DAZING
DEFINE
DEKING
DEVINE
DEWING
DICING
DIKING
DINING
DIVINE
DIVING
DIVINO
DOLING
DOMINE
DOMING
DOMINI
DOMINO
DOPING
DOSING
DOTING
DOZING
DRAINS
DRYING
DRYINK
DUKING
DUPING
DURING
DYEING
EALING
EARING
EASING
EATING
EBBING
ECHINO
EDGING
EGGING
ELAINE
ELNINO
ENCINA
ENCINO
ENDING
ENGINE
EOSINS
EPPING
EQUINE
ERMINE
ERRING
ERVING
EYEING
FACING
FADING
FAKING
FALINE
FAMINE
FARINA
FARING
FAXING
FAZING
FEEING
FELINE
FETING
FIFING
FILING
FINING
FIRING
FIXING
FLYING
FLYINS
FORINT
FOXING
FRYING
FUMING
FUSING
FUZING
GAGING
GAMINE
GAMING
GAMINS
GAPING
GATING
GAZING
GEEING
GEMINI
GHAINS
GIBING
GIVING
GLUING
GOLINO
GORING
GRAINS
GRAINY
GROINS
GUYING
GYBING
HALING
HARING
HATING
HAVING
HAWING
HAYING
HAZING
HEWING
HEXING
HIDING
HIEING
HIKING
HIRING
HIVING
HOEING
HOLING
HOMING
HOMINY
HONING
HOPING
HOSING
HYPING
ICHING
IDLING
ILLINI
IMFINE
IMPING
INKIND
INKING
INLINE
INNING
INTINE
IODINE
IRKING
IRVINE
IRVING
JADING
JANINE
JAPING
JAWING
JIBING
JIMINY
JIVING
JOKING
JUKING
KALINE
KEYING
KITING
LACING
LADING
LADINO
LAMINA
LAMING
LAPINS
LATINA
LATINI
LATINO
LATINS
LAVING
LAWING
LAYING
LAZING
LEVINE
LIKING
LIMING
LINING
LIVING
LOPING
LOSING
LOVING
LOWING
LUBING
LUMINA
LUPINE
LUPINO
LURING
LUTING
LYSINE
LYSINS
MAKING
MARINA
MARINE
MARINO
MATING
MATINS
MAXINE
MEDINA
MELINA
MENINX
MERINO
METING
MEWING
MIKING
MIMING
MINING
MIRING
MIXING
MODINE
MOLINE
MOOING
MOPING
MOVING
MOWING
MUCINS
MURINE
MUSING
MUTING
MUTINY
NADINE
NAMING
NEVINS
NIMINY
NIXING
NOMINE
NOSING
NOTING
NUKING
NUMINA
OARING
OFFING
OGLING
OILING
ONDINE
ONLINE
OOHING
OOZING
OPTING
ORBING
ORPINE
ORSINO
OSCINE
OUTING
OWNING
PACING
PACINO
PAGING
PALING
PARING
PATINA
PATINE
PAVING
PAWING
PAYING
PEKING
PEKINS
PEPINO
PIKING
PILING
PIMINY
PINING
PIPING
PLAINS
PLAINT
PLYING
POKING
POLING
PORING
POSING
PRYING
PULING
PURINA
PURINE
QUAINT
QUOINS
RACINE
RACING
RAGING
RAKING
RAPINE
RAPINI
RARING
RASING
RATINE
RATING
RAVINE
RAVING
RAZING
REBIND
REDING
REDINK
REFINE
REGINA
RELINE
REMIND
REPINE
REPINS
RESING
RESINS
RESINY
RETINA
REWIND
REWINS
RICING
RIDING
RILING
RIMING
RIMINI
RISING
RIVING
ROBING
ROBINS
ROPING
ROSINS
ROSINY
ROTINI
ROVING
ROWING
RULING
RUMINA
RUNINS
SABINE
SABINS
SALINA
SALINE
SATING
SATINS
SATINY
SAVING
SAWING
SAYING
SEEING
SERINE
SERINS
SETINS
SEWING
SHRINE
SHRINK
SHYING
SIDING
SIRING
SITING
SITINS
SIXING
SIZING
SKEINS
SKIING
SKYING
SLUING
SOFINE
SOLING
SOWING
SPHINX
SPLINE
SPLINT
SPRING
SPRINT
SPYING
SQUINT
STAINS
STEINS
STRINE
STRING
SUPINE
SWAINS
SYRINX
TAHINI
TAKING
TAKINS
TAMING
TAPING
TAPINS
TARING
TAWING
TAXING
TEEING
TIDING
TIEING
TIEINS
TILING
TIMING
TIPINS
TIRING
TOEING
TOEINS
TONING
TORINO
TOTING
TOWING
TOXINS
TOYING
TRAINS
TRUING
TRYING
TUBING
TUNING
TURING
TYPING
UNBIND
UNDINE
UNKIND
UNKINK
UNLINK
UNPINS
UNWIND
UPLINK
UPPING
UPWIND
URGING
URSINE
VEXING
VIKING
VINING
VISINE
VOTING
VOWING
WADING
WAGING
WAHINE
WAKING
WANING
WARING
WAVING
WAXING
WILING
WINING
WIPING
WIRING
WOOING
WOWING
YAWING
YOGINI
YOKING
ZAYINS
ZONING

•••I•N

ACTION
ADRIAN
ADRIEN
ALBION
AMNION
ANCIEN
APPIAN
ASSIGN
BAHIAN
BENIGN
BUNION
CAMION
CATION
COSIGN
DAMIEN
DARIEN
DESIGN
DIDION
DORIAN
DURIAN
ELOIGN
ENSIGN
EOLIAN
EONIAN
FABIAN
FANION
FENIAN
FIJIAN
FUJIAN
FUSION
GABION
INDIAN
IONIAN
JOVIAN
JULIAN
LEGION
LOGION
LOTION
LUCIAN
MALIGN
MARIAN
MARION
MEDIAN
MIDIAN
MINION
MORION
MOTION
NATION
NOTION
NUBIAN
OBRIAN
OBRIEN
OPTION
OSSIAN
PELION
PINION
POTION
RADIAN
RATION
REGION
RESIGN
SIMIAN
SYRIAN
TALION
TITIAN
TUPIAN
TYRIAN
UGRIAN
VISION
VIVIAN
VIVIEN

••••IN

ADDSIN
ADJOIN
ALBOIN
ALCUIN
ALDRIN
AMBLIN
ANACIN
ASKSIN
ATTAIN
AUSTIN
AZORIN
BACKIN
BAFFIN
BARKIN
BERLIN
BIDSIN
BIOTIN
BLOWIN
BOBBIN
BODKIN
BOFFIN
BOUDIN
BOWFIN
BROLIN
BUSKIN
BUSTIN
BUTTIN
CALLIN
CALVIN
CAMEIN
CARDIN
CARLIN
CASHIN
CATKIN
CAVEIN
CHAPIN
CHEMIN
CHENIN
CHIPIN
CHITIN
CHOPIN
CLAVIN
CLUEIN
COCHIN
COMEIN
CORBIN
COUSIN
CRETIN
CRONIN
CULKIN
CURTIN
CUTSIN

DARWIN
DASSIN
DEALIN
DENTIN
DETAIN
DEVEIN
DIGSIN
DINEIN
DIOXIN
DIVEIN
DOBBIN
DOBLIN
DOESIN
DOMAIN
DONEIN
DOVEIN
DRAGIN
DRAWIN
DREWIN
DROPIN
DUBBIN
DUBLIN
DUCHIN
DUNLIN
DURBIN
DUSTIN
EASEIN
EATSIN
EDGEIN
ENJOIN
FADEIN
FALLIN
FELLIN
FIBRIN
FILLIN
FIRKIN
FITSIN
FLEWIN
FLORIN
FOGSIN
GAIJIN
GASKIN
GATLIN
GAVEIN
GAWAIN
GETSIN
GIVEIN
GLOBIN
GOBLIN
GODWIN
GOESIN
GRADIN
GRATIN
GRODIN
HAMLIN
HANDIN
HANGIN
HARBIN
HARLIN
HATPIN
HEADIN
HEFLIN
HELDIN
HEMSIN
HENNIN
HEREIN
HOLDIN
HOPSIN
HORNIN
HOWLIN
HUNGIN
ICEDIN
ICESIN
ILORIN
INVAIN
IRISIN
ISELIN
JAMSIN
JERKIN
JOININ
JOPLIN
JOSKIN
JUMPIN
JUSTIN
KAOLIN
KEEPIN
KELVIN
KEYSIN
KICKIN
LAIDIN
LANVIN
LAYSIN
LEADIN
LEFTIN
LEGUIN
LETSIN
LIESIN
LIGNIN
LIVEIN
LOCKIN
LOGSIN
LOMEIN
LOOKIN
LORAIN
LOVEIN
LUBLIN
MAILIN
MALKIN
MALTIN
MARGIN
MARLIN
MARTIN
MARVIN
MATLIN
MCBAIN
MCLAIN
MELVIN
MERLIN
MOULIN
MOVEIN
MUFFIN
MUNTIN
MUSLIN
MYELIN
MYOSIN
NAILIN
NAPKIN
NIACIN
NOGGIN
NUBBIN
NUTKIN
OBTAIN
OLEFIN
ORDAIN
ORIGIN
OSSEIN
PAIDIN
PAPAIN
PAQUIN
PAYSIN
PECTIN
PEERIN
PEPSIN
PETAIN
PIDGIN
PIETIN
PILEIN
PINYIN
PIPKIN
PIPPIN
PLUGIN
POPLIN
POPSIN
POURIN
PREVIN
PUFFIN
PULLIN
PURLIN
PUTSIN
RAISIN
RAKEIN
RANKIN
RATLIN
READIN
REDFIN
REELIN
REGAIN
REININ
REJOIN
REMAIN
RENNIN
RESPIN
RETAIN
ROLLIN
ROPEIN
RUBSIN
RUNSIN
RUSKIN
SEENIN
SEEPIN
SEESIN
SENDIN
SENTIN
SEQUIN
SERKIN
SETSIN
SHOOIN
SHOWIN
SHUTIN
SIGNIN
SINGIN
SINKIN
SISKIN
SITSIN
SLIDIN
SLIPIN
SMILIN
SNOWIN
SOCKIN
SPAVIN
SPRAIN
STALIN
STEPIN
STIRIN
STOPIN
STOTIN
STRAIN
SUCKIN
TAKEIN
TANNIN
TENPIN
TIEDIN
TIEPIN
TIESIN
TIFFIN
TIPSIN
TOCSIN
TOEDIN
TOESIN
TOMLIN
TONKIN
TOOKIN
TUCKIN
TUNEIN
TURNIN
TURPIN
UJJAIN
URCHIN
VERDIN
VERMIN
VIOLIN
VIRGIN
VOTEIN
WADEIN
WALKIN
WANTIN
WAVEIN
WELKIN
WENTIN
WINWIN
WITHIN
WORKIN
XINGIN
ZEROIN
ZOOMIN

I0••••

IODATE
IODIDE
IODINE
IODISE
IODIZE
IOLITE
IOMOTH
IONIAN
IONICS
IONISE
IONIUM
IONIZE
IOWANS

I•0•••

ICONIC
IDOIDO
IGOTIT
ILOILO
ILORIN
IMOGEN
INOUYE
IROBOT
IRONED
IRONER
IRONIC
IRONON
ISOBAR
ISOGON
ISOHEL
ISOLDE
ISOMER
ISOPOD

I••0••

ICEOUT
IDIOCY
IDIOMS
IDIOTS
IGLOOS
IGNORE
IMPORT
IMPOSE
IMPOST
INBORN
INCOME
INDOOR
INDORE
INFOLD
INFORM
INGOTS
INIONS
INJOKE
INLOVE
INMOST
INPORT
INPOUR
INROAD
INSOLE
INTONE
INTOTO
INTOWN
INVOKE
IOMOTH

I•••0•

ICEBOX
ICEFOG
IGLOOS
IMPROV
INAFOG
INAROW
INCHON
INDOOR
INFLOW
INTROS
IROBOT
IRONON
ISADOR
ISOGON
ISOPOD

I••••0

IBIBIO
IDOIDO
ILOILO
IMMUNO
INDIGO
INITIO
INTOTO
INVIVO

•I0•••

BIOBIO
BIOGAS
BIOMES
BIONDI
BIONIC
BIOTAS
BIOTIC
BIOTIN
DIODES
DIONEB
DIONNE
DIOXIN
FIORDS
GIOTTO
KIOSKS
KIOWAS
LIONEL
LIONET
LIONLY
LIOTTA
MIOSIS
PIOLET
RIOJAS
RIOTED
RIOTER
SIOUAN
VIOLAS
VIOLET
VIOLIN

•I•0••

AIROUT
BICORN
BIFOLD
BIGOTS
BIJOUX
BILOXI
BIPODS
BISONS
BITOFF
BITOLA
CIBOLA
DICOTS
DIEOFF
DIEOUT
DIGOUT
DIMOUT
DIPODY
DIPOLE
DISOWN
DIVOTS
EIDOLA
FILOSE
GIGOLO
GIGOTS
GIJOES
HIDOUT
HITOUT
KIBOSH
KIDORY
KIMONO
LIPOID
LITOUT
MIDORI
MILORD
MILOSZ
MIMOSA
MINOAN
MINORS
MIWOKS
NICOLA
NICOLE
NICOLO
NIKOLA
PICOTS
PIGOUT
PILOSE
PILOTI
PILOTS
PINOAK
PINOLE
PINONS
PINOTS
PITONS
PIVOTS
RIBOSE
RIGORS
RIGOUR
RIMOSE
RIPOFF
RIPOUT
SILOAM
SILOED
SILONE
SIMONE
SIMONY
SITOUT
TIPOFF
TIVOLI
VIGODA
VIGORS
VIGOUR
VINOUS
VISORS
WICOPY
WIDOWS
WIGOUT
WINONA
WINOUT

•I••0•

AIMFOR
BIDSON
BIGBOY
BIGTOE
BIGTOP
BILLON
BILLOW
BISHOP
CISCOS
CITRON
DIALOG
DIATOM
DIDION
DIGLOT
DILLON
DINEON
DISCOS
DITTOS
GIBBON
GIBSON
GIDEON
GIZMOS
HICKOK
HIERON
HILTON
HINTON
HIPHOP
HIPPOS
HIREON
HITSON
HIVAOA
JIMSON
KILROY
KINDOF
KITFOX
LICTOR
LIELOW
LIMBOS
LIPTON
LIQUOR
LISBOA
LISBON
LISTON
LITHOG
LITHOS
LIVEON
MICRON
MICROS
MIGNON
MILTON
MIMEOS
MINION
MINNOW
MIRROR
NIMROD
NIPPON
PIANOS
PICKON
PIGEON
PILEON
PILLOW
PINION
PINSON
PINTOS
PINYON
PINZON
PISTOL
PISTON
RIBBON
RIDSOF
SIGNON
SIGNOR
SIMEON
SIPHON
SITCOM
SITSON
TIEROD
TIGLON
TINGOD
TINPOT
TIPTOE
TIPTOP
VIACOM
VICTOR
VIDEOS
VILLON
VINTON
VIREOS
VISION
WILCOX
WILLOW
WILSON
WILTON
WINDOM
WINDOW
WINNOW
WINSOR
WISDOM
ZIPLOC
ZIRCON

•I•••0

AIELLO
AIKIDO
AIMSTO
BIBLIO
BILBAO
BIOBIO
BISTRO
CICERO
CITATO
DIABLO
DINERO
DIRIGO
DIVINO
FIASCO
FIGARO
FINITO
GIGOLO
GINKGO
GIOTTO
GITANO
GIVETO
HIDEHO
KIMONO
LIBIDO
LIESTO
MIKADO
MILANO
NICOLO
NIELLO
NIHILO
NINGBO
PICABO
PICARO
PIETRO
PINERO
PISANO
RIALTO
RIGHTO
RIZZIO
SIDERO
SINGTO
TIEDTO
TIESTO
VIRAGO
WISETO

••I0••

ALIOTO
ANIONS
ARIOSE
ARIOSO
AXIOMS
AXIONS
GRIOTS
IDIOCY
IDIOMS
IDIOTS
INIONS
ODIOUS
OHIOAN
ONIONS
ONIONY
ORIOLE
OTIOSE
PRIONS
PRIORI
PRIORS
PRIORY
SCIONS
TRIODE
UNIONS

••I•0•

ALISON
AMIDOL
AMIGOS
AMINOR

ASIMOV
AVISOS
BAILOR
BMINOR
BRITON
CAICOS
CHIGOE
CHILOE
CHINOS
CHIRON
CHISOX
CHITON
CLIPON
CMINOR
DAIKON
DAIMON
DEIMOS
DMINOR
EDISON
EDITOR
EJIDOS
ELINOR
EMINOR
EPILOG
FMINOR
FRIJOL
FRITOS
GAINON
GMINOR
GRISON
GUIDON
GUIROS
LAIDON
NOIRON
ORISON
PAILOU
PHILOL
PHILOS
POIROT
POISON
PRIMOS
PRISON
QUINOA
RHINOS
SAIGON
SAILOR
SHILOH
SHIMON
SKIBOB
SKIROS
SKITOW
SLIPON
SPIGOT
SPIROS
SUITOR
TAILOR
TAINOS
TRICOT
TRIGON
TRIPOD
TRIPOS
TRITON
UNIPOD
UNISON
WAITON
WHILOM

••I••O

AKIMBO
ALIOTO
ARIOSO
ARISTO
BOINGO
BRILLO
CRISCO
CRISTO
DAIMYO
EDITIO
EMILIO
EOIPSO
FRISCO
GOINTO
GRINGO
HAIRDO
IBIBIO
INITIO
LAIDTO
OBISPO
OLINGO
OVIEDO
SCIPIO
SEISMO
SHINTO
SPINTO
STINGO
TRICHO
WEIRDO
WHIZZO

•••IO•

ACTION
ALBION
AMNION
AUDIOS
BUNION
CAMION
CATION
CURIOS
DIDION
ELLIOT
FANION
FOLIOS
FUSION
GABION
HELIOS
HERIOT
HESIOD
JOLIOT
JUNIOR
LEGION
LOGION
LOTION
MANIOC
MARION
MINION
MORION
MOTION
NATION
NOTION
OPTION
PATIOS
PELION
PERIOD
PINION
POTION
RADIOS
RATION
RATIOS
REGION
SAVIOR
SENIOR
TALION
VISION

•••I•O

ACTINO
AIKIDO
ALBINO
ALNICO
AQUINO
BENITO
BONITO
CALICO
CAMINO
CASINO
COGITO
DENIRO
DEVITO
DIRIGO
DIVINO
DOMINO
DOSIDO
ECHINO
ELNINO
ENCINO
ENRICO
ESKIMO
FINITO
GOLINO
IDOIDO
ILOILO
INDIGO
INVIVO
LADINO
LATIGO
LATINO
LIBIDO
LUPINO
MARIKO
MARINO
MEDICO
MEJICO
MERINO
MEXICO
NIHILO
ORSINO
PACINO
PEPINO
SUBITO
TORINO
ULTIMO

••••IO

ADAGIO
AFLCIO
BAGUIO
BARRIO
BIBLIO
BIOBIO
CARDIO
CASSIO
CRANIO
DELRIO
EDITIO
EMILIO
FLORIO
IBIBIO
INITIO
KUOPIO
LASHIO
MACEIO
MAGGIO
NUNCIO
PERNIO
PHYSIO
PLAGIO
RIZZIO
SCIPIO
SERGIO
STUDIO

IP••••

IPECAC

I•P•••

IMPACT
IMPAIR
IMPALA
IMPALE
IMPART
IMPEDE
IMPELS
IMPEND
IMPERF
IMPING
IMPISH
IMPORT
IMPOSE
IMPOST
IMPROV
IMPUGN
IMPURE
IMPUTE
INPART
INPLAY
INPORT
INPOUR
INPUTS

I••P••

INAPET
INSPAN
ISOPOD

I•••P•

INCEPT
IRRUPT

I••••P

ICECAP
ICEDUP
ICESUP
INSTEP

•IP•••

BIPEDS
BIPODS
CIPHER
DIPODY
DIPOLE
DIPPED
DIPPER
FIPPLE
GIPPED
GIPPER
HIPHOP
HIPPED
HIPPER
HIPPIE
HIPPOS
KIPPER
KIPPUR
LIPASE
LIPENG
LIPIDE
LIPIDS
LIPOID
LIPPED
LIPTON
NIPPED
NIPPER
NIPPON
NIPPUR
NIPSAT
NIPSEY
NIPUPS
PIPALS
PIPERS
PIPEUP
PIPIER
PIPING
PIPITS
PIPKIN
PIPPED
PIPPIN
RIPELY
RIPENS
RIPEST
RIPKEN
RIPLEY
RIPOFF
RIPOUT
RIPPED
RIPPER
RIPPLE
RIPPLY
RIPRAP
RIPSAW
RIPSUP
SIPHON
SIPPED
SIPPER
SIPPET
TIPINS
TIPOFF
TIPPED
TIPPER
TIPPET
TIPPLE
TIPSIN
TIPTOE
TIPTOP
TIPUPS
VIPERS
WIPERS
WIPEUP
WIPING
YIPPED
YIPPEE
ZIPLOC
ZIPPED
ZIPPER
ZIPSUP

•I•P••

DIAPER
DIEPPE
DIMPLE
DIMPLY
DIPPED
DIPPER
DISPEL
FIPPLE
GIPPED
GIPPER
HIPPED
HIPPER
HIPPIE
HIPPOS
HISPID
KIPPER
KIPPUR
LIMPED
LIMPER
LIMPET
LIMPID
LIMPLY
LIPPED
LISPED
MILPAS
NIPPED
NIPPER
NIPPON
NIPPUR
OILPAN
PIEPAN
PIGPEN
PIPPED
PIPPIN
RIMPLE
RIPPED
RIPPER
RIPPLE
RIPPLY
SIMPER
SIMPLE
SIMPLY
SIPPED
SIPPER
SIPPET
TIEPIN
TINPAN
TINPOT
TIPPED
TIPPER
TIPPET
TIPPLE
WIMPLE
WISPED
YIPPED
YIPPEE
ZILPAH
ZIPPED
ZIPPER

•I••P•

BICEPS
DIEPPE
FIVEPM
FIXUPS
MIXUPS
NINEPM
NIPUPS
PINUPS
SITUPS
TIEUPS
TIPUPS
WICOPY

•I•••P

BIDSUP
BIGTOP
BINDUP
BISHOP
BITMAP
DIALUP
DIGSUP
FILLIP
FILLUP
FIREUP
FIRMUP
GIVEUP
HICCUP
HIGHUP
HIKEUP
HIPHOP
HITSUP
KICKUP
KIDNAP
LIFTUP
LINEUP
LINKUP
MILSAP
MISHAP
PICKUP
PILEUP
PIPEUP
PIRRIP
RIGSUP
RILEUP
RINGUP
RIPRAP
RIPSUP
SIGNUP
SITSUP
SIZEUP
TIDYUP
TIEDUP
TIESUP
TIPTOP
TITTUP
WINDUP
WIPEUP
WISEUP
ZIPSUP

••IP••

CHIPIN
CLIPON
CRIPES
DRIPPY
EOIPSO
FLIPUP
GRIPED
GRIPER
GRIPES
GRIPPE
JAIPUR
PRIPET
QUIPPY
QUIPUS
RAIPUR
SAIPAN
SCIPIO
SKIPIT
SKIPPY
SLIPIN
SLIPON
SLIPPY
SLIPUP
SNIPED
SNIPER
SNIPES
SNIPPY
STIPEL
STIPES
SWIPED
SWIPER
SWIPES
TAIPAN
TAIPEI
TRIPLE
TRIPLY
TRIPOD
TRIPOS
TRIPUP
UNIPOD
WHIPPY
WHIPUP

••I•P•

BLIMPS
CHIMPS
CHIRPS
CHIRPY
CRIMPS
CRIMPY
CRISPS
CRISPY
DRIPPY
GRIPPE
GUIMPE
OBISPO
PRIMPS
QUIPPY
SKIMPS
SKIMPY
SKIPPY
SLIPPY
SNIPPY
STIMPY
WHIPPY

••I••P

CHINUP
COILUP
FAIRUP
FLIPUP
JOINUP
LAIDUP
PAIDUP
PAIRUP
PHILIP
SLIPUP
STIRUP
SUITUP
TRICEP
TRIPUP
WAITUP
WHIPUP

•••IP•

CALIPH
CERIPH
EQUIPS
FELIPE
OXLIPS
RECIPE
SCRIPS
SCRIPT
STRIPE
STRIPS
STRIPY
THRIPS
TULIPS
UNRIPE
UNZIPS
VCHIPS

•••I•P

MEGILP
SCRIMP
SHRIMP

••••IP

BUNYIP
CATNIP
FILLIP
GOSSIP
HOTTIP
PHILIP
PIRRIP
RESHIP
THELIP
TURNIP

IQ••••

IQTEST

I••Q••

IRAQIS

•IQ•••

LIQUID
LIQUOR
PIQUED
PIQUES
PIQUET

•I•Q••

BISQUE
CINQUE
CIRQUE
RISQUE

•I•••Q

HIGHIQ

••IQ••

CAIQUE
CLIQUE
CLIQUY
CUIQUE
UBIQUE
UNIQUE

•••I•Q

SUSIEQ

••••IQ

HIGHIQ

IR••••

IRANIS
IRAQIS
IRATER
IREFUL
IRENES
IRENIC
IRIDES

IRIDIC
IRISES
IRISIN
IRKING
IRLENE
IROBOT
IRONED
IRONER
IRONIC
IRONON
IRREAL
IRRUPT
IRTYSH
IRVINE
IRVING

I•R•••

INROAD
INRUSH
IRREAL
IRRUPT
ISRAEL

I••R••

IATRIC
IBERIA
ICARIA
ICARUS
ILORIN
IMARET
IMBRUE
IMPROV
INARCH
INAROW
INARUT
INBRED
INDRIS
INGRAM
INGRES
INGRID
INTROS
INURED
INURES
ISTRIA
ITURBI

I•••R•

IDCARD
IDLERS
IGNORE
IMMURE
IMPART
IMPERF
IMPORT
IMPURE
INBORN
INCURS
INDIRA
INDORE
INFERS
INFIRM
INFORM
INHERE
INJURE
INJURY
INKERS
INPART
INPORT
INSERT
INSURE
INTERJ
INTERN
INTURN
INVERT
INWARD
IZZARD

I••••R

ICKIER
IFFIER
IMAGER
IMPAIR
INANER
INDOOR
INGEAR
INGMAR
INKIER
INPOUR
INSTAR
IRATER
IRONER
ISADOR
ISHTAR
ISOBAR
ISOMER
ISSUER

•IR•••

AIRARM
AIRBAG
AIRBUS
AIRDAM
AIRDRY
AIRGUN
AIRIER
AIRILY
AIRING
AIRMAN
AIRMEN
AIROUT
AIRSAC
AIRWAY
BIRDED
BIRDER
BIRDIE
BIREME
BIRGIT
BIRLED
BIRNEY
BIRTHS
CIRCLE
CIRCUM
CIRCUS
CIRQUE
CIRRUS
DIRECT
DIRELY
DIREST
DIRGES
DIRHAM
DIRIGE
DIRIGO
DIRNDL
FIRERS
FIREUP
FIRING
FIRKIN
FIRMAN
FIRMED
FIRMER
FIRMLY
FIRMUP
FIRSTS
FIRTHS
GIRARD
GIRDED
GIRDER
GIRDLE
GIRNED
GIRTED
GIRTHS
HIREON
HIRERS
HIRING
HIRSCH
KIRMAN
KIRSCH
KIRTLE
MIRAGE
MIRIAM
MIRIER
MIRING
MIRREN
MIRROR
PIRACY
PIRANA
PIRATE
PIRRIP
SIRDAR
SIRENS
SIRICA
SIRING
SIRIUS
SIRRAH
SIRREE
TIRADE
TIRANA
TIRANE
TIRING
VIRAGO
VIREOS
VIRGIL
VIRGIN
VIRILE
VIRTUE
VIRTUS
WIRERS
WIRIER
WIRILY
WIRING
ZIRCON

•I•R••

AIGRET
BIERCE
BIGRED
CIARDI
CIRRUS
CITRIC
CITRON
CITRUS
DIGRAM
FIBRES
FIBRIL
FIBRIN
FIERCE
FIORDS
GIBRAN
HIERON
HIJRAH
KILROY
LIBRIS
LIERNE
LITRES
LIVRES
MICRON
MICROS
MIDRIB
MIHRAB
MIRREN
MIRROR
MITRAL
MITRED
MITRES
NIMROD
NITRES
NITRIC
OILRIG
PIERCE
PIERRE
PIRRIP
RIPRAP
SIERRA
SIRRAH
SIRREE
TIARAS
TIERCE
TIERED
TIEROD
TIERRA
TIGRIS
TITRED
TITRES
VITRIC

•I••R•

AIDERS
AILERS
AIRARM
AIRDRY
BIAFRA
BICARB
BICORN
BIHARI
BIKERS
BINARY
BISTRO
BITERS
CICERO
CIDERS
CIGARS
CITERS
DICERS
DINARS
DINERO
DINERS
DISARM
DIVERS
DIVERT
DIYERS
EIDERS
FIACRE
FIBERS
FIFERS
FIGARO
FIGURE
FILERS
FINERY
FIRERS
FIVERS
FIXERS
GIBERS
GIRARD
GIVERS
HIDERS
HIKERS
HILARY
HIRERS
JIVERS
KIDORY
KITERS
LIBERI
LIFERS
LIGERS
LIGURE
LINERS
LITERS
LIVERS
LIVERY
LIZARD
MIDORI
MILERS
MILORD
MIMERS
MINERS
MINORS
MISERS
MISERY
MITERS
MIXERS
NINERS
NITERS
NITERY
OILERS
PICARA
PICARD
PICARO
PIERRE
PIETRO
PIKERS
PINERO
PINERY
PIPERS
RICERS
RIDERS
RIGORS
RISERS
RITARD
RIVERA
RIVERS
SIDERO
SIDERS
SIERRA
SIGURD
SISERA
SISTRA
SITARS
SIXERS
SIZERS
TIERRA
TIGERS
TILERS
TIMBRE
TIMERS
TISHRI
TITERS
UIGURS
VICARS
VIDERI
VIGORS
VINERY
VIPERS
VISORS
WINERY
WINTRY
WIPERS
WIRERS
WIZARD

•I•••R

AIMFOR
AIRIER
BICKER
BIDDER
BIGGER
BIGSUR
BINDER
BIRDER
BITTER
CINDER
CIPHER
DIALER
DIAPER
DICIER
DICKER
DIETER
DIFFER
DIGGER
DILLER
DIMMER
DINNER
DIPPER
DISBAR
DITHER
EISNER
EITHER
FIBBER
FILLER
FILTER
FINDER
FINGER
FIRMER
FISHER
FITTER
GIBBER
GILDER
GINGER
GIPPER
GIRDER
HIGHER
HILLER
HINDER
HINTER
HIPPER
HISSER
HITHER
HITTER
JIGGER
JITTER
JIVIER
KICKER
KIDDER
KIEFER
KILLER
KILMER
KILTER
KINDER
KIPPER
KIPPUR
KISSER
LIBBER
LICTOR
LIEDER
LIEFER
LIFTER
LIMBER
LIMIER
LIMNER
LIMPER
LINEAR
LINGER
LINIER
LINKER
LINTER
LIQUOR
LISTER
LITTER
MIDAIR
MIDLER
MILDER
MILKER
MILLER
MILNER
MINCER
MINDER
MINTER
MIRIER
MIRROR
MISTER
NICKER
NIGHER
NIPPER
NIPPUR
OILIER
PICKER
PIECER
PIETER
PILFER
PILLAR
PINCER
PINDAR
PINIER
PINKER
PINNER
PINTER
PIPIER
PITIER
PITTER
QINTAR
RICHER
RIFLER
RIGGER
RIGOUR
RIMIER
RINGER
RIOTER
RIPPER
RISKER
RITTER
SICKER
SIDDUR
SIFTER
SIGHER
SIGNER
SIGNOR
SILVER
SIMMER
SIMPER
SINGER
SINKER
SINNER
SINTER
SIPPER
SIRDAR
SISLER
SISTER
SITTER
TICKER
TIDIER
TIGGER
TILLER
TILTER
TIMBER
TINDER
TINEAR
TINIER
TINKER
TINNER
TINTER
TIPPER
TITFER
TITHER
TITTER
VICTOR
VIEWER
VIGOUR
VINIER
VIZIER
WICKER
WIENER
WILBUR
WILDER
WILIER
WINCER
WINDER
WINGER
WINIER
WINKER
WINNER
WINSOR
WINTER
WIRIER
WISHER
WISTER
WITHER
ZIMMER
ZINGER
ZIPPER
ZITHER

••IR••

BAIRNS
BEIRUT
BGIRLS
CAIRNS
CHIRAC
CHIRON
CHIRPS
CHIRPY
CHIRRS
DAIREN
EPIRUS
FAIRED
FAIRER
FAIRLY
FAIRUP
FLIRTS
FLIRTY
GUIROS
HAIRDO
HAIRED
LAIRDS
MOIRES
NAIRAS
NOIRON
OSIRIS
PAIRED
PAIRUP
POIROT
QUIRES
QUIRKS
QUIRKY
QUIRTS
SHIRAZ
SHIRER
SHIRES
SHIRKS
SHIRRS
SHIRTS
SHIRTY
SKIRLS
SKIROS
SKIRRS
SKIRTS
SKIRUN
SMIRCH
SMIRKS
SMIRKY
SOIREE
SPIRAL
SPIREA
SPIRED
SPIRES
SPIRIT
SPIROS
STIRIN
STIRKS
STIRUP
SWIRLS
SWIRLY
TBIRDS
THIRDS
THIRST
THIRTY
TWIRLS
WEIRDO
WEIRDY
WHIRLS
WHIRLY
WHIRRS
ZAIRES

••I•R•

ANITRA
APIARY
AVIARY
BRIARD
BRIARS
BRIERS
BRIERY
CHIRRS
CRIERS
DEIDRE
DMITRI
DRIERS
EMIGRE
FLIERS
FRIARS
FRIARY
FRIERS

GRIGRI
GUITRY
MAITRE
OSIERS
PLIERS
PRIERS
PRIORI
PRIORS
PRIORY
SHIRRS
SKIERS
SKIRRS
SPIERS
TRIERS
WHIRRS

••I••R
ALITER
AMINOR
BAILER
BAILOR
BMINOR
BOILER
CHIDER
CMINOR
COINER
DEICER
DMINOR
DRIVER
DUIKER
EDITOR
ELINOR
ELIXIR
EMINOR
EVILER
FAIRER
FMINOR
GAINER
GAITER
GEIGER
GLIDER
GMINOR
GRIPER
GUITAR
HEIFER
JAILER
JAIPUR
JOINER
JUICER
KAISER
LOITER
MAILER
MOILER
NAILER
OBITER
OLIVER
OPINER
PFIZER
PRICER
PRIMER
QUIVER
RAIDER
RAILER
RAINER
RAIPUR
RAISER
REINER
RUINER
SAILOR
SEINER
SEIZER
SHIKAR
SHINER
SHIRER
SHIVER
SKIVER
SLICER
SLIDER
SLIVER
SMILER
SNIDER
SNIPER
SPIDER
SPIKER
STIVER
SUITOR
SWIPER
TAILOR
TOILER
TRITER
UNITER
VAINER
WAILER
WAITER
WAIVER
WEIMAR
WHINER
WHITER
WRITER
ZUIDER

•••IR•
ADMIRE
AFFIRM
ALHIRT
ASPIRE
ASWIRL
ATTIRE
AWHIRL
BEMIRE
CHAIRS
CHOIRS
CLAIRE
DENIRO
DESIRE
ELMIRA
ELVIRA
EMPIRE
ENGIRD
ENGIRT
ENTIRE
EXPIRE
EXPIRY
FAKIRS
FLAIRS
GEZIRA
GLAIRS
GLAIRY
HEGIRA
INDIRA
INFIRM
JABIRU
KAFIRS
KEFIRS
MYGIRL
NADIRS
ONFIRE
PAMIRS
REAIRS
REHIRE
RETIRE
REWIRE
SAFIRE
SATIRE
SQUIRE
SQUIRM
SQUIRT
STAIRS
TAPIRS
THEIRS
TSHIRT
UMPIRE
UNGIRD
UNGIRT
VENIRE

•••I•R
ACHIER
AIRIER
ARTIER
ASHIER
BONIER
BOXIER
BUSIER
CAGIER
CAHIER
CAKIER
CANIER
CAVIAR
COKIER
COPIER
COSIER
COZIER
DENIER
DEWIER
DICIER
DOPIER
DOZIER
EASIER
EDGIER
EELIER
EERIER
EGGIER
ENVIER
FOLIAR
FOXIER
FUMIER
GAMIER
GLUIER
GOOIER
GORIER
HAZIER
HOKIER
HOLIER
HOMIER
HOSIER
ICKIER
IFFIER
INKIER
JAVIER
JIVIER
JOKIER
JUNIOR
LACIER
LAKIER
LANIER
LAZIER
LEVIER
LIMIER
LINIER
LOGIER
MAZIER
METIER
MIRIER
MOPIER
NAPIER
NOSIER
OATIER
OILIER
OOZIER
PALIER
PAPIER
PINIER
PIPIER
PITIER
POKIER
PUNIER
RACIER
RAPIER
RIMIER
ROPIER
ROSIER
SAVIOR
SENIOR
SEXIER
SPRIER
TIDIER
TINIER
TONIER
TYPIER
UGLIER
VANIER
VINIER
VIZIER
WANIER
WARIER
WAVIER
WAXIER
WILIER
WINIER
WIRIER
XAVIER
ZANIER

••••IR
AAFAIR
ABUKIR
AFFAIR
AGADIR
ALTAIR
AUPAIR
BELAIR
BESTIR
COHEIR
DEVOIR
ECLAIR
ELIXIR
FAFNIR
HOTAIR
IMPAIR
KAFFIR
MCNAIR
MEMOIR
MENHIR
MIDAIR
MOHAIR
REDFIR
RENOIR
REPAIR
REVOIR
SANTIR
SAVOIR
SHAMIR
UNFAIR
YESSIR

IS••••
ISABEL
ISADOR
ISAIAH
ISCHIA
ISELIN
ISEULT
ISHTAR
ISLAND
ISLETS
ISMENE
ISOBAR
ISOGON
ISOHEL
ISOLDE
ISOMER
ISOPOD
ISRAEL
ISSUED
ISSUER
ISSUES
ISTHMI
ISTLES
ISTRIA

I•S•••
IJSSEL
INSANE
INSEAM
INSECT
INSERT
INSETS
INSIDE
INSIST
INSITU
INSOLE
INSPAN
INSTAL
INSTAR
INSTEP
INSTIL
INSULT
INSURE
INSYNC
ISSUED
ISSUER
ISSUES
ITSELF

I••S••
IBISES
ICESIN
ICESUP
IJSSEL
ILESHA
ILLSAY
INESSE
IRISES
IRISIN
ITASCA

I•••S•
ICIEST
IDLEST
ILLEST
ILLUSE
IMPISH
IMPOSE
IMPOST
INCASE
INCASH
INCISE
INCUSE
INESSE
INFEST
INFUSE
INGEST
INJEST
INMOST
INNESS
INRUSH
INSIST
INVEST
IODISE
IONISE
IQTEST
IRTYSH

I••••S
IBEAMS
IBEXES
IBISES
ICARUS
ICINGS
IDEALS
IDIOMS
IDIOTS
IDLERS
IDTAGS
IDYLLS
IGLOOS
ILEXES
IMAGES
IMBUES
IMPELS
INCANS
INCHES
INCURS
INDIES
INDRIS
INFERS
INGLES
INGOTS
INGRES
INIONS
INKERS
INKLES
INLAWS
INLAYS
INLETS
INNESS
INPUTS
INSETS
INTENS
INTROS
INUITS
INURES
IONICS
IOWANS
IRANIS
IRAQIS
IRENES
IRIDES
IRISES
ISLETS
ISSUES
ISTLES
ITCHES

•IS•••
AISLES
BISCAY
BISECT
BISHOP
BISONS
BISQUE
BISSAU
BISSET
BISTRO
CISCOS
CISKEI
DISANT
DISARM
DISBAR
DISCOS
DISCUS
DISHED
DISHES
DISKED
DISMAL
DISMAY
DISMES
DISNEY
DISOWN
DISPEL
DISSED
DISTAL
DISTIL
DISUSE
EISNER
FISCAL
FISHED
FISHER
FISHES
FISTED
FISTIC
HISPID
HISSAT
HISSED
HISSER
HISSES
KISHKE
KISLEV
KISMET
KISSED
KISSER
KISSES
LISBOA
LISBON
LISLES
LISPED
LISTED
LISTEE
LISTEL
LISTEN
LISTER
LISTON
MISCHA
MISCUE
MISDID
MISERS
MISERY
MISFIT
MISHAP
MISHIT
MISLAY
MISLED
MISSAL
MISSAY
MISSED
MISSES
MISSIS
MISSUS
MISTED
MISTER
MISUSE
NISSAN
NISSEN
PISANO
PISANS
PISCES
PISGAH
PISTES
PISTIL
PISTOL
PISTON
RISERS
RISING
RISKED
RISKER
RISQUE
SISALS
SISERA
SISKEL
SISKIN
SISLER
SISLEY
SISTER
SISTRA
TISANE
TISHRI
TISSUE
VISAED
VISAGE
VISCID
VISHNU
VISINE
VISION
VISITS
VISORS
VISTAS
VISUAL
WISDOM
WISELY
WISENT
WISEST
WISETO
WISEUP
WISHED
WISHER
WISHES
WISPED
WISTER

•I•S••
AIMSAT
AIMSTO
AIRSAC
BIASED
BIASES
BIDSIN
BIDSON
BIDSUP
BIGSUR
BISSAU
BISSET
DIESEL
DIESES
DIESIS
DIGSIN
DIGSUP
DILSEY
DIMSUM
DISSED
FIASCO
FIESTA
FIRSTS
FITSIN
GIBSON
HIRSCH
HISSAT
HISSED
HISSER
HISSES
HITSIT
HITSON
HITSUP
JIGSAW
JIMSON
KINSEY
KINSKI
KIOSKS
KIRSCH
KISSED
KISSER
KISSES
KITSCH
LIESIN
LIESTO
LINSEY
MIASMA
MILSAP
MIOSIS
MISSAL
MISSAY
MISSED
MISSES
MISSIS
MISSUS
NIPSAT
NIPSEY
NISSAN
NISSEN
PIGSTY
PINSON
PITSAW
RIDSOF
RIGSUP
RIMSKY
RINSED
RINSES
RIPSAW
RIPSUP
SIESTA
SITSBY
SITSIN
SITSON
SITSUP
TIESIN
TIESTO
TIESUP
TILSIT
TINSEL
TIPSIN

TISSUE
VIZSLA
WIESEL
WILSON
WIMSEY
WINSOR
ZIPSUP

•I••S•

DIGEST
DIREST
DISUSE
DIVEST
FILOSE
FINEST
FINISH
KIBOSH
LIAISE
LIPASE
MILOSZ
MIMOSA
MISUSE
NICEST
PILOSE
RIBOSE
RIFEST
RIMOSE
RIPEST
SINISE
SIWASH
VILEST
WIDEST
WIDISH
WINISH
WISEST

•I•••S

AIDERS
AILERS
AIRBUS
AISLES
BIASES
BIBLES
BICEPS
BIGHTS
BIGOTS
BIKERS
BILGES
BINGES
BIOGAS
BIOMES
BIOTAS
BIPEDS
BIPODS
BIRTHS
BISONS
BITERS
CIDERS
CIGARS
CIRCUS
CIRRUS
CISCOS
CITERS
CITIES
CITIUS
CITRUS
CIVETS
CIVICS
DICERS
DICOTS
DICTUS
DIDIES
DIESES
DIESIS
DIGITS
DINARS
DINERS
DINGUS
DIODES
DIRGES
DISCOS
DISCUS
DISHES
DISMES
DITTOS
DITZES
DIVANS
DIVERS
DIVOTS
DIXITS
DIYERS
DIZENS
EIDERS
EIGHTS
FIBERS
FIBRES
FICHES
FICHUS
FIELDS
FIENDS
FIFERS
FIFTHS
FIGHTS
FILERS
FILETS
FILIUS
FILLES
FINALS
FIORDS
FIRERS
FIRSTS
FIRTHS
FISHES
FIVERS
FIVEWS
FIXERS
FIXUPS
FIZZES
GIANTS
GIBERS
GIGOTS
GIGUES
GIJOES
GILLIS
GIMELS
GIMMES
GIRTHS
GIVENS
GIVERS
GIZMOS
HIATUS
HIDERS
HIKERS
HINDUS
HINGES
HINGIS
HIPPOS
HIRERS
HISSES
JIHADS
JINXES
JIVERS
KIANGS
KILIMS
KIOSKS
KIOWAS
KISSES
KITERS
LIANAS
LIANES
LIANGS
LIBELS
LIBRIS
LIEBYS
LIEGES
LIEUTS
LIFERS
LIGERS
LIGHTS
LIKENS
LILACS
LILIES
LIMBOS
LIMBUS
LIMENS
LIMEYS
LIMITS
LINENS
LINERS
LIPIDS
LISLES
LITERS
LITHOS
LITMUS
LITRES
LIVENS
LIVERS
LIVRES
MICROS
MIDGES
MILERS
MILPAS
MIMEOS
MIMERS
MIMICS
MINCES
MINERS
MINIMS
MINKES
MINORS
MINXES
MIOSIS
MISERS
MISSES
MISSIS
MISSUS
MITERS
MITRES
MIWOKS
MIXERS
MIXUPS
MIZENS
NICHES
NIECES
NIGHTS
NIMBUS
NINERS
NINJAS
NINTHS
NIPUPS
NITERS
NITRES
NIXIES
OILERS
PIANOS
PICOTS
PICULS
PIECES
PIETAS
PIKERS
PILAFS
PILEUS
PILOTS
PINDUS
PINNAS
PINONS
PINOTS
PINTOS
PINUPS
PIPALS
PIPERS
PIPITS
PIQUES
PISANS
PISCES
PISTES
PITIES
PITONS
PIVOTS
PIXELS
PIXIES
PIZZAS
RIATAS
RICERS
RICHES
RIDERS
RIDGES
RIFLES
RIGHTS
RIGORS
RILLES
RINSES
RIOJAS
RIPENS
RISERS
RIVALS
RIVERS
RIVETS
RIYALS
SIBYLS
SIDERS
SIDLES
SIEGES
SIEVES
SIGHTS
SIGILS
SIGMAS
SILVAS
SINEWS
SINGES
SIRENS
SIRIUS
SISALS
SITARS
SITINS
SITUPS
SIXERS
SIXTHS
SIXTUS
SIZERS
TIARAS
TIBIAS
TICALS
TIDIES
TIEINS
TIEUPS
TIGERS
TIGHTS
TIGRIS
TILAKS
TILDES
TILERS
TILLIS
TIMERS
TINCTS
TINGES
TIPINS
TIPUPS
TITANS
TITERS
TITHES
TITLES
TITRES
UIGURS
UINTAS
VIANDS
VICARS
VICTIS
VIDEOS
VIGILS
VIGORS
VILLAS
VILLUS
VINCES
VINOUS
VINYLS
VIOLAS
VIPERS
VIREOS
VIRTUS
VISITS
VISORS
VISTAS
VITALS
VIXENS
WIDENS
WIDOWS
WIDTHS
WIELDS
WIGHTS
WILKES
WILLIS
WINCES
WINZES
WIPERS
WIRERS
WISHES
WITHES
WIZENS
YIELDS
ZIBETS

••IS••

ALISON
ARISEN
ARISES
ARISTA
ARISTO
AVISOS
CHISEL
CHISOX
CRISCO
CRISES
CRISIS
CRISPS
CRISPY
CRISTO
CUISSE
DAISES
DEISTS
EDISON
ELISHA
ELISSA
ENISLE
EXISTS
FAISAL
FEISTY
FOISTS
FRISCO
FRISEE
FRISES
FRISKS
FRISKY
GEISEL
GEISHA
GRISLY
GRISON
GRISTS
GUISES
HEISTS
HOISTS
IBISES
IRISES
IRISIN
JOISTS
KAISER
MAISIE
NEISSE
NOISED
NOISES
OBISPO
ODISTS
ORISON
ORISSA
OVISAC
PAISAS
PLISSE
POISED
POISES
POISON
PRISMS
PRISON
PRISSY
PUISNE
RAISED
RAISER
RAISES
RAISIN
SEISMO
SEISMS
SUISSE
THISBE
TRISHA
TRISTE
TWISTS
TWISTY
UNISEX
UNISON
UNISYS
VAISYA
WAISTS
WHISKS
WHISKY
WRISTS

••I•S•

AHIMSA
AMIDST
ARIOSE
ARIOSO
CUISSE
DRIEST
ELISSA
EOIPSO
FLIMSY
GAINST
GRILSE
ICIEST
NEISSE
ORISSA
OTIOSE
PLISSE
PRIEST
PRISSY
SHIEST
SHIISM
SLIEST
SLIMSY
SUISSE
THIRST
WHILST
WHIMSY
WRIEST

••I••S

ABIDES
ACINUS
ADIDAS
ADIEUS
AKITAS
ALIBIS
ALIENS
ALIGNS
ALINES
AMICES
AMICUS
AMIDES
AMIENS
AMIGAS
AMIGOS
AMINES
AMINUS
ANIMAS
ANIMES
ANIMUS
ANIONS
APICES
ARISES
ASIANS
ASIDES
AVIANS
AVISOS
AXIOMS
AXIONS
AZIDES
AZINES
BAINES
BAIRNS
BAIZAS
BEIGES
BEINGS
BGIRLS
BLIMPS
BLINDS
BLINIS
BLINKS
BMINUS
BOITES
BRIANS
BRIARS
BRIBES
BRICKS
BRIDES
BRIEFS
BRIERS
BRIGGS
BRILLS
BRINES
BRINGS
BRINKS
BSIDES
BUILDS
CAICOS
CAIRNS
CEIBAS
CHIAUS
CHICKS
CHIDES
CHIEFS
CHILDS
CHILLS
CHIMES
CHIMPS
CHINES
CHINKS
CHINOS
CHIRPS
CHIRRS
CHIVES
CLICKS
CLIFFS
CLIMBS
CLIMES
CLINES
CLINGS
CLINKS
CMINUS
CNIDUS
COIGNS
CRICKS
CRIERS
CRIMES
CRIMPS
CRIPES
CRISES
CRISIS
CRISPS
DAISES
DEICES
DEIGNS
DEIMOS
DEISTS
DMINUS
DOINGS
DRIERS
DRIFTS
DRILLS
DRINGS
DRINKS
DRIVES
EDICTS
EDILES
EJIDOS
ELIDES
ELITES
EPIRUS
ERINYS
EVICTS
EXILES
EXISTS
FAINTS
FAITHS
FEIGNS
FEINTS
FLICKS
FLIERS
FLINGS
FLINTS
FLIRTS
FOISTS
FRIARS
FRIERS
FRILLS
FRISES
FRISKS
FRITOS
GLIDES
GLINTS
GOINGS
GRIEFS
GRIFTS
GRILLS
GRIMES
GRINDS
GRIOTS
GRIPES
GRISTS
GUIDES
GUILDS
GUILES
GUIROS
GUISES
HAIDAS
HAIKUS
HAINES
HEISTS
HOISTS
IBISES
ICINGS
IDIOMS
IDIOTS
INIONS
IRIDES
IRISES
JOINTS
JOISTS
JUICES
KNICKS
KNIFES
KNIVES
LAIRDS
MAIDUS
MAILES
MAIZES
MOINES
MOIRES
NAIADS
NAIRAS
NEIGHS
NOISES

ODIOUS
ODISTS
ODIUMS
OGIVES
OLIVES
ONIONS
OPINES
ORIBIS
ORIELS
ORINGS
OSIERS
OSIRIS
OTITIS
OXIDES
PAINTS
PAISAS
PHIALS
PHILOS
PLIERS
PLINKS
POILUS
POINTS
POISES
PRICES
PRICKS
PRIDES
PRIERS
PRIMES
PRIMOS
PRIMPS
PRIMUS
PRINKS
PRINTS
PRIONS
PRIORS
PRISMS
PRIZES
QUIETS
QUILLS
QUILTS
QUINTS
QUIPUS
QUIRES
QUIRKS
QUIRTS
RAINES
RAISES
REIGNS
REINAS
REINKS
RHINOS
SAIGAS
SAINTS
SCIFIS
SCIONS
SEINES
SEISMS
SEIZES
SHIFTS
SHILLS
SHINES
SHIRES
SHIRKS
SHIRRS
SHIRTS
SKIERS
SKIFFS
SKILLS
SKIMPS
SKINKS
SKIRLS
SKIROS
SKIRRS
SKIRTS
SKIVES
SLICES
SLICKS
SLIDES
SLIMES
SLINGS
SLINKS
SMILES
SMIRKS
SMITES
SMITHS
SNICKS
SNIFFS
SNIPES
SPICAS
SPICES
SPIELS
SPIERS
SPIFFS
SPIKES
SPILES
SPILLS
SPINES
SPINKS
SPIRES
SPIROS
SPITES
STICKS
STIFFS
STILES
STILLS
STILTS
STINGS
STINKS
STINTS
STIPES
STIRKS
SUITES
SWIFTS
SWILLS
SWINGS
SWIPES
SWIRLS
TAIGAS
TAINOS
TAINTS
TBILLS
TBIRDS
THIGHS
THILLS
THINGS
THINKS
THIRDS
TOILES
TRIADS
TRIALS
TRIBES
TRICES
TRICKS
TRIERS
TRIKES
TRILLS
TRINES
TRIPOS
TWILLS
TWINES
TWIRLS
TWISTS
UMIAKS
UNIATS
UNIONS
UNISYS
UNITAS
UNITES
URIALS
VOICES
VOILES
VSIGNS
VSIXES
WAISTS
WAIVES
WEIGHS
WHIFFS
WHILES
WHINES
WHIRLS
WHIRRS
WHISKS
WHITES
WRINGS
WRISTS
WRITES
XFILES
YOICKS
ZAIRES

•••IS•

ADVISE
AGEISM
AGEIST
AGUISH
AORIST
ARLISS
ARTIST
ASPISH
ASSISI
ASSIST
ATRISK
BANISH
BARISH
BETISE
BLAISE
BLUISH
BOYISH
BRAISE
BRUISE
CAMISE
CERISE
CHAISE
CHRISM
COYISH
CRUISE
CUBISM
CUBIST
DANISH
DELIST
DEMISE
DENISE
DESIST
DEVISE
DOVISH
DUDISH
EGOISM
EGOIST
ELFISH
ELOISE
ELVISH
ENLIST
EXCISE
FAMISH
FETISH
FINISH
FRAISE
GARISH
GNEISS
GOFISH
HOLISM
HOLIST
IMPISH
INCISE
INSIST
IODISE
IONISE
JADISH
JEWISH
JURIST
JUTISH
KLEIST
KUMISS
KWEISI
LATISH
LAVISH
LEGIST
LIAISE
LOUISA
LOUISE
LOWISH
LUTIST
LYRIST
MAOISM
MAOIST
MARISA
MARISH
MARIST
MODISH
MONISM
MONIST
MOPISH
MULISH
NEWISH
NOWISE
NUDIST
OAFISH
OBOIST
OFFISH
OGRISH
OLDISH
OWLISH
PALISH
PARISH
PERISH
POLISH
PRAISE
PUNISH
PURISM
PURIST
RADISH
RAKISH
RAVISH
RAWISH
RELISH
RELIST
REMISE
REMISS
RESIST
REVISE
SALISH
SCHISM
SCHIST
SEXIST
SHIISM
SINISE
SQUISH
SUFISM
TANIST
TAOISM
TAOIST
THEISM
THEIST
TONISH
TRUISM
TUBIST
TYPIST
UNWISE
UNWISH
UPPISH
UPRISE
VALISE
VANISH
VERISM
WIDISH
WINISH
YOGISM

•••I•S

ADLIBS
ADMITS
AERIES
AFRITS
AGGIES
ALLIES
ALOINS
ALTIUS
AMBITS
ANTICS
ANVILS
APHIDS
ARLISS
ARMIES
AROIDS
ASDICS
ASPICS
ATKINS
ATTICS
AUDIOS
AUDITS
AUXINS
AVAILS
AVOIDS
AWAITS
BABIES
BASICS
BASINS
BATIKS
BEDIMS
BEFITS
BEGINS
BELIES
BEVIES
BODIES
BOGIES
BOVIDS
BRAIDS
BRAILS
BRAINS
BROILS
BRUINS
BRUITS
BURIES
BURINS
BUSIES
CABINS
CANIDS
CAPIAS
CARIBS
CARIES
CAVILS
CHAINS
CHAIRS
CHOIRS
CITIES
CITIUS
CIVICS
CLAIMS
COBIAS
COLIES
COMICS
CONICS
CONIES
COPIES
COSIES
COZIES
CUBICS
CUBITS
CUPIDS
CURIOS
CUTIES
CUTINS
CYNICS
DARIUS
DAVIES
DAVITS
DEBITS
DEFIES
DELIUS
DEMIES
DEMITS
DENIES
DENIMS
DEVILS
DIDIES
DIGITS
DIXITS
DOGIES
DORIES
DRAILS
DRAINS
DROIDS
DROITS
DRUIDS
DUTIES
EDDIES
EMAILS
ENNIUS
ENVIES
EOSINS
EQUIPS
ESPIES
ETHICS
EYRIES
FACIAS
FACIES
FAKIRS
FERIAS
FILIUS
FLAILS
FLAIRS
FLUIDS
FLYINS
FOGIES
FOLIOS
FRUITS
FURIES
FUSILS
GABIES
GAMINS
GENIES
GENIUS
GHAINS
GLAIRS
GNEISS
GOBIES
GRAILS
GRAINS
GROINS
GSUITS
HABITS
HAKIMS
HELIOS
INDIES
INUITS
IONICS
JULIUS
JURIES
KAFIRS
KEFIRS
KILIMS
KRAITS
KUMISS
LADIES
LAMIAS
LAPINS
LATINS
LEVIES
LILIES
LIMITS
LIPIDS
LOOIES
LORIES
LUCIUS
LYRICS
LYSINS
MANIAS
MARIUS
MATINS
MAXIMS
MEDIAS
MEDICS
MERITS
MIMICS
MINIMS
MOBIUS
MONIES
MOTIFS
MOVIES
MUCINS
NADIRS
NAVIES
NEVINS
NIXIES
NOHITS
NORIAS
OLDIES
OPTICS
ORBITS
ORGIES
OSMICS
OVOIDS
OXLIPS
PAMIRS
PANICS
PATIOS
PEKINS
PERILS
PEWITS
PIPITS
PITIES
PIXIES
PLAIDS
PLAINS
PLAITS
POGIES
PONIES
POSIES
POSITS
PUPILS
PYXIES
QUAILS
QUOINS
QUOITS
RABIES
RADIOS
RADIUS
RAMIES
RANIDS
RAPIDS
RATIOS
REAIMS
REAIRS
REBIDS
REFITS
REGIUS
RELICS
RELIES
REMISS
REMITS
REOILS
REPINS
RESINS
RETIES
REWINS
ROBINS
ROSINS
RUBIES
RUNINS
SABINS
SAHIBS
SATINS
SCRIMS
SCRIPS
SEPIAS
SERIES
SERIFS
SERINS
SETINS
SHEIKS
SIGILS
SIRIUS
SITINS
SKEINS
SNAILS
SOLIDS
SONICS
SPLITS
SPOILS
SPRIGS
SPRITS
SQUIBS
SQUIDS
STAINS
STAIRS
STEINS
STOICS
STRIPS
SWAINS
TAKINS
TAMILS
TAPINS
TAPIRS
TAXIES
THEIRS
THRIPS
TIBIAS
TIDIES
TIEINS
TIPINS
TOBIAS
TOBIES
TOEINS
TONICS
TOPICS
TORIES
TOXICS
TOXINS
TRAILS
TRAINS
TRAITS
TULIPS
TUNICS
UGLIES
UNDIES
UNFITS
UNPINS
UNRIGS
UNTIES
UNZIPS
URSIDS
VARIES
VCHIPS
VIGILS
VISITS
YALIES
ZAMIAS
ZANIES
ZAYINS
ZOOIDS
ZORILS

••••IS

ABATIS
ADONIS
ALANIS
ALEXIS
ALIBIS
AMADIS
AMATIS
ANUBIS
AODAIS
ARAMIS
ARTOIS
BARRIS
BAUCIS
BEAVIS
BLINIS
BREVIS
CADDIS

CALAIS
CAPRIS
CASSIS
CLEVIS
CLORIS
CLOVIS
COATIS
CORGIS
CRISIS
CULLIS
CURTIS
CUSTIS
DASHIS
DEBRIS
DENNIS
DERMIS
DERRIS
DHOTIS
DIESIS
DUBOIS
ECESIS
ELEMIS
ENOKIS
ENOSIS
ENVOIS
FERRIS
GALOIS
GHAZIS
GILLIS
GLACIS
GLYNIS
GNOSIS
GRATIS
HADJIS
HAGGIS
HAJJIS
HARRIS
HINGIS
HOURIS
HUBRIS
INDRIS
IRANIS
IRAQIS
KAURIS
KEMPIS
KERMIS
KHAKIS
KUKRIS
LANAIS
LANDIS
LIBRIS
MAHDIS
MAJLIS
MANTIS
MAORIS
MAQUIS
MASAIS
MATHIS
MENTIS
MIOSIS
MISSIS
MORRIS
MUFTIS
MYOSIS
NEREIS
NOESIS
NORRIS
OKAPIS
OMANIS
ORIBIS
OSIRIS
OTITIS
OXALIS
PARNIS
PARRIS
PARVIS
PASTIS
PATOIS
PAUCIS
PELVIS
PENNIS
PHOCIS
PRAXIS
PRECIS
RABBIS
RACHIS
SARDIS
SAUDIS
SCIFIS
SERAIS
SHOJIS
SPAHIS
STASIS
SUNNIS
SWAMIS
SWAZIS
TENNIS
TETRIS
THATIS
THESIS
THETIS
TIGRIS
TILLIS
TMESIS
TRAVIS
TSURIS
UNGUIS
VALOIS
VERBIS
VICTIS
WALLIS
WILLIS
YAQUIS
ZEUXIS

IT••••

ITALIA
ITALIC
ITASCA
ITCHED
ITCHES
ITHACA
ITHAKI
ITSELF
ITURBI
ITZHAK

I•T•••

IATRIC
IDTAGS
INTACT
INTAKE
INTEND
INTENS
INTENT
INTERJ
INTERN
INTIMA
INTIME
INTINE
INTONE
INTOTO
INTOWN
INTROS
INTUIT
INTUNE
INTURN
IQTEST
IRTYSH
ISTHMI
ISTLES
ISTRIA

I••T••

ICHTHY
IGETIT
IGOTIT
INITIO
INSTAL
INSTAR
INSTEP
INSTIL
IRATER
ISHTAR

I•••T•

IDEATE
IDIOTS
IGNATZ
IGNITE
IMPUTE
INCITE
INDITE
INGOTS
INLETS
INMATE
INNATE
INPUTS
INSETS
INSITU
INTOTO
INUITS
INVITE
INWITH
IODATE
IOLITE
IOMOTH
ISLETS

I••••T

ICEOUT
ICIEST
IDLEST
IGETIT
IGOTIT
ILLEST
ILLMET
IMARET
IMPACT
IMPART
IMPORT
IMPOST
INAPET
INARUT
INCEPT
INCULT
INDEBT
INDENT
INDICT
INDUCT
INFACT
INFANT
INFECT
INFEST
INGEST
INJECT
INJEST
INKJET
INMOST
INPART
INPORT
INSECT
INSERT
INSIST
INSULT
INTACT
INTENT
INTUIT
INVENT
INVERT
INVEST
IQTEST
IROBOT
IRRUPT
ISEULT

•IT•••

BITERS
BITING
BITMAP
BITOFF
BITOLA
BITTED
BITTEN
BITTER
CITATO
CITERS
CITIES
CITIFY
CITING
CITIUS
CITRIC
CITRON
CITRUS
DITHER
DITTOS
DITZES
EITHER
FITFUL
FITSIN
FITTED
FITTER
GITANO
HITECH
HITHER
HITMAN
HITMEN
HITOUT
HITSIT
HITSON
HITSUP
HITTER
JITNEY
JITTER
KITBAG
KITERS
KITFOX
KITING
KITKAT
KITSCH
KITTEN
LITANY
LITCHI
LITERS
LITHIC
LITHOG
LITHOS
LITMUS
LITOUT
LITRES
LITTER
LITTLE
MITERS
MITRAL
MITRED
MITRES
MITTEN
NITERS
NITERY
NITRES
NITRIC
NITWIT
PITCHY
PITHED
PITIED
PITIER
PITIES
PITMAN
PITMEN
PITONS
PITSAW
PITTED
PITTER
RITARD
RITTER
RITUAL
SITARS
SITCOM
SITING
SITINS
SITOUT
SITSBY
SITSIN
SITSON
SITSUP
SITTER
SITUPS
TITANS
TITBIT
TITERS
TITFER
TITHED
TITHER
TITHES
TITIAN
TITLED
TITLES
TITRED
TITRES
TITTER
TITTLE
TITTUP
VITALE
VITALS
VITRIC
WITCHY
WITHAL
WITHED
WITHER
WITHES
WITHIN
WITHIT
WITTED
ZITHER

•I•T••

BIGTEN
BIGTOE
BIGTOP
BIOTAS
BIOTIC
BIOTIN
BIRTHS
BISTRO
BITTED
BITTEN
BITTER
DIATOM
DICTUM
DICTUS
DIETED
DIETER
DIKTAT
DINTED
DISTAL
DISTIL
DITTOS
FIFTHS
FILTER
FILTHY
FIRTHS
FISTED
FISTIC
FITTED
FITTER
GIFTED
GIOTTO
GIRTED
GIRTHS
HIATAL
HIATUS
HILTON
HINTAT
HINTED
HINTER
HINTON
HITTER
JILTED
JITTER
KILTED
KILTER
KILTIE
KIRTLE
KITTEN
LICTOR
LIFTED
LIFTER
LIFTUP
LILTED
LINTEL
LINTER
LIOTTA
LIPTON
LISTED
LISTEE
LISTEL
LISTEN
LISTER
LISTON
LITTER
LITTLE
MILTIE
MILTON
MINTED
MINTER
MISTED
MISTER
MITTEN
MIXTEC
NINTHS
PIETAS
PIETER
PIETIN
PIETRO
PINTER
PINTLE
PINTOS
PISTES
PISTIL
PISTOL
PISTON
PITTED
PITTER
QINTAR
RIATAS
RIFTED
RIOTED
RIOTER
RITTER
SIFTED
SIFTER
SILTED
SINTAX
SINTER
SISTER
SISTRA
SITTER
SIXTHS
SIXTUS
TICTAC
TILTED
TILTER
TINTED
TINTER
TIPTOE
TIPTOP
TITTER
TITTLE
TITTUP
UINTAS
VICTIM
VICTIS
VICTOR
VINTON
VIRTUE
VIRTUS
VISTAS
WIDTHS
WILTED
WILTON
WINTER
WINTRY
WISTER
WITTED

•I••T•

AIMSTO
BIGHTS
BIGOTS
BINATE
CITATO
CIVETS
DICOTS
DIGITS
DILATE
DILUTE
DIMITY
DIVOTS
DIXITS
EIGHTH
EIGHTS
EIGHTY
FICHTE
FIESTA
FIGHTS
FILETS
FINITE
FINITO
FIRSTS
FIXATE
FIXITY
GIANTS
GIGOTS
GIOTTO
GIVETO
HINCTY
KIBITZ
LIESTO
LIEUTS
LIGATE
LIGHTS
LILITH
LIMITS
LIOTTA
MIGHTY
MIKITA
MINUTE
NICETY
NIGHTS
NIGHTY
NIKITA
NIMITZ
NINETY
PICOTS
PIGSTY
PILATE
PILOTI
PILOTS
PINATA
PINITE
PINOTS
PIPITS
PIRATE
PIVOTS
RIALTO
RIGHTO
RIGHTS
RIGHTY
RIVETS
SIESTA
SIGHTS
SINGTO
TIEDTO
TIESTO
TIGHTS
TINCTS
VISITS
WIGHTS
WISETO
ZIBETS
ZIZITH

•I•••T

AIGRET
AIMSAT
AIROUT
BILLET
BIRGIT
BISECT
BISSET
DIDACT
DIEOUT
DIGEST
DIGLOT
DIGOUT
DIKTAT
DIMOUT
DIMWIT
DIRECT
DIREST
DISANT
DIVERT
DIVEST
FIDGET
FILLET
FINEST
GIBBET
GIBLET
GIDGET
GIMLET
HIDOUT
HINTAT
HISSAT
HITOUT
HITSIT
KISMET
KITKAT
LIMPET
LINNET
LIONET
LITOUT
MIDGET
MILLET
MINUET
MINUIT
MISFIT
MISHIT
NICEST
NIPSAT
NITWIT
PIAGET
PICKAT
PICKET
PIGLET
PIGNUT
PIGOUT
PINXIT
PIOLET
PIQUET
QIVIUT
RIDENT
RIFEST
RILLET
RIPEST
RIPOUT
SIGNET
SILENT
SIPPET
SITOUT
TICKET

TIDBIT
TILSIT
TINHAT
TINPOT
TIPPET
TITBIT
VILEST
VINCIT
VIOLET
VIVANT
WICKET
WIDEST
WIDGET
WIGLET
WIGOUT
WILLET
WINGIT
WINKAT
WINOUT
WISENT
WISEST
WITHIT

••IT••

AKITAS
ALITER
ANITRA
BAITED
BLITHE
BOITES
BRITON
CHITIN
CHITON
CRITIC
DMITRI
EDITED
EDITIO
EDITOR
ELITES
EXITED
FAITHS
FLITCH
FRITOS
GAITED
GAITER
GLITCH
GLITZY
GRITTY
GUITAR
GUITRY
INITIO
KEITEL
LOITER
MAITAI
MAITRE
OBITER
OTITIC
OTITIS
QUITIT
SKITCH
SKITOW
SLITHY
SLITTY
SMITES
SMITHS
SMITHY
SNITCH
SPITED
SPITES
STITCH
STITHY
SUITED
SUITES
SUITOR
SUITUP
SWITCH
TRITER
TRITON
TWITCH
TWITTY
UNITAL
UNITAS
UNITED
UNITER
UNITES
WAITED
WAITER
WAITON
WAITUP
WHITEN
WHITER
WHITES
WHITTY
WRITER
WRITES
WRITHE

••I•T•

ALIOTO
ARISTA
ARISTO
AVIATE
BLINTZ
CHINTZ
CRISTO
DAINTY
DEISTS
DRIFTS
DRIFTY
EDICTS
EVICTS
EXISTS
FAINTS
FEINTS
FEISTY
FLINTS
FLINTY
FLIRTS
FLIRTY
FOISTS
GAIETY
GLINTS
GOINTO
GRIFTS
GRIOTS
GRISTS
GRITTY
GUILTY
HEISTS
HOISTS
IDIOTS
JOINTS
JOISTS
LAIDTO
MOIETY
ODISTS
OPIATE
PAINTS
PAINTY
PAIUTE
PLINTH
POINTE
POINTS
POINTY
PRINTS
QUIETS
QUILTS
QUINTS
QUIRTS
SAINTE
SAINTS
SHIFTS
SHIFTY
SHIITE
SHINTO
SHIRTS
SHIRTY
SKIRTS
SLITTY
SPILTH
SPINTO
STILTS
STINTS
SWIFTS
TAINTS
THIRTY
TRISTE
TWISTS
TWISTY
TWITTY
UBIETY
UNIATE
UNIATS
WAISTS
WHITTY
WRISTS

••I••T

ALIGHT
AMIDST
ARIGHT
BEIRUT
BLIGHT
BRIGHT
CLIENT
DRIEST
DWIGHT
ELICIT
FLIGHT
FRIGHT
GAINST
GRIVET
HAIGHT
HEIGHT
ICIEST
KNIGHT
ORIENT
PLIANT
PLIGHT
POIROT
PRIEST
PRIPET
PRIVET
QUITIT
RAILAT
SHIEST
SKIPIT
SLIEST
SLIGHT
SPIGOT
SPINET
SPIRIT
SWIVET
THIRST
TOILET
TRICOT
TRIJET
TRIVET
TWILIT
VEIGHT
VOIGHT
WEIGHT
WHILST
WRIEST
WRIGHT

•••IT•

ACUITY
ADMITS
AFRITS
AMBITS
APLITE
ASEITY
AUDITS
AWAITS
BARITE
BEFITS
BENITO
BONITO
BRUITS
CAPITA
CAVITY
COGITO
COMITY
CUBITS
DAMITA
DAVITS
DEBITS
DEMITS
DEVITO
DEWITT
DIGITS
DIMITY
DIXITS
DONITZ
DROITS
ENMITY
ENTITY
EOLITH
EQUITY
EXCITE
FAJITA
FERITY
FINITE
FINITO
FIXITY
FRUITS
FRUITY
GOWITH
GSUITS
GUNITE
HABITS
HALITE
HAMITE
IGNITE
INCITE
INDITE
INSITU
INUITS
INVITE
INWITH
IOLITE
JUDITH
KIBITZ
KRAITS
LAXITY
LENITY
LEVITE
LEVITY
LILITH
LIMITS
LOLITA
LUCITE
MERITS
MIKITA
MORITA
MORITZ
NIKITA
NIMITZ
NOHITS
NUDITY
ODDITY
ONSITE
OOLITE
OOLITH
OPHITE
ORBITS
ORNITH
PARITY
PEPITA
PETITE
PEWITS
PINITE
PIPITS
PLAITS
POLITE
POLITY
POSITS
PURITY
PYRITE
QUOITS
RARITY
RATITE
RECITE
REFITS
REMITS
ROSITA
SAMITE
SANITY
SEMITE
SENITI
SHIITE
SPLITS
SPRITE
SPRITS
SPRITZ
SUBITO
TAHITI
TONITE
TRAITS
UNFITS
UPPITY
VANITY
VENITE
VERITE
VERITY
VISITS
WAPITI
WRAITH
ZENITH
ZIZITH

•••I•T

ADRIFT
AGEIST
AGLINT
ALHIRT
ANOINT
AORIST
ARTIST
ASSIST
CUBIST
DELICT
DELIST
DEPICT
DESIST
DEWITT
EGOIST
ELLIOT
ENGIRT
ENLIST
FORINT
HERIOT
HOLIST
INDICT
INSIST
JOLIET
JOLIOT
JULIET
JURIST
KLEIST
LARIAT
LEGIST
LUTIST
LYRIST
MAOIST
MARIST
MONIST
NUDIST
OBOIST
PLAINT
PURIST
QIVIUT
QUAINT
RELICT
RELIST
RESIST
SCHIST
SCRIPT
SEXIST
SHRIFT
SOVIET
SPLINT
SPOILT
SPRINT
SQUINT
SQUIRT
STRICT
TANIST
TAOIST
THEIST
THRIFT
TSHIRT
TUBIST
TYPIST
UNGIRT
UPLIFT

••••IT

ACQUIT
ADROIT
ALBEIT
ANNUIT
ARMPIT
ATTRIT
AUFAIT
AULAIT
BAGSIT
BANDIT
BEATIT
BELOIT
BENOIT
BIRGIT
BLEWIT
BLOWIT
CANLIT
COEDIT
COMFIT
COMMIT
COOLIT
CREDIT
DACOIT
DARNIT
DAYLIT
DECEIT
DIMWIT
DOGSIT
DORRIT
DROPIT
ELEGIT
ELICIT
ESPRIT
GAMBIT
GASLIT
GETSIT
GODWIT
GOTOIT
HENBIT
HERMIT
HITSIT
HOBBIT
HOLDIT
HOOFIT
IGETIT
IGOTIT
INTUIT
JESUIT
KERMIT
KUWAIT
LOSEIT
LOSTIT
MADEIT
MAKEIT
MINUIT
MISFIT
MISHIT
NITWIT
NOEXIT
OUTFIT
OUTHIT
OUTWIT
PANDIT
PERMIT
PETTIT
PINXIT
POSTIT
PROFIT
PROSIT
PULPIT
PUNDIT
QUITIT
RABBIT
REEDIT
SAWFIT
SEEFIT
SENNIT
SKIPIT
SOBEIT
SOFFIT
SPIRIT
STOPIT
STRAIT
SUBMIT
SUMMIT
SUNLIT
TARPIT
TIDBIT
TILSIT
TITBIT
TOMTIT
TOOKIT
TURBIT
TWILIT
TWOBIT
UNKNIT
VINCIT
WESKIT
WINGIT
WITHIT

I•U•••

IGUACU
IGUANA
INUITS
INURED
INURES
ITURBI

I••U••

ILLUME
ILLUSE
IMBUED
IMBUES
IMMUNE
IMMUNO
IMMURE
IMPUGN
IMPURE
IMPUTE
INBULK
INCULT
INCURS
INCUSE
INDUCE
INDUCT
INFULL
INFUSE
INJURE
INJURY
INLUCK
INOUYE
INPUTS
INRUSH
INSULT
INSURE
INTUIT
INTUNE
INTURN
IRRUPT
ISEULT
ISSUED
ISSUER
ISSUES

I•••U•

ICARUS
ICEDUP
ICEOUT
ICESUP
IMBRUE
INARUT
INDIUM
INFLUX
INHAUL
INPOUR
IONIUM
IREFUL

I••••U

IGUACU
INSITU

•IU•••

CIUDAD

•I•U••

DILUTE
DISUSE
FIBULA
FIGURE
FIXUPS
GIGUES
KIKUYU
LIEUTS
LIGULA
LIGURE
LIQUID
LIQUOR
MIFUNE
MIGUEL
MINUET
MINUIT
MINUTE
MISUSE
MIXUPS
NIPUPS
PICULS
PINUPS
PIQUED
PIQUES
PIQUET
RITUAL
SIGURD
SIOUAN
SITUPS
TIEUPS
TIPUPS
UIGURS
VICUNA
VISUAL

•I••U•

AIDFUL
AIMFUL
AIRBUS
AIRGUN
AIROUT
BIDSUP
BIGGUN
BIGSUR

BIJOUX
BINDUP
BISQUE
CILIUM
CINQUE
CIRCUM
CIRCUS
CIRQUE
CIRRUS
CITIUS
CITRUS
DIALUP
DICTUM
DICTUS
DIEOUT
DIGOUT
DIGSUP
DIMOUT
DIMSUM
DINGUS
DISCUS
FICHUS
FILIUS
FILLUP
FIREUP
FIRMUP
FITFUL
GILGUY
GIVEUP
HIATUS
HICCUP
HIDOUT
HIGHUP
HIKEUP
HINDUS
HITOUT
HITSUP
KICKUP
KIPPUR
LIFTUP
LIMBUS
LINEUP
LINGUA
LINKUP
LITMUS
LITOUT
MINIUM
MISCUE
MISSUS
NIMBUS
NIPPUR
PICKUP
PIGNUT
PIGOUT
PILEUM
PILEUP
PILEUS
PINDUS
PIPEUP
QIVIUT
RIGOUR
RIGSUP
RILEUP
RINGUP
RIPOUT
RIPSUP
RISQUE
SIDDUR
SIGNUP
SINFUL
SIRIUS
SITOUT
SITSUP
SIXGUN
SIXTUS
SIZEUP
TIDYUP
TIEDUP
TIESUP
TISSUE
TITTUP
VIGOUR
VILLUS
VINOUS
VIRTUE
VIRTUS
WIGOUT
WILBUR
WILFUL
WINDUP
WINOUT
WIPEUP
WISEUP
ZIPSUP

•I•••U
BISSAU
KIKUYU
MILIEU
NIIHAU
PICCHU
VISHNU

••IU••
ODIUMS
PAIUTE
TRIUNE

••I•U•
ACINUS
ADIEUS
ADIEUX
AMICUS
AMINUS
ANIMUS
BEIRUT
BMINUS
CAIQUE
CHIAUS
CHINUP
CLIQUE
CLIQUY
CMINUS
CNIDUS
COILUP
CUIQUE
DMINUS
EPIRUS
FAIRUP
FAIYUM
FLIPUP
HAIKUS
JAIPUR
JOINUP
KAILUA
LAIDUP
MAIDUS
ODIOUS
PAIDUP
PAIRUP
POILUS
PRIMUM
PRIMUS
QUIPUS
RAIPUR
SKIRUN
SLIPUP
STIRUP
SUITUP
TRIPUP
UBIQUE
UNIQUE
WAITUP
WHIPUP

••I••U
NIIHAU
PAILOU

•••IU•
ACTIUM
ALLIUM
ALTIUS
ATRIUM
BARIUM
CERIUM
CESIUM
CILIUM
CITIUS
CONIUM
CORIUM
CURIUM
DARIUS
DELIUS
ENNIUS
ERBIUM
FILIUS
FOLIUM
GENIUS
HELIUM
INDIUM
IONIUM
JULIUS
LATIUM
LUCIUS
MARIUS
MEDIUM
MINIUM
MOBIUS
OMNIUM
OSMIUM
OSTIUM
PODIUM
QIVIUT
RADIUM
RADIUS
REGIUS
SIRIUS
SODIUM
TEDIUM
VALIUM

•••I•U
DESILU
INSITU
JABIRU
MALIBU
MARILU
MILIEU

I•V•••
INVADE
INVAIN
INVENT
INVERT
INVEST
INVITE
INVIVO
INVOKE
IRVINE
IRVING

I•••V•
INLOVE
INVIVO

I••••V
IMPROV

•IV•••
CIVETS
CIVICS
DIVANS
DIVEIN
DIVERS
DIVERT
DIVEST
DIVIDE
DIVINE
DIVING
DIVINO
DIVOTS
FIVEAM
FIVEPM
FIVERS
FIVEWS
GIVEIN
GIVENS
GIVERS
GIVETO
GIVEUP
GIVING
HIVAOA
HIVING
JIVERS
JIVIER
JIVING
LIVEIN
LIVELY
LIVENS
LIVEON
LIVERS
LIVERY
LIVING
LIVRES
PIVOTS
QIVIUT
RIVALS
RIVERA
RIVERS
RIVETS
RIVING
TIVOLI
VIVACE
VIVANT
VIVIAN
VIVIEN
VIVIFY

•I•V••
KIDVID
SIEVED
SIEVES
SILVAS
SILVER

•I•••V
KISLEV

••IV••
CHIVES
DRIVEL
DRIVEN
DRIVER
DRIVES
GRIVET
KNIVES
OGIVES
OLIVER
OLIVES
OLIVIA
PRIVET
QUIVER
SHIVER
SKIVED
SKIVER
SKIVES
SKIVVY
SLIVER
SNIVEL
SPIVAK
SPIVVY
STIVER
STIVIC
SWIVEL
SWIVET
TRIVET
TRIVIA
UNIVAC
WAIVED
WAIVER
WAIVES

••I•V•
GRIEVE
SKIVVY
SPIVVY
THIEVE

••I••V
ASIMOV

•••IV•
ACTIVE
ARGIVE
ARRIVE
DATIVE
DERIVE
ENDIVE
GODIVA
INVIVO
MOTIVE
NATIVE
RELIVE
REVIVE
SALIVA
SHRIVE
STRIVE
THRIVE
VOTIVE

I•W•••
INWARD
INWITH
IOWANS

I••W••
INAWAY

I•••W•
INLAWS
INTOWN

I••••W
INAROW
INFLOW

•IW•••
MIWOKS
SIWASH

•I•W••
AIRWAY
BIGWIG
DIMWIT
KIOWAS
MIDWAY
NITWIT
VIEWED
VIEWER
WIGWAG
WIGWAM
WINWIN

•I••W•
DISOWN
FIVEWS
SINEWS
SINEWY
WIDOWS

•I•••W
BILLOW
JIGSAW
LIELOW
MILDEW
MINNOW
PILLOW
PITSAW
RIPSAW
WILLOW
WINDOW
WINNOW

••IW••
OBIWAN
TAIWAN

••I•W•
OJIBWA

••I••W
SKITOW

•••I•W
ONVIEW
REVIEW

I••X••
IBEXES
ILEXES

I••••X
ICEBOX
INAFIX
INFLUX

•IX•••
DIXITS
FIXATE
FIXERS
FIXING
FIXITY
FIXUPS
MIXERS
MIXING
MIXTEC
MIXUPS
NIXIES
NIXING
PIXELS
PIXIES
SIXERS
SIXGUN
SIXING
SIXTHS
SIXTUS
VIXENS

•I•X••
DIOXIN
JINXED
JINXES
MINXES
PINXIT

•I••X•
BILOXI

•I•••X
BIJOUX
KITFOX
PICKAX
SINTAX
WILCOX
WINDEX

••IX••
BLIXEN
ELIXIR
TRIXIE
VSIXES

••I••X
ADIEUX
CHISOX
CLIMAX
SMILAX
UNISEX

•••IX•
MAXIXE

•••I•X
MENINX
SPHINX
SYRINX

••••IX
BENDIX
BOLLIX
COMMIX
INAFIX
MANNIX
MATRIX
PREFIX
PROLIX
SPADIX
SUFFIX
THESIX
TOMMIX

I•Y•••
IDYLLS

I••Y••
INSYNC
IRTYSH

I•••Y•
INLAYS
INOUYE

I••••Y
ICHTHY
IDIOCY
ILLSAY
INAWAY
INFAMY
INJURY
INPLAY

•IY•••
DIYERS
RIYADH
RIYALS

•I•Y••
LIBYAN
MINYAN
PINYIN
PINYON
SIBYLS
TIDYUP
VINYLS

•I••Y•
KIKUYU
LIEBYS
LIMEYS
RIBEYE
TIEDYE

•I•••Y
AIRDRY
AIRILY
AIRWAY
BIGAMY
BIGBOY
BINARY
BIRNEY
BISCAY
CICELY
CITIFY
DICKEY
DIDDLY
DILSEY
DIMITY
DIMPLY
DINGHY
DINKEY
DIPODY
DIRELY
DISMAY
DISNEY
EIGHTY
FILTHY
FINELY
FINERY
FINNEY
FIRMLY
FIXITY
GIGGLY
GILGUY
HICKEY
HIGHLY
HILARY
HINCTY
JIGGLY
JIMINY
JINGLY
JITNEY
KIDNEY
KIDORY
KILROY
KINDLY
KINGLY
KINSEY
LIEFLY
LIKELY
LIMPLY
LINENY
LINNEY
LINSEY
LIONLY
LITANY
LIVELY
LIVERY
MICKEY
MIDDAY
MIDWAY
MIGHTY
MILADY
MILDLY
MILLAY
MINIFY
MISERY
MISLAY
MISSAY
NIAMEY
NICELY
NICETY
NIDIFY
NIGHTY
NIMBLY
NIMINY
NINETY
NIPSEY
NITERY
OILILY
PIGSTY
PIMINY
PINERY
PIRACY
PITCHY
RICHLY
RICKEY
RIDLEY
RIFELY
RIGHTY
RIMSKY

RIPELY
RIPLEY
RIPPLY
SICILY
SICKLY
SIDNEY
SIMONY
SIMPLY
SINEWY
SINGLY
SISLEY
SITSBY
TICKLY
TIDDLY
TIDILY
TIMELY
TINGLY
TINILY
TINKLY
VIABLY
VILELY
VILIFY
VINERY
VINIFY
VIVIFY
WICOPY
WIDELY
WIFELY
WIGGLY
WILDLY
WILILY
WIMSEY
WINERY
WINTRY
WIRILY
WISELY
WITCHY

••IY••
FAIYUM

••I•Y•
DAIMYO
ERINYS
UNISYS
VAISYA

••I••Y
ACIDLY
APIARY
ARIDLY
AVIARY
AVIDLY
BAILEY
BLIMEY
BOIGNY
BRICKY
BRIERY
CHICLY
CHILLY
CHINKY
CHIRPY
CLIFFY
CLINGY
CLIQUY
CRIKEY
CRIMPY
CRISPY
DAILEY
DAINTY
DRIFTY
DRIPPY
EVILLY
FAIRLY
FEISTY
FLIMSY
FLINTY
FLIRTY
FRIARY
FRIDAY
FRILLY
FRINGY
FRISKY
FRIZZY
GAIETY
GAINLY
GLIBLY
GLITZY
GRIMLY
GRISLY
GRITTY
GUILTY
GUITRY
HAILEY
IDIOCY
LAIDBY
MAINLY
MOIETY
ONIONY
PAINTY
PHILBY
PHILLY
POINTY
PRICEY
PRIMLY
PRIORY
PRISSY
QUINCY
QUIPPY
QUIRKY
RAINEY
REILLY
SHIFTY
SHILLY
SHIMMY
SHINDY
SHINNY
SHIRTY
SKIDDY
SKIMPY
SKINNY
SKIPPY
SKIVVY
SLIMLY
SLIMSY
SLINKY
SLIPPY
SLITHY
SLITTY
SMILEY
SMIRKY
SMITHY
SNIFFY
SNIPPY
SPIFFY
SPIVVY
STICKY
STILLY
STIMPY
STINGY
STINKY
STITHY
SWINGY
SWIRLY
THINGY
THINLY
THIRTY
TRICKY
TRIGLY
TRILBY
TRIMLY
TRIPLY
TWIGGY
TWISTY
TWITTY
UBIETY
VAINLY
WEIRDY
WHIMSY
WHINEY
WHINNY
WHIPPY
WHIRLY
WHISKY
WHITTY

•••I•Y
ACUITY
AERIFY
AERILY
AIRILY
ARTILY
ASEITY
AURIFY
BASIFY
BODILY
BRAINY
BUSILY
CAGILY
CAVITY
CECILY
CITIFY
CODIFY
COMITY
COSILY
COZILY
DEWILY
DIMITY
DOZILY
EASILY
EDGILY
EERILY
EFFIGY
ENMITY
ENTITY
EQUITY
EXPIRY
FAMILY
FERITY
FIXITY
FOXILY
FRAIDY
FRUITY
GAMILY
GASIFY
GLAIRY
GORILY
GRAINY
HAZILY
HOLILY
HOMILY
HOMINY
JIMINY
JOKILY
LACILY
LAXITY
LAZILY
LENITY
LEVITY
LOGILY
MAZILY
MINIFY
MODIFY
MUTINY
NIDIFY
NIMINY
NOSILY
NOTIFY
NUDITY
ODDITY
OILILY
OOZILY
OSSIFY
PACIFY
PARITY
PIMINY
POKILY
POLICY
POLITY
PUNILY
PURIFY
PURITY
RACILY
RAMIFY
RARIFY
RARITY
RATIFY
RESINY
ROSILY
ROSINY
RUBIFY
SALIFY
SANITY
SATINY
SCHIZY
SEXILY
SICILY
STRIPY
TIDILY
TINILY
TYPIFY
UGLIFY
UGLILY
UNOILY
UNTIDY
UNWILY
UPPITY
VANITY
VERIFY
VERILY
VERITY
VILIFY
VINIFY
VIVIFY
WARILY
WAVILY
WAXILY
WILILY
WIRILY
ZANILY

IZ••••
IZABAL
IZZARD

I•Z•••
ITZHAK
IZZARD

I•••Z•
IODIZE
IONIZE

I••••Z
IGNATZ

•IZ•••
DIZENS
FIZGIG
FIZZED
FIZZES
FIZZLE
GIZMOS
LIZARD
LIZZIE
MIZENS
MIZZEN
MIZZLE
PIZAZZ
PIZZAS
RIZZIO
SIZERS
SIZEUP
SIZING
SIZZLE
VIZIER
VIZSLA
WIZARD
WIZENS
ZIZITH

•I•Z••
DITZES
FIZZED
FIZZES
FIZZLE
LIZZIE
MIZZEN
MIZZLE
PIAZZA
PINZON
PIZZAS
RIZZIO
SIZZLE
WINZES
ZIGZAG

•I••Z•
PIAZZA
PIZAZZ
RIENZI

•I•••Z
KIBITZ
MILOSZ
NIMITZ
PIZAZZ

••IZ••
BAIZAS
FRIZZY
MAIZES
PFIZER
PRIZED
PRIZES
SEIZED
SEIZER
SEIZES
WHIZZO

••I•Z•
FRIEZE
FRIZZY
GLITZY
WHIZZO

••I••Z
BLINTZ
BRIENZ
CHINTZ
SHIRAZ

•••IZ•
ASSIZE
BELIZE
IODIZE
IONIZE
SCHIZY

•••I•Z
DONITZ
KIBITZ
MORITZ
NIMITZ
SPRITZ

••••IZ
CURTIZ
TABRIZ
THEWIZ

JA••••
JABBAR
JABBED
JABBER
JABIRU
JABOTS
JACALS
JACANA
JACKAL
JACKED
JACKET
JACKEY
JACKIE
JACKUP
JACLYN
JACOBI
JADING
JADISH
JAEGER
JAGGED
JAGGER
JAGUAR
JAILED
JAILER
JAIPUR
JALAPA
JALOPY
JAMAAL
JAMMED
JAMMER
JAMOKE
JAMSIN
JAMSUP
JAMUPS
JANGLE
JANGLY
JANHUS
JANICE
JANINE
JANSEN
JANSKY
JAPANS
JAPERS
JAPERY
JAPING
JARFUL
JARGON
JARRAH
JARRED
JASCHA
JASEYS
JASPER
JAUNTS
JAUNTY
JAURES
JAVARI
JAVIER
JAWING
JAWOHL
JAYCEE
JAYVEE
JAZZED
JAZZES
JAZZUP

J•A•••
JEANNE
JOANIE
JOANNA
JOANNE
JUAREZ

J••A••
JACALS
JACANA
JALAPA
JAMAAL
JAPANS
JAVARI
JICAMA
JIHADS
JOHANN
JONAHS
JUDAEA
JUDAIC
JUMADA
JURADO
JURATS

J•••A•
JABBAR
JACKAL
JAGUAR
JAMAAL
JARRAH
JEERAT
JETLAG
JETSAM
JETWAY
JIGSAW
JINNAH
JORDAN
JOSIAH
JOVIAL
JOVIAN
JUBBAH
JULIAN
JUMPAT
JUNEAU
JUNTAS

J••••A
JACANA
JALAPA
JASCHA
JERBOA
JICAMA
JOANNA
JOJOBA
JOSHUA
JUDAEA
JUDOKA
JUMADA

•JA•••
AJANTA

•J•A••
UJJAIN

•J•••A
AJANTA
DJERBA
EJECTA
OJIBWA

••JA••
ADJANI
DEJAVU
HIJACK
MOJAVE
PAJAMA
PYJAMA
RAJAHS
SEJANT
TEJANO
UJJAIN
UNJAMS

••J•A•
FIJIAN
FUJIAN
HIJRAH
STJOAN

••J••A
ARJUNA
FAJITA
JOJOBA
PAJAMA
PYJAMA

•••JA•
DEEJAY
ELIJAH
INAJAM
LOGJAM
NINJAS
PUNJAB
RIOJAS
THUJAS
TRAJAN
TROJAN
VEEJAY

•••J•A
PRAJNA

••••JA
BAROJA

J•B•••
JABBAR
JABBED
JABBER
JABIRU
JABOTS
JIBBED
JIBING
JOBBED
JOBBER
JOBETH
JOBHOP
JOBLOT
JUBBAH

J••B••
JABBAR
JABBED
JABBER
JERBOA
JIBBED
JOBBED
JOBBER
JUBBAH
JUMBLE
JUMBOS

J•••B•
JACOBI
JOJOBA
JUJUBE

•J•B••
OJIBWA

•J••B•
DJERBA

••J•B•
JOJOBA
JUJUBE
MCJOBS

•••J•B
CONJOB
DAYJOB
ODDJOB
PUNJAB
TOPJOB

J•C•••
JACALS
JACANA
JACKAL
JACKED
JACKET
JACKEY
JACKIE
JACKUP
JACLYN

JACOBI
JECKLE
JICAMA
JOCKEY
JOCOSE
JOCUND

J••C••
JASCHA
JAYCEE
JUICED
JUICER
JUICES
JUNCOS

J•••C•
JANICE
JOUNCE
JOUNCY

J••••C
JUDAIC

•J•C••
EJECTA
EJECTS

••J•C•
ABJECT
DEJECT
HIJACK
INJECT
MEJICO
OBJECT
REJECT

J•D•••
JADING
JADISH
JUDAEA
JUDAIC
JUDDER
JUDGED
JUDGES
JUDITH
JUDOKA

J••D••
JORDAN
JUDDER

J•••D•
JIHADS
JUMADA
JURADO

J••••D
JABBED
JACKED
JAGGED
JAILED
JAMMED
JARRED
JAZZED
JEERED
JELLED
JERKED
JESTED
JETTED
JIBBED
JIGGED
JILTED
JINKED
JINXED
JOBBED
JOCUND
JOGGED
JOINED
JOLTED
JOSHED
JOTTED
JUDGED
JUGGED
JUICED
JUMPED
JUNKED
JUTTED

•J•D••
EJIDOS

•J••D•
FJELDS
FJORDS

••J••D
BUJOLD

JE••••
JEANNE
JECKLE
JEERAT
JEERED
JEERER
JEETER
JEEVES
JEJUNE
JEKYLL
JELLED
JENNER
JENNET
JENNEY
JENNIE
JENSEN
JERBOA
JEREMY
JERKED
JERKIN
JEROME
JERSEY
JESSEL
JESSIE
JESTED
JESTER
JESUIT
JETGUN
JETHRO
JETLAG
JETSAM
JETSET
JETSKI
JETSON
JETTED
JETWAY
JEWELS
JEWETT
JEWISH

J•E•••
JAEGER
JEERAT
JEERED
JEERER
JEETER
JEEVES
JOETEX

J••E••
JAPERS
JAPERY
JASEYS
JEREMY
JEWELS
JEWETT
JIVERS
JOBETH
JOKERS
JOLENE
JOSEPH
JOWETT
JULEPS
JUNEAU

J•••E•
JABBED
JABBER
JACKED
JACKET
JACKEY
JAEGER
JAGGED
JAGGER
JAILED
JAILER
JAMMED
JAMMER
JANSEN
JARRED
JASPER
JAURES
JAVIER
JAYCEE
JAYVEE
JAZZED
JAZZES
JEERED
JEERER
JEETER
JEEVES
JELLED
JENNER
JENNET
JENNEY
JENSEN
JERKED
JERSEY
JESSEL
JESTED
JESTER
JETSET
JETTED
JIBBED
JIGGED
JIGGER
JILTED
JINKED
JINXED
JINXES
JITNEY
JITTER
JIVIER
JOBBED
JOBBER
JOCKEY
JOETEX
JOGGED
JOGGER
JOINED
JOINER
JOKIER
JOLIET
JOLTED
JOSHED
JOSHES
JOSSER
JOSSES
JOTTED
JOULES
JOYNER
JUAREZ
JUDAEA
JUDDER
JUDGED
JUDGES
JUGGED
JUICED
JUICER
JUICES
JULIET
JUMPED
JUMPER
JUNKED
JUNKER
JUNKET
JURIES
JUSTER
JUTTED

J••••E
JACKIE
JAMOKE
JANGLE
JANICE
JANINE
JAYCEE
JAYVEE
JEANNE
JECKLE
JEJUNE
JENNIE
JEROME
JESSIE
JIGGLE
JIMMIE
JINGLE
JOANIE
JOANNE
JOCOSE
JOGGLE
JOHORE
JOLENE
JOSTLE
JOUNCE
JUGGLE
JUJUBE
JUMBLE
JUNGLE
JUNKIE

•JE•••
DJERBA
EJECTA
EJECTS
FJELDS

•J••E•
IJSSEL
KJOLEN

••JE••
ABJECT
DEJECT
INJECT
INJEST
OBJECT
REJECT

••J•E•
GIJOES
HAJJES
MAJGEN

••J••E
ABJURE
ADJURE
BYJOVE
CAJOLE
DEJURE
INJOKE
INJURE
JEJUNE
JUJUBE
MOJAVE

•••JE•
FANJET
GASJET
HADJES
HAJJES
INKJET
KOPJES
RAMJET
TRIJET

••••JE
SKOPJE

J••F••
JARFUL
JOYFUL
JUGFUL

•JF•••
AJFOYT

J•G•••
JAGGED
JAGGER
JAGUAR
JIGGED
JIGGER
JIGGLE
JIGGLY
JIGSAW
JOGGED
JOGGER
JOGGLE
JUGFUL
JUGGED
JUGGLE

J••G••
JAEGER
JAGGED
JAGGER
JANGLE
JANGLY
JARGON
JETGUN
JIGGED
JIGGER
JIGGLE
JIGGLY
JINGLE
JINGLY
JOGGED
JOGGER
JOGGLE
JUDGED
JUDGES
JUGGED
JUGGLE
JUNGLE
JUNGLY

J••••G
JADING
JAPING
JAWING
JETLAG
JIBING
JIVING
JOKING
JUKING

••JG••
MAJGEN

J•H•••
JIHADS
JOHANN
JOHNNY
JOHORE

J••H••
JANHUS
JETHRO
JOBHOP
JOSHED
JOSHES
JOSHUA

J•••H•
JASCHA
JAWOHL
JONAHS

J••••H
JADISH
JARRAH
JEWISH
JINNAH
JOBETH
JOSEPH
JOSIAH
JUBBAH
JUDITH
JUTISH

••J•H•
RAJAHS
STJOHN
UPJOHN

••J••H
HIJRAH

•••J•H
ELIJAH

JI••••
JIBBED
JIBING
JICAMA
JIGGED
JIGGER
JIGGLE
JIGGLY
JIGSAW
JIHADS
JILTED
JIMINY
JIMMIE
JIMSON
JINGLE
JINGLY
JINKED
JINNAH
JINXED
JINXES
JITNEY
JITTER
JIVERS
JIVIER
JIVING

J•I•••
JAILED
JAILER
JAIPUR
JOINED
JOINER
JOININ
JOINTS
JOINUP
JOISTS
JUICED
JUICER
JUICES

J••I••
JABIRU
JADING
JADISH
JANICE
JANINE
JAPING
JAVIER
JAWING
JEWISH
JIBING
JIMINY
JIVIER
JIVING
JOKIER
JOKILY
JOKING
JOLIET
JOLIOT
JOSIAH
JOVIAL
JOVIAN
JUDITH
JUKING
JULIAN
JULIET
JULIUS
JUNIOR
JURIES
JURIST
JUTISH

J•••I•
JACKIE
JAMSIN
JENNIE
JERKIN
JESSIE
JESUIT
JIMMIE
JOANIE
JOININ
JOPLIN
JOSKIN
JUDAIC
JUMPIN
JUNKIE
JUSTIN

J••••I
JACOBI
JAVARI
JETSKI

•JI•••
EJIDOS
OJIBWA

•J••I•
UJJAIN

••JI••
FAJITA
FIJIAN
FUJIAN
MEJICO

••J•I•
ADJOIN
ENJOIN
HAJJIS
MAJLIS
REJOIN
UJJAIN

••J••I
ADJANI

•••JI•
GAIJIN
HADJIS
HAJJIS
SHOJIS

••••JI
ROMAJI

J•J•••
JEJUNE
JOJOBA
JUJUBE

•JJ•••
UJJAIN

••JJ••
HAJJES
HAJJIS

J•K•••
JEKYLL
JOKERS
JOKIER
JOKILY
JOKING
JUKING

J••K••
JACKAL
JACKED
JACKET
JACKEY
JACKIE
JACKUP
JECKLE
JERKED
JERKIN
JINKED
JOCKEY
JOSKIN
JUNKED
JUNKER
JUNKET
JUNKIE

J•••K•
JAMOKE
JANSKY
JETSKI
JUDOKA

••J•K•
INJOKE

••J••K
HIJACK

•••JK•
STOJKO

•••J•K
SELJUK

J•L•••
JALAPA
JALOPY
JELLED
JILTED
JOLENE
JOLIET
JOLIOT
JOLSON
JOLTED
JULEPS
JULIAN
JULIET
JULIUS

J••L••
JACLYN
JAILED
JAILER
JELLED
JETLAG
JOBLOT
JOPLIN
JOULES

J•••L•
JACALS
JANGLE
JANGLY
JECKLE
JEKYLL
JEWELS
JIGGLE
JIGGLY
JINGLE
JINGLY
JOGGLE
JOKILY
JOSTLE
JUGGLE
JUMBLE
JUNGLE
JUNGLY
JUSTLY

J••••L
JACKAL
JAMAAL
JARFUL
JAWOHL
JEKYLL
JESSEL
JOVIAL
JOYFUL
JUGFUL

•J•L••
FJELDS
KJOLEN

•J•••L
IJSSEL

••JL••
MAJLIS

••J•L•
BUJOLD
CAJOLE

•••J•L
BANJUL
FRIJOL

J•M•••
JAMAAL
JAMMED
JAMMER
JAMOKE
JAMSIN
JAMSUP
JAMUPS
JIMINY
JIMMIE
JIMSON
JUMADA
JUMBLE
JUMBOS
JUMPAT
JUMPED
JUMPER
JUMPIN
JUMPON
JUMPUP

J••M••
JAMMED
JAMMER
JIMMIE

J•••M•
JEREMY
JEROME
JICAMA
JORUMS

J••••M
JETSAM

••J•M•
PAJAMA
PYJAMA
UNJAMS

•••J•M
BOOJUM
INAJAM
LOGJAM

J•N•••
JANGLE
JANGLY
JANHUS
JANICE
JANINE
JANSEN
JANSKY
JENNER
JENNET
JENNEY
JENNIE
JENSEN
JINGLE
JINGLY
JINKED
JINNAH
JINXED
JINXES
JONAHS
JONSON
JUNCOS
JUNEAU
JUNGLE
JUNGLY
JUNIOR
JUNKED
JUNKER
JUNKET
JUNKIE
JUNTAS
JUNTOS

J••N••
JAUNTS
JAUNTY
JEANNE
JENNER
JENNET
JENNEY
JENNIE
JINNAH
JITNEY
JOANIE
JOANNA
JOANNE
JOHNNY
JOINED
JOINER
JOININ
JOINTS
JOINUP
JOUNCE
JOUNCY
JOYNER

J•••N•
JACANA
JADING
JANINE
JAPANS
JAPING
JAWING
JEANNE
JEJUNE
JIBING
JIMINY
JIVING
JOANNA
JOANNE
JOCUND
JOHANN
JOHNNY
JOKING
JOLENE
JOURNO
JUKING

J••••N
JACLYN
JAMSIN
JANSEN
JARGON
JENSEN
JERKIN
JETGUN
JETSON
JIMSON
JOHANN
JOININ
JOLSON
JONSON
JOPLIN
JORDAN
JOSKIN
JOVIAN
JULIAN
JUMPIN
JUMPON
JUSTIN

•J•N••
AJANTA

•J•••N
KJOLEN
UJJAIN

••J•N•
ADJANI
ARJUNA
CAJUNS
JEJUNE
SEJANT
TEJANO

••J••N
ADJOIN
ENJOIN
FIJIAN
FUJIAN
MAJGEN
REJOIN
STJOAN
STJOHN
UJJAIN
UPJOHN

•••JN•
PRAJNA

•••J•N
DONJON
GAIJIN
TRAJAN
TROJAN

JO••••
JOANIE
JOANNA
JOANNE
JOBBED
JOBBER
JOBETH
JOBHOP
JOBLOT
JOCKEY
JOCOSE
JOCUND
JOETEX
JOGGED
JOGGER
JOGGLE
JOHANN
JOHNNY
JOHORE
JOINED
JOINER
JOININ
JOINTS
JOINUP
JOISTS
JOJOBA
JOKERS
JOKIER
JOKILY
JOKING
JOLENE
JOLIÉT
JOLIOT
JOLSON
JOLTED
JONAHS
JONSON
JOPLIN
JORDAN
JORUMS
JOSEPH
JOSHED
JOSHES
JOSHUA
JOSIAH
JOSKIN
JOSSER
JOSSES
JOSTLE
JOTTED
JOULES
JOUNCE
JOUNCY
JOURNO
JOUSTS
JOVIAL
JOVIAN
JOWETT
JOYFUL
JOYNER
JOYOUS

J••O••
JABOTS
JACOBI
JALOPY
JAMOKE
JAWOHL
JEROME
JOCOSE
JOHORE
JOJOBA
JOYOUS
JUDOKA
JURORS

J•••O•
JARGON
JERBOA
JETSON
JIMSON
JOBHOP
JOBLOT
JOLIOT
JOLSON
JONSON
JUMBOS
JUMPON
JUNCOS
JUNIOR
JUNTOS

J••••O
JETHRO
JOURNO
JURADO

•JO•••
FJORDS
KJOLEN

•J•O••
AJFOYT

•J••O•
EJIDOS

••JO••
ADJOIN
ANJOUS
BIJOUX
BUJOLD
BYJOVE
CAJOLE
ENJOIN
ENJOYS
GIJOES
INJOKE
JOJOBA
MAJORS
MCJOBS
REJOIN
STJOAN
STJOHN
UPJOHN

••J••O
MEJICO
TEJANO

•••JO•
ACAJOU
AMAJOR
BANJOS
BMAJOR
CMAJOR
CONJOB
DAYJOB
DMAJOR
DONJON
EMAJOR
FMAJOR
FRIJOL
GMAJOR
MENJOU
ODDJOB
TOPJOB

•••J•O
STOJKO

••••JO
NAVAJO

J•P•••
JAPANS
JAPERS
JAPERY
JAPING
JOPLIN

J••P••
JAIPUR
JASPER
JUMPAT
JUMPED
JUMPER
JUMPIN
JUMPON
JUMPUP

J•••P•
JALAPA
JALOPY
JAMUPS
JOSEPH
JULEPS

J••••P
JACKUP
JAMSUP
JAZZUP
JOBHOP
JOINUP
JUMPUP

••JP••
RAJPUT

J•R•••
JARFUL
JARGON
JARRAH
JARRED
JERBOA
JEREMY
JERKED
JERKIN
JEROME
JERSEY
JORDAN
JORUMS
JURADO
JURATS
JURIES
JURIST
JURORS

J••R••
JARRAH
JARRED
JAURES
JEERAT
JEERED
JEERER
JOURNO
JUAREZ

J•••R•
JABIRU
JAPERS
JAPERY
JAVARI
JETHRO
JIVERS
JOHORE
JOKERS
JURORS

J••••R
JABBAR
JABBER
JAEGER
JAGGER
JAGUAR
JAILER
JAIPUR
JAMMER
JASPER
JAVIER
JEERER
JEETER
JENNER
JESTER
JIGGER
JITTER
JIVIER
JOBBER
JOGGER
JOINER
JOKIER
JOSSER
JOYNER
JUDDER
JUICER
JUMPER
JUNIOR
JUNKER
JUSTER

•J•R••
DJERBA
FJORDS

••JR••
HIJRAH

••J•R•
ABJURE
ADJURE
DEJURE
INJURE
INJURY
MAJORS

•••J•R
AMAJOR
BMAJOR
CMAJOR
DMAJOR
EMAJOR
FMAJOR
GMAJOR

J•S•••
JASCHA
JASEYS
JASPER
JESSEL
JESSIE
JESTED
JESTER
JESUIT
JOSEPH
JOSHED
JOSHES
JOSHUA
JOSIAH
JOSKIN
JOSSER
JOSSES
JOSTLE
JUSTER
JUSTIN
JUSTLY

J••S••
JAMSIN
JAMSUP
JANSEN
JANSKY
JENSEN
JERSEY
JESSEL
JESSIE
JETSAM
JETSET
JETSKI
JETSON
JIGSAW
JIMSON
JOISTS
JOLSON
JONSON
JOSSER
JOSSES
JOUSTS

J•••S•
JADISH
JEWISH
JOCOSE
JURIST
JUTISH

J••••S
JABOTS
JACALS
JAMUPS
JANHUS
JAPANS
JAPERS
JASEYS
JAUNTS
JAURES
JAZZES
JEEVES
JEWELS
JIHADS
JINXES
JIVERS
JOINTS
JOISTS
JOKERS
JONAHS
JORUMS
JOSHES
JOSSES
JOULES
JOUSTS
JOYOUS
JUDGES
JUICES
JULEPS
JULIUS
JUMBOS
JUNCOS
JUNTAS
JUNTOS
JURATS
JURIES
JURORS

•JS•••
IJSSEL

•J•S••
IJSSEL

•J•••S
EJECTS
EJIDOS
FJELDS
FJORDS

••J•S•
ADJUST
INJEST
UNJUST

••J••S
ANJOUS
CAJUNS
ENJOYS
GIJOES
HAJJES
HAJJIS
MAJLIS
MAJORS
MCJOBS
RAJAHS
UNJAMS

•••J•S
BANJOS
HADJES
HADJIS
HAJJES
HAJJIS
KOPJES
NINJAS
RIOJAS
SHOJIS
THUJAS

J•T•••
JETGUN
JETHRO
JETLAG
JETSAM
JETSET
JETSKI
JETSON
JETTED
JETWAY
JITNEY
JITTER
JOTTED
JUTISH
JUTTED

J••T••
JEETER
JESTED
JESTER
JETTED
JILTED
JITTER
JOETEX
JOLTED
JOSTLE
JOTTED
JUNTAS
JUNTOS
JUSTER
JUSTIN
JUSTLY
JUTTED

J•••T•
JABOTS
JAUNTS
JAUNTY
JEWETT
JOBETH
JOINTS
JOISTS
JOUSTS
JOWETT
JUDITH
JURATS

J••••T
JACKET
JEERAT
JENNET
JESUIT
JETSET
JEWETT
JOBLOT
JOLIET
JOLIOT
JOWETT
JULIET
JUMPAT
JUNKET
JURIST

•J••T•
AJANTA
EJECTA
EJECTS

•J•••T
AJFOYT

••J•T•
FAJITA

••J••T
ABJECT
ADJUST
DEJECT
INJECT
INJEST
OBJECT
RAJPUT
REJECT
SEJANT
UNJUST

•••J•T
FANJET
GASJET
INKJET
RAMJET
TRIJET

JU••••
JUAREZ
JUBBAH
JUDAEA
JUDAIC
JUDDER
JUDGED
JUDGES
JUDITH
JUDOKA
JUGFUL
JUGGED
JUGGLE
JUICED
JUICER
JUICES
JUJUBE
JUKING
JULEPS
JULIAN
JULIET
JULIUS
JUMADA
JUMBLE
JUMBOS
JUMPAT
JUMPED
JUMPER
JUMPIN
JUMPON
JUMPUP
JUNCOS
JUNEAU
JUNGLE
JUNGLY
JUNIOR
JUNKED
JUNKER
JUNKET
JUNKIE
JUNTAS
JUNTOS
JURADO
JURATS
JURIES
JURIST
JURORS
JUSTER
JUSTIN
JUSTLY
JUTISH
JUTTED

J•U•••
JAUNTS
JAUNTY
JAURES
JOULES
JOUNCE
JOUNCY
JOURNO
JOUSTS

J••U••
JAGUAR
JAMUPS
JEJUNE
JESUIT
JOCUND
JORUMS
JUJUBE

J•••U•
JACKUP
JAIPUR
JAMSUP
JANHUS
JARFUL
JAZZUP
JETGUN
JOINUP
JOSHUA
JOYFUL
JOYOUS
JUGFUL
JULIUS
JUMPUP

J••••U
JABIRU
JUNEAU

••JU••
ABJURE
ADJURE
ADJUST
ARJUNA
CAJUNS
DEJURE
INJURE
INJURY
JEJUNE
JUJUBE
UNJUST

••J•U•
ANJOUS
BIJOUX
RAJPUT

••J••U
DEJAVU

•••JU•
BANJUL
BOOJUM
SELJUK

•••J•U
ACAJOU
MENJOU

••••JU
CHONJU

J•V•••
JAVARI
JAVIER
JIVERS
JIVIER
JIVING
JOVIAL
JOVIAN

J••V••
JAYVEE
JEEVES

••J•V•
BYJOVE
DEJAVU
MOJAVE

J•W•••
JAWING
JAWOHL
JEWELS
JEWETT
JEWISH
JOWETT

J••W••
JETWAY

J••••W
JIGSAW

•J••W•
OJIBWA

J••X••
JINXED
JINXES

J••••X
JOETEX

••J••X
BIJOUX

J•Y•••
JAYCEE
JAYVEE
JOYFUL
JOYNER
JOYOUS

J••Y••
JEKYLL

J•••Y•
JACLYN
JASEYS

J••••Y
JACKEY
JALOPY
JANGLY
JANSKY
JAPERY
JAUNTY
JENNEY
JEREMY
JERSEY
JETWAY
JIGGLY
JIMINY
JINGLY
JITNEY
JOCKEY
JOHNNY
JOKILY
JOUNCY
JUNGLY
JUSTLY

•J••Y•
AJFOYT

••J•Y•
ENJOYS

••J••Y
INJURY

•••J•Y
DEEJAY
VEEJAY

J•Z•••
JAZZED
JAZZES
JAZZUP

J••Z••
JAZZED
JAZZES
JAZZUP

J••••Z
JUAREZ

KA••••
KABOBS
KABOOM
KABUKI
KAFFIR
KAFIRS
KAGERA
KAHLIL
KAHLUA
KAHUNA
KAILUA
KAISER
KAKAPO
KALAKH
KALINE
KALKAN
KALMAR
KAMALA
KANAKA
KANDER
KANSAN
KANSAS
KANTOR
KAOLIN
KAPLAN
KAPPAS
KARATE
KARATS
KAREEM
KARIBA
KARMIC
KARNAK
KAROSS
KARPOV
KARRAS
KARROO
KARSTS
KASBAH
KASDAN
KATHIE
KATMAI
KAUNAS
KAUNDA
KAURIS
KAVNER
KAYAKS
KAYOED
KAZAKH
KAZAKS
KAZOOS

K•A•••
KEARNY
KEATON
KHAFRE
KHAKIS
KHALID
KIANGS
KLATCH
KLAXON
KNACKS
KNAGGY
KNARRY
KNAVES
KOALAS
KRAALS
KRAITS
KRAKEN
KRAKOW
KRAMER
KRANTZ
KRASNY
KRATER
KWACHA
KWANZA
KYACKS

K••A••
KAKAPO
KALAKH
KAMALA
KANAKA
KARATE
KARATS
KAYAKS
KAZAKH
KAZAKS
KDLANG
KEBABS
KERALA
KIGALI
KNEADS
KODALY
KORATS
KOVACS
KRAALS
KULAKS
KURALT
KUVASZ
KUWAIT

K•••A•
KALKAN
KALMAR
KANSAN
KANSAS
KAPLAN
KAPPAS
KARNAK
KARRAS
KASBAH
KASDAN
KATMAI
KAUNAS
KEENAN
KEEPAT
KENYAN
KEPTAT
KERMAN
KEVLAR
KEYPAD
KEYWAY
KIDMAN
KIDNAP
KIOWAS
KIRMAN
KITBAG
KITKAT
KLIBAN
KOALAS
KODIAK
KOMBAT
KONRAD
KOREAN
KORMAN
KOUFAX
KUBLAI
KURGAN

K••••A
KAGERA
KAHLUA
KAHUNA
KAILUA
KAMALA
KANAKA
KARIBA
KAUNDA
KERALA
KESHIA
KINEMA
KONICA
KORUNA
KWACHA
KWANZA

•KA•••
OKAPIS
OKAYED
SKALDS
SKANKS
SKATED
SKATER
SKATES
UKASES

•K•A••
AKUAKU
OKSANA
SKEANS
SKOALS

•K••A•
AKELAS
AKITAS
SKYCAP
SKYLAB
SKYWAY

•K•••A
OKSANA

••KA••
ACKACK
ALKALI
ANKARA
ASKARI
DEKALB
GOKART
KAKAPO
MAKALU
MIKADO
PIKAKE
TOKAYS
UAKARI
YUKATA
YUKAWA

••K•A•
DIKTAT
LEKVAR
POKEAT
SUKKAH
TOKLAS

••K••A
ANKARA
BAKULA
BIKILA
DAKOTA
LAKOTA
MAKEBA
MAKUTA
MIKITA
NIKITA
NIKOLA
PAKULA
YAKIMA
YAKUZA
YUKATA
YUKAWA

•••KA•
BABKAS
BAIKAL
BALKAN
BARKAT
BROKAW
CHUKAR
HOOKAH
JACKAL
KALKAN
KITKAT
LOOKAT
PARKAS
PARKAY
PECKAT
PEEKAT
PICKAT
PICKAX
POLKAS
PUNKAH
RYOKAN
SHIKAR
SUCKAS
SUKKAH
TALKAT
TANKAS
VODKAS
WINKAT

•••K•A
CHUKKA
GURKHA
MARKKA
MOSKVA
QUOKKA

••••KA
ALASKA
ANNIKA
BANGKA
CHUKKA
EUREKA
FLICKA
GLINKA
JUDOKA
KANAKA
LUSAKA
MARKKA
MEDAKA
NOOTKA
QUOKKA
SEDAKA
TANAKA
TOPEKA
TROIKA
WOVOKA

K•B•••
KABOBS
KABOOM
KABUKI
KEBABS
KEBOBS
KIBBLE
KIBITZ
KIBOSH
KOBOLD
KUBLAI

K••B••
KASBAH
KHYBER
KIBBLE
KITBAG
KLIBAN
KNOBBY
KOMBAT
KORBUT

K•••B•
KABOBS
KARIBA
KEBABS
KEBOBS
KNOBBY

•KB•••
EKBERG

•K•B••
SKIBOB
SKYBOX

•K••B•
AKIMBO

•K•••B
SKIBOB
SKYLAB

••K•B•
MAKEBA

••K••B
DEKALB

K•C•••
KICKED
KICKER
KICKIN
KICKUP
KUCHEN

K••C••
KIMCHI
KNACKS
KNICKS
KNOCKS
KWACHA
KYACKS

K•••C•
KIRSCH
KITSCH
KLATCH
KONICA
KOPECK
KOVACS
KVETCH

K••••C
KARMIC

•K•C••
SKYCAP

•K••C•
SKETCH
SKITCH

••K•C•
ACKACK
EDKOCH

••K••C
PYKNIC

•••K•C
TURKIC

KD••••
KDLANG

K•D•••
KEDGED
KEDGES
KIDDED
KIDDER
KIDDIE
KIDMAN
KIDNAP
KIDNEY
KIDORY
KIDVID
KODALY
KODIAK
KUDROW
KUDZUS

K••D••
KANDER
KASDAN
KIDDED
KIDDER
KIDDIE
KINDER
KINDLE
KINDLY
KINDOF
KLUDGE

K•••D•
KAUNDA
KNEADS
KOMODO

K••••D
KAYOED
KEDGED
KEELED
KEENED
KEGGED
KENNED
KERNED
KEYPAD
KHALID
KICKED
KIDDED
KIDVID
KILLED
KILNED
KILTED
KINGED
KINKED
KISSED
KNIFED
KOBOLD
KONRAD

•K•D••
SKIDDY

•K••D•
SKALDS
SKIDDY

•K•••D
OKAYED
SKATED
SKEWED
SKIVED

••KD••
DIKDIK

••K•D•
AIKIDO
ALKYDS
MAKEDO
MIKADO

••K••D
ANKLED
INKIND
UNKIND
YAKKED
YUKKED

•••K•D
AWAKED
BACKED
BALKED
BANKED
BARKED
BASKED
BEAKED
BILKED
BOOKED
BRAKED
BUCKED
BULKED
BUNKED
BUSKED
CALKED
CARKED
CHOKED
COCKED
CONKED
COOKED
CORKED
DECKED
DISKED
DOCKED
DUCKED
DUNKED
EVOKED
FINKED
FLAKED
FORKED
FUNKED
GAWKED
HACKED
HARKED
HAWKED
HOCKED
HONKED
HOOKED
HULKED
HUSKED
JACKED
JERKED
JINKED
JUNKED
KICKED
KINKED
LACKED
LARKED
LEAKED
LICKED
LINKED
LOCKED
LOOKED
LUCKED
LURKED
MARKED
MASKED
MILKED
MOCKED
MUCKED
NECKED
NICKED
OINKED
PACKED
PARKED
PEAKED
PECKED
PEEKED
PERKED
PICKED
PINKED
QUAKED
RACKED
RANKED
REEKED
RICKED
RISKED
ROCKED
ROOKED
RUCKED
SACKED
SILKED
SLAKED
SMOKED
SNAKED
SOAKED
SOCKED
SPIKED
SPOKED
STAKED
STOKED
SUCKED
SULKED
TACKED
TALKED
TANKED
TASKED
THEKID
TICKED
TUCKED
TUSKED
WALKED
WICKED
WINKED
WORKED
YACKED
YAKKED
YANKED
YERKED
YOLKED
YUKKED
ZONKED

KE••••
KEARNY
KEATON
KEBABS
KEBOBS
KEDGED
KEDGES
KEELED
KEELER
KEENAN
KEENED
KEENEN
KEENER
KEENLY
KEEPAT
KEEPER
KEEPIN
KEEPON
KEEPTO
KEEPUP
KEFIRS
KEGGED
KEGLER
KEITEL
KELLER
KELLEY
KELPIE
KELSEY
KELVIN
KEMPIS
KENNED
KENNEL
KENNER
KENNYG
KENTON
KENYAN
KEPLER
KEPTAT
KEPTON
KEPTUP
KERALA
KERMAN
KERMES
KERMIS
KERMIT
KERNED
KERNEL
KERNOI
KERNOS
KERSEE
KERSEY
KESHIA
KETONE
KETTLE
KEVELS
KEVLAR
KEWPIE
KEYING
KEYNES
KEYPAD
KEYSIN
KEYSUP
KEYWAY

K•E•••
KEELED
KEELER
KEENAN
KEENED
KEENEN
KEENER
KEENLY
KEEPAT
KEEPER
KEEPIN
KEEPON
KEEPTO
KEEPUP
KIEFER
KLEIST
KMESON
KNEADS
KNEELS
KNELLS
KOENIG
KPELLE
KRESGE
KVELLS
KVETCH
KWEISI

K••E••
KAGERA
KAREEM
KEVELS
KHMERS
KINEMA
KITERS
KNEELS
KOPECK
KOPEKS
KOREAN

K•••E•
KAISER
KANDER
KAREEM
KAVNER
KAYOED
KEDGED
KEDGES
KEELED
KEELER
KEENED
KEENEN
KEENER
KEEPER
KEGGED
KEGLER
KEITEL
KELLER
KELLEY
KELSEY
KENNED
KENNEL
KENNER
KEPLER
KERMES
KERNED
KERNEL
KERSEE
KERSEY
KEYNES
KHYBER
KICKED
KICKER
KIDDED
KIDDER
KIDNEY
KIEFER
KILLED
KILLER
KILMER
KILNED
KILTED
KILTER
KINDER
KINGED
KINKED
KINSEY
KIPPER
KISLEV
KISMET
KISSED
KISSER
KISSES
KITTEN
KJOLEN
KNAVES
KNIFED
KNIFES
KNIVES
KNOWER
KOHLER
KOPJES
KOPPEL
KOSHER
KOTTER
KRAKEN
KRAMER
KRATER
KRONER
KRUGER
KUCHEN
KUMMEL

K••••E
KALINE
KARATE
KATHIE
KELPIE
KERSEE
KETONE
KETTLE
KEWPIE
KHAFRE
KIBBLE
KIDDIE
KILTIE
KINDLE
KINGME
KIRTLE
KISHKE
KLUDGE
KOOKIE
KPELLE
KRESGE
KURILE

•KE•••
AKELAS
AKENES
EKEOUT
OKEEFE
OKELLY
SKEANS
SKEINS
SKERRY
SKETCH
SKEWED
SKEWER

•K•E••
EKBERG
OKEEFE
SKIERS

•K••E•
AKENES
OKAYED
SKATED
SKATER
SKATES
SKEWED
SKEWER
SKIVED
SKIVER
SKIVES
UKASES

•K•••E
OKEEFE
SKOKIE
SKOPJE

••KE••
ALKENE
ASKERS
BAKERS
BAKERY
BEKESY
BIKERS
ESKERS
FAKERS
FAKERY
HIKERS
HIKEUP
INKERS
JOKERS
LAKERS
LIKELY
LIKENS
MAKEBA
MAKEDO
MAKEIT
MAKERS
MAKEUP
PIKERS
POKEAT
POKERS
POKERY
POKEYS
RAKEIN
RAKERS
RAKEUP
REKEYS
SAKERS
TAKEIN
TAKEON
TAKERS
TAKETH
TAKETO
TAKEUP
TOKENS
UPKEEP
WAKENS
WAKEUP
WOKEUP
YOKELS

••K•E•
ANKLED
ANKLES
ANKLET
AUKLET
CAKIER
COKIER
FOKKER
HOKIER
ICKIER
INKIER
INKJET
INKLES
JOKIER
LAKIER
MCKUEN
NIKKEI
OAKLEY
ORKNEY
PEKOES
POKIER
UPKEEP
YAKKED
YAKKER
YUKKED

••K••E
ALKENE
PIKAKE

•••KE•
AWAKED
AWAKEN
AWAKES
AWOKEN
BACKED
BACKER
BALKED
BANKED
BANKER
BARKED
BARKER
BASKED
BASKET
BEAKED
BEAKER
BECKER
BECKET
BICKER
BILKED
BLOKES
BOOKED
BOOKER
BOSKET
BRAKED
BRAKES

BROKEN
BROKER
BUCKED
BUCKET
BULKED
BUNKED
BUNKER
BUSKED
CALKED
CANKER
CARKED
CHOKED
CHOKER
CHOKES
CISKEI
COCKED
COCKER
CONKED
CONKER
COOKED
COOKER
CORKED
CORKER
CRAKES
CRIKEY
DANKER
DARKEN
DARKER
DECKED
DECKER
DICKER
DICKEY
DINKEY
DISKED
DOCKED
DOCKER
DOCKET
DONKEY
DRAKES
DUCKED
DUIKER
DUNKED
DUNKER
EVOKED
EVOKER
EVOKES
FAWKES
FINKED
FLAKED
FLAKER
FLAKES
FLAKEY
FLUKES
FLUKEY
FOKKER
FORKED
FORKER
FUNKED
GASKET
GAWKED
GAWKER
HACKED
HACKER
HANKER
HARKED
HARKEN
HARKER
HAWKED
HAWKER
HICKEY
HOCKED
HOCKEY
HONKED
HONKER
HOOKED
HULKED
HUNKER
HUSKED
HUSKER
JACKED
JACKET
JACKEY
JERKED
JINKED
JOCKEY
JUNKED
JUNKER
JUNKET
KICKED
KICKER
KINKED
KRAKEN
LACKED
LACKEY
LANKER
LARKED
LATKES
LEAKED
LEAKER
LEAKEY
LICKED
LINKED
LINKER
LOCKED
LOCKER
LOCKET
LOOKED
LOOKER
LOWKEY
LUCKED
LUNKER
LURKED
MARKED
MARKER
MARKET
MASKED
MASKER
MEEKER
MENKEN
MERKEL
MICKEY
MILKED
MILKER
MINKES
MOCKED
MOCKER
MONKEY
MUCKED
MUSKEG
MUSKET
NECKED
NICKED
NICKEL
NICKER
NIKKEI
OFFKEY
OINKED
PACKED
PACKER
PACKET
PARKED
PARKER
PEAKED
PECKED
PEEKED
PERKED
PICKED
PICKER
PICKET
PINKED
PINKEN
PINKER
POCKET
PORKER
PUCKER
PUNKER
QUAKED
QUAKER
QUAKES
RACKED
RACKET
RANKED
RANKER
REEKED
RICKED
RICKEY
RIPKEN
RISKED
RISKER
ROCKED
ROCKER
ROCKET
ROOKED
RUCKED
SACKED
SACKER
SECKEL
SEEKER
SHAKEN
SHAKER
SHAKES
SHEKEL
SICKEN
SICKER
SILKED
SILKEN
SINKER
SISKEL
SLAKED
SLAKES
SMOKED
SMOKER
SMOKES
SMOKEY
SNAKED
SNAKES
SOAKED
SOAKER
SOCKED
SOCKET
SPIKED
SPIKER
SPIKES
SPOKED
SPOKEN
SPOKES
STAKED
STAKES
STOKED
STOKER
STOKES
SUCKED
SUCKER
SULKED
SULKER
SUNKEN
TACKED
TACKER
TALKED
TALKER
TANKED
TANKER
TASKED
TEDKEY
TERKEL
TICKED
TICKER
TICKET
TINKER
TRIKES
TUCKED
TUCKER
TUCKET
TURKEY
TUSKED
TUSKER
WALKED
WALKEN
WALKER
WEAKEN
WEAKER
WICKED
WICKER
WICKET
WILKES
WINKED
WINKER
WORKED
WORKER
YACKED
YAKKED
YAKKER
YANKED
YANKEE
YERKED
YERKES
YOLKED
YORKER
YUKKED
ZONKED
ZONKER

•••K•E
BOOKIE
BUCKLE
CACKLE
COCKLE
COOKIE
DARKLE
DECKLE
FICKLE
FOLKIE
HACKIE
HACKLE
HANKIE
HECKLE
JACKIE
JECKLE
JUNKIE
KOOKIE
MUSKIE
PICKLE
PINKIE
PUNKIE
RANKLE
ROCKNE
ROOKIE
SICKLE
SKOKIE
TACKLE
TALKIE
TICKLE
TINKLE
WALKIE
WINKIE
WINKLE
WOOKIE
YANKEE
YORKIE

••••KE
AXLIKE
BELIKE
BETAKE
BOURKE
BROOKE
CLARKE
GRIMKE
INJOKE
INTAKE
INVOKE
JAMOKE
KISHKE
MOLTKE
OXLIKE
PELIKE
PERUKE
PIKAKE
REBUKE
REMAKE
RETAKE
REVOKE
ROURKE
SHRIKE
STLUKE
STRAKE
STRIKE
STROKE
THICKE
UNLIKE
UNMAKE
UNYOKE
UPDIKE
UPTAKE

K•F•••
KAFFIR
KAFIRS
KEFIRS

K••F••
KAFFIR
KHAFRE
KIEFER
KITFOX
KNIFED
KNIFES
KOUFAX

K•••F•
KLOOFS
KUNGFU

K••••F
KINDOF

•K•F••
SKIFFS

•K••F•
OKEEFE
SKIFFS

••KF••
ASKFOR

K•G•••
KAGERA
KEGGED
KEGLER
KIGALI

K••G••
KEDGED
KEDGES
KEGGED
KINGED
KINGLY
KINGME
KNAGGY
KNIGHT
KRUGER
KUNGFU
KURGAN

K•••G•
KIANGS
KLUDGE
KNAGGY
KRESGE

K••••G
KDLANG
KENNYG
KEYING
KITBAG
KITING
KOENIG

•K•••G
EKBERG
SKIING
SKYING

••K••G
ASKING
BAKING
BBKING
BIKING
CAKING
DEKING
DIKING
DUKING
FAKING
HIKING
INKING
IRKING
JOKING
JUKING
LIKING
MAKING
MEKONG
MIKING
NUKING
PEKING
PIKING
POKING
RAKING
TAKING
VIKING
WAKING
YOKING

•••KG•
GINKGO

•••K•G
MUSKEG

KH••••
KHAFRE
KHAKIS
KHALID
KHMERS
KHOUMS
KHYBER

K•H•••
KAHLIL
KAHLUA
KAHUNA
KOHLER

K••H••
KATHIE
KESHIA
KISHKE
KOSHER
KUCHEN

K•••H•
KIMCHI
KNIGHT
KWACHA
KYUSHU

K••••H
KALAKH
KASBAH
KAZAKH
KIBOSH
KIRSCH
KITSCH
KLATCH
KVETCH

•K•••H
SKETCH
SKITCH

••K••H
EDKOCH
RAKISH
SUKKAH
TAKETH

•••KH•
GURKHA

•••K•H
HOOKAH
PUNKAH
SUKKAH

••••KH
KALAKH
KAZAKH
SAMEKH

KI••••
KIANGS
KIBBLE
KIBITZ
KIBOSH
KICKED
KICKER
KICKIN
KICKUP
KIDDED
KIDDER
KIDDIE
KIDMAN
KIDNAP
KIDNEY
KIDORY
KIDVID
KIEFER
KIGALI
KIKUYU
KILIMS
KILLED
KILLER
KILMER
KILNED
KILROY
KILTED
KILTER
KILTIE
KIMCHI
KIMONO
KINDER
KINDLE
KINDLY
KINDOF
KINEMA
KINGED
KINGLY
KINGME
KINKED
KINSEY
KINSKI
KIOSKS
KIOWAS
KIPPER
KIPPUR
KIRMAN
KIRSCH
KIRTLE
KISHKE
KISLEV
KISMET
KISSED
KISSER
KISSES
KITBAG
KITERS
KITFOX
KITING
KITKAT
KITSCH
KITTEN

K•I•••
KAILUA
KAISER
KEITEL
KLIBAN
KNICKS
KNIFED
KNIFES
KNIGHT
KNIVES

K••I••
KAFIRS
KALINE
KARIBA
KEFIRS
KEYING
KIBITZ
KILIMS
KITING
KLEIST
KODIAK
KONICA
KRAITS
KUMISS
KURILE
KWEISI

K•••I•
KAFFIR
KAHLIL
KAOLIN
KARMIC
KATHIE
KAURIS
KEEPIN
KELPIE
KELVIN
KEMPIS
KERMIS
KERMIT
KESHIA
KEWPIE
KEYSIN
KHAKIS
KHALID
KICKIN
KIDDIE
KIDVID
KILTIE
KOENIG
KOOKIE
KUKRIS
KUOPIO
KUWAIT

K••••I
KABUKI
KATMAI
KERNOI
KIGALI
KIMCHI
KINSKI
KUBLAI
KWEISI

•KI•••
AKIMBO

AKITAS
SKIBOB
SKIDDY
SKIERS
SKIFFS
SKIING
SKILLS
SKIMPS
SKIMPY
SKINKS
SKINNY
SKIPIT
SKIPPY
SKIRLS
SKIROS
SKIRRS
SKIRTS
SKIRUN
SKITCH
SKITOW
SKIVED
SKIVER
SKIVES
SKIVVY

•K•I••
SKEINS
SKIING
SKYING

•K••I•
OKAPIS
SKIPIT
SKOKIE

••KI••
AIKIDO
ASKING
ATKINS
BAKING
BBKING
BIKILA
BIKING
BIKINI
CAKIER
CAKING
COKIER
DEKING
DIKING
DUKING
ESKIMO
FAKING
FAKIRS
HAKIMS
HIKING
HOKIER
ICKIER
INKIER
INKIND
INKING
IRKING
JOKIER
JOKILY
JOKING
JUKING
LAKIER
LIKING
MAKING
MIKING
MIKITA
NIKITA
NUKING
PEKING
PEKINS
PIKING
POKIER
POKILY
POKING
RAKING
RAKISH
TAKING
TAKINS
UNKIND
UNKINK
VIKING
WAKING
YAKIMA
YOKING

••K•I•
ASKSIN
DIKDIK
KUKRIS
MAKEIT
PYKNIC
RAKEIN
SIKKIM
TAKEIN
UNKNIT

••K••I
ALKALI
ASKARI
BIKINI
NIKKEI
UAKARI

•••KI•
ABUKIR
BACKIN
BARKIN
BODKIN
BOOKIE
BUSKIN
CATKIN
COOKIE
CULKIN
ENOKIS
FIRKIN
FOLKIE
GASKIN
HACKIE
HANKIE
JACKIE
JERKIN
JOSKIN
JUNKIE
KHAKIS
KICKIN
KOOKIE
LOCKIN
LOOKIN
MALKIN
MUSKIE
NAPKIN
NUTKIN
PINKIE
PIPKIN
PUNKIE
RANKIN
ROOKIE
RUSKIN
SERKIN
SIKKIM
SINKIN
SISKIN
SKOKIE
SOCKIN
SUCKIN
TALKIE
THEKID
TONKIN
TOOKIN
TOOKIT
TUCKIN
TURKIC
WALKIE
WALKIN
WELKIN
WESKIT
WINKIE
WOOKIE
WORKIN
YORKIE

•••K•I
BHAKTI
CISKEI
NIKKEI
SHAKTI

••••KI
ADZUKI
EVENKI
HIDEKI
ITHAKI
JETSKI
KABUKI
KINSKI
SALUKI
SUZUKI

KJ••••
KJOLEN

K••J••
KOPJES

•K••J•
SKOPJE

••KJ••
INKJET

K•K•••
KAKAPO
KIKUYU
KOKOMO
KUKRIS

K••K••
KALKAN
KHAKIS
KICKED
KICKER
KICKIN
KICKUP
KINKED
KITKAT
KOOKIE
KRAKEN
KRAKOW

K•••K•
KABUKI
KALAKH
KANAKA
KAYAKS
KAZAKH
KAZAKS
KINSKI
KIOSKS
KISHKE
KNACKS
KNICKS
KNOCKS
KOPEKS
KULAKS
KYACKS

K••••K
KARNAK
KODIAK
KOPECK
KUSPUK

•K•K••
SKOKIE

•K••K•
AKUAKU
SKANKS
SKINKS
SKULKS
SKUNKS
SKUNKY

••KK••
DEKKOS
FOKKER
NIKKEI
SIKKIM
SUKKAH
YAKKED
YAKKER
YUKKED

••K•K•
PIKAKE

••K••K
ACKACK
DIKDIK
MUKLUK
UNKINK

•••KK•
CHUKKA
MARKKA
QUOKKA

•••K•K
HICKOK

KL••••
KLATCH
KLAXON
KLEIST
KLIBAN
KLOOFS
KLUDGE
KLUTZY

K•L•••
KALAKH
KALINE
KALKAN
KALMAR
KDLANG
KELLER
KELLEY
KELPIE
KELSEY
KELVIN
KILIMS
KILLED
KILLER
KILMER
KILNED
KILROY
KILTED
KILTER
KILTIE
KULAKS
KULTUR

K••L••
KAHLIL
KAHLUA
KAILUA
KAOLIN
KAPLAN
KEELED
KEELER
KEGLER
KELLER
KELLEY
KEPLER
KEVLAR
KHALID
KILLED
KILLER
KISLEV
KJOLEN
KNELLS
KNOLLS
KNOLLY
KOALAS
KOHLER
KPELLE
KUBLAI
KUNLUN
KVELLS

K•••L•
KAMALA
KEENLY
KERALA
KETTLE
KEVELS
KIBBLE
KIGALI
KINDLE
KINDLY
KINGLY
KIRTLE
KNEELS
KNELLS
KNOLLS
KNOLLY
KNURLS
KNURLY
KOBOLD
KODALY
KPELLE
KRAALS
KURALT
KURILE
KVELLS

K••••L
KAHLIL
KEITEL
KENNEL
KERNEL
KOPPEL
KUMMEL

•K•L••
AKELAS
OKELLY
SKALDS
SKILLS
SKULKS
SKULLS
SKYLAB

•K••L•
OKELLY
SKILLS
SKIRLS
SKOALS
SKULLS

••KL••
ANKLED
ANKLES
ANKLET
AUKLET
INKLES
MUKLUK
OAKLEY
TOKLAS

••K•L•
ALKALI
ALKYLS
BAKULA
BIKILA
DEKALB
JEKYLL
JOKILY
LIKELY
MAKALU
NIKOLA
PAKULA
POKILY
YOKELS

••K••L
JEKYLL

•••KL•
BUCKLE
CACKLE
COCKLE
DANKLY
DARKLE
DARKLY
DECKLE
FICKLE
HACKLE
HACKLY
HECKLE
JECKLE
LANKLY
MEEKLY
PICKLE
RANKLE
RANKLY
SICKLE
SICKLY
TACKLE
TICKLE
TICKLY
TINKLE
TINKLY
WEAKLY
WEEKLY
WINKLE

•••K•L
BAIKAL
JACKAL
MERKEL
NICKEL
SECKEL
SHEKEL
SISKEL
TERKEL

KM••••
KMESON

K•M•••
KAMALA
KEMPIS
KHMERS
KIMCHI
KIMONO
KOMBAT
KOMODO
KUMISS
KUMMEL

K••M••
KALMAR
KARMIC
KATMAI
KERMAN
KERMES
KERMIS
KERMIT
KIDMAN
KILMER
KIRMAN
KISMET
KORMAN
KRAMER
KUMMEL

K•••M•
KHOUMS
KILIMS
KINEMA
KINGME
KOKOMO

K••••M
KABOOM
KAREEM

•K•M••
AKIMBO
SKIMPS
SKIMPY

••K•M•
ESKIMO
HAKIMS
KOKOMO
YAKIMA

••K••M
SIKKIM

•••K•M
BUNKUM
SIKKIM

KN••••
KNACKS
KNAGGY
KNARRY
KNAVES
KNEADS
KNEELS
KNELLS
KNICKS
KNIFED
KNIFES
KNIGHT
KNIVES
KNOBBY
KNOCKS
KNOLLS
KNOLLY
KNOTTS
KNOTTY
KNOUTS
KNOWER
KNOWNS
KNURLS
KNURLY

K•N•••
KANAKA
KANDER
KANSAN
KANSAS
KANTOR
KENNED
KENNEL
KENNER
KENNYG
KENTON
KENYAN
KINDER
KINDLE
KINDLY
KINDOF
KINEMA
KINGED
KINGLY
KINGME
KINKED
KINSEY
KINSKI
KONICA
KONRAD
KUNGFU
KUNLUN

K••N••
KARNAK
KAUNAS
KAUNDA
KAVNER
KEENAN
KEENED
KEENEN
KEENER
KEENLY
KENNED
KENNEL
KENNER
KENNYG
KERNED
KERNEL
KERNOI
KERNOS
KEYNES
KIANGS
KIDNAP
KIDNEY
KILNED
KOENIG
KOONTZ
KRANTZ
KRONER
KRONOR
KRONUR
KWANZA

K•••N•
KAHUNA
KALINE
KDLANG
KEARNY
KETONE
KEYING
KIMONO
KITING
KNOWNS
KORUNA
KRASNY

K••••N
KALKAN
KANSAN
KAOLIN
KAPLAN
KASDAN
KEATON
KEENAN
KEENEN
KEEPIN
KEEPON
KELVIN
KENTON
KENYAN
KEPTON
KERMAN
KEYSIN
KICKIN
KIDMAN
KIRMAN
KITTEN
KJOLEN

KLAXON
KLIBAN
KMESON
KOREAN
KORMAN
KRAKEN
KUCHEN
KUNLUN
KURGAN

•KN•••
SKNXXX

•K•N••
AKENES
SKANKS
SKINKS
SKINNY
SKUNKS
SKUNKY

•K••N•
OKSANA
SKEANS
SKEINS
SKIING
SKINNY
SKYING

•K•••N
SKIRUN

••KN••
ORKNEY
PYKNIC
UNKNIT
UNKNOT

••K•N•
ALKENE
ASKING
ATKINS
BAKING
BBKING
BIKING
BIKINI
CAKING
DEKING
DIKING
DUKING
FAKING
HIKING
INKIND
INKING
IRKING
JOKING
JUKING
LIKENS
LIKING
MAKING
MEKONG
MIKING
NUKING
PEKING
PEKINS
PIKING
POKING
RAKING
TAKING
TAKINS
TOKENS
UNKIND
UNKINK
VIKING
WAKENS
WAKING
YOKING

••K••N
ASKSIN
MCKUEN
NEKTON
RAKEIN
TAKEIN
TAKEON

•••KN•
ROCKNE

•••K•N
AWAKEN
AWOKEN
BACKIN
BALKAN
BANKON
BARKIN
BECKON
BODKIN
BROKEN
BUSKIN
CATKIN
CULKIN
DAIKON
DARKEN
FIRKIN
GASKIN
HARKEN
JERKIN
JOSKIN
KALKAN
KICKIN
KRAKEN
LOCKIN
LOCKON
LOOKIN
LOOKON
MALKIN
MENKEN
NAPKIN
NUTKIN
PICKON
PINKEN
PIPKIN
RANKIN
RECKON
RIPKEN
RUSKIN
RYOKAN
SERKIN
SHAKEN
SICKEN
SILKEN
SINKIN
SISKIN
SOCKIN
SPOKEN
SUCKIN
SUNKEN
TACKON
TONKIN
TOOKIN
TOOKON
TUCKIN
WALKEN
WALKIN
WALKON
WEAKEN
WELKIN
WORKIN
WORKON

KO••••
KOALAS
KOBOLD
KODALY
KODIAK
KOENIG
KOHLER
KOKOMO
KOMBAT
KOMODO
KONICA
KONRAD
KOOKIE
KOONTZ
KOPECK
KOPEKS
KOPJES
KOPPEL
KORATS
KORBUT
KOREAN
KORMAN
KORUNA
KOSHER
KOSOVO
KOTTER
KOUFAX
KOVACS
KOWTOW

K•O•••
KAOLIN
KHOUMS
KIOSKS
KIOWAS
KJOLEN
KLOOFS
KNOBBY
KNOCKS
KNOLLS
KNOLLY
KNOTTS
KNOTTY
KNOUTS
KNOWER
KNOWNS
KOOKIE
KOONTZ
KRONER
KRONOR
KRONUR
KUOPIO

K••O••
KABOBS
KABOOM
KAROSS
KAYOED
KAZOOS
KEBOBS
KETONE
KIBOSH
KIDORY
KIMONO
KLOOFS
KOBOLD
KOKOMO
KOMODO
KOSOVO

K•••O•
KABOOM
KANTOR
KARPOV
KARROO
KAZOOS
KEATON
KEEPON
KENTON
KEPTON
KERNOI
KERNOS
KILROY
KINDOF
KITFOX
KLAXON
KMESON
KOWTOW
KRAKOW
KRONOR
KUDROW

K••••O
KAKAPO
KARROO
KEEPTO
KIMONO
KOKOMO
KOMODO
KOSOVO
KUOPIO

•KO•••
SKOALS
SKOKIE
SKOPJE
SKORTS

•K•O••
EKEOUT

•K••O•
SKIBOB
SKIROS
SKITOW
SKYBOX

•K•••O
AKIMBO

••KO••
ASKOUT
DAKOTA
EDKOCH
KOKOMO
LAKOTA
MEKONG
NIKOLA
PEKOES

••K•O•
ASKFOR
DEKKOS
HYKSOS
NEKTON
TAKEON
UNKNOT

••K••O
AIKIDO
ESKIMO
KAKAPO
KOKOMO
MAKEDO
MIKADO
TAKETO

•••KO•
ANGKOR
BANKON
BECKON
BUNKOS
CHEKOV
CUCKOO
DAIKON
DEKKOS
GECKOS
HICKOK
KRAKOW
LOCKON
LOOKON
MUSKOX
PICKON
RECKON
SHAKOS
TACKON
TOOKON
WACKOS
WALKON
WORKON
ZHUKOV

•••K•O
CUCKOO
GINKGO
LOOKTO
TALKTO
TOOKTO

••••KO
BAMAKO
MARIKO
ROTHKO
STOJKO

KP••••
KPELLE

K•P•••
KAPLAN
KAPPAS
KEPLER
KEPTAT
KEPTON
KEPTUP
KIPPER
KIPPUR
KOPECK
KOPEKS
KOPJES
KOPPEL

K••P••
KAPPAS
KARPOV
KEEPAT
KEEPER
KEEPIN
KEEPON
KEEPTO
KEEPUP
KELPIE
KEMPIS
KEWPIE
KEYPAD
KIPPER
KIPPUR
KOPPEL
KUOPIO
KUSPUK

K•••P•
KAKAPO

K••••P
KEEPUP
KEPTUP
KEYSUP
KICKUP
KIDNAP

•K•P••
OKAPIS
SKIPIT
SKIPPY
SKOPJE

•K••P•
SKIMPS
SKIMPY
SKIPPY

•K•••P
SKYCAP

••K•P•
KAKAPO

••K••P
HIKEUP
MAKEUP
RAKEUP
TAKEUP
UPKEEP
WAKEUP
WOKEUP

•••K•P
BACKUP
BUCKUP
COOKUP
HOOKUP
JACKUP
KICKUP
LINKUP
LOCKUP
LOOKUP
MARKUP
MOCKUP
MUCKUP
PACKUP
PERKUP
PICKUP
RACKUP
SOAKUP
TALKUP
TANKUP
TOOKUP
WALKUP
WORKUP

KR••••
KRAALS
KRAITS
KRAKEN
KRAKOW
KRAMER
KRANTZ
KRASNY
KRATER
KRESGE
KRONER
KRONOR
KRONUR
KRUGER

K•R•••
KARATE
KARATS
KAREEM
KARIBA
KARMIC
KARNAK
KAROSS
KARPOV
KARRAS
KARROO
KARSTS
KERALA
KERMAN
KERMES
KERMIS
KERMIT
KERNED
KERNEL
KERNOI
KERNOS
KERSEE
KERSEY
KIRMAN
KIRSCH
KIRTLE
KORATS
KORBUT
KOREAN
KORMAN
KORUNA
KURALT
KURGAN
KURILE

K••R••
KARRAS
KARROO
KAURIS
KEARNY
KILROY
KNARRY
KNURLS
KNURLY
KONRAD
KUDROW
KUKRIS

K•••R•
KAFIRS
KAGERA
KEFIRS
KHAFRE
KHMERS
KIDORY
KITERS
KNARRY

K••••R
KAFFIR
KAISER
KALMAR
KANDER
KANTOR
KAVNER
KEELER
KEENER
KEEPER
KEGLER
KELLER
KENNER
KEPLER
KEVLAR
KHYBER
KICKER
KIDDER
KIEFER
KILLER
KILMER
KILTER
KINDER
KIPPER
KIPPUR
KISSER
KNOWER
KOHLER
KOSHER
KOTTER
KRAMER
KRATER
KRONER
KRONOR
KRONUR
KRUGER
KULTUR

•K•R••
SKERRY
SKIRLS
SKIROS
SKIRRS
SKIRTS
SKIRUN
SKORTS

•K••R•
EKBERG
SKERRY
SKIERS
SKIRRS

•K•••R
SKATER
SKEWER
SKIVER

••KR••
KUKRIS

••K•R•
ANKARA
ASKARI
ASKERS
BAKERS
BAKERY
BIKERS
ESKERS
FAKERS
FAKERY
FAKIRS
GOKART
HIKERS
INKERS
JOKERS
LAKERS
MAKERS
PIKERS
POKERS
POKERY
RAKERS
SAKERS
TAKERS
UAKARI

••K••R
ASKFOR
CAKIER
COKIER
FOKKER
HOKIER
ICKIER
INKIER
JOKIER
LAKIER
LEKVAR
POKIER
YAKKER

•••K•R
ABUKIR
ANGKOR
BACKER
BANKER
BARKER
BEAKER
BECKER
BICKER
BOOKER
BROKER
BUNKER
CANKER
CHOKER
CHUKAR
COCKER
CONKER
COOKER
CORKER
DANKER
DARKER
DECKER
DICKER
DOCKER
DUIKER
DUNKER

EVOKER
FLAKER
FOKKER
FORKER
GAWKER
HACKER
HANKER
HARKER
HAWKER
HONKER
HUNKER
HUSKER
JUNKER
KICKER
LANKER
LEAKER
LINKER
LOCKER
LOOKER
LUNKER
MARKER
MASKER
MEEKER
MILKER
MOCKER
NICKER
PACKER
PARKER
PICKER
PINKER
PORKER
PUCKER
PUNKER
QUAKER
RANKER
RISKER
ROCKER
SACKER
SEEKER
SHAKER
SHIKAR
SICKER
SINKER
SMOKER
SOAKER
SPIKER
STOKER
SUCKER
SULKER
TACKER
TALKER
TANKER
TICKER
TINKER
TUCKER
TUSKER
WALKER
WEAKER
WICKER
WINKER
WORKER
YAKKER
YORKER
ZONKER

K•S•••

KASBAH
KASDAN
KESHIA
KISHKE
KISLEV
KISMET
KISSED
KISSER
KISSES
KOSHER
KOSOVO
KUSPUK

K••S••

KAISER
KANSAN
KANSAS
KARSTS
KELSEY
KERSEE
KERSEY
KEYSIN
KEYSUP
KINSEY
KINSKI
KIOSKS
KIRSCH
KISSED
KISSER
KISSES
KITSCH
KMESON
KRASNY
KRESGE
KYUSHU

K•••S•

KAROSS
KIBOSH
KLEIST
KUMISS
KUVASZ
KWEISI

K••••S

KABOBS
KAFIRS
KANSAS
KAPPAS
KARATS
KAROSS
KARRAS
KARSTS
KAUNAS
KAURIS
KAYAKS
KAZAKS
KAZOOS
KEBABS
KEBOBS
KEDGES
KEFIRS
KEMPIS
KERMES
KERMIS
KERNOS
KEVELS
KEYNES
KHAKIS
KHMERS
KHOUMS
KIANGS
KILIMS
KIOSKS
KIOWAS
KISSES
KITERS
KLOOFS
KNACKS
KNAVES
KNEADS
KNEELS
KNELLS
KNICKS
KNIFES
KNIVES
KNOCKS
KNOLLS
KNOTTS
KNOUTS
KNOWNS
KNURLS
KOALAS
KOPEKS
KOPJES
KORATS
KOVACS
KRAALS
KRAITS
KUDZUS
KUKRIS
KULAKS
KUMISS
KVELLS
KYACKS

•KS•••

OKSANA

•K•S••

UKASES

•K•••S

AKELAS
AKENES
AKITAS
OKAPIS
SKALDS
SKANKS
SKATES
SKEANS
SKEINS
SKIERS
SKIFFS
SKILLS
SKIMPS
SKINKS
SKIRLS
SKIROS
SKIRRS
SKIRTS
SKIVES
SKOALS
SKORTS
SKULKS
SKULLS
SKUNKS
UKASES

••KS••

ASKSIN
HYKSOS

••K•S•

BEKESY
RAKISH

••K••S

ALKYDS
ALKYLS
ANKLES
ASKERS
ATKINS
BAKERS
BIKERS
DEKKOS
ESKERS
FAKERS
FAKIRS
HAKIMS
HIKERS
HYKSOS
INKERS
INKLES
JOKERS
KUKRIS
LAKERS
LIKENS
MAKERS
PEKINS
PEKOES
PIKERS
POKERS
POKEYS
RAKERS
REKEYS
SAKERS
TAKERS
TAKINS
TOKAYS
TOKENS
TOKLAS
WAKENS
YAKUTS
YOKELS
YOKUTS

•••KS•

FOLKSY

•••K•S

AWAKES
BABKAS
BACKUS
BLOKES
BRAKES
BUNKOS
CHOKES
CRAKES
DEKKOS
DRAKES
ENOKIS
EVOKES
FAWKES
FLAKES
FLUKES
GECKOS
HAIKUS
KHAKIS
LATKES
MINKES
PARKAS
POLKAS
QUAKES
RUCKUS
SHAKES
SHAKOS
SLAKES
SMOKES
SNAKES
SPIKES
SPOKES
STAKES
STOKES
SUCKAS
TANKAS
TRIKES
VODKAS
WACKOS
WILKES
YERKES

••••KS

BATIKS
BAULKS
BLACKS
BLANKS
BLINKS
BLOCKS
BREAKS
BRICKS
BRINKS
BROOKS
CAULKS
CHALKS
CHECKS
CHEEKS
CHICKS
CHINKS
CHOCKS
CHUCKS
CHUNKS
CLACKS
CLANKS
CLEEKS
CLERKS
CLICKS
CLINKS
CLOAKS
CLOCKS
CLONKS
CLUCKS
CLUNKS
CRACKS
CRANKS
CREAKS
CREEKS
CRICKS
CROAKS
CROCKS
CROOKS
DMARKS
DRINKS
FLACKS
FLANKS
FLASKS
FLECKS
FLICKS
FLOCKS
FLUNKS
FRANKS
FREAKS
FRISKS
FROCKS
GREEKS
HACEKS
KAYAKS
KAZAKS
KIOSKS
KNACKS
KNICKS
KNOCKS
KOPEKS
KULAKS
KYACKS
MIWOKS
OZARKS
PLANKS
PLINKS
PLONKS
PLUCKS
PLUNKS
PRANKS
PRICKS
PRINKS
QUACKS
QUARKS
QUIRKS
REINKS
SHACKS
SHANKS
SHARKS
SHEIKS
SHIRKS
SHOCKS
SHOOKS
SHUCKS
SKANKS
SKINKS
SKULKS
SKUNKS
SLACKS
SLEEKS
SLICKS
SLINKS
SMACKS
SMIRKS
SMOCKS
SNACKS
SNEAKS
SNICKS
SNOOKS
SPANKS
SPARKS
SPEAKS
SPECKS
SPINKS
SPOOKS
STACKS
STALKS
STEAKS
STICKS
STINKS
STIRKS
STOCKS
STOOKS
STORKS
SWANKS
THANKS
THINKS
THUNKS
TILAKS
TRACKS
TRICKS
TRUCKS
TRUNKS
TWEAKS
UMIAKS
UZBEKS
VNECKS
WHACKS
WHELKS
WHISKS
WRACKS
WREAKS
WRECKS
YAPOKS
YOICKS
YUROKS

K•T•••

KATHIE
KATMAI
KETONE
KETTLE
KITBAG
KITERS
KITFOX
KITING
KITKAT
KITSCH
KITTEN
KOTTER

K••T••

KANTOR
KEATON
KEITEL
KENTON
KEPTAT
KEPTON
KEPTUP
KETTLE
KILTED
KILTER
KILTIE
KIRTLE
KITTEN
KLATCH
KLUTZY
KNOTTS
KNOTTY
KOTTER
KOWTOW
KRATER
KULTUR
KVETCH

K•••T•

KARATE
KARATS
KARSTS
KEEPTO
KIBITZ
KNOTTS
KNOTTY
KNOUTS
KOONTZ
KORATS
KRAITS
KRANTZ

K••••T

KEEPAT
KEPTAT
KERMIT
KISMET
KITKAT
KLEIST
KNIGHT
KOMBAT
KORBUT
KURALT
KUWAIT

•K•T••

AKITAS
SKATED
SKATER
SKATES
SKETCH
SKITCH
SKITOW

•K••T•

SKIRTS
SKORTS

•K•••T

EKEOUT
SKIPIT

••KT••

DIKTAT
NEKTON

••K•T•

DAKOTA
LAKOTA
MAKUTA
MIKITA
NIKITA
TAKETH
TAKETO
YAKUTS
YOKUTS
YUKATA

••K••T

ANKLET
ASKOUT
AUKLET
DIKTAT
GOKART
INKJET
MAKEIT
POKEAT
UNKNIT
UNKNOT

•••KT•

BHAKTI
LOOKTO
SHAKTI
TALKTO
TOOKTO

•••K•T

BARKAT
BASKET
BECKET
BOSKET
BUCKET
DOCKET
GASKET
JACKET
JUNKET
KITKAT
LOCKET
LOOKAT
MARKET
MUSKET
PACKET
PECKAT
PEEKAT
PICKAT
PICKET
POCKET
RACKET
ROCKET
SOCKET
TALKAT
TICKET
TOOKIT
TUCKET
WESKIT
WICKET
WINKAT

KU••••

KUBLAI
KUCHEN
KUDROW
KUDZUS
KUKRIS
KULAKS
KULTUR
KUMISS
KUMMEL
KUNGFU
KUNLUN
KUOPIO
KURALT
KURGAN
KURILE
KUSPUK
KUVASZ
KUWAIT

K•U•••

KAUNAS
KAUNDA
KAURIS
KLUDGE
KLUTZY
KNURLS
KNURLY
KOUFAX
KRUGER
KYUSHU

K••U••

KABUKI
KAHUNA
KHOUMS
KIKUYU
KNOUTS
KORUNA

K•••U•

KAHLUA
KAILUA
KEEPUP
KEPTUP
KEYSUP

KICKUP
KIPPUR
KORBUT
KRONUR
KUDZUS
KULTUR
KUNLUN
KUSPUK

K••••U
KIKUYU
KUNGFU
KYUSHU

•KU•••
AKUAKU
SKULKS
SKULLS
SKUNKS
SKUNKY

•K••U•
EKEOUT
SKIRUN

•K•••U
AKUAKU

••KU••
BAKULA
KIKUYU
MAKUTA
MCKUEN
PAKULA
YAKUTS
YAKUZA
YOKUTS

••K•U•
ASKOUT
HIKEUP
MAKEUP
MUKLUK
RAKEUP
TAKEUP
WAKEUP
WOKEUP

••K••U
KIKUYU
MAKALU

•••KU•
BACKUP
BACKUS
BUCKUP
BUNKUM
COOKUP
HAIKUS
HOOKUP
JACKUP
KICKUP
LINKUP
LOCKUP
LOOKUP
MARKUP
MOCKUP
MUCKUP
PACKUP
PERKUP
PICKUP
RACKUP
RUCKUS
SOAKUP
TALKUP
TANKUP
TOOKUP
WALKUP
WORKUP

•••K•U
RYUKYU

••••KU
AKUAKU

KV••••
KVELLS
KVETCH

K•V•••
KAVNER
KEVELS
KEVLAR
KOVACS
KUVASZ

K••V••
KELVIN
KIDVID
KNAVES
KNIVES

K•••V•
KOSOVO

K••••V
KARPOV
KISLEV

•K•V••
SKIVED
SKIVER
SKIVES
SKIVVY

•K••V•
SKIVVY

••KV••
LEKVAR

•••KV•
MOSKVA

•••K•V
CHEKOV
ROCKYV
ZHUKOV

KW••••
KWACHA
KWANZA
KWEISI

K•W•••
KEWPIE
KOWTOW
KUWAIT

K••W••
KEYWAY
KIOWAS
KNOWER
KNOWNS

K••••W
KOWTOW
KRAKOW
KUDROW

•K•W••
SKEWED
SKEWER
SKYWAY

•K•••W
SKITOW

••K•W•
YUKAWA

•••K•W
BROKAW
KRAKOW

K••X••
KLAXON

K••••X
KITFOX
KOUFAX

•K•X••
SKNXXX

•K••X•
SKNXXX

•K•••X
SKNXXX
SKYBOX

•••K•X
MUSKOX
PICKAX

KY••••
KYACKS
KYUSHU

K•Y•••
KAYAKS
KAYOED
KEYING
KEYNES
KEYPAD
KEYSIN
KEYSUP
KEYWAY
KHYBER

K••Y••
KENYAN

K•••Y•
KENNYG
KIKUYU

K••••Y
KEARNY
KEENLY
KELLEY
KELSEY
KERSEY
KEYWAY
KIDNEY
KIDORY
KILROY
KINDLY
KINGLY
KINSEY
KLUTZY
KNAGGY
KNARRY
KNOBBY
KNOLLY
KNOTTY
KNURLY
KODALY
KRASNY

•KY•••
SKYBOX
SKYCAP
SKYING
SKYLAB
SKYWAY

•K•Y••
OKAYED

•K•••Y
OKELLY
SKERRY
SKIDDY
SKIMPY
SKINNY
SKIPPY
SKIVVY
SKUNKY
SKYWAY

••KY••
ALKYDS
ALKYLS
JEKYLL

••K•Y•
KIKUYU
POKEYS
REKEYS
TOKAYS

••K••Y
BAKERY
BEKESY
FAKERY
JOKILY
LIKELY
OAKLEY
ORKNEY
POKERY
POKILY

•••KY•
ROCKYV
RYUKYU

•••K•Y
CRIKEY
DANKLY
DARKLY
DICKEY
DINKEY
DONKEY
FLAKEY
FLUKEY
FOLKSY
HACKLY
HICKEY
HOCKEY
JACKEY
JOCKEY
LACKEY
LANKLY
LEAKEY
LOWKEY
MEEKLY
MICKEY
MONKEY
OFFKEY
PARKAY
RANKLY
RICKEY
SICKLY
SMOKEY
TEDKEY
TICKLY
TINKLY
TURKEY
WEAKLY
WEEKLY

••••KY
ALECKY
BLOCKY
BRICKY
BROOKY
CHALKY
CHEEKY
CHINKY
CHUNKY
CLANKY
CLUNKY
CRACKY
CRANKY
CREAKY
CROAKY
FLECKY
FLOCKY
FLUNKY
FREAKY
FRISKY
JANSKY
NEVSKY
PLUCKY
PROSKY
QUIRKY
RIMSKY
SKUNKY
SLEEKY
SLINKY
SMIRKY
SNEAKY
SNOOKY
SPANKY
SPARKY
SPOOKY
SPUNKY
STALKY
STANKY
STICKY
STINKY
STOCKY
SWANKY
TRICKY
WHACKY
WHISKY

K•Z•••
KAZAKH
KAZAKS
KAZOOS

K••Z••
KUDZUS

K•••Z•
KLUTZY
KWANZA

K••••Z
KIBITZ
KOONTZ
KRANTZ
KUVASZ

••K•Z•
YAKUZA

LA••••
LAAGER
LABELS
LABIAL
LABILE
LABORS
LABOUR
LABREA
LABRET
LABRUM
LACERS
LACEUP
LACHES
LACIER
LACILY
LACING
LACKED
LACKEY
LACTIC
LACUNA
LADDER
LADDIE
LADERS
LADIDA
LADIES
LADING
LADINO
LADLED
LADLER
LADLES
LADOGA
LAFFER
LAGASH
LAGERS
LAGGED
LAGGER
LAGOON
LAGUNA
LAHORE
LAIDBY
LAIDIN
LAIDON
LAIDTO
LAIDUP
LAINIE
LAIRDS
LAKERS
LAKIER
LAKOTA
LALALA
LAMARR
LAMAZE
LAMBDA
LAMBED
LAMECH
LAMEDH
LAMEDS
LAMELY
LAMENT
LAMESA
LAMEST
LAMIAS
LAMINA
LAMING
LAMMAS
LAMMED
LAMONT
LAMOUR
LANAIS
LANARK
LANATE
LANCED
LANCER
LANCES
LANCET
LANDAU
LANDED
LANDER
LANDHO
LANDIS
LANDON
LANDRY
LANGUR
LANIER
LANKER
LANKLY
LANOSE
LANSON
LANVIN
LAOTSE
LAOTZU
LAPDOG
LAPELS
LAPFUL
LAPHAM
LAPINS
LAPPED
LAPPET
LAPSED
LAPSES
LAPSUP
LAPTEV
LAPTOP
LAPUTA
LARAMS
LARDED
LARDER
LARDON
LAREDO
LARGER
LARGES
LARGOS
LARIAT
LARKED
LAROSA
LARRUP
LARSEN
LARSON
LARVAE
LARVAL
LARVAS
LARYNX
LASCAR
LASERS
LASHED
LASHER
LASHES
LASHIO
LASHUP
LASSEN
LASSER
LASSES
LASSIE
LASSOS
LASTED
LASTEX
LASTLY
LATEEN
LATELY
LATENE
LATENS
LATENT
LATEST
LATHED
LATHER
LATHES
LATIGO
LATINA
LATINI
LATINO
LATINS
LATISH
LATIUM
LATKES
LATONA
LATOUR
LATOYA
LATTEN
LATTER
LATVIA
LAUDED
LAUDER
LAUGHS
LAUNCH
LAUPER
LAUREL
LAUREN
LAURIE
LAVABO
LAVAGE
LAVERS
LAVING
LAVISH
LAWFUL
LAWING
LAWMAN
LAWMEN
LAWSON
LAWTON
LAWYER
LAXEST
LAXITY
LAYBYS
LAYERS
LAYFOR
LAYING
LAYLOW
LAYMAN
LAYMEN
LAYOFF
LAYOUT
LAYSBY
LAYSIN
LAYSON
LAYSTO
LAYSUP
LAYUPS
LAZBOY
LAZIER
LAZILY
LAZING
LAZULI

L•A•••
LAAGER
LEACHY
LEADED
LEADEN
LEADER
LEADIN
LEADON
LEADTO
LEADUP
LEAFED
LEAGUE
LEAKED
LEAKER
LEAKEY
LEALTY
LEANED
LEANER
LEANLY
LEANON
LEANTO
LEAPED
LEAPER
LEARNS
LEARNT
LEASED
LEASER
LEASES
LEAVED
LEAVEN
LEAVES
LIABLE
LIAISE
LIANAS
LIANES
LIANGS
LLAMAS
LLANOS
LOADED
LOADER
LOAFED
LOAFER
LOAMED
LOANED
LOANER
LOATHE

LOAVES
LUANDA

L••A••
LAGASH
LALALA
LAMARR
LAMAZE
LANAIS
LANARK
LANATE
LARAMS
LAVABO
LAVAGE
LCHAIM
LEGACY
LEGALS
LEGATE
LEGATO
LELAND
LEMANS
LENAPE
LESAGE
LEVANT
LIGAND
LIGATE
LILACS
LINAGE
LIPASE
LITANY
LIZARD
LOBATE
LOCALE
LOCALS
LOCATE
LORAIN
LOTAHS
LOVAGE
LUNACY
LUNATE
LUSAKA
LUXATE

L•••A•
LABIAL
LAMIAS
LAMMAS
LANDAU
LAPHAM
LARIAT
LARVAE
LARVAL
LARVAS
LASCAR
LAWMAN
LAYMAN
LEERAT
LEEWAY
LEGMAN
LEHUAS
LEKVAR
LEMMAS
LESTAT
LETHAL
LETSAT
LIANAS
LIBYAN
LINEAL
LINEAR
LLAMAS
LLBEAN
LOGJAM
LONGAN
LOOFAH
LOOFAS
LOOKAT
LOQUAT
LOREAL
LOTHAR
LOWCAL
LOWFAT
LUCIAN
LUMBAR

L••••A
LABREA
LACUNA
LADIDA
LADOGA
LAGUNA
LAKOTA
LALALA
LAMBDA
LAMESA
LAMINA
LAPUTA
LAROSA
LATINA
LATONA
LATOYA
LATVIA
LERIDA
LEXICA
LIGULA
LINGUA
LIOTTA
LISBOA
LOGGIA
LOLITA
LORICA
LOUISA
LOYOLA
LUANDA
LUMINA
LUNULA
LUSAKA

•LA•••
ALAMOS
ALANIS
ALANON
ALARIC
ALARMS
ALARUM
ALASKA
ALATAU
ALATED
BLABBY
BLACKS
BLADED
BLADER
BLADES
BLAINE
BLAISE
BLAMED
BLAMES
BLANCA
BLANCH
BLANDA
BLANKS
BLARED
BLARES
BLASTS
BLATTY
BLAZED
BLAZER
BLAZES
BLAZON
CLACKS
CLAIMS
CLAIRE
CLAMMY
CLAMOR
CLAMPS
CLAMUP
CLANCY
CLANGS
CLANKS
CLANKY
CLAQUE
CLARET
CLARKE
CLAROS
CLASPS
CLASSY
CLAUDE
CLAUSE
CLAVES
CLAVIN
CLAWED
CLAWER
CLAYEY
DLAYER
ELAINE
ELANDS
ELAPID
ELAPSE
ELATED
ELATER
ELATES
ELAYER
ELAYNE
FLABBY
FLACKS
FLACON
FLAGGY
FLAGON
FLAILS
FLAIRS
FLAKED
FLAKER
FLAKES
FLAKEY
FLAMBE
FLAMED
FLAMES
FLANGE
FLANKS
FLAPPY
FLARED
FLARES
FLASHY
FLASKS
FLATLY
FLAUNT
FLAVIA
FLAVOR
FLAWED
FLAXEN
FLAXES
FLAYED
FLAYER
GLACES
GLACIS
GLADES
GLADLY
GLADYS
GLAIRS
GLAIRY
GLAMOR
GLANCE
GLANDS
GLARED
GLARES
GLASER
GLASSY
GLAZED
GLAZER
GLAZES
KLATCH
KLAXON
LLAMAS
LLANOS
PLACED
PLACER
PLACES
PLACET
PLACID
PLAGAL
PLAGES
PLAGIO
PLAGUE
PLAICE
PLAIDS
PLAINS
PLAINT
PLAITS
PLANAR
PLANCK
PLANED
PLANER
PLANES
PLANET
PLANKS
PLANON
PLANTE
PLANTS
PLAQUE
PLASHY
PLASMA
PLASMO
PLASTY
PLATED
PLATEN
PLATER
PLATES
PLATTE
PLAYAS
PLAYAT
PLAYED
PLAYER
PLAYON
PLAYUP
PLAZAS
SLACKS
SLAGGY
SLAKED
SLAKES
SLALOM
SLANGS
SLANGY
SLANTS
SLAPPY
SLAPUP
SLATED
SLATER
SLATES
SLAVED
SLAVER
SLAVES
SLAVEY
SLAVIC
SLAYED
SLAYER
TLALOC

•L•A••
ALBANO
ALBANY
ALCAPP
ALEAST
ALKALI
ALLAYS
ALMATY
ALPACA
ALSACE
ALTAIC
ALTAIR
ALTARS
ALWAYS
BLEACH
BLEARS
BLEARY
BLEATS
BLOATS
CLEANS
CLEARS
CLEATS
CLEAVE
CLOACA
CLOAKS
ELPASO
FLOATS
FLOATY
GLEAMS
GLEAMY
GLEANS
GLOATS
ILEANA
NLEAST
OLDAGE
OLEARY
OLEATE
PLEACH
PLEADS
PLEASE
PLEATS
PLIANT
SLEAVE
SLEAZE
SLEAZY
SLOANE
ULLAGE

•L••A•
ALATAU
ALEGAR
ALEMAN
ALLDAY
ALLMAN
ALOHAS
ALOMAR
ALPHAS
ALTMAN
ALULAE
ALULAR
CLIMAX
ELFMAN
ELIJAH
FLEWAT
FLORAE
FLORAL
FLORAS
FLYMAN
FLYWAY
GLOBAL
ILLSAY
KLIBAN
LLAMAS
LLBEAN
OLDHAM
OLDHAT
OLDMAN
OLDSAW
PLAGAL
PLANAR
PLAYAS
PLAYAT
PLAZAS
PLEIAD
PLEXAL
PLICAE
PLURAL
SLEZAK
SLOGAN
SLOVAK
ULLMAN
ULTRAS

•L•••A
ALASKA
ALEXIA
ALICIA
ALPACA
ALTHEA
ALTIMA
ALUMNA
ALYSSA
BLANCA
BLANDA
CLOACA
ELISHA
ELISSA
ELMIRA
ELVIRA
FLAVIA
FLICKA
GLENDA
GLINKA
GLORIA
GLOSSA
ILEANA
ILESHA
OLINDA
OLIVIA
PLASMA
PLEURA
ULTIMA

••LA••
ABLATE
ABLAUT
ABLAZE
AFLAME
AFLATS
AGLAIA
AGLARE
ALLAYS
ASLANT
ATLAST
ATLATL
AULAIT
BALAAM
BALATA
BELAIR
BELAYS
BYLAWS
CALAIS
CALASH
CCLAMP
COLADA
DALASI
DELANO
DELANY
DELATE
DELAYS
DILATE
ECLAIR
ECLATS
EFLATS
ENLACE
FALANA
FULANI
GALAGO
GALAHS
GALATA
GALAXY
GELADA
GELATI
GELATO
GULAGS
HILARY
INLAID
INLAND
INLAWS
INLAYS
ISLAND
JALAPA
KALAKH
KDLANG
KULAKS
LALALA
LELAND
LILACS
MALABO
MALADY
MALAGA
MALATE
MALAWI
MALAYA
MALAYS
MCLAIN
MELANO
MILADY
MILANO
MOLARS
OBLAST
OBLATE
OFLATE
OGLALA
ONLAND
OOLALA
PALACE
PALAEO
PALATE
PELAGE
PILAFS
PILATE
POLAND
RELACE
RELAID
RELATE
RELAYS
ROLAND
SALAAM
SALADO
SALADS
SALALS
SALAMI
SALARY
SCLAFF
SILAGE
SOLACE
SOLANS
SOLARS
SPLASH
SPLATS
SPLAYS
TILAKS
TULANE
TULARE
UCLANS
UHLANS
ULLAGE
UMLAUT
UNLACE
UNLADE
UNLAID
UNLASH
UPLAND
VOLANS
VOLANT
VOLARE

••L•A•
AFLOAT
AGLEAM
ALLDAY
ALLMAN
BALAAM
BALKAN
BALLAD
BALSAM
BALZAC
BELDAM
BELIAL
BELLAY
BILBAO
BULGAR
BULLAE
CALLAO
CALLAS
CALPAC
CELLAE
CELLAR
COLFAX
COLLAR
COLMAN
DALLAS
DELMAR
DELRAY
DELTAS
DOLLAR
DOLMAN
DOLMAS
EOLIAN
FELLAH
FELLAS
FILIAL
FOLIAR
FULMAR
GALEAE
GALPAL
GALWAY
GALYAK
GILEAD
GULLAH
HALVAH
HELLAS
ILLSAY
JULIAN
KALKAN
KALMAR
MCLEAN
MELMAC
MILLAY
MILPAS
MILSAP
MOLDAU
MOLNAR
MULLAH
MULLAS
NILGAI
NOLEAD
NOLOAD
NULLAH
OILCAN
OILMAN
OILPAN
ONLOAN
PALEAE
PALLAS
PALMAS
PILLAR
POLEAX
POLKAS
PULSAR
RELOAD
SALAAM
SALMAN
SALSAS
SILOAM
SILVAS
SOLDAN
SOLFAS
SULTAN
SYLVAN
TALKAT
TULSAN
ULLMAN
UNLEAD
UNLOAD
UPLOAD
VILLAS
VOLVAS
VULCAN
VULGAR
ZILPAH

••L••A
AGLAIA
BALATA
BALBOA
BELUGA
BULOVA
COLADA
COLIMA
DULLEA
FALANA
FULCRA
GALATA
GALENA
GALLIA
GELADA
HELENA
HULLOA
JALAPA
LALALA
LOLITA
MALAGA
MALAYA
MELINA
MULETA
OGLALA
OOLALA
PALLIA
PALOMA
PELOTA
SALINA
SALIVA
SALVIA
SCLERA
SELENA
SILICA
SYLVIA
TOLUCA
WALESA

•••LA•
AKELAS
ALULAE
ALULAR
ASHLAR
BALLAD
BEDLAM
BELLAY
BEULAH
BULLAE
BURLAP
BYPLAY
CALLAO
CALLAS
CELLAE
CELLAR
CHELAE
CHELAS
COLLAR
CYCLAS
DALLAS
DEWLAP
DOBLAS
DOLLAR
EARLAP
FELLAH
FELLAS
GAGLAW
GULLAH
HARLAN
HELLAS
INPLAY
JETLAG
KAPLAN
KEVLAR
KOALAS
KUBLAI
MEDLAR
MEDLAT
MILLAY
MISLAY
MOOLAH
MULLAH
MULLAS
NULLAH
NYALAS
OCULAR
OUTLAW
OUTLAY
OVULAR
PALLAS
PARLAY
PEDLAR
PHILAE
PHYLAE
PILLAR
POPLAR
PRELAW
RAGLAN
RAILAT
REFLAG
REPLAN
REPLAY
SCALAR
SEALAB
SENLAC
SKYLAB
SMILAX
STALAG
STELAE
STELAR
TABLAS
TESLAS
TOKLAS
UNCLAD
UVULAE
UVULAR
UVULAS
VACLAV
VASLAV
VILLAS
VIOLAS
WAYLAY

•••L•A
ABOLLA
AEOLIA
AMELIA
ANGLIA
APULIA
ARALIA
AXILLA
AZALEA
CHOLLA
COULDA
DAHLIA
DEFLEA
DULLEA
EMILIA
ETALIA
GALLIA
HULLOA
IMELDA
ITALIA
KAHLUA
KAILUA
OBELIA
PAELLA
PALLIA
PSYLLA
REALIA
SCALIA
SCYLLA
STELLA
THALIA
THELMA

••••LA
ABOLLA
ANGELA
ANGOLA
AQUILA
ARBELA
AREOLA
ATTILA
AXILLA
BAKULA
BIKILA
BITOLA
BRAILA
CABALA
CANOLA
CHOLLA
CIBOLA
COPULA
CUPOLA
DOUALA
EIDOLA
FACULA
FIBULA
HOOPLA
IMPALA
KAMALA
KERALA
LALALA
LIGULA
LOYOLA
LUNULA
MACULA
MANILA
MAZOLA
MODELA
NEBULA
NICOLA
NIKOLA
OGLALA
OOLALA
OSCULA
PAELLA
PAKULA
PAMELA
PARULA
PAYOLA
PETULA
PSYLLA
PUEBLA
RADULA
RAMBLA
RCCOLA
ROMOLA
SCYLLA
SHEILA
STELLA
TABULA
URSULA
VIZSLA

L•B•••
LABELS
LABIAL
LABILE
LABORS
LABOUR
LABREA
LABRET
LABRUM
LEBRUN
LIBBED
LIBBER
LIBELS
LIBERI
LIBIDO
LIBRIS
LIBYAN
LLBEAN
LOBATE
LOBBED
LOBBER
LOBULE
LUBBER
LUBECK
LUBING
LUBLIN

L••B••
LAMBDA
LAMBED
LAYBYS
LAZBOY
LESBOS
LIABLE
LIBBED
LIBBER
LIEBIG
LIEBYS
LIMBED
LIMBER
LIMBOS
LIMBUS
LISBOA
LISBON
LOBBED
LOBBER
LOMBOK
LOWBOY
LUBBER
LUMBAR
LUMBER

L•••B•
LAIDBY
LAVABO
LAYSBY
LETSBE

•LB•••
ALBANO
ALBANY
ALBEDO
ALBEIT
ALBERT
ALBINO
ALBION
ALBOIN
ALBORG
ALBUMS
ELBERT
ELBOWS
ELBRUS
LLBEAN

•L•B••
ALIBIS
ALIBLE
ALLBUT
BLABBY
CLUBBY
FLABBY
FLYBOY
FLYBYS
GLEBES
GLIBLY
GLOBAL
GLOBED
GLOBES
GLOBIN
KLIBAN
OLDBOY
PLEBES
SLOBBY

•L••B•
BLABBY
BLURBS
CLIMBS
CLUBBY
FLABBY
FLAMBE
PLUMBS
SLOBBY

••LB••
ALLBUT
BALBOA
BILBAO
BULBIL
BULBUL
TALBOT
WILBUR

••L•B•
ADLIBS
CELEBS
MALABO
MALIBU
PHLEBO

••L••B
APLOMB

•••LB•
PHILBY
TRILBY

•••L•B
SEALAB
SKYLAB

••••LB
DEKALB

LC••••
LCHAIM

L•C•••
LACERS
LACEUP
LACHES
LACIER
LACILY
LACING
LACKED
LACKEY
LACTIC
LACUNA
LECTER
LECTOR
LICHEN
LICKED
LICTOR
LOCALE
LOCALS
LOCATE
LOCKED
LOCKER
LOCKET
LOCKIN
LOCKON
LOCKUP
LOCUST
LUCENT
LUCIAN
LUCITE
LUCIUS
LUCKED
LYCEES
LYCEUM

L••C••
LANCED
LANCER
LANCES
LANCET
LASCAR
LEACHY
LITCHI
LOUCHE
LOWCAL
LUNCHY

L•••C•
LAMECH
LAUNCH
LEGACY
LEXICA
LILACS
LORICA
LUBECK
LUNACY
LYRICS

L••••C
LACTIC
LITHIC

•LC•••
ALCAPP
ALCOTT
ALCOVE
ALCUIN
ULCERS

•L•C••
ALECKY
ALECTO
ALICIA
BLACKS
BLOCKS
BLOCKY
CLACKS
CLICHE
CLICKS
CLOCHE
CLOCKS
CLUCKS
ELECTS
ELICIT
FLACKS
FLACON
FLECHE
FLECKS
FLECKY
FLICKA
FLICKS
FLOCKS
FLOCKY
GLACES
GLACIS
GLYCOL
PLACED
PLACER
PLACES
PLACET
PLACID
PLICAE
PLUCKS
PLUCKY
SLACKS
SLICED
SLICER
SLICES
SLICKS

•L••C•
ALNICO
ALPACA
ALSACE
BLANCA
BLANCH
BLEACH
BLENCH
BLOTCH
CLANCY
CLENCH
CLINCH
CLOACA
CLUTCH
ELLICE
FLEECE
FLEECY
FLETCH
FLINCH
FLITCH
GLANCE
GLITCH
KLATCH
OLMECS
PLAICE
PLANCK
PLEACH
SLOUCH
SLUICE

•L•••C
ALARIC
ALTAIC
CLERIC
CLINIC
OLDVIC
SLAVIC
TLALOC

••LC••
AFLCIO
CALCES
DULCET
FALCES
FALCON
FULCRA
MULCTS
OILCAN
SULCUS
TALCED
TALCUM
VELCRO
VULCAN
WILCOX

••L•C•
CALICO
DELICT
ELLICE
ENLACE
INLUCK
LILACS
MALICE
MOLOCH
OCLOCK
PALACE
POLICE
POLICY
RELACE
RELICS
RELICT
RELOCK
RELUCT
SELECT
SILICA
SOLACE
SPLICE
TOLUCA
UNLACE
UNLOCK
VELOCE

••L••C
BALTIC
BALZAC
BELLOC
CALPAC
CELTIC
CULTIC
DELTIC
GALLIC
MELMAC
PELVIC
TOLTEC

•••LC•
CHALCO

•••L•C
AEOLIC
ANGLIC
BELLOC
CYCLIC
ENBLOC
EXILIC
FROLIC
GAELIC
GALLIC
GARLIC
ITALIC
PUBLIC
SENLAC
TLALOC
URALIC
ZIPLOC

L•D•••
LADDER
LADDIE
LADERS
LADIDA
LADIES
LADING
LADINO
LADLED
LADLER
LADLES
LADOGA
LEDGER
LEDGES
LEDOFF
LEDOUT
LIDDED
LODENS
LODGED
LODGER
LODGES
LUDDEN
LUDENS
LUDLUM
LUDWIG

L••D••
LADDER
LADDIE
LAIDBY
LAIDIN
LAIDON
LAIDTO
LAIDUP
LANDAU
LANDED
LANDER
LANDHO
LANDIS
LANDON
LANDRY
LAPDOG
LARDED
LARDER
LARDON
LAUDED
LAUDER
LEADED
LEADEN
LEADER
LEADIN
LEADON

LEADTO
LEADUP
LEIDEN
LENDER
LEWDER
LEWDLY
LEYDEN
LIDDED
LIEDER
LINDEN
LOADED
LOADER
LONDON
LORDED
LORDLY
LOUDEN
LOUDER
LOUDLY
LUDDEN
LUNDEN
LYNDON

L•••D•

LADIDA
LAIRDS
LAMBDA
LAMEDH
LAMEDS
LAREDO
LERIDA
LIBIDO
LIPIDE
LIPIDS
LLOYDS
LUANDA

L••••D

LACKED
LADLED
LAGGED
LAMBED
LAMMED
LANCED
LANDED
LAPPED
LAPSED
LARDED
LARKED
LASHED
LASTED
LATHED
LAUDED
LEADED
LEAFED
LEAKED
LEANED
LEAPED
LEASED
LEAVED
LEERED
LEGEND
LEGGED
LELAND
LEMOND
LENSED
LEONID
LETTED
LEVEED
LEVIED
LIBBED
LICKED
LIDDED
LIFTED
LIGAND
LILTED
LIMBED
LIMNED
LIMPED
LIMPID
LINKED
LIPOID
LIPPED
LIQUID
LISPED
LISTED
LIZARD
LOADED
LOAFED
LOAMED
LOANED
LOBBED
LOCKED
LODGED
LOFTED
LOGGED
LOLLED
LOMOND
LONGED
LOOKED
LOOMED
LOOPED
LOOSED
LOOTED
LOPPED
LORDED
LOTTED
LOUSED
LOWEND
LUCKED
LUFFED
LUGGED
LULLED
LUMPED
LUNGED
LURKED
LUSTED
LYNYRD

•LD•••

ALDERS
ALDINE
ALDOSE
ALDOUS
ALDRIN
ELDERS
ELDEST
OLDAGE
OLDBOY
OLDEST
OLDHAM
OLDHAT
OLDIES
OLDISH
OLDMAN
OLDMEN
OLDPRO
OLDSAW
OLDVIC

•L•D••

ALLDAY
BLADED
BLADER
BLADES
CLODDY
ELIDED
ELIDES
ELUDED
ELUDER
ELUDES
FLEDGE
FLEDGY
GLADES
GLADLY
GLADYS
GLIDED
GLIDER
GLIDES
KLUDGE
PLEDGE
SLEDGE
SLIDER
SLIDES
SLIDIN
SLUDGE
SLUDGY

•L••D•

ALBEDO
ALKYDS
ALLUDE
BLANDA
BLEEDS
BLENDE
BLENDS
BLINDS
BLONDE
BLONDS
BLOODY
CLAUDE
CLODDY
CLOUDS
CLOUDY
ELANDS
FLOODS
FLUIDS
GLANDS
GLENDA
LLOYDS
OLINDA
PLAIDS
PLEADS

•L•••D

ALATED
ALFRED
ALLIED
ALMOND
BLADED
BLAMED
BLARED
BLAZED
CLAWED
CLEPED
CLEWED
CLONED
CLOSED
CLOYED
ELAPID
ELATED
ELIDED
ELOPED
ELUDED
ELUTED
ELWOOD
FLAKED
FLAMED
FLARED
FLAWED
FLAYED
FLEXED
FLEYED
FLORID
FLOWED
FLUTED
FLUXED
FLYROD
GLARED
GLAZED
GLIDED
GLOBED
GLOVED
GLOWED
GLOZED
ILLFED
PLACED
PLACID
PLANED
PLATED
PLAYED
PLEIAD
PLOWED
PLUMED
SLAKED
SLATED
SLAVED
SLAYED
SLEWED
SLICED
SLIMED
SLOPED
SLOWED

••LD••

ALLDAY
BALDER
BALDLY
BELDAM
BOLDER
BOLDLY
CALDER
COLDER
COLDLY
FELDON
FOLDED
FOLDER
FOLDUP
GILDED
GILDER
GOLDEN
GOLDIE
HELDIN
HELDON
HELDTO
HELDUP
HOLDEN
HOLDER
HOLDIN
HOLDIT
HOLDON
HOLDTO
HOLDUP
MALDEN
MELDED
MILDER
MILDEW
MILDLY
MOLDAU
MOLDED
MOLDER
POLDER
SELDOM
SOLDAN
SOLDER
SOLDON
TILDEN
TILDES
TOLDOF
TOLDON
VALDEZ
VELDTS
WALDEN
WELDED
WELDER
WILDER
WILDLY

••L•D•

ALLUDE
BOLIDE
COLADA
DELUDE
GELADA
HALIDE
MALADY
MELODY
MILADY
SALADO
SALADS
SOLIDI
SOLIDS
TELEDU
TOLEDO
UNLADE

••L••D

ALLIED
BALKED
BALLAD
BELIED
BELLED
BELTED
BILKED
BILLED
BOLTED
BULGED
BULKED
BULLED
CALKED
CALLED
CALMED
CALVED
CELLED
CULLED
DELVED
DOLLED
DULLED
FELLED
FELTED
FILLED
FILMED
FOLDED
GALLED
GELLED
GILDED
GILEAD
GILLED
GOLFED
GULFED
GULLED
GULPED
HALOED
HALOID
HALTED
HALVED
HELMED
HELPED
HILLED
HULKED
HULLED
ILLFED
INLAID
INLAND
ISLAND
JELLED
JILTED
JOLTED
KILLED
KILNED
KILTED
LELAND
LILTED
LOLLED
LULLED
MALTED
MELDED
MELTED
MILKED
MILLED
MILORD
MOLDED
MOLTED
MULLED
NOLEAD
NOLOAD
NULLED
ONLAND
PALLED
PALLID
PALMED
PELTED
PILLED
POLAND
POLLED
PULLED
PULPED
PULSED
RELAID
RELIED
RELOAD
ROLAND
ROLLED
SALTED
SALVED
SILKED
SILOED
SILTED
SOLOED
SOLVED
SULKED
TALCED
TALKED
TALMUD
TILLED
TILTED
TOLLED
UNLAID
UNLEAD
UNLOAD
UPLAND
UPLOAD
VALUED
VALVED
WALKED
WALLED
WELDED
WELLED
WELTED
WILLED
WILTED
WOLFED
XYLOID
YELLED
YELPED
YOLKED

•••LD•

BUILDS
CHILDE
CHILDS
COULDA
FIELDS
FJELDS
GUILDS
IMELDA
ISOLDE
MOULDS
MOULDY
SCALDS
SCOLDS
SKALDS
WIELDS
WORLDS
YIELDS

•••L•D

ADDLED
AMBLED
ANELED
ANGLED
ANKLED
BAILED
BALLAD
BAWLED
BELLED
BILLED
BIRLED
BOILED
BOWLED
BUGLED
BULLED
BURLED
CABLED
CALLED
CEILED
CELLED
COILED
COOLED
COWLED
CULLED
CURLED
CYCLED
DIALED
DOLLED
DUELED
DULLED
EAGLED
EUCLID
EXILED
EYELID
FABLED
FAILED
FELLED
FILLED
FOALED
FOILED
FOOLED
FOULED
FOWLED
FUELED
FURLED
GABLED
GALLED
GAOLED
GELLED
GILLED
GULLED
HAILED
HAULED
HEALED
HEELED
HILLED
HOWLED
HULLED
HURLED
JAILED
JELLED
KEELED
KHALID
KILLED
LADLED
LOLLED
LULLED
MAILED
MARLED
MAULED
MEWLED
MILLED
MISLED
MOILED
MULLED
NAILED
NULLED
PALLED
PALLID
PEALED
PEELED
PILLED
POLLED
POOLED
PULLED
PURLED
RAILED
REELED
RIFLED
ROILED
ROLLED
SAILED
SCALED
SEALED
SIDLED
SMILED
SOILED
STALED
STOLID
STYLED
TABLED
TAILED
TILLED
TITLED
TOILED
TOLLED
TOOLED
UNCLAD
VEILED
WAILED
WALLED
WELLED
WHILED
WILLED
YELLED
YOWLED

••••LD

AFIELD
AGEOLD
ARNOLD
BEHELD
BEHOLD
BIFOLD
BUJOLD
DONALD
ENFOLD
GERALD
GOWILD
HARALD
HAROLD
HERALD
INFOLD
KOBOLD
ONHOLD
OSWALD
REHELD
REMOLD
RESOLD
RETOLD
REWELD
RIBALD
RONALD
SHIELD
SHOULD
UNFOLD
UNSOLD
UNTOLD
UPHELD
UPHOLD

LE••••

LEACHY
LEADED
LEADEN
LEADER
LEADIN
LEADON
LEADTO
LEADUP
LEAFED
LEAGUE
LEAKED
LEAKER
LEAKEY

LEALTY
LEANED
LEANER
LEANLY
LEANON
LEANTO
LEAPED
LEAPER
LEARNS
LEARNT
LEASED
LEASER
LEASES
LEAVED
LEAVEN
LEAVES
LEBRUN
LECTER
LECTOR
LEDGER
LEDGES
LEDOFF
LEDOUT
LEERAT
LEERED
LEERER
LEEWAY
LEFTIE
LEFTIN
LEGACY
LEGALS
LEGATE
LEGATO
LEGEND
LEGGED
LEGION
LEGIST
LEGMAN
LEGMEN
LEGREE
LEGUIN
LEGUME
LEHIGH
LEHRER
LEHUAS
LEIDEN
LEKVAR
LELAND
LEMANS
LEMMAS
LEMMON
LEMNOS
LEMOND
LEMONS
LEMONY
LEMUEL
LEMURS
LENAPE
LENDER
LENGTH
LENITY
LENNIE
LENNON
LENNOX
LENORE
LENSED
LENSES
LENTEN
LENTIL
LEONES
LEONID
LEONIE
LEPTON
LERIDA
LERNER
LESAGE
LESBOS
LESLEY
LESLIE
LESSEE
LESSEN
LESSER
LESSON
LESSOR
LESTAT
LESTER
LETFLY
LETHAL
LETOFF
LETOUT
LETSAT
LETSBE
LETSGO
LETSIN
LETSON
LETSUP
LETTED
LETTER
LETUPS
LEVANT
LEVEED
LEVEES
LEVELS
LEVENE
LEVERS
LEVIED
LEVIER
LEVIES
LEVINE
LEVITE
LEVITY
LEWDER
LEWDLY
LEXEME
LEXICA
LEYDEN

L•E•••

LEERAT
LEERED
LEERER
LEEWAY
LIEBIG
LIEBYS
LIEDER
LIEFER
LIEFLY
LIEGES
LIELOW
LIENEE
LIERNE
LIESIN
LIESTO
LIEUTS

L••E••

LABELS
LACERS
LACEUP
LADERS
LAGERS
LAKERS
LAMECH
LAMEDH
LAMEDS
LAMELY
LAMENT
LAMESA
LAMEST
LAPELS
LAREDO
LASERS
LATEEN
LATELY
LATENE
LATENS
LATENT
LATEST
LAVERS
LAXEST
LAYERS
LEGEND
LEVEED
LEVEES
LEVELS
LEVENE
LEVERS
LEXEME
LIBELS
LIBERI
LIFERS
LIGERS
LIKELY
LIKENS
LIMENS
LIMEYS
LINEAL
LINEAR
LINENS
LINENY
LINERS
LINEUP
LIPENG
LITERS
LIVEIN
LIVELY
LIVENS
LIVEON
LIVERS
LIVERY
LLBEAN
LODENS
LOMEIN
LONELY
LONERS
LOPERS
LOREAL
LORENZ
LOSEIT
LOSERS
LOVEIN
LOVELL
LOVELY
LOVERS
LOVETT
LOWELL
LOWEND
LOWERS
LOWERY
LOWEST
LUBECK
LUCENT
LUDENS
LUGERS
LUMENS
LYCEES
LYCEUM

L•••E•

LAAGER
LABREA
LABRET
LACHES
LACIER
LACKED
LACKEY
LADDER
LADIES
LADLED
LADLER
LADLES
LAFFER
LAGGED
LAGGER
LAKIER
LAMBED
LAMMED
LANCED
LANCER
LANCES
LANCET
LANDED
LANDER
LANIER
LANKER
LAPPED
LAPPET
LAPSED
LAPSES
LAPTEV
LARDED
LARDER
LARGER
LARGES
LARKED
LARSEN
LASHED
LASHER
LASHES
LASSEN
LASSER
LASSES
LASTED
LASTEX
LATEEN
LATHED
LATHER
LATHES
LATKES
LATTEN
LATTER
LAUDED
LAUDER
LAUPER
LAUREL
LAUREN
LAWMEN
LAWYER
LAYMEN
LAZIER
LEADED
LEADEN
LEADER
LEAFED
LEAKED
LEAKER
LEAKEY
LEANED
LEANER
LEAPED
LEAPER
LEASED
LEASER
LEASES
LEAVED
LEAVEN
LEAVES
LECTER
LEDGER
LEDGES
LEERED
LEERER
LEGGED
LEGMEN
LEGREE
LEHRER
LEIDEN
LEMUEL
LENDER
LENSED
LENSES
LENTEN
LEONES
LERNER
LESLEY
LESSEE
LESSEN
LESSER
LESTER
LETTED
LETTER
LEVEED
LEVEES
LEVIED
LEVIER
LEVIES
LEWDER
LEYDEN
LIANES
LIBBED
LIBBER
LICHEN
LICKED
LIDDED
LIEDER
LIEFER
LIEGES
LIENEE
LIFTED
LIFTER
LILIES
LILTED
LIMBED
LIMBER
LIMIER
LIMNED
LIMNER
LIMPED
LIMPER
LIMPET
LINDEN
LINGER
LINIER
LINKED
LINKER
LINNET
LINNEY
LINSEY
LINTEL
LINTER
LIONEL
LIONET
LIPPED
LISLES
LISPED
LISTED
LISTEE
LISTEL
LISTEN
LISTER
LITRES
LITTER
LIVRES
LOADED
LOADER
LOAFED
LOAFER
LOAMED
LOANED
LOANER
LOAVES
LOBBED
LOBBER
LOCKED
LOCKER
LOCKET
LODGED
LODGER
LODGES
LOFTED
LOGGED
LOGGER
LOGIER
LOITER
LOLLED
LONGED
LONGER
LONGES
LOOIES
LOOKED
LOOKER
LOOMED
LOONEY
LOOPED
LOOPER
LOOSED
LOOSEN
LOOSER
LOOSES
LOOTED
LOOTER
LOPPED
LOPPER
LORDED
LORIES
LOSSES
LOTTED
LOUDEN
LOUDER
LOUPES
LOUSED
LOUSES
LOUVER
LOWKEY
LUBBER
LUCKED
LUDDEN
LUFFED
LUGGED
LUGGER
LULLED
LUMBER
LUMPED
LUMPEN
LUMPER
LUNDEN
LUNGED
LUNGES
LUNKER
LURKED
LUSHER
LUSTED
LUSTER
LUTHER
LUTZES
LYCEES
LYNLEY
LYNXES

L••••E

LABILE
LADDIE
LAHORE
LAINIE
LAMAZE
LANATE
LANOSE
LAOTSE
LARVAE
LASSIE
LATENE
LAURIE
LAVAGE
LEAGUE
LEFTIE
LEGATE
LEGREE
LEGUME
LENAPE
LENNIE
LENORE
LEONIE
LESAGE
LESLIE
LESSEE
LETSBE
LEVENE
LEVINE
LEVITE
LEXEME
LHOTSE
LIABLE
LIAISE
LIENEE
LIERNE
LIGATE
LIGURE
LILLIE
LINAGE
LIPASE
LIPIDE
LISTEE
LITTLE
LIZZIE
LOATHE
LOBATE
LOBULE
LOCALE
LOCATE
LONGUE
LOONIE
LOUCHE
LOUISE
LOUNGE
LOUVRE
LOVAGE
LUCITE
LUNATE
LUPINE
LUPONE
LUSTRE
LUXATE
LYSINE

•LE•••

ALEAST
ALECKY
ALECTO
ALEGAR
ALEGRE
ALEMAN
ALEPHS
ALEPPO
ALERTS
ALEUTS
ALEVEL
ALEXEI
ALEXIA
ALEXIS
BLEACH
BLEARS
BLEARY
BLEATS
BLEEDS
BLEEPS
BLENCH
BLENDE
BLENDS
BLENNY
BLEWIT
BLEWUP
CLEANS
CLEARS
CLEATS
CLEAVE
CLEEKS
CLEESE
CLEFTS
CLENCH
CLEPED
CLERGY
CLERIC
CLERKS
CLEVER
CLEVES
CLEVIS
CLEWED
ELECTS
ELEGIT
ELEMIS
ELEVEN
ELEVES
FLECHE
FLECKS
FLECKY
FLEDGE
FLEDGY
FLEECE
FLEECY
FLEERS
FLEETS
FLENSE
FLESHY
FLETCH
FLEURY
FLEWAT
FLEWIN
FLEXED
FLEXES
FLEXOR
FLEYED
GLEAMS
GLEAMY
GLEANS
GLEBES
GLENDA
GLENNE
ILEANA
ILESHA
ILEXES
KLEIST
NLEAST
OLEARY
OLEATE
OLEFIN
OLESON
OLEVEL
PLEACH
PLEADS
PLEASE
PLEATS
PLEBES
PLEDGE
PLEIAD
PLENTY
PLENUM
PLEURA
PLEXAL
PLEXOR
PLEXUS
SLEAVE
SLEAZE
SLEAZY
SLEDGE
SLEEKS
SLEEKY
SLEEPS
SLEEPY
SLEETS
SLEETY
SLEEVE
SLEIGH
SLEUTH
SLEWED
SLEZAK

•L•E••

ALBEDO
ALBEIT
ALBERT

ALDERS
ALIENS
ALKENE
ALLEES
ALLEGE
ALLELE
ALLEYS
ALPERT
ALTERS
ALWEST
BLEEDS
BLEEPS
BLUELY
BLUEOX
BLUEST
BLUESY
BLUETS
BLUEYS
CLEEKS
CLEESE
CLIENT
CLUEIN
ELBERT
ELDERS
ELDEST
ELLERY
ELVERS
FLEECE
FLEECY
FLEERS
FLEETS
FLIERS
FLUENT
FLYERS
GLUERS
ILLEST
LLBEAN
NLWEST
OLDEST
OLMECS
PLIERS
SLEEKS
SLEEKY
SLEEPS
SLEEPY
SLEETS
SLEETY
SLEEVE
SLIEST
SLYEST
ULCERS

•L••E•

ALATED
ALEVEL
ALEXEI
ALFRED
ALFVEN
ALINES
ALITER
ALLEES
ALLIED
ALLIES
ALLSET
ALLWET
ALTHEA
BLADED
BLADER
BLADES
BLAMED
BLAMES
BLARED
BLARES
BLAZED
BLAZER
BLAZES
BLIMEY
BLIXEN
BLOKES
BLOOEY
BLOWER
CLARET
CLAVES
CLAWED
CLAWER
CLAYEY
CLEPED
CLEVER
CLEVES
CLEWED
CLIMES
CLINES
CLONED
CLONES
CLOSED
CLOSER
CLOSES
CLOSET
CLOVEN
CLOVER
CLOVES
CLOYED
DLAYER
ELATED
ELATER
ELATES
ELAYER
ELEVEN
ELEVES
ELIDED
ELIDES
ELITES
ELOPED
ELOPER
ELOPES
ELUDED
ELUDER
ELUDES
ELUTED
ELUTES
ELYSEE
FLAKED
FLAKER
FLAKES
FLAKEY
FLAMED
FLAMES
FLARED
FLARES
FLAWED
FLAXEN
FLAXES
FLAYED
FLAYER
FLEXED
FLEXES
FLEYED
FLOOEY
FLORES
FLORET
FLOWED
FLOWER
FLUKES
FLUKEY
FLUMES
FLUTED
FLUTES
FLUTEY
FLUXED
FLUXES
FLYMEN
FLYNET
GLACES
GLADES
GLARED
GLARES
GLASER
GLAZED
GLAZER
GLAZES
GLEBES
GLIDED
GLIDER
GLIDES
GLOBED
GLOBES
GLOVED
GLOVER
GLOVES
GLOWED
GLOWER
GLOZED
GLOZES
GLUIER
GLUTEI
GLUTEN
GLUTES
ILEXES
ILLFED
ILLMET
OLDIES
OLDMEN
OLEVEL
OLIVER
OLIVES
PLACED
PLACER
PLACES
PLACET
PLAGES
PLANED
PLANER
PLANES
PLANET
PLATED
PLATEN
PLATER
PLATES
PLAYED
PLAYER
PLEBES
PLOVER
PLOWED
PLOWER
PLUMED
PLUMES
PLUSES
SLAKED
SLAKES
SLATED
SLATER
SLATES
SLAVED
SLAVER
SLAVES
SLAVEY
SLAYED
SLAYER
SLEWED
SLICED
SLICER
SLICES
SLIDER
SLIDES
SLIMED
SLIMES
SLIVER
SLOPED
SLOPES
SLOVEN
SLOWED
SLOWER
SLYPES
ULSTER

•L•••E

ALCOVE
ALDINE
ALDOSE
ALEGRE
ALFINE
ALGORE
ALIBLE
ALKENE
ALLEGE
ALLELE
ALLUDE
ALLURE
ALPINE
ALSACE
ALULAE
BLAINE
BLAISE
BLENDE
BLITHE
BLONDE
BLOUSE
BLYTHE
CLAIRE
CLAQUE
CLARKE
CLAUDE
CLAUSE
CLEAVE
CLEESE
CLICHE
CLIQUE
CLOCHE
CLOQUE
CLOTHE
ELAINE
ELAPSE
ELAYNE
ELLICE
ELMORE
ELOISE
ELYSEE
FLAMBE
FLANGE
FLECHE
FLEDGE
FLEECE
FLENSE
FLORAE
GLANCE
GLENNE
ILLUME
ILLUSE
KLUDGE
OLDAGE
OLEATE
PLAGUE
PLAICE
PLANTE
PLAQUE
PLATTE
PLEASE
PLEDGE
PLICAE
PLISSE
PLUNGE
SLEAVE
SLEAZE
SLEDGE
SLEEVE
SLOANE
SLUDGE
SLUICE
ULLAGE

••LE••

ABLEST
AGLEAM
AGLETS
AILEEN
AILERS
ALLEES
ALLEGE
ALLELE
ALLEYS
ARLEEN
ARLENE
ASLEEP
BALEEN
BALERS
BOLERO
BOLEYN
CELEBS
CELERY
COLEUS
CULETS
DALETH
DELEON
DELETE
DOLENZ
EELERS
EILEEN
ELLERY
EXLEGE
FILENE
FILERS
FILETS
GALEAE
GALENA
GELEES
GILEAD
GOLEMS
HALERS
HALERU
HALEST
HALEVY
HELENA
HELENE
HELENS
HOLEUP
IDLERS
IDLEST
ILLEST
INLETS
IRLENE
ISLETS
JOLENE
JULEPS
MCLEAN
MELEES
MILERS
MOLEST
MULETA
MULEYS
NFLERS
NHLERS
NOLEAD
NOLENS
NOLESS
OGLERS
OILERS
OWLETS
PALEAE
PALELY
PALEST
PELEUS
PHLEBO
PHLEGM
PILEIN
PILEON
PILEUM
PILEUP
PILEUS
POLEAX
POLERS
POLEYN
RELENT
RELETS
RELEVY
RILEUP
ROLEOS
RULEON
RULERS
SCLERA
SCLERO
SELECT
SELENA
SELENE
SELENO
SILENI
SILENT
SOLEIL
SOLELY
SOLEMN
SOLENT
SOLERS
SOLEUS
SPLEEN
TALENT
TALERS
TALESE
TELEDU
TILERS
TOLEDO
UNLEAD
UNLESS
VALENS
VALENT
VALERY
VALETS
VILELY
VILEST
VOLENS
WALERS
WALESA
XYLENE

••L•E•

AILEEN
ALLEES
ALLIED
ALLIES
ALLSET
ALLWET
ARLEEN
ASLEEP
BALDER
BALEEN
BALKED
BALLET
BELIED
BELIEF
BELIES
BELLED
BELLES
BELTED
BILGES
BILKED
BILLED
BILLET
BOLDER
BOLGER
BOLTED
BULGED
BULGES
BULKED
BULLED
BULLET
BULWER
CALCES
CALDER
CALKED
CALLED
CALLER
CALLES
CALMED
CALMER
CALVED
CALVES
CALXES
CELLED
COLDER
COLIES
COLLET
COLTER
CULLED
CULLEN
CULLER
CULLET
CULVER
DALLES
DELVED
DELVER
DELVES
DILLER
DILSEY
DOLLED
DOLMEN
DULCET
DULLEA
DULLED
DULLER
DULLES
EELIER
EILEEN
FALCES
FALLEN
FALSER
FALTER
FELLED
FELLER
FELTED
FILLED
FILLER
FILLES
FILLET
FILMED
FILTER
FOLDED
FOLDER
FULLER
GALLED
GALLEY
GELEES
GELLED
GELSEY
GILDED
GILDER
GILLED
GOLDEN
GOLFED
GOLFER
GULFED
GULLED
GULLET
GULPED
GULPER
HALLEL
HALLEY
HALOED
HALOES
HALSEY
HALTED
HALTER
HALVED
HALVES
HELLER
HELMED
HELMET
HELPED
HELPER
HELTER
HELVES
HILLED
HILLEL
HILLER
HOLDEN
HOLDER
HOLIER
HOLLER
HOLMES
HULKED
HULLED
HULLER
ILLFED
ILLMET
JELLED
JILTED
JOLIET
JOLTED
JULIET
KELLER
KELLEY
KELSEY
KILLED
KILLER
KILMER
KILNED
KILTED
KILTER
LILIES
LILTED
LOLLED
LULLED
MALDEN
MALLEE
MALLEI
MALLET
MALTED
MELDED
MELEES
MELTED
MILDER
MILDEW
MILIEU
MILKED
MILKER
MILLED
MILLER
MILLET
MILNER
MOLDED
MOLDER
MOLTED
MOLTEN
MOLTER
MULLED
MULLER
MULLET
NULLED
OILIER
OILMEN
PALAEO
PALIER
PALLED
PALLET
PALMED
PALMER
PALTER
PELLET
PELMET
PELTED
PELTER
PHLOEM
PILFER
PILLED
POLDER
POLLED
POLLEN
POLLER
POLLEX
PULLED
PULLET
PULLEY
PULPED

PULSED
PULSES
RELIED
RELIEF
RELIES
RILLES
RILLET
ROLLED
ROLLER
SALLET
SALTED
SALTEN
SALTER
SALVED
SALVER
SALVES
SELLER
SELVES
SILKED
SILKEN
SILOED
SILTED
SILVER
SOLDER
SOLOED
SOLVED
SOLVER
SOLVES
SPLEEN
SULKED
SULKER
SULLEN
TALCED
TALKED
TALKER
TALLER
TELLER
TILDEN
TILDES
TILLED
TILLER
TILTED
TILTER
TOLLED
TOLTEC
TULLES
UGLIER
UGLIES
VALDEZ
VALLEE
VALLEY
VALUED
VALUES
VALVED
VALVES
VELVET
VOLLEY
WALDEN
WALKED
WALKEN
WALKER
WALLED
WALLER
WALLET
WALTER
WELDED
WELDER
WELLED
WELLER
WELLES
WELTED
WELTER
WILDER
WILIER
WILKES
WILLED
WILLEM
WILLET
WILTED
WOLFED
WOLPER
WOLSEY
WOLVES
YALIES
YELLED
YELLER
YELPED
YELPER
YOLKED

••L••E

ABLATE
ABLAZE
AFLAME
AGLARE
ALLEGE
ALLELE
ALLUDE
ALLURE
APLITE
ARLENE
ASLOPE
AXLIKE
BELIKE
BELIZE
BILLIE
BOLIDE
BULLAE
BYLINE
CALQUE
CELINE
CELLAE
COLLIE
DELATE
DELETE
DELUDE
DELUGE
DELUXE
DILATE
DILUTE
ELLICE
ENLACE
EXLEGE
FALINE
FELINE
FELIPE
FELLOE
FILENE
FILOSE
FOLKIE
GALEAE
GALORE
GILLIE
GOLDIE
HALIDE
HALITE
HELENE
ILLUME
ILLUSE
INLINE
INLOVE
IOLITE
IRLENE
JOLENE
KALINE
KELPIE
KILTIE
LILLIE
MALATE
MALICE
MALLEE
MALONE
MILLIE
MILTIE
MOLINE
MOLTKE
NELLIE
NOLOSE
OBLATE
OBLIGE
OFLATE
ONLINE
OOLITE
OXLIKE
PALACE
PALATE
PALEAE
PELAGE
PELIKE
PILATE
PILOSE
POLICE
POLITE
PULQUE
RELACE
RELATE
RELINE
RELIVE
RELUME
ROLLIE
SALINE
SALOME
SALUTE
SELENE
SILAGE
SILONE
SOLACE
SOLUTE
SPLICE
SPLINE
STLUKE
TALESE
TALKIE
TILLIE
TOLIFE
TULANE
TULARE
ULLAGE
UNLACE
UNLADE
UNLIKE
VALISE
VALLEE
VELOCE
VOLARE
VOLUME
VOLUTE
WALKIE
WILLIE
XYLENE

•••LE•

ABELES
ADDLED
ADDLES
AISLES
AMBLED
AMBLER
AMBLES
AMOLES
AMPLER
AMULET
ANELED
ANELES
ANGLED
ANGLER
ANGLES
ANKLED
ANKLES
ANKLET
ANNLEE
ANOLES
ANTLER
APPLES
APPLET
ARMLET
ASHLEY
ATTLEE
AUKLET
AZALEA
BAILED
BAILEE
BAILER
BAILEY
BALLET
BARLEY
BAWLED
BAWLER
BEGLEY
BELLED
BELLES
BIBLES
BILLED
BILLET
BIRLED
BOGLES
BOILED
BOILER
BOSLEY
BOULES
BOULEZ
BOWLED
BOWLER
BOWLES
BRULES
BUGLED
BUGLER
BUGLES
BULLED
BULLET
BURLED
BURLEY
BUTLER
CABLED
CABLER
CABLES
CALLED
CALLER
CALLES
CAMLET
CAPLET
CEILED
CELLED
CHALET
CHOLER
COALER
COILED
COLLET
COOLED
COOLER
COPLEY
COULEE
COWLED
COWLEY
CULLED
CULLEN
CULLER
CULLET
CURLED
CURLER
CURLEW
CURLEY
CUTLER
CUTLET
CYCLED
CYCLER
CYCLES
DAILEY
DALLES
DEALER
DEFLEA
DHOLES
DIALED
DIALER
DILLER
DOGLEG
DOLLED
DOOLEY
DUDLEY
DUELED
DUELER
DULLEA
DULLED
DULLER
DULLES
DUPLEX
EAGLED
EAGLES
EAGLET
ECCLES
ECOLES
EDILES
EMBLEM
EVILER
EXILED
EXILES
EYELET
FABLED
FABLER
FABLES
FAILED
FALLEN
FARLEY
FEELER
FELLED
FELLER
FILLED
FILLER
FILLES
FILLET
FOALED
FOILED
FOOLED
FOOLER
FOULED
FOULER
FOWLED
FOWLER
FOWLES
FUELED
FUELER
FULLER
FURLED
GABLED
GABLER
GABLES
GALLED
GALLEY
GAOLED
GAOLER
GELLED
GIBLET
GILLED
GIMLET
GOBLET
GOULET
GUILES
GULLED
GULLET
GURLEY
HAILED
HAILEY
HALLEL
HALLEY
HAMLET
HANLEY
HAOLES
HARLEM
HARLEY
HAULED
HAULER
HAYLEY
HEALED
HEALER
HEELED
HEELER
HELLER
HENLEY
HILLED
HILLEL
HILLER
HOLLER
HOWLED
HOWLER
HULLED
HULLER
HURLED
HURLER
HURLEY
HUXLEY
INGLES
INKLES
ISTLES
JAILED
JAILER
JELLED
JOULES
KEELED
KEELER
KEGLER
KELLER
KELLEY
KEPLER
KILLED
KILLER
KISLEV
KJOLEN
KOHLER
LADLED
LADLER
LADLES
LESLEY
LISLES
LOLLED
LULLED
LYNLEY
MAHLER
MAILED
MAILER
MAILES
MALLEE
MALLEI
MALLET
MAPLES
MARLED
MARLEE
MARLEY
MAULED
MAULER
MEDLEY
MEWLED
MEWLER
MIDLER
MILLED
MILLER
MILLET
MISLED
MOBLEY
MOILED
MOILER
MORLEY
MOSLEM
MOTLEY
MULLED
MULLER
MULLET
NAILED
NAILER
NAPLES
NEWLEY
NOBLER
NOBLES
NUCLEI
NUCLEO
NULLED
NUTLET
OAKLEY
OMELET
OODLES
ORALES
ORTLES
OSTLER
OUTLET
OVULES
PALLED
PALLET
PARLEY
PAULEY
PEALED
PEELED
PEELER
PEGLER
PELLET
PIGLET
PILLED
PIOLET
POLLED
POLLEN
POLLER
POLLEX
POOLED
PROLES
PULLED
PULLET
PULLEY
PURLED
RAILED
RAILER
REALER
REALES
REELED
REFLEX
REGLET
RIDLEY
RIFLED
RIFLER
RIFLES
RILLES
RILLET
RIPLEY
ROBLES
ROILED
ROLLED
ROLLER
RUBLES
RUBLEV
RUNLET
SABLES
SAILED
SALLET
SAMLET
SAYLES
SCALED
SCALER
SCALES
SCHLEP
SEALED
SEALER
SEELEY
SELLER
SHALES
SHALEY
SHOLEM
SIDLED
SIDLES
SISLER
SISLEY
SMILED
SMILER
SMILES
SMILEY
SOCLES
SOILED
SPILES
STALED
STALER
STALES
STELES
STILES
STOLEN
STOLES
STYLED
STYLER
STYLES
STYLET
SUBLET
SULLEN
SUTLER
SWALES
TABLED
TABLES
TABLET
TAILED
TALLER
TELLER
THALER
THALES
THOLES
TILLED
TILLER
TITLED
TITLES
TOILED
TOILER
TOILES
TOILET
TOLLED
TOOLED
TRALEE
TULLES
UNCLES
VALLEE
VALLEY
VARLET
VEBLEN
VEILED
VIOLET
VOILES
VOLLEY
WAILED
WAILER
WALLED
WALLER
WALLET
WELLED
WELLER
WELLES
WESLEY
WHALER
WHALES
WHILED
WHILES
WHOLES
WIGLET
WILLED
WILLEM
WILLET
WOHLER
WOOLEN
WOOLEY
WURLEY
XFILES
YELLED
YELLER
YOWLED

•••L•E

ADELIE
ADELLE
ALULAE

AMALIE
ANNLEE
ATTLEE
AVULSE
BAILEE
BIGLIE
BILLIE
BOULLE
BULLAE
CELLAE
CHELAE
CHILDE
CHILOE
COLLIE
COULEE
EVOLVE
EVULSE
FAILLE
FELLOE
GILLIE
GOALIE
GRILLE
GRILSE
ISOLDE
KPELLE
LESLIE
LILLIE
MALLEE
MARLEE
MEALIE
MILLIE
MRBLUE
NELLIE
ORELSE
PHILAE
PHYLAE
REGLUE
ROLLIE
RVALUE
SHELVE
STELAE
STOLLE
SVELTE
TAILLE
TILLIE
TRALEE
TUILLE
TWELVE
UNGLUE
UVALUE
UVULAE
VALLEE
WILLIE

••••LE

ADELLE
AEDILE
ALIBLE
ALLELE
AMPULE
ARABLE
ARGYLE
AUDILE
AWHILE
BABBLE
BAFFLE
BANGLE
BATTLE
BAUBLE
BEADLE
BEAGLE
BEATLE
BEETLE
BIDDLE
BOBBLE
BOGGLE
BOODLE
BOTTLE
BOUCLE
BOULLE
BRIDLE
BUBBLE
BUCKLE
BUMBLE
BUNDLE
BUNGLE
BURBLE
BURGLE
BUSTLE
CACKLE
CAJOLE
CANDLE
CANTLE
CAROLE
CASTLE
CATTLE
CAUDLE
CECILE
CHICLE
CIRCLE
COBBLE
COCKLE
CODDLE
COUPLE
CRADLE
CREOLE
CUDDLE
CURDLE
CURULE
CYBELE
DABBLE
DANDLE
DANGLE
DAPPLE
DARKLE
DAWDLE
DAZZLE
DECKLE
DEFILE
DIBBLE
DIDDLE
DIMPLE
DINGLE
DIPOLE
DOABLE
DOCILE
DONGLE
DOODLE
DOTTLE
DOUBLE
EDERLE
EDIBLE
ENABLE
ENISLE
ENSILE
ETOILE
EXHALE
FACILE
FAILLE
FATALE
FEEBLE
FEMALE
FERULE
FETTLE
FICKLE
FIDDLE
FINALE
FIPPLE
FIZZLE
FOCSLE
FOIBLE
FONDLE
FOOZLE
FUDDLE
FUMBLE
FUTILE
GABBLE
GAGGLE
GAMBLE
GANGLE
GARBLE
GARGLE
GENTLE
GIGGLE
GIRDLE
GOBBLE
GOGGLE
GOOGLE
GRABLE
GRILLE
GURGLE
GUZZLE
HABILE
HACKLE
HAGGLE
HANDLE
HASSLE
HECKLE
HEDDLE
HIGGLE
HOBBLE
HOOPLE
HOPPLE
HUBBLE
HUDDLE
HUMBLE
HURDLE
HURTLE
HUSTLE
ICICLE
IMPALE
INHALE
INSOLE
JANGLE
JECKLE
JIGGLE
JINGLE
JOGGLE
JOSTLE
JUGGLE
JUMBLE
JUNGLE
KETTLE
KIBBLE
KINDLE
KIRTLE
KPELLE
KURILE
LABILE
LIABLE
LITTLE
LOBULE
LOCALE
MANGLE
MANTLE
MARBLE
MARPLE
MCHALE
MEDDLE
METTLE
MIDDLE
MIGGLE
MINGLE
MIZZLE
MOBILE
MODULE
MORALE
MOTILE
MOTTLE
MUDDLE
MUFFLE
MUMBLE
MUSCLE
MUZZLE
MYRTLE
NEEDLE
NESTLE
NETTLE
NIBBLE
NICOLE
NIGGLE
NIMBLE
NOBBLE
NODDLE
NODULE
NOODLE
NOSALE
NOZZLE
NUBBLE
NUBILE
NUZZLE
ONFILE
ONSALE
ORACLE
ORIOLE
OTOOLE
PADDLE
PAROLE
PEBBLE
PEDDLE
PEOPLE
PESTLE
PICKLE
PIFFLE
PINOLE
PINTLE
POODLE
POPPLE
POTTLE
PUDDLE
PURFLE
PURPLE
PUZZLE
QUAYLE
RABBLE
RADDLE
RAFFLE
RAMBLE
RANKLE
RASSLE
RATTLE
RAZZLE
REFILE
REGALE
RESALE
RESILE
RESOLE
RETILE
REVILE
RIDDLE
RIFFLE
RIMPLE
RIPPLE
ROUBLE
ROYALE
RUBBLE
RUDDLE
RUFFLE
RUMBLE
RUMPLE
RUNDLE
RUSTLE
RUTILE
SADDLE
SAMPLE
SEARLE
SEDILE
SEMELE
SETTLE
SICKLE
SIECLE
SIMILE
SIMPLE
SINGLE
SIZZLE
STABLE
STAPLE
STEELE
STIFLE
STOLLE
SUBTLE
SUPPLE
TACKLE
TAILLE
TAMALE
TANGLE
TATTLE
TEMPLE
THRALE
TICKLE
TINGLE
TINKLE
TIPPLE
TITTLE
TODDLE
TOGGLE
TOOTLE
TOPPLE
TOUSLE
TREBLE
TRIFLE
TRIPLE
TUILLE
TUMBLE
TURTLE
TUSSLE
UNABLE
UNPILE
USABLE
VIABLE
VIRILE
VITALE
WADDLE
WAFFLE
WAGGLE
WAMBLE
WANGLE
WARBLE
WATTLE
WIGGLE
WIMBLE
WIMPLE
WINKLE
WOBBLE

L•F•••

LAFFER
LEFTIE
LEFTIN
LIFERS
LIFTED
LIFTER
LIFTUP
LOFTED
LUFFED

L••F••

LAFFER
LAPFUL
LAWFUL
LAYFOR
LEAFED
LETFLY
LIEFER
LIEFLY
LOAFED
LOAFER
LOOFAH
LOOFAS
LOWFAT
LUFFED

L•••F•

LAYOFF
LEDOFF
LETOFF
LOGOFF

L••••F

LAYOFF
LEDOFF
LETOFF
LOGOFF

•LF•••

ALFINE
ALFRED
ALFVEN
ELFISH
ELFMAN

•L•F••

ALLFOR
BLUFFS
CLEFTS
CLIFFS
CLIFFY
FLUFFS
FLUFFY
ILLFED
OLEFIN

•L••F•

BLUFFS
CLIFFS
CLIFFY
FLUFFS
FLUFFY
KLOOFS

••LF••

ALLFOR
BELFRY
COLFAX
DELFTS
FULFIL
GOLFED
GOLFER
GULFED
ILLFED
PILFER
SOLFAS
SULFUR
WILFUL
WOLFED

••L•F•

PILAFS
SALIFY
SCLAFF
TOLIFE
UGLIFY
UPLIFT
VILIFY

••L••F

BELIEF
RELIEF
SCLAFF
TELLOF
TOLDOF

•••LF•

AMALFI

•••L•F

TELLOF

••••LF

BEHALF
ENGULF
INHALF
ITSELF
MYSELF
RUDOLF

L•G•••

LAGASH
LAGERS
LAGGED
LAGGER
LAGOON
LAGUNA
LEGACY
LEGALS
LEGATE
LEGATO
LEGEND
LEGGED
LEGION
LEGIST
LEGMAN
LEGMEN
LEGREE
LEGUIN
LEGUME
LIGAND
LIGATE
LIGERS
LIGHTS
LIGNIN
LIGULA
LIGURE
LOGGED
LOGGER
LOGGIA
LOGIER
LOGILY
LOGION
LOGJAM
LOGOFF
LOGOUT
LOGSIN
LOGSON
LUGERS
LUGGED
LUGGER
LUGNUT
LUGOSI

L••G••

LAAGER
LAGGED
LAGGER
LANGUR
LARGER
LARGES
LARGOS
LAUGHS
LEAGUE
LEDGER
LEDGES
LEGGED
LENGTH
LIEGES
LINGER
LINGUA
LODGED
LODGER
LODGES
LOGGED
LOGGER
LOGGIA
LONGAN
LONGED
LONGER
LONGES
LONGLY
LONGUE
LOUGHS
LUGGED
LUGGER
LUNGED
LUNGES

L•••G•

LADOGA
LATIGO
LAVAGE
LEHIGH
LESAGE
LETSGO
LIANGS
LINAGE
LOUNGE
LOVAGE

L••••G

LACING
LADING
LAMING
LAPDOG
LAVING
LAWING
LAYING
LAZING
LIEBIG
LIKING
LIMING
LINING
LIPENG
LITHOG
LIVING
LOPING
LOSING
LOVING
LOWING
LUBING
LUDWIG
LURING
LUTING

•LG•••

ALGORE

•L•G••

ALEGAR
ALEGRE
ALIGHT
ALIGNS
BLIGHT
CLOGGY
CLOGUP
ELEGIT
FLAGGY
FLAGON
FLIGHT
GLOGGS
PLAGAL
PLAGES
PLAGIO
PLAGUE
PLIGHT
PLUGIN
SLAGGY
SLIGHT
SLOGAN
SLUGGO

•L••G•

ALLEGE
CLANGS
CLERGY
CLINGS
CLINGY
CLOGGY
ELOIGN
FLAGGY
FLANGE
FLEDGE

FLEDGY
FLINGS
GLOGGS
KLUDGE
OLDAGE
OLINGO
PLEDGE
PLOUGH
PLUNGE
SLAGGY
SLANGS
SLANGY
SLEDGE
SLEIGH
SLINGS
SLOUGH
SLUDGE
SLUDGY
SLUGGO
ULLAGE

•L•••G
ALBORG
BLUING
CLUING
FLYING
GLUING
PLYING
SLUING

••LG••
BILGES
BOLGER
BULGAR
BULGED
BULGES
BULGUR
GILGUY
NILGAI
VULGAR

••L•G•
ALLEGE
BELUGA
COLUGO
DELUGE
EULOGY
EXLEGE
GALAGO
GULAGS
MALAGA
MALIGN
OBLIGE
OOLOGY
PELAGE
PHLEGM
SILAGE
TELUGU
ULLAGE

••L••G
AILING
BALING
BELONG
DELONG
DOLING
EALING
FILING
HALING
HOLING
IDLING
KDLANG
OBLONG
OGLING
OILING
OILRIG
OOLONG
PALING
PILING
POLING
PULING
RILING
RULING
SOLING
SOLONG
TILING
WILING

•••L•G
ANALOG
DIALOG
DOGLEG
EPILOG
GASLOG
JETLAG
PROLOG
REFLAG
SAWLOG
STALAG
UNCLOG
UNPLUG

LH••••
LHOTSE

L•H•••
LAHORE
LCHAIM
LEHIGH
LEHRER
LEHUAS

L••H••
LACHES
LAPHAM
LASHED
LASHER
LASHES
LASHIO
LASHUP
LATHED
LATHER
LATHES
LETHAL
LICHEN
LIGHTS
LITHIC
LITHOG
LITHOS
LOTHAR
LUSHER
LUSHLY
LUTHER
LUTHOR

L•••H•
LANDHO
LAUGHS
LEACHY
LITCHI
LOATHE
LOTAHS
LOUCHE
LOUGHS
LUNCHY
LYMPHS

L••••H
LAGASH
LAMECH
LAMEDH
LATISH
LAUNCH
LAVISH
LEHIGH
LENGTH
LILITH
LOOFAH
LOWISH

•LH•••
ALHIRT
HLHUNT

•L•H••
ALOHAS
ALPHAS
ALTHEA
ELOHIM
OLDHAM
OLDHAT

•L••H•
ALEPHS
ALIGHT
BLIGHT
BLITHE
BLYTHE
CLICHE
CLOCHE
CLOTHE
CLOTHO
CLOTHS
ELISHA
FLASHY
FLECHE
FLESHY
FLIGHT
GLYPHS
ILESHA
PLASHY
PLIGHT
PLUSHY
SLIGHT
SLITHY
SLOSHY
SLOTHS
SLUSHY

•L•••H
BLANCH
BLEACH
BLENCH
BLOTCH
BLUISH
CLENCH
CLINCH
CLUTCH
ELFISH
ELIJAH
ELVISH
FLETCH
FLINCH
FLITCH
GLITCH
KLATCH
OLDISH
PLEACH
PLINTH
PLOUGH
SLEIGH
SLEUTH
SLOUCH
SLOUGH

••L•H•
BOLSHY
DELPHI
FILTHY
GALAHS
SYLPHS

••L••H
ABLUSH
CALASH
CALIPH
DALETH
DULUTH
EOLITH
FELLAH
GALOSH
GULLAH
HALVAH
KALAKH
LILITH
MOLOCH
MULISH
MULLAH
NULLAH
OOLITH
OWLISH
PALISH
POLISH
RELISH
SALISH
SPLASH
SPLOSH
UNLASH
ZILPAH

•••L•H
ADOLPH
BEULAH
FELLAH
GUELPH
GULLAH
HEALTH
MOOLAH
MULLAH
NULLAH
SHILOH
SPILTH
WEALTH

LI••••
LIABLE
LIAISE
LIANAS
LIANES
LIANGS
LIBBED
LIBBER
LIBELS
LIBERI
LIBIDO
LIBRIS
LIBYAN
LICHEN
LICKED
LICTOR
LIDDED
LIEBIG
LIEBYS
LIEDER
LIEFER
LIEFLY
LIEGES
LIELOW
LIENEE
LIERNE
LIESIN
LIESTO
LIEUTS
LIFERS
LIFTED
LIFTER
LIFTUP
LIGAND
LIGATE
LIGERS
LIGHTS
LIGNIN
LIGULA
LIGURE
LIKELY
LIKENS
LIKING
LILACS
LILIES
LILITH
LILLIE
LILTED
LIMBED
LIMBER
LIMBOS
LIMBUS
LIMENS
LIMEYS
LIMIER
LIMING
LIMITS
LIMNED
LIMNER
LIMPED
LIMPER
LIMPET
LIMPID
LIMPLY
LINAGE
LINDEN
LINEAL
LINEAR
LINENS
LINENY
LINERS
LINEUP
LINGER
LINGUA
LINIER
LINING
LINKED
LINKER
LINKUP
LINNET
LINNEY
LINSEY
LINTEL
LINTER
LIONEL
LIONET
LIONLY
LIOTTA
LIPASE
LIPENG
LIPIDE
LIPIDS
LIPOID
LIPPED
LIPTON
LIQUID
LIQUOR
LISBOA
LISBON
LISLES
LISPED
LISTED
LISTEE
LISTEL
LISTEN
LISTER
LISTON
LITANY
LITCHI
LITERS
LITHIC
LITHOG
LITHOS
LITMUS
LITOUT
LITRES
LITTER
LITTLE
LIVEIN
LIVELY
LIVENS
LIVEON
LIVERS
LIVERY
LIVING
LIVRES
LIZARD
LIZZIE

L•I•••
LAIDBY
LAIDIN
LAIDON
LAIDTO
LAIDUP
LAINIE
LAIRDS
LEIDEN
LOITER

L••I••
LABIAL
LABILE
LACIER
LACILY
LACING
LADIDA
LADIES
LADING
LADINO
LAKIER
LAMIAS
LAMINA
LAMING
LANIER
LAPINS
LARIAT
LATIGO
LATINA
LATINI
LATINO
LATINS
LATISH
LATIUM
LAVING
LAVISH
LAWING
LAXITY
LAYING
LAZIER
LAZILY
LAZING
LEGION
LEGIST
LEHIGH
LENITY
LERIDA
LEVIED
LEVIER
LEVIES
LEVINE
LEVITE
LEVITY
LEXICA
LIAISE
LIBIDO
LIKING
LILIES
LILITH
LIMIER
LIMING
LIMITS
LINIER
LINING
LIPIDE
LIPIDS
LIVING
LOGIER
LOGILY
LOGION
LOLITA
LOOIES
LOPING
LORICA
LORIES
LOSING
LOTION
LOUISA
LOUISE
LOVING
LOWING
LOWISH
LUBING
LUCIAN
LUCITE
LUCIUS
LUMINA
LUPINE
LUPINO
LURING
LUTING
LUTIST
LYRICS
LYRIST
LYSINE
LYSINS

L•••I•
LACTIC
LADDIE
LAIDIN
LAINIE
LANAIS
LANDIS
LANVIN
LASHIO
LASSIE
LATVIA
LAURIE
LAYSIN
LCHAIM
LEADIN
LEFTIE
LEFTIN
LEGUIN
LENNIE
LENTIL
LEONID
LEONIE
LESLIE
LETSIN
LIBRIS
LIEBIG
LIESIN
LIGNIN
LILLIE
LIMPID
LIPOID
LIQUID
LITHIC
LIVEIN
LIZZIE
LOCKIN
LOGGIA
LOGSIN
LOMEIN
LOOKIN
LOONIE
LORAIN
LOSEIT
LOSTIT
LOVEIN
LUBLIN
LUDWIG

L••••I
LATINI
LAZULI
LIBERI
LITCHI
LUGOSI

•LI•••
ALIBIS
ALIBLE
ALICIA
ALIENS
ALIGHT
ALIGNS
ALINES
ALIOTO
ALISON
ALITER
BLIGHT
BLIMEY
BLIMPS
BLINDS
BLINIS
BLINKS
BLINTZ
BLITHE
BLIXEN
CLICHE
CLICKS
CLIENT
CLIFFS
CLIFFY
CLIMAX
CLIMBS
CLIMES
CLINCH
CLINES
CLINGS
CLINGY
CLINIC
CLINKS
CLIPON
CLIQUE
CLIQUY
ELICIT
ELIDED
ELIDES
ELIJAH
ELINOR
ELISHA
ELISSA
ELITES
ELIXIR
FLICKA
FLICKS
FLIERS
FLIGHT
FLIMSY
FLINCH
FLINGS
FLINTS
FLINTY
FLIPUP
FLIRTS
FLIRTY
FLITCH
GLIBLY
GLIDED
GLIDER
GLIDES
GLINKA
GLINTS
GLITCH
GLITZY
KLIBAN
OLINDA
OLINGO
OLIVER
OLIVES
OLIVIA
PLIANT

PLICAE
PLIERS
PLIGHT
PLINKS
PLINTH
PLISSE
SLICED
SLICER
SLICES
SLICKS
SLIDER
SLIDES
SLIDIN
SLIEST
SLIGHT
SLIMED
SLIMES
SLIMLY
SLIMSY
SLINGS
SLINKS
SLINKY
SLIPIN
SLIPON
SLIPPY
SLIPUP
SLITHY
SLITTY
SLIVER

•L•I••

ALBINO
ALBION
ALDINE
ALFINE
ALHIRT
ALLIED
ALLIES
ALLIUM
ALNICO
ALOINS
ALPINE
ALTIMA
ALTIUS
BLAINE
BLAISE
BLUING
BLUISH
CLAIMS
CLAIRE
CLUING
ELAINE
ELFISH
ELLICE
ELLIOT
ELMIRA
ELNINO
ELOIGN
ELOISE
ELVIRA
ELVISH
FLAILS
FLAIRS
FLUIDS
FLYING
FLYINS
GLAIRS
GLAIRY
GLUIER
GLUING
ILLINI
ILOILO
KLEIST
OLDIES
OLDISH
PLAICE
PLAIDS
PLAINS
PLAINT
PLAITS
PLEIAD
PLYING
SLEIGH
SLUICE
SLUING
ULTIMA
ULTIMO

•L••I•

ALANIS
ALARIC
ALBEIT
ALBOIN
ALCUIN
ALDRIN
ALEXIA
ALEXIS
ALIBIS
ALICIA
ALTAIC
ALTAIR
BLEWIT
BLINIS
BLOWIN
BLOWIT
CLAVIN
CLERIC
CLEVIS
CLINIC
CLORIS
CLOVIS
CLUEIN
ELAPID
ELEGIT
ELEMIS
ELICIT
ELIXIR
ELOHIM
FLAVIA
FLEWIN
FLORID
FLORIN
FLORIO
GLACIS
GLOBIN
GLORIA
GLYNIS
ILORIN
OLDVIC
OLEFIN
OLIVIA
PLACID
PLAGIO
PLUGIN
SLAVIC
SLIDIN
SLIPIN
SLOVIK

•L•••I

ALEXEI
ALKALI
ALUMNI
GLUTEI
ILLINI

••LI••

ADLIBS
AGLINT
AILING
ALLIED
ALLIES
ALLIUM
APLITE
ARLISS
AXLIKE
BALING
BELIAL
BELIED
BELIEF
BELIES
BELIKE
BELIZE
BOLIDE
BYLINE
CALICO
CALIPH
CELINE
CILIUM
COLIES
COLIMA
DELICT
DELIST
DELIUS
DOLING
EALING
EELIER
ELLICE
ELLIOT
ENLIST
EOLIAN
EOLITH
FALINE
FELINE
FELIPE
FILIAL
FILING
FILIUS
FOLIAR
FOLIOS
FOLIUM
GOLINO
HALIDE
HALING
HALITE
HELIOS
HELIUM
HOLIER
HOLILY
HOLING
HOLISM
HOLIST
IDLING
ILLINI
INLINE
IOLITE
JOLIET
JOLIOT
JULIAN
JULIET
JULIUS
KALINE
KILIMS
LILIES
LILITH
LOLITA
MALIBU
MALICE
MALIGN
MELINA
MILIEU
MOLINE
MULISH
OBLIGE
OGLING
OILIER
OILILY
OILING
ONLINE
OOLITE
OOLITH
OWLISH
OXLIKE
OXLIPS
PALIER
PALING
PALISH
PELIKE
PELION
PILING
POLICE
POLICY
POLING
POLISH
POLITE
POLITY
PULING
RELICS
RELICT
RELIED
RELIEF
RELIES
RELINE
RELISH
RELIST
RELIVE
RILING
RULING
SALIFY
SALINA
SALINE
SALISH
SALIVA
SILICA
SOLIDI
SOLIDS
SOLING
SPLICE
SPLINE
SPLINT
SPLITS
TALION
TILING
TOLIFE
TULIPS
UGLIER
UGLIES
UGLIFY
UGLILY
UNLIKE
UNLINK
UPLIFT
UPLINK
VALISE
VALIUM
VILIFY
WILIER
WILILY
WILING
YALIES

••L•I•

AFLCIO
AGLAIA
AULAIT
BALTIC
BELAIR
BELOIT
BILLIE
BOLLIX
BULBIL
CALAIS
CALLIN
CALVIN
CELTIC
COLLIE
CULKIN
CULLIS
CULTIC
DELRIO
DELTIC
ECLAIR
FALLIN
FELLIN
FILLIN
FILLIP
FOLKIE
FULFIL
GALLIA
GALLIC
GALOIS
GILLIE
GILLIS
GOLDIE
HALOID
HELDIN
HOLDIN
HOLDIT
INLAID
KELPIE
KELVIN
KILTIE
LILLIE
MALKIN
MALTIN
MCLAIN
MELVIL
MELVIN
MILLIE
MILTIE
NELLIE
OILRIG
PALLIA
PALLID
PELVIC
PELVIS
PILEIN
PULLIN
PULPIT
RELAID
ROLLIE
ROLLIN
SALVIA
SOLEIL
SYLVIA
TALKIE
TILLIE
TILLIS
TILSIT
UNLAID
VALOIS
WALKIE
WALKIN
WALLIS
WELKIN
WILLIE
WILLIS
XYLOID

••L••I

BILOXI
DALASI
DELPHI
FULANI
GELATI
ILLINI
MALAWI
MALLEI
MALOTI
NILGAI
PILOTI
POLLOI
SALAMI
SALUKI
SILENI
SOLIDI

•••LI•

ADELIE
AEOLIA
AEOLIC
AMALIE
AMBLIN
AMELIA
ANGLIA
ANGLIC
APULIA
ARALIA
BERLIN
BIBLIO
BIGLIE
BILLIE
BOLLIX
BROLIN
CALLIN
CANLIT
CARLIN
COLLIE
COOLIT
CULLIS
CYCLIC
DAHLIA
DAYLIT
DEALIN
DOBLIN
DUBLIN
DUNLIN
EMILIA
EMILIO
ETALIA
ETALII
EUCLID
EXILIC
EYELID
FALLIN
FELLIN
FILLIN
FILLIP
FROLIC
GAELIC
GALLIA
GALLIC
GARLIC
GASLIT
GATLIN
GILLIE
GILLIS
GOALIE
GOBLIN
HAMLIN
HARLIN
HEFLIN
HOWLIN
ISELIN
ITALIA
ITALIC
JOPLIN
KAHLIL
KAOLIN
KHALID
LESLIE
LILLIE
LUBLIN
MAILIN
MAJLIS
MARLIN
MATLIN
MEALIE
MERLIN
MILLIE
MOULIN
MUSLIM
MUSLIN
MYELIN
NAILIN
NELLIE
OBELIA
OXALIS
PALLIA
PALLID
PHILIP
POPLIN
PRELIM
PROLIX
PUBLIC
PULLIN
PURLIN
RATLIN
REALIA
REELIN
ROLLIE
ROLLIN
SCALIA
SMILIN
STALIN
STOLID
SUNLIT
SUSLIK
THALIA
THELIP
TILLIE
TILLIS
TOMLIN
TWILIT
URALIC
VIOLIN
WALLIS
WILLIE
WILLIS

•••L•I

AMALFI
CHILLI
ETALII
KUBLAI
MALLEI
NIELLI
NUCLEI
OCELLI
POLLOI
SMALTI

••••LI

ALKALI
ANGELI
ANNULI
ARGALI
CHILLI
CUMULI
DENALI
KIGALI
LAZULI
MOWGLI
NAPOLI
NEPALI
NEROLI
NIELLI
OCELLI
POPULI
SNUGLI
SOMALI
TIVOLI
TUMULI

L••J••

LOGJAM

•L•J••

ELIJAH

••LJ••

SELJUK

L•K•••

LAKERS
LAKIER
LAKOTA
LEKVAR
LIKELY
LIKENS
LIKING

L••K••

LACKED
LACKEY
LANKER
LANKLY
LARKED
LATKES
LEAKED
LEAKER
LEAKEY
LICKED
LINKED
LINKER
LINKUP
LOCKED
LOCKER
LOCKET
LOCKIN
LOCKON
LOCKUP
LOOKAT
LOOKED
LOOKER
LOOKIN
LOOKON
LOOKTO
LOOKUP
LOWKEY
LUCKED
LUNKER
LURKED

L•••K•

LUSAKA

L••••K

LANARK
LOMBOK
LUBECK

•LK•••

ALKALI
ALKENE
ALKYDS
ALKYLS

•L•K••

BLOKES
FLAKED
FLAKER
FLAKES
FLAKEY
FLUKES
FLUKEY
SLAKED
SLAKES

•L••K•

ALASKA
ALECKY
BLACKS
BLANKS
BLINKS
BLOCKS
BLOCKY
CLACKS
CLANKS
CLANKY
CLARKE
CLEEKS
CLERKS
CLICKS
CLINKS
CLOAKS
CLOCKS
CLONKS
CLUCKS
CLUNKS

CLUNKY
FLACKS
FLANKS
FLASKS
FLECKS
FLECKY
FLICKA
FLICKS
FLOCKS
FLOCKY
FLUNKS
FLUNKY
GLINKA
PLANKS
PLINKS
PLONKS
PLUCKS
PLUCKY
PLUNKS
SLACKS
SLEEKS
SLEEKY
SLICKS
SLINKS
SLINKY

•L•••K
PLANCK
SLEZAK
SLOVAK
SLOVIK

••LK••
BALKAN
BALKED
BILKED
BULKED
CALKED
CULKIN
FOLKIE
FOLKSY
HULKED
KALKAN
MALKIN
MILKED
MILKER
POLKAS
SILKED
SILKEN
SULKED
SULKER
TALKAT
TALKED
TALKER
TALKIE
TALKTO
TALKUP
WALKED
WALKEN
WALKER
WALKIE
WALKIN
WALKON
WALKUP
WELKIN
WILKES
YOLKED

••L•K•
AXLIKE
BELIKE
KALAKH
KULAKS
MOLTKE
OXLIKE
PELIKE
SALUKI
STLUKE
TILAKS
UNLIKE

••L••K
GALYAK
INLUCK
OCLOCK
RELOCK
SELJUK
UNLINK
UNLOCK
UPLINK

•••LK•
BAULKS
CAULKS
CHALKS
CHALKY
SKULKS
STALKS
STALKY
WHELKS

•••L•K
MUKLUK
SUSLIK
URALSK

••••LK
BYTALK
INBULK
UPTALK

LL••••
LLAMAS
LLANOS
LLBEAN
LLOYDS

L•L•••
LALALA
LELAND
LILACS
LILIES
LILITH
LILLIE
LILTED
LOLITA
LOLLED
LOLLOP
LULLED

L••L••
LADLED
LADLER
LADLES
LAYLOW
LEALTY
LESLEY
LESLIE
LIELOW
LILLIE
LISLES
LOLLED
LOLLOP
LUBLIN
LUDLUM
LULLED
LYNLEY

L•••L•
LABELS
LABILE
LACILY
LALALA
LAMELY
LANKLY
LAPELS
LASTLY
LATELY
LAZILY
LAZULI
LEANLY
LEGALS
LETFLY
LEVELS
LEWDLY
LIABLE
LIBELS
LIEFLY
LIGULA
LIKELY
LIMPLY
LIONLY
LITTLE
LIVELY
LOBULE
LOCALE
LOCALS
LOGILY
LONELY
LONGLY
LORDLY
LOUDLY
LOVELL
LOVELY
LOWELL
LOYOLA
LUNULA
LUSHLY

L••••L
LABIAL
LAPFUL
LARVAL
LAUREL
LAWFUL
LEMUEL
LENTIL
LETHAL
LINEAL
LINTEL
LIONEL
LISTEL
LONNOL
LOREAL
LOVELL
LOWCAL
LOWELL

•LL•••
ALLAYS
ALLBUT
ALLDAY
ALLEES
ALLEGE
ALLELE
ALLEYS
ALLFOR
ALLIED
ALLIES
ALLIUM
ALLMAN
ALLOTS
ALLOUT
ALLOWS
ALLOYS
ALLPRO
ALLSET
ALLUDE
ALLURE
ALLWET
ELLERY
ELLICE
ELLIOT
ILLEST
ILLFED
ILLINI
ILLMET
ILLSAY
ILLUME
ILLUSE
ULLAGE
ULLMAN

•L•L••
ALULAE
ALULAR
SLALOM
TLALOC

•L••L•
ALIBLE
ALKALI
ALKYLS
ALLELE
BLUELY
FLAILS
FLATLY
GLADLY
GLIBLY
GLUMLY
ILOILO
SLIMLY
SLOWLY

•L•••L
ALEVEL
FLORAL
GLOBAL
GLYCOL
OLEVEL
PLAGAL
PLEXAL
PLURAL

••LL••
BALLAD
BALLET
BALLON
BALLOT
BALLOU
BALLUP
BELLAY
BELLED
BELLES
BELLOC
BELLOW
BILLED
BILLET
BILLIE
BILLON
BILLOW
BOLLIX
BULLAE
BULLED
BULLET
CALLAO
CALLAS
CALLED
CALLER
CALLES
CALLIN
CALLON
CALLOW
CALLUP
CALLUS
CELLAE
CELLAR
CELLED
CELLOS
COLLAR
COLLET
COLLIE
COLLOP
COLLOQ
CULLED
CULLEN
CULLER
CULLET
CULLIS
DALLAS
DALLES
DILLER
DILLON
DOLLAR
DOLLED
DOLLOP
DOLLUP
DULLEA
DULLED
DULLER
DULLES
FALLEN
FALLIN
FALLON
FALLOW
FALLTO
FELLAH
FELLAS
FELLED
FELLER
FELLIN
FELLOE
FELLON
FELLOW
FELLTO
FILLED
FILLER
FILLES
FILLET
FILLIN
FILLIP
FILLUP
FOLLOW
FULLER
GALLED
GALLEY
GALLIA
GALLIC
GALLON
GALLOP
GALLUP
GELLED
GILLED
GILLIE
GILLIS
GOLLUM
GULLAH
GULLED
GULLET
HALLEL
HALLEY
HALLOO
HALLOS
HALLOW
HALLUX
HELLAS
HELLER
HELLOS
HILLED
HILLEL
HILLER
HOLLER
HOLLOW
HULLED
HULLER
HULLOA
HULLOS
JELLED
KELLER
KELLEY
KILLED
KILLER
LILLIE
LOLLED
LOLLOP
LULLED
MALLEE
MALLEI
MALLET
MALLOW
MELLON
MELLOW
MILLAY
MILLED
MILLER
MILLET
MILLIE
MULLAH
MULLAS
MULLED
MULLER
MULLET
NELLIE
NULLAH
NULLED
PALLAS
PALLED
PALLET
PALLIA
PALLID
PALLOR
PELLET
PILLAR
PILLED
PILLOW
POLLED
POLLEN
POLLER
POLLEX
POLLOI
POLLUX
PULLED
PULLET
PULLEY
PULLIN
PULLON
PULLUP
RILLES
RILLET
ROLLED
ROLLER
ROLLIE
ROLLIN
ROLLON
ROLLUP
SALLET
SALLOW
SELLER
SULLEN
TALLER
TALLOW
TELLER
TELLOF
TELLON
TILLED
TILLER
TILLIE
TILLIS
TOLLED
TULLES
VALLEE
VALLEY
VELLUM
VILLAS
VILLON
VILLUS
VOLLEY
WALLED
WALLER
WALLET
WALLIS
WALLOP
WALLOW
WALLUP
WELLED
WELLER
WELLES
WELLUP
WILLED
WILLEM
WILLET
WILLIE
WILLIS
WILLOW
YELLED
YELLER
YELLOW

••L•L•
ALLELE
BALDLY
BOLDLY
CALMLY
COLDLY
HOLILY
LALALA
MILDLY
OGLALA
OILILY
OOLALA
PALELY
SALALS
SOLELY
UGLILY
VILELY
WILDLY
WILILY

••L••L
ATLATL
BELIAL
BULBIL
BULBUL
FILIAL
FULFIL
GALPAL
HALLEL
HILLEL
MELVIL
SOLEIL
WILFUL

•••LL•
ABOLLA
ADELLE
AIELLO
APOLLO
ARALLU
ATOLLS
AXILLA
BCELLS
BOULLE
BRILLO
BRILLS
BROLLY
CHILLI
CHILLS
CHILLY
CHOLLA
COOLLY
DRILLS
DROLLS
DROLLY
DUALLY
DUELLO
DWELLS
EVILLY
FAILLE
FOULLY
FRILLS
FRILLY
GRILLE
GRILLS
IDYLLS
KNELLS
KNOLLS
KNOLLY
KPELLE
KVELLS
NIELLI
NIELLO
OCELLI
OKELLY
ORALLY
OTELLO
OVALLY
PAELLA
PHILLY
PHYLLO
PSYLLA
QUELLS
QUILLS
REALLY
REILLY
SCULLS
SCULLY
SCYLLA
SHALLY
SHELLS
SHELLY
SHILLS
SHILLY
SKILLS
SKULLS
SMALLS
SMELLS
SMELLY
SNELLS
SPALLS
SPELLS
SPILLS
STALLS
STELLA
STILLS
STILLY
STOLLE
STULLS
SWELLS
SWILLS
TAILLE
TBILLS
THILLS
TRILLS
TROLLS
TUILLE
TWILLS
WHOLLY
WOOLLY

•••L•L
HALLEL
HILLEL
KAHLIL
PHILOL

••••LL
ANGELL
APPALL
ARGYLL
ASWELL
ATWILL
BACALL
BEFALL
BEFELL
CAVELL
COSELL
CYBILL
DOTELL
DUVALL
ENDALL

ENROLL
ERROLL
GIBILL
HAMILL
HOWELL
INFULL
JEKYLL
LOVELL
LOWELL
MABELL
OHWELL
ONCALL
ONEILL
ORWELL
POWELL
RECALL
REFILL
REPOLL
RESELL
RETELL
RYDELL
SCHELL
SCROLL
SEWELL
SHRILL
SQUALL
SQUILL
STROLL
THATLL
THEYLL
THRALL
THRILL
UNROLL
UNWELL
UPHILL
UPWELL
WHATLL
YOUALL

L•M•••

LAMARR
LAMAZE
LAMBDA
LAMBED
LAMECH
LAMEDH
LAMEDS
LAMELY
LAMENT
LAMESA
LAMEST
LAMIAS
LAMINA
LAMING
LAMMAS
LAMMED
LAMONT
LAMOUR
LEMANS
LEMMAS
LEMMON
LEMNOS
LEMOND
LEMONS
LEMONY
LEMUEL
LEMURS
LIMBED
LIMBER
LIMBOS
LIMBUS
LIMENS
LIMEYS
LIMIER
LIMING
LIMITS
LIMNED
LIMNER
LIMPED
LIMPER
LIMPET
LIMPID
LIMPLY
LOMBOK
LOMEIN
LOMOND
LUMBAR
LUMBER
LUMENS
LUMINA
LUMMOX
LUMPED
LUMPEN
LUMPER
LUMPUR
LYMPHS

L••M••

LAMMAS
LAMMED
LAWMAN
LAWMEN
LAYMAN
LAYMEN
LEGMAN
LEGMEN
LEMMAS
LEMMON
LITMUS
LLAMAS
LOAMED
LOOMED
LUMMOX

L•••M•

LARAMS
LEGUME
LEXEME

L••••M

LABRUM
LAPHAM
LATIUM
LCHAIM
LOGJAM
LUDLUM
LYCEUM

•LM•••

ALMATY
ALMOND
ALMOST
ELMIRA
ELMORE
OLMECS

•L•M••

ALAMOS
ALEMAN
ALLMAN
ALOMAR
ALTMAN
ALUMNA
ALUMNI
BLAMED
BLAMES
BLIMEY
BLIMPS
CLAMMY
CLAMOR
CLAMPS
CLAMUP
CLIMAX
CLIMBS
CLIMES
CLOMPS
CLUMPS
CLUMPY
CLUMSY
ELEMIS
ELFMAN
FLAMBE
FLAMED
FLAMES
FLIMSY
FLUMES
FLYMAN
FLYMEN
GLAMOR
GLUMLY
ILLMET
LLAMAS
OLDMAN
OLDMEN
PLUMBS
PLUMED
PLUMES
PLUMMY
PLUMPS
SLIMED
SLIMES
SLIMLY
SLIMSY
SLUMMY
SLUMPS
ULLMAN

•L••M•

ALARMS
ALBUMS
ALTIMA
BLOOMS
BLOOMY
CLAIMS
CLAMMY
GLEAMS
GLEAMY
GLOOMS
GLOOMY
ILLUME
PLASMA
PLASMO
PLUMMY
SLUMMY
ULTIMA
ULTIMO

•L•••M

ALARUM
ALLIUM
ELOHIM
OLDHAM
PLENUM
SLALOM

••LM••

ALLMAN
CALMED
CALMER
CALMLY
COLMAN
DELMAR
DOLMAN
DOLMAS
DOLMEN
FILMED
FULMAR
HELMED
HELMET
HELMUT
HOLMES
ILLMET
KALMAR
KILMER
MELMAC
OILMAN
OILMEN
PALMAS
PALMED
PALMER
PELMET
SALMAN
SALMON
TALMUD
ULLMAN

••L•M•

AFLAME
APLOMB
CCLAMP
COLIMA
COLUMN
GOLEMS
ILLUME
KILIMS
PALOMA
RELUME
SALAMI
SALOME
SOLEMN
VOLUME

••L••M

ABLOOM
AGLEAM
ALLIUM
BALAAM
BALSAM
BELDAM
CILIUM
FOLIUM
FOLSOM
GOLLUM
HELIUM
HOLISM
MULTUM
PHLEGM
PHLOEM
PILEUM
SALAAM
SALTUM
SELDOM
SILOAM
TALCUM
VALIUM
VELLUM
WILLEM

•••LM•

HAULMS
PSALMS
QUALMS
REALMS
STELMO
THELMA
WHELMS

•••L•M

ASYLUM
BEDLAM
COELOM
EMBLEM
GOLLUM
HARLEM
LUDLUM
MOSLEM
MUSLIM
PABLUM
PEPLUM
PHYLUM
PRELIM
SHALOM
SHOLEM
SHOLOM
SLALOM
VELLUM
WHILOM
WILLEM

••••LM

ANSELM
BECALM

L•N•••

LANAIS
LANARK
LANATE
LANCED
LANCER
LANCES
LANCET
LANDAU
LANDED
LANDER
LANDHO
LANDIS
LANDON
LANDRY
LANGUR
LANIER
LANKER
LANKLY
LANOSE
LANSON
LANVIN
LENAPE
LENDER
LENGTH
LENITY
LENNIE
LENNON
LENNOX
LENORE
LENSED
LENSES
LENTEN
LENTIL
LINAGE
LINDEN
LINEAL
LINEAR
LINENS
LINENY
LINERS
LINEUP
LINGER
LINGUA
LINIER
LINING
LINKED
LINKER
LINKUP
LINNET
LINNEY
LINSEY
LINTEL
LINTER
LONDON
LONELY
LONERS
LONGAN
LONGED
LONGER
LONGES
LONGLY
LONGUE
LONNOL
LUNACY
LUNATE
LUNCHY
LUNDEN
LUNGED
LUNGES
LUNKER
LUNULA
LYNDON
LYNLEY
LYNXES
LYNYRD

L••N••

LAINIE
LAUNCH
LEANED
LEANER
LEANLY
LEANON
LEANTO
LEMNOS
LENNIE
LENNON
LENNOX
LEONES
LEONID
LEONIE
LERNER
LIANAS
LIANES
LIANGS
LIENEE
LIGNIN
LIMNED
LIMNER
LINNET
LINNEY
LIONEL
LIONET
LIONLY
LLANOS
LOANED
LOANER
LONNOL
LOONEY
LOONIE
LOUNGE
LUANDA
LUGNUT

L•••N•

LACING
LACUNA
LADING
LADINO
LAGUNA
LAMENT
LAMINA
LAMING
LAMONT
LAPINS
LARYNX
LATENE
LATENS
LATENT
LATINA
LATINI
LATINO
LATINS
LATONA
LAVING
LAWING
LAYING
LAZING
LEARNS
LEARNT
LEGEND
LELAND
LEMANS
LEMOND
LEMONS
LEMONY
LEVANT
LEVENE
LEVINE
LIERNE
LIGAND
LIKENS
LIKING
LIMENS
LIMING
LINENS
LINENY
LINING
LIPENG
LITANY
LIVENS
LIVING
LODENS
LOMOND
LOPING
LORENZ
LOSING
LOVING
LOWEND
LOWING
LUBING
LUCENT
LUDENS
LUMENS
LUMINA
LUPINE
LUPINO
LUPONE
LURING
LUTING
LYSINE
LYSINS

L••••N

LAGOON
LAIDIN
LAIDON
LANDON
LANSON
LANVIN
LARDON
LARSEN
LARSON
LASSEN
LATEEN
LATTEN
LAUREN
LAWMAN
LAWMEN
LAWSON
LAWTON
LAYMAN
LAYMEN
LAYSIN
LAYSON
LEADEN
LEADIN
LEADON
LEANON
LEAVEN
LEBRUN
LEFTIN
LEGION
LEGMAN
LEGMEN
LEGUIN
LEIDEN
LEMMON
LENNON
LENTEN
LEPTON
LESSEN
LESSON
LETSIN
LETSON
LEYDEN
LIBYAN
LICHEN
LIESIN
LIGNIN
LINDEN
LIPTON
LISBON
LISTEN
LISTON
LIVEIN
LIVEON
LLBEAN
LOCKIN
LOCKON
LOGION
LOGSIN
LOGSON
LOMEIN
LONDON
LONGAN
LOOKIN
LOOKON
LOOSEN
LORAIN
LOTION
LOUDEN
LOVEIN
LUBLIN
LUCIAN
LUDDEN
LUMPEN
LUNDEN
LYNDON
LYTTON

•LN•••

ALNICO
ELNINO

•L•N••

ALANIS
ALANON
ALINES
ALONSO
ALONZO
BLANCA
BLANCH
BLANDA
BLANKS
BLENCH
BLENDE
BLENDS
BLENNY
BLINDS
BLINIS
BLINKS
BLINTZ
BLONDE
BLONDS
BLUNTS
CLANCY
CLANGS
CLANKS
CLANKY
CLENCH
CLINCH
CLINES
CLINGS
CLINGY
CLINIC
CLINKS
CLONED
CLONES
CLONKS
CLONUS
CLUNKS
CLUNKY
ELANDS
ELINOR
FLANGE

FLANKS
FLENSE
FLINCH
FLINGS
FLINTS
FLINTY
FLUNKS
FLUNKY
FLYNET
GLANCE
GLANDS
GLENDA
GLENNE
GLINKA
GLINTS
GLYNIS
LLANOS
OLINDA
OLINGO
PLANAR
PLANCK
PLANED
PLANER
PLANES
PLANET
PLANKS
PLANON
PLANTE
PLANTS
PLENTY
PLENUM
PLINKS
PLINTH
PLONKS
PLUNGE
PLUNKS
SLANGS
SLANGY
SLANTS
SLINGS
SLINKS
SLINKY

•L••N•

ALBANO
ALBANY
ALBINO
ALDINE
ALFINE
ALIENS
ALIGNS
ALKENE
ALMOND
ALOINS
ALPINE
ALUMNA
ALUMNI
BLAINE
BLENNY
BLUING
CLEANS
CLIENT
CLOWNS
CLUING
ELAINE
ELAYNE
ELNINO
FLAUNT
FLUENT
FLYING
FLYINS
GLEANS
GLENNE
GLUING
GLUONS
HLHUNT
ILEANA
ILLINI
PLAINS
PLAINT
PLIANT
PLYING
SLOANE
SLUING

•L•••N

ALANON
ALBION
ALBOIN
ALCUIN
ALDRIN
ALEMAN
ALFVEN
ALISON
ALLMAN
ALTMAN
BLAZON
BLIXEN
BLOWIN
CLAVIN
CLIPON
CLOVEN
CLUEIN
ELEVEN
ELFMAN
ELOIGN
FLACON
FLAGON
FLAXEN
FLEWIN
FLORIN
FLYMAN
FLYMEN
GLOBIN
GLUTEN
ILORIN
KLAXON
KLIBAN
LLBEAN
OLDMAN
OLDMEN
OLEFIN
OLESON
PLANON
PLATEN
PLAYON
PLUGIN
SLIDIN
SLIPIN
SLIPON
SLOGAN
SLOVEN
ULLMAN

••LN••

KILNED
MILNER
MOLNAR
WALNUT

••L•N•

AGLINT
AILING
ARLENE
ASLANT
BALING
BELONG
BYLINE
CELINE
COLONS
COLONY
DELANO
DELANY
DELONG
DOLENZ
DOLING
EALING
FALANA
FALINE
FELINE
FELONS
FELONY
FILENE
FILING
FULANI
GALENA
GOLINO
HALING
HELENA
HELENE
HELENS
HOLING
IDLING
ILLINI
INLAND
INLINE
IRLENE
ISLAND
JOLENE
KALINE
KDLANG
LELAND
MALONE
MELANO
MELINA
MELONS
MILANO
MOLINE
NOLENS
NYLONS
OBLONG
OGLING
OILING
ONLAND
ONLINE
OOLONG
PALING
PILING
POLAND
POLING
PULING
PYLONS
RELENT
RELINE
RILING
ROLAND
RULING
SALINA
SALINE
SALONS
SELENA
SELENE
SELENO
SILENI
SILENT
SILONE
SOLANS
SOLENT
SOLING
SOLONG
SPLINE
SPLINT
TALENT
TALONS
TILING
TULANE
UCLANS
UHLANS
UNLINK
UPLAND
UPLINK
VALENS
VALENT
VOLANS
VOLANT
VOLENS
WILING
XYLENE

••L••N

AILEEN
ALLMAN
ARLEEN
BALEEN
BALKAN
BALLON
BILLON
BOLEYN
BOLTON
CALLIN
CALLON
CALVIN
COLMAN
COLUMN
CULKIN
CULLEN
DALTON
DELEON
DILLON
DOLMAN
DOLMEN
EILEEN
EOLIAN
FALCON
FALLEN
FALLIN
FALLON
FELDON
FELLIN
FELLON
FILLIN
FULTON
GALLON
GOLDEN
HELDIN
HELDON
HILTON
HOLDEN
HOLDIN
HOLDON
JOLSON
JULIAN
KALKAN
KELVIN
MALDEN
MALIGN
MALKIN
MALTIN
MCLAIN
MCLEAN
MELLON
MELTON
MELVIN
MELVYN
MILTON
MOLTEN
NELSON
OILCAN
OILMAN
OILMEN
OILPAN
ONLOAN
PELION
PILEIN
PILEON
POLEYN
POLLEN
PULLIN
PULLON
ROLLIN
ROLLON
RULEON
SALMAN
SALMON
SALOON
SALTEN
SALTON
SILKEN
SOLDAN
SOLDON
SOLEMN
SPLEEN
SULLEN
SULTAN
SYLVAN
TALION
TELLON
TILDEN
TOLDON
TULSAN
ULLMAN
VILLON
VULCAN
WALDEN
WALKEN
WALKIN
WALKON
WALTON
WELKIN
WILSON
WILTON

•••L•N

AMBLIN
AVALON
BALLON
BANLON
BERLIN
BILLON
BROLIN
CALLIN
CALLON
CARLIN
CEYLON
CULLEN
DEALIN
DILLON
DOBLIN
DUBLIN
DUNLIN
EVELYN
FALLEN
FALLIN
FALLON
FELLIN
FELLON
FILLIN
GALLON
GATLIN
GOBLIN
HAMLIN
HARLAN
HARLIN
HEFLIN
HOWLIN
ISELIN
JACLYN
JOPLIN
KAOLIN
KAPLAN
KJOLEN
KUNLUN
LUBLIN
MAILIN
MARLIN
MARLON
MATLIN
MELLON
MERLIN
MERLON
MOULIN
MUSLIN
MYELIN
NAILIN
POLLEN
POPLIN
PULLIN
PULLON
PURLIN
RAGLAN
RATLIN
REELIN
REPLAN
REVLON
ROLLIN
ROLLON
SMILIN
STALIN
STOLEN
STOLON
SULLEN
TEFLON
TELLON
TIGLON
TOMLIN
TOULON
TRYLON
VEBLEN
VILLON
VIOLIN
WAYLON
WOOLEN

••••LN

HAMELN
WEDELN

LO••••

LOADED
LOADER
LOAFED
LOAFER
LOAMED
LOANED
LOANER
LOATHE
LOAVES
LOBATE
LOBBED
LOBBER
LOBULE
LOCALE
LOCALS
LOCATE
LOCKED
LOCKER
LOCKET
LOCKIN
LOCKON
LOCKUP
LOCUST
LODENS
LODGED
LODGER
LODGES
LOFTED
LOGGED
LOGGER
LOGGIA
LOGIER
LOGILY
LOGION
LOGJAM
LOGOFF
LOGOUT
LOGSIN
LOGSON
LOITER
LOLITA
LOLLED
LOLLOP
LOMBOK
LOMEIN
LOMOND
LONDON
LONELY
LONERS
LONGAN
LONGED
LONGER
LONGES
LONGLY
LONGUE
LONNOL
LOOFAH
LOOFAS
LOOIES
LOOKAT
LOOKED
LOOKER
LOOKIN
LOOKON
LOOKTO
LOOKUP
LOOMED
LOONEY
LOONIE
LOOPED
LOOPER
LOOSED
LOOSEN
LOOSER
LOOSES
LOOTED
LOOTER
LOPERS
LOPING
LOPPED
LOPPER
LOQUAT
LORAIN
LORDED
LORDLY
LOREAL
LORENZ
LORICA
LORIES
LOSEIT
LOSERS
LOSING
LOSSES
LOSTIT
LOTAHS
LOTHAR
LOTION
LOTTED
LOTTOS
LOUCHE
LOUDEN
LOUDER
LOUDLY
LOUGHS
LOUISA
LOUISE
LOUNGE
LOUPES
LOUSED
LOUSES
LOUVER
LOUVRE
LOVAGE
LOVEIN
LOVELL
LOVELY
LOVERS
LOVETT
LOVING
LOWBOY
LOWCAL
LOWELL
LOWEND
LOWERS
LOWERY
LOWEST
LOWFAT
LOWING
LOWISH
LOWKEY
LOYOLA

L•O•••

LAOTSE
LAOTZU
LEONES
LEONID
LEONIE
LHOTSE
LIONEL
LIONET
LIONLY
LIOTTA
LLOYDS
LOOFAH
LOOFAS
LOOIES
LOOKAT
LOOKED
LOOKER
LOOKIN
LOOKON
LOOKTO
LOOKUP
LOOMED
LOONEY
LOONIE
LOOPED
LOOPER
LOOSED
LOOSEN
LOOSER
LOOSES
LOOTED
LOOTER

L••O••

LABORS
LABOUR
LADOGA
LAGOON
LAHORE
LAKOTA
LAMONT
LAMOUR
LANOSE
LAROSA
LATONA
LATOUR
LATOYA
LAYOFF
LAYOUT
LEDOFF
LEDOUT
LEMOND
LEMONS
LEMONY
LENORE
LETOFF
LETOUT
LIPOID
LITOUT
LOGOFF
LOGOUT
LOMOND
LOYOLA
LUGOSI
LUPONE

L•••O•

LAGOON
LAIDON

LANDON
LANSON
LAPDOG
LAPTOP
LARDON
LARGOS
LARSON
LASSOS
LAWSON
LAWTON
LAYFOR
LAYLOW
LAYSON
LAZBOY
LEADON
LEANON
LECTOR
LEGION
LEMMON
LEMNOS
LENNON
LENNOX
LEPTON
LESBOS
LESSON
LESSOR
LETSON
LICTOR
LIELOW
LIMBOS
LIPTON
LIQUOR
LISBOA
LISBON
LISTON
LITHOG
LITHOS
LIVEON
LLANOS
LOCKON
LOGION
LOGSON
LOLLOP
LOMBOK
LONDON
LONNOL
LOOKON
LOTION
LOTTOS
LOWBOY
LUMMOX
LUTHOR
LYNDON
LYTTON

L••••O

LADINO
LAIDTO
LANDHO
LAREDO
LASHIO
LATIGO
LATINO
LAVABO
LAYSTO
LEADTO
LEANTO
LEGATO
LETSGO
LIBIDO
LIESTO
LOOKTO
LUPINO

•LO•••

ALOHAS
ALOINS
ALOMAR
ALONSO
ALONZO
BLOATS
BLOCKS
BLOCKY
BLOKES
BLONDE
BLONDS
BLOODY
BLOOEY
BLOOMS
BLOOMY
BLOOPS
BLOTCH
BLOTTO
BLOTTY
BLOUSE
BLOWER
BLOWIN
BLOWIT
BLOWSY
BLOWUP
BLOWZY
CLOACA
CLOAKS
CLOCHE
CLOCKS
CLODDY
CLOGGY
CLOGUP
CLOMPS
CLONED
CLONES
CLONKS
CLONUS
CLOQUE
CLORIS
CLOROX
CLOSED
CLOSER
CLOSES
CLOSET
CLOTHE
CLOTHO
CLOTHS
CLOTTY
CLOUDS
CLOUDY
CLOUTS
CLOVEN
CLOVER
CLOVES
CLOVIS
CLOWNS
CLOYED
ELOHIM
ELOIGN
ELOISE
ELOPED
ELOPER
ELOPES
FLOATS
FLOATY
FLOCKS
FLOCKY
FLOODS
FLOOEY
FLOORS
FLOPPY
FLOPSY
FLORAE
FLORAL
FLORAS
FLORES
FLORET
FLORID
FLORIN
FLORIO
FLOSSY
FLOURS
FLOURY
FLOUTS
FLOWED
FLOWER
GLOATS
GLOBAL
GLOBED
GLOBES
GLOBIN
GLOGGS
GLOOMS
GLOOMY
GLOPPY
GLORIA
GLOSSA
GLOSSO
GLOSSY
GLOVED
GLOVER
GLOVES
GLOWED
GLOWER
GLOZED
GLOZES
ILOILO
ILORIN
KLOOFS
LLOYDS
PLONKS
PLOTTY
PLOUGH
PLOVER
PLOWED
PLOWER
SLOANE
SLOBBY
SLOGAN
SLOOPS
SLOPED
SLOPES
SLOPPY
SLOSHY
SLOTHS
SLOUCH
SLOUGH
SLOVAK
SLOVEN
SLOVIK
SLOWED
SLOWER
SLOWLY
SLOWUP
ZLOTYS

•L•O••

ALBOIN
ALBORG
ALCOTT
ALCOVE
ALDOSE
ALDOUS
ALGORE
ALIOTO
ALLOTS
ALLOUT
ALLOWS
ALLOYS
ALMOND
ALMOST
BLOODY
BLOOEY
BLOOMS
BLOOMY
BLOOPS
ELBOWS
ELMORE
ELWOOD
FLOODS
FLOOEY
FLOORS
FLUORO
FLYOUT
GLOOMS
GLOOMY
GLUONS
KLOOFS
SLOOPS

•L••O•

ALAMOS
ALANON
ALBION
ALISON
ALLFOR
BLAZON
BLUEOX
CLAMOR
CLAROS
CLIPON
CLOROX
ELINOR
ELLIOT
ELWOOD
FLACON
FLAGON
FLAVOR
FLEXOR
FLYBOY
FLYROD
GLAMOR
GLYCOL
KLAXON
LLANOS
OLDBOY
OLESON
PLANON
PLAYON
PLEXOR
SLALOM
SLIPON
TLALOC

•L•••O

ALBANO
ALBEDO
ALBINO
ALECTO
ALEPPO
ALIOTO
ALLPRO
ALNICO
ALONSO
ALONZO
BLOTTO
CLOTHO
ELNINO
ELPASO
FLORIO
FLUORO
GLOSSO
ILOILO
OLDPRO
OLINGO
PLAGIO
PLASMO
SLUGGO
ULTIMO

••LO••

ABLOOM
AFLOAT
ALLOTS
ALLOUT
ALLOWS
ALLOYS
APLOMB
ASLOPE
BELOIT
BELONG
BILOXI
BULOVA
CHLORO
COLONS
COLONY
COLORS
COLOUR
DELONG
DOLORS
DOLOUR
EULOGY
FELONS
FELONY
FILOSE
GALOIS
GALOOT
GALOPS
GALORE
GALOSH
HALOED
HALOES
HALOID
HELOTS
IGLOOS
INLOVE
JALOPY
MALONE
MALORY
MALOTI
MELODY
MELONS
MELOTT
MILORD
MILOSZ
MOLOCH
MOLOPO
NOLOAD
NOLOSE
NYLONS
OBLONG
OCLOCK
ONLOAN
OOLOGY
OOLONG
ORLOPS
PALOMA
PELOPS
PELOTA
PHLOEM
PILOSE
PILOTI
PILOTS
PYLONS
RELOAD
RELOCK
SALOME
SALONS
SALOON
SILOAM
SILOED
SILONE
SOLOED
SOLONG
SPLOSH
TALONS
UNLOAD
UNLOCK
UPLOAD
VALOIS
VALOUR
VELOCE
VELOUR
XYLOID

••L•O•

ABLOOM
ALLFOR
BALBOA
BALLON
BALLOT
BALLOU
BELLOC
BELLOW
BILLON
BILLOW
BOLTON
CALLON
CALLOW
CELLOS
COLLOP
COLLOQ
DALTON
DELEON
DELROY
DILLON
DOLLOP
ELLIOT
FALCON
FALLON
FALLOW
FELDON
FELLOE
FELLON
FELLOW
FOLIOS
FOLLOW
FOLSOM
FULTON
GALLON
GALLOP
GALOOT
HALLOO
HALLOS
HALLOW
HELDON
HELIOS
HELLOS
HILTON
HOLDON
HOLLOW
HULLOA
HULLOS
IGLOOS
JOLIOT
JOLSON
KILROY
LOLLOP
MALLOW
MELLON
MELLOW
MELTON
MILTON
NELSON
PALLOR
PELION
PILEON
PILLOW
POLLOI
POLPOT
PULLON
ROLEOS
ROLLON
RULEON
SALLOW
SALMON
SALOON
SALTON
SALVOR
SALVOS
SELDOM
SOLDON
TALBOT
TALION
TALLOW
TELLOF
TELLON
TOLDOF
TOLDON
VILLON
VOLVOX
WALKON
WALLOP
WALLOW
WALTON
WILCOX
WILLOW
WILSON
WILTON
YELLOW

••L••O

AFLCIO
ALLPRO
BILBAO
BOLERO
CALICO
CALLAO
CHLORO
COLUGO
DELANO
DELRIO
FALLTO
FELLTO
GALAGO
GELATO
GOLINO
HALLOO
HELDTO
HOLDTO
MALABO
MELANO
MILANO
MOLOPO
PALAEO
PHLEBO
SALADO
SCLERO
SELENO
TALKTO
TOLEDO
VELCRO

•••LO•

ANALOG
ANGLOS
AVALON
BADLOT
BAILOR
BALLON
BALLOT
BALLOU
BANLON
BAYLOR
BELLOC
BELLOW
BILLON
BILLOW
CALLON
CALLOW
CARLOS
CARLOT
CELLOS
CEYLON
CHILOE
CHOLOS
COELOM
COLLOP
COLLOQ
CYCLOS
DEPLOY
DIALOG
DIGLOT
DILLON
DOLLOP
DUNLOP
DYELOT
EMPLOY
ENBLOC
EPILOG
FALLON
FALLOW
FARLOW
FELLOE
FELLON
FELLOW
FOLLOW
GALLON
GALLOP
GASLOG
GOSLOW
HALLOO
HALLOS
HALLOW
HARLOW
HELLOS
HOLLOW
HULLOA
HULLOS
INFLOW
JOBLOT
LAYLOW
LIELOW
LOLLOP
MALLOW
MARLON
MELLON
MELLOW
MERLON
MERLOT
OCELOT
ODDLOT
PAILOU
PALLOR
PARLOR
PAVLOV
PEPLOS
PHILOL
PHILOS
PILLOW
POLLOI
PROLOG
PULLON
REPLOW
REVLON
ROLLON
SAILOR
SALLOW
SAWLOG
SHALOM
SHILOH
SHOLOM
SLALOM
STOLON
TAILOR
TALLOW
TAYLOR
TEFLON
TELLOF
TELLON
TIGLON
TLALOC
TOULON
TRYLON
UNCLOG
VILLON
WALLOP
WALLOW
WAYLON
WHILOM
WILLOW
YELLOW
ZEALOT
ZIPLOC

•••L•O
AIELLO
APOLLO
BIBLIO
BRILLO
CALLAO
CHALCO
DUELLO
EMILIO
FALLTO
FELLTO
HALLOO
NIELLO
NUCLEO
OTELLO
PHYLLO
RIALTO
SMALTO
STELMO

••••LO
AIELLO
ANGELO
APOLLO
BAROLO
BRILLO
CUMULO
DAYGLO
DIABLO
DUELLO
ENHALO
GIGOLO
ILOILO
MEGALO
MODULO
NICOLO
NIELLO
NIHILO
OTELLO
PHYLLO
POMELO
PUEBLO
ROBALO
STMALO
TUPELO
YUNGLO

L•P•••
LAPDOG
LAPELS
LAPFUL
LAPHAM
LAPINS
LAPPED
LAPPET
LAPSED
LAPSES
LAPSUP
LAPTEV
LAPTOP
LAPUTA
LEPTON
LIPASE
LIPENG
LIPIDE
LIPIDS
LIPOID
LIPPED
LIPTON
LOPERS
LOPING
LOPPED
LOPPER
LUPINE
LUPINO
LUPONE

L••P••
LAPPED
LAPPET
LAUPER
LEAPED
LEAPER
LIMPED
LIMPER
LIMPET
LIMPID
LIMPLY
LIPPED
LISPED
LOOPED
LOOPER
LOPPED
LOPPER
LOUPES
LUMPED
LUMPEN
LUMPER
LUMPUR
LYMPHS

L•••P•
LAYUPS
LENAPE
LETUPS

L••••P
LACEUP
LAIDUP
LAPSUP
LAPTOP
LARRUP
LASHUP
LAYSUP
LEADUP
LETSUP
LIFTUP
LINEUP
LINKUP
LOCKUP
LOLLOP
LOOKUP

•LP•••
ALPACA
ALPERT
ALPHAS
ALPINE
ELPASO

•L•P••
ALEPHS
ALEPPO
ALLPRO
CLEPED
CLIPON
ELAPID
ELAPSE
ELOPED
ELOPER
ELOPES
FLAPPY
FLIPUP
FLOPPY
FLOPSY
GLOPPY
GLYPHS
OLDPRO
SLAPPY
SLAPUP
SLIPIN
SLIPON
SLIPPY
SLIPUP
SLOPED
SLOPES
SLOPPY
SLYPES

•L••P•
ALCAPP
ALEPPO
BLEEPS
BLIMPS
BLOOPS
CLAMPS
CLASPS
CLOMPS
CLUMPS
CLUMPY
FLAPPY
FLOPPY
GLOPPY
PLUMPS
SLAPPY
SLEEPS
SLEEPY
SLIPPY
SLOOPS
SLOPPY
SLUMPS
SLURPS

•L•••P
ALCAPP
BLEWUP
BLOWUP
CLAMUP
CLOGUP
FLIPUP
PLAYUP
SLAPUP
SLIPUP
SLOWUP

••LP••
ALLPRO
CALPAC
DELPHI
GALPAL
GULPED
GULPER
HELPED
HELPER
KELPIE
MILPAS
OILPAN
PALPUS
POLPOT
PULPED
PULPIT
SYLPHS
WOLPER
YELPED
YELPER
ZILPAH

••L•P•
ASLOPE
CALIPH
FELIPE
GALOPS
JALAPA
JALOPY
JULEPS
MOLOPO
ORLOPS
OXLIPS
PELOPS
POLYPS
TULIPS

••L••P
ASLEEP
BALLUP
CALLUP
CCLAMP
COLLOP
DOLLOP
DOLLUP
FILLIP
FILLUP
FOLDUP
GALLOP
GALLUP
HELDUP
HOLDUP
HOLEUP
LOLLOP
MILSAP
PILEUP
PULLUP
RILEUP
ROLLUP
TALKUP
WALKUP
WALLOP
WALLUP
WELLUP

•••LP•
ADOLPH
GUELPH
SCALPS
SCULPT
WHELPS

•••L•P
BALLUP
BURLAP
CALLUP
COILUP
COLLOP
CURLUP
DEWLAP
DIALUP
DOLLOP
DOLLUP
DUNLOP
EARLAP
FILLIP
FILLUP
FOULUP
GALLOP
GALLUP
HAULUP
LOLLOP
PHILIP
PULLUP
ROLLUP
SCHLEP
SEALUP
THELIP
TOOLUP
WALLOP
WALLUP
WELLUP

••••LP
MEGILP

L•Q•••
LIQUID
LIQUOR
LOQUAT

•L•Q••
CLAQUE
CLIQUE
CLIQUY
CLOQUE
PLAQUE

••LQ••
CALQUE
PULQUE

••L••Q
COLLOQ

•••L•Q
COLLOQ

••••LQ
POSSLQ

L•R•••
LARAMS
LARDED
LARDER
LARDON
LAREDO
LARGER
LARGES
LARGOS
LARIAT
LARKED
LAROSA
LARRUP
LARSEN
LARSON
LARVAE
LARVAL
LARVAS
LARYNX
LERIDA
LERNER
LORAIN
LORDED
LORDLY
LOREAL
LORENZ
LORICA
LORIES
LURING
LURKED
LYRICS
LYRIST

L••R••
LABREA
LABRET
LABRUM
LAIRDS
LARRUP
LAUREL
LAUREN
LAURIE
LEARNS
LEARNT
LEBRUN
LEERAT
LEERED
LEERER
LEGREE
LEHRER
LIBRIS
LIERNE
LITRES
LIVRES

L•••R•
LABORS
LACERS
LADERS
LAGERS
LAHORE
LAKERS
LAMARR
LANARK
LANDRY
LASERS
LAVERS
LAYERS
LEMURS
LENORE
LEVERS
LIBERI
LIFERS
LIGERS
LIGURE
LINERS
LITERS
LIVERS
LIVERY
LIZARD
LONERS
LOPERS
LOSERS
LOUVRE
LOVERS
LOWERS
LOWERY
LUGERS
LUSTRE
LUXURY
LYNYRD

L••••R
LAAGER
LABOUR
LACIER
LADDER
LADLER
LAFFER
LAGGER
LAKIER
LAMARR
LAMOUR
LANCER
LANDER
LANGUR
LANIER
LANKER
LARDER
LARGER
LASCAR
LASHER
LASSER
LATHER
LATOUR
LATTER
LAUDER
LAUPER
LAWYER
LAYFOR
LAZIER
LEADER
LEAKER
LEANER
LEAPER
LEASER
LECTER
LECTOR
LEDGER
LEERER
LEHRER
LEKVAR
LENDER
LERNER
LESSER
LESSOR
LESTER
LETTER
LEVIER
LEWDER
LIBBER
LICTOR
LIEDER
LIEFER
LIFTER
LIMBER
LIMIER
LIMNER
LIMPER
LINEAR
LINGER
LINIER
LINKER
LINTER
LIQUOR
LISTER
LITTER
LOADER
LOAFER
LOANER
LOBBER
LOCKER
LODGER
LOGGER
LOGIER
LOITER
LONGER
LOOKER
LOOPER
LOOSER
LOOTER
LOPPER
LOTHAR
LOUDER
LOUVER
LUBBER
LUGGER
LUMBAR
LUMBER
LUMPER
LUMPUR
LUNKER
LUSHER
LUSTER
LUTHER
LUTHOR

•L•R••
ALARIC
ALARMS
ALARUM
ALDRIN
ALERTS
ALFRED
BLARED
BLARES
BLURBS
BLURRY
BLURTS
CLARET
CLARKE
CLAROS
CLERGY
CLERIC
CLERKS
CLORIS
CLOROX
ELBRUS
FLARED
FLARES
FLIRTS
FLIRTY
FLORAE
FLORAL
FLORAS
FLORES
FLORET
FLORID
FLORIN
FLORIO
FLURRY
FLYROD
GLARED
GLARES
GLORIA
ILORIN
PLURAL
SLURPS
SLURRY
ULTRAS

•L••R•
ALBERT
ALBORG
ALDERS
ALEGRE
ALGORE
ALHIRT
ALLPRO
ALLURE
ALPERT
ALTARS
ALTERS
BLEARS
BLEARY
BLURRY
CLAIRE
CLEARS
ELBERT
ELDERS
ELLERY
ELMIRA
ELMORE
ELVERS
ELVIRA
FLAIRS
FLEERS
FLEURY
FLIERS
FLOORS
FLOURS
FLOURY
FLUORO
FLURRY
FLYERS
GLAIRS
GLAIRY
GLUERS
OLDPRO
OLEARY
PLEURA
PLIERS
SLURRY
ULCERS

•L•••R
ALEGAR
ALITER
ALLFOR
ALOMAR
ALTAIR
ALULAR
BLADER
BLAZER
BLOWER
CLAMOR
CLAWER
CLEVER
CLOSER
CLOVER
DLAYER
ELATER
ELAYER
ELINOR
ELIXIR
ELOPER
ELUDER
FLAKER
FLAVOR
FLAYER
FLEXOR
FLOWER
GLAMOR
GLASER

GLAZER
GLIDER
GLOVER
GLOWER
GLUIER
OLIVER
PLACER
PLANAR
PLANER
PLATER
PLAYER
PLEXOR
PLOVER
PLOWER
SLATER
SLAVER
SLAYER
SLICER
SLIDER
SLIVER
SLOWER
ULSTER

••LR••
DELRAY
DELRIO
DELROY
KILROY
OILRIG
WALRUS

••L•R•
AGLARE
AILERS
ALLPRO
ALLURE
BALERS
BELFRY
BOLERO
CELERY
CHLORO
COLORS
DOLORS
EELERS
ELLERY
FILERS
FULCRA
GALORE
HALERS
HALERU
HILARY
IDLERS
MALORY
MILERS
MILORD
MOLARS
NFLERS
NHLERS
OGLERS
OILERS
PALTRY
PELTRY
POLERS
RULERS
SALARY
SCLERA
SCLERO
SOLARS
SOLERS
SULTRY
TALERS
TILERS
TULARE
VALERY
VELCRO
VOLARE
WALERS

••L••R
ALLFOR
BALDER
BELAIR
BOLDER
BOLGER
BULGAR
BULGUR
BULWER
CALDER
CALLER
CALMER
CELLAR
COLDER
COLLAR
COLOUR
COLTER
CULLER
CULVER
DELMAR
DELVER
DILLER
DOLLAR
DOLOUR
DULLER
ECLAIR
EELIER
FALSER
FALTER
FELLER
FILLER
FILTER
FOLDER
FOLIAR
FULLER
FULMAR
GILDER
GOLFER
GULPER
HALTER
HELLER
HELPER
HELTER
HILLER
HOLDER
HOLIER
HOLLER
HULLER
KALMAR
KELLER
KILLER
KILMER
KILTER
KULTUR
MILDER
MILKER
MILLER
MILNER
MOLDER
MOLNAR
MOLTER
MULLER
OILIER
PALIER
PALLOR
PALMER
PALTER
PELTER
PILFER
PILLAR
POLDER
POLLER
PULSAR
ROLLER
SALTER
SALVER
SALVOR
SELLER
SILVER
SOLDER
SOLVER
SULFUR
SULKER
TALKER
TALLER
TELLER
TILLER
TILTER
UGLIER
VALOUR
VELOUR
VULGAR
WALKER
WALLER
WALTER
WELDER
WELLER
WELTER
WILBUR
WILDER
WILIER
WOLPER
YELLER
YELPER

•••L•R
ALULAR
AMBLER
AMPLER
ANGLER
ANTLER
ASHLAR
BAILER
BAILOR
BAWLER
BAYLOR
BOILER
BOWLER
BUGLER
BUTLER
CABLER
CALLER
CELLAR
CHOLER
COALER
COLLAR
COOLER
CULLER
CURLER
CUTLER
CYCLER
DEALER
DIALER
DILLER
DOLLAR
DUELER
DULLER
EVILER
FABLER
FEELER
FELLER
FILLER
FOOLER
FOULER
FOWLER
FUELER
FULLER
GABLER
GAOLER
HAULER
HEALER
HEELER
HELLER
HILLER
HOLLER
HOWLER
HULLER
HURLER
JAILER
KEELER
KEGLER
KELLER
KEPLER
KEVLAR
KILLER
KOHLER
LADLER
MAHLER
MAILER
MAULER
MEDLAR
MEWLER
MIDLER
MILLER
MOILER
MULLER
NAILER
NOBLER
OCULAR
OSTLER
OVULAR
PALLOR
PARLOR
PEDLAR
PEELER
PEGLER
PILLAR
POLLER
POPLAR
RAILER
REALER
RIFLER
ROLLER
SAILOR
SCALAR
SCALER
SEALER
SELLER
SISLER
SMILER
STALER
STELAR
STYLER
SUTLER
TAILOR
TALLER
TAYLOR
TELLER
THALER
TILLER
TOILER
UVULAR
WAILER
WALLER
WELLER
WHALER
WOHLER
YELLER

L•S•••
LASCAR
LASERS
LASHED
LASHER
LASHES
LASHIO
LASHUP
LASSEN
LASSER
LASSES
LASSIE
LASSOS
LASTED
LASTEX
LASTLY
LESAGE
LESBOS
LESLEY
LESLIE
LESSEE
LESSEN
LESSER
LESSON
LESSOR
LESTAT
LESTER
LISBOA
LISBON
LISLES
LISPED
LISTED
LISTEE
LISTEL
LISTEN
LISTER
LISTON
LOSEIT
LOSERS
LOSING
LOSSES
LOSTIT
LUSAKA
LUSHER
LUSHLY
LUSTED
LUSTER
LUSTRE
LYSINE
LYSINS

L••S••
LANSON
LAPSED
LAPSES
LAPSUP
LARSEN
LARSON
LASSEN
LASSER
LASSES
LASSIE
LASSOS
LAWSON
LAYSBY
LAYSIN
LAYSON
LAYSTO
LAYSUP
LEASED
LEASER
LEASES
LENSED
LENSES
LESSEE
LESSEN
LESSER
LESSON
LESSOR
LETSAT
LETSBE
LETSGO
LETSIN
LETSON
LETSUP
LIESIN
LIESTO
LINSEY
LOGSIN
LOGSON
LOOSED
LOOSEN
LOOSER
LOOSES
LOSSES
LOUSED
LOUSES

L•••S•
LAGASH
LAMESA
LAMEST
LANOSE
LAOTSE
LAROSA
LATEST
LATISH
LAVISH
LAXEST
LEGIST
LHOTSE
LIAISE
LIPASE
LOCUST
LOUISA
LOUISE
LOWEST
LOWISH
LUGOSI
LUTIST
LYRIST

L••••S
LABELS
LABORS
LACERS
LACHES
LADERS
LADIES
LADLES
LAGERS
LAIRDS
LAKERS
LAMEDS
LAMIAS
LAMMAS
LANAIS
LANCES
LANDIS
LAPELS
LAPINS
LAPSES
LARAMS
LARGES
LARGOS
LARVAS
LASERS
LASHES
LASSES
LASSOS
LATENS
LATHES
LATINS
LATKES
LAUGHS
LAVERS
LAYBYS
LAYERS
LAYUPS
LEARNS
LEASES
LEAVES
LEDGES
LEGALS
LEHUAS
LEMANS
LEMMAS
LEMNOS
LEMONS
LEMURS
LENSES
LEONES
LESBOS
LETUPS
LEVEES
LEVELS
LEVERS
LEVIES
LIANAS
LIANES
LIANGS
LIBELS
LIBRIS
LIEBYS
LIEGES
LIEUTS
LIFERS
LIGERS
LIGHTS
LIKENS
LILACS
LILIES
LIMBOS
LIMBUS
LIMENS
LIMEYS
LIMITS
LINENS
LINERS
LIPIDS
LISLES
LITERS
LITHOS
LITMUS
LITRES
LIVENS
LIVERS
LIVRES
LLAMAS
LLANOS
LLOYDS
LOAVES
LOCALS
LODENS
LODGES
LONERS
LONGES
LOOFAS
LOOIES
LOOSES
LOPERS
LORIES
LOSERS
LOSSES
LOTAHS
LOTTOS
LOUGHS
LOUPES
LOUSES
LOVERS
LOWERS
LUCIUS
LUDENS
LUGERS
LUMENS
LUNGES
LUTZES
LYCEES
LYMPHS
LYNXES
LYRICS
LYSINS

•LS•••
ALSACE
ULSTER

•L•S••
ALASKA
ALISON
ALLSET
ALYSSA
BLASTS
CLASPS
CLASSY
CLOSED
CLOSER
CLOSES
CLOSET
ELISHA
ELISSA
ELYSEE
FLASHY
FLASKS
FLESHY
FLOSSY
GLASER
GLASSY
GLOSSA
GLOSSO
GLOSSY
ILESHA
ILLSAY
OLDSAW
OLESON
PLASHY
PLASMA
PLASMO
PLASTY
PLISSE
PLUSES
PLUSHY
SLOSHY
SLUSHY

•L••S•
ALDOSE
ALEAST
ALMOST
ALONSO
ALWEST
ALYSSA
BLAISE
BLOUSE
BLOWSY
BLUEST
BLUESY
BLUISH
CLASSY
CLAUSE
CLEESE
CLUMSY
ELAPSE
ELDEST
ELFISH
ELISSA
ELOISE
ELPASO
ELVISH
FLENSE
FLIMSY
FLOPSY
FLOSSY
GLASSY
GLOSSA
GLOSSO
GLOSSY
ILLEST
ILLUSE
KLEIST
NLEAST
NLWEST
OLDEST
OLDISH
PLEASE
PLISSE
SLIEST
SLIMSY
SLYEST

•L•••S
ALAMOS
ALANIS

ALARMS
ALBUMS
ALDERS
ALDOUS
ALEPHS
ALERTS
ALEUTS
ALEXIS
ALIBIS
ALIENS
ALIGNS
ALINES
ALKYDS
ALKYLS
ALLAYS
ALLEES
ALLEYS
ALLIES
ALLOTS
ALLOWS
ALLOYS
ALOHAS
ALOINS
ALPHAS
ALTARS
ALTERS
ALTIUS
ALWAYS
BLACKS
BLADES
BLAMES
BLANKS
BLARES
BLASTS
BLAZES
BLEARS
BLEATS
BLEEDS
BLEEPS
BLENDS
BLIMPS
BLINDS
BLINIS
BLINKS
BLOATS
BLOCKS
BLOKES
BLONDS
BLOOMS
BLOOPS
BLUETS
BLUEYS
BLUFFS
BLUNTS
BLURBS
BLURTS
CLACKS
CLAIMS
CLAMPS
CLANGS
CLANKS
CLAROS
CLASPS
CLAVES
CLEANS
CLEARS
CLEATS
CLEEKS
CLEFTS
CLERKS
CLEVES
CLEVIS
CLICKS
CLIFFS
CLIMBS
CLIMES
CLINES
CLINGS
CLINKS
CLOAKS
CLOCKS
CLOMPS
CLONES
CLONKS
CLONUS
CLORIS
CLOSES
CLOTHS
CLOUDS
CLOUTS
CLOVES
CLOVIS
CLOWNS
CLUCKS
CLUMPS
CLUNKS
ELANDS
ELATES
ELBOWS
ELBRUS
ELDERS
ELECTS
ELEMIS
ELEVES
ELIDES
ELITES
ELOPES
ELUDES
ELUTES
ELVERS
FLACKS
FLAILS
FLAIRS
FLAKES
FLAMES
FLANKS
FLARES
FLASKS
FLAXES
FLECKS
FLEERS
FLEETS
FLEXES
FLICKS
FLIERS
FLINGS
FLINTS
FLIRTS
FLOATS
FLOCKS
FLOODS
FLOORS
FLORAS
FLORES
FLOURS
FLOUTS
FLUFFS
FLUIDS
FLUKES
FLUMES
FLUNKS
FLUTES
FLUXES
FLYBYS
FLYERS
FLYINS
GLACES
GLACIS
GLADES
GLADYS
GLAIRS
GLANDS
GLARES
GLAZES
GLEAMS
GLEANS
GLEBES
GLIDES
GLINTS
GLOATS
GLOBES
GLOGGS
GLOOMS
GLOVES
GLOZES
GLUERS
GLUONS
GLUTES
GLYNIS
GLYPHS
ILEXES
KLOOFS
LLAMAS
LLANOS
LLOYDS
OLDIES
OLIVES
OLMECS
PLACES
PLAGES
PLAIDS
PLAINS
PLAITS
PLANES
PLANKS
PLANTS
PLATES
PLAYAS
PLAZAS
PLEADS
PLEATS
PLEBES
PLEXUS
PLIERS
PLINKS
PLONKS
PLUCKS
PLUMBS
PLUMES
PLUMPS
PLUNKS
PLUSES
SLACKS
SLAKES
SLANGS
SLANTS
SLATES
SLAVES
SLEEKS
SLEEPS
SLEETS
SLICES
SLICKS
SLIDES
SLIMES
SLINGS
SLINKS
SLOOPS
SLOPES
SLOTHS
SLUMPS
SLURPS
SLYPES
ULCERS
ULTRAS
ZLOTYS

••LS••

ALLSET
BALSAM
BOLSHY
DILSEY
FALSER
FOLSOM
GELSEY
HALSEY
ILLSAY
JOLSON
KELSEY
MILSAP
NELSON
PULSAR
PULSED
PULSES
SALSAS
TILSIT
TULSAN
WILSON
WOLSEY

••L•S•

ABLEST
ABLUSH
ARLISS
ATLAST
CALASH
DALASI
DELIST
ENLIST
FILOSE
FOLKSY
GALOSH
HALEST
HOLISM
HOLIST
IDLEST
ILLEST
ILLUSE
MILOSZ
MOLEST
MULISH
NOLESS
NOLOSE
OBLAST
OWLISH
PALEST
PALISH
PILOSE
POLISH
RELISH
RELIST
SALISH
SPLASH
SPLOSH
TALESE
UNLASH
UNLESS
VALISE
VILEST
WALESA

••L••S

ADLIBS
AFLATS
AGLETS
AILERS
ALLAYS
ALLEES
ALLEYS
ALLIES
ALLOTS
ALLOWS
ALLOYS
ARLISS
BALERS
BELAYS
BELIES
BELLES
BILGES
BULGES
BYLAWS
CALAIS
CALCES
CALLAS
CALLES
CALLUS
CALVES
CALXES
CELEBS
CELLOS
COLEUS
COLIES
COLONS
COLORS
CULETS
CULLIS
DALLAS
DALLES
DELAYS
DELFTS
DELIUS
DELTAS
DELVES
DOLMAS
DOLORS
DULLES
ECLATS
EELERS
EFLATS
FALCES
FELLAS
FELONS
FILERS
FILETS
FILIUS
FILLES
FOLIOS
GALAHS
GALOIS
GALOPS
GELEES
GILLIS
GOLEMS
GULAGS
HALERS
HALLOS
HALOES
HALVES
HELENS
HELIOS
HELLAS
HELLOS
HELOTS
HELVES
HOLMES
HULLOS
IDLERS
IGLOOS
INLAWS
INLAYS
INLETS
ISLETS
JULEPS
JULIUS
KILIMS
KULAKS
LILACS
LILIES
MALAYS
MELEES
MELONS
MILERS
MILPAS
MOLARS
MULCTS
MULEYS
MULLAS
NFLERS
NHLERS
NOLENS
NOLESS
NYLONS
OGLERS
OILERS
ORLOPS
OWLETS
OXLIPS
PALLAS
PALMAS
PALPUS
PELEUS
PELOPS
PELVIS
PILAFS
PILEUS
PILOTS
POLERS
POLKAS
POLYPS
PULSES
PYLONS
RELAYS
RELETS
RELICS
RELIES
RILLES
ROLEOS
RULERS
SALADS
SALALS
SALONS
SALSAS
SALVES
SALVOS
SELVES
SILVAS
SOLANS
SOLARS
SOLERS
SOLEUS
SOLFAS
SOLIDS
SOLVES
SPLATS
SPLAYS
SPLITS
SULCUS
SYLPHS
TALERS
TALONS
TILAKS
TILDES
TILERS
TILLIS
TULIPS
TULLES
UCLANS
UGLIES
UHLANS
UNLESS
VALENS
VALETS
VALOIS
VALUES
VALVES
VELDTS
VILLAS
VILLUS
VOLANS
VOLENS
VOLVAS
WALERS
WALLIS
WALRUS
WELLES
WILKES
WILLIS
WOLVES
YALIES

•••LS•

AVULSE
EVULSE
GRILSE
ORELSE
URALSK
WHILST

•••L•S

ABELES
ADDLES
ADULTS
AEOLUS
AISLES
AKELAS
AMBLES
AMOLES
ANELES
ANGLES
ANGLOS
ANKLES
ANOLES
APPLES
ATOLLS
BAULKS
BCELLS
BELLES
BIBLES
BOGLES
BOULES
BOWLES
BRILLS
BRULES
BUGLES
BUILDS
CABLES
CALLAS
CALLES
CALLUS
CARLOS
CAULKS
CELLOS
CHALKS
CHELAS
CHILDS
CHILLS
CHOLOS
CULLIS
CYCLAS
CYCLES
CYCLOS
DALLAS
DALLES
DHOLES
DOBLAS
DRILLS
DROLLS
DULLES
DWELLS
EAGLES
ECCLES
ECOLES
EDILES
EXALTS
EXILES
EXULTS
FABLES
FAULTS
FELLAS
FIELDS
FILLES
FJELDS
FOWLES
FRILLS
GABLES
GILLIS
GRILLS
GUILDS
GUILES
HALLOS
HAOLES
HAULMS
HELLAS
HELLOS
HULLOS
IDYLLS
INGLES
INKLES
ISTLES
JOULES
KNELLS
KNOLLS
KOALAS
KVELLS
LADLES
LISLES
MAILES
MAJLIS
MAPLES
MOULDS
MOULTS
MULLAS
NAPLES
NOBLES
NYALAS
OBELUS
OODLES
ORALES
ORTLES
OVULES
OXALIS
PALLAS
PEPLOS
PHILOS
POILUS
POULTS
PROLES
PSALMS
QUALMS
QUELLS
QUILLS
QUILTS
REALES
REALMS
RIFLES
RILLES
ROBLES
RUBLES
SABLES
SAULTS
SAYLES
SCALDS
SCALES
SCALPS
SCOLDS
SCULLS
SHALES
SHELLS
SHILLS
SIDLES
SKALDS
SKILLS
SKULKS
SKULLS
SMALLS
SMELLS
SMELTS
SMILES
SMOLTS
SNELLS
SOCLES
SPALLS
SPELLS
SPILES
SPILLS
STALES
STALKS
STALLS
STELES
STILES

STILLS
STILTS
STOLES
STULLS
STYLES
STYLUS
SWALES
SWELLS
SWILLS
TABLAS
TABLES
TBILLS
TESLAS
THALES
THILLS
THOLES
TILLIS
TITLES
TOILES
TOKLAS
TRILLS
TROLLS
TULLES
TWILLS
UBOLTS
UNCLES
UVULAS
VAULTS
VILLAS
VILLUS
VIOLAS
VOILES
WALLIS
WELLES
WHALES
WHELKS
WHELMS
WHELPS
WHILES
WHOLES
WIELDS
WILLIS
WORLDS
XFILES
YIELDS

••••LS

ALKYLS
AMPULS
ANGELS
ANNALS
ANNULS
ANVILS
APPALS
ARTELS
ATOLLS
AVAILS
BABELS
BABULS
BAGELS
BCELLS
BETELS
BEVELS
BEZELS
BGIRLS
BOTELS
BRAILS
BRAWLS
BRILLS
BROILS
CABALS
CAMELS
CANALS
CAROLS
CASALS
CAVILS
CEORLS
CHILLS
CHURLS
CORALS
CRAWLS
CREELS
CUPELS
DECALS
DEVILS
DOWELS
DRAILS
DRAWLS
DRILLS
DROLLS
DROOLS
DWELLS
EASELS
EDSELS
EMAILS
ENGELS
ENROLS
EQUALS
EXCELS
EXPELS
EXTOLS
FINALS
FLAILS
FRILLS
FUSILS
GAVELS
GAYALS
GHOULS
GIMELS
GNARLS
GORALS
GRAILS
GRILLS
GROWLS
GRUELS
HAMALS
HAZELS
HOSELS
HOTELS
HOVELS
IDEALS
IDYLLS
IMPELS
JACALS
JEWELS
KEVELS
KNEELS
KNELLS
KNOLLS
KNURLS
KRAALS
KVELLS
LABELS
LAPELS
LEGALS
LEVELS
LIBELS
LOCALS
MEDALS
METALS
MODELS
MOGULS
MORALS
MORELS
MOTELS
MURALS
NASALS
NAVELS
NEWELS
NOVELS
ORIELS
OUSELS
OUZELS
PANELS
PEARLS
PEDALS
PERILS
PETALS
PHIALS
PICULS
PIPALS
PIXELS
PROWLS
PUPILS
QUAILS
QUELLS
QUILLS
RATELS
RAVELS
REBELS
REOILS
REPELS
REVELS
RIVALS
RIYALS
ROWELS
ROYALS
SALALS
SCOWLS
SCULLS
SEPALS
SHAWLS
SHELLS
SHILLS
SHOALS
SIBYLS
SIGILS
SISALS
SKILLS
SKIRLS
SKOALS
SKULLS
SMALLS
SMELLS
SNAILS
SNARLS
SNELLS
SOTOLS
SPALLS
SPELLS
SPIELS
SPILLS
SPOILS
SPOOLS
STALLS
STEALS
STEELS
STILLS
STOOLS
STULLS
SWELLS
SWILLS
SWIRLS
TAMILS
TBILLS
TEPALS
THILLS
TICALS
TOTALS
TOWELS
TRAILS
TRAWLS
TRIALS
TRILLS
TROLLS
TWILLS
TWIRLS
UMBELS
URIALS
USUALS
VIGILS
VINYLS
VITALS
VOCALS
VOWELS
WHEALS
WHEELS
WHIRLS
WHORLS
YODELS
YOKELS
ZORILS

L•T•••

LATEEN
LATELY
LATENE
LATENS
LATENT
LATEST
LATHED
LATHER
LATHES
LATIGO
LATINA
LATINI
LATINO
LATINS
LATISH
LATIUM
LATKES
LATONA
LATOUR
LATOYA
LATTEN
LATTER
LATVIA
LETFLY
LETHAL
LETOFF
LETOUT
LETSAT
LETSBE
LETSGO
LETSIN
LETSON
LETSUP
LETTED
LETTER
LETUPS
LITANY
LITCHI
LITERS
LITHIC
LITHOG
LITHOS
LITMUS
LITOUT
LITRES
LITTER
LITTLE
LOTAHS
LOTHAR
LOTION
LOTTED
LOTTOS
LUTHER
LUTHOR
LUTING
LUTIST
LUTZES
LYTTON

L••T••

LACTIC
LAOTSE
LAOTZU
LAPTEV
LAPTOP
LASTED
LASTEX
LASTLY
LATTEN
LATTER
LAWTON
LECTER
LECTOR
LEFTIE
LEFTIN
LENTEN
LENTIL
LEPTON
LESTAT
LESTER
LETTED
LETTER
LHOTSE
LICTOR
LIFTED
LIFTER
LIFTUP
LILTED
LINTEL
LINTER
LIOTTA
LIPTON
LISTED
LISTEE
LISTEL
LISTEN
LISTER
LISTON
LITTER
LITTLE
LOATHE
LOFTED
LOITER
LOOTED
LOOTER
LOSTIT
LOTTED
LOTTOS
LUSTED
LUSTER
LUSTRE
LYTTON

L•••T•

LAIDTO
LAKOTA
LANATE
LAPUTA
LAXITY
LAYSTO
LEADTO
LEALTY
LEANTO
LEGATE
LEGATO
LENGTH
LENITY
LEVITE
LEVITY
LIESTO
LIEUTS
LIGATE
LIGHTS
LILITH
LIMITS
LIOTTA
LOBATE
LOCATE
LOLITA
LOOKTO
LOVETT
LUCITE
LUNATE
LUXATE

L••••T

LABRET
LAMENT
LAMEST
LAMONT
LANCET
LAPPET
LARIAT
LATENT
LATEST
LAXEST
LAYOUT
LEARNT
LEDOUT
LEERAT
LEGIST
LESTAT
LETOUT
LETSAT
LEVANT
LIMPET
LINNET
LIONET
LITOUT
LOCKET
LOCUST
LOGOUT
LOOKAT
LOQUAT
LOSEIT
LOSTIT
LOVETT
LOWEST
LOWFAT
LUCENT
LUGNUT
LUTIST
LYRIST

•LT•••

ALTAIC
ALTAIR
ALTARS
ALTERS
ALTHEA
ALTIMA
ALTIUS
ALTMAN
ULTIMA
ULTIMO
ULTRAS

•L•T••

ALATAU
ALATED
ALITER
BLATTY
BLITHE
BLOTCH
BLOTTO
BLOTTY
BLYTHE
CLOTHE
CLOTHO
CLOTHS
CLOTTY
CLUTCH
ELATED
ELATER
ELATES
ELITES
ELUTED
ELUTES
FLATLY
FLETCH
FLITCH
FLUTED
FLUTES
FLUTEY
GLITCH
GLITZY
GLUTEI
GLUTEN
GLUTES
KLATCH
KLUTZY
PLATED
PLATEN
PLATER
PLATES
PLATTE
PLOTTY
SLATED
SLATER
SLATES
SLITHY
SLITTY
SLOTHS
ULSTER
ZLOTYS

•L••T•

ALCOTT
ALECTO
ALERTS
ALEUTS
ALIOTO
ALLOTS
ALMATY
BLASTS
BLATTY
BLEATS
BLINTZ
BLOATS
BLOTTO
BLOTTY
BLUETS
BLUNTS
BLURTS
CLEATS
CLEFTS
CLOTTY
CLOUTS
ELECTS
FLEETS
FLINTS
FLINTY
FLIRTS
FLIRTY
FLOATS
FLOATY
FLOUTS
GLINTS
GLOATS
OLEATE
PLAITS
PLANTE
PLANTS
PLASTY
PLATTE
PLEATS
PLENTY
PLINTH
PLOTTY
SLANTS
SLEETS
SLEETY
SLEUTH
SLITTY

•L•••T

ALBEIT
ALBERT
ALCOTT
ALEAST
ALHIRT
ALIGHT
ALLBUT
ALLOUT
ALLSET
ALLWET
ALMOST
ALPERT
ALWEST
BLEWIT
BLIGHT
BLOWIT
BLUEST
CLARET
CLIENT
CLOSET
ELBERT
ELDEST
ELEGIT
ELICIT
ELLIOT
FLAUNT
FLEWAT
FLIGHT
FLORET
FLUENT
FLYNET
FLYOUT
HLHUNT
ILLEST
ILLMET
KLEIST
NLEAST
NLWEST
OLDEST
OLDHAT
PLACET
PLAINT
PLANET
PLAYAT
PLIANT
PLIGHT
SLIEST
SLIGHT
SLYEST

••LT••

BALTIC
BELTED
BOLTED
BOLTON
CELTIC
COLTER
CULTIC
DALTON
DELTAS
DELTIC
FALTER
FELTED
FILTER
FILTHY
FULTON
HALTED
HALTER
HELTER
HILTON
JILTED
JOLTED
KILTED
KILTER
KILTIE
KULTUR
LILTED
MALTED
MALTIN
MELTED
MELTON
MILTIE
MILTON
MOLTED
MOLTEN
MOLTER
MOLTKE
MULTUM
PALTER
PALTRY

PELTED
PELTER
PELTRY
SALTED
SALTEN
SALTER
SALTON
SALTUM
SILTED
SULTAN
SULTRY
TILTED
TILTER
TOLTEC
WALTER
WALTON
WELTED
WELTER
WILTED
WILTON

••L•T•

ABLATE
AFLATS
AGLETS
ALLOTS
APLITE
ATLATL
BALATA
CULETS
DALETH
DELATE
DELETE
DELFTS
DILATE
DILUTE
DULUTH
ECLATS
EFLATS
EOLITH
FALLTO
FELLTO
FILETS
GALATA
GELATI
GELATO
HALITE
HELDTO
HELOTS
HOLDTO
INLETS
IOLITE
ISLETS
LILITH
LOLITA
MALATE
MALOTI
MELOTT
MULCTS
MULETA
OBLATE
OFLATE
OOLITE
OOLITH
OWLETS
PALATE
PELOTA
PILATE
PILOTI
PILOTS
POLITE
POLITY
RELATE
RELETS
SALUTE
SOLUTE
SPLATS
SPLITS
TALKTO
VALETS
VELDTS
VOLUTE

••L••T

ABLAUT
ABLEST
AFLOAT
AGLINT
ALLBUT
ALLOUT
ALLSET
ALLWET
ASLANT
ATLAST
AULAIT
BALLET
BALLOT
BELOIT
BILLET
BULLET
COLLET
CULLET
DELICT
DELIST
DULCET
ELLIOT
ENLIST
FILLET
GALOOT
GULLET
HALEST
HELMET
HELMUT
HOLDIT
HOLIST
IDLEST
ILLEST
ILLMET
JOLIET
JOLIOT
JULIET
MALLET
MELOTT
MILLET
MOLEST
MULLET
OBLAST
PALEST
PALLET
PELLET
PELMET
POLPOT
PULLET
PULPIT
RELENT
RELICT
RELIST
RELUCT
RILLET
SALLET
SALYUT
SELECT
SILENT
SOLENT
SPLINT
TALBOT
TALENT
TALKAT
TILSIT
UMLAUT
UPLIFT
VALENT
VELVET
VILEST
VOLANT
WALLET
WALNUT
WILLET

•••LT•

ADULTS
EXALTS
EXULTS
FALLTO
FAULTS
FAULTY
FAWLTY
FEALTY
FELLTO
GUILTY
HEALTH
LEALTY
MOULTS
POULTS
QUILTS
REALTY
RIALTO
SAULTS
SHELTY
SMALTI
SMALTO
SMELTS
SMOLTS
SPILTH
STILTS
SVELTE
UBOLTS
VAULTS
VAULTY
WEALTH

•••L•T

AMULET
ANKLET
APPLET
ARMLET
AUKLET
BADLOT
BALLET
BALLOT
BILLET
BULLET
CAMLET
CANLIT
CAPLET
CARLOT
CHALET
COLLET
COOLIT
CULLET
CUTLET
DAYLIT
DIGLOT
DYELOT
EAGLET
ENGLUT
EYELET
FILLET
GASLIT
GIBLET
GIMLET
GOBLET
GOULET
GULLET
HAMLET
JOBLOT
MALLET
MEDLAT
MERLOT
MILLET
MULLET
NUTLET
OCELOT
ODDLOT
OMELET
OUTLET
PALLET
PELLET
PIGLET
PIOLET
PULLET
RAILAT
REGLET
RILLET
RUNLET
SALLET
SAMLET
SCULPT
STYLET
SUBLET
SUNLIT
TABLET
TOILET
TWILIT
VARLET
VIOLET
WALLET
WHILST
WIGLET
WILLET
ZEALOT

••••LT

BASALT
COBALT
DESALT
INCULT
INSULT
ISEULT
KURALT
MODELT
OCCULT
PENULT
REBOLT
REMELT
RESALT
RESULT
REVOLT
SPOILT
TUMULT
TYBALT
UNBELT
UNBOLT

LU••••

LUANDA
LUBBER
LUBECK
LUBING
LUBLIN
LUCENT
LUCIAN
LUCITE
LUCIUS
LUCKED
LUDDEN
LUDENS
LUDLUM
LUDWIG
LUFFED
LUGERS
LUGGED
LUGGER
LUGNUT
LUGOSI
LULLED
LUMBAR
LUMBER
LUMENS
LUMINA
LUMMOX
LUMPED
LUMPEN
LUMPER
LUMPUR
LUNACY
LUNATE
LUNCHY
LUNDEN
LUNGED
LUNGES
LUNKER
LUNULA
LUPINE
LUPINO
LUPONE
LURING
LURKED
LUSAKA
LUSHER
LUSHLY
LUSTED
LUSTER
LUSTRE
LUTHER
LUTHOR
LUTING
LUTIST
LUTZES
LUXATE
LUXURY

L•U•••

LAUDED
LAUDER
LAUGHS
LAUNCH
LAUPER
LAUREL
LAUREN
LAURIE
LOUCHE
LOUDEN
LOUDER
LOUDLY
LOUGHS
LOUISA
LOUISE
LOUNGE
LOUPES
LOUSED
LOUSES
LOUVER
LOUVRE

L••U••

LACUNA
LAGUNA
LAPUTA
LAYUPS
LAZULI
LEGUIN
LEGUME
LEHUAS
LEMUEL
LEMURS
LETUPS
LIEUTS
LIGULA
LIGURE
LIQUID
LIQUOR
LOBULE
LOCUST
LOQUAT
LUNULA
LUXURY

L•••U•

LABOUR
LABRUM
LACEUP
LAIDUP
LAMOUR
LANGUR
LAPFUL
LAPSUP
LARRUP
LASHUP
LATIUM
LATOUR
LAWFUL
LAYOUT
LAYSUP
LEADUP
LEAGUE
LEBRUN
LEDOUT
LETOUT
LETSUP
LIFTUP
LIMBUS
LINEUP
LINGUA
LINKUP
LITMUS
LITOUT
LOCKUP
LOGOUT
LONGUE
LOOKUP
LUCIUS
LUDLUM
LUGNUT
LUMPUR
LYCEUM

L••••U

LANDAU
LAOTZU

•LU•••

ALULAE
ALULAR
ALUMNA
ALUMNI
BLUELY
BLUEOX
BLUEST
BLUESY
BLUETS
BLUEYS
BLUFFS
BLUING
BLUISH
BLUNTS
BLURBS
BLURRY
BLURTS
CLUBBY
CLUCKS
CLUEIN
CLUING
CLUMPS
CLUMPY
CLUMSY
CLUNKS
CLUNKY
CLUTCH
ELUDED
ELUDER
ELUDES
ELUTED
ELUTES
FLUENT
FLUFFS
FLUFFY
FLUIDS
FLUKES
FLUKEY
FLUMES
FLUNKS
FLUNKY
FLUORO
FLURRY
FLUTED
FLUTES
FLUTEY
FLUXED
FLUXES
GLUERS
GLUIER
GLUING
GLUMLY
GLUONS
GLUTEI
GLUTEN
GLUTES
KLUDGE
KLUTZY
PLUCKS
PLUCKY
PLUGIN
PLUMBS
PLUMED
PLUMES
PLUMMY
PLUMPS
PLUNGE
PLUNKS
PLURAL
PLUSES
PLUSHY
SLUDGE
SLUDGY
SLUGGO
SLUICE
SLUING
SLUMMY
SLUMPS
SLURPS
SLURRY
SLUSHY

•L•U••

ALBUMS
ALCUIN
ALEUTS
ALLUDE
ALLURE
BLOUSE
CLAUDE
CLAUSE
CLOUDS
CLOUDY
CLOUTS
FLAUNT
FLEURY
FLOURS
FLOURY
FLOUTS
HLHUNT
ILLUME
ILLUSE
PLEURA
PLOUGH
SLEUTH
SLOUCH
SLOUGH

•L••U•

ALARUM
ALDOUS
ALLBUT
ALLIUM
ALLOUT
ALTIUS
BLEWUP
BLOWUP
CLAMUP
CLAQUE
CLIQUE
CLIQUY
CLOGUP
CLONUS
CLOQUE
ELBRUS
FLIPUP
FLYOUT
PLAGUE
PLAQUE
PLAYUP
PLENUM
PLEXUS
SLAPUP
SLIPUP
SLOWUP

•L•••U

ALATAU

••LU••

ABLUSH
ALLUDE
ALLURE
BELUGA
COLUGO
COLUMN
DELUDE
DELUGE
DELUXE
DILUTE
DULUTH
ILLUME
ILLUSE
INLUCK
RELUCT
RELUME
SALUKI
SALUTE
SOLUTE
STLUKE
TELUGU
TOLUCA
VALUED
VALUES
VOLUME
VOLUTE

••L•U•

ABLAUT
ALLBUT
ALLIUM
ALLOUT
BALLUP
BULBUL
BULGUR
CALLUP
CALLUS
CALQUE
CILIUM
COLEUS
COLOUR
DELIUS
DOLLUP
DOLOUR
FILIUS
FILLUP
FOLDUP
FOLIUM
GALLUP
GILGUY
GOLLUM
HALLUX
HELDUP
HELIUM
HELMUT
HOLDUP
HOLEUP
JULIUS
KULTUR

MULTUM
PALPUS
PELEUS
PILEUM
PILEUP
PILEUS
POLLUX
PULLUP
PULQUE
RILEUP
ROLLUP
SALTUM
SALYUT
SELJUK
SOLEUS
SULCUS
SULFUR
TALCUM
TALKUP
TALMUD
UMLAUT
VALIUM
VALOUR
VELLUM
VELOUR
VILLUS
WALKUP
WALLUP
WALNUT
WALRUS
WELLUP
WILBUR
WILFUL

••L••U

BALLOU
HALERU
MALIBU
MILIEU
MOLDAU
TELEDU
TELUGU

•••LU•

AEOLUS
ASYLUM
BALLUP
CALLUP
CALLUS
COILUP
CURLUP
DIALUP
DOLLUP
EFFLUX
ENGLUT
FILLUP
FOULUP
GALLUP
GOLLUM
HALLUX
HAULUP
INFLUX
KAHLUA
KAILUA
KUNLUN
LUDLUM
MRBLUE
MUKLUK
OBELUS
PABLUM
PEPLUM
PHYLUM
POILUS
POLLUX
PULLUP
REFLUX
REGLUE
ROLLUP
RVALUE
SEALUP
STYLUS
TOOLUP
UNGLUE
UNPLUG
UVALUE
VELLUM
VILLUS
WALLUP
WELLUP

•••L•U

ARALLU
BALLOU
PAILOU

••••LU

ARALLU
BABALU
DESILU
MAKALU
MARILU
ORMOLU
TUVALU

L•V•••

LAVABO
LAVAGE
LAVERS
LAVING
LAVISH
LEVANT
LEVEED
LEVEES
LEVELS
LEVENE
LEVERS
LEVIED
LEVIER
LEVIES
LEVINE
LEVITE
LEVITY
LIVEIN
LIVELY
LIVENS
LIVEON
LIVERS
LIVERY
LIVING
LIVRES
LOVAGE
LOVEIN
LOVELL
LOVELY
LOVERS
LOVETT
LOVING

L••V••

LANVIN
LARVAE
LARVAL
LARVAS
LATVIA
LEAVED
LEAVEN
LEAVES
LEKVAR
LOAVES
LOUVER
LOUVRE

L••••V

LAPTEV

•LV•••

ELVERS
ELVIRA
ELVISH

•L•V••

ALEVEL
ALFVEN
CLAVES
CLAVIN
CLEVER
CLEVES
CLEVIS
CLOVEN
CLOVER
CLOVES
CLOVIS
ELEVEN
ELEVES
FLAVIA
FLAVOR
GLOVED
GLOVER
GLOVES
OLDVIC
OLEVEL
OLIVER
OLIVES
OLIVIA
PLOVER
SLAVED
SLAVER
SLAVES
SLAVEY
SLAVIC
SLIVER
SLOVAK
SLOVEN
SLOVIK

•L••V•

ALCOVE
CLEAVE
SLEAVE
SLEEVE

••LV••

CALVED
CALVES
CALVIN
CULVER
DELVED
DELVER
DELVES
HALVAH
HALVED
HALVES
HELVES
KELVIN
MELVIL
MELVIN
MELVYN
PELVIC
PELVIS
SALVED
SALVER
SALVES
SALVIA
SALVOR
SALVOS
SELVES
SILVAS
SILVER
SOLVED
SOLVER
SOLVES
SYLVAN
SYLVIA
VALVED
VALVES
VELVET
VOLVAS
VOLVOX
WOLVES

••L•V•

BULOVA
HALEVY
INLOVE
RELEVY
RELIVE
SALIVA

•••LV•

EVOLVE
SHELVE
TWELVE

•••L•V

KISLEV
PAVLOV
RUBLEV
VACLAV
VASLAV

L•W•••

LAWFUL
LAWING
LAWMAN
LAWMEN
LAWSON
LAWTON
LAWYER
LEWDER
LEWDLY
LOWBOY
LOWCAL
LOWELL
LOWEND
LOWERS
LOWERY
LOWEST
LOWFAT
LOWING
LOWISH
LOWKEY

L••W••

LEEWAY
LUDWIG

L••••W

LAYLOW
LIELOW

•LW•••

ALWAYS
ALWEST
ELWOOD
NLWEST

•L•W••

ALLWET
BLEWIT
BLEWUP
BLOWER
BLOWIN
BLOWIT
BLOWSY
BLOWUP
BLOWZY
CLAWED
CLAWER
CLEWED
CLOWNS
FLAWED
FLEWAT
FLEWIN
FLOWED
FLOWER
FLYWAY
GLOWED
GLOWER
PLOWED
PLOWER
SLEWED
SLOWED
SLOWER
SLOWLY
SLOWUP

•L••W•

ALLOWS
ELBOWS

•L•••W

OLDSAW

••LW••

ALLWET
BULWER
GALWAY

••L•W•

ALLOWS
BYLAWS
INLAWS
MALAWI

••L••W

BELLOW
BILLOW
CALLOW
FALLOW
FELLOW
FOLLOW
HALLOW
HOLLOW
MALLOW
MELLOW
MILDEW
PILLOW
SALLOW
TALLOW
WALLOW
WILLOW
YELLOW

•••L•W

BELLOW
BILLOW
CALLOW
CURLEW
FALLOW
FARLOW
FELLOW
FOLLOW
GAGLAW
GOSLOW
HALLOW
HARLOW
HOLLOW
INFLOW
LAYLOW
LIELOW
MALLOW
MELLOW
OUTLAW
PILLOW
PRELAW
REPLOW
SALLOW
TALLOW
WALLOW
WILLOW
YELLOW

L•X•••

LAXEST
LAXITY
LEXEME
LEXICA
LUXATE
LUXURY

L••X••

LYNXES

L••••X

LARYNX
LASTEX
LENNOX
LUMMOX

•L•X••

ALEXEI
ALEXIA
ALEXIS
BLIXEN
ELIXIR
FLAXEN
FLAXES
FLEXED
FLEXES
FLEXOR
FLUXED
FLUXES
ILEXES
KLAXON
PLEXAL
PLEXOR
PLEXUS

•L•••X

BLUEOX
CLIMAX
CLOROX

••LX••

CALXES

••L•X•

BILOXI
DELUXE
GALAXY

••L••X

BOLLIX
COLFAX
HALLUX
POLEAX
POLLEX
POLLUX
VOLVOX
WILCOX

•••L•X

BOLLIX
DUPLEX
EFFLUX
HALLUX
INFLUX
POLLEX
POLLUX
PROLIX
REFLEX
REFLUX
SMILAX

LY••••

LYCEES
LYCEUM
LYMPHS
LYNDON
LYNLEY
LYNXES
LYNYRD
LYRICS
LYRIST
LYSINE
LYSINS
LYTTON

L•Y•••

LAYBYS
LAYERS
LAYFOR
LAYING
LAYLOW
LAYMAN
LAYMEN
LAYOFF
LAYOUT
LAYSBY
LAYSIN
LAYSON
LAYSTO
LAYSUP
LAYUPS
LEYDEN
LOYOLA

L••Y••

LARYNX
LAWYER
LIBYAN
LLOYDS
LYNYRD

L•••Y•

LATOYA
LAYBYS
LIEBYS
LIMEYS

L••••Y

LACILY
LACKEY
LAIDBY
LAMELY
LANDRY
LANKLY
LASTLY
LATELY
LAXITY
LAYSBY
LAZBOY
LAZILY
LEACHY
LEAKEY
LEALTY
LEANLY
LEEWAY
LEGACY
LEMONY
LENITY
LESLEY
LETFLY
LEVITY
LEWDLY
LIEFLY
LIKELY
LIMPLY
LINENY
LINNEY
LINSEY
LIONLY
LITANY
LIVELY
LIVERY
LOGILY
LONELY
LONGLY
LOONEY
LORDLY
LOUDLY
LOVELY
LOWBOY
LOWERY
LOWKEY
LUNACY
LUNCHY
LUSHLY
LUXURY
LYNLEY

•LY•••

ALYSSA
BLYTHE
ELYSEE
FLYBOY
FLYBYS
FLYERS
FLYING
FLYINS
FLYMAN
FLYMEN
FLYNET
FLYOUT
FLYROD
FLYWAY
GLYCOL
GLYNIS
GLYPHS
PLYING
SLYEST
SLYPES

•L•Y••

ALKYDS
ALKYLS
CLAYEY
CLOYED
DLAYER
ELAYER
ELAYNE
FLAYED
FLAYER
FLEYED
LLOYDS
PLAYAS
PLAYAT
PLAYED
PLAYER
PLAYON
PLAYUP
SLAYED
SLAYER

•L••Y•

ALLAYS
ALLEYS
ALLOYS
ALWAYS
BLUEYS
FLYBYS
GLADYS
ZLOTYS

•L•••Y

ALBANY
ALECKY
ALLDAY
ALMATY
BLABBY
BLATTY
BLEARY
BLENNY
BLIMEY
BLOCKY
BLOODY
BLOOEY
BLOOMY
BLOTTY
BLOWSY

BLOWZY
BLUELY
BLUESY
BLURRY
CLAMMY
CLANCY
CLANKY
CLASSY
CLAYEY
CLERGY
CLIFFY
CLINGY
CLIQUY
CLODDY
CLOGGY
CLOTTY
CLOUDY
CLUBBY
CLUMPY
CLUMSY
CLUNKY
ELLERY
FLABBY
FLAGGY
FLAKEY
FLAPPY
FLASHY
FLATLY
FLECKY
FLEDGY
FLEECY
FLESHY
FLEURY
FLIMSY
FLINTY
FLIRTY
FLOATY
FLOCKY
FLOOEY
FLOPPY
FLOPSY
FLOSSY
FLOURY
FLUFFY
FLUKEY
FLUNKY
FLURRY
FLUTEY
FLYBOY
FLYWAY
GLADLY
GLAIRY
GLASSY
GLEAMY
GLIBLY
GLITZY
GLOOMY
GLOPPY
GLOSSY
GLUMLY
ILLSAY
KLUTZY
OLDBOY
OLEARY
PLASHY
PLASTY
PLENTY
PLOTTY
PLUCKY
PLUMMY
PLUSHY
SLAGGY
SLANGY
SLAPPY
SLAVEY
SLEAZY
SLEEKY
SLEEPY
SLEETY
SLIMLY
SLIMSY
SLINKY
SLIPPY
SLITHY
SLITTY
SLOBBY
SLOPPY
SLOSHY
SLOWLY
SLUDGY
SLUMMY
SLURRY
SLUSHY

••LY••

GALYAK
POLYPS
SALYUT

••L•Y•

ALLAYS
ALLEYS
ALLOYS
BELAYS
BOLEYN
DELAYS
INLAYS
MALAYA
MALAYS
MELVYN
MULEYS
POLEYN
RELAYS
SPLAYS

••L••Y

ALLDAY
BALDLY
BELFRY
BELLAY
BOLDLY
BOLSHY
CALMLY
CELERY
COLDLY
COLONY
DELANY
DELRAY
DELROY
DILSEY
ELLERY
EULOGY
FELONY
FILTHY
FOLKSY
GALAXY
GALLEY
GALWAY
GELSEY
GILGUY
HALEVY
HALLEY
HALSEY
HILARY
HOLILY
ILLSAY
JALOPY
KELLEY
KELSEY
KILROY
MALADY
MALORY
MELODY
MILADY
MILDLY
MILLAY
OILILY
OOLOGY
PALELY
PALTRY
PELTRY
POLICY
POLITY
PULLEY
RELEVY
SALARY
SALIFY
SOLELY
SULTRY
UGLIFY
UGLILY
VALERY
VALLEY
VILELY
VILIFY
VOLLEY
WILDLY
WILILY
WOLSEY

•••LY•

EVELYN
JACLYN

•••L•Y

ASHLEY
BAILEY
BARLEY
BEGLEY
BELLAY
BOSLEY
BROLLY
BURLEY
BYPLAY
CHALKY
CHILLY
COOLLY
COPLEY
COWLEY
CURLEY
DAILEY
DEPLOY
DOOLEY
DROLLY
DUALLY
DUDLEY
EMPLOY
EVILLY
FARLEY
FAULTY
FAWLTY
FEALTY
FOULLY
FRILLY
GALLEY
GUILTY
GURLEY
HAILEY
HALLEY
HANLEY
HARLEY
HAYLEY
HENLEY
HURLEY
HUXLEY
INPLAY
KELLEY
KNOLLY
LEALTY
LESLEY
LYNLEY
MARLEY
MEDLEY
MILLAY
MISLAY
MOBLEY
MORLEY
MOTLEY
MOULDY
NEWLEY
OAKLEY
OKELLY
ORALLY
OUTLAY
OVALLY
PARLAY
PARLEY
PAULEY
PHILBY
PHILLY
PULLEY
REALLY
REALTY
REILLY
REPLAY
RIDLEY
RIPLEY
SCULLY
SEELEY
SHALEY
SHALLY
SHELLY
SHELTY
SHILLY
SISLEY
SMELLY
SMILEY
STALKY
STILLY
TRILBY
VALLEY
VAULTY
VOLLEY
WAYLAY
WESLEY
WHOLLY
WOOLEY
WOOLLY
WURLEY

••••LY

ACIDLY
AERILY
AIRILY
ARCHLY
ARIDLY
ARTILY
AVIDLY
AWEDLY
BALDLY
BARELY
BARFLY
BASELY
BASSLY
BLUELY
BODILY
BOLDLY
BOTFLY
BROLLY
BUBBLY
BURBLY
BUSILY
CAGILY
CALMLY
CECILY
CHARLY
CHICLY
CHILLY
CICELY
COLDLY
COMELY
COMPLY
COOLLY
COSILY
COSTLY
COZILY
CRAWLY
CUDDLY
CURTLY
CUTELY
DAFTLY
DAMPLY
DANGLY
DANKLY
DARKLY
DEADLY
DEAFLY
DEARLY
DEEPLY
DEFTLY
DEWILY
DIDDLY
DIMPLY
DIRELY
DOUBLY
DOURLY
DOZILY
DRABLY
DRAWLY
DROLLY
DROOLY
DRYFLY
DUALLY
DUMBLY
EASILY
EBERLY
EDGILY
EERILY
EVENLY
EVERLY
EVILLY
FAIRLY
FAMILY
FEATLY
FEEBLY
FINELY
FIRMLY
FLATLY
FONDLY
FOULLY
FOXILY
FREELY
FRILLY
GADFLY
GAINLY
GAMELY
GAMILY
GANGLY
GENTLY
GIGGLY
GLADLY
GLIBLY
GLUMLY
GNARLY
GOGGLY
GOODLY
GOOGLY
GORILY
GRAYLY
GREYLY
GRIMLY
GRISLY
GROWLY
HACKLY
HARDLY
HAZILY
HIGHLY
HOLILY
HOMELY
HOMILY
HOSTLY
HOURLY
HUBBLY
HUGELY
HUMBLY
JANGLY
JIGGLY
JINGLY
JOKILY
JUNGLY
JUSTLY
KEENLY
KINDLY
KINGLY
KNOLLY
KNURLY
KODALY
LACILY
LAMELY
LANKLY
LASTLY
LATELY
LAZILY
LEANLY
LETFLY
LEWDLY
LIEFLY
LIKELY
LIMPLY
LIONLY
LIVELY
LOGILY
LONELY
LONGLY
LORDLY
LOUDLY
LOVELY
LUSHLY
MAINLY
MARBLY
MAYFLY
MAZILY
MEANLY
MEASLY
MEDFLY
MEEKLY
MEETLY
MERELY
MILDLY
MOSTLY
MUMBLY
MUSCLY
MUTELY
NAMELY
NEARLY
NEATLY
NETTLY
NICELY
NIMBLY
NOSILY
NUBBLY
NUDELY
NUMBLY
OILILY
OKELLY
OOZILY
OPENLY
ORALLY
OUTFLY
OVALLY
OVERLY
PALELY
PARTLY
PEARLY
PEBBLY
PERTLY
PHILLY
POKILY
POORLY
POPFLY
PORTLY
POSHLY
PRIMLY
PUDDLY
PUNILY
PURELY
PURPLY
RACILY
RANKLY
RAPTLY
RARELY
RASHLY
RATTLY
REALLY
REILLY
RICHLY
RIFELY
RIPELY
RIPPLY
RONELY
ROSILY
RUBBLY
RUDELY
RUFFLY
RUMBLY
RUMPLY
SAFELY
SAGELY
SANELY
SCULLY
SEEMLY
SEXILY
SHALLY
SHELLY
SHILLY
SHOALY
SICILY
SICKLY
SIMPLY
SINGLY
SLIMLY
SLOWLY
SMELLY
SMUGLY
SNARLY
SNUGLY
SOFTLY
SOLELY
SORELY
SOURLY
SPRYLY
STABLY
STEELY
STILLY
STOOLY
SUBTLY
SUPPLY
SURELY
SWIRLY
TAMELY
TANGLY
TARTLY
TAUTLY
THEFLY
THINLY
THUSLY
TICKLY
TIDDLY
TIDILY
TIMELY
TINGLY
TINILY
TINKLY
TREBLY
TRIGLY
TRIMLY
TRIPLY
TWOPLY
UGLILY
UNDULY
UNHOLY
UNOILY
UNRULY
UNWILY
USABLY
VAINLY
VASTLY
VERILY
VIABLY
VILELY
VOWELY
WADDLY
WAFFLY
WAGGLY
WAMBLY
WARILY
WARMLY
WAVILY
WAXILY
WEAKLY
WEEKLY
WETFLY
WHIRLY
WHOLLY
WIDELY
WIFELY
WIGGLY
WILDLY
WILILY
WIRILY
WISELY
WOBBLY
WOOLLY
YARELY
YEARLY
ZANILY

L•Z•••

LAZBOY
LAZIER
LAZILY
LAZING
LAZULI
LIZARD
LIZZIE

L••Z••

LIZZIE
LUTZES

L•••Z•

LAMAZE
LAOTZU

L••••Z

LORENZ

•L•Z••

BLAZED
BLAZER
BLAZES
BLAZON
GLAZED
GLAZER
GLAZES
GLOZED
GLOZES
PLAZAS
SLEZAK

•L••Z•

ALONZO
BLOWZY
GLITZY
KLUTZY
SLEAZE
SLEAZY

•L•••Z

BLINTZ

••LZ••
BALZAC

••L•Z•
ABLAZE
BELIZE

••L••Z
DOLENZ
MILOSZ
VALDEZ

•••L•Z
BOULEZ

••••LZ
SCHULZ

MA••••
MABELL
MACACO
MACAWS
MACEIO
MACHES
MACHOS
MACOUN
MACRAE
MACRON
MACROS
MACULA
MADAME
MADAMS
MADCAP
MADDEN
MADDER
MADDIE
MADEDO
MADEIT
MADERO
MADEUP
MADMAN
MADMAX
MADMEN
MADRAS
MADRES
MADRID
MADSEN
MADTOM
MADURA
MADURO
MAENAD
MAGGIE
MAGGIO
MAGMAS
MAGNET
MAGNON
MAGNUM
MAGNUS
MAGPIE
MAGUEY
MAGYAR
MAHDIS
MAHLER
MAHOUT
MAHZOR
MAIDEN
MAIDUS
MAILED
MAILER
MAILES
MAILIN
MAINLY
MAISIE
MAITAI
MAITRE
MAIZES
MAJGEN
MAJLIS
MAJORS
MAKALU
MAKEBA
MAKEDO
MAKEIT
MAKERS
MAKEUP
MAKING
MAKUTA
MALABO
MALADY
MALAGA
MALATE
MALAWI
MALAYA
MALAYS
MALDEN
MALIBU
MALICE
MALIGN
MALKIN
MALLEE
MALLEI
MALLET
MALLOW
MALONE
MALORY
MALOTI
MALTED
MALTIN
MAMBAS
MAMBOS
MAMMAL
MAMMAS
MAMMON
MANAGE
MANAMA
MANANA
MANAUS
MANCHA
MANCHU
MANDAN
MANDAY
MANEGE
MANFUL
MANGER
MANGLE
MANGOS
MANIAC
MANIAS
MANILA
MANIOC
MANNED
MANNER
MANNIX
MANORS
MANQUE
MANRAY
MANSES
MANTAS
MANTEL
MANTIC
MANTIS
MANTLE
MANTRA
MANTUA
MANUAL
MANUEL
MAOISM
MAOIST
MAORIS
MAOTAI
MAPLES
MAPPED
MAPPER
MAPUTO
MAQUIS
MARACA
MARAUD
MARBLE
MARBLY
MARCEL
MARCHE
MARCIA
MARCIE
MARCOS
MARCUS
MARDUK
MARGAY
MARGES
MARGIE
MARGIN
MARGOT
MARIAH
MARIAN
MARIEL
MARIKO
MARILU
MARINA
MARINE
MARINO
MARION
MARISA
MARISH
MARIST
MARIUS
MARKED
MARKER
MARKET
MARKKA
MARKUP
MARLED
MARLEE
MARLEY
MARLIN
MARLON
MARMEE
MARMOT
MARNER
MARNIE
MAROON
MARPLE
MARQUE
MARRED
MARRON
MARROW
MARSHA
MARSHY
MARTEL
MARTEN
MARTHA
MARTIN
MARTYR
MARVEL
MARVIN
MASADA
MASAIS
MASCOT
MASERS
MASERU
MASHED
MASHER
MASHES
MASHIE
MASKED
MASKER
MASONS
MASQUE
MASSED
MASSES
MASSEY
MASSIF
MASTER
MASTIC
MATERS
MATEYS
MATHER
MATHIS
MATING
MATINS
MATLIN
MATRIX
MATRON
MATTEA
MATTED
MATTEL
MATTER
MATTES
MATTIE
MATURE
MATZOH
MATZOS
MAULED
MAULER
MAUMAU
MAUMEE
MAUNDY
MAURYA
MAUSER
MAUVES
MAVENS
MAXENE
MAXIMA
MAXIMS
MAXINE
MAXIXE
MAXOUT
MAYANS
MAYBES
MAYDAY
MAYFLY
MAYHAP
MAYHEM
MAYORS
MAYPOP
MAYTAG
MAZERS
MAZIER
MAZILY
MAZOLA
MAZUMA

M•A•••
MCADAM
MCADOO
MEADOW
MEAGER
MEAGRE
MEALIE
MEANER
MEANIE
MEANLY
MEASLY
MIAMIA
MIASMA
MOANED
MOANER
MOATED

M••A••
MACACO
MACAWS
MADAME
MADAMS
MAKALU
MALABO
MALADY
MALAGA
MALATE
MALAWI
MALAYA
MALAYS
MANAGE
MANAMA
MANANA
MANAUS
MARACA
MARAUD
MASADA
MASAIS
MAYANS
MCBAIN
MCCABE
MCCANN
MCHALE
MCLAIN
MCNAIR
MEDAKA
MEDALS
MEGALO
MEGARA
MELANO
MENACE
MENADO
MENAGE
MESABI
METALS
METATE
MIDAIR
MIKADO
MILADY
MILANO
MIRAGE
MOHAIR
MOHAVE
MOHAWK
MOJAVE
MOLARS
MONACO
MONADS
MORALE
MORALS
MORANT
MORASS
MORAVA
MORAYS
MOSAIC
MOZART
MUFASA
MUGABE
MURALS
MURANO
MUTANT
MUTATE
MUTATO
MYNAHS

M•••A•
MACRAE
MADCAP
MADMAN
MADMAX
MADRAS
MAENAD
MAGMAS
MAGYAR
MAITAI
MAMBAS
MAMMAL
MAMMAS
MANDAN
MANDAY
MANIAC
MANIAS
MANRAY
MANTAS
MANUAL
MAOTAI
MARGAY
MARIAH
MARIAN
MAUMAU
MAYDAY
MAYHAP
MAYTAG
MCADAM
MCGRAW
MCLEAN
MECCAS
MEDGAR
MEDIAL
MEDIAN
MEDIAS
MEDLAR
MEDLAT
MELMAC
MENIAL
MENSAE
MENSAL
MENSAS
MENTAL
MERMAN
MESCAL
MICMAC
MIDDAY
MIDIAN
MIDWAY
MIHRAB
MILLAY
MILPAS
MILSAP
MINOAN
MINYAN
MIRIAM
MISHAP
MISLAY
MISSAL
MISSAY
MITRAL
MOBCAP
MOCHAS
MOLDAU
MOLNAR
MOMMAS
MONDAY
MOOLAH
MOREAU
MORGAN
MORNAY
MORTAL
MORTAR
MOSHAV
MSQUAD
MUDCAT
MUDRAS
MULLAH
MULLAS
MURRAY
MUSCAT
MUSIAL
MUTUAL
MYRDAL
MYRIAD

M••••A
MACULA
MADURA
MAKEBA
MAKUTA
MALAGA
MALAYA
MANAMA
MANANA
MANCHA
MANILA
MANTRA
MANTUA
MARACA
MARCIA
MARINA
MARISA
MARKKA
MARSHA
MARTHA
MASADA
MATTEA
MAURYA
MAXIMA
MAZOLA
MAZUMA
MCCREA
MEDAKA
MEDINA
MEDUSA
MEGARA
MELINA
MERIDA
MIAMIA
MIASMA
MIKITA
MIMOSA
MINIMA
MISCHA
MODELA
MODENA
MONERA
MONETA
MONICA
MORAVA
MORITA
MOSKVA
MOTHRA
MUCOSA
MUFASA
MULETA
MURCIA
MYOPIA

•MA•••
AMADIS
AMADOU
AMAJOR
AMALFI
AMALIE
AMANDA
AMATIS
AMATOL
AMAZED
AMAZES
AMAZON
BMAJOR
CMAJOR
DMAJOR
DMARKS
EMAILS
EMAJOR
FMAJOR
GMAJOR
IMAGED
IMAGER
IMAGES
IMAMAN
IMARET
OMAHAN
OMAHAS
OMANIS
OMASUM
SMACKS
SMALLS
SMALTI
SMALTO
SMARMY
SMARTS
SMARTY

•M•A••
AMBATO
AMHARA
EMBANK
EMBARK
EMBAYS
EMDASH
IMPACT
IMPAIR
IMPALA
IMPALE
IMPART
SMEARS
SMEARY
UMIAKS
UMLAUT
UMTATA

•M••A•
AMEBAE
AMEBAS
AMIGAS
AMORAL
AMTRAC
AMTRAK
AMYTAN
EMQUAD
IMAMAN
OMAHAN
OMAHAS
OMEGAS
SMILAX
UMBRAE
UMBRAL
UMBRAS

•M•••A
AMANDA
AMELIA
AMENRA
AMHARA
AMOEBA
EMILIA
IMELDA
IMPALA
OMERTA
SMYRNA
UMBRIA
UMTATA

••MA••
ADMASS
ALMATY
ARMADA
ARMAGH
ARMAND
ARMANI
ASMARA
AYMARA
BAMAKO
BEMATA
CAMARO
COMATE
DAMAGE
DAMASK
DAMATO
DEMAND
DOMAIN
DOMANI
FEMALE
GAMAYS
GEMARA
HAMALS
HEMATO
HOMAGE
HUMANE
HUMANS
INMATE
JAMAAL
JUMADA
KAMALA
LAMARR
LAMAZE
LEMANS
NAMATH
NEMATO
NOMADS

POMACE
POMADE
RAMADA
RAMATE
REMADE
REMAIL
REMAIN
REMAKE
REMAND
REMANS
REMAPS
REMARK
ROMAIC
ROMAJI
ROMANO
ROMANS
ROMANY
SAMARA
SOMALI
SOMANY
SOMATA
SOMATO
STMALO
STMARK
SUMACS
TAMALE
TAMARA
TAMAYO
TOMATO
UNMADE
UNMAKE
UNMANS
UNMASK
USMAIL
YAMAHA
ZYMASE

••M•A•
AIMSAT
BEMOAN
BOMBAY
BUMRAP
CAMEAT
COMBAT
COMEAT
COMMAS
COMPAQ
COMSAT
CYMBAL
DAMMAR
DEMEAN
GAMMAS
GEMMAE
GIMBAL
GYMBAG
HYMNAL
JAMAAL
JUMPAT
KOMBAT
LAMIAS
LAMMAS
LEMMAS
LUMBAR
MAMBAS
MAMMAL
MAMMAS
MOMMAS
NUMBAT
OOMPAH
PAMPAS
QUMRAN
RAMEAU
RAMSAY
RUMBAS
SAMBAL
SAMBAR
SAMBAS
SAMIAM
SAMOAN
SAMPAN
SIMIAN
SUMMAE
SUMMAS
TAMTAM
TIMBAL
TOMBAC
TOMCAT
WOMBAT
ZAMIAS

••M••A
ARMADA
ASMARA
AYMARA
BEMATA
CAMERA
DAMITA
ELMIRA
FEMORA
GAMBIA
GEMARA
JUMADA
KAMALA
LAMBDA
LAMESA
LAMINA
LUMINA
MIMOSA
NUMINA
PAMELA
POMONA
RAMADA
RAMBLA
RAMONA
REMORA
REMUDA
ROMOLA
RUMINA
SAMARA
SAMOSA
SOMATA
TAMARA
XIMENA
YAMAHA
ZAMBIA

•••MA•
AGAMAS
AIRMAN
ALEMAN
ALLMAN
ALOMAR
ALTMAN
ANIMAL
ANIMAS
APEMAN
AROMAS
ATAMAN
BADMAN
BARMAN
BATMAN
BIGMAC
BITMAP
BORMAN
BOWMAN
BRUMAL
BURMAN
BUSMAN
CAIMAN
CARMAN
CAYMAN
CLIMAX
COLMAN
COMMAS
CONMAN
CORMAN
COWMAN
DAGMAR
DAMMAR
DELMAR
DERMAL
DESMAN
DISMAL
DISMAY
DOGMAS
DOLMAN
DOLMAS
DRAMAS
ELFMAN
ENDMAN
FBIMAN
FENMAN
FERMAT
FIRMAN
FLYMAN
FORMAL
FORMAN
FORMAT
FULMAR
GAGMAN
GAMMAS
GASMAN
GEMMAE
GERMAN
GETMAD
GOTMAD
GRAMAS
GUNMAN
HAEMAT
HAGMAN
HERMAN
HETMAN
HIEMAL
HITMAN
ICEMAN
IMAMAN
INGMAR
KALMAR
KATMAI
KERMAN
KIDMAN
KIRMAN
KORMAN
LAMMAS
LAWMAN
LAYMAN
LEGMAN
LEMMAS
LLAMAS
MADMAN
MADMAX
MAGMAS
MAMMAL
MAMMAS
MAUMAU
MELMAC
MERMAN
MICMAC
MOMMAS
NETMAN
NEUMAN
NEWMAN
NEWMAR
NORMAL
NORMAN
OILMAN
OLDMAN
ONEMAN
PACMAN
PALMAS
PENMAN
PIEMAN
PITMAN
PRIMAL
RAGMAN
RODMAN
RUDMAN
SALMAN
SEAMAN
SGTMAJ
SHAMAN
SIGMAS
STOMAS
STOMAT
SUMMAE
SUMMAS
TARMAC
TASMAN
TAXMAN
THOMAS
TINMAN
TOAMAN
TODMAN
TRUMAN
TUBMAN
ULLMAN
WEIMAR
YEOMAN
YESMAN
ZEEMAN

•••M•A
AHIMSA
ALUMNA
ANEMIA
CRIMEA
GRAMPA
MIAMIA
NOUMEA
RHUMBA

••••MA
ALTIMA
BAHAMA
BRAHMA
CHACMA
CHROMA
CINEMA
COLIMA
DAGAMA
DHARMA
DODOMA
ENIGMA
FATIMA
INTIMA
JICAMA
KINEMA
MANAMA
MAXIMA
MAZUMA
MIASMA
MINIMA
OEDEMA
OPTIMA
PAJAMA
PALOMA
PANAMA
PLASMA
PNEUMA
PYJAMA
SCHEMA
SONOMA
STIGMA
TACOMA
THELMA
TRAUMA
ULTIMA
YAKIMA
YOYOMA
ZEUGMA

MB••••
MBUNDU

M•B•••
MABELL
MCBAIN
MOBBED
MOBCAP
MOBILE
MOBIUS
MOBLEY
MRBLUE

M••B••
MAMBAS
MAMBOS
MARBLE
MARBLY
MAYBES
MEMBER
MOBBED
MORBID
MUMBLE
MUMBLY

M•••B•
MAKEBA
MALABO
MALIBU
MCCABE
MCJOBS
MESABI
MUGABE

M••••B
MIDRIB
MIHRAB

•MB•••
AMBATO
AMBERS
AMBERY
AMBITS
AMBLED
AMBLER
AMBLES
AMBLIN
AMBUSH
EMBANK
EMBARK
EMBAYS
EMBDEN
EMBEDS
EMBERS
EMBLEM
EMBODY
EMBOSS
EMBRYO
IMBIBE
IMBRUE
IMBUED
IMBUES
UMBELS
UMBERS
UMBRAE
UMBRAL
UMBRAS
UMBRIA

•M•B••
AMEBAE
AMEBAS
AMEBIC

•M••B•
AMOEBA
IMBIBE

••MB••
BAMBOO
BOMBAY
BOMBED
BOMBER
BOMBES
BUMBLE
BUMBRY
CAMBER
COMBAT
COMBED
COMBER
COMBES
COMBOS
CUMBER
CYMBAL
DUMBER
DUMBLY
FUMBLE
GAMBIA
GAMBIT
GAMBLE
GAMBOL
GIMBAL
GIMBEL
GUMBEL
GUMBOS
GYMBAG
HOMBRE
HUMBLE
HUMBLY
HUMBUG
IAMBIC
JUMBLE
JUMBOS
KOMBAT
LAMBDA
LAMBED
LIMBED
LIMBER
LIMBOS
LIMBUS
LOMBOK
LUMBAR
LUMBER
MAMBAS
MAMBOS
MEMBER
MUMBLE
MUMBLY
NIMBLE
NIMBLY
NIMBUS
NUMBAT
NUMBED
NUMBER
NUMBLY
RAMBLA
RAMBLE
RUMBAS
RUMBLE
RUMBLY
SAMBAL
SAMBAR
SAMBAS
SIMBEL
SOMBER
SOMBRE
SYMBOL
TIMBAL
TIMBER
TIMBRE
TOMBAC
TOMBOY
TUMBLE
WAMBLE
WAMBLY
WIMBLE
WOMBAT
ZAMBIA
ZOMBIE

••M•B•
CAMEBY
COMEBY
DEMOBS

•••MB•
ABOMBS
AKIMBO
BRUMBY
CLIMBS
CRAMBO
CRUMBS
CRUMBY
FLAMBE
HBOMBS
PLUMBS
RHOMBI
RHOMBS
RHUMBA
RHUMBS
THUMBS

••••MB
APLOMB
BENUMB

MC••••
MCADAM
MCADOO
MCBAIN
MCCABE
MCCANN
MCCREA
MCGRAW
MCGREW
MCHALE
MCHUGH
MCJOBS
MCKUEN
MCLAIN
MCLEAN
MCNAIR

M•C•••
MACACO
MACAWS
MACEIO
MACHES
MACHOS
MACOUN
MACRAE
MACRON
MACROS
MACULA
MCCABE
MCCANN
MCCREA
MECCAS
MICHEL
MICKEY
MICMAC
MICRON
MICROS
MOCHAS
MOCKED
MOCKER
MOCKUP
MRCOOL
MUCINS
MUCKED
MUCKUP
MUCOSA
MUCOUS

M••C••
MADCAP
MANCHA
MANCHU
MARCEL
MARCHE
MARCIA
MARCIE
MARCOS
MARCUS
MASCOT
MECCAS
MERCED
MERCER
MESCAL
MINCED
MINCER
MINCES
MISCHA
MISCUE
MOBCAP
MOSCOW
MUDCAT
MULCTS
MUNCHY
MUNCIE
MURCIA
MUSCAT
MUSCLE
MUSCLY

M•••C•
MACACO
MALICE
MARACA
MEDICI
MEDICO
MEDICS
MEJICO
MENACE
MENSCH
MEXICO
MIMICS
MODOCS
MOHOCK
MOLOCH
MONACO
MONICA
MUNICH

M••••C
MANIAC
MANIOC
MANTIC
MASTIC
MELMAC
METRIC
MICMAC
MIXTEC
MOSAIC
MYOPIC
MYSTIC
MYTHIC

•MC•••
EMCEED
EMCEES

•M•C••
AMECHE
AMICES
AMICUS
SMACKS
SMOCKS

•M••C•
AMERCE
IMPACT
SMIRCH
SMOOCH
SMUTCH

•M•••C
AMEBIC

AMTRAC

••MC••
KIMCHI
TOMCAT

••M•C•
COMICS
LAMECH
MIMICS
OLMECS
OSMICS
POMACE
PUMICE
REMICK
SAMECH
SUMACS

••M••C
CYMRIC
HOMEEC
IAMBIC
ROMAIC
TOMBAC

•••M•C
ANEMIC
ANOMIC
ATOMIC
BIGMAC
CADMIC
COSMIC
FORMIC
GNOMIC
KARMIC
MELMAC
MICMAC
TARMAC

••••MC
RUNDMC

M•D•••
MADAME
MADAMS
MADCAP
MADDEN
MADDER
MADDIE
MADEDO
MADEIT
MADERO
MADEUP
MADMAN
MADMAX
MADMEN
MADRAS
MADRES
MADRID
MADSEN
MADTOM
MADURA
MADURO
MEDAKA
MEDALS
MEDDLE
MEDFLY
MEDGAR
MEDIAL
MEDIAN
MEDIAS
MEDICI
MEDICO
MEDICS
MEDINA
MEDIUM
MEDLAR
MEDLAT
MEDLEY
MEDUSA
MIDAIR
MIDDAY
MIDDEN
MIDDLE
MIDGES
MIDGET
MIDIAN
MIDLER
MIDORI
MIDRIB
MIDWAY
MODELA
MODELS
MODELT
MODEMS
MODENA
MODERN
MODEST
MODIFY
MODINE
MODISH
MODOCS
MODULE
MODULO
MUDCAT
MUDDED
MUDDER
MUDDLE
MUDEEL
MUDHEN
MUDPIE
MUDRAS

M••D••
MADDEN
MADDER
MADDIE
MAHDIS
MAIDEN
MAIDUS
MALDEN
MANDAN
MANDAY
MARDUK
MAYDAY
MCADAM
MCADOO
MEADOW
MEDDLE
MELDED
MENDED
MENDEL
MENDER
MENDES
MIDDAY
MIDDEN
MIDDLE
MILDER
MILDEW
MILDLY
MINDED
MINDER
MISDID
MOLDAU
MOLDED
MOLDER
MONDAY
MUDDED
MUDDER
MUDDLE
MURDER
MYRDAL

M•••D•
MADEDO
MAKEDO
MALADY
MASADA
MAUNDY
MBUNDU
MELODY
MENADO
MERIDA
MIKADO
MILADY
MONADS
MONODY
MOPEDS
MOULDS
MOULDY
MOUNDS
MRHYDE

M••••D
MADRID
MAENAD
MAILED
MALTED
MANNED
MAPPED
MARAUD
MARKED
MARLED
MARRED
MASHED
MASKED
MASSED
MATTED
MAULED
MELDED
MELTED
MENDED
MEOWED
MERCED
MERGED
MESHED
MESSED
METHOD
MEWLED
MIFFED
MILKED
MILLED
MILORD
MINCED
MINDED
MINTED
MISDID
MISLED
MISSED
MISTED
MITRED
MOANED
MOATED
MOBBED
MOCKED
MOILED
MOLDED
MOLTED
MONIED
MOONED
MOORED
MOOTED
MOPPED
MORBID
MOSHED
MOSSED
MOUSED
MSQUAD
MUCKED
MUDDED
MUFFED
MUGGED
MULLED
MUMMED
MUMPED
MUSHED
MUSSED
MUZZED
MYRIAD
MYWORD

•MD•••
EMDASH

•M•D••
AMADIS
AMADOU
AMEDEO
AMIDES
AMIDOL
AMIDST
EMBDEN
SMUDGE
SMUDGY

•M••D•
AMANDA
AMENDS
EMBEDS
EMBODY
EMENDS
IMELDA
IMPEDE

•M•••D
AMAZED
AMBLED
AMPHID
AMUSED
EMCEED
EMOTED
EMQUAD
IMAGED
IMBUED
IMPEND
SMILED
SMOKED

••MD••
CAMDEN
DUMDUM

••M•D•
ARMADA
COMEDY
DEMODE
JUMADA
KOMODO
LAMBDA
LAMEDH
LAMEDS
NOMADS
POMADE
RAMADA
REMADE
REMEDY
REMUDA
UNMADE

••M••D
ALMOND
ARMAND
BOMBED
BUMMED
BUMPED
CAMPED
COMBED
DAMMED
DAMNED
DAMPED
DEMAND
DEMOND
DIMMED
DUMPED
EDMOND
EDMUND
GAMMED
GEMMED
GUMMED
HAMMED
HEMMED
HUMMED
HUMPED
HYMNED
JAMMED
JUMPED
LAMBED
LAMMED
LEMOND
LIMBED
LIMNED
LIMPED
LIMPID
LOMOND
LUMPED
MUMMED
MUMPED
NIMROD
NUMBED
ORMOND
OSMOND
OSMUND
PUMPED
RAMMED
RAMPED
RAMROD
REMAND
REMEND
REMIND
REMOLD
RIMMED
ROMPED
SUMMED
TAMPED
TEMPED
TUMMED
VAMPED

•••M•D
BEAMED
BLAMED
BOOMED
BUMMED
CALMED
CHIMED
DAMMED
DEEMED
DIMMED
DOOMED
FARMED
FILMED
FIRMED
FLAMED
FOAMED
FORMED
FRAMED
GAMMED
GAUMED
GEMMED
GETMAD
GOTMAD
GRIMED
GUMMED
HAMMED
HARMED
HELMED
HEMMED
HUMMED
JAMMED
LAMMED
LOAMED
LOOMED
MUMMED
PALMED
PERMED
PLUMED
PREMED
PRIMED
RAMMED
REAMED
RHYMED
RIMMED
ROAMED
ROOMED
SEAMED
SEEMED
SHAMED
SLIMED
SPUMED
SUMMED
TALMUD
TEAMED
TEEMED
TERMED
THEMED
TUMMED
WARMED
WORMED
ZOOMED

ME••••
MEADOW
MEAGER
MEAGRE
MEALIE
MEANER
MEANIE
MEANLY
MEASLY
MECCAS
MEDAKA
MEDALS
MEDDLE
MEDFLY
MEDGAR
MEDIAL
MEDIAN
MEDIAS
MEDICI
MEDICO
MEDICS
MEDINA
MEDIUM
MEDLAR
MEDLAT
MEDLEY
MEDUSA
MEEKER
MEEKLY
MEERUT
MEETER
MEETLY
MEGALO
MEGARA
MEGILP
MEGOHM
MEJICO
MEKONG
MELANO
MELDED
MELEES
MELINA
MELLON
MELLOW
MELMAC
MELODY
MELONS
MELOTT
MELTED
MELTON
MELVIL
MELVIN
MELVYN
MEMBER
MEMNON
MEMOIR
MEMORY
MENACE
MENADO
MENAGE
MENDED
MENDEL
MENDER
MENDES
MENHIR
MENIAL
MENINX
MENJOU
MENKEN
MENNEN
MENSAE
MENSAL
MENSAS
MENSCH
MENTAL
MENTIS
MENTOR
MEOWED
MERCED
MERCER
MERELY
MEREST
MERGED
MERGER
MERGES
MERIDA
MERINO
MERITS
MERKEL
MERLIN
MERLON
MERLOT
MERMAN
MERMEN
MEROPE
MERSEY
MERTON
MERVYN
MESABI
MESCAL
MESHED
MESHES
MESMER
MESONS
MESSED
MESSES
MESSRS
MESSUP
METALS
METATE
METEOR
METERS
METHOD
METHYL
METIER
METING
METOPE
METRES
METRIC
METROS
METTLE
MEWING
MEWLED
MEWLER
MEXICO
MEZZOS

M•E•••
MAENAD
MEEKER
MEEKLY
MEERUT
MEETER
MEETLY
MYELIN

M••E••
MABELL
MACEIO
MADEDO
MADEIT
MADERO
MADEUP
MAKEBA
MAKEDO
MAKEIT
MAKERS
MAKEUP
MANEGE
MASERS
MASERU
MATERS
MATEYS
MAVENS
MAXENE
MAZERS
MCLEAN
MELEES
MERELY
MEREST
METEOR
METERS
MILERS
MIMEOS
MIMERS
MINERS
MISERS
MISERY
MITERS
MIXERS
MIZENS
MODELA
MODELS
MODELT
MODEMS
MODENA
MODERN
MODEST
MOIETY
MOLEST
MOMENT
MONERA
MONETA
MONEYS
MOPEDS
MOPERS
MOPERY
MOREAU
MOREEN
MORELS
MORENO
MOSEYS
MOTELS
MOTETS
MOVEIN
MOVEON
MOVERS
MOVEUP
MOWERS
MOYERS
MUDEEL
MULETA
MULEYS
MUSERS
MUSEUM
MUTELY
MUTEST
MYSELF

M•••E•
MACHES
MADDEN
MADDER
MADMEN
MADRES
MADSEN
MAGNET
MAGUEY
MAHLER
MAIDEN
MAILED
MAILER
MAILES
MAIZES
MAJGEN
MALDEN
MALLEE
MALLEI
MALLET
MALTED
MANGER
MANNED
MANNER
MANSES
MANTEL
MANUEL
MAPLES
MAPPED
MAPPER
MARCEL
MARGES
MARIEL
MARKED
MARKER
MARKET
MARLED
MARLEE
MARLEY
MARMEE
MARNER
MARRED
MARTEL
MARTEN
MARVEL
MASHED
MASHER
MASHES
MASKED
MASKER
MASSED
MASSES
MASSEY
MASTER
MATHER
MATTEA
MATTED
MATTEL
MATTER
MATTES
MAULED
MAULER
MAUMEE
MAUSER
MAUVES
MAYBES
MAYHEM
MAZIER
MCCREA
MCGREW
MCKUEN
MEAGER
MEANER
MEDLEY
MEEKER
MEETER
MELDED
MELEES
MELTED
MEMBER
MENDED
MENDEL
MENDER
MENDES
MENKEN
MENNEN
MEOWED
MERCED
MERCER
MERGED
MERGER
MERGES
MERKEL
MERMEN
MERSEY
MESHED
MESHES
MESMER
MESSED
MESSES
METIER
METRES
MEWLED
MEWLER
MICHEL
MICKEY
MIDDEN
MIDGES
MIDGET
MIDLER
MIFFED
MIGUEL
MILDER
MILDEW
MILIEU
MILKED
MILKER
MILLED
MILLER
MILLET
MILNER
MINCED
MINCER
MINCES
MINDED
MINDER
MINKES
MINTED
MINTER
MINUET
MINXES
MIRIER
MIRREN
MISLED
MISSED
MISSES
MISTED
MISTER
MITRED
MITRES
MITTEN
MIXTEC
MIZZEN
MOANED
MOANER
MOATED
MOBBED
MOBLEY
MOCKED
MOCKER
MOILED
MOILER
MOINES
MOIRES
MOLDED
MOLDER
MOLTED
MOLTEN
MOLTER
MONGER
MONIED
MONIES
MONKEY
MONTEL
MONTES
MONTEZ
MOONED
MOONEY
MOORED
MOOTED
MOPIER
MOPPED
MOPPER
MOPPET
MOREEN
MORGEN
MORLEY
MORSEL
MOSHED
MOSHER
MOSHES
MOSLEM
MOSSED
MOSSES
MOSTEL
MOTHER
MOTLEY
MOUSED
MOUSER
MOUSES
MOUSEY
MOVIES
MUCKED
MUDDED
MUDDER
MUDEEL
MUDHEN
MUFFED
MUGGED
MUGGER
MULLED
MULLER
MULLET
MUMMED
MUMMER
MUMPED
MUPPET
MURDER
MURIEL
MURRES
MURREY
MUSHED
MUSHER
MUSHES
MUSKEG
MUSKET
MUSSED
MUSSEL
MUSSES
MUSTER
MUTTER
MUZZED
MUZZES
MYOPES

M••••E
MACRAE
MADAME
MADDIE
MAGGIE
MAGPIE
MAISIE
MAITRE
MALATE
MALICE
MALLEE
MALONE
MANAGE
MANEGE
MANGLE
MANQUE
MANTLE
MARBLE
MARCHE
MARCIE
MARGIE
MARINE
MARLEE
MARMEE
MARNIE
MARPLE
MARQUE
MASHIE
MASQUE
MATTIE
MATURE
MAUMEE
MAXENE
MAXINE
MAXIXE
MCCABE
MCHALE
MEAGRE
MEALIE
MEANIE
MEDDLE
MENACE
MENAGE
MENSAE
MEROPE
METATE
METOPE
METTLE
MIDDLE
MIFUNE
MIGGLE
MILLIE
MILTIE
MINGLE
MINNIE
MINUTE
MIRAGE
MISCUE
MISUSE
MIZZLE
MOBILE
MODINE
MODULE
MOHAVE
MOJAVE
MOLINE
MOLTKE
MOMMIE
MONROE
MORALE
MOROSE
MOSQUE
MOTILE
MOTIVE
MOTTLE
MOUSSE
MRBLUE
MRHYDE
MUDDLE
MUDPIE
MUFFLE
MUGABE
MUMBLE
MUNCIE
MURINE
MUSCLE
MUSKIE
MUTATE
MUZZLE
MYRTLE
MYSORE

•ME•••
AMEBAE
AMEBAS
AMEBIC
AMECHE
AMEDEO
AMEERS
AMELIA
AMENDS
AMENRA
AMENTS
AMERCE
AMERSP
EMEERS
EMENDS
EMERGE
EMEUTE
IMELDA
KMESON
OMEGAS
OMELET
OMERTA
SMEARS
SMEARY
SMELLS
SMELLY
SMELTS
SMERSH
TMESIS

•M•E••
AMBERS
AMBERY
AMEERS
AMIENS
AMOEBA
AMPERE
AMVETS
EMBEDS
EMBERS
EMCEED
EMCEES
EMEERS
EMMETS
EMMETT
EMPERY
IMPEDE
IMPELS
IMPEND
IMPERF
UMBELS
UMBERS

•M••E•
AMAZED
AMAZES
AMBLED
AMBLER
AMBLES
AMEDEO
AMICES
AMIDES
AMINES
AMOLES
AMPLER
AMSTEL
AMULET
AMUSED
AMUSES
EMBDEN
EMBLEM
EMCEED
EMCEES
EMOTED
EMOTER
EMOTES
IMAGED
IMAGER
IMAGES
IMARET
IMBUED
IMBUES
IMOGEN
OMELET
SMILED
SMILER
SMILES
SMILEY
SMITES
SMOKED
SMOKER
SMOKES
SMOKEY

•M•••E
AMALIE
AMEBAE
AMECHE
AMERCE
AMPERE
AMPULE
BMOVIE
EMERGE
EMEUTE
EMIGRE
EMPIRE
IMBIBE
IMBRUE
IMFINE
IMMUNE
IMMURE
IMPALE
IMPEDE
IMPOSE
IMPURE
IMPUTE
SMUDGE
UMBRAE
UMPIRE

••ME••
ARMETS
CAMEAT
CAMEBY
CAMEIN
CAMELS
CAMEON
CAMEOS
CAMERA
CAMETO
CAMEUP
CEMENT
COMEAT
COMEBY
COMEDY
COMEIN
COMELY
COMEON
COMERS
COMETH
COMETO
COMETS
COMEUP
DEMEAN
EMMETS
EMMETT
ENMESH
FOMENT
GAMELY
GAMEST
GAMETE
GIMELS
HAMELN
HOMEEC
HOMELY
HOMERS
HUMERI
ISMENE
KHMERS
LAMECH
LAMEDH
LAMEDS
LAMELY
LAMENT
LAMESA
LAMEST
LIMENS
LIMEYS
LOMEIN
LUMENS
MIMEOS
MIMERS
MOMENT
NAMELY
NAMERS
NUMERO
NYMETS
OLMECS
PAMELA
POMELO
RAMEAU
RAMETS
REMEDY
REMELT
REMEND
ROMEOS
ROMERO
RUMENS
SAMECH
SAMEKH
SEMELE
SIMEON
SOMERS
TAMELY
TAMERS
TAMEST
TIMELY
TIMERS
TUMEFY
UNMEET
UNMESH
WOMENS
XIMENA
YEMENI

••M•E•
ARMIES
ARMLET
BOMBED
BOMBER
BOMBES
BUMMED
BUMMER
BUMPED
BUMPER
CAMBER
CAMDEN
CAMLET
CAMPED
CAMPER
COMBED
COMBER
COMBES
COMPEL
COMTES
CUMBER
DAMIEN
DAMMED
DAMNED
DAMPED
DAMPEN
DAMPER
DAMSEL
DEMIES
DIMMED
DIMMER
DOMREP
DUMBER
DUMPED
DUMPER
FEMMES
FUMIER
GAMIER
GAMMED
GAMMER
GEMMED
GIMBEL
GIMLET
GIMMES
GUMBEL
GUMMED
HAMLET
HAMMED
HAMMER
HAMPER
HEMMED
HEMMER
HOMEEC
HOMIER
HUMMED
HUMMER
HUMPED
HUMVEE
HYMNED
JAMMED
JAMMER
JUMPED
JUMPER
KUMMEL
LAMBED
LAMMED
LEMUEL
LIMBED
LIMBER
LIMIER
LIMNED
LIMNER
LIMPED
LIMPER
LIMPET
LUMBER
LUMPED
LUMPEN
LUMPER
MEMBER
MUMMED
MUMMER
MUMPED
NUMBED
NUMBER
PAMPER
POMMEE
POMMEL
POMPEY
PUMMEL
PUMPED
PUMPER
RAMIES
RAMJET
RAMMED
RAMPED
RAMSES
RAMSEY
RIMIER
RIMMED
ROMMEL
ROMNEY
ROMPED
ROMPER
RUMMER
SAMLET
SAMUEL
SEMPER

SIMBEL
SIMMER
SIMNEL
SIMPER
SOMBER
SOMMER
SUMMED
SUMMER
SUMNER
SUMTER
TAMPED
TAMPER
TEMPED
TEMPEH
TEMPER
TIMBER
TUMMED
UNMEET
VAMPED
VAMPER
WIMSEY
YAMMER
ZIMMER

••M••E

ADMIRE
ARMURE
BEMINE
BEMIRE
BEMUSE
BUMBLE
CAMISE
COMATE
DAMAGE
DAMONE
DAMORE
DEMISE
DEMODE
DEMOTE
DEMURE
DIMPLE
DOMINE
ELMORE
ERMINE
EXMORE
FAMINE
FEMALE
FUMBLE
GAMBLE
GAMETE
GAMINE
GEMMAE
GEMOTE
HAMITE
HOMAGE
HOMBRE
HUMANE
HUMBLE
HUMVEE
IMMUNE
IMMURE
INMATE
ISMENE
JAMOKE
JIMMIE
JUMBLE
LAMAZE
MOMMIE
MUMBLE
NIMBLE
NOMINE
NOMORE
OSMOSE
POMACE
POMADE
POMMEE
PUMICE
RAMATE
RAMBLE
RAMONE
RAMOSE
REMADE
REMAKE
REMISE
REMOTE
REMOVE
RIMOSE
RIMPLE
RUMBLE
RUMPLE
SAMITE
SAMMIE
SAMPLE
SEMELE
SEMITE
SEMPRE
SIMILE
SIMONE
SIMPLE
SOMBRE
SUMMAE
TAMALE
TEMPLE
TIMBRE
TUMBLE
UNMADE
UNMAKE
WAMBLE
WIMBLE
WIMPLE
ZOMBIE
ZYMASE

•••ME•

ACUMEN
AIRMEN
ANIMES
APEMEN
BADMEN
BARMEN
BATMEN
BEAMED
BIOMES
BLAMED
BLAMES
BLIMEY
BOOMED
BOOMER
BOWMEN
BREMEN
BRUMES
BUMMED
BUMMER
BUSMEN
CALMED
CALMER
CARMEL
CARMEN
CERMET
CHIMED
CHIMES
CLIMES
CONMEN
COWMEN
CREMES
CRIMEA
CRIMES
DAMMED
DEEMED
DIMMED
DIMMER
DISMES
DOLMEN
DOOMED
DORMER
EDAMES
ENAMEL
ENDMEN
FARMED
FARMER
FBIMEN
FEMMES
FENMEN
FILMED
FIRMED
FIRMER
FLAMED
FLAMES
FLUMES
FLYMEN
FOAMED
FORMED
FORMER
FRAMED
FRAMES
GAGMEN
GAMMED
GAMMER
GASMEN
GAUMED
GEMMED
GIMMES
GNOMES
GRIMED
GRIMES
GUMMED
GUNMEN
HAMMED
HAMMER
HARMED
HELMED
HELMET
HEMMED
HEMMER
HERMES
HITMEN
HOLMES
HORMEL
HUMMED
HUMMER
ICEMEN
ILLMET
ISOMER
JAMMED
JAMMER
KERMES
KILMER
KISMET
KRAMER
KUMMEL
LAMMED
LAWMEN
LAYMEN
LEGMEN
LOAMED
LOOMED
MADMEN
MARMEE
MAUMEE
MERMEN
MESMER
MUMMED
MUMMER
NETMEN
NEUMES
NIAMEY
NOUMEA
NUTMEG
OILMEN
OLDMEN
PALMED
PALMER
PELMET
PENMEN
PERMED
PIEMEN
PITMEN
PLUMED
PLUMES
POMMEE
POMMEL
PREMED
PRIMED
PRIMER
PRIMES
PUMMEL
RAGMEN
RAMMED
REAMED
REAMER
RHAMES
RHYMED
RHYMER
RHYMES
RIMMED
ROAMED
ROAMER
ROHMER
ROMMEL
ROOMED
ROOMER
RUMMER
SEAMED
SEAMEN
SEEMED
SHAMED
SHAMES
SIMMER
SLIMED
SLIMES
SOMMER
SPUMED
SPUMES
STAMEN
STUMER
SUMMED
SUMMER
TAXMEN
TEAMED
TEEMED
TERMED
TEXMEX
THAMES
THEMED
THEMES
TINMEN
TUMMED
WARMED
WARMER
WORMED
XIAMEN
YAMMER
YEOMEN
YESMEN
ZIMMER
ZOOMED

•••M•E

ANOMIE
FLAMBE
GEMMAE
GRAMME
GRIMKE
GUIMPE
JIMMIE
MARMEE
MAUMEE
MOMMIE
POMMEE
PREMIE
ROOMIE
SAMMIE
STYMIE
SUMMAE
TROMPE

••••ME

AFLAME
AFRAME
ASSUME
ATHOME
BECAME
BECOME
BIREME
BYNAME
CHROME
DANGME
DEARME
DEFAME
ENZYME
GENOME
GOHOME
GRAMME
ILLUME
INCOME
INTIME
JEROME
KINGME
LEGUME
LEXEME
MADAME
NONAME
ONTIME
RACEME
RADOME
REGIME
RELUME
RENAME
RESUME
RETIME
SALOME
SCHEME
SESAME
SHOWME
UGSOME
UPTIME
VOLUME

M•F•••

MIFFED
MIFUNE
MUFASA
MUFFED
MUFFIN
MUFFLE
MUFTIS

M••F••

MANFUL
MAYFLY
MEDFLY
MIFFED
MISFIT
MUFFED
MUFFIN
MUFFLE

M•••F•

MINIFY
MODIFY
MOTIFS

M••••F

MASSIF
MYSELF

•MF•••

IMFINE

•M••F•

AMALFI
SMURFS

•M•••F

IMPERF

••MF••

AIMFOR
AIMFUL
ARMFUL
COMFIT

••M•F•

RAMIFY
TUMEFY

M•G•••

MAGGIE
MAGGIO
MAGMAS
MAGNET
MAGNON
MAGNUM
MAGNUS
MAGPIE
MAGUEY
MAGYAR
MCGRAW
MCGREW
MEGALO
MEGARA
MEGILP
MEGOHM
MIGGLE
MIGHTY
MIGNON
MIGUEL
MOGULS
MUGABE
MUGGED
MUGGER
MUGHOS
MYGIRL

M••G••

MAGGIE
MAGGIO
MAJGEN
MANGER
MANGLE
MANGOS
MARGAY
MARGES
MARGIE
MARGIN
MARGOT
MEAGER
MEAGRE
MEDGAR
MERGED
MERGER
MERGES
MIDGES
MIDGET
MIGGLE
MINGLE
MONGER
MONGOL
MORGAN
MORGEN
MOWGLI
MUGGED
MUGGER
MUNGOS

M•••G•

MALAGA
MALIGN
MANAGE
MANEGE
MCHUGH
MENAGE
MIRAGE

M••••G

MAKING
MATING
MAYTAG
MEKONG
METING
MEWING
MIKING
MIMING
MINING
MIRING
MIXING
MOOING
MOPING
MOVING
MOWING
MUSING
MUSKEG
MUTING

•M•G••

AMIGAS
AMIGOS
EMIGRE
IMAGED
IMAGER
IMAGES
IMOGEN
OMEGAS
SMOGGY
SMUGLY

•M••G•

EMERGE
HMONGS
IMPUGN
SMOGGY
SMUDGE
SMUDGY

•M•••G

IMPING

••M•G•

ARMAGH
DAMAGE
HOMAGE

••M••G

AIMING
ARMING
COMING
DOMING
FUMING
GAMING
GYMBAG
HOMING
HUMBUG
LAMING
LIMING
MIMING
NAMING
RIMING
TAMING
TIMING

•••M•G

NUTMEG
WONMUG

M•H•••

MAHDIS
MAHLER
MAHOUT
MAHZOR
MCHALE
MCHUGH
MIHRAB
MOHAIR
MOHAVE
MOHAWK
MOHOCK
MOHURS
MRHYDE

M••H••

MACHES
MACHOS
MASHED
MASHER
MASHES
MASHIE
MATHER
MATHIS
MAYHAP
MAYHEM
MENHIR
MESHED
MESHES
METHOD
METHYL
MICHEL
MIGHTY
MISHAP
MISHIT
MOCHAS
MOSHAV
MOSHED
MOSHER
MOSHES
MOTHER
MOTHRA
MUDHEN
MUGHOS
MUSHED
MUSHER
MUSHES
MUZHIK
MYOHMY
MYTHIC
MYTHOI
MYTHOL
MYTHOS

M•••H•

MANCHA
MANCHU
MARCHE
MARSHA
MARSHY
MARTHA
MEGOHM
MISCHA
MONTHS
MORPHO
MORPHS
MORPHY
MOUTHS
MOUTHY
MUNCHY
MURPHY
MYNAHS
MYRRHS

M••••H

MARIAH
MARISH
MATZOH
MCHUGH
MENSCH
MODISH
MOLOCH
MOOLAH
MOPISH
MULISH
MULLAH
MUNICH

•MH•••
AMHARA

•M•H••
AMPHID
OMAHAN
OMAHAS

•M••H•
AMECHE
SMITHS
SMITHY

•M•••H
AMBUSH
EMDASH
IMPISH
SMERSH
SMIRCH
SMOOCH
SMOOTH
SMUTCH

••M•H•
HUMPHS
KIMCHI
LYMPHS
NYMPHS
YAMAHA

••M••H
ARMAGH
COMETH
ENMESH
FAMISH
IOMOTH
LAMECH
LAMEDH
NAMATH
OOMPAH
SAMECH
SAMEKH
TEMPEH
UNMESH

•••M•H
WARMTH

MI••••
MIAMIA
MIASMA
MICHEL
MICKEY
MICMAC
MICRON
MICROS
MIDAIR
MIDDAY
MIDDEN
MIDDLE
MIDGES
MIDGET
MIDIAN
MIDLER
MIDORI
MIDRIB
MIDWAY
MIFFED
MIFUNE
MIGGLE
MIGHTY
MIGNON
MIGUEL
MIHRAB
MIKADO
MIKING
MIKITA
MILADY
MILANO
MILDER
MILDEW
MILDLY
MILERS
MILIEU
MILKED
MILKER
MILLAY
MILLED
MILLER
MILLET
MILLIE
MILNER
MILORD
MILOSZ
MILPAS
MILSAP
MILTIE
MILTON
MIMEOS
MIMERS
MIMICS
MIMING
MIMOSA
MINCED
MINCER
MINCES
MINDED
MINDER
MINERS
MINGLE
MINIFY
MINIMA
MINIMS
MINING
MINION
MINIUM
MINKES
MINNIE
MINNOW
MINOAN
MINORS
MINTED
MINTER
MINUET
MINUIT
MINUTE
MINXES
MINYAN
MIOSIS
MIRAGE
MIRIAM
MIRIER
MIRING
MIRREN
MIRROR
MISCHA
MISCUE
MISDID
MISERS
MISERY
MISFIT
MISHAP
MISHIT
MISLAY
MISLED
MISSAL
MISSAY
MISSED
MISSES
MISSIS
MISSUS
MISTED
MISTER
MISUSE
MITERS
MITRAL
MITRED
MITRES
MITTEN
MIWOKS
MIXERS
MIXING
MIXTEC
MIXUPS
MIZENS
MIZZEN
MIZZLE

M•I•••
MAIDEN
MAIDUS
MAILED
MAILER
MAILES
MAILIN
MAINLY
MAISIE
MAITAI
MAITRE
MAIZES
MOIETY
MOILED
MOILER
MOINES
MOIRES

M••I••
MAKING
MALIBU
MALICE
MALIGN
MANIAC
MANIAS
MANILA
MANIOC
MAOISM
MAOIST
MARIAH
MARIAN
MARIEL
MARIKO
MARILU
MARINA
MARINE
MARINO
MARION
MARISA
MARISH
MARIST
MARIUS
MATING
MATINS
MAXIMA
MAXIMS
MAXINE
MAXIXE
MAZIER
MAZILY
MEDIAL
MEDIAN
MEDIAS
MEDICI
MEDICO
MEDICS
MEDINA
MEDIUM
MEGILP
MEJICO
MELINA
MENIAL
MENINX
MERIDA
MERINO
MERITS
METIER
METING
MEWING
MEXICO
MIDIAN
MIKING
MIKITA
MILIEU
MIMICS
MIMING
MINIFY
MINIMA
MINIMS
MINING
MINION
MINIUM
MIRIAM
MIRIER
MIRING
MIXING
MOBILE
MOBIUS
MODIFY
MODINE
MODISH
MOLINE
MONICA
MONIED
MONIES
MONISM
MONIST
MOOING
MOPIER
MOPING
MOPISH
MORION
MORITA
MORITZ
MOTIFS
MOTILE
MOTION
MOTIVE
MOVIES
MOVING
MOWING
MUCINS
MULISH
MUNICH
MURIEL
MURINE
MUSIAL
MUSING
MUTING
MUTINY
MYGIRL
MYRIAD

M•••I•
MACEIO
MADDIE
MADEIT
MADRID
MAGGIE
MAGGIO
MAGPIE
MAHDIS
MAILIN
MAISIE
MAJLIS
MAKEIT
MALKIN
MALTIN
MANNIX
MANTIC
MANTIS
MAORIS
MAQUIS
MARCIA
MARCIE
MARGIE
MARGIN
MARLIN
MARNIE
MARTIN
MARVIN
MASAIS
MASHIE
MASSIF
MASTIC
MATHIS
MATLIN
MATRIX
MATTIE
MCBAIN
MCLAIN
MCNAIR
MEALIE
MEANIE
MELVIL
MELVIN
MEMOIR
MENHIR
MENTIS
MERLIN
METRIC
MIAMIA
MIDAIR
MIDRIB
MILLIE
MILTIE
MINNIE
MINUIT
MIOSIS
MISDID
MISFIT
MISHIT
MISSIS
MOHAIR
MOMMIE
MORBID
MORRIS
MOSAIC
MOULIN
MOVEIN
MUDPIE
MUFFIN
MUFTIS
MUNCIE
MUNTIN
MURCIA
MUSKIE
MUSLIM
MUSLIN
MUZHIK
MYELIN
MYOPIA
MYOPIC
MYOSIN
MYOSIS
MYSTIC
MYTHIC

M••••I
MAITAI
MALAWI
MALLEI
MALOTI
MAOTAI
MEDICI
MESABI
MIDORI
MORONI
MOWGLI
MYTHOI

•MI•••
AMICES
AMICUS
AMIDES
AMIDOL
AMIDST
AMIENS
AMIGAS
AMIGOS
AMINES
AMINOR
AMINUS
BMINOR
BMINUS
CMINOR
CMINUS
DMINOR
DMINUS
DMITRI
EMIGRE
EMILIA
EMILIO
EMINOR
FMINOR
GMINOR
SMILAX
SMILED
SMILER
SMILES
SMILEY
SMILIN
SMIRCH
SMIRKS
SMIRKY
SMITES
SMITHS
SMITHY
UMIAKS

•M•I••
AMBITS
AMNION
EMAILS
EMPIRE
IMBIBE
IMFINE
IMPING
IMPISH
OMNIUM
UMPIRE

•M••I•
AMADIS
AMALIE
AMATIS
AMBLIN
AMEBIC
AMELIA
AMPHID
BMOVIE
EMILIA
EMILIO
IMPAIR
OMANIS
SMILIN
TMESIS
UMBRIA

•M•••I
AMALFI
DMITRI
SMALTI

••MI••
ADMIRE
ADMITS
AIMING
ARMIES
ARMING
BEMINE
BEMIRE
BIMINI
CAMINO
CAMION
CAMISE
COMICS
COMING
COMITY
DAMIEN
DAMITA
DEMIES
DEMISE
DEMITS
DIMITY
DOMINE
DOMING
DOMINI
DOMINO
ELMIRA
ENMITY
ERMINE
FAMILY
FAMINE
FAMISH
FUMIER
FUMING
GAMIER
GAMILY
GAMINE
GAMING
GAMINS
GEMINI
HAMILL
HAMITE
HOMIER
HOMILY
HOMING
HOMINY
JIMINY
KUMISS
LAMIAS
LAMINA
LAMING
LIMIER
LIMING
LIMITS
LUMINA
MIMICS
MIMING
NAMING
NIMINY
NIMITZ
NOMINE
NUMINA
OSMICS
OSMIUM
PAMIRS
PIMINY
PUMICE
RAMIES
RAMIFY
REMICK
REMIND
REMISE
REMISS
REMITS
RIMIER
RIMING
RIMINI
RUMINA
SAMIAM
SAMITE
SEMITE
SIMIAN
SIMILE
TAMILS
TAMING
TIMING
ZAMIAS

••M•I•
ARMPIT
CAMEIN
COMEIN
COMFIT
COMMIT
COMMIX
CYMRIC
DIMWIT
DOMAIN
GAMBIA
GAMBIT
HAMLIN
HEMSIN
IAMBIC
JAMSIN
JIMMIE
JUMPIN
KEMPIS
LIMPID
LOMEIN
MEMOIR
MOMMIE
REMAIL
REMAIN
ROMAIC
SAMMIE
SUMMIT
TOMLIN
TOMMIX
TOMTIT
USMAIL
ZAMBIA
ZOMBIE

••M••I
ARMANI
BIMINI
CUMULI
DOMANI
DOMINI
GEMINI
HUMERI
KIMCHI
RIMINI
ROMAJI
SOMALI
TUMULI
YEMENI

•••MI•
ANEMIA
ANEMIC
ANOMIC
ANOMIE
ARAMIS
ATOMIC
CADMIC
CHEMIN
COMMIT
COMMIX
COSMIC
DERMIS
ELEMIS
FORMIC
GNOMIC
HERMIT
JIMMIE
KARMIC
KERMIS
KERMIT
MIAMIA
MOMMIE
PERMIT
PREMIE
ROOMIE
SAMMIE
SHAMIR
STYMIE
SUBMIT

SUMMIT
SWAMIS
TOMMIX
VERMIN
ZOOMIN

•••M•I
ALUMNI
DROMOI
KATMAI
RHOMBI
SCAMPI

••••MI
BATUMI
BONAMI
DOREMI
ISTHMI
SALAMI
SURIMI
TATAMI

M•J•••
MAJGEN
MAJLIS
MAJORS
MCJOBS
MEJICO
MOJAVE

M••J••
MENJOU

•M•J••
AMAJOR
BMAJOR
CMAJOR
DMAJOR
EMAJOR
FMAJOR
GMAJOR

••MJ••
RAMJET

••M•J•
ROMAJI

•••M•J
SGTMAJ

M•K•••
MAKALU
MAKEBA
MAKEDO
MAKEIT
MAKERS
MAKEUP
MAKING
MAKUTA
MCKUEN
MEKONG
MIKADO
MIKING
MIKITA
MUKLUK

M••K••
MALKIN
MARKED
MARKER
MARKET
MARKKA
MARKUP
MASKED
MASKER
MEEKER
MEEKLY
MENKEN
MERKEL
MICKEY
MILKED
MILKER
MINKES
MOCKED
MOCKER
MOCKUP
MONKEY
MOSKVA
MUCKED
MUCKUP
MUSKEG
MUSKET
MUSKIE
MUSKOX

M•••K•
MARIKO
MARKKA
MEDAKA
MIWOKS
MOLTKE

M••••K
MARDUK
MOHAWK
MOHOCK
MUKLUK
MUZHIK

•M•K••
SMOKED
SMOKER
SMOKES
SMOKEY

•M••K•
DMARKS
SMACKS
SMIRKS
SMIRKY
SMOCKS
UMIAKS

•M•••K
AMTRAK
EMBANK
EMBARK

••M•K•
BAMAKO
JAMOKE
REMAKE
RIMSKY
SAMEKH
UNMAKE

••M••K
DAMASK
LOMBOK
REMARK
REMICK
STMARK
UNMASK

•••MK•
GRIMKE

M•L•••
MALABO
MALADY
MALAGA
MALATE
MALAWI
MALAYA
MALAYS
MALDEN
MALIBU
MALICE
MALIGN
MALKIN
MALLEE
MALLEI
MALLET
MALLOW
MALONE
MALORY
MALOTI
MALTED
MALTIN
MCLAIN
MCLEAN
MELANO
MELDED
MELEES
MELINA
MELLON
MELLOW
MELMAC
MELODY
MELONS
MELOTT
MELTED
MELTON
MELVIL
MELVIN
MELVYN
MILADY
MILANO
MILDER
MILDEW
MILDLY
MILERS
MILIEU
MILKED
MILKER
MILLAY
MILLED
MILLER
MILLET
MILLIE
MILNER
MILORD
MILOSZ
MILPAS
MILSAP
MILTIE
MILTON
MOLARS
MOLDAU
MOLDED
MOLDER
MOLEST
MOLINE
MOLNAR
MOLOCH
MOLOPO
MOLTED
MOLTEN
MOLTER
MOLTKE
MULCTS
MULETA
MULEYS
MULISH
MULLAH
MULLAS
MULLED
MULLER
MULLET
MULTUM

M••L••
MAHLER
MAILED
MAILER
MAILES
MAILIN
MAJLIS
MALLEE
MALLEI
MALLET
MALLOW
MAPLES
MARLED
MARLEE
MARLEY
MARLIN
MARLON
MATLIN
MAULED
MAULER
MEALIE
MEDLAR
MEDLAT
MEDLEY
MELLON
MELLOW
MERLIN
MERLON
MERLOT
MEWLED
MEWLER
MIDLER
MILLAY
MILLED
MILLER
MILLET
MILLIE
MISLAY
MISLED
MOBLEY
MOILED
MOILER
MOOLAH
MORLEY
MOSLEM
MOTLEY
MOULDS
MOULDY
MOULIN
MOULTS
MRBLUE
MUKLUK
MULLAH
MULLAS
MULLED
MULLER
MULLET
MUSLIM
MUSLIN
MYELIN

M•••L•
MABELL
MACULA
MAINLY
MAKALU
MANGLE
MANILA
MANTLE
MARBLE
MARBLY
MARILU
MARPLE
MAYFLY
MAZILY
MAZOLA
MCHALE
MEANLY
MEASLY
MEDALS
MEDDLE
MEDFLY
MEEKLY
MEETLY
MEGALO
MEGILP
MERELY
METALS
METTLE
MIDDLE
MIGGLE
MILDLY
MINGLE
MIZZLE
MOBILE
MODELA
MODELS
MODELT
MODULE
MODULO
MOGULS
MORALE
MORALS
MORELS
MOSTLY
MOTELS
MOTILE
MOTTLE
MOWGLI
MUDDLE
MUFFLE
MUMBLE
MUMBLY
MURALS
MUSCLE
MUSCLY
MUTELY
MUZZLE
MYRTLE
MYSELF

M••••L
MABELL
MAMMAL
MANFUL
MANTEL
MANUAL
MANUEL
MARCEL
MARIEL
MARTEL
MARVEL
MATTEL
MEDIAL
MELVIL
MENDEL
MENIAL
MENSAL
MENTAL
MERKEL
MESCAL
METHYL
MICHEL
MIGUEL
MISSAL
MITRAL
MONGOL
MONTEL
MORSEL
MORTAL
MOSTEL
MRCOOL
MUDEEL
MURIEL
MUSIAL
MUSSEL
MUTUAL
MYGIRL
MYRDAL
MYTHOL

•ML•••
UMLAUT

•M•L••
AMALFI
AMALIE
AMBLED
AMBLER
AMBLES
AMBLIN
AMELIA
AMOLES
AMPLER
AMULET
EMBLEM
EMILIA
EMILIO
EMPLOY
IMELDA
OMELET
SMALLS
SMALTI
SMALTO
SMELLS
SMELLY
SMELTS
SMILAX
SMILED
SMILER
SMILES
SMILEY
SMILIN
SMOLTS

•M••L•
AMPULE
AMPULS
EMAILS
IMPALA
IMPALE
IMPELS
SMALLS
SMELLS
SMELLY
SMUGLY
UMBELS

•M•••L
AMATOL
AMIDOL
AMORAL
AMSTEL
UMBRAL

••ML••
ARMLET
CAMLET
GIMLET
HAMLET
HAMLIN
SAMLET
TOMLIN

••M•L•
BUMBLE
CAMELS
COMELY
COMPLY
CUMULI
CUMULO
DAMPLY
DIMPLE
DIMPLY
DUMBLY
FAMILY
FEMALE
FUMBLE
GAMBLE
GAMELY
GAMILY
GIMELS
HAMALS
HAMELN
HAMILL
HOMELY
HOMILY
HUMBLE
HUMBLY
JUMBLE
KAMALA
LAMELY
LIMPLY
MUMBLE
MUMBLY
NAMELY
NIMBLE
NIMBLY
NUMBLY
ORMOLU
PAMELA
POMELO
RAMBLA
RAMBLE
REMELT
REMOLD
RIMPLE
ROMOLA
RUMBLE
RUMBLY
RUMPLE
RUMPLY
SAMPLE
SEMELE
SIMILE
SIMPLE
SIMPLY
SOMALI
STMALO
TAMALE
TAMELY
TAMILS
TEMPLE
TIMELY
TUMBLE
TUMULI
TUMULT
WAMBLE
WAMBLY
WIMBLE
WIMPLE

••M••L
AIMFUL
ARMFUL
COMPEL
CYMBAL
DAMSEL
GAMBOL
GIMBAL
GIMBEL
GUMBEL
HAMILL
HYMNAL
JAMAAL
KUMMEL
LEMUEL
MAMMAL
POMMEL
PUMMEL
REMAIL
ROMMEL
SAMBAL
SAMUEL
SIMBEL
SIMNEL
SYMBOL
TIMBAL
USMAIL

•••ML•
CALMLY
FIRMLY
GLUMLY
GRIMLY
PRIMLY
SEEMLY
SLIMLY
TRIMLY
WARMLY

•••M•L
ANIMAL
BRUMAL
CARMEL
DERMAL
DISMAL
ENAMEL
ETYMOL
FORMAL
HIEMAL
HORMEL
KUMMEL
MAMMAL
NORMAL
POMMEL
PRIMAL
PUMMEL
ROMMEL

M•M•••
MAMBAS
MAMBOS
MAMMAL
MAMMAS
MAMMON
MEMBER
MEMNON
MEMOIR
MEMORY
MIMEOS
MIMERS
MIMICS
MIMING
MIMOSA
MOMENT
MOMMAS
MOMMIE
MRMOTO
MUMBLE
MUMBLY
MUMMED
MUMMER
MUMPED

M••M••
MADMAN
MADMAX
MADMEN
MAGMAS
MAMMAL
MAMMAS
MAMMON
MARMEE
MARMOT
MAUMAU
MAUMEE
MELMAC
MERMAN
MERMEN
MESMER
MIAMIA
MICMAC
MOMMAS
MOMMIE
MORMON
MOTMOT

MUMMED
MUMMER
MURMUR
MUUMUU

M•••M•
MADAME
MADAMS
MANAMA
MAXIMA
MAXIMS
MAZUMA
MIASMA
MINIMA
MINIMS
MODEMS
MYOHMY

M••••M
MADTOM
MAGNUM
MAOISM
MAYHEM
MCADAM
MEDIUM
MEGOHM
MINIUM
MIRIAM
MONISM
MOSLEM
MULTUM
MUSEUM
MUSLIM

•MM•••
EMMETS
EMMETT
IMMUNE
IMMUNO
IMMURE

•M•M••
IMAMAN

•M••M•
SMARMY

•M•••M
EMBLEM
OMASUM
OMNIUM

••MM••
BUMMED
BUMMER
COMMAS
COMMIT
COMMIX
COMMON
DAMMAR
DAMMED
DIMMED
DIMMER
FEMMES
GAMMAS
GAMMED
GAMMER
GAMMON
GEMMAE
GEMMED
GIMMES
GUMMED
HAMMED
HAMMER
HEMMED
HEMMER
HUMMED
HUMMER
HUMMUS
JAMMED
JAMMER
JIMMIE
KUMMEL
LAMMAS
LAMMED
LEMMAS
LEMMON
LUMMOX
MAMMAL
MAMMAS
MAMMON
MOMMAS
MOMMIE
MUMMED
MUMMER
POMMEE
POMMEL
PUMMEL
RAMMED
RIMMED
ROMMEL
RUMMER
SAMMIE
SIMMER
SOMMER
SUMMAE
SUMMAS
SUMMED
SUMMER
SUMMIT
SUMMON
TAMMUZ
TOMMIX
TUMMED
YAMMER
ZIMMER

••M••M
DIMSUM
DUMDUM
OSMIUM
POMPOM
SAMIAM
TAMTAM
TOMTOM
WAMPUM
YUMYUM

•••MM•
CHAMMY
CHUMMY
CLAMMY
CRUMMY
GRAMME
GRAMMY
PLUMMY
SCUMMY
SHIMMY
SLUMMY
WHAMMO
WHAMMY

•••M•M
PRIMUM

M•N•••
MANAGE
MANAMA
MANANA
MANAUS
MANCHA
MANCHU
MANDAN
MANDAY
MANEGE
MANFUL
MANGER
MANGLE
MANGOS
MANIAC
MANIAS
MANILA
MANIOC
MANNED
MANNER
MANNIX
MANORS
MANQUE
MANRAY
MANSES
MANTAS
MANTEL
MANTIC
MANTIS
MANTLE
MANTRA
MANTUA
MANUAL
MANUEL
MCNAIR
MENACE
MENADO
MENAGE
MENDED
MENDEL
MENDER
MENDES
MENHIR
MENIAL
MENINX
MENJOU
MENKEN
MENNEN
MENSAE
MENSAL
MENSAS
MENSCH
MENTAL
MENTIS
MENTOR
MINCED
MINCER
MINCES
MINDED
MINDER
MINERS
MINGLE
MINIFY
MINIMA
MINIMS
MINING
MINION
MINIUM
MINKES
MINNIE
MINNOW
MINOAN
MINORS
MINTED
MINTER
MINUET
MINUIT
MINUTE
MINXES
MINYAN
MONACO
MONADS
MONDAY
MONERA
MONETA
MONEYS
MONGER
MONGOL
MONICA
MONIED
MONIES
MONISM
MONIST
MONKEY
MONODY
MONROE
MONTEL
MONTES
MONTEZ
MONTHS
MUNCHY
MUNCIE
MUNGOS
MUNICH
MUNTIN
MYNAHS

M••N••
MAENAD
MAGNET
MAGNON
MAGNUM
MAGNUS
MAINLY
MANNED
MANNER
MANNIX
MARNER
MARNIE
MAUNDY
MBUNDU
MEANER
MEANIE
MEANLY
MEMNON
MENNEN
MIGNON
MILNER
MINNIE
MINNOW
MOANED
MOANER
MOINES
MOLNAR
MOONED
MOONEY
MORNAY
MOUNDS
MOUNTS
MOUNTY

M•••N•
MAKING
MALONE
MANANA
MARINA
MARINE
MARINO
MASONS
MATING
MATINS
MAVENS
MAXENE
MAXINE
MAYANS
MCCANN
MEDINA
MEKONG
MELANO
MELINA
MELONS
MENINX
MERINO
MESONS
METING
MEWING
MIFUNE
MIKING
MILANO
MIMING
MINING
MIRING
MIXING
MIZENS
MODENA
MODINE
MOLINE
MOMENT
MOOING
MOPING
MORANT
MORENO
MORONI
MORONS
MOURNS
MOVING
MOWING
MUCINS
MURANO
MURINE
MUSING
MUSTNT
MUTANT
MUTING
MUTINY

M••••N
MACOUN
MACRON
MADDEN
MADMAN
MADMEN
MADSEN
MAGNON
MAIDEN
MAILIN
MAJGEN
MALDEN
MALIGN
MALKIN
MALTIN
MAMMON
MANDAN
MARGIN
MARIAN
MARION
MARLIN
MARLON
MAROON
MARRON
MARTEN
MARTIN
MARVIN
MATLIN
MATRON
MCBAIN
MCCANN
MCKUEN
MCLAIN
MCLEAN
MEDIAN
MELLON
MELTON
MELVIN
MELVYN
MEMNON
MENKEN
MENNEN
MERLIN
MERLON
MERMAN
MERMEN
MERTON
MERVYN
MICRON
MIDDEN
MIDIAN
MIGNON
MILTON
MINION
MINOAN
MINYAN
MIRREN
MITTEN
MIZZEN
MODERN
MOLTEN
MOREEN
MORGAN
MORGEN
MORION
MORMON
MORTON
MOTION
MOTOWN
MOULIN
MOUTON
MOVEIN
MOVEON
MUDHEN
MUFFIN
MUNTIN
MUSLIN
MUTTON
MYELIN
MYOSIN

•MN•••
AMNION
OMNIUM

•M•N••
AMANDA
AMENDS
AMENRA
AMENTS
AMINES
AMINOR
AMINUS
BMINOR
BMINUS
CMINOR
CMINUS
DMINOR
DMINUS
EMENDS
EMINOR
FMINOR
GMINOR
HMONGS
OMANIS

•M••N•
AMIENS
AMOUNT
EMBANK
IMFINE
IMMUNE
IMMUNO
IMPEND
IMPING
SMYRNA

•M•••N
AMAZON
AMBLIN
AMNION
AMYTAN
EMBDEN
IMAMAN
IMOGEN
IMPUGN
KMESON
OMAHAN
SMILIN

••MN••
DAMNED
HYMNAL
HYMNED
LEMNOS
LIMNED
LIMNER
MEMNON
ROMNEY
SIMNEL
SUMNER

••M•N•
AIMING
ALMOND
ARMAND
ARMANI
ARMING
AUMONT
BEMINE
BIMINI
CAMINO
CEMENT
COMING
DAMONE
DEMAND
DEMOND
DEMONS
DOMANI
DOMINE
DOMING
DOMINI
DOMINO
DUMONT
EDMOND
EDMUND
EGMONT
ERMINE
FAMINE
FOMENT
FUMING
GAMINE
GAMING
GAMINS
GEMINI
HOMING
HOMINY
HUMANE
HUMANS
IMMUNE
IMMUNO
ISMENE
JIMINY
KIMONO
LAMENT
LAMINA
LAMING
LAMONT
LEMANS
LEMOND
LEMONS
LEMONY
LIMENS
LIMING
LOMOND
LUMENS
LUMINA
MIMING
MOMENT
NAMING
NIMINY
NOMINE
NUMINA
ORMOND
OSMOND
OSMUND
PIMINY
POMONA
RAMONA
RAMONE
REMAND
REMANS
REMEND
REMIND
RIMING
RIMINI
ROMANO
ROMANS
ROMANY
RUMENS
RUMINA
SIMONE
SIMONY
SOMANY
TAMING
TIMING
UNMANS
WOMENS
XIMENA
YEMENI

••M••N
BEMOAN
CAMDEN
CAMEIN
CAMEON
CAMION
COMEIN
COMEON
COMMON
DAMIEN
DAMPEN
DAMSON
DEMEAN
DOMAIN
GAMMON
HAMELN
HAMLIN
HEMSIN
JAMSIN
JIMSON
JUMPIN
JUMPON
LEMMON
LOMEIN
LUMPEN
MAMMON
MEMNON
POMPON
QUMRAN
RAMSON
REMAIN
REMOWN
SAMOAN
SAMPAN
SAMSON
SIMEON
SIMIAN
SUMMON
TOMLIN

•••MN•
ALUMNA
ALUMNI

•••M•N
ACUMEN
AIRMAN
AIRMEN
ALEMAN
ALLMAN
ALTMAN
APEMAN
APEMEN
ATAMAN
BADMAN
BADMEN
BARMAN
BARMEN

BATMAN
BATMEN
BEAMON
BORMAN
BOWMAN
BOWMEN
BREMEN
BURMAN
BUSMAN
BUSMEN
CAIMAN
CARMAN
CARMEN
CAYMAN
CHEMIN
COLMAN
COMMON
CONMAN
CONMEN
CORMAN
COWMAN
COWMEN
DAIMON
DESMAN
DOLMAN
DOLMEN
ELFMAN
ENDMAN
ENDMEN
ETYMON
FBIMAN
FBIMEN
FENMAN
FENMEN
FIRMAN
FLYMAN
FLYMEN
FORMAN
GAGMAN
GAGMEN
GAMMON
GASMAN
GASMEN
GERMAN
GNOMON
GUNMAN
GUNMEN
HAEMON
HAGMAN
HARMON
HERMAN
HERMON
HETMAN
HITMAN
HITMEN
ICEMAN
ICEMEN
IMAMAN
KERMAN
KIDMAN
KIRMAN
KORMAN
LAWMAN
LAWMEN
LAYMAN
LAYMEN
LEGMAN
LEGMEN
LEMMON
MADMAN
MADMEN
MAMMON
MERMAN
MERMEN
MORMON
NETMAN
NETMEN
NEUMAN
NEWMAN
NORMAN
OILMAN
OILMEN
OLDMAN
OLDMEN
ONEMAN
PACMAN
PENMAN
PENMEN
PIEMAN
PIEMEN
PITMAN
PITMEN
RAGMAN
RAGMEN
RODMAN
RUDMAN
SALMAN
SALMON
SEAMAN
SEAMEN
SERMON
SHAMAN
SHIMON
STAMEN
SUMMON
TASMAN
TAXMAN
TAXMEN
TINMAN
TINMEN
TOAMAN
TODMAN
TRUMAN
TUBMAN
ULLMAN
VERMIN
XIAMEN
YEOMAN
YEOMEN
YESMAN
YESMEN
ZEEMAN
ZOOMIN

••••MN
AUTUMN
COLUMN
SOLEMN

MO••••
MOANED
MOANER
MOATED
MOBBED
MOBCAP
MOBILE
MOBIUS
MOBLEY
MOCHAS
MOCKED
MOCKER
MOCKUP
MODELA
MODELS
MODELT
MODEMS
MODENA
MODERN
MODEST
MODIFY
MODINE
MODISH
MODOCS
MODULE
MODULO
MOGULS
MOHAIR
MOHAVE
MOHAWK
MOHOCK
MOHURS
MOIETY
MOILED
MOILER
MOINES
MOIRES
MOJAVE
MOLARS
MOLDAU
MOLDED
MOLDER
MOLEST
MOLINE
MOLNAR
MOLOCH
MOLOPO
MOLTED
MOLTEN
MOLTER
MOLTKE
MOMENT
MOMMAS
MOMMIE
MONACO
MONADS
MONDAY
MONERA
MONETA
MONEYS
MONGER
MONGOL
MONICA
MONIED
MONIES
MONISM
MONIST
MONKEY
MONODY
MONROE
MONTEL
MONTES
MONTEZ
MONTHS
MOOING
MOOLAH
MOONED
MOONEY
MOORED
MOOTED
MOPEDS
MOPERS
MOPERY
MOPIER
MOPING
MOPISH
MOPPED
MOPPER
MOPPET
MOPSUP
MOPTOP
MOPUPS
MORALE
MORALS
MORANT
MORASS
MORAVA
MORAYS
MORBID
MOREAU
MOREEN
MORELS
MORENO
MORGAN
MORGEN
MORION
MORITA
MORITZ
MORLEY
MORMON
MORNAY
MORONI
MORONS
MOROSE
MORPHO
MORPHS
MORPHY
MORRIS
MORROW
MORSEL
MORTAL
MORTAR
MORTON
MOSAIC
MOSCOW
MOSEYS
MOSHAV
MOSHED
MOSHER
MOSHES
MOSKVA
MOSLEM
MOSQUE
MOSSED
MOSSES
MOSTEL
MOSTLY
MOTELS
MOTETS
MOTHER
MOTHRA
MOTIFS
MOTILE
MOTION
MOTIVE
MOTLEY
MOTMOT
MOTORS
MOTOWN
MOTTLE
MOTTOS
MOULDS
MOULDY
MOULIN
MOULTS
MOUNDS
MOUNTS
MOUNTY
MOURNS
MOUSED
MOUSER
MOUSES
MOUSEY
MOUSSE
MOUTHS
MOUTHY
MOUTON
MOVEIN
MOVEON
MOVERS
MOVEUP
MOVIES
MOVING
MOWERS
MOWGLI
MOWING
MOYERS
MOZART

M•O•••
MAOISM
MAOIST
MAORIS
MAOTAI
MEOWED
MIOSIS
MOOING
MOOLAH
MOONED
MOONEY
MOORED
MOOTED
MYOHMY
MYOPES
MYOPIA
MYOPIC
MYOSIN
MYOSIS

M••O••
MACOUN
MAHOUT
MAJORS
MALONE
MALORY
MALOTI
MANORS
MAROON
MASONS
MAXOUT
MAYORS
MAZOLA
MCJOBS
MEGOHM
MEKONG
MELODY
MELONS
MELOTT
MEMOIR
MEMORY
MEROPE
MESONS
METOPE
MIDORI
MILORD
MILOSZ
MIMOSA
MINOAN
MINORS
MIWOKS
MODOCS
MOHOCK
MOLOCH
MOLOPO
MONODY
MORONI
MORONS
MOROSE
MOTORS
MOTOWN
MRCOOL
MRMOTO
MUCOSA
MUCOUS
MYSORE
MYWORD

M•••O•
MACHOS
MACRON
MACROS
MADTOM
MAGNON
MAHZOR
MALLOW
MAMBOS
MAMMON
MANGOS
MANIOC
MARCOS
MARGOT
MARION
MARLON
MARMOT
MAROON
MARRON
MARROW
MASCOT
MATRON
MATZOH
MATZOS
MAYPOP
MCADOO
MEADOW
MELLON
MELLOW
MELTON
MEMNON
MENJOU
MENTOR
MERLON
MERLOT
MERTON
METEOR
METHOD
METROS
MEZZOS
MICRON
MICROS
MIGNON
MILTON
MIMEOS
MINION
MINNOW
MIRROR
MONGOL
MONROE
MOPTOP
MORION
MORMON
MORROW
MORTON
MOSCOW
MOTION
MOTMOT
MOTTOS
MOUTON
MOVEON
MRCOOL
MUGHOS
MUNGOS
MURROW
MUSKOX
MUTTON
MYTHOI
MYTHOL
MYTHOS

M••••O
MACACO
MACEIO
MADEDO
MADERO
MADURO
MAGGIO
MAKEDO
MALABO
MAPUTO
MARIKO
MARINO
MCADOO
MEDICO
MEGALO
MEJICO
MELANO
MENADO
MERINO
MEXICO
MIKADO
MILANO
MODULO
MOLOPO
MONACO
MORENO
MORPHO
MRMOTO
MURANO
MUTATO

•MO•••
AMOEBA
AMOLES
AMORAL
AMOSOZ
AMOUNT
AMOURS
BMOVIE
EMOTED
EMOTER
EMOTES
HMONGS
IMOGEN
SMOCKS
SMOGGY
SMOKED
SMOKER
SMOKES
SMOKEY
SMOLTS
SMOOCH
SMOOTH

•M•O••
EMBODY
EMBOSS
IMPORT
IMPOSE
IMPOST
SMOOCH
SMOOTH

•M••O•
AMADOU
AMAJOR
AMATOL
AMAZON
AMIDOL
AMIGOS
AMINOR
AMNION
AMOSOZ
BMAJOR
BMINOR
CMAJOR
CMINOR
DMAJOR
DMINOR
EMAJOR
EMINOR
EMPLOY
EMPTOR
FMAJOR
FMINOR
GMAJOR
GMINOR
IMPROV
KMESON

•M•••O
AMBATO
AMEDEO
EMBRYO
EMILIO
IMMUNO
SMALTO

••MO••
ALMOND
ALMOST
ARMORS
ARMORY
ARMOUR
ATMOST
AUMONT
BEMOAN
BUMOUT
DAMONE
DAMORE
DAMOUR
DEMOBS
DEMODE
DEMOND
DEMONS
DEMOTE
DIMOUT
DUMONT
EDMOND
EGMONT
ELMORE
EXMOOR
EXMORE
FAMOUS
FEMORA
GEMOTE
GEMOTS
HUMORS
HUMOUR
INMOST
IOMOTH
JAMOKE
KIMONO
KOMODO
LAMONT
LAMOUR
LEMOND
LEMONS
LEMONY
LOMOND
MEMOIR
MEMORY
MIMOSA
MRMOTO
NOMORE
ORMOLU
ORMOND
OSMOND
OSMOSE
POMONA
RAMONA
RAMONE
RAMOSE
RAMOUS
REMOLD
REMOPS
REMORA
REMOTE
REMOVE
REMOWN
REMOWS
RIMOSE
ROMOLA
RUMORS
RUMOUR
SAMOAN
SAMOSA
SIMONE
SIMONY
UNMOOR
UPMOST
UTMOST

••M•O•
AIMFOR
BAMBOO
CAMEON
CAMEOS
CAMION
CAMPOS
COMBOS
COMEON
COMMON

COMPOS
DAMSON
EXMOOR
GAMBOL
GAMMON
GUMBOS
JIMSON
JUMBOS
JUMPON
LEMMON
LEMNOS
LIMBOS
LOMBOK
LUMMOX
MAMBOS
MAMMON
MEMNON
MIMEOS
NIMROD
POMPOM
POMPON
RAMROD
RAMSON
ROMEOS
SAMSON
SIMEON
SUMMON
SYMBOL
TEMPOS
TOMBOY
TOMTOM
UNMOOR
YOMTOV

••M••O
AIMSTO
BAMAKO
BAMBOO
BUMPPO
CAMARO
CAMETO
CAMINO
COMETO
CUMULO
DAMATO
DOMINO
HEMATO
IMMUNO
KIMONO
KOMODO
MRMOTO
NEMATO
NUMERO
POMELO
ROMANO
ROMERO
SOMATO
STMALO
TAMAYO
TOMATO

•••MO•
ALAMOS
ASIMOV
BEAMON
BONMOT
CLAMOR
COMMON
COSMOS
DAIMON
DEIMOS
DROMOI
DROMOS
DUOMOS
ENAMOR
ETYMOL
ETYMON
GAMMON
GIZMOS
GLAMOR
GNOMON
HAEMON
HARMON
HAYMOW
HERMON
LEMMON
LUMMOX
MAMMON
MARMOT
MORMON
MOTMOT
OROMOS
PATMOS
PRIMOS
PROMOS
QUEMOY
RAGMOP
SALMON
SCHMOO
SCHMOS
SERMON
SHIMON
SUMMON
TREMOR
WETMOP

•••M•O
AKIMBO
ATEMPO
CRAMBO
DAIMYO
SCHMOO
WHAMMO
WHOMSO

••••MO
CHROMO
DYNAMO
ENTOMO
ESKIMO
KOKOMO
PLASMO
SEISMO
STELMO
THERMO
ULTIMO
WHAMMO

M•P•••
MAPLES
MAPPED
MAPPER
MAPUTO
MOPEDS
MOPERS
MOPERY
MOPIER
MOPING
MOPISH
MOPPED
MOPPER
MOPPET
MOPSUP
MOPTOP
MOPUPS
MUPPET

M••P••
MAGPIE
MAPPED
MAPPER
MARPLE
MAYPOP
MILPAS
MOPPED
MOPPER
MOPPET
MORPHO
MORPHS
MORPHY
MUDPIE
MUMPED
MUPPET
MURPHY
MYOPES
MYOPIA
MYOPIC

M•••P•
MEROPE
METOPE
MIXUPS
MOLOPO
MOPUPS

M••••P
MADCAP
MADEUP
MAKEUP
MARKUP
MAYHAP
MAYPOP
MEGILP
MESSUP
MILSAP
MISHAP
MOBCAP
MOCKUP
MOPSUP
MOPTOP
MOVEUP
MUCKUP
MUSSUP

•MP•••
AMPERE
AMPHID
AMPLER
AMPULE
AMPULS
EMPERY
EMPIRE
EMPLOY
EMPTOR
IMPACT
IMPAIR
IMPALA
IMPALE
IMPART
IMPEDE
IMPELS
IMPEND
IMPERF
IMPING
IMPISH
IMPORT
IMPOSE
IMPOST
IMPROV
IMPUGN
IMPURE
IMPUTE
UMPIRE

•M•••P
AMERSP

••MP••
ARMPIT
BUMPED
BUMPER
BUMPPO
BUMPUP
CAMPED
CAMPER
CAMPOS
CAMPUS
COMPAQ
COMPEL
COMPLY
COMPOS
DAMPED
DAMPEN
DAMPER
DAMPLY
DIMPLE
DIMPLY
DUMPED
DUMPER
HAMPER
HUMPED
HUMPHS
JUMPAT
JUMPED
JUMPER
JUMPIN
JUMPON
JUMPUP
KEMPIS
LIMPED
LIMPER
LIMPET
LIMPID
LIMPLY
LUMPED
LUMPEN
LUMPER
LUMPUR
LYMPHS
MUMPED
NYMPHS
OOMPAH
PAMPAS
PAMPER
POMPEY
POMPOM
POMPON
PUMPED
PUMPER
PUMPUP
RAMPED
RIMPLE
ROMPED
ROMPER
RUMPLE
RUMPLY
RUMPUS
SAMPAN
SAMPLE
SEMPER
SEMPRE
SIMPER
SIMPLE
SIMPLY
TAMPED
TAMPER
TEMPED
TEMPEH
TEMPER
TEMPLE
TEMPOS
TEMPTS
TEMPUS
VAMPED
VAMPER
WAMPUM
WIMPLE

••M•P•
BUMPPO
JAMUPS
REMAPS
REMOPS
SUMUPS

••M••P
BUMPUP
BUMRAP
CAMEUP
COMEUP
DAMSUP
DOMREP
GUMSUP
JAMSUP
JUMPUP
PUMPUP
SUMSUP

•••MP•
ATEMPO
BLIMPS
CHAMPS
CHIMPS
CHOMPS
CHUMPS
CLAMPS
CLOMPS
CLUMPS
CLUMPY
CRAMPS
CRIMPS
CRIMPY
EXEMPT
FRUMPS
FRUMPY
GRAMPA
GRAMPS
GRUMPS
GRUMPY
GUIMPE
PLUMPS
PRIMPS
PROMPT
SCAMPI
SCAMPS
SKIMPS
SKIMPY
SLUMPS
STAMPS
STIMPY
STOMPS
STUMPS
STUMPY
SWAMPS
SWAMPY
THUMPS
TRAMPS
TROMPE
TROMPS
TRUMPS
WHOMPS

•••M•P
BEAMUP
BITMAP
CLAMUP
DRUMUP
FIRMUP
RAGMOP
TEAMUP
WARMUP
WETMOP

••••MP
CCLAMP
DECAMP
ENCAMP
GAZUMP
PREAMP
REVAMP
SCRIMP
SHRIMP

M•Q•••
MAQUIS
MSQUAD

M••Q••
MANQUE
MARQUE
MASQUE
MOSQUE

•MQ•••
EMQUAD

••M••Q
COMPAQ

MR••••
MRBLUE
MRCOOL
MRHYDE
MRMOTO

M•R•••
MARACA
MARAUD
MARBLE
MARBLY
MARCEL
MARCHE
MARCIA
MARCIE
MARCOS
MARCUS
MARDUK
MARGAY
MARGES
MARGIE
MARGIN
MARGOT
MARIAH
MARIAN
MARIEL
MARIKO
MARILU
MARINA
MARINE
MARINO
MARION
MARISA
MARISH
MARIST
MARIUS
MARKED
MARKER
MARKET
MARKKA
MARKUP
MARLED
MARLEE
MARLEY
MARLIN
MARLON
MARMEE
MARMOT
MARNER
MARNIE
MAROON
MARPLE
MARQUE
MARRED
MARRON
MARROW
MARSHA
MARSHY
MARTEL
MARTEN
MARTHA
MARTIN
MARTYR
MARVEL
MARVIN
MERCED
MERCER
MERELY
MEREST
MERGED
MERGER
MERGES
MERIDA
MERINO
MERITS
MERKEL
MERLIN
MERLON
MERLOT
MERMAN
MERMEN
MEROPE
MERSEY
MERTON
MERVYN
MIRAGE
MIRIAM
MIRIER
MIRING
MIRREN
MIRROR
MORALE
MORALS
MORANT
MORASS
MORAVA
MORAYS
MORBID
MOREAU
MOREEN
MORELS
MORENO
MORGAN
MORGEN
MORION
MORITA
MORITZ
MORLEY
MORMON
MORNAY
MORONI
MORONS
MOROSE
MORPHO
MORPHS
MORPHY
MORRIS
MORROW
MORSEL
MORTAL
MORTAR
MORTON
MURALS
MURANO
MURCIA
MURDER
MURIEL
MURINE
MURMUR
MURPHY
MURRAY
MURRES
MURREY
MURROW
MYRDAL
MYRIAD
MYRRHS
MYRTLE

M••R••
MACRAE
MACRON
MACROS
MADRAS
MADRES
MADRID
MANRAY
MAORIS
MARRED
MARRON
MARROW
MATRIX
MATRON
MAURYA
MCCREA
MCGRAW
MCGREW
MEERUT
METRES
METRIC
METROS
MICRON
MICROS
MIDRIB
MIHRAB
MIRREN
MIRROR
MITRAL
MITRED
MITRES
MOIRES
MONROE
MOORED
MORRIS
MORROW
MOURNS
MUDRAS
MURRAY
MURRES
MURREY
MURROW
MYRRHS

M•••R•
MADERO
MADURA
MADURO
MAITRE
MAJORS
MAKERS
MALORY
MANORS
MANTRA
MASERS
MASERU
MATERS
MATURE
MAYORS
MAZERS
MEAGRE
MEGARA
MEMORY
MESSRS
METERS
MIDORI
MILERS
MILORD
MIMERS
MINERS
MINORS
MISERS
MISERY
MITERS
MIXERS
MODERN
MOHURS
MOLARS
MONERA
MOPERS
MOPERY
MOTHRA

MOTORS
MOVERS
MOWERS
MOYERS
MOZART
MUSERS
MYGIRL
MYSORE
MYWORD

M••••R
MADDER
MAGYAR
MAHLER
MAHZOR
MAILER
MANGER
MANNER
MAPPER
MARKER
MARNER
MARTYR
MASHER
MASKER
MASTER
MATHER
MATTER
MAULER
MAUSER
MAZIER
MCNAIR
MEAGER
MEANER
MEDGAR
MEDLAR
MEEKER
MEETER
MEMBER
MEMOIR
MENDER
MENHIR
MENTOR
MERCER
MERGER
MESMER
METEOR
METIER
MEWLER
MIDAIR
MIDLER
MILDER
MILKER
MILLER
MILNER
MINCER
MINDER
MINTER
MIRIER
MIRROR
MISTER
MOANER
MOCKER
MOHAIR
MOILER
MOLDER
MOLNAR
MOLTER
MONGER
MOPIER
MOPPER
MORTAR
MOSHER
MOTHER
MOUSER
MUDDER
MUGGER
MULLER
MUMMER
MURDER
MURMUR
MUSHER
MUSTER
MUTTER

•M•R••
AMERCE
AMERSP
AMORAL
AMTRAC
AMTRAK
DMARKS
EMBRYO
EMERGE
IMARET
IMBRUE
IMPROV
OMERTA
SMARMY
SMARTS
SMARTY
SMERSH
SMIRCH
SMIRKS
SMIRKY
SMURFS
SMYRNA
UMBRAE
UMBRAL
UMBRAS
UMBRIA

•M••R•
AMBERS
AMBERY
AMEERS
AMENRA
AMHARA
AMOURS
AMPERE
DMITRI
EMBARK
EMBERS
EMEERS
EMIGRE
EMPERY
EMPIRE
IMMURE
IMPART
IMPERF
IMPORT
IMPURE
SMEARS
SMEARY
UMBERS
UMPIRE

•M•••R
AMAJOR
AMBLER
AMINOR
AMPLER
BMAJOR
BMINOR
CMAJOR
CMINOR
DMAJOR
DMINOR
EMAJOR
EMINOR
EMOTER
EMPTOR
FMAJOR
FMINOR
GMAJOR
GMINOR
IMAGER
IMPAIR
SMILER
SMOKER

••MR••
BUMRAP
CYMRIC
DOMREP
NIMROD
QUMRAN
RAMROD

••M•R•
ADMIRE
ARMORS
ARMORY
ARMURE
ASMARA
AYMARA
BEMIRE
BUMBRY
CAMARO
CAMERA
COMERS
DAMORE
DEMURE
DEMURS
ELMIRA
ELMORE
EXMORE
FEMORA
FEMURS
GEMARA
HOMBRE
HOMERS
HUMERI
HUMORS
IMMURE
KHMERS
LAMARR
LEMURS
MEMORY
MIMERS
NAMERS
NOMORE
NUMERO
PAMIRS
REMARK
REMORA
ROMERO
RUMORS
SAMARA
SEMPRE
SOMBRE
SOMERS
STMARK
TAMARA
TAMERS
TIMBRE
TIMERS

••M••R
AIMFOR
ARMOUR
BOMBER
BUMMER
BUMPER
CAMBER
CAMPER
COMBER
CUMBER
DAMMAR
DAMOUR
DAMPER
DIMMER
DUMBER
DUMPER
EXMOOR
FUMIER
GAMIER
GAMMER
HAMMER
HAMPER
HEMMER
HOMIER
HUMMER
HUMOUR
JAMMER
JUMPER
LAMARR
LAMOUR
LIMBER
LIMIER
LIMNER
LIMPER
LUMBAR
LUMBER
LUMPER
LUMPUR
MEMBER
MEMOIR
MUMMER
NUMBER
PAMPER
PUMPER
RIMIER
ROMPER
RUMMER
RUMOUR
SAMBAR
SEMPER
SIMMER
SIMPER
SOMBER
SOMMER
SUMMER
SUMNER
SUMTER
TAMPER
TEMPER
TIMBER
UNMOOR
VAMPER
YAMMER
ZIMMER

•••M•R
ALOMAR
BOOMER
BUMMER
CALMER
CLAMOR
DAGMAR
DAMMAR
DELMAR
DIMMER
DORMER
ENAMOR
FARMER
FIRMER
FORMER
FULMAR
GAMMER
GLAMOR
HAMMER
HEMMER
HUMMER
INGMAR
ISOMER
JAMMER
KALMAR
KILMER
KRAMER
MESMER
MUMMER
MURMUR
NEWMAR
PALMER
PRIMER
REAMER
RHYMER
ROAMER
ROHMER
ROOMER
RUMMER
SHAMIR
SIMMER
SOMMER
STUMER
SUMMER
TREMOR
WARMER
WEIMAR
YAMMER
ZIMMER

MS••••
MSQUAD

M•S•••
MASADA
MASAIS
MASCOT
MASERS
MASERU
MASHED
MASHER
MASHES
MASHIE
MASKED
MASKER
MASONS
MASQUE
MASSED
MASSES
MASSEY
MASSIF
MASTER
MASTIC
MESABI
MESCAL
MESHED
MESHES
MESMER
MESONS
MESSED
MESSES
MESSRS
MESSUP
MISCHA
MISCUE
MISDID
MISERS
MISERY
MISFIT
MISHAP
MISHIT
MISLAY
MISLED
MISSAL
MISSAY
MISSED
MISSES
MISSIS
MISSUS
MISTED
MISTER
MISUSE
MOSAIC
MOSCOW
MOSEYS
MOSHAV
MOSHED
MOSHER
MOSHES
MOSKVA
MOSLEM
MOSQUE
MOSSED
MOSSES
MOSTEL
MOSTLY
MUSCAT
MUSCLE
MUSCLY
MUSERS
MUSEUM
MUSHED
MUSHER
MUSHES
MUSIAL
MUSING
MUSKEG
MUSKET
MUSKIE
MUSKOX
MUSLIM
MUSLIN
MUSSED
MUSSEL
MUSSES
MUSSUP
MUSTER
MUSTNT
MYSELF
MYSORE
MYSTIC

M••S••
MADSEN
MAISIE
MANSES
MARSHA
MARSHY
MASSED
MASSES
MASSEY
MASSIF
MAUSER
MEASLY
MENSAE
MENSAL
MENSAS
MENSCH
MERSEY
MESSED
MESSES
MESSRS
MESSUP
MIASMA
MILSAP
MIOSIS
MISSAL
MISSAY
MISSED
MISSES
MISSIS
MISSUS
MOPSUP
MORSEL
MOSSED
MOSSES
MOUSED
MOUSER
MOUSES
MOUSEY
MOUSSE
MUSSED
MUSSEL
MUSSES
MUSSUP
MYOSIN
MYOSIS

M•••S•
MAOISM
MAOIST
MARISA
MARISH
MARIST
MEDUSA
MEREST
MILOSZ
MIMOSA
MISUSE
MODEST
MODISH
MOLEST
MONISM
MONIST
MOPISH
MORASS
MOROSE
MOUSSE
MUCOSA
MUFASA
MULISH
MUTEST

M••••S
MACAWS
MACHES
MACHOS
MACROS
MADAMS
MADRAS
MADRES
MAGMAS
MAGNUS
MAHDIS
MAIDUS
MAILES
MAIZES
MAJLIS
MAJORS
MAKERS
MALAYS
MAMBAS
MAMBOS
MAMMAS
MANAUS
MANGOS
MANIAS
MANORS
MANSES
MANTAS
MANTIS
MAORIS
MAPLES
MAQUIS
MARCOS
MARCUS
MARGES
MARIUS
MASAIS
MASERS
MASHES
MASONS
MASSES
MATERS
MATEYS
MATHIS
MATINS
MATTES
MATZOS
MAUVES
MAVENS
MAXIMS
MAYANS
MAYBES
MAYORS
MAZERS
MCJOBS
MECCAS
MEDALS
MEDIAS
MEDICS
MELEES
MELONS
MENDES
MENSAS
MENTIS
MERGES
MERITS
MESHES
MESONS
MESSES
MESSRS
METALS
METERS
METRES
METROS
MEZZOS
MICROS
MIDGES
MILERS
MILPAS
MIMEOS
MIMERS
MIMICS
MINCES
MINERS
MINIMS
MINKES
MINORS
MINXES
MIOSIS
MISERS
MISSES
MISSIS
MISSUS
MITERS
MITRES
MIWOKS
MIXERS
MIXUPS
MIZENS
MOBIUS
MOCHAS
MODELS
MODEMS
MODOCS
MOGULS
MOHURS
MOINES
MOIRES
MOLARS
MOMMAS
MONADS
MONEYS
MONIES
MONTES
MONTHS
MOPEDS
MOPERS
MOPUPS
MORALS
MORASS
MORAYS
MORELS
MORONS
MORPHS
MORRIS
MOSEYS
MOSHES
MOSSES
MOTELS
MOTETS
MOTIFS
MOTORS
MOTTOS
MOULDS
MOULTS
MOUNDS

MOUNTS MOURNS MOUSES MOUTHS MOVERS MOVIES MOWERS MOYERS MUCINS MUCOUS MUDRAS MUFTIS MUGHOS MULCTS MULEYS MULLAS MUNGOS MURALS MURRES MUSERS MUSHES MUSSES MUZZES MYNAHS MYOPES MYOSIS MYRRHS MYTHOS

•MS•••

AMSTEL

•M•S••

AMOSOZ AMUSED AMUSES KMESON OMASUM TMESIS

•M••S•

AMBUSH AMERSP AMIDST EMBOSS EMDASH IMPISH IMPOSE IMPOST SMERSH

•M•••S

AMADIS AMATIS AMAZES AMBERS AMBITS AMBLES AMEBAS AMEERS AMENDS AMENTS AMICES AMICUS AMIDES AMIENS AMIGAS AMIGOS AMINES AMINUS AMOLES AMOURS AMPULS AMUSES AMVETS BMINUS CMINUS DMARKS DMINUS EMAILS EMBAYS EMBEDS EMBERS EMBOSS EMCEES EMEERS EMENDS EMMETS EMOTES HMONGS IMAGES IMBUES IMPELS OMAHAS OMANIS OMEGAS SMACKS SMALLS SMARTS SMEARS SMELLS SMELTS SMILES SMIRKS SMITES SMITHS SMOCKS SMOKES SMOLTS SMURFS TMESIS UMBELS UMBERS UMBRAS UMIAKS

••MS••

AIMSAT AIMSTO COMSAT DAMSEL DAMSON DAMSUP DIMSUM GUMSUP HEMSIN JAMSIN JAMSUP JIMSON RAMSAY RAMSES RAMSEY RAMSON RIMSKY SAMSON SUMSUP WIMSEY

••M•S•

ADMASS ALMOST ATMOST BEMUSE CAMISE DAMASK DEMISE ENMESH FAMISH GAMEST INMOST KUMISS LAMESA LAMEST MIMOSA OSMOSE RAMOSE REMISE REMISS RIMOSE SAMOSA TAMEST UNMASK UNMESH UPMOST UTMOST ZYMASE

••M••S

ADMASS ADMITS ARMETS ARMIES ARMORS BOMBES CAMELS CAMEOS CAMPOS CAMPUS COMBES COMBOS COMERS COMETS COMICS COMMAS COMPOS COMTES DEMIES DEMITS DEMOBS DEMONS DEMURS EMMETS FAMOUS FEMMES FEMURS GAMAYS GAMINS GAMMAS GAMUTS GEMOTS GIMELS GIMMES GUMBOS HAMALS HOMERS HUMANS HUMMUS HUMORS HUMPHS JAMUPS JUMBOS KEMPIS KHMERS KUMISS LAMEDS LAMIAS LAMMAS LEMANS LEMMAS LEMNOS LEMONS LEMURS LIMBOS LIMBUS LIMENS LIMEYS LIMITS LUMENS LYMPHS MAMBAS MAMBOS MAMMAS MIMEOS MIMERS MIMICS MOMMAS NAMERS NIMBUS NOMADS NYMETS NYMPHS OLMECS OSMICS PAMIRS PAMPAS RAMETS RAMIES RAMOUS RAMSES REMANS REMAPS REMISS REMITS REMOPS REMOWS ROMANS ROMEOS RUMBAS RUMENS RUMORS RUMPUS SAMBAS SOMERS SUMACS SUMMAS SUMUPS TAMERS TAMILS TEMPOS TEMPTS TEMPUS TIMERS UNMANS WOMENS ZAMIAS

•••MS•

AHIMSA CLUMSY FLIMSY SLIMSY WHIMSY WHOMSO

•••M•S

ABOMBS AGAMAS ALAMOS ANIMAS ANIMES ANIMUS ARAMIS AROMAS BIOMES BLAMES BLIMPS BRUMES CADMUS CHAMPS CHIMES CHIMPS CHOMPS CHUMPS CLAMPS CLIMBS CLIMES CLOMPS CLUMPS COMMAS COSMOS CRAMPS CREMES CRIMES CRIMPS CRUMBS DEIMOS DERMIS DISMES DOGMAS DOLMAS DRAMAS DROMOS DUOMOS EDAMES ELEMIS FEMMES FLAMES FLUMES FRAMES FRUMPS GAMMAS GIMMES GIZMOS GNOMES GRAMAS GRAMPS GRIMES GRUMPS HBOMBS HERMES HOLMES HUMMUS KERMES KERMIS LAMMAS LEMMAS LITMUS LLAMAS MAGMAS MAMMAS MOMMAS NEUMES OROMOS PALMAS PATMOS PLUMBS PLUMES PLUMPS PRIMES PRIMOS PRIMPS PRIMUS PROMOS RHAMES RHOMBS RHUMBS RHYMES SCAMPS SCHMOS SEAMUS SHAMES SHAMUS SIGMAS SKIMPS SLIMES SLUMPS SPUMES STAMPS STOMAS STOMPS STUMPS SUMMAS SWAMIS SWAMPS THAMES THEMES THOMAS THUMBS THUMPS THYMUS TRAMPS TROMPS TRUMPS WHOMPS

••••MS

ABOHMS ABRAMS ABYSMS ADDAMS ADEEMS ALARMS ALBUMS ATEAMS AXIOMS BEDIMS BEGUMS BESOMS BLOOMS BRAHMS BREAMS BROOMS CAROMS CDROMS CHARMS CHASMS CLAIMS CREAMS DENIMS DREAMS EPROMS FORUMS GLEAMS GLOOMS GOLEMS GROOMS HAKIMS HAREMS HAULMS HBEAMS IBEAMS IDIOMS JORUMS KHOUMS KILIMS LARAMS MADAMS MAXIMS MINIMS MODEMS ODIUMS OGHAMS PRISMS PROAMS PROEMS PSALMS QUALMS REAIMS REALMS REARMS REHEMS RHEUMS SCRAMS SCRIMS SCRUMS SEDUMS SEISMS SERUMS SHAWMS SPASMS STEAMS STORMS STRUMS SWARMS THERMS THRUMS TOTEMS UGGAMS UNARMS UNJAMS VENOMS VROOMS WHELMS

M•T•••

MATERS MATEYS MATHER MATHIS MATING MATINS MATLIN MATRIX MATRON MATTEA MATTED MATTEL MATTER MATTES MATTIE MATURE MATZOH MATZOS METALS METATE METEOR METERS METHOD METHYL METIER METING METOPE METRES METRIC METROS METTLE MITERS MITRAL MITRED MITRES MITTEN MOTELS MOTETS MOTHER MOTHRA MOTIFS MOTILE MOTION MOTIVE MOTLEY MOTMOT MOTORS MOTOWN MOTTLE MOTTOS MUTANT MUTATE MUTATO MUTELY MUTEST MUTING MUTINY MUTTER MUTTON MUTUAL MYTHIC MYTHOI MYTHOL MYTHOS

M••T••

MADTOM MAITAI MAITRE MALTED MALTIN MANTAS MANTEL MANTIC MANTIS MANTLE MANTRA MANTUA MAOTAI MARTEL MARTEN MARTHA MARTIN MARTYR MASTER MASTIC MATTEA MATTED MATTEL MATTER MATTES MATTIE MAYTAG MEETER MEETLY MELTED MELTON MENTAL MENTIS MENTOR MERTON METTLE MILTIE MILTON MINTED MINTER MISTED MISTER MITTEN MIXTEC MOATED MOLTED MOLTEN MOLTER MOLTKE MONTEL MONTES MONTEZ MONTHS MOOTED MOPTOP MORTAL MORTAR MORTON MOSTEL MOSTLY MOTTLE MOTTOS MOUTHS MOUTHY MOUTON MUFTIS MULTUM MUNTIN MUSTER MUSTNT MUTTER MUTTON MYRTLE MYSTIC

M•••T•

MAKUTA MALATE MALOTI MAPUTO MELOTT MERITS METATE MIGHTY MIKITA MINUTE MOIETY MONETA MORITA

MORITZ MOTETS MOULTS MOUNTS MOUNTY MRMOTO MULCTS MULETA MUTATE MUTATO

M••••T
MADEIT MAGNET MAHOUT MAKEIT MALLET MAOIST MARGOT MARIST MARKET MARMOT MASCOT MAXOUT MEDLAT MEERUT MELOTT MEREST MERLOT MIDGET MILLET MINUET MINUIT MISFIT MISHIT MODELT MODEST MOLEST MOMENT MONIST MOPPET MORANT MOTMOT MOZART MUDCAT MULLET MUPPET MUSCAT MUSKET MUSTNT MUTANT MUTEST

•MT•••
AMTRAC AMTRAK UMTATA

•M•T••
AMATIS AMATOL AMSTEL AMYTAN

DMITRI EMOTED EMOTER EMOTES EMPTOR SMITES SMITHS SMITHY SMUTCH SMUTTY

•M••T•
AMBATO AMBITS AMENTS AMVETS EMEUTE EMMETS EMMETT IMPUTE OMERTA SMALTI SMALTO SMARTS SMARTY SMELTS SMOLTS SMOOTH SMUTTY UMTATA

•M•••T
AMIDST AMOUNT AMULET EMMETT IMARET IMPACT IMPART IMPORT IMPOST OMELET UMLAUT

••MT••
COMTES SUMTER TAMTAM TOMTIT TOMTOM YOMTOV

••M•T•
ADMITS AIMSTO ALMATY ARMETS BEMATA CAMETO COMATE COMETH COMETO COMETS COMITY DAMATO DAMITA DEMITS DEMOTE DIMITY EMMETS EMMETT ENMITY GAMETE GAMUTS GEMOTE GEMOTS HAMITE HEMATO INMATE IOMOTH LIMITS MRMOTO NAMATH NEMATO NIMITZ NYMETS RAMATE RAMETS REMITS REMOTE SAMITE SEMITE SOMATA SOMATO TEMPTS TOMATO

••M••T
AIMSAT ALMOST ARMLET ARMPIT ATMOST AUMONT BUMOUT CAMEAT CAMLET CEMENT COMBAT COMEAT COMFIT COMMIT COMSAT DIMOUT DIMWIT DUMONT EGMONT EMMETT FOMENT GAMBIT GAMEST GIMLET HAMLET INMOST JUMPAT KOMBAT LAMENT LAMEST LAMONT LIMPET MOMENT NUMBAT RAMJET REMELT SAMLET SUMMIT TAMEST TOMCAT TOMTIT TUMULT UNMEET UPMOST UTMOST WOMBAT

•••MT•
WARMTH

•••M•T
BONMOT CERMET COMMIT EXEMPT FERMAT FORMAT HAEMAT HELMET HELMUT HERMIT ILLMET KERMIT KISMET MARMOT MOTMOT PELMET PERMIT PROMPT STOMAT SUBMIT SUMMIT

••••MT
DREAMT

MU••••
MUCINS MUCKED MUCKUP MUCOSA MUCOUS MUDCAT MUDDED MUDDER MUDDLE MUDEEL MUDHEN MUDPIE MUDRAS MUFASA MUFFED MUFFIN MUFFLE MUFTIS MUGABE MUGGED MUGGER MUGHOS MUKLUK MULCTS MULETA MULEYS MULISH MULLAH MULLAS MULLED MULLER MULLET MULTUM MUMBLE MUMBLY MUMMED MUMMER MUMPED MUNCHY MUNCIE MUNGOS MUNICH MUNTIN MUPPET MURALS MURANO MURCIA MURDER MURIEL MURINE MURMUR MURPHY MURRAY MURRES MURREY MURROW MUSCAT MUSCLE MUSCLY MUSERS MUSEUM MUSHED MUSHER MUSHES MUSIAL MUSING MUSKEG MUSKET MUSKIE MUSKOX MUSLIM MUSLIN MUSSED MUSSEL MUSSES MUSSUP MUSTER MUSTNT MUTANT MUTATE MUTATO MUTELY MUTEST MUTING MUTINY MUTTER MUTTON MUTUAL MUUMUU MUZHIK MUZZED MUZZES MUZZLE

M•U•••
MAULED MAULER MAUMAU MAUMEE MAUNDY MAURYA MAUSER MAUVES MBUNDU MOULDS MOULDY MOULIN MOULTS MOUNDS MOUNTS MOUNTY MOURNS MOUSED MOUSER MOUSES MOUSEY MOUSSE MOUTHS MOUTHY MOUTON MUUMUU

M••U••
MACULA MADURA MADURO MAGUEY MAKUTA MANUAL MANUEL MAPUTO MAQUIS MATURE MAZUMA MCHUGH MCKUEN MEDUSA MIFUNE MIGUEL MINUET MINUIT MINUTE MISUSE MIXUPS MODULE MODULO MOGULS MOHURS MOPUPS MSQUAD MUTUAL

M•••U•
MACOUN MADEUP MAGNUM MAGNUS MAHOUT MAIDUS MAKEUP MANAUS MANFUL MANQUE MANTUA MARAUD MARCUS MARDUK MARIUS MARKUP MARQUE MASQUE MAXOUT MEDIUM MEERUT MESSUP MINIUM MISCUE MISSUS MOBIUS MOCKUP MOPSUP MOSQUE MOVEUP MRBLUE MUCKUP MUCOUS MUKLUK MULTUM MURMUR MUSEUM MUSSUP MUUMUU

M••••U
MAKALU MALIBU MANCHU MARILU MASERU MAUMAU MBUNDU MENJOU MILIEU MOLDAU MOREAU MUUMUU

•MU•••
AMULET AMUSED AMUSES SMUDGE SMUDGY SMUGLY SMURFS SMUTCH SMUTTY

•M•U••
AMBUSH AMOUNT AMOURS AMPULE AMPULS EMEUTE EMQUAD IMBUED IMBUES IMMUNE IMMUNO IMMURE IMPUGN IMPURE IMPUTE

•M••U•
AMICUS AMINUS BMINUS CMINUS DMINUS IMBRUE OMASUM OMNIUM UMLAUT

•M•••U
AMADOU

••MU••
ARMURE BEMUSE CUMULI CUMULO DEMURE DEMURS EDMUND FEMURS GAMUTS IMMUNE IMMUNO IMMURE JAMUPS LEMUEL LEMURS OSMUND REMUDA SAMUEL SUMUPS TUMULI TUMULT

••M•U•
AIMFUL ARMFUL ARMOUR BUMOUT BUMPUP CAMEUP CAMPUS COMEUP DAMOUR DAMSUP DIMOUT DIMSUM DUMDUM FAMOUS GUMSUP HUMBUG HUMMUS HUMOUR JAMSUP JUMPUP LAMOUR LIMBUS LUMPUR NIMBUS OSMIUM PUMPUP RAMOUS RUMOUR RUMPUS SUMSUP TAMMUZ TEMPUS WAMPUM YUMYUM

••M••U
ORMOLU RAMEAU

•••MU•
ANIMUS BEAMUP CADMUS CLAMUP DRUMUP FIRMUP HELMUT HORMUZ HUMMUS LITMUS MURMUR MUUMUU PRIMUM PRIMUS SEAMUS SHAMUS TALMUD TAMMUZ TEAMUP THYMUS WARMUP WONMUG

•••M•U
MAUMAU MUUMUU

M•V•••
MAVENS MOVEIN MOVEON MOVERS MOVEUP MOVIES MOVING

M••V••
MARVEL MARVIN MAUVES MELVIL MELVIN MELVYN MERVYN

M•••V•
MOHAVE MOJAVE MORAVA MOSKVA MOTIVE

M••••V
MOSHAV

•MV•••
AMVETS

•M•V••
BMOVIE

•M•••V
IMPROV

••MV••
HUMVEE

••M•V•
REMOVE

••M••V
YOMTOV

•••M•V
ASIMOV

M•W•••
MEWING MEWLED

MEWLER
MIWOKS
MOWERS
MOWGLI
MOWING
MYWORD

M••W••
MEOWED
MIDWAY

M•••W•
MACAWS
MALAWI
MOHAWK
MOTOWN

M••••W
MALLOW
MARROW
MCGRAW
MCGREW
MEADOW
MELLOW
MILDEW
MINNOW
MORROW
MOSCOW
MURROW

••MW••
DIMWIT

••M•W•
REMOWN
REMOWS

•••M•W
HAYMOW

M•X•••
MAXENE
MAXIMA
MAXIMS
MAXINE
MAXIXE
MAXOUT
MEXICO
MIXERS
MIXING
MIXTEC
MIXUPS

M••X••
MINXES

M•••X•
MAXIXE

M••••X
MADMAX
MANNIX
MATRIX
MENINX
MUSKOX

•M•••X
SMILAX

••M••X
COMMIX
LUMMOX
TOMMIX

•••M•X
CLIMAX
COMMIX
LUMMOX
MADMAX
TEXMEX
TOMMIX

MY••••
MYELIN
MYGIRL
MYNAHS
MYOHMY
MYOPES
MYOPIA
MYOPIC
MYOSIN
MYOSIS
MYRDAL
MYRIAD
MYRRHS
MYRTLE
MYSELF
MYSORE
MYSTIC
MYTHIC
MYTHOI
MYTHOL
MYTHOS
MYWORD

M•Y•••
MAYANS
MAYBES
MAYDAY
MAYFLY
MAYHAP
MAYHEM
MAYORS
MAYPOP
MAYTAG
MOYERS

M••Y••
MAGYAR
MINYAN
MRHYDE

M•••Y•
MALAYA
MALAYS
MARTYR
MATEYS
MAURYA
MELVYN
MERVYN
METHYL
MONEYS
MORAYS
MOSEYS
MULEYS

M••••Y
MAGUEY
MAINLY
MALADY
MALORY
MANDAY
MANRAY
MARBLY
MARGAY
MARLEY
MARSHY
MASSEY
MAUNDY
MAYDAY
MAYFLY
MAZILY
MEANLY
MEASLY
MEDFLY
MEDLEY
MEEKLY
MEETLY
MELODY
MEMORY
MERELY
MERSEY
MICKEY
MIDDAY
MIDWAY
MIGHTY
MILADY
MILDLY
MILLAY
MINIFY
MISERY
MISLAY
MISSAY
MOBLEY
MODIFY
MOIETY
MONDAY
MONKEY
MONODY
MOONEY
MOPERY
MORLEY
MORNAY
MORPHY
MOSTLY
MOTLEY
MOULDY
MOUNTY
MOUSEY
MOUTHY
MUMBLY
MUNCHY
MURPHY
MURRAY
MURREY
MUSCLY
MUTELY
MUTINY
MYOHMY

•MY•••
AMYTAN
SMYRNA

•M••Y•
EMBAYS
EMBRYO

•M•••Y
AMBERY
EMBODY
EMPERY
EMPLOY
SMARMY
SMARTY
SMEARY
SMELLY
SMILEY
SMIRKY
SMITHY
SMOGGY
SMOKEY
SMUDGY
SMUGLY
SMUTTY

••MY••
YUMYUM

••M•Y•
GAMAYS
LIMEYS
TAMAYO

••M••Y
ALMATY
ARMORY
BOMBAY
BUMBRY
CAMEBY
COMEBY
COMEDY
COMELY
COMITY
COMPLY
DAMPLY
DIMITY
DIMPLY
DUMBLY
ENMITY
FAMILY
GAMELY
GAMILY
HOMELY
HOMILY
HOMINY
HUMBLY
JIMINY
LAMELY
LEMONY
LIMPLY
MEMORY
MUMBLY
NAMELY
NIMBLY
NIMINY
NUMBLY
PIMINY
POMPEY
RAMIFY
RAMSAY
RAMSEY
REMEDY
RIMSKY
ROMANY
ROMNEY
RUMBLY
RUMPLY
SIMONY
SIMPLY
SOMANY
TAMELY
TIMELY
TOMBOY
TUMEFY
WAMBLY
WIMSEY

•••MY•
DAIMYO

•••M•Y
BLIMEY
BRUMBY
CALMLY
CHAMMY
CHUMMY
CLAMMY
CLUMPY
CLUMSY
CRIMPY
CRUMBY
CRUMMY
DISMAY
FIRMLY
FLIMSY
FRUMPY
GLUMLY
GRAMMY
GRIMLY
GRUMPY
NIAMEY
PLUMMY
PRIMLY
QUEMOY
SCUMMY
SEEMLY
SHIMMY
SKIMPY
SLIMLY
SLIMSY
SLUMMY
STIMPY
STUMPY
SWAMPY
TRIMLY
WARMLY
WHAMMY
WHIMSY

••••MY
BIGAMY
BLOOMY
BROOMY
CHAMMY
CHROMY
CHUMMY
CLAMMY
CREAMY
CRUMMY
DREAMY
GLEAMY
GLOOMY
GRAMMY
INFAMY
JEREMY
MYOHMY
PLUMMY
RHEUMY
SCUMMY
SHIMMY
SLUMMY
SMARMY
STEAMY
STORMY
WHAMMY

M•Z•••
MAZERS
MAZIER
MAZILY
MAZOLA
MAZUMA
MEZZOS
MIZENS
MIZZEN
MIZZLE
MOZART
MUZHIK
MUZZED
MUZZES
MUZZLE

M••Z••
MAHZOR
MAIZES
MATZOH
MATZOS
MEZZOS
MIZZEN
MIZZLE
MUZZED
MUZZES
MUZZLE

M••••Z
MILOSZ
MONTEZ
MORITZ

•M•Z••
AMAZED
AMAZES
AMAZON

•M•••Z
AMOSOZ

••M•Z•
LAMAZE

••M••Z
NIMITZ
TAMMUZ

•••M•Z
HORMUZ
TAMMUZ

NA••••
NABBED
NABBER
NABOBS
NABORS
NACHOS
NACRES
NADINE
NADIRS
NAGANO
NAGGED
NAGGER
NAGOYA
NAIADS
NAILED
NAILER
NAILIN
NAIRAS
NAMATH
NAMELY
NAMERS
NAMING
NANNIE
NANOOK
NANSEN
NANTES
NAPERY
NAPIER
NAPKIN
NAPLES
NAPOLI
NAPPED
NAPPER
NAPPES
NAPPIE
NARIAL
NARNIA
NARROW
NARVIK
NARWAL
NASALS
NASCAR
NASDAQ
NASEBY
NASHUA
NASSAU
NASSER
NATANT
NATHAN
NATICK
NATION
NATIVE
NATRON
NATTER
NATURA
NATURE
NAUGHT
NAUSEA
NAUTCH
NAVAHO
NAVAJO
NAVELS
NAVIES
NAWABS
NAYSAY

N•A•••
NEARBY
NEARED
NEARER
NEARLY
NEARTO
NEATEN
NEATER
NEATLY
NIACIN
NIAMEY
NUANCE
NYALAS
NYASSA

N••A••
NAGANO
NAIADS
NAMATH
NASALS
NATANT
NAVAHO
NAVAJO
NAWABS
NEGATE
NEMATO
NEPALI
NEVADA
NEWAGE
NEWARK
NICAEA
NLEAST
NOMADS
NONAGE
NONAME
NONARY
NOSALE
NOTARY
NOTATE
NOVATO
NUTATE

N•••A•
NAIRAS
NARIAL
NARWAL
NASCAR
NASDAQ
NASSAU
NATHAN
NAYSAY
NECTAR
NETMAN
NETPAY
NEUMAN
NEURAL
NEWMAN
NEWMAR
NICEAN
NIIHAU
NILGAI
NINEAM
NINJAS
NIPSAT
NISSAN
NOLEAD
NOLOAD
NONFAT
NOONAN
NORGAY
NORIAS
NORMAL
NORMAN
NORWAY
NOSOAP
NOTBAD
NOUGAT
NUBIAN
NUCHAE
NUCHAL
NULLAH
NUMBAT
NYALAS

N••••A
NAGOYA
NARNIA
NASHUA
NATURA
NAUSEA
NEBULA
NERUDA
NESTEA
NEVADA
NICAEA
NICOLA
NIKITA
NIKOLA
NOOTKA
NOUMEA
NOVENA
NUMINA
NUTRIA
NYASSA

•NA•••
ANACIN
ANADEM
ANALOG
ANANDA
ANATTO
ENABLE
ENACTS
ENAMEL
ENAMOR
ENATES
GNARLS
GNARLY
GNATTY
GNAWED
GNAWER
INAFIX
INAFOG
INAJAM
INANER
INAPET
INARCH
INAROW
INARUT
INAWAY
KNACKS
KNAGGY
KNARRY
KNAVES
ONAGER
SNACKS
SNAFUS
SNAGGY
SNAILS
SNAKED
SNAKES
SNAPAT
SNAPPY
SNAPTO
SNAPUP
SNARED
SNARES
SNARLS
SNARLY
SNATCH
SNATHE
SNATHS
SNAZZY
UNABLE
UNAGED

UNARMS
UNAWED

•N•A••

ANKARA
ANNABA
ANNALS
ANSARA
ANSATE
ANWANG
ANYANG
ENCAGE
ENCAMP
ENCASE
ENDALL
ENDASH
ENFANT
ENGAGE
ENHALO
ENLACE
ENRAGE
ENRAPT
ENTAIL
INCANS
INCASE
INCASH
INDABA
INFACT
INFAMY
INFANT
INHALE
INHALF
INHAND
INHAUL
INLAID
INLAND
INLAWS
INLAYS
INMATE
INNAGE
INNATE
INPART
INSANE
INTACT
INTAKE
INVADE
INVAIN
INWARD
KNEADS
ONCALL
ONEACT
ONHAND
ONLAND
ONSALE
ONTAPE
ONWARD
SNEAKS
SNEAKY
UNBARS
UNCAGE
UNCAPS
UNCASE
UNEASE
UNEASY
UNFAIR
UNHAND
UNIATE
UNIATS
UNJAMS
UNLACE
UNLADE
UNLAID
UNLASH
UNMADE
UNMAKE
UNMANS
UNMASK
UNPACK
UNPAID
UNSAFE
UNSAID
UNSAYS
UNTACK
UNWARY

•N••A•

ANDEAN
ANIMAL
ANIMAS
ANNEAL
ANNUAL
ANORAK
ANSGAR
ANURAN
ANYDAY
ANYWAY
CNIDAE
ENDEAR
ENDMAN
ENGRAM
ENNEAD
ENQUAD
ENTRAP
ENWRAP
INAJAM
INAWAY
INDIAN
INGEAR
INGMAR
INGRAM
INPLAY
INROAD
INSEAM
INSPAN
INSTAL
INSTAR
ONEDAY
ONEMAN
ONEWAY
ONLOAN
SNAPAT
SNOCAT
UNCIAL
UNCLAD
UNDRAW
UNGUAL
UNITAL
UNITAS
UNIVAC
UNLEAD
UNLOAD
UNOCAL
UNREAD
UNREAL
UNSEAL
UNSEAT
UNSNAG
UNSNAP
UNTRAP
UNWRAP

•N•••A

ANANDA
ANCONA
ANDREA
ANEMIA
ANGELA
ANGLIA
ANGOLA
ANGORA
ANITRA
ANKARA
ANNABA
ANNIKA
ANSARA
ENCINA
ENDORA
ENIGMA
INDABA
INDIRA
INTIMA
ONEIDA
PNEUMA

••NA••

ADNATE
AGNATE
ANNABA
ANNALS
BANANA
BINARY
BINATE
BONAMI
BYNAME
CANAAN
CANADA
CANALS
CANAPE
CANARD
CANARY
CONANT
CUNARD
CUNAXA
DANANG
DANAUS
DENALI
DENARY
DINARS
DONALD
DONATE
DUNANT
DYNAMO
DYNAST
ERNANI
FINALE
FINALS
IGNACE
IGNATZ
INNAGE
INNATE
JONAHS
KANAKA
LANAIS
LANARK
LANATE
LENAPE
LINAGE
LUNACY
LUNATE
MANAGE
MANAMA
MANANA
MANAUS
MCNAIR
MENACE
MENADO
MENAGE
MONACO
MONADS
MYNAHS
NONAGE
NONAME
NONARY
ORNATE
OXNARD
PANADA
PANAMA
PENANG
PINATA
RENAIL
RENAME
RENATA
RONALD
SENARY
SENATE
SONANT
SONATA
TANAKA
TANANA
TENACE
TENANT
XANADU
ZENANA
ZONATE

••N•A•

AENEAS
ANNEAL
ANNUAL
BANTAM
BANYAN
BANZAI
BENDAY
BENGAL
BENGAY
BONSAI
BUNYAN
CANAAN
CANCAN
CANNAE
CANTAB
CANVAS
CONFAB
CONGAS
CONMAN
CONRAD
CONTAC
CONWAY
CUNEAL
DANNAY
DENIAL
DENTAL
DONNAS
DUNBAR
DUNCAN
DUNHAM
ENNEAD
EONIAN
FANTAN
FENIAN
FENMAN
FENWAY
FINIAL
FINNAN
FONTAL
GENIAL
GENOAN
GENUAL
GUNMAN
GUNNAR
HANGAR
HANNAH
HENNAS
HINTAT
IONIAN
JINNAH
JUNEAU
JUNTAS
KANSAN
KANSAS
KENYAN
KONRAD
LANDAU
LINEAL
LINEAR
LONGAN
MANDAN
MANDAY
MANIAC
MANIAS
MANRAY
MANTAS
MANUAL
MENIAL
MENSAE
MENSAL
MENSAS
MENTAL
MINOAN
MINYAN
MONDAY
NINEAM
NINJAS
NONFAT
PANDAS
PENMAN
PENNAE
PENPAL
PENTAD
PINDAR
PINEAL
PINNAE
PINNAS
PINOAK
PUNJAB
PUNKAH
QANTAS
QINTAR
RENTAL
RUNSAT
RUNWAY
SANDAL
SENDAK
SENLAC
SENNAS
SINBAD
SINEAD
SINTAX
SONTAG
SUNDAE
SUNDAY
SUNRAY
SUNTAN
SYNTAX
TANKAS
TANOAK
TANOAN
TINCAL
TINCAN
TINEAR
TINHAT
TINMAN
TINPAN
TONGAN
UINTAS
VANDAL
VENIAL
WANTAD
WENTAT
WINKAT
YENTAS
YUNNAN

••N••A

ADNEXA
ANNABA
ANNIKA
ARNICA
BANANA
BANGKA
CANADA
CANOLA
CANOVA
CINEMA
CONCHA
CONTRA
CUNAXA
DUNERA
GENERA
GENEVA
KANAKA
KINEMA
KONICA
LINGUA
LUNULA
MANAMA
MANANA
MANCHA
MANILA
MANTRA
MANTUA
MINIMA
MONERA
MONETA
MONICA
PANADA
PANAMA
PENNIA
PINATA
RENATA
SANCTA
SANDIA
SANDRA
SENECA
SENEGA
SENORA
SENTRA
SONATA
SONOMA
SONORA
TANAKA
TANANA
TANTRA
TUNDRA
TUNICA
WINONA
ZENANA
ZINNIA

•••NA•

ADONAI
AGENAS
ARENAS
ASANAS
ATONAL
AXONAL
BWANAS
CANNAE
CARNAL
CATNAP
COGNAC
DANNAY
DARNAY
DONNAS
EPINAL
FAUNAE
FAUNAL
FAUNAS
FINNAN
GUNNAR
HAINAN
HANNAH
HENNAS
HYENAS
HYMNAL
JINNAH
KARNAK
KAUNAS
KEENAN
KIDNAP
LIANAS
MAENAD
MOLNAR
MORNAY
NOONAN
PENNAE
PINNAE
PINNAS
PLANAR
PUTNAM
REGNAL
REGNAT
REINAS
RHINAL
RUANAS
SAUNAS
SCENAS
SENNAS
SIGNAL
SPINAL
SRANAN
TAINAN
THENAR
TRINAL
UNSNAG
UNSNAP
VARNAS
VEINAL
VERNAL
YUNNAN

•••N•A

AGENDA
AJANTA
AMANDA
AMENRA
ANANDA
BIANCA
BLANCA
BLANDA
BOSNIA
BRENDA
CORNEA
CRANIA
CRENNA
DEANNA
DUENNA
EUPNEA
FAENZA
FRANCA
GLENDA
GLINKA
GOANNA
GUINEA
JOANNA
KAUNDA
KWANZA
LUANDA
NARNIA
OLINDA
PAANGA
PENNIA
QUANTA
QUINOA
RHONDA
RUANDA
RWANDA
SARNIA
SHANIA
SIENNA
STANZA
UGANDA
URANIA
VIENNA
ZINNIA

••••NA

ALUMNA
ANCONA
ARCANA
ARJUNA
ATHENA
BANANA
CABANA
CARINA
CATENA
CESSNA
CORONA
COVINA
CRENNA
DEANNA
DUENNA
ENCINA
ESPANA
FALANA
FARINA
GALENA
GOANNA
GRETNA
GUIANA
GUYANA
HABANA
HAVANA
HELENA
IGUANA
ILEANA
JACANA
JOANNA
KAHUNA
KORUNA
LACUNA
LAGUNA
LAMINA
LATINA
LATONA
LUMINA
MANANA
MARINA
MEDINA
MELINA
MODENA
NOVENA
NUMINA
OKSANA
ORGANA
ORIANA
PARANA
PATINA
PIRANA
POMONA
PRAJNA
PURINA
RAMONA
REGINA
RETINA
ROWENA
ROXANA
RUMINA
SABENA
SALINA
SELENA
SERENA
SHEENA
SIENNA
SMYRNA
STERNA
TANANA
TIRANA
TUCANA
URBANA
VARUNA
VERONA
VICUNA
VIENNA
WINONA
XIMENA
ZENANA

N•B•••

NABBED
NABBER
NABOBS
NABORS
NEBULA
NIBBLE
NOBBLE
NOBLER
NOBLES
NOBODY
NUBBED

NUBBIN
NUBBLE
NUBBLY
NUBIAN
NUBILE

N••B••
NABBED
NABBER
NIBBLE
NIMBLE
NIMBLY
NIMBUS
NOBBLE
NOTBAD
NUBBED
NUBBIN
NUBBLE
NUBBLY
NUMBAT
NUMBED
NUMBER
NUMBLY

N•••B•
NABOBS
NASEBY
NAWABS
NEARBY
NINGBO

•NB•••
ENBLOC
INBORN
INBRED
INBULK
UNBARS
UNBELT
UNBEND
UNBENT
UNBIND
UNBOLT
UNBORN
UNBUSY

•N•B••
ANUBIS
ENABLE
KNOBBY
SNOBBY
SNUBBY
UNABLE

•N••B•
ANNABA
ENROBE
INDABA
INDEBT
KNOBBY
SNOBBY
SNUBBY
UNROBE

••NB••
BONBON
DUNBAR
HENBIT
SINBAD

••N•B•
ANNABA
DANUBE
GONEBY
NINGBO
WENTBY

••N••B
BENUMB
CANTAB
CONFAB
CONJOB
PUNJAB

•••N•B
DIONEB
HOBNOB

N•C•••
NACHOS
NACRES
NECKED
NECTAR
NICAEA
NICEAN
NICELY
NICENE
NICEST
NICETY
NICHES
NICKED
NICKEL
NICKER
NICOLA
NICOLE
NICOLO
NOCENT
NUCHAE
NUCHAL
NUCLEI
NUCLEO

N••C••
NASCAR
NIACIN
NIECES
NONCOM
NOTCHY
NUECES
NUNCIO

N•••C•
NATICK
NAUTCH
NODICE
NOTICE
NOVICE
NUANCE

N••••C
NITRIC
NOETIC
NORDIC

•NC•••
ANCHOR
ANCIEN
ANCONA
ENCAGE
ENCAMP
ENCASE
ENCINA
ENCINO
ENCODE
ENCORE
INCANS
INCASE
INCASH
INCEPT
INCHED
INCHES
INCHON
INCISE
INCITE
INCOME
INCULT
INCURS
INCUSE
ONCALL
UNCAGE
UNCAPS
UNCASE
UNCHIC
UNCIAL
UNCLAD
UNCLES
UNCLOG
UNCOIL
UNCOOL
UNCORK
UNCURL

•N•C••
ANACIN
ANTCOW
ENACTS
KNACKS
KNICKS
KNOCKS
SNACKS
SNICKS
SNOCAT
UNICEF
UNOCAL
VNECKS

•N••C•
ANTICS
ENESCO
ENLACE
ENRICH
ENRICO
ENTICE
INARCH
INDICT
INDUCE
INDUCT
INFACT
INFECT
INJECT
INLUCK
INSECT
INTACT
ONDECK
ONEACT
SNATCH
SNITCH
UNESCO
UNLACE
UNLOCK
UNPACK
UNTACK

•N•••C
ANEMIC
ANGLIC
ANODIC
ANOMIC
ENBLOC
GNOMIC
INSYNC
ONSPEC
UNCHIC
UNIFIC
UNIVAC

••NC••
BONCES
BUNCHE
BUNCHY
BUNCOS
CANCAN
CANCEL
CANCUN
CONCHA
CONCHS
CONCUR
DANCED
DANCER
DANCES
DUNCAN
DUNCES
FENCED
FENCER
FENCES
HINCTY
HONCHO
JUNCOS
LANCED
LANCER
LANCES
LANCET
LUNCHY
MANCHA
MANCHU
MINCED
MINCER
MINCES
MUNCHY
MUNCIE
NONCOM
NUNCIO
OUNCES
PANCHO
PENCEL
PENCIL
PINCER
PONCES
PONCHO
PUNCHY
RANCHO
RANCID
RANCOR
RUNCIE
SANCHO
SANCTA
SYNCED
TINCAL
TINCAN
TINCTS
VINCES
VINCIT
WENCES
WINCED
WINCER
WINCES

••N•C•
ALNICO
ARNICA
CONICS
CONOCO
CYNICS
EUNICE
IGNACE
IONICS
JANICE
KONICA
LUNACY
MENACE
MENSCH
MONACO
MONICA
MUNICH
PANICS
SENECA
SONICS
SUNOCO
TENACE
TONICS
TUNICA
TUNICS
VENICE
ZANUCK

••N••C
CONTAC
FENNEC
FINNIC
MANIAC
MANIOC
MANTIC
PONTIC
RUNDMC
SENLAC
SYNDIC
TANNIC
TENREC
ZENDIC

•••NC•
AGENCY
ATONCE
BIANCA
BLANCA
BLANCH
BLENCH
BOUNCE
BOUNCY
BRANCH
BRONCO
BRONCS
BRUNCH
CHANCE
CHANCY
CHINCH
CLANCY
CLENCH
CLINCH
CRUNCH
DRENCH
EVINCE
FIANCE
FLINCH
FRANCA
FRANCE
FRANCK
FRANCO
FRANCS
FRENCH
GLANCE
GRINCH
HAUNCH
JOUNCE
JOUNCY
LAUNCH
NUANCE
PAUNCH
PLANCK
POUNCE
PRANCE
PRINCE
QUENCH
QUINCE
QUINCY
SCONCE
SEANCE
STANCE
STANCH
STENCH
THENCE
TRANCE
TRENCH
USANCE
WHENCE
WRENCH

•••N•C
ATONIC
BIONIC
CLINIC
COGNAC
CYANIC
EDENIC
ETHNIC
ETONIC
FENNEC
FINNIC
ICONIC
IRENIC
IRONIC
OZONIC
PHONIC
PICNIC
PYKNIC
SCENIC
TANNIC
URANIC

••••NC
FERENC
INSYNC

N•D•••
NADINE
NADIRS
NIDIFY
NODDED
NODDLE
NODICE
NODOFF
NODOSE
NODULE
NUDELY
NUDEST
NUDGED
NUDGER
NUDGES
NUDIST
NUDITY
NUDNIK

N••D••
NASDAQ
NEEDED
NEEDLE
NEEDNT
NODDED
NODDLE
NOODLE
NORDIC

N•••D•
NAIADS
NERUDA
NEVADA
NOBODY
NOMADS

N••••D
NABBED
NAGGED
NAILED
NAPPED
NEARED
NECKED
NEEDED
NEREID
NESTED
NETTED
NICKED
NIMROD
NIPPED
NODDED
NOGOOD
NOISED
NOLEAD
NOLOAD
NOOSED
NOSHED
NOTBAD
NUBBED
NUDGED
NULLED
NUMBED
NURSED
NUTTED

•ND•••
ANDEAN
ANDHOW
ANDREA
ANDREI
ANDRES
ANDREW
ANDREY
ANDROS
ENDALL
ENDASH
ENDEAR
ENDERS
ENDING
ENDIVE
ENDMAN
ENDMEN
ENDORA
ENDOWS
ENDRUN
ENDSUP
ENDUED
ENDUES
ENDURE
ENDURO
ENDUSE
INDABA
INDEBT
INDEED
INDENE
INDENT
INDIAN
INDICT
INDIES
INDIGO
INDIRA
INDITE
INDIUM
INDOOR
INDORE
INDRIS
INDUCE
INDUCT
ONDECK
ONDINE
UNDIES
UNDINE
UNDOER
UNDOES
UNDONE
UNDRAW
UNDULY
UNDYED

•N•D••
ANADEM
ANODES
ANODIC
ANYDAY
CNIDAE
CNIDUS
ONEDAY
ONEDGE
SNIDER
SNYDER

•N••D•
ANANDA
ANHYDR
ENCODE
INSIDE
INVADE
KNEADS
ONEIDA
ONSIDE
SNOODS
UNLADE
UNMADE
UNTIDY

•N•••D
ANELED
ANGLED
ANKLED
ANTEED
ENDUED
ENFOLD
ENGIRD
ENNEAD
ENQUAD
ENSUED
ENURED
ENVIED
GNAWED
INBRED
INCHED
INDEED
INFOLD
INGRID
INHAND
INKIND
INLAID
INLAND
INNEED
INROAD
INTEND
INURED
INWARD
KNIFED
ONHAND
ONHOLD
ONLAND
ONWARD
SNAKED
SNARED
SNIPED
SNORED
SNOWED
UNAGED
UNAWED
UNBEND
UNBIND
UNCLAD
UNDYED
UNFOLD
UNGIRD
UNHAND
UNHEED
UNIPOD
UNITED
UNKIND
UNLAID
UNLEAD
UNLOAD
UNPAID
UNREAD
UNSAID
UNSHED
UNSHOD
UNSOLD
UNTIED
UNTOLD
UNTROD
UNUSED
UNWIND

••ND••
BANDED
BANDIT
BANDOG
BENDAY
BENDED
BENDER

BENDIX
BINDER
BINDUP
BONDED
BUNDLE
CANDID
CANDLE
CANDOR
CINDER
CONDOR
CONDOS
DANDER
DANDIE
DANDLE
DENDRI
DENDRO
DONDER
DUNDEE
FANDOM
FENDED
FENDER
FINDER
FONDER
FONDLE
FONDLY
FONDUE
FUNDED
GANDER
GANDHI
GENDER
GUNDOG
HANDED
HANDEL
HANDIN
HANDLE
HANDON
HANDUP
HINDER
HINDUS
KANDER
KINDER
KINDLE
KINDLY
KINDOF
LANDAU
LANDED
LANDER
LANDHO
LANDIS
LANDON
LANDRY
LENDER
LINDEN
LONDON
LUNDEN
LYNDON
MANDAN
MANDAY
MENDED
MENDEL
MENDER
MENDES
MINDED
MINDER
MONDAY
PANDAS
PANDER
PANDIT
PENDED
PINDAR
PINDUS
PONDER
PUNDIT
RANDOM
RANDRY
RENDER
RONDEL
RONDOS
RUNDLE
RUNDMC
RUNDRY
SANDAL
SANDED
SANDER
SANDIA
SANDRA
SENDAK
SENDER
SENDIN
SENDUP
SONDES
SUNDAE
SUNDAY
SUNDER
SUNDEW
SUNDOG
SUNDRY
SYNDIC
TANDEM
TENDED
TENDER
TENDON
TENDTO
TINDER
TONDOS
TUNDRA
VANDAL
VENDED
VENDEE
VENDOR
WANDER
WENDED
WINDED
WINDER
WINDEX
WINDOM
WINDOW
WINDUP
WONDER
YONDER
ZANDER
ZENDIC
ZENDOS

••N•D•

CANADA
CANIDS
DENUDE
MENADO
MONADS
MONODY
PANADA
RANIDS
SYNODS
XANADU

••N••D

AENEID
ARNOLD
BANDED
BANGED
BANKED
BANNED
BENDED
BINGED
BINNED
BONDED
BONGED
BUNGED
BUNKED
BUNTED
CANARD
CANDID
CANNED
CANOED
CANTED
CENSED
CONFED
CONKED
CONNED
CONOID
CONRAD
CUNARD
DANCED
DENIED
DENNED
DENTED
DINGED
DINNED
DINTED
DONALD
DONNED
DUNKED
DUNNED
ENNEAD
FANGED
FANNED
FENCED
FENDED
FINKED
FINNED
FUNDED
FUNKED
FUNNED
GANGED
GINNED
GONGED
GUNNED
HANDED
HANGED
HENTED
HINGED
HINTED
HONIED
HONKED
HUNTED
INNEED
JINKED
JINXED
JUNKED
KENNED
KINGED
KINKED
KONRAD
LANCED
LANDED
LENSED
LINKED
LONGED
LUNGED
LYNYRD
MANNED
MENDED
MINCED
MINDED
MINTED
MONIED
OINKED
OXNARD
PANNED
PANTED
PENDED
PENNED
PENROD
PENTAD
PINGED
PINKED
PINNED
PONGED
PONGID
PONIED
PUNNED
PUNTED
RANCID
RANGED
RANKED
RANTED
RENTED
RINGED
RINSED
RONALD
SANDED
SENSED
SINBAD
SINEAD
SINGED
SINNED
SUNGOD
SUNNED
SYNCED
TANGED
TANKED
TANNED
TENDED
TENSED
TENTED
TINGED
TINGOD
TINNED
TINTED
VANNED
VENDED
VENTED
WANNED
WANTAD
WANTED
WENDED
WINCED
WINDED
WINGED
WINKED
WONNED
WONTED
YANKED
YENNED
ZINGED
ZONKED

•••ND•

AGENDA
AMANDA
AMENDS
ANANDA
ARENDT
BIONDI
BLANDA
BLENDE
BLENDS
BLINDS
BLONDE
BLONDS
BOUNDS
BRANDO
BRANDS
BRANDT
BRANDX
BRANDY
BRENDA
DIRNDL
EBONDS
ELANDS
EMENDS
FIENDS
FOUNDS
FRONDS
GLANDS
GLENDA
GRANDE
GRANDS
GRINDS
GRUNDY
HOUNDS
HOUNDY
KAUNDA
LUANDA
MAUNDY
MBUNDU
MOUNDS
OLINDA
POUNDS
RHONDA
ROUNDS
RUANDA
RWANDA
SCENDS
SHANDY
SHINDY
SOUNDS
SPENDS
STANDS
TBONDS
TRENDS
TRENDY
UGANDA
UPENDS
VIANDS
WOUNDS
ZOUNDS

•••N•D

ATONED
BANNED
BEANED
BINNED
BRINED
BURNED
CANNED
CLONED
COINED
CONNED
CORNED
CRANED
DAMNED
DARNED
DAWNED
DENNED
DINNED
DONNED
DOWNED
DRONED
DUNNED
DURNED
EARNED
EVENED
FANNED
FAWNED
FINNED
FOINED
FUNNED
GAINED
GINNED
GIRNED
GOUNOD
GOWNED
GUNNED
HORNED
HYMNED
IRONED
JOINED
KEENED
KENNED
KERNED
KILNED
LEANED
LEONID
LIMNED
LOANED
MAENAD
MANNED
MOANED
MOONED
OPENED
OPINED
PAINED
PANNED
PAWNED
PEENED
PENNED
PERNOD
PHONED
PINNED
PLANED
PRUNED
PUNNED
RAINED
REINED
RUINED
SEINED
SHINED
SIGNED
SINNED
SPINED
STONED
SUNNED
TANNED
TINNED
TURNED
TWINED
VANNED
VEINED
WANNED
WARNED
WEANED
WHINED
WONNED
YARNED
YAWNED
YEANED
YENNED

••••ND

ABOUND
ADDEND
ALMOND
APPEND
ARMAND
AROUND
ASCEND
ATHAND
ATTEND
AUFOND
AUGEND
BEHIND
BEYOND
BRIAND
BYHAND
DEFEND
DEMAND
DEMOND
DEPEND
EDMOND
EDMUND
ERRAND
EXPAND
EXPEND
EXTEND
FAGEND
FECUND
FRIEND
GERUND
GROUND
IMPEND
INHAND
INKIND
INLAND
INTEND
ISLAND
JOCUND
LEGEND
LELAND
LEMOND
LIGAND
LOMOND
LOWEND
OBTUND
OFFEND
ONHAND
ONLAND
ORMOND
OSMOND
OSMUND
OSTEND
POLAND
REBEND
REBIND
REFUND
REMAND
REMEND
REMIND
REPAND
RESAND
RESEND
REWIND
RIBAND
ROLAND
ROTUND
SECOND
STRAND
TAGEND
THEEND
UNBEND
UNBIND
UNHAND
UNKIND
UNWIND
UPLAND
UPWIND

NE••••

NEARBY
NEARED
NEARER
NEARLY
NEARTO
NEATEN
NEATER
NEATLY
NEBULA
NECKED
NECTAR
NEEDED
NEEDLE
NEEDNT
NEESON
NEGATE
NEIGHS
NEISSE
NEKTON
NELLIE
NELSON
NEMATO
NENETS
NEPALI
NEPHEW
NEPHRO
NEREID
NEREIS
NEREUS
NEROLI
NERUDA
NERVES
NESSES
NESSIE
NESTEA
NESTED
NESTER
NESTLE
NESTOR
NETHER
NETMAN
NETMEN
NETPAY
NETTED
NETTLE
NETTLY
NETTON
NEUMAN
NEUMES
NEURAL
NEUROL
NEURON
NEUTER
NEVADA
NEVERS
NEVINS
NEVSKY
NEWAGE
NEWARK
NEWELS
NEWEST
NEWISH
NEWLEY
NEWMAN
NEWMAR
NEWTON
NEXTTO

N•E•••

NEEDED
NEEDLE
NEEDNT
NEESON
NIECES
NIELLI
NIELLO
NLEAST
NOESIS
NOETIC
NOEXIT
NUECES

N••E••

NAMELY
NAMERS
NAPERY
NASEBY
NAVELS
NENETS
NEREID
NEREIS
NEREUS
NEVERS
NEWELS
NEWEST
NFLERS
NHLERS
NICEAN
NICELY
NICENE
NICEST
NICETY
NINEAM
NINEPM
NINERS
NINETY
NITERS
NITERY
NLWEST
NOCENT
NOLEAD
NOLENS
NOLESS
NONEGO
NONETS
NOPETS
NOTERS
NOVELS
NOVENA
NUDELY
NUDEST

NUGENT
NUMERO
NYMETS

N•••E•

NABBED
NABBER
NACRES
NAGGED
NAGGER
NAILED
NAILER
NANSEN
NANTES
NAPIER
NAPLES
NAPPED
NAPPER
NAPPES
NASSER
NATTER
NAUSEA
NAVIES
NEARED
NEARER
NEATEN
NEATER
NECKED
NEEDED
NEPHEW
NERVES
NESSES
NESTEA
NESTED
NESTER
NETHER
NETMEN
NETTED
NEUMES
NEUTER
NEWLEY
NGUYEN
NIAMEY
NICAEA
NICHES
NICKED
NICKEL
NICKER
NIECES
NIGHER
NIKKEI
NIPPED
NIPPER
NIPSEY
NISSEN
NITRES
NIXIES
NOBLER
NOBLES
NODDED
NOISED
NOISES
NOONES
NOOSED
NOOSES
NOSHED
NOSHER
NOSHES
NOSIER
NOTYET
NOUMEA
NUBBED
NUCLEI
NUCLEO
NUDGED
NUDGER
NUDGES
NUECES
NUGGET
NULLED
NUMBED
NUMBER
NURSED
NURSER
NURSES
NUTLET
NUTMEG
NUTTED
NUTTER

N••••E

NADINE
NANNIE
NAPPIE
NATIVE
NATURE
NEEDLE
NEGATE
NEISSE
NELLIE
NESSIE
NESTLE
NETTLE
NEWAGE
NIBBLE
NICENE
NICOLE
NIGGLE
NIMBLE
NOBBLE
NODDLE
NODICE
NODOSE
NODULE
NOLOSE
NOMINE
NOMORE
NONAGE
NONAME
NOODLE
NOSALE
NOTATE
NOTICE
NOVICE
NOWISE
NOZZLE
NUANCE
NUBBLE
NUBILE
NUCHAE
NUTATE
NUZZLE

•NE•••

ANELED
ANELES
ANEMIA
ANEMIC
ANERGY
ENERGY
ENESCO
GNEISS
INESSE
KNEADS
KNEELS
KNELLS
ONEACT
ONEDAY
ONEDGE
ONEIDA
ONEILL
ONEMAN
ONETWO
ONEUPS
ONEWAY
PNEUMA
SNEAKS
SNEAKY
SNEERS
SNEERY
SNEEZE
SNEEZY
SNELLS
UNEASE
UNEASY
UNESCO
UNEVEN
VNECKS

•N•E••

ANDEAN
ANGELA
ANGELI
ANGELL
ANGELO
ANGELS
ANGERS
ANNEAL
ANNEXE
ANSELM
ANTEED
ANTERO
ANTEUP
ENDEAR
ENDERS
ENGELS
ENMESH
ENNEAD
ENTERO
ENTERS
INCEPT
INDEBT
INDEED
INDENE
INDENT
INFECT
INFERS
INFEST
INGEAR
INGEST
INHERE
INJECT
INJEST
INKERS
INLETS
INNEED
INNESS
INSEAM
INSECT
INSERT
INSETS
INTEND
INTENS
INTENT
INTERJ
INTERN
INVENT
INVERT
INVEST
KNEELS
ONDECK
ONSETS
SNEERS
SNEERY
SNEEZE
SNEEZY
UNBELT
UNBEND
UNBENT
UNHEED
UNLEAD
UNLESS
UNMEET
UNMESH
UNPEGS
UNPENS
UNREAD
UNREAL
UNREEL
UNREST
UNSEAL
UNSEAT
UNSEEN
UNSEWN
UNSEWS
UNVEIL
UNWELL

•N••E•

ANADEM
ANCIEN
ANDREA
ANDREI
ANDRES
ANDREW
ANDREY
ANELED
ANELES
ANGLED
ANGLER
ANGLES
ANIMES
ANKLED
ANKLES
ANKLET
ANNLEE
ANODES
ANOLES
ANSWER
ANTEED
ANTHEM
ANTHER
ANTLER
ANTRES
CNOTES
ENAMEL
ENATES
ENDMEN
ENDUED
ENDUES
ENSUED
ENSUES
ENTREE
ENURED
ENURES
ENVIED
ENVIER
ENVIES
GNAWED
GNAWER
GNOMES
INANER
INAPET
INBRED
INCHED
INCHES
INDEED
INDIES
INGLES
INGRES
INKIER
INKJET
INKLES
INNEED
INSTEP
INURED
INURES
KNAVES
KNIFED
KNIFES
KNIVES
KNOWER
ONAGER
ONSPEC
ONUSES
ONVIEW
ONYXES
SNAKED
SNAKES
SNARED
SNARES
SNIDER
SNIPED
SNIPER
SNIPES
SNIVEL
SNOPES
SNORED
SNORER
SNORES
SNOWED
SNYDER
TNOTES
UNAGED
UNAWED
UNCLES
UNDIES
UNDOER
UNDOES
UNDYED
UNEVEN
UNFREE
UNGUES
UNHEED
UNICEF
UNISEX
UNITED
UNITER
UNITES
UNMEET
UNOPEN
UNREEL
UNSEEN
UNSHED
UNTIED
UNTIES
UNUSED

•N•••E

ANNEXE
ANNLEE
ANOMIE
ANSATE
ANYONE
CNIDAE
ENABLE
ENCAGE
ENCASE
ENCODE
ENCORE
ENDIVE
ENDURE
ENDUSE
ENGAGE
ENGINE
ENISLE
ENLACE
ENRAGE
ENROBE
ENSILE
ENSURE
ENTICE
ENTIRE
ENTREE
ENZYME
INCASE
INCISE
INCITE
INCOME
INCUSE
INDENE
INDITE
INDORE
INDUCE
INESSE
INFUSE
INHALE
INHERE
INJOKE
INJURE
INLINE
INLOVE
INMATE
INNAGE
INNATE
INOUYE
INSANE
INSIDE
INSOLE
INSURE
INTAKE
INTIME
INTINE
INTONE
INTUNE
INVADE
INVITE
INVOKE
ONDINE
ONEDGE
ONFILE
ONFIRE
ONLINE
ONSALE
ONSIDE
ONSITE
ONTAPE
ONTIME
SNATHE
SNEEZE
SNOOZE
UNABLE
UNCAGE
UNCASE
UNDINE
UNDONE
UNEASE
UNFREE
UNGLUE
UNIATE
UNIQUE
UNLACE
UNLADE
UNLIKE
UNMADE
UNMAKE
UNPILE
UNRIPE
UNROBE
UNSAFE
UNSURE
UNTRUE
UNTUNE
UNWISE
UNWOVE
UNYOKE

••NE••

ADNEXA
AENEAS
AENEID
ANNEAL
ANNEXE
ARNESS
ARNETT
BONERS
BONEUP
CANERS
CINEMA
CONEYS
CUNEAL
DINEIN
DINEON
DINERO
DINERS
DONEES
DONEIN
DONETS
DONEUP
DUNERA
ENNEAD
ERNEST
FINELY
FINERY
FINEST
GENERA
GENETS
GENEVA
GENEVE
GONEBY
GONERS
HONEST
HONEYS
INNEED
INNESS
JUNEAU
KINEMA
LINEAL
LINEAR
LINENS
LINENY
LINERS
LINEUP
LONELY
LONERS
MANEGE
MINERS
MONERA
MONETA
MONEYS
NENETS
NINEAM
NINEPM
NINERS
NINETY
NONEGO
NONETS
ORNERY
OWNERS
PANELS
PINEAL
PINERO
PINERY
RANEES
RENEGE
RENEWS
RONELY
SANELY
SANEST
SENECA
SENEGA
SINEAD
SINEWS
SINEWY
TENENS
TENETS
TINEAR
TONERS
TONEUP
TUNEIN
TUNERS
TUNEUP
VENEER
VENETO
VINERY
WANERS
WINERY

••N•E•

ANNLEE
ARNHEM
BANDED
BANGED
BANGER
BANKED
BANKER
BANNED
BANNER
BANTER
BENDED
BENDER
BINDER
BINGED
BINGES
BINNED
BONCES
BONDED
BONGED
BONIER
BONNES
BONNET
BONZES
BUNGED
BUNGEE
BUNKED
BUNKER
BUNSEN
BUNTED
BUNTER
BUNUEL
CANCEL
CANIER
CANKER
CANNED
CANNEL
CANNER
CANNES
CANOED
CANOES
CANTED
CANTER
CENSED
CENSER
CENSES
CENTER
CINDER
CONFED
CONFER
CONGER
CONIES
CONKED
CONKER
CONMEN
CONNED
CONNER
CONTES
CONVEX
CONVEY
DANCED
DANCER
DANCES
DANDER
DANGER
DANIEL
DANKER
DANNER
DANTES
DENIED
DENIER
DENIES
DENNED
DENSER
DENTED
DENVER
DENZEL
DINGED
DINKEY
DINNED
DINNER
DINTED

DONDER
DONEES
DONKEY
DONNED
DONNEE
DONNER
DUNCES
DUNDEE
DUNKED
DUNKER
DUNNED
FANGED
FANJET
FANNED
FENCED
FENCER
FENCES
FENDED
FENDER
FENMEN
FENNEC
FENNEL
FINDER
FINGER
FINKED
FINNED
FINNEY
FONDER
FUNDED
FUNKED
FUNNED
FUNNEL
GANDER
GANGED
GANGER
GANGES
GANNET
GENDER
GENIES
GENRES
GINGER
GINNED
GONGED
GUNMEN
GUNNED
GUNNEL
GUNNER
GUNTER
HANDED
HANDEL
HANGED
HANGER
HANKER
HANLEY
HANSEL
HENLEY
HENNER
HENTED
HINDER
HINGED
HINGES
HINTED
HINTER

HONIED
HONKED
HONKER
HUNGER
HUNKER
HUNTED
HUNTER
INNEED
JANSEN
JENNER
JENNET
JENNEY
JENSEN
JINKED
JINXED
JINXES
JUNKED
JUNKER
JUNKET
KANDER
KENNED
KENNEL
KENNER
KINDER
KINGED
KINKED
KINSEY
LANCED
LANCER
LANCES
LANCET
LANDED
LANDER
LANIER
LANKER
LENDER
LENSED
LENSES
LENTEN
LINDEN
LINGER
LINIER
LINKED
LINKER
LINNET
LINNEY
LINSEY
LINTEL
LINTER
LONGED
LONGER
LONGES
LUNDEN
LUNGED
LUNGES
LUNKER
LYNLEY
LYNXES
MANGER
MANNED
MANNER
MANSES
MANTEL

MANUEL
MENDED
MENDEL
MENDER
MENDES
MENKEN
MENNEN
MINCED
MINCER
MINCES
MINDED
MINDER
MINKES
MINTED
MINTER
MINUET
MINXES
MONGER
MONIED
MONIES
MONKEY
MONTEL
MONTES
MONTEZ
NANSEN
NANTES
OINKED
OUNCES
PANDER
PANNED
PANNER
PANNES
PANTED
PANZER
PENCEL
PENDED
PENMEN
PENNED
PENNER
PENNEY
PENSEE
PINCER
PINGED
PINIER
PINKED
PINKEN
PINKER
PINNED
PINNER
PINTER
PONCES
PONDER
PONGED
PONGEE
PONIED
PONIES
PONTES
PUNIER
PUNKER
PUNNED
PUNNET
PUNTED
PUNTER

RANEES
RANGED
RANGER
RANGES
RANKED
RANKER
RANTED
RANTER
RENDER
RENNES
RENNET
RENTED
RENTER
RINGED
RINGER
RINSED
RINSES
RONDEL
RUNLET
RUNNEL
RUNNER
SANDED
SANDER
SANGER
SANSEI
SANTEE
SENDER
SENNET
SENSED
SENSEI
SENSES
SINGED
SINGER
SINGES
SINKER
SINNED
SINNER
SINTER
SONDES
SONNET
SUNDER
SUNDEW
SUNKEN
SUNNED
SUNSET
SYNCED
TANDEM
TANGED
TANKED
TANKER
TANNED
TANNER
TANTES
TENDED
TENDER
TENREC
TENSED
TENSER
TENSES
TENTED
TENTER
TINDER
TINGED

TINGES
TINIER
TINKER
TINMEN
TINNED
TINNER
TINSEL
TINTED
TINTER
TONIER
TONNES
TUNNEL
TUNNEY
VANIER
VANNED
VENDED
VENDEE
VENEER
VENTED
VENTER
VENUES
VINCES
VINIER
WANDER
WANIER
WANNED
WANNER
WANTED
WENCES
WENDED
WINCED
WINCER
WINCES
WINDED
WINDER
WINDEX
WINGED
WINGER
WINIER
WINKED
WINKER
WINNER
WINTER
WINZES
WONDER
WONNED
WONTED
WYNTER
YANKED
YANKEE
YENNED
YONDER
ZANDER
ZANIER
ZANIES
ZENGER
ZINGED
ZINGER
ZONKED
ZONKER

••N••E

ADNATE
AGNATE
ANNEXE
ANNLEE
AUNTIE
BANGLE
BINATE
BONNIE
BUNCHE
BUNDLE
BUNGEE
BUNGLE
BYNAME
CANAPE
CANDLE
CANINE
CANNAE
CANTLE
CANUTE
CENOTE
CENTRE
CINQUE
CONNIE
CONTRE
CONURE
DANDIE
DANDLE
DANGLE
DANGME
DANUBE
DENGUE
DENISE
DENOTE
DENUDE
DINGLE
DONATE
DONGLE
DONNEE
DUNDEE
EUNICE
FANNIE
FINALE
FINITE
FONDLE
FONDUE
GANGLE
GANGUE
GENEVE
GENOME
GENTLE
GUNITE
HANDLE
HANKIE
HONORE
IGNACE
IGNITE
IGNORE
INNAGE
INNATE
IONISE
IONIZE
JANGLE
JANICE
JANINE

JENNIE
JINGLE
JUNGLE
JUNKIE
KINDLE
KINGME
LANATE
LANOSE
LENAPE
LENNIE
LENORE
LINAGE
LONGUE
LUNATE
MANAGE
MANEGE
MANGLE
MANQUE
MANTLE
MENACE
MENAGE
MENSAE
MINGLE
MINNIE
MINUTE
MONROE
MUNCIE
NANNIE
NONAGE
NONAME
OENONE
ORNATE
PENNAE
PENSEE
PINITE
PINKIE
PINNAE
PINOLE
PINTLE
PONGEE
PUNKIE
RANKLE
RENAME
RENEGE
RENNIE
RENOTE
RONNIE
RUNCIE
RUNDLE
SANTEE
SENATE
SINGLE
SINISE
SUNDAE
TANGLE
TENACE
TENURE
TINGLE
TINKLE
TONGUE
TONITE
VENDEE
VENICE

VENIRE
VENITE
VINNIE
WANGLE
WINKIE
WINKLE
WINNIE
YANKEE
ZONATE

•••NE•

AKENES
ALINES
AMINES
ATONED
ATONES
AZINES
BAINES
BANNED
BANNER
BARNES
BARNEY
BEANED
BINNED
BIRNEY
BONNES
BONNET
BORNEO
BOWNET
BRINED
BRINES
BRUNEI
BRUNET
BURNED
BURNER
BURNET
BURNEY
BYRNES
CAGNEY
CANNED
CANNEL
CANNER
CANNES
CARNES
CARNET
CARNEY
CHANEL
CHANEY
CHINES
CLINES
CLONED
CLONES
COINED
COINER
CONNED
CONNER
COONEY
CORNEA
CORNED
CORNEL
CORNER
CORNET
CRANED

CRANES
CRENEL
CRONES
CYGNET
DABNEY
DAMNED
DANNER
DARNED
DARNEL
DARNER
DAWNED
DENNED
DINNED
DINNER
DIONEB
DISNEY
DONNED
DONNEE
DONNER
DOWNED
DOWNER
DOWNEY
DRONED
DRONER
DRONES
DUNNED
DURNED
EARNED
EARNER
EISNER
EUPNEA
EVENED
EVENER
FANNED
FAWNED
FAWNER
FENNEC
FENNEL
FINNED
FINNEY
FLYNET
FOINED
FUNNED
FUNNEL
GAINED
GAINER
GANNET
GARNER
GARNET
GINNED
GIRNED
GOWNED
GUINEA
GUNNED
GUNNEL
GUNNER
GURNEY
HAINES
HEANEY
HEFNER
HENNER
HORNED
HORNER

HORNET
HORNEY
HYMNED
INANER
IRENES
IRONED
IRONER
JENNER
JENNET
JENNEY
JITNEY
JOINED
JOINER
JOYNER
KAVNER
KEENED
KEENEN
KEENER
KENNED
KENNEL
KENNER
KERNED
KERNEL
KEYNES
KIDNEY
KILNED
KRONER
LEANED
LEANER
LEONES
LERNER
LIANES
LIENEE
LIMNED
LIMNER
LINNET
LINNEY
LIONEL
LIONET
LOANED
LOANER
LOONEY
MAGNET
MANNED
MANNER
MARNER
MEANER
MENNEN
MILNER
MOANED
MOANER
MOINES
MOONED
MOONEY
NOONES
OPENED
OPENER
OPINED
OPINER
OPINES
ORKNEY
PAINED
PANNED

PANNER
PANNES
PAWNED
PAWNEE
PAWNER
PEENED
PENNED
PENNER
PENNEY
PHONED
PHONES
PHONEY
PINNED
PINNER
PLANED
PLANER
PLANES
PLANET
PRUNED
PRUNER
PRUNES
PUNNED
PUNNET
RADNER
RAINED
RAINER
RAINES
RAINEY
REINED
REINER
RENNES
RENNET
REUNES
RODNEY
ROMNEY
ROONEY
RUINED
RUINER
RUNNEL
RUNNER
SCENES
SCONES
SEINED
SEINER
SEINES
SENNET
SHINED
SHINER
SHINES
SIDNEY
SIGNED
SIGNEE
SIGNER
SIGNET
SIMNEL
SINNED
SINNER
SONNET
SOONER
SPINED
SPINEL
SPINES
SPINET

STONED
STONER
STONES
SUMNER
SUNNED
SWANEE
SYDNEY
TANNED
TANNER
TBONES
TEENER
TERNES
THANES
TINNED
TINNER
TONNES
TOWNER
TRINES
TUNNEL
TUNNEY
TURNED
TURNER
TWINED
TWINES
USENET
VAINER
VANNED
VARNEY
VEINED
WAGNER
WANNED
WANNER
WAPNER
WARNED
WARNER
WATNEY
WEANED
WERNER
WHINED
WHINER
WHINES
WHINEY
WIENER
WINNER
WONNED
YARNED
YAWNED
YAWNER
YEANED
YENNED

•••N•E
ATONCE
AVENGE
AVENUE
BEANIE
BERNIE
BLENDE
BLONDE
BONNIE
BOUNCE
BRONTE
BRONZE
CANNAE
CHANCE
CHANGE
CONNIE
CRINGE
DIANNE
DIONNE
DONNEE
EVINCE
EVONNE
FANNIE
FAUNAE
FIANCE
FLANGE
FLENSE
FRANCE
FRINGE
GLANCE
GLENNE
GRANDE
GRANGE
GRUNGE
GWYNNE
JEANNE
JENNIE
JOANIE
JOANNE
JOUNCE
LAINIE
LENNIE
LEONIE
LIENEE
LOONIE
LOUNGE
MARNIE
MEANIE
MINNIE
NANNIE
NUANCE
ODENSE
ORANGE
PAWNEE
PENNAE
PINNAE
PLANTE
PLUNGE
POINTE
POUNCE
PRANCE
PRINCE
PRYNNE
PUENTE
QUINCE
RENNIE
RONNIE
SAINTE
SCONCE
SEANCE
SIGNEE
SPONGE
STANCE
SWANEE
THENCE
TOONIE
TOWNIE
TRANCE
TWINGE
USANCE
VIENNE
VINNIE
WEENIE
WHENCE
WINNIE
YVONNE

••••NE
ACHENE
ACTONE
AFFINE
AHERNE
ALDINE
ALFINE
ALKENE
ALPINE
ANYONE
ARCANE
ARLENE
ARSENE
ATHENE
ATTUNE
BEGONE
BEMINE
BLAINE
BOURNE
BOVINE
BROWNE
BUTANE
BUTENE
BYGONE
BYLINE
CANINE
CAPONE
CELINE
CETANE
CHAINE
COHUNE
COSINE
DAMONE
DAPHNE
DAYONE
DEBONE
DEFINE
DEPONE
DEVINE
DIANNE
DIONNE
DIVINE
DOMINE
DWAYNE
ELAINE
ELAYNE
ENGINE
EOCENE
EQUINE
ERMINE
ESSENE
ETERNE
ETHANE
ETHENE
EUGENE
EVONNE
EVZONE
FALINE
FAMINE
FELINE
FILENE
GAMINE
GLENNE
GREENE
GWYNNE
GYRENE
HELENE
HUMANE
IMFINE
IMMUNE
INDENE
INLINE
INSANE
INTINE
INTONE
INTUNE
IODINE
IRLENE
IRVINE
ISMENE
JANINE
JEANNE
JEJUNE
JOANNE
JOLENE
KALINE
KETONE
LATENE
LEVENE
LEVINE
LIERNE
LUPINE
LUPONE
LYSINE
MALONE
MARINE
MAXENE
MAXINE
MIFUNE
MODINE
MOLINE
MURINE
NADINE
NICENE
NOMINE
OCTANE
OENONE
ONDINE
ONLINE
ORPINE
OSCINE
PATINE
PAVANE
PROCNE
PRYNNE
PUISNE
PURINE
RACINE
RAMONE
RAPINE
RATINE
RAVINE
RECANE
REDONE
REFINE
RELINE
REPINE
RETENE
RETUNE
REZONE
ROCKNE
ROXANE
SABINE
SALINE
SCARNE
SELENE
SERENE
SERINE
SHAYNE
SHRINE
SILONE
SIMONE
SLOANE
SOFINE
SOIGNE
SPLINE
STERNE
STRINE
SUPINE
THRONE
TIRANE
TISANE
TRIUNE
TULANE
TYRONE
UNDINE
UNDONE
UNTUNE
URBANE
URSINE
VIENNE
VISINE
WAHINE
XYLENE
YVONNE

NF••••
NFLERS

N••F••
NONFAT

N•••F•
NIDIFY
NODOFF
NOTIFY

N••••F
NODOFF

•NF•••
ENFANT
ENFOLD
INFACT
INFAMY
INFANT
INFECT
INFERS
INFEST
INFIRM
INFLOW
INFLUX
INFOLD
INFORM
INFULL
INFUSE
ONFILE
ONFIRE
ONFOOT
UNFAIR
UNFITS
UNFOLD
UNFREE
UNFURL

•N•F••
INAFIX
INAFOG
KNIFED
KNIFES
SNAFUS
SNIFFS
SNIFFY
SNUFFS
SNUFFY
UNIFIC

•N••F•
SNIFFS
SNIFFY
SNUFFS
SNUFFY
UNSAFE

•N•••F
ENGULF
INHALF
UNICEF

••NF••
CANFUL
CONFAB
CONFED
CONFER
GUNFOR
MANFUL
NONFAT
PANFRY
PANFUL
RANFOR
RUNFOR
SINFUL

••N•F•
CANIFF
KUNGFU
MINIFY
RANOFF
RUNOFF
SENUFO
VINIFY

••N••F
CANIFF
KINDOF
RANOFF
RUNOFF

NG••••
NGUYEN

N•G•••
NAGANO
NAGGED
NAGGER
NAGOYA
NEGATE
NIGGLE
NIGHER
NIGHTS
NIGHTY
NOGGIN
NOGOOD
NUGENT
NUGGET

N••G••
NAGGED
NAGGER
NAUGHT
NEIGHS
NIGGLE
NILGAI
NINGBO
NOGGIN
NORGAY
NOUGAT
NOUGHT
NUDGED
NUDGER
NUDGES
NUGGET

N•••G•
NEWAGE
NONAGE
NONEGO

N••••G
NAMING
NIXING
NOSING
NOTING
NUKING
NUTMEG

•NG•••
ANGELA
ANGELI
ANGELL
ANGELO
ANGELS
ANGERS
ANGKOR
ANGLED
ANGLER
ANGLES
ANGLIA
ANGLIC
ANGLOS
ANGOLA
ANGORA
ENGAGE
ENGELS
ENGINE
ENGIRD
ENGIRT
ENGLUT
ENGRAM
ENGULF
INGEAR
INGEST
INGLES
INGMAR
INGOTS
INGRAM
INGRES
INGRID
UNGIRD
UNGIRT
UNGLUE
UNGUAL
UNGUES
UNGUIS

•N•G••
ANSGAR
ENIGMA
KNAGGY
KNIGHT
ONAGER
SNAGGY
SNUGLI
SNUGLY
UNAGED

•N••G•
ANERGY
ENCAGE
ENERGY
ENGAGE
ENOUGH
ENRAGE
ENSIGN
INDIGO
INNAGE
KNAGGY
ONEDGE
ONHIGH
SNAGGY
UNCAGE
UNPEGS
UNRIGS

•N•••G
ANALOG
ANWANG
ANYANG
ENDING
INAFOG
INKING
INNING
UNCLOG
UNPLUG
UNSNAG
UNSUNG

••NG••
BANGED
BANGER
BANGKA
BANGLE
BANGOR
BANGUI
BANGUP
BENGAL
BENGAY
BINGED
BINGES
BONGED
BONGOS
BUNGED
BUNGEE
BUNGLE
CONGAS
CONGER
CONGOU
DANGER
DANGLE
DANGLY
DANGME
DENGUE
DINGED
DINGHY
DINGLE
DINGUS
DONGLE
FANGED
FINGER
FUNGUS
GANGED
GANGER
GANGES
GANGLE
GANGLY
GANGUE
GANGUP
GINGER
GONGED

GUNGHO
HANGAR
HANGED
HANGER
HANGIN
HANGON
HANGUL
HANGUP
HINGED
HINGES
HINGIS
HUNGER
HUNGIN
HUNGON
HUNGRY
HUNGUP
HUNGWU
JANGLE
JANGLY
JINGLE
JINGLY
JUNGLE
JUNGLY
KINGED
KINGLY
KINGME
KUNGFU
LANGUR
LENGTH
LINGER
LINGUA
LONGAN
LONGED
LONGER
LONGES
LONGLY
LONGUE
LUNGED
LUNGES
MANGER
MANGLE
MANGOS
MINGLE
MONGER
MONGOL
MUNGOS
NINGBO
PENGHU
PINGED
PONGED
PONGEE
PONGID
RANGED
RANGER
RANGES
RANGUP
RINGED
RINGER
RINGUP
RUNGUP
SANGER
SANGTO
SINGED
SINGER
SINGES
SINGIN
SINGLE
SINGLY
SINGTO
SUNGOD
TANGED
TANGLE
TANGLY
TANGOS
TANGUY
TINGED
TINGES
TINGLE
TINGLY
TINGOD
TONGAN
TONGUE
WANGLE
WINGED
WINGER
WINGIT
XINGIN
YANGON
YUNGLO
ZENGER
ZINGED
ZINGER

••N•G•

BENIGN
GINKGO
GONOGO
INNAGE
LINAGE
MANAGE
MANEGE
MENAGE
NONAGE
NONEGO
RENEGE
SENEGA

••N••G

AWNING
BANDOG
BENING
BONING
CANING
DANANG
DANZIG
DINING
FINING
GUNDOG
HONING
INNING
KENNYG
LINING
MINING
OWNING
PENANG
PINING
SONTAG
SUNDOG
TONING
TUNING
VINING
WANING
WINING
WONMUG
ZONING

•••NG•

AVENGE
BEINGS
BOINGO
BRINGS
CHANGE
CLANGS
CLINGS
CLINGY
CRINGE
DOINGS
DRINGS
ERYNGO
FLANGE
FLINGS
FRINGE
FRINGY
GOINGS
GRANGE
GRINGO
GRUNGE
GRUNGY
HMONGS
ICINGS
KIANGS
LIANGS
LOUNGE
OLINGO
ORANGE
ORANGS
ORANGY
ORINGS
PAANGA
PLUNGE
PRANGS
PRONGS
QUANGO
SLANGS
SLANGY
SLINGS
SPONGE
SPONGY
STINGO
STINGS
STINGY
SWINGS
SWINGY
THINGS
THINGY
THONGS
TWANGS
TWANGY
TWINGE
UBANGI
WHANGS
WRINGS
WRONGS

•••N•G

EGGNOG
KENNYG
KOENIG
STENOG
UNSNAG

••••NG

AAHING
ABYING
ACHING
ACTING
ADDING
AGEING
AIDING
AILING
AIMING
AIRING
ANWANG
ANYANG
ARCING
ARMING
ASKING
AWNING
BAAING
BAKING
BALING
BARING
BARONG
BASING
BATING
BAYING
BBKING
BELONG
BENING
BERING
BIDING
BIKING
BITING
BLUING
BODING
BOEING
BOGONG
BONING
BOOING
BORING
BOWING
BOXING
BUSING
BUTUNG
BUYING
CAGING
CAKING
CANING
CARING
CASING
CAVING
CAWING
CEDING
CHIANG
CITING
CLUING
CODING
COMING
COOING
COPING
CORING
COWING
CRYING
CUBING
CURING
DANANG
DARING
DATING
DATONG
DAZING
DEKING
DELONG
DEWING
DICING
DIKING
DINING
DIVING
DOLING
DOMING
DOPING
DOSING
DOTING
DOZING
DRYING
DUGONG
DUKING
DUPING
DURING
DYEING
EALING
EARING
EASING
EATING
EBBING
EDGING
EGGING
ENDING
EPPING
ERRING
ERVING
EYEING
FACING
FADING
FAKING
FARING
FAXING
FAZING
FEEING
FETING
FIFING
FILING
FINING
FIRING
FIXING
FLYING
FOXING
FRYING
FUMING
FUSING
FUZING
GAGING
GAMING
GAPING
GATING
GAZING
GEEING
GIBING
GIVING
GLUING
GORING
GUYING
GYBING
HALING
HARING
HATING
HAVING
HAWING
HAYING
HAZING
HEWING
HEXING
HIDING
HIEING
HIKING
HIRING
HIVING
HOEING
HOLING
HOMING
HONING
HOPING
HOSING
HYPING
ICHING
IDLING
IMPING
INKING
INNING
IRKING
IRVING
JADING
JAPING
JAWING
JIBING
JIVING
JOKING
JUKING
KDLANG
KEYING
KITING
LACING
LADING
LAMING
LAVING
LAWING
LAYING
LAZING
LIKING
LIMING
LINING
LIPENG
LIVING
LOPING
LOSING
LOVING
LOWING
LUBING
LURING
LUTING
MAKING
MATING
MEKONG
METING
MEWING
MIKING
MIMING
MINING
MIRING
MIXING
MOOING
MOPING
MOVING
MOWING
MUSING
MUTING
NAMING
NIXING
NOSING
NOTING
NUKING
OARING
OBLONG
OFFING
OGLING
OILING
OOHING
OOLONG
OOZING
OPTING
ORBING
OUTING
OWNING
PACING
PADANG
PAGING
PAHANG
PALING
PARANG
PARING
PAVING
PAWING
PAYING
PEKING
PENANG
PIKING
PILING
PINING
PIPING
PLYING
POKING
POLING
PORING
POSING
PRYING
PULING
RACING
RAGING
RAKING
RARING
RASING
RATING
RAVING
RAZING
REDING
REHANG
REHUNG
RESING
RICING
RIDING
RILING
RIMING
RISING
RIVING
ROBING
ROPING
ROVING
ROWING
RULING
SARONG
SATANG
SATING
SAVING
SAWING
SAYING
SEEING
SEWING
SHYING
SIDING
SIRING
SITING
SIXING
SIZING
SKIING
SKYING
SLUING
SOLING
SOLONG
SOWING
SPRANG
SPRING
SPRUNG
SPYING
STRING
STRONG
STRUNG
TAKING
TAMING
TAPING
TARING
TAWING
TAXING
TEEING
THRONG
TIDING
TIEING
TILING
TIMING
TIRING
TOEING
TONING
TOTING
TOWING
TOYING
TRUING
TRYING
TUBING
TUNING
TURING
TYPING
UNSUNG
UPPING
URGING
VEXING
VIKING
VINING
VOTING
VOWING
WADING
WAGING
WAKING
WANING
WARING
WAVING
WAXING
WILING
WINING
WIPING
WIRING
WOOING
WOWING
YAWING
YOKING
ZONING

NH••••

NHLERS

N•H•••

NIHILO
NOHITS

N••H••

NACHOS
NASHUA
NATHAN
NEPHEW
NEPHRO
NETHER
NICHES
NIGHER
NIGHTS
NIGHTY
NIIHAU
NOSHED
NOSHER
NOSHES
NOSHOW
NUCHAE
NUCHAL

N•••H•

NAUGHT
NAVAHO
NEIGHS
NINTHS
NORTHS
NOTCHY
NOUGHT
NYMPHS

N••••H

NAMATH
NAUTCH
NEWISH
NULLAH

•NH•••

ANHYDR
ENHALO
INHALE
INHALF
INHAND
INHAUL
INHERE
ONHAND
ONHIGH
ONHOLD
UNHAND
UNHEED
UNHOLY
UNHOOK
UNHURT

•N•H••

ANCHOR
ANDHOW
ANNHON
ANTHEM
ANTHER
ANYHOW
INCHED
INCHES
INCHON
UNCHIC
UNSHED
UNSHOD

•N••H•

KNIGHT
SNATHE
SNATHS

•N•••H

ENDASH
ENMESH
ENOUGH
ENRICH
INARCH
INCASH
INRUSH

INWITH
ONHIGH
ONRUSH
SNATCH
SNITCH
UNLASH
UNMESH
UNWISH

••NH••
ANNHON
ARNHEM
BENHUR
DUNHAM
JANHUS
MENHIR
SENHOR
TINHAT

••N•H•
BUNCHE
BUNCHY
CANTHI
CONCHA
CONCHS
DINGHY
GANDHI
GUNGHO
GUNSHY
HONCHO
HONSHU
JONAHS
LANDHO
LUNCHY
MANCHA
MANCHU
MONTHS
MUNCHY
MYNAHS
NINTHS
PANCHO
PENGHU
PONCHO
PUNCHY
RANCHO
SANCHO
TENTHS
XANTHO

••N••H
BANISH
DANISH
FINISH
HANNAH
JINNAH
LENGTH
MENSCH
MUNICH
ORNITH
PUNISH
PUNKAH
TONISH
VANISH
WINISH
ZENITH

•••N•H
BLANCH
BLENCH
BRANCH
BRUNCH
CHINCH
CLENCH
CLINCH
CRUNCH
DRENCH
FLINCH
FRENCH
GRINCH
HANNAH
HAUNCH
JINNAH
LAUNCH
PAUNCH
PLINTH
QUENCH
STANCH
STENCH
TRENCH
WRENCH

NI••••
NIACIN
NIAMEY
NIBBLE
NICAEA
NICEAN
NICELY
NICENE
NICEST
NICETY
NICHES
NICKED
NICKEL
NICKER
NICOLA
NICOLE
NICOLO
NIDIFY
NIECES
NIELLI
NIELLO
NIGGLE
NIGHER
NIGHTS
NIGHTY
NIHILO
NIIHAU
NIKITA
NIKKEI
NIKOLA
NILGAI
NIMBLE
NIMBLY
NIMBUS
NIMINY
NIMITZ
NIMROD
NINEAM
NINEPM
NINERS
NINETY
NINGBO
NINJAS
NINTHS
NIPPED
NIPPER
NIPPON
NIPPUR
NIPSAT
NIPSEY
NIPUPS
NISSAN
NISSEN
NITERS
NITERY
NITRES
NITRIC
NITWIT
NIXIES
NIXING

N•I•••
NAIADS
NAILED
NAILER
NAILIN
NAIRAS
NEIGHS
NEISSE
NIIHAU
NOIRON
NOISED
NOISES

N••I••
NADINE
NADIRS
NAMING
NAPIER
NARIAL
NATICK
NATION
NATIVE
NAVIES
NEVINS
NEWISH
NIDIFY
NIHILO
NIKITA
NIMINY
NIMITZ
NIXIES
NIXING
NODICE
NOHITS
NOMINE
NORIAS
NOSIER
NOSILY
NOSING
NOTICE
NOTIFY
NOTING
NOTION
NOVICE
NOWISE
NUBIAN
NUBILE
NUDIST
NUDITY
NUKING
NUMINA

N•••I•
NAILIN
NANNIE
NAPKIN
NAPPIE
NARNIA
NARVIK
NELLIE
NEREID
NEREIS
NESSIE
NIACIN
NITRIC
NITWIT
NOESIS
NOETIC
NOEXIT
NOGGIN
NORDIC
NORRIS
NUBBIN
NUDNIK
NUNCIO
NUTKIN
NUTRIA
NYQUIL

N••••I
NAPOLI
NEPALI
NEROLI
NIELLI
NIKKEI
NILGAI
NUCLEI

•NI•••
ANIMAL
ANIMAS
ANIMES
ANIMUS
ANIONS
ANITRA
CNIDAE
CNIDUS
ENIGMA
ENISLE
INIONS
INITIO
KNICKS
KNIFED
KNIFES
KNIGHT
KNIVES
ONIONS
ONIONY
SNICKS
SNIDER
SNIFFS
SNIFFY
SNIPED
SNIPER
SNIPES
SNIPPY
SNITCH
SNIVEL
UNIATE
UNIATS
UNICEF
UNIFIC
UNIONS
UNIPOD
UNIQUE
UNISEX
UNISON
UNISYS
UNITAL
UNITAS
UNITED
UNITER
UNITES
UNIVAC

•N•I••
ANCIEN
ANNIKA
ANOINT
ANTICS
ANVILS
ENCINA
ENCINO
ENDING
ENDIVE
ENGINE
ENGIRD
ENGIRT
ENLIST
ENMITY
ENNIUS
ENRICH
ENRICO
ENSIGN
ENSILE
ENTICE
ENTIRE
ENTITY
ENVIED
ENVIER
ENVIES
GNEISS
INCISE
INCITE
INDIAN
INDICT
INDIES
INDIGO
INDIRA
INDITE
INDIUM
INFIRM
INKIER
INKIND
INKING
INLINE
INNING
INSIDE
INSIST
INSITU
INTIMA
INTIME
INTINE
INUITS
INVITE
INVIVO
INWITH
ONDINE
ONEIDA
ONEILL
ONFILE
ONFIRE
ONHIGH
ONLINE
ONSIDE
ONSITE
ONTIME
ONVIEW
SNAILS
UNBIND
UNCIAL
UNDIES
UNDINE
UNFITS
UNGIRD
UNGIRT
UNKIND
UNKINK
UNLIKE
UNLINK
UNOILY
UNPILE
UNPINS
UNRIGS
UNRIPE
UNTIDY
UNTIED
UNTIES
UNWILY
UNWIND
UNWISE
UNWISH
UNZIPS

•N••I•
ANACIN
ANEMIA
ANEMIC
ANGLIA
ANGLIC
ANNUIT
ANODIC
ANOMIC
ANOMIE
ANTRIM
ANUBIS
ENJOIN
ENOKIS
ENOSIS
ENTAIL
ENVOIS
GNOMIC
GNOSIS
INAFIX
INDRIS
INGRID
INITIO
INLAID
INSTIL
INTUIT
INVAIN
SNOWIN
UNCHIC
UNCOIL
UNFAIR
UNGUIS
UNIFIC
UNKNIT
UNLAID
UNPAID
UNSAID
UNVEIL

•N•••I
ANDREI
ANGELI
ANNULI
SNUGLI

••NI••
ALNICO
AMNION
ANNIKA
ARNICA
AWNING
BANISH
BENIGN
BENING
BENITO
BONIER
BONING
BONITO
BUNION
CANIDS
CANIER
CANIFF
CANINE
CANING
CONICS
CONIES
CONIUM
CYNICS
DANIEL
DANISH
DENIAL
DENIED
DENIER
DENIES
DENIMS
DENIRO
DENISE
DINING
DONITZ
ELNINO
ENNIUS
EONIAN
EUNICE
FANION
FENIAN
FINIAL
FINING
FINISH
FINITE
FINITO
GENIAL
GENIES
GENIUS
GUNITE
HONIED
HONING
IGNITE
INNING
IONIAN
IONICS
IONISE
IONIUM
IONIZE
JANICE
JANINE
JUNIOR
KONICA
LANIER
LENITY
LINIER
LINING
MANIAC
MANIAS
MANILA
MANIOC
MENIAL
MENINX
MINIFY
MINIMA
MINIMS
MINING
MINION
MINIUM
MONICA
MONIED
MONIES
MONISM
MONIST
MUNICH
OMNIUM
ORNITH
OWNING
PANICS
PINIER
PINING
PINION
PINITE
PONIED
PONIES
PUNIER
PUNILY
PUNISH
RANIDS
RUNINS
SANITY
SENIOR
SENITI
SINISE
SONICS
TANIST
TINIER
TINILY
TONICS
TONIER
TONING
TONISH
TONITE
TUNICA
TUNICS
TUNING
VANIER
VANISH
VANITY
VENIAL
VENICE
VENIRE
VENITE
VINIER
VINIFY
VINING
WANIER
WANING
WINIER
WINING
WINISH
ZANIER
ZANIES
ZANILY
ZENITH
ZONING

••N•I•
AENEID
ANNUIT
AUNTIE
BANDIT
BENDIX
BENOIT
BONNIE
BUNYIP
CANDID
CANLIT
CONNIE
CONOID
DANDIE
DANZIG
DENNIS
DENTIL
DENTIN
DINEIN
DONEIN
DUNLIN
FANNIE
FINNIC
HANDIN
HANGIN
HANKIE
HENBIT
HENNIN
HENRIK
HINGIS
HUNGIN
JENNIE
JUNKIE
LANAIS
LANDIS
LANVIN
LENNIE
LENTIL
MANNIX
MANTIC
MANTIS
MCNAIR
MENHIR
MENTIS
MINNIE
MINUIT
MUNCIE
MUNTIN
NANNIE
NUNCIO
PANDIT
PENCIL
PENNIA
PENNIS
PINKIE
PINXIT
PINYIN
PONGID
PONTIC
PUNDIT
PUNKIE
RANCID
RANKIN
RENAIL
RENNIE
RENNIN
RENOIR
RONNIE
RUNCIE
RUNSIN
SANDIA
SANTIR
SENDIN

SENNIT
SENTIN
SINGIN
SINKIN
SUNLIT
SUNNIS
SYNDIC
TANNIC
TANNIN
TENNIS
TENPIN
TONKIN
TONSIL
TUNEIN
VINCIT
VINNIE
WANTIN
WENTIN
WINGIT
WINKIE
WINNIE
WINWIN
XINGIN
ZENDIC
ZINNIA

••N••I

ANNULI
BANGUI
BANZAI
BENONI
BONAMI
BONSAI
CANTHI
CENTRI
DENALI
DENDRI
ERNANI
GANDHI
KINSKI
SANSEI
SENITI
SENSEI
YANQUI

•••NI•

ADONIS
ALANIS
ATONIC
BEANIE
BERNIE
BIONIC
BLINIS
BONNIE
BOSNIA
CATNIP
CHENIN
CLINIC
CONNIE
CRANIA
CRANIO
CRONIN
CYANIC
DARNIT
DENNIS
EDENIC
ETHNIC
ETONIC
FAFNIR
FANNIE
FINNIC
GLYNIS
HENNIN
HORNIN
ICONIC
IRANIS
IRENIC
IRONIC
JENNIE
JOANIE
JOININ
KOENIG
LAINIE
LENNIE
LEONID
LEONIE
LIGNIN
LOONIE
MANNIX
MARNIE
MEANIE
MINNIE
NANNIE
NARNIA
NUDNIK
OMANIS
OZONIC
PARNIS
PENNIA
PENNIS
PERNIO
PHONIC
PICNIC
PYKNIC
REININ
RENNIE
RENNIN
RESNIK
RONNIE
SARNIA
SCENIC
SEENIN
SENNIT
SHANIA
SIGNIN
SUNNIS
TANNIC
TANNIN
TENNIS
TOONIE
TOWNIE
TURNIN
TURNIP
UNKNIT
URANIA
URANIC
VINNIE
WEENIE
WINNIE
ZINNIA

•••N•I

ADONAI
AVANTI
BIONDI
BRUNEI
EVENKI
KERNOI
RIENZI
UBANGI

••••NI

ADJANI
ALUMNI
ARMANI
BENONI
BIKINI
BIMINI
BODONI
BUSONI
CARONI
DOMANI
DOMINI
ERNANI
FULANI
GEMINI
ILLINI
LATINI
MORONI
RAPINI
RIMINI
ROTINI
SILENI
TAHINI
YEMENI
YOGINI

N••J••

NINJAS

N•••J•

NAVAJO

•NJ•••

ANJOUS
ENJOIN
ENJOYS
INJECT
INJEST
INJOKE
INJURE
INJURY
UNJAMS
UNJUST

•N•J••

INAJAM
INKJET

•N•••J

INTERJ

••NJ••

BANJOS
BANJUL
CONJOB
DONJON
FANJET
MENJOU
NINJAS
PUNJAB

•••NJ•

CHONJU

N•K•••

NEKTON
NIKITA
NIKKEI
NIKOLA
NUKING

N••K••

NAPKIN
NECKED
NICKED
NICKEL
NICKER
NIKKEI
NUTKIN

N•••K•

NEVSKY
NOOTKA

N••••K

NANOOK
NARVIK
NATICK
NEWARK
NUDNIK

•NK•••

ANKARA
ANKLED
ANKLES
ANKLET
INKERS
INKIER
INKIND
INKING
INKJET
INKLES
UNKIND
UNKINK
UNKNIT
UNKNOT

•N•K••

ANGKOR
ENOKIS
SNAKED
SNAKES

•N••K•

ANNIKA
INJOKE
INTAKE
INVOKE
KNACKS
KNICKS
KNOCKS
SNACKS
SNEAKS
SNEAKY
SNICKS
SNOOKS
SNOOKY
UNLIKE
UNMAKE
UNYOKE
VNECKS

•N•••K

ANORAK
INBULK
INLUCK
ONDECK
UNCORK
UNHOOK
UNKINK
UNLINK
UNLOCK
UNMASK
UNPACK
UNTACK

••NK••

BANKED
BANKER
BANKON
BUNKED
BUNKER
BUNKOS
BUNKUM
CANKER
CONKED
CONKER
DANKER
DANKLY
DINKEY
DONKEY
DUNKED
DUNKER
FINKED
FUNKED
GINKGO
HANKER
HANKIE
HONKED
HONKER
HUNKER
JINKED
JUNKED
JUNKER
JUNKET
JUNKIE
KINKED
LANKER
LANKLY
LINKED
LINKER
LINKUP
LUNKER
MENKEN
MINKES
MONKEY
OINKED
PINKED
PINKEN
PINKER
PINKIE
PUNKAH
PUNKER
PUNKIE
RANKED
RANKER
RANKIN
RANKLE
RANKLY
SINKER
SINKIN
SUNKEN
TANKAS
TANKED
TANKER
TANKUP
TINKER
TINKLE
TINKLY
TONKIN
WINKAT
WINKED
WINKER
WINKIE
WINKLE
YANKED
YANKEE
ZONKED
ZONKER

••N•K•

ANNIKA
BANGKA
JANSKY
KANAKA
KINSKI
TANAKA

••N••K

HENRIK
LANARK
NANOOK
PINOAK
SENDAK
TANOAK
ZANUCK

•••NK•

BLANKS
BLINKS
BRINKS
CHINKS
CHINKY
CHUNKS
CHUNKY
CLANKS
CLANKY
CLINKS
CLONKS
CLUNKS
CLUNKY
CRANKS
CRANKY
DRINKS
EVENKI
FLANKS
FLUNKS
FLUNKY
FRANKS
GLINKA
PLANKS
PLINKS
PLONKS
PLUNKS
PRANKS
PRINKS
REINKS
SHANKS
SKANKS
SKINKS
SKUNKS
SKUNKY
SLINKS
SLINKY
SPANKS
SPANKY
SPINKS
SPUNKY
STANKY
STINKS
STINKY
SWANKS
SWANKY
THANKS
THINKS
THUNKS
TRUNKS

•••N•K

FRANCK
GDANSK
KARNAK
NUDNIK
PLANCK
RESNIK

••••NK

DEBUNK
DRYINK
EMBANK
PODUNK
REDINK
SHRANK
SHRINK
SHRUNK
UNKINK
UNLINK
UPLINK

NL••••

NLEAST
NLWEST

N•L•••

NELLIE
NELSON
NFLERS
NHLERS
NILGAI
NOLEAD
NOLENS
NOLESS
NOLOAD
NOLOSE
NULLAH
NULLED
NYLONS

N••L••

NAILED
NAILER
NAILIN
NAPLES
NELLIE
NEWLEY
NIELLI
NIELLO
NOBLER
NOBLES
NUCLEI
NUCLEO
NULLAH
NULLED
NUTLET
NYALAS

N•••L•

NAMELY
NAPOLI
NASALS
NAVELS
NEARLY
NEATLY
NEBULA
NEEDLE
NEPALI
NEROLI
NESTLE
NETTLE
NETTLY
NEWELS
NIBBLE
NICELY
NICOLA
NICOLE
NICOLO
NIELLI
NIELLO
NIGGLE
NIHILO
NIKOLA
NIMBLE
NIMBLY
NOBBLE
NODDLE
NODULE
NOODLE
NOSALE
NOSILY
NOVELS
NOZZLE
NUBBLE
NUBBLY
NUBILE
NUDELY
NUMBLY
NUZZLE

N••••L

NARIAL
NARWAL
NEURAL
NEUROL
NICKEL
NORMAL
NUCHAL
NYQUIL

•NL•••

ENLACE
ENLIST
INLAID
INLAND
INLAWS
INLAYS
INLETS
INLINE
INLOVE
INLUCK
ONLAND
ONLINE
ONLOAN
UNLACE
UNLADE
UNLAID
UNLASH
UNLEAD
UNLESS
UNLIKE
UNLINK
UNLOAD
UNLOCK

•N•L••

ANALOG
ANELED
ANELES
ANGLED
ANGLER
ANGLES
ANGLIA
ANGLIC
ANGLOS
ANKLED
ANKLES
ANKLET
ANNLEE
ANOLES
ANTLER
ENBLOC
ENGLUT
INFLOW
INFLUX
INGLES
INKLES
INPLAY
KNELLS
KNOLLS
KNOLLY
SNELLS
UNCLAD
UNCLES
UNCLOG
UNGLUE
UNPLUG

•N••L•

ANGELA
ANGELI
ANGELL
ANGELO
ANGELS
ANGOLA
ANNALS
ANNULI
ANNULS
ANSELM
ANVILS
ENABLE
ENDALL
ENFOLD
ENGELS
ENGULF
ENHALO
ENISLE
ENROLL
ENROLS
ENSILE
GNARLS
GNARLY
INBULK
INCULT
INFOLD
INFULL
INHALE
INHALF
INSOLE
INSULT
KNEELS

KNELLS
KNOLLS
KNOLLY
KNURLS
KNURLY
ONCALL
ONEILL
ONFILE
ONHOLD
ONSALE
SNAILS
SNARLS
SNARLY
SNELLS
SNUGLI
SNUGLY
UNABLE
UNBELT
UNBOLT
UNDULY
UNFOLD
UNHOLY
UNOILY
UNPILE
UNROLL
UNRULY
UNSOLD
UNTOLD
UNWELL
UNWILY

•N•••L
ANGELL
ANIMAL
ANNEAL
ANNUAL
ENAMEL
ENDALL
ENROLL
ENSOUL
ENTAIL
INFULL
INHAUL
INSTAL
INSTIL
ONCALL
ONEILL
SNIVEL
UNCIAL
UNCOIL
UNCOOL
UNCURL
UNFURL
UNGUAL
UNITAL
UNOCAL
UNREAL
UNREEL
UNROLL
UNSEAL
UNVEIL
UNWELL

••NL••
ANNLEE
BANLON
CANLIT
DUNLIN
DUNLOP
HANLEY
HENLEY
KUNLUN
LYNLEY
RUNLET
SENLAC
SUNLIT

••N•L•
ANNALS
ANNULI
ANNULS
ARNOLD
BANGLE
BUNDLE
BUNGLE
CANALS
CANDLE
CANOLA
CANTLE
DANDLE
DANGLE
DANGLY
DANKLY
DENALI
DINGLE
DONALD
DONGLE
FINALE
FINALS
FINELY
FONDLE
FONDLY
GANGLE
GANGLY
GENTLE
GENTLY
HANDLE
JANGLE
JANGLY
JINGLE
JINGLY
JUNGLE
JUNGLY
KINDLE
KINDLY
KINGLY
LANKLY
LONELY
LONGLY
LUNULA
MANGLE
MANILA
MANTLE
MINGLE
PANELS
PENULT

PINOLE
PINTLE
PUNILY
RANKLE
RANKLY
RONALD
RONELY
RUNDLE
SANELY
SINGLE
SINGLY
TANGLE
TANGLY
TINGLE
TINGLY
TINILY
TINKLE
TINKLY
VINYLS
WANGLE
WINKLE
YUNGLO
ZANILY

••N••L
ANNEAL
ANNUAL
BANJUL
BENGAL
BENZOL
BUNUEL
CANCEL
CANFUL
CANNEL
CONSUL
CUNEAL
DANIEL
DENIAL
DENTAL
DENTIL
DENZEL
FENNEL
FINIAL
FONTAL
FUNNEL
GENIAL
GENUAL
GUNNEL
HANDEL
HANGUL
HANSEL
KENNEL
LENTIL
LINEAL
LINTEL
LONNOL
MANFUL
MANTEL
MANUAL
MANUEL
MENDEL
MENIAL
MENSAL

MENTAL
MONGOL
MONTEL
PANFUL
PENCEL
PENCIL
PENPAL
PINEAL
RENAIL
RENTAL
RONDEL
RUNNEL
SANDAL
SINFUL
TINCAL
TINSEL
TONSIL
TUNNEL
VANDAL
VENIAL

•••NL•
EVENLY
GAINLY
KEENLY
LEANLY
LIONLY
MAINLY
MEANLY
OPENLY
THINLY
VAINLY

•••N•L
ATONAL
AXONAL
CANNEL
CARNAL
CHANEL
CORNEL
CRENEL
DARNEL
DIRNDL
EPINAL
FAUNAL
FENNEL
FUNNEL
GUNNEL
HYMNAL
KENNEL
KERNEL
LIONEL
LONNOL
PHENOL
PHENYL
REGNAL
RHINAL
RUNNEL
SIGNAL
SIMNEL
SPINAL
SPINEL
TRINAL

TUNNEL
VEINAL
VERNAL

N•M•••
NAMATH
NAMELY
NAMERS
NAMING
NEMATO
NIMBLE
NIMBLY
NIMBUS
NIMINY
NIMITZ
NIMROD
NOMADS
NOMINE
NOMORE
NUMBAT
NUMBED
NUMBER
NUMBLY
NUMERO
NUMINA
NYMETS
NYMPHS

N••M••
NETMAN
NETMEN
NEUMAN
NEUMES
NEWMAN
NEWMAR
NIAMEY
NORMAL
NORMAN
NOUMEA
NUTMEG

N•••M•
NONAME

N••••M
NINEAM
NINEPM
NONCOM

•NM•••
ENMESH
ENMITY
INMATE
INMOST
UNMADE
UNMAKE
UNMANS
UNMASK
UNMEET
UNMESH
UNMOOR

•N•M••
ANEMIA
ANEMIC
ANIMAL
ANIMAS
ANIMES
ANIMUS
ANOMIC
ANOMIE
ENAMEL
ENAMOR
ENDMAN
ENDMEN
GNOMES
GNOMIC
GNOMON
INGMAR
ONEMAN

•N••M•
ENCAMP
ENIGMA
ENTOMO
ENZYME
INCOME
INFAMY
INTIMA
INTIME
ONTIME
PNEUMA
UNARMS
UNJAMS

•N•••M
ANADEM
ANONYM
ANSELM
ANTHEM
ANTRIM
ANTRUM
ENGRAM
INAJAM
INDIUM
INFIRM
INFORM
INGRAM
INSEAM

••NM••
BONMOT
CONMAN
CONMEN
FENMAN
FENMEN
GUNMAN
GUNMEN
PENMAN
PENMEN
TINMAN
TINMEN
WONMUG

••N•M•
BENUMB
BONAMI
BYNAME
CINEMA
DANGME
DENIMS
DYNAMO
GENOME
KINEMA
KINGME
MANAMA
MINIMA
MINIMS
NONAME
PANAMA
RENAME
RUNDMC
SONOMA
VENOMS

••N••M
ARNHEM
BANTAM
BUNKUM
CONIUM
DUNHAM
FANDOM
HANSOM
IONIUM
MINIUM
MONISM
NINEAM
NINEPM
NONCOM
OMNIUM
RANDOM
RANSOM
TANDEM
WINDOM

•••N•M
ANONYM
BARNUM
EPONYM
FRENUM
MAGNUM
PHENOM
PLENUM
PUTNAM

N•N•••
NANNIE
NANOOK
NANSEN
NANTES
NENETS
NINEAM
NINEPM
NINERS
NINETY
NINGBO
NINJAS

NINTHS
NONAGE
NONAME
NONARY
NONCOM
NONEGO
NONETS
NONFAT
NUNCIO

N••N••
NANNIE
NARNIA
NOONAN
NOONES
NOTNOW
NUANCE
NUDNIK

N•••N•
NADINE
NAGANO
NAMING
NATANT
NEEDNT
NEVINS
NICENE
NIMINY
NIXING
NOCENT
NOLENS
NOMINE
NOSING
NOTING
NOVENA
NUGENT
NUKING
NUMINA
NYLONS

N••••N
NAILIN
NANSEN
NAPKIN
NATHAN
NATION
NATRON
NEATEN
NEESON
NEKTON
NELSON
NETMAN
NETMEN
NETTON
NEUMAN
NEURON
NEWMAN
NEWTON
NGUYEN
NIACIN
NICEAN
NIPPON
NISSAN

NISSEN
NOGGIN
NOIRON
NOONAN
NORMAN
NORTON
NOTION
NUBBIN
NUBIAN
NUTKIN

•NN•••
ANNABA
ANNALS
ANNEAL
ANNEXE
ANNHON
ANNIKA
ANNLEE
ANNOYS
ANNUAL
ANNUIT
ANNULI
ANNULS
ENNEAD
ENNIUS
INNAGE
INNATE
INNEED
INNESS
INNING

•N•N••
ANANDA
ANONYM
INANER
UNKNIT
UNKNOT
UNSNAG
UNSNAP

•N••N•
ANCONA
ANIONS
ANOINT
ANTONY
ANWANG
ANYANG
ANYONE
ENCINA
ENCINO
ENDING
ENFANT
ENGINE
INCANS
INDENE
INDENT
INFANT
INHAND
INIONS
INKIND
INKING
INLAND

INLINE
INNING
INSANE
INSYNC
INTEND
INTENS
INTENT
INTINE
INTONE
INTUNE
INVENT
KNOWNS
ONDINE
ONHAND
ONIONS
ONIONY
ONLAND
ONLINE
UNBEND
UNBENT
UNBIND
UNDINE
UNDONE
UNHAND
UNIONS
UNKIND
UNKINK
UNLINK
UNMANS
UNPENS
UNPINS
UNSUNG
UNTUNE
UNWIND

•N•••N
ANACIN
ANCIEN
ANDEAN
ANNHON
ANTRON
ANURAN
ENDMAN
ENDMEN
ENDRUN
ENJOIN
ENSIGN
GNOMON
INBORN
INCHON
INDIAN
INSPAN
INTERN
INTOWN
INTURN
INVAIN
ONEMAN
ONLOAN
SNOWIN
UNBORN
UNEVEN
UNISON
UNOPEN

UNSEEN
UNSEWN
UNSOWN
UNTORN
UNWORN

••NN••
BANNED
BANNER
BINNED
BONNES
BONNET
BONNIE
CANNAE
CANNED
CANNEL
CANNER
CANNES
CANNON
CANNOT
CONNED
CONNER
CONNIE
CONNOR
DANNAY
DANNER
DENNED
DENNIS
DINNED
DINNER
DONNAS
DONNED
DONNEE
DONNER
DUNNED
FANNED
FANNIE
FENNEC
FENNEL
FINNAN
FINNED
FINNEY
FINNIC
FUNNED
FUNNEL
GANNET
GINNED
GUNNAR
GUNNED
GUNNEL
GUNNER
HANNAH
HENNAS
HENNER
HENNIN
JENNER
JENNET
JENNEY
JENNIE
JINNAH
KENNED
KENNEL
KENNER
KENNYG
LENNIE
LENNON
LENNOX
LINNET
LINNEY
LONNOL
MANNED
MANNER
MANNIX
MENNEN
MINNIE
MINNOW
NANNIE
PANNED
PANNER
PANNES
PENNAE
PENNED
PENNER
PENNEY
PENNIA
PENNIS
PENNON
PINNAE
PINNAS
PINNED
PINNER
PUNNED
PUNNET
RENNES
RENNET
RENNIE
RENNIN
RONNIE
RUNNEL
RUNNER
SANNUP
SENNAS
SENNET
SENNIT
SINNED
SINNER
SONNET
SUNNED
SUNNIS
TANNED
TANNER
TANNIC
TANNIN
TENNIS
TINNED
TINNER
TONNES
TUNNEL
TUNNEY
VANNED
VINNIE
WANNED
WANNER
WINNER
WINNIE
WINNOW
WONNED
YENNED
YUNNAN
ZINNIA

••N•N•
AWNING
BANANA
BENING
BENONI
BONING
CANINE
CANING
CANONS
CONANT
DANANG
DINING
DUNANT
ELNINO
ERNANI
FANONS
FINING
HONING
INNING
JANINE
LINENS
LINENY
LINING
MANANA
MENINX
MINING
OENONE
OWNING
PENANG
PINING
PINONS
RUNINS
RUNONS
SONANT
SUNUNU
TANANA
TENANT
TENENS
TENONS
TONING
TUNING
VINING
WANING
WINING
WINONA
ZENANA
ZONING

••N••N
AMNION
ANNHON
BANKON
BANLON
BANYAN
BENIGN
BENSON
BENTON
BONBON
BONTON
BUNION
BUNSEN
BUNYAN
CANAAN
CANCAN
CANCUN
CANNON
CANTON
CANYON
CONMAN
CONMEN
DANSON
DANTON
DENTIN
DENTON
DINEIN
DINEON
DONEIN
DONJON
DUNCAN
DUNLIN
EONIAN
FANION
FANTAN
FENIAN
FENMAN
FENMEN
FINNAN
GENOAN
GUNMAN
GUNMEN
HANDIN
HANDON
HANGIN
HANGON
HANSON
HENNIN
HENSON
HINTON
HUNGIN
HUNGON
IONIAN
JANSEN
JENSEN
JONSON
KANSAN
KENTON
KENYAN
KUNLUN
LANDON
LANSON
LANVIN
LENNON
LENTEN
LINDEN
LONDON
LONGAN
LUNDEN
LYNDON
MANDAN
MENKEN
MENNEN
MINION
MINOAN
MINYAN
MUNTIN
NANSEN
PENMAN
PENMEN
PENNON
PINION
PINKEN
PINSON
PINYIN
PINYON
PINZON
RANKIN
RENNIN
RENOWN
RUNSIN
RUNSON
RUNYON
SENDIN
SENTIN
SINGIN
SINKIN
SUNKEN
SUNTAN
TANNIN
TANOAN
TENDON
TENPIN
TINCAN
TINMAN
TINMEN
TINPAN
TONGAN
TONKIN
TUNEIN
VANRYN
VINTON
WANTIN
WANTON
WENTIN
WENTON
WINWIN
WONTON
WYNTON
XINGIN
YANGON
YUNNAN

•••NN•
BLENNY
BRANNY
CRANNY
CRENNA
DEANNA
DIANNE
DIONNE
DUENNA
EVONNE
FRANNY
GLENNE
GOANNA
GRANNY
GWYNNE
JEANNE
JOANNA
JOANNE
JOHNNY
PRYNNE
SHANNY
SHINNY
SIENNA
SKINNY
VIENNA
VIENNE
WHINNY
YVONNE

•••N•N
ALANON
CANNON
CHENIN
CRONIN
CRONYN
DAWNON
DOWNON
FINNAN
GAINON
GUENON
HAINAN
HENNIN
HORNIN
IRONON
JOININ
KEENAN
KEENEN
LEANON
LENNON
LIGNIN
MAGNON
MEMNON
MENNEN
MIGNON
NOONAN
PENNON
PHONON
PLANON
REININ
RENNIN
SEENIN
SEWNON
SIGNIN
SIGNON
SRANAN
TAINAN
TANNIN
TURNIN
TURNON
VERNON
YUNNAN

••••NN
EDWYNN
JOHANN
MCCANN
SUSANN

NO••••
NOBBLE
NOBLER
NOBLES
NOBODY
NOCENT
NODDED
NODDLE
NODICE
NODOFF
NODOSE
NODULE
NOESIS
NOETIC
NOEXIT
NOGGIN
NOGOOD
NOHITS
NOIRON
NOISED
NOISES
NOLEAD
NOLENS
NOLESS
NOLOAD
NOLOSE
NOMADS
NOMINE
NOMORE
NONAGE
NONAME
NONARY
NONCOM
NONEGO
NONETS
NONFAT
NOODLE
NOONAN
NOONES
NOOSED
NOOSES
NOOTKA
NOPETS
NORDIC
NORGAY
NORIAS
NORMAL
NORMAN
NORRIS
NORTHS
NORTON
NORWAY
NOSALE
NOSHED
NOSHER
NOSHES
NOSHOW
NOSIER
NOSILY
NOSING
NOSOAP
NOTARY
NOTATE
NOTBAD
NOTCHY
NOTERS
NOTICE
NOTIFY
NOTING
NOTION
NOTNOW
NOTYET
NOUGAT
NOUGHT
NOUMEA
NOVATO
NOVELS
NOVENA
NOVICE
NOWISE
NOZZLE

N•O•••
NOODLE
NOONAN
NOONES
NOOSED
NOOSES
NOOTKA

N••O••
NABOBS
NABORS
NAGOYA
NANOOK
NAPOLI
NEROLI
NICOLA
NICOLE
NICOLO
NIKOLA
NOBODY
NODOFF
NODOSE
NOGOOD
NOLOAD
NOLOSE
NOMORE
NOSOAP
NYLONS

N•••O•
NACHOS
NANOOK
NARROW
NATION
NATRON
NEESON
NEKTON
NELSON
NESTOR
NETTON
NEUROL
NEURON
NEWTON
NIMROD
NIPPON
NOGOOD
NOIRON
NONCOM
NORTON
NOSHOW
NOTION
NOTNOW

N••••O
NAGANO
NAVAHO
NAVAJO
NEARTO
NEMATO
NEPHRO
NEXTTO
NICOLO
NIELLO
NIHILO
NINGBO
NONEGO
NOVATO
NUCLEO
NUMERO
NUNCIO

•NO•••
ANODES
ANODIC
ANOINT
ANOLES
ANOMIC
ANOMIE
ANONYM
ANORAK
CNOTES
ENOKIS
ENOSIS
ENOUGH
GNOMES
GNOMIC
GNOMON
GNOSIS
INOUYE
KNOBBY
KNOCKS
KNOLLS
KNOLLY
KNOTTS
KNOTTY
KNOUTS
KNOWER
KNOWNS
SNOBBY
SNOCAT
SNOODS
SNOOKS
SNOOKY
SNOOPS
SNOOPY
SNOOTS
SNOOTY
SNOOZE
SNOOZY
SNOPES
SNORED
SNORER
SNORES
SNORTS
SNOTTY
SNOUTS
SNOWED
SNOWIN
TNOTES
UNOCAL
UNOILY
UNOPEN

•N•O••
ANCONA
ANGOLA
ANGORA
ANIONS
ANJOUS
ANNOYS
ANTONY
ANYONE
ENCODE
ENCORE
ENDORA
ENDOWS
ENFOLD
ENJOIN
ENJOYS
ENROBE
ENROLL
ENROLS
ENROOT
ENSOUL
ENTOMO
ENVOIS
ENVOYS
INBORN
INCOME
INDOOR
INDORE
INFOLD
INFORM
INGOTS
INIONS
INJOKE
INLOVE
INMOST
INPORT
INPOUR
INROAD
INSOLE
INTONE
INTOTO
INTOWN
INVOKE
ONFOOT
ONHOLD

ONIONS
ONIONY
ONLOAN
ONTOUR
SNOODS
SNOOKS
SNOOKY
SNOOPS
SNOOPY
SNOOTS
SNOOTY
SNOOZE
SNOOZY
UNBOLT
UNBORN
UNCOIL
UNCOOL
UNCORK
UNDOER
UNDOES
UNDONE
UNFOLD
UNHOLY
UNHOOK
UNIONS
UNLOAD
UNLOCK
UNMOOR
UNROBE
UNROLL
UNROOT
UNSOLD
UNSOWN
UNTOLD
UNTORN
UNWORN
UNWOVE
UNYOKE

•N••O•

ANALOG
ANCHOR
ANDHOW
ANDROS
ANGKOR
ANGLOS
ANNHON
ANTCOW
ANTRON
ANYHOW
ENAMOR
ENBLOC
ENROOT
GNOMON
INAFOG
INAROW
INCHON
INDOOR
INFLOW
INTROS
ONFOOT
UNCLOG
UNCOOL
UNHOOK
UNIPOD
UNISON
UNKNOT
UNMOOR
UNROOT
UNSHOD
UNSTOP
UNTROD

•N•••O

ANATTO
ANGELO
ANTERO
ENCINO
ENDURO
ENESCO
ENHALO
ENRICO
ENTERO
ENTOMO
INDIGO
INITIO
INTOTO
INVIVO
ONETWO
SNAPTO
UNESCO

••NO••

ANNOYS
ARNOLD
BENOIT
BENONI
CANOED
CANOES
CANOLA
CANONS
CANOPY
CANOVA
CENOTE
CONOCO
CONOID
DENOTE
DENOVO
DONORS
FANONS
FANOUT
GENOAN
GENOME
GONOGO
HONORE
HONORS
HONOUR
IGNORE
LANOSE
LENORE
MANORS
MINOAN
MINORS
MONODY
NANOOK
OENONE
PANOUT
PINOAK
PINOLE
PINONS
PINOTS
RANOFF
RANOUT
RENOIR
RENOTE
RENOWN
RUNOFF
RUNONS
RUNOUT
SENORA
SENORS
SONOMA
SONORA
SUNOCO
SYNODS
TANOAK
TANOAN
TENONS
TENORS
VENOMS
VENOUS
VINOUS
WINONA
WINOUT
WONOUT

••N•O•

AMNION
ANNHON
BANDOG
BANGOR
BANJOS
BANKON
BANLON
BENSON
BENTON
BENZOL
BONBON
BONGOS
BONMOT
BONTON
BUNCOS
BUNION
BUNKOS
CANDOR
CANNON
CANNOT
CANTON
CANTOR
CANTOS
CANYON
CENSOR
CENTOS
CONDOR
CONDOS
CONGOU
CONJOB
CONNOR
CONROY
CONVOY
DANSON
DANTON
DENTON
DINEON
DONJON
DUNLOP
FANDOM
FANION
GUNDOG
GUNFOR
HANDON
HANGON
HANSOM
HANSON
HENSON
HINTON
HUNGON
JONSON
JUNCOS
JUNIOR
JUNTOS
KANTOR
KENTON
KINDOF
LANDON
LANSON
LENNON
LENNOX
LONDON
LONNOL
LYNDON
MANGOS
MANIOC
MENJOU
MENTOR
MINION
MINNOW
MONGOL
MONROE
MUNGOS
NANOOK
NONCOM
PANTOS
PENNON
PENROD
PINION
PINSON
PINTOS
PINYON
PINZON
RANCOR
RANDOM
RANFOR
RANSOM
RONDOS
RUNFOR
RUNSON
RUNYON
SANTOS
SENHOR
SENIOR
SENSOR
SUNDOG
SUNGOD
TANGOS
TENDON
TENSOR
TINGOD
TINPOT
TONDOS
VENDOR
VINTON
WANTON
WENTON
WINDOM
WINDOW
WINNOW
WINSOR
WONTON
WYNTON
YANGON
ZENDOS

••N••O

ALNICO
BANQUO
BENITO
BONITO
CENTRO
CONOCO
DENDRO
DENIRO
DENOVO
DINERO
DYNAMO
ELNINO
FINITO
GINKGO
GONOGO
GUNGHO
HONCHO
LANDHO
MENADO
MONACO
NINGBO
NONEGO
NUNCIO
PANCHO
PINERO
PONCHO
RANCHO
RUNSTO
SANCHO
SANGTO
SENUFO
SINGTO
SUNOCO
TENDTO
TENUTO
VENETO
WANTTO
XANTHO
YUNGLO

•••NO•

ALANON
AMINOR
BEANOS
BMINOR
BUENOS
CANNON
CANNOT
CARNOT
CHINOS
CMINOR
CONNOR
CPSNOW
DAWNON
DMINOR
DOWNON
EGGNOG
ELINOR
EMINOR
ERENOW
ETHNOS
FMINOR
GAINON
GAYNOR
GMINOR
GOUNOD
GUENON
HOBNOB
HOWNOW
HYPNOS
IRONON
KERNOI
KERNOS
KRONOR
LEANON
LEMNOS
LENNON
LENNOX
LLANOS
LONNOL
MAGNON
MEMNON
MIGNON
MINNOW
NOTNOW
PENNON
PERNOD
PHENOL
PHENOM
PHONON
PHONOS
PIANOS
PLANON
QUINOA
RHINOS
SCHNOZ
SEWNON
SIGNON
SIGNOR
STENOG
STENOS
TAINOS
TURNON
UNKNOT
VERNON
WHYNOT
WINNOW

•••N•O

ALONSO
ALONZO
BOINGO
BORNEO
BRANDO
BRONCO
CRANIO
ERYNGO
EVENSO
FRANCO
GOINTO
GRINGO
LEANTO
ODONTO
OLINGO
OPENTO
PERNIO
PRONTO
QUANGO
SEENTO
SHINTO
SPINTO
STINGO
TURNTO

••••NO

ACTINO
ADRENO
ALBANO
ALBINO
AQUINO
AVERNO
CAMINO
CASINO
CHRONO
CYRANO
DELANO
DIVINO
DOMINO
ECHINO
ELNINO
ENCINO
FRESNO
GITANO
GOLINO
GRODNO
IMMUNO
JOURNO
KIMONO
LADINO
LATINO
LUPINO
MARINO
MELANO
MERINO
MILANO
MORENO
MURANO
NAGANO
ORSINO
PACINO
PEPINO
PISANO
POCONO
ROMANO
SELENO
STERNO
STHENO
TECHNO
TEJANO
TORINO

N•P•••

NAPERY
NAPIER
NAPKIN
NAPLES
NAPOLI
NAPPED
NAPPER
NAPPES
NAPPIE
NEPALI
NEPHEW
NEPHRO
NIPPED
NIPPER
NIPPON
NIPPUR
NIPSAT
NIPSEY
NIPUPS
NOPETS

N••P••

NAPPED
NAPPER
NAPPES
NAPPIE
NETPAY
NIPPED
NIPPER
NIPPON
NIPPUR
NYMPHS

N•••P•

NINEPM
NIPUPS

N••••P

NOSOAP

•NP•••

INPART
INPLAY
INPORT
INPOUR
INPUTS
UNPACK
UNPAID
UNPEGS
UNPENS
UNPILE
UNPINS
UNPLUG

•N•P••

INAPET
INSPAN
ONSPEC
SNAPAT
SNAPPY
SNAPTO
SNAPUP
SNIPED
SNIPER
SNIPES
SNIPPY
SNOPES
UNIPOD
UNOPEN

•N••P•

ENRAPT
INCEPT
ONEUPS
ONTAPE
SNAPPY
SNIPPY
SNOOPS
SNOOPY
UNCAPS
UNRIPE
UNZIPS

•N•••P

ANTEUP
ENCAMP
ENDSUP
ENTRAP
ENWRAP
INSTEP
SNAPUP
UNSNAP
UNSTOP
UNTRAP
UNWRAP

••NP••

PENPAL
TENPIN
TINPAN
TINPOT

••N•P•

CANAPE
CANOPY
LENAPE
NINEPM
PINUPS
RUNUPS
SUNUPS

••N••P

BANGUP
BINDUP
BONEUP
BUNYIP
DONEUP
DUNLOP
GANGUP
HANDUP
HANGUP
HUNGUP
LINEUP
LINKUP
OWNSUP
PENTUP
PONYUP
RANGUP
RINGUP
RUNGUP
RUNSUP
SANNUP
SENDUP
SENTUP
TANKUP
TONEUP
TUNEUP
WENTUP
WINDUP

•••N•P

BURNUP
CATNAP
CATNIP
CHINUP
EVENUP
JOINUP
KIDNAP
OPENUP
PRENUP
SANNUP
SEWNUP
SIGNUP
TURNIP
TURNUP
UNSNAP

N•Q•••

NYQUIL

N••••Q

NASDAQ

•NQ•••

ENQUAD

•N•Q••

UNIQUE

••NQ••

BANQUO
CINQUE
MANQUE
YANQUI

N•R•••
NARIAL
NARNIA
NARROW
NARVIK
NARWAL
NEREID
NEREIS
NEREUS
NEROLI
NERUDA
NERVES
NORDIC
NORGAY
NORIAS
NORMAL
NORMAN
NORRIS
NORTHS
NORTON
NORWAY
NURSED
NURSER
NURSES

N••R••
NACRES
NAIRAS
NARROW
NATRON
NEARBY
NEARED
NEARER
NEARLY
NEARTO
NEURAL
NEUROL
NEURON
NIMROD
NITRES
NITRIC
NOIRON
NORRIS
NUTRIA

N•••R•
NABORS
NADIRS
NAMERS
NAPERY
NATURA
NATURE
NEPHRO
NEVERS
NEWARK
NFLERS
NHLERS
NINERS
NITERS
NITERY
NOMORE
NONARY
NOTARY
NOTERS
NUMERO

N••••R
NABBER
NAGGER
NAILER
NAPIER
NAPPER
NASCAR
NASSER
NATTER
NEARER
NEATER
NECTAR
NESTER
NESTOR
NETHER
NEUTER
NEWMAR
NICKER
NIGHER
NIPPER
NIPPUR
NOBLER
NOSHER
NOSIER
NUDGER
NUMBER
NURSER
NUTTER

•NR•••
ENRAGE
ENRAPT
ENRICH
ENRICO
ENROBE
ENROLL
ENROLS
ENROOT
INROAD
INRUSH
ONRUSH
UNREAD
UNREAL
UNREEL
UNREST
UNRIGS
UNRIPE
UNROBE
UNROLL
UNROOT
UNRULY

•N•R••
ANDREA
ANDREI
ANDRES
ANDREW
ANDREY
ANDROS
ANERGY
ANORAK
ANTRES
ANTRIM
ANTRON
ANTRUM
ANURAN
ENDRUN
ENERGY
ENGRAM
ENTRAP
ENTREE
ENURED
ENURES
ENWRAP
GNARLS
GNARLY
INARCH
INAROW
INARUT
INBRED
INDRIS
INGRAM
INGRES
INGRID
INTROS
INURED
INURES
KNARRY
KNURLS
KNURLY
SNARED
SNARES
SNARLS
SNARLY
SNORED
SNORER
SNORES
SNORTS
UNARMS
UNDRAW
UNFREE
UNTRAP
UNTROD
UNTRUE
UNWRAP

•N••R•
ANGERS
ANGORA
ANITRA
ANKARA
ANSARA
ANTERO
ENCORE
ENDERS
ENDORA
ENDURE
ENDURO
ENGIRD
ENGIRT
ENSURE
ENTERO
ENTERS
ENTIRE
INBORN
INCURS
INDIRA
INDORE
INFERS
INFIRM
INFORM
INHERE
INJURE
INJURY
INKERS
INPART
INPORT
INSERT
INSURE
INTERJ
INTERN
INTURN
INVERT
INWARD
KNARRY
ONFIRE
ONWARD
SNEERS
SNEERY
UNBARS
UNBORN
UNCORK
UNCURL
UNFURL
UNGIRD
UNGIRT
UNHURT
UNSURE
UNTORN
UNWARY
UNWORN

•N•••R
ANCHOR
ANGKOR
ANGLER
ANHYDR
ANSGAR
ANSWER
ANTHER
ANTLER
ENAMOR
ENDEAR
ENVIER
GNAWER
INANER
INDOOR
INGEAR
INGMAR
INKIER
INPOUR
INSTAR
KNOWER
ONAGER
ONTOUR
SNIDER
SNIPER
SNORER
SNYDER
UNDOER
UNFAIR
UNITER
UNMOOR

••NR••
CONRAD
CONROY
GENRES
HENRIK
HENRYV
KONRAD
MANRAY
MONROE
PENROD
SUNRAY
TENREC
VANRYN

••N•R•
BINARY
BONERS
CANARD
CANARY
CANERS
CENTRE
CENTRI
CENTRO
CONTRA
CONTRE
CONURE
CUNARD
DENARY
DENDRI
DENDRO
DENIRO
DINARS
DINERO
DINERS
DONORS
DUNERA
FINERY
GANTRY
GENERA
GENTRY
GONERS
HONORE
HONORS
HUNGRY
IGNORE
LANARK
LANDRY
LENORE
LINERS
LONERS
LYNYRD
MANORS
MANTRA
MINERS
MINORS
MONERA
NINERS
NONARY
ORNERY
OWNERS
OXNARD
PANFRY
PANTRY
PENURY
PINERO
PINERY
RANDRY
RUNDRY
SANDRA
SENARY
SENORA
SENORS
SENTRA
SENTRY
SONORA
SUNDRY
TANTRA
TENORS
TENURE
TONERS
TUNDRA
TUNERS
VENIRE
VINERY
WANERS
WINERY
WINTRY

••N••R
BANGER
BANGOR
BANKER
BANNER
BANTER
BENDER
BENHUR
BINDER
BONIER
BUNKER
BUNTER
CANDOR
CANIER
CANKER
CANNER
CANTER
CANTOR
CENSER
CENSOR
CENTER
CINDER
CONCUR
CONDOR
CONFER
CONGER
CONKER
CONNER
CONNOR
DANCER
DANDER
DANGER
DANKER
DANNER
DENIER
DENSER
DENVER
DINNER
DONDER
DONNER
DUNBAR
DUNKER
FENCER
FENDER
FINDER
FINGER
FONDER
GANDER
GANGER
GENDER
GINGER
GUNFOR
GUNNAR
GUNNER
GUNTER
HANGAR
HANGER
HANKER
HENNER
HINDER
HINTER
HONKER
HONOUR
HUNGER
HUNKER
HUNTER
JENNER
JUNIOR
JUNKER
KANDER
KANTOR
KENNER
KINDER
LANCER
LANDER
LANGUR
LANIER
LANKER
LENDER
LINEAR
LINGER
LINIER
LINKER
LINTER
LONGER
LUNKER
MANGER
MANNER
MCNAIR
MENDER
MENHIR
MENTOR
MINCER
MINDER
MINTER
MONGER
PANDER
PANNER
PANZER
PENNER
PINCER
PINDAR
PINIER
PINKER
PINNER
PINTER
PONDER
PUNIER
PUNKER
PUNTER
QINTAR
RANCOR
RANFOR
RANGER
RANKER
RANTER
RENDER
RENOIR
RENTER
RINGER
RUNFOR
RUNNER
SANDER
SANGER
SANTIR
SENDER
SENHOR
SENIOR
SENSOR
SINGER
SINKER
SINNER
SINTER
SUNDER
TANKER
TANNER
TENDER
TENSER
TENSOR
TENTER
TINDER
TINEAR
TINIER
TINKER
TINNER
TINTER
TONIER
VANIER
VENDOR
VENEER
VENTER
VINIER
WANDER
WANIER
WANNER
WINCER
WINDER
WINGER
WINIER
WINKER
WINNER
WINSOR
WINTER
WONDER
WYNTER
YONDER
ZANDER
ZANIER
ZENGER
ZINGER
ZONKER

•••NR•
AMENRA
OHENRY

•••N•R
AMINOR
BANNER
BMINOR
BURNER
CANNER
CMINOR
COINER
CONNER
CONNOR
CORNER
DANNER
DARNER
DINNER
DMINOR
DONNER
DOWNER
DRONER
EARNER
EISNER
ELINOR
EMINOR
EVENER
FAFNIR
FAWNER
FMINOR
GAINER
GARNER
GAYNOR
GMINOR
GUNNAR
GUNNER
HEFNER
HENNER
HORNER
INANER
IRONER
JENNER
JOINER
JOYNER
KAVNER
KEENER
KENNER
KRONER
KRONOR
KRONUR
LEANER
LERNER
LIMNER
LOANER
MANNER
MARNER
MEANER
MILNER
MOANER
MOLNAR
OPENER
OPINER
PANNER
PAWNER
PENNER
PINNER
PLANAR
PLANER
PRUNER
RADNER
RAINER
REINER
RUINER
RUNNER
SEINER
SHINER
SIGNER
SIGNOR
SINNER
SOONER
STONER
SUMNER
TANNER
TEENER
THENAR
TINNER
TOWNER
TURNER
VAINER
WAGNER
WANNER
WAPNER
WARNER
WERNER
WHINER
WIENER
WINNER
YAWNER

N•S•••
NASALS
NASCAR
NASDAQ
NASEBY
NASHUA
NASSAU
NASSER
NESSES
NESSIE
NESTEA

NESTED
NESTER
NESTLE
NESTOR
NISSAN
NISSEN
NOSALE
NOSHED
NOSHER
NOSHES
NOSHOW
NOSIER
NOSILY
NOSING
NOSOAP

N••S••
NANSEN
NASSAU
NASSER
NAUSEA
NAYSAY
NEESON
NEISSE
NELSON
NESSES
NESSIE
NEVSKY
NIPSAT
NIPSEY
NISSAN
NISSEN
NOESIS
NOISED
NOISES
NOOSED
NOOSES
NURSED
NURSER
NURSES
NYASSA

N•••S•
NEISSE
NEWEST
NEWISH
NICEST
NLEAST
NLWEST
NODOSE
NOLESS
NOLOSE
NOWISE
NUDEST
NUDIST
NYASSA

N••••S
NABOBS
NABORS
NACHOS
NACRES
NADIRS
NAIADS
NAIRAS
NAMERS
NANTES
NAPLES
NAPPES
NASALS
NAVELS
NAVIES
NAWABS
NEIGHS
NENETS
NEREIS
NEREUS
NERVES
NESSES
NEUMES
NEVERS
NEVINS
NEWELS
NFLERS
NHLERS
NICHES
NIECES
NIGHTS
NIMBUS
NINERS
NINJAS
NINTHS
NIPUPS
NITERS
NITRES
NIXIES
NOBLES
NOESIS
NOHITS
NOISES
NOLENS
NOLESS
NOMADS
NONETS
NOONES
NOOSES
NOPETS
NORIAS
NORRIS
NORTHS
NOSHES
NOTERS
NOVELS
NUDGES
NUECES
NURSES
NYALAS
NYLONS
NYMETS
NYMPHS

•NS•••
ANSARA
ANSATE
ANSELM
ANSGAR
ANSWER
ENSIGN
ENSILE
ENSOUL
ENSUED
ENSUES
ENSURE
INSANE
INSEAM
INSECT
INSERT
INSETS
INSIDE
INSIST
INSITU
INSOLE
INSPAN
INSTAL
INSTAR
INSTEP
INSTIL
INSULT
INSURE
INSYNC
ONSALE
ONSETS
ONSIDE
ONSITE
ONSPEC
UNSAFE
UNSAID
UNSAYS
UNSEAL
UNSEAT
UNSEEN
UNSEWN
UNSEWS
UNSHED
UNSHOD
UNSNAG
UNSNAP
UNSOLD
UNSOWN
UNSTOP
UNSUNG
UNSURE

•N•S••
ENDSUP
ENESCO
ENISLE
ENOSIS
GNOSIS
INESSE
ONUSES
UNESCO
UNISEX
UNISON
UNISYS
UNUSED

•N••S•
ENCASE
ENDASH
ENDUSE
ENLIST
ENMESH
GNEISS
INCASE
INCASH
INCISE
INCUSE
INESSE
INFEST
INFUSE
INGEST
INJEST
INMOST
INNESS
INRUSH
INSIST
INVEST
ONRUSH
UNBUSY
UNCASE
UNEASE
UNEASY
UNJUST
UNLASH
UNLESS
UNMASK
UNMESH
UNREST
UNWISE
UNWISH

•N•••S
ANDRES
ANDROS
ANELES
ANGELS
ANGERS
ANGLES
ANGLOS
ANIMAS
ANIMES
ANIMUS
ANIONS
ANJOUS
ANKLES
ANNALS
ANNOYS
ANNULS
ANODES
ANOLES
ANTICS
ANTRES
ANUBIS
ANVILS
CNIDUS
CNOTES
ENACTS
ENATES
ENDERS
ENDOWS
ENDUES
ENGELS
ENJOYS
ENNIUS
ENOKIS
ENOSIS
ENROLS
ENSUES
ENTERS
ENURES
ENVIES
ENVOIS
ENVOYS
GNARLS
GNEISS
GNOMES
GNOSIS
INCANS
INCHES
INCURS
INDIES
INDRIS
INFERS
INGLES
INGOTS
INGRES
INIONS
INKERS
INKLES
INLAWS
INLAYS
INLETS
INNESS
INPUTS
INSETS
INTENS
INTROS
INUITS
INURES
KNACKS
KNAVES
KNEADS
KNEELS
KNELLS
KNICKS
KNIFES
KNIVES
KNOCKS
KNOLLS
KNOTTS
KNOUTS
KNOWNS
KNURLS
ONEUPS
ONIONS
ONSETS
ONUSES
ONYXES
SNACKS
SNAFUS
SNAILS
SNAKES
SNARES
SNARLS
SNATHS
SNEAKS
SNEERS
SNELLS
SNICKS
SNIFFS
SNIPES
SNOODS
SNOOKS
SNOOPS
SNOOTS
SNOPES
SNORES
SNORTS
SNOUTS
SNUFFS
TNOTES
UNARMS
UNBARS
UNCAPS
UNCLES
UNDIES
UNDOES
UNFITS
UNGUES
UNGUIS
UNIATS
UNIONS
UNISYS
UNITAS
UNITES
UNJAMS
UNLESS
UNMANS
UNPEGS
UNPENS
UNPINS
UNRIGS
UNSAYS
UNSEWS
UNTIES
UNZIPS
VNECKS

••NS••
BENSON
BONSAI
BUNSEN
CENSED
CENSER
CENSES
CENSOR
CENSUS
CONSUL
DANSON
DENSER
GUNSHY
HANSEL
HANSOM
HANSON
HENSON
HONSHU
JANSEN
JANSKY
JENSEN
JONSON
KANSAN
KANSAS
KINSEY
KINSKI
LANSON
LENSED
LENSES
LINSEY
MANSES
MENSAE
MENSAL
MENSAS
MENSCH
NANSEN
OWNSUP
PENSEE
PINSON
RANSOM
RINSED
RINSES
RUNSAT
RUNSIN
RUNSON
RUNSTO
RUNSUP
SANSEI
SENSED
SENSEI
SENSES
SENSOR
SUNSET
TENSED
TENSER
TENSES
TENSOR
TINSEL
TONSIL
WINSOR

••N•S•
ARNESS
BANISH
DANISH
DENISE
DYNAST
ERNEST
FINEST
FINISH
HONEST
INNESS
IONISE
LANOSE
MONISM
MONIST
PUNISH
SANEST
SINISE
TANIST
TONISH
VANISH
WINISH

••N••S
AENEAS
ANNALS
ANNOYS
ANNULS
ARNESS
BANJOS
BANTUS
BINGES
BONCES
BONERS
BONGOS
BONNES
BONZES
BUNCOS
BUNKOS
CANALS
CANERS
CANIDS
CANNES
CANOES
CANONS
CANTOS
CANVAS
CENSES
CENSUS
CENTOS
CONCHS
CONDOS
CONEYS
CONGAS
CONICS
CONIES
CONTES
CYNICS
DANAUS
DANCES
DANTES
DENIES
DENIMS
DENNIS
DINARS
DINERS
DINGUS
DONEES
DONETS
DONNAS
DONORS
DONUTS
DUNCES
ENNIUS
FANONS
FENCES
FINALS
FUNGUS
GANGES
GENETS
GENIES
GENIUS
GENRES
GONERS
HENNAS
HINDUS
HINGES
HINGIS
HONEYS
HONORS
INNESS
IONICS
JANHUS
JINXES
JONAHS
JUNCOS
JUNTAS
JUNTOS
KANSAS
LANAIS
LANCES
LANDIS
LENSES
LINENS
LINERS
LONERS
LONGES
LUNGES
LYNXES
MANAUS
MANGOS
MANIAS
MANORS
MANSES
MANTAS
MANTIS
MENDES
MENSAS
MENTIS
MINCES
MINERS
MINIMS
MINKES
MINORS
MINXES
MONADS
MONEYS
MONIES
MONTES
MONTHS
MUNGOS
MYNAHS
NANTES
NENETS
NINERS
NINJAS
NINTHS
NONETS
OUNCES
OWNERS
PANDAS
PANELS
PANICS
PANNES
PANTOS
PENNIS
PINDUS
PINNAS
PINONS
PINOTS
PINTOS
PINUPS
PONCES
PONIES
PONTES
PONTUS
QANTAS
RANEES
RANGES
RANIDS
RENEWS
RENNES
RINSES
RONDOS
RUNINS
RUNONS
RUNUPS
SANTOS
SENNAS
SENORS
SENSES
SINEWS
SINGES
SONDES
SONICS
SUNNIS
SUNUPS
SYNODS
TANGOS
TANKAS
TANTES
TENENS
TENETS
TENNIS
TENONS
TENORS
TENSES
TENTHS
TINCTS
TINGES
TONDOS
TONERS
TONICS
TONNES
TUNERS
TUNICS
UINTAS
VENOMS
VENOUS
VENUES
VINCES
VINOUS
VINYLS
WANERS
WENCES
WINCES
WINZES
YENTAS
ZANIES
ZENDOS

•••NS•
ALONSO
EVENSO
FLENSE
GAINST
GDANSK
ODENSE
TEENSY
WEENSY

•••N•S
ACINUS
ADONIS
AGENAS
AGENTS
AKENES
ALANIS
ALINES
AMENDS
AMENTS
AMINES
AMINUS
ARENAS
ASANAS
ATONES
AZINES
BAINES
BARNES
BEANOS
BEINGS
BLANKS
BLENDS
BLINDS
BLINIS
BLINKS
BLONDS
BLUNTS
BMINUS
BONNES
BOUNDS
BRANDS
BRANTS
BRENTS
BRINES
BRINGS
BRINKS
BRONCS
BRUNTS
BUENOS
BWANAS
BYRNES
CANNES
CARNES
CHANTS
CHINES
CHINKS
CHINOS
CHUNKS
CLANGS
CLANKS
CLINES
CLINGS
CLINKS
CLONES
CLONKS
CLONUS
CLUNKS
CMINUS
COUNTS
CRANES
CRANKS
CRONES
CRONUS
CYGNUS
DAUNTS
DENNIS
DMINUS
DOINGS
DONNAS
DRINGS
DRINKS
DRONES
EBONDS
ELANDS
EMENDS
ERINYS
ETHNOS
EVENTS
FAINTS
FAUNAS
FAUNUS
FEINTS
FIENDS
FLANKS
FLINGS
FLINTS
FLUNKS
FOUNDS
FOUNTS
FRANCS
FRANKS
FRONDS
FRONTS
GIANTS
GLANDS
GLINTS
GLYNIS
GOINGS
GRANDS
GRANTS
GRINDS
GRUNTS
HAINES
HAUNTS
HENNAS
HMONGS
HOUNDS
HYENAS
HYPNOS
ICINGS
IRANIS
IRENES
JAUNTS
JOINTS
KAUNAS
KERNOS
KEYNES
KIANGS
LEMNOS
LEONES
LIANAS
LIANES
LIANGS
LLANOS
MAGNUS
MOINES
MOUNDS
MOUNTS
NOONES
OMANIS
OPINES
ORANGS
ORANTS
ORINGS
PAINTS
PANNES
PARNIS
PENNIS
PHONES
PHONOS
PIANOS
PINNAS
PLANES
PLANKS
PLANTS
PLINKS
PLONKS
PLUNKS
POINTS
POUNDS
PRANGS
PRANKS
PRINKS
PRINTS
PRONGS
PRUNES
QUINTS
RAINES
REINAS
REINKS
RENNES
REUNES
RHINOS
ROUNDS
RUANAS
SAINTS
SAUNAS
SCANTS
SCENAS
SCENDS
SCENES
SCENTS
SCONES
SEINES
SENNAS
SHANKS
SHINES
SHUNTS
SKANKS
SKINKS
SKUNKS
SLANGS
SLANTS
SLINGS
SLINKS
SOUNDS
SPANKS
SPENDS
SPINES
SPINKS
STANDS
STENOS
STINGS
STINKS
STINTS
STONES
STUNTS
SUNNIS
SWANKS
SWINGS
TAINOS
TAINTS
TAUNTS
TBONDS
TBONES
TENNIS
TERNES
THANES
THANKS
THINGS
THINKS
THONGS
THUNKS
TONNES
TRENDS
TRINES
TRUNKS
TWANGS
TWINES
UPENDS
URANUS
VARNAS
VAUNTS
VIANDS
WHANGS
WHINES
WOUNDS
WRINGS
WRONGS
ZOUNDS

••••NS
ACORNS
ADDONS
ADORNS
ALIENS
ALIGNS
ALOINS
AMIENS
ANIONS
APRONS
ARSONS
ARYANS
ASIANS
ASPENS
ATHENS
ATKINS
AUDENS
AUXINS
AVIANS
AXIONS
BAIRNS
BARONS
BASINS
BATONS
BEGINS
BISONS
BOSONS
BOSUNS
BRAINS
BRIANS
BROWNS
BRUINS
BURINS
CABINS
CAIRNS
CAJUNS
CANONS
CAPONS
CHAINS
CHURNS
CLEANS
CLOWNS
CODONS
COIGNS
COLONS
COVENS
COWENS
COZENS
CROONS
CROWNS
CUTINS
DEIGNS
DEMONS
DIVANS
DIZENS
DOGONS
DOYENS
DOZENS
DRAINS
DROWNS
EOSINS
FANONS
FEIGNS
FELONS
FLYINS
FOEHNS
FROWNS
FUTONS
GAMINS
GHAINS
GIVENS
GLEANS
GLUONS
GRAINS
GREENS
GROANS
GROINS
GYRONS
HAVENS
HAZANS
HELENS
HERONS
HOGANS
HUMANS
HURONS
INCANS
INIONS
INTENS
IOWANS
JAPANS
KNOWNS
LAPINS
LATENS
LATINS
LEARNS
LEMANS
LEMONS
LIKENS
LIMENS
LINENS
LIVENS
LODENS
LUDENS
LUMENS
LYSINS
MASONS
MATINS
MAVENS
MAYANS
MELONS
MESONS
MIZENS
MORONS
MOURNS
MUCINS
NEVINS
NOLENS
NYLONS
OCEANS
ONIONS
ORGANS
PAEANS
PAEONS
PAGANS
PARENS
PATENS
PECANS
PEKINS
PINONS
PISANS
PITONS
PLAINS
PRAWNS
PREENS
PRIONS
PUTONS
PYLONS
QUEENS
QUERNS
QUOINS
RACONS
RAVENS
RAYONS
RECONS
REIGNS
REMANS
REPINS
RERUNS
RESINS
REWINS
RIPENS
ROBINS
ROMANS
ROSINS
ROWENS
RUBENS
RUMENS
RUNINS
RUNONS
SABINS
SALONS
SARANS
SATINS
SAXONS
SCIONS
SCORNS
SEDANS
SERINS
SETINS
SEVENS
SHEENS
SIRENS
SITINS
SKEANS
SKEINS
SOLANS
SPAWNS
SPOONS
SPURNS
STAINS
STEINS
STERNS
SWAINS
SWOONS
TAKINS
TALONS
TAPINS
TAUONS
TENENS
TENONS
TETONS
TEXANS
THORNS
TIEINS
TIPINS
TITANS
TOEINS
TOKENS
TOXINS
TOYONS
TRAINS
TWEENS
UCLANS
UHLANS
UNIONS
UNMANS
UNPENS
UNPINS
UTURNS
VALENS
VEGANS
VIXENS
VOLANS
VOLENS
VSIGNS
WAGONS
WAKENS
WAYANS
WIDENS
WIZENS
WOMENS
YEARNS
ZAYINS
ZAZENS

N•T•••
NATANT
NATHAN
NATICK
NATION
NATIVE
NATRON
NATTER
NATURA
NATURE
NETHER
NETMAN
NETMEN
NETPAY
NETTED
NETTLE
NETTLY
NETTON
NITERS
NITERY
NITRES
NITRIC
NITWIT
NOTARY
NOTATE
NOTBAD
NOTCHY
NOTERS
NOTICE
NOTIFY
NOTING
NOTION
NOTNOW
NOTYET
NUTATE
NUTKIN
NUTLET
NUTMEG
NUTRIA
NUTTED
NUTTER

N••T••
NANTES
NATTER
NAUTCH
NEATEN
NEATER
NEATLY
NECTAR
NEKTON
NESTEA
NESTED
NESTER
NESTLE
NESTOR
NETTED
NETTLE
NETTLY
NETTON
NEUTER
NEWTON
NEXTTO
NINTHS
NOETIC
NOOTKA
NORTHS
NORTON
NUTTED
NUTTER

N•••T•
NAMATH
NEARTO
NEGATE
NEMATO
NENETS
NEXTTO
NICETY
NIGHTS
NIGHTY
NIKITA
NIMITZ
NINETY
NOHITS
NONETS
NOPETS
NOTATE
NOVATO
NUDITY
NUTATE
NYMETS

N••••T
NATANT
NAUGHT
NEEDNT
NEWEST
NICEST
NIPSAT
NITWIT
NLEAST
NLWEST
NOCENT
NOEXIT
NONFAT
NOTYET
NOUGAT
NOUGHT
NUDEST
NUDIST
NUGENT
NUGGET
NUMBAT
NUTLET

•NT•••
ANTCOW
ANTEED
ANTERO
ANTEUP
ANTHEM
ANTHER
ANTICS
ANTLER
ANTONY
ANTRES
ANTRIM
ANTRON
ANTRUM
ENTAIL
ENTERO
ENTERS
ENTICE
ENTIRE
ENTITY
ENTOMO
ENTRAP
ENTREE
INTACT
INTAKE
INTEND
INTENS
INTENT
INTERJ
INTERN
INTIMA
INTIME
INTINE
INTONE
INTOTO
INTOWN
INTROS
INTUIT
INTUNE
INTURN
ONTAPE
ONTIME
ONTOUR
UNTACK
UNTIDY
UNTIED
UNTIES
UNTOLD

UNTORN
UNTRAP
UNTROD
UNTRUE
UNTUNE

•N•T••
ANATTO
ANITRA
CNOTES
ENATES
GNATTY
INITIO
INSTAL
INSTAR
INSTEP
INSTIL
KNOTTS
KNOTTY
ONETWO
SNATCH
SNATHE
SNATHS
SNITCH
SNOTTY
TNOTES
UNITAL
UNITAS
UNITED
UNITER
UNITES
UNSTOP

•N••T•
ANATTO
ANSATE
ENACTS
ENMITY
ENTITY
GNATTY
INCITE
INDITE
INGOTS
INLETS
INMATE
INNATE
INPUTS
INSETS
INSITU
INTOTO
INUITS
INVITE
INWITH
KNOTTS
KNOTTY
KNOUTS
ONSETS
ONSITE
SNAPTO
SNOOTS
SNOOTY
SNORTS
SNOTTY
SNOUTS
UNFITS
UNIATE
UNIATS

•N•••T
ANKLET
ANNUIT
ANOINT
ENFANT
ENGIRT
ENGLUT
ENLIST
ENRAPT
ENROOT
INAPET
INARUT
INCEPT
INCULT
INDEBT
INDENT
INDICT
INDUCT
INFACT
INFANT
INFECT
INFEST
INGEST
INJECT
INJEST
INKJET
INMOST
INPART
INPORT
INSECT
INSERT
INSIST
INSULT
INTACT
INTENT
INTUIT
INVENT
INVERT
INVEST
KNIGHT
ONEACT
ONFOOT
SNAPAT
SNOCAT
UNBELT
UNBENT
UNBOLT
UNGIRT
UNHURT
UNJUST
UNKNIT
UNKNOT
UNMEET
UNREST
UNROOT
UNSEAT

••NT••
AUNTIE
BANTAM
BANTER
BANTUS
BENTON
BONTON
BUNTED
BUNTER
CANTAB
CANTED
CANTER
CANTHI
CANTLE
CANTON
CANTOR
CANTOS
CENTER
CENTOS
CENTRE
CENTRI
CENTRO
CONTAC
CONTES
CONTRA
CONTRE
DANTES
DANTON
DENTAL
DENTED
DENTIL
DENTIN
DENTON
DINTED
FANTAN
FONTAL
GANTRY
GENTLE
GENTLY
GENTRY
GUNTER
HENTED
HINTAT
HINTED
HINTER
HINTON
HUNTED
HUNTER
JUNTAS
JUNTOS
KANTOR
KENTON
LENTEN
LENTIL
LINTEL
LINTER
MANTAS
MANTEL
MANTIC
MANTIS
MANTLE
MANTRA
MANTUA
MENTAL
MENTIS
MENTOR
MINTED
MINTER
MONTEL
MONTES
MONTEZ
MONTHS
MUNTIN
NANTES
NINTHS
PANTED
PANTOS
PANTRY
PENTAD
PENTUP
PINTER
PINTLE
PINTOS
PONTES
PONTIC
PONTUS
PUNTED
PUNTER
QANTAS
QINTAR
RANTED
RANTER
RENTAL
RENTED
RENTER
SANTEE
SANTIR
SANTOS
SENTIN
SENTRA
SENTRY
SENTUP
SINTAX
SINTER
SONTAG
SUNTAN
SYNTAX
TANTES
TANTRA
TENTED
TENTER
TENTHS
TINTED
TINTER
UINTAS
VENTED
VENTER
VINTON
WANTAD
WANTED
WANTIN
WANTON
WANTTO
WENTAT
WENTBY
WENTIN
WENTON
WENTUP
WINTER
WINTRY
WONTED
WONTON
WYNTER
WYNTON
XANTHO
YENTAS

••N•T•
ADNATE
AGNATE
ARNETT
BENITO
BINATE
BONITO
CANUTE
CENOTE
DENOTE
DONATE
DONETS
DONITZ
DONUTS
FINITE
FINITO
GENETS
GUNITE
HINCTY
IGNATZ
IGNITE
INNATE
LANATE
LENGTH
LENITY
LUNATE
MINUTE
MONETA
NENETS
NINETY
NONETS
ORNATE
ORNITH
PINATA
PINITE
PINOTS
RENATA
RENOTE
RUNSTO
SANCTA
SANGTO
SANITY
SENATE
SENITI
SINGTO
SONATA
TENDTO
TENETS
TENUTO
TINCTS
TONITE
VANITY
VENETO
VENITE
WANTTO
ZENITH
ZONATE

••N••T
ANNUIT
ARNETT
BANDIT
BENOIT
BONMOT
BONNET
CANLIT
CANNOT
CONANT
DUNANT
DYNAST
ERNEST
FANJET
FANOUT
FINEST
GANNET
HENBIT
HINTAT
HONEST
JENNET
JUNKET
LANCET
LINNET
MINUET
MINUIT
MONIST
NONFAT
PANDIT
PANOUT
PENULT
PINXIT
PUNDIT
PUNNET
RANOUT
RENNET
RUNLET
RUNOUT
RUNSAT
SANEST
SENNET
SENNIT
SONANT
SONNET
SUNLIT
SUNSET
TANIST
TENANT
TINHAT
TINPOT
VINCIT
WENTAT
WINGIT
WINKAT
WINOUT
WONOUT

•••NT•
AGENTS
AJANTA
AMENTS
AVANTI
BLINTZ
BLUNTS
BOUNTY
BRANTS
BRENTS
BRONTE
BRUNTS
CHANTS
CHINTZ
COUNTS
COUNTY
DAINTY
DAUNTS
EVENTS
FAINTS
FEINTS
FLINTS
FLINTY
FOUNTS
FRONTS
GIANTS
GLINTS
GOINTO
GRANTS
GRUNTS
HAUNTS
JAUNTS
JAUNTY
JOINTS
KOONTZ
KRANTZ
LEANTO
MOUNTS
MOUNTY
ODONTO
OPENTO
ORANTS
PAINTS
PAINTY
PLANTE
PLANTS
PLENTY
PLINTH
POINTE
POINTS
POINTY
PRINTS
PRONTO
PUENTE
QUANTA
QUINTS
SAINTE
SAINTS
SCANTS
SCANTY
SCENTS
SEENTO
SHANTY
SHINTO
SHUNTS
SLANTS
SPINTO
STINTS
STUNTS
STUNTY
TAINTS
TAUNTS
TURNTO
TWENTY
VAUNTS

•••N•T
ARENDT
BONNET
BOWNET
BRANDT
BRUNET
BURNET
CANNOT
CAPNUT
CARNET
CARNOT
CORNET
CYGNET
DARNIT
FLYNET
GAINST
GANNET
GARNET
HEXNUT
HORNET
JENNET
LINNET
LIONET
LUGNUT
MAGNET
PEANUT
PIGNUT
PLANET
PUNNET
REGNAT
RENNET
SENNET
SENNIT
SIGNET
SONNET
SPINET
UNKNIT
UNKNOT
USENET
WALNUT
WHYNOT

••••NT
ABSENT
ACCENT
ADVENT
AGLINT
AMOUNT
ANOINT
ARDENT
ARGENT
ARPENT
ARRANT
ASCENT
ASLANT
ASSENT
AUMONT
AVAUNT
BESANT
BEZANT
BRYANT
CADENT
CEDANT
CEMENT
CLIENT
COGENT
CONANT
COVENT
DARENT
DECANT
DECENT
DETENT
DISANT
DOCENT
DOESNT
DOPANT
DUMONT
DUNANT
DUPONT
DURANT
EGMONT
ENFANT
ERRANT
ESCENT
EXEUNT
EXTANT
EXTENT
FLAUNT
FLUENT
FOMENT
FORINT
GERENT
GERONT
HAVENT
HLHUNT
INDENT
INFANT
INTENT
INVENT
LAMENT
LAMONT
LATENT
LEARNT
LEVANT
LUCENT
MOMENT
MORANT
MUSTNT
MUTANT
NATANT
NEEDNT
NOCENT
NUGENT
OCTANT
ORIENT
PARENT
PATENT
PEDANT
PLAINT
PLIANT
POTENT
QUAINT
REBENT
RECANT
RECENT
REDANT
REGENT
RELENT
REPENT
RERENT
RESENT
RIDENT
RODENT
SAVANT
SECANT
SEJANT
SILENT
SOLENT
SONANT
SPLINT
SPRINT
SQUINT
TALENT
TENANT
TRUANT
TYRANT
UNBENT
URGENT
UTHANT
VACANT
VALENT
VIVANT
VOLANT
WERENT
WISENT

NU••••
NUANCE
NUBBED
NUBBIN
NUBBLE
NUBBLY
NUBIAN
NUBILE
NUCHAE
NUCHAL
NUCLEI
NUCLEO
NUDELY
NUDEST
NUDGED
NUDGER
NUDGES
NUDIST
NUDITY
NUDNIK

NUECES
NUGENT
NUGGET
NUKING
NULLAH
NULLED
NUMBAT
NUMBED
NUMBER
NUMBLY
NUMERO
NUMINA
NUNCIO
NURSED
NURSER
NURSES
NUTATE
NUTKIN
NUTLET
NUTMEG
NUTRIA
NUTTED
NUTTER
NUZZLE

N•U•••
NAUGHT
NAUSEA
NAUTCH
NEUMAN
NEUMES
NEURAL
NEUROL
NEURON
NEUTER
NGUYEN
NOUGAT
NOUGHT
NOUMEA

N••U••
NATURA
NATURE
NEBULA
NERUDA
NIPUPS
NODULE
NYQUIL

N•••U•
NASHUA
NEREUS
NIMBUS
NIPPUR

N••••U
NASSAU
NIIHAU

•NU•••
ANUBIS
ANURAN
ENURED
ENURES
INUITS
INURED
INURES
KNURLS
KNURLY
ONUSES
SNUBBY
SNUFFS
SNUFFY
SNUGLI
SNUGLY
UNUSED

•N•U••
ANNUAL
ANNUIT
ANNULI
ANNULS
ENDUED
ENDUES
ENDURE
ENDURO
ENDUSE
ENGULF
ENOUGH
ENQUAD
ENSUED
ENSUES
ENSURE
INBULK
INCULT
INCURS
INCUSE
INDUCE
INDUCT
INFULL
INFUSE
INJURE
INJURY
INLUCK
INOUYE
INPUTS
INRUSH
INSULT
INSURE
INTUIT
INTUNE
INTURN
KNOUTS
ONEUPS
ONRUSH
PNEUMA
SNOUTS
UNBUSY
UNCURL
UNDULY
UNFURL
UNGUAL
UNGUES
UNGUIS
UNHURT
UNJUST
UNRULY
UNSUNG
UNSURE
UNTUNE

•N••U•
ANIMUS
ANJOUS
ANTEUP
ANTRUM
CNIDUS
ENDRUN
ENDSUP
ENGLUT
ENNIUS
ENSOUL
INARUT
INDIUM
INFLUX
INHAUL
INPOUR
ONTOUR
SNAFUS
SNAPUP
UNGLUE
UNIQUE
UNPLUG
UNTRUE

•N•••U
INSITU

••NU••
ANNUAL
ANNUIT
ANNULI
ANNULS
BENUMB
BUNUEL
CANUTE
CONURE
DANUBE
DENUDE
DONUTS
GENUAL
LUNULA
MANUAL
MANUEL
MINUET
MINUIT
MINUTE
PENULT
PENURY
PINUPS
RUNUPS
SENUFO
SUNUNU
SUNUPS
TENURE
TENUTO
VENUES
ZANUCK

••N•U•
BANGUI
BANGUP
BANJUL
BANQUO
BANTUS
BENHUR
BINDUP
BONEUP
BUNKUM
CANCUN
CANFUL
CENSUS
CINQUE
CONCUR
CONIUM
CONSUL
DANAUS
DENGUE
DINGUS
DONEUP
ENNIUS
FANOUT
FONDUE
FUNGUS
GANGUE
GANGUP
GENIUS
HANDUP
HANGUL
HANGUP
HINDUS
HONOUR
HUNGUP
IONIUM
JANHUS
KUNLUN
LANGUR
LINEUP
LINGUA
LINKUP
LONGUE
MANAUS
MANFUL
MANQUE
MANTUA
MINIUM
OMNIUM
OWNSUP
PANFUL
PANOUT
PENTUP
PINDUS
PONTUS
PONYUP
RANGUP
RANOUT
RINGUP
RUNGUP
RUNOUT
RUNSUP
SANNUP
SENDUP
SENTUP
SINFUL
TANGUY
TANKUP
TONEUP
TONGUE
TUNEUP
VENOUS
VINOUS
WENTUP
WINDUP
WINOUT
WONMUG
WONOUT
YANQUI

••N••U
CONGOU
HONSHU
HUNGWU
JUNEAU
KUNGFU
LANDAU
MANCHU
MENJOU
PENGHU
SUNUNU
XANADU

•••NU•
ACINUS
AMINUS
AVENUE
BARNUM
BMINUS
BURNUP
CAPNUT
CHINUP
CLONUS
CMINUS
CRONUS
CYGNUS
DMINUS
EVENUP
FAUNUS
FRENUM
HEXNUT
JOINUP
KRONUR
LUGNUT
MAGNUM
MAGNUS
OPENUP
PEANUT
PIGNUT
PLENUM
PRENUP
SANNUP
SEWNUP
SIGNUP
TURNUP
URANUS
WALNUT

•••N•U
CHONJU
MBUNDU

••••NU
SUNUNU
VISHNU

N•V•••
NAVAHO
NAVAJO
NAVELS
NAVIES
NEVADA
NEVERS
NEVINS
NEVSKY
NOVATO
NOVELS
NOVENA
NOVICE

N••V••
NARVIK
NERVES

N•••V•
NATIVE

•NV•••
ANVILS
ENVIED
ENVIER
ENVIES
ENVOIS
ENVOYS
INVADE
INVAIN
INVENT
INVERT
INVEST
INVITE
INVIVO
INVOKE
ONVIEW
UNVEIL

•N•V••
KNAVES
KNIVES
SNIVEL
UNEVEN
UNIVAC

•N••V•
ENDIVE
INLOVE
INVIVO
UNWOVE

••NV••
CANVAS
CONVEX
CONVEY
CONVOY
DENVER
LANVIN

••N•V•
CANOVA
DENOVO
GENEVA
GENEVE

••N••V
HENRYV

N•W•••
NAWABS
NEWAGE
NEWARK
NEWELS
NEWEST
NEWISH
NEWLEY
NEWMAN
NEWMAR
NEWTON
NLWEST
NOWISE

N••W••
NARWAL
NITWIT
NORWAY

N••••W
NARROW
NEPHEW
NOSHOW
NOTNOW

•NW•••
ANWANG
ENWRAP
INWARD
INWITH
ONWARD
UNWARY
UNWELL
UNWILY
UNWIND
UNWISE
UNWISH
UNWORN
UNWOVE
UNWRAP

•N•W••
ANSWER
ANYWAY
GNAWED
GNAWER
INAWAY
KNOWER
KNOWNS
ONEWAY
SNOWED
SNOWIN
UNAWED

•N••W•
ENDOWS
INLAWS
INTOWN
ONETWO
UNSEWN
UNSEWS
UNSOWN

•N•••W
ANDHOW
ANDREW
ANTCOW
ANYHOW
INAROW
INFLOW
ONVIEW
UNDRAW

••NW••
CONWAY
FENWAY
RUNWAY
WINWIN

••N•W•
HUNGWU
RENEWS
RENOWN
SINEWS
SINEWY

••N••W
MINNOW
SUNDEW
WINDOW
WINNOW

•••N•W
CPSNOW
ERENOW
HOWNOW
MINNOW
NOTNOW
WINNOW

N•X•••
NEXTTO
NIXIES
NIXING

N••X••
NOEXIT

•N•X••
ONYXES

•N••X•
ANNEXE

•N•••X
INAFIX
INFLUX
UNISEX

••NX••
JINXED
JINXES
LYNXES
MINXES
PINXIT
SKNXXX

••N•X•
ADNEXA
ANNEXE
CUNAXA
SKNXXX

••N••X
BENDIX
CONVEX
LENNOX
MANNIX
MENINX
SINTAX
SKNXXX
SYNTAX
WINDEX

•••N•X
BRANDX
LENNOX
MANNIX

••••NX
LARYNX
MENINX
SPHINX
SYRINX

NY••••
NYALAS
NYASSA
NYLONS
NYMETS
NYMPHS
NYQUIL

N•Y•••
NAYSAY

N••Y••
NGUYEN
NOTYET

N•••Y•
NAGOYA

N••••Y
NAMELY
NAPERY
NASEBY
NAYSAY
NEARBY
NEARLY
NEATLY
NETPAY
NETTLY
NEVSKY
NEWLEY
NIAMEY
NICELY
NICETY
NIDIFY
NIGHTY
NIMBLY
NIMINY
NINETY
NIPSEY
NITERY
NOBODY
NONARY
NORGAY
NORWAY
NOSILY
NOTARY
NOTCHY
NOTIFY
NUBBLY
NUDELY
NUDITY
NUMBLY

•NY•••
ANYANG
ANYDAY
ANYHOW
ANYONE
ANYWAY
ONYXES
SNYDER
UNYOKE

•N•Y••
ANHYDR
ENZYME
INSYNC
UNDYED

•N••Y•
ANNOYS
ANONYM
ENJOYS
ENVOYS
INLAYS
INOUYE
UNISYS
UNSAYS

•N•••Y
ANDREY

ANERGY
ANTONY
ANYDAY
ANYWAY
ENERGY
ENMITY
ENTITY
GNARLY
GNATTY
INAWAY
INFAMY
INJURY
INPLAY
KNAGGY
KNARRY
KNOBBY
KNOLLY
KNOTTY
KNURLY
ONEDAY
ONEWAY
ONIONY
SNAGGY
SNAPPY
SNARLY
SNAZZY
SNEAKY
SNEERY
SNEEZY
SNIFFY
SNIPPY
SNOBBY
SNOOKY
SNOOPY
SNOOTY
SNOOZY
SNOTTY
SNUBBY
SNUFFY
SNUGLY
UNBUSY
UNDULY
UNEASY
UNHOLY
UNOILY
UNRULY
UNTIDY
UNWARY
UNWILY

••NY••
BANYAN
BUNYAN
BUNYIP
CANYON
KENYAN
LYNYRD
MINYAN
PINYIN
PINYON
PONYUP
RUNYON
VINYLS

••N•Y•
ANNOYS
CONEYS
HENRYV
HONEYS
KENNYG
MONEYS
VANRYN

••N••Y
BENDAY
BENGAY
BINARY
BUNCHY
CANARY
CANOPY
CONROY
CONVEY
CONVOY
CONWAY
DANGLY
DANKLY
DANNAY
DENARY
DINGHY
DINKEY
DONKEY
FENWAY
FINELY
FINERY
FINNEY
FONDLY
GANGLY
GANTRY
GENTLY
GENTRY
GONEBY
GUNSHY
HANLEY
HENLEY
HINCTY
HUNGRY
JANGLY
JANSKY
JENNEY
JINGLY
JUNGLY
KINDLY
KINGLY
KINSEY
LANDRY
LANKLY
LENITY
LINENY
LINNEY
LINSEY
LONELY
LONGLY
LUNACY
LUNCHY
LYNLEY
MANDAY
MANRAY
MINIFY
MONDAY
MONKEY
MONODY
MUNCHY
NINETY
NONARY
ORNERY
PANFRY
PANTRY
PENNEY
PENURY
PINERY
PUNCHY
PUNILY
RANDRY
RANKLY
RONELY
RUNDRY
RUNWAY
SANELY
SANITY
SENARY
SENTRY
SINEWY
SINGLY
SUNDAY
SUNDRY
SUNRAY
TANGLY
TANGUY
TINGLY
TINILY
TINKLY
TUNNEY
VANITY
VINERY
VINIFY
WENTBY
WINERY
WINTRY
ZANILY

•••NY•
ANONYM
CRONYN
EPONYM
ERINYS
KENNYG
PHENYL

•••N•Y
AGENCY
BARNEY
BIRNEY
BLENNY
BOUNCY
BOUNTY
BRANDY
BRANNY
BRONZY
BURNEY
CAGNEY
CARNEY
CHANCY
CHANEY
CHINKY
CHUNKY
CLANCY
CLANKY
CLINGY
CLUNKY
COONEY
COUNTY
CRANKY
CRANNY
DABNEY
DAINTY
DANNAY
DARNAY
DISNEY
DOWNEY
EVENLY
FINNEY
FLINTY
FLUNKY
FRANNY
FRENZY
FRINGY
GAINLY
GRANNY
GRUNDY
GRUNGY
GURNEY
HEANEY
HORNEY
HOUNDY
JAUNTY
JENNEY
JITNEY
JOHNNY
JOUNCY
KEENLY
KIDNEY
LEANLY
LINNEY
LIONLY
LOONEY
MAINLY
MAUNDY
MEANLY
MOONEY
MORNAY
MOUNTY
OHENRY
OPENLY
ORANGY
ORKNEY
PAINTY
PENNEY
PHONEY
PLENTY
POINTY
QUINCY
RAINEY
RODNEY
ROMNEY
ROONEY
SCANTY
SHANDY
SHANNY
SHANTY
SHINDY
SHINNY
SIDNEY
SKINNY
SKUNKY
SLANGY
SLINKY
SPANKY
SPONGY
SPUNKY
STANKY
STINGY
STINKY
STUNTY
SWANKY
SWINGY
SYDNEY
TEENSY
THINGY
THINLY
TRENDY
TUNNEY
TWANGY
TWENTY
VAINLY
VARNEY
WATNEY
WEENSY
WHINEY
WHINNY

••••NY
ALBANY
ANTONY
BARONY
BETONY
BLENNY
BOIGNY
BOTANY
BRAINY
BRANNY
BRAWNY
BROWNY
BRYONY
COLONY
CRANNY
CZERNY
DELANY
FELONY
FRANNY
GRAINY
GRANNY
GREENY
GROZNY
HOMINY
JIMINY
JOHNNY
KEARNY
KRASNY
LEMONY
LINENY
LITANY
MUTINY
NIMINY
ONIONY
PIMINY
REDENY
RESINY
ROMANY
ROSINY
SATINY
SAXONY
SHANNY
SHINNY
SIMONY
SKINNY
SOMANY
SPOONY
THORNY
TWEENY
WHINNY

N•Z•••
NOZZLE
NUZZLE

N••Z••
NOZZLE
NUZZLE

N••••Z
NIMITZ

•NZ•••
ENZYME
UNZIPS

•N•Z••
SNAZZY

•N••Z•
SNAZZY
SNEEZE
SNEEZY
SNOOZE
SNOOZY

••NZ••
BANZAI
BENZOL
BONZES
DANZIG
DENZEL
PANZER
PINZON
WINZES

••N•Z•
IONIZE

••N••Z
DONITZ
IGNATZ
MONTEZ

•••NZ•
ALONZO
BRONZE
BRONZY
FAENZA
FRENZY
KWANZA
RIENZI
STANZA

•••N•Z
BLINTZ
CHINTZ
KOONTZ
KRANTZ
SCHNOZ

••••NZ
BRIENZ
DOLENZ
LORENZ

OA••••
OAFISH
OAKLEY
OARING
OATERS
OATIER
OAXACA

O•A•••
OCASEK
OCASEY
OKAPIS
OKAYED
OMAHAN
OMAHAS
OMANIS
OMASUM
ONAGER
OPAQUE
ORACHS
ORACLE
ORALES
ORALLY
ORANGE
ORANGS
ORANGY
ORANTS
ORATED
ORATES
ORATOR
OSAGES
OVALLY
OXALIS
OZARKS

O••A••
OAXACA
OBEAHS
OBLAST
OBLATE
OBTAIN
OCEANS
OCTADS
OCTANE
OCTANT
OCTAVE
OCTAVO
OFLATE
OGHAMS
OGLALA
OKSANA
OLDAGE
OLEARY
OLEATE
ONCALL
ONEACT
ONHAND
ONLAND
ONSALE
ONTAPE
ONWARD
OOLALA
OPIATE
ORBACH
ORDAIN
OREADS
ORGANA
ORGANS
ORGATE
ORIANA
ORNATE
OSCARS
OSHAWA
OSWALD
OTTAVA
OTTAWA
OUTACT
OUTAGE
OUTATE
OXCART
OXNARD
OXTAIL

O•••A•
OBIWAN
OBRIAN
OCREAE
OCULAR
OFFDAY
OGDOAD
OHIOAN
OHYEAH
OILCAN
OILMAN
OILPAN
OLDHAM
OLDHAT
OLDMAN
OLDSAW
OMAHAN
OMAHAS
OMEGAS
ONEDAY
ONEMAN
ONEWAY
ONLOAN
OOMPAH
OPERAS
ORDEAL
ORGEAT
ORPHAN
OSSIAN
OSTEAL
OUTEAT
OUTLAW
OUTLAY
OUTRAN
OVISAC
OVULAR

O••••A
OAXACA
OBELIA
ODESSA
ODETTA
OEDEMA
OGLALA
OJIBWA
OKSANA
OLINDA
OLIVIA
OMERTA
ONEIDA
OOLALA
OPTIMA
OREIDA
ORGANA
ORIANA
ORISSA
ORTEGA
OSCULA
OSHAWA
OTTAVA
OTTAWA

•OA•••
BOARDS
BOASTS
BOATED
BOATEL
BOATER
COALER
COAPTS
COARSE
COASTS
COATED
COATIS
COAXED
COAXER
COAXES
DOABLE
FOALED
FOAMED
GOADED
GOALIE
GOANNA
GOATEE
GOAWAY
GOAWRY
HOAGIE
HOARDS
HOARSE
HOAXED
HOAXER
HOAXES
JOANIE
JOANNA
JOANNE
KOALAS
LOADED
LOADER
LOAFED
LOAFER
LOAMED
LOANED
LOANER
LOATHE
LOAVES
MOANED
MOANER
MOATED
POACHY
ROADIE
ROAMED
ROAMER
ROARED
ROARER
ROASTS
SOAKED
SOAKER
SOAKUP
SOAPED
SOAPER
SOARED
SOARER
SOARES
SOASTO
SOAVES
TOAMAN
TOASTS
TOASTY
TOATEE

•O•A••
AODAIS
BOGART
BONAMI
BORAGE
BORATE
BORAXO
BOTANY
BOVARY
BOYARS
COBALT

COLADA
COMATE
CONANT
COPAYS
CORALS
COWARD
DOMAIN
DOMANI
DONALD
DONATE
DOPANT
DORADO
DORAGS
DORATI
DOSAGE
DOTAGE
DOTARD
DOUALA
FORAGE
FORAYS
GOBACK
GOCART
GODARD
GOEASY
GOKART
GORALS
HOBART
HODADS
HOGANS
HOMAGE
HORACE
HOTAIR
HOWARD
IODATE
IOWANS
JOHANN
JONAHS
KODALY
KORATS
KOVACS
LOBATE
LOCALE
LOCALS
LOCATE
LORAIN
LOTAHS
LOVAGE
MOHAIR
MOHAVE
MOHAWK
MOJAVE
MOLARS
MONACO
MONADS
MORALE
MORALS
MORANT
MORASS
MORAVA
MORAYS
MOSAIC
MOZART
NOMADS
NONAGE
NONAME
NONARY
NOSALE
NOTARY
NOTATE
NOVATO
OOLALA
POLAND
POMACE
POMADE
POPART
POSADA
POTAGE
POTASH
POTATO
ROBALO
ROLAND
ROMAIC
ROMAJI
ROMANO
ROMANS
ROMANY
RONALD
ROSARY
ROTARY
ROTATE
ROXANA
ROXANE
ROYALE
ROYALS
SOCAGE
SOLACE
SOLANS
SOLARS
SOMALI
SOMANY
SOMATA
SOMATO
SONANT
SONATA
SOUARI
TOBAGO
TODATE
TOGAED
TOKAYS
TOMATO
TORAHS
TOTALS
TOWAGE
TOWARD
VOCALS
VOLANS
VOLANT
VOLARE
VOTARY
VOYAGE
YOUALL
ZONATE
ZOUAVE

•O••A•

AORTAE
AORTAL
AORTAS
AOUDAD
BOBCAT
BOMBAY
BONSAI
BOREAL
BOREAS
BORMAN
BOWMAN
BOWOAR
BOWSAW
BOXCAR
COBHAM
COBIAS
COBRAS
COCOAS
COEVAL
COGNAC
COLFAX
COLLAR
COLMAN
COMBAT
COMEAT
COMMAS
COMPAQ
COMSAT
CONFAB
CONGAS
CONMAN
CONRAD
CONTAC
CONWAY
COOGAN
CORBAN
CORDAY
CORMAN
CORRAL
COSTAE
COSTAL
COSTAR
COSTAS
COTTAS
COUGAR
COWMAN
DOBLAS
DOBRAS
DOGDAY
DOGEAR
DOGMAS
DOGSAT
DOGTAG
DOLLAR
DOLMAN
DOLMAS
DONNAS
DOODAD
DOODAH
DORCAS
DORIAN
DORSAL
DOSSAL
DOTHAN
EOLIAN
EONIAN
FOETAL
FOGHAT
FOLIAR
FONTAL
FORBAD
FORMAL
FORMAN
FORMAT
FORTAS
FOSSAE
FOSSAS
FOURAM
FOVEAE
GOAWAY
GOESAT
GOSTAG
GOTHAM
GOTMAD
HOOHAH
HOOHAS
HOOKAH
HOORAH
HOORAY
HOOTAT
HOSTAS
HOTCAP
HOTCAR
HOTWAR
HOWDAH
IONIAN
JORDAN
JOSIAH
JOVIAL
JOVIAN
KOALAS
KODIAK
KOMBAT
KONRAD
KOREAN
KORMAN
KOUFAX
LOGJAM
LONGAN
LOOFAH
LOOFAS
LOOKAT
LOQUAT
LOREAL
LOTHAR
LOWCAL
LOWFAT
MOBCAP
MOCHAS
MOLDAU
MOLNAR
MOMMAS
MONDAY
MOOLAH
MOREAU
MORGAN
MORNAY
MORTAL
MORTAR
MOSHAV
NOLEAD
NOLOAD
NONFAT
NOONAN
NORGAY
NORIAS
NORMAL
NORMAN
NORWAY
NOSOAP
NOTBAD
NOUGAT
OOMPAH
POKEAT
POLEAX
POLKAS
POPLAR
POPPAS
PORTAL
POSTAL
RODHAM
RODMAN
ROSEAU
SOCIAL
SOLDAN
SOLFAS
SONTAG
SOTHAT
SOWHAT
TOAMAN
TOBIAS
TODDAO
TODMAN
TOECAP
TOETAP
TOKLAS
TOMBAC
TOMCAT
TONGAN
TOOBAD
TOPCAT
TOPHAT
TOREAT
TOUCAN
TOWCAR
VODKAS
VOLVAS
WOMBAT
ZODIAC

•O•••A

BODEGA
BOGOTA
BORGIA
BOSNIA
COLADA
COLIMA
CONCHA
CONTRA
COPULA
CORNEA
CORONA
CORYZA
COULDA
COVINA
COWPEA
DODECA
DODOMA
DOUALA
GOANNA
GODIVA
GOTCHA
HOOPLA
HOTTEA
JOANNA
JOJOBA
JOSHUA
KONICA
KORUNA
LOGGIA
LOLITA
LORICA
LOUISA
LOYOLA
MODELA
MODENA
MONERA
MONETA
MONICA
MORAVA
MORITA
MOSKVA
MOTHRA
NOOTKA
NOUMEA
NOVENA
OOLALA
POMONA
PORTIA
POSADA
ROBBIA
ROMOLA
ROSITA
ROSTRA
ROWENA
ROXANA
SOMATA
SONATA
SONOMA
SONORA
SOPHIA
TOLUCA
TOPEKA
TOYOTA
WOVOKA
YORUBA
YOYOMA
ZOYSIA

••OA••

ABOARD
BLOATS
BROACH
BROADS
CHOATE
CLOACA
CLOAKS
CROAKS
CROAKY
CROATS
EBOATS
FLOATS
FLOATY
GLOATS
GROANS
GROATS
PROAMS
SHOALS
SHOALY
SHOATS
SKOALS
SLOANE
STOATS
UBOATS

••O•A•

ABORAL
ADONAI
AGORAE
AGORAS
ALOHAS
ALOMAR
AMORAL
ANORAK
APODAL
AROMAS
ASOSAN
ATONAL
AVOWAL
AXONAL
BAOBAB
BHOPAL
BIOGAS
BIOTAS
BROGAN
BROKAW
CHORAL
COOGAN
DEODAR
DOODAD
DOODAH
DVORAK
FLORAE
FLORAL
FLORAS
GLOBAL
HOOHAH
HOOHAS
HOOKAH
HOORAH
HOORAY
HOOTAT
ISOBAR
KIOWAS
LOOFAH
LOOFAS
LOOKAT
MAOTAI
MOOLAH
NOONAN
PROTAX
PROZAC
QUOTAS
RIOJAS
RYOKAN
SHOFAR
SHORAN
SHOTAT
SIOUAN
SLOGAN
SLOVAK
SNOCAT
STOMAS
STOMAT
THOMAS
THORAX
TOOBAD
TROCAR
TROJAN
TWOWAY
UNOCAL
VIOLAS
XHOSAS
YEOMAN

••O••A

ABOLLA
AEOLIA
AMOEBA
CHOLLA
CHOPRA
CLOACA
EROICA
GLORIA
GLOSSA
HOOPLA
LIOTTA
MYOPIA
NOOTKA
PEORIA
PHOBIA
QUOKKA
QUOTHA
RHONDA
SCORIA
SCOTIA
SFORZA
SHORTA
TROIKA
UTOPIA

•••OA•

ABROAD
AFLOAT
BEMOAN
BOWOAR
BUROAK
BYROAD
COCOAS
GENOAN
INROAD
MINOAN
NOLOAD
NOSOAP
OGDOAD
OHIOAN
ONLOAN
PINOAK
PTBOAT
RECOAT
REDOAK
RELOAD
SAMOAN
SILOAM
STJOAN
TANOAK
TANOAN
THROAT
UNLOAD
UPLOAD
UPROAR

•••O•A

ANCONA
ANGOLA
ANGORA
AREOLA
ARROBA
AURORA
BAROJA
BITOLA
BOGOTA
BULOVA
CANOLA
CANOVA
CHROMA
CIBOLA
CORONA
CUPOLA
DAKOTA
DODOMA
EIDOLA
ENDORA
ESPOSA
EUBOEA
EUDORA
EUROPA
FEDORA
FEMORA
JOJOBA
JUDOKA
LADOGA
LAKOTA
LAROSA
LATONA
LATOYA
LOYOLA
MAZOLA
MIMOSA
MUCOSA
NAGOYA
NICOLA
NIKOLA
PAGODA
PALOMA
PAYOLA
PELOTA
POMONA
RAMONA
RCCOLA
REMORA
ROMOLA
SAMOSA
SENORA
SEROSA
SONOMA
SONORA
TACOMA
TOYOTA
VERONA
VIGODA
WINONA
WOVOKA
YOYOMA
ZADORA

••••OA

BALBOA
HIVAOA
HULLOA
JERBOA
LISBOA
QUINOA

OB••••

OBEAHS
OBELIA
OBELUS
OBERON
OBEYED
OBISPO
OBITER
OBIWAN
OBJECT
OBLAST
OBLATE
OBLIGE
OBLONG
OBOIST
OBRIAN
OBRIEN
OBSESS
OBSTET
OBTAIN
OBTEST
OBTUND
OBTUSE
OBVERT

O•B•••

ORBACH
ORBING
ORBITS
OSBORN
OXBOWS

O••B••
OJIBWA
OLDBOY
ORIBIS
OUTBID
OUTBOX

O••••B
ODDJOB

•OB•••
BOBBED
BOBBER
BOBBIE
BOBBIN
BOBBLE
BOBCAT
BOBSUP
COBALT
COBBLE
COBHAM
COBIAS
COBRAS
COBURG
COBURN
COBWEB
DOBBER
DOBBIN
DOBLAS
DOBLIN
DOBRAS
DOBROS
DOBSON
FOBBED
FOBOFF
GOBACK
GOBBLE
GOBIES
GOBLET
GOBLIN
GOBUST
HOBART
HOBBES
HOBBIT
HOBBLE
HOBNOB
HOBOES
HOBSON
JOBBED
JOBBER
JOBETH
JOBHOP
JOBLOT
KOBOLD
LOBATE
LOBBED
LOBBER
LOBULE
MOBBED
MOBCAP
MOBILE
MOBIUS
MOBLEY
NOBBLE
NOBLER
NOBLES
NOBODY
POBOYS
ROBALO
ROBBED
ROBBER
ROBBIA
ROBBIE
ROBERT
ROBING
ROBINS
ROBLES
ROBOTS
ROBROY
ROBSON
ROBUST
SOBBED
SOBBER
SOBEIT
SOBERS
SOBFUL
TOBAGO
TOBIAS
TOBIES
TOBOOT
TOBRUK
WOBBLE
WOBBLY
YOBBOS

•O•B••
BOBBED
BOBBER
BOBBIE
BOBBIN
BOBBLE
BOMBAY
BOMBED
BOMBER
BOMBES
BONBON
BOOBOO
BOUBOU
BOXBOY
COBBLE
COMBAT
COMBED
COMBER
COMBES
COMBOS
CORBAN
CORBEL
CORBIN
COWBOY
DOABLE
DOBBER
DOBBIN
DOOBIE
DOUBLE
DOUBLY
DOUBTS
FOBBED
FOGBOW
FOIBLE
FORBAD
FORBES
FORBID
GOBBLE
GOOBER
HOBBES
HOBBIT
HOBBLE
HOMBRE
HOTBED
HOTBOX
JOBBED
JOBBER
KOMBAT
KORBUT
LOBBED
LOBBER
LOMBOK
LOWBOY
MOBBED
MORBID
NOBBLE
NOTBAD
ROBBED
ROBBER
ROBBIA
ROBBIE
ROUBLE
SOBBED
SOBBER
SOMBER
SOMBRE
SORBET
SORBIC
SOWBUG
TOMBAC
TOMBOY
TOOBAD
WOBBLE
WOBBLY
WOMBAT
YOBBOS
YOUBET
ZOMBIE

•O••B•
COMEBY
DOESBY
GOESBY
GONEBY
GOODBY
JOJOBA
YORUBA

•O•••B
COBWEB
CONFAB
CONJOB
HOBNOB
HOTTUB
TOPJOB

••OB••
ADOBES
BAOBAB
BIOBIO
BOOBOO
DOOBIE
GLOBAL
GLOBED
GLOBES
GLOBIN
GOOBER
IROBOT
ISOBAR
KNOBBY
PHOBIA
PHOBIC
PHOBOS
PROBED
PROBER
PROBES
SLOBBY
SNOBBY
TOOBAD
TWOBIT

••O•B•
ABOMBS
AMOEBA
CROSBY
DROPBY
GOODBY
HBOMBS
KNOBBY
PHOEBE
RHOMBI
RHOMBS
SLOBBY
SNOBBY

••O••B
BAOBAB
DIONEB

•••OB•
AEROBE
ARROBA
CAROBS
DEMOBS
ENROBE
JACOBI
JOJOBA
KABOBS
KEBOBS
MCJOBS
NABOBS
STROBE
THROBS
TYCOBB
UNROBE

•••O•B
ABSORB
ADSORB
APLOMB
RESORB
TYCOBB

••••OB
CONJOB
DAYJOB
HOBNOB
ODDJOB
SKIBOB
TOPJOB

OC••••
OCASEK
OCASEY
OCCULT
OCCUPY
OCCURS
OCEANS
OCELLI
OCELOT
OCHERS
OCHERY
OCHRES
OCLOCK
OCREAE
OCTADS
OCTANE
OCTANT
OCTAVE
OCTAVO
OCTETS
OCTOPI
OCTROI
OCULAR

O•C•••
OCCULT
OCCUPY
OCCURS
ONCALL
OOCYTE
ORCHID
ORCHIL
OSCARS
OSCINE
OSCULA
OXCART

O••C••
OILCAN
ORACHS
ORACLE
OUNCES
OUTCRY

O•••C•
OAXACA
OBJECT
OCLOCK
OFFICE
OLMECS
ONDECK
ONEACT
OPTICS
ORBACH
OROZCO
OSMICS
OUTACT

O••••C
OLDVIC
ONSPEC
ORPHIC
OTITIC
OVISAC
OXIDIC
OZONIC

•OC•••
BOCCIE
BOCHCO
COCCID
COCCUS
COCCYX
COCHIN
COCKED
COCKER
COCKLE
COCOAS
COCOON
DOCENT
DOCILE
DOCKED
DOCKER
DOCKET
DOCTOR
EOCENE
FOCSLE
GOCART
HOCKED
HOCKEY
JOCKEY
JOCOSE
JOCUND
LOCALE
LOCALS
LOCATE
LOCKED
LOCKER
LOCKET
LOCKIN
LOCKON
LOCKUP
LOCUST
MOCHAS
MOCKED
MOCKER
MOCKUP
NOCENT
OOCYTE
POCKET
POCONO
ROCHET
ROCKED
ROCKER
ROCKET
ROCKNE
ROCKYV
ROCOCO
SOCAGE
SOCCER
SOCIAL
SOCKED
SOCKET
SOCKIN
SOCLES
TOCSIN
VOCALS

•O•C••
BOBCAT
BOCCIE
BONCES
BOTCHY
BOUCLE
BOXCAR
COCCID
COCCUS
COCCYX
CONCHA
CONCHS
CONCUR
DORCAS
FORCED
FORCER
FORCES
GOTCHA
HONCHO
HOTCAP
HOTCAR
LOUCHE
LOWCAL
MOBCAP
MOSCOW
NONCOM
NOTCHY
POACHY
PONCES
PONCHO
POUCHY
ROSCOE
SOCCER
TOECAP
TOMCAT
TOPCAT
TORCHY
TOUCAN
TOUCHE
TOUCHY
TOWCAR
VOICED
VOICES
YOICKS

•O••C•
BOCHCO
BODICE
BORSCH
BOUNCE
BOUNCY
COERCE
COMICS
CONICS
CONOCO
DODECA
GOBACK
HOOTCH
HORACE
IONICS
JOUNCE
JOUNCY
KONICA
KOPECK
KOVACS
LORICA
MODOCS
MOHOCK
MOLOCH
MONACO
MONICA
NODICE
NOTICE
NOVICE
POLICE
POLICY
POMACE
POUNCE
ROCOCO
SOLACE
SONICS
SOURCE
TOLUCA
TONICS
TOPICS
TOXICS
VOTECH
YORICK

•O•••C
AORTIC
COGNAC
CONTAC
COPTIC
COSMIC
COURIC
FORMIC
GOTHIC
HOMEEC
MOSAIC
NOETIC
NORDIC
POETIC
PONTIC
ROMAIC
SORBIC
TOLTEC
TOMBAC
ZODIAC

••OC••
AVOCET
BLOCKS
BLOCKY
CHOCKS
CLOCHE
CLOCKS
CROCKS
CROCUS
EPOCHS
FLOCKS
FLOCKY
FROCKS
GROCER
KNOCKS
PHOCIS
PROCNE
SHOCKS
SMOCKS
SNOCAT
STOCKS
STOCKY
TROCAR
TROCHE
UNOCAL

••O•C•
ATONCE
AVOUCH
BLOTCH
BROACH
BRONCO
BRONCS
BROOCH
CHOICE
CLOACA
CROUCH
EROICA
GROUCH
HOOTCH
OROZCO
SCONCE
SCORCH
SCOTCH
SLOUCH
SMOOCH
STOICS
STORCH

••O••C
AEOLIC
ANODIC
ANOMIC
ATOMIC
ATONIC
BIONIC
BIOTIC
EROTIC
ETONIC
EXOTIC
FROLIC
GNOMIC
ICONIC
IRONIC
MYOPIC
OZONIC
PHOBIC
PHONIC
PHOTIC
PROZAC
TROPIC

•••OC•
BROOCH
CONOCO
DECOCT
DUROCS
EDKOCH
HAVOCS
IDIOCY
MODOCS
MOHOCK
MOLOCH
OCLOCK
RELOCK
ROCOCO
SMOOCH
SUNOCO
UNLOCK
VELOCE

•••O•C
ECHOIC
HEROIC

••••OC
BELLOC
ENBLOC
MANIOC
TLALOC
ZIPLOC

OD••••
ODDEST
ODDITY
ODDJOB
ODDLOT
ODDSON
ODENSE
ODESSA
ODETTA
ODETTE
ODIOUS
ODISTS
ODIUMS
ODONTO
ODOURS

O•D•••
ODDEST
ODDITY
ODDJOB
ODDLOT
ODDSON

OEDEMA
OGDOAD
OLDAGE
OLDBOY
OLDEST
OLDHAM
OLDHAT
OLDIES
OLDISH
OLDMAN
OLDMEN
OLDPRO
OLDSAW
OLDVIC
ONDECK
ONDINE
OODLES
ORDAIN
ORDEAL
ORDERS
ORDURE

O••D••

OFFDAY
ONEDAY
ONEDGE
OUTDID
OXIDES
OXIDIC
OXYDOL

O•••D•

OCTADS
OLINDA
ONEIDA
ONSIDE
OREADS
OREIDA
OROIDE
OVERDO
OVIEDO
OVOIDS

O••••D

OBEYED
OBTUND
OFFEND
OGDOAD
OINKED
OKAYED
ONHAND
ONHOLD
ONLAND
ONWARD
OPENED
OPINED
ORATED
ORCHID
ORMOND
OSGOOD
OSMOND
OSMUND
OSTEND
OSWALD
OUSTED
OUTBID
OUTDID
OXFORD
OXNARD

•OD•••

AODAIS
BODEGA
BODICE
BODIED
BODIES
BODILY
BODING
BODKIN
BODONI
CODDLE
CODERS
CODGER
CODIFY
CODING
CODONS
DODDER
DODECA
DODGED
DODGER
DODGES
DODODO
DODOES
DODOMA
FODDER
GODARD
GODETS
GODIVA
GODOWN
GODSON
GODWIN
GODWIT
HODADS
HODGES
IODATE
IODIDE
IODINE
IODISE
IODIZE
KODALY
KODIAK
LODENS
LODGED
LODGER
LODGES
MODELA
MODELS
MODELT
MODEMS
MODENA
MODERN
MODEST
MODIFY
MODINE
MODISH
MODOCS
MODULE
MODULO
NODDED
NODDLE
NODICE
NODOFF
NODOSE
NODULE
OODLES
PODDED
PODIUM
PODUNK
RODDED
RODENT
RODEOS
RODHAM
RODMAN
RODNEY
SODDED
SODDEN
SODIUM
TODATE
TODDAO
TODDLE
TODMAN
VODKAS
WODGES
YODELS
ZODIAC

•O•D••

AOUDAD
BOLDER
BOLDLY
BONDED
BOODLE
BORDEN
BORDER
BOUDIN
CODDLE
COEDIT
COLDER
COLDLY
CONDOR
CONDOS
COODER
CORDAY
CORDED
CORDON
DODDER
DOGDAY
DOGDOM
DONDER
DOODAD
DOODAH
DOODLE
FODDER
FOLDED
FOLDER
FOLDUP
FONDER
FONDLE
FONDLY
FONDUE
FOODIE
FORDED
GOADED
GOLDEN
GOLDIE
GOODBY
GOODEN
GOODIE
GOODLY
GOODOH
GORDIE
GORDON
HOLDEN
HOLDER
HOLDIN
HOLDIT
HOLDON
HOLDTO
HOLDUP
HOODED
HOODOO
HORDES
HOTDOG
HOWDAH
HOYDEN
JORDAN
LOADED
LOADER
LONDON
LORDED
LORDLY
LOUDEN
LOUDER
LOUDLY
MOLDAU
MOLDED
MOLDER
MONDAY
NODDED
NODDLE
NOODLE
NORDIC
PODDED
POLDER
PONDER
POODLE
POWDER
ROADIE
RODDED
RONDEL
RONDOS
SODDED
SODDEN
SOLDAN
SOLDER
SOLDON
SONDES
SORDID
TODDAO
TODDLE
TOEDIN
TOLDOF
TOLDON
TONDOS
TOPDOG
TOYDOG
VOIDED
VOODOO
WONDER
WOODED
WOODEN
WOODSY
WORDED
YONDER

•O••D•

BOARDS
BOLIDE
BORIDE
BOUNDS
BOVIDS
COLADA
COMEDY
COULDA
DODODO
DORADO
DOSIDO
FOUNDS
GOURDE
GOURDS
HOARDS
HODADS
HOUNDS
HOUNDY
IODIDE
KOMODO
MONADS
MONODY
MOPEDS
MOULDS
MOULDY
MOUNDS
NOBODY
NOMADS
POMADE
POSADA
POUNDS
ROUNDS
SOLIDI
SOLIDS
SOUNDS
TOLEDO
WORLDS
WOUNDS
ZOOIDS
ZOUNDS

•O•••D

AOUDAD
BOATED
BOBBED
BODIED
BOFFED
BOGGED
BOILED
BOLTED
BOMBED
BONDED
BONGED
BOOKED
BOOMED
BOOTED
BOPPED
BOSSED
BOUSED
BOWLED
COATED
COAXED
COCCID
COCKED
COGGED
COIFED
COILED
COINED
COMBED
CONFED
CONKED
CONNED
CONOID
CONRAD
COOKED
COOLED
COOPED
COPIED
COPPED
CORDED
CORKED
CORNED
COSHED
COSIED
COWARD
COWLED
COZIED
DOCKED
DODGED
DOFFED
DOGGED
DOGOOD
DOLLED
DONALD
DONNED
DOODAD
DOOMED
DOSSED
DOTARD
DOTTED
DOUSED
DOWNED
DOWSED
FOALED
FOAMED
FOBBED
FOETID
FOGGED
FOILED
FOINED
FOLDED
FOOLED
FOOTED
FORBAD
FORBID
FORCED
FORDED
FORGED
FORKED
FORMED
FOULED
FOWLED
GOADED
GODARD
GOLFED
GONGED
GOOFED
GOOSED
GORGED
GOTMAD
GOUGED
GOUNOD
GOWILD
GOWNED
HOAXED
HOCKED
HOGGED
HONIED
HONKED
HOODED
HOOFED
HOOKED
HOOPED
HOOTED
HOPPED
HORNED
HORRID
HORSED
HOSTED
HOTBED
HOTROD
HOUSED
HOWARD
HOWLED
JOBBED
JOCUND
JOGGED
JOINED
JOLTED
JOSHED
JOTTED
KOBOLD
KONRAD
LOADED
LOAFED
LOAMED
LOANED
LOBBED
LOCKED
LODGED
LOFTED
LOGGED
LOLLED
LOMOND
LONGED
LOOKED
LOOMED
LOOPED
LOOSED
LOOTED
LOPPED
LORDED
LOTTED
LOUSED
LOWEND
MOANED
MOATED
MOBBED
MOCKED
MOILED
MOLDED
MOLTED
MONIED
MOONED
MOORED
MOOTED
MOPPED
MORBID
MOSHED
MOSSED
MOUSED
NODDED
NOGOOD
NOISED
NOLEAD
NOLOAD
NOOSED
NOSHED
NOTBAD
PODDED
POISED
POLAND
POLLED
PONGED
PONGID
PONIED
POOHED
POOLED
POOPED
POPPED
PORTED
POSTED
POTTED
POURED
POUTED
ROAMED
ROARED
ROBBED
ROCKED
RODDED
ROILED
ROLAND
ROLLED
ROMPED
RONALD
ROOFED
ROOKED
ROOMED
ROOTED
ROTTED
ROTUND
ROUGED
ROUSED
ROUTED
SOAKED
SOAPED
SOARED
SOBBED
SOCKED
SODDED
SOILED
SOLOED
SOLVED
SOPPED
SORDID
SORTED
SOTTED
SOURED
SOUSED
TOGAED
TOGGED
TOILED
TOLLED
TOOBAD
TOOLED
TOOTED
TOPPED
TOROID
TORPID
TORRID
TOSSED
TOTTED
TOURED
TOUTED
TOWARD
VOICED
VOIDED
WOLFED
WONNED
WONTED
WOODED
WOOFED
WORDED
WORKED
WORMED
YOLKED
YOWLED
YOYOED
ZONKED
ZOOMED

••OD••

ABODES
ANODES
ANODIC
APODAL
ATODDS
AZODYE
BOODLE
BRODIE
CLODDY
COODER
DEODAR
DIODES
DOODAD
DOODAH
DOODLE
EPODES
ERODED
ERODES
EXODUS
FOODIE
FYODOR
GEODES
GOODBY
GOODEN
GOODIE
GOODLY
GOODOH
GRODIN
GRODNO
HOODED
HOODOO
NOODLE
POODLE
RHODES
SHODDY
STODGE
STODGY
VOODOO
WOODED
WOODEN
WOODSY

••O•D•

AROIDS
ATODDS
AVOIDS
BIONDI
BLONDE
BLONDS
BLOODY
BROADS
BROODS
BROODY
CHORDS
CLODDY
CLOUDS
CLOUDY
CROWDS
DROIDS
EBONDS
FIORDS
FJORDS
FLOODS
FRONDS
IDOIDO
ISOLDE
LLOYDS
OROIDE
OVOIDS
RHONDA
SCOLDS
SHODDY

SNOODS
SWORDS
TBONDS
ZOOIDS

••O••D

ABOARD
ABOUND
ADORED
AROUND
ATONED
AVOWED
BOOKED
BOOMED
BOOTED
BUOYED
CHOKED
CHOWED
CLONED
CLOSED
CLOYED
COOKED
COOLED
COOPED
CROWED
DOODAD
DOOMED
DRONED
ELOPED
EMOTED
ERODED
EVOKED
FLORID
FLOWED
FOOLED
FOOTED
GAOLED
GLOBED
GLOVED
GLOWED
GLOZED
GOOFED
GOOSED
GROPED
GROUND
HOODED
HOOFED
HOOKED
HOOPED
HOOTED
IRONED
ISOPOD
LEONID
LOOKED
LOOMED
LOOPED
LOOSED
LOOTED
MEOWED
MOONED
MOORED
MOOTED
NOOSED
PHONED
PLOWED
POOHED
POOLED
POOPED
PROBED
PROSED
PROVED
QUOTED
RIOTED
ROOFED
ROOKED
ROOMED
ROOTED
SCOPED
SCORED
SHOOED
SHORED
SHOULD
SHOVED
SHOWED
SLOPED
SLOWED
SMOKED
SNORED
SNOWED
SPOKED
STOKED
STOLID
STONED
STORED
STOWED
TOOBAD
TOOLED
TOOTED
TROWED
WOODED
WOOFED
ZOOMED

•••OD•

BIPODS
BLOODY
BROODS
BROODY
DECODE
DEMODE
DIPODY
DODODO
EMBODY
ENCODE
EPHODS
FLOODS
KOMODO
MELODY
MONODY
NOBODY
PAGODA
PARODY
RECODE
RESODS
SARODS
SCRODS
SNOODS
STRODE
SYNODS
TRIODE
VIGODA

•••O•D

ABROAD
ACCORD
AFFORD
AGEOLD
ALMOND
ARNOLD
ATWOOD
AUFOND
BEHOLD
BEYOND
BIFOLD
BUJOLD
BYROAD
BYWORD
CANOED
CONOID
CUBOID
DADOED
DEMOND
DEVOID
DOGOOD
ECHOED
EDMOND
EDWOOD
ELWOOD
ENFOLD
HALOED
HALOID
HAROLD
HYPOED
INFOLD
INROAD
KAYOED
KOBOLD
LEMOND
LIPOID
LOMOND
MILORD
MYWORD
NOGOOD
NOLOAD
OGDOAD
ONHOLD
ORMOND
OSGOOD
OSMOND
OXFORD
RECORD
RELOAD
REMOLD
RESOLD
RETOLD
REWORD
SECOND
SHOOED
SHROUD
SILOED
SOLOED
STROUD
TOROID
UNFOLD
UNLOAD
UNSOLD
UNTOLD
UPHOLD
UPLOAD
VETOED
XYLOID
YOYOED
ZEROED

••••OD

ATWOOD
DOGOOD
EDWOOD
ELWOOD
FLYROD
GOUNOD
HESIOD
HOTROD
ISOPOD
METHOD
NIMROD
NOGOOD
OSGOOD
PEAPOD
PENROD
PEQUOD
PERIOD
PERNOD
RAMROD
RESHOD
SUNGOD
TIEROD
TINGOD
TRIPOD
UNIPOD
UNSHOD
UNTROD
WARGOD

OE••••

OEDEMA
OENONE
OERTER
OEUVRE

O•E•••

OBEAHS
OBELIA
OBELUS
OBERON
OBEYED
OCEANS
OCELLI
OCELOT
ODENSE
ODESSA
ODETTA
ODETTE
OHENRY
OKEEFE
OKELLY
OLEARY
OLEATE
OLEFIN
OLESON
OLEVEL
OMEGAS
OMELET
OMERTA
ONEACT
ONEDAY
ONEDGE
ONEIDA
ONEILL
ONEMAN
ONETWO
ONEUPS
ONEWAY
OPENED
OPENER
OPENLY
OPENTO
OPENUP
OPERAS
OREADS
OREGON
OREIDA
ORELSE
OTELLO
OVERDO
OVERLY
OXEYES

O••E••

OATERS
OBJECT
OBSESS
OBTEST
OBVERT
OCHERS
OCHERY
OCREAE
OCTETS
ODDEST
OEDEMA
OFFEND
OFFERS
OGLERS
OGRESS
OHWELL
OHYEAH
OILERS
OKEEFE
OLDEST
OLMECS
ONDECK
ONSETS
ORDEAL
ORDERS
ORGEAT
ORIELS
ORIENT
ORNERY
ORRERY
ORTEGA
ORWELL
OSIERS
OSSEIN
OSSETE
OSTEAL
OSTEND
OSWEGO
OTHERS
OTTERS
OUSELS
OUTEAT
OUZELS
OVIEDO
OWLETS
OWNERS

O•••E•

OAKLEY
OATIER
OBEYED
OBITER
OBRIEN
OBSTET
OCASEK
OCASEY
OCHRES
OERTER
OFFKEY
OFFSET
OGIVES
OILIER
OILMEN
OINKED
OKAYED
OLDIES
OLDMEN
OLEVEL
OLIVER
OLIVES
OMELET
ONAGER
ONSPEC
ONUSES
ONVIEW
ONYXES
OODLES
OOZIER
OPENED
OPENER
OPINED
OPINER
OPINES
OPUSES
ORALES
ORATED
ORATES
ORGIES
ORIGEN
ORKNEY
ORTLES
ORYXES
OSAGES
OSPREY
OSTLER
OUNCES
OUSTED
OUSTER
OUTLET
OUTSET
OVULES
OXEYES
OXIDES
OXYGEN
OYSTER

O••••E

OBLATE
OBLIGE
OBTUSE
OCREAE
OCTANE
OCTAVE
ODENSE
ODETTE
OENONE
OEUVRE
OFFICE
OFLATE
OKEEFE
OLDAGE
OLEATE
ONDINE
ONEDGE
ONFILE
ONFIRE
ONLINE
ONSALE
ONSIDE
ONSITE
ONTAPE
ONTIME
OOCYTE
OOLITE
OPAQUE
OPHITE
OPIATE
OPPOSE
ORACLE
ORANGE
ORDURE
ORELSE
ORGATE
ORIOLE
ORNATE
OROIDE
ORPINE
OSCINE
OSMOSE
OSSETE
OTIOSE
OTOOLE
OUTAGE
OUTATE
OXLIKE

•OE•••

BOEING
COEDIT
COELOM
COERCE
COEVAL
DOESBY
DOESIN
DOESNT
DOESUP
FOEHNS
FOETAL
FOETID
FOETOR
FOETUS
GOEASY
GOESAT
GOESBY
GOESIN
GOESON
GOESUP
GOETHE
HOEING
JOETEX
KOENIG
NOESIS
NOETIC
NOEXIT
POETIC
POETRY
SOEURS
TOECAP
TOEDIN
TOEING
TOEINS
TOESIN
TOETAP
WOEFUL

•O•E••

BODEGA
BOGEYS
BOLERO
BOLEYN
BONERS
BONEUP
BOPEEP
BOREAL
BOREAS
BOREON
BORERS
BOREUP
BOTELS
BOWERS
BOWERY
BOXERS
CODERS
COGENT
COHEIR
COHERE
COLEUS
COMEAT
COMEBY
COMEDY
COMEIN
COMELY
COMEON
COMERS
COMETH
COMETO
COMETS
COMEUP
CONEYS
COOERS
CORERS
COSELL
COVENS
COVENT
COVERS
COVERT
COVETS
COVEYS
COWENS
COWERS
COYEST
COZENS
DOCENT
DODECA
DOGEAR
DOGEYS
DOLENZ
DONEES
DONEIN
DONETS
DONEUP
DOREMI
DOSERS
DOTELL
DOTEON
DOVEIN
DOWELS
DOWERS
DOWERY
DOYENS
DOZENS
DOZERS
EOCENE
FOGEYS
FOMENT
FOREGO
FOREST
FOVEAE
FOYERS
GODETS
GOFERS
GOLEMS
GONEBY
GONERS
GOVERN
GOWEST
HOLEUP
HOMEEC
HOMELY
HOMERS
HONEST
HONEYS
HOPERS
HOSELS
HOTELS
HOVELS
HOVERS
HOVETO
HOWELL
JOBETH
JOKERS
JOLENE
JOSEPH
JOWETT
KOPECK
KOPEKS
KOREAN
LODENS
LOMEIN
LONELY
LONERS
LOPERS
LOREAL
LORENZ
LOSEIT
LOSERS
LOVEIN
LOVELL
LOVELY
LOVERS
LOVETT
LOWELL
LOWEND
LOWERS
LOWERY
LOWEST
MODELA
MODELS
MODELT
MODEMS
MODENA
MODERN
MODEST
MOIETY
MOLEST
MOMENT
MONERA
MONETA
MONEYS
MOPEDS
MOPERS
MOPERY
MOREAU
MOREEN
MORELS
MORENO
MOSEYS
MOTELS
MOTETS
MOVEIN
MOVEON

MOVERS
MOVEUP
MOWERS
MOYERS
NOCENT
NOLEAD
NOLENS
NOLESS
NONEGO
NONETS
NOPETS
NOTERS
NOVELS
NOVENA
POKEAT
POKERS
POKERY
POKEYS
POLEAX
POLERS
POLEYN
POMELO
POPEYE
POSERS
POSEUR
POTEEN
POTENT
POWELL
POWERS
ROBERT
RODENT
RODEOS
ROGERS
ROLEOS
ROMEOS
ROMERO
RONELY
ROPEIN
ROPERS
ROSEAU
ROVERS
ROWELS
ROWENA
ROWENS
ROWERS
SOBEIT
SOBERS
SOLEIL
SOLELY
SOLEMN
SOLENT
SOLERS
SOLEUS
SOMERS
SORELY
SOREST
SOWERS
SOWETO
SOXERS
TOKENS
TOLEDO
TONERS
TONEUP
TOPEKA
TOPERS
TOREAT
TORERO
TOREUP
TOTEMS
TOTERS
TOWELS
TOWERS
TOWERY
VOLENS
VOTECH
VOTEIN
VOTERS
VOWELS
VOWELY
VOWERS
WOKEUP
WOMENS
WOOERS
WOREON
YODELS
YOKELS

•O••E•

BOATED
BOATEL
BOATER
BOBBED
BOBBER
BODIED
BODIES
BOFFED
BOGGED
BOGIES
BOGLES
BOILED
BOILER
BOITES
BOLDER
BOLGER
BOLTED
BOMBED
BOMBER
BOMBES
BONCES
BONDED
BONGED
BONIER
BONNES
BONNET
BONZES
BOOKED
BOOKER
BOOMED
BOOMER
BOOTED
BOOTEE
BOOTES
BOPEEP
BOPPED
BOPPER
BORDEN
BORDER
BORNEO
BOSKET
BOSLEY
BOSSED
BOSSES
BOTHER
BOTREE
BOULES
BOULEZ
BOUSED
BOUSES
BOVVER
BOWLED
BOWLER
BOWLES
BOWMEN
BOWNET
BOWSER
BOWYER
BOXIER
BOXSET
COALER
COATED
COAXED
COAXER
COAXES
COBWEB
COCKED
COCKER
CODGER
COFFEE
COFFER
COGGED
COIFED
COILED
COINED
COINER
COKIER
COLDER
COLIES
COLLET
COLTER
COMBED
COMBER
COMBES
COMPEL
COMTES
CONFED
CONFER
CONGER
CONIES
CONKED
CONKER
CONMEN
CONNED
CONNER
CONTES
CONVEX
CONVEY
COODER
COOKED
COOKER
COOLED
COOLER
COONEY
COOPED
COOPER
COOTER
COPIED
COPIER
COPIES
COPLEY
COPPED
COPPER
COPSES
COPTER
COQUET
CORBEL
CORDED
CORKED
CORKER
CORNEA
CORNED
CORNEL
CORNER
CORNET
CORREL
CORSET
CORTES
CORTEX
CORTEZ
CORVEE
CORVES
COSHED
COSHES
COSIED
COSIER
COSIES
COSSET
COTTEN
COTTER
COULEE
COUPES
COUTER
COWLED
COWLEY
COWMEN
COWPEA
COWPER
COZIED
COZIER
COZIES
DOBBER
DOCKED
DOCKER
DOCKET
DODDER
DODGED
DODGER
DODGES
DODOES
DOFFED
DOGGED
DOGGER
DOGIES
DOGLEG
DOLLED
DOLMEN
DOMREP
DONDER
DONEES
DONKEY
DONNED
DONNEE
DONNER
DOOLEY
DOOMED
DOPIER
DORIES
DORMER
DORSET
DORSEY
DOSSED
DOSSEL
DOSSER
DOSSES
DOTTED
DOURER
DOUSED
DOUSES
DOWNED
DOWNER
DOWNEY
DOWSED
DOWSER
DOWSES
DOZIER
FOALED
FOAMED
FOBBED
FODDER
FOGGED
FOGGER
FOGIES
FOILED
FOINED
FOKKER
FOLDED
FOLDER
FONDER
FOOLED
FOOLER
FOOTED
FOOTER
FORBES
FORCED
FORCER
FORCES
FORDED
FORGED
FORGER
FORGES
FORGET
FORKED
FORKER
FORMED
FORMER
FORTES
FOSSES
FOSSEY
FOSTER
FOULED
FOULER
FOWLED
FOWLER
FOWLES
FOXIER
GOADED
GOATEE
GOBIES
GOBLET
GOLDEN
GOLFED
GOLFER
GONGED
GOOBER
GOODEN
GOOFED
GOOIER
GOOSED
GOOSES
GOOSEY
GOOVER
GOPHER
GORGED
GORGES
GORGET
GORIER
GORSES
GOSHEN
GOSPEL
GOTSET
GOTTEN
GOUGED
GOUGER
GOUGES
GOULET
GOWNED
HOAXED
HOAXER
HOAXES
HOBBES
HOBOES
HOCKED
HOCKEY
HODGES
HOGGED
HOGGET
HOKIER
HOLDEN
HOLDER
HOLIER
HOLLER
HOLMES
HOMEEC
HOMIER
HONIED
HONKED
HONKER
HOODED
HOOFED
HOOFER
HOOKED
HOOPED
HOOPER
HOOTED
HOOTER
HOOVER
HOOVES
HOPPED
HOPPER
HORDES
HORMEL
HORNED
HORNER
HORNET
HORNEY
HORSED
HORSES
HORSEY
HOSIER
HOSTED
HOSTEL
HOTBED
HOTTEA
HOTTER
HOUSED
HOUSES
HOWLED
HOWLER
HOYDEN
JOBBED
JOBBER
JOCKEY
JOETEX
JOGGED
JOGGER
JOINED
JOINER
JOKIER
JOLIET
JOLTED
JOSHED
JOSHES
JOSSER
JOSSES
JOTTED
JOULES
JOYNER
KOHLER
KOPJES
KOPPEL
KOSHER
KOTTER
LOADED
LOADER
LOAFED
LOAFER
LOAMED
LOANED
LOANER
LOAVES
LOBBED
LOBBER
LOCKED
LOCKER
LOCKET
LODGED
LODGER
LODGES
LOFTED
LOGGED
LOGGER
LOGIER
LOITER
LOLLED
LONGED
LONGER
LONGES
LOOIES
LOOKED
LOOKER
LOOMED
LOONEY
LOOPED
LOOPER
LOOSED
LOOSEN
LOOSER
LOOSES
LOOTED
LOOTER
LOPPED
LOPPER
LORDED
LORIES
LOSSES
LOTTED
LOUDEN
LOUDER
LOUPES
LOUSED
LOUSES
LOUVER
LOWKEY
MOANED
MOANER
MOATED
MOBBED
MOBLEY
MOCKED
MOCKER
MOILED
MOILER
MOINES
MOIRES
MOLDED
MOLDER
MOLTED
MOLTEN
MOLTER
MONGER
MONIED
MONIES
MONKEY
MONTEL
MONTES
MONTEZ
MOONED
MOONEY
MOORED
MOOTED
MOPIER
MOPPED
MOPPER
MOPPET
MOREEN
MORGEN
MORLEY
MORSEL
MOSHED
MOSHER
MOSHES
MOSLEM
MOSSED
MOSSES
MOSTEL
MOTHER
MOTLEY
MOUSED
MOUSER
MOUSES
MOUSEY
MOVIES
NOBLER
NOBLES
NODDED
NOISED
NOISES
NOONES
NOOSED
NOOSES
NOSHED
NOSHER
NOSHES
NOSIER
NOTYET
NOUMEA
OODLES
OOZIER
POCKET
PODDED
POGIES
POISED
POISES
POKIER
POLDER
POLLED
POLLEN
POLLER
POLLEX
POMMEE
POMMEL
POMPEY
PONCES
PONDER
PONGED
PONGEE
PONIED
PONIES
PONTES
POOHED
POOLED
POOPED
POORER
POPPED
POPPER
POPPET
PORKER
PORTED
PORTER
POSHER
POSIES
POSSES
POSSET
POSTED
POSTER
POTEEN
POTHER
POTTED
POTTER
POURED
POURER
POUTED
POUTER
POWDER
ROAMED
ROAMER
ROARED
ROARER
ROBBED
ROBBER
ROBLES
ROCHET
ROCKED
ROCKER
ROCKET
RODDED
RODNEY
ROGUES
ROHMER
ROILED
ROLLED
ROLLER
ROMMEL
ROMNEY
ROMPED
ROMPER
RONDEL
ROOFED
ROOFER
ROOKED
ROOMED
ROOMER
ROONEY
ROOTED
ROOTER
ROPIER
ROSIER
ROSTER
ROTTED
ROTTEN
ROTTER

ROUGED
ROUGES
ROUSED
ROUSER
ROUSES
ROUTED
ROUTER
ROUTES
ROZZER
SOAKED
SOAKER
SOAPED
SOAPER
SOARED
SOARER
SOARES
SOAVES
SOBBED
SOBBER
SOCCER
SOCKED
SOCKET
SOCLES
SODDED
SODDEN
SOFTEN
SOFTER
SOILED
SOIREE
SOLDER
SOLOED
SOLVED
SOLVER
SOLVES
SOMBER
SOMMER
SONDES
SONNET
SOONER
SOPPED
SORBET
SORREL
SORTED
SORTER
SOTTED
SOURED
SOURER
SOUSED
SOUSES
SOUTER
SOVIET
TOATEE
TOBIES
TOFFEE
TOGAED
TOGGED
TOILED
TOILER
TOILES
TOILET
TOLLED
TOLTEC
TONIER
TONNES
TOOLED
TOOTED
TOOTER
TOPPED
TOPPER
TOPTEN
TOQUES
TORIES
TORRES
TORREY
TORTES
TOSSED
TOSSER
TOSSES
TOTHER
TOTTED
TOTTER
TOUPEE
TOURED
TOURER
TOUTED
TOUTER
TOWHEE
TOWNER
VOGUES
VOICED
VOICES
VOIDED
VOILES
VOLLEY
VORTEX
VOSGES
WODGES
WOHLER
WOLFED
WOLPER
WOLSEY
WOLVES
WONDER
WONNED
WONTED
WOODED
WOODEN
WOOFED
WOOFER
WOOLEN
WOOLEY
WORDED
WORKED
WORKER
WORMED
WORSEN
WOWSER
YOLKED
YONDER
YORKER
YOUBET
YOWLED
YOYOED
ZONKED
ZONKER
ZOOMED

•O•••E

AORTAE
BOBBIE
BOBBLE
BOCCIE
BODICE
BOGGLE
BOLIDE
BONNIE
BOODLE
BOOGIE
BOOKIE
BOOTEE
BOOTHE
BOOTIE
BORAGE
BORATE
BORIDE
BOTREE
BOTTLE
BOUCLE
BOUFFE
BOULLE
BOUNCE
BOURKE
BOURNE
BOURSE
BOVINE
BOWTIE
COARSE
COBBLE
COCKLE
CODDLE
COERCE
COFFEE
COHERE
COHUNE
COLLIE
COMATE
CONNIE
CONTRE
CONURE
COOKIE
COOTIE
CORVEE
COSINE
COSTAE
COULEE
COUPLE
COURSE
COWRIE
COYOTE
DOABLE
DOCILE
DOGGIE
DOMINE
DONATE
DONGLE
DONNEE
DOOBIE
DOODLE
DOOGIE
DOOZIE
DOSAGE
DOTAGE
DOTTIE
DOTTLE
DOUBLE
EOCENE
FOCSLE
FOIBLE
FOLKIE
FONDLE
FONDUE
FOODIE
FOOZLE
FORAGE
FOSSAE
FOVEAE
FOZZIE
GOALIE
GOATEE
GOBBLE
GOETHE
GOGGLE
GOHOME
GOLDIE
GOODIE
GOOGLE
GORDIE
GOURDE
HOAGIE
HOARSE
HOBBLE
HOGTIE
HOMAGE
HOMBRE
HONORE
HOOPLE
HOOPOE
HOOTIE
HOPPLE
HORACE
IODATE
IODIDE
IODINE
IODISE
IODIZE
IOLITE
IONISE
IONIZE
JOANIE
JOANNE
JOCOSE
JOGGLE
JOHORE
JOLENE
JOSTLE
JOUNCE
KOOKIE
LOATHE
LOBATE
LOBULE
LOCALE
LOCATE
LONGUE
LOONIE
LOUCHE
LOUISE
LOUNGE
LOUVRE
LOVAGE
MOBILE
MODINE
MODULE
MOHAVE
MOJAVE
MOLINE
MOLTKE
MOMMIE
MONROE
MORALE
MOROSE
MOSQUE
MOTILE
MOTIVE
MOTTLE
MOUSSE
NOBBLE
NODDLE
NODICE
NODOSE
NODULE
NOLOSE
NOMINE
NOMORE
NONAGE
NONAME
NOODLE
NOSALE
NOTATE
NOTICE
NOVICE
NOWISE
NOZZLE
OOCYTE
OOLITE
POINTE
POLICE
POLITE
POMACE
POMADE
POMMEE
PONGEE
POODLE
POPEYE
POPPLE
POTAGE
POTPIE
POTTLE
POUNCE
POUSSE
ROADIE
ROBBIE
ROCKNE
ROLLIE
RONNIE
ROOKIE
ROOMIE
ROSCOE
ROTATE
ROUBLE
ROURKE
ROXANE
ROYALE
SOCAGE
SOFINE
SOFTIE
SOIGNE
SOIREE
SOLACE
SOLUTE
SOMBRE
SOOTHE
SOPHIE
SORTIE
SOURCE
TOATEE
TODATE
TODDLE
TOFFEE
TOGGLE
TOLIFE
TONGUE
TONITE
TOONIE
TOOTLE
TOPPLE
TOROSE
TORQUE
TOUCHE
TOUPEE
TOUSLE
TOWAGE
TOWHEE
TOWNIE
VOLARE
VOLUME
VOLUTE
VOTIVE
VOYAGE
WOBBLE
WOOGIE
WOOKIE
YORKIE
ZOMBIE
ZONATE
ZOUAVE

••OE••

AMOEBA
COOERS
PHOEBE
PROEMS
SHOERS
WOOERS

••O•E•

ABODES
ADOBES
ADORED
ADOREE
ADORER
ADORES
AMOLES
ANODES
ANOLES
APOGEE
ATONED
ATONES
AVOCET
AVOWED
AVOWER
AWOKEN
AZORES
BIOMES
BLOKES
BLOOEY
BLOWER
BOOKED
BOOKER
BOOMED
BOOMER
BOOTED
BOOTEE
BOOTES
BROKEN
BROKER
BUOYED
CHOKED
CHOKER
CHOKES
CHOLER
CHORES
CHOSEN
CHOWED
CLONED
CLONES
CLOSED
CLOSER
CLOSES
CLOSET
CLOVEN
CLOVER
CLOVES
CLOYED
CNOTES
COODER
COOKED
COOKER
COOLED
COOLER
COONEY
COOPED
COOPER
COOTER
CRONES
CROWED
CROWER
CROZES
DHOLES
DHOTEL
DIODES
DIONEB
DOOLEY
DOOMED
DRONED
DRONER
DRONES
DROVER
DROVES
ECOLES
ELOPED
ELOPER
ELOPES
EMOTED
EMOTER
EMOTES
EPODES
EPOPEE
ERODED
ERODES
EVOKED
EVOKER
EVOKES
FLOOEY
FLORES
FLORET
FLOWED
FLOWER
FOOLED
FOOLER
FOOTED
FOOTER
FROZEN
GAOLED
GAOLER
GEODES
GLOBED
GLOBES
GLOVED
GLOVER
GLOVES
GLOWED
GLOWER
GLOZED
GLOZES
GNOMES
GOOBER
GOODEN
GOOFED
GOOIER
GOOSED
GOOSES
GOOSEY
GOOVER
GROCER
GROPED
GROPES
GROVEL
GROVER
GROVES
GROWER
HAOLES
HOODED
HOOFED
HOOFER
HOOKED
HOOPED
HOOPER
HOOTED
HOOTER
HOOVER
HOOVES
IMOGEN
IRONED
IRONER
ISOHEL
ISOMER
KJOLEN
KNOWER
KRONER
LEONES
LIONEL
LIONET
LOOIES
LOOKED
LOOKER
LOOMED
LOONEY
LOOPED
LOOPER
LOOSED
LOOSEN
LOOSER
LOOSES
LOOTED
LOOTER
MEOWED
MOONED
MOONEY
MOORED
MOOTED
MYOPES
NOONES
NOOSED
NOOSES
PHONED
PHONES
PHONEY
PHOOEY
PIOLET
PLOVER
PLOWED
PLOWER
POOHED
POOLED
POOPED
POORER
PROBED
PROBER
PROBES
PROLES
PROPEL
PROPER
PROSED
PROSER
PROSES
PROTEI
PROTEM
PROVED
PROVEN
PROVER
PROVES
QUOTED
QUOTER
QUOTES
REOPEN
RHODES
RIOTED
RIOTER
ROOFED
ROOFER
ROOKED
ROOMED
ROOMER
ROONEY
ROOTED
ROOTER
SCONES
SCOPED
SCOPES
SCORED
SCORER
SCORES
SCOTER
SHOLEM
SHOOED
SHORED
SHORES
SHOVED
SHOVEL
SHOVER
SHOVES
SHOWED
SHOWER
SLOPED
SLOPES
SLOVEN
SLOWED
SLOWER
SMOKED
SMOKER
SMOKES
SMOKEY
SNOPES
SNORED
SNORER
SNORES
SNOWED
SOONER
SPOKED
SPOKEN
SPOKES
SPORES
STOKED
STOKER
STOKES
STOLEN
STOLES
STONED
STONER
STONES
STOPES

STORED
STORER
STORES
STOREY
STOVER
STOVES
STOWED
TBONES
THOLES
TNOTES
TOOLED
TOOTED
TOOTER
TROPES
TROPEZ
TROVES
TROWED
TROWEL
TWOFER
UNOPEN
USOPEN
VIOLET
WHOLES
WOODED
WOODEN
WOOFED
WOOFER
WOOLEN
WOOLEY
YEOMEN
ZOOMED

••O••E

ADOREE
AGORAE
ANOMIE
APOGEE
AROUSE
ATONCE
AZODYE
BLONDE
BLOUSE
BMOVIE
BOODLE
BOOGIE
BOOKIE
BOOTEE
BOOTHE
BOOTIE
BRODIE
BROGUE
BRONTE
BRONZE
BROOKE
BROWNE
BROWSE
CHOATE
CHOICE
CHOOSE
CLOCHE
CLOQUE
CLOTHE
COOKIE
COOTIE
CROSSE
CROUSE
CROUTE
DIONNE
DOOBIE
DOODLE
DOOGIE
DOOZIE
DROGUE
DROWSE
ELOISE
EPOPEE
ETOILE
EVOLVE
EVONNE
FLORAE
FOODIE
FOOZLE
GEORGE
GOODIE
GOOGLE
GROOVE
GROSSE
GROUSE
HOOPLE
HOOPOE
HOOTIE
INOUYE
ISOLDE
KOOKIE
LAOTSE
LEONIE
LHOTSE
LOONIE
NOODLE
OROIDE
OTOOLE
PEOPLE
PHOEBE
POODLE
PROCNE
PROPRE
PROWSE
QUOQUE
ROOKIE
ROOMIE
SCONCE
SCOUSE
SHOPPE
SHORTE
SHOWME
SKOKIE
SKOPJE
SLOANE
SNOOZE
SOOTHE
SPONGE
SPOUSE
STODGE
STOGIE
STOLLE
STOOGE
THORPE
TOONIE
TOOTLE
TROCHE
TROMPE
TROUPE
TROUVE
WOOGIE
WOOKIE
YVONNE

•••OE•

BLOOEY
CANOED
CANOES
DADOED
DADOES
DODOES
ECHOED
ECHOES
EDDOES
EUBOEA
FLOOEY
GIJOES
HALOED
HALOES
HEROES
HOBOES
HYPOED
KAYOED
PEKOES
PHLOEM
PHOOEY
REDOES
SHOOED
SILOED
SOLOED
THROES
UNDOER
UNDOES
VETOED
VETOER
VETOES
YOYOED
ZEROED
ZEROES

•••O•E

ACTONE
AEROBE
ALCOVE
ALDOSE
ALGORE
ANYONE
APPOSE
ARIOSE
ASHORE
ASLOPE
ATHOME
BECOME
BEFORE
BEGONE
BEHOVE
BROOKE
BYGONE
BYJOVE
BYROTE
CAJOLE
CAPONE
CAPOTE
CAROLE
CENOTE
CHOOSE
CHROME
COYOTE
CREOLE
DAMONE
DAMORE
DAYONE
DEBONE
DECODE
DEMODE
DEMOTE
DENOTE
DEPONE
DEPOSE
DEVOTE
DIPOLE
EEYORE
ELMORE
ENCODE
ENCORE
ENROBE
EUROPE
EVZONE
EXMORE
EXPOSE
FILOSE
FURORE
GALORE
GEMOTE
GENOME
GOHOME
GROOVE
GYROSE
HONORE
IGNORE
IMPOSE
INCOME
INDORE
INJOKE
INLOVE
INSOLE
INTONE
INVOKE
JAMOKE
JEROME
JOCOSE
JOHORE
KETONE
LAHORE
LANOSE
LENORE
LUPONE
MALONE
MEROPE
METOPE
MOROSE
MYSORE
NICOLE
NODOSE
NOLOSE
NOMORE
OENONE
OPPOSE
ORIOLE
OSMOSE
OTIOSE
OTOOLE
PAROLE
PEYOTE
PILOSE
PINOLE
RADOME
RAMONE
RAMOSE
RECODE
REDONE
REMOTE
REMOVE
RENOTE
REPOSE
RESOLE
REVOKE
REWOVE
REZONE
RIBOSE
RIMOSE
RUGOSE
SALOME
SAVOIE
SETOSE
SHROVE
SILONE
SIMONE
SNOOZE
STOOGE
STROBE
STRODE
STROKE
STROVE
TAGORE
THRONE
THROVE
TOROSE
TRIODE
TYRONE
UGSOME
UNDONE
UNROBE
UNWOVE
UNYOKE
UPROSE
VADOSE
VELOCE
ZYGOTE

••••OE

BIGTOE
CHIGOE
CHILOE
CRUSOE
FAEROE
FELLOE
HOOPOE
MONROE
RESHOE
ROSCOE
TIPTOE
WASHOE

OF••••

OFFDAY
OFFEND
OFFERS
OFFICE
OFFING
OFFISH
OFFKEY
OFFSET
OFLATE

O•F•••

OAFISH
OFFDAY
OFFEND
OFFERS
OFFICE
OFFING
OFFISH
OFFKEY
OFFSET
ONFILE
ONFIRE
ONFOOT
OXFORD

O••F••

OLEFIN
OPTFOR
OUTFIT
OUTFLY
OUTFOX

O•••F•

OKEEFE
OSSIFY

•OF•••

BOFFED
BOFFIN
BOFFOS
COFFEE
COFFER
DOFFED
GOFERS
GOFISH
LOFTED
SOFFIT
SOFINE
SOFTEN
SOFTER
SOFTIE
SOFTLY
TOFFEE

•O•F••

BOFFED
BOFFIN
BOFFOS
BOTFLY
BOUFFE
BOWFIN
BOXFUL
COFFEE
COFFER
COIFED
COLFAX
COMFIT
CONFAB
CONFED
CONFER
DOFFED
DOOFUS
GOLFED
GOLFER
GOOFED
GOOFUP
HOOFED
HOOFER
HOOFIT
JOYFUL
KOUFAX
LOAFED
LOAFER
LOOFAH
LOOFAS
LOWFAT
NONFAT
POPFLY
POTFUL
ROOFED
ROOFER
SOBFUL
SOFFIT
SOLFAS
TOFFEE
WOEFUL
WOLFED
WOOFED
WOOFER

•O••F•

BOUFFE
CODIFY
FOBOFF
GOSOFT
GOTOFF
HOPOFF
LOGOFF
MODIFY
MOTIFS
NODOFF
NOTIFY
POPOFF
TOLIFE
TOPOFF

•O•••F

FOBOFF
GOTOFF
HOPOFF
LOGOFF
NODOFF
POPOFF
SORTOF
TOLDOF
TOPOFF

••OF••

CROFTS
DOOFUS
GOOFED
GOOFUP
HOOFED
HOOFER
HOOFIT
LOOFAH
LOOFAS
PROFIT
ROOFED
ROOFER
SCOFFS
SHOFAR
TWOFER
WOOFED
WOOFER

••O•F•

KLOOFS
PROOFS
SCOFFS
SPOOFS
WHOOFS

•••OF•

BEGOFF
BITOFF
BUGOFF
BUYOFF
CRYOFF
CUTOFF
DIEOFF
DRYOFF
FAROFF
FOBOFF
GETOFF
GOSOFT
GOTOFF
HOPOFF
KLOOFS
LAYOFF
LEDOFF
LETOFF
LOGOFF
NODOFF
PAYOFF
POPOFF
PROOFS
PUTOFF
RANOFF
RIPOFF
RUBOFF
RUNOFF
SAWOFF
SEEOFF
SETOFF
SPOOFS
TAPOFF
TEEOFF
TIPOFF
TOPOFF
WHOOFS

•••O•F

BEGOFF
BEHOOF
BITOFF
BUGOFF
BUYOFF
CRYOFF
CUTOFF
DIEOFF
DRYOFF
FAROFF
FOBOFF
GETOFF
GOTOFF
HOPOFF
LAYOFF
LEDOFF
LETOFF
LOGOFF
NODOFF
PAYOFF
POPOFF
PUTOFF
RANOFF
RIPOFF
RUBOFF
RUDOLF
RUNOFF
SAWOFF
SEEOFF
SETOFF
TAPOFF
TEEOFF
TIPOFF
TOPOFF

••••OF

BEHOOF
HEAROF
HEREOF
KINDOF
RIDSOF
SORTOF
TELLOF
TOLDOF

OG••••

OGDOAD
OGHAMS
OGIVES
OGLALA
OGLERS
OGLING
OGRESS
OGRISH

O•G•••

ORGANA
ORGANS
ORGATE
ORGEAT
ORGIES
OSGOOD
OUGHTS

O••G••

OMEGAS
ONAGER
OREGON
ORIGEN
ORIGIN
OSAGES
OUTGUN
OXYGEN

O•••G•

OBLIGE
OLDAGE
OLINGO
ONEDGE
ONHIGH
OOLOGY
OPPUGN
ORANGE
ORANGS
ORANGY
ORINGS
ORTEGA
OSWEGO
OUTAGE

O••••G

OARING
OBLONG
OFFING
OGLING
OILING
OILRIG
OOHING
OOLONG
OOZING
OPTING
ORBING
OUTING
OWNING

•OG•••

BOGART
BOGEYS

BOGGED
BOGGLE
BOGIES
BOGLES
BOGONG
BOGOTA
COGENT
COGGED
COGITO
COGNAC
DOGDAY
DOGDOM
DOGEAR
DOGEYS
DOGGED
DOGGER
DOGGIE
DOGIES
DOGLEG
DOGMAS
DOGONS
DOGOOD
DOGSAT
DOGSIT
DOGTAG
FOGBOW
FOGEYS
FOGGED
FOGGER
FOGHAT
FOGIES
FOGSIN
FOGSUP
GOGGLE
GOGGLY
HOGANS
HOGGED
HOGGET
HOGTIE
JOGGED
JOGGER
JOGGLE
LOGGED
LOGGER
LOGGIA
LOGIER
LOGILY
LOGION
LOGJAM
LOGOFF
LOGOUT
LOGSIN
LOGSON
MOGULS
NOGGIN
NOGOOD
POGIES
ROGERS
ROGUES
TOGAED
TOGGED
TOGGLE
VOGUES
YOGINI
YOGISM
YOGURT

•O•G••

BOGGED
BOGGLE
BOIGNY
BOLGER
BONGED
BONGOS
BOOGIE
BORGIA
BOUGHS
BOUGHT
CODGER
COGGED
COIGNS
CONGAS
CONGER
CONGOU
COOGAN
CORGIS
COUGAR
COUGHS
DODGED
DODGER
DODGES
DOGGED
DOGGER
DOGGIE
DONGLE
DOOGIE
DOUGHS
DOUGHY
FOGGED
FOGGER
FORGED
FORGER
FORGES
FORGET
FORGOT
FOUGHT
GOGGLE
GOGGLY
GONGED
GOOGLE
GOOGLY
GOOGOL
GOOGOO
GORGED
GORGES
GORGET
GORGON
GOUGED
GOUGER
GOUGES
HOAGIE
HODGES
HOGGED
HOGGET
HOUGHS
JOGGED
JOGGER
JOGGLE
LODGED
LODGER
LODGES
LOGGED
LOGGER
LOGGIA
LONGAN
LONGED
LONGER
LONGES
LONGLY
LONGUE
LOUGHS
MONGER
MONGOL
MORGAN
MORGEN
MOWGLI
NOGGIN
NORGAY
NOUGAT
NOUGHT
PONGED
PONGEE
PONGID
POPGUN
ROTGUT
ROUGED
ROUGES
ROUGHS
ROUGHY
SOIGNE
SOUGHS
SOUGHT
TOGGED
TOGGLE
TONGAN
TONGUE
TOPGUN
TOUGHS
TOUGHY
VOIGHT
VOSGES
WODGES
WOOGIE

•O••G•

BODEGA
BOINGO
BORAGE
COLUGO
COSIGN
DOINGS
DORAGS
DOSAGE
DOTAGE
FORAGE
FOREGO
GOINGS
GONOGO
HOMAGE
LOUNGE
LOVAGE
NONAGE
NONEGO
OOLOGY
POTAGE
SOCAGE
TOBAGO
TOWAGE
VOYAGE

•O•••G

BODING
BOEING
BOGONG
BONING
BOOING
BORING
BOWING
BOXING
COBURG
CODING
COMING
COOING
COPING
CORING
COWING
DOGLEG
DOGTAG
DOLING
DOMING
DOPING
DOSING
DOTING
DOZING
FOXING
GORING
GOSTAG
HOEING
HOLING
HOMING
HONING
HOPING
HOSING
HOTDOG
JOKING
KOENIG
LOPING
LOSING
LOVING
LOWING
MOOING
MOPING
MOVING
MOWING
NOSING
NOTING
OOHING
OOLONG
OOZING
POKING
POLING
PORING
POSING
ROBING
ROPING
ROVING
ROWING
SOLING
SOLONG
SONTAG
SOWBUG
SOWING
TOEING
TONING
TOPDOG
TOTING
TOWING
TOYDOG
TOYING
VOTING
VOWING
WONMUG
WOOING
WOWING
YOKING
ZONING

••OG••

APOGEE
BIOGAS
BOOGIE
BROGAN
BROGUE
CLOGGY
CLOGUP
COOGAN
DOOGIE
DROGUE
FROGGY
GLOGGS
GOOGLE
GOOGLY
GOOGOL
GOOGOO
GROGGY
IMOGEN
ISOGON
SHOGUN
SLOGAN
SMOGGY
STOGIE
TROGON
WOOGIE

••O•G•

CHOUGH
CLOGGY
ELOIGN
ENOUGH
FROGGY
GEORGE
GEORGY
GLOGGS
GROGGY
HMONGS
PLOUGH
PRONGS
SLOUGH
SMOGGY
SPONGE
SPONGY
STODGE
STODGY
STOOGE
THONGS
THOUGH
TROUGH
WRONGS

••O••G

BOOING
COOING
MOOING
PHOTOG
PROLOG
WOOING

•••OG•

BEFOGS
DEFOGS
EULOGY
GONOGO
LADOGA
OOLOGY
STOOGE

•••O•G

ALBORG
BARONG
BELONG
BOGONG
CYBORG
DATONG
DELONG
DUGONG
MEKONG
OBLONG
OOLONG
SARONG
SOLONG
STRONG
THRONG
VYBORG

••••OG

ANALOG
BANDOG
DIALOG
EGGNOG
EPILOG
GASLOG
GUNDOG
HERZOG
HOTDOG
ICEFOG
INAFOG
LAPDOG
LITHOG
PETROG
PHOTOG
PROLOG
PYEDOG
QUAHOG
REDDOG
SAWLOG
SEADOG
STENOG
SUNDOG
TAUTOG
TOPDOG
TOYDOG
UNCLOG

OH••••

OHENRY
OHIOAN
OHWELL
OHYEAH

O•H•••

OCHERS
OCHERY
OCHRES
OGHAMS
ONHAND
ONHIGH
ONHOLD
OOHING
OPHITE
OSHAWA
OTHERS

O••H••

OLDHAM
OLDHAT
OMAHAN
OMAHAS
ORCHID
ORCHIL
ORPHAN
ORPHIC
OUGHTS
OUTHIT

O•••H•

OBEAHS
ORACHS

O••••H

OAFISH
OFFISH
OGRISH
OHYEAH
OLDISH
ONHIGH
ONRUSH
OOLITH
OOMPAH
ORBACH
ORNITH
OWLISH

•OH•••

COHEIR
COHERE
COHORT
COHOST
COHUNE
GOHOME
HOHOHO
JOHANN
JOHNNY
JOHORE
KOHLER
MOHAIR
MOHAVE
MOHAWK
MOHOCK
MOHURS
NOHITS
OOHING
ROHMER
WOHLER
YOHOHO

•O•H••

BOCHCO
BOOHOO
BOTHER
COBHAM
COCHIN
COSHED
COSHES
DOTHAN
FOEHNS
FOGHAT
GOPHER
GOSHEN
GOTHAM
GOTHIC
HOOHAH
HOOHAS
JOBHOP
JOSHED
JOSHES
JOSHUA
KOSHER
LOTHAR
MOCHAS
MOSHAV
MOSHED
MOSHER
MOSHES
MOTHER
MOTHRA
NOSHED
NOSHER
NOSHES
NOSHOW
POOHED
POSHER
POSHLY
POTHER
ROCHET
RODHAM
ROTHKO
SOPHIA
SOPHIE
SOTHAT
SOWHAT
TOPHAT
TOPHUS
TOTHER
TOWHEE
YOOHOO

•O••H•

BOLSHY
BOOTHE
BOOTHS
BOTCHY
BOUGHS
BOUGHT
CONCHA
CONCHS
COUGHS
DOUGHS
DOUGHY
FOUGHT
GOETHE
GOTCHA
HOHOHO
HONCHO
HONSHU
HOUGHS
JONAHS
LOATHE
LOTAHS
LOUCHE
LOUGHS
MONTHS
MORPHO
MORPHS
MORPHY
MOUTHS
MOUTHY
NORTHS
NOTCHY
NOUGHT
POACHY
PONCHO
POUCHY
ROUGHS
ROUGHY
SOOTHE
SOUGHS
SOUGHT
SOUTHS
TOOTHY
TORAHS
TORCHY
TOUCHE
TOUCHY
TOUGHS
TOUGHY
VOIGHT
WORTHS
WORTHY
YOHOHO
YOUTHS

•O•••H

BORSCH
BOYISH
COMETH
COYISH
DOODAH
DOVISH
EOLITH
FOURTH
GOFISH
GOODOH
GOWITH
HOOHAH
HOOKAH
HOORAH
HOOTCH
HOWDAH
IOMOTH
JOBETH
JOSEPH
JOSIAH
LOOFAH
LOWISH
MODISH
MOLOCH
MOOLAH
MOPISH
OOLITH
OOMPAH
POLISH
POTASH
TONISH
VOTECH

••OH••

ABOHMS
ALOHAS
BOOHOO
ELOHIM
HOOHAH
HOOHAS
ISOHEL
MYOHMY
POOHED
YOOHOO

••O•H•

BOOTHE
BOOTHS
BROTHS
CLOCHE
CLOTHE
CLOTHO
CLOTHS
EPOCHS
FROTHS
FROTHY
QUOTHA
SLOSHY
SLOTHS

SOOTHE
TOOTHY
TROCHE
TROPHY
TROTHS

••O••H
ADOLPH
AVOUCH
BLOTCH
BROACH
BROOCH
CHOUGH
CROUCH
DOODAH
ENOUGH
GOODOH
GROUCH
GROWTH
HOOHAH
HOOKAH
HOORAH
HOOTCH
LOOFAH
MOOLAH
PLOUGH
SCORCH
SCOTCH
SLOUCH
SLOUGH
SMOOCH
SMOOTH
STORCH
SWOOSH
THOUGH
TROUGH
WHOOSH

•••OH•
HOHOHO
JAWOHL
MEGOHM
STJOHN
UPJOHN
YOHOHO

•••O•H
BROOCH
BYGOSH
EDKOCH
GALOSH
IOMOTH
KIBOSH
MOLOCH
SMOOCH
SMOOTH
SPLOSH
SWOOSH
WHOOSH
ZEROTH

••••OH
GOODOH
MATZOH
SHILOH

OI••••
OILCAN
OILERS
OILIER
OILILY
OILING
OILMAN
OILMEN
OILPAN
OILRIG
OINKED

O•I•••
OBISPO
OBITER
OBIWAN
ODIOUS
ODISTS
ODIUMS
OGIVES
OHIOAN
OJIBWA
OLINDA
OLINGO
OLIVER
OLIVES
OLIVIA
ONIONS
ONIONY
OPIATE
OPINED
OPINER
OPINES
ORIANA
ORIBIS
ORIELS
ORIENT
ORIGEN
ORIGIN
ORINGS
ORIOLE
ORISON
ORISSA
OSIERS
OSIRIS
OTIOSE
OTITIC
OTITIS
OVIEDO
OVISAC
OXIDES
OXIDIC

O••I••
OAFISH
OARING
OATIER
OBLIGE
OBOIST
OBRIAN
OBRIEN
ODDITY
OFFICE
OFFING
OFFISH
OGLING
OGRISH
OILIER
OILILY
OILING
OLDIES
OLDISH
OMNIUM
ONDINE
ONEIDA
ONEILL
ONFILE
ONFIRE
ONHIGH
ONLINE
ONSIDE
ONSITE
ONTIME
ONVIEW
OOHING
OOLITE
OOLITH
OOZIER
OOZILY
OOZING
OPHITE
OPTICS
OPTIMA
OPTING
OPTION
ORBING
ORBITS
OREIDA
ORGIES
ORNITH
OROIDE
ORPINE
ORSINO
OSCINE
OSMICS
OSMIUM
OSSIAN
OSSIFY
OSTIUM
OUTING
OVOIDS
OWLISH
OWNING
OXLIKE
OXLIPS

O•••I•
OBELIA
OBTAIN
OILRIG
OKAPIS
OLDVIC
OLEFIN
OLIVIA
OMANIS
ORCHID
ORCHIL
ORDAIN
ORIBIS
ORIGIN
ORPHIC
OSIRIS
OSSEIN
OTITIC
OTITIS
OUTBID
OUTDID
OUTFIT
OUTHIT
OUTWIT
OXALIS
OXIDIC
OXTAIL
OZONIC

O••••I
OCELLI
OCTOPI
OCTROI

•OI•••
BOIGNY
BOILED
BOILER
BOINGO
BOITES
COIFED
COIGNS
COILED
COILUP
COINED
COINER
DOINGS
EOIPSO
FOIBLE
FOILED
FOINED
FOISTS
GOINGS
GOINTO
HOISTS
JOINED
JOINER
JOININ
JOINTS
JOINUP
JOISTS
LOITER
MOIETY
MOILED
MOILER
MOINES
MOIRES
NOIRON
NOISED
NOISES
POILUS
POINTE
POINTS
POINTY
POIROT
POISED
POISES
POISON
ROILED
SOIGNE
SOILED
SOIREE
TOILED
TOILER
TOILES
TOILET
VOICED
VOICES
VOIDED
VOIGHT
VOILES
YOICKS

•O•I••
AORIST
BODICE
BODIED
BODIES
BODILY
BODING
BOEING
BOGIES
BOLIDE
BONIER
BONING
BONITO
BOOING
BORIDE
BORING
BOVIDS
BOVINE
BOWING
BOXIER
BOXING
BOYISH
COBIAS
CODIFY
CODING
COGITO
COKIER
COLIES
COLIMA
COMICS
COMING
COMITY
CONICS
CONIES
CONIUM
COOING
COPIED
COPIER
COPIES
COPING
CORING
CORIUM
COSIED
COSIER
COSIES
COSIGN
COSILY
COSINE
COVINA
COWING
COYISH
COZIED
COZIER
COZIES
COZILY
DOCILE
DOGIES
DOLING
DOMINE
DOMING
DOMINI
DOMINO
DONITZ
DOPIER
DOPING
DORIAN
DORIES
DOSIDO
DOSING
DOTING
DOVISH
DOZIER
DOZILY
DOZING
EOLIAN
EOLITH
EONIAN
EOSINS
FOGIES
FOLIAR
FOLIOS
FOLIUM
FORINT
FOXIER
FOXILY
FOXING
GOBIES
GODIVA
GOFISH
GOLINO
GOOIER
GORIER
GORILY
GORING
GOWILD
GOWITH
HOEING
HOKIER
HOLIER
HOLILY
HOLING
HOLISM
HOLIST
HOMIER
HOMILY
HOMING
HOMINY
HONIED
HONING
HOPING
HOSIER
HOSING
IODIDE
IODINE
IODISE
IODIZE
IOLITE
IONIAN
IONICS
IONISE
IONIUM
IONIZE
JOKIER
JOKILY
JOKING
JOLIET
JOLIOT
JOSIAH
JOVIAL
JOVIAN
KODIAK
KONICA
LOGIER
LOGILY
LOGION
LOLITA
LOOIES
LOPING
LORICA
LORIES
LOSING
LOTION
LOUISA
LOUISE
LOVING
LOWING
LOWISH
MOBILE
MOBIUS
MODIFY
MODINE
MODISH
MOLINE
MONICA
MONIED
MONIES
MONISM
MONIST
MOOING
MOPIER
MOPING
MOPISH
MORION
MORITA
MORITZ
MOTIFS
MOTILE
MOTION
MOTIVE
MOVIES
MOVING
MOWING
NODICE
NOHITS
NOMINE
NORIAS
NOSIER
NOSILY
NOSING
NOTICE
NOTIFY
NOTING
NOTION
NOVICE
NOWISE
OOHING
OOLITE
OOLITH
OOZIER
OOZILY
OOZING
PODIUM
POGIES
POKIER
POKILY
POKING
POLICE
POLICY
POLING
POLISH
POLITE
POLITY
PONIED
PONIES
PORING
POSIES
POSING
POSITS
POTION
ROBING
ROBINS
ROPIER
ROPING
ROSIER
ROSILY
ROSINS
ROSINY
ROSITA
ROTINI
ROVING
ROWING
SOCIAL
SODIUM
SOFINE
SOLIDI
SOLIDS
SOLING
SONICS
SOVIET
SOWING
TOBIAS
TOBIES
TOEING
TOEINS
TOLIFE
TONICS
TONIER
TONING
TONISH
TONITE
TOPICS
TORIES
TORINO
TOTING
TOWING
TOXICS
TOXINS
TOYING
VOTING
VOTIVE
VOWING
WOOING
WOWING
YOGINI
YOGISM
YOKING
YORICK
ZODIAC
ZONING
ZOOIDS
ZORILS

•O••I•
AODAIS
AORTIC
BOBBIE
BOBBIN
BOCCIE
BODKIN
BOFFIN
BOLLIX
BONNIE
BOOGIE
BOOKIE
BOOTIE
BORGIA
BOSNIA
BOUDIN
BOWFIN
BOWTIE
COATIS
COCCID
COCHIN
COEDIT
COHEIR
COLLIE
COMEIN
COMFIT
COMMIT
COMMIX
CONNIE
CONOID
COOKIE
COOLIT
COOTIE
COPTIC
CORBIN
CORGIS
COSMIC
COURIC
COUSIN
COWRIE
DOBBIN
DOBLIN
DOESIN
DOGGIE
DOGSIT
DOMAIN
DONEIN
DOOBIE
DOOGIE
DOOZIE
DORRIT
DOTTIE
DOVEIN
FOETID
FOGSIN
FOLKIE
FOODIE
FORBID
FORMIC
FOSSIL
FOZZIE
GOALIE
GOBLIN
GODWIN
GODWIT
GOESIN
GOLDIE
GOODIE
GORDIE
GOSSIP
GOTHIC
GOTOIT
HOAGIE
HOBBIT
HOGTIE
HOLDIN
HOLDIT
HOOFIT
HOOTIE
HOPSIN
HORNIN
HORRID
HOTAIR
HOTTIP
HOURIS
HOWLIN
JOANIE
JOININ
JOPLIN
JOSKIN
KOENIG
KOOKIE
LOCKIN

LOGGIA
LOGSIN
LOMEIN
LOOKIN
LOONIE
LORAIN
LOSEIT
LOSTIT
LOVEIN
MOHAIR
MOMMIE
MORBID
MORRIS
MOSAIC
MOULIN
MOVEIN
NOESIS
NOETIC
NOEXIT
NOGGIN
NORDIC
NORRIS
POETIC
PONGID
PONTIC
POPLIN
POPSIN
PORTIA
POSTIT
POTPIE
POURIN
ROADIE
ROBBIA
ROBBIE
ROLLIE
ROLLIN
ROMAIC
RONNIE
ROOKIE
ROOMIE
ROPEIN
SOBEIT
SOCKIN
SOFFIT
SOFTIE
SOLEIL
SOPHIA
SOPHIE
SORBIC
SORDID
SORTIE
TOCSIN
TOEDIN
TOESIN
TOMLIN
TOMMIX
TOMTIT
TONKIN
TONSIL
TOOKIN
TOOKIT
TOONIE
TOROID
TORPID
TORRID
TOWNIE
VOTEIN
WOOGIE
WOOKIE
WORKIN
YORKIE
ZOMBIE
ZOOMIN
ZOYSIA

•O•••I

BODONI
BONAMI
BONSAI
BORZOI
DOMANI
DOMINI
DORATI
DOREMI
MORONI
MOWGLI
POLLOI
POPULI
POTOSI
ROMAJI
ROTINI
SOLIDI
SOMALI
SOUARI
YOGINI

••OI••

ALOINS
ANOINT
AROIDS
AVOIDS
BOOING
BROILS
CHOICE
CHOIRS
COOING
DROIDS
DROITS
EGOISM
EGOIST
ELOIGN
ELOISE
EROICA
ETOILE
GOOIER
GROINS
IDOIDO
ILOILO
LOOIES
MAOISM
MAOIST
MOOING
OBOIST
OROIDE
OVOIDS
QUOINS
QUOITS
REOILS
SPOILS
SPOILT
STOICS
TAOISM
TAOIST
TROIKA
UNOILY
WOOING
ZOOIDS

••O•I•

ADONIS
AEOLIA
AEOLIC
ANODIC
ANOMIC
ANOMIE
ATOMIC
ATONIC
AZORIN
BIOBIO
BIONIC
BIOTIC
BIOTIN
BLOWIN
BLOWIT
BMOVIE
BOOGIE
BOOKIE
BOOTIE
BRODIE
BROLIN
CHOPIN
CLORIS
CLOVIS
COOKIE
COOLIT
COOTIE
CRONIN
DHOTIS
DIOXIN
DOOBIE
DOOGIE
DOOZIE
DROPIN
DROPIT
ELOHIM
ENOKIS
ENOSIS
EROTIC
ETONIC
EXOTIC
FLORID
FLORIN
FLORIO
FOODIE
FROLIC
GLOBIN
GLORIA
GNOMIC
GNOSIS
GOODIE
GRODIN
HOOFIT
HOOTIE
ICONIC
IGOTIT
ILORIN
IRONIC
KAOLIN
KOOKIE
KUOPIO
LEONID
LEONIE
LOOKIN
LOONIE
MAORIS
MIOSIS
MYOPIA
MYOPIC
MYOSIN
MYOSIS
OZONIC
PEORIA
PHOBIA
PHOBIC
PHOCIS
PHONIC
PHOTIC
PROFIT
PROLIX
PROSIT
ROOKIE
ROOMIE
SCORIA
SCOTIA
SHOJIS
SHOOIN
SHOWIN
SKOKIE
SLOVIK
SNOWIN
STOGIE
STOLID
STOPIN
STOPIT
STOTIN
TOOKIN
TOOKIT
TOONIE
TROPIC
TWOBIT
UTOPIA
VIOLIN
WOOGIE
WOOKIE
ZOOMIN

••O••I

ADONAI
AGOUTI
BIONDI
DROMOI
MAOTAI
PROTEI
RHOMBI
SHORTI
WHOOPI

•••OI•

ADJOIN
ADROIT
ALBOIN
ARTOIS
BELOIT
BENOIT
CONOID
CUBOID
DACOIT
DEVOID
DEVOIR
DUBOIS
ECHOIC
ENJOIN
ENVOIS
GALOIS
GOTOIT
HALOID
HEROIC
LIPOID
MEMOIR
PATOIS
REBOIL
RECOIL
REJOIN
RENOIR
REVOIR
SAVOIE
SAVOIR
SHOOIN
TOROID
UNCOIL
VALOIS
XYLOID
ZEROIN

•••O•I

BENONI
BILOXI
BODONI
BUSONI
CARONI
EPHORI
JACOBI
LUGOSI
MALOTI
MIDORI
MORONI
NAPOLI
NEROLI
OCTOPI
PILOTI
POTOSI
PRIORI
SATORI
TIVOLI
WHOOPI

••••OI

BORZOI
DROMOI
KERNOI
MYTHOI
OCTROI
POLLOI

OJ••••

OJIBWA

O•J•••

OBJECT

O••J••

ODDJOB

•OJ•••

JOJOBA
MOJAVE

•O•J••

BOOJUM
CONJOB
DONJON
KOPJES
LOGJAM
TOPJOB

•O••J•

ROMAJI

••OJ••

BOOJUM
RIOJAS
SHOJIS
STOJKO
TROJAN

••O•J•

CHONJU
SKOPJE

•••OJ•

BAROJA

OK••••

OKAPIS
OKAYED
OKEEFE
OKELLY
OKSANA

O•K•••

OAKLEY
ORKNEY

O••K••

OFFKEY
OINKED

O•••K•

OXLIKE
OZARKS

O••••K

OCASEK
OCLOCK
ONDECK

•OK•••

COKIER
FOKKER
GOKART
HOKIER
JOKERS
JOKIER
JOKILY
JOKING
KOKOMO
POKEAT
POKERS
POKERY
POKEYS
POKIER
POKILY
POKING
TOKAYS
TOKENS
TOKLAS
WOKEUP
YOKELS
YOKING
YOKUTS

•O•K••

BODKIN
BOOKED
BOOKER
BOOKIE
BOSKET
COCKED
COCKER
COCKLE
CONKED
CONKER
COOKED
COOKER
COOKIE
COOKUP
CORKED
CORKER
DOCKED
DOCKER
DOCKET
DONKEY
FOKKER
FOLKIE
FOLKSY
FORKED
FORKER
HOCKED
HOCKEY
HONKED
HONKER
HOOKAH
HOOKED
HOOKUP
JOCKEY
JOSKIN
KOOKIE
LOCKED
LOCKER
LOCKET
LOCKIN
LOCKON
LOCKUP
LOOKAT
LOOKED
LOOKER
LOOKIN
LOOKON
LOOKTO
LOOKUP
LOWKEY
MOCKED
MOCKER
MOCKUP
MONKEY
MOSKVA
POCKET
POLKAS
PORKER
ROCKED
ROCKER
ROCKET
ROCKNE
ROCKYV
ROOKED
ROOKIE
SOAKED
SOAKER
SOAKUP
SOCKED
SOCKET
SOCKIN
TONKIN
TOOKIN
TOOKIT
TOOKON
TOOKTO
TOOKUP
VODKAS
WOOKIE
WORKED
WORKER
WORKIN
WORKON
WORKUP
YOLKED
YORKER
YORKIE
ZONKED
ZONKER

•O••K•

BOURKE
KOPEKS
MOLTKE
NOOTKA
ROTHKO
ROURKE
TOPEKA
WOVOKA
YOICKS

•O•••K

GOBACK
KODIAK
KOPECK
LOMBOK
MOHAWK
MOHOCK
PODUNK
TOBRUK
VOSTOK
YORICK

••OK••

AWOKEN
BLOKES
BOOKED
BOOKER
BOOKIE
BROKAW
BROKEN
BROKER
CHOKED
CHOKER
CHOKES
COOKED
COOKER
COOKIE
COOKUP
ENOKIS
EVOKED
EVOKER
EVOKES
HOOKAH
HOOKED
HOOKUP
KOOKIE
LOOKAT
LOOKED
LOOKER
LOOKIN
LOOKON
LOOKTO
LOOKUP
QUOKKA
ROOKED
ROOKIE
RYOKAN
SKOKIE
SMOKED
SMOKER
SMOKES
SMOKEY
SPOKED
SPOKEN
SPOKES
STOKED
STOKER
STOKES
TOOKIN
TOOKIT
TOOKON
TOOKTO
TOOKUP
WOOKIE

••O•K•

BLOCKS
BLOCKY
BROOKE
BROOKS
BROOKY
CHOCKS
CLOAKS
CLOCKS
CLONKS
CROAKS
CROAKY
CROCKS
CROOKS
FLOCKS
FLOCKY
FROCKS
KIOSKS
KNOCKS
NOOTKA
PLONKS
PROSKY
QUOKKA
SHOCKS
SHOOKS
SMOCKS
SNOOKS
SNOOKY
SPOOKS
SPOOKY
STOCKS
STOCKY
STOJKO
STOOKS
STORKS
TROIKA

••O••K

ANORAK
DVORAK
SLOVAK
SLOVIK

•••OK•

BROOKE
BROOKS
BROOKY
CROOKS
INJOKE
INVOKE
JAMOKE
JUDOKA
MIWOKS
REVOKE

SHOOKS
SNOOKS
SNOOKY
SPOOKS
SPOOKY
STOOKS
STROKE
UNYOKE
WOVOKA
YAPOKS
YUROKS

•••O•K

ATWORK
BETOOK
BUROAK
DRHOOK
FAROUK
MOHOCK
NANOOK
OCLOCK
PINOAK
RECORK
REDOAK
REHOOK
RELOCK
RETOOK
REWORK
TANOAK
UNCORK
UNHOOK
UNLOCK

••••OK

BARTOK
BETOOK
DRHOOK
HICKOK
LOMBOK
NANOOK
REEBOK
REHOOK
RETOOK
RHEBOK
UNHOOK
VOSTOK

OL••••

OLDAGE
OLDBOY
OLDEST
OLDHAM
OLDHAT
OLDIES
OLDISH
OLDMAN
OLDMEN
OLDPRO
OLDSAW
OLDVIC
OLEARY
OLEATE
OLEFIN
OLESON
OLEVEL
OLINDA
OLINGO
OLIVER
OLIVES
OLIVIA
OLMECS

O•L•••

OBLAST
OBLATE
OBLIGE
OBLONG
OCLOCK
OFLATE
OGLALA
OGLERS
OGLING
OILCAN
OILERS
OILIER
OILILY
OILING
OILMAN
OILMEN
OILPAN
OILRIG
ONLAND
ONLINE
ONLOAN
OOLALA
OOLITE
OOLITH
OOLOGY
OOLONG
ORLOPS
OWLETS
OWLISH
OXLIKE
OXLIPS

O••L••

OAKLEY
OBELIA
OBELUS
OCELLI
OCELOT
OCULAR
ODDLOT
OKELLY
OMELET
OODLES
ORALES
ORALLY
ORELSE
ORTLES
OSTLER
OTELLO
OUTLAW
OUTLAY
OUTLET
OVALLY
OVULAR
OVULES
OXALIS

O•••L•

OCCULT
OCELLI
OGLALA
OHWELL
OILILY
OKELLY
ONCALL
ONEILL
ONFILE
ONHOLD
ONSALE
OOLALA
OOZILY
OPENLY
ORACLE
ORALLY
ORIELS
ORIOLE
ORMOLU
ORWELL
OSCULA
OSWALD
OTELLO
OTOOLE
OUSELS
OUTFLY
OUZELS
OVALLY
OVERLY

O••••L

OHWELL
OLEVEL
ONCALL
ONEILL
ORCHIL
ORDEAL
ORWELL
OSTEAL
OXTAIL
OXYDOL

•OL•••

BOLDER
BOLDLY
BOLERO
BOLEYN
BOLGER
BOLIDE
BOLLIX
BOLSHY
BOLTED
BOLTON
COLADA
COLDER
COLDLY
COLEUS
COLFAX
COLIES
COLIMA
COLLAR
COLLET
COLLIE
COLLOP
COLLOQ
COLMAN
COLONS
COLONY
COLORS
COLOUR
COLTER
COLUGO
COLUMN
DOLENZ
DOLING
DOLLAR
DOLLED
DOLLOP
DOLLUP
DOLMAN
DOLMAS
DOLMEN
DOLORS
DOLOUR
EOLIAN
EOLITH
FOLDED
FOLDER
FOLDUP
FOLIAR
FOLIOS
FOLIUM
FOLKIE
FOLKSY
FOLLOW
FOLSOM
GOLDEN
GOLDIE
GOLEMS
GOLFED
GOLFER
GOLINO
GOLLUM
HOLDEN
HOLDER
HOLDIN
HOLDIT
HOLDON
HOLDTO
HOLDUP
HOLEUP
HOLIER
HOLILY
HOLING
HOLISM
HOLIST
HOLLER
HOLLOW
HOLMES
IOLITE
JOLENE
JOLIET
JOLIOT
JOLSON
JOLTED
LOLITA
LOLLED
LOLLOP
MOLARS
MOLDAU
MOLDED
MOLDER
MOLEST
MOLINE
MOLNAR
MOLOCH
MOLOPO
MOLTED
MOLTEN
MOLTER
MOLTKE
NOLEAD
NOLENS
NOLESS
NOLOAD
NOLOSE
OOLALA
OOLITE
OOLITH
OOLOGY
OOLONG
POLAND
POLDER
POLEAX
POLERS
POLEYN
POLICE
POLICY
POLING
POLISH
POLITE
POLITY
POLKAS
POLLED
POLLEN
POLLER
POLLEX
POLLOI
POLLUX
POLPOT
POLYPS
ROLAND
ROLEOS
ROLLED
ROLLER
ROLLIE
ROLLIN
ROLLON
ROLLUP
SOLACE
SOLANS
SOLARS
SOLDAN
SOLDER
SOLDON
SOLEIL
SOLELY
SOLEMN
SOLENT
SOLERS
SOLEUS
SOLFAS
SOLIDI
SOLIDS
SOLING
SOLOED
SOLONG
SOLUTE
SOLVED
SOLVER
SOLVES
TOLDOF
TOLDON
TOLEDO
TOLIFE
TOLLED
TOLTEC
TOLUCA
VOLANS
VOLANT
VOLARE
VOLENS
VOLLEY
VOLUME
VOLUTE
VOLVAS
VOLVOX
WOLFED
WOLPER
WOLSEY
WOLVES
YOLKED

•O•L••

BOGLES
BOILED
BOILER
BOLLIX
BOSLEY
BOULES
BOULEZ
BOULLE
BOWLED
BOWLER
BOWLES
COALER
COELOM
COILED
COILUP
COLLAR
COLLET
COLLIE
COLLOP
COLLOQ
COOLED
COOLER
COOLIT
COOLLY
COPLEY
COULDA
COULEE
COWLED
COWLEY
DOBLAS
DOBLIN
DOGLEG
DOLLAR
DOLLED
DOLLOP
DOLLUP
DOOLEY
FOALED
FOILED
FOLLOW
FOOLED
FOOLER
FOULED
FOULER
FOULLY
FOULUP
FOWLED
FOWLER
FOWLES
GOALIE
GOBLET
GOBLIN
GOLLUM
GOSLOW
GOULET
HOLLER
HOLLOW
HOWLED
HOWLER
HOWLIN
JOBLOT
JOPLIN
JOULES
KOALAS
KOHLER
LOLLED
LOLLOP
MOBLEY
MOILED
MOILER
MOOLAH
MORLEY
MOSLEM
MOTLEY
MOULDS
MOULDY
MOULIN
MOULTS
NOBLER
NOBLES
OODLES
POILUS
POLLED
POLLEN
POLLER
POLLEX
POLLOI
POLLUX
POOLED
POPLAR
POPLIN
POULTS
ROBLES
ROILED
ROLLED
ROLLER
ROLLIE
ROLLIN
ROLLON
ROLLUP
SOCLES
SOILED
TOILED
TOILER
TOILES
TOILET
TOKLAS
TOLLED
TOMLIN
TOOLED
TOOLUP
TOULON
VOILES
VOLLEY
WOHLER
WOOLEN
WOOLEY
WOOLLY
WORLDS
YOWLED

•O••L•

BOBBLE
BODILY
BOGGLE
BOLDLY
BOODLE
BOTELS
BOTFLY
BOTTLE
BOUCLE
BOULLE
COBALT
COBBLE
COCKLE
CODDLE
COLDLY
COMELY
COMPLY
COOLLY
COPULA
CORALS
COSELL
COSILY
COSTLY
COUPLE
COZILY
DOABLE
DOCILE
DONALD
DONGLE
DOODLE
DOTELL
DOTTLE
DOUALA
DOUBLE
DOUBLY
DOURLY
DOWELS
DOZILY
FOCSLE
FOIBLE
FONDLE
FONDLY
FOOZLE
FOULLY
FOXILY
GOBBLE
GOGGLE
GOGGLY
GOODLY
GOOGLE
GOOGLY
GORALS
GORILY
GOWILD
HOBBLE
HOLILY
HOMELY
HOMILY
HOOPLA
HOOPLE
HOPPLE
HOSELS
HOSTLY
HOTELS
HOURLY
HOVELS
HOWELL
JOGGLE
JOKILY
JOSTLE
KOBOLD
KODALY
LOBULE
LOCALE
LOCALS
LOGILY
LONELY
LONGLY
LORDLY
LOUDLY
LOVELL
LOVELY
LOWELL
LOYOLA
MOBILE
MODELA
MODELS
MODELT
MODULE
MODULO
MOGULS
MORALE
MORALS
MORELS
MOSTLY
MOTELS
MOTILE
MOTTLE
MOWGLI
NOBBLE
NODDLE
NODULE
NOODLE
NOSALE
NOSILY
NOVELS
NOZZLE
OOLALA
OOZILY
POKILY
POMELO
POODLE
POORLY
POPFLY
POPPLE
POPULI
PORTLY
POSHLY
POSSLQ
POTTLE
POWELL
ROBALO
ROMOLA
RONALD
RONELY
ROSILY
ROUBLE
ROWELS
ROYALE
ROYALS
SOFTLY
SOLELY
SOMALI
SORELY
SOTOLS
SOURLY
TODDLE
TOGGLE
TOOTLE
TOPPLE
TOTALS
TOUSLE
TOWELS
VOCALS
VOWELS
VOWELY
WOBBLE
WOBBLY
WOOLLY
YODELS
YOKELS
YOUALL
ZORILS

•O•••L
AORTAL
BOATEL
BOREAL
BOXFUL
COEVAL
COMPEL
CONSUL
CORBEL
CORNEL
CORRAL
CORREL
COSELL
COSTAL
DORSAL
DOSSAL
DOSSEL
DOTELL
FOETAL
FONTAL
FORMAL
FOSSIL
GOOGOL
GOSPEL
HORMEL
HOSTEL
HOWELL
JOVIAL
JOYFUL
KOPPEL
LONNOL
LOREAL
LOVELL
LOWCAL
LOWELL
MONGOL
MONTEL
MORSEL
MORTAL
MOSTEL
NORMAL
POMMEL
PORTAL
POSTAL
POTFUL
POWELL
ROMMEL
RONDEL
SOBFUL
SOCIAL
SOLEIL
SORREL
TONSIL
WOEFUL
YOUALL

••OL••
ABOLLA
ADOLPH
AEOLIA
AEOLIC
AEOLUS
AMOLES
ANOLES
APOLLO
ATOLLS
BROLIN
BROLLY
CHOLER
CHOLLA
CHOLOS
COOLED
COOLER
COOLIT
COOLLY
DHOLES
DOOLEY
DROLLS
DROLLY
ECOLES
EVOLVE
FOOLED
FOOLER
FROLIC
GAOLED
GAOLER
HAOLES
ISOLDE
KAOLIN
KJOLEN
KNOLLS
KNOLLY
MOOLAH
PIOLET
POOLED
PROLES
PROLIX
PROLOG
SCOLDS
SHOLEM
SHOLOM
SMOLTS
STOLEN
STOLES
STOLID
STOLLE
STOLON
THOLES
TOOLED
TOOLUP
TROLLS
UBOLTS
VIOLAS
VIOLET
VIOLIN
WHOLES
WHOLLY
WOOLEN
WOOLEY
WOOLLY

••O•L•
ABOLLA
APOLLO
ATOLLS
BOODLE
BROILS
BROLLY
CEORLS
CHOLLA
COOLLY
DOODLE
DROLLS
DROLLY
DROOLS
DROOLY
ETOILE
FOOZLE
GHOULS
GOODLY
GOOGLE
GOOGLY
GROWLS
GROWLY
HOOPLA
HOOPLE
ILOILO
KNOLLS
KNOLLY
LIONLY
NOODLE
OTOOLE
PEOPLE
POODLE
POORLY
PROWLS
REOILS
SCOWLS
SHOALS
SHOALY
SHOULD
SKOALS
SLOWLY
SPOILS
SPOILT
SPOOLS
STOLLE
STOOLS
STOOLY
TOOTLE
TROLLS
TWOPLY
UNOILY
WHOLLY
WHORLS
WOOLLY

••O••L
ABORAL
AMORAL
APODAL
ATONAL
AVOWAL
AXONAL
BHOPAL
CHORAL
DHOTEL
FLORAL
GLOBAL
GOOGOL
GROVEL
ISOHEL
LIONEL
PROPEL
SHOVEL
TROWEL
UNOCAL

•••OL•
AGEOLD
ANGOLA
AREOLA
ARNOLD
BAROLO
BEHOLD
BIFOLD
BITOLA
BUJOLD
CAJOLE
CANOLA
CAROLE
CAROLS
CIBOLA
CREOLE
CUPOLA
DIPOLE
DROOLS
DROOLY
EIDOLA
ENFOLD
ENROLL
ENROLS
ERROLL
EXTOLS
GIGOLO
HAROLD
INFOLD
INSOLE
KOBOLD
LOYOLA
MAZOLA
NAPOLI
NEROLI
NICOLA
NICOLE
NICOLO
NIKOLA
ONHOLD
ORIOLE
ORMOLU
OTOOLE
PAROLE
PAYOLA
PINOLE
RCCOLA
REBOLT
REMOLD
REPOLL
RESOLD
RESOLE
RETOLD
REVOLT
ROMOLA
RUDOLF
SCROLL
SOTOLS
SPOOLS
STOOLS
STOOLY
STROLL
TIVOLI
UNBOLT
UNFOLD
UNHOLY
UNROLL
UNSOLD
UNTOLD
UPHOLD

•••O•L
BEFOUL
ENROLL
ENSOUL
ERROLL
FAZOOL
JAWOHL
MRCOOL
REBOIL
RECOIL
REPOLL
RETOOL
SCHOOL
SCHORL
SCROLL
STROLL
UNCOIL
UNCOOL
UNROLL

••••OL
AMATOL
AMIDOL
BENZOL
CARROL
CRESOL
ETYMOL
FAZOOL
FRIJOL
GAMBOL
GLYCOL
GOOGOL
LONNOL
MONGOL
MRCOOL
MYTHOL
NEUROL
OXYDOL
PATHOL
PATROL
PETROL
PHENOL
PHILOL
PISTOL
RETOOL
SCHOOL
STEROL
SYMBOL
TYDBOL
UNCOOL
WARHOL

OM••••
OMAHAN
OMAHAS
OMANIS
OMASUM
OMEGAS
OMELET
OMERTA
OMNIUM

O•M•••
OLMECS
OOMPAH
ORMOLU
ORMOND
OSMICS
OSMIUM
OSMOND
OSMOSE
OSMUND

O••M••
OILMAN
OILMEN
OLDMAN
OLDMEN
ONEMAN
OROMOS

O•••M•
ODIUMS
OEDEMA
OGHAMS
ONTIME
OPTIMA

O••••M
OLDHAM
OMASUM
OMNIUM
OSMIUM
OSTIUM

•OM•••
BOMBAY
BOMBED
BOMBER
BOMBES
COMATE
COMBAT
COMBED
COMBER
COMBES
COMBOS
COMEAT
COMEBY
COMEDY
COMEIN
COMELY
COMEON
COMERS
COMETH
COMETO
COMETS
COMEUP
COMFIT
COMICS
COMING
COMITY
COMMAS
COMMIT
COMMIX
COMMON
COMPAQ
COMPEL
COMPLY
COMPOS
COMSAT
COMTES
DOMAIN
DOMANI
DOMINE
DOMING
DOMINI
DOMINO
DOMREP
FOMENT
HOMAGE
HOMBRE
HOMEEC
HOMELY
HOMERS
HOMIER
HOMILY
HOMING
HOMINY
IOMOTH
KOMBAT
KOMODO
LOMBOK
LOMEIN
LOMOND
MOMENT
MOMMAS
MOMMIE
NOMADS
NOMINE
NOMORE
OOMPAH
POMACE
POMADE
POMELO
POMMEE
POMMEL
POMONA
POMPEY
POMPOM
POMPON
ROMAIC
ROMAJI
ROMANO
ROMANS
ROMANY
ROMEOS
ROMERO
ROMMEL
ROMNEY
ROMOLA
ROMPED
ROMPER
SOMALI
SOMANY
SOMATA
SOMATO
SOMBER
SOMBRE
SOMERS
SOMMER
TOMATO
TOMBAC
TOMBOY
TOMCAT
TOMLIN
TOMMIX
TOMTIT
TOMTOM
WOMBAT
WOMENS
YOMTOV
ZOMBIE

•O•M••
BONMOT
BOOMED
BOOMER
BORMAN
BOWMAN
BOWMEN
COLMAN
COMMAS
COMMIT
COMMIX
COMMON
CONMAN
CONMEN
CORMAN
COSMIC
COSMOS
COWMAN
COWMEN
DOGMAS
DOLMAN
DOLMAS
DOLMEN
DOOMED
DORMER
FOAMED
FORMAL
FORMAN
FORMAT
FORMED
FORMER
FORMIC
GOTMAD
HOLMES
HORMEL
HORMUZ
KORMAN
LOAMED
LOOMED
MOMMAS
MOMMIE
MORMON
MOTMOT
NORMAL
NORMAN
NOUMEA
POMMEE
POMMEL
ROAMED
ROAMER
RODMAN
ROHMER
ROMMEL
ROOMED
ROOMER
ROOMIE
SOMMER
TOAMAN
TODMAN
TOMMIX
WONMUG
WORMED
ZOOMED
ZOOMIN

•O••M•
BONAMI
COLIMA
COLUMN
DODOMA
DOREMI
FORUMS
GOHOME
GOLEMS
JORUMS
KOKOMO
MODEMS
NONAME
SOLEMN
SONOMA
TOTEMS
VOLUME
YOYOMA

•O•••M
BOOJUM
BOTTOM
COBHAM
COELOM
CONIUM
CORIUM
DOGDOM
DORSUM
FOLIUM
FOLSOM
FOURAM
FOURPM
GOLLUM
GOTHAM
HOLISM
IONIUM
LOGJAM
MONISM
MOSLEM
NONCOM
PODIUM
POMPOM
POSSUM
RODHAM
SODIUM
TOMTOM
YOGISM

••OM••
ABOMBS
ALOMAR
ANOMIC
ANOMIE
AROMAS
ATOMIC
BIOMES
BOOMED
BOOMER
CHOMPS
CLOMPS
DOOMED
DROMOI
DROMOS
DUOMOS
GNOMES
GNOMIC
GNOMON
HBOMBS
ISOMER
LOOMED
OROMOS
PROMOS
PROMPT
RHOMBI
RHOMBS
ROOMED
ROOMER
ROOMIE
STOMAS
STOMAT
STOMPS
THOMAS
TROMPE
TROMPS
WHOMPS
WHOMSO
YEOMAN
YEOMEN
ZOOMED
ZOOMIN

••O•M•
ABOHMS

BLOOMS
BLOOMY
BROOMS
BROOMY
GLOOMS
GLOOMY
GROOMS
KHOUMS
MYOHMY
PROAMS
PROEMS
SHOWME
STORMS
STORMY
VROOMS

••O••M

ANONYM
BOOJUM
EGOISM
ELOHIM
EPONYM
MAOISM
PROTEM
QUORUM
SHOLEM
SHOLOM
TAOISM

•••OM•

APLOMB
ATHOME
AXIOMS
BECOME
BESOMS
BLOOMS
BLOOMY
BROOMS
BROOMY
CAROMS
CDROMS
CHROMA
CHROME
CHROMO
CHROMY
DODOMA
ENTOMO
EPROMS
GENOME
GLOOMS
GLOOMY
GOHOME
GROOMS
IDIOMS
INCOME
JEROME
KOKOMO
PALOMA
RADOME
SALOME
SONOMA
TACOMA
UGSOME
VENOMS
VROOMS
YOYOMA

•••O•M

ABLOOM
DEFORM
INFORM
KABOOM
MEGOHM
PHLOEM
REFORM
SHBOOM
SILOAM

••••OM

ABLOOM
BOTTOM
COELOM
CUSTOM
DIATOM
DOGDOM
FANDOM
FATHOM
FOLSOM
HANSOM
KABOOM
MADTOM
NONCOM
PHENOM
POMPOM
RANDOM
RANSOM
SELDOM
SHALOM
SHBOOM
SHOLOM
SITCOM
SLALOM
TOMTOM
VIACOM
WHILOM
WINDOM
WISDOM

ON••••

ONAGER
ONCALL
ONDECK
ONDINE
ONEACT
ONEDAY
ONEDGE
ONEIDA
ONEILL
ONEMAN
ONETWO
ONEUPS
ONEWAY
ONFILE
ONFIRE
ONFOOT
ONHAND
ONHIGH
ONHOLD
ONIONS
ONIONY
ONLAND
ONLINE
ONLOAN
ONRUSH
ONSALE
ONSETS
ONSIDE
ONSITE
ONSPEC
ONTAPE
ONTIME
ONTOUR
ONUSES
ONVIEW
ONWARD
ONYXES

O•N•••

OENONE
OINKED
OMNIUM
ORNATE
ORNERY
ORNITH
OUNCES
OWNERS
OWNING
OWNSUP
OXNARD

O••N••

ODENSE
ODONTO
OHENRY
OLINDA
OLINGO
OMANIS
OPENED
OPENER
OPENLY
OPENTO
OPENUP
OPINED
OPINER
OPINES
ORANGE
ORANGS
ORANGY
ORANTS
ORINGS
ORKNEY
OZONIC

O•••N•

OARING
OBLONG
OBTUND
OCEANS
OCTANE
OCTANT
OENONE
OFFEND
OFFING
OGLING
OILING
OKSANA
ONDINE
ONHAND
ONIONS
ONIONY
ONLAND
ONLINE
OOHING
OOLONG
OOZING
OPTING
ORBING
ORGANA
ORGANS
ORIANA
ORIENT
ORMOND
ORPINE
ORSINO
OSCINE
OSMOND
OSMUND
OSTEND
OUTING
OWNING

O••••N

OBERON
OBIWAN
OBRIAN
OBRIEN
OBTAIN
ODDSON
OHIOAN
OILCAN
OILMAN
OILMEN
OILPAN
OLDMAN
OLDMEN
OLEFIN
OLESON
OMAHAN
ONEMAN
ONLOAN
OPPUGN
OPTION
ORDAIN
OREGON
ORIGEN
ORIGIN
ORISON
ORPHAN
OSBORN
OSSEIN
OSSIAN
OUTGUN
OUTRAN
OUTRUN
OXYGEN

•ON•••

BONAMI
BONBON
BONCES
BONDED
BONERS
BONEUP
BONGED
BONGOS
BONIER
BONING
BONITO
BONMOT
BONNES
BONNET
BONNIE
BONSAI
BONTON
BONZES
CONANT
CONCHA
CONCHS
CONCUR
CONDOR
CONDOS
CONEYS
CONFAB
CONFED
CONFER
CONGAS
CONGER
CONGOU
CONICS
CONIES
CONIUM
CONJOB
CONKED
CONKER
CONMAN
CONMEN
CONNED
CONNER
CONNIE
CONNOR
CONOCO
CONOID
CONRAD
CONROY
CONSUL
CONTAC
CONTES
CONTRA
CONTRE
CONURE
CONVEX
CONVEY
CONVOY
CONWAY
DONALD
DONATE
DONDER
DONEES
DONEIN
DONETS
DONEUP
DONGLE
DONITZ
DONJON
DONKEY
DONNAS
DONNED
DONNEE
DONNER
DONORS
DONUTS
EONIAN
FONDER
FONDLE
FONDLY
FONDUE
FONTAL
GONEBY
GONERS
GONGED
GONOGO
HONCHO
HONEST
HONEYS
HONIED
HONING
HONKED
HONKER
HONORE
HONORS
HONOUR
HONSHU
IONIAN
IONICS
IONISE
IONIUM
IONIZE
JONAHS
JONSON
KONICA
KONRAD
LONDON
LONELY
LONERS
LONGAN
LONGED
LONGER
LONGES
LONGLY
LONGUE
LONNOL
MONACO
MONADS
MONDAY
MONERA
MONETA
MONEYS
MONGER
MONGOL
MONICA
MONIED
MONIES
MONISM
MONIST
MONKEY
MONODY
MONROE
MONTEL
MONTES
MONTEZ
MONTHS
NONAGE
NONAME
NONARY
NONCOM
NONEGO
NONETS
NONFAT
PONCES
PONCHO
PONDER
PONGED
PONGEE
PONGID
PONIED
PONIES
PONTES
PONTIC
PONTUS
PONYUP
RONALD
RONDEL
RONDOS
RONELY
RONNIE
SONANT
SONATA
SONDES
SONICS
SONNET
SONOMA
SONORA
SONTAG
TONDOS
TONERS
TONEUP
TONGAN
TONGUE
TONICS
TONIER
TONING
TONISH
TONITE
TONKIN
TONNES
TONSIL
WONDER
WONMUG
WONNED
WONOUT
WONTED
WONTON
YONDER
ZONATE
ZONING
ZONKED
ZONKER

•O•N••

BOINGO
BONNES
BONNET
BONNIE
BORNEO
BOSNIA
BOUNCE
BOUNCY
BOUNDS
BOUNTY
BOWNET
COGNAC
COINED
COINER
CONNED
CONNER
CONNIE
CONNOR
COONEY
CORNEA
CORNED
CORNEL
CORNER
CORNET
COUNTS
COUNTY
DOINGS
DONNAS
DONNED
DONNEE
DONNER
DOWNED
DOWNER
DOWNEY
DOWNON
FOINED
FOUNDS
FOUNTS
GOANNA
GOINGS
GOINTO
GOUNOD
GOWNED
HOBNOB
HORNED
HORNER
HORNET
HORNEY
HORNIN
HOUNDS
HOUNDY
HOWNOW
JOANIE
JOANNA
JOANNE
JOHNNY
JOINED
JOINER
JOININ
JOINTS
JOINUP
JOUNCE
JOUNCY
JOYNER
KOENIG
KOONTZ
LOANED
LOANER
LONNOL
LOONEY
LOONIE
LOUNGE
MOANED
MOANER
MOINES
MOLNAR
MOONED
MOONEY
MORNAY
MOUNDS
MOUNTS
MOUNTY
NOONAN
NOONES
NOTNOW
POINTE
POINTS
POINTY
POUNCE
POUNDS
RODNEY
ROMNEY
RONNIE
ROONEY
ROUNDS
SONNET
SOONER
SOUNDS
TONNES
TOONIE
TOWNER
TOWNIE
WONNED
WOUNDS
ZOUNDS

•O••N•

BODING
BODONI
BOEING
BOGONG
BOIGNY
BONING
BOOING
BORING
BOSONS
BOSUNS
BOTANY
BOURNE
BOVINE
BOWING
BOXING
CODING
CODONS
COGENT
COHUNE
COIGNS
COLONS
COLONY
COMING
CONANT
COOING
COPING
CORING
CORONA
COSINE
COVENS
COVENT
COVINA
COWENS
COWING
COZENS
DOCENT
DOESNT
DOGONS
DOLENZ
DOLING
DOMANI
DOMINE
DOMING
DOMINI
DOMINO
DOPANT
DOPING
DOSING
DOTING
DOYENS
DOZENS
DOZING
EOCENE
EOSINS
FOEHNS
FOMENT
FORINT
FOXING
GOANNA
GOLINO
GORING
HOEING
HOGANS
HOLING
HOMING
HOMINY
HONING
HOPING
HOSING
IODINE
IOWANS
JOANNA
JOANNE
JOCUND

JOHANN
JOHNNY
JOKING
JOLENE
JOURNO
KORUNA
LODENS
LOMOND
LOPING
LORENZ
LOSING
LOVING
LOWEND
LOWING
MODENA
MODINE
MOLINE
MOMENT
MOOING
MOPING
MORANT
MORENO
MORONI
MORONS
MOURNS
MOVING
MOWING
NOCENT
NOLENS
NOMINE
NOSING
NOTING
NOVENA
OOHING
OOLONG
OOZING
POCONO
PODUNK
POKING
POLAND
POLING
POMONA
PORING
POSING
POTENT
ROBING
ROBINS
ROCKNE
RODENT
ROLAND
ROMANO
ROMANS
ROMANY
ROPING
ROSINS
ROSINY
ROTINI
ROTUND
ROVING
ROWENA
ROWENS
ROWING
ROXANA
ROXANE
SOFINE
SOIGNE
SOLANS
SOLENT
SOLING
SOLONG
SOMANY
SONANT
SOWING
TOEING
TOEINS
TOKENS
TONING
TORINO
TOTING
TOWING
TOXINS
TOYING
TOYONS
VOLANS
VOLANT
VOLENS
VOTING
VOWING
WOMENS
WOOING
WOWING
YOGINI
YOKING
ZONING

•O•••N

BOBBIN
BODKIN
BOFFIN
BOLEYN
BOLTON
BONBON
BONTON
BORDEN
BOREON
BORMAN
BOSTON
BOUDIN
BOWFIN
BOWMAN
BOWMEN
COBURN
COCHIN
COCOON
COLMAN
COLUMN
COMEIN
COMEON
COMMON
CONMAN
CONMEN
COOGAN
CORBAN
CORBIN
CORDON
CORMAN
COSIGN
COTTEN
COTTON
COUPON
COUSIN
COWMAN
COWMEN
DOBBIN
DOBLIN
DOBSON
DOESIN
DOLMAN
DOLMEN
DOMAIN
DONEIN
DONJON
DORIAN
DOTEON
DOTHAN
DOVEIN
DOWNON
EOLIAN
EONIAN
FOGSIN
FORMAN
GOBLIN
GODOWN
GODSON
GODWIN
GOESIN
GOESON
GOLDEN
GOODEN
GORDON
GORGON
GOSHEN
GOTTEN
GOVERN
HOBSON
HOLDEN
HOLDIN
HOLDON
HOPSIN
HORNIN
HORTON
HOWLIN
HOYDEN
IONIAN
JOHANN
JOININ
JOLSON
JONSON
JOPLIN
JORDAN
JOSKIN
JOVIAN
KOREAN
KORMAN
LOCKIN
LOCKON
LOGION
LOGSIN
LOGSON
LOMEIN
LONDON
LONGAN
LOOKIN
LOOKON
LOOSEN
LORAIN
LOTION
LOUDEN
LOVEIN
MODERN
MOLTEN
MOREEN
MORGAN
MORGEN
MORION
MORMON
MORTON
MOTION
MOTOWN
MOULIN
MOUTON
MOVEIN
MOVEON
NOGGIN
NOIRON
NOONAN
NORMAN
NORTON
NOTION
POISON
POLEYN
POLLEN
POMPON
POPGUN
POPLIN
POPSIN
POSTON
POTEEN
POTION
POURIN
ROBSON
RODMAN
ROLLIN
ROLLON
ROPEIN
ROTTEN
SOCKIN
SODDEN
SOFTEN
SOLDAN
SOLDON
SOLEMN
SOSOON
TOAMAN
TOCSIN
TODMAN
TOEDIN
TOESIN
TOLDON
TOMLIN
TONGAN
TONKIN
TOOKIN
TOOKON
TOPGUN
TOPTEN
TOUCAN
TOULON
VOTEIN
WONTON
WOODEN
WOOLEN
WOREON
WORKIN
WORKON
WORSEN
ZOOMIN

••ON••

ADONAI
ADONIS
ALONSO
ALONZO
ANONYM
ATONAL
ATONCE
ATONED
ATONES
ATONIC
AXONAL
BIONDI
BIONIC
BLONDE
BLONDS
BRONCO
BRONCS
BRONTE
BRONZE
BRONZY
CHONJU
CLONED
CLONES
CLONKS
CLONUS
COONEY
CRONES
CRONIN
CRONUS
CRONYN
DIONEB
DIONNE
DRONED
DRONER
DRONES
EBONDS
EPONYM
ETONIC
EVONNE
FRONDS
FRONTS
HMONGS
ICONIC
IRONED
IRONER
IRONIC
IRONON
KOONTZ
KRONER
KRONOR
KRONUR
LEONES
LEONID
LEONIE
LIONEL
LIONET
LIONLY
LOONEY
LOONIE
MOONED
MOONEY
NOONAN
NOONES
ODONTO
OZONIC
PHONED
PHONES
PHONEY
PHONIC
PHONON
PHONOS
PLONKS
PRONGS
PRONTO
RHONDA
ROONEY
SCONCE
SCONES
SOONER
SPONGE
SPONGY
STONED
STONER
STONES
TBONDS
TBONES
THONGS
TOONIE
WRONGS
YVONNE

••O•N•

ABOUND
ACORNS
ADORNS
ALOINS
AMOUNT
ANOINT
AROUND
BOOING
BROWNE
BROWNS
BROWNY
CLOWNS
COOING
CROONS
CROWNS
DIONNE
DROWNS
EVONNE
FROWNS
GROANS
GRODNO
GROINS
GROUND
GROZNY
KNOWNS
MOOING
PROCNE
QUOINS
SCORNS
SLOANE
SPOONS
SPOONY
SWOONS
THORNS
THORNY
WOOING
YVONNE

••O••N

ASOSAN
AWOKEN
AZORIN
BIOTIN
BLOWIN
BROGAN
BROKEN
BROLIN
CHOPIN
CHOSEN
CLOVEN
COOGAN
CRONIN
CRONYN
CROTON
DIOXIN
DROPIN
ELOIGN
FLORIN
FROZEN
GLOBIN
GNOMON
GOODEN
GRODIN
GROTON
GROWON
ILORIN
IMOGEN
IRONON
ISOGON
KAOLIN
KJOLEN
LOOKIN
LOOKON
LOOSEN
MYOSIN
NOONAN
PHONON
PHOTON
PROTON
PROVEN
REOPEN
RYOKAN
SHOGUN
SHOOIN
SHORAN
SHOWIN
SIOUAN
SLOGAN
SLOVEN
SNOWIN
SPOKEN
STOLEN
STOLON
STOPIN
STOTIN
TOOKIN
TOOKON
TROGON
TROJAN
UNOPEN
USOPEN
VIOLIN
WOODEN
WOOLEN
YEOMAN
YEOMEN
ZOOMIN

•••ON•

ACTONE
ADDONS
ALMOND
ANCONA
ANIONS
ANTONY
ANYONE
APRONS
ARSONS
AUFOND
AUMONT
AXIONS
BARONG
BARONS
BARONY
BATONS
BEGONE
BELONG
BENONI
BETONY
BEYOND
BISONS
BODONI
BOGONG
BOSONS
BRYONY
BUSONI
BYGONE
CANONS
CAPONE
CAPONS
CARONI
CHRONO
CODONS
COLONS
COLONY
CORONA
CROONS
DAMONE
DATONG
DAYONE
DEBONE
DELONG
DEMOND
DEMONS
DEPONE
DOGONS
DUGONG
DUMONT
DUPONT
EDMOND
EGMONT
EVZONE
FANONS
FELONS
FELONY
FUTONS
GERONT
GLUONS
GYRONS
HERONS
HURONS
INIONS
INTONE
KETONE
KIMONO
LAMONT
LATONA
LEMOND
LEMONS
LEMONY
LOMOND
LUPONE
MALONE
MASONS
MEKONG
MELONS
MESONS
MORONI
MORONS
NYLONS
OBLONG
OENONE
ONIONS
ONIONY
OOLONG
ORMOND
OSMOND
PAEONS
PINONS
PITONS
POCONO
POMONA
PRIONS
PUTONS
PYLONS
RACONS
RAMONA
RAMONE
RAYONS
RECONS
REDONE
REZONE
RUNONS
SALONS
SARONG
SAXONS
SAXONY
SCIONS
SECOND
SILONE
SIMONE
SIMONY
SOLONG
SPOONS
SPOONY
STRONG
SWOONS
TALONS
TAUONS
TENONS
TETONS
THRONE
THRONG
TOYONS
TYRONE
UNDONE
UNIONS
VERONA
WAGONS
WINONA

•••O•N

ADJOIN
ALBOIN
ASWOON
BABOON
BEMOAN
BICORN
COCOON
DEHORN
DISOWN
ENJOIN
GENOAN
GODOWN
INBORN
INTOWN
LAGOON
MACOUN
MAROON
MINOAN
MOTOWN
OHIOAN
ONLOAN
OSBORN
REBORN
REJOIN
REMOWN
RENOWN
SALOON

SAMOAN
SHOOIN
SOSOON
STJOAN
STJOHN
SUBORN
TANOAN
THROWN
TYCOON
UNBORN
UNSOWN
UNTORN
UNWORN
UPJOHN
UPTOWN
ZEROIN

••••ON

ACTION
ACTSON
ADDSON
ALANON
ALBION
ALISON
AMAZON
AMNION
ANNHON
ANTRON
ARAGON
ARCHON
ASWOON
AVALON
AVEDON
BABOON
BABSON
BALLON
BANKON
BANLON
BARRON
BARTON
BARYON
BEACON
BEAMON
BEARON
BEATON
BECKON
BENSON
BENTON
BETSON
BIDSON
BILLON
BLAZON
BOLTON
BONBON
BONTON
BOREON
BOSTON
BRETON
BRITON
BRYSON
BUFFON
BUNION
BURTON
BUTTON
CALLON
CAMEON
CAMION
CANNON
CANTON
CANYON
CARBON
CARSON
CARTON
CASTON
CATION
CATTON
CAXTON
CEYLON
CHARON
CHIRON
CHITON
CHYRON
CITRON
CLIPON
COCOON
COMEON
COMMON
CORDON
COTTON
COUPON
CRAYON
CROTON
CURZON
DACRON
DAIKON
DAIMON
DALTON
DAMSON
DANSON
DANTON
DAWNON
DAWSON
DAYTON
DEACON
DEADON
DELEON
DENTON
DIDION
DILLON
DINEON
DOBSON
DONJON
DOTEON
DOWNON
DRAGON
DRAWON
DREWON
EASTON
EDISON
EGGSON
EPHRON
ETYMON
FALCON
FALLON
FANION
FEEDON
FELDON
FELLON
FLACON
FLAGON
FULTON
FUSION
GABION
GAINON
GALLON
GAMMON
GARCON
GARSON
GASCON
GASTON
GETSON
GIBBON
GIBSON
GIDEON
GNOMON
GODSON
GOESON
GORDON
GORGON
GREWON
GRISON
GROTON
GROWON
GUENON
GUIDON
HADRON
HAEMON
HAGDON
HANDON
HANGON
HANSON
HARMON
HARPON
HAVEON
HEADON
HEBRON
HEDRON
HELDON
HENSON
HEREON
HERMON
HESTON
HIERON
HILTON
HINTON
HIREON
HITSON
HOBSON
HOLDON
HORTON
HUDSON
HUNGON
HUSTON
HUTTON
INCHON
IRONON
ISOGON
JARGON
JETSON
JIMSON
JOLSON
JONSON
JUMPON
KEATON
KEEPON
KENTON
KEPTON
KLAXON
KMESON
LAGOON
LAIDON
LANDON
LANSON
LARDON
LARSON
LAWSON
LAWTON
LAYSON
LEADON
LEANON
LEGION
LEMMON
LENNON
LEPTON
LESSON
LETSON
LIPTON
LISBON
LISTON
LIVEON
LOCKON
LOGION
LOGSON
LONDON
LOOKON
LOTION
LYNDON
LYTTON
MACRON
MAGNON
MAMMON
MARION
MARLON
MAROON
MARRON
MATRON
MELLON
MELTON
MEMNON
MERLON
MERTON
MICRON
MIGNON
MILTON
MINION
MORION
MORMON
MORTON
MOTION
MOUTON
MOVEON
MUTTON
NATION
NATRON
NEESON
NEKTON
NELSON
NETTON
NEURON
NEWTON
NIPPON
NOIRON
NORTON
NOTION
OBERON
ODDSON
OLESON
OPTION
OREGON
ORISON
PARDON
PARSON
PARTON
PASSON
PATRON
PATTON
PAXTON
PAYSON
PELION
PENNON
PERSON
PEYTON
PHONON
PHOTON
PICKON
PIGEON
PILEON
PINION
PINSON
PINYON
PINZON
PISTON
PLANON
PLAYON
POISON
POMPON
POSTON
POTION
PREYON
PRISON
PROTON
PULLON
PUSHON
PUTSON
PYTHON
QUEZON
RAMSON
RATION
RATSON
REASON
RECKON
REGION
RESTON
RETTON
REVLON
REVSON
RHYTON
RIBBON
ROBSON
ROLLON
RULEON
RUNSON
RUNYON
SAIGON
SALMON
SALOON
SALTON
SAMSON
SARGON
SARTON
SEASON
SEATON
SERMON
SETSON
SEWNON
SEWSON
SEXTON
SHARON
SHIMON
SIGNON
SIMEON
SIPHON
SITSON
SLIPON
SOLDON
SOSOON
SPURON
STAYON
STEPON
STOLON
STYRON
SUMMON
SUTTON
SYPHON
TACKON
TAKEON
TALION
TARPON
TEFLON
TELLON
TENDON
TEUTON
TIGLON
TOLDON
TOOKON
TOULON
TRIGON
TRITON
TROGON
TRYLON
TUCSON
TURNON
TYCOON
UNISON
VERDON
VERNON
VILLON
VINTON
VISION
WAGGON
WAITON
WALKON
WALTON
WANTON
WATSON
WAYLON
WEAPON
WENTON
WESSON
WILSON
WILTON
WONTON
WOREON
WORKON
WYNTON
YANGON
YAUPON
ZIRCON

OO••••

OOCYTE
OODLES
OOHING
OOLALA
OOLITE
OOLITH
OOLOGY
OOLONG
OOMPAH
OOZIER
OOZILY
OOZING

O•O•••

OBOIST
ODONTO
ODOURS
OPORTO
OROIDE
OROMOS
OROZCO
OTOOLE
OVOIDS
OZONIC

O••O••

OBLONG
OCLOCK
OCTOPI
ODIOUS
OENONE
OGDOAD
OHIOAN
ONFOOT
ONHOLD
ONIONS
ONIONY
ONLOAN
ONTOUR
OOLOGY
OOLONG
OPPOSE
OPTOUT
ORIOLE
ORLOPS
ORMOLU
ORMOND
OSBORN
OSGOOD
OSMOND
OSMOSE
OTIOSE
OTOOLE
OXBOWS
OXFORD

O•••O•

OBERON
OCELOT
OCTROI
ODDJOB
ODDLOT
ODDSON
OLDBOY
OLESON
ONFOOT
OPTFOR
OPTION
ORATOR
OREGON
ORISON
OROMOS
OSGOOD
OUTBOX
OUTFOX
OXYDOL

O••••O

OBISPO
OCTAVO
ODONTO
OLDPRO
OLINGO
ONETWO
OPENTO
OPORTO
OROZCO
ORSINO
OSWEGO
OTELLO
OVERDO
OVIEDO

•OO•••

BOOBOO
BOODLE
BOOGIE
BOOHOO
BOOING
BOOJUM
BOOKED
BOOKER
BOOKIE
BOOMED
BOOMER
BOOSTS
BOOTED
BOOTEE
BOOTES
BOOTHE
BOOTHS
BOOTIE
BOOTSY
BOOTUP
COODER
COOERS
COOGAN
COOING
COOKED
COOKER
COOKIE
COOKUP
COOLED
COOLER
COOLIT
COOLLY
COONEY
COOPED
COOPER
COOPTS
COOPUP
COOTER
COOTIE
DOOBIE
DOODAD
DOODAH
DOODLE
DOOFUS
DOOGIE
DOOLEY
DOOMED
DOOWOP
DOOZIE
FOODIE
FOOLED
FOOLER
FOOTED
FOOTER
FOOZLE
GOOBER
GOODBY
GOODEN
GOODIE
GOODLY
GOODOH
GOOFED
GOOFUP
GOOGLE
GOOGLY
GOOGOL
GOOGOO
GOOIER
GOOSED
GOOSES
GOOSEY
GOOVER
HOODED
HOODOO
HOOFED
HOOFER
HOOFIT
HOOHAH
HOOHAS
HOOKAH
HOOKED
HOOKUP
HOOPED
HOOPER
HOOPLA
HOOPLE
HOOPOE
HOORAH
HOORAY
HOOTAT
HOOTCH
HOOTED
HOOTER
HOOTIE
HOOVER
HOOVES
KOOKIE
KOONTZ
LOOFAH
LOOFAS
LOOIES
LOOKAT
LOOKED
LOOKER
LOOKIN
LOOKON
LOOKTO
LOOKUP
LOOMED
LOONEY
LOONIE
LOOPED
LOOPER
LOOSED
LOOSEN
LOOSER
LOOSES
LOOTED
LOOTER
MOOING
MOOLAH
MOONED
MOONEY
MOORED
MOOTED
NOODLE
NOONAN
NOONES
NOOSED
NOOSES
NOOTKA
POODLE
POOHED
POOLED
POOPED
POORER

POORLY
ROOFED
ROOFER
ROOKED
ROOKIE
ROOMED
ROOMER
ROOMIE
ROONEY
ROOSTS
ROOTED
ROOTER
SOONER
SOOTHE
TOOBAD
TOOKIN
TOOKIT
TOOKON
TOOKTO
TOOKUP
TOOLED
TOOLUP
TOONIE
TOOTED
TOOTER
TOOTHY
TOOTLE
TOOTOO
TOOTSY
VOODOO
WOODED
WOODEN
WOODSY
WOOERS
WOOFED
WOOFER
WOOGIE
WOOING
WOOKIE
WOOLEN
WOOLEY
WOOLLY
YOOHOO
ZOOIDS
ZOOMED
ZOOMIN

•0•0••

BODONI
BOGONG
BOGOTA
BOSONS
BOWOAR
BOWOUT
COCOAS
COCOON
CODONS
COHORT
COHOST
COLONS
COLONY
COLORS
COLOUR
CONOCO
CONOID
COPOUT
CORONA
COYOTE
DODODO
DODOES
DODOMA
DOGONS
DOGOOD
DOLORS
DOLOUR
DONORS
FOBOFF
GODOWN
GOHOME
GONOGO
GOSOFT
GOTOFF
GOTOIT
GOTOUT
HOBOES
HOHOHO
HONORE
HONORS
HONOUR
HOPOFF
IOMOTH
JOCOSE
JOHORE
JOJOBA
JOYOUS
KOBOLD
KOKOMO
KOMODO
KOSOVO
LOGOFF
LOGOUT
LOMOND
LOYOLA
MODOCS
MOHOCK
MOLOCH
MOLOPO
MONODY
MORONI
MORONS
MOROSE
MOTORS
MOTOWN
NOBODY
NODOFF
NODOSE
NOGOOD
NOLOAD
NOLOSE
NOMORE
NOSOAP
OOLOGY
OOLONG
POBOYS
POCONO
POMONA
POPOFF
POPOUT
POROUS
POTOSI
ROBOTS
ROCOCO
ROMOLA
ROTORS
SOLOED
SOLONG
SONOMA
SONORA
SOPORS
SOSOON
SOTOLS
TOBOOT
TOPOFF
TOPOUT
TOROID
TOROSE
TOYONS
TOYOTA
VOROUS
WONOUT
WOVOKA
YOHOHO
YOYOED
YOYOMA

•0••0•

BOFFOS
BOLTON
BONBON
BONGOS
BONMOT
BONTON
BOOBOO
BOOHOO
BOREON
BORROW
BORZOI
BOSTON
BOTTOM
BOUBOU
BOWWOW
BOXBOY
BOXTOP
COCOON
COELOM
COLLOP
COLLOQ
COMBOS
COMEON
COMMON
COMPOS
CONDOR
CONDOS
CONGOU
CONJOB
CONNOR
CONROY
CONVOY
CORDON
COSMOS
COTTON
COUPON
COWBOY
COWPOX
DOBROS
DOBSON
DOCTOR
DOGDOM
DOGOOD
DOLLOP
DONJON
DOOWOP
DOTEON
DOWNON
FOETOR
FOGBOW
FOLIOS
FOLLOW
FOLSOM
FORGOT
GODSON
GOESON
GOODOH
GOOGOL
GOOGOO
GORDON
GORGON
GOSLOW
GOUNOD
HOBNOB
HOBSON
HOLDON
HOLLOW
HOODOO
HOOPOE
HORROR
HORTON
HOTBOX
HOTDOG
HOTPOT
HOTROD
HOWNOW
HOWTOS
JOBHOP
JOBLOT
JOLIOT
JOLSON
JONSON
KOWTOW
LOCKON
LOGION
LOGSON
LOLLOP
LOMBOK
LONDON
LONNOL
LOOKON
LOTION
LOTTOS
LOWBOY
MONGOL
MONROE
MOPTOP
MORION
MORMON
MORROW
MORTON
MOSCOW
MOTION
MOTMOT
MOTTOS
MOUTON
MOVEON
NOGOOD
NOIRON
NONCOM
NORTON
NOSHOW
NOTION
NOTNOW
POIROT
POISON
POLLOI
POLPOT
POMPOM
POMPON
POPTOP
POSTON
POTION
POTTOS
POWWOW
ROBROY
ROBSON
RODEOS
ROLEOS
ROLLON
ROMEOS
RONDOS
ROSCOE
ROSTOV
SOLDON
SORROW
SORTOF
SOSOON
TOBOOT
TOLDOF
TOLDON
TOMBOY
TOMTOM
TONDOS
TOOKON
TOOTOO
TOPDOG
TOPJOB
TORPOR
TORSOS
TOULON
TOYDOG
VOLVOX
VOODOO
VOSTOK
VOXPOP
WONTON
WOREON
WORKON
YOBBOS
YOMTOV
YOOHOO

•0•••0

BOCHCO
BOINGO
BOLERO
BONITO
BOOBOO
BOOHOO
BORAXO
BORNEO
COGITO
COLUGO
COMETO
CONOCO
DODODO
DOMINO
DORADO
DOSIDO
EOIPSO
FOREGO
GOINTO
GOLINO
GONOGO
GOOGOO
HOHOHO
HOLDTO
HONCHO
HOODOO
HOVETO
JOURNO
KOKOMO
KOMODO
KOSOVO
LOOKTO
MODULO
MOLOPO
MONACO
MORENO
MORPHO
NONEGO
NOVATO
POCONO
POMELO
PONCHO
POTATO
ROBALO
ROCOCO
ROMANO
ROMERO
ROTHKO
SOASTO
SOMATO
SOWETO
TOBAGO
TODDAO
TOLEDO
TOMATO
TOOKTO
TOOTOO
TORERO
TORINO
VOODOO
YOHOHO
YOOHOO

••00••

BLOODY
BLOOEY
BLOOMS
BLOOMY
BLOOPS
BROOCH
BROODS
BROODY
BROOKE
BROOKS
BROOKY
BROOMS
BROOMY
CHOOSE
CHOOSY
CHOOYU
CROOKS
CROONS
DROOLS
DROOLY
DROOPS
DROOPY
FLOODS
FLOOEY
FLOORS
GLOOMS
GLOOMY
GROOMS
GROOVE
GROOVY
KLOOFS
OTOOLE
PHOOEY
PROOFS
SCOOPS
SCOOTS
SHOOED
SHOOIN
SHOOKS
SHOOTS
SLOOPS
SMOOCH
SMOOTH
SNOODS
SNOOKS
SNOOKY
SNOOPS
SNOOPY
SNOOTS
SNOOTY
SNOOZE
SNOOZY
SPOOFS
SPOOKS
SPOOKY
SPOOLS
SPOONS
SPOONY
SPOORS
STOOGE
STOOKS
STOOLS
STOOLY
STOOPS
SWOONS
SWOOPS
SWOOSH
TROOPS
VROOMS
WHOOFS
WHOOPI
WHOOPS
WHOOSH

••0•0•

AGOROT
AMOSOZ
BOOBOO
BOOHOO
CHOLOS
CLOROX
CROTON
DOOWOP
DROMOI
DROMOS
DUOMOS
FYODOR
GNOMON
GOODOH
GOOGOL
GOOGOO
GROTON
GROWON
HOODOO
HOOPOE
IROBOT
IRONON
ISOGON
ISOPOD
KRONOR
LOOKON
OROMOS
PHOBOS
PHONON
PHONOS
PHOTOG
PHOTON
PHOTOS
PROLOG
PROMOS
PROTON
SHOLOM
STOLON
TOOKON
TOOTOO
TROGON
VOODOO
YOOHOO

••0••0

ALONSO
ALONZO
APOLLO
BIOBIO
BLOTTO
BOOBOO
BOOHOO
BRONCO
CLOTHO
FLORIO
GIOTTO
GLOSSO
GOOGOO
GRODNO
GROSSO
GROTTO
HOODOO
IDOIDO
ILOILO
KUOPIO
LOOKTO
ODONTO
OPORTO
OROZCO
PRONTO
SCOTTO
SHORTO
STOJKO
TOOKTO
TOOTOO
TROPPO
VOODOO
WHOMSO
YOOHOO

•••00•

ABLOOM
ASWOON
ATWOOD
BABOON
BEHOOF
BETOOK
COCOON
DOGOOD
DRHOOK
EDWOOD
ELWOOD
ENROOT
EXMOOR
FAZOOL
FTROOP
GALOOT
IGLOOS
INDOOR
KABOOM
KAZOOS
LAGOON
MAROON
MRCOOL
NANOOK
NOGOOD
ONFOOT
OSGOOD
REBOOT
REHOOK
RETOOK
RETOOL
SALOON
SCHOOL
SCROOP
SHBOOM
SOSOON
TABOOS
TOBOOT
TYCOON
UNCOOL
UNHOOK
UNMOOR
UNROOT
UPROOT
WAHOOS
YAHOOS

•••0•0

ALIOTO
ARIOSO
ARROYO
BAROLO
CHLORO
CHROMO
CHRONO
CONOCO
DENOVO
DESOTO
DEVOTO
DODODO
ENTOMO
ESPOSO
EXVOTO
FLUORO
GIGOLO
GONOGO
HOHOHO
INTOTO
KIMONO
KOKOMO
KOMODO
KOSOVO
MOLOPO
MRMOTO
NICOLO
POCONO
REBOZO
ROCOCO
SUNOCO
YOHOHO

••••00

AHCHOO
BAMBOO
BOOBOO
BOOHOO
BURGOO
CUCKOO
GOOGOO

HALLOO
HOODOO
KARROO
MCADOO
SCHMOO
TATTOO
TOOTOO
VOODOO
YOOHOO

OP••••
OPAQUE
OPENED
OPENER
OPENLY
OPENTO
OPENUP
OPERAS
OPHITE
OPIATE
OPINED
OPINER
OPINES
OPORTO
OPPOSE
OPPUGN
OPTFOR
OPTICS
OPTIMA
OPTING
OPTION
OPTOUT
OPUSES

O•P•••
OPPOSE
OPPUGN
ORPHAN
ORPHIC
ORPINE
OSPREY

O••P••
OILPAN
OKAPIS
OLDPRO
ONSPEC
OOMPAH
OUTPUT

O•••P•
OBISPO
OCCUPY
OCTOPI
ONEUPS
ONTAPE
ORLOPS
OXLIPS

O••••P
OPENUP
OWNSUP

•OP•••
BOPEEP
BOPPED
BOPPER
COPAYS
COPIED
COPIER
COPIES
COPING
COPLEY
COPOUT
COPPED
COPPER
COPSES
COPTER
COPTIC
COPULA
DOPANT
DOPIER
DOPING
GOPHER
HOPERS
HOPING
HOPOFF
HOPPED
HOPPER
HOPPLE
HOPSIN
HOPSUP
JOPLIN
KOPECK
KOPEKS
KOPJES
KOPPEL
LOPERS
LOPING
LOPPED
LOPPER
MOPEDS
MOPERS
MOPERY
MOPIER
MOPING
MOPISH
MOPPED
MOPPER
MOPPET
MOPSUP
MOPTOP
MOPUPS
NOPETS
POPART
POPEYE
POPFLY
POPGUN
POPLAR
POPLIN
POPOFF
POPOUT
POPPAS
POPPED
POPPER
POPPET
POPPLE
POPSIN
POPSUP
POPTOP
POPULI
POPUPS
ROPEIN
ROPERS
ROPIER
ROPING
SOPHIA
SOPHIE
SOPORS
SOPPED
SOPSUP
TOPCAT
TOPDOG
TOPEKA
TOPERS
TOPGUN
TOPHAT
TOPHUS
TOPICS
TOPJOB
TOPOFF
TOPOUT
TOPPED
TOPPER
TOPPLE
TOPTEN

•O•P••
BOPPED
BOPPER
COAPTS
COMPAQ
COMPEL
COMPLY
COMPOS
COOPED
COOPER
COOPTS
COOPUP
COPPED
COPPER
CORPUS
COUPES
COUPLE
COUPON
COWPEA
COWPER
COWPOX
COYPUS
EOIPSO
GOSPEL
HOOPED
HOOPER
HOOPLA
HOOPLE
HOOPOE
HOPPED
HOPPER
HOPPLE
HOTPOT
KOPPEL
LOOPED
LOOPER
LOPPED
LOPPER
LOUPES
MOPPED
MOPPER
MOPPET
MORPHO
MORPHS
MORPHY
OOMPAH
POLPOT
POMPEY
POMPOM
POMPON
POOPED
POPPAS
POPPED
POPPER
POPPET
POPPLE
POTPIE
ROMPED
ROMPER
SOAPED
SOAPER
SOPPED
SOUPUP
TOPPED
TOPPER
TOPPLE
TORPID
TORPOR
TOUPEE
VOXPOP
WOLPER

•O••P•
FOURPM
JOSEPH
MOLOPO
MOPUPS
POLYPS
POPUPS

•O•••P
BOBSUP
BONEUP
BOOTUP
BOPEEP
BOREUP
BOXTOP
COILUP
COLLOP
COMEUP
COOKUP
COOPUP
DOESUP
DOLLOP
DOLLUP
DOMREP
DONEUP
DOOWOP
FOGSUP
FOLDUP
FOULUP
GOESUP
GOOFUP
GOSSIP
HOLDUP
HOLEUP
HOOKUP
HOPSUP
HOTCAP
HOTTIP
JOBHOP
JOINUP
LOCKUP
LOLLOP
LOOKUP
MOBCAP
MOCKUP
MOPSUP
MOPTOP
MOVEUP
NOSOAP
PONYUP
POPSUP
POPTOP
ROLLUP
SOAKUP
SOPSUP
SOUPUP
TOECAP
TOETAP
TONEUP
TOOKUP
TOOLUP
TOREUP
TOSSUP
TOTSUP
VOXPOP
WOKEUP
WORKUP

••OP••
ADOPTS
BHOPAL
CHOPIN
CHOPPY
CHOPRA
COOPED
COOPER
COOPTS
COOPUP
CROPUP
DROPBY
DROPIN
DROPIT
ELOPED
ELOPER
ELOPES
EPOPEE
FLOPPY
FLOPSY
GLOPPY
GROPED
GROPES
HOOPED
HOOPER
HOOPLA
HOOPLE
HOOPOE
ISOPOD
KUOPIO
LOOPED
LOOPER
MYOPES
MYOPIA
MYOPIC
PEOPLE
POOPED
PROPEL
PROPER
PROPRE
PROPUP
REOPEN
SCOPED
SCOPES
SHOPPE
SKOPJE
SLOPED
SLOPES
SLOPPY
SNOPES
STOPES
STOPIN
STOPIT
STOPUP
TROPES
TROPEZ
TROPHY
TROPIC
TROPPO
TWOPLY
UNOPEN
USOPEN
UTOPIA

••O•P•
ADOLPH
BLOOPS
CHOMPS
CHOPPY
CLOMPS
CROUPY
DROOPS
DROOPY
FLOPPY
GLOPPY
GROUPS
PROMPT
SCOOPS
SHOPPE
SLOOPS
SLOPPY
SNOOPS
SNOOPY
STOMPS
STOOPS
STOUPS
SWOOPS
THORPE
THORPS
TROMPE
TROMPS
TROOPS
TROPPO
TROUPE
WHOMPS
WHOOPI
WHOOPS

••O••P
BLOWUP
BOOTUP
BUOYUP
CLOGUP
COOKUP
COOPUP
CROPUP
DOOWOP
GOOFUP
GROWUP
HOOKUP
LOOKUP
PROPUP
SHOTUP
SHOWUP
SLOWUP
STOPUP
TOOKUP
TOOLUP

•••OP•
ASLOPE
BEBOPS
BLOOPS
CANOPY
CHEOPS
DROOPS
DROOPY
ESTOPS
EUROPA
EUROPE
FSTOPS
GALOPS
JALOPY
MEROPE
METOPE
MOLOPO
OCTOPI
ORLOPS
PELOPS
RECOPY
REMOPS
RETOPS
SCOOPS
SLOOPS
SNOOPS
SNOOPY
STOOPS
STROPS
SWOOPS
SYSOPS
TROOPS
WHOOPI
WHOOPS
WICOPY

•••O•P
FTROOP
NOSOAP
RECOUP
SCROOP

••••OP
BARHOP
BIGTOP
BISHOP
BOXTOP
CARHOP
COLLOP
DETROP
DOLLOP
DOOWOP
DUNLOP
FTROOP
GALLOP
HIPHOP
HYSSOP
JOBHOP
LAPTOP
LOLLOP
MAYPOP
MOPTOP
PEGTOP
POPTOP
RAGMOP
RAGTOP
REDTOP
SCROOP
TIPTOP
UNSTOP
VOXPOP
WALLOP
WETMOP

O••Q••
OPAQUE

•OQ•••
COQUET
LOQUAT
TOQUES

•O•Q••
MOSQUE
TORQUE

•O•••Q
COLLOQ
COMPAQ
POSSLQ

••OQ••
CLOQUE
QUOQUE

••••OQ
COLLOQ

OR••••
ORACHS
ORACLE
ORALES
ORALLY
ORANGE
ORANGS
ORANGY
ORANTS
ORATED
ORATES
ORATOR
ORBACH
ORBING
ORBITS
ORCHID
ORCHIL
ORDAIN
ORDEAL
ORDERS
ORDURE
OREADS
OREGON
OREIDA
ORELSE
ORGANA
ORGANS
ORGATE
ORGEAT
ORGIES
ORIANA
ORIBIS
ORIELS
ORIENT
ORIGEN
ORIGIN
ORINGS
ORIOLE
ORISON
ORISSA
ORKNEY
ORLOPS
ORMOLU
ORMOND
ORNATE
ORNERY
ORNITH
OROIDE
OROMOS
OROZCO
ORPHAN
ORPHIC
ORPINE
ORRERY
ORSINO
ORTEGA
ORTLES
ORWELL
ORYXES

O•R•••
OARING
OBRIAN
OBRIEN
OCREAE
OERTER
OGRESS
OGRISH
ONRUSH
ORRERY

O••R••
OBERON
OCHRES
OCTROI
OILRIG
OMERTA
OPERAS
OPORTO
OSIRIS
OSPREY
OUTRAN
OUTRUN
OVERDO
OVERLY
OZARKS

O•••R•
OATERS
OBVERT
OCCURS
OCHERS
OCHERY
ODOURS
OEUVRE
OFFERS
OGLERS
OHENRY
OILERS
OLDPRO
OLEARY
ONFIRE
ONWARD
ORDERS
ORDURE
ORNERY
ORRERY
OSBORN
OSCARS
OSIERS
OTHERS
OTTERS
OUTCRY
OWNERS
OXCART
OXFORD

OXNARD

O••••R

OATIER
OBITER
OCULAR
OERTER
OILIER
OLIVER
ONAGER
ONTOUR
OOZIER
OPENER
OPINER
OPTFOR
ORATOR
OSTLER
OUSTER
OVULAR
OYSTER

•OR•••

AORIST
AORTAE
AORTAL
AORTAS
AORTIC
BORAGE
BORATE
BORAXO
BORDEN
BORDER
BOREAL
BOREAS
BOREON
BORERS
BOREUP
BORGIA
BORIDE
BORING
BORMAN
BORNEO
BORROW
BORSCH
BORZOI
CORALS
CORBAN
CORBEL
CORBIN
CORDAY
CORDED
CORDON
CORERS
CORGIS
CORING
CORIUM
CORKED
CORKER
CORMAN
CORNEA
CORNED
CORNEL
CORNER
CORNET
CORONA
CORPUS
CORRAL
CORREL
CORSET
CORTES
CORTEX
CORTEZ
CORVEE
CORVES
CORYZA
DORADO
DORAGS
DORATI
DORCAS
DOREMI
DORIAN
DORIES
DORMER
DORRIT
DORSAL
DORSET
DORSEY
DORSUM
FORAGE
FORAYS
FORBAD
FORBES
FORBID
FORCED
FORCER
FORCES
FORDED
FOREGO
FOREST
FORGED
FORGER
FORGES
FORGET
FORGOT
FORINT
FORKED
FORKER
FORMAL
FORMAN
FORMAT
FORMED
FORMER
FORMIC
FORTAS
FORTES
FORUMS
GORALS
GORDIE
GORDON
GORGED
GORGES
GORGET
GORGON
GORIER
GORILY
GORING
GORSES
HORACE
HORDES
HORMEL
HORMUZ
HORNED
HORNER
HORNET
HORNEY
HORNIN
HORRID
HORROR
HORSED
HORSES
HORSEY
HORTON
JORDAN
JORUMS
KORATS
KORBUT
KOREAN
KORMAN
KORUNA
LORAIN
LORDED
LORDLY
LOREAL
LORENZ
LORICA
LORIES
MORALE
MORALS
MORANT
MORASS
MORAVA
MORAYS
MORBID
MOREAU
MOREEN
MORELS
MORENO
MORGAN
MORGEN
MORION
MORITA
MORITZ
MORLEY
MORMON
MORNAY
MORONI
MORONS
MOROSE
MORPHO
MORPHS
MORPHY
MORRIS
MORROW
MORSEL
MORTAL
MORTAR
MORTON
NORDIC
NORGAY
NORIAS
NORMAL
NORMAN
NORRIS
NORTHS
NORTON
NORWAY
PORING
PORKER
POROUS
PORTAL
PORTED
PORTER
PORTIA
PORTLY
SORBET
SORBIC
SORDID
SORELY
SOREST
SORREL
SORROW
SORTED
SORTER
SORTIE
SORTOF
TORAHS
TORCHY
TOREAT
TORERO
TOREUP
TORIES
TORINO
TOROID
TOROSE
TORPID
TORPOR
TORQUE
TORRES
TORREY
TORRID
TORSOS
TORTES
VOROUS
VORTEX
WORDED
WOREON
WORKED
WORKER
WORKIN
WORKON
WORKUP
WORLDS
WORMED
WORSEN
WORSTS
WORTHS
WORTHY
YORICK
YORKER
YORKIE
YORUBA
ZORILS

•O•R••

BOARDS
BORROW
BOTREE
BOURKE
BOURNE
BOURSE
COARSE
COBRAS
COERCE
CONRAD
CONROY
CORRAL
CORREL
COURIC
COURSE
COURTS
COWRIE
DOBRAS
DOBROS
DOMREP
DORRIT
DOURER
DOURLY
FOURAM
FOURPM
FOURTH
GOURDE
GOURDS
HOARDS
HOARSE
HOORAH
HOORAY
HORRID
HORROR
HOTROD
HOURIS
HOURLY
JOURNO
KONRAD
MOIRES
MONROE
MOORED
MORRIS
MORROW
MOURNS
NOIRON
NORRIS
POIROT
POORER
POORLY
POURED
POURER
POURIN
ROARED
ROARER
ROBROY
ROURKE
SOARED
SOARER
SOARES
SOIREE
SORREL
SORROW
SOURCE
SOURED
SOURER
SOURLY
TOBRUK
TORRES
TORREY
TORRID
TOURED
TOURER

•O••R•

BOGART
BOLERO
BONERS
BORERS
BOVARY
BOWERS
BOWERY
BOXERS
BOYARS
COBURG
COBURN
CODERS
COHERE
COHORT
COLORS
COMERS
CONTRA
CONTRE
CONURE
COOERS
CORERS
COVERS
COVERT
COWARD
COWERS
DOLORS
DONORS
DOSERS
DOTARD
DOWERS
DOWERY
DOZERS
FOYERS
GOAWRY
GOCART
GODARD
GOFERS
GOKART
GONERS
GOVERN
HOBART
HOMBRE
HOMERS
HONORE
HONORS
HOPERS
HOVERS
HOWARD
JOHORE
JOKERS
LONERS
LOPERS
LOSERS
LOUVRE
LOVERS
LOWERS
LOWERY
MODERN
MOHURS
MOLARS
MONERA
MOPERS
MOPERY
MOTHRA
MOTORS
MOVERS
MOWERS
MOYERS
MOZART
NOMORE
NONARY
NOTARY
NOTERS
POETRY
POKERS
POKERY
POLERS
POPART
POSERS
POWERS
ROBERT
ROGERS
ROMERO
ROPERS
ROSARY
ROSTRA
ROTARY
ROTORS
ROVERS
ROWERS
SOBERS
SOEURS
SOLARS
SOLERS
SOMBRE
SOMERS
SONORA
SOPORS
SOUARI
SOWERS
SOXERS
TONERS
TOPERS
TORERO
TOTERS
TOWARD
TOWERS
TOWERY
VOLARE
VOTARY
VOTERS
VOWERS
WOOERS
YOGURT

•O•••R

BOATER
BOBBER
BOILER
BOLDER
BOLGER
BOMBER
BONIER
BOOKER
BOOMER
BOPPER
BORDER
BOTHER
BOVVER
BOWLER
BOWOAR
BOWSER
BOWYER
BOXCAR
BOXIER
COALER
COAXER
COCKER
CODGER
COFFER
COHEIR
COINER
COKIER
COLDER
COLLAR
COLOUR
COLTER
COMBER
CONCUR
CONDOR
CONFER
CONGER
CONKER
CONNER
CONNOR
COODER
COOKER
COOLER
COOPER
COOTER
COPIER
COPPER
COPTER
CORKER
CORNER
COSIER
COSTAR
COTTER
COUGAR
COUTER
COWPER
COZIER
DOBBER
DOCKER
DOCTOR
DODDER
DODGER
DOGEAR
DOGGER
DOLLAR
DOLOUR
DONDER
DONNER
DOPIER
DORMER
DOSSER
DOURER
DOWNER
DOWSER
DOZIER
FODDER
FOETOR
FOGGER
FOKKER
FOLDER
FOLIAR
FONDER
FOOLER
FOOTER
FORCER
FORGER
FORKER
FORMER
FOSTER
FOULER
FOWLER
FOXIER
GOLFER
GOOBER
GOOIER
GOOVER
GOPHER
GORIER
GOUGER
HOAXER
HOKIER
HOLDER
HOLIER
HOLLER
HOMIER
HONKER
HONOUR
HOOFER
HOOPER
HOOTER
HOOVER
HOPPER
HORNER
HORROR
HOSIER
HOTAIR
HOTCAR
HOTTER
HOTWAR
HOWLER
JOBBER
JOGGER
JOINER
JOKIER
JOSSER
JOYNER
KOHLER
KOSHER
KOTTER
LOADER
LOAFER
LOANER
LOBBER
LOCKER
LODGER
LOGGER
LOGIER
LOITER
LONGER
LOOKER
LOOPER
LOOSER
LOOTER
LOPPER
LOTHAR
LOUDER
LOUVER
MOANER
MOCKER
MOHAIR
MOILER
MOLDER
MOLNAR
MOLTER
MONGER
MOPIER
MOPPER
MORTAR
MOSHER
MOTHER
MOUSER
NOBLER
NOSHER
NOSIER
OOZIER
POKIER
POLDER
POLLER
PONDER
POORER
POPLAR
POPPER
PORKER
PORTER
POSEUR
POSHER
POSTER
POTHER
POTTER
POURER
POUTER
POWDER
ROAMER
ROARER
ROBBER
ROCKER
ROHMER

ROLLER
ROMPER
ROOFER
ROOMER
ROOTER
ROPIER
ROSIER
ROSTER
ROTTER
ROUSER
ROUTER
ROZZER
SOAKER
SOAPER
SOARER
SOBBER
SOCCER
SOFTER
SOLDER
SOLVER
SOMBER
SOMMER
SOONER
SORTER
SOURER
SOUTER
TOILER
TONIER
TOOTER
TOPPER
TORPOR
TOSSER
TOTHER
TOTTER
TOURER
TOUTER
TOWCAR
TOWNER
WOHLER
WOLPER
WONDER
WOOFER
WORKER
WOWSER
YONDER
YORKER
ZONKER

••OR••

ABORAL
ABORTS
ACORNS
ADORED
ADOREE
ADORER
ADORES
ADORNS
AGORAE
AGORAS
AGOROT
AMORAL
ANORAK
AZORES
AZORIN
CEORLS
CHORAL
CHORDS
CHORES
CHORUS
CLORIS
CLOROX
DVORAK
FIORDS
FJORDS
FLORAE
FLORAL
FLORAS
FLORES
FLORET
FLORID
FLORIN
FLORIO
GEORGE
GEORGY
GLORIA
HOORAH
HOORAY
ILORIN
MAORIS
MOORED
OPORTO
PEORIA
POORER
POORLY
QUORUM
SCORCH
SCORED
SCORER
SCORES
SCORIA
SCORNS
SFORZA
SHORAN
SHORED
SHORES
SHORTA
SHORTE
SHORTI
SHORTO
SHORTS
SHORTU
SHORTY
SKORTS
SNORED
SNORER
SNORES
SNORTS
SPORES
SPORTS
SPORTY
STORCH
STORED
STORER
STORES
STOREY
STORKS
STORMS
STORMY
STORRS
SWORDS
THORAX
THORNS
THORNY
THORPE
THORPS
WHORLS

••O•R•

ABOARD
AMOURS
CHOIRS
CHOPRA
COOERS
FLOORS
FLOURS
FLOURY
ODOURS
PROPRE
SCOURS
SHOERS
SPOORS
STORRS
WOOERS

••O••R

ADORER
ALOMAR
AVOWER
BLOWER
BOOKER
BOOMER
BROKER
CHOKER
CHOLER
CLOSER
CLOVER
COODER
COOKER
COOLER
COOPER
COOTER
CROWER
DEODAR
DRONER
DROVER
ELOPER
EMOTER
EVOKER
FLOWER
FOOLER
FOOTER
FYODOR
GAOLER
GLOVER
GLOWER
GOOBER
GOOIER
GOOVER
GROCER
GROVER
GROWER
HOOFER
HOOPER
HOOTER
HOOVER
IRONER
ISOBAR
ISOMER
KNOWER
KRONER
KRONOR
KRONUR
LOOKER
LOOPER
LOOSER
LOOTER
PLOVER
PLOWER
POORER
PROBER
PROPER
PROSER
PROVER
QUOTER
RIOTER
ROOFER
ROOMER
ROOTER
SCORER
SCOTER
SHOFAR
SHOVER
SHOWER
SLOWER
SMOKER
SNORER
SOONER
STOKER
STONER
STORER
STOVER
TOOTER
TROCAR
TWOFER
WOOFER

•••OR•

ABHORS
ABSORB
ACCORD
ACTORS
ADSORB
AFFORD
ALBORG
ALGORE
ANGORA
ARBORS
ARDORS
ARMORS
ARMORY
ASHORE
ASSORT
ATWORK
AURORA
BEFORE
BICORN
BYWORD
CAVORT
CHLORO
COHORT
COLORS
CYBORG
DAMORE
DECORS
DEFORM
DEHORN
DEPORT
DOLORS
DONORS
EEYORE
EFFORT
ELMORE
ENCORE
ENDORA
EPHORI
EPHORS
ERRORS
ESCORT
EUDORA
EXHORT
EXMORE
EXPORT
EXTORT
FAVORS
FEDORA
FEMORA
FLOORS
FLUORO
FURORE
FURORS
GALORE
GATORS
HONORE
HONORS
HUMORS
IGNORE
IMPORT
INBORN
INDORE
INFORM
INPORT
JOHORE
JURORS
KIDORY
LABORS
LAHORE
LENORE
MAJORS
MALORY
MANORS
MAYORS
MEMORY
MIDORI
MILORD
MINORS
MOTORS
MYSORE
MYWORD
NABORS
NOMORE
OSBORN
OXFORD
PRIORI
PRIORS
PRIORY
RAZORS
REBORN
RECORD
RECORK
REFORM
REMORA
REPORT
RESORB
RESORT
RETORT
REWORD
REWORK
RIGORS
ROTORS
RUMORS
SAPORS
SATORI
SAVORS
SAVORY
SCHORL
SENORA
SENORS
SONORA
SOPORS
SPOORS
SUBORN
TABORS
TAGORE
TENORS
THEORY
TUDORS
TUTORS
UNBORN
UNCORK
UNTORN
UNWORN
VAPORS
VAPORY
VIGORS
VISORS
VYBORG
ZADORA

•••O•R

ARBOUR
ARDOUR
ARMOUR
BOWOAR
COLOUR
DAMOUR
DETOUR
DEVOIR
DEVOUR
DOLOUR
EXMOOR
FAVOUR
HONOUR
HUMOUR
INDOOR
INPOUR
LABOUR
LAMOUR
LATOUR
MEMOIR
ONTOUR
RENOIR
RETOUR
REVOIR
RIGOUR
RUMOUR
SAVOIR
SAVOUR
UNDOER
UNMOOR
UPROAR
VALOUR
VAPOUR
VELOUR
VETOER
VIGOUR

••••OR

AIMFOR
ALLFOR
AMAJOR
AMINOR
ANCHOR
ANGKOR
ASKFOR
AUTHOR
BAILOR
BANGOR
BAYLOR
BETTOR
BMAJOR
BMINOR
CANDOR
CANTOR
CAPTOR
CASTOR
CAWDOR
CENSOR
CHADOR
CLAMOR
CMAJOR
CMINOR
CONDOR
CONNOR
CURSOR
DEBTOR
DMAJOR
DMINOR
DOCTOR
EDITOR
ELINOR
EMAJOR
EMINOR
EMPTOR
ENAMOR
ETUXOR
EXMOOR
FACTOR
FERVOR
FLAVOR
FLEXOR
FMAJOR
FMINOR
FOETOR
FYODOR
GAYNOR
GLAMOR
GMAJOR
GMINOR
GREGOR
GUNFOR
HARBOR
HATHOR
HECTOR
HORROR
INDOOR
ISADOR
JUNIOR
KANTOR
KRONOR
LAYFOR
LECTOR
LESSOR
LICTOR
LIQUOR
LUTHOR
MAHZOR
MENTOR
METEOR
MIRROR
NESTOR
OPTFOR
ORATOR
PALLOR
PARLOR
PASTOR
PAYFOR
PLEXOR
RANCOR
RANFOR
RAPTOR
RECTOR
RHETOR
RUNFOR
SAILOR
SALVOR
SAVIOR
SECTOR
SENHOR
SENIOR
SENSOR
SIGNOR
STATOR
STUPOR
SUCCOR
SUITOR
TAILOR
TAYLOR
TENSOR
TERROR
TORPOR
TREMOR
TREVOR
TRYFOR
TURGOR
UNMOOR
VECTOR
VENDOR
VICTOR
WINSOR

OS••••

OSAGES
OSBORN
OSCARS
OSCINE
OSCULA
OSGOOD
OSHAWA
OSIERS
OSIRIS
OSMICS
OSMIUM
OSMOND
OSMOSE
OSMUND
OSPREY
OSSEIN
OSSETE
OSSIAN
OSSIFY
OSTEAL
OSTEND
OSTIUM
OSTLER
OSWALD
OSWEGO

O•S•••

OBSESS
OBSTET
OKSANA
ONSALE
ONSETS
ONSIDE
ONSITE
ONSPEC
ORSINO
OSSEIN
OSSETE
OSSIAN
OSSIFY
OUSELS
OUSTED
OUSTER
OYSTER

O••S••

OBISPO
OCASEK
OCASEY
ODDSON
ODESSA
ODISTS
OFFSET
OLDSAW
OLESON
OMASUM
ONUSES
OPUSES
ORISON
ORISSA
OUTSET
OVISAC
OWNSUP

O•••S•

OAFISH
OBLAST
OBOIST
OBSESS
OBTEST
OBTUSE
ODDEST
ODENSE
ODESSA
OFFISH
OGRESS
OGRISH
OLDEST
OLDISH
ONRUSH
OPPOSE
ORELSE
ORISSA
OSMOSE
OTIOSE
OWLISH

O••••S

OATERS
OBEAHS
OBELUS
OBSESS
OCCURS
OCEANS
OCHERS
OCHRES
OCTADS
OCTETS
ODIOUS
ODISTS
ODIUMS
ODOURS
OFFERS
OGHAMS
OGIVES
OGLERS
OGRESS
OILERS

OKAPIS
OLDIES
OLIVES
OLMECS
OMAHAS
OMANIS
OMEGAS
ONEUPS
ONIONS
ONSETS
ONUSES
ONYXES
OODLES
OPERAS
OPINES
OPTICS
OPUSES
ORACHS
ORALES
ORANGS
ORANTS
ORATES
ORBITS
ORDERS
OREADS
ORGANS
ORGIES
ORIBIS
ORIELS
ORINGS
ORLOPS
OROMOS
ORTLES
ORYXES
OSAGES
OSCARS
OSIERS
OSIRIS
OSMICS
OTHERS
OTITIS
OTTERS
OUGHTS
OUNCES
OUSELS
OUZELS
OVOIDS
OVULES
OWLETS
OWNERS
OXALIS
OXBOWS
OXEYES
OXIDES
OXLIPS
OZARKS

•OS•••

BOSKET
BOSLEY
BOSNIA
BOSONS
BOSSED
BOSSES
BOSTON
BOSUNS
COSELL
COSHED
COSHES
COSIED
COSIER
COSIES
COSIGN
COSILY
COSINE
COSMIC
COSMOS
COSSET
COSTAE
COSTAL
COSTAR
COSTAS
COSTLY
DOSAGE
DOSERS
DOSIDO
DOSING
DOSSAL
DOSSED
DOSSEL
DOSSER
DOSSES
EOSINS
FOSSAE
FOSSAS
FOSSES
FOSSEY
FOSSIL
FOSTER
GOSHEN
GOSLOW
GOSOFT
GOSPEL
GOSSIP
GOSTAG
HOSELS
HOSIER
HOSING
HOSTAS
HOSTED
HOSTEL
HOSTLY
JOSEPH
JOSHED
JOSHES
JOSHUA
JOSIAH
JOSKIN
JOSSER
JOSSES
JOSTLE
KOSHER
KOSOVO
LOSEIT
LOSERS
LOSING
LOSSES
LOSTIT
MOSAIC
MOSCOW
MOSEYS
MOSHAV
MOSHED
MOSHER
MOSHES
MOSKVA
MOSLEM
MOSQUE
MOSSED
MOSSES
MOSTEL
MOSTLY
NOSALE
NOSHED
NOSHER
NOSHES
NOSHOW
NOSIER
NOSILY
NOSING
NOSOAP
POSADA
POSERS
POSEUR
POSHER
POSHLY
POSIES
POSING
POSITS
POSSES
POSSET
POSSLQ
POSSUM
POSTAL
POSTED
POSTER
POSTIT
POSTON
ROSARY
ROSCOE
ROSEAU
ROSIER
ROSILY
ROSINS
ROSINY
ROSITA
ROSTER
ROSTOV
ROSTRA
SOSOON
TOSSED
TOSSER
TOSSES
TOSSUP
VOSGES
VOSTOK

•O•S••

BOASTS
BOBSUP
BOLSHY
BONSAI
BOOSTS
BORSCH
BOSSED
BOSSES
BOUSED
BOUSES
BOWSAW
BOWSER
BOXSET
COASTS
COMSAT
CONSUL
COPSES
CORSET
COSSET
COUSIN
DOBSON
DOESBY
DOESIN
DOESNT
DOESUP
DOGSAT
DOGSIT
DORSAL
DORSET
DORSEY
DORSUM
DOSSAL
DOSSED
DOSSEL
DOSSER
DOSSES
DOUSED
DOUSES
DOWSED
DOWSER
DOWSES
FOCSLE
FOGSIN
FOGSUP
FOISTS
FOLSOM
FOSSAE
FOSSAS
FOSSES
FOSSEY
FOSSIL
GODSON
GOESAT
GOESBY
GOESIN
GOESON
GOESUP
GOOSED
GOOSES
GOOSEY
GORSES
GOSSIP
GOTSET
HOBSON
HOISTS
HONSHU
HOPSIN
HOPSUP
HORSED
HORSES
HORSEY
HOUSED
HOUSES
JOISTS
JOLSON
JONSON
JOSSER
JOSSES
JOUSTS
LOGSIN
LOGSON
LOOSED
LOOSEN
LOOSER
LOOSES
LOSSES
LOUSED
LOUSES
MOPSUP
MORSEL
MOSSED
MOSSES
MOUSED
MOUSER
MOUSES
MOUSEY
MOUSSE
NOESIS
NOISED
NOISES
NOOSED
NOOSES
POISED
POISES
POISON
POPSIN
POPSUP
POSSES
POSSET
POSSLQ
POSSUM
POUSSE
ROASTS
ROBSON
ROOSTS
ROUSED
ROUSER
ROUSES
ROUSTS
SOASTO
SOPSUP
SOUSED
SOUSES
TOASTS
TOASTY
TOCSIN
TOESIN
TONSIL
TORSOS
TOSSED
TOSSER
TOSSES
TOSSUP
TOTSUP
TOUSLE
WOLSEY
WORSEN
WORSTS
WOWSER
ZOYSIA

•O••S•

AORIST
BOOTSY
BOURSE
BOYISH
COARSE
COHOST
COURSE
COYEST
COYISH
DOVISH
EOIPSO
FOLKSY
FOREST
GOBUST
GOEASY
GOFISH
GOWEST
HOARSE
HOLISM
HOLIST
HONEST
IODISE
IONISE
JOCOSE
LOCUST
LOUISA
LOUISE
LOWEST
LOWISH
MODEST
MODISH
MOLEST
MONISM
MONIST
MOPISH
MORASS
MOROSE
MOUSSE
NODOSE
NOLESS
NOLOSE
NOWISE
POLISH
POTASH
POTOSI
POUSSE
ROBUST
SOREST
TONISH
TOOTSY
TOROSE
WOODSY
YOGISM

•O•••S

AODAIS
AORTAS
BOARDS
BOASTS
BODIES
BOFFOS
BOGEYS
BOGIES
BOGLES
BOITES
BOMBES
BONCES
BONERS
BONGOS
BONNES
BONZES
BOOSTS
BOOTES
BOOTHS
BOREAS
BORERS
BOSONS
BOSSES
BOSUNS
BOTELS
BOUGHS
BOULES
BOUNDS
BOUSES
BOVIDS
BOWERS
BOWLES
BOXERS
BOYARS
COAPTS
COASTS
COATIS
COAXES
COBIAS
COBRAS
COCCUS
COCOAS
CODERS
CODONS
COIGNS
COLEUS
COLIES
COLONS
COLORS
COMBES
COMBOS
COMERS
COMETS
COMICS
COMMAS
COMPOS
COMTES
CONCHS
CONDOS
CONEYS
CONGAS
CONICS
CONIES
CONTES
COOERS
COOPTS
COPAYS
COPIES
COPSES
CORALS
CORERS
CORGIS
CORPUS
CORTES
CORVES
COSHES
COSIES
COSMOS
COSTAS
COTTAS
COUGHS
COUNTS
COUPES
COURTS
COVENS
COVERS
COVETS
COVEYS
COWENS
COWERS
COYPUS
COZENS
COZIES
DOBLAS
DOBRAS
DOBROS
DODGES
DODOES
DOGEYS
DOGIES
DOGMAS
DOGONS
DOINGS
DOLMAS
DOLORS
DONEES
DONETS
DONNAS
DONORS
DONUTS
DOOFUS
DORAGS
DORCAS
DORIES
DOSERS
DOSSES
DOUBTS
DOUGHS
DOUSES
DOWELS
DOWERS
DOWSES
DOYENS
DOZENS
DOZERS
EOSINS
FOEHNS
FOETUS
FOGEYS
FOGIES
FOISTS
FOLIOS
FORAYS
FORBES
FORCES
FORGES
FORTAS
FORTES
FORUMS
FOSSAS
FOSSES
FOUNDS
FOUNTS
FOWLES
FOYERS
GOBIES
GODETS
GOFERS
GOINGS
GOLEMS
GONERS
GOOSES
GORALS
GORGES
GORSES
GOUGES
GOURDS
HOARDS
HOAXES
HOBBES
HOBOES
HODADS
HODGES
HOGANS
HOISTS
HOLMES
HOMERS
HONEYS
HONORS
HOOHAS
HOOVES
HOPERS
HORDES
HORSES
HOSELS
HOSTAS
HOTELS
HOUGHS
HOUNDS
HOURIS
HOUSES
HOVELS
HOVERS
HOWTOS
IONICS
IOWANS
JOINTS
JOISTS
JOKERS
JONAHS
JORUMS
JOSHES
JOSSES
JOULES
JOUSTS
JOYOUS
KOALAS
KOPEKS
KOPJES
KORATS
KOVACS
LOAVES
LOCALS
LODENS
LODGES
LONERS
LONGES
LOOFAS
LOOIES
LOOSES
LOPERS
LORIES
LOSERS
LOSSES
LOTAHS
LOTTOS
LOUGHS
LOUPES
LOUSES
LOVERS
LOWERS
MOBIUS
MOCHAS
MODELS
MODEMS
MODOCS
MOGULS
MOHURS
MOINES
MOIRES
MOLARS
MOMMAS
MONADS
MONEYS
MONIES
MONTES
MONTHS
MOPEDS
MOPERS
MOPUPS
MORALS
MORASS
MORAYS
MORELS
MORONS

MORPHS
MORRIS
MOSEYS
MOSHES
MOSSES
MOTELS
MOTETS
MOTIFS
MOTORS
MOTTOS
MOULDS
MOULTS
MOUNDS
MOUNTS
MOURNS
MOUSES
MOUTHS
MOVERS
MOVIES
MOWERS
MOYERS
NOBLES
NOESIS
NOHITS
NOISES
NOLENS
NOLESS
NOMADS
NONETS
NOONES
NOOSES
NOPETS
NORIAS
NORRIS
NORTHS
NOSHES
NOTERS
NOVELS
OODLES
POBOYS
POGIES
POILUS
POINTS
POISES
POKERS
POKEYS
POLERS
POLKAS
POLYPS
PONCES
PONIES
PONTES
PONTUS
POPPAS
POPUPS
POROUS
POSERS
POSIES
POSITS
POSSES
POTTOS
POULTS
POUNDS
POWERS
ROASTS
ROBINS
ROBLES
ROBOTS
RODEOS
ROGERS
ROGUES
ROLEOS
ROMANS
ROMEOS
RONDOS
ROOSTS
ROPERS
ROSINS
ROTORS
ROUGES
ROUGHS
ROUNDS
ROUSES
ROUSTS
ROUTES
ROVERS
ROWELS
ROWENS
ROWERS
ROYALS
SOARES
SOAVES
SOBERS
SOCLES
SOEURS
SOLANS
SOLARS
SOLERS
SOLEUS
SOLFAS
SOLIDS
SOLVES
SOMERS
SONDES
SONICS
SOPORS
SOTOLS
SOUGHS
SOUNDS
SOUSES
SOUTHS
SOWERS
SOXERS
TOASTS
TOBIAS
TOBIES
TOEINS
TOILES
TOKAYS
TOKENS
TOKLAS
TONDOS
TONERS
TONICS
TONNES
TOPERS
TOPHUS
TOPICS
TOQUES
TORAHS
TORIES
TORRES
TORSOS
TORTES
TOSSES
TOTALS
TOTEMS
TOTERS
TOUGHS
TOWELS
TOWERS
TOXICS
TOXINS
TOYONS
VOCALS
VODKAS
VOGUES
VOICES
VOILES
VOLANS
VOLENS
VOLVAS
VOROUS
VOSGES
VOTERS
VOWELS
VOWERS
WODGES
WOLVES
WOMENS
WOOERS
WORLDS
WORSTS
WORTHS
WOUNDS
YOBBOS
YODELS
YOICKS
YOKELS
YOKUTS
YOUTHS
ZOOIDS
ZORILS
ZOUNDS

••OS••

AMOSOZ
ASOSAN
BOOSTS
CHOSEN
CLOSED
CLOSER
CLOSES
CLOSET
CROSBY
CROSSE
ENOSIS
FLOSSY
FROSTS
FROSTY
GHOSTS
GLOSSA
GLOSSO
GLOSSY
GNOSIS
GOOSED
GOOSES
GOOSEY
GROSSE
GROSSO
GROSZY
KIOSKS
LOOSED
LOOSEN
LOOSER
LOOSES
MIOSIS
MYOSIN
MYOSIS
NOOSED
NOOSES
PROSED
PROSER
PROSES
PROSIT
PROSKY
ROOSTS
SLOSHY
XHOSAS

••O•S•

ALONSO
AROUSE
BLOUSE
BLOWSY
BOOTSY
BROWSE
CHOOSE
CHOOSY
CROSSE
CROUSE
DROWSE
DROWSY
EGOISM
EGOIST
ELOISE
FLOPSY
FLOSSY
GLOSSA
GLOSSO
GLOSSY
GROSSE
GROSSO
GROUSE
LAOTSE
LHOTSE
MAOISM
MAOIST
OBOIST
PROUST
PROWSE
SCOUSE
SPOUSE
SWOOSH
TAOISM
TAOIST
TOOTSY
WHOMSO
WHOOSH
WOODSY

••O••S

ABODES
ABOHMS
ABOMBS
ABORTS
ACORNS
ADOBES
ADONIS
ADOPTS
ADORES
ADORNS
AEOLUS
AGORAS
ALOHAS
ALOINS
AMOLES
AMOURS
ANODES
ANOLES
AROIDS
AROMAS
ATODDS
ATOLLS
ATONES
AVOIDS
AZORES
BIOGAS
BIOMES
BIOTAS
BLOATS
BLOCKS
BLOKES
BLONDS
BLOOMS
BLOOPS
BOOSTS
BOOTES
BOOTHS
BROADS
BROILS
BRONCS
BROODS
BROOKS
BROOMS
BROTHS
BROWNS
CEORLS
CHOCKS
CHOIRS
CHOKES
CHOLOS
CHOMPS
CHORDS
CHORES
CHORUS
CLOAKS
CLOCKS
CLOMPS
CLONES
CLONKS
CLONUS
CLORIS
CLOSES
CLOTHS
CLOUDS
CLOUTS
CLOVES
CLOVIS
CLOWNS
CNOTES
COOERS
COOPTS
CROAKS
CROATS
CROCKS
CROCUS
CROFTS
CRONES
CRONUS
CROOKS
CROONS
CROWDS
CROWNS
CROZES
DHOLES
DHOTIS
DIODES
DOOFUS
DROIDS
DROITS
DROLLS
DROMOS
DRONES
DROOLS
DROOPS
DROVES
DROWNS
DUOMOS
EBOATS
EBONDS
ECOLES
ELOPES
EMOTES
ENOKIS
ENOSIS
EPOCHS
EPODES
ERODES
EVOKES
EXODUS
FIORDS
FJORDS
FLOATS
FLOCKS
FLOODS
FLOORS
FLORAS
FLORES
FLOURS
FLOUTS
FROCKS
FRONDS
FRONTS
FROSTS
FROTHS
FROWNS
GEODES
GHOSTS
GHOULS
GLOATS
GLOBES
GLOGGS
GLOOMS
GLOVES
GLOZES
GNOMES
GNOSIS
GOOSES
GROANS
GROATS
GROINS
GROOMS
GROPES
GROUPS
GROUTS
GROVES
GROWLS
HAOLES
HBOMBS
HMONGS
HOOHAS
HOOVES
KHOUMS
KIOSKS
KIOWAS
KLOOFS
KNOCKS
KNOLLS
KNOTTS
KNOUTS
KNOWNS
LEONES
LLOYDS
LOOFAS
LOOIES
LOOSES
MAORIS
MIOSIS
MYOPES
MYOSIS
NOONES
NOOSES
ODOURS
OROMOS
OVOIDS
PHOBOS
PHOCIS
PHONES
PHONOS
PHOTOS
PLONKS
PROAMS
PROBES
PROEMS
PROLES
PROMOS
PRONGS
PROOFS
PROSES
PROVES
PROWLS
QUOINS
QUOITS
QUOTAS
QUOTES
REOILS
RHODES
RHOMBS
RIOJAS
ROOSTS
SCOFFS
SCOLDS
SCONES
SCOOPS
SCOOTS
SCOPES
SCORES
SCORNS
SCOURS
SCOUTS
SCOWLS
SHOALS
SHOATS
SHOCKS
SHOERS
SHOJIS
SHOOKS
SHOOTS
SHORES
SHORTS
SHOUTS
SHOVES
SKOALS
SKORTS
SLOOPS
SLOPES
SLOTHS
SMOCKS
SMOKES
SMOLTS
SNOODS
SNOOKS
SNOOPS
SNOOTS
SNOPES
SNORES
SNORTS
SNOUTS
SPOILS
SPOKES
SPOOFS
SPOOKS
SPOOLS
SPOONS
SPOORS
SPORES
SPORTS
SPOUTS
STOATS
STOCKS
STOICS
STOKES
STOLES
STOMAS
STOMPS
STONES
STOOKS
STOOLS
STOOPS
STOPES
STORES
STORKS
STORMS
STORRS
STOUPS
STOUTS
STOVES
SWOONS
SWOOPS
SWORDS
TBONDS
TBONES
THOLES
THOMAS
THONGS
THORNS
THORPS
TNOTES
TROLLS
TROMPS
TROOPS
TROPES
TROTHS
TROUTS
TROVES
UBOATS
UBOLTS
VIOLAS
VROOMS
WHOLES
WHOMPS
WHOOFS
WHOOPS
WHORLS
WOOERS
WRONGS
XHOSAS
ZLOTYS
ZOOIDS

•••OS•

ACCOST
ACROSS
ALDOSE
ALMOST
APPOSE
ARGOSY
ARIOSE
ARIOSO
ATCOST
ATMOST
BYGOSH
CHOOSE
CHOOSY
COHOST
DEPOSE
EMBOSS
ESPOSA
ESPOSO
EXPOSE
EXPOST
FILOSE
GALOSH
GYROSE
IMPOSE
IMPOST
INMOST
JOCOSE
KAROSS
KIBOSH
LANOSE
LAROSA
LUGOSI
MILOSZ
MIMOSA
MOROSE
MUCOSA
NODOSE
NOLOSE
OPPOSE
OSMOSE
OTIOSE
PILOSE
POTOSI
RAMOSE
REPOSE
REPOST
RIBOSE
RIMOSE
RUGOSE
SAMOSA
SEROSA
SETOSE
SPLOSH
SWOOSH
TOROSE
UPMOST
UPROSE
UTMOST
VADOSE
WHOOSH

•••O•S

ABBOTS
ABHORS
ACEOUS
ACROSS
ACTORS
ADDONS

ALDOUS
ALLOTS
ALLOWS
ALLOYS
ANIONS
ANJOUS
ANNOYS
APRONS
ARBORS
ARDORS
ARGOTS
ARMORS
ARROWS
ARSONS
ARTOIS
ASCOTS
AUROUS
AXIOMS
AXIONS
BARONS
BATONS
BAYOUS
BEBOPS
BEFOGS
BESOMS
BESOTS
BIGOTS
BIPODS
BISONS
BLOOMS
BLOOPS
BOSONS
BROODS
BROOKS
BROOMS
CAHOWS
CANOES
CANONS
CAPONS
CAROBS
CAROLS
CAROMS
CDROMS
CHEOPS
COCOAS
CODONS
COLONS
COLORS
CROOKS
CROONS
CSPOTS
DADOES
DECORS
DECOYS
DEFOGS
DEMOBS
DEMONS
DEPOTS
DICOTS
DIVOTS
DODOES
DOGONS
DOLORS
DONORS
DROOLS
DROOPS
DUBOIS
DUROCS
ECHOES
EDDOES
ELBOWS
EMBOSS
ENDOWS
ENJOYS
ENROLS
ENVOIS
ENVOYS
EPHODS
EPHORS
EPROMS
ERGOTS
ERRORS
ESTOPS
EXTOLS
FAGOTS
FAMOUS
FANONS
FAVORS
FELONS
FLOODS
FLOORS
FSTOPS
FURORS
FUTONS
GALOIS
GALOPS
GATORS
GEMOTS
GIGOTS
GIJOES
GLOOMS
GLUONS
GRIOTS
GROOMS
GUYOTS
GYRONS
HALOES
HAVOCS
HELOTS
HEROES
HERONS
HOBOES
HONORS
HUMORS
HURONS
IDIOMS
IDIOTS
IGLOOS
INGOTS
INIONS
JABOTS
JOYOUS
JURORS
KABOBS
KAROSS
KAZOOS
KEBOBS
KLOOFS
LABORS
LEMONS
MAJORS
MANORS
MASONS
MAYORS
MCJOBS
MELONS
MESONS
MINORS
MIWOKS
MODOCS
MORONS
MOTORS
MUCOUS
NABOBS
NABORS
NYLONS
ODIOUS
ONIONS
ORLOPS
OXBOWS
PAEONS
PATOIS
PEKOES
PELOPS
PICOTS
PILOTS
PINONS
PINOTS
PITONS
PIVOTS
POBOYS
POROUS
PRIONS
PRIORS
PROOFS
PUTONS
PYLONS
RACONS
RAMOUS
RAYONS
RAZORS
RECONS
REDOES
REMOPS
REMOWS
REPOTS
RESODS
RETOPS
RETOWS
RIGORS
ROBOTS
ROTORS
RUFOUS
RUMORS
RUNONS
SABOTS
SALONS
SAPORS
SARODS
SAVORS
SAXONS
SCIONS
SCOOPS
SCOOTS
SCRODS
SENORS
SEPOYS
SEROUS
SEROWS
SHOOKS
SHOOTS
SLOOPS
SNOODS
SNOOKS
SNOOPS
SNOOTS
SOPORS
SOTOLS
SPOOFS
SPOOKS
SPOOLS
SPOONS
SPOORS
STOOKS
STOOLS
STOOPS
STROPS
SWOONS
SWOOPS
SYNODS
SYSOPS
TABOOS
TABORS
TALONS
TAROTS
TAUONS
TENONS
TENORS
TETONS
THROBS
THROES
THROWS
TOYONS
TROOPS
TUDORS
TUTORS
UNDOES
UNIONS
UPBOWS
VALOIS
VAPORS
VENOMS
VENOUS
VETOES
VIGORS
VINOUS
VISORS
VOROUS
VROOMS
WAGONS
WAHOOS
WHOOFS
WHOOPS
WIDOWS
YAHOOS
YAPOKS
YUROKS
ZEROES

••••OS

ABYDOS
AGGROS
ALAMOS
AMIGOS
ANDROS
ANGLOS
ARCCOS
ASTROS
AUDIOS
AVISOS
BANJOS
BASSOS
BATHOS
BEANOS
BOFFOS
BONGOS
BRAVOS
BRAZOS
BUENOS
BUFFOS
BUNCOS
BUNKOS
BURGOS
BURROS
BUTEOS
CACAOS
CAICOS
CAMEOS
CAMPOS
CANTOS
CARBOS
CARGOS
CARLOS
CELLOS
CENTOS
CERROS
CESTOS
CHINOS
CHOLOS
CISCOS
CLAROS
COMBOS
COMPOS
CONDOS
COSMOS
CREDOS
CURIOS
CUSTOS
CYCLOS
DEIMOS
DEKKOS
DISCOS
DITTOS
DOBROS
DROMOS
DUOMOS
EJIDOS
ETHNOS
FOLIOS
FRITOS
GECKOS
GIZMOS
GUACOS
GUIROS
GUMBOS
HALLOS
HELIOS
HELLOS
HIPPOS
HOWTOS
HUEVOS
HULLOS
HYDROS
HYKSOS
HYPNOS
IGLOOS
INTROS
JUMBOS
JUNCOS
JUNTOS
KAZOOS
KERNOS
LARGOS
LASSOS
LEMNOS
LESBOS
LIMBOS
LITHOS
LLANOS
LOTTOS
MACHOS
MACROS
MAMBOS
MANGOS
MARCOS
MATZOS
METROS
MEZZOS
MICROS
MIMEOS
MOTTOS
MUGHOS
MUNGOS
MYTHOS
NACHOS
OROMOS
PANTOS
PASEOS
PATHOS
PATIOS
PATMOS
PEPLOS
PESTOS
PHAROS
PHILOS
PHOBOS
PHONOS
PHOTOS
PIANOS
PINTOS
POTTOS
PRIMOS
PROMOS
RADIOS
RATIOS
RECTOS
REPROS
RETROS
RHINOS
RODEOS
ROLEOS
ROMEOS
RONDOS
SALVOS
SANTOS
SARGOS
SAYSOS
SCHMOS
SERVOS
SESTOS
SETTOS
SHAKOS
SKIROS
SPIROS
STENOS
TABOOS
TAINOS
TANGOS
TEMPOS
TONDOS
TORSOS
TRIPOS
TURBOS
VERSOS
VIDEOS
VIREOS
WACKOS
WAHOOS
YAHOOS
YOBBOS
ZENDOS

OT••••

OTELLO
OTHERS
OTIOSE
OTITIC
OTITIS
OTOOLE
OTTAVA
OTTAWA
OTTERS

O•T•••

OATERS
OATIER
OBTAIN
OBTEST
OBTUND
OBTUSE
OCTADS
OCTANE
OCTANT
OCTAVE
OCTAVO
OCTETS
OCTOPI
OCTROI
ONTAPE
ONTIME
ONTOUR
OPTFOR
OPTICS
OPTIMA
OPTING
OPTION
OPTOUT
ORTEGA
ORTLES
OSTEAL
OSTEND
OSTIUM
OSTLER
OTTAVA
OTTAWA
OTTERS
OUTACT
OUTAGE
OUTATE
OUTBID
OUTBOX
OUTCRY
OUTDID
OUTEAT
OUTFIT
OUTFLY
OUTFOX
OUTGUN
OUTHIT
OUTING
OUTLAW
OUTLAY
OUTLET
OUTPUT
OUTRAN
OUTRUN
OUTSET
OUTWIT
OXTAIL

O••T••

OBITER
OBSTET
ODETTA
ODETTE
OERTER
ONETWO
ORATED
ORATES
ORATOR
OTITIC
OTITIS
OUSTED
OUSTER
OYSTER

O•••T•

OBLATE
OCTETS
ODDITY
ODETTA
ODETTE
ODISTS
ODONTO
OFLATE
OLEATE
OMERTA
ONSETS
ONSITE
OOCYTE
OOLITE
OOLITH
OPENTO
OPHITE
OPIATE
OPORTO
ORANTS
ORBITS
ORGATE
ORNATE
ORNITH
OSSETE
OUGHTS
OUTATE
OWLETS

O••••T

OBJECT
OBLAST
OBOIST
OBSTET
OBTEST
OBVERT
OCCULT
OCELOT
OCTANT
ODDEST
ODDLOT
OFFSET
OLDEST
OLDHAT
OMELET
ONEACT
ONFOOT
OPTOUT
ORGEAT
ORIENT
OUTACT
OUTEAT
OUTFIT
OUTHIT
OUTLET
OUTPUT
OUTSET
OUTWIT
OXCART

•OT•••

BOTANY
BOTCHY
BOTELS
BOTFLY
BOTHER
BOTREE
BOTTLE
BOTTOM
COTTAS
COTTEN
COTTER
COTTON
DOTAGE
DOTARD
DOTELL
DOTEON
DOTHAN
DOTING
DOTTED
DOTTIE
DOTTLE
GOTCHA
GOTHAM
GOTHIC
GOTMAD
GOTOFF
GOTOIT
GOTOUT
GOTSET
GOTTEN
HOTAIR
HOTBED
HOTBOX
HOTCAP
HOTCAR
HOTDOG
HOTELS
HOTPOT
HOTROD
HOTTEA
HOTTER
HOTTIP
HOTTUB
HOTWAR
JOTTED
KOTTER
LOTAHS
LOTHAR
LOTION
LOTTED
LOTTOS
MOTELS
MOTETS
MOTHER
MOTHRA
MOTIFS
MOTILE
MOTION
MOTIVE
MOTLEY
MOTMOT
MOTORS

MOTOWN
MOTTLE
MOTTOS
NOTARY
NOTATE
NOTBAD
NOTCHY
NOTERS
NOTICE
NOTIFY
NOTING
NOTION
NOTNOW
NOTYET
POTAGE
POTASH
POTATO
POTEEN
POTENT
POTFUL
POTHER
POTION
POTOSI
POTPIE
POTTED
POTTER
POTTLE
POTTOS
ROTARY
ROTATE
ROTGUT
ROTHKO
ROTINI
ROTORS
ROTTED
ROTTEN
ROTTER
ROTUND
SOTHAT
SOTOLS
SOTTED
TOTALS
TOTEMS
TOTERS
TOTHER
TOTING
TOTSUP
TOTTED
TOTTER
VOTARY
VOTECH
VOTEIN
VOTERS
VOTING
VOTIVE

•O•T••

AORTAE
AORTAL
AORTAS
AORTIC
BOATED
BOATEL
BOATER
BOITES
BOLTED
BOLTON
BONTON
BOOTED
BOOTEE
BOOTES
BOOTHE
BOOTHS
BOOTIE
BOOTSY
BOOTUP
BOSTON
BOTTLE
BOTTOM
BOWTIE
BOXTOP
COATED
COATIS
COLTER
COMTES
CONTAC
CONTES
CONTRA
CONTRE
COOTER
COOTIE
COPTER
COPTIC
CORTES
CORTEX
CORTEZ
COSTAE
COSTAL
COSTAR
COSTAS
COSTLY
COTTAS
COTTEN
COTTER
COTTON
COUTER
DOCTOR
DOGTAG
DOTTED
DOTTIE
DOTTLE
FOETAL
FOETID
FOETOR
FOETUS
FONTAL
FOOTED
FOOTER
FORTAS
FORTES
FOSTER
GOATEE
GOETHE
GOSTAG
GOTTEN
HOGTIE
HOOTAT
HOOTCH
HOOTED
HOOTER
HOOTIE
HORTON
HOSTAS
HOSTED
HOSTEL
HOSTLY
HOTTEA
HOTTER
HOTTIP
HOTTUB
HOWTOS
JOETEX
JOLTED
JOSTLE
JOTTED
KOTTER
KOWTOW
LOATHE
LOFTED
LOITER
LOOTED
LOOTER
LOSTIT
LOTTED
LOTTOS
MOATED
MOLTED
MOLTEN
MOLTER
MOLTKE
MONTEL
MONTES
MONTEZ
MONTHS
MOOTED
MOPTOP
MORTAL
MORTAR
MORTON
MOSTEL
MOSTLY
MOTTLE
MOTTOS
MOUTHS
MOUTHY
MOUTON
NOETIC
NOOTKA
NORTHS
NORTON
POETIC
POETRY
PONTES
PONTIC
PONTUS
POPTOP
PORTAL
PORTED
PORTER
PORTIA
PORTLY
POSTAL
POSTED
POSTER
POSTIT
POSTON
POTTED
POTTER
POTTLE
POTTOS
POUTED
POUTER
ROOTED
ROOTER
ROSTER
ROSTOV
ROSTRA
ROTTED
ROTTEN
ROTTER
ROUTED
ROUTER
ROUTES
SOFTEN
SOFTER
SOFTIE
SOFTLY
SONTAG
SOOTHE
SORTED
SORTER
SORTIE
SORTOF
SOTTED
SOUTER
SOUTHS
TOATEE
TOETAP
TOLTEC
TOMTIT
TOMTOM
TOOTED
TOOTER
TOOTHY
TOOTLE
TOOTOO
TOOTSY
TOPTEN
TORTES
TOTTED
TOTTER
TOUTED
TOUTER
VORTEX
VOSTOK
WONTED
WONTON
WORTHS
WORTHY
YOMTOV
YOUTHS

•O••T•

BOASTS
BOGOTA
BONITO
BOOSTS
BORATE
BOUNTY
COAPTS
COASTS
COGITO
COMATE
COMETH
COMETO
COMETS
COMITY
COOPTS
COUNTS
COUNTY
COURTS
COVETS
COYOTE
DONATE
DONETS
DONITZ
DONUTS
DORATI
DOUBTS
EOLITH
FOISTS
FOUNTS
FOURTH
GODETS
GOINTO
GOWITH
HOISTS
HOLDTO
HOVETO
IODATE
IOLITE
IOMOTH
JOBETH
JOINTS
JOISTS
JOUSTS
JOWETT
KOONTZ
KORATS
LOBATE
LOCATE
LOLITA
LOOKTO
LOVETT
MOIETY
MONETA
MORITA
MORITZ
MOTETS
MOULTS
MOUNTS
MOUNTY
NOHITS
NONETS
NOPETS
NOTATE
NOVATO
OOCYTE
OOLITE
OOLITH
POINTE
POINTS
POINTY
POLITE
POLITY
POSITS
POTATO
POULTS
ROASTS
ROBOTS
ROOSTS
ROSITA
ROTATE
ROUSTS
SOASTO
SOLUTE
SOMATA
SOMATO
SONATA
SOWETO
TOASTS
TOASTY
TODATE
TOMATO
TONITE
TOOKTO
TOYOTA
VOLUTE
WORSTS
YOKUTS
ZONATE

•O•••T

AORIST
BOBCAT
BOGART
BONMOT
BONNET
BOSKET
BOUGHT
BOWNET
BOWOUT
BOXSET
COBALT
COEDIT
COGENT
COHORT
COHOST
COLLET
COMBAT
COMEAT
COMFIT
COMMIT
COMSAT
CONANT
COOLIT
COPOUT
COQUET
CORNET
CORSET
COSSET
COVENT
COVERT
COYEST
DOCENT
DOCKET
DOESNT
DOGSAT
DOGSIT
DOPANT
DORRIT
DORSET
FOGHAT
FOMENT
FOREST
FORGET
FORGOT
FORINT
FORMAT
FOUGHT
GOBLET
GOBUST
GOCART
GODWIT
GOESAT
GOKART
GORGET
GOSOFT
GOTOIT
GOTOUT
GOTSET
GOULET
GOWEST
HOBART
HOBBIT
HOGGET
HOLDIT
HOLIST
HONEST
HOOFIT
HOOTAT
HORNET
HOTPOT
JOBLOT
JOLIET
JOLIOT
JOWETT
KOMBAT
KORBUT
LOCKET
LOCUST
LOGOUT
LOOKAT
LOQUAT
LOSEIT
LOSTIT
LOVETT
LOWEST
LOWFAT
MODELT
MODEST
MOLEST
MOMENT
MONIST
MOPPET
MORANT
MOTMOT
MOZART
NOCENT
NOEXIT
NONFAT
NOTYET
NOUGAT
NOUGHT
POCKET
POIROT
POKEAT
POLPOT
POPART
POPOUT
POPPET
POSSET
POSTIT
POTENT
ROBERT
ROBUST
ROCHET
ROCKET
RODENT
ROTGUT
SOBEIT
SOCKET
SOFFIT
SOLENT
SONANT
SONNET
SORBET
SOREST
SOTHAT
SOUGHT
SOVIET
SOWHAT
TOBOOT
TOILET
TOMCAT
TOMTIT
TOOKIT
TOPCAT
TOPHAT
TOPOUT
TOREAT
VOIGHT
VOLANT
WOMBAT
WONOUT
YOGURT
YOUBET

••OT••

BIOTAS
BIOTIC
BIOTIN
BLOTCH
BLOTTO
BLOTTY
BOOTED
BOOTEE
BOOTES
BOOTHE
BOOTHS
BOOTIE
BOOTSY
BOOTUP
BROTHS
CLOTHE
CLOTHO
CLOTHS
CLOTTY
CNOTES
COOTER
COOTIE
CROTON
DHOTEL
DHOTIS
EMOTED
EMOTER
EMOTES
EROTIC
EXOTIC
FOOTED
FOOTER
FROTHS
FROTHY
GIOTTO
GROTON
GROTTO
GROTTY
HOOTAT
HOOTCH
HOOTED
HOOTER
HOOTIE
IGOTIT
KNOTTS
KNOTTY
LAOTSE
LAOTZU
LHOTSE
LIOTTA
LOOTED
LOOTER
MAOTAI
MOOTED
NOOTKA
PHOTIC
PHOTOG
PHOTON
PHOTOS
PLOTTY
PROTAX
PROTEI
PROTEM
PROTON
QUOTAS
QUOTED
QUOTER
QUOTES
QUOTHA
RIOTED
RIOTER
ROOTED
ROOTER
SCOTCH
SCOTER
SCOTIA
SCOTTO
SCOTTY
SHOTAT
SHOTUP
SLOTHS
SNOTTY
SOOTHE
SPOTTY
STOTIN
TNOTES
TOOTED
TOOTER
TOOTHY
TOOTLE
TOOTOO
TOOTSY
TROTHS
ZLOTYS

••O•T•

ABORTS
ADOPTS
AGOUTI
BLOATS
BLOTTO
BLOTTY
BOOSTS
BRONTE
CHOATE
CLOTTY
CLOUTS
COOPTS
CROATS
CROFTS
CROUTE
DROITS
EBOATS
FLOATS
FLOATY
FLOUTS
FRONTS
FROSTS
FROSTY
GHOSTS
GIOTTO
GLOATS
GROATS
GROTTO
GROTTY
GROUTS
GROUTY
GROWTH
KNOTTS
KNOTTY
KNOUTS

KOONTZ
LIOTTA
LOOKTO
ODONTO
OPORTO
PLOTTY
PRONTO
QUOITS
ROOSTS
SCOOTS
SCOTTO
SCOTTY
SCOUTS
SHOATS
SHOOTS
SHORTA
SHORTE
SHORTI
SHORTO
SHORTS
SHORTU
SHORTY
SHOUTS
SKORTS
SMOLTS
SMOOTH
SNOOTS
SNOOTY
SNORTS
SNOTTY
SNOUTS
SPORTS
SPORTY
SPOTTY
SPOUTS
STOATS
STOUTS
TOOKTO
TROUTS
UBOATS
UBOLTS

••O••T
AGOROT
AMOUNT
ANOINT
AVOCET
BLOWIT
CLOSET
COOLIT
DROPIT
EGOIST
FLORET
HOOFIT
HOOTAT
IGOTIT
IROBOT
LIONET
LOOKAT
MAOIST
OBOIST
PIOLET
PROFIT
PROMPT
PROSIT
PROUST
SHOTAT
SNOCAT
SPOILT
STOMAT
STOPIT
TAOIST
TOOKIT
TWOBIT
VIOLET

•••OT•
ABBOTS
ABBOTT
ALCOTT
ALIOTO
ALLOTS
ARGOTS
ASCOTS
BESOTS
BIGOTS
BOGOTA
BYROTE
CAPOTE
CENOTE
COYOTE
CSPOTS
DAKOTA
DEMOTE
DENOTE
DEPOTS
DESOTO
DEVOTE
DEVOTO
DICOTS
DIVOTS
ERGOTS
EXVOTO
FAGOTS
GEMOTE
GEMOTS
GIGOTS
GRIOTS
GUYOTS
HELOTS
IDIOTS
INGOTS
INTOTO
IOMOTH
JABOTS
LAKOTA
MALOTI
MELOTT
MRMOTO
PELOTA
PEYOTE
PICOTS
PILOTI
PILOTS
PINOTS
PIVOTS
REMOTE
RENOTE
REPOTS
ROBOTS
SABOTS
SCOOTS
SHOOTS
SMOOTH
SNOOTS
SNOOTY
TAROTS
TOYOTA
ZEROTH
ZYGOTE

•••O•T
ABBOTT
ACCOST
ACEOUT
ACTOUT
ADROIT
AFLOAT
AIROUT
AJFOYT
ALCOTT
ALLOUT
ALMOST
ASKOUT
ASSORT
ATCOST
ATEOUT
ATMOST
AUMONT
BELOIT
BENOIT
BOWOUT
BUGOUT
BUMOUT
BUYOUT
CAVORT
COHORT
COHOST
COPOUT
CUTOUT
DACOIT
DECOCT
DEPORT
DEVOUT
DIEOUT
DIGOUT
DIMOUT
DRYOUT
DUGOUT
DUMONT
DUPONT
EATOUT
EFFORT
EGMONT
EKEOUT
ENROOT
ESCORT
EXHORT
EXPORT
EXPOST
EXTORT
FANOUT
FAROUT
FLYOUT
GALOOT
GERONT
GETOUT
GOSOFT
GOTOIT
GOTOUT
HIDOUT
HITOUT
ICEOUT
IMPORT
IMPOST
INMOST
INPORT
LAMONT
LAYOUT
LEDOUT
LETOUT
LITOUT
LOGOUT
MAHOUT
MAXOUT
MELOTT
ONFOOT
OPTOUT
PANOUT
PAYOUT
PIGOUT
POPOUT
PTBOAT
PUTOUT
RAGOUT
RANOUT
REBOLT
REBOOT
RECOAT
REPORT
REPOST
RESORT
RETORT
REVOLT
RIPOUT
RUBOUT
RUNOUT
SATOUT
SAWOUT
SEEOUT
SETOUT
SITOUT
SPROUT
TAGOUT
TAPOUT
THROAT
TOBOOT
TOPOUT
TRYOUT
UNBOLT
UNROOT
UPMOST
UPROOT
UTMOST
WAYOUT
WIGOUT
WINOUT
WONOUT
XEDOUT

••••OT
AGOROT
BADLOT
BALLOT
BARDOT
BONMOT
BURBOT
CANNOT
CARLOT
CARNOT
CARROT
DESPOT
DIGLOT
DRYROT
DYELOT
ELLIOT
ENROOT
FORGOT
GALOOT
HERIOT
HOTPOT
IROBOT
JOBLOT
JOLIOT
MARGOT
MARMOT
MASCOT
MERLOT
MOTMOT
OCELOT
ODDLOT
ONFOOT
PARROT
PEQUOT
PERROT
POIROT
POLPOT
REBOOT
REDHOT
RESHOT
SPIGOT
TALBOT
TEAPOT
TINPOT
TOBOOT
TRICOT
TURBOT
UNKNOT
UNROOT
UPROOT
UPSHOT
WHYNOT
ZEALOT

OU••••
OUGHTS
OUNCES
OUSELS
OUSTED
OUSTER
OUTACT
OUTAGE
OUTATE
OUTBID
OUTBOX
OUTCRY
OUTDID
OUTEAT
OUTFIT
OUTFLY
OUTFOX
OUTGUN
OUTHIT
OUTING
OUTLAW
OUTLAY
OUTLET
OUTPUT
OUTRAN
OUTRUN
OUTSET
OUTWIT
OUZELS

O•U•••
OCULAR
OEUVRE
ONUSES
OPUSES
OVULAR
OVULES

O••U••
OBTUND
OBTUSE
OCCULT
OCCUPY
OCCURS
ODIUMS
ODOURS
ONEUPS
ONRUSH
OPPUGN
ORDURE
OSCULA
OSMUND

O•••U•
OBELUS
ODIOUS
OMASUM
OMNIUM
ONTOUR
OPAQUE
OPENUP
OPTOUT
OSMIUM
OSTIUM
OUTGUN
OUTPUT
OUTRUN
OWNSUP

O••••U
ORMOLU

•OU•••
AOUDAD
BOUBOU
BOUCLE
BOUDIN
BOUFFE
BOUGHS
BOUGHT
BOULES
BOULEZ
BOULLE
BOUNCE
BOUNCY
BOUNDS
BOUNTY
BOURKE
BOURNE
BOURSE
BOUSED
BOUSES
COUGAR
COUGHS
COULDA
COULEE
COUNTS
COUNTY
COUPES
COUPLE
COUPON
COURIC
COURSE
COURTS
COUSIN
COUTER
DOUALA
DOUBLE
DOUBLY
DOUBTS
DOUGHS
DOUGHY
DOURER
DOURLY
DOUSED
DOUSES
FOUGHT
FOULED
FOULER
FOULLY
FOULUP
FOUNDS
FOUNTS
FOURAM
FOURPM
FOURTH
GOUGED
GOUGER
GOUGES
GOULET
GOUNOD
GOURDE
GOURDS
HOUGHS
HOUNDS
HOUNDY
HOURIS
HOURLY
HOUSED
HOUSES
JOULES
JOUNCE
JOUNCY
JOURNO
JOUSTS
KOUFAX
LOUCHE
LOUDEN
LOUDER
LOUDLY
LOUGHS
LOUISA
LOUISE
LOUNGE
LOUPES
LOUSED
LOUSES
LOUVER
LOUVRE
MOULDS
MOULDY
MOULIN
MOULTS
MOUNDS
MOUNTS
MOUNTY
MOURNS
MOUSED
MOUSER
MOUSES
MOUSEY
MOUSSE
MOUTHS
MOUTHY
MOUTON
NOUGAT
NOUGHT
NOUMEA
POUCHY
POULTS
POUNCE
POUNDS
POURED
POURER
POURIN
POUSSE
POUTED
POUTER
ROUBLE
ROUGED
ROUGES
ROUGHS
ROUGHY
ROUNDS
ROURKE
ROUSED
ROUSER
ROUSES
ROUSTS
ROUTED
ROUTER
ROUTES
SOUARI
SOUGHS
SOUGHT
SOUNDS
SOUPUP
SOURCE
SOURED
SOURER
SOURLY
SOUSED
SOUSES
SOUTER
SOUTHS
TOUCAN
TOUCHE
TOUCHY
TOUGHS
TOUGHY
TOULON
TOUPEE
TOURED
TOURER
TOUSLE
TOUTED
TOUTER
WOUNDS
YOUALL
YOUBET
YOUTHS
ZOUAVE
ZOUNDS

•O•U••
BOSUNS
COBURG
COBURN
COHUNE
COLUGO
COLUMN
CONURE
COPULA
COQUET
DONUTS
FORUMS
GOBUST
JOCUND
JORUMS
KORUNA
LOBULE
LOCUST
LOQUAT
MODULE
MODULO
MOGULS
MOHURS
MOPUPS
NODULE
PODUNK
POPULI
POPUPS
ROBUST
ROGUES
ROTUND
SOEURS
SOLUTE
TOLUCA
TOQUES
VOGUES
VOLUME
VOLUTE
YOGURT
YOKUTS
YORUBA

•O••U•
BOBSUP
BONEUP
BOOJUM
BOOTUP
BOREUP
BOWOUT
BOXFUL
COCCUS
COILUP
COLEUS
COLOUR
COMEUP
CONCUR
CONIUM
CONSUL
COOKUP
COOPUP
COPOUT
CORIUM
CORPUS
COYPUS
DOESUP
DOLLUP
DOLOUR
DONEUP
DOOFUS
DORSUM
FOETUS
FOGSUP
FOLDUP
FOLIUM
FONDUE
FOULUP
GOESUP
GOLLUM
GOOFUP
GOTOUT
HOLDUP

HOLEUP
HONOUR
HOOKUP
HOPSUP
HORMUZ
HOTTUB
IONIUM
JOINUP
JOSHUA
JOYFUL
JOYOUS
KORBUT
LOCKUP
LOGOUT
LONGUE
LOOKUP
MOBIUS
MOCKUP
MOPSUP
MOSQUE
MOVEUP
PODIUM
POILUS
POLLUX
PONTUS
PONYUP
POPGUN
POPOUT
POPSUP
POROUS
POSEUR
POSSUM
POTFUL
ROLLUP
ROTGUT
SOAKUP
SOBFUL
SODIUM
SOLEUS
SOPSUP
SOUPUP
SOWBUG
TOBRUK
TONEUP
TONGUE
TOOKUP
TOOLUP
TOPGUN
TOPHUS
TOPOUT
TOREUP
TORQUE
TOSSUP
TOTSUP
VOROUS
WOEFUL
WOKEUP
WONMUG
WONOUT
WORKUP

•O•••U

BOUBOU
CONGOU
HONSHU
MOLDAU
MOREAU
ROSEAU

••OU••

ABOUND
AGOUTI
AMOUNT
AMOURS
AROUND
AROUSE
AVOUCH
BLOUSE
CHOUGH
CLOUDS
CLOUDY
CLOUTS
CROUCH
CROUPY
CROUSE
CROUTE
ENOUGH
FLOURS
FLOURY
FLOUTS
GHOULS
GROUCH
GROUND
GROUPS
GROUSE
GROUTS
GROUTY
INOUYE
KHOUMS
KNOUTS
ODOURS
PLOUGH
PROUST
SCOURS
SCOUSE
SCOUTS
SHOULD
SHOUTS
SIOUAN
SLOUCH
SLOUGH
SNOUTS
SPOUSE
SPOUTS
STOUPS
STOUTS
THOUGH
TROUGH
TROUPE
TROUTS
TROUVE

••O•U•

AEOLUS
BLOWUP
BOOJUM
BOOTUP
BROGUE
BUOYUP
CHORUS
CLOGUP
CLONUS
CLOQUE
COOKUP
COOPUP
CROCUS
CRONUS
CROPUP
DOOFUS
DROGUE
EXODUS
GOOFUP
GROWUP
HOOKUP
KRONUR
LOOKUP
PROPUP
QUOQUE
QUORUM
SHOGUN
SHOTUP
SHOWUP
SLOWUP
STOPUP
TOOKUP
TOOLUP

••O••U

CHONJU
CHOOYU
LAOTZU
SHORTU

•••OU•

ACEOUS
ACEOUT
ACTOUT
AIROUT
ALDOUS
ALLOUT
ANJOUS
ARBOUR
ARDOUR
ARMOUR
ASKOUT
ATEOUT
AUROUS
BAYOUS
BEFOUL
BIJOUX
BOWOUT
BUGOUT
BUMOUT
BUYOUT
COLOUR
COPOUT
CUTOUT
DAMOUR
DETOUR
DEVOUR
DEVOUT
DIEOUT
DIGOUT
DIMOUT
DOLOUR
DRYOUT
DUGOUT
EATOUT
EKEOUT
ENSOUL
FAMOUS
FANOUT
FAROUK
FAROUT
FAVOUR
FLYOUT
GETOUT
GOTOUT
HIDOUT
HITOUT
HONOUR
HUMOUR
ICEOUT
INPOUR
JOYOUS
LABOUR
LAMOUR
LATOUR
LAYOUT
LEDOUT
LETOUT
LITOUT
LOGOUT
MACOUN
MAHOUT
MAXOUT
MUCOUS
ODIOUS
ONTOUR
OPTOUT
PANOUT
PAYOUT
PIGOUT
POPOUT
POROUS
PUTOUT
RAGOUT
RAMOUS
RANOUT
RECOUP
RETOUR
RIGOUR
RIPOUT
RUBOUT
RUFOUS
RUMOUR
RUNOUT
SATOUT
SAVOUR
SAWOUT
SEEOUT
SEROUS
SETOUT
SHROUD
SITOUT
SPROUT
STROUD
TAGOUT
TAPOUT
TOPOUT
TRYOUT
VALOUR
VAPOUR
VELOUR
VENOUS
VIGOUR
VINOUS
VOROUS
WAYOUT
WIGOUT
WINOUT
WONOUT
XEDOUT

•••O•U

CHOOYU
ORMOLU

••••OU

ACAJOU
AMADOU
BALLOU
BOUBOU
CACHOU
CONGOU
FUZHOU
HEYYOU
MENJOU
PAILOU

OV••••

OVALLY
OVERDO
OVERLY
OVIEDO
OVISAC
OVOIDS
OVULAR
OVULES

O•V•••

OBVERT
ONVIEW

O••V••

OEUVRE
OGIVES
OLDVIC
OLEVEL
OLIVER
OLIVES
OLIVIA

O•••V•

OCTAVE
OCTAVO
OTTAVA

•OV•••

BOVARY
BOVIDS
BOVINE
BOVVER
COVENS
COVENT
COVERS
COVERT
COVETS
COVEYS
COVINA
DOVEIN
DOVISH
FOVEAE
GOVERN
HOVELS
HOVERS
HOVETO
JOVIAL
JOVIAN
KOVACS
LOVAGE
LOVEIN
LOVELL
LOVELY
LOVERS
LOVETT
LOVING
MOVEIN
MOVEON
MOVERS
MOVEUP
MOVIES
MOVING
NOVATO
NOVELS
NOVENA
NOVICE
ROVERS
ROVING
SOVIET
WOVOKA

•O•V••

BOVVER
COEVAL
CONVEX
CONVEY
CONVOY
CORVEE
CORVES
GOOVER
HOOVER
HOOVES
LOAVES
LOUVER
LOUVRE
SOAVES
SOLVED
SOLVER
SOLVES
VOLVAS
VOLVOX
WOLVES

•O••V•

GODIVA
KOSOVO
MOHAVE
MOJAVE
MORAVA
MOSKVA
MOTIVE
VOTIVE
ZOUAVE

•O•••V

MOSHAV
ROCKYV
ROSTOV
YOMTOV

••OV••

BMOVIE
CLOVEN
CLOVER
CLOVES
CLOVIS
DROVER
DROVES
GLOVED
GLOVER
GLOVES
GOOVER
GROVEL
GROVER
GROVES
HOOVER
HOOVES
PLOVER
PROVED
PROVEN
PROVER
PROVES
SHOVED
SHOVEL
SHOVER
SHOVES
SLOVAK
SLOVEN
SLOVIK
STOVER
STOVES
TROVES

••O•V•

EVOLVE
GROOVE
GROOVY
TROUVE

•••OV•

ALCOVE
BEHOVE
BULOVA
BYJOVE
CANOVA
DENOVO
GROOVE
GROOVY
INLOVE
KOSOVO
REMOVE
REWOVE
SHROVE
STROVE
THROVE
UNWOVE

••••OV

ASIMOV
BRASOV
CHEKOV
IMPROV
KARPOV
PAVLOV
ROSTOV
YOMTOV
ZHUKOV

OW••••

OWLETS
OWLISH
OWNERS
OWNING
OWNSUP

O•W•••

OHWELL
ONWARD
ORWELL
OSWALD
OSWEGO

O••W••

OBIWAN
ONEWAY
OUTWIT

O•••W•

OJIBWA
ONETWO
OSHAWA
OTTAWA
OXBOWS

O••••W

OLDSAW
ONVIEW
OUTLAW

•OW•••

BOWERS
BOWERY
BOWFIN
BOWING
BOWLED
BOWLER
BOWLES
BOWMAN
BOWMEN
BOWNET
BOWOAR
BOWOUT
BOWSAW
BOWSER
BOWTIE
BOWWOW
BOWYER
COWARD
COWBOY
COWENS
COWERS
COWING
COWLED
COWLEY
COWMAN
COWMEN
COWPEA
COWPER
COWPOX
COWRIE
DOWELS
DOWERS
DOWERY
DOWNED
DOWNER
DOWNEY
DOWNON
DOWSED
DOWSER
DOWSES
FOWLED
FOWLER
FOWLES
GOWEST
GOWILD
GOWITH
GOWNED
HOWARD
HOWDAH
HOWELL
HOWLED
HOWLER
HOWLIN
HOWNOW
HOWTOS
IOWANS
JOWETT
KOWTOW
LOWBOY
LOWCAL
LOWELL
LOWEND
LOWERS
LOWERY
LOWEST
LOWFAT
LOWING
LOWISH
LOWKEY
MOWERS
MOWGLI
MOWING
NOWISE
POWDER
POWELL
POWERS
POWWOW
ROWELS
ROWENA
ROWENS
ROWERS
ROWING
SOWBUG
SOWERS
SOWETO
SOWHAT
SOWING
TOWAGE
TOWARD
TOWCAR
TOWELS
TOWERS
TOWERY
TOWHEE
TOWING
TOWNER
TOWNIE
VOWELS
VOWELY
VOWERS
VOWING
WOWING
WOWSER
YOWLED

•O•W••

BOWWOW
COBWEB
CONWAY
DOOWOP
GOAWAY
GOAWRY
GODWIN
GODWIT
HOTWAR
NORWAY
POWWOW

•O••W•

GODOWN
MOHAWK
MOTOWN

•O•••W

BORROW
BOWSAW
BOWWOW
FOGBOW

FOLLOW
GOSLOW
HOLLOW
HOWNOW
KOWTOW
MORROW
MOSCOW
NOSHOW
NOTNOW
POWWOW
SORROW

••OW••
AVOWAL
AVOWED
AVOWER
BLOWER
BLOWIN
BLOWIT
BLOWSY
BLOWUP
BLOWZY
BROWNE
BROWNS
BROWNY
BROWSE
CHOWED
CLOWNS
CROWDS
CROWED
CROWER
CROWNS
DOOWOP
DROWNS
DROWSE
DROWSY
FLOWED
FLOWER
FROWNS
FROWZY
GLOWED
GLOWER
GROWER
GROWLS
GROWLY
GROWON
GROWTH
GROWUP
KIOWAS
KNOWER
KNOWNS
MEOWED
PLOWED
PLOWER
PROWLS
PROWSE
SCOWLS
SHOWED
SHOWER
SHOWIN
SHOWME
SHOWUP
SLOWED
SLOWER
SLOWLY
SLOWUP
SNOWED
SNOWIN
STOWED
TROWED
TROWEL
TWOWAY

••O••W
BROKAW

•••OW•
ALLOWS
ARROWS
CAHOWS
DISOWN
ELBOWS
ENDOWS
GODOWN
INTOWN
MOTOWN
OXBOWS
REMOWN
REMOWS
RENOWN
RETOWS
SEROWS
THROWN
THROWS
UNSOWN
UPBOWS
UPTOWN
WIDOWS

••••OW
ANDHOW
ANTCOW
ANYHOW
BARROW
BELLOW
BESTOW
BILLOW
BORROW
BOWWOW
BURROW
CALLOW
CPSNOW
DARROW
ERENOW
ESCROW
FALLOW
FARLOW
FARROW
FELLOW
FOGBOW
FOLLOW
FURROW
GOSLOW
HALLOW
HARLOW
HARROW
HAYMOW
HOLLOW
HOWNOW
INAROW
INFLOW
KOWTOW
KRAKOW
KUDROW
LAYLOW
LIELOW
MALLOW
MARROW
MEADOW
MELLOW
MINNOW
MORROW
MOSCOW
MURROW
NARROW
NOSHOW
NOTNOW
PESCOW
PILLOW
POWWOW
REPLOW
SALLOW
SEACOW
SHADOW
SKITOW
SORROW
TALLOW
TVSHOW
WALLOW
WILLOW
WINDOW
WINNOW
YARROW
YELLOW

OX••••
OXALIS
OXBOWS
OXCART
OXEYES
OXFORD
OXIDES
OXIDIC
OXLIKE
OXLIPS
OXNARD
OXTAIL
OXYDOL
OXYGEN

O•X•••
OAXACA

O••X••
ONYXES
ORYXES

O••••X
OUTBOX
OUTFOX

•OX•••
BOXBOY
BOXCAR
BOXERS
BOXFUL
BOXIER
BOXING
BOXSET
BOXTOP
FOXIER
FOXILY
FOXING
ROXANA
ROXANE
SOXERS
TOXICS
TOXINS
VOXPOP

•O•X••
COAXED
COAXER
COAXES
HOAXED
HOAXER
HOAXES
NOEXIT

•O••X•
BORAXO

•O•••X
BOLLIX
COCCYX
COLFAX
COMMIX
CONVEX
CORTEX
COWPOX
HOTBOX
JOETEX
KOUFAX
POLEAX
POLLEX
POLLUX
TOMMIX
VOLVOX
VORTEX

••OX••
DIOXIN

••O••X
CLOROX
PROLIX
PROTAX
THORAX

•••OX•
BILOXI

•••O•X
BIJOUX

••••OX
BLUEOX
CHISOX
CLOROX
COWPOX
HATBOX
HOTBOX
ICEBOX
KITFOX
LENNOX
LUMMOX
MUSKOX
OUTBOX
OUTFOX
PAYBOX
REDFOX
REDSOX
SEAFOX
SKYBOX
VOLVOX
WILCOX

OY••••
OYSTER

O•Y•••
OHYEAH
ONYXES
ORYXES
OXYDOL
OXYGEN

O••Y••
OBEYED
OKAYED
OOCYTE
OXEYES

O••••Y
OAKLEY
OCASEY
OCCUPY
OCHERY
ODDITY
OFFDAY
OFFKEY
OHENRY
OILILY
OKELLY
OLDBOY
OLEARY
ONEDAY
ONEWAY
ONIONY
OOLOGY
OOZILY
OPENLY
ORALLY
ORANGY
ORKNEY
ORNERY
ORRERY
OSPREY
OSSIFY
OUTCRY
OUTFLY
OUTLAY
OVALLY
OVERLY

•OY•••
BOYARS
BOYISH
COYEST
COYISH
COYOTE
COYPUS
DOYENS
FOYERS
HOYDEN
JOYFUL
JOYNER
JOYOUS
LOYOLA
MOYERS
ROYALE
ROYALS
TOYDOG
TOYING
TOYONS
TOYOTA
VOYAGE
YOYOED
YOYOMA
ZOYSIA

•O•Y••
BOWYER
CORYZA
NOTYET
OOCYTE
POLYPS
PONYUP

•O••Y•
BOGEYS
BOLEYN
COCCYX
CONEYS
COPAYS
COVEYS
DOGEYS
FOGEYS
FORAYS
HONEYS
MONEYS
MORAYS
MOSEYS
POBOYS
POKEYS
POLEYN
POPEYE
ROCKYV
TOKAYS

•O•••Y
BODILY
BOIGNY
BOLDLY
BOLSHY
BOMBAY
BOOTSY
BOSLEY
BOTANY
BOTCHY
BOTFLY
BOUNCY
BOUNTY
BOVARY
BOWERY
BOXBOY
CODIFY
COLDLY
COLONY
COMEBY
COMEDY
COMELY
COMITY
COMPLY
CONROY
CONVEY
CONVOY
CONWAY
COOLLY
COONEY
COPLEY
CORDAY
COSILY
COSTLY
COUNTY
COWBOY
COWLEY
COZILY
DOESBY
DOGDAY
DONKEY
DOOLEY
DORSEY
DOUBLY
DOUGHY
DOURLY
DOWERY
DOWNEY
DOZILY
FOLKSY
FONDLY
FOSSEY
FOULLY
FOXILY
GOAWAY
GOAWRY
GOEASY
GOESBY
GOGGLY
GONEBY
GOODBY
GOODLY
GOOGLY
GOOSEY
GORILY
HOCKEY
HOLILY
HOMELY
HOMILY
HOMINY
HOORAY
HORNEY
HORSEY
HOSTLY
HOUNDY
HOURLY
JOCKEY
JOHNNY
JOKILY
JOUNCY
KODALY
LOGILY
LONELY
LONGLY
LOONEY
LORDLY
LOUDLY
LOVELY
LOWBOY
LOWERY
LOWKEY
MOBLEY
MODIFY
MOIETY
MONDAY
MONKEY
MONODY
MOONEY
MOPERY
MORLEY
MORNAY
MORPHY
MOSTLY
MOTLEY
MOULDY
MOUNTY
MOUSEY
MOUTHY
NOBODY
NONARY
NORGAY
NORWAY
NOSILY
NOTARY
NOTCHY
NOTIFY
OOLOGY
OOZILY
POACHY
POETRY
POINTY
POKERY
POKILY
POLICY
POLITY
POMPEY
POORLY
POPFLY
PORTLY
POSHLY
POUCHY
ROBROY
RODNEY
ROMANY
ROMNEY
RONELY
ROONEY
ROSARY
ROSILY
ROSINY
ROTARY
ROUGHY
SOFTLY
SOLELY
SOMANY
SORELY
SOURLY
TOASTY
TOMBOY
TOOTHY
TOOTSY
TORCHY
TORREY
TOUCHY
TOUGHY
TOWERY
VOLLEY
VOTARY
VOWELY
WOBBLY
WOLSEY
WOODSY
WOOLEY
WOOLLY
WORTHY

••OY••
BUOYED
BUOYUP
CLOYED
LLOYDS

••O•Y•
ANONYM
AZODYE
CHOOYU
CRONYN
EPONYM
INOUYE
ZLOTYS

••O••Y
BLOCKY
BLOODY
BLOOEY
BLOOMY
BLOTTY
BLOWSY
BLOWZY
BOOTSY
BROLLY
BRONZY
BROODY
BROOKY
BROOMY
BROWNY
CHOOSY
CHOPPY
CLODDY
CLOGGY
CLOTTY
CLOUDY
COOLLY
COONEY
CROAKY
CROSBY
CROUPY
DOOLEY
DROLLY
DROOLY
DROOPY
DROPBY
DROWSY
FLOATY
FLOCKY
FLOOEY
FLOPPY
FLOPSY
FLOSSY
FLOURY
FROGGY
FROSTY
FROTHY
FROWZY
GEORGY
GLOOMY
GLOPPY
GLOSSY
GOODBY
GOODLY
GOOGLY
GOOSEY
GROGGY
GROOVY
GROSZY
GROTTY
GROUTY
GROWLY
GROZNY
HOORAY
KNOBBY
KNOLLY
KNOTTY
LIONLY
LOONEY
MOONEY
MYOHMY
PHONEY
PHOOEY
PLOTTY

POORLY
PROSKY
ROONEY
SCOTTY
SHOALY
SHODDY
SHORTY
SLOBBY
SLOPPY
SLOSHY
SLOWLY
SMOGGY
SMOKEY
SNOBBY
SNOOKY
SNOOPY
SNOOTY
SNOOZY
SNOTTY
SPONGY
SPOOKY
SPOONY
SPORTY
SPOTTY
STOCKY
STODGY
STOOLY
STOREY
STORMY
THORNY
TOOTHY
TOOTSY
TROPHY
TWOPLY
TWOWAY
UNOILY
WHOLLY
WOODSY
WOOLEY
WOOLLY

•••OY•
AJFOYT
ALLOYS
ANNOYS
ARROYO
CHOOYU
DECOYS
ENJOYS
ENVOYS
LATOYA
NAGOYA
POBOYS
SEPOYS

•••O•Y
ANTONY
ARGOSY
ARMORY
BARONY
BETONY
BLOODY
BLOOEY
BLOOMY
BROODY
BROOKY
BROOMY
BRYONY
CANOPY
CHOOSY
CHROMY
COLONY
DIPODY
DROOLY
DROOPY
EMBODY
EULOGY
FELONY
FLOOEY
GLOOMY
GROOVY
IDIOCY
JALOPY
KIDORY
LEMONY
MALORY
MELODY
MEMORY
MONODY
NOBODY
ONIONY
OOLOGY
PARODY
PHOOEY
PRIORY
RECOPY
SAVORY
SAXONY
SIMONY
SNOOKY
SNOOPY
SNOOTY
SNOOZY
SPOOKY
SPOONY
STOOLY
THEORY
UNHOLY
VAPORY
WICOPY

••••OY
BADBOY
BATBOY
BIGBOY
BOXBOY
BUSBOY
CARBOY
CONROY
CONVOY
COWBOY
DAYBOY
DELROY
DEPLOY
EMPLOY
FLYBOY
KILROY
LAZBOY
LOWBOY
OLDBOY
QUEMOY
ROBROY
STEFOY
TEAPOY
THETOY
TOMBOY

OZ••••
OZARKS
OZONIC

O•Z•••
OOZIER
OOZILY
OOZING
OUZELS

O••Z••
OROZCO

•OZ•••
COZENS
COZIED
COZIER
COZIES
COZILY
DOZENS
DOZERS
DOZIER
DOZILY
DOZING
FOZZIE
MOZART
NOZZLE
OOZIER
OOZILY
OOZING
ROZZER

•O•Z••
BONZES
BORZOI
DOOZIE
FOOZLE
FOZZIE
NOZZLE
ROZZER

•O••Z•
CORYZA
IODIZE
IONIZE

•O•••Z
BOULEZ
CORTEZ
DOLENZ
DONITZ
HORMUZ
KOONTZ
LORENZ
MONTEZ
MORITZ

••OZ••
CROZES
DOOZIE
FOOZLE
FROZEN
GLOZED
GLOZES
GROZNY
OROZCO
PROZAC

••O•Z•
ALONZO
BLOWZY
BRONZE
BRONZY
FROWZY
GROSZY
LAOTZU
SFORZA
SNOOZE
SNOOZY

••O••Z
AMOSOZ
KOONTZ
TROPEZ

•••OZ•
REBOZO
SNOOZE
SNOOZY

•••O•Z
MILOSZ

••••OZ
AMOSOZ
SCHNOZ

PA••••
PAANGA
PABLUM
PACERS
PACIFY
PACING
PACINO
PACKED
PACKER
PACKET
PACKUP
PACMAN
PADANG
PADDED
PADDER
PADDLE
PADRES
PADUAN
PAEANS
PAELLA
PAEONS
PAGANS
PAGERS
PAGING
PAGODA
PAHANG
PAHARI
PAIDIN
PAIDUP
PAILOU
PAINED
PAINTS
PAINTY
PAIRED
PAIRUP
PAISAS
PAIUTE
PAJAMA
PAKULA
PALACE
PALAEO
PALATE
PALEAE
PALELY
PALEST
PALIER
PALING
PALISH
PALLAS
PALLED
PALLET
PALLIA
PALLID
PALLOR
PALMAS
PALMED
PALMER
PALOMA
PALPUS
PALTER
PALTRY
PAMELA
PAMIRS
PAMPAS
PAMPER
PANADA
PANAMA
PANCHO
PANDAS
PANDER
PANDIT
PANELS
PANFRY
PANFUL
PANICS
PANNED
PANNER
PANNES
PANOUT
PANTED
PANTOS
PANTRY
PANZER
PAPACY
PAPAGO
PAPAIN
PAPAWS
PAPAYA
PAPERS
PAPERY
PAPIER
PAPPAS
PAPPUS
PAPUAN
PAPYRI
PAQUIN
PARADE
PARANA
PARANG
PARAPH
PARCAE
PARCEL
PARDON
PARENS
PARENT
PARERS
PARETO
PAREVE
PARGET
PARIAH
PARING
PARISH
PARITY
PARKAS
PARKAY
PARKED
PARKER
PARLAY
PARLEY
PARLOR
PARNIS
PARODY
PAROLE
PARRED
PARREL
PARRIS
PARROT
PARSEC
PARSED
PARSEE
PARSER
PARSES
PARSON
PARTED
PARTLY
PARTON
PARULA
PARURE
PARVIS
PASCAL
PASEOS
PASHAS
PASHTO
PASSBY
PASSED
PASSEL
PASSER
PASSES
PASSIM
PASSON
PASSUP
PASTAS
PASTED
PASTEL
PASTES
PASTIS
PASTOR
PASTRY
PATACA
PATCHY
PATENS
PATENT
PATERS
PATHAN
PATHOL
PATHOS
PATINA
PATINE
PATIOS
PATMOS
PATOIS
PATROL
PATRON
PATTED
PATTEN
PATTER
PATTON
PAUCIS
PAULEY
PAUNCH
PAUPER
PAUSED
PAUSES
PAVANE
PAVERS
PAVING
PAVLOV
PAWERS
PAWING
PAWNED
PAWNEE
PAWNER
PAWPAW
PAWSAT
PAXTON
PAYBOX
PAYDAY
PAYEES
PAYERS
PAYFOR
PAYING
PAYOFF
PAYOLA
PAYOUT
PAYSIN
PAYSON
PAYSUP

P•A•••
PAANGA
PEACHY
PEAHEN
PEAKED
PEALED
PEANUT
PEAPOD
PEARLS
PEARLY
PEAVEY
PHAGES
PHAROS
PHASED
PHASER
PHASES
PHATIC
PIAFFE
PIAGET
PIANOS
PIAZZA
PLACED
PLACER
PLACES
PLACET
PLACID
PLAGAL
PLAGES
PLAGIO
PLAGUE
PLAICE
PLAIDS
PLAINS
PLAINT
PLAITS
PLANAR
PLANCK
PLANED
PLANER
PLANES
PLANET
PLANKS
PLANON
PLANTE
PLANTS
PLAQUE
PLASHY
PLASMA
PLASMO
PLASTY
PLATED
PLATEN
PLATER
PLATES
PLATTE
PLAYAS
PLAYAT
PLAYED
PLAYER
PLAYON
PLAYUP
PLAZAS
POACHY
PRAGUE
PRAISE
PRAJNA
PRANCE
PRANGS
PRANKS
PRASES
PRATED
PRATER
PRATES
PRAVDA
PRAWNS
PRAXES
PRAXIS
PRAYED
PRAYER
PSALMS

P••A••
PADANG
PAEANS
PAGANS
PAHANG
PAHARI
PAJAMA
PALACE
PALAEO
PALATE
PANADA
PANAMA
PAPACY
PAPAGO
PAPAIN
PAPAWS
PAPAYA
PARADE
PARANA
PARANG
PARAPH
PATACA
PAVANE
PECANS
PEDALS
PEDANT
PEDATE
PELAGE
PENANG
PESACH
PESAWA
PETAIN
PETALS
PETARD
PHIALS
PHRASE
PICABO
PICARA
PICARD
PICARO
PIKAKE
PILAFS
PILATE
PINATA
PIPALS
PIRACY
PIRANA
PIRATE
PISANO
PISANS
PIZAZZ
PLEACH
PLEADS
PLEASE
PLEATS
PLIANT
POLAND
POMACE
POMADE
POPART
POSADA
POTAGE
POTASH
POTATO
PREACH
PREAMP
PROAMS
PTRAPS
PURACE
PYJAMA

P•••A•
PACMAN
PADUAN
PAISAS
PALEAE
PALLAS
PALMAS
PAMPAS
PANDAS
PAPPAS
PAPUAN
PARCAE
PARIAH
PARKAS
PARKAY
PARLAY
PASCAL
PASHAS
PASTAS
PATHAN
PAWPAW
PAWSAT
PAYDAY
PECKAT
PEDLAR
PEDWAY
PEEKAT
PEERAT
PENMAN
PENNAE
PENPAL
PENTAD
PHILAE
PHYLAE
PICKAT
PICKAX
PIEMAN

PIEPAN
PIETAS
PILLAR
PINDAR
PINEAL
PINNAE
PINNAS
PINOAK
PISGAH
PITMAN
PITSAW
PIZZAS
PLAGAL
PLANAR
PLAYAS
PLAYAT
PLAZAS
PLEIAD
PLEXAL
PLICAE
PLURAL
POKEAT
POLEAX
POLKAS
POPLAR
POPPAS
PORTAL
POSTAL
PREFAB
PRELAW
PREPAY
PRETAX
PREWAR
PRIMAL
PROTAX
PROZAC
PSYWAR
PTBOAT
PULSAR
PUNJAB
PUNKAH
PURDAH
PUTNAM

P••••A
PAANGA
PAELLA
PAGODA
PAJAMA
PAKULA
PALLIA
PALOMA
PAMELA
PANADA
PANAMA
PAPAYA
PARANA
PARULA
PATACA
PATINA
PAYOLA
PELOTA
PENNIA
PEORIA
PEPITA
PERCHA
PERSIA
PERUGA
PESAWA
PESETA
PETULA
PHOBIA
PIAZZA
PICARA
PINATA
PIRANA
PLASMA
PLEURA
PNEUMA
POMONA
PORTIA
POSADA
PRAJNA
PRAVDA
PSYLLA
PUEBLA
PURINA
PYJAMA
PYTHIA

•PA•••
APACHE
APATHY
EPARCH
OPAQUE
SPACED
SPACEK
SPACER
SPACES
SPACEY
SPADED
SPADER
SPADES
SPADIX
SPAHIS
SPALLS
SPANKS
SPANKY
SPARED
SPARER
SPARES
SPARGE
SPARKS
SPARKY
SPARSE
SPARTA
SPASMS
SPATES
SPATHE
SPAVIN
SPAWNS
SPAYED
UPASES

•P•A••
APIARY
APPALL
APPALS
EPHAHS
OPIATE
SPEAKS
SPEARS
SPLASH
SPLATS
SPLAYS
SPRAGS
SPRAIN
SPRANG
SPRATS
SPRAWL
SPRAYS
UPCAST
UPDATE
UPLAND
UPTAKE
UPTALK
UPWARD

•P••A•
APEMAN
APICAL
APODAL
APPEAL
APPEAR
APPIAN
EPICAL
EPINAL
IPECAC
OPERAS
SPICAS
SPINAL
SPIRAL
SPIVAK
SPREAD
UPBEAT
UPLOAD
UPROAR

•P•••A
APULIA
OPTIMA
SPARTA
SPIREA

••PA••
ALPACA
APPALL
APPALS
AUPAIR
BYPASS
BYPAST
BYPATH
COPAYS
DEPART
DEPAUL
DEPAUW
DOPANT
ELPASO
ESPANA
EXPAND
IMPACT
IMPAIR
IMPALA
IMPALE
IMPART
INPART
JAPANS
LIPASE
NEPALI
PAPACY
PAPAGO
PAPAIN
PAPAWS
PAPAYA
PIPALS
POPART
REPADS
REPAID
REPAIR
REPAND
REPAST
REPAVE
REPAYS
RUPAUL
SEPALS
STPAUL
TEPALS
UNPACK
UNPAID
ZAPATA

••P•A•
ALPHAS
APPEAL
APPEAR
APPIAN
BYPLAY
CAPIAS
CAPTAN
CUPPAS
ESPIAL
HEPCAT
HEPTAD
INPLAY
KAPLAN
KAPPAS
KEPTAT
LAPHAM
NIPSAT
ORPHAN
PAPPAS
PAPUAN
POPLAR
POPPAS
REPEAL
REPEAT
REPLAN
REPLAY
RIPRAP
RIPSAW
RUPIAH
SEPIAS
SEPTAL
TAPPAN
TOPCAT
TOPHAT
TUPIAN

••P••A
ALPACA
ASPERA
CAPITA
COPULA
CUPOLA
ESPANA
ESPOSA
EUPNEA
IMPALA
LAPUTA
PAPAYA
PEPITA
SOPHIA
TEPHRA
TOPEKA
ZAPATA

•••PA•
BHOPAL
CALPAC
CARPAL
CASPAR
COMPAQ
CUPPAS
DEEPAK
FRYPAN
GALPAL
GASPAR
INSPAN
JUMPAT
KAPPAS
KEEPAT
KEYPAD
MILPAS
NETPAY
OILPAN
OOMPAH
PAMPAS
PAPPAS
PAWPAW
PENPAL
PIEPAN
POPPAS
PREPAY
SAIPAN
SAMPAN
SNAPAT
STUPAS
SUBPAR
TAIPAN
TAPPAN
TARPAN
TINPAN
TREPAN
ZILPAH

•••P•A
CHOPRA
COWPEA
GRAPPA
HOOPLA
MYOPIA
UTOPIA

••••PA
EUROPA
GRAMPA
GRAPPA
JALAPA
SHERPA

P•B•••
PABLUM
PEBBLE
PEBBLY
POBOYS
PTBOAT
PUBLIC

P••B••
PAYBOX
PEBBLE
PEBBLY
PHOBIA
PHOBIC
PHOBOS
PLEBES
PROBED
PROBER
PROBES
PUEBLA
PUEBLO

P•••B•
PASSBY
PHILBY
PHLEBO
PHOEBE
PICABO
PLUMBS
PUTSBY

P••••B
PREFAB
PUNJAB

•PB•••
UPBEAT
UPBOWS

•P••B•
EPHEBE

•P•••B
APLOMB

••P••B
SUPERB
TOPJOB

•••PB•
DROPBY

P•C•••
PACERS
PACIFY
PACING
PACINO
PACKED
PACKER
PACKET
PACKUP
PACMAN
PECANS
PECKAT
PECKED
PECTIC
PECTIN
PICABO
PICARA
PICARD
PICARO
PICCHU
PICKAT
PICKAX
PICKED
PICKER
PICKET
PICKLE
PICKON
PICKUP
PICNIC
PICOTS
PICULS
POCKET
POCONO
PUCKER

P••C••
PANCHO
PARCAE
PARCEL
PASCAL
PATCHY
PAUCIS
PEACHY
PENCEL
PENCIL
PERCHA
PESCOW
PHOCIS
PICCHU
PIECED
PIECER
PIECES
PINCER
PISCES
PITCHY
PLACED
PLACER
PLACES
PLACET
PLACID
PLICAE
PLUCKS
PLUCKY
POACHY
PONCES
PONCHO
POUCHY
PRECIS
PRICED
PRICER
PRICES
PRICEY
PRICKS
PROCNE
PSYCHE
PSYCHO
PSYCHS
PUNCHY

P•••C•
PALACE
PANICS
PAPACY
PATACA
PAUNCH
PEERCE
PESACH
PIERCE
PIRACY
PLAICE
PLANCK
PLEACH
POLICE
POLICY
POMACE
POUNCE
PRANCE
PREACH
PRINCE
PUMICE
PURACE
PUTSCH

P••••C
PARSEC
PECTIC
PELVIC
PEPTIC
PHATIC
PHOBIC
PHONIC
PHOTIC
PICNIC
POETIC
PONTIC
PROZAC
PUBLIC
PYKNIC

•PC•••
UPCAST

•P•C••
APACHE
APICAL
APICES
EPICAL
EPOCHS
IPECAC
SPACED
SPACEK
SPACER
SPACES
SPACEY
SPECIE
SPECKS
SPICAS
SPICED
SPICES

•P••C•
APERCU
APIECE
EPARCH
OPTICS
SPEECH
SPLICE
SPRUCE
UPTICK

•P•••C
IPECAC

••PC••
HEPCAT
TOPCAT

••P•C•
ALPACA
ASPECT
ASPICS
DEPICT
EXPECT
IMPACT
KOPECK
PAPACY
TOPICS
UNPACK

••P••C
COPTIC
CUPRIC
ORPHIC
PEPTIC
SEPTIC
ZIPLOC

•••P•C
CALPAC
MYOPIC
ONSPEC
TROPIC

P•D•••
PADANG
PADDED
PADDER
PADDLE
PADRES
PADUAN
PEDALS
PEDANT
PEDATE
PEDDLE
PEDLAR
PEDWAY
PIDGIN
PODDED
PODIUM
PODUNK
PUDDLE
PUDDLY

P••D••
PADDED
PADDER
PADDLE
PAIDIN
PAIDUP
PANDAS
PANDER
PANDIT
PARDON
PAYDAY
PEDDLE
PEEDEE
PENDED
PERDUE
PHEDRE
PINDAR
PINDUS
PLEDGE
PODDED
POLDER
PONDER
POODLE
POWDER
PRIDED
PRIDES
PRUDES
PUDDLE
PUDDLY
PUNDIT
PURDAH
PURDUE
PYEDOG

P•••D•
PAGODA
PANADA
PARADE
PARODY
PLAIDS
PLEADS
POMADE
POSADA
POUNDS
PRAVDA

PSEUDO
PSEUDS

P••••D

PACKED
PADDED
PAINED
PAIRED
PALLED
PALLID
PALMED
PANNED
PANTED
PARKED
PARRED
PARSED
PARTED
PASSED
PASTED
PATTED
PAUSED
PAWNED
PEAKED
PEALED
PEAPOD
PECKED
PEEKED
PEELED
PEENED
PEEPED
PEERED
PEEVED
PEGGED
PELTED
PENDED
PENNED
PENROD
PENTAD
PEPPED
PEQUOD
PERIOD
PERKED
PERMED
PERNOD
PETARD
PETTED
PHASED
PHONED
PHYSED
PICARD
PICKED
PIECED
PIGGED
PILLED
PINGED
PINKED
PINNED
PIPPED
PIQUED
PITHED
PITIED
PITTED
PLACED
PLACID
PLANED
PLATED
PLAYED
PLEIAD
PLOWED
PLUMED
PODDED
POISED
POLAND
POLLED
PONGED
PONGID
PONIED
POOHED
POOLED
POOPED
POPPED
PORTED
POSTED
POTTED
POURED
POUTED
PRATED
PRAYED
PREMED
PREYED
PRICED
PRIDED
PRIMED
PRIZED
PROBED
PROSED
PROVED
PRUNED
PUFFED
PUGGED
PULLED
PULPED
PULSED
PUMPED
PUNNED
PUNTED
PUREED
PURGED
PURLED
PURRED
PURSED
PUSHED
PUTRID
PUTTED

•PD•••

UPDATE
UPDIKE

•P•D••

APODAL
EPODES
SPADED
SPADER
SPADES
SPADIX
SPEDUP
SPIDER

•P••D•

APHIDS
EPHODS
SPEEDO
SPEEDS
SPEEDY
SPENDS
UPENDS
UPSIDE

•P•••D

APPEND
OPENED
OPINED
SPACED
SPADED
SPARED
SPAYED
SPEWED
SPICED
SPIKED
SPINED
SPIRED
SPITED
SPOKED
SPREAD
SPUMED
UPHELD
UPHOLD
UPLAND
UPLOAD
UPWARD
UPWIND

••PD••

LAPDOG
TOPDOG

••P•D•

BIPEDS
BIPODS
CUPIDS
DIPODY
IMPEDE
LIPIDE
LIPIDS
MOPEDS
RAPIDS
REPADS

••P••D

AMPHID
APPEND
BOPPED
CAPPED
CAPSID
COPIED
COPPED
CUPPED
DAPPED
DEPEND
DIPPED
ESPIED
EXPAND
EXPEND
GAPPED
GIPPED
GYPPED
HAPPED
HEPTAD
HIPPED
HOPPED
HYPOED
IMPEND
LAPPED
LAPSED
LIPOID
LIPPED
LOPPED
MAPPED
MOPPED
NAPPED
NIPPED
PEPPED
PIPPED
POPPED
RAPPED
REPAID
REPAND
RIPPED
SAPPED
SIPPED
SOPPED
SUPPED
TAPPED
TIPPED
TOPPED
UNPAID
YAPPED
YIPPED
ZAPPED
ZIPPED

•••P•D

BEEPED
BOPPED
BUMPED
BURPED
CAMPED
CAPPED
CARPED
CLEPED
COOPED
COPPED
CUPPED
CUSPED
CUSPID
DAMPED
DAPPED
DIPPED
DRAPED
DUMPED
ELAPID
ELOPED
GAPPED
GASPED
GAWPED
GIPPED
GRIPED
GROPED
GULPED
GYPPED
HAPPED
HARPED
HASPED
HEAPED
HELPED
HIPPED
HISPID
HOOPED
HOPPED
HUMPED
ISOPOD
JUMPED
KEYPAD
LAPPED
LEAPED
LIMPED
LIMPID
LIPPED
LISPED
LOOPED
LOPPED
LUMPED
MAPPED
MOPPED
MUMPED
NAPPED
NIPPED
PEAPOD
PEEPED
PEPPED
PIPPED
POOPED
POPPED
PULPED
PUMPED
RAMPED
RAPPED
RASPED
REAPED
RIPPED
ROMPED
RSVPED
SAPPED
SCAPED
SCOPED
SEEPED
SHAPED
SIPPED
SLOPED
SNIPED
SOAPED
SOPPED
STUPID
SUPPED
SWIPED
TAMPED
TAPPED
TEMPED
TIPPED
TOPPED
TORPID
TREPID
TRIPOD
UNIPOD
VAMPED
VESPID
WARPED
WISPED
YAPPED
YAWPED
YELPED
YIPPED
ZAPPED
ZIPPED

PE••••

PEACHY
PEAHEN
PEAKED
PEALED
PEANUT
PEAPOD
PEARLS
PEARLY
PEAVEY
PEBBLE
PEBBLY
PECANS
PECKAT
PECKED
PECTIC
PECTIN
PEDALS
PEDANT
PEDATE
PEDDLE
PEDLAR
PEDWAY
PEEDEE
PEEKAT
PEEKED
PEELED
PEELER
PEENED
PEEPED
PEEPER
PEERAT
PEERCE
PEERED
PEERIN
PEEVED
PEEVES
PEEWEE
PEGGED
PEGLER
PEGTOP
PEKING
PEKINS
PEKOES
PELAGE
PELEUS
PELIKE
PELION
PELLET
PELMET
PELOPS
PELOTA
PELTED
PELTER
PELTRY
PELVIC
PELVIS
PENANG
PENCEL
PENCIL
PENDED
PENGHU
PENMAN
PENMEN
PENNAE
PENNED
PENNER
PENNEY
PENNIA
PENNIS
PENNON
PENPAL
PENROD
PENSEE
PENTAD
PENTUP
PENULT
PENURY
PEOPLE
PEORIA
PEPFUL
PEPINO
PEPITA
PEPLOS
PEPLUM
PEPPED
PEPPER
PEPSIN
PEPSUP
PEPTIC
PEQUOD
PEQUOT
PERCHA
PERDUE
PERILS
PERIOD
PERISH
PERKED
PERKUP
PERMED
PERMIT
PERNIO
PERNOD
PERROT
PERSIA
PERSON
PERTER
PERTLY
PERUGA
PERUKE
PERUSE
PESACH
PESAWA
PESCOW
PESETA
PESTER
PESTLE
PESTOS
PETAIN
PETALS
PETARD
PETERS
PETITE
PETREL
PETRIE
PETROG
PETROL
PETTED
PETTER
PETTIT
PETULA
PEWEES
PEWITS
PEWTER
PEYOTE
PEYTON

P•E•••

PAEANS
PAELLA
PAEONS
PEEDEE
PEEKAT
PEEKED
PEELED
PEELER
PEENED
PEEPED
PEEPER
PEERAT
PEERCE
PEERED
PEERIN
PEEVED
PEEVES
PEEWEE
PHEDRE
PHENOL
PHENOM
PHENYL
PIECED
PIECER
PIECES
PIEMAN
PIEMEN
PIEPAN
PIERCE
PIERRE
PIETAS
PIETER
PIETIN
PIETRO
PLEACH
PLEADS
PLEASE
PLEATS
PLEBES
PLEDGE
PLEIAD
PLENTY
PLENUM
PLEURA
PLEXAL
PLEXOR
PLEXUS
PNEUMA
POETIC
POETRY
PREACH
PREAMP
PRECIS
PREENS
PREFAB
PREFER
PREFIX
PRELAW
PRELIM
PREMED
PREMIE
PRENUP
PREPAY
PREPPY
PRESET
PRESTO
PRETAX
PRETER
PRETTY
PREVIN
PREWAR
PREYED
PREYON
PSEUDO
PSEUDS
PUEBLA
PUEBLO
PUENTE
PUERTO
PYEDOG

P••E••

PACERS
PAGERS
PALEAE
PALELY
PALEST
PAMELA
PANELS
PAPERS
PAPERY
PARENS
PARENT
PARERS
PARETO
PAREVE
PASEOS
PATENS
PATENT
PATERS
PAVERS
PAWERS
PAYEES
PAYERS
PELEUS
PESETA
PETERS
PEWEES
PHLEBO
PHLEGM
PHOEBE
PIGEON
PIKERS
PILEIN
PILEON
PILEUM
PILEUP
PILEUS
PINEAL
PINERO
PINERY
PIPERS
PIPEUP
PIXELS
PLIERS
POKEAT
POKERS
POKERY
POKEYS
POLEAX
POLERS
POLEYN
POMELO
POPEYE
POSERS
POSEUR
POTEEN
POTENT
POWELL
POWERS
PREENS
PRIERS
PRIEST
PROEMS
PUREED
PUREES
PURELY
PUREST

P•••E•

PACKED
PACKER
PACKET
PADDED
PADDER
PADRES

PAINED
PAIRED
PALAEO
PALIER
PALLED
PALLET
PALMED
PALMER
PALTER
PAMPER
PANDER
PANNED
PANNER
PANNES
PANTED
PANZER
PAPIER
PARCEL
PARGET
PARKED
PARKER
PARLEY
PARRED
PARREL
PARSEC
PARSED
PARSEE
PARSER
PARSES
PARTED
PASSED
PASSEL
PASSER
PASSES
PASTED
PASTEL
PASTES
PATTED
PATTEN
PATTER
PAULEY
PAUPER
PAUSED
PAUSES
PAWNED
PAWNEE
PAWNER
PAYEES
PEAHEN
PEAKED
PEALED
PEAVEY
PECKED
PEEDEE
PEEKED
PEELED
PEELER
PEENED
PEEPED
PEEPER
PEERED
PEEVED
PEEVES
PEEWEE
PEGGED
PEGLER
PEKOES
PELLET
PELMET
PELTED
PELTER
PENCEL
PENDED
PENMEN
PENNED
PENNER
PENNEY
PENSEE
PEPPED
PEPPER
PERKED
PERMED
PERTER
PESTER
PETREL
PETTED
PETTER
PEWEES
PEWTER
PFIZER
PHAGES
PHASED
PHASER
PHASES
PHLOEM
PHONED
PHONES
PHONEY
PHOOEY
PHYSED
PIAGET
PICKED
PICKER
PICKET
PIECED
PIECER
PIECES
PIEMEN
PIETER
PIGGED
PIGLET
PIGPEN
PILFER
PILLED
PINCER
PINGED
PINIER
PINKED
PINKEN
PINKER
PINNED
PINNER
PINTER
PIOLET
PIPIER
PIPPED
PIQUED
PIQUES
PIQUET
PISCES
PISTES
PITHED
PITIED
PITIER
PITIES
PITMEN
PITTED
PITTER
PIXIES
PLACED
PLACER
PLACES
PLACET
PLAGES
PLANED
PLANER
PLANES
PLANET
PLATED
PLATEN
PLATER
PLATES
PLAYED
PLAYER
PLEBES
PLOVER
PLOWED
PLOWER
PLUMED
PLUMES
PLUSES
POCKET
PODDED
POGIES
POISED
POISES
POKIER
POLDER
POLLED
POLLEN
POLLER
POLLEX
POMMEE
POMMEL
POMPEY
PONCES
PONDER
PONGED
PONGEE
PONIED
PONIES
PONTES
POOHED
POOLED
POOPED
POORER
POPPED
POPPER
POPPET
PORKER
PORTED
PORTER
POSHER
POSIES
POSSES
POSSET
POSTED
POSTER
POTEEN
POTHER
POTTED
POTTER
POURED
POURER
POUTED
POUTER
POWDER
PRASES
PRATED
PRATER
PRATES
PRAXES
PRAYED
PRAYER
PREFER
PREMED
PRESET
PRETER
PREYED
PRICED
PRICER
PRICES
PRICEY
PRIDED
PRIDES
PRIMED
PRIMER
PRIMES
PRIPET
PRIVET
PRIZED
PRIZES
PROBED
PROBER
PROBES
PROLES
PROPEL
PROPER
PROSED
PROSER
PROSES
PROTEI
PROTEM
PROVED
PROVEN
PROVER
PROVES
PRUDES
PRUNED
PRUNER
PRUNES
PUCKER
PUFFED
PUFFER
PUGGED
PUGREE
PULLED
PULLET
PULLEY
PULPED
PULSED
PULSES
PUMMEL
PUMPED
PUMPER
PUNIER
PUNKER
PUNNED
PUNNET
PUNTED
PUNTER
PUPPET
PUREED
PUREES
PURGED
PURGES
PURLED
PURRED
PURRER
PURSED
PURSER
PURSES
PURVEY
PUSHED
PUSHES
PUSSES
PUTTED
PUTTEE
PUTTER
PYXIES

P••••E

PADDLE
PAIUTE
PALACE
PALATE
PALEAE
PARADE
PARCAE
PAREVE
PAROLE
PARSEE
PARURE
PATINE
PAVANE
PAWNEE
PEBBLE
PEDATE
PEDDLE
PEEDEE
PEERCE
PEEWEE
PELAGE
PELIKE
PENNAE
PENSEE
PEOPLE
PERDUE
PERUKE
PERUSE
PESTLE
PETITE
PETRIE
PEYOTE
PHEDRE
PHILAE
PHOEBE
PHRASE
PHYLAE
PIAFFE
PICKLE
PIERCE
PIERRE
PIFFLE
PIGGIE
PIKAKE
PILATE
PILOSE
PINITE
PINKIE
PINNAE
PINOLE
PINTLE
PIRATE
PLAGUE
PLAICE
PLANTE
PLAQUE
PLATTE
PLEASE
PLEDGE
PLICAE
PLISSE
PLUNGE
POINTE
POLICE
POLITE
POMACE
POMADE
POMMEE
PONGEE
POODLE
POPEYE
POPPLE
POTAGE
POTPIE
POTTLE
POUNCE
POUSSE
PRAGUE
PRAISE
PRANCE
PREMIE
PRINCE
PROCNE
PROPRE
PROWSE
PRYNNE
PSYCHE
PUDDLE
PUENTE
PUGREE
PUISNE
PULQUE
PUMICE
PUNKIE
PURACE
PURDUE
PURFLE
PURINE
PURPLE
PURSUE
PUTTEE
PUZZLE
PYRITE

•PE•••

APEMAN
APEMEN
APERCU
APEXES
IPECAC
KPELLE
OPENED
OPENER
OPENLY
OPENTO
OPENUP
OPERAS
SPEAKS
SPEARS
SPECIE
SPECKS
SPEDUP
SPEECH
SPEEDO
SPEEDS
SPEEDY
SPELLS
SPENDS
SPERRY
SPEWED
UPENDS

•P•E••

APIECE
APPEAL
APPEAR
APPEND
APTEST
EPHEBE
SPEECH
SPEEDO
SPEEDS
SPEEDY
SPHERE
SPHERY
SPIELS
SPIERS
SPLEEN
SPREAD
SPREES
UPBEAT
UPHELD
UPKEEP
UPPERS
UPSETS
UPWELL

•P••E•

APEMEN
APEXES
APICES
APOGEE
APPLES
APPLET
EPODES
EPOPEE
OPENED
OPENER
OPINED
OPINER
OPINES
OPUSES
SPACED
SPACEK
SPACER
SPACES
SPACEY
SPADED
SPADER
SPADES
SPARED
SPARER
SPARES
SPATES
SPAYED
SPEWED
SPICED
SPICES
SPIDER
SPIKED
SPIKER
SPIKES
SPILES
SPINED
SPINEL
SPINES
SPINET
SPIREA
SPIRED
SPIRES
SPITED
SPITES
SPLEEN
SPOKED
SPOKEN
SPOKES
SPORES
SPREES
SPRIER
SPRUES
SPRYER
SPUMED
SPUMES
UPASES
UPKEEP

•P•••E

APACHE
APIECE
APLITE
APOGEE
APPOSE
EPHEBE
EPOPEE
KPELLE
OPAQUE
OPHITE
OPIATE
OPPOSE
SPARGE
SPARSE
SPATHE
SPECIE
SPHERE
SPLICE
SPLINE
SPONGE
SPOUSE
SPRITE
SPRUCE
SPURGE
UPDATE
UPDIKE
UPRISE
UPROSE
UPSIDE
UPTAKE
UPTIME

••PE••

ALPERT
AMPERE
APPEAL
APPEAR
APPEND
ARPENT
ASPECT
ASPENS
ASPERA
BIPEDS
BOPEEP
CAPERS
CUPELS
DEPEND
DUPERY
EMPERY
EXPECT
EXPELS
EXPEND
EXPERT
GAPERS
HOPERS
HYPEUP
IMPEDE
IMPELS
IMPEND
IMPERF
JAPERS
JAPERY
KOPECK
KOPEKS
LAPELS
LIPENG
LOPERS
MOPEDS
MOPERS
MOPERY
NAPERY
NOPETS
PAPERS
PAPERY
PIPERS
PIPEUP
POPEYE
REPEAL
REPEAT
REPEGS
REPELS
REPENT
RIPELY
RIPENS
RIPEST
ROPEIN
ROPERS
RUPEES
RUPERT
STPETE
SUPERB
SUPERS
TAPERS
TEPEES
TOPEKA
TOPERS
TUPELO
TYPERS
TYPEUP
UNPEGS
UNPENS
UPPERS
VIPERS
WIPERS
WIPEUP

••P•E•

AMPLER
APPLES
APPLET
BOPEEP
BOPPED
BOPPER
CAPLET
CAPPED
CAPPER
CIPHER
COPIED
COPIER
COPIES
COPLEY

COPPED
COPPER
COPSES
COPTER
CUPPED
CYPHER
DAPPED
DAPPER
DIPPED
DIPPER
DOPIER
DUPLEX
ESPIED
ESPIES
EUPNEA
GAPPED
GIPPED
GIPPER
GOPHER
GYPPED
GYPPER
HAPPED
HAPPEN
HEPPER
HIPPED
HIPPER
HOPPED
HOPPER
HYPHEN
HYPOED
KEPLER
KIPPER
KOPJES
KOPPEL
LAPPED
LAPPET
LAPSED
LAPSES
LAPTEV
LIPPED
LOPPED
LOPPER
MAPLES
MAPPED
MAPPER
MOPIER
MOPPED
MOPPER
MOPPET
MUPPET
NAPIER
NAPLES
NAPPED
NAPPER
NAPPES
NEPHEW
NIPPED
NIPPER
NIPSEY
OSPREY
PAPIER
PEPPED
PEPPER
PIPIER
PIPPED
POPPED
POPPER
POPPET
PUPPET
RAPIER
RAPPED
RAPPEE
RAPPEL
RAPPER
RIPKEN
RIPLEY
RIPPED
RIPPER
ROPIER
RUPEES
SAPPED
SAPPER
SEPTET
SIPPED
SIPPER
SIPPET
SOPPED
SUPPED
SUPPER
TAPPED
TAPPER
TAPPET
TEPEES
TIPPED
TIPPER
TIPPET
TOPPED
TOPPER
TOPTEN
TYPIER
WAPNER
YAPPED
YIPPED
YIPPEE
ZAPPED
ZAPPER
ZIPPED
ZIPPER

••P••E

ALPINE
AMPERE
AMPULE
APPOSE
ASPIRE
CAPONE
CAPOTE
DAPHNE
DAPPLE
DEPONE
DEPOSE
DEPUTE
DIPOLE
EMPIRE
EXPIRE
EXPOSE
FIPPLE
HIPPIE
HOPPLE
IMPALE
IMPEDE
IMPOSE
IMPURE
IMPUTE
LIPASE
LIPIDE
LUPINE
LUPONE
NAPPIE
OPPOSE
ORPINE
POPEYE
POPPLE
RAPINE
RAPPEE
REPAVE
REPINE
REPOSE
REPUTE
RIPPLE
SOPHIE
STPETE
SUPINE
SUPPLE
TIPPLE
TIPTOE
TOPPLE
UMPIRE
UNPILE
YIPPEE
YUPPIE

•••PE•

AUSPEX
BEEPED
BEEPER
BOPPED
BOPPER
BUMPED
BUMPER
BURPED
CAMPED
CAMPER
CAPPED
CAPPER
CARPED
CARPEL
CARPER
CARPET
CASPER
CHAPEL
CLEPED
COMPEL
COOPED
COOPER
COPPED
COPPER
COUPES
COWPEA
COWPER
CRAPES
CREPES
CRIPES
CUPPED
CUSPED
DAMPED
DAMPEN
DAMPER
DAPPED
DAPPER
DEEPEN
DEEPER
DIAPER
DIPPED
DIPPER
DISPEL
DRAPED
DRAPER
DRAPES
DRUPES
DUMPED
DUMPER
ELOPED
ELOPER
ELOPES
EPOPEE
ETAPES
GAPPED
GASPED
GASPER
GAWPED
GIPPED
GIPPER
GOSPEL
GRAPES
GRAPEY
GRIPED
GRIPER
GRIPES
GROPED
GROPES
GULPED
GULPER
GYPPED
GYPPER
HAMPER
HAPPED
HAPPEN
HARPED
HARPER
HASPED
HEAPED
HELPED
HELPER
HEPPER
HIPPED
HIPPER
HOOPED
HOOPER
HOPPED
HOPPER
HUMPED
INAPET
JASPER
JUMPED
JUMPER
KEEPER
KIPPER
KOPPEL
LAPPED
LAPPET
LAUPER
LEAPED
LEAPER
LIMPED
LIMPER
LIMPET
LIPPED
LISPED
LOOPED
LOOPER
LOPPED
LOPPER
LOUPES
LUMPED
LUMPEN
LUMPER
MAPPED
MAPPER
MOPPED
MOPPER
MOPPET
MUMPED
MUPPET
MYOPES
NAPPED
NAPPER
NAPPES
NIPPED
NIPPER
ONSPEC
PAMPER
PAUPER
PEEPED
PEEPER
PEPPED
PEPPER
PIGPEN
PIPPED
POMPEY
POOPED
POPPED
POPPER
POPPET
PRIPET
PROPEL
PROPER
PULPED
PUMPED
PUMPER
PUPPET
RAMPED
RAPPED
RAPPEE
RAPPEL
RAPPER
RASPED
RASPER
REAPED
REAPER
REOPEN
RIPPED
RIPPER
ROMPED
ROMPER
RSVPED
SAPPED
SAPPER
SCAPED
SCAPES
SCOPED
SCOPES
SEEPED
SEMPER
SHAPED
SHAPER
SHAPES
SIMPER
SIPPED
SIPPER
SIPPET
SLOPED
SLOPES
SLYPES
SNIPED
SNIPER
SNIPES
SNOPES
SOAPED
SOAPER
SOPPED
STAPES
STIPEL
STIPES
STOPES
STUPES
SUPPED
SUPPER
SWIPED
SWIPER
SWIPES
TAIPEI
TAMPED
TAMPER
TAPPED
TAPPER
TAPPET
TAUPES
TEMPED
TEMPEH
TEMPER
TIPPED
TIPPER
TIPPET
TOPPED
TOPPER
TOUPEE
TROPES
TROPEZ
UNOPEN
USOPEN
VAMPED
VAMPER
VESPER
WARPED
WEEPER
WISPED
WOLPER
YAPPED
YAWPED
YAWPER
YELPED
YELPER
YIPPED
YIPPEE
ZAPPED
ZAPPER
ZIPPED
ZIPPER

•••P•E

COUPLE
DAPPLE
DIEPPE
DIMPLE
ELAPSE
EPOPEE
FIPPLE
FRAPPE
GRIPPE
HIPPIE
HOOPLE
HOOPOE
HOPPLE
KELPIE
KEWPIE
MAGPIE
MARPLE
MUDPIE
NAPPIE
PEOPLE
POPPLE
POTPIE
PROPRE
PURPLE
RAPPEE
RIMPLE
RIPPLE
RUMPLE
SAMPLE
SEMPRE
SHOPPE
SIMPLE
SKOPJE
STAPLE
STEPPE
SUPPLE
TEMPLE
TIPPLE
TOPPLE
TOUPEE
TRIPLE
WEEPIE
WIMPLE
YIPPEE
YUPPIE

••••PE

ASLOPE
CANAPE
DIEPPE
ECTYPE
ESCAPE
EUROPE
FELIPE
FRAPPE
GRIPPE
GUIMPE
LENAPE
MEROPE
METOPE
ONTAPE
RECIPE
RETAPE
RETYPE
SCRAPE
SERAPE
SHOPPE
STEPPE
STRIPE
THORPE
TROMPE
TROUPE
UNRIPE

PF••••

PFIZER

P•F•••

PIFFLE
PUFFED
PUFFER
PUFFIN

P••F••

PANFRY
PANFUL
PAYFOR
PEPFUL
PIAFFE
PIFFLE
PILFER
POPFLY
POTFUL
PREFAB
PREFER
PREFIX
PROFIT
PUFFED
PUFFER
PUFFIN
PURFLE

P•••F•

PACIFY
PAYOFF
PIAFFE
PILAFS
POPOFF
PROOFS
PURIFY
PUTOFF

P••••F

PAYOFF
POPOFF
PUTOFF

•P•F••

OPTFOR
SPIFFS
SPIFFY

•P••F•

SPIFFS
SPIFFY
SPOOFS
UPLIFT

••PF••

CAPFUL
CUPFUL
LAPFUL
PEPFUL
POPFLY

••P•F•

HOPOFF
POPOFF
RIPOFF
TAPOFF
TIPOFF
TOPOFF
TYPIFY

••P••F

HOPOFF
IMPERF
POPOFF
RIPOFF
TAPOFF
TIPOFF
TOPOFF

•••P•F

STAPUF

P•G•••

PAGANS
PAGERS
PAGING
PAGODA
PEGGED
PEGLER
PEGTOP
PIGEON
PIGGED
PIGGIE
PIGLET
PIGNUT
PIGOUT
PIGPEN
PIGSTY
POGIES
PUGGED
PUGREE

P••G••

PARGET
PEGGED
PENGHU
PHAGES
PIAGET
PIDGIN
PIGGED
PIGGIE
PINGED
PISGAH
PLAGAL
PLAGES
PLAGIO
PLAGUE
PLIGHT
PLUGIN
PONGED
PONGEE
PONGID
POPGUN
PRAGUE
PUGGED
PURGED
PURGES

P•••G•

PAANGA
PAPAGO
PELAGE
PERUGA
PHLEGM
PLEDGE
PLOUGH
PLUNGE
POTAGE
PRANGS
PRONGS

P••••G

PACING
PADANG
PAGING
PAHANG
PALING
PARANG
PARING
PAVING
PAWING
PAYING
PEKING
PENANG

PETROG
PHOTOG
PIKING
PILING
PINING
PIPING
PLYING
POKING
POLING
PORING
POSING
PROLOG
PRYING
PULING
PYEDOG

•P•G••
APOGEE
SPIGOT

•P••G•
OPPUGN
SPARGE
SPONGE
SPONGY
SPRAGS
SPRIGS
SPURGE

•P•••G
EPILOG
EPPING
OPTING
SPRANG
SPRING
SPRUNG
SPYING
UPPING

••PG••
CAPGUN
POPGUN
TOPGUN

••P•G•
IMPUGN
OPPUGN
PAPAGO
REPEGS
REPUGN
UNPEGS

••P••G
COPING
DOPING
DUPING
EPPING
GAPING
HOPING
HYPING
IMPING
JAPING
LAPDOG
LIPENG
LOPING
MOPING
PIPING
ROPING
TAPING
TOPDOG
TYPING
UNPLUG
UPPING
WIPING

PH••••
PHAGES
PHAROS
PHASED
PHASER
PHASES
PHATIC
PHEDRE
PHENOL
PHENOM
PHENYL
PHIALS
PHILAE
PHILBY
PHILIP
PHILLY
PHILOL
PHILOS
PHLEBO
PHLEGM
PHLOEM
PHOBIA
PHOBIC
PHOBOS
PHOCIS
PHOEBE
PHONED
PHONES
PHONEY
PHONIC
PHONON
PHONOS
PHOOEY
PHOTIC
PHOTOG
PHOTON
PHOTOS
PHRASE
PHYLAE
PHYLLO
PHYLUM
PHYSED
PHYSIO

P•H•••
PAHANG
PAHARI

P••H••
PASHAS
PASHTO
PATHAN
PATHOL
PATHOS
PEAHEN
PITHED
POOHED
POSHER
POSHLY
POTHER
PUSHED
PUSHES
PUSHON
PUSHUP
PYTHIA
PYTHON

P•••H•
PANCHO
PATCHY
PEACHY
PENGHU
PERCHA
PICCHU
PITCHY
PLASHY
PLIGHT
PLUSHY
POACHY
PONCHO
POUCHY
PSYCHE
PSYCHO
PSYCHS
PUNCHY

P••••H
PALISH
PARAPH
PARIAH
PARISH
PAUNCH
PERISH
PESACH
PISGAH
PLEACH
PLINTH
PLOUGH
POLISH
POTASH
PREACH
PUNISH
PUNKAH
PURDAH
PUTSCH

•PH•••
APHIDS
EPHAHS
EPHEBE
EPHODS
EPHORI
EPHORS
EPHRON
OPHITE
SPHERE
SPHERY
SPHINX
UPHELD
UPHILL
UPHOLD

•P•H••
SPAHIS
UPSHOT

•P••H•
APACHE
APATHY
EPHAHS
EPOCHS
SPATHE
UPJOHN

•P•••H
EPARCH
SPEECH
SPILTH
SPLASH
SPLOSH
UPPISH
UPRUSH

••PH••
ALPHAS
AMPHID
CIPHER
CYPHER
DAPHNE
GOPHER
HIPHOP
HYPHEN
LAPHAM
NEPHEW
NEPHRO
ORPHAN
ORPHIC
SIPHON
SOPHIA
SOPHIE
SYPHON
TEPHRA
TOPHAT
TOPHUS
TYPHUS
ZEPHYR

••P•H•
DEPTHS
SAPPHO

••P••H
ASPISH
BYPATH
IMPISH
MOPISH
RUPIAH
UPPISH

•••PH•
ALEPHS
DELPHI
GLYPHS
GRAPHS
GRAPHY
HUMPHS
LYMPHS
MORPHO
MORPHS
MORPHY
MURPHY
NYMPHS
SAPPHO
SYLPHS
TROPHY

•••P•H
OOMPAH
TEMPEH
ZILPAH

••••PH
ADOLPH
CALIPH
CERIPH
GUELPH
JOSEPH
PARAPH
SERAPH
TERAPH

PI••••
PIAFFE
PIAGET
PIANOS
PIAZZA
PICABO
PICARA
PICARD
PICARO
PICCHU
PICKAT
PICKAX
PICKED
PICKER
PICKET
PICKLE
PICKON
PICKUP
PICNIC
PICOTS
PICULS
PIDGIN
PIECED
PIECER
PIECES
PIEMAN
PIEMEN
PIEPAN
PIERCE
PIERRE
PIETAS
PIETER
PIETIN
PIETRO
PIFFLE
PIGEON
PIGGED
PIGGIE
PIGLET
PIGNUT
PIGOUT
PIGPEN
PIGSTY
PIKAKE
PIKERS
PIKING
PILAFS
PILATE
PILEIN
PILEON
PILEUM
PILEUP
PILEUS
PILFER
PILING
PILLAR
PILLED
PILLOW
PILOSE
PILOTI
PILOTS
PIMINY
PINATA
PINCER
PINDAR
PINDUS
PINEAL
PINERO
PINERY
PINGED
PINIER
PINING
PINION
PINITE
PINKED
PINKEN
PINKER
PINKIE
PINNAE
PINNAS
PINNED
PINNER
PINOAK
PINOLE
PINONS
PINOTS
PINSON
PINTER
PINTLE
PINTOS
PINUPS
PINXIT
PINYIN
PINYON
PINZON
PIOLET
PIPALS
PIPERS
PIPEUP
PIPIER
PIPING
PIPITS
PIPKIN
PIPPED
PIPPIN
PIQUED
PIQUES
PIQUET
PIRACY
PIRANA
PIRATE
PIRRIP
PISANO
PISANS
PISCES
PISGAH
PISTES
PISTIL
PISTOL
PISTON
PITCHY
PITHED
PITIED
PITIER
PITIES
PITMAN
PITMEN
PITONS
PITSAW
PITTED
PITTER
PIVOTS
PIXELS
PIXIES
PIZAZZ
PIZZAS

P•I•••
PAIDIN
PAIDUP
PAILOU
PAINED
PAINTS
PAINTY
PAIRED
PAIRUP
PAISAS
PAIUTE
PFIZER
PHIALS
PHILAE
PHILBY
PHILIP
PHILLY
PHILOL
PHILOS
PLIANT
PLICAE
PLIERS
PLIGHT
PLINKS
PLINTH
PLISSE
POILUS
POINTE
POINTS
POINTY
POIROT
POISED
POISES
POISON
PRICED
PRICER
PRICES
PRICEY
PRICKS
PRIDED
PRIDES
PRIERS
PRIEST
PRIMAL
PRIMED
PRIMER
PRIMES
PRIMLY
PRIMOS
PRIMPS
PRIMUM
PRIMUS
PRINCE
PRINKS
PRINTS
PRIONS
PRIORI
PRIORS
PRIORY
PRIPET
PRISMS
PRISON
PRISSY
PRIVET
PRIZED
PRIZES
PUISNE

P••I••
PACIFY
PACING
PACINO
PAGING
PALIER
PALING
PALISH
PAMIRS
PANICS
PAPIER
PARIAH
PARING
PARISH
PARITY
PATINA
PATINE
PATIOS
PAVING
PAWING
PAYING
PEKING
PEKINS
PELIKE
PELION
PEPINO
PEPITA
PERILS
PERIOD
PERISH
PETITE
PEWITS
PIKING
PILING
PIMINY
PINIER
PINING
PINION
PINITE
PIPIER
PIPING
PIPITS
PITIED
PITIER
PITIES
PIXIES
PLAICE
PLAIDS
PLAINS
PLAINT
PLAITS
PLEIAD
PLYING
PODIUM
POGIES
POKIER
POKILY
POKING
POLICE
POLICY
POLING
POLISH
POLITE
POLITY
PONIED
PONIES
PORING
POSIES
POSING
POSITS
POTION
PRAISE
PRYING
PULING
PUMICE
PUNIER
PUNILY
PUNISH
PUPILS
PURIFY
PURINA
PURINE
PURISM
PURIST
PURITY
PYRITE
PYXIES

P•••I•
PAIDIN
PALLIA
PALLID
PANDIT
PAPAIN
PAQUIN
PARNIS
PARRIS
PARVIS
PASSIM
PASTIS
PATOIS
PAUCIS
PAYSIN
PECTIC
PECTIN
PEERIN
PELVIC
PELVIS
PENCIL
PENNIA
PENNIS
PEORIA
PEPSIN
PEPTIC
PERMIT
PERNIO
PERSIA
PETAIN
PETRIE
PETTIT
PHATIC
PHILIP
PHOBIA
PHOBIC
PHOCIS
PHONIC
PHOTIC
PHYSIO
PICNIC
PIDGIN
PIETIN
PIGGIE
PILEIN
PINKIE
PINXIT
PINYIN
PIPKIN
PIPPIN
PIRRIP

PISTIL
PLACID
PLAGIO
PLUGIN
POETIC
PONGID
PONTIC
POPLIN
POPSIN
PORTIA
POSTIT
POTPIE
POURIN
PRAXIS
PRECIS
PREFIX
PRELIM
PREMIE
PREVIN
PROFIT
PROLIX
PROSIT
PUBLIC
PUFFIN
PULLIN
PULPIT
PUNDIT
PUNKIE
PURLIN
PUTRID
PUTSIN
PYKNIC
PYTHIA

P••••I

PAHARI
PAPYRI
PILOTI
POLLOI
POPULI
POTOSI
PRIORI
PROTEI

•PI•••

APIARY
APICAL
APICES
APIECE
EPICAL
EPILOG
EPINAL
EPIRUS
OPIATE
OPINED
OPINER
OPINES
SPICAS
SPICED
SPICES
SPIDER
SPIELS
SPIERS
SPIFFS
SPIFFY
SPIGOT
SPIKED
SPIKER
SPIKES
SPILES
SPILLS
SPILTH
SPINAL
SPINED
SPINEL
SPINES
SPINET
SPINKS
SPINTO
SPIRAL
SPIREA
SPIRED
SPIRES
SPIRIT
SPIROS
SPITED
SPITES
SPIVAK
SPIVVY

•P•I••

APHIDS
APLITE
APPIAN
EPPING
OPHITE
OPTICS
OPTIMA
OPTING
OPTION
SPHINX
SPLICE
SPLINE
SPLINT
SPLITS
SPOILS
SPOILT
SPRIER
SPRIGS
SPRING
SPRINT
SPRITE
SPRITS
SPRITZ
SPYING
UPDIKE
UPHILL
UPLIFT
UPLINK
UPPING
UPPISH
UPPITY
UPRISE
UPSIDE
UPTICK
UPTIME
UPWIND

•P••I•

APULIA
SPADIX
SPAHIS
SPAVIN
SPECIE
SPIRIT
SPRAIN

•P•••I

EPHORI

••PI••

ALPINE
APPIAN
ASPICS
ASPIRE
ASPISH
CAPIAS
CAPITA
COPIED
COPIER
COPIES
COPING
CUPIDS
DEPICT
DOPIER
DOPING
DUPING
EMPIRE
EPPING
ESPIAL
ESPIED
ESPIES
EXPIRE
EXPIRY
GAPING
HOPING
HYPING
IMPING
IMPISH
JAPING
LAPINS
LIPIDE
LIPIDS
LOPING
LUPINE
LUPINO
MOPIER
MOPING
MOPISH
NAPIER
ORPINE
PAPIER
PEPINO
PEPITA
PIPIER
PIPING
PIPITS
PUPILS
RAPIDS
RAPIER
RAPINE
RAPINI
REPINE
REPINS
ROPIER
ROPING
RUPIAH
SEPIAS
SUPINE
TAPING
TAPINS
TAPIRS
TIPINS
TOPICS
TUPIAN
TYPIER
TYPIFY
TYPING
TYPIST
UMPIRE
UNPILE
UNPINS
UPPING
UPPISH
UPPITY
WAPITI
WIPING

••P•I•

AMPHID
AUPAIR
CAPRIS
CAPSID
COPTIC
CUPRIC
ESPRIT
HIPPIE
HOPSIN
IMPAIR
JOPLIN
LIPOID
NAPKIN
NAPPIE
ORPHIC
PAPAIN
PEPSIN
PEPTIC
PIPKIN
PIPPIN
POPLIN
POPSIN
REPAID
REPAIR
ROPEIN
SEPTIC
SOPHIA
SOPHIE
TIPSIN
UNPAID
YUPPIE

••P••I

NAPOLI
NEPALI
PAPYRI
POPULI
RAPINI
WAPITI

•••PI•

ARMPIT
CHAPIN
CHIPIN
CHOPIN
CUSPID
DROPIN
DROPIT
ELAPID
HATPIN
HIPPIE
HISPID
JUMPIN
KEEPIN
KELPIE
KEMPIS
KEWPIE
KUOPIO
LIMPID
MAGPIE
MUDPIE
MYOPIA
MYOPIC
NAPPIE
OKAPIS
PIPPIN
POTPIE
PULPIT
RESPIN
SCIPIO
SEEPIN
SKIPIT
SLIPIN
STEPIN
STOPIN
STOPIT
STUPID
TARPIT
TENPIN
TIEPIN
TORPID
TREPID
TROPIC
TURPIN
UTOPIA
VESPID
WEEPIE
YUPPIE

•••P•I

DELPHI
TAIPEI

••••PI

OCTOPI
SCAMPI
WHOOPI

P•J•••

PAJAMA
PYJAMA

P••J••

PRAJNA
PUNJAB

•PJ•••

UPJOHN

••PJ••

KOPJES
TOPJOB

•••PJ•

SKOPJE

P•K•••

PAKULA
PEKING
PEKINS
PEKOES
PIKAKE
PIKERS
PIKING
POKEAT
POKERS
POKERY
POKEYS
POKIER
POKILY
POKING
PYKNIC

P••K••

PACKED
PACKER
PACKET
PACKUP
PARKAS
PARKAY
PARKED
PARKER
PEAKED
PECKAT
PECKED
PEEKAT
PEEKED
PERKED
PERKUP
PICKAT
PICKAX
PICKED
PICKER
PICKET
PICKLE
PICKON
PICKUP
PINKED
PINKEN
PINKER
PINKIE
PIPKIN
POCKET
POLKAS
PORKER
PUCKER
PUNKAH
PUNKER
PUNKIE

P•••K•

PELIKE
PERUKE
PIKAKE
PLANKS
PLINKS
PLONKS
PLUCKS
PLUCKY
PLUNKS
PRANKS
PRICKS
PRINKS
PROSKY

P••••K

PINOAK
PLANCK
PODUNK

•PK•••

UPKEEP

•P•K••

SPIKED
SPIKER
SPIKES
SPOKED
SPOKEN
SPOKES

•P••K•

SPANKS
SPANKY
SPARKS
SPARKY
SPEAKS
SPECKS
SPINKS
SPOOKS
SPOOKY
SPUNKY
UPDIKE
UPTAKE

•P•••K

SPACEK
SPIVAK
UPLINK
UPTALK
UPTICK

••PK••

NAPKIN
PIPKIN
RIPKEN

••P•K•

KOPEKS
TOPEKA
YAPOKS

••P••K

KOPECK
UNPACK

•••P•K

DEEPAK
KUSPUK

PL••••

PLACED
PLACER
PLACES
PLACET
PLACID
PLAGAL
PLAGES
PLAGIO
PLAGUE
PLAICE
PLAIDS
PLAINS
PLAINT
PLAITS
PLANAR
PLANCK
PLANED
PLANER
PLANES
PLANET
PLANKS
PLANON
PLANTE
PLANTS
PLAQUE
PLASHY
PLASMA
PLASMO
PLASTY
PLATED
PLATEN
PLATER
PLATES
PLATTE
PLAYAS
PLAYAT
PLAYED
PLAYER
PLAYON
PLAYUP
PLAZAS
PLEACH
PLEADS
PLEASE
PLEATS
PLEBES
PLEDGE
PLEIAD
PLENTY
PLENUM
PLEURA
PLEXAL
PLEXOR
PLEXUS
PLIANT
PLICAE
PLIERS
PLIGHT
PLINKS
PLINTH
PLISSE
PLONKS
PLOTTY
PLOUGH
PLOVER
PLOWED
PLOWER
PLUCKS
PLUCKY
PLUGIN
PLUMBS
PLUMED
PLUMES
PLUMMY
PLUMPS
PLUNGE
PLUNKS
PLURAL
PLUSES
PLUSHY
PLYING

P•L•••

PALACE
PALAEO
PALATE
PALEAE
PALELY
PALEST
PALIER
PALING
PALISH
PALLAS
PALLED
PALLET
PALLIA
PALLID
PALLOR
PALMAS
PALMED
PALMER
PALOMA
PALPUS
PALTER
PALTRY
PELAGE
PELEUS
PELIKE
PELION
PELLET
PELMET
PELOPS
PELOTA
PELTED
PELTER
PELTRY
PELVIC
PELVIS
PHLEBO
PHLEGM
PHLOEM
PILAFS
PILATE
PILEIN
PILEON
PILEUM
PILEUP
PILEUS
PILFER
PILING
PILLAR
PILLED
PILLOW
PILOSE
PILOTI
PILOTS
POLAND
POLDER
POLEAX
POLERS
POLEYN
POLICE
POLICY
POLING
POLISH
POLITE
POLITY
POLKAS
POLLED
POLLEN
POLLER
POLLEX
POLLOI
POLLUX
POLPOT
POLYPS
PULING
PULLED
PULLET
PULLEY
PULLIN
PULLON
PULLUP
PULPED
PULPIT
PULQUE
PULSAR
PULSED
PULSES
PYLONS

P••L••
PABLUM
PAELLA
PAILOU
PALLAS
PALLED
PALLET
PALLIA
PALLID
PALLOR
PARLAY
PARLEY
PARLOR
PAULEY
PAVLOV
PEALED
PEDLAR
PEELED
PEELER
PEGLER
PELLET
PEPLOS
PEPLUM
PHILAE
PHILBY
PHILIP
PHILLY
PHILOL
PHILOS
PHYLAE
PHYLLO
PHYLUM
PIGLET
PILLAR
PILLED
PILLOW
PIOLET
POILUS
POLLED
POLLEN
POLLER
POLLEX
POLLOI
POLLUX
POOLED
POPLAR
POPLIN
POULTS
PRELAW
PRELIM
PROLES
PROLIX
PROLOG
PSALMS
PSYLLA
PUBLIC
PULLED
PULLET
PULLEY
PULLIN
PULLON
PULLUP
PURLED
PURLIN

P•••L•
PADDLE
PAELLA
PAKULA
PALELY
PAMELA
PANELS
PAROLE
PARTLY
PARULA
PAYOLA
PEARLS
PEARLY
PEBBLE
PEBBLY
PEDALS
PEDDLE
PENULT
PEOPLE
PERILS
PERTLY
PESTLE
PETALS
PETULA
PHIALS
PHILLY
PHYLLO
PICKLE
PICULS
PIFFLE
PINOLE
PINTLE
PIPALS
PIXELS
POKILY
POMELO
POODLE
POORLY
POPFLY
POPPLE
POPULI
PORTLY
POSHLY
POSSLQ
POTTLE
POWELL
PRIMLY
PROWLS
PSYLLA
PUDDLE
PUDDLY
PUEBLA
PUEBLO
PUNILY
PUPILS
PURELY
PURFLE
PURPLE
PURPLY
PUZZLE

P••••L
PANFUL
PARCEL
PARREL
PASCAL
PASSEL
PASTEL
PATHOL
PATROL
PENCEL
PENCIL
PENPAL
PEPFUL
PETREL
PETROL
PHENOL
PHENYL
PHILOL
PINEAL
PISTIL
PISTOL
PLAGAL
PLEXAL
PLURAL
POMMEL
PORTAL
POSTAL
POTFUL
POWELL
PRIMAL
PROPEL
PUMMEL

•PL•••
APLITE
APLOMB
SPLASH
SPLATS
SPLAYS
SPLEEN
SPLICE
SPLINE
SPLINT
SPLITS
SPLOSH
UPLAND
UPLIFT
UPLINK
UPLOAD

•P•L••
APOLLO
APPLES
APPLET
APULIA
EPILOG
KPELLE
SPALLS
SPELLS
SPILES
SPILLS
SPILTH

•P••L•
APOLLO
APPALL
APPALS
KPELLE
OPENLY
SPALLS
SPELLS
SPIELS
SPILLS
SPOILS
SPOILT
SPOOLS
SPRYLY
UPHELD
UPHILL
UPHOLD
UPTALK
UPWELL

•P•••L
APICAL
APODAL
APPALL
APPEAL
EPICAL
EPINAL
SPINAL
SPINEL
SPIRAL
SPRAWL
UPHILL
UPWELL

••PL••
AMPLER
APPLES
APPLET
BYPLAY
CAPLET
COPLEY
DEPLOY
DUPLEX
EMPLOY
INPLAY
JOPLIN
KAPLAN
KEPLER
MAPLES
NAPLES
PEPLOS
PEPLUM
POPLAR
POPLIN
REPLAN
REPLAY
REPLOW
RIPLEY
UNPLUG
ZIPLOC

••P•L•
AMPULE
AMPULS
APPALL
APPALS
COPULA
CUPELS
CUPOLA
DAPPLE
DIPOLE
EXPELS
FIPPLE
HOPPLE
IMPALA
IMPALE
IMPELS
LAPELS
NAPOLI
NEPALI
PIPALS
POPFLY
POPPLE
POPULI
PUPILS
RAPTLY
REPELS
REPOLL
RIPELY
RIPPLE
RIPPLY
SEPALS
SUPPLE
SUPPLY
TEPALS
TIPPLE
TOPPLE
TUPELO
UNPILE

••P••L
APPALL
APPEAL
CAPFUL
CUPFUL
DEPAUL
ESPIAL
KOPPEL
LAPFUL
PEPFUL
RAPPEL
REPEAL
REPOLL
RUPAUL
SEPTAL
STPAUL

•••PL•
COMPLY
COUPLE
DAMPLY
DAPPLE
DEEPLY
DIMPLE
DIMPLY
FIPPLE
HOOPLA
HOOPLE
HOPPLE
LIMPLY
MARPLE
PEOPLE
POPPLE
PURPLE
PURPLY
RIMPLE
RIPPLE
RIPPLY
RUMPLE
RUMPLY
SAMPLE
SIMPLE
SIMPLY
STAPLE
SUPPLE
SUPPLY
TEMPLE
TIPPLE
TOPPLE
TRIPLE
TRIPLY
TWOPLY
WIMPLE

•••P•L
BHOPAL
CARPAL
CARPEL
CHAPEL
COMPEL
DISPEL
GALPAL
GOSPEL
KOPPEL
PENPAL
PROPEL
RAPPEL
STIPEL

P•M•••
PAMELA
PAMIRS
PAMPAS
PAMPER
PIMINY
POMACE
POMADE
POMELO
POMMEE
POMMEL
POMONA
POMPEY
POMPOM
POMPON
PUMICE
PUMMEL
PUMPED
PUMPER
PUMPUP

P••M••
PACMAN
PALMAS
PALMED
PALMER
PATMOS
PELMET
PENMAN
PENMEN
PERMED
PERMIT
PIEMAN
PIEMEN
PITMAN
PITMEN
PLUMBS
PLUMED
PLUMES
PLUMMY
PLUMPS
POMMEE
POMMEL
PREMED
PREMIE
PRIMAL
PRIMED
PRIMER
PRIMES
PRIMLY
PRIMOS
PRIMPS
PRIMUM
PRIMUS
PROMOS
PROMPT
PUMMEL

P•••M•
PAJAMA
PALOMA
PANAMA
PLASMA
PLASMO
PLUMMY
PNEUMA
PREAMP
PRISMS
PROAMS
PROEMS
PSALMS
PYJAMA

P••••M
PABLUM
PASSIM
PEPLUM
PHENOM
PHLEGM
PHLOEM
PHYLUM
PILEUM
PLENUM
PODIUM
POMPOM
POSSUM
PRELIM
PRIMUM
PROTEM
PURISM
PUTNAM

•PM•••
UPMOST

•P•M••
APEMAN
APEMEN
SPUMED
SPUMES

•P••M•
APLOMB
EPROMS
OPTIMA
SPASMS
UPTIME

•P•••M
EPONYM

••P••M
GYPSUM
LAPHAM
PEPLUM
SEPTUM

•••P•M
POMPOM
WAMPUM

••••PM
FIVEPM
FOURPM
NINEPM

PN••••
PNEUMA

P•N•••
PANADA
PANAMA
PANCHO
PANDAS
PANDER
PANDIT
PANELS
PANFRY
PANFUL
PANICS
PANNED
PANNER
PANNES
PANOUT
PANTED
PANTOS
PANTRY
PANZER
PENANG
PENCEL
PENCIL
PENDED
PENGHU
PENMAN
PENMEN
PENNAE
PENNED
PENNER
PENNEY
PENNIA
PENNIS
PENNON
PENPAL
PENROD
PENSEE
PENTAD
PENTUP
PENULT
PENURY
PINATA
PINCER
PINDAR
PINDUS
PINEAL
PINERO
PINERY
PINGED
PINIER
PINING
PINION
PINITE
PINKED
PINKEN
PINKER
PINKIE
PINNAE
PINNAS
PINNED
PINNER
PINOAK
PINOLE
PINONS
PINOTS
PINSON
PINTER
PINTLE
PINTOS
PINUPS
PINXIT
PINYIN
PINYON
PINZON
PONCES
PONCHO
PONDER
PONGED
PONGEE
PONGID
PONIED
PONIES
PONTES
PONTIC
PONTUS
PONYUP
PUNCHY
PUNDIT
PUNIER
PUNILY
PUNISH
PUNJAB
PUNKAH
PUNKER
PUNKIE
PUNNED
PUNNET
PUNTED
PUNTER

P••N••
PAANGA
PAINED
PAINTS
PAINTY
PANNED
PANNER
PANNES
PARNIS
PAUNCH
PAWNED
PAWNEE
PAWNER
PEANUT
PEENED
PENNAE
PENNED
PENNER
PENNEY
PENNIA
PENNIS
PENNON
PERNIO
PERNOD
PHENOL
PHENOM
PHENYL
PHONED
PHONES
PHONEY
PHONIC
PHONON
PHONOS
PIANOS
PICNIC
PIGNUT
PINNAE
PINNAS
PINNED
PINNER
PLANAR
PLANCK
PLANED
PLANER
PLANES

PLANET
PLANKS
PLANON
PLANTE
PLANTS
PLENTY
PLENUM
PLINKS
PLINTH
PLONKS
PLUNGE
PLUNKS
POINTE
POINTS
POINTY
POUNCE
POUNDS
PRANCE
PRANGS
PRANKS
PRENUP
PRINCE
PRINKS
PRINTS
PRONGS
PRONTO
PRUNED
PRUNER
PRUNES
PRYNNE
PUENTE
PUNNED
PUNNET
PUTNAM
PYKNIC

P•••N•

PACING
PACINO
PADANG
PAEANS
PAEONS
PAGANS
PAGING
PAHANG
PALING
PARANA
PARANG
PARENS
PARENT
PARING
PATENS
PATENT
PATINA
PATINE
PAVANE
PAVING
PAWING
PAYING
PECANS
PEDANT
PEKING
PEKINS
PENANG
PEPINO
PIKING
PILING
PIMINY
PINING
PINONS
PIPING
PIRANA
PISANO
PISANS
PITONS
PLAINS
PLAINT
PLIANT
PLYING
POCONO
PODUNK
POKING
POLAND
POLING
POMONA
PORING
POSING
POTENT
PRAJNA
PRAWNS
PREENS
PRIONS
PROCNE
PRYING
PRYNNE
PUISNE
PULING
PURINA
PURINE
PUTONS
PYLONS

P••••N

PACMAN
PADUAN
PAIDIN
PAPAIN
PAPUAN
PAQUIN
PARDON
PARSON
PARTON
PASSON
PATHAN
PATRON
PATTEN
PATTON
PAXTON
PAYSIN
PAYSON
PEAHEN
PECTIN
PEERIN
PELION
PENMAN
PENMEN
PENNON
PEPSIN
PERSON
PETAIN
PEYTON
PHONON
PHOTON
PICKON
PIDGIN
PIEMAN
PIEMEN
PIEPAN
PIETIN
PIGEON
PIGPEN
PILEIN
PILEON
PINION
PINKEN
PINSON
PINYIN
PINYON
PINZON
PIPKIN
PIPPIN
PISTON
PITMAN
PITMEN
PLANON
PLATEN
PLAYON
PLUGIN
POISON
POLEYN
POLLEN
POMPON
POPGUN
POPLIN
POPSIN
POSTON
POTEEN
POTION
POURIN
PREVIN
PREYON
PRISON
PROTON
PROVEN
PUFFIN
PULLIN
PULLON
PURLIN
PUSHON
PUTSIN
PUTSON
PYTHON

•P•N••

CPSNOW
EPINAL
EPONYM
OPENED
OPENER
OPENLY
OPENTO
OPENUP
OPINED
OPINER
OPINES
SPANKS
SPANKY
SPENDS
SPINAL
SPINED
SPINEL
SPINES
SPINET
SPINKS
SPINTO
SPONGE
SPONGY
SPUNKY
UPENDS

•P••N•

APPEND
APRONS
EPPING
OPTING
SPAWNS
SPHINX
SPLINE
SPLINT
SPOONS
SPOONY
SPRANG
SPRING
SPRINT
SPRUNG
SPURNS
SPYING
UPLAND
UPLINK
UPPING
UPWIND

•P•••N

APEMAN
APEMEN
APPIAN
EPHRON
OPPUGN
OPTION
SPAVIN
SPLEEN
SPOKEN
SPRAIN
SPURON
UPJOHN
UPTOWN
UPTURN

••PN••

CAPNUT
EUPNEA
HYPNOS
WAPNER

••P•N•

ALPINE
APPEND
ARPENT
ASPENS
CAPONE
CAPONS
COPING
DAPHNE
DEPEND
DEPONE
DOPANT
DOPING
DUPING
DUPONT
EPPING
ESPANA
EXPAND
EXPEND
GAPING
HOPING
HYPING
IMPEND
IMPING
JAPANS
JAPING
LAPINS
LIPENG
LOPING
LUPINE
LUPINO
LUPONE
MOPING
ORPINE
PEPINO
PIPING
RAPINE
RAPINI
REPAND
REPENT
REPINE
REPINS
RIPENS
ROPING
SUPINE
TAPING
TAPINS
TIPINS
TYPING
UNPENS
UNPINS
UPPING
WIPING

••P••N

APPIAN
CAPGUN
CAPTAN
HAPPEN
HOPSIN
HYPHEN
IMPUGN
JOPLIN
KAPLAN
KEPTON
LEPTON
LIPTON
NAPKIN
NIPPON
OPPUGN
ORPHAN
PAPAIN
PAPUAN
PEPSIN
PIPKIN
PIPPIN
POPGUN
POPLIN
POPSIN
REPLAN
REPUGN
RIPKEN
ROPEIN
SIPHON
SYPHON
TAPPAN
TIPSIN
TOPGUN
TOPTEN
TUPIAN

•••P•N

CHAPIN
CHIPIN
CHOPIN
CLIPON
COUPON
DAMPEN
DEEPEN
DROPIN
FRYPAN
HAPPEN
HARPON
HATPIN
INSPAN
JUMPIN
JUMPON
KEEPIN
KEEPON
LUMPEN
NIPPON
OILPAN
PIEPAN
PIGPEN
PIPPIN
POMPON
REOPEN
RESPIN
SAIPAN
SAMPAN
SEEPIN
SLIPIN
SLIPON
STEPIN
STEPON
STOPIN
TAIPAN
TAPPAN
TARPAN
TARPON
TENPIN
TIEPIN
TINPAN
TREPAN
TURPIN
UNOPEN
USOPEN
WEAPON
YAUPON

PO••••

POACHY
POBOYS
POCKET
POCONO
PODDED
PODIUM
PODUNK
POETIC
POETRY
POGIES
POILUS
POINTE
POINTS
POINTY
POIROT
POISED
POISES
POISON
POKEAT
POKERS
POKERY
POKEYS
POKIER
POKILY
POKING
POLAND
POLDER
POLEAX
POLERS
POLEYN
POLICE
POLICY
POLING
POLISH
POLITE
POLITY
POLKAS
POLLED
POLLEN
POLLER
POLLEX
POLLOI
POLLUX
POLPOT
POLYPS
POMACE
POMADE
POMELO
POMMEE
POMMEL
POMONA
POMPEY
POMPOM
POMPON
PONCES
PONCHO
PONDER
PONGED
PONGEE
PONGID
PONIED
PONIES
PONTES
PONTIC
PONTUS
PONYUP
POODLE
POOHED
POOLED
POOPED
POORER
POORLY
POPART
POPEYE
POPFLY
POPGUN
POPLAR
POPLIN
POPOFF
POPOUT
POPPAS
POPPED
POPPER
POPPET
POPPLE
POPSIN
POPSUP
POPTOP
POPULI
POPUPS
PORING
PORKER
POROUS
PORTAL
PORTED
PORTER
PORTIA
PORTLY
POSADA
POSERS
POSEUR
POSHER
POSHLY
POSIES
POSING
POSITS
POSSES
POSSET
POSSLQ
POSSUM
POSTAL
POSTED
POSTER
POSTIT
POSTON
POTAGE
POTASH
POTATO
POTEEN
POTENT
POTFUL
POTHER
POTION
POTOSI
POTPIE
POTTED
POTTER
POTTLE
POTTOS
POUCHY
POULTS
POUNCE
POUNDS
POURED
POURER
POURIN
POUSSE
POUTED
POUTER
POWDER
POWELL
POWERS
POWWOW

P•O•••

PEOPLE
PEORIA
PHOBIA
PHOBIC
PHOBOS
PHOCIS
PHOEBE
PHONED
PHONES
PHONEY
PHONIC
PHONON
PHONOS
PHOOEY
PHOTIC
PHOTOG
PHOTON
PHOTOS
PIOLET
PLONKS
PLOTTY
PLOUGH
PLOVER
PLOWED
PLOWER
POODLE
POOHED
POOLED
POOPED
POORER
POORLY
PROAMS
PROBED
PROBER
PROBES
PROCNE
PROEMS
PROFIT
PROLES
PROLIX
PROLOG
PROMOS
PROMPT
PRONGS
PRONTO
PROOFS
PROPEL
PROPER
PROPRE
PROPUP
PROSED
PROSER
PROSES
PROSIT
PROSKY
PROTAX
PROTEI
PROTEM
PROTON
PROUST
PROVED
PROVEN
PROVER
PROVES
PROWLS
PROWSE
PROZAC

P••O••

PAEONS
PAGODA
PALOMA
PANOUT
PARODY
PAROLE
PATOIS
PAYOFF
PAYOLA
PAYOUT
PEKOES
PELOPS
PELOTA
PEYOTE
PHLOEM
PHOOEY
PICOTS
PIGOUT
PILOSE
PILOTI
PILOTS

PINOAK
PINOLE
PINONS
PINOTS
PITONS
PIVOTS
POBOYS
POCONO
POMONA
POPOFF
POPOUT
POROUS
POTOSI
PRIONS
PRIORI
PRIORS
PRIORY
PROOFS
PTBOAT
PUTOFF
PUTONS
PUTOUT
PYLONS

P•••O•
PAILOU
PALLOR
PANTOS
PARDON
PARLOR
PARROT
PARSON
PARTON
PASEOS
PASSON
PASTOR
PATHOL
PATHOS
PATIOS
PATMOS
PATROL
PATRON
PATTON
PAVLOV
PAXTON
PAYBOX
PAYFOR
PAYSON
PEAPOD
PEGTOP
PELION
PENNON
PENROD
PEPLOS
PEQUOD
PEQUOT
PERIOD
PERNOD
PERROT
PERSON
PESCOW
PESTOS
PETROG
PETROL
PEYTON
PHAROS
PHENOL
PHENOM
PHILOL
PHILOS
PHOBOS
PHONON
PHONOS
PHOTOG
PHOTON
PHOTOS
PIANOS
PICKON
PIGEON
PILEON
PILLOW
PINION
PINSON
PINTOS
PINYON
PINZON
PISTOL
PISTON
PLANON
PLAYON
PLEXOR
POIROT
POISON
POLLOI
POLPOT
POMPOM
POMPON
POPTOP
POSTON
POTION
POTTOS
POWWOW
PREYON
PRIMOS
PRISON
PROLOG
PROMOS
PROTON
PULLON
PUSHON
PUTSON
PYEDOG
PYTHON

P••••O
PACINO
PALAEO
PANCHO
PAPAGO
PARETO
PASHTO
PEPINO
PERNIO
PHLEBO
PHYLLO
PHYSIO
PICABO
PICARO
PIETRO
PINERO
PISANO
PLAGIO
PLASMO
POCONO
POMELO
PONCHO
POTATO
PRESTO
PRONTO
PSEUDO
PSYCHO
PUEBLO
PUERTO
PUTSTO

•PO•••
APODAL
APOGEE
APOLLO
EPOCHS
EPODES
EPONYM
EPOPEE
OPORTO
SPOILS
SPOILT
SPOKED
SPOKEN
SPOKES
SPONGE
SPONGY
SPOOFS
SPOOKS
SPOOKY
SPOOLS
SPOONS
SPOONY
SPOORS
SPORES
SPORTS
SPORTY
SPOTTY
SPOUSE
SPOUTS

•P•O••
APLOMB
APPOSE
APRONS
EPHODS
EPHORI
EPHORS
EPROMS
OPPOSE
OPTOUT
SPLOSH
SPOOFS
SPOOKS
SPOOKY
SPOOLS
SPOONS
SPOONY
SPOORS
SPROUT
UPBOWS
UPHOLD
UPJOHN
UPLOAD
UPMOST
UPROAR
UPROOT
UPROSE
UPTOWN

•P••O•
CPSNOW
EPHRON
EPILOG
OPTFOR
OPTION
SPIGOT
SPIROS
SPURON
UPROOT
UPSHOT

•P•••O
APOLLO
OPENTO
OPORTO
SPEEDO
SPINTO

••PO••
APPOSE
BIPODS
CAPONE
CAPONS
CAPOTE
COPOUT
CSPOTS
CUPOLA
DEPONE
DEPORT
DEPOSE
DEPOTS
DIPODY
DIPOLE
DUPONT
ESPOSA
ESPOSO
EXPORT
EXPOSE
EXPOST
HOPOFF
HYPOED
IMPORT
IMPOSE
IMPOST
INPORT
INPOUR
LIPOID
LUPONE
NAPOLI
OPPOSE
POPOFF
POPOUT
REPOLL
REPORT
REPOSE
REPOST
REPOTS
RIPOFF
RIPOUT
SAPORS
SEPOYS
SOPORS
TAPOFF
TAPOUT
TIPOFF
TOPOFF
TOPOUT
VAPORS
VAPORY
VAPOUR
YAPOKS

••P•O•
CAPTOR
DEPLOY
EMPLOY
EMPTOR
HIPHOP
HIPPOS
HYPNOS
IMPROV
KEPTON
LAPDOG
LAPTOP
LEPTON
LIPTON
MOPTOP
NIPPON
PEPLOS
POPTOP
RAPTOR
REPLOW
REPROS
SIPHON
SYPHON
TIPTOE
TIPTOP
TOPDOG
TOPJOB
ZIPLOC

••P••O
ELPASO
ESPOSO
LUPINO
MAPUTO
NEPHRO
PAPAGO
PEPINO
SAPPHO
TUPELO

•••PO•
CAMPOS
CLIPON
COMPOS
COUPON
COWPOX
DESPOT
HARPON
HIPPOS
HOOPOE
HOTPOT
ISOPOD
JUMPON
KARPOV
KEEPON
MAYPOP
NIPPON
PEAPOD
POLPOT
POMPOM
POMPON
SLIPON
STEPON
STUPOR
TARPON
TEAPOT
TEAPOY
TEMPOS
TINPOT
TORPOR
TRIPOD
TRIPOS
UNIPOD
VOXPOP
WEAPON
YAUPON

•••P•O
ALEPPO
ALLPRO
BUMPPO
CRYPTO
EOIPSO
KEEPTO
KUOPIO
MORPHO
OLDPRO
SAPPHO
SCIPIO
SNAPTO
TROPPO

••••PO
ALEPPO
ATEMPO
BUMPPO
CHEAPO
DACAPO
KAKAPO
MOLOPO
OBISPO
TROPPO

P•P•••
PAPACY
PAPAGO
PAPAIN
PAPAWS
PAPAYA
PAPERS
PAPERY
PAPIER
PAPPAS
PAPPUS
PAPUAN
PAPYRI
PEPFUL
PEPINO
PEPITA
PEPLOS
PEPLUM
PEPPED
PEPPER
PEPSIN
PEPSUP
PEPTIC
PIPALS
PIPERS
PIPEUP
PIPIER
PIPING
PIPITS
PIPKIN
PIPPED
PIPPIN
POPART
POPEYE
POPFLY
POPGUN
POPLAR
POPLIN
POPOFF
POPOUT
POPPAS
POPPED
POPPER
POPPET
POPPLE
POPSIN
POPSUP
POPTOP
POPULI
POPUPS
PUPILS
PUPPET

P••P••
PALPUS
PAMPAS
PAMPER
PAPPAS
PAPPUS
PAUPER
PAWPAW
PEAPOD
PEEPED
PEEPER
PENPAL
PEOPLE
PEPPED
PEPPER
PIEPAN
PIGPEN
PIPPED
PIPPIN
POLPOT
POMPEY
POMPOM
POMPON
POOPED
POPPAS
POPPED
POPPER
POPPET
POPPLE
POTPIE
PREPAY
PREPPY
PRIPET
PROPEL
PROPER
PROPRE
PROPUP
PULPED
PULPIT
PUMPED
PUMPER
PUMPUP
PUPPET
PURPLE
PURPLY
PUTPUT

P•••P•
PARAPH
PELOPS
PINUPS
PLUMPS
POLYPS
POPUPS
PREPPY
PRIMPS
PROMPT
PTRAPS

P••••P
PACKUP
PAIDUP
PAIRUP
PASSUP
PAYSUP
PEGTOP
PENTUP
PEPSUP
PERKUP
PHILIP
PICKUP
PILEUP
PIPEUP
PIRRIP
PLAYUP
PONYUP
POPSUP
POPTOP
PREAMP
PRENUP
PROPUP
PULLUP
PUMPUP
PUSHUP
PUTSUP

•PP•••
APPALL
APPALS
APPEAL
APPEAR
APPEND
APPIAN
APPLES
APPLET
APPOSE
EPPING
OPPOSE
OPPUGN
UPPERS
UPPING
UPPISH
UPPITY

•P•P••
EPOPEE

•P•••P
OPENUP
SPEDUP
UPKEEP

••PP••
BOPPED
BOPPER
CAPPED
CAPPER
COPPED
COPPER
CUPPAS
CUPPED
DAPPED
DAPPER
DAPPLE
DIPPED
DIPPER
FIPPLE
GAPPED
GIPPED
GIPPER
GYPPED
GYPPER
HAPPED
HAPPEN
HEPPER
HIPPED
HIPPER
HIPPIE
HIPPOS
HOPPED
HOPPER
HOPPLE
KAPPAS
KIPPER
KIPPUR
KOPPEL
LAPPED
LAPPET
LIPPED
LOPPED
LOPPER
MAPPED
MAPPER
MOPPED
MOPPER
MOPPET
MUPPET
NAPPED
NAPPER
NAPPES
NAPPIE
NIPPED
NIPPER
NIPPON
NIPPUR
PAPPAS
PAPPUS
PEPPED
PEPPER
PIPPED
PIPPIN
POPPAS
POPPED
POPPER
POPPET
POPPLE
PUPPET
RAPPED
RAPPEE
RAPPEL
RAPPER
RIPPED
RIPPER
RIPPLE
RIPPLY
SAPPED
SAPPER
SAPPHO
SIPPED
SIPPER
SIPPET
SOPPED
SUPPED
SUPPER
SUPPLE
SUPPLY
TAPPAN

TAPPED
TAPPER
TAPPET
TIPPED
TIPPER
TIPPET
TIPPLE
TOPPED
TOPPER
TOPPLE
YAPPED
YIPPED
YIPPEE
YUPPIE
ZAPPED
ZAPPER
ZIPPED
ZIPPER

••P•P•
MOPUPS
NIPUPS
POPUPS
TIPUPS

••P••P
BOPEEP
HIPHOP
HOPSUP
HYPEUP
KEPTUP
LAPSUP
LAPTOP
MOPSUP
MOPTOP
PEPSUP
PIPEUP
POPSUP
POPTOP
RIPRAP
RIPSUP
SOPSUP
TIPTOP
TYPEUP
WIPEUP
ZIPSUP

•••PP•
ALEPPO
BUMPPO
CHOPPY
DIEPPE
DRIPPY
FLAPPY
FLOPPY
FRAPPE
GLOPPY
GRAPPA
GRIPPE
PREPPY
QUIPPY
SHOPPE
SKIPPY
SLAPPY
SLIPPY
SLOPPY
SNAPPY
SNIPPY
STEPPE
TRAPPY
TROPPO
WHIPPY

•••P•P
BUMPUP
COOPUP
CROPUP
FLIPUP
JUMPUP
KEEPUP
MAYPOP
PROPUP
PUMPUP
SLAPUP
SLIPUP
SNAPUP
SOUPUP
STEPUP
STOPUP
TRIPUP
VOXPOP
WHIPUP
WRAPUP

••••PP
ALCAPP

P•Q•••
PAQUIN
PEQUOD
PEQUOT
PIQUED
PIQUES
PIQUET

P••Q••
PLAQUE
PULQUE

P••••Q
POSSLQ

•P•Q••
OPAQUE

•••P•Q
COMPAQ

PR••••
PRAGUE
PRAISE
PRAJNA
PRANCE
PRANGS
PRANKS
PRASES
PRATED
PRATER
PRATES
PRAVDA
PRAWNS
PRAXES
PRAXIS
PRAYED
PRAYER
PREACH
PREAMP
PRECIS
PREENS
PREFAB
PREFER
PREFIX
PRELAW
PRELIM
PREMED
PREMIE
PRENUP
PREPAY
PREPPY
PRESET
PRESTO
PRETAX
PRETER
PRETTY
PREVIN
PREWAR
PREYED
PREYON
PRICED
PRICER
PRICES
PRICEY
PRICKS
PRIDED
PRIDES
PRIERS
PRIEST
PRIMAL
PRIMED
PRIMER
PRIMES
PRIMLY
PRIMOS
PRIMPS
PRIMUM
PRIMUS
PRINCE
PRINKS
PRINTS
PRIONS
PRIORI
PRIORS
PRIORY
PRIPET
PRISMS
PRISON
PRISSY
PRIVET
PRIZED
PRIZES
PROAMS
PROBED
PROBER
PROBES
PROCNE
PROEMS
PROFIT
PROLES
PROLIX
PROLOG
PROMOS
PROMPT
PRONGS
PRONTO
PROOFS
PROPEL
PROPER
PROPRE
PROPUP
PROSED
PROSER
PROSES
PROSIT
PROSKY
PROTAX
PROTEI
PROTEM
PROTON
PROUST
PROVED
PROVEN
PROVER
PROVES
PROWLS
PROWSE
PROZAC
PRUDES
PRUNED
PRUNER
PRUNES
PRYING
PRYNNE

P•R•••
PARADE
PARANA
PARANG
PARAPH
PARCAE
PARCEL
PARDON
PARENS
PARENT
PARERS
PARETO
PAREVE
PARGET
PARIAH
PARING
PARISH
PARITY
PARKAS
PARKAY
PARKED
PARKER
PARLAY
PARLEY
PARLOR
PARNIS
PARODY
PAROLE
PARRED
PARREL
PARRIS
PARROT
PARSEC
PARSED
PARSEE
PARSER
PARSES
PARSON
PARTED
PARTLY
PARTON
PARULA
PARURE
PARVIS
PERCHA
PERDUE
PERILS
PERIOD
PERISH
PERKED
PERKUP
PERMED
PERMIT
PERNIO
PERNOD
PERROT
PERSIA
PERSON
PERTER
PERTLY
PERUGA
PERUKE
PERUSE
PHRASE
PIRACY
PIRANA
PIRATE
PIRRIP
PORING
PORKER
POROUS
PORTAL
PORTED
PORTER
PORTIA
PORTLY
PTRAPS
PURACE
PURDAH
PURDUE
PUREED
PUREES
PURELY
PUREST
PURFLE
PURGED
PURGES
PURIFY
PURINA
PURINE
PURISM
PURIST
PURITY
PURLED
PURLIN
PURPLE
PURPLY
PURRED
PURRER
PURSED
PURSER
PURSES
PURSUE
PURVEY
PYRITE

P••R••
PADRES
PAIRED
PAIRUP
PARRED
PARREL
PARRIS
PARROT
PATROL
PATRON
PEARLS
PEARLY
PEERAT
PEERCE
PEERED
PEERIN
PENROD
PEORIA
PERROT
PETREL
PETRIE
PETROG
PETROL
PHAROS
PIERCE
PIERRE
PIRRIP
PLURAL
POIROT
POORER
POORLY
POURED
POURER
POURIN
PUERTO
PUGREE
PURRED
PURRER
PUTRID

P•••R•
PACERS
PAGERS
PAHARI
PALTRY
PAMIRS
PANFRY
PANTRY
PAPERS
PAPERY
PAPYRI
PARERS
PARURE
PASTRY
PATERS
PAVERS
PAWERS
PAYERS
PELTRY
PENURY
PETARD
PETERS
PHEDRE
PICARA
PICARD
PICARO
PIERRE
PIETRO
PIKERS
PINERO
PINERY
PIPERS
PLEURA
PLIERS
POETRY
POKERS
POKERY
POLERS
POPART
POSERS
POWERS
PRIERS
PRIORI
PRIORS
PRIORY
PROPRE

P••••R
PACKER
PADDER
PALIER
PALLOR
PALMER
PALTER
PAMPER
PANDER
PANNER
PANZER
PAPIER
PARKER
PARLOR
PARSER
PASSER
PASTOR
PATTER
PAUPER
PAWNER
PAYFOR
PEDLAR
PEELER
PEEPER
PEGLER
PELTER
PENNER
PEPPER
PERTER
PESTER
PETTER
PEWTER
PFIZER
PHASER
PICKER
PIECER
PIETER
PILFER
PILLAR
PINCER
PINDAR
PINIER
PINKER
PINNER
PINTER
PIPIER
PITIER
PITTER
PLACER
PLANAR
PLANER
PLATER
PLAYER
PLEXOR
PLOVER
PLOWER
POKIER
POLDER
POLLER
PONDER
POORER
POPLAR
POPPER
PORKER
PORTER
POSEUR
POSHER
POSTER
POTHER
POTTER
POURER
POUTER
POWDER
PRATER
PRAYER
PREFER
PRETER
PREWAR
PRICER
PRIMER
PROBER
PROPER
PROSER
PROVER
PRUNER
PSYWAR
PUCKER
PUFFER
PULSAR
PUMPER
PUNIER
PUNKER
PUNTER
PURRER
PURSER
PUTTER

•PR•••
APRONS
EPROMS
SPRAGS
SPRAIN
SPRANG
SPRATS
SPRAWL
SPRAYS
SPREAD
SPREES
SPRIER
SPRIGS
SPRING
SPRINT
SPRITE
SPRITS
SPRITZ
SPROUT
SPRUCE
SPRUES
SPRUNG
SPRYER
SPRYLY
UPRISE
UPROAR
UPROOT
UPROSE
UPRUSH

•P•R••
APERCU
EPARCH
EPHRON
EPIRUS
OPERAS
OPORTO
SPARED
SPARER
SPARES
SPARGE
SPARKS
SPARKY
SPARSE
SPARTA
SPERRY
SPIRAL
SPIREA
SPIRED
SPIRES
SPIRIT
SPIROS
SPORES
SPORTS
SPORTY
SPURGE
SPURNS
SPURON
SPURRY
SPURTS

•P••R•
APIARY
EPHORI
EPHORS
SPEARS
SPERRY
SPHERE
SPHERY
SPIERS
SPOORS
SPURRY
UPPERS
UPTURN
UPWARD

•P•••R
APPEAR
OPENER
OPINER
OPTFOR
SPACER
SPADER
SPARER
SPIDER
SPIKER
SPRIER
SPRYER
UPROAR

••PR••
CAPRIS
CUPRIC
CYPRUS
ESPRIT
IMPROV
OSPREY
REPROS
RIPRAP

••P•R•
ALPERT
AMPERE
ASPERA
ASPIRE
CAPERS
DEPART
DEPORT

DUPERY
EMPERY
EMPIRE
EXPERT
EXPIRE
EXPIRY
EXPORT
GAPERS
HOPERS
IMPART
IMPERF
IMPORT
IMPURE
INPART
INPORT
JAPERS
JAPERY
LOPERS
MOPERS
MOPERY
NAPERY
NEPHRO
PAPERS
PAPERY
PAPYRI
PIPERS
POPART
REPORT
ROPERS
RUPERT
SAPORS
SOPORS
SUPERB
SUPERS
TAPERS
TAPIRS
TEPHRA
TOPERS
TYPERS
UMPIRE
UPPERS
VAPORS
VAPORY
VIPERS
WIPERS

••P••R

AMPLER
APPEAR
AUPAIR
BOPPER
CAPPER
CAPTOR
CIPHER
COPIER
COPPER
COPTER
CYPHER
DAPPER
DIPPER
DOPIER
EMPTOR
GIPPER
GOPHER
GYPPER
HEPPER
HIPPER
HOPPER
IMPAIR
INPOUR
KEPLER
KIPPER
KIPPUR
LOPPER
MAPPER
MOPIER
MOPPER
NAPIER
NAPPER
NIPPER
NIPPUR
PAPIER
PEPPER
PIPIER
POPLAR
POPPER
RAPIER
RAPPER
RAPTOR
REPAIR
RIPPER
ROPIER
SAPPER
SIPPER
SUPPER
TAPPER
TIPPER
TOPPER
TYPIER
VAPOUR
WAPNER
ZAPPER
ZEPHYR
ZIPPER

•••PR•

ALLPRO
CHOPRA
OLDPRO
PROPRE
SEMPRE

•••P•R

BEEPER
BOPPER
BUMPER
CAMPER
CAPPER
CARPER
CASPAR
CASPER
COOPER
COPPER
COWPER
DAMPER
DAPPER
DEEPER
DIAPER
DIPPER
DRAPER
DUMPER
ELOPER
GASPAR
GASPER
GIPPER
GRIPER
GULPER
GYPPER
HAMPER
HARPER
HELPER
HEPPER
HIPPER
HOOPER
HOPPER
JAIPUR
JASPER
JUMPER
KEEPER
KIPPER
KIPPUR
LAUPER
LEAPER
LIMPER
LOOPER
LOPPER
LUMPER
LUMPUR
MAPPER
MOPPER
NAPPER
NIPPER
NIPPUR
PAMPER
PAUPER
PEEPER
PEPPER
POPPER
PROPER
PUMPER
RAIPUR
RAPPER
RASPER
REAPER
RIPPER
ROMPER
SAPPER
SEMPER
SHAPER
SIMPER
SIPPER
SNIPER
SOAPER
STUPOR
SUBPAR
SUPPER
SWIPER
TAMPER
TAPPER
TEMPER
TIPPER
TOPPER
TORPOR
VAMPER
VESPER
WEEPER
WOLPER
YAWPER
YELPER
ZAPPER
ZIPPER

PS••••

PSALMS
PSEUDO
PSEUDS
PSYCHE
PSYCHO
PSYCHS
PSYLLA
PSYWAR

P•S•••

PASCAL
PASEOS
PASHAS
PASHTO
PASSBY
PASSED
PASSEL
PASSER
PASSES
PASSIM
PASSON
PASSUP
PASTAS
PASTED
PASTEL
PASTES
PASTIS
PASTOR
PASTRY
PESACH
PESAWA
PESCOW
PESETA
PESTER
PESTLE
PESTOS
PISANO
PISANS
PISCES
PISGAH
PISTES
PISTIL
PISTOL
PISTON
POSADA
POSERS
POSEUR
POSHER
POSHLY
POSIES
POSING
POSITS
POSSES
POSSET
POSSLQ
POSSUM
POSTAL
POSTED
POSTER
POSTIT
POSTON
PUSHED
PUSHES
PUSHON
PUSHUP
PUSSES

P••S••

PAISAS
PARSEC
PARSED
PARSEE
PARSER
PARSES
PARSON
PASSBY
PASSED
PASSEL
PASSER
PASSES
PASSIM
PASSON
PASSUP
PAUSED
PAUSES
PAWSAT
PAYSIN
PAYSON
PAYSUP
PENSEE
PEPSIN
PEPSUP
PERSIA
PERSON
PHASED
PHASER
PHASES
PHYSED
PHYSIO
PIGSTY
PINSON
PITSAW
PLASHY
PLASMA
PLASMO
PLASTY
PLISSE
PLUSES
PLUSHY
POISED
POISES
POISON
POPSIN
POPSUP
POSSES
POSSET
POSSLQ
POSSUM
POUSSE
PRASES
PRESET
PRESTO
PRISMS
PRISON
PRISSY
PROSED
PROSER
PROSES
PROSIT
PROSKY
PUISNE
PULSAR
PULSED
PULSES
PURSED
PURSER
PURSES
PURSUE
PUSSES
PUTSBY
PUTSCH
PUTSIN
PUTSON
PUTSTO
PUTSUP

P•••S•

PALEST
PALISH
PARISH
PERISH
PERUSE
PHRASE
PILOSE
PLEASE
PLISSE
POLISH
POTASH
POTOSI
POUSSE
PRAISE
PRIEST
PRISSY
PROUST
PROWSE
PUNISH
PUREST
PURISM
PURIST

P••••S

PACERS
PADRES
PAEANS
PAEONS
PAGANS
PAGERS
PAINTS
PAISAS
PALLAS
PALMAS
PALPUS
PAMIRS
PAMPAS
PANDAS
PANELS
PANICS
PANNES
PANTOS
PAPAWS
PAPERS
PAPPAS
PAPPUS
PARENS
PARERS
PARKAS
PARNIS
PARRIS
PARSES
PARVIS
PASEOS
PASHAS
PASSES
PASTAS
PASTES
PASTIS
PATENS
PATERS
PATHOS
PATIOS
PATMOS
PATOIS
PAUCIS
PAUSES
PAVERS
PAWERS
PAYEES
PAYERS
PEARLS
PECANS
PEDALS
PEEVES
PEKINS
PEKOES
PELEUS
PELOPS
PELVIS
PENNIS
PEPLOS
PERILS
PESTOS
PETALS
PETERS
PEWEES
PEWITS
PHAGES
PHAROS
PHASES
PHIALS
PHILOS
PHOBOS
PHOCIS
PHONES
PHONOS
PHOTOS
PIANOS
PICOTS
PICULS
PIECES
PIETAS
PIKERS
PILAFS
PILEUS
PILOTS
PINDUS
PINNAS
PINONS
PINOTS
PINTOS
PINUPS
PIPALS
PIPERS
PIPITS
PIQUES
PISANS
PISCES
PISTES
PITIES
PITONS
PIVOTS
PIXELS
PIXIES
PIZZAS
PLACES
PLAGES
PLAIDS
PLAINS
PLAITS
PLANES
PLANKS
PLANTS
PLATES
PLAYAS
PLAZAS
PLEADS
PLEATS
PLEBES
PLEXUS
PLIERS
PLINKS
PLONKS
PLUCKS
PLUMBS
PLUMES
PLUMPS
PLUNKS
PLUSES
POBOYS
POGIES
POILUS
POINTS
POISES
POKERS
POKEYS
POLERS
POLKAS
POLYPS
PONCES
PONIES
PONTES
PONTUS
POPPAS
POPUPS
POROUS
POSERS
POSIES
POSITS
POSSES
POTTOS
POULTS
POUNDS
POWERS
PRANGS
PRANKS
PRASES
PRATES
PRAWNS
PRAXES
PRAXIS
PRECIS
PREENS
PRICES
PRICKS
PRIDES
PRIERS
PRIMES
PRIMOS
PRIMPS
PRIMUS
PRINKS
PRINTS
PRIONS
PRIORS
PRISMS
PRIZES
PROAMS
PROBES
PROEMS
PROLES
PROMOS
PRONGS
PROOFS
PROSES
PROVES
PROWLS
PRUDES
PRUNES
PSALMS
PSEUDS
PSYCHS
PTRAPS
PULSES
PUPILS
PUREES
PURGES
PURSES
PUSHES
PUSSES
PUTONS
PYLONS
PYXIES

•PS•••

CPSNOW
UPSETS
UPSHOT
UPSIDE

•P•S••

OPUSES
SPASMS
UPASES

•P••S•

APPOSE
APTEST
OPPOSE
SPARSE
SPLASH
SPLOSH
SPOUSE
UPCAST
UPMOST
UPPISH
UPRISE
UPROSE
UPRUSH

•P•••S

APEXES
APHIDS
APICES
APPALS
APPLES
APRONS
EPHAHS
EPHODS
EPHORS
EPIRUS
EPOCHS
EPODES
EPROMS
OPERAS
OPINES
OPTICS
OPUSES
SPACES
SPADES
SPAHIS
SPALLS
SPANKS
SPARES
SPARKS
SPASMS
SPATES
SPAWNS
SPEAKS

SPEARS
SPECKS
SPEEDS
SPELLS
SPENDS
SPICAS
SPICES
SPIELS
SPIERS
SPIFFS
SPIKES
SPILES
SPILLS
SPINES
SPINKS
SPIRES
SPIROS
SPITES
SPLATS
SPLAYS
SPLITS
SPOILS
SPOKES
SPOOFS
SPOOKS
SPOOLS
SPOONS
SPOORS
SPORES
SPORTS
SPOUTS
SPRAGS
SPRATS
SPRAYS
SPREES
SPRIGS
SPRITS
SPRUES
SPUMES
SPURNS
SPURTS
UPASES
UPBOWS
UPENDS
UPPERS
UPSETS

••PS••
CAPSID
COPSES
GYPSUM
HOPSIN
HOPSUP
LAPSED
LAPSES
LAPSUP
MOPSUP
NIPSAT
NIPSEY
PEPSIN
PEPSUP
POPSIN
POPSUP

RIPSAW
RIPSUP
SOPSUP
TIPSIN
ZIPSUP

••P•S•
APPOSE
ASPISH
BYPASS
BYPAST
DEPOSE
ELPASO
ESPOSA
ESPOSO
EXPOSE
EXPOST
IMPISH
IMPOSE
IMPOST
LIPASE
MOPISH
OPPOSE
REPAST
REPOSE
REPOST
RIPEST
TYPIST
UPPISH

••P••S
ALPHAS
AMPULS
APPALS
APPLES
ASPENS
ASPICS
BIPEDS
BIPODS
BYPASS
CAPERS
CAPIAS
CAPONS
CAPRIS
COPAYS
COPIES
COPSES
CSPOTS
CUPELS
CUPIDS
CUPPAS
CYPRUS
DEPOTS
DEPTHS
ESPIES
EXPELS
GAPERS
HIPPOS
HOPERS
HYPNOS
IMPELS
INPUTS
JAPANS
JAPERS
KAPPAS
KOPEKS
KOPJES
LAPELS
LAPINS
LAPSES
LIPIDS
LOPERS
MAPLES
MOPEDS
MOPERS
MOPUPS
NAPLES
NAPPES
NIPUPS
NOPETS
PAPAWS
PAPERS
PAPPAS
PAPPUS
PEPLOS
PIPALS
PIPERS
PIPITS
POPPAS
POPUPS
PUPILS
RAPIDS
REPADS
REPAYS
REPEGS
REPELS
REPINS
REPOTS
REPROS
RIPENS
ROPERS
RUPEES
SAPORS
SEPALS
SEPIAS
SEPOYS
SOPORS
SUPERS
TAPERS
TAPINS
TAPIRS
TEPALS
TEPEES
TIPINS
TIPUPS
TOPERS
TOPHUS
TOPICS
TYPERS
TYPHUS
UNPEGS
UNPENS
UNPINS
UPPERS
VAPORS
VIPERS
WIPERS
YAPOKS

•••PS•
ELAPSE
EOIPSO
FLOPSY

•••P•S
ADAPTS
ADEPTS
ADOPTS
ALEPHS
CAMPOS
CAMPUS
CARPUS
COAPTS
COMPOS
COOPTS
CORPUS
COUPES
COYPUS
CRAPES
CREPES
CRIPES
CRYPTS
CUPPAS
DRAPES
DRUPES
ELOPES
ERUPTS
ETAPES
GLYPHS
GRAPES
GRAPHS
GRIPES
GROPES
HIPPOS
HUMPHS
KAPPAS
KEMPIS
LOUPES
LYMPHS
MILPAS
MORPHS
MYOPES
NAPPES
NYMPHS
OKAPIS
PALPUS
PAMPAS
PAPPAS
PAPPUS
POPPAS
QUIPUS
RUMPUS
SCAPES
SCOPES
SHAPES
SLOPES
SLYPES
SNIPES
SNOPES
STAPES
STIPES
STOPES
STUPAS
STUPES
SWIPES
SYLPHS
TAUPES
TEMPOS
TEMPTS
TEMPUS
TRIPOS
TROPES

••••PS
BEBOPS
BICEPS
BLEEPS
BLIMPS
BLOOPS
CHAMPS
CHEEPS
CHEOPS
CHIMPS
CHIRPS
CHOMPS
CHUMPS
CLAMPS
CLASPS
CLOMPS
CLUMPS
CRAMPS
CREEPS
CRIMPS
CRISPS
CUTUPS
DROOPS
EQUIPS
ESTOPS
FIXUPS
FRUMPS
FSTOPS
GALOPS
GETUPS
GRAMPS
GRASPS
GROUPS
GRUMPS
JAMUPS
JULEPS
LAYUPS
LETUPS
MIXUPS
MOPUPS
NIPUPS
ONEUPS
ORLOPS
OXLIPS
PELOPS
PINUPS
PLUMPS
POLYPS
POPUPS
PRIMPS
PTRAPS
RECAPS
REMAPS
REMOPS
RETAPS
RETOPS
RUNUPS
SCALPS
SCAMPS
SCARPS
SCAUPS
SCOOPS
SCRAPS
SCRIPS
SETUPS
SHARPS
SHEEPS
SITUPS
SKIMPS
SLEEPS
SLOOPS
SLUMPS
SLURPS
SNOOPS
STAMPS
STEEPS
STOMPS
STOOPS
STOUPS
STRAPS
STRIPS
STROPS
STUMPS
SUMUPS
SUNUPS
SWAMPS
SWEEPS
SWOOPS
SYRUPS
SYSOPS
THORPS
THRIPS
THUMPS
TIEUPS
TIPUPS
TRAMPS
TROMPS
TROOPS
TRUMPS
TULIPS
TWERPS
UNCAPS
UNZIPS
USURPS
VCHIPS
WHELPS
WHOMPS
WHOOPS

PT••••
PTBOAT
PTRAPS

P•T•••
PATACA
PATCHY
PATENS
PATENT
PATERS
PATHAN
PATHOL
PATHOS
PATINA
PATINE
PATIOS
PATMOS
PATOIS
PATROL
PATRON
PATTED
PATTEN
PATTER
PATTON
PETAIN
PETALS
PETARD
PETERS
PETITE
PETREL
PETRIE
PETROG
PETROL
PETTED
PETTER
PETTIT
PETULA
PITCHY
PITHED
PITIED
PITIER
PITIES
PITMAN
PITMEN
PITONS
PITSAW
PITTED
PITTER
POTAGE
POTASH
POTATO
POTEEN
POTENT
POTFUL
POTHER
POTION
POTOSI
POTPIE
POTTED
POTTER
POTTLE
POTTOS
PUTNAM
PUTOFF
PUTONS
PUTOUT
PUTPUT
PUTRID
PUTSBY
PUTSCH
PUTSIN
PUTSON
PUTSTO
PUTSUP
PUTTED
PUTTEE
PUTTER
PYTHIA
PYTHON

P••T••
PALTER
PALTRY
PANTED
PANTOS
PANTRY
PARTED
PARTLY
PARTON
PASTAS
PASTED
PASTEL
PASTES
PASTIS
PASTOR
PASTRY
PATTED
PATTEN
PATTER
PATTON
PAXTON
PECTIC
PECTIN
PEGTOP
PELTED
PELTER
PELTRY
PENTAD
PENTUP
PEPTIC
PERTER
PERTLY
PESTER
PESTLE
PESTOS
PETTED
PETTER
PETTIT
PEWTER
PEYTON
PHATIC
PHOTIC
PHOTOG
PHOTON
PHOTOS
PIETAS
PIETER
PIETIN
PIETRO
PINTER
PINTLE
PINTOS
PISTES
PISTIL
PISTOL
PISTON
PITTED
PITTER
PLATED
PLATEN
PLATER
PLATES
PLATTE
PLOTTY
POETIC
POETRY
PONTES
PONTIC
PONTUS
POPTOP
PORTAL
PORTED
PORTER
PORTIA
PORTLY
POSTAL
POSTED
POSTER
POSTIT
POSTON
POTTED
POTTER
POTTLE
POTTOS
POUTED
POUTER
PRATED
PRATER
PRATES
PRETAX
PRETER
PRETTY
PROTAX
PROTEI
PROTEM
PROTON
PUNTED
PUNTER
PUTTED
PUTTEE
PUTTER

P•••T•
PAINTS
PAINTY
PAIUTE
PALATE
PARETO
PARITY
PASHTO
PEDATE
PELOTA
PEPITA
PESETA
PETITE
PEWITS
PEYOTE
PICOTS
PIGSTY
PILATE
PILOTI
PILOTS
PINATA
PINITE
PINOTS
PIPITS
PIRATE
PIVOTS
PLAITS
PLANTE
PLANTS
PLASTY
PLATTE
PLEATS
PLENTY
PLINTH
PLOTTY
POINTE
POINTS
POINTY
POLITE
POLITY
POSITS
POTATO
POULTS
PRESTO
PRETTY
PRINTS
PRONTO
PUENTE
PUERTO
PURITY
PUTSTO
PYRITE

P••••T
PACKET
PALEST
PALLET
PANDIT
PANOUT
PARENT
PARGET
PARROT
PATENT
PAWSAT
PAYOUT
PEANUT
PECKAT
PEDANT
PEEKAT
PEERAT
PELLET
PELMET
PENULT
PEQUOT

PERMIT
PERROT
PETTIT
PIAGET
PICKAT
PICKET
PIGLET
PIGNUT
PIGOUT
PINXIT
PIOLET
PIQUET
PLACET
PLAINT
PLANET
PLAYAT
PLIANT
PLIGHT
POCKET
POIROT
POKEAT
POLPOT
POPART
POPOUT
POPPET
POSSET
POSTIT
POTENT
PRESET
PRIEST
PRIPET
PRIVET
PROFIT
PROMPT
PROSIT
PROUST
PTBOAT
PULLET
PULPIT
PUNDIT
PUNNET
PUPPET
PUREST
PURIST
PUTOUT
PUTPUT

•PT•••
APTEST
OPTFOR
OPTICS
OPTIMA
OPTING
OPTION
OPTOUT
UPTAKE
UPTALK
UPTICK
UPTIME
UPTOWN
UPTURN

•P•T••
APATHY
SPATES
SPATHE
SPITED
SPITES
SPOTTY

•P••T•
APLITE
OPENTO
OPHITE
OPIATE
OPORTO
SPARTA
SPILTH
SPINTO
SPLATS
SPLITS
SPORTS
SPORTY
SPOTTY
SPOUTS
SPRATS
SPRITE
SPRITS
SPRITZ
SPURTS
UPDATE
UPPITY
UPSETS

•P•••T
APPLET
APTEST
OPTOUT
SPIGOT
SPINET
SPIRIT
SPLINT
SPOILT
SPRINT
SPROUT
UPBEAT
UPCAST
UPLIFT
UPMOST
UPROOT
UPSHOT

••PT••
CAPTAN
CAPTOR
COPTER
COPTIC
DEPTHS
EMPTOR
HEPTAD
KEPTAT
KEPTON
KEPTUP
LAPTEV
LAPTOP
LEPTON
LIPTON
MOPTOP
PEPTIC
POPTOP
RAPTLY
RAPTOR
SEPTAL
SEPTET
SEPTIC
SEPTUM
TIPTOE
TIPTOP
TOPTEN

••P•T•
BYPATH
CAPITA
CAPOTE
CSPOTS
DEPOTS
DEPUTE
DEPUTY
IMPUTE
INPUTS
LAPUTA
MAPUTO
NOPETS
PEPITA
PIPITS
REPOTS
REPUTE
STPETE
UPPITY
WAPITI
ZAPATA

••P••T
ALPERT
APPLET
ARPENT
ASPECT
BYPAST
CAPLET
CAPNUT
COPOUT
DEPART
DEPICT
DEPORT
DOPANT
DUPONT
ESPRIT
EXPECT
EXPERT
EXPORT
EXPOST
HEPCAT
IMPACT
IMPART
IMPORT
IMPOST
INPART
INPORT
KEPTAT
LAPPET
MOPPET
MUPPET
NIPSAT
POPART
POPOUT
POPPET
PUPPET
REPAST
REPEAT
REPENT
REPORT
REPOST
RIPEST
RIPOUT
RUPERT
SEPTET
SIPPET
TAPOUT
TAPPET
TIPPET
TOPCAT
TOPHAT
TOPOUT
TYPIST

•••PT•
ADAPTS
ADEPTS
ADOPTS
COAPTS
COOPTS
CRYPTO
CRYPTS
ERUPTS
KEEPTO
SNAPTO
TEMPTS

•••P•T
ARMPIT
CARPET
DESPOT
DROPIT
HOTPOT
INAPET
JUMPAT
KEEPAT
LAPPET
LIMPET
MOPPET
MUPPET
OUTPUT
POLPOT
POPPET
PRIPET
PULPIT
PUPPET
PUTPUT
RAJPUT
SIPPET
SKIPIT
SNAPAT
STOPIT
TAPPET
TARPIT
TEAPOT
TINPOT
TIPPET

••••PT
ABRUPT
ACCEPT
ENRAPT
EXCEPT
EXEMPT
INCEPT
IRRUPT
PROMPT
SCRIPT
SCULPT

PU••••
PUBLIC
PUCKER
PUDDLE
PUDDLY
PUEBLA
PUEBLO
PUENTE
PUERTO
PUFFED
PUFFER
PUFFIN
PUGGED
PUGREE
PUISNE
PULING
PULLED
PULLET
PULLEY
PULLIN
PULLON
PULLUP
PULPED
PULPIT
PULQUE
PULSAR
PULSED
PULSES
PUMICE
PUMMEL
PUMPED
PUMPER
PUMPUP
PUNCHY
PUNDIT
PUNIER
PUNILY
PUNISH
PUNJAB
PUNKAH
PUNKER
PUNKIE
PUNNED
PUNNET
PUNTED
PUNTER
PUPILS
PUPPET
PURACE
PURDAH
PURDUE
PUREED
PUREES
PURELY
PUREST
PURFLE
PURGED
PURGES
PURIFY
PURINA
PURINE
PURISM
PURIST
PURITY
PURLED
PURLIN
PURPLE
PURPLY
PURRED
PURRER
PURSED
PURSER
PURSES
PURSUE
PURVEY
PUSHED
PUSHES
PUSHON
PUSHUP
PUSSES
PUTNAM
PUTOFF
PUTONS
PUTOUT
PUTPUT
PUTRID
PUTSBY
PUTSCH
PUTSIN
PUTSON
PUTSTO
PUTSUP
PUTTED
PUTTEE
PUTTER
PUZZLE

P•U•••
PAUCIS
PAULEY
PAUNCH
PAUPER
PAUSED
PAUSES
PLUCKS
PLUCKY
PLUGIN
PLUMBS
PLUMED
PLUMES
PLUMMY
PLUMPS
PLUNGE
PLUNKS
PLURAL
PLUSES
PLUSHY
POUCHY
POULTS
POUNCE
POUNDS
POURED
POURER
POURIN
POUSSE
POUTED
POUTER
PRUDES
PRUNED
PRUNER
PRUNES

P••U••
PADUAN
PAIUTE
PAKULA
PAPUAN
PAQUIN
PARULA
PARURE
PENULT
PENURY
PEQUOD
PEQUOT
PERUGA
PERUKE
PERUSE
PETULA
PICULS
PINUPS
PIQUED
PIQUES
PIQUET
PLEURA
PLOUGH
PNEUMA
PODUNK
POPULI
POPUPS
PROUST
PSEUDO
PSEUDS

P•••U•
PABLUM
PACKUP
PAIDUP
PAIRUP
PALPUS
PANFUL
PANOUT
PAPPUS
PASSUP
PAYOUT
PAYSUP
PEANUT
PELEUS
PENTUP
PEPFUL
PEPLUM
PEPSUP
PERDUE
PERKUP
PHYLUM
PICKUP
PIGNUT
PIGOUT
PILEUM
PILEUP
PILEUS
PINDUS
PIPEUP
PLAGUE
PLAQUE
PLAYUP
PLENUM
PLEXUS
PODIUM
POILUS
POLLUX
PONTUS
PONYUP
POPGUN
POPOUT
POPSUP
POROUS
POSEUR
POSSUM
POTFUL
PRAGUE
PRENUP
PRIMUM
PRIMUS
PROPUP
PULLUP
PULQUE
PUMPUP
PURDUE
PURSUE
PUSHUP
PUTOUT
PUTPUT
PUTSUP

P••••U
PAILOU
PENGHU
PICCHU

•PU•••
APULIA
OPUSES
SPUMED
SPUMES
SPUNKY
SPURGE
SPURNS
SPURON
SPURRY
SPURTS

•P•U••
OPPUGN
SPOUSE
SPOUTS
SPRUCE
SPRUES
SPRUNG
UPRUSH
UPTURN

•P••U•
EPIRUS
OPAQUE
OPENUP
OPTOUT
SPEDUP
SPROUT

•P•••U
APERCU

••PU••
AMPULE
AMPULS
COPULA
DEPUTE
DEPUTY
IMPUGN
IMPURE
IMPUTE
INPUTS
LAPUTA
MAPUTO
MOPUPS
NIPUPS
OPPUGN
PAPUAN
POPULI
POPUPS
REPUGN
REPUTE
TIPUPS

••P•U•
CAPFUL
CAPGUN
CAPNUT
COPOUT
CUPFUL
CYPRUS
DEPAUL
DEPAUW
GYPSUM
HOPSUP
HYPEUP
INPOUR
KEPTUP
KIPPUR
LAPFUL
LAPSUP
MOPSUP
NIPPUR
PAPPUS
PEPFUL
PEPLUM
PEPSUP
PIPEUP
POPGUN
POPOUT
POPSUP
RIPOUT
RIPSUP
RUPAUL
SEPTUM
SOPSUP
STPAUL
TAPOUT
TOPGUN
TOPHUS
TOPOUT
TYPEUP
TYPHUS
UNPLUG
VAPOUR
WIPEUP
ZIPSUP

•••PU•
BUMPUP
CAMPUS
CARPUS
COOPUP
CORPUS
COYPUS
CROPUP
FLIPUP
JAIPUR
JUMPUP
KEEPUP
KIPPUR
KUSPUK
LUMPUR
NIPPUR
OUTPUT
PALPUS
PAPPUS
PROPUP
PUMPUP
PUTPUT
QUIPUS
RAIPUR
RAJPUT
RUMPUS
SLAPUP
SLIPUP
SNAPUP
SOUPUP

STAPUF
STEPUP
STOPUP
TEMPUS
TRIPUP
WAMPUM
WHIPUP
WRAPUP

P•V•••
PAVANE
PAVERS
PAVING
PAVLOV
PIVOTS

P••V••
PARVIS
PEAVEY
PEEVED
PEEVES
PELVIC
PELVIS
PLOVER
PRAVDA
PREVIN
PRIVET
PROVED
PROVEN
PROVER
PROVES
PURVEY

P•••V•
PAREVE

P••••V
PAVLOV

•P•V••
SPAVIN
SPIVAK
SPIVVY

•P••V•
SPIVVY

••P•V•
REPAVE

••P••V
IMPROV
LAPTEV

•••P•V
KARPOV

P•W•••
PAWERS
PAWING
PAWNED
PAWNEE
PAWNER
PAWPAW
PAWSAT
PEWEES
PEWITS
PEWTER
POWDER
POWELL
POWERS
POWWOW

P••W••
PEDWAY
PEEWEE
PLOWED
PLOWER
POWWOW
PRAWNS
PREWAR
PROWLS
PROWSE
PSYWAR

P•••W•
PAPAWS
PESAWA

P••••W
PAWPAW
PESCOW
PILLOW
PITSAW
POWWOW
PRELAW

•PW•••
UPWARD
UPWELL
UPWIND

•P•W••
SPAWNS
SPEWED

•P••W•
SPRAWL
UPBOWS
UPTOWN

•P•••W
CPSNOW

••P•W•
PAPAWS

••P••W
DEPAUW
NEPHEW
REPLOW
RIPSAW

•••P•W
PAWPAW

P•X•••
PAXTON
PIXELS
PIXIES
PYXIES

P••X••
PINXIT
PLEXAL
PLEXOR
PLEXUS
PRAXES
PRAXIS

P••••X
PAYBOX
PICKAX
POLEAX
POLLEX
POLLUX
PREFIX
PRETAX
PROLIX
PROTAX

•P•X••
APEXES

•P•••X
SPADIX
SPHINX

••P••X
DUPLEX

•••P•X
AUSPEX
COWPOX

PY••••
PYEDOG
PYJAMA
PYKNIC
PYLONS
PYRITE
PYTHIA
PYTHON
PYXIES

P•Y•••
PAYBOX
PAYDAY
PAYEES
PAYERS
PAYFOR
PAYING
PAYOFF
PAYOLA
PAYOUT
PAYSIN
PAYSON
PAYSUP
PEYOTE
PEYTON
PHYLAE
PHYLLO
PHYLUM
PHYSED
PHYSIO
PLYING
PRYING
PRYNNE
PSYCHE
PSYCHO
PSYCHS
PSYLLA
PSYWAR

P••Y••
PAPYRI
PINYIN
PINYON
PLAYAS
PLAYAT
PLAYED
PLAYER
PLAYON
PLAYUP
POLYPS
PONYUP
PRAYED
PRAYER
PREYED
PREYON

P•••Y•
PAPAYA
PHENYL
POBOYS
POKEYS
POLEYN
POPEYE

P••••Y
PACIFY
PAINTY
PALELY
PALTRY
PANFRY
PANTRY
PAPACY
PAPERY
PARITY
PARKAY
PARLAY
PARLEY
PARODY
PARTLY
PASSBY
PASTRY
PATCHY
PAULEY
PAYDAY
PEACHY
PEARLY
PEAVEY
PEBBLY
PEDWAY
PELTRY
PENNEY
PENURY
PERTLY
PHILBY
PHILLY
PHONEY
PHOOEY
PIGSTY
PIMINY
PINERY
PIRACY
PITCHY
PLASHY
PLASTY
PLENTY
PLOTTY
PLUCKY
PLUMMY
PLUSHY
POACHY
POETRY
POINTY
POKERY
POKILY
POLICY
POLITY
POMPEY
POORLY
POPFLY
PORTLY
POSHLY
POUCHY
PREPAY
PREPPY
PRETTY
PRICEY
PRIMLY
PRIORY
PRISSY
PROSKY
PUDDLY
PULLEY
PUNCHY
PUNILY
PURELY
PURIFY
PURITY
PURPLY
PURVEY
PUTSBY

•PY•••
SPYING

•P•Y••
SPAYED
SPRYER
SPRYLY

•P••Y•
EPONYM
SPLAYS
SPRAYS

•P•••Y
APATHY
APIARY
OPENLY
SPACEY
SPANKY
SPARKY
SPEEDY
SPERRY
SPHERY
SPIFFY
SPIVVY
SPONGY
SPOOKY
SPOONY
SPORTY
SPOTTY
SPRYLY
SPUNKY
SPURRY
UPPITY

••PY••
PAPYRI

••P•Y•
COPAYS
PAPAYA
POPEYE
REPAYS
SEPOYS
ZEPHYR

••P••Y
BYPLAY
COPLEY
DEPLOY
DEPUTY
DIPODY
DUPERY
EMPERY
EMPLOY
EXPIRY
INPLAY
JAPERY
MOPERY
NAPERY
NIPSEY
OSPREY
PAPACY
PAPERY
POPFLY
RAPTLY
REPLAY
RIPELY
RIPLEY
RIPPLY
SUPPLY
TYPIFY
UPPITY
VAPORY

•••P•Y
CHOPPY
COMPLY
DAMPLY
DEEPLY
DIMPLY
DRIPPY
DROPBY
FLAPPY
FLOPPY
FLOPSY
GLOPPY
GRAPEY
GRAPHY
LIMPLY
MORPHY
MURPHY
NETPAY
POMPEY
PREPAY
PREPPY
PURPLY
QUIPPY
RIPPLY
RUMPLY
SIMPLY
SKIPPY
SLAPPY
SLIPPY
SLOPPY
SNAPPY
SNIPPY
SUPPLY
TEAPOY
TRAPPY
TRIPLY
TROPHY
TWOPLY
WHIPPY

••••PY
CANOPY
CHIRPY
CHOPPY
CLUMPY
CREEPY
CRIMPY
CRISPY
CROUPY
DRIPPY
DROOPY
FLAPPY
FLOPPY
FRUMPY
GLOPPY
GRUMPY
JALOPY
OCCUPY
PREPPY
QUIPPY
RECOPY
SKIMPY
SKIPPY
SLAPPY
SLEEPY
SLIPPY
SLOPPY
SNAPPY
SNIPPY
SNOOPY
STIMPY
STRIPY
STUMPY
SWAMPY
SYRUPY
TRAPPY
WHIPPY
WICOPY

P•Z•••
PIZAZZ
PIZZAS
PUZZLE

P••Z••
PANZER
PFIZER
PIAZZA
PINZON
PIZZAS
PLAZAS
PRIZED
PRIZES
PROZAC
PUZZLE

P•••Z•
PIAZZA
PIZAZZ

P••••Z
PIZAZZ

•P•••Z
SPRITZ

•••P•Z
TROPEZ

QA••••
QANTAS
QATARI

Q•A•••
QUACKS
QUADRI
QUAFFS
QUAGGA
QUAGGY
QUAHOG
QUAILS
QUAINT
QUAKED
QUAKER
QUAKES
QUALMS
QUANGO
QUANTA
QUARKS
QUARRY
QUARTO
QUARTS
QUARTZ
QUASAR
QUAVER
QUAYLE

Q••A••
QATARI
QUEASY

Q•••A•
QANTAS
QINTAR
QUASAR
QUMRAN
QUOTAS

Q••••A
QUAGGA
QUANTA
QUETTA
QUINOA
QUOKKA
QUOTHA

•Q•A••
AQUATE
EQUALS
EQUATE
SQUABS
SQUADS
SQUALL
SQUARE
SQUASH
SQUATS
SQUAWK

•Q••A•
SQUEAK
SQUEAL

•Q•••A
AQUILA

••Q•A•
EMQUAD
ENQUAD
LOQUAT
MSQUAD

••Q••A
BUQSHA

Q••B••
QUEBEC

•Q••B•
SQUABS
SQUIBB
SQUIBS

•Q•••B
SQUIBB

Q••C••
QUACKS
QUICHE

Q•••C•
QUENCH
QUINCE
QUINCY

Q••••C
QUEBEC

Q••D••
QUADRI
QUIDDE

Q•••D•
QUIDDE

Q••••D
QUAKED
QUEUED
QUOTED

•Q••D•
SQUADS
SQUIDS

••Q••D
EMQUAD
ENQUAD
LIQUID
MSQUAD
PEQUOD
PIQUED

Q•E•••
QUEASY
QUEBEC
QUEENS
QUELLS
QUEMOY
QUENCH
QUERNS
QUESTS
QUETTA
QUEUED
QUEUER
QUEUES
QUEZON
QWERTY

Q••E••
QUEENS
QUIETS

Q•••E•
QUAKED
QUAKER
QUAKES
QUAVER
QUEBEC
QUEUED
QUEUER
QUEUES
QUIRES
QUIVER
QUOTED
QUOTER
QUOTES

Q••••E
QUAYLE
QUICHE
QUIDDE
QUINCE
QUOQUE

•Q•E••
IQTEST
SQUEAK
SQUEAL

•Q•••E
AQUATE
EQUATE
EQUINE
SQUARE
SQUIRE

••Q•E•
COQUET
PIQUED
PIQUES
PIQUET
RAQUEL
SEQUEL
TOQUES
TUQUES

•••Q•E
BARQUE
BASQUE
BISQUE
BRAQUE
CAIQUE
CALQUE
CASQUE
CHEQUE
CINQUE
CIRQUE
CLAQUE
CLIQUE
CLOQUE
CUIQUE
MANQUE
MARQUE
MASQUE
MOSQUE
OPAQUE
PLAQUE
PULQUE
QUOQUE
RISQUE
SACQUE
TORQUE
UBIQUE
UNIQUE

Q••F••
QUAFFS

Q•••F•
QUAFFS

Q••G••
QUAGGA
QUAGGY

Q•••G•
QUAGGA
QUAGGY
QUANGO

Q••••G
QUAHOG

Q••H••
QUAHOG

Q•••H•
QUICHE
QUOTHA

Q••••H
QUENCH
QURUSH

•Q•••H
SQUASH
SQUISH
SQUUSH

••Q•H•
BUQSHA

QI••••
QINTAR
QIVIUT

Q•I•••
QUICHE
QUIDDE
QUIETS
QUILLS
QUILTS
QUINCE
QUINCY
QUINOA
QUINTS
QUIPPY
QUIPUS
QUIRES
QUIRKS
QUIRKY
QUIRTS
QUITIT
QUIVER

Q••I••
QIVIUT
QUAILS
QUAINT
QUOINS
QUOITS

Q•••I•
QUITIT

Q••••I
QATARI
QUADRI

•Q•I••
AQUILA
AQUINO
EQUINE
EQUIPS
EQUITY
SQUIBB
SQUIBS
SQUIDS
SQUILL
SQUINT
SQUIRE
SQUIRM
SQUIRT
SQUISH

••Q•I•
ACQUIT
LIQUID
MAQUIS
NYQUIL
PAQUIN
SEQUIN
YAQUIS

•••QI•
IRAQIS

•••Q•I
SESQUI
YANQUI

Q••K••
QUAKED
QUAKER
QUAKES
QUOKKA

Q•••K•
QUACKS
QUARKS
QUIRKS
QUIRKY
QUOKKA

•Q•••K
SQUAWK
SQUEAK

Q••L••
QUALMS
QUELLS
QUILLS
QUILTS

Q•••L•
QUAILS
QUAYLE
QUELLS
QUILLS

•Q••L•
AQUILA
EQUALS
SQUALL
SQUILL

•Q•••L
SQUALL
SQUEAL
SQUILL

••Q••L
NYQUIL
RAQUEL
SEQUEL

Q•M•••
QUMRAN

Q••M••
QUEMOY

Q•••M•
QUALMS

Q••••M
QUORUM

•Q•••M
SQUIRM

Q•N•••
QANTAS
QINTAR

Q••N••
QUANGO
QUANTA
QUENCH
QUINCE
QUINCY
QUINOA
QUINTS

Q•••N•
QUAINT
QUEENS
QUERNS
QUOINS

Q••••N
QUEZON
QUMRAN

•Q••N•
AQUINO
EQUINE
SQUINT

••Q••N
PAQUIN
SEQUIN

Q•O•••
QUOINS
QUOITS
QUOKKA
QUOQUE
QUORUM
QUOTAS
QUOTED
QUOTER
QUOTES
QUOTHA

Q•••O•
QUAHOG
QUEMOY
QUEZON
QUINOA

Q••••O
QUANGO
QUARTO

•Q•••O
AQUINO

••Q•O•
LIQUOR
PEQUOD
PEQUOT

•••Q•O
BANQUO

Q••P••
QUIPPY
QUIPUS

Q•••P•
QUIPPY

•Q••P•
EQUIPS

Q••Q••
QUOQUE

••••QQ
ETSEQQ

Q•R•••
QURUSH

Q••R••
QUARKS
QUARRY
QUARTO
QUARTS
QUARTZ
QUERNS
QUIRES
QUIRKS
QUIRKY
QUIRTS
QUMRAN
QUORUM
QWERTY

Q•••R•
QATARI
QUADRI
QUARRY

Q••••R
QINTAR
QUAKER
QUASAR
QUAVER
QUEUER
QUIVER
QUOTER

•Q••R•
SQUARE
SQUIRE
SQUIRM
SQUIRT

••Q••R
LIQUOR

Q••S••
QUASAR
QUESTS

Q•••S•
QUEASY
QURUSH

Q••••S
QANTAS
QUACKS
QUAFFS
QUAILS
QUAKES
QUALMS
QUARKS
QUARTS
QUEENS
QUELLS
QUERNS
QUESTS
QUEUES
QUIETS
QUILLS
QUILTS
QUINTS
QUIPUS
QUIRES
QUIRKS
QUIRTS
QUOINS
QUOITS
QUOTAS
QUOTES

•Q••S•
IQTEST
SQUASH
SQUISH
SQUUSH

•Q•••S
EQUALS
EQUIPS
SQUABS
SQUADS
SQUATS
SQUIBS
SQUIDS

••QS••
BUQSHA

••Q••S
MAQUIS
PIQUES
TOQUES
TUQUES
YAQUIS

•••Q•S
IRAQIS

Q•T•••
QATARI

Q••T••
QANTAS
QINTAR
QUETTA
QUITIT
QUOTAS
QUOTED
QUOTER
QUOTES
QUOTHA

Q•••T•
QUANTA
QUARTO
QUARTS
QUARTZ
QUESTS
QUETTA
QUIETS
QUILTS
QUINTS
QUIRTS
QUOITS
QWERTY

Q••••T
QIVIUT
QUAINT
QUITIT

•QT•••
IQTEST

•Q••T•
AQUATE
EQUATE
EQUITY
SQUATS

•Q•••T
IQTEST
SQUINT
SQUIRT

••Q••T
ACQUIT
COQUET
LOQUAT
PEQUOT
PIQUET

QU••••
QUACKS
QUADRI
QUAFFS
QUAGGA
QUAGGY
QUAHOG
QUAILS
QUAINT
QUAKED
QUAKER
QUAKES
QUALMS
QUANGO
QUANTA
QUARKS
QUARRY
QUARTO
QUARTS
QUARTZ
QUASAR
QUAVER
QUAYLE
QUEASY
QUEBEC
QUEENS
QUELLS
QUEMOY
QUENCH
QUERNS
QUESTS
QUETTA
QUEUED
QUEUER
QUEUES
QUEZON
QUICHE
QUIDDE
QUIETS
QUILLS
QUILTS
QUINCE
QUINCY
QUINOA
QUINTS
QUIPPY
QUIPUS
QUIRES
QUIRKS
QUIRKY
QUIRTS
QUITIT
QUIVER
QUMRAN
QUOINS
QUOITS
QUOKKA
QUOQUE
QUORUM
QUOTAS
QUOTED
QUOTER
QUOTES
QUOTHA
QURUSH

Q••U••
QUEUED
QUEUER
QUEUES
QURUSH

Q•••U•
QIVIUT
QUIPUS
QUOQUE
QUORUM

•QU•••
AQUATE
AQUILA
AQUINO
EQUALS
EQUATE
EQUINE
EQUIPS
EQUITY
SQUABS
SQUADS
SQUALL
SQUARE
SQUASH
SQUATS
SQUAWK
SQUEAK
SQUEAL
SQUIBB
SQUIBS
SQUIDS
SQUILL
SQUINT
SQUIRE
SQUIRM
SQUIRT
SQUISH
SQUUSH

•Q•U••
SQUUSH

••QU••
ACQUIT
COQUET
EMQUAD
ENQUAD
LIQUID
LIQUOR
LOQUAT
MAQUIS
MSQUAD
NYQUIL
PAQUIN
PEQUOD
PEQUOT
PIQUED
PIQUES
PIQUET
RAQUEL
SEQUEL
SEQUIN
TOQUES
TUQUES
YAQUIS

•••QU•
BANQUO
BARQUE
BASQUE
BISQUE
BRAQUE
CAIQUE
CALQUE
CASQUE
CHEQUE
CINQUE
CIRQUE
CLAQUE
CLIQUE
CLIQUY

CLOQUE
CUIQUE
MANQUE
MARQUE
MASQUE
MOSQUE
OPAQUE
PLAQUE
PULQUE
QUOQUE
RISQUE
SACQUE
SESQUI
TORQUE
UBIQUE
UNIQUE
YANQUI

Q•V•••
QIVIUT

Q••V••
QUAVER
QUIVER

QW••••
QWERTY

•Q••W•
SQUAWK

Q••Y••
QUAYLE

Q••••Y
QUAGGY
QUARRY
QUEASY
QUEMOY
QUINCY
QUIPPY
QUIRKY
QWERTY

•Q•••Y
EQUITY

•••Q•Y
CLIQUY

Q••Z••
QUEZON

Q••••Z
QUARTZ

RA••••
RABATO
RABBET
RABBIS
RABBIT
RABBLE
RABIES
RACEME
RACERS
RACHEL
RACHIS
RACIAL
RACIER
RACILY
RACINE
RACING
RACKED
RACKET
RACKUP
RACONS
RADDLE
RADIAL
RADIAN
RADIOS
RADISH
RADIUM
RADIUS
RADNER
RADOME
RADULA
RAFAEL
RAFFIA
RAFFLE
RAFTED
RAFTER
RAGBAG
RAGGED
RAGING
RAGLAN
RAGMAN
RAGMEN
RAGMOP
RAGOUT
RAGRUG
RAGTAG
RAGTOP
RAHRAH
RAIDED
RAIDER
RAILAT
RAILED
RAILER
RAINED
RAINER
RAINES
RAINEY
RAIPUR
RAISED
RAISER
RAISES
RAISIN
RAJAHS
RAJPUT
RAKEIN
RAKERS
RAKEUP
RAKING
RAKISH
RAMADA
RAMATE
RAMBLA
RAMBLE
RAMEAU
RAMETS
RAMIES
RAMIFY
RAMJET
RAMMED
RAMONA
RAMONE
RAMOSE
RAMOUS
RAMPED
RAMROD
RAMSAY
RAMSES
RAMSEY
RAMSON
RANCHO
RANCID
RANCOR
RANDOM
RANDRY
RANEES
RANFOR
RANGED
RANGER
RANGES
RANGUP
RANIDS
RANKED
RANKER
RANKIN
RANKLE
RANKLY
RANOFF
RANOUT
RANSOM
RANTED
RANTER
RAPIDS
RAPIER
RAPINE
RAPINI
RAPPED
RAPPEE
RAPPEL
RAPPER
RAPTLY
RAPTOR
RAQUEL
RAREFY
RARELY
RAREST
RARIFY
RARING
RARITY
RASCAL
RASERS
RASHAD
RASHER
RASHES
RASHID
RASHLY
RASING
RASPED
RASPER
RASSLE
RASTER
RATEDG
RATEDR
RATEDX
RATELS
RATERS
RATHER
RATIFY
RATINE
RATING
RATION
RATIOS
RATITE
RATLIN
RATSON
RATTAN
RATTED
RATTER
RATTLE
RATTLY
RAVAGE
RAVELS
RAVENS
RAVERS
RAVEUP
RAVINE
RAVING
RAVISH
RAWEGG
RAWEST
RAWISH
RAYGUN
RAYONS
RAZING
RAZORS
RAZZED
RAZZES
RAZZLE

R•A•••
REACTS
READER
READIN
REAGAN
REAIMS
REAIRS
REALER
REALES
REALIA
REALLY
REALMS
REALTY
REAMED
REAMER
REAPED
REAPER
REARED
REARER
REARMS
REARUP
REASON
REATAS
RHABDO
RHAMES
RIALTO
RIATAS
ROADIE
ROAMED
ROAMER
ROARED
ROARER
ROASTS
RRATED
RUANAS
RUANDA
RVALUE
RWANDA
RYAZAN

R••A••
RABATO
RAFAEL
RAJAHS
RAMADA
RAMATE
RAVAGE
REBAGS
REBARS
REBATE
RECALL
RECANE
RECANT
RECAPS
RECAST
REDACT
REDANT
REDATE
REFACE
REGAIN
REGALE
REGARD
REHABS
REHANG
REHASH
RELACE
RELAID
RELATE
RELAYS
REMADE
REMAIL
REMAIN
REMAKE
REMAND
REMANS
REMAPS
REMARK
RENAIL
RENAME
RENATA
REPADS
REPAID
REPAIR
REPAND
REPAST
REPAVE
REPAYS
RERATE
RESALE
RESALT
RESAND
RESAWN
RESAWS
RETAGS
RETAIL
RETAIN
RETAKE
RETAPE
RETAPS
RETARD
RETARS
REVAMP
REWARD
REWARM
REWASH
RIBALD
RIBAND
RITARD
RIVALS
RIYADH
RIYALS
ROBALO
ROLAND
ROMAIC
ROMAJI
ROMANO
ROMANS
ROMANY
RONALD
ROSARY
ROTARY
ROTATE
ROXANA
ROXANE
ROYALE
ROYALS
RUBATI
RUBATO
RUGATE
RUPAUL

R•••A•
RACIAL
RADIAL
RADIAN
RAGBAG
RAGLAN
RAGMAN
RAGTAG
RAHRAH
RAILAT
RAMEAU
RAMSAY
RASCAL
RASHAD
RATTAN
REAGAN
REATAS
RECOAT
REDBAY
REDCAP
REDEAL
REDHAT
REDIAL
REDOAK
REDRAW
REDTAG
REFLAG
REGGAE
REGNAL
REGNAT
REHEAL
REHEAR
REHEAT
REINAS
RELOAD
RENTAL
REPEAL
REPEAT
REPLAN
REPLAY
REREAD
RESEAL
RESEAT
RESEAU
RETEAR
RETIAL
RETRAL
REVEAL
REWRAP
REXCAT
RHINAL
RIATAS
RIOJAS
RIPRAP
RIPSAW
RITUAL
RODHAM
RODMAN
ROSEAU
RUANAS
RUDMAN
RUMBAS
RUNSAT
RUNWAY
RUPIAH
RUTTAN
RYAZAN
RYOKAN

R••••A
RADULA
RAFFIA
RAMADA
RAMBLA
RAMONA
RCCOLA
REALIA
REDSEA
REGINA
REMORA
REMUDA
RENATA
RESEDA
RETINA
RHONDA
RHUMBA
RIVERA
ROBBIA
ROMOLA
ROSITA
ROSTRA
ROWENA
ROXANA
RUANDA
RUMINA
RUSSIA
RWANDA

•RA•••
ARABIA
ARABIC
ARABLE
ARAFAT
ARAGON
ARALIA
ARALLU
ARAMIS
ARARAT
ARAWAK
BRACED
BRACER
BRACES
BRACHY
BRACTS
BRAHMA
BRAHMS
BRAIDS
BRAILA
BRAILS
BRAINS
BRAINY
BRAISE
BRAKED
BRAKES
BRANCH
BRANDO
BRANDS
BRANDT
BRANDX
BRANDY
BRANNY
BRANTS
BRAQUE
BRASHY
BRASOV
BRASSY
BRATSK
BRATTY
BRAVAS
BRAVED
BRAVER
BRAVES
BRAVOS
BRAWLS
BRAWNY
BRAYED
BRAYER
BRAZED
BRAZEN
BRAZER
BRAZES
BRAZIL
BRAZOS
BRAZZA
BRAZZI
CRABBE
CRABBY
CRACKS
CRACKY
CRADLE
CRAFTS
CRAFTY
CRAGGY
CRAKES
CRAMBO
CRAMPS
CRANED
CRANES
CRANIA
CRANIO
CRANKS
CRANKY
CRANNY
CRAPES
CRATED
CRATER
CRATES
CRAVAT
CRAVED
CRAVEN
CRAVER
CRAVES
CRAWLS
CRAWLY
CRAYON
CRAZED
CRAZES
DRABLY
DRACHM
DRAFTS
DRAFTY
DRAGEE
DRAGGY
DRAGIN
DRAGON
DRAILS
DRAINS
DRAKES
DRAMAS
DRAPED
DRAPER
DRAPES
DRAWER
DRAWIN
DRAWLS
DRAWLY
DRAWON
DRAWUP
DRAYED
ERASED
ERASER
ERASES
FRACAS
FRAIDY
FRAISE
FRAMED
FRAMES
FRANCA
FRANCE
FRANCK
FRANCO
FRANCS
FRANKS
FRANNY
FRAPPE
FRASER
FRAUDS
FRAUEN
FRAYED
FRAZER
GRABAT
GRABBY
GRABEN
GRABLE
GRACED
GRACES
GRACIE
GRADEA
GRADED
GRADER
GRADES
GRADIN
GRADUS
GRAECO
GRAFTS
GRAHAM
GRAILS
GRAINS
GRAINY
GRAMAS
GRAMME
GRAMMY
GRAMPA
GRAMPS
GRANDE
GRANDS
GRANGE
GRANNY
GRANTS
GRAPES
GRAPEY
GRAPHS
GRAPHY
GRAPPA
GRASPS
GRASSO

GRASSY
GRATED
GRATER
GRATES
GRATIA
GRATIN
GRATIS
GRAVED
GRAVEL
GRAVEN
GRAVER
GRAVES
GRAVID
GRAYED
GRAYER
GRAYLY
GRAZED
GRAZER
GRAZES
IRANIS
IRAQIS
IRATER
KRAALS
KRAITS
KRAKEN
KRAKOW
KRAMER
KRANTZ
KRASNY
KRATER
ORACHS
ORACLE
ORALES
ORALLY
ORANGE
ORANGS
ORANGY
ORANTS
ORATED
ORATES
ORATOR
PRAGUE
PRAISE
PRAJNA
PRANCE
PRANGS
PRANKS
PRASES
PRATED
PRATER
PRATES
PRAVDA
PRAWNS
PRAXES
PRAXIS
PRAYED
PRAYER
RRATED
SRANAN
TRACED
TRACER
TRACES
TRACEY
TRACHY
TRACKS
TRACTS
TRADED
TRADER
TRADES
TRAGIC
TRAILS
TRAINS
TRAITS
TRAJAN
TRALEE
TRAMPS
TRANCE
TRAPPY
TRASHY
TRAUMA
TRAVEL
TRAVES
TRAVIS
TRAWLS
URACIL
URAEUS
URALIC
URALSK
URANIA
URANIC
URANUS
WRACKS
WRAITH
WRAPUP
WRASSE
WRATHS
WRATHY
XRATED
XRAYED

•R•A••

ARCADE
ARCANA
ARCANE
ARCARO
ARGALI
ARMADA
ARMAGH
ARMAND
ARMANI
ARRACK
ARRANT
ARRAYS
ARVADA
ARYANS
BREACH
BREADS
BREAKS
BREAMS
BREAST
BREATH
BRIAND
BRIANS
BRIARD
BRIARS
BROACH
BROADS
BRYANT
CREAKS
CREAKY
CREAMS
CREAMY
CREASE
CREASY
CREATE
CROAKS
CROAKY
CROATS
DREADS
DREAMS
DREAMT
DREAMY
DREARY
DRYADS
ERGATE
ERHARD
ERNANI
ERRAND
ERRANT
ERRARE
ERRATA
ERSATZ
FREAKS
FREAKY
FRIARS
FRIARY
GREASE
GREASY
GREATS
GREAVE
GROANS
GROATS
KRAALS
ORBACH
ORDAIN
OREADS
ORGANA
ORGANS
ORGATE
ORIANA
ORNATE
PREACH
PREAMP
PROAMS
TREADS
TREATS
TREATY
TRIADS
TRIAGE
TRIALS
TRUANT
URBANA
URBANE
URIALS
WREAKS
WREATH

•R••A•

ARAFAT
ARARAT
ARAWAK
ARCTAN
ARECAS
ARENAS
AROMAS
ARREAR
ARUBAN
BRAVAS
BRIDAL
BROGAN
BROKAW
BRUMAL
BRUTAL
CRAVAT
CRETAN
CRURAL
DRAMAS
FRACAS
FRIDAY
FRUGAL
FRYPAN
GRABAT
GRAHAM
GRAMAS
IRREAL
ORDEAL
ORGEAT
ORPHAN
PREFAB
PRELAW
PREPAY
PRETAX
PREWAR
PRIMAL
PROTAX
PROZAC
SRANAN
TRAJAN
TREPAN
TRIBAL
TRINAL
TROCAR
TROJAN
TRUMAN

•R•••A

ARABIA
ARALIA
ARBELA
ARCANA
AREOLA
ARETHA
ARISTA
ARJUNA
ARMADA
ARNICA
ARRIBA
ARROBA
ARVADA
BRAHMA
BRAILA
BRAZZA
BRENDA
CRANIA
CRENNA
CREUSA
CRIMEA
EROICA
ERRATA
FRANCA
FRESCA
GRADEA
GRAMPA
GRAPPA
GRATIA
GRETNA
OREIDA
ORGANA
ORIANA
ORISSA
ORTEGA
PRAJNA
PRAVDA
TRAUMA
TREDIA
TRICIA
TRISHA
TRIVIA
TROIKA
URANIA
URBANA
URSULA

••RA••

ABRADE
ABRAMS
AERATE
AFRAID
AFRAME
AIRARM
ARRACK
ARRANT
ARRAYS
BERATE
BORAGE
BORATE
BORAXO
CARAFE
CARATS
CERATE
CORALS
CURACY
CURARE
CURATE
CYRANO
DERAIL
DORADO
DORAGS
DORATI
DURANT
ENRAGE
ENRAPT
ERRAND
ERRANT
ERRARE
ERRATA
EURAIL
FARADS
FORAGE
FORAYS
GARAGE
GERAHS
GERALD
GERARD
GIRARD
GORALS
GYRATE
HARALD
HARARE
HARASS
HERALD
HORACE
ISRAEL
JURADO
JURATS
KARATE
KARATS
KERALA
KORATS
KURALT
LARAMS
LORAIN
MARACA
MARAUD
MIRAGE
MORALE
MORALS
MORANT
MORASS
MORAVA
MORAYS
MURALS
MURANO
PARADE
PARANA
PARANG
PARAPH
PHRASE
PIRACY
PIRANA
PIRATE
PTRAPS
PURACE
RERATE
SARANS
SCRAGS
SCRAMS
SCRAPE
SCRAPS
SCRAWL
SERACS
SERAIS
SERAPE
SERAPH
SHRANK
SPRAGS
SPRAIN
SPRANG
SPRATS
SPRAWL
SPRAYS
STRABO
STRADS
STRAFE
STRAIN
STRAIT
STRAKE
STRAND
STRAPS
STRASS
STRATA
STRATI
STRATO
STRAUB
STRAUS
STRAWS
STRAWY
STRAYS
SURAHS
TARAWA
TERAPH
TERATO
THRACE
THRALE
THRALL
THRASH
TIRADE
TIRANA
TIRANE
TORAHS
TYRANT
VIRAGO

••R•A•

ABROAD
ADRIAN
AERIAL
AIRBAG
AIRDAM
AIRMAN
AIRSAC
AIRWAY
AORTAE
AORTAL
AORTAS
ARREAR
ATRIAL
BARCAR
BARKAT
BARMAN
BARTAB
BOREAL
BOREAS
BORMAN
BUREAU
BURGAS
BURLAP
BURMAN
BUROAK
BURSAE
BURSAL
BURSAR
BURSAS
BYROAD
CARMAN
CARNAL
CARPAL
CEREAL
CORBAN
CORDAY
CORMAN
CORRAL
CURIAE
CURIAL
DARNAY
DERMAL
DIRHAM
DORCAS
DORIAN
DORSAL
DURBAN
DURBAR
DURHAM
DURIAN
EARLAP
EARWAX
FARRAH
FARRAR
FERIAL
FERIAS
FERMAT
FIRMAN
FORBAD
FORMAL
FORMAN
FORMAT
FORTAS
GERMAN
HARLAN
HERBAL
HEREAT
HERMAN
HURRAH
HURRAY
INROAD
IRREAL
JARRAH
JORDAN
KARNAK
KARRAS
KERMAN
KIRMAN
KOREAN
KORMAN
KURGAN
LARIAT
LARVAE
LARVAL
LARVAS
LOREAL
MARGAY
MARIAH
MARIAN
MERMAN
MIRIAM
MOREAU
MORGAN
MORNAY
MORTAL
MORTAR
MURRAY
MYRDAL
MYRIAD
NARIAL
NARWAL
NORGAY
NORIAS
NORMAL
NORMAN
NORWAY
OBRIAN
OCREAE
PARCAE
PARIAH
PARKAS
PARKAY
PARLAY
PORTAL
PURDAH
REREAD
SCREAK
SCREAM
SERIAL
SERVAL
SIRDAR
SIRRAH
SPREAD
STREAK
STREAM
STRIAE
SURTAX
SYRIAN
TARMAC
TARPAN
TARSAL
TARTAN
TARTAR
TARZAN
TERRAN
THREAD
THREAT
THROAT
TOREAT
TURBAN
TYRIAN
UGRIAN
UNREAD
UNREAL
UPROAR
VARNAS
VERBAL
VERNAL
WARSAW

••R••A

AFRICA
ARRIBA
ARROBA
AURIGA
AURORA
BARBRA
BAROJA
BERTHA
BORGIA
CARINA
CHROMA
CORNEA
CORONA
CORYZA
DURYEA
EARTHA
ERRATA
EUREKA
EUROPA
FARINA
GARCIA
GURKHA
JERBOA
KARIBA
KERALA
KORUNA
LAROSA
LERIDA
LORICA
MARACA
MARCIA
MARINA
MARISA
MARKKA
MARSHA
MARTHA
MERIDA
MORAVA
MORITA
MURCIA
NARNIA
NERUDA
PARANA
PARULA
PERCHA
PERSIA
PERUGA
PIRANA
PORTIA
PURINA
SARNIA
SERBIA
SERENA
SEROSA
SIRICA
STRATA
TARAWA
TERESA
TIRANA
VARUNA
VERONA
YORUBA
ZAREBA

•••RA•

ABORAL
AFFRAY
AGORAE
AGORAS
AMORAL
AMTRAC
AMTRAK
ANORAK
ANURAN
ARARAT
ASHRAM
ASTRAL
ASTRAY
BETRAY
BEWRAY
BUMRAP
CHIRAC
CHORAL
COBRAS
CONRAD
CORRAL
CRURAL
DEBRAS
DEFRAY
DELRAY
DIGRAM
DOBRAS
DVORAK
ENGRAM
ENTRAP
ENWRAP
ESDRAS
ESTRAY
EXTRAS
FABRAY
FARRAH
FARRAR
FLORAE
FLORAL
FLORAS
FOURAM
GIBRAN
HIJRAH
HOORAH
HOORAY
HURRAH
HURRAY
HYDRAE
HYDRAS
INGRAM
JARRAH
JEERAT
KARRAS
KONRAD
LEERAT
MACRAE
MADRAS
MANRAY
MCGRAW
MIHRAB
MITRAL
MUDRAS
MURRAY
NAIRAS
NEURAL
OPERAS
OUTRAN
PEERAT
PLURAL
QUMRAN
RAHRAH
REDRAW
RETRAL
REWRAP
RIPRAP
SABRAS
SACRAL
SATRAP
SCARAB
SEURAT
SHIRAZ
SHORAN
SIRRAH
SPIRAL
SUDRAS
SUNRAY
SUTRAS
SWARAJ
TAYRAS
TEARAT
TERRAN
TETRAD
TETRAS
THORAX
TIARAS
ULTRAS
UMBRAE
UMBRAL
UMBRAS
UNDRAW
UNTRAP
UNWRAP
ZEBRAS

•••R•A

ANDREA
DHARMA
DJERBA
EGERIA
GLORIA
IBERIA
ICARIA
ISTRIA
LABREA
MAURYA
MCCREA
NUTRIA
OMERTA
PEORIA
SCORIA
SFORZA
SHARIA
SHERPA
SHORTA
SIERRA
SMYRNA
SPARTA
SPIREA
STERNA
STYRIA
TIERRA
UMBRIA

••••RA

AMENRA
AMHARA
ANGORA
ANITRA
ANKARA
ANSARA
ASMARA
ASPERA
AURORA
AYMARA
BARBRA
BIAFRA
CAMERA
CETERA
CHOPRA
CONTRA
DATURA
DUNERA
ELMIRA
ELVIRA
ENDORA
EUDORA
EXEDRA
FEDORA
FEMORA
FULCRA
GEMARA
GENERA
GEZIRA
HEGIRA
INDIRA
KAGERA
MADURA
MANTRA
MEGARA
MONERA
MOTHRA
NATURA
PICARA
PLEURA
REMORA
RIVERA
ROSTRA
SAHARA
SAMARA
SANDRA
SCLERA
SEGURA
SENORA
SENTRA
SIERRA
SISERA
SISTRA
SONORA
TAMARA
TANTRA
TEPHRA
TIERRA
TUNDRA
ZADORA

R•B•••

RABATO
RABBET
RABBIS
RABBIT
RABBLE
RABIES
REBAGS
REBARS
REBATE
REBBES
REBECS
REBELS
REBEND
REBENT
REBIDS
REBIND
REBOIL
REBOLT
REBOOT
REBORN
REBOZO
REBUFF
REBUKE
REBURY
REBUTS
RIBALD
RIBAND
RIBBED
RIBBON
RIBEYE
RIBOSE
ROBALO
ROBBED
ROBBER
ROBBIA
ROBBIE
ROBERT
ROBING
ROBINS
ROBLES
ROBOTS
ROBROY
ROBSON
ROBUST
RUBATI
RUBATO
RUBBED
RUBBER
RUBBLE
RUBBLY
RUBENS
RUBIED
RUBIES
RUBIFY
RUBLES
RUBLEV
RUBOFF
RUBOUT
RUBRIC
RUBSIN

R••B••

RABBET
RABBIS
RABBIT
RABBLE
RAGBAG
RAMBLA
RAMBLE
REBBES
REDBAY
REDBUD
REEBOK
REUBEN
RHABDO
RHEBOK
RIBBED
RIBBON
ROBBED
ROBBER
ROBBIA
ROBBIE
ROUBLE
RUBBED
RUBBER
RUBBLE
RUBBLY
RUMBAS
RUMBLE
RUMBLY

R•••B•

REDUBS
REHABS
RHOMBI
RHOMBS
RHUMBA
RHUMBS

R••••B

RESORB
REVERB

•RB•••

ARBELA
ARBORS
ARBOUR
ERBIUM
MRBLUE
ORBACH
ORBING
ORBITS
URBANA
URBANE

•R•B••

ARABIA
ARABIC
ARABLE
ARUBAN
BRIBED
BRIBES
CRABBE
CRABBY
DRABLY
EREBUS
GRABAT
GRABBY
GRABEN
GRABLE
GREBES
GRUBBY
IROBOT
ORIBIS
PROBED
PROBER
PROBES
TREBEK
TREBLE
TREBLY
TRIBAL
TRIBES

•R••B•

ARDEBS
ARRIBA
ARROBA
BRUMBY
CRABBE
CRABBY
CRAMBO
CROSBY
CRUMBS
CRUMBY
DROPBY
GRABBY
GRUBBY
TRILBY

•R•••B

PREFAB

••RB••

AIRBAG
AIRBUS
BARBED
BARBEL
BARBER
BARBET
BARBIE
BARBRA
BERBER
BURBLE
BURBLY
BURBOT
CARBON
CARBOS
CARBOY
CORBAN
CORBEL
CORBIN
CURBED
DURBAN
DURBAR
DURBIN
FERBER
FORBAD
FORBES
FORBID
GARBED
GARBLE
GERBER
GERBIL
HARBIN
HARBOR
HERBAL
HERBIE
JERBOA
KORBUT
MARBLE
MARBLY
MORBID
SERBIA
SORBET
SORBIC
TURBAN
TURBID
TURBIT
TURBOS
TURBOT
VERBAL
VERBIS
WARBLE

••R•B•

AEROBE
ARRIBA
ARROBA
CARIBE
CARIBS
CAROBS
ENROBE
HARDBY
HEREBY
KARIBA
SCRIBE
SCRUBS
SHRUBS
STRABO
STROBE
THROBS
UNROBE
YORUBA
ZAREBA

••R••B

BARTAB
STRAUB

•••RB•

BLURBS
DJERBA
EXURBS
ITURBI
NEARBY

•••R•B

CHERUB
MIDRIB
MIHRAB
SCARAB
ZAGREB

••••RB

ABSORB
ADSORB
ADVERB
BICARB
RESORB
REVERB
SUBURB
SUPERB

RC••••

RCCOLA

R•C•••

RACEME
RACERS
RACHEL
RACHIS
RACIAL
RACIER
RACILY
RACINE
RACING
RACKED
RACKET
RACKUP
RACONS
RCCOLA
RECALL
RECANE
RECANT
RECAPS
RECAST
RECEDE
RECENT
RECESS
RECIFE
RECIPE
RECITE
RECKON
RECOAT
RECODE
RECOIL
RECONS
RECOPY
RECORD
RECORK
RECOUP
RECTOR
RECTOS
RECTUS
RECURS
RECUSE
RICERS
RICHEN
RICHER
RICHES
RICHIE
RICHLY
RICING
RICKED
RICKEY
ROCHET
ROCKED
ROCKER
ROCKET
ROCKNE
ROCKYV
ROCOCO
RUCHES
RUCKED
RUCKUS

R••C••

RANCHO
RANCID
RANCOR
RASCAL
REACTS
REDCAP
REECHO
RESCUE
REXCAT
ROSCOE
RUNCIE

R•••C•

REBECS
REDACT
REDUCE
REFACE
REJECT
RELACE
RELICS
RELICT
RELOCK
RELUCT
REMICK
RESECT
ROCOCO

R••••C

ROMAIC
RUBRIC
RUNDMC
RUSTIC

•RC•••

ARCADE
ARCANA
ARCANE
ARCARO
ARCCOS
ARCHED
ARCHER
ARCHES
ARCHIE
ARCHLY
ARCHON
ARCING
ARCTAN
ARCTIC
MRCOOL
ORCHID
ORCHIL
URCHIN

•R•C••

ARCCOS
ARECAS
BRACED
BRACER
BRACES
BRACHY
BRACTS
BRECHT
BRICKS
BRICKY
CRACKS
CRACKY
CRECHE
CRICKS
CROCKS
CROCUS
CRUCES
DRACHM
ERECTS
ERUCTS
FRACAS
FROCKS
GRACED
GRACES
GRACIE
GROCER
ORACHS
ORACLE
PRECIS
PRICED
PRICER
PRICES
PRICEY
PRICKS
PROCNE
TRACED
TRACER
TRACES
TRACEY
TRACHY
TRACKS
TRACTS
TRICED
TRICEP
TRICES
TRICHO
TRICIA
TRICKS
TRICKY
TRICOT
TROCAR
TROCHE

TRUCES
TRUCKS
URACIL
WRACKS
WRECKS

•R••C•
ARNICA
ARRACK
BRANCH
BREACH
BREECH
BROACH
BRONCO
BRONCS
BROOCH
BRUNCH
CRISCO
CROUCH
CRUNCH
CRUTCH
DRENCH
DRYICE
EROICA
FRANCA
FRANCE
FRANCK
FRANCO
FRANCS
FRENCH
FRESCA
FRESCO
FRISCO
GRAECO
GREECE
GRINCH
GROUCH
ORBACH
OROZCO
PRANCE
PREACH
PRINCE
TRANCE
TRENCH
WRENCH
WRETCH

•R•••C
ARABIC
ARCTIC
CRITIC
EROTIC
FROLIC
IRENIC
IRIDIC
IRONIC
ORPHIC
PROZAC
TRAGIC
TROPIC
URALIC
URANIC

••RC••
BARCAR
CIRCLE
CIRCUM
CIRCUS
DORCAS
FARCED
FARCES
FARCRY
FORCED
FORCER
FORCES
GARCIA
GARCON
MARCEL
MARCHE
MARCIA
MARCIE
MARCOS
MARCUS
MERCED
MERCER
MURCIA
PARCAE
PARCEL
PERCHA
TERCEL
TERCET
TORCHY
WARCRY
ZIRCON

••R•C•
AFRICA
ARRACK
BARUCH
BORSCH
CURACY
DIRECT
DUROCS
ENRICH
ENRICO
HIRSCH
HORACE
KIRSCH
LORICA
LYRICS
MARACA
PIRACY
PURACE
SERACS
SIRICA
SPRUCE
STRICK
STRICT
STRUCK
THRACE
THRICE
YORICK
ZURICH

••R••C
AIRSAC
AORTIC
BARDIC
FERENC
FERRIC
FORMIC
GARLIC
HEROIC
KARMIC
NORDIC
PARSEC
SORBIC
TARMAC
TURKIC

•••RC•
AMERCE
APERCU
BIERCE
CHURCH
COERCE
EPARCH
EXARCH
FIERCE
INARCH
PEERCE
PIERCE
SCARCE
SCORCH
SEARCH
SMIRCH
SOURCE
STARCH
STORCH
TIERCE

•••R•C
AGARIC
ALARIC
AMTRAC
CEDRIC
CHIRAC
CITRIC
CLERIC
COURIC
CUPRIC
CYMRIC
FABRIC
FERRIC
IATRIC
METRIC
NITRIC
RUBRIC
TENREC
VITRIC

R•D•••
RADDLE
RADIAL
RADIAN
RADIOS
RADISH
RADIUM
RADIUS
RADNER
RADOME
RADULA
REDACT
REDANT
REDATE
REDBAY
REDBUD
REDCAP
REDDEN
REDDER
REDDOG
REDEAL
REDEEM
REDENY
REDEYE
REDFIN
REDFIR
REDFOX
REDGUM
REDHAT
REDHOT
REDIAL
REDING
REDINK
REDOAK
REDOES
REDONE
REDRAW
REDREW
REDSEA
REDSOX
REDTAG
REDTOP
REDUBS
REDUCE
REDYED
REDYES
RIDDED
RIDDEN
RIDDLE
RIDENT
RIDERS
RIDGED
RIDGES
RIDING
RIDLEY
RIDSOF
RODDED
RODENT
RODEOS
RODHAM
RODMAN
RODNEY
RUDDER
RUDDLE
RUDELY
RUDEST
RUDMAN
RUDOLF
RYDELL

R••D••
RADDLE
RAIDED
RAIDER
RANDOM
RANDRY
READER
READIN
REDDEN
REDDER
REDDOG
REEDIT
RENDER
RHODES
RIDDED
RIDDEN
RIDDLE
ROADIE
RODDED
RONDEL
RONDOS
RUDDER
RUDDLE
RUNDLE
RUNDMC
RUNDRY

R•••D•
RAMADA
RANIDS
RAPIDS
RATEDG
RATEDR
RATEDX
REBIDS
RECEDE
RECODE
REMADE
REMEDY
REMUDA
REPADS
RESEDA
RESIDE
RESODS
REWEDS
RHABDO
RHONDA
RIYADH
ROUNDS
RUANDA
RWANDA

R••••D
RACKED
RAFTED
RAGGED
RAIDED
RAILED
RAINED
RAISED
RAMMED
RAMPED
RAMROD
RANCID
RANGED
RANKED
RANTED
RAPPED
RASHAD
RASHID
RASPED
RATTED
RAZZED
REAMED
REAPED
REARED
REBEND
REBIND
RECORD
REDBUD
REDYED
REEFED
REEKED
REELED
REEVED
REFFED
REFUND
REGARD
REHELD
REINED
RELAID
RELIED
RELOAD
REMAND
REMEND
REMIND
REMOLD
RENTED
REPAID
REPAND
REREAD
RESAND
RESEED
RESEND
RESHOD
RESOLD
RESTED
RETARD
RETIED
RETOLD
REUSED
REVVED
REWARD
REWELD
REWIND
REWORD
RHYMED
RIBALD
RIBAND
RIBBED
RICKED
RIDDED
RIDGED
RIFFED
RIFLED
RIFTED
RIGGED
RIMMED
RINGED
RINSED
RIOTED
RIPPED
RISKED
RITARD
ROAMED
ROARED
ROBBED
ROCKED
RODDED
ROILED
ROLAND
ROLLED
ROMPED
RONALD
ROOFED
ROOKED
ROOMED
ROOTED
ROTTED
ROTUND
ROUGED
ROUSED
ROUTED
RRATED
RSVPED
RUBBED
RUBIED
RUCKED
RUFFED
RUGGED
RUINED
RUSHED
RUSTED
RUTTED

•RD•••
ARDEBS
ARDENT
ARDORS
ARDOUR
ORDAIN
ORDEAL
ORDERS
ORDURE

•R•D••
ARIDLY
BRIDAL
BRIDES
BRIDGE
BRIDLE
BRODIE
BRUDER
CRADLE
CREDIT
CREDOS
CRUDDY
CRUDER
DREDGE
DRUDGE
DRYDEN
ERODED
ERODES
FREDDY
FRIDAY
FRIDGE
GRADEA
GRADED
GRADER
GRADES
GRADIN
GRADUS
GRODIN
GRODNO
GRUDGE
IRIDES
IRIDIC
PRIDED
PRIDES
PRUDES
TRADED
TRADER
TRADES
TREDIA
TRUDGE

•R••D•
ARCADE
ARENDT
ARMADA
AROIDS
ARVADA
BRAIDS
BRANDO
BRANDS
BRANDT
BRANDX
BRANDY
BREADS
BREEDS
BRENDA
BROADS
BROODS
BROODY
CREEDS
CROWDS
CRUDDY
DREADS
DROIDS
DRUIDS
DRYADS
FRAIDY
FRAUDS
FREDDY
FRONDS
GRANDE
GRANDS
GREEDY
GRINDS
GRUNDY
MRHYDE
OREADS
OREIDA
OROIDE
PRAVDA
TREADS
TRENDS
TRENDY
TRIADS
TRIODE
URSIDS

•R•••D
ARCHED
ARGUED
ARMAND
ARNOLD
AROUND
BRACED
BRAKED
BRAVED
BRAYED
BRAZED
BREWED
BRIAND
BRIARD
BRIBED
BRIGID
BRINED
BRUXED
CRANED
CRATED
CRAVED
CRAZED
CREWED
CROWED
DRAPED
DRAYED
DRONED
ERASED
ERHARD
ERODED
ERRAND
FRAMED
FRAYED
FRIEND
FRIGID
GRACED
GRADED
GRATED
GRAVED
GRAVID
GRAYED
GRAZED
GREYED
GRIMED
GRIPED
GROPED
GROUND
IRONED
ORATED
ORCHID
ORMOND
PRATED
PRAYED
PREMED
PREYED
PRICED
PRIDED
PRIMED
PRIZED
PROBED
PROSED
PROVED
PRUNED
RRATED
TRACED
TRADED
TREPID
TRICED
TRIFID
TRIPOD
TROWED
XRATED
XRAYED

••RD••
AIRDAM
AIRDRY
BARDIC
BARDOT
BIRDED
BIRDER
BIRDIE
BORDEN
BORDER
BURDEN
CARDED
CARDER
CARDIN
CARDIO
CORDAY
CORDED
CORDON
CURDED
CURDLE
FORDED
GARDEN
GIRDED
GIRDER
GIRDLE
GORDIE
GORDON
HARDBY
HARDEN
HARDER
HARDLY
HARDUP
HERDED
HERDER
HORDES
HURDLE
JORDAN
LARDED
LARDER
LARDON
LORDED
LORDLY

MARDUK
MURDER
MYRDAL
NORDIC
PARDON
PERDUE
PURDAH
PURDUE
SARDIS
SIRDAR
SORDID
VARDEN
VERDIN
VERDON
VERDUN
WARDED
WARDEN
WARDER
WORDED
YARDED

••R•D•

ABRADE
BORIDE
DERIDE
DIRNDL
DORADO
FARADS
JURADO
LAREDO
LERIDA
MERIDA
NERUDA
PARADE
PARODY
SARODS
SCRODS
SHREDS
STRADS
STRIDE
STRODE
TEREDO
TIRADE
WORLDS

••R••D

ABROAD
AFRAID
AGREED
BARBED
BARGED
BARKED
BARRED
BIRDED
BIRLED
BURIED
BURLED
BURNED
BURPED
BURRED
BYROAD
CARDED
CARKED
CARPED
CARTED
CARVED
CERVID
CORDED
CORKED
CORNED
CURBED
CURDED
CURLED
CURRED
CURSED
CURVED
DARNED
DARTED
DURNED
EARNED
ERRAND
FARCED
FARMED
FERVID
FIRMED
FORBAD
FORBID
FORCED
FORDED
FORGED
FORKED
FORMED
FURLED
FURRED
GARBED
GERALD
GERARD
GERUND
GIRARD
GIRDED
GIRNED
GIRTED
GORGED
HARALD
HARKED
HARMED
HAROLD
HARPED
HERALD
HERDED
HORNED
HORRID
HORSED
HURLED
INROAD
JARRED
JERKED
KERNED
LARDED
LARKED
LORDED
LURKED
MARAUD
MARKED
MARLED
MARRED
MERCED
MERGED
MORBID
MYRIAD
NEREID
NURSED
PARKED
PARRED
PARSED
PARTED
PERIOD
PERKED
PERMED
PERNOD
PORTED
PUREED
PURGED
PURLED
PURRED
PURSED
REREAD
SCREED
SERVED
SHREWD
SHROUD
SORDID
SORTED
SPREAD
STRAND
STROUD
SURFED
SURGED
TARRED
TERMED
THREAD
THREED
TOROID
TORPID
TORRID
TURBID
TURFED
TURGID
TURNED
UNREAD
VARIED
VERGED
VERSED
WARDED
WARGOD
WARMED
WARNED
WARPED
WARRED
WORDED
WORKED
WORMED
YARDED
YARNED
YERKED
ZEROED

•••RD•

AWARDS
BEARDS
BOARDS
CHORDS
CIARDI
FIORDS
FJORDS
GOURDE
GOURDS
GUARDS
HAIRDO
HOARDS
LAIRDS
OVERDO
SHARDS
STURDY
SWARDS
SWORDS
TBIRDS
THIRDS
WEIRDO
WEIRDY

•••R•D

ACARID
ADORED
ALFRED
ASTRID
BARRED
BIGRED
BLARED
BURRED
CONRAD
CURRED
ENURED
FAIRED
FEARED
FLARED
FLORID
FLYROD
FURRED
GEARED
GLARED
HAIRED
HATRED
HORRID
HOTROD
HYBRID
INBRED
INGRID
INURED
JARRED
JEERED
KONRAD
LEERED
MADRID
MARRED
MITRED
MOORED
NEARED
NIMROD
PAIRED
PARRED
PEERED
PENROD
POURED
PURRED
PUTRID
RAMROD
REARED
ROARED
SACRED
SAWRED
SCARED
SCORED
SEARED
SEERED
SHARED
SHORED
SNARED
SNORED
SOARED
SOURED
SPARED
SPIRED
STARED
STORED
TARRED
TEARED
TETRAD
TIERED
TIEROD
TITRED
TORRID
TOURED
UNTROD
USERID
VEERED
WARRED
WHERED

••••RD

ABOARD
ABSURD
ACCORD
AFEARD
AFFORD
ASGARD
BAYARD
BRIARD
BYWORD
CANARD
COWARD
CUNARD
DOTARD
EDGARD
EDUARD
EDVARD
EDWARD
ENGIRD
ERHARD
EZZARD
FUGARD
GERARD
GIRARD
GODARD
HAZARD
HOWARD
IDCARD
INWARD
IZZARD
LIZARD
LYNYRD
MILORD
MYWORD
ONWARD
OXFORD
OXNARD
PETARD
PICARD
RECORD
REGARD
RETARD
REWARD
REWORD
RITARD
SEWARD
SIGURD
TABARD
TOWARD
UNGIRD
UPWARD
WIZARD

RE••••

REACTS
READER
READIN
REAGAN
REAIMS
REAIRS
REALER
REALES
REALIA
REALLY
REALMS
REALTY
REAMED
REAMER
REAPED
REAPER
REARED
REARER
REARMS
REARUP
REASON
REATAS
REBAGS
REBARS
REBATE
REBBES
REBECS
REBELS
REBEND
REBENT
REBIDS
REBIND
REBOIL
REBOLT
REBOOT
REBORN
REBOZO
REBUFF
REBUKE
REBURY
REBUTS
RECALL
RECANE
RECANT
RECAPS
RECAST
RECEDE
RECENT
RECESS
RECIFE
RECIPE
RECITE
RECKON
RECOAT
RECODE
RECOIL
RECONS
RECOPY
RECORD
RECORK
RECOUP
RECTOR
RECTOS
RECTUS
RECURS
RECUSE
REDACT
REDANT
REDATE
REDBAY
REDBUD
REDCAP
REDDEN
REDDER
REDDOG
REDEAL
REDEEM
REDENY
REDEYE
REDFIN
REDFIR
REDFOX
REDGUM
REDHAT
REDHOT
REDIAL
REDING
REDINK
REDOAK
REDOES
REDONE
REDRAW
REDREW
REDSEA
REDSOX
REDTAG
REDTOP
REDUBS
REDUCE
REDYED
REDYES
REEBOK
REECHO
REEDIT
REEFED
REEFER
REEKED
REELED
REELIN
REESES
REEVED
REEVES
REFACE
REFERS
REFFED
REFILE
REFILL
REFINE
REFITS
REFLAG
REFLEX
REFLUX
REFORM
REFUEL
REFUGE
REFUND
REFUSE
REFUTE
REGAIN
REGALE
REGARD
REGENT
REGGAE
REGGIE
REGIME
REGINA
REGION
REGIUS
REGLET
REGLUE
REGNAL
REGNAT
REGRET
REHABS
REHANG
REHASH
REHEAL
REHEAR
REHEAT
REHEEL
REHELD
REHEMS
REHIRE
REHOOK
REHUNG
REIGNS
REILLY
REINAS
REINED
REINER
REININ
REINKS
REJECT
REJOIN
REKEYS
RELACE
RELAID
RELATE
RELAYS
RELENT
RELETS
RELEVY
RELICS
RELICT
RELIED
RELIEF
RELIES
RELINE
RELISH
RELIST
RELIVE
RELOAD
RELOCK
RELUCT
RELUME
REMADE
REMAIL
REMAIN
REMAKE
REMAND
REMANS
REMAPS
REMARK
REMEDY
REMELT
REMEND
REMICK
REMIND
REMISE
REMISS
REMITS
REMOLD
REMOPS
REMORA
REMOTE
REMOVE
REMOWN
REMOWS
REMUDA
RENAIL
RENAME
RENATA
RENDER
RENEGE
RENEWS
RENNES
RENNET
RENNIE
RENNIN
RENOIR
RENOTE
RENOWN
RENTAL
RENTED
RENTER
REOILS
REOPEN
REPADS
REPAID
REPAIR
REPAND
REPAST
REPAVE
REPAYS
REPEAL
REPEAT
REPEGS
REPELS
REPENT
REPINE
REPINS
REPLAN
REPLAY
REPLOW
REPOLL
REPORT
REPOSE
REPOST
REPOTS
REPROS
REPUGN
REPUTE
RERATE
REREAD
RERENT
RERUNS
RESALE
RESALT
RESAND
RESAWN
RESAWS
RESCUE
RESEAL
RESEAT
RESEAU
RESECT
RESEDA
RESEED
RESEEN
RESEES
RESELL
RESEND
RESENT
RESETS
RESEWN
RESEWS
RESHES
RESHIP
RESHOD
RESHOE
RESHOT
RESIDE
RESIGN
RESILE
RESING
RESINS
RESINY

RESIST
RESNIK
RESODS
RESOLD
RESOLE
RESORB
RESORT
RESPIN
RESTED
RESTER
RESTON
RESTUP
RESULT
RESUME
RETAGS
RETAIL
RETAIN
RETAKE
RETAPE
RETAPS
RETARD
RETARS
RETEAR
RETELL
RETENE
RETEST
RETIAL
RETIED
RETIES
RETILE
RETIME
RETINA
RETIRE
RETOLD
RETOOK
RETOOL
RETOPS
RETORT
RETOUR
RETOWS
RETRAL
RETRIM
RETROS
RETTON
RETUNE
RETURN
RETYPE
REUBEN
REUNES
REUSED
REUSES
REUTER
REVAMP
REVEAL
REVELS
REVERB
REVERE
REVERS
REVERT
REVETS
REVIEW
REVILE
REVISE
REVIVE
REVLON
REVOIR
REVOKE
REVOLT
REVSON
REVSUP
REVUES
REVVED
REWARD
REWARM
REWASH
REWEDS
REWELD
REWIND
REWINS
REWIRE
REWORD
REWORK
REWOVE
REWRAP
REXCAT
REZONE

R•E•••

REEBOK
REECHO
REEDIT
REEFED
REEFER
REEKED
REELED
REELIN
REESES
REEVED
REEVES
RHEBOK
RHESUS
RHETOR
RHEUMS
RHEUMY
RIENZI
RUEFUL

R••E••

RACEME
RACERS
RAKEIN
RAKERS
RAKEUP
RAMEAU
RAMETS
RANEES
RAREFY
RARELY
RAREST
RASERS
RATEDG
RATEDR
RATEDX
RATELS
RATERS
RAVELS
RAVENS
RAVERS
RAVEUP
RAWEGG
RAWEST
REBECS
REBELS
REBEND
REBENT
RECEDE
RECENT
RECESS
REDEAL
REDEEM
REDENY
REDEYE
REFERS
REGENT
REHEAL
REHEAR
REHEAT
REHEEL
REHELD
REHEMS
REJECT
REKEYS
RELENT
RELETS
RELEVY
REMEDY
REMELT
REMEND
RENEGE
RENEWS
REPEAL
REPEAT
REPEGS
REPELS
REPENT
REREAD
RERENT
RESEAL
RESEAT
RESEAU
RESECT
RESEDA
RESEED
RESEEN
RESEES
RESELL
RESEND
RESENT
RESETS
RESEWN
RESEWS
RETEAR
RETELL
RETENE
RETEST
REVEAL
REVELS
REVERB
REVERE
REVERS
REVERT
REVETS
REWEDS
REWELD
RIBEYE
RICERS
RIDENT
RIDERS
RIFELY
RIFEST
RILEUP
RIPELY
RIPENS
RIPEST
RISERS
RIVERA
RIVERS
RIVETS
ROBERT
RODENT
RODEOS
ROGERS
ROLEOS
ROMEOS
ROMERO
RONELY
ROPEIN
ROPERS
ROSEAU
ROVERS
ROWELS
ROWENA
ROWENS
ROWERS
RUBENS
RUDELY
RUDEST
RULEON
RULERS
RUMENS
RUPEES
RUPERT
RYDELL

R•••E•

RABBET
RABIES
RACHEL
RACIER
RACKED
RACKET
RADNER
RAFAEL
RAFTED
RAFTER
RAGGED
RAGMEN
RAIDED
RAIDER
RAILED
RAILER
RAINED
RAINER
RAINES
RAINEY
RAISED
RAISER
RAISES
RAMIES
RAMJET
RAMMED
RAMPED
RAMSES
RAMSEY
RANEES
RANGED
RANGER
RANGES
RANKED
RANKER
RANTED
RANTER
RAPIER
RAPPED
RAPPEE
RAPPEL
RAPPER
RAQUEL
RASHER
RASHES
RASPED
RASPER
RASTER
RATHER
RATTED
RATTER
RAZZED
RAZZES
READER
REALER
REALES
REAMED
REAMER
REAPED
REAPER
REARED
REARER
REBBES
REDDEN
REDDER
REDEEM
REDOES
REDREW
REDSEA
REDYED
REDYES
REEFED
REEFER
REEKED
REELED
REESES
REEVED
REEVES
REFFED
REFLEX
REFUEL
REGLET
REGRET
REHEEL
REINED
REINER
RELIED
RELIEF
RELIES
RENDER
RENNES
RENNET
RENTED
RENTER
REOPEN
RESEED
RESEEN
RESEES
RESHES
RESTED
RESTER
RETIED
RETIES
REUBEN
REUNES
REUSED
REUSES
REUTER
REVIEW
REVUES
REVVED
RHAMES
RHODES
RHYMED
RHYMER
RHYMES
RIBBED
RICHEN
RICHER
RICHES
RICKED
RICKEY
RIDDED
RIDDEN
RIDGED
RIDGES
RIDLEY
RIFFED
RIFLED
RIFLER
RIFLES
RIFTED
RIGGED
RIGGER
RILLES
RILLET
RIMIER
RIMMED
RINGED
RINGER
RINSED
RINSES
RIOTED
RIOTER
RIPKEN
RIPLEY
RIPPED
RIPPER
RISKED
RISKER
RITTER
ROAMED
ROAMER
ROARED
ROARER
ROBBED
ROBBER
ROBLES
ROCHET
ROCKED
ROCKER
ROCKET
RODDED
RODNEY
ROGUES
ROHMER
ROILED
ROLLED
ROLLER
ROMMEL
ROMNEY
ROMPED
ROMPER
RONDEL
ROOFED
ROOFER
ROOKED
ROOMED
ROOMER
ROONEY
ROOTED
ROOTER
ROPIER
ROSIER
ROSTER
ROTTED
ROTTEN
ROTTER
ROUGED
ROUGES
ROUSED
ROUSER
ROUSES
ROUTED
ROUTER
ROUTES
ROZZER
RRATED
RSVPED
RUBBED
RUBBER
RUBIED
RUBIES
RUBLES
RUBLEV
RUCHES
RUCKED
RUDDER
RUFFED
RUGGED
RUINED
RUINER
RUMMER
RUNLET
RUNNEL
RUNNER
RUPEES
RUSHED
RUSHEE
RUSHES
RUSSET
RUSTED
RUTGER
RUTTED

R••••E

RABBLE
RACEME
RACINE
RADDLE
RADOME
RAFFLE
RAMATE
RAMBLE
RAMONE
RAMOSE
RANKLE
RAPINE
RAPPEE
RASSLE
RATINE
RATITE
RATTLE
RAVAGE
RAVINE
RAZZLE
REBATE
REBUKE
RECANE
RECEDE
RECIFE
RECIPE
RECITE
RECODE
RECUSE
REDATE
REDEYE
REDONE
REDUCE
REFACE
REFILE
REFINE
REFUGE
REFUSE
REFUTE
REGALE
REGGAE
REGGIE
REGIME
REGLUE
REHIRE
RELACE
RELATE
RELINE
RELIVE
RELUME
REMADE
REMAKE
REMISE
REMOTE
REMOVE
RENAME
RENEGE
RENNIE
RENOTE
REPAVE
REPINE
REPOSE
REPUTE
RERATE
RESALE
RESCUE
RESHOE
RESIDE
RESILE
RESOLE
RESUME
RETAKE
RETAPE
RETENE
RETILE
RETIME
RETIRE
RETUNE
RETYPE
REVERE
REVILE
REVISE
REVIVE
REVOKE
REWIRE
REWOVE
REZONE
RIBEYE
RIBOSE
RICHIE
RIDDLE
RIFFLE
RIMOSE
RIMPLE
RIPPLE
RISQUE
ROADIE
ROBBIE
ROCKNE
ROLLIE
RONNIE
ROOKIE
ROOMIE
ROSCOE
ROTATE
ROUBLE
ROURKE
ROXANE
ROYALE
RUBBLE
RUDDLE
RUFFLE
RUGATE
RUGOSE
RUMBLE
RUMPLE
RUNCIE
RUNDLE
RUSHEE
RUSTLE
RUTILE
RVALUE

•RE•••

ARECAS
ARENAS
ARENDT
AREOLA
ARETES
ARETHA
AREZZO
BREACH
BREADS
BREAKS
BREAMS
BREAST
BREATH
BRECHT
BREECH
BREEDS
BREEZE
BREEZY
BREMEN
BRENDA
BRENTS
BRETON
BREUER
BREVES
BREVET
BREVIS
BREWED
BREWER
BREYER
CREAKS
CREAKY
CREAMS
CREAMY
CREASE
CREASY
CREATE
CRECHE
CREDIT
CREDOS
CREEDS
CREEKS
CREELS
CREEPS
CREEPY
CREMES

CRENEL
CRENNA
CREOLE
CREPES
CRESOL
CRESTS
CRETAN
CRETIN
CREUSA
CREWED
CREWEL
DREADS
DREAMS
DREAMT
DREAMY
DREARY
DREDGE
DRENCH
DRESSY
DREWIN
DREWON
DREWUP
DREXEL
EREBUS
ERECTS
ERENOW
ERESTU
FREAKS
FREAKY
FREDDY
FREELY
FREEST
FREEZE
FRENCH
FRENUM
FRENZY
FRESCA
FRESCO
FRESNO
FRETTY
GREASE
GREASY
GREATS
GREAVE
GREBES
GREECE
GREEDY
GREEKS
GREENE
GREENS
GREENY
GREETS
GREGOR
GREIGE
GRETEL
GRETNA
GREWON
GREWUP
GREYED
GREYER
GREYLY
IREFUL
IRENES
IRENIC
KRESGE
OREADS
OREGON
OREIDA
ORELSE
PREACH
PREAMP
PRECIS
PREENS
PREFAB
PREFER
PREFIX
PRELAW
PRELIM
PREMED
PREMIE
PRENUP
PREPAY
PREPPY
PRESET
PRESTO
PRETAX
PRETER
PRETTY
PREVIN
PREWAR
PREYED
PREYON
TREADS
TREATS
TREATY
TREBEK
TREBLE
TREBLY
TREDIA
TREMOR
TRENCH
TRENDS
TRENDY
TREPAN
TREPID
TREVOR
WREAKS
WREATH
WRECKS
WRENCH
WRESTS
WRETCH

•R•E••

ARBELA
ARDEBS
ARDENT
ARGENT
ARLEEN
ARLENE
ARMETS
ARNESS
ARNETT
ARPENT
ARREAR
ARREST
ARSENE
ARTELS
ARTERY
BREECH
BREEDS
BREEZE
BREEZY
BRIEFS
BRIENZ
BRIERS
BRIERY
CREEDS
CREEKS
CREELS
CREEPS
CREEPY
CRIERS
CRUETS
CRYERS
DRIERS
DRIEST
DRYERS
DRYEST
ERNEST
FREELY
FREEST
FREEZE
FRIEND
FRIERS
FRIEZE
FRYERS
GRAECO
GREECE
GREEDY
GREEKS
GREENE
GREENS
GREENY
GREETS
GRIEFS
GRIEVE
GRUELS
IRLENE
IRREAL
ORDEAL
ORDERS
ORGEAT
ORIELS
ORIENT
ORNERY
ORRERY
ORTEGA
ORWELL
PREENS
PRIERS
PRIEST
PROEMS
TRIERS
TRUEST
URAEUS
URGENT
URGERS
URTEXT
WRIEST
WRYEST

•R••E•

ARCHED
ARCHER
ARCHES
ARETES
ARGUED
ARGUER
ARGUES
ARISEN
ARISES
ARLEEN
ARMIES
ARMLET
ARNHEM
ARTIER
BRACED
BRACER
BRACES
BRAKED
BRAKES
BRAVED
BRAVER
BRAVES
BRAYED
BRAYER
BRAZED
BRAZEN
BRAZER
BRAZES
BREMEN
BREUER
BREVES
BREVET
BREWED
BREWER
BREYER
BRIBED
BRIBES
BRIDES
BRINED
BRINES
BROKEN
BROKER
BRUDER
BRUGES
BRULES
BRUMES
BRUNEI
BRUNET
BRUTES
BRUXED
BRUXES
CRAKES
CRANED
CRANES
CRAPES
CRATED
CRATER
CRATES
CRAVED
CRAVEN
CRAVER
CRAVES
CRAZED
CRAZES
CREMES
CRENEL
CREPES
CREWED
CREWEL
CRIKEY
CRIMEA
CRIMES
CRIPES
CRISES
CRONES
CROWED
CROWER
CROZES
CRUCES
CRUDER
CRUSES
CRUXES
DRAGEE
DRAKES
DRAPED
DRAPER
DRAPES
DRAWER
DRAYED
DREXEL
DRIVEL
DRIVEN
DRIVER
DRIVES
DRONED
DRONER
DRONES
DROVER
DROVES
DRUPES
DRUZES
DRYDEN
ERASED
ERASER
ERASES
ERODED
ERODES
FRAMED
FRAMES
FRASER
FRAUEN
FRAYED
FRAZER
FRISEE
FRISES
FROZEN
GRABEN
GRACED
GRACES
GRADEA
GRADED
GRADER
GRADES
GRAPES
GRAPEY
GRATED
GRATER
GRATES
GRAVED
GRAVEL
GRAVEN
GRAVER
GRAVES
GRAYED
GRAYER
GRAZED
GRAZER
GRAZES
GREBES
GRETEL
GREYED
GREYER
GRIMED
GRIMES
GRIPED
GRIPER
GRIPES
GRIVET
GROCER
GROPED
GROPES
GROVEL
GROVER
GROVES
GROWER
IRATER
IRENES
IRIDES
IRISES
IRONED
IRONER
KRAKEN
KRAMER
KRATER
KRONER
KRUGER
ORALES
ORATED
ORATES
ORGIES
ORIGEN
ORKNEY
ORTLES
ORYXES
PRASES
PRATED
PRATER
PRATES
PRAXES
PRAYED
PRAYER
PREFER
PREMED
PRESET
PRETER
PREYED
PRICED
PRICER
PRICES
PRICEY
PRIDED
PRIDES
PRIMED
PRIMER
PRIMES
PRIPET
PRIVET
PRIZED
PRIZES
PROBED
PROBER
PROBES
PROLES
PROPEL
PROPER
PROSED
PROSER
PROSES
PROTEI
PROTEM
PROVED
PROVEN
PROVER
PROVES
PRUDES
PRUNED
PRUNER
PRUNES
RRATED
TRACED
TRACER
TRACES
TRACEY
TRADED
TRADER
TRADES
TRALEE
TRAVEL
TRAVES
TREBEK
TRIBES
TRICED
TRICEP
TRICES
TRIJET
TRIKES
TRINES
TRITER
TRIVET
TROPES
TROPEZ
TROVES
TROWED
TROWEL
TRUCES
URUSES
WRITER
WRITES
XRATED
XRAYED

•R•••E

ARABLE
ARCADE
ARCANE
ARCHIE
ARGIVE
ARGYLE
ARIOSE
ARLENE
ARMURE
AROUSE
ARRIVE
ARSENE
BRAISE
BRAQUE
BREEZE
BRIDGE
BRIDLE
BRODIE
BROGUE
BRONTE
BRONZE
BROOKE
BROWNE
BROWSE
BRUISE
CRABBE
CRADLE
CREASE
CREATE
CRECHE
CREOLE
CRINGE
CROSSE
CROUSE
CROUTE
CRUISE
CRUSOE
DRAGEE
DREDGE
DROGUE
DROWSE
DRUDGE
DRYICE
ERGATE
ERMINE
ERRARE
FRAISE
FRANCE
FRAPPE
FREEZE
FRIDGE
FRIEZE
FRINGE
FRISEE
GRABLE
GRACIE
GRAMME
GRANDE
GRANGE
GREASE
GREAVE
GREECE
GREENE
GREIGE
GRIEVE
GRILLE
GRILSE
GRIMKE
GRIPPE
GROOVE
GROSSE
GROUSE
GRUDGE
GRUNGE
IRLENE
IRVINE
KRESGE
MRBLUE
MRHYDE
ORACLE
ORANGE
ORDURE
ORELSE
ORGATE
ORIOLE
ORNATE
OROIDE
ORPINE
PRAGUE
PRAISE
PRANCE
PREMIE
PRINCE
PROCNE
PROPRE
PROWSE
PRYNNE
TRALEE
TRANCE
TREBLE
TRIAGE
TRIFLE
TRIODE
TRIPLE
TRISTE
TRIUNE
TRIXIE
TROCHE
TROMPE
TROUPE
TROUVE
TRUDGE
URBANE
URSINE
WRASSE
WRITHE

••RE••

ADRENO
AFREET
AFRESH
AGREED
AGREES
ARREAR
ARREST
ATREST
ATREUS
AUREUS
BAREGE
BARELY
BAREST
BEREFT
BERETS
BIREME
BOREAL
BOREAS
BOREON
BORERS
BOREUP
BUREAU
CAREEN
CAREER
CARESS
CARETO
CARETS
CEREAL
CEREUS
CORERS
CURERS
DARENT
DARETO
DIRECT
DIRELY
DIREST
DOREMI
DURESS
EGRESS
EGRETS
EUREKA
FARERS
FERENC
FIRERS
FIREUP
FOREGO
FOREST
GARETH
GERENT
GYRENE
HAREMS
HEREAT
HEREBY
HEREIN
HEREOF
HEREON
HERESY
HERETO
HIREON
HIRERS
IRREAL
JEREMY
KAREEM
KOREAN
LAREDO
LOREAL
LORENZ

MERELY
MEREST
MOREAU
MOREEN
MORELS
MORENO
NEREID
NEREIS
NEREUS
OCREAE
OGRESS
ORRERY
PARENS
PARENT
PARERS
PARETO
PAREVE
PUREED
PUREES
PURELY
PUREST
RAREFY
RARELY
RAREST
REREAD
RERENT
SCREAK
SCREAM
SCREED
SCREEN
SCREES
SCREWS
SCREWY
SERENA
SERENE
SHREDS
SHREWD
SHREWS
SIRENS
SORELY
SOREST
SPREAD
SPREES
STREAK
STREAM
STREEP
STREET
STRESS
STREWN
STREWS
SURELY
SUREST
SURETE
SURETY
TEREDO
TERESA
TERETE
TEREUS
THREAD
THREAT
THREED
THREES
THRESH
TOREAT
TORERO
TOREUP
TUREEN
UNREAD
UNREAL
UNREEL
UNREST
VARESE
VEREEN
VIREOS
WERENT
WIRERS
WOREON
YARELY
YAREST
ZAREBA

••R•E•

ADRIEN
AERIES
AFREET
AGREED
AGREES
AIRIER
AIRMEN
BARBED
BARBEL
BARBER
BARBET
BARGED
BARGES
BARKED
BARKER
BARLEY
BARMEN
BARNES
BARNEY
BARRED
BARREL
BARREN
BARRES
BARTER
BERBER
BERGEN
BIRDED
BIRDER
BIRLED
BIRNEY
BORDEN
BORDER
BORNEO
BURDEN
BURGEE
BURGER
BURIED
BURIES
BURLED
BURLEY
BURNED
BURNER
BURNET
BURNEY
BURPED
BURRED
BURSES
BYRNES
CARDED
CARDER
CAREEN
CAREER
CARIES
CARKED
CARMEL
CARMEN
CARNES
CARNET
CARNEY
CARPED
CARPEL
CARPER
CARPET
CARREL
CARREY
CARTED
CARTEL
CARTER
CARTES
CARVED
CARVER
CARVES
CARVEY
CERMET
CORBEL
CORDED
CORKED
CORKER
CORNEA
CORNED
CORNEL
CORNER
CORNET
CORREL
CORSET
CORTES
CORTEX
CORTEZ
CORVEE
CORVES
CURBED
CURDED
CURFEW
CURLED
CURLER
CURLEW
CURLEY
CURRED
CURSED
CURSES
CURTER
CURVED
CURVES
CURVET
DARIEN
DARKEN
DARKER
DARNED
DARNEL
DARNER
DARREN
DARTED
DARTER
DIRGES
DORIES
DORMER
DORSET
DORSEY
DURFEY
DURNED
DURYEA
EARNED
EARNER
EERIER
EYRIES
FARCED
FARCES
FARLEY
FARMED
FARMER
FERBER
FERRER
FERRET
FIRMED
FIRMER
FORBES
FORCED
FORCER
FORCES
FORDED
FORGED
FORGER
FORGES
FORGET
FORKED
FORKER
FORMED
FORMER
FORTES
FURIES
FURLED
FURRED
FURZES
GARBED
GARDEN
GARNER
GARNET
GARRET
GARTER
GARVEY
GERBER
GIRDED
GIRDER
GIRNED
GIRTED
GORGED
GORGES
GORGET
GORIER
GORSES
GURLEY
GURNEY
HARDEN
HARDER
HARKED
HARKEN
HARKER
HARLEM
HARLEY
HARMED
HARPED
HARPER
HARVEY
HERDED
HERDER
HERMES
HEROES
HERSEY
HORDES
HORMEL
HORNED
HORNER
HORNET
HORNEY
HORSED
HORSES
HORSEY
HURLED
HURLER
HURLEY
ISRAEL
JARRED
JERKED
JERSEY
JURIES
KAREEM
KERMES
KERNED
KERNEL
KERSEE
KERSEY
LARDED
LARDER
LARGER
LARGES
LARKED
LARSEN
LERNER
LORDED
LORIES
LURKED
MARCEL
MARGES
MARIEL
MARKED
MARKER
MARKET
MARLED
MARLEE
MARLEY
MARMEE
MARNER
MARRED
MARTEL
MARTEN
MARVEL
MERCED
MERCER
MERGED
MERGER
MERGES
MERKEL
MERMEN
MERSEY
MIRIER
MIRREN
MOREEN
MORGEN
MORLEY
MORSEL
MURDER
MURIEL
MURRES
MURREY
NERVES
NURSED
NURSER
NURSES
OBRIEN
OERTER
PARCEL
PARGET
PARKED
PARKER
PARLEY
PARRED
PARREL
PARSEC
PARSED
PARSEE
PARSER
PARSES
PARTED
PERKED
PERMED
PERTER
PORKER
PORTED
PORTER
PUREED
PUREES
PURGED
PURGES
PURLED
PURRED
PURRER
PURSED
PURSER
PURSES
PURVEY
SARGES
SCREED
SCREEN
SCREES
SERGEI
SERGES
SERIES
SERVED
SERVER
SERVES
SHRIEK
SIRREE
SORBET
SORREL
SORTED
SORTER
SPREES
SPRIER
SPRUES
SPRYER
STREEP
STREET
SURFED
SURFER
SURGED
SURGES
SURREY
SURVEY
TARGES
TARGET
TARRED
TARTER
TERCEL
TERCET
TERKEL
TERMED
TERNES
TERRET
TERSER
THREED
THREES
THROES
TORIES
TORRES
TORREY
TORTES
TUREEN
TURFED
TURKEY
TURNED
TURNER
TURRET
TURVES
UNREEL
VARDEN
VARIED
VARIES
VARLET
VARNEY
VEREEN
VERGED
VERGER
VERGES
VERSED
VERSES
VERTEX
VERVES
VERVET
VORTEX
WARDED
WARDEN
WARDER
WARIER
WARMED
WARMER
WARNED
WARNER
WARPED
WARRED
WARREN
WERFEL
WERNER
WIRIER
WORDED
WORKED
WORKER
WORMED
WORSEN
WURLEY
XERXES
YARDED
YARNED
YERKED
YERKES
YORKER
ZEROED
ZEROES

••R••E

ABRADE
AERATE
AEROBE
AFRAME
AORTAE
ARRIVE
BARBIE
BAREGE
BARITE
BARQUE
BARRIE
BERATE
BERNIE
BERTIE
BIRDIE
BIREME
BORAGE
BORATE
BORIDE
BURBLE
BURGEE
BURGLE
BURSAE
BYROTE
CARAFE
CARIBE
CAROLE
CARRIE
CERATE
CERISE
CERUSE
CHROME
CIRCLE
CIRQUE
CORVEE
CURARE
CURATE
CURDLE
CURIAE
CURULE
DARKLE
DERIDE
DERIVE
DIRIGE
ENRAGE
ENROBE
ERRARE
EUROPE
FERGIE
FERULE
FORAGE
FURORE
GARAGE
GARBLE
GARGLE
GERTIE
GIRDLE
GORDIE
GURGLE
GYRATE
GYRENE
GYROSE
HARARE
HERBIE
HORACE
HURDLE
HURTLE
JEROME
KARATE
KERSEE
KIRTLE
KURILE
LARVAE
MARBLE
MARCHE
MARCIE
MARGIE
MARINE
MARLEE
MARMEE
MARNIE
MARPLE
MARQUE
MEROPE
MIRAGE
MORALE
MOROSE
MURINE
MYRTLE
OCREAE
PARADE
PARCAE
PAREVE
PAROLE
PARSEE
PARURE
PERDUE
PERUKE
PERUSE
PHRASE
PIRATE
PURACE
PURDUE
PURFLE
PURINE
PURPLE
PURSUE
PYRITE
RERATE
SARTRE
SCRAPE
SCRIBE
SERAPE
SERENE
SERINE
SHRIKE
SHRINE
SHRIVE
SHROVE
SIRREE
SORTIE
SPRITE
SPRUCE
STRAFE
STRAKE
STRIAE
STRIDE
STRIFE
STRIKE
STRINE
STRIPE
STRIVE
STROBE
STRODE
STROKE
STROVE
SURETE
TERETE
THRACE
THRALE
THRICE
THRIVE
THRONE
THROVE
TIRADE
TIRANE
TOROSE
TORQUE
TURTLE
TYRONE
UNRIPE
UNROBE
UPRISE
UPROSE
VARESE
VERITE
VIRILE
VIRTUE
WARBLE

YORKIE

•••RE•
ADORED
ADOREE
ADORER
ADORES
AIGRET
ALFRED
ANDREA
ANDREI
ANDRES
ANDREW
ANDREY
ANTRES
AUBREY
AUDREY
AZORES
BARRED
BARREL
BARREN
BARRES
BEARER
BIGRED
BLARED
BLARES
BOTREE
BURRED
CADRES
CARREL
CARREY
CHORES
CLARET
CORREL
CURRED
DAIREN
DARREN
DEARER
DECREE
DEGREE
DOMREP
DOURER
EAGRES
ENTREE
ENURED
ENURES
FAIRED
FAIRER
FEARED
FEARER
FERRER
FERRET
FIBRES
FLARED
FLARES
FLORES
FLORET
FURRED
GARRET
GEARED
GENRES
GLARED
GLARES
HAIRED
HATRED
HEARER
HEBREW
HEDREN
IMARET
INBRED
INGRES
INURED
INURES
JARRED
JAURES
JEERED
JEERER
JUAREZ
LABREA
LABRET
LAUREL
LAUREN
LEERED
LEERER
LEGREE
LEHRER
LITRES
LIVRES
MADRES
MARRED
MCCREA
MCGREW
METRES
MIRREN
MITRED
MITRES
MOIRES
MOORED
MURRES
MURREY
NACRES
NEARED
NEARER
NITRES
OCHRES
OSPREY
PADRES
PAIRED
PARRED
PARREL
PEERED
PETREL
POORER
POURED
POURER
PUGREE
PURRED
PURRER
QUIRES
REARED
REARER
REDREW
REGRET
ROARED
ROARER
SABRES
SACRED
SAUREL
SAWRED
SCARED
SCARER
SCARES
SCORED
SCORER
SCORES
SEARED
SECRET
SEERED
SEVRES
SHARED
SHARER
SHARES
SHEREE
SHIRER
SHIRES
SHORED
SHORES
SIRREE
SNARED
SNARES
SNORED
SNORER
SNORES
SOARED
SOARER
SOARES
SOIREE
SORREL
SOURED
SOURER
SPARED
SPARER
SPARES
SPIREA
SPIRED
SPIRES
SPORES
STARED
STARER
STARES
STEREO
STERES
STORED
STORER
STORES
STOREY
SURREY
TARRED
TEARED
TENREC
TERRET
THERES
TIERED
TITRED
TITRES
TORRES
TORREY
TOURED
TOURER
TUAREG
TURRET
UNFREE
USURER
VEERED
WARRED
WARREN
WEARER
WHERED
WHERES
ZAGREB
ZAIRES

•••R•E
ACCRUE
ADOREE
AGORAE
AHERNE
AMERCE
AVERSE
BARRIE
BEURRE
BIERCE
BOTREE
BOURKE
BOURNE
BOURSE
CARRIE
CHARGE
CHERIE
CLARKE
COARSE
COERCE
COURSE
COWRIE
DEARIE
DEARME
DECREE
DEGREE
DUARTE
ECARTE
EDERLE
EMERGE
ENTREE
ETERNE
FAERIE
FAEROE
FIERCE
FLORAE
GEORGE
GOURDE
GUERRE
HEARYE
HOARSE
HYDRAE
IMBRUE
LAURIE
LEGREE
LIERNE
MACRAE
MONROE
PEERCE
PETRIE
PIERCE
PIERRE
PUGREE
ROURKE
SCARCE
SCARNE
SCURVE
SEARLE
SHEREE
SHORTE
SIRREE
SOIREE
SOURCE
SPARGE
SPARSE
SPURGE
STARVE
STERNE
SWERVE
THORPE
TIERCE
UMBRAE
UNFREE
UNTRUE

••••RE
ABJURE
ADHERE
ADJURE
ADMIRE
AGLARE
ALEGRE
ALGORE
ALLURE
AMPERE
ARMURE
ASHORE
ASPIRE
ASSURE
ATTIRE
BEFORE
BEMIRE
BEURRE
BEWARE
CENTRE
CESARE
CHEVRE
CLAIRE
COHERE
CONTRE
CONURE
CURARE
DAMORE
DEIDRE
DEJURE
DEMURE
DESIRE
EEYORE
ELMORE
EMIGRE
EMPIRE
ENCORE
ENDURE
ENSURE
ENTIRE
ERRARE
EUCHRE
EXMORE
EXPIRE
FIACRE
FIGURE
FURORE
FUTURE
GALORE
GUERRE
HARARE
HOMBRE
HONORE
IGNORE
IMMURE
IMPURE
INDORE
INHERE
INJURE
INSURE
JOHORE
KHAFRE
LAHORE
LENORE
LIGURE
LOUVRE
LUSTRE
MAITRE
MATURE
MEAGRE
MYSORE
NATURE
NOMORE
OEUVRE
ONFIRE
ORDURE
PARURE
PHEDRE
PIERRE
PROPRE
REHIRE
RETIRE
REVERE
REWIRE
SAFIRE
SARTRE
SATIRE
SECURE
SEMPRE
SEVERE
SOMBRE
SPHERE
SQUARE
SQUIRE
SUTURE
TAGORE
TENURE
THEYRE
TIMBRE
TULARE
TUYERE
UMPIRE
UNSURE
VENIRE
VOLARE

R•F•••
RAFAEL
RAFFIA
RAFFLE
RAFTED
RAFTER
REFACE
REFERS
REFFED
REFILE
REFILL
REFINE
REFITS
REFLAG
REFLEX
REFLUX
REFORM
REFUEL
REFUGE
REFUND
REFUSE
REFUTE
RIFELY
RIFEST
RIFFED
RIFFLE
RIFIFI
RIFLED
RIFLER
RIFLES
RIFTED
RUFFED
RUFFLE
RUFFLY
RUFOUS

R••F••
RAFFIA
RAFFLE
RANFOR
REDFIN
REDFIR
REDFOX
REEFED
REEFER
REFFED
RIFFED
RIFFLE
ROOFED
ROOFER
RUEFUL
RUFFED
RUFFLE
RUFFLY
RUNFOR

R•••F•
RAMIFY
RANOFF
RAREFY
RARIFY
RATIFY
REBUFF
RECIFE
RIFIFI
RIPOFF
RUBIFY
RUBOFF
RUNOFF

R••••F
RANOFF
REBUFF
RELIEF
RIDSOF
RIPOFF
RUBOFF
RUDOLF
RUNOFF

•RF•••
ERFURT

•R•F••
ARAFAT
ARMFUL
ARTFUL
CRAFTS
CRAFTY
CROFTS
DRAFTS
DRAFTY
DRIFTS
DRIFTY
DRYFLY
GRAFTS
GRIFTS
IREFUL
PREFAB
PREFER
PREFIX
PROFIT
TRIFID
TRIFLE
TRYFOR

•R••F•
ARGUFY
BRIEFS
CRYOFF
DRYOFF
GRIEFS
PROOFS

•R•••F
CRYOFF
DRYOFF

••RF••
BARFLY
CARFUL
CURFEW
DURFEY
EARFUL
JARFUL
PURFLE
SURFED
SURFER
TURFED
WERFEL

••R•F•
ADRIFT
AERIFY
AURIFY
BEREFT
CARAFE
FAROFF
PURIFY
RAREFY
RARIFY
SCRUFF
SERIFS
SHRIFT
STRAFE
STRIFE
TARIFF
THRIFT
VERIFY

••R••F
CERTIF
FAROFF
HEREOF
SCRUFF
SORTOF
TARIFF

•••RF•
DWARFS
SCARFS
SCURFY
SMURFS
WHARFS

•••R•F
HEAROF
SHARIF
SHERIF

••••RF
IMPERF

R•G•••
RAGBAG
RAGGED
RAGING
RAGLAN
RAGMAN
RAGMEN
RAGMOP
RAGOUT
RAGRUG
RAGTAG
RAGTOP
REGAIN
REGALE
REGARD
REGENT
REGGAE
REGGIE
REGIME
REGINA
REGION
REGIUS
REGLET
REGLUE
REGNAL
REGNAT
REGRET
RIGGED
RIGGER
RIGHTO
RIGHTS
RIGHTY
RIGORS
RIGOUR
RIGSUP
ROGERS
ROGUES
RUGATE
RUGGED
RUGOSE

R••G••
RAGGED
RANGED
RANGER
RANGES
RANGUP
RAYGUN
REAGAN
REDGUM
REGGAE
REGGIE
REIGNS
RIDGED
RIDGES
RIGGED
RIGGER
RINGED
RINGER
RINGUP
ROTGUT
ROUGED
ROUGES
ROUGHS
ROUGHY
RUGGED
RUNGUP
RUTGER

R•••G•
RAVAGE
RAWEGG
REBAGS
REFUGE

RENEGE
REPEGS
REPUGN
RESIGN
RETAGS

R••••G
RACING
RAGBAG
RAGING
RAGRUG
RAGTAG
RAKING
RARING
RASING
RATEDG
RATING
RAVING
RAWEGG
RAZING
REDDOG
REDING
REDTAG
REFLAG
REHANG
REHUNG
RESING
RICING
RIDING
RILING
RIMING
RISING
RIVING
ROBING
ROPING
ROVING
ROWING
RULING

•RG•••
ARGALI
ARGENT
ARGIVE
ARGOSY
ARGOTS
ARGUED
ARGUER
ARGUES
ARGUFY
ARGYLE
ARGYLL
ERGATE
ERGOTS
ORGANA
ORGANS
ORGATE
ORGEAT
ORGIES
URGENT
URGERS
URGING

•R•G••
ARAGON
ARIGHT
ARTGUM
BRIGGS
BRIGHT
BRIGID
BROGAN
BROGUE
BRUGES
CRAGGY
DRAGEE
DRAGGY
DRAGIN
DRAGON
DROGUE
FRIGHT
FRIGID
FROGGY
FRUGAL
GREGOR
GRIGRI
GROGGY
KRUGER
OREGON
ORIGEN
ORIGIN
PRAGUE
TRAGIC
TRIGLY
TRIGON
TROGON
WRIGHT

•R••G•
ARMAGH
BRIDGE
BRIGGS
BRINGS
CRAGGY
CRINGE
DRAGGY
DREDGE
DRINGS
DRUDGE
ERYNGO
FRIDGE
FRINGE
FRINGY
FROGGY
GRANGE
GREIGE
GRINGO
GROGGY
GRUDGE
GRUNGE
GRUNGY
KRESGE
ORANGE
ORANGS
ORANGY
ORINGS
ORTEGA
PRANGS
PRONGS
TRIAGE
TROUGH
TRUDGE
WRINGS
WRONGS

•R•••G
ARCING
ARMING
CRYING
DRYING
ERRING
ERVING
FRYING
IRKING
IRVING
ORBING
PROLOG
PRYING
TRUING
TRYING
URGING

••RG••
AIRGUN
BARGED
BARGES
BERGEN
BIRGIT
BORGIA
BURGAS
BURGEE
BURGER
BURGHS
BURGLE
BURGOO
BURGOS
CARGOS
CORGIS
DIRGES
FERGIE
FERGUS
FORGED
FORGER
FORGES
FORGET
FORGOT
GARGLE
GORGED
GORGES
GORGET
GORGON
GURGLE
JARGON
KURGAN
LARGER
LARGES
LARGOS
MARGAY
MARGES
MARGIE
MARGIN
MARGOT
MERGED
MERGER
MERGES
MORGAN
MORGEN
NORGAY
PARGET
PURGED
PURGES
SARGES
SARGON
SARGOS
SERGEI
SERGES
SERGIO
SURGED
SURGES
TARGES
TARGET
TURGID
TURGOR
VERGED
VERGER
VERGES
VIRGIL
VIRGIN
WARGOD

••R•G•
AURIGA
BAREGE
BORAGE
DIRIGE
DIRIGO
DORAGS
ENRAGE
FORAGE
FOREGO
GARAGE
MIRAGE
PERUGA
SCRAGS
SHRUGS
SPRAGS
SPRIGS
UNRIGS
VIRAGO

••R••G
AIRBAG
AIRING
BARING
BARONG
BERING
BORING
CARING
CORING
CURING
DARING
DURING
EARING
EARWIG
ERRING
FARING
FIRING
GORING
HARING
HERZOG
HIRING
LURING
MIRING
OARING
PARANG
PARING
PORING
RARING
SARONG
SIRING
SPRANG
SPRING
SPRUNG
STRING
STRONG
STRUNG
TARING
THRONG
TIRING
TURING
WARING
WIRING

•••RG•
ANERGY
ATERGO
CHARGE
CLERGY
EMERGE
ENERGY
GEORGE
GEORGY
SPARGE
SPURGE

•••R•G
CATRIG
GEHRIG
OILRIG
PETROG
RAGRUG
TUAREG

••••RG
ALBORG
COBURG
CYBORG
EDBERG
EKBERG
SEBERG
VYBORG

RH••••
RHABDO
RHAMES
RHEBOK
RHESUS
RHETOR
RHEUMS
RHEUMY
RHINAL
RHINOS
RHODES
RHOMBI
RHOMBS
RHONDA
RHUMBA
RHUMBS
RHYMED
RHYMER
RHYMES
RHYTHM
RHYTON

R•H•••
RAHRAH
REHABS
REHANG
REHASH
REHEAL
REHEAR
REHEAT
REHEEL
REHELD
REHEMS
REHIRE
REHOOK
REHUNG
ROHMER

R••H••
RACHEL
RACHIS
RASHAD
RASHER
RASHES
RASHID
RASHLY
RATHER
REDHAT
REDHOT
RESHES
RESHIP
RESHOD
RESHOE
RESHOT
RICHEN
RICHER
RICHES
RICHIE
RICHLY
RIGHTO
RIGHTS
RIGHTY
ROCHET
RODHAM
ROTHKO
RUCHES
RUSHED
RUSHEE
RUSHES

R•••H•
RAJAHS
RANCHO
REECHO
RHYTHM
ROUGHS
ROUGHY

R••••H
RADISH
RAHRAH
RAKISH
RAVISH
RAWISH
REHASH
RELISH
REWASH
RIYADH
RUPIAH

•RH•••
DRHOOK
ERHARD
MRHYDE

•R•H••
ARCHED
ARCHER
ARCHES
ARCHIE
ARCHLY
ARCHON
ARNHEM
ARTHRO
ARTHUR
BRAHMA
BRAHMS
GRAHAM
ORCHID
ORCHIL
ORPHAN
ORPHIC
URCHIN

•R••H•
ARETHA
ARIGHT
BRACHY
BRASHY
BRECHT
BRIGHT
BROTHS
BRUSHY
CRECHE
DRACHM
FRIGHT
FROTHS
FROTHY
GRAPHS
GRAPHY
ORACHS
TRACHY
TRASHY
TRICHO
TRISHA
TROCHE
TROPHY
TROTHS
TRUTHS
WRATHS
WRATHY
WRIGHT
WRITHE

•R•••H
ARMAGH
BRANCH
BREACH
BREATH
BREECH
BROACH
BROOCH
BRUNCH
CROUCH
CRUNCH
CRUTCH
DRENCH
FRENCH
GRINCH
GROUCH
GROWTH
IRTYSH
ORBACH
ORNITH
PREACH
TRENCH
TROUGH
WRAITH
WREATH
WRENCH
WRETCH

••RH••
BARHOP
CARHOP
DIRHAM
DURHAM
WARHOL

••R•H•
BERTHA
BERTHS
BIRTHS
BURGHS
EARTHA
EARTHY
FIRTHS
GARTHS
GERAHS
GIRTHS
GURKHA
MARCHE
MARSHA
MARSHY
MARTHA
MORPHO
MORPHS
MORPHY
MURPHY
MYRRHS
NORTHS
PERCHA
SURAHS
TORAHS
TORCHY
WORTHS
WORTHY

••R••H
AFRESH
BARISH
BARUCH
BORSCH
CERIPH
ENRICH
FARRAH
GARETH
GARISH
HIRSCH
HURRAH
INRUSH
JARRAH
KIRSCH
MARIAH
MARISH
OGRISH
ONRUSH
PARAPH
PARIAH
PARISH
PERISH
PURDAH
QURUSH
SERAPH
SIRRAH
TERAPH
THRASH
THRESH
THRUSH
UPRUSH
WARMTH
ZEROTH
ZURICH

•••RH•
MYRRHS

•••R•H
CHURCH
DEARTH
EPARCH
EXARCH
FARRAH
FOURTH
HEARTH
HIJRAH
HOORAH
HURRAH
INARCH
JARRAH
RAHRAH
SCORCH
SEARCH
SIRRAH
SMERSH
SMIRCH
STARCH
STORCH
SWARTH

RI••••
RIALTO
RIATAS
RIBALD
RIBAND
RIBBED
RIBBON
RIBEYE
RIBOSE
RICERS
RICHEN
RICHER
RICHES
RICHIE
RICHLY
RICING
RICKED
RICKEY
RIDDED
RIDDEN
RIDDLE
RIDENT
RIDERS
RIDGED
RIDGES
RIDING
RIDLEY
RIDSOF
RIENZI
RIFELY
RIFEST
RIFFED
RIFFLE
RIFIFI
RIFLED
RIFLER
RIFLES
RIFTED
RIGGED
RIGGER
RIGHTO
RIGHTS
RIGHTY
RIGORS
RIGOUR
RIGSUP
RILEUP
RILING
RILLES

RILLET
RIMIER
RIMING
RIMINI
RIMMED
RIMOSE
RIMPLE
RIMSKY
RINGED
RINGER
RINGUP
RINSED
RINSES
RIOJAS
RIOTED
RIOTER
RIPELY
RIPENS
RIPEST
RIPKEN
RIPLEY
RIPOFF
RIPOUT
RIPPED
RIPPER
RIPPLE
RIPPLY
RIPRAP
RIPSAW
RIPSUP
RISERS
RISING
RISKED
RISKER
RISQUE
RITARD
RITTER
RITUAL
RIVALS
RIVERA
RIVERS
RIVETS
RIVING
RIYADH
RIYALS
RIZZIO

R•I•••

RAIDED
RAIDER
RAILAT
RAILED
RAILER
RAINED
RAINER
RAINES
RAINEY
RAIPUR
RAISED
RAISER
RAISES
RAISIN
REIGNS
REILLY
REINAS
REINED
REINER
REININ
REINKS
RHINAL
RHINOS
ROILED
RUINED
RUINER

R••I••

RABIES
RACIAL
RACIER
RACILY
RACINE
RACING
RADIAL
RADIAN
RADIOS
RADISH
RADIUM
RADIUS
RAGING
RAKING
RAKISH
RAMIES
RAMIFY
RANIDS
RAPIDS
RAPIER
RAPINE
RAPINI
RARIFY
RARING
RARITY
RASING
RATIFY
RATINE
RATING
RATION
RATIOS
RATITE
RAVINE
RAVING
RAVISH
RAWISH
RAZING
REAIMS
REAIRS
REBIDS
REBIND
RECIFE
RECIPE
RECITE
REDIAL
REDING
REDINK
REFILE
REFILL
REFINE
REFITS
REGIME
REGINA
REGION
REGIUS
REHIRE
RELICS
RELICT
RELIED
RELIEF
RELIES
RELINE
RELISH
RELIST
RELIVE
REMICK
REMIND
REMISE
REMISS
REMITS
REOILS
REPINE
REPINS
RESIDE
RESIGN
RESILE
RESING
RESINS
RESINY
RESIST
RETIAL
RETIED
RETIES
RETILE
RETIME
RETINA
RETIRE
REVIEW
REVILE
REVISE
REVIVE
REWIND
REWINS
REWIRE
RICING
RIDING
RIFIFI
RILING
RIMIER
RIMING
RIMINI
RISING
RIVING
ROBING
ROBINS
ROPIER
ROPING
ROSIER
ROSILY
ROSINS
ROSINY
ROSITA
ROTINI
ROVING
ROWING
RUBIED
RUBIES
RUBIFY
RULING
RUMINA
RUNINS
RUPIAH
RUTILE

R•••I•

RABBIS
RABBIT
RACHIS
RAFFIA
RAISIN
RAKEIN
RANCID
RANKIN
RASHID
RATLIN
READIN
REALIA
REBOIL
RECOIL
REDFIN
REDFIR
REEDIT
REELIN
REGAIN
REGGIE
REININ
REJOIN
RELAID
REMAIL
REMAIN
RENAIL
RENNIE
RENNIN
RENOIR
REPAID
REPAIR
RESHIP
RESNIK
RESPIN
RETAIL
RETAIN
RETRIM
REVOIR
RICHIE
RIZZIO
ROADIE
ROBBIA
ROBBIE
ROLLIE
ROLLIN
ROMAIC
RONNIE
ROOKIE
ROOMIE
ROPEIN
RUBRIC
RUBSIN
RUNCIE
RUNSIN
RUSKIN
RUSSIA
RUSTIC

R••••I

RAPINI
RHOMBI
RIENZI
RIFIFI
RIMINI
ROMAJI
ROTINI
RUBATI

•RI•••

ARIDLY
ARIGHT
ARIOSE
ARIOSO
ARISEN
ARISES
ARISTA
ARISTO
BRIAND
BRIANS
BRIARD
BRIARS
BRIBED
BRIBES
BRICKS
BRICKY
BRIDAL
BRIDES
BRIDGE
BRIDLE
BRIEFS
BRIENZ
BRIERS
BRIERY
BRIGGS
BRIGHT
BRIGID
BRILLO
BRILLS
BRINED
BRINES
BRINGS
BRINKS
BRITON
CRICKS
CRIERS
CRIKEY
CRIMEA
CRIMES
CRIMPS
CRIMPY
CRINGE
CRIPES
CRISCO
CRISES
CRISIS
CRISPS
CRISPY
CRISTO
CRITIC
DRIERS
DRIEST
DRIFTS
DRIFTY
DRILLS
DRINGS
DRINKS
DRIPPY
DRIVEL
DRIVEN
DRIVER
DRIVES
ERINYS
FRIARS
FRIARY
FRIDAY
FRIDGE
FRIEND
FRIERS
FRIEZE
FRIGHT
FRIGID
FRIJOL
FRILLS
FRILLY
FRINGE
FRINGY
FRISCO
FRISEE
FRISES
FRISKS
FRISKY
FRITOS
FRIZZY
GRIEFS
GRIEVE
GRIFTS
GRIGRI
GRILLE
GRILLS
GRILSE
GRIMED
GRIMES
GRIMKE
GRIMLY
GRINCH
GRINDS
GRINGO
GRIOTS
GRIPED
GRIPER
GRIPES
GRIPPE
GRISLY
GRISON
GRISTS
GRITTY
GRIVET
IRIDES
IRIDIC
IRISES
IRISIN
ORIANA
ORIBIS
ORIELS
ORIENT
ORIGEN
ORIGIN
ORINGS
ORIOLE
ORISON
ORISSA
PRICED
PRICER
PRICES
PRICEY
PRICKS
PRIDED
PRIDES
PRIERS
PRIEST
PRIMAL
PRIMED
PRIMER
PRIMES
PRIMLY
PRIMOS
PRIMPS
PRIMUM
PRIMUS
PRINCE
PRINKS
PRINTS
PRIONS
PRIORI
PRIORS
PRIORY
PRIPET
PRISMS
PRISON
PRISSY
PRIVET
PRIZED
PRIZES
TRIADS
TRIAGE
TRIALS
TRIBAL
TRIBES
TRICED
TRICEP
TRICES
TRICHO
TRICIA
TRICKS
TRICKY
TRICOT
TRIERS
TRIFID
TRIFLE
TRIGLY
TRIGON
TRIJET
TRIKES
TRILBY
TRILLS
TRIMLY
TRINAL
TRINES
TRIODE
TRIPLE
TRIPLY
TRIPOD
TRIPOS
TRIPUP
TRISHA
TRISTE
TRITER
TRITON
TRIUNE
TRIVET
TRIVIA
TRIXIE
URIALS
WRIEST
WRIGHT
WRINGS
WRISTS
WRITER
WRITES
WRITHE

•R•I••

ARCING
ARGIVE
ARLISS
ARMIES
ARMING
ARNICA
AROIDS
ARRIBA
ARRIVE
ARTIER
ARTILY
ARTIST
BRAIDS
BRAILA
BRAILS
BRAINS
BRAINY
BRAISE
BROILS
BRUINS
BRUISE
BRUITS
CRUISE
CRYING
DRAILS
DRAINS
DROIDS
DROITS
DRUIDS
DRYICE
DRYING
DRYINK
ERBIUM
ERMINE
EROICA
ERRING
ERVING
FRAIDY
FRAISE
FRUITS
FRUITY
FRYING
GRAILS
GRAINS
GRAINY
GREIGE
GROINS
IRKING
IRVINE
IRVING
KRAITS
ORBING
ORBITS
OREIDA
ORGIES
ORNITH
OROIDE
ORPINE
ORSINO
PRAISE
PRYING
TRAILS
TRAINS
TRAITS
TROIKA
TRUING
TRUISM
TRYING
URGING
URSIDS
URSINE
WRAITH

•R••I•

ARABIA
ARABIC
ARALIA
ARAMIS
ARCHIE
ARCTIC
ARMPIT
ARTOIS
BRAZIL
BREVIS
BRIGID
BRODIE
BROLIN
CRANIA
CRANIO
CREDIT
CRETIN
CRISIS
CRITIC
CRONIN
DRAGIN
DRAWIN
DREWIN
DROPIN
DROPIT
EROTIC
FRIGID
FROLIC
GRACIE
GRADIN
GRATIA
GRATIN
GRATIS
GRAVID
GRODIN
IRANIS
IRAQIS
IRENIC
IRIDIC
IRISIN
IRONIC
ORCHID
ORCHIL
ORDAIN
ORIBIS
ORIGIN
ORPHIC
PRAXIS
PRECIS
PREFIX
PRELIM
PREMIE
PREVIN
PROFIT
PROLIX
PROSIT
TRAGIC
TRAVIS
TREDIA
TREPID
TRICIA
TRIFID
TRIVIA
TRIXIE
TROPIC
URACIL
URALIC
URANIA
URANIC
URCHIN

•R•••I

ARGALI
ARMANI
BRAZZI
BRUNEI
DROMOI
ERNANI
FRUTTI
GRIGRI
PRIORI
PROTEI

••RI••
ADRIAN
ADRIEN
ADRIFT
AERIAL
AERIES
AERIFY
AERILY
AFRICA
AFRITS
AIRIER
AIRILY
AIRING
AORIST
ARRIBA
ARRIVE
ATRIAL
ATRISK
ATRIUM
AURIFY
AURIGA
BARING
BARISH
BARITE
BARIUM
BERING
BORIDE
BORING
BURIED
BURIES
BURINS
CARIBE
CARIBS
CARIES
CARINA
CARING
CERIPH
CERISE
CERIUM
CHRISM
CORING
CORIUM
CURIAE
CURIAL
CURING
CURIOS
CURIUM
DARIEN
DARING
DARIUS
DERIDE
DERIVE
DIRIGE
DIRIGO
DORIAN
DORIES
DURIAN
DURING
EARING
EERIER
EERILY
ENRICH
ENRICO
ERRING
EYRIES
FARINA
FARING
FERIAL
FERIAS
FERITY
FIRING
FORINT
FURIES
GARISH
GORIER
GORILY
GORING
HARING
HERIOT
HIRING
JURIES
JURIST
KARIBA
KURILE
LARIAT
LERIDA
LORICA
LORIES
LURING
LYRICS
LYRIST
MARIAH
MARIAN
MARIEL
MARIKO
MARILU
MARINA
MARINE
MARINO
MARION
MARISA
MARISH
MARIST
MARIUS
MERIDA
MERINO
MERITS
MIRIAM
MIRIER
MIRING
MORION
MORITA
MORITZ
MURIEL
MURINE
MYRIAD
NARIAL
NORIAS
OARING
OBRIAN
OBRIEN
OGRISH
PARIAH
PARING
PARISH
PARITY
PERILS
PERIOD
PERISH
PORING
PURIFY
PURINA
PURINE
PURISM
PURIST
PURITY
PYRITE
RARIFY
RARING
RARITY
SCRIBE
SCRIMP
SCRIMS
SCRIPS
SCRIPT
SERIAL
SERIES
SERIFS
SERINE
SERINS
SHRIEK
SHRIFT
SHRIKE
SHRILL
SHRIMP
SHRINE
SHRINK
SHRIVE
SIRICA
SIRING
SIRIUS
SPRIER
SPRIGS
SPRING
SPRINT
SPRITE
SPRITS
SPRITZ
STRIAE
STRICK
STRICT
STRIDE
STRIFE
STRIKE
STRINE
STRING
STRIPE
STRIPS
STRIPY
STRIVE
SURIMI
SYRIAN
SYRINX
TARIFF
TARING
THRICE
THRIFT
THRILL
THRIPS
THRIVE
TIRING
TORIES
TORINO
TURING
TYRIAN
UGRIAN
UNRIGS
UNRIPE
UPRISE
VARIED
VARIES
VERIFY
VERILY
VERISM
VERITE
VERITY
VIRILE
WARIER
WARILY
WARING
WIRIER
WIRILY
WIRING
YORICK
ZORILS
ZURICH

••R•I•
ADROIT
AFRAID
AORTIC
BARBIE
BARDIC
BARKIN
BARRIE
BARRIO
BARRIS
BERLIN
BERNIE
BERTIE
BIRDIE
BIRGIT
BORGIA
CARDIN
CARDIO
CARLIN
CARRIE
CERTIF
CERVID
CORBIN
CORGIS
CURTIN
CURTIS
CURTIZ
DARNIT
DARWIN
DERAIL
DERMIS
DERRIS
DORRIT
DURBIN
EARWIG
EURAIL
FERGIE
FERRIC
FERRIS
FERVID
FIRKIN
FORBID
FORMIC
GARCIA
GARLIC
GERBIL
GERTIE
GORDIE
HARBIN
HARLIN
HARRIS
HERBIE
HEREIN
HERMIT
HEROIC
HORNIN
HORRID
JERKIN
KARMIC
KERMIS
KERMIT
LORAIN
MARCIA
MARCIE
MARGIE
MARGIN
MARLIN
MARNIE
MARTIN
MARVIN
MERLIN
MORBID
MORRIS
MURCIA
NARNIA
NARVIK
NEREID
NEREIS
NORDIC
NORRIS
PARNIS
PARRIS
PARVIS
PERMIT
PERNIO
PERSIA
PIRRIP
PORTIA
PURLIN
SARDIS
SARNIA
SERAIS
SERBIA
SERGIO
SERKIN
SORBIC
SORDID
SORTIE
SPRAIN
STRAIN
STRAIT
TARPIT
TOROID
TORPID
TORRID
TURBID
TURBIT
TURGID
TURKIC
TURNIN
TURNIP
TURPIN
VERBIS
VERDIN
VERMIN
VIRGIL
VIRGIN
WORKIN
YORKIE
ZEROIN

••R••I
BORZOI
CARONI
DORATI
DOREMI
KERNOI
MORONI
NEROLI
SERGEI
STRATI
SURIMI

•••RI•
ACARID
AGARIC
ALARIC
ALDRIN
ANTRIM
ASTRID
ATTRIT
AZORIN
BARRIE
BARRIO
BARRIS
CAPRIS
CARRIE
CATRIG
CEDRIC
CHERIE
CITRIC
CLERIC
CLORIS
COURIC
COWRIE
CUPRIC
CYMRIC
DEARIE
DEBRIS
DELRIO
DERRIS
DORRIT
EGERIA
ESPRIT
FABRIC
FAERIE
FERRIC
FERRIS
FIBRIL
FIBRIN
FLORID
FLORIN
FLORIO
GEHRIG
GLORIA
HARRIS
HENRIK
HORRID
HOURIS
HUBRIS
HYBRID
IATRIC
IBERIA
ICARIA
ILORIN
INDRIS
INGRID
ISTRIA
KAURIS
KUKRIS
LAURIE
LIBRIS
MADRID
MAORIS
MATRIX
METRIC
MIDRIB
MORRIS
NITRIC
NORRIS
NUTRIA
OILRIG
OSIRIS
PARRIS
PEERIN
PEORIA
PETRIE
PIRRIP
POURIN
PUTRID
RETRIM
RUBRIC
SCORIA
SHARIA
SHARIF
SHERIF
SPIRIT
STIRIN
STYRIA
TABRIZ
TETRIS
TIGRIS
TORRID
TSURIS
TUGRIK
UMBRIA
USERID
VITRIC

•••R•I
ANDREI
CIARDI
ITURBI
OCTROI
SHORTI
THYRSI

••••RI
ASKARI
BIHARI
CENTRI
DENDRI
DMITRI
EPHORI
GRIGRI
HATARI
HEGARI
HUMERI
JAVARI
LIBERI
MIDORI
PAHARI
PAPYRI
PRIORI
QATARI
QUADRI
SAFARI
SATORI
SOUARI
TISHRI
UAKARI
VIDERI

R•J•••
RAJAHS
RAJPUT
REJECT
REJOIN

R••J••
RAMJET
RIOJAS

R•••J•
ROMAJI

•RJ•••
ARJUNA

•R•J••
FRIJOL
PRAJNA
TRAJAN
TRIJET
TROJAN

••R•J•
BAROJA

•••R•J
SWARAJ

••••RJ
INTERJ

R•K•••
RAKEIN
RAKERS
RAKEUP
RAKING
RAKISH
REKEYS

R••K••
RACKED
RACKET
RACKUP
RANKED
RANKER
RANKIN
RANKLE
RANKLY
RECKON
REEKED
RICKED
RICKEY
RIPKEN
RISKED
RISKER
ROCKED
ROCKER
ROCKET
ROCKNE
ROCKYV
ROOKED
ROOKIE
RUCKED
RUCKUS
RUSKIN
RYOKAN
RYUKYU

R•••K•
REBUKE
REINKS
REMAKE
RETAKE
REVOKE
RIMSKY
ROTHKO
ROURKE

R••••K
RECORK
REDINK
REDOAK
REEBOK
REHOOK
RELOCK
REMARK
REMICK
RESNIK
RETOOK
REWORK
RHEBOK

•RK•••
IRKING
ORKNEY

•R•K••
BRAKED
BRAKES
BROKAW
BROKEN
BROKER
CRAKES
CRIKEY
DRAKES
KRAKEN
KRAKOW
TRIKES

•R••K•
BREAKS
BRICKS
BRICKY
BRINKS
BROOKE
BROOKS
BROOKY
CRACKS
CRACKY
CRANKS
CRANKY
CREAKS
CREAKY
CREEKS
CRICKS
CROAKS
CROAKY
CROCKS
CROOKS
DRINKS
FRANKS
FREAKS
FREAKY
FRISKS
FRISKY
FROCKS
GREEKS
GRIMKE
PRANKS
PRICKS
PRINKS
PROSKY
TRACKS
TRICKS
TRICKY
TROIKA
TRUCKS
TRUNKS

WRACKS
WREAKS
WRECKS

•R•••K
ARAWAK
ARRACK
BRATSK
DRHOOK
DRYINK
FRANCK
TREBEK
URALSK

••RK••
BARKAT
BARKED
BARKER
BARKIN
CARKED
CORKED
CORKER
DARKEN
DARKER
DARKLE
DARKLY
FIRKIN
FORKED
FORKER
GURKHA
HARKED
HARKEN
HARKER
JERKED
JERKIN
LARKED
LURKED
MARKED
MARKER
MARKET
MARKKA
MARKUP
MERKEL
PARKAS
PARKAY
PARKED
PARKER
PERKED
PERKUP
PORKER
SERKIN
TERKEL
TURKEY
TURKIC
WORKED
WORKER
WORKIN
WORKON
WORKUP
YERKED
YERKES
YORKER
YORKIE

••R•K•
EUREKA
MARIKO
MARKKA
PERUKE
SHRIKE
STRAKE
STRIKE
STROKE
YUROKS

••R••K
ARRACK
ATRISK
BARTOK
BUROAK
FAROUK
KARNAK
MARDUK
NARVIK
SCREAK
SHRANK
SHRIEK
SHRINK
SHRUNK
STREAK
STRICK
STRUCK
YORICK

•••RK•
BOURKE
CLARKE
CLERKS
DMARKS
OZARKS
QUARKS
QUIRKS
QUIRKY
ROURKE
SHARKS
SHIRKS
SMIRKS
SMIRKY
SPARKS
SPARKY
STIRKS
STORKS

•••R•K
AMTRAK
ANORAK
DVORAK
HENRIK
TOBRUK
TUGRIK

••••RK
ATWORK
DEBARK
EMBARK
LANARK
NEWARK
RECORK
REMARK
REWORK
STMARK
UNCORK

R•L•••
RELACE
RELAID
RELATE
RELAYS
RELENT
RELETS
RELEVY
RELICS
RELICT
RELIED
RELIEF
RELIES
RELINE
RELISH
RELIST
RELIVE
RELOAD
RELOCK
RELUCT
RELUME
RILEUP
RILING
RILLES
RILLET
ROLAND
ROLEOS
ROLLED
ROLLER
ROLLIE
ROLLIN
ROLLON
ROLLUP
RULEON
RULERS
RULING

R••L••
RAGLAN
RAILAT
RAILED
RAILER
RATLIN
REALER
REALES
REALIA
REALLY
REALMS
REALTY
REELED
REELIN
REFLAG
REFLEX
REFLUX
REGLET
REGLUE
REILLY
REPLAN
REPLAY
REPLOW
REVLON
RIALTO
RIDLEY
RIFLED
RIFLER
RIFLES
RILLES
RILLET
RIPLEY
ROBLES
ROILED
ROLLED
ROLLER
ROLLIE
ROLLIN
ROLLON
ROLLUP
RUBLES
RUBLEV
RUNLET
RVALUE

R•••L•
RABBLE
RACILY
RADDLE
RADULA
RAFFLE
RAMBLA
RAMBLE
RANKLE
RANKLY
RAPTLY
RARELY
RASHLY
RASSLE
RATELS
RATTLE
RATTLY
RAVELS
RAZZLE
RCCOLA
REALLY
REBELS
REBOLT
RECALL
REFILE
REFILL
REGALE
REHELD
REILLY
REMELT
REMOLD
REOILS
REPELS
REPOLL
RESALE
RESALT
RESELL
RESILE
RESOLD
RESOLE
RESULT
RETELL
RETILE
RETOLD
REVELS
REVILE
REVOLT
REWELD
RIBALD
RICHLY
RIDDLE
RIFELY
RIFFLE
RIMPLE
RIPELY
RIPPLE
RIPPLY
RIVALS
RIYALS
ROBALO
ROMOLA
RONALD
RONELY
ROSILY
ROUBLE
ROWELS
ROYALE
ROYALS
RUBBLE
RUBBLY
RUDDLE
RUDELY
RUDOLF
RUFFLE
RUFFLY
RUMBLE
RUMBLY
RUMPLE
RUMPLY
RUNDLE
RUSTLE
RUTILE
RYDELL

R••••L
RACHEL
RACIAL
RADIAL
RAFAEL
RAPPEL
RAQUEL
RASCAL
REBOIL
RECALL
RECOIL
REDEAL
REDIAL
REFILL
REFUEL
REGNAL
REHEAL
REHEEL
REMAIL
RENAIL
RENTAL
REPEAL
REPOLL
RESEAL
RESELL
RETAIL
RETELL
RETIAL
RETOOL
RETRAL
REVEAL
RHINAL
RITUAL
ROMMEL
RONDEL
RUEFUL
RUNNEL
RUPAUL
RYDELL

•RL•••
ARLEEN
ARLENE
ARLISS
IRLENE
ORLOPS

•R•L••
ARALIA
ARALLU
ARMLET
BRILLO
BRILLS
BROLIN
BROLLY
BRULES
DRILLS
DROLLS
DROLLY
FRILLS
FRILLY
FROLIC
GRILLE
GRILLS
GRILSE
MRBLUE
ORALES
ORALLY
ORELSE
ORTLES
PRELAW
PRELIM
PROLES
PROLIX
PROLOG
TRALEE
TRILBY
TRILLS
TROLLS
TRYLON
URALIC
URALSK

•R••L•
ARABLE
ARALLU
ARBELA
ARCHLY
AREOLA
ARGALI
ARGYLE
ARGYLL
ARIDLY
ARNOLD
ARTELS
ARTILY
BRAILA
BRAILS
BRAWLS
BRIDLE
BRILLO
BRILLS
BROILS
BROLLY
CRADLE
CRAWLS
CRAWLY
CREELS
CREOLE
DRABLY
DRAILS
DRAWLS
DRAWLY
DRILLS
DROLLS
DROLLY
DROOLS
DROOLY
DRYFLY
ERROLL
FREELY
FRILLS
FRILLY
GRABLE
GRAILS
GRAYLY
GREYLY
GRILLE
GRILLS
GRIMLY
GRISLY
GROWLS
GROWLY
GRUELS
KRAALS
ORACLE
ORALLY
ORIELS
ORIOLE
ORMOLU
ORWELL
PRIMLY
PROWLS
TRAILS
TRAWLS
TREBLE
TREBLY
TRIALS
TRIFLE
TRIGLY
TRILLS
TRIMLY
TRIPLE
TRIPLY
TROLLS
URIALS
URSULA

•R•••L
ARGYLL
ARMFUL
ARTFUL
BRAZIL
BRIDAL
BRUMAL
BRUTAL
CRENEL
CRESOL
CREWEL
CRURAL
DREXEL
DRIVEL
ERROLL
FRIJOL
FRUGAL
GRAVEL
GRETEL
GROVEL
IREFUL
IRREAL
MRCOOL
ORCHIL
ORDEAL
ORWELL
PRIMAL
PROPEL
TRAVEL
TRIBAL
TRINAL
TROWEL
URACIL

••RL••
BARLEY
BERLIN
BIRLED
BURLAP
BURLED
BURLEY
CARLIN
CARLOS
CARLOT
CURLED
CURLER
CURLEW
CURLEY
CURLUP
EARLAP
FARLEY
FARLOW
FURLED
GARLIC
GURLEY
HARLAN
HARLEM
HARLEY
HARLIN
HARLOW
HURLED
HURLER
HURLEY
MARLED
MARLEE
MARLEY
MARLIN
MARLON
MERLIN
MERLON
MERLOT
MORLEY
PARLAY
PARLEY
PARLOR
PURLED
PURLIN
VARLET
WORLDS
WURLEY

••R•L•
AERILY
AIRILY
BARELY
BARFLY
BAROLO
BURBLE
BURBLY
BURGLE
CAROLE
CAROLS
CIRCLE
CORALS
CURDLE
CURTLY
CURULE
DARKLE
DARKLY
DIRELY
EERILY
ENROLL
ENROLS
ERROLL
FERULE
FIRMLY
GARBLE
GARGLE
GERALD
GIRDLE
GORALS
GORILY
GURGLE
HARALD
HARDLY
HAROLD
HERALD
HURDLE
HURTLE
KERALA
KIRTLE
KURALT
KURILE
LORDLY
MARBLE
MARBLY
MARILU
MARPLE
MERELY
MORALE
MORALS
MORELS
MURALS
MYRTLE
NEROLI
PAROLE
PARTLY
PARULA
PERILS
PERTLY
PORTLY
PURELY
PURFLE
PURPLE
PURPLY
RARELY
SCROLL
SHRILL
SORELY
SPRYLY
STROLL
SURELY
TARTLY
THRALE
THRALL
THRILL
TURTLE
UNROLL
UNRULY
VERILY
VIRILE
WARBLE
WARILY
WARMLY
WIRILY
YARELY
ZORILS

••R••L
AERIAL
AORTAL
ATRIAL
BARBEL
BARREL

BOREAL
BURSAL
CARFUL
CARMEL
CARNAL
CARPAL
CARPEL
CARREL
CARROL
CARTEL
CEREAL
CORBEL
CORNEL
CORRAL
CORREL
CURIAL
DARNEL
DARRYL
DERAIL
DERMAL
DIRNDL
DORSAL
EARFUL
ENROLL
ERROLL
EURAIL
FERIAL
FORMAL
GERBIL
HERBAL
HORMEL
IRREAL
ISRAEL
JARFUL
KERNEL
LARVAL
LOREAL
MARCEL
MARIEL
MARTEL
MARVEL
MERKEL
MORSEL
MORTAL
MURIEL
MYRDAL
NARIAL
NARWAL
NORMAL
PARCEL
PARREL
PORTAL
SCRAWL
SCROLL
SERIAL
SERVAL
SHRILL
SORREL
SPRAWL
STROLL
TARSAL
TERCEL
TERKEL
THRALL
THRILL
UNREAL
UNREEL
UNROLL
VERBAL
VERNAL
VIRGIL
WARHOL
WERFEL

•••RL•
BGIRLS
CEORLS
CHARLY
CHURLS
DEARLY
DOURLY
EBERLY
EDERLE
EVERLY
FAIRLY
GNARLS
GNARLY
HOURLY
KNURLS
KNURLY
NEARLY
OVERLY
PEARLS
PEARLY
POORLY
SEARLE
SKIRLS
SNARLS
SNARLY
SOURLY
SWIRLS
SWIRLY
TWIRLS
WHIRLS
WHIRLY
WHORLS
YEARLY

•••R•L
ABORAL
AMORAL
ASTRAL
BARREL
CARREL
CARROL
CHERYL
CHORAL
CORRAL
CORREL
CRURAL
DARRYL
FIBRIL
FLORAL
LAUREL
MITRAL
NEURAL
NEUROL
PARREL
PATROL
PETREL
PETROL
PLURAL
RETRAL
SACRAL
SAUREL
SHERYL
SORREL
SPIRAL
STEROL
UMBRAL

••••RL
ASWIRL
AWHIRL
MYGIRL
SCHORL
UNCURL
UNFURL

R•M•••
RAMADA
RAMATE
RAMBLA
RAMBLE
RAMEAU
RAMETS
RAMIES
RAMIFY
RAMJET
RAMMED
RAMONA
RAMONE
RAMOSE
RAMOUS
RAMPED
RAMROD
RAMSAY
RAMSES
RAMSEY
RAMSON
REMADE
REMAIL
REMAIN
REMAKE
REMAND
REMANS
REMAPS
REMARK
REMEDY
REMELT
REMEND
REMICK
REMIND
REMISE
REMISS
REMITS
REMOLD
REMOPS
REMORA
REMOTE
REMOVE
REMOWN
REMOWS
REMUDA
RIMIER
RIMING
RIMINI
RIMMED
RIMOSE
RIMPLE
RIMSKY
ROMAIC
ROMAJI
ROMANO
ROMANS
ROMANY
ROMEOS
ROMERO
ROMMEL
ROMNEY
ROMOLA
ROMPED
ROMPER
RUMBAS
RUMBLE
RUMBLY
RUMENS
RUMINA
RUMMER
RUMORS
RUMOUR
RUMPLE
RUMPLY
RUMPUS

R••M••
RAGMAN
RAGMEN
RAGMOP
RAMMED
REAMED
REAMER
RHAMES
RHOMBI
RHOMBS
RHUMBA
RHUMBS
RHYMED
RHYMER
RHYMES
RIMMED
ROAMED
ROAMER
RODMAN
ROHMER
ROMMEL
ROOMED
ROOMER
ROOMIE
RUDMAN
RUMMER

R•••M•
RACEME
RADOME
REAIMS
REALMS
REARMS
REGIME
REHEMS
RELUME
RENAME
RESUME
RETIME
REVAMP
RHEUMS
RHEUMY
RUNDMC

R••••M
RADIUM
RANDOM
RANSOM
REDEEM
REDGUM
REFORM
RETRIM
REWARM
RHYTHM
RODHAM

•RM•••
ARMADA
ARMAGH
ARMAND
ARMANI
ARMETS
ARMFUL
ARMIES
ARMING
ARMLET
ARMORS
ARMORY
ARMOUR
ARMPIT
ARMURE
ERMINE
MRMOTO
ORMOLU
ORMOND

•R•M••
ARAMIS
AROMAS
BREMEN
BRUMAL
BRUMBY
BRUMES
CRAMBO
CRAMPS
CREMES
CRIMEA
CRIMES
CRIMPS
CRIMPY
CRUMBS
CRUMBY
CRUMMY
DRAMAS
DROMOI
DROMOS
DRUMUP
FRAMED
FRAMES
FRUMPS
FRUMPY
GRAMAS
GRAMME
GRAMMY
GRAMPA
GRAMPS
GRIMED
GRIMES
GRIMKE
GRIMLY
GRUMPS
GRUMPY
KRAMER
OROMOS
PREMED
PREMIE
PRIMAL
PRIMED
PRIMER
PRIMES
PRIMLY
PRIMOS
PRIMPS
PRIMUM
PRIMUS
PROMOS
PROMPT
TRAMPS
TREMOR
TRIMLY
TROMPE
TROMPS
TRUMAN
TRUMPS

•R••M•
BRAHMA
BRAHMS
BREAMS
BROOMS
BROOMY
CREAMS
CREAMY
CRUMMY
DREAMS
DREAMT
DREAMY
GRAMME
GRAMMY
GROOMS
PREAMP
PRISMS
PROAMS
PROEMS
TRAUMA
VROOMS

•R•••M
ARNHEM
ARTGUM
DRACHM
ERBIUM
FRENUM
GRAHAM
PRELIM
PRIMUM
PROTEM
TRUISM

••RM••
AIRMAN
AIRMEN
BARMAN
BARMEN
BORMAN
BURMAN
CARMAN
CARMEL
CARMEN
CERMET
CORMAN
DERMAL
DERMIS
DORMER
FARMED
FARMER
FERMAT
FIRMAN
FIRMED
FIRMER
FIRMLY
FIRMUP
FORMAL
FORMAN
FORMAT
FORMED
FORMER
FORMIC
GERMAN
HARMED
HARMON
HERMAN
HERMES
HERMIT
HERMON
HORMEL
HORMUZ
KARMIC
KERMAN
KERMES
KERMIS
KERMIT
KIRMAN
KORMAN
MARMEE
MARMOT
MERMAN
MERMEN
MORMON
MURMUR
NORMAL
NORMAN
PERMED
PERMIT
SERMON
TARMAC
TERMED
VERMIN
WARMED
WARMER
WARMLY
WARMTH
WARMUP
WORMED

••R•M•
ABRAMS
AFRAME
BIREME
CAROMS
CDROMS
CHROMA
CHROME
CHROMO
CHROMY
DOREMI
EPROMS
FORUMS
HAREMS
JEREMY
JEROME
JORUMS
LARAMS
SCRAMS
SCRIMP
SCRIMS
SCRUMS
SERUMS
SHRIMP
STRUMS
SURIMI
THRUMS

••R••M
AIRARM
AIRDAM
ATRIUM
BARIUM
BARNUM
CERIUM
CHRISM
CIRCUM
CORIUM
CURIUM
DIRHAM
DORSUM
DURHAM
HARLEM
KAREEM
MIRIAM
PURISM
SCREAM
STREAM
VERISM

•••RM•
ALARMS
CHARMS
DEARME
DHARMA
REARMS
SMARMY
STORMS
STORMY
SWARMS
THERMO
THERMS
UNARMS

•••R•M
ALARUM
ANTRIM
ANTRUM
ASHRAM
BAYRUM
DIGRAM
ENGRAM
FOURAM
FOURPM
INGRAM
LABRUM
QUORUM
RETRIM
SACRUM
SCARUM

••••RM
AFFIRM
AIRARM
DEFORM
DISARM
INFIRM
INFORM
REFORM
REWARM
SQUIRM

R•N•••
RANCHO
RANCID
RANCOR
RANDOM
RANDRY
RANEES
RANFOR
RANGED
RANGER
RANGES
RANGUP
RANIDS
RANKED
RANKER
RANKIN
RANKLE
RANKLY
RANOFF
RANOUT
RANSOM
RANTED
RANTER
RENAIL
RENAME
RENATA
RENDER
RENEGE
RENEWS
RENNES
RENNET
RENNIE
RENNIN
RENOIR
RENOTE
RENOWN
RENTAL
RENTED
RENTER
RINGED
RINGER
RINGUP
RINSED
RINSES
RONALD
RONDEL
RONDOS
RONELY
RONNIE
RUNCIE
RUNDLE
RUNDMC
RUNDRY
RUNFOR
RUNGUP
RUNINS
RUNLET
RUNNEL
RUNNER
RUNOFF
RUNONS
RUNOUT
RUNSAT
RUNSIN
RUNSON
RUNSTO
RUNSUP
RUNUPS
RUNWAY
RUNYON

R••N••
RADNER
RAINED
RAINER
RAINES
RAINEY
REGNAL

REGNAT
REINAS
REINED
REINER
REININ
REINKS
RENNES
RENNET
RENNIE
RENNIN
RESNIK
REUNES
RHINAL
RHINOS
RHONDA
RIENZI
RODNEY
ROMNEY
RONNIE
ROONEY
ROUNDS
RUANAS
RUANDA
RUINED
RUINER
RUNNEL
RUNNER
RWANDA

R••N•

RACINE
RACING
RACONS
RAGING
RAKING
RAMONA
RAMONE
RAPINE
RAPINI
RARING
RASING
RATINE
RATING
RAVENS
RAVINE
RAVING
RAYONS
RAZING
REBEND
REBENT
REBIND
RECANE
RECANT
RECENT
RECONS
REDANT
REDENY
REDING
REDINK
REDONE
REFINE
REFUND
REGENT
REGINA
REHANG
REHUNG
REIGNS
RELENT
RELINE
REMAND
REMANS
REMEND
REMIND
REPAND
REPENT
REPINE
REPINS
RERENT
RERUNS
RESAND
RESEND
RESENT
RESING
RESINS
RESINY
RETENE
RETINA
RETUNE
REWIND
REWINS
REZONE
RIBAND
RICING
RIDENT
RIDING
RILING
RIMING
RIMINI
RIPENS
RISING
RIVING
ROBING
ROBINS
ROCKNE
RODENT
ROLAND
ROMANO
ROMANS
ROMANY
ROPING
ROSINS
ROSINY
ROTINI
ROTUND
ROVING
ROWENA
ROWENS
ROWING
ROXANA
ROXANE
RUBENS
RULING
RUMENS
RUMINA
RUNINS
RUNONS

R••••N

RADIAN
RAGLAN
RAGMAN
RAGMEN
RAISIN
RAKEIN
RAMSON
RANKIN
RATION
RATLIN
RATSON
RATTAN
RAYGUN
READIN
REAGAN
REASON
REBORN
RECKON
REDDEN
REDFIN
REELIN
REGAIN
REGION
REININ
REJOIN
REMAIN
REMOWN
RENNIN
RENOWN
REOPEN
REPLAN
REPUGN
RESAWN
RESEEN
RESEWN
RESIGN
RESPIN
RESTON
RETAIN
RETTON
RETURN
REUBEN
REVLON
REVSON
RHYTON
RIBBON
RICHEN
RIDDEN
RIPKEN
ROBSON
RODMAN
ROLLIN
ROLLON
ROPEIN
ROTTEN
RUBSIN
RUDMAN
RULEON
RUNSIN
RUNSON
RUNYON
RUSKIN
RUTTAN
RYAZAN
RYOKAN

•RN•••

ARNESS
ARNETT
ARNHEM
ARNICA
ARNOLD
ERNANI
ERNEST
ORNATE
ORNERY
ORNITH

•R•N••

ARENAS
ARENDT
BRANCH
BRANDO
BRANDS
BRANDT
BRANDX
BRANDY
BRANNY
BRANTS
BRENDA
BRENTS
BRINED
BRINES
BRINGS
BRINKS
BRONCO
BRONCS
BRONTE
BRONZE
BRONZY
BRUNCH
BRUNEI
BRUNET
BRUNTS
CRANED
CRANES
CRANIA
CRANIO
CRANKS
CRANKY
CRANNY
CRENEL
CRENNA
CRINGE
CRONES
CRONIN
CRONUS
CRONYN
CRUNCH
DRENCH
DRINGS
DRINKS
DRONED
DRONER
DRONES
ERENOW
ERINYS
ERYNGO
FRANCA
FRANCE
FRANCK
FRANCO
FRANCS
FRANKS
FRANNY
FRENCH
FRENUM
FRENZY
FRINGE
FRINGY
FRONDS
FRONTS
GRANDE
GRANDS
GRANGE
GRANNY
GRANTS
GRINCH
GRINDS
GRINGO
GRUNDY
GRUNGE
GRUNGY
GRUNTS
IRANIS
IRENES
IRENIC
IRONED
IRONER
IRONIC
IRONON
KRANTZ
KRONER
KRONOR
KRONUR
ORANGE
ORANGS
ORANGY
ORANTS
ORINGS
ORKNEY
PRANCE
PRANGS
PRANKS
PRENUP
PRINCE
PRINKS
PRINTS
PRONGS
PRONTO
PRUNED
PRUNER
PRUNES
PRYNNE
SRANAN
TRANCE
TRENCH
TRENDS
TRENDY
TRINAL
TRINES
TRUNKS
URANIA
URANIC
URANUS
WRENCH
WRINGS
WRONGS

•R••N•

ARCANA
ARCANE
ARCING
ARDENT
ARGENT
ARJUNA
ARLENE
ARMAND
ARMANI
ARMING
AROUND
ARPENT
ARRANT
ARSENE
ARSONS
ARYANS
BRAINS
BRAINY
BRANNY
BRAWNY
BRIAND
BRIANS
BRIENZ
BROWNE
BROWNS
BROWNY
BRUINS
BRYANT
BRYONY
CRANNY
CRENNA
CROONS
CROWNS
CRYING
DRAINS
DROWNS
DRYING
DRYINK
ERMINE
ERNANI
ERRAND
ERRANT
ERRING
ERVING
FRANNY
FRESNO
FRIEND
FROWNS
FRYING
GRAINS
GRAINY
GRANNY
GREENE
GREENS
GREENY
GRETNA
GROANS
GRODNO
GROINS
GROUND
GROZNY
IRKING
IRLENE
IRVINE
IRVING
KRASNY
ORBING
ORGANA
ORGANS
ORIANA
ORIENT
ORMOND
ORPINE
ORSINO
PRAJNA
PRAWNS
PREENS
PRIONS
PROCNE
PRYING
PRYNNE
TRAINS
TRIUNE
TRUANT
TRUING
TRYING
URBANA
URBANE
URGENT
URGING
URSINE

•R•••N

ARAGON
ARCHON
ARCTAN
ARISEN
ARLEEN
ARUBAN
BRAZEN
BREMEN
BRETON
BRITON
BROGAN
BROKEN
BROLIN
BRYSON
CRAVEN
CRAYON
CRETAN
CRETIN
CRONIN
CRONYN
CROTON
DRAGIN
DRAGON
DRAWIN
DRAWON
DREWIN
DREWON
DRIVEN
DROPIN
DRYDEN
DRYRUN
FRAUEN
FROZEN
FRYPAN
GRABEN
GRADIN
GRATIN
GRAVEN
GREWON
GRISON
GRODIN
GROTON
GROWON
IRISIN
IRONON
KRAKEN
ORDAIN
OREGON
ORIGEN
ORIGIN
ORISON
ORPHAN
PREVIN
PREYON
PRISON
PROTON
PROVEN
SRANAN
TRAJAN
TREPAN
TRIGON
TRITON
TROGON
TROJAN
TRUMAN
TRYLON
URCHIN

••RN••

BARNES
BARNEY
BARNUM
BERNIE
BIRNEY
BORNEO
BURNED
BURNER
BURNET
BURNEY
BURNUP
BYRNES
CARNAL
CARNES
CARNET
CARNEY
CARNOT
CORNEA
CORNED
CORNEL
CORNER
CORNET
DARNAY
DARNED
DARNEL
DARNER
DARNIT
DIRNDL
DURNED
EARNED
EARNER
GARNER
GARNET
GIRNED
GURNEY
HORNED
HORNER
HORNET
HORNEY
HORNIN
KARNAK
KERNED
KERNEL
KERNOI
KERNOS
LERNER
MARNER
MARNIE
MORNAY
NARNIA
PARNIS
PERNIO
PERNOD
SARNIA
TERNES
TURNED
TURNER
TURNIN
TURNIP
TURNON
TURNTO
TURNUP
VARNAS
VARNEY
VERNAL
VERNON
WARNED
WARNER
WERNER
YARNED

••R•N•

ADRENO
AIRING
APRONS
ARRANT
BARING
BARONG
BARONS
BARONY
BERING
BORING
BURINS
CARINA
CARING
CARONI
CHRONO
CORING
CORONA
CURING
CYRANO
DARENT
DARING
DURANT
DURING
EARING
ERRAND
ERRANT
ERRING
FARINA
FARING
FERENC
FIRING
FORINT
GERENT
GERONT
GERUND
GORING
GYRENE
GYRONS
HARING
HERONS
HIRING
HURONS
KORUNA
LARYNX
LORENZ
LURING
MARINA
MARINE
MARINO
MERINO
MIRING
MORANT
MORENO
MORONI
MORONS
MURANO
MURINE
OARING
PARANA
PARANG
PARENS
PARENT
PARING
PIRANA
PORING
PURINA
PURINE
RARING
RERENT

RERUNS
SARANS
SARONG
SERENA
SERENE
SERINE
SERINS
SHRANK
SHRINE
SHRINK
SHRUNK
SIRENS
SIRING
SPRANG
SPRING
SPRINT
SPRUNG
STRAND
STRINE
STRING
STRONG
STRUNG
SYRINX
TARING
THRONE
THRONG
TIRANA
TIRANE
TIRING
TORINO
TURING
TYRANT
TYRONE
VARUNA
VERONA
WARING
WERENT
WIRING

••R••N

ADRIAN
ADRIEN
AIRGUN
AIRMAN
AIRMEN
BARKIN
BARMAN
BARMEN
BARREN
BARRON
BARTON
BARYON
BARZUN
BERGEN
BERLIN
BORDEN
BOREON
BORMAN
BURDEN
BURMAN
BURTON
CARBON
CARDIN
CAREEN
CARLIN
CARMAN
CARMEN
CARSON
CARTON
CORBAN
CORBIN
CORDON
CORMAN
CURTIN
CURZON
DARIEN
DARKEN
DARREN
DARWIN
DORIAN
DURBAN
DURBIN
DURIAN
FIRKIN
FIRMAN
FORMAN
GARCON
GARDEN
GARSON
GERMAN
GORDON
GORGON
HARBIN
HARDEN
HARKEN
HARLAN
HARLIN
HARMON
HARPON
HEREIN
HEREON
HERMAN
HERMON
HIREON
HORNIN
HORTON
JARGON
JERKIN
JORDAN
KERMAN
KIRMAN
KOREAN
KORMAN
KURGAN
LARDON
LARSEN
LARSON
LORAIN
MARGIN
MARIAN
MARION
MARLIN
MARLON
MAROON
MARRON
MARTEN
MARTIN
MARVIN
MERLIN
MERLON
MERMAN
MERMEN
MERTON
MERVYN
MIRREN
MOREEN
MORGAN
MORGEN
MORION
MORMON
MORTON
NORMAN
NORTON
OBRIAN
OBRIEN
PARDON
PARSON
PARTON
PERSON
PURLIN
SARGON
SARTON
SCREEN
SERKIN
SERMON
SPRAIN
STRAIN
STREWN
SYRIAN
TARPAN
TARPON
TARTAN
TARZAN
TERRAN
THROWN
TURBAN
TUREEN
TURNIN
TURNON
TURPIN
TYRIAN
UGRIAN
VARDEN
VERDIN
VERDON
VERDUN
VEREEN
VERMIN
VERNON
VIRGIN
WARDEN
WARREN
WOREON
WORKIN
WORKON
WORSEN
ZEROIN
ZIRCON

•••RN•

ACORNS
ADORNS
AHERNE
AVERNO
BAIRNS
BOURNE
CAIRNS
CHURNS
CZERNY
ETERNE
JOURNO
KEARNY
LEARNS
LEARNT
LIERNE
MOURNS
QUERNS
SCARNE
SCORNS
SMYRNA
SPURNS
STERNA
STERNE
STERNO
STERNS
THORNS
THORNY
UTURNS
YEARNS

•••R•N

ALDRIN
ANTRON
ANURAN
AZORIN
BARREN
BARRON
BEARON
CHARON
CHIRON
CHYRON
CITRON
DACRON
DAIREN
DARREN
DRYRUN
ENDRUN
EPHRON
FIBRIN
FLORIN
GIBRAN
GUDRUN
HADRON
HEBRON
HEDREN
HEDRON
HIERON
ILORIN
LAUREN
LEBRUN
MACRON
MARRON
MATRON
MICRON
MIRREN
NATRON
NEURON
NOIRON
OBERON
OUTRAN
OUTRUN
PATRON
PEERIN
POURIN
QUMRAN
SHARON
SHORAN
SKIRUN
SPURON
STIRIN
STYRON
TERRAN
VANRYN
WARREN

••••RN

ASTERN
AUBURN
BICORN
CASERN
CAVERN
COBURN
DEHORN
EXTERN
GOVERN
INBORN
INTERN
INTURN
MODERN
OSBORN
REBORN
RETURN
SATURN
SECERN
SEVERN
SUBORN
TAVERN
UNBORN
UNTORN
UNWORN
UPTURN
WEBERN
WYVERN

RO••••

ROADIE
ROAMED
ROAMER
ROARED
ROARER
ROASTS
ROBALO
ROBBED
ROBBER
ROBBIA
ROBBIE
ROBERT
ROBING
ROBINS
ROBLES
ROBOTS
ROBROY
ROBSON
ROBUST
ROCHET
ROCKED
ROCKER
ROCKET
ROCKNE
ROCKYV
ROCOCO
RODDED
RODENT
RODEOS
RODHAM
RODMAN
RODNEY
ROGERS
ROGUES
ROHMER
ROILED
ROLAND
ROLEOS
ROLLED
ROLLER
ROLLIE
ROLLIN
ROLLON
ROLLUP
ROMAIC
ROMAJI
ROMANO
ROMANS
ROMANY
ROMEOS
ROMERO
ROMMEL
ROMNEY
ROMOLA
ROMPED
ROMPER
RONALD
RONDEL
RONDOS
RONELY
RONNIE
ROOFED
ROOFER
ROOKED
ROOKIE
ROOMED
ROOMER
ROOMIE
ROONEY
ROOSTS
ROOTED
ROOTER
ROPEIN
ROPERS
ROPIER
ROPING
ROSARY
ROSCOE
ROSEAU
ROSIER
ROSILY
ROSINS
ROSINY
ROSITA
ROSTER
ROSTOV
ROSTRA
ROTARY
ROTATE
ROTGUT
ROTHKO
ROTINI
ROTORS
ROTTED
ROTTEN
ROTTER
ROTUND
ROUBLE
ROUGED
ROUGES
ROUGHS
ROUGHY
ROUNDS
ROURKE
ROUSED
ROUSER
ROUSES
ROUSTS
ROUTED
ROUTER
ROUTES
ROVERS
ROVING
ROWELS
ROWENA
ROWENS
ROWERS
ROWING
ROXANA
ROXANE
ROYALE
ROYALS
ROZZER

R•O•••

REOILS
REOPEN
RHODES
RHOMBI
RHOMBS
RHONDA
RIOJAS
RIOTED
RIOTER
ROOFED
ROOFER
ROOKED
ROOKIE
ROOMED
ROOMER
ROOMIE
ROONEY
ROOSTS
ROOTED
ROOTER
RYOKAN

R••O••

RACONS
RADOME
RAGOUT
RAMONA
RAMONE
RAMOSE
RAMOUS
RANOFF
RANOUT
RAYONS
RAZORS
RCCOLA
REBOIL
REBOLT
REBOOT
REBORN
REBOZO
RECOAT
RECODE
RECOIL
RECONS
RECOPY
RECORD
RECORK
RECOUP
REDOAK
REDOES
REDONE
REFORM
REHOOK
REJOIN
RELOAD
RELOCK
REMOLD
REMOPS
REMORA
REMOTE
REMOVE
REMOWN
REMOWS
RENOIR
RENOTE
RENOWN
REPOLL
REPORT
REPOSE
REPOST
REPOTS
RESODS
RESOLD
RESOLE
RESORB
RESORT
RETOLD
RETOOK
RETOOL
RETOPS
RETORT
RETOUR
RETOWS
REVOIR
REVOKE
REVOLT
REWORD
REWORK
REWOVE
REZONE
RIBOSE
RIGORS
RIGOUR
RIMOSE
RIPOFF
RIPOUT
ROBOTS
ROCOCO
ROMOLA
ROTORS
RUBOFF
RUBOUT
RUDOLF
RUFOUS
RUGOSE
RUMORS
RUMOUR
RUNOFF
RUNONS
RUNOUT

R•••O•

RADIOS
RAGMOP
RAGTOP
RAMROD
RAMSON
RANCOR
RANDOM
RANFOR
RANSOM
RAPTOR
RATION
RATIOS
RATSON
REASON
REBOOT
RECKON
RECTOR
RECTOS
REDDOG
REDFOX
REDHOT
REDSOX
REDTOP
REEBOK
REGION
REHOOK
REPLOW
REPROS
RESHOD
RESHOE
RESHOT
RESTON
RETOOK
RETOOL
RETROS
RETTON
REVLON
REVSON
RHEBOK
RHETOR
RHINOS
RHYTON
RIBBON
RIDSOF
ROBROY
ROBSON
RODEOS
ROLEOS
ROLLON
ROMEOS
RONDOS
ROSCOE
ROSTOV
RULEON
RUNFOR
RUNSON
RUNYON

R••••O

RABATO
RANCHO
REBOZO
REECHO
RHABDO
RIALTO
RIGHTO
RIZZIO
ROBALO
ROCOCO
ROMANO
ROMERO
ROTHKO
RUBATO
RUNSTO

•RO•••

AROIDS
AROMAS
AROUND
AROUSE
BROACH
BROADS
BRODIE
BROGAN
BROGUE
BROILS
BROKAW
BROKEN

BROKER
BROLIN
BROLLY
BRONCO
BRONCS
BRONTE
BRONZE
BRONZY
BROOCH
BROODS
BROODY
BROOKE
BROOKS
BROOKY
BROOMS
BROOMY
BROTHS
BROWNE
BROWNS
BROWNY
BROWSE
CROAKS
CROAKY
CROATS
CROCKS
CROCUS
CROFTS
CRONES
CRONIN
CRONUS
CRONYN
CROOKS
CROONS
CROPUP
CROSBY
CROSSE
CROTON
CROUCH
CROUPY
CROUSE
CROUTE
CROWDS
CROWED
CROWER
CROWNS
CROZES
DROGUE
DROIDS
DROITS
DROLLS
DROLLY
DROMOI
DROMOS
DRONED
DRONER
DRONES
DROOLS
DROOLY
DROOPS
DROOPY
DROPBY
DROPIN
DROPIT
DROVER
DROVES
DROWNS
DROWSE
DROWSY
ERODED
ERODES
EROICA
EROTIC
FROCKS
FROGGY
FROLIC
FRONDS
FRONTS
FROSTS
FROSTY
FROTHS
FROTHY
FROWNS
FROWZY
FROZEN
GROANS
GROATS
GROCER
GRODIN
GRODNO
GROGGY
GROINS
GROOMS
GROOVE
GROOVY
GROPED
GROPES
GROSSE
GROSSO
GROSZY
GROTON
GROTTO
GROTTY
GROUCH
GROUND
GROUPS
GROUSE
GROUTS
GROUTY
GROVEL
GROVER
GROVES
GROWER
GROWLS
GROWLY
GROWON
GROWTH
GROWUP
GROZNY
IROBOT
IRONED
IRONER
IRONIC
IRONON
KRONER
KRONOR
KRONUR
OROIDE
OROMOS
OROZCO
PROAMS
PROBED
PROBER
PROBES
PROCNE
PROEMS
PROFIT
PROLES
PROLIX
PROLOG
PROMOS
PROMPT
PRONGS
PRONTO
PROOFS
PROPEL
PROPER
PROPRE
PROPUP
PROSED
PROSER
PROSES
PROSIT
PROSKY
PROTAX
PROTEI
PROTEM
PROTON
PROUST
PROVED
PROVEN
PROVER
PROVES
PROWLS
PROWSE
PROZAC
TROCAR
TROCHE
TROGON
TROIKA
TROJAN
TROLLS
TROMPE
TROMPS
TROOPS
TROPES
TROPEZ
TROPHY
TROPIC
TROPPO
TROTHS
TROUGH
TROUPE
TROUTS
TROUVE
TROVES
TROWED
TROWEL
VROOMS
WRONGS

•R•O••

ARBORS
ARBOUR
ARDORS
ARDOUR
AREOLA
ARGOSY
ARGOTS
ARIOSE
ARIOSO
ARMORS
ARMORY
ARMOUR
ARNOLD
ARROBA
ARROWS
ARROYO
ARSONS
ARTOIS
BROOCH
BROODS
BROODY
BROOKE
BROOKS
BROOKY
BROOMS
BROOMY
BRYONY
CREOLE
CROOKS
CROONS
CRYOFF
DRHOOK
DROOLS
DROOLY
DROOPS
DROOPY
DRYOFF
DRYOUT
ERGOTS
ERROLL
ERRORS
GRIOTS
GROOMS
GROOVE
GROOVY
MRCOOL
MRMOTO
ORIOLE
ORLOPS
ORMOLU
ORMOND
PRIONS
PRIORI
PRIORS
PRIORY
PROOFS
TRIODE
TROOPS
TRYOUT
VROOMS

•R••O•

ARAGON
ARCCOS
ARCHON
BRASOV
BRAVOS
BRAZOS
BRETON
BRITON
BRYSON
CRAYON
CREDOS
CRESOL
CROTON
CRUSOE
DRAGON
DRAWON
DREWON
DRHOOK
DROMOI
DROMOS
DRYROT
ERENOW
FRIJOL
FRITOS
GREGOR
GREWON
GRISON
GROTON
GROWON
IROBOT
IRONON
KRAKOW
KRONOR
MRCOOL
ORATOR
OREGON
ORISON
OROMOS
PREYON
PRIMOS
PRISON
PROLOG
PROMOS
PROTON
TREMOR
TREVOR
TRICOT
TRIGON
TRIPOD
TRIPOS
TRITON
TROGON
TRYFOR
TRYLON

•R•••O

ARCARO
AREZZO
ARIOSO
ARISTO
ARROYO
ARTHRO
ARTURO
BRANDO
BRILLO
BRONCO
CRAMBO
CRANIO
CRISCO
CRISTO
CRYPTO
ERYNGO
FRANCO
FRESCO
FRESNO
FRISCO
GRAECO
GRASSO
GRINGO
GRODNO
GROSSO
GROTTO
MRMOTO
OROZCO
ORSINO
PRESTO
PRONTO
TRICHO
TROPPO

••RO••

ABROAD
ACROSS
ADROIT
AEROBE
AIROUT
APRONS
ARROBA
ARROWS
ARROYO
AURORA
AUROUS
BAROJA
BAROLO
BARONG
BARONS
BARONY
BUROAK
BYROAD
BYROTE
CAROBS
CAROLE
CAROLS
CAROMS
CARONI
CDROMS
CHROMA
CHROME
CHROMO
CHROMY
CHRONO
CORONA
DUROCS
ENROBE
ENROLL
ENROLS
ENROOT
EPROMS
ERROLL
ERRORS
EUROPA
EUROPE
FAROFF
FAROUK
FAROUT
FTROOP
FURORE
FURORS
GERONT
GYRONS
GYROSE
HAROLD
HEROES
HEROIC
HERONS
HURONS
INROAD
JEROME
JURORS
KAROSS
LAROSA
MAROON
MEROPE
MORONI
MORONS
MOROSE
NEROLI
PARODY
PAROLE
POROUS
SARODS
SARONG
SCRODS
SCROLL
SCROOP
SEROSA
SEROUS
SEROWS
SHROUD
SHROVE
SPROUT
STROBE
STRODE
STROKE
STROLL
STRONG
STROPS
STROUD
STROVE
TAROTS
THROAT
THROBS
THROES
THRONE
THRONG
THROVE
THROWN
THROWS
TOROID
TOROSE
TYRONE
UNROBE
UNROLL
UNROOT
UPROAR
UPROOT
UPROSE
VERONA
VOROUS
YUROKS
ZEROED
ZEROES
ZEROIN
ZEROTH

••R•O•

BARDOT
BARHOP
BARRON
BARROW
BARTOK
BARTON
BARYON
BOREON
BORROW
BORZOI
BURBOT
BURGOO
BURGOS
BURROS
BURROW
BURTON
CARBON
CARBOS
CARBOY
CARGOS
CARHOP
CARLOS
CARLOT
CARNOT
CARROL
CARROT
CARSON
CARTON
CERROS
CORDON
CURIOS
CURSOR
CURZON
DARROW
ENROOT
FARLOW
FARROW
FERVOR
FORGOT
FTROOP
FURROW
GARCON
GARSON
GORDON
GORGON
HARBOR
HARLOW
HARMON
HARPON
HARROW
HEREOF
HEREON
HERIOT
HERMON
HERZOG
HIREON
HORROR
HORTON
JARGON
JERBOA
KARPOV
KARROO
KERNOI
KERNOS
LARDON
LARGOS
LARSON
MARCOS
MARGOT
MARION
MARLON
MARMOT
MAROON
MARRON
MARROW
MERLON
MERLOT
MERTON
MIRROR
MORION
MORMON
MORROW
MORTON
MURROW
NARROW
NORTON
PARDON
PARLOR
PARROT
PARSON
PARTON
PERIOD
PERNOD
PERROT
PERSON
SARGON
SARGOS
SARTON
SCROOP
SERMON
SERVOS
SORROW
SORTOF
TARPON
TERROR
TORPOR
TORSOS
TURBOS
TURBOT
TURGOR
TURNON
UNROOT
UPROOT
VERDON
VERNON
VERSOS
VIREOS
WARGOD
WARHOL
WOREON
WORKON
YARROW
ZIRCON

••R••O

ADRENO
ARROYO
BAROLO
BARRIO
BORAXO
BORNEO
BURGOO
CARDIO
CARETO
CARUSO
CHROMO
CHRONO
CYRANO
DARETO
DIRIGO
DORADO
ENRICO
FOREGO
HERETO
JURADO
KARROO
LAREDO
MARIKO
MARINO
MERINO
MORENO
MORPHO
MURANO
PARETO
PERNIO
SERGIO
STRABO
STRATO
TERATO
TEREDO
TORERO
TORINO
TURNTO
VIRAGO

•••RO•

AGGROS
AGOROT
ANDROS
ANTRON
ASTROS

BARRON
BARROW
BEARON
BORROW
BURROS
BURROW
CARROL
CARROT
CERROS
CHARON
CHIRON
CHYRON
CITRON
CLAROS
CLOROX
CONROY
DACRON
DARROW
DELROY
DETROP
DOBROS
DRYROT
EPHRON
ESCROW
FAEROE
FARROW
FLYROD
FURROW
GUIROS
HADRON
HARROW
HEAROF
HEBRON
HEDRON
HIERON
HORROR
HOTROD
HYDROS
IMPROV
INAROW
INTROS
KARROO
KILROY
KUDROW
MACRON
MACROS
MARRON
MARROW
MATRON
METROS
MICRON
MICROS
MIRROR
MONROE
MORROW
MURROW
NARROW
NATRON
NEUROL
NEURON
NIMROD
NOIRON
OBERON
OCTROI
PARROT
PATROL
PATRON
PENROD
PERROT
PETROG
PETROL
PHAROS
POIROT
RAMROD
REPROS
RETROS
ROBROY
SHARON
SKIROS
SORROW
SPIROS
SPURON
STEROL
STYRON
TERROR
TIEROD
UNTROD
YARROW

•••R•O
ATERGO
AVERNO
BARRIO
CHARRO
CHURRO
DELRIO
EMBRYO
EVERSO
FLORIO
GEARTO
HAIRDO
JOURNO
KARROO
NEARTO
OPORTO
OVERDO
PUERTO
QUARTO
SHORTO
STEREO
STERNO
THERMO
WEIRDO

••••RO
ALLPRO
ANTERO
ARCARO
ARTHRO
ARTURO
AUSTRO
BISTRO
BOLERO
CAMARO
CASTRO
CENTRO
CHARRO
CHLORO
CHURRO
CICERO
DENDRO
DENIRO
DEXTRO
DINERO
ENDURO
ENTERO
FIGARO
FLUORO
GABBRO
GASTRO
HASBRO
HETERO
JETHRO
MADERO
MADURO
NEPHRO
NUMERO
OLDPRO
PICARO
PIETRO
PINERO
ROMERO
SCLERO
SIDERO
TORERO
VELCRO

R•P•••
RAPIDS
RAPIER
RAPINE
RAPINI
RAPPED
RAPPEE
RAPPEL
RAPPER
RAPTLY
RAPTOR
REPADS
REPAID
REPAIR
REPAND
REPAST
REPAVE
REPAYS
REPEAL
REPEAT
REPEGS
REPELS
REPENT
REPINE
REPINS
REPLAN
REPLAY
REPLOW
REPOLL
REPORT
REPOSE
REPOST
REPOTS
REPROS
REPUGN
REPUTE
RIPELY
RIPENS
RIPEST
RIPKEN
RIPLEY
RIPOFF
RIPOUT
RIPPED
RIPPER
RIPPLE
RIPPLY
RIPRAP
RIPSAW
RIPSUP
ROPEIN
ROPERS
ROPIER
ROPING
RUPAUL
RUPEES
RUPERT
RUPIAH

R••P••
RAIPUR
RAJPUT
RAMPED
RAPPED
RAPPEE
RAPPEL
RAPPER
RASPED
RASPER
REAPED
REAPER
REOPEN
RESPIN
RIMPLE
RIPPED
RIPPER
RIPPLE
RIPPLY
ROMPED
ROMPER
RSVPED
RUMPLE
RUMPLY
RUMPUS

R•••P•
RECAPS
RECIPE
RECOPY
REMAPS
REMOPS
RETAPE
RETAPS
RETOPS
RETYPE
RUNUPS

R••••P
RACKUP
RAGMOP
RAGTOP
RAKEUP
RANGUP
RAVEUP
REARUP
RECOUP
REDCAP
REDTOP
RESHIP
RESTUP
REVAMP
REVSUP
REWRAP
RIGSUP
RILEUP
RINGUP
RIPRAP
RIPSUP
ROLLUP
RUNGUP
RUNSUP

•RP•••
ARPENT
ORPHAN
ORPHIC
ORPINE

•R•P••
ARMPIT
CRAPES
CREPES
CRIPES
CROPUP
CRYPTO
CRYPTS
DRAPED
DRAPER
DRAPES
DRIPPY
DROPBY
DROPIN
DROPIT
DRUPES
ERUPTS
FRAPPE
FRYPAN
GRAPES
GRAPEY
GRAPHS
GRAPHY
GRAPPA
GRIPED
GRIPER
GRIPES
GRIPPE
GROPED
GROPES
PREPAY
PREPPY
PRIPET
PROPEL
PROPER
PROPRE
PROPUP
TRAPPY
TREPAN
TREPID
TRIPLE
TRIPLY
TRIPOD
TRIPOS
TRIPUP
TROPES
TROPEZ
TROPHY
TROPIC
TROPPO
WRAPUP

•R••P•
CRAMPS
CREEPS
CREEPY
CRIMPS
CRIMPY
CRISPS
CRISPY
CROUPY
DRIPPY
DROOPS
DROOPY
FRAPPE
FRUMPS
FRUMPY
GRAMPA
GRAMPS
GRAPPA
GRASPS
GRIPPE
GROUPS
GRUMPS
GRUMPY
IRRUPT
ORLOPS
PREPPY
PRIMPS
PROMPT
TRAMPS
TRAPPY
TROMPE
TROMPS
TROOPS
TROPPO
TROUPE
TRUMPS

•R•••P
CROPUP
DRAWUP
DREWUP
DRUMUP
GREWUP
GROWUP
PREAMP
PRENUP
PROPUP
TRICEP
TRIPUP
WRAPUP

••RP••
BURPED
CARPAL
CARPED
CARPEL
CARPER
CARPET
CARPUS
CORPUS
HARPED
HARPER
HARPON
KARPOV
MARPLE
MORPHO
MORPHS
MORPHY
MURPHY
PURPLE
PURPLY
TARPAN
TARPIT
TARPON
TORPID
TORPOR
TURPIN
WARPED

••R•P•
ABRUPT
CERIPH
ENRAPT
EUROPA
EUROPE
IRRUPT
MEROPE
PARAPH
PTRAPS
SCRAPE
SCRAPS
SCRIPS
SCRIPT
SERAPE
SERAPH
STRAPS
STRIPE
STRIPS
STRIPY
STROPS
SYRUPS
SYRUPY
TERAPH
THRIPS
UNRIPE

••R••P
BARHOP
BOREUP
BURLAP
BURNUP
CARHOP
CURLUP
EARLAP
FIREUP
FIRMUP
FTROOP
HARDUP
LARRUP
MARKUP
PERKUP
PIRRIP
SCRIMP
SCROOP
SHRIMP
STREEP
TOREUP
TURNIP
TURNUP
WARMUP
WORKUP

•••RP•
CHIRPS
CHIRPY
FOURPM
SCARPS
SHARPS
SHERPA
SLURPS
THORPE
THORPS
TWERPS
USURPS

•••R•P
AMERSP
BEARUP
BUMRAP
DETROP
DOMREP
ENTRAP
ENWRAP
FAIRUP
GEARUP
LARRUP
PAIRUP
PIRRIP
REARUP
REWRAP
RIPRAP
SATRAP
STIRUP
TEARUP
UNTRAP
UNWRAP

••••RP
ASHARP
BSHARP
CSHARP
DSHARP
ESCARP
ESHARP
FSHARP
GSHARP

R•Q•••
RAQUEL

R••Q••
RISQUE

•R•Q••
BRAQUE
IRAQIS

••RQ••
BARQUE
CIRQUE
MARQUE
TORQUE

RR••••
RRATED

R•R•••
RAREFY
RARELY
RAREST
RARIFY
RARING
RARITY
RERATE
REREAD
RERENT
RERUNS

R••R••
RAGRUG
RAHRAH
RAMROD
REARED
REARER
REARMS
REARUP
REDRAW
REDREW
REGRET
REPROS
RETRAL
RETRIM
RETROS
REWRAP
RIPRAP
ROARED
ROARER
ROBROY
ROURKE
RUBRIC

R•••R•
RACERS
RAKERS
RANDRY
RASERS
RATERS
RAVERS
RAZORS
REAIRS
REBARS
REBORN
REBURY
RECORD
RECORK
RECURS
REFERS
REFORM
REGARD
REHIRE
REMARK
REMORA
REPORT
RESORB
RESORT
RETARD
RETARS
RETIRE
RETORT
RETURN
REVERB
REVERE
REVERS
REVERT
REWARD
REWARM
REWIRE
REWORD
REWORK
RICERS
RIDERS
RIGORS
RISERS
RITARD
RIVERA
RIVERS
ROBERT
ROGERS
ROMERO
ROPERS
ROSARY
ROSTRA
ROTARY
ROTORS
ROVERS
ROWERS
RULERS
RUMORS
RUNDRY
RUPERT

R••••R
RACIER
RADNER

RAFTER
RAIDER
RAILER
RAINER
RAIPUR
RAISER
RANCOR
RANFOR
RANGER
RANKER
RANTER
RAPIER
RAPPER
RAPTOR
RASHER
RASPER
RASTER
RATEDR
RATHER
RATTER
READER
REALER
REAMER
REAPER
REARER
RECTOR
REDDER
REDFIR
REEFER
REHEAR
REINER
RENDER
RENOIR
RENTER
REPAIR
RESTER
RETEAR
RETOUR
REUTER
REVOIR
RHETOR
RHYMER
RICHER
RIFLER
RIGGER
RIGOUR
RIMIER
RINGER
RIOTER
RIPPER
RISKER
RITTER
ROAMER
ROARER
ROBBER
ROCKER
ROHMER
ROLLER
ROMPER
ROOFER
ROOMER
ROOTER
ROPIER
ROSIER
ROSTER
ROTTER
ROUSER
ROUTER
ROZZER
RUBBER
RUDDER
RUINER
RUMMER
RUMOUR
RUNFOR
RUNNER
RUTGER

•RR•••

ARRACK
ARRANT
ARRAYS
ARREAR
ARREST
ARRIBA
ARRIVE
ARROBA
ARROWS
ARROYO
ERRAND
ERRANT
ERRARE
ERRATA
ERRING
ERROLL
ERRORS
IRREAL
IRRUPT
ORRERY

•R•R••

ARARAT
CRURAL
DRYROT
DRYRUN

•R••R•

ARBORS
ARCARO
ARDORS
ARMORS
ARMORY
ARMURE
ARTERY
ARTHRO
ARTURO
BRIARD
BRIARS
BRIERS
BRIERY
CRIERS
CRYERS
DREARY
DRIERS
DRYERS
ERFURT
ERHARD
ERRARE
ERRORS
FRIARS
FRIARY
FRIERS
FRYERS
GRIGRI
ORDERS
ORDURE
ORNERY
ORRERY
PRIERS
PRIORI
PRIORS
PRIORY
PROPRE
TRIERS
URGERS

•R•••R

ARBOUR
ARCHER
ARDOUR
ARGUER
ARMOUR
ARREAR
ARTHUR
ARTIER
BRACER
BRAVER
BRAYER
BRAZER
BREUER
BREWER
BREYER
BROKER
BRUDER
CRATER
CRAVER
CROWER
CRUDER
DRAPER
DRAWER
DRIVER
DRONER
DROVER
ERASER
FRASER
FRAZER
GRADER
GRATER
GRAVER
GRAYER
GRAZER
GREGOR
GREYER
GRIPER
GROCER
GROVER
GROWER
IRATER
IRONER
KRAMER
KRATER
KRONER
KRONOR
KRONUR
KRUGER
ORATOR
PRATER
PRAYER
PREFER
PRETER
PREWAR
PRICER
PRIMER
PROBER
PROPER
PROSER
PROVER
PRUNER
TRACER
TRADER
TREMOR
TREVOR
TRITER
TROCAR
TRYFOR
WRITER

••RR••

BARRED
BARREL
BARREN
BARRES
BARRIE
BARRIO
BARRIS
BARRON
BARROW
BORROW
BURRED
BURROS
BURROW
CARREL
CARREY
CARRIE
CARROL
CARROT
CERROS
CIRRUS
CORRAL
CORREL
CURRED
DARREN
DARROW
DARRYL
DERRIS
DORRIT
FARRAH
FARRAR
FARROW
FERRER
FERRET
FERRIC
FERRIS
FURRED
FURROW
GARRET
HARRIS
HARROW
HORRID
HORROR
HURRAH
HURRAY
JARRAH
JARRED
KARRAS
KARROO
LARRUP
MARRED
MARRON
MARROW
MIRREN
MIRROR
MORRIS
MORROW
MURRAY
MURRES
MURREY
MURROW
MYRRHS
NARROW
NORRIS
PARRED
PARREL
PARRIS
PARROT
PERROT
PIRRIP
PURRED
PURRER
SIRRAH
SIRREE
SORREL
SORROW
SURREY
TARRED
TERRAN
TERRET
TERROR
TORRES
TORREY
TORRID
TURRET
WARRED
WARREN
YARROW

••R•R•

AIRARM
AIRDRY
AURORA
BARBRA
BORERS
CORERS
CURARE
CURERS
ERRARE
ERRORS
FARCRY
FARERS
FIRERS
FURORE
FURORS
GERARD
GIRARD
HARARE
HIRERS
JURORS
ORRERY
PARERS
PARURE
SARTRE
TORERO
WARCRY
WIRERS

••R••R

AIRIER
ARREAR
BARBER
BARCAR
BARKER
BARTER
BERBER
BIRDER
BORDER
BURGER
BURNER
BURSAR
CARDER
CAREER
CARPER
CARTER
CARVER
CORKER
CORNER
CURLER
CURSOR
CURTER
DARKER
DARNER
DARTER
DORMER
DURBAR
EARNER
EERIER
FARMER
FARRAR
FERBER
FERRER
FERVOR
FIRMER
FORCER
FORGER
FORKER
FORMER
GARNER
GARTER
GERBER
GIRDER
GORIER
HARBOR
HARDER
HARKER
HARPER
HERDER
HORNER
HORROR
HURLER
LARDER
LARGER
LERNER
MARKER
MARNER
MARTYR
MERCER
MERGER
MIRIER
MIRROR
MORTAR
MURDER
MURMUR
NURSER
OERTER
PARKER
PARLOR
PARSER
PERTER
PORKER
PORTER
PURRER
PURSER
SERVER
SIRDAR
SORTER
SPRIER
SPRYER
SURFER
TARTAR
TARTER
TERROR
TERSER
TORPOR
TURGOR
TURNER
UPROAR
VERGER
WARDER
WARIER
WARMER
WARNER
WERNER
WIRIER
WORKER
YORKER

•••RR•

BEURRE
BLURRY
CHARRO
CHERRY
CHIRRS
CHURRO
CHURRS
FLURRY
GHARRY
GUERRE
KNARRY
PIERRE
QUARRY
SCARRY
SCURRY
SHERRY
SHIRRS
SIERRA
SKERRY
SKIRRS
SLURRY
SPERRY
SPURRY
STARRY
STORRS
TIERRA
WHERRY
WHIRRS

•••R•R

ADORER
BEARER
DEARER
DOURER
FAIRER
FARRAR
FEARER
FERRER
HEARER
HORROR
JEERER
LEERER
LEHRER
MIRROR
NEARER
POORER
POURER
PURRER
REARER
ROARER
SCARER
SCORER
SHARER
SHIRER
SNORER
SOARER
SOURER
SPARER
STARER
STORER
TERROR
TOURER
USURER
WEARER

••••RR

LAMARR

RS••••

RSVPED

R•S•••

RASCAL
RASERS
RASHAD
RASHER
RASHES
RASHID
RASHLY
RASING
RASPED
RASPER
RASSLE
RASTER
RESALE
RESALT
RESAND
RESAWN
RESAWS
RESCUE
RESEAL
RESEAT
RESEAU
RESECT
RESEDA
RESEED
RESEEN
RESEES
RESELL
RESEND
RESENT
RESETS
RESEWN
RESEWS
RESHES
RESHIP
RESHOD
RESHOE
RESHOT
RESIDE
RESIGN
RESILE
RESING
RESINS
RESINY
RESIST
RESNIK
RESODS
RESOLD
RESOLE
RESORB
RESORT
RESPIN
RESTED
RESTER
RESTON
RESTUP
RESULT
RESUME
RISERS
RISING
RISKED
RISKER
RISQUE
ROSARY
ROSCOE
ROSEAU
ROSIER
ROSILY
ROSINS
ROSINY
ROSITA
ROSTER
ROSTOV
ROSTRA
RUSHED
RUSHEE
RUSHES
RUSKIN
RUSSET
RUSSIA
RUSTED
RUSTIC
RUSTLE

R••S••

RAISED
RAISER
RAISES
RAISIN
RAMSAY
RAMSES
RAMSEY
RAMSON
RANSOM
RASSLE
RATSON
REASON
REDSEA
REDSOX
REESES
REUSED
REUSES
REVSON
REVSUP
RHESUS
RIDSOF
RIGSUP
RIMSKY
RINSED
RINSES
RIPSAW
RIPSUP
ROASTS
ROBSON
ROOSTS
ROUSED
ROUSER
ROUSES
ROUSTS
RUBSIN
RUNSAT
RUNSIN
RUNSON

RUNSTO
RUNSUP
RUSSET
RUSSIA

R•••S•

RADISH
RAKISH
RAMOSE
RAREST
RAVISH
RAWEST
RAWISH
RECAST
RECESS
RECUSE
REFUSE
REHASH
RELISH
RELIST
REMISE
REMISS
REPAST
REPOSE
REPOST
RESIST
RETEST
REVISE
REWASH
RIBOSE
RIFEST
RIMOSE
RIPEST
ROBUST
RUDEST
RUGOSE

R••••S

RABBIS
RABIES
RACERS
RACHIS
RACONS
RADIOS
RADIUS
RAINES
RAISES
RAJAHS
RAKERS
RAMETS
RAMIES
RAMOUS
RAMSES
RANEES
RANGES
RANIDS
RAPIDS
RASERS
RASHES
RATELS
RATERS
RATIOS
RAVELS
RAVENS
RAVERS
RAYONS
RAZORS
RAZZES
REACTS
REAIMS
REAIRS
REALES
REALMS
REARMS
REATAS
REBAGS
REBARS
REBBES
REBECS
REBELS
REBIDS
REBUTS
RECAPS
RECESS
RECONS
RECTOS
RECTUS
RECURS
REDOES
REDUBS
REDYES
REESES
REEVES
REFERS
REFITS
REGIUS
REHABS
REHEMS
REIGNS
REINAS
REINKS
REKEYS
RELAYS
RELETS
RELICS
RELIES
REMANS
REMAPS
REMISS
REMITS
REMOPS
REMOWS
RENEWS
RENNES
REOILS
REPADS
REPAYS
REPEGS
REPELS
REPINS
REPOTS
REPROS
RERUNS
RESAWS
RESEES
RESETS
RESEWS
RESHES
RESINS
RESODS
RETAGS
RETAPS
RETARS
RETIES
RETOPS
RETOWS
RETROS
REUNES
REUSES
REVELS
REVERS
REVETS
REVUES
REWEDS
REWINS
RHAMES
RHESUS
RHEUMS
RHINOS
RHODES
RHOMBS
RHUMBS
RHYMES
RIATAS
RICERS
RICHES
RIDERS
RIDGES
RIFLES
RIGHTS
RIGORS
RILLES
RINSES
RIOJAS
RIPENS
RISERS
RIVALS
RIVERS
RIVETS
RIYALS
ROASTS
ROBINS
ROBLES
ROBOTS
RODEOS
ROGERS
ROGUES
ROLEOS
ROMANS
ROMEOS
RONDOS
ROOSTS
ROPERS
ROSINS
ROTORS
ROUGES
ROUGHS
ROUNDS
ROUSES
ROUSTS
ROUTES
ROVERS
ROWELS
ROWENS
ROWERS
ROYALS
RUANAS
RUBENS
RUBIES
RUBLES
RUCHES
RUCKUS
RUFOUS
RULERS
RUMBAS
RUMENS
RUMORS
RUMPUS
RUNINS
RUNONS
RUNUPS
RUPEES
RUSHES

•RS•••

ARSENE
ARSONS
ERSATZ
ORSINO
URSIDS
URSINE
URSULA

•R•S••

ARISEN
ARISES
ARISTA
ARISTO
BRASHY
BRASOV
BRASSY
BRUSHY
BRYSON
CRESOL
CRESTS
CRISCO
CRISES
CRISIS
CRISPS
CRISPY
CRISTO
CROSBY
CROSSE
CRUSES
CRUSOE
CRUSTS
CRUSTY
DRESSY
ERASED
ERASER
ERASES
ERESTU
FRASER
FRESCA
FRESCO
FRESNO
FRISCO
FRISEE
FRISES
FRISKS
FRISKY
FROSTS
FROSTY
GRASPS
GRASSO
GRASSY
GRISLY
GRISON
GRISTS
GROSSE
GROSSO
GROSZY
IRISES
IRISIN
KRASNY
KRESGE
ORISON
ORISSA
PRASES
PRESET
PRESTO
PRISMS
PRISON
PRISSY
PROSED
PROSER
PROSES
PROSIT
PROSKY
TRASHY
TRISHA
TRISTE
TRUSTS
TRUSTY
TRYSTS
URUSES
WRASSE
WRESTS
WRISTS

•R••S•

ARGOSY
ARIOSE
ARIOSO
ARLISS
ARNESS
AROUSE
ARREST
ARTIST
BRAISE
BRASSY
BRATSK
BREAST
BROWSE
BRUISE
CREASE
CREASY
CREUSA
CROSSE
CROUSE
CRUISE
DRESSY
DRIEST
DROWSE
DROWSY
DRYEST
ERNEST
FRAISE
FREEST
GRASSO
GRASSY
GREASE
GREASY
GRILSE
GROSSE
GROSSO
GROUSE
IRTYSH
ORELSE
ORISSA
PRAISE
PRIEST
PRISSY
PROUST
PROWSE
TRUEST
TRUISM
URALSK
WRASSE
WRIEST
WRYEST

•R•••S

ARAMIS
ARBORS
ARCCOS
ARCHES
ARDEBS
ARDORS
ARECAS
ARENAS
ARETES
ARGOTS
ARGUES
ARISES
ARLISS
ARMETS
ARMIES
ARMORS
ARNESS
AROIDS
AROMAS
ARRAYS
ARROWS
ARSONS
ARTELS
ARTOIS
ARYANS
BRACES
BRACTS
BRAHMS
BRAIDS
BRAILS
BRAINS
BRAKES
BRANDS
BRANTS
BRAVAS
BRAVES
BRAVOS
BRAWLS
BRAZES
BRAZOS
BREADS
BREAKS
BREAMS
BREEDS
BRENTS
BREVES
BREVIS
BRIANS
BRIARS
BRIBES
BRICKS
BRIDES
BRIEFS
BRIERS
BRIGGS
BRILLS
BRINES
BRINGS
BRINKS
BROADS
BROILS
BRONCS
BROODS
BROOKS
BROOMS
BROTHS
BROWNS
BRUGES
BRUINS
BRUITS
BRULES
BRUMES
BRUNTS
BRUTES
BRUTUS
BRUXES
CRACKS
CRAFTS
CRAKES
CRAMPS
CRANES
CRANKS
CRAPES
CRATES
CRAVES
CRAWLS
CRAZES
CREAKS
CREAMS
CREDOS
CREEDS
CREEKS
CREELS
CREEPS
CREMES
CREPES
CRESTS
CRICKS
CRIERS
CRIMES
CRIMPS
CRIPES
CRISES
CRISIS
CRISPS
CROAKS
CROATS
CROCKS
CROCUS
CROFTS
CRONES
CRONUS
CROOKS
CROONS
CROWDS
CROWNS
CROZES
CRUCES
CRUETS
CRUMBS
CRUSES
CRUSTS
CRUXES
CRYERS
CRYPTS
DRAFTS
DRAILS
DRAINS
DRAKES
DRAMAS
DRAPES
DRAWLS
DREADS
DREAMS
DRIERS
DRIFTS
DRILLS
DRINGS
DRINKS
DRIVES
DROIDS
DROITS
DROLLS
DROMOS
DRONES
DROOLS
DROOPS
DROVES
DROWNS
DRUIDS
DRUPES
DRUZES
DRYADS
DRYERS
ERASES
EREBUS
ERECTS
ERGOTS
ERINYS
ERODES
ERRORS
ERUCTS
ERUPTS
FRACAS
FRAMES
FRANCS
FRANKS
FRAUDS
FREAKS
FRIARS
FRIERS
FRILLS
FRISES
FRISKS
FRITOS
FROCKS
FRONDS
FRONTS
FROSTS
FROTHS
FROWNS
FRUITS
FRUMPS
FRYERS
GRACES
GRADES
GRADUS
GRAFTS
GRAILS
GRAINS
GRAMAS
GRAMPS
GRANDS
GRANTS
GRAPES
GRAPHS
GRASPS
GRATES
GRATIS
GRAVES
GRAZES
GREATS
GREBES
GREEKS
GREENS
GREETS
GRIEFS
GRIFTS
GRILLS
GRIMES
GRINDS
GRIOTS
GRIPES
GRISTS
GROANS
GROATS
GROINS
GROOMS
GROPES
GROUPS
GROUTS
GROVES
GROWLS
GRUELS
GRUMPS
GRUNTS
IRANIS
IRAQIS
IRENES
IRIDES
IRISES
KRAALS
KRAITS
ORACHS
ORALES
ORANGS
ORANTS
ORATES
ORBITS
ORDERS
OREADS
ORGANS
ORGIES
ORIBIS
ORIELS
ORINGS
ORLOPS
OROMOS
ORTLES
ORYXES
PRANGS
PRANKS
PRASES
PRATES
PRAWNS
PRAXES
PRAXIS
PRECIS
PREENS
PRICES
PRICKS
PRIDES
PRIERS
PRIMES
PRIMOS
PRIMPS
PRIMUS
PRINKS
PRINTS
PRIONS
PRIORS
PRISMS
PRIZES
PROAMS
PROBES
PROEMS
PROLES

PROMOS
PRONGS
PROOFS
PROSES
PROVES
PROWLS
PRUDES
PRUNES
TRACES
TRACKS
TRACTS
TRADES
TRAILS
TRAINS
TRAITS
TRAMPS
TRAVES
TRAVIS
TRAWLS
TREADS
TREATS
TRENDS
TRIADS
TRIALS
TRIBES
TRICES
TRICKS
TRIERS
TRIKES
TRILLS
TRINES
TRIPOS
TROLLS
TROMPS
TROOPS
TROPES
TROTHS
TROUTS
TROVES
TRUCES
TRUCKS
TRUMPS
TRUNKS
TRUSTS
TRUTHS
TRYSTS
URAEUS
URANUS
URGERS
URIALS
URSIDS
URUSES
VROOMS
WRACKS
WRATHS
WREAKS
WRECKS
WRESTS
WRINGS
WRISTS
WRITES
WRONGS

••RS••

AIRSAC
BORSCH
BURSAE
BURSAL
BURSAR
BURSAS
BURSES
BURSTS
CARSON
CORSET
CURSED
CURSES
CURSOR
DORSAL
DORSET
DORSEY
DORSUM
FIRSTS
GARSON
GORSES
HERSEY
HIRSCH
HORSED
HORSES
HORSEY
JERSEY
KARSTS
KERSEE
KERSEY
KIRSCH
LARSEN
LARSON
MARSHA
MARSHY
MERSEY
MORSEL
NURSED
NURSER
NURSES
PARSEC
PARSED
PARSEE
PARSER
PARSES
PARSON
PERSIA
PERSON
PURSED
PURSER
PURSES
PURSUE
TARSAL
TARSUS
TERSER
TORSOS
VERSED
VERSES
VERSOS
VERSTS
VERSUS
WARSAW
WORSEN
WORSTS
WURSTS

••R•S•

ACROSS
AFRESH
AORIST
ARREST
ATREST
ATRISK
BAREST
BARISH
CARESS
CARUSO
CERISE
CERUSE
CHRISM
CURTSY
DIREST
DURESS
EGRESS
FOREST
GARISH
GYROSE
HARASS
HERESY
INRUSH
JURIST
KAROSS
LAROSA
LYRIST
MARISA
MARISH
MARIST
MEREST
MORASS
MOROSE
OGRESS
OGRISH
ONRUSH
PARISH
PERISH
PERUSE
PHRASE
PUREST
PURISM
PURIST
QURUSH
RAREST
SEROSA
SOREST
STRASS
STRESS
SUREST
TERESA
THRASH
THRESH
THRUSH
THRUST
TOROSE
UNREST
UPRISE
UPROSE
UPRUSH
VARESE
VERISM
YAREST

••R••S

ABRAMS
ACROSS
AERIES
AFRITS
AGREES
AIRBUS
AORTAS
APRONS
ARRAYS
ARROWS
ATREUS
AUREUS
AUROUS
BARGES
BARNES
BARONS
BARRES
BARRIS
BERETS
BERTHS
BIRTHS
BOREAS
BORERS
BURGAS
BURGHS
BURGOS
BURIES
BURINS
BURROS
BURSAS
BURSES
BURSTS
BYRNES
CARATS
CARBOS
CARESS
CARETS
CARGOS
CARIBS
CARIES
CARLOS
CARNES
CAROBS
CAROLS
CAROMS
CARPUS
CARTES
CARVES
CDROMS
CEREUS
CERROS
CIRCUS
CIRRUS
CORALS
CORERS
CORGIS
CORPUS
CORTES
CORVES
CURERS
CURIOS
CURSES
CURTIS
CURVES
DARIUS
DERMIS
DERRIS
DIRGES
DORAGS
DORCAS
DORIES
DURESS
DUROCS
EGRESS
EGRETS
ENROLS
EPROMS
ERRORS
EYRIES
FARADS
FARCES
FARERS
FERGUS
FERIAS
FERRIS
FIRERS
FIRSTS
FIRTHS
FORAYS
FORBES
FORCES
FORGES
FORTAS
FORTES
FORUMS
FURIES
FURORS
FURZES
GARTHS
GERAHS
GIRTHS
GORALS
GORGES
GORSES
GYRONS
HARASS
HAREMS
HARRIS
HERMES
HEROES
HERONS
HIRERS
HORDES
HORSES
HURONS
JORUMS
JURATS
JURIES
JURORS
KARATS
KAROSS
KARRAS
KARSTS
KERMES
KERMIS
KERNOS
KORATS
LARAMS
LARGES
LARGOS
LARVAS
LORIES
LYRICS
MARCOS
MARCUS
MARGES
MARIUS
MERGES
MERITS
MORALS
MORASS
MORAYS
MORELS
MORONS
MORPHS
MORRIS
MURALS
MURRES
MYRRHS
NEREIS
NEREUS
NERVES
NORIAS
NORRIS
NORTHS
NURSES
OGRESS
PARENS
PARERS
PARKAS
PARNIS
PARRIS
PARSES
PARVIS
PERILS
POROUS
PTRAPS
PUREES
PURGES
PURSES
RERUNS
SARANS
SARDIS
SARGES
SARGOS
SARODS
SCRAGS
SCRAMS
SCRAPS
SCREES
SCREWS
SCRIMS
SCRIPS
SCRODS
SCRUBS
SCRUMS
SERACS
SERAIS
SERGES
SERIES
SERIFS
SERINS
SEROUS
SEROWS
SERUMS
SERVES
SERVOS
SHREDS
SHREWS
SHRUBS
SHRUGS
SIRENS
SIRIUS
SPRAGS
SPRATS
SPRAYS
SPREES
SPRIGS
SPRITS
SPRUES
STRADS
STRAPS
STRASS
STRAUS
STRAWS
STRAYS
STRESS
STREWS
STRIPS
STROPS
STRUMS
STRUTS
SURAHS
SURGES
SYRUPS
TARGES
TAROTS
TARSUS
TEREUS
TERNES
THREES
THRIPS
THROBS
THROES
THROWS
THRUMS
TORAHS
TORIES
TORRES
TORSOS
TORTES
TURBOS
TURVES
UNRIGS
VARIES
VARNAS
VERBIS
VERGES
VERSES
VERSOS
VERSTS
VERSUS
VERVES
VIREOS
VIRTUS
VOROUS
WIRERS
WORLDS
WORSTS
WORTHS
WURSTS
XERXES
YERKES
YUROKS
ZEROES
ZORILS

•••RS•

AMERSP
AVERSE
BOURSE
COARSE
COURSE
EVERSO
HEARST
HOARSE
SMERSH
SPARSE
THIRST
THYRSI

•••R•S

ABORTS
ACARUS
ACORNS
ADORES
ADORNS
AGGROS
AGORAS
ALARMS
ALERTS
ANDRES
ANDROS
ANTRES
ASTROS
AVERTS
AWARDS
AZORES
BAIRNS
BARRES
BARRIS
BEARDS
BGIRLS
BLARES
BLURBS
BLURTS
BOARDS
BURROS
CADRES
CAIRNS
CAPRIS
CEORLS
CERROS
CHARMS
CHARTS
CHIRPS
CHIRRS
CHORDS
CHORES
CHORUS
CHURLS
CHURNS
CHURRS
CIRRUS
CITRUS
CLAROS
CLERKS
CLORIS
COBRAS
COURTS
CYPRUS
DEBRAS
DEBRIS
DERRIS
DMARKS
DOBRAS
DOBROS
DWARFS
EAGRES
ELBRUS
ENURES
EPIRUS
ESDRAS
EVERTS
EXERTS
EXTRAS
EXURBS
FERRIS
FIBRES
FIORDS
FJORDS
FLARES
FLIRTS
FLORAS
FLORES
GENRES
GLARES
GNARLS
GOURDS
GUARDS
GUIROS
HARRIS
HEARTS
HOARDS
HOURIS
HUBRIS
HYDRAS
HYDROS
ICARUS
INDRIS
INGRES
INTROS
INURES
JAURES
KARRAS
KAURIS
KNURLS
KUKRIS
LAIRDS
LEARNS
LIBRIS
LITRES
LIVRES
MACROS
MADRAS
MADRES
MAORIS
METRES
METROS
MICROS
MITRES
MOIRES
MORRIS
MOURNS
MUDRAS
MURRES
MYRRHS
NACRES
NAIRAS
NITRES
NORRIS
OCHRES
OPERAS
OSIRIS
OZARKS
PADRES
PARRIS
PEARLS
PHAROS
QUARKS
QUARTS
QUERNS
QUIRES
QUIRKS
QUIRTS
REARMS
REPROS
RETROS
SABRAS
SABRES
SCARES
SCARFS
SCARPS
SCORES
SCORNS
SEVRES
SHARDS
SHARES
SHARKS
SHARPS
SHIRES
SHIRKS
SHIRRS
SHIRTS
SHORES

SHORTS
SKIRLS
SKIROS
SKIRRS
SKIRTS
SKORTS
SLURPS
SMARTS
SMIRKS
SMURFS
SNARES
SNARLS
SNORES
SNORTS
SOARES
SPARES
SPARKS
SPIRES
SPIROS
SPORES
SPORTS
SPURNS
SPURTS
STARES
STARTS
STERES
STERNS
STIRKS
STORES
STORKS
STORMS
STORRS
SUDRAS
SUTRAS
SWARDS
SWARMS
SWIRLS
SWORDS
TAURUS
TAYRAS
TBIRDS
TETRAS
TETRIS
THERES
THERMS
THIRDS
THORNS
THORPS
TIARAS
TIGRIS
TITRES
TORRES
TSURIS
TWERPS
TWIRLS
ULTRAS
UMBRAS
UNARMS
USURPS
UTURNS
WALRUS
WHARFS
WHERES
WHIRLS
WHIRRS
WHORLS
YEARNS
ZAIRES
ZEBRAS

••••RS

ABHORS
ACTORS
ADDERS
AIDERS
AILERS
ALDERS
ALTARS
ALTERS
AMBERS
AMEERS
AMOURS
ANGERS
ARBORS
ARDORS
ARMORS
ASKERS
ASTERS
ATTARS
AUGERS
AUGURS
BAKERS
BALERS
BIKERS
BITERS
BLEARS
BONERS
BORERS
BOWERS
BOXERS
BOYARS
BRIARS
BRIERS
BUYERS
CABERS
CAGERS
CANERS
CAPERS
CATERS
CAVERS
CEDARS
CHAIRS
CHEERS
CHIRRS
CHOIRS
CHURRS
CIDERS
CIGARS
CITERS
CLEARS
CODERS
COLORS
COMERS
COOERS
CORERS
COVERS
COWERS
CRIERS
CRYERS
CURERS
CYDERS
DATERS
DEBARS
DECORS
DEFERS
DEMURS
DETERS
DICERS
DINARS
DINERS
DIVERS
DIYERS
DOLORS
DONORS
DOSERS
DOWERS
DOZERS
DRIERS
DRYERS
EATERS
EDGARS
EDGERS
EELERS
EIDERS
ELDERS
ELVERS
EMBERS
EMEERS
ENDERS
ENTERS
EPHORS
ERRORS
ESKERS
ESTERS
ETHERS
FAKERS
FAKIRS
FARERS
FAVORS
FEMURS
FEVERS
FIBERS
FIFERS
FILERS
FIRERS
FIVERS
FIXERS
FLAIRS
FLEERS
FLIERS
FLOORS
FLOURS
FLYERS
FOYERS
FRIARS
FRIERS
FRYERS
FURORS
GAPERS
GATERS
GATORS
GIBERS
GIVERS
GLAIRS
GLUERS
GOFERS
GONERS
HALERS
HATERS
HAVERS
HAZERS
HEWERS
HEXERS
HIDERS
HIKERS
HIRERS
HOMERS
HONORS
HOPERS
HOVERS
HUMORS
IDLERS
INCURS
INFERS
INKERS
JAPERS
JIVERS
JOKERS
JURORS
KAFIRS
KEFIRS
KHMERS
KITERS
LABORS
LACERS
LADERS
LAGERS
LAKERS
LASERS
LAVERS
LAYERS
LEMURS
LEVERS
LIFERS
LIGERS
LINERS
LITERS
LIVERS
LONERS
LOPERS
LOSERS
LOVERS
LOWERS
LUGERS
MAJORS
MAKERS
MANORS
MASERS
MATERS
MAYORS
MAZERS
MESSRS
METERS
MILERS
MIMERS
MINERS
MINORS
MISERS
MITERS
MIXERS
MOHURS
MOLARS
MOPERS
MOTORS
MOVERS
MOWERS
MOYERS
MUSERS
NABORS
NADIRS
NAMERS
NEVERS
NFLERS
NHLERS
NINERS
NITERS
NOTERS
OATERS
OCCURS
OCHERS
ODOURS
OFFERS
OGLERS
OILERS
ORDERS
OSCARS
OSIERS
OTHERS
OTTERS
OWNERS
PACERS
PAGERS
PAMIRS
PAPERS
PARERS
PATERS
PAVERS
PAWERS
PAYERS
PETERS
PIKERS
PIPERS
PLIERS
POKERS
POLERS
POSERS
POWERS
PRIERS
PRIORS
RACERS
RAKERS
RASERS
RATERS
RAVERS
RAZORS
REAIRS
REBARS
RECURS
REFERS
RETARS
REVERS
RICERS
RIDERS
RIGORS
RISERS
RIVERS
ROGERS
ROPERS
ROTORS
ROVERS
ROWERS
RULERS
RUMORS
SABERS
SAKERS
SAPORS
SATYRS
SAVERS
SAVORS
SAYERS
SCOURS
SEDERS
SENORS
SEVERS
SEWERS
SHEARS
SHEERS
SHIRRS
SHOERS
SIDERS
SITARS
SIXERS
SIZERS
SKIERS
SKIRRS
SMEARS
SNEERS
SOBERS
SOEURS
SOLARS
SOLERS
SOMERS
SOPORS
SOWERS
SOXERS
SPEARS
SPIERS
SPOORS
STAIRS
STEERS
STORRS
SUGARS
SUPERS
SWEARS
TABORS
TAKERS
TALERS
TAMERS
TAPERS
TAPIRS
TASERS
TATARS
TATERS
TAXERS
TENORS
THEIRS
TIGERS
TILERS
TIMERS
TITERS
TONERS
TOPERS
TOTERS
TOWERS
TRIERS
TUBERS
TUDORS
TUNERS
TUTORS
TYPERS
UDDERS
UIGURS
ULCERS
UMBERS
UNBARS
UPPERS
URGERS
USHERS
UTTERS
VAPORS
VEXERS
VICARS
VIGORS
VIPERS
VISORS
VOTERS
VOWERS
WADERS
WAFERS
WAGERS
WALERS
WANERS
WATERS
WAVERS
WAXERS
WHIRRS
WIPERS
WIRERS
WOOERS

R•T•••

RATEDG
RATEDR
RATEDX
RATELS
RATERS
RATHER
RATIFY
RATINE
RATING
RATION
RATIOS
RATITE
RATLIN
RATSON
RATTAN
RATTED
RATTER
RATTLE
RATTLY
RETAGS
RETAIL
RETAIN
RETAKE
RETAPE
RETAPS
RETARD
RETARS
RETEAR
RETELL
RETENE
RETEST
RETIAL
RETIED
RETIES
RETILE
RETIME
RETINA
RETIRE
RETOLD
RETOOK
RETOOL
RETOPS
RETORT
RETOUR
RETOWS
RETRAL
RETRIM
RETROS
RETTON
RETUNE
RETURN
RETYPE
RITARD
RITTER
RITUAL
ROTARY
ROTATE
ROTGUT
ROTHKO
ROTINI
ROTORS
ROTTED
ROTTEN
ROTTER
ROTUND
RUTGER
RUTILE
RUTTAN
RUTTED

R••T••

RAFTED
RAFTER
RAGTAG
RAGTOP
RANTED
RANTER
RAPTLY
RAPTOR
RASTER
RATTAN
RATTED
RATTER
RATTLE
RATTLY
REATAS
RECTOR
RECTOS
RECTUS
REDTAG
REDTOP
RENTAL
RENTED
RENTER
RESTED
RESTER
RESTON
RESTUP
RETTON
REUTER
RHETOR
RHYTHM
RHYTON
RIATAS
RIFTED
RIOTED
RIOTER
RITTER
ROOTED
ROOTER
ROSTER
ROSTOV
ROSTRA
ROTTED
ROTTEN
ROTTER
ROUTED
ROUTER
ROUTES
RRATED
RUSTED
RUSTIC
RUSTLE
RUTTAN
RUTTED

R•••T•

RABATO
RAMATE
RAMETS
RARITY
RATITE
REACTS
REALTY
REBATE
REBUTS
RECITE
REDATE
REFITS
REFUTE
RELATE
RELETS
REMITS
REMOTE
RENATA
RENOTE
REPOTS
REPUTE
RERATE
RESETS
REVETS
RIALTO
RIGHTO
RIGHTS
RIGHTY
RIVETS
ROASTS
ROBOTS
ROOSTS
ROSITA
ROTATE
ROUSTS
RUBATI
RUBATO
RUGATE
RUNSTO

R••••T

RABBET
RABBIT
RACKET
RAGOUT
RAILAT
RAJPUT
RAMJET
RANOUT
RAREST
RAWEST
REBENT
REBOLT
REBOOT
RECANT
RECAST
RECENT
RECOAT
REDACT
REDANT
REDHAT
REDHOT
REEDIT
REGENT
REGLET
REGNAT
REGRET
REHEAT
REJECT
RELENT
RELICT
RELIST

RELUCT
REMELT
RENNET
REPAST
REPEAT
REPENT
REPORT
REPOST
RERENT
RESALT
RESEAT
RESECT
RESENT
RESHOT
RESIST
RESORT
RESULT
RETEST
RETORT
REVERT
REVOLT
REXCAT
RIDENT
RIFEST
RILLET
RIPEST
RIPOUT
ROBERT
ROBUST
ROCHET
ROCKET
RODENT
ROTGUT
RUBOUT
RUDEST
RUNLET
RUNOUT
RUNSAT
RUPERT
RUSSET

•RT•••

ARTELS
ARTERY
ARTFUL
ARTGUM
ARTHRO
ARTHUR
ARTIER
ARTILY
ARTIST
ARTOIS
ARTURO
IRTYSH
ORTEGA
ORTLES
URTEXT

•R•T••

ARCTAN
ARCTIC
ARETES
ARETHA
BRATSK
BRATTY
BRETON
BRITON
BROTHS
BRUTAL
BRUTES
BRUTUS
CRATED
CRATER
CRATES
CRETAN
CRETIN
CRITIC
CROTON
CRUTCH
EROTIC
FRETTY
FRITOS
FROTHS
FROTHY
FRUTTI
GRATED
GRATER
GRATES
GRATIA
GRATIN
GRATIS
GRETEL
GRETNA
GRITTY
GROTON
GROTTO
GROTTY
IRATER
KRATER
ORATED
ORATES
ORATOR
PRATED
PRATER
PRATES
PRETAX
PRETER
PRETTY
PROTAX
PROTEI
PROTEM
PROTON
RRATED
TRITER
TRITON
TROTHS
TRUTHS
WRATHS
WRATHY
WRETCH
WRITER
WRITES
WRITHE
XRATED

•R••T•

ARGOTS
ARISTA
ARISTO
ARMETS
ARNETT
BRACTS
BRANTS
BRATTY
BREATH
BRENTS
BRONTE
BRUITS
BRUNTS
CRAFTS
CRAFTY
CREATE
CRESTS
CRISTO
CROATS
CROFTS
CROUTE
CRUETS
CRUSTS
CRUSTY
CRYPTO
CRYPTS
DRAFTS
DRAFTY
DRIFTS
DRIFTY
DROITS
ERECTS
ERESTU
ERGATE
ERGOTS
ERRATA
ERSATZ
ERUCTS
ERUPTS
FRETTY
FRONTS
FROSTS
FROSTY
FRUITS
FRUITY
FRUTTI
GRAFTS
GRANTS
GREATS
GREETS
GRIFTS
GRIOTS
GRISTS
GRITTY
GROATS
GROTTO
GROTTY
GROUTS
GROUTY
GROWTH
GRUNTS
KRAITS
KRANTZ
MRMOTO
ORANTS
ORBITS
ORGATE
ORNATE
ORNITH
PRESTO
PRETTY
PRINTS
PRONTO
TRACTS
TRAITS
TREATS
TREATY
TRISTE
TROUTS
TRUSTS
TRUSTY
TRYSTS
WRAITH
WREATH
WRESTS
WRISTS

•R•••T

ARAFAT
ARARAT
ARDENT
ARENDT
ARGENT
ARIGHT
ARMLET
ARMPIT
ARNETT
ARPENT
ARRANT
ARREST
ARTIST
BRANDT
BREAST
BRECHT
BREVET
BRIGHT
BRUNET
BRYANT
CRAVAT
CREDIT
DREAMT
DRIEST
DROPIT
DRYEST
DRYOUT
DRYROT
ERFURT
ERNEST
ERRANT
FREEST
FRIGHT
GRABAT
GRIVET
IROBOT
IRRUPT
ORGEAT
ORIENT
PRESET
PRIEST
PRIPET
PRIVET
PROFIT
PROMPT
PROSIT
PROUST
TRICOT
TRIJET
TRIVET
TRUANT
TRUEST
TRYOUT
URGENT
URTEXT
WRIEST
WRIGHT
WRYEST

••RT••

AORTAE
AORTAL
AORTAS
AORTIC
BARTAB
BARTER
BARTOK
BARTON
BERTHA
BERTHS
BERTIE
BIRTHS
BURTON
CARTED
CARTEL
CARTER
CARTES
CARTON
CERTIF
CORTES
CORTEX
CORTEZ
CURTER
CURTIN
CURTIS
CURTIZ
CURTLY
CURTSY
DARTED
DARTER
EARTHA
EARTHY
FIRTHS
FORTAS
FORTES
GARTER
GARTHS
GERTIE
GIRTED
GIRTHS
HORTON
HURTLE
KIRTLE
MARTEL
MARTEN
MARTHA
MARTIN
MARTYR
MERTON
MORTAL
MORTAR
MORTON
MYRTLE
NORTHS
NORTON
OERTER
PARTED
PARTLY
PARTON
PERTER
PERTLY
PORTAL
PORTED
PORTER
PORTIA
PORTLY
SARTON
SARTRE
SORTED
SORTER
SORTIE
SORTOF
SURTAX
TARTAN
TARTAR
TARTER
TARTLY
TORTES
TURTLE
VERTEX
VIRTUE
VIRTUS
VORTEX
WORTHS
WORTHY

••R•T•

AERATE
AFRITS
BARITE
BERATE
BERETS
BORATE
BURSTS
BYROTE
CARATS
CARETO
CARETS
CERATE
CURATE
DARETO
DORATI
EGRETS
ERRATA
FERITY
FIRSTS
GARETH
GYRATE
HERETO
JURATS
KARATE
KARATS
KARSTS
KORATS
MERITS
MORITA
MORITZ
PARETO
PARITY
PIRATE
PURITY
PYRITE
RARITY
RERATE
SPRATS
SPRITE
SPRITS
SPRITZ
STRATA
STRATI
STRATO
STRUTS
SURETE
SURETY
TAROTS
TERATO
TERETE
TURNTO
VERITE
VERITY
VERSTS
WARMTH
WORSTS
WURSTS
ZEROTH

••R••T

ABRUPT
ADRIFT
ADROIT
AFREET
AIROUT
AORIST
ARRANT
ARREST
ATREST
BARBET
BARDOT
BAREST
BARKAT
BEREFT
BIRGIT
BURBOT
BURNET
CARLOT
CARNET
CARNOT
CARPET
CARROT
CERMET
CORNET
CORSET
CURVET
DARENT
DARNIT
DIRECT
DIREST
DORRIT
DORSET
DURANT
ENRAPT
ENROOT
ERRANT
FAROUT
FERMAT
FERRET
FOREST
FORGET
FORGOT
FORINT
FORMAT
GARNET
GARRET
GERENT
GERONT
GORGET
HEREAT
HERIOT
HERMIT
HORNET
IRRUPT
JURIST
KERMIT
KORBUT
KURALT
LARIAT
LYRIST
MARGOT
MARIST
MARKET
MARMOT
MEREST
MERLOT
MORANT
PARENT
PARGET
PARROT
PERMIT
PERROT
PUREST
PURIST
RAREST
RERENT
SCRIPT
SHRIFT
SORBET
SOREST
SPRINT
SPROUT
STRAIT
STREET
STRICT
SUREST
TARGET
TARPIT
TERCET
TERRET
THREAT
THRIFT
THROAT
THRUST
TOREAT
TURBIT
TURBOT
TURRET
TYRANT
UNREST
UNROOT
UPROOT
VARLET
VERVET
WERENT
YAREST

•••RT•

ABORTS
ALERTS
AVERTS
BLURTS
CHARTS
CHERTY
COURTS
DEARTH
DUARTE
ECARTE
EVERTS
EXERTS
FLIRTS
FLIRTY
FOURTH
GEARTO
HEARTH
HEARTS
HEARTY
NEARTO
OMERTA
OPORTO
PUERTO
QUARTO
QUARTS
QUARTZ
QUIRTS
QWERTY
SHIRTS
SHIRTY
SHORTA
SHORTE
SHORTI
SHORTO
SHORTS
SHORTU
SHORTY
SKIRTS
SKORTS
SMARTS
SMARTY
SNORTS
SPARTA
SPORTS
SPORTY
SPURTS
STARTS
SWARTH
THIRTY

•••R•T

AGOROT
AIGRET
ARARAT
ATTRIT
BEIRUT
CARROT
CLARET
DORRIT
DRYROT
ESPRIT
FERRET
FLORET
GARRET
HEARST
IMARET
INARUT
JEERAT
LABRET
LEARNT
LEERAT
MEERUT
PARROT
PEERAT
PERROT
POIROT
REGRET
SECRET
SEURAT
SPIRIT
TEARAT
TERRET
THIRST
TURRET

••••RT

ADVERT
ALBERT
ALHIRT
ALPERT
ASSERT
ASSORT
BOGART
CAVORT
COHORT
COVERT
DEPART
DEPORT
DESERT
DIVERT

EFFORT
EGBERT
ELBERT
ENGIRT
ERFURT
ESCORT
EXHORT
EXPERT
EXPORT
EXSERT
EXTORT
GOCART
GOKART
HOBART
HUBERT
IMPART
IMPORT
INPART
INPORT
INSERT
INVERT
MOZART
OBVERT
OXCART
POPART
REPORT
RESORT
RETORT
REVERT
ROBERT
RUPERT
SQUIRT
STUART
THWART
TSHIRT
UNGIRT
UNHURT
YOGURT

RU••••
RUANAS
RUANDA
RUBATI
RUBATO
RUBBED
RUBBER
RUBBLE
RUBBLY
RUBENS
RUBIED
RUBIES
RUBIFY
RUBLES
RUBLEV
RUBOFF
RUBOUT
RUBRIC
RUBSIN
RUCHES
RUCKED
RUCKUS
RUDDER
RUDDLE
RUDELY
RUDEST
RUDMAN
RUDOLF
RUEFUL
RUFFED
RUFFLE
RUFFLY
RUFOUS
RUGATE
RUGGED
RUGOSE
RUINED
RUINER
RULEON
RULERS
RULING
RUMBAS
RUMBLE
RUMBLY
RUMENS
RUMINA
RUMMER
RUMORS
RUMOUR
RUMPLE
RUMPLY
RUMPUS
RUNCIE
RUNDLE
RUNDMC
RUNDRY
RUNFOR
RUNGUP
RUNINS
RUNLET
RUNNEL
RUNNER
RUNOFF
RUNONS
RUNOUT
RUNSAT
RUNSIN
RUNSON
RUNSTO
RUNSUP
RUNUPS
RUNWAY
RUNYON
RUPAUL
RUPEES
RUPERT
RUPIAH
RUSHED
RUSHEE
RUSHES
RUSKIN
RUSSET
RUSSIA
RUSTED
RUSTIC
RUSTLE
RUTGER
RUTILE
RUTTAN
RUTTED

R•U•••
REUBEN
REUNES
REUSED
REUSES
REUTER
RHUMBA
RHUMBS
ROUBLE
ROUGED
ROUGES
ROUGHS
ROUGHY
ROUNDS
ROURKE
ROUSED
ROUSER
ROUSES
ROUSTS
ROUTED
ROUTER
ROUTES
RYUKYU

R••U••
RADULA
RAQUEL
REBUFF
REBUKE
REBURY
REBUTS
RECURS
RECUSE
REDUBS
REDUCE
REFUEL
REFUGE
REFUND
REFUSE
REFUTE
REHUNG
RELUCT
RELUME
REMUDA
REPUGN
REPUTE
RERUNS
RESULT
RESUME
RETUNE
RETURN
REVUES
RHEUMS
RHEUMY
RITUAL
ROBUST
ROGUES
ROTUND
RUNUPS

R•••U•
RACKUP
RADIUM
RADIUS
RAGOUT
RAGRUG
RAIPUR
RAJPUT
RAKEUP
RAMOUS
RANGUP
RANOUT
RAVEUP
RAYGUN
REARUP
RECOUP
RECTUS
REDBUD
REDGUM
REFLUX
REGIUS
REGLUE
RESCUE
RESTUP
RETOUR
REVSUP
RHESUS
RIGOUR
RIGSUP
RILEUP
RINGUP
RIPOUT
RIPSUP
RISQUE
ROLLUP
ROTGUT
RUBOUT
RUCKUS
RUEFUL
RUFOUS
RUMOUR
RUMPUS
RUNGUP
RUNOUT
RUNSUP
RUPAUL
RVALUE

R••••U
RAMEAU
RESEAU
ROSEAU
RYUKYU

•RU•••
ARUBAN
BRUDER
BRUGES
BRUINS
BRUISE
BRUITS
BRULES
BRUMAL
BRUMBY
BRUMES
BRUNCH
BRUNEI
BRUNET
BRUNTS
BRUSHY
BRUTAL
BRUTES
BRUTUS
BRUXED
BRUXES
CRUCES
CRUDDY
CRUDER
CRUETS
CRUISE
CRUMBS
CRUMBY
CRUMMY
CRUNCH
CRURAL
CRUSES
CRUSOE
CRUSTS
CRUSTY
CRUTCH
CRUXES
DRUDGE
DRUIDS
DRUMUP
DRUPES
DRUZES
ERUCTS
ERUPTS
FRUGAL
FRUITS
FRUITY
FRUMPS
FRUMPY
FRUTTI
GRUBBY
GRUDGE
GRUELS
GRUMPS
GRUMPY
GRUNDY
GRUNGE
GRUNGY
GRUNTS
KRUGER
PRUDES
PRUNED
PRUNER
PRUNES
TRUANT
TRUCES
TRUCKS
TRUDGE
TRUEST
TRUING
TRUISM
TRUMAN
TRUMPS
TRUNKS
TRUSTS
TRUSTY
TRUTHS
URUSES

•R•U••
ARGUED
ARGUER
ARGUES
ARGUFY
ARJUNA
ARMURE
AROUND
AROUSE
ARTURO
BREUER
CREUSA
CROUCH
CROUPY
CROUSE
CROUTE
ERFURT
FRAUDS
FRAUEN
GROUCH
GROUND
GROUPS
GROUSE
GROUTS
GROUTY
IRRUPT
ORDURE
PROUST
TRAUMA
TRIUNE
TROUGH
TROUPE
TROUTS
TROUVE
URSULA

•R••U•
ARBOUR
ARDOUR
ARMFUL
ARMOUR
ARTFUL
ARTGUM
ARTHUR
BRAQUE
BROGUE
BRUTUS
CROCUS
CRONUS
CROPUP
DRAWUP
DREWUP
DROGUE
DRUMUP
DRYOUT
DRYRUN
ERBIUM
EREBUS
FRENUM
GRADUS
GREWUP
GROWUP
IREFUL
KRONUR
MRBLUE
PRAGUE
PRENUP
PRIMUM
PRIMUS
PROPUP
TRIPUP
TRYOUT
URAEUS
URANUS
WRAPUP

•R•••U
ARALLU
ERESTU
ORMOLU

••RU••
ABRUPT
BARUCH
CARUSO
CERUSE
CURULE
FERULE
FORUMS
GERUND
INRUSH
IRRUPT
JORUMS
KORUNA
NERUDA
ONRUSH
PARULA
PARURE
PERUGA
PERUKE
PERUSE
QURUSH
RERUNS
SCRUBS
SCRUFF
SCRUMS
SERUMS
SHRUBS
SHRUGS
SHRUNK
SPRUCE
SPRUES
SPRUNG
STRUCK
STRUMS
STRUNG
STRUTS
SYRUPS
SYRUPY
THRUMS
THRUSH
THRUST
UNRULY
UPRUSH
VARUNA
YORUBA

••R•U•
AIRBUS
AIRGUN
AIROUT
ATREUS
ATRIUM
AUREUS
AUROUS
BARIUM
BARNUM
BARQUE
BARZUN
BOREUP
BURNUP
CARFUL
CARPUS
CEREUS
CERIUM
CIRCUM
CIRCUS
CIRQUE
CIRRUS
CORIUM
CORPUS
CURIUM
CURLUP
DARIUS
DORSUM
EARFUL
FAROUK
FAROUT
FERGUS
FIREUP
FIRMUP
HARDUP
HORMUZ
JARFUL
KORBUT
LARRUP
MARAUD
MARCUS
MARDUK
MARIUS
MARKUP
MARQUE
MURMUR
NEREUS
PERDUE
PERKUP
POROUS
PURDUE
PURSUE
SEROUS
SHROUD
SIRIUS
SPROUT
STRAUB
STRAUS
STROUD
TARSUS
TEREUS
TOREUP
TORQUE
TURNUP
VERDUN
VERSUS
VIRTUE
VIRTUS
VOROUS
WARMUP
WORKUP

••R••U
BUREAU
MARILU
MOREAU

•••RU•
ACARUS
ACCRUE
ALARUM
ANTRUM
BAYRUM
BEARUP
BEIRUT
CHERUB
CHORUS
CIRRUS
CITRUS
CYPRUS
DRYRUN
ELBRUS
ENDRUN
EPIRUS
FAIRUP
GEARUP
GUDRUN
ICARUS
IMBRUE
INARUT
LABRUM
LARRUP
LEBRUN
MEERUT
OUTRUN
PAIRUP
QUORUM
RAGRUG
REARUP
SACRUM
SCARUM
SKIRUN
STIRUP
TAURUS
TEARUP
TOBRUK
UNTRUE
WALRUS

•••R•U
APERCU
SHORTU

••••RU
HALERU
JABIRU
MASERU
SUBARU

RV••••
RVALUE

R•V•••
RAVAGE
RAVELS
RAVENS
RAVERS
RAVEUP
RAVINE
RAVING
RAVISH
REVAMP
REVEAL
REVELS
REVERB
REVERE
REVERS
REVERT
REVETS
REVIEW
REVILE
REVISE
REVIVE
REVLON
REVOIR
REVOKE
REVOLT
REVSON
REVSUP
REVUES
REVVED
RIVALS
RIVERA
RIVERS
RIVETS
RIVING
ROVERS
ROVING
RSVPED

R••V••
REEVED
REEVES
REVVED

R•••V•
RELEVY
RELIVE
REMOVE
REPAVE
REVIVE
REWOVE

R••••V
ROCKYV
ROSTOV
RUBLEV

•RV•••
ARVADA
ERVING
IRVINE
IRVING

•R•V••
BRAVAS
BRAVED
BRAVER
BRAVES
BRAVOS
BREVES
BREVET
BREVIS
CRAVAT
CRAVED
CRAVEN
CRAVER
CRAVES
DRIVEL
DRIVEN
DRIVER
DRIVES
DROVER
DROVES
GRAVED
GRAVEL
GRAVEN
GRAVER
GRAVES
GRAVID
GRIVET
GROVEL
GROVER
GROVES
PRAVDA
PREVIN
PRIVET
PROVED
PROVEN
PROVER
PROVES
TRAVEL
TRAVES
TRAVIS
TREVOR
TRIVET
TRIVIA
TROVES

•R••V•
ARGIVE
ARRIVE
GREAVE
GRIEVE
GROOVE
GROOVY
TROUVE

•R•••V
BRASOV

••RV••
CARVED
CARVER
CARVES
CARVEY
CERVID
CORVEE
CORVES
CURVED
CURVES
CURVET
FERVID
FERVOR
GARVEY
HARVEY
LARVAE
LARVAL
LARVAS
MARVEL
MARVIN
MERVYN
NARVIK
NERVES
PARVIS
PURVEY
SERVAL
SERVED
SERVER
SERVES
SERVOS
SURVEY
TURVES
VERVES
VERVET

••R•V•
ARRIVE
DERIVE
MORAVA
PAREVE
SHRIVE
SHROVE
STRIVE
STROVE
THRIVE
THROVE

••R••V
KARPOV

•••RV•
SCURVE
SCURVY
STARVE
SWERVE

•••R•V
HENRYV
IMPROV

RW••••
RWANDA

R•W•••
RAWEGG
RAWEST
RAWISH
REWARD
REWARM
REWASH
REWEDS
REWELD
REWIND
REWINS
REWIRE
REWORD
REWORK
REWOVE
REWRAP
ROWELS
ROWENA
ROWENS
ROWERS
ROWING

R••W••
RUNWAY

R•••W•
REMOWN
REMOWS
RENEWS
RENOWN
RESAWN
RESAWS
RESEWN
RESEWS
RETOWS

R••••W
REDRAW
REDREW
REPLOW
REVIEW
RIPSAW

•RW•••
ORWELL

•R•W••
ARAWAK
BRAWLS
BRAWNY
BREWED
BREWER
BROWNE
BROWNS
BROWNY
BROWSE
CRAWLS
CRAWLY
CREWED
CREWEL
CROWDS
CROWED
CROWER
CROWNS
DRAWER
DRAWIN
DRAWLS
DRAWLY
DRAWON
DRAWUP
DREWIN
DREWON
DREWUP
DROWNS
DROWSE
DROWSY
FROWNS
FROWZY
GREWON
GREWUP
GROWER
GROWLS
GROWLY
GROWON
GROWTH
GROWUP
PRAWNS
PREWAR
PROWLS
PROWSE
TRAWLS
TROWED
TROWEL

•R••W•
ARROWS

•R•••W
BROKAW
ERENOW
KRAKOW
PRELAW

••RW••
AIRWAY
DARWIN
EARWAX
EARWIG
NARWAL
NORWAY

••R•W•
ARROWS
SCRAWL
SCREWS
SCREWY
SEROWS
SHREWD
SHREWS
SPRAWL
STRAWS
STRAWY
STREWN
STREWS
TARAWA
THROWN
THROWS

••R••W
BARROW
BORROW
BURROW
CURFEW
CURLEW
DARROW
FARLOW
FARROW
FURROW
HARLOW
HARROW
MARROW
MORROW
MURROW
NARROW
SORROW
WARSAW
YARROW

•••R•W
ANDREW
BARROW
BORROW
BURROW
DARROW
ESCROW
FARROW
FURROW
HARROW
HEBREW
INAROW
KUDROW
MARROW
MCGRAW
MCGREW
MORROW
MURROW
NARROW
REDRAW
REDREW
SORROW
UNDRAW
YARROW

R•X•••
REXCAT
ROXANA
ROXANE

R••••X
RATEDX
REDFOX
REDSOX
REFLEX
REFLUX

•R•X••
BRUXED
BRUXES
CRUXES
DREXEL
ORYXES
PRAXES
PRAXIS
TRIXIE

•R••X•
URTEXT

•R•••X
BRANDX
PREFIX
PRETAX
PROLIX
PROTAX

••RX••
XERXES

••R•X•
BORAXO

••R••X
CORTEX
EARWAX
LARYNX
SURTAX
SYRINX
VERTEX
VORTEX

•••R•X
CLOROX
MATRIX
THORAX

RY••••
RYAZAN
RYDELL
RYOKAN
RYUKYU

R•Y•••
RAYGUN
RAYONS
RHYMED
RHYMER
RHYMES
RHYTHM
RHYTON
RIYADH
RIYALS
ROYALE
ROYALS

R••Y••
REDYED
REDYES
RETYPE
RUNYON

R•••Y•
REDEYE
REKEYS
RELAYS
REPAYS
RIBEYE
ROCKYV
RYUKYU

R••••Y
RACILY
RAINEY
RAMIFY
RAMSAY
RAMSEY
RANDRY
RANKLY
RAPTLY
RAREFY
RARELY
RARIFY
RARITY
RASHLY
RATIFY
RATTLY
REALLY
REALTY
REBURY
RECOPY
REDBAY
REDENY
REILLY
RELEVY
REMEDY
REPLAY
RESINY
RHEUMY
RICHLY
RICKEY
RIDLEY
RIFELY
RIGHTY
RIMSKY
RIPELY
RIPLEY
RIPPLY
ROBROY
RODNEY
ROMANY
ROMNEY
RONELY
ROONEY
ROSARY
ROSILY
ROSINY
ROTARY
ROUGHY
RUBBLY
RUBIFY
RUDELY
RUFFLY
RUMBLY
RUMPLY
RUNDRY
RUNWAY

•RY•••
ARYANS
BRYANT
BRYONY
BRYSON
CRYERS
CRYING
CRYOFF
CRYPTO
CRYPTS
DRYADS
DRYDEN
DRYERS
DRYEST
DRYFLY
DRYICE
DRYING
DRYINK
DRYOFF
DRYOUT
DRYROT
DRYRUN
ERYNGO
FRYERS
FRYING
FRYPAN
ORYXES
PRYING
PRYNNE
TRYFOR
TRYING
TRYLON
TRYOUT
TRYSTS
WRYEST

•R•Y••
ARGYLE
ARGYLL
BRAYED
BRAYER
BREYER
CRAYON
DRAYED
FRAYED
GRAYED
GRAYER
GRAYLY
GREYED
GREYER
GREYLY
IRTYSH
MRHYDE
PRAYED
PRAYER
PREYED
PREYON
XRAYED

•R••Y•
ARRAYS
ARROYO
CRONYN
ERINYS

•R•••Y
ARCHLY
ARGOSY
ARGUFY
ARIDLY
ARMORY
ARTERY
ARTILY
BRACHY
BRAINY
BRANDY
BRANNY
BRASHY
BRASSY
BRATTY
BRAWNY
BREEZY
BRICKY
BRIERY
BROLLY
BRONZY
BROODY
BROOKY
BROOMY
BROWNY
BRUMBY
BRUSHY
BRYONY
CRABBY
CRACKY
CRAFTY
CRAGGY
CRANKY
CRANNY
CRAWLY
CREAKY
CREAMY
CREASY
CREEPY
CRIKEY
CRIMPY
CRISPY
CROAKY
CROSBY
CROUPY
CRUDDY
CRUMBY
CRUMMY
CRUSTY
DRABLY
DRAFTY
DRAGGY
DRAWLY
DREAMY
DREARY
DRESSY
DRIFTY
DRIPPY
DROLLY
DROOLY
DROOPY
DROPBY
DROWSY
DRYFLY
FRAIDY
FRANNY
FREAKY
FREDDY
FREELY
FRENZY
FRETTY
FRIARY
FRIDAY
FRILLY
FRINGY
FRISKY
FRIZZY
FROGGY
FROSTY
FROTHY
FROWZY
FRUITY
FRUMPY
GRABBY
GRAINY
GRAMMY
GRANNY
GRAPEY
GRAPHY
GRASSY
GRAYLY
GREASY
GREEDY
GREENY
GREYLY
GRIMLY
GRISLY
GRITTY
GROGGY
GROOVY
GROSZY
GROTTY
GROUTY
GROWLY
GROZNY
GRUBBY
GRUMPY
GRUNDY
GRUNGY
KRASNY
ORALLY
ORANGY
ORKNEY
ORNERY
ORRERY
PREPAY
PREPPY
PRETTY
PRICEY
PRIMLY

PRIORY
PRISSY
PROSKY
TRACEY
TRACHY
TRAPPY
TRASHY
TREATY
TREBLY
TRENDY
TRICKY
TRIGLY
TRILBY
TRIMLY
TRIPLY
TROPHY
TRUSTY
WRATHY

••RY••
BARYON
CORYZA
DURYEA
LARYNX
SPRYER
SPRYLY

••R•Y•
ARRAYS
ARROYO
DARRYL
FORAYS
MARTYR
MERVYN
MORAYS
SPRAYS
STRAYS

••R••Y
AERIFY
AERILY
AIRDRY
AIRILY
AIRWAY
AURIFY
BARELY
BARFLY
BARLEY
BARNEY
BARONY
BIRNEY
BURBLY
BURLEY
BURNEY
CARBOY
CARNEY
CARREY
CARVEY
CHROMY
CORDAY
CURACY
CURLEY
CURTLY
CURTSY
DARKLY
DARNAY
DIRELY
DORSEY
DURFEY
EARTHY
EERILY
FARCRY
FARLEY
FERITY
FIRMLY
GARVEY
GORILY
GURLEY
GURNEY
HARDBY
HARDLY
HARLEY
HARVEY
HEREBY
HERESY
HERSEY
HORNEY
HORSEY
HURLEY
HURRAY
JEREMY
JERSEY
KERSEY
LORDLY
MARBLY
MARGAY
MARLEY
MARSHY
MERELY
MERSEY
MORLEY
MORNAY
MORPHY
MURPHY
MURRAY
MURREY
NORGAY
NORWAY
ORRERY
PARITY
PARKAY
PARLAY
PARLEY
PARODY
PARTLY
PERTLY
PIRACY
PORTLY
PURELY
PURIFY
PURITY
PURPLY
PURVEY
RAREFY
RARELY
RARIFY
RARITY
SCREWY
SORELY
SPRYLY
STRAWY
STRIPY
SURELY
SURETY
SURREY
SURVEY
SYRUPY
TARTLY
TORCHY
TORREY
TURKEY
UNRULY
VARNEY
VERIFY
VERILY
VERITY
WARCRY
WARILY
WARMLY
WIRILY
WORTHY
WURLEY
YARELY

•••RY•
CHERYL
DARRYL
EMBRYO
HEARYE
HENRYV
MAURYA
SHERYL
VANRYN

•••R•Y
AFFRAY
ANDREY
ANERGY
ASTRAY
AUBREY
AUDREY
BETRAY
BEWRAY
BLURRY
CARREY
CHARLY
CHERRY
CHERTY
CHIRPY
CLERGY
CONROY
CZERNY
DEARLY
DEFRAY
DELRAY
DELROY
DOURLY
EBERLY
ENERGY
ESTRAY
EVERLY
FABRAY
FAIRLY
FLIRTY
FLURRY
GEORGY
GHARRY
GNARLY
HEARTY
HOORAY
HOURLY
HURRAY
KEARNY
KILROY
KNARRY
KNURLY
MANRAY
MURRAY
MURREY
NEARBY
NEARLY
OSPREY
OVERLY
PEARLY
POORLY
QUARRY
QUIRKY
QWERTY
ROBROY
SCARRY
SCURFY
SCURRY
SCURVY
SHERRY
SHIRTY
SHORTY
SKERRY
SLURRY
SMARMY
SMARTY
SMIRKY
SNARLY
SOURLY
SPARKY
SPERRY
SPORTY
SPURRY
STARRY
STOREY
STORMY
STURDY
SUNRAY
SURREY
SWIRLY
THIRTY
THORNY
TORREY
WEIRDY
WHERRY
WHIRLY
YEARLY

••••RY
AIRDRY
AMBERY
APIARY
ARMORY
ARTERY
ASBURY
AUGURY
AVIARY
AWEARY
BAKERY
BELFRY
BINARY
BLEARY
BLURRY
BOVARY
BOWERY
BRIERY
BUMBRY
CANARY
CELERY
CHEERY
CHERRY
DATARY
DENARY
DESCRY
DESTRY
DOWERY
DREARY
DUPERY
EATERY
ELLERY
EMPERY
EXPIRY
FAKERY
FARCRY
FINERY
FLEURY
FLOURY
FLURRY
FRIARY
GANTRY
GENTRY
GHARRY
GLAIRY
GOAWRY
GUITRY
HILARY
HUNGRY
INJURY
JAPERY
KIDORY
KNARRY
LANDRY
LIVERY
LOWERY
LUXURY
MALORY
MEMORY
MISERY
MOPERY
NAPERY
NITERY
NONARY
NOTARY
OCHERY
OHENRY
OLEARY
ORNERY
ORRERY
OUTCRY
PALTRY
PANFRY
PANTRY
PAPERY
PASTRY
PELTRY
PENURY
PINERY
POETRY
POKERY
PRIORY
QUARRY
RANDRY
REBURY
ROSARY
ROTARY
RUNDRY
SALARY
SAVORY
SCARRY
SCURRY
SENARY
SENTRY
SEVERY
SHERRY
SKERRY
SLURRY
SMEARY
SNEERY
SPERRY
SPHERY
SPURRY
STARRY
SUGARY
SULTRY
SUNDRY
TAWDRY
THEORY
TOWERY
UNWARY
VAGARY
VALERY
VAPORY
VESTRY
VINERY
VOTARY
WAFERY
WARCRY
WATERY
WAVERY
WHERRY
WINERY
WINTRY

R•Z•••
RAZING
RAZORS
RAZZED
RAZZES
RAZZLE
REZONE
RIZZIO
ROZZER

R••Z••
RAZZED
RAZZES
RAZZLE
RIZZIO
ROZZER
RYAZAN

R•••Z•
REBOZO
RIENZI

•R•Z••
AREZZO
BRAZED
BRAZEN
BRAZER
BRAZES
BRAZIL
BRAZOS
BRAZZA
BRAZZI
CRAZED
CRAZES
CROZES
DRUZES
FRAZER
FRIZZY
FROZEN
GRAZED
GRAZER
GRAZES
GROZNY
OROZCO
PRIZED
PRIZES
PROZAC

•R••Z•
AREZZO
BRAZZA
BRAZZI
BREEZE
BREEZY
BRONZE
BRONZY
FREEZE
FRENZY
FRIEZE
FRIZZY
FROWZY
GROSZY

•R•••Z
BRIENZ
ERSATZ
KRANTZ
TROPEZ

••RZ••
BARZUN
BORZOI
CURZON
FURZES
HERZOG
TARZAN

••R•Z•
CORYZA

••R••Z
CORTEZ
CURTIZ
HORMUZ
LORENZ
MORITZ
SPRITZ

•••RZ•
SFORZA

•••R•Z
JUAREZ
QUARTZ
SHIRAZ
TABRIZ

SA••••
SABATO
SABENA
SABERS
SABINE
SABINS
SABLES
SABOTS
SABRAS
SABRES
SACHEM
SACHET
SACKED
SACKER
SACQUE
SACRAL
SACRED
SACRUM
SADDAM
SADDEN
SADDER
SADDLE
SADHES
SADHUS
SAFARI
SAFELY
SAFEST
SAFETY
SAFIRE
SAGELY
SAGEST
SAGGED
SAHARA
SAHIBS
SAIGAS
SAIGON
SAILED
SAILOR
SAINTE
SAINTS
SAIPAN
SAKERS
SALAAM
SALADO
SALADS
SALALS
SALAMI
SALARY
SALIFY
SALINA
SALINE
SALISH
SALIVA
SALLET
SALLOW
SALMAN
SALMON
SALOME
SALONS
SALOON
SALSAS
SALTED
SALTEN
SALTER
SALTON
SALTUM
SALUKI
SALUTE
SALVED
SALVER
SALVES
SALVIA
SALVOR
SALVOS
SALYUT
SAMARA
SAMBAL
SAMBAR
SAMBAS
SAMECH
SAMEKH
SAMIAM
SAMITE
SAMLET
SAMMIE
SAMOAN
SAMOSA
SAMPAN
SAMPLE
SAMSON
SAMUEL
SANCHO
SANCTA
SANDAL
SANDED
SANDER
SANDIA
SANDRA
SANELY
SANEST
SANGER
SANGTO
SANITY
SANNUP
SANSEI
SANTEE
SANTIR
SANTOS
SAPORS
SAPPED
SAPPER
SAPPHO
SARANS
SARDIS
SARGES
SARGON
SARGOS
SARNIA
SARODS
SARONG
SARTON
SARTRE
SASEBO
SASHAY
SASHED
SASHES
SASSED
SASSER
SASSES
SATANG
SATEEN
SATING
SATINS
SATINY
SATIRE
SATORI
SATOUT
SATRAP
SATURN
SATYRS
SAUCED
SAUCER
SAUCES
SAUDIS
SAUGER
SAULTS
SAUNAS
SAUREL
SAUTES
SAVAGE
SAVAII
SAVANT
SAVATE
SAVERS
SAVEUP

SAVING
SAVIOR
SAVOIE
SAVOIR
SAVORS
SAVORY
SAVOUR
SAWFIT
SAWING
SAWLOG
SAWOFF
SAWOUT
SAWRED
SAWYER
SAXONS
SAXONY
SAYERS
SAYING
SAYLES
SAYSOS
SAYYES
SAYYID

S•A•••

SCABBY
SCALAR
SCALDS
SCALED
SCALER
SCALES
SCALIA
SCALPS
SCAMPI
SCAMPS
SCANTS
SCANTY
SCAPED
SCAPES
SCARAB
SCARCE
SCARED
SCARER
SCARES
SCARFS
SCARNE
SCARPS
SCARRY
SCARUM
SCATHE
SCATTY
SCAUPS
SEABAG
SEABED
SEABEE
SEACOW
SEADOG
SEAFAN
SEAFOX
SEAGAL
SEALAB
SEALED
SEALER
SEALUP
SEAMAN
SEAMED
SEAMEN
SEAMUS
SEANCE
SEARCH
SEARED
SEARLE
SEASON
SEATED
SEATER
SEATON
SEAWAY
SHABAN
SHABBY
SHACKS
SHADED
SHADES
SHADOW
SHAFTS
SHAGGY
SHAKEN
SHAKER
SHAKES
SHAKOS
SHAKTI
SHALES
SHALEY
SHALLY
SHALOM
SHAMAN
SHAMED
SHAMES
SHAMIR
SHAMUS
SHANDY
SHANIA
SHANKS
SHANNY
SHANTY
SHAPED
SHAPER
SHAPES
SHARDS
SHARED
SHARER
SHARES
SHARIA
SHARIF
SHARKS
SHARON
SHARPS
SHASTA
SHAVED
SHAVEN
SHAVER
SHAVES
SHAWLS
SHAWMS
SHAYNE
SHAZAM
SKALDS
SKANKS
SKATED
SKATER
SKATES
SLACKS
SLAGGY
SLAKED
SLAKES
SLALOM
SLANGS
SLANGY
SLANTS
SLAPPY
SLAPUP
SLATED
SLATER
SLATES
SLAVED
SLAVER
SLAVES
SLAVEY
SLAVIC
SLAYED
SLAYER
SMACKS
SMALLS
SMALTI
SMALTO
SMARMY
SMARTS
SMARTY
SNACKS
SNAFUS
SNAGGY
SNAILS
SNAKED
SNAKES
SNAPAT
SNAPPY
SNAPTO
SNAPUP
SNARED
SNARES
SNARLS
SNARLY
SNATCH
SNATHE
SNATHS
SNAZZY
SOAKED
SOAKER
SOAKUP
SOAPED
SOAPER
SOARED
SOARER
SOARES
SOASTO
SOAVES
SPACED
SPACEK
SPACER
SPACES
SPACEY
SPADED
SPADER
SPADES
SPADIX
SPAHIS
SPALLS
SPANKS
SPANKY
SPARED
SPARER
SPARES
SPARGE
SPARKS
SPARKY
SPARSE
SPARTA
SPASMS
SPATES
SPATHE
SPAVIN
SPAWNS
SPAYED
SRANAN
STABAT
STABLE
STABLY
STACEY
STACKS
STACTE
STADIA
STAFFS
STAGED
STAGER
STAGES
STAINS
STAIRS
STAKED
STAKES
STALAG
STALED
STALER
STALES
STALIN
STALKS
STALKY
STALLS
STAMEN
STAMPS
STANCE
STANCH
STANDS
STANKY
STANZA
STAPES
STAPLE
STAPUF
STARCH
STARED
STARER
STARES
STARRY
STARTS
STARVE
STASES
STASIS
STATED
STATEN
STATER
STATES
STATIC
STATOR
STATUE
STATUS
STAVED
STAVES
STAYED
STAYON
STAYUP
SUAVER
SWABBY
SWAGED
SWAGES
SWAINS
SWALES
SWAMIS
SWAMPS
SWAMPY
SWANEE
SWANKS
SWANKY
SWARAJ
SWARDS
SWARMS
SWARTH
SWATCH
SWATHE
SWATHS
SWAYED
SWAYER
SWAYZE
SWAZIS

S••A••

SABATO
SAFARI
SAHARA
SALAAM
SALADO
SALADS
SALALS
SALAMI
SALARY
SAMARA
SARANS
SATANG
SAVAGE
SAVAII
SAVANT
SAVATE
SCLAFF
SCRAGS
SCRAMS
SCRAPE
SCRAPS
SCRAWL
SECANT
SEDAKA
SEDANS
SEDATE
SEJANT
SENARY
SENATE
SEPALS
SERACS
SERAIS
SERAPE
SERAPH
SESAME
SEWAGE
SEWARD
SHEAFS
SHEARS
SHEATH
SHEAVE
SHOALS
SHOALY
SHOATS
SHRANK
SILAGE
SISALS
SITARS
SIWASH
SKEANS
SKOALS
SLEAVE
SLEAZE
SLEAZY
SLOANE
SMEARS
SMEARY
SNEAKS
SNEAKY
SOCAGE
SOLACE
SOLANS
SOLARS
SOMALI
SOMANY
SOMATA
SOMATO
SONANT
SONATA
SOUARI
SPEAKS
SPEARS
SPLASH
SPLATS
SPLAYS
SPRAGS
SPRAIN
SPRANG
SPRATS
SPRAWL
SPRAYS
SQUABS
SQUADS
SQUALL
SQUARE
SQUASH
SQUATS
SQUAWK
STEADS
STEADY
STEAKS
STEALS
STEAMS
STEAMY
STMALO
STMARK
STOATS
STPAUL
STRABO
STRADS
STRAFE
STRAIN
STRAIT
STRAKE
STRAND
STRAPS
STRASS
STRATA
STRATI
STRATO
STRAUB
STRAUS
STRAWS
STRAWY
STRAYS
STUART
SUBARU
SUGARS
SUGARY
SUMACS
SURAHS
SUSANN
SWEARS
SWEATS
SWEATY

S•••A•

SABRAS
SACRAL
SADDAM
SAIGAS
SAIPAN
SALAAM
SALMAN
SALSAS
SAMBAL
SAMBAR
SAMBAS
SAMIAM
SAMOAN
SAMPAN
SANDAL
SASHAY
SATRAP
SAUNAS
SCALAR
SCARAB
SCENAS
SCHWAB
SCHWAS
SCREAK
SCREAM
SCUBAS
SEABAG
SEAFAN
SEAGAL
SEALAB
SEAMAN
SEAWAY
SEESAW
SENDAK
SENLAC
SENNAS
SEPIAS
SEPTAL
SERIAL
SERVAL
SETSAT
SEURAT
SGTMAJ
SHABAN
SHAMAN
SHAZAM
SHEVAT
SHIKAR
SHIRAZ
SHOFAR
SHORAN
SHOTAT
SIGMAS
SIGNAL
SILOAM
SILVAS
SIMIAN
SINBAD
SINEAD
SINTAX
SIOUAN
SIRDAR
SIRRAH
SKYCAP
SKYLAB
SKYWAY
SLEZAK
SLOGAN
SLOVAK
SMILAX
SNAPAT
SNOCAT
SOCIAL
SOLDAN
SOLFAS
SONTAG
SOTHAT
SOWHAT
SPICAS
SPINAL
SPIRAL
SPIVAK
SPREAD
SQUEAK
SQUEAL
SRANAN
STABAT
STALAG
STEFAN
STELAE
STELAR
STJOAN
STOMAS
STOMAT
STREAK
STREAM
STRIAE
STUPAS
SUBPAR
SUBWAY
SUCHAS
SUCKAS
SUDRAS
SUKKAH
SULTAN
SUMMAE
SUMMAS
SUNDAE
SUNDAY
SUNRAY
SUNTAN
SURTAX
SUTRAS
SWARAJ
SYLVAN
SYNTAX
SYRIAN

S••••A

SABENA
SAHARA
SALINA
SALIVA
SALVIA
SAMARA
SAMOSA
SANCTA
SANDIA
SANDRA
SARNIA
SCALIA
SCHEMA
SCLERA
SCORIA
SCOTIA
SCYLLA
SEDAKA
SEGURA
SELENA
SENECA
SENEGA
SENORA
SENTRA
SERBIA
SERENA
SEROSA
SFORZA
SHANIA
SHARIA
SHASTA
SHEENA
SHEILA
SHERPA
SHORTA
SIENNA
SIERRA
SIESTA
SILICA
SIRICA
SISERA
SISTRA
SMYRNA
SOMATA
SONATA
SONOMA
SONORA
SOPHIA
SPARTA
SPIREA
STADIA
STANZA
STELLA
STERNA
STIGMA
STRATA
STYRIA
SYLVIA

•SA•••

ASANAS
ISABEL
ISADOR
ISAIAH
OSAGES
PSALMS
USABLE
USABLY
USAGES
USANCE
ZSAZSA

•S•A••

ASGARD
ASHARP
ASIANS
ASKARI
ASLANT
ASMARA
ASSAIL
ASSAYS
BSHARP
CSHARP
DSHARP
ESCAPE
ESCARP
ESHARP
ESPANA
ESSAYS
ESTATE
FSHARP
GSHARP

GSTAAD
ISLAND
ISRAEL
OSCARS
OSHAWA
OSWALD
USMAIL
USUALS

•S••A•

ASANAS
ASCHAM
ASHCAN
ASHLAR
ASHRAM
ASOSAN
ASTRAL
ASTRAY
ESDRAS
ESPIAL
ESTRAY
GSTAAD
ISAIAH
ISHTAR
ISOBAR
MSQUAD
OSSIAN
OSTEAL
PSYWAR

•S•••A

ASMARA
ASPERA
ESPANA
ESPOSA
ISCHIA
ISTRIA
OSCULA
OSHAWA
PSYLLA
ZSAZSA

••SA••

ALSACE
ANSARA
ANSATE
ASSAIL
ASSAYS
BASALT
BESANT
CASABA
CASALS
CASAVA
CESARE
CUSACK
DESALT
DISANT
DISARM
DOSAGE
ERSATZ
ESSAYS
INSANE
LESAGE
LUSAKA
MASADA
MASAIS
MESABI
MOSAIC
NASALS
NOSALE
OKSANA
ONSALE
PESACH
PESAWA
PISANO
PISANS
POSADA
RESALE
RESALT
RESAND
RESAWN
RESAWS
ROSARY
SESAME
SISALS
SUSANN
TISANE
UNSAFE
UNSAID
UNSAYS
VISAED
VISAGE
WASABI

••S•A•

ABSCAM
ANSGAR
BISCAY
BISSAU
BUSBAR
BUSMAN
CASBAH
CASPAR
CASUAL
CESTAS
COSTAE
COSTAL
COSTAR
COSTAS
CUSHAW
DESMAN
DISBAR
DISMAL
DISMAY
DISTAL
DOSSAL
FESTAL
FESTAS
FISCAL
FOSSAE
FOSSAS
GASBAG
GASCAP
GASMAN
GASPAR
GOSTAG
GUSTAV
HASSAM
HASSAN
HISSAT
HOSTAS
HUSSAR
INSEAM
INSPAN
INSTAL
INSTAR
JOSIAH
KASBAH
KASDAN
LASCAR
LESTAT
MESCAL
MISHAP
MISLAY
MISSAL
MISSAY
MOSHAV
MUSCAT
MUSIAL
NASCAR
NASDAQ
NASSAU
NISSAN
NOSOAP
OSSIAN
PASCAL
PASHAS
PASTAS
PISGAH
POSTAL
RASCAL
RASHAD
RESEAL
RESEAT
RESEAU
ROSEAU
SASHAY
TASMAN
TESLAS
TESTAE
TUSCAN
TUSSAH
UNSEAL
UNSEAT
UNSNAG
UNSNAP
VASLAV
VASSAL
VASSAR
VESTAL
VESTAS
VISTAS
VISUAL
WYSTAN
YESMAN

••S••A

ANSARA
BOSNIA
BUSHWA
CASABA
CASAVA
CASSIA
CESSNA
DESICA
FASCIA
HESTIA
JASCHA
JOSHUA
KESHIA
LISBOA
LUSAKA
MASADA
MISCHA
MOSKVA
NASHUA
NESTEA
OKSANA
PESAWA
PESETA
POSADA
RESEDA
ROSITA
ROSTRA
RUSSIA
SISERA
SISTRA
URSULA

•••SA•

ACTSAS
AIMSAT
AIRSAC
ASOSAN
BALSAM
BISSAU
BONSAI
BOWSAW
BURSAE
BURSAL
BURSAR
BURSAS
CAESAR
CAUSAL
COMSAT
DOGSAT
DORSAL
DOSSAL
EATSAT
FAISAL
FOSSAE
FOSSAS
GETSAT
GOESAT
HASSAM
HASSAN
HAUSAS
HISSAT
HUSSAR
ILLSAY
JETSAM
JIGSAW
KANSAN
KANSAS
LETSAT
MENSAE
MENSAL
MENSAS
MILSAP
MISSAL
MISSAY
NASSAU
NAYSAY
NIPSAT
NISSAN
OLDSAW
OVISAC
PAISAS
PAWSAT
PITSAW
PULSAR
QUASAR
RAMSAY
RIPSAW
RUNSAT
SALSAS
SEESAW
SETSAT
TARSAL
TULSAN
TUSSAH
VASSAL
VASSAR
WARSAW
WAUSAU
XHOSAS

•••S•A

ALASKA
ALYSSA
ARISTA
AVESTA
AYESHA
BUQSHA
CASSIA
CESSNA
CUESTA
EDESSA
EGESTA
ELISHA
ELISSA
FIESTA
FRESCA
GEISHA
GLOSSA
ILESHA
ITASCA
MARSHA
MIASMA
NAUSEA
NYASSA
ODESSA
ORISSA
PERSIA
PLASMA
REDSEA
RUSSIA
SHASTA
SIESTA
THESEA
TRISHA
VAISYA
VIZSLA
ZOYSIA

••••SA

AHIMSA
ALYSSA
CREUSA
EDESSA
ELISSA
ESPOSA
GLOSSA
LAMESA
LAROSA
LOUISA
MARISA
MEDUSA
MIMOSA
MUCOSA
MUFASA
NYASSA
ODESSA
ORISSA
SAMOSA
SEROSA
TERESA
WALESA
ZSAZSA

S•B•••

SABATO
SABENA
SABERS
SABINE
SABINS
SABLES
SABOTS
SABRAS
SABRES
SEBERG
SHBOOM
SIBYLS
SOBBED
SOBBER
SOBEIT
SOBERS
SOBFUL
SUBARU
SUBBED
SUBDEB
SUBDUE
SUBGUM
SUBITO
SUBLET
SUBMIT
SUBORN
SUBPAR
SUBSET
SUBTLE
SUBTLY
SUBURB
SUBWAY

S••B••

SAMBAL
SAMBAR
SAMBAS
SCABBY
SCUBAS
SEABAG
SEABED
SEABEE
SERBIA
SHABAN
SHABBY
SIMBEL
SINBAD
SKIBOB
SKYBOX
SLOBBY
SNOBBY
SNUBBY
SOBBED
SOBBER
SOMBER
SOMBRE
SORBET
SORBIC
SOWBUG
STABAT
STABLE
STABLY
STUBBY
SUBBED
SWABBY
SYMBOL

S•••B•

SAHIBS
SASEBO
SCABBY
SCRIBE
SCRUBS
SETSBY
SHABBY
SHRUBS
SITSBY
SLOBBY
SNOBBY
SNUBBY
SQUABS
SQUIBB
SQUIBS
STRABO
STROBE
STUBBY
SWABBY

S••••B

SCARAB
SCHWAB
SEALAB
SKIBOB
SKYLAB
SQUIBB
STRAUB
SUBDEB
SUBURB
SUPERB

•SB•••

ASBURY
OSBORN

•S•B••

ISABEL
ISOBAR
USABLE
USABLY

••SB••

BUSBAR
BUSBOY
CASBAH
DISBAR
GASBAG
HASBRO
KASBAH
LESBOS
LISBOA
LISBON

••S•B•

CASABA
MESABI
NASEBY
PASSBY
SASEBO
WASABI

••S••B

ABSORB
ADSORB
RESORB

•••SB•

CROSBY
DOESBY
GATSBY
GETSBY
GOESBY
LAYSBY
LETSBE
PASSBY
PUTSBY
SETSBY
SITSBY
THISBE

SC••••

SCABBY
SCALAR
SCALDS
SCALED
SCALER
SCALES
SCALIA
SCALPS
SCAMPI
SCAMPS
SCANTS
SCANTY
SCAPED
SCAPES
SCARAB
SCARCE
SCARED
SCARER
SCARES
SCARFS
SCARNE
SCARPS
SCARRY
SCARUM
SCATHE
SCATTY
SCAUPS
SCENAS
SCENDS
SCENES
SCENIC
SCENTS
SCHELL
SCHEMA
SCHEME
SCHICK
SCHIFF
SCHISM
SCHIST
SCHIZY
SCHLEP
SCHMOO
SCHMOS
SCHNOZ
SCHOOL
SCHORL
SCHULZ
SCHUSS
SCHWAB
SCHWAS
SCIFIS
SCIONS
SCIPIO
SCLAFF
SCLERA
SCLERO
SCOFFS
SCOLDS
SCONCE
SCONES
SCOOPS
SCOOTS
SCOPED
SCOPES
SCORCH
SCORED
SCORER
SCORES
SCORIA
SCORNS
SCOTCH
SCOTER
SCOTIA
SCOTTO
SCOTTY
SCOURS
SCOUSE
SCOUTS
SCOWLS
SCRAGS
SCRAMS
SCRAPE
SCRAPS
SCRAWL
SCREAK
SCREAM
SCREED
SCREEN
SCREES
SCREWS
SCREWY
SCRIBE
SCRIMP
SCRIMS
SCRIPS
SCRIPT
SCRODS
SCROLL
SCROOP
SCRUBS
SCRUFF
SCRUMS
SCUBAS
SCUFFS
SCULLS
SCULLY
SCULPT
SCUMMY
SCURFY
SCURRY
SCURVE
SCURVY
SCUTCH
SCUTES
SCUZZY
SCYLLA
SCYTHE

S•C•••

SACHEM
SACHET
SACKED
SACKER
SACQUE
SACRAL
SACRED
SACRUM
SECANT
SECEDE

SECERN
SECKEL
SECOND
SECRET
SECTOR
SECURE
SICCED
SICILY
SICKEN
SICKER
SICKLE
SICKLY
SOCAGE
SOCCER
SOCIAL
SOCKED
SOCKET
SOCKIN
SOCLES
SUCCES
SUCCOR
SUCHAS
SUCKAS
SUCKED
SUCKER
SUCKIN

S••C••

SANCHO
SANCTA
SAUCED
SAUCER
SAUCES
SEACOW
SEICHE
SHACKS
SHOCKS
SHUCKS
SICCED
SIECLE
SITCOM
SKYCAP
SLACKS
SLICED
SLICER
SLICES
SLICKS
SMACKS
SMOCKS
SNACKS
SNICKS
SNOCAT
SOCCER
SPACED
SPACEK
SPACER
SPACES
SPACEY
SPECIE
SPECKS
SPICAS
SPICED
SPICES
STACEY
STACKS
STACTE
STICKS
STICKY
STOCKS
STOCKY
STUCCO
SUCCES
SUCCOR
SULCUS
SYNCED

S•••C•

SAMECH
SCARCE
SCHICK
SCONCE
SCORCH
SCOTCH
SCUTCH
SEANCE
SEARCH
SEDUCE
SELECT
SENECA
SERACS
SHTICK
SILICA
SIRICA
SKETCH
SKITCH
SLOUCH
SLUICE
SMIRCH
SMOOCH
SMUTCH
SNATCH
SNITCH
SOLACE
SONICS
SOURCE
SPEECH
SPLICE
SPRUCE
STANCE
STANCH
STARCH
STENCH
STITCH
STOICS
STORCH
STRICK
STRICT
STRUCK
STUCCO
SUMACS
SUNOCO
SWATCH
SWITCH

S••••C

SCENIC
SENLAC
SEPTIC
SLAVIC
SORBIC
STATIC
STIVIC
SYNDIC

•SC•••

ASCEND
ASCENT
ASCHAM
ASCOTS
ESCAPE
ESCARP
ESCENT
ESCHER
ESCHEW
ESCORT
ESCROW
ESCUDO
ISCHIA
OSCARS
OSCINE
OSCULA

•S•C••

ASHCAN
PSYCHE
PSYCHO
PSYCHS

•S••C•

ASDICS
ASPECT
ASPICS
OSMICS
USANCE

••SC••

ABSCAM
BISCAY
CISCOS
DESCRY
DISCOS
DISCUS
FASCES
FASCIA
FESCUE
FISCAL
GASCAP
GASCON
JASCHA
LASCAR
MASCOT
MESCAL
MISCHA
MISCUE
MOSCOW
MUSCAT
MUSCLE
MUSCLY
NASCAR
PASCAL
PESCOW
PISCES
RASCAL
RESCUE
ROSCOE
TUSCAN
VISCID

••S•C•

ALSACE
BASICS
BISECT
CUSACK
DESICA
INSECT
PESACH
RESECT

••S••C

COSMIC
FISTIC
FUSTIC
GESTIC
INSYNC
MASTIC
MOSAIC
MYSTIC
ONSPEC
RUSTIC

•••SC•

BORSCH
CRISCO
ENESCO
FIASCO
FRESCA
FRESCO
FRISCO
HIRSCH
ITASCA
KIRSCH
KITSCH
MENSCH
PUTSCH
UNESCO

•••S•C

AIRSAC
ECESIC
OVISAC
PARSEC

S•D•••

SADDAM
SADDEN
SADDER
SADDLE
SADHES
SADHUS
SEDAKA
SEDANS
SEDATE
SEDERS
SEDGES
SEDILE
SEDUCE
SEDUMS
SIDDUR
SIDERO
SIDERS
SIDING
SIDLED
SIDLES
SIDNEY
SODDED
SODDEN
SODIUM
SUDDEN
SUDRAS
SUDSED
SUDSES
SYDNEY

S••D••

SADDAM
SADDEN
SADDER
SADDLE
SANDAL
SANDED
SANDER
SANDIA
SANDRA
SARDIS
SAUDIS
SEADOG
SEEDED
SEEDER
SEIDEL
SELDOM
SENDAK
SENDER
SENDIN
SENDUP
SHADED
SHADES
SHADOW
SHODDY
SIDDUR
SIRDAR
SKIDDY
SLEDGE
SLIDER
SLIDES
SLIDIN
SLUDGE
SLUDGY
SMUDGE
SMUDGY
SNIDER
SNYDER
SODDED
SODDEN
SOLDAN
SOLDER
SOLDON
SONDES
SORDID
SPADED
SPADER
SPADES
SPADIX
SPEDUP
SPIDER
STADIA
STODGE
STODGY
STUDIO
SUBDEB
SUBDUE
SUDDEN
SUEDES
SUNDAE
SUNDAY
SUNDER
SUNDEW
SUNDOG
SUNDRY
SWEDEN
SWEDES
SYNDIC

S•••D•

SALADO
SALADS
SARODS
SCALDS
SCENDS
SCOLDS
SCRODS
SECEDE
SHANDY
SHARDS
SHEEDY
SHINDY
SHODDY
SHREDS
SKALDS
SKIDDY
SNOODS
SOLIDI
SOLIDS
SOUNDS
SPEEDO
SPEEDS
SPEEDY
SPENDS
SQUADS
SQUIDS
STANDS
STEADS
STEADY
STEEDS
STRADS
STRIDE
STRODE
STURDY
SWARDS
SWORDS
SYNODS

S••••D

SACKED
SACRED
SAGGED
SAILED
SALTED
SALVED
SANDED
SAPPED
SASHED
SASSED
SAUCED
SAWRED
SAYYID
SCALED
SCAPED
SCARED
SCOPED
SCORED
SCREED
SEABED
SEALED
SEAMED
SEARED
SEATED
SECOND
SEEDED
SEEMED
SEEPED
SEERED
SEGUED
SEINED
SEIZED
SENSED
SERVED
SEWARD
SHADED
SHAMED
SHAPED
SHARED
SHAVED
SHIELD
SHINED
SHOOED
SHORED
SHOULD
SHOVED
SHOWED
SHREWD
SHROUD
SICCED
SIDLED
SIEGED
SIEVED
SIFTED
SIGHED
SIGNED
SIGURD
SILKED
SILOED
SILTED
SINBAD
SINEAD
SINGED
SINNED
SIPPED
SKATED
SKEWED
SKIVED
SLAKED
SLATED
SLAVED
SLAYED
SLEWED
SLICED
SLIMED
SLOPED
SLOWED
SMILED
SMOKED
SNAKED
SNARED
SNIPED
SNORED
SNOWED
SOAKED
SOAPED
SOARED
SOBBED
SOCKED
SODDED
SOILED
SOLOED
SOLVED
SOPPED
SORDID
SORTED
SOTTED
SOURED
SOUSED
SPACED
SPADED
SPARED
SPAYED
SPEWED
SPICED
SPIKED
SPINED
SPIRED
SPITED
SPOKED
SPREAD
SPUMED
STAGED
STAKED
STALED
STARED
STATED
STAVED
STAYED
STEWED
STOKED
STOLID
STONED
STORED
STOWED
STRAND
STROUD
STUPID
STYLED
SUBBED
SUCKED
SUDSED
SUITED
SULKED
SUMMED
SUNGOD
SUNNED
SUPPED
SURFED
SURGED
SUSSED
SWAGED
SWAYED
SWIPED
SYNCED

•SD•••

ASDICS
ESDRAS

•S•D••

ASIDES
BSIDES
ISADOR
USEDTO
USEDUP

•S••D•

ESCUDO
ISOLDE
PSEUDO
PSEUDS

•S•••D

ASCEND
ASGARD
ASTRID
ESPIED
GSTAAD
ISLAND
ISOPOD
ISSUED
MSQUAD
OSGOOD
OSMOND
OSMUND
OSTEND
OSWALD
RSVPED
USERID

••SD••

KASDAN
MISDID
NASDAQ
WISDOM

••S•D•

BESIDE
DOSIDO
INSIDE
MASADA
ONSIDE
POSADA
RESEDA
RESIDE
RESODS
UPSIDE
URSIDS

••S••D

ABSURD
ATSTUD
AXSEED
BASHED
BASKED
BASTED
BESTED
BOSSED
BUSHED
BUSIED
BUSKED
BUSSED
BUSTED
CASHED
CESSED
COSHED
COSIED
CUSPED
CUSPID
CUSSED
DASHED
DISHED
DISKED
DISSED
DOSSED
DUSTED
ENSUED
FASTED
FESSED
FISHED
FISTED
FUSSED
GASHED
GASPED
GASSED
GUSHED
GUSTED
HASHED
HASPED
HESIOD
HISPID
HISSED
HOSTED
HUSHED
HUSKED
ISSUED
JESTED

JOSHED
KISSED
LASHED
LASTED
LISPED
LISTED
LUSTED
MASHED
MASKED
MASSED
MESHED
MESSED
MISDID
MISLED
MISSED
MISTED
MOSHED
MOSSED
MUSHED
MUSSED
NESTED
NOSHED
OUSTED
PASSED
PASTED
POSTED
PUSHED
RASHAD
RASHID
RASPED
RESAND
RESEED
RESEND
RESHOD
RESOLD
RESTED
RISKED
RUSHED
RUSTED
SASHED
SASSED
SUSSED
TASKED
TASTED
TESTED
TOSSED
TUSKED
UNSAID
UNSHED
UNSHOD
UNSOLD
VESPID
VESTED
VISAED
VISCID
WASHED
WASTED
WISHED
WISPED
YESSED
ZESTED

•••S•D

ABASED
ABUSED
AMUSED
BIASED
BOSSED
BOUSED
BUSSED
CAPSID
CAUSED
CEASED
CENSED
CESSED
CHASED
CLOSED
CURSED
CUSSED
DISSED
DOSSED
DOUSED
DOWSED
ERASED
FESSED
FUSSED
GASSED
GOOSED
HISSED
HORSED
HOUSED
KISSED
LAPSED
LEASED
LENSED
LOOSED
LOUSED
MASSED
MESSED
MISSED
MOSSED
MOUSED
MUSSED
NOISED
NOOSED
NURSED
PARSED
PASSED
PAUSED
PHASED
PHYSED
POISED
PROSED
PULSED
PURSED
RAISED
REUSED
RINSED
ROUSED
SASSED
SENSED
SOUSED
SUDSED
SUSSED
TEASED
TENSED
TOSSED
UNUSED
VERSED
YESSED

SE••••

SEABAG
SEABED
SEABEE
SEACOW
SEADOG
SEAFAN
SEAFOX
SEAGAL
SEALAB
SEALED
SEALER
SEALUP
SEAMAN
SEAMED
SEAMEN
SEAMUS
SEANCE
SEARCH
SEARED
SEARLE
SEASON
SEATED
SEATER
SEATON
SEAWAY
SEBERG
SECANT
SECEDE
SECERN
SECKEL
SECOND
SECRET
SECTOR
SECURE
SEDAKA
SEDANS
SEDATE
SEDERS
SEDGES
SEDILE
SEDUCE
SEDUMS
SEEDED
SEEDER
SEEFIT
SEEGER
SEEING
SEEKER
SEELEY
SEEMED
SEEMLY
SEENIN
SEENTO
SEEOFF
SEEOUT
SEEPED
SEEPIN
SEERED
SEESAW
SEESIN
SEESTO
SEETHE
SEGUED
SEGUES
SEGURA
SEICHE
SEIDEL
SEINED
SEINER
SEINES
SEISMO
SEISMS
SEIZED
SEIZER
SEIZES
SEJANT
SELDOM
SELECT
SELENA
SELENE
SELENO
SELJUK
SELLER
SELVES
SEMELE
SEMITE
SEMPER
SEMPRE
SENARY
SENATE
SENDAK
SENDER
SENDIN
SENDUP
SENECA
SENEGA
SENHOR
SENIOR
SENITI
SENLAC
SENNAS
SENNET
SENNIT
SENORA
SENORS
SENSED
SENSEI
SENSES
SENSOR
SENTIN
SENTRA
SENTRY
SENTUP
SENUFO
SEPALS
SEPIAS
SEPOYS
SEPTAL
SEPTET
SEPTIC
SEPTUM
SEQUEL
SEQUIN
SERACS
SERAIS
SERAPE
SERAPH
SERBIA
SERENA
SERENE
SERGEI
SERGES
SERGIO
SERIAL
SERIES
SERIFS
SERINE
SERINS
SERKIN
SERMON
SEROSA
SEROUS
SEROWS
SERUMS
SERVAL
SERVED
SERVER
SERVES
SERVOS
SESAME
SESQUI
SESTET
SESTOS
SETINS
SETOFF
SETOSE
SETOUT
SETSAT
SETSBY
SETSIN
SETSON
SETSUP
SETTEE
SETTER
SETTLE
SETTOS
SETUPS
SEURAT
SEVENS
SEVERE
SEVERN
SEVERS
SEVERY
SEVRES
SEWAGE
SEWARD
SEWELL
SEWERS
SEWING
SEWNON
SEWNUP
SEWSON
SEWSUP
SEXIER
SEXILY
SEXIST
SEXTET
SEXTON

S•E•••

SCENAS
SCENDS
SCENES
SCENIC
SCENTS
SEEDED
SEEDER
SEEFIT
SEEGER
SEEING
SEEKER
SEELEY
SEEMED
SEEMLY
SEENIN
SEENTO
SEEOFF
SEEOUT
SEEPED
SEEPIN
SEERED
SEESAW
SEESIN
SEESTO
SEETHE
SHEAFS
SHEARS
SHEATH
SHEAVE
SHEEDY
SHEEHY
SHEENA
SHEENS
SHEEPS
SHEERS
SHEETS
SHEIKS
SHEILA
SHEKEL
SHELLS
SHELLY
SHELTY
SHELVE
SHEREE
SHERIF
SHERPA
SHERRY
SHERYL
SHEVAT
SIECLE
SIEGED
SIEGEL
SIEGES
SIENNA
SIERRA
SIESTA
SIEVED
SIEVES
SKEANS
SKEINS
SKERRY
SKETCH
SKEWED
SKEWER
SLEAVE
SLEAZE
SLEAZY
SLEDGE
SLEEKS
SLEEKY
SLEEPS
SLEEPY
SLEETS
SLEETY
SLEEVE
SLEIGH
SLEUTH
SLEWED
SLEZAK
SMEARS
SMEARY
SMELLS
SMELLY
SMELTS
SMERSH
SNEAKS
SNEAKY
SNEERS
SNEERY
SNEEZE
SNEEZY
SNELLS
SOEURS
SPEAKS
SPEARS
SPECIE
SPECKS
SPEDUP
SPEECH
SPEEDO
SPEEDS
SPEEDY
SPELLS
SPENDS
SPERRY
SPEWED
STEADS
STEADY
STEAKS
STEALS
STEAMS
STEAMY
STEEDS
STEELE
STEELS
STEELY
STEEPS
STEERS
STEEVE
STEFAN
STEFFI
STEFOY
STEINS
STELAE
STELAR
STELES
STELLA
STELMO
STENCH
STENOG
STENOS
STEPIN
STEPON
STEPPE
STEPUP
STEREO
STERES
STERNA
STERNE
STERNO
STERNS
STEROL
STEVEN
STEVIE
STEWED
STEWER
SUEDES
SVELTE
SWEARS
SWEATS
SWEATY
SWEDEN
SWEDES
SWEEPS
SWEETS
SWELLS
SWERVE

S••E••

SABENA
SABERS
SAFELY
SAFEST
SAFETY
SAGELY
SAGEST
SAKERS
SAMECH
SAMEKH
SANELY
SANEST
SASEBO
SATEEN
SAVERS
SAVEUP
SAYERS
SCHELL
SCHEMA
SCHEME
SCLERA
SCLERO
SCREAK
SCREAM
SCREED
SCREEN
SCREES
SCREWS
SCREWY
SEBERG
SECEDE
SECERN
SEDERS
SELECT
SELENA
SELENE
SELENO
SEMELE
SENECA
SENEGA
SERENA
SERENE
SEVENS
SEVERE
SEVERN
SEVERS
SEVERY
SEWELL
SEWERS
SHEEDY
SHEEHY
SHEENA
SHEENS
SHEEPS
SHEERS
SHEETS
SHIELD
SHIEST
SHOERS
SHREDS
SHREWD
SHREWS
SHTETL
SHYEST
SIDERO
SIDERS
SILENI
SILENT
SIMEON
SINEAD
SINEWS
SINEWY
SIRENS
SISERA
SIXERS
SIZERS
SIZEUP
SKIERS
SLEEKS
SLEEKY
SLEEPS
SLEEPY
SLEETS
SLEETY
SLEEVE
SLIEST
SLYEST
SNEERS
SNEERY
SNEEZE
SNEEZY
SOBEIT
SOBERS
SOLEIL
SOLELY
SOLEMN
SOLENT
SOLERS
SOLEUS
SOMERS
SORELY
SOREST
SOWERS
SOWETO
SOXERS
SPEECH
SPEEDO
SPEEDS
SPEEDY
SPHERE
SPHERY
SPIELS
SPIERS
SPLEEN
SPREAD
SPREES
SQUEAK
SQUEAL
STEEDS
STEELE
STEELS
STEELY
STEEPS
STEERS
STEEVE
STHENO
STPETE
STREAK
STREAM
STREEP
STREET
STRESS
STREWN
STREWS
SUPERB
SUPERS
SURELY
SUREST
SURETE
SURETY
SWEEPS
SWEETS

S•••E•

SABLES
SABRES
SACHEM
SACHET

SACKED
SACKER
SACRED
SADDEN
SADDER
SADHES
SAGGED
SAILED
SALLET
SALTED
SALTEN
SALTER
SALVED
SALVER
SALVES
SAMLET
SAMUEL
SANDED
SANDER
SANGER
SANSEI
SANTEE
SAPPED
SAPPER
SARGES
SASHED
SASHES
SASSED
SASSER
SASSES
SATEEN
SAUCED
SAUCER
SAUCES
SAUGER
SAUREL
SAUTES
SAWRED
SAWYER
SAYLES
SAYYES
SCALED
SCALER
SCALES
SCAPED
SCAPES
SCARED
SCARER
SCARES
SCENES
SCHLEP
SCONES
SCOPED
SCOPES
SCORED
SCORER
SCORES
SCOTER
SCREED
SCREEN
SCREES
SCUTES
SEABED

SEABEE
SEALED
SEALER
SEAMED
SEAMEN
SEARED
SEATED
SEATER
SECKEL
SECRET
SEDGES
SEEDED
SEEDER
SEEGER
SEEKER
SEELEY
SEEMED
SEEPED
SEERED
SEGUED
SEGUES
SEIDEL
SEINED
SEINER
SEINES
SEIZED
SEIZER
SEIZES
SELLER
SELVES
SEMPER
SENDER
SENNET
SENSED
SENSEI
SENSES
SEPTET
SEQUEL
SERGEI
SERGES
SERIES
SERVED
SERVER
SERVES
SESTET
SETTEE
SETTER
SEVRES
SEXIER
SEXTET
SHADED
SHADES
SHAKEN
SHAKER
SHAKES
SHALES
SHALEY
SHAMED
SHAMES
SHAPED
SHAPER
SHAPES
SHARED

SHARER
SHARES
SHAVED
SHAVEN
SHAVER
SHAVES
SHEKEL
SHEREE
SHINED
SHINER
SHINES
SHIRER
SHIRES
SHIVER
SHOLEM
SHOOED
SHORED
SHORES
SHOVED
SHOVEL
SHOVER
SHOVES
SHOWED
SHOWER
SHRIEK
SICCED
SICKEN
SICKER
SIDLED
SIDLES
SIDNEY
SIEGED
SIEGEL
SIEGES
SIEVED
SIEVES
SIFTED
SIFTER
SIGHED
SIGHER
SIGNED
SIGNEE
SIGNER
SIGNET
SILKED
SILKEN
SILOED
SILTED
SILVER
SIMBEL
SIMMER
SIMNEL
SIMPER
SINGED
SINGER
SINGES
SINKER
SINNED
SINNER
SINTER
SIPPED
SIPPER
SIPPET

SIRREE
SISKEL
SISLER
SISLEY
SISTER
SITTER
SKATED
SKATER
SKATES
SKEWED
SKEWER
SKIVED
SKIVER
SKIVES
SLAKED
SLAKES
SLATED
SLATER
SLATES
SLAVED
SLAVER
SLAVES
SLAVEY
SLAYED
SLAYER
SLEWED
SLICED
SLICER
SLICES
SLIDER
SLIDES
SLIMED
SLIMES
SLIVER
SLOPED
SLOPES
SLOVEN
SLOWED
SLOWER
SLYPES
SMILED
SMILER
SMILES
SMILEY
SMITES
SMOKED
SMOKER
SMOKES
SMOKEY
SNAKED
SNAKES
SNARED
SNARES
SNIDER
SNIPED
SNIPER
SNIPES
SNIVEL
SNOPES
SNORED
SNORER
SNORES
SNOWED

SNYDER
SOAKED
SOAKER
SOAPED
SOAPER
SOARED
SOARER
SOARES
SOAVES
SOBBED
SOBBER
SOCCER
SOCKED
SOCKET
SOCLES
SODDED
SODDEN
SOFTEN
SOFTER
SOILED
SOIREE
SOLDER
SOLOED
SOLVED
SOLVER
SOLVES
SOMBER
SOMMER
SONDES
SONNET
SOONER
SOPPED
SORBET
SORREL
SORTED
SORTER
SOTTED
SOURED
SOURER
SOUSED
SOUSES
SOUTER
SOVIET
SPACED
SPACEK
SPACER
SPACES
SPACEY
SPADED
SPADER
SPADES
SPARED
SPARER
SPARES
SPATES
SPAYED
SPEWED
SPICED
SPICES
SPIDER
SPIKED
SPIKER
SPIKES

SPILES
SPINED
SPINEL
SPINES
SPINET
SPIREA
SPIRED
SPIRES
SPITED
SPITES
SPLEEN
SPOKED
SPOKEN
SPOKES
SPORES
SPREES
SPRIER
SPRUES
SPRYER
SPUMED
SPUMES
STACEY
STAGED
STAGER
STAGES
STAKED
STAKES
STALED
STALER
STALES
STAMEN
STAPES
STARED
STARER
STARES
STASES
STATED
STATEN
STATER
STATES
STAVED
STAVES
STAYED
STELES
STEREO
STERES
STEVEN
STEWED
STEWER
STILES
STIPEL
STIPES
STIVER
STOKED
STOKER
STOKES
STOLEN
STOLES
STONED
STONER
STONES
STOPES
STORED

STORER
STORES
STOREY
STOVER
STOVES
STOWED
STREEP
STREET
STUMER
STUPES
STYLED
STYLER
STYLES
STYLET
SUAVER
SUBBED
SUBDEB
SUBLET
SUBSET
SUCCES
SUCKED
SUCKER
SUDDEN
SUDSED
SUDSES
SUEDES
SUFFER
SUITED
SUITES
SULKED
SULKER
SULLEN
SUMMED
SUMMER
SUMNER
SUMTER
SUNDER
SUNDEW
SUNKEN
SUNNED
SUNSET
SUPPED
SUPPER
SURFED
SURFER
SURGED
SURGES
SURREY
SURVEY
SUSIEQ
SUSSED
SUSSES
SUSSEX
SUTLER
SUTTER
SWAGED
SWAGES
SWALES
SWANEE
SWAYED
SWAYER
SWEDEN
SWEDES

SWIPED
SWIPER
SWIPES
SWIVEL
SWIVET
SYDNEY
SYNCED
SYSTEM

S••••E

SABINE
SACQUE
SADDLE
SAFIRE
SAINTE
SALINE
SALOME
SALUTE
SAMITE
SAMMIE
SAMPLE
SANTEE
SARTRE
SATIRE
SAVAGE
SAVATE
SAVOIE
SCARCE
SCARNE
SCATHE
SCHEME
SCONCE
SCOUSE
SCRAPE
SCRIBE
SCURVE
SCYTHE
SEABEE
SEANCE
SEARLE
SECEDE
SECURE
SEDATE
SEDILE
SEDUCE
SEETHE
SEICHE
SELENE
SEMELE
SEMITE
SEMPRE
SENATE
SERAPE
SERENE
SERINE
SESAME
SETOSE
SETTEE
SETTLE
SEVERE
SEWAGE
SHAYNE
SHEAVE

SHELVE
SHEREE
SHIITE
SHOPPE
SHORTE
SHOWME
SHRIKE
SHRINE
SHRIVE
SHROVE
SICKLE
SIECLE
SIGNEE
SILAGE
SILONE
SIMILE
SIMONE
SIMPLE
SINGLE
SINISE
SIRREE
SIZZLE
SKOKIE
SKOPJE
SLEAVE
SLEAZE
SLEDGE
SLEEVE
SLOANE
SLUDGE
SLUICE
SMUDGE
SNATHE
SNEEZE
SNOOZE
SOCAGE
SOFINE
SOFTIE
SOIGNE
SOIREE
SOLACE
SOLUTE
SOMBRE
SOOTHE
SOPHIE
SORTIE
SOURCE
SPARGE
SPARSE
SPATHE
SPECIE
SPHERE
SPLICE
SPLINE
SPONGE
SPOUSE
SPRITE
SPRUCE
SPURGE
SQUARE
SQUIRE
STABLE
STACTE

STANCE
STAPLE
STARVE
STATUE
STEELE
STEEVE
STELAE
STEPPE
STERNE
STEVIE
STIFLE
STLUKE
STODGE
STOGIE
STOLLE
STOOGE
STPETE
STRAFE
STRAKE
STRIAE
STRIDE
STRIFE
STRIKE
STRINE
STRIPE
STRIVE
STROBE
STRODE
STROKE
STROVE
STYMIE
SUBDUE
SUBTLE
SUISSE
SUMMAE
SUNDAE
SUPINE
SUPPLE
SURETE
SUTURE
SVELTE
SWANEE
SWATHE
SWAYZE
SWERVE

•SE•••

ASEITY
ASEVER
ISELIN
ISEULT
PSEUDO
PSEUDS
TSETSE
USEDTO
USEDUP
USEFUL
USENET
USERID
USESUP

•S•E••

ASCEND

ASCENT
ASKERS
ASLEEP
ASPECT
ASPENS
ASPERA
ASSENT
ASSERT
ASSESS
ASSETS
ASTERN
ASTERS
ASWELL
ESCENT
ESKERS
ESSENE
ESTEEM
ESTERS
ISLETS
ISMENE
OSIERS
OSSEIN
OSSETE
OSTEAL
OSTEND
OSWEGO
USHERS

•S••E•

ASEVER
ASHIER
ASHLEY
ASIDES
ASLEEP
BSIDES
ESCHER
ESCHEW
ESPIED
ESPIES
ESTEEM
ESTHER
ISABEL
ISOHEL
ISOMER
ISRAEL
ISSUED
ISSUER
ISSUES
ISTLES
OSAGES
OSPREY
OSTLER
RSVPED
USAGES
USENET
USOPEN
USURER
VSIXES

•S•••E

ASHORE
ASLOPE
ASPIRE
ASSIZE
ASSUME
ASSURE
ASTUTE
ESCAPE
ESSENE
ESTATE
ISMENE
ISOLDE
OSCINE
OSMOSE
OSSETE
PSYCHE
TSETSE
USABLE
USANCE

••SE••

ABSENT
ANSELM
ARSENE
ASSENT
ASSERT
ASSESS
ASSETS
AXSEED
BASELY
BASEST
BESETS
BISECT
CASEFY
CASERN
COSELL
DESERT
DOSERS
EASEIN
EASELS
EASEUP
EDSELS
ESSENE
ETSEQQ
EXSERT
FUSEES
HOSELS
INSEAM
INSECT
INSERT
INSETS
ITSELF
JASEYS
JOSEPH
LASERS
LOSEIT
LOSERS
MASERS
MASERU
MISERS
MISERY
MOSEYS
MUSERS
MUSEUM
MYSELF
NASEBY
OBSESS
ONSETS
OSSEIN
OSSETE
OUSELS
PASEOS
PESETA
POSERS
POSEUR
RASERS
RESEAL
RESEAT
RESEAU
RESECT
RESEDA
RESEED
RESEEN
RESEES
RESELL
RESEND
RESENT
RESETS
RESEWN
RESEWS
RISERS
ROSEAU
SASEBO
SISERA
TASERS
TVSETS
UNSEAL
UNSEAT
UNSEEN
UNSEWN
UNSEWS
UPSETS
WISELY
WISENT
WISEST
WISETO
WISEUP

••S•E•

AISLES
AMSTEL
ANSWER
AUSPEX
AUSTEN
AXSEED
BASHED
BASHES
BASKED
BASKET
BASSES
BASSET
BASTED
BASTER
BASTES
BESSER
BESTED
BISSET
BOSKET
BOSLEY
BOSSED
BOSSES
BUSHED
BUSHEL
BUSHES
BUSIED
BUSIER
BUSIES
BUSKED
BUSMEN
BUSSED
BUSSES
BUSTED
BUSTER
CASHED
CASHES
CASHEW
CASPER
CASTER
CASTES
CESSED
CESSES
CISKEI
COSHED
COSHES
COSIED
COSIER
COSIES
COSSET
CUSPED
CUSSED
CUSSES
CUSTER
DASHED
DASHER
DASHES
DISHED
DISHES
DISKED
DISMES
DISNEY
DISPEL
DISSED
DOSSED
DOSSEL
DOSSER
DOSSES
DUSTED
DUSTER
EASIER
EASTER
EISNER
ENSUED
ENSUES
FASCES
FASTED
FASTEN
FASTER
FESSED
FESSES
FESTER
FISHED
FISHER
FISHES
FISTED
FOSSES
FOSSEY
FOSTER
FUSEES
FUSSED
FUSSES
GASHED
GASHES
GASJET
GASKET
GASMEN
GASPED
GASPER
GASSED
GASSER
GASSES
GESTES
GOSHEN
GOSPEL
GUSHED
GUSHER
GUSHES
GUSSET
GUSTED
HASHED
HASHES
HASPED
HASTEN
HASTES
HESTER
HISSED
HISSER
HISSES
HOSIER
HOSTED
HOSTEL
HUSHED
HUSHES
HUSKED
HUSKER
HUSSEY
IJSSEL
INSTEP
ISSUED
ISSUER
ISSUES
JASPER
JESSEL
JESTED
JESTER
JOSHED
JOSHES
JOSSER
JOSSES
JUSTER
KISLEV
KISMET
KISSED
KISSER
KISSES
KOSHER
LASHED
LASHER
LASHES
LASSEN
LASSER
LASSES
LASTED
LASTEX
LESLEY
LESSEE
LESSEN
LESSER
LESTER
LISLES
LISPED
LISTED
LISTEE
LISTEL
LISTEN
LISTER
LOSSES
LUSHER
LUSTED
LUSTER
MASHED
MASHER
MASHES
MASKED
MASKER
MASSED
MASSES
MASSEY
MASTER
MESHED
MESHES
MESMER
MESSED
MESSES
MISLED
MISSED
MISSES
MISTED
MISTER
MOSHED
MOSHER
MOSHES
MOSLEM
MOSSED
MOSSES
MOSTEL
MUSHED
MUSHER
MUSHES
MUSKEG
MUSKET
MUSSED
MUSSEL
MUSSES
MUSTER
NASSER
NESSES
NESTEA
NESTED
NESTER
NISSEN
NOSHED
NOSHER
NOSHES
NOSIER
OBSTET
ONSPEC
OUSTED
OUSTER
OYSTER
PASSED
PASSEL
PASSER
PASSES
PASTED
PASTEL
PASTES
PESTER
PISCES
PISTES
POSHER
POSIES
POSSES
POSSET
POSTED
POSTER
PUSHED
PUSHES
PUSSES
RASHER
RASHES
RASPED
RASPER
RASTER
RESEED
RESEEN
RESEES
RESHES
RESTED
RESTER
RISKED
RISKER
ROSIER
ROSTER
RUSHED
RUSHEE
RUSHES
RUSSET
RUSTED
SASHED
SASHES
SASSED
SASSER
SASSES
SESTET
SISKEL
SISLER
SISLEY
SISTER
SUSIEQ
SUSSED
SUSSES
SUSSEX
SYSTEM
TASKED
TASSEL
TASSES
TASTED
TASTER
TASTES
TESTED
TESTEE
TESTER
TOSSED
TOSSER
TOSSES
TUSKED
TUSKER
ULSTER
UNSEEN
UNSHED
VASTER
VESPER
VESSEL
VESTED
VESTEE
VISAED
VOSGES
WASHED
WASHER
WASHES
WASTED
WASTER
WASTES
WESLEY
WESSEX
WISHED
WISHER
WISHES
WISPED
WISTER
WUSSES
XYSTER
YASSER
YESMEN
YESSED
YESSES
YESTER
ZESTED

••S••E

ALSACE
ANSATE
ARSENE
ASSIZE
ASSUME
ASSURE
AUSSIE
BASQUE
BESIDE
BESSIE
BISQUE
BUSTLE
BYSSHE
CASQUE
CASTLE
CESARE
COSINE
COSTAE
DESIRE
DISUSE
DOSAGE
ENSILE
ENSURE
ESSENE
FESCUE
FOSSAE
HASSLE
HUSTLE
INSANE
INSIDE
INSOLE
INSURE
JESSIE
JOSTLE
KISHKE
LASSIE
LESAGE
LESLIE
LESSEE
LISTEE
LUSTRE
LYSINE
MASHIE
MASQUE
MISCUE
MISUSE
MOSQUE
MUSCLE
MUSKIE
MYSORE
NESSIE
NESTLE
NOSALE
ONSALE
ONSIDE
ONSITE
OSSETE
PESTLE
RASSLE
RESALE
RESCUE
RESHOE
RESIDE
RESILE
RESOLE
RESUME
RISQUE
ROSCOE
RUSHEE
RUSTLE
SESAME
TESSIE
TESTAE
TESTEE
TISANE
TISSUE
TUSSLE
UGSOME
UNSAFE
UNSURE
UPSIDE
URSINE
VESTEE
VISAGE
VISINE
WASHOE

•••SE•

ABASED
ABASES
ABUSED
ABUSER
ABUSES
ALLSET
AMUSED
AMUSES
ARISEN
ARISES
BASSES
BASSET
BESSER
BETSEY
BIASED
BIASES
BISSET
BOSSED
BOSSES
BOUSED
BOUSES
BOWSER
BOXSET
BUNSEN
BURSES
BUSSED
BUSSES
CAUSED
CAUSES
CEASED
CEASES
CENSED
CENSER
CENSES
CESSED
CESSES
CHASED
CHASER
CHASES
CHISEL
CHOSEN
CLOSED
CLOSER
CLOSES
CLOSET
COPSES
CORSET
COSSET
CRISES
CRUSES
CURSED
CURSES

CUSSED
CUSSES
DAISES
DAMSEL
DENSER
DIESEL
DIESES
DILSEY
DISSED
DORSET
DORSEY
DOSSED
DOSSEL
DOSSER
DOSSES
DOUSED
DOUSES
DOWSED
DOWSER
DOWSES
ELYSEE
ERASED
ERASER
ERASES
FALSER
FESSED
FESSES
FOSSES
FOSSEY
FRASER
FRISEE
FRISES
FUSSED
FUSSES
GASSED
GASSER
GASSES
GEISEL
GELSEY
GETSET
GEYSER
GLASER
GOOSED
GOOSES
GOOSEY
GORSES
GOTSET
GUISES
GUSSET
HALSEY
HANSEL
HAWSER
HAWSES
HERSEY
HISSED
HISSER
HISSES
HORSED
HORSES
HORSEY
HOUSED
HOUSES
HUSSEY
IBISES
IJSSEL
IRISES
JANSEN
JENSEN
JERSEY
JESSEL
JETSET
JOSSER
JOSSES
KAISER
KELSEY
KERSEE
KERSEY
KINSEY
KISSED
KISSER
KISSES
LAPSED
LAPSES
LARSEN
LASSEN
LASSER
LASSES
LEASED
LEASER
LEASES
LENSED
LENSES
LESSEE
LESSEN
LESSER
LINSEY
LOOSED
LOOSEN
LOOSER
LOOSES
LOSSES
LOUSED
LOUSES
MADSEN
MANSES
MASSED
MASSES
MASSEY
MAUSER
MERSEY
MESSED
MESSES
MISSED
MISSES
MORSEL
MOSSED
MOSSES
MOUSED
MOUSER
MOUSES
MOUSEY
MUSSED
MUSSEL
MUSSES
NANSEN
NASSER
NAUSEA
NESSES
NIPSEY
NISSEN
NOISED
NOISES
NOOSED
NOOSES
NURSED
NURSER
NURSES
OCASEK
OCASEY
OFFSET
ONUSES
OPUSES
OUTSET
PARSEC
PARSED
PARSEE
PARSER
PARSES
PASSED
PASSEL
PASSER
PASSES
PAUSED
PAUSES
PENSEE
PHASED
PHASER
PHASES
PHYSED
PLUSES
POISED
POISES
POSSES
POSSET
PRASES
PRESET
PROSED
PROSER
PROSES
PULSED
PULSES
PURSED
PURSER
PURSES
PUSSES
RAISED
RAISER
RAISES
RAMSES
RAMSEY
REDSEA
REESES
REUSED
REUSES
RINSED
RINSES
ROUSED
ROUSER
ROUSES
RUSSET
SANSEI
SASSED
SASSER
SASSES
SENSED
SENSEI
SENSES
SOUSED
SOUSES
STASES
SUBSET
SUDSED
SUDSES
SUNSET
SUSSED
SUSSES
SUSSEX
TASSEL
TASSES
TEASED
TEASEL
TEASER
TEASES
TEASET
TENSED
TENSER
TENSES
TERSER
THESEA
THESES
TINSEL
TOSSED
TOSSER
TOSSES
UKASES
UNISEX
UNUSED
UPASES
URUSES
VERSED
VERSES
VESSEL
WEASEL
WESSEX
WIESEL
WIMSEY
WOLSEY
WORSEN
WOWSER
WUSSES
YASSER
YESSED
YESSES

•••S•E

ABESSE
ADESTE
AUSSIE
BESSIE
BURSAE
BYSSHE
CHASSE
CHASTE
CROSSE
CRUSOE
CUISSE
ELYSEE
ENISLE
FOCSLE
FOSSAE
FRISEE
GROSSE
HASSLE
INESSE
JESSIE
KERSEE
KRESGE
LASSIE
LESSEE
LETSBE
MAISIE
MENSAE
MOUSSE
NEISSE
NESSIE
PARSEE
PENSEE
PLISSE
POUSSE
PUISNE
PURSUE
RASSLE
SUISSE
TESSIE
THISBE
TISSUE
TOUSLE
TRISTE
TUSSLE
WRASSE

••••SE

ABESSE
ACCUSE
ADVISE
ALDOSE
APPOSE
ARIOSE
AROUSE
ATEASE
AVERSE
AVULSE
BEMUSE
BETISE
BLAISE
BLOUSE
BOURSE
BRAISE
BROWSE
BRUISE
CAMISE
CAYUSE
CERISE
CERUSE
CHAISE
CHASSE
CHEESE
CHOOSE
CLAUSE
CLEESE
COARSE
COURSE
CREASE
CROSSE
CROUSE
CRUISE
CUISSE
DEBASE
DEFUSE
DEMISE
DENISE
DEPOSE
DEVISE
DISUSE
DROWSE
EFFUSE
ELAPSE
ELOISE
ENCASE
ENDUSE
EVULSE
EXCISE
EXCUSE
EXPOSE
FILOSE
FLENSE
FRAISE
GREASE
GRILSE
GROSSE
GROUSE
GYROSE
HOARSE
ILLUSE
IMPOSE
INCASE
INCISE
INCUSE
INESSE
INFUSE
IODISE
IONISE
JOCOSE
LANOSE
LAOTSE
LHOTSE
LIAISE
LIPASE
LOUISE
MISUSE
MOROSE
MOUSSE
NEISSE
NODOSE
NOLOSE
NOWISE
OBTUSE
ODENSE
OPPOSE
ORELSE
OSMOSE
OTIOSE
PERUSE
PHRASE
PILOSE
PLEASE
PLISSE
POUSSE
PRAISE
PROWSE
RAMOSE
RECUSE
REFUSE
REMISE
REPOSE
REVISE
RIBOSE
RIMOSE
RUGOSE
SCOUSE
SETOSE
SINISE
SPARSE
SPOUSE
SUISSE
TALESE
TOROSE
TSETSE
UNCASE
UNEASE
UNWISE
UPRISE
UPROSE
VADOSE
VALISE
VARESE
WRASSE
ZYMASE

SF••••

SFORZA

S•F•••

SAFARI
SAFELY
SAFEST
SAFETY
SAFIRE
SIFTED
SIFTER
SOFFIT
SOFINE
SOFTEN
SOFTER
SOFTIE
SOFTLY
SUFFER
SUFFIX
SUFISM

S••F••

SAWFIT
SCIFIS
SCOFFS
SCUFFS
SEAFAN
SEAFOX
SEEFIT
SHAFTS
SHIFTS
SHIFTY
SHOFAR
SINFUL
SKIFFS
SNAFUS
SNIFFS
SNIFFY
SNUFFS
SNUFFY
SOBFUL
SOFFIT
SOLFAS
SPIFFS
SPIFFY
STAFFS
STEFAN
STEFFI
STEFOY
STIFFS
STIFLE
STUFFS
STUFFY
SUFFER
SUFFIX
SULFUR
SURFED
SURFER
SWIFTS

S•••F•

SALIFY
SAWOFF
SCARFS
SCHIFF
SCLAFF
SCOFFS
SCRUFF
SCUFFS
SCURFY
SEEOFF
SENUFO
SERIFS
SETOFF
SHEAFS
SHRIFT
SKIFFS
SMURFS
SNIFFS
SNIFFY
SNUFFS
SNUFFY
SPIFFS
SPIFFY
SPOOFS
STAFFS
STEFFI
STIFFS
STRAFE
STRIFE
STUFFS
STUFFY

S••••F

SAWOFF
SCHIFF
SCLAFF
SCRUFF
SEEOFF
SETOFF
SHARIF
SHERIF
SORTOF
STAPUF

•S•F••

ASKFOR
USEFUL

•S••F•

OSSIFY

••SF••

MISFIT

••S•F•

BASIFY
CASEFY
GASIFY
GOSOFT
OSSIFY
UNSAFE

••S••F

ITSELF
MASSIF
MYSELF

•••S•F

MASSIF
RIDSOF

SG••••

SGTMAJ

S•G•••

SAGELY
SAGEST
SAGGED
SEGUED
SEGUES
SEGURA
SIGHED
SIGHER
SIGHTS
SIGILS
SIGMAS
SIGNAL
SIGNED
SIGNEE
SIGNER
SIGNET
SIGNIN
SIGNON
SIGNOR
SIGNUP
SIGURD
SUGARS
SUGARY

S••G••

SAGGED
SAIGAS
SAIGON
SANGER
SANGTO
SARGES
SARGON
SARGOS
SAUGER
SEAGAL
SEDGES
SEEGER
SERGEI
SERGES
SERGIO
SHAGGY
SHOGUN
SIEGED
SIEGEL
SIEGES
SINGED
SINGER
SINGES
SINGIN
SINGLE
SINGLY
SINGTO
SIXGUN
SLAGGY
SLIGHT
SLOGAN
SLUGGO
SMOGGY
SMUGLY
SNAGGY
SNUGLI
SNUGLY
SOIGNE
SOUGHS
SOUGHT
SPIGOT
STAGED
STAGER
STAGES
STIGMA
STOGIE
SUBGUM
SUNGOD
SURGED

SURGES
SWAGED
SWAGES

S•••G•
SAVAGE
SCRAGS
SENEGA
SEWAGE
SHAGGY
SHRUGS
SILAGE
SLAGGY
SLANGS
SLANGY
SLEDGE
SLEIGH
SLINGS
SLOUGH
SLUDGE
SLUDGY
SLUGGO
SMOGGY
SMUDGE
SMUDGY
SNAGGY
SOCAGE
SPARGE
SPONGE
SPONGY
SPRAGS
SPRIGS
SPURGE
STINGO
STINGS
STINGY
STODGE
STODGY
STOOGE
SWINGS
SWINGY
SYZYGY

S••••G
SARONG
SATANG
SATING
SAVING
SAWING
SAWLOG
SAYING
SEABAG
SEADOG
SEBERG
SEEING
SEWING
SHYING
SIDING
SIRING
SITING
SIXING
SIZING
SKIING
SKYING
SLUING
SOLING
SOLONG
SONTAG
SOWBUG
SOWING
SPRANG
SPRING
SPRUNG
SPYING
STALAG
STENOG
STRING
STRONG
STRUNG
SUNDOG

•SG•••
ASGARD
OSGOOD

•S•G••
ISOGON
OSAGES
USAGES
VSIGNS

•S••G•
ASSIGN
OSWEGO

•S•••G
ASKING

••SG••
ANSGAR
PISGAH
VOSGES

••S•G•
ASSIGN
COSIGN
DESIGN
DOSAGE
ENSIGN
LESAGE
RESIGN
VISAGE

••S••G
BASING
BUSING
CASING
DOSING
EASING
FUSING
GASBAG
GASLOG
GOSTAG
HOSING
LOSING
MUSING
MUSKEG
NOSING
POSING
RASING
RESING
RISING
UNSNAG
UNSUNG

•••SG•
KRESGE
LETSGO

SH••••
SHABAN
SHABBY
SHACKS
SHADED
SHADES
SHADOW
SHAFTS
SHAGGY
SHAKEN
SHAKER
SHAKES
SHAKOS
SHAKTI
SHALES
SHALEY
SHALLY
SHALOM
SHAMAN
SHAMED
SHAMES
SHAMIR
SHAMUS
SHANDY
SHANIA
SHANKS
SHANNY
SHANTY
SHAPED
SHAPER
SHAPES
SHARDS
SHARED
SHARER
SHARES
SHARIA
SHARIF
SHARKS
SHARON
SHARPS
SHASTA
SHAVED
SHAVEN
SHAVER
SHAVES
SHAWLS
SHAWMS
SHAYNE
SHAZAM
SHBOOM
SHEAFS
SHEARS
SHEATH
SHEAVE
SHEEDY
SHEEHY
SHEENA
SHEENS
SHEEPS
SHEERS
SHEETS
SHEIKS
SHEILA
SHEKEL
SHELLS
SHELLY
SHELTY
SHELVE
SHEREE
SHERIF
SHERPA
SHERRY
SHERYL
SHEVAT
SHIELD
SHIEST
SHIFTS
SHIFTY
SHIISM
SHIITE
SHIKAR
SHILLS
SHILLY
SHILOH
SHIMMY
SHIMON
SHINDY
SHINED
SHINER
SHINES
SHINNY
SHINTO
SHIRAZ
SHIRER
SHIRES
SHIRKS
SHIRRS
SHIRTS
SHIRTY
SHIVER
SHOALS
SHOALY
SHOATS
SHOCKS
SHODDY
SHOERS
SHOFAR
SHOGUN
SHOJIS
SHOLEM
SHOLOM
SHOOED
SHOOIN
SHOOKS
SHOOTS
SHOPPE
SHORAN
SHORED
SHORES
SHORTA
SHORTE
SHORTI
SHORTO
SHORTS
SHORTU
SHORTY
SHOTAT
SHOTUP
SHOULD
SHOUTS
SHOVED
SHOVEL
SHOVER
SHOVES
SHOWED
SHOWER
SHOWIN
SHOWME
SHOWUP
SHRANK
SHREDS
SHREWD
SHREWS
SHRIEK
SHRIFT
SHRIKE
SHRILL
SHRIMP
SHRINE
SHRINK
SHRIVE
SHROUD
SHROVE
SHRUBS
SHRUGS
SHRUNK
SHTETL
SHTICK
SHUCKS
SHUNTS
SHUTIN
SHUTUP
SHYEST
SHYING

S•H•••
SAHARA
SAHIBS
SCHELL
SCHEMA
SCHEME
SCHICK
SCHIFF
SCHISM
SCHIST
SCHIZY
SCHLEP
SCHMOO
SCHMOS
SCHNOZ
SCHOOL
SCHORL
SCHULZ
SCHUSS
SCHWAB
SCHWAS
SPHERE
SPHERY
SPHINX
STHENO

S••H••
SACHEM
SACHET
SADHES
SADHUS
SASHAY
SASHED
SASHES
SENHOR
SIGHED
SIGHER
SIGHTS
SIPHON
SOPHIA
SOPHIE
SOTHAT
SOWHAT
SPAHIS
SUCHAS
SYPHON

S•••H•
SANCHO
SAPPHO
SCATHE
SCYTHE
SEETHE
SEICHE
SHEEHY
SIXTHS
SLIGHT
SLITHY
SLOSHY
SLOTHS
SLUSHY
SMITHS
SMITHY
SNATHE
SNATHS
SOOTHE
SOUGHS
SOUGHT
SOUTHS
SPATHE
STITHY
STJOHN
SURAHS
SWATHE
SWATHS
SYLPHS

S••••H
SALISH
SAMECH
SAMEKH
SCORCH
SCOTCH
SCUTCH
SEARCH
SERAPH
SHEATH
SHILOH
SIRRAH
SIWASH
SKETCH
SKITCH
SLEIGH
SLEUTH
SLOUCH
SLOUGH
SMERSH
SMIRCH
SMOOCH
SMOOTH
SMUTCH
SNATCH
SNITCH
SPEECH
SPILTH
SPLASH
SPLOSH
SQUASH
SQUISH
SQUUSH
STANCH
STARCH
STENCH
STITCH
STORCH
SUKKAH
SWARTH
SWATCH
SWITCH
SWOOSH

•SH•••
ASHARP
ASHCAN
ASHIER
ASHLAR
ASHLEY
ASHORE
ASHRAM
BSHARP
CSHARP
DSHARP
ESHARP
FSHARP
GSHARP
ISHTAR
OSHAWA
TSHIRT
USHERS

•S•H••
ASCHAM
ESCHER
ESCHEW
ESTHER
ISCHIA
ISOHEL
ISTHMI

•S••H•
PSYCHE
PSYCHO
PSYCHS

•S•••H
ASPISH
ISAIAH

••SH••
BASHED
BASHES
BISHOP
BUSHED
BUSHEL
BUSHES
BUSHWA
CASHED
CASHES
CASHEW
CASHIN
COSHED
COSHES
CUSHAW
DASHED
DASHER
DASHES
DASHIS
DISHED
DISHES
FISHED
FISHER
FISHES
GASHED
GASHES
GOSHEN
GUSHED
GUSHER
GUSHES
HASHED
HASHES
HUSHED
HUSHES
JOSHED
JOSHES
JOSHUA
KESHIA
KISHKE
KOSHER
LASHED
LASHER
LASHES
LASHIO
LASHUP
LUSHER
LUSHLY
MASHED
MASHER
MASHES
MASHIE
MESHED
MESHES
MISHAP
MISHIT
MOSHAV
MOSHED
MOSHER
MOSHES
MUSHED
MUSHER
MUSHES
NASHUA
NOSHED
NOSHER
NOSHES
NOSHOW
PASHAS
PASHTO
POSHER
POSHLY
PUSHED
PUSHES
PUSHON
PUSHUP
RASHAD
RASHER
RASHES
RASHID
RASHLY
RESHES
RESHIP
RESHOD
RESHOE
RESHOT
RUSHED
RUSHEE
RUSHES
SASHAY
SASHED
SASHES
TISHRI
TVSHOW
UNSHED
UNSHOD
UPSHOT
VASHTI
VISHNU
WASHED
WASHER
WASHES
WASHOE
WASHUP
WISHED
WISHER
WISHES

••S•H•
BYSSHE
JASCHA
MISCHA

••S••H
CASBAH
JOSEPH
JOSIAH
KASBAH
PESACH
PISGAH
TUSSAH

•••SH•
AYESHA
BOLSHY
BRASHY
BRUSHY
BUQSHA
BYSSHE
ELISHA
FLASHY
FLESHY
GEISHA
GUNSHY
HONSHU
ILESHA
KYUSHU
MARSHA
MARSHY
PLASHY
PLUSHY
SLOSHY
SLUSHY
TRASHY
TRISHA

•••S•H
BORSCH
HIRSCH
KIRSCH
KITSCH
MENSCH
PUTSCH
TUSSAH

••••SH
ABLUSH
AFRESH
AGUISH
AMBUSH
ASPISH
BANISH
BARISH
BLUISH
BOYISH
BYGOSH
CALASH
COYISH
DANISH

DOVISH
DUDISH
ELFISH
ELVISH
EMDASH
ENDASH
ENMESH
FAMISH
FETISH
FINISH
GALOSH
GARISH
GOFISH
IMPISH
INCASH
INRUSH
IRTYSH
JADISH
JEWISH
JUTISH
KIBOSH
LAGASH
LATISH
LAVISH
LOWISH
MARISH
MODISH
MOPISH
MULISH
NEWISH
OAFISH
OFFISH
OGRISH
OLDISH
ONRUSH
OWLISH
PALISH
PARISH
PERISH
POLISH
POTASH
PUNISH
QURUSH
RADISH
RAKISH
RAVISH
RAWISH
REHASH
RELISH
REWASH
SALISH
SIWASH
SMERSH
SPLASH
SPLOSH
SQUASH
SQUISH
SQUUSH
SWOOSH
THRASH
THRESH
THRUSH
TONISH
UNLASH
UNMESH
UNWISH
UPPISH
UPRUSH
VANISH
WABASH
WHOOSH
WIDISH
WINISH

SI••••

SIBYLS
SICCED
SICILY
SICKEN
SICKER
SICKLE
SICKLY
SIDDUR
SIDERO
SIDERS
SIDING
SIDLED
SIDLES
SIDNEY
SIECLE
SIEGED
SIEGEL
SIEGES
SIENNA
SIERRA
SIESTA
SIEVED
SIEVES
SIFTED
SIFTER
SIGHED
SIGHER
SIGHTS
SIGILS
SIGMAS
SIGNAL
SIGNED
SIGNEE
SIGNER
SIGNET
SIGNIN
SIGNON
SIGNOR
SIGNUP
SIGURD
SIKKIM
SILAGE
SILENI
SILENT
SILICA
SILKED
SILKEN
SILOAM
SILOED
SILONE
SILTED
SILVAS
SILVER
SIMBEL
SIMEON
SIMIAN
SIMILE
SIMMER
SIMNEL
SIMONE
SIMONY
SIMPER
SIMPLE
SIMPLY
SINBAD
SINEAD
SINEWS
SINEWY
SINFUL
SINGED
SINGER
SINGES
SINGIN
SINGLE
SINGLY
SINGTO
SINISE
SINKER
SINKIN
SINNED
SINNER
SINTAX
SINTER
SIOUAN
SIPHON
SIPPED
SIPPER
SIPPET
SIRDAR
SIRENS
SIRICA
SIRING
SIRIUS
SIRRAH
SIRREE
SISALS
SISERA
SISKEL
SISKIN
SISLER
SISLEY
SISTER
SISTRA
SITARS
SITCOM
SITING
SITINS
SITOUT
SITSBY
SITSIN
SITSON
SITSUP
SITTER
SITUPS
SIWASH
SIXERS
SIXGUN
SIXING
SIXTHS
SIXTUS
SIZERS
SIZEUP
SIZING
SIZZLE

S•I•••

SAIGAS
SAIGON
SAILED
SAILOR
SAINTE
SAINTS
SAIPAN
SCIFIS
SCIONS
SCIPIO
SEICHE
SEIDEL
SEINED
SEINER
SEINES
SEISMO
SEISMS
SEIZED
SEIZER
SEIZES
SHIELD
SHIEST
SHIFTS
SHIFTY
SHIISM
SHIITE
SHIKAR
SHILLS
SHILLY
SHILOH
SHIMMY
SHIMON
SHINDY
SHINED
SHINER
SHINES
SHINNY
SHINTO
SHIRAZ
SHIRER
SHIRES
SHIRKS
SHIRRS
SHIRTS
SHIRTY
SHIVER
SKIBOB
SKIDDY
SKIERS
SKIFFS
SKIING
SKILLS
SKIMPS
SKIMPY
SKINKS
SKINNY
SKIPIT
SKIPPY
SKIRLS
SKIROS
SKIRRS
SKIRTS
SKIRUN
SKITCH
SKITOW
SKIVED
SKIVER
SKIVES
SKIVVY
SLICED
SLICER
SLICES
SLICKS
SLIDER
SLIDES
SLIDIN
SLIEST
SLIGHT
SLIMED
SLIMES
SLIMLY
SLIMSY
SLINGS
SLINKS
SLINKY
SLIPIN
SLIPON
SLIPPY
SLIPUP
SLITHY
SLITTY
SLIVER
SMILAX
SMILED
SMILER
SMILES
SMILEY
SMILIN
SMIRCH
SMIRKS
SMIRKY
SMITES
SMITHS
SMITHY
SNICKS
SNIDER
SNIFFS
SNIFFY
SNIPED
SNIPER
SNIPES
SNIPPY
SNITCH
SNIVEL
SOIGNE
SOILED
SOIREE
SPICAS
SPICED
SPICES
SPIDER
SPIELS
SPIERS
SPIFFS
SPIFFY
SPIGOT
SPIKED
SPIKER
SPIKES
SPILES
SPILLS
SPILTH
SPINAL
SPINED
SPINEL
SPINES
SPINET
SPINKS
SPINTO
SPIRAL
SPIREA
SPIRED
SPIRES
SPIRIT
SPIROS
SPITED
SPITES
SPIVAK
SPIVVY
STICKS
STICKY
STIFFS
STIFLE
STIGMA
STILES
STILLS
STILLY
STILTS
STIMPY
STINGO
STINGS
STINGY
STINKS
STINKY
STINTS
STIPEL
STIPES
STIRIN
STIRKS
STIRUP
STITCH
STITHY
STIVER
STIVIC
SUISSE
SUITED
SUITES
SUITOR
SUITUP
SWIFTS
SWILLS
SWINGS
SWINGY
SWIPED
SWIPER
SWIPES
SWIRLS
SWIRLY
SWITCH
SWIVEL
SWIVET

S••I••

SABINE
SABINS
SAFIRE
SAHIBS
SALIFY
SALINA
SALINE
SALISH
SALIVA
SAMIAM
SAMITE
SANITY
SATING
SATINS
SATINY
SATIRE
SAVING
SAVIOR
SAWING
SAYING
SCHICK
SCHIFF
SCHISM
SCHIST
SCHIZY
SCRIBE
SCRIMP
SCRIMS
SCRIPS
SCRIPT
SEDILE
SEEING
SEMITE
SENIOR
SENITI
SEPIAS
SERIAL
SERIES
SERIFS
SERINE
SERINS
SETINS
SEWING
SEXIER
SEXILY
SEXIST
SHEIKS
SHEILA
SHIISM
SHIITE
SHRIEK
SHRIFT
SHRIKE
SHRILL
SHRIMP
SHRINE
SHRINK
SHRIVE
SHTICK
SHYING
SICILY
SIDING
SIGILS
SILICA
SIMIAN
SIMILE
SINISE
SIRICA
SIRING
SIRIUS
SITING
SITINS
SIXING
SIZING
SKEINS
SKIING
SKYING
SLEIGH
SLUICE
SLUING
SNAILS
SOCIAL
SODIUM
SOFINE
SOLIDI
SOLIDS
SOLING
SONICS
SOVIET
SOWING
SPHINX
SPLICE
SPLINE
SPLINT
SPLITS
SPOILS
SPOILT
SPRIER
SPRIGS
SPRING
SPRINT
SPRITE
SPRITS
SPRITZ
SPYING
SQUIBB
SQUIBS
SQUIDS
SQUILL
SQUINT
SQUIRE
SQUIRM
SQUIRT
SQUISH
STAINS
STAIRS
STEINS
STOICS
STRIAE
STRICK
STRICT
STRIDE
STRIFE
STRIKE
STRINE
STRING
STRIPE
STRIPS
STRIPY
STRIVE
SUBITO
SUFISM
SUPINE
SURIMI
SUSIEQ
SWAINS
SYRIAN
SYRINX

S•••I•

SALVIA
SAMMIE
SANDIA
SANTIR
SARDIS
SARNIA
SAUDIS
SAVAII
SAVOIE
SAVOIR
SAWFIT
SAYYID
SCALIA
SCENIC
SCIFIS
SCIPIO
SCORIA
SCOTIA
SEEFIT
SEENIN
SEEPIN
SEESIN
SENDIN
SENNIT
SENTIN
SEPTIC
SEQUIN
SERAIS
SERBIA
SERGIO
SERKIN
SETSIN
SHAMIR
SHANIA
SHARIA
SHARIF
SHERIF
SHOJIS
SHOOIN
SHOWIN
SHUTIN
SIGNIN
SIKKIM
SINGIN
SINKIN
SISKIN
SITSIN
SKIPIT
SKOKIE
SLAVIC
SLIDIN
SLIPIN
SLOVIK
SMILIN
SNOWIN
SOBEIT
SOCKIN
SOFFIT
SOFTIE
SOLEIL
SOPHIA
SOPHIE
SORBIC
SORDID
SORTIE
SPADIX
SPAHIS
SPAVIN
SPECIE
SPIRIT
SPRAIN
STADIA
STALIN
STASIS
STATIC
STEPIN
STEVIE
STIRIN
STIVIC
STOGIE
STOLID
STOPIN
STOPIT
STOTIN
STRAIN
STRAIT
STUDIO
STUPID
STYMIE
STYRIA
SUBMIT
SUCKIN
SUFFIX
SUMMIT
SUNLIT
SUNNIS

SUSLIK
SWAMIS
SWAZIS
SYLVIA
SYNDIC

S••••I
SAFARI
SALAMI
SALUKI
SANSEI
SATORI
SAVAII
SCAMPI
SENITI
SENSEI
SERGEI
SESQUI
SHAKTI
SHORTI
SILENI
SMALTI
SNUGLI
SOLIDI
SOMALI
SOUARI
STEFFI
STRATI
SURIMI
SUZUKI

•SI•••
ASIANS
ASIDES
ASIMOV
BSIDES
OSIERS
OSIRIS
VSIGNS
VSIXES

•S•I••
ASDICS
ASEITY
ASHIER
ASKING
ASPICS
ASPIRE
ASPISH
ASSIGN
ASSISI
ASSIST
ASSIZE
ASWIRL
ESKIMO
ESPIAL
ESPIED
ESPIES
GSUITS
ISAIAH
OSCINE
OSMICS
OSMIUM
OSSIAN
OSSIFY
OSTIUM
TSHIRT

•S••I•
ASKSIN
ASSAIL
ASTRID
ESPRIT
ISCHIA
ISELIN
ISTRIA
OSIRIS
OSSEIN
TSURIS
USERID
USMAIL

•S•••I
ASKARI
ASSISI
ISTHMI

••SI••
ASSIGN
ASSISI
ASSIST
ASSIZE
BASICS
BASIFY
BASING
BASINS
BESIDE
BUSIED
BUSIER
BUSIES
BUSILY
BUSING
CASING
CASINO
CESIUM
COSIED
COSIER
COSIES
COSIGN
COSILY
COSINE
DESICA
DESIGN
DESILU
DESIRE
DESIST
DOSIDO
DOSING
EASIER
EASILY
EASING
ENSIGN
ENSILE
EOSINS
FUSILS
FUSING
FUSION
GASIFY
HESIOD
HOSIER
HOSING
INSIDE
INSIST
INSITU
JOSIAH
LOSING
LYSINE
LYSINS
MUSIAL
MUSING
NOSIER
NOSILY
NOSING
ONSIDE
ONSITE
ORSINO
OSSIAN
OSSIFY
POSIES
POSING
POSITS
RASING
RESIDE
RESIGN
RESILE
RESING
RESINS
RESINY
RESIST
RISING
ROSIER
ROSILY
ROSINS
ROSINY
ROSITA
SUSIEQ
UPSIDE
URSIDS
URSINE
VISINE
VISION
VISITS

••S•I•
ASSAIL
AUSSIE
AUSTIN
BESSIE
BESTIR
BOSNIA
BUSKIN
BUSTIN
CASHIN
CASSIA
CASSIO
CASSIS
COSMIC
CUSPID
CUSTIS
DASHIS
DASSIN
DISTIL
DUSTIN
EASEIN
FASCIA
FISTIC
FOSSIL
FUSTIC
GASKIN
GASLIT
GESTIC
GOSSIP
HESTIA
HISPID
INSTIL
JESSIE
JESUIT
JOSKIN
JUSTIN
KESHIA
LASHIO
LASSIE
LESLIE
LOSEIT
LOSTIT
MASAIS
MASHIE
MASSIF
MASTIC
MISDID
MISFIT
MISHIT
MISSIS
MOSAIC
MUSKIE
MUSLIM
MUSLIN
MYSTIC
NESSIE
OSSEIN
PASSIM
PASTIS
PISTIL
POSTIT
RASHID
RESHIP
RESNIK
RESPIN
RUSKIN
RUSSIA
RUSTIC
SISKIN
SUSLIK
TESSIE
UNSAID
VESPID
VISCID
WESKIT
YESSIR

••S••I
ASSISI
BUSONI
CISKEI
MESABI
SESQUI
TISHRI
VASHTI
WASABI

•••SI•
ADDSIN
ASKSIN
AUSSIE
BAGSIT
BESSIE
BIDSIN
CAPSID
CASSIA
CASSIO
CASSIS
COUSIN
CRISIS
CUTSIN
DASSIN
DEASIL
DIESIS
DIGSIN
DOESIN
DOGSIT
EATSIN
ECESIC
ECESIS
ENOSIS
FITSIN
FOGSIN
FOSSIL
GETSIN
GETSIT
GNOSIS
GOESIN
GOSSIP
HEMSIN
HITSIT
HOPSIN
ICESIN
IRISIN
JAMSIN
JESSIE
KEYSIN
LASSIE
LAYSIN
LETSIN
LIESIN
LOGSIN
MAISIE
MASSIF
MIOSIS
MISSIS
MYOSIN
MYOSIS
NESSIE
NOESIS
PASSIM
PAYSIN
PEPSIN
PERSIA
PHYSIO
POPSIN
PROSIT
PUTSIN
RAISIN
RUBSIN
RUNSIN
RUSSIA
SEESIN
SETSIN
SITSIN
STASIS
TESSIE
THESIS
THESIX
TIESIN
TILSIT
TIPSIN
TMESIS
TOCSIN
TOESIN
TONSIL
YESSIR
ZOYSIA

•••S•I
AGASSI
BONSAI
JETSKI
KINSKI
SANSEI
SENSEI

••••SI
AGASSI
ASSISI
CHUHSI
DALASI
KWEISI
LUGOSI
POTOSI
THYRSI
TZUHSI
WATUSI

S•J•••
SEJANT
STJOAN
STJOHN

S••J••
SELJUK
SHOJIS
STOJKO

S•••J•
SKOPJE

S••••J
SGTMAJ
SWARAJ

••SJ••
GASJET

SK••••
SKALDS
SKANKS
SKATED
SKATER
SKATES
SKEANS
SKEINS
SKERRY
SKETCH
SKEWED
SKEWER
SKIBOB
SKIDDY
SKIERS
SKIFFS
SKIING
SKILLS
SKIMPS
SKIMPY
SKINKS
SKINNY
SKIPIT
SKIPPY
SKIRLS
SKIROS
SKIRRS
SKIRTS
SKIRUN
SKITCH
SKITOW
SKIVED
SKIVER
SKIVES
SKIVVY
SKNXXX
SKOALS
SKOKIE
SKOPJE
SKORTS
SKULKS
SKULLS
SKUNKS
SKUNKY
SKYBOX
SKYCAP
SKYING
SKYLAB
SKYWAY

S•K•••
SAKERS
SIKKIM
SUKKAH

S••K••
SACKED
SACKER
SECKEL
SEEKER
SERKIN
SHAKEN
SHAKER
SHAKES
SHAKOS
SHAKTI
SHEKEL
SHIKAR
SICKEN
SICKER
SICKLE
SICKLY
SIKKIM
SILKED
SILKEN
SINKER
SINKIN
SISKEL
SISKIN
SKOKIE
SLAKED
SLAKES
SMOKED
SMOKER
SMOKES
SMOKEY
SNAKED
SNAKES
SOAKED
SOAKER
SOAKUP
SOCKED
SOCKET
SOCKIN
SPIKED
SPIKER
SPIKES
SPOKED
SPOKEN
SPOKES
STAKED
STAKES
STOKED
STOKER
STOKES
SUCKAS
SUCKED
SUCKER
SUCKIN
SUKKAH
SULKED
SULKER
SUNKEN

S•••K•
SALUKI
SAMEKH
SEDAKA
SHACKS
SHANKS
SHARKS
SHEIKS
SHIRKS
SHOCKS
SHOOKS
SHRIKE
SHUCKS
SKANKS
SKINKS
SKULKS
SKUNKS
SKUNKY
SLACKS
SLEEKS
SLEEKY
SLICKS
SLINKS
SLINKY
SMACKS
SMIRKS
SMIRKY
SMOCKS
SNACKS
SNEAKS
SNEAKY
SNICKS
SNOOKS
SNOOKY
SPANKS
SPANKY
SPARKS
SPARKY
SPEAKS
SPECKS
SPINKS
SPOOKS
SPOOKY
SPUNKY
STACKS
STALKS
STALKY
STANKY
STEAKS
STICKS
STICKY
STINKS
STINKY
STIRKS
STLUKE
STOCKS
STOCKY
STOJKO
STOOKS
STORKS
STRAKE
STRIKE
STROKE
SUZUKI
SWANKS
SWANKY

S••••K
SCHICK
SCREAK
SELJUK
SENDAK
SHRANK
SHRIEK
SHRINK
SHRUNK
SHTICK
SLEZAK
SLOVAK
SLOVIK
SPACEK
SPIVAK
SQUAWK
SQUEAK
STMARK
STREAK
STRICK
STRUCK
SUSLIK

•SK•••
ASKARI
ASKERS
ASKFOR
ASKING
ASKOUT
ASKSIN
ESKERS
ESKIMO

••SK••
BASKED
BASKET
BOSKET
BUSKED
BUSKIN
CISKEI
DISKED
GASKET
GASKIN
HUSKED
HUSKER
JOSKIN
MASKED
MASKER
MOSKVA
MUSKEG
MUSKET
MUSKIE
MUSKOX
RISKED
RISKER
RUSKIN
SISKEL
SISKIN
TASKED
TUSKED
TUSKER
WESKIT

••S•K•
KISHKE
LUSAKA

••S••K

CUSACK
KUSPUK
RESNIK
SUSLIK
VOSTOK

•••SK•

ALASKA
FLASKS
FRISKS
FRISKY
JANSKY
JETSKI
KINSKI
KIOSKS
NEVSKY
PROSKY
RIMSKY
WHISKS
WHISKY

•••S•K

OCASEK

••••SK

ATRISK
BRATSK
DAMASK
GDANSK
UNMASK
URALSK

SL••••

SLACKS
SLAGGY
SLAKED
SLAKES
SLALOM
SLANGS
SLANGY
SLANTS
SLAPPY
SLAPUP
SLATED
SLATER
SLATES
SLAVED
SLAVER
SLAVES
SLAVEY
SLAVIC
SLAYED
SLAYER
SLEAVE
SLEAZE
SLEAZY
SLEDGE
SLEEKS
SLEEKY
SLEEPS
SLEEPY
SLEETS
SLEETY
SLEEVE
SLEIGH
SLEUTH
SLEWED
SLEZAK
SLICED
SLICER
SLICES
SLICKS
SLIDER
SLIDES
SLIDIN
SLIEST
SLIGHT
SLIMED
SLIMES
SLIMLY
SLIMSY
SLINGS
SLINKS
SLINKY
SLIPIN
SLIPON
SLIPPY
SLIPUP
SLITHY
SLITTY
SLIVER
SLOANE
SLOBBY
SLOGAN
SLOOPS
SLOPED
SLOPES
SLOPPY
SLOSHY
SLOTHS
SLOUCH
SLOUGH
SLOVAK
SLOVEN
SLOVIK
SLOWED
SLOWER
SLOWLY
SLOWUP
SLUDGE
SLUDGY
SLUGGO
SLUICE
SLUING
SLUMMY
SLUMPS
SLURPS
SLURRY
SLUSHY
SLYEST
SLYPES

S•L•••

SALAAM
SALADO
SALADS
SALALS
SALAMI
SALARY
SALIFY
SALINA
SALINE
SALISH
SALIVA
SALLET
SALLOW
SALMAN
SALMON
SALOME
SALONS
SALOON
SALSAS
SALTED
SALTEN
SALTER
SALTON
SALTUM
SALUKI
SALUTE
SALVED
SALVER
SALVES
SALVIA
SALVOR
SALVOS
SALYUT
SCLAFF
SCLERA
SCLERO
SELDOM
SELECT
SELENA
SELENE
SELENO
SELJUK
SELLER
SELVES
SILAGE
SILENI
SILENT
SILICA
SILKED
SILKEN
SILOAM
SILOED
SILONE
SILTED
SILVAS
SILVER
SOLACE
SOLANS
SOLARS
SOLDAN
SOLDER
SOLDON
SOLEIL
SOLELY
SOLEMN
SOLENT
SOLERS
SOLEUS
SOLFAS
SOLIDI
SOLIDS
SOLING
SOLOED
SOLONG
SOLUTE
SOLVED
SOLVER
SOLVES
SPLASH
SPLATS
SPLAYS
SPLEEN
SPLICE
SPLINE
SPLINT
SPLITS
SPLOSH
STLUKE
SULCUS
SULFUR
SULKED
SULKER
SULLEN
SULTAN
SULTRY
SYLPHS
SYLVAN
SYLVIA

S••L••

SABLES
SAILED
SAILOR
SALLET
SALLOW
SAMLET
SAULTS
SAWLOG
SAYLES
SCALAR
SCALDS
SCALED
SCALER
SCALES
SCALIA
SCALPS
SCHLEP
SCOLDS
SCULLS
SCULLY
SCULPT
SCYLLA
SEALAB
SEALED
SEALER
SEALUP
SEELEY
SELLER
SENLAC
SHALES
SHALEY
SHALLY
SHALOM
SHELLS
SHELLY
SHELTY
SHELVE
SHILLS
SHILLY
SHILOH
SHOLEM
SHOLOM
SIDLED
SIDLES
SISLER
SISLEY
SKALDS
SKILLS
SKULKS
SKULLS
SKYLAB
SLALOM
SMALLS
SMALTI
SMALTO
SMELLS
SMELLY
SMELTS
SMILAX
SMILED
SMILER
SMILES
SMILEY
SMILIN
SMOLTS
SNELLS
SOCLES
SOILED
SPALLS
SPELLS
SPILES
SPILLS
SPILTH
STALAG
STALED
STALER
STALES
STALIN
STALKS
STALKY
STALLS
STELAE
STELAR
STELES
STELLA
STELMO
STILES
STILLS
STILLY
STILTS
STOLEN
STOLES
STOLID
STOLLE
STOLON
STULLS
STYLED
STYLER
STYLES
STYLET
STYLUS
SUBLET
SULLEN
SUNLIT
SUSLIK
SUTLER
SVELTE
SWALES
SWELLS
SWILLS

S•••L•

SADDLE
SAFELY
SAGELY
SALALS
SAMPLE
SANELY
SCHELL
SCHULZ
SCOWLS
SCROLL
SCULLS
SCULLY
SCYLLA
SEARLE
SEDILE
SEEMLY
SEMELE
SEPALS
SETTLE
SEWELL
SEXILY
SHALLY
SHAWLS
SHEILA
SHELLS
SHELLY
SHIELD
SHILLS
SHILLY
SHOALS
SHOALY
SHOULD
SHRILL
SIBYLS
SICILY
SICKLE
SICKLY
SIECLE
SIGILS
SIMILE
SIMPLE
SIMPLY
SINGLE
SINGLY
SISALS
SIZZLE
SKILLS
SKIRLS
SKOALS
SKULLS
SLIMLY
SLOWLY
SMALLS
SMELLS
SMELLY
SMUGLY
SNAILS
SNARLS
SNARLY
SNELLS
SNUGLI
SNUGLY
SOFTLY
SOLELY
SOMALI
SORELY
SOTOLS
SOURLY
SPALLS
SPELLS
SPIELS
SPILLS
SPOILS
SPOILT
SPOOLS
SPRYLY
SQUALL
SQUILL
STABLE
STABLY
STALLS
STAPLE
STEALS
STEELE
STEELS
STEELY
STELLA
STIFLE
STILLS
STILLY
STMALO
STOLLE
STOOLS
STOOLY
STROLL
STULLS
SUBTLE
SUBTLY
SUPPLE
SUPPLY
SURELY
SWELLS
SWILLS
SWIRLS
SWIRLY

S••••L

SACRAL
SAMBAL
SAMUEL
SANDAL
SAUREL
SCHELL
SCHOOL
SCHORL
SCRAWL
SCROLL
SEAGAL
SECKEL
SEIDEL
SEPTAL
SEQUEL
SERIAL
SERVAL
SEWELL
SHEKEL
SHERYL
SHOVEL
SHRILL
SHTETL
SIEGEL
SIGNAL
SIMBEL
SIMNEL
SINFUL
SISKEL
SNIVEL
SOBFUL
SOCIAL
SOLEIL
SORREL
SPINAL
SPINEL
SPIRAL
SPRAWL
SQUALL
SQUEAL
SQUILL
STEROL
STIPEL
STPAUL
STROLL
SWIVEL
SYMBOL

•SL•••

ASLANT
ASLEEP
ASLOPE
ISLAND
ISLETS

•S•L••

ASHLAR
ASHLEY
ASYLUM
ISELIN
ISOLDE
ISTLES
OSTLER
PSALMS
PSYLLA

•S••L•

ASWELL
ISEULT
OSCULA
OSWALD
PSYLLA
USABLE
USABLY
USUALS

•S•••L

ASSAIL
ASTRAL
ASWELL
ASWIRL
ESPIAL
ISABEL
ISOHEL
ISRAEL
OSTEAL
USEFUL
USMAIL

••SL••

AISLES
BOSLEY
GASLIT
GASLOG
GOSLOW
KISLEV
LESLEY
LESLIE
LISLES
MISLAY
MISLED
MOSLEM
MUSLIM
MUSLIN
SISLER
SISLEY
SUSLIK
TESLAS
VASLAV
WESLEY

••S•L•

ANSELM
BASALT
BASELY
BASSLY
BUSILY
BUSTLE
CASALS
CASTLE
COSELL
COSILY
COSTLY
DESALT
DESILU
EASELS
EASILY
EDSELS
ENSILE
FUSILS
HASSLE
HOSELS
HOSTLY
HUSTLE
INSOLE
INSULT
ITSELF
JOSTLE
JUSTLY
LASTLY
LUSHLY
MOSTLY
MUSCLE
MUSCLY
MYSELF
NASALS
NESTLE
NOSALE
NOSILY
ONSALE
OUSELS
PESTLE
POSHLY
POSSLQ
RASHLY
RASSLE
RESALE
RESALT
RESELL
RESILE
RESOLD
RESOLE
RESULT
ROSILY
RUSTLE
SISALS
TUSSLE
UNSOLD
URSULA
VASTLY
WISELY

••S••L

AMSTEL
ASSAIL
BUSHEL
CASUAL
COSELL
COSTAL
DISMAL
DISPEL
DISTAL
DISTIL
DOSSAL
DOSSEL
ENSOUL
FESTAL
FISCAL

FOSSIL
GOSPEL
HOSTEL
IJSSEL
INSTAL
INSTIL
JESSEL
LISTEL
MESCAL
MISSAL
MOSTEL
MUSIAL
MUSSEL
PASCAL
PASSEL
PASTEL
PISTIL
PISTOL
POSTAL
RASCAL
RESEAL
RESELL
SISKEL
TASSEL
UNSEAL
VASSAL
VESSEL
VESTAL
VISUAL

•••SL•
BASSLY
ENISLE
FOCSLE
GRISLY
HASSLE
MEASLY
POSSLQ
RASSLE
THUSLY
TOUSLE
TUSSLE
VIZSLA

•••S•L
BURSAL
CAUSAL
CHISEL
CONSUL
CRESOL
DAMSEL
DEASIL
DIESEL
DORSAL
DOSSAL
DOSSEL
FAISAL
FOSSIL
GEISEL
HANSEL
IJSSEL
JESSEL
MENSAL
MISSAL
MORSEL
MUSSEL
PASSEL
TARSAL
TASSEL
TEASEL
TINSEL
TONSIL
VASSAL
VESSEL
WEASEL
WIESEL

SM••••
SMACKS
SMALLS
SMALTI
SMALTO
SMARMY
SMARTS
SMARTY
SMEARS
SMEARY
SMELLS
SMELLY
SMELTS
SMERSH
SMILAX
SMILED
SMILER
SMILES
SMILEY
SMILIN
SMIRCH
SMIRKS
SMIRKY
SMITES
SMITHS
SMITHY
SMOCKS
SMOGGY
SMOKED
SMOKER
SMOKES
SMOKEY
SMOLTS
SMOOCH
SMOOTH
SMUDGE
SMUDGY
SMUGLY
SMURFS
SMUTCH
SMUTTY
SMYRNA

S•M•••
SAMARA
SAMBAL
SAMBAR
SAMBAS
SAMECH
SAMEKH
SAMIAM
SAMITE
SAMLET
SAMMIE
SAMOAN
SAMOSA
SAMPAN
SAMPLE
SAMSON
SAMUEL
SEMELE
SEMITE
SEMPER
SEMPRE
SIMBEL
SIMEON
SIMIAN
SIMILE
SIMMER
SIMNEL
SIMONE
SIMONY
SIMPER
SIMPLE
SIMPLY
SOMALI
SOMANY
SOMATA
SOMATO
SOMBER
SOMBRE
SOMERS
SOMMER
STMALO
STMARK
SUMACS
SUMMAE
SUMMAS
SUMMED
SUMMER
SUMMIT
SUMMON
SUMNER
SUMSUP
SUMTER
SUMUPS
SYMBOL

S••M••
SALMAN
SALMON
SAMMIE
SCAMPI
SCAMPS
SCHMOO
SCHMOS
SCUMMY
SEAMAN
SEAMED
SEAMEN
SEAMUS
SEEMED
SEEMLY
SERMON
SGTMAJ
SHAMAN
SHAMED
SHAMES
SHAMIR
SHAMUS
SHIMMY
SHIMON
SIGMAS
SIMMER
SKIMPS
SKIMPY
SLIMED
SLIMES
SLIMLY
SLIMSY
SLUMMY
SLUMPS
SOMMER
SPUMED
SPUMES
STAMEN
STAMPS
STIMPY
STOMAS
STOMAT
STOMPS
STUMER
STUMPS
STUMPY
STYMIE
SUBMIT
SUMMAE
SUMMAS
SUMMED
SUMMER
SUMMIT
SUMMON
SWAMIS
SWAMPS
SWAMPY

S•••M•
SALAMI
SALOME
SCHEMA
SCHEME
SCRAMS
SCRIMP
SCRIMS
SCRUMS
SCUMMY
SEDUMS
SEISMO
SEISMS
SERUMS
SESAME
SHAWMS
SHIMMY
SHOWME
SHRIMP
SLUMMY
SMARMY
SOLEMN
SONOMA
SPASMS
STEAMS
STEAMY
STELMO
STIGMA
STORMS
STORMY
STRUMS
SURIMI
SWARMS

S••••M
SACHEM
SACRUM
SADDAM
SALAAM
SALTUM
SAMIAM
SCARUM
SCHISM
SCREAM
SELDOM
SEPTUM
SHALOM
SHAZAM
SHBOOM
SHIISM
SHOLEM
SHOLOM
SIKKIM
SILOAM
SITCOM
SLALOM
SODIUM
SQUIRM
STREAM
SUBGUM
SUFISM
SYSTEM

•SM•••
ASMARA
ISMENE
OSMICS
OSMIUM
OSMOND
OSMOSE
OSMUND
USMAIL

•S•M••
ASIMOV
ISOMER

•S••M•
ASSUME
ESKIMO
ISTHMI
PSALMS

•S•••M
ASCHAM
ASHRAM
ASYLUM
ESTEEM
OSMIUM
OSTIUM

••SM••
BUSMAN
BUSMEN
COSMIC
COSMOS
DESMAN
DISMAL
DISMAY
DISMES
GASMAN
GASMEN
KISMET
MESMER
TASMAN
YESMAN
YESMEN

••S•M•
ASSUME
BESOMS
RESUME
SESAME
UGSOME

••S••M
ABSCAM
ANSELM
CESIUM
CUSTOM
DISARM
HASSAM
INSEAM
MOSLEM
MUSEUM
MUSLIM
PASSIM
POSSUM
SYSTEM
WISDOM

•••SM•
ABYSMS
CHASMS
MIASMA
PLASMA
PLASMO
PRISMS
SEISMO
SEISMS
SPASMS

•••S•M
BALSAM
DIMSUM
DORSUM
FOLSOM
GYPSUM
HANSOM
HASSAM
JETSAM
OMASUM
PASSIM
POSSUM
RANSOM

••••SM
AGEISM
CHRISM
CUBISM
EGOISM
HOLISM
MAOISM
MONISM
PURISM
SCHISM
SHIISM
SUFISM
TAOISM
THEISM
TRUISM
VERISM
YOGISM

SN••••
SNACKS
SNAFUS
SNAGGY
SNAILS
SNAKED
SNAKES
SNAPAT
SNAPPY
SNAPTO
SNAPUP
SNARED
SNARES
SNARLS
SNARLY
SNATCH
SNATHE
SNATHS
SNAZZY
SNEAKS
SNEAKY
SNEERS
SNEERY
SNEEZE
SNEEZY
SNELLS
SNICKS
SNIDER
SNIFFS
SNIFFY
SNIPED
SNIPER
SNIPES
SNIPPY
SNITCH
SNIVEL
SNOBBY
SNOCAT
SNOODS
SNOOKS
SNOOKY
SNOOPS
SNOOPY
SNOOTS
SNOOTY
SNOOZE
SNOOZY
SNOPES
SNORED
SNORER
SNORES
SNORTS
SNOTTY
SNOUTS
SNOWED
SNOWIN
SNUBBY
SNUFFS
SNUFFY
SNUGLI
SNUGLY
SNYDER

S•N•••
SANCHO
SANCTA
SANDAL
SANDED
SANDER
SANDIA
SANDRA
SANELY
SANEST
SANGER
SANGTO
SANITY
SANNUP
SANSEI
SANTEE
SANTIR
SANTOS
SENARY
SENATE
SENDAK
SENDER
SENDIN
SENDUP
SENECA
SENEGA
SENHOR
SENIOR
SENITI
SENLAC
SENNAS
SENNET
SENNIT
SENORA
SENORS
SENSED
SENSEI
SENSES
SENSOR
SENTIN
SENTRA
SENTRY
SENTUP
SENUFO
SINBAD
SINEAD
SINEWS
SINEWY
SINFUL
SINGED
SINGER
SINGES
SINGIN
SINGLE
SINGLY
SINGTO
SINISE
SINKER
SINKIN
SINNED
SINNER
SINTAX
SINTER
SKNXXX
SONANT
SONATA
SONDES
SONICS
SONNET
SONOMA
SONORA
SONTAG
SUNDAE
SUNDAY
SUNDER
SUNDEW
SUNDOG
SUNDRY
SUNGOD
SUNKEN
SUNLIT
SUNNED
SUNNIS
SUNOCO
SUNRAY
SUNSET
SUNTAN
SUNUNU
SUNUPS
SYNCED
SYNDIC
SYNODS
SYNTAX

S••N••
SAINTE
SAINTS
SANNUP
SARNIA
SAUNAS
SCANTS
SCANTY
SCENAS
SCENDS
SCENES
SCENIC
SCENTS
SCHNOZ
SCONCE
SCONES
SEANCE
SEENIN
SEENTO
SEINED
SEINER
SEINES
SENNAS
SENNET
SENNIT
SEWNON
SEWNUP
SHANDY
SHANIA
SHANKS
SHANNY
SHANTY
SHINDY
SHINED
SHINER
SHINES
SHINNY
SHINTO
SHUNTS
SIDNEY
SIENNA
SIGNAL
SIGNED
SIGNEE
SIGNER
SIGNET
SIGNIN
SIGNON
SIGNOR
SIGNUP
SIMNEL
SINNED
SINNER
SKANKS
SKINKS
SKINNY
SKUNKS
SKUNKY
SLANGS
SLANGY
SLANTS
SLINGS
SLINKS
SLINKY
SONNET
SOONER
SOUNDS

SPANKS
SPANKY
SPENDS
SPINAL
SPINED
SPINEL
SPINES
SPINET
SPINKS
SPINTO
SPONGE
SPONGY
SPUNKY
SRANAN
STANCE
STANCH
STANDS
STANKY
STANZA
STENCH
STENOG
STENOS
STINGO
STINGS
STINGY
STINKS
STINKY
STINTS
STONED
STONER
STONES
STUNTS
STUNTY
SUMNER
SUNNED
SUNNIS
SWANEE
SWANKS
SWANKY
SWINGS
SWINGY
SYDNEY

S•••N•

SABENA
SABINE
SABINS
SALINA
SALINE
SALONS
SARANS
SARONG
SATANG
SATING
SATINS
SATINY
SAVANT
SAVING
SAWING
SAXONS
SAXONY
SAYING
SCARNE
SCIONS
SCORNS
SECANT
SECOND
SEDANS
SEEING
SEJANT
SELENA
SELENE
SELENO
SERENA
SERENE
SERINE
SERINS
SETINS
SEVENS
SEWING
SHANNY
SHAYNE
SHEENA
SHEENS
SHINNY
SHRANK
SHRINE
SHRINK
SHRUNK
SHYING
SIDING
SIENNA
SILENI
SILENT
SILONE
SIMONE
SIMONY
SIRENS
SIRING
SITING
SITINS
SIXING
SIZING
SKEANS
SKEINS
SKIING
SKINNY
SKYING
SLOANE
SLUING
SMYRNA
SOFINE
SOIGNE
SOLANS
SOLENT
SOLING
SOLONG
SOMANY
SONANT
SOWING
SPAWNS
SPHINX
SPLINE
SPLINT
SPOONS
SPOONY
SPRANG
SPRING
SPRINT
SPRUNG
SPURNS
SPYING
SQUINT
STAINS
STEINS
STERNA
STERNE
STERNO
STERNS
STHENO
STRAND
STRINE
STRING
STRONG
STRUNG
SUNUNU
SUPINE
SUSANN
SWAINS
SWOONS
SYRINX

S••••N

SADDEN
SAIGON
SAIPAN
SALMAN
SALMON
SALOON
SALTEN
SALTON
SAMOAN
SAMPAN
SAMSON
SARGON
SARTON
SATEEN
SATURN
SCREEN
SEAFAN
SEAMAN
SEAMEN
SEASON
SEATON
SECERN
SEENIN
SEEPIN
SEESIN
SENDIN
SENTIN
SEQUIN
SERKIN
SERMON
SETSIN
SETSON
SEVERN
SEWNON
SEWSON
SEXTON
SHABAN
SHAKEN
SHAMAN
SHARON
SHAVEN
SHIMON
SHOGUN
SHOOIN
SHORAN
SHOWIN
SHUTIN
SICKEN
SIGNIN
SIGNON
SILKEN
SIMEON
SIMIAN
SINGIN
SINKIN
SIOUAN
SIPHON
SISKIN
SITSIN
SITSON
SIXGUN
SKIRUN
SLIDIN
SLIPIN
SLIPON
SLOGAN
SLOVEN
SMILIN
SNOWIN
SOCKIN
SODDEN
SOFTEN
SOLDAN
SOLDON
SOLEMN
SOSOON
SPAVIN
SPLEEN
SPOKEN
SPRAIN
SPURON
SRANAN
STALIN
STAMEN
STATEN
STAYON
STEFAN
STEPIN
STEPON
STEVEN
STIRIN
STJOAN
STJOHN
STOLEN
STOLON
STOPIN
STOTIN
STRAIN
STREWN
STYRON
SUBORN
SUCKIN
SUDDEN
SULLEN
SULTAN
SUMMON
SUNKEN
SUNTAN
SUSANN
SUTTON
SWEDEN
SYLVAN
SYPHON
SYRIAN

•S•N••

ASANAS
USANCE
USENET

•S••N•

ASCEND
ASCENT
ASIANS
ASKING
ASLANT
ASPENS
ASSENT
ESCENT
ESPANA
ESSENE
ISLAND
ISMENE
OSCINE
OSMOND
OSMUND
OSTEND
VSIGNS

•S•••N

ASHCAN
ASKSIN
ASOSAN
ASSIGN
ASTERN
ASWOON
ISELIN
ISOGON
OSBORN
OSSEIN
OSSIAN
USOPEN

••SN••

BOSNIA
CPSNOW
DISNEY
EISNER
RESNIK
UNSNAG
UNSNAP

••S•N•

ABSENT
ARSENE
ARSONS
ASSENT
BASING
BASINS
BESANT
BISONS
BOSONS
BOSUNS
BUSING
BUSONI
CASING
CASINO
CESSNA
COSINE
DISANT
DOSING
EASING
EOSINS
ESSENE
FUSING
HOSING
INSANE
INSYNC
LOSING
LYSINE
LYSINS
MASONS
MESONS
MUSING
MUSTNT
NOSING
OKSANA
ORSINO
PISANO
PISANS
POSING
RASING
RESAND
RESEND
RESENT
RESING
RESINS
RESINY
RISING
ROSINS
ROSINY
SUSANN
TISANE
UNSUNG
URSINE
VISHNU
VISINE
WISENT

••S••N

ASSIGN
AUSTEN
AUSTIN
BOSTON
BUSKIN
BUSMAN
BUSMEN
BUSTIN
CASERN
CASHIN
CASTON
COSIGN
DASSIN
DESIGN
DESMAN
DISOWN
DUSTIN
EASEIN
EASTON
ENSIGN
FASTEN
FUSION
GASCON
GASKIN
GASMAN
GASMEN
GASTON
GOSHEN
HASSAN
HASTEN
HESTON
HUSTON
INSPAN
JOSKIN
JUSTIN
KASDAN
LASSEN
LESSEN
LESSON
LISBON
LISTEN
LISTON
MUSLIN
NISSAN
NISSEN
OSSEIN
OSSIAN
PASSON
PISTON
POSTON
PUSHON
RESAWN
RESEEN
RESEWN
RESIGN
RESPIN
RESTON
RUSKIN
SISKIN
SOSOON
SUSANN
TASMAN
TUSCAN
UNSEEN
UNSEWN
UNSOWN
VISION
WESSON
WYSTAN
YESMAN
YESMEN

•••SN•

CESSNA
DOESNT
FRESNO
KRASNY
PUISNE

•••S•N

ACTSON
ADDSIN
ADDSON
ALISON
ARISEN
ASKSIN
ASOSAN
BABSON
BENSON
BETSON
BIDSIN
BIDSON
BRYSON
BUNSEN
CARSON
CHOSEN
COUSIN
CUTSIN
DAMSON
DANSON
DASSIN
DATSUN
DAWSON
DIGSIN
DOBSON
DOESIN
EATSIN
EDISON
EGGSON
FITSIN
FOGSIN
GARSON
GETSIN
GETSON
GIBSON
GODSON
GOESIN
GOESON
GRISON
HANSON
HASSAN
HEMSIN
HENSON
HITSON
HOBSON
HOPSIN
HUDSON
ICESIN
IRISIN
JAMSIN
JANSEN
JENSEN
JETSON
JIMSON
JOLSON
JONSON
KANSAN
KEYSIN
KMESON
LANSON
LARSEN
LARSON
LASSEN
LAWSON
LAYSIN
LAYSON
LESSEN
LESSON
LETSIN
LETSON
LIESIN
LOGSIN
LOGSON
LOOSEN
MADSEN
MYOSIN
NANSEN
NEESON
NELSON
NISSAN
NISSEN
ODDSON
OLESON
ORISON
PARSON
PASSON
PAYSIN
PAYSON
PEPSIN
PERSON
PINSON
POISON
POPSIN
PRISON
PUTSIN
PUTSON
RAISIN
RAMSON
RATSON
REASON
REVSON
ROBSON
RUBSIN
RUNSIN
RUNSON
SAMSON
SEASON
SEESIN
SETSIN
SETSON
SEWSON
SITSIN
SITSON
TIESIN
TIPSIN
TOCSIN
TOESIN
TUCSON
TULSAN
UNISON
WATSON
WESSON
WILSON
WORSEN

SO••••

SOAKED
SOAKER
SOAKUP
SOAPED
SOAPER
SOARED
SOARER
SOARES
SOASTO
SOAVES
SOBBED
SOBBER
SOBEIT
SOBERS
SOBFUL
SOCAGE
SOCCER
SOCIAL
SOCKED
SOCKET
SOCKIN
SOCLES
SODDED
SODDEN
SODIUM
SOEURS
SOFFIT
SOFINE
SOFTEN
SOFTER
SOFTIE
SOFTLY
SOIGNE
SOILED
SOIREE
SOLACE
SOLANS
SOLARS
SOLDAN
SOLDER
SOLDON
SOLEIL
SOLELY
SOLEMN
SOLENT
SOLERS
SOLEUS
SOLFAS
SOLIDI
SOLIDS
SOLING

SOLOED
SOLONG
SOLUTE
SOLVED
SOLVER
SOLVES
SOMALI
SOMANY
SOMATA
SOMATO
SOMBER
SOMBRE
SOMERS
SOMMER
SONANT
SONATA
SONDES
SONICS
SONNET
SONOMA
SONORA
SONTAG
SOONER
SOOTHE
SOPHIA
SOPHIE
SOPORS
SOPPED
SOPSUP
SORBET
SORBIC
SORDID
SORELY
SOREST
SORREL
SORROW
SORTED
SORTER
SORTIE
SORTOF
SOSOON
SOTHAT
SOTOLS
SOTTED
SOUARI
SOUGHS
SOUGHT
SOUNDS
SOUPUP
SOURCE
SOURED
SOURER
SOURLY
SOUSED
SOUSES
SOUTER
SOUTHS
SOVIET
SOWBUG
SOWERS
SOWETO
SOWHAT
SOWING
SOXERS

S•O•••

SCOFFS
SCOLDS
SCONCE
SCONES
SCOOPS
SCOOTS
SCOPED
SCOPES
SCORCH
SCORED
SCORER
SCORES
SCORIA
SCORNS
SCOTCH
SCOTER
SCOTIA
SCOTTO
SCOTTY
SCOURS
SCOUSE
SCOUTS
SCOWLS
SFORZA
SHOALS
SHOALY
SHOATS
SHOCKS
SHODDY
SHOERS
SHOFAR
SHOGUN
SHOJIS
SHOLEM
SHOLOM
SHOOED
SHOOIN
SHOOKS
SHOOTS
SHOPPE
SHORAN
SHORED
SHORES
SHORTA
SHORTE
SHORTI
SHORTO
SHORTS
SHORTU
SHORTY
SHOTAT
SHOTUP
SHOULD
SHOUTS
SHOVED
SHOVEL
SHOVER
SHOVES
SHOWED
SHOWER
SHOWIN
SHOWME
SHOWUP
SIOUAN
SKOALS
SKOKIE
SKOPJE
SKORTS
SLOANE
SLOBBY
SLOGAN
SLOOPS
SLOPED
SLOPES
SLOPPY
SLOSHY
SLOTHS
SLOUCH
SLOUGH
SLOVAK
SLOVEN
SLOVIK
SLOWED
SLOWER
SLOWLY
SLOWUP
SMOCKS
SMOGGY
SMOKED
SMOKER
SMOKES
SMOKEY
SMOLTS
SMOOCH
SMOOTH
SNOBBY
SNOCAT
SNOODS
SNOOKS
SNOOKY
SNOOPS
SNOOPY
SNOOTS
SNOOTY
SNOOZE
SNOOZY
SNOPES
SNORED
SNORER
SNORES
SNORTS
SNOTTY
SNOUTS
SNOWED
SNOWIN
SOONER
SOOTHE
SPOILS
SPOILT
SPOKED
SPOKEN
SPOKES
SPONGE
SPONGY
SPOOFS
SPOOKS
SPOOKY
SPOOLS
SPOONS
SPOONY
SPOORS
SPORES
SPORTS
SPORTY
SPOTTY
SPOUSE
SPOUTS
STOATS
STOCKS
STOCKY
STODGE
STODGY
STOGIE
STOICS
STOJKO
STOKED
STOKER
STOKES
STOLEN
STOLES
STOLID
STOLLE
STOLON
STOMAS
STOMAT
STOMPS
STONED
STONER
STONES
STOOGE
STOOKS
STOOLS
STOOLY
STOOPS
STOPES
STOPIN
STOPIT
STOPUP
STORCH
STORED
STORER
STORES
STOREY
STORKS
STORMS
STORMY
STORRS
STOTIN
STOUPS
STOUTS
STOVER
STOVES
STOWED
SWOONS
SWOOPS
SWOOSH
SWORDS

S••O••

SABOTS
SALOME
SALONS
SALOON
SAMOAN
SAMOSA
SAPORS
SARODS
SARONG
SATORI
SATOUT
SAVOIE
SAVOIR
SAVORS
SAVORY
SAVOUR
SAWOFF
SAWOUT
SAXONS
SAXONY
SCHOOL
SCHORL
SCIONS
SCOOPS
SCOOTS
SCRODS
SCROLL
SCROOP
SECOND
SEEOFF
SEEOUT
SENORA
SENORS
SEPOYS
SEROSA
SEROUS
SEROWS
SETOFF
SETOSE
SETOUT
SHBOOM
SHOOED
SHOOIN
SHOOKS
SHOOTS
SHROUD
SHROVE
SILOAM
SILOED
SILONE
SIMONE
SIMONY
SITOUT
SLOOPS
SMOOCH
SMOOTH
SNOODS
SNOOKS
SNOOKY
SNOOPS
SNOOPY
SNOOTS
SNOOTY
SNOOZE
SNOOZY
SOLOED
SOLONG
SONOMA
SONORA
SOPORS
SOSOON
SOTOLS
SPLOSH
SPOOFS
SPOOKS
SPOOKY
SPOOLS
SPOONS
SPOONY
SPOORS
SPROUT
STJOAN
STJOHN
STOOGE
STOOKS
STOOLS
STOOLY
STOOPS
STROBE
STRODE
STROKE
STROLL
STRONG
STROPS
STROUD
STROVE
SUBORN
SUNOCO
SWOONS
SWOOPS
SWOOSH
SYNODS
SYSOPS

S•••O•

SAIGON
SAILOR
SALLOW
SALMON
SALOON
SALTON
SALVOR
SALVOS
SAMSON
SANTOS
SARGON
SARGOS
SARTON
SAVIOR
SAWLOG
SAYSOS
SCHMOO
SCHMOS
SCHNOZ
SCHOOL
SCROOP
SEACOW
SEADOG
SEAFOX
SEASON
SEATON
SECTOR
SELDOM
SENHOR
SENIOR
SENSOR
SERMON
SERVOS
SESTOS
SETSON
SETTOS
SEWNON
SEWSON
SEXTON
SHADOW
SHAKOS
SHALOM
SHARON
SHBOOM
SHILOH
SHIMON
SHOLOM
SIGNON
SIGNOR
SIMEON
SIPHON
SITCOM
SITSON
SKIBOB
SKIROS
SKITOW
SKYBOX
SLALOM
SLIPON
SOLDON
SORROW
SORTOF
SOSOON
SPIGOT
SPIROS
SPURON
STATOR
STAYON
STEFOY
STENOG
STENOS
STEPON
STEROL
STOLON
STUPOR
STYRON
SUCCOR
SUITOR
SUMMON
SUNDOG
SUNGOD
SUTTON
SYMBOL
SYPHON

S••••O

SABATO
SALADO
SANCHO
SANGTO
SAPPHO
SASEBO
SCHMOO
SCIPIO
SCLERO
SCOTTO
SEENTO
SEESTO
SEISMO
SELENO
SENUFO
SERGIO
SHINTO
SHORTO
SIDERO
SINGTO
SLUGGO
SMALTO
SNAPTO
SOASTO
SOMATO
SOWETO
SPEEDO
SPINTO
STELMO
STEREO
STERNO
STHENO
STINGO
STMALO
STOJKO
STRABO
STRATO
STUCCO
STUDIO
SUBITO
SUNOCO

•SO•••

ASOSAN
ISOBAR
ISOGON
ISOHEL
ISOLDE
ISOMER
ISOPOD
USOPEN

•S•O••

ASCOTS
ASHORE
ASKOUT
ASLOPE
ASSORT
ASWOON
CSPOTS
ESCORT
ESPOSA
ESPOSO
ESTOPS
FSTOPS
OSBORN
OSGOOD
OSMOND
OSMOSE

•S••O•

ASIMOV
ASKFOR
ASTROS
ASWOON
ESCROW
ISADOR
ISOGON
ISOPOD
OSGOOD

•S•••O

ESCUDO
ESKIMO
ESPOSO
OSWEGO
PSEUDO
PSYCHO
USEDTO

••SO••

ABSORB
ADSORB
ARSONS
ASSORT
BESOMS
BESOTS
BISONS
BOSONS
BUSONI
DESOTO
DISOWN
ENSOUL
GOSOFT
INSOLE
KOSOVO
MASONS
MESONS
MYSORE
NOSOAP
RESODS
RESOLD
RESOLE
RESORB
RESORT
SOSOON
SYSOPS
UGSOME
UNSOLD
UNSOWN
VISORS

••S•O•

BASSOS
BESTOW
BISHOP
BOSTON
BUSBOY
CASTON
CASTOR
CESTOS
CISCOS
COSMOS
CPSNOW
CUSTOM
CUSTOS
DESPOT
DISCOS
EASTON
FUSION
GASCON
GASLOG
GASTON
GOSLOW
HESIOD
HESTON
HUSTON
HYSSOP
LASSOS
LESBOS
LESSON
LESSOR
LISBOA
LISBON
LISTON
MASCOT
MOSCOW
MUSKOX
NESTOR
NOSHOW
PASEOS
PASSON
PASTOR
PESCOW
PESTOS
PISTOL
PISTON
POSTON
PUSHON
RESHOD
RESHOE
RESHOT
RESTON
ROSCOE
ROSTOV
SESTOS
SOSOON
TVSHOW
UNSHOD
UNSTOP
UPSHOT
VISION
VOSTOK
WASHOE
WESSON

WISDOM

••S••O

AUSTRO
BISTRO
CASINO
CASSIO
CASTRO
DESOTO
DOSIDO
GASTRO
HASBRO
KOSOVO
LASHIO
ORSINO
PASHTO
PISANO
SASEBO
WISETO

•••SO•

ACTSON
ADDSON
ALISON
AMOSOZ
AVISOS
BABSON
BASSOS
BENSON
BETSON
BIDSON
BRASOV
BRYSON
CARSON
CENSOR
CHISOX
CRESOL
CRUSOE
CURSOR
DAMSON
DANSON
DAWSON
DOBSON
EDISON
EGGSON
FOLSOM
GARSON
GETSON
GIBSON
GODSON
GOESON
GRISON
HANSOM
HANSON
HENSON
HITSON
HOBSON
HUDSON
HYKSOS
HYSSOP
JETSON
JIMSON
JOLSON
JONSON
KMESON
LANSON
LARSON
LASSOS
LAWSON
LAYSON
LESSON
LESSOR
LETSON
LOGSON
NEESON
NELSON
ODDSON
OLESON
ORISON
PARSON
PASSON
PAYSON
PERSON
PINSON
POISON
PRISON
PUTSON
RAMSON
RANSOM
RATSON
REASON
REDSOX
REVSON
RIDSOF
ROBSON
RUNSON
SAMSON
SAYSOS
SEASON
SENSOR
SETSON
SEWSON
SITSON
TENSOR
TORSOS
TUCSON
UNISON
VERSOS
WATSON
WESSON
WILSON
WINSOR

•••S•O

ADDSTO
AIMSTO
ARISTO
CASSIO
CRISCO
CRISTO
ENESCO
FIASCO
FRESCO
FRESNO
FRISCO
GETSTO
GLOSSO
GRASSO
GROSSO
LAYSTO
LETSGO
LIESTO
OBISPO
PHYSIO
PLASMO
PRESTO
PUTSTO
RUNSTO
SEESTO
SEISMO
SOASTO
TIESTO
UNESCO

••••SO

ALONSO
ARIOSO
CARUSO
ELPASO
EOIPSO
ESPOSO
EVENSO
EVERSO
GLOSSO
GRASSO
GROSSO
WHOMSO

SP••••

SPACED
SPACEK
SPACER
SPACES
SPACEY
SPADED
SPADER
SPADES
SPADIX
SPAHIS
SPALLS
SPANKS
SPANKY
SPARED
SPARER
SPARES
SPARGE
SPARKS
SPARKY
SPARSE
SPARTA
SPASMS
SPATES
SPATHE
SPAVIN
SPAWNS
SPAYED
SPEAKS
SPEARS
SPECIE
SPECKS
SPEDUP
SPEECH
SPEEDO
SPEEDS
SPEEDY
SPELLS
SPENDS
SPERRY
SPEWED
SPHERE
SPHERY
SPHINX
SPICAS
SPICED
SPICES
SPIDER
SPIELS
SPIERS
SPIFFS
SPIFFY
SPIGOT
SPIKED
SPIKER
SPIKES
SPILES
SPILLS
SPILTH
SPINAL
SPINED
SPINEL
SPINES
SPINET
SPINKS
SPINTO
SPIRAL
SPIREA
SPIRED
SPIRES
SPIRIT
SPIROS
SPITED
SPITES
SPIVAK
SPIVVY
SPLASH
SPLATS
SPLAYS
SPLEEN
SPLICE
SPLINE
SPLINT
SPLITS
SPLOSH
SPOILS
SPOILT
SPOKED
SPOKEN
SPOKES
SPONGE
SPONGY
SPOOFS
SPOOKS
SPOOKY
SPOOLS
SPOONS
SPOONY
SPOORS
SPORES
SPORTS
SPORTY
SPOTTY
SPOUSE
SPOUTS
SPRAGS
SPRAIN
SPRANG
SPRATS
SPRAWL
SPRAYS
SPREAD
SPREES
SPRIER
SPRIGS
SPRING
SPRINT
SPRITE
SPRITS
SPRITZ
SPROUT
SPRUCE
SPRUES
SPRUNG
SPRYER
SPRYLY
SPUMED
SPUMES
SPUNKY
SPURGE
SPURNS
SPURON
SPURRY
SPURTS
SPYING

S•P•••

SAPORS
SAPPED
SAPPER
SAPPHO
SEPALS
SEPIAS
SEPOYS
SEPTAL
SEPTET
SEPTIC
SEPTUM
SIPHON
SIPPED
SIPPER
SIPPET
SOPHIA
SOPHIE
SOPORS
SOPPED
SOPSUP
STPAUL
STPETE
SUPERB
SUPERS
SUPINE
SUPPED
SUPPER
SUPPLE
SUPPLY
SYPHON

S••P••

SAIPAN
SAMPAN
SAMPLE
SAPPED
SAPPER
SAPPHO
SCAPED
SCAPES
SCIPIO
SCOPED
SCOPES
SEEPED
SEEPIN
SEMPER
SEMPRE
SHAPED
SHAPER
SHAPES
SHOPPE
SIMPER
SIMPLE
SIMPLY
SIPPED
SIPPER
SIPPET
SKIPIT
SKIPPY
SKOPJE
SLAPPY
SLAPUP
SLIPIN
SLIPON
SLIPPY
SLIPUP
SLOPED
SLOPES
SLOPPY
SLYPES
SNAPAT
SNAPPY
SNAPTO
SNAPUP
SNIPED
SNIPER
SNIPES
SNIPPY
SNOPES
SOAPED
SOAPER
SOPPED
SOUPUP
STAPES
STAPLE
STAPUF
STEPIN
STEPON
STEPPE
STEPUP
STIPEL
STIPES
STOPES
STOPIN
STOPIT
STOPUP
STUPAS
STUPES
STUPID
STUPOR
SUBPAR
SUPPED
SUPPER
SUPPLE
SUPPLY
SWIPED
SWIPER
SWIPES
SYLPHS

S•••P•

SCALPS
SCAMPI
SCAMPS
SCARPS
SCAUPS
SCOOPS
SCRAPE
SCRAPS
SCRIPS
SCRIPT
SCULPT
SERAPE
SERAPH
SETUPS
SHARPS
SHEEPS
SHERPA
SHOPPE
SITUPS
SKIMPS
SKIMPY
SKIPPY
SLAPPY
SLEEPS
SLEEPY
SLIPPY
SLOOPS
SLOPPY
SLUMPS
SLURPS
SNAPPY
SNIPPY
SNOOPS
SNOOPY
STAMPS
STEEPS
STEPPE
STIMPY
STOMPS
STOOPS
STOUPS
STRAPS
STRIPE
STRIPS
STRIPY
STROPS
STUMPS
STUMPY
SUMUPS
SUNUPS
SWAMPS
SWAMPY
SWEEPS
SWOOPS
SYRUPS
SYRUPY
SYSOPS

S••••P

SANNUP
SATRAP
SAVEUP
SCHLEP
SCRIMP
SCROOP
SEALUP
SENDUP
SENTUP
SETSUP
SEWNUP
SEWSUP
SHOTUP
SHOWUP
SHRIMP
SHUTUP
SIGNUP
SITSUP
SIZEUP
SKYCAP
SLAPUP
SLIPUP
SLOWUP
SNAPUP
SOAKUP
SOPSUP
SOUPUP
SPEDUP
STAYUP
STEPUP
STIRUP
STOPUP
STREEP
SUITUP
SUMSUP

•SP•••

ASPECT
ASPENS
ASPERA
ASPICS
ASPIRE
ASPISH
CSPOTS
ESPANA
ESPIAL
ESPIED
ESPIES
ESPOSA
ESPOSO
ESPRIT
OSPREY

•S•P••

ISOPOD
RSVPED
USOPEN

•S••P•

ASLOPE
ESCAPE
ESTOPS
FSTOPS
USURPS

•S•••P

ASHARP
ASLEEP
BSHARP
CSHARP
DSHARP
ESCARP
ESHARP
FSHARP
GSHARP
USEDUP
USESUP

••SP••

AUSPEX
CASPAR
CASPER
CUSPED
CUSPID
DESPOT
DISPEL
GASPAR
GASPED
GASPER
GOSPEL
HASPED
HISPID
INSPAN
JASPER
KUSPUK
LISPED
ONSPEC
RASPED
RASPER
RESPIN
VESPER
VESPID
WISPED

••S•P•

JOSEPH
SYSOPS

••S••P

BISHOP
DUSTUP
EASEUP
FESSUP
GASCAP
GOSSIP
HYSSOP
INSTEP
LASHUP
MESSUP
MISHAP
MUSSUP
NOSOAP
PASSUP
PUSHUP
RESHIP
RESTUP
TOSSUP
UNSNAP
UNSTOP
WASHUP
WISEUP

•••SP•

CLASPS
CRISPS
CRISPY
GRASPS
OBISPO

•••S•P

ACESUP
ACTSUP
ADDSUP
BIDSUP
BOBSUP
BUYSUP
CATSUP
CUTSUP
DAMSUP
DIGSUP
DOESUP
EATSUP
ENDSUP
FESSUP
FOGSUP
GETSUP
GOESUP
GOSSIP
GUMSUP
HITSUP
HOPSUP
HYSSOP
ICESUP
JAMSUP
KEYSUP

LAPSUP
LAYSUP
LETSUP
MESSUP
MILSAP
MOPSUP
MUSSUP
OWNSUP
PASSUP
PAYSUP
PEPSUP
POPSUP
PUTSUP
REVSUP
RIGSUP
RIPSUP
RUNSUP
SETSUP
SEWSUP
SITSUP
SOPSUP
SUMSUP
TAGSUP
TEESUP
TIESUP
TOSSUP
TOTSUP
USESUP
WADSUP
ZIPSUP

••••SP
AMERSP

SQ••••
SQUABS
SQUADS
SQUALL
SQUARE
SQUASH
SQUATS
SQUAWK
SQUEAK
SQUEAL
SQUIBB
SQUIBS
SQUIDS
SQUILL
SQUINT
SQUIRE
SQUIRM
SQUIRT
SQUISH
SQUUSH

S•Q•••
SEQUEL
SEQUIN

S••Q••
SACQUE
SESQUI

S••••Q
SUSIEQ

•SQ•••
MSQUAD

••SQ••
BASQUE
BISQUE
CASQUE
MASQUE
MOSQUE
RISQUE
SESQUI

••S•Q•
ETSEQQ

••S••Q
ETSEQQ
NASDAQ
POSSLQ
SUSIEQ

•••S•Q
POSSLQ

SR••••
SRANAN

S•R•••
SARANS
SARDIS
SARGES
SARGON
SARGOS
SARNIA
SARODS
SARONG
SARTON
SARTRE
SCRAGS
SCRAMS
SCRAPE
SCRAPS
SCRAWL
SCREAK
SCREAM
SCREED
SCREEN
SCREES
SCREWS
SCREWY
SCRIBE
SCRIMP
SCRIMS
SCRIPS
SCRIPT
SCRODS
SCROLL
SCROOP
SCRUBS
SCRUFF
SCRUMS
SERACS
SERAIS
SERAPE
SERAPH
SERBIA
SERENA
SERENE
SERGEI
SERGES
SERGIO
SERIAL
SERIES
SERIFS
SERINE
SERINS
SERKIN
SERMON
SEROSA
SEROUS
SEROWS
SERUMS
SERVAL
SERVED
SERVER
SERVES
SERVOS
SHRANK
SHREDS
SHREWD
SHREWS
SHRIEK
SHRIFT
SHRIKE
SHRILL
SHRIMP
SHRINE
SHRINK
SHRIVE
SHROUD
SHROVE
SHRUBS
SHRUGS
SHRUNK
SIRDAR
SIRENS
SIRICA
SIRING
SIRIUS
SIRRAH
SIRREE
SORBET
SORBIC
SORDID
SORELY
SOREST
SORREL
SORROW
SORTED
SORTER
SORTIE
SORTOF
SPRAGS
SPRAIN
SPRANG
SPRATS
SPRAWL
SPRAYS
SPREAD
SPREES
SPRIER
SPRIGS
SPRING
SPRINT
SPRITE
SPRITS
SPRITZ
SPROUT
SPRUCE
SPRUES
SPRUNG
SPRYER
SPRYLY
STRABO
STRADS
STRAFE
STRAIN
STRAIT
STRAKE
STRAND
STRAPS
STRASS
STRATA
STRATI
STRATO
STRAUB
STRAUS
STRAWS
STRAWY
STRAYS
STREAK
STREAM
STREEP
STREET
STRESS
STREWN
STREWS
STRIAE
STRICK
STRICT
STRIDE
STRIFE
STRIKE
STRINE
STRING
STRIPE
STRIPS
STRIPY
STRIVE
STROBE
STRODE
STROKE
STROLL
STRONG
STROPS
STROUD
STROVE
STRUCK
STRUMS
STRUNG
STRUTS
SURAHS
SURELY
SUREST
SURETE
SURETY
SURFED
SURFER
SURGED
SURGES
SURIMI
SURREY
SURTAX
SURVEY
SYRIAN
SYRINX
SYRUPS
SYRUPY

S••R••
SABRAS
SABRES
SACRAL
SACRED
SACRUM
SATRAP
SAUREL
SAWRED
SCARAB
SCARCE
SCARED
SCARER
SCARES
SCARFS
SCARNE
SCARPS
SCARRY
SCARUM
SCORCH
SCORED
SCORER
SCORES
SCORIA
SCORNS
SCURFY
SCURRY
SCURVE
SCURVY
SEARCH
SEARED
SEARLE
SECRET
SEERED
SEURAT
SEVRES
SFORZA
SHARDS
SHARED
SHARER
SHARES
SHARIA
SHARIF
SHARKS
SHARON
SHARPS
SHEREE
SHERIF
SHERPA
SHERRY
SHERYL
SHIRAZ
SHIRER
SHIRES
SHIRKS
SHIRRS
SHIRTS
SHIRTY
SHORAN
SHORED
SHORES
SHORTA
SHORTE
SHORTI
SHORTO
SHORTS
SHORTU
SHORTY
SIERRA
SIRRAH
SIRREE
SKERRY
SKIRLS
SKIROS
SKIRRS
SKIRTS
SKIRUN
SKORTS
SLURPS
SLURRY
SMARMY
SMARTS
SMARTY
SMERSH
SMIRCH
SMIRKS
SMIRKY
SMURFS
SMYRNA
SNARED
SNARES
SNARLS
SNARLY
SNORED
SNORER
SNORES
SNORTS
SOARED
SOARER
SOARES
SOIREE
SORREL
SORROW
SOURCE
SOURED
SOURER
SOURLY
SPARED
SPARER
SPARES
SPARGE
SPARKS
SPARKY
SPARSE
SPARTA
SPERRY
SPIRAL
SPIREA
SPIRED
SPIRES
SPIRIT
SPIROS
SPORES
SPORTS
SPORTY
SPURGE
SPURNS
SPURON
SPURRY
SPURTS
STARCH
STARED
STARER
STARES
STARRY
STARTS
STARVE
STEREO
STERES
STERNA
STERNE
STERNO
STERNS
STEROL
STIRIN
STIRKS
STIRUP
STORCH
STORED
STORER
STORES
STOREY
STORKS
STORMS
STORMY
STORRS
STURDY
STYRIA
STYRON
SUDRAS
SUNRAY
SURREY
SUTRAS
SWARAJ
SWARDS
SWARMS
SWARTH
SWERVE
SWIRLS
SWIRLY
SWORDS

S•••R•
SABERS
SAFARI
SAFIRE
SAHARA
SAKERS
SALARY
SAMARA
SANDRA
SAPORS
SARTRE
SATIRE
SATORI
SATURN
SATYRS
SAVERS
SAVORS
SAVORY
SAYERS
SCARRY
SCHORL
SCLERA
SCLERO
SCOURS
SCURRY
SEBERG
SECERN
SECURE
SEDERS
SEGURA
SEMPRE
SENARY
SENORA
SENORS
SENTRA
SENTRY
SEVERE
SEVERN
SEVERS
SEVERY
SEWARD
SEWERS
SHEARS
SHEERS
SHERRY
SHIRRS
SHOERS
SIDERO
SIDERS
SIERRA
SIGURD
SISERA
SISTRA
SITARS
SIXERS
SIZERS
SKERRY
SKIERS
SKIRRS
SLURRY
SMEARS
SMEARY
SNEERS
SNEERY
SOBERS
SOEURS
SOLARS
SOLERS
SOMBRE
SOMERS
SONORA
SOPORS
SOUARI
SOWERS
SOXERS
SPEARS
SPERRY
SPHERE
SPHERY
SPIERS
SPOORS
SPURRY
SQUARE
SQUIRE
SQUIRM
SQUIRT
STAIRS
STARRY
STEERS
STMARK
STORRS
STUART
SUBARU
SUBORN
SUBURB
SUGARS
SUGARY
SULTRY
SUNDRY
SUPERB
SUPERS
SUTURE
SWEARS

S••••R
SACKER
SADDER
SAILOR
SALTER
SALVER
SALVOR
SAMBAR
SANDER
SANGER
SANTIR
SAPPER
SASSER
SAUCER
SAUGER
SAVIOR
SAVOIR
SAVOUR
SAWYER
SCALAR
SCALER
SCARER
SCORER
SCOTER
SEALER
SEATER
SECTOR
SEEDER
SEEGER
SEEKER
SEINER
SEIZER
SELLER
SEMPER
SENDER
SENHOR
SENIOR
SENSOR
SERVER
SETTER
SEXIER
SHAKER
SHAMIR
SHAPER
SHARER
SHAVER
SHIKAR
SHINER
SHIRER
SHIVER
SHOFAR
SHOVER
SHOWER
SICKER
SIDDUR
SIFTER
SIGHER
SIGNER
SIGNOR
SILVER
SIMMER
SIMPER
SINGER
SINKER
SINNER
SINTER
SIPPER
SIRDAR
SISLER
SISTER
SITTER
SKATER
SKEWER
SKIVER
SLATER
SLAVER
SLAYER
SLICER
SLIDER

SLIVER
SLOWER
SMILER
SMOKER
SNIDER
SNIPER
SNORER
SNYDER
SOAKER
SOAPER
SOARER
SOBBER
SOCCER
SOFTER
SOLDER
SOLVER
SOMBER
SOMMER
SOONER
SORTER
SOURER
SOUTER
SPACER
SPADER
SPARER
SPIDER
SPIKER
SPRIER
SPRYER
STAGER
STALER
STARER
STATER
STATOR
STELAR
STEWER
STIVER
STOKER
STONER
STORER
STOVER
STUMER
STUPOR
STYLER
SUAVER
SUBPAR
SUCCOR
SUCKER
SUFFER
SUITOR
SULFUR
SULKER
SUMMER
SUMNER
SUMTER
SUNDER
SUPPER
SURFER
SUTLER
SUTTER
SWAYER
SWIPER

•SR•••
ISRAEL

•S•R••
ASHRAM
ASTRAL
ASTRAY
ASTRID
ASTROS
ESCROW
ESDRAS
ESPRIT
ESTRAY
ISTRIA
OSIRIS
OSPREY
TSURIS
USERID
USURER
USURPS

•S••R•
ASBURY
ASGARD
ASHARP
ASHORE
ASKARI
ASKERS
ASMARA
ASPERA
ASPIRE
ASSERT
ASSORT
ASSURE
ASTERN
ASTERS
ASWIRL
BSHARP
CSHARP
DSHARP
ESCARP
ESCORT
ESHARP
ESKERS
ESTERS
FSHARP
GSHARP
OSBORN
OSCARS
OSIERS
TSHIRT
USHERS

•S•••R
ASEVER
ASHIER
ASHLAR
ASKFOR
ESCHER
ESTHER
ISADOR
ISHTAR
ISOBAR
ISOMER
ISSUER
OSTLER
PSYWAR
USURER

••S•R•
ABSORB
ABSURD
ADSORB
ANSARA
ASSERT
ASSORT
ASSURE
AUSTRO
BISTRO
CASERN
CASTRO
CESARE
DESCRY
DESERT
DESIRE
DESTRY
DISARM
DOSERS
ENSURE
EXSERT
GASTRO
HASBRO
INSERT
INSURE
LASERS
LOSERS
LUSTRE
MASERS
MASERU
MESSRS
MISERS
MISERY
MUSERS
MYSORE
PASTRY
POSERS
RASERS
RESORB
RESORT
RISERS
ROSARY
ROSTRA
SISERA
SISTRA
TASERS
TISHRI
UNSURE
VESTRY
VISORS

••S••R
ANSGAR
ANSWER
BASTER
BESSER
BESTIR
BUSBAR
BUSIER
BUSTER
CASPAR
CASPER
CASTER
CASTOR
COSIER
COSTAR
CUSTER
DASHER
DISBAR
DOSSER
DUSTER
EASIER
EASTER
EISNER
FASTER
FESTER
FISHER
FOSTER
GASPAR
GASPER
GASSER
GUSHER
HESTER
HISSER
HOSIER
HUSKER
HUSSAR
INSTAR
ISSUER
JASPER
JESTER
JOSSER
JUSTER
KISSER
KOSHER
LASCAR
LASHER
LASSER
LESSER
LESSOR
LESTER
LISTER
LUSHER
LUSTER
MASHER
MASKER
MASTER
MESMER
MISTER
MOSHER
MUSHER
MUSTER
NASCAR
NASSER
NESTER
NESTOR
NOSHER
NOSIER
OUSTER
OYSTER
PASSER
PASTOR
PESTER
POSEUR
POSHER
POSTER
RASHER
RASPER
RASTER
RESTER
RISKER
ROSIER
ROSTER
SASSER
SISLER
SISTER
TASTER
TESTER
TOSSER
TUSKER
ULSTER
VASSAR
VASTER
VESPER
WASHER
WASTER
WISHER
WISTER
XYSTER
YASSER
YESSIR
YESTER

•••SR•
MESSRS

•••S•R
ABUSER
BESSER
BIGSUR
BOWSER
BURSAR
CAESAR
CENSER
CENSOR
CHASER
CLOSER
CURSOR
DENSER
DOSSER
DOWSER
ERASER
FALSER
FRASER
GASSER
GEYSER
GLASER
HAWSER
HISSER
HUSSAR
JOSSER
KAISER
KISSER
LASSER
LEASER
LESSER
LESSOR
LOOSER
MAUSER
MOUSER
NASSER
NURSER
PARSER
PASSER
PHASER
PROSER
PULSAR
PURSER
QUASAR
RAISER
ROUSER
SASSER
SENSOR
TEASER
TENSER
TENSOR
TERSER
TOSSER
VASSAR
WINSOR
WOWSER
YASSER
YESSIR

S•S•••
SASEBO
SASHAY
SASHED
SASHES
SASSED
SASSER
SASSES
SESAME
SESQUI
SESTET
SESTOS
SISALS
SISERA
SISKEL
SISKIN
SISLER
SISLEY
SISTER
SISTRA
SOSOON
SUSANN
SUSIEQ
SUSLIK
SUSSED
SUSSES
SUSSEX
SYSOPS
SYSTEM

S••S••
SALSAS
SAMSON
SANSEI
SASSED
SASSER
SASSES
SAYSOS
SEASON
SEESAW
SEESIN
SEESTO
SEISMO
SEISMS
SENSED
SENSEI
SENSES
SENSOR
SETSAT
SETSBY
SETSIN
SETSON
SETSUP
SEWSON
SEWSUP
SHASTA
SIESTA
SITSBY
SITSIN
SITSON
SITSUP
SLOSHY
SLUSHY
SOASTO
SOPSUP
SOUSED
SOUSES
SPASMS
STASES
STASIS
SUBSET
SUDSED
SUDSES
SUISSE
SUMSUP
SUNSET
SUSSED
SUSSES
SUSSEX

S•••S•
SAFEST
SAGEST
SALISH
SAMOSA
SANEST
SCHISM
SCHIST
SCHUSS
SCOUSE
SEROSA
SETOSE
SEXIST
SHIEST
SHIISM
SHYEST
SINISE
SIWASH
SLIEST
SLIMSY
SLYEST
SMERSH
SOREST
SPARSE
SPLASH
SPLOSH
SPOUSE
SQUASH
SQUISH
SQUUSH
STRASS
STRESS
SUFISM
SUISSE
SUREST
SWOOSH

S••••S
SABERS
SABINS
SABLES
SABOTS
SABRAS
SABRES
SADHES
SADHUS
SAHIBS
SAIGAS
SAINTS
SAKERS
SALADS
SALALS
SALONS
SALSAS
SALVES
SALVOS
SAMBAS
SANTOS
SAPORS
SARANS
SARDIS
SARGES
SARGOS
SARODS
SASHES
SASSES
SATINS
SATYRS
SAUCES
SAUDIS
SAULTS
SAUNAS
SAUTES
SAVERS
SAVORS
SAXONS
SAYERS
SAYLES
SAYSOS
SAYYES
SCALDS
SCALES
SCALPS
SCAMPS
SCANTS
SCAPES
SCARES
SCARFS
SCARPS
SCAUPS
SCENAS
SCENDS
SCENES
SCENTS
SCHMOS
SCHUSS
SCHWAS
SCIFIS
SCIONS
SCOFFS
SCOLDS
SCONES
SCOOPS
SCOOTS
SCOPES
SCORES
SCORNS
SCOURS
SCOUTS
SCOWLS
SCRAGS
SCRAMS
SCRAPS
SCREES
SCREWS
SCRIMS
SCRIPS
SCRODS
SCRUBS
SCRUMS
SCUBAS
SCUFFS
SCULLS
SCUTES
SEAMUS
SEDANS
SEDERS
SEDGES
SEDUMS
SEGUES
SEINES
SEISMS
SEIZES
SELVES
SENNAS
SENORS
SENSES
SEPALS
SEPIAS
SEPOYS
SERACS
SERAIS
SERGES
SERIES
SERIFS
SERINS
SEROUS
SEROWS
SERUMS
SERVES
SERVOS
SESTOS
SETINS
SETTOS
SETUPS
SEVENS
SEVERS
SEVRES
SEWERS
SHACKS
SHADES
SHAFTS
SHAKES
SHAKOS
SHALES
SHAMES
SHAMUS
SHANKS
SHAPES
SHARDS
SHARES
SHARKS
SHARPS
SHAVES
SHAWLS
SHAWMS
SHEAFS
SHEARS
SHEENS
SHEEPS
SHEERS
SHEETS
SHEIKS
SHELLS
SHIFTS
SHILLS
SHINES
SHIRES
SHIRKS
SHIRRS
SHIRTS
SHOALS
SHOATS
SHOCKS
SHOERS
SHOJIS
SHOOKS
SHOOTS
SHORES
SHORTS
SHOUTS
SHOVES
SHREDS
SHREWS

SHRUBS	SLUMPS	SPADES	STALKS	STROPS	ASSERT	OSAGES	HASSAM	POSSES	BISONS
SHRUGS	SLURPS	SPAHIS	STALLS	STRUMS	ASSESS	OSCARS	HASSAN	POSSET	BOSONS
SHUCKS	SLYPES	SPALLS	STAMPS	STRUTS	ASSETS	OSIERS	HASSLE	POSSLQ	BOSSES
SHUNTS	SMACKS	SPANKS	STANDS	STUFFS	ASSIGN	OSIRIS	HISSAT	POSSUM	BOSUNS
SIBYLS	SMALLS	SPARES	STAPES	STULLS	ASSISI	OSMICS	HISSED	PUSSES	BUSHES
SIDERS	SMARTS	SPARKS	STARES	STUMPS	ASSIST	PSALMS	HISSER	RASSLE	BUSIES
SIDLES	SMEARS	SPASMS	STARTS	STUNTS	ASSIZE	PSEUDS	HISSES	RUSSET	BUSSES
SIEGES	SMELLS	SPATES	STASES	STUPAS	ASSORT	PSYCHS	HUSSAR	RUSSIA	BYSSUS
SIEVES	SMELTS	SPAWNS	STASIS	STUPES	ASSUME	TSURIS	HUSSEY	SASSED	CASALS
SIGHTS	SMILES	SPEAKS	STATES	STYLES	ASSURE	USAGES	HYSSOP	SASSER	CASHES
SIGILS	SMIRKS	SPEARS	STATUS	STYLUS	ESSAYS	USHERS	IJSSEL	SASSES	CASSIS
SIGMAS	SMITES	SPECKS	STAVES	SUCCES	ESSENE	USUALS	JESSEL	SUSSED	CASTES
SILVAS	SMITHS	SPEEDS	STEADS	SUCHAS	ISSUED	USURPS	JESSIE	SUSSES	CESSES
SINEWS	SMOCKS	SPELLS	STEAKS	SUCKAS	ISSUER	VSIGNS	JOSSER	SUSSEX	CESTAS
SINGES	SMOKES	SPENDS	STEALS	SUDRAS	ISSUES	VSIXES	JOSSES	TASSEL	CESTOS
SIRENS	SMOLTS	SPICAS	STEAMS	SUDSES	OSSEIN		KISSED	TASSES	CESTUS
SIRIUS	SMURFS	SPICES	STEEDS	SUEDES	OSSETE	••SS••	KISSER	TESSIE	CISCOS
SISALS	SNACKS	SPIELS	STEELS	SUGARS	OSSIAN	AUSSIE	KISSES	TISSUE	COSHES
SITARS	SNAFUS	SPIERS	STEEPS	SUITES	OSSIFY	BASSES	LASSEN	TOSSED	COSIES
SITINS	SNAILS	SPIFFS	STEERS	SULCUS		BASSET	LASSER	TOSSER	COSMOS
SITUPS	SNAKES	SPIKES	STEINS	SUMACS	•S•S••	BASSLY	LASSES	TOSSES	COSTAS
SIXERS	SNARES	SPILES	STELES	SUMMAS	ASKSIN	BASSOS	LASSIE	TOSSUP	CUSSES
SIXTHS	SNARLS	SPILLS	STENOS	SUMUPS	ASOSAN	BESSER	LASSOS	TUSSAH	CUSTIS
SIXTUS	SNATHS	SPINES	STERES	SUNNIS	USESUP	BESSIE	LESSEE	TUSSLE	CUSTOS
SIZERS	SNEAKS	SPINKS	STERNS	SUNUPS		BISSAU	LESSEN	VASSAL	DASHES
SKALDS	SNEERS	SPIRES	STICKS	SUPERS	•S••S•	BISSET	LESSER	VASSAR	DASHIS
SKANKS	SNELLS	SPIROS	STIFFS	SURAHS	ASPISH	BOSSED	LESSON	VESSEL	DISCOS
SKATES	SNICKS	SPITES	STILES	SURGES	ASSESS	BOSSES	LESSOR	WESSEX	DISCUS
SKEANS	SNIFFS	SPLATS	STILLS	SUSSES	ASSISI	BUSSED	LOSSES	WESSON	DISHES
SKEINS	SNIPES	SPLAYS	STILTS	SUTRAS	ASSIST	BUSSES	MASSED	WUSSES	DISMES
SKIERS	SNOODS	SPLITS	STINGS	SWAGES	ESPOSA	BYSSHE	MASSES	YASSER	DOSERS
SKIFFS	SNOOKS	SPOILS	STINKS	SWAINS	ESPOSO	BYSSUS	MASSEY	YESSED	DOSSES
SKILLS	SNOOPS	SPOKES	STINTS	SWALES	OSMOSE	CASSIA	MASSIF	YESSES	EASELS
SKIMPS	SNOOTS	SPOOFS	STIPES	SWAMIS	TSETSE	CASSIO	MESSED	YESSIR	EDSELS
SKINKS	SNOPES	SPOOKS	STIRKS	SWAMPS	ZSAZSA	CASSIS	MESSES		ENSUES
SKIRLS	SNORES	SPOOLS	STOATS	SWANKS		CESSED	MESSRS	••S•S•	EOSINS
SKIROS	SNORTS	SPOONS	STOCKS	SWARDS	•S•••S	CESSES	MESSUP	ASSESS	ESSAYS
SKIRRS	SNOUTS	SPOORS	STOICS	SWARMS	ASANAS	CESSNA	MISSAL	ASSISI	FASCES
SKIRTS	SNUFFS	SPORES	STOKES	SWATHS	ASCOTS	COSSET	MISSAY	ASSIST	FESSES
SKIVES	SOARES	SPORTS	STOLES	SWAZIS	ASDICS	CUSSED	MISSED	BASEST	FESTAS
SKOALS	SOAVES	SPOUTS	STOMAS	SWEARS	ASIANS	CUSSES	MISSES	DESIST	FESTUS
SKORTS	SOBERS	SPRAGS	STOMPS	SWEATS	ASIDES	DASSIN	MISSIS	DISUSE	FISHES
SKULKS	SOCLES	SPRATS	STONES	SWEDES	ASKERS	DISSED	MISSUS	INSIST	FOSSAS
SKULLS	SOEURS	SPRAYS	STOOKS	SWEEPS	ASPENS	DOSSAL	MOSSED	MISUSE	FOSSES
SKUNKS	SOLANS	SPREES	STOOLS	SWEETS	ASPICS	DOSSED	MOSSES	OBSESS	FUSEES
SLACKS	SOLARS	SPRIGS	STOOPS	SWELLS	ASSAYS	DOSSEL	MUSSED	RESIST	FUSILS
SLAKES	SOLERS	SPRITS	STOPES	SWIFTS	ASSESS	DOSSER	MUSSEL	WISEST	FUSSES
SLANGS	SOLEUS	SPRUES	STORES	SWILLS	ASSETS	DOSSES	MUSSES		GASHES
SLANTS	SOLFAS	SPUMES	STORKS	SWINGS	ASTERS	FESSED	MUSSUP	••S••S	GASSES
SLATES	SOLIDS	SPURNS	STORMS	SWIPES	ASTROS	FESSES	NASSAU	AISLES	GESTES
SLAVES	SOLVES	SPURTS	STORRS	SWIRLS	BSIDES	FESSUP	NASSER	ARSONS	GUSHES
SLEEKS	SOMERS	SQUABS	STOUPS	SWOONS	CSPOTS	FOSSAE	NESSES	ASSAYS	HASHES
SLEEPS	SONDES	SQUADS	STOUTS	SWOOPS	ESDRAS	FOSSAS	NESSIE	ASSESS	HASTES
SLEETS	SONICS	SQUATS	STOVES	SWORDS	ESKERS	FOSSES	NISSAN	ASSETS	HISSES
SLICES	SOPORS	SQUIBS	STRADS	SYLPHS	ESPIES	FOSSEY	NISSEN	BASHES	HOSELS
SLICKS	SOTOLS	SQUIDS	STRAPS	SYNODS	ESSAYS	FOSSIL	PASSBY	BASICS	HOSTAS
SLIDES	SOUGHS	STACKS	STRASS	SYRUPS	ESTERS	FUSSED	PASSED	BASINS	HUSHES
SLIMES	SOUNDS	STAFFS	STRAUS	SYSOPS	ESTOPS	FUSSES	PASSEL	BASSES	INSETS
SLINGS	SOUSES	STAGES	STRAWS		FSTOPS	GASSED	PASSER	BASSOS	ISSUES
SLINKS	SOUTHS	STAINS	STRAYS	•SS•••	GSUITS	GASSER	PASSES	BASTES	JASEYS
SLOOPS	SOWERS	STAIRS	STRESS	ASSAIL	ISLETS	GASSES	PASSIM	BESETS	JOSHES
SLOPES	SOXERS	STAKES	STREWS	ASSAYS	ISSUES	GOSSIP	PASSON	BESOMS	JOSSES
SLOTHS	SPACES	STALES	STRIPS	ASSENT	ISTLES	GUSSET	PASSUP	BESOTS	KISSES

LASERS
LASHES
LASSES
LASSOS
LESBOS
LISLES
LOSERS
LOSSES
LYSINS
MASAIS
MASERS
MASHES
MASONS
MASSES
MESHES
MESONS
MESSES
MESSRS
MISERS
MISSES
MISSIS
MISSUS
MOSEYS
MOSHES
MOSSES
MUSERS
MUSHES
MUSSES
NASALS
NESSES
NOSHES
OBSESS
ONSETS
OUSELS
PASEOS
PASHAS
PASSES
PASTAS
PASTES
PASTIS
PESTOS
PISANS
PISCES
PISTES
POSERS
POSIES
POSITS
POSSES
PUSHES
PUSSES
RASERS
RASHES
RESAWS
RESEES
RESETS
RESEWS
RESHES
RESINS
RESODS
RISERS
ROSINS
RUSHES
SASHES
SASSES
SESTOS
SISALS
SUSSES
SYSOPS
TASERS
TASSES
TASTES
TESLAS
TOSSES
TVSETS
UNSAYS
UNSEWS
UPSETS
URSIDS
VESTAS
VISITS
VISORS
VISTAS
VOSGES
WASHES
WASTES
WISHES
WUSSES
YESSES

•••SS•

ABESSE
AGASSI
ALYSSA
BRASSY
CHASSE
CLASSY
CROSSE
CUISSE
DRESSY
EDESSA
ELISSA
FLOSSY
GLASSY
GLOSSA
GLOSSO
GLOSSY
GRASSO
GRASSY
GROSSE
GROSSO
INESSE
MOUSSE
NEISSE
NYASSA
ODESSA
ORISSA
PLISSE
POUSSE
PRISSY
SUISSE
WRASSE

•••S•S

ABASES
ABUSES
ABYSMS
ACTSAS
AMUSES
ARISES
ATESTS
AVISOS
BASSES
BASSOS
BEASTS
BIASES
BLASTS
BOASTS
BOOSTS
BOSSES
BOUSES
BURSAS
BURSES
BURSTS
BUSSES
BYSSUS
CASSIS
CAUSES
CEASES
CENSES
CENSUS
CESSES
CHASES
CHASMS
CHESTS
CLASPS
CLOSES
COASTS
COPSES
CRESTS
CRISES
CRISIS
CRISPS
CRUSES
CRUSTS
CURSES
CUSSES
DAISES
DEISTS
DIESES
DIESIS
DOSSES
DOUSES
DOWSES
ECESIS
EGESTS
ENOSIS
ERASES
EXISTS
FEASTS
FESSES
FIRSTS
FLASKS
FOISTS
FOSSAS
FOSSES
FRISES
FRISKS
FROSTS
FUSSES
GASSES
GHOSTS
GNOSIS
GOOSES
GORSES
GRASPS
GRISTS
GUESTS
GUISES
HAUSAS
HAWSES
HEISTS
HISSES
HOISTS
HORSES
HOUSES
HYKSOS
IBISES
IRISES
JOISTS
JOSSES
JOUSTS
KANSAS
KARSTS
KIOSKS
KISSES
LAPSES
LASSES
LASSOS
LEASES
LENSES
LOOSES
LOSSES
LOUSES
MANSES
MASSES
MENSAS
MESSES
MESSRS
MIOSIS
MISSES
MISSIS
MISSUS
MOSSES
MOUSES
MUSSES
MYOSIS
NESSES
NOESIS
NOISES
NOOSES
NURSES
ODISTS
ONUSES
OPUSES
PAISAS
PARSES
PASSES
PAUSES
PHASES
PLUSES
POISES
POSSES
PRASES
PRISMS
PROSES
PULSES
PURSES
PUSSES
QUESTS
RAISES
RAMSES
REESES
REUSES
RHESUS
RINSES
ROASTS
ROOSTS
ROUSES
ROUSTS
SALSAS
SASSES
SAYSOS
SEISMS
SENSES
SOUSES
SPASMS
STASES
STASIS
SUDSES
SUSSES
TARSUS
TASSES
TEASES
TENSES
THESES
THESIS
TMESIS
TOASTS
TORSOS
TOSSES
TRUSTS
TRYSTS
TWISTS
UKASES
UNISYS
UPASES
URUSES
VERSES
VERSOS
VERSTS
VERSUS
WAISTS
WHISKS
WORSTS
WRESTS
WRISTS
WURSTS
WUSSES
XHOSAS
YEASTS
YESSES

••••SS

ABBESS
ACCESS
ACROSS
ADMASS
ARLISS
ARNESS
ASSESS
BYPASS
CARESS
DURESS
EGRESS
EMBOSS
EXCESS
GNEISS
HARASS
INNESS
KAROSS
KUMISS
MORASS
NOLESS
OBSESS
OGRESS
RECESS
REMISS
SCHUSS
STRASS
STRESS
UNLESS

ST••••

STABAT
STABLE
STABLY
STACEY
STACKS
STACTE
STADIA
STAFFS
STAGED
STAGER
STAGES
STAINS
STAIRS
STAKED
STAKES
STALAG
STALED
STALER
STALES
STALIN
STALKS
STALKY
STALLS
STAMEN
STAMPS
STANCE
STANCH
STANDS
STANKY
STANZA
STAPES
STAPLE
STAPUF
STARCH
STARED
STARER
STARES
STARRY
STARTS
STARVE
STASES
STASIS
STATED
STATEN
STATER
STATES
STATIC
STATOR
STATUE
STATUS
STAVED
STAVES
STAYED
STAYON
STAYUP
STEADS
STEADY
STEAKS
STEALS
STEAMS
STEAMY
STEEDS
STEELE
STEELS
STEELY
STEEPS
STEERS
STEEVE
STEFAN
STEFFI
STEFOY
STEINS
STELAE
STELAR
STELES
STELLA
STELMO
STENCH
STENOG
STENOS
STEPIN
STEPON
STEPPE
STEPUP
STEREO
STERES
STERNA
STERNE
STERNO
STERNS
STEROL
STEVEN
STEVIE
STEWED
STEWER
STHENO
STICKS
STICKY
STIFFS
STIFLE
STIGMA
STILES
STILLS
STILLY
STILTS
STIMPY
STINGO
STINGS
STINGY
STINKS
STINKY
STINTS
STIPEL
STIPES
STIRIN
STIRKS
STIRUP
STITCH
STITHY
STIVER
STIVIC
STJOAN
STJOHN
STLUKE
STMALO
STMARK
STOATS
STOCKS
STOCKY
STODGE
STODGY
STOGIE
STOICS
STOJKO
STOKED
STOKER
STOKES
STOLEN
STOLES
STOLID
STOLLE
STOLON
STOMAS
STOMAT
STOMPS
STONED
STONER
STONES
STOOGE
STOOKS
STOOLS
STOOLY
STOOPS
STOPES
STOPIN
STOPIT
STOPUP
STORCH
STORED
STORER
STORES
STOREY
STORKS
STORMS
STORMY
STORRS
STOTIN
STOUPS
STOUTS
STOVER
STOVES
STOWED
STPAUL
STPETE
STRABO
STRADS
STRAFE
STRAIN
STRAIT
STRAKE
STRAND
STRAPS
STRASS
STRATA
STRATI
STRATO
STRAUB
STRAUS
STRAWS
STRAWY
STRAYS
STREAK
STREAM
STREEP
STREET
STRESS
STREWN
STREWS
STRIAE
STRICK
STRICT
STRIDE
STRIFE
STRIKE
STRINE
STRING
STRIPE
STRIPS
STRIPY
STRIVE
STROBE
STRODE
STROKE
STROLL
STRONG
STROPS
STROUD
STROVE
STRUCK
STRUMS
STRUNG
STRUTS
STUART
STUBBY
STUCCO
STUDIO
STUFFS
STUFFY
STULLS
STUMER
STUMPS
STUMPY
STUNTS
STUNTY
STUPAS
STUPES
STUPID
STUPOR
STURDY
STYLED
STYLER
STYLES
STYLET
STYLUS
STYMIE
STYRIA
STYRON

S•T•••

SATANG
SATEEN
SATING
SATINS
SATINY
SATIRE
SATORI
SATOUT
SATRAP
SATURN
SATYRS
SETINS
SETOFF
SETOSE
SETOUT
SETSAT
SETSBY
SETSIN
SETSON
SETSUP
SETTEE
SETTER
SETTLE
SETTOS
SETUPS
SGTMAJ
SHTETL
SHTICK
SITARS
SITCOM
SITING
SITINS
SITOUT
SITSBY
SITSIN
SITSON
SITSUP
SITTER

SITUPS
SOTHAT
SOTOLS
SOTTED
SUTLER
SUTRAS
SUTTER
SUTTON
SUTURE

S••T••

SALTED
SALTEN
SALTER
SALTON
SALTUM
SANTEE
SANTIR
SANTOS
SARTON
SARTRE
SAUTES
SCATHE
SCATTY
SCOTCH
SCOTER
SCOTIA
SCOTTO
SCOTTY
SCUTCH
SCUTES
SCYTHE
SEATED
SEATER
SEATON
SECTOR
SEETHE
SENTIN
SENTRA
SENTRY
SENTUP
SEPTAL
SEPTET
SEPTIC
SEPTUM
SESTET
SESTOS
SETTEE
SETTER
SETTLE
SETTOS
SEXTET
SEXTON
SHOTAT
SHOTUP
SHUTIN
SHUTUP
SIFTED
SIFTER
SILTED
SINTAX
SINTER
SISTER
SISTRA
SITTER
SIXTHS
SIXTUS
SKATED
SKATER
SKATES
SKETCH
SKITCH
SKITOW
SLATED
SLATER
SLATES
SLITHY
SLITTY
SLOTHS
SMITES
SMITHS
SMITHY
SMUTCH
SMUTTY
SNATCH
SNATHE
SNATHS
SNITCH
SNOTTY
SOFTEN
SOFTER
SOFTIE
SOFTLY
SONTAG
SOOTHE
SORTED
SORTER
SORTIE
SORTOF
SOTTED
SOUTER
SOUTHS
SPATES
SPATHE
SPITED
SPITES
SPOTTY
STATED
STATEN
STATER
STATES
STATIC
STATOR
STATUE
STATUS
STITCH
STITHY
STOTIN
SUBTLE
SUBTLY
SUITED
SUITES
SUITOR
SUITUP
SULTAN
SULTRY
SUMTER
SUNTAN
SURTAX
SUTTER
SUTTON
SWATCH
SWATHE
SWATHS
SWITCH
SYNTAX
SYSTEM

S•••T•

SABATO
SABOTS
SAFETY
SAINTE
SAINTS
SALUTE
SAMITE
SANCTA
SANGTO
SANITY
SAULTS
SAVATE
SCANTS
SCANTY
SCATTY
SCENTS
SCOOTS
SCOTTO
SCOTTY
SCOUTS
SEDATE
SEENTO
SEESTO
SEMITE
SENATE
SENITI
SHAFTS
SHAKTI
SHANTY
SHASTA
SHEATH
SHEETS
SHELTY
SHIFTS
SHIFTY
SHIITE
SHINTO
SHIRTS
SHIRTY
SHOATS
SHOOTS
SHORTA
SHORTE
SHORTI
SHORTO
SHORTS
SHORTU
SHORTY
SHOUTS
SHTETL
SHUNTS
SIESTA
SIGHTS
SINGTO
SKIRTS
SKORTS
SLANTS
SLEETS
SLEETY
SLEUTH
SLITTY
SMALTI
SMALTO
SMARTS
SMARTY
SMELTS
SMOLTS
SMOOTH
SMUTTY
SNAPTO
SNOOTS
SNOOTY
SNORTS
SNOTTY
SNOUTS
SOASTO
SOLUTE
SOMATA
SOMATO
SONATA
SOWETO
SPARTA
SPILTH
SPINTO
SPLATS
SPLITS
SPORTS
SPORTY
SPOTTY
SPOUTS
SPRATS
SPRITE
SPRITS
SPRITZ
SPURTS
SQUATS
STACTE
STARTS
STILTS
STINTS
STOATS
STOUTS
STPETE
STRATA
STRATI
STRATO
STRUTS
STUNTS
STUNTY
SUBITO
SURETE
SURETY
SVELTE
SWARTH
SWEATS
SWEATY
SWEETS
SWIFTS

S••••T

SACHET
SAFEST
SAGEST
SALLET
SALYUT
SAMLET
SANEST
SATOUT
SAVANT
SAWFIT
SAWOUT
SCHIST
SCRIPT
SCULPT
SECANT
SECRET
SEEFIT
SEEOUT
SEJANT
SELECT
SENNET
SENNIT
SEPTET
SESTET
SETOUT
SETSAT
SEURAT
SEXIST
SEXTET
SHEVAT
SHIEST
SHOTAT
SHRIFT
SHYEST
SIGNET
SILENT
SIPPET
SITOUT
SKIPIT
SLIEST
SLIGHT
SLYEST
SNAPAT
SNOCAT
SOBEIT
SOCKET
SOFFIT
SOLENT
SONANT
SONNET
SORBET
SOREST
SOTHAT
SOUGHT
SOVIET
SOWHAT
SPIGOT
SPINET
SPIRIT
SPLINT
SPOILT
SPRINT
SPROUT
SQUINT
SQUIRT
STABAT
STOMAT
STOPIT
STRAIT
STREET
STRICT
STUART
STYLET
SUBLET
SUBMIT
SUBSET
SUMMIT
SUNLIT
SUNSET
SUREST
SWIVET

•ST•••

ASTERN
ASTERS
ASTRAL
ASTRAY
ASTRID
ASTROS
ASTUTE
ESTATE
ESTEEM
ESTERS
ESTHER
ESTOPS
ESTRAY
FSTOPS
GSTAAD
ISTHMI
ISTLES
ISTRIA
OSTEAL
OSTEND
OSTIUM
OSTLER

•S•T••

ISHTAR
TSETSE

•S••T•

ASCOTS
ASEITY
ASSETS
ASTUTE
CSPOTS
ESTATE
GSUITS
ISLETS
OSSETE
USEDTO

•S•••T

ASCENT
ASKOUT
ASLANT
ASPECT
ASSENT
ASSERT
ASSIST
ASSORT
ESCENT
ESCORT
ESPRIT
ISEULT
TSHIRT
USENET

••ST••

AMSTEL
ATSTUD
AUSTEN
AUSTIN
AUSTRO
BASTED
BASTER
BASTES
BESTED
BESTIR
BESTOW
BISTRO
BOSTON
BUSTED
BUSTER
BUSTIN
BUSTLE
CASTER
CASTES
CASTLE
CASTON
CASTOR
CASTRO
CESTAS
CESTOS
CESTUS
COSTAE
COSTAL
COSTAR
COSTAS
COSTLY
CUSTER
CUSTIS
CUSTOM
CUSTOS
DESTRY
DISTAL
DISTIL
DUSTED
DUSTER
DUSTIN
DUSTUP
EASTER
EASTON
FASTED
FASTEN
FASTER
FESTAL
FESTAS
FESTER
FESTUS
FISTED
FISTIC
FOSTER
FUSTIC
GASTON
GASTRO
GESTES
GESTIC
GOSTAG
GUSTAV
GUSTED
HASTEN
HASTES
HESTER
HESTIA
HESTON
HOSTAS
HOSTED
HOSTEL
HOSTLY
HUSTLE
HUSTON
INSTAL
INSTAR
INSTEP
INSTIL
JESTED
JESTER
JOSTLE
JUSTER
JUSTIN
JUSTLY
LASTED
LASTEX
LASTLY
LESTAT
LESTER
LISTED
LISTEE
LISTEL
LISTEN
LISTER
LISTON
LOSTIT
LUSTED
LUSTER
LUSTRE
MASTER
MASTIC
MISTED
MISTER
MOSTEL
MOSTLY
MUSTER
MUSTNT
MYSTIC
NESTEA
NESTED
NESTER
NESTLE
NESTOR
OBSTET
OUSTED
OUSTER
OYSTER
PASTAS
PASTED
PASTEL
PASTES
PASTIS
PASTOR
PASTRY
PESTER
PESTLE
PESTOS
PISTES
PISTIL
PISTOL
PISTON
POSTAL
POSTED
POSTER
POSTIT
POSTON
RASTER
RESTED
RESTER
RESTON
RESTUP
ROSTER
ROSTOV
ROSTRA
RUSTED
RUSTIC
RUSTLE
SESTET
SESTOS
SISTER
SISTRA
SYSTEM
TASTED
TASTER
TASTES
TESTAE
TESTED
TESTEE
TESTER
ULSTER
UNSTOP
VASTER
VASTLY
VESTAL
VESTAS
VESTED
VESTEE
VESTRY
VISTAS
VOSTOK
WASTED
WASTER
WASTES
WISTER
WYSTAN
XYSTER
YESTER
ZESTED

••S•T•

ANSATE
ASSETS
BESETS
BESOTS
DESOTO
ERSATZ
INSETS
INSITU
ONSETS
ONSITE
OSSETE
PASHTO
PESETA
POSITS
RESETS
ROSITA
TVSETS
UPSETS
VASHTI
VISITS
WISETO

••S••T

ABSENT
ASSENT
ASSERT
ASSIST
ASSORT
BASALT
BASEST
BASKET
BASSET
BESANT
BISECT
BISSET
BOSKET
COSSET
DESALT
DESERT
DESIST
DESPOT
DISANT
EXSERT
GASJET
GASKET
GASLIT
GOSOFT
GUSSET
HISSAT
INSECT
INSERT
INSIST
INSULT

JESUIT
KISMET
LESTAT
LOSEIT
LOSTIT
MASCOT
MISFIT
MISHIT
MUSCAT
MUSKET
MUSTNT
OBSTET
POSSET
POSTIT
RESALT
RESEAT
RESECT
RESENT
RESHOT
RESIST
RESORT
RESULT
RUSSET
SESTET
UNSEAT
UPSHOT
WESKIT
WISENT
WISEST

•••ST•

ADDSTO
ADESTE
AIMSTO
ARISTA
ARISTO
ATESTS
AVESTA
BEASTS
BLASTS
BOASTS
BOOSTS
BURSTS
CHASTE
CHESTS
CHESTY
COASTS
CRESTS
CRISTO
CRUSTS
CRUSTY
CUESTA
DEISTS
EGESTA
EGESTS
ERESTU
EXISTS
FEASTS
FEISTY
FIESTA
FIRSTS
FOISTS
FROSTS
FROSTY
GETSTO
GHOSTS
GRISTS
GUESTS
HEISTS
HOISTS
JOISTS
JOUSTS
KARSTS
LAYSTO
LIESTO
ODISTS
PIGSTY
PLASTY
PRESTO
PUTSTO
QUESTS
ROASTS
ROOSTS
ROUSTS
RUNSTO
SEESTO
SHASTA
SIESTA
SOASTO
TIESTO
TOASTS
TOASTY
TRISTE
TRUSTS
TRUSTY
TRYSTS
TWISTS
TWISTY
VERSTS
WAISTS
WORSTS
WRESTS
WRISTS
WURSTS
YEASTS
YEASTY

•••S•T

AIMSAT
ALLSET
BAGSIT
BASSET
BISSET
BOXSET
CLOSET
COMSAT
CORSET
COSSET
DOESNT
DOGSAT
DOGSIT
DORSET
EATSAT
GETSAT
GETSET
GETSIT
GOESAT
GOTSET
GUSSET
HISSAT
HITSIT
JETSET
LETSAT
NIPSAT
OFFSET
OUTSET
PAWSAT
POSSET
PRESET
PROSIT
RUNSAT
RUSSET
SETSAT
SUBSET
SUNSET
TEASET
TILSIT

••••ST

ABLEST
ACCOST
ADJUST
AGEIST
AGHAST
ALEAST
ALMOST
ALWEST
AMIDST
AORIST
APTEST
ARREST
ARTIST
ASSIST
ATBEST
ATCOST
ATLAST
ATMOST
ATREST
ATTEST
AUGUST
BAREST
BASEST
BEHEST
BLUEST
BREAST
BYPAST
COHOST
COYEST
CUBIST
CUTEST
DEGUST
DELIST
DESIST
DETEST
DEVEST
DIGEST
DIREST
DIVEST
DRIEST
DRYEST
DYNAST
EGOIST
ELDEST
ENLIST
ERNEST
EXPOST
FEWEST
FEYEST
FINEST
FOREST
FREEST
GAINST
GAMEST
GAYEST
GOBUST
GOWEST
HALEST
HEARST
HOLIST
HONEST
HUGEST
ICIEST
IDLEST
ILLEST
IMPOST
INFEST
INGEST
INJEST
INMOST
INSIST
INVEST
IQTEST
JURIST
KLEIST
LAMEST
LATEST
LAXEST
LEGIST
LOCUST
LOWEST
LUTIST
LYRIST
MAOIST
MARIST
MEREST
MODEST
MOLEST
MONIST
MUTEST
NEWEST
NICEST
NLEAST
NLWEST
NUDEST
NUDIST
OBLAST
OBOIST
OBTEST
ODDEST
OLDEST
PALEST
PRIEST
PROUST
PUREST
PURIST
RAREST
RAWEST
RECAST
RELIST
REPAST
REPOST
RESIST
RETEST
RIFEST
RIPEST
ROBUST
RUDEST
SAFEST
SAGEST
SANEST
SCHIST
SEXIST
SHIEST
SHYEST
SLIEST
SLYEST
SOREST
SUREST
TAMEST
TANIST
TAOIST
THEIST
THIRST
THRUST
TRUEST
TUBIST
TWEEST
TYPIST
UNJUST
UNREST
UPCAST
UPMOST
UTMOST
VILEST
WHILST
WIDEST
WISEST
WRIEST
WRYEST
YAREST

SU••••

SUAVER
SUBARU
SUBBED
SUBDEB
SUBDUE
SUBGUM
SUBITO
SUBLET
SUBMIT
SUBORN
SUBPAR
SUBSET
SUBTLE
SUBTLY
SUBURB
SUBWAY
SUCCES
SUCCOR
SUCHAS
SUCKAS
SUCKED
SUCKER
SUCKIN
SUDDEN
SUDRAS
SUDSED
SUDSES
SUEDES
SUFFER
SUFFIX
SUFISM
SUGARS
SUGARY
SUISSE
SUITED
SUITES
SUITOR
SUITUP
SUKKAH
SULCUS
SULFUR
SULKED
SULKER
SULLEN
SULTAN
SULTRY
SUMACS
SUMMAE
SUMMAS
SUMMED
SUMMER
SUMMIT
SUMMON
SUMNER
SUMSUP
SUMTER
SUMUPS
SUNDAE
SUNDAY
SUNDER
SUNDEW
SUNDOG
SUNDRY
SUNGOD
SUNKEN
SUNLIT
SUNNED
SUNNIS
SUNOCO
SUNRAY
SUNSET
SUNTAN
SUNUNU
SUNUPS
SUPERB
SUPERS
SUPINE
SUPPED
SUPPER
SUPPLE
SUPPLY
SURAHS
SURELY
SUREST
SURETE
SURETY
SURFED
SURFER
SURGED
SURGES
SURIMI
SURREY
SURTAX
SURVEY
SUSANN
SUSIEQ
SUSLIK
SUSSED
SUSSES
SUSSEX
SUTLER
SUTRAS
SUTTER
SUTTON
SUTURE
SUZUKI

S•U•••

SAUCED
SAUCER
SAUCES
SAUDIS
SAUGER
SAULTS
SAUNAS
SAUREL
SAUTES
SCUBAS
SCUFFS
SCULLS
SCULLY
SCULPT
SCUMMY
SCURFY
SCURRY
SCURVE
SCURVY
SCUTCH
SCUTES
SCUZZY
SEURAT
SHUCKS
SHUNTS
SHUTIN
SHUTUP
SKULKS
SKULLS
SKUNKS
SKUNKY
SLUDGE
SLUDGY
SLUGGO
SLUICE
SLUING
SLUMMY
SLUMPS
SLURPS
SLURRY
SLUSHY
SMUDGE
SMUDGY
SMUGLY
SMURFS
SMUTCH
SMUTTY
SNUBBY
SNUFFS
SNUFFY
SNUGLI
SNUGLY
SOUARI
SOUGHS
SOUGHT
SOUNDS
SOUPUP
SOURCE
SOURED
SOURER
SOURLY
SOUSED
SOUSES
SOUTER
SOUTHS
SPUMED
SPUMES
SPUNKY
SPURGE
SPURNS
SPURON
SPURRY
SPURTS
SQUABS
SQUADS
SQUALL
SQUARE
SQUASH
SQUATS
SQUAWK
SQUEAK
SQUEAL
SQUIBB
SQUIBS
SQUIDS
SQUILL
SQUINT
SQUIRE
SQUIRM
SQUIRT
SQUISH
SQUUSH
STUART
STUBBY
STUCCO
STUDIO
STUFFS
STUFFY
STULLS
STUMER
STUMPS
STUMPY
STUNTS
STUNTY
STUPAS
STUPES
STUPID
STUPOR
STURDY

S••U••

SALUKI
SALUTE
SAMUEL
SATURN
SCAUPS
SCHULZ
SCHUSS
SCOURS
SCOUSE
SCOUTS
SCRUBS
SCRUFF
SCRUMS
SECURE
SEDUCE
SEDUMS
SEGUED
SEGUES
SEGURA
SENUFO
SEQUEL
SEQUIN
SERUMS
SETUPS
SHOULD
SHOUTS
SHRUBS
SHRUGS
SHRUNK
SIGURD
SIOUAN
SITUPS
SLEUTH
SLOUCH
SLOUGH
SNOUTS
SOEURS
SOLUTE
SPOUSE
SPOUTS
SPRUCE
SPRUES
SPRUNG
SQUUSH
STLUKE
STOUPS
STOUTS
STRUCK
STRUMS
STRUNG
STRUTS
SUBURB
SUMUPS
SUNUNU
SUNUPS
SUTURE
SUZUKI
SYRUPS
SYRUPY

S•••U•

SACQUE
SACRUM
SADHUS
SALTUM
SALYUT
SANNUP
SATOUT
SAVEUP
SAVOUR
SAWOUT
SCARUM
SEALUP
SEAMUS
SEEOUT
SELJUK
SENDUP
SENTUP
SEPTUM
SEROUS
SESQUI
SETOUT
SETSUP
SEWNUP
SEWSUP
SHAMUS
SHOGUN
SHOTUP
SHOWUP
SHROUD
SHUTUP
SIDDUR
SIGNUP
SINFUL
SIRIUS
SITOUT
SITSUP
SIXGUN
SIXTUS
SIZEUP
SKIRUN
SLAPUP
SLIPUP
SLOWUP
SNAFUS
SNAPUP
SOAKUP
SOBFUL
SODIUM

SOLEUS
SOPSUP
SOUPUP
SOWBUG
SPEDUP
SPROUT
STAPUF
STATUE
STATUS
STAYUP
STEPUP
STIRUP
STOPUP
STPAUL
STRAUB
STRAUS
STROUD
STYLUS
SUBDUE
SUBGUM
SUITUP
SULCUS
SULFUR
SUMSUP

S••••U
SHORTU
SUBARU
SUNUNU

•SU•••
GSUITS
TSURIS
USUALS
USURER
USURPS

•S•U••
ASBURY
ASSUME
ASSURE
ASTUTE
ESCUDO
ISEULT
ISSUED
ISSUER
ISSUES
MSQUAD
OSCULA
OSMUND
PSEUDO
PSEUDS

•S••U•
ASKOUT
ASYLUM
OSMIUM
OSTIUM
USEDUP
USEFUL
USESUP

••SU••
ABSURD
ASSUME
ASSURE
BOSUNS
CASUAL
DISUSE
ENSUED
ENSUES
ENSURE
INSULT
INSURE
ISSUED
ISSUER
ISSUES
JESUIT
MISUSE
RESULT
RESUME
UNSUNG
UNSURE
URSULA
VISUAL

••S•U•
ATSTUD
BASQUE
BISQUE
BYSSUS
CASQUE
CESIUM
CESTUS
DISCUS
DUSTUP
EASEUP
ENSOUL
FESCUE
FESSUP
FESTUS
JOSHUA
KUSPUK
LASHUP
MASQUE
MESSUP
MISCUE
MISSUS
MOSQUE
MUSEUM
MUSSUP
NASHUA
PASSUP
POSEUR
POSSUM
PUSHUP
RESCUE
RESTUP
RISQUE
SESQUI
TISSUE
TOSSUP
WASHUP
WISEUP

••S••U
BISSAU
DESILU
INSITU
MASERU
NASSAU
RESEAU
ROSEAU
VISHNU

•••SU•
ACESUP
ACTSUP
ADDSUP
BIDSUP
BIGSUR
BOBSUP
BUYSUP
BYSSUS
CATSUP
CENSUS
CONSUL
CUTSUP
DAMSUP
DATSUN
DIGSUP
DIMSUM
DOESUP
DORSUM
EATSUP
ENDSUP
FESSUP
FOGSUP
GETSUP
GOESUP
GUMSUP
GYPSUM
HITSUP
HOPSUP
ICESUP
JAMSUP
KEYSUP
LAPSUP
LAYSUP
LETSUP
MESSUP
MISSUS
MOPSUP
MUSSUP
OMASUM
OWNSUP
PASSUP
PAYSUP
PEPSUP
POPSUP
POSSUM
PURSUE
PUTSUP
REVSUP
RHESUS
RIGSUP
RIPSUP
RUNSUP
SETSUP
SEWSUP
SITSUP
SOPSUP
SUMSUP
TAGSUP
TARSUS
TEESUP
TIESUP
TISSUE
TOSSUP
TOTSUP
USESUP
VERSUS
WADSUP
ZIPSUP

•••S•U
BISSAU
ERESTU
HONSHU
KYUSHU
NASSAU
WAUSAU

••••SU
HAVASU

SV••••
SVELTE

S•V•••
SAVAGE
SAVAII
SAVANT
SAVATE
SAVERS
SAVEUP
SAVING
SAVIOR
SAVOIE
SAVOIR
SAVORS
SAVORY
SAVOUR
SEVENS
SEVERE
SEVERN
SEVERS
SEVERY
SEVRES
SOVIET

S••V••
SALVED
SALVER
SALVES
SALVIA
SALVOR
SALVOS
SELVES
SERVAL
SERVED
SERVER
SERVES
SERVOS
SHAVED
SHAVEN
SHAVER
SHAVES
SHEVAT
SHIVER
SHOVED
SHOVEL
SHOVER
SHOVES
SIEVED
SIEVES
SILVAS
SILVER
SKIVED
SKIVER
SKIVES
SKIVVY
SLAVED
SLAVER
SLAVES
SLAVEY
SLAVIC
SLIVER
SLOVAK
SLOVEN
SLOVIK
SNIVEL
SOAVES
SOLVED
SOLVER
SOLVES
SPAVIN
SPIVAK
SPIVVY
STAVED
STAVES
STEVEN
STEVIE
STIVER
STIVIC
STOVER
STOVES
SUAVER
SURVEY
SWIVEL
SWIVET
SYLVAN
SYLVIA

S•••V•
SALIVA
SCURVE
SCURVY
SHEAVE
SHELVE
SHRIVE
SHROVE
SKIVVY
SLEAVE
SLEEVE
SPIVVY
STARVE
STEEVE
STRIVE
STROVE
SWERVE

•SV•••
RSVPED

•S•V••
ASEVER

•S•••V
ASIMOV

••S•V•
CASAVA
KOSOVO
MOSKVA

••S••V
GUSTAV
KISLEV
MOSHAV
ROSTOV
VASLAV

•••S•V
BRASOV

SW••••
SWABBY
SWAGED
SWAGES
SWAINS
SWALES
SWAMIS
SWAMPS
SWAMPY
SWANEE
SWANKS
SWANKY
SWARAJ
SWARDS
SWARMS
SWARTH
SWATCH
SWATHE
SWATHS
SWAYED
SWAYER
SWAYZE
SWAZIS
SWEARS
SWEATS
SWEATY
SWEDEN
SWEDES
SWEEPS
SWEETS
SWELLS
SWERVE
SWIFTS
SWILLS
SWINGS
SWINGY
SWIPED
SWIPER
SWIPES
SWIRLS
SWIRLY
SWITCH
SWIVEL
SWIVET
SWOONS
SWOOPS
SWOOSH
SWORDS

S•W•••
SAWFIT
SAWING
SAWLOG
SAWOFF
SAWOUT
SAWRED
SAWYER
SEWAGE
SEWARD
SEWELL
SEWERS
SEWING
SEWNON
SEWNUP
SEWSON
SEWSUP
SIWASH
SOWBUG
SOWERS
SOWETO
SOWHAT
SOWING

S••W••
SCHWAB
SCHWAS
SCOWLS
SEAWAY
SHAWLS
SHAWMS
SHOWED
SHOWER
SHOWIN
SHOWME
SHOWUP
SKEWED
SKEWER
SKYWAY
SLEWED
SLOWED
SLOWER
SLOWLY
SLOWUP
SNOWED
SNOWIN
SPAWNS
SPEWED
STEWED
STEWER
STOWED
SUBWAY

S•••W•
SCRAWL
SCREWS
SCREWY
SEROWS
SHREWD
SHREWS
SINEWS
SINEWY
SPRAWL
SQUAWK
STRAWS
STRAWY
STREWN
STREWS

S••••W
SALLOW
SEACOW
SEESAW
SHADOW
SKITOW
SORROW
SUNDEW

•SW•••
ASWELL
ASWIRL
ASWOON
OSWALD
OSWEGO

•S•W••
PSYWAR

•S••W•
OSHAWA

•S•••W
ESCHEW
ESCROW

••SW••
ANSWER

••S•W•
BUSHWA
DISOWN
PESAWA
RESAWN
RESAWS
RESEWN
RESEWS
UNSEWN
UNSEWS
UNSOWN

••S••W
BESTOW
CASHEW
CPSNOW
CUSHAW
GOSLOW
MOSCOW
NOSHOW
PESCOW
TVSHOW

•••S•W
BOWSAW
JIGSAW
OLDSAW
PITSAW
RIPSAW
SEESAW
WARSAW

S•X•••
SAXONS
SAXONY
SEXIER
SEXILY
SEXIST
SEXTET
SEXTON
SIXERS
SIXGUN
SIXING
SIXTHS
SIXTUS
SOXERS

S••X••
SKNXXX

S•••X•
SKNXXX

S••••X
SEAFOX
SINTAX
SKNXXX
SKYBOX
SMILAX
SPADIX
SPHINX
SUFFIX
SURTAX
SUSSEX
SYNTAX
SYRINX

•S•X••
VSIXES

••S••X
AUSPEX
LASTEX
MUSKOX
SUSSEX
WESSEX

•••S•X
CHISOX
REDSOX
SUSSEX
THESIX
UNISEX
WESSEX

SY••••
SYDNEY
SYLPHS
SYLVAN
SYLVIA
SYMBOL
SYNCED
SYNDIC
SYNODS
SYNTAX
SYPHON
SYRIAN
SYRINX
SYRUPS
SYRUPY
SYSOPS
SYSTEM
SYZYGY

S•Y•••
SAYERS
SAYING
SAYLES
SAYSOS
SAYYES
SAYYID
SCYLLA
SCYTHE
SHYEST
SHYING
SKYBOX
SKYCAP
SKYING
SKYLAB
SKYWAY
SLYEST
SLYPES
SMYRNA
SNYDER
SPYING
STYLED
STYLER
STYLES
STYLET
STYLUS
STYMIE
STYRIA
STYRON

S••Y••
SALYUT

SATYRS
SAWYER
SAYYES
SAYYID
SHAYNE
SIBYLS
SLAYED
SLAYER
SPAYED
SPRYER
SPRYLY
STAYED
STAYON
STAYUP
SWAYED
SWAYER
SWAYZE
SYZYGY

S•••Y•

SEPOYS
SHERYL
SPLAYS
SPRAYS
STRAYS

S••••Y

SAFELY
SAFETY
SAGELY
SALARY
SALIFY
SANELY
SANITY
SASHAY
SATINY
SAVORY
SAXONY
SCABBY
SCANTY
SCARRY
SCATTY
SCHIZY
SCOTTY
SCREWY
SCULLY
SCUMMY
SCURFY
SCURRY
SCURVY
SCUZZY
SEAWAY
SEELEY
SEEMLY
SENARY
SENTRY
SETSBY
SEVERY
SEXILY
SHABBY
SHAGGY
SHALEY
SHALLY
SHANDY
SHANNY
SHANTY
SHEEDY
SHEEHY
SHELLY
SHELTY
SHERRY
SHIFTY
SHILLY
SHIMMY
SHINDY
SHINNY
SHIRTY
SHOALY
SHODDY
SHORTY
SICILY
SICKLY
SIDNEY
SIMONY
SIMPLY
SINEWY
SINGLY
SISLEY
SITSBY
SKERRY
SKIDDY
SKIMPY
SKINNY
SKIPPY
SKIVVY
SKUNKY
SKYWAY
SLAGGY
SLANGY
SLAPPY
SLAVEY
SLEAZY
SLEEKY
SLEEPY
SLEETY
SLIMLY
SLIMSY
SLINKY
SLIPPY
SLITHY
SLITTY
SLOBBY
SLOPPY
SLOSHY
SLOWLY
SLUDGY
SLUMMY
SLURRY
SLUSHY
SMARMY
SMARTY
SMEARY
SMELLY
SMILEY
SMIRKY
SMITHY
SMOGGY
SMOKEY
SMUDGY
SMUGLY
SMUTTY
SNAGGY
SNAPPY
SNARLY
SNAZZY
SNEAKY
SNEERY
SNEEZY
SNIFFY
SNIPPY
SNOBBY
SNOOKY
SNOOPY
SNOOTY
SNOOZY
SNOTTY
SNUBBY
SNUFFY
SNUGLY
SOFTLY
SOLELY
SOMANY
SORELY
SOURLY
SPACEY
SPANKY
SPARKY
SPEEDY
SPERRY
SPHERY
SPIFFY
SPIVVY
SPONGY
SPOOKY
SPOONY
SPORTY
SPOTTY
SPRYLY
SPUNKY
SPURRY
STABLY
STACEY
STALKY
STANKY
STARRY
STEADY
STEAMY
STEELY
STEFOY
STICKY
STILLY
STIMPY
STINGY
STINKY
STITHY
STOCKY
STODGY
STOOLY
STOREY
STORMY
STRAWY
STRIPY
STUBBY
STUFFY
STUMPY
STUNTY
STURDY
SUBTLY
SUBWAY
SUGARY
SULTRY
SUNDAY
SUNDRY
SUNRAY
SUPPLY
SURELY
SURETY
SURREY
SURVEY
SWABBY
SWAMPY
SWANKY
SWEATY
SWINGY
SWIRLY
SYDNEY
SYRUPY
SYZYGY

•SY•••

ASYLUM
PSYCHE
PSYCHO
PSYCHS
PSYLLA
PSYWAR

•S••Y•

ASSAYS
ESSAYS

•S•••Y

ASBURY
ASEITY
ASHLEY
ASTRAY
ESTRAY
OSPREY
OSSIFY
USABLY

••SY••

INSYNC

••S•Y•

ASSAYS
ESSAYS
JASEYS
MOSEYS
UNSAYS

••S••Y

BASELY
BASIFY
BASSLY
BISCAY
BOSLEY
BUSBOY
BUSILY
CASEFY
COSILY
COSTLY
DESCRY
DESTRY
DISMAY
DISNEY
EASILY
FOSSEY
GASIFY
HOSTLY
HUSSEY
JUSTLY
LASTLY
LESLEY
LUSHLY
MASSEY
MISERY
MISLAY
MISSAY
MOSTLY
MUSCLY
NASEBY
NOSILY
OSSIFY
PASSBY
PASTRY
POSHLY
RASHLY
RESINY
ROSARY
ROSILY
ROSINY
SASHAY
SISLEY
VASTLY
VESTRY
WESLEY
WISELY

•••SY•

UNISYS
VAISYA

•••S•Y

BASSLY
BETSEY
BOLSHY
BRASHY
BRASSY
BRUSHY
CHESTY
CLASSY
CRISPY
CROSBY
CRUSTY
DILSEY
DOESBY
DORSEY
DRESSY
FEISTY
FLASHY
FLESHY
FLOSSY
FOSSEY
FRISKY
FROSTY
GATSBY
GELSEY
GETSBY
GLASSY
GLOSSY
GOESBY
GOOSEY
GRASSY
GRISLY
GROSZY
GUNSHY
HALSEY
HERSEY
HORSEY
HUSSEY
ILLSAY
JANSKY
JERSEY
KELSEY
KERSEY
KINSEY
KRASNY
LAYSBY
LINSEY
MARSHY
MASSEY
MEASLY
MERSEY
MISSAY
MOUSEY
NAYSAY
NEVSKY
NIPSEY
OCASEY
PASSBY
PIGSTY
PLASHY
PLASTY
PLUSHY
PRISSY
PROSKY
PUTSBY
RAMSAY
RAMSEY
RIMSKY
SETSBY
SITSBY
SLOSHY
SLUSHY
THUSLY
TOASTY
TRASHY
TRUSTY
TWISTY
WHISKY
WIMSEY
WOLSEY
YEASTY

••••SY

ARGOSY
BEKESY
BLOWSY
BLUESY
BOOTSY
BRASSY
CHEESY
CHOOSY
CLASSY
CLUMSY
CREASY
CURTSY
CUTESY
DRESSY
DROWSY
FLIMSY
FLOPSY
FLOSSY
FOLKSY
GLASSY
GLOSSY
GOEASY
GRASSY
GREASY
HERESY
PRISSY
QUEASY
SLIMSY
TEENSY
TOOTSY
UNBUSY
UNEASY
WEENSY
WHIMSY
WOODSY

S•Z•••

SIZERS
SIZEUP
SIZING
SIZZLE
SUZUKI
SYZYGY

S••Z••

SCUZZY
SEIZED
SEIZER
SEIZES
SHAZAM
SIZZLE
SLEZAK
SNAZZY
SWAZIS

S•••Z•

SCHIZY
SCUZZY
SFORZA
SLEAZE
SLEAZY
SNAZZY
SNEEZE
SNEEZY
SNOOZE
SNOOZY
STANZA
SWAYZE

S••••Z

SCHNOZ
SCHULZ
SHIRAZ
SPRITZ

•S•Z••

ZSAZSA

•S••Z•

ASSIZE

••S•Z•

ASSIZE

••S••Z

ERSATZ

•••SZ•

GROSZY

•••S•Z

AMOSOZ

••••SZ

KUVASZ
MILOSZ

TA••••

TABARD
TABBED
TABLAS
TABLED
TABLES
TABLET
TABOOS
TABORS
TABRIZ
TABULA
TACKED
TACKER
TACKLE
TACKON
TACOMA
TACTIC
TAGDAY
TAGEND
TAGGED
TAGORE
TAGOUT
TAGSUP
TAHINI
TAHITI
TAICHI
TAIGAS
TAILED
TAILLE
TAILOR
TAINAN
TAINOS
TAINTS
TAIPAN
TAIPEI
TAIWAN
TAKEIN
TAKEON
TAKERS
TAKETH
TAKETO
TAKEUP
TAKING
TAKINS
TALBOT
TALCED
TALCUM
TALENT
TALERS
TALESE
TALION
TALKAT
TALKED
TALKER
TALKIE
TALKTO
TALKUP
TALLER
TALLOW
TALMUD
TALONS
TAMALE
TAMARA
TAMAYO
TAMELY
TAMERS
TAMEST
TAMILS
TAMING
TAMMUZ
TAMPED
TAMPER
TAMTAM
TANAKA
TANANA
TANDEM
TANGED
TANGLE
TANGLY
TANGOS
TANGUY
TANIST
TANKAS
TANKED
TANKER
TANKUP
TANNED
TANNER
TANNIC
TANNIN
TANOAK
TANOAN
TANTES
TANTRA
TAOISM
TAOIST
TAPERS
TAPING
TAPINS
TAPIRS
TAPOFF
TAPOUT
TAPPAN
TAPPED
TAPPER
TAPPET
TARAWA
TARGES
TARGET
TARIFF
TARING
TARMAC
TAROTS
TARPAN
TARPIT
TARPON
TARRED
TARSAL
TARSUS
TARTAN
TARTAR
TARTER
TARTLY
TARZAN
TASERS
TASKED
TASMAN
TASSEL
TASSES
TASTED
TASTER
TASTES
TATAMI
TATARS
TATERS
TATTED
TATTER
TATTLE
TATTOO
TAUGHT
TAUNTS
TAUONS
TAUPES
TAURUS
TAUTEN
TAUTER
TAUTLY

TAUTOG
TAVERN
TAWDRY
TAWING
TAXERS
TAXIED
TAXIES
TAXING
TAXMAN
TAXMEN
TAYLOR
TAYRAS
TAZZAS

T•A•••

TEABAG
TEACUP
TEAMED
TEAMUP
TEAPOT
TEAPOY
TEARAT
TEARED
TEARUP
TEASED
TEASEL
TEASER
TEASES
TEASET
THALER
THALES
THALIA
THAMES
THANES
THANKS
THATCH
THATIS
THATLL
THAWED
THAYER
TIARAS
TLALOC
TOAMAN
TOASTS
TOASTY
TOATEE
TRACED
TRACER
TRACES
TRACEY
TRACHY
TRACKS
TRACTS
TRADED
TRADER
TRADES
TRAGIC
TRAILS
TRAINS
TRAITS
TRAJAN
TRALEE
TRAMPS
TRANCE
TRAPPY
TRASHY
TRAUMA
TRAVEL
TRAVES
TRAVIS
TRAWLS
TUAREG
TWANGS
TWANGY

T••A••

TABARD
TAMALE
TAMARA
TAMAYO
TANAKA
TANANA
TARAWA
TATAMI
TATARS
TEJANO
TENACE
TENANT
TEPALS
TERAPH
TERATO
TEXACO
TEXANS
THRACE
THRALE
THRALL
THRASH
THWACK
THWART
TICALS
TILAKS
TIRADE
TIRANA
TIRANE
TISANE
TITANS
TOBAGO
TODATE
TOGAED
TOKAYS
TOMATO
TORAHS
TOTALS
TOWAGE
TOWARD
TREADS
TREATS
TREATY
TRIADS
TRIAGE
TRIALS
TRUANT
TUBATE
TUCANA
TULANE
TULARE
TUVALU
TWEAKS
TYBALT
TYRANT

T•••A•

TABLAS
TAGDAY
TAIGAS
TAINAN
TAIPAN
TAIWAN
TALKAT
TAMTAM
TANKAS
TANOAK
TANOAN
TAPPAN
TARMAC
TARPAN
TARSAL
TARTAN
TARTAR
TARZAN
TASMAN
TAXMAN
TAYRAS
TAZZAS
TEABAG
TEARAT
TERRAN
TESLAS
TESTAE
TETRAD
TETRAS
THECAE
THECAL
THEHAJ
THENAR
THETAS
THOMAS
THORAX
THREAD
THREAT
THROAT
THUJAS
TIARAS
TIBIAE
TIBIAL
TIBIAS
TICTAC
TIMBAL
TINCAL
TINCAN
TINEAR
TINHAT
TINMAN
TINPAN
TITIAN
TOAMAN
TOBIAS
TODDAO
TODMAN
TOECAP
TOETAP
TOKLAS
TOMBAC
TOMCAT
TONGAN
TOOBAD
TOPCAT
TOPHAT
TOREAT
TOUCAN
TOWCAR
TRAJAN
TREPAN
TRIBAL
TRINAL
TROCAR
TROJAN
TRUMAN
TUBMAN
TULSAN
TUPIAN
TURBAN
TUSCAN
TUSSAH
TWOWAY
TYRIAN

T••••A

TABULA
TACOMA
TAMARA
TANAKA
TANANA
TANTRA
TARAWA
TEPHRA
TERESA
THALIA
THELMA
THESEA
TIERRA
TIRANA
TOLUCA
TOPEKA
TOYOTA
TRAUMA
TREDIA
TRICIA
TRISHA
TRIVIA
TROIKA
TUCANA
TUNDRA
TUNICA

•TA•••

ATAMAN
ETALIA
ETALII
ETAPES
ITALIA
ITALIC
ITASCA
STABAT
STABLE
STABLY
STACEY
STACKS
STACTE
STADIA
STAFFS
STAGED
STAGER
STAGES
STAINS
STAIRS
STAKED
STAKES
STALAG
STALED
STALER
STALES
STALIN
STALKS
STALKY
STALLS
STAMEN
STAMPS
STANCE
STANCH
STANDS
STANKY
STANZA
STAPES
STAPLE
STAPUF
STARCH
STARED
STARER
STARES
STARRY
STARTS
STARVE
STASES
STASIS
STATED
STATEN
STATER
STATES
STATIC
STATOR
STATUE
STATUS
STAVED
STAVES
STAYED
STAYON
STAYUP
UTAHAN

•T•A••

ATBATS
ATEAMS
ATEASE
ATHAND
ATLAST
ATLATL
ATTACH
ATTACK
ATTAIN
ATTARS
ETHANE
ITHACA
ITHAKI
OTTAVA
OTTAWA
PTRAPS
STEADS
STEADY
STEAKS
STEALS
STEAMS
STEAMY
STMALO
STMARK
STOATS
STPAUL
STRABO
STRADS
STRAFE
STRAIN
STRAIT
STRAKE
STRAND
STRAPS
STRASS
STRATA
STRATI
STRATO
STRAUB
STRAUS
STRAWS
STRAWY
STRAYS
STUART
UTHANT

•T••A•

ATAMAN
ATONAL
ATRIAL
ATTHAT
ITZHAK
PTBOAT
STABAT
STALAG
STEFAN
STELAE
STELAR
STJOAN
STOMAS
STOMAT
STREAK
STREAM
STRIAE
STUPAS
UTAHAN

•T•••A

ATHENA
ATTICA
ATTILA
ETALIA
ITALIA
ITASCA
ITHACA
OTTAVA
OTTAWA
STADIA
STANZA
STELLA
STERNA
STIGMA
STRATA
STYRIA
UTOPIA

••TA••

ALTAIC
ALTAIR
ALTARS
ATTACH
ATTACK
ATTAIN
ATTARS
BATAAN
BETAKE
BOTANY
BUTANE
BYTALK
CETANE
CITATO
DATARY
DETACH
DETAIL
DETAIN
DOTAGE
DOTARD
ENTAIL
ESTATE
EUTAXY
EXTANT
FATALE
GITANO
GSTAAD
HATARI
HOTAIR
IDTAGS
INTACT
INTAKE
LITANY
LOTAHS
METALS
METATE
MUTANT
MUTATE
MUTATO
NATANT
NOTARY
NOTATE
NUTATE
OBTAIN
OCTADS
OCTANE
OCTANT
OCTAVE
OCTAVO
ONTAPE
OTTAVA
OTTAWA
OUTACT
OUTAGE
OUTATE
OXTAIL
PATACA
PETAIN
PETALS
PETARD
POTAGE
POTASH
POTATO
QATARI
RETAGS
RETAIL
RETAIN
RETAKE
RETAPE
RETAPS
RETARD
RETARS
RITARD
ROTARY
ROTATE
SATANG
SITARS
TATAMI
TATARS
TITANS
TOTALS
UMTATA
UNTACK
UPTAKE
UPTALK
VITALE
VITALS
VOTARY

••T•A•

ACTSAS
ACTUAL
ALTMAN
AMTRAC
AMTRAK
ASTRAL
ASTRAY
ATTHAT
BATAAN
BATEAU
BATMAN
BATYAM
BETRAY
BETTAS
BITMAP
CATHAY
CATNAP
COTTAS
DOTHAN
EATSAT
ENTRAP
ESTRAY
EXTRAS
FATCAT
FATWAS
GATEAU
GETMAD
GETSAT
GOTHAM
GOTMAD
GSTAAD
GUTTAE
HETMAN
HITMAN
HOTCAP
HOTCAR
HOTWAR
JETLAG
JETSAM
JETWAY
KATMAI
KITBAG
KITKAT
LETHAL
LETSAT
LOTHAR
MITRAL
MUTUAL
NATHAN
NETMAN
NETPAY
NOTBAD
OSTEAL
OUTEAT
OUTLAW
OUTLAY
OUTRAN
PATHAN
PITMAN
PITSAW
PUTNAM
RATTAN
RETEAR
RETIAL
RETRAL
RITUAL
RUTTAN
SATRAP
SETSAT
SGTMAJ
SOTHAT
SUTRAS
TETRAD
TETRAS
TITIAN
ULTRAS
UNTRAP
WETBAR
WITHAL

••T••A

ALTHEA
ALTIMA
ATTICA
ATTILA
BETCHA
BITOLA
CATENA
CETERA
DATURA
FATIMA
GOTCHA
HOTTEA
INTIMA
ISTRIA
LATINA
LATONA
LATOYA
LATVIA
MATTEA
MOTHRA
NATURA
NUTRIA
OPTIMA
ORTEGA
OTTAVA
OTTAWA
PATACA
PATINA
PETULA
PYTHIA
RETINA
ULTIMA
UMTATA

•••TA•

ACETAL
AKITAS
ALATAU
AMYTAN
AORTAE
AORTAL
AORTAS
ARCTAN
AVATAR
BANTAM
BARTAB
BETTAS
BHUTAN
BIOTAS
BRUTAL
CAFTAN
CANTAB
CAPTAN
CESTAS
CONTAC
COSTAE
COSTAL
COSTAR
COSTAS
COTTAS
CRETAN
DELTAS

DENTAL
DIKTAT
DISTAL
DOGTAG
DUCTAL
FANTAN
FESTAL
FESTAS
FOETAL
FONTAL
FORTAS
GOSTAG
GUITAR
GUSTAV
GUTTAE
HEPTAD
HIATAL
HINTAT
HOOTAT
HOSTAS
HYETAL
INSTAL
INSTAR
ISHTAR
JUNTAS
KEPTAT
LESTAT
MAITAI
MANTAS
MAOTAI
MAYTAG
MENTAL
MORTAL
MORTAR
NECTAR
PASTAS
PENTAD
PIETAS
PORTAL
POSTAL
PRETAX
PROTAX
QANTAS
QINTAR
QUOTAS
RAGTAG
RATTAN
REATAS
REDTAG
RENTAL
RIATAS
RUTTAN
SEPTAL
SHOTAT
SINTAX
SONTAG
SULTAN
SUNTAN
SURTAX
SYNTAX
TAMTAM
TARTAN
TARTAR
TESTAE
THETAS
TICTAC
TOETAP
UINTAS
UNITAL
UNITAS
VESTAL
VESTAS
VISTAS
WANTAD
WENTAT
WYSTAN
YENTAS

•••T•A

AGATHA
ANITRA
ARETHA
BERTHA
CONTRA
EARTHA
GRATIA
GRETNA
HESTIA
HOTTEA
LIOTTA
MANTRA
MANTUA
MARTHA
MATTEA
NESTEA
NOOTKA
ODETTA
PORTIA
QUETTA
QUOTHA
ROSTRA
SCOTIA
SENTRA
SISTRA
TANTRA

••••TA

AJANTA
ARISTA
AVESTA
BALATA
BEMATA
BOGOTA
CAPITA
CUESTA
DAKOTA
DAMITA
EGESTA
EJECTA
ERRATA
EXACTA
FAJITA
FIESTA
GALATA
LAKOTA
LAPUTA
LIOTTA
LOLITA
MAKUTA
MIKITA
MONETA
MORITA
MULETA
NIKITA
ODETTA
OMERTA
PELOTA
PEPITA
PESETA
PINATA
QUANTA
QUETTA
RENATA
ROSITA
SANCTA
SHASTA
SHORTA
SIESTA
SOMATA
SONATA
SPARTA
STRATA
TOYOTA
UMTATA
YUKATA
ZAPATA

TB••••

TBILLS
TBIRDS
TBONDS
TBONES

T•B•••

TABARD
TABBED
TABLAS
TABLED
TABLES
TABLET
TABOOS
TABORS
TABRIZ
TABULA
TIBIAE
TIBIAL
TIBIAS
TOBAGO
TOBIAS
TOBIES
TOBOOT
TOBRUK
TUBATE
TUBBED
TUBERS
TUBING
TUBIST
TUBMAN
TYBALT

T••B••

TABBED
TALBOT
TEABAG
THEBES
TIDBIT
TIMBAL
TIMBER
TIMBRE
TITBIT
TOMBAC
TOMBOY
TOOBAD
TREBEK
TREBLE
TREBLY
TRIBAL
TRIBES
TUBBED
TUMBLE
TURBAN
TURBID
TURBIT
TURBOS
TURBOT
TWOBIT
TYDBOL

T•••B•

THISBE
THROBS
THUMBS
TRILBY
TYCOBB

T••••B

THEWEB
TOPJOB
TYCOBB

•TB•••

ATBATS
ATBEST
PTBOAT

•T•B••

STABAT
STABLE
STABLY
STUBBY

•T••B•

ITURBI
STRABO
STROBE
STUBBY

•T•••B

STRAUB

••TB••

BATBOY
HATBOX
HOTBED
HOTBOX
KITBAG
NOTBAD
OUTBID
OUTBOX
TITBIT
WETBAR

••T•B•

GATSBY
GETSBY
LETSBE
PUTSBY
SETSBY
SITSBY

••T••B

HOTTUB

•••TB•

WENTBY

•••T•B

BARTAB
CANTAB
HOTTUB

T•C•••

TACKED
TACKER
TACKLE
TACKON
TACOMA
TACTIC
TECHIE
TECHNO
TICALS
TICKED
TICKER
TICKET
TICKLE
TICKLY
TICTAC
TOCSIN
TUCANA
TUCHUN
TUCKED
TUCKER
TUCKET
TUCKIN
TUCSON
TYCOBB
TYCOON

T••C••

TAICHI
TALCED
TALCUM
TEACUP
TERCEL
TERCET
TETCHY
THECAE
THECAL
THICKE
TINCAL
TINCAN
TINCTS
TOECAP
TOMCAT
TOPCAT
TORCHY
TOUCAN
TOUCHE
TOUCHY
TOWCAR
TRACED
TRACER
TRACES
TRACEY
TRACHY
TRACKS
TRACTS
TRICED
TRICEP
TRICES
TRICHO
TRICIA
TRICKS
TRICKY
TRICOT
TROCAR
TROCHE
TRUCES
TRUCKS
TUSCAN

T•••C•

TENACE
TEXACO
THATCH
THENCE
THRACE
THRICE
THWACK
TIERCE
TOLUCA
TONICS
TOPICS
TOXICS
TRANCE
TRENCH
TUNICA
TUNICS
TWITCH

T••••C

TACTIC
TANNIC
TARMAC
TENREC
THETIC
TICTAC
TLALOC
TOLTEC
TOMBAC
TRAGIC
TROPIC
TURKIC

•TC•••

ATCOST
ETCHED
ETCHER
ETCHES
ITCHED
ITCHES

•T•C••

STACEY
STACKS
STACTE
STICKS
STICKY
STOCKS
STOCKY
STUCCO

•T••C•

ATONCE
ATTACH
ATTACK
ATTICA
ATTICS
ETHICS
ITASCA
ITHACA
STANCE
STANCH
STARCH
STENCH
STITCH
STOICS
STORCH
STRICK
STRICT
STRUCK
STUCCO

•T•••C

ATOMIC
ATONIC
ETHNIC
ETONIC
ITALIC
OTITIC
STATIC
STIVIC

••TC••

ANTCOW
BETCHA
BOTCHY
CATCHY
FATCAT
GOTCHA
HOTCAP
HOTCAR
LITCHI
NOTCHY
OUTCRY
PATCHY
PITCHY
SITCOM
TETCHY
WITCHY

••T•C•

ANTICS
ATTACH
ATTACK
ATTICA
ATTICS
AZTECS
DETACH
DETECT
ENTICE
HITECH
INTACT
KITSCH
NATICK
NOTICE
OPTICS
OUTACT
PATACA
PUTSCH
SHTICK
UNTACK
UPTICK
VOTECH

••T••C

ALTAIC
AMTRAC
CITRIC
GOTHIC
IATRIC
LITHIC
METRIC
MYTHIC
NITRIC
VITRIC

•••TC•

BLOTCH
CLUTCH
CRUTCH
FLETCH
FLITCH
GLITCH
HOOTCH
KLATCH
KVETCH
NAUTCH
SCOTCH
SCUTCH
SKETCH
SKITCH
SMUTCH
SNATCH
SNITCH
STITCH
SWATCH
SWITCH
THATCH
TWITCH
WRETCH

•••T•C

ACETIC
AORTIC
ARCTIC
BALTIC
BIOTIC
CELTIC
CONTAC
COPTIC
CRITIC
CULTIC
DELTIC
EROTIC
EXOTIC
FISTIC
FUSTIC
GESTIC
HECTIC
LACTIC
MANTIC
MASTIC
MIXTEC
MYSTIC
NOETIC
OTITIC
PECTIC
PEPTIC
PHATIC
PHOTIC
POETIC
PONTIC
RUSTIC
SEPTIC
STATIC
TACTIC
THETIC
TICTAC
TOLTEC

T•D•••

TEDDED
TEDDER
TEDEUM
TEDIUM
TEDKEY
TIDBIT
TIDDLY
TIDIED
TIDIER
TIDIES
TIDILY
TIDING
TIDYUP
TODATE
TODDAO
TODDLE
TODMAN
TUDORS
TYDBOL

T••D••

TAGDAY
TANDEM
TAWDRY
TEDDED
TEDDER
TEEDUP
TENDED
TENDER
TENDON
TENDTO
TIDDLY
TIEDIN
TIEDTO
TIEDUP
TIEDYE
TILDEN
TILDES
TINDER
TODDAO
TODDLE
TOEDIN
TOLDOF
TOLDON
TONDOS
TOPDOG
TOYDOG
TRADED
TRADER
TRADES
TREDIA
TRUDGE
TUNDRA

T•••D•

TBIRDS
TBONDS
TELEDU
TEREDO
THIRDS
TIRADE
TOLEDO
TREADS
TRENDS
TRENDY
TRIADS
TRIODE
TUXEDO
TWEEDS
TWEEDY

T••••D

TABARD
TABBED
TABLED
TACKED
TAGEND
TAGGED
TAILED

TALCED
TALKED
TALMUD
TAMPED
TANGED
TANKED
TANNED
TAPPED
TARRED
TASKED
TASTED
TATTED
TAXIED
TEAMED
TEARED
TEASED
TEDDED
TEEMED
TEHEED
TEMPED
TENDED
TENSED
TENTED
TERMED
TESTED
TETRAD
THAWED
THEEND
THEFED
THEKID
THEMED
THREAD
THREED
TICKED
TIDIED
TIERED
TIEROD
TIFFED
TILLED
TILTED
TINGED
TINGOD
TINNED
TINTED
TIPPED
TITHED
TITLED
TITRED
TOGAED
TOGGED
TOILED
TOLLED
TOOBAD
TOOLED
TOOTED
TOPPED
TOROID
TORPID
TORRID
TOSSED
TOTTED
TOURED
TOUTED
TOWARD
TRACED
TRADED
TREPID
TRICED
TRIFID
TRIPOD
TROWED
TUBBED
TUCKED
TUFTED
TUGGED
TUMMED
TURBID
TURFED
TURGID
TURNED
TUSKED
TUTUED
TWINED

•T•D••

ATODDS
ETUDES
STADIA
STODGE
STODGY
STUDIO

•T••D•

ATODDS
STANDS
STEADS
STEADY
STEEDS
STRADS
STRIDE
STRODE
STURDY

•T•••D

ATHAND
ATONED
ATSTUD
ATTEND
ATWOOD
ETCHED
ITCHED
STAGED
STAKED
STALED
STARED
STATED
STAVED
STAYED
STEWED
STOKED
STOLID
STONED
STORED
STOWED
STRAND
STROUD
STUPID
STYLED

••TD••

HOTDOG
OUTDID

••T•D•

BETIDE
OCTADS
RATEDG
RATEDR
RATEDX
UNTIDY

••T••D

ANTEED
ASTRID
ATTEND
BATHED
BATTED
BITTED
BUTTED
CATTED
DOTARD
DOTTED
EXTEND
FATTED
FITTED
FUTZED
GETMAD
GOTMAD
GSTAAD
GUTTED
HATRED
HATTED
HOTBED
HOTROD
HUTTED
INTEND
JETTED
JOTTED
JUTTED
LATHED
LETTED
LOTTED
MATTED
METHOD
MITRED
NETTED
NOTBAD
NUTTED
OBTUND
OSTEND
OUTBID
OUTDID
PATTED
PETARD
PETTED
PITHED
PITIED
PITTED
POTTED
PUTRID
PUTTED
RATTED
RETARD
RETIED
RETOLD
RITARD
ROTTED
ROTUND
RUTTED
SOTTED
TATTED
TETRAD
TITHED
TITLED
TITRED
TOTTED
TUTUED
UNTIED
UNTOLD
UNTROD
VATTED
VETOED
VETTED
WETTED
WITHED
WITTED

•••T•D

ABATED
ALATED
ATSTUD
BAITED
BASTED
BATTED
BELTED
BESTED
BITTED
BOATED
BOLTED
BOOTED
BUNTED
BUSTED
BUTTED
CANTED
CARTED
CATTED
CHUTED
COATED
CRATED
DARTED
DENTED
DIETED
DINTED
DOTTED
DUSTED
EDITED
ELATED
ELUTED
EMOTED
EXITED
FASTED
FATTED
FELTED
FISTED
FITTED
FLUTED
FOETID
FOOTED
GAITED
GIFTED
GIRTED
GRATED
GUSTED
GUTTED
HAFTED
HALTED
HATTED
HEATED
HEFTED
HENTED
HEPTAD
HINTED
HOOTED
HOSTED
HUNTED
HUTTED
JESTED
JETTED
JILTED
JOLTED
JOTTED
JUTTED
KILTED
LASTED
LETTED
LIFTED
LILTED
LISTED
LOFTED
LOOTED
LOTTED
LUSTED
MALTED
MATTED
MELTED
MINTED
MISTED
MOATED
MOLTED
MOOTED
NESTED
NETTED
NUTTED
ORATED
OUSTED
PANTED
PARTED
PASTED
PATTED
PELTED
PENTAD
PETTED
PITTED
PLATED
PORTED
POSTED
POTTED
POUTED
PRATED
PUNTED
PUTTED
QUOTED
RAFTED
RANTED
RATTED
RENTED
RESTED
RIFTED
RIOTED
ROOTED
ROTTED
ROUTED
RRATED
RUSTED
RUTTED
SALTED
SEATED
SIFTED
SILTED
SKATED
SLATED
SORTED
SOTTED
SPITED
STATED
SUITED
TASTED
TATTED
TENTED
TESTED
TILTED
TINTED
TOOTED
TOTTED
TOUTED
TUFTED
UNITED
VATTED
VENTED
VESTED
VETTED
WAFTED
WAITED
WANTAD
WANTED
WASTED
WELTED
WETTED
WILTED
WITTED
WONTED
XRATED
ZESTED

TE••••

TEABAG
TEACUP
TEAMED
TEAMUP
TEAPOT
TEAPOY
TEARAT
TEARED
TEARUP
TEASED
TEASEL
TEASER
TEASES
TEASET
TECHIE
TECHNO
TEDDED
TEDDER
TEDEUM
TEDIUM
TEDKEY
TEEDUP
TEEHEE
TEEING
TEEMED
TEENER
TEENSY
TEEOFF
TEESUP
TEETER
TEETHE
TEEVEE
TEFLON
TEHEED
TEHEES
TEJANO
TELEDU
TELLER
TELLOF
TELLON
TELUGU
TEMPED
TEMPEH
TEMPER
TEMPLE
TEMPOS
TEMPTS
TEMPUS
TENACE
TENANT
TENDED
TENDER
TENDON
TENDTO
TENENS
TENETS
TENNIS
TENONS
TENORS
TENPIN
TENREC
TENSED
TENSER
TENSES
TENSOR
TENTED
TENTER
TENTHS
TENURE
TENUTO
TEPALS
TEPEES
TEPHRA
TERAPH
TERATO
TERCEL
TERCET
TEREDO
TERESA
TERETE
TEREUS
TERKEL
TERMED
TERNES
TERRAN
TERRET
TERROR
TERSER
TESLAS
TESSIE
TESTAE
TESTED
TESTEE
TESTER
TETCHY
TETHER
TETHYS
TETONS
TETRAD
TETRAS
TETRIS
TETZEL
TEUTON
TEXACO
TEXANS
TEXMEX

T•E•••

TEEDUP
TEEHEE
TEEING
TEEMED
TEENER
TEENSY
TEEOFF
TEESUP
TEETER
TEETHE
TEEVEE
THEBES
THECAE
THECAL
THEEND
THEFED
THEFLY
THEFTS
THEHAJ
THEIRS
THEISM
THEIST
THEKID
THELIP
THELMA
THEMED
THEMES
THENAR
THENCE
THEORY
THERES
THERMO
THERMS
THESEA
THESES
THESIS
THESIX
THETAS
THETIC
THETIS
THETOY
THEWEB
THEWIZ
THEYLL
THEYRE
THEYVE
TIEDIN
TIEDTO
TIEDUP
TIEDYE
TIEING
TIEINS
TIEPIN
TIERCE
TIERED
TIEROD
TIERRA
TIESIN
TIESTO
TIESUP
TIEUPS
TMESIS
TOECAP
TOEDIN
TOEING
TOEINS
TOESIN
TOETAP
TREADS
TREATS
TREATY
TREBEK
TREBLE
TREBLY
TREDIA
TREMOR
TRENCH
TRENDS
TRENDY
TREPAN
TREPID
TREVOR
TSETSE
TWEAKS
TWEEDS
TWEEDY
TWEENS
TWEENY
TWEEST
TWEETS
TWEETY
TWEEZE
TWELVE
TWENTY
TWERPS

T••E••

TAGEND
TAKEIN
TAKEON
TAKERS
TAKETH
TAKETO
TAKEUP
TALENT
TALERS
TALESE
TAMELY
TAMERS
TAMEST
TAPERS
TASERS
TATERS
TAVERN
TAXERS
TEDEUM
TEHEED
TEHEES
TELEDU
TENENS
TENETS
TEPEES
TEREDO
TERESA
TERETE
TEREUS
THEEND
THIEVE
THREAD
THREAT
THREED
THREES
THRESH
TIGERS
TILERS
TIMELY
TIMERS
TINEAR
TITERS
TOKENS
TOLEDO
TONERS
TONEUP
TOPEKA
TOPERS
TOREAT
TORERO

TOREUP
TOTEMS
TOTERS
TOWELS
TOWERS
TOWERY
TRIERS
TRUEST
TUBERS
TUMEFY
TUNEIN
TUNERS
TUNEUP
TUPELO
TUREEN
TUXEDO
TUYERE
TVSETS
TWEEDS
TWEEDY
TWEENS
TWEENY
TWEEST
TWEETS
TWEETY
TWEEZE
TYPERS
TYPEUP

T•••E•

TABBED
TABLED
TABLES
TABLET
TACKED
TACKER
TAGGED
TAILED
TAIPEI
TALCED
TALKED
TALKER
TALLER
TAMPED
TAMPER
TANDEM
TANGED
TANKED
TANKER
TANNED
TANNER
TANTES
TAPPED
TAPPER
TAPPET
TARGES
TARGET
TARRED
TARTER
TASKED
TASSEL
TASSES
TASTED
TASTER
TASTES
TATTED
TATTER
TAUPES
TAUTEN
TAUTER
TAXIED
TAXIES
TAXMEN
TBONES
TEAMED
TEARED
TEASED
TEASEL
TEASER
TEASES
TEASET
TEDDED
TEDDER
TEDKEY
TEEHEE
TEEMED
TEENER
TEETER
TEEVEE
TEHEED
TEHEES
TELLER
TEMPED
TEMPEH
TEMPER
TENDED
TENDER
TENREC
TENSED
TENSER
TENSES
TENTED
TENTER
TEPEES
TERCEL
TERCET
TERKEL
TERMED
TERNES
TERRET
TERSER
TESTED
TESTEE
TESTER
TETHER
TETZEL
TEXMEX
THALER
THALES
THAMES
THANES
THAWED
THAYER
THEBES
THEFED
THEMED
THEMES
THERES
THESEA
THESES
THEWEB
THOLES
THREED
THREES
THROES
TICKED
TICKER
TICKET
TIDIED
TIDIER
TIDIES
TIERED
TIFFED
TIGGER
TILDEN
TILDES
TILLED
TILLER
TILTED
TILTER
TIMBER
TINDER
TINGED
TINGES
TINIER
TINKER
TINMEN
TINNED
TINNER
TINSEL
TINTED
TINTER
TIPPED
TIPPER
TIPPET
TITFER
TITHED
TITHER
TITHES
TITLED
TITLES
TITRED
TITRES
TITTER
TNOTES
TOATEE
TOBIES
TOFFEE
TOGAED
TOGGED
TOILED
TOILER
TOILES
TOILET
TOLLED
TOLTEC
TONIER
TONNES
TOOLED
TOOTED
TOOTER
TOPPED
TOPPER
TOPTEN
TOQUES
TORIES
TORRES
TORREY
TORTES
TOSSED
TOSSER
TOSSES
TOTHER
TOTTED
TOTTER
TOUPEE
TOURED
TOURER
TOUTED
TOUTER
TOWHEE
TOWNER
TRACED
TRACER
TRACES
TRACEY
TRADED
TRADER
TRADES
TRALEE
TRAVEL
TRAVES
TREBEK
TRIBES
TRICED
TRICEP
TRICES
TRIJET
TRIKES
TRINES
TRITER
TRIVET
TROPES
TROPEZ
TROVES
TROWED
TROWEL
TRUCES
TUAREG
TUBBED
TUCKED
TUCKER
TUCKET
TUFFET
TUFTED
TUGGED
TUGGER
TULLES
TUMMED
TUNNEL
TUNNEY
TUQUES
TUREEN
TURFED
TURKEY
TURNED
TURNER
TURRET
TURVES
TUSKED
TUSKER
TUTUED
TWINED
TWINES
TWOFER
TYPIER

T••••E

TACKLE
TAGORE
TAILLE
TALESE
TALKIE
TAMALE
TANGLE
TATTLE
TECHIE
TEEHEE
TEETHE
TEEVEE
TEMPLE
TENACE
TENURE
TERETE
TESSIE
TESTAE
TESTEE
THECAE
THENCE
THEYRE
THEYVE
THICKE
THIEVE
THISBE
THORPE
THRACE
THRALE
THRICE
THRIVE
THRONE
THROVE
TIBIAE
TICKLE
TIEDYE
TIERCE
TILLIE
TIMBRE
TINGLE
TINKLE
TIPPLE
TIPTOE
TIRADE
TIRANE
TISANE
TISSUE
TITTLE
TOATEE
TODATE
TODDLE
TOFFEE
TOGGLE
TOLIFE
TONGUE
TONITE
TOONIE
TOOTLE
TOPPLE
TOROSE
TORQUE
TOUCHE
TOUPEE
TOUSLE
TOWAGE
TOWHEE
TOWNIE
TRALEE
TRANCE
TREBLE
TRIAGE
TRIFLE
TRIODE
TRIPLE
TRISTE
TRIUNE
TRIXIE
TROCHE
TROMPE
TROUPE
TROUVE
TRUDGE
TSETSE
TUBATE
TUILLE
TULANE
TULARE
TUMBLE
TURTLE
TUSSLE
TUYERE
TWEEZE
TWELVE
TWINGE
TYRONE

•TE•••

ATEAMS
ATEASE
ATEMPO
ATEOUT
ATERGO
ATESTS
ETERNE
OTELLO
STEADS
STEADY
STEAKS
STEALS
STEAMS
STEAMY
STEEDS
STEELE
STEELS
STEELY
STEEPS
STEERS
STEEVE
STEFAN
STEFFI
STEFOY
STEINS
STELAE
STELAR
STELES
STELLA
STELMO
STENCH
STENOG
STENOS
STEPIN
STEPON
STEPPE
STEPUP
STEREO
STERES
STERNA
STERNE
STERNO
STERNS
STEROL
STEVEN
STEVIE
STEWED
STEWER

•T•E••

ATBEST
ATHENA
ATHENE
ATHENS
ATREST
ATREUS
ATTEND
ATTEST
ETHENE
ETHERS
ETSEQQ
ITSELF
OTHERS
OTTERS
STEEDS
STEELE
STEELS
STEELY
STEEPS
STEERS
STEEVE
STHENO
STPETE
STREAK
STREAM
STREEP
STREET
STRESS
STREWN
STREWS
UTTERS

•T••E•

ATONED
ATONES
ATTLEE
ETAPES
ETCHED
ETCHER
ETCHES
ETUDES
ITCHED
ITCHES
STACEY
STAGED
STAGER
STAGES
STAKED
STAKES
STALED
STALER
STALES
STAMEN
STAPES
STARED
STARER
STARES
STASES
STATED
STATEN
STATER
STATES
STAVED
STAVES
STAYED
STELES
STEREO
STERES
STEVEN
STEWED
STEWER
STILES
STIPEL
STIPES
STIVER
STOKED
STOKER
STOKES
STOLEN
STOLES
STONED
STONER
STONES
STOPES
STORED
STORER
STORES
STOREY
STOVER
STOVES
STOWED
STREEP
STREET
STUMER
STUPES
STYLED
STYLER
STYLES
STYLET

•T•••E

ATEASE
ATHENE
ATHOME
ATONCE
ATTIRE
ATTLEE
ATTUNE
ETERNE
ETHANE
ETHENE
ETOILE
OTIOSE
OTOOLE
STABLE
STACTE
STANCE
STAPLE
STARVE
STATUE
STEELE
STEEVE
STELAE
STEPPE
STERNE
STEVIE
STIFLE
STLUKE
STODGE
STOGIE
STOLLE
STOOGE
STPETE
STRAFE
STRAKE
STRIAE
STRIDE
STRIFE
STRIKE
STRINE
STRIPE
STRIVE
STROBE
STRODE
STROKE
STROVE
STYMIE

••TE••

ALTERS
ANTEED
ANTERO
ANTEUP
APTEST
ARTELS
ARTERY
ASTERN
ASTERS
ATTEND
ATTEST
AUTEUR
AZTECS
BATEAU
BETELS
BITERS
BOTELS
BUTENE
BUTEOS
CATENA
CATERS
CETERA
CITERS
CUTELY
CUTEST
CUTESY
DATERS
DETECT
DETENT
DETERS
DETEST
DOTELL
DOTEON
EATERS
EATERY
ENTERO
ENTERS
ESTEEM
ESTERS
EXTEND
EXTENT
EXTERN
GATEAU
GATERS
HATERS
HETERO
HITECH
HOTELS
INTEND
INTENS
INTENT
INTERJ
INTERN
IQTEST
KITERS
LATEEN
LATELY
LATENE
LATENS
LATENT
LATEST
LITERS
MATERS
MATEYS
METEOR
METERS

MITERS
MOTELS
MOTETS
MUTELY
MUTEST
NITERS
NITERY
NOTERS
OATERS
OBTEST
OCTETS
ORTEGA
OSTEAL
OSTEND
OTTERS
OUTEAT
PATENS
PATENT
PATERS
PETERS
POTEEN
POTENT
RATEDG
RATEDR
RATEDX
RATELS
RATERS
RETEAR
RETELL
RETENE
RETEST
SATEEN
SHTETL
TATERS
TITERS
TOTEMS
TOTERS
URTEXT
UTTERS
VOTECH
VOTEIN
VOTERS
WATERS
WATERY

••T•E•

AETHER
ALTHEA
ANTEED
ANTHEM
ANTHER
ANTLER
ANTRES
ARTIER
ATTLEE
BATHED
BATHER
BATHES
BATMEN
BATTED
BATTEL
BATTEN
BATTER
BETHEL
BETSEY
BETTER
BITTED
BITTEN
BITTER
BOTHER
BOTREE
BUTLER
BUTTED
BUTTER
BUTTES
CATHER
CATTED
CITIES
COTTEN
COTTER
CUTIES
CUTLER
CUTLET
CUTTER
DITHER
DITZES
DOTTED
DUTIES
EITHER
ENTREE
ESTEEM
ESTHER
FATHER
FATTED
FATTEN
FATTER
FETTER
FITTED
FITTER
FUTZED
FUTZES
GATHER
GETSET
GETTER
GOTSET
GOTTEN
GUTTED
GUTTER
HATRED
HATTED
HATTER
HITHER
HITMEN
HITTER
HOTBED
HOTTEA
HOTTER
HUTTED
ISTLES
JETSET
JETTED
JITNEY
JITTER
JOTTED
JUTTED
KITTEN
KOTTER
LATEEN
LATHED
LATHER
LATHES
LATKES
LATTEN
LATTER
LETTED
LETTER
LITRES
LITTER
LOTTED
LUTHER
LUTZES
MATHER
MATTEA
MATTED
MATTEL
MATTER
MATTES
METIER
METRES
MITRED
MITRES
MITTEN
MOTHER
MOTLEY
MUTTER
NATTER
NETHER
NETMEN
NETTED
NITRES
NOTYET
NUTLET
NUTMEG
NUTTED
NUTTER
OATIER
ORTLES
OSTLER
OUTLET
OUTSET
PATTED
PATTEN
PATTER
PETREL
PETTED
PETTER
PITHED
PITIED
PITIER
PITIES
PITMEN
PITTED
PITTER
POTEEN
POTHER
POTTED
POTTER
PUTTED
PUTTEE
PUTTER
RATHER
RATTED
RATTER
RETIED
RETIES
RITTER
ROTTED
ROTTEN
ROTTER
RUTGER
RUTTED
SATEEN
SETTEE
SETTER
SITTER
SOTTED
SUTLER
SUTTER
TATTED
TATTER
TETHER
TETZEL
TITFER
TITHED
TITHER
TITHES
TITLED
TITLES
TITRED
TITRES
TITTER
TOTHER
TOTTED
TOTTER
TUTUED
UNTIED
UNTIES
VATTED
VETOED
VETOER
VETOES
VETTED
WATNEY
WETHER
WETTED
WETTER
WITHED
WITHER
WITHES
WITTED
ZITHER

••T••E

ACTIVE
ACTONE
ASTUTE
ATTIRE
ATTLEE
ATTUNE
BATTLE
BATTUE
BETAKE
BETIDE
BETISE
BOTREE
BOTTLE
BUTANE
BUTENE
CATTLE
CETANE
DATIVE
DOTAGE
DOTTIE
DOTTLE
ECTYPE
ENTICE
ENTIRE
ENTREE
ESTATE
FATALE
FETTLE
FUTILE
FUTURE
GUTTAE
HATTIE
HETTIE
INTAKE
INTIME
INTINE
INTONE
INTUNE
KATHIE
KETONE
KETTLE
LATENE
LETSBE
LITTLE
MATTIE
MATURE
METATE
METOPE
METTLE
MOTILE
MOTIVE
MOTTLE
MUTATE
NATIVE
NATURE
NETTLE
NOTATE
NOTICE
NUTATE
OBTUSE
OCTANE
OCTAVE
ONTAPE
ONTIME
OUTAGE
OUTATE
PATINE
PETITE
PETRIE
POTAGE
POTPIE
POTTLE
PUTTEE
RATINE
RATITE
RATTLE
RETAKE
RETAPE
RETENE
RETILE
RETIME
RETIRE
RETUNE
RETYPE
ROTATE
RUTILE
SATIRE
SETOSE
SETTEE
SETTLE
SUTURE
TATTLE
TITTLE
UNTRUE
UNTUNE
UPTAKE
UPTIME
VITALE
VOTIVE
WATTLE

•••TE•

ABATED
ABATES
AEETES
AGATES
ALATED
ALITER
AMSTEL
ARETES
AUSTEN
BAITED
BANTER
BARTER
BASTED
BASTER
BASTES
BATTED
BATTEL
BATTEN
BATTER
BAXTER
BEATEN
BEATER
BELTED
BESTED
BETTER
BIGTEN
BITTED
BITTEN
BITTER
BOATED
BOATEL
BOATER
BOITES
BOLTED
BOOTED
BOOTEE
BOOTES
BRUTES
BUNTED
BUNTER
BUSTED
BUSTER
BUTTED
BUTTER
BUTTES
CANTED
CANTER
CARTED
CARTEL
CARTER
CARTES
CASTER
CASTES
CATTED
CENTER
CHUTED
CHUTES
CNOTES
COATED
COLTER
COMTES
CONTES
COOTER
COPTER
CORTES
CORTEX
CORTEZ
COTTEN
COTTER
COUTER
CRATED
CRATER
CRATES
CURTER
CUSTER
CUTTER
DAFTER
DANTES
DARTED
DARTER
DEFTER
DENTED
DEXTER
DHOTEL
DIETED
DIETER
DINTED
DOTTED
DUSTED
DUSTER
EASTER
EDITED
ELATED
ELATER
ELATES
ELITES
ELUTED
ELUTES
EMOTED
EMOTER
EMOTES
ENATES
EXETER
EXITED
FALTER
FASTED
FASTEN
FASTER
FATTED
FATTEN
FATTER
FELTED
FESTER
FETTER
FILTER
FISTED
FITTED
FITTER
FLUTED
FLUTES
FLUTEY
FOOTED
FOOTER
FORTES
FOSTER
GAITED
GAITER
GARTER
GESTES
GETTER
GIFTED
GIRTED
GLUTEI
GLUTEN
GLUTES
GOATEE
GOTTEN
GRATED
GRATER
GRATES
GRETEL
GUNTER
GUSTED
GUTTED
GUTTER
HAFTED
HALTED
HALTER
HASTEN
HASTES
HATTED
HATTER
HEATED
HEATER
HEFTED
HELTER
HENTED
HESTER
HINTED
HINTER
HITTER
HOOTED
HOOTER
HOSTED
HOSTEL
HOTTEA
HOTTER
HUNTED
HUNTER
HUTTED
INSTEP
IRATER
JEETER
JESTED
JESTER
JETTED
JILTED
JITTER
JOETEX
JOLTED
JOTTED
JUSTER
JUTTED
KEITEL
KILTED
KILTER
KITTEN
KOTTER
KRATER
LAPTEV
LASTED
LASTEX
LATTEN
LATTER
LECTER
LENTEN
LESTER
LETTED
LETTER
LIFTED
LIFTER
LILTED
LINTEL
LINTER
LISTED
LISTEE
LISTEL
LISTEN
LISTER
LITTER
LOFTED
LOITER
LOOTED
LOOTER
LOTTED
LUSTED
LUSTER
MALTED
MANTEL
MARTEL
MARTEN
MASTER
MATTEA
MATTED
MATTEL
MATTER
MATTES
MEETER
MELTED
MINTED
MINTER
MISTED
MISTER
MITTEN
MIXTEC
MOATED
MOLTED
MOLTEN
MOLTER
MONTEL
MONTES
MONTEZ
MOOTED
MOSTEL
MUSTER
MUTTER
NANTES
NATTER
NEATEN
NEATER
NESTEA
NESTED
NESTER
NETTED
NEUTER
NUTTED
NUTTER
OBITER
OBSTET
OERTER
ORATED
ORATES
OUSTED
OUSTER
OYSTER
PALTER
PANTED
PARTED
PASTED
PASTEL
PASTES
PATTED
PATTEN
PATTER
PELTED
PELTER
PERTER
PESTER
PETTED
PETTER
PEWTER
PIETER
PINTER
PISTES
PITTED

PITTER
PLATED
PLATEN
PLATER
PLATES
PONTES
PORTED
PORTER
POSTED
POSTER
POTTED
POTTER
POUTED
POUTER
PRATED
PRATER
PRATES
PRETER
PROTEI
PROTEM
PUNTED
PUNTER
PUTTED
PUTTEE
PUTTER
QUOTED
QUOTER
QUOTES
RAFTED
RAFTER
RANTED
RANTER
RASTER
RATTED
RATTER
RENTED
RENTER
RESTED
RESTER
REUTER
RIFTED
RIOTED
RIOTER
RITTER
ROOTED
ROOTER
ROSTER
ROTTED
ROTTEN
ROTTER
ROUTED
ROUTER
ROUTES
RRATED
RUSTED
RUTTED
SALTED
SALTEN
SALTER
SANTEE
SAUTES
SCOTER
SCUTES
SEATED
SEATER
SEPTET
SESTET
SETTEE
SETTER
SEXTET
SIFTED
SIFTER
SILTED
SINTER
SISTER
SITTER
SKATED
SKATER
SKATES
SLATED
SLATER
SLATES
SMITES
SOFTEN
SOFTER
SORTED
SORTER
SOTTED
SOUTER
SPATES
SPITED
SPITES
STATED
STATEN
STATER
STATES
SUITED
SUITES
SUMTER
SUTTER
SYSTEM
TANTES
TARTER
TASTED
TASTER
TASTES
TATTED
TATTER
TAUTEN
TAUTER
TEETER
TENTED
TENTER
TESTED
TESTEE
TESTER
TILTED
TILTER
TINTED
TINTER
TITTER
TNOTES
TOATEE
TOLTEC
TOOTED
TOOTER
TOPTEN
TORTES
TOTTED
TOTTER
TOUTED
TOUTER
TRITER
TUFTED
ULSTER
UNITED
UNITER
UNITES
VASTER
VATTED
VENTED
VENTER
VERTEX
VESTED
VESTEE
VETTED
VORTEX
WAFTED
WAITED
WAITER
WALTER
WANTED
WASTED
WASTER
WASTES
WELTED
WELTER
WETTED
WETTER
WHITEN
WHITER
WHITES
WILTED
WINTER
WISTER
WITTED
WONTED
WRITER
WRITES
WYNTER
XRATED
XYSTER
YESTER
ZESTED

•••T•E

AORTAE
AUNTIE
BATTLE
BATTUE
BEATLE
BEETLE
BERTIE
BIGTOE
BLITHE
BLYTHE
BOOTEE
BOOTHE
BOOTIE
BOTTLE
BOWTIE
BUSTLE
CANTLE
CASTLE
CATTLE
CENTRE
CLOTHE
CONTRE
COOTIE
COSTAE
DOTTIE
DOTTLE
FETTLE
GENTLE
GERTIE
GOATEE
GOETHE
GUTTAE
HATTIE
HETTIE
HOGTIE
HOOTIE
HURTLE
HUSTLE
JOSTLE
KETTLE
KILTIE
KIRTLE
LAOTSE
LEFTIE
LHOTSE
LISTEE
LITTLE
LOATHE
LUSTRE
MAITRE
MANTLE
MATTIE
METTLE
MILTIE
MOLTKE
MOTTLE
MYRTLE
NESTLE
NETTLE
ODETTE
PESTLE
PINTLE
PLATTE
POTTLE
PUTTEE
RATTLE
RUSTLE
SANTEE
SARTRE
SCATHE
SCYTHE
SEETHE
SETTEE
SETTLE
SNATHE
SOFTIE
SOOTHE
SORTIE
SPATHE
STATUE
SUBTLE
SWATHE
TATTLE
TEETHE
TESTAE
TESTEE
TIPTOE
TITTLE
TOATEE
TOOTLE
TSETSE
TURTLE
VESTEE
VIRTUE
WATTLE
WHATVE
WRITHE
YVETTE

••••TE

ABLATE
ACUATE
ADESTE
ADNATE
AERATE
AGNATE
ANSATE
APLITE
AQUATE
ASTUTE
AVIATE
BARITE
BERATE
BINATE
BORATE
BRONTE
BYROTE
CANUTE
CAPOTE
CENOTE
CERATE
CHASTE
CHOATE
COMATE
COYOTE
CREATE
CROUTE
CURATE
DEBATE
DELATE
DELETE
DEMOTE
DENOTE
DEPUTE
DEVOTE
DILATE
DILUTE
DONATE
DUARTE
ECARTE
EFFETE
EMEUTE
EQUATE
ERGATE
ESTATE
EXCITE
FICHTE
FINITE
FIXATE
GAMETE
GEMOTE
GUNITE
GYRATE
HALITE
HAMITE
HECATE
IDEATE
IGNITE
IMPUTE
INCITE
INDITE
INMATE
INNATE
INVITE
IODATE
IOLITE
KARATE
LANATE
LEGATE
LEVITE
LIGATE
LOBATE
LOCATE
LUCITE
LUNATE
LUXATE
MALATE
METATE
MINUTE
MUTATE
NEGATE
NOTATE
NUTATE
OBLATE
ODETTE
OFLATE
OLEATE
ONSITE
OOCYTE
OOLITE
OPHITE
OPIATE
ORGATE
ORNATE
OSSETE
OUTATE
PAIUTE
PALATE
PEDATE
PETITE
PEYOTE
PILATE
PINITE
PIRATE
PLANTE
PLATTE
POINTE
POLITE
PUENTE
PYRITE
RAMATE
RATITE
REBATE
RECITE
REDATE
REFUTE
RELATE
REMOTE
RENOTE
REPUTE
RERATE
ROTATE
RUGATE
SAINTE
SALUTE
SAMITE
SAVATE
SEDATE
SEMITE
SENATE
SHIITE
SHORTE
SOLUTE
SPRITE
STACTE
STPETE
SURETE
SVELTE
TERETE
TODATE
TONITE
TRISTE
TUBATE
UNIATE
UPDATE
VACATE
VENITE
VERITE
VOLUTE
YVETTE
ZONATE
ZYGOTE

T•F•••

TEFLON
TIFFED
TIFFIN
TOFFEE
TUFFET
TUFTED

T••F••

THEFED
THEFLY
THEFTS
TIFFED
TIFFIN
TITFER
TOFFEE
TRIFID
TRIFLE
TRYFOR
TUFFET
TURFED
TWOFER

T•••F•

TAPOFF
TARIFF
TEEOFF
THRIFT
TIPOFF
TOLIFE
TOPOFF
TUMEFY
TYPIFY

T••••F

TAPOFF
TARIFF
TEEOFF
TELLOF
TIPOFF
TOLDOF
TOPOFF

•T•F••

STAFFS
STEFAN
STEFFI
STEFOY
STIFFS
STIFLE
STUFFS
STUFFY

•T••F•

STAFFS
STEFFI
STIFFS
STRAFE
STRIFE
STUFFS
STUFFY

•T•••F

ITSELF
STAPUF

••TF••

ARTFUL
BOTFLY
FITFUL
HATFUL
KITFOX
LETFLY
OPTFOR
OUTFIT
OUTFLY
OUTFOX
POTFUL
TITFER
VATFUL
WETFLY

••T•F•

BITOFF
CITIFY
CUTOFF
GETOFF
GOTOFF
LETOFF
MOTIFS
NOTIFY
PUTOFF
RATIFY
SETOFF

••T••F

BITOFF
CUTOFF
GETOFF
GOTOFF
LETOFF
PUTOFF
SETOFF

•••T•F

CERTIF
SORTOF
WHATIF

T•G•••

TAGDAY
TAGEND
TAGGED
TAGORE
TAGOUT
TAGSUP
TIGERS
TIGGER
TIGHTS
TIGLON
TIGRIS
TOGAED
TOGGED
TOGGLE
TUGGED
TUGGER
TUGRIK

T••G••

TAGGED
TAIGAS
TANGED
TANGLE
TANGLY
TANGOS
TANGUY
TARGES
TARGET
TAUGHT
THIGHS
TIGGER
TINGED
TINGES
TINGLE
TINGLY
TINGOD
TOGGED
TOGGLE
TONGAN
TONGUE
TOPGUN
TOUGHS
TOUGHY
TRAGIC
TRIGLY
TRIGON
TROGON
TUGGED
TUGGER
TURGID
TURGOR
TWIGGY

T•••G•

TELUGU
THINGS
THINGY
THONGS
THOUGH
TOBAGO
TOWAGE
TRIAGE
TROUGH
TRUDGE
TWANGS
TWANGY
TWIGGY
TWINGE

T••••G

TAKING
TAMING
TAPING
TARING
TAUTOG
TAWING
TAXING
TEABAG
TEEING
THRONG
TIDING
TIEING
TILING
TIMING
TIRING
TOEING
TONING
TOPDOG
TOTING
TOWING
TOYDOG

TOYING
TRUING
TRYING
TUAREG
TUBING
TUNING
TURING
TYPING

•T•G••
STAGED
STAGER
STAGES
STIGMA
STOGIE

•T••G•
ATERGO
STINGO
STINGS
STINGY
STODGE
STODGY
STOOGE

•T•••G
STALAG
STENOG
STRING
STRONG
STRUNG

••TG••
ARTGUM
CATGUT
JETGUN
OUTGUN
ROTGUT
RUTGER

••T•G•
DOTAGE
IDTAGS
LATIGO
LETSGO
ORTEGA
OUTAGE
POTAGE
RETAGS

••T••G
ACTING
BATING
BITING
BUTUNG
CATRIG
CITING
DATING
DATONG
DOTING
EATING
FETING
GATING
HATING
HOTDOG
JETLAG
KITBAG
KITING
LITHOG
LUTING
MATING
METING
MUTING
NOTING
NUTMEG
OPTING
OUTING
PETROG
RATEDG
RATING
SATANG
SATING
SITING
TOTING
VOTING
WETTIG

•••T•G
DOGTAG
GOSTAG
MAYTAG
PHOTOG
RAGTAG
REDTAG
SONTAG
TAUTOG
WETTIG
ZAFTIG

TH••••
THALER
THALES
THALIA
THAMES
THANES
THANKS
THATCH
THATIS
THATLL
THAWED
THAYER
THEBES
THECAE
THECAL
THEEND
THEFED
THEFLY
THEFTS
THEHAJ
THEIRS
THEISM
THEIST
THEKID
THELIP
THELMA
THEMED
THEMES
THENAR
THENCE
THEORY
THERES
THERMO
THERMS
THESEA
THESES
THESIS
THESIX
THETAS
THETIC
THETIS
THETOY
THEWEB
THEWIZ
THEYLL
THEYRE
THEYVE
THICKE
THIEVE
THIGHS
THILLS
THINGS
THINGY
THINKS
THINLY
THIRDS
THIRST
THIRTY
THISBE
THOLES
THOMAS
THONGS
THORAX
THORNS
THORNY
THORPE
THORPS
THOUGH
THRACE
THRALE
THRALL
THRASH
THREAD
THREAT
THREED
THREES
THRESH
THRICE
THRIFT
THRILL
THRIPS
THRIVE
THROAT
THROBS
THROES
THRONE
THRONG
THROVE
THROWN
THROWS
THRUMS
THRUSH
THRUST
THUJAS
THUMBS
THUMPS
THUNKS
THUSLY
THWACK
THWART
THYMUS
THYRSI

T•H•••
TAHINI
TAHITI
TEHEED
TEHEES
TSHIRT

T••H••
TECHIE
TECHNO
TEEHEE
TEPHRA
TETHER
TETHYS
THEHAJ
TIGHTS
TINHAT
TISHRI
TITHED
TITHER
TITHES
TOPHAT
TOPHUS
TOTHER
TOWHEE
TUCHUN
TVSHOW
TYPHUS
TZUHSI

T•••H•
TAICHI
TAUGHT
TEETHE
TENTHS
TETCHY
THIGHS
TOOTHY
TORAHS
TORCHY
TOUCHE
TOUCHY
TOUGHS
TOUGHY
TRACHY
TRASHY
TRICHO
TRISHA
TROCHE
TROPHY
TROTHS
TRUTHS

T••••H
TAKETH
TEMPEH
TERAPH
THATCH
THOUGH
THRASH
THRESH
THRUSH
TONISH
TRENCH
TROUGH
TUSSAH
TWITCH

•TH•••
ATHAND
ATHENA
ATHENE
ATHENS
ATHOME
ETHANE
ETHENE
ETHERS
ETHICS
ETHNIC
ETHNOS
ITHACA
ITHAKI
OTHERS
STHENO
UTHANT

•T•H••
ATTHAT
ETCHED
ETCHER
ETCHES
ITCHED
ITCHES
ITZHAK
UTAHAN

•T••H•
STITHY
STJOHN

•T•••H
ATTACH
STANCH
STARCH
STENCH
STITCH
STORCH

••TH••
AETHER
ALTHEA
ANTHEM
ANTHER
ARTHRO
ARTHUR
ATTHAT
AUTHOR
BATHED
BATHER
BATHES
BATHOS
BETHEL
BOTHER
CATHAY
CATHER
DITHER
DOTHAN
EITHER
ESTHER
FATHER
FATHOM
GATHER
GOTHAM
GOTHIC
HATHOR
HITHER
ISTHMI
JETHRO
KATHIE
LATHED
LATHER
LATHES
LETHAL
LITHIC
LITHOG
LITHOS
LOTHAR
LUTHER
LUTHOR
MATHER
MATHIS
METHOD
METHYL
MOTHER
MOTHRA
MYTHIC
MYTHOI
MYTHOL
MYTHOS
NATHAN
NETHER
OUTHIT
PATHAN
PATHOL
PATHOS
PITHED
POTHER
PYTHIA
PYTHON
RATHER
ROTHKO
SOTHAT
TETHER
TETHYS
TITHED
TITHER
TITHES
TOTHER
WETHER
WITHAL
WITHED
WITHER
WITHES
WITHIN
WITHIT
ZITHER

••T•H•
BETCHA
BOTCHY
CATCHY
GOTCHA
LITCHI
LOTAHS
NOTCHY
PATCHY
PITCHY
TETCHY
WITCHY

••T••H
ATTACH
DETACH
FETISH
HITECH
IRTYSH
JUTISH
KITSCH
LATISH
MATZOH
POTASH
PUTSCH
VOTECH

•••TH•
AGATHA
APATHY
ARETHA
BERTHA
BERTHS
BIRTHS
BLITHE
BLYTHE
BOOTHE
BOOTHS
BROTHS
CANTHI
CHETHS
CLOTHE
CLOTHO
CLOTHS
DEPTHS
EARTHA
EARTHY
FAITHS
FIFTHS
FILTHY
FIRTHS
FROTHS
FROTHY
GARTHS
GIRTHS
GOETHE
HEATHS
HEATHY
ICHTHY
LOATHE
MARTHA
MONTHS
MOUTHS
MOUTHY
NINTHS
NORTHS
QUOTHA
RHYTHM
SCATHE
SCYTHE
SEETHE
SIXTHS
SLITHY
SLOTHS
SMITHS
SMITHY
SNATHE
SNATHS
SOOTHE
SOUTHS
SPATHE
STITHY
SWATHE
SWATHS
TEETHE
TENTHS
TOOTHY
TROTHS
TRUTHS
WIDTHS
WORTHS
WORTHY
WRATHS
WRATHY
WRITHE
XANTHO
YOUTHS

•••T•H
BLOTCH
CLUTCH
CRUTCH
FLETCH
FLITCH
GLITCH
HOOTCH
KLATCH
KVETCH
NAUTCH
SCOTCH
SCUTCH
SKETCH
SKITCH
SMUTCH
SNATCH
SNITCH
STITCH
SWATCH
SWITCH
THATCH
TWITCH
WRETCH

••••TH
BREATH
BYPATH
COMETH
DALETH
DEARTH
DULUTH
EIGHTH
EOLITH
FOURTH
GARETH
GOWITH
GROWTH
HEALTH
HEARTH
INWITH
IOMOTH
JOBETH
JUDITH
LENGTH
LILITH
NAMATH
OOLITH
ORNITH
PLINTH
SHEATH
SLEUTH
SMOOTH
SPILTH
SWARTH
TAKETH
WARMTH
WEALTH
WRAITH
WREATH
ZENITH
ZEROTH
ZIZITH

TI••••
TIARAS
TIBIAE
TIBIAL
TIBIAS
TICALS
TICKED
TICKER
TICKET
TICKLE
TICKLY
TICTAC
TIDBIT
TIDDLY
TIDIED
TIDIER
TIDIES
TIDILY
TIDING
TIDYUP
TIEDIN
TIEDTO
TIEDUP
TIEDYE
TIEING
TIEINS
TIEPIN
TIERCE
TIERED
TIEROD
TIERRA
TIESIN
TIESTO
TIESUP
TIEUPS
TIFFED
TIFFIN
TIGERS
TIGGER
TIGHTS
TIGLON
TIGRIS
TILAKS
TILDEN
TILDES
TILERS
TILING
TILLED
TILLER
TILLIE
TILLIS
TILSIT
TILTED
TILTER
TIMBAL
TIMBER
TIMBRE
TIMELY
TIMERS
TIMING
TINCAL
TINCAN
TINCTS
TINDER
TINEAR
TINGED
TINGES
TINGLE
TINGLY
TINGOD
TINHAT
TINIER
TINILY
TINKER
TINKLE
TINKLY
TINMAN
TINMEN
TINNED

TINNER
TINPAN
TINPOT
TINSEL
TINTED
TINTER
TIPINS
TIPOFF
TIPPED
TIPPER
TIPPET
TIPPLE
TIPSIN
TIPTOE
TIPTOP
TIPUPS
TIRADE
TIRANA
TIRANE
TIRING
TISANE
TISHRI
TISSUE
TITANS
TITBIT
TITERS
TITFER
TITHED
TITHER
TITHES
TITIAN
TITLED
TITLES
TITRED
TITRES
TITTER
TITTLE
TITTUP
TIVOLI

T•I•••

TAICHI
TAIGAS
TAILED
TAILLE
TAILOR
TAINAN
TAINOS
TAINTS
TAIPAN
TAIPEI
TAIWAN
TBILLS
TBIRDS
THICKE
THIEVE
THIGHS
THILLS
THINGS
THINGY
THINKS
THINLY
THIRDS
THIRST
THIRTY
THISBE
TOILED
TOILER
TOILES
TOILET
TRIADS
TRIAGE
TRIALS
TRIBAL
TRIBES
TRICED
TRICEP
TRICES
TRICHO
TRICIA
TRICKS
TRICKY
TRICOT
TRIERS
TRIFID
TRIFLE
TRIGLY
TRIGON
TRIJET
TRIKES
TRILBY
TRILLS
TRIMLY
TRINAL
TRINES
TRIODE
TRIPLE
TRIPLY
TRIPOD
TRIPOS
TRIPUP
TRISHA
TRISTE
TRITER
TRITON
TRIUNE
TRIVET
TRIVIA
TRIXIE
TUILLE
TWIGGY
TWILIT
TWILLS
TWINED
TWINES
TWINGE
TWIRLS
TWISTS
TWISTY
TWITCH
TWITTY

T••I••

TAHINI
TAHITI
TAKING
TAKINS
TALION
TAMILS
TAMING
TANIST
TAOISM
TAOIST
TAPING
TAPINS
TAPIRS
TARIFF
TARING
TAWING
TAXIED
TAXIES
TAXING
TEDIUM
TEEING
THEIRS
THEISM
THEIST
THRICE
THRIFT
THRILL
THRIPS
THRIVE
TIBIAE
TIBIAL
TIBIAS
TIDIED
TIDIER
TIDIES
TIDILY
TIDING
TIEING
TIEINS
TILING
TIMING
TINIER
TINILY
TIPINS
TIRING
TITIAN
TOBIAS
TOBIES
TOEING
TOEINS
TOLIFE
TONICS
TONIER
TONING
TONISH
TONITE
TOPICS
TORIES
TORINO
TOTING
TOWING
TOXICS
TOXINS
TOYING
TRAILS
TRAINS
TRAITS
TROIKA
TRUING
TRUISM
TRYING
TSHIRT
TUBING
TUBIST
TULIPS
TUNICA
TUNICS
TUNING
TUPIAN
TURING
TYPIER
TYPIFY
TYPING
TYPIST
TYRIAN

T•••I•

TABRIZ
TACTIC
TAKEIN
TALKIE
TANNIC
TANNIN
TARPIT
TECHIE
TENNIS
TENPIN
TESSIE
TETRIS
THALIA
THATIS
THEKID
THELIP
THESIS
THESIX
THETIC
THETIS
THEWIZ
TIDBIT
TIEDIN
TIEPIN
TIESIN
TIFFIN
TIGRIS
TILLIE
TILLIS
TILSIT
TIPSIN
TITBIT
TMESIS
TOCSIN
TOEDIN
TOESIN
TOMLIN
TOMMIX
TOMTIT
TONKIN
TONSIL
TOOKIN
TOOKIT
TOONIE
TOROID
TORPID
TORRID
TOWNIE
TRAGIC
TRAVIS
TREDIA
TREPID
TRICIA
TRIFID
TRIVIA
TRIXIE
TROPIC
TSURIS
TUCKIN
TUGRIK
TUNEIN
TURBID
TURBIT
TURGID
TURKIC
TURNIN
TURNIP
TURPIN
TWILIT
TWOBIT

T••••I

TAHINI
TAHITI
TAICHI
TAIPEI
TATAMI
THYRSI
TISHRI
TIVOLI
TUMULI
TZUHSI

•TI•••

OTIOSE
OTITIC
OTITIS
STICKS
STICKY
STIFFS
STIFLE
STIGMA
STILES
STILLS
STILLY
STILTS
STIMPY
STINGO
STINGS
STINGY
STINKS
STINKY
STINTS
STIPEL
STIPES
STIRIN
STIRKS
STIRUP
STITCH
STITHY
STIVER
STIVIC

•T•I••

ATKINS
ATRIAL
ATRISK
ATRIUM
ATTICA
ATTICS
ATTILA
ATTIRE
ATWILL
ETHICS
ETOILE
STAINS
STAIRS
STEINS
STOICS
STRIAE
STRICK
STRICT
STRIDE
STRIFE
STRIKE
STRINE
STRING
STRIPE
STRIPS
STRIPY
STRIVE

•T••I•

ATOMIC
ATONIC
ATTAIN
ATTRIT
ETALIA
ETALII
ETHNIC
ETONIC
ITALIA
ITALIC
OTITIC
OTITIS
STADIA
STALIN
STASIS
STATIC
STEPIN
STEVIE
STIRIN
STIVIC
STOGIE
STOLID
STOPIN
STOPIT
STOTIN
STRAIN
STRAIT
STUDIO
STUPID
STYMIE
STYRIA
UTOPIA

•T•••I

ETALII
ITHAKI
ITURBI
STEFFI
STRATI

••TI••

ACTIII
ACTING
ACTINO
ACTION
ACTIUM
ACTIVE
ALTIMA
ALTIUS
ANTICS
ARTIER
ARTILY
ARTIST
ATTICA
ATTICS
ATTILA
ATTIRE
BATIKS
BATING
BETIDE
BETISE
BITING
CATION
CITIES
CITIFY
CITING
CITIUS
CUTIES
CUTINS
DATING
DATIVE
DOTING
DUTIES
EATING
ENTICE
ENTIRE
ENTITY
FATIMA
FETING
FETISH
FUTILE
GATING
HATING
INTIMA
INTIME
INTINE
JUTISH
KITING
LATIGO
LATINA
LATINI
LATINO
LATINS
LATISH
LATIUM
LOTION
LUTING
LUTIST
MATING
MATINS
METIER
METING
MOTIFS
MOTILE
MOTION
MOTIVE
MUTING
MUTINY
NATICK
NATION
NATIVE
NOTICE
NOTIFY
NOTING
NOTION
OATIER
ONTIME
OPTICS
OPTIMA
OPTING
OPTION
OSTIUM
OUTING
PATINA
PATINE
PATIOS
PETITE
PITIED
PITIER
PITIES
POTION
RATIFY
RATINE
RATING
RATION
RATIOS
RATITE
RETIAL
RETIED
RETIES
RETILE
RETIME
RETINA
RETIRE
ROTINI
RUTILE
SATING
SATINS
SATINY
SATIRE
SETINS
SHTICK
SITING
SITINS
TITIAN
TOTING
ULTIMA
ULTIMO
UNTIDY
UNTIED
UNTIES
UPTICK
UPTIME
VOTING
VOTIVE

••T•I•

ACTIII
ALTAIC
ALTAIR
ANTRIM
ARTOIS
ASTRID
ATTAIN
ATTRIT
BUTTIN
CATKIN
CATNIP
CATRIG
CITRIC
CUTSIN
DETAIL
DETAIN
DOTTIE
EATSIN
ENTAIL
FITSIN
GATLIN
GETSIN
GETSIT
GOTHIC
GOTOIT
HATPIN
HATTIE
HETTIE
HITSIT
HOTAIR
HOTTIP
IATRIC
INTUIT
ISTRIA
KATHIE
LATVIA
LETSIN
LITHIC
MATHIS
MATLIN
MATRIX
MATTIE
METRIC
MYTHIC
NITRIC
NITWIT
NUTKIN
NUTRIA
OBTAIN
OUTBID
OUTDID
OUTFIT
OUTHIT
OUTWIT
OXTAIL
PATOIS
PETAIN
PETRIE
PETTIT
POTPIE
PUTRID
PUTSIN
PYTHIA
RATLIN
RETAIL
RETAIN
RETRIM
SETSIN
SITSIN
TETRIS
TITBIT
VITRIC
VOTEIN
WETTIG
WITHIN
WITHIT

••T••I

ACTIII
BATUMI
HATARI
ISTHMI
JETSKI
KATMAI
LATINI
LITCHI
MYTHOI
OCTOPI
OCTROI
POTOSI
QATARI
ROTINI
SATORI
TATAMI
WATUSI

•••TI•

ABATIS
ACETIC
AMATIS
AORTIC
ARCTIC
AUNTIE
AUSTIN
BALTIC
BEATIT
BERTIE
BESTIR
BIOTIC
BIOTIN

BOOTIE
BOWTIE
BUSTIN
BUTTIN
CELTIC
CERTIF
CHITIN
COATIS
COOTIE
COPTIC
CRETIN
CRITIC
CULTIC
CURTIN
CURTIS
CURTIZ
CUSTIS
DELTIC
DENTIL
DENTIN
DHOTIS
DISTIL
DOTTIE
DUSTIN
EDITIO
EROTIC
EXOTIC
FISTIC
FOETID
FUSTIC
GERTIE
GESTIC
GRATIA
GRATIN
GRATIS
HATTIE
HECTIC
HESTIA
HETTIE
HOGTIE
HOOTIE
HOTTIP
IGETIT
IGOTIT
INITIO
INSTIL
JUSTIN
KILTIE
LACTIC
LEFTIE
LEFTIN
LENTIL
LOSTIT
MALTIN
MANTIC
MANTIS
MARTIN
MASTIC
MATTIE
MENTIS
MILTIE
MUFTIS
MUNTIN
MYSTIC
NOETIC
OTITIC
OTITIS
PASTIS
PECTIC
PECTIN
PEPTIC
PETTIT
PHATIC
PHOTIC
PIETIN
PISTIL
POETIC
PONTIC
PORTIA
POSTIT
QUITIT
RUSTIC
SANTIR
SCOTIA
SENTIN
SEPTIC
SHUTIN
SOFTIE
SORTIE
STATIC
STOTIN
TACTIC
THATIS
THETIC
THETIS
TOMTIT
VICTIM
VICTIS
WANTIN
WENTIN
WETTIG
WHATIF
ZAFTIG

•••T•I
CANTHI
CENTRI
DMITRI
FRUTTI
GLUTEI
MAITAI
MAOTAI
PROTEI

••••TI
AGOUTI
AVANTI
BHAKTI
DORATI
FRUTTI
GELATI
MALOTI
PILOTI
RUBATI
SENITI
SHAKTI
SHORTI
SMALTI
STRATI
TAHITI
VASHTI
WAPITI

T•J•••
TEJANO

T••J••
THUJAS
TOPJOB
TRAJAN
TRIJET
TROJAN

T••••J
THEHAJ

•TJ•••
STJOAN
STJOHN

•T•J••
STOJKO

••T••J
INTERJ
SGTMAJ

T•K•••
TAKEIN
TAKEON
TAKERS
TAKETH
TAKETO
TAKEUP
TAKING
TAKINS
TOKAYS
TOKENS
TOKLAS

T••K••
TACKED
TACKER
TACKLE
TACKON
TALKAT
TALKED
TALKER
TALKIE
TALKTO
TALKUP
TANKAS
TANKED
TANKER
TANKUP
TASKED
TEDKEY
TERKEL
THEKID
TICKED
TICKER
TICKET
TICKLE
TICKLY
TINKER
TINKLE
TINKLY
TONKIN
TOOKIN
TOOKIT
TOOKON
TOOKTO
TOOKUP
TRIKES
TUCKED
TUCKER
TUCKET
TUCKIN
TURKEY
TURKIC
TUSKED
TUSKER

T•••K•
TANAKA
THANKS
THICKE
THINKS
THUNKS
TILAKS
TOPEKA
TRACKS
TRICKS
TRICKY
TROIKA
TRUCKS
TRUNKS
TWEAKS

T••••K
TANOAK
THWACK
TOBRUK
TREBEK
TUGRIK

•TK•••
ATKINS

•T•K••
STAKED
STAKES
STOKED
STOKER
STOKES

•T••K•
ITHAKI
STACKS
STALKS
STALKY
STANKY
STEAKS
STICKS
STICKY
STINKS
STINKY
STIRKS
STLUKE
STOCKS
STOCKY
STOJKO
STOOKS
STORKS
STRAKE
STRIKE
STROKE

•T•••K
ATRISK
ATTACK
ATWORK
ITZHAK
STMARK
STREAK
STRICK
STRUCK

••TK••
CATKIN
KITKAT
LATKES
NUTKIN

••T•K•
BATIKS
BETAKE
INTAKE
JETSKI
RETAKE
ROTHKO
UPTAKE

••T••K
AMTRAK
ATTACK
BETOOK
BYTALK
NATICK
RETOOK
SHTICK
UNTACK
UPTALK
UPTICK

•••TK•
MOLTKE
NOOTKA

•••T•K
BARTOK
BRATSK
VOSTOK

TL••••
TLALOC

T•L•••
TALBOT
TALCED
TALCUM
TALENT
TALERS
TALESE
TALION
TALKAT
TALKED
TALKER
TALKIE
TALKTO
TALKUP
TALLER
TALLOW
TALMUD
TALONS
TELEDU
TELLER
TELLOF
TELLON
TELUGU
TILAKS
TILDEN
TILDES
TILERS
TILING
TILLED
TILLER
TILLIE
TILLIS
TILSIT
TILTED
TILTER
TOLDOF
TOLDON
TOLEDO
TOLIFE
TOLLED
TOLTEC
TOLUCA
TULANE
TULARE
TULIPS
TULLES
TULSAN

T••L••
TABLAS
TABLED
TABLES
TABLET
TAILED
TAILLE
TAILOR
TALLER
TALLOW
TAYLOR
TBILLS
TEFLON
TELLER
TELLOF
TELLON
TESLAS
THALER
THALES
THALIA
THELIP
THELMA
THILLS
THOLES
TIGLON
TILLED
TILLER
TILLIE
TILLIS
TITLED
TITLES
TLALOC
TOILED
TOILER
TOILES
TOILET
TOKLAS
TOLLED
TOMLIN
TOOLED
TOOLUP
TOULON
TRALEE
TRILBY
TRILLS
TROLLS
TRYLON
TUILLE
TULLES
TWELVE
TWILIT
TWILLS

T•••L•
TABULA
TACKLE
TAILLE
TAMALE
TAMELY
TAMILS
TANGLE
TANGLY
TARTLY
TATTLE
TAUTLY
TBILLS
TEMPLE
TEPALS
THATLL
THEFLY
THEYLL
THILLS
THINLY
THRALE
THRALL
THRILL
THUSLY
TICALS
TICKLE
TICKLY
TIDDLY
TIDILY
TIMELY
TINGLE
TINGLY
TINILY
TINKLE
TINKLY
TIPPLE
TITTLE
TIVOLI
TODDLE
TOGGLE
TOOTLE
TOPPLE
TOTALS
TOUSLE
TOWELS
TRAILS
TRAWLS
TREBLE
TREBLY
TRIALS
TRIFLE
TRIGLY
TRILLS
TRIMLY
TRIPLE
TRIPLY
TROLLS
TUILLE
TUMBLE
TUMULI
TUMULT
TUPELO
TURTLE
TUSSLE
TUVALU
TWILLS
TWIRLS
TWOPLY
TYBALT

T••••L
TARSAL
TASSEL
TEASEL
TERCEL
TERKEL
TETZEL
THATLL
THECAL
THEYLL
THRALL
THRILL
TIBIAL
TIMBAL
TINCAL
TINSEL
TONSIL
TRAVEL
TRIBAL
TRINAL
TROWEL
TUNNEL
TYDBOL

•TL•••
ATLAST
ATLATL
STLUKE

•T•L••
ATOLLS
ATTLEE
ETALIA
ETALII
ITALIA
ITALIC
OTELLO
STALAG
STALED
STALER
STALES
STALIN
STALKS
STALKY
STALLS
STELAE
STELAR
STELES
STELLA
STELMO
STILES
STILLS
STILLY
STILTS
STOLEN
STOLES
STOLID
STOLLE
STOLON
STULLS
STYLED
STYLER
STYLES
STYLET
STYLUS

•T••L•
ATOLLS
ATTILA
ATWILL
ETOILE
ITSELF
OTELLO
OTOOLE
STABLE
STABLY
STALLS
STAPLE
STEALS
STEELE
STEELS
STEELY
STELLA
STIFLE
STILLS
STILLY
STMALO
STOLLE
STOOLS
STOOLY
STROLL
STULLS

•T•••L
ATLATL
ATONAL
ATRIAL
ATWILL
ETYMOL
STEROL
STIPEL
STPAUL
STROLL

••TL••
ANTLER
ATTLEE
BUTLER
CUTLER
CUTLET
GATLIN
ISTLES
JETLAG
MATLIN
MOTLEY
NUTLET
ORTLES
OSTLER
OUTLAW
OUTLAY
OUTLET
RATLIN
SUTLER
TITLED
TITLES

••T•L•
ARTELS
ARTILY
ATTILA
BATTLE
BETELS
BITOLA
BOTELS
BOTFLY
BOTTLE
BYTALK
CATTLE
CUTELY
DOTELL
DOTTLE

EXTOLS FATALE FETTLE FUTILE HOTELS KETTLE LATELY LETFLY LITTLE METALS METTLE MOTELS MOTILE MOTTLE MUTELY NETTLE NETTLY OUTFLY PETALS PETULA POTTLE RATELS RATTLE RATTLY RETELL RETILE RETOLD RUTILE SETTLE SOTOLS TATTLE TITTLE TOTALS UNTOLD UPTALK VITALE VITALS WATTLE WETFLY

••T••L

ACTUAL ARTFUL ASTRAL BATTEL BETHEL DETAIL DOTELL ENTAIL FITFUL HATFUL LETHAL MATTEL METHYL MITRAL MUTUAL MYTHOL OSTEAL OXTAIL PATHOL PATROL PETREL PETROL POTFUL RETAIL RETELL RETIAL RETOOL RETRAL RITUAL SHTETL TETZEL VATFUL WITHAL

•••TL•

BATTLE BEATLE BEETLE BOTTLE BUSTLE CANTLE CASTLE CATTLE COSTLY CURTLY DAFTLY DEFTLY DOTTLE FEATLY FETTLE FLATLY GENTLE GENTLY HOSTLY HURTLE HUSTLE JOSTLE JUSTLY KETTLE KIRTLE LASTLY LITTLE MANTLE MEETLY METTLE MOSTLY MOTTLE MYRTLE NEATLY NESTLE NETTLE NETTLY PARTLY PERTLY PESTLE PINTLE PORTLY POTTLE RAPTLY RATTLE RATTLY RUSTLE SETTLE SOFTLY SUBTLE SUBTLY TARTLY TATTLE TAUTLY THATLL TITTLE TOOTLE TURTLE VASTLY WATTLE WHATLL

•••T•L

ACETAL ACETYL AMATOL AMSTEL AORTAL BATTEL BOATEL BRUTAL CARTEL COSTAL DACTYL DENTAL DENTIL DHOTEL DISTAL DISTIL DUCTAL FESTAL FOETAL FONTAL GRETEL HIATAL HOSTEL HYETAL INSTAL INSTIL KEITEL LENTIL LINTEL LISTEL MANTEL MARTEL MATTEL MENTAL MONTEL MORTAL MOSTEL PASTEL PISTIL PISTOL PORTAL POSTAL RENTAL SEPTAL THATLL UNITAL VESTAL WHATLL

••••TL

ATLATL SHTETL

TM••••

TMESIS

T•M•••

TAMALE TAMARA TAMAYO TAMELY TAMERS TAMEST TAMILS TAMING TAMMUZ TAMPED TAMPER TAMTAM TEMPED TEMPEH TEMPER TEMPLE TEMPOS TEMPTS TEMPUS TIMBAL TIMBER TIMBRE TIMELY TIMERS TIMING TOMATO TOMBAC TOMBOY TOMCAT TOMLIN TOMMIX TOMTIT TOMTOM TUMBLE TUMEFY TUMMED TUMULI TUMULT

T••M••

TALMUD TAMMUZ TARMAC TASMAN TAXMAN TAXMEN TEAMED TEAMUP TEEMED TERMED TEXMEX THAMES THEMED THEMES THOMAS THUMBS THUMPS THYMUS TINMAN TINMEN TOAMAN TODMAN TOMMIX TRAMPS TREMOR TRIMLY TROMPE TROMPS TRUMAN TRUMPS TUBMAN TUMMED

T•••M•

TACOMA TATAMI THELMA THERMO THERMS THRUMS TOTEMS TRAUMA

T••••M

TALCUM TAMTAM TANDEM TAOISM TEDEUM TEDIUM THEISM TOMTOM TRUISM

•TM•••

ATMOST STMALO STMARK UTMOST

•T•M••

ATAMAN ATEMPO ATOMIC ETYMOL ETYMON STAMEN STAMPS STIMPY STOMAS STOMAT STOMPS STUMER STUMPS STUMPY STYMIE

•T••M•

ATEAMS ATHOME STEAMS STEAMY STELMO STIGMA STORMS STORMY STRUMS

•T•••M

ATRIUM STREAM

••TM••

ALTMAN BATMAN BATMEN BITMAP GETMAD GOTMAD HETMAN HITMAN HITMEN KATMAI LITMUS MOTMOT NETMAN NETMEN NUTMEG PATMOS PITMAN PITMEN SGTMAJ WETMOP

••T•M•

ALTIMA AUTUMN BATUMI ENTOMO FATIMA INTIMA INTIME ISTHMI ONTIME OPTIMA RETIME TATAMI TOTEMS ULTIMA ULTIMO UPTIME

••T••M

ACTIUM ANTHEM ANTRIM ANTRUM ARTGUM BATYAM BOTTOM ESTEEM FATHOM GOTHAM JETSAM LATIUM OSTIUM PUTNAM RETRIM SITCOM

•••T•M

ADYTUM BANTAM BOTTOM CUSTOM DIATOM DICTUM MADTOM MULTUM PROTEM RHYTHM SALTUM SEPTUM SYSTEM TAMTAM TOMTOM VICTIM

TN••••

TNOTES

T•N•••

TANAKA TANANA TANDEM TANGED TANGLE TANGLY TANGOS TANGUY TANIST TANKAS TANKED TANKER TANKUP TANNED TANNER TANNIC TANNIN TANOAK TANOAN TANTES TANTRA TENACE TENANT TENDED TENDER TENDON TENDTO TENENS TENETS TENNIS TENONS TENORS TENPIN TENREC TENSED TENSER TENSES TENSOR TENTED TENTER TENTHS TENURE TENUTO TINCAL TINCAN TINCTS TINDER TINEAR TINGED TINGES TINGLE TINGLY TINGOD TINHAT TINIER TINILY TINKER TINKLE TINKLY TINMAN TINMEN TINNED TINNER TINPAN TINPOT TINSEL TINTED TINTER TONDOS TONERS TONEUP TONGAN TONGUE TONICS TONIER TONING TONISH TONITE TONKIN TONNES TONSIL TUNDRA TUNEIN TUNERS TUNEUP TUNICA TUNICS TUNING TUNNEL TUNNEY

T••N••

TAINAN TAINOS TAINTS TANNED TANNER TANNIC TANNIN TAUNTS TBONDS TBONES TEENER TEENSY TENNIS TERNES THANES THANKS THENAR THENCE THINGS THINGY THINKS THINLY THONGS THUNKS TINNED TINNER TONNES TOONIE TOWNER TOWNIE TRANCE TRENCH TRENDS TRENDY TRINAL TRINES TRUNKS TUNNEL TUNNEY TURNED TURNER TURNIN TURNIP TURNON TURNTO TURNUP TWANGS TWANGY TWENTY TWINED TWINES TWINGE

T•••N•

TAGEND TAHINI TAKING TAKINS TALENT TALONS TAMING TANANA TAPING TAPINS TARING TAUONS TAWING TAXING TECHNO TEEING TEJANO TENANT TENENS TENONS TETONS TEXANS THEEND THORNS THORNY THRONE THRONG TIDING TIEING TIEINS TILING TIMING TIPINS TIRANA TIRANE TIRING TISANE TITANS TOEING TOEINS TOKENS TONING TORINO TOTING TOWING TOXINS TOYING TOYONS TRAINS TRIUNE TRUANT TRUING TRYING TUBING TUCANA TULANE TUNING TURING TWEENS TWEENY TYPING TYRANT TYRONE

T••••N

TACKON TAINAN TAIPAN TAIWAN TAKEIN TAKEON TALION TANNIN TANOAN

TAPPAN
TARPAN
TARPON
TARTAN
TARZAN
TASMAN
TAUTEN
TAVERN
TAXMAN
TAXMEN
TEFLON
TELLON
TENDON
TENPIN
TERRAN
TEUTON
THROWN
TIEDIN
TIEPIN
TIESIN
TIFFIN
TIGLON
TILDEN
TINCAN
TINMAN
TINMEN
TINPAN
TIPSIN
TITIAN
TOAMAN
TOCSIN
TODMAN
TOEDIN
TOESIN
TOLDON
TOMLIN
TONGAN
TONKIN
TOOKIN
TOOKON
TOPGUN
TOPTEN
TOUCAN
TOULON
TRAJAN
TREPAN
TRIGON
TRITON
TROGON
TROJAN
TRUMAN
TRYLON
TUBMAN
TUCHUN
TUCKIN
TUCSON
TULSAN
TUNEIN
TUPIAN
TURBAN
TUREEN
TURNIN
TURNON
TURPIN
TUSCAN
TYCOON
TYRIAN

•T•N••

ATONAL
ATONCE
ATONED
ATONES
ATONIC
ETHNIC
ETHNOS
ETONIC
STANCE
STANCH
STANDS
STANKY
STANZA
STENCH
STENOG
STENOS
STINGO
STINGS
STINGY
STINKS
STINKY
STINTS
STONED
STONER
STONES
STUNTS
STUNTY

•T••N•

ATHAND
ATHENA
ATHENE
ATHENS
ATKINS
ATTEND
ATTUNE
ETERNE
ETHANE
ETHENE
STAINS
STEINS
STERNA
STERNE
STERNO
STERNS
STHENO
STRAND
STRINE
STRING
STRONG
STRUNG
UTHANT
UTURNS

•T•••N

ATAMAN
ATTAIN
ETYMON
STALIN
STAMEN
STATEN
STAYON
STEFAN
STEPIN
STEPON
STEVEN
STIRIN
STJOAN
STJOHN
STOLEN
STOLON
STOPIN
STOTIN
STRAIN
STREWN
STYRON
UTAHAN

••TN••

CATNAP
CATNIP
JITNEY
NOTNOW
PUTNAM
WATNEY

••T•N•

ACTING
ACTINO
ACTONE
ANTONY
ATTEND
ATTUNE
BATING
BATONS
BETONY
BITING
BOTANY
BUTANE
BUTENE
BUTUNG
CATENA
CETANE
CITING
CUTINS
DATING
DATONG
DETENT
DOTING
EATING
EXTANT
EXTEND
EXTENT
FETING
FUTONS
GATING
GITANO
HATING
INTEND
INTENS
INTENT
INTINE
INTONE
INTUNE
KETONE
KITING
LATENE
LATENS
LATENT
LATINA
LATINI
LATINO
LATINS
LATONA
LITANY
LUTING
MATING
MATINS
METING
MUTANT
MUTING
MUTINY
NATANT
NOTING
OBTUND
OCTANE
OCTANT
OPTING
OSTEND
OUTING
PATENS
PATENT
PATINA
PATINE
PITONS
POTENT
PUTONS
RATINE
RATING
RETENE
RETINA
RETUNE
ROTINI
ROTUND
SATANG
SATING
SATINS
SATINY
SETINS
SITING
SITINS
TETONS
TITANS
TOTING
UNTUNE
VOTING

••T••N

ACTION
ACTSON
ALTMAN
ANTRON
ASTERN
ATTAIN
AUTUMN
BATAAN
BATMAN
BATMEN
BATTEN
BETSON
BITTEN
BUTTIN
BUTTON
CATION
CATKIN
CATTON
CITRON
COTTEN
COTTON
CUTSIN
DATSUN
DETAIN
DOTEON
DOTHAN
EATSIN
EXTERN
FATTEN
FITSIN
GATLIN
GETSIN
GETSON
GOTTEN
HATPIN
HETMAN
HITMAN
HITMEN
HITSON
HUTTON
INTERN
INTOWN
INTURN
JETGUN
JETSON
KITTEN
LATEEN
LATTEN
LETSIN
LETSON
LOTION
LYTTON
MATLIN
MATRON
MITTEN
MOTION
MOTOWN
MUTTON
NATHAN
NATION
NATRON
NETMAN
NETMEN
NETTON
NOTION
NUTKIN
OBTAIN
OPTION
OUTGUN
OUTRAN
OUTRUN
PATHAN
PATRON
PATTEN
PATTON
PETAIN
PITMAN
PITMEN
POTEEN
POTION
PUTSIN
PUTSON
PYTHON
RATION
RATLIN
RATSON
RATTAN
RETAIN
RETTON
RETURN
ROTTEN
RUTTAN
SATEEN
SATURN
SETSIN
SETSON
SITSIN
SITSON
SUTTON
TITIAN
UNTORN
UPTOWN
UPTURN
VOTEIN
WATSON
WITHIN

•••TN•

GRETNA
MUSTNT

•••T•N

AMYTAN
ARCTAN
AUSTEN
AUSTIN
BARTON
BATTEN
BEATEN
BEATON
BENTON
BHUTAN
BIGTEN
BIOTIN
BITTEN
BOLTON
BONTON
BOSTON
BRETON
BRITON
BURTON
BUSTIN
BUTTIN
BUTTON
CAFTAN
CANTON
CAPTAN
CARTON
CASTON
CATTON
CAXTON
CHITIN
CHITON
COTTEN
COTTON
CRETAN
CRETIN
CROTON
CURTIN
DALTON
DANTON
DAYTON
DENTIN
DENTON
DUSTIN
EASTON
FANTAN
FASTEN
FATTEN
FULTON
GASTON
GLUTEN
GOTTEN
GRATIN
GROTON
HASTEN
HESTON
HILTON
HINTON
HORTON
HUSTON
HUTTON
JUSTIN
KEATON
KENTON
KEPTON
KITTEN
LATTEN
LAWTON
LEFTIN
LENTEN
LEPTON
LIPTON
LISTEN
LISTON
LYTTON
MALTIN
MARTEN
MARTIN
MELTON
MERTON
MILTON
MITTEN
MOLTEN
MORTON
MOUTON
MUNTIN
MUTTON
NEATEN
NEKTON
NETTON
NEWTON
NORTON
PARTON
PATTEN
PATTON
PAXTON
PECTIN
PEYTON
PHOTON
PIETIN
PISTON
PLATEN
POSTON
PROTON
RATTAN
RESTON
RETTON
RHYTON
ROTTEN
RUTTAN
SALTEN
SALTON
SARTON
SEATON
SENTIN
SEXTON
SHUTIN
SOFTEN
STATEN
STOTIN
SULTAN
SUNTAN
SUTTON
TARTAN
TAUTEN
TEUTON
TOPTEN
TRITON
VINTON
WAITON
WALTON
WANTIN
WANTON
WENTIN
WENTON
WHITEN
WILTON
WONTON
WYNTON
WYSTAN

TO••••

TOAMAN
TOASTS
TOASTY
TOATEE
TOBAGO
TOBIAS
TOBIES
TOBOOT
TOBRUK
TOCSIN
TODATE
TODDAO
TODDLE
TODMAN
TOECAP
TOEDIN
TOEING
TOEINS
TOESIN
TOETAP
TOFFEE
TOGAED
TOGGED
TOGGLE
TOILED
TOILER
TOILES
TOILET
TOKAYS
TOKENS
TOKLAS
TOLDOF
TOLDON
TOLEDO
TOLIFE
TOLLED
TOLTEC
TOLUCA
TOMATO
TOMBAC
TOMBOY
TOMCAT
TOMLIN
TOMMIX
TOMTIT
TOMTOM
TONDOS
TONERS
TONEUP
TONGAN
TONGUE
TONICS
TONIER
TONING
TONISH
TONITE
TONKIN
TONNES
TONSIL
TOOBAD
TOOKIN
TOOKIT
TOOKON
TOOKTO
TOOKUP
TOOLED
TOOLUP
TOONIE
TOOTED
TOOTER
TOOTHY
TOOTLE
TOOTOO
TOOTSY
TOPCAT
TOPDOG
TOPEKA
TOPERS
TOPGUN
TOPHAT
TOPHUS
TOPICS
TOPJOB
TOPOFF
TOPOUT
TOPPED
TOPPER
TOPPLE
TOPTEN
TOQUES
TORAHS
TORCHY
TOREAT
TORERO
TOREUP
TORIES
TORINO
TOROID
TOROSE
TORPID
TORPOR
TORQUE
TORRES
TORREY
TORRID
TORSOS
TORTES
TOSSED
TOSSER
TOSSES
TOSSUP
TOTALS
TOTEMS
TOTERS
TOTHER
TOTING
TOTSUP
TOTTED
TOTTER
TOUCAN
TOUCHE
TOUCHY
TOUGHS
TOUGHY
TOULON
TOUPEE
TOURED
TOURER
TOUSLE
TOUTED

TOUTER
TOWAGE
TOWARD
TOWCAR
TOWELS
TOWERS
TOWERY
TOWHEE
TOWING
TOWNER
TOWNIE
TOXICS
TOXINS
TOYDOG
TOYING
TOYONS
TOYOTA

T•O•••

TAOISM
TAOIST
TBONDS
TBONES
THOLES
THOMAS
THONGS
THORAX
THORNS
THORNY
THORPE
THORPS
THOUGH
TNOTES
TOOBAD
TOOKIN
TOOKIT
TOOKON
TOOKTO
TOOKUP
TOOLED
TOOLUP
TOONIE
TOOTED
TOOTER
TOOTHY
TOOTLE
TOOTOO
TOOTSY
TROCAR
TROCHE
TROGON
TROIKA
TROJAN
TROLLS
TROMPE
TROMPS
TROOPS
TROPES
TROPEZ
TROPHY
TROPIC
TROPPO
TROTHS
TROUGH
TROUPE
TROUTS
TROUVE
TROVES
TROWED
TROWEL
TWOBIT
TWOFER
TWOPLY
TWOWAY

T••O••

TABOOS
TABORS
TACOMA
TAGORE
TAGOUT
TALONS
TANOAK
TANOAN
TAPOFF
TAPOUT
TAROTS
TAUONS
TEEOFF
TENONS
TENORS
TETONS
THEORY
THROAT
THROBS
THROES
THRONE
THRONG
THROVE
THROWN
THROWS
TIPOFF
TIVOLI
TOBOOT
TOPOFF
TOPOUT
TOROID
TOROSE
TOYONS
TOYOTA
TRIODE
TROOPS
TRYOUT
TUDORS
TUTORS
TYCOBB
TYCOON
TYRONE

T•••O•

TABOOS
TACKON
TAILOR
TAINOS
TAKEON
TALBOT
TALION
TALLOW
TANGOS
TARPON
TATTOO
TAUTOG
TAYLOR
TEAPOT
TEAPOY
TEFLON
TELLOF
TELLON
TEMPOS
TENDON
TENSOR
TERROR
TEUTON
THETOY
TIEROD
TIGLON
TINGOD
TINPOT
TIPTOE
TIPTOP
TLALOC
TOBOOT
TOLDOF
TOLDON
TOMBOY
TOMTOM
TONDOS
TOOKON
TOOTOO
TOPDOG
TOPJOB
TORPOR
TORSOS
TOULON
TOYDOG
TREMOR
TREVOR
TRICOT
TRIGON
TRIPOD
TRIPOS
TRITON
TROGON
TRYFOR
TRYLON
TUCSON
TURBOS
TURBOT
TURGOR
TURNON
TVSHOW
TYCOON
TYDBOL

T••••O

TAKETO
TALKTO
TAMAYO
TATTOO
TECHNO
TEJANO
TENDTO
TENUTO
TERATO
TEREDO
TEXACO
THERMO
TIEDTO
TIESTO
TOBAGO
TODDAO
TOLEDO
TOMATO
TOOKTO
TOOTOO
TORERO
TORINO
TRICHO
TROPPO
TUPELO
TURNTO
TUXEDO

•TO•••

ATODDS
ATOLLS
ATOMIC
ATONAL
ATONCE
ATONED
ATONES
ATONIC
ETOILE
ETONIC
OTOOLE
STOATS
STOCKS
STOCKY
STODGE
STODGY
STOGIE
STOICS
STOJKO
STOKED
STOKER
STOKES
STOLEN
STOLES
STOLID
STOLLE
STOLON
STOMAS
STOMAT
STOMPS
STONED
STONER
STONES
STOOGE
STOOKS
STOOLS
STOOLY
STOOPS
STOPES
STOPIN
STOPIT
STOPUP
STORCH
STORED
STORER
STORES
STOREY
STORKS
STORMS
STORMY
STORRS
STOTIN
STOUPS
STOUTS
STOVER
STOVES
STOWED
UTOPIA

•T•O••

ATCOST
ATEOUT
ATHOME
ATMOST
ATWOOD
ATWORK
FTROOP
OTIOSE
OTOOLE
PTBOAT
STJOAN
STJOHN
STOOGE
STOOKS
STOOLS
STOOLY
STOOPS
STROBE
STRODE
STROKE
STROLL
STRONG
STROPS
STROUD
STROVE
UTMOST

•T••O•

ATWOOD
ETHNOS
ETUXOR
ETYMOL
ETYMON
FTROOP
STATOR
STAYON
STEFOY
STENOG
STENOS
STEPON
STEROL
STOLON
STUPOR
STYRON

•T•••O

ATEMPO
ATERGO
OTELLO
STELMO
STEREO
STERNO
STHENO
STINGO
STMALO
STOJKO
STRABO
STRATO
STUCCO
STUDIO

••TO••

ACTONE
ACTORS
ACTOUT
ANTONY
ARTOIS
BATONS
BETONY
BETOOK
BITOFF
BITOLA
CUTOFF
CUTOUT
DATONG
DETOUR
EATOUT
ENTOMO
ESTOPS
EXTOLS
EXTORT
FSTOPS
FUTONS
GATORS
GETOFF
GETOUT
GOTOFF
GOTOIT
GOTOUT
HITOUT
INTONE
INTOTO
INTOWN
KETONE
LATONA
LATOUR
LATOYA
LETOFF
LETOUT
LITOUT
METOPE
MOTORS
MOTOWN
OCTOPI
ONTOUR
OPTOUT
PATOIS
PITONS
POTOSI
PUTOFF
PUTONS
PUTOUT
RETOLD
RETOOK
RETOOL
RETOPS
RETORT
RETOUR
RETOWS
ROTORS
SATORI
SATOUT
SETOFF
SETOSE
SETOUT
SITOUT
SOTOLS
TETONS
TUTORS
UNTOLD
UNTORN
UPTOWN
VETOED
VETOER
VETOES

••T•O•

ACTION
ACTSON
ANTCOW
ANTRON
ASTROS
AUTHOR
BATBOY
BATHOS
BETOOK
BETSON
BETTOR
BOTTOM
BUTEOS
BUTTON
CATION
CATTON
CITRON
COTTON
DETROP
DITTOS
DOTEON
FATHOM
GETSON
HATBOX
HATHOR
HITSON
HOTBOX
HOTDOG
HOTPOT
HOTROD
HUTTON
INTROS
JETSON
KITFOX
LETSON
LITHOG
LITHOS
LOTION
LOTTOS
LUTHOR
LYTTON
MATRON
MATZOH
MATZOS
METEOR
METHOD
METROS
MOTION
MOTMOT
MOTTOS
MUTTON
MYTHOI
MYTHOL
MYTHOS
NATION
NATRON
NETTON
NOTION
NOTNOW
OCTROI
OPTFOR
OPTION
OUTBOX
OUTFOX
PATHOL
PATHOS
PATIOS
PATMOS
PATROL
PATRON
PATTON
PETROG
PETROL
POTION
POTTOS
PUTSON
PYTHON
RATION
RATIOS
RATSON
RETOOK
RETOOL
RETROS
RETTON
SETSON
SETTOS
SITCOM
SITSON
SUTTON
TATTOO
UNTROD
WATSON
WETMOP

••T••O

ACTINO
ACTTWO
ANTERO
ARTHRO
ARTURO
CITATO
ENTERO
ENTOMO
GETSTO
GITANO
HETERO
INTOTO
JETHRO
LATIGO
LATINO
LETSGO
MUTATO
OCTAVO
POTATO
PUTSTO
ROTHKO
TATTOO
ULTIMO

•••TO•

AMATOL
BARTOK
BARTON
BEATON
BENTON
BESTOW
BETTOR
BIGTOE
BIGTOP
BOLTON
BONTON
BOSTON
BOTTOM
BOXTOP
BRETON
BRITON
BURTON
BUTTON
CANTON
CANTOR
CANTOS
CAPTOR
CARTON
CASTON
CASTOR
CATTON
CAXTON
CENTOS
CESTOS
CHITON
COTTON
CROTON
CUSTOM
CUSTOS
DALTON
DANTON
DAYTON
DEBTOR
DENTON
DIATOM
DITTOS
DOCTOR
EASTON
EDITOR
EMPTOR
FACTOR
FOETOR
FRITOS
FULTON
GASTON
GROTON
HECTOR
HESTON
HILTON
HINTON
HORTON
HOWTOS
HUSTON
HUTTON
JUNTOS
KANTOR
KEATON
KENTON
KEPTON
KOWTOW
LAPTOP
LAWTON
LECTOR
LEPTON
LICTOR
LIPTON
LISTON
LOTTOS
LYTTON
MADTOM
MELTON
MENTOR
MERTON
MILTON
MOPTOP
MORTON
MOTTOS
MOUTON
MUTTON
NEKTON
NESTOR
NETTON
NEWTON
NORTON
ORATOR
PANTOS
PARTON
PASTOR
PATTON
PAXTON
PEGTOP
PESTOS
PEYTON
PHOTOG
PHOTON

PHOTOS
PINTOS
PISTOL
PISTON
POPTOP
POSTON
POTTOS
PROTON
RAGTOP
RAPTOR
RECTOR
RECTOS
REDTOP
RESTON
RETTON
RHETOR
RHYTON
ROSTOV
SALTON
SANTOS
SARTON
SEATON
SECTOR
SESTOS
SETTOS
SEXTON
SKITOW
SORTOF
STATOR
SUITOR
SUTTON
TATTOO
TAUTOG
TEUTON
THETOY
TIPTOE
TIPTOP
TOMTOM
TOOTOO
TRITON
UNSTOP
VECTOR
VICTOR
VINTON
VOSTOK
WAITON
WALTON
WANTON
WENTON
WILTON
WONTON
WYNTON
YOMTOV

•••T•O
ACTTWO
ANATTO
AUSTRO
BHUTTO
BISTRO
BLOTTO
CASTRO
CENTRO
CLOTHO
DEXTRO
EDITIO
GASTRO
GHETTO
GIOTTO
GROTTO
INITIO
NEXTTO
ONETWO
PIETRO
SCOTTO
TATTOO
TOOTOO
WANTTO
XANTHO

••••TO
ADDSTO
AIMSTO
ALECTO
ALIOTO
AMBATO
ANATTO
ARISTO
BENITO
BHUTTO
BLOTTO
BONITO
CAMETO
CARETO
CITATO
COGITO
COMETO
CRISTO
CRYPTO
DAMATO
DARETO
DESOTO
DEVITO
DEVOTO
EXACTO
EXVOTO
FALLTO
FELLTO
FINITO
GEARTO
GELATO
GETSTO
GHETTO
GIOTTO
GIVETO
GOINTO
GROTTO
HELDTO
HEMATO
HERETO
HOLDTO
HOVETO
INTOTO
KEEPTO
LAIDTO
LAYSTO
LEADTO
LEANTO
LEGATO
LIESTO
LOOKTO
MAPUTO
MRMOTO
MUTATO
NEARTO
NEMATO
NEXTTO
NOVATO
ODONTO
OPENTO
OPORTO
PARETO
PASHTO
POTATO
PRESTO
PRONTO
PUERTO
PUTSTO
QUARTO
RABATO
RIALTO
RIGHTO
RUBATO
RUNSTO
SABATO
SANGTO
SCOTTO
SEENTO
SEESTO
SHINTO
SHORTO
SINGTO
SMALTO
SNAPTO
SOASTO
SOMATO
SOWETO
SPINTO
STRATO
SUBITO
TAKETO
TALKTO
TENDTO
TENUTO
TERATO
TIEDTO
TIESTO
TOMATO
TOOKTO
TURNTO
USEDTO
VENETO
WANTTO
WISETO

T•P•••
TAPERS
TAPING
TAPINS
TAPIRS
TAPOFF
TAPOUT
TAPPAN
TAPPED
TAPPER
TAPPET
TEPALS
TEPEES
TEPHRA
TIPINS
TIPOFF
TIPPED
TIPPER
TIPPET
TIPPLE
TIPSIN
TIPTOE
TIPTOP
TIPUPS
TOPCAT
TOPDOG
TOPEKA
TOPERS
TOPGUN
TOPHAT
TOPHUS
TOPICS
TOPJOB
TOPOFF
TOPOUT
TOPPED
TOPPER
TOPPLE
TOPTEN
TUPELO
TUPIAN
TYPERS
TYPEUP
TYPHUS
TYPIER
TYPIFY
TYPING
TYPIST

T••P••
TAIPAN
TAIPEI
TAMPED
TAMPER
TAPPAN
TAPPED
TAPPER
TAPPET
TARPAN
TARPIT
TARPON
TAUPES
TEAPOT
TEAPOY
TEMPED
TEMPEH
TEMPER
TEMPLE
TEMPOS
TEMPTS
TEMPUS
TENPIN
TIEPIN
TINPAN
TINPOT
TIPPED
TIPPER
TIPPET
TIPPLE
TOPPED
TOPPER
TOPPLE
TORPID
TORPOR
TOUPEE
TRAPPY
TREPAN
TREPID
TRIPLE
TRIPLY
TRIPOD
TRIPOS
TRIPUP
TROPES
TROPEZ
TROPHY
TROPIC
TROPPO
TURPIN
TWOPLY

T•••P•
TERAPH
THORPE
THORPS
THRIPS
THUMPS
TIEUPS
TIPUPS
TRAMPS
TRAPPY
TROMPE
TROMPS
TROOPS
TROPPO
TROUPE
TRUMPS
TULIPS
TWERPS

T••••P
TAGSUP
TAKEUP
TALKUP
TANKUP
TEACUP
TEAMUP
TEARUP
TEEDUP
TEESUP
THELIP
TIDYUP
TIEDUP
TIESUP
TIPTOP
TITTUP
TOECAP
TOETAP
TONEUP
TOOKUP
TOOLUP
TOREUP
TOSSUP
TOTSUP
TRICEP
TRIPUP
TUNEUP
TURNIP
TURNUP
TYPEUP

•TP•••
STPAUL
STPETE

•T•P••
ETAPES
STAPES
STAPLE
STAPUF
STEPIN
STEPON
STEPPE
STEPUP
STIPEL
STIPES
STOPES
STOPIN
STOPIT
STOPUP
STUPAS
STUPES
STUPID
STUPOR
UTOPIA

•T••P•
ATEMPO
PTRAPS
STAMPS
STEEPS
STEPPE
STIMPY
STOMPS
STOOPS
STOUPS
STRAPS
STRIPE
STRIPS
STRIPY
STROPS
STUMPS
STUMPY

•T•••P
FTROOP
STAYUP
STEPUP
STIRUP
STOPUP
STREEP

••TP••
HATPIN
HOTPOT
NETPAY
OUTPUT
POTPIE
PUTPUT

••T•P•
CUTUPS
ECTYPE
ESTOPS
FSTOPS
GETUPS
LETUPS
METOPE
OCTOPI
ONTAPE
RETAPE
RETAPS
RETOPS
RETYPE
SETUPS
SITUPS

••T••P
ACTSUP
ANTEUP
BITMAP
CATNAP
CATNIP
CATSUP
CUTSUP
DETROP
EATSUP
ENTRAP
GETSUP
HITSUP
HOTCAP
HOTTIP
LETSUP
PUTSUP
SATRAP
SETSUP
SITSUP
TITTUP
TOTSUP
UNTRAP
WETMOP

•••T•P
BEATUP
BIGTOP
BOOTUP
BOXTOP
CHATUP
DUSTUP
HEATUP
HOTTIP
INSTEP
KEPTUP
LAPTOP
LIFTUP
MOPTOP
PEGTOP
PENTUP
POPTOP
RAGTOP
REDTOP
RESTUP
SENTUP
SHOTUP
SHUTUP
SUITUP
TIPTOP
TITTUP
TOETAP
UNSTOP
WAITUP
WENTUP

T•Q•••
TOQUES
TUQUES

T••Q••
TORQUE

•T••Q•
ETSEQQ

•T•••Q
ETSEQQ

TR••••
TRACED
TRACER
TRACES
TRACEY
TRACHY
TRACKS
TRACTS
TRADED
TRADER
TRADES
TRAGIC
TRAILS
TRAINS
TRAITS
TRAJAN
TRALEE
TRAMPS
TRANCE
TRAPPY
TRASHY
TRAUMA
TRAVEL
TRAVES
TRAVIS
TRAWLS
TREADS
TREATS
TREATY
TREBEK
TREBLE
TREBLY
TREDIA
TREMOR
TRENCH
TRENDS
TRENDY
TREPAN
TREPID
TREVOR
TRIADS
TRIAGE
TRIALS
TRIBAL
TRIBES
TRICED
TRICEP
TRICES
TRICHO
TRICIA
TRICKS
TRICKY
TRICOT
TRIERS
TRIFID
TRIFLE
TRIGLY
TRIGON
TRIJET
TRIKES
TRILBY
TRILLS
TRIMLY
TRINAL
TRINES
TRIODE
TRIPLE
TRIPLY
TRIPOD
TRIPOS
TRIPUP
TRISHA
TRISTE
TRITER
TRITON
TRIUNE
TRIVET
TRIVIA
TRIXIE
TROCAR
TROCHE
TROGON
TROIKA
TROJAN
TROLLS
TROMPE
TROMPS
TROOPS
TROPES
TROPEZ
TROPHY
TROPIC
TROPPO
TROTHS
TROUGH
TROUPE
TROUTS
TROUVE
TROVES
TROWED
TROWEL
TRUANT
TRUCES
TRUCKS
TRUDGE
TRUEST
TRUING
TRUISM
TRUMAN
TRUMPS
TRUNKS
TRUSTS
TRUSTY
TRUTHS
TRYFOR
TRYING
TRYLON
TRYOUT
TRYSTS

T•R•••
TARAWA
TARGES
TARGET
TARIFF
TARING
TARMAC
TAROTS
TARPAN
TARPIT
TARPON
TARRED
TARSAL
TARSUS
TARTAN
TARTAR
TARTER
TARTLY
TARZAN
TERAPH
TERATO
TERCEL
TERCET
TEREDO
TERESA
TERETE
TEREUS
TERKEL
TERMED
TERNES

TERRAN
TERRET
TERROR
TERSER
THRACE
THRALE
THRALL
THRASH
THREAD
THREAT
THREED
THREES
THRESH
THRICE
THRIFT
THRILL
THRIPS
THRIVE
THROAT
THROBS
THROES
THRONE
THRONG
THROVE
THROWN
THROWS
THRUMS
THRUSH
THRUST
TIRADE
TIRANA
TIRANE
TIRING
TORAHS
TORCHY
TOREAT
TORERO
TOREUP
TORIES
TORINO
TOROID
TOROSE
TORPID
TORPOR
TORQUE
TORRES
TORREY
TORRID
TORSOS
TORTES
TURBAN
TURBID
TURBIT
TURBOS
TURBOT
TUREEN
TURFED
TURGID
TURGOR
TURING
TURKEY
TURKIC
TURNED
TURNER
TURNIN
TURNIP
TURNON
TURNTO
TURNUP
TURPIN
TURRET
TURTLE
TURVES
TYRANT
TYRIAN
TYRONE

T••R••

TABRIZ
TARRED
TAURUS
TAYRAS
TBIRDS
TEARAT
TEARED
TEARUP
TENREC
TERRAN
TERRET
TERROR
TETRAD
TETRAS
TETRIS
THERES
THERMO
THERMS
THIRDS
THIRST
THIRTY
THORAX
THORNS
THORNY
THORPE
THORPS
THYRSI
TIARAS
TIERCE
TIERED
TIEROD
TIERRA
TIGRIS
TITRED
TITRES
TOBRUK
TORRES
TORREY
TORRID
TOURED
TOURER
TSURIS
TUAREG
TUGRIK
TURRET
TWERPS
TWIRLS

T•••R•

TABARD
TABORS
TAGORE
TAKERS
TALERS
TAMARA
TAMERS
TANTRA
TAPERS
TAPIRS
TASERS
TATARS
TATERS
TAVERN
TAWDRY
TAXERS
TENORS
TENURE
TEPHRA
THEIRS
THEORY
THEYRE
THWART
TIERRA
TIGERS
TILERS
TIMBRE
TIMERS
TISHRI
TITERS
TONERS
TOPERS
TORERO
TOTERS
TOWARD
TOWERS
TOWERY
TRIERS
TSHIRT
TUBERS
TUDORS
TULARE
TUNDRA
TUNERS
TUTORS
TUYERE
TYPERS

T••••R

TACKER
TAILOR
TALKER
TALLER
TAMPER
TANKER
TANNER
TAPPER
TARTAR
TARTER
TASTER
TATTER
TAUTER
TAYLOR
TEASER
TEDDER
TEENER
TEETER
TELLER
TEMPER
TENDER
TENSER
TENSOR
TENTER
TERROR
TERSER
TESTER
TETHER
THALER
THAYER
THENAR
TICKER
TIDIER
TIGGER
TILLER
TILTER
TIMBER
TINDER
TINEAR
TINIER
TINKER
TINNER
TINTER
TIPPER
TITFER
TITHER
TITTER
TOILER
TONIER
TOOTER
TOPPER
TORPOR
TOSSER
TOTHER
TOTTER
TOURER
TOUTER
TOWCAR
TOWNER
TRACER
TRADER
TREMOR
TREVOR
TRITER
TROCAR
TRYFOR
TUCKER
TUGGER
TURGOR
TURNER
TUSKER
TWOFER
TYPIER

•TR•••

ATREST
ATREUS
ATRIAL
ATRISK
ATRIUM
FTROOP
PTRAPS
STRABO
STRADS
STRAFE
STRAIN
STRAIT
STRAKE
STRAND
STRAPS
STRASS
STRATA
STRATI
STRATO
STRAUB
STRAUS
STRAWS
STRAWY
STRAYS
STREAK
STREAM
STREEP
STREET
STRESS
STREWN
STREWS
STRIAE
STRICK
STRICT
STRIDE
STRIFE
STRIKE
STRINE
STRING
STRIPE
STRIPS
STRIPY
STRIVE
STROBE
STRODE
STROKE
STROLL
STRONG
STROPS
STROUD
STROVE
STRUCK
STRUMS
STRUNG
STRUTS

•T•R••

ATERGO
ATTRIT
ETERNE
ITURBI
STARCH
STARED
STARER
STARES
STARRY
STARTS
STARVE
STEREO
STERES
STERNA
STERNE
STERNO
STERNS
STEROL
STIRIN
STIRKS
STIRUP
STORCH
STORED
STORER
STORES
STOREY
STORKS
STORMS
STORMY
STORRS
STURDY
STYRIA
STYRON
UTURNS

•T••R•

ATTARS
ATTIRE
ATWORK
ETHERS
OTHERS
OTTERS
STAIRS
STARRY
STEERS
STMARK
STORRS
STUART
UTTERS

•T•••R

ETCHER
ETUXOR
STAGER
STALER
STARER
STATER
STATOR
STELAR
STEWER
STIVER
STOKER
STONER
STORER
STOVER
STUMER
STUPOR
STYLER

••TR••

AMTRAC
AMTRAK
ANTRES
ANTRIM
ANTRON
ANTRUM
ASTRAL
ASTRAY
ASTRID
ASTROS
ATTRIT
BETRAY
BOTREE
CATRIG
CITRIC
CITRON
CITRUS
DETROP
ENTRAP
ENTREE
ESTRAY
EXTRAS
HATRED
HOTROD
IATRIC
INTROS
ISTRIA
LITRES
MATRIX
MATRON
METRES
METRIC
METROS
MITRAL
MITRED
MITRES
NATRON
NITRES
NITRIC
NUTRIA
OCTROI
OUTRAN
OUTRUN
PATROL
PATRON
PETREL
PETRIE
PETROG
PETROL
PUTRID
RETRAL
RETRIM
RETROS
SATRAP
SUTRAS
TETRAD
TETRAS
TETRIS
TITRED
TITRES
ULTRAS
UNTRAP
UNTROD
UNTRUE
VITRIC

••T•R•

ACTORS
ALTARS
ALTERS
ANTERO
ARTERY
ARTHRO
ARTURO
ASTERN
ASTERS
ATTARS
ATTIRE
BITERS
CATERS
CETERA
CITERS
DATARY
DATERS
DATURA
DETERS
DOTARD
EATERS
EATERY
ENTERO
ENTERS
ENTIRE
ESTERS
EXTERN
EXTORT
FUTURE
GATERS
GATORS
HATARI
HATERS
HETERO
INTERJ
INTERN
INTURN
JETHRO
KITERS
LITERS
MATERS
MATURE
METERS
MITERS
MOTHRA
MOTORS
NATURA
NATURE
NITERS
NITERY
NOTARY
NOTERS
OATERS
OTTERS
OUTCRY
PATERS
PETARD
PETERS
QATARI
RATERS
RETARD
RETARS
RETIRE
RETORT
RETURN
RITARD
ROTARY
ROTORS
SATIRE
SATORI
SATURN
SATYRS
SITARS
SUTURE
TATARS
TATERS
TITERS
TOTERS
TUTORS
UNTORN
UPTURN
UTTERS
VOTARY
VOTERS
WATERS
WATERY

••T••R

AETHER
ALTAIR
ANTHER
ANTLER
ARTHUR
ARTIER
AUTEUR
AUTHOR
BATHER
BATTER
BETTER
BETTOR
BITTER
BOTHER
BUTLER
BUTTER
CATHER
COTTER
CUTLER
CUTTER
DETOUR
DITHER
EITHER
ESTHER
FATHER
FATTER
FETTER
FITTER
GATHER
GETTER
GUTTER
HATHOR
HATTER
HITHER
HITTER
HOTAIR
HOTCAR
HOTTER
HOTWAR
JITTER
KOTTER
LATHER
LATOUR
LATTER
LETTER
LITTER
LOTHAR
LUTHER
LUTHOR
MATHER
MATTER
METEOR
METIER
MOTHER
MUTTER
NATTER
NETHER
NUTTER
OATIER
ONTOUR
OPTFOR
OSTLER
PATTER
PETTER
PITIER
PITTER
POTHER
POTTER
PUTTER
RATEDR
RATHER
RATTER
RETEAR
RETOUR
RITTER
ROTTER
RUTGER
SETTER
SITTER
SUTLER
SUTTER
TATTER
TETHER
TITFER
TITHER
TITTER
TOTHER
TOTTER
VETOER
WETBAR
WETHER
WETTER
WITHER
ZITHER

•••TR•
ANITRA
AUSTRO
BISTRO
CASTRO
CENTRE
CENTRI
CENTRO
CONTRA
CONTRE
DESTRY
DEXTRO
DMITRI
GANTRY
GASTRO
GENTRY
GUITRY
LUSTRE
MAITRE
MANTRA
PALTRY
PANTRY
PASTRY
PELTRY
PIETRO
POETRY
ROSTRA
SARTRE
SENTRA
SENTRY
SISTRA
SULTRY
TANTRA
VESTRY
WINTRY

•••T•R
ALITER
AVATAR
BANTER
BARTER
BASTER
BATTER
BAXTER
BEATER
BESTIR
BETTER
BETTOR
BITTER
BOATER
BUNTER
BUSTER
BUTTER
CANTER
CANTOR
CAPTOR
CARTER
CASTER
CASTOR
CENTER
COLTER
COOTER
COPTER
COSTAR
COTTER
COUTER
CRATER
CURTER
CUSTER
CUTTER
DAFTER
DARTER
DEBTOR
DEFTER
DEXTER
DIETER
DOCTOR
DUSTER
EASTER
EDITOR
ELATER
EMOTER
EMPTOR
EXETER
FACTOR
FALTER
FASTER
FATTER
FESTER
FETTER
FILTER
FITTER
FOETOR
FOOTER
FOSTER
GAITER
GARTER
GETTER
GRATER
GUITAR
GUNTER
GUTTER
HALTER
HATTER
HEATER
HECTOR
HELTER
HESTER
HINTER
HITTER
HOOTER
HOTTER
HUNTER
INSTAR
IRATER
ISHTAR
JEETER
JESTER
JITTER
JUSTER
KANTOR
KILTER
KOTTER
KRATER
KULTUR
LATTER
LECTER
LECTOR
LESTER
LETTER
LICTOR
LIFTER
LINTER
LISTER
LITTER
LOITER
LOOTER
LUSTER
MARTYR
MASTER
MATTER
MEETER
MENTOR
MINTER
MISTER
MOLTER
MORTAR
MUSTER
MUTTER
NATTER
NEATER
NECTAR
NESTER
NESTOR
NEUTER
NUTTER
OBITER
OERTER
ORATOR
OUSTER
OYSTER
PALTER
PASTOR
PATTER
PELTER
PERTER
PESTER
PETTER
PEWTER
PIETER
PINTER
PITTER
PLATER
PORTER
POSTER
POTTER
POUTER
PRATER
PRETER
PUNTER
PUTTER
QINTAR
QUOTER
RAFTER
RANTER
RAPTOR
RASTER
RATTER
RECTOR
RENTER
RESTER
REUTER
RHETOR
RIOTER
RITTER
ROOTER
ROSTER
ROTTER
ROUTER
SALTER
SANTIR
SCOTER
SEATER
SECTOR
SETTER
SIFTER
SINTER
SISTER
SITTER
SKATER
SLATER
SOFTER
SORTER
SOUTER
STATER
STATOR
SUITOR
SUMTER
SUTTER
TARTAR
TARTER
TASTER
TATTER
TAUTER
TEETER
TENTER
TESTER
TILTER
TINTER
TITTER
TOOTER
TOTTER
TOUTER
TRITER
ULSTER
UNITER
VASTER
VECTOR
VENTER
VICTOR
WAITER
WALTER
WASTER
WELTER
WETTER
WHITER
WINTER
WISTER
WRITER
WYNTER
XYSTER
YESTER

TS••••
TSETSE
TSHIRT
TSURIS

T•S•••
TASERS
TASKED
TASMAN
TASSEL
TASSES
TASTED
TASTER
TASTES
TESLAS
TESSIE
TESTAE
TESTED
TESTEE
TESTER
TISANE
TISHRI
TISSUE
TOSSED
TOSSER
TOSSES
TOSSUP
TUSCAN
TUSKED
TUSKER
TUSSAH
TUSSLE
TVSETS
TVSHOW

T••S••
TAGSUP
TARSAL
TARSUS
TASSEL
TASSES
TEASED
TEASEL
TEASER
TEASES
TEASET
TEESUP
TENSED
TENSER
TENSES
TENSOR
TERSER
TESSIE
THESEA
THESES
THESIS
THESIX
THISBE
THUSLY
TIESIN
TIESTO
TIESUP
TILSIT
TINSEL
TIPSIN
TISSUE
TMESIS
TOASTS
TOASTY
TOCSIN
TOESIN
TONSIL
TORSOS
TOSSED
TOSSER
TOSSES
TOSSUP
TOTSUP
TOUSLE
TRASHY
TRISHA
TRISTE
TRUSTS
TRUSTY
TRYSTS
TUCSON
TULSAN
TUSSAH
TUSSLE
TWISTS
TWISTY

T•••S•
TALESE
TAMEST
TANIST
TAOISM
TAOIST
TEENSY
TERESA
THEISM
THEIST
THIRST
THRASH
THRESH
THRUSH
THRUST
THYRSI
TONISH
TOOTSY
TOROSE
TRUEST
TRUISM
TSETSE
TUBIST
TWEEST
TYPIST
TZUHSI

T••••S
TABLAS
TABLES
TABOOS
TABORS
TAIGAS
TAINOS
TAINTS
TAKERS
TAKINS
TALERS
TALONS
TAMERS
TAMILS
TANGOS
TANKAS
TANTES
TAPERS
TAPINS
TAPIRS
TARGES
TAROTS
TARSUS
TASERS
TASSES
TASTES
TATARS
TATERS
TAUNTS
TAUONS
TAUPES
TAURUS
TAXERS
TAXIES
TAYRAS
TAZZAS
TBILLS
TBIRDS
TBONDS
TBONES
TEASES
TEHEES
TEMPOS
TEMPTS
TEMPUS
TENENS
TENETS
TENNIS
TENONS
TENORS
TENSES
TENTHS
TEPALS
TEPEES
TEREUS
TERNES
TESLAS
TETHYS
TETONS
TETRAS
TETRIS
TEXANS
THALES
THAMES
THANES
THANKS
THATIS
THEBES
THEFTS
THEIRS
THEMES
THERES
THERMS
THESES
THESIS
THETAS
THETIS
THIGHS
THILLS
THINGS
THINKS
THIRDS
THOLES
THOMAS
THONGS
THORNS
THORPS
THREES
THRIPS
THROBS
THROES
THROWS
THRUMS
THUJAS
THUMBS
THUMPS
THUNKS
THYMUS
TIARAS
TIBIAS
TICALS
TIDIES
TIEINS
TIEUPS
TIGERS
TIGHTS
TIGRIS
TILAKS
TILDES
TILERS
TILLIS
TIMERS
TINCTS
TINGES
TIPINS
TIPUPS
TITANS
TITERS
TITHES
TITLES
TITRES
TMESIS
TNOTES
TOASTS
TOBIAS
TOBIES
TOEINS
TOILES
TOKAYS
TOKENS
TOKLAS
TONDOS
TONERS
TONICS
TONNES
TOPERS
TOPHUS
TOPICS
TOQUES
TORAHS
TORIES
TORRES
TORSOS
TORTES
TOSSES
TOTALS
TOTEMS
TOTERS
TOUGHS
TOWELS
TOWERS
TOXICS
TOXINS
TOYONS
TRACES
TRACKS
TRACTS
TRADES
TRAILS
TRAINS
TRAITS
TRAMPS
TRAVES
TRAVIS
TRAWLS
TREADS
TREATS
TRENDS
TRIADS
TRIALS
TRIBES
TRICES
TRICKS
TRIERS
TRIKES
TRILLS
TRINES
TRIPOS
TROLLS
TROMPS
TROOPS
TROPES
TROTHS
TROUTS
TROVES
TRUCES
TRUCKS
TRUMPS
TRUNKS
TRUSTS
TRUTHS
TRYSTS
TSURIS
TUBERS
TUDORS
TULIPS
TULLES
TUNERS
TUNICS
TUQUES
TURBOS
TURVES
TUTORS
TVSETS
TWANGS
TWEAKS
TWEEDS
TWEENS
TWEETS
TWERPS
TWILLS
TWINES
TWIRLS
TWISTS
TYPERS
TYPHUS

•TS•••
ATSTUD
ETSEQQ
ITSELF

•T•S••
ATESTS
ITASCA
STASES
STASIS

•T••S•
ATBEST
ATCOST
ATEASE
ATLAST
ATMOST
ATREST
ATRISK
ATTEST
OTIOSE
STRASS
STRESS
UTMOST

•T•••S
ATBATS
ATEAMS
ATESTS
ATHENS
ATKINS
ATODDS
ATOLLS
ATONES
ATREUS
ATTARS
ATTICS
ETAPES
ETCHES
ETHERS
ETHICS
ETHNOS

ETUDES
ITCHES
OTHERS
OTITIS
OTTERS
PTRAPS
STACKS
STAFFS
STAGES
STAINS
STAIRS
STAKES
STALES
STALKS
STALLS
STAMPS
STANDS
STAPES
STARES
STARTS
STASES
STASIS
STATES
STATUS
STAVES
STEADS
STEAKS
STEALS
STEAMS
STEEDS
STEELS
STEEPS
STEERS
STEINS
STELES
STENOS
STERES
STERNS
STICKS
STIFFS
STILES
STILLS
STILTS
STINGS
STINKS
STINTS
STIPES
STIRKS
STOATS
STOCKS
STOICS
STOKES
STOLES
STOMAS
STOMPS
STONES
STOOKS
STOOLS
STOOPS
STOPES
STORES
STORKS
STORMS
STORRS
STOUPS
STOUTS
STOVES
STRADS
STRAPS
STRASS
STRAUS
STRAWS
STRAYS
STRESS
STREWS
STRIPS
STROPS
STRUMS
STRUTS
STUFFS
STULLS
STUMPS
STUNTS
STUPAS
STUPES
STYLES
STYLUS
UTTERS
UTURNS

••TS••

ACTSAS
ACTSON
ACTSUP
BETSEY
BETSON
CATSUP
CUTSIN
CUTSUP
DATSUN
EATSAT
EATSIN
EATSUP
FITSIN
GATSBY
GETSAT
GETSBY
GETSET
GETSIN
GETSIT
GETSON
GETSTO
GETSUP
GOTSET
HITSIT
HITSON
HITSUP
JETSAM
JETSET
JETSKI
JETSON
KITSCH
LETSAT
LETSBE
LETSGO
LETSIN
LETSON
LETSUP
OUTSET
PITSAW
PUTSBY
PUTSCH
PUTSIN
PUTSON
PUTSTO
PUTSUP
RATSON
SETSAT
SETSBY
SETSIN
SETSON
SETSUP
SITSBY
SITSIN
SITSON
SITSUP
TOTSUP
WATSON

••T•S•

APTEST
ARTIST
ATTEST
BETISE
CUTEST
CUTESY
DETEST
FETISH
IQTEST
IRTYSH
JUTISH
LATEST
LATISH
LUTIST
MUTEST
OBTEST
OBTUSE
POTASH
POTOSI
RETEST
SETOSE
WATUSI

••T••S

ACTORS
ACTSAS
ALTARS
ALTERS
ALTIUS
ANTICS
ANTRES
ARTELS
ARTOIS
ASTERS
ASTROS
ATTARS
ATTICS
AZTECS
BATHES
BATHOS
BATIKS
BATONS
BETELS
BETTAS
BITERS
BOTELS
BUTEOS
BUTTES
BUTUTS
CATERS
CITERS
CITIES
CITIUS
CITRUS
COTTAS
CUTIES
CUTINS
CUTUPS
DATERS
DETERS
DITTOS
DITZES
DUTIES
EATERS
ENTERS
ESTERS
ESTOPS
EXTOLS
EXTRAS
FATWAS
FSTOPS
FUTONS
FUTZES
GATERS
GATORS
GETUPS
HATERS
HOTELS
IDTAGS
INTENS
INTROS
ISTLES
KITERS
LATENS
LATHES
LATINS
LATKES
LETUPS
LITERS
LITHOS
LITMUS
LITRES
LOTAHS
LOTTOS
LUTZES
MATERS
MATEYS
MATHIS
MATINS
MATTES
MATZOS
METALS
METERS
METRES
METROS
MITERS
MITRES
MOTELS
MOTETS
MOTIFS
MOTORS
MOTTOS
MYTHOS
NITERS
NITRES
NOTERS
OATERS
OCTADS
OCTETS
OPTICS
ORTLES
OTTERS
PATENS
PATERS
PATHOS
PATIOS
PATMOS
PATOIS
PETALS
PETERS
PITIES
PITONS
POTTOS
PUTONS
RATELS
RATERS
RATIOS
RETAGS
RETAPS
RETARS
RETIES
RETOPS
RETOWS
RETROS
ROTORS
SATINS
SATYRS
SETINS
SETTOS
SETUPS
SITARS
SITINS
SITUPS
SOTOLS
SUTRAS
TATARS
TATERS
TETHYS
TETONS
TETRAS
TETRIS
TITANS
TITERS
TITHES
TITLES
TITRES
TOTALS
TOTEMS
TOTERS
TUTORS
ULTRAS
UNTIES
UTTERS
VETOES
VITALS
VOTERS
WATERS
WITHES

•••TS•

BOOTSY
BRATSK
CURTSY
LAOTSE
LHOTSE
TOOTSY
TSETSE

•••T•S

ABATES
ABATIS
AEETES
AGATES
AKITAS
AMATIS
AORTAS
ARETES
BANTUS
BASTES
BERTHS
BETTAS
BIÓTAS
BIRTHS
BOITES
BOOTES
BOOTHS
BROTHS
BRUTES
BRUTUS
BUTTES
CACTUS
CANTOS
CARTES
CASTES
CENTOS
CESTAS
CESTOS
CESTUS
CHETHS
CHUTES
CLOTHS
CNOTES
COATIS
COMTES
CONTES
CORTES
COSTAS
COTTAS
CRATES
CURTIS
CUSTIS
CUSTOS
DANTES
DELTAS
DEPTHS
DHOTIS
DICTUS
DITTOS
ELATES
ELITES
ELUTES
EMOTES
ENATES
FAITHS
FESTAS
FESTUS
FIFTHS
FIRTHS
FLUTES
FOETUS
FORTAS
FORTES
FRITOS
FROTHS
GARTHS
GESTES
GIRTHS
GLUTES
GRATÉS
GRATIS
HASTES
HEATHS
HIATUS
HOSTAS
HOWTOS
JUNTAS
JUNTOS
KNOTTS
LOTTOS
MANTAS
MANTIS
MATTES
MENTIS
MONTES
MONTHS
MOTTOS
MOUTHS
MUFTIS
NANTES
NINTHS
NORTHS
ORATES
OTITIS
PANTOS
PASTAS
PASTES
PASTIS
PESTOS
PHOTOS
PIETAS
PINTOS
PISTES
PLATES
PONTES
PONTUS
POTTOS
PRATES
QANTAS
QUOTAS
QUOTES
REATAS
RECTOS
RECTUS
RIATAS
ROUTES
SANTOS
SAUTES
SCUTES
SESTOS
SETTOS
SIXTHS
SIXTUS
SKATES
SLATES
SLOTHS
SMITES
SMITHS
SNATHS
SOUTHS
SPATES
SPITES
STATES
STATUS
SUITES
SWATHS
TANTES
TASTES
TENTHS
THATIS
THETAS
THETIS
TNOTES
TORTES
TROTHS
TRUTHS
UINTAS
UNITAS
UNITES
VESTAS
VICTIS
VIRTUS
VISTAS
WASTES
WHITES
WIDTHS
WORTHS
WRATHS
WRITES
YENTAS
YOUTHS
ZLOTYS

••••TS

ABBOTS
ABORTS
ADAPTS
ADEPTS
ADMITS
ADOPTS
ADULTS
AFLATS
AFRITS
AGENTS
AGLETS
ALERTS
ALEUTS
ALLOTS
AMBITS
AMENTS
AMVETS
ARGOTS
ARMETS
ASCOTS
ASSETS
ATBATS
ATESTS
AUDITS
AUGHTS
AVERTS
AWAITS
BEASTS
BEAUTS
BEFITS
BEGETS
BERETS
BESETS
BESOTS
BIGHTS
BIGOTS
BLASTS
BLEATS
BLOATS
BLUETS
BLUNTS
BLURTS
BOASTS
BOOSTS
BRACTS
BRANTS
BRENTS
BRUITS
BRUNTS
BURSTS
BUTUTS
CADETS
CARATS
CARETS
CHANTS
CHARTS
CHEATS
CHESTS
CIVETS
CLEATS
CLEFTS
CLOUTS
COAPTS
COASTS
COMETS
COOPTS
COUNTS
COURTS
COVETS
CRAFTS
CRESTS
CROATS
CROFTS
CRUETS
CRUSTS
CRYPTS
CSPOTS
CUBITS
CULETS
DAUNTS
DAVITS
DEBITS
DEBUTS
DEFATS
DEISTS
DELFTS
DEMITS
DEPOTS
DICOTS
DIGITS
DIVOTS
DIXITS
DONETS
DONUTS
DOUBTS
DRAFTS
DRIFTS
DROITS
DUCATS
DUVETS
EBOATS
ECLATS
EDICTS
EFLATS
EGESTS
EGRETS
EIGHTS
EJECTS
ELECTS
EMMETS
ENACTS
ERECTS
ERGOTS
ERUCTS
ERUPTS
EVENTS
EVERTS
EVICTS
EXACTS
EXALTS
EXERTS
EXISTS
EXULTS
FACETS
FAGOTS
FAINTS
FAULTS

FEASTS
FEINTS
FIGHTS
FILETS
FIRSTS
FLEETS
FLINTS
FLIRTS
FLOATS
FLOUTS
FOISTS
FOUNTS
FRONTS
FROSTS
FRUITS
GAMUTS
GEMOTS
GENETS
GHOSTS
GIANTS
GIGOTS
GLINTS
GLOATS
GODETS
GRAFTS
GRANTS
GREATS
GREETS
GRIFTS
GRIOTS
GRISTS
GROATS
GROUTS
GRUNTS
GSUITS
GUESTS
GUYOTS
HABITS
HAUNTS
HEARTS
HEISTS
HELOTS
HOISTS
IDIOTS
INGOTS
INLETS
INPUTS
INSETS
INUITS
ISLETS
JABOTS
JAUNTS
JOINTS
JOISTS
JOUSTS
JURATS
KARATS
KARSTS
KNOTTS
KNOUTS
KORATS
KRAITS
LIEUTS
LIGHTS
LIMITS
MERITS
MOTETS
MOULTS
MOUNTS
MULCTS
NENETS
NIGHTS
NOHITS
NONETS
NOPETS
NYMETS
OCTETS
ODISTS
ONSETS
ORANTS
ORBITS
OUGHTS
OWLETS
PAINTS
PEWITS
PICOTS
PILOTS
PINOTS
PIPITS
PIVOTS
PLAITS
PLANTS
PLEATS
POINTS
POSITS
POULTS
PRINTS
QUARTS
QUESTS
QUIETS
QUILTS
QUINTS
QUIRTS
QUOITS
RAMETS
REACTS
REBUTS
REFITS
RELETS
REMITS
REPOTS
RESETS
REVETS
RIGHTS
RIVETS
ROASTS
ROBOTS
ROOSTS
ROUSTS
SABOTS
SAINTS
SAULTS
SCANTS
SCENTS
SCOOTS
SCOUTS
SHAFTS
SHEETS
SHIFTS
SHIRTS
SHOATS
SHOOTS
SHORTS
SHOUTS
SHUNTS
SIGHTS
SKIRTS
SKORTS
SLANTS
SLEETS
SMARTS
SMELTS
SMOLTS
SNOOTS
SNORTS
SNOUTS
SPLATS
SPLITS
SPORTS
SPOUTS
SPRATS
SPRITS
SPURTS
SQUATS
STARTS
STILTS
STINTS
STOATS
STOUTS
STRUTS
STUNTS
SWEATS
SWEETS
SWIFTS
TAINTS
TAROTS
TAUNTS
TEMPTS
TENETS
THEFTS
TIGHTS
TINCTS
TOASTS
TRACTS
TRAITS
TREATS
TROUTS
TRUSTS
TRYSTS
TVSETS
TWEETS
TWISTS
UBOATS
UBOLTS
UNFITS
UNIATS
UPSETS
VALETS
VAULTS
VAUNTS
VELDTS
VERSTS
VISITS
WAISTS
WHEATS
WIGHTS
WORSTS
WRESTS
WRISTS
WURSTS
YACHTS
YAKUTS
YEASTS
YOKUTS
ZIBETS

T•T•••

TATAMI
TATARS
TATERS
TATTED
TATTER
TATTLE
TATTOO
TETCHY
TETHER
TETHYS
TETONS
TETRAD
TETRAS
TETRIS
TETZEL
TITANS
TITBIT
TITERS
TITFER
TITHED
TITHER
TITHES
TITIAN
TITLED
TITLES
TITRED
TITRES
TITTER
TITTLE
TITTUP
TOTALS
TOTEMS
TOTERS
TOTHER
TOTING
TOTSUP
TOTTED
TOTTER
TUTORS
TUTTUT
TUTUED

T••T••

TACTIC
TAMTAM
TANTES
TANTRA
TARTAN
TARTAR
TARTER
TARTLY
TASTED
TASTER
TASTES
TATTED
TATTER
TATTLE
TATTOO
TAUTEN
TAUTER
TAUTLY
TAUTOG
TEETER
TEETHE
TENTED
TENTER
TENTHS
TESTAE
TESTED
TESTEE
TESTER
TEUTON
THATCH
THATIS
THATLL
THETAS
THETIC
THETIS
THETOY
TICTAC
TILTED
TILTER
TINTED
TINTER
TIPTOE
TIPTOP
TITTER
TITTLE
TITTUP
TNOTES
TOATEE
TOETAP
TOLTEC
TOMTIT
TOMTOM
TOOTED
TOOTER
TOOTHY
TOOTLE
TOOTOO
TOOTSY
TOPTEN
TORTES
TOTTED
TOTTER
TOUTED
TOUTER
TRITER
TRITON
TROTHS
TRUTHS
TSETSE
TUFTED
TURTLE
TUTTUT
TWITCH
TWITTY

T•••T•

TAHITI
TAINTS
TAKETH
TAKETO
TALKTO
TAROTS
TAUNTS
TEMPTS
TENDTO
TENETS
TENUTO
TERATO
TERETE
THEFTS
THIRTY
TIEDTO
TIESTO
TIGHTS
TINCTS
TOASTS
TOASTY
TODATE
TOMATO
TONITE
TOOKTO
TOYOTA
TRACTS
TRAITS
TREATS
TREATY
TRISTE
TROUTS
TRUSTS
TRUSTY
TRYSTS
TUBATE
TURNTO
TVSETS
TWEETS
TWEETY
TWENTY
TWISTS
TWISTY
TWITTY

T••••T

TABLET
TAGOUT
TALBOT
TALENT
TALKAT
TAMEST
TANIST
TAOIST
TAPOUT
TAPPET
TARGET
TARPIT
TAUGHT
TEAPOT
TEARAT
TEASET
TENANT
TERCET
TERRET
THEIST
THIRST
THREAT
THRIFT
THROAT
THRUST
THWART
TICKET
TIDBIT
TILSIT
TINHAT
TINPOT
TIPPET
TITBIT
TOBOOT
TOILET
TOMCAT
TOMTIT
TOOKIT
TOPCAT
TOPHAT
TOPOUT
TOREAT
TRICOT
TRIJET
TRIVET
TRUANT
TRUEST
TRYOUT
TSHIRT
TUBIST
TUCKET
TUFFET
TUMULT
TURBIT
TURBOT
TURRET
TUTTUT
TWEEST
TWILIT
TWOBIT
TYBALT
TYPIST
TYRANT

•TT•••

ATTACH
ATTACK
ATTAIN
ATTARS
ATTEND
ATTEST
ATTHAT
ATTICA
ATTICS
ATTILA
ATTIRE
ATTLEE
ATTRIT
ATTUNE
OTTAVA
OTTAWA
OTTERS
UTTERS

•T•T••

ATSTUD
OTITIC
OTITIS
STATED
STATEN
STATER
STATES
STATIC
STATOR
STATUE
STATUS
STITCH
STITHY
STOTIN

•T••T•

ATBATS
ATESTS
ATLATL
STACTE
STARTS
STILTS
STINTS
STOATS
STOUTS
STPETE
STRATA
STRATI
STRATO
STRUTS
STUNTS
STUNTY

•T•••T

ATBEST
ATCOST
ATEOUT
ATLAST
ATMOST
ATREST
ATTEST
ATTHAT
ATTRIT
PTBOAT
STABAT
STOMAT
STOPIT
STRAIT
STREET
STRICT
STUART
STYLET
UTHANT
UTMOST

••TT••

ACTTWO
BATTED
BATTEL
BATTEN
BATTER
BATTLE
BATTUE
BETTAS
BETTER
BETTOR
BITTED
BITTEN
BITTER
BOTTLE
BOTTOM
BUTTED
BUTTER
BUTTES
BUTTIN
BUTTON
CATTED
CATTLE
CATTON
COTTAS
COTTEN
COTTER
COTTON
CUTTER
DITTOS
DOTTED
DOTTIE
DOTTLE
FATTED
FATTEN
FATTER
FETTER
FETTLE
FITTED
FITTER
GETTER
GOTTEN
GUTTAE
GUTTED
GUTTER
HATTED
HATTER
HATTIE
HETTIE
HITTER
HOTTEA
HOTTER
HOTTIP
HOTTUB
HUTTED
HUTTON
JETTED
JITTER
JOTTED
JUTTED
KETTLE
KITTEN
KOTTER
LATTEN
LATTER
LETTED
LETTER
LITTER
LITTLE
LOTTED
LOTTOS
LYTTON
MATTEA
MATTED
MATTEL
MATTER
MATTES
MATTIE
METTLE
MITTEN
MOTTLE
MOTTOS
MUTTER
MUTTON
NATTER
NETTED
NETTLE
NETTLY
NETTON
NUTTED
NUTTER
PATTED
PATTEN
PATTER
PATTON
PETTED
PETTER
PETTIT
PITTED
PITTER
POTTED
POTTER
POTTLE
POTTOS
PUTTED
PUTTEE
PUTTER
RATTAN
RATTED
RATTER
RATTLE
RATTLY
RETTON
RITTER
ROTTED
ROTTEN
ROTTER
RUTTAN

RUTTED
SETTEE
SETTER
SETTLE
SETTOS
SITTER
SOTTED
SUTTER
SUTTON
TATTED
TATTER
TATTLE
TATTOO
TITTER
TITTLE
TITTUP
TOTTED
TOTTER
TUTTUT
VATTED
VETTED
WATTLE
WETTED
WETTER
WETTIG
WITTED

••T•T•
ASTUTE
BUTUTS
CITATO
ENTITY
ESTATE
GETSTO
INTOTO
METATE
MOTETS
MUTATE
MUTATO
NOTATE
NUTATE
OCTETS
OUTATE
PETITE
POTATO
PUTSTO
RATITE
ROTATE
SHTETL
UMTATA

••T••T
ACTOUT
APTEST
ARTIST
ATTEST
ATTHAT
ATTRIT
CATGUT
CUTEST
CUTLET
CUTOUT
DETECT
DETENT
DETEST
EATOUT
EATSAT
EXTANT
EXTENT
EXTORT
FATCAT
GETOUT
GETSAT
GETSET
GETSIT
GOTOIT
GOTOUT
GOTSET
HITOUT
HITSIT
HOTPOT
INTACT
INTENT
INTUIT
IQTEST
JETSET
KITKAT
LATENT
LATEST
LETOUT
LETSAT
LITOUT
LUTIST
MOTMOT
MUTANT
MUTEST
NATANT
NITWIT
NOTYET
NUTLET
OBTEST
OCTANT
OPTOUT
OUTACT
OUTEAT
OUTFIT
OUTHIT
OUTLET
OUTPUT
OUTSET
OUTWIT
PATENT
PETTIT
POTENT
PUTOUT
PUTPUT
RETEST
RETORT
ROTGUT
SATOUT
SETOUT
SETSAT
SITOUT
SOTHAT
TITBIT
TUTTUT
URTEXT
WITHIT

•••TT•
ANATTO
BEATTY
BHUTTO
BLATTY
BLOTTO
BLOTTY
BRATTY
CHATTY
CLOTTY
FRETTY
FRUTTI
GHETTO
GIOTTO
GNATTY
GRITTY
GROTTO
GROTTY
KNOTTS
KNOTTY
LIOTTA
NEXTTO
ODETTA
ODETTE
PLATTE
PLOTTY
PRETTY
QUETTA
SCATTY
SCOTTO
SCOTTY
SLITTY
SMUTTY
SNOTTY
SPOTTY
TWITTY
WANTTO
WHITTY
YVETTE

•••T•T
BEATIT
DIKTAT
HINTAT
HOOTAT
IGETIT
IGOTIT
KEPTAT
LESTAT
LOSTIT
MUSTNT
OBSTET
PETTIT
POSTIT
QUITIT
SEPTET
SESTET
SEXTET
SHOTAT
TOMTIT
TUTTUT
WENTAT

••••TT
ABBOTT
ALCOTT
ARNETT
CAVETT
DEWITT
EMMETT
JEWETT
JOWETT
LOVETT
MELOTT

TU••••
TUAREG
TUBATE
TUBBED
TUBERS
TUBING
TUBIST
TUBMAN
TUCANA
TUCHUN
TUCKED
TUCKER
TUCKET
TUCKIN
TUCSON
TUDORS
TUFFET
TUFTED
TUGGED
TUGGER
TUGRIK
TUILLE
TULANE
TULARE
TULIPS
TULLES
TULSAN
TUMBLE
TUMEFY
TUMMED
TUMULI
TUMULT
TUNDRA
TUNEIN
TUNERS
TUNEUP
TUNICA
TUNICS
TUNING
TUNNEL
TUNNEY
TUPELO
TUPIAN
TUQUES
TURBAN
TURBID
TURBIT
TURBOS
TURBOT
TUREEN
TURFED
TURGID
TURGOR
TURING
TURKEY
TURKIC
TURNED
TURNER
TURNIN
TURNIP
TURNON
TURNTO
TURNUP
TURPIN
TURRET
TURTLE
TURVES
TUSCAN
TUSKED
TUSKER
TUSSAH
TUSSLE
TUTORS
TUTTUT
TUTUED
TUVALU
TUXEDO
TUYERE

T•U•••
TAUGHT
TAUNTS
TAUONS
TAUPES
TAURUS
TAUTEN
TAUTER
TAUTLY
TAUTOG
TEUTON
THUJAS
THUMBS
THUMPS
THUNKS
THUSLY
TOUCAN
TOUCHE
TOUCHY
TOUGHS
TOUGHY
TOULON
TOUPEE
TOURED
TOURER
TOUSLE
TOUTED
TOUTER
TRUANT
TRUCES
TRUCKS
TRUDGE
TRUEST
TRUING
TRUISM
TRUMAN
TRUMPS
TRUNKS
TRUSTS
TRUSTY
TRUTHS
TSURIS
TZUHSI

T••U••
TABULA
TELUGU
TENURE
TENUTO
THOUGH
THRUMS
THRUSH
THRUST
TIEUPS
TIPUPS
TOLUCA
TOQUES
TRAUMA
TRIUNE
TROUGH
TROUPE
TROUTS
TROUVE
TUMULI
TUMULT
TUQUES
TUTUED

T•••U•
TAGOUT
TAGSUP
TAKEUP
TALCUM
TALKUP
TALMUD
TAMMUZ
TANGUY
TANKUP
TAPOUT
TARSUS
TAURUS
TEACUP
TEAMUP
TEARUP
TEDEUM
TEDIUM
TEEDUP
TEESUP
TEMPUS
TEREUS
THYMUS
TIDYUP
TIEDUP
TIESUP
TISSUE
TITTUP
TOBRUK
TONEUP
TONGUE
TOOKUP
TOOLUP
TOPGUN
TOPHUS
TOPOUT
TOREUP
TORQUE
TOSSUP
TOTSUP
TRIPUP
TRYOUT
TUCHUN
TUNEUP
TURNUP
TUTTUT
TYPEUP
TYPHUS

T••••U
TELEDU
TELUGU
TUVALU

•TU•••
ETUDES
ETUXOR
ITURBI
STUART
STUBBY
STUCCO
STUDIO
STUFFS
STUFFY
STULLS
STUMER
STUMPS
STUMPY
STUNTS
STUNTY
STUPAS
STUPES
STUPID
STUPOR
STURDY
UTURNS

•T•U••
ATTUNE
STLUKE
STOUPS
STOUTS
STRUCK
STRUMS
STRUNG
STRUTS

•T••U•
ATEOUT
ATREUS
ATRIUM
ATSTUD
STAPUF
STATUE
STATUS
STAYUP
STEPUP
STIRUP
STOPUP
STPAUL
STRAUB
STRAUS
STROUD
STYLUS

••TU••
ACTUAL
ARTURO
ASTUTE
ATTUNE
AUTUMN
BATUMI
BUTUNG
BUTUTS
CUTUPS
DATURA
FUTURE
GETUPS
INTUIT
INTUNE
INTURN
LETUPS
MATURE
MUTUAL
NATURA
NATURE
OBTUND
OBTUSE
PETULA
RETUNE
RETURN
RITUAL
ROTUND
SATURN
SETUPS
SITUPS
SUTURE
TUTUED
UNTUNE
UPTURN
WATUSI

••T•U•
ACTIUM
ACTOUT
ACTSUP
ALTIUS
ANTEUP
ANTRUM
ARTFUL
ARTGUM
ARTHUR
AUTEUR
BATTUE
CATGUT
CATSUP
CITIUS
CITRUS
CUTOUT
CUTSUP
DATSUN
DETOUR
EATOUT
EATSUP
FITFUL
GETOUT
GETSUP
GOTOUT
HATFUL
HITOUT
HITSUP
HOTTUB
JETGUN
LATIUM
LATOUR
LETOUT
LETSUP
LITMUS
LITOUT
ONTOUR
OPTOUT
OSTIUM
OUTGUN
OUTPUT
OUTRUN
POTFUL
PUTOUT
PUTPUT
PUTSUP
RETOUR
ROTGUT
SATOUT
SETOUT
SETSUP
SITOUT
SITSUP
TITTUP
TOTSUP
TUTTUT
UNTRUE
VATFUL

••T••U
BATEAU
GATEAU

•••TU•
ADYTUM
ATSTUD
BANTUS
BATTUE
BEATUP
BOOTUP
BRUTUS
CACTUS
CESTUS
CHATUP
DICTUM
DICTUS
DUSTUP
FESTUS
FOETUS
HEATUP
HIATUS
HOTTUB
KEPTUP
KULTUR
LIFTUP
MANTUA
MULTUM
PENTUP
PONTUS
RECTUS
RESTUP
SALTUM
SENTUP
SEPTUM
SHOTUP
SHUTUP
SIXTUS
STATUE
STATUS
SUITUP
TITTUP
TUTTUT
VIRTUE
VIRTUS
WAITUP
WENTUP

•••T•U
ALATAU
LAOTZU

••••TU
ERESTU
INSITU
SHORTU

TV••••
TVSETS
TVSHOW

T•V•••
TAVERN
TIVOLI
TUVALU

T••V••
TEEVEE
TRAVEL
TRAVES
TRAVIS
TREVOR
TRIVET
TRIVIA
TROVES
TURVES

T••V•
THEYVE
THIEVE
THRIVE
THROVE
TROUVE
TWELVE

•T•V••
STAVED
STAVES
STEVEN
STEVIE
STIVER
STIVIC
STOVER
STOVES

•T••V•
OTTAVA
STARVE
STEEVE
STRIVE
STROVE

••TV••
LATVIA

••T•V•
ACTIVE
DATIVE
MOTIVE
NATIVE
OCTAVE
OCTAVO
OTTAVA
VOTIVE

•••TV•
WHATVE

•••T•V
GUSTAV
LAPTEV
ROSTOV
YOMTOV

TW••••
TWANGS
TWANGY
TWEAKS
TWEEDS
TWEEDY
TWEENS
TWEENY
TWEEST
TWEETS
TWEETY
TWEEZE
TWELVE
TWENTY
TWERPS
TWIGGY
TWILIT
TWILLS
TWINED
TWINES
TWINGE
TWIRLS
TWISTS
TWISTY
TWITCH
TWITTY
TWOBIT
TWOFER
TWOPLY
TWOWAY

T•W•••
TAWDRY
TAWING
THWACK
THWART
TOWAGE
TOWARD
TOWCAR
TOWELS
TOWERS
TOWERY
TOWHEE
TOWING
TOWNER
TOWNIE

T••W••
TAIWAN
THAWED
THEWEB
THEWIZ
TRAWLS
TROWED
TROWEL
TWOWAY

T•••W•
TARAWA
THROWN
THROWS

T••••W
TALLOW
TVSHOW

•TW•••
ATWILL
ATWOOD
ATWORK

•T•W••
STEWED
STEWER
STOWED

•T••W•
OTTAWA
STRAWS
STRAWY
STREWN
STREWS

••TW••
FATWAS
HOTWAR
JETWAY
NITWIT
OUTWIT

••T•W•
ACTTWO
INTOWN
MOTOWN
OTTAWA
RETOWS
UPTOWN

••T••W
ANTCOW
NOTNOW
OUTLAW
PITSAW

•••TW•
ACTTWO
ONETWO

•••T•W
BESTOW
KOWTOW
SKITOW

T•X•••
TAXERS
TAXIED
TAXIES
TAXING
TAXMAN
TAXMEN
TEXACO
TEXANS
TEXMEX
TOXICS
TOXINS
TUXEDO

T••X••
TRIXIE

T••••X
TEXMEX
THESIX
THORAX
TOMMIX

•T•X••
ETUXOR

••T•X•
EUTAXY
URTEXT

••T••X
HATBOX
HOTBOX
KITFOX
MATRIX
OUTBOX
OUTFOX
RATEDX

•••T•X
CORTEX
JOETEX
LASTEX
PRETAX
PROTAX
SINTAX
SURTAX
SYNTAX
VERTEX
VORTEX

TY••••
TYBALT
TYCOBB
TYCOON
TYDBOL
TYPERS
TYPEUP
TYPHUS
TYPIER
TYPIFY
TYPING
TYPIST
TYRANT
TYRIAN
TYRONE

T•Y•••
TAYLOR
TAYRAS
THYMUS
THYRSI
TOYDOG
TOYING
TOYONS
TOYOTA
TRYFOR
TRYING
TRYLON
TRYOUT
TRYSTS
TUYERE

T••Y••
THAYER
THEYLL
THEYRE
THEYVE
TIDYUP

T•••Y•
TAMAYO
TETHYS
TIEDYE
TOKAYS

T••••Y
TAGDAY
TAMELY
TANGLY
TANGUY
TARTLY
TAUTLY
TAWDRY
TEAPOY
TEDKEY
TEENSY
TETCHY
THEFLY
THEORY
THETOY
THINGY
THINLY
THIRTY
THORNY
THUSLY
TICKLY
TIDDLY
TIDILY
TIMELY
TINGLY
TINILY
TINKLY
TOASTY
TOMBOY
TOOTHY
TOOTSY
TORCHY
TORREY
TOUCHY
TOUGHY
TOWERY
TRACEY
TRACHY
TRAPPY
TRASHY
TREATY
TREBLY
TRENDY
TRICKY
TRIGLY
TRILBY
TRIMLY
TRIPLY
TROPHY
TRUSTY
TUMEFY
TUNNEY
TURKEY
TWANGY
TWEEDY
TWEENY
TWEETY
TWENTY
TWIGGY
TWISTY
TWITTY
TWOPLY
TWOWAY
TYPIFY

•TY•••
ETYMOL
ETYMON
STYLED
STYLER
STYLES
STYLET
STYLUS
STYMIE
STYRIA
STYRON

•T•Y••
STAYED
STAYON
STAYUP

•T••Y•
STRAYS

•T•••Y
STABLY
STACEY
STALKY
STANKY
STARRY
STEADY
STEAMY
STEELY
STEFOY
STICKY
STILLY
STIMPY
STINGY
STINKY
STITHY
STOCKY
STODGY
STOOLY
STOREY
STORMY
STRAWY
STRIPY
STUBBY
STUFFY
STUMPY
STUNTY
STURDY

••TY••
BATYAM
ECTYPE
IRTYSH
NOTYET
RETYPE
SATYRS

••T•Y•
LATOYA
MATEYS
METHYL
TETHYS

••T••Y
ANTONY
ARTERY
ARTILY
ASTRAY
BATBOY
BETONY
BETRAY
BETSEY
BOTANY
BOTCHY
BOTFLY
CATCHY
CATHAY
CITIFY
CUTELY
CUTESY
DATARY
EATERY
ENTITY
ESTRAY
EUTAXY
GATSBY
GETSBY
JETWAY
JITNEY
LATELY
LETFLY
LITANY
MOTLEY
MUTELY
MUTINY
NETPAY
NETTLY
NITERY
NOTARY
NOTCHY
NOTIFY
OUTCRY
OUTFLY
OUTLAY
PATCHY
PITCHY
PUTSBY
RATIFY
RATTLY
ROTARY
SATINY
SETSBY
SITSBY
TETCHY
UNTIDY
VOTARY
WATERY
WATNEY
WETFLY
WITCHY

•••TY•
ACETYL
DACTYL
MARTYR
ZLOTYS

•••T•Y
APATHY
BEATTY
BLATTY
BLOTTY
BOOTSY
BRATTY
CHATTY
CLOTTY
COSTLY
CURTLY
CURTSY
DAFTLY
DEFTLY
DESTRY
EARTHY
FEATLY
FILTHY
FLATLY
FLUTEY
FRETTY
FROTHY
GANTRY
GENTLY
GENTRY
GLITZY
GNATTY
GRITTY
GROTTY
GUITRY
HEATHY
HOSTLY
ICHTHY
JUSTLY
KLUTZY
KNOTTY
LASTLY
MEETLY
MOSTLY
MOUTHY
NEATLY
NETTLY
PALTRY
PANTRY
PARTLY
PASTRY
PELTRY
PERTLY
PLOTTY
POETRY
PORTLY
PRETTY
RAPTLY
RATTLY
SCATTY
SCOTTY
SENTRY
SLITHY
SLITTY
SMITHY
SMUTTY
SNOTTY
SOFTLY
SPOTTY
STITHY
SUBTLY
SULTRY
TARTLY
TAUTLY
THETOY
TOOTHY
TOOTSY
TWITTY
VASTLY
VESTRY
WENTBY
WHITTY
WINTRY
WORTHY
WRATHY

••••TY
ACUITY
ALMATY
ASEITY
BEATTY
BEAUTY
BLATTY
BLOTTY
BOUNTY
BRATTY
CAVITY
CHATTY
CHERTY
CHESTY
CLOTTY
COMITY
COUNTY
CRAFTY
CRUSTY
DAINTY
DEPUTY
DIMITY
DRAFTY
DRIFTY
EIGHTY
ENMITY
ENTITY
EQUITY
FAULTY
FAWLTY
FEALTY
FEISTY
FERITY
FIXITY
FLINTY
FLIRTY
FLOATY
FRETTY
FROSTY
FRUITY
GAIETY
GNATTY
GRITTY
GROTTY
GROUTY
GUILTY
HEARTY
HINCTY
JAUNTY
KNOTTY
LAXITY
LEALTY
LENITY
LEVITY
MIGHTY
MOIETY
MOUNTY
NICETY
NIGHTY
NINETY
NUDITY
ODDITY
PAINTY
PARITY
PIGSTY
PLASTY
PLENTY
PLOTTY
POINTY
POLITY
PRETTY
PURITY
QWERTY
RARITY
REALTY
RIGHTY
SAFETY
SANITY
SCANTY
SCATTY
SCOTTY
SHANTY
SHELTY
SHIFTY
SHIRTY
SHORTY
SLEETY
SLITTY
SMARTY
SMUTTY
SNOOTY
SNOTTY
SPORTY
SPOTTY
STUNTY
SURETY
SWEATY
THIRTY
TOASTY
TREATY
TRUSTY
TWEETY

TWENTY
TWISTY
TWITTY
UBIETY
UPPITY
VANITY
VAULTY
VERITY
WHITTY
YEASTY

TZ••••
TZUHSI

T•Z•••
TAZZAS

T••Z••
TARZAN
TAZZAS
TETZEL

T•••Z•
TWEEZE

T••••Z
TABRIZ
TAMMUZ
THEWIZ
TROPEZ

•TZ•••
ITZHAK

•T••Z•
STANZA

••TZ••
DITZES
FUTZED
FUTZES
LUTZES
MATZOH
MATZOS
TETZEL

•••TZ•
GLITZY
KLUTZY
LAOTZU

•••T•Z
CORTEZ
CURTIZ
MONTEZ

••••TZ
BLINTZ
CHINTZ
DONITZ
ERSATZ
IGNATZ
KIBITZ
KOONTZ
KRANTZ
MORITZ
NIMITZ
QUARTZ
SPRITZ

UA••••
UAKARI

U•A•••
UBANGI
UGANDA
UKASES
UNABLE
UNAGED
UNARMS
UNAWED
UPASES
URACIL
URAEUS
URALIC
URALSK
URANIA
URANIC
URANUS
USABLE
USABLY
USAGES
USANCE
UTAHAN
UVALUE

U••A••
UAKARI
UBOATS
UCLANS
UGGAMS
UHLANS
UJJAIN
ULLAGE
UMIAKS
UMLAUT
UMTATA
UNBARS
UNCAGE
UNCAPS
UNCASE
UNEASE
UNEASY
UNFAIR
UNHAND
UNIATE
UNIATS
UNJAMS
UNLACE
UNLADE
UNLAID
UNLASH
UNMADE
UNMAKE
UNMANS
UNMASK
UNPACK
UNPAID
UNSAFE
UNSAID
UNSAYS
UNTACK
UNWARY
UPCAST
UPDATE
UPLAND
UPTAKE
UPTALK
UPWARD
URBANA
URBANE
URIALS
USMAIL
USUALS
UTHANT

U•••A•
UGRIAN
UINTAS
ULLMAN
ULTRAS
UMBRAE
UMBRAL
UMBRAS
UNCIAL
UNCLAD
UNDRAW
UNGUAL
UNITAL
UNITAS
UNIVAC
UNLEAD
UNLOAD
UNOCAL
UNREAD
UNREAL
UNSEAL
UNSEAT
UNSNAG
UNSNAP
UNTRAP
UNWRAP
UPBEAT
UPLOAD
UPROAR
UTAHAN
UVULAE
UVULAR
UVULAS
UZZIAH

U••••A
UGANDA
ULTIMA
UMBRIA
UMTATA
URANIA
URBANA
URSULA
UTOPIA

•UA•••
DUALLY
DUARTE
GUACOS
GUARDS
GUAVAS
JUAREZ
LUANDA
NUANCE
QUACKS
QUADRI
QUAFFS
QUAGGA
QUAGGY
QUAHOG
QUAILS
QUAINT
QUAKED
QUAKER
QUAKES
QUALMS
QUANGO
QUANTA
QUARKS
QUARRY
QUARTO
QUARTS
QUARTZ
QUASAR
QUAVER
QUAYLE
RUANAS
RUANDA
SUAVER
TUAREG

•U•A••
AUBADE
AUFAIT
AULAIT
AUPAIR
BUTANE
CUBAGE
CUIABA
CUNARD
CUNAXA
CURACY
CURARE
CURATE
CUSACK
DUCATS
DUNANT
DURANT
DUVALL
EURAIL
EUTAXY
FUGARD
FULANI
GUIANA
GULAGS
GUYANA
HUMANE
HUMANS
JUDAEA
JUDAIC
JUMADA
JURADO
JURATS
KULAKS
KURALT
KUVASZ
KUWAIT
LUNACY
LUNATE
LUSAKA
LUXATE
MUFASA
MUGABE
MURALS
MURANO
MUTANT
MUTATE
MUTATO
NUTATE
OUTACT
OUTAGE
OUTATE
PURACE
QUEASY
RUBATI
RUBATO
RUGATE
RUPAUL
SUBARU
SUGARS
SUGARY
SUMACS
SURAHS
SUSANN
TUBATE
TUCANA
TULANE
TULARE
TUVALU
YUKATA
YUKAWA

•U••A•
AUDIAL
AUGEAN
BUCCAL
BUCHAN
BULGAR
BULLAE
BUMRAP
BUNYAN
BUREAU
BURGAS
BURLAP
BURMAN
BUROAK
BURSAE
BURSAL
BURSAR
BURSAS
BUSBAR
BUSMAN
CUNEAL
CUPPAS
CURIAE
CURIAL
CUSHAW
DUCTAL
DUNBAR
DUNCAN
DUNHAM
DURBAN
DURBAR
DURHAM
DURIAN
FUJIAN
FULMAR
GUAVAS
GUFFAW
GUITAR
GULLAH
GUNMAN
GUNNAR
GUSTAV
GUTTAE
HUBCAP
HURRAH
HURRAY
HUSSAR
HUZZAH
HUZZAS
JUBBAH
JULIAN
JUMPAT
JUNEAU
JUNTAS
KUBLAI
KURGAN
LUCIAN
LUMBAR
MUDCAT
MUDRAS
MULLAH
MULLAS
MURRAY
MUSCAT
MUSIAL
MUTUAL
NUBIAN
NUCHAE
NUCHAL
NULLAH
NUMBAT
OUTEAT
OUTLAW
OUTLAY
OUTRAN
PULSAR
PUNJAB
PUNKAH
PURDAH
PUTNAM
QUASAR
QUMRAN
QUOTAS
RUANAS
RUDMAN
RUMBAS
RUNSAT
RUNWAY
RUPIAH
RUTTAN
SUBPAR
SUBWAY
SUCHAS
SUCKAS
SUDRAS
SUKKAH
SULTAN
SUMMAE
SUMMAS
SUNDAE
SUNDAY
SUNRAY
SUNTAN
SURTAX
SUTRAS
TUBMAN
TULSAN
TUPIAN
TURBAN
TUSCAN
TUSSAH
VULCAN
VULGAR
YUCCAS
YUNNAN

•U•••A
AURIGA
AURORA
BUDDHA
BULOVA
BUQSHA
BUSHWA
CUESTA
CUIABA
CUNAXA
CUPOLA
DUENNA
DULLEA
DUNERA
DURYEA
EUBOEA
EUDORA
EUPNEA
EUREKA
EUROPA
FULCRA
GUIANA
GUINEA
GURKHA
GUYANA
HULLOA
JUDAEA
JUDOKA
JUMADA
LUANDA
LUMINA
LUNULA
LUSAKA
MUCOSA
MUFASA
MULETA
MURCIA
NUMINA
NUTRIA
PUEBLA
PURINA
QUAGGA
QUANTA
QUETTA
QUINOA
QUOKKA
QUOTHA
RUANDA
RUMINA
RUSSIA
TUCANA
TUNDRA
TUNICA
YUKATA
YUKAWA

••UA••
ACUATE
AKUAKU
AQUATE
DOUALA
EDUARD
EQUALS
EQUATE
IGUACU
IGUANA
SOUARI
SQUABS
SQUADS
SQUALL
SQUARE
SQUASH
SQUATS
SQUAWK
STUART
TRUANT
USUALS
YOUALL
ZOUAVE

••U•A•
ALULAE
ALULAR
ANURAN
AOUDAD
ARUBAN
BEULAH
BHUTAN
BRUMAL
BRUTAL
CAUDAL
CAUSAL
CHUKAR
CIUDAD
COUGAR
CRURAL
FAUNAE
FAUNAL
FAUNAS
FEUDAL
FOURAM
FRUGAL
HAUSAS
KAUNAS
KOUFAX
MAUMAU
NEUMAN
NEURAL
NOUGAT
OCULAR
OVULAR
PLURAL
SAUNAS
SCUBAS
SEURAT
SQUEAK
SQUEAL
STUPAS
THUJAS
TOUCAN
TRUMAN
UVULAE
UVULAR
UVULAS
WAUSAU

••U••A
ALUMNA
APULIA
AQUILA
CHUKKA
COULDA
DOUALA
IGUANA
KAUNDA
LOUISA
MAURYA
NAUSEA
NOUMEA
RHUMBA
ZEUGMA

•••UA•
ACTUAL
ANNUAL
CAGUAS
CASUAL
EMQUAD
ENQUAD
GENUAL
JAGUAR
LEHUAS
LOQUAT
MANUAL
MSQUAD
MUTUAL
PADUAN
PAPUAN
RITUAL
SIOUAN
UNGUAL
VISUAL

•••U•A
ARJUNA
BAKULA
BELUGA
CAYUGA
COPULA
CREUSA
DATURA
FACULA
FIBULA
HECUBA
KAHUNA
KORUNA
LACUNA
LAGUNA
LAPUTA
LIGULA
LUNULA
MACULA
MADURA
MAKUTA
MAZUMA
MEDUSA
NATURA
NEBULA
NERUDA
OSCULA
PAKULA
PARULA
PERUGA
PETULA
PLEURA
PNEUMA
RADULA
REMUDA
SEGURA
TABULA
TOLUCA
TRAUMA
URSULA
VARUNA
VICUNA
YAKUZA
YORUBA

••••UA
JOSHUA
KAHLUA
KAILUA
LINGUA
MANTUA
NASHUA

UB••••
UBANGI
UBIETY
UBIQUE
UBOATS
UBOLTS

U•B•••
UMBELS
UMBERS
UMBRAE
UMBRAL
UMBRAS
UMBRIA
UNBARS
UNBELT
UNBEND
UNBENT
UNBIND
UNBOLT
UNBORN
UNBUSY
UPBEAT
UPBOWS
URBANA
URBANE
UZBEKS

U••B••
UNABLE
USABLE
USABLY

U•••B•
UNROBE

•UB•••
AUBADE
AUBREY
AUBURN
BUBBLE
BUBBLY
CUBAGE
CUBEBS
CUBICS
CUBING
CUBISM
CUBIST
CUBITS
CUBOID
DUBBED
DUBBIN
DUBCEK
DUBLIN
DUBOIS
EUBOEA
FUBBED
HUBBLE
HUBBLY
HUBBUB
HUBCAP
HUBERT
HUBRIS
JUBBAH
KUBLAI
LUBBER
LUBECK
LUBING
LUBLIN
NUBBED
NUBBIN
NUBBLE
NUBBLY
NUBIAN
NUBILE
PUBLIC
RUBATI
RUBATO
RUBBED
RUBBER
RUBBLE
RUBBLY
RUBENS
RUBIED
RUBIES
RUBIFY
RUBLES
RUBLEV
RUBOFF
RUBOUT
RUBRIC
RUBSIN
SUBARU
SUBBED
SUBDEB
SUBDUE
SUBGUM
SUBITO
SUBLET
SUBMIT
SUBORN
SUBPAR
SUBSET
SUBTLE
SUBTLY
SUBURB
SUBWAY
TUBATE
TUBBED
TUBERS
TUBING
TUBIST
TUBMAN

•U•B••
BUBBLE
BUBBLY
BULBIL
BULBUL
BUMBLE
BUMBRY
BURBLE
BURBLY
BURBOT
BUSBAR
BUSBOY
CUMBER
CURBED
DUBBED
DUBBIN
DUMBER
DUMBLY
DUNBAR
DURBAN
DURBAR
DURBIN
FUBBED
FUMBLE
GUMBEL
GUMBOS
HUBBLE
HUBBLY
HUBBUB
HUMBLE
HUMBLY
HUMBUG
JUBBAH
JUMBLE
JUMBOS
LUBBER
LUMBAR
LUMBER
MUMBLE
MUMBLY
NUBBED
NUBBIN
NUBBLE
NUBBLY
NUMBAT
NUMBED
NUMBER
NUMBLY
OUTBID
OUTBOX
PUEBLA
PUEBLO
QUEBEC
RUBBED
RUBBER
RUBBLE
RUBBLY
RUMBAS
RUMBLE
RUMBLY
SUBBED
TUBBED
TUMBLE
TURBAN
TURBID
TURBIT
TURBOS
TURBOT

•U••B•
CUBEBS
CUIABA
JUJUBE
MUGABE
PUTSBY

•U•••B
HUBBUB
PUNJAB
SUBDEB
SUBURB
SUPERB

••UB••
ANUBIS
ARUBAN
BAUBLE
BOUBOU
CHUBBY
CLUBBY
DAUBED
DAUBER
DAUBES
DOUBLE
DOUBLY
DOUBTS
GRUBBY
REUBEN
ROUBLE
SCUBAS
SNUBBY
STUBBY
YOUBET

••U•B•
BLURBS
BRUMBY
CHUBBY
CLUBBY
CRUMBS
CRUMBY
EXURBS
GRUBBY
ITURBI
PLUMBS
RHUMBA
RHUMBS
SNUBBY
SQUABS
SQUIBB
SQUIBS
STUBBY
THUMBS

••U••B
SQUIBB

•••UB•
DANUBE
HECUBA
JUJUBE
REDUBS
SCRUBS
SHRUBS
YORUBA

•••U•B
BENUMB
SUBURB

••••UB
BEDAUB
CHERUB
HOTTUB
HUBBUB
STRAUB

UC••••
UCLANS

U•C•••
ULCERS
UNCAGE
UNCAPS
UNCASE
UNCHIC
UNCIAL
UNCLAD
UNCLES
UNCLOG
UNCOIL
UNCOOL
UNCORK
UNCURL
UPCAST
URCHIN

U••C••
UNICEF
UNOCAL
URACIL

U•••C•
UNESCO
UNLACE
UNLOCK
UNPACK
UNTACK
UPTICK
USANCE

U••••C
UNCHIC
UNIFIC
UNIVAC
URALIC
URANIC

•UC•••
BUCCAL
BUCHAN
BUCKED
BUCKET
BUCKLE
BUCKUP
CUCKOO
DUCATS
DUCHIN
DUCKED
DUCTAL
EUCHRE
EUCLID
KUCHEN
LUCENT
LUCIAN
LUCITE
LUCIUS
LUCKED
MUCINS
MUCKED
MUCKUP
MUCOSA
MUCOUS
NUCHAE
NUCHAL
NUCLEI
NUCLEO
PUCKER
RUCHES
RUCKED
RUCKUS
SUCCES
SUCCOR
SUCHAS
SUCKAS
SUCKED
SUCKER
SUCKIN
TUCANA
TUCHUN
TUCKED
TUCKER
TUCKET
TUCKIN
TUCSON
YUCCAS

•U•C••
BUCCAL
BUNCHE
BUNCHY
BUNCOS
DUBCEK
DULCET
DUNCAN
DUNCES
FULCRA
GUACOS
HUBCAP
JUICED
JUICER
JUICES
JUNCOS
LUNCHY
MUDCAT
MULCTS
MUNCHY
MUNCIE
MURCIA
MUSCAT
MUSCLE
MUSCLY
NUECES
NUNCIO
OUNCES
OUTCRY
PUNCHY
QUACKS
QUICHE
RUNCIE
SUCCES
SUCCOR
SULCUS
TUSCAN
VULCAN
YUCCAS

•U••C•
CUBICS
CURACY
CUSACK
DUROCS
EUNICE
LUBECK
LUNACY
MUNICH
NUANCE
OUTACT
PUMICE
PURACE
PUTSCH
QUENCH
QUINCE
QUINCY
SUMACS
SUNOCO
TUNICA
TUNICS
ZURICH

•U•••C
CULTIC
CUPRIC
FUSTIC
JUDAIC
PUBLIC
QUEBEC
RUBRIC
RUNDMC
RUSTIC
TURKIC

••UC••
BAUCIS
BOUCLE
CAUCHO
CAUCHY
CAUCUS
CHUCKS
CLUCKS
CRUCES
DEUCED
DEUCES
EDUCED
EDUCES
ERUCTS
FAUCES
FAUCET
GAUCHE
GAUCHO
LOUCHE
PAUCIS
PLUCKS
PLUCKY
POUCHY
SAUCED
SAUCER
SAUCES
SHUCKS
STUCCO
TOUCAN
TOUCHE
TOUCHY
TRUCES
TRUCKS

••U•C•
BOUNCE
BOUNCY
BRUNCH
CHURCH
CLUTCH
CRUNCH
CRUTCH
HAUNCH
IGUACU
JOUNCE
JOUNCY
LAUNCH
NAUTCH
PAUNCH
POUNCE
SCUTCH
SLUICE
SMUTCH
SOURCE
STUCCO

••U••C
COURIC

•••UC•
ABDUCT
ADDUCE
ADDUCT
AVOUCH
BARUCH
CROUCH
DEDUCE
DEDUCT
GROUCH
INDUCE
INDUCT
INLUCK
REDUCE
RELUCT
SEDUCE
SLOUCH
SPRUCE
STRUCK
TOLUCA
ZANUCK

UD••••
UDDERS

U•D•••
UDDERS
UNDIES
UNDINE
UNDOER
UNDOES
UNDONE
UNDRAW
UNDULY
UNDYED
UPDATE
UPDIKE

U••D••
USEDTO
USEDUP

U•••D•
UGANDA
UNLADE
UNMADE
UNTIDY
UPENDS
UPSIDE
URSIDS

U••••D
UNAGED
UNAWED
UNBEND
UNBIND
UNCLAD
UNDYED
UNFOLD
UNGIRD
UNHAND
UNHEED
UNIPOD
UNITED
UNKIND
UNLAID
UNLEAD
UNLOAD
UNPAID
UNREAD
UNSAID
UNSHED
UNSHOD
UNSOLD
UNTIED
UNTOLD
UNTROD
UNUSED
UNWIND
UPHELD
UPHOLD
UPLAND
UPLOAD
UPWARD
UPWIND
USERID

•UD•••
AUDENS
AUDIAL
AUDILE
AUDIOS
AUDITS
AUDREY
BUDDED
BUDDHA
BUDGED
BUDGES
BUDGET
BUDGIE
CUDDLE
CUDDLY
CUDGEL
DUDEEN
DUDISH
DUDLEY
EUDORA
FUDDLE
FUDGED
FUDGES
GUDRUN
HUDDLE
HUDSON
JUDAEA
JUDAIC
JUDDER
JUDGED
JUDGES
JUDITH
JUDOKA
KUDROW
KUDZUS
LUDDEN
LUDENS
LUDLUM
LUDWIG
MUDCAT
MUDDED
MUDDER
MUDDLE
MUDEEL
MUDHEN
MUDPIE
MUDRAS
NUDELY
NUDEST
NUDGED
NUDGER
NUDGES
NUDIST
NUDITY
NUDNIK
PUDDLE
PUDDLY
RUDDER
RUDDLE
RUDELY
RUDEST

RUDMAN
RUDOLF
SUDDEN
SUDRAS
SUDSED
SUDSES
TUDORS

•U•D••

BUDDED
BUDDHA
BUNDLE
BURDEN
CUDDLE
CUDDLY
CURDED
CURDLE
DUMDUM
DUNDEE
FUDDLE
FUNDED
GUIDED
GUIDES
GUIDON
GUNDOG
HUDDLE
HURDLE
JUDDER
LUDDEN
LUNDEN
MUDDED
MUDDER
MUDDLE
MURDER
OUTDID
PUDDLE
PUDDLY
PUNDIT
PURDAH
PURDUE
QUADRI
QUIDDE
RUDDER
RUDDLE
RUNDLE
RUNDMC
RUNDRY
SUBDEB
SUBDUE
SUDDEN
SUEDES
SUNDAE
SUNDAY
SUNDER
SUNDEW
SUNDOG
SUNDRY
TUNDRA
ZUIDER

•U••D•

AUBADE
BUILDS
CUPIDS
GUARDS
GUILDS
JUMADA
JURADO
LUANDA
QUIDDE
RUANDA
TUXEDO

•U•••D

AUFOND
AUGEND
BUCKED
BUDDED
BUDGED
BUFFED
BUGGED
BUGLED
BUJOLD
BULGED
BULKED
BULLED
BUMMED
BUMPED
BUNGED
BUNKED
BUNTED
BUOYED
BURIED
BURLED
BURNED
BURPED
BURRED
BUSHED
BUSIED
BUSKED
BUSSED
BUSTED
BUTTED
BUZZED
CUBOID
CUFFED
CULLED
CUNARD
CUPPED
CURBED
CURDED
CURLED
CURRED
CURSED
CURVED
CUSPED
CUSPID
CUSSED
DUBBED
DUCKED
DUELED
DULLED
DUMPED
DUNKED
DUNNED
DURNED
DUSTED
EUCLID
FUBBED
FUDGED
FUELED
FUGARD
FUNDED
FUNKED
FUNNED
FURLED
FURRED
FUSSED
FUTZED
FUZZED
GUIDED
GULFED
GULLED
GULPED
GUMMED
GUNNED
GUSHED
GUSTED
GUTTED
HUFFED
HUGGED
HULKED
HULLED
HUMMED
HUMPED
HUNTED
HURLED
HUSHED
HUSKED
HUTTED
JUDGED
JUGGED
JUICED
JUMPED
JUNKED
JUTTED
LUCKED
LUFFED
LUGGED
LULLED
LUMPED
LUNGED
LURKED
LUSTED
MUCKED
MUDDED
MUFFED
MUGGED
MULLED
MUMMED
MUMPED
MUSHED
MUSSED
MUZZED
NUBBED
NUDGED
NULLED
NUMBED
NURSED
NUTTED
OUSTED
OUTBID
OUTDID
PUFFED
PUGGED
PULLED
PULPED
PULSED
PUMPED
PUNNED
PUNTED
PUREED
PURGED
PURLED
PURRED
PURSED
PUSHED
PUTRID
PUTTED
QUAKED
QUEUED
QUOTED
RUBBED
RUBIED
RUCKED
RUFFED
RUGGED
RUINED
RUSHED
RUSTED
RUTTED
SUBBED
SUCKED
SUDSED
SUITED
SULKED
SUMMED
SUNGOD
SUNNED
SUPPED
SURFED
SURGED
SUSSED
TUBBED
TUCKED
TUFTED
TUGGED
TUMMED
TURBID
TURFED
TURGID
TURNED
TUSKED
TUTUED
YUKKED

••UD••

AOUDAD
BOUDIN
BRUDER
CAUDAL
CAUDEX
CAUDLE
CIUDAD
CRUDDY
CRUDER
DRUDGE
ELUDED
ELUDER
ELUDES
ETUDES
EXUDED
EXUDES
FEUDAL
FEUDED
GRUDGE
KLUDGE
LAUDED
LAUDER
LOUDEN
LOUDER
LOUDLY
PRUDES
SAUDIS
SLUDGE
SLUDGY
SMUDGE
SMUDGY
STUDIO
TRUDGE

••U•D•

BOUNDS
COULDA
CRUDDY
DRUIDS
FLUIDS
FOUNDS
GOURDE
GOURDS
GRUNDY
HOUNDS
HOUNDY
KAUNDA
MAUNDY
MBUNDU
MOULDS
MOULDY
MOUNDS
POUNDS
ROUNDS
SOUNDS
SQUADS
SQUIDS
STURDY
WOUNDS
ZOUNDS

••U••D

ABUSED
AMUSED
AOUDAD
BOUSED
BRUXED
CAUSED
CHUTED
CIUDAD
DAUBED
DEUCED
DOUSED
EDUARD
EDUCED
ELUDED
ELUTED
ENURED
EXUDED
FEUDED
FLUTED
FLUXED
FOULED
GAUGED
GAUMED
GOUGED
GOUNOD
HAULED
HOUSED
INURED
LAUDED
LOUSED
MAULED
MOUSED
PAUSED
PLUMED
POURED
POUTED
PRUNED
REUSED
ROUGED
ROUSED
ROUTED
SAUCED
SOURED
SOUSED
SPUMED
STUPID
TOURED
TOUTED
UNUSED

•••UD•

ALLUDE
CLAUDE
CLOUDS
CLOUDY
DELUDE
DENUDE
ESCUDO
FRAUDS
NERUDA
PSEUDO
PSEUDS
REMUDA
YEHUDI

•••U•D

ABOUND
ABSURD
ARGUED
AROUND
EDMUND
EMQUAD
ENDUED
ENQUAD
ENSUED
FECUND
GERUND
GROUND
IMBUED
ISSUED
JOCUND
LIQUID
MSQUAD
OBTUND
OSMUND
PEQUOD
PIQUED
QUEUED
REFUND
ROTUND
SEGUED
SHOULD
SIGURD
TUTUED
VALUED

••••UD

ATSTUD
MARAUD
REDBUD
SHROUD
STROUD
TALMUD

U•E•••

UNEASE
UNEASY
UNESCO
UNEVEN
UNEVEN
UPENDS
USEDTO
USEDUP
USEFUL
USENET
USERID
USESUP

U••E••

UBIETY
UDDERS
ULCERS
UMBELS
UMBERS
UNBELT
UNBEND
UNBENT
UNHEED
UNLEAD
UNLESS
UNMEET
UNMESH
UNPEGS
UNPENS
UNREAD
UNREAL
UNREEL
UNREST
UNSEAL
UNSEAT
UNSEEN
UNSEWN
UNSEWS
UNVEIL
UNWELL
UPBEAT
UPHELD
UPKEEP
UPPERS
UPSETS
UPWELL
URAEUS
URGENT
URGERS
URTEXT
USHERS
UTTERS
UZBEKS

U•••E•

UGLIER
UGLIES
UKASES
ULSTER
UNAGED
UNAWED
UNCLES
UNDIES
UNDOER
UNDOES
UNDYED
UNEVEN
UNFREE
UNGUES
UNHEED
UNICEF
UNISEX
UNITED
UNITER
UNITES
UNMEET
UNOPEN
UNREEL
UNSEEN
UNSHED
UNTIED
UNTIES
UNUSED
UPASES
UPKEEP
URUSES
USAGES
USENET
USOPEN
USURER

U••••E

UBIQUE
UGSOME
ULLAGE
UMBRAE
UMPIRE
UNABLE
UNCAGE
UNCASE
UNDINE
UNDONE
UNEASE
UNFREE
UNGLUE
UNIATE
UNIQUE
UNLACE
UNLADE
UNLIKE
UNMADE
UNMAKE
UNPILE
UNRIPE
UNROBE
UNSAFE
UNSURE
UNTRUE
UNTUNE
UNWISE
UNWOVE
UNYOKE
UPDATE
UPDIKE
UPRISE
UPROSE
UPSIDE
UPTAKE
UPTIME
URBANE
URSINE
USABLE
USANCE
UVALUE
UVULAE

•UE•••

BUENOS
CUESTA
DUELED
DUELER
DUELLO
DUENNA
FUELED
FUELER
GUELPH
GUENON
GUERRE
GUESTS
HUEVOS
NUECES
PUEBLA
PUEBLO
PUENTE
PUERTO
QUEASY
QUEBEC
QUEENS
QUELLS
QUEMOY
QUENCH
QUERNS
QUESTS
QUETTA
QUEUED
QUEUER
QUEUES
QUEZON
RUEFUL
SUEDES

•U•E••

AUDENS
AUGEAN
AUGEND
AUGERS
AUREUS
AUTEUR
BUREAU
BUTENE
BUTEOS
BUYERS
CUBEBS
CULETS
CUNEAL
CUPELS
CURERS
CUTELY
CUTEST
CUTESY
CUVEES
DUDEEN
DUNERA
DUPERY
DURESS
DUVETS
EUGENE
EUREKA
FUSEES
FUZEES
HUBERT
HUGELY
HUGEST
HUMERI
JULEPS
JUNEAU
LUBECK
LUCENT
LUDENS
LUGERS
LUMENS
MUDEEL
MULETA
MULEYS
MUSERS
MUSEUM
MUTELY

MUTEST
NUDELY
NUDEST
NUGENT
NUMERO
OUSELS
OUTEAT
OUZELS
PUREED
PUREES
PURELY
PUREST
QUEENS
QUIETS
RUBENS
RUDELY
RUDEST
RULEON
RULERS
RUMENS
RUPEES
RUPERT
SUPERB
SUPERS
SURELY
SUREST
SURETE
SURETY
TUBERS
TUMEFY
TUNEIN
TUNERS
TUNEUP
TUPELO
TUREEN
TUXEDO
TUYERE

•U••E•
AUBREY
AUDREY
AUKLET
AUSPEX
AUSTEN
BUCKED
BUCKET
BUDDED
BUDGED
BUDGES
BUDGET
BUFFED
BUFFER
BUFFET
BUGGED
BUGLED
BUGLER
BUGLES
BULGED
BULGES
BULKED
BULLED
BULLET
BULWER
BUMMED
BUMMER
BUMPED
BUMPER
BUNGED
BUNGEE
BUNKED
BUNKER
BUNSEN
BUNTED
BUNTER
BUNUEL
BUOYED
BURDEN
BURGEE
BURGER
BURIED
BURIES
BURLED
BURLEY
BURNED
BURNER
BURNET
BURNEY
BURPED
BURRED
BURSES
BUSHED
BUSHEL
BUSHES
BUSIED
BUSIER
BUSIES
BUSKED
BUSMEN
BUSSED
BUSSES
BUSTED
BUSTER
BUTLER
BUTTED
BUTTER
BUTTES
BUZZED
BUZZER
BUZZES
CUDGEL
CUFFED
CULLED
CULLEN
CULLER
CULLET
CULVER
CUMBER
CUPPED
CURBED
CURDED
CURFEW
CURLED
CURLER
CURLEW
CURLEY
CURRED
CURSED
CURSES
CURTER
CURVED
CURVES
CURVET
CUSPED
CUSSED
CUSSES
CUSTER
CUTIES
CUTLER
CUTLET
CUTTER
CUVEES
DUBBED
DUBCEK
DUCKED
DUDEEN
DUDLEY
DUELED
DUELER
DUFFEL
DUFFER
DUIKER
DULCET
DULLEA
DULLED
DULLER
DULLES
DUMBER
DUMPED
DUMPER
DUNCES
DUNDEE
DUNKED
DUNKER
DUNNED
DUPLEX
DURFEY
DURNED
DURYEA
DUSTED
DUSTER
DUTIES
EUBOEA
EUPNEA
FUBBED
FUDGED
FUDGES
FUELED
FUELER
FUGUES
FULLER
FUMIER
FUNDED
FUNKED
FUNNED
FUNNEL
FURIES
FURLED
FURRED
FURZES
FUSEES
FUSSED
FUSSES
FUTZED
FUTZES
FUZEES
FUZZED
FUZZES
GUIDED
GUIDES
GUILES
GUINEA
GUISES
GULFED
GULLED
GULLET
GULPED
GULPER
GUMBEL
GUMMED
GUNMEN
GUNNED
GUNNEL
GUNNER
GUNTER
GURLEY
GURNEY
GUSHED
GUSHER
GUSHES
GUSSET
GUSTED
GUTTED
GUTTER
HUFFED
HUGGED
HUGGER
HUGHES
HULKED
HULLED
HULLER
HUMMED
HUMMER
HUMPED
HUMVEE
HUNGER
HUNKER
HUNTED
HUNTER
HURLED
HURLER
HURLEY
HUSHED
HUSHES
HUSKED
HUSKER
HUSSEY
HUTTED
HUXLEY
JUAREZ
JUDAEA
JUDDER
JUDGED
JUDGES
JUGGED
JUICED
JUICER
JUICES
JULIET
JUMPED
JUMPER
JUNKED
JUNKER
JUNKET
JURIES
JUSTER
JUTTED
KUCHEN
KUMMEL
LUBBER
LUCKED
LUDDEN
LUFFED
LUGGED
LUGGER
LULLED
LUMBER
LUMPED
LUMPEN
LUMPER
LUNDEN
LUNGED
LUNGES
LUNKER
LURKED
LUSHER
LUSTED
LUSTER
LUTHER
LUTZES
MUCKED
MUDDED
MUDDER
MUDEEL
MUDHEN
MUFFED
MUGGED
MUGGER
MULLED
MULLER
MULLET
MUMMED
MUMMER
MUMPED
MUPPET
MURDER
MURIEL
MURRES
MURREY
MUSHED
MUSHER
MUSHES
MUSKEG
MUSKET
MUSSED
MUSSEL
MUSSES
MUSTER
MUTTER
MUZZED
MUZZES
NUBBED
NUCLEI
NUCLEO
NUDGED
NUDGER
NUDGES
NUECES
NUGGET
NULLED
NUMBED
NUMBER
NURSED
NURSER
NURSES
NUTLET
NUTMEG
NUTTED
NUTTER
OUNCES
OUSTED
OUSTER
OUTLET
OUTSET
PUCKER
PUFFED
PUFFER
PUGGED
PUGREE
PULLED
PULLET
PULLEY
PULPED
PULSED
PULSES
PUMMEL
PUMPED
PUMPER
PUNIER
PUNKER
PUNNED
PUNNET
PUNTED
PUNTER
PUPPET
PUREED
PUREES
PURGED
PURGES
PURLED
PURRED
PURRER
PURSED
PURSER
PURSES
PURVEY
PUSHED
PUSHES
PUSSES
PUTTED
PUTTEE
PUTTER
QUAKED
QUAKER
QUAKES
QUAVER
QUEBEC
QUEUED
QUEUER
QUEUES
QUIRES
QUIVER
QUOTED
QUOTER
QUOTES
RUBBED
RUBBER
RUBIED
RUBIES
RUBLES
RUBLEV
RUCHES
RUCKED
RUDDER
RUFFED
RUGGED
RUINED
RUINER
RUMMER
RUNLET
RUNNEL
RUNNER
RUPEES
RUSHED
RUSHEE
RUSHES
RUSSET
RUSTED
RUTGER
RUTTED
SUAVER
SUBBED
SUBDEB
SUBLET
SUBSET
SUCCES
SUCKED
SUCKER
SUDDEN
SUDSED
SUDSES
SUEDES
SUFFER
SUITED
SUITES
SULKED
SULKER
SULLEN
SUMMED
SUMMER
SUMNER
SUMTER
SUNDER
SUNDEW
SUNKEN
SUNNED
SUNSET
SUPPED
SUPPER
SURFED
SURFER
SURGED
SURGES
SURREY
SURVEY
SUSIEQ
SUSSED
SUSSES
SUSSEX
SUTLER
SUTTER
TUAREG
TUBBED
TUCKED
TUCKER
TUCKET
TUFFET
TUFTED
TUGGED
TUGGER
TULLES
TUMMED
TUNNEL
TUNNEY
TUQUES
TUREEN
TURFED
TURKEY
TURNED
TURNER
TURRET
TURVES
TUSKED
TUSKER
TUTUED
WURLEY
WUSSES
YUKKED
ZUIDER

•U•••E
AUBADE
AUDILE
AUNTIE
AUSSIE
BUBBLE
BUCKLE
BUDGIE
BULLAE
BUMBLE
BUNCHE
BUNDLE
BUNGEE
BUNGLE
BURBLE
BURGEE
BURGLE
BURSAE
BUSTLE
BUTANE
BUTENE
CUBAGE
CUDDLE
CUIQUE
CUISSE
CURARE
CURATE
CURDLE
CURIAE
CURULE
DUARTE
DUNDEE
EUCHRE
EUGENE
EUNICE
EUROPE
FUDDLE
FUMBLE
FURORE
FUTILE
FUTURE
GUERRE
GUIMPE
GUNITE
GURGLE
GUTTAE
GUZZLE
HUBBLE
HUDDLE
HUMANE
HUMBLE
HUMVEE
HURDLE
HURTLE
HUSTLE
JUGGLE
JUJUBE
JUMBLE
JUNGLE
JUNKIE
KURILE
LUCITE
LUNATE
LUPINE
LUPONE
LUSTRE
LUXATE
MUDDLE
MUDPIE
MUFFLE
MUGABE
MUMBLE
MUNCIE
MURINE
MUSCLE
MUSKIE
MUTATE
MUZZLE
NUANCE
NUBBLE
NUBILE
NUCHAE
NUTATE
NUZZLE
OUTAGE
OUTATE
PUDDLE
PUENTE
PUGREE
PUISNE
PULQUE
PUMICE
PUNKIE
PURACE
PURDUE
PURFLE
PURINE
PURPLE
PURSUE
PUTTEE
PUZZLE
QUAYLE
QUICHE
QUIDDE
QUINCE
QUOQUE
RUBBLE
RUDDLE
RUFFLE
RUGATE
RUGOSE
RUMBLE
RUMPLE
RUNCIE
RUNDLE
RUSHEE
RUSTLE
RUTILE
SUBDUE
SUBTLE
SUISSE
SUMMAE
SUNDAE
SUPINE
SUPPLE
SURETE
SUTURE
TUBATE
TUILLE
TULANE
TULARE
TUMBLE
TURTLE
TUSSLE
TUYERE
YUPPIE

••UE••
BLUELY
BLUEOX
BLUEST

BLUESY
BLUETS
BLUEYS
CLUEIN
CRUETS
FLUENT
GLUERS
GRUELS
SQUEAK
SQUEAL
TRUEST

••U•E•

ABUSED
ABUSER
ABUSES
ACUMEN
AMULET
AMUSED
AMUSES
BOULES
BOULEZ
BOUSED
BOUSES
BRUDER
BRUGES
BRULES
BRUMES
BRUNEI
BRUNET
BRUTES
BRUXED
BRUXES
CAUDEX
CAUSED
CAUSES
CHUTED
CHUTES
COULEE
COUPES
COUTER
CRUCES
CRUDER
CRUSES
CRUXES
DAUBED
DAUBER
DAUBES
DEUCED
DEUCES
DOURER
DOUSED
DOUSES
DRUPES
DRUZES
EDUCED
EDUCES
ELUDED
ELUDER
ELUDES
ELUTED
ELUTES
ENURED
ENURES
ETUDES
EXUDED
EXUDES
FAUCES
FAUCET
FEUDED
FLUKES
FLUKEY
FLUMES
FLUTED
FLUTES
FLUTEY
FLUXED
FLUXES
FOULED
FOULER
GAUGED
GAUGER
GAUGES
GAUMED
GAUZES
GLUIER
GLUTEI
GLUTEN
GLUTES
GOUGED
GOUGER
GOUGES
GOULET
HAULED
HAULER
HOUSED
HOUSES
INURED
INURES
JAURES
JOULES
KRUGER
LAUDED
LAUDER
LAUPER
LAUREL
LAUREN
LOUDEN
LOUDER
LOUPES
LOUSED
LOUSES
LOUVER
MAULED
MAULER
MAUMEE
MAUSER
MAUVES
MOUSED
MOUSER
MOUSES
MOUSEY
NAUSEA
NEUMES
NEUTER
NGUYEN
NOUMEA
ONUSES
OPUSES
OVULES
PAULEY
PAUPER
PAUSED
PAUSES
PLUMED
PLUMES
PLUSES
POURED
POURER
POUTED
POUTER
PRUDES
PRUNED
PRUNER
PRUNES
REUBEN
REUNES
REUSED
REUSES
REUTER
ROUGED
ROUGES
ROUSED
ROUSER
ROUSES
ROUTED
ROUTER
ROUTES
SAUCED
SAUCER
SAUCES
SAUGER
SAUREL
SAUTES
SCUTES
SOURED
SOURER
SOUSED
SOUSES
SOUTER
SPUMED
SPUMES
STUMER
STUPES
TAUPES
TAUTEN
TAUTER
TOUPEE
TOURED
TOURER
TOUTED
TOUTER
TRUCES
UNUSED
URUSES
USURER
YOUBET

••U••E

ACUATE
ALULAE
AQUATE
AVULSE
BAUBLE
BEURRE
BOUCLE
BOUFFE
BOULLE
BOUNCE
BOURKE
BOURNE
BOURSE
BRUISE
CAUDLE
COULEE
COUPLE
COURSE
CRUISE
CRUSOE
DOUBLE
DRUDGE
EQUATE
EQUINE
EVULSE
FAUNAE
GAUCHE
GOURDE
GRUDGE
GRUNGE
JOUNCE
KLUDGE
LAURIE
LOUCHE
LOUISE
LOUNGE
LOUVRE
MAUMEE
MOUSSE
OEUVRE
PLUNGE
POUNCE
POUSSE
ROUBLE
ROURKE
SCURVE
SLUDGE
SLUICE
SMUDGE
SOURCE
SPURGE
SQUARE
SQUIRE
TOUCHE
TOUPEE
TOUSLE
TRUDGE
UVULAE
ZOUAVE

•••UE•

ARGUED
ARGUER
ARGUES
BREUER
BUNUEL
COQUET
ENDUED
ENDUES
ENSUED
ENSUES
FRAUEN
FUGUES
GIGUES
IMBUED
IMBUES
ISSUED
ISSUER
ISSUES
LEMUEL
MAGUEY
MANUEL
MCKUEN
MIGUEL
MINUET
PIQUED
PIQUES
PIQUET
QUEUED
QUEUER
QUEUES
RAQUEL
REFUEL
REVUES
ROGUES
SAMUEL
SEGUED
SEGUES
SEQUEL
SPRUES
TOQUES
TUQUES
TUTUED
UNGUES
VAGUER
VALUED
VALUES
VENUES
VOGUES

•••U•E

ABJURE
ACCUSE
ADDUCE
ADJURE
ALLUDE
ALLURE
AMPULE
ARMURE
AROUSE
ASSUME
ASSURE
ASTUTE
ATTUNE
BEMUSE
BLOUSE
CANUTE
CAYUSE
CERUSE
CLAUDE
CLAUSE
COHUNE
CONURE
CROUSE
CROUTE
CURULE
DANUBE
DEDUCE
DEFUSE
DEJURE
DELUDE
DELUGE
DELUXE
DEMURE
DENUDE
DEPUTE
DILUTE
DISUSE
EFFUSE
EMEUTE
ENDURE
ENDUSE
ENSURE
EXCUSE
FERULE
FIGURE
FUTURE
GROUSE
ILLUME
ILLUSE
IMMUNE
IMMURE
IMPURE
IMPUTE
INCUSE
INDUCE
INFUSE
INJURE
INOUYE
INSURE
INTUNE
JEJUNE
JUJUBE
LEGUME
LIGURE
LOBULE
MATURE
MIFUNE
MINUTE
MISUSE
MODULE
NATURE
NODULE
OBTUSE
ORDURE
PAIUTE
PARURE
PERUKE
PERUSE
REBUKE
RECUSE
REDUCE
REFUGE
REFUSE
REFUTE
RELUME
REPUTE
RESUME
RETUNE
SALUTE
SCOUSE
SECURE
SEDUCE
SOLUTE
SPOUSE
SPRUCE
STLUKE
SUTURE
TENURE
TRIUNE
TROUPE
TROUVE
UNSURE
UNTUNE
VOLUME
VOLUTE

••••UE

ACCRUE
AVENUE
BARQUE
BASQUE
BATTUE
BISQUE
BRAQUE
BROGUE
CAIQUE
CALQUE
CASQUE
CHEQUE
CINQUE
CIRQUE
CLAQUE
CLIQUE
CLOQUE
CUIQUE
DENGUE
DROGUE
FESCUE
FONDUE
GANGUE
IMBRUE
LEAGUE
LONGUE
MANQUE
MARQUE
MASQUE
MISCUE
MOSQUE
MRBLUE
OPAQUE
PERDUE
PLAGUE
PLAQUE
PRAGUE
PULQUE
PURDUE
PURSUE
QUOQUE
REGLUE
RESCUE
RISQUE
RVALUE
SACQUE
STATUE
SUBDUE
TISSUE
TONGUE
TORQUE
UBIQUE
UNGLUE
UNIQUE
UNTRUE
UVALUE
VIRTUE

U•F•••

UNFAIR
UNFITS
UNFOLD
UNFREE
UNFURL

U••F••

UNIFIC
USEFUL

U•••F•

UGLIFY
UNSAFE
UPLIFT

U••••F

UNICEF

•UF•••

AUFAIT
AUFOND
BUFFED
BUFFER
BUFFET
BUFFON
BUFFOS
CUFFED
DUFFEL
DUFFER
GUFFAW
HUFFED
LUFFED
MUFASA
MUFFED
MUFFIN
MUFFLE
MUFTIS
PUFFED
PUFFER
PUFFIN
RUFFED
RUFFLE
RUFFLY
RUFOUS
SUFFER
SUFFIX
SUFISM
TUFFET
TUFTED

•U•F••

BUFFED
BUFFER
BUFFET
BUFFON
BUFFOS
CUFFED
CUPFUL
CURFEW
DUFFEL
DUFFER
DURFEY
FULFIL
GUFFAW
GULFED
GUNFOR
HUFFED
JUGFUL
LUFFED
MUFFED
MUFFIN
MUFFLE
OUTFIT
OUTFLY
OUTFOX
PUFFED
PUFFER
PUFFIN
PURFLE
QUAFFS
RUEFUL
RUFFED
RUFFLE
RUFFLY
RUNFOR
SUFFER
SUFFIX
SULFUR
SURFED
SURFER
TUFFET
TURFED

•U••F•

AURIFY
BUGOFF
BUYOFF
CUTOFF
KUNGFU
PURIFY
PUTOFF
QUAFFS
RUBIFY
RUBOFF
RUNOFF
TUMEFY

•U•••F

BUGOFF
BUYOFF
CUTOFF
PUTOFF
RUBOFF
RUDOLF
RUNOFF

••UF••

BLUFFS
BOUFFE
CHUFFY
FLUFFS
FLUFFY
KOUFAX
SCUFFS
SNUFFS
SNUFFY
STUFFS
STUFFY

••U•F•

BLUFFS
BOUFFE
CHUFFY
FLUFFS
FLUFFY
SCUFFS
SCURFY
SMURFS
SNUFFS
SNUFFY
STUFFS
STUFFY

•••UF•

ARGUFY
REBUFF
SCRUFF
SENUFO

•••U•F

ENGULF
REBUFF
SCRUFF

••••UF

STAPUF

UG••••

UGANDA
UGGAMS
UGLIER
UGLIES
UGLIFY

UGLILY
UGRIAN
UGSOME

U•G•••
UGGAMS
UIGURS
UNGIRD
UNGIRT
UNGLUE
UNGUAL
UNGUES
UNGUIS
URGENT
URGERS
URGING

U••G••
UNAGED
USAGES

U•••G•
UBANGI
ULLAGE
UNCAGE
UNPEGS
UNRIGS

U••••G
UNCLOG
UNPLUG
UNSNAG
UNSUNG
UPPING
URGING

•UG•••
AUGEAN
AUGEND
AUGERS
AUGHTS
AUGURS
AUGURY
AUGUST
BUGGED
BUGLED
BUGLER
BUGLES
BUGOFF
BUGOUT
DUGONG
DUGOUT
EUGENE
FUGARD
FUGUES
HUGELY
HUGEST
HUGGED
HUGGER
HUGHES
JUGFUL
JUGGED
JUGGLE
LUGERS
LUGGED
LUGGER
LUGNUT
LUGOSI
MUGABE
MUGGED
MUGGER
MUGHOS
NUGENT
NUGGET
OUGHTS
PUGGED
PUGREE
RUGATE
RUGGED
RUGOSE
SUGARS
SUGARY
TUGGED
TUGGER
TUGRIK

•U•G••
BUDGED
BUDGES
BUDGET
BUDGIE
BUGGED
BULGAR
BULGED
BULGES
BULGUR
BUNGED
BUNGEE
BUNGLE
BURGAS
BURGEE
BURGER
BURGHS
BURGLE
BURGOO
BURGOS
CUDGEL
FUDGED
FUDGES
FUNGUS
GUNGHO
GURGLE
HUGGED
HUGGER
HUNGER
HUNGIN
HUNGON
HUNGRY
HUNGUP
HUNGWU
JUDGED
JUDGES
JUGGED
JUGGLE
JUNGLE
JUNGLY
KUNGFU
KURGAN
LUGGED
LUGGER
LUNGED
LUNGES
MUGGED
MUGGER
MUNGOS
NUDGED
NUDGER
NUDGES
NUGGET
OUTGUN
PUGGED
PURGED
PURGES
QUAGGA
QUAGGY
RUGGED
RUNGUP
RUTGER
SUBGUM
SUNGOD
SURGED
SURGES
TUGGED
TUGGER
TURGID
TURGOR
VULGAR
YUNGLO

•U••G•
AURIGA
CUBAGE
EULOGY
GULAGS
OUTAGE
QUAGGA
QUAGGY
QUANGO

•U•••G
BUSING
BUTUNG
BUYING
CUBING
CURING
DUGONG
DUKING
DUPING
DURING
FUMING
FUSING
FUZING
GUNDOG
GUYING
HUMBUG
JUKING
LUBING
LUDWIG
LURING
LUTING
MUSING
MUSKEG
MUTING
NUKING
NUTMEG
OUTING
PULING
QUAHOG
RULING
SUNDOG
TUAREG
TUBING
TUNING
TURING

••UG••
BOUGHS
BOUGHT
BRUGES
CAUGHT
COUGAR
COUGHS
DOUGHS
DOUGHY
FOUGHT
FRUGAL
GAUGED
GAUGER
GAUGES
GOUGED
GOUGER
GOUGES
HOUGHS
KRUGER
LAUGHS
LOUGHS
NAUGHT
NOUGAT
NOUGHT
PLUGIN
ROUGED
ROUGES
ROUGHS
ROUGHY
SAUGER
SLUGGO
SMUGLY
SNUGLI
SNUGLY
SOUGHS
SOUGHT
TAUGHT
TOUGHS
TOUGHY
VAUGHN
ZEUGMA

••U•G•
DRUDGE
GRUDGE
GRUNGE
GRUNGY
KLUDGE
LOUNGE
PLUNGE
SLUDGE
SLUDGY
SLUGGO
SMUDGE
SMUDGY
SPURGE
TRUDGE

••U••G
BLUING
CLUING
GLUING
SLUING
TAUTOG
TRUING

•••UG•
BELUGA
CAYUGA
CHOUGH
COLUGO
DEBUGS
DELUGE
ENOUGH
IMPUGN
MCHUGH
OPPUGN
PERUGA
PLOUGH
REFUGE
REPUGN
SHRUGS
SLOUGH
TELUGU
THOUGH
TROUGH

•••U•G
BUTUNG
COBURG
REHUNG
SPRUNG
STRUNG
UNSUNG

••••UG
BEDBUG
HUMBUG
RAGRUG
SOWBUG
UNPLUG
WONMUG

UH••••
UHLANS

U•H•••
UNHAND
UNHEED
UNHOLY
UNHOOK
UNHURT
UPHELD
UPHILL
UPHOLD
USHERS
UTHANT

U••H••
UNCHIC
UNSHED
UNSHOD
UPSHOT
URCHIN
UTAHAN

U•••H•
UPJOHN

U••••H
UNLASH
UNMESH
UNWISH
UPPISH
UPRUSH
UZZIAH

•U•H••
AUGHTS
AUTHOR
BUCHAN
BUSHED
BUSHEL
BUSHES
BUSHWA
CUSHAW
DUCHIN
DUNHAM
DURHAM
EUCHRE
FUZHOU
GUSHED
GUSHER
GUSHES
HUGHES
HUSHED
HUSHES
KUCHEN
LUSHER
LUSHLY
LUTHER
LUTHOR
MUDHEN
MUGHOS
MUSHED
MUSHER
MUSHES
MUZHIK
NUCHAE
NUCHAL
OUGHTS
OUTHIT
PUSHED
PUSHES
PUSHON
PUSHUP
QUAHOG
RUCHES
RUSHED
RUSHEE
RUSHES
SUCHAS
TUCHUN

•U••H•
BUDDHA
BUNCHE
BUNCHY
BUQSHA
BURGHS
GUNGHO
GUNSHY
GURKHA
HUMPHS
LUNCHY
MUNCHY
MURPHY
PUNCHY
QUICHE
QUOTHA
SURAHS

•U•••H
DUDISH
DULUTH
GUELPH
GULLAH
HURRAH
HUZZAH
JUBBAH
JUDITH
JUTISH
MULISH
MULLAH
MUNICH
NULLAH
PUNISH
PUNKAH
PURDAH
PUTSCH
QUENCH
QURUSH
RUPIAH
SUKKAH
TUSSAH
ZURICH

••UH••
CHUHSI
TZUHSI

••U•H•
BOUGHS
BOUGHT
BRUSHY
CAUCHO
CAUCHY
CAUGHT
COUGHS
DOUGHS
DOUGHY
FOUGHT
GAUCHE
GAUCHO
HOUGHS
KYUSHU
LAUGHS
LOUCHE
LOUGHS
MOUTHS
MOUTHY
NAUGHT
NOUGHT
PLUSHY
POUCHY
ROUGHS
ROUGHY
SLUSHY
SOUGHS
SOUGHT
SOUTHS
TAUGHT
TOUCHE
TOUCHY
TOUGHS
TOUGHY
TRUTHS
VAUGHN
YOUTHS

••U••H
AGUISH
BEULAH
BLUISH
BRUNCH
CHURCH
CLUTCH
CRUNCH
CRUTCH
FOURTH
HAUNCH
LAUNCH
NAUTCH
PAUNCH
SCUTCH
SMUTCH
SQUASH
SQUISH
SQUUSH

•••U•H
ABLUSH
AMBUSH
AVOUCH
BARUCH
CHOUGH
CROUCH
DULUTH
ENOUGH
GROUCH
INRUSH
MCHUGH
ONRUSH
PLOUGH
QURUSH
SLEUTH
SLOUCH
SLOUGH
SQUUSH
THOUGH
THRUSH
TROUGH
UPRUSH

UI••••
UIGURS
UINTAS

U•I•••
UBIETY
UBIQUE
UMIAKS
UNIATE
UNIATS
UNICEF
UNIFIC
UNIONS
UNIPOD
UNIQUE
UNISEX
UNISON
UNISYS
UNITAL
UNITAS
UNITED
UNITER
UNITES
UNIVAC
URIALS

U••I••
UGLIER
UGLIES
UGLIFY
UGLILY
UGRIAN
ULTIMA
ULTIMO
UMPIRE
UNBIND
UNCIAL
UNDIES
UNDINE
UNFITS
UNGIRD
UNGIRT
UNKIND
UNKINK
UNLIKE
UNLINK
UNOILY
UNPILE
UNPINS
UNRIGS
UNRIPE
UNTIDY
UNTIED
UNTIES
UNWILY
UNWIND
UNWISE
UNWISH
UNZIPS
UPDIKE
UPHILL
UPLIFT
UPLINK
UPPING
UPPISH
UPPITY
UPRISE
UPSIDE
UPTICK
UPTIME
UPWIND
URGING
URSIDS
URSINE
UZZIAH

U•••I•
UJJAIN
UMBRIA
UNCHIC
UNCOIL
UNFAIR
UNGUIS
UNIFIC
UNKNIT
UNLAID
UNPAID
UNSAID
UNVEIL
URACIL
URALIC
URANIA
URANIC
URCHIN
USERID
USMAIL
UTOPIA

U••••I
UAKARI
UBANGI

•UI•••
BUILDS
CUIABA
CUIQUE
CUISSE
DUIKER
GUIANA
GUIDED
GUIDES

GUIDON
GUILDS
GUILES
GUILTY
GUIMPE
GUINEA
GUIROS
GUISES
GUITAR
GUITRY
JUICED
JUICER
JUICES
PUISNE
QUICHE
QUIDDE
QUIETS
QUILLS
QUILTS
QUINCE
QUINCY
QUINOA
QUINTS
QUIPPY
QUIPUS
QUIRES
QUIRKS
QUIRKY
QUIRTS
QUITIT
QUIVER
RUINED
RUINER
SUISSE
SUITED
SUITES
SUITOR
SUITUP
TUILLE
ZUIDER

•U•I••
AUDIAL
AUDILE
AUDIOS
AUDITS
AURIFY
AURIGA
AUXINS
BUNION
BURIED
BURIES
BURINS
BUSIED
BUSIER
BUSIES
BUSILY
BUSING
BUYING
CUBICS
CUBING
CUBISM
CUBIST
CUBITS
CUPIDS
CURIAE
CURIAL
CURING
CURIOS
CURIUM
CUTIES
CUTINS
DUDISH
DUKING
DUPING
DURIAN
DURING
DUTIES
EUNICE
FUJIAN
FUMIER
FUMING
FURIES
FUSILS
FUSING
FUSION
FUTILE
FUZING
GUNITE
GUYING
JUDITH
JUKING
JULIAN
JULIET
JULIUS
JUNIOR
JURIES
JURIST
JUTISH
KUMISS
KURILE
LUBING
LUCIAN
LUCITE
LUCIUS
LUMINA
LUPINE
LUPINO
LURING
LUTING
LUTIST
MUCINS
MULISH
MUNICH
MURIEL
MURINE
MUSIAL
MUSING
MUTING
MUTINY
NUBIAN
NUBILE
NUDIST
NUDITY
NUKING
NUMINA
OUTING
PULING
PUMICE
PUNIER
PUNILY
PUNISH
PUPILS
PURIFY
PURINA
PURINE
PURISM
PURIST
PURITY
QUAILS
QUAINT
QUOINS
QUOITS
RUBIED
RUBIES
RUBIFY
RULING
RUMINA
RUNINS
RUPIAH
RUTILE
SUBITO
SUFISM
SUPINE
SURIMI
SUSIEQ
TUBING
TUBIST
TULIPS
TUNICA
TUNICS
TUNING
TUPIAN
TURING
ZURICH

•U••I•
AUFAIT
AULAIT
AUNTIE
AUPAIR
AUSSIE
AUSTIN
BUDGIE
BULBIL
BUNYIP
BUSKIN
BUSTIN
BUTTIN
CUBOID
CULKIN
CULLIS
CULTIC
CUPRIC
CURTIN
CURTIS
CURTIZ
CUSPID
CUSTIS
CUTSIN
DUBBIN
DUBLIN
DUBOIS
DUCHIN
DUNLIN
DURBIN
DUSTIN
EUCLID
EURAIL
FULFIL
FUSTIC
HUBRIS
HUNGIN
JUDAIC
JUMPIN
JUNKIE
JUSTIN
KUKRIS
KUOPIO
KUWAIT
LUBLIN
LUDWIG
MUDPIE
MUFFIN
MUFTIS
MUNCIE
MUNTIN
MURCIA
MUSKIE
MUSLIM
MUSLIN
MUZHIK
NUBBIN
NUDNIK
NUNCIO
NUTKIN
NUTRIA
OUTBID
OUTDID
OUTFIT
OUTHIT
OUTWIT
PUBLIC
PUFFIN
PULLIN
PULPIT
PUNDIT
PUNKIE
PURLIN
PUTRID
PUTSIN
QUITIT
RUBRIC
RUBSIN
RUNCIE
RUNSIN
RUSKIN
RUSSIA
RUSTIC
SUBMIT
SUCKIN
SUFFIX
SUMMIT
SUNLIT
SUNNIS
SUSLIK
TUCKIN
TUGRIK
TUNEIN
TURBID
TURBIT
TURGID
TURKIC
TURNIN
TURNIP
TURPIN
YUPPIE

•U•••I
BUSONI
CUMULI
FULANI
HUMERI
KUBLAI
LUGOSI
NUCLEI
QUADRI
RUBATI
SURIMI
SUZUKI
TUMULI

••UI••
ACUITY
AGUISH
AQUILA
AQUINO
BLUING
BLUISH
BRUINS
BRUISE
BRUITS
CLUING
CRUISE
DRUIDS
EQUINE
EQUIPS
EQUITY
FLUIDS
FRUITS
FRUITY
GLUIER
GLUING
GSUITS
INUITS
LOUISA
LOUISE
SLUICE
SLUING
SQUIBB
SQUIBS
SQUIDS
SQUILL
SQUINT
SQUIRE
SQUIRM
SQUIRT
SQUISH
TRUING
TRUISM

••U•I•
ABUKIR
ANUBIS
APULIA
BAUCIS
BOUDIN
CLUEIN
COURIC
COUSIN
HOURIS
KAURIS
LAURIE
MOULIN
PAUCIS
PLUGIN
POURIN
SAUDIS
SHUTIN
STUDIO
STUPID
TSURIS
ZEUXIS

••U••I
ALUMNI
BRUNEI
CHUHSI
FRUTTI
GLUTEI
ITURBI
SNUGLI
SOUARI
TZUHSI

•••UI•
ACQUIT
ALCUIN
ANNUIT
BAGUIO
INTUIT
JESUIT
LEGUIN
LIQUID
MAQUIS
MINUIT
NYQUIL
PAQUIN
SEQUIN
UNGUIS
YAQUIS

•••U•I
ADZUKI
AGOUTI
ANNULI
BATUMI
CUMULI
KABUKI
LAZULI
POPULI
SALUKI
SUZUKI
TUMULI
WATUSI
YEHUDI

••••UI
BANGUI
SESQUI
YANQUI

UJ••••
UJJAIN

U•J•••
UJJAIN
UNJAMS
UNJUST
UPJOHN

•UJ•••
BUJOLD
FUJIAN
JUJUBE

•U•J••
PUNJAB

••UJ••
THUJAS

UK••••
UKASES

U•K•••
UAKARI
UNKIND
UNKINK
UNKNIT
UNKNOT
UPKEEP

U•••K•
UMIAKS
UNLIKE
UNMAKE
UNYOKE
UPDIKE
UPTAKE
UZBEKS

U••••K
UNCORK
UNHOOK
UNKINK
UNLINK
UNLOCK
UNMASK
UNPACK
UNTACK
UPLINK
UPTALK
UPTICK
URALSK

•UK•••
AUKLET
DUKING
JUKING
KUKRIS
MUKLUK
NUKING
SUKKAH
YUKATA
YUKAWA
YUKKED

•U•K••
BUCKED
BUCKET
BUCKLE
BUCKUP
BULKED
BUNKED
BUNKER
BUNKOS
BUNKUM
BUSKED
BUSKIN
CUCKOO
CULKIN
DUCKED
DUIKER
DUNKED
DUNKER
FUNKED
GURKHA
HULKED
HUNKER
HUSKED
HUSKER
JUNKED
JUNKER
JUNKET
JUNKIE
LUCKED
LUNKER
LURKED
MUCKED
MUCKUP
MUSKEG
MUSKET
MUSKIE
MUSKOX
NUTKIN
PUCKER
PUNKAH
PUNKER
PUNKIE
QUAKED
QUAKER
QUAKES
QUOKKA
RUCKED
RUCKUS
RUSKIN
SUCKAS
SUCKED
SUCKER
SUCKIN
SUKKAH
SULKED
SULKER
SUNKEN
TUCKED
TUCKER
TUCKET
TUCKIN
TURKEY
TURKIC
TUSKED
TUSKER
YUKKED

•U••K•
EUREKA
JUDOKA
KULAKS
LUSAKA
QUACKS
QUARKS
QUIRKS
QUIRKY
QUOKKA
SUZUKI
YUROKS

•U•••K
BUROAK
CUSACK
DUBCEK
KUSPUK
LUBECK
MUKLUK
MUZHIK
NUDNIK
SUSLIK
TUGRIK

••UK••
ABUKIR
CHUKAR
CHUKKA
FLUKES
FLUKEY
RYUKYU
ZHUKOV

••U•K•
AKUAKU
BAULKS
BOURKE
CAULKS
CHUCKS
CHUKKA
CHUNKS
CHUNKY
CLUCKS
CLUNKS
CLUNKY
FLUNKS
FLUNKY
PLUCKS
PLUCKY
PLUNKS
ROURKE
SHUCKS
SKULKS
SKUNKS
SKUNKY
SPUNKY
THUNKS
TRUCKS
TRUNKS

••U••K
SQUAWK
SQUEAK

•••UK•
ADZUKI
KABUKI
PERUKE
REBUKE
SALUKI
STLUKE
SUZUKI

•••U•K
DEBUNK
INBULK
INLUCK
PODUNK
SHRUNK
STRUCK
ZANUCK

••••UK
DYBBUK
FAROUK
KUSPUK
MARDUK
MUKLUK
SELJUK
TOBRUK

UL••••
ULCERS
ULLAGE
ULLMAN
ULSTER
ULTIMA
ULTIMO
ULTRAS

U•L•••
UCLANS
UGLIER
UGLIES

UGLIFY
UGLILY
UHLANS
ULLAGE
ULLMAN
UMLAUT
UNLACE
UNLADE
UNLAID
UNLASH
UNLEAD
UNLESS
UNLIKE
UNLINK
UNLOAD
UNLOCK
UPLAND
UPLIFT
UPLINK
UPLOAD

U••L••

UBOLTS
UNCLAD
UNCLES
UNCLOG
UNGLUE
UNPLUG
URALIC
URALSK
UVALUE
UVULAE
UVULAR
UVULAS

U•••L•

UGLILY
UMBELS
UNABLE
UNBELT
UNBOLT
UNDULY
UNFOLD
UNHOLY
UNOILY
UNPILE
UNROLL
UNRULY
UNSOLD
UNTOLD
UNWELL
UNWILY
UPHELD
UPHILL
UPHOLD
UPTALK
UPWELL
URIALS
URSULA
USABLE
USABLY
USUALS

U••••L

UMBRAL
UNCIAL
UNCOIL
UNCOOL
UNCURL
UNFURL
UNGUAL
UNITAL
UNOCAL
UNREAL
UNREEL
UNROLL
UNSEAL
UNVEIL
UNWELL
UPHILL
UPWELL
URACIL
USEFUL
USMAIL

•UL•••

AULAIT
BULBIL
BULBUL
BULGAR
BULGED
BULGES
BULGUR
BULKED
BULLAE
BULLED
BULLET
BULOVA
BULWER
CULETS
CULKIN
CULLED
CULLEN
CULLER
CULLET
CULLIS
CULTIC
CULVER
DULCET
DULLEA
DULLED
DULLER
DULLES
DULUTH
EULOGY
FULANI
FULCRA
FULFIL
FULLER
FULMAR
FULTON
GULAGS
GULFED
GULLAH
GULLED
GULLET
GULPED
GULPER
HULKED
HULLED
HULLER
HULLOA
HULLOS
JULEPS
JULIAN
JULIET
JULIUS
KULAKS
KULTUR
LULLED
MULCTS
MULETA
MULEYS
MULISH
MULLAH
MULLAS
MULLED
MULLER
MULLET
MULTUM
NULLAH
NULLED
PULING
PULLED
PULLET
PULLEY
PULLIN
PULLON
PULLUP
PULPED
PULPIT
PULQUE
PULSAR
PULSED
PULSES
RULEON
RULERS
RULING
SULCUS
SULFUR
SULKED
SULKER
SULLEN
SULTAN
SULTRY
TULANE
TULARE
TULIPS
TULLES
TULSAN
VULCAN
VULGAR

•U•L••

AUKLET
BUGLED
BUGLER
BUGLES
BUILDS
BULLAE
BULLED
BULLET
BURLAP
BURLED
BURLEY
BUTLER
CULLED
CULLEN
CULLER
CULLET
CULLIS
CURLED
CURLER
CURLEW
CURLEY
CURLUP
CUTLER
CUTLET
DUALLY
DUBLIN
DUDLEY
DUELED
DUELER
DUELLO
DULLEA
DULLED
DULLER
DULLES
DUNLIN
DUNLOP
DUPLEX
EUCLID
FUELED
FUELER
FULLER
FURLED
GUELPH
GUILDS
GUILES
GUILTY
GULLAH
GULLED
GULLET
GURLEY
HULLED
HULLER
HULLOA
HULLOS
HURLED
HURLER
HURLEY
HUXLEY
KUBLAI
KUNLUN
LUBLIN
LUDLUM
LULLED
MUKLUK
MULLAH
MULLAS
MULLED
MULLER
MULLET
MUSLIM
MUSLIN
NUCLEI
NUCLEO
NULLAH
NULLED
NUTLET
OUTLAW
OUTLAY
OUTLET
PUBLIC
PULLED
PULLET
PULLEY
PULLIN
PULLON
PULLUP
PURLED
PURLIN
QUALMS
QUELLS
QUILLS
QUILTS
RUBLES
RUBLEV
RUNLET
SUBLET
SULLEN
SUNLIT
SUSLIK
SUTLER
TUILLE
TULLES
WURLEY

•U••L•

AUDILE
BUBBLE
BUBBLY
BUCKLE
BUJOLD
BUMBLE
BUNDLE
BUNGLE
BURBLE
BURBLY
BURGLE
BUSILY
BUSTLE
CUDDLE
CUDDLY
CUMULI
CUMULO
CUPELS
CUPOLA
CURDLE
CURTLY
CURULE
CUTELY
DUALLY
DUELLO
DUMBLY
DUVALL
FUDDLE
FUMBLE
FUSILS
FUTILE
GURGLE
GUZZLE
HUBBLE
HUBBLY
HUDDLE
HUGELY
HUMBLE
HUMBLY
HURDLE
HURTLE
HUSTLE
JUGGLE
JUMBLE
JUNGLE
JUNGLY
JUSTLY
KURALT
KURILE
LUNULA
LUSHLY
MUDDLE
MUFFLE
MUMBLE
MUMBLY
MURALS
MUSCLE
MUSCLY
MUTELY
MUZZLE
NUBBLE
NUBBLY
NUBILE
NUDELY
NUMBLY
NUZZLE
OUSELS
OUTFLY
OUZELS
PUDDLE
PUDDLY
PUEBLA
PUEBLO
PUNILY
PUPILS
PURELY
PURFLE
PURPLE
PURPLY
PUZZLE
QUAILS
QUAYLE
QUELLS
QUILLS
RUBBLE
RUBBLY
RUDDLE
RUDELY
RUDOLF
RUFFLE
RUFFLY
RUMBLE
RUMBLY
RUMPLE
RUMPLY
RUNDLE
RUSTLE
RUTILE
SUBTLE
SUBTLY
SUPPLE
SUPPLY
SURELY
TUILLE
TUMBLE
TUMULI
TUMULT
TUPELO
TURTLE
TUSSLE
TUVALU
YUNGLO

•U•••L

AUDIAL
BUCCAL
BULBIL
BULBUL
BUNUEL
BURSAL
BUSHEL
CUDGEL
CUNEAL
CUPFUL
CURIAL
DUCTAL
DUFFEL
DUVALL
EURAIL
FULFIL
FUNNEL
GUMBEL
GUNNEL
JUGFUL
KUMMEL
MUDEEL
MURIEL
MUSIAL
MUSSEL
MUTUAL
NUCHAL
PUMMEL
RUEFUL
RUNNEL
RUPAUL
TUNNEL

••UL••

ADULTS
ALULAE
ALULAR
AMULET
APULIA
AVULSE
BAULKS
BEULAH
BOULES
BOULEZ
BOULLE
BRULES
CAULKS
COULDA
COULEE
EVULSE
EXULTS
FAULTS
FAULTY
FOULED
FOULER
FOULLY
FOULUP
GOULET
HAULED
HAULER
HAULMS
HAULUP
JOULES
MAULED
MAULER
MOULDS
MOULDY
MOULIN
MOULTS
OCULAR
OVULAR
OVULES
PAULEY
POULTS
SAULTS
SCULLS
SCULLY
SCULPT
SKULKS
SKULLS
STULLS
TOULON
UVULAE
UVULAR
UVULAS
VAULTS
VAULTY

••U•L•

AQUILA
BAUBLE
BLUELY
BOUCLE
BOULLE
CAUDLE
CHURLS
COUPLE
DOUALA
DOUBLE
DOUBLY
DOURLY
EQUALS
FOULLY
GLUMLY
GRUELS
HOURLY
KNURLS
KNURLY
LOUDLY
ROUBLE
SCULLS
SCULLY
SKULLS
SMUGLY
SNUGLI
SNUGLY
SOURLY
SQUALL
SQUILL
STULLS
TAUTLY
THUSLY
TOUSLE
USUALS
YOUALL

••U••L

BRUMAL
BRUTAL
CAUDAL
CAUSAL
CRURAL
FAUNAL
FEUDAL
FRUGAL
LAUREL
NEURAL
NEUROL
PLURAL
SAUREL
SQUALL
SQUEAL
SQUILL
YOUALL

•••UL•

AMPULE
AMPULS
ANNULI
ANNULS
BABULS
BAKULA
COPULA
CUMULI
CUMULO
CURULE
ENGULF
FACULA
FERULE
FIBULA
GHOULS
INBULK
INCULT
INFULL
INSULT
ISEULT
LAZULI
LIGULA
LOBULE
LUNULA
MACULA
MODULE
MODULO
MOGULS
NEBULA
NODULE
OCCULT
OSCULA
PAKULA
PARULA
PENULT
PETULA
PICULS
POPULI
RADULA
RESULT
SCHULZ
SHOULD
TABULA
TUMULI
TUMULT
UNDULY
UNRULY
URSULA

•••U•L

ACTUAL
ANNUAL
BUNUEL
CASUAL
GENUAL
INFULL
LEMUEL
MANUAL
MANUEL
MIGUEL
MUTUAL
NYQUIL
RAQUEL
REFUEL
RITUAL
SAMUEL
SEQUEL
UNCURL
UNFURL
UNGUAL
VISUAL

••••UL

AIDFUL
AIMFUL
ARMFUL
ARTFUL
BAGFUL
BANJUL
BEFOUL
BOXFUL

BULBUL
CANFUL
CAPFUL
CARFUL
CONSUL
CUPFUL
DEPAUL
EARFUL
ENSOUL
EYEFUL
FITFUL
HANGUL
HATFUL
INHAUL
IREFUL
JARFUL
JOYFUL
JUGFUL
LAPFUL
LAWFUL
MANFUL
PANFUL
PEPFUL
POTFUL
RUEFUL
RUPAUL
SINFUL
SOBFUL
STPAUL
USEFUL
VATFUL
WILFUL
WOEFUL

UM••••

UMBELS
UMBERS
UMBRAE
UMBRAL
UMBRAS
UMBRIA
UMIAKS
UMLAUT
UMPIRE
UMTATA

U•M•••

UNMADE
UNMAKE
UNMANS
UNMASK
UNMEET
UNMESH
UNMOOR
UPMOST
USMAIL
UTMOST

U••M••

ULLMAN

U•••M•

UGGAMS
UGSOME
ULTIMA
ULTIMO
UNARMS
UNJAMS
UPTIME

•UM•••

AUMONT
BUMBLE
BUMBRY
BUMMED
BUMMER
BUMOUT
BUMPED
BUMPER
BUMPPO
BUMPUP
BUMRAP
CUMBER
CUMULI
CUMULO
DUMBER
DUMBLY
DUMDUM
DUMONT
DUMPED
DUMPER
FUMBLE
FUMIER
FUMING
GUMBEL
GUMBOS
GUMMED
GUMSUP
HUMANE
HUMANS
HUMBLE
HUMBLY
HUMBUG
HUMERI
HUMMED
HUMMER
HUMMUS
HUMORS
HUMOUR
HUMPED
HUMPHS
HUMVEE
JUMADA
JUMBLE
JUMBOS
JUMPAT
JUMPED
JUMPER
JUMPIN
JUMPON
JUMPUP
KUMISS
KUMMEL
LUMBAR
LUMBER
LUMENS
LUMINA
LUMMOX
LUMPED
LUMPEN
LUMPER
LUMPUR
MUMBLE
MUMBLY
MUMMED
MUMMER
MUMPED
NUMBAT
NUMBED
NUMBER
NUMBLY
NUMERO
NUMINA
PUMICE
PUMMEL
PUMPED
PUMPER
PUMPUP
QUMRAN
RUMBAS
RUMBLE
RUMBLY
RUMENS
RUMINA
RUMMER
RUMORS
RUMOUR
RUMPLE
RUMPLY
RUMPUS
SUMACS
SUMMAE
SUMMAS
SUMMED
SUMMER
SUMMIT
SUMMON
SUMNER
SUMSUP
SUMTER
SUMUPS
TUMBLE
TUMEFY
TUMMED
TUMULI
TUMULT
YUMYUM

•U•M••

BUMMED
BUMMER
BURMAN
BUSMAN
BUSMEN
DUOMOS
FULMAR
GUIMPE
GUMMED
GUNMAN
GUNMEN
HUMMED
HUMMER
HUMMUS
KUMMEL
LUMMOX
MUMMED
MUMMER
MURMUR
MUUMUU
NUTMEG
PUMMEL
QUEMOY
RUDMAN
RUMMER
SUBMIT
SUMMAE
SUMMAS
SUMMED
SUMMER
SUMMIT
SUMMON
TUBMAN
TUMMED

•U••M•

AUTUMN
QUALMS
RUNDMC
SURIMI

•U•••M

BUNKUM
CUBISM
CURIUM
CUSTOM
DUMDUM
DUNHAM
DURHAM
LUDLUM
MULTUM
MUSEUM
MUSLIM
PURISM
PUTNAM
QUORUM
SUBGUM
SUFISM
YUMYUM

••UM••

ACUMEN
ALUMNA
ALUMNI
BRUMAL
BRUMBY
BRUMES
CHUMMY
CHUMPS
CLUMPS
CLUMPY
CLUMSY
CRUMBS
CRUMBY
CRUMMY
DRUMUP
FLUMES
FRUMPS
FRUMPY
GAUMED
GLUMLY
GRUMPS
GRUMPY
MAUMAU
MAUMEE
MUUMUU
NEUMAN
NEUMES
NOUMEA
PLUMBS
PLUMED
PLUMES
PLUMMY
PLUMPS
RHUMBA
RHUMBS
SCUMMY
SLUMMY
SLUMPS
SPUMED
SPUMES
STUMER
STUMPS
STUMPY
THUMBS
THUMPS
TRUMAN
TRUMPS

••U•M•

CHUMMY
CRUMMY
HAULMS
PLUMMY
SCUMMY
SLUMMY
ZEUGMA

••U••M

FOURAM
FOURPM
SQUIRM
TRUISM

•••UM•

ALBUMS
ASSUME
AUTUMN
BATUMI
BEGUMS
BENUMB
COLUMN
FORUMS
GAZUMP
ILLUME
JORUMS
KHOUMS
LEGUME
MAZUMA
ODIUMS
PNEUMA
RELUME
RESUME
RHEUMS
RHEUMY
SCRUMS
SEDUMS
SERUMS
STRUMS
THRUMS
TRAUMA
VOLUME

•••U•M

VACUUM

••••UM

ACTIUM
ADYTUM
ALARUM
ALLIUM
ANTRUM
ARTGUM
ASYLUM
ATRIUM
BARIUM
BARNUM
BAYRUM
BEEGUM
BOOJUM
BUNKUM
CERIUM
CESIUM
CILIUM
CIRCUM
CONIUM
CORIUM
CURIUM
DICTUM
DIMSUM
DORSUM
DUMDUM
ERBIUM
FAIYUM
FOLIUM
FRENUM
GOLLUM
GYPSUM
HELIUM
INDIUM
IONIUM
LABRUM
LATIUM
LUDLUM
LYCEUM
MAGNUM
MEDIUM
MINIUM
MULTUM
MUSEUM
OMASUM
OMNIUM
OSMIUM
OSTIUM
PABLUM
PEPLUM
PHYLUM
PILEUM
PLENUM
PODIUM
POSSUM
PRIMUM
QUORUM
RADIUM
REDGUM
SACRUM
SALTUM
SCARUM
SEPTUM
SODIUM
SUBGUM
TALCUM
TEDEUM
TEDIUM
VACUUM
VALIUM
VELLUM
WAMPUM
YUMYUM

UN••••

UNABLE
UNAGED
UNARMS
UNAWED
UNBARS
UNBELT
UNBEND
UNBENT
UNBIND
UNBOLT
UNBORN
UNBUSY
UNCAGE
UNCAPS
UNCASE
UNCHIC
UNCIAL
UNCLAD
UNCLES
UNCLOG
UNCOIL
UNCOOL
UNCORK
UNCURL
UNDIES
UNDINE
UNDOER
UNDOES
UNDONE
UNDRAW
UNDULY
UNDYED
UNEASE
UNEASY
UNESCO
UNEVEN
UNFAIR
UNFITS
UNFOLD
UNFREE
UNFURL
UNGIRD
UNGIRT
UNGLUE
UNGUAL
UNGUES
UNGUIS
UNHAND
UNHEED
UNHOLY
UNHOOK
UNHURT
UNIATE
UNIATS
UNICEF
UNIFIC
UNIONS
UNIPOD
UNIQUE
UNISEX
UNISON
UNISYS
UNITAL
UNITAS
UNITED
UNITER
UNITES
UNIVAC
UNJAMS
UNJUST
UNKIND
UNKINK
UNKNIT
UNKNOT
UNLACE
UNLADE
UNLAID
UNLASH
UNLEAD
UNLESS
UNLIKE
UNLINK
UNLOAD
UNLOCK
UNMADE
UNMAKE
UNMANS
UNMASK
UNMEET
UNMESH
UNMOOR
UNOCAL
UNOILY
UNOPEN
UNPACK
UNPAID
UNPEGS
UNPENS
UNPILE
UNPINS
UNPLUG
UNREAD
UNREAL
UNREEL
UNREST
UNRIGS
UNRIPE
UNROBE
UNROLL
UNROOT
UNRULY
UNSAFE
UNSAID
UNSAYS
UNSEAL
UNSEAT
UNSEEN
UNSEWN
UNSEWS
UNSHED
UNSHOD
UNSNAG
UNSNAP
UNSOLD
UNSOWN
UNSTOP
UNSUNG
UNSURE
UNTACK
UNTIDY
UNTIED
UNTIES
UNTOLD
UNTORN
UNTRAP
UNTROD
UNTRUE
UNTUNE
UNUSED
UNVEIL
UNWARY
UNWELL
UNWILY
UNWIND
UNWISE
UNWISH
UNWORN
UNWOVE
UNWRAP
UNYOKE
UNZIPS

U•N•••

UINTAS

U••N••

UBANGI
UGANDA
UNKNIT
UNKNOT
UNSNAG
UNSNAP
UPENDS
URANIA
URANIC
URANUS
USANCE
USENET

U•••N•

UCLANS
UHLANS
UNBEND
UNBENT
UNBIND
UNDINE
UNDONE
UNHAND
UNIONS
UNKIND
UNKINK
UNLINK
UNMANS
UNPENS
UNPINS
UNSUNG
UNTUNE
UNWIND
UPLAND
UPLINK
UPPING
UPWIND
URBANA
URBANE
URGENT
URGING
URSINE
UTHANT
UTURNS

U••••N

UGRIAN
UJJAIN
ULLMAN
UNBORN
UNEVEN
UNISON
UNOPEN
UNSEEN
UNSEWN
UNSOWN
UNTORN
UNWORN
UPJOHN
UPTOWN
UPTURN
URCHIN
USOPEN
UTAHAN

•UN•••
AUNTIE
BUNCHE
BUNCHY
BUNCOS
BUNDLE
BUNGED
BUNGEE
BUNGLE
BUNION
BUNKED
BUNKER
BUNKOS
BUNKUM
BUNSEN
BUNTED
BUNTER
BUNUEL
BUNYAN
BUNYIP
CUNARD
CUNAXA
CUNEAL
DUNANT
DUNBAR
DUNCAN
DUNCES
DUNDEE
DUNERA
DUNHAM
DUNKED
DUNKER
DUNLIN
DUNLOP
DUNNED
EUNICE
FUNDED
FUNGUS
FUNKED
FUNNED
FUNNEL
GUNDOG
GUNFOR
GUNGHO
GUNITE
GUNMAN
GUNMEN
GUNNAR
GUNNED
GUNNEL
GUNNER
GUNSHY
GUNTER
HUNGER
HUNGIN
HUNGON
HUNGRY
HUNGUP
HUNGWU
HUNKER
HUNTED
HUNTER
JUNCOS
JUNEAU
JUNGLE
JUNGLY
JUNIOR
JUNKED
JUNKER
JUNKET
JUNKIE
JUNTAS
JUNTOS
KUNGFU
KUNLUN
LUNACY
LUNATE
LUNCHY
LUNDEN
LUNGED
LUNGES
LUNKER
LUNULA
MUNCHY
MUNCIE
MUNGOS
MUNICH
MUNTIN
NUNCIO
OUNCES
PUNCHY
PUNDIT
PUNIER
PUNILY
PUNISH
PUNJAB
PUNKAH
PUNKER
PUNKIE
PUNNED
PUNNET
PUNTED
PUNTER
RUNCIE
RUNDLE
RUNDMC
RUNDRY
RUNFOR
RUNGUP
RUNINS
RUNLET
RUNNEL
RUNNER
RUNOFF
RUNONS
RUNOUT
RUNSAT
RUNSIN
RUNSON
RUNSTO
RUNSUP
RUNUPS
RUNWAY
RUNYON
SUNDAE
SUNDAY
SUNDER
SUNDEW
SUNDOG
SUNDRY
SUNGOD
SUNKEN
SUNLIT
SUNNED
SUNNIS
SUNOCO
SUNRAY
SUNSET
SUNTAN
SUNUNU
SUNUPS
TUNDRA
TUNEIN
TUNERS
TUNEUP
TUNICA
TUNICS
TUNING
TUNNEL
TUNNEY
YUNGLO
YUNNAN

•U•N••
BUENOS
BURNED
BURNER
BURNET
BURNEY
BURNUP
DUENNA
DUNNED
DURNED
EUPNEA
FUNNED
FUNNEL
GUENON
GUINEA
GUNNAR
GUNNED
GUNNEL
GUNNER
GURNEY
LUANDA
LUGNUT
NUANCE
NUDNIK
PUENTE
PUNNED
PUNNET
PUTNAM
QUANGO
QUANTA
QUENCH
QUINCE
QUINCY
QUINOA
QUINTS
RUANAS
RUANDA
RUINED
RUINER
RUNNEL
RUNNER
SUMNER
SUNNED
SUNNIS
TUNNEL
TUNNEY
TURNED
TURNER
TURNIN
TURNIP
TURNON
TURNTO
TURNUP
YUNNAN

•U••N•
AUDENS
AUFOND
AUGEND
AUMONT
AUXINS
BURINS
BUSING
BUSONI
BUTANE
BUTENE
BUTUNG
BUYING
CUBING
CURING
CUTINS
DUENNA
DUGONG
DUKING
DUMONT
DUNANT
DUPING
DUPONT
DURANT
DURING
EUGENE
FULANI
FUMING
FUSING
FUTONS
FUZING
GUIANA
GUYANA
GUYING
HUMANE
HUMANS
HURONS
JUKING
LUBING
LUCENT
LUDENS
LUMENS
LUMINA
LUPINE
LUPINO
LUPONE
LURING
LUTING
MUCINS
MURANO
MURINE
MUSING
MUSTNT
MUTANT
MUTING
MUTINY
NUGENT
NUKING
NUMINA
OUTING
PUISNE
PULING
PURINA
PURINE
PUTONS
QUAINT
QUEENS
QUERNS
QUOINS
RUBENS
RULING
RUMENS
RUMINA
RUNINS
RUNONS
SUNUNU
SUPINE
SUSANN
TUBING
TUCANA
TULANE
TUNING
TURING

•U•••N
AUBURN
AUGEAN
AUSTEN
AUSTIN
AUTUMN
BUCHAN
BUFFON
BUNION
BUNSEN
BUNYAN
BURDEN
BURMAN
BURTON
BUSKIN
BUSMAN
BUSMEN
BUSTIN
BUTTIN
BUTTON
CULKIN
CULLEN
CURTIN
CURZON
CUTSIN
DUBBIN
DUBLIN
DUCHIN
DUDEEN
DUNCAN
DUNLIN
DURBAN
DURBIN
DURIAN
DUSTIN
FUJIAN
FULTON
FUSION
GUDRUN
GUENON
GUIDON
GUNMAN
GUNMEN
HUDSON
HUNGIN
HUNGON
HUSTON
HUTTON
JULIAN
JUMPIN
JUMPON
JUSTIN
KUCHEN
KUNLUN
KURGAN
LUBLIN
LUCIAN
LUDDEN
LUMPEN
LUNDEN
MUDHEN
MUFFIN
MUNTIN
MUSLIN
MUTTON
NUBBIN
NUBIAN
NUTKIN
OUTGUN
OUTRAN
OUTRUN
PUFFIN
PULLIN
PULLON
PURLIN
PUSHON
PUTSIN
PUTSON
QUEZON
QUMRAN
RUBSIN
RUDMAN
RULEON
RUNSIN
RUNSON
RUNYON
RUSKIN
RUTTAN
SUBORN
SUCKIN
SUDDEN
SULLEN
SULTAN
SUMMON
SUNKEN
SUNTAN
SUSANN
SUTTON
TUBMAN
TUCHUN
TUCKIN
TUCSON
TULSAN
TUNEIN
TUPIAN
TURBAN
TUREEN
TURNIN
TURNON
TURPIN
TUSCAN
VULCAN
YUNNAN

••UN••
BLUNTS
BOUNCE
BOUNCY
BOUNDS
BOUNTY
BRUNCH
BRUNEI
BRUNET
BRUNTS
CHUNKS
CHUNKY
CLUNKS
CLUNKY
COUNTS
COUNTY
CRUNCH
DAUNTS
FAUNAE
FAUNAL
FAUNAS
FAUNUS
FLUNKS
FLUNKY
FOUNDS
FOUNTS
GOUNOD
GRUNDY
GRUNGE
GRUNGY
GRUNTS
HAUNCH
HAUNTS
HOUNDS
HOUNDY
JAUNTS
JAUNTY
JOUNCE
JOUNCY
KAUNAS
KAUNDA
LAUNCH
LOUNGE
MAUNDY
MBUNDU
MOUNDS
MOUNTS
MOUNTY
PAUNCH
PLUNGE
PLUNKS
POUNCE
POUNDS
PRUNED
PRUNER
PRUNES
REUNES
ROUNDS
SAUNAS
SHUNTS
SKUNKS
SKUNKY
SOUNDS
SPUNKY
STUNTS
STUNTY
TAUNTS
THUNKS
TRUNKS
VAUNTS
WOUNDS
ZOUNDS

••U•N•
ALUMNA
ALUMNI
AQUINO
BLUING
BOURNE
BRUINS
CHURNS
CLUING
EQUINE
FLUENT
GLUING
GLUONS
IGUANA
JOURNO
MOURNS
SLUING
SPURNS
SQUINT
TAUONS
TRUANT
TRUING
UTURNS

••U••N
ACUMEN
ANURAN
ARUBAN
BHUTAN
BOUDIN
CLUEIN
COUPON
COUSIN
GLUTEN
LAUREN
LOUDEN
MOULIN
MOUTON
NEUMAN
NEURON
NGUYEN
PLUGIN
POURIN
REUBEN
SHUTIN
SPURON
TAUTEN
TEUTON
TOUCAN
TOULON
TRUMAN
VAUGHN
YAUPON

•••UN•
ABOUND
AMOUNT
ARJUNA
AROUND
ATTUNE
AVAUNT
BOSUNS
BUTUNG
CAJUNS
COHUNE
DEBUNK
EDMUND
EXEUNT
FECUND
FLAUNT
GERUND
GROUND
HLHUNT
IMMUNE
IMMUNO
INTUNE
JEJUNE
JOCUND
KAHUNA
KORUNA
LACUNA
LAGUNA
MIFUNE
OBTUND
OSMUND
PODUNK
REFUND
REHUNG
RERUNS
RETUNE
ROTUND
SHRUNK
SPRUNG
STRUNG
SUNUNU
TRIUNE
UNSUNG
UNTUNE
VARUNA
VICUNA

•••U•N
ALCUIN
AUBURN
AUTUMN
COBURN
COLUMN
FRAUEN
IMPUGN
INTURN
LEGUIN
MCKUEN
OPPUGN
PADUAN
PAPUAN
PAQUIN
REPUGN
RETURN
SATURN
SEQUIN
SIOUAN
UPTURN

••••UN
AIRGUN
BARZUN
BIGGUN
CANCUN
CAPGUN
DATSUN
DRYRUN
ENDRUN
GUDRUN
JETGUN
KUNLUN
LEBRUN
MACOUN
OUTGUN
OUTRUN
POPGUN
RAYGUN
SHOGUN
SIXGUN
SKIRUN
TOPGUN
TUCHUN
VERDUN

U•O•••
UBOATS

UBOLTS
UNOCAL
UNOILY
UNOPEN
USOPEN
UTOPIA

U••O••
UGSOME
UNBOLT
UNBORN
UNCOIL
UNCOOL
UNCORK
UNDOER
UNDOES
UNDONE
UNFOLD
UNHOLY
UNHOOK
UNIONS
UNLOAD
UNLOCK
UNMOOR
UNROBE
UNROLL
UNROOT
UNSOLD
UNSOWN
UNTOLD
UNTORN
UNWORN
UNWOVE
UNYOKE
UPBOWS
UPHOLD
UPJOHN
UPLOAD
UPMOST
UPROAR
UPROOT
UPROSE
UPTOWN
UTMOST

U•••O•
UNCLOG
UNCOOL
UNHOOK
UNIPOD
UNISON
UNKNOT
UNMOOR
UNROOT
UNSHOD
UNSTOP
UNTROD
UPROOT
UPSHOT

U••••O
ULTIMO
UNESCO
USEDTO

•UO•••
BUOYED
BUOYUP
DUOMOS
KUOPIO
QUOINS
QUOITS
QUOKKA
QUOQUE
QUORUM
QUOTAS
QUOTED
QUOTER
QUOTES
QUOTHA

•U•O••
AUFOND
AUMONT
AURORA
AUROUS
BUGOFF
BUGOUT
BUJOLD
BULOVA
BUMOUT
BUROAK
BUSONI
BUYOFF
BUYOUT
CUBOID
CUPOLA
CUTOFF
CUTOUT
DUBOIS
DUGONG
DUGOUT
DUMONT
DUPONT
DUROCS
EUBOEA
EUDORA
EULOGY
EUROPA
EUROPE
FURORE
FURORS
FUTONS
GUYOTS
HUMORS
HUMOUR
HURONS
JUDOKA
JURORS
LUGOSI
LUPONE
MUCOSA
MUCOUS
PUTOFF
PUTONS
PUTOUT
RUBOFF
RUBOUT
RUDOLF
RUFOUS
RUGOSE
RUMORS
RUMOUR
RUNOFF
RUNONS
RUNOUT
SUBORN
SUNOCO
TUDORS
TUTORS
YUROKS

•U••O•
AUDIOS
AUTHOR
BUENOS
BUFFON
BUFFOS
BUNCOS
BUNION
BUNKOS
BURBOT
BURGOO
BURGOS
BURROS
BURROW
BURTON
BUSBOY
BUTEOS
BUTTON
CUCKOO
CURIOS
CURSOR
CURZON
CUSTOM
CUSTOS
DUNLOP
DUOMOS
FULTON
FURROW
FUSION
FUZHOU
GUACOS
GUENON
GUIDON
GUIROS
GUMBOS
GUNDOG
GUNFOR
HUDSON
HUEVOS
HULLOA
HULLOS
HUNGON
HUSTON
HUTTON
JUMBOS
JUMPON
JUNCOS
JUNIOR
JUNTOS
KUDROW
LUMMOX
LUTHOR
MUGHOS
MUNGOS
MURROW
MUSKOX
MUTTON
OUTBOX
OUTFOX
PULLON
PUSHON
PUTSON
QUAHOG
QUEMOY
QUEZON
QUINOA
RULEON
RUNFOR
RUNSON
RUNYON
SUCCOR
SUITOR
SUMMON
SUNDOG
SUNGOD
SUTTON
TUCSON
TURBOS
TURBOT
TURGOR
TURNON

•U•••O
AUSTRO
BUMPPO
BURGOO
CUCKOO
CUMULO
DUELLO
GUNGHO
JURADO
KUOPIO
LUPINO
MURANO
MUTATO
NUCLEO
NUMERO
NUNCIO
PUEBLO
PUERTO
PUTSTO
QUANGO
QUARTO
RUBATO
RUNSTO
SUBITO
SUNOCO
TUPELO
TURNTO
TUXEDO
YUNGLO

••UO••
FLUORO
GLUONS
TAUONS

••U•O•
BLUEOX
BOUBOU
COUPON
CRUSOE
ETUXOR
GOUNOD
MOUTON
NEUROL
NEURON
SPURON
STUPOR
TAUTOG
TEUTON
TOULON
YAUPON
ZHUKOV

••U••O
AQUINO
BHUTTO
CAUCHO
CHURRO
FLUORO
GAUCHO
JOURNO
SLUGGO
STUCCO
STUDIO

•••UO•
LIQUOR
PEQUOD
PEQUOT

•••U•O
ARTURO
BAGUIO
CARUSO
COLUGO
CUMULO
ENDURO
ESCUDO
IMMUNO
MADURO
MAPUTO
MODULO
PSEUDO
SENUFO
TENUTO

••••UO
BANQUO

UP••••
UPASES
UPBEAT
UPBOWS
UPCAST
UPDATE
UPDIKE
UPENDS
UPHELD
UPHILL
UPHOLD
UPJOHN
UPKEEP
UPLAND
UPLIFT
UPLINK
UPLOAD
UPMOST
UPPERS
UPPING
UPPISH
UPPITY
UPRISE
UPROAR
UPROOT
UPROSE
UPRUSH
UPSETS
UPSHOT
UPSIDE
UPTAKE
UPTALK
UPTICK
UPTIME
UPTOWN
UPTURN
UPWARD
UPWELL
UPWIND

U•P•••
UMPIRE
UNPACK
UNPAID
UNPEGS
UNPENS
UNPILE
UNPINS
UNPLUG
UPPERS
UPPING
UPPISH
UPPITY

U••P••
UNIPOD
UNOPEN
USOPEN
UTOPIA

U•••P•
UNCAPS
UNRIPE
UNZIPS
USURPS

U••••P
UNSNAP
UNSTOP
UNTRAP
UNWRAP
UPKEEP
USEDUP
USESUP

•UP•••
AUPAIR
CUPELS
CUPFUL
CUPIDS
CUPOLA
CUPPAS
CUPPED
CUPRIC
DUPERY
DUPING
DUPLEX
DUPONT
EUPNEA
LUPINE
LUPINO
LUPONE
MUPPET
PUPILS
PUPPET
RUPAUL
RUPEES
RUPERT
RUPIAH
SUPERB
SUPERS
SUPINE
SUPPED
SUPPER
SUPPLE
SUPPLY
TUPELO
TUPIAN
YUPPIE

•U•P••
AUSPEX
BUMPED
BUMPER
BUMPPO
BUMPUP
BURPED
CUPPAS
CUPPED
CUSPED
CUSPID
DUMPED
DUMPER
GULPED
GULPER
HUMPED
HUMPHS
JUMPAT
JUMPED
JUMPER
JUMPIN
JUMPON
JUMPUP
KUOPIO
KUSPUK
LUMPED
LUMPEN
LUMPER
LUMPUR
MUDPIE
MUMPED
MUPPET
MURPHY
OUTPUT
PULPED
PULPIT
PUMPED
PUMPER
PUMPUP
PUPPET
PURPLE
PURPLY
PUTPUT
QUIPPY
QUIPUS
RUMPLE
RUMPLY
RUMPUS
SUBPAR
SUPPED
SUPPER
SUPPLE
SUPPLY
TURPIN
YUPPIE

•U••P•
BUMPPO
CUTUPS
EUROPA
EUROPE
GUELPH
GUIMPE
JULEPS
QUIPPY
RUNUPS
SUMUPS
SUNUPS
TULIPS

•U•••P
BUCKUP
BUMPUP
BUMRAP
BUNYIP
BUOYUP
BURLAP
BURNUP
BUYSUP
CURLUP
CUTSUP
DUNLOP
DUSTUP
GUMSUP
HUBCAP
HUNGUP
JUMPUP
MUCKUP
MUSSUP
PULLUP
PUMPUP
PUSHUP
PUTSUP
RUNGUP
RUNSUP
SUITUP
SUMSUP
TUNEUP
TURNIP
TURNUP

••UP••
COUPES
COUPLE
COUPON
DRUPES
ERUPTS
LAUPER
LOUPES
PAUPER
SOUPUP
STUPAS
STUPES
STUPID
STUPOR
TAUPES
TOUPEE
YAUPON

••U•P•
CHUMPS
CLUMPS
CLUMPY
EQUIPS
FOURPM
FRUMPS
FRUMPY
GRUMPS
GRUMPY
PLUMPS
SCULPT
SLUMPS
SLURPS
STUMPS
STUMPY
THUMPS
TRUMPS
USURPS

••U••P
DRUMUP
FOULUP
HAULUP
SHUTUP
SOUPUP

•••UP•
ABRUPT
CROUPY
CUTUPS
FIXUPS
GETUPS
GROUPS
IRRUPT
JAMUPS
LAYUPS
LETUPS
MIXUPS
MOPUPS
NIPUPS
OCCUPY
ONEUPS
PINUPS
POPUPS
RUNUPS
SCAUPS
SETUPS
SITUPS
STOUPS
SUMUPS
SUNUPS
SYRUPS
SYRUPY
TIEUPS
TIPUPS
TROUPE

•••U•P
GAZUMP

••••UP
ACESUP
ACTSUP
ADDSUP
ANTEUP
BACKUP
BALLUP
BANGUP
BEADUP
BEAMUP
BEARUP
BEATUP
BEEFUP
BIDSUP
BINDUP
BLEWUP
BLOWUP
BOBSUP
BONEUP
BOOTUP
BOREUP
BUCKUP
BUMPUP
BUOYUP
BURNUP
BUYSUP
CALLUP
CAMEUP
CATSUP

CHATUP
CHEWUP
CHINUP
CLAMUP
CLOGUP
COILUP
COMEUP
COOKUP
COOPUP
CROPUP
CURLUP
CUTSUP
DAMSUP
DIALUP
DIGSUP
DOESUP
DOLLUP
DONEUP
DRAWUP
DREWUP
DRUMUP
DUSTUP
EASEUP
EATSUP
EGGCUP
ENDSUP
EVENUP
EYECUP
FACEUP
FAIRUP
FESSUP
FILLUP
FIREUP
FIRMUP
FLIPUP
FOGSUP
FOLDUP
FOULUP
GALLUP
GANGUP
GAVEUP
GEARUP
GETSUP
GIVEUP
GOESUP
GOOFUP
GREWUP
GROWUP
GUMSUP
HANDUP
HANGUP
HARDUP
HAULUP
HEADUP
HEATUP
HELDUP
HICCUP
HIGHUP
HIKEUP
HITSUP
HOLDUP
HOLEUP
HOOKUP
HOPSUP
HUNGUP
HYPEUP
ICEDUP
ICESUP
JACKUP
JAMSUP
JAZZUP
JOINUP
JUMPUP
KEEPUP
KEPTUP
KEYSUP
KICKUP
LACEUP
LAIDUP
LAPSUP
LARRUP
LASHUP
LAYSUP
LEADUP
LETSUP
LIFTUP
LINEUP
LINKUP
LOCKUP
LOOKUP
MADEUP
MAKEUP
MARKUP
MESSUP
MOCKUP
MOPSUP
MOVEUP
MUCKUP
MUSSUP
OPENUP
OWNSUP
PACKUP
PAIDUP
PAIRUP
PASSUP
PAYSUP
PENTUP
PEPSUP
PERKUP
PICKUP
PILEUP
PIPEUP
PLAYUP
PONYUP
POPSUP
PRENUP
PROPUP
PULLUP
PUMPUP
PUSHUP
PUTSUP
RACKUP
RAKEUP
RANGUP
RAVEUP
REARUP
RECOUP
RESTUP
REVSUP
RIGSUP
RILEUP
RINGUP
RIPSUP
ROLLUP
RUNGUP
RUNSUP
SANNUP
SAVEUP
SEALUP
SENDUP
SENTUP
SETSUP
SEWNUP
SEWSUP
SHOTUP
SHOWUP
SHUTUP
SIGNUP
SITSUP
SIZEUP
SLAPUP
SLIPUP
SLOWUP
SNAPUP
SOAKUP
SOPSUP
SOUPUP
SPEDUP
STAYUP
STEPUP
STIRUP
STOPUP
SUITUP
SUMSUP
TAGSUP
TAKEUP
TALKUP
TANKUP
TEACUP
TEAMUP
TEARUP
TEEDUP
TEESUP
TIDYUP
TIEDUP
TIESUP
TITTUP
TONEUP
TOOKUP
TOOLUP
TOREUP
TOSSUP
TOTSUP
TRIPUP
TUNEUP
TURNUP
TYPEUP
USEDUP
USESUP
WADSUP
WAITUP
WAKEUP
WALKUP
WALLUP
WARMUP
WASHUP
WELLUP
WENTUP
WHIPUP
WINDUP
WIPEUP
WISEUP
WOKEUP
WORKUP
WRAPUP
ZIPSUP

U••Q••

UBIQUE
UNIQUE

•UQ•••

BUQSHA
TUQUES

•U•Q••

CUIQUE
PULQUE
QUOQUE

•U•••Q

SUSIEQ

UR••••

URACIL
URAEUS
URALIC
URALSK
URANIA
URANIC
URANUS
URBANA
URBANE
URCHIN
URGENT
URGERS
URGING
URIALS
URSIDS
URSINE
URSULA
URTEXT
URUSES

U•R•••

UGRIAN
UNREAD
UNREAL
UNREEL
UNREST
UNRIGS
UNRIPE
UNROBE
UNROLL
UNROOT
UNRULY
UPRISE
UPROAR
UPROOT
UPROSE
UPRUSH

U••R••

ULTRAS
UMBRAE
UMBRAL
UMBRAS
UMBRIA
UNARMS
UNDRAW
UNFREE
UNTRAP
UNTROD
UNTRUE
UNWRAP
USERID
USURER
USURPS
UTURNS

U•••R•

UAKARI
UDDERS
UIGURS
ULCERS
UMBERS
UMPIRE
UNBARS
UNBORN
UNCORK
UNCURL
UNFURL
UNGIRD
UNGIRT
UNHURT
UNSURE
UNTORN
UNWARY
UNWORN
UPPERS
UPTURN
UPWARD
URGERS
USHERS
UTTERS

U••••R

UGLIER
ULSTER
UNDOER
UNFAIR
UNITER
UNMOOR
UPROAR
USURER
UVULAR

•UR•••

AUREUS
AURIFY
AURIGA
AURORA
AUROUS
BURBLE
BURBLY
BURBOT
BURDEN
BUREAU
BURGAS
BURGEE
BURGER
BURGHS
BURGLE
BURGOO
BURGOS
BURIED
BURIES
BURINS
BURLAP
BURLED
BURLEY
BURMAN
BURNED
BURNER
BURNET
BURNEY
BURNUP
BUROAK
BURPED
BURRED
BURROS
BURROW
BURSAE
BURSAL
BURSAR
BURSAS
BURSES
BURSTS
BURTON
CURACY
CURARE
CURATE
CURBED
CURDED
CURDLE
CURERS
CURFEW
CURIAE
CURIAL
CURING
CURIOS
CURIUM
CURLED
CURLER
CURLEW
CURLEY
CURLUP
CURRED
CURSED
CURSES
CURSOR
CURTER
CURTIN
CURTIS
CURTIZ
CURTLY
CURTSY
CURULE
CURVED
CURVES
CURVET
CURZON
DURANT
DURBAN
DURBAR
DURBIN
DURESS
DURFEY
DURHAM
DURIAN
DURING
DURNED
DUROCS
DURYEA
EURAIL
EUREKA
EUROPA
EUROPE
FURIES
FURLED
FURORE
FURORS
FURRED
FURROW
FURZES
GURGLE
GURKHA
GURLEY
GURNEY
HURDLE
HURLED
HURLER
HURLEY
HURONS
HURRAH
HURRAY
HURTLE
JURADO
JURATS
JURIES
JURIST
JURORS
KURALT
KURGAN
KURILE
LURING
LURKED
MURALS
MURANO
MURCIA
MURDER
MURIEL
MURINE
MURMUR
MURPHY
MURRAY
MURRES
MURREY
MURROW
NURSED
NURSER
NURSES
PURACE
PURDAH
PURDUE
PUREED
PUREES
PURELY
PUREST
PURFLE
PURGED
PURGES
PURIFY
PURINA
PURINE
PURISM
PURIST
PURITY
PURLED
PURLIN
PURPLE
PURPLY
PURRED
PURRER
PURSED
PURSER
PURSES
PURSUE
PURVEY
QURUSH
SURAHS
SURELY
SUREST
SURETE
SURETY
SURFED
SURFER
SURGED
SURGES
SURIMI
SURREY
SURTAX
SURVEY
TURBAN
TURBID
TURBIT
TURBOS
TURBOT
TUREEN
TURFED
TURGID
TURGOR
TURING
TURKEY
TURKIC
TURNED
TURNER
TURNIN
TURNIP
TURNON
TURNTO
TURNUP
TURPIN
TURRET
TURTLE
TURVES
WURLEY
WURSTS
YUROKS
ZURICH

•U•R••

AUBREY
AUDREY
BUMRAP
BURRED
BURROS
BURROW
CUPRIC
CURRED
DUARTE
FURRED
FURROW
GUARDS
GUDRUN
GUERRE
GUIROS
HUBRIS
HURRAH
HURRAY
JUAREZ
KUDROW
KUKRIS
MUDRAS
MURRAY
MURRES
MURREY
MURROW
NUTRIA
OUTRAN
OUTRUN
PUERTO
PUGREE
PURRED
PURRER
PUTRID
QUARKS
QUARRY
QUARTO
QUARTS
QUARTZ
QUERNS
QUIRES
QUIRKS
QUIRKY
QUIRTS
QUMRAN
QUORUM
RUBRIC
SUDRAS
SUNRAY
SURREY
SUTRAS
TUAREG
TUGRIK
TURRET

•U••R•

AUBURN
AUGERS
AUGURS
AUGURY
AURORA
AUSTRO
BUMBRY
BUYERS
CUNARD
CURARE
CURERS
DUNERA
DUPERY
EUCHRE
EUDORA
FUGARD
FULCRA
FURORE
FURORS
FUTURE
GUERRE
GUITRY
HUBERT
HUMERI
HUMORS
HUNGRY
JURORS
LUGERS
LUSTRE
LUXURY
MUSERS
NUMERO
OUTCRY
QUADRI
QUARRY
RULERS
RUMORS
RUNDRY
RUPERT
SUBARU
SUBORN
SUBURB
SUGARS
SUGARY
SULTRY
SUNDRY
SUPERB
SUPERS
SUTURE
TUBERS
TUDORS
TULARE

TUNDRA
TUNERS
TUTORS
TUYERE

•U•••R

AUPAIR
AUTEUR
AUTHOR
BUFFER
BUGLER
BULGAR
BULGUR
BULWER
BUMMER
BUMPER
BUNKER
BUNTER
BURGER
BURNER
BURSAR
BUSBAR
BUSIER
BUSTER
BUTLER
BUTTER
BUZZER
CULLER
CULVER
CUMBER
CURLER
CURSOR
CURTER
CUSTER
CUTLER
CUTTER
DUELER
DUFFER
DUIKER
DULLER
DUMBER
DUMPER
DUNBAR
DUNKER
DURBAR
DUSTER
FUELER
FULLER
FULMAR
FUMIER
GUITAR
GULPER
GUNFOR
GUNNAR
GUNNER
GUNTER
GUSHER
GUTTER
HUGGER
HULLER
HUMMER
HUMOUR
HUNGER
HUNKER
HUNTER
HURLER
HUSKER
HUSSAR
JUDDER
JUICER
JUMPER
JUNIOR
JUNKER
JUSTER
KULTUR
LUBBER
LUGGER
LUMBAR
LUMBER
LUMPER
LUMPUR
LUNKER
LUSHER
LUSTER
LUTHER
LUTHOR
MUDDER
MUGGER
MULLER
MUMMER
MURDER
MURMUR
MUSHER
MUSTER
MUTTER
NUDGER
NUMBER
NURSER
NUTTER
OUSTER
PUCKER
PUFFER
PULSAR
PUMPER
PUNIER
PUNKER
PUNTER
PURRER
PURSER
PUTTER
QUAKER
QUASAR
QUAVER
QUEUER
QUIVER
QUOTER
RUBBER
RUDDER
RUINER
RUMMER
RUMOUR
RUNFOR
RUNNER
RUTGER
SUAVER
SUBPAR
SUCCOR
SUCKER
SUFFER
SUITOR
SULFUR
SULKER
SUMMER
SUMNER
SUMTER
SUNDER
SUPPER
SURFER
SUTLER
SUTTER
TUCKER
TUGGER
TURGOR
TURNER
TUSKER
VULGAR
ZUIDER

••UR••

ANURAN
BEURRE
BLURBS
BLURRY
BLURTS
BOURKE
BOURNE
BOURSE
CHURCH
CHURLS
CHURNS
CHURRO
CHURRS
COURIC
COURSE
COURTS
CRURAL
DOURER
DOURLY
ENURED
ENURES
EXURBS
FLURRY
FOURAM
FOURPM
FOURTH
GOURDE
GOURDS
HOURIS
HOURLY
INURED
INURES
ITURBI
JAURES
JOURNO
KAURIS
KNURLS
KNURLY
LAUREL
LAUREN
LAURIE
MAURYA
MOURNS
NEURAL
NEUROL
NEURON
PLURAL
POURED
POURER
POURIN
ROURKE
SAUREL
SCURFY
SCURRY
SCURVE
SCURVY
SEURAT
SLURPS
SLURRY
SMURFS
SOURCE
SOURED
SOURER
SOURLY
SPURGE
SPURNS
SPURON
SPURRY
SPURTS
STURDY
TAURUS
TOURED
TOURER
TSURIS
USURER
USURPS
UTURNS

••U•R•

BEURRE
BLURRY
CHURRO
CHURRS
EDUARD
FLUORO
FLURRY
GLUERS
LOUVRE
OEUVRE
SCURRY
SLURRY
SOUARI
SPURRY
SQUARE
SQUIRE
SQUIRM
SQUIRT
STUART

••U••R

ABUKIR
ABUSER
ALULAR
BRUDER
CHUKAR
COUGAR
COUTER
CRUDER
DAUBER
DOURER
ELUDER
ETUXOR
FOULER
GAUGER
GLUIER
GOUGER
HAULER
KRUGER
LAUDER
LAUPER
LOUDER
LOUVER
MAULER
MAUSER
MOUSER
NEUTER
OCULAR
OVULAR
PAUPER
POURER
POUTER
PRUNER
REUTER
ROUSER
ROUTER
SAUCER
SAUGER
SOURER
SOUTER
STUMER
STUPOR
TAUTER
TOURER
TOUTER
USURER
UVULAR

•••UR•

ABJURE
ABSURD
ADJURE
ALLURE
AMOURS
ARMURE
ARTURO
ASBURY
ASSURE
AUBURN
AUGURS
AUGURY
COBURG
COBURN
CONURE
DATURA
DEJURE
DEMURE
DEMURS
ENDURE
ENDURO
ENSURE
ERFURT
FEMURS
FIGURE
FLEURY
FLOURS
FLOURY
FUTURE
IMMURE
IMPURE
INCURS
INJURE
INJURY
INSURE
INTURN
LEMURS
LIGURE
LUXURY
MADURA
MADURO
MATURE
MOHURS
NATURA
NATURE
OCCURS
ODOURS
ORDURE
PARURE
PENURY
PLEURA
REBURY
RECURS
RETURN
SATURN
SCOURS
SECURE
SEGURA
SIGURD
SOEURS
SUBURB
SUTURE
TENURE
UIGURS
UNCURL
UNFURL
UNHURT
UNSURE
UPTURN
YOGURT

•••U•R

ARGUER
BREUER
ISSUER
JAGUAR
LIQUOR
QUEUER
VAGUER

••••UR

ARBOUR
ARDOUR
ARMOUR
ARTHUR
AUTEUR
BENHUR
BIGSUR
BULGUR
COLOUR
CONCUR
DAMOUR
DETOUR
DEVOUR
DOLOUR
FAVOUR
HONOUR
HUMOUR
INPOUR
JAIPUR
KIPPUR
KRONUR
KULTUR
LABOUR
LAMOUR
LANGUR
LATOUR
LUMPUR
MURMUR
NIPPUR
ONTOUR
POSEUR
RAIPUR
RETOUR
RIGOUR
RUMOUR
SAVOUR
SIDDUR
SULFUR
VALOUR
VAPOUR
VELOUR
VIGOUR
WILBUR

US••••

USABLE
USABLY
USAGES
USANCE
USEDTO
USEDUP
USEFUL
USENET
USERID
USESUP
USHERS
USMAIL
USOPEN
USUALS
USURER
USURPS

U•S•••

UGSOME
ULSTER
UNSAFE
UNSAID
UNSAYS
UNSEAL
UNSEAT
UNSEEN
UNSEWN
UNSEWS
UNSHED
UNSHOD
UNSNAG
UNSNAP
UNSOLD
UNSOWN
UNSTOP
UNSUNG
UNSURE
UPSETS
UPSHOT
UPSIDE
URSIDS
URSINE
URSULA

U••S••

UKASES
UNESCO
UNISEX
UNISON
UNISYS
UNUSED
UPASES
URUSES
USESUP

U•••S•

UNBUSY
UNCASE
UNEASE
UNEASY
UNJUST
UNLASH
UNLESS
UNMASK
UNMESH
UNREST
UNWISE
UNWISH
UPCAST
UPMOST
UPPISH
UPRISE
UPROSE
UPRUSH
URALSK
UTMOST

U••••S

UBOATS
UBOLTS
UCLANS
UDDERS
UGGAMS
UGLIES
UHLANS
UIGURS
UINTAS
UKASES
ULCERS
ULTRAS
UMBELS
UMBERS
UMBRAS
UMIAKS
UNARMS
UNBARS
UNCAPS
UNCLES
UNDIES
UNDOES
UNFITS
UNGUES
UNGUIS
UNIATS
UNIONS
UNISYS
UNITAS
UNITES
UNJAMS
UNLESS
UNMANS
UNPEGS
UNPENS
UNPINS
UNRIGS
UNSAYS
UNSEWS
UNTIES
UNZIPS
UPASES
UPBOWS
UPENDS
UPPERS
UPSETS
URAEUS
URANUS
URGERS
URIALS
URSIDS
URUSES
USAGES
USHERS
USUALS
USURPS
UTTERS
UTURNS
UVULAS
UZBEKS

•US•••

AUSPEX
AUSSIE
AUSTEN
AUSTIN
AUSTRO
BUSBAR
BUSBOY
BUSHED
BUSHEL
BUSHES
BUSHWA
BUSIED
BUSIER
BUSIES
BUSILY
BUSING
BUSKED
BUSKIN
BUSMAN
BUSMEN
BUSONI
BUSSED
BUSSES
BUSTED
BUSTER
BUSTIN
BUSTLE
CUSACK
CUSHAW
CUSPED
CUSPID
CUSSED
CUSSES
CUSTER
CUSTIS
CUSTOM
CUSTOS
DUSTED
DUSTER
DUSTIN
DUSTUP
FUSEES
FUSILS
FUSING
FUSION
FUSSED
FUSSES
FUSTIC
GUSHED
GUSHER
GUSHES
GUSSET
GUSTAV
GUSTED
HUSHED
HUSHES
HUSKED
HUSKER
HUSSAR
HUSSEY
HUSTLE
HUSTON
JUSTER
JUSTIN
JUSTLY
KUSPUK

LUSAKA
LUSHER
LUSHLY
LUSTED
LUSTER
LUSTRE
MUSCAT
MUSCLE
MUSCLY
MUSERS
MUSEUM
MUSHED
MUSHER
MUSHES
MUSIAL
MUSING
MUSKEG
MUSKET
MUSKIE
MUSKOX
MUSLIM
MUSLIN
MUSSED
MUSSEL
MUSSES
MUSSUP
MUSTER
MUSTNT
OUSELS
OUSTED
OUSTER
PUSHED
PUSHES
PUSHON
PUSHUP
PUSSES
RUSHED
RUSHEE
RUSHES
RUSKIN
RUSSET
RUSSIA
RUSTED
RUSTIC
RUSTLE
SUSANN
SUSIEQ
SUSLIK
SUSSED
SUSSES
SUSSEX
TUSCAN
TUSKED
TUSKER
TUSSAH
TUSSLE
WUSSES

•U•S••

AUSSIE
BUNSEN
BUQSHA
BURSAE
BURSAL
BURSAR
BURSAS
BURSES
BURSTS
BUSSED
BUSSES
BUYSUP
CUESTA
CUISSE
CURSED
CURSES
CURSOR
CUSSED
CUSSES
CUTSIN
CUTSUP
FUSSED
FUSSES
GUESTS
GUISES
GUMSUP
GUNSHY
GUSSET
HUDSON
HUSSAR
HUSSEY
MUSSED
MUSSEL
MUSSES
MUSSUP
NURSED
NURSER
NURSES
OUTSET
PUISNE
PULSAR
PULSED
PULSES
PURSED
PURSER
PURSES
PURSUE
PUSSES
PUTSBY
PUTSCH
PUTSIN
PUTSON
PUTSTO
PUTSUP
QUASAR
QUESTS
RUBSIN
RUNSAT
RUNSIN
RUNSON
RUNSTO
RUNSUP
RUSSET
RUSSIA
SUBSET
SUDSED
SUDSES
SUISSE
SUMSUP
SUNSET
SUSSED
SUSSES
SUSSEX
TUCSON
TULSAN
TUSSAH
TUSSLE
WURSTS
WUSSES

•U••S•

AUGUST
CUBISM
CUBIST
CUISSE
CURTSY
CUTEST
CUTESY
DUDISH
DURESS
HUGEST
JURIST
JUTISH
KUMISS
KUVASZ
LUGOSI
LUTIST
MUCOSA
MUFASA
MULISH
MUTEST
NUDEST
NUDIST
PUNISH
PUREST
PURISM
PURIST
QUEASY
QURUSH
RUDEST
RUGOSE
SUFISM
SUISSE
SUREST
TUBIST

•U•••S

AUDENS
AUDIOS
AUDITS
AUGERS
AUGHTS
AUGURS
AUREUS
AUROUS
AUXINS
BUDGES
BUENOS
BUFFOS
BUGLES
BUILDS
BULGES
BUNCOS
BUNKOS
BURGAS
BURGHS
BURGOS
BURIES
BURINS
BURROS
BURSAS
BURSES
BURSTS
BUSHES
BUSIES
BUSSES
BUTEOS
BUTTES
BUTUTS
BUYERS
BUZZES
CUBEBS
CUBICS
CUBITS
CULETS
CULLIS
CUPELS
CUPIDS
CUPPAS
CURERS
CURIOS
CURSES
CURTIS
CURVES
CUSSES
CUSTIS
CUSTOS
CUTIES
CUTINS
CUTUPS
CUVEES
DUBOIS
DUCATS
DULLES
DUNCES
DUOMOS
DURESS
DUROCS
DUTIES
DUVETS
FUDGES
FUGUES
FUNGUS
FURIES
FURORS
FURZES
FUSEES
FUSILS
FUSSES
FUTONS
FUTZES
FUZEES
FUZZES
GUACOS
GUARDS
GUAVAS
GUESTS
GUIDES
GUILDS
GUILES
GUIROS
GUISES
GULAGS
GUMBOS
GUSHES
GUYOTS
HUBRIS
HUEVOS
HUGHES
HULLOS
HUMANS
HUMMUS
HUMORS
HUMPHS
HURONS
HUSHES
HUZZAS
JUDGES
JUICES
JULEPS
JULIUS
JUMBOS
JUNCOS
JUNTAS
JUNTOS
JURATS
JURIES
JURORS
KUDZUS
KUKRIS
KULAKS
KUMISS
LUCIUS
LUDENS
LUGERS
LUMENS
LUNGES
LUTZES
MUCINS
MUCOUS
MUDRAS
MUFTIS
MUGHOS
MULCTS
MULEYS
MULLAS
MUNGOS
MURALS
MURRES
MUSERS
MUSHES
MUSSES
MUZZES
NUDGES
NUECES
NURSES
OUGHTS
OUNCES
OUSELS
OUZELS
PULSES
PUPILS
PUREES
PURGES
PURSES
PUSHES
PUSSES
PUTONS
QUACKS
QUAFFS
QUAILS
QUAKES
QUALMS
QUARKS
QUARTS
QUEENS
QUELLS
QUERNS
QUESTS
QUEUES
QUIETS
QUILLS
QUILTS
QUINTS
QUIPUS
QUIRES
QUIRKS
QUIRTS
QUOINS
QUOITS
QUOTAS
QUOTES
RUANAS
RUBENS
RUBIES
RUBLES
RUCHES
RUCKUS
RUFOUS
RULERS
RUMBAS
RUMENS
RUMORS
RUMPUS
RUNINS
RUNONS
RUNUPS
RUPEES
RUSHES
SUCCES
SUCHAS
SUCKAS
SUDRAS
SUDSES
SUEDES
SUGARS
SUITES
SULCUS
SUMACS
SUMMAS
SUMUPS
SUNNIS
SUNUPS
SUPERS
SURAHS
SURGES
SUSSES
SUTRAS
TUBERS
TUDORS
TULIPS
TULLES
TUNERS
TUNICS
TUQUES
TURBOS
TURVES
TUTORS
WURSTS
WUSSES
YUCCAS
YUROKS

••US••

ABUSED
ABUSER
ABUSES
AMUSED
AMUSES
BOUSED
BOUSES
BRUSHY
CAUSAL
CAUSED
CAUSES
COUSIN
CRUSES
CRUSOE
CRUSTS
CRUSTY
DOUSED
DOUSES
HAUSAS
HOUSED
HOUSES
JOUSTS
KYUSHU
LOUSED
LOUSES
MAUSER
MOUSED
MOUSER
MOUSES
MOUSEY
MOUSSE
NAUSEA
ONUSES
OPUSES
PAUSED
PAUSES
PLUSES
PLUSHY
POUSSE
REUSED
REUSES
ROUSED
ROUSER
ROUSES
ROUSTS
SLUSHY
SOUSED
SOUSES
THUSLY
TOUSLE
TRUSTS
TRUSTY
UNUSED
URUSES
WAUSAU

••U•S•

AGUISH
AVULSE
BLUEST
BLUESY
BLUISH
BOURSE
BRUISE
CHUHSI
CLUMSY
COURSE
CRUISE
EVULSE
LOUISA
LOUISE
MOUSSE
POUSSE
SQUASH
SQUISH
SQUUSH
TRUEST
TRUISM
TZUHSI

••U••S

ABUSES
ADULTS
AMUSES
ANUBIS
BAUCIS
BAULKS
BLUETS
BLUEYS
BLUFFS
BLUNTS
BLURBS
BLURTS
BOUGHS
BOULES
BOUNDS
BOUSES
BRUGES
BRUINS
BRUITS
BRULES
BRUMES
BRUNTS
BRUTES
BRUTUS
BRUXES
CAUCUS
CAULKS
CAUSES
CHUCKS
CHUMPS
CHUNKS
CHURLS
CHURNS
CHURRS
CHUTES
CLUCKS
CLUMPS
CLUNKS
COUGHS
COUNTS
COUPES
COURTS
CRUCES
CRUETS
CRUMBS
CRUSES
CRUSTS
CRUXES
DAUBES
DAUNTS
DEUCES
DOUBTS
DOUGHS
DOUSES
DRUIDS
DRUPES
DRUZES
EDUCES
ELUDES
ELUTES
ENURES
EQUALS
EQUIPS
ERUCTS
ERUPTS
ETUDES
EXUDES
EXULTS
EXURBS
FAUCES
FAULTS
FAUNAS
FAUNUS
FLUFFS
FLUIDS
FLUKES
FLUMES
FLUNKS
FLUTES
FLUXES
FOUNDS
FOUNTS
FRUITS
FRUMPS
GAUGES
GAUZES
GLUERS
GLUONS
GLUTES
GOUGES
GOURDS
GRUELS
GRUMPS
GRUNTS
GSUITS
HAULMS
HAUNTS
HAUSAS
HOUGHS
HOUNDS
HOURIS
HOUSES
INUITS
INURES
JAUNTS
JAURES
JOULES
JOUSTS
KAUNAS
KAURIS
KNURLS
LAUGHS
LOUGHS
LOUPES
LOUSES
MAUVES
MOULDS
MOULTS
MOUNDS
MOUNTS
MOURNS
MOUSES
MOUTHS
NEUMES
ONUSES
OPUSES
OVULES
PAUCIS
PAUSES
PLUCKS
PLUMBS
PLUMES
PLUMPS
PLUNKS
PLUSES
POULTS
POUNDS
PRUDES
PRUNES
REUNES
REUSES
RHUMBS
ROUGES
ROUGHS
ROUNDS
ROUSES

ROUSTS
ROUTES
SAUCES
SAUDIS
SAULTS
SAUNAS
SAUTES
SCUBAS
SCUFFS
SCULLS
SCUTES
SHUCKS
SHUNTS
SKULKS
SKULLS
SKUNKS
SLUMPS
SLURPS
SMURFS
SNUFFS
SOUGHS
SOUNDS
SOUSES
SOUTHS
SPUMES
SPURNS
SPURTS
SQUABS
SQUADS
SQUATS
SQUIBS
SQUIDS
STUFFS
STULLS
STUMPS
STUNTS
STUPAS
STUPES
TAUNTS
TAUONS
TAUPES
TAURUS
THUJAS
THUMBS
THUMPS
THUNKS
TOUGHS
TRUCES
TRUCKS
TRUMPS
TRUNKS
TRUSTS
TRUTHS
TSURIS
URUSES
USUALS
USURPS
UTURNS
UVULAS
VAULTS
VAUNTS
WOUNDS
YOUTHS

ZEUXIS
ZOUNDS

•••US•

ABLUSH
ACCUSE
ADJUST
AMBUSH
AROUSE
AUGUST
BEMUSE
BLOUSE
CARUSO
CAYUSE
CERUSE
CLAUSE
CREUSA
CROUSE
DEFUSE
DEGUST
DISUSE
EFFUSE
ENDUSE
EXCUSE
GOBUST
GROUSE
ILLUSE
INCUSE
INFUSE
INRUSH
LOCUST
MEDUSA
MISUSE
OBTUSE
ONRUSH
PERUSE
PROUST
QURUSH
RECUSE
REFUSE
ROBUST
SCHUSS
SCOUSE
SPOUSE
SQUUSH
THRUSH
THRUST
UNBUSY
UNJUST
UPRUSH
WATUSI

•••U•S

ALBUMS
ALEUTS
AMOURS
AMPULS
ANNULS
ARGUES
AUGURS
BABULS
BEAUTS
BEGUMS
BOSUNS
BUTUTS
CAGUAS
CAJUNS
CLOUDS
CLOUTS
CUTUPS
DEBUGS
DEBUTS
DEMURS
DONUTS
ENDUES
ENSUES
FEMURS
FIXUPS
FLOURS
FLOUTS
FORUMS
FRAUDS
FUGUES
GAMUTS
GETUPS
GHOULS
GIGUES
GROUPS
GROUTS
IMBUES
INCURS
INPUTS
ISSUES
JAMUPS
JORUMS
KHOUMS
KNOUTS
LAYUPS
LEHUAS
LEMURS
LETUPS
LIEUTS
MAQUIS
MIXUPS
MOGULS
MOHURS
MOPUPS
NIPUPS
OCCURS
ODIUMS
ODOURS
ONEUPS
PICULS
PINUPS
PIQUES
POPUPS
PSEUDS
QUEUES
REBUTS
RECURS
REDUBS
RERUNS
REVUES
RHEUMS
ROGUES
RUNUPS
SCAUPS
SCHUSS
SCOURS
SCOUTS
SCRUBS
SCRUMS
SEDUMS
SEGUES
SERUMS
SETUPS
SHOUTS
SHRUBS
SHRUGS
SITUPS
SNOUTS
SOEURS
SPOUTS
SPRUES
STOUPS
STOUTS
STRUMS
STRUTS
SUMUPS
SUNUPS
SYRUPS
THRUMS
TIEUPS
TIPUPS
TOQUES
TROUTS
TUQUES
UIGURS
UNGUES
UNGUIS
VALUES
VENUES
VOGUES
YAKUTS
YAQUIS
YOKUTS

••••US

ABACUS
ACARUS
ACEOUS
ACINUS
ADIEUS
AEOLUS
AIRBUS
ALDOUS
ALTIUS
AMICUS
AMINUS
ANIMUS
ANJOUS
ATREUS
AUREUS
AUROUS
BACKUS
BANTUS
BAYOUS
BMINUS
BRUTUS
BYSSUS
CACTUS
CADMUS
CALLUS
CAMPUS
CARPUS
CAUCUS
CENSUS
CEREUS
CESTUS
CHIAUS
CHORUS
CIRCUS
CIRRUS
CITIUS
CITRUS
CLONUS
CMINUS
CNIDUS
COCCUS
COLEUS
CORPUS
COYPUS
CROCUS
CRONUS
CYGNUS
CYPRUS
DANAUS
DARIUS
DELIUS
DICTUS
DINGUS
DISCUS
DMINUS
DOOFUS
ELBRUS
ENNIUS
EPIRUS
EREBUS
EXODUS
FAMOUS
FAUNUS
FERGUS
FESTUS
FICHUS
FILIUS
FOETUS
FUNGUS
GENIUS
GRADUS
HAIKUS
HIATUS
HINDUS
HUMMUS
ICARUS
JANHUS
JOYOUS
JULIUS
KUDZUS
LIMBUS
LITMUS
LUCIUS
MAGNUS
MAIDUS
MANAUS
MARCUS
MARIUS
MISSUS
MOBIUS
MUCOUS
NEREUS
NIMBUS
OBELUS
ODIOUS
PALPUS
PAPPUS
PELEUS
PILEUS
PINDUS
PLEXUS
POILUS
PONTUS
POROUS
PRIMUS
QUIPUS
RADIUS
RAMOUS
RECTUS
REGIUS
RHESUS
RUCKUS
RUFOUS
RUMPUS
SADHUS
SEAMUS
SEROUS
SHAMUS
SIRIUS
SIXTUS
SNAFUS
SOLEUS
STATUS
STRAUS
STYLUS
SULCUS
TARSUS
TAURUS
TEMPUS
TEREUS
THYMUS
TOPHUS
TYPHUS
URAEUS
URANUS
VENOUS
VERSUS
VILLUS
VINOUS
VIRTUS
VOROUS
WALRUS

UT••••

UTAHAN
UTHANT
UTMOST
UTOPIA
UTTERS
UTURNS

U•T•••

ULTIMA
ULTIMO
ULTRAS
UMTATA
UNTACK
UNTIDY
UNTIED
UNTIES
UNTOLD
UNTORN
UNTRAP
UNTROD
UNTRUE
UNTUNE
UPTAKE
UPTALK
UPTICK
UPTIME
UPTOWN
UPTURN
URTEXT
UTTERS

U••T••

UINTAS
ULSTER
UNITAL
UNITAS
UNITED
UNITER
UNITES
UNSTOP

U•••T•

UBIETY
UBOATS
UBOLTS
UMTATA
UNFITS
UNIATE
UNIATS
UPDATE
UPPITY
UPSETS
USEDTO

U••••T

UMLAUT
UNBELT
UNBENT
UNBOLT
UNGIRT
UNHURT
UNJUST
UNKNIT
UNKNOT
UNMEET
UNREST
UNROOT
UNSEAT
UPBEAT
UPCAST
UPLIFT
UPMOST
UPROOT
UPSHOT
URGENT
URTEXT
USENET
UTHANT
UTMOST

•UT•••

AUTEUR
AUTHOR
AUTUMN
BUTANE
BUTENE
BUTEOS
BUTLER
BUTTED
BUTTER
BUTTES
BUTTIN
BUTTON
BUTUNG
BUTUTS
CUTELY
CUTEST
CUTESY
CUTIES
CUTINS
CUTLER
CUTLET
CUTOFF
CUTOUT
CUTSIN
CUTSUP
CUTTER
CUTUPS
DUTIES
EUTAXY
FUTILE
FUTONS
FUTURE
FUTZED
FUTZES
GUTTAE
GUTTED
GUTTER
HUTTED
HUTTON
JUTISH
JUTTED
LUTHER
LUTHOR
LUTING
LUTIST
LUTZES
MUTANT
MUTATE
MUTATO
MUTELY
MUTEST
MUTING
MUTINY
MUTTER
MUTTON
MUTUAL
NUTATE
NUTKIN
NUTLET
NUTMEG
NUTRIA
NUTTED
NUTTER
OUTACT
OUTAGE
OUTATE
OUTBID
OUTBOX
OUTCRY
OUTDID
OUTEAT
OUTFIT
OUTFLY
OUTFOX
OUTGUN
OUTHIT
OUTING
OUTLAW
OUTLAY
OUTLET
OUTPUT
OUTRAN
OUTRUN
OUTSET
OUTWIT
PUTNAM
PUTOFF
PUTONS
PUTOUT
PUTPUT
PUTRID
PUTSBY
PUTSCH
PUTSIN
PUTSON
PUTSTO
PUTSUP
PUTTED
PUTTEE
PUTTER
RUTGER
RUTILE
RUTTAN
RUTTED
SUTLER
SUTRAS
SUTTER
SUTTON
SUTURE
TUTORS
TUTTUT
TUTUED

•U•T••

AUNTIE
AUSTEN
AUSTIN
AUSTRO
BUNTED
BUNTER
BURTON
BUSTED
BUSTER
BUSTIN
BUSTLE
BUTTED
BUTTER
BUTTES
BUTTIN
BUTTON
CULTIC
CURTER
CURTIN
CURTIS
CURTIZ
CURTLY
CURTSY
CUSTER
CUSTIS
CUSTOM
CUSTOS
CUTTER
DUCTAL
DUSTED
DUSTER
DUSTIN
DUSTUP
FULTON
FUSTIC
GUITAR
GUITRY
GUNTER
GUSTAV
GUSTED
GUTTAE
GUTTED
GUTTER
HUNTED
HUNTER
HURTLE
HUSTLE
HUSTON
HUTTED
HUTTON
JUNTAS
JUNTOS
JUSTER
JUSTIN
JUSTLY
JUTTED
KULTUR
LUSTED
LUSTER
LUSTRE

MUFTIS
MULTUM
MUNTIN
MUSTER
MUSTNT
MUTTER
MUTTON
NUTTED
NUTTER
OUSTED
OUSTER
PUNTED
PUNTER
PUTTED
PUTTEE
PUTTER
QUETTA
QUITIT
QUOTAS
QUOTED
QUOTER
QUOTES
QUOTHA
RUSTED
RUSTIC
RUSTLE
RUTTAN
RUTTED
SUBTLE
SUBTLY
SUITED
SUITES
SUITOR
SUITUP
SULTAN
SULTRY
SUMTER
SUNTAN
SURTAX
SUTTER
SUTTON
TUFTED
TURTLE
TUTTUT

•U••T•

AUDITS
AUGHTS
BURSTS
BUTUTS
CUBITS
CUESTA
CULETS
CURATE
DUARTE
DUCATS
DULUTH
DUVETS
GUESTS
GUILTY
GUNITE
GUYOTS
JUDITH
JURATS
LUCITE
LUNATE
LUXATE
MULCTS
MULETA
MUTATE
MUTATO
NUDITY
NUTATE
OUGHTS
OUTATE
PUENTE
PUERTO
PURITY
PUTSTO
QUANTA
QUARTO
QUARTS
QUARTZ
QUESTS
QUETTA
QUIETS
QUILTS
QUINTS
QUIRTS
QUOITS
RUBATI
RUBATO
RUGATE
RUNSTO
SUBITO
SURETE
SURETY
TUBATE
TURNTO
WURSTS
YUKATA

•U•••T

AUFAIT
AUGUST
AUKLET
AULAIT
AUMONT
BUCKET
BUDGET
BUFFET
BUGOUT
BULLET
BUMOUT
BURBOT
BURNET
BUYOUT
CUBIST
CULLET
CURVET
CUTEST
CUTLET
CUTOUT
DUGOUT
DULCET
DUMONT
DUNANT
DUPONT
DURANT
GULLET
GUSSET
HUBERT
HUGEST
JULIET
JUMPAT
JUNKET
JURIST
KURALT
KUWAIT
LUCENT
LUGNUT
LUTIST
MUDCAT
MULLET
MUPPET
MUSCAT
MUSKET
MUSTNT
MUTANT
MUTEST
NUDEST
NUDIST
NUGENT
NUGGET
NUMBAT
NUTLET
OUTACT
OUTEAT
OUTFIT
OUTHIT
OUTLET
OUTPUT
OUTSET
OUTWIT
PULLET
PULPIT
PUNDIT
PUNNET
PUPPET
PUREST
PURIST
PUTOUT
PUTPUT
QUAINT
QUITIT
RUBOUT
RUDEST
RUNLET
RUNOUT
RUNSAT
RUPERT
RUSSET
SUBLET
SUBMIT
SUBSET
SUMMIT
SUNLIT
SUNSET
SUREST
TUBIST
TUCKET
TUFFET
TUMULT
TURBIT
TURBOT
TURRET
TUTTUT

••UT••

BHUTAN
BHUTTO
BRUTAL
BRUTES
BRUTUS
CHUTED
CHUTES
CLUTCH
COUTER
CRUTCH
ELUTED
ELUTES
FLUTED
FLUTES
FLUTEY
FRUTTI
GLUTEI
GLUTEN
GLUTES
KLUTZY
MOUTHS
MOUTHY
MOUTON
NAUTCH
NEUTER
POUTED
POUTER
REUTER
ROUTED
ROUTER
ROUTES
SAUTES
SCUTCH
SCUTES
SHUTIN
SHUTUP
SMUTCH
SMUTTY
SOUTER
SOUTHS
TAUTEN
TAUTER
TAUTLY
TAUTOG
TEUTON
TOUTED
TOUTER
TRUTHS
YOUTHS

••U•T•

ACUATE
ACUITY
ADULTS
AQUATE
BHUTTO
BLUETS
BLUNTS
BLURTS
BOUNTY
BRUITS
BRUNTS
COUNTS
COUNTY
COURTS
CRUETS
CRUSTS
CRUSTY
DAUNTS
DOUBTS
EQUATE
EQUITY
ERUCTS
ERUPTS
EXULTS
FAULTS
FAULTY
FOUNTS
FOURTH
FRUITS
FRUITY
FRUTTI
GRUNTS
GSUITS
HAUNTS
INUITS
JAUNTS
JAUNTY
JOUSTS
MOULTS
MOUNTS
MOUNTY
POULTS
ROUSTS
SAULTS
SHUNTS
SMUTTY
SPURTS
SQUATS
STUNTS
STUNTY
TAUNTS
TRUSTS
TRUSTY
VAULTS
VAULTY
VAUNTS

••U••T

AMULET
BLUEST
BOUGHT
BRUNET
CAUGHT
FAUCET
FLUENT
FOUGHT
GOULET
NAUGHT
NOUGAT
NOUGHT
SCULPT
SEURAT
SOUGHT
SQUINT
SQUIRT
STUART
TAUGHT
TRUANT
TRUEST
YOUBET

•••UT•

AGOUTI
ALEUTS
ASTUTE
BEAUTS
BEAUTY
BUTUTS
CANUTE
CLOUTS
CROUTE
DEBUTS
DEPUTE
DEPUTY
DILUTE
DONUTS
DULUTH
EMEUTE
FLOUTS
GAMUTS
GROUTS
GROUTY
IMPUTE
INPUTS
KNOUTS
LAPUTA
LIEUTS
MAKUTA
MAPUTO
MINUTE
PAIUTE
REBUTS
REFUTE
REPUTE
SALUTE
SCOUTS
SHOUTS
SLEUTH
SNOUTS
SOLUTE
SPOUTS
STOUTS
STRUTS
TENUTO
TROUTS
VOLUTE
YAKUTS
YOKUTS

•••U•T

ABDUCT
ABRUPT
ACQUIT
ADDUCT
ADJUST
AMOUNT
ANNUIT
AUGUST
AVAUNT
COQUET
DEDUCT
DEGUST
ERFURT
EXEUNT
FLAUNT
GOBUST
HLHUNT
INCULT
INDUCT
INSULT
INTUIT
IRRUPT
ISEULT
JESUIT
LOCUST
LOQUAT
MINUET
MINUIT
OCCULT
PENULT
PEQUOT
PIQUET
PROUST
RELUCT
RESULT
ROBUST
THRUST
TUMULT
UNHURT
UNJUST
YOGURT

••••UT

ABLAUT
ACEOUT
ACTOUT
AIROUT
ALLBUT
ALLOUT
ASKOUT
ATEOUT
BEIRUT
BOWOUT
BUGOUT
BUMOUT
BUYOUT
CAPNUT
CATGUT
COPOUT
CUTOUT
DEVOUT
DIEOUT
DIGOUT
DIMOUT
DRYOUT
DUGOUT
EATOUT
EKEOUT
ENGLUT
FANOUT
FAROUT
FLYOUT
GETOUT
GOTOUT
HELMUT
HEXNUT
HIDOUT
HITOUT
ICEOUT
INARUT
KORBUT
LAYOUT
LEDOUT
LETOUT
LITOUT
LOGOUT
LUGNUT
MAHOUT
MAXOUT
MEERUT
OPTOUT
OUTPUT
PANOUT
PAYOUT
PEANUT
PIGNUT
PIGOUT
POPOUT
PUTOUT
PUTPUT
QIVIUT
RAGOUT
RAJPUT
RANOUT
RIPOUT
ROTGUT
RUBOUT
RUNOUT
SALYUT
SATOUT
SAWOUT
SEEOUT
SETOUT
SITOUT
SPROUT
TAGOUT
TAPOUT
TOPOUT
TRYOUT
TUTTUT
UMLAUT
WALNUT
WAYOUT
WIGOUT
WINOUT
WONOUT
XEDOUT

U•U•••

UNUSED
URUSES
USUALS
USURER
USURPS
UTURNS
UVULAE
UVULAR
UVULAS

U••U••

UIGURS
UNBUSY
UNCURL
UNDULY
UNFURL
UNGUAL
UNGUES
UNGUIS
UNHURT
UNJUST
UNRULY
UNSUNG
UNSURE
UNTUNE
UPRUSH
UPTURN
URSULA

U•••U•

UBIQUE
UMLAUT
UNGLUE
UNIQUE
UNPLUG
UNTRUE
URAEUS
URANUS
USEDUP
USEFUL
USESUP
UVALUE

•UU•••

MUUMUU

•U•U••

AUBURN
AUGURS
AUGURY
AUGUST
AUTUMN
BUNUEL
BUTUNG
BUTUTS
CUMULI
CUMULO
CURULE
CUTUPS
DULUTH
FUGUES
FUTURE
JUJUBE
LUNULA
LUXURY
MUTUAL
QUEUED
QUEUER
QUEUES
QURUSH
RUNUPS
SUBURB
SUMUPS
SUNUNU
SUNUPS
SUTURE
SUZUKI
TUMULI
TUMULT
TUQUES
TUTUED

•U••U•

AUREUS
AUROUS
AUTEUR
BUCKUP
BUGOUT
BULBUL
BULGUR
BUMOUT
BUMPUP
BUNKUM
BUOYUP
BURNUP
BUYOUT
BUYSUP
CUIQUE
CUPFUL
CURIUM
CURLUP
CUTOUT
CUTSUP
DUGOUT
DUMDUM
DUSTUP
FUNGUS
GUDRUN
GUMSUP
HUBBUB
HUMBUG
HUMMUS
HUMOUR
HUNGUP
JUGFUL
JULIUS
JUMPUP
KUDZUS
KULTUR
KUNLUN
KUSPUK
LUCIUS

LUDLUM
LUGNUT
LUMPUR
MUCKUP
MUCOUS
MUKLUK
MULTUM
MURMUR
MUSEUM
MUSSUP
MUUMUU
OUTGUN
OUTPUT
OUTRUN
PULLUP
PULQUE
PUMPUP
PURDUE
PURSUE
PUSHUP
PUTOUT
PUTPUT
PUTSUP
QUIPUS
QUOQUE
QUORUM
RUBOUT
RUCKUS
RUEFUL
RUFOUS
RUMOUR
RUMPUS
RUNGUP
RUNOUT
RUNSUP
RUPAUL
SUBDUE
SUBGUM
SUITUP
SULCUS
SULFUR
SUMSUP
TUCHUN
TUNEUP
TURNUP
TUTTUT
YUMYUM

•U•••U
BUREAU
FUZHOU
HUNGWU
JUNEAU
KUNGFU
MUUMUU
SUBARU
SUNUNU
TUVALU

••UU••
SQUUSH

••U•U•
BRUTUS
CAUCUS
DRUMUP
FAUNUS
FOULUP
HAULUP
MUUMUU
SHUTUP
SOUPUP
TAURUS

••U••U
AKUAKU
BOUBOU
IGUACU
KYUSHU
MAUMAU
MBUNDU
MUUMUU
RYUKYU
WAUSAU

•••UU•
VACUUM

•••U•U
KIKUYU
SUNUNU
TELUGU

••••UU
MUUMUU

UV••••
UVALUE
UVULAE
UVULAR
UVULAS

U•V•••
UNVEIL

U••V••
UNEVEN
UNIVAC

U•••V•
UNWOVE

•UV•••
CUVEES
DUVALL
DUVETS
KUVASZ
TUVALU

•U•V••
CULVER
CURVED
CURVES
CURVET
GUAVAS
HUEVOS
HUMVEE
PURVEY
QUAVER
QUIVER
SUAVER
SURVEY
TURVES

•U••V•
BULOVA

•U•••V
GUSTAV
RUBLEV

••UV••
LOUVER
LOUVRE
MAUVES
OEUVRE

••U•V•
SCURVE
SCURVY
ZOUAVE

••U••V
ZHUKOV

•••UV•
TROUVE

U•W•••
UNWARY
UNWELL
UNWILY
UNWIND
UNWISE
UNWISH
UNWORN
UNWOVE
UNWRAP
UPWARD
UPWELL
UPWIND

U••W••
UNAWED

U•••W•
UNSEWN
UNSEWS
UNSOWN
UPBOWS
UPTOWN

U••••W
UNDRAW

•UW•••
KUWAIT

•U•W••
BULWER
LUDWIG
OUTWIT
RUNWAY
SUBWAY

•U••W•
BUSHWA
HUNGWU
YUKAWA

•U•••W
BURROW
CURFEW
CURLEW
CUSHAW
FURROW
GUFFAW
KUDROW
MURROW
OUTLAW
SUNDEW

••U•W•
SQUAWK

••••UW
DEPAUW

U•••X•
URTEXT

U••••X
UNISEX

•UX•••
AUXINS
HUXLEY
LUXATE
LUXURY
TUXEDO

•U••X•
CUNAXA
EUTAXY

•U•••X
AUSPEX
DUPLEX
LUMMOX
MUSKOX
OUTBOX
OUTFOX
SUFFIX
SURTAX
SUSSEX

••UX••
BRUXED
BRUXES
CRUXES
ETUXOR
FLUXED
FLUXES
ZEUXIS

••U••X
BLUEOX
CAUDEX
KOUFAX

•••UX•
DELUXE

••••UX
ADIEUX
BAYEUX
BIJOUX
EFFLUX
HALLUX
INFLUX
POLLUX
REFLUX

U•Y•••
UNYOKE

U••Y••
UNDYED

U•••Y•
UNISYS
UNSAYS

U••••Y
UBIETY
UGLIFY
UGLILY
UNBUSY
UNDULY
UNEASY
UNHOLY
UNOILY
UNRULY
UNTIDY
UNWARY
UNWILY
UPPITY
USABLY

•UY•••
BUYERS
BUYING
BUYOFF
BUYOUT
BUYSUP
GUYANA
GUYING
GUYOTS
TUYERE

•U•Y••
BUNYAN
BUNYIP
BUOYED
BUOYUP
DURYEA
QUAYLE
RUNYON
YUMYUM

•U••Y•
MULEYS

•U•••Y
AUBREY
AUDREY
AUGURY
AURIFY
BUBBLY
BUMBRY
BUNCHY
BURBLY
BURLEY
BURNEY
BUSBOY
BUSILY
CUDDLY
CURACY
CURLEY
CURTLY
CURTSY
CUTELY
CUTESY
DUALLY
DUDLEY
DUMBLY
DUPERY
DURFEY
EULOGY
EUTAXY
GUILTY
GUITRY
GUNSHY
GURLEY
GURNEY
HUBBLY
HUGELY
HUMBLY
HUNGRY
HURLEY
HURRAY
HUSSEY
HUXLEY
JUNGLY
JUSTLY
LUNACY
LUNCHY
LUSHLY
LUXURY
MUMBLY
MUNCHY
MURPHY
MURRAY
MURREY
MUSCLY
MUTELY
MUTINY
NUBBLY
NUDELY
NUDITY
NUMBLY
OUTCRY
OUTFLY
OUTLAY
PUDDLY
PULLEY
PUNCHY
PUNILY
PURELY
PURIFY
PURITY
PURPLY
PURVEY
PUTSBY
QUAGGY
QUARRY
QUEASY
QUEMOY
QUINCY
QUIPPY
QUIRKY
RUBBLY
RUBIFY
RUDELY
RUFFLY
RUMBLY
RUMPLY
RUNDRY
RUNWAY
SUBTLY
SUBWAY
SUGARY
SULTRY
SUNDAY
SUNDRY
SUNRAY
SUPPLY
SURELY
SURETY
SURREY
SURVEY
TUMEFY
TUNNEY
TURKEY
WURLEY

••UY••
NGUYEN

••U•Y•
BLUEYS
MAURYA
RYUKYU

••U••Y
ACUITY
BLUELY
BLUESY
BLURRY
BOUNCY
BOUNTY
BRUMBY
BRUSHY
CAUCHY
CHUBBY
CHUFFY
CHUMMY
CHUNKY
CLUBBY
CLUMPY
CLUMSY
CLUNKY
COUNTY
CRUDDY
CRUMBY
CRUMMY
CRUSTY
DOUBLY
DOUGHY
DOURLY
EQUITY
FAULTY
FLUFFY
FLUKEY
FLUNKY
FLURRY
FLUTEY
FOULLY
FRUITY
FRUMPY
GLUMLY
GRUBBY
GRUMPY
GRUNDY
GRUNGY
HOUNDY
HOURLY
JAUNTY
JOUNCY
KLUTZY
KNURLY
LOUDLY
MAUNDY
MOULDY
MOUNTY
MOUSEY
MOUTHY
PAULEY
PLUCKY
PLUMMY
PLUSHY
POUCHY
ROUGHY
SCULLY
SCUMMY
SCURFY
SCURRY
SCURVY
SCUZZY
SKUNKY
SLUDGY
SLUMMY
SLURRY
SLUSHY
SMUDGY
SMUGLY
SMUTTY
SNUBBY
SNUFFY
SNUGLY
SOURLY
SPUNKY
SPURRY
STUBBY
STUFFY
STUMPY
STUNTY
STURDY
TAUTLY
THUSLY
TOUCHY
TOUGHY
TRUSTY
VAULTY

•••UY•
INOUYE
KIKUYU

•••U•Y
ARGUFY
ASBURY
AUGURY
BEAUTY
CLOUDY
CROUPY
DEPUTY
FLEURY
FLOURY
GROUTY
INJURY
LUXURY
MAGUEY
OCCUPY
PENURY
REBURY
RHEUMY
SYRUPY
UNBUSY
UNDULY
UNRULY

••••UY
BADGUY
CLIQUY
GILGUY
TANGUY

UZ••••
UZBEKS
UZZIAH

U•Z•••
UNZIPS
UZZIAH

•UZ•••
BUZZED
BUZZER
BUZZES
FUZEES
FUZHOU
FUZING
FUZZED
FUZZES
GUZZLE
HUZZAH
HUZZAS
MUZHIK
MUZZED
MUZZES
MUZZLE
NUZZLE
OUZELS
PUZZLE
SUZUKI

•U•Z••
BUZZED
BUZZER
BUZZES
CURZON
FURZES
FUTZED
FUTZES
FUZZED
FUZZES
GUZZLE
HUZZAH
HUZZAS
KUDZUS
LUTZES
MUZZED
MUZZES
MUZZLE
NUZZLE
PUZZLE
QUEZON

•U•••Z
CURTIZ
JUAREZ
KUVASZ
QUARTZ

••UZ••
DRUZES
GAUZES
SCUZZY

••U•Z•
KLUTZY
SCUZZY

••U••Z
BOULEZ

•••UZ•
YAKUZA

•••U•Z
SCHULZ

••••UZ
HORMUZ
TAMMUZ

VA••••
VACANT
VACATE
VACHEL
VACLAV
VACUUM
VADOSE
VAGARY
VAGUER
VAINER
VAINLY
VAISYA
VALDEZ
VALENS
VALENT
VALERY
VALETS
VALISE
VALIUM
VALLEE
VALLEY
VALOIS
VALOUR
VALUED
VALUES
VALVED
VALVES
VAMPED
VAMPER
VANDAL
VANIER
VANISH
VANITY
VANNED
VANRYN
VAPORS
VAPORY
VAPOUR
VARDEN
VARESE
VARIED
VARIES
VARLET
VARNAS
VARNEY
VARUNA
VASHTI
VASLAV
VASSAL
VASSAR
VASTER
VASTLY
VATFUL
VATTED
VAUGHN
VAULTS
VAULTY
VAUNTS

V•A•••
VIABLE
VIABLY
VIACOM
VIANDS

V••A••
VACANT
VACATE
VAGARY
VEGANS
VICARS
VIRAGO
VISAED
VISAGE
VITALE
VITALS
VIVACE
VIVANT
VOCALS
VOLANS
VOLANT
VOLARE
VOTARY
VOYAGE

V•••A•
VACLAV
VANDAL
VARNAS
VASLAV
VASSAL
VASSAR
VEEJAY
VEINAL
VENIAL
VERBAL
VERNAL
VESTAL
VESTAS
VILLAS
VIOLAS
VISTAS
VISUAL
VIVIAN
VODKAS
VOLVAS
VULCAN
VULGAR

V••••A
VAISYA
VARUNA
VERONA
VICUNA
VIENNA
VIGODA
VIZSLA

•VA•••
AVAILS
AVALON
AVANTI
AVATAR
AVAUNT
EVADED
EVADER
EVADES
OVALLY
RVALUE
UVALUE

•V•A••
AVIANS
AVIARY
AVIATE

•V••A•
AVATAR
AVOWAL
DVORAK
OVISAC
OVULAR
UVULAE
UVULAR
UVULAS

•V•••A
AVESTA

••VA••
ARVADA
BOVARY
DIVANS
DUVALL
EDVARD
HAVANA
HAVASU
HIVAOA
INVADE
INVAIN
JAVARI
KOVACS
KUVASZ
LAVABO
LAVAGE
LEVANT
LOVAGE
NAVAHO
NAVAJO
NEVADA
NOVATO
PAVANE
RAVAGE
REVAMP
RIVALS
SAVAGE
SAVAII
SAVANT
SAVATE
TUVALU
VIVACE
VIVANT

••V•A•
CAVEAT
CAVIAR
FIVEAM
FOVEAE
GAVIAL
HAVEAT
JOVIAL
JOVIAN
KEVLAR
REVEAL
VIVIAN

••V••A
ARVADA
COVINA
ELVIRA
HAVANA
HIVAOA
NEVADA
NOVENA
RIVERA
WOVOKA

•••VA•
BRAVAS
CANVAS
CHEVAL
COEVAL
CRAVAT
GUAVAS
HALVAH
LARVAE
LARVAL
LARVAS
LEKVAR
SERVAL
SHEVAT
SILVAS
SLOVAK
SPIVAK
SYLVAN
UNIVAC
VOLVAS

•••V•A
FLAVIA
LATVIA
OLIVIA
PRAVDA
SALVIA
SYLVIA
TRIVIA

••••VA
BULOVA
CANOVA
CASAVA
GENEVA
GODIVA
MORAVA
MOSKVA
OTTAVA
SALIVA

V•B•••
VEBLEN
VYBORG

V••B••
VERBAL
VERBIS
VIABLE
VIABLY

••V•B•
LAVABO

••V••B
ADVERB
REVERB

VC••••
VCHIPS

V•C•••
VACANT
VACATE
VACHEL
VACLAV
VACUUM
VECTOR
VICARS
VICTIM
VICTIS
VICTOR
VICUNA
VOCALS

V••C••
VELCRO
VIACOM
VINCES
VINCIT
VISCID
VNECKS
VOICED
VOICES
VULCAN

V•••C•
VELOCE
VENICE
VIVACE
VOTECH

V••••C
VITRIC

•V•C••
AVOCET
EVICTS

•V••C•
AVOUCH
EVINCE
KVETCH

•V•••C
OVISAC

••V•C•
ADVICE
CIVICS
DEVICE
HAVOCS
KOVACS
NOVICE
VIVACE

•••V•C
OLDVIC
PELVIC
SLAVIC
STIVIC
UNIVAC

V•D•••
VADOSE
VEDDER
VIDEOS
VIDERI
VODKAS

V••D••
VALDEZ
VANDAL
VARDEN
VEDDER
VELDTS
VENDED
VENDEE
VENDOR
VERDIN
VERDON
VERDUN
VOIDED
VOODOO

V•••D•
VIANDS
VIGODA

V••••D
VALUED
VALVED
VAMPED
VANNED
VARIED
VATTED
VEERED
VEGGED
VEILED
VEINED
VENDED
VENTED
VERGED
VERSED
VESPID
VESTED
VETOED
VETTED
VIEWED
VISAED
VISCID
VOICED
VOIDED

•V•D••
AVEDON
AVIDLY
EVADED
EVADER
EVADES

•V••D•
AVOIDS
OVERDO
OVIEDO
OVOIDS

•V•••D
AVOWED
EVADED
EVENED
EVOKED

••V•D•
ARVADA
BOVIDS
DIVIDE
INVADE
NEVADA

••V••D
DEVOID
EDVARD
ENVIED
LEVEED
LEVIED
REVVED
RSVPED

•••VD•
PRAVDA

•••V•D
BRAVED
CALVED
CARVED
CERVID
CRAVED
CURVED
DELVED
FERVID
GLOVED
GRAVED
GRAVID
HALVED
HEAVED
KIDVID
LEAVED
PEEVED
PROVED
REEVED
REVVED
SALVED
SERVED
SHAVED
SHOVED
SIEVED
SKIVED
SLAVED
SOLVED
STAVED
VALVED
WAIVED
WEAVED

VE••••
VEBLEN
VECTOR
VEDDER
VEEJAY
VEERED
VEGANS
VEGGED
VEGGIE
VEIGHT
VEILED
VEINAL
VEINED
VELCRO
VELDTS
VELLUM
VELOCE
VELOUR
VELVET
VENDED
VENDEE
VENDOR
VENEER
VENETO
VENIAL
VENICE
VENIRE
VENITE
VENOMS
VENOUS
VENTED
VENTER
VENUES
VERBAL
VERBIS
VERDIN
VERDON
VERDUN
VEREEN
VERGED
VERGER
VERGES
VERIFY
VERILY
VERISM
VERITE
VERITY
VERMIN
VERNAL
VERNON
VERONA
VERSED
VERSES
VERSOS
VERSTS
VERSUS
VERTEX
VERVES
VERVET
VESPER
VESPID
VESSEL
VESTAL
VESTAS
VESTED
VESTEE
VESTRY
VETOED
VETOER
VETOES
VETTED
VEXERS
VEXING

V•E•••
VEEJAY
VEERED
VIENNA
VIENNE
VIEWED
VIEWER
VNECKS

V••E••
VALENS
VALENT
VALERY
VALETS
VARESE
VENEER
VENETO
VEREEN
VEXERS
VIDEOS
VIDERI
VILELY
VILEST
VINERY
VIPERS
VIREOS
VIXENS
VOLENS
VOTECH
VOTEIN
VOTERS
VOWELS
VOWELY
VOWERS

V•••E•
VACHEL
VAGUER
VAINER
VALDEZ
VALLEE
VALLEY
VALUED
VALUES
VALVED
VALVES
VAMPED
VAMPER
VANIER
VANNED
VARDEN
VARIED
VARIES
VARLET
VARNEY
VASTER
VATTED
VEBLEN
VEDDER
VEERED
VEGGED
VEILED
VEINED
VELVET
VENDED
VENDEE
VENEER
VENTED
VENTER
VENUES
VEREEN
VERGED
VERGER
VERGES
VERSED
VERSES
VERTEX
VERVES
VERVET
VESPER
VESSEL
VESTED
VESTEE
VETOED
VETOER
VETOES
VETTED
VIEWED
VIEWER
VINCES
VINIER
VIOLET
VISAED
VIVIEN
VIZIER

VOGUES
VOICED
VOICES
VOIDED
VOILES
VOLLEY
VORTEX
VOSGES
VSIXES

V••••E
VACATE
VADOSE
VALISE
VALLEE
VARESE
VEGGIE
VELOCE
VENDEE
VENICE
VENIRE
VENITE
VERITE
VESTEE
VIABLE
VIENNE
VINNIE
VIRILE
VIRTUE
VISAGE
VISINE
VITALE
VIVACE
VOLARE
VOLUME
VOLUTE
VOTIVE
VOYAGE

•VE•••
AVEDON
AVENGE
AVENUE
AVERNO
AVERSE
AVERTS
AVESTA
EVELYN
EVENED
EVENER
EVENKI
EVENLY
EVENSO
EVENTS
EVENUP
EVERLY
EVERSO
EVERTS
KVELLS
KVETCH
OVERDO
OVERLY
SVELTE
YVETTE

•V•E••
OVIEDO
TVSETS

•V••E•
AVOCET
AVOWED
AVOWER
EVADED
EVADER
EVADES
EVENED
EVENER
EVILER
EVOKED
EVOKER
EVOKES
OVULES

•V•••E
AVENGE
AVENUE
AVERSE
AVIATE
AVULSE
EVINCE
EVOLVE
EVONNE
EVULSE
EVZONE
RVALUE
SVELTE
UVALUE
UVULAE
YVETTE
YVONNE

••VE••
ADVENT
ADVERB
ADVERT
AMVETS
BEVELS
CAVEAT
CAVEIN
CAVELL
CAVERN
CAVERS
CAVETT
CIVETS
COVENS
COVENT
COVERS
COVERT
COVETS
COVEYS
CUVEES
DEVEIN
DEVEST
DIVEIN
DIVERS
DIVERT
DIVEST
DOVEIN
DUVETS
ELVERS
FEVERS
FIVEAM
FIVEPM
FIVERS
FIVEWS
FOVEAE
GAVEIN
GAVELS
GAVEUP
GIVEIN
GIVENS
GIVERS
GIVETO
GIVEUP
GOVERN
HAVEAT
HAVENS
HAVENT
HAVEON
HAVERS
HOVELS
HOVERS
HOVETO
INVENT
INVERT
INVEST
JIVERS
KEVELS
LAVERS
LEVEED
LEVEES
LEVELS
LEVENE
LEVERS
LIVEIN
LIVELY
LIVENS
LIVEON
LIVERS
LIVERY
LOVEIN
LOVELL
LOVELY
LOVERS
LOVETT
MAVENS
MOVEIN
MOVEON
MOVERS
MOVEUP
NAVELS
NEVERS
NOVELS
NOVENA
OBVERT
PAVERS
RAVELS
RAVENS
RAVERS
RAVEUP
REVEAL
REVELS
REVERB
REVERE
REVERS
REVERT
REVETS
RIVERA
RIVERS
RIVETS
ROVERS
SAVERS
SAVEUP
SEVENS
SEVERE
SEVERN
SEVERS
SEVERY
TAVERN
UNVEIL
WAVEIN
WAVERS
WAVERY
WYVERN

••V•E•
BEVIES
BOVVER
CUVEES
DAVIES
ENVIED
ENVIER
ENVIES
JAVIER
JIVIER
KAVNER
LEVEED
LEVEES
LEVIED
LEVIER
LEVIES
LIVRES
MOVIES
NAVIES
ONVIEW
REVIEW
REVUES
REVVED
RSVPED
SEVRES
SOVIET
VIVIEN
WAVIER
XAVIER

••V••E
ADVICE
ADVISE
BOVINE
DEVICE
DEVINE
DEVISE
DEVOTE
DIVIDE
DIVINE
FOVEAE
INVADE
INVITE
INVOKE
IRVINE
LAVAGE
LEVENE
LEVINE
LEVITE
LOVAGE
NOVICE
PAVANE
RAVAGE
RAVINE
REVERE
REVILE
REVISE
REVIVE
REVOKE
SAVAGE
SAVATE
SAVOIE
SEVERE
VIVACE

•••VE•
AGAVES
ALEVEL
ALFVEN
ASEVER
BEAVER
BEEVES
BOVVER
BRAVED
BRAVER
BRAVES
BREVES
BREVET
CALVED
CALVES
CARVED
CARVER
CARVES
CARVEY
CHAVEZ
CHEVET
CHIVES
CLAVES
CLEVER
CLEVES
CLOVEN
CLOVER
CLOVES
CONVEX
CONVEY
CORVEE
CORVES
CRAVED
CRAVEN
CRAVER
CRAVES
CULVER
CURVED
CURVES
CURVET
DELVED
DELVER
DELVES
DENVER
DRIVEL
DRIVEN
DRIVER
DRIVES
DROVER
DROVES
ELEVEN
ELEVES
GARVEY
GLOVED
GLOVER
GLOVES
GOOVER
GRAVED
GRAVEL
GRAVEN
GRAVER
GRAVES
GRIVET
GROVEL
GROVER
GROVES
HALVED
HALVES
HARVEY
HEAVED
HEAVEN
HEAVER
HEAVES
HELVES
HOOVER
HOOVES
HUMVEE
JAYVEE
JEEVES
KNAVES
KNIVES
LEAVED
LEAVEN
LEAVES
LOAVES
LOUVER
MARVEL
MAUVES
NERVES
OGIVES
OLEVEL
OLIVER
OLIVES
PEAVEY
PEEVED
PEEVES
PLOVER
PRIVET
PROVED
PROVEN
PROVER
PROVES
PURVEY
QUAVER
QUIVER
REEVED
REEVES
REVVED
SALVED
SALVER
SALVES
SELVES
SERVED
SERVER
SERVES
SHAVED
SHAVEN
SHAVER
SHAVES
SHIVER
SHOVED
SHOVEL
SHOVER
SHOVES
SIEVED
SIEVES
SILVER
SKIVED
SKIVER
SKIVES
SLAVED
SLAVER
SLAVES
SLAVEY
SLIVER
SLOVEN
SNIVEL
SOAVES
SOLVED
SOLVER
SOLVES
STAVED
STAVES
STEVEN
STIVER
STOVER
STOVES
SUAVER
SURVEY
SWIVEL
SWIVET
TEEVEE
TRAVEL
TRAVES
TRIVET
TROVES
TURVES
UNEVEN
VALVED
VALVES
VELVET
VERVES
VERVET
WAIVED
WAIVER
WAIVES
WEAVED
WEAVER
WEAVES
WOLVES

•••V•E
BMOVIE
CHEVRE
CORVEE
HUMVEE
JAYVEE
LARVAE
LOUVRE
OEUVRE
STEVIE
TEEVEE

••••VE
ACTIVE
ALCOVE
ARGIVE
ARRIVE
BEHAVE
BEHOVE
BYJOVE
CLEAVE
DATIVE
DERIVE
ENDIVE
EVOLVE
GENEVE
GREAVE
GRIEVE
GROOVE
INLOVE
MOHAVE
MOJAVE
MOTIVE
NATIVE
OCTAVE
PAREVE
RELIVE
REMOVE
REPAVE
REVIVE
REWOVE
SCURVE
SHEAVE
SHELVE
SHRIVE
SHROVE
SLEAVE
SLEEVE
STARVE
STEEVE
STRIVE
STROVE
SWERVE
THEYVE
THIEVE
THRIVE
THROVE
TROUVE
TWELVE
UNWOVE
VOTIVE
WHATVE
ZOUAVE

V••F••
VATFUL

V•••F•
VERIFY
VILIFY
VINIFY
VIVIFY

••V•F•
VIVIFY

V•G•••
VAGARY
VAGUER
VEGANS
VEGGED
VEGGIE
VIGILS
VIGODA
VIGORS
VIGOUR
VOGUES

V••G••
VAUGHN
VEGGED
VEGGIE
VEIGHT
VERGED
VERGER
VERGES
VIRGIL
VIRGIN
VOIGHT
VOSGES
VSIGNS
VULGAR

V•••G•
VIRAGO
VISAGE
VOYAGE

V••••G
VEXING
VIKING
VINING
VOTING
VOWING
VYBORG

•V••G•
AVENGE

••V•G•
LAVAGE
LOVAGE
RAVAGE
SAVAGE

••V••G
CAVING
DIVING
ERVING
GIVING
HAVING
HIVING
IRVING
JIVING
LAVING
LIVING
LOVING
MOVING
PAVING
RAVING
RIVING
ROVING
SAVING
WAVING

V•H•••
VCHIPS

V••H••
VACHEL
VASHTI
VISHNU

V•••H•
VAUGHN
VEIGHT
VOIGHT

V••••H
VANISH
VOTECH

•V•H••
TVSHOW

•V•••H
AVOUCH
KVETCH

••V•H•
NAVAHO

••V••H
DOVISH
ELVISH
LAVISH
RAVISH

•••V•H
HALVAH

VI••••
VIABLE
VIABLY
VIACOM
VIANDS
VICARS
VICTIM
VICTIS
VICTOR
VICUNA
VIDEOS
VIDERI
VIENNA
VIENNE
VIEWED
VIEWER
VIGILS
VIGODA
VIGORS
VIGOUR
VIKING
VILELY
VILEST
VILIFY
VILLAS
VILLON
VILLUS
VINCES
VINCIT
VINERY
VINIER
VINIFY
VINING
VINNIE
VINOUS
VINTON
VINYLS
VIOLAS
VIOLET
VIOLIN
VIPERS
VIRAGO
VIREOS
VIRGIL
VIRGIN
VIRILE
VIRTUE
VIRTUS
VISAED
VISAGE
VISCID
VISHNU
VISINE
VISION
VISITS
VISORS
VISTAS
VISUAL
VITALE
VITALS
VITRIC
VIVACE
VIVANT
VIVIAN
VIVIEN
VIVIFY
VIXENS
VIZIER
VIZSLA

V•I•••
VAINER
VAINLY
VAISYA
VEIGHT
VEILED
VEINAL
VEINED
VOICED
VOICES
VOIDED
VOIGHT
VOILES
VSIGNS
VSIXES

V••I••
VALISE
VALIUM
VANIER
VANISH
VANITY
VARIED
VARIES
VCHIPS
VENIAL
VENICE
VENIRE
VENITE
VERIFY
VERILY
VERISM
VERITE
VERITY
VEXING
VIGILS
VIKING
VILIFY
VINIER
VINIFY
VINING
VIRILE
VISINE
VISION
VISITS
VIVIAN
VIVIEN
VIVIFY
VIZIER
VOTING
VOTIVE
VOWING

V•••I•
VALOIS
VEGGIE
VERBIS
VERDIN
VERMIN
VESPID
VICTIM
VICTIS
VINCIT
VINNIE
VIOLIN
VIRGIL
VIRGIN
VISCID
VITRIC
VOTEIN

V••••I
VASHTI
VIDERI

•VI•••
AVIANS
AVIARY
AVIATE
AVIDLY
AVISOS
EVICTS
EVILER
EVILLY
EVINCE
OVIEDO
OVISAC

•V•I••
AVAILS
AVOIDS
OVOIDS

•V•••I
AVANTI
EVENKI

••VI••
ADVICE
ADVISE
ANVILS
BEVIES
BOVIDS
BOVINE
CAVIAR
CAVILS
CAVING
CAVITY
CIVICS
COVINA
DAVIES
DAVITS
DEVICE
DEVILS
DEVINE
DEVISE
DEVITO
DIVIDE
DIVINE
DIVING
DIVINO
DOVISH
ELVIRA
ELVISH
ENVIED
ENVIER
ENVIES
ERVING
GAVIAL
GIVING
HAVING
HIVING
INVITE
INVIVO
IRVINE
IRVING
JAVIER
JIVIER
JIVING
JOVIAL
JOVIAN
LAVING
LAVISH
LEVIED
LEVIER
LEVIES
LEVINE
LEVITE
LEVITY
LIVING
LOVING
MOVIES
MOVING
NAVIES
NEVINS
NOVICE
ONVIEW
PAVING
QIVIUT
RAVINE
RAVING
RAVISH
REVIEW
REVILE
REVISE
REVIVE
RIVING
ROVING
SAVING
SAVIOR
SOVIET
VIVIAN
VIVIEN
VIVIFY
WAVIER
WAVILY
WAVING
XAVIER

••V•I•
CAVEIN
DEVEIN
DEVOID
DEVOIR
DIVEIN
DOVEIN
ENVOIS
GAVEIN
GIVEIN
INVAIN
LIVEIN
LOVEIN
MOVEIN
REVOIR
SAVAII
SAVOIE
SAVOIR
UNVEIL
WAVEIN

••V••I
JAVARI
SAVAII
TIVOLI

•••VI•
BEAVIS
BMOVIE
BREVIS
CALVIN
CERVID
CLAVIN
CLEVIS
CLOVIS
FERVID
FLAVIA
GRAVID
KELVIN
KIDVID
LANVIN
LATVIA
MARVIN
MELVIL
MELVIN
NARVIK
OLDVIC
OLIVIA
PARVIS
PELVIC
PELVIS
PREVIN
SALVIA
SLAVIC
SLOVIK
SPAVIN
STEVIE
STIVIC
SYLVIA
TRAVIS
TRIVIA
WEEVIL

V••J••
VEEJAY

••V•J•
NAVAJO

V•K•••
VIKING

V••K••
VODKAS

V•••K•
VNECKS

V••••K
VOSTOK

•V•K••
EVOKED
EVOKER
EVOKES

•V••K•
EVENKI

•V•••K
DVORAK

••V•K•
INVOKE
NEVSKY
REVOKE
WOVOKA

•••V•K
NARVIK
SLOVAK
SLOVIK
SPIVAK

V•L•••
VALDEZ
VALENS
VALENT
VALERY
VALETS
VALISE
VALIUM
VALLEE
VALLEY
VALOIS
VALOUR
VALUED
VALUES
VALVED
VALVES
VELCRO
VELDTS
VELLUM
VELOCE
VELOUR
VELVET
VILELY
VILEST
VILIFY
VILLAS
VILLON
VILLUS
VOLANS
VOLANT
VOLARE
VOLENS
VOLLEY
VOLUME
VOLUTE
VOLVAS
VOLVOX
VULCAN
VULGAR

V••L••
VACLAV
VALLEE
VALLEY
VARLET
VASLAV
VAULTS
VAULTY
VEBLEN
VEILED
VELLUM
VILLAS
VILLON
VILLUS
VIOLAS
VIOLET
VIOLIN
VOILES
VOLLEY

V•••L•
VAINLY
VASTLY
VERILY
VIABLE
VIABLY
VIGILS
VILELY
VINYLS
VIRILE
VITALE
VITALS
VIZSLA
VOCALS
VOWELS
VOWELY

V••••L
VACHEL
VANDAL
VASSAL
VATFUL
VEINAL
VENIAL
VERBAL
VERNAL
VESSEL
VESTAL
VIRGIL
VISUAL

•V•L••
AVALON
AVULSE
EVELYN
EVILER
EVILLY
EVOLVE
EVULSE
KVELLS
OVALLY
OVULAR
OVULES
RVALUE
SVELTE
UVALUE
UVULAE
UVULAR
UVULAS

•V••L•
AVAILS
AVIDLY
EVENLY
EVERLY
EVILLY
KVELLS
OVALLY
OVERLY

•V•••L
AVOWAL

••VL••
KEVLAR
PAVLOV
REVLON

••V•L•
ANVILS
BEVELS
CAVELL
CAVILS
DEVILS
DUVALL
GAVELS
HOVELS
KEVELS
LEVELS
LIVELY
LOVELL
LOVELY
NAVELS
NOVELS
RAVELS
REVELS
REVILE
REVOLT
RIVALS
TIVOLI
TUVALU
WAVILY

••V••L
CAVELL
DUVALL
GAVIAL
JOVIAL
LOVELL
REVEAL
UNVEIL

•••V•L
ALEVEL
CHEVAL
COEVAL
DRIVEL
GRAVEL
GROVEL
LARVAL
MARVEL
MELVIL
OLEVEL
SERVAL
SHOVEL
SNIVEL
SWIVEL
TRAVEL
WEEVIL

V•M•••
VAMPED
VAMPER

V••M••
VERMIN

V•••M•
VENOMS
VOLUME
VROOMS

V••••M
VACUUM
VALIUM
VELLUM
VERISM
VIACOM
VICTIM

••V•M•
REVAMP

••V••M
FIVEAM
FIVEPM

VN••••
VNECKS

V•N•••
VANDAL
VANIER
VANISH
VANITY
VANNED
VANRYN
VENDED
VENDEE
VENDOR
VENEER
VENETO
VENIAL
VENICE
VENIRE
VENITE
VENOMS
VENOUS
VENTED
VENTER
VENUES
VINCES
VINCIT
VINERY
VINIER
VINIFY
VINING
VINNIE
VINOUS
VINTON
VINYLS

V••N••
VAINER

VAINLY
VANNED
VARNAS
VARNEY
VAUNTS
VEINAL
VEINED
VERNAL
VERNON
VIANDS
VIENNA
VIENNE
VINNIE

V•••N•
VACANT
VALENS
VALENT
VARUNA
VEGANS
VERONA
VEXING
VICUNA
VIENNA
VIENNE
VIKING
VINING
VISHNU
VISINE
VIVANT
VIXENS
VOLANS
VOLANT
VOLENS
VOTING
VOWING
VSIGNS

V••••N
VANRYN
VARDEN
VAUGHN
VEBLEN
VERDIN
VERDON
VERDUN
VEREEN
VERMIN
VERNON
VILLON
VINTON
VIOLIN
VIRGIN
VISION
VIVIAN
VIVIEN
VOTEIN
VULCAN

•V•N••
AVANTI
AVENGE
AVENUE
EVENED
EVENER
EVENKI
EVENLY
EVENSO
EVENTS
EVENUP
EVINCE
EVONNE
YVONNE

•V••N•
AVAUNT
AVERNO
AVIANS
EVONNE
EVZONE
YVONNE

•V•••N
AVALON
AVEDON
EVELYN

••VN••
KAVNER

••V•N•
ADVENT
BOVINE
CAVING
COVENS
COVENT
COVINA
DEVINE
DIVANS
DIVINE
DIVING
DIVINO
ERVING
GIVENS
GIVING
HAVANA
HAVENS
HAVENT
HAVING
HIVING
INVENT
IRVINE
IRVING
JIVING
LAVING
LEVANT
LEVENE
LEVINE
LIVENS
LIVING
LOVING
MAVENS
MOVING
NEVINS
NOVENA
PAVANE
PAVING
RAVENS
RAVINE
RAVING
RIVING
ROVING
SAVANT
SAVING
SEVENS
VIVANT
WAVING

••V••N
CAVEIN
CAVERN
DEVEIN
DIVEIN
DOVEIN
GAVEIN
GIVEIN
GOVERN
HAVEON
INVAIN
JOVIAN
LIVEIN
LIVEON
LOVEIN
MOVEIN
MOVEON
REVLON
REVSON
SEVERN
TAVERN
VIVIAN
VIVIEN
WAVEIN
WYVERN

•••V•N
ALFVEN
CALVIN
CLAVIN
CLOVEN
CRAVEN
DRIVEN
ELEVEN
GRAVEN
HEAVEN
KELVIN
LANVIN
LEAVEN
MARVIN
MELVIN
MELVYN
MERVYN
PREVIN
PROVEN
SHAVEN
SLOVEN
SPAVIN
STEVEN
SYLVAN
UNEVEN

VO••••
VOCALS
VODKAS
VOGUES
VOICED
VOICES
VOIDED
VOIGHT
VOILES
VOLANS
VOLANT
VOLARE
VOLENS
VOLLEY
VOLUME
VOLUTE
VOLVAS
VOLVOX
VOODOO
VOROUS
VORTEX
VOSGES
VOSTOK
VOTARY
VOTECH
VOTEIN
VOTERS
VOTING
VOTIVE
VOWELS
VOWELY
VOWERS
VOWING
VOXPOP
VOYAGE

V•O•••
VIOLAS
VIOLET
VIOLIN
VOODOO
VROOMS

V••O••
VADOSE
VALOIS
VALOUR
VAPORS
VAPORY
VAPOUR
VELOCE
VELOUR
VENOMS
VENOUS
VERONA
VETOED
VETOER
VETOES
VIGODA
VIGORS
VIGOUR
VINOUS
VISORS
VOROUS
VROOMS
VYBORG

V•••O•
VECTOR
VENDOR
VERDON
VERNON
VERSOS
VIACOM
VICTOR
VIDEOS
VILLON
VINTON
VIREOS
VISION
VOLVOX
VOODOO
VOSTOK
VOXPOP

V••••O
VELCRO
VENETO
VIRAGO
VOODOO

•VO•••
AVOCET
AVOIDS
AVOUCH
AVOWAL
AVOWED
AVOWER
DVORAK
EVOKED
EVOKER
EVOKES
EVOLVE
EVONNE
OVOIDS
YVONNE

•V•O••
EVZONE

•V••O•
AVALON
AVEDON
AVISOS
TVSHOW

•V•••O
AVERNO
EVENSO
EVERSO
OVERDO
OVIEDO

••VO••
CAVORT
DEVOID
DEVOIR
DEVOTE
DEVOTO
DEVOUR
DEVOUT
DIVOTS
ENVOIS
ENVOYS
EXVOTO
FAVORS
FAVOUR
HAVOCS
INVOKE
PIVOTS
REVOIR
REVOKE
REVOLT
SAVOIE
SAVOIR
SAVORS
SAVORY
SAVOUR
TIVOLI
WOVOKA

••V•O•
HAVEON
HIVAOA
LIVEON
MOVEON
PAVLOV
REVLON
REVSON
SAVIOR

••V••O
DEVITO
DEVOTO
DIVINO
EXVOTO
GIVETO
HOVETO
INVIVO
LAVABO
NAVAHO
NAVAJO
NOVATO

•••VO•
BRAVOS
CONVOY
FERVOR
FLAVOR
HUEVOS
SALVOR
SALVOS
SERVOS
TREVOR
VOLVOX

••••VO
DENOVO
INVIVO
KOSOVO
OCTAVO

V•P•••
VAPORS
VAPORY
VAPOUR
VIPERS

V••P••
VAMPED
VAMPER
VESPER
VESPID
VOXPOP

V•••P•
VCHIPS

V••••P
VOXPOP

•V•••P
EVENUP

••VP••
RSVPED

••V•P•
FIVEPM

••V••P
GAVEUP
GIVEUP
MOVEUP
RAVEUP
REVAMP
REVSUP
SAVEUP

VR••••
VROOMS

V•R•••
VARDEN
VARESE
VARIED
VARIES
VARLET
VARNAS
VARNEY
VARUNA
VERBAL
VERBIS
VERDIN
VERDON
VERDUN
VEREEN
VERGED
VERGER
VERGES
VERIFY
VERILY
VERISM
VERITE
VERITY
VERMIN
VERNAL
VERNON
VERONA
VERSED
VERSES
VERSOS
VERSTS
VERSUS
VERTEX
VERVES
VERVET
VIRAGO
VIREOS
VIRGIL
VIRGIN
VIRILE
VIRTUE
VIRTUS
VOROUS
VORTEX

V••R••
VANRYN
VEERED
VITRIC

V•••R•
VAGARY
VALERY
VAPORS
VAPORY
VELCRO
VENIRE
VESTRY
VEXERS
VICARS
VIDERI
VIGORS
VINERY
VIPERS
VISORS
VOLARE
VOTARY
VOTERS
VOWERS
VYBORG

V••••R
VAGUER
VAINER
VALOUR
VAMPER
VANIER
VAPOUR
VASSAR
VASTER
VECTOR
VEDDER
VELOUR
VENDOR
VENEER
VENTER
VERGER
VESPER
VETOER
VICTOR
VIEWER
VIGOUR
VINIER
VIZIER
VULGAR

•V•R••
AVERNO
AVERSE
AVERTS
DVORAK
EVERLY
EVERSO
EVERTS
OVERDO
OVERLY

•V••R•
AVIARY

•V•••R
AVATAR
AVOWER
EVADER
EVENER
EVILER
EVOKER
OVULAR
UVULAR

••VR••
LIVRES
SEVRES

••V•R•
ADVERB
ADVERT
BOVARY
CAVERN
CAVERS
CAVORT
COVERS
COVERT
DIVERS
DIVERT
EDVARD
ELVERS
ELVIRA
FAVORS
FEVERS
FIVERS
GIVERS
GOVERN
HAVERS
HOVERS
INVERT
JAVARI
JIVERS
LAVERS
LEVERS
LIVERS
LIVERY
LOVERS
MOVERS
NEVERS
OBVERT
PAVERS
RAVERS
REVERB
REVERE
REVERS
REVERT
RIVERA
RIVERS
ROVERS
SAVERS
SAVORS
SAVORY
SEVERE
SEVERN
SEVERS
SEVERY
TAVERN
WAVERS
WAVERY
WYVERN

••V••R
BOVVER CAVIAR DEVOIR DEVOUR ENVIER FAVOUR JAVIER JIVIER KAVNER KEVLAR LEVIER REVOIR SAVIOR SAVOIR SAVOUR WAVIER XAVIER

•••VR•
CHEVRE LOUVRE OEUVRE

•••V•R
ASEVER BEAVER BOVVER BRAVER CARVER CLEVER CLOVER CRAVER CULVER DELVER DENVER DRIVER DROVER FERVOR FLAVOR GLOVER GOOVER GRAVER GROVER HEAVER HOOVER LEKVAR LOUVER OLIVER PLOVER PROVER QUAVER QUIVER SALVER SALVOR SERVER SHAVER SHIVER SHOVER SILVER SKIVER SLAVER SLIVER SOLVER STIVER STOVER SUAVER TREVOR WAIVER WEAVER

VS••••
VSIGNS VSIXES

V•S•••
VASHTI VASLAV VASSAL VASSAR VASTER VASTLY VESPER VESPID VESSEL VESTAL VESTAS VESTED VESTEE VESTRY VISAED VISAGE VISCID VISHNU VISINE VISION VISITS VISORS VISTAS VISUAL VOSGES VOSTOK

V••S••
VAISYA VASSAL VASSAR VERSED VERSES VERSOS VERSTS VERSUS VESSEL VIZSLA

V•••S•
VADOSE VALISE VANISH VARESE VERISM VILEST

V••••S
VALENS VALETS VALOIS VALUES VALVES VAPORS VARIES VARNAS VAULTS VAUNTS VCHIPS VEGANS VELDTS VENOMS VENOUS VENUES VERBIS VERGES VERSES VERSOS VERSTS VERSUS VERVES VESTAS VETOES VEXERS VIANDS VICARS VICTIS VIDEOS VIGILS VIGORS VILLAS VILLUS VINCES VINOUS VINYLS VIOLAS VIPERS VIREOS VIRTUS VISITS VISORS VISTAS VITALS VIXENS VNECKS VOCALS VODKAS VOGUES VOICES VOILES VOLANS VOLENS VOLVAS VOROUS VOSGES VOTERS VOWELS VOWERS VROOMS VSIGNS VSIXES

•VS•••
TVSETS TVSHOW

•V•S••
AVESTA AVISOS OVISAC

•V••S•
AVERSE AVULSE EVENSO EVERSO EVULSE

•V•••S
AVAILS AVERTS AVIANS AVISOS AVOIDS EVADES EVENTS EVERTS EVICTS EVOKES KVELLS OVOIDS OVULES TVSETS UVULAS

••VS••
NEVSKY REVSON REVSUP

••V•S•
ADVISE DEVEST DEVISE DIVEST DOVISH ELVISH HAVASU INVEST KUVASZ LAVISH RAVISH REVISE

••V••S
AMVETS ANVILS BEVELS BEVIES BOVIDS CAVERS CAVILS CIVETS CIVICS COVENS COVERS COVETS COVEYS CUVEES DAVIES DAVITS DEVILS DIVANS DIVERS DIVOTS DUVETS ELVERS ENVIES ENVOIS ENVOYS FAVORS FEVERS FIVERS FIVEWS GAVELS GIVENS GIVERS HAVENS HAVERS HAVOCS HOVELS HOVERS JIVERS KEVELS KOVACS LAVERS LEVEES LEVELS LEVERS LEVIES LIVENS LIVERS LIVRES LOVERS MAVENS MOVERS MOVIES NAVELS NAVIES NEVERS NEVINS NOVELS PAVERS PIVOTS RAVELS RAVENS RAVERS REVELS REVERS REVETS REVUES RIVALS RIVERS RIVETS ROVERS SAVERS SAVORS SEVENS SEVERS SEVRES WAVERS

•••V•S
AGAVES BEAVIS BEEVES BRAVAS BRAVES BRAVOS BREVES BREVIS CALVES CANVAS CARVES CHIVES CLAVES CLEVES CLEVIS CLOVES CLOVIS CORVES CRAVES CURVES DELVES DRIVES DROVES ELEVES GLOVES GRAVES GROVES GUAVAS HALVES HEAVES HELVES HOOVES HUEVOS JEEVES KNAVES KNIVES LARVAS LEAVES LOAVES MAUVES NERVES OGIVES OLIVES PARVIS PEEVES PELVIS PROVES REEVES SALVES SALVOS SELVES SERVES SERVOS SHAVES SHOVES SIEVES SILVAS SKIVES SLAVES SOAVES SOLVES STAVES STOVES TRAVES TRAVIS TROVES TURVES VALVES VERVES VOLVAS WAIVES WEAVES WOLVES

V•T•••
VATFUL VATTED VETOED VETOER VETOES VETTED VITALE VITALS VITRIC VOTARY VOTECH VOTEIN VOTERS VOTING VOTIVE

V••T••
VASTER VASTLY VATTED VECTOR VENTED VENTER VERTEX VESTAL VESTAS VESTED VESTEE VESTRY VETTED VICTIM VICTIS VICTOR VINTON VIRTUE VIRTUS VISTAS VORTEX VOSTOK

V•••T•
VACATE VALETS VANITY VASHTI VAULTS VAULTY VAUNTS VELDTS VENETO VENITE VERITE VERITY VERSTS VISITS VOLUTE

V••••T
VACANT VALENT VARLET VEIGHT VELVET VERVET VILEST VINCIT VIOLET VIVANT VOIGHT VOLANT

•V•T••
AVATAR KVETCH YVETTE

•V••T•
AVANTI AVERTS AVESTA AVIATE EVENTS EVERTS EVICTS SVELTE TVSETS YVETTE

•V•••T
AVAUNT AVOCET

••V•T•
AMVETS CAVETT CAVITY CIVETS COVETS DAVITS DEVITO DEVOTE DEVOTO DIVOTS DUVETS EXVOTO GIVETO HOVETO INVITE LEVITE LEVITY LOVETT NOVATO PIVOTS REVETS RIVETS SAVATE

••V••T
ADVENT ADVERT CAVEAT CAVETT CAVORT COVENT COVERT DEVEST DEVOUT DIVERT DIVEST HAVEAT HAVENT INVENT INVERT INVEST LEVANT LOVETT OBVERT QIVIUT REVERT REVOLT SAVANT SOVIET VIVANT

•••V•T
BREVET CHEVET CRAVAT CURVET GRIVET PRIVET SHEVAT SWIVET TRIVET VELVET VERVET

VU••••
VULCAN VULGAR

V•U•••
VAUGHN VAULTS VAULTY VAUNTS

V••U••
VACUUM VAGUER VALUED VALUES VARUNA VENUES VICUNA VISUAL VOGUES VOLUME VOLUTE

V•••U•
VACUUM VALIUM VALOUR VAPOUR VATFUL VELLUM VELOUR VENOUS VERDUN VERSUS VIGOUR VILLUS VINOUS VIRTUE VIRTUS VOROUS

V••••U
VISHNU

•VU•••
AVULSE EVULSE OVULAR OVULES

UVULAE
UVULAR
UVULAS

•V•U••
AVAUNT
AVOUCH

•V••U•
AVENUE
EVENUP
RVALUE
UVALUE

••VU••
REVUES

••V•U•
DEVOUR
DEVOUT
FAVOUR
GAVEUP
GIVEUP
MOVEUP
QIVIUT
RAVEUP
REVSUP
SAVEUP
SAVOUR

••V••U
HAVASU
TUVALU

••••VU
DEJAVU

V•V•••
VIVACE
VIVANT
VIVIAN
VIVIEN
VIVIFY

V••V••
VALVED
VALVES
VELVET
VERVES
VERVET
VOLVAS
VOLVOX

V•••V•
VOTIVE

V••••V
VACLAV
VASLAV

•V••V•
EVOLVE

••VV••
BOVVER
REVVED

••V•V•
INVIVO
REVIVE

••V••V
PAVLOV

•••VV•
SKIVVY
SPIVVY

V•W•••
VOWELS
VOWELY
VOWERS
VOWING

V••W••
VIEWED
VIEWER

•V•W••
AVOWAL
AVOWED
AVOWER

•V•••W
TVSHOW

••V•W•
FIVEWS

••V••W
ONVIEW
REVIEW

V•X•••
VEXERS
VEXING
VIXENS
VOXPOP

V••X••
VSIXES

V••••X
VERTEX
VOLVOX
VORTEX

•••V•X
CONVEX
VOLVOX

VY••••
VYBORG

V•Y•••
VOYAGE

V••Y••
VINYLS

V•••Y•
VAISYA
VANRYN

V••••Y
VAGARY
VAINLY
VALERY
VALLEY
VANITY
VAPORY
VARNEY
VASTLY
VAULTY
VEEJAY
VERIFY
VERILY
VERITY
VESTRY
VIABLY
VILELY
VILIFY
VINERY
VINIFY
VIVIFY
VOLLEY
VOTARY
VOWELY

•V••Y•
EVELYN

•V•••Y
AVIARY
AVIDLY
EVENLY
EVERLY
EVILLY
OVALLY
OVERLY

••V•Y•
COVEYS
ENVOYS

••V••Y
BOVARY
CAVITY
LEVITY
LIVELY
LIVERY
LOVELY
NEVSKY
SAVORY
SEVERY
VIVIFY
WAVERY
WAVILY

•••VY•
MELVYN
MERVYN

•••V•Y
CARVEY
CONVEY
CONVOY
GARVEY
HARVEY
PEAVEY
PURVEY
SKIVVY
SLAVEY
SPIVVY
SURVEY

••••VY
GROOVY
HALEVY
RELEVY
SCURVY
SKIVVY
SPIVVY

V•Z•••
VIZIER
VIZSLA

V••••Z
VALDEZ

•VZ•••
EVZONE

••V••Z
KUVASZ

•••V•Z
CHAVEZ

WA••••
WABASH
WACKOS
WADDED
WADDLE
WADDLY
WADEIN
WADERS
WADING
WADSUP
WAFERS
WAFERY
WAFFLE
WAFFLY
WAFTED
WAGERS
WAGGED
WAGGLE
WAGGLY
WAGGON
WAGING
WAGNER
WAGONS
WAHINE
WAHOOS
WAHWAH
WAILED
WAILER
WAISTS
WAITED
WAITER
WAITON
WAITUP
WAIVED
WAIVER
WAIVES
WAKENS
WAKEUP
WAKING
WALDEN
WALERS
WALESA
WALKED
WALKEN
WALKER
WALKIE
WALKIN
WALKON
WALKUP
WALLED
WALLER
WALLET
WALLIS
WALLOP
WALLOW
WALLUP
WALNUT
WALRUS
WALTER
WALTON
WAMBLE
WAMBLY
WAMPUM
WANDER
WANERS
WANGLE
WANIER
WANING
WANNED
WANNER
WANTAD
WANTED
WANTIN
WANTON
WANTTO
WAPITI
WAPNER
WARBLE
WARCRY
WARDED
WARDEN
WARDER
WARGOD
WARHOL
WARIER
WARILY
WARING
WARMED
WARMER
WARMLY
WARMTH
WARMUP
WARNED
WARNER
WARPED
WARRED
WARREN
WARSAW
WASABI
WASHED
WASHER
WASHES
WASHOE
WASHUP
WASTED
WASTER
WASTES
WATERS
WATERY
WATNEY
WATSON
WATTLE
WATUSI
WAUSAU
WAVEIN
WAVERS
WAVERY
WAVIER
WAVILY
WAVING
WAXERS
WAXIER
WAXILY
WAXING
WAYANS
WAYLAY
WAYLON
WAYOUT

W•A•••
WEAKEN
WEAKER
WEAKLY
WEALTH
WEANED
WEAPON
WEARER
WEASEL
WEAVED
WEAVER
WEAVES
WHACKS
WHACKY
WHALER
WHALES
WHAMMO
WHAMMY
WHANGS
WHARFS
WHATIF
WHATLL
WHATVE
WRACKS
WRAITH
WRAPUP
WRASSE
WRATHS
WRATHY

W••A••
WABASH
WASABI
WAYANS
WHEALS
WHEATS
WIZARD
WREAKS
WREATH

W•••A•
WAHWAH
WANTAD
WARSAW
WAUSAU
WAYLAY
WEIMAR
WENTAT
WETBAR
WHYDAH
WICCAN
WIGWAG
WIGWAM
WINKAT
WITHAL
WOMBAT
WYSTAN

W••••A
WALESA
WINONA
WOVOKA

•WA•••
AWAITS
AWAKED
AWAKEN
AWAKES
AWARDS
BWANAS
DWARFS
DWAYNE
KWACHA
KWANZA
RWANDA
SWABBY
SWAGED
SWAGES
SWAINS
SWALES
SWAMIS
SWAMPS
SWAMPY
SWANEE
SWANKS
SWANKY
SWARAJ
SWARDS
SWARMS
SWARTH
SWATCH
SWATHE
SWATHS
SWAYED
SWAYER
SWAYZE
SWAZIS
TWANGS
TWANGY

•W•A••
AWEARY
SWEARS
SWEATS
SWEATY
TWEAKS

•W••A•
BWANAS
SWARAJ
TWOWAY

•W•••A
KWACHA
KWANZA
RWANDA

••WA••
ALWAYS
ANWANG
BEWAIL
BEWARE
BYWAYS
COWARD
EDWARD
GAWAIN
HAWAII
HOWARD
INWARD
IOWANS
KUWAIT
NAWABS
NEWAGE
NEWARK
ONWARD
OSWALD
REWARD
REWARM
REWASH
SEWAGE
SEWARD
SIWASH
THWACK
THWART
TOWAGE
TOWARD
UNWARY
UPWARD

••W•A•
BEWRAY
BOWMAN
BOWOAR
BOWSAW
COWMAN
DEWLAP
ENWRAP
GEWGAW
HAWHAW
HOWDAH
LAWMAN
LOWCAL
LOWFAT
NEWMAN
NEWMAR
PAWPAW
PAWSAT
REWRAP
SOWHAT
TOWCAR
UNWRAP

••W••A
COWPEA
ROWENA

•••WA•
AIRWAY
ANYWAY
ARAWAK
AVOWAL
CONWAY
EARWAX
FATWAS
FENWAY
FLEWAT
FLYWAY
GALWAY
GOAWAY
HOTWAR
INAWAY
JETWAY
KEYWAY
KIOWAS
LEEWAY
MIDWAY
NARWAL
NORWAY
OBIWAN
ONEWAY
PEDWAY
PREWAR
PSYWAR
RUNWAY
SCHWAB
SCHWAS
SEAWAY
SKYWAY
SUBWAY
TAIWAN
TWOWAY
WAHWAH
WIGWAG
WIGWAM

••••WA
BUSHWA
OJIBWA
OSHAWA
OTTAWA
PESAWA
TARAWA
YUKAWA

W•B•••
WABASH
WEBBED
WEBBER
WEBERN
WOBBLE
WOBBLY

W••B••
WAMBLE
WAMBLY
WARBLE
WEBBED
WEBBER
WETBAR
WILBUR
WIMBLE
WOBBLE
WOBBLY

WOMBAT

W•••B•
WASABI
WENTBY

•W•B••
SWABBY
TWOBIT

•W••B•
DWEEBS
SWABBY

••WB••
COWBOY
LOWBOY
SOWBUG

••W•B•
NAWABS

•••W•B
COBWEB
SCHWAB
THEWEB

W•C•••
WACKOS
WICCAN
WICKED
WICKER
WICKET
WICOPY

W••C••
WARCRY
WENCES
WHACKS
WHACKY
WICCAN
WILCOX
WINCED
WINCER
WINCES
WITCHY
WRACKS
WRECKS

W•••C•
WHENCE
WRENCH
WRETCH

•W•C••
KWACHA

•W••C•
SWATCH
SWITCH
TWITCH

••WC••
LOWCAL
TOWCAR

••W•C•
THWACK

W•D•••
WADDED
WADDLE
WADDLY
WADEIN
WADERS
WADING
WADSUP
WEDDED
WEDELN
WEDGED
WEDGES
WEDGIE
WIDELY
WIDENS
WIDEST
WIDGET
WIDISH
WIDOWS
WIDTHS
WODGES

W••D••
WADDED
WADDLE
WADDLY
WALDEN
WANDER
WARDED
WARDEN
WARDER
WEDDED
WEEDED
WEEDER
WELDED
WELDER
WENDED
WHYDAH
WILDER
WILDLY
WINDED
WINDER
WINDEX
WINDOM
WINDOW
WINDUP
WISDOM
WONDER
WOODED
WOODEN
WOODSY
WORDED

W•••D•
WEIRDO
WEIRDY
WIELDS
WORLDS
WOUNDS

W••••D
WADDED
WAFTED
WAGGED
WAILED
WAITED
WAIVED
WALKED
WALLED
WANNED
WANTAD
WANTED
WARDED
WARGOD
WARMED
WARNED
WARPED
WARRED
WASHED
WASTED
WEANED
WEAVED
WEBBED
WEDDED
WEDGED
WEEDED
WELDED
WELLED
WELTED
WENDED
WETTED
WHERED
WHILED
WHINED
WICKED
WIGGED
WILLED
WILTED
WINCED
WINDED
WINGED
WINKED
WISHED
WISPED
WITHED
WITTED
WIZARD
WOLFED
WONNED
WONTED
WOODED
WOOFED
WORDED
WORKED
WORMED

•W•D••
AWEDLY
SWEDEN
SWEDES

•W••D•
AWARDS
RWANDA
SWARDS
SWORDS
TWEEDS
TWEEDY

•W•••D
AWAKED
SWAGED
SWAYED
SWIPED
TWINED

••WD••
CAWDOR
DAWDLE
HOWDAH
LEWDER
LEWDLY
POWDER
TAWDRY

••W•D•
REWEDS

••W••D
ATWOOD
BAWLED
BOWLED
BYWORD
COWARD
COWLED
DAWNED
DOWNED
DOWSED
EDWARD
EDWOOD
ELWOOD
FAWNED
FOWLED
GAWKED
GAWPED
GOWILD
GOWNED
HAWKED
HOWARD
HOWLED
INWARD
LOWEND
MEWLED
MYWORD
ONWARD
OSWALD
PAWNED
REWARD
REWELD
REWIND
REWORD
SAWRED
SEWARD
TOWARD
UNWIND
UPWARD
UPWIND
YAWNED
YAWPED
YOWLED

•••WD•
CROWDS

•••W•D
AVOWED
BREWED
CHEWED
CHOWED
CLAWED
CLEWED
CREWED
CROWED
FLAWED
FLOWED
GLOWED
GNAWED
MEOWED
PLOWED
SHOWED
SKEWED
SLEWED
SLOWED
SNOWED
SPEWED
STEWED
STOWED
THAWED
TROWED
UNAWED
VIEWED

••••WD
SHREWD

WE••••
WEAKEN
WEAKER
WEAKLY
WEALTH
WEANED
WEAPON
WEARER
WEASEL
WEAVED
WEAVER
WEAVES
WEBBED
WEBBER
WEBERN
WEDDED
WEDELN
WEDGED
WEDGES
WEDGIE
WEEDED
WEEDER
WEEKLY
WEENIE
WEENSY
WEEPER
WEEPIE
WEEVIL
WEIGHS
WEIGHT
WEIMAR
WEIRDO
WEIRDY
WELDED
WELDER
WELKIN
WELLED
WELLER
WELLES
WELLUP
WELTED
WELTER
WENCES
WENDED
WENTAT
WENTBY
WENTIN
WENTON
WENTUP
WERENT
WERFEL
WERNER
WESKIT
WESLEY
WESSEX
WESSON
WETBAR
WETFLY
WETHER
WETMOP
WETTED
WETTER
WETTIG

W•E•••
WEEDED
WEEDER
WEEKLY
WEENIE
WEENSY
WEEPER
WEEPIE
WEEVIL
WHEALS
WHEATS
WHEELS
WHEEZE
WHEEZY
WHELKS
WHELMS
WHELPS
WHENCE
WHERED
WHERES
WHERRY
WIELDS
WIENER
WIESEL
WOEFUL
WREAKS
WREATH
WRECKS
WRENCH
WRESTS
WRETCH

W••E••
WADEIN
WADERS
WAFERS
WAFERY
WAGERS
WAKENS
WAKEUP
WALERS
WALESA
WANERS
WATERS
WATERY
WAVEIN
WAVERS
WAVERY
WAXERS
WEBERN
WEDELN
WERENT
WHEELS
WHEEZE
WHEEZY
WIDELY
WIDENS
WIDEST
WIFELY
WINERY
WIPERS
WIPEUP
WIRERS
WISELY
WISENT
WISEST
WISETO
WISEUP
WIZENS
WOKEUP
WOMENS
WOOERS
WOREON
WRIEST
WRYEST
WYVERN

W•••E•
WADDED
WAFTED
WAGGED
WAGNER
WAILED
WAILER
WAITED
WAITER
WAIVED
WAIVER
WAIVES
WALDEN
WALKED
WALKEN
WALKER
WALLED
WALLER
WALLET
WALTER
WANDER
WANIER
WANNED
WANNER
WANTED
WAPNER
WARDED
WARDEN
WARDER
WARIER
WARMED
WARMER
WARNED
WARNER
WARPED
WARRED
WARREN
WASHED
WASHER
WASHES
WASTED
WASTER
WASTES
WATNEY
WAVIER
WAXIER
WEAKEN
WEAKER
WEANED
WEARER
WEASEL
WEAVED
WEAVER
WEAVES
WEBBED
WEBBER
WEDDED
WEDGED
WEDGES
WEEDED
WEEDER
WEEPER
WELDED
WELDER
WELLED
WELLER
WELLES
WELTED
WELTER
WENCES
WENDED
WERFEL
WERNER
WESLEY
WESSEX
WETHER
WETTED
WETTER
WHALER
WHALES
WHERED
WHERES
WHILED
WHILES
WHINED
WHINER
WHINES
WHINEY
WHITEN
WHITER
WHITES
WHOLES
WICKED
WICKER
WICKET
WIDGET
WIENER
WIESEL
WIGGED
WIGLET
WILDER
WILIER
WILKES
WILLED
WILLEM
WILLET
WILTED
WIMSEY
WINCED
WINCER
WINCES
WINDED
WINDER
WINDEX
WINGED
WINGER
WINIER
WINKED
WINKER
WINNER
WINTER
WINZES
WIRIER
WISHED
WISHER
WISHES
WISPED
WISTER
WITHED
WITHER
WITHES
WITTED
WODGES
WOHLER
WOLFED
WOLPER
WOLSEY
WOLVES
WONDER
WONNED
WONTED
WOODED
WOODEN
WOOFED
WOOFER
WOOLEN
WOOLEY
WORDED
WORKED
WORKER
WORMED
WORSEN
WOWSER
WRITER
WRITES
WURLEY
WUSSES
WYNTER

W••••E
WADDLE
WAFFLE
WAGGLE
WAHINE
WALKIE

WAMBLE
WANGLE
WARBLE
WASHOE
WATTLE
WEDGIE
WEENIE
WEEPIE
WHATVE
WHEEZE
WHENCE
WIGGLE
WILLIE
WIMBLE
WIMPLE
WINKIE
WINKLE
WINNIE
WOBBLE
WOOGIE
WOOKIE
WRASSE
WRITHE

•WE•••
AWEARY
AWEDLY
AWEIGH
DWEEBS
DWELLS
KWEISI
QWERTY
SWEARS
SWEATS
SWEATY
SWEDEN
SWEDES
SWEEPS
SWEETS
SWELLS
SWERVE
TWEAKS
TWEEDS
TWEEDY
TWEENS
TWEENY
TWEEST
TWEETS
TWEETY
TWEEZE
TWELVE
TWENTY
TWERPS

•W•E••
DWEEBS
OWLETS
OWNERS
SWEEPS
SWEETS
TWEEDS
TWEEDY
TWEENS
TWEENY
TWEEST
TWEETS
TWEETY
TWEEZE

•W••E•
AWAKED
AWAKEN
AWAKES
AWOKEN
SWAGED
SWAGES
SWALES
SWANEE
SWAYED
SWAYER
SWEDEN
SWEDES
SWIPED
SWIPER
SWIPES
SWIVEL
SWIVET
TWINED
TWINES
TWOFER

•W•••E
AWHILE
DWAYNE
GWYNNE
SWANEE
SWATHE
SWAYZE
SWERVE
TWEEZE
TWELVE
TWINGE

••WE••
ADWEEK
ALWEST
ASWELL
BOWERS
BOWERY
COWENS
COWERS
DOWELS
DOWERS
DOWERY
FEWEST
GOWEST
HEWERS
HOWELL
JEWELS
JEWETT
JOWETT
LOWELL
LOWEND
LOWERS
LOWERY
LOWEST
MOWERS
NEWELS
NEWEST
NLWEST
OHWELL
ORWELL
OSWEGO
PAWERS
PEWEES
POWELL
POWERS
RAWEGG
RAWEST
REWEDS
REWELD
ROWELS
ROWENA
ROWENS
ROWERS
SEWELL
SEWERS
SOWERS
SOWETO
TOWELS
TOWERS
TOWERY
UNWELL
UPWELL
VOWELS
VOWELY
VOWERS

••W•E•
ADWEEK
BAWLED
BAWLER
BOWLED
BOWLER
BOWLES
BOWMEN
BOWNET
BOWSER
BOWYER
COWLED
COWLEY
COWMEN
COWPEA
COWPER
DAWNED
DEWIER
DOWNED
DOWNER
DOWNEY
DOWSED
DOWSER
DOWSES
FAWKES
FAWNED
FAWNER
FOWLED
FOWLER
FOWLES
GAWKED
GAWKER
GAWPED
GOWNED
HAWKED
HAWKER
HAWSER
HAWSES
HOWLED
HOWLER
LAWMEN
LAWYER
LEWDER
LOWKEY
MEWLED
MEWLER
NEWLEY
PAWNED
PAWNEE
PAWNER
PEWEES
PEWTER
POWDER
SAWRED
SAWYER
TOWHEE
TOWNER
WOWSER
YAWNED
YAWNER
YAWPED
YAWPER
YOWLED

••W••E
BEWARE
BOWTIE
COWRIE
DAWDLE
EXWIFE
KEWPIE
NEWAGE
NOWISE
PAWNEE
REWIRE
REWOVE
SEWAGE
TOWAGE
TOWHEE
TOWNIE
UNWISE
UNWOVE

•••WE•
ALLWET
ANSWER
AVOWED
AVOWER
BLOWER
BREWED
BREWER
BULWER
CHEWED
CHEWER
CHOWED
CLAWED
CLAWER
CLEWED
COBWEB
CREWED
CREWEL
CROWED
CROWER
DRAWER
FLAWED
FLOWED
FLOWER
GLOWED
GLOWER
GNAWED
GNAWER
GROWER
KNOWER
MEOWED
PEEWEE
PLOWED
PLOWER
SHOWED
SHOWER
SKEWED
SKEWER
SLEWED
SLOWED
SLOWER
SNOWED
SPEWED
STEWED
STEWER
STOWED
THAWED
THEWEB
TROWED
TROWEL
UNAWED
VIEWED
VIEWER
YAHWEH

•••W•E
BROWNE
BROWSE
DROWSE
PEEWEE
PROWSE
SHOWME

W•F•••
WAFERS
WAFERY
WAFFLE
WAFFLY
WAFTED
WIFELY

W••F••
WAFFLE
WAFFLY
WERFEL
WETFLY
WHIFFS
WILFUL
WOEFUL
WOLFED
WOOFED
WOOFER

W•••F•
WHARFS
WHIFFS
WHOOFS

W••••F
WHATIF

•W•F••
SWIFTS
TWOFER

•W••F•
DWARFS

••WF••
BOWFIN
LAWFUL
LOWFAT
SAWFIT

••W•F•
EXWIFE
SAWOFF

••W••F
SAWOFF

W•G•••
WAGERS
WAGGED
WAGGLE
WAGGLY
WAGGON
WAGING
WAGNER
WAGONS
WIGGED
WIGGLE
WIGGLY
WIGHTS
WIGLET
WIGOUT
WIGWAG
WIGWAM

W••G••
WAGGED
WAGGLE
WAGGLY
WAGGON
WANGLE
WARGOD
WEDGED
WEDGES
WEDGIE
WEIGHS
WEIGHT
WIDGET
WIGGED
WIGGLE
WIGGLY
WINGED
WINGER
WINGIT
WODGES
WOOGIE
WRIGHT

W•••G•
WHANGS
WRINGS
WRONGS

W••••G
WADING
WAGING
WAKING
WANING
WARING
WAVING
WAXING
WETTIG
WIGWAG
WILING
WINING
WIPING
WIRING
WONMUG
WOOING
WOWING

•W•G••
DWIGHT
SWAGED
SWAGES
TWIGGY

•W••G•
AWEIGH
SWINGS
SWINGY
TWANGS
TWANGY
TWIGGY
TWINGE

•W•••G
AWNING
OWNING

••WG••
GEWGAW
MOWGLI

••W•G•
NEWAGE
OSWEGO
RAWEGG
SEWAGE
TOWAGE

••W••G
ANWANG
BOWING
CAWING
COWING
DEWING
HAWING
HEWING
JAWING
LAWING
LOWING
MEWING
MOWING
PAWING
RAWEGG
ROWING
SAWING
SAWLOG
SEWING
SOWBUG
SOWING
TAWING
TOWING
VOWING
WOWING
YAWING

•••W•G
BIGWIG
EARWIG
LUDWIG
WIGWAG

WH••••
WHACKS
WHACKY
WHALER
WHALES
WHAMMO
WHAMMY
WHANGS
WHARFS
WHATIF
WHATLL
WHATVE
WHEALS
WHEATS
WHEELS
WHEEZE
WHEEZY
WHELKS
WHELMS
WHELPS
WHENCE
WHERED
WHERES
WHERRY
WHIFFS
WHILED
WHILES
WHILOM
WHILST
WHIMSY
WHINED
WHINER
WHINES
WHINEY
WHINNY
WHIPPY
WHIPUP
WHIRLS
WHIRLY
WHIRRS
WHISKS
WHISKY
WHITEN
WHITER
WHITES
WHITTY
WHIZZO
WHOLES
WHOLLY
WHOMPS
WHOMSO
WHOOFS
WHOOPI
WHOOPS
WHOOSH
WHORLS
WHYDAH
WHYNOT

W•H•••
WAHINE
WAHOOS
WAHWAH
WOHLER

W••H••
WARHOL
WASHED
WASHER
WASHES
WASHOE
WASHUP
WETHER
WIGHTS
WISHED
WISHER
WISHES
WITHAL
WITHED
WITHER
WITHES
WITHIN
WITHIT

W•••H•
WEIGHS
WEIGHT
WIDTHS
WITCHY
WORTHS
WORTHY
WRATHS
WRATHY
WRIGHT
WRITHE

W••••H
WABASH
WAHWAH
WARMTH
WEALTH
WHOOSH
WHYDAH
WIDISH
WINISH
WRAITH
WREATH
WRENCH
WRETCH

•WH•••
AWHILE
AWHIRL

•W••H•
DWIGHT
KWACHA
SWATHE
SWATHS

•W•••H
AWEIGH
OWLISH

SWARTH
SWATCH
SWITCH
SWOOSH
TWITCH

••WH••
HAWHAW
SOWHAT
TOWHEE

••W•H•
JAWOHL

••W••H
GOWITH
HOWDAH
INWITH
JEWISH
LOWISH
NEWISH
RAWISH
REWASH
SIWASH
UNWISH

•••W•H
GROWTH
WAHWAH
YAHWEH

WI••••
WICCAN
WICKED
WICKER
WICKET
WICOPY
WIDELY
WIDENS
WIDEST
WIDGET
WIDISH
WIDOWS
WIDTHS
WIELDS
WIENER
WIESEL
WIFELY
WIGGED
WIGGLE
WIGGLY
WIGHTS
WIGLET
WIGOUT
WIGWAG
WIGWAM
WILBUR
WILCOX
WILDER
WILDLY
WILFUL
WILIER
WILILY
WILING
WILKES
WILLED
WILLEM
WILLET
WILLIE
WILLIS
WILLOW
WILSON
WILTED
WILTON
WIMBLE
WIMPLE
WIMSEY
WINCED
WINCER
WINCES
WINDED
WINDER
WINDEX
WINDOM
WINDOW
WINDUP
WINERY
WINGED
WINGER
WINGIT
WINIER
WINING
WINISH
WINKAT
WINKED
WINKER
WINKIE
WINKLE
WINNER
WINNIE
WINNOW
WINONA
WINOUT
WINSOR
WINTER
WINTRY
WINWIN
WINZES
WIPERS
WIPEUP
WIPING
WIRERS
WIRIER
WIRILY
WIRING
WISDOM
WISELY
WISENT
WISEST
WISETO
WISEUP
WISHED
WISHER
WISHES
WISPED
WISTER
WITCHY
WITHAL
WITHED
WITHER
WITHES
WITHIN
WITHIT
WITTED
WIZARD
WIZENS

W•I•••
WAILED
WAILER
WAISTS
WAITED
WAITER
WAITON
WAITUP
WAIVED
WAIVER
WAIVES
WEIGHS
WEIGHT
WEIMAR
WEIRDO
WEIRDY
WHIFFS
WHILED
WHILES
WHILOM
WHILST
WHIMSY
WHINED
WHINER
WHINES
WHINEY
WHINNY
WHIPPY
WHIPUP
WHIRLS
WHIRLY
WHIRRS
WHISKS
WHISKY
WHITEN
WHITER
WHITES
WHITTY
WHIZZO
WRIEST
WRIGHT
WRINGS
WRISTS
WRITER
WRITES
WRITHE

W••I••
WADING
WAGING
WAHINE
WAKING
WANIER
WANING
WAPITI
WARIER
WARILY
WARING
WAVIER
WAVILY
WAVING
WAXIER
WAXILY
WAXING
WIDISH
WILIER
WILILY
WILING
WINIER
WINING
WINISH
WIPING
WIRIER
WIRILY
WIRING
WOOING
WOWING
WRAITH

W•••I•
WADEIN
WALKIE
WALKIN
WALLIS
WANTIN
WAVEIN
WEDGIE
WEENIE
WEEPIE
WEEVIL
WELKIN
WENTIN
WESKIT
WETTIG
WHATIF
WILLIE
WILLIS
WINGIT
WINKIE
WINNIE
WINWIN
WITHIN
WITHIT
WOOGIE
WOOKIE
WORKIN

W••••I
WAPITI
WASABI
WATUSI
WHOOPI

•WI•••
DWIGHT
SWIFTS
SWILLS
SWINGS
SWINGY
SWIPED
SWIPER
SWIPES
SWIRLS
SWIRLY
SWITCH
SWIVEL
SWIVET
TWIGGY
TWILIT
TWILLS
TWINED
TWINES
TWINGE
TWIRLS
TWISTS
TWISTY
TWITCH
TWITTY

•W•I••
AWAITS
AWEIGH
AWHILE
AWHIRL
AWNING
KWEISI
OWLISH
OWNING
SWAINS

•W••I•
SWAMIS
SWAZIS
TWILIT
TWOBIT

•W•••I
KWEISI

••WI••
ASWIRL
ATWILL
BOWING
CAWING
COWING
DEWIER
DEWILY
DEWING
DEWITT
EXWIFE
GOWILD
GOWITH
HAWING
HEWING
INWITH
JAWING
JEWISH
LAWING
LOWING
LOWISH
MEWING
MOWING
NEWISH
NOWISE
PAWING
PEWITS
RAWISH
REWIND
REWINS
REWIRE
ROWING
SAWING
SEWING
SOWING
TAWING
TOWING
UNWILY
UNWIND
UNWISE
UNWISH
UPWIND
VOWING
WOWING
YAWING

••W•I•
BEWAIL
BOWFIN
BOWTIE
COWRIE
GAWAIN
HAWAII
HOWLIN
KEWPIE
KUWAIT
SAWFIT
TOWNIE

••W••I
HAWAII
MOWGLI

•••WI•
BIGWIG
BLEWIT
BLOWIN
BLOWIT
DARWIN
DIMWIT
DRAWIN
DREWIN
EARWIG
FLEWIN
GODWIN
GODWIT
LUDWIG
NITWIT
OUTWIT
SHOWIN
SNOWIN
THEWIZ
WINWIN

••••WI
MALAWI

•W•••J
SWARAJ

W•K•••
WAKENS
WAKEUP
WAKING
WOKEUP

W••K••
WACKOS
WALKED
WALKEN
WALKER
WALKIE
WALKIN
WALKON
WALKUP
WEAKEN
WEAKER
WEAKLY
WEEKLY
WELKIN
WESKIT
WICKED
WICKER
WICKET
WILKES
WINKAT
WINKED
WINKER
WINKIE
WINKLE
WOOKIE
WORKED
WORKER
WORKIN
WORKON
WORKUP

W•••K•
WHACKS
WHACKY
WHELKS
WHISKS
WHISKY
WOVOKA
WRACKS
WREAKS
WRECKS

•W•K••
AWAKED
AWAKEN
AWAKES
AWOKEN

•W••K•
SWANKS
SWANKY
TWEAKS

••WK••
FAWKES
GAWKED
GAWKER
HAWKED
HAWKER
LOWKEY

••W•K•
MIWOKS

••W••K
ADWEEK
ATWORK
NEWARK
REWORK
THWACK

•••W•K
ARAWAK

••••WK
MOHAWK
SQUAWK

W•L•••
WALDEN
WALERS
WALESA
WALKED
WALKEN
WALKER
WALKIE
WALKIN
WALKON
WALKUP
WALLED
WALLER
WALLET
WALLIS
WALLOP
WALLOW
WALLUP
WALNUT
WALRUS
WALTER
WALTON
WELDED
WELDER
WELKIN
WELLED
WELLER
WELLES
WELLUP
WELTED
WELTER
WILBUR
WILCOX
WILDER
WILDLY
WILFUL
WILIER
WILILY
WILING
WILKES
WILLED
WILLEM
WILLET
WILLIE
WILLIS
WILLOW
WILSON
WILTED
WILTON
WOLFED
WOLPER
WOLSEY
WOLVES

W••L••
WAILED
WAILER
WALLED
WALLER
WALLET
WALLIS
WALLOP
WALLOW
WALLUP
WAYLAY
WAYLON
WEALTH
WELLED
WELLER
WELLES
WELLUP
WESLEY
WHALER
WHALES
WHELKS
WHELMS
WHELPS
WHILED
WHILES
WHILOM
WHILST
WHOLES
WHOLLY
WIELDS
WIGLET
WILLED
WILLEM
WILLET
WILLIE
WILLIS
WILLOW
WOHLER
WOOLEN
WOOLEY
WOOLLY
WORLDS
WURLEY

W•••L•
WADDLE
WADDLY
WAFFLE
WAFFLY
WAGGLE
WAGGLY
WAMBLE
WAMBLY
WANGLE
WARBLE
WARILY
WARMLY
WATTLE
WAVILY
WAXILY
WEAKLY
WEDELN
WEEKLY
WETFLY
WHATLL
WHEALS
WHEELS
WHIRLS
WHIRLY
WHOLLY
WHORLS
WIDELY
WIFELY
WIGGLE
WIGGLY

WILDLY
WILILY
WIMBLE
WIMPLE
WINKLE
WIRILY
WISELY
WOBBLE
WOBBLY
WOOLLY

W••••L
WARHOL
WEASEL
WEEVIL
WERFEL
WHATLL
WIESEL
WILFUL
WITHAL
WOEFUL

•WL•••
OWLETS
OWLISH

•W•L••
DWELLS
SWALES
SWELLS
SWILLS
TWELVE
TWILIT
TWILLS

•W••L•
AWEDLY
AWHILE
DWELLS
SWELLS
SWILLS
SWIRLS
SWIRLY
TWILLS
TWIRLS
TWOPLY

•W•••L
AWHIRL
SWIVEL

••WL••
BAWLED
BAWLER
BOWLED
BOWLER
BOWLES
COWLED
COWLEY
DEWLAP
FAWLTY
FOWLED
FOWLER
FOWLES
HOWLED
HOWLER
HOWLIN
MEWLED
MEWLER
NEWLEY
SAWLOG
YOWLED

••W•L•
ASWELL
ATWILL
DAWDLE
DEWILY
DOWELS
GOWILD
HOWELL
JEWELS
LEWDLY
LOWELL
MOWGLI
NEWELS
OHWELL
ORWELL
OSWALD
POWELL
REWELD
ROWELS
SEWELL
TOWELS
UNWELL
UNWILY
UPWELL
VOWELS
VOWELY

••W••L
ASWELL
ASWIRL
ATWILL
BEWAIL
HOWELL
JAWOHL
LAWFUL
LOWCAL
LOWELL
OHWELL
ORWELL
POWELL
SEWELL
UNWELL
UPWELL

•••WL•
BRAWLS
CRAWLS
CRAWLY
DRAWLS
DRAWLY
GROWLS
GROWLY
PROWLS
SCOWLS
SHAWLS
SLOWLY
TRAWLS

•••W•L
AVOWAL
CREWEL
NARWAL
TROWEL

••••WL
SCRAWL
SPRAWL

W•M•••
WAMBLE
WAMBLY
WAMPUM
WIMBLE
WIMPLE
WIMSEY
WOMBAT
WOMENS

W••M••
WARMED
WARMER
WARMLY
WARMTH
WARMUP
WEIMAR
WETMOP
WHAMMO
WHAMMY
WHIMSY
WHOMPS
WHOMSO
WONMUG
WORMED

W•••M•
WHAMMO
WHAMMY
WHELMS

W••••M
WAMPUM
WHILOM
WIGWAM
WILLEM
WINDOM
WISDOM

•W•M••
SWAMIS
SWAMPS
SWAMPY

•W••M•
SWARMS

••WM••
BOWMAN
BOWMEN
COWMAN
COWMEN
LAWMAN
LAWMEN
NEWMAN
NEWMAR

••W••M
REWARM

•••WM•
SHAWMS
SHOWME

•••W•M
WIGWAM

W•N•••
WANDER
WANERS
WANGLE
WANIER
WANING
WANNED
WANNER
WANTAD
WANTED
WANTIN
WANTON
WANTTO
WENCES
WENDED
WENTAT
WENTBY
WENTIN
WENTON
WENTUP
WINCED
WINCER
WINCES
WINDED
WINDER
WINDEX
WINDOM
WINDOW
WINDUP
WINERY
WINGED
WINGER
WINGIT
WINIER
WINING
WINISH
WINKAT
WINKED
WINKER
WINKIE
WINKLE
WINNER
WINNIE
WINNOW
WINONA
WINOUT
WINSOR
WINTER
WINTRY
WINWIN
WINZES
WONDER
WONMUG
WONNED
WONOUT
WONTED
WONTON
WYNTER
WYNTON

W••N••
WAGNER
WALNUT
WANNED
WANNER
WAPNER
WARNED
WARNER
WATNEY
WEANED
WEENIE
WEENSY
WERNER
WHANGS
WHENCE
WHINED
WHINER
WHINES
WHINEY
WHINNY
WHYNOT
WIENER
WINNER
WINNIE
WINNOW
WONNED
WOUNDS
WRENCH
WRINGS
WRONGS

W•••N•
WADING
WAGING
WAGONS
WAHINE
WAKENS
WAKING
WANING
WARING
WAVING
WAXING
WAYANS
WERENT
WHINNY
WIDENS
WILING
WINING
WINONA
WIPING
WIRING
WISENT
WIZENS
WOMENS
WOOING
WOWING

W••••N
WADEIN
WAGGON
WAITON
WALDEN
WALKEN
WALKIN
WALKON
WALTON
WANTIN
WANTON
WARDEN
WARREN
WATSON
WAVEIN
WAYLON
WEAKEN
WEAPON
WEBERN
WEDELN
WELKIN
WENTIN
WENTON
WESSON
WHITEN
WICCAN
WILSON
WILTON
WINWIN
WITHIN
WONTON
WOODEN
WOOLEN
WOREON
WORKIN
WORKON
WORSEN
WYNTON
WYSTAN
WYVERN

•WN•••
AWNING
OWNERS
OWNING
OWNSUP

•W•N••
BWANAS
GWYNNE
KWANZA
RWANDA
SWANEE
SWANKS
SWANKY
SWINGS
SWINGY
TWANGS
TWANGY
TWENTY
TWINED
TWINES
TWINGE

•W••N•
AWNING
DWAYNE
GWYNNE
OWNING
SWAINS
SWOONS
TWEENS
TWEENY

•W•••N
AWAKEN
AWOKEN
SWEDEN

••WN••
BOWNET
DAWNED
DAWNON
DOWNED
DOWNER
DOWNEY
DOWNON
FAWNED
FAWNER
GOWNED
HOWNOW
PAWNED
PAWNEE
PAWNER
SEWNON
SEWNUP
TOWNER
TOWNIE
YAWNED
YAWNER

••W•N•
ANWANG
BOWING
CAWING
COWENS
COWING
DEWING
EDWYNN
HAWING
HEWING
IOWANS
JAWING
LAWING
LOWEND
LOWING
MEWING
MOWING
PAWING
REWIND
REWINS
ROWENA
ROWENS
ROWING
SAWING
SEWING
SOWING
TAWING
TOWING
UNWIND
UPWIND
VOWING
WOWING
YAWING

••W••N
ASWOON
BOWFIN
BOWMAN
BOWMEN
COWMAN
COWMEN
DAWNON
DAWSON
DOWNON
EDWYNN
GAWAIN
HOWLIN
LAWMAN
LAWMEN
LAWSON
LAWTON
NEWMAN
NEWTON
SEWNON
SEWSON
UNWORN

•••WN•
BRAWNY
BROWNE
BROWNS
BROWNY
CLOWNS
CROWNS
DROWNS
FROWNS
KNOWNS
PRAWNS
SPAWNS

•••W•N
BLOWIN
DARWIN
DRAWIN
DRAWON
DREWIN
DREWON
FLEWIN
GODWIN
GREWON
GROWON
OBIWAN
SHOWIN
SNOWIN
TAIWAN
WINWIN

••••WN
DISOWN
GODOWN
INTOWN
MOTOWN
REMOWN
RENOWN
RESAWN
RESEWN
STREWN
THROWN
UNSEWN
UNSOWN
UPTOWN

WO••••
WOBBLE
WOBBLY
WODGES
WOEFUL
WOHLER
WOKEUP
WOLFED
WOLPER
WOLSEY
WOLVES
WOMBAT
WOMENS
WONDER
WONMUG
WONNED
WONOUT
WONTED
WONTON
WOODED
WOODEN
WOODSY
WOOERS
WOOFED
WOOFER
WOOGIE
WOOING
WOOKIE
WOOLEN
WOOLEY
WOOLLY
WORDED
WOREON
WORKED
WORKER
WORKIN
WORKON
WORKUP
WORLDS
WORMED
WORSEN
WORSTS
WORTHS
WORTHY
WOUNDS
WOVOKA
WOWING
WOWSER

W•O•••
WHOLES
WHOLLY
WHOMPS
WHOMSO
WHOOFS
WHOOPI
WHOOPS
WHOOSH
WHORLS
WOODED
WOODEN
WOODSY
WOOERS
WOOFED
WOOFER
WOOGIE
WOOING
WOOKIE
WOOLEN
WOOLEY
WOOLLY

WRONGS

W••O••
WAGONS
WAHOOS
WAYOUT
WHOOFS
WHOOPI
WHOOPS
WHOOSH
WICOPY
WIDOWS
WIGOUT
WINONA
WINOUT
WONOUT
WOVOKA

W•••O•
WACKOS
WAGGON
WAHOOS
WAITON
WALKON
WALLOP
WALLOW
WALTON
WANTON
WARGOD
WARHOL
WASHOE
WATSON
WAYLON
WEAPON
WENTON
WESSON
WETMOP
WHILOM
WHYNOT
WILCOX
WILLOW
WILSON
WILTON
WINDOM
WINDOW
WINNOW
WINSOR
WISDOM
WONTON
WOREON
WORKON
WYNTON

W••••O
WANTTO
WEIRDO
WHAMMO
WHIZZO
WHOMSO
WISETO

•WO•••
AWOKEN
SWOONS
SWOOPS
SWOOSH
SWORDS
TWOBIT
TWOFER
TWOPLY
TWOWAY

•W•O••
SWOONS
SWOOPS
SWOOSH

••WO••
ASWOON
ATWOOD
ATWORK
BOWOAR
BOWOUT
BYWORD
EDWOOD
ELWOOD
JAWOHL
MIWOKS
MYWORD
REWORD
REWORK
REWOVE
SAWOFF
SAWOUT
UNWORN
UNWOVE

••W•O•
ASWOON
ATWOOD
BOWWOW
CAWDOR
COWBOY
COWPOX
DAWNON
DAWSON
DOWNON
EDWOOD
ELWOOD
HOWNOW
HOWTOS
KOWTOW
LAWSON
LAWTON
LOWBOY
NEWTON
POWWOW
SAWLOG
SEWNON
SEWSON

••W••O
OSWEGO
SOWETO

•••WO•
BOWWOW
DOOWOP
DRAWON
DREWON
GREWON
GROWON
POWWOW

••••WO
ACTTWO
ONETWO

W•P•••
WAPITI
WAPNER
WIPERS
WIPEUP
WIPING

W••P••
WAMPUM
WARPED
WEAPON
WEEPER
WEEPIE
WHIPPY
WHIPUP
WIMPLE
WISPED
WOLPER
WRAPUP

W•••P•
WHELPS
WHIPPY
WHOMPS
WHOOPI
WHOOPS
WICOPY

W••••P
WADSUP
WAITUP
WAKEUP
WALKUP
WALLOP
WALLUP
WARMUP
WASHUP
WELLUP
WENTUP
WETMOP
WHIPUP
WINDUP
WIPEUP
WISEUP
WOKEUP
WORKUP
WRAPUP

•W•P••
SWIPED
SWIPER
SWIPES
TWOPLY

•W••P•
SWAMPS
SWAMPY
SWEEPS
SWOOPS
TWERPS

•W•••P
OWNSUP

••WP••
COWPEA
COWPER
COWPOX
GAWPED
KEWPIE
PAWPAW
YAWPED
YAWPER

••W••P
DEWLAP
ENWRAP
REWRAP
SEWNUP
SEWSUP
UNWRAP

•••W•P
BLEWUP
BLOWUP
CHEWUP
DOOWOP
DRAWUP
DREWUP
GREWUP
GROWUP
SHOWUP
SLOWUP

WR••••
WRACKS
WRAITH
WRAPUP
WRASSE
WRATHS
WRATHY
WREAKS
WREATH
WRECKS
WRENCH
WRESTS
WRETCH
WRIEST
WRIGHT
WRINGS
WRISTS
WRITER
WRITES
WRITHE
WRONGS
WRYEST

W•R•••
WARBLE
WARCRY
WARDED
WARDEN
WARDER
WARGOD
WARHOL
WARIER
WARILY
WARING
WARMED
WARMER
WARMLY
WARMTH
WARMUP
WARNED
WARNER
WARPED
WARRED
WARREN
WARSAW
WERENT
WERFEL
WERNER
WIRERS
WIRIER
WIRILY
WIRING
WORDED
WOREON
WORKED
WORKER
WORKIN
WORKON
WORKUP
WORLDS
WORMED
WORSEN
WORSTS
WORTHS
WORTHY
WURLEY
WURSTS

W••R••
WALRUS
WARRED
WARREN
WEARER
WEIRDO
WEIRDY
WHARFS
WHERED
WHERES
WHERRY
WHIRLS
WHIRLY
WHIRRS
WHORLS

W•••R•
WADERS
WAFERS
WAFERY
WAGERS
WALERS
WANERS
WARCRY
WATERS
WATERY
WAVERS
WAVERY
WAXERS
WEBERN
WHERRY
WHIRRS
WINERY
WINTRY
WIPERS
WIRERS
WIZARD
WOOERS
WYVERN

W••••R
WAGNER
WAILER
WAITER
WAIVER
WALKER
WALLER
WALTER
WANDER
WANIER
WANNER
WAPNER
WARDER
WARIER
WARMER
WARNER
WASHER
WASTER
WAVIER
WAXIER
WEAKER
WEARER
WEAVER
WEBBER
WEEDER
WEEPER
WEIMAR
WELDER
WELLER
WELTER
WERNER
WETBAR
WETHER
WETTER
WHALER
WHINER
WHITER
WICKER
WIENER
WILBUR
WILDER
WILIER
WINCER
WINDER
WINGER
WINIER
WINKER
WINNER
WINSOR
WINTER
WIRIER
WISHER
WISTER
WITHER
WOHLER
WOLPER
WONDER
WOOFER
WORKER
WOWSER
WRITER
WYNTER

•W•R••
AWARDS
DWARFS
QWERTY
SWARAJ
SWARDS
SWARMS
SWARTH
SWERVE
SWIRLS
SWIRLY
SWORDS
TWERPS
TWIRLS

•W••R•
AWEARY
AWHIRL
OWNERS
SWEARS

•W•••R
SWAYER
SWIPER
TWOFER

••WR••
BEWRAY
COWRIE
ENWRAP
REWRAP
SAWRED
UNWRAP

••W•R•
ASWIRL
ATWORK
BEWARE
BOWERS
BOWERY
BYWORD
COWARD
COWERS
DOWERS
DOWERY
EDWARD
HEWERS
HOWARD
INWARD
LOWERS
LOWERY
MOWERS
MYWORD
NEWARK
ONWARD
PAWERS
POWERS
REWARD
REWARM
REWIRE
REWORD
REWORK
ROWERS
SEWARD
SEWERS
SOWERS
TAWDRY
THWART
TOWARD
TOWERS
TOWERY
UNWARY
UNWORN
UPWARD
VOWERS

••W••R
BAWLER
BOWLER
BOWOAR
BOWSER
BOWYER
CAWDOR
COWPER
DEWIER
DOWNER
DOWSER
FAWNER
FOWLER
GAWKER
HAWKER
HAWSER
HOWLER
LAWYER
LEWDER
MEWLER
NEWMAR
PAWNER
PEWTER
POWDER
SAWYER
TOWCAR
TOWNER
WOWSER
YAWNER
YAWPER

•••WR•
GOAWRY

•••W•R
ANSWER
AVOWER
BLOWER
BREWER
BULWER
CHEWER
CLAWER
CROWER
DRAWER
FLOWER
GLOWER
GNAWER
GROWER
HOTWAR
KNOWER
PLOWER
PREWAR
PSYWAR
SHOWER
SKEWER
SLOWER
STEWER
VIEWER

W•S•••
WASABI
WASHED
WASHER
WASHES
WASHOE
WASHUP
WASTED
WASTER
WASTES
WESKIT
WESLEY
WESSEX
WESSON
WISDOM
WISELY
WISENT
WISEST
WISETO
WISEUP
WISHED
WISHER
WISHES
WISPED
WISTER
WUSSES
WYSTAN

W••S••
WADSUP
WAISTS
WARSAW
WATSON
WAUSAU
WEASEL
WESSEX
WESSON
WHISKS
WHISKY
WIESEL
WILSON
WIMSEY
WINSOR
WOLSEY
WORSEN
WORSTS
WOWSER
WRASSE
WRESTS
WRISTS
WURSTS
WUSSES

W•••S•
WABASH
WALESA
WATUSI
WEENSY
WHILST
WHIMSY

WHOMSO
WHOOSH
WIDEST
WIDISH
WINISH
WISEST
WOODSY
WRASSE
WRIEST
WRYEST

W••••S
WACKOS
WADERS
WAFERS
WAGERS
WAGONS
WAHOOS
WAISTS
WAIVES
WAKENS
WALERS
WALLIS
WALRUS
WANERS
WASHES
WASTES
WATERS
WAVERS
WAXERS
WAYANS
WEAVES
WEDGES
WEIGHS
WELLES
WENCES
WHACKS
WHALES
WHANGS
WHARFS
WHEALS
WHEATS
WHEELS
WHELKS
WHELMS
WHELPS
WHERES
WHIFFS
WHILES
WHINES
WHIRLS
WHIRRS
WHISKS
WHITES
WHOLES
WHOMPS
WHOOFS
WHOOPS
WHORLS
WIDENS
WIDOWS
WIDTHS
WIELDS
WIGHTS
WILKES
WILLIS
WINCES
WINZES
WIPERS
WIRERS
WISHES
WITHES
WIZENS
WODGES
WOLVES
WOMENS
WOOERS
WORLDS
WORSTS
WORTHS
WOUNDS
WRACKS
WRATHS
WREAKS
WRECKS
WRESTS
WRINGS
WRISTS
WRITES
WRONGS
WURSTS
WUSSES

•W•S••
OWNSUP
TWISTS
TWISTY

•W••S•
KWEISI
OWLISH
SWOOSH
TWEEST

•W•••S
AWAITS
AWAKES
AWARDS
BWANAS
DWARFS
DWEEBS
DWELLS
OWLETS
OWNERS
SWAGES
SWAINS
SWALES
SWAMIS
SWAMPS
SWANKS
SWARDS
SWARMS
SWATHS
SWAZIS
SWEARS
SWEATS
SWEDES
SWEEPS
SWEETS
SWELLS
SWIFTS
SWILLS
SWINGS
SWIPES
SWIRLS
SWOONS
SWOOPS
SWORDS
TWANGS
TWEAKS
TWEEDS
TWEENS
TWEETS
TWERPS
TWILLS
TWINES
TWIRLS
TWISTS

••WS••
BOWSAW
BOWSER
DAWSON
DOWSED
DOWSER
DOWSES
HAWSER
HAWSES
LAWSON
PAWSAT
SEWSON
SEWSUP
WOWSER

••W•S•
ALWEST
FEWEST
GOWEST
JEWISH
LOWEST
LOWISH
NEWEST
NEWISH
NLWEST
NOWISE
RAWEST
RAWISH
REWASH
SIWASH
UNWISE
UNWISH

••W••S
ALWAYS
BOWERS
BOWLES
BYWAYS
COWENS
COWERS
DOWELS
DOWERS
DOWSES
FAWKES
FOWLES
HAWSES
HEWERS
HOWTOS
IOWANS
JEWELS
LOWERS
MIWOKS
MOWERS
NAWABS
NEWELS
PAWERS
PEWEES
PEWITS
POWERS
REWEDS
REWINS
ROWELS
ROWENS
ROWERS
SEWERS
SOWERS
TOWELS
TOWERS
VOWELS
VOWERS

•••WS•
BLOWSY
BROWSE
DROWSE
DROWSY
PROWSE

•••W•S
BRAWLS
BROWNS
CLOWNS
CRAWLS
CROWDS
CROWNS
DRAWLS
DROWNS
FATWAS
FROWNS
GROWLS
KIOWAS
KNOWNS
PRAWNS
PROWLS
SCHWAS
SCOWLS
SHAWLS
SHAWMS
SPAWNS
TRAWLS

••••WS
ALLOWS
ARROWS
BEDEWS
BYLAWS
CAHOWS
ELBOWS
ENDOWS
FIVEWS
INLAWS
MACAWS
OXBOWS
PAPAWS
REMOWS
RENEWS
RESAWS
RESEWS
RETOWS
SCREWS
SEROWS
SHREWS
SINEWS
STRAWS
STREWS
THROWS
UNSEWS
UPBOWS
WIDOWS

W•T•••
WATERS
WATERY
WATNEY
WATSON
WATTLE
WATUSI
WETBAR
WETFLY
WETHER
WETMOP
WETTED
WETTER
WETTIG
WITCHY
WITHAL
WITHED
WITHER
WITHES
WITHIN
WITHIT
WITTED

W••T••
WAFTED
WAITED
WAITER
WAITON
WAITUP
WALTER
WALTON
WANTAD
WANTED
WANTIN
WANTON
WANTTO
WASTED
WASTER
WASTES
WATTLE
WELTED
WELTER
WENTAT
WENTBY
WENTIN
WENTON
WENTUP
WETTED
WETTER
WETTIG
WHATIF
WHATLL
WHATVE
WHITEN
WHITER
WHITES
WHITTY
WIDTHS
WILTED
WILTON
WINTER
WINTRY
WISTER
WITTED
WONTED
WONTON
WORTHS
WORTHY
WRATHS
WRATHY
WRETCH
WRITER
WRITES
WRITHE
WYNTER
WYNTON
WYSTAN

W•••T•
WAISTS
WANTTO
WAPITI
WARMTH
WEALTH
WHEATS
WHITTY
WIGHTS
WISETO
WORSTS
WRAITH
WREATH
WRESTS
WRISTS
WURSTS

W••••T
WALLET
WALNUT
WAYOUT
WEIGHT
WENTAT
WERENT
WESKIT
WHILST
WHYNOT
WICKET
WIDEST
WIDGET
WIGLET
WIGOUT
WILLET
WINGIT
WINKAT
WINOUT
WISENT
WISEST
WITHIT
WOMBAT
WONOUT
WRIEST
WRIGHT
WRYEST

•W•T••
SWATCH
SWATHE
SWATHS
SWITCH
TWITCH
TWITTY

•W••T•
AWAITS
OWLETS
QWERTY
SWARTH
SWEATS
SWEATY
SWEETS
SWIFTS
TWEETS
TWEETY
TWENTY
TWISTS
TWISTY
TWITTY

•W•••T
DWIGHT
SWIVET
TWEEST
TWILIT
TWOBIT

••WT••
BOWTIE
HOWTOS
KOWTOW
LAWTON
NEWTON
PEWTER

••W•T•
DEWITT
FAWLTY
GOWITH
INWITH
JEWETT
JOWETT
PEWITS
SOWETO

••W••T
ALWEST
BOWNET
BOWOUT
DEWITT
FEWEST
GOWEST
JEWETT
JOWETT
KUWAIT
LOWEST
LOWFAT
NEWEST
NLWEST
PAWSAT
RAWEST
SAWFIT
SAWOUT
SOWHAT
THWART

•••WT•
GROWTH

•••W•T
ALLWET
BLEWIT
BLOWIT
DIMWIT
FLEWAT
GODWIT
NITWIT
OUTWIT

WU••••
WURLEY
WURSTS
WUSSES

W•U•••
WAUSAU
WOUNDS

W••U••
WATUSI

W•••U•
WADSUP
WAITUP
WAKEUP
WALKUP
WALLUP
WALNUT
WALRUS
WAMPUM
WARMUP
WASHUP
WAYOUT
WELLUP
WENTUP
WHIPUP
WIGOUT
WILBUR
WILFUL
WINDUP
WINOUT
WIPEUP
WISEUP
WOEFUL
WOKEUP
WONMUG
WONOUT
WORKUP
WRAPUP

W••••U
WAUSAU

•W••U•
OWNSUP

••W•U•
BOWOUT
LAWFUL
SAWOUT
SEWNUP
SEWSUP
SOWBUG

•••WU•
BLEWUP
BLOWUP
CHEWUP
DRAWUP
DREWUP
GREWUP
GROWUP
SHOWUP
SLOWUP

••••WU
HUNGWU

W•V•••
WAVEIN
WAVERS
WAVERY
WAVIER
WAVILY
WAVING
WOVOKA
WYVERN

W••V••
WAIVED
WAIVER
WAIVES
WEAVED
WEAVER
WEAVES
WEEVIL
WOLVES

W•••V•
WHATVE

•W•V••
SWIVEL
SWIVET

•W••V•
SWERVE
TWELVE

••W•V•
REWOVE
UNWOVE

W•W•••
WOWING
WOWSER

W••W••
WAHWAH
WIGWAG
WIGWAM
WINWIN

W•••W•
WIDOWS

W••••W
WALLOW
WARSAW
WILLOW
WINDOW
WINNOW

•W•W••
TWOWAY

••WW••
BOWWOW
POWWOW

••W••W
BOWSAW
BOWWOW
GEWGAW
HAWHAW
HOWNOW
KOWTOW
PAWPAW
POWWOW

•••W•W
BOWWOW
POWWOW

W•X•••
WAXERS
WAXIER
WAXILY
WAXING

W••••X
WESSEX
WILCOX
WINDEX

••W••X
COWPOX

•••W•X
EARWAX

WY••••
WYNTER
WYNTON
WYSTAN
WYVERN

W•Y•••
WAYANS
WAYLAY
WAYLON
WAYOUT
WHYDAH
WHYNOT
WRYEST

W••••Y
WADDLY
WAFERY
WAFFLY
WAGGLY
WAMBLY
WARCRY
WARILY
WARMLY
WATERY
WATNEY
WAVERY
WAVILY
WAXILY
WAYLAY
WEAKLY
WEEKLY
WEENSY
WEIRDY
WENTBY
WESLEY
WETFLY
WHACKY
WHAMMY
WHEEZY
WHERRY
WHIMSY
WHINEY
WHINNY
WHIPPY
WHIRLY
WHISKY
WHITTY
WHOLLY
WICOPY
WIDELY
WIFELY
WIGGLY
WILDLY
WILILY
WIMSEY
WINERY
WINTRY
WIRILY
WISELY
WITCHY
WOBBLY
WOLSEY
WOODSY
WOOLEY
WOOLLY
WORTHY
WRATHY
WURLEY

•WY•••
GWYNNE

•W•Y••
DWAYNE
SWAYED
SWAYER
SWAYZE

•W•••Y
AWEARY
AWEDLY
QWERTY
SWABBY
SWAMPY
SWANKY
SWEATY
SWINGY
SWIRLY
TWANGY
TWEEDY
TWEENY
TWEETY
TWENTY
TWIGGY
TWISTY
TWITTY
TWOPLY
TWOWAY

••WY••
BOWYER
EDWYNN
LAWYER
SAWYER

••W•Y•
ALWAYS
BYWAYS

••W••Y
BEWRAY
BOWERY
COWBOY
COWLEY
DEWILY
DOWERY
DOWNEY
FAWLTY
LEWDLY
LOWBOY
LOWERY
LOWKEY
NEWLEY
TAWDRY
TOWERY
UNWARY
UNWILY
VOWELY

•••W•Y
AIRWAY
ANYWAY
BLOWSY
BLOWZY
BRAWNY
BROWNY
CONWAY
CRAWLY
DRAWLY
DROWSY
FENWAY
FLYWAY
FROWZY
GALWAY
GOAWAY
GOAWRY
GROWLY
INAWAY
JETWAY
KEYWAY
LEEWAY
MIDWAY
NORWAY
ONEWAY
PEDWAY
RUNWAY
SEAWAY
SKYWAY
SLOWLY
SUBWAY
TWOWAY

••••WY
SCREWY
SINEWY
STRAWY

W•Z•••
WIZARD
WIZENS

W••Z••
WHIZZO
WINZES

W•••Z•
WHEEZE
WHEEZY
WHIZZO

•W•Z••
SWAZIS

•W••Z•
KWANZA
SWAYZE
TWEEZE

•••WZ•
BLOWZY
FROWZY

•••W•Z
THEWIZ

XA••••
XANADU
XANTHO
XAVIER

X•A•••
XIAMEN
XRATED
XRAYED

X••A••
XANADU

X•••A•
XHOSAS

X••••A
XIMENA

•XA•••
EXACTA
EXACTO
EXACTS
EXALTS
EXARCH
OXALIS

•X•A••
EXHALE
EXPAND
EXTANT
OXCART
OXNARD
OXTAIL

•X••A•
AXONAL
EXTRAS

•X•••A
AXILLA
EXACTA
EXEDRA

••XA••
FIXATE
HEXADS
LUXATE
OAXACA
ROXANA
ROXANE
TEXACO
TEXANS

••X•A•
BOXCAR
REXCAT
TAXMAN

••X••A
LEXICA
MAXIMA
OAXACA
ROXANA

•••XA•
PLEXAL

•••X•A
ALEXIA

••••XA
ADNEXA
CUNAXA

X•B•••
XEBECS

•XB•••
OXBOWS

•X••B•
EXURBS

••XB••
BOXBOY

X•••C•
XEBECS

•XC•••
EXCEED
EXCELS
EXCEPT
EXCESS
EXCISE
EXCITE
EXCUSE
OXCART

•X•C••
EXACTA
EXACTO
EXACTS

•X••C•
EXARCH
EXPECT

•X•••C
EXILIC
EXOTIC
OXIDIC

••XC••
BOXCAR
REXCAT

••X•C•
LEXICA
MEXICO
OAXACA
TEXACO
TOXICS

••X••C
MIXTEC

X•D•••
XEDOUT

X•••D•
XANADU

X••••D
XRATED
XRAYED
XYLOID

•X•D••
EXEDRA
EXODUS
EXUDED
EXUDES
OXIDES
OXIDIC
OXYDOL

•X•••D
AXSEED
EXCEED
EXILED
EXITED
EXPAND
EXPEND
EXTEND
EXUDED
OXFORD
OXNARD

••X•D•
HEXADS
TUXEDO

••X••D
TAXIED

•••X•D
BRUXED
COAXED
FLEXED
FLUXED
HOAXED
JINXED

XE••••
XEBECS
XEDOUT
XERXES

X••E••
XEBECS
XIMENA
XYLENE

X•••E•
XAVIER
XERXES
XFILES
XIAMEN
XRATED
XRAYED
XYSTER

X••••E
XYLENE

•XE•••
EXEDRA
EXEMPT
EXERTS
EXETER
EXEUNT
OXEYES

•X•E••
AXSEED
EXCEED
EXCELS
EXCEPT
EXCESS
EXLEGE
EXPECT
EXPELS
EXPEND
EXPERT
EXSERT
EXTEND
EXTENT
EXTERN

•X••E•
AXSEED
EXCEED
EXETER
EXILED
EXILES
EXITED
EXUDED
EXUDES
OXEYES
OXIDES
OXYGEN

•X•••E
AXLIKE
EXCISE
EXCITE
EXCUSE
EXHALE
EXLEGE
EXMORE
EXPIRE
EXPOSE
EXWIFE
OXLIKE

••XE••
BOXERS
FIXERS
HEXERS
LAXEST
LEXEME
MAXENE
MIXERS
PIXELS
SIXERS
SOXERS
TAXERS
TUXEDO
VEXERS
VIXENS
WAXERS

••X•E•
BAXTER
BOXIER
BOXSET
DEXTER
FOXIER
HUXLEY
MIXTEC
NIXIES
PIXIES
PYXIES
SEXIER
SEXTET
TAXIED
TAXIES
TAXMEN
TEXMEX
WAXIER

••X••E
FIXATE
LEXEME
LUXATE
MAXENE
MAXINE
MAXIXE
ROXANE

•••XE•
ALEXEI
APEXES
BLIXEN
BRUXED
BRUXES
CALXES
COAXED
COAXER
COAXES
CRUXES
DREXEL
FLAXEN
FLAXES
FLEXED
FLEXES
FLUXED
FLUXES
HOAXED
HOAXER
HOAXES
IBEXES
ILEXES
JINXED
JINXES
LYNXES
MINXES
ONYXES
ORYXES
PRAXES
VSIXES
XERXES

•••X•E
TRIXIE

••••XE
ANNEXE
DELUXE
MAXIXE

XF••••
XFILES

•XF•••
OXFORD

•X••F•
EXWIFE

••XF••
BOXFUL

X••G••
XINGIN

•X•G••
OXYGEN

•X••G•
EXLEGE

••XG••
SIXGUN

••X••G
BOXING
FAXING
FIXING
FOXING
HEXING
MIXING
NIXING
SIXING
TAXING
VEXING
WAXING

XH••••
XHOSAS

X•••H•
XANTHO

•XH•••
EXHALE
EXHORT

•X•••H
EXARCH

••X•H•
SIXTHS

XI••••
XIAMEN
XIMENA
XINGIN

X•I•••
XFILES

X••I••
XAVIER

X•••I•
XINGIN
XYLOID

•XI•••
AXILLA
AXIOMS
AXIONS
EXILED
EXILES
EXILIC
EXISTS
EXITED
OXIDES
OXIDIC

•X•I••
AXLIKE
EXCISE
EXCITE
EXPIRE
EXPIRY
EXWIFE
OXLIKE
OXLIPS

•X••I•
EXILIC
EXOTIC
OXALIS
OXIDIC
OXTAIL

••XI••
AUXINS
BOXIER
BOXING
DIXITS
FAXING
FIXING
FIXITY
FOXIER
FOXILY
FOXING
HEXING
LAXITY
LEXICA
MAXIMA
MAXIMS
MAXINE
MAXIXE
MEXICO
MIXING
NIXIES
NIXING
PIXIES
PYXIES
SEXIER
SEXILY
SEXIST
SIXING
TAXIED
TAXIES
TAXING
TOXICS
TOXINS
VEXING
WAXIER
WAXILY
WAXING

•••XI•
ALEXIA
ALEXIS
DIOXIN
ELIXIR
NOEXIT
PINXIT
PRAXIS
TRIXIE
ZEUXIS

•••X•I
ALEXEI

••••XI
BILOXI

•X••K•
AXLIKE
OXLIKE

X•L•••
XYLENE
XYLOID

X••L••
XFILES

•XL•••
AXLIKE
EXLEGE
OXLIKE
OXLIPS

•X•L••
AXILLA
EXALTS
EXILED
EXILES
EXILIC
EXULTS
OXALIS

•X••L•
AXILLA
EXCELS
EXHALE
EXPELS
EXTOLS

•X•••L
AXONAL
OXTAIL
OXYDOL

••XL••
HUXLEY

••X•L•
FOXILY
PIXELS
SEXILY
WAXILY

••X••L
BOXFUL

•••X•L
DREXEL
PLEXAL

X•M•••
XIMENA

X••M••
XIAMEN

•XM•••
EXMOOR
EXMORE

•X•M••
EXEMPT

•X••M•
AXIOMS

••XM••
TAXMAN
TAXMEN
TEXMEX

••X•M•
LEXEME
MAXIMA
MAXIMS

X•N•••
XANADU
XANTHO
XINGIN

X•••N•
XIMENA
XYLENE

X••••N
XIAMEN
XINGIN

•XN•••
OXNARD

•X•N••
AXONAL

•X••N•
AXIONS
EXEUNT
EXPAND
EXPEND
EXTANT
EXTEND
EXTENT

•X•••N
EXTERN
OXYGEN

••XN••
HEXNUT

••X•N•
AUXINS
BOXING
FAXING
FIXING
FOXING
HEXING
MAXENE
MAXINE
MIXING
NIXING
ROXANA
ROXANE
SAXONS
SAXONY
SIXING
TAXING
TEXANS
TOXINS
VEXING
VIXENS
WAXING

••X••N
CAXTON
PAXTON
SEXTON
SIXGUN
TAXMAN
TAXMEN

•••X•N
BLIXEN
DIOXIN
FLAXEN
KLAXON

X•O•••
XHOSAS

X••O••
XEDOUT
XYLOID

X••••O
XANTHO

•XO•••
AXONAL
EXODUS
EXOTIC

•X•O••
AXIOMS
AXIONS
EXHORT
EXMOOR
EXMORE
EXPORT
EXPOSE
EXPOST
EXTOLS
EXTORT
EXVOTO
OXBOWS
OXFORD

•X••O•
EXMOOR
OXYDOL

•X•••O
EXACTO
EXVOTO

••XO••
MAXOUT
SAXONS
SAXONY

••X•O•
BOXBOY
BOXTOP
CAXTON
PAXTON
SEXTON
VOXPOP

••X••O
DEXTRO
MEXICO
NEXTTO
TEXACO
TUXEDO

•••XO•
ETUXOR
FLEXOR
KLAXON
PLEXOR

••••XO
BORAXO

•XP•••
EXPAND
EXPECT
EXPELS
EXPEND
EXPERT
EXPIRE
EXPIRY
EXPORT
EXPOSE
EXPOST

•X••P•
EXCEPT
EXEMPT
OXLIPS

••XP••
VOXPOP

••X•P•
FIXUPS
MIXUPS

••X••P
BOXTOP
VOXPOP

XR••••
XRATED
XRAYED

X•R•••
XERXES

X••••R
XAVIER
XYSTER

•X•R••
EXARCH
EXERTS
EXTRAS
EXURBS

•X••R•
EXEDRA
EXHORT
EXMORE
EXPERT
EXPIRE
EXPIRY
EXPORT
EXSERT
EXTERN
EXTORT
OXCART
OXFORD
OXNARD

•X•••R
EXETER
EXMOOR

••X•R•
BOXERS
DEXTRO
FIXERS
HEXERS
LUXURY
MIXERS
SIXERS
SOXERS
TAXERS
VEXERS
WAXERS

••X••R
BAXTER
BOXCAR
BOXIER
DEXTER
FOXIER
SEXIER
WAXIER

•••X•R
COAXER
ELIXIR
ETUXOR
FLEXOR
HOAXER
PLEXOR

X•S•••
XYSTER

X••S••
XHOSAS

X••••S
XEBECS
XERXES
XFILES
XHOSAS

•XS•••
AXSEED
EXSERT

•X•S••
EXISTS

•X••S•
EXCESS
EXCISE
EXCUSE
EXPOSE
EXPOST

•X•••S
AXIOMS
AXIONS
EXACTS
EXALTS
EXCELS
EXCESS
EXERTS
EXILES
EXISTS
EXODUS
EXPELS
EXTOLS
EXTRAS
EXUDES
EXULTS
EXURBS
OXALIS
OXBOWS
OXEYES
OXIDES
OXLIPS

••XS••
BOXSET

••X•S•
LAXEST
SEXIST

••X••S
AUXINS
BOXERS
DIXITS
FIXERS
FIXUPS
HEXADS
HEXERS
MAXIMS
MIXERS
MIXUPS
NIXIES
PIXELS
PIXIES
PYXIES
SAXONS
SIXERS
SIXTHS
SIXTUS
SOXERS
TAXERS
TAXIES
TEXANS
TOXICS
TOXINS
VEXERS
VIXENS
WAXERS

•••X•S
ALEXIS
APEXES
BRUXES
CALXES
COAXES
CRUXES
FLAXES
FLEXES
FLUXES
HOAXES
IBEXES
ILEXES
JINXES
LYNXES
MINXES
ONYXES
ORYXES
PLEXUS
PRAXES
PRAXIS
VSIXES
XERXES
ZEUXIS

X••T••
XANTHO
XRATED
XYSTER

X••••T
XEDOUT

•XT•••
EXTANT
EXTEND
EXTENT
EXTERN
EXTOLS
EXTORT
EXTRAS
OXTAIL

•X•T••
EXETER
EXITED
EXOTIC

•X••T•
EXACTA
EXACTO
EXACTS
EXALTS
EXCITE
EXERTS
EXISTS
EXULTS
EXVOTO

•X•••T
EXCEPT
EXEMPT
EXEUNT
EXHORT
EXPECT
EXPERT
EXPORT
EXPOST
EXSERT
EXTANT
EXTENT
EXTORT
OXCART

••XT••
BAXTER
BOXTOP
CAXTON
DEXTER
DEXTRO
MIXTEC
NEXTTO
PAXTON
SEXTET
SEXTON
SIXTHS
SIXTUS

••X•T•
DIXITS
FIXATE
FIXITY
LAXITY
LUXATE
NEXTTO

••X••T
BOXSET
HEXNUT
LAXEST
MAXOUT
REXCAT
SEXIST
SEXTET

•••X•T
NOEXIT
PINXIT

••••XT
URTEXT

X•••U•
XEDOUT

X••••U
XANADU

•XU•••
EXUDED
EXUDES
EXULTS
EXURBS

•X•U••
EXCUSE
EXEUNT

•X••U•
EXODUS

••XU••
FIXUPS
LUXURY
MIXUPS

••X•U•
BOXFUL
HEXNUT
MAXOUT
SIXGUN
SIXTUS

•••XU•
PLEXUS

X•V•••
XAVIER

•XV•••
EXVOTO

•XW•••
EXWIFE

•X••W•
OXBOWS

X••X••
XERXES

••X•X•
MAXIXE

••X••X
TEXMEX

•••XX•
SKNXXX

•••X•X
SKNXXX

••••XX
SKNXXX

XY••••
XYLENE
XYLOID
XYSTER

X••Y••
XRAYED

•XY•••
OXYDOL
OXYGEN

•X•Y••
OXEYES

•X•••Y
EXPIRY

••X••Y
BOXBOY
FIXITY
FOXILY
HUXLEY
LAXITY
LUXURY
SAXONY
SEXILY
WAXILY

••••XY
EUTAXY
GALAXY

YA••••
YABBER
YACHTS
YACKED
YAHOOS
YAHWEH
YAKIMA
YAKKED
YAKKER
YAKUTS
YAKUZA
YALIES
YAMAHA
YAMMER
YANGON
YANKED
YANKEE
YANQUI
YAPOKS
YAPPED
YAQUIS
YARDED
YARELY
YAREST
YARNED
YARROW
YASSER
YAUPON
YAWING
YAWNED
YAWNER
YAWPED
YAWPER

Y•A•••
YEAGER
YEANED
YEARLY
YEARNS
YEASTS
YEASTY

Y••A••
YAMAHA
YOUALL
YUKATA
YUKAWA

Y•••A•
YENTAS
YEOMAN
YESMAN
YUCCAS
YUNNAN

Y••••A
YAKIMA
YAKUZA
YAMAHA
YORUBA
YOYOMA
YUKATA
YUKAWA

•YA•••
CYANIC
DYADIC
HYADES
KYACKS
NYALAS
NYASSA
RYAZAN

•Y•A••
AYEAYE
AYMARA
BYHAND
BYLAWS
BYNAME
BYPASS
BYPAST
BYPATH
BYTALK
BYWAYS
CYCADS
CYRANO
DYNAMO
DYNAST
GYRATE
MYNAHS
PYJAMA
TYBALT
TYRANT
ZYMASE

•Y••A•
BYPLAY
BYROAD
CYCLAS
CYMBAL
GYMBAG
HYDRAE
HYDRAS
HYENAS
HYETAL
HYMNAL
MYRDAL
MYRIAD
NYALAS
RYAZAN
RYOKAN
SYLVAN
SYNTAX
SYRIAN
TYRIAN
WYSTAN

•Y•••A
AYESHA
AYMARA
MYOPIA
NYASSA
PYJAMA
PYTHIA
SYLVIA

••YA••
ANYANG
ARYANS
BAYARD
BOYARS
BRYANT
DRYADS
GAYALS
GUYANA
KAYAKS
MAYANS
RIYADH
RIYALS
ROYALE
ROYALS
VOYAGE
WAYANS

••Y•A•
AMYTAN
ANYDAY
ANYWAY
CAYMAN
FLYMAN
FLYWAY
FRYPAN
HEYDAY
KEYPAD
KEYWAY
LAYMAN
MAYDAY
MAYHAP
MAYTAG
NAYSAY
OHYEAH
PAYDAY
PHYLAE
PSYWAR
SKYCAP
SKYLAB
SKYWAY
TAYRAS
WAYLAY
WHYDAH

••Y••A
ALYSSA
CAYUGA
GUYANA
LOYOLA
PAYOLA
PSYLLA
SCYLLA
SMYRNA
STYRIA
TOYOTA
YOYOMA
ZOYSIA

•••YA•
BANYAN
BATYAM
BUNYAN
GALYAK
KENYAN
LIBYAN
MAGYAR
MINYAN
PLAYAS
PLAYAT

•••Y•A
CORYZA
DURYEA

••••YA
LATOYA
MALAYA
MAURYA
NAGOYA
PAPAYA
VAISYA

Y•B•••
YABBER
YOBBOS

Y••B••
YABBER
YOBBOS
YOUBET

Y•••B•
YORUBA

•YB•••
CYBELE
CYBILL
CYBORG
DYBBUK
GYBING
HYBRID
TYBALT
VYBORG

•Y•B••
BYEBYE
CYMBAL
DYBBUK
GYMBAG
SYMBOL
TYDBOL

•Y••B•
TYCOBB

•Y•••B
TYCOBB

••YB••
DAYBED
DAYBOY
FLYBOY
FLYBYS
KHYBER
LAYBYS
MAYBES
PAYBOX
SKYBOX

••Y•B•
LAYSBY

••Y••B
DAYJOB
SKYLAB

Y•C•••
YACHTS
YACKED
YUCCAS

Y••C••
YOICKS
YUCCAS

Y•••C•
YORICK

•YC•••
CYCADS
CYCLAS
CYCLED
CYCLER
CYCLES
CYCLIC
CYCLOS
LYCEES
LYCEUM
TYCOBB
TYCOON

•Y•C••
EYECUP
KYACKS
SYNCED

•Y••C•
CYNICS
LYRICS
ZYDECO

•Y•••C
CYANIC
CYCLIC
CYMRIC
DYADIC
MYOPIC
MYSTIC
MYTHIC
PYKNIC
SYNDIC

••YC••
GLYCOL
JAYCEE
PSYCHE
PSYCHO
PSYCHS
SKYCAP

••Y•C•
DRYICE

•••Y•C
INSYNC

Y•D•••
YODELS

Y••D••
YARDED
YONDER

Y•••D•
YEHUDI
YIELDS

Y••••D
YACKED
YAKKED
YANKED
YAPPED
YARDED
YARNED
YAWNED
YAWPED
YEANED
YELLED
YELPED
YENNED
YERKED
YESSED
YIPPED
YOLKED
YOWLED
YOYOED
YUKKED

•YD•••
CYDERS
HYDRAE
HYDRAS
HYDROS
RYDELL
SYDNEY
TYDBOL
ZYDECO

•Y•D••
DYADIC
FYODOR
HYADES
LYNDON
MYRDAL
PYEDOG
SYNDIC

•Y••D•
CYCADS
SYNODS

•Y•••D
BYHAND
BYROAD
BYWORD
CYCLED
EYELID
GYPPED
HYBRID
HYMNED
HYPOED
LYNYRD
MYRIAD
MYWORD
SYNCED
XYLOID

••YD••
ABYDOS
ANYDAY
DRYDEN
HAYDEN
HEYDAY
HOYDEN
LEYDEN
MAYDAY
OXYDOL
PAYDAY
SNYDER
TOYDOG
WHYDAH

••Y•D•
DRYADS
RIYADH

••Y••D
BAYARD
BEYOND
DAYBED
FLYROD
KAYOED
KEYPAD
PHYSED
RHYMED
SAYYID
STYLED
YOYOED

•••YD•
ALKYDS
ANHYDR
LLOYDS
MRHYDE

•••Y•D
BRAYED
BUOYED
CLOYED
DRAYED
FLAYED
FLEYED
FRAYED
GRAYED
GREYED
LYNYRD
OBEYED
OKAYED
PLAYED
PRAYED
PREYED
REDYED
SAYYID
SLAYED
SPAYED
STAYED
SWAYED
UNDYED
XRAYED

YE••••
YEAGER
YEANED
YEARLY
YEARNS
YEASTS
YEASTY
YEHUDI

YELLED
YELLER
YELLOW
YELPED
YELPER
YEMENI
YENNED
YENTAS
YEOMAN
YEOMEN
YERKED
YERKES
YESMAN
YESMEN
YESSED
YESSES
YESSIR
YESTER

Y•E•••

YIELDS
YVETTE

Y••E••

YARELY
YAREST
YEMENI
YODELS
YOKELS

Y•••E•

YABBER
YACKED
YAHWEH
YAKKED
YAKKER
YALIES
YAMMER
YANKED
YANKEE
YAPPED
YARDED
YARNED
YASSER
YAWNED
YAWNER
YAWPED
YAWPER
YEAGER
YEANED
YELLED
YELLER
YELPED
YELPER
YENNED
YEOMEN
YERKED
YERKES
YESMEN
YESSED
YESSES
YESTER
YIPPED
YIPPEE
YOLKED
YONDER
YORKER
YOUBET
YOWLED
YOYOED
YUKKED

Y••••E

YANKEE
YIPPEE
YORKIE
YUPPIE
YVETTE
YVONNE

•YE•••

AYEAYE
AYESHA
BYEBYE
DYEING
DYELOT
EYECUP
EYEFUL
EYEING
EYELET
EYELID
HYENAS
HYETAL
MYELIN
PYEDOG

•Y•E••

CYBELE
CYDERS
GYRENE
HYPEUP
LYCEES
LYCEUM
MYSELF
NYMETS
RYDELL
TYPERS
TYPEUP
WYVERN
XYLENE
ZYDECO

•Y••E•

BYRNES
CYCLED
CYCLER
CYCLES
CYGNET
CYPHER
EYELET
EYRIES
GYPPED
GYPPER
HYADES
HYMNED
HYPHEN
HYPOED
LYCEES
LYNLEY
LYNXES
MYOPES
OYSTER
PYXIES
SYDNEY
SYNCED
SYSTEM
TYPIER
WYNTER
XYSTER

•Y•••E

AYEAYE
BYEBYE
BYGONE
BYJOVE
BYLINE
BYNAME
BYROTE
BYSSHE
CYBELE
GYRATE
GYRENE
GYROSE
HYDRAE
LYSINE
MYRTLE
MYSORE
PYRITE
TYRONE
XYLENE
ZYGOTE
ZYMASE

••YE••

BAYEUX
BUYERS
COYEST
CRYERS
DIYERS
DOYENS
DRYERS
DRYEST
FEYEST
FLYERS
FOYERS
FRYERS
GAYEST
LAYERS
MOYERS
OHYEAH
PAYEES
PAYERS
SAYERS
SHYEST
SLYEST
TUYERE
WRYEST

••Y•E•

DAYBED
DRYDEN
ELYSEE
FLYMEN
FLYNET
GEYSER
HAYDEN
HAYLEY
HOYDEN
JAYCEE
JAYVEE
JOYNER
KAYOED
KEYNES
KHYBER
LAYMEN
LEYDEN
MAYBES
MAYHEM
ONYXES
ORYXES
OXYGEN
PAYEES
PHYSED
RHYMED
RHYMER
RHYMES
SAYLES
SAYYES
SLYPES
SNYDER
STYLED
STYLER
STYLES
STYLET
YOYOED

••Y••E

ANYONE
BLYTHE
CAYUSE
COYOTE
DAYONE
DRYICE
EEYORE
ELYSEE
GWYNNE
JAYCEE
JAYVEE
PEYOTE
PHYLAE
PRYNNE
PSYCHE
ROYALE
SCYTHE
STYMIE
TUYERE
UNYOKE
VOYAGE

•••YE•

BOWYER
BRAYED
BRAYER
BREYER
BUOYED
CLAYEY
CLOYED
DLAYER
DRAYED
DURYEA
ELAYER
FLAYED
FLAYER
FLEYED
FRAYED
GRAYED
GRAYER
GREYED
GREYER
LAWYER
NGUYEN
NOTYET
OBEYED
OKAYED
OXEYES
PLAYED
PLAYER
PRAYED
PRAYER
PREYED
REDYED
REDYES
SAWYER
SAYYES
SLAYED
SLAYER
SPAYED
SPRYER
STAYED
SWAYED
SWAYER
THAYER
UNDYED
XRAYED

•••Y•E

ARGYLE
DWAYNE
ECTYPE
ELAYNE
ENZYME
MRHYDE
OOCYTE
QUAYLE
RETYPE
SHAYNE
SWAYZE
THEYRE
THEYVE

••••YE

AYEAYE
AZODYE
BYEBYE
HEARYE
INOUYE
POPEYE
REDEYE
RIBEYE
TIEDYE

•Y•F••

EYEFUL

•Y••F•

TYPIFY

•Y•••F

MYSELF

••YF••

DRYFLY
JOYFUL
LAYFOR
MAYFLY
PAYFOR
TRYFOR

••Y•F•

BUYOFF
CRYOFF
DRYOFF
LAYOFF
PAYOFF

••Y••F

BUYOFF
CRYOFF
DRYOFF
LAYOFF
PAYOFF

Y•G•••

YOGINI
YOGISM
YOGURT

Y••G••

YANGON
YEAGER
YUNGLO

Y••••G

YAWING
YOKING

•YG•••

BYGONE
BYGOSH
CYGNET
CYGNUS
MYGIRL
ZYGOTE

•Y••G•

SYZYGY

•Y•••G

CYBORG
DYEING
EYEING
GYBING
GYMBAG
HYPING
PYEDOG
TYPING
VYBORG

••YG••

DAYGLO
OXYGEN
RAYGUN

••Y•G•

CAYUGA
ERYNGO
VOYAGE

••Y••G

ABYING
ANYANG
BAYING
BUYING
CRYING
DRYING
FLYING
FRYING
GUYING
HAYING
KEYING
LAYING
MAYTAG
PAYING
PLYING
PRYING
SAYING
SHYING
SKYING
SPYING
TOYDOG
TOYING
TRYING

•••YG•

SYZYGY

••••YG

KENNYG

Y•H•••

YAHOOS
YAHWEH
YEHUDI
YOHOHO

Y••H••

YACHTS
YOOHOO

Y•••H•

YAMAHA
YOHOHO
YOUTHS

Y••••H

YAHWEH

•YH•••

BYHAND

•Y•H••

CYPHER
HYPHEN
MYOHMY
MYTHIC
MYTHOI
MYTHOL
MYTHOS
PYTHIA
PYTHON
SYPHON
TYPHUS

•Y••H•

AYESHA
BYSSHE
KYUSHU
LYMPHS
MYNAHS
MYRRHS
NYMPHS
SYLPHS

•Y•••H

BYGOSH
BYPATH

••YH••

ANYHOW
MAYHAP
MAYHEM

••Y•H•

BLYTHE
GLYPHS
PSYCHE
PSYCHO
PSYCHS
RHYTHM
SCYTHE

••Y••H

BOYISH
COYISH
OHYEAH
RIYADH
WHYDAH

•••Y•H

IRTYSH

YI••••

YIELDS
YIPPED
YIPPEE

Y•I•••

YOICKS

Y••I••

YAKIMA
YALIES
YAWING
YOGINI
YOGISM
YOKING
YORICK

Y•••I•

YAQUIS
YESSIR
YORKIE
YUPPIE

Y••••I

YANQUI
YEHUDI
YEMENI
YOGINI

•Y•I••

BYLINE
CYBILL
CYNICS
DYEING
EYEING
EYRIES
GYBING
HYPING
LYRICS
LYRIST
LYSINE
LYSINS
MYGIRL
MYRIAD
PYRITE
PYXIES
SYRIAN
SYRINX
TYPIER
TYPIFY
TYPING
TYPIST
TYRIAN

•Y••I•

CYANIC
CYCLIC
CYMRIC
DYADIC
EYELID
HYBRID
MYELIN
MYOPIA
MYOPIC
MYOSIN
MYOSIS
MYSTIC
MYTHIC
NYQUIL
PYKNIC
PYTHIA
SYLVIA
SYNDIC
XYLOID

•Y•••I

MYTHOI

••YI••

ABYING
BAYING
BOYISH
BUYING
COYISH
CRYING
DRYICE
DRYING
DRYINK
FLYING
FLYINS
FRYING
GUYING
HAYING
KEYING
LAYING
PAYING
PLYING
PRYING
SAYING

SHYING
SKYING
SPYING
TOYING
TRYING
ZAYINS

••Y•I•
DAYLIT
GLYNIS
KEYSIN
LAYSIN
PAYSIN
PHYSIO
SAYYID
STYMIE
STYRIA
ZOYSIA

••Y••I
THYRSI

•••YI•
BUNYIP
PINYIN
SAYYID

•••Y•I
PAPYRI

•YJ•••
BYJOVE
PYJAMA

••YJ••
DAYJOB

Y•K•••
YAKIMA
YAKKED
YAKKER
YAKUTS
YAKUZA
YOKELS
YOKING
YOKUTS
YUKATA
YUKAWA
YUKKED

Y••K••
YACKED
YAKKED
YAKKER
YANKED
YANKEE
YERKED
YERKES
YOLKED
YORKER
YORKIE
YUKKED

Y•••K•
YAPOKS
YOICKS
YUROKS

Y••••K
YORICK

•YK•••
HYKSOS
PYKNIC

•Y•K••
RYOKAN
RYUKYU

•Y••K•
KYACKS

•Y•••K
BYTALK
DYBBUK

••Y•K•
KAYAKS
UNYOKE

••Y••K
DRYINK

•••Y•K
GALYAK

Y•L•••
YALIES
YELLED
YELLER
YELLOW
YELPED
YELPER
YOLKED

Y••L••
YELLED
YELLER
YELLOW
YIELDS
YOWLED

Y•••L•
YARELY
YEARLY
YODELS
YOKELS
YOUALL
YUNGLO

Y••••L
YOUALL

•YL•••
BYLAWS
BYLINE
NYLONS
PYLONS
SYLPHS
SYLVAN
SYLVIA
XYLENE
XYLOID

•Y•L••
BYPLAY
CYCLAS
CYCLED
CYCLER
CYCLES
CYCLIC
CYCLOS
DYELOT
EYELET
EYELID
LYNLEY
MYELIN
NYALAS

•Y••L•
BYTALK
CYBELE
CYBILL
MYRTLE
MYSELF
RYDELL
TYBALT

•Y•••L
CYBILL
CYMBAL
EYEFUL
HYETAL
HYMNAL
MYGIRL
MYRDAL
MYTHOL
NYQUIL
RYDELL
SYMBOL
TYDBOL

••YL••
ASYLUM
BAYLOR
CEYLON
DAYLIT
HAYLEY
IDYLLS
LAYLOW
PHYLAE
PHYLLO
PHYLUM
PSYLLA
SAYLES
SCYLLA
SKYLAB
STYLED
STYLER
STYLES
STYLET
STYLUS
TAYLOR
TRYLON
WAYLAY
WAYLON

••Y•L•
DAYGLO
DRYFLY
GAYALS
IDYLLS
LOYOLA
MAYFLY
PAYOLA
PHYLLO
PSYLLA
RIYALS
ROYALE
ROYALS
SCYLLA

••Y••L
ETYMOL
GLYCOL
JOYFUL
OXYDOL

•••YL•
ALKYLS
ARGYLE
ARGYLL
GRAYLY
GREYLY
JEKYLL
QUAYLE
SIBYLS
SPRYLY
THEYLL
VINYLS

•••Y•L
ARGYLL
JEKYLL
THEYLL

••••YL
ACETYL
CHERYL
DACTYL
DARRYL
METHYL
PHENYL
SHERYL

Y•M•••
YAMAHA
YAMMER
YEMENI
YOMTOV
YUMYUM

Y••M••
YAMMER
YEOMAN
YEOMEN
YESMAN
YESMEN

Y•••M•
YAKIMA
YOYOMA

Y••••M
YOGISM
YUMYUM

•YM•••
AYMARA
CYMBAL
CYMRIC
GYMBAG
HYMNAL
HYMNED
LYMPHS
NYMETS
NYMPHS
SYMBOL
ZYMASE

•Y••M•
BYNAME
DYNAMO
MYOHMY
PYJAMA

•Y•••M
GYPSUM
LYCEUM
SYSTEM

••YM••
CAYMAN
ETYMOL
ETYMON
FLYMAN
FLYMEN
HAYMOW
LAYMAN
LAYMEN
RHYMED
RHYMER
RHYMES
STYMIE
THYMUS

••Y•M•
ABYSMS
YOYOMA

••Y••M
ADYTUM
ASYLUM
BAYRUM
MAYHEM
PHYLUM
RHYTHM

•••YM•
ENZYME

•••Y•M
BATYAM
FAIYUM
YUMYUM

••••YM
ANONYM
EPONYM

Y•N•••
YANGON
YANKED
YANKEE
YANQUI
YENNED
YENTAS
YONDER
YUNGLO
YUNNAN

Y••N••
YARNED
YAWNED
YAWNER
YEANED
YENNED
YUNNAN
YVONNE

Y•••N•
YAWING
YEARNS
YEMENI
YOGINI
YOKING
YVONNE

Y••••N
YANGON
YAUPON
YEOMAN
YEOMEN
YESMAN
YESMEN
YUNNAN

•YN•••
BYNAME
CYNICS
DYNAMO
DYNAST
LYNDON
LYNLEY
LYNXES
LYNYRD
MYNAHS
SYNCED
SYNDIC
SYNODS
SYNTAX
WYNTER
WYNTON

•Y•N••
BYRNES
CYANIC
CYGNET
CYGNUS
HYENAS
HYMNAL
HYMNED
HYPNOS
PYKNIC
SYDNEY

•Y••N•
BYGONE
BYHAND
BYLINE
CYRANO
DYEING
EYEING
GYBING
GYRENE
GYRONS
HYPING
LYSINE
LYSINS
NYLONS
PYLONS
SYRINX
TYPING
TYRANT
TYRONE
XYLENE

•Y•••N
HYPHEN
LYNDON
LYTTON
MYELIN
MYOSIN
PYTHON
RYAZAN
RYOKAN
SYLVAN
SYPHON
SYRIAN
TYCOON
TYRIAN
WYNTON
WYSTAN
WYVERN

••YN••
ERYNGO
FLYNET
GAYNOR
GLYNIS
GWYNNE
JOYNER
KEYNES
PRYNNE
WHYNOT

••Y•N•
ABYING
ANYANG
ANYONE
ARYANS
BAYING
BEYOND
BRYANT
BRYONY
BUYING
CRYING
DAYONE
DOYENS
DRYING
DRYINK
FLYING
FLYINS
FRYING
GUYANA
GUYING
GWYNNE
HAYING
KEYING
LAYING
MAYANS
PAYING
PLYING
PRYING
PRYNNE
RAYONS
SAYING
SHYING
SKYING
SMYRNA
SPYING
TOYING
TOYONS
TRYING
WAYANS
ZAYINS

••Y••N
AMYTAN
BRYSON
CAYMAN
CEYLON
CHYRON
DAYTON
DRYDEN
DRYRUN
ETYMON
FLYMAN
FLYMEN
FRYPAN
HAYDEN
HOYDEN
KEYSIN
LAYMAN
LAYMEN
LAYSIN
LAYSON
LEYDEN
OXYGEN
PAYSIN
PAYSON
PEYTON
RAYGUN
RHYTON
STYRON
TRYLON
WAYLON

•••YN•
DWAYNE
EDWYNN
ELAYNE
INSYNC
LARYNX
SHAYNE

•••Y•N
BANYAN
BARYON
BUNYAN
CANYON
CRAYON
EDWYNN
KENYAN
LIBYAN
MINYAN
NGUYEN
PINYIN
PINYON
PLAYON
PREYON
RUNYON
STAYON

••••YN
BOLEYN
CRONYN
EVELYN
JACLYN
MELVYN
MERVYN
POLEYN
VANRYN

YO••••
YOBBOS
YODELS
YOGINI
YOGISM
YOGURT
YOHOHO
YOICKS
YOKELS
YOKING
YOKUTS
YOLKED
YOMTOV
YONDER
YOOHOO
YORICK
YORKER
YORKIE
YORUBA
YOUALL
YOUBET
YOUTHS
YOWLED
YOYOED
YOYOMA

Y•O•••
YEOMAN
YEOMEN
YOOHOO
YVONNE

Y••O••
YAHOOS
YAPOKS
YOHOHO
YOYOED
YOYOMA
YUROKS

Y•••O•
YAHOOS
YANGON
YARROW
YAUPON
YELLOW

YOBBOS
YOMTOV
YOOHOO

Y••••O
YOHOHO
YOOHOO
YUNGLO

•YO•••
FYODOR
MYOHMY
MYOPES
MYOPIA
MYOPIC
MYOSIN
MYOSIS
RYOKAN

•Y•O••
BYGONE
BYGOSH
BYJOVE
BYROAD
BYROTE
BYWORD
CYBORG
GYRONS
GYROSE
HYPOED
MYSORE
MYWORD
NYLONS
PYLONS
SYNODS
SYSOPS
TYCOBB
TYCOON
TYRONE
VYBORG
XYLOID
ZYGOTE

•Y••O•
CYCLOS
DYELOT
FYODOR
HYDROS
HYKSOS
HYPNOS
HYSSOP
LYNDON
LYTTON
MYTHOI
MYTHOL
MYTHOS
PYEDOG
PYTHON
SYMBOL
SYPHON
TYCOON
TYDBOL
WYNTON

•Y•••O
CYRANO
DYNAMO
ZYDECO

••YO••
ANYONE
BAYOUS
BEYOND
BRYONY
BUYOFF
BUYOUT
COYOTE
CRYOFF
DAYONE
DRYOFF
DRYOUT
EEYORE
FLYOUT
GUYOTS
JOYOUS
KAYOED
LAYOFF
LAYOUT
LOYOLA
MAYORS
PAYOFF
PAYOLA
PAYOUT
PEYOTE
RAYONS
TOYONS
TOYOTA
TRYOUT
UNYOKE
WAYOUT
YOYOED
YOYOMA

••Y•O•
ABYDOS
ANYHOW
BAYLOR
BRYSON
CEYLON
CHYRON
DAYBOY
DAYJOB
DAYTON
DRYROT
ETYMOL
ETYMON
FLYBOY
FLYROD
GAYNOR
GLYCOL
HAYMOW
HEYYOU
LAYFOR
LAYLOW
LAYSON
MAYPOP
OXYDOL
PAYBOX
PAYFOR
PAYSON
PEYTON
RHYTON
SAYSOS
SKYBOX
STYRON
TAYLOR
TOYDOG
TRYFOR
TRYLON
WAYLON
WHYNOT

••Y••O
CRYPTO
DAYGLO
ERYNGO
LAYSTO
PHYLLO
PHYSIO
PSYCHO

•••YO•
BARYON
CANYON
CRAYON
HEYYOU
PINYON
PLAYON
PREYON
RUNYON
STAYON

••••YO
ARROYO
DADDYO
DAIMYO
EMBRYO
TAMAYO

Y•P•••
YAPOKS
YAPPED
YIPPED
YIPPEE
YUPPIE

Y••P••
YAPPED
YAUPON
YAWPED
YAWPER
YELPED
YELPER
YIPPED
YIPPEE
YUPPIE

•YP•••
BYPASS
BYPAST
BYPATH
BYPLAY
CYPHER
CYPRUS
GYPPED
GYPPER
GYPSUM
HYPEUP
HYPHEN
HYPING
HYPNOS
HYPOED
SYPHON
TYPERS
TYPEUP
TYPHUS
TYPIER
TYPIFY
TYPING
TYPIST

•Y•P••
GYPPED
GYPPER
LYMPHS
MYOPES
MYOPIA
MYOPIC
NYMPHS
SYLPHS

•Y••P•
SYRUPS
SYRUPY
SYSOPS

•Y•••P
EYECUP
HYPEUP
HYSSOP
TYPEUP

••YP••
COYPUS
CRYPTO
CRYPTS
FRYPAN
GLYPHS
KEYPAD
MAYPOP
SLYPES

••Y•P•
LAYUPS

••Y••P
BUYSUP
KEYSUP
LAYSUP
MAYHAP
MAYPOP
PAYSUP
SKYCAP

•••YP•
ECTYPE
POLYPS
RETYPE

•••Y•P
BUNYIP
BUOYUP
PLAYUP
PONYUP
STAYUP
TIDYUP

Y•Q•••
YAQUIS

Y••Q••
YANQUI

•YQ•••
NYQUIL

Y•R•••
YARDED
YARELY
YAREST
YARNED
YARROW
YERKED
YERKES
YORICK
YORKER
YORKIE
YORUBA
YUROKS

Y••R••
YARROW
YEARLY
YEARNS

Y•••R•
YOGURT

Y••••R
YABBER
YAKKER
YAMMER
YASSER
YAWNER
YAWPER
YEAGER
YELLER
YELPER
YESSIR
YESTER
YONDER
YORKER

•YR•••
BYRNES
BYROAD
BYROTE
CYRANO
EYRIES
GYRATE
GYRENE
GYRONS
GYROSE
LYRICS
LYRIST
MYRDAL
MYRIAD
MYRRHS
MYRTLE
PYRITE
SYRIAN
SYRINX
SYRUPS
SYRUPY
TYRANT
TYRIAN
TYRONE

•Y•R••
CYMRIC
CYPRUS
HYBRID
HYDRAE
HYDRAS
HYDROS
MYRRHS

•Y••R•
AYMARA
BYWORD
CYBORG
CYDERS
LYNYRD
MYGIRL
MYSORE
MYWORD
TYPERS
VYBORG
WYVERN

•Y•••R
CYCLER
CYPHER
FYODOR
GYPPER
OYSTER
TYPIER
WYNTER
XYSTER

••YR••
BAYRUM
CHYRON
DRYROT
DRYRUN
FLYROD
SMYRNA
STYRIA
STYRON
TAYRAS
THYRSI

••Y•R•
BAYARD
BOYARS
BUYERS
CRYERS
DIYERS
DRYERS
EEYORE
FLYERS
FOYERS
FRYERS
LAYERS
MAYORS
MOYERS
PAYERS
SAYERS
TUYERE

••Y••R
BAYLOR
GAYNOR
GEYSER
JOYNER
KHYBER
LAYFOR
PAYFOR
PSYWAR
RHYMER
SNYDER
STYLER
TAYLOR
TRYFOR

•••YR•
LYNYRD
PAPYRI
SATYRS
THEYRE

•••Y•R
ANHYDR
BOWYER
BRAYER
BREYER
DLAYER
ELAYER
FLAYER
GRAYER
GREYER
LAWYER
MAGYAR
PLAYER
PRAYER
SAWYER
SLAYER
SPRYER
SWAYER
THAYER

••••YR
MARTYR
ZEPHYR

Y•S•••
YASSER
YESMAN
YESMEN
YESSED
YESSES
YESSIR
YESTER

Y••S••
YASSER
YEASTS
YEASTY
YESSED
YESSES
YESSIR

Y•••S•
YAREST
YOGISM

Y••••S
YACHTS
YAHOOS
YAKUTS
YALIES
YAPOKS
YAQUIS
YEARNS
YEASTS
YENTAS
YERKES
YESSES
YIELDS
YOBBOS
YODELS
YOICKS
YOKELS
YOKUTS
YOUTHS
YUCCAS
YUROKS

•YS•••
BYSSHE
BYSSUS
HYSSOP
LYSINE
LYSINS
MYSELF
MYSORE
MYSTIC
OYSTER
SYSOPS
SYSTEM
WYSTAN
XYSTER

•Y•S••
AYESHA
BYSSHE
BYSSUS
GYPSUM
HYKSOS
HYSSOP
KYUSHU
MYOSIN
MYOSIS
NYASSA

•Y••S•
BYGOSH
BYPASS
BYPAST
DYNAST
GYROSE
LYRIST
NYASSA
TYPIST
ZYMASE

•Y•••S
BYLAWS
BYPASS
BYRNES
BYSSUS
BYWAYS
CYCADS
CYCLAS
CYCLES
CYCLOS
CYDERS
CYGNUS
CYNICS
CYPRUS
EYRIES
GYRONS
HYADES
HYDRAS
HYDROS
HYENAS
HYKSOS
HYPNOS
KYACKS
LYCEES
LYMPHS
LYNXES
LYRICS
LYSINS
MYNAHS
MYOPES
MYOSIS
MYRRHS
MYTHOS
NYALAS
NYLONS
NYMETS
NYMPHS
PYLONS
PYXIES
SYLPHS
SYNODS
SYRUPS
SYSOPS
TYPERS
TYPHUS

••YS••
ABYSMS
ALYSSA
BRYSON
BUYSUP
ELYSEE
GEYSER
KEYSIN
KEYSUP
LAYSBY
LAYSIN
LAYSON
LAYSTO
LAYSUP
NAYSAY
PAYSIN
PAYSON
PAYSUP
PHYSED
PHYSIO
SAYSOS
TRYSTS
ZOYSIA

••Y•S•
ALYSSA
BOYISH
CAYUSE
COYEST

COYISH
DRYEST
FEYEST
GAYEST
SHYEST
SLYEST
THYRSI
WRYEST

••Y••S
ABYDOS
ABYSMS
ARYANS
BAYOUS
BOYARS
BUYERS
COYPUS
CRYERS
CRYPTS
DIYERS
DOYENS
DRYADS
DRYERS
FLYBYS
FLYERS
FLYINS
FOYERS
FRYERS
GAYALS
GLYNIS
GLYPHS
GUYOTS
IDYLLS
JOYOUS
KAYAKS
KEYNES
LAYBYS
LAYERS
LAYUPS
MAYANS
MAYBES
MAYORS
MOYERS
ONYXES
ORYXES
PAYEES
PAYERS
PSYCHS
RAYONS
RHYMES
RIYALS
ROYALS
SAYERS
SAYLES
SAYSOS
SAYYES
SLYPES
STYLES
STYLUS
TAYRAS

THYMUS
TOYONS
TRYSTS
WAYANS
ZAYINS

•••YS•
IRTYSH

•••Y•S
ALKYDS
ALKYLS
LLOYDS
OXEYES
PLAYAS
POLYPS
REDYES
SATYRS
SAYYES
SIBYLS
VINYLS

••••YS
ABBEYS
ALLAYS
ALLEYS
ALLOYS
ALWAYS
ANNOYS
ARRAYS
ASSAYS
BELAYS
BLUEYS
BOGEYS
BYWAYS
CONEYS
COPAYS
COVEYS
DECAYS
DECOYS
DELAYS
DOGEYS
EMBAYS
ENJOYS
ENVOYS
ERINYS
ESSAYS
FLYBYS
FOGEYS
FORAYS
GAMAYS
GLADYS
HONEYS
INLAYS
JASEYS
LAYBYS
LIEBYS
LIMEYS
MALAYS
MATEYS

MONEYS
MORAYS
MOSEYS
MULEYS
POBOYS
POKEYS
REKEYS
RELAYS
REPAYS
SEPOYS
SPLAYS
SPRAYS
STRAYS
TETHYS
TOKAYS
UNISYS
UNSAYS
ZLOTYS

Y••T••
YENTAS
YESTER
YOMTOV
YOUTHS
YVETTE

Y•••T•
YACHTS
YAKUTS
YEASTS
YEASTY
YOKUTS
YUKATA
YVETTE

Y••••T
YAREST
YOGURT
YOUBET

•YT•••
BYTALK
LYTTON
MYTHIC
MYTHOI
MYTHOL
MYTHOS
PYTHIA
PYTHON

•Y•T••
HYETAL
LYTTON
MYRTLE
MYSTIC
OYSTER
SYNTAX
SYSTEM
WYNTER
WYNTON

WYSTAN
XYSTER

•Y••T•
BYPATH
BYROTE
GYRATE
NYMETS
PYRITE
ZYGOTE

•Y•••T
BYPAST
CYGNET
DYELOT
DYNAST
EYELET
LYRIST
TYBALT
TYPIST
TYRANT

••YT••
ADYTUM
AMYTAN
BLYTHE
DAYTON
MAYTAG
PEYTON
RHYTHM
RHYTON
SCYTHE

••Y•T•
COYOTE
CRYPTO
CRYPTS
GUYOTS
LAYSTO
PEYOTE
TOYOTA
TRYSTS

••Y••T
BRYANT
BUYOUT
COYEST
DAYLIT
DRYEST
DRYOUT
DRYROT
FEYEST
FLYNET
FLYOUT
GAYEST
LAYOUT
PAYOUT
SHYEST
SLYEST
STYLET

TRYOUT
WAYOUT
WHYNOT
WRYEST

•••YT•
OOCYTE

•••Y•T
NOTYET
PLAYAT
SALYUT

••••YT
AJFOYT

YU••••
YUCCAS
YUKATA
YUKAWA
YUKKED
YUMYUM
YUNGLO
YUNNAN
YUPPIE
YUROKS

Y•U•••
YAUPON
YOUALL
YOUBET
YOUTHS

Y••U••
YAKUTS
YAKUZA
YAQUIS
YEHUDI
YOGURT
YOKUTS
YORUBA

Y•••U•
YANQUI
YUMYUM

•YU•••
KYUSHU
RYUKYU

•Y•U••
NYQUIL
SYRUPS
SYRUPY

•Y••U•
BYSSUS
CYGNUS
CYPRUS
DYBBUK

EYECUP
EYEFUL
GYPSUM
HYPEUP
LYCEUM
TYPEUP
TYPHUS

•Y•••U
KYUSHU
RYUKYU

••YU••
CAYUGA
CAYUSE
LAYUPS

••Y•U•
ADYTUM
ASYLUM
BAYEUX
BAYOUS
BAYRUM
BUYOUT
BUYSUP
COYPUS
DRYOUT
DRYRUN
FLYOUT
JOYFUL
JOYOUS
KEYSUP
LAYOUT
LAYSUP
PAYOUT
PAYSUP
PHYLUM
RAYGUN
STYLUS
THYMUS
TRYOUT
WAYOUT

••Y••U
HEYYOU

•••YU•
BUOYUP
FAIYUM
PLAYUP
PONYUP
SALYUT
STAYUP
TIDYUP
YUMYUM

•••Y•U
HEYYOU

••••YU
CHOOYU
KIKUYU
RYUKYU

YV••••
YVETTE
YVONNE

Y••••V
YOMTOV

•YV•••
WYVERN

•Y•V••
SYLVAN
SYLVIA

•Y••V•
BYJOVE

••YV••
JAYVEE

•••YV•
THEYVE

••••YV
HENRYV
ROCKYV

Y•W•••
YAWING
YAWNED
YAWNER
YAWPED
YAWPER
YOWLED

Y••W••
YAHWEH

Y•••W•
YUKAWA

Y••••W
YARROW
YELLOW

•YW•••
BYWAYS
BYWORD
MYWORD

•Y••W•
BYLAWS

••YW••
ANYWAY

FLYWAY
KEYWAY
PSYWAR
SKYWAY

••Y••W
ANYHOW
HAYMOW
LAYLOW

•YX•••
PYXIES

•Y•X••
LYNXES

•Y•••X
SYNTAX
SYRINX

••YX••
ONYXES
ORYXES

••Y••X
BAYEUX
PAYBOX
SKYBOX

•••Y•X
LARYNX

••••YX
COCCYX

Y•Y•••
YOYOED
YOYOMA

Y••Y••
YUMYUM

Y••••Y
YARELY
YEARLY
YEASTY

•Y•Y••
LYNYRD
SYZYGY

•Y••Y•
AYEAYE
BYEBYE
BYWAYS
RYUKYU

•Y•••Y
BYPLAY
LYNLEY

MYOHMY
SYDNEY
SYRUPY
SYZYGY
TYPIFY

••YY••
HEYYOU
SAYYES
SAYYID

••Y•Y•
FLYBYS
LAYBYS

••Y••Y
ANYDAY
ANYWAY
BRYONY
DAYBOY
DRYFLY
FLYBOY
FLYWAY
HAYLEY
HEYDAY
KEYWAY
LAYSBY
MAYDAY
MAYFLY
NAYSAY
PAYDAY
SKYWAY
WAYLAY

•••Y•Y
CLAYEY
GRAYLY
GREYLY
SPRYLY
SYZYGY

Y•••Z•
YAKUZA

•YZ•••
SYZYGY

•Y•Z••
RYAZAN

•••YZ•
CORYZA
SWAYZE

ZA••••
ZADDIK
ZADORA
ZAFFER
ZAFTIG
ZAGGED

ZAGREB
ZAIRES
ZAMBIA
ZAMIAS
ZANDER
ZANIER
ZANIES
ZANILY
ZANUCK
ZAPATA
ZAPPED
ZAPPER
ZAREBA
ZAYINS
ZAZENS

Z•A•••
ZEALOT
ZSAZSA

Z••A••
ZAPATA
ZENANA
ZONATE
ZOUAVE
ZYMASE

Z•••A•
ZAMIAS
ZEBRAS
ZEDBAR
ZEEMAN
ZIGZAG
ZILPAH
ZODIAC

Z••••A
ZADORA
ZAMBIA
ZAPATA
ZAREBA
ZENANA
ZEUGMA
ZINNIA
ZOYSIA
ZSAZSA

•ZA•••
AZALEA
IZABAL
OZARKS

•Z•A••
EZZARD
IZZARD

•Z••A•
IZABAL
UZZIAH

•Z•••A
AZALEA

••ZA••
BAZAAR
BEZANT
EZZARD
HAZANS
HAZARD
IZZARD
KAZAKH
KAZAKS
LIZARD
MOZART
PIZAZZ
WIZARD

••Z•A•
BAZAAR
FEZZAN
HUZZAH
HUZZAS
ITZHAK
PIZZAS
TAZZAS
UZZIAH

••Z••A
GEZIRA
MAZOLA
MAZUMA
VIZSLA

•••ZA•
BAIZAS
BALZAC
BANZAI
FEZZAN
HUZZAH
HUZZAS
PIZZAS
PLAZAS
PROZAC
RYAZAN
SHAZAM
SLEZAK
TARZAN
TAZZAS
ZIGZAG

•••Z•A
BRAZZA
PIAZZA
ZSAZSA

••••ZA
BRAZZA
CORYZA
FAENZA
KWANZA
PIAZZA
SFORZA
STANZA
YAKUZA

Z•B•••
ZEBRAS
ZIBETS

Z••B••
ZAMBIA
ZEDBAR
ZOMBIE

Z•••B•
ZAREBA

Z••••B
ZAGREB

•ZB•••
UZBEKS

•Z•B••
IZABAL

••ZB••
LAZBOY

••Z•B•
GAZEBO

Z••C••
ZIRCON

Z•••C•
ZANUCK
ZURICH
ZYDECO

Z••••C
ZENDIC
ZIPLOC
ZODIAC

•Z•C••
CZECHS

•Z••C•
AZTECS

•Z•••C
OZONIC

•••ZC•
OROZCO

•••Z•C
BALZAC
PROZAC

Z•D•••
ZADDIK
ZADORA
ZEDBAR
ZODIAC
ZYDECO

Z••D••
ZADDIK
ZANDER
ZENDIC
ZENDOS
ZUIDER

Z•••D•
ZOOIDS
ZOUNDS

Z••••D
ZAGGED
ZAPPED
ZEROED
ZESTED
ZIGGED
ZINGED
ZIPPED
ZONKED
ZOOMED

•Z•D••
AZIDES
AZODYE

•Z•••D
EZZARD
IZZARD

••Z••D
BUZZED
COZIED
EZZARD
FIZZED
FUZZED
HAZARD
IZZARD
JAZZED
LIZARD
MUZZED
RAZZED
WIZARD

•••Z•D
AMAZED
BLAZED
BRAZED
BUZZED
CRAZED
FIZZED
FUTZED
FUZZED
GLAZED
GLOZED
GRAZED
JAZZED
MUZZED
PRIZED
RAZZED
SEIZED

ZE••••
ZEALOT
ZEBRAS
ZEDBAR
ZEEMAN
ZENANA
ZENDIC
ZENDOS
ZENGER
ZENITH
ZEPHYR
ZEROED
ZEROES
ZEROIN
ZEROTH
ZESTED
ZEUGMA
ZEUXIS

Z•E•••
ZEEMAN

Z••E••
ZAREBA
ZAZENS
ZIBETS
ZYDECO

Z•••E•
ZAFFER
ZAGGED
ZAGREB
ZAIRES
ZANDER
ZANIER
ZANIES
ZAPPED
ZAPPER
ZENGER
ZEROED
ZEROES
ZESTED
ZIGGED
ZIMMER
ZINGED
ZINGER
ZIPPED
ZIPPER
ZITHER
ZONKED
ZONKER
ZOOMED
ZUIDER

Z••••E
ZOMBIE
ZONATE
ZOUAVE
ZYGOTE
ZYMASE

•ZE•••
CZECHS
CZERNY

•Z•E••
AZTECS
UZBEKS

•Z••E•
AZALEA
AZIDES
AZINES
AZORES

•Z•••E
AZODYE

••ZE••
BEZELS
COZENS
DIZENS
DOZENS
DOZERS
FUZEES
GAZEBO
HAZELS
HAZERS
MAZERS
MIZENS
OUZELS
SIZERS
SIZEUP
WIZENS
ZAZENS

••Z•E•
BUZZED
BUZZER
BUZZES
COZIED
COZIER
COZIES
DOZIER
FEZZES
FIZZED
FIZZES
FUZEES
FUZZED
FUZZES
HAZIER
JAZZED
JAZZES
LAZIER
MAZIER
MIZZEN
MUZZED
MUZZES
OOZIER
RAZZED
RAZZES
ROZZER
VIZIER

••Z••E
DAZZLE
ENZYME
EVZONE
FIZZLE
FOZZIE
GUZZLE
LIZZIE
MIZZLE
MUZZLE
NOZZLE
NUZZLE
PUZZLE
RAZZLE
REZONE
SIZZLE

•••ZE•
AMAZED
AMAZES
BLAZED
BLAZER
BLAZES
BONZES
BRAZED
BRAZEN
BRAZER
BRAZES
BUZZED
BUZZER
BUZZES
CRAZED
CRAZES
CROZES
DENZEL
DITZES
DRUZES
FEZZES
FIZZED
FIZZES
FRAZER
FROZEN
FURZES
FUTZED
FUTZES
FUZZED
FUZZES
GAUZES
GEEZER
GLAZED
GLAZER
GLAZES
GLOZED
GLOZES
GRAZED
GRAZER
GRAZES
JAZZED
JAZZES
LUTZES
MAIZES
MIZZEN
MUZZED
MUZZES
PANZER
PFIZER
PRIZED
PRIZES
RAZZED
RAZZES
ROZZER
SEIZED
SEIZER
SEIZES
TETZEL
WINZES

•••Z•E
DAZZLE
DOOZIE
FIZZLE
FOOZLE
FOZZIE
GUZZLE
LIZZIE
MIZZLE
MUZZLE
NOZZLE
NUZZLE
PUZZLE
RAZZLE
SIZZLE

••••ZE
ABLAZE
ASSIZE
BEDAZE
BELIZE
BREEZE
BRONZE
FREEZE
FRIEZE
IODIZE
IONIZE
LAMAZE
SLEAZE
SNEEZE
SNOOZE
SWAYZE
TWEEZE
WHEEZE

Z•F•••
ZAFFER
ZAFTIG

Z••F••
ZAFFER

Z•G•••
ZAGGED
ZAGREB
ZIGGED
ZIGZAG
ZYGOTE

Z••G••
ZAGGED
ZENGER
ZEUGMA
ZIGGED
ZINGED
ZINGER

Z••••G
ZAFTIG
ZIGZAG
ZONING

••ZG••
FIZGIG

••Z•G•
SYZYGY

••Z••G
DAZING
DOZING
FAZING
FIZGIG
FUZING
GAZING
HAZING
LAZING
OOZING
RAZING
SIZING

•••Z•G
DANZIG
HERZOG
ZIGZAG

ZH••••
ZHUKOV

Z••H••
ZEPHYR
ZITHER

Z••••H
ZENITH
ZEROTH
ZILPAH
ZIZITH
ZURICH

•Z•H••
TZUHSI

•Z••H•
CZECHS

•Z•••H
UZZIAH

••ZH••
FUZHOU
ITZHAK
MUZHIK

••Z••H
HUZZAH
KAZAKH
UZZIAH
ZIZITH

•••Z•H
HUZZAH
MATZOH

ZI••••
ZIBETS
ZIGGED
ZIGZAG
ZILPAH
ZIMMER
ZINGED
ZINGER
ZINNIA
ZIPLOC
ZIPPED
ZIPPER
ZIPSUP
ZIRCON
ZITHER
ZIZITH

Z•I•••
ZAIRES
ZUIDER

Z••I••
ZAMIAS
ZANIER
ZANIES
ZANILY
ZAYINS
ZENITH
ZIZITH
ZODIAC
ZONING
ZOOIDS
ZORILS
ZURICH

Z•••I•
ZADDIK
ZAFTIG
ZAMBIA
ZENDIC
ZEROIN
ZEUXIS
ZINNIA
ZOMBIE
ZOOMIN
ZOYSIA

•ZI•••
AZIDES
AZINES

•Z•I••
UZZIAH

•Z••I•
AZORIN
OZONIC

•Z•••I
TZUHSI

••ZI••
COZIED
COZIER
COZIES
COZILY
DAZING
DOZIER
DOZILY
DOZING
FAZING
FUZING
GAZING
GEZIRA
HAZIER
HAZILY
HAZING
LAZIER
LAZILY
LAZING
MAZIER
MAZILY
OOZIER
OOZILY
OOZING

RAZING
SIZING
UNZIPS
UZZIAH
VIZIER
ZIZITH

••Z•I•
FIZGIG
FOZZIE
LIZZIE
MUZHIK
RIZZIO

••Z••I
ADZUKI
LAZULI
SUZUKI

•••ZI•
BRAZIL
DANZIG
DOOZIE
FOZZIE
GHAZIS
LIZZIE
RIZZIO
SWAZIS

•••Z•I
BANZAI
BORZOI
BRAZZI

••••ZI
BRAZZI
RIENZI

Z••K••
ZHUKOV
ZONKED
ZONKER

Z••••K
ZADDIK
ZANUCK

•Z••K•
OZARKS
UZBEKS

••Z•K•
ADZUKI
KAZAKH
KAZAKS
SUZUKI

••Z••K
ITZHAK
MUZHIK

•••Z•K
SLEZAK

ZL••••
ZLOTYS

Z•L•••
ZILPAH

Z••L••
ZEALOT
ZIPLOC

Z•••L•
ZANILY
ZORILS

•Z•L••
AZALEA

•Z•••L
IZABAL

••Z•L•
BEZELS
COZILY
DAZZLE
DOZILY
FIZZLE
GUZZLE
HAZELS
HAZILY
LAZILY
LAZULI
MAZILY
MAZOLA
MIZZLE
MUZZLE
NOZZLE
NUZZLE
OOZILY
OUZELS
PUZZLE
RAZZLE
SIZZLE
VIZSLA

••Z••L
FAZOOL

•••ZL•
DAZZLE
FIZZLE
FOOZLE
GUZZLE
MIZZLE
MUZZLE
NOZZLE
NUZZLE
PUZZLE
RAZZLE
SIZZLE

•••Z•L
BENZOL
BRAZIL
DENZEL
TETZEL

Z•M•••
ZAMBIA
ZAMIAS
ZIMMER
ZOMBIE
ZYMASE

Z••M••
ZEEMAN
ZIMMER
ZOOMED
ZOOMIN

Z•••M•
ZEUGMA

••ZM••
GIZMOS

••Z•M•
ENZYME
GAZUMP
MAZUMA

•••Z•M
SHAZAM

Z•N•••
ZANDER
ZANIER
ZANIES
ZANILY
ZANUCK
ZENANA
ZENDIC
ZENDOS
ZENGER
ZENITH
ZINGED
ZINGER
ZINNIA
ZONATE
ZONING
ZONKED
ZONKER

Z••N••
ZINNIA
ZOUNDS

Z•••N•
ZAYINS
ZAZENS
ZENANA
ZONING

Z••••N
ZEEMAN
ZEROIN
ZIRCON
ZOOMIN

•Z•N••
AZINES
OZONIC

•Z••N•
CZERNY

•Z•••N
AZORIN

••Z•N•
BEZANT
COZENS
DAZING
DIZENS
DOZENS
DOZING
EVZONE
FAZING
FUZING
GAZING
HAZANS
HAZING
LAZING
MIZENS
OOZING
RAZING
REZONE
SIZING
WIZENS
ZAZENS

••Z••N
FEZZAN
MIZZEN

•••ZN•
GROZNY

•••Z•N
AMAZON
BARZUN
BLAZON
BRAZEN
CURZON
FEZZAN
FROZEN
MIZZEN
PINZON
QUEZON
RYAZAN
TARZAN

ZO••••
ZODIAC
ZOMBIE
ZONATE
ZONING
ZONKED
ZONKER
ZOOIDS
ZOOMED
ZOOMIN
ZORILS
ZOUAVE
ZOUNDS
ZOYSIA

Z•O•••
ZLOTYS
ZOOIDS
ZOOMED
ZOOMIN

Z••O••
ZADORA
ZEROED
ZEROES
ZEROIN
ZEROTH
ZYGOTE

Z•••O•
ZEALOT
ZENDOS
ZHUKOV
ZIPLOC
ZIRCON

Z••••O
ZYDECO

•ZO•••
AZODYE
AZORES
AZORIN
OZONIC

••ZO••
EVZONE
FAZOOL
KAZOOS
MAZOLA
RAZORS
REZONE

••Z•O•
FAZOOL
FUZHOU
GIZMOS
KAZOOS
LAZBOY
MEZZOS

••Z••O
GAZEBO
RIZZIO

•••ZO•
AMAZON
BENZOL
BLAZON
BORZOI
BRAZOS
CURZON
HERZOG
MAHZOR
MATZOH
MATZOS
MEZZOS
PINZON
QUEZON

•••Z•O
AREZZO
OROZCO
RIZZIO
WHIZZO

••••ZO
ALONZO
AREZZO
REBOZO
WHIZZO

Z•P•••
ZAPATA
ZAPPED
ZAPPER
ZEPHYR
ZIPLOC
ZIPPED
ZIPPER
ZIPSUP

Z••P••
ZAPPED
ZAPPER
ZILPAH
ZIPPED
ZIPPER

Z••••P
ZIPSUP

••Z•P•
UNZIPS

••Z••P
GAZUMP
JAZZUP
SIZEUP

•••Z•P
JAZZUP

Z•R•••
ZAREBA
ZEROED
ZEROES
ZEROIN
ZEROTH
ZIRCON
ZORILS
ZURICH

Z••R••
ZAGREB
ZAIRES
ZEBRAS

Z•••R•
ZADORA

Z••••R
ZAFFER
ZANDER
ZANIER
ZAPPER
ZEDBAR
ZENGER
ZEPHYR
ZIMMER
ZINGER
ZIPPER
ZITHER
ZONKER
ZUIDER

•Z•R••
AZORES
AZORIN
CZERNY
OZARKS

•Z••R•
EZZARD
IZZARD

••Z•R•
DOZERS
EZZARD
GEZIRA
HAZARD
HAZERS
IZZARD
LIZARD
MAZERS
MOZART
RAZORS
SIZERS
WIZARD

••Z••R
BAZAAR
BUZZER
COZIER
DOZIER
HAZIER
LAZIER
MAZIER
OOZIER
ROZZER
VIZIER

•••Z•R
BLAZER
BRAZER
BUZZER
FRAZER
GEEZER
GLAZER
GRAZER
MAHZOR
PANZER
PFIZER
ROZZER
SEIZER

ZS••••
ZSAZSA

Z•S•••
ZESTED

Z••S••
ZIPSUP
ZOYSIA

Z•••S•
ZSAZSA
ZYMASE

Z••••S
ZAIRES
ZAMIAS
ZANIES
ZAYINS
ZAZENS
ZEBRAS
ZENDOS
ZEROES
ZEUXIS
ZIBETS
ZLOTYS
ZOOIDS
ZORILS
ZOUNDS

•Z••S•
TZUHSI

•Z•••S
AZIDES
AZINES
AZORES
AZTECS
CZECHS
OZARKS
UZBEKS

••ZS••
VIZSLA

••Z••S
BEZELS
BUZZES
COZENS
COZIES
DIZENS
DOZENS
DOZERS
FEZZES
FIZZES
FUZEES
FUZZES
GIZMOS
HAZANS
HAZELS
HAZERS
HUZZAS
JAZZES
KAZAKS
KAZOOS
MAZERS
MEZZOS
MIZENS
MUZZES
OUZELS
PIZZAS
RAZORS
RAZZES
SIZERS
TAZZAS
UNZIPS
WIZENS
ZAZENS

•••ZS•
ZSAZSA

•••Z•S
AMAZES
BAIZAS
BLAZES
BONZES
BRAZES
BRAZOS
BUZZES
CRAZES
CROZES
DITZES
DRUZES
FEZZES
FIZZES
FURZES
FUTZES
FUZZES
GAUZES
GHAZIS
GLAZES
GLOZES
GRAZES
HUZZAS
JAZZES
KUDZUS
LUTZES
MAIZES
MATZOS
MEZZOS
MUZZES
PIZZAS
PLAZAS
PRIZES
RAZZES
SEIZES
SWAZIS
TAZZAS
WINZES

Z•T•••
ZITHER

Z••T••
ZAFTIG
ZESTED
ZLOTYS

Z•••T•
ZAPATA
ZENITH
ZEROTH
ZIBETS
ZIZITH
ZONATE
ZYGOTE

Z••••T
ZEALOT

•ZT•••
AZTECS

••Z•T•
ZIZITH

••Z••T
BEZANT
MOZART

ZU••••
ZUIDER
ZURICH

Z•U•••
ZEUGMA
ZEUXIS
ZHUKOV
ZOUAVE
ZOUNDS

Z••U••
ZANUCK

Z•••U•
ZIPSUP

•ZU•••
TZUHSI

••ZU••
ADZUKI
GAZUMP
LAZULI
MAZUMA
SUZUKI

••Z•U•
JAZZUP
SIZEUP

••Z••U
FUZHOU

•••ZU•
BARZUN
JAZZUP
KUDZUS

••••ZU
LAOTZU

Z•••V•
ZOUAVE

Z••••V
ZHUKOV

Z••X••
ZEUXIS

ZY••••
ZYDECO
ZYGOTE
ZYMASE

Z•Y•••
ZAYINS
ZOYSIA

Z•••Y•
ZEPHYR
ZLOTYS

Z••••Y
ZANILY

•Z••Y•
AZODYE

•Z•••Y
CZERNY

••ZY••
ENZYME
SYZYGY

••Z••Y
COZILY
DOZILY
HAZILY
LAZBOY
LAZILY
MAZILY
OOZILY
SYZYGY

•••Z•Y
FRIZZY
GROZNY
SCUZZY

SNAZZY

••••ZY
BLOWZY
BREEZY
BRONZY
FRENZY
FRIZZY
FROWZY
GLITZY
GROSZY
KLUTZY
SCHIZY
SCUZZY
SLEAZY
SNAZZY
SNEEZY
SNOOZY
WHEEZY

Z•Z•••
ZAZENS
ZIZITH

Z••Z••
ZIGZAG
ZSAZSA

•ZZ•••
EZZARD
IZZARD
UZZIAH

••ZZ••
BUZZED
BUZZER
BUZZES
DAZZLE
FEZZAN
FEZZES
FIZZED
FIZZES
FIZZLE
FOZZIE
FUZZED
FUZZES
GUZZLE
HUZZAH
HUZZAS
JAZZED
JAZZES
JAZZUP
LIZZIE
MEZZOS
MIZZEN
MIZZLE
MUZZED
MUZZES
MUZZLE
NOZZLE
NUZZLE
PIZZAS
PUZZLE
RAZZED
RAZZES
RAZZLE
RIZZIO
ROZZER
SIZZLE
TAZZAS

••Z•Z•
PIZAZZ

••Z••Z
PIZAZZ

•••ZZ•
AREZZO
BRAZZA
BRAZZI
FRIZZY
PIAZZA
SCUZZY
SNAZZY
WHIZZO

••••ZZ
PIZAZZ